Aak to Zumbra

A Dictionary of the World's Watercraft

The Mariners' Museum

with contributions by M.H. Parry and others
Illustrations by M.H. Parry

The Mariners' Museum Newport News, Virginia

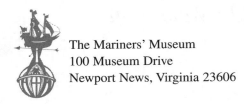

The Mariners' Museum
100 Museum Drive
Newport News, Virginia 23606

Executive Editor: Beverly McMillan
Managing Editor: Susannah Livingston
Editor: Susan Beaven Rutter
Design and Composition: sbR Graphic Design
Cover Design: Kelly O'Neill

Printed in the United States of America

Library of Congress Cataloging-in-Publication Data is available.

ISBN 0-917376-46-3

Contents

Foreword *by Basil Greenhill* i

Introduction iii

Acknowledgments ix

Dictionary of the World's Watercraft 1

Selected Reading 653

Geographical Index 655

✍ Foreword ✍

The modern history of the development of serious academic interest in the ethnography of boats and vessels began with worldwide studies by James Hornell, who set out "to marshal in due order the major part of the knowledge within our ken concerning the origins of the many devices upon which one, living in varying stages of culture, launched themselves afloat upon rivers, lakes and sea." Hornell published widely in academic journals between 1919 and 1943. Jointly with A. C. Haddon he produced three volumes of studies of Pacific canoes, most conveniently available in a combined reprint, *Canoes of Oceania* (Honolulu, Bishop Museum Press, 1975). The descriptions of canoes in this monumental work are of great and enduring value. Inevitably, as the authors themselves recognized, some of the conclusions were to prove subject to refinement based on later research. The same may be said of Hornell's last publication, *Water Transport* (Cambridge, England, 1946; second ed., Newton Abbot, England, 1970), which encapsulated much of his life's work. It still remains, as the American nautical historian Edwin Doran, Jr., said many years ago, the place to begin with any study of what in Hornell's day were called "primitive craft."

Although a great deal of work has been done since Hornell, he has had no real successor in the global comparative study of boats. In the archaeological field Professor Sean McGrail's *Ancient Boats of the World* offers similar breadth of treatment, but most subsequent studies have been regional, or of one group of boats, or of one boat type. In this respect Muriel Parry's work is comparable with Hornell's in its breadth. The problems of nomenclature, with which this dictionary so ably and comprehensively deals, will become even greater as terms drop out of use and students of the history of the boat become more and more dependent on literary sources rather than current examples.

The development of serious study of the boat as an important cultural artifact is a product of the twentieth century. In the United States, wide interest perhaps can be dated from the publication of Howard Irving Chapelle's *American Sailing Craft* in New York in 1936. Chapelle was a naval architect turned naval architecture historian. In that book, as well as in *American Small Sailing Craft* (New York, 1951) and in many articles, he recorded the results of assiduous travel on the east coast of the United States and Canada from Florida to Labrador. He was an excellent draftsman, and his work is an invaluable record. He was appointed curator of the National Watercraft Collection, and he used his position, quite correctly, to present the history of American working vessels as what a contemporary journalist described as "a doctoral tract in a graduate school."

Despite the high level of originality in much of his work, Chapelle has been criticized for his lack of scholarly apparatus. He was not a man to indicate his sources, and he was inclined to decorate his drawings with charming details for which there was perhaps little historical evidence. To a degree it was these decorations that made the drawings so attractive, and they played their part in converting many a layman into a boat buff, or often into something more serious. At the end of his working life Chapelle confounded us all by producing in *American Fishing Schooners* (New York, 1973), possibly his best work of all, no fewer than 371 pages of notes and source material in a book of 893 pages.

I knew Howard Chapelle well in the 1950s and 1960s. He was intolerant of some aspects of American—we might now say Western—life as it was developing at that period. He would have been surprised, I think, at the extent to which his work was taken up on the grounds that it provided an escape from such developments. His St. Paul, if I may use such a term, was John Gardner, a practical boatbuilder who in the 1960s began writing for the regional monthly trade newspaper *The Maine Coast Fisherman*, later the *National Fisherman*. John Gardner himself was a very able practical boatbuilder, and his excellent writing, aided by such factors as the studiously accurate and very attractive drawings of Sam Manning, did a great deal to stimulate interest in boat ethnography in the United States.

Interest in working boats developed in Scandinavia, Finland, and north Germany and Poland in the first half of the twentieth century and steadily widened as the century progressed. This interest was firmly founded on an awareness of the historical significance of indigenous boats—an awareness that stretched back into the nineteenth century. In this region boats developed in different forms from those in North America. The last generation of wooden boats in this part of Europe tended to be the direct descendants of boats dating back to the era of the Scandinavian expansion—the so-called Viking Age—and even earlier in Sweden and Finland. These boats retain structural features, and even design characteristics, going back many centuries.

It can be said, though perhaps not too seriously, that there has perhaps always been an element of nationalism at work in the enthusiasm with which maritime ethnographic and archaeological studies have been pursued in the Baltic region. This is, of course, combined with the fascination of the study of people utterly remote from us today whose maritime achievements were, in terms of the range of their voyaging—from Newfoundland in the West to the Bosporus in the East—utterly astonishing. Moreover, their boats were the results of extremely sophisticated "engineering in wood," as Ole Crumlin-Pedersen has put it, and objects of great beauty and specialized functional efficiency.

A comprehensive pioneering study of the working boats of many areas of a whole geographical region was completed by Bernhard Færøyvik, his wife, Aletta, and his son, Øystein, in Norway and the extreme north of Fenno Scandia in the 1920s, 1930s, and 1940s. Færøyvik, a fisherman by origin, trained as a schoolteacher and made full use of his origins and practical knowledge to produce, latterly with official financial support, a remarkable compendium of information in notes and drawings. The material is now deposited in the Maritime Museum in Bergen and partly published in English in *Inshore Craft of Norway* (London, 1979), edited by Arne Christensen. Færøyvik is notable for recording the local names of boats and their constituent parts. He felt that this philological material would prove of historical value. He believed, in the words of Øystein Færøyvik, that "the only way in which it would be possible to reconstruct the origin and evolution of Norwegian boats, and to understand the part played by local conditions in this process, was by documenting the local craft in use along the coastal and inland waterways."

In Britain quite a lot of, by modern standards, fairly rough and ready recording work was done in the 1930s by Phillip Oak, H. Oliver Hill, and others. But the importance of working boats to the society as a whole was not sufficient to ensure the preservation of any significant collection of samples at that time. The work of Phillip Oak was, indeed, never published in its entirety, but was to have great long-term influence. British interest in the ethnography of working boats followed the American and Scandinavian movements some ten or more years later. Eric McKee's *Working Boats of Britain* (London, 1983) set new international standards in the treatment of its subject. Above all, McKee's book made it clear, as has McGrail's work in the field of maritime archaeology, that the boat herself cannot be studied in isolation. McGrail defines maritime archaeology as having at its core the professional study of the building techniques and the materials used in the construction of vessels, but including also the consideration of the whole operation of boats and ships, their equipment, cargoes, the economic and social background of their operation, their performance, and the way they were handled. To have reality, the study of the ethnography of the boat must be similarly broadly based.

The boat is part of an economic, social, cultural, and geographical complex. She is intelligible only in that context. To understand her you must understand the ways in which the people who built and used her lived and thought, and usually they lived and thought in ways quite remote from those of late-twentieth-century Westerners. The results achieved will always have to be assessed against the standard of the society that created the boat. This fact is very vividly brought out in Jon Crondal's "Researching Living Traditions of Square-sail Rigged Norwegian Boats" in *Sailing Into The Past* (Ole Crumlin-Pedersen and Max Vinner, eds., Roskilde, Denmark, 1986). Crondal talked with men whose working conditions in their youth were little different from those of the Viking era. They revealed "a wealth of experience and insight that most of us can only dream of attaining…it is the boat that tells a sailor how it should be trimmed. The problem cannot be solved on an intellectual level alone…The whole way of thinking about boat and rig has its starting point in circumstances that would seem extreme…to ordinary seafaring people today."

It is within this context, so briefly and selectively indicated, of developing international interest in the ethnography of the boat and the withering away of the maritime cultures that this work is to be appreciated. Its value to ethnographers, historians, and archaeologists will increase as the years go by.

Basil Greenhill, CB, CMG, FSA, FRHistS

Introduction

Over time people have used great ingenuity to meet the challenge of getting from one shore to another. They have been motivated by the desire to conquer, for whatever reason, the peoples living across the river, the lake, the bay, the ocean, and by the tantalizing wealth of resources to be found beneath these waters. The countless watercraft types found around the world—each type adapting to unique environmental conditions, using available construction materials, and capitalizing on the successes and failures of earlier boatbuilders—attest to our success in meeting these challenges. Watercraft evolve over time; a totally new type would indeed be a rarity.

The more than 5,600 entries contained in this dictionary were selected from a file of over 19,000 terms gathered between 1974 and 1995. The content evolved as burgeoning interest in indigenous watercraft produced new basic data, and as enticing leads and relationships beckoned. As work proceeded, it became evident that existing maritime dictionaries rarely made more than a token effort to provide researchers with the alternate names and spellings by which a particular craft may have been known. The inclusion of these variants will assist researchers in identifying duplicated types under different names or spellings.

Some well-known types were not included—this is not an unabridged dictionary—but with the world to select from, it was possible to include many little-known types. The emphasis is on working watercraft built by local craftsmen. No attempt was made to distinguish between boat, vessel, and ship, as such terms are too imprecise to give more than a very general indication of size.

The often detailed entries found in this volume will enable the reader to identify the multiple boat types known by a particular word, some of the activities undertaken by watercraft around the world, and some of the unique construction materials used. It is also hoped that the dictionary, with its thousands of cross-references, will provide the impetus and foundation for investigation and interpretation of type and linguistic correlations.

Boat Evolution and Names

Long ago, a person was content to lie astride a fallen log and paddle by hand to cross a quiet stream or a small lake. But restless and visionary locals in many parts of the world began to recognize the desirability of greater mobility, safety, and passenger and cargo capacity, and in time great ships evolved.

Limited materials for construction in some areas of the world created pockets of uniquely adapted watercraft: the Inuit skin boats where no trees exist; reed balsas and woven reed-bottomed craft; bowl-shaped coracles using twigs and easily secured skins; hewn logs; and multiple logs lashed to form rafts, both for cargo transport and to transport the logs themselves. Many of these seemingly primitive craft represent such a perfect balance between need and available resources that they exist today almost unchanged. Tradition-strong, self-sufficient cultures tend to retain their boat types, despite the availability of newer designs.

Economics played an important role in how and how far each basic craft developed. When fishing close inshore no longer provided an adequate catch to feed a growing population, more stable boats were needed to venture farther offshore and return safely. When the peoples on an opposite shore could provide special foods, raw materials, or utensils, it became desirable to have boats sufficiently large and sturdy to permit trade for these items. Modifications often resulted from harbor development or from shifting trade routes due to new product demands. For those engaged mainly in fishing, changes resulted from the fluctuations in numbers and location of the primary catch.

Geographic factors greatly affected how water transport evolved. A transportation-poor, rugged hinterland encouraged coastal inhabitants to look seaward, and boats evolved relatively quickly. The shore itself-steep or flat, sandy or cobbly, soft or firm, narrow or wide, marshy, protected or open-directly affected how a boat type evolved. Tide rise, currents, prevailing winds, sea and surf, ice conditions, water temperature, marked seasonal changes—each in its own way has had a bearing on the watercraft we see today, and in many craft we no longer see. Limited land resources encouraged peoples to investigate what the sea could provide-sealskins, whale oil, seaweed for fertilizer, salt, oysters, and, of course, fish. Diminished resources sometimes prompted the development of boats capable of moving whole communities to distant areas, seasonally or permanently.

The hazards of open water presented special problems to be overcome, and contributed to resistance to major changes. Lives and boats could be lost quickly at sea, and radical innovations in boat design were usually viewed with suspicion. But builders continued to seek the most weatherly design, the best arrangement of equipment, the greatest cost effectiveness, and the design best suited for a vessel's primary mission. Occasionally hybrids were produced, taking features from two types. Both mechanization and the use of synthetic materials profoundly influenced hull design and ultimately the names given to a type; changes that were slow to gain acceptance in the past are now considered routine. Only a few types of boats have remained essentially unchanged for centuries, having achieved a balance between materials and use.

Wars, local or widespread, have presented special needs that also have affected boat design. Long wars doomed some vessel types engaged in marginal activities. Watercraft to wage war require special modifications and improvements, and experience with these vessels has often resulted in a new type for peacetime use.

Exploration and colonization presented demands for long-range vessels, and the new immigrants in turn often provided the indigenous peoples with new construction ideas and sailing techniques, frequently thoroughly diluting the indigenous craft and, in some cases, causing the adoption of a westernized term for the watercraft. More recently, efforts to improve the living standard in areas where fish provide an important source of protein have resulted in major modifications of existing types or in the development of new ones.

Committees have established uniform terminology in geography, ornithology, and botany, but there is rarely a consensus on what to call a particular boat type. A waterman takes a casual approach to boat identification, perhaps merely referring to his "20-footer" or to his "big boat"; only the scholar or lexicographer feels the need to be specific. But from the beginning man has referred to watercraft by some name, a term that is often merely a generic word

for "boat." What seems to be a unique type and term on one island may be given another name on an adjacent island. As new features are incorporated, a totally new term may be required to clarify which type is being discussed. Or a boat might be altered to undertake a special activity and might consequently need a modifier to specify this special use; in a few places exactly the same boat will have different names depending on its current, often seasonal, use.

A boat name also may change as a craft moves from one river system or even one part of a river to another. Or a generic term might no longer be suitable for a modified type being used farther down the coast. Even so, there tends to be a lingua franca within sea and ocean basins, the principal term for a vessel type correlating with political dominance at any one time.

Some boat terms have evolved from the principal function of a type, e.g., shrimper, collier. Mariners do not usually use a place name as a modifier, though such modifiers are frequently seen in the literature.

Many terms assigned to vernacular watercraft came from explorers and missionaries who tended to be casual about spelling, usually relying on phonetics. They often assigned a term that described a seemingly similar type of vessel known at home. Explorers rarely had the opportunity to put the craft they were describing in context with related craft in adjacent areas. The language of the traveler and its pronunciation greatly affected the resulting spelling; later travelers from another country often assigned a different name or spelling to the same boat type. Also, if one asked the natives on the beach what their boat type was called, the answer was often the equivalent of "boat"; not recognizing this, the traveler sometimes provided a detailed description for what is essentially a generic term.

Customs officials were generally casual about recording names for vessels, often assigning different names to the same type. To further complicate terminology, some boats, such as canoes, bore the names of their owners. Pronunciation of dialects in major widespread languages, such as Arabic, produced different-sounding names and suggested (often wrongly) different craft. Large vessel types tended to be assigned a term popular in a country at a given time, but the adjacent country might describe the same vessel with a term or spelling popular there. As people emigrated to distant lands, they tended to employ terms they knew at home.

Source materials

Traditional watercraft are fast disappearing in the face of modern technologies, and the term "traditional" has become too diluted to have real meaning. In many instances, scholars have had to work with the last remaining hulk, which may be disintegrating rapidly and may or may not be typical of the type. For many boat types, the reports, and sometimes the artwork, of early travelers and missionaries (both of varying reliability) are all that will ever be available.

Still, the burgeoning interest in traditional watercraft and their preservation and replication has produced a plethora of recent sources. In the past, common workboats were rarely described in detail. They were usually built by eye, based on experience and simple traditional rules, and reflected the reference of the builder or owner. They followed no set design, but their features and variations were adequately understood locally. Newer studies that recognize variables have made it possible here to include details not previously available for the preparation of maritime dictionaries.

Drawings, hull lines, and photographs were examined where available. These varied considerably in detail and reliability, and again may not even be typical. In some instances, such sources corroborated each other and confirmed the available textual material. Differences in dates of the available sources caused the greatest disparity-not necessarily because of original inaccuracies, but because each source tended to reflect one period and failed to acknowledge changing technologies and increasingly rapid evolution. Models were also a significant source, but their dependability rests on the modelmaker's care and the depth of the preliminary research. Often these were our only source.

Supplemental information for this dictionary was found in journals and monographs on fishing, transportation, inland waterways, ports, local history, regional and material culture studies, modelmaking, geography and exploration, boats and yachting, naval history, and underwater archaeology. Regional dictionaries were a significant source; although useful in establishing preferred spellings, a few of them provided surprising details. Many of them contributed new types not noted elsewhere.

Watercraft selection

With over 19,000 recorded working watercraft to choose from, it was necessary to be selective about watercraft types described here. Most, but not all, major types have been included; those omitted are described in standard nautical dictionaries. This volume also includes many lesser-known but interesting boats rarely cited in nautical dictionaries, and often previously described only in material culture studies.

Some boats that are not necessarily unusual in themselves engage in unusual activities: dredging for starfish, transporting night soil, providing a riverside work area for laundresses, conveying churchgoers, ferrying cattle to outlying pastures. Some of these are included for general interest and to indicate the diversity of uses to which boats can be put.

Watercraft with the same or similar names are often found in far-flung geographic areas. They are included here to aid readers in recognizing that there may be more than one craft by the same or similar name. The overlap of terminology may encourage further research.

Some types have been included because their names cry out to be cited. How can one resist such whimsy as lemon squeezer, male boat, toothpick, blobber, goat boat, bread pan, goozing boat, coffin ship, cadger, or buffalo boat?

It is harder to explain what has been omitted. With a few exceptions, boats designed to be propelled solely by an engine (as opposed to those converted from sail), pleasure and racing craft, and classes of the larger naval vessels have been bypassed. When included, they relate linguistically to some particular vernacular watercraft. Also excluded are archaeological finds, which frequently bear the name of the location of the find, the original name usually being unknown.

Descriptions

In general, each boat term is followed by the name of the country or region where the vessel was constructed, its primary function, period of operation, visual appearance, means of propulsion, crew size, dimensions, and other recorded names and spellings. Terms that are described elsewhere in the dictionary are printed in boldface and marked with a star; interested researchers may follow this lead.

Entry term

For local watercraft, the vernacular term is the primary entry. Where there was a choice of term or spelling, the one used by the most authoritative source was adopted. In some regions, word stems remain the same but the endings vary markedly. In such cases each term might refer to different craft, as with gabara, gabare, gabareau, gabaret, gabarot, gabarra. It is also not unknown for a writer to coin a term to describe a boat when the local term is not available. And there is evidence that a few indigenous peoples may have no term for a type, using only their hands to identify it.

Generic terms for widely known watercraft are usually entered under the English spelling. In practice, people have often assigned generic labels to quite distinct craft, producing an erroneous mental picture of the boat. Where a generic term also applies to unique local craft, there is a subhead under the generic term. In some cases, descriptions are combined under a broad term such as "kayak," where several ethnic subgroups use the same basic type of boat; local names are given as variants. In other cases, a term may define a particular sail plan used with non-specific hull types.

The etymology of terms is generally omitted because it is often controversial. On occasion, a direct translation is provided as a matter of general interest.

Insofar as possible, diacritic marks were added to terms since these typically affect pronunciation. Diacritic marks alter the alphabetical position of a word in some indigenous dictionaries, but such distinctions have not been honored in this maritime dictionary, the arrangement being letter by letter. In some languages, such as Arabic, various diacritics may be employed for a single letter, depending on the region or country and the particular system of transliteration. The diacritic marks used by the principal source are the ones used here. For the People's Republic of China, all boat and place names have been converted to Pinyin, with the Wade Giles and French transliterations added as variants. A few languages use multiple diacritics on a single letter, and reproducing some of these was not feasible.

Geographical designations

Present-day place names and political entities are used in most cases, even though the particular watercraft may be from a period when the locality or country was known by another name. The older, often more familiar, place name for newly renamed entities is provided in parentheses. Conventional spellings are used for major cities, countries, and international bodies of water.

Function

Generally the primary use to which a particular boat is put is the one cited. Such use affects its design, equipment, and crew size. Few watercraft have a single function, and many serve various uses from one season to another. Local tradition is often significant, with each area retaining its preferred type for a particular use, while elsewhere the same function is undertaken with a different craft.

Period of use

Where possible, this dictionary specifies the period during which a particular craft was (or is) in use. Occasionally it gives the date of the last one built. If the boat type was verified as extinct, this is stated, and the resurgence of some previously extinct working types as pleasure craft is also noted.

Physical characteristics

This volume emphasizes the form and design features of each watercraft-type of planking (flush-laid carvel or overlapping clinker); transverse framing on open boats; bow, stern, and bottom shapes; degree of decking, with cabin location; and rudder and stabilizing elements such as centerboard, leeboards, outriggers, sponsons. It is not always possible to determine whether a foreign technical term has the same meaning as it does in English; in general the one used is that of the source.

Methods of construction are omitted except for a few small, exotic types of relatively simple construction. Ships are described only briefly, since the emphasis is on smaller craft.

Major watercraft that have worked over an extended period naturally evolve, and sometimes only the name remains the same. Of particular concern are vessels of the fifteenth and sixteenth centuries; they are poorly known and their descriptions must be viewed with caution.

A visit to a crowded harbor reveals that seemingly similar workboats often differ in minor details. It is thus extremely difficult to describe a "typical" boat. Readers are advised that the descriptions provide only a general indication of what the watercraft are or were like. For some, greater attention may be paid to hull than to rigging, or vice versa, usually reflecting the particular emphasis of the original source.

Methods of propulsion

Most of the watercraft described herein worked primarily under sail, and sail type is given in general terms. Vessel types that survived over a long period usually underwent changes in sails and rigging, either to improve efficiency or to conform to the latest fashion. Frequently when rigging was altered on larger vessels of a particular hull type, the term by which the type was identified also changed. Until the mid-nineteenth century, the rig was the principal criterion for assigning a name to a vessel type.

Many fishing boats adopted auxiliary engines in the nineteenth century, but continued to employ sails as the primary method of propulsion, especially while actually fishing. In time this was reversed, with a sail used mainly for steadying the vessel while riding to the nets.

With small, manually propelled craft, sources are not always specific as to whether a vessel worked or works with oars or paddles. When illustrative material is available, the probable method can be deduced. Most sailing craft can be rowed in calms or when maneuvering in close quarters. Small inland craft are frequently poled or propelled by some similar device. Larger types used on rivers and canals were once towed by animals or humans; now, except in less developed areas, most are motorized.

Crew

Crew size provides an indication of the requirements for handling a particular craft, either to propel it or to perform its primary activity. In this volume, the range given usually correlates with the range of vessel sizes, but may reflect seasonal requirements for a particular type of fishing. Square and lateen sails require larger crews than fore-and-aft sails. Evolving modifications in sail type often reduced the number of crew members required, making the vessel more economical to operate, as did the adoption of auxiliary engines. Unless stated separately, crew figures may be a composite of those required to operate the vessel and those needed to handle nets, armament, reserve rowers, etc. These figures must be viewed as a guideline only.

Dimensions

Boat and vessel dimensions are given in metric units, the most common system of measurement. A range of recorded lengths provides a general idea of how large or small a craft is or was, although ranges varied where a type was used over a long period. It is not unusual for an existing boat to be lengthened to increase capacity or to provide for an additional mast. The dimensions should not be viewed as definitive since sources are not always precise in stating which measurements are being cited— length overall, length on the waterline, length on the keel, length between perpendiculars, or whether the length included the rudder or both rudder and bowsprit. Sources may have unwittingly combined various criteria. Also, reliability of lengths is suspect in places where local taxes are based on length features, the builder and owner naturally being anxious to keep within certain parameters.

When available, a single set of dimensions is included to indicate probable relative length/width/depth. Ideally, such figures are for a typical craft, but often only a single set of figures was available. If known, the date of this specific vessel is provided since vessels of different periods may vary in their proportions. Draft is given when known, but records do not always indicate whether such a figure is maximum or minimum draft, and (when appropriate) whether it includes a dropped centerboard.

Tonnage ranges are given only when other dimensions were unavailable. These may reflect displacement tonnage or cargo capacity. Since it is frequently impossible to determine which type a source cited, it is unwise to combine figures from different sources. When a specific tonnage figure is given, it relates directly to the dimensions to which it is appended. The abbreviation "rt" stands for "register tonnage"; "grt" stands for "gross register tonnage."

Notes to the entries

In most cases, there are multiple spellings for a given watercraft as well as local and colloquial names. Variable spellings may reflect dialects; phonetic spellings; the casual approach to spelling in earlier times and among semi-literate watermen; the way in which a particular word is spelled or pronounced in other languages; and sometimes poor orthography in a printed source.

In areas using a non-Roman alphabet, varying transliteration systems result in different spellings. When the plural is markedly different from the singular form of the noun, the plural is given. For widely used generic terms, such as schooner or lighter, the word in other languages is usually limited to the more common European languages.

Some watercraft bear colorful colloquial names, assigned by local watermen or often by competing watermen, and these have been included when reported in the sources. All terms listed are cross-referenced.

While every effort, within time constraints, has been made to ensure the accuracy of the cross-referencing in this dictionary, some cross-references may have been missed. In many cases, the spelling of a cross-reference will not include diacritical marks that are represented in an actual entry, particularly when a vessel is found in more that one country. Readers who are looking for a very specific spelling are urged to read through an entire referenced entry.

Name variations and/or alternative spellings follow the appropriate description. When such a listing immediately follows the entry term, these names and spellings apply to each of the subheads that follow.

Boat terms listed in "Note also" have some connection with the entry word, be it a type belonging to the same family, a comparable construction or building material, similar activity, or closely allied spelling that might confuse a researcher. The reader is left to follow these leads if desired. "See also" and "Further reference" refer the reader to descriptions of other, sometimes unrelated, boats known by the term just defined.

We have relied heavily on René de Kerchove's *International Maritime Dictionary* (2nd edition) for consistency of terminology. In some cases, however, source descriptions vary; we have followed the original sources when in doubt.

Further reading

When a substantial article or a book provides significant details of construction or historical background for a particular type of boat, a reference is included under this heading. These citations are not to be construed as a definitive bibliography for a particular description, since most descriptions are a synthesis of many sources, some providing only a single piece of data.

Illustrations

The drawings illustrate a few of the fascinating boat types found around the world. Some continue in use in much the same form as that portrayed, representing important means of transportation or livelihood in balance with need, materials, and economics. Readers are cautioned that design limitations preclude showing each boat in its relative size, each being reduced to fit the page format.

The sources for the drawings include illustrations in works of early travelers that were deemed reasonably accurate; well-proportioned museum models; and photographs of actual boats in situ. Each captures the boat at a particular place at a particular time; a date is provided when possible. Any particular illustration does not necessarily include all of the features listed within the description or, conversely, may show attributes that are not mentioned; the intention is simply to show one example of the vessel under consideration.

General reading list

A bibliography of sources used in compiling this dictionary would be unmanageable, since thousands have been consulted. However, this section lists some of the standard works on traditional watercraft. Some of these provide an overview of a specific geographic area, others discuss a major category of watercraft, and some are important general works on watercraft. These studies will enable a reader to gain an appreciation of the interrelationships of associated types and regional variations.

Geographical Index

This index is for readers interested in ascertaining which watercraft from a particular country or major region have been included in this dictionary. Variant names and spellings are not included, only the term under which the watercraft is entered.

★ ★ ★ ★

Readers who find errors in this work or who would like to offer suggestions for improvements may contact The Mariners' Museum Publications Department, 100 Museum Drive, Newport News, Virginia 23606. We welcome your thoughtful comments and wish you many hours of happy discovery with *Aak to Zumbra*.

Acknowledgments

In the course of 20 years of research for this dictionary innumerable people and organizations have made important contributions to its content.

Many people devoted considerable time to reviewing parts of the manuscript. Special note should be made of the following people:

Michael Alford (U.S.)
David Baumer (U.S.)
François Beaudouin (France)
Hallie Bond (U.S.)
Maynard Bray (U.S.)
Arne Emil Christensen (Norway)
Kelvin Duarte (Brazil)
John Gardner (U.S.)
Basil Greenhill (England)
Frits Hengeveld (Netherlands)
Jim Holt (U.S.)
Manuel Leitão (Portugal)
Jerzy Litwin (Poland)
Michael McCaughan (Northern Ireland)
Eric McKee (England)
Jules Van Beylen (Belgium)

Assistance in various ways was provided by the staffs of the following museums and organizations:

Instituto Nacional de Anthropologia (Argentina)
Schiffahrtsmuseum, Spits an der Donau (Austria)
National Scheepvaartmuseum (Belgium)
Museu Naval (Brazil)
Hudson's Bay Company (Canada)
Manitoba Museum of Man & Nature (Canada)
Maritime Museum of British Columbia (Canada)
Maritime Museum of the Atlantic (Canada)
National Museum of Man (Canada)
Provincial Museum of Alberta (Canada)
Vancouver Maritime Museum (Canada)
Fiskeri-og Sjøfartmuseum (Denmark)
Handels-og Søfartmuseum pa Kronborg (Denmark)
Museum de la Marine, Paris and Marseille (France)
Deutsches Schiffahrtsmuseum (Germany)
Food and Agriculture Organization (Italy)
Kobe Maritime Museum (Japan)
Maritiem Museum "Prins Hendrik" (Netherlands)
Nederlands Scheepvaart Museum (Netherlands)
Rijksmuseum voor Volkenkunde (Netherlands)
Visserijmuseum (Netherlands)
Zuiderzeemuseum (Netherlands)
Fiskerei Museet (Norway)
Bergens Sjøfartsmuseum (Norway)
Stavanger Sjøfartsmuseum (Norway)
Museum de Marinha (Portugal)
National Archives and Museum (Seychelles)
Seychelles Maritime School (Seychelles)
Maritime Museum (Singapore)
National Museum (Singapore)
Museo Maritimo de Barcelona (Spain)
Sjöfartsmuseum i Göteborg (Sweden)
Deniz Müzei (Turkey)
Cambridge University Museum of Archaeology and Ethnology (England)
Exeter Maritime Museum (England)
Falmouth Maritime Museum (England)
Merseyside Museum (England)
Museum of Mankind (England)
National Maritime Museum (England)
Science Museum (England)
Welsh Folk Museum (Wales)
United States:
Adirondack Museum
Antique Boat Museum
Bernice P. Bishop Museum
Calvert Marine Museum
Center for Wooden Boats
Chesapeake Bay Maritime Museum
Hudson River Maritime Museum
Library of Congress
Long Island Maritime Museum
Maine Maritime Museum
Mystic Seaport Museum
National Maritime Museum
Navy Library and Museum
New Jersey Historical Society
Peabody Museum
Penobscot Marine Museum
Princeton University Library
Radcliffe Maritime Museum
Rock Hall Waterman's Museum
Smithsonian Institution
Society of American Foresters
U.S. Naval Academy Museum
Ward Foundation

Individuals from around the world generously shared their knowledge and resources:

Gösta Ågren (Finland)
Eric Alfred (Singapore)
Béat Arnold (Switzerland)
William A. Baker (U.S.)
George Barrett (U.S.)

Basil W. Bathe (England)
Poul Bloesch (Switzerland)
Douglas Brooks (U.S.)
Edwin Doran, Jr. (U.S.)
Somasiri Devendra (Sri Lanka)
Kelvin Rother Duarte (Brazil)
Theodor Elsing (Netherlands)
Octávio Lixa Filgueiras (Portugal)
William C. Fleetwood, Jr. (U.S.)
Benjamin Fuller (U.S.)
Morton Gotchche (Denmark)
Henning Henningsen (Denmark)
Neil Hollander (France)
G. Adrian Horridge (Australia)
Robin Inglis (Canada)
Erick Jansen (Norway)
Eric Kentley (England)
L. Th. Lehmann (Netherlands)
Michael E. Martin (England)
José-Maria Martinez-Hidalgo (Spain)
Armando Reis Moura (Portugal)
Christian Nielsen (Denmark)
Gunnar Nordliner (Sweden)
Davil Olsen (Canada)
Pete McCurdy (New Zealand)
A. H. J. Prins (Netherlands)
Bill Reid (Canada)
Edoardo Ricardi (Italy)
Michael Sanderson (England)
William Scott (Philippines)
George Selim (U.S.)
William Shank (U.S.)
Peter Skanse (Sweden)
J. E. Spencer (U.S.)

Roger Taylor (U.S.)
Anastasios Tzamtzis (Greece)
Marguerite Verkade (Netherlands)
G. D. Von der Heide (Netherlands)
David Zimmerly (Canada)
Tom Zydler (U.S.)

Special mention must be made of Honor Johnson, who meticulously compiled the Geographical Index.

In a long-term project such as this, it is inevitable that a number of individuals who made significant contributions are not around to see that their efforts were not in vain. They have not been forgotten and are included in the above listings.

No book of broad scope and massive detail comes into being without the efforts of many dedicated people. Executive Editor Beverly McMillan directed the process of fashioning *Aak to Zumbra* from computer files and original artwork. As the manuscript evolved into its final form, Ben A.G. Fuller provided an invaluable, expert review. The cadre of proofreaders included Elizabeth C. Dudley and Ruth Bizot. Zac Rutter also read the entire manuscript, providing especially noteworthy assistance in the editing process. Some twenty-five years in the making, *Aak to Zumbra* simply could not have reached fruition without the dedication of editor Susan Rutter and managing editor Susannah Livingston, whose thoughtful contributions have improved every page.

John B. Hightower, President and CEO
The Mariners' Museum, August 2000

aack, aacken See **aak**

aaddaarit See **umiak-3**

Aafjord baat, Aafjordsbaad See **åfjordsbåt**

aak *Belgium/Germany/Netherlands:* Very old Germanic term for a river **barge***, inland vessel, or **boat***; associated principally with Belgian, Dutch, and German rivers. Carried mainly wine, as well as wood and general bulk cargo from the 17th into the 20th century. Local variations sometimes bore the name of the place of origin, as **Dorsten'sche Aak*** (from Dorsten), **Kölner Aak*** (from Cologne), **Neckaraak***, **Rheinaak***, **Ruhraak*** (from the Neckar, Rhein, and Ruhr Valleys, respectively). Some were disparaging terms, as **herna*** and **schouw***, while others reflected some special feature, as **beitelaak***, **stevenaak**, **klipperaak***. Built of wood; some of iron in the 19th century. Wooden vessels snub-bowed, with a flat bottom turning up to the edge of the gunwale, forming a raking triangle, square, or trapezoid. No stem or sternpost initially; then superimposed; rudder hung on sternpost. Iron **aken** had a normal stem. Sharp chines on the wooden vessels, including the bow and stern; wall-sided, rounded on the iron **barges**; flat sheer. Clipper bow and counter stern on the **stevenaak**. River vessels usually decked at ends, the open hatches covered by cambered or roof-shaped hatch covers. Normally, cabin abaft the central hatches. Large rudder with wide blade below the waterline; in the late 18th century, tiller activated a balanced rudder to the outside edge. Some employed leeboards. Small **aken** stepped one mast; the larger, two (the **zeilaak**). Set gaff sails, gaff topsails, staysails, 1-2 jibs. Early **barges** set a tall sprit mainsail and rectangular mizzen. Masts could be struck. Some towed. Reported lengths 25-43m; length-to-beam ratio to 8:1. The **Hollandse aak** (**Hollandse slechtaak** or **Hollandse zoomaak**) was built mainly in Noordbrabant. Generally in the shorter range, more rounded, greater sheer; stern more vertical than the German type. Many ran the upper reaches of the rivers and, accordingly, were usually called **bovenlanders** (see **Bovenmaase aak**). Other recorded names: **aack**, **aake(s)**, **Aakschiff**, **Achen**, **a(c)que**, **aek(en)**, **Ak**, **âk**, **ake**, **aquo**, **Haak**, **Nachen***; pl. **aacken, aken, Haaken**; **Holländisches Aak**, **Hollandsche Sch(l)echtaak**, **slechtaak**. Note also **baggeraak**, **boeieraak**, **griendaak**, **lemmeraak**, **praamaak**, **Samoreus**, **visaak**, **walenmajol**, **Wasser-Diligence**, **zalmschouw**, **Zeeuwse schouw**.

aake, aakes See **aak**

aakje See **visaak**

Aakschiff See **aak, Ruhraak**

aakschip See **visaak**

aaktjalk *Germany/Netherlands:* Hybrid vessel with the flat bow of the **aak*** and the vertical sternpost of the **tjalk***. Worked the lower Rhine River area from early in the 19th century to at least the 1960s. Late boats of iron or steel. Flat bottom curved up to form the full cut bow; soft turn of the bilges; rounded stern. Top strake has tumble home at the ends above the wale. Decked, with a long central hatch; cuddy aft. Leeboards on those that sailed; now motorized. Wide fin to the rudder. Sailing **aaktjalken** were gaff-rigged to a single mast. Crewed by a family. Length with rudder 22m, beam 4.3m, depth 2m, draft laden 1.45m.

aalaak, aalaken See **palingaak**

aalax-ulax̂tax̂ See **kayak-9**

aalboeier See **Fries Jacht**

aaledrivkvase See **drivkvase**

Aalsmeerer Punter See **Aalsmeerse punter**

Aalsmeersche grundel See **grundel**

Aalsmeersche punter See **Aalsmeerse punter**

Aalsmeerse grundel See **grundel**

Aalsmeerse punter *Netherlands, SW:* A member of the **punter*** family that serves the agricultural region around Aalsmeer, southwest of Amsterdam. Very few extant. Flat bottom, with slight fore-and-aft rocker; heels of stem and sternpost extend under the bottom for a short distance. Sharply raked, straight ends. Strong sheer; top strake's tumble home is shallower near the ends; flared sides. Short end decks; open waist. Wide rudder, especially below the waterline; downsloping tiller slots over the hooked rudderhead. One or 2 leeboards employed when sailing. Single mast, slightly aft-raking, steps against the foredeck. Sets either a spritsail or a loose-footed, boomed leg-of-mutton mainsail and a foresail to a bumkin. Reported lengths 5.5-7m; e.g., length 7m, beam 1.5m, depth 0.45m. Other recorded names: **Aalsmeerer Punter**, **Aalsmeersche punter**, **landschuit**, **weyschuit**, **weyschuytje**

aankun-ulux̂tax̂ See **kayak-9**

aardappelboeier See **boeier**

aardappelskûtsje See **skûtsje**

aardappelsnik See **snik-3**

aattring See **åttring**

ab See **ap**

Abaco dinghy, Abaco skiff See **Bahama dinghy**

'abādīje See **chalabiya**

abak *Indonesia, W:* Term for **canoe*** in the Mentawai Islands off the west coast of Sumatra. Mostly a well-shaped, round-bottomed dugout; tapered ends turn up slightly. May lack outriggers or employ a single or double outrigger, each with 2 booms lashed directly to the float. Simple canoe ca. 4m long.

Abanaki canoe See **Abenaki canoe**

'abari *Arabian Peninsula:* All-purpose craft of varied design. Some served as **ship's boats***; Omani boats fished for sharks. Popular with smugglers. Many on the south coast were 1- or 2-masted, double-ended boats; elongated straight stem; raised deck aft, light deck forward; removable weathercloths. Arabian Peninsula boats generally sewn; Somali boats nailed. Rudder inserted through metal rings on the stern. Those now serving as **ferries*** on Dubai Creek in the United Arab Emirates mainly motorized, only the smaller being rowed; rudder extends forward under the square stern. 5-15t. Spelling variants: **'abariyah, abra, 'abrah, 'abri, ebri, ibri**. Note also **baghla**.

'abariyah See **'abari**

Abenaki canoe *Canada, E/United States, NE:* Birchbark **canoe*** of the Abenaki of southern Quebec Province and northern New England; used mostly for hunting and fishing. Became popular with European sportsmen. Bow and stern either swept

Abenaki canoe

up quickly to a high peak or rose gently toward the ends; stem rounded sharply from the bottom to a straight vertical or reverse curving stem line. Bottom flat longitudinally and athwartships, with slight rocker at ends. Sides straight or slightly rounded; quick turn of the bilges. Sheathing of short lengths; ribs ca. 5cm wide; thwarts evenly spaced. Bark covering often of a single piece; usually a supplemental protective strip along the gunwale; caulked with pitch, in later years with rosin. Reported lengths 3.7-4.9m, widths 0.81-0.84m, depths 0.31-0.36m; hunting **canoes** as short as 3.1m. Other recorded names: **Abanaki canoe, Abnaki canoe, St. Francis canoe, wiguaol**. See also **wabânäki tcîmân**.

Aberdeen boat See **herring boat**

Aberystwyth beach boat *Wales, W:* **1.** Open **rowing boat*** developed in the 1890s for coastal line fishing and as a waterman's boat for summer tourists. Used along Cardigan Bay until the mid-20th century. Sharp ends but fuller at the stern to enable the boat to remain dry while nosed onto the steeply shelving beach to take on passengers. Sternpost raked initially, later vertical; stem slightly raked; well-rounded forefoot. Clinker-built; flat floors with strong turn of the bilges. Ornamental ironwork around the stern sheets on the older boats;

Aberystwyth beach boat-1

later only a wooden board or none. Mainly rowed, but those that fished set a lugsail to an aft-raking mast. Crew of 2 when herring fishing. Reported lengths 4.9-6.4m; e.g., length 5.54m, beam 1.67m, depth 0.97m.
2. Also an open, 3-masted sprit-rigged boat that worked out of Aberystwyth in the mid-19th century. Clinker

planking; long straight keel; fairly straight stem, plumb transom. The mainmast was struck when fishing. Reported lengths on keel 7-7.6m.

abiso See **advice boat**

ablâm See **belem**

Abnaki canoe See **Abenaki canoe**

Abortschiff See **Leibschiff**

ābra See **shū·ai**

abra, 'abrah, 'abri See **'abari**

abubuz *Oman, SE:* Cargo vessel, mainly from Sur; last built in the mid-1960s. Characterized by a straight stem terminating in a clipper-type bow; tip often painted black, with a white band. Square, slightly raked, and undecorated stern; upper strakes extend beyond the stern, creating an overhang; carved stern rail on some. Caulked with fiber or raw cotton, saturated with fish, coconut, or simsim oil. Flat sheer. Long rudder; tiller comes inboard below a stern railing. Now mainly motorized, but carries a slightly forward-raking mast to which a lateen sail may be raised. Crew of ca. 7. Length ca. 18m.

abwâm See **boom**

acal *Mexico, central:* Aztec term for **dugout canoe***, with 6,000-7,000 reportedly provisioning Mexico City. Flat bottom and narrow bow. Some appear to have had high, outward-flaring ends; special **canoes** had animal or bird figureheads. Held as many as 60 people, some serving as **houseboats***; small boats fished. Paddled, standing; paddles square-ended. Poled in shallow water. Reported lengths 4.3-5.6m, although some reported to have been 15m long; e.g., length 5.6m, beam 0.7m, depth 0.35m. Also reported as a 1-man reed **balsa***. Other recorded names: **acala, acal(l)e, acalli, aecaler; tahucup** in Tabasco

acala, acale, acalle, acalli See **acal**

Acapulco galleon See **galleon-3**

accident boat A **ship's boat***, especially on a passenger vessel, that is swung out on its davits for immediate lowering in case of an emergency. Usually one of the smaller boats. Other recorded names: **alarm boat, battello di emergenza** (or **soccorso**), **Berichtschaftsboot, bote de salvamento, canot de secours, embarcation de secours, emergency boat, man over boord boot** (or **m.o.b. boat**), **Notfallboot, rescue båd** (or **boat**), **reserve boat, sea boat, spare boat, stand-by boat, Unfallboot**. Note also **lifeboat**.

accommodation boat *Bangladesh/India:* A **barge***-like vessel towed by a **paddle wheel steamer** on the Hooghly, Ganges, and Brahmaputra Rivers in the early 19th century. The **steamer** and **accommodation boat** carried the cargo; officers and passengers lived aboard the **barge**; on some, meals were taken aboard the **steamer** and later aboard the **barge**. **Barge** rigged with 2 masts that carried square and spritsails. The **barge** was so connected to the **steamer** that if the latter grounded, the **barge** could be instantly detached and swung free. Length 38m, beam 6m. In some cases, the **steamer** carried the officers and fuel, while the cargo was stowed in the **accommodation** or **baggage boat** being towed behind. Both ca. 36m long. Name variant: **accommodation flat**. Note also **flat-4**.

accommodation flat See **accommodation boat**
accon **1.** Small box-like boat, a **punt***.

2. _France, W:_ Used in gathering mussels at low tide; dates from at least the 11th century. Rectangular, with flat bottom and flat vertical or flaring sides. One or both ends higher than the sides; bow generally raked. Today often of molded fiberglass or aluminum. Propelled by kneeling occupant, who pushes the craft over the mud with one foot using the mussel scoop as a paddle; sometimes towed. May set a small standing

accon-2

lugsail; mast stepped through the forward thwart; rudder shipped when sailing. Capacity ca. 300kg. Closely allied to the **galupe***. Note also **mud sled**, **ni mo chuan**, **pousse-pied**, **Schuiten**.

3. _France, Mediterranean coast/adjacent Italy:_ Open **lighter*** or **scow*** used in quiet waters and harbors to provision ships, off-load cargo, and transport workers in shipyards. Generally towed. In Roman times, ferried passengers, soldiers, and animals across rivers.

4. _West Indies:_ French term applied to an 18th-century **barge***-like craft. Often supplied fresh water to naval vessels. Large **accons** set a square sail. Reported lengths 6-9m, widths 1.2-1.5m.
Other recorded names: **accone**, **ackon**, **acom**, **aco(u)n**, **hacon**, **laccon**, **laccun**, **lacoun**. Further references: **gros bois**, **punt-1**
accone See **accon**
Achen See **aak**
Achill Island curragh _Ireland, W:_ Cloth-covered, planked boat used mainly for coastal fishing. Characterized by a double gunwale in which upper and lower gunwales are separated by wooden blocks. Thwart ends rest on lower gunwale. A pair of tholepins fit into rowlock cleats abaft each thwart. Aft seat used by steersman and as a knee rest when hauling up lobster pots. Ribs generally double for most of the boat's length. Sheers up in straight line to a pointed bow; square stern. Calico covering, applied in 3 longitudinal strips or multiple transverse strips; edges covered by narrow battens; waterproofed with tar. Crew of 3-4. Two sizes—2 or 3 rowing thwarts; 3-thwart boat averages 6.2m long, 1.9m wide, and 0.56m deep. Further reading: James Hornell, _British Coracles and Irish Curraghs,_ Pt. III (London: Society for Nautical Research, 1938), 8-12. Note also **curragh**.
Achter See **shell-2**
Achterhang See **Bock**

Achterin, Achterzille See **Salzzille**
achtriemsgiek See **shell-2**
ackon, acom See **accon**
acon See **accon**, **pousse-pied**
acone See **galupe**
acostado See **barca da arte xávega**, **enviada**
acoun See **accon**
acque See **aak**
acque de Cologne See **Kölner Aak**
ac-so-molth See **tci'k'Enō**
aḍagu See **padagu-1**
ad balam See **balam**
a death See **death galley**
adii canoe See **ahima**
Adirāmpatnam boat _India, SE:_ Lug-sailed **fishing boat*** that worked out of Adirāmpatnam on Palk

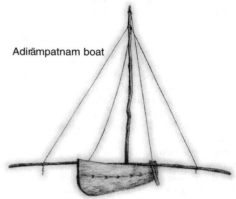

Adirāmpatnam boat

Strait. Plank-extended **dugout canoe***; planking sewn on; sides have slight tumble home; double-ended; sheer sweeps up at ends. Open except for short stern deck. Steered with a pair of narrow quarter rudders worked by foot; dropped a leeboard forward. A long (to 11.3m), drooping balance board crossed the boat just forward of the mast; made in 3 pieces, the outer pieces twisted so that the leading edge dipped slightly; stayed from the mast; 1-2 crew members sat out on the weather side. Mast stepped amidships; stayed aft, the stay looping through a hole in the hull. Length 10m, beam and depth 0.7m. Spelling variant: **Atirāmpatnam boat**. Note also **palagai kattu vattai**.
Adirondack guideboat _United States, NE:_ Light boat designed for easy portaging between lakes in the Adirondack Mountains. Used primarily for fishing, hunting, and camping from ca. 1835; fell into disuse by the turn of the century. Transom-sterned to the 1870s, then mostly sharp-ended. Recurving stem and sternpost on the **Long Lake** and **Saranac boats**; raked outward on some **Brown's Tract boats**. Marked sheer at ends; flat elliptical bottom board. Strakes beveled at top and bottom and fastened with hundreds of copper tacks to form a smooth skin. Narrow sawn ribs, set 15cm apart, strongly curved. Flat bottom board. Working boats mainly painted, pleasure boats varnished. Carrying yoke for portaging. Rowed with a

pair of long oars; standard boats had 2 rowing stations—one amidships, one at the bow. Paddled when sneaking up on a deer. Reported lengths 3.7-6.7m;

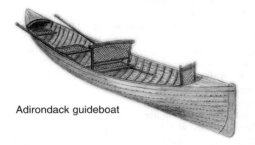

Adirondack guideboat

e.g., length 4.9m, beam 1.0m, depth 0.3m; weight to ca. 32kg; the heavier **freight boat**★ (**church boat**★, or **tote boat**) was as long as 6.38m and 1.1m wide. Other recorded names: **Adirondack skiff** (early term); familiarly **cockleshell**★, **fairy boat**, **Long-Laker**, **Saranac Laker** (or **skiff**). Further reading: Kenneth and Helen Durant, *The Adirondack Guide-Boat* (Camden, Maine: International Marine Publishing Co., 1980); Hallie E. Bond, *Boats and Boating in the Adirondacks* (Syracuse, N.Y.: Syracuse University Press and The Adirondack Museum, 1995).

Adirondack skiff See **Adirondack guide-boat**

adjong See **junk**

adjung See **galleon-3**

admiraalschip See **flagship**

admiral *Canada, E:* In the late 18th and early 19th centuries, the **admiral** was the 1st English cod-fishing vessel of the season to arrive at a Newfoundland harbor. Her captain administered justice among the later-arriving vessels to this harbor. The same applied in Nova Scotia, but here the captain had less judicial power. Name variant: **admiral ship**

admiral class *England, NW:* Class of **narrow boats**★ characterized by blunt, plumb bows, a small stem that flared at the top to merge with the gunwale, and oval steel hoops over the hold to support the tarpaulins. Last built in early 1960s.

admiral's barge See **barge-2**, **barge-11b**

admiralsbåt, Admiralsboot See **barge-2**

Admiralschiff See **flagship**

admiral ship See **admiral**

Admiralsschiff, admiral's ship See **flagship**

Admiralty cutter See **cutter-7**

adrya *Cyprus:* Hollowed out from a tree trunk. Used at least until the 18th century.

advice See **advice boat**

advice boat Small, fast boat for conveying orders and intelligence between ships, usually in a **fleet**★; might also conduct scouting missions and transfer personnel. Mainly rowed, but when sailed, rigged as a **brig**★, **cutter**★, **lugger**★, or **schooner**★; adopted motors during the 19th century. In time of war, generally armed. Term used from the late 17th century, but in classical times they were called **naves tabellariae**. In the French navy they were lightly armed coastal convoy escorts. Selected name variants: **abiso**, **advice**, **adviesboot** (**jacht, jagt, yacht**), **advieso**,

advijsvaartuig, advisbaad (**båt, boot, jacht, jagt**), **adviso, Advisschiff, avis, Avisjacht aviso, avisobrik** (**fartyg, jacht, schoener**), **Avisoschiff, avviso** (pl. **avvisi**), **barca d'avviso, barque d'avis, croiseur d'escadre, depechebaad, depeschbåt, Depeschenboot, despatch boat** (or **vessel**), **dispatch boat, éclaireur, mōsca, navis tabellaria, Postjacht, tabellaria** (**navis**). Note also **corvette-1, mouche, patache-2a**.

adviesboot See **advice boat**

adviesjacht See **advice boat, cruiser-2**

adviesjagt, advieso, adviesyacht, advijsvaartuig, advisbaad, advisbåt, advisboot, Advisjacht, advisjagt, adviso, Advisschiff See **advice boat**

aecaler See **acal**

aek See **aak, visaak**

aeken See **aak**

aekje See **visaak**

affréteur See **freighter-1**

åfjordsbåt *Norway, N:* Åfjorden was a main boat-building center for the coast to the north and south; boats built in the area were called **åfjordsbåter**. Those built in Trondheimfjorden were also called **åfjordsbåter**. Classified by the number of pairs of oars or the number of oars used, e.g., **færing**★ (2 pairs), **seksæring**★ (3 pairs), **firing**★ (4 pairs), **åttring**★ (8 pairs), **fembøring**★ (10 oars). A large boat going to the Lofoten Islands to fish would be called a **storbåt**★. Open boats, used mainly for fishing. Rowed and sailed. Name variants: **Aafjord baat, Aafjordsbaad, Åfording**. Further reading: Gunnar Eldjarn and Jon Godal, *Nordlandsbåten og Åfjordsbåten, Bind 3, Åfjordsbåten* (Lesja: A. Kjellands Forlag, 1988). Note also **grisbåt**.

åfjordsbåter See **åfjordsbåt**

åfjordsfæring See **færing-5**

åfjordsfembøring See **fembøring-1**

åfjordsseksring See **seksæring-6**

Åfording See **åfjordsbåt**

African trader See **slaver-1**

after boat See **eftirbátur**

aftrhlestr See **skipsbåt-1**

agai-ni-waiau *Solomon Islands, western Pacific:* A special ceremonial and sacred **bonito canoe** of Santa Ana Island at the south end of the archipelago; used in the initiation rites of young boys. Plank-built canoe of the **ora**★ type, with high, curved ends and washstrakes forward. A carved bird's head with a fish in its mouth tops the bow erection, a small crouching dog decorates the inward slope of the stern erection; further carvings embellish the inner ends of the washstrakes. Two bottom

agai-ni-waiau

and 2 side planks; end pieces created with separate planking. Open; sides often ornamented with inlaid shell. Paddles used for propulsion and steering. Length 6.1m, beam 0.58m, depth 0.38m. Note also **'iola**.

age See **aka-2**

aġerrābo See **agherrabo**

agetaguri-ami-bune *Japan, northern Honshu:* Net-tending boat of Aomori Prefecture. Three transverse beams project from the starboard side, 2 from the port side. Square sail set to a single mast. Crew of 9. Length 11m, beam 2.2m, depth 0.82m.

agherrabo *Morocco, S:* Berber **fishing boat★** that works from the beaches at Safi south to Cap Juby; considered an old type. Robust but supple; sharp, curved ends, sometimes with a tall, slender stemhead; keel; strong sheer. Rudder hung out with 2 pintles and gudgeons. A low cuddy abaft a small foredeck, level with the rowing thwarts, holds the net; helmsman's seat is flush with the stern gunwale, forward of which is a 2nd low cuddy for the helmsman. Exterior coated with pitch except for a wide band at the sheer line that is painted white, with a spiral decoration in color; the low decking and the bulkhead supporting the stern seat are decorated. Rowed, double-banked, to the cadence of chanting; oars worked against a single tholepin, secured by a leather thong. Occasionally a temporary sail might be created by stretching a robe between 2

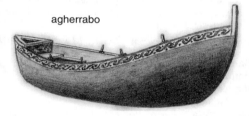

agherrabo

oars. Crew of 6 oarsmen, 1 or 2 fishermen, and the helmsman. Reported lengths 7.5-9m; e.g., length ca. 8m, beam 1.6m. Other recorded names: **aġerrābo, aguerrabo, cárabo, gharrabu, gherrabu, lgāreb**; pl. **igherruba, iguerruba**. Note also **qârĕb**.

aghribah See **grab-1**

aguerrabo See **agherrabo**

agyakruk See **kayak-4**

ahangada *Paraguay, E:* **Raft★** for ferrying passengers and goods. Bamboo poles lashed together, light transverse sticks tied on top. Poled mainly but might use a liana strung across a stream as a ferrying wire. Reported lengths 4-5m.

ahima *Ghana/Togo:* Open sailing **dugout canoe★** for working at sea with lines or a drift net (the *ali* or *adii* net). Roughly hewn in the interior and hauled to the coast to be completed. Pointed ends, strong sheer, no keel. Series of narrow thwarts lashed in; weatherboards added at the bow of the larger boats. Tarred inside and out; decorated along the sheerline, often with proverbs; occasionally fitted with leeboards. Steered with a long sweep or a paddle. Mast, stepped to bottom with long iron nails and raking to windward, is restepped when going about. Square sail, extended with 2 bamboo spars. Halyard carried to windward as a stay; tack made fast to the bow. Vang from the head and sheet from the clew lead to the stern. May be paddled, using 3-pronged paddles; now generally equipped with an outboard motor. Crew of 5-7, but some large boats take

10-14. Reported lengths 7-9m, widths 1.4-1.5m, depths 0.66-1.2m. Other recorded names: **ahlima** (in Togo); **adii canoe, ali canoe, ali lele**

ahlima See **ahima**

aiala See **aiola**

aidedeya *Papua New Guinea, SE:* Large sailing **outrigger canoe★** of the Amphlett Group, lying between the D'Entrecasteaux and Trobriand Islands. Transports local produce and pottery. Dugout hull raised with 2-3 strakes, planked clinker-fashion; bow enclosed by a breakwater. Vertical prow; bow and breakwater carved and painted. Twelve booms (attached with crossed sticks) extend to the heavy float. A platform of thin rods is constructed across the booms; when heavy loads of pottery carried, another platform is built out on the lee side. Steered with a large oar thrust through the platform near the stern; a smaller oar works in a fulcrum on the lee side. Single forward-raking mast stepped well forward, the forked end held against the 3rd boom by a mast shore. Two stays—one to bow of the float, the other to the weather end of the 7th boom. Triangular lateen-type pandanus-leaf sail; boomed at the bottom. Also paddled or rowed. Crew of 4. Reported lengths overall 4.5-8m. Name variant: **oga**. Further reading: P. K. Lauer, "Sailing with the Amphlett Islanders," *Journal of the Polynesian Society* (December 1970), 381-398.

aiola *Portugal, south-central coast:* Small, beamy boat used in octopus fishing at Sesimbra. Wide transom stern; tall stemhead; short foredeck. Rowed by single occupant. Length overall 3.9m, beam 1.52m. Spelling variant: **aiala**. Note also **canoa da picada**.

aissaugue See **palangrier**

aixàvega See **jábega**

'aiyassa See **gaiassa**

aiyebu *Papua New Guinea, SE:* A **dugout canoe★** of the D'Entrecasteaux Islands that is stabilized by an outrigger. The float, as long as the hull, is connected by groupings of 3-5 booms at each end and sometimes a central boom; undercrossed connectives used at the float end; sticks laid atop the booms form a platform to carry nets, fishtraps, food, etc. Hull has similar elongated ends and tumble home sides. With favorable winds sets a long rectangular sail of woven coconut leaves; supported by a thin pole that passes through one side of the sail. Carries up to 8 people.

ajong See **junk**

ak 1. *Fiji Islands, central Pacific:* At Rotuma Island, north of the main group, the generic term for a **boat★**.
2. *Papua New Guinea, NE:* Term for **canoe★** at Molot in the eastern Bismarck Archipelago. Most canoes of the area use a single outrigger.
See also **aak, ok**.

aka 1. *Kiribati (Gilbert) Islands, central Pacific:* Term, used in combined form, signifies **canoe★**, including legendary **canoes** such as **aka-aka** and **aka-bu-toatoa**.
2. *Papua New Guinea, Bismarck Archipelago:* Generic term for a **boat★** in the Duke of York Islands. The

indigenous **canoes** of the area employ a single outrigger. Spelling variant: **age**

3. *Vanuatu (New Hebrides), western Pacific:* Generic term for **canoe** on several islands in the archipelago. On Mota in the Banks group, an **aka** is a single-**outrigger canoe**★. Dugout hull; sharp, overhanging ends, which are planked over. Low washstrakes and weatherboards sewn on amidships, onto which a platform is laid with an open cockpit-type area. Three straight booms, attached with undercrossed sticks, extend to a long, flat float. Steered with a long oar, using a vertical fulcrum piece attached to the stern. Sail, forming a wide "V," set up amidships; horizontal cloths; spars along each side. Name variant: **na-tiaka**. Note also **eka-3, ok**.

aka-aka See **aka-1**

akaala See **äkälla**

aka-bu-toatoa See **aka-1**

akada hodi See **akada hody**

akada hody *India, W:* Used for shooting shore seines on the Konkan and Malabar coasts. May be either a **dugout canoe**★ with low vertical sides or a plank-built boat with 3 planks each on the sides and bottom. Lengths 5-6m. Name variants: **akada hodi, padavu**★ (on Malabar Coast). Note also **hody, padagu**.

äkälla *Australia, NE:* Aboriginal **dugout canoe**★ of the northeast coast of Queensland; used primarily to hunt turtles, dugongs, and eggs of sea birds and turtles. Bow and stern raked, especially the stern, which has a shelf-like overhang; rounded forefoot.

äkälla

Washboard lashed to the outside of each gunwale; joint caulked with rolled pads of tea-tree bark. Single outrigger, generally to starboard; 4-7 pairs of sticks pass through the washboard to the opposite side of the boat; these booms are secured one above the other to 2 pegs inserted into the float; float ca. 3.66m long and set ca. 61cm from the hull. Staging formed by booms, houses, harpoons, and spears. Reported hull lengths 4.9-5.8m, widths 0.41-0.56m. Name variant: **akaala**

äkatos See **launch**

ake See **aak**

'ākea See **wa'a kaulua**

aken See **aak**

akit See **rakit**

aklāk See **kelek**

aktarma *Greece/Turkey:* Type of **trechandiri**★ used by sponge divers, especially in the Dodecanese Islands off the southwest Turkish coast. Heavy forward, the bow higher than the stern. Note also **sponge boat-2**.

a kuba See **oánga**

alaalafaga See **va'a alo**

alagulot See **kayak-9**

alamana 1. *Bulgaria:* **Fishing boat**★ with a mast at the bow on which the captain stands to locate schools of fish, especially mackerel, which stir phosphorescence at night. Work in pairs with a long net between. High, curved, sharp ends; lightly built; decked at stern. May be decorated at the ends and along the sides. Mainly rowed, with 4 pairs of oars. Sometimes sets a small sail. Pair of boats requires 19 men. Reported lengths 12-13.7m; e.g., length 12m, beam 2m. Spelling variants: **alamanata**; pl. **alamani**

2. *Turkey:* **a.** Double-ended **fishing boat** that works out of the Black and Marmara Seas. Deep hull; curved, raked ends; sheer sweeps up at the bow. Ends decked. In the Black Sea the fishing master stands on a pole at the bow and sights schools of bonito. Mainly rowed, employing 3-6 pairs of oars; in the Black Sea rowed double-banked; in the Sea of Marmara, single-banked. In the Istanbul area, auxiliary sails may be used. Reported lengths 9-12m. Other recorded names: **alamana kaighi, alamena qaighy, alamona**; pl. **alamanalar**. Note also **balıkçı kayığı**. **b.** Also reported as a **coaster**★ with a straight raked stem, less-raked square stern, strong sheer, outboard rudder with tiller. Set a lateen sail and a large jib to a rising bowsprit. Crew of 20. Length ca. 15m.

alamana kaighi, alamanalar See **alamana-2**

alamanata, alamani See **alamana-1**

alamena qaïghy, alamona See **alamana-2**

ålandsgaleas See **galeas-1**

ålandsskuta *Gulf of Bothnia, S:* Refers to 3 types of craft that sailed regularly between the Finnish Ahvenanmaa (Åland Islands) and Stockholm—the **galeas**★, **jakt**★, and **segelsump**★.

ålandssnipa See **snipa**

Ålands sumpar See **segelsump**

alarm boat See **accident boat**

Alaska dory See **dory-5**

Alaskan canoe See **northern-style canoe**

alax-uluẍtaẍ See **kayak-9**

Albemarle Sound shad boat See **North Carolina shad boat**

Albemarle Sound skiff See **sharpie-4**

albuferenc *Spain, E:* Transports local produce on Albufera de Valencia, a lagoon south of Valencia. Double-ended; bold sheer; curving stem with raised stemhead; flat bottom. Cambered decks at bow and stern; side decks. Large lateen sail set to stout, forward-raking mast. Yard hung with double halyard rove through sheaves set in masthead. No standing rigging. Poled in shallows; may use a

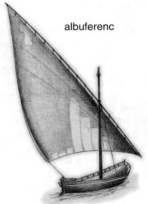

albuferenc

motor in deeper areas. Reported lengths 7.6-9.1m; shallow draft. Other recorded names: **albuferench, alijador del lago**

albuferench See **albuferenc**
Aldeburgh beach boat See **beach punt-1**
Aldeburgh smack See **cod smack-1**
Aldeburgh sprat boat See **beach punt-1**
al''dija See **ládija**
åledrivkvase See **drivkvase**
alège See **allège**
aleggio See **lighter**
alèuge See **allège**
Algonkin canoe *Canada, E:* Old-style birchbark **canoe★** of the Algonkin tribes of the Ottawa River basin. High ends, narrow bottom, flaring sides; sharp ends at the cutwater. Flat sheer amidships, rising toward ends, then almost vertical at the ends. Stem pieces rounded up from the bottom, recurved slightly toward the top, and then usually rounded inboard sharply so that stem turned downward to the gunwale cap; in some areas the gunwale cap swept up smoothly to a vertical stem piece. Crooked stick created the high flattened or recurved tops to the stem pieces; notched headboard lashed and tenoned to the end pieces to form a unit.

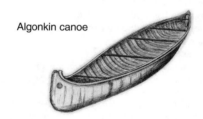

Algonkin canoe

Bark covering secured to gunwales with group lashings, the thong carried from group to group with a long stitch. Reported lengths 3.65-4.88m; e.g., length 4m, beam 0.8m, depth 0.29m. Name variant: **wigwass tciman**. Further reading: E. T. Adney and H. I. Chapelle, *The Bark Canoes and Skin Boats of North America* (Washington, D.C.: Smithsonian Institution, 1964), 113-122. See also **wabânäki tcîmân**.
Algonquin canoe See **wabânäki tcîmân**
'alia *Samoa, central Pacific:* Double **canoe★** that strongly resembled the Tongan **kalia★** and the Fijian **drua★**. Frequently used by raiding parties in the 19th century. Hulls were planked up from a keel; end pieces were solid. Hulls of different lengths, with elongated pointed ends on the shorter hull and vertical ends on the main hull. Stout crosspieces secured the 2 hulls; a platform, on which a house was usually erected, crossed the hulls. A boomed lateen-type sail was set from the main hull. Forward-raking mast stayed fore and aft; stays slacked off and the mast inclined to the opposite end when going about. Characteristically stepped the yard into a hole in the "bow" end. Now built of marine plywood and equipped with an outboard motor. Reported lengths 5.8-8.5m.
alibbo, alibo See **lighter-1**
ali canoe See **ahima**
alijador See **lighter-l**
alijador del lago See **albuferenc**

ali lele See **ahima**
alis-alis *Indonesia, central:* Plank-built boat used for fishing, transporting the catch to market, and carrying cargo and passengers. Found mainly along part of the north coast of eastern Java, especially in Madura Strait. On Madura, **alis-alis** is the general term for a **boat★**. Characteristically, keel extends beyond the raked ends, which terminate in flat Y- or

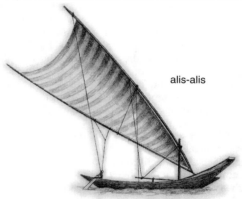

alis-alis

T-shaped surfaces. Framing sparse; thwarts (which project through the hull) provide the main strengthening; bottom flat; sheer strong. Some highly decorated, especially on the flat ends. Loosely decked; may have a peaked deckhouse of matting; small boats open. Employs a heavy quarter rudder; double outriggers common in the 19th century. Most have 2 stubby masts, stepped in forward third of the boat, to which triangular sails are hung from the forward part of the yard; apex tacked down; lightly boomed at the foot. Position of the yard may be regulated by a line to an outrigger boom. Madura boats generally single-masted. Also paddled. Reported lengths 5-12m; e.g., length 9m, beam 2.5m, depth 0.8m. Other recorded names: **alis-2, lis-alis** (on Madura), **perahu** (or **prahoe**) **alis-alis**
alis-2 See **alis-alis**
aljibe *Spain:* A boat fitted with tanks to carry fresh water or fuel to ships at anchor. Note also **gabarrón, tank boat, water boat.**
alleague See **allège**
alleague d'Arles See **allège d'Arles**
allèche See **allège**
allège French term for a **lighter★**, especially one used to transfer cargo at ports lacking docking facilities and, in river mouths, to receive discharged cargo and ballast from oceangoing ships so that they might proceed upriver. Term dates at least to the 15th century. Generally towed. Large sailing **allèges** also served as **coasters★**, and some served as **ship's boats★** on river craft. Other recorded names: **alè(u)ge, alleauge, allèche, alleggio, allegium, allegre, alleige, ballast boat, barca d'allegio, bateau (d') allège, embarcación de alijo, lèuge.** Note also **allège d'Arles, ballast barge, chaland.** Further reference: **train de bateaux**
allège d'amarrage See **anchor hoy**

allège d'Arles *France, S:* Clipper-bowed vessel of the Rhône River. Dates from at least the 17th century. During the 18th and early 19th centuries, transported stone from Arles, lumber and hay along the lower river and adjacent Mediterranean coast, and munitions to naval vessels at Toulon. Evolved considerably during the period. Primarily sharp-ended; flat bottom, longitudinally planked; small plank keel. High sheer; sides flare, then have tumble home. Recurved stem with high head; bulwarks carried beyond the sharp stern; raked sternpost. Set a large lateen mainsail, small square topsail, and boomed-out headsail that was generally not tacked to the bowsprit. Those of the late 17th century set 2 lateen sails; foremast in the bow, raking forward. In addition to the supporting gammon knee, a triangular lattice framework ran out on the bowsprit from the forward part of the bow. Dimensions (1840): length 23.2m, beam 7.33m, depth 2.43m; shallow draft. Spelling variant: **alleague d'Arles**

alleggio See **allège, lighter-1**

Alleghany skiff See **Allegheny skiff**

Allegheny skiff *United States, north-central:* Carried 8-12t of cargo on the Allegheny River to Pittsburgh and into the Ohio River until ca. 1915. Those used in Illinois trade and on the upper Mississippi and Missouri Rivers might be called **Mackinaw skiffs**. Flat bottom; covered; steered with a long sweep; shallow draft. Spelling variant: **Alleghany skiff**

allegium, allegre, alleige See **allège**

allibo, allievo See **lighter-1**

almaadia, almaadya See **almady**

almache See **mashua-3**

almade, almadi See **almady**

almadia 1. *Mozambique, N:* General term applied to all small boats. One type, in the Matibane Bay area, engages in net fishing. U- or V-shaped cross section; alternating frames support sides, but are not secured to the false keelson; no keel. Ends similar, flattened and raked, each with a short horizontal extension. Six thwarts on which the crew of 12 sit to paddle; steered with a paddle. Also poled, and at times sets a small lateen sail to a mast stepped about a third in from the bow. Reported lengths 6-7m; e.g., length 7m, beam 0.8m, depth 0.6m; shallow draft. Spelling variant: **almodia**

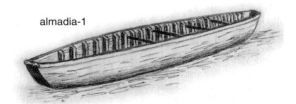

almadia-1

2. *Switzerland:* On Lake of Lucerne, an **almadia** was used for fishing. This **dugout canoe★** was sometimes known by its early term, **monòssilo**.
See also **almady, catur-1, ekem.**

almadie See **almady, catur-1**

al-ma 'dīya See **almady**

almady 1. Word applied by early explorers to a **canoe★**, usually a large **dugout canoe★**. Term found in literature in West Africa, India, and Latin America. Some in Africa, especially in Guinea, were square-sterned bark **canoes** ca. 7.3m long and 2.1m wide; others were dugouts that might carry as many as 50 people. The **almady** of Calicut on the Indian Malabar Coast had sewn-on planks to raise the sides; also called a **catur★**. Note also **canoa, ekem, maddia.**

2. Word also described a **raft★**, probably from the Arabic **al-ma'dia.** Used to ferry people and merchandise, but some were **timber rafts★** floated downstream. Other recorded names: **almaadia, almaadya, almade, almadi, almadía, almadie, al-ma 'dīya, almadye, almaid(i)a, almedya, almodia, armadia, aumedia, navata, negro boat**

almadye, almaida, almaidia See **almady**

al-mashueh See **mashua-3**

almedya See **almady**

almodia See **almadia, almady**

aloet See **alut**

alo folafolau See **te-puke**

alogocharavo, alogokharavo See **horse carrier**

aloi, alôt djoewééng, alôt soĕlôk See **alut**

Alsterschute See **Schute-1**

Altenwerder Eiskahn See **Eiskahn**

Altenwerder Ewer See **Ewer**

alud See **alut**

alūdiya See **ládija**

alut *Indonesia, Kalimantan (Borneo)/East Malaysia:* Plank-extended **dugout canoe★** used by several ethnic groups in the border area between the 2 countries. Called **alut** (or **alôt soĕlôk**) by the Kenyah, **aloi** by the Bukutan Dayak, **alud** by the Dusun and the Balud-Opie, **arud** by the Land Dayak, and **aruk** or **harok** by the Kayan. Bottom sweeps up at each end to form a long overhang; sharp ends; fairly flat floors. Added strake may be lashed on with rotan, and seam caulked with the center rib of a palm. A wide plank may further extend the bow. Some groups add a bark weathercloth to the sides and bow when running rapids. The Dusun carve residual blocks into the sides to support the seats (2 bamboo poles with lacings between) and at times raise an awning and the weathercloth. Some that have a cloverleaf decoration at the ends are called **alôt djoewééng** by the Kenyans. A popular craft, they are procured by coastal Malay and Chinese traders, who add an outboard motor. Reported lengths 3-46m; the latter size sometimes employs 100 men, paddling 2 abreast; the Kayan call a smaller **canoe**, with 20 paddlers, a **temoi**. Other recorded names: **aloet, arut.** Note also **jalor-3.**

alut

alvarenga 1. Portuguese generic term for a **barge★** or **lighter★.**

2. *Brazil, E:* Used particularly at Recife, Salvador, and Rio de Janeiro (where it is called **saveiro★**) for ship-to-shore cargo transfer. Solidly constructed; flat to

alvarenga-2

moderate sheer; some double-ended, others square-sterned; often a deep keel aft; frequently ship a large triangular rudder. May be open or have a covered hold; early types had a slanting wooden roof on one side and a removable tarpaulin on the other side. Generally poled, by 2 men; sometimes set a gaff sail to an aft-raking mast stepped well forward; occasionally seen with a lateen sail. Now mostly towed. Reported lengths 10-20m, widths 4.4-5.7m, depth ca. 1.5m. Name variant: **batelão**

älvbåt *Sweden, central and N:* Designation for a type of river (*älv*) boat that traverses the quieter rivers. Smooth-skinned, with 3-4 strakes, the top strake filling in the midship sheer and phasing out before the ends. Sharp ends; stem and sternpost curved or raking; may have a stemband. Wide keelson; rounded, flaring sides; frames scarfed on the bottom. Rowing benches set low, and raised flooring may be placed at the stern. Employs 1-3 pairs of oarlocks; in some areas, the oarlock is an inverted crescent with a circle cut out on the top; elsewhere, a natural crook is used. Poled upstream. When conditions suitable, may set a small spritsail and be steered with a paddle. Reported lengths 6.1-9.7m; length to breadth ca. 4:1. Name variant: **Lima-båt** (in west-central Sweden). Note also **elvebåt**.

alzacaballo See **pontoon-1**

ama **1.** *Iraq, S:* Babylonian term for a **raft★** constructed of reeds. Spelling variant: **amû**

2. *United States, SW:* **Áma** is used by the Yavapai Native Americans of central Arizona for a **boat★** or **canoe★**.
See also **wa'a kaulua, waka ama**.

ama-bune See **ami-bune**

amatasi **1.** *Samoa, central Pacific:* Deep-sea fishing and traveling **canoe★** that became extinct toward the mid-19th century. Multipiece strakes added to keel piece, sewn so that stitching showed only on the inside; U-shaped in cross section; hull deepest near the bow. Raked concave stem, with gripe at forefoot; stern elongated, terminating in a small notched piece. Ends decked; tops decorated with a line of cowrie shells. Multiple outrigger booms lashed across the gunwales; long float, extended farther forward than aft; float and booms attached by divergent stanchions and lashings. Balance board opposite outrigger. Steered with a paddle. Single forward-raking mast stepped on the bottom and lashed to a thwart. Triangular mat sail; apex tacked either to bow or stern; boomed at foot, with streamers.

Reported lengths 15-30m. The term is also applied to toy **canoes**. Name variant: **pirogue de voyage**

2. *Tuvalu (Ellice) Islands, western Pacific:* Large, single-outrigger traveling **canoe**; extinct. Built with short planks sewn together onto a dugout base. Sharp ends; bottom rounded in cross section and longitudinally. Decked at ends. Three straight booms extended to the float, each attached with 2 pairs of divergent stanchions; light platform across the booms. Balance board extended out the side opposite the outrigger. Short mast stepped in thwart, raking forward. Set a triangular sail, apex tacked just abaft the foredeck; boomed at foot. Reported to have carried 100 people.

amatiatia *New Zealand:* **1.** Maori term for a **canoe★** with an outrigger, which was also called *amatiatia*.

2. The word also described a **raft★** with an outrigger that was used on the east coast of North Island. Main component (called **mokihi★**) composed of 4-6 poles of a very buoyant wood, laid side-by-side, the narrower ends forward; pinned with trunnels; 2nd layer lashed on top. The outrigger part similarly made, but with fewer poles. Set ca. 90-120cm apart and joined by 3 transverse booms. Platform might be laid across the booms for cargo. Supported 2 people.

ambarcaţiune See **boat-1**

américain *West Indies:* Term sometimes applied in the French-speaking islands to a vessel rigged as a **fore-and-aft schooner** (see **schooner**), lacking a square topsail on the foremast. Spelling variant: **méricain**

américaine See **fisherman-1**

American shooting yacht See **scow-11a**

Amesbury dory See **Banks dory**

Amesbury dory-skiff, Amesbury skiff See **dory-skiff**

ami-bune *Japan:* A boat that tends fish nets (*ami*). Most open; crew of 6 on some. Other recorded names: **ama-bune, net boat★**

amiraalschip, amiral See **flagship**

amiral filikası See **barge-2**

amiraljica See **flagship**

amiralsbåt See **barge-2**

amiralskepp, ammiraglia See **flagship**

Amoy fisher *China, E:* Especially seaworthy **fishing boat★** that works out of the Xiamen (Amoy) area with nets. Strong sheer terminated in a bluff flat bow and an oval transom; ends raked sharply. Flat bottom, transversely planked; small protective keel. Stern wings support a hand windlass for the retractable rudder; some have a small gallery. Three conspicuous wales. Decked; gaps in bulwarks abaft the mainmast provide an opening for launching the 8-10 bamboo **rafts** used in fishing (see **zhu pai**). Below decks divided into 12 compartments for supplies and living quarters. Small type lacks deckhouse; has large hatch. Hull painted white, with colored bulwarks; yin and yang symbol on the bow transom; stern transom gaily painted; oculi near the bows. Holes in the sides permit flooding of 2 compartments for the catch. Generally 3-masted; small foremast and mainmast raked forward; mizzen stepped on the starboard quarter. Until World War I, set flat-headed split-bamboo sails with a straight leech; thereafter mainsail peaked and mizzen square-headed, both of brown cloth; foresail remained a mat sail. Some single-masted. Now motorized. Crew of 5-7, plus the crews for the **zhu pai**. Reported lengths 12-21m; e.g., length overall 16.8m, beam 5.2m, depth 1.8m. Other recorded names: **Amoy junk, bai di chuan, Hsiamen chuan, pai-tai ch'uan, pe-ti tch'ouan, white-bottomed boat, Xiamen chuan.** Note also **pai ti chuan.**

Amoy junk See **Amoy fisher, Fukien trader**
'Ampton boat, 'Ampton flat See **wharf boat**
Amsterdamer Samoreus See **Samoreus**
Amsterdamsche dekschuit, Amsterdamsche zolder-schuit See **dekschuit**
amû See **ama-1**
anak bedar *Peninsular Malaysia:* Small version of the cargo **bedar★**. Works along the east coast, serving principally as a **ferryboat★**, but also used for estuary fishing. Raked stem extends forward in duck-bill projection, rounded forefoot; raked stern. Steered with a rudder. Those used for fishing have spar rests for the lowered mast and yard. Sets standing lugsail from a mast stepped about a third of the distance in from the bow. About 8.5m long. Name variant: **ano' bedar**

anak bedar

anan *Chile, S:* Bark **canoe★** of the Yahgan of southern Tierra del Fuego; used for fishing and sealing until the end of the 19th century. Three to 5 large slabs of ever-green beech bark, softened by water, were sewn together with thin strips of whalebone or shredded saplings to form a cigar-shaped **canoe**. Slender upturned ends tied with whalebone or braced by a thong running back to the nearest thwart. Smooth overhang from the bottom; some had 2 short exten-sions at the bow. Caulked with mixture of mud and grass, wild celery, or moss, but leaked badly. Ribs of split winters-bark were held in position by the gun-wales, which were sewn on; 5 or 6 thwarts inserted or fastened across the gunwales. Layer of bark on the bottom; sod fireplace set in the bottom. Paddles (2-4) had long, slender blades attached to a short, round loom; occasionally set a crude sealskin sail. Reported lengths 4-6.7m, widths 0.7-1.2m, depth ca. 0.6m. Other recorded names: **annan, auchtagorun anèn,**

e(e)n-anan or **een-anèn** (winter **canoe**); the better canoe was the **hacua** or **kakua anèn** (spring or sum-mer **canoe**); **canoa de corteza; dalca★**. Further read-ing: Jean-Pierre Caille, "Dans les Canaux de Patagonie," *Chasse-Marée* 42 (1989), 40-41; Carlos-Pedro Vairo, "Reconstitution d'un Canot Fuegien à Ushuaia," ibid., 46-47.

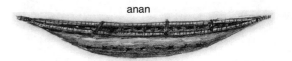

anan

anatkuat See **kayak-11**
anchor boat 1. One of a pair of **rowing boats★** that alternately dropped an anchor ahead on a long warp from a river vessel, which then kedged itself upstream. Note also **horse-machine boat**.
2. *United States, central:* Name given to a small boat at Waukegan on the southwestern shore of Lake Michigan. Used to remove fish from nets and with-draw the stakes supporting the nets.
Further reference: **anchor hoy**
anchor hoy A heavily constructed, beamy boat that raised or transported anchors and anchor chains and set harbor moorings. Usually equipped with suitable der-rick or special davits and capstans. Those that carried fresh water to ships had tanks below decks. Early boats, transporting anchors, were towed by **rowboats★** to off-lying ships that had lost theirs. Some **sloop★**-rigged. Other recorded names: **allège d'amarrage, anchor boat★, Ankerleichter, Ankerpünte, barca per salpare, bateau corps-mort, chain boat** (or **lighter**), **mooring boat** (**hulk** or **lighter**), **peata da ormeggio, pontone a salpare, pontone d'ormeggio, pontone salpa-ancore, ponton mouilleur, Vertäuboot, Vertäuungsprahm**. Note also **lancione-2**.
Anderhalbmaster, anderhalfmaster See **ketch**
Angelboot, Angelfischerboot See **hooker-2**
Angelfischereifahrzeug See **tuna boat**
Angelkahn, Angelkähne See **barkas-3**
Angelleinfahrzeug See **longliner-1**
angiak See **angyaq**
angiapik See **baidara**
angiaq See **angyaq**
an·giar· See **umiak-1**
angioq See **angyaq**
äng-oru See **äng-oruwa**
äng-oruwa *Sri Lanka, S:* Rowing **canoe★** used to catch bait (**äng**) with a net and to catch lobsters. Special modification made to the more common **oruwa★**. Forward on the outrigger (port) side a short rail runs parallel to the hull to the forward outrigger boom and aft to a crossbeam lashed athwartships; a 2nd rail par-allels the starboard side, lashed forward to the cross-beam and aft to the outboard extension of the after boom. Loops on the rails secure the oars. Outrigger booms and crossbeam lashed to rods that extend out through the side planking. Plank depth varies, some-times being equal to that of the dugout hull. Generally 2 slender oars; 2 pieces fixed to the loom where it is

inserted through the loop. May erect a stick with a hook on which to hang an oil lamp. Steered with a short paddle. Crew of 3 generally, 4-5 on larger **canoes**. Average length 7m, beam 0.6m, depth 0.8m. Other recorded names: pl. **äng-oru**; **pokrissa** (lobster)-**oruwa**

angul See **angula**

angula *Sri Lanka:* Sinhala term for a double **canoe** that ferries passengers across streams and carries produce downriver. Two **dugout canoes***, generally flat-bottomed, secured by transverse beams with a platform laid across them. Paddled or poled. Size varies with importance of the crossing; reported lengths 7.6-9.1m; e.g., length 8.5m, combined width 2.6m. Other recorded names: **anjeela**, **saṁghāṭi** (Pali), **sangadam*** (Tamil), **saṅghāṭa*** (Sanskrit); pl. **angul**. Note also **padda boat**.

angyak See **angyaq**

angyapiget, angyapik See **umiak-4**

angyaq *Alaska, W:* Siberian Yupik (or Yuit) term on St. Lawrence Island for a **boat*** in general, while a **skin boat*** is called **angyapik** (see **umiak-4**). Spelling variants: **angiak, angiaq, angioq, angyak, anijak, anijuk**; pl. **angyat**

angyat See **angyaq**

Anha See **jangada-4**

anijak, anijuk See **angyaq**

anime perse See **gozzo**

anjeela See **angula**

Ankerleichter See **anchor hoy**

Ankermutzen See **Mutzen-3**

Ankernachen See **Rheinfloss**

Ankerpünte See **anchor hoy**

ankerschip *Belgium, NW:* Small 15th-century Flemish **fishing boat***, mainly from Antwerp. Its fishing gear was anchored in the river. The **ankerschuit** was probably similar but smaller.

ankerschuit See **ankerschip**

ankun-ulux̂tax̂ See **kayak-9**

Anlegeponton See **dummy barge-1**

annan See **anan**

Annan whammel-net boat See **whammel boat**

annexe *France:* A small, sturdy boat annexed to a larger vessel; generally too large to be carried on board, so is towed. May be used by fishermen working lobster pots and inshore nets; some serve as training craft for naval cadets. Frequently used with a 2nd **annexe** by a **sardinier*** to shoot the nets; on cod grounds, an **annexe** also fishes some distance from the **mother ship***. Mainly rowed, single-banked, by 2 men toward the bow, a 3rd manning a scull at the stern. When sailed, sets a gaff, lug-, or spritsail. Motors now common. Reported lengths 2.4-6.9m; e.g., length 3.5m, beam 1.5m. Other recorded names: **canot***, **canot annexe**. See also **tender**.

annisaq See **umiak-1**

ano' bedar See **anak bedar**

ansjovisjol See **Staverse jol**

antàn See **sandón**

Antigua sloop See **Tortola sloop**

antillais Term given to sailing ships that worked between French ports and the Antilles until World War I. Most were **barks***, **brigs***, **brigantines***, and **schooners***.

Antung trader See **da hong chuan**

Antwerpse sloep *Belgium:* **Cutter***-rigged **fishing boat*** that worked out of Antwerp, fishing for herring and cod on the North Sea's Dogger Bank and off Iceland.

Antwerpse sloep

Last built in 1895. Carvel-planked with a heavy, slightly curved stem; flat stern; round bilges; vertical sides; straight keel. Decked; live well amidships. Large, loose-footed, boomed gaff mainsail; gaff topsail; staysail; and jib to a long running bowsprit. Toward the end of the century, some set a small lug mizzen. Crew of 11-14 when fishing for cod and herring and 6-8 for other fishing. Length 19.5m, beam 6m, depth 3.58m; 30-120t, the larger **schooner***-rigged. Note also **sloep**.

ao tsêng See **ao zeng**

ao'txs See **West Coast canoe**

ao zeng *China, SE:* **Fishing boat*** of the Shantou (Swatow) area that employed a dip net hung from a movable bowsprit-like projection. Crew of 4. Length 7.6m, beam 2.6m. Spelling variants: **ao tsêng, o tsang**

ap *India, Bay of Bengal:* Expanded **dugout canoes*** of Car Nicobar in the northern Nicobar Islands that were purchased from Chowra islanders in the central Nicobars, where they are called **düe***. The Car Nicobar islanders race a particularly long variety, using 18-20

ap

paddlers. Long single-outrigger float attached by 2 booms; multiple crossed-stick attachments pass beneath each boom. Numerous thwarts sit atop the gunwales, capped by longitudinal pieces, the assemblage providing a platform for cargo. Bow might turn up higher than stern and, on occasion, was ornamented with feathers and flags. One to 4 rectangular palm lugsails were set to short masts of about equal height; later, cloth lateen-type sails used. Lancet-shaped paddle blades. Reported lengths 12-30m; e.g., length 13m, beam and depth 0.9m. Spelling variants: **ab, app**

Apol-bolle See **bol-2**

app See **ap**

Appledore gravel barge See **gravel barge**

ap-t'eang See **ya ze chuan**

'aqaba See **harrâqa**

aqrab See **qārib**

aque See **aak**

aquillado See **quillat**

aquo See **aak**

Aran Islands canoe *Ireland, NW:* **Curragh★** of the Aran Islanders; used for sea fishing, kelp gathering, and lightering. Formerly, hides covered the withe framework; now 1-2 layers of tarred canvas cover a lath frame. Swept-up bow ends in a point; low, square stern; straight and nearly parallel sides. Framework composed of upper and lower gunwales strung with the thwarts and steadied by knees; closely spaced longitudinal laths form the rounded bottom. Rowed single-banked, with 2-4 pairs of oars; a triangular board attached to the loom fits over the tholepin. Helmsman works a steering oar against stern tholepins. Movable ballast of beach sand or boulders. Also sailed, using a low, wide lugsail, hoisted to a short, unstayed mast. Outboard motor now used on long trips. Lengths

Aran Islands canoe

range from 2-man boats of 4.5-4.9m to 4-man boats of 6.7-7.6m; width 0.9-1.1m; depth 66-68cm. Name variant: **Aran Islands curragh**. Further reading: James Hornell, *British Coracles and Irish Curraghs*, Pt. III (London: Society for Nautical Research, 1938), 16-23.

Aran Islands curragh See **Aran Islands canoe**

Arbeitboot, Arbeitsbeiboot See **Arbeitsboot**

Arbeitsboot *Germany:* **1.** Term for a general-purpose boat, especially for harbor work—moving other craft, laying out anchors, cleaning hulls, etc. Usually a sturdy boat, with a flat bottom and wide transom. Other recorded names: **Arbeitboot, Arbeitsbeiboot**

2. The **Arbeitsboot** of the lower Weser River in northwestern Germany is a small, slender boat, with low sheer, rising floors, and transom stern.

arbor-bot See **lambo-1**

ar c'hanot See **sardinier breton**

Archerskjøite, Archerskøyte See **losbåt-2**

arégolou See **coracle-4**

arendalspram See **pram-6a**

arendalssjægte, arendalssjekte See **sjekte**

arendalsskøyte See **skøyte-3**

Arendal yol See **Norway yawl-1**

aragagua See **argosy**

argīlī See **coracle-4**

argose, argosea, argosey, argosies See **argosy**

argosy Large, burdensome 16th- and 17th-century **merchantman★** considered to have been either a **carrack★** or a **galleon★**. Built mainly at Ragusa (now Dubrovnik) on the Dalmatian coast, but frequently used by Venetian merchants. Many traded with England, where the term **argosy** was a corruption of Ragusa, their place of origin. Other recorded names: **argagua, argose(a), argosey, argozee, argozie, argusa, arguze, ragosie, ragusa, ragusce, ragusea, ragusy(e), rhaguse**; pl. **argosies**

argozee, argozie, argusa, arguze See **argosy**

arigōlu See **coracle-4**

ark **1.** General term for a large, cumbersome vessel, usually enclosed. May also describe a **houseboat★** used for commercial purposes. Note also **Arke**.

2. *Canada:* **a.** Special flat-bottomed **arks** carried flour on the Grand River from Galt to Dunnville in southern Ontario in the 1830s. Poled by 6-7 men. Length 24.4m, width 4.9m; shallow draft. Name variant: **Shade's ark**. **b.** In southwestern British Columbia, an experimental **ark** served as a floating cannery in the latter half of the 19th century. Equipped with an engine and mainsail and jib. Designed to accompany the fishing **fleets★**. Unsuccessful in that activity, partly because of poor maneuverability, but later freighted after a 2nd engine was added, especially for carrying bricks. Two-story building had the canning equipment on the lower floor and accommodations above. Length 43m, beam 10m.

3. *United States, NE:* In Connecticut oystering areas, the **ark** was a **scow★** or other **hulk★** on which a house had been built, serving as a work area and storehouse. Other recorded names: **scow, scow house**

4. *United States, E:* **a.** A roughly built **barge★**-like craft that carried coal and general merchandise on the Lehigh, Delaware, and Susquehanna Rivers in the early 19th century. Run singly or strung together to make a flexible train as long as 55m. Originally a rectangular box of heavy planking spiked together, the lead boat of a train having a sharp bow. Later boats were sharp at each end. Decked; a house might be built amidships. Steered with a long oar at each end. Sold for lumber after being unloaded. As many as 4 **arks** hitched together could be handled by one man on the Lehigh. Reported lengths 6.1-7.6m, widths 4.9-5.5m. **b.** In the 1760s, **arks** on the Susquehanna and Delaware Rivers were topheavy grain **barges**; coal was also a prominent cargo. Later, the term was taken over by settlers for a boat that had sharp ends and used a steering oar at each end. In the mid-19th century, the **Susquehanna ark** was a **flatboat★**-type craft that followed timber drives; one provided sleeping and eating quarters; another housed horses. Some simple **arks** were loaded with lumber and shingles. Reported lengths 6-27m, widths to 6.1m, depths 0.9-1.5m, draft ca. 0.6m. Other recorded name: **Susquehanna boat**. **c.** On the Potomac River, **arks** served as stores for rivermen, as cover-up craft for moonshiners, as brothels, and as floating homes for shad gill-net fishermen and shipyard workers. Usually anchored on the western shore and secluded inlets. The **ark** colonies were disbanded after World War II. Flat bottom, flat sides, square raked ends. House covered most of the **barge**-like hull. Reported lengths 6-18m; standard model 6m long, beam 3m, draft 0.3m. Name variant: **Potomac ark**

5. *United States, W:* **Houseboat** of the San Francisco Bay area; became popular in the 1880s, originally as fishing and duck-hunting clubs, later as homes; only a few remain. Hulls of the early **houseboats** were derived from **scow-schooners***; flat bottom, square raking ends. Area below the waterline covered with Irish felt and a sheath of redwood, then tarred. Flat-roofed house covered most or all of the hull; porch frequently extended beyond the sides. Note also **scow-11g**.

Further references: **flatboat-4**, **oyster barge**, **shanty boat**, **wanigan**

Arkansas boat See **flatboat-4**

Arke *Germany, central:* Flat-bottomed boat of the upper Elbe River. Sharp bow, square stern.

armadia See **almady**

Arnemuidenaar See **Arnemuidense hoogaars**

Arnemuidense hoogaars *Netherlands, SW:* **1. Fishing boat*** of the **hoogaars*** type built at Arnemuiden, but sometimes at other yards. Plied the waters of the Scheldt Estuary and coastal waters off Walcheren, fishing mainly for shrimp. Probably existed in the 17th century; extinct by 1930. Fished with 2 boomed trawl nets, drifting with wind and stream. Clinker-planked to the wale, flaring sides, top strake had strong tumble home. Flat bottom with rocker; greatest draft beneath the mast. Bluff bow with long, straight raking stem; sharp stern, with short sternpost. Top strake formed a pointed bow and rounded stern. Strong sheer. Early 19th-century boats had removable foredeck, later fixed. Open waist, steering well aft. Cauldron in the waist used for cooking the shrimp. Early 19th-century type had wide, rounded leeboards, later narrow. Rudder extended below the bottom, easily lifted. Stepped a pole mast abaft the foredeck, with forestay only. Set a spritsail canted toward the stern, with a long, heavy sprit. Also set a jib, auxiliary storm jib, staysail. A ringtail sail was hung from the top of the sprit and boomed on the leech of the mainsail. Mainsail and staysail tanned. Crew of 4 men and a boy. Reported lengths 12.5-14m; e.g., length 12.5m, beam 4.1m, depth 1.6m. Other recorded names: **Arnemuidenaar, Arnemuider** (or **Arnemuidse**) **hoogaars**
2. In the 19th century, a smaller type was used mainly for fishing in protected waters, but also as a **ferry***, a produce carrier, and a pleasure craft. Similar to the above, but more simply produced and generally less sturdy, with fewer and lighter ribs. Entirely open, or with a small cuddy in front of the steering well; some had a windlass at the forward end. Round leeboards. Mast stepped in heavy thwart. Rigged in a similar manner as the larger type, but mainsail more vertical. Length ca. 9.5m.

Arnemuider hoogaars, Arnemuidse hoogaars See **Arnemuidense hoogaars**

ắrŏ *Indonesia, E:* Jirewatao **outrigger canoe*** of the Lake Sentani area of northern Irian Jaya. Dugout hull. Paddled and sailed.

aro See **arụ**

arobail, aroebai, āròebäil, aroembai, aroepae, aroepai See **orembai**

aroet See **arut**

arosutáhu See **falca**

arot See **arut**

arpai See **orembai**

ar plato See **plate-6**

arrastrero, arrostrero, arrostrero, arrostrero por el costado, arrastrero por popa See **trawler**

arte, arte de chovega See **barca da arte xávega**

articulated junk See **liang jie tou**

arụ *Nigeria, S:* **Dugout canoe*** of the Niger Delta, adjacent rivers, and the coastal lagoon. Used for family transportation, to carry local products, and for fishing. Hewn in the bush, using fire, from several types of trees; 2-4 **canoes** may be made from a single tree trunk. Elongated ends square-cut and rise above the water; stern paddler sits on the flattened, somewhat wider end. Sides expanded by heat; the result may be asymmetrical; thwarts help retain the shape. Paddled; occasionally sailed. Lance-shaped blades generally colorfully painted. Small sprit- or triangular sail may be set to a mast stepped through a thwart well forward. Reported lengths 3.7-7.3m; some communally owned; may range to 16m. Spelling variant: **aro**. Further reading: Jean-Louis Tallec, "Les Pirogues du Niger," *Chasse-Marée* 56 (1991), 40-53.

arua See **oruwa-1**

arubai, arubaillo See **orembai**

aru balikkandathu See **odam-1b**

arud, aruk See **alut**

arumbae, arumbai See **orembai**

Arun spritsail barge *England, S:* Plied the Arun Navigation and some of the connecting canals until the late 19th century, carrying chalk, timber, stone. Sharp bow; square or sharp stern; flat bottom; rounded bilges; outboard rudder with wide blade below the waterline; tiller. Fore- and stern decks, narrow side decks; some had a small cabin at the stern. Single mast in a tabernacle, stepped amidships. Spritsail brailed to the short mast; foresail. Crew of 2-3. Reported lengths 12-21m, beam 3.7m.

arut *Indonesia, central:* Plank-built craft of southeastern Kalimantan (Borneo). Mainly used for trading, but a small type, the **arut tambangan**, serves as a **ferry***. Ends curved, frequently recurving above the gunwale line; stern might be broad or often shaped like a bird's head. Numerous thwarts. Thatched hut, open along the sides or with portable mat sides; some have a loose deck. Paddled, using round-bladed paddles. **Ferry** type is ca. 7.5m long, 0.94m wide. Other recorded names: **aroet, arot, arut pongkoh**. Note also **alut**.

arut pongkoh, arut tambangan See **arut**

aruvalikkunna thoni See **dhoni-5**

ar vag See **sardinier breton**

Aschenboot, Aschenprahm See **ash boat**

ash boat Designated to collect ashes from coal-burning ships in a port; some also collected rubbish. Other recorded names: **Aschenboot, Aschenprahm, ash lighter, askbåt, asu-bune, bette à escarbilles***, **sullage lighter**

ashi-buné *Japan:* Term for a very early craft built of bundles of reeds or bamboo stems. Believed to have been capable of transporting people and cargo both on rivers and at sea. Other recorded names: **reed canoe** (or **ship**)

ash lighter See **ash boat**

Ash Point wherry See **salmon wherry**

asi See **lakatoi**

askbåt See **ash boat**

aspen See **äsping**

äsping *Sweden:* **1.** Specifically, a boat hollowed out of an aspen (*asp*) log; or the term can signify a small planked boat.

2. Small undecked warship that was designed mainly to be rowed. Used as late as the 1780s. Name variant: **galäräsping**

3. Later, a ship's **longboat**. Towed the ship at times, and maintained communication with shore. Ends full; stem plumb, with cutaway forefoot; sternpost raked. Four thwarts. Rowed between double tholepins. Length ca. 6m, beam 1.8m. Name variant: **skeppsäsping**

4. A small cargo vessel. Heavy, curved stem and sternpost; undecked except at the stern. Gaff-rigged with boomed mainsail, 1-2 headsails; sharply steeved-up

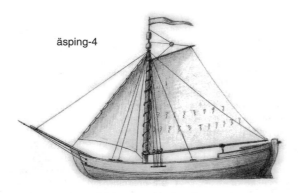

äsping-4

bowsprit. Some were 3-masted, sprit-rigged vessels, a type that was also reported as part of the Brandenburg-Prussian **fleet**.

Spelling variants: **aspen**, **esping**, **espink**. See also **haapio-1**.

Assendelfter melkschuitje See **melkschuitje**

Astrakhan river smack See **prorěz**

asu-bune See **ash boat**

atcheen See **banting-2**

atech qaïghy, at echek qaïghy See **at kayığı**

at gemisi See **huissier**

Athabascan canoe See **kayak-form canoe**

Athabasca scow See **scow-5**

Atirāmpatnam boat See **Adirāmpatnam boat**

at kayığı *Turkey, NW:* Type of **kayık*** that transported horses (*at*) and other cargo on the Bosporus and Dardanelles. Wider than other boats of the type. Other recorded names: **atech qaïghy, at (echek) qaïghy, horse boat***

atkuat See **baidara**

Atlantic City skiff See **Sea Bright skiff**

at qaïghy See **at kayığı**

a'tqEs See **West Coast canoe**

atrah See **qatrah**

åttæring, åttæringr See **åttring**

attamanmad See **woodskin**

áttamannafar *Denmark, Faroe Islands:* Double-ended open boat rowed by 8 (*átta*) men. Used for fishing and pilot whale-hunting. Clinker-built; strong curve to ends; deep keel; 4 thwarts. Early helmsmen steered with a short oar placed to leeward, but

held to windward in bad weather. Later, a curved rudder was hung on the sternpost, extending well

áttamannafar

below the keel. Rudder maneuvered by short lines attached to each end of a wooden bar or short rod inserted into one side of the bar. Rowed double-banked, each man with a single oar. When handline fishing, specific positions are assumed: the starboard oarsman on the 2nd thwart moves to the bow seat; the other man on this thwart works both oars; the 3rd thwart-man on the port side goes aft and his partner rows with both oars; the remaining men on the port side turn and face forward. Each man pulls his handline over the top of the oarlock. When sailing, sets a lug mainsail and sprit mizzen. Depending on the wind, mainmast stepped at the 1st or 2nd thwart. Some set a single lugsail just forward of amidships. Reported lengths overall 7.3-9.7m, widths 1.93-2.45m, depths 0.8-0.9m. Other recorded names: **eightereen**, **eight-man boat**, **otteman(d)sfar**. Further reading: C. V. Sølver, "Færingerbåde" in: *Årbog* (Helsingør: Handels-og Søfartsmuseet, 1957), 139-155; Morten Gøthche, *Færøbåden* (Roskilde: Vikingskibshallen, 1985). Note also **færobåd**.

attirah See **gaţîra**

åttring *Norway, W and N:* Correctly, a boat propelled by 8 (*åtte*) oars; in some areas a later type used 10 oars, but was still called an **åttring**. Engaged mainly in fishing, but many were general-purpose boats. Dates from at least the mid-18th century; generally gone by the early 20th century. Open; clinker-planked, with sharp ends; widely flaring sides; long keel. Outboard rudder worked with a single-arm yoke to a long, slender tiller. Several varieties have been identified. A small type is a **små-åttring**; a large type might be called a **stor-åttring**. Other recorded names: **aattring**, **åttæring**, **åttæringr**, **åttringen**, **ottring(sbaad)**; pl. **åttringane**, **åttringar**, **åttringene**, **åttringer**

1. The **åttring** of Sognefjord was used only in the fjord, carrying churchgoers, hay, produce, etc. Planked with 4 strakes to each side; beam slightly greater forward; strong sheer toward the bow. Ends curved, merging with a long keel. Set a square sail. 1840 boat measured 7.44m long, 1.92m wide, and 0.58m deep. Name variant: **sogneåttring**

2. The **åttring** of Sunnmøre (Sondmøre) District originally employed 8 oars, but later used 10 oars, retaining the **åttring** name. Used for high-seas fishing, some sailed as far as Iceland and England. Extra fullness forward achieved by pairs of narrow strakes in the bow scarfed with a single strake extending aft to the sternpost; special strengthening provided by 2 pairs of diagonal ribs. Mast stepped against the midships thwart; set a trapezoidal sail with a long, angled luff tacked directly to the stem. When fishing offshore in summer, stepped a foremast in the bow and a mizzenmast, both setting trapezoidal sails, the foresail tacked to a jibboom. Crew of 7-8. Reported lengths 12.1-15.8m; e.g., length 12.44m, beam 1.98m, depth 0.98m. Other recorded names: **Söndmöersk ottringsbaad, sondmør-ottring, sunnmørsåttring** (or **ottring**)

3. The **nordlandsottring** was made in Bindal, Salten, and Rana (where it was known as **ranværsottring**). Used for fishing and carrying people and provisions. Here, too, the boats became 10-oared but retained the 8-oar designation, **ottring** or **åttring**. The boat might also be called a **femrømming** (see **fem-roms båt**), having 5 "rooms." Ends straight and plumb, the stem lightly recurved. Wide top strake, usually painted white; strong sheer toward the ends. The large **storottring** (**stor-åttring** or **storbåt***) that went to the Lofoten Islands to fish had a cuddy aft; some carried a **jolle***. Mast lowered while fishing, sometimes to an athwartship crutch behind the stem. Set a square sail and square topsail; a few later boats converted to gaff rig, with staysail. By 1914, most had installed an inboard engine (**motoråttring**). Rowed single-banked. Crew of 4-6. Reported lengths 8.58-11m; an 1800 Salten boat was 8.58m long, 2.02m wide, and 0.66m deep. Some northern Norway boats are built for specific uses—**sommar-åttring** (or **sommer-åttring**) is lightly built for summer fishing; the **vinter-åttring** is heavier than the regular **åttring**, fishing mainly in the winter; the **garn-åttring** employs nets (*garn*) and is wider and beamier. The **lin-åttring** (or **line-åttring**) fishes with lines; tall ends, heavy sternpost, often a forehold. In the Lofoten Islands, the **Yttersi-åttring** is 6-oared and the **Innersi-åttring** is smaller and has lower ends. The **Finnmarks-åttring** was large, 9.4m long. Other recorded names: **nordlandsåttring, ranværings-åttring**

åttringane, åttringar, åttringen, åttringene, åttringer See **åttring**

atuneira *Madeira:* Open **whaleboat***-type craft used in the tuna fisheries. Motorized. Spelling variant: pl. **atuneiros**. Further reference: **tuna boat**

atuneiros See **atuneira**

atunero See **tuna boat**

auang-galay See **panco-2**

auchtagorun anèn See **anan**

auchtoaring See **great boat-5**

Aufklärer, Aufklärungsfahrzeug, Aufklärungsschiff See **scout-1**

aumedia See **almady**

Au Sable River drift boat *United States, north-central:* Designed to float down this river in the northern part of the Lower Peninsula of Michigan. Originally used by loggers for hauling and transportation in the late 19th century; now used by trout fishermen. Drifts downstream, controlled by poles and sometimes by logging chains used as drags. Sharp raked ends, although for a short period built with a transom stern to support an outboard motor; transom extension above the gunwale for the motor retained as a back rest for the poler. Flat bottom with rocker toward the ends, flat athwartships; hard chines; sides vertical or flared; low freeboard; early boats had a fairly flat sheer, now moderate. Originally of white pine, most now of plywood. Pivoting seat set atop a live well at the bow; space for gear on either side of the box. Short foredeck; flooring on bottom, now sometimes carpeted. Frames notched to hold the poles (often 3 of different lengths). Reported lengths 4.9-7.3m; e.g., length 7.16m, beam on bottom 0.66m, on top 0.97m, depth ca. 0.4m. Other recorded names: **Au Sable River skiff, drift boat★, pole boat★**

Au Sable River skiff See **Au Sable River drift boat**

Ausleger gig See **wherry-2**

Auslegerkanu See **outrigger canoe**

Ausleger wherry See **wherry-2**

Auslieger See **caper**

Aussenmotte See **Mutte**

auto boat See **motor boat-1**

Autofähre, auto ferry See **ferryboat-1**

automobile See **motor boat-1**

automoteur *France:* Term given to a self-propelled inland waterways craft, as opposed to one towed by animals or a tractor. Most often a **péniche★**. Other recorded names: **bateau automoteur, motor** (in Alsace), **Motorschiff**

auvergnat *France, south-central:* General term given to the inland vessels that operated in the Auvergne region, especially on the upper Loire and Allier Rivers. See also **berrichon, chênière, salembarde, sapine**.

aveiro *Portugal:* General term given to the various boat types that originated in the Aveiro area of the central coast. They were one of the major categories traveling to, and sometimes remaining in, the Lisbon area in the mid-19th century. Spelling variant: **avieiro**

aveka See **vaka-7a**

avieiro See **aveiro**

avis, Avisjacht, aviso, avisobrik, avisofartyg, avisojacht, Avisschiff, avisoschoener See **advice boat**

Avon tar boat *England, SW:* A variety of **trow⋆** that carried tar on the western part of the Avon River to ports in the Bristol Channel. Worked from the 1860s to the late 1960s. Bluff bow, raised foredeck, rounded counter stern. Small wheelhouse aft. Sailed until converted to diesel in the early 1920s.

avvisi, avviso See **advice boat**

awā'n *United States, SW:* General term of the Karankawa of southwest Texas for a **boat⋆**, **vessel⋆**, or **ship⋆**. More specifically, the term described their **dugout canoes⋆**, which had bluntly pointed ends and residual decking at each end; bark was left on the outside; poled; ca. 6m long, narrow. **Awā'n** might also apply to the small, cast-off, flat-bottomed boats the Karankawa obtained from the Europeans; also poled, or might set a small sail.

a waqa See **waqa-2**

ax·ut See **kayak-8**

ayasah, ayassa See **gaiassa**

ayssangue See **palangrier**

azabra See **zabra**

baad See **bad**, **båt**
baair See **baris**
baard Reported as a medieval transport.
baardse Used in northwestern Europe from the 14th to
the 16th century, initially as an oared naval vessel; by
the mid-15th century also carried sails. Full-bodied,
double-ended, clinker-planked; several heavy wales.
Forecastle, with quarter-deck abaft an open waist. A
1343 vessel employed 12 oarsmen, a steersman, 4
marksmen, and a standard bearer; reported with as
many as 40 oarsmen. Sailing **baardsen** (pl.) set
square sails to 2 masts, each with a square topsail;
lateen mizzen. Built with castles at bow and stern.
150-500t. Other recorded names: **baardze, baartse,
baartze, baerdse, baergie, baerd(t)ze, baertse, bairdse,
bairdze, barge*, bargie** (pl. **bargiën**), **barghe, barse*,
berge, roeibaarze, roeibaerdtze, zeebargie**. Note
also **galley-5, rowbarge**. Further reference: **trekschuit**
baardsen, baardze, baartse, baartze See **baardse**
babao See **baobao**
bac *France:* **1.** French term for a **ferryboat***. Generally
low-sided; bow and stern often blunt to permit riding
up onto the bank. Propelled by pole, oars, swimmer,
sail, a rope stretched across a stream, or motor.
  2. A **punt*** of shipwrights that carries tar, pitch, etc.
  3. At Bassin d'Arcachon (embayment) on the coast
southwest of Bordeaux, special **bacs** aid in the local
oyster industry and in transporting wood. Last one still
sailing in mid-1950s. Design not standardized, but in
general they are shallow draft, with a centerboard
when sailed; decked, cuddy below. Bulwarks stop just
short of the stern, leaving the square stern area open;
bulwark sections removable. Bows vary but often cutaway sharply above and below the waterline; stern
overhanging. Flat floors, hard chines, vertical sides.

bac-3

Bottom rounded or slightly V-sectioned; no frames,
but heavy scantlings and numerous braces. Sometimes uses a sweep-type rudder fixed to a pintle on
the after deck, with an oarlock device; broad blade
flares down into the water. Most **sloop***-rigged, jib to

stemhead; some lug-rigged. Now motorized. Many
modified to pleasure craft. Size range: length 9.4m,
beam 2.8m, depth 0.6m to 15.5m by 4m by 2m; draft
0.25-0.30m. Name variants: **bac (à voile) d'Arcachon,
bac ostréicole**
  4. In Morbihan Department in northwest France, the
oyster **bac** of the early 20th century was an open, double-ended **scow***. Flat bottom, with long, sloping
ends; straight vertical sides. Fully decked. Originally
maneuvered by 3 men using 2 oars and a scull; now
motorized. Reported lengths 7-10m. Name variants:
bac d'ostrique, bac du Morbihan
  5. Term has also been applied to small vessels plying
rivers and canals.
Spelling variants: **bach, bachot*** (dim.), **Back, bacq(ue),
bag*, bag-treiz, bak*, barco à traio.** Further references:
bak, chaland-3a, ferryboat-1, waal
baca Low Latin term for a **boat***. See also **bou**.
bacalhoeiro *Portugal:* Cod-fishing boats, mainly **schooners***,
that went annually to the Grand Banks off Newfound-
land. Fish caught from **dories** (see **banks dory**). A
1937 4-masted steel **schooner**: length overall 63.5m,
beam 10m, 665grt. Other recorded names: **baccalao**
(or **baccalau**) **schooner, lugre bacalhoeiro**
bacassa *West Indies, E:* Term most often used to
describe a Carib **dugout canoe*** of the late 17th and
early 18th centuries, but sometimes considered a general term for a **lighter***. Dugout hull of a type of cedar,
hewn with fire, 4cm on the bottom, 3cm on the sides.
Planking, sewn on with bark fiber, raised the sides 20-
40cm. Pointed bow, flat stern, sheer sweeps up forward. Mat shelter might be provided toward the stern.
Steered with a long paddle. Sailed and paddled.
Portrayed with a single spritsail and jib, or with 3
masts, plus topsails. Large boats might carry 50 people. Reported lengths 10-13m; e.g., length 12.8m,
beam 2m. Spelling variants: **barcas(s)as**
bac à voile de'Arcachon See **bac-3**
baccalao schooner, baccalhau schooner See **bacalhoeiro**
Baccalieu skiff *Canada, E:* Small 2-masted **schooner***
that fished for cod off Baccalieu Island, northeast of
Winterton on the east coast of Newfoundland. Boat
anchored off the island and deployed 2-man
rodneys* which had been carried on board; the
schooner was called a **floater*** when anchored.
Boats returned to Winterton every 2-3 weeks with
salted cod. Open; high sides, transom stern. Gaff
sails set to 2 light polemasts; jib to short bowsprit.
Also rowed. Crew of 5. Reported lengths 10.7-13.7m.
Note also **cod-seine skiff**.
bac d'Arcachon See **bac-3**
bac de Charleroi See **baquet de Charleroi**
bac de moulin See **moulin-bateau**
bac d'ostrique, bac du Morbihan See **bac-4**
bach See **bac**
bach de moulin See **moulin-bateau**
bache 1. *Belgium, E/France, NE:* Important early **ferry-
boat*** on the Meuse River. Most capable of carrying

10 passengers, sometimes with a horse or cart. Flat bottom, undecked; stability maintained by a sweep. Reported lengths 15-18m, widths 2-2.7m.
2. *France, east-central:* **a.** The **bâche** was a small **passage boat★** or **ferry★** used on the Saône River, especially at Lyon. Reported as early as the 14th century. Rowed, often by women. Spelling variants: **bachot★**, **baicha★** (pl. **baichae**), **baiche**. Note also **bèche-1**. **b.** **Barge★** of the Saône that transported construction materials, especially sand, during the 19th century; built until 1960. Those built upstream from Port-Rivière (north of Villefranche) were called **bâches**, while those built downstream were called **sapines★**. Flat plumb stern; blunt bow that turned up from a flat, longitudinally planked bottom. Sides flat but flared on some. Carvel-planked; last boats of iron or steel. Those of wood after 1940 were called **sabliers non ponté** or **petit bateaux de dragages**. No rudder; maneuvered by a sweep, 15-20m long, at the stern, and a shorter one at the bow. Reported lengths 10-26m, widths 3.5-5.2m.

bachet *France, SW:* **1.** Carried heavy bulk cargo, produce, and passengers in the mouth of the Adour, on the southwest coast, and along the middle river, mainly from the 2nd half of the 19th into the early 20th century; some motorized versions still operate, carrying sand. One type had a counter stern (**bachet à voûte** or **bachet cabané**), another a high transom (**bachet à tableau**); the former had a raised cabin abaft the mast and a steering hatch at the stern. The transom-sterned boat was decked at the bow and stern. Keel, round bilges, curved stem; carvel-planked over frames. Inboard or outboard rudder. Bent a wide lugsail on a horizontal yard; mast stepped well forward. Also towed, poled, or rowed. Reported lengths 12-18m. **2.** In the Garonne Estuary, the **bachet** was reportedly a lifesaving craft.
Spelling variant: **bachette**. See also **bachot**.

bachet à tableau, bachet à voûte, bachet cabané, bachette See **bachet**

bachot 1. Small boat used on rivers and sheltered waters to ferry foot passengers, transport provisions, or handle lines for large vessels. In general roughly built, clinker- or carvel-planked, square stern, square or pointed bow, flat bottom, straight or slightly curved sides. Some 7-10m long, 1-2m wide, shallow draft. Name variant: **bachot de service**
2. *Belgium:* The **bachot belge** performed the same functions. Clinker-planked, with **pram★** bow, bottom rocker forward, small skeg, slightly raked stern.
3. *France:* **a.** In 18th-century Paris, special **bachots**, called **batelets★**, ran scheduled trips to Saint-Cloud, southwest of Paris. **b.** The **bachot** of the upper Seine, at Saint Mammès, had a straight elongated bow, plumb stern, marked sheer toward the bow. **c.** An old **bachot** type on the Seine had 2 elongated straight ends, flat bottom, flaring sides. **d.** The **bachot** at Jantelle on the Oise River had a straight raked stem, nearly plumb sternpost, flat bottom, carvel planking. **e.** The **bachot normand** was a small boat that belonged to the **besogne★**. **Pram★**-ended; bottom flat, curved up at the ends; decked at bow and stern. Length

ca. 4m. **f.** Those on the Loire River might be maneuvered by a sweep with a triangular blade at the end (the **bachot à piautre**). **g.** **Ship's boat★** towed or carried aboard a **péniche★**. Some accompanied a **train de bateaux★**, performing sounding duties and reconnoitering channels. **h.** Small **fishing boat★**, especially one that has a perforated compartment for holding live fish. Note also **vivier**.
Spelling variants: **bachet★**, **baiche**, **barcot★**. Note also **barcote**. Further references: **bac**, **bâche-2**, **baicha**, **bêche-2**, **plate-1**

bachot à piautre See **bachot-3**
bachot belge See **bachot-2**
bachot de service See **bachot-1**
bachot normand See **bachot-3**
bacik, bacisko See **bat-2**
Back See **bac**
Bäckenschiff See **leibschiff-1**
backwater boat, backwater boatt See **Fleet trow**
bacoli, bacolo See **trabaccolo**
bacon box See **zeeschouw**
bacop *France, N:* Open boat that transports local produce in the marshy areas off the Aa River in French Flanders. Sharp, overhanging and rising bow; small, high transom; flat bottom. Wide lapped planking, flaring sides. Small foredeck. Mainly poled, but some fitted for an outboard motor. Length ca. 4.5m, beam ca. 1.0m, depth ca. 0.3m; early boats larger and might set a sail. Note also **scute-2a**.
bac ostréicole See **bac-3**
bacq, bacque See **bac**
bad 1. *Denmark:* **Båd** is the Danish generic for **boat★**. Spelling variant: **baad**.
2. *Ireland:* **Bád** in Gaelic means **boat★**.
3. *Wales:* Term for **boat★** in Welsh.
badaini See **bedan-1**
badan See **bedan-1, beden-2**
badane, badani See **bedan-1**
badan-safar See **bedan-safar**
badan-seyad See **bedan-seyad**
baddi See **bhedi**
baden, badeni, badini See **bedan-1**
bád iomara See **bád iomartha**
bád iomartha *Ireland, W:* Heavy boat of the **hooker★** family. Used for short-haul work. Originally propelled by long oars; now some have engines. Oak hull; deep plumb stem; narrow, raked transom; heavily timbered; sides have tumble home. Some converted to leisure sailing. Other recorded names: **bád iomara, carrying boat★**
badjera See **badjra**
badjra *Bangladesh/India:* **Houseboat★** on the Ganges River and delta area that was used initially mainly by local officials and for ceremonial purposes; some types carried cargo. Reported from at least the 16th century; still in use today, not only for living quarters but as mobile cinemas, for educational purposes, and by holy men collecting donations. Spoon-shaped with a high stern and low bow; bottom either flat or rounded, no keel. Large, low cabin aft, the amenities and construction commensurate with the status of the user. When used as a cook boat, 2 brick hearths incorporated.

Rowers, as many as 16, worked forward of or above the cabin using bamboo oars with disc-shaped blades.

badjra

Steered with a huge oar from the roof or by a large, tri-angular balanced rudder. When sailed, set a square mainsail with a bamboo yard and a topsail; mast stepped amidships. Crew of 9-16. Often accompanied by a **fleet*** of smaller boats, e.g., a **pallar*** as a kitchen boat and a small **panshi*** as a **tender***. Reported lengths 7.6-18.2m, widths 2.44-5m, depths 1.22-1.88m; shallow draft. Other recorded names: **badjera, bajara, bajra(h), bazra, Bengalee boat, budgaro(o), budgarow, budgerow, budgra, budjerow, bu(d)jra, buggalow, green boat**. Note also **pinash**.
bád móna, bád mór See **Galway hooker**
bæltbåd, bæltbådene See **bæltsbåd**
bæltsbåd *Denmark, central:* **Cutter***-rigged herring fishing and cargo boat built in the Storebælt area. Clinker-planked until the late 19th century, then carvel. Sides rounded above the waterline, sharp and deep below; maximum beam abreast the mast; bar keel, which projects beyond the sternpost to protect the rudder. Stem curved. Prior to 1870, transom-sterned; later modified to a sharp or rounded stern. Hull tarred. Decked with standing well for helmsman, or half-decked; fish well. Outboard rudder; tiller may come in below gunwale. Gaff mainsail loose-footed with boom; gaff topsail, 2 headsails. Mast stepped about a third of distance in from the bow. Crew of 3 when fishing. Reported lengths 7.6-10.8m; e.g., length

bæltsbåd

overall 8.3m, on keel 6.3m, beam 2.8m, depth 1.3m. Name variants: **bæltbåd, Belt boat**; pl. **bæltbådene**
bæltsmakke See **smakke-2**
baerdse, baerdtze, baerdze, baergie, baertse, baertze See **baardse**
baer-warn See **bärwän**
bæt See **boat-1**

bag *France, W:* In Brittany, a general term for a **boat***, **canot***, or **chaloupe***. Other recorded names: **bak***, **vag**; pl. **bageier, bagou, bigi**. Further reference: **bac**
Bagageschiff See **Leibschiff-1**
bagala See **baghla-1, bangala, kotia**
bagalla See **baghla-1**
bagalo See **baghla-1, kotia**
bag and spoon dredger See **spoon dridger**
bage See **bak-2**
bageier See **bag**
baggage boat See **accommodation boat, kettuvallam, patela, ulakh**
baggala See **baghla-1, bangala, kotia**
baggalat, baggalo, baggalow, baggara See **baghla-1**
baggārah See **belem-3, shahuf**
bagger See **dredger-1, sandbagger**
baggeraak *Netherlands:* A vessel of the **aak*** family that dredged in tidal rivers of South Holland. Some later craft transported local produce. Built of wood, iron, or steel, mainly at Sliedrecht. Flat bottom plank-ing turned up at the bow to gunwale level; some had a false stem ending in a point. Shallow, narrow transom; sternpost continued under stern as deadwood. Sheer sweeps up at the bow. Open except for cuddy forward and steering cockpit; hold covered by curved hatches on some; movable washboards. Outboard rudder; tiller; tall leeboards. Set a spritsail or loose-footed, boomed gaff sail. Reported length 12.55m, beam one-quarter. Other recorded names: **flat***, **flette***, **Sliedrechter aak** (or **aakje**), **Sliedrechtse aak, vlet***; pl. **baggeraken**. Note also **bovenmaase aak**.
baggeraken See **baggeraak**
baggermachine, Baggermaschine, baggermolen, baggermoolen See **dredger-1**
Baggerprahm See **hopper-1, Prahm-2**
baggerschuit See **dredger-1**
Baggerschute See **hopper-1**
baghala See **baghla-1**
baghalah *Iraq, S:* Used for lightering on the Shatt-al-Arab River. A large one was capable of carrying 100 men or 20 horses. Generally poled, but with a follow-ing wind, set a sail to a small mast. See also **baghla-1**.
baghela See **baghla-1**
baghla 1. *Arabian Peninsula:* Built mainly at Persian (Arabian) Gulf ports, but carried cargo to the east coast of Africa, the Red Sea, and India; still occasion-ally seen in the 1960s. Early vessels armed and often manned by pirates. Distinguished from other so-called **dhows*** by a stem extension surmounted by a bitt with a truncated peg and curved ring; by the 5 windows on an elaborately carved, arched transom; and by quarter galleries. The long stem raked forward from a short straight keel that was deeper forward. Truncated stern ended in a slightly raked counter and a high poop. Carvel-planked; double hull with a composition layer between; sides had tumble home aft of amidships; considerable rise to the floors. Some had copper sheathing on the bottom, other bottoms sheathed with thin planking. Coated above the waterline with fish oil, whitened below with a mixture of sheep's tail fat, lime, and paraffin. Massive rudder came inboard through rudder trunk; tiller controlled with chains

leading to the barrel of a steering wheel. Generally fully decked, the largest having 2 decks; large stern cabin; sometimes mat weather cloths installed. Some carried a **jalbūt**★ or an **'abari**★ from the stern and a **mashua**★ on deck. Stepped 1-3 masts, but most 2-masted. Heavy, forward-raking mainmast, equal to the ship's length, was stepped amidships on the 2-masted vessels; multipiece yard fished together. Mizzenmast,

baghla

stepped at forward end of poop, shorter and less raked. Quadrilateral lateen-type sail with a short luff, of coarse canvas. Occasionally set a topsail to a temporary topmast and a jigger. Sails set outside the standing rigging. Vessels from Masqat (Muscat) had a short curved bowsprit. Crew of 20-50. Reported lengths 12-55m; e.g., length 22.6m, beam 7.6m, depth 4.5m. Other recorded names: **bagalla, bag(g)ala, bagalo, baggalat, baggalo(w), baggara, baghala, baghalah**★, **baghela, baghlah, baglah, baġle** (pl. **biġâl**), **baglos, baḳalā, bakele, bhagla** (erroneously), **bugal(l)a, buggalah, buggalow, buggelah, bughalah, bugla, bungalow, el-běġáleh** (pl. **el-beġál**), **khasaba** (at Sur), **shuwai'ai** or **shuwai'i** (in Oman); **bagla** (pl. **bagol**) by the Afar. Note also **bugalilo, ganja, khashabah**.
2. *Tanzania:* A variety of the Persian Gulf **baghla** was built at Zanzibar. Single-masted with no bowsprit. Spelling variant: pl. **mabagala**
Further reference: **kotia**

baghlah See **baghla-1**
bagik See **batelet**
bag-kregina See **coquillier**
bagla See **baghla-1**, **kotia**
baglah, baġle See **baghla-1**
bag-lestr See **chaloupe-6**
baglos See **baghla-1**
bag-net coble See **coble-5**
bago *Indonesia:* **1.** On the west coast of Sulawesi (Celebes), the smaller **bago** is generally a **fishing boat**★, the larger a trader. Basically a **pajala**★-type hull, to which a pole mast is stepped. Straight or curved raking stem; square or sharp raking stern; pointed stem and sternpost generally rise above the gunwales. Rounded hull; marked sheer; low freeboard. Steered with quarter rudders permanently fixed to crossbeams that form part of a framework out over the stern. Mostly open, with a small, mat, peaked-roof house aft; traders have a wooden cabin. Mast stepped in forward third. Early boats set a rectangular lug-type sail; more recently a long-boomed gaff or leg-of-mutton

sail. Large boomed jib to bowsprit, staysail. Crew of 7 on 33t trader. Reported length 11m, beam ca. one-quarter. Name variant: **West Sulawesi lambo**
2. The term **bago** is used at Bali for a **lambo**★-type boat, usually with a western Sulawesi crew. Hunts turtles, mainly for Balinese consumption.
3. The trading **bago** is commonly found at Java and to the east. Sharp ends. Flat-roofed cabin, sides slope inward from the top strake. Stern extension for the quarter rudder may be box-like or a framework. Mast stepped forward of the cabin or in a tabernacle on the cabin roof. Boomed gaff sail; large jib to a bowsed-down bowsprit that reaches back to the cabin, supported by trailboards. Other recorded names: **bago prahu, prau bago**
bagol See **baghla-1**
bago prahu See **bago-3**
bagou See **bag**
bagouigou See **batelet**
bag Plougastel See **chaloupe de Plougastel**
bag-rouederez See **chalutier**
bag-treiz See **bac**
baguik See **batelet**
bag-wagon See **sandbagger**
Bahama dinghy *Bahamas:* **1.** Small, heavy family boat that varies slightly with the builder and from island to island, but essentially unchanged since the 18th century. Those servicing larger off-lying boats or providing transportation between settlements generally open; the **fishing boats**★ are larger, often decked forward and along the sides, and equipped with a well amidships. Those used for sponging work out from a **smack boat**★ or **schooner**★ with 2 men. Built by eye from sawn frames; greatest beam (one-half keel length) forward of amidships. Most have a heart-shaped transom that curves above the sheer strake; those from Abaco and Cays have fuller transoms and a marked rise of floors. Bow sharp, with a straight raking stem. Keel long, straight,

Bahama dinghy-1

and with drag. Heavy caprail. Outboard rudder; tiller slots into rudderhead. The Andros Island **dinghy**★ has sharper lines than the Abaco and Cays boat, and a flat or hogged sheer. Sets a large, baggy, modified leg-of-mutton sail, loose-footed but with a very long boom. Sail originally had a short gaff but now has a large headboard; sail of heavy canvas. Mast flexible, unstayed, and rakes aft; halyard run from masthead block to stemhead, through a block and aft to a cleat, to form a headstay. Uses a sculling oar in a notch in the port side of the transom; slight curve to the loom. Most now equipped with an outboard motor.

Reported lengths 2.7-6m; e.g., length 4.4m, beam 1.64m, depth 0.76m. Other recorded names: **Abaco dinghy** (or **skiff**)

2. A recent type of **dinghy** on Eleuthera is narrow, has a transversely planked flat bottom, pleasing sheer, and a high, raked, square transom stern. Mostly sculled or poled. Reported lengths 2.7-5.5m.

Bahama sloop See **sharpshooter-1, smack boat-1**

Bahama smack See **smack boat-1**

Bahama sponge schooner See **sponge schooner-1**

bai ao ch'iao, bai ao qiao See **lorcha-3**

bai-ao-shiao See **lorcha-7**

baicha *France, east-central:* Small **passage boat*** of the Saône River. Some had a cloth-covered canopy. Rowed, mainly by women. Other recorded names: **bachot***, **besche**; at Lyon, **baiche** or **bèche**. Further reference: **bache-2**

baichae See **bache-2**

baiche See **bache-2, bachot, baicha**

baida **1.** *Bangladesh:* A gypsy **houseboat***. Long, narrow, and usually poorly maintained. Most of hull covered by an arched roof.

2. *Russia, SW/Ukraine, SE:* A **fishing boat*** that could be sailed and rowed. Native to the Sea of Azov.

3. *Russia, SW:* A 19th-century **ferryboat*** on the Don River. Elongated raking ends enabled the boat to run onto banks; shallow stern transom. Sailed, with a lateen-type sail to a short mast, or poled. Could carry 10-12 people. Length ca. 32m, width ca. 8m. Name variant: **baidarka**

baidac, baidak See **baidaka**

baidaka *Ukraine, W:* **Barge***-type vessel that navigated on the western rivers, especially in the Dnieper Basin. Large rudder. Single mast, setting a spritsail, or 2 masts, setting lugsails. Reported lengths 21-49m, widths 4.27-14.3m, depths 1-2.56m, draft 0.71-1.87m; some to 60m long. Spelling variants: **baidac, baidak, baidake, bajdak**; pl. **baidaki**

baidake, baidaki See **baidaka**

baidar *Russia, E:* Term applied to various types of small boats or **canoes***, sometimes to a **dugout canoe***. Note also **baidara, kayak**.

baidara *Russia, eastern Siberia:* Walrus-skin **umiak*** of the Chukchi peoples. Bow and stern pointed, the former raked, with rounded forefoot; stern more vertical; sides flared. Gunwales extended beyond the headboards. Larger boats had as many as 21 frames on each side and across the bottom; framework bound together with skin thongs or strings of whalebone; 4 thwarts. One-and-one-half to 2 skins used; edges brought over the gunwale and laced to the middle stringer; skins removed and stored in winter and oiled each year. Originally paddled; later adopted long narrow oars, and rowed one person to a thwart. Sometimes set a square sail; later gaff or spritsail. Sail originally of reindeer skins; later of cloth. Pole mast stepped just forward of amidships into a block on the keelson. Smallest used single-handed; largest worked with 6-12 people. Reported lengths 5.5-18.2m; e.g., length 10.7m, beam at gunwales 1.37m, on bottom 0.76m, depth 0.8m. Other recorded names: **angiapik**, **atkuat** (by the Chukchi), **baidar***, **baidarrah**,

bajdara, baydar(a), bidar*, **bidara, bidarra(h), haitara**. Further references: **ga'twaat, umiak-1, umiak-4**

baidarka See **baida-3, kayak-9, kayak-11**

baidarrah See **baidara**

bai di chuan See **Amoy fisher**

bai du chuan *China, E:* Three-masted **coaster*** built at Shantou (Swatow). Broad bow that narrowed slightly at the waterline, painted red and blue with a white chevron; highly ornamented oval stern. Sheered up toward the ends, especially at the stern. Gangway port amidships. Foremast raked over the bow, mainmast and mizzen vertical. Set high-peaked, balance lugsails of cloth. Length 19m, beam 4.6m. Name variants: **pai-tu ch'uan, white bottomed junk**

Bailey bridging pontoon See **pontoon-7**

bai mu chuan See **shou kou ma yang zi**

bàirc See **bàrc**

bairdse, bairdze See **baardse**

bait See **boat-1**

bait boat **1.** A boat that uses bait, such as cut-up fish or shellfish, to lure fish to the lines.

2. *United States, E:* On the Virginia side of Chesapeake Bay, **bait boats** catch bait, chiefly menhaden, for use by the various bay crab boats. A **purse boat** (ca. 11m long) works with a larger boat (14-18m long) to set a purse seine, called a **snapper rig**. Motorized, with characteristic tall exhaust stack and high sheer forward; plumb rounded stern.

See also **Bermuda dinghy, striker boat-2**.

baiter **1.** *Canada, E:* The Newfoundland **baiter** catches capelin, herring, and squid for use as bait in the cod fishery. Note also **baitskif, capelanier**.

2. *England, E:* Vessel that caught whitebait, especially on the lower Thames River and estuary. Caught with a type of stow net. Used until at least the mid-1960s.

baitskiff *Canada, E:* Open boat of Newfoundland that netted capelin for bait in the cod fishery. Reported as early as the late 18th century and still used in the 1960s. Might tow a **punt***. Rowed and sailed. Crew of 5-7. Note also **baiter-1, capelanier**.

bajara See **badjra**

bajarka See **kayak-11**

Bajau houseboat See **djènging**

bajbot See **lifeboat**

bajdak See **baidaka**

bajdara See **baidara**

bajdarka See **kayak-9**

ba jiang chuan *China:* **1.** Early patrol and reconnaissance boat used mainly in southwest China and in Bo Hai in the north. Low bow, very high curving stern. Decked. Rowed with 4 oars per side. Also sailed; battened lugsails set to 2 strikable masts, the mainmast amidships, the foremast well forward.

2. Coaster* that worked at least to the mid-20th century in the Shantou (Swatow) area on the southeast coast. Bluff bow, transom stern, both raked; sheer sweeps up at the ends. Flush deck; portable mat house. Hull decorated, especially the bow. Rowed and sailed; 8 oars. Mainmast stepped amidships; forward-raking foremast well forward. Battened lugsails, with curved leech and medium peak, set to starboard. Length 18m, beam 4.6m; size varied widely.

Other recorded names: **eight-oared boat, pa-chiang chhuan** (or **ch'uan**), **pa tsiang tch'ouan**

bajitpuri See **patam-1**

bajra, bajrah See **badjra**

bak 1. *Belgium:* Boxy river and **canal barge***. Flat bottom; bluff slightly raking bow, straight sides, vertical stern, low sheer. Small flat bow "moustache"; lacks the usual rubbing strakes along the sides. Single towing bitt at each side of the bow; pairs of mooring bitts on the fore- and after decks. Low cabin amidships. Rudder extension can be raised in confined spaces. Reported lengths 37.5-39m, beam 5m, draft 1.8-2.3m. Spelling variants: **bac***; pl. **bakken.** Note also **kantelbak, waal, zolderbak.**
2. *Haiti:* Creole term for a **ferryboat*** or a **raft***. Spelling variants: **bac*, bage.** Further references: **bac, bag, baquet de Charleroi**

báka *Easter Island, southern Pacific:* General term for a **boat***. Spelling variants: **vahka, vaka***

baḳalā See **baghla-1**

bakanawa See **ulatoka-1**

báka póe-póe *Easter Island, southern Pacific:* **1.** Generic term for a **boat*** or **canoe***. Term has also been applied to a **whaleboat***-type boat.
2. Originally an **outrigger canoe*** composed of many short lengths, possibly of driftwood, laced together. Ends sweep up sharply, terminating in slender, flattened extensions. Caulked with moss or earth. A single, and possibly double, outrigger comprised 2 widely spaced light booms that attached directly to 1 or more slender floats. Paddled. Reported lengths 1.5-6.1m, very narrow. Other recorded names: **poepoe, vaka poepoe**

bakele See **baghla-1**

Bakenboot See **beacon boat**

bakigi caighi See **balıkçı kayığı**

bakkebåd *Denmark, W:* Fished for cod and haddock out of Esbjerg in the late 19th and early 20th centuries. Carvel-planked. Bluff bow; stem curved above the waterline, strongly raked below. Stern rounded, raked below the waterline, or rounded counter. Drag to straight keel, steep rise to the floors, flaring sides. Decked; inboard rudder on counter-sterned vessels. **Cutter***- or **ketch***-rigged; gaff sails, loose-footed, boomed; topsails; long bowsprit; multiple headsails. Reported lengths 11-20m; **cutter** 11.5m long, 4.2m wide, 2m deep. Other recorded names: **Esbjerd cod-fishing boat, Esbjerg (fiske)kutter.** Note also **kutter-1.**

bakken See **bak-1, baquet de Charleroi**

bak van Charleroi See **baquet de Charleroi**

balance canoe See **canoe**

balahú *Spain, N:* Small ship of the Vizcaya coast. Spelling variant: **balajú.** See also **ballahou.**

balajú See **balahú**

balam *Bangladesh:* Term, which dates from at least the mid-17th century, applied to a variety of craft ranging from small river fishing **canoes*** to large **coasters***. Now rarely seen. Characterized by blunt, raked ends and a plank-extended dugout hull. Stern may be as much as 1.22m higher than the bow; round bottom. On

some, beams lashed athwartships and heavy floors help maintain the dugout shape. On the southeast coast, the boats are officially designated by the number of planks added on, although local usage varies: an **ad balam** has 1, the **balam proper** 2, the **gadu** 3, and the **jalyanao** 4; however, the number of planks may actually vary on each side. Originally, planks sewn on

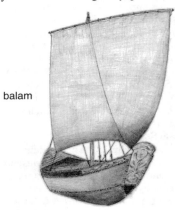

balam

with cane and caulked with false hemp or straw, but metal fastenings now common. Some **balams** remove their planking during the monsoon season, engaging in interior fishing with only the dugout hull. Many brightly painted with geometric designs. Rudder, partly balanced, worked on the quarters, or the boat may be steered with long oars controlled by a rope traveler or crossbar. Sailing **balams** set a large square sail from a yard. Mast usually stepped into a tabernacle; numerous shrouds, backstays, and a forestay. Rowed from loose planks laid in the bow; oars of bamboo with plank blade. Crew of 5-20. Reported lengths 9-24.4m, widths 2.44-4.27m, depths 1.83-2.44m. Other recorded names: **balam nauka, balaum, bulam boat, gadhu.** Note also **bara balam, modhyam balam, teddy balam, trawler-2.** Further reference: **belem**

balam nauka See **balam**

balanay See **barangay**

balance canoe See **canoe-1**

balancela *Spain:* Trader and **fishing boat*** of the Mediterranean coast and the Balearic Islands. Originally double-ended, but later had a rounded stern

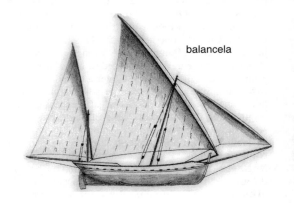

balancela

or a square counter; cutaway forefoot; stem recurved slightly at the top. Washstrake from just aft of the bow to beyond the stern. Flat floors; grounding keels. Curved rudder extends below the bottom on some boats. Also built of iron or steel. Decked. Lateen-rigged with 2-3 masts, the primary masts raking strongly forward. On the 2-masted boats, the foot of the mainsail extends the length of the vessel. Small jigger sheeted to an outrigger; foresail tacked to a long rising bowsprit. Also rowed. Reported lengths 12-18m, widths 3.51-4.78m, depths 1.22-1.46m. Spelling variants: **balancelle★**, **balanci**, **blanenca**. Note also **bilancella**, **pilobote**.

balancella See **bilancella**

balancelle 1. *Algeria:* Used in pairs with a *bœuf* net, especially off the eastern coast, where the boats were called **pareilles**. At Algiers, the boats were heavier and stayed at sea as long as a week. In both areas the catch was transferred to shore by a small 3-man boat called a **porte-poisson** (or **caique★**). Slender bow; formerly square-sterned, later sharp. Some continued to sail until the mid-1920s, but by then most were motorized. Crew of 5-12. 15-30t, greater at Algiers. Note also **bateau bœuf**.

2. *France, Mediterranean coast:* 19th-century **fishing boat★**, **coaster★**, **advice boat★**, and armed **patrol boat★** that protected fishing rights. Sharp ends; curved stem extended above the gunwales; straight sternpost; strong sheer. Decked forward, rowing benches abaft the forecastle. Railing along each side on some types. One to 3 masts, setting lateen sails or quadrilateral lateen-type sails with a short luff. Mainmast raked forward; mizzen smaller and vertical, stepped well inboard, or raked aft and sheeted to a jiggerboom. Some required as many as 20 rowers. Length to ca. 25m. Name variant: **balânsi** (in Tunisia)

Further references: **balancela**, **bilancella**, **paranza**, **pilobote**

balance-log canoe See **outrigger canoe**

balanci See **balancela**

Balander See **bilander-1**

balandra 1. Spanish and Portuguese word for a **cutter★**- or **sloop★**-rigged fishing, pleasure, and general transport craft; at times used for privateering. Reported lengths 14-18m; e.g., length 16.2m, beam 4.38m, depth 1.6m. Other recorded names: **balandre**, **balandro★** (a small **balandra** or sometimes reserved for a **sloop**-rigged boat), **ballandra**, **bélandre**, **masta-bakar** (Basque)

2. Also, in Spanish and Italian, a vessel that serves as a **guard ship★** at a naval arsenal or off the entrance to a port, especially to guard against importation of contraband. Other recorded names: **balandra de arsenal**, **guardaporto**, **patache★**. Note also **coast guard ship**.

3. *Argentina/Uruguay:* Cargo **lighter★** of the Río Uruguay. Raked stem; low freeboard; sheer sweeps up toward the bow. Boomed gaff mainsail, staysail, jib to rising bowsprit, topsail.

4. *Brazil:* A decked cargo boat with a single lateen sail.

5. *Canary Islands:* **Yawl★**- or **ketch★**-rigged fishing vessel that usually worked off Western Sahara. Some had a live well. Boomed gaff mainsail and mizzen, gaff topsails; jibboom. Crew of 8-12. 50-100t.

6. *Ecuador:* **Sloop**-rigged cargo carrier. Rounded bottom, with keel; generally high prow. Decked; small forecastle, and sometimes a small poop. Length 12m, beam 4.5m, freeboard ca. 1.5m.

balandra-6

7. *Peru:* Small decked boat that transported supplies between the Lobos Islands and the northern mainland coast and engaged in fishing off Callao. Generally a clipper bow, transom stern, and small cabin. Gaff mainsail; boom lacing knotted separately at each tie. Two headsails tacked to a very long bowsprit. Reported lengths 7.6-10m, widths 2.13-3m, depths 1.07-1.83m.

8. *Philippines, central:* Double-**outrigger canoe★** used for fishing, and being fast, for transporting fresh fish, passengers, and produce to urban centers. Plank-extended **dugout canoe★** with sharp, strongly raked bow and stern; sheer sweeps up at ends. Three booms pierce the hull and connect on each side directly to the long thin floats. Quarter rudder. Sets a high-peaked standing lugsail, foot laced to a very long boom; staysail tacked to stem. Reported lengths 9-12m, narrow. Another type attributed to this part of the Philippines is 3-masted and ca. 24m long. Spelling variant: **balanra**

balandra-8

9. *Puerto Rico, N West Indies:* Heavily canvassed, **sloop**-rigged boat. Originally a trader, now small types fish and others participate in local regattas. Carvel-planked; floor timbers, aprons, ribs, stem, and sternpost hand-hewn natural crooks; heavily timbered; 1.5m-deep fixed keel. Overhanging bow and stern; sharp entry; small raked transom; strong sheer. Flush-decked, low bulwarks; small cargo hatch (replaced by shallow cockpit on small boats); helmsman braces against a wooden cleat. Tall, sharply raked mast. Mainsail laced to long boom and to the mast. Jib to headstay. Crew of 6. Lengths mostly 5-6m, some to 9m. Note also **navito barco**.

Further references: **bilander-1**, **falua-2**, **imbabura**

balandra de arsenal See **balandra-2**

balandre See **balandra-1**, **balandro**, **bilander-1**

balandro 1. In Spanish-speaking areas, frequently designates a **sloop***-rigged boat. Fine lines, especially those that race; fuller lines on traders and **fishing boats***. Name variant: **balandre** (Catalan)

2. *Canary Islands:* **Fishing boat** that usually worked off the African coast. Generally transported salted fish, but some had a live well. Plumb, slightly curved stem; transom or counter stern. **Cutter***-rigged with large boomed gaff sail, gaff topsail; jibboom, 3 jibs. Those fitted with a wet well generally had a gaff mizzen. Crew of 10. 25-30t.

3. *Cuba:* A **sloop**-rigged **fishing boat**.

See also **balandra**.

balandro vivero See **vivero-3a**

balangai See **barangay**

balangar See **balinger-1**

baláñgay See **barangay**

balangha See **balinger-2**

balanghai, balanghay See **barangay**

balanra See **balandra-8**

balanselle See **bilancella**

balânsi See **balancelle-2**

balão See **ballahou, balon-1, vallam-1a**

balaon See **ballahou**

bala-oruwa See **varakan-oruwa**

balaou *Iceland:* Early **schooner*** employed in fishing. Masts heavily raked. Further reference: **ballahou**

balaşkerma See **palischermo-1**

balato See **barato**

balau See **ballahou**

balaum See **balam, vallam-1a**

balc yawl See **baulk yawl**

bald-headed schooner See **schooner-1, schooner-barge-2**

baldheader 1. A boat lacking headsails.

2. Vessel with no sails above the mainsail(s), or a square-rigged vessel with no topsails above the topgallants. See also **schooner-1**.

baldie *Scotland, east coast:* Inshore line-**fishing boat*** of the late 19th and early 20th centuries; related to the larger **fifie***. Double-ended with vertical or slightly raking, straight ends; clinker-built originally, later carvel; sharply rising floors. Early boats open, then decked forward and aft, with open waist; some fully decked, with a large hatch. Smaller boats had a single mast stepped well forward and a lofty dipping lugsail tacked to the stemhead. Larger boats also set a standing lug mizzen, sheeted to an outrigger, and a jib on a long bowsprit. Also rowed, using 2 pairs of 3.66m-long oars. Auxiliaries on some. Crew of 2-5. Sizes varied with local conditions, those working out of harbors being the largest and more heavily built. Reported keel lengths 6.4-12.2m; e.g., length overall 7.5m, on keel 6.4m, beam 2.5m, depth 1.0m. Other recorded names: **baldy, bauldie, garibaldie (Leith baldie), Newhaven yawl, skiff*** (in Banffshire)

baldus See **balsa**

baldy See **baldie**

baleazalea See **whaleboat-1**

baleeira *Brazil:* 1. The **baleeira** of Bahia State in northeastern Brazil was used solely for whaling; worked until ca. 1910. Flexible carvel planking. Harpoonist stood on a small forecastle. Double-ended; bow and stern raked; high stemhead; little sheer except toward

baleeira-1

the bow. Oars worked against tholepins, secured by leather loops. Set a large lugsail on an aft-raking mast; sail extended by a bowline to the 1st thwart. Crew of 10-16. Reported lengths 10-18m, widths 2-3.5m, depths 1.0-1.8m, draft 0.85-0.9m.

2. The **baleeira** of the southern coast was modelled after the American **whaleboat*** and was clinker-built. Used solely for whaling until the mid-19th century; thereafter for both whaling and cargo; still used in the 1940s. Set 1-2 spritsails.

Spelling variant: **baleira**. See also **canoa do baleeiro, whaleboat-1**.

Baleiner See **baleinier**

baleinier *France:* Small, swift vessel of the 13th-16th centuries used primarily for privateering and scouting. In the 15th century, some engaged in commerce on the high seas. Worked with oars and sail. Ca. 100t. Spelling variants: **Baleiner, baleinière, balener, baleney, baleng(h)ier, balenièr(a), balinger***, **balinier, ballen(n)ier, ballinger**. See also **whaleboat-1, whaler-1**.

baleinière See **baleinier, canoa do baleeiro, whaleboat-1, whaleboat-7b**

baleinière de barre *West Africa:* **Whaleboat***-type craft employed by the Kru of the West African coast as **lighters*** to transfer heavy cargo and passengers to and from off-lying ships. Work through the surf off beaches. Sharp and slightly curved ends; open; relatively high-sided. Paddled by 8 men sitting on the gunwales, using short paddles with serrated, leaf-shaped blades. Sometimes 2 men in the bow row, single-banked. Steered with a sweep. Reported lengths 9-13.7m. Other recorded names: **pirogue de barre, surfboat***. Note also **bar boat**.

baleinière de Gaspé *Canada, E:* **Whaleboat*** used in Gaspé Bay during the 19th century. Sharp, raked, and slightly curved ends; lapped planking; top strake cut down slightly amidships; bilge keels along central part.

baleinière de sauvetage See **lifeboat**

baleinière du calfat See **plate-3**

baleinier-usine See **whaler-1**
baleira See **baleeira**
balenario See **whaler-1**
balener See **baleinier**
balenera See **whaleboat-1**
baleney See **baleinier**
balenger See **balinger-1**
balenghier See **baleinier**
balengier See **baleinier**, **balinger-1**
balengner See **ballinier**
balenier See **baleinier**, **ballinier**
balenièra See **baleinier**, **whaleboat-1**
balenière, **balenista** See **whaler-1**
bale-ontzi See **whaleboat-1**
balham See **vallam-3**
balıkçı kayığı *Turkey, NW:* Fishing (*balıkçı*) **boat*** of the **kayık*** type, used in the Istanbul area, mainly with nets. Carvel-planked; flat floors; straight block keel. Strongly curved stem and sternpost; sheer swept up; stem sometimes widened and recurved toward the top. Stem, sternpost, and top strakes often elaborately carved. Foredeck ended in a carved breakwater; longer stern deck for nets also terminated in a breakwater. Steered with a sweep or rudder. Mast near the bow often used by a fish spotter. Mainly rowed, using 4-6 oars, with 1 man to each oar; oars bulbous toward the inner end, blades often crescent-shaped at the bottom. Might also set a sail, usually a short-luffed dipping lugsail. Reported lengths 7-13.3m; e.g., length 13.3m, beam 2.3m, depth 0.9m. Other recorded names: **bakigi caighi**, **balikdja kaighi**, **caique***. Note also **alamana-2**.
balikdja kaighi See **balıkçı kayığı**
balingaria, **balingario** See **whaler-1**
balinger 1. *British Isles/France/Germany/Netherlands:* Variously reported between the 14th and late 17th centuries. In the early period, the vessels were long, narrow-oared, **galley***-type naval and cargo craft that frequented the North Sea, as well as the Bay of Biscay, where they probably engaged in whaling. Some traveled in concert with naval ships, conveying messages, passengers, and undertaking reconnaissance. Sharp ends. Set 1-3 sails, probably square, when conditions warranted; ranged from 16-160t, with 30-62 oars, 1 man per oar. Later reported as a small single-masted **coaster*** that set a square- or spritsail and had no forecastle, or as a 2-masted vessel, probably with square sails or a sprit mainsail and a lateen mizzen. Crew varied with vessel size and use; as many as 146 reported for those engaging in warlike activities. Shallow draft. Spelling variants: **balangar**, **bal(l)enger**, **balengier**, **ballinger**, **ballunger**, **balyngar**, **balynger**
2. *Indonesia (Moluccas)/Philippines:* Term used by early travelers for a large trading vessel. Spelling variant: **balangha**
Further references: **baleinier**, **nef-1**
balingera See **whaler-1**
balinier See **baleinier**
baliseur, **balizador**, **balizeur** See **beacon boat**
balk yawl See **baulk yawl**
ballaho, **ballahoe**, **ballahoo** See **ballahou**

ballahou 1. Term sometimes given to a slovenly vessel, to one that maneuvers poorly, or to a **man-of-war*** with poorly stayed masts.
2. *Bermuda and West Indies:* A locally built **schooner***-type vessel used mainly in the 19th century. Principally a trader, but its speed made it popular for piracy and smuggling. Characterized by tall masts, with the foremast near vertical or sometimes forward-raking, and the mainmast raking sharply aft. Tall, narrow gaff sails; foresail overlapped the main; mainsail boomed and gaff peaked-up sharply. A large full-cut jib ran to a long bowsprit. In Bermuda, this rig was popular in the 1830s and was sometimes also called a **Bermuda schooner***. In general, the vessels had a plumb stem, wide shallow counter, raked sternpost, sharply rising floors, and little sheer. Reported lengths 25-29m; draft 3.9-4.2m.
Spelling variants: **balahú***, **balão**, **balaon**, **bala(o)u**, **ballaho(e)**, **ballahoo**, **ballauro**, **ballyhou**, **bullahoo**
ballahou schooner See **Bermuda schooner-1**
ballam See **belem**, **vallam-1a**, **vallam-2**
ballam ·ashuri See **belem-1**
ballam nassūri See **belem-2**
ballam suffina See **belem-1**
ballandra See **balandra-1**
ballanero See **whaler-1**
ballang See **rua ballang**
ballao See **padow**
ballast barge 1. Vessel that dredges for sand and gravel ballast, generally from rivers and harbors, and transports it to ships. A vessel in ballast may be called a **bateau lesteur**. Note also **dredger-1**.
2. *British Isles:* Those on the Thames in the early 19th century had bluff rounded ends and massive stem and sternpost; primarily open, non-sailing craft worked by 2 men. Very low freeboard when loaded. Later boats square-ended, and employed steam-operated dredging buckets. Those near Portsmouth on the south coast were often **ketch***-rigged. On the east coast, many coal-carrying vessels earned the name **ballast barge** because their inability to sail well when light made it desirable, and profitable, to carry ballast sand on their return trip.
Selected name variants: **ballast boat** (or **dredger**, **lighter**), **ballaster**, **Ballastever**, **Ballastewer**, **Ballastleichter**, **ballastlichter**, **balastman**, **ballastschuit***, **Ballastschute**, **barca da zavorra**, **barca zavorriera**, **barco de lastre**, **bateau délasteur** (or **délesteur**), **bote de lastrar**, **chalana para lestre**, **chiatta da zavorra**, **délasteur**, **dirt gab(b)ard**. Note also **allège**.
ballast boat, **ballast dredger**, **ballaster**, **Ballastever**, **Ballastewer**, **Ballastleichter** See **ballast barge**
ballastlicher See **ballast barge**, **ballastschuit**
ballast lighter, **ballastman** See **ballast barge**
ballast punt *England, SE:* Dredged gravel from along much of the Thames River and many canals for use as road material, for riverbank maintenance, and to clear the channels. Heavily constructed. Square raked ends; small end decks. One man guided the boat with a long pole; the 2nd handled a pole with a wire basket on one end or worked a small winch along one side, which raised the scoop. Name variant: **dredging punt**

ballastschuit *Belgium, N:* Type of **schuit**★ used on the Scheldt River to transport ballast materials to and from ships at Antwerp. Heavily built, with bluff ends, flat floors, curved sides; leeboards. Name variant: **ballastlichter**. Note also **ballast barge**.

ballastschute See **ballast barge**

ballast trow See **trow-1**

ballauro See **ballahou**

ballenera *Argentina/Uruguay:* Fast vessel that carried passengers and cargo between Buenos Aires and Montevideo in the 19th century. The larger boats had a railing above the deck, the smaller only a molding; loaded, their decks were almost awash. Variously rigged as a **sloop**★, **cutter**★, **ketch**★, or **schooner**★. One to 3 in crew, more on the **topsail schooner**. From 10-60t, the largest single-masters being ca. 40t. See also **whaleboat-1**.

ballenero See **whaler-1**

ballenger See **balinger-1**

ballenier, ballennier See **baleinier, whaleboat-1**

balley See **bawley**

ballinger See **baleinier, balinger-1**

ballinier *Seychelles:* The **whaleboat**★ was probably introduced to these Indian Ocean islands in the early 1900s. Now used for line fishing, mainly for the locally popular *karang*. Clinker-planked; grown or sawn timbers; copper-fastened with nails and roves; rounded bilges. Some builders now use laminated frames and other structural members. Sharp ends; straight, mildly raked stem; sternpost similar but now cutaway for a propeller. Decked at the ends, under which the crew may sleep. Mast and sails lowered when not in use. Most have a diesel engine. Average length 9m. Other recorded names: **balengner, balenier, welbot**

balloen See **rua ballang**

ballon *Peninsular Malaysia:* Reported in the 17th century as a fishing or river **dugout canoe**★. Propelled by small paddles, paddler standing. Further references: **balon, rua ballang**

ballong See **vallam-1a**

balloni See **rua ballang**

balloon See **rua ballang, vallam-1a**

ballum See **vallam-1a**

ballunger See **balinger-1**

bally See **bawley**

ballyhou See **ballahou**

baloa See **vallam-1a**

balolang See **bilolang**

balon *India:* Official **barge**★ and pleasure craft of the states bordering the west coast. Used to the end of the 19th century. Long, narrow boat carved from a single tree trunk; rounded hull; raised ends; some boats gilded. Rowed. Spelling variants: **balão, ballon**★, **baloon**. Note also **vallam-1a**. Further references: **balsa-6, rua ballang**

baloon See **balon, vallam-1a**

balos See **balsa-6**

balóto See **baroto**

balsa 1. Term loosely applied to a **float**★ or **raft**★ constructed of logs, especially of balsa wood, or of such objects as inflated skins, rubber bags, or casks, held together by a light framework. May also be constructed of bound rolls of a local grass or reed. Further reading: J. G. Nelson, "The Geography of the Balsa," *American Neptune* XXI (1961), 157-195. Note also **chiatta, jangada, life raft, reed boat-1, zaima-2, zattera**.

2. *Argentina:* A craft that transported cargo on the Paraná River from Asunción in Paraguay, where most were constructed, to Buenos Aires. Consisted of 2-3 heavy **canoes**★, across which a platform was lashed. Cargo placed on the platform and in the **canoes**. House added on deck. Propelled by oars and a large square sail; maneuvered by a long sweep. The **canoes** served as **tenders**★ for other boats on completion of the trip.

3. *Argentina, west-central:* One-man reed **balsa** used for fishing in the former marshes of Guanacache. Large oval central bundle formed the bottom, and 2-3 small tubes created the sides. Blunt ends, which turned up only slightly, were lashed tightly together; the rest of the hull was secured with sharp stakes. Poled. Length 4.3m, width 1.15m.

4. *Bolivia/Peru:* General term applied to several models of reed boat used on Lake Titicaca and nearby lakes. Vary from 1-man craft composed of 2 cigar-shaped bundles to sturdy 5-bundle **balsas**; the largest are produced by the Uru of the Bay of Puno in the northwestern part of the lake. When large loads must be transported, 2 boats may be lashed together with a platform between to form a **catamaran**★ or very long boats are used to provide extra buoyancy. Large **balsas** may have a mat shelter. The bundles, all of the giant *totora* sedge, may be 30cm in diameter; bound into shape with braided rope of *ichu* grass. On some, a

balsa-4

thin tubular roll wedged between the 2 large rolls creates a "keel," and a small tube on top of each large roll forms "gunwales." The Uru peoples lash the 2 main bundles to a thinner "keel" and not to each other. Bow and stern designs vary with tribal custom and the number of bundles that make up the boat; some ends blunt, others rake up smartly to a point, some turn up sharply and are then cut off blunt, and still others turn up and recurve slightly. Curvature achieved solely by gradual shaping and lacing. Propelled by double-bladed paddles, a trident-ended pole, or sail. The multipiece mast is usually an inverted "V," with the lower ends resting on the top bundles, secured by lashings, and stayed by another pole; some masts rake sharply forward. The lugsails are of reeds, with top and bottom yards, and may be rectangular, trapezoidal, or hexagonal; the thicker bottom ends of the reeds are aligned to form the leech. Many now use cloth sails. A short oar, tucked under the helmsman's leg, serves as a rudder when sailing. Reported lengths 1.8-8m; e.g., length 5.2m, beam 1.32m, depth 0.66m. Other recorded names: **huampu***, **jamppu**, **yampa**, **yuampu** (Aymará), **oca** (by the Uru)

5. *Brazil:* **a.** In the Rio de São Francisco Basin in eastern Brazil, **balsas** are composed of bundles of the buoyant *buriti* palm. May have low railings and a palm awning to protect passengers in the central area. Parts of a large **balsa** may be sold en route and the remainder sold on arrival at its destination. Maneuvered by a crew of 2, steering at the bow and stern. Reported lengths 12-40m; e.g., length 12m, width 2.5m, depth 1.0m. **b.** A 7-log **balsa** is used in the Acre area, in southwestern Brazil.

6. *Chile, N:* **a.** Skin **raft** that passed through the surf in order to unload passengers and baggage from ships lying offshore; also used for coastal travel and fishing. Two inflated skins of seal, sea lion, or other animals

balsa-6a

were placed parallel or drawn together at the front end to form a triangle. One or more platforms of cane or poles were lashed across the skins. Skins sewn, usually with seal intestines, so that the ends curved upwards; inflated through a tube at one end. Propelled by 1-3 persons using double-bladed paddles; occasionally hoisted a small sail. Reported by early explorers and used in isolated locations at least as late as the 1940s. Ca. 2.4m long. Other recorded names: **balon***, **balos**, **balza**. **b.** In the area of Arica, some fishermen use a log **balsa**, working out through the surf with a long net. Net hauled ashore by a team of men. Constructed of *magué* wood from Peru. Each of the three 4.7m-long logs has a diameter of 20cm; lashed together in several places. Three short logs are lashed on to form a raised bow ca. 50cm long. Rowed with a short bamboo oar. Crew of 2. Width ca. 1.0m.

7. *Mexico, NW:* Flexible reed **balsa** of the Seri of the eastern Gulf of California; last made ca. 1922. Composed of 3 bundles of overlapping reeds, as long

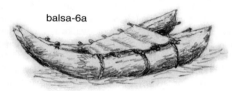

balsa-7

as 9m, with the butt ends amidships. Each bundle tied internally as construction proceeded and then wound spirally with a thin cord on completion. The 3 bundles were lashed together on the same plane, the long tapered ends tied securely. Appearance in the water

varied with number of persons (1-4) using the craft; the more people the higher the ends. Propelled by double-bladed paddle, harpoon, hands, or swimmer. Length 9m, beam 1.2m, depth 0.5m. Name variants: **grass boat***, **hascám**. Further reading: W. J. McGee, "The Seri Indians" in: *Seventeenth Annual Report of the Bureau of American Ethnology, 1895-1896* (Washington, D.C.: Government Printing Office, 1898), 215-221.

8. *Mexico, SW:* Gourd **raft** of the Río de las Balsas. Sealed, bottle-shaped gourds lashed together with a network of rope and logs. Transports people, but especially fruit, to market. On the return trip, the **raft** is disassembled; the gourds, and sometimes the logs, are carried home on foot. Small **rafts** used for fishing were ca. 1.0m square. Note also **calabaza**.

9. *Peru, north-central:* The cargo-carrying **balsas** of the swift Río Mayo are constructed of light tree trunks. The larger ends of the trunks are placed forward. Lashed with lianas and bark fiber. Cargo and passengers placed on a raised platform of crossed palm branches set on a network of struts ca. 45cm above the **raft** itself. Paddled and maneuvered by several men at the square bow end. Generally used only for a single downstream trip.

10. *Philippines:* An assemblage of logs, planks, or bamboo poles fastened together to form a **raft** for the transport of goods and passengers, especially on Luzon. Sometimes the logs and bamboo poles are themselves the cargo.

11. *South America, west coast:* Indigenous log **raft** reported by early travelers, principally from southern Colombia to central Peru. All made of Ecuadorian

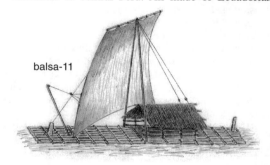

balsa-11

balsa logs. Size, shape, and rigging varied, indicating adaptations to meet special uses and geographical conditions. Modified by the colonial Spanish, who found them useful as river craft in lowland Ecuador, where they were sometimes 24m long and outfitted for comfortable travel. Some only a skeletal framework; others solidly built surfaces of 2 layers of logs; 2-deck seagoing **rafts** also reported. Small **balsas** used mainly for ferrying and cargo transport, and some constructed as 1-way **timber rafts*** that floated downstream. Many equipped with sails, and 2-masted types were seen. The masts often the inverted "V" type. Then, as now, the sailing **balsas** used one or more daggerboards at each end to control direction under sail. On the smaller unrigged craft, a plank aft maneuvered in a sculling motion propels the craft. Recent **balsas** are recorded as having 5-11 logs and up to 18m long, but most are shorter. Shaped bows on some; others squared off. On the sailing craft, the mast is placed in a hardwood step and sets either a lug-, sprit-, or gaff sail. A light spar may extend the lugsail. Large Ecuadorian **balsas** were in use until about 1920, often aiding in lightering from ships; some small fishing craft are still found in isolated communities, and some of these have plank sides. Other recorded names: **balza**, **jaguanda**, **jangada***, **jangu(a)da**. Note also **balsilla**, **balsita**, **bongo-3**, **Sechuras**.

12. *United States:* A class of boat in the U.S. Navy. Two cigar-shaped, airtight cylinders are held parallel by an open wooden framework. Equipped with oarlocks for rowing or sculling and eyebolts for lifting to and from a ship. May also set a spritsail. Serves as a floating stage for those painting a ship's hull; also important as a **life raft***. Length 5.5m, width 2m. Name variant: **catamaran**. Note also **balsa raft**.

13. *Uruguay:* Vessel of the peoples living along the Uruguay River. Two large boats were joined together with crossplanks. Reeds strewn over the decking; a small, hide-covered hut, set in the middle, provided shelter. Rowed, both upstream and down. Length to ca. 21m.

14. *Venezuela, W:* The **balsa** was still seen occasionally on Lake Maracaibo in the late 19th century. Some constructed of tree trunks, but most were of bundles of reeds, to which crosspoles were fastened.

Other recorded names: **baldus**, **balse**, **balsilla***, **balza**, **balze**, **vals(s)a**. Further references: **caballito**, **chinchorro**, **life raft**, **nu-2a**, **pelota-2**, **tõ´ xana**, **wo´te**

balsa de juncos See **caballito**
balsa de salvamento See **life raft**
balsa dos Paymarys See **ytapá**
balsa punt See **balsa raft**
balsa raft British navy term for a light **raft*** composed of 2 connected wooden floats. Used for cutting in the waterline on ships, and painting. In former days used for refastening the copper sheathing, hence also called **copper punt***; the **punt*** was more boat-like and varied during the 19th century in shape and size. Reported lengths 3-4.3m, widths 1.4-1.7m. Name variant: **balsa punt**. Note also **balsa-12**, **plate-3**, **vlot-1**.
balsa salvavidas See **life raft**
balse See **balsa**
balsilla *Ecuador, S/Peru, N:* Term applied to a small sailing balsa-log **raft*** still used for ferrying to large offshore craft and for fishing. Word may also apply to smaller craft made from discarded logs of larger **rafts**. Vary from 4-5 logs, the 4-log **balsilla** favored in Ecuador since the early 20th century. The 4-log **raft** has 2 large, slightly longer logs outside and 2 smaller logs in the center; each log tapered at the ends, then cut blunt. In 5-log **rafts**, the logs are of roughly equal diameter (15-30cm), tapered to form a bow or cut square. Logs are bound at the bow and stern and held rigid by hardwood crossties. Centerboard on some, placed just abaft the mast. Steered with a sculling oar or plank. When beyond the surf, the oar is slipped between the logs aft and serves to propel the craft, using a special rhythmic

motion—set, twist, push. A short mast steps between 2 logs directly behind the forward crosstie, stayed forward with 2 stays to the outside logs; single stay aft. Off Ecuador, the **rafts** now use a gaff sail with bamboo gaff and boom; prior to the 20th century, they set a spritsail, as they still do in Peru. Mast struck while fishing. Crew of 1-2. Reported lengths 2.7-4.9m; e.g., length 4.9m, beam 3.25m, depth 0.3m. Note also **balsa-11**. Further reference: **balsa**
balsita *Peru:* Small, crude non-sailing **raft***. Used mainly by fishermen who work out from the northern beaches, but also found as **tenders*** on **botes*** and powered craft. The balsa logs are joined by 2-3 crosspieces

balsita

of special shape so that the longitudinal logs are depressed to form a uniform bottom surface. Forward ends of logs sweep up on the bottom to provide a planing surface; aft ends left blunt. Propelled by a wide-bladed, tapered plank that is maneuvered in a peculiar fashion, using a log aft as a fulcrum. Note also **balsa-11**.
Baltic dandy, **Baltic ketch** See **galeass-4**
Baltic trader **Coaster*** that works from Swedish ports. Bow reinforced to provide ice-breaking capabilities. Further references: **easterling**, **galeass-4**
Baltimore buckeye See **bugeye**
Baltimore clipper *United States:* Fast, weatherly **schooner*** popular in the 1st half of the 19th century. Term not used until ca. 1825, but the type had been evolving before then. Most of the better-known vessels built at Baltimore, but also constructed elsewhere on Chesapeake Bay and as far north as New England. Popular as armed **privateers*** and blockade runners, as **slavers***, and as coastal passenger vessels. Limited cargo space caused their demise. Rounded, raking, slightly curved stem; raking square counter stern. Considerable deadrise, slack bilges, deep drag aft; greatest beam about one-quarter in from the bow, clean run aft; low freeboard. Generally painted black; high bulwarks, pierced for gun ports on those that were armed. Decked; generally a flush deck. The 2 tall, slender masts raked sharply aft, setting gaff sails. Square topsails set to one or both masts. Long bowsprit carried 2 or more jibs. A few **brig***-rigged. Crew of 20-30. Reported lengths 16.6-35m; e.g., length 28.3m, beam 7.3m, depth at stern 4m. Other recorded names: **Baltimore clipper-schooner**, **Chesapeake Bay schooner** (**clipper-schooner** or **schooner-clipper**), **clipper-goélette**, **heeler***. Further reading: Howard Irving Chapelle, *The Baltimore Clipper, Its Origin and Development* (New York: Dover Publishers, 1930; reprint 1988). Note also **clipper**, **fruit schooner**, **pilot boat model**, **Virginia model**.
Baltimore clipper-schooner See **Baltimore clipper**
balyngar, **balynger** See **balinger-1**
balza, **balze** See **balsa**
bamboo cargo-carrying raft See **fa zi**

bamboo-carrying pole junk See **bian zi**
bamboo-leaf boat See **sasa-buné**
bambot, bambott See **bumboat-1**
banama See **banawa**
banana boat 1. A ship constructed or modified to transport bananas. Usually fast. Cargo holds heated or cooled as necessary to bring the green stalks to near-ripe stage by arrival in port. Other recorded names: **Bananaschiff, bananier(a)**. Note also **fruit ship**.
2. During World War II converted **banana boats** were used as escorts. In the British Royal Navy, invasion **barges** might be called **banana boats**.
3. *Zambia, N:* Plank boat, so called because of its banana-like shape. New type designed to supplement the **dugout canoes★** on Lake Mweru as fishing craft. Clinker-planked; rounded flaring sides; numerous ribs; strong bottom rocker; bow transoms. Propelled mainly by an outboard motor. Length 7m, beam 1.35m, depth 0.56m.
Further reference: **surfboat-2**
Bananenschiff, bananier, bananiera See **banana boat**
banawa *Indonesia, E/central:* **1.** General term for **boat★** or **vessel★**.
2. Term once used specifically for a beamy trader from the southwestern part of Sulawesi (Celebes), designed to carry horses and buffalo. Extinct. Plank-built of short lengths; sharp ends; keel with strong rocker merged into curved and raked ends. Gangways out over the sides provided a route around the open hold; they also supported a lattice deck over the hold, which was partitioned into stables. Square-ended poop deck continued outboard on the quarters. Pivoting quarter rudders worked from lower outboard galleries. Two tripod masts; the taller forward mast stepped in forward third; the aftermast stepped at the break in the poop. Elongated lug-type mat sails bent to top and bottom yards. Small jib held by a light spar.
Other recorded names: **banama** (by the Dayak), **bĕnaoe** or **benau** (by the Timorese)
banca *Philippines:* The universal craft of the islands—a simple or plank-extended **dugout canoe★** that serves for fishing, pearling, cargo transport, and as a water taxi, etc. Most **bancas** are known by the use to which they are put; a few of the more important types are listed below under "note also." Usually have double outriggers, with direct connectives, but many work with only one or none; the floats may "toe in" at the bow end; on some large **bancas**, sponsons along the hull just above the waterline increase stability. Generally sharp-ended, but many have square ends; bow usually rises in a long overhang; ends may turn up; on some a platform at the bow serves as a fishing stage. Large **bancas** with a narrow mat-roofed cabin are often called **banquillas**. Paddled, rowed, or set a rectangular sail to a demountable tripod mast or a pole mast; modern types sometimes attach an outboard motor to a sawed-off transom; a few have a small inboard engine and are known as **pump boats★**. Reported lengths 5-22m; average length 10m, beam 1.0m, depth 0.6m. Other recorded names: **bangca, bangka', banka, bogo**. Further reading: T. L. Sinclair, Jr., "You Can't Beat the Banca," *American Neptune*

XIX (1932), 257-264. Note also **baroto, boteng pamunuanam, chinchorrohan, dinalapang, panca, vinta**.
band See **crib-1, shot**
bandar manché See **manji**
bander boat See **bunder boat**
bandoeng See **bandong**
bandong 1. *Indonesia, NW/Singapore:* Transported firewood and charcoal from the Riau Archipelago to Singapore. Lug-rigged on 1-2 masts; also rowed. Crew of 5. Length ca. 16.5m, beam 4m, depth 1.8m; cap. 4.8-9.5t.
2. *Indonesia, north-central/East Malaysia:* Flat-bottomed boat that carried cargo on western Kalimantan (Borneo) and southwestern Sarawak rivers. Plank-built; ends raked; multiple thwarts; outboard gangway for polers. Partly decked; remainder loosely covered with bamboo; steered with an oar. Paddled and poled. Cap. ca. 2t.
3. *East Malaysia:* Used for fishing and trading, especially in the southwestern part of Sarawak. The **bandong peranto** uses drift nets. Plank-built onto a dugout keel piece; sharp ends, raked; clipper bow, sometimes with vestiges of a carved figurehead; strong sheer; quarter rudder. **Fishing boats★** open except for short end decking; awning amidships on small types; large traders decked, with an open-ended cabin over the hold. **Fishing boats** and small traders set a lugsail to a pole mast stepped through a thwart, the trader adding a staysail. Large traders set a gaff (usually standing) mainsail, jib to a bowsprit, and staysail. Also paddled. Reported lengths 9-14m; fishing boats ca. 9m, beam and depth 1.0m.
Other recorded names: **bandoeng, perahoe bandoeng, perahu bandong**
bandong peranto See **bandong-3**
bandong temuai See **peleleh**
baṇḍūqī śikӧri See **shikara**
bangala *Maldives:* Interisland trader, built in India, that worked as far as Sri Lanka; none owned after 1960. Considered to be a **kotia★**, but known in the Maldives as a **bangala**. High poop with carved counter stern, considerable sheer, strongly raked bow. Lateen-rigged on 2-3 masts; some set a square topsail on the fore-

bangala

mast. Reported lengths 24-25m, widths 6.1-6.4m. Other recorded names: **bag(g)ala, buggalow, na, nau★**
bangarā See **ekta**
bangca See **banca**

bang choon See **phang chun**

bangga See **bangka**

bangka *Indonesia, central:* General term for **boat**★ or **canoe**★ in parts of Sulawesi (Celebes) and Kalimantan (Borneo). Spelling variants: **bangga, bongka, obangga**. Note also **bangko**. Further references: **banca, baroto, tongkang-2, wangka**

bàngka rī nīngkē *Indonesia, central:* **Raft**★ used by the Padoé people, near Lakes Matana and Towuti in southeastern Sulawesi (Celebes).

bangko *Indonesia, NE:* Generic term for **boat**★ at Ternate in the Moluccas. A special type of **bangko** provides interisland transport for passengers, livestock, and merchandise. Lightly constructed plankbuilt boat; sharp ends turn up. Two heavy outriggers; 4 booms cross to the floats. House amidships. Paddled or sailed. Other recorded names: **prahoe** (or **proa**) **bangko, prahoe kagoena, proa kaguna**. Note also **bangka**.

bangkong 1. *Indonesia, central:* Term for a **canoe**★ in the Semitau dialect in Kalimantan Barat (western Borneo).
2. *East Malaysia:* Very long, heavy plank-extended **dugout canoe**★ used on Sarawak rivers by the Sea Dayak peoples. Square overhanging ends; planking terminates short of each end in a square breakwater. On early boats, each plank had a ledge on which succeeding planks were lashed with rattan. The Chinese adaptation has a square raked bow that sweeps up sharply. Awning covers all or part of the hull. May be fancifully painted. Paddled. Length over 15m. Those used for war and piracy (the **bangkong** or **perau' pengayau**) are reported to have carried as many as 80 warriors who stood atop the long, flat roof that covered most of the hull; 60-80 men might paddle below, but the average was ca. 30 men. May have employed a rudder in addition to paddles. Plank extensions sewn on; tall curved stern; low overhanging bow on which brass swivels were placed. Reported lengths 21-30m; e.g., length 30m, beam 3m. Other recorded names: **bankong, bantang, rangkang**

Bangor coracle See **Dee coracle**

bangué *Brazil, E:* Skin **pelota**★ of the interior rivers of Bahia State. On square types, sticks are laced along each side to reinforce the top; on circular types, curved sticks are used. Sometimes a few branches are laid across the bottom.

banka *Indonesia, central:* Generic term for a **perahu**★ in the Padoe dialect of southwestern Sulawesi (Celebes). Further reference: **banca**

bank boat *England:* **Punt**★-type craft for trimming hedges and weeds along canals; carries clay to plug leaks. A small shelter contains a few amenities. Towed by the workers. Note also **weed cutter**.

bank dory See **Banks dory**

banker *Canada, E/United States, E:* **1.** Term sometimes applied loosely to vessels that work the offshore fishing banks, staying out for periods of time and salting (**salt banker**) or freezing the catch, as opposed to the **market boat**★ that brings the catch in fresh. Now motorized.

2. Vessel that fished for cod on the fishing banks off Nova Scotia and Newfoundland, as well as Georges Bank off eastern Massachusetts. Generally **schooners**★ out of New England and Nova Scotian ports. Greatest concentration during the 19th century. Those used prior to the late 19th century were strongly built, round-bottomed, straight-keeled, apple-bowed, square-sterned, beamy; moderate drag. Quarter-deck; accommodations forward and aft. By the early 20th century, **bankers** were sleek, fast **schooners**. Early **bankers** anchored and fished directly from the side; later fishing done from 2-man **dories** (see **Banks dory**), up to 10-12 nested on deck. Mainly 2-masted; a few 3-masted **schooners** built toward the end of the century. Some early single-masted vessels used a gaff mainsail and 1-2 headsails, and often a square topsail. Crew of 20-24. Typically 18m long, 5.5m wide, 2.2m deep. Other recorded names: **banking schooner** (or **vessel**), **bankke shippe, bank(s)man, bank ship, banquais, banqué, banquier, clipper banker, grand banker, (Grand) Banks schooner, Neufundlandschoner**. Note also **canadienne, côtier, dory trawler, fisherman-1, Georgesman, knockabout-3b, morutier, sharpshooter-2, terreneuvier**.

bankeskuta See **bankskuta**

Bank fisherman See **fisherman-1**

bankfiskersköite See **bankskøyte**

banking dory See **Banks dory**

banking schooner, banking vessel, bankke ship, bankman See **banker-2**

bankong See **bangkong-2**

Banks dory *Canada, E/United States, NE:* Small open boat that revolutionized hook-and-line fishing in the mid-19th century, working mainly from **schooners**★ fishing the banks between Massachusetts and Newfoundland. Also popular for inshore fishing and as **lifeboats**★. Classified by bottom lengths, as **12-foot** (3.7m) **dory, 15-foot** (4.6m) **dory**. Narrow, flat, longitudinally planked bottom with rocker; straight flared sides, strakes half-lapped, the laps phasing out at the ends. Strong sheer, less on the inshore boats. Sharp bow, slightly curved raked stem; narrow, raked, wedge-shaped transom, curved on top, with notch for a sculling or steering oar. Three to 5 thwarts, removable to permit nesting on deck. Rowed, using 1-2 pairs of oars. Occasionally set a small loose-footed spritsail or a gaff sail, with standing gaff and fixed boom, set to a short mast stepped in the forward thwart. The 12- to 14-ft. **dories** are 1-man boats; the 15- and 16-ft. boats are 2-man. Bottom lengths 12-16 ft. (3.7-4.9m); e.g., length overall 5.5m, on bottom 4.3m, maximum beam 1.5m, depth 0.53m. Large banks-type **dories** are used by herring and mackerel **seine boats**★ along the Maine and Nova Scotian coasts, especially to carry nets. Length overall ca. 6.4m. Other recorded names: **bank** (or **banking**) **dory, cod dory, doris des Bancs, fisherman's dory, haddock dory, halibut dory** (16 ft.), **nesting dory, trawl dory**★ (14 and 15 ft.); also **Amesbury, Cape Cod, Gloucester,** and **Grand Banks dory**. Further reading: John Gardner, *The Dory Book* (Camden, Maine:

International Marine Publishing Co., 1978). Note also **banker, doris, dory, Lunenburg dory, Shelburne dory.**

Banks fisherman See **fisherman-1**

bank ship See **banker-2**

bankskjøite, banksköite See **bankskøyte**

bankskøyte *Norway, W:* Fishes for cod on the banks off the west coast. Carvel-planked, with full bow and stern and considerable rise to the hollow floors from a deep keel. Sharp ends; stem curved, sternpost straight, both raked. Decked, hatch amidships; outboard square-heeled rudder; tiller. Carries boats on deck, often nested **doryer** (see **dory**). **Ketch***-rigged, with loose-footed gaff mainsail, boomed mizzen. Topsails to one or both pole masts, forestaysail, jib to bowsprit. Now motorized. Sailing vessels had crew of 10-12 in summer, more in winter. Average length overall 18.2m, on keel 10.4m, beam 6.4m, hold depth 2.4m, draft 1.7m. Other recorded names: **bankfiskersköite, bankskjøite, banksköite.** Note also **bankskuta, skøyte.**

bankskuta *Sweden, SW:* Built on the Bohuslän coast for longline fishing on the banks of the Skagerak and North Sea. Worked to the end of the 19th century. Clinker- or carvel-planked, strongly raked ends to a comparatively short keel; steep rise to the floors, soft turn of the bilges; strong sheer. Full ends; stem curved above the waterline, straight below; sternpost sharply raked and straight. Narrow outboard rudder; tiller. Decked; raised bulwark at bow. Carried 2 boats from which the crew fished. Early boats 2- or 3-masted, setting square sails. By the 19th century, adopted spritsails; ca. 1860, used gaff sails and foremast abolished. Yard topsails, forestaysail, jib to bowsprit, sometimes a watersail below the bowsprit. Crew of 8-14, depending on boat size. Reported lengths overall 12.8-19.8m; e.g., length overall 19.2m, on keel 12.8m, beam 8.13m, hold depth 2.7m. Spelling variants: **bankeskuta**; pl. **bankskutor.** Note also **bankskøyte, hvassing.**

bankskutor See **bankskuta**

banksman, banks schooner See **banker-2**

banneton See **vivier-2**

banouche See **sambūq-2**

banquais, banqué See **banker-2**

banquetier See **terreneuvier**

banquier See **banker-2, terreneuvier**

banquilla See **banca**

bantang See **bangkong-2, banting-2**

bantim Early Malay term for a **brig*** or **brigantine***. Spelling variant: pl. **bantins**. Further reference: **banting-1**

bantin See **banting-1**

banting 1. *Indonesia:* Beamy trading vessel, dating from the 17th century, built mainly at Atjeh in northwestern Sumatra and on the north coast of Java. Probably armed. Stem recurved at stemhead; top strake continued aft at the stern to form wings; quarter rudders. Central hold; low house. Stepped 2-3 slender masts. The forward mast(s) set 2 square sails, the mizzenmast a boomed gaff sail. Crew of 6. One reported as 27m long, 8.2m wide, and 2.1m deep. Other recorded names: **bantim*, bantin, bantis**

2. *Peninsular Malaysia:* Open dugout-hulled craft used at the southern end of the Malay Peninsula. Sharp ends;

projecting concave stem; sharply rising floors formed a keel; strong frames. Bulwarks at each end; inside gunwale fitted with tholepins; sheer swept up at bow. Balance lugsails set to 2 masts; small jib run to bowsprit. Reported length 10.2m, beam 1.8m, depth 1.0m. Other recorded names: **atcheen, bantang, fast boat***

bantingan *Indonesia:* **Pram***-like boat towed behind a larger boat.

bantins See **bantim**

bantis See **banting-1**

baobao *Tonga, central Pacific:* Roughly hewn single-outrigger paddling **canoe*** used for inshore fishing. Details vary somewhat from island to island. Dugout hull, slight tumble home to sides; bottom rounded transversely with rocker fore-and-aft, with stern ending above the waterline. Solid vertical ends; break in the sheer line near ends. Two or 3 straight booms, lashed atop the gunwales, cross to the pointed float.

baobao

Booms and float attached by pairs of over-crossed stanchions, or by double U-shaped flexible withes. Carries 1-2 people. Reported lengths 3-5m, beam at bilges 0.3-0.4m, depth 0.31-0.38m. Spelling variants: **babao, bo(o)bao, boopaa, boopah, bopao, bopau, bou(paa), bupaa, papao, popao**

baptiau See **bateau**

baqqarah See **belem-3**

baquet See **baquet de Charleroi**

baquet de Charleroi *Belgium:* Box-shaped **canal barge*** built to transport coal from Charleroi to Brussels and grain on the return trip. Operated during the latter half of the 19th century and the 1st half of the 20th. Constructed of wood, iron, or steel; bow and stern usually vertical; straight sides, with tumble home at ends; no rubbing wales; low sheer. Short end decks; long central hatch, cambered hatch cover; narrow gangway along each side; very small, low cabin aft. Wide-bladed rudder with a folding extension that could be raised in locks; long tiller. Leeboards used when sailing. Towed along the canal by a horse, a family, or later by tractor. Mast stepped forward of the hatch; struck during canal passages. Set a loose-footed, boomed (with a punting pole) gaff sail; boom could be set into different loops in the leech. Gaff topsail; sometimes a foresail. When empty, 2-3 were lashed together to prevent capsizing. Reported lengths 18-20m; e.g., length with rudder extension 19.5m, beam 2.62-2.65m, depth ca. 2m, draft loaded 1.8m. Cap. 67-72t. Other recorded names: **bac de Charleroi, bak*** (pl. **bakken**), **bak van Charleroi, baquet, Charleroi bak** (or **baquet**)

baquet wallon See **waal**

bara balam *Bangladesh:* **Coaster*** that also fishes. Built up from a dugout base, the planking lashed on with rattan.

Raked bow transom; sharp, raked stern. Fore- and stern decks; open waist raised by portable washstrakes when underway. Sets a square sail. Crew of 14 when fishing. Length 15m, beam 4.3m, depth 1.8-2.4m. Note also **balam**.

baragóso, baragozzo See **bragozzo**

barakas *India, NW:* Refers mainly to a coastal vessel and may apply to both large and small vessels. Spelling variants: **barkas★, barkūs, bharakas, varkkas**

baranay See **barangay**

baranette See **barquerole**

barangai, barangar See **barangay**

barangay *Philippines:* **1.** Fast seagoing vessel of the early indigenous peoples, especially those of northern Mindanao; dated from at least the 3rd century. Apparently armed. Planking joined edge-to-edge with wooden pegs; additional strength provided by pliant wooden strips sewn to raised lugs spaced at intervals on the inside; caulked with fiber and resin. Sharp ends, flat floors amidships; semicircular in cross section; plank keel; low sides. Reported as undecked or with multiple decks. It is uncertain whether the vessel used double outriggers that rested on the water or outliers for balance. Longitudinal poles across the outrigger booms provided seating for paddlers, sitting in 2-6 rows on each outrigger; also rowed from the boat itself. When sailed, set a square sail to 1-2 collapsible bipod or tripod mast(s). Some carried 60-90 people; house or awning amidships and sometimes at stern; platform above the rowers, which might be used by warriors. Estimated lengths 14-20m; beam ca. 4m.

2. Long, narrow river craft for transporting freight and passengers in northern Luzon. Plank-built, the planking fastened with dowels or secured on the inside with rattan lacing; sometimes constructed of bamboo. The planked boats had sharp ends, rounded bottom with keel, low freeboard; caulked with coconut fiber. Often had a house with a rounded roof at the stern for the family and crew. Bamboo outriggers might be used. Poled, paddled, or sailed. The numerous short paddles had elongated blades that were pointed at the ends. Some set a trapezoidal sail to a single mast. As many as 20 men might work the iron-tipped poles. Name variant: **baraŋay** (a communal boat)

3. In the same area, a **barangay** may be a coastal **fishing boat★** using the *chinchorro* net. Sharp, raked bow; counter-like stern; bottom rocker.

4. A small type was built up from a dugout bottom that curved athwartships with rocker fore-and-aft. Lapped planking, probably sewn on; top strake very wide. Ends raked up in a curve; thick stem; small stern transom to which a rudder might be fixed, or a paddle used. A bamboo platform extended outboard on each side and projected forward and aft at the ends; paddlers, at least 4 to each side, sat on a low rail on the outer edge of the crossbeams. Arched mat house covered most of the hull. Mast stepped on block on the bottom, setting a battened balance lugsail.

Spelling variants: **balanay, balang(h)ai, baláñgay, balanghay, baranay, barangai, barangar, barangayan, baranggay, biniday, varangay**

barangayan, baranggay See **barangay**

baransèlla See **paranza**

barato See **baroto**

Barbados flying-fish boat *West Indies:* A good sailer that fished for flying fish off Barbados. Baggy leg-of-mutton mainsail and a very large, baggy jib to a short down-curved bowsprit. Open, sharp bow, recurved stem, transom stern, flat sheer. Crew of ca. 3. Length ca. 9m, deep hull. Sailing type extinct since the 1930s. Those now used for this purpose have a low trunk cabin amidships and a motor, but may step a mast.

Barbados schooner *West Indies:* Barbadian **schooners★** vary somewhat, depending on their intended mission—interisland trade, fishing, or coastal traffic. All are fast and fine-lined. Only a few remain. Note also **West Indies schooner**.

1. The fishing vessels have a plumb stem, short raking counter, flat sheer with low freeboard. Masts nearly equal height; loose-footed gaff foresail, sheeted well aft; mainsail with a gunter yard, set almost parallel to the mast, long boom. Sail laced to the masts. Bowsed-down bowsprit secures a large jib with a heavy roach to the foot.

2. The now-extinct type, which carried supplies and passengers between Bridgetown on the southwest coast and Speightstown on the northwest coast, was similar except that the foresail was boomed and the gaff was set almost horizontally. Masts vertical, the

Barbados schooner-2

mainmast taller. Reported lengths 24-30m. Early 19th-century boats depicted with aft-raking masts setting leg-of-mutton sails, the mainsail loose-footed and boomed. Name variant: **Speightstown schooner**

3. On the interisland traders, both masts may be vertical or the mainmast rakes aft. Foresail boomed or loose-footed, and the gaff has little peak. Mainsail, with a long boom, employs a regular, a high-peaked, or a gunter gaff. Long bowsprit uses a very large jib or a smaller jib and staysail. Plumb or curved stem, flat or counter stern, sharp deadrise, little sheer.

barbareske, barbaresque See **xebec-2**

barbariccio See **cabanella**

Barbary galiote See **galiot-7**

bar boat *Nigeria, SW:* Used in the late 19th century at Lagos to transfer cargo to and from ships. 7-8t. Note also **baleinière de barre**. Further reference: **masula**

bàrc *Ireland/Scotland:* Early Gaelic generic term for a **vessel★, boat★, skiff★**. May also designate a wooden **coaster★**. Name variants: **bàirc**; pl. **bàrca★**

barc See **barco-1**, **bark-1**

barca **1.** In Latin-derived languages, **barca** refers generally to a **boat**★ or a small **ship**★. However, the word may imply definite limitations, as in Italy today, where it is a craft under 100t cap. and, in size, falls between the smaller **battello**★ and the larger **barco**★. In many places, the word describes a precise craft, often local. Some of these follow. **2.** In a pejorative sense, a **barca** is a badly outfitted and unseaworthy vessel. **3.** *Brazil, east-central:* A **lighter**★-type vessel used on the middle São Francisco River from the end of the 17th to the mid-20th century. Distinguished by its carved figurehead of an animal, bird, or young woman; others painted. An arched housing of palm thatching protected the cargo and sheltered the family. Bottom flat, with keel. With favorable winds set 2 triangular sails, one laced to the mast and sheeted aft, the

barca-3

other boomed out forward; might set a jib similar to a spinnaker. Also rowed by 6-12; oars ca. 6m long. Sometimes used a type of boathook to grab branches and work upstream. Reported lengths 13.2-24.6m, widths 2.6-3.5m, depths 0.77-1.76m; shallow draft. A **barca** that transported cattle also plied the river, the **barca de passagem do gado**. This vessel lacked the figurehead and sails. A railing surrounding the hold prevented the cattle from jumping overboard. **4.** *Ecuador:* Three-masted cargo vessel. Rounded bottom with keel, high prow. Decked; small forecastle; holds and hatches; small poop on some. Length ca. 12.2m, beam 4.6m. **5.** *France:* The **barca** of 6th- to 9th-century Gallic sailors was a large, sturdy, carvel-built, flat-floored merchant vessel. **6.** *Italy:* **a.** The Venetian **barca** (or **barza**) of the late 15th and early 16th centuries was a round-bottomed sailing vessel with a low, narrow bow. Armed and often used to convoy other vessels or to engage in piracy; also served as a cargo carrier and in coastal defense. Cap. ca. 600t. Additional recorded names: **barzot(t)o**; pl. **barce**★, **barche**★, **barze**, **barzot(t)i**. **b.** In the Gulf of Venice and the adjacent lagoons, the **barca** is a long, narrow **fishing boat**★. Flat bottom, no keel; curved stem, rounded or sharp stern; large rudder. Decked, with a central hatch, or open, with a cuddy at each end. Rowed or sets a small lugsail to a short mast stepped through a thwart in the after third of the boat. Crew of 1-20, the larger crew required for trawling operations. Reported lengths 8-12m; e.g., length 9.9m, beam 2m, inside depth 0.5m. Name variant: **barca di Grado**. **c.** The fisherman's **barca** of Lago di Piediluco, south of Terni in Umbria, is a simple **punt**★. Shallow square ends; flat bottom, curves up at the stern, which is slightly higher than the bow. Two curved juniper-branch ribs

cross gunwale-to-gunwale. Coverboard at each end. Length 4m, beam 1.0m, depth 0.25m. **7.** *Italy, Sicily:* This **barca** has an exceptionally tall, inward-raking sternpost with the rudder following the sternpost's curve. Tiller cants downward sharply. Plumb stem with a high stemhead; straight keel has a slight drag; rounded stern. The cuddy forward creates a break in the bulwarks. Rowed, with 3 pairs of oars. Also sets a sail, usually lateen. Length ca. 10m. **8.** *Mozambique:* 15th-century **coaster**★. Strongly curved stem with high stemhead, considerable sheer; tall rudder. Mast, stepped just forward of amidships, set a large square sail. **9.** *Portugal:* **a.** Early **barcas** were small shallow-draft craft engaged in fishing and in river and coastal traffic; single-masted, with a quadrilateral sail; under 30t. The 15th-century **barca** was 2- or 3-masted, often serving as a reconnaissance vessel accompanying Portuguese explorers. Small square foresail, square mainsail, and on 3-masted types, a gaff mizzen; 1-2 topsails per mast. Sometimes rowed. The term **barca** now often refers to a vessel with more than 3 masts, having square sails on the 2 forward masts and lateen sails on the after masts. **b.** A **raft**★ used in collecting shellfish, seaweed, and octopus in rocky areas near Apulia, in the north. A wooden frame of poplar logs is filled with strips of cork. To help transport the catch from the beach, some **rafts** have 2 wooden wheels at one end and handles at the other. Poled by 1-man crew. Length 2m, width 0.85m, depth 0.37m. **c.** The small open **barca** of the upper Rio Lima in northwestern Portugal is used for local fishing and ferrying. Flat bottom, straight raked stem, wide transom. Straight sides, flared toward the stern. Rowed with single pair of oars. Length ca. 6m. **d.** On several Douro River tributaries in northeastern Portugal, the **barca** is a primitive box-shaped craft. Used mainly for fishing and light cargo transfer. Flat bottom, square ends, flat sides. Strengthening treads across the bottom. Poled. Length ca. 2.8m, beam 1.65m, depth 0.45m. **e.** Operates the *armação à valenciana*, a stationary fish trap, off beaches in the Tagus Estuary and in the Sesimbra area to the south. Three **barcas** work with a **batel**★. Each **barca** has a special duty and, accordingly, is given an identifying name: those at each end (the **barcas das portas**★) are the **barca da gacha da terra** (land side) and the **barca da gacha do mar** (seaward side). Extinct as a sailing craft. The rowing/sailing boats were sharp-ended, the stern slightly fuller; slightly curved stem, curved sternpost; shallow keel, bilge strakes, 2 wales along each side. A shredded wool ball topped the stemhead to reduce chafing of the sail. Open, with 5 thwarts and short forward and stern decks. Anchor davits at bow and stern, some had a small capstan. Steered with a sweep when rowed; shipped a rudder while sailing. Tarred hull, often with white triangle at the bows; identifying symbol also at the bows. Unstayed, forward-raking mast stepped in forward thwart; large quadrilateral lateen-type sail with a short luff. When rowed, usually employed 3 oars to a side, but could use 5. Crew of 10-11. Reported lengths 7.4-10m; average 8.6m long, 2.56m wide, 0.77m deep.

Modern motorized **barcas** are decked and have a wheelhouse; the wool ball on the stemhead has been retained. Other recorded names: **barca de armação**; pl. **barcas das armações. f.** Large double-ended **rowing boat★** used to transport the sardine catch from boats working out of Nazaré on the central coast. Carvel-planked, keel, strong sheer, open. Length 10.5m, beam 3.4m, depth 1.0m. Name variant: **barco★**
10. *Turkey:* The Turkish **barça** was a large sailing **merchantman★** of the late 15th into the 17th century. Relatively narrow bow; 2-3 masts set square sails.
Spelling variants: **barcaccia★, barcha, barka★, barqua, barxa, barza★, berca, varca, varke;** pl. **barcae, barche**. Note also **barco, bark, barque**. Further references: **bàrc, barcaccia, barco-4, barco de lavrador, barka-2, barke, barque-4, boat-1, jábega, jangada-4**
barca à brick-barca See **bark-1**
barca a tramoggia See **marie-salope**
barca a vela Italian term meaning not only a **sailboat★**, but also the largest of the **ship's boats★** on Italian naval vessels. Note also **scialuppa**.
barca bestia See **barkentine**
barca bombardiera See **bomb vessel**
barcaça 1. Portuguese word signifying a wooden or metal **barge★** or **lighter★** used to transport supplies, fuel, water, etc., especially on rivers. One type was designed to assist in maneuvering ships to be careened. Generally beamy, flat-bottomed, shallow depth; large hold area. Mostly towed. Spelling variants: **barquaca, barquaza**. Note also **batelão-1**.
2. *Brazil, E:* Transported produce from upriver and along the coast to ports between Salvador (Bahia) and

barcaça-2

Fortaleza. Still used in the early 1940s. Wall-sided, with hard turn of the bilge; mostly flat-bottomed; some larger vessels had keels; planking up to 7cm thick; copper-bottomed at Salvador. Long projecting bow on some facilitated grounding onto riverbanks; marked sheer toward the square, raked stem. Transom stern; outboard rudder; tiller; some used a steering oar. Straw-roofed cuddy forward or low cabin aft; large hatch amidships, coaming above gunwale level. Carried 2-3 pole masts; number and position depended on preference of owner rather than vessel size. No standing rigging. Small foremast stepped in eyes; mainmast about a third of the way aft, and in the 3-

masted type, the after mast was about a third in from the stern. At Salvador, foremast vertical and others raked aft; elsewhere all raked aft. Set gaff sails, most baggy with no reef points; or set leg-of-mutton sails. Forward boom topped at every tack, with boom overlapping mainmast by 1.8-2.4m. Sails laced to gaff, boom, and mast. Most had a bowsprit. Carried a **catraia★** as a **tender★**. Lengths 15-21m, widths 3-4m; e.g., length 21m, beam 4m, depth 1.3m, draft 1.5m laden, 45t. Spelling variant: **barcazar**. Note also **barcachina**.
3. *Portugal, Madeira:* The **barcaça** of these islands provided fresh water and coal to ships at Funchal.
Further reference: **barcaccia**
barcaça d'agua See **water boat-1**
barca cannoniera See **gunboat**
barca canterii, barca cantherii See **barge de cantier**
barca catalana, barca catalanesche See **catalane**
barcaçca See **barcaccia**
barcaccia *Italy:* **1.** Italian term for an unseaworthy boat, a craft that assisted in caulking a ship, a **ferry★** for transporting horses and wagons, or the largest of a **ship's boats★** on a merchant vessel (see **launch** and **scialuppa**). Spelling variants: **barcaç(ç)a, barcacia, barcazza, barchaca, barchaçia;** pl. **barcaccie**
2. Three-masted vessel of the northern Adriatic. Carried diverse cargoes from the late 17th into the 18th century. Curved stem, counter stern, poop deck. Stepped a sharply raking foremast in the eyes, a lightly raked mainmast amidships, and a vertical mizzen on the poop. Set lateen sails. Other recorded names: **barca★, bargòzzo**
Further references: **barca, barkaca, launch**
barcaccie See **barcaccia**
barcachina *Brazil, E:* A small **barcaça★** that traded off the Alagoas and Pernambuco coasts. Gaff-rigged; stepped 2 masts, both well forward, with the foremast in the eyes. Name variant: **lancha★**

barcachina

barcacia See **barcaccia**
barca cisterna See **water boat-1**
barca copriruota See **paddle-box boat**
barca corallina See **corallina**
barca correire *Italy, N:* Carried mail, passengers, and light merchandise on northern rivers and canals during the 19th century. On the Grand Canal, where it was called a **barchetto★**, the vessel had a sharp overhanging bow; stern also strongly raked, sharp below, flared

toward the top and cut square at top strake. Very strong sheer at ends; flat bottom; straight flaring sides. Decked at ends; house amidships extended to gunwales. Towed by a horse; steered with a long sweep.

barca correire

Length overall 16.25m, on keel 14.1m, beam 3.45m, depth amidships 1.0m. Name variant: **correira**

barca corridoia See **scorridora**

barca da arte de chávega, barca da arte de xávega See **barca da arte xávega**

barca da arte xávega *Portugal, S:* Fished, mainly for sardines, off the Algarve coast. Worked out from the beaches with a bag net (*xávega*). Assisted by a small open **calimeira** (or **calima**) that attached itself to the seaward end of the net to signal the direction to pull the net; square stern; 3 oars per side. An **acostado** (see **enviada**) transported the catch to shore, and at times towed the **barca★**. Elongated raised bow supported by a gammon knee; curved tall stemhead, with knob on top, sometimes covered with wool. Sternpost curved and also tall, but with a fiddlehead at the top. Similar but lower fiddleheads at the bow, sometimes considered to be stylized snake heads. Carvel-planked, flat floors, long straight keel, rounded bilges, bilge keels, stern fuller than bow. Open, moderate sheer. Steered with an oar. Employed 5-10 oars per side; single tholepins. Reported lengths 9-10m; e.g., length 9.7m, beam 2.5m, depth 0.7m. Other recorded names: **arte (de chovega), barca da arte de chávega** (or **xávega**), **barco de arte de xávega**. Further reading: Paul Delerue, "The 'Barca da Arte Xávega'" in: *Local Boats*, Part i, International Symposium on Boat and Ship Archaeology, 4th, Porto, 1985 (Oxford: 1988 [BAR International Series, 438(i)]), 221-252. Note also **jábega**.

barca da caçada See **barca do alto**

barca da casada See **puparin**

barca da gacha *Portugal:* One of 2 boats used in tunny fishing, and for working the *armaçao* net for sardines. Positioned along the sides near the front of the net to help the **barca das portas★**.

barca da gacha da terra, barca da gacha do mar See **barca-9**

barca d'allegio See **allège**

barca da portas See **barca das portas**

barca das portas *Portugal:* Open boat positioned at the opening of a net used for sardines and tunny to draw up the net to close it. Sharp, tall ends. Tunny fishermen stand on a platform along one side while gaffing the fish. Sprit-rigged. Name variant: **barca da portas**. Note also **barca-9, barca da gacha**. Further reference: **tuna boat**

barca da traghetto See **ferryboat-1**

barca d'avviso See **advice boat**

barca da zavorra See **ballast barge**

barca de agua abaixo See **fragata-2**

barca de armação See **barca-9**

barca de atoage de Viscaya See **trincadura**

barca de bou See **barca del bou**

barca de cantaria, barca de canterio, barca de cantherii, barca de cantherio See **barge de cantier**

barca de carga, barca de carreto See **batelão-1**

barca de falca *Spain:* Boat with sides raised by wash-strakes that extend almost to each end. The ribs project above the top strakes to support the washstrakes; further strengthened by a stringer and a caprail along each side. Stem and sternpost commonly strongly curved, the stem tall and cut at an angle. Note also **falca**.

barca de jábega See **jábega**

barca del bou *Spain, E:* Works with a trawl net, drifting with the wind, the net (*bou*) connected to a spar at each end of the boat. Sharp bow; tall curved stem, cutaway forefoot; sharp or transom stern; sternpost vertical or recurved; flaring sides. Outboard rudder projects below the deep keel, worked with tiller or yoke and lines; grounding keels; some with a daggerboard. Highly cambered deck; washboards extend from stem, or just aft of it, almost to the sternpost, or they are

barca del bou

lacking amidships to provide space for the tholepins. A forward-raking mainmast sets a large lateen sail; usually a bowsprit is run out for a small jib. Some also have a vertical mizzenmast with a lateen sail sheeted to an outrigger. Reported lengths 11.5-13m; e.g., length 13m, width 3m, depth 0.6m. Other recorded names: **barca de bou, barque del bou, bastiment** (at Villanueva y Geltrú)

barca del Gozo See **dghajsa tal-pass**

barca del passo See **dghajsa-1**

barca del passo grande See **dghajsa tal-pass**

barca de menaide See **manaide**

barca de mitjana *Spain, E:* Type of **falucho★** used until the 1st quarter of the 20th century on the Mediterranean coast and in the Balearic Islands for fishing and transporting agricultural produce. Full bow, curved stem, with high head; straight keel; elliptical counter stern; short grounding keels; rounded bilges. Cambered deck; deep bulwarks; cuddy for crew forward, captain's cabin aft. Set a large lateen sail on a stocky, forward-raking mainmast, stepped forward of amidships, and a smaller lateen to a mizzenmast (*mitjana*) stepped against the sternpost, sheeted to an outrigger. Jib to long steeved-up jibboom. 60-100t disp. Other recorded names: **falutx(o), haloque**

barca de palangra, barca de palangre, barca de palengre de mallorquina See **palangrero-1**

barca de paliscalmo, barca de panescal, barca de parascalmo See **palischermo-1**

barca de pareja, barca de parella See **pareja**

barca de parescalmo, barca de parischalmo See **palischermo-1**

barca de passagem See **valboeiro**

barca de passagem do gado See **barca-2**

barca de penescalm See **palischermo-1**

barca de sardinal, barca de sardinals See **barco de sardinal**

barcă de serviciu See **pinnace-1**

barca de trafégo *Portugal, N:* Sturdy open **lighter★** used to load and unload ships anchored at the mouth of the Douro River. Raked stem, vertical sternpost; ends extend ca. 20cm above the gunwales. Rowed by crew of 2, or towed. Length 25m, beam 7m, depth 2.5m.

barca di Grado See **barca-6**

barca di guardia *Italy:* **1.** In the tuna fisheries of Naples and ports to the south, a small open boat that monitors the entrance to the large rectangular net. Called a **coalannito** in the south, where a 2nd boat, the **portanova**, is also used. Rowed by 1 man. Note also **bastardo**.
  2. Open boat used at Naples to set trammel nets. Portable mast; lateen sail; jib.

barca di piloti See **pilot boat**

barca di ronda See **guard boat-1**

barca do alto *Portugal, south-central:* Fine-lined, sprit-rigged boat that engages in offshore line fishing out of Sesimbra. Bow sharp, stern slightly rounded; stem lightly raked, with rounded forefoot; wool ball on tall stemhead reduces sail chafing; plumb sternpost; shallow keel. Open; 4-5 thwarts; narrow outboard rudder; tiller; floorboards; stern sheets. Sides on most blue, bottom reddish brown, yellow sheer strake; oculi or star on white patch at the bows. Steps 1-2 unstayed masts; the taller (or single) mast stepped in the eyes; the aft-raking mizzenmast approximately amidships. Rowed in calms, 4-5 oars per side. Crew of 12, plus 1 or 2 boys. Reported lengths 7.7-9m, average 8.8m long, 2.7m wide, 0.94m deep, 5.34rt. Name variant: **barca da caçada**

barcae See **barca**

barca incendiaria See **fire ship**

barca local See **shore boat-1**

barcalonga See **barcolongo, barque longue**

barca mercantil See **bateira mercantel**

barcane See **barcone**

barca netta, barcanette See **barquerole**

barca paranza See **paranza**

barca per salpare See **anchor hoy**

barca pescantina See **pescantina**

barca peschereccia See **fishing boat**

barca piloti See **pilot boat**

barca pompa See **fire boat**

barca quillada See **quillat**

barcareccio *Italy:* **1.** Generic term for a local **fleet★** of small boats that serve the same purpose, e.g., **fishing boats★**, small harbor craft, etc.
  2. Collective term for the open boats that engage in a tuna trap operation. Note also **cabanella, caporais, musciara, vascello**.

barcarolă, barcarolle, barcarolo, barcaruolo See **barquerole**

barca sardinal, barca sardinalera See **barco de sardinal**

barcasas See **bacassa**

barcas das armações See **barca-9**

barca solera See **rai-2**

barcass See **launch**

barcassa See **lighter-1**

barcassas See **bacassa**

barcasse 1. French term for a bad vessel, especially one that sails poorly close to the wind. Sometimes, however, the word may refer simply to a ship of large tonnage. Spelling variant: **barcasso**
  2. *France, S:* Double-ended **fishing boat★** of the Côte d'Azur.
See also **barcaza, barkaca, launch, mahonne-4**.

barcasso See **barcasse-1**

bar cat See **crab scraper**

barcata See **barqueta-1**

barca tamburo See **paddle-box boat**

barca tramoggia See **hopper**

barcaz See **barge-1**

barcaza 1. *Spain, SW:* Reported by 18th- and 19th-century writers as a strong open vessel used particularly in the Cádiz area. Sharp ends; slender raised bow; strong sheer; heavily ballasted. Rudder hung on long pintle below and hooked to gudgeon above. Mast, stepped amidships, set a large square sail with a bonnet; yard hung off center, lugsail fashion; sail extended by a bowline. For long trips, a 2nd mast might be stepped forward; in heavy weather the mainmast was struck and a small sail set to the foremast. By removing the washstrakes, the vessel could be rowed, using as many as 16 oars. Crew of 10-14. Reported lengths 9-12m, widths 2.4-2.7m, depth ca. 1.5m. Can also refer to a bad vessel. Spelling variants: **barcasse★, bécass(e), beccaccia, Bekasse**. Note also **gabarra-5a**.
  2. *Spain, NW:* The long, narrow **barcaza de carga** traverses the Río Miño (Minho) on the Spain/Portugal border. Salt and lumber are primary cargoes. Sharp bow; slightly curved stem; narrow square stern; fairly flat floors amidships; keel. Decked, 2 large holds, accommodations between decks. Outboard rudder; tiller. Mast stepped approximately amidships, setting a quadrilateral lateen-type sail with a short luff. Length 20m, beam 5m, freeboard when loaded 0.2m, 45t disp. Name variants: **barcaza (or barco) de cargo del Río Miño**
See also **lighter-1**.

barcaza de carga, barcaza de carga del Río Miño See **barcaza-2**

barcazar See **barcaça-2**

barca zavorriera See **ballast barge**

barcazza See **barcaccia**

barc-bestija See **barkentine**

barce 1. *Italy, NW:* The **barcé** is used along the upper Po River. Open boat, with sharp elongated bow; curved sternpost ends above the sheer strake; flat bottom, low sides. Maneuvered by a sweep on the quarter and an oar forward. Length 6.8m, beam 1.4m, depth 1.0m.
  2. *Turkey:* **Barçe** is an old term for a **galley★** or naval **launch★**.
Further reference: **barca-6**

barce de canterio See **barge de cantier**

barce de parischalmo See **palischermo-1**

barcha See **barca, barka-7, barkë-2**
barchaça, barchacia See **barcaccia**
barcha de canterii, barcha de canterio, barcha de cantherii, barcha de cantherio See **barge de cantier**
barcha de parescalmo See **palischermo-1**
barchalonga See **barque longue**
barcham de canterio See **barge de cantier**
barche An old French term for a small, flat-floored vessel. In the 16th century, it was an important type, setting a square sail. A small type was called a **barchot**. See also **barca, barca-6, barque**.
Barche longe See **barque longue**
barchentina See **barkentine**
barche paranze See **paranza**
barcheruolo See **barquerole**
barchèt See **trabaccolo**
barcheta, barchetinha See **barchetta**
barchètt *Italy, N:* Small, double-ended passenger boat of Lago d'Orta. Flat bottom rises toward the ends to meet the gunwales. Passengers protected by an arched awning. Rowed. Length 6.15m, beam 1.95m, depth 0.7m.
barchetta *Italy:* **1.** Italian diminutive for a small ship or boat used for transportation or pleasure. Both rowed and sailed. Some forms of the word, such as **barchettuccia** and **barchettucio**, are deprecatory.
2. Small boat used by Sicilians in sponge fishing off Tunisia. Several work from a **mother ship***, a **bovo***, either carried aboard the ship or towed behind. Sharp ends; stem may extend well above the gunwale; rounded forefoot; slightly raked sternpost; flat sheer; straight keel. Two demountable benches; small stern deck; larger foredeck. Rowed by one man while engaged in fishing and by two when going to and from the **mother ship**; oars have counterbalance block. Crew of 2-4. Reported lengths 4.2-6.5m; e.g., length 4.2m, beam 1.55m, depth 0.7m.
3. A large, sturdy type of **gondola*** that ferried between the islands and the mainland and between Venice and the beach; some carried the mail, others the sick, and still others the dead to the cemetery. Dates at least to the 15th century but now extinct. More symmetrical longitudinally than the **gondola** and with a simple iron sheath on the prow; stem and sternpost extend above the top strake and recurve slightly. Decked at the ends. Generally rowed, employing a tall oarlock as a fulcrum. Occasionally set a small lugsail, at which times a rudder was shipped. Other recorded names: **batelo, gondola da fresco, mezza gondola**
Spelling variants: **barcheta, barchetinha, barchettella, barchettina, barchettino, barchetto*, barchighèdda, barchina, barchit(t)a, barčica, barketa, barketta*, barquetta**; pl. **barchette, barchetti, barquette***
barchette, barchettella See **barchetta**
barchetti See **barchetta, barchetto, trabaccolo**
barchettina, barchettino See **barchetta**
barchetto *Italy:* **1.** River craft of the Tevere (Tiber) River in west-central Italy that can carry ca. 50t. Upturned ends terminate in a point.
2. Lightly built vessel of the Lombardy lakes area in northern Italy. In the 15th century, reported as carrying mail and messages. On Lago de Garda, the **barchetto**

was the largest and most numerous of the **fishing boats***; used a large net. Flat bottom; ends elevated. Rowed.
3. Term **barchètto** is also used in the Marches of eastern Italy.
Spelling variant: pl. **barchetti**. See also **barca correire, barchetta, trabaccolo-2**.
barchettuccia, barchettucio See **barchetta**
barchi See **barco-1**
barchica See **barka-7**
barchighèdda, barchina, barchita, barchitta See **barchetta**
barchot See **barche**
barchote See **barcote**
barčica See **barchetta, barka-7**
Barckelonge See **barque longue-1**
barco **1.** Italian, Portuguese, and Spanish word, loosely used to designate many types of watercraft—from small **rowing boats*** to **ships***. Formerly the word applied specifically to a small **coaster*** that had a topmast and topsails. In some cases, the word refers to a unique type, a few of which follow. Other recorded names: **barc*, barcone*, barçonis, barçonus, barcu*, bárkŭ, itsasontzi, ontzi, untzi** (Basque); **vaixell** (Catalan); Italian pl. **barchi**. Note also **barca, barcote, barquete**.
2. *Argentina/Paraguay:* Vessel that transported cargo on the Paraná River between Buenos Aires and Asunción. Generally undecked except for a small cabin with limited accommodations. An arched cover protected the cargo. Employed a square sail set in the forward part. Also rowed, the oarsmen seated on the many benches that spanned the hull. Rudder and tiller controlled from the cabin. Reported lengths on keel 17-18m, beam 7.5m, draft 1.9-2.5m.
3. *Brazil, E:* **a.** Heavy 3-masted **coaster** from Bahia State, dating from the late 16th century. Foremast set a lugsail, extended by spar and bowline; after 2 masts set gaff sails. Now mostly 1- and 2-masted. Flat bottom, square stern. Reported lengths 11-22m; beam one-third. **b.** Two-masted open boat that served the coastal area around Vitoria. Dugout hull, with raised sides; thwarts. Set lateen sails. Rowed when necessary. **c.** **Coaster** from the southern state of Santa Catarina. Rig varied with wind conditions. **d.** On the north coast the **barco** set a square sail. Note also **batelão**.
4. *Portugal, N:* **a.** Small, open coastal **fishing boat*** found along the estuary at Caminha on the northern border. Clinker-planked, sharp-ended, curved and raked stem; keel. Black hull. Rowed and sailed, setting a spritsail. Crew of 2-3. Length 6m, beam 2m, depth 0.65m. **b.** The **barco** on the Rio Lima above Ponte de Lima is used for fishing and ferrying. Clinker-planked, flat bottom, wide transom, heavy straight stem, open. Rowed. Length 4.3m, beam 1.4m, depth 0.38m. **c.** On the lower Rio Lima, the **barco** is an open, flat-bottomed, clinker-built boat used for transporting cargo and ferrying. Two planks form the straight, flared sides; wide bottom doubled; rabbetted stem straight and raked; very narrow transom; ribs paired. Wide-bladed rudder; tiller slots over rudderhead. Single mast secured to the bulkhead amidships; square- or sprit-rigged. Also poled. Crew of 2. Length

16m, beam 3.5m, depth 0.7m. Other recorded names: **barca***, **barco de carga. d.** The sturdy open **barco** of the Douro River engages in local traffic. Ends raked; sternpost capped with a curved iron piece. Rowed by its 2-man crew, 1 oar each; often towed. Maximum length 24m, beam 7m, depth 2.5m.

5. Two-masted **fishing boat** that worked out of Sesimbra south of Lisbon. Plumb, sharp bow, rounded stern. Foremast raked aft; sprit-rigged. Also rowed.

Further references: **barca-9**, **bark**, **batelão-4**, **chinchorro-2**, **saveiro-2**, **vigilenga**

barco à traio See **bac**

barco ballenero See **whaleboat-1**

barco bèstia See **barkentine**

barco cañonero See **gunboat**

barco catalano See **catalane**

barco copriruota See **paddle-box boat**

barco correo See **mail boat-1**

barco costeño See **coaster**

barco crucero See **cruiser-2**

barco da neta See **catraia-7**

barco da pescada *Portugal, central:* Large 2-masted boat that fished for a type of hake (*pescada*) from Buarcos. Sharp ends, curved stem, straight raked sternpost; outboard rudder, worked with lines. Small cuddy forward, decked at stern, open waist. Oculi on bows. Mainmast stepped amidships and sharply raked forward; less raked after mast stepped midway between mainmast and stern. Both set lateen sails. Rowed in calms, with 10 oars, 5 per side. Crew varied with number of nets carried, but usually 10-25. Reported lengths 10-13m, depths 1.2-1.4m. Name variant: **lancha da pescada**

barco da rede See **bateira ílhava**

barco da roça See **perua**

barco das padeiras See **valboeiro**

barco da xávega See **xávega**

barco de arrastre, barco de arresto See **trawler-1**

barco de arte de xávega See **barca da arte xávega, catraia-7**

barco de bico See **netinha**

barco de carga See **barco-4**

barco de carga del Río Miño See **barcaza-2**

barco de correo See **packet boat-1**

barco de dornas See **dorna-2**

barco de duas proas See **meia lua-2**

barco de festejos See **chi-tong-t'eang**

barco de frete See **valboeiro**

barco de fundo de prato See **canote**

barco de lastre See **ballast boat**

barco de lavrador *Portugal, central:* **1.** Long, narrow boat used by the farmers (*lavradores*) of the Mondego River above Coimbra to carry produce and to ferry across the river. Carvel-planked; sharp bow overhangs and sheer sweeps up to a vertical point; stern also sharp but lower and terminates in a block. Flat bottom, with rocker toward the ends. Short end decking. Bench amidships supports the mast when used. Hull blackened with tar. Also poled. Length 8m, beam 1.2m, depth 0.48m. Name variant: **barco dos lavradores**
2. On the Lavos lagoon near the mouth of the Mondego there is another black-hulled "farmer's boat," called

here a **barca***. Serves for general transportation and to carry produce. Double-ended; stem and sternpost of equal height and curve up smoothly from the bottom. Decked at the ends, with a very small cuddy. Sailed and poled. Length 8.15m, beam 2.5m, depth 1.1m.

barco del práctico See **pilot boat**

barco de mar See **saveiro-2**

barco de palangre mallorquina See **palangrero**

barco de pareja See **pareja**

barco de pasage See **passage boat**

barco de pesca See **fishing boat**

barco de pesca de alto See **caique-8**

barco de pilotes See **pilot boat**

barco de ruedas See **paddle boat-3**

barco de sardinal *Spain, N/NE:* Sardine **fishing boat*** on the Bay of Biscay and Catalan coasts. Characterized by washstrakes that extended from abaft the stem to near the sternpost, often deeper forward of amidships; tholepins recessed into the strakes. Straight or curved, vertical stem ends in high, obliquely cut stemhead; sternpost rounded. Flat floors; straight keel and grounding keels. Double-ended; decked at bow and stern and along the sides. S-curve to rudder; light tiller slotted over rudderhead. Often brightly painted and decorated with designs and figures. Stepped a single forward-raking mast amidships; lateen sail. Also rowed; auxiliary common. Crew of 4-6, plus the captain. Reported lengths 6-8m; e.g., length 7.6m, beam 2.4m, depth 1.0m. Other recorded names: **barca de sardinal(s)**, **barca sardinal(era)**, **barco de sardinel**, **barque de sardinal**, **barqueta de sardinal**, **sardinera**. Further reading: L. Bellón, "Pesca y Utilización del Boquerón y de la Sardina en las Costas de Málaga," *Boletin del Instituto Español de Oceanografía* 30 (1950). Note also **barquilla de sardinal**, **sardinal**.

barco de sardinel See **barco de sardinal**

barco de toucinheiro See **valboeiro**

barco de vela See **sailboat**

barco do candil *Portugal, central:* **Fishing boat*** launched from the beach at Nazaré in support of the seining operation; a smaller variety also found at São Martinho do Porto. Use phosphorescent lures to attract fish. Flat bottom curves up sharply forward to a wedge; stem, starting well above the waterline, continues up vertically, terminating in a square stemhead. Flat stern, vertically planked, rounds up from the bottom.

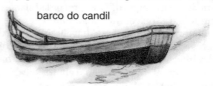
barco do candil

Carvel-planked, heavy gunwales, bold sheer. Open except for short foredeck; 2 benches. Painted black below the waterline, variously painted above; stylized oculi. Rowed, double-banked, with 4 oars. Reported lengths 4.7-5.7m; e.g., length 5.7m, beam 2m, depth 0.8m. Other recorded names: **barquinha de pesca com engodo**, **barquinho do candil**, **candil**

barco do mar See **meia lua-2**, **saveiro-2**

barco do pilado *Portugal, N:* Open boat that collects the swimming crab (*pilado*) for fertilizer in the area north of Póvoa de Varzim. Operates with a small **caique** (see **caique-8**). Carvel-planked; shallow keel; flat floors amidships; flaring sides; moderate sheer. Raked ends; sharp entrance, fuller stern. Narrow, raked rudder extends well below the bottom; tiller slots over rudderhead. Four rowing thwarts, wide bench forward, small seat aft. Winched up onto the beach on a ladder-type framework. Mast stepped into a block and braced between 2 thwarts. Sets a lateen sail; spar rest along the port side. The type at Âncora, called a **bolantim**, is rowed only. Length 8m, beam 3m, depth ca. 1.4m. Note also **bateira do mar, bateira mercantel**.

barco dos lavradores See **barco de lavrador-1**

barco faro, barco farol See **lightship**

barco ílhavo See **bateira ílhava**

barcolongo *Spain:* **1.** Fast **coaster★** of early origin. Described in the 17th century as long, low, with a high bluff bow, and decked or open; used to the 19th century. Rowed and sailed. Set 1-3 square sails; bowlines to a long, curved spar rigged beyond the bow; or set a long lateen sail to a central pole mast. Those fishing out of Cadiz were 2- or 3-masted, lug-rigged vessels. **2.** Term also applied to armed **sloops★** of the Spanish navy.
Spelling variants: **barcalonga, barcoluengo, barkalonga, barqualonga**. Note also **barque longue, double shallop**. Further reference: **long ship**

barcoluengo See **barcolongo**

barco mineiro *Brazil, S:* Large vessel that transported cargo at high water on western Minas Gerais rivers, especially the Araguaia and Tocantins. Rounded bottom, keel, strengthened with frames; bow turned up sharply. Palm thatch awning protected the cargo. Large rudder worked from the roof. Low freeboard permitted paddlers (12-50) to sit along the sides. Name variant: **bote mineiro**

barco moliceiro See **moliceiro**

barcòn *Italy, north-central:* Large half-decked boat that came from the northern lakes to the Piedmont, via canals, carrying construction materials, combustibles, etc. Sharp ends; bow raked up, stern more rounded; flat bottom. Outboard rudder worked with a long tiller. Black hull. Towed, sometimes rowed. Length 16m, beam 4m at gunwales, on bottom 3.8m, depth amidships 1.25m. Note also **barcone**. Further reference: **lighter-1**

barcone *Italy:* **1.** Generic for **barge★** or **lighter★**. Generally decked. Some specifically transported materiel. Sometimes described as a 2- or 3-masted fishing vessel of the Mediterranean, ca. 20m long; or a motorized **fishing boat★**.
2. The **barcone** of Lake Como in northern Italy carried sand, heavy cargo, livestock. Sharp overhanging bow, sharp or rounded stern; sheer swept up at the ends, the bow lower than the stern. Undecked; arched, canvas-covered awning extended over most of the hull. Steered with a quarter rudder on the starboard side or a midline rudder. Set a very tall square sail to a mast stepped well forward; mast stayed aft. Some had an auxiliary motor. Length ca. 9m.

3. On the Volturno and Sarno Rivers, in the Naples area on the west coast, the **barcone** of the beginning of the 20th century was an open, square-ended, flat-bottomed craft. Bottom curves up at the ends; marked sheer. Sides vertical and nearly parallel; 5 bottom cleats; sides supported only toward each end. Poled. Length 4.2m, beam 1.0m, depth amidships 0.32m.
Spelling variants: **barcane, barcon★**; pl. **barconi**. Further reference: **barco-1**

barcone a remi, barcone d'allibo See **dumb barge**

barconi See **barcone**

barçonis, barçonus See **barco-1**

barco pescador See **fishing boat**

barco poveiro See **poveiro-2**

barco rabão See **rabão**

barco rabelo, barco rebello See **rabelo**

barco salvavidas See **lifeboat**

barco savaleiro See **saveiro-2**

barcos das padeiras See **valboeiro**

barcosi See **barcoso**

barcoso *Italy:* Reported in the 14th century, and again in the 17th, as a large naval vessel, about which little is known. Spelling variant: pl. **barcosi**. See also **bragozzo**.

barcos semanais See **valboeiro**

barcos trainones See **traiña**

barcot *France, S:* Small double-ended boat that served as a **ship's boat★** for vessels on the Rhône and Saône Rivers during the 18th and 19th centuries. Capable of carrying 5-6 men. See also **bachot**.

barco tamburo See **paddle-box boat**

barcote In Portuguese, a diminutive of **barco★**, namely a small boat. Spelling variant: **barchote**. Note also **bachot**.

barco traiñon See **traiña**

barcotta In 15th-century Italy, a vessel of medium size. Spelling variant: **barcotto**

barcotto See **barcotta**

barco velera See **sailboat**

barco vivero See **vivero-1**

barcque See **bark**

barcu **1.** *France, Corsica:* Narrow open boat ca. 10m long. **2.** *Italy, N:* The **barcù** of Lago d'Iseo carries cargo. Flat bottom, sharp ends, strongly curved stem and sternpost. Decked at ends. Steering oar on the quarter, worked with a pin from the loom, aided by lines and pulleys from a post on the stern deck. Mast stepped through a thwart in the forward quarter; set a rectangular sail, controlled by bowlines. Length 17.6m, beam 5.2m, depth 1.0m.
See also **barco-1**.

bărcuta See **jolly boat-1**

Bardese See **Barse**

barečka See **barka-1**

bareczka See **barka-4**

bare flat See **Mersey flat**

bare-head smack See **sharpshooter-1**

barga See **barge-1, bargia**

barga de canthero, barga de quanterio See **barge de cantier**

barga domini See **nacelle-5**

bargae See **bargia**

bargagno See **bragagna**, **dredger-1**
bargantí See **brigantine**
bargantim See **bargatim**, **brigantine**
bargantin See **bargatim-1**
bargatim **1.** *India:* Reported as an indigenous, shallow-draft, light **rowing boat★**. Probably a Portuguese term. Spelling variant: **bargantin**
  2. *Mediterranean:* A similiar description was applied in the 16th century to a coastal boat. Spelling variant: **bargantim**
barge **1.** Bulk-cargo craft of rivers and canals, but may also engage in limited coastwise traffic. Distinguished from a **lighter★** by working over longer distances and transporting the load directly to its destination. Usually flat-bottomed and full-bodied; constructed of wood, steel, or concrete. Ends usually square above and raked below, at one end or both, and lack stem and sternpost; slab-sided. May be rigged or unrigged, and either towed, pushed, or self-propelled. Additional selected names: **barcaz**, **barga**, **bargea**, **bargie**, **barica**, **baris★**, **barja**, **barka★**, **baržha★**, **chaland★**, **deregiye**, **deregli(j)a**, **dereglja**, **flodpråm**, **Kahn★**, **läktare**, **šlep** (and **şlep**), **téglenica**. Note also **dumb barge**, **gabare**, **scow**, **tug-2**.
  2. A long, light **pulling boat★** used as a **tender★** to a **man-of-war★**, especially to convey the flag officer. Pulled 10-14 oars, double-banked. **Barges** also carried sails. Clinker- or carvel-built, small high transom stern; soft bilges; some had a drop keel; might have a rudder. Often richly ornamented; stern bench; some had a small cabin. Use in England dates from at least the early 16th century; that of an admiral was painted green, earning the nickname **green parrot**. Now powered. Reported lengths 8.5-14.4m. Other recorded names: **admiralsbåt**, **Admiralsboot**, **canot d'apparat**, **canot de parade**, **galaboot**, **gro(o)te sloep**, **Labberboot**, **Labberlot**, **service barge**, **admiral's barge**, **amiral filikası**, **bote de almirante**, **canot de l'amiral**, **Chefboot**, **escaler do almirante**, **falúa del almirante**, **lancia ammiraglio**, **vedette (de l')** **amiral**, **yole de l'amiral**. Note also **canot-2**, **ship's boat**.
  3. An elegantly furnished ceremonial vessel, used from Roman times as a state **barge** or as a conveyance for high-ranking government officials or visiting dignitaries. Most long, narrow, and shallow. A shelter usually covers part of the boat. Rowed, paddled, or mechanically propelled. Used in several parts of Europe and in south and southeastern Asia. In 17th-century England, guilds and livery companies owned **barges** for ceremonial use. Other recorded names: **bargie**, **bateau de parade**, **procession barge**, **royal barge**, **state barge**. Note also **bucintoro**, **falua-1**, **Fishmongers' Company barge**, **rua ballang**, **stadsbarge**, **Stationers' barge**, **Trinity House barge**.
  4. An ornamental **houseboat★**, especially one permanently moored. Note also **college barge**.
  5. Officially, in the United States, any vessel (except for a **dredger★** or **houseboat★**) that has no propulsion power of its own.
  6. *Australia, S:* **a.** A seaworthy working **ketch★** of the Hobart area of Tasmania. Evolved in the mid-1800s to provide communication to the southern part of the

island, and especially to carry lumber. When roads made these activities unprofitable, they engaged in crayfishing. Essentially extinct. Early **barges** were similar to the **Thames sailing barge★**, having a bluff bow and transom stern, and being steered with a long tiller to an outboard rudder. Evolved into a beamier vessel with a fine entrance, clipper bow, counter stern, stiff round bilges, wide keel that extended ca. 15cm below the garboard strakes and tapered to the stem and sternpost. Steered with a wheel; centerboard ca. 3.05m wide, 3.66m long, and extended 2.44m below the keel. Flush deck; main cabin generally aft; crew housed in forecastle. Set large boomed gaff sails, large jackyard topsails, jib and staysail. Auxiliaries installed early in the 20th century. Average length overall 20.7m, on keel 16.8m, width 5.18m, molded depth 1.52m, draft light 1.22m aft. Name variants: **Hobart ketch**, **Tasmanian ketch**. **b.** Cargo **barges** were towed by small **sidewheelers** on the Murray River and its tributaries bordering New South Wales and Victoria. Worked mainly in the 2nd half of the 19th century, carrying bales of wool and timber downstream and stores upstream. A **steamer** would tow one or more **barges**, although on some tributaries, timber-carrying **barges** would drift downstream, controlled by poling and a drag chain. Built entirely of wood or a combination of wood and iron. Sharp ends, some with a rounded stern. Flat bottom, with keelson. Towing pole of the **steamer** located amidships, reducing the whipping effect of the tow on sharp river bends. **Barge** steered by a large wheel mounted on a portable platform that could be raised as the cargo piled up; steering cables ran from the wheelhouse to the aft end of the rudder. Some steered by dragging a chain over the stern. Very shallow draft.
  7. *Canada, E:* **a.** Ancillary craft of fishing **schooners★**, working during the 19th century in the Strait of Belle Isle and off Labrador. Aided in collecting, holding, and processing the catch, and carrying the cod-seine. Several might be carried on board, being sold later to local fishermen. One type described as sharp-ended; mainly rowed, by 2-6 men, but also sailed, setting a mainsail, foresail, and jib. Recent citations refer to a **barge** as a floating fish-handling facility; flat-bottomed. Name variant: **fishing barge**. **b.** The 19th-century **barge** of the cod fishermen of Gaspé Bay was an open **whaleboat★**-type. Strongly raked sternpost; outboard rudder; downward-sloping tiller. Rigged as a **schooner★**, with 2 fore-and-aft sails and a jib. Some were 3-masted sprit-rigged boats, the mizzen loose-footed but boomed. Crew of 2. Reported lengths on keel 5.5-6.7m, widths 1.5-2m. **c.** At Cape Breton Island, a **barge** is a sharp-ended **fishing boat★**, varying in length from 6-18.2m. Name variant: **boat★**. **d.** A wooden boat used by the Escoumins of the north shore of the St. Lawrence River estuary to hunt beluga whales with spears. Rowed; 2 oars. Trapezoidal sail also used. Crew of 2. Length ca. 5m. **e.** Assists in the Magdalen Islands' herring net operation. Paired with a 2nd **barge**. Carvel-planked, closely spaced ribs, sharp ends. Open, painted gray. Towed to the site, but maneuvered thereafter by oars. Crew of 2-3. Note also

gabarre. f. The small Labrador fishing **barge** was sharp-sterned. **g. Fleets** of **barges** carried lumber on the Ottawa River in the 19th century. Made in Ottawa and Hull in large numbers. The lumber might go via the Rideau Canal to Oswego for connection with the Erie Canal system; some went through the Richelieu River, Lake Champlain, and the Hudson River Canal. Simply constructed, bluff ends; square stern on some; 3 rubbing strakes. Living accommodations for the operator and his family. The **white barges** carried up to 175,000 board feet, a limitation imposed by the Erie Canal system. The **blue barges** carried up to 300,000 board feet and could traverse the Ottawa River locks.

8. *England:* **a.** Reported as flat-bottomed and carrying leeboards; listed as early as the 13th century. Frequently used to transport cargo from seagoing vessels to towns upstream. Many **ketch**-rigged, others as **sloops⋆**. Masts usually in tabernacles for ease of lowering when passing under bridges. Some rowed; one in the mid-13th century employed 32 oars and in the early 15th century carried 48 oars. About 100t; shallow draft. Spelling variants: **bargi**; pl. **bargiis. b.** Small cargo vessel of the Rivers Severn and Wye in western England; the last on the Severn carried stone until the early 20th century. On the Wye, the term was used synonymously with **trow⋆**, while on the Severn above Gloucester, **barge** and **frigate⋆** were synonymous. Flat bottom, no keel; bluff bow; probably overhanging square stern with dummy quarter galleries and stern windows. Large open hold. Square-sailed in the 18th century; later some adopted spritsails, and in the 19th century most were **ketch**-rigged. Reported lengths 12-18m; e.g., length 15.2m, beam 4.6m, draft loaded 0.9m, cap. 30t. Further name variant: **up-river trow**

9. *France:* **a.** The **barge** of the lower Loire River and nearby offshore islands in western France is a flat-bottomed **fishing boat⋆**. Dates to at least the early 18th century, but nearly extinct. Clinker-built, beamy, sharp ends, keelless, partly decked. Tall mast, stepped amidships, sets a square sail. Also rowed; 2 oars from one side, the 3rd used on the opposite side, toward the stern, as a rudder. Crew of 3-4. About 6m long. Name variant: **barge nantaise. b.** The large Normandy **barge** of the 14th and 16th centuries required as many as 100 men. Some engaged in herring and mackerel fishing and in transporting salt; in the mid-16th century, Dieppe armed some of its fishing **barges** for war purposes. Clinker-built; decked; poop aft and raised deck forward. Set a square sail. 50-100t. **c.** Old term for a **skiff⋆** or **yawl⋆**. **d.** The term **barge** is given to the 2 special vessels of the Seine River that are rigidly coupled end-to-end and pushed by a specially designed **push boat⋆**, the **pousseur**; the combined unit is 127.5m long. Built of steel; double-ended and propelled in either direction; interior partitioned into 3 compartments, the end compartments serving as buffers. Two engines propel the unit. Crew of 5 operate the **pousseur**; none needed on the **barges**. Each **barge** 54.4m long and 9.5m wide. Name variant: **pousseur-barge**

10. *Ireland/United Kingdom:* The term **barge** sometimes applied to a canal or river craft with a beam twice that of a **narrow boat⋆**. On the Thames, the word was reserved for vessels exceeding 70t, smaller working craft being called merely **boat**.

11. *United States:* **a.** Long, narrow boat of the late 18th century. Frequently used for ceremonial purposes, but also functioned as a **gunboat⋆**, making inshore raids. Saw service until ca. 1825. Round or flat bottom, square stern; some double-ended, resembling oversized **whaleboats⋆**. Weather cloths screened the crew from small-arms fire. When sailed, set 1-2 leg-of-mutton, sprit-, or lateen sails. Smaller types rowed only, using as many as 32 oars. Length to 23m; 1776 barge 12.5m long, 2.2m wide, 0.86m deep, 0.3m draft. Name variant: **rowboat⋆. b.** The U. S. Navy **barge** was a class of **ship's boat⋆** between 1830 and 1865. Sharp-ended. Lengths 8.5-10.4m; e.g., length 8.5m, beam 1.8m, depth 0.7m. By 1870, one type of **ship's boat** was the 9m-long **schooner⋆**-rigged **barge**, which could be rowed by 12 oarsmen. Oared **barges** for flag officers were retained into the early 20th century as carvel-planked, plumb-stemmed, counter-sterned boats. Pulled 6-7 pairs of oars (double-banked), or set 2 sliding gunter lugsails and a foresail; mainsail boomed. Length 9m, beam 2m, depth 0.8m. By 1910, motorized **barges** were authorized to convey the admiral and his staff. Capable of being stowed aboard a ship. Cabins forward and aft, with an open raised cockpit between. Black hull. 9-12m long. Name variant: **admiral's barge**. Note also **canot-2. c.** During the War of 1812, rowing **galleys⋆**, designated **barges**, were used on Lakes Champlain and Erie. Had bow cannon. Name variant: **barge-of-war**. Note also **row galley. d.** Armed **scow**-like vessel used by the Americans during the War of 1812 on the Patuxent River, a western arm of Chesapeake Bay. Square ends; deep bulwarks. **Schooner**- or **sloop**-rigged; also used sweeps. Reported lengths 12-23m, beamy, shallow draft. The opposing British **barges** were open, round-bottomed vessels with a sharp stern. Worked with oars and sail. **e.** Type of racing boat. Mid-19th-century boats were probably modified naval **barges**. Some **four-** and **six-oared barges** of the late 19th century had a very sharp bow, plumb stem, and a high narrow transom. Decked at the ends; the 6-oared boat had 2 seats at the stern. Outboard rudder. Six-oared boat: length ca. 13.4m, beam 1.37m. **f.** Used on the Hudson River and water links to Philadelphia in the 1820s during the period when steam engines were prone to explode and catch fire; this so-called **safety barge** was towed behind a **steamboat**. Similar in design to the **steamboat** of the period but without an engine. Some were connected by a long hawser, others by a gangway on a floating swivel. Generally a resplendent craft, running on a regular schedule or as a chartered excursion boat. Had 2 open decks, or the lower deck might have staterooms and dining facilities; some also carried freight, as did the **steamboat** itself. Later, some relegated to carrying animals, hay, ice, or to serving as floating theaters. One was 33m long, 6.8m wide, and 2.3m deep. Name variant: **ladies' barge**, **tow boat⋆. g.** In colonial mid-Atlantic states a **barge** was a **ship's boat**, or it was a roomy flat-bottomed boat that employed oars and sail. Some were **water-taxis**, with a cabin aft and, in some places, were rowed by slave oarsmen with a white coxswain. Small high transom. Steered with a rudder and tiller. Reported lengths of the **water-taxis** 8.3-12.2m. Also called **colonial barge** or **gentleman's pulling boat. h.** Sharp-ended **keelboat★** type, used on the larger rivers, especially the Ohio and Mississippi; dated from ca. 1800. Very early **barges** square-ended. Being relatively fast, they were popular with businessmen, officials, and land speculators; also carried cargo. Sheer swept up slightly at the ends; steered with a rudder or sweep. House arrangements varied from a simple cabin amidships to a fully covered hull that was bullet-proof and might have ports for small cannon. Walkway along the sides for poling; seats forward for rowers. Stepped 1-2 masts and were rigged with square sails and topsail, as a **schooner,** or with square sails on the foremast and a fore-and-aft sail on the mainmast. Maneuvered with long oars on downstream run, poled or warped upstream. Crew of 4 plus helmsman downstream, 8-50 upstream. Reported lengths 9-36m, widths 2-7m; draft 0.9-1.22m. Name variant: **berge**; previously called **row galleys★. i.** Vessel anchored at popular sport fishing sites off southern California. A floating hotel for day fishermen, with amenities, food, and sometimes accommodations. Majority are converted **yachts★. j.** Special **barges** transport logs from the cutting area to a mill. Wood or steel; flat-topped or open, depending on the type of loading or unloading used. Log **barges** generally towed in a line, but on the Mississippi River, they are lashed end-to-end and pushed. On Lake Superior, some cargo vessels with engines removed have been converted for transporting pulpwood, as much as 2,500 peeled cords. Pulpwood **barges** on the South Atlantic and Gulf Coasts are flat-topped and generally unloaded by a derrick or crane. Self-dumping **barges** are used in coastal British Columbia. Towed in strings of 3-5 by a **tug★**. Tipped to 30° by flooding special tanks; designed to be self-draining so the **barge** rights itself when light waterline reached. May carry a **boom boat★** on board. Length 104m, beam 18m, cap. 7,000t. **k. Barges** on Coos Bay in southwestern Oregon transported both mature and seed oysters. Rectangular, with raked ends. Small **barges** might have an outboard motor; larger towed.

12. *West Indies:* An armed **dugout canoe★**. Best known around the island of Hispaniola.

Further references: **baardse, barque, boat-4, coal bunker, doghole schooner, esquif-2, Gravesend barge, Mackinaw boat, Potomac fish lighter, punt-7, rowing lighter, schooner-barge-2, scow-1, scow-7, snik-2, Thames sailing barge, trekschuit-1, wide boat**

bargea See **barge-1, bargia**

barge à morue See **cod-fishing boat**

bargea cantharia See **barge de cantier**

barge à rames See **rowbarge**

barge de cantier A 13th-century **ship's boat★**, especially of a Mediterranean **nef★**, that was towed behind the main vessel. Sometimes used as a brig for recalcitrant sailors. Generally decked. One carried 52 oars; others

had as few as 8 oars. Steered with a long sweep mounted on the sternpost. Might raise a lateen sail. Calculated length 14.3m. Other recorded names: **barca cant(h)erii, barca de cantaria (cantherii, cant(h)erio), barce de canterio, barcha cant(h)erii, barcha de cant(h)erio (or de cantherii), barcham de canterio, barga de canthero (or quanterio), bargea de cantharia, bargue de cantier, barque de cantier, cantherius**

barge ketch See **boomy**

barge nantaise See **barge-9**

barge-of-war See **barge-11c**

barge-yacht Flat-bottomed, shallow-draft **barge★**-type craft built or converted for use as a **yacht★**. Those used in the British Isles were usually converted **Thames sailing barges★**. From the late 19th century to the present, smaller **barge-yachts** have been specially built as pleasure craft. Usually employ leeboards. Most have a square or counter stern. The converted **sailing barges** generally retain the sprit mainsail and gaff mizzen rig, but others employ a gaff main and mizzen. The smaller **yachts** are usually **sloop★-, cutter★-,** or **yawl★**-rigged. The smaller types are ca. 6.4-9.1m long. Name variant: **yacht-barge**

barghe See **baardse**

bargi See **barge-8**

bargia An early Italian **galley★**-type vessel used for war and cargo transport. Some required a crew of 250. Spelling variants: **barga(e), bargea**

bargie See **baardse, barge-1, barge-3, trekschuit-1**

bargiën See **baardse**

bargiis See **barge-8**

bargio *Italy, NW:* Early term given to a small boat used to communicate with ships lying at anchor; also a **ship's boat★**. Long, narrow, and often highly decorated. In some areas of Tuscany, may be a pleasure craft. Name variant: **bargiola** (dim.)

bargiola See **bargio**

bargogno See **dredger-1**

bargóso, bargózo See **bragozzo**

bargozzo See **barcaccia-2, bragozzo**

bargue See **barque**

bargue de cantier See **barge de cantier**

bari See **baris**

barica See **barge-1**

baride See **baris**

baris *Egypt:* **1.** Term applied loosely to any type of ancient water craft constructed of papyrus, as well as to plank-built boats. Word has also been applied to early Egyptian funerary boats.
  2. Cargo vessel of the Nile that dates from early times. Plank-built in short lengths of acacia; little or no framing; caulked with papyrus (thought sometimes to have been bound with papyrus). Towed upstream; downstream, to control the boat, a hurdle of tamarisk, reinforced by wattle work, was suspended at the bow and a stone was hung from the stern. Steered with a type of quarter rudder fashioned from boards ca. 1.0m long laid side by side and fastened with strong wooden crooks. Square papyrus sails might be used on upriver trip.
  Other recorded names: **baair, bari, baride, barit.** See also **barge-1.**

barit See **baris**

barja See **barge-1**, **barzha**

bark Term variously applied to a hull or rig type. **Barque★** generally the British and French spelling; **bark** the American; also **barcque**, **barke★**.
1. Although cited as early as the 14th century, by the 17th century a **bark** was a medium-sized **coaster★** or fishing vessel. Most often cited as an 18th- and 19th-century 3-masted **merchantman★** rigged with square sails on the fore- and mainmasts and a fore-and-aft sail and a gaff topsail on the mizzenmast; 3 headsails to a long rising bowsprit. In later years, increased to 4 masts (**four-masted bark★** or **barque**, **quatre-mâts barque**, **Viermastbark**, **four poster**) or 5 masts. Other recorded names: **barc★**, **barco★**, **barka★**, **barken**, **barkèya̧t**, **barko★**, **Barkschiff**, **barkschip**, **barkskepp**, **barrik**, **bricbarca**, (**barca à**) **brick-barca**, **brigantino a palo**, **dreimastbark**, **gambara**, **trei-mat**, **tres-mast**, **trois-mâts** (**barque**); Arab pl. **ba̧rka̧wa̧t**, **ba̧rkuwa̧t**. Note also **barca**, **jackass bark**, **polacre**, **ship**, **shipentine**.
2. Word **bark** originally used loosely for a small decked vessel of any rig, or for a **rowing boat★**, and still so-used in poetry.
3. *Guinea:* General term given to the many small coastal and riverine **fishing boats★**. Large **barks** sail- or motor-equipped. Crew of 1-6.
4. *North America:* An early nickname for a birchbark **canoe**.
5. *United States:* In colonial America, a small, heavily built **coaster★** with a square or rounded stern, flush deck; might be rigged as a **brigantine★**, **ketch★**, or **ship★**, or with square sails on the mainmast and the shorter foremast, and a square topsail on the mainmast. Another type was smaller, double-ended, and set square sails to the 2 masts, the foremast being quite small; length on keel 10.7m, beam 4.2m, depth 1.8m. Other recorded names: **barcque**, **barke**. Further reading: William A. Baker, *The 'Mayflower' and Other Colonial Vessels* (Annapolis, Md.: Naval Institute Press, 1983; London: Conway Maritime Press, 1983), 95-118. Further references: **bark boat**, **cat-2**, **hoy-1**, **trekschuit-1**

barka 1. In the Czech language, **bárka** means a **boat★** or **vessel★**. Name variant: **barečka** (dim.)
2. *France, Corsica:* Open boat that fished with nets or baskets to catch octopuses along the northern part of the island. Sharp ends, slightly raked; stem head angled; carvel-planked. Foredeck; comparatively deep bulwarks; 2 thwarts; engine housing amidships. Single tholepins for 5 pairs of oars, secured by strops; some oars square-loomed. Rowed to maneuver while setting and hauling nets and baskets. Length ca. 5m. Spelling variant: **barca★**
3. *Hungary:* **Bárka** may designate a boat-shaped container in which to keep live fish. Dates to the 13th century. Note also **fish car**.
4. *Poland:* Word loosely applied to a **boat** and especially to a **barge★**. A type of **barka** transported grain on Polish rivers; crew of 3-4. Other recorded names: **barki**, **bareczka** (dim.)
5. *Russia:* **a.** A large, flat-bottomed **raft★**-like craft used to carry cargo downstream. Dismantled on arriving at its destination. Planked-up sides and roofed

over. Propelled by oars; controlled by sweeps at each end or by a wide-bladed rudder. Reported lengths 21-85m, widths 6.4-12m. **b.** On the Yenisei River in Siberia, the **barka** was a **passage boat★**, maneuvered mainly by women. Spelling variant: **barké**
6. *Switzerland:* Romande term for a decked sailing vessel used on some Swiss lakes.
7. Croatian term for a small **boat** or **skiff★**; the word also can mean **ship★**; an 1869 **barka** was deep-hulled with 3 masts. Other recorded names: **barcha**, **bârkica** (Slovenian); dim. **barchica** or **barčica**; pl. **barke** Further references: **barca**, **barge**, **bark**

barkaca Large cargo vessel of the Dalmatian coast. Commonly had a small engine. Other recorded names: **barcaccia★**, **barcasse★**, **barkača**, **barkasa**

barkača See **launch**

barkalonga See **barcolongo**, **barque longue**

barkantina, **barkantine** See **barkentine**

Barkarole, **barkarolle** See **barquerole**

barkas 1. *Lithuania/Russia:* A naval vessel's **longboat★** or **launch★**; a **lighter★**. Reported lengths 9-12m. Spelling variant: **barkaz** (Russian)
2. *Netherlands:* **Fishing boat★** of the Zuiderzee that was both rowed and sailed. Crew of 2.
3. *Poland, E:* Square-sailed **trawler★** that fished in pairs on Zalew Wiślany (Frisches Haff or Vistula Bay) for eel and whitefish. Dated from the early 14th century to the early 1970s. Also used on the northern part of the bay, but probably extinct there. Clinker-planked of oak; sharp, raked ends; straight keel; soft turn of the bilges. Built to work either to right or left, with appropriate side strengthening. Waist open between 2 bulkheads, live well between, decked at ends. Outboard rudder; tiller unshipped when trawling. Mast stepped just forward of amidships against the forward bulkhead. Forestay and 2 asymmetrically placed shrouds. Set a very tall square sail with reef points in upper half. One boat of the pair permitted to have an engine (after 1955); used for going to and from port only. Crew of ca. 5. Reported lengths 9-11m; e.g., length ca. 10m, beam 3.5m, depth 1.5m, draft 1.0m. The smaller **półbarkas** (or **pówbarkas**) was 8-9m long; used to the early 1970s. Other recorded names: **barkasa** (pl. **barkasy**); **Angelkahn**, pl. **Angelkähne** (German); pl. **półbarkasy**. Further reading: Alexander Celarek, "The Barkas of Vistula Bay," *Classic Boat* 35 (1991), 59-65. Note also **Garnsicken**.
4. *Poland:* Small motorized vessel that engages in harbor work.
Further references: **barakas**, **launch**, **longboat-1**, **mashhûf**, **sloep-2**

barkasa See **barkaca**, **barkas-3**, **launch**

Barkass, **Barkasse** See **launch**, **longboat-1**

barkasy See **barkas-3**

ba̧rka̧wât See **bark-1**

barkaz See **barkas-1**, **launch**

bark-beštija See **barkentine**

bark boat A general term given to small boats made from tree bark. May employ sophisticated construction, as with the Native American birchbark, spruce-bark, or elmbark **canoes★**, or be quite primitive. Elmbark used inside out. Generally closed at the ends, but some have sheer that sweeps up and are open-ended. Shape retained by ribs or by athwartships cording or sticks. Usually long and narrow. Other recorded names: **bark★, bark canoe, boomschorskano; canoa de corteza, canot d'écorce, Rindenboot, schorsboot; birch(bark) canoe, birch rinde cannoe, Birkenrindenboot; elm canoe; sprucebark canoe★**. Note also **almady, anan, bärwän, concha-2, gre, guli, ichikondo, igat, muterere, ngarawa, ngardän, woodskin, yachip**.

Barkboat See **barque**

bark canoe See **bark boat**

barke 1. In German, **Barke** is variously attributed to a **skiff★** or small **boat★**, a **ship's boat★**, or a sailless Mediterranean **fishing boat★**. Spelling variant: pl. **Barken**
2. In Albania, **barkë** is a general term for a small boat. Spelling variants: **barca★, barcha, barkha, varke, varkha**
3. *Switzerland:* **a.** On the Lake of Biel in western Switzerland, a **Barke** was a cargo vessel. Cap. 20-80t. **b.** The **Holzbarke** of Lake Lugano on the Swiss/Italian border carried firewood. Faggots were placed at the ends and split logs amidships. Sharp overhanging ends; arched house. Rowed (**Ruderbarke**) and sailed, by 2-3 women. Cap. 1,000-15,000 kilos. Name variant: **barca★**
Further references: **bark, bark-5, barka-5, barka-6, barque-4, barque du Léman, Barse, trap**

Barke à tchauque See **grande barque-2**

Barke des marmets See **barque des marmets**

Barkelonge See **barque longue**

barken See **bark-1, barke**

barkenteen, barkentijn See **barkentine**

barkentine Distinguished by its rig—square sails on its foremast and fore-and-aft sails on the main and mizzenmasts; additional masts also fore-and-aft rigged. Sometimes called a **three-masted schooner**, but the **schooner★** type had only a fore lower and topmast and no lower square sail. Primarily a merchant vessel; term reported as early as the late 17th century, but was mainly used in the latter part of the 19th century. Some had 4, 5, or 6 masts. Usually a clipper bow and counter stern; flat floors; some of steel. Those built for the Great Lakes were narrower than the seagoing ships. By the early 20th century, some had an auxiliary engine. Most 45-53m long. Selected name variants: **barchentina, barkantina, barkantine, barkenteen, barkentijn, barkentyna, barkentyne, barkschoener, Barkschoner, barque-goëlette, barquentin(e), barquentina, barquentyne, bergantin goleta de tres palos, dreimastschoener(brik), nave goletta (pl. navi golette), Scho(o)nerbark, schoenerbark, three-masted brig, trois-mâts goëlette, barca (or barco) bestia, barc-beštija, bárko beştya, bark-beštija, bark-mato, barkobestia**

barkentyna, barkentyne See **barkentine**

barketa See **barchetta**

barketta *Switzerland, S:* A **boat★** or small **vessel★** in the dialect of the Swiss Romande. See also **barchetta**.

barkêyật See **bark-1**

barkha See **barke-2**

barki 1. *Bangladesh, NE:* Long, slender open craft of the Sylhet area that transports sand and produce. Flat

bottom turns up at each end, creating a long overhang and flattened spade-like ends. Top strake stops short of the ends. Steered with a long paddle. Mainly poled, but may set a light spritsail to a slender mast stepped through a forward thwart. Average ca. 8m long. Spelling variant: **burki** (erroneously)
2. *Europe, NW:* In Viking and Irish literature a **barki** is described as a **ship's boat★**.
See also **bark-4**.

bârkica See **barka-6**

băṛkîṇǎ See **barquinha-1**

Barking smack See **cod smack-1**

Barking tartar See **cruiser-4**

Barking well smack See **cod smack-1**

Barkkuff See **Kuff**

bark-mato See **barkentine**

bârko Arabic generic term for a small open **boat★**, a **launch★**. Spelling variant: pl. **baṛkůwật**. See also **bark-1**.

barkobestia, bárko beştya See **barkentine**

barkos See **launch**

Barkschiff, barkschip, barkskepp See **bark-1**

barkschoener, Barkschoner See **barkentine**

bárkŭ See **barco-1**

barkūs See **barakas**

barkuwat See **bark-1, bârko**

Barlow boat See **narrow boat**

barmenskjøite, barmensköite See **skøyte-2**

Bar muffie See **polacca**

Barnegat Bay boat See **Barnegat sneakbox**

Barnegat Bay catboat See **catboat-2**

Barnegat cruiser, Barnegat duck boat See **Barnegat sneakbox**

Barnegat sneakbox *United States, E:* Used from the mid-1830s by private and commercial hunters on the creeks and marshes of southern New Jersey, later on Long Island Sound and elsewhere along the east coast. In the latter half of the 19th century, evolved into a popular racing craft, which they still are today in places. Also used by oyster tongers and as transportation in the Barnegat Bay area. Early boats of cedar and oak, later of plywood. Spoon-shaped, with bottom curving upward in a smooth, flat arc to meet the deck; longitudinally planked; wide and shallow, vertical or slightly raked transom, attached with natural knees; small skeg; flat or reverse sheer. Deck cambered from just above the waterline; temporary washboards on after deck for decoy stowage. Might have a canvas spray hood forward of the small rectangular cockpit. Originally used a leeboard, then a scimitar-shaped daggerboard, later a centerboard and, occasionally, a longer daggerboard as well. Initially steered with an oar, then by a shallow rudder worked primarily by lines. Pair of runners on the bottom enabled the boat to be pulled over the ice or onto the shore. Early racing craft carried movable ballast. Short unstayed mast. Set a boomed spritsail originally, later a gaff or balanced lugsail. Also rowed, using oarlocks on movable stanchions. Some now use an outboard motor to reach hunting grounds. Reported lengths 3.7-6m, the longer boats being racing classes; e.g., length 3.7m, width 1.0m, depth 0.25m, draft ca. 15cm. Other recorded names: **Barnegat Bay boat, Barnegat cruiser**

(modified gunning model), **Barnegat duck boat, box, devil's coffin, Jersey Coast sneakbox, melon seed*, New Jersey sneakbox, sneak boat*, sneakbox; Perrine** (for racing). The **St. Francis sneakbox** was built on the St. Lawrence as a pleasure craft. Note also **dink**.

Barnegatter See **catboat-2**

Barnsley keel See **Humber keel**

baroto *Philippines, central:* Important **fishing boat*, ferry***, and cargo transport of the islands bordering the Visayan Sea and in the Zamboanga area of Mindanao. Vary from 1-man craft to those capable of carrying 10. Most have double outriggers, some a single outrigger, while the beamier cargo boats have none. Adzed dugout hull extended by a single strake; sides may be raised further by bamboo matting coated with a waterproofing compound. In some areas the sides consisted of 2 rows of vertically placed palm stalks inserted into light stringers. Sharp-ended; vertical bow and stern scarfed onto the dugout section; bow higher and more overhanging than the stern; bottom flattened. Thwarts attached to residual lugs. Larger boats had a temporary house; most are now entirely open. Steered with an oar or midline rudder. Small boats use 2 outrigger booms, larger 3-4. Mainly sculled but also paddled, poled, rowed, or sailed. Paddles have an oblong blade. Short mast supports a boomed triangular sail, hung with apex down, and a spritsail or square sail. Large plank-extended **barotos** called **tinimbaos** or **tinimbaws**. Reported lengths 4-12m; e.g., length 4m, beam 0.4m, depth 0.5m. In some fishing operations, **barotos** may be given special names. A large **baroto**, called a **pukutan**, carries the large *panikirkinia* net; a small **baroto** holds one end of the net and is called a **lawitan**. Other recorded names: **barato, barroto, boroto, Balóto, balato,** or **boloto** by the Visayan Islands peoples; **bangka** (Tagalog). Note also **banca, dalámas, sibidsibiran, salispan**.

barqua See **barca**

barquaca See **barcaça-1**

barqualonga See **barcolongo**

barquaza See **barcaça-1**

barque French term that has numerous imprecise meanings, ranging from **dugout canoe*, fishing boat***, and **lighter***, to a large 5-masted vessel. The word has also been applied to vessels of less than 150t cap., regardless of rig type.

1. *Canada:* Single-decked vessel used by the French during the 18th century. Square sails on mainmast or forward 2 masts, lateen mizzen. Capacity under 100t.

2. *France:* **a.** Term used for large Norman naval vessels. **b.** Type of vessel used on canals in the south. Those of the 19th and 20th centuries on the Canal du Midi were flat-bottomed, decked vessels 25.7m long and 4.34m wide. Those of the late 18th century were from 10-24.3m long and 2-5.5m wide. **c.** Rhône River **barques** of southeastern France have 320-625t cap. Generally have a steel hull, deck, and hatches. Towed. Reported lengths 55-65m, widths 7-8m, draft 1.4-1.8m. **d.** The **barque-amirale** of the late 17th century was a **galley*** type, with cabins at bow and stern for the sailors and a large cabin amidships. Length 17m, beam 3.7m. Accompanied by smaller **barques** for servants and

lesser dignitaries. **e.** The 19th-century **barque de poste** had a flat bottom; curved, sharp, plumb, or counter stern; curved stem. Service dated from the mid-17th century. The **barque de poste rapide** had finer lines, flat floors, keel, rounded bilges. A passenger cabin covered most of the hull. Towed by 2-4 horses. Rudder wide-bladed below the waterline; tiller. Reported lengths 8-22m; e.g., length 20m, beam 4.4m, draft 0.6m. **f.** In speaking of a **ship***, the term **barque** may be derisive.

3. *Mediterranean:* In the 17th and 18th centuries, a **barque** could be a small, round-bottomed ship or a **galley*** for either war or commerce. On the round vessels, the bows were full, stem curved, sheer strong, poop overhanging. Might set square sails to the main- and mizzenmasts and a lateen on the foremast; or the mizzen might carry a spritsail and topsail. One setting square sails on all masts was called a **barque vaisseau**; a fully lateen-rigged vessel was a **barque latine**. 18th-century lengths ca. 21-30m, breadth ca. one-third, depth to breadth less than one-half; tonnage of late 17th century French **barques** ranged between 10 and 120t. Name variant: **barque italienne**. Note also **caique-4**.

4. *Switzerland:* **Barques** were found on many Swiss lakes. Early vessels on Lake of Geneva (Lake Léman) carried merchandise; others in the 17th and 18th centuries were armed vessels. One late 18th-century naval craft had a sharp concave bow and square stern; 2 masts, the foremast raking forward in the eyes, the vertical mainmast amidships, set lateen sails. Some fished (note also **barque du Léman**). On Lake of Biel, northeast of Lake of Neuchâtel, the cargo **barque** (or **Barke***) had a flat bottom, high sharp bow, lower plumb stern. Open; arched covering forward. Set a single sail: square, sprit, or triangular. Crew of 5. Lengths overall 12-16m, beam ca. 2m. The **barque** (also **Barke** or **barca**) of Lake Lugano on the Italian border carried coal and wood. Overhanging ends. Arched covering aft. Steered with a sweep. Mainly rowed with 2-3 pairs of oars; also sailed. Cap. 1-15t.

5. *Uganda, NW/Zaire, NE:* Planked **canoe***, used mainly for fishing, especially on Lake Albert. Slab sides, flat bottom, vertical stem, transom stern. Name variant: **Congo barque**

6. *United States, SE:* Word sometimes used in the early 18th century by Native Americans of the southern Atlantic coast to describe a log **raft***.

7. *United States, central:* Early 18th-century sailing vessel that carried merchandise on the Mississippi River and in the Gulf of Mexico. The river **barques** also had oars. Reported cap. 45-50t.

Other recorded names: **barche*, barge*, bargue, barkboat***. Note also **barca, bark, demi-barque**. Further references: **barque du Léman, bette, saettia-2**

barque à barrière See **navis baragniata**

barque-amirale See **barque-2d**

barque à tchauque See **grande barque-2**

barque catalane See **catalane**

barque chênière See **chênière**

barque cochère See **cochère**

barque d'avis See **advice boat**

barque de cantier See **barge de cantier**
barque del bou See **barca del bou**
barque de mer *France, S:* Small cargo **tartane*** that traversed the Canal du Midi until the beginning of the 20th century. Also used at sea. Sharp ends, flat floors. Length to 15m, beam ca. 5m. Further reference: **ghe biê'n**
barque de palangre See **palangrero-1**
barque de parascalme See **palischermo-1**
barque de poste, barque de poste rapide See **barque-2e**
barque de promenade See **yacht-2**
barque de sardinal See **barco de sardinal**
barque des marmets *Switzerland, W:* Carried merchandise on Neuchâtel and adjacent lakes. Sharp high bow, raked stem, plumb transom stern, little sheer except at the bow, flat keelless bottom. Open except for foredeck; 2 thwarts forward of the mast. Rudder hung with rings and angle hook; sometimes a side rudder was suspended from a willow ring; centerboard. Early boats set a quadrilateral sail, later a square sail. Length overall ca. 17m, on bottom 15m, beam 4m, depth forward 2.5m, aft 1.1m. Other recorded names: **Barke des marmets, barquette*, Schiff***
barque de vivandier See **bumboat-1**
barque Djenné *Mali, central:* General term for the slender plank-built boats used by various groups in the inner Niger Delta area. The smallest, to ca. 10m long, are used mainly for fishing, the harpooner standing at the bow. The next larger category, to ca. 20m long, is mainly a family craft, but also used for fishing. The largest, ca. 40m long, transports people and cargo between markets and carries salt. Constructed of a mosaic of irregular planking, often salvaged from old boats. Slender, elongated solid ends slot onto the bottom. Bottom flat athwartships, with fore-and-aft rocker. Ends forced up with stones before sides attached. Side and bottom planking nailed, except amidships where the 2 halves are sewn together, but now commonly pegged rather than sewn. Maximum beam amidships; flared sides; sometimes the boat is taken apart at the center stitching and transoms are attached, forming 2 separate boats. Caulked with fiber from the fruit of the baobab tree. Open; numerous thwarts; platform at the stern; firebox on larger boats, because the family may live aboard for as long as a week. Propelled by paddles, oars, sail; poled, sculled, or towed in narrow areas. Might employ a small square mat sail. More recently the larger boats motorized; these are called **pinasses*** and have a flat stern for the outboard motor and cables that lead forward to the steersman. Other recorded names: **djenné, pirogue de Djenné; hulu, kii, kin, kun, kūū** by the Bozo; **holi** in the Kelinga dialect of the Bozo; **kulu** or **xulū** in the Diafarabé dialect of the Bozo; **kuni** or **kuru** by the Bambara. Those used for hunting are called **pénhulu**. Further reading: A. Pitot and J. Daget, *Les Barques du Moyen Niger* (Paris: Gauthier-Villars, 1948 [Documents d'Ethnographie Naval, Fasc. 5]).
barque du Léman *France, E/Switzerland, W:* Lateen-rigged vessel of Lakes of Geneva (Léman) and Annecy. Transported stone, sand, and firewood on deck. Last one constructed in 1906. Carvel-planked;

rounded flaring sides; maximum beam amidships; flat sheer except for sharp rise at the bow; very low freeboard. Flat bottom with only a slight rise to the floors; straight keel. Concave curve to the bow, high stemhead; narrow transom. Wide-bladed rudder hung well below the keel; long up-turned tiller. Cabin forward. Narrow walkways ran outboard along each side, providing access to bow and stern around the deck cargo, and for poling. Several transverse chains prevented the hull from expanding under heavy loads. Stepped 2 pole masts of equal height, the foremast close to the bow and raked slightly forward. Lateen sails bent to 1-piece yards; set goose-winged when running before the wind. Jib run to a light bowsprit since the end of

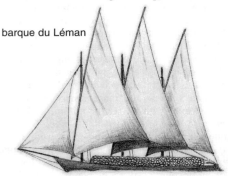

barque du Léman

the 19th century. Lacking wind, the **barques** were poled, towed from shore, or in open water, towed by the vessel's **naviot***. Very large **barques** had as many as 4 masts. These were also rowed or sculled. Later vessels motorized. Crew of 4, later 5. Reported lengths 26-35m; e.g., length on deck 26.8m, beam 7.4m, depth 2m, draft loaded 2.25m. Smaller 2-masted **barques**, called **bricks**, were built until 1931, most often by the Swiss. Crew of 3. Reported lengths on keel 16-18m, length-to-beam ratio 3.5:1. Formerly called **brigantins***. Other recorded names: **barke*, barque*, barque latine, barque lémanique, Latin barge**. Further reading: Gérard Cornaz, *Les Barques du Léman*, 2nd ed. (Grenoble: Éditions des 4 Seigneurs, 1976). Note also **cochère**.
barque du Rhône See **penelle**
barque du seigneur See **nacelle-5**
barque flibustière See **freebooter**
barque-goëlette See **barkentine**
barqueirolo See **barquerole**
barque italienne See **barque-3**
barque jackass See **jackass bark**
barque latine See **barque-3, barque du Léman**
barque lémanique See **barque du Léman**
barque longue 1. Long, low, narrow vessel designed to be both rowed and sailed. Used in northern Europe, on the Danube River, and in France, mainly in the 17th and early 18th centuries, as an armed escort, **advice boat***, or reconnaissance boat. Sharp ends or a stern transom. Open, with as many as 14 rowing benches; larger vessels fully decked. Stepped 1-2 masts; set square sails and sometimes topsails; some lateen-rigged. Might have a spritsail below a bowsprit. Those that were armed carried 15-50 men. Reported lengths

12-15m, widths 2.7-4.5m, depths 1.37-1.75m. Other recorded names: **barcalonga, Barchalonga, Barche longe, Bar(c)kelonge, chaloupe double, corvette★, dobbele chaloupe, double chaloupe, double sloop, galléole, long barque**. Note also **barcolongo, double shallop, senau**.

2. *Belgium:* Small **galley★**-type **man-of-war★** used by Flemish privateers in the 17th and 18th centuries. Low sides, moderate sheer, higher top strake aft. Slightly curved raking stem, raking heart-shaped transom with sternpost for an outboard rudder. Thwarts for 25-44 oarsmen. Small types open, larger decked, with hatches fore and aft. Armed with 2-10 cannon, a canon-perier or swivel gun, axes, and pikes. Stepped 1-2 masts. Single-masted vessels rigged with square sail, staysail, spritsail beneath a small bowsprit. The 2-masted vessels stepped the foremast close to the stem, mainmast amidships; set square sails and a square topsail. Staysails between the masts; also might rig studding sails. Crew of ca. 50-70. Length on keel 15m, beam 5.2m, depth 2m. Other recorded names: **barcalongo, barkalonga**

3. *France, N:* The 18th-century **barque longue** of the Dunkerque area was a **brigantine★**-rigged **fishing boat★**. Some worked as cargo vessels. Originally square-sterned, later round-sterned. Decked to the mainmast; cargo vessels fully decked and might step a mizzenmast. Reported lengths 17-18.5m; beam 5.2-5.85m, on bottom 2.6-3m; depth 3.58-3.9m; draft 2.28-2.6m.

barque morutière See **cod-fishing boat**

barquentin, barquentina, barquentine, barquentyna, barquentyne See **barkentine**

barque olonnoise See **barque sablaise**

barque pannoise See **panneschuit**

barque perlière See **pearling lugger**

barque provençale *France, Mediterranean coast:* 18th-century **coaster★**. Characterized by a tall pole mainmast that carried 3 square sails, a forward-raking foremast to which a large lateen sail was fitted, small lateen sail to the mizzenmast, plus 1-2 square sails to a topmast. The forward lateen yard was tacked to a slender spar running out from the false stem or beak; the after lateen sheeted to an outrigger. Decked; large poop ran from just abaft the mainmast to beyond the sternpost. Hatches amidships, sometimes equipped with special chains for the barrels of wine carried in the hold.

barquerol See **barquerole**

barquerole **1.** French term for a small **boat★**, generally without sails, used in quiet waters as a **passage boat★** or pleasure craft. Cap. 4-6 persons.
2. Sometimes attributed to a **barge★** of the northern Adriatic lagoons, but word has wider meaning elsewhere in the Mediterranean.
3. *Turkey, west coast:* In the Izmir (Smyrna) area, a small seaworthy boat.
Other recorded names: **baranette, barca netta, barcanette, barcarolă, barcarolle, barcar(u)olo, barcheruolo, Barkarole, barkarolle, barqueirolo, barquerol(le), barquette★**

barquerolle See **barquerole**

barque sablaise *France, Bay of Biscay coast:* Inshore **fishing boat★**, especially for sardines, that was developed at Les Sables-d'Olonne ca. 1900 and was an active sailer until 1930, when motors were installed. Characterized by an elongated rounded stern; sharply raked straight sternpost came to just above the deck. S-shaped tiller passed through a hole in the bulwark or below the railing that surrounded the vessel. Plumb stem extended above the bulwarks. Straight keel with marked drag. Decked; cabin aft, entered through a raised hatch. Painted with a wide red or black band that followed the sheer, white below.

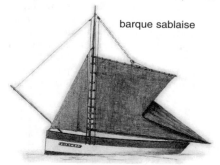

barque sablaise

Carried or towed a **tender★**, called a **canot★** or **canotte★**, on deck; 2.6-3.5m long. Rigged with loose-footed, boomed gaff mainsail, staysail, one or more jibs, and yard topsail; 2 or 3 shrouds. Sails might be ochre, blue, yellow, red; some had a decorative emblem. Crew of 5-6. Length 16m, beam 5m, draft 2m; 7-30t. Other recorded names: **barque olonnoise, barquette sablaise, gazelle des sables, sloop sablaise**. Further reading: Dominique Duviard and Noël Gruet, *Histoire d'un Bateau de Pêche: La Gazelle des Sables d'Olonne* (Aubin à Poitiers: Éditions Gallimard, 1981).

barque sétoise See **bateau sétois**

barquet *France, Mediterranean:* A **skiff★** or **wherry★**-type boat; term dates from at least the 16th century. Used mainly for fishing on bays and in river mouths. Sharp, strongly raked ends; flat bottom with strong rocker; straight flaring sides; strong sheer. Generally rowed with 2-3 pairs of oars, but also sailed. Reported lengths 3.7-5.5m. Note also **barqueta, barquette-4, bette**

barqueta **1.** Catalan, Portuguese, and Spanish term for a very small **boat★** or **skiff★**. Other recorded names: **barcata, barquet★, barquita; ontziño, ontziska** (Basque); **barqueto** (in Provence). Note also **barquete, barquette**.
2. *Madeira Islands:* Small boat used to convey passengers from ships lying in a roadstead. Rowed solo.
Further reference: **canoa-6**

barqueta de sardinal See **barco de sardinal**

barque tartane See **tartane de Marseille**

barquete Spanish diminutive for a **barco★**. Note also **barqueta**. Further reference: **barquette**

barqueto See **barqueta**

barquetta See **barchetta**

barquette **1.** French term for a small **ship★** or **rowing boat★**; occasionally a **fishing boat★**; sometimes a small **ferryboat★**. Note also **barquet, barqueta, demi-barque**.

2. *France, Mediterranean coast:* General-purpose and **fishing boat** seen mainly at Marseille; some formed a racing class. Evolved from the Italian **barchetta**★ in the 19th century, but also reported as an inshore **fishing boat** of the 17th-18th centuries. Some variation by builder and locality, but most sharp-ended; straight stem, rounded forefoot; tall stemhead, characteristically capped with a carved bulging decoration; curved sternpost; fine entrance; flat floors; straight or slightly curved keel. High washboards on some; sections removable for rowing. Decked, half-decked, or open. Generally set a lateen sail, sometimes a lugsail, to a vertical mast amidships. Some stepped a short mast in the bow, setting a small sail that was boomed out forward with a sprit. Jib run to a small jibboom that passed through an iron loop on the stem. Now motorized. Crew of 2

barquette-2

when fishing, 3 when racing. Reported lengths 3.5-10m; e.g., length 5m, beam 1.83m, depth 0.86m. Other recorded names: **barquette marseillaise**; racing boats: **barquette de régate**, **ciotaden**, **gourse de régate**

3. *St. Pierre and Miquelon:* Open boat that engaged in coastal cod fishing off this French Overseas Territory south of Newfoundland. Crew of 2. Reported lengths 7.3-8m.

4. *Switzerland:* **a.** During the 18th century, the **barquette** was a naval vessel on several lakes. One in the latter part of the century had a crew of 12. Probably lateen-rigged. Spelling variants: **barquet**★, **barquot**★. **b.** Small **fishing boat** in use on rivers reported in the late 18th and early 19th centuries.
Spelling variant: **barquete**★. Further references: **barchetta**, **barque des marmets**, **barquerole**, **demi-barque**

barquette de régate, **barquette marseillaise** See **bar-quette-2**

barquette sablaise See **barque sablaise**

barque vaisseau See **barque-3**

barquilla 1. Generic term in Spanish for small open **boats**★, especially those used in ports, on rivers, and close inshore. May be propelled by oars, sail, or motor. Other recorded names: **barquillo**, **barquito**; **barxete** and **barxot** (Catalan)

2. *Spain:* A small **falucho**★ that guarded Spanish ports. Manned by 8-10.

3. *Spain, north coast:* Small **fishing boat**★ that was both rowed and sailed. Set a single lugsail, well forward. Note also **barquilla de sardinel**. Further reference: **barquille**

barquilla de sardinal *Spain, E:* Double-ended sardine **trawler**★. Bow slightly sharper than stern; stem straight

barquilla de sardinal

and vertical, high stemhead cut to oblique point; sternpost strongly curved. Straight keel; grounding keels. Washstrakes extend from stem aft to an athwartships board just forward of the sternpost. Decked, cuddy forward; wide side decks; steering well just forward of the transverse board; 3 thwarts. Forward-raking mast stepped amidships, setting a lateen sail; spar rest just aft of the transverse board. Also rowed, sometimes with 7-9 oars; auxiliaries in some boats. Crew of 4-6, plus captain. Reported lengths 6-8m; e.g., length 7, beam 2.6m, depth 1.0m. Further reading: L. Bellón, "Pesca y Utilización del Boquerón y de la Sardina en las Costas de Málaga," *Boletin del Instituto Español de Oceanografía* 30 (1950). Note also **barco de sardinal**.

barquille In 17th-century French usage, a small vessel, usually spoken of disparagingly. Other recorded names: **barquilla**★ (Spanish), **barr-amzer** (Breton)

barquillo 1. Spanish diminutive of **barco**★. Small boat used on rivers, in nearshore areas, and in ports.

2. *Canary Islands, eastern Atlantic Ocean:* Small lateen-sailed boat used for inshore fishing. Also rowed. Ca. 1.0t.
Further reference: **barquilla-1**

barquinha 1. *Cape Verde Islands:* In their Creole language, **bǎṛkîňǎ** means **barquinha**.

2. *Portugal:* **a.** In general, a little **boat**★ or small **barge**★. Considered a diminutive of **barca**★. **b.** Open boat of the lower Rio Lima in northern Portugal; used for cargo transport, ferrying, and fishing. Clinker-planked; sharp bow, raked stem; transom stern; sides nearly plumb. Flat bottom, longitudinally planked, no keel; paired ribs, each running down one side and across the bottom; slightly raised flooring at the stern. Poled or set a spritsail or square sail. Crew of 1-2, 4 when fishing. Reported lengths 9-10m; e.g., length 10m, beam 2.18m, depth 0.6m. Spelling variant: **barquinho**★

barquinha de pesca com engodo See **barco do candil**

barquinha rabela See **rabelo**

barquinho *Portugal, central:* Small open **fishing boat**★ found at the mouth of the Rio Alcoa at Nazaré and at São Martinho do Porto. The boats in both areas are similar, the latter often called a **barquinho-vigia**. Carvel-planked, transom stern, flat bottom. Rowed.

Length ca. 3m, beam 1.3m, depth 0.3m. See also **barquinha-2**.

barquinho do candil See **barco do candil**

barquinho do coberto *Portugal, central:* Fishes for whiting and eels in calm waters off the beach at Buarcos. Carvel-planked, flat floors, raked ends, narrow transom. Rowed. Crew of 1-2. Length 5m, beam 1.43m, depth 0.45m.

barquinho-vigia See **barquinho**

barquita See **barqueta-1**

barquito See **barquilla-1**

barquito de pesca See **rabão**

barquot Term used by French travelers of the late 17th century for a 2-man **fishing boat★**. Note also **barquet**. Further reference: **barquette-4**

Barra canoe *Gambia:* Large boat that could ferry as many as 50 people across the Gambia River between Bathurst (now Banjul) and Barra. Set 2 large spritsails. Also rowed.

barracouta boat *Australia, S:* Trolls for barracouta and pots for lobsters in Tasmanian waters. Evolved in the latter half of the 19th century, spreading from the Victorian coast. A few motorized boats remain. Some restored sailing craft participate in regattas. Some also engaged in crayfishing, the larger of these having a wet well. Hull form ranged from narrow with hollow garboards to beamy with full bilges; the older boats tended to have a straighter stem and keel. Clinker-built on steam-bent frames prior to 1900, both clinker and carvel to 1920, then mainly carvel. Smaller boats uncaulked except for garboard strakes. Transom stern; smaller boats had a temporary counter-like platform from which to fish. Drag to the curved keel; steep rise to the floors; massive centerboard in later years. Large cockpit; decked to just abaft the mast, short stern deck, narrow side decks. Outboard rudder; tiller. Mast stepped about a third in from the bow. Early boats employed a standing lugsail, some boomed but laced only at the clew. Gaff on the later gaff-rigged boats high-peaked; the gaff fitted to a well-greased metal collar on the mast. Jib set flying or on a traveler that hauled out on the bowsed-down bowsprit. Rowed when necessary, often for long distances. Crew of 1-2. Reported lengths 6-15m; average length 8m, beam 2.8m, draft 1.0m. Other recorded names: **'cliff boat**, **'couta boat**, **Queenscliff couta boat**, **Tasmanian barracouta boat**

barr-amzer See **barquille**

barrik See **bark-1**

barroto See **baroto**

Barse *Germany:* May have designated a small cargo vessel (1767), a vessel without a mast (1879), or a naval vessel serving guard duty in a harbor; also used at the mouth of the Weser River as a channel-marking ship during the 17th-18th centuries. Spelling variants: **Bardese, Barke★, Ba(r)sse, Barze**. See also **baardse**.

barsera See **brazzera**

Barsse See **Barse**

Bartholomew's bread pan See **compartment boat**

Barton horse boat *England, NE:* A **ferry★** that conveyed passengers and livestock across the Humber Estuary between Barton-upon-Humber and Hull.

Operated from the 14th century. By the mid-19th century, it was a **cutter★**-rigged, transom-sterned craft. Note also **horse boat**.

Barton sloop See **Humber sloop**

barudel paruwa See **paruwa-2**

bärwän *Australia, N:* Bark **canoe★** of the eastern side of Arnhem Land on the Gulf of Carpentaria. Constructed of a single sheet of eucalyptus bark, flattened by smoking to prevent cracking, and turned so that the inner surface becomes the outside of the **canoe**. Ends similar, formed by stitching with a grass fiber down the inner edge of the bow and stern and laced along the outer edges. Rounded bottom; stringers prevent craft from collapsing; grass ropes prevent spreading; sides strengthened by light gunwale poles. Paddled. Large size: length overall 4.6m, on bottom 4m, width 0.9m, depth 0.58m. Spelling variant: **baer-warn**

barxa See **barca**

barxete, barxot See **barquilla-1**

barza See **barca, barca-6, barzha**

barze See **barca-6, Barse**

barzha *Russia:* **Barge★**-like craft that may be towed or that tows another vessel. Earlier **barzhas** on the Volga River were 2-masted and characteristically carried pennants with wind vanes on both the main- and mizzenmasts. Spelling variants: **barja, barža**

baržha See **barge-1, hopper-1**

barzha plashkoum See **dummy barge-1**

barzoti, barzoto, barzotti, barzotto See **barca-6**

bã:s *South Africa:* A swimming log employed by the Korana of the Orange River basin to cross rivers. Generally 1 person lies alongside or astride the willow log, grasping a peg near the forward end and propelling the log by kicking; if used by more than 1 person, each has a peg to grasp. Reported lengths 1.22-4.57m. Another version is composed of 2 parallel logs connected by a transverse log, with 2 people holding the crossbar and others at each end of the longitudinal logs. Other recorded names: **dã:s; houte-paard** or **wooden horse** (by the Klaarwater Hottentots)

bascule, basculle See **vivier-1**

basin boat See **tarai-bune**

bask *Norway, NE:* Small open boat of the northern Lapps (Same) of the eastern region of Finnmark, including northeast Finland and the northwest corner of Russia. Employed in estuary and lake fishing and for travel. Lapped strakes of pine, originally sewn with reindeer sinews, later nailed; ribs also of pine, ca. 50cm apart. Caulked with moss. Wide low keel; fairly flat floors, soft turn of the bilges. Sharp ends; stemhead recurved; sternpost lightly curved and plumb to strongly raked. Narrow rudder; tiller. Rowed, punted, and sailed. Rowed with 1-4 pairs of oars between double tholepins or a shaped block and loop. Might set a tall square sail originally; later a spritsail. Reported lengths 3.3-4.85m; e.g., length 4.85m, width 1.27-1.32m, depth 0.37m. Other recorded names: **baskebåt, Lapp boat**; pl. **baskene, basker**. One used by the Skolte Lapps may be called a **Skoltebask**; one from the Tana Fjord, a **Tanabask**. Note also **elvebåt, Lappbåt, Skoltelapsbåt**.

baş kanca See **cangia**

baskebåt, baskene, basker See **bask**

basket An old, leaky, worn-out vessel, usually requiring constant pumping.

basket boat A boat with a shell formed by woven leaves or split branches. Generally round or roughly oval and keelless. Coated with a waterproof material. Paddled or poled. Best known are the **coracle★** of Wales, the **quffa★** of Iraq, and the **ghe nang★** of Vietnam. Other recorded names: **Korbboot, Korbgeflechtboot**

basket canoe *Canada, E:* Roundish boat used by the Micmac of the Maritime Provinces for lake-to-lake travel. Skins covered a wickerwork frame.

basnig See **basnigan**

basnigan *Philippines:* Uses a bag net (the *basnig*) in night fishing; may also serve as a trader. Large double-outrigger canoe★; often a plank-extended dugout. Bow sharp and high, may recurve at the head; stern lower but also sheers up; "U" or "V" in cross section. Ribs mortised in. Platform amidships for shooting and stowing the net; lamp at bow to attract fish. Bamboo outrigger floats, booms of a pliable wood. Some colorfully painted. Employs a triangular sail and foresail; multiple shrouds to the outriggers. Crew of 18-25 on the large boats. Large vessels now mainly motorized and without outriggers. Reported lengths 9-15m; some to 41m; very narrow. Other recorded names: **basnig, parao★** or **parau★** (in Visayan dialect of central Philippines)

basouille See **vivier-1**

basquine See **bisquine**

Bass See **Buttjolle**

Basse See **Barse**

baştarda *Turkey:* A very large naval **galley★** that served as vessel of the commander in the16th-17th centuries. The sultan's **galley** was the **baştarda-i humayun**. High bulging poop; 36 rowing benches. Spelling variants: **baştarde, bastarda hümayün, baştarde-i hümâyun**

bastarda See **bastardo, bâtard-1**

bastarda hümayün, baştarda-i humayun See **baştarda**

bastard boat See **wide boat**

bastard canoe See **canot bâtard**

bastarde See **ba tarda, bastardo**

baştarde-i hümâyun See **baştarda**

bastardella, bastardelle See **row galley-1**

bastardo *Italy:* **1.** One of 4-6 small boats used in the tuna fisheries out of Naples on the west coast. Positioned on each side of a quadrangle. A capstan handles the net. Length ca. 10m. Name variant: **bastarda** (Sardinia). Note also **barca di guarda**.
2. Flat-bottomed cargo craft of the Po and Panaro Rivers in northern Italy. Sharp upturned bow; slightly rounded stern; maximum beam well forward; hard chines; flared sides; low freeboard; outboard rudder. Decked at bow and stern; open waist, protected by a light arched covering. Length 25.4m, beam 5.87m, depth 1.45m; cap. 90t.
Spelling variant: pl. **bastarde**

basteau See **bateau**

bastimen See **ship**

bastiment See **barca del bou, bastimento**

bastimento Generic term in Italian and Spanish for a **boat★, vessel★,** or **ship★.** Generally refers to one not armed for war, although in Greece the word was usually reserved for a warship. Spelling variants: **bastiment, vastimento**

bastimento di dogana, bastimento doganale See **revenue cutter-1**

bastimento filibustiere See **freebooter**

bastimento guardaporto See **guard ship**

bat 1. *Norway/Sweden:* **Båt** is the generic term for **boat★.** Spelling variants: Norwegian—**baad, båten,** pl. **båtane, båtene, båtar, båter;** Old Norse—**båtr;** Swedish—**båten,** pl. **båtar, båtarna**
2. *Poland:* Term for a **boat★** or **vessel★.** Early references cite the **bat** as a **ship's boat★.** A small boat is a **bacik,** while an old and unsightly craft may be called a **bacisko.** Further name variants: **bata★, batka**
3. *Russia, E:* The **bat'** was a **dugout canoe★** used by the indigenous peoples of the Kamchatka Peninsula, Sakhalin Island, and the lower Amur River area, primarily for transportation but also for fishing. Heavy, roughly hewn; often topsides with tumble home.

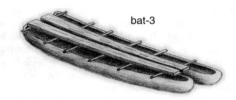

bat-3

Pointed or square at the ends, or had a spoon-shaped bow and squared stern. When carrying bulky loads or numerous people, 2 **canoes** were placed side by side and joined by poles and a platform. Drifted with the current, or was poled. Reported lengths ca. 8-15m; narrow. Other recorded names: **bate, batnik, baty, botnik, elle´ut** (by the Koryaks)
4. *United States, E:* Term given to the flat-bottomed boat used in haul-seining operations on western beaches of southern Chesapeake Bay. Probably a dialect form of **bateau** (see **bateau-7**). The **bat** secured the seaward end of the net and housed it when not in use. Sharp bow, wide transom stern, open except for narrow side decks. Powered by a Model A engine. Length 7.6m.
Further reference: **boat-1**

bata 1. *Poland:* A large craft used on the Warta River until the 1940s as a **fish car★.**
2. *Scotland:* **Bàta** is a Gaelic term for a **boat★, pinnace★,** or **barge★.** Other recorded names: **bàtacha(i)n** (dim.), **bhàta;** pl. **bàtaichean.** Further reference: **bat-2**

bàtachain, bàtachan See **bàta**

bàtà da chroinn See **wherry**

bàtaichean See **bàta**

bat' aiseig See **ferryboat-1**

batalya See **patalya**

batana *Croatia:* **1.** At Rovigno d'Istria, a seaport on the northwest coast, a craft similar to the Venetian **sanpierota★.** Flat bottom; straight flared sides; sharp bow with strongly raked stem; square raking stern; sheer sweeps up toward the bow. Brightly painted; outboard rudder. Sets a lug mainsail and a jib. Reported length 6-7m; e.g., length 6.6m, beam 1.74m.

2. Elsewhere, the **batana** may be a small boat used in coastal fishing. Flat bottom, transversely planked; straight flaring sides; hard chines; 10-12 ribs. Sharp raking stem; wide, slightly raked transom stern, external sternpost. Rowed with 2-4 oars against single tholepins. Reported lengths 3-4m, beam ca. 1.5m, depth ca. 0.5m.
Other recorded names: **batel***; **ploščak** (Slovenian). Further references: **battana-1**, **battana-5**

bâtane, bâtar See **bât-1**

bâtard 1. Large, square-sterned **galleys*** that were placed on either side of the larger and stronger **flagship***. Name variants: **bastarda***, **bâtarde**, **bâtardelle**. Note also **capitane**, **patronne**, **real**.
2. *France:* An inland waterway **barge*** that transported merchandise until the mid-20th century, especially on the canals of Orléans and Nivernais. Flat bottom; symmetrical rounded ends, sheer swept up at bow and stern; wide-bladed rudder. Decked; steering cockpit; cabin amidships. Reported lengths 19.5-30.5m; e.g., length 21.4m, beam 3m, depth 1.0m. Note also **bateau bâtard**.

batardate See **row galley-1**

batard canoe See **canot bâtard**

bâtard du Pollet See **quenouille**

bâtarde See **bâtard-1**, **pinasse-1a**

batardelle See **bâtard-1**, **row galley-1**

bâtarna See **bât-1**

batātîl See **batil-1**

batau See **bateau**

bate See **bat-3**, **boat-1**

batea Spanish term for a boxy craft found at shipyards, arsenals, and ports. By extension, a vessel that, because of its shallow draft, navigates on rivers, especially to ferry. When decked, may be used for lightering, and locally called a **pasacaballo**. Square ends, flat bottom and sides. Other name variant: **bot***. Further reference: **punt-2**

bateau 1. French word for a **boat***, especially one that is open, lightly constructed, narrow-beamed, and mainly used on protected waters or near the coast. Now a general term for any small boat. May be rowed, sculled, sailed, or motorized.
2. *Barbados, West Indies:* Small flat-bottomed boats used by pairs of boys or young men who row out to anchored ships in order to dive for coins. Roughly constructed.
3. *Canada, E:* **a.** Three-man boat used for inshore fishing on the northern peninsula of Newfoundland and on Labrador. Employed a lugsail. **b.** Term given to a **rowboat*** by 18th-century French-Canadians. Sharp ends; flat bottom, sheer swept up at ends; top sheer less; vertical sides. Rowed by 4 men, poled, or set a square sail. Spelling variant: **battoe**. **c.** In the same period, a **bateau** (or **batteau***) might be used in a general sense to designate any sailing vessel. **d.** In Quebec, the classification for a fishing **bateau** is a boat less than 10grt and 4-12m long. May be rowed or have a motor.
4. *Haiti:* In Creole dialect, a type of decked **barge***. Spelling variant: **bato**
5. *Honduras/Nicaragua:* Transports freight on rivers bordering the Caribbean. Constructed by halving a local **dugout canoe***, the **pitpan***, lengthwise and inserting planking for a new bottom. Planks raise the sides. Large boats have a small stern cabin of bamboo and thatch. Steered with a large paddle. Manned by 6-12. Lengths to 18.2m; widths 1.22-1.83m; cap. 2.5-5t.
6. *Jamaica, NE:* A fishing **raft***, more or less substantial. Found particularly between Priestmans River and Port Antonio. May be of loosely secured branches, of bamboo, or of a half dozen well-lashed logs. Spelling variants: **bato**, **batu**
7. *United States:* **a.** In some places a **scow*** is called a **bateau**. In the southern states, a **bateau** may be an old and clumsy boat. **b.** Half-decked crabbing boat with a V-bottom and centerboard. Mainmast stepped at the bow, mizzen on the counter. Length 6.4m, beam 2.5m, depth 0.6m. Note also **crabbing bateau**. **c.** Armed craft used on Lake Champlain in northern New York State and other northern lakes during the American Revolution. Flat bottom, generally sharp ends, wide strakes; weather cloths protected crew from small-arms fire. Rowed and sailed, setting a single lateen, spritsail, or 2 leg-of-mutton sails. Lengths to 18m. Note also **batoe**. **d.** Cargo carried by **Durham boats*** on the Oswego River in western New York State in the early 19th century had to be transported over the falls at Fulton. It was then carried in **bateaux** the 19km to Oswego on Lake Ontario. Salt in barrels was an important cargo. Lightly built open boats about half the size of the local **Durham boats** and lacked their running boards. Sharp, raked ends. Usually propelled by oars or setting poles; with favorable winds raised a square sail and, at times, a square topsail. Crew of 3. **e.** The **Mohawk River bateau** in central New York State of the 17th and early 18th centuries was an open, sharp-ended cargo boat. Mainly built at Schenectady. Flat bottom, slight rocker toward the ends; plank keel and keelson; raked stem and sternpost. Sides straight and slightly flared; hull fuller forward than aft. Steered with a 5.5-6.1m-long sweep. Rowed and sailed; upstream employed sett poles. Square sail and topsail set to a light mast stepped in the forward thwart. Length dictated the number in crew: **three-handed bateau**, **five-handed bateau**, and the largest, the **eight-handed bateau**. Lengths mostly 9-9.8m, some as short as 5.5m, a few as long as 15.2m; e.g., length 9.8m, beam 1.8m, depth 0.76m. Further reading: Robert E. Hager, *Mohawk River Boats and Navigation Before 1820* (Syracuse, N.Y.: Canal Society of New York State, 1987). Note also **batteau-4b**. **f.** Flatiron-shaped boat of the oyster tonging fleet of Staten Island in the New York Bay area. **g.** Some local peoples of the Chesapeake Bay area call anything that floats a **bateau**, but more precisely, any V-bottom craft. Note also **bat-4**, **crabbing skiff**, **one-sail bateau**, **pound boat**, **skipjack**. **h.** Boat that followed **timber rafts*** on the Susquehanna River in eastern Pennsylvania. Held 20 people. Length 9m; beam 1.5m. Name variant: **bateaus**. **i.** Transported freight and passengers on Pennsylvania and West Virginia rivers during the 19th and early 20th centuries. Relatively flat craft with decks at each end; rounded or square at bow and stern. Rudder at each end; some

maneuvered by sweeps. The men who poled the **bateau** upstream walked half the length of the boat on each side before resetting the pole; later a **skiff**★ with a motor pushed the boat. Length ca. 18.2m, beam 3m, depth 0.6m; shallow draft. **j.** In Georgia, South Carolina, and northern Florida, a **bateau** is an open, plank-built craft that is individually built, varying in shape and size accordingly. Now frequently constructed of plywood. Multipurpose boats, although some serve specifically as **ferries**★, as craft for wildfowlers, and the larger, as freight carriers. In coastal areas, the **bateau** is most often a small, flat-bottomed **skiff**★. Bottom cross-planked, flat forward of amidships, then curves up to a wide transom; plank keel and skeg added on. Plumb stem; each side of a single cypress or pine plank; chine pieces nailed in place; short side frames; knees at the bow and each corner of the transom. Primarily rowed, but a few set a spritsail, and some larger boats were **sloop**★-rigged; most now have outboard motors. Average lengths 4.3-4.9m, beam 1.2-1.5m. The inland river **bateau** was a narrow, shallow, square-ended craft. Used until the late 1930s for ferrying and fishing. Also flat-bottomed but longitudinally planked and curved up at each end; framed across the bottom. Single side planks nailed directly to the bottom plank edges; sides straight with little flare and only slight curvature at the ends; bow end narrower and shallower than stern. Seats and end decking nailed to top of side strakes. Mainly paddled. Reported lengths 4.6-6.7m, beam ca. 0.9m, depth 0.3. Other recorded names: **batteau**, **battoe**, **riverboat**★. Note also **diamond bottom bateau**. **k.** In the French province along the Mississippi, during the 1st half of the 18th century, the term was applied indiscriminately to private and government vessels of 25-100t that sailed to the West Indies and along the Gulf of Mexico coast; others, in the range of 12-16t, plied the Mississippi River. **l.** In the central United States, a **bateau** was a large planked **skiff**★-type boat used by the early settlers, often moving whole families up and down major rivers. The first were built in 1787, near Pittsburgh, to move government provisions and troops. Flat bottom, no keel, tapered ends; awning or cabin aft. Maneuvered downstream by pairs of sweeps; another sweep served as a rudder. Poled upstream generally. Sometimes they were part of a large convoy that rowed and sailed up the Mississippi River in late winter and early spring. Some set a square or lugsail. Reported lengths 6-12m. Spelling variant: **batteau**. Note also **Mackinaw boat-2**, **skiff-10**. **m.** In parts of Louisiana, **bateau** may designate any flat-bottomed, blunt-ended vessel, although most are small and paddled. **n.** A heavy, square-ended **fishing boat**★ of the Louisiana bayous popular in the 1st half of the 20th century. Some mainly transported iced fish to market; still used by the lumber industry in the Atchafalaya Basin. Flat bottom has slight rocker at bow, as does the sheer; bow narrower than stern. Decked forward and aft, open waist; several transverse bulkheads. Inboard motor. Reported lengths 6-7m, beam ca. 1.5m; shallow draft. Other recorded names: **bateau putt-putt**, **gas boat**★; **Joe boat**, **johnboat**★ in the northeastern

part of the state. **o.** A **scow**★-like **bateau** was built in the Straits of Mackinac area between Lakes Michigan and Huron in the days of the fur traders. Carried mainly bulk cargo, cordwood, produce, etc. Flat bottom, hard chines, straight flaring sides, square ends. Crew of 3-4. Propelled by sweeps or a makeshift square sail. **p.** A 19th- and early 20th-century oyster-tonging **bateau** of Shoalwater Bay at the south end of Willapa Bay in southwestern Washington State. Also used on Coos Bay in southwestern Oregon. Flatiron shape, with wide flat bottom and flaring sides; washboards along the sides, set well inboard; occasionally a centerboard. Some fully decked. Lug- or cat-rigged, or towed, often in strings. Reported lengths 7.3-9m, widths 3.4-3.7m; shallow draft. Name variants: **Shoalwater Bay boat** (name applied to those used in the San Francisco Bay area), **Shoalwater oyster bateau**. **q.** On the Columbia River in the northwest, in the 1840s, the **bateau** was a clinker-built boat with a slightly rounded bottom, sharp ends, low sheer. Paddled. Length ca. 9m. Spelling variant: **batteau**
8. *Virgin Islands, West Indies:* Small, flat-bottomed **skiff** widely used for fishing on the island of St. Croix. Spelling variants: **baptiau**, **basteau**, **batau**, **batel**★, **batèli**, **batèt**, **batè(o)u**, **batiau**, **batoe**★, **batteau**★, **batto**★, **battoe**, **batty**; pl. **bateaux**, **batteaus**, **batteaux**. Further references: **batoe**, **batteau**, **boat-1**, **Charleston bateau**, **crabbing skiff**, **flat-6**, **flatboat-6**, **float-6**, **gabare-6b**, **goélette-2**, **James River bateau**, **launch-7**, **Mackinaw boat-1**, **boat-2**, **one-sail bateau**, **oyster sloop-3**, **pound boat-2**, **St. Lawrence barge**, **St. Lawrence bateau**, **skipjack-1**, **sloop-6**, **small bateau**, **timber raft-2a**, **timber raft-4**, **York boat**

bateau à aubes See **paddle boat-3**
bateau à canards See **ya ze chuan**
bateau à eau See **water boat-1**
bateau à éperon See **mourre de pouar**
bateau à franc-bord See **chaloupe-6**
bateau à laver See **bateau lavoir**
bateau allège See **allège**
bateau à marché See **market boat-4**
bateau à moteur See **motor boat-1**
bateau-annexe See **tender**
bateau à roues See **paddle boat-3**
bateau à tête rouge See **hong tou chuan**
bateau automobile See **motor boat-1**
bateau automoteur See **automoteur**
bateau à voiles See **sailboat**
bateau balise See **beacon boat**
bateau bâtard *France:* Handline **fishing boat**★ that was extinct by the early 19th century. Square stern; half-decked or decked, with cockpit; cuddy. Tall mainmast, foremast half the height. Set square sails and topsails. Reported lengths overall 9.1-9.7m, on keel 7.8-8.45m, beam 2.92m.
bateau berckois See **bateau de Berck**
bateau bermudien See **Bermudian**
bateau berrichon See **berrichon**
bateau bête See **bette**
bateau bœuf *France, Mediterranean coast:* Lateen-rigged **fishing boat**★ that worked in pairs suspending a trawl net of the *bœuf* type between them; also found

in Algeria and Tunisia. Used from the 18th century until World War II. Type evolved during this period, but later boats had a sharp stern and bluff bows with generally curved stem; loose wool topped taller stemheads to reduce sail chafing. Rounded stern, raked sternpost; flat floors; slight drag to the straight keel.

bateau bœuf

On some, rudder hung below the keel; tiller slotted over rudderhead. Decked; shallow steering well aft. Hull colorfully painted. Carried a transom-sterned **chaloupe**★ on board. Vertical mast stepped a little forward of amidships with no standing rigging; 2 halyards to a side, 1 to the yard and 1 to the mast. Generally 2 jibs or 1 very large jib; long bowsprit. In strong winds, mainsail taken down and a small triangular sail bent to a shorter yard. Early boats required a crew of 16-18, later only 5 or 6. Reported lengths 11-16m; e.g., length on deck 15.8m, beam 5m, depth 2.25m; draft 1.6-1.7m. Name variant: **bœuf**. Further reading: Bernard Vigne, "Les Bateaux-Bœufs de Sète," *Chasse-Marée* 89 (1995), 30-45. Note also **balancelle-1**, **bovo**, **chalutier**, **nacelle-2**, **tartane de l'Estaque**, **tartane de Marseille**.

bateau bombe See **bomb vessel**
bateau borneur See **borneur**
bateau brabaçon See **schuit-2**
bateau breton See **chaloupe de Plougastel**
bateau brise-glace See **iceboat-1**
bateau cabine See **moulin-bateau**
bateau cannonier See **gunboat**
bateau catalan See **catalane**
bateau charroi *France:* General term for a small boat that transports people, produce, animals, etc. Generally a river craft. Note also **charoi**.
bateau citerne See **tanker, water boat**
bateau coche See **coche d'eau**
bateau collecteur See **packer**
bateau cordier See **cordier**
bateau cormoran See **lu ci chuan**
bateau corps-morts See **anchor hoy**
bateau couvert See **tilt boat**
bateau d'allège See **allège**
bateau d'Amerique See **Bermudian**
bateau de Berck *France, N:* Collective term for beamy, flat-floored **fishing boats**★ that worked from the shingle beach at Berck, evolving in design from the mid-19th to the mid-20th century. The original open boat and a later half-decked boat were called **cordiers**★; another type was fully decked. This decked boat was large, clinker-built, had a strongly raked, wide tran-

som stern and flat floors, and employed a long daggerboard through the garboard strake in the forward third. Characteristically bluff-bowed with maximum beam about one-third in from the bow. Frames installed after planking completed. Hull blackened with coal tar, except for a white top strake. A larger type that fished for herring or mackerel had a small forward cabin, then a room for net floats, followed by the fish hold, the net room, rope room, and finally a gear room. A large capstan aft hauled the net. Rigged with lugsails on the main- and mizzenmasts; 1-2 jibs set to a long bowsprit. Mainmast lowered to a crutch tall enough to clear the capstan. Engine installed on some later boats. Crew of 22 on large boats, 5-6 on the smaller. Reported lengths 4-20m; e.g., length overall 12m, beam 5.3m, depth 2m, draft 1.35m; small boats beamier in proportion to length. The early open type had a unique rowing arrangement: each side had 2-8 oar ports that could be closed by sliding doors. The fishermen rowed, double-banked, from benches, sitting with their heads just above gunwale level. Set a large standing lugsail to the mainmast, stepped on the stem. Mizzenmast stepped against the port side of the

bateau de Berck

transom, setting a small lugsail sheeted to a long outrigger. Estimated lengths of this early boat: 2 oar ports, 4.5m; 5 oar ports, 7.8m; 8 oar ports, 11.8m. Additional recorded names: **bateau berckois**, **Berck lugger**, **Berckois**, **chalutier de Berck**, **cordier berckois**, **scute**★. Further reading: François Beaudouin, *Le Bateau de Berck* (Paris: Institut d'Ethnologie, 1970).
bateau de canal See **péniche-4a**
bateau de charge de Cochin See **manji**
bateau de Colgone See **Samoreus**
bateau de fleurs See **hua chuan**
bateau de la douane See **revenue cutter-1**
bateau de la marchande See **bumboat**
bateau de Lannion *France, NW:* Lug-sailed boat from Lannion on the north coast of Brittany used to catch fish and crustaceans, and to gather seaweed. Curved stem, straight raked transom, straight keel. Originally decked only at stern; outboard rudder; tiller. Taller foremast stepped in the eyes, mainmast amidships; later the foremast was shorter and jib was set to a bowsprit. Mainsail loose-footed and boomed; foresail loose-footed. Also rowed. Length 8.8m, beam 2.78m, depth 1.0m.
bateau de Lanvéoc See **traversier-2**
bateau délasteur, bateau délesteur See **ballast barge**
bateau de mât See **train de bateaux**

bateau de messagerie See **beurtschip**
bateau de parade See **barge-3**
bateau de passage See **chaloupe de Plougastel**, **hoy**, **passage boat-1**, **traversier-l**
bateau de patrouille See **fishery guard ship**
bateau de patrouilleur See **patrol boat**
bateau de pêche See **fishing boat**
bateau de pêche à la traine See **troller**
bateau de plaisance See **yacht-2**
bateau de Plougastel See **chaloupe de Plougastel**
bateau de promenade See **day boat-1**
bateau de provisions See **bumboat-1**
bateau d'Equihen *France, N:* Robust 2-masted boat that worked off the beach at Equihen, just south of Boulogne. Fished for mackerel in summer and herring in winter. Some worn-out boats were turned over and used as dwellings. Clinker construction; strong frames. Flat floors, deep keel, sharp turn of the bilges, plumb sides, moderate to strong sheer. Straight stem, slightly raked; bluff bow tapered to a strongly raking transom. Partly decked; open area, roughly amidships, extended from side to side; centerboard about a third in from the bow, open on either side. Outboard rudder, with extension below the waterline; tiller slotted through the rudderhead. Mainmast stepped well forward, raking slightly aft, set a dipping lugsail. Mizzenmast, generally vertical, set a standing lugsail sheeted to a long outrigger; occasionally raised a lug topsail. Jib ran out on a long, slender, rising bowsprit. Crew of 4-5 for mackerel, up to 11 for herring. Reported lengths overall 9-10m; e.g., length overall 9.5m, on keel 7.94m, beam 3.84m, depth 1.35m, draft 0.95m. Name variant: **Equihen fishing boat**
bateau dériveur See **drift boat**
bateau de sauvetage See **lifeboat**
bateau de selle See **bateau lavoir**
bateau de service See **beurtschip**
bateau de terre See **shore boat-1**
bateau de tête See **train de bateaux**
bateau de Tournai See **waal**
bateau de transport See **packer**
bateau d'interior See **riverboat**
bateau d'office See **bumboat-1**
bateau dragueur See **dredger-1**
bateau du large See **moulin-bateau**
bateau faucher *France, NE:* **Catamaran***-type craft that cut bank and bottom weeds on some French tributaries of the Rhine River. Powerful engine permitted it to work both upstream and down. Propelled by 1-2 paddle wheels that also activated a scythe suspended at the stern. Length 6.5m, beam 1.6m. Note also **weed cutter**.
bateau feu See **lightship**
bateau fluvial See **riverboat**
bateau foncet See **foncet**
bateau fruitier See **fruit ship**
bateau gigogne See **mother ship**
bateau goémonier See **canot goëmonier**
bateau harenguier See **harenguier**
bateau jack See **jack**
bateau jumeau See **mother**
bateau lavoir *France:* A public wash house moored along the riverbank of a city, where laundresses went

to wash the family linens. Some operated as late as the 1970s. In the early 19th century there were as many as 91 in the Nantes area. Flat-bottomed **barge***, generally covered. Some had accommodation for the manager and his family. In the Rhône Basin, they were usually called **plates*** (or **plattes**). Those with facilities for heating water were called **plates chaudes**, those without were **plates froides**. Reported lengths 10-35m, widths 5-6m, shallow draft. A 25-place boat on the Loire at Nantes was 27.6m long, 5.4m wide, 0.8m deep. Other recorded names: **bateau à laver**, **bateau de selle**, **laundry barge**. Further reading: André Péron, "Les Bateaux-lavoirs à Nantes..." *Chasse-Marée* 46 (1990), 18-27.
bateau lesteur See **ballast barge**
bateau logement See **houseboat-1**
bateaulx flobars See **flambart**
bateau Mackinaw See **Mackinaw boat**
bateau maison See **houseboat-1**
bateau mère See **mother ship**
bateau mi-ponté See **half-decker**
bateau mouche *France:* Developed in the mid-1800s to provide water transportation in urban areas, were 1st constructed in the Mouche Quarter at Lyons. Best known in Paris where, at one time, as many as 107 boats operated, averaging 270 passengers per vessel. Employed steam engines, and operated at ca. 16km per hour. Fell into disuse during World War I due to the improvement of metropolitan land transportation systems, but revived as a popular tourist craft in Paris. Name variant: **mouche***. Note also **coche d'eau**.
bateau nantais See **chaland de Loire**
bateau normand See **besogne**
bateau pannier See **ghe nang**
bateau pêcheur See **fishing boat**
bateau pédale See **jiao hua chuan**
bateau phare See **lightship**
bateau picard See **picard-2**
bateau pied See **jiao hua chuan**
bateau pilote *France:* 18th-century term for vessels that preceded the main naval fleet to determine the best route. See also **pilot boat**.
bateau plat **1.** *Canada, E:* Built at Quebec in the late 17th and early 18th centuries to provide provisions and troops to distant French posts. Reported lengths on keel 7-9m.
   2. *United States, central:* Shallow-draft boat of the French colonists in the Mississippi Valley during the 18th century. Carried cargo such as buffalo hides, transferred settlers from arriving ships to shore, and provided general transportation. Plank-built, with a flat bottom and sharp ends. Reported length 12m, beam 2.7m, depth 1.2m; 2-15t burden. Spelling variant: **batteau plat**. Note also **chaland-5**.
   Further references: **bette**, **flatboat-6**, **plate**
bateau pointu See **spits**
bateau pompe See **fire boat**
bateau porte-feu See **light boat-2**
bateau poste See **jiao hua chuan**
bateau putt-putt See **bateau-7n**
bateau rapide See **fast boat-2**
bateau remorqueur See **tug**

bateaus See **bateau-7**

bateau sardinal See **sardinal-2**

bateau secondaire See **moulin-bateau**

bateau senneur See **seine boat-1**

bateau serpent See **pambán-manché**

bateau sétois *France, S:* Transported wine on the Étang de Thau from the Sète area to ports near Marseille. Sharp ends; heavy stem that projected forward near the top; keel on early vessels, later flat-bottomed. Casks stored in the hold and on deck. Large lateen sail, jib. Last boats motorized and without sails. Length 20m, beam 5.4m; shallow draft. Name variant: **barque sétoise**. See also **bateau bœuf**.

bateau sonnette See **pile driver-1**

bateau soulier See **shoe dhoni**

bateau thonier See **thonier**

bateau toulonnaise See **rafiau-1**

bateau traineau See **iceboat-1**

bateau transporteur See **carrying boat**

bateau vivier See **vivier-1**, **well boat-1**

bateau Wallon See **waal**

bateaux See **bateau**

bateel See **batil-1**

bateele See **batelo**

bateira **1.** Generic term in Portuguese for a small, flat-bottomed workboat used mainly on rivers. Some propelled by oars alone; others may set a sail. Also reported as a **ship's boat★** serving a **galley★**. **2.** *Brazil:* **a.** Flat-bottomed, unrigged **lighter★** used particularly in shallow lagoons and rivers. Hull forms vary, but show European influence. **b.** In some areas, as in the state of Rio de Janeiro, the **bateira** may be a small **fishing boat★**. Some have a wide transom and plumb stem; others double-ended. Employs a quadrilateral lateen-type sail with a short luff. **3.** *Portugal:* **a.** Small 2-man boat that fishes for shad on the Tagus River in the Lisbon area with a trammel net or shore seine; also used for recreation. Carvel-planked; flat keelless bottom, curves up at the bow, progressively narrowing toward the sharp, raked bow; narrow, plumb transom; strong sheer. Foredeck, with 2 bitts. May set a spritsail. Also rowed with 2 oars. Length 5.8m, beam 1.5m, depth 0.46m. **b.** Fishing boat of Óbidos Lagoon on the central coast. Carvel-planked; chine plank protrudes slightly; flat bottom, turns up to an overhanging stern, square on top; raked stem; flat sheer. Decked in forward third; locker aft. Coated with pitch. Propelled by 2 oars or poles; single tholepin. Length 6.75m, beam 1.65m, depth 0.5m. **c.** At Buarcos on the central coast, the **bateira** engages in fishing and crabbing off the beach. Carvel-planked, flat bottom, flared sides. Raised, but relatively low bow; low, raked sharp stern. Wale borders top strake. Decked forward, with small cuddy, and at the stern. Worked with 2 narrow oars, one at each of the 2 thwarts; block on oar loom fits over tholepin. Occasionally sails, with the mast braced against the cuddy bulkhead. Length 7.3m, beam 2.1m, depth 0.5m. **d.** In the north, a type of **bateira** works in the Rio Douro estuary and along the neighboring coast. Flat bottom rises at the bow, terminating in a point and continuing as a rising stem. Low, sharp, curved sternpost. Carvel-planked, lightly curved flaring sides. Cambered foredeck. Ships a rudder while sailing; rudder extends below the bottom; tiller slips over rudderhead. Employs 2 narrow-bladed, beveled oars; block on loom slips onto tholepin. Mast stepped through thwart into block on the bottom; 2 positions. Square sail. Crew of 3. Length ca. 8m, beam 2m, depth 0.6m. Name variant: **bateira da Afurada** Further references: **bateira do Mondego**, **chalana-8**, **labrega**

bateira caçadeira See **caçadeira**

bateira chinchorro See **chinchorro-2**

bateira da Afurada See **bateira-3**

bateira de mar See **bateira do mar-1**

bateira do mar *Portugal:* **1.** Open boat used for beach seining off the mouth of the Douro and at other coastal locations to the south. Initially caught crabs for use as fertilizer. Carvel-planked; crescent sheer but stern low; sharp ends; flat bottom with rocker. Two half-bulkheads fitted abaft the 1st and 2nd thwarts. Generally sides painted with contrasting sheer strake, and bow decorated with a simple design. Rowed with a pair of oars, 3 men to each 6.5m-long oar when rowing, 2 when shooting the net. Reported lengths 7.5-9m; e.g., length 9m, beam 2.18m, on bottom 1.4m, depth 0.64m; draft 0.3m. Name variants: **bateira de mar**, **bateira do Rio Douro**. Note also **barco do pilado**. **2.** On the coast south of Figueira da Foz, the **bateira do mar** engages in fishing and crabbing. Crescent-shaped, being of the **meia lua★** type. Flat bottom curves up to the high, elongated bow and to the lower sharp stern; diamond-shaped stemhead. Sides flare; maximum beam amidships, curving immediately to the narrow ends. Small arched foredeck; raised flooring just abaft the foredeck and at the stern. Rowed with a single oar from each of the 2 thwarts. Length 8m, beam 2.4m.

bateira do Mondego *Portugal, central:* Flat-bottomed river craft used for fishing at the mouth of the Mondego River. Somewhat flattened bow, rounded forefoot; sharp stern. Mast stepped through a bench; sets a lateen sail. Also rowed, with 1-2 pairs of oars. Crew of 3-4. Reported lengths 6-10m; e.g., length 6.7m, beam 1.68m, depth 0.5m. Other recorded names: **bateira★**, **chinchorro★** (at Gala), **muleta★**

bateira do Mondego

bateira do pilado See **bateira mercantel**
bateira do Rio Douro See **bateira do mar**
bateira ílhava *Portugal, central:* Narrow boat that
works out of Ílhavo and beaches to the north, and in
the fall and early winter, fishes for sardines in the area
of the Tagus Estuary. Often engages in net fishing
locally, and collects seaweed in the Ria de Aveiro.
When working in pairs for sardines, using the *tarrafa*
net, the boat transporting the gear is called the **barco
da rede**; the other, called the **caique***, hauls in the net
and carries the fish to market. Large boats that went to
Lisbon with general cargo were called **enviadas***; they
were then sold there and known as **varinos**. Carvel-
planked; sharp ends; flat floors with rocker; plank
keel; curved bow and stern, the bow slightly higher;
plumb stemhead. Open, cuddy below the cambered
foredeck; seat at the stern; wide-bladed rudder. Hull
blackened with tar after a year. Tall standing lugsail
set to a mast stepped through a thwart amidships;
some reported to have set a lateen sail. Also rowed and
poled; 2 long oars; loom fitted with a block that fits
over the single tholepin. Crew of 2-7, but requires 16
when sardine fishing. Reported lengths 7.3-14m; e.g.,
length 8.2m, beam 1.45m, depth 0.5m; shallow draft.
Other recorded names: **barco ílhavo**, **ílhava**, **ílhavo**,
ílhavo da tarrafa
bateira labrega See **labrega**
bateira marinhoa *Portugal, central:* Small flat-bottomed boat used on the lagoon at Aveiro (Ria de
Aveiro) for cargo and to transport salt workers to and
from their homes. Sharp ends, with a long curve from
the bottom to an overhanging bow; curved sternpost;
straight stem; cuddy forward. Some hulls blackened
with pitch. Generally poled but may be rowed. Length
8.75m, beam 1.75m, depth 0.55m.
bateira mercantel *Portugal, central:* Operates mainly
in the lagoon at Aveiro (Ria de Aveiro), carrying merchandise, construction materials, and fish, and also
dredging for cockles. At Ariao, where they catch
swimming crabs (*pilado*), they are called **bateiras do
pilado**. Carvel planking; sharp ends; flat bottom that
rises at the bow to merge with the tall curved stem;
sternpost curved. Sharp sheer toward the stern, more
elongated at the bow. Flared sides raised by a low
washstrake above the wale, terminating at the end of
the foredeck; strake braced by the ribs. For cockling,
long boards placed inside the washstrake serve as
walkways. Decked at the bow; some have benches
along the sides for passengers in addition to those
athwartships. Tall, curved and raked rudder, worked
with yoke and lines. When cockling, a type of windlass draws the anchored boat with its rake and bag net
up toward the anchor. Poled, rowed, and sailed. Tall
vertical mast stepped about a third of the way in from
the bow, sets a trapezoidal sail and sometimes a foresail. Crew of 2-3. Reported lengths 10.6-14.5m; e.g.,
length 10.6m, beam 1.75m, depth 0.64m, draft 0.3m.
The larger **mercanteis** are very similar, but lack side
benches and washstrake. Transport cargo on the Vouga
and the Agueda Rivers from the mountains to Aveiro.
On occasion, in good weather, they carry wood or salt
down the coast to Lisbon. Poled when wind adverse.

Additional recorded names: **mercante**, **mercantel**; pl.
bateiras mercanteis, **mercanteis**; **barca mercantil**.
Note also **barco do pilado**. Further reference: **labrega**
bateira murtoseira See **chinchorro-2**, **labrega**
bateiras mercanteis See **bateira mercantel**
bateis See **batel**
bateis do Seixal See **batel do Seixal**
bâteka See **eka-1**
batel **1.** In Portuguese, a small **boat*** or **skiff***. Also a
small, open, double-ended craft used in port traffic,
especially in Spanish ports.
2. In the 15th and 16th centuries, a **batel** was a small
double-ended vessel that accompanied a large ship.
Those accompanying the Portuguese or Spanish **nau***
were similar to, but proportionately smaller than, the
ship, generally one-third its keel length, although
those carried on board were obviously smaller. The
batel might tow the ship in calms; laying anchors was
another important function. In Portugal, some of those
that escorted local **galleys*** were elegantly appointed
and used by royalty. The term is also reported from
Normandy and Brittany in the 14th and 15th centuries;
these did not exceed 10t.
3. *India, NW:* Roughly built cargo carrier that trades
mainly from Bombay (Mumbai) into the Gulf of
Kutch. Long and slightly curved raking stem; shield-
shaped raked transom. Straight keel; S-curve to the
flat floors; maximum beam abaft amidships; ribs
extend above side planking at ends; strong sheer at
the bow. Fore- and stern decks, open waist; sides
raised above gunwale level at the stern; area forward
of this break protected by bamboo weather screens.
Rails at the stern support main yard when lowered.
Outboard rudder; tiller. Topsides oiled and varnished, bottom coated with oil or grease and chunam.
Carries a **muchwa***. One to 3 forward-raking masts;
mainmast very heavy, mizzen smaller and lighter;
sometimes a small jigger stepped at the stern. Hoists
a quadrilateral lateen-type sail with a short luff and
sometimes a shallow topsail to the mainmast; jib set
flying to a long steeved-up bowsprit. Crew of 5-8.
Reported lengths overall 14.5-24.4m, between perpendiculars 9-20.4m; widths 4.6-6.4m; depths 1.8-
3.2m. Other recorded names: **batille**, **butille**,
Jafarabadi hody (or **nauri**), **Verāval baghla**.
Further reading: N. F. J. Wilson, *The Native Craft, a
General Description of the Native Craft Visiting
Bombay Harbour* (Bombay: Bombay Port Trust,
1909), 11-19, 71-74. Note also **battela**.
4. *Italy, N:* The **batèl** of the middle Po Valley is an open
boat used for fishing. Symmetrical ends, including the
sheer and height of the ends. Ends sharp, flat bottom
longitudinally planked, floor frames and ribs separate.
Low, slightly flaring sides constructed of 3 flush-laid
planks. Poled or rowed standing at the stern; oar against
an oar fork. Length 6.9m, beam 2m, depth 1.35m.
5. *Philippines:* Variously reported as a small **dugout
canoe*** with double outriggers that served as a **ship's
boat*** in the 17th century; as a sailing craft that plied
navigable rivers and sheltered coastal waters of
Batangas and Quezon Provinces in southern Luzon;
and as a present-day interisland trader. This later vessel

is heavily built, beamy, counter-sterned, flat-floored; has a trunk cabin aft, and works under a large sail.

6. *Portugal*: **a.** Open **fishing boat★** that worked off beaches on the central coast, mainly netting sardines.

batel-6a

Double-ended, flat floors, keel; slightly curved, plumb ends; pointed stemhead often sheathed in metal. Some had washstrakes; an opening amidships aided net handling. A few set a spritsail, but more commonly a single quadrilateral lateen-type sail with a short luff. Those going farther offshore often set 2 sails. Also rowed; a block with a hole affixed to the loom slotted over the single tholepin. Crew of 10-18. Reported lengths 10-11m, beam to 3.5m, depth 1.3m. Note also **barca-9. b.** On the northern coast, especially at Póvoa de Varzim, the **batel** also engaged in sardine fishing; at Buarcos, farther south, the last boats of the type tended sardine **trawlers★**, especially to transport the catch to shore. Carvel-planked, sharp ends, flat bottom, open. Sailed and rowed, with as many as 12 oars. Crew of 7-16. Reported lengths 8-10m; e.g., length 9.45m, beam 2.5m, depth 1.3m. Name variant: **batel poveiro. c.** The **batel** of the lower Cávado River, in the north, is completely open with strongly flared sides. Used for local transportation and fishing. Carvel-planked, sharp raking stem and sternpost, flat bottom, flat sheer. Stringers extend along each side and join at bow and stern; 3 benches. Sides painted, and a white stripe bands each side, stem, and sternpost. Rowed or sets a spritsail. Crew of 2. Length 5.68m, beam 1.64m, depth 0.4m. Name variant: **batel do rio. d.** The **batel** found in Lavos Lagoon at the mouth of the Mondego on the north-central coast transports salt and sand. Carvel-planked, flat bottom, flared sides, blunt bow; stern curves up. Decked at bow, with door in bulkhead; stern deck forms a small compartment and seat for helmsman. Rowed and sailed, setting a lugsail. Length 23.5m, beam 2.5m, depth 1.0m. **e.** A **batel** fished inside river mouths on the Algarve coast in the south. Sharp ends, tall stemhead, oculi. Rowed and sailed. Length 6.8m, beam 2.2m, depth 1.0m.

7. *Spain, north coast:* Small inshore **fishing boat.** Double-ended, 3 thwarts. Rowed with a pair of oars; also sculled. May be rigged with a lugsail. Generally operated by 1 person. Reported lengths 4.6-6.5m; e.g., length 6.5m, beam 1.2m. Name variants: **bateljo** (deprecatory); **txanel** (Basque)

Spelling variants: **batela★**, **batell(a)**, **bateu**; Portuguese pl. **bateis.** Further references: **batana, bateau, batel da testa, batil-1, battela-1, battello veneto, bedi, canote**

batela 1. *India, W:* Single-masted trader of the Malabar Coast. Cap. 30-85t. Name variant: **botilla.** Note also **battela-1.**

2. *Italy, NE:* Carried produce and passengers across the lagoons at the northen end of the Adriatic. Two principal types: the **prawn-tailed batela** (**batela a coa de gambero**, **batela a pinzo**) with a curved, upturned sternpost extending higher than the bow, and a long overhanging stem; and the **batela buranela**, from Burano, with low, elongated ends. A pointed iron decoration fit onto the stem; at the stern an iron band capped the sternpost and extended out onto the deck. Flat bottom, sharp raked bow, flat or rounded stern, flat or curved sides, moderate sheer, curved ribs, strong floor timbers. Cambered decks at each end, narrow side decks. Mainly rowed, standing on a block on the port gunwale of the after deck. Sometimes set a single lugsail to a mast stepped abaft amidships. Worked by 1-2 men. Reported lengths 8-12m; e.g., length 11m, beam 2m, depth 0.68m. Other recorded names: **batela di Burano, bat(t)ella, batello, battello★, buranella**; pl. **batel(l)e, battelle**

3. *Portugal, N/Spain, NW:* Small open boat that tended fish traps along the middle part of the Minho River, on the border with Spain; also engaged in smuggling. Flat bottom, planked fore-and-aft; sharp raked bow; wide raked transom. Rowed, paddled, or poled; may now employ an outboard motor. Reported lengths 4.1-4.5m; e.g., length 4.3m, beam 1.5m, depth 0.5m.

Further references: **batel, batil-1, battela-1**

batela a coa de gambero, batela a pinzo, batela buranela, batela di Burano See **batela-2**

batela istriana See **battana-2**

batelão 1. Portuguese word for a **lighter★** that aids in discharging ships, transporting heavy objects in a port, or handling sand and mud from dredging operations. Early 17th-century usage merely refers to **batelão** as a large vessel. Iron or wood, flat bottom, shallow draft. Usually towed, poled, or rowed. Note also **alvarenga, barcaça, barca de carga, barca de carreto.**

2. *Brazil, SE:* Multipurpose **dugout canoe★** used on the Lagoa dos Patos in Rio Grande do Sul. Short, narrow. Bluff, raked ends. Rowed with short oars or poled.

3. *Brazil, E:* On the Rio São Francisco, the term may apply to an undecked **lighter**-type vessel or to a large **dugout canoe**, especially one that has been split longitudinally, with one or more planks inserted to widen the hull. An arched mat hut might cover most of the hull. Some newer types on the middle section of the river stepped 1-2 masts, each setting a triangular sail. Above Juàzeiro, the **batelão** was called a **paquete★.** Long, narrow, and low-sided.

4. *Brazil, Amazon Basin:* Designed to carry heavy cargoes on the larger tributary rivers. Principally a built-up

batelão-4

dugout canoe. Generally undecked, but covered partially or entirely by an arched thatched house; when decked, called a **barco★.** Mainly rowed, but may be tracked from shore or poled; poled types had planks on the gunwale for the poler; fixed helm. The heavily planked **batelões** of the upper Rio Negro were designed to carry 30-100t of local products on a 1-way trip down through the rapids. The larger boats navigated the rapids by means of long sweeps operated from a platform built above the barrel-shaped thatched hut that covered part or all of the craft. Once downstream, these were rigged with a square sail, or **schooner***-rigged, and used as freight carriers until the advent of steam vessels in the mid-19th century; these lower **riverboats*** were popularly known as Spanish vessels. Those that transported cattle on the lower Amazon set a square sail; similar craft were used on some of the southern tributaries of the Amazon. Crew of 4-12. Reported lengths 7.6-12.2m. Name variant: **iar-uhu** (in Tupí dialect)

5. *Brazil, SW:* An early 19th-century variety of **batelão** on the Rio Paraguai (Paraguay) in Mato Grosso was a large **dugout canoe** with a keel. Poled or rowed with short oars. Length 12m, beam 1.2m, draft 0.4m; cap. 3t. Spelling variants: **bateloe**; pl. **batelões**. Further references: **alvarenga-2**, **batil-1**, **canoa-3**

batelão-regatão *Brazil, N:* Itinerant **store boat*** that works on the rivers of Amazonas. Plank-built on frames. Open except for shelters that protect merchandise. Originally propelled by oars, now by motor. Note also **regatão**.

batel da testa *Portugal, central:* Moored at the seaward end of the *armações à valenciana*, a stationary fish trap for sardines in the Tagus Estuary. Part of a 4-boat team that includes 3 **barcas*** (see **barca-9**). During the twice-daily raising of the net, the boat holds extra gear, but may transfer excess fish to shore; otherwise permanently stationed at the net during the fishing season. Sharp ends, plumb stem, rounded forefoot, curved sternpost; full forward to support the gear; strong sheer. Open except for short fore- and stern decks. Tarred black; usually a white triangle on each bow is decorated with a symbol identifying ownership. Typically rowed; steered with a sweep. Operated by crew from the **barcas**. Reported lengths 8.4-9.5m; average length 8.8m, beam 2.55m, depth 0.84m. Name variant: **batel***

batel do rio See **batel-6**

batel do Seixal *Portugal, central:* Drift **trawler*** that worked with a bag net (the *tar taranha*) around the Tagus Estuary; extinct by World War II. Its special feature was its sail arrangement. When underway, a single lateen sail was set to a slightly aft-raking pole mast and a small square headsail was tacked to the masthead; while fishing, up to 8 special drift sails were fitted to 2 very long outriggers, 1 at the bow and 1 at the stern. Sails sewn with narrow cloths. Carvel-planked; plumb stem with rounded forefoot; raked transom stern; marked sheer toward the bow; straight keel; high rounded bilges; tiller slotted over the rudder. Fully decked, large hatch amidships; single bit on each bow, a pair on each quarter. Two heavy wales ran along each side; above them 2-3 characteristic half circles were painted at the bow and stern; triangular patch painted at the bows. Oars used when becalmed. Reported

lengths 9.6-12.25m; e.g., length 12.25m, beam 4.4m, depth 1.86m. Other recorded names: **bote da (arte da) tartaranha**, **bote do Seixal**; pl. **bateis do Seixal**

batele *Indonesia, central:* Designation for a boat that was rowed on Muna and Butan Islands off the southeastern tip of Sulawesi (Celebes). See also **batela-2**, **batelet**, **coquet**.

batelet *France:* **1.** General term, dating to the 12th century, for a small **boat***. Some reported to have been made of boiled leather. Principally rowed. Other recorded names: **batelé**, **batelon***, **batelou(n)**; in Breton, **bagik** or **baguik**, pl. **bagouigou**

2. In 18th-century Paris, **batelets** provided transportation on the Seine. Some could be boarded with horse and carriage, but generally they accommodated 5 passengers.

3. At Pollet, across from Dieppe on the Normandy coast, **batelets** served as **ship's boats*** to **fishing boats***, transferring the catch to shore and, at times, engaging in line fishing. Sharp ends; small cuddy. Rowed with 4-6 oars; might also set a sail to a small mast. Reported lengths 4.88-5.2m, widths and depths 1.3-1.65m.

Further references: **bachot-3**, **quenouille**

batel flambart See **flambart**

batèli See **bateau**

batêlica See **battellina**

batelin **1.** *Croatia/Italy, NW:* Local term for a small, light, open boat at Muggia near Trieste and at Novigrad on the Istrian Peninsula.

2. At Piran, on the Istrian Peninsula, the **batelin** is a flat-bottomed boat with a curved stem. Employs a rudder and tiller.

See also **battello-1**.

batelîna See **battellina**

bateljo See **batel-7**

batell See **batel**, **battello**

batella See **batel**, **batela-2**, **battela-1**, **battello**

batelle *England:* Old term for a small **boat*** or **skiff***; first cited in the 14th century. Spelling variant: **battle**. Further references: **batela-2**, **batil-1**

batello See **batela-2**, **batil-1**, **battana-2**, **battello**

batelluccio da sardelle See **battelluccio**

batelo *East Africa:* Lateen-rigged boat with a sharp bow, square stern with poop, strong sheer. Forward-raking mast. Length 15.5m, beam 3m, depth 1.4m. Name variant: **bateele**. See also **barchetta-3**, **battela-1**, **battello**.

batelo a pizzo, **batelo col fio** See **topo**

bateloe, **batelões** See **batelão**

batelon *Italy, NE:* Small cargo boat of the canals of Venice; nearly extinct. Identified by heavy metal bands capping the stem and sternpost. Long and low; double-ended but stern narrower and more tapered; flat bottom curves up at the ends; sheer follows this curve. Decked at bow and stern. Narrow side decks; rudder, hung by gudgeons and pintles, drops well below the bottom; tall rudderhead; long tiller slopes downward. Mainly rowed; now most are motorized. Crew of 2. Length 12m, beam 2.26m, depth ca. 1.0m. Spelling variants: **battelon**; pl. **bateloni**. See also **batelet**.

bateloni See **batelon**

batelou, **bateloun** See **batelet**

batel poveiro See **batel-6**

batelu *Equatorial Guinea:* **Dugout canoe⋆** of Pagalu (Annobón) Island in the Gulf of Guinea used mainly to hunt young whales. Manned by a harpooner and 2 paddlers. Length ca. 6m. Name variant: **cayuco⋆**

bateluccio See **battelluccio**

båten See **båt-1**, **boat-1**

båtene See **båt-1**

bateo a Chioggia, bateo a pisso See **topo**

batèou See **bateau**, **rafiau-1**

båter See **båt-1**

batèt See **bateau**

bateu See **bateau**, **batel**

batiau See **bateau**

batiau flambars See **flambart**

batil 1. *Persian (Arabian) Gulf and Oman:* Fast, low **coaster⋆** that was once a dreaded pirate craft; later, large types were used by Arab chiefs for state occasions. Prior to their demise in the 2nd half of the 20th century, they were mainly pearling vessels. Details vary, but characteristically had an elongated, straight raking bow with an oval disc atop the stemhead, except on Iranian vessels. Sharp stern with high vertical sternpost that, in some areas, carried a forward-projecting ornament resembling a dog's head. After third of the keel sloped upward and extended beyond the sternpost; keel on some roughly one-third the length of the vessel. Rudder hung below and under the keel; worked with lines that ran from the quarters to a short spar affixed to the outer edge of the rudder just above the waterline; tall rudderhead. Decked at ends, larger sizes fully decked; ribs at waist extended above the top strake. Hull oiled and varnished; stylized decorations at bow and stern. Small types hoisted a single quadrilateral lateen-type sail with a short luff to a forward-raking mast; larger vessels, especially of the Iranian coast, also had a similar but smaller mizzen. In calms, propelled by sweeps. Crew of 10-20, to 30-45 when pearling. Reported lengths 14.6-23m, widths 2.8-4.9m, depths 1.2-2.1m. A type of **batil** is still found on Musandan Peninsula beaches of northern Oman. Stemhead covered in goatskin; tall planked fin at stern; strongly curved keel toward the stern; steep rise to the floors. Length overall 11.6m, between perpendiculars 10.5m. Spelling variants: **bat(t)eel**, **batel⋆**, **batela⋆**, **batelão⋆**, **batelle**, **batello**, **batili**, **batilla**, **battela**, **battil** (pl. **batātī l** or **beṭôṭel**), **betela**, **betil(i)**, **beṫṫīl**, **bittīl**, **buteel**).
2. *Philippines:* Sturdy coastal cargo and passenger vessel used around some of the central islands. Double-ended; straight, almost vertical stem and sternpost; narrow keel. Outboard rudder hung by eyes and pintles; tiller. Employed double outriggers; 3 booms connected directly to long, thin floats. Decked; cabin house aft. Set 2 large boomed standing lugsails and a jib. Reported lengths 13.7-18.2m.
Further references: **sampan batil**, **zaruq**

batila See **battela-1**

batili See **batil-1**

batilla See **batil-1**, **battela-1**

batille See **batel-3**

batimâ See **batiman**

batiman *Haiti:* Creole term for a **boat⋆** or **ship⋆**, especially one that sails. Spelling variants: **batimâ**, **bâtiment**

batimen See **ship**

bâtiment See **batiman**, **ship**

bâtiment amiral See **flagship**

bâtiment canard See **pile driver-2**

bâtiment charbonnier See **collier-1**

bâtiment chasseur See **chasseur**

bâtiment croiseur See **cruiser-2**

bâtiment de commerce See **merchantman**

bâtiment de douane See **revenue cutter-1**

bâtiment de guerre See **man-of-war**

bâtiment dépôt See **mother ship**

bâtiment de servitude See **plate-3**

bâtiment écurie See **horse carrier**

bâtiment latin See **lateener**

bâtiment long See **long ship**

bâtiment marchand See **merchantman**

bâtiment négrier See **slaver-1**

bâtiment usine See **factory ship**

batis See **boat-1**

batiste See **batteau-2a**

batka See **bat-2**

batnik See **bat-3**

bato *Réunion:* Creole term for **boat⋆** on this western Indian Ocean island. See also **bateau-4**, **bateau-6**.

batoe *Canada/United States:* Spelling used in the British colonies in America for the earlier fur-trading **batteau⋆**. Important for river and lake transportation in the St. Lawrence valley and northern New York State from the mid-17th century to the latter part of the 18th. During the French and Indian Wars of 1756-1763, many thousands of the boats were employed, and a British group of that period was called the Battoe Service. The British **batoe** was considered better suited for lake work, the French for fast water. Flat bottom, curved sides, sharp ends, raking curved stem, raked straight sternpost. Rowed; steered with a sweep. Length ca. 10m, beam 2m, depth 1.0m. Other recorded names: **bateau⋆**, **battoe**

batr See **båt-1**, **boat-1**

battal See **schooner-4**

battana *Italy:* 1. Generic term for a flat-bottomed boat. Spelling variants: **batàna⋆**; pl. **battane**. Note also **burchio-2**.
2. Small **fishing boat⋆** that engaged in sardine and anchovy fishing off the west coast of Istria and in the lagoon at Grado at the head of the Adriatic. Sharp bow with raked stem, narrow rounded and raked stern, flat bottom, straight sides. Decked at ends with open waist, or fully decked with a large central hatch or 2 smaller hatches. Stepped 1-2 masts, setting boomed lugsails. The smaller foremast unshipped when sailing close-hauled and a jib-headed sail set between the mainmast and stemhead. Generally 6 in crew. Reported lengths 4-10m; e.g., length 6m, beam 1.4m, hold depth 0.3m; Istrian boats beamier. Other recorded names: **batela istriana**, **batello**, **battello⋆**, **battelluccio⋆**, **sandolo⋆**
3. The **battàna** is also found from Venice south to Fano on the east side of the Italian peninsula. Most engage

in coastal fishing, but at Ravenna they also carry assorted cargo, especially refuse. Sharp ends, the stern fuller; straight, sharply raked stem; sternpost slightly raked; flat bottom; sharp chines; slight sheer. Larger boats decked with central hatch; may have washboards that terminate just before the ends; smaller types half-decked or open. Rudder hangs well below the bottom, bulging out forward under the stern; long tiller slotted over rudderhead. Sides brightly painted, and stars on the bows replace the traditional oculi. Sets 1-2 boomed yellow-orange lugsails with a short luff. Jib tacked to stemhead on single-masted type. Single vertical mast stepped amidships through a thwart; mast could be struck. On 2-masted boats, both masts rake slightly forward, the foremast having the greater rake. Also rowed, using 1-2 oars that work against a tall hook-shaped fulcrum. Now mainly motorized. Reported lengths 3.8-9.7m; e.g., length overall 5.95m; beam 1.78m, on bottom 1.35m; depth ca. 0.52m. Name variants: **battàna romagnola**, **Romagna battàna**

4. In the Senigallia area on the east coast, the **battàna** may be a small flatiron-shaped **rowboat★**. Flat bottom with rocker, cross-planked. Raked stem; square stern, nearly plumb; sides straight and slightly flared; ribs and chine pieces; maximum beam in forward third; strong sheer. Three longitudinal floor battens, 3 grounding keels. Fore- and stern decks. Two single tholepins paired at thwart, another forward, and one farther aft. May step a mast through a thwart and set a lateen sail. Length 3.8m, beam 1.5m, depth 1.0m. Name variant: **battàna di Senigallia**

5. The **battana aconitana** is found from Fano south to Ancona. Open **lighter★**-type craft, with a sharp bow, straight stem, transom stern, flat bottom. Decked at stern, short foredeck. Uses a rudder. Spelling variant: **batana★**

6. The **battàna fiumaròla** is used on rivers in the central part of the country. Sharp bow, transom stern; cross-planked, flat bottom. Seldom uses a rudder.

battana aconitana See **battana-5**
battàna di Senigallia See **battana-4**
battàna fiumaròla See **battana-6**
battàna romagnola See **battana-3**
battane See **battana-1**
batteau **1.** *Belize:* Term applied to a **pitpan★** that has been enlarged by sawing it in half longitudinally and inserting a wide plank. May require up to 40 paddlers.
2. *Canada:* **a.** An important craft of 17th-century Canadian and Great Lakes fur traders. Used in various other capacities into the 19th century. Initially, the French boat was more heavily built and the English **batteau** was larger. Specially adapted for running rapids, they were the principal means of transportation up the St. Lawrence River into the Great Lakes, traveling in flotillas of over 400 boats. Sharp, raked ends; flat bottom, longitudinally planked, some rocker; flared, carvel-planked sides; chine-built; strong sheer. Generally paddled, but larger boats were rowed and steered with a paddle; also poled or tracked from shore. In open water a triangular sail set, using an oar as a temporary mast. Crew of 5-6. Reported lengths 5.4-12.2m, widths 1-2.4m; cap. to 4.5t. Other recorded names: **bateau★**, **batiste**, **Canadian boat**, **Great**

Lakes bateau, **River dory**, **St. Lawrence River dory**. **b.** Those on the Ottawa River in eastern Canada in the early 19th century carried cargo, generally flour. Length 25m, width 3-3.7m, hold depth 1.5m. Decked for about 3.7m at each end; covering board ran along the side for polers. Small size completely open. Set a large lug- or square sail. Crew of 5—a helmsman and 4 rowers.
3. *United States, E:* **a.** On Chesapeake Bay this term dates to the colonial period, designating a variety of small **skiff★**-type craft. Generally double-ended, with a V-bottomed hull. Early boats mostly poled or rowed along tributary creeks. Some to 15m long. Spelling variant: **bateau★**. Note also **skipjack**. **b.** An early version of the **Durham boat★**, the Delaware River **batteau** carried freight and passengers. Strongly planked and framed. A stern canopy protected the captain and passengers, who camped ashore at night. Downstream, boat guided by 8-10 oarsmen; upstream, sett poles used. **c.** In Delaware Bay, a **sharpie★**-type boat known as a **batteau** was used in gill net and seine fisheries. Built by the fishermen themselves. Most flat-bottomed, sharp-bowed, and wide-sterned. Rowed. Reported lengths 3.7-6m, the larger carrying the seine nets.
4. *United States, NE:* **a.** The colonial **batteau** played an important role in the American Revolution, particularly on northeastern rivers and lakes. These were similar to the **batteau** of the fur traders and lumbermen, being flat-bottomed and double-ended. Stem raked and forefoot curved, sternpost straight and raked. Paddled and poled. Generally carried 6-7 men; could be portaged by 4 men. Length 9.2m, beam 2m, depth 0.86m; shallow draft. Note also **batoe**, **flat batteau**, **lumberman's batteau**, **Quebec batteau**. **b.** The colonial **batteau** was also a square-ended, flat-bottomed boat used to traverse such rivers as the Mohawk and the Connecticut. These carried mainly freight and produce, having a capacity of 1-2t. Floated downstream, controlled by long sweeps. Poled upstream, the poleman setting the ironshod pole and walking on a plank along each gunwale. Crew of 3-6. Shallow draft. Name variant: **flatboat★**. Note also **bateau-7e**.
Further references: **bateau**, **bateau-7j**, **bateau-7l**, **bateau-7q**, **Durham boat**, **James River bateau**, **skipjack-1**, **square-ender**
batteau plat See **bateau plat**
batteaus See **bateau**, **lumberman's batteau**
batteaux See **bateau**, **batteau**
batteel See **batil-1**
battèj See **battèll**
battela **1.** *India, W:* **Coaster★** built mainly at Gujarat ports; old vessels modified to handle coal and heavy cargo at Bombay (Mumbai). Some early vessels may have been small fighting craft. Characterized by a slightly curved, sharply raking stem and raised side strakes at bow and stern, with the intervening open area protected by portable bamboo weather screens. Early vessels carried a circular stemhead ornament. Roughly constructed; square stern; some large vessels have carved and painted counters. Strong sheer at bow and stern; flat floors. Tiller slotted over a tall rudderhead. Temporary decking protects the cargo; crew live aft. Carries a **muchwa★** that may be swung out over

the weather side, supported by the masthead, to act as ballast. Steps 1-2 forward-raking masts, each setting a high-peaked, baggy quadrilateral lateen-type sail with a short luff; topsail sometimes set to mainmast; larger vessels also use a jigger mast. Sails boomed out when required. Long bowsprit angles up sharply, holding a large jib. Crew of 7-30. Reported lengths 10.7-26.8m; e.g., length overall 18.2m, on keel 13.7m; beam 4.6m; hold depth 3m. Other recorded names: **batel***, **batela***, **batella**, **batelo***, **batil(l)a**, **batteloe**, **battila**, **betillo**, **botella**, **boutilla**

2. *Spain, N:* Long, narrow Basque **fishing boat***. Plumb stem; curved sternpost that recurves somewhat; rounded stern. Open except for seats at bow and stern; 4 thwarts. Brightly painted. Rowed with 3 pairs of oars; single tholepins. Helmsman works a sweep against a tholepin. Also sails, setting a lugsail to an aft-raking mast stepped at the bow. Length ca. 5.5m.
Further reference: **batil-1**

battelina See **battellina**

battèll *Italy, N:* Small open boat of Lake Como (Lario) used for passenger transport and fishing. Dates at least to the 16th century. Sharp, raking bow, terminating with a small knob; sharp but fuller stern. Flat bottom with slight rocker; straight flaring sides; moderate sheer. Small end decks; bench along each side; arched canvas-covered roof over most of hull. **Fishing boats*** black; tourist boats blue and white with tarred bottom. Rowed with 2 pairs of oars. Length 6.35m, beam 2.2m, depth 0.57m. Other recorded names: **batel***, **lucìa**; pl. **battèj**. Note also **batello-2**.

battella *Italy:* **1.** General term for a small **boat***.
2. In the Pavia area of northwestern Italy, the **battèlla** is a long, narrow, open boat used for transporting sand and gravel. Similar ends sharp, and the stem and sternpost curl up above the sheer strake. Flat bottom; ribs and floor frames separate. Length 13.5m, beam 3.2m, depth 2.7m.
Further references: **batela-2**, **cumacèna**

battelle See **batela-2**

battelletti, battelletto, battelli See **battello**

battelli comacchiesi See **cumacèna**

battellina 1. *Croatia/Italy:* Small inshore **fishing boat*** used at the head of the Adriatic Sea and along the

battellina-1

Dalmatian coast. Sharp bow, with overhanging, slightly curved stem. Stern generally full and rounded, but in some Italian areas it may have a transom stern. Flat bottom, slightly flared sides. Rudder hangs well below

the bottom. Half-decked. Boomed, trapezoidal, balance lugsail set to a portable mast that is stepped abaft amidships against the thwart. More generally rowed. Crew of 2-3. Reported lengths 4-5.4m, widths 1.45-1.7m, depths 0.45-0.6m.
2. The Venetian **battellina** is similar to the **gondola***. Bow is slightly recurved and a metal band is fixed to the stem. Decked at bow and stern. A flat decorative piece follows the sheer line at each end. Rowed; also steps 2 masts. Length ca. 7m, beam 1.2m; a similar larger type, the **battellona**, was ca. 10.4m long and 2m wide.
Spelling variants: **batêlica, batelîna, battelina;** pl. **battelline, battelon** (Venetian), **battellone**

battelline See **battellina**

battellino Italian term for a small wooden boat used in cleaning and repairing ships' hulls. Propelled by 2 oars. See also **battello, trabaccolo-2.**

battello 1. An Italian generic for a small **boat*** or **dinghy***. Sometimes specified as a small **ship's boat*** on a **man-of-war***, merchant vessel, or **fishing boat***, used to transport people, baggage, or fish to shore. Rowed, sailed, or motorized. In the Italian navy, the word may indicate a **submarine**. Name variant: **batelin*** (Venetian dialect)
2. *Italy, N:* Cargo, fishing, and passenger boat of Lake Como and other Lombardy lakes. Sharp ends; flat bottom; lightly curved, flared sides; slight sheer, the bow higher than the stern. Arched awning over the central part; small foredeck. Rowed, generally by a single oarsman, working a pair of oars; a forward pair of oarforks used when the boat is light, an after pair when carrying cargo. Some set a square sail, steering with an oar. Length 8m, beam 2.7m. A small size is a **luzía**, ca. 6m long. Other recorded names: **nav*, nave*** (pl. **navi**)
Spelling variants: **batell, batella, batello, batèo, battelletto, battellino*;** pl. **battelletti, battelli.** Further references: **batela-2, battana-2, caorlina**

battello a slitta See **iceboat-1**

battello cannoniere See **gunboat**

battello carbonaio, battello carboniere See **collier-1**

battèllo comacchiese See **cumacèna**

battello da crociera See **cruiser-1**

battello da ghiaccio See **iceboat-1**

battello da pesca See **fishing boat**

battello della dogana See **revenue cutter-1**

battello di emergenza See **accident boat**

battello di piloti See **pilot boat**

battello di provviste See **bumboat-1**

battello di salvamento, battello di salvataggio See **lifeboat**

battello di soccorso See **accident boat**

battello giudice See **mark boat-1**

battello meda See **beacon boat**

battellon, battellona, battellone See **battellina**

battello pilota See **pilot boat**

battello pompa See **fire boat**

battello ponzese *Italy, Sardinia:* Double-ended boat employed in shellfishing. Raked stem, flat floors, outboard rudder. Ca. 6m long.

battello segnale See **beacon boat**

battello veneto *Italy, NE:* Open boat for fishing and local transport in the Po Delta area northwest of the Adriatic Sea. Double-ended, with full lines at bow and stern; almost rectangular along the central section; flat bottom; 3-piece frames; a thwart near each end. A narrower and less boxy type found in the area is called a **sandolo★**. Rowed with 2 oars; tall fulcrum-type oarlocks used, 3 on the left and 1 on the right. Length 7m, beam 1.62m, depth 0.4m. Further name variant: **batel★**

battellucci See **battelluccio**

battelluccio *Italy, NE:* **Fishing boat★** of the **bragozzo★** type that originated in the Chioggia area in the northwestern part of the Adriatic Sea; used mainly to trawl for sardines. Curved stem and sternpost, bluff bow, rounded stern; flat bottom; deep rudder. Decked or partly decked, with cuddy forward; a single bitt on each side of the bow; bow and stern painted with figures and designs. Single trapezoidal lugsail set to a mast stepped toward the stern; sometimes employs a special jib-type sail. Sails painted with distinctive designs. Also rowed from the stern, using a tall fulcrum-type oarlock. Reported lengths 9-13m; e.g., length 11m, beam 2.8m, depth 0.97m. Name variants: **batelluccio da sardelle, bateluccio;** pl. **battellucci.** Further reference: **battana-2**

batteloe See **battela-1**

battelon See **batelon**

batteria, batteria galleggiante, Batterie, batterie flottante See **floating battery**

battery See **floating battery, shad battery, sinkbox**

battery boat *United States, E:* A boat that transported and aided in setting the **batteries** (see **sinkbox**) used by waterfowl hunters on the North Carolina coastal bays. Often had a boom for loading and unloading the **battery**.

battil See **batil-1**

battila See **battela-1**

battipalo See **pile driver-1**

battis See **boat-1**

battle See **batelle**

battle cruiser See **cruiser-3**

batto 14th-century Italian word that described a type of **rowboat★**. See also **bateau**.

battoe See **bateau, bateau-3, bateau-7j, batoe**

batty See **bateau**

batu See **bateau-6**

batwing boat See **Saint Lawrence skiff**

baty See **bat-3**

baudarka See **boudarka**

baul See **bāūlīa**

bauldie See **baldie**

baulea See **bāūlīa, shoe dhoni**

bauleah See **bāūlīa**

bāūlīa *India, NE:* Bengal vessel that has been variously reported as a passenger craft, a cargo carrier and, on the Kosi River, a **fishing boat★**. In the Calcutta area, the **bāūlīa** was a **passage boat★** for Europeans and wealthy Indians and also served for up-country journeys; 1-2 cabins provided amenities. Generally white inside and green outside. On cargo carriers, cargo stowed beneath an arched awning above which was a platform for the helmsman. Bottom flat with no keel;

side planks "stapled" on, often to a dugout base. Strong fore-and-aft rocker; sharp ends were overhanging, the stern higher than the bow. Generally steered

bāūlīa

with a sweep. Mostly rowed, the oarsmen forward of the cabin. When sailed used a lugsail. Crew of 4-8 mostly. Reported lengths 11-20m; length 6-10 times the width. Other recorded names: **baoulya, baul, bauléa, bauleah, bawaleea, bhaolia, bhāle, bhaulea(h), bháulía, bhauliya, bholiah, bhouliya, bol★, bole★, bolea(h), boli, bolia(h), bolio, boulia, Ganges boat**

baulk yawl *United Kingdom:* Open boat of the Isle of Man and Northern Ireland that engaged in longline (baulk) and herring fishing with nets until the 1930s. Worked mainly off beaches. Clinker-built, with elm frames; 4 thwarts. Sharp-sterned until the mid-19th century, when a square raked transom became more common; stem fairly straight. Light gunwales slotted for the 2 pairs of square-loomed oars; rowlocks later. Open until the late 19th century, then half-decked; the last boats had

baulk yawl

a cabin. Many rigged with a standing lugsail with its clew hauled out on a traveler to the end of the boom; a foresail ran to the top of the mast and was hauled out on an iron bumkin. Short mast stepped against the 2nd bench. Others set a square dipping lugsail, tacked to a hook at the bow; halyard secured to a cleat on the weather side of the 2nd thwart, the only stay. Crew of 4-7. Reported lengths on keel 5.2-5.5m, beam 1.73m. Other recorded names: **balc yawl, balk yawl, Manx yawl**

Baumfloss See **timber raft-1**

Baumkahn, Baumschiff See **dugout canoe**

baurua *Kiribati (Gilbert Islands), central Pacific:* Large interisland voyaging and **war canoe**; extinct except for reproductions. Early boats double-hulled. Double-ended hull, planked up from a sharp keel piece that curved up at the ends to the top strake. Keel convex longitudinally; lee side of hull flattened, weather side rounded. Strakes of short lengths butted end-to-end and lashed on edge-to-edge; strakes followed keel line and truncated at sheer line; 2-piece frames inserted. Flat sheer on top strake except at ends, which swept up. Long, heavy torpedo-shaped float attached to 5 long, downward-curving outrigger booms by forked-stick connectives; braced by stringers from the ends of the **canoe*** and across the booms. One or 2 large triangular sails: apex tacked to forward end of boat, boomed at the foot. Forward-raking mast set into step on the central boom close inboard; multi-holed in order to adjust positions. Mast shored by brace from the boom, stayed fore-and-aft and from the end of the boom. A modern reproduction steps 3 masts. Also paddled. Reported lengths 18-30m; e.g., length 18.2m, beam 2m, depth 1.8m. Name variant: **te baurua**

bawaleea See **bāūlīa**

bawley *England, SE:* Beamy **cutter***-rigged boat of the Thames Estuary. Renowned shrimpers, but they also trawled, dredged for oysters, stowboated for whitebait, whelked, cockled, provisioned ships, and ran the catch from **smacks*** to shore. Used from the early 19th century. A few reproductions now in use, but their main period was from the 1870s to World War I. Later boats had engines and typically were not **bawley**-rigged. **Bawleys** sailed out of several ports, varying slightly in size and construction details. Generally a high bow, low stern, straight plumb stem with slightly raked forefoot. Wide, shallow, and lightly raked transom, although at Leigh and on the River Medway the transom was usually nearly vertical; at Leigh it was painted white; some early boats pink-sterned. Deep, straight keel with drag; rounded bilges; fine entry and long run. Initially clinker-built, later carvel. Open originally, half-decked in mid-19th century, then decked except for a narrow hatch that extended almost to the sternpost; the hatch on **Medway bawleys** ended forward of a small steering cockpit; deep bulwarks. A tarred canvas tent provided protection on early boats, later a cuddy installed. Early **bawleys** had a wet well; later employed a cauldron to boil the shrimp immediately. Outboard rudder; tiller might extend through the top strake. Most black-hulled with a white line around the rubbing strake. The **dinghy*** may be called a **foot boat*** or **skiff**. Lofty boomless gaff sail, with luff and leech almost parallel, set to a short mast; sail fitted with a brail leading to the throat. Long standing gaff, peaked up; sheeted to a horse. Very tall topmast set a jackyard, and later a jib-headed topsail; topmast taken down in winter. **Medway bawleys** stepped mast in a tabernacle. One or 2 headsails; long, heavy bowsprit. Some early **bawleys** set spritsails; a few **Margate** and **Whitstable bawleys** used a standing lug mizzen. A pair of oars was set in lumber irons on deck. Crew of 2-4. Reported lengths 6-15m, the smaller size generally built earlier; 1880s boat 9.8m long, 3.5m wide, 1.2m draft aft. Other recorded names: **ball(e)y, bawley-boat, boiler boat, boily boat, borl(e)y, Leigh** (and **Thames**) **shrimper, whitebaiter**; also **Blackwater, Essex, Gravesend, Harwich, Leigh, Maldon,**

Rochester, Southend, Thames bawley. Further reading: John Leather, *Smacks and Bawleys* (Lavenham: Terence Dalton Ltd., 1991). Note also **cockle galley, Peter boat-2, stowboat**.

bawley-boat See **bawley**

bay boat 1. *Australia:* One of a group of vessels of the Australian Commonwealth Shipping Line; each named after one of Australia's bays. **2.** *Canada, E:* A vessel that puts in at settlements on the Newfoundland and Labrador coasts with supplies, mail, and passengers. **3.** *United States, E:* **a.** Term given to boats that harvested oysters, clams, and fish from Great South Bay on Long Island in New York State. In the early part of the 20th century, most were either cat- or **sloop***-rigged. Generally low-sided, beamy, and shallow draft. Other recorded names: **clam boat, oyster boat***. Note also **catboat-2d, oyster sloop-1. b.** A **bay boat** on Chesapeake Bay is a locally built workboat. Further references: **buy boat-2, Morecambe Bay prawner, Parrett flatner**

Bay coaster *United States, NE:* Small **schooner*** that carried pulpwood and cordwood locally in Penobscot Bay and upriver to Bangor. Some ran as **packet boats*** to Portland. A **yawlboat*** provided power when needed; auxiliaries on some later vessels. 30-70t.

bay craft Vessel that confines its activity to a bay and lower tributaries.

baydar, baydara See **baidara**

baydarka See **kayak-9, kayak-11**

baydarque See **kayak-9**

Bay Islands dorey *Honduras, E:* Large, beamy **dugout canoe*** of the Bay Islands (Islas de la Bahía) off the northwest Caribbean coast of Honduras. Originally sailed; engines now installed, modifying the original design to include decking forward and coaming around a cockpit. Fine entrance. Note also **dori**.

bayman *United States, NE:* Early northern Maine term for local **schooners*** that fished within Chaleur Bay in southwestern Gulf of St. Lawrence.

Bay of Fundy shad boat *Canada, E:* **Fishing boat*** of the late 19th and early 20th centuries. Sharply raked stem; full bow; maximum beam well forward; originally sharp-sterned, later a high, raked transom; drag to the straight plank keel; steep, straight rise to the floors. Outboard rudder flared below the waterline. Forward third decked, cuddy below; stern bench. Mast stepped about a fourth of the distance from the bow. Set a boomed gaff mainsail; jib to a short bowsprit. Later motorized. Length ca. 7.5m, beam 2.4m, depth aft 1.7m. Those of Cobequid Bay, Nova Scotia, at the eastern end of the Bay of Fundy, had lapstrake topsides and carvel below; bluff, recurving bow; raked transom above deep deadwood or pink-sterned; narrow, flat bottom; grounding keels along the chines; some had a centerboard. Open. These boats set 1-2 spritsails and sometimes a small jib to a light bowsprit; masts unstayed so they could be unstepped, with sail wrapped around them. Length 7.6m, beam 2.44m.

bayoux See **bisquine**

bay punt *Canada, E:* Newfoundland boat used in winter to hunt sea birds and seals. Due to occasional need to haul it onto the ice, had thin, narrow planking for lightness, tin sheathing at the bow, and an ironshod keel. Similar to the **rodney★** in shape, with round bottom, curved stem, raked transom stern, open. Propelled by oars, sail, and later by small outboard motor. Crew of 4. Reported lengths 5.5-5.8m. Note also **sealing punt**.

bayt See **boat-1**

bazar caique, **Bazar-Kaik**, **bazar qaïghy** See **pazar kayığı**

bazitpuri See **patam-1**

bazra See **badjra**

bbrahòzzë, **bbrayòzzë** See **bragozzo**

beach boat In general, any boat designed to operate off an open beach. Each site has its own peculiar beach and water conditions, and the boats have been adapted to meet them. Most open and rowed or sailed; some fully motorized and decked. Strongly built, beamy, mainly flat-floored with shallow or no keel; may have side keels. Sharp-ended or with a transom. Rudder easily shipped or unshipped; propeller (if any) protected by an extension running between rudder heel and sternpost. Launched and retrieved bow or stern first. Handling may be suitable only at certain tide stages. On steep beaches, gravity may assist launching; some rely on a cable attached to an offshore piling or anchored buoy to get through the surf. Hauled ashore by animals, rollers, winches, tractors, wheelbarrow devices. Name variant: **Strandboot★**. Note also **Aberystwyth beach boat**, **Brighton beach boat**. Further reference: **surfboat-6a**

beach dory See **Sea Bright skiff**

beach gig *United Kingdom:* Long, narrow **pulling boat★** popular at beach resorts. Usually sturdy and well-built. Sometimes sets a small lugsail. Lengths to 9m. Further reference: **Yarmouth pilot gig**

beach launch See **launch-6**

beach lighter See **beach punt-3**

beach punt **1.** *England, E:* Small, beamy inshore **fishing boat★** used off Suffolk and east-facing Norfolk beaches. Heavily built with clinker planking; flat floors; bottom protected by doublings or beach keels. Upright stem, rounded forefoot; straight keel, deadwood aft; wide, vertical transom stern, although double-ended in Norfolk until the 1920s. Usually undecked; 3-4 thwarts; partitioned for fish sorting. Beach shingle ballast carried in sacks, jettisoned as catch brought aboard.

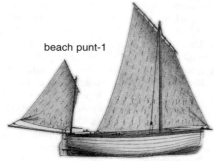

beach punt-1

Tarred hulls on early 19th-century boats, white since the latter part of the century. Dipping lugsail forward,

hooked to short iron bumkin. Standing lug aft, mast stepped against the transom to starboard of rudder, foot extended by long outrigger. No shrouds, but halyard set to weather side. Masts could be stowed. Some smaller Norfolk boats set a single dipping lugsail. The larger 2-masted boats might use a **sloop★** rig when bottom trawling. Cockerel vane traditional on mizzen masthead. Also rowed, standing, using 2-4 pairs of oars, worked in double tholepins; sculling notch on the transom. Now have a small engine. Crew of 2-4. Reported lengths 4.3-7.6m, the longer in Norfolk; e.g., length 5.2m, beam 2.13m, depth 0.76m. Other recorded names: **Aldeburgh beach** (or **sprat**) **boat**, **longshore punt**, **Norfolk** (and **Southwold**) **beach punt**, **Norfolk fishing punt**, **punt★**, **spratter**, **Suffolk beach boat**, **Suffolk** (**beach**) **punt**, **trim-tram** (at Yarmouth), **Yarmouth punt**. Note also **Norfolk crabber**.

2. *United States, E:* The **beach punt** of the watermen of Virginia's Eastern Shore of Chesapeake Bay was a **scow★**-like craft. Flat bottom with equally curved ends. Propelled by a sculling oar. Length 7.3m, beam 1.8m.

3. *West Indies:* Term often applied to any small **boat★**. A few worked as **lighters★** from beaches off some islands. Flat bottom, planked longitudinally; strong fore-and-aft bottom rocker that continued up to gunwale level at the ends; straight flared sides; strong sheer. Partly floored; house amidships, to protect the cargo, supported on outriggers along each side; small boats open. Steered and sculled by an oar that passed through a hole in the stern; also rowed, with the oarlocks on the outriggers. Small boats: length 7m, beam 2m, draft 0.6m. Other recorded names: **beach lighter**, **West Indian beach lighter**

Further reference: **Hastings lugger**

beach skiff *England, E:* Clinker-built **pulling boat★** that worked drift nets close inshore in the Yarmouth area. Crew of 2. On the central Suffolk coast some tended lobster pots. Reported lengths 3.7-4.3m, beam 1.0m. Further reference: **Sea Bright skiff**

beach yawl *England, E:* **1.** Long, lean boat that tended ships lying off the East Anglia coast; removed salvage from wrecked vessels, put pilots aboard ships and, in fine weather, carried fish from **smacks★** to shore. First reported ca. 1770; last built in the 1890s. Many of the later boats were adapted for pleasure trips from the

beach yawl-1

beach. Clinker-built, steamed oak frames, close-timbered; most double-ended; fine entry and run; on some, midship section noticeably flat, easy rise of the floors on others. Vertical stem; nearly vertical sternpost; straight keel, up to 15cm deep; considerable sheer; rudder might hang below keel. Ballast usually bags of beach shingle, shifted as needed. **Pilot yawls** were fine-lined and exceptionally fast; salvage and supply **yawls*** slower. Until the mid-19th century, set 2 dipping lugsails and a standing lug mizzen; thereafter mainmast discarded and the fore- and mizzen sails enlarged. Foresail tacked to a short iron bumkin, one sheet leading through a ringbolt outside the rail, the 2nd carried to a samson post on the tabernacle. Mizzen sheeted to a very long outrigger. Mizzenmast stayed forward by a rope and tackle made fast to an eyebolt through the keelson. In light weather ran out a bowsprit and jib. Rowed in calms and while putting about; 8-14 pairs of oars, some double-banked; oarports often cut into washstrakes. Small **beach yawls** had crew of 8-12, the larger 25-30; 40 might be employed in salvage work. Reported lengths 12.2-24.4m; e.g., length 15m, beam 3m, depth 1.0m. Other recorded names: **jol**, **Lowestoft yawl** (or **yoll**), **Norfolk beach yawl** (or **yoll**), **yol**, **yoll***; also **East Anglia**, **Southwold**, **Suffolk**, **Walberswick**, **Winterton**, and **Yarmouth beach yawl**. Note also **ferryboat-2**. **2.** Those used in The Wash by King's Lynn cockle fishermen were half-decked, **cutter***-rigged craft. Flexible boats designed to withstand pounding on sandbanks. Double-ended, clinker-built. Towed a large **rowboat***. Crew of 3-4. Reported lengths 9-12m; e.g., length 11m, beam 3.4m, draft 1.0m.

beacon boat **1.** A vessel that supplies **lightships*** and lighthouses and transports the crews back and forth. Some equipped to place and service channel buoys and light beacons. Crews may be sent ashore in small boats to maintain shore-based navigation aids. Other recorded names: **Bakenboot**, **baliseur**, **balizador**, **balizeur**, **bateau balise**, **battello meda** (or **segnale**), **bote valiza**, **buoy boat** (**tender** or **yacht**), **buoy-laying boat**, **Leuchtturm-Tender**, **lighthouse tender**, **Tonnenleger**; in England: **Trinity House boat** (**tender** or **yacht**), **Trinity buoy yacht**, **Trinity sloop** or **yacht**. **2.** A small unattended **lightship***.

beam float See **camakau**
beam trawler See **trawler**
bean cod See **muleta-1**
beanie See **pungy**
Beaufort skiff See **North Carolina sail skiff**
Beaver canoe See **kayak-form canoe**
becandre See **waal**
bécass, bécasse, beccaccia See **barcaza**
bec de canard, bec de canne See **bé de cane**
bèche *France, east-central:* **1.** In the 16th century, the **bèche** of the Saône River was a small boat with an arched canopy that covered most of the hull. Note also **bâche-2**.
  2. A small **fishing boat*** used on rivers, especially the Saône. Most have a perforated compartment to hold the catch alive and some small types are anchored in the river to serve as a holding tank for fish. In the Mâcon area, the **bèche** of the early 20th century was 10-20m long and held ca. 4t of fish; sharp ends, flat bottom, decked at bow and stern. A smaller type, still in use, serves mainly as a **vivier***. Wide square stern; narrower sloping bow, cut square; flat, longitudinally planked bottom. Most of hull occupied by the fish

well. Caulked with moss. Name variant: **bachot*** Spelling variant: **besche**. Further reference: **baicha**
bech tchiftè See **kayık-2**
beda *Malaysia:* **Schooner***-rigged vessel with 3 pole masts. See also **bedar**, **bidar-3**.
bedan **1.** *Arabian Peninsula, S:* Fast, low-lying vessel engaged in freighting, smuggling and, in early days, transporting slaves. A small type is still found fishing near shore and a few traders work from the central Oman coast, but both types now mainly raced. Originally sewn teak planking, later nailed; sharp ends; end pieces may still be sewn on; flat sheer; slack bilges. Vertically

bedan-1

planked false stem piece added above the vertical cutwater, creating a clipper-bow appearance. Vertical timbering, secured by battens, added to the sternpost, terminating in a tall secondary post. To this an equally tall rudder is secured by coir rope at top and bottom; rudder, which extends below the bottom, is unshipped and hung from the quarter when in port. Rudder worked by lines from a peg-like tiller fixed to its outer edge near the waterline; lines lead to intricate system of ropes and beams, and lead aft to the helmsman. No centerline keel; 2 grounding keels common. Open except for deck aft and tiny foredeck; large vessels might be fully decked; matting often lashed to sides to increase freeboard. Might have a stylized figurehead at the stern. Most single-masted, although those that engaged in East African trade had 2 masts (the extinct **'uwaisiyyah**); masts vertical and supported by athwartship beams. Lateen or quadrilateral lateen-type sail with a short luff; some with heavy bowsprit and jib. Also rowed, using square-bladed oars on tholepins. Crew of 4-10. Reported lengths 6-15m for fishing type; trader exceeds 15m. Other recorded names: **badaini**, **badan(e)**, **badani**, **baden(i)**, **badini**, **bedani**, **bedeen**, **beden***, **bedeni**, **buden**, **zaruq***, **zaruqah**
  2. *Kenya:* Trading **bedans** that reached Mombasa were locally called **samaki** (fish) **dhows** because they arrived with salted fish caught en route and laid out on board to dry; also, their high rudderpost gave the stern a fishtail appearance. Further name variant: **fish dhow**
bedang See **beduang**
bedani See **bedan-1**
bedan-safar *Oman, NE:* Originated on the Muscat coast, but traveled widely, trading and fishing for tuna in the Persian (Arabian) Gulf and reportedly going as far as the East Indies. Double-ended; sharp bow, false convex stem; wide sternpost swept up at outer end. Narrow flat bottom, with strong fore-and-aft rocker; bilge keels, which sometimes joined at the bow and

stern. Strongly flared sides, slightly rounded; marked sheer. Planking originally sewn. Narrow rudder, worked with multiple lines, extended below the bottom; tall rudderhead. Decked at bow and stern. Hull treated with a reddish resin. Large quadrilateral lateen-type sail with a short luff hung from a forward-raking mast; luff boomed out. Also rowed, using scoop-bladed oars worked against tholepins. Reported lengths 12-18m; shallow draft. Spelling variants: **badan-safar**, **béden-safar**

bedan-seyad *Oman, NE:* **Fishing boat*** of the Batinah coast, northwest of Muscat; some went as far as Bombay (Mumbai). A few still work. Double-ended; planking of early boats sewn, 2 strakes to each side; flat bottom, with rocker, formed from a narrow single plank; bilge keels; sides flare at about 45°; no ribs. Sharp bow, with convex stem; very wide vertical sternpost extends above the gunwale. Narrow rudder projects beyond the top of the sternpost and well below the bottom; worked by a series of lines. Caulked with oakum saturated with a reddish resinous compound, which is also used on the hull. Partly decked at the stern; loose decking laid on the thwarts over remaining area; thwarts pierce the hull. A wide lugsail set to a slightly forward-raking mast. Sail boomed out forward. Also rowed. Length ca. 10m, narrow. Spelling variants: **badan-seyad**, **béden-sayad**

bedar 1. *Indonesia, W:* Boat type in the Sakai dialect of Rokan River area on the west coast of central Sumatra. **2.** *Indonesia, peninsular:* **a.** Lug-rigged craft that carries cargo along the east coast of the Malay Peninsula. Varies in size and design, but most have sharp ends, a long straight keel, raked ends, elongated bow. Rudder and tiller. Rounded mat-roofed house at the stern. One or 2 masts. Foremast on 2-masted vessels steps in the bow and rakes forward; mainmast amidships is only slightly raked. Sets mat, Chinese-type, polygonal lugsails or wide standing lugsails of cloth. Long bowsprit, bowsed down. Also rowed. Mostly 9-11m long; shallow draft. **b.** Small open boat that engages in line and net fishing at several east coast localities. Sharp ends, concave stem has a flattened, elongated bow piece; full raked stern, with a short platform. Those that sail have crutches set at right angles out over the side near the bow and stern to support the lowered mast and spars while fishing; crutches carved as stylized birds' heads or demons. Standing lugsail set to a light mast. Reported lengths 7.3-9m; e.g., length 7.3m, beam 1.2m, depth 0.6m. **c.** The **bedar** was also used by local rajahs, sometimes as a state craft. One such boat had a long sharp bow, concave stem with carved fiddlehead at the end; steep rise to the floors; sharp stern, with square overhanging poop. Narrow rudder extended up through poop deck. Decked; cabin aft. Lugsail set to a single mast stepped well forward. Also rowed or paddled. Length overall 10.4m, beam 2m, depth 0.9m. **d.** Small, narrow **galley***-type boat. Some used for warfare, others as pleasure craft by local rulers. Sharp bow. Propelled by paddlers along the middle. Name variant: **sampan bidar** Other recorded names: **beda***, **bidaar**, **bidar***, **perahu beda**, **perahu bedar.** Note also **anak bedar.**

bed boat See **narrow boat**

bé de cane *France, central:* Clinker-planked vessel of the Canal du Berry that transported merchandise during the mid-19th century. A modified **chaland de Loire***, adapted to fit canal size. Wide strakes, pegged; ribs alternated with floor frames; straight sides, narrowing quickly at the bow. Flat bottom, longitudinally planked; turned up at the bow to form a flat raking surface, said to resemble a duck's bill. Flat stern, vertically planked, often decorated with scroll work. Cabin aft, stable amidships, open holds. Steered with twin rudders plus a very long sweep. Crew of 2-3. Length to 28m, beam 2.5m, depth 1.5m. Other recorded names: **bec de canard**, **bec de canne**; pl. **bés de cane.** Note also **berrichon.**

bedeen See **bedan-1**

beden 1. *Iran, SE:* Deep-hulled trader working out of Bandar 'Abbās. Raked, relatively straight stem to the top, where it projects forward for ca. 2m in a nearly horizontal position; flat floors amidships. Transom stern, although small types can be sharp-sterned. Sets a large single lateen sail. **2.** *Somalia:* Sewn boat used particularly by shark fishermen along the east-facing coast. Sharp ends; strongly raked stem extends well above the gunwale; sternpost less raked and not as tall. Hull sewn with coir rope or, more recently, fishing line; stitches cross on the inside, vertical outside; 5 main strakes; some treenailed. Heavy gunwale pegged to top strake; full ribs alternate with half ribs. Caulked during sewing, using pitch in the seam and a strip of beaten fiber sewn into position. Keel; straight flaring sides; strong sheer; thwarts sewn to the hull. Small rudder attached to lower half of the post with grommets; worked with lines from the outer edge. Uses sweeps consisting of a long pole to which a round blade is attached. Quadrilateral lateen-type sail with a short luff may be set to a short, stout mast. Crew of ca. 8. Reported lengths 6-10m; e.g., length 10m, beam 1.82m. Spelling variant: **badan.** Further reading: N. Chittick, "Sewn Boats in the Western Indian Ocean, and a Survival in Somalia," *International Journal of Nautical Archaeology* 9 (1980), 1-19. Note also **bedan.** Further reference: **bedan-1**

bedeni See **bedan-1**

béden-safar See **bedan-safar**

béden-sayad See **bedan-seyad**

bedi *India, NW/Pakistan, SE:* Vessel from Karachi, the

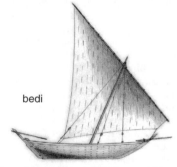

bedi

Indus River delta area, and Gujarat. Although originally designed for fishing offshore with large gill nets, the remaining boats mainly transport cargo and generally are called **muchewa**. Carvel-planked, with long overhanging bow; short, straight keel, parallel to the waterline; square sloping transom. Nearly straight sheer; strong rise to the floors; waterlines often hollow at bow and in the run; full quarters with flat buttocks. Fixed deck at bow and stern, open amidships. Narrow rudder, with high head. Employs rock ballast in hull and movable ballast in sandbags on deck; small boats may use a balance board. Generally sets a quadrilateral lateen-type sail with a short luff to a forward-raking mast. A mizzenmast may also be stepped. Usually crew of 12. Reported lengths 10.7-23m; e.g., length overall 20.9m, beam 4.48m, molded depth 1.87m. Other recorded names: **batel*** (on Makran coast), **bheddi**, **máhi-kush batél** (large size on Makran coast, where they may work beach seines with a crew of 6-10). Further reading: *Food and Agriculture Organization, Fishing Boats of the World*, Vol.1 (London: The Fishing News, 1955), 28, 30, 38, 39-50. Note also **berí**, **bhedi**, **bunder boat-2**.

bedienschuit See **bumboat-1**

bedoeang See **beduang**

beduang *Indonesia, central:* Double-outrigger craft that was mainly a **fishing boat***, but larger sizes served as traders. Found along the northeast coast of Java and on Madura. Built up from a dugout base with 1-2 planks and sometimes a washstrake. Hull narrow in proportion to depth. Sharp ends; bottom curved up smoothly at bow, which raked inward sharply at the top. Stern higher; rounded up to a tall projection or was cut to a sharp, straight raking end. Two booms crossed the hull to long bamboo floats set well away from the hull; booms anchored by double lashings that passed under a crosspiece wedged beneath protuberances left in the hull. Forward boom attached directly to each float. After boom secured by a vertical stanchion and an angle brace; boom stayed from the mast. Rudder secured against a transverse piece on the windward quarter. Stepped a very short, fixed foremast in the bow. Removable mainmast stepped close to the stern. Triangular mat sails hung from a yard, lug-fashion; boomed at the foot; mainsail tacked to the bow. Small size ca. 5m long, largest to ca. 16m; e.g., length ca. 9.75m, beam 0.6m, depth 0.7m. Other recorded names: **bedang**, **bedoeang**, **peduang**, **prahu peduang**, **prao bedouang**, **prau bed(u)ang**, **prau beduwang**

beef boat 1. *United Kingdom:* A boat, sometimes a small **fishing smack***, that supplied provisions, especially fresh meat, and powder to ships of the Royal Navy. Note also **market boat-4**.
2. *United States:* A slang term for a cargo or supply boat.

Beer Head lugger See **Beer lugger**

Beer lugger *England, SW:* Beamy **fishing boat*** that worked off the eastern beaches of the south Devon coast from at least the mid-18th century. Three-masted until World War I; afterwards auxiliaries were introduced, the mainmast omitted, and the size reduced. Clinker-built, with rather flat floors and rounded bilges; straight keel, with drag. Straight, vertical stem; raked stern, with wide transom, tucked up slightly at the heel. Some older boats had a washstrake above the

gunwale; oarport cut in just abaft the foremast; later boats had chocks for oarlocks. Open initially, later small cuddy forward; movable partition below the 2nd and 3rd thwarts created a fishhold and place for gear.

Beer lugger

Hull generally tarred inside and out, with a white streak below gunwale strake; Sidmouth boats varnished. Unique, long iron bumkin on the stemhead, bowsed down sharply by a bobstay. Dipping lug foresail, nearly as large as the mainsail, overlapped it by a third of its area; luff strongly angled; spar from mast held the luff taut. Mainsail luff made fast to the foremast by a bowline. Mizzenmast, setting a standing lugsail, was stepped through the top of the transom, just clear of the rudderhead. A 4th sail, a fore mizzen, used in hard weather, was set as a foresail. The masts were light spars; the mizzen raked aft slightly, the fore- and mainmasts sometimes bowed forward slightly by the weight of the sails. Sidmouth boats generally set a large dipping lugsail forward and, in later years, a small standing lug mizzen. Crew of 3-4. Reported lengths 4.6-8.5m, widths 2.54-6m, depths 1.27-1.52m; shallow draft. Sidmouth boats smaller and slightly beamier than those from Beer. Other recorded names: **Beer Head lugger**, **Beer trawler**, **Sidmouth lugger**

beerotter *Belgium:* Wooden vessel of the **otter*** family built for the Antwerp Public Cleaning Department to transport sewage and refuse to Antwerp dumps and to Zeeland farmers for use on their fields. Worked until World War II. Carvel-planked; flat bottom, with keel; bluff bow; flat sheer. Rubbing strake did not parallel the sheer but turned up higher at the ends. Decked, raised deck aft, with cuddy below; narrow gangway along the low, flat hatches; deckhouse abaft the hold on some. Equipped with pumps. Lightly rigged with a loose-footed, boomed gaff sail, headsails, and sometimes a jigger mizzenmast on the rudderhead. Strike masts. Later boats motorized. Other recorded names: **dung otter**, **sump otter**

Beer trawler See **Beer lugger**

beet See **bette**

beetle boat *United Kingdom:* Beetle-shaped armored landing craft of the Royal Navy. First used in World War I. Capable of carrying 500 men. Shallow draft. See also **whaleboat-7a**.

Beetle cat or **catboat** See **catboat-2c**
Beetle whaleboat See **whaleboat-7a**
Befrachter See **freighter-1**
Beiboot *Germany:* A **ship's boat**★, without reference to type. May be rowed, sailed, or motorized. Note also **Arbeitsboot, kleiner Kahn**.
Beichväterschiff See **Leibschiff**
beira, beiro See **bero**
beitel See **beitelaak**
beitelaak *Germany/Netherlands:* Vessel of the lower Rhine River that carried bulk cargo; operated into the 17th century. Characterized by a narrow bow that raked up in a flat surface as wide as the flat bottom, earning the name *beitel* (chisel) **aak**★. Stern plumb, with a sternpost on some; others had a stern similar to the bow. Clinker-planked straight sides. Decked at the ends; central area covered by a cambered hatch. Outboard rudder; 2 or sometimes 4 narrow leeboards. On single-masted vessels, the tall pole mast set a square sail. The short mizzen on the 2-masted vessels set a type of spritsail. Towed upstream by horses. Other recorded names: **beitel, Beitelschiff, beitelschip**; pl. **beitelaken**
beitelaken, Beitelschiff, beitelschip See **beitelaak**
Beizhili junk See **Kiangsu trader**
bejú See **chalana-8**
Bekasse See **barcaza**
bélăm, belan See **bélang**
belande See **bilander**
belander See **bijlander, bilander-1**
belandra, belandra pequena See **bilander-1**
bélandre See **balandra, bijlander, bilander-1, waal**
bélandre hollandais See **pleit**
bélang *Indonesia, E:* **1.** Plank-built general-purpose craft from Banda, Kai, Tanimbar, and Aru Islands. Early boats used for war; some popular for regattas; Kai islanders used them for pearling. Some still built in the Aru Islands. Sharp ends; keel follows a smooth line into the curved stem and sternpost that terminate in sharp, vertical pieces as high as 1.0m above the gunwale. Strakes abut against the ends rather than turning up; top strake terminates before reaching the ends; flat sheer; curved flare to the sides. Strakes now doweled edge-to-edge, previously sewn. In the Aru Islands, flexible ribs lashed to residual lugs on the inside of the strakes. Square gunwale planks join outside the stem and sternpost. Vertical poles support split-bamboo decking; pearling boats had solid end decks; some had a high steering bench aft. Might have a saddle-shaped house. Sailed and paddled. One or 2 masts. Reported lengths 10-18m; e.g., length 10m, beam 2m, depth 0.75m. On Banda, the large festival boats carry 30-80 passengers.
2. The **prahu belan** (or **bélang**) at Ambon is reported as a large **outrigger canoe**★.
Other recorded names: **bélăm, belan, perahu belan, prahu bélang**. Note also **orembai belan**.
bélebois See **billyboy**
belem *Arabian Peninsula/Iran/Iraq:* Term applied to a number of vaguely defined Persian (Arabian) Gulf and Red Sea craft, often with local names. Generic term for **boat**★ in Kurdish. Descriptions of a few of the better known follow.

1. A sharp-ended, open, round-bottomed boat, especially in southern Iraq (**belem irāqī**) and at Bahrain. In Kuwait, it is called a **ketīre**. Originally a **dugout canoe**★ imported from India (see **houri** and **vallam**) or may be of similar design but plank-built. Sometimes carried aboard a **dhow**★ as a **ship's boat**★. At Basra, the white-painted **belem ·ashuri** (also **ballam ·ashuri, belem 'išāri, bellam Ashāri**, or **bellum ashari**) is used to ferry passengers, or as a **tender**★ or **lighter**★. High ends terminate in a scroll design. Poled from platforms at bow and stern, rowed, towed, or sailed. Length ca. 6m, beam 1.0m. The **belem saffara** is a sailing cargo vessel of ca. l00t that plies lower Iraqi rivers; double-ended but with a flat bottom and end decking. A smaller size is called **belem suffina** (or **ballam suffina**).
2. A larger type of **belem** carried freight from Basra to Kuwait and was called **belem nasari** (or **ballam nassūri, bellum nassari**). Reported lengths 12-15m.
3. In Bushire, Iran, a **belem** is a small, broad-beamed cargo boat. Called **baggārah** (or **baqqarah**) in Kuwait. In Bahrain, a small type may be called a **mashueh**.
4. A small open **belem** that is used for fishing, but powered by an outboard motor, is now in use in some Persian Gulf areas.
5. Double-ended **coaster**★ of the Persian Gulf; distinguished by a curved raking stem, a straight raking sternpost, and no stemhead projection. Steered with a yoke and lines. Often decked aft, with a railing. Sets a quadrilateral lateen-type sail with a short luff to a slightly forward-raking mast.
6. Fishing **belems** of 6-9m were double-ended, with an extended stemhead, curved stem, straight raking sternpost.
7. A Red Sea **belem** was reported to be double-ended with stem and sternposts that stopped short of the top strake. Steered with yoke and lines. Set a single quadrilateral lateen-type sail with a short luff.
Spelling variants: **balam**★, **ballam, bellam, bellem, bellum**; pl. **ablâm, iblâm**. Further reference: **mahaila-2**
belem ·ashuri See **belem-1, mahaila-2**
belem irāqī, belem 'išāri See **belem-1**
belem nasari See **belem-2**
belem saffara, belem suffina See **belem-1**
Belfast yawl See **Groomsport yawl**
bélibois See **billyboy**
belingiero See **whaler-1**
Belizean smack *Belize:* Plank-built **fishing boat**★ introduced from Cuba in 1911. Built on natural crook

Belizean smack

frames; deep, long, narrow bilge keel. Double-ended until ca. 1925; now has raked transom stern. Steered with a yoke on the rudder. Utilizes a sliding gunter rig and boomed foresail. Crew of 3-5. Reported lengths 6.7-9m. Called a **smack*** when fitted with a wet well, **dry boat*** when the well is a dry type, and **sloop*** when there is no well.

Bella Bella canoe See **northern-style canoe**

bellam See **belem**

bellam Ashāri See **belem-1**

bellande See **bilander**

bellem See **belem**

bellum See **belem, vallam-1a**

bellum ashari See **belem-1**

bellum nassari See **belem-2**

bélo See **bero**

beloengkang See **belongkang**

belongkang *Indonesia, W:* Large **canoe** used on the rivers of central and southeastern Sumatra, mainly transporting cargo, but also military personnel and others. **Dugout canoe*** with extended sides to increase capacity; flat bottom, curved up toward truncated ends. Wooden deck at ends, bamboo decking amidships; large house covered the after part of the hull; in rainy weather an awning protected the bow paddlers. Two curved pieces extended beyond the stern to support a bench for the helmsman and the roof over him. Quarter rudders with trapezoidal blades. Poled upstream, rowed downstream. Other recorded names: **beloengkang, biloengkang, bloenkang, perahu bĕlungkang, praauw (prahoe) bloengkang**. Note also **perahu bĕlongkang**.

Belt boat See **bæltsbåd**

bena See **roko-2**

benaoe, benau See **banawa**

Benedenlander See **klipper**

Bengalee boat See **badjra**

béntjalang See **pencalang**

benzaisen See **sengoku bune**

Beothuc canoe, Beothuck canoe See **Beothuk canoe**

Beothuk canoe *Canada, E:* Birchbark **canoe** of the Beothuk of Newfoundland, who were exterminated in the early 19th century. Probably used for coastal travel, inshore fishing, sealing, and collecting eggs of sea birds. Characterized by a sharp V-section and hogged sheer; shape preserved by thwarts at midship peak. Ends peaked up; stick at each end aided transfer of the **canoe** to and from the water. Bottom straight, with a keelson, but also

Beothuk canoe

reported as curved. Ballasted with stones or cargo. Sheathing of 2-3 lengths of bark; lath-like ribs; gunwale formed by in- and outwales. Seams sewn with split spruce root; caulked with mixture of turpentine, oil, and ochre. Used long, narrow-bladed paddles; probably also sailed, with the mast lashed to the center thwart. Capacity of 4-5. Reported lengths 4.3-6.7m; e.g., length 4.57m, beam 1.0m, depth amidships 0.56m. Other recorded names: **Beothuc(k) canoe**. Further reading: Ingeborg Marshall, *Beothuk Canoes: An Analysis and Comparative Study* (Ottowa: National Museum of Man, 1985 [Canadian Ethnology Service, Mercury Series, Paper 102]).

beppu See **beppu tōni**

beppu tōni *India, SW:* Open boat used for longline fishing and setting gill nets on the Kerala coast. Basically a **dugout canoe***; some plank-extended; others have a stabilizing device. Sharp ends curve and sweep up; 8-9 thwarts. Steered with a paddle. Two masts, stepped through thwarts, the mizzen well inboard. Fitted with 2 spritsails and a foresail boomed out off the bow quarter. Crew of 4-8. Reported lengths 7.6-9.8m; e.g., length 8.4m, depth 0.58m. Other recorded names: **beppu, beputhoni, vallam*, veppu tōni**. Note also **tony**.

beputhoni See **beppu tōni**

ber *India, NE:* In part of northeastern Bihar state, 2 **canoes*** were connected, **catamaran***-fashion, by a bamboo platform. Used in the dry season when water levels were low. Crew of 2. Cap. ca. 4,000kg. Name variant: **singri**. See also **masula**.

beṛá *Bangladesh/India:* **1.** A **raft*** in Hindi.
2. Ceremonial **float*** set on Bengali rivers by Muslims to honor the saint, Khaja Khizr, especially on Thursday evenings in summer. Presented in consequence of a vow, a special benefit, birth of a child, etc. A paper and tinsel boat is set onto the float, the face of a female and crest and breast of a peacock at the bow. Accompanied by lights and music.

berca See **barca**

Berchtesgadener Plätte See **Plätte-1**

Berck lugger, Berckois See **bateau de Berck**

berdí See **chalana-8**

bereme See **perama-2**

bergantí See **brigantine, brigantino**

bergantí-goleta See **hermaphrodite brig**

bergantim See **brigantine** and **brigantine-5**

bergantim real See **real-2**

bergantín *Peru, south-central coast:* Two-masted **fishing boat*** used in the Pisco area prior to 1950. Ends rounded. Loose-footed, boomed spritsails with sprits set well up the masts. Small jib tacked to short bowsprit. Ca. 9m long. See also **brig, brigantine, brigantino**.

bergantina See **brigantine**

bergantín cántabro See **zabra**

bergantine See **brigantino**

bergantinejo See **brig**

bergantine reaes See **real-2**

bergantín-goleta See **hermaphrodite brig**

bergantin goleta de tres palos See **barkentine**

bergantini See **brigantine**

bergantino See **brigantino**

bergantino del passo del Canale See **madia-1**

bergantín redondo See **brig**

bergantinus See **brigantino**

bergantí rodó See **brig**

bĕrgas *Indonesia, central:* A boat type in the Sasak dialect on Lombok.

berge See **barge-11h, whaleboat-7b**

berge baleinière See **goelette-1c**

Bergenaar See **zalmschouw**

Bergense schouw See **Zeeuwse schouw**

Berghe *Austria, NE:* A 16th-century term for boats used on the Danube River at Vienna.

bergozzo See **bragozzo**

Bergse schouw See **Zeeuwse schouw**

berí *Pakistan, E:* Cargo vessel of the upper Indus River and its tributaries, the Ravi, Chenab, and Jhelum. Plank-built of irregular deodar pieces that were scarfed, joined on bamboo pegs on the edge, and fastened outside with iron clamps; sides vertical. Flat bottom joined to the sides with large iron clamps; longitudinal beams strengthened bottom. Ribs stopped short of the gunwales. Square ends, with bottom rounding up obliquely; in some places, sides tapered slightly at the bow and stern. A sort of poop constructed at the stern below which crew slept; some decked at bow. Set an oblong cloth sail, with yard at top and bottom, to a mast stepped through a thwart about a third abaft the bow. Mast stayed forward and aft, 2 shrouds at the side. Cap. 20-40t. Note also **bedi**.

Bereitschaftsboot See **accident boat**

berk See **hoy-1**

Berliner Zille See **Zille**

Bermuda boat See **Bermudian**

Bermuda cutter See **Bermuda sloop-2**

Bermuda dinghy Small type of the later **Bermuda sloop⋆**; especially popular in the 19th century. Open boat with a curved fin keel—a small keel of iron or wood for general use and a temporary large one of iron for racing. The special racing class (**Bermuda fitted dinghies**) were half-decked. Raked stem, with cutaway forefoot; tucked-up transom stern; rounded bilges. Set a loose-footed leg-of-mutton sail with a horizontal sprit; about half the sprit extended beyond the stern. Jib set flying to a long bowsprit. Mast raked aft. Also rowed or sculled. Reported lengths 3.7-4.3m, beam ca. 1.42m. Other recorded names: **bait boat⋆**, **dinkeye**, **off-and-on boat⋆**

Bermuda fitted dinghy See **Bermuda dinghy**

Bermuda schooner 1. *Bermuda/West Indies:* Fast 3-masted vessel, built mainly at Bermuda in the 1st quarter of the 19th century. Used mostly for running blockades and piracy; carried as many as 10 guns. Curved stem with cutaway forefoot; full transom, either flush or overhanging; steep deadrise. Narrow rudder; tiller came up either below or through the transom. Decked; long, low quarter-deck. Gaff-rigged to aft-raking masts; leg-of-mutton sails used between 1820 and 1850. Crew of ca. 50. Length on deck 24.3m, on keel 18.5m, beam 6.4m, depth 2.4m. Other recorded names: **ballahou schooner**, **Bermudian⋆**. Note also **ballahou**.

2. Term now applied to 2-masted **schooner⋆**-rigged pleasure craft with leg-of-mutton sails, hoisted by single halyard, with luff rope fitted in a groove in the tall masts. Roach commonly battened. Other recorded names: **goëlette Bermudienne**, **Hochtakeltschuner**

Bermuda sloop 1. Topsail **sloop⋆** of the **Jamaica sloop⋆** type that was built in Bermuda from the late 1600s to the early 1900s, evolving into a separate type by the mid-18th century. Used by traders, smugglers, privateers, and for fishing; in the early years of the 19th century, became a small cruiser class of the British Royal Navy. Type also built and used in the United States in the early 18th century, especially on Chesapeake Bay. The **Chesapeake Bay sloop** became popular during the 19th century and was the precursor of the **skipjack⋆**. Built of local red cedar, with steeply rising floors and well-rounded bilges; deep drag to the keel, later a curved keel; heavily ballasted. Square, raking counter; raked stem with cutaway forefoot; early boats had strong sheer with low freeboard. Cambered deck; high, short quarter-deck; stern cabin; later flush-decked. **Fishing boats⋆** had a wet well. Long, sharply raking mast stepped just over the forefoot. Boomed mainsail loose-footed. At times set a square course, topsail, and topgallant. Long, fixed rising bowsprit with 2 or more headsails. Reported lengths 18-23m; e.g., length on deck 20m, on keel 15m, beam 6.4m, hold depth 2.7m. Name variant: **Jamaica sloop**. Note also **Bermudian**.

2. About 1830, a leg-of-mutton **sloop** rig was adopted so successfully on the smaller local **schooners⋆** and gaff **sloops** that these **Bermuda sloops** became a popular racing **yacht⋆** in England until the late 19th century. In Bermuda, they both raced and worked. Mainsail loose-footed with an overhanging boom. Jib ran to a stay or set flying; jib topsail set to a jibboom. Stem either straight or clipper; counter stern; drag to keel. Reported lengths 7-12m; e.g., length 11.4m, beam 3.5m, draft 2m. Name variant: **Bermuda cutter**. Note also **Bermuda dinghy**.

3. The fishing **sloop** of the early part of the 20th century caught mostly rockfish and grouper. Rounded counter stern; half-decked, with wide side decks; live well. Very tall pole mast set a leg-of-mutton sail with a long boom. When engines installed, the drive shaft passed through the well. Crew of 2-3. Average length 9m.

Bermudian 1. Word applies loosely to Bermuda-built vessels of the 18th-19th centuries, particularly to the **Bermuda sloops⋆** and the **Bermuda schooners⋆**. Other recorded names: **bateau bermudien**, **bateau d'Amerique**, **Bermuda boat**, **Bermudiana**, **Bermudiano**, **bermudien**, **bot⋆**, **mudian**, **mugian**

2. 19th-century British Royal Navy term for a wet ship. The Bermuda-built naval **sloops⋆** and **schooners⋆** of the early 1800s were wet vessels due to their tall masts, heavy armament, and light displacement.

Bermudiana See **Bermudian**

Bermudian ketch See **ketch-2**

Bermudiano See **Bermudian**

Bermudian yawl See **yawl-2**

bermudien See **Bermudian**

Berner Schiff, **Berner Weidling** See **Weidling-3**

bero *Indonesia, SE:* Double-**outrigger canoe⋆** of Timor, Solor, Wetar, and Tanimbar Islands. Fishes and collects mother-of-pearl shells. Dugout with sides raised by a washstrake of wood or palm leaves, or planks deepen a shallow dugout hull, above which a narrow washstrake is fitted. At the bow, hull rounds up gradually, ending in a V-shaped decoration; stern rises more abruptly. Two outriggers, each consisting of 2 booms, one set over the other; long, sturdy floats, or 2 bamboo poles may comprise each float. A Timor **bero** without outriggers is a **bero liman**. Paddled; larger **canoes⋆** sailed. Tripod mast, stepped well forward, sets a rectangular sail of cloth or matting. Mast stayed aft. Reported lengths 6-8m. Other recorded names: **beira**, **beiro**, **bélo**, **bérok**, **prahu bérok**, **proa bero**. See also **roh**.

bérok See **bero**

béroko See **roko-2**

bero liman See **bero**

berrichon *France, central:* General term for boats that carried local industrial products on the Canal du Berry and adjacent waterways until the early 20th century. Best known are the **bé de cane★** and the **flûte du Berry★**. Flat bottom, straight sides, square stern, sharp or blunt bow. Twin rudders, or a midline rudder that could be folded in two. Narrowness made them unstable with a light cargo. Mainly horse-drawn; some later boats motorized. Lock dimensions limited length to 28m and beam to 2.6m. Other recorded names: **auvergnat, bateau berrichon, Berry, boîte à horloge, guenille, mille-(guenille), mon(t)luçon**

Berry See **berrichon**

Berwick sea salmon coble See **coble-4**

Besahn-Ewer, Besan-Ever See **Besan-Ewer**

Besan-Ewer *Germany, NW:* A 2-masted **Ewer★**; basically a **ketch★** rig. Developed in the mid-19th century and used as **coasters★** and **fishing boats★** on the lower Elbe and Weser Rivers, and in the Frisian Islands. Worked until mid-20th century. Flat-bottomed until ca. 1870, after which some had a keel, earning the name **Kiel-Ewer**. Carvel-planked; flat floors, sharp bilges. Wide raked transom; curved stem, some clipper-bowed. Decked, central hatch, cabin forward and aft; might have a deckhouse forward of the mizzenmast. Wet well on fishing vessels. Leeboards abandoned when keel added; centerboard substituted. Outboard rudder; black hull. Set loose-footed, boomed gaff sails; gaff topsails, 2-3 headsails. Reported lengths 14.6-29m; e.g., length 17.2m, beam 5.3m, depth 2m, draft 1.7m. Other recorded names: **Besahn-Ewer, Besan-Ever, Besooneeber, bezaanever, Blankeneser Besahnewer, Zweimastewer**. Note also **Giek-Ewer**.

Besankutter See **ketch**

Besanschute See **bezaanschuit**

besanyacht See **bezaanjacht**

besche See **baicha, bèche**

beş çifte See **kayık-2**

beş çifte piyade See **piyade**

bés de cane See **bé de cane**

besogne *France, N:* Large river vessel dating from the 17th century. Those used on the lower Seine and the Oise Rivers in the 1st half of the 19th century carried merchandise and heavy cargo, such as stone. Exaggerated sheer at the ends. Huge trapezoidal rudder continued well above the raking sternpost; long tiller extended over the house at the stern. Sharp overhanging bow; stern blunt. Flat bottom, longitudinally planked; turned up in flat surface to a point at the bow. Decked at bow and stern. Some had a short towing mast. The large decked **besognes** on the Canal Saint-Denis carried 500t and required 4 horses. Reported lengths 30-45m, beam 6-7m, draft 1.85-2m. Other recorded names: **bateau normand, chaland normand**. Note also **bachot-3**.

Besooneeber See **Besan-Ewer**

besquine *Mediterranean:* Three-masted fishing vessel and **coaster★**. Rounded stern. Mainmast a pole mast;

carried a bowsprit. Also rowed. Cap. ca. 40t. Further reference: **bisquine**.

best and best boat In a race between 2 groups, each team picks its fastest boat to participate. Usually applied to rowing races, formerly in England, now mainly in Australia and New Zealand. Name variant: **wager boat**. Note also **best and best punt, best boat, shell**.

best and best punt *England:* A class of racing **punts★** that, although not necessarily standard, were usually lighter and narrower than those in other **punt** classes. Only a few built since 1914, but interest is being revived. Characteristically had a chine piece for strengthening in addition to the usual knees and transverse treads. Completely double-ended, and punted from the center in either direction. Square ends sloped up from the flat bottom; oiled canvas deck at each end. Lengths to 10.46m, widths as little as 27cm, but generally ca. 40cm. Note also **punt-7**.

best boat *United Kingdom:* Initially, the best available boat for a sculling race; now usually an approved type for a particular race. **Best boats** used by professionals were sometimes called **wager boats** since wagers were placed by the backers. Most were semicircular in cross section; type of fin placed aft of the sculler. Sliding seat, oars outrigged. Reported lengths 7.6-9.7m, width 0.3m, depth 0.15m. Further name variant: **toothpick★**. Note also **shell**.

beta *Italy, NE:* In Venice the word may be used generically for a **barge★** or, more specifically, for one that dredges in the lagoons. Trap door in the bottom opens to empty the load into the sea. Note also **hopper, marie-salope**.

betala *Tanzania, Zanzibar:* A type of medium-sized **dhow★** that was typical of those built on the island. Narrow curved bow; square plumb stern; lofty poop; single vertical mast. Spelling variant: **betela**; **kiBatela, kibetala** (dims.)

bête See **bette**

betela See **batil-1, betala**

bethel ship See **church boat, gospel ship, mission smack**

betil, betili See **batil-1**

betillo See **battela-1**

betộtel See **batil-1**

betta *Italy:* **1.** At Ancona on the central Adriatic coast, a **barge★** or **lighter★**.
2. At Genoa on the northwest coast, the word is used pejoratively to describe an unseaworthy boat.
3. In the Italian navy, a vessel adapted to the transport of materiel and provisions.

bette *France, S:* **Dory★**-like boat of the lagoons of the Mediterranean coast; used for fishing, transportation, and recreation. Those used at sea, the **bettes marines**, are more sturdily constructed. Probably dates from the mid-19th century; only small examples survive. The large **bette de Martigues** is able to fish at sea as well as proceed under sail on the canal to Martigues. Raked, sharp ends; flat bottom athwartships, longitudinally planked, fore-and-aft rocker; broad plank keel; straight flaring sides; marked sheer, stern slightly higher than bow. Open, often with a short deck at each end; may have a locker beneath the stern bench.

Supplemental washstrakes have tumble home on larger boats; panels removable for rowing; one with no washstrakes generally called a **barquet*** (or **barquè**).

bette

Narrow rudder extends below the keel; can be set higher in shallow water; short tiller. Generally brightly painted. Short mast stepped in center thwart. Lateen mainsail bent to 1- or 2-piece yard. Small jib tacked to stemhead; those used for racing (**bette de course**) set a large boomed-out jib. Also rowed, with 3-4 pairs of oars worked against a tholepin. Workboats now motorized. Reported lengths 3-8.5m; typical: length overall 5.7m, on bottom 4.75m, beam 1.85m, depth 0.57m; shallow draft. The decked type, the **bette pontée**, is 8.5m long. Other recorded names: **bateau bête**, **bateau plat**, **beet**, **bête**, **bette martégale**, **bette provençale**, **betto**, **Marseille dory**. Further reading: Jules Vence, *Construction & Manœuvre des Bateaux & Embarcations à Voilure Latine* (Grenoble: Terre et Mer, 1982 [reprint of 1897 ed.]), 87-101. Further reference: **marie-salope**

bette à detritus See **bette à escarbilles**

bette à escarbilles *France:* Small **barge*** that cleared ports of refuse, especially ashes and garbage from anchored ships. Other recorded names: **bette à detritus**, **escarbilleur**. Note also **ash boat**, **marie-salope**.

bette de course, **bette de Martigues**, **bette marine**, **bette martégale**, **bette pontée**, **bette provençale** See **bette**

bettīl See **batil-1**

betto See **bette**

beugschip See **longliner-1**

beugsloep See **sloep-3**

beugvisser See **longliner-1**

beun See **kaar**

beunschepen See **beunschip**

beunschip *Belgium/Netherlands:* **1.** A **fishing boat*** with a live fish well (the *beun* or *bun*) that water enters through holes in the bottom. Ca. 16t. Other recorded names: **bunschip**, **bunschuit**; pl. **beunschepen**. Note also **sloep-3**, **waterschip**, **well boat**.

  2. A vessel designed to carry dredged sand, mud, stone, etc. Double hull. Discharges load by opening valves in the bottom. The cargo may be replaced by water. Usually towed (**beunsleepschip** or **sleep-beunschip**), but some now motorized.

3. Some early **beunschepen** transported sea water to salt evaporation ponds.

beunsleepschip See **beunschip-2**

beunsloep See **sloep-3**

beurtkaag See **kaag**

beurtman, **beurtscheepje**, **beurtschepen**, **Beurtschiff** See **beurtschip**

beurtschip *Belgium/Netherlands:* Generic term for a freight boat that made regular trips between designated inland points from the Middle Ages into the 20th century. One early type, the **marktschip** (**market boat***), transported produce and people on market days in the late 15th century. One carrying passengers was known as a **veerschip***. Through the years various types of vessels provided these services. In general, they were sturdy with a flat floor, bluff bow, and leeboards. Decked; generally had a forecastle and deckhouse; covered hold. Late 18th-century **beurtschepen** (pl.) on the Zuiderzee had space for a few 1st-class passengers, special sleeping areas for others, and as many as 130 traveled in the hold. Early boats sprit-rigged, with windlasses to manage the heavy sprit; later gaff- or **ketch***-rigged. Engines adopted by the 19th century. An early 17th-century vessel measured 18m long and 5.5m wide. Other recorded names: **bateau de messagerie** (or **de service**), **beurtman**, **beurtscheepje** (dim.), **beurtveer** (erroneously), **Brabantsch beurtschip** (or **gaffelaar**), **Lemmer beurtschip** (or **beurtman**). Note also **markschuit**. Further reference: **beurtschuit**

beurtschuit *Belgium:* Carried cargo on inland waterways of Flanders and Brabant until the 1st quarter of the 20th century. Some could accommodate a few passengers. Carvel-planked, with full lines; deep gunwale strake; slightly curved stem ended in a sharp point. Decked; long covered hold amidships; wide leeboards. Painted rudderhead rounded, with a knob on forward part; tiller slotted over rudder. Most carried 3 gaily painted barrels at the stern. Mast stepped in a tabernacle well forward. Set a loose-footed, boomed gaff sail with a short curved gaff, staysail, and sometimes a jib. Crew of 1-2. Reported lengths 14-17m, width 5m, depths 1.5-1.8m. Other recorded names: **beurtschip***, **Vlaamse beurtschuit**. Note also **Brabantse schuit**.

beurtsnik See **snik-3**

beurtsomp *Netherlands, NE:* 19th-century vessel that regularly carried wood, tiles, and peat on the inland waterways. Ends rounded, bottom flat, sides curved with tumble home at topsides; slight sheer with wales curving up at the stem, elsewhere following the sheer line. Decked, cuddy forward, covered hatch bordered by side decks; steering deck, then raised deck with cabin below. Medium width leeboards. Mast could be struck. Set a gaff sail with a short gaff. Reported lengths 15.5-16.7m; e.g., length 16.7m, beam 3.4m, depth 1.7m; shallow draft. Other recorded names: **Rangschiff**; pl. **beurtsompen**. Note also **somp**.

beurtsompen See **beurtsomp**

beurtveer See **beurtschip**

bevaia See **lakatoi**

Beverley keel See **Humber keel**

bezaan See **bezaanschuit**

bezaanever See **Besan-Ewer**

bezaanjacht *Netherlands:* Luxurious pleasure craft from the 17th into the 19th century. Rigged with a loose-footed, boomed gaff mainsail; long gaff; forestaysail; jib to a detachable jibboom. Some set a square topsail and stepped a small mizzenmast. Carvel-built; bluff bow; decorative flat stern with 2 large windows at the sides. Foredeck; open abaft the mast. Wide leeboards. Ca. 35t burden, shallow draft. Other recorded names: **besanyacht, bezaan yacht; bezan(t)** (incorrectly); pl. **bezanen, bizan**. Note also **jacht-3**.

bezaanschuit *Netherlands, S:* Beamy boat of the southwestern islands. Used in the 2nd half of the 18th and the 19th centuries, especially for line fishing for plaice (*schol*). Characterized by its boomed, loose-footed gaff rig, supplemented by jib and staysail. Strong carvel-planked vessel; marked sheer; curved plumb stem; straight, slightly raked sternpost; bluff bow; full buttocks; flat floors; keel; rounded bilges. Flush deck; fish well abaft the mast, surrounded by 4 hatches; standing room for helmsman; capstan forward of the cockpit. Slender leeboards; tall-headed outboard rudder; 3 tiny barrels painted on the head. On the larger boats, the tiller passed through the wide top strake.

bezaanschuit

Crew of 5. Reported lengths 10-12m. Other recorded names: **Besanschute, bezaan,** pl. **bezanen; bezanschuit, schollenschute, scholschuit, scholschuyte.** Note also **pink, schuit.**

bezaan yacht See **bezaanjacht**

bezaisen See **sengoku bune**

bezan See **bezaanjacht**

bezanen See **bezaanjacht, bezaanschuit**

bezanschuit See **bezaanschuit**

bezant See **bezaanjacht**

bhagla See **baghla-1**

bhala See **bhelā**

bhaolia See **baūlīa**

bhar, bhara See **bhur**

bharakas See **barakas**

bhart *Pakistan, SE:* Local trader and, at times, a **fishing boat***, especially in the Indus Delta and Karachi area. Double-ended, strong sheer, deep hull, strong rise to the floors, high stemhead. Movable sideboards installed when carrying high deck cargo. Tall rudderhead; tiller slopes downward, frequently painted in white bands. Well-maintained, often with decorated stem and sternpost and patterns along sheer line. Lateen sails set to main- and mizzenmasts.

bhata See **bàta**

bhaulea, bhauleah, bháulía, bhauliya See **baūlīa**

bheddi See **bedi, bhedi**

bhedi *Bangladesh:* **Panshi*** type on the lower Ganges River. Carries produce and sand; when carrying pottery, open lath structures extend out each side. Heavy, raked block stem extends well above the top strake; sternpost higher. Propelled by 3-6 oarsmen; often towed. Steered with a long sweep. Reported lengths 5.5-9m, some much larger, widths 1.5-2.4m, depths 0.9-1.2m. Spelling variants: **baddi, bheddi**. Note also **bedi**.

bhel See **bhelā**

bhelā *Bangladesh/India, NE:* **Raft*** of bundles of banana or plantain stems, shola or bans sticks, or light

bhelā

wood. Used for ferrying and for cast or drag net and line fishing. The **plantain raft (kalār bhelā)** comprises 4-5 stems skewered together with bamboo and lashed transversely on top and bottom. The **shola raft (shola bhelā)** is constructed with 3-4 bundles of sticks tied at intervals and secured on top and bottom with athwartships sticks. About 1.22-2.74m long and 0.91-1.22m wide. Local name variants: **bhala, bhel, bhe(u)ra, bhewra, chali, dongá*, dongi**

bhera See **bhelā**

bhesal dingi See **dingi-2**

bheura, bhewra See **bhelā**

bhim *India, NE:* Small **lighter*** that aided in loading and unloading cargo for seagoing ships anchored off Calcutta in the early 19th century. Note also **bhimā, bhur**.

bhim *India, W:* One of a class of ordinary ships of the early Hindu period. Not very seaworthy and, consequently, considered a bad luck vessel. Length ca. 20m; length-to-beam-to-depth 2:1:1. Note also **bhim**.

bhir See **bhur**

bholiah See **baūlīa**

bhoot See **bot-4**

bhooti See **buti-1b**

bhōt See **bot-4**

bhouliya See **baūlīa**

bhūm See **boom-1**

bhur 1. *Bangladesh/India, NE:* Cargo **lighter*** of the Ganges Delta area; transported jute, timber, coal, stone. Participated in river naval operations in the mid-17th century. Low, blunt bluff bow; elevated stern; sides parallel for most of length. Small cabin at stern; waist open or covered with thatching; high cargoes contained by a bamboo framework along the sides. Helmsman worked from a platform, manning a huge triangular balanced rudder at the port quarter; rotated

around a vertical axis by a tiller. Rowed from atop the cargo using long sweeps with small round blades. Set a large square mainsail and sometimes a topsail to a mast of 2 pieces spliced together. Often tracked upstream from shore by a rope to the masthead. Length-to-beam ratio 3:1; cap. 20-100t. Spelling variants: **bhar, bharra, bhir, b·hur, boeri, boora, borae, borr, bouri(e), Buri**. Note also **bhim, bouri de nage**.
2. *India, NE:* In Assam, may refer to a **raft★** of wood or bamboo.

biabina See **binabina**

biade See **piyade**

Biancella See **bilancella**

bian zi *China, central:* A class of cargo **junks★**, mainly of the waterways of Hunan, Jiangxi (Kiangsi), and Hubei (Hupeh) Provinces and the middle Chang Jiang (Yangtze) from Yichang (I-Chang) to Wuhan. Carried produce, cotton cloth, charcoal, paper, stone. Some old boats might be coupled side-by-side to carry long reeds for fuel, blinds, and mats. Sheer swept up at stern; ends cut square and, in the case of the **tuo bian zi** of Yichang, a heavy beam was built into the bow.

bian zi

Heavy wales along the sides. Hull divided into watertight compartments. Mat- or wooden-roofed houses covered the midship and after decks. Tall mainmast stepped amidships; shorter foremast, raked slightly forward, stepped in the bow. Set rectangular lugsails. Also poled, and some towed by a steam launch. Crew of ca. 6. Reported lengths 12.2-19.8m, widths 2-3.7m, depths 1-1.37m; shallow draft. Other recorded names: **bamboo-carrying pole junk, flat boat★, Hsiang-yang pien tzŭ, pien-tan, pien-tzŭ, Xiang-yang bian zi, t'o-pien tzŭ**

bidaar See **bedar, bidar-2, bidar-3**

bidai-ontzi See **mail boat-1**

bidar 1. *Brunei/East Malaysia:* Small general-purpose boat of the Brunei Bay area. One type, the **perau' bidar**, is used for racing. Planked-up sides on dugout base; sharp "V" in cross section; double-ended. Lightly constructed house often runs full-length, especially when used as a family boat. At sea, a light spritsail set. Stern or quarter rudder used when sailing; when paddled, a paddle serves as a rudder.
2. *Indonesia, W, Riau Archipelago:* **Bidar** may describe 3 types of craft used in these islands off the east coast of Sumatra. One was an interisland 2-masted boat of local viceroys (the **bidar kadjang serong**). Awning

covered part of the hull. Employed 20-30 rowers; set square mat sails; reported lengths 9-14m, widths 1.8-3.7m, depths 1-2.13m. A 2nd type was a small **fishing boat★** that used cast nets or shore seines. A 3rd was a single-masted, decked, seagoing craft with a clipper bow and square galleries aft. Spelling variant: **bidaar**
3. *Indonesia, W:* At Palembang and elsewhere in southern Sumatra, the **bidar** conveyed local colonial personages; less elaborate types transferred passengers to and from ships, and some made coastal journeys (the

bidar-3

reis-bidar). Dugout hull, raised by a single strake along each side. Forward end projected over the water, ending in a blunt raked bow. On some, the stern swept up sharply, and had 2 extensions resembling a swallow's tail. Decked throughout; stern area decked for the helmsman, or he might stand on a crossbeam to work the quarter rudder. Most of hull covered by a saddle-shaped board and palm-leaf roof; on some, only a simple awning covered the after end (the **tent-bidar**); others had an enclosed house. Thwarts for paddlers forward. Triangular-bladed paddle. Smaller types 3.7-7.6m long; larger to ca. 12.2m; widths roughly 1.2-1.8m. Other recorded names: **beda★, bidaar, prāhu bīdar, sampan bidar**
4. *Indonesia, central:* Plank-extended **dugout canoe★** employed on large rivers on the west coast of Kalimantan (Borneo). Separate stem pieces, flattened bottom. Decked; generally a house covers most of the hull. Paddled; leaf-shaped blades, crossbar grip. Reported lengths 15-18m, narrow. Name variant: **sampan bidar**
Further references: **baidara, bedar**

bidara See **baidara**

bidarka See **kayak-9**

bidar kadjang serong See **bidar-2**

bidarkee, bidarki, bidarky See **kayak-9**

bidarra, bidarrah See **baidara**

Bideford polacca, Bideford polacker See **polacca**

Bideford sand barge See **gravel barge**

bidu' See **bilo'**

biel biel See **kaloa**

Biesboschaak See **griendaak**

Biesbosschuitje *Netherlands, SW:* Small open **fishing boat★** from the Biesbosch area, southeast of Rotterdam. Clinker-built with wide planks; sharp ends; strongly raked stem; lightly raked sternpost; flat floors. Wet well; tent rigged up forward to protect the crew; leeboards. Outboard rudder with wide blade below the waterline; tiller slotted over rudderhead. Reported lengths 6-9m, widths 2-3m.

bi fa zi *China, N:* **Raft★** of inflated skins that ran tributaries of the Huang He (Hwang Ho or Yellow River) and parts of the river itself during spring and fall. Smaller **rafts** generally of 9-15 goat or sheep skins, but might be combined to form **rafts** of as many as

800 skins. Small rafts still served as local transportation in the 1990s. Cured skins (the section from forward of the hind legs to the neck) are tied, legs up, to poles which, in turn, are lashed to crosspieces to form a raft. Some **rafts** were made from 125-150 yak or bullock skins stuffed with much of the cargo, generally with wool, then tied together with a platform set on top. At its destination, the **raft** components and cargo were sold; or just the cargo and poles were sold, the dried skins carried back to their starting point; for small **rafts**, the poles and skins were packed together and shouldered home. Generally controlled by bow and stern sweeps. Small **rafts** ca. 3m long by 1.8m wide; large **rafts** ca. 23m by 15m. Other recorded names: **ch'i-fa, fa tzǔ, phi-fa tzǔ, pi-fa (-tzǔ), sheepskin raft**

biǧâl See **baghla-1**

bigalet See **bugalet**

big bird boat See **green eyebrow**

big boat See **Galway hooker, Hastings lugger, lang boomer, longboat-7, seine boat-5a, storbåt-2**

big canoe See **West Coast canoe**

big coble See **coble-1a, coble-1b**

bigi See **bag**

big mizzener See **dandy**

big punt See **motor boat-2**

big red boat, big red-headed oceangoing boat See **da hong chuan**

big-river canoe *Canada, E:* Birchbark **canoe*** of the Micmac of the Gaspé Peninsula and parts of the Maritime Provinces. Light, well-constructed **canoe** with sharp torpedo lines; circular bow and stern profile, with no break in the sheer line; sheer nearly straight or slightly hogged; strong tumble home; slightly rounded bottom athwartships. No framework at ends, stiffness created by battens placed inside the bark; ends stuffed with moss and shavings. Light gunwale; headboards provided tension for the bark cover. Five to 7 thwarts, thin ribs and sheathing. Hogging achieved by treating the gunwales with boiling water before assembly and staking them out to dry in desired sheer curves. Bark gores laced without overlap. Lengths generally 4.57-6.1m; e.g., length 5.49m, beam 0.94m, depth 0.33m. Name variant: **Micmac big-river canoe**

big salmon boat See **drontheim**

big skiff See **skiff-3**

big sloop See **Brixham smack**

bijboot, bijboten See **ship's boat, tender**

bijlander *Belgium/France:* Box-shaped inland **barge*** that plied canals and rivers of Flanders and northern France (where it was called a **bélandre**) into the 20th century. Flat bottom, sharp chines; straight sides, straight, raking stem, raked square ends, rounded forefoot; vertical sternpost; light sheer. Distinctive rub strakes formed a continuous horizontal line across the bow and stern. Originally built of wood, later of iron or steel. Short foredeck with single bitt behind the stempost; cambered hatch covers; decked at stern. Early vessels had leeboards; broad trapezoidal rudder could be raised in confined spaces. Strikable mast stepped about a third in from the bow; **cutter***- or **sloop***-rigged. Towed by horses when not sailing. Crew of 3. Reported lengths 28-34m, widths 4.6-5m.

Other recorded names: **belander, billander, binlander, binne(n)lander, binnelandries, bylander; dubbel** (and **halve**) **binlander**. Seagoing vessels called **zeebijlander**. Further references: **bilander-1, waal**

bik See **pink-2**

bilancella *Italy, W:* A poorly defined term, but usually describes a **fishing boat*** or small **coaster***. Mainly from the Naples area, but found all along the west coast and at Sicily and Sardinia. The **fishing boat** works with a type of drag net, often in pairs and, in this connection, closely resembles the **paranza***. Sharp ends, tall stemhead or concave stem, terminating below bowsprit (Sardinia); ends slightly raked; flat floors; moderate sheer. Decked, but waist often open. Most set a quadrilateral lateen-type sail with a short luff or lateen sail to a forward-raking mast. Flying jib to a long rising bowsprit. Also rowed, employing as many as 10 oars to a side. Reported lengths 8-20m; e.g., length 17m, beam 4.55m, depth 1.5m. Other recorded names: **balancella, balanselle, Biancella, bilancella peschereccia, bilancelo, rivano-bilancella**; pl. **balancelle***, **bilancelle**; **laccone** (on Elba). Note also **balancela**.

bilancella da pesca See **paranza**

bilancella peschereccia, bilancelle, bilancelo See **bilancella**

bilander **1.** *Belgium/France/Netherlands/United Kingdom:* Reported as both a small **coaster*** and an inland craft; early references to **binlanders** (see **bijlander**) date from the Middle Ages, but cited most frequently during the 18th and 19th centuries. English **bilanders** carried passengers to America in the 1st half of the 18th century. Carvel-planked. **Coasters** mainly 2-masted, with square sails on the foremast and a lateen-type sail on the mainmast, above which were 1-2 square topsails; some employed leeboards. Inland vessels were flat-bottomed, single-masted, and **sloop***- or lug-rigged; to ca. 24t. Other recorded names: **Balander, balandra***, **balandre, bel(l)ande, belander, belandra, bélandre, bijlander***, **bilandre, billander, billender, hukare***, **salanda; palandra*** (erroneously). One of small size called a **belandra pequena, demi-bélandre**, or **demy bellandre**.

2. *United States, NE:* Also built in New England in the early 18th century, serving the colonists as codfishing boats off Newfoundland and as cargo vessels. Bluff bow; counter stern; raised quarter-deck, windows on the quarter. Stepped a main- and foremast, the latter carrying square sails, the mainmast an inclined lugsail with a long yard set fore-and-aft, above which was a square topsail. Length ca. 23m.

bilandre See **bilander-1**

bilge board scow See **scow-11b**

bilibili **1.** *Fiji, central Pacific:* Bamboo **raft*** used mainly on rivers of the principal islands. Makes a one-way trip downstream, carrying passengers and local products, especially bananas. Style varies with the locale and function, some requiring greater freeboard and a protective thatched hut. Bamboo poles arranged so that the narrower ends lie at the bow, creating a wedge-shaped craft. Bow lashed with vines; transverse pieces secure the poles at widely spaced intervals.

Sides raised by bundles of poles; on some, a 2nd layer of poles serves as a light deck. Punted, generally by 2 men. Reported lengths 5.5-9.5m. A large seagoing **raft**, able to ferry 5-6t, was used at one time. These had a 2-story hut and might transport 20-30 people. Name variant: **waqa bilibili**

2. *Vanuatu (New Hebrides), western Pacific:* Single-**outrigger canoe**★ of Espiritu Santo Island. Wide dugout hull, slightly oval in cross section. Ends elongated, shelf-like; may be serrated or decorated in some manner. Early boats had washstrakes amidships. Three outrigger booms cross the hull and extend to the float, which is club-shaped with the narrow end forward; under-crossed sticks connect float and booms. Movable platform of broad planks lashed atop the gunwales, secured by gunwale poles. Seats forward and abaft the platform. Paddled, 2 abreast.

billander See **bijlander**, **bilander-1**

billender See **bilander-1**

billieboat *West Indies, SE:* Popular **whaleboat**★-type of **fishing boat**★ of St. Vincent, Grenada, and the Grenadines. Strongly built double-ender. Rowed or sailed. Length overall 4m, on keel 2.7m. Note also **billyboy**.

bill raft See **timber raft-2a**

billuga *France, Corsica:* **Fishing boat**★ of the southwest coast, used mainly by the local Napolitans. Sharp, slender bow; cutwater often sculpted. Mast stepped amidships; lateen mainsail, jib. Some motorized. Other recorded names: **felouque**★, **villuga**. Note also **felouque corse**.

billyboat See **billyboy**

billyboy *England, E and S:* Boxy **coaster**★ that worked from the 18th to the early 20th century, operating well inland or off the beaches if necessary. Mainly built in Yorkshire (**Yorkshire billyboy**), but some built as far south as Essex. The term has been applied mostly to **ketch**★-rigged **coasters**, but the true **billyboy** set a

billyboy

gaff sail with 1-2 headsails. Double-ended with full bow and stern; relatively fine run; ends plumb, the stem slightly curved, some clipper-bowed. Flat floors enabled vessel to dry out; long straight keel; slab-sided; rounded bilges; considerable sheer, especially on early vessels; high bulwarks. Early wooden vessels clinker-built, usually carvel later, then iron or steel; some appear to have had upper strakes lapped, carvel below. Cabin forward of the binnacle, 2-3 hatches, forecastle. Narrow outboard rudder; rudderhead cut

off short, the curved tiller piercing the taffrail; some used a wheel. Most had leeboards; later vessels raised and lowered leeboards and halyards by crab winches forward of the masts (Westcountrymen called this vessel a **crab wincher**). Bulwarks painted black, with a white riband; hull tarred black, except for varnished strake. Rigged as **sloops**★ of the period until the beginning of the 19th century, setting at times 4 headsails, gaff and square topsail, and topgallant in addition to the loose-footed boomed gaff mainsail. **Ketches**★ gradually supplanted the single-masted vessels, sometimes setting a square or jib-headed topsail and topgallants; a **ketch**-rigged vessel was called a **dickie**, the dickie being the forward-raking mizzenmast. Some rigged as **topsail schooners** (**billyboy** or **jackass schooners**). Masts stepped in tabernacles on those making inland trips, for lowering at bridges. Bowsprit steeved up sharply. Often operated by a family; those with long booms required 4 men and a boy; **ketches** used 2-3 men and a boy. Reported lengths 17-28m; e.g., length 19.2m, beam 4.88m, depth 2.6m. Other recorded names: **bélebois**, **bélibois**, **billyboat**. Note also **billieboat**.

billyboy schooner See **billyboy**

bilo' *Indonesia, W:* Large sailing vessel of Simeulue (Simalur) Island off northwestern Sumatra; carries copra, rattan, and coconuts locally. Usually decked at bow and stern, with a house of matting and bamboo aft. Sets 1-2 sails. Spelling variants: **bidu'**, **biloe'**, **bilu'**; **bilō** (Salang and Sigulè Islands). See also **bilus**.

biloe' See **bilo'**

biloengkang See **belongkang**

bilolang *Indonesia, central:* Double-**outrigger canoe**★ used by the Bugis and Makassarese peoples of southwestern Sulawesi (Celebes) for fishing, trading, and racing; term may also merely designate an **outrigger canoe**. Dugout with a flattened bottom; straight, blunt end pieces. Two booms connect with long floats; at the end of each boom, a hockey stick-shaped piece is lashed on, the longer end angling down to the float; longitudinal stringers across the booms provide strengthening. Floats set ca. 3.2m out from the hull, the forward ends toeing out slightly. Trading boats have a shelter built out on the booms. Very tall mast stepped about a third in from the bow; movable stays run to the after booms, fixed stays to the forward booms. Sets a triangular or elongated rectangular sail. When racing, the crew may serve as live ballast, standing on a special stringer attached to the outrigger component, holding ropes from the mast. **Fishing boats**★ also rowed. One racing **canoe** reported as 8.7m long, 0.56m wide, and 0.79m deep. Other recorded names: **balolang**, **todi-todi**. Note also **birowang**.

bilos See **bilus**

bilu' See **bilo'**

bilus *Philippines, central:* Fast double-**outrigger canoe**★ used for interisland transport, trading, and tending fish corrals, especially on the islands of Panay and Negros. Dugout hull raised by 1-2 strakes; ends raked, bow sharp, stern cut square. Sometimes bark used for washstrakes. Three equally spaced booms connect directly with the long, sturdy floats. Steered with a quarter rudder. Rowed or sailed. Set a type of spritsail that is essentially triangular; boomed at the foot; sprit, held by sling at the mast, extends the upper side. Sail rove through a hole in the masthead or through a suspended block. Jib to stemhead. Length to ca. 16m. Spelling variants: **bilo(s)**

bimbá *Angola, W:* **Raft★** used along the central coast to ferry people and cattle across shallow rivers and for fishing offshore and inshore. Composed of slender strips of bimba wood lashed, pegged, and weighted

bimbá

so that the bow end curves up markedly. Some square-ended, others sharp-bowed. May be concave athwartships, with the outside poles forming gunwales that extend beyond the stern; type of shoe keel in forward part onto which a small stem is socketed. Some at Novo Redondo are so deeply concave that the open end is almost a half circle. The square-ended **tchimbala** has a framework set onto the **raft** to provide a bench for rowing. Poled and rowed; those used for fishing step a bamboo mast through a thwart, setting a spritsail. Lobita area boat length 1.5m, width 0.75m. Spelling variant: **mbimba**. Further reading: Luis Taveira, "Bimbá," *Geographica* (Lisbon), 1/3 and 4 (1965), 87-106, 63-82; 2/2 and 3 (1966), 47-66, 38-56.

binabaeng parao See **parao-3**

binabina *Solomon Islands, western Pacific:* Type of plank-extended paddling **canoe★** that ranges from a 1-person **canoe** to one capable of holding 50 paddlers. Found mainly on Santa Isabel, Guadalcanal, and Florida Islands. Identified by their high curved stern, low bow, and washstrakes that extend for only a short distance in from the bow. Four strakes raise each side above the keel piece; residual ridges on the inside of each strake serve for strengthening; ribs are lashed through holes in these ridges. Sharp ends; steep rise to the floors. Bottom rocker rounds up to the tall, curved stern piece; bow rises more gradually in a straight line, terminating at an oblique, inward-raking angle. Washstrakes have a concave sheer line, ending in a vertical break; flare out slightly. Open; 5-6 thwarts rest on stringers. Hull stained black; may be plain or elegantly decorated with mother of pearl. Paddles have lanceolate blades and shovel-headed grip; paddlers sit 2 abreast on the larger **canoes**. Occasionally sailed, the mast lashed to the forward thwart. Reported lengths 4.6-18.2m; e.g., length 6.7m, beam 0.7m, height at stern 1.14m. Other recorded names: **biabina**, **mbinambina**, **na binabina**. Note also **roko-2**.

bindal, bindaling, bindall See **bindalsbåt**

bindalsbåt *Norway, N:* General term given to a category of **nordlandsbåt** built in the important boatbuilding center of Bindalen. The boats are lightly built with sharp entrance and run; easily rowed. Best-known are the 4-oared **færing★** (**bindalsfæring**) and the 6-oared **fembøring★** (**bindalsfembøring**). Other recorded names: **bindal(l)**, **bindaling**

bindalsfæring, bindalsfembøring See **bindalsbåt**

bing xian chuan See **Chênhai chuan**

biniday See **barangay**

bink See **pink-2**

binlander, binnelander, binnelandries See **bijlander**

Binnenbulle See **Eiderschnigge**

Binnenfahrer See **Mutte**

Binnenfahrzeug See **riverboat**

binnenlander See **bijlander**

binnenmot, Binnenmotte, Binnenmutte See **Mutte**

binnenpleit See **pleit-1, pleit-3**

Binnenschiff, binnenschip See **riverboat**

Binnenschlup See **Schlup-2**

binnentjalk See **tjalk-2, tjalk-3**

binnenvaartuig See **riverboat**

Binsen-Floss See **caballito, reed boat**

binta *Indonesia, central:* Pirate craft of the Bugis peoples of southwest Sulawesi (Celebes) Island. Prominent in the early 19th century, when the Bugis used their rowing prowess to overtake becalmed ships. Oarsmen worked from decks that projected from each side of the hull; one group of oarsmen sat, working oars against a forked post, a 2nd group stood, working their oars from atop a rail laid onto the outer fork of the posts. Upper oars had rectangular blades; the lower, long, narrow blades; both types had an enlarged loom at the inboard end. Plank-built, deep hull; heavy beams athwartships supported the overhanging deck; bottom had rocker; bow curved up smoothly from the bottom, raking forward; sharp stern, but planking ran aft as an extension to the sides, creating a gallery. Heavy bulkhead forward protected the pirates; 1-2 cannon. Two houses, one amidships, the other aft, or one large house extending over the after two-thirds of the hull. Quarter rudders, worked from within the gallery. Two bipod masts, the forward mast taller. Set boomed, oblong lugsails; luff crescentic. One or 2 headsails to a long spar. Crew of 25-30. Other recorded names: **bintak★**, **perahu binta**. Further reading: C. Nooteboom, "Diremen in den Indischen Archipel," *Cultureel Indie* I (1939), 347-51. See also **vinta**.

bintak *Malaysia/Philippines, S:* A type of pirate ship. Those in the Sulu Sea area had 2 rows of oars on each side, one above the other, with 12 oars to each row. Name variant: **perahu bintak**. See also **binta**.

bintas See **vinta**

birchbark, birch canoe, birch rinde cannoe See **bark boat**

bird caique See **saltanat kayığı**

birgende See **brigantine**

bir juftah See **kayık-2**

Birkenrindenboot See **bark boat**

birkindi, birkinti See **brigantine**

biroang, birorang See **birowang**

birowah *Indonesia, central:* An **outrigger canoe⋆** in the Kambang dialect of Kangean Island, east of Madura. Very long outrigger booms. Deep hull, beam ca. 90cm. Note also **birowang**.

birowang *Indonesia, central:* One of the double-**outrigger canoes⋆** of the Buginese and Makassarese of southern Sulawesi (Celebes). Flat bottom with rocker; straight, raking, heavy stem and sternpost. Dugout hull with flattened sides. Framework of booms and stringers extends out each side, with 2 booms terminating in curved pieces that connect directly with the slender floats; floats flare outward at the bow ends. Steered with a quarter rudder braced against a Y-shaped crossbeam. Tripod mast; 2 legs, stepped athwartships on an inboard part of the outrigger framework, can pivot aft. Third leg, stepped near the bow, steadies the other legs and holds the foot of the sail boom. Masthead hooked. Sail a wide, tilted rectangle; tacked to forward boom, sheeted to after boom. Slender hull. Spelling variants: **biroang**, **birorang**. Note also **bilolang**, **birowah**.

bir tchiftè See **kayık-2**

biscaïen, **biscaïenne**, **biscaïn**, **biscaïne**, **biscaisk båd**, **Biscayan** See **biscayenne**

Biscayan boat See **trincadura**

Biscayan shallop, **Biscayaslup**, **Biscayen**, **Biscayen boat** See **biscayenne**

biscayenne *France, SW:* Basque boat used along the French coast, but mainly in the southern part of the Bay of Biscay to fish for mackerel and sardines and for lightering. Dated from at least the 16th century; only replicas remain. Narrow sharp ends; straight keel. Early boats open; later decked. Outboard rudder; tiller. Set 2 quadrilateral lugsails; mainsail twice the size of the foresail. Foremast stepped in the eyes, sometimes raking forward; mainmast amidships. Also rowed with 3-6 pairs of oars. Reported lengths 13.3-13.76m, beam ca. 3m. Other recorded names: **biscaïen(ne)**, **biscaïn(ne)**, **biscaisk båd**, **Biscayan (shallop)**, **Biscayaslup**, **Biscayen (boat)**, **Biskaaise sloep**, **biskajski**, **byscayenne**, **chaloupe biscayenne**, **trincadour(e)**, **txalupa**. Note also **trincadura**. Further references: **bisquine**, **whaler-2**

Biscayne Bay sharpie See **sharpie-5**

Biskaaise sloep, **biskajski** See **biscayenne**

bisquine *France, N:* Best-known is the 3-masted **lugger⋆** of the Normandy and eastern Brittany coasts, especially from Cancale, Granville, Saint-Vaast, Saint-Malo, and Trouville. The term, however, may designate several boat types similarly rigged. Some worked out of the British Channel Islands. Used for fishing and oyster dredging and, at times, as an **advice boat⋆** or a **pilot boat⋆**. Larger versions served as **coasters⋆**. Often transported the catch to market from a **fishing boat⋆** working on the grounds. Term used since the 18th century; boat rare after World War II. Carvel-planked, with a fine run; moderate sheer, high freeboard forward. Short straight keel with deep drag; steep floors; early boats had marked tumble home and less fine run. Stem straight and vertical. Originally, sternpost straight and raked and stern square or rounded; long, narrow counter adopted at the end of the 19th

century. Small boats open; larger decked; small cabin aft, storage area forward, fish hold amidships. Large **bisquines** carried a **doris⋆** and 2 **canots de ligne** of ca. 5m on board. Boomless standing lugsails and topsails set from 2 very tall pole masts; when racing, also set topgallants. Later boats had a mizzenmast, also with a standing lug and a topsail. Foremast stepped in the eyes, mainmast about amidships, both raking aft but at different angles; largely unstayed, being supported by whip and runner tackle. On one mast, yards hung abaft the mast; on the other, forward of the mast. Full-cut deep jib to a long bowsprit. Auxiliaries on most later boats. Crew on fishing boats 5-7, plus captain and a boy; those dredging oysters had a crew of 11-12. Early boats ca. 6.7-8.6m long, later 12-25m; e.g., length overall 12m, on keel 8.75m, beam 3.3m, depth aft 2.88m; draft aft 2.5m. Other recorded names: **basquine**, **besquine⋆**, **biscayenne⋆**, **bisquine de Granville** (**Cotentin**, **de Barfleur**, and **de Cancale**), **Cancale bisquine**, **Granville bisquine**; **bayoux** (small **bisquines**). Further reading: Jean Le Bot, *La Bisquine de Cancale et de Granville* (Grenoble: Éditions des 4-Seigneurs, 1979); Denis-Michel Boell, *Les Bisquines, Chalutiers et Ligneurs de Granville et Cancale* (Douarnenez: Chasse-Marée, 1989); François Renault, *Bateaux de Normandie* (Rennes: Éditions de l'Estran, 1984). Note also **chalutier**.

bisquine de Cancale, **bisquine Cotentin**, **bisquine de Barfleur**, **bisquine de Granville** See **bisquine**

bittīl See **batil-1**

bitumen carrier See **tanker**

bizan See **bezaanjacht**

black boat *England, central:* **Narrow boat⋆** that carries tar on the Midlands canal network. Term refers to black sides on its small cabin as well as to its cargo. Other recorded names: **day tar boat**, **tar boat⋆**. Further reference: **tarrāda**

Black Country day boat See **day boat-2**

black cutter *England, SW:* The service **cutters⋆** used by Dartmouth naval cadets on the River Dart.

black eyebrow See **green eyebrow**

black flat See **packet**

black nancy See **nancy**

black-sailed trader See **Norfolk wherry**

Blackwater bawley See **bawley**

Blackwater punt See **gun punt**

Blackwater watch boat See **watch boat**

blaes See **blazer**

blanenca See **balancela**

Blankeboetje, **Blankenberg barge**, **Blankenbergsche schuit** See **Blankenbergse schuit**

Blankenbergse schuit *Belgium, SW:* Strongly built lug-rigged boat depicted as early as 1460; fished since the 18th century for herring and cod, working from the sandy beach at Blankenberge out into the North Sea; last one sailed until 1904. Clinker-built with broad strakes, the top strake very wide amidships. Heavy, flat bottom, mostly carvel-planked; rounded bilges. Full bow with curved, raked stem; narrower rounded stern; straight, raked sternpost. Strong sheer toward the bow; maximum beam well forward, wall-sided. Outboard rudder that extended well below keel was taken aboard when beaching. Heavy, wide, deep lee-boards. Most half-decked, with windlass; accommodations forward; open waist; side decks. Foremast stepped against the stem and lashed to the stemhead. Heavy mainmast stepped through a strong thwart amidships. Forward lugsail almost square, with shorter luff; boomed out with a spar. Tall lug mainsail loose-footed and boomed. Masts could be struck. Crew of 5. Dimension range: length 10m, beam 4m, depth ca. 2m to 11.8m by 5.05m by 2m; draft ca. 0.2m. Cap. 15-21t. Later boats fully decked and **cutter**★-rigged; many transferred their home port to neighboring Heist (now Zeebrugge). Other recorded names: **Blankeboetje, Blankenberg barge, Blankenbergsche schuit, Blanken-boet(je), Blankenburg brig** (erroneously), **scute de Blankenberge, scutte de Blankenberghe.** Note also **Heistse schuit.**

Blankenboet, Blankenboetje, Blankenburg brig See **Blankenbergse schuit**

Blankeneser Besahnewer See **Besan-Ewer**

Blankeneser Ewer See **Ewer, Pfahl-Ewer**

Blankeneser Pfahl-Ewer See **Pfahl-Ewer**

Blasket Island curragh See **naomóg-2**

Blätte See **Plätte-1**

blazer *Belgium/Netherlands, W and N:* Heavily built **fishing boat**★ developed in the 19th century, sailing off the coasts and the Scheldt River. Also used as a **coaster**★, **lighter**★, and for rescue work. Initially clink-er-built, then carvel. Flat floors; angular chines; straight keel. Bluff bows, curved stem ending in a point; full stern; straight, raking sternpost. Low sheer; wide bulwark, increased by a washboard. Decked over forward cuddy; waist; live fish well. Crew of 2-3. Narrow leeboards; outboard rudder; tiller slotted over rudderhead. Unstayed mast, setting loose-footed gaff mainsail; staysail; jib to bowsprit. Large boats **ketch**★-rigged. Reported lengths 13.7m; e.g. length 13.7m, beam 4.1m, depth 1.7m. Other recorded names: **blaes, blazerschuit**

blazerschuit See **blazer**

Blekingeeka, Blekinger Kahn See **blekingseka**

blekingseka *Sweden, S:* General term for a small **fish-ing boat**★ that operates out of the south coast province of Blekinge. Good sailer. Clinker-built of wide oak (*ek*) strakes, with few or no frames. Full bow on early types; sharper more recently; beamy, tapering toward the stern; curved stem, cutaway forefoot; shallow, raked transom, strongly raked sternpost. Deep T-shaped keel, with drag; flat floors amidships; curving flared sides; moderate sheer. Narrow rudder; curved tiller; some used a centerboard. Older boats open, later decked. Smaller types step a light mast about one-third in from the bow. Sets a spritsail, staysail, jib to light bowsprit, and sometimes a yard topsail; some set a sprit mizzen. Also rowed with 2-4 pairs of oars; double tholepins. Recent boats may be modified for a motor. Crew of 3-5. Reported lengths overall 4-10.7m, beam one-third, depth one-eighth. Other recorded names: **Blekingeeka, Blekinger Kahn**. Note also **Bornholmsk ege, eka, vrakeka**.

Blette See **Plätte-1**

blind boat See **kamé-no-ko-bune**

blobber *England, E:* A trawler's boat that had been retired and later modified for use as a **houseboat**★ or for pleasure or fishing (especially eel blobbing); found in the early 20th century on the Rivers Hull and Humber. Original boats open, chubby, and sturdily

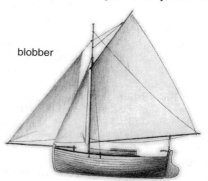

blobber

built; clinker planking; closely spaced timbers; narrow transom; straight vertical stem. Remodeled in various ways, but often by internal strengthening, adding a top strake or bolting on a curved keel, or adding decking along the sides and forward for a trunk cabin. The **houseboats** had higher cabins and were sculled or towed. Those that sailed were mostly **cutter**★-rigged, with a loose-footed boomed mainsail; boom extended well outboard. Reported lengths 5.2-5.5m, widths 1.98-2.13m, depth ca. 0.76m. Other recorded names: **blobbing boat, Yorkshire blobber**

blobbing boat See **blobber**

block See **Cumberland River drift**

blockade runner See **runner**

Block Island boat *United States, NE:* Beamy **double-ender**★ used for fishing and traveling between Block Island and the mainland coast of Rhode Island. In the 1st half of the 19th century, they were small, open,

Block Island boat

high-sheer boats (earning the nickname **cowhorn**); these worked off beaches until 1873. Construction of a harbor permitted use of larger, half-decked boats. Lapstrake planking; nearly straight stem and stern-post, both raked; steep deadrise. Long straight keel, with drag; iron shoe on stem and keel; low freeboard amidships. Rudder, which had a notch that aided in boarding the boat, hung on sternpost; long tiller could be set between pegs, enabling it to be left unattended.

Open waist partitioned for cargo; narrow waterways; freeboard raised with portable washboards; beach stone ballast. Foremast stepped well forward, mainmast about amidships; both tapered and raked aft; mast partners on early boats had hinged iron collars for easy unstepping; no standing rigging. Loose-footed foresail overlapped the main; mainsail loose-footed but boomed, the boom extending well beyond the stern and sheeted to a traveler. Both sails had very short gaffs and several rows of reef points. Crew of 2-5. Reported lengths 4.9-12.2m; e.g., length 9.8m, beam 3.5m, depth 1.3m, draft 1.2m. Further name variant: **Block Island double-ender**

Block Island double-ender See **Block Island boat**
Blockschiff See **hulk-3**
Blödte See **Plätte-1**
bloenkang See **belongkang**
blokschiv See **hulk-3**
Blokzijlder jacht *Netherlands:* Fast sailing 19th-century cargo vessel out of Blokzijl on the east side of the Zuiderzee. Rounded bow and stern; heavy curved stem, particularly below the waterline; straight, almost vertical sternpost. Carvel-planked, flat bottom, straight keel; rounded bilges; slight tumble home to top strakes, pronounced at ends; moderate sheer, heavy rubbing strake. Rudder fixed to a wide, slightly raked sternpost; tiller set over rudderhead. Rounded leeboards. Decked; windlass on foredeck; central hatch, cambered cover; narrow waterways; cabin aft; steering cockpit. Gaff-rigged; short curved gaff; 1-2 headsails; mast could be struck. Length 13m, beam 3.6m, depth 1.6m. Other recorded names: **Blokzijlder jagt**, **Blokzijler jacht**, **Blokzijl yacht**. Note also **jacht-3**.

Blokzijlder jagt, Blokzijler jacht, Blokzijl yacht See **Blokzijlder jacht**
blood boat **1.** Colloquial term for a British navy **jolly boat** of the 1st half of the 19th century; so called because it was often used to bring fresh meat to the ship. Later, term might apply to any harbor craft serving this purpose.
2. During World Wars I and II, the term was given to a small vessel that sank mines brought to the surface by a mine sweeper.
3. *United States:* Disparaging term given to United States merchant vessels of the mid-19th century because of their poor living conditions. Other recorded name: **blood packet**. Those running from the east coast to Pacific ports might be called **Down East blood boats**.

blood packet See **blood boat-3**
blubber hunter, blubber ship See **whaler-1**
blue barge See **barge-7**
Blue Elvan barge See **Plymouth barge**
blue-horse junk See **ma lan**
boanga See **juanga**
boarding boat **1.** Any boat used to transfer crew from shore to an offlying vessel. May also carry the catch from a **fishing boat** to shore.
2. *United Kingdom:* Special boats of the Royal National Lifeboat Institution that convey the crew from the beach to a moored **lifeboat**. Designed as **pulling boats**, but may be warped out to the **lifeboat**, or may

use an engine. Carvel- or clinker-planked; sharp-ended or with a tucked-up transom; low rise to the floors. Lengths 3-7.6m; e.g., length 5m, beam 1.8m.
3. *United States, central:* Ohio **canal boat** that accompanied maintenance dredges of the late 19th and early 20th centuries. Housed the foreman and his family in a 5.5m forward cabin and the work crew in an after cabin. Decked between cabins. Flat floors, bluff ends. This type of boat was also used by state inspectors, various officials, and politicians and went by the term **state boat**. Length 23m, beam 4m.
boarding punt See **punt-9**
boat **1.** To landsmen the word usually denotes any craft used on the water; to seamen a **boat** is distinguished from a **ship** by being small and generally open; propelled by oars, sail, or a small motor; constructed of wood, metal, cloth, cement, or synthetics; and unsuited for living aboard for long periods. A yachtsman refers to his craft as a **boat**. A ship's **lifeboat** may be loosely called a **boat**. In naval parlance, a **boat** is one capable of being carried aboard a ship, although some large naval craft may be known as **boats**, e.g., **destroyers**, **submarines**, and **torpedo boats**. Other exceptions include inland vessels, such as **steamboats**; vessels designed for a particular service, such as **ferryboats**, **mail boats**, and **night boats**; and small ships that engage in a regular run, such as the **Boston boat**. In the United States, a **boat** is one used for non-commercial purposes, or one for hire carrying 6 passengers or fewer. Selected name variants: **ambarcaiune, bad, bæt, bait, barca, bat(e), bât** or **båten, bateau, bat(t)is, batr, bayt, boate, boitt, Boot, boote, bot, bote, both, botte, canoe, qārib, sea-bat, zawraq**
2. *Canada, E:* Small 17th- and 18th-century sailing vessel used for inshore cod fishing off Newfoundland. Open or partly decked. Generally 2-masted, lug-rigged. Crew of 5, 3 to fish and 2 to process the catch. Some 12m long on the keel. In the early 19th century, **boats** were decked **schooners** of ca. 12-20t; crew of 2-4.
3. *England, E:* Vessel built on the lines of the **Humber keel**, but which had no masts or sails and generally did not navigate tidal waters. Open hold with no hatch coverings.
4. *England, SE:* On the Thames, a **boat** is any craft smaller than ca. 70t; those larger are called **barges**.
5. *England, W:* On the Mersey waterway in the 18th century, a **boat** was less than 4.3m wide, while a **flat** was wider.
6. *Eastern Pacific:* Local name for a flat-bottomed fishing **launch** in French Polynesia. Powered by an outboard or inboard motor. Reported lengths 4-7m.
7. *United Kingdom:* The term **boat** may be used by fishermen to distinguish between a fishing **smack** and a **fishing boat**, the former being decked, the latter only half-decked. Generally 20-40t burden.
8. *West Indies:* In the Netherlands Antilles, the term **boat** may designate a locally constructed, **sloop**-rigged fishing craft. Transom stern, narrow keel, decked or open. Long, overhanging boom to mainsail, short bowsprit. Average 4 in crew. Length 6m; 4-6rt. Name variant: **sailboat**

Further references: **barge-7c, barge-10, Humber keel, narrow boat, smack-1, whaler-2, West Country boat, Yorkshire keel**

boat-canoe *United States, E:* A **dugout canoe**★ produced by early settlers in New England and elsewhere along the Atlantic coast; the term was used in South Carolina at least into the early 20th century. Constructed along European lines with sharp bow and high-tucked transom; sometimes plank-extended. Small rudder; some may have used leeboards; a 19th-century example had a centerboard. Principally rowed, but might set a spritsail. Early boats probably 7.6-9.1m long; a 19th-century boat was 4.9m long, 1.25m wide, 0.36m deep. See also **vallam-2**.

boat-catamaran *India, SW:* A 3-log **raft**★ used by the Parawa peoples for ocean fishing, working in pairs. The larger center log forms a keel piece set between 2 logs placed to form a trough and held in position at

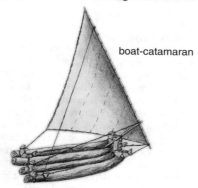

boat-catamaran

each end by a horn-shaped crosspiece. Ends planed flush on the bottom to provide a smooth overhanging bow and stern. When sailed, the larger of the 2 **rafts** steps a small, forward-raking spar backstayed to the 2 aft crosspieces. A small tanned triangular sail is bent to a light bamboo yard, tacked to the 2 bow crosspieces, and sheeted to an after crosspiece. The 2 **rafts** are not parallel, the bow ends being closer together. Steered with a large paddle. Propelled also with short split-bamboo pieces, the paddlers standing. Crew of 2. The larger **raft** 7m long, 0.9m wide; the smaller 6m long, 0.8m wide. A 4-log **boat-catamaran** is used in the lobster fishery of this area. Construction similar to those above. A triangular sail also used; while sailing, a plank inserted between the 2 inner logs serves as a centerboard and a split-bamboo paddle serves as a rudder. Length 6.4m, width 0.6m. Note also **catamaran**.

boate See **boat-1**

boatie *Scotland, NE:* Term given to the small, clinker-built **rowing boat**★ used as a **ship's boat**★ aboard a Fraserburgh's steam **drifter**★.

boatila manché See **kalla dhoni**

boat of the gods See **shen bo zi**

boat-pinnace See **pinnace-1**

boatu See **dhoni-2**

bobao See **baobao**

boçentòro See **bucintoro**

bo chuan *China:* **1.** A **junk**★-type **lighter**★. Style varies somewhat from port to port. Other recorded names:

po-ch'uan, transfer boat, wharf boat★. Note also ma tou chuan.

2. The **bo chuan** at Yichang (I-Ch'ang) on the central Chang Jiang (Yangtze) must adapt to seasonal water level changes. Square ends, stern sweeps up. Heavily planked, with 3 wales running full length, flat bottom, 15 bulkheads. Partly decked. Large balanced rudder, with rudder stock coming up inboard; long tiller. Length 24m, beam 4.6m, depth ca. 1.2m, cap. ca. 60t. Other recorded names: **I-Ch'ang bo chuan, I-Ch'ang po-ch'uan**

Further reference: **long chuan**

Bock *Germany, W:* Largest of the 19th-century **Weser barges**★ towed to Bremen by horses or by 40-70 runners. In order to make up a full load for an oceangoing ship, 3 types were coupled—the **Bock**, the smaller **Achterhang** (or **Hinterhang**), and the small **Bulle**★. Open; spritsail set to a single mast. Length 36m, beam 2.7m, cap. 80t. Spelling variant: pl. **Böcke**★

Böcke *Switzerland, central:* 19th-century square-ended vessel found on Lakes Thun and Brienzer. Carried bulk cargo. Low-sided. Cap. 10-30t. See also **Bock**.

Bockkahn See **Kaffenkahn**

Bockkranhulk, Bockprahm, Bockschiff See **sheer hulk**

bodemschuit See **bom-1**

boeier *Belgium/Netherlands:* **1. Coaster**★, mainly of the 16th-17th centuries, but mentioned as early as the 15th century. Some German-built. Also sailed to the British Isles, France, and into the Baltic. Shallow draft enabled them to proceed to river ports. Frequently armed with as many as 8 guns. Probably carvel planking, flat floors with keel, curved stem, straight raking sternpost. Most round-sterned; 2 or more heavy wales along the gunwales continued aft to form a narrow triangular counter for a helm. Foredeck with windlass, cabin house aft, cambered hatches, steering platform. Small vessels had leeboards after ca. 1600; tiller came inboard below the gunwale. Larger 16th-century vessels sometimes had a transom, 2-3 heavy strakes, poop deck or large cabin. Early **boeiers** sprit- or lug-rigged. Later, the smaller vessels set a loose-footed gaff sail with a long standing gaff, a staysail, square topsail and sometimes a watersail. Larger vessels were square-rigged and also stepped a lateen-rigged mizzenmast just inboard of the sternpost, and a jib ran to a jib-boom; sometimes used a watersail. Crew of 5-8. Reported lengths 20-24m; e.g., length 20m, width 6.66m, depth 3.44m, draft 3.1m. Medium-sized **boeiers** 50-100t cap., small 30t. Name variant: **karveel**★. Note also **ever**.

2. In the 17th century, the **boeier** was revived, in name at least, as an inland vessel used for carrying produce and forage (**vrachtboeier**) and church goers (**kerkscheepje**) until the 19th century; later became a pleasure craft (**boeierjacht**). The latter remains a popular **yacht**★ and is built in sizes ranging from 6-20m. Clinker-built until the 19th century, then carvel; now generally of steel. Double-ended, with rounded bow and stern; deep plumb or curved stem ending in a high point; often has a gripe; plumb or raked sternpost. Flat floors; rounded bilges; strong sheer, low freeboard.

Decked, central cabin, steering well aft. Long-bladed rudder, often with carving at its head and ensign staff on its outer edge; tiller sweeps downward. Early boats with a carved head affixed to the rudder went by the term **kopjacht**; these generally had a deeper hull, narrow rudder, iron tiller. Broad leeboards, shape varies locally. Originally raised a spritsail, then a loose-footed gaff sail laced to the unstayed mast, which is stepped in a tabernacle; jib to an iron bumkin, staysail. Permanent pennant flies from the masthead. Reported lengths 6-12m, occasionally to 18m; beam ca. one-third. Other recorded names: **aardappelboeier** (potato carrier), **kopboot, kopjagt.** Note also **Fries jacht.** Other recorded names: **boeierscepe, boeijer, boëjer, boeyer, boeyjer, boi(er), bojart, bojer*, booyer, bouier, bouyer, boyer*, bu(j)er, Schnigge***

boeieraak *Belgium, N/Netherlands, SW and central:* Boat that combined features of the **boeier*** and the **aak*.**

1. Used from the mid-19th to the mid-20th century to work oyster and mussel beds in protected waters. One type dredged, others transported fish. Carvel-planked, with wide strakes; later boats iron or steel; the wale ran horizontal to the waterline before turning up at the ends; little sheer. Flat bottom, planked fore-and-aft, continued as a flat surface almost to the gunwale; angular bilges; sides flared to the wale, then had slight tumble home. A false stem added on; at the stern a skeg supported the rudder, which extended below the bottom; curved tiller slotted over the rudderhead. Long, narrow leeboards. Decked to mast and at stern; generally had a live well; many had a steering well; open amidships. Loose-footed, boomed gaff sail set to a lowering mast stepped well forward; narrow staysail; sometimes a large jib run to a jibboom. Crew of 2-3. Reported lengths 10-16m, iron vessels to 20m; e.g., length 11.3m, beam 3.3m, depth 1.6m. Other recorded names: **boeieraakje** (dim.), **vischboeieraakje**; pl. **boeieraken**

2. A **boeieraak** was also a wooden river **barge***, carrying sand, gravel, stone, reeds, and wood on the IJssel River.

boeieraakje, boeieraken See **boeieraak**
boeierjacht See **boeier-2**
boeierscepe See **boeier**
boeiertje See **tjotter**
boeijer, boëjer See **boeier**
boerenjol See **jol**
boerenplat *Netherlands:* Open farmer's boat for transporting produce, cattle, flowers, dung, and mud on lakes in the northern and southern part of the country. Double-ended; straight raking stem and sternpost; slight rocker to bottom, with forefoot and skeg. Wide, rounded bow and stern connected by low, straight, flaring sides; light sheer. Short end decks. Rudder follows stern rake, wide blade aft. Rowed, poled, or sailed with small spritsail. Mast stepped at end of foredeck. Length 8m, beam 2.75m, depth 0.5m. Name variant: **schuit***

boerenpunter See **Giethoornse punter**
boerenschouw *Netherlands:* Open **punt***-type farm (*boeren*) boat found in a small area of central Netherlands. Flat bottom with rocker, longitudinally

planked; ends rise in long overhang to a shallow transom; athwartships flooring. Flat sides, generally a single plank, curving inward toward the ends; strengthened with pairs of natural frames; flat sheer. Poled. Length ca. 4.6m, beam 0.9m. Note also **schouw.**

boeri See **bhur**
boëtteur *Canada, E:* Name given to a Newfoundland boat that procured bait for other fishermen. People of French St. Pierre and Miquelon Islands generally called such boats **galopers**, but this name was also given to the boats that brought provisions from Newfoundland. Spelling variant: **galopper.** Note also **bait boat, bait skiff, galloper.**

bœuf See **bateau bœuf**
bœurtun See **mahonne-2**
boëyer, boeyjer See **boeier**
bog See **Hastings lugger**
bogeyman See **fishery guard ship**
bognono See **waka-3**
bogo See **banca**
bogserbåt, bogserfartyg See **tug**
bohatja *Pakistan:* Large cargo boat of the middle Indus River. Flat ends round up scroll fashion. Bottom flat; sides parallel at bottom but flare out above because deck beams are wider. Sides built first, then bottom and sides joined to transverse floor beams. Frequently decorated at the bow with metal, mirrors, carvings, etc. Family generally lives aboard. Pulled with long 15cm-thick sweeps by 3-4 crew on each sweep; fitted with jackstay to serve as a grip. Use rudder when running downstream. Also tracked from shore. May set shallow square sail with its foot extended by a light spar, or a tall lateen sail. Name variant: **darewal battella**

Böhmisch Zille See **Zille**
bohmschep See **dugout canoe**
Bohne See **Meppler praam**
Bohrmachen, Bohrnachen See **Bornachen**
bohuseka See **orusteka**
bohusjolle See **bohusjulle**
bohusjulle *Sweden, W:* Open, beamy boat of the Bohus area developed in the mid-19th century, mainly for inshore fishing. Clinker-planked; full bow, stem curved and cutaway below the waterline; stern raked, wineglass transom; considerable sheer. Straight keel, with slight drag aft; S-curve to the floors; maximum beam forward of amidships. Three or 4 thwarts; small foredeck and stern seat on some. Downward-sloping tiller slots over the outboard rudder. Rowed, oars against 3-4 double tholepins. Those that sailed stepped a mast against the forward thwart. Set a boomless spritsail with the sprit snotter well up the mast; jib to stemhead or a small iron jibboom. Some set a small yard topsail, the long yard held by the lower part of the sprit. Often built with motors after 1920. Those that are mainly rowed (the **roddjulle***) range between 3.7-4.6m in length; the sailing type (**segeljulle**) is 4.6-6m long; the motor type (**motorjulle**) from 4-9m long; e.g., length 4.6m, beam ca. 2m, depth ca. 0.75m. Other recorded names: **bohusjolle, julle, julle från Orust.** Note also **jolle-7.**

bohuslämska See **orusteka**
boi, boier See **boeier**

boiler boat, boily boat See **bawley**
bois fouillé See **boumba**
boîte à horloge See **berrichon**
boitt See **boat-1**
bojart See **boeier**
Bojer *Germany, NW:* Transported firewood, peat, and produce along the lower rivers on the North Sea coast of Schleswig-Holstein from the late 18th through the 19th century. Slender vessel, designed to negotiate locks, earning the nickname **Slüsenkrüper** or **Sleusenkriecher**, a "lock-crawler." Full bow; rounded stern, broad above the waterline; lightly curved stem with a small gripe; vertical sternpost. Flat floors; long, straight, shallow keel; rounded bilges and straight sides. Decked; hatch amidships extended almost to bulwarks; steering well at stern. Leeboards, detached in narrow locks. Outboard rudder; tiller slotted over rudderhead. Low pole mast, stepped about one-third in from the bow; mast could be struck. Set a loose-footed, boomed gaff mainsail and large staysail. Crew of 2. Length 12.4m, beam 2.8m, hold depth 1.2m. Other recorded names: **Boyer, Eiderbojer, Torfboyer.** See also **boeier.**
bol *Netherlands:* **1.** Chubby boat that originated around 1900 as a **fishing boat**★ on the Zuiderzee and the protected waters along the north coast. Last **fishing boat** built in the 1920s, but the type is now a popular motorized pleasure boat. Originally built of wood, carvel-planked; now steel. Full round bow; curved stem ends in a point; stern narrower, raked sternpost, with deadwood. Round bottom; shallow keel; slight rocker. Sides have tumble home above the wale; moderate sheer, rising toward the bow. Long, narrow leeboards; wide rudder. Most **fishing boats** decked in forward half; usually a live fish well; cabin aft on pleasure craft. Strike mast stepped through deck just forward of amidships; sets a loose-footed, boomed gaff sail with a short curved gaff, staysail to jibboom, and jib to bowsprit; occasionally a topsail. Crew of 2. Reported lengths 7-10m, widths 1.8-3.5m. Other recorded names: **bolle, bolle van Urk**; pl. **bollen.** Note also **Boll, Vollenhovense bol.**
2. Bollen are also a large **barge**★ type of the Groningen and Drenthe Canals in the northeast. Two types are the **opgeboeide bol** and the **platte bol.** The **opgeboeide bol** (**bolle met boord**) has a single top strake that becomes wider and has tumble home toward the ends; wale at lower edge runs full length; flat sheer. Slightly raked stem, with gripe; flat floors, rounded bilges. Decked at ends, hatch between; low cabin near the stern, bordered by a low railing. Winch on foredeck used in kedging over mudbanks that form below locks. Narrow leeboards just abaft the mast. Rudder wide-bladed below the waterline; tiller arches up slightly. Short, strikable mast stepped just forward of the hatch; boomed, loose-footed gaff sail, with very long boom and short S-curved gaff. 1928 vessel: 21.4m long, 4.36m wide, 1.15m deep. The **platte bol** is similar except for a blunter bow, and it lacks the top strake, the wale running at deck level. Steel leeboards. A sub-type, the **Apol-bolle**, was built by A. Apol in Wirdum, south of Groningen; characteristically boxy and clumsy; oval portholes in the cabin;

marked flattened hump to tiller. Cap. 50-60t.
Further reference: **bāūlīa**
bolantim See **barco do pilado**
bole A small boat. See also **bāūlīa.**
bolea, boleah, boli, bolia, boliah, bolio See **bāūlīa**
Boll *Germany, NW:* **Fishing boat**★ of the Ems Estuary. Flat bottom, decked forward, leeboards. Gaff mainsail, foresail, and topsail. Length 8.5m, beam 2.7m. Note also **bol.**
bolle See **bol, Bulle, Eiderschnigge**
bolle met boord See **bol-2**
bollen See **bol, Bulle**
bolle van Urk See **bol**
boloto See **baroto**
bolpraam *Netherlands, N:* Long, low metal-hulled vessel that carried produce, especially potatoes, and other bulk cargoes such as peat, dung, and straw. Still used for repairing locks. Rounded ends, false stem and gripe; straight sternpost. No bulwarks; flat sheer except at the bow, which curves up slightly. Flat bottom; rounded bilges. Decked only at ends; long central covered hatch, bordered by narrow gangways; very small raised cabin aft. Small iron, or occasionally wooden, leeboards; large fin to the rudder; long curved tiller slotted over rudderhead. A simplified **bolpraam**, called a **schuit**★ or **open bolpraam**, had no deck or only short end decks, no leeboards; thwart across the open hold supported a short mast with spritsail; mostly poled. Although a poor sailer, a few **bolpramen** (pl.) stepped a lowering mast forward of the hatch, setting a loose-footed, boomed gaff sail with a slightly curved gaff, and sometimes a staysail. Reported lengths 15-22m; e.g., length 22m, beam 4.5m, depth 1.4m; shallow draft. Name variant: **platte bolle.** Note also **praam.**
bolpramen See **bolpraam**
bom *Netherlands, W:* **1.** Boxy **fishing boat**★ that worked from the flat beaches bordering the coast north of the mouth of the Maas River during the 18th and 19th centuries; extinct by 1919. Primarily drifted for herring, but in winter fished for flounder, plaice, and ray. Clinker-built, with an exceptionally heavy flat bottom; the few with a keel were called **kielbommen.** Double-ended with bluff bow and stern; heavy stem and sternpost. Decked, large cabin for the crew; leeboards on those with no keel; live well. Mainsail, just forward of amidships, set a loose-footed, boomed gaff sail and often a topsail. Many also used a small mizzenmast, stepped on the starboard quarter, setting a similar gaff sail. Two or 3 headsails. Mainmast generally struck while drifting. Crew of 6-10, the larger number when drifting. Length about twice the beam; reported lengths 8.8-16.6m; e.g., length 13m, beam 6m, depth 1.84m; shallow draft. Other recorded names: **bodemschuit, bomb, bom(b)schuit, bomme, bomschip, bonscheep, dum, Katwijk-pom, Katwijkse bom(schuit), Scheveningische bom, Zijdse bom, Zijdtsche bom**; pl. **bommen, bomschuiten.** Further reading: E. W. Petrejus, *De Bomschuit, Een Verwenden Scheepstype* (Rotterdam: Prins Hendrik Museum, 1954).
2. After the harbor at Scheveningen was built in 1899, a new type of **bom** was developed, the **loggerbom.**

This larger, narrower vessel had a deep keel, rising floors, rounded bilges, counter stern with inboard rudder, straight lightly raked stern, but was clinker-built. **Ketch***-rigged. Length 22m, beam 7.2m, depth 3m. Name variant: **Lelybom**

bomb See **bom-1**, **bomb vessel**

bombard See **bomb vessel**

bombarda *Greece:* Seaworthy **coaster*** that stepped 2 masts of almost equal height, the pole foremast often raking slightly aft, the mainmast vertical. Extinct. On one type, the foremast was fitted with 4 square sails, the after mast with a large, loose-footed, boomed gaff sail and gaff topsail. Another type carried 3 square sails on the foremast and a lugsail on the after mast. Three jibs to a rising bowsprit on both types. Square stern, sharp bow, strong sheer. Length 15.5m, beam 5m, depth 2.7m; usually 65-150t burden, some to 250t. Those with a sharp stern and lugsail on the mainmast were called **bombarda sambatiera**. Spelling variant: **bombartha**. Further references: **bombarde**, **bomb vessel**

bombarda sambatiera See **bombarda**

bombarde *Mediterranean:* Small merchant vessel of the mid-18th to early 20th century. Sharp bow, some with a fiddle-headed beak; transom or counter stern; flat floors. Decked. Set square sails on the pole mainmast; lateen or gaff sails on the mizzenmast, and sometimes a mizzen topsail; 2 headsails to a long rising bowsprit. Topsail and topgallant. Crew of 6. Reported lengths 14-22m; e.g., length 20m, beam 6.6m, depth 3.54m. Spelling variant: **bombarda***. See also **bomb vessel**

bombardeer galioot, **Bombardeerschip**, **bombardeira**, **bombardera**, **bombarderfartøj**, **bombarder galiot**, **bombardero**, **bombardier galiote**, **Bombardierketsch**, **bombardirnoe sudno**, **bombardiskov korabl'**, **bombarta** See **bomb vessel**

bombartha See **bombarda**

Bombay bark See **dinghy-4**

Bombenfahrzeug, **bombe vessel**, **bomb ketch**, **bombkits** See **bomb vessel**

bomboat See **boom boat**, **bumboat-1**

bombot See **bombotte**

bombote *Venezuela, E:* At shallow ports on Isla Margarita, a small boat that transfers passengers from off-lying vessels to the quay.

bombotte *France, W:* Small open boat of the Vendée coast. Served as an **annexe*** to **sardiniers***, to ferry tourists and villagers between communities, and for fishing. Name derived from its likeness to a wooden shoe (*botte*). Keel turned up forward to a small bow transom; maximum beam amidships, tapering to a slightly raked wineglass transom; high curved bilges. Small foredeck; steered with an oar. Mainmast stepped through forward thwart, setting a standing lugsail. Spritsail set to a slightly aft-raking mizzenmast at the transom. Jib tacked to bow. Also rowed. Reported lengths 4-5m; e.g., length ca. 4.3m, beam 1.5m, depth 0.6m. Spelling variant: **bombot**

bombschuit See **bom-1**

bomb vessel Strongly built vessel of the late 17th to early 19th century. Used mainly to bombard coastal installations; a few also served on Arctic expeditions.

Popular with the French and English, but also found in Scandinavia and Russia. Square or rounded stern; curved stem or beakhead; mainly flat-floored, others had a round hull; heavily timbered. Principal distinction between the French and English vessels was the position of the mortars; on the French, the 2 mortars were placed abreast forward of the mainmast; the English placed one forward of the mainmast, the other abaft of it; the Swedish placed one on the quarterdeck. Some early 19th-century French vessels had a single mortar and were called **bateaux bombes**. An accompanying **tender***, aboard which the artillery personnel lived, transported the powder and empty shells. Early vessels were rigged in the manner of the 17th-century **ketch***, the **bomb ketch**; later the English, while retaining the term **bomb ketch**, removed the foremast and adopted square sails on the midship mainmast, and a lateen or gaff mizzen. Lengths in the 17th century ranged from 16-26m; widths 7.7-8.7m; shallow draft permitted close approach to shore. Selected name variants: **barca bombardiera**, **bomb(ard)**, **bombarda***, **bombarde***, **bombardeer galioot**, **Bombaardeerschip**, **bombarde(i)ra**, **bombarderfartøj**, **bombarder galiot**, **bombardero**, **bombardier galiote**, **Bombardierketsch**, **bombardirnoe sudno**, **bombardiskov korabl'**, **bombarta**, **Bombenfahrzeug**, **bombe vessel**, **bom(b)kits**, **bumbarda**, **bumbarta**, **galeotta bombardiera**, **galeotta da bombe**, **galiota de bombas**, **gal(l)iote à bombes**, **galiote à mortiers**, **lancha bombarde(i)ra**, **mörsarfartyg**, **mortar boat***, **mortar vessel**, **morteerchaloupe**, **nave bombardier(a)**. Note also **gondola-7**.

bomkane See **dugout canoe**

bomkits See **bomb vessel**

bomme, **bommen**, **bomschip**, **bomschuit**, **bomschuiten** See **bom-1**

bomsegljakt, **bomseil-jægt**, **bomseiljakt**, **bomseiljekt**, **bomsiglar**, **bomsiglarjekt** See **jakt**

bon boat See **bumboat-1**

bond See **crib**

Bönder *Germany, W:* Operated on the middle and lower Rhine River from the 1st half of the 18th century to the end of the 19th, carrying freight and passengers. Strongly built with clinker planking originally, later carvel. Flat bottom; bilges rounded into curved sides; bottom planking continued up at the ends to form a flat bow and stern; maximum beam in forward third, tapering toward the stern. Tiller worked a large outboard rudder; employed leeboards, except for some upriver vessels. In the 18th century, some had gangboards outside the hull. Decked at ends; long covered hatch; some had a cabin below decks aft, others a large deckhouse forward of the mizzenmast. Most stepped 2 masts, the 18th-century vessels setting a large square mainsail, topsail, and a large spritsail abaft the mast; mizzen set a spritsail. Later, only spritsails used, and still later gaff sails adopted. Reported lengths 22-36m; e.g., length 31m, beam 6.2m, depth 2.8m. Spelling variants: **Bönn(d)er**, **Bunder**

bondo See **falucho-3**

bōnga *Solomon Islands, western Pacific:* **Outrigger canoe*** of the Lau peoples of Malaita Island in the central islands.

bonga See **bongo-1**, **bongo-5**, **juanga**, **wom**
bonggi, **bonggy** See **bungay-2**
bongka See **bangka**
bongo 1. *Latin America/United States, S:* Large **dugout canoe**★ used on rivers and along adjacent coasts. Usually hewn from the bongo tree. Center generally protected by a palm-leaf shelter. Mainly paddled or poled, both while standing. Lined through difficult rapids. In some areas, served in cargo handling at major ports. Those in Colombia reported as capable of transporting 5-6t of produce or cattle, and the largest carry 20-25 people, although 5 or 6 is more usual. Spelling variants: **bonga**★, **bunga**, **bungo**, **ponga**, **pongo**★
2. *Chile:* Open **fishing boat**★ launched through the surf. Sharp bow with curved stem, narrow square stern, wide rounded bottom, no keel. Propelled by oars or an outboard motor. Crew of 2-4. Reported lengths 3-7m; e.g., length 7m, beam 1.4m, depth 0.6m. Name variant: **bote**★. Note also **canoa-4**.
3. *Ecuador:* **a.** Plank-extended **dugout canoe**★ used mainly for fishing; some transport the catch and some are carried aboard local **tuna boats**★. Sides raised by a single strake, fixed outside the hull, supported by 3-5 ribs that meet at the midline. Sharp, curved bow; stern mostly sharp, some square; bottom flat; sheer

bongo-3a

sweeps up at the ends. In some areas, a thick balsa log fixed along each side increases stability. Some still sail, employing a gunter-type triangular sail, boomed at the foot. Earlier **bongos** square-sailed. Mast stepped into block on the bottom. Most now modified for an outboard motor by cutting the top strake at the stern and adding a crosspiece. To support the motor, a pair of short planks extend aft on each side of the dugout hull, braced by a crossbeam above the sharp stern. Also rowed or paddled. Crew of 1-3. Reported lengths 5-12m; e.g., length 7.85m, beam 0.86m, depth 0.68m. Name variant: **canoa**★ (usually the smaller non-motorized boat, but in at least one area, the **canoa** is the larger boat with an outboard). Further reading: Eva König, *Traditionelle Küstenfischerei Ecuadors, am Beispiel van San Pedro/Guayas* (Bonn: Holos, 1990). **b.** Also reported as a **raft**★ that fishes off Playas on the central coast. Center hollowed out for a rattan cage to hold the catch. Collapsible mast sets a triangular sail. A small size is called a **bonquito**. Note also **balsa-11**.
4. *El Salvador:* Coastal fishermen use the dugout **bongo** with a trammel net. Propelled by oar and sail. Reported lengths 7.6-9m.
5. *Panama:* **a.** Large 18th-century **dugout canoe** that carried passengers and cargo on the Río Chagres across the isthmus from Panama City to Portobelo. Decked; house aft. Paddled by crew of 18-20. Length ca. 37m. Other recorded names: **bonga**★, **bonque**. **b.**

Also reported as a **schooner**★-rigged **coaster**★. Modified dugout with vertical washstrakes.
6. *Venezuela:* Term applies to several types of boats. Those used upstream on the larger rivers are **dugout canoes** capable of carrying from 3-5t; flat sheer; mostly poled, lined through rapids; ca. 12m long, 3m wide. On the lower Orinoco River, the term applies to a shallow-draft dugout that is half covered with a thatched roof; usually motorized. The Lake Maracaibo **bongo** is a motorized **launch**★-type craft used for transportation and fishing; flat bottom, no keel, square stern, sharp raked bow.
7. *West Africa:* **Boñgo** may describe a **canoe**★ or large **raft**.
Further references: **canoa-4**, **panga-1**
bonitera l. *Peru:* A copy of the double-ended American **whaleboat**★ adopted by Peruvian fishermen in the 19th century. Still used, especially for catching bonito. Present-day **boniteras** are decked and ca. 10m long.
2. *Spain, N:* Old coastal **fishing boat**★; replaced by steam **launches**★. Primarily used for summer bonito fishing, but also for tuna, cod, bream, and conger eels. When used for winter fishing with multi-hook lines, the boat may be called a **lancha calera** (see **calera**). Raked and slightly curved stem, tall stemhead; transom or sharp stern. Centerboard; outboard rudder; tiller. Open or half-decked. Five to 10 rowing thwarts; rowed double-banked. Set 2 dipping lugsails, the foresail quite small. Foremast vertical, mainmast raked aft. Reported lengths 11-16.7m; e.g., length 16.7m, beam 3.7m, depth 1.7m. Other recorded names: **bonitera vizcaina**, **lancha bonitera**
bonitera vizcaina See **bonitera-2**
bonito canoe See **agai-ni-waiau**, **'iola**, **va'a alo**, **waka tiu**
Bönnder See **Bönder**
bonne See **pointer**
Bönner See **Bönder**
bonque See **bongo-5**
bonquito See **bongo-3**
bons *Netherlands, NE:* Small flat-bottomed boat of the **schokker**★ family that was built until ca. 1910 at ports on the east side of the Zuiderzee, notably at Vollenhove and Elburg. Engaged mainly in herring and anchovy fishing. Maximum beam well forward, tapering to a narrow rounded stern. Prominent, strongly raked, straight stem, cut at right angle at the top where it is doubled for the anchor hawser; raked sternpost. Skeg in after third; angular bilges with curving flared sides up to the wale, very wide garboard strake. Wide washstrakes with tumble home that extend from just abaft the stem to aft of amidships; marked sheer toward bow. Open or half-decked; fish well abaft amidships. Narrow leeboards; large-bladed outboard rudder with a recurved head; tiller slotted over rudderhead. Mast raked slightly aft; loose-footed, boomed gaff sail with curved gaff; large staysail; jib to reefing bowsprit, which was run out through a ring on the stemhead. When running before the wind, a tall, narrow square sail could be boomed out from the mainmast. Some motorized. Generally crew of 2. Reported lengths 10-12.2m; e.g., length 10.75m, beam at wales

3.56m, depth 1.28m; shallow draft. Other recorded names: **bonsien, bonsje, Elburger bons, kleine schokker** (**schuit** or **schute**), **Vollenhovense bons** (or **schokker** or **schuit**), **Vollenhover bonsje**; pl. **bonzen**. Further reading: Peter Dorleijn, *Van Gaand en Staand Want, De Zeilvisserij Voor en Na de Afsluiting van de Zuiderzee*, vol. IV (Weesp: Van Kampen & Zn., 1985), 268-273.

bon-scheep See **bom-1**

bonsien, bonsje See **bons**

bony boat See **menhaden boat**

bony-fish boat *United States, NE:* Local term in the Mystic, Connecticut, area for boats engaging in menhaden ("bony-fish") fishing. Note also **menhaden boat, sail gear**.

bonzen See **bons**

booanga See **juanga-1**

boobao See **baobao**

boom *Arabian Peninsula/Iran:* Trading vessel found in the Persian (Arabian) Gulf and on the Oman coast. Largest carried cargo to Africa and India. Still built in a few areas, often on the west coast of India. Now entirely motorized. Distinctive feature is the tall, straight, plank-like stemhead that rises at an angle of ca. 45°; tip usually painted black, often with a white band below. Characteristically double-ended, although motorized **booms** built in the United Arab Emirates have a square stern; sternpost raked, markedly on the sharp-sterned type. Straight keel; slight sheer, but rising to the low poop. Usually decked; space below the awning-sheltered poop may be used for cargo, for special passengers, or for any women on board; now often have wooden deckhouse aft. Toilet box generally outboard on each side of the rudder. Sturdy rudder hung on sternpost; colorful yoke connected by lines to a wheel; older types used a tiller. Usually carries a **mashua**⋆ on board and, on some, a small **ka'it** hangs on davits. Topsides oiled, bottom coated with a mixture of lime and animal fat or fish oil; often had a painted design atop the sternpost. Most 2-masted with no standing rigging, the main halyard serving as a backstay. A few large vessels were 3-masted. Mainmast tall and thick, raking slightly forward and stepped just forward of amidships. Light, almost vertical mizzenmast at end of the poop deck. Both set quadrilateral lateen-type sails with a short luff or the mizzen might be a lateen sail. Jib boomed out by a spar against the stem projection. Crew of 15-40. Reported lengths 11-100m; the longest found in Iran; e.g., length overall 33.7m, on keel 20m, beam 7.7m, depth ca. 3m. Other recorded names: **bhūm, boum, būm, Kuwait boat**; pl. **abwâm**. Note also **dangi, schooner-4**.

2. *Canada/United States:* In the lumbering industry, a **raft**⋆ of logs or squared timber used to control the movement of logs. In places, such as the Erie Canal in central New York State, such **log booms** had to be cast free, sluiced through the locks, and regrouped below. Further references: **dhangi, timber raft-1**

boom-barge See **boomy**

boom boat 1. A **ship's boat**⋆ stowed in the space between the fore- and mainmasts (the boom), where the spare spars were stored. Rowed with 2-4 oars. Other recorded names: **bomboat, Decksboot**

2. *Canada/United States:* Used to sort and corral logs, separate bunched-up logs, assist in towing log **rafts**⋆, units, etc. Originally merely 2 logs lashed together, propelled by a powerful outboard motor. Beamy, short, and highly maneuverable. Some have "teeth" on their bow to help gain a good grip on logs. Other recorded names: **boom dozer, booming beaver, boom scooter, bulldozer boat, dozer boat, log bronc, pond boat**. Note also **barge-11j**. Further references: **bumboat-1, boom defense vessel**

boom defense vessel Small armed craft that, by means of a chain, closed off a port in time of war. Vessels working with anti-**submarine** nets had a crane to move the nets. One British Royal Navy boat 5.2m long, 2.2m wide. Other recorded names: **boom boat**⋆, **gate ship** (or **vessel**), **guardaostruzioni, Sperr-bewachter, Sperrfahrzeug, Sperrwaffenschiff**

boom dozer See **boom boat-2**

boomey See **boomy**

boomie See **boomy, Channel barge**

booming beaver See **boom boat-2**

Boomkahn See **dugout canoe**

boom of logs See **crib**

boomsail barge See **boomy**

boomsail boat See **Essex smack**

boomschip, boomschipp See **dugout canoe**

boomschorskano See **bark boat**

boom scooter See **boom boat-2**

boomstamkano See **dugout canoe**

boomy *England, S and E:* Flat-bottomed **coaster**⋆ that carried bulk cargoes mostly in and out of estuaries and shallow coastal creeks from the mid-19th century until World War II. The last reportedly built in 1919. Box-like hull, square chines; strong bottom, longitudinally planked; heavy keel. Bow often fitted with a false stem to form a clipper-type bow; generally rounded counter stern, although some had a square transom; bold sheer. Low freeboard. Decked; roomy forecastle, large cabin aft, wheelhouse; large hatches with meter-high coamings. Early vessels steered with a tiller, later by a wheel. Leeboards used when traveling light; heavy rudder. Boomed gaff sails, either loose-footed or laced; roller reefing frequently used; some non-boomed types kept the main gaff standing and brailed in the sail. Mainmast often raked forward and stepped in a tabernacle; pronounced curve to topmast. Fitted with gaff or jib-headed topsails; topsails characteristically set to port side. Sometimes set 2 square topsails forward of the mainmast. The mizzenmast on **boomies** was relatively large and stepped well inboard; earlier, stepped on the rudderhead; set a lug- or spritsail. Originally a running bowsprit, later fixed bowsprit; 3-4 headsails. Foresails sheeted to a short iron horse or chain. Sails white except for a brown foresail. Crew of 3-5. Reported lengths 25-31m; e.g., length 29m, beam 7m, depth of hold 2.5m; shallow draft. Other recorded names: **barge ketch** (south coast term), **boom-barge, boomey, boomie, boomsail barge, boomy barge, ketch-barge**⋆. Note also **Thames sailing barge**.

boomy barge See **boomy**

boopaa, boopah See **baobao**

boora See **bhur**

boot **1.** *Belgium/Netherlands:* Generic term for a small open **boat★**, usually serving as a **tender★** to river craft or as a **ship's boat★** on **fishing boats★**, **ferries★**, **yachts★**, or ships. Rowed, sailed, or motorized. Spelling variant: pl. **booten**

2. *Germany, N:* Along the Baltic coast, it is common among local peoples to use the term **Boot** for numerous boat types. Frequently refers to boats on Rügen Island. Most often small, open, and roughly built. Clinker-planked; plank keel common. Sharp bow, some with an inner stem. Stern sharp or a U-shaped transom; an inserted block may form a narrow transom. Some use a centerboard. Rowed or sailed. Set 1-2 spritsails. Other recorded names: **bot, but, Roonboot** Further references: **boat-1, kutter-2, Sandboot, tjotter**

boote See **boat-1**

booten See **boot-1**

booti See **buti-1b**

Boot mit Zweimannduchten See **double-banked boat**

booyer See **boeier**

bopao, bopau See **baobao**

borae See **bhur**

borcèj, borcèll See **burchièllo-2**

borcelli, borcello See **burchièllo-1**

Bordfloss See **Bretterfloss**

bordhaugskøyte See **skøyte-4**

bordonaro See **gozzo**

borgantin See **brigantine**

børing See **byrding**

borley, borly See **bawley**

borneur *France:* Term given to a small **coaster★** limited legally to working over short distances, carrying diverse cargoes into small ports and inlets. The term **écraseur de crabes** used derogatorily by high seas sailors for these craft. Name variant: **bateau borneur**

Bornachen *Germany, SW:* Powerfully built vessel that transported grapes on the Mosel River. Sharp bow, rounded stern, relatively narrow bottom. Length to ca. 24m, beam 6m; cap. 30-50t. Other recorded names: **Bohrmachen, Bohrnachen, champ de vigne**. Note also **Nachen-1**.

Bornholmerbåd, Bornholm salmon boat, Bornholmsk dæksbåd See **Bornholmsk laksebåd**

Bornholmsk ege *Denmark, E:* Small 3-masted herring and salmon **fishing boat★** from the Baltic island of Bornholm; adopted on the south coast of Sweden,

Bornholmsk ege

where it is known as a **blekingseka★**. Clinker-built, keel, straight raking stem and sternpost, mostly transom-sterned. Early boats set a lugsail on the mainmast and spritsails on mizzen- and foremasts, the former raked forward. Later boats set 3 spritsails. Also rowed. Crew of 2-3. Reported lengths 7-9m, widths 2.4-3m, depth 1.0m; a smaller size, the **halvege**, is ca. 5.5m long. Other recorded names: **ege**; pl. **eger**

Bornholmsk halvdækbåd See **Bornholmsk laksebåd**

Bornholmsk laksebåd *Denmark, E:* **Fishing boat★** from Bornholm Island; in winter fished for salmon (*laks*), in summer for herring. Developed in the mid-19th century. Clinker-built double-ender with full lines. Ends curved above the waterline, raked below; moderate sheer. Flush deck; 2 hatches forward, small trunk cabin aft; cockpit for helmsman; some half-decked. High stem; open railing on some. Both tiller and rudder curved. Mainmast about length of boat; some stepped a mizzenmast. Mostly **cutter★**-rigged, with boomless gaff mainsail, high-peaked yard topsail, and 2 foresails. Early boats often set spritsails on the main- and mizzenmasts. Motorized early in the 20th century. Crew of 2-4. Reported lengths 7.3-10.3m, widths 3-4m, depths 1.2-1.5m, draft 1.1-1.6m. Other recorded names: **Bornholmerbåd, Bornholm salmon boat, Bornholmsk dæksbåd, Bornholmsk halvdækbåd, laxfiskbåt, rundstævnede**

boro nouka See **nouka**

boroto See **baroto**

borr See **bhur**

Boston cutter, Boston fishing cutter See **Boston hooker-1**

Boston hooker *United States, NE:* **1.** Adapted in the 1850s by Irish fishermen from boats on the west coast of Ireland (see **Galway hooker**). Lines sharper, with greater deadrise than the Irish boats. Extinct by the early 20th century. Carvel-planked, some roughly built; near-vertical stem; stern sharp below the waterline, raking sternpost, heart-shaped transom above or stern full-ended. Straight keel with drag; sharply rising floors to full bilges; wall-sided or has tumble home. Low monkey rails from stern to abreast the mast; characteristically, hawser chock fastened outside the rail forward and to one side of the stemhead. Open abaft the cuddy; fish hold or a fish well amidships; steering well aft; topsides coated with tar. Outboard rudder; short heavy tiller. Bald-headed **cutter★** rig, with 2 headsails. Long gaff; mainsail laced to mast; running bowsprit to port of stem. Crew of 4. Reported lengths 9-11.6m; e.g., length overall 11m, on keel 8.8m, beam 2.82m, draft aft 1.75m. Other recorded names: **Boston (fishing) cutter, dundavoe, Irish boat (cutter or hooker)**

2. Similar were the Boston **Dungarvan boats**; also used by Irish market fishermen, perhaps primarily by those from Dungarvan on the south coast of Ireland. Sharp but rounded bow with wide stem, square stern, deep keel, deep hull. Interior layout similar to the **Boston hooker**. Length on deck averaged 9m. Name variant: **Boston market cutter**

Boston market cutter See **Boston hooker-2**

Boston pilot schooner *United States, NE:* Fast, deep-hulled vessel of the 19th century. Boston retained its

schooners* until the 1960s. Considerable variation between vessels, resulting from attempts to achieve speed and easy motion. Stem shape ranged from slightly rounded to strongly cutaway to concave. High counter stern prevalent above a plumb or raking sternpost. Deep drag to the keel, sharply rising floors to high bilges, low freeboard. Most flush-decked, others had a raised quarter-deck. Carried a so-called **canoe*** or **yawl*** on either side of the forward hatch for the pilots' use; rowed. Two masts, either nearly vertical or raking aft. Generally narrow foresail, large mainsail; both boomed. Several headsails and usually topsails. Crew of 4-6, plus 4-6 pilots. Reported lengths 19-34m; an 1876 vessel was 22.5m long on the rail, 20.4m between perpendiculars, 6m wide, 3m deep. Note also **pilot yawl**.

Boston whaler Popular open craft with square ends, straight sides, flat bottom specially shaped for planing. Constructed of fiberglass. Used with an outboard motor.

Boston Whitehall See **Whitehall boat**

bot 1. *France:* In the mid-19th century, a boat rigged as a **cutter*** or **sloop***.
2. *France, SW:* Small Dordogne River **gabare*** of the 18th-19th centuries.
3. *India, W:* Term for a small **galbat*** or **canoe***. Spelling variants: **bôt**, **bote*** (in Konkani); **bota*** (in Marathi).
4. *Indonesia/Malaysia:* General term for a western-type **boat***. In northern Sumatra and the Riau Archipelago, the **bot** was an undecked **sloop**-rigged craft. May also refer to a boat that is mainly rowed. Other recorded names: **bhōt**, **sambo*** (at Atjeh)
5. *Papua New Guinea:* In Pidgin English, the word for **boat**.
6. *Papua New Guinea, Bismarck Archipelago:* In the Rabaul area on New Britain Island, a **bōt** is a western-style boat. A large boat is called a **bōt-i-tǎ**.
7. *Poland, N:* **Bôt** is a popular Kashubian term for a **boat**, especially one used for fishing in the Gulf of Danzig (Gdańsk). Rowed or sailed, usually setting a spritsail. Spelling variant: **but**
8. Russian word for **boat**. May refer to a wooden **fishing boat*** (**rybolovniya bot**), 15-20m long. Usually single-masted or motorized. Might also be a flat-bottomed freight boat, with one mast. Name variant: **botik** (dim.)
9. *Vanuatu (New Hebrides), western Pacific:* **Boat** in Bichelamar, the lingua franca of the islands. Spelling variant: **pot**
Further references: **batea**, **Bermudian**, **boat-1**, **Boot**, **bote-8**, **botr**, **botter**

bota *Italy, NW:* Type of **fishing boat*** in the dialect of the Liguria area. See also **bot-3**.
botaak See **botter**
bota da popa See **quarter boat-1**
botboot See **botter**
bot de llum See **lamparo**
bote 1. Non-specific Spanish and Portuguese term for a small, all-purpose boat that is open, solidly constructed, and relatively beamy. Mostly rowed but may set a small sail, such as a spritsail, or operate by motor. May also

denote a naval **ship's boat***, setting 1-3 leg-of-mutton, sprit-, or lugsails. Name variant: **botecillo** (dim.)
2. *Argentina:* One of the sailing cargo vessels reported in use on the Río Paraná in the late 18th century. Reported keel lengths 8.4-13.4m; draft 1.9-2.5m.
3. *Brazil:* **a. Fishing boat*** of the northeastern coastal area. Carvel planking, straight flaring sides, sharp deadrise amidships, deep skeg. Raked stem; raked transom is generally two-thirds of the beam; reverse sheer toward the bow. Decked; may have a fish hold. Sailing type still predominant. Usually sets a single triangular sail and jib when trolling for tuna. Many motorized. Reported lengths 6-9m, beam one-third length, depth one-third beam. Further reading: John Patrick Sarsfield, "Master Frame and Ribbands, A Brazilian Case Study..." in: *International Symposium on Boat and Ship Archaeology*, 5th, Amsterdam, 1988; *Carvel Construction Technique* (Oxford: Oxbow Books, 1991), 137-145. **b. Canoe***-type craft that plied the tributaries of the Amazon Basin. Characterized by arched mat-roofed cabins at each end, with an open space between. Sharp bow, square stern. Helmsman sat atop the after cabin to work the tiller. Paddled and poled; up to 6 oarsmen sat on each of the side decks. Reported lengths 26-32m; 1761 **bote** in Pará in the eastern basin was 26.4m long and 3m wide. Name variant: **canoa*** (in Pará)
4. *Colombia:* **a.** On the Caribbean coast, a **bote** is a single-piece **dugout canoe*** used mainly for fishing. Sharp, plumb cutwater with marked flare toward the gunwales; sharp sheer at bow; sharp stern. One with a rounded bow is called a **potrillo**. Thwart supporting the mast set onto residual ledges in the dugout sides. Lengths 3-8m, widths 1-2m, depth ca. 0.4m. **b.** On the inland waterways of central Colombia, the **bote** has wider uses and is plank-built; sharp bow. On the lower Río Magdalena, some have 2 decks and a shelter. Generally employ a motor; those with outboard motors go by the name **yonson** in places; others are towed. May have a capacity of 8-9t of livestock and cargo. Other recorded names: **falca***, **lancha***
5. *Peru:* **a.** Small, heavily constructed **fishing boat** found along the entire coast. Although design and rig vary slightly from place to place, certain characteristics prevail. A full bluff bow terminates in a heavy, straight stem, sometimes with a slight clipper-bow overhang. Wide, shallow wineglass transom, slightly raked. Rounded bottom, with shallow keel; short skeg to which the lower gudgeon of the outboard rudder is fitted. Most open except for a small cuddy; others decked, with a large central hatch and a small one at the stern. Often carried a small **balsa*** (**balsita**) as a **tender***. Mast steps

bote-5a

into a heavy block fastened to the keelson and passes through the after part of the cuddy. Standing rigging—forestay, 2 shrouds, 2 backstays. Sets a lugsail, leg-of-mutton, or gaff sail. Crew of 4-7. Reported lengths 5-8m, widths 1.7-2.7m, depths 1-1.7m, draft 0.45-1.0m. Name variant: **bote pescador. b.** A 19th-century type of **longboat**★ launched from beaches in the Pisco area of the central coast, originally for ship-to-shore work and later for fishing. Carvel-built on a keel, with light frames; strengthened by heavy knees and thwarts. Easy lines and short run. Wide wineglass transom. Formerly rigged as a spritsail **schooner**★ with short, easily unstepped masts; also set a small jib. Later used leg-of-mutton or gaff sails or a single spritsail. Also rowed; now use outboard motors. Ca. 6m long.

6. *Poland, N:* The indigenous **Böte** of the Elbing River was an oak and spruce vessel with a keel. Reported lengths 15-18m, beam 3.7-4.3m.

7. *Portugal:* **a.** Open boat with straight vertical stem, raked square stern. Engaged in coastal hook-and-line fishing out of Sesimbra, south of Lisbon. High-peaked spritsails; forward mast inclined slightly aft; after mast smaller and vertical. Also rowed. **b. Fishing boat** that works out of Ericeira, north of Lisbon. Carvel-planked, upright stem, elliptical transom stern. Sets a lateen sail to a single mast. Also rowed. Ca. 4.5m long. **c.** A type of cargo vessel of the Tagus River area that still serves Lisbon and outlying towns. Carvel-planked; flat floors amidships, S-curve aft, rounded bilges; graceful sheer; solid bulwarks, 2 bollards at bow and on the stern quarters; washboards may be installed. Plumb stem, raked rectangular transom; stem and rudderhead of similar height, shape, and decoration; tiller slots over rudderhead. Open waist, decked at bow and stern. Two heavy wales (*cintas*) on each side; light-colored bow patch, formerly with floral motifs; 2-3 overlapping half circles decorate bow and stern quarters between the wales and cap rail. Pole mast rakes slightly forward. Early vessels set a quadrilateral lateen-type sail with a short luff, now fitted with a loose-footed gaff sail and 1-2 headsails. Also rowed. Reported lengths 9-20m; e.g., length 15m, beam 4.3m, depth 1.85m. Name variant: **bote de quatro cintas.** The **bote de meia-quilha** is essentially the same except for concave floors with accentuated bilges and a shallower keel. Sometimes runs out a short bowsprit for a flying jib. Note also **bote fragata. d.** Serves as an **enviada**★ for **muletas**★ working out of the Tagus, carrying the catch to Lisbon markets. Slightly curved stem, square stern, maximum beam well forward, single wale. Decked, central hatch; 2 bollards forward and 4 aft for use in tying up alongside the **muleta.** Outboard rudder; tiller. Slightly forward-raking mast stepped about a quarter in from the bow. Sets a quadrilateral lateen-type sail with short luff that can be brailed; small jib to a rising bowsprit. Crew of 4. Length 8.8m, beam 2.6m, depth 1.0m; 4.5rt. Name variant: **bote do Seixal. e.** Common type in the southern coastal zone; works with the *xávega* net. Rowed with as many as 8 oars, and some set a lateen sail or quadrilateral lateen-type sail with a short luff. Recently adopted an outboard motor. Length 6m, beam 2m, depth 0.6m. Name variant: **bote da calima**

8. *Spain:* General term for a small **fishing boat**, often serving as an auxiliary to a larger boat. Construction details vary widely with locale and designated activity. Ends may be sharp, or the stern rounded

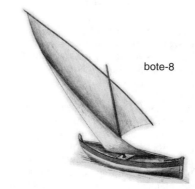

bote-8

and raked to varying degrees. Floors often flat. Essentially open, but may have small end and side decks. Outboard rudder, often hanging well below the bottom; tiller. Rowed and sailed. Dipping lug- or lateen sail is set to a single mast. Those fishing for lobster may have 6 in crew. Reported lengths 3.8-8.8m; e.g., length 6.5m, beam 2.76m, depth 0.85m. Other recorded names: **bote de pesca, bot**★ (in Cataluña and Valencia), **pirlo** (in Galicia)

9. *Thailand:* Term that may merely mean **boat**★.

10. *Venezuela:* Small **fishing boat** of Isla de Margarita, off the mainland coast. Mainly rowed, but sailed occasionally. Some had a live well.

Further references: **boat-1, bongo-2, bot-3, canoa do baleeiro, catraia-3, Erdlomme, galeão-1, lifeboat**

bote cacilheiro *Portugal, central:* Vessel that moved passengers and cargo across the Tagus River to and from Lisbon. Carvel-planked; straight stem with high stemhead; raked transom stern; rounded bilges; keel; single thin wale along each side. Light-colored, wedge-shaped decoration at the bows, stripe along upper edge and in the interior. Single gaff sail and headsails; early boats set a quadrilateral lateen-type sail with a short luff. Also rowed. Reported lengths 9.8-12.2m; e.g., length 10.2m, beam 3m, depth 1.37m. Name variant: **cacilheiro.** Note also **canoa cacilheira.**

bote-canoa See **canoa-12**

bote catraio *Portugal, central:* Popular water taxi in the Lisbon area; sometimes used for fishing and cargo. Common early in the 20th century. Carvel-planked; straight stem, cutaway forefoot; long keel; transom stern. Single light wale along each side; open. Generally set spritsails on the mainmast and small mizzenmast, sheeted to an outrigger; jib set flying from the bowsprit. Sometimes lacked mizzenmast. Early boats set a quadrilateral lateen-type sail with a short luff as a mainsail. Also rowed with 2-6 oars. Crew of 1-3; could carry 25 passengers. Reported lengths 5.5-8m; e.g., length 6.45m, beam 2.14m, depth 0.7m. Other recorded names: **bote de catraiar, catraieiro, catraio**★, **catrajo.** Note also **catraia.**

bote chalana See **chalana-6**

botecillo See **bote-1**

bote da arte de tartaranha See **batel do Seixal**
bote da calima See **bote-7**
bote da tartaranha See **batel do Seixal**
bote de almirante See **barge-2**
bote de carroza See **houseboat-1**
bote de catraiar See **bote catraio**
bote de lastrar See **ballast boat**
bote de los pescantes del costado See **quarter boat**
bote de los pescantes de popa See **stern boat**
bote de meia-quilha See **bote-7**
bote de pesca See **bote-8**
bote de pescador See **fishing boat**
bote de pinho *Portugal, central:* Beamy vessel of the Tagus River that specialized in transporting pine branches for Lisbon bakeries and, at times, freighted straw upriver for the army, earning the additional name of **straw boat★**. No longer needed in these capacities, the few remaining boats carry general cargoes. Carvel-planked; flat floors with full bilges; keel; open. Plumb stem with high stemhead; raked transom stern. Two heavy wales along each side; 2 bollards at bow and aft quarters. Tiller slotted over the tall rudderhead; heel of rudder slopes downward and aft, below the keel line. Loads of branches were often so wide that the excess was supported by the vessel's 2 **tenders★** tied one to each side. Set a lateen sail or loose-footed gaff sail, with 2 headsails. Reported lengths 13.3-14.2m; e.g., length 14.2m, beam 4m, depth 1.75m. Other recorded names: **bote do pinho, pine boat**
bote de popa See **quarter boat**
bote de práctico See **pilot boat**
bote de quatro cintas See **bote-7**
bote de rancheros See **bumboat-1**
bote de remo See **catraia-3**
bote de remos See **rowboat-1**
bote de remos pareles See **double-banked boat**
bote de ronda See **guard boat-1**
bote de rueda a popa See **paddle-box boat**
bote de salvamento See **accident boat**
bote de vela *Puerto Rico:* Term used on this West Indian island for the local **schooners★**. Further references: **catraia-3, sailboat**
bote do arrasto See **muleta**
bote do camarão *Portugal, central:* Small, fine-lined boat that fishes for shrimp (*camarão*) with a beam trawl along the north shore of the Tagus River. Carvel-planked; vertical stem, cutaway forefoot; wide, raked transom; single wale along each side; short bilge keel. Open except for short fore- and stern decks. Rowed with single pair of oars. Worked by 1 man. Length 3.8m, beam 1.4m, depth 0.56m.
bote do pinho See **bote de pinho**
bote do Seixal See **batel do Seixal, bote-7**
bote falucho See **falucho-4**
bote fragata *Portugal, central:* Cargo vessel of the Tagus Estuary that has features of both the **bote★** and the **fragata★**. Carvel-planked with continuous, graceful sheer; 2 wales extend along each side; sometimes washboards added; a pair of bitts on each quarter. Slight rise to the floors, rounded bilges. Straight vertical stem with high stemhead; rounded gripe; flat,

raked transom. Tiller slotted through rudderhead. Bulwarks and transom painted black; half-circle decoration at bows and on stern quarters, between wales and cap rail; sometimes lack bow patches. Loose-footed gaff sail set to a slightly aft-raking mast; tall staysail. Length overall 11.5m, between perpendiculars 10.2m, beam 3.76m, depth 1.7m; some much smaller.
bote lancha See **longboat-1, ship's boat**
botella See **battela-1**
Botel Tobago canoe See **chinedkulan**
bote mineiro See **barco mineiro**
boteng pamunuanan *Philippines, central:* General-purpose boat originally designed to work the *pamunuanan* fish corral, but it became popular for other uses, including as an important **ship's boat★** for larger craft. Dugout hull; sharp bow, straight above the waterline, curved below; moderate bow flare; tucked-up plumb transom; strong sheer. Open; short foredeck and stern bench. Outboard rudder; tiller. Rowed, paddled, or sailed, setting a spritsail. Those used to tow **bancas★** to fishing grounds are motorized. Crew of 5 oarsmen or 10 paddlers.
bote pescador See **bote-5**
bote salvavidas See **lifeboat**
bote salvavidas de los tambores See **paddle-box boat**
bote valiza See **beacon boat-1**
bote vivandero See **bumboat-1**
bote vivero See **vivero-3b**
bote volanteiro See **bote xeiteiro**
bote xeiteiro *Spain, NW:* Fished with the *xeito* net out of ports in southwestern Galicia. Also built in northern Portugal. Open; sharp, raked ends; stem and sternpost curved or straight; bow higher than stern. Narrow rudder, drops below keel; short tiller. Mast, stepped through a thwart, rakes sharply aft. Sets a lugsail, either rectangular or square; tacked to stemhead, sheeted aft. Also rowed, 6 oars per side. Crew of 6-7. Reported lengths 4.2-6m; e.g., length 4.2m, beam 1.68m, depth 1.0m. Name variant: **bote volanteiro**. Note also **xeito**.
both See **boat-1**
bother See **botter**
bothome See **bottoms-3**
botik See **bot-8**
botilla See **batela-1**
bōt-i-tǎ See **bot-6**
botnik See **bat-3**
botome See **bottoms-1**
botr *Loyalty Islands, New Caledonia, western Pacific:* Term for **boat★** in the Nengone dialect of Mare Island. In the Dehi dialect on Lifou, it is **bot★**.
bòtry See **boutre**
botschuit, botsleeper See **botter**
botte *Canada, E:* In the Magdalen Islands in the Gulf of St. Lawrence, **botte** can be generic for **boat★**, but generally refers to a specific type of coastal lobstering and **fishing boat★**. Now motorized (**botte à moteur**), but originally rowed or sailed, setting a loose-footed gaff sail and using a centerboard. Early boats mainly clinker-planked, now carvel. The sharp-ended type (**botte pointu**) superseded by a flat-sterned type suitable for handling lobster traps; some counter-sterned. Open or

has a small rough cabin. Note also **gabarre**. Further reference: **boat-1**

botte à moteur See **botte**

bōttelammañci See **kalla dhoni**

bottengarnprâm See **pålpråm**

botte pointu See **botte**

botter *Netherlands:* Zuiderzee, North Sea, and south-western Zeeland **fishing boat*** that worked until ca. 1966. Dates back ca. 400 years. The **Zuidwalbotter** of the south shore of the Zuiderzee is considered to have the most pleasing lines. The **Westwalbotter** of the western shore had a fuller build. The **botter van**

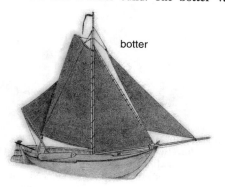

botter

Baasrode was built on the Scheldt River southwest of Antwerp. Some worked in pairs, and some were specifically built to work left or right. Heavily constructed of oak, carvel-planked; narrow bulwarks with sharp tumble home above the wale. Bottom flat or has a slight rise to the floors; bottom about half the maximum beam. Hard chine at the bilges; shallow keel; wide deadwood. Bold sheer forward, merging to a point at the stemhead; stem curved and raked, sometimes with a small gripe at the foot; bluff bow. Low stern, rounded with narrow quarters; raked sternpost. Prominent hatchet-shaped rudder; tiller. Greatest beam about one-third from the bow. Long, narrow leeboards. Decked forward; small stern deck. Live well amidships. **Botters** working on the North Sea were fully decked, with steering cockpit. Heavy pole mast set a narrow, loose-footed, boomed mainsail; short gaff, either straight or curved. Mast stepped in tabernacle; iron rod forestay. Large fore staysail often overlapped the mast. Long, light reefing bowsprit and jib run out when fishing and on **yachts**. Long, triangular sail (often an old jib) hoisted to the mast and boomed out aft for added speed, especially on runs home after fishing. Motors installed beginning ca. 1915. Crew of 2-5. Reported lengths 9-18m; the **Zuiderzeebotter** was generally shorter than 13.5m; e.g., length overall 10.6m, beam 3.66m, depth 0.95m. **Zuidwalbotters** carried more sail and were 12.45-13.5m long, 4.3-4.4m wide, 1.0m deep. The more heavily built **Noordzeebotter** from Urk Island was fully decked, with steering cockpit, and had a higher counter, partial washboard on top strake, fuller body underwater, and narrower rudder. Usually 12.8-19m long; e.g., length 18m, beam 5.3m, depth 2.2m. The **botter van Baasrode** was similar. **Botters** are still seen converted

to, or specially designed as, **yachts*** (**botterjacht**). Name variants: **Nordzeebotter, North Sea botter, Oostwalbotter, Urker botter**. Other recorded names: **bot***, **botaak, botboot, bother, botschuit, botsleeper, botterje** (dim.), **botting, Fischerbotter, visbotter, Zuyderzeebotter**; from the south coast, the **Bunschoter** (**botter**) (from Bunschoter), **Gooise** (or **Gooier**) **botter, Gooysche vischbotter, Huizer botter** (from Huizen). Further reading: Peter Dorleijn, *Geen Moed Vist Ook, Fragmenten Uit de Zuiderzeevisserij* (Bussum: Uniboek, 1977); Jules Van Beylen, *De Botter: Geschiednis en Bouwbeschrijving van een Nederlands Visserschip* (Weesp: De Boer Maritiem, 1985). Note also **koopbotter, kwak, Marker botter, Waalschokker.**

botterjacht, botterje, botter van Baasrode, botting See **botter**

bottoms 1. Maritime term, often legal, for **ships***, **vessels***, **boats***. Often referred to in association with ships of another country, e.g., **foreign bottoms, stranger's bottoms, Dutch bottoms**. Term used at least as early as the early 16th century. Spelling variant: **botome**

2. Term may apply to **lighters*** lying side-by-side on the mud.

3. *England:* **a. Hereditary bottoms** were ships chartered to the East India Company, which had the proprietary right to replace them when they became unseaworthy. **b.** Term given to small boats that ferried passengers. Cited from The Fens and the Thames. Spelling variant: **bothome**

botvissertje See **Zeeuwse schouw**

bou *Spain:* Term applied to a boat that trawls with a *bou* net. Name variant: **baca***. See also **baobao, buey.**

bouafouyé See **boumba**

bouanga See **juanga-l**

boucanier See **buccaneer**

boucaut See **bullboat-2**

bouco *United States, central:* Temporary craft used by early settlers to cross streams. Two hides were stretched over a pole framework, creating a tub-like boat. Name variant: **coracle***. Note also **bullboat, pelota.**

boudarka *Russia, central:* Open **fishing boat*** of the Caspian Sea, especially in the Astrakhan area. Light construction, flat floors, rounded bilges, flaring sides, strong sheer. Long, sharply raked straight stem; narrow V-transom, less raked than the bow. One to 2 masts setting lug- or spritsail(s). Also rowed. Reported lengths 6.3-7.6m, beam ca. 1.5m. Spelling variant: **baudarka**

bou-écran See **ni mo chuan**

bougalet See **bugalet**

bouier See **boeier**

boulter boat See **Plymouth hooker**

boum See **boom**

boumba *Haiti:* A **dugout canoe***, especially one that carries provisions. Some engage in fishing, using handlines and lobster baskets. Bow wide, blunt, and sweeps up; stern low. Reported lengths 4.6-5.5m. Other recorded names: **bois fouillé, bouafouyé, bounba**. Note also **bumboat.**

boumkane See **dugout canoe**

bounba See **boumba**

bounty boat A **fishing boat**★ or **merchantman**★ built or operated with a bounty or subsidy from the government. The bounty was employed most often in times of war, and was awarded to vessels suitable for defense purposes. Term used most often in Great Britain and France. Name variant: **bounty ship**. Note also **buss**.

bounty buss See **buss-2**

bounty ship See **bounty boat**

boupaa See **baobao**

bouri See **bhur**

bouri de nage *Bangladesh, S/India, NE:* **Canoe**★-like boat that preceded the large **bouri** (see **bhur**) as it traveled, mainly in the Ganges Delta. Planked hull, cone-shaped raised ends. Rowed and sailed, but a poor sailer. Spelling variant: pl. **bouris de nage**

bourie See **bhur**

bouris de nage See **bouri de nage**

bout *Papua New Guinea, E:* Generic term for **boat**★; not applied to local **canoes**★ or to a **ship**★. Word used on Buka Island and northern Bougainville in the northern Solomon chain. See also **dhow**.

bouticlar, bouticlard See **vivier-2**

boutilla See **battela-1**

boutique See **vivier-2**

boutre *Malagasy Republic:* On the northwest coast, where Arabs intermixed with the Malagasy peoples, these **dhow**★-type vessels were built as early as the 17th century. Mostly smaller and of poorer construction than similar boats elsewhere. Sharp bow, with curved and strongly raked stem; lightly raked square stern; maximum beam well aft; straight sides; shallow rise to the floors. Usually undecked; when decked called a **kotia**★; low mat house covered midship area. Carried a single-**outrigger canoe**★ as a **ship's boat**★. Caulked with cotton saturated with fish oil; hull coated with lime, fat, and tallow. Two sharply raking masts set lateen sails. The small mizzenmast was counterbalanced from a stubby post above the deck level. Ranged from ca. 150-200t. Spelling variants: **bòtry**, **butri**. Further references: **dao, dhow-1**

bouyer See **boeier**

bovenlander See **aak, herna, Oberländer-1, spitsbek**

bovenlandsche baggeraakje, bovenmaasche aak, bovenmaasche baggeraak See **bovenmaase aak**

bovenmaase aak *Netherlands, S:* An **aak**★-type vessel of the middle and upper Maas River that dredged sandflats and transported merchandise; some still working in the 1960s. Flat bottom turns up at the overhanging bow to form a flat surface that tapers to a point at the gunwales; angular chines. Sharp stern, small sternpost and skeg. Carvel planking, with top strake clinker; flat sheer, with some rise at the ends. Some, as at Hedel (the similar **Hedelse aak**), employed leeboards. Some used a special rudder in which the post passed up through the stern; tiller activated the post as well as a curved wooden beam attached to the outer edge of the blade. Cuddy forward or aft; open waist. Spritsail to a lowering mast common, or set a loose-footed, boomed gaff mainsail and staysail. Reported lengths 12-16m; e.g., length ca. 15.5m, beam 3.4m, depth ca. 1.0m. Other recorded

names: **bovenlandsche baggeraakje, bovenmaasche (bagger)aak, Hedelsche aak**. Note also **baggeraak**.

bovi See **bovo**

bovo *Italy, west coast and Sicily:* Two-masted vessel that evolved in the 18th century, worked during the 19th century, but is now extinct. Early vessels were **corsairs**★, later used for cargo, notably to carry grain and wine from Sicily, or as a **fishing boat**★, often

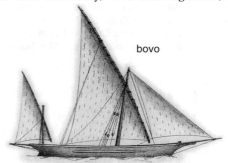

bovo

going to North Africa. Off Tunisia some served as **mother ships**★ for the small sponge-seeking **barchetti** (see **barchetta**). Curved, raked stem; sharp bow; sometimes clipper-bowed; square or rounded counter stern; slight sheer. Decked, pronounced camber to the deck. Large lateen sail set to the mainmast; early vessels might add a small square topsail, later a yard topsail. Short mizzenmast set a lateen or gaff sail sheeted to an outrigger. Long bowsprit carried 1 large or 2 small jibs. Towed a **canotto**★ or carried it on deck. **Fishing boats** had a crew of 6-7. Reported lengths of cargo vessels 16.5-25.2m, widths 4.8-7m, depths 2.18-2.95m; **fishing boats** were 11.4-15m by 3.3-4.3m by 0.9-1.54m. Spelling variant: pl. **bovi**. Note also **bateau bœuf**. Further reference: **pareggia**

bow boat *United States:* Lumber industry term for a small boat placed at the forward end of a **lumber** or **log raft** (see **timber raft**) as a steering aid. Also, in the mid- to late 19th century in the Mississippi basin, **bow boats** were secured to the front of a long string of **barges**★ that were being pushed by a **push boat**★. This **steamer** was lashed "athwartships." Also aided in organizing the tow and catching runaway **barges**. Length ca. 15m, beam 3m. See also **whaler-3**.

bow box See **hinge boat**

bow picker See **gillnetter-1**

bowsprit sloop See **smack boat-1**

box See **Barnegat sneakbox, flatboat-4, sinkbox**

box boat 1. *England, central:* Type of **canal boat**★ that transported coal from the mines in open iron boxes; others carried limestone and ironstone. At the terminal the boxes were lifted to the quay by a dockside crane. The boxes emptied their load through doors on the bottom. Some worked into the 1950s. In one area, a modern type still carries automobile components. Original boats were sharp-ended, slab-sided, decked at the ends, and had a large rudder. Rowed. Reported lengths 20.7-21.3m; e.g., length 21.3m, beam 2m. Note also **coal box-1**.

2. *United States, E:* **a.** Box boats were used on the "Main Line" canal system across Pennsylvania. Cargo

carried in special boxes on decks of canal **barges** in the 1st half of the 19th century. **b.** Chesapeake Bay term for a plank-built, hard-chine **freight boat★**.
Further reference: **flatboat-5**

box-built boat See **skipjack-1**

box cabin boat See **day boat-2**

box float 1. *United Kingdom:* A British navy service **float★** made of rubber covered with plywood. Cap. 8 people.
2. *United States, E:* **Punt★**-type craft of colonial Virginia. Flat bottom, curved up to end transoms; near-vertical sides, narrowing toward the ends. Short end decks, side decks. Rowed, double tholepins. Name variant: **scow★**

boxman See **fleeter**

box in wood for a clock See **berrichon**

box trow See **trow-1**

boyart See **hoy**

boyer Flat-floored vessel common in the Baltic Sea during the 18th century. Set a gaff and square sail to the mainmast and square topsails; gaff mizzen. Shallow draft. See also **boeier**, **Bojer**.

boyert *Sweden:* 17th-century pleasure craft. Rounded bow and stern, raked ends, straight keel, rising floors, rounded bilges; sides had tumble home. Decked forward, cabin and cockpit abaft the mast. Carvings at bow and stern and on rudderhead. Gaff-rigged with 2 headsails. Length 11m, beam 3.8m, depth 1.3m.

Boyne coracle See **Boyne curragh**

Boyne curragh *Ireland, E:* **Coracle★**-shaped salmon **fishing boat★** of the Boyne River valley; still used. Steep-sided, oval or nearly round. Constructed upside down by inserting the ends of hazel rods into the ground—7 set longitudinally and 8 set transversely; rods arched to opposite side and tied where they cross. Gunwale formed by several rows of rods with a thick rim of rods added to protect the top against the nets. Crossbraces of withes provided further support. Softened skin, usually tanned oxhide, was laced to the gunwale at short intervals; tarred canvas more prevalent later. Paddler kneels in the bow while a 2nd person sits on a wooden seat tending the net. Seat slung from rope or withe braces attached to sides and rear of the frame. Paddle blade flat on one side, curved on the other, spade-shaped handle. Reported lengths 1.8-1.9m, widths 1.16-

Boyne curragh

1.9m, depth ca. 0.43m. Name variant: **Boyne coracle**. Further reading: James Hornell, *British Coracles and Irish Curraghs*, Pt. II (London: Society for Nautical Research, 1938), 154-161. Note also **curragh**.

Brabantsch beurtschip, Brabantsch gaffelaar See **beurtschip**

Brabantse beurtschuit See **beurtschuit**

Brabantse schoenerkof See **kof**

Brabantse schuit See **beurtschuit**, **schuit-2**

bracera, bracere, bracerica, bracerina, bracerota See **brazzera**

bracózzo See **bragozzo**

Braddenkahn See **kurnevalts**

bragagna *Italy, NE:* Long, narrow 3-masted vessel that engaged mainly in lagoon and marsh fishing from March to October, working mainly out of Chioggia at the southern end of the Lagoon of Venice. Drifted broadside with a *bragagna* net. Replaced toward the end of the 19th century by the **bragozetto**, which may still be called a **bragagna** since it uses the same net. Sharp bow, curved stem; sharp or rounded stern, curved sternpost. Flat bottom, longitudinally planked. Ribs and floor timbers abut; slightly curved sides. Decked at the ends, narrow side decks. Three strong crossbeams flush with the top strake. In calms, windlass amidships used to winch the vessel toward a pole that has been carried forward and driven into the mud. Very deep rudder; long tiller slotted over the rudderhead. Decorated with a design at the bows or with white circular oculi. Carried a **burchiello★** or a small **maròta★** (boat-like fish tanks for the catch) outboard over the bow or stern. Fore- and aft masts raked outward. Mainmast either vertical or raked aft, braced against the center beam, stepped on the midline or just off to port; other masts stepped through beams. Set large rectangular lugsails, hung from the center of the yard, boomed at the foot, and generally overlapping. Forward 2 sails trapezoidal, after sail roughly square. Also rowed, using the local type of hooked oar rest, the central 2 notched on both sides so the vessel could be rowed in either direction. Crew of 2-4. Reported lengths 9-15m; e.g., length 11.13m, beam 1.76m, depth 0.7m. Other recorded names: **bargagno**, **bragagnello, braganja, bragozzetto**; pl. **bragagne**; **bragoz(z)etti**. Further reading: M. Marzari, "The Bragagna," *The Mariner's Mirror* 69 (1983), 143-155. Note also **portolata**.

bragagne, bragagnello See **bragagna**

bragamtim See **brigantine**

braganja See **bragagna**

bragantym See **brigantine**

bragazzo, bragoc, bragoci, brago da pesca, bragóso, bragósso See **bragozzo**

bragozetti, bragozetto See **bragagna**

bragózo, bragozze See **bragozzo**

bragozzetto See **bragagna**, **bragozzo**

bragozzetto chiogiotto, bragozo, bragozze, bragozzi, bragozzija See **bragozzo**

bragozzo *Italy, NW:* Lug-sailed **fishing boat★** of the Adriatic, most working out of Chioggia at the south end of the Lagoon of Venice, but also found along the Istrian Peninsula. Tows trawl nets, the smaller types often working in pairs; some small boats still operate. Heavily constructed and boxy in appearance; generally have a flat bottom with no keel, although some Istrian boats have a shallow keel; slight fore-and-aft rocker. Bluff bow; strongly curved stem; sternpost less curved or may be straight; wide flat stern. Very large rudder, almost half of which extends below the bottom, serving in lieu of a centerboard; in shallow water rudder triced up with heavy tackle from the masthead; long tiller. Originally open, but later decked, with one or more small cockpits; deck cambered. Hull painted black, but many had distinctive and intricate paintings, often religious, at the bows; oculi common. An elaborate and individual wind vane carried on the mainmast. When working alone, the boat may tow a live fish box, either a 8.7-14m long **maròta**★ or a 3.8m **burchiello**★. Boomed balance lugsails set to port on a tall mainmast and shorter foremast, the latter raking forward. Occasionally a jib might run to a jibboom. Smaller boats single-masted.

bragozzo

Sails colorful, often with paintings and geometric designs. At times employ 2-4 oars, using the tall fulcrum-type oarlock of the Venetian area. Auxiliaries now common. Crew mostly 2-4, plus a boy. Reported lengths 8-22m; e.g., length 13m, beam 3.3m, depth 1.0m; length-to-beam ratio generally not greater than 4:1. The longer, heavier type, the **bragozzo d'altura**, engaged in deep-sea fishing and had a crew of 6-8. The small, single-masted **bragozzetto chiogiotto** was constructed along similar lines. Mast stepped about two-thirds back from the bow. Reported lengths 8-10m; e.g., length 9m, beam 2.6m, depth 1.0m. Other recorded names: **bar(a)góso, bar(a)gozzo, barcóso**★, **bargózo, bbràhozzë, bbrayòzzë, bergozzo, bracózzo, bragazzo, bragoc(i), brago da pesca, bragós(s)o, brágózo, bragozze, bragozzija, bragozzo cervesi, bragozzo chioggiotto, bragozzo istriano, bragozzo romagnolo, braguc, braguoso, braguzo; shiletto** (at Ancona); **trabaccolo da pesca** (erroneously); pl. **bragozzi**. Further reading: Mario Mazari, *Il Bragozzo, Storiae Tradizioni della Tipica Barca da Pescadell'Adriatico* (Milan: U. Mursia Editore, 1982). Note also **battelluccio, portolata**.

bragozzo cervesi, bragozzo chiogiotto, bragozzo d'altura, bragozzo istriano, bragozzo romagnolo, braguc, braguoso, braguzo See **bragozzo**

brail See **timber raft-3**

brakeka See **vrakeka**

brama See **shnyaka-2**

Bramsegelschoner, bramsejlskonnert See **schooner-1**

Brancaster canoe, Brancaster flatty See **flattie-2**

brander See **fire ship**

brandschip, brandschiff See **fire ship**

brandschuit See **somp**

Brandungsboot See **surfboat-1**

bränuare See **fire ship**

brasiera, brassera See **brazzera**

bratsera *Greece:* Fishing and cargo vessel, the term referring primarily to its lug rig, although the word may be used locally for any 2-masted vessel rigged

similarly. Most sharp-ended, with curved stem and straight raked sternpost, but some have a counter stern and clipper bow, and others a transom stern. Strong sheer, especially forward. Cambered deck, deckhouse on some. Most have a forward-raking foremast and an aft-raking mainmast. Set a boomed trapezoidal balance lug foresail and standing lug mainsail. Two or 3 jibs run to a long rising bowsprit, sometimes bowsed down; may set a small yard topsail on the mainmast. Auxiliaries common after World War I. Crew of 3-4. Reported lengths 15-17.5m; e.g., length 17.5m, beam 5.2m, depth 2.75m. Other recorded names: **brazzera**★, **vratsera**. Note also **kaiki, trechandiri**.

brazèra, brazèra da Comisa, brazèra istriana, brazèra piranse See **brazzera**

brazzera *Croatia/Italy, NE:* A small **fishing boat**★ or a larger robust **coaster**★ of the Adriatic; reported from the early 18th century, having originated at the island of Brazza (Brac) on the central Dalmatian coast. Extinct. Sharp ends; flat floors; keel; bold sheer; curved stem which may be strongly recurved, sometimes with a knob on the stemhead. Open except at ends. Mainly sailed but might be rowed, double-banked, with 6 pairs of oars. Early boats set square sails, later lug, lateen, or gaff. Crew of 2-6. Reported lengths 7-12m, widths 3-4m, depths 0.5-2m. Several local variations of Istrian Peninsula vessels have been identified: The **brazzera di Capodistria** (Koper) had a sharp bow and full stern; stepped 2 masts, close together forward, setting lateen sails; fixed bowsprit; sometimes a mizzenmast. The **brazzera Istriana** had oculi at the bows, a single mast setting a lugsail, and flying jib to a reefing bowsprit. The economically constructed **brazzera di Pirano** set a single lugsail and a small jib. On the Dalmatian coast, the elegant **brazzera Dalmata** had a full stern and sharp bow with hollow entrance, clipper stem, and set a lugsail and flying jib to a fixed bowsprit; later a gaff sail common, long gaff. Other recorded names: **barsera, bracera, brasiera, brassera, brazèra, brazèra da Comisa, brazèra istriana, brazèra piranse**; pl. **bracere, brazzero**; dim. **bracerica, bracerina, bracerota**. Further reference: **bratsera**

brazzera Dalmata, brazzera di Capodistria, brazzera di Pirano, brazzera Istriana, brazzero See **brazzera**

bread pan See **compartment boat**

Brëëm *Switzerland, north-central:* On Lake of Zurich, a **dumb barge**★ that transports gravel, mud, etc. Square ends, flat bottom, open; currently of steel. The **Fale-Brëëm** has a trap door in the bottom to release dredged materials. Maneuvered by a **tug**★. Cap. 100-250t. Other recorded names: pl. **Brëëme; Prahm**★

bregada See **frigate-4**

bregandine, bregantin See **brigantine**

bregantini, bregantino See **brigantino**

Breitlingslomme See **żakówka**

brêk See **brig**

brelle See **train de bois**

Bremerkahn See **Kahn-2**

Breton tunnyman See **thonier**

Bretterfloss *Austria/Germany:* **Rafts**★ composed of sawn lumber that ran numerous rivers since at least the 16th century. Those on the Danube River composed of multiple units, each unit of 10-20 boards connected by special planks that enabled the units to swivel as demanded by the current. Along the side of each **raft** a board flared outward to deflect the water. Steered with multiple sweeps. Lengths to 100m, 20m wide, 1.0m deep. Other recorded names: **Bordfloss, Dielenfloss; Ladenkarl** (in the Danube area); **Sägewarenfloss** (in the Black Forest); **Stümmel** (on the Main); pl. **Bretterflösse.** Note also **timber raft.**

Bretterflösse See **Bretterfloss**

breu *Brazil:* A **dinghy★** or **bumboat★.**

bribane, bribenne See **gribane**

bric See **brig**

bricbarca See **bark-1**

bric-goeletă See **hermaphrodite brig**

brick See **barque du Léman, brig**

brick-barca See **bark-1**

brick barge See **brickie**

bricker See **Hudson River brick schooner**

brick-goélette See **hermaphrodite brig, skûna**

brickie *England, SE:* A **Thames sailing barge★** that carried bricks from sites on the north shore of Kent to London, returning with refuse to be used in brick making. Operated from the 19th to the mid-20th century. Boxy shape; extremely flat sheer; often awash in a seaway. Very long wooden tiller. Most employed a stumpy **barge★** rig, with a large, high-peaked sprit mainsail and a small sprit mizzen. Some set a topsail; a few were **schooner★**-rigged. Sails tanned. Averaged 100t of bricks. Name variant: **brick barge.** Further reference: **Brixham smack**

brick schooner See **Hudson River brick schooner**

brick scow See **scow schooner-3**

brick scuner See **hermaphrodite brig**

bricq See **brig**

bridge of boats See **pontoon-2**

Bridgwater barge See **Bridgwater boat**

Bridgwater boat *England, W:* Flat-bottomed **barge★** designed to work siliceous deposits from the banks of the River Parrett on the south shore of the Bristol Channel, and transport the mud to kilns at Bridgwater. Used from the 19th to the mid-20th century. Clinker-built, little sheer, deep stem, narrow tombstone stern, raked ends, bow fuller than stern, overlapping frames. Decked at ends; large-bladed rudder. Three forked sticks fitted into forecastle bulkhead for the towing chains. Steered by sweeps. Propelled by tide, tug, or tracked from shore. Length 16.8m, beam 4m, depth 1.3m. Other recorded names: **Bridgwater barge, flatner★**

Bridgwater flatner See **Parrett flatner**

Bridgwater trow See **trow-1**

brig Small 2-masted 18th- and 19th-century vessel of commerce and war (**brig of war**) that, for most of the period, set square sails on the fore- and mainmasts and multiple headsails. Some early vessels carried a lateen mainsail. **Brig** rig still found on some naval training ships. Bowsprit and jibboom. Term sometimes considered an abbreviation of **brigantine★**, or, erroneously, as a diminutive of that term. Selected name variants: **bergantín★, bergantí rodó; bergantinejo** (dim.); **bergantín redondo, brêk, bric, brick, bricq, brigg(en); brigger** (Norwegian pl.); **Briggschiff,**

brigue, brik(k), brug, bryg, langard, ybrgq. Note also **bantim, briki, cutter-brig, gun brig, hermaphrodite brig, snow.** Further reference: **winkle brig**

briga, brigandin, brigandine, brigantijn, brigantil See **brigantine**

brigantin 1. *Canada:* Small, slender ship used by the 16th- and 17th-century French, often as a naval vessel. Low sides with one deck. Carried a square sail on the foremast and lateen on the after mast. Vessels so rigged also engaged in offshore banks fishing.
2. *France/Switzerland:* A keel-built vessel of the **galley★** type used on Lake of Geneva (Lake Léman) in the 17th century. Equipped with 1-2 cannon. Had a cabin. Rowed with 5-8 oars per side, 1 man to each oar. Early **brigantins** had a single mast; by the end of the 19th century carried 2 lateen sails. Crew of 25-50 men, including the soldiers. Reported lengths 14.6-20m; e.g., length 14.6m, beam 3m.
3. *United States, south-central:* The French in Louisiana used the **brigantin** as a cargo vessel during the early 18th century, both in the Gulf of Mexico and on the Mississippi. Crew of 12. Cap. 15-70t. Further references: **barque du Léman, brigantine**

brigantina See **brigantine**

brigantine 1. Relatively small 2-masted vessel, mainly of the late 17th to the 19th century. Describes a rig type rather than the hull. Square sails set to the foremast, sometimes with a gaff sail behind. Mainmast originally set a tall square sail and later a boomed gaff or leg-of-mutton sail; topsails gaff or square; often one or more main staysails. In the late 17th century, square sails were set to both masts. Modern **brigantines** carry a fore-and-aft mainsail, a square main topsail and topgallant sail, but no sail on the lower yard. **Brig★** often used as a shortened form of **brigantine**, but the **brig** evolved into a separate type.
2. In the Mediterranean, the **brigantine** was a small **galley★** working under oars or sail. Also used during the 16th century on the Danube. It was a favorite of the sea brigands of the 17th and early 18th centuries, but during the 14th-16th centuries, the vessels engaged in reconnaissance work, often towed astern or carried knocked down aboard exploration vessels, including those of Christopher Columbus. Open or decked, some with a poop deck; flat-bottomed; often a ram bow. Steered with rudder and tiller. Employed 8-28 oars to a side, with 1 man to each long, slender oar. Lateen sails set to 1-2 masts, the foremast stepped well forward and the mainmast a little forward of amidships. Some used lateen sails on the foremast; mizzen and square sails on the mainmast. Reported lengths 12-19m; e.g., length 14m, beam 2.7m; shallow draft. Other recorded names: **bergantina** (small size), **caravenne.** Note also **half galley, real.**
3. *Argentina, NE:* A type of **brigantine** traded upriver to Paraguay until ca. 1940. Exceptionally tall masts, the fore topmast setting 2 square sails. Long rising bowsprit; main boom extended beyond the rounded counter stern. Built of local hardwoods *quebracho* and *viraco.* Rudder came up inboard.
4. *Maldive Islands:* Vessels with this rig sailed until at least the mid-20th century. Some had a deckhouse aft. Ca. 200t.

5. *Portugal:* The **bergantim** of the 16th-century Portuguese in South and Southeast Asia was a small **galeota**★. Lateen sail set to a single mast. Also rowed, employing 8-10 oars, with one man to an oar.

6. *Sri Lanka:* Locally owned **brigantine**-rigged vessels sailed, mostly out of Jaffna, until at least World War II. Traded mainly in the Gulf of Mannar area, but some made 3 trips annually to Myanmar (Burma) for rice. Built of teak, including the spars.

Selected name variants: **bargantí, bargantim, berganti, bergantim, bergantín★, bergantina, bergantini, birgende, birkindi, birkinti, borgantin, bragamtim, bragantym, bregandine, bregantin, briga, brigandin(e), brigantijn, brigantil, brigantin★, brigantina, brigantino★** (pl. **brigantini**), **brigantinus, brigantyn, brigentin, briguantin, bringantin, fregatim, Kruisbrik, Mufferdeibrigg, pergantini, pergende, vergantin.** Note also **bantim, hermaphrodite brig, polacre.**

brigantini See **brigantine, brigantino**

brigantino *Italy:* Venetian **galley**★ dating to the 13th century; carried letters around the **fleet**★, transported emissaries, etc. Rowed from 14-16 rowing benches, 2 men per oar. On some, a lateen sail set to a single mast. Spelling variants: **bergantin★, bergantine, bergantino, bergantinus, bregantino;** pl. **berganti, bregantini, brigantini.** Further reference: **brigantine**

brigantino a palo See **bark-1**

brigantino goletta See **hermaphrodite brig**

brigantinus, brigantyn See **brigantine**

brig corvette See **corvette-1**

brig-cutter See **cutter-brig**

brigentin See **brigantine**

brigg, briggen, brigger See **brig**

Briggkutter See **cutter-brig**

brig goélette, brig goletta See **hermaphrodite brig**

Briggschiff See **brig**

Briggschoner, Brigg-schoner See **hermaphrodite brig**

Brightlingsea oyster boat See **Essex smack**

Brighton beach boat *England, S:* Worked off the beach of this south coast town; hauled up by capstan originally, later onto ways. Generally clinker-built, some carvel. Flat floors originally, later greater rise; strong bilge keels; straight keel with some drag. Plumb stem, square counter above a raking sternpost. Centerboard; slot in counter admitted rudder when beaching. Decked to mast and at the counter; waterways along the open waist. **Cutter**★-rigged; large headsails. Length 6.4m, beam 2m, depth ca. 1.3m; shallow draft.

Brighton hog boat See **hog boat**

brigkutter See **cutter-brig**

brigoletta See **hermaphrodite brig**

brig of war See **brig**

brig polacre See **polacre**

brig schooner, brigškuner See **hermaphrodite brig**

brig-slaver See **slaver-1**

brig-sloop See **sloop-1**

briguantin See **brigantine**

brigue See **brig**

brigue-escuna See **hermaphrodite brig**

brik See **brig**

briki Greek term for a **brig**★. Important early 19th-century Greek-built ship during the Turkish occupation.

Clipper bow, counter stern. Long rising bowsprit for the 3 headsails. Gaff spanker boomed but loose-footed. Crew of 40-50, although armed vessels carried as many as 100 men. Mainly 200-350t. Name variants: **brikion, paron★**

brikion See **briki**

brikk See **brig**

brikškuna See **hermaphrodite brig**

brillsicken See **zig**

bringantin See **brigantine**

brise glace See **ice breaker**

brisse See **bucia, buss**

Bristol Bay gillnetter See **gillnetter-2**

British Columbia double-ender, British Columbia gillnet boat, British Columbia gillnetter See **gillnetter-2**

Brixham cutter, Brixham dandy, Brixham sloop See **Brixham smack**

Brixham smack *England, SW:* Red-sailed, deep-sea **trawler**★ of Brixham, in use from the latter part of the 18th to the mid-20th century; during this period, hull and rigging were altered to meet demands of new technologies. In general, the later **smacks**★ had a high bow with straight stem and cutaway forefoot, sharply raked sternpost, square or elliptical counter, fine entrance. Straight keel with drag, and sharp rise to the floors. Decked; forecastle held gear; fish hold abaft the mainmast; cabin aft; **ship's boat**★, called a **punt**★, carried on deck. Hand winch used for the beam trawl until the 1880s, when steam capstan installed. Mainmast stepped well aft and usually raked forward. **Cutter**★-rigged to turn of the century, **ketches**★ began coming into prominence ca. 1875. Sail plan varied with the season—in winter they used a heavy, loose-footed boomed mainsail and mizzen and a triangular main

Brixham smack

topsail, very large foresail, and multiple jibs. In summer the mainsail was lighter, mizzen larger, and topsails jib-headed or yard. Jibs set flying to a running bowsprit. Sails tanned. Engines installed later. Crew of 4-6. Reported lengths 11-30m; e.g., length 21.7m, beam 5.36m, depth 2.77m. **Brixham trawlers** were locally called **smacks**; those under 48t were designated **mules**★ (or **mulies**); large **ketch**-rigged vessels were called **big sloops**. Before World War I, the smaller **cutter**-rigged boats, under 25t, were known as **mumble bees**; crew of 2, plus a boy. Other recorded names: **brickie★, Brixham cutter** (or **dandy, sloop**), **long boomer, mumbleby, mumbles bee** (or **boat**). Further reading: John Corin, *"Provident" and the Story of the Brixham Smacks* (Reading, England: Tops'l Books, 1980).

Brixham trawler See **Brixham smack**

broadbeam See **flatboat-4**

broadhorn *United States, central:* A type of **flatboat★** that carried coal on the rivers in the Pittsburgh area of western Pennsylvania in the 19th century. Some proceeded to New Orleans; if the coal was unloaded at Vicksburg or Natchez, the boat was sold to a lumber yard where it was then loaded with wood for the rest of the trip, to be broken up upon arrival. Because of water levels and ice, ran only in the spring and late autumn. Built of 4cm lumber; flat bottom; straight sides; square ends. Operated in pairs, lashed side-by-side. House built on one of the boats was almost completely covered by coal when loaded. Accompanied by two 6-oared **skiffs★**. Crew of 12-20. Reported lengths 18-53m, beam ca. 7.3m, depth 2.4m. Other recorded names: **coal boat** (or **flat**). Note also **tow boat-4**. Further reference: **flatboat-4**

broadhorse See **flatboat-4**

Broadland wherry See **Norfolk wherry**

broadside sailing boat See **utase-ami gyosen**

Broads lateener *England, E:* Lateen-rigged boat mainly raced on the Norfolk Broads during the 19th century.

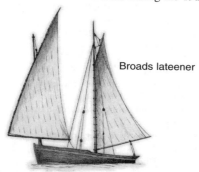

Broads lateener

Clinker-built with mildly curved and raking stem; low counter stern; steep rise to the floors; deep keel, with gripe forward. Rudderpost came up through the counter. Decked at bow and stern and along the sides. Initially lateen sails on fore- and mainmasts, modified to various combinations of lug-, lateen-, and gaff sails. Reported lengths 4.27-7.92m; e.g., length 6.7m, beam 2.44m, draft 0.96m. Name variant: **lateener★**

Broads wherry See **Norfolk wherry**

brod na točkove See **paddle boat-3**

brod plivari ar See **seine boat-1**

brogan *United States, E:* Evolved in the mid-19th century from the **Chesapeake Bay log canoe★** to meet the need for a larger and more seaworthy craft capable of pulling an oyster dredge and transporting the haul to distant markets on the bay. Bottom sometimes a single log that formed both the keel and floors; the remainder of the hull framed and planked; last boats of at least 5 logs. Sharp, raked ends, clipper bow. Open initially, with side decks, then fully decked with open hatches or half-decked; cuddy forward. Centerboard on most. Tiller used until the early 1890s, then a wheel. Boomed leg-of-mutton sails set to 2 heavy masts. Smaller mainmast raked farther aft than the foremast, which had an adjustable rake. Shrouds and forestay on foremast; mainmast removable. Jib, with partial club, ran to a short fixed bowsprit. Early boats set a square foresail; gaff foresail adopted in the late 19th century. Crew of 2-3. Reported lengths 10.6-17m; e.g., length 13m, beam 3.7m, draft 0.84m.

brønnbåt See **well boat-1**

Brown's Tract boat See **Adirondack guideboat**

bruchiello See **burchiello**

Brückenkahn, Brückenpontoon, Brückenschiff See **pontoon-2**

brug See **brig**

Bruinisser jacht See **lemmeraak**

bruletto, brûlot, brulote, brulotte, bruloto, brulotti, brulotto See **fire ship**

bryg See **brig**

buanga See **juanga-1**

Bubfisch Boot The German version of the **catboat★**. A pleasure craft. Note also **una boat**.

bucca See **bucia**

buccaneer Term sometimes given to a pre-18th-century vessel manned by pirates or buccaneers. Term popular in the West Indies. Spelling variant: **boucanier**. Note also **corsair**.

buccentoro See **bucintoro**

buccia, buccio See **bucia**

buce See **bucia, buss**

bucea, bucee See **bucia**

bucentarius See **bucintoro**

Bucentaur *Germany, S:* An elegant vessel (**Leibschiff★**) of the **bucintoro★** type built for the electors of Bavaria. Used from the latter part of the 17th into the 18th century on Starnberger See. Depicted as having a rounded bow from which 2 decorative rams projected, one above the other. Flat stern with 2 stairways leading to the dock or shore. Flat floors. Three decks, the lowest deck for the oarsmen, who numbered as many as 150. Usually armed. Set 1-2 large square sails. Length ca. 29m, beam 7.5m. Accompanied by a **fleet** of other craft, including smaller **galleys★** belonging to court members (as long as 23.5m) and Venetian-type **gondolas★**. Various support vessels were needed: the **cook boats** (**Küchenschiffe★** or **Küchlschiffe**), 20-25m long; the **beverage boat** (**Getränkschiff** or **Kellerschiff**), 15.7m long; a boat for the silver and tableware (**Silberschiff** or **Silberkammerschiff**), 13m long; the **Musikschiff** for the musicians. Small, flat, beamy boats (the **Farmschiffe, Fahrn,** or **Faren**) ferried furniture, firewood, ammunition for hunting; some were merely lake boats of the dugout type. Additional name variant: **Bucintoro★**. Further reading: Gerhard Schober, *Prunkschiffe auf dem Starnberger See* (Munich: Suddeutscher Verlag, 1982). Further reference: **bucintoro**

bucentaure, bucentauro, bucentaurum, bucentaurus, bucentorio, bucentoro, bucentorus See **bucintoro**

buceta *Spain:* **1.** A boat that engaged in port traffic; elevated and slightly raking bow; lateen-rigged.

2. Flat-bottomed craft used while cleaning and painting the sides of ships. Also aided in the transfer of small vessels from one site to another.

3. In northwestern Spain, a small, sharp-ended **fishing boat★**. In some areas, engages in line fishing for conger eels; elsewhere they fish for pout, octopus, or shellfish. Carvel-planked; slightly raked stem and sternpost;

curved sides; keel ca. 10cm deep. Mainly open, with bench around the stern; may have short end decks, with cuddy. Painted white or green, tarred below the waterline. May set a lateen sail or a tall rectangular lugsail to a single sharply raking mast. Also rowed. Crew of 2-4. Reported lengths 4.35-6.5m; e.g., length 5m, beam 1.75m, depth 0.6m.

buche See **bucia, buss**

bucia *Mediterranean:* Sailing vessel of 12th- and 13th-century crusaders and merchants; reported from Venice, Genoa, and Syria. Physical descriptions conflict; variously cited as a cargo, naval, or transport vessel, and as an Italian fishing craft. Two decks; castles at each end were common. Steered with quarter rudders. Stepped 2-3 masts usually setting lateen sails, although mainmast might set a square sail. Also rowed, employing as many as 112 oars on 13th-century Catalan ships. Reported lengths 20-37.4m; Catalan ship 37.4m long, 10m wide. Other recorded names: **brisse, bucc(i)a, buc(c)io, bucea, buche, bucioletto, bucius, bugaletto, burchio*, burcia, burcio, bús, buscia, buscio, buse, buso, buss*, bussa*, bussanave, busus, buza*, buz(z)o, nave buzio;** pl. **buce(e), bucii, busi*, buzi**

bucii See **bucia**

bucintori See **bucintoro**

bucintoro **1.** *Austria:* A **Bucintoro** belonging to Graf Batthyány in the early 19th century was used on the Danube in the vicinity of Vienna for pleasure outings. Inward-raking sharp ends and sides. Hull fully covered, with tower amidships.

2. *Italy:* **a.** Ceremonial state **barge* (galera da cerimonia)** of the Doge of Venice. Last, and most sumptuous, launched in 1729. Principally used to convey the Doge and his entourage to the coast on Ascension Day to perform the traditional "Marriage of Venice to the Sea" ceremony, carrying as many as 600 people aboard. This last **barge** had 2 decks, the passengers on the upper deck and the oarsmen below. The upper room was roofed over with a silk tent. Elaborately decorated inside and out with carvings and gilded figures; the bow carried the figure of Justice and a long beak on which a carved lion crouched. The 168 oarsmen rowed 4 to each of the 42 oars. Bow and stern rounded, sternpost very curved, stem less curved, outboard rudder. Length 34.8m, beam 7.3m, height 8.3m. Similar but probably less ornate state **barges** reported from Ferrara, Bologna, Rome, and Ludovico Sforza. Spelling variants: **boçentòro, buccentoro, bucentarius; Bucentaur*** (the proper name given to each boat, dating from 1311); **bucentaure, bucentauro, bucentaurum, bucentaurus, bucentor(i)o, bucentorus, buciontòro;** pl. **buciontori. b.** Along the central Po River in northern Italy, especially between Cremona and Ostiglia, the **bucintoro** was a flat-bottomed cargo boat. Bottom curved up to the top strake forming a flat "V"; strong sheer toward the high bow; square stern. Decked at bow and stern. Outboard rudder; tiller. Mast stepped just abaft the foredeck setting a boomed lugsail. Also rowed. Length 20m, beam 4.7m, depth 3.6m.

bucintoro del Panaro *Italy, N:* Flat-bottomed cargo craft of the lower Po River and the Panaro, a right-bank tributary. Sharp bow with strongly curved stem;

rounded stern and curved sternpost; straight flared sides; strong sheer at the bow merges with the upturned stem. Decked at ends; arched covering over the waist. Wide outboard rudder; S-shaped tiller. Length 22.25m, beam 4.52m, depth 1.52m, cap. 52t.

bucio See **bucia, buss**

bucioletto See **bucia**

buciontòro See **bucintoro**

bucius See **bucia**

buck See **buckie, Kaffenkahn**

Bücke *Poland:* Long, low-sided **riverboat***. Flat bottom; elongated ends terminating in small square transoms; lightly curved sides. House amidships. Steered with a sweep. Raised oar blocks, 1 pair forward of the house, 2 abaft the house. Length ca. 30m.

bucket Colloquial term for an old, worn-out ship.

bucket dredger See **dredger-1**

buckeye, buckeye schooner See **bugeye**

buckie *Northern Ireland:* Term formerly given in the Mourne area on the southeast coast to the decked **fishing boats*** of the Scottish east coast. Other recorded names: **buck, buckie boat, Scotch buck, Scots buck.** See also **scaffie.**

buckie boat See **buckie, lang boomer, scaffie**

Buckie herring boat See **scaffie**

buckie schooner boat See **bugeye**

Buckkahn See **Kaffenkahn**

bucze See **buss**

buden See **bedan-1**

budgaro, budgaroo, budgarow See **badjra**

budgerow See **badjra, kotia**

budget barge, budgett barge, budgett stern See **swim-headed barge**

budgra, budjerow, budjra See **badjra**

buer See **boeier**

Buesenzille See **Plätte-1**

buey *Spain, SW:* Fishing **boat*** of the Bay of Cádiz that works in pairs with a net. Sailed. Name variant: **bou*** (along the northeastern coast)

buffalo boat *China, east-central:* A special breed of water buffalo was used to tow a train of small **salt boats*** on canals in northern Zhejiang (Che-chiang) Province. A swimming buffalo could tow at least 6 boats, at a speed of ca. 6km per hour. See also **bullboat-2, mussuck.**

buffalo-skin coracle See **bullboat-1**

bugai See **bugeye**

bugala See **baghla-1**

bugale See **bugalet**

bugalet *France:* **1.** Small craft that transported passengers and provisions to ships lying in roadsteads off Brittany from the 17th to the mid-19th century; the larger sizes also employed as **coasters***. Built on the lines of the large ships of the period, having a figurehead at the bow, a bridgehouse, sides of a **frigate***, and decorative quarter galleries. Short foremast set a square sail; mainmast set a large square sail plus a topsail; generally 2 jibs. Reported lengths 10.7-11.6m.

2. A small **cutter***-rigged **barge* (gabare*)** that transported munitions for the Marine militaire. Full lines, bluff bows, broad stern. Decked; long covered hatch amidships. Spelling variants: **bigalet, bougalet, bugale**

bugaletto See **bucia**

bugalilo *Arabian Peninsula:* Large vessel of the Persian (Arabian) Gulf; possibly the **baghla★**. Name variant: **buglo**. Further reference: **kotia**

bugalla See **baghla-1**

bugeye *United States, E:* Two-masted oyster dredger and **buy boat★** of Chesapeake Bay; some worked on the Potomac River. Developed in the late 1860s; built mainly between 1880 and 1900. Some remain; most converted to pleasure craft, or have been built recently as **yachts★** (**bugeye yacht**). In late spring and summer, carried produce, timber, and occasionally passengers. Originally built of 5-11 shaped logs called chunks. The shaped logs were pinned together. Later only keelson and bottom fashioned from the logs (the **chunk boat★**); finally, as suitable logs became scarce, built as plank-and-frame vessels (**frame boat**). Sharp ends; clipper bow; the **patent-stern bugeye** had a framework built out over the stern to provide more deck space and to support stern davits for the **push boat★**. A few were round-sterned (**round-stern bugeye** or **bugeye with a bustle**). Flat floors, flatter on the log type; rounded bilges, the 3rd log usually forming the bilge. Strong sheer, low sides. Originally a keel, later a heavy centerboard. Decked; cuddy just abaft the mainmast and sometimes a raised cabin aft; hold amidships; log rail. Outboard rudder; tiller initially, sometimes carved; later a wheel. Two masts raked aft; the mainmast was the shorter; on most **bugeyes**, the foremast, stepped well forward, equaled the length of the vessel. Set boomed leg-of-mutton sails; multiple reef points to help maintain dredging speed. Jib had a short club, and some had a bonnet. Bowsprit fixed between a heavy pair of knightheads, with the heel let into a sampson post; graceful longhead and decorated trailboards. A few single-masted. Crew of as many as 10 when oystering; at other times 2 men or a man and a boy. Lengths mainly between 15-18m; range: 9m long, 3m wide, 0.76m deep to 25.9m by 7m by 1.8m; shallow draft. Other recorded names: **Baltimore buckeye, buckeye (schooner), buckie schooner boat, bugai, bugy, Chesapeake Bay bugeye, oyster buckeye**. Further reading: M. V. Brewington, *Chesapeake Bay Log Canoes and Bugeyes* (Cambridge, Md.: Cornell Maritime Press, 1963). Note also **pungy**.

bugeye with a bustle, bugeye yacht See **bugeye**

buggalah See **baghla-1**

buggalow See **badjra, baghla-1, bangala, kotia**

buggelah See **baghla-1**

buggelow See **kotia**

bughalah See **baghla-1**

Bugis paduakan See **padewakang**

Bugis prahu, Bugis schooner See **pinisi**

bugla See **baghla-1**

buglo See **bugalilo**

bugy See **bugeye**

buis **1.** *Belgium/France, N:* 12th-century open **fishing boat★** of the Flanders coast. The type was probably used by Flemish crusaders. Rounded ends, flat floors. Equipped with rowing benches; also sailed. Other recorded names: **busch(e), buza★**

2. *Netherlands:* The Dutch **buis**, or **haringbuis**, which dominated North Sea herring fisheries in the 14th-17th

centuries, was made more efficient in the early 15th century by the use of a specially designed net. In its various forms, the vessel endured until the mid-19th century. Some served armed convoy duty with the **fishing fleet** (the **buisconvoyer**) and some carried cargo in the off-season. Little is known about the 15th-century vessel. By the 16th century, when the **buis** was solely a **fishing boat**, it was carvel-planked (the **kraveelbuis**), had a keel, square or rounded stern, bluff bow, curved stem, and nearly perpendicular sides. Strong sternpost supported a heavy rudder, which came up inboard. Small decks fore and aft; some larger types fully decked. Vessels of the 17th century had a rounded stern below a high, narrow counter. Tiller passed through the counter or beneath the raised top strakes; a type without this feature was called a **kwee** (pl. **kweden**). The **buis** was 2-masted (**tweemastbuis**) in the 14th century, then 3-masted (**dreimastbuis**) until ca. 1700, each mast setting deep, narrow square sails; the mainmast frequently set a topsail. Fore- and mainmasts hinged so they could be lowered to a lateral rack just forward of the mizzenmast while fishing. On some, the mizzenmast carried a lateen sail. During the 18th century, adopted the 2-masted **hoeker** rig (the **hoekerbuis★**); eliminating the foremast left the forward area clear for net handling; both masts generally carried a square sail, later a gaff mizzen. Crew of 8-15. The earlier vessels were larger, as long as 30m. By the 17th century, they ranged between ca. 14-22m; e.g., length overall 21.6m, beam 5.6m, draft 1.8m. Other recorded names: **buis-convooier, buise★, buisse, buse, buss★, buys(schip), buys(s)e, buza★, harinck-buyse, convoyer, Häringbüse, Heringbüse, herring buss, touque**; pl. **buizen, Büsen, buysen**. The French sometimes called the Dutch vessel a **nevre** or **neur(r)e**. Further reading: Heinrich Stettner, "Die Niederländsche und Emder Fischerei mit Büsen und Ihre Darstellung Inbesondere auf Alten Fliesen, Giebelsteinen und Grafiken," *Deutsches Schiffahrtsarchiv* 2 (1978), 165-180. Note also **buyscarveel**.

buis-convooier, buisconvoyer See **buis-2**

Buise *Germany, NW:* Engaged in herring fishing in the North Sea. Early vessels followed the general lines and rig of the Dutch **buis★**. In time they became a separate German type, working until the mid-1850s. Decked, with deep bulwarks; bluff bow and curved stem; rounded stern; marked sheer toward the stern; tiller came inboard below the gunwales. Set a large square sail, with bonnet, to an aft-raking mainmast; mizzenmast carried a small square sail. Staysail; jib to a long running bowsprit. Early vessels generally 3-masted. 1806 dimensions: length 18.9m, beam 5.16m, hold depth 2.58m, cap. 108t. Other recorded names: **Büse, Emder Häringsbuise, Häringbuise, Heringbuise, Hering(s)buyse, Heringsbüse**; pl. **Buisen, Buizen buise**. Note also **buis-2**.

Buisen See **Buise**

buisse See **buis-2**

Buitenmot, Buitenmutte See **Mutte**

buizen See **buis-2, Buise**

bujer See **boeier**

bujra See **badjra**

Bukkahn See **Kaffenkahn**

bukser, bukserbåt, buksir See **tug**

buksir-tolkach See **push boat**

bulam boat See **balam**

bulkhead See **live barge**

bullahoo See **ballahou**

bullboat *Canada, central/United States, central:* **1.** Bowl-shaped craft covered with the hide of a bull buffalo. Used by the Native Americans of the central plains, mainly to cross streams. Found from south-central Canada almost to the Gulf of Mexico; also used by the Sauk of Wisconsin and several of the Ohio River basin tribes. Usually of a single hide, but some used as many as 6 hides; bull hides preferred because they leaked less. Hide untanned; hair might be either inside or out; hide coated daily with a mixture of fat and ashes. Tail retained on some to serve as a tow rope. Willow frame withes set widely apart, half one way, the other half at right angles; circular gunwale of withes. Flattened on the bottom, sides vertical or flared. Poled, paddled with hands, or towed by walker or swimmer. Carried 1-4 persons. Reported diameter 1.2-2.4m, depth ca. 0.46m. Other recorded names: **buffalo-skin coracle**, **máh-ṭi** (Hidatsa), **menaka** or **mĭ-ná-ki** (Mandan), **skin canoe**. Note also **coracle, pelota, skin boat**.
2. A modification of the round **bullboat** was made by some tribes and by early traders, especially to transport bales of fur down the usually shallow tributaries of the central plains. Stout willow or cottonwood poles were laid lengthwise and crosswise and lashed together with rawhide to create an elongated, round-ended, flexible craft. Side frames of willow twigs, the smaller ends lashed to the crosspieces and the larger ends bent vertically to support the sides, then secured to the gunwale pole. The buffalo hides were dressed, the hair removed. Hides were sewn together with buffalo sinew to form a continuous sheet; hide covering soaked before being put onto the frame so it would shrink while drying. Seams coated with mixture of buffalo tallow and ashes. Cargo laid onto loose pole flooring. Boat brought ashore to dry at night, serving as a shelter at the same time. Crew of 2 poled the boat. Length ca. 9m, width 3.7m, depth 0.5m; draft dry ca. 10cm, 15-20cm by the end of the day. Other recorded names: **boucaut, buffalo boat★, bull-hide boat**. Note also **bouco**.
3. In areas where moose and caribou were prevalent, tribes constructed so-called **parchment canoes** for temporary use. De-haired, stretched, and dried skins fastened over a willow framework in the manner of the **bullboat**. Further references: **bullhead boat, corita**

bulldozer boat See **boom boat-2**

Bulle *Germany, NW:* Squat, compact boat that often served as a **lighter★**, transporting cargoes from larger vessels up the smaller tributaries. Some were square-ended **barges★** specially fitted for careening sailing ships. Open; rounded bow and stern. On the Ems River, the boat was notably chubby and beamy; some sailed. On the upper reaches of the Weser River, the **Bullen** (pl.) were towed by horses. Cap. ca. 20t. Other recorded names: **Bolle** (pl. **Bollen**), **Schute★**. Note also **Bock, Boll, Ostebulle**. Further reference: **Eiderschnigge**

Bullen See **Bulle**

bullhead See **busthead**

bullhead boat *United States, NE:* Small, well-built **barge★** of the Erie Canal in central New York State; used in the 19th century to transport dry cargoes such as flour and grain. Rounded bow and stern, straight sides, flat bottom turned up at ends. Housed over from end to end, but open below; very narrow side decks. Steered from stern cabin roof; mule housed in the bow cabin. Name variant: **bullboat★**

bull-hide boat See **bullboat-2**

bullock boat See **ferryboat-2**

Bullom boat *Sierra Leone:* Well-built **dugout canoe★** from the Bullom coast northwest of Freetown. Used

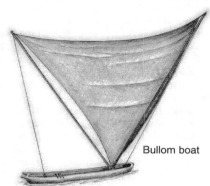

Bullom boat

for fishing and to transport produce and passengers to Freetown. May be steered by rudder. Propelled by spade-bladed paddles or sail. Employs a spritsail or a V-shaped sail supported by 2 long, pliant bamboo spars. Crew of 3-5. Reported lengths 6.1-10.67m, widths 1.68-1.98m, draft 0.76-0.9m. Name variant: **mampaboot** (by the Temne)

būm See **boom**

bumbarda, bumbarta See **bomb vessel**

bumboat 1. Any small shore-based boat that peddles fresh produce, small articles, clothing, tobacco, and often illicit goods, to ships in a harbor. Generally rowed. Those on the Hudson River in New York State were steam-powered, but attached themselves to **barge** units. In the 17th century, they were the boats of scavengers, and were also called **dirt boats★** on the Thames in southeast England. Some boats that supplied fresh water to ships were also known as **bumboats**. Selected further name variants: **bambot(t), barque de vivandier, bateau de la marchande, bateau de provisions** (or **bateau d'office), battello di provviste, bedienschuit, bomboat, bon boat, boomboat★, bote de rancheros, bote vivandero, breu★, Bumboot★, goofer, Kajedraier, kattrejarbåt, proviantbåt, vivandier, Wasserboot**. Note also **boumba, bumboat, kadraai, kadrejerjolle, parlevinker**.
2. *Grenada, southern Windward Islands:* Open workboat that has become a popular regatta craft. Carvel-planked, sharp bow, plumb stem, short foredeck, wide transom, no keel, rudder. Boomed spritsail set to a light mast; bamboo sprit set high, held by a free-moving jaw; jib to stemhead. Reported lengths 4.27-5.5m, beamy, shallow hull.
3. *Trinidad:* In some parts of this West Indian island, a clinker-built **dinghy★**-type boat used in pot fishing. Further references: **dinghy-4, dirt boat**

Bumboot See **bumboat-1, bunboot**

bumkin See **winkle brig**

bummer See **jack**

bumming yawl See **buyer smack**

bumkin See **winkle brig**

bun See **pointer**

bunboot *Belgium/Netherlands, SW:* **1.** General term for a boat with a live fish well (*bun*).
2. Small beamy **fishing boat★** of South Holland and Flanders dating from at least the late 18th century. Had a *bun* or box in which to keep fish alive. Some conveyed pilots to and from ships. Mainly rowed. Name variant: **Bumboot.** Note also **bumboat, kaarboot.**

Bunder See **Bönder**

bunder boat **1.** One that plies between vessels at anchor and the bunder (dock or harbor). Well known in Bombay (Mumbai) Harbor. Some used as **coasters★.** Generally sturdy, undecked, and fitted with a shelter. Sometimes sets 1-2 sails. Spelling variant: **bander boat.** Note also **shore boat-1.**
2. *Pakistan, SE:* Those at Karachi are the smallest of the **bedi★** type of boat. Overhanging bow and transom stern. Awning covers the aft benches; bow usually gaily painted, remainder of hull oiled and varnished. In addition to rock ballast, employs a balance board on which 2 men may sit. Quadrilateral lateen-type sail with a short luff set to a forward-raking mast. Yard rigged inside the shrouds. Crew of 3 and sometimes a boy. Length ca. 7.6m, beamy. Note also **jālibōt.**

bundūqī shikarī See **shikara**

bune, buney See **fune**

bunga See **bongo-1**

bungalow See **baghla-1**

bungay **1.** *Belize/Honduras:* Small **schooner★**-rigged **coaster★** that traded between Belize and northern Honduras. Two headsails.
2. *Jamaica:* Large **dugout canoe★** that carried as many as 5-6 hogsheads down rivers. Originally hewn from a cotton tree; later plank-built with flat bottom. Spelling variants: **bonggi, bonggy, bungey, bungy** (pl. **bungies**)

bungey, bungies See **bungay-2**

bungo See **bongo-1**

bungy See **bungay-2**

bunhoeker See **hoekerbuis, vishoeker**

bunker boat See **menhaden boat**

Bünn-Ewer See **Pfahl-ewer, well boat**

Bünnschiff See **well boat-1**

bünnsloep See **sloep-3**

bunschip See **beunschip-1**

Bunschoter See **botter**

bunschouw See **schouw**

bunschuit See **beunschip-1, schuit**

bunsloep See **sloep-3**

buoy boat, buoy-laying boat, buoy tender, buoy yacht
See **beacon boat-1**

bupaa See **baobao**

buque **1.** In Spanish, **buque** means a **ship★** or **vessel★.** In Portuguese, it may mean a **jolly boat★** or a **cutter★.** Name variant: **vaixell** (Catalan)
2. *Portugal, central:* Three or 4 **buques** aid the team of boats working a ring net, looking for shoals of fish,

driving them into the net, helping to close the net, and transporting the catch to market. Sharp bow, straight or slightly curved stem; ball of shredded wool on the stemhead reduces chafing of the sail. Fuller stern, curved sternpost; keel; low sides; single wale along each side. Early boats open; later decked with long central hatch; outboard rudder; short tiller. Quadrilateral lateen-type sail with a short luff set to a forward-raking mast. Rowed in calms and when helping to close the net; 2 oars per side, stropped to single tholepins; rowed standing, facing forward. Crew of 4-5. Length 12.3m, beam 3.45m, depth 1.0m, 9.65rt. Note also **galeão.**
3. *Portugal, S:* A type of **buque** still carries fruit from Alcoutim on the Guadiana River on the southeast border to ports along the Algarve coast.
Further reference: **ship**

buque almirante, buque amirante See **flagship**

buque armado en corso See **privateer**

buque camaronero See **shrimper**

buque carbonero See **collier-1**

buque costero See **coaster**

buque de guarda-costas See **coast guard ship**

buque de guardia See **guard ship**

buque de guerra See **man-of-war**

buque de palangrero See **palangrero**

buque de pesca See **fishing boat**

buque de pesca al cerco de jareta See **seine boat-1**

buque de ruedas See **paddle boat-3**

buque faro See **lightship**

buque gemelo See **mother**

buque guardapesca See **fishery guard ship**

buque insignia See **flagship**

buque negrero See **slaver-1**

buque nodriza See **mother ship**

buque palangrero See **palangrero**

buque para pesca con caña See **tuna boat**

buque remolcador See **tug-1**

buque valiza See **lightship**

burai See **moto-moto**

buralan *Philippines, central:* Single-outrigger **banca★** of Laguna de Bay on Luzon, south of Manila. Aids in driving bamboo poles into the lake bottom to support the *pukot* bag net. Length ca. 9m, beam 1.0m, depth 0.5m. Name variant: **pangititan**

buranella See **batela-2**

buranja *Turkey, NW:* Dugout canoe★ of European Turkey used for river fishing.

burceli See **burchièllo-2**

burcèlo See **burchièllo-1**

burchi See **burchio, maròta**

burchia See **burchio**

burchiela See **burchièlla**

burchiela da fango, burchiele da fango See **burchio-2**

burchieli See **burchièllo-1**

burchièlla *Italy, E:* **1.** In Venice, a 17th-century service boat to a **burchio★;** farther south, a beamy flat-bottomed cargo boat similar to the **burchio,** working under oars and ca. 12m long. The name has also been applied to **fishing boats★** on the Po River and in the lagoons at the north end of the Adriatic, and to craft that carried reeds. Spelling variants: **burchiela, burchielus;** pl. **burchièlle.** Note also **burchièllo.**

2. The late 16th-century **burchièlla** at Ancona was a naval vessel that served as a port **lighter★**. Similar **burchièlle** served other ports on the east coast. Flat bottom, slight rocker at the ends; rounded sides; 3-piece frames. Curved stem and sternpost, the forefoot cutaway. Open except for foredeck and a short stern deck where the top strake formed a shallow transom.
Further reference: **burchio-2**

burchièlle See **burchièlla**

burchielletto, burchièlli, burchiellino See **burchièllo-1**

burchièllo *Italy:* **1.** Primarily a passenger craft on inland waterways, although some carried merchandise. Found as far south as Rome, on several northern lakes, and at Venice. Considered to have been a small **burchio★**. Dates to at least the 17th century; now extinct. The lake craft were open and double-ended, with a strong sheer at the ends, flat bottom, vertical sides; steered with a very long sweep counterpoised with a stone. At Venice, early **burchièlli** (pl.) ran daily to Padua, while others could be hired to transport families to their country homes; these had a house amidships, often richly furnished. Towed by horses or rowed, or set 1-2 sails. Reported dimensions of the lake boats were 18-23.8m, widths 4.75-4.9m, depths 1.32-1.38m. At Chioggia, south of Venice, the **burchièlli** were 16-20m long, 2.5-3.5m wide, and had a crew of 3. One Venetian craft was 13.7m long, 2.4m wide, and 0.91m deep. Another type brought bulk cargo and produce by river and canals from Lake Como (Lario) to Milan. Flat bottom turned up at the ends to form flat surfaces up to the top of the sheer strake. Sheer strake lapped. Steered with a sweep, the helmsman seated on a bench. Other recorded names: **borcèll** (pl. **borcèj**), **borcello, bruchiello, burcèlo, burchielo, burcièlo; burchielletto, burchiellino** (dims.); further plurals: **borcelli, burchieli**. Note also **burchièlla**.
2. In northeastern Italy, a **burchièllo** is a boat-shaped, perforated fish tank carried aboard several types of **fishing boats★**. Ca. 3.8m long. Other recorded names: **burcelo**; pl. **burceli**. Note also **bragagna, bragozzo**.

burchièlo See **burchièllo-1**

burchielus See **burchièlla**

burchieto See **burchio**

burchio *Italy:* **1.** Name applied to a heavy **barge★**-like craft that plied rivers, canals, lakes, and lagoons in several Italian areas, notably the Tiber, Arno, and Po Rivers, the northern lakes, and the Lagoon of Venice. Early reports indicate they also crossed the Adriatic to the Dalmatian coast. Some were cargo carriers, others carried passengers. Flat bottom; decked; cabins at stern and amidships. In confined waters, they were towed by 1 or more horses or drifted with the current; in open waters they were sailed or rowed; following World War II, engines employed. Stepped 1-2 masts setting large lateen sails. Crew of 3. Reported lengths 22-35m; e.g., length 25m, beam 5.7m, depth 1.6m. Other recorded names: **burchia, burchione, burcho★, burcio, burcla, burclellus, burclus**; pl. **burchi(ioni), burci**; dim. **burchieto**
2. Best-known were those of the Venice area. Most carried heavy cargoes, including silica sand for the

Murano glass works (**burchio da sabbia**), produce, forage (**burchio da fieno**), and some (**burchio da fango**) moved dredged mud and silt. One type, with suitable amenities, ran regular passenger schedules to nearby towns. Flat bottom; longitudinal planking turned up to form a flat wedge-shaped bow; at top of the raked bow a knob projected forward to protect the bow from bridge abutments, etc. Rounded stern with vertical sternpost; outboard rudder; long tiller. Low freeboard; sheer swept up, sometimes abruptly at bow. Decked forward and aft; cargo boats had 1-2 holds; some housed the owner's family in part of the boat; passenger craft had a cabin amidships, sometimes with two rooms, one above the other. Hull painted black. Towed a **battana★**, a diminutive **burchio**; one type of service boat was called **burchièlla★** in the 17th century. Later sailing vessels set ochre lugsails to 2 masts, one forward of the hatch or cabin, the other aft; foremast was taller; both could be struck. One or both sails often had a design. Early types set square or lateen sails. Lengths mostly under 9m, but some to 33m; e.g., length 18m, beam 4m, depth 1.48m. Other recorded names: **burchiela da fango**; pl. **burchiele da fango**
Note also **burchièlla, burchièllo**. Further references: **bucia, maròta**

burchio da fango, burchio da fieno, burchio da sabbia See **burchio-2**

burchione, burchioni See **burchio**

burcho Spanish term for a large **barge★**-type craft. Generally rowed. Further reference: **burchio**

Burchzille See **Waidzille**

burci See **burchio, maròta**

burcia See **bucia**

burcièl, burcièli See **maròta**

burcio See **bucia, burchio, maròta**

burcla, burclellus, burclus See **burchio**

burdjik See **burdjuk**

burdjuk **1.** *Iraq, S:* Term sometimes given to an inflated goat skin used for ferrying across rivers. Name variant: **mussuck★**
2. *Turkmenistan/Uzbekistan:* Inflated skin or skins used along the Amu Darya River and its tributaries and in the Aral Sea. Sometimes employed in piracy, attacking craft rowing along the river. Spelling variant: **burdjik**

Bure wherry See **Norfolk wherry**

Buri See **bhur**

Burma rice boat See **laung-zat**

burrinha *Brazil, E:* Small **jangada★** used for inshore fishing along the coast of Bahia. Sets a square sail.

burro *Spain, NE:* A small type of **xeito★** used for river fishing in the interior. Further reference: **coble-1d**

burse See **buss**

bus See **bucia, buss**

busce See **buss**

busch, busche See **buis, buss**

buscia See **bucia**

buscie See **buss**

buscio See **bucia**

buse See **bucia, buis-2, Buise, buss**

büsen See **buis-2, buss**

bush, bushe See **buss**

bushwack boat *United States, E:* Used by waterfowl hunters on upper Chesapeake Bay. Flat bottom, skeg; sharp bow; wide, raked transom, straight flared sides. Hunters camouflaged by canvas secured along the gunwales; white hull; lantern used for night hunting. Rowed to general area with 2 pairs of oars; leather on oarlocks muffled sound. Sculled approaching the waterfowl; sculling oar worked through a hole low in the transom, the sculler lying on the bottom, sculling over his shoulder. Two men operated the guns. As geese became plentiful, largely replacing the ducks, sides of the boats were cut lower, enabling large goose decoys to provide more concealment for the boat; eventually a law was passed requiring sides at least 50cm high. This was countered by **layout boats**★ that carried more gunners and lay lower in the water. Reported lengths of the **bushwack boats** 3.7-5.3m; e.g., length 4.7m, beam 1.2m. Other recorded names: **bushwack skiff, bushwhack boat, run boat**★, **sneak boat**★. Note also **cabin boat-3**.

bushwack skiff, bushwhack boat See **bushwack boat**

busi 1. The word **būsi** was used by early Arabian poets to mean a **boat**★.
  2. *Spain:* Small double-ended boat that may serve as a **dinghy**★, as a **shore boat**★, or for fishing. Tall stemhead, lower sternpost; grounding keels; decked aft, short foredeck. Mainly rowed. Other recorded names: **buso, buzo**
  Further references: **bucia, gussi**

buso See **bucia, busi-2, gussi**

buss 1. Two or 3-masted oceangoing cargo vessel, dating from the 12th-14th centuries, mainly in northern Europe. Round-hulled.
  2. *United Kingdom:* **a.** Heavy **fishing boat**★ first reported in the 14th century as a single-masted boat. Best known from the mid-17th century when the English modified the successful Dutch **buis**★ in order to compete for herring in English waters. Remained basically the same, with rigging modifications, until the mid-19th century. Carvel-planked; bluff bow, mildly curved stem. Originally vertical sternpost, then raked; rounded stern; later vessels had a high counter-type stern through which the rudder extended. Straight keel; fairly vertical sides; sheer swept up toward the stern; high freeboard. Early vessels basically open; later, cabins forward and aft, decked between. Carried 3 boats for net tending. Large ensign flew at the stern. The single-masted vessel stepped its heavy mast amidships and set a square sail; bowsprit used to extend bowlines. When adapting the Dutch type, the **buss** became 3-masted, with square sails on the masts and a square topsail on the main topmast; no bowsprit. Later boats might employ a leg-of-mutton mizzen. Abandoned the foremast by 1840s, and ran jib to a bowsprit, large staysail to stemhead, and a flying jib to a jibboom lashed to the bowsprit. Still others adopted lugsails. Boats of 20t required crew of 5, and for every 5t in size, another hand was needed; largest required 18 men. Reported lengths 15-24m; 1768 vessel 20m long overall, 17m on keel, 5m wide, 2.6m hold depth. Other recorded names: **bounty buss, flibot**★, **flyboat**★, **herring buss**. Note also **bounty boat, jagger**. **b.** The

nickname **buss** has been applied to east coast **drifters**★ by Mounts Bay fishermen of the southwest coast.
  Selected name variants: **brisse, buc(h)e, bucio, bucze, buis**★, **burse, bus, busch(e), busc(i)e, Büse** (pl. **Büsen), bush(e), bussa**★, **busse, butse, buza**★, **buz(z)e, buzo**. Further references: **bucia, buis-2, buza**

bússa Icelandic designation for a heavy vessel of ample proportions; may derive from their disparaging assessment of the Dutch **buis**★. Other recorded names: **bússu(r), buza**★, **buzu-skip**. Note also **hafskip**. Further references: **bucia, buss**

bussanave See **bucia**

busse See **buss, búza**

bussi See **gussi**

bússu, bússur See **bússa**

busthead *United States, central:* Plank-built boat of the upper Tennessee River used mainly for fishing. Flat bottom rose above the waterline at the stern; hexagonal transom. A special rudder device, fixed to the transom and called a tail oar, kept the boat aligned with the current; could be flipped up when not needed. Other recorded names: **bullhead**★, **Tennessee River busthead**

busus See **bucia**

but See **boot-2, bot-7**

buteel See **batil-1**

Butenbulle See **Eiderschnigge**

Butenmutte See **Mutte**

buti 1. *East Africa:* **a.** Predecessor of the **Lamu jahazi**★. Single-masted **coaster**★ with a mildly curved, upright stem; square stern; undecked; sides raised by mat weather screens. Lateen sail. 20-60t. **b.** Term may now designate any small **boat**★. Spelling variants: **b(h)ooti, mabuti**
  2. *Philippines, S:* The word **bu-ti** is applied to a European-type boat by peoples of the Sulu Archipelago.
  Further reference: **Lamu jahazi**

butille See **batel-3**

Buton lambo See **lambo-1**

butră See **dhow-1**

butri See **boutre**

butse See **buss**

butt boat See **Fenland lighter**

butterbox 1. A lumbering, inelegant vessel.
  2. *United Kingdom:* **Coaster**★ that had full lines. Rigged as a **brig**★ with square sails on the fore- and mainmasts, plus a gaff sail abaft the mainmast.
  Further reference: **kof**

butthead 1. Term sometimes given to a small square-bowed boat suitable for quiet waters. Other recorded names: **square-toe frigate, swim bow**
  2. *United States, SE:* Powered **scow**★ used in South Carolina to transport oysters to canneries. Oysters piled high on the deck, and held in by planks along each side. Square bow, flat floors. Length 5.2m, beam 1.0m. Note also **oyster scow**.
  Further reference: **chalan**

Butt head See **scow-schooner-2**

buṭṭi See **coracle-4**

Buttjill See **Buttjolle**

Buttjolle *Germany, North Sea coast:* Full-bodied boat that fished for flounder (*Butt*), especially out of the

Elbe Estuary. Extinct by 1900. Carvel planking; sharp ends; strongly curved stem ending in a bold sheer at the bow; keel; considerable rise to the floors. Fish well; leeboards, later centerboard; outboard rudder. Open until the mid-19th century; later half-decked with open waist. Originally set a square sail; then a high-peaked boomed lugsail or gaff sail to a light mast; staysail. Reported lengths 7.8-8.5m; e.g., length 7.8m, beam 2.57m, depth 1.0m; shallow draft. Name variant: **Buttjill, Finkenwerder Buttjolle**; a small one, in jest, **Bass**

butty See **josher-2**

butty boat, **butty collier**, **butty gang**, **butty pal** See **narrow boat**

Butung lambo See **lambo-1**

buy boat *United States, E:* **1.** On Chesapeake Bay, the Potomac River, and the New Jersey coast, a craft whose captain buys oysters, crabs, and fish directly from fishermen and sells the catch ashore. Off-season the boat may haul produce, cordwood, etc. Some bought seed oysters and hauled them to oystermen to plant. Several local types of boats—sailing and/or motorized—are used for this purpose, sometimes an enlarged-capacity boat of the type used for fishing. On Chesapeake Bay, some oyster **buy boats** have distinctive high, plumb bows, round sterns, low freeboard aft; pilot houses aft. Name variants: **carrier boat**, **market (boat★)**. Note also **Chesapeake Bay schooner, freight boat**, **oyster sloop-1**.
2. Today on the Chesapeake, the term **buy** or **deck boat** has been retained for **deadrise boats★** engaged in crab dredging; these boats deliver their catch directly to crab-picking houses. Some trawl in the Atlantic or haul grain locally in the off-season; others dredge and plant seed oysters. All motorized. Average length 12.8m. Other recorded names: **bay boat★**, **runner★**
Further references: **garvey**, **koopbotter**

buyer smack *British Isles:* Late 18th- and early 19th-century vessel that cruised through the herring **fleet** off the Isle of Man in the Irish Sea buying the catch and transporting it to market. Some of the larger vessels were known to have gone into the Mediterranean. Name variants: **bumming yawl**, **fresh-buyer**. Note also **Manx wherry**, **smack-5**.

buys See **buis-2**

buyscarveel *Netherlands:* Some Dutch shipbuilders of the 16th century developed a hybrid vessel, the **buyscarveel**, that had a **buis★** hull and **caravel★** rigging, both modified; was probably a bulk carrier. Bow lower than the regular **buis**; fully decked.

buyse, **buysen**, **buysschip**, **buysse** See **buis-2**

búza *Scandinavia:* An oceangoing vessel of the 12th-13th centuries that served first as a fighting ship and later as a **merchantman★**. Primarily a sailing vessel. Name variant: **buss★**, **bussa★**, **busse**; pl. **búzur**. Note also **hafskip**.

buza See **bucia**, **buis**, **bússa**

buze See **buss**

buzi See **bucia**

buzo *Italy, Sicily:* Small lateen-rigged boat that works out of south coast ports, going particularly to Tunisia

for sponges. Partly decked; standing well for the helmsman, a well forward for the crew member who adjusts the jib, and a central hatch for the oarmen; when closed, the hatch serves as a temporary cabin. Reported lengths 6-8m. See also **bucia**, **busi-1**, **buss**.

búzur See **búza**

buzu-skip See **bússa**

buzze See **buss**

buzzo See **bucia**

by-boat **1.** *Canada, E:* Term used in 17th- and 18th-century Newfoundland for independently owned inshore **fishing boats★**. Such boats were monitored and frequently outfitted and provided with crews by the so-called **by-boat** keepers, men sent to Newfoundland each season for this purpose. The catch was sold to **sack ships★** for transport to Europe. Size, design, and rig varied; generally open. Spelling variant: **bye-boat**
2. *United Kingdom:* An extra or supplementary vessel, that is, one that worked independently of established companies or lines. Such vessels were often smaller.

by-darkey See **kayak-9**

bye-boat See **by-boat**

bylander See **bijlander**

byrding **1.** *Scandinavia:* The Viking coasting **byrðing** carried supplies and fish, sometimes traveling as far as Iceland and England. Also used for escort duty with **fleets**. Short and beamy; decked at bow and stern; hull ceiled. Might be lengthened and converted to a **langskip★**. Generally sailed, but when rowed, oars worked through oar ports. Crew of ca. 12-30. Other recorded names: **byrdinge(n)**, **byrðingr**, **byrðingur★**, **byrthingur**; pl. **byrðingar**, **byrthinger**; **vista-byrðngr**. Note also **hafskip**.
2. *Norway, W:* Type of light cargo boat. Open; usually rowed with 2 oars from the bow and 2 from the stern. Cap. ca. 36t. Name variant: **børing** (carried wheat)

byrðingar See **byrding**, **byrðdingur**

byrdinge, **byrdingen**, **byrðdingr** See **byrding**

bryðdingur *Iceland:* Adapted in Iceland from the Viking **byrding★** as a sturdy fishing and cargo boat. Transporting driftwood and shark fishing were important activities, at least toward the end of the 19th century. Clinker-planked, rounded bottom eased into flaring sides, straight keel. Sharp ends, with strongly curved and cutaway stem and sternpost. Low flooring permitted rowing from the 5 thwarts; storage areas below the flooring. Outboard rudder; tiller. Employed 10 oars. Mast stepped amidships; quadrilateral main- and topsails hung from centered yards. Mainsail boomed out forward. 1875 boat 11.9m long overall, 7.34m on keel, 3.3m wide, 1.08m deep. Spelling variants: **byrðingr**; pl. **byrðdingar**.

byrðingr, **byrðingur** See **byrding**

byrogoe See **purgoo**

byrthinger, **brythingur** See **byrding-1**

byscayenne See **biscayenne**

bysse *Denmark:* 17th-century vessel of ca. 64-120t. Spelling variant: pl. **bysser**. Note also **buss**.

bysser See **bysse**

caano See **canoe**

caballito *Peru:* **1.** One-man reed boat used for coastal fishing since the pre-Columbian period, but now found only in isolated communities. Launched and landed through the surf. The northern **caballito** is composed of 2 bundles of totora reeds, tapered to form a pointed, upturned bow. A small cockpit to hold the catch is created just forward of the square stern. In Asia on the south-central coast, a large 3-bundle **caballito**, called a **balsa**★, assists with the chinchorro

caballito-1

net, and a smaller type, the **patache**★, carries the hauling ropes. The reed bundles, ca. 30-40cm in diameter, are bound tightly with rope. To increase freeboard, several layers of reeds may be laid on top. Set against racks to dry after each trip. Lifespan ranges from one month to a year. Paddled, double-bladed fashion, using a long bladeless split-bamboo pole or sometimes a paddle with pointed blades. Paddler sits with his legs along the side or kneels, but while passing through the surf, he may sit astride with legs in the water. Reported lengths 2.4-4.6m, widths 0.5-1.4m. Other recorded names: **balsa de juncos, Binsen-Floss, caballito** (pony) **del mar, potrillo**
2. Another **caballito** uses 3 balsa logs, lashed so that 2 form the bottom and a 3rd the top. Paddler sits astride the bundle to paddle. Worked in pairs, towing a small net.

caballito del mar See **caballito-1**

caballito de totora *Ecuador, north-central:* One-man reed craft found on several mountain lakes. Constructed of 3 bundles of totora reeds, the central keel bundle bound tightly to form a lightly upturned point at the bow; the outer 2 bundles create the sides; truncated stern. Platform of reeds laid on the after half. Paddle has a very slender loom to which a spade-shaped blade is attached. Length ca. 2.5m.

cabana *Spain:* **1.** A small flat-bottomed, square-ended boat that conveyed workmen and materials to ships under repair at Spanish arsenals.
2. Rectangular **raft**★-like craft with a small house that, in earlier days, served as an office for customs or revenue guards at ports.

cabane 1. *Canada, E:* High-sided vessel used by early fishermen from France as living quarters on coastal Newfoundland. The smaller types housed the fishermen; the larger, the captain and officers.
2. *France:* Transported passengers until the early 19th century, particularly in the Loire Basin of western and central France. Flat-bottomed, decked, large passenger cabin amidships. A large size was sometimes called a **cabanistes**, while another large one with elaborate accommodations for important personages was a **cabane royale**. Towed or rowed. Length in 17th century ca. 19m. Spelling variant: **cabanne**. Note also **coche d'eau**.
Further reference: **toue**

cabanella *Italy:* Small boat placed inside the net for the use of the master of a tuna fishing operation or positioned to guard the entrance to the quadrangle. Double-ended; decked at bow and stern, narrow side decks. Rowed. Length ca. 5m, narrow. Other recorded names: **barbariccio** (Sardinia), **cabanne(lla)**, **misciaretta, musciaretta**. Note also **barcareccio, caporais, musciara, vascello**.

cabane royale, cabanistes See **cabane-2**

cabanne See **cabane-2, cabanella**

cabannella See **cabanella**

cabin boat 1. *England, central:* On Birmingham and Black Country canals, a **narrow boat**★ that had sleeping or family accommodations might be called a **cabin boat** in contrast to a **day boat**★. Generally long-distance carriers, and some might be **flyboats**★, running non-stop. Name variant: **high deck boat**
2. *India, W:* Term given to fast-traveling boats that plied the backwaters and rivers in the Cochin and Quilon areas. Usually 10-14 rowers occupied the open front half of the boat. The back half had 2 cabins, the aftermost cabin for women and children, the more forward cabin for the men; sparse amenities. Sharp bow; high, narrow transom stern. Awning might be placed over the rowers. Bamboo oars with saucer-shaped blades. Length ca. 9m, beam 1.5m.
3. *United States, E:* A **scow-schooner** (see **scow-11**) or **scow-sloop**★ that had been converted with suitable living amenities for the use of waterfowl hunters of the late 19th century on upper Chesapeake Bay. Accompanied by a **bushwack boat**★ and **sinkbox**★. Other recorded names: **gunning scow, lay boat**★. Note also **down-the-bay sharpie**.
Further reference: **layout boat-1**

cabin cruiser See **cruiser-1**

cabin dram See **dram**

cabin skiff *United States, E:* Sharp-ended oystering boat of the Miles River area on the eastern side of Chesapeake Bay. Developed in the 1880s; used until the early 20th century. Slight "V" bottom; planked fore-and-aft; planks as thick as 8cm; slight rocker created by stones placed amidships. Hard chine to slightly flaring sides that were often of a single plank. Raked, straight ends; longhead supported the bowsprit. Outboard rudder; tiller; centerboard. Small trunk cabin forward for the 2-man crew. Stepped 1-2 unstayed masts, raking aft. Set leg-of-mutton sails, with club to the clew. Very long boom on the single-masted boats. Jib to bowsprit. Reported lengths 9.4-9.8m, beam 2m. Other recorded names: **cabin skift, clipper skiff, Miles River cabin skiff**

cabin skift See **cabin skiff**

cable ferry *United States, E:* At New Hope, Pennsylvania, on the Delaware River, **canal boats***, transferring between the Delaware and Raritan Canal on the east side of the river and the Delaware Canal on the west side, were attached with pulleys at bow and stern to a cable stretched from towers on each bank. The boats were angled at 45° to take advantage of water pressure to "ferry" across the river. Operated in the 19th century. A similer arrangement at Easton at the north end of the Delaware Canal aided the transfer to and from the Morris Canal. Further reference: **ferryboat**

caboteur *Canada, E:* French-Canadian term for a wooden **coaster***; term dates to early Canadian history. Now may be 30m long and 500t, but as little as 50t.

cabotier See **cabotière**, **coaster**

cabotière *France, N:* Long, narrow, flat cargo craft used mainly on Normandy rivers during the mid-18th century. Very long sweep-type rudder. Spelling variants: **cabotier**, **cabottière**

cabotiero, **cabotor** See **coaster**

cabottière See **cabotière**

caçadeira *Portugal, central:* Fishing and wildfowling boat of the coastal lagoon at Aveiro; may also provide transportation between marinas and the widespread canal network. Flat bottom; straight flaring sides;

caçadeira

overhanging bow; curved ends; sheer strake extends beyond stem forming a low beak; sharp stern. Washboards amidships; demountable rudder. Cuddy beneath foredeck; short floorboard aft. Coated with pitch; small white triangles at bow and stern. Sailed, rowed, or poled. A lug- or small lateen sail set to a short mast stepped in the single thwart. Crew of 2. Reported lengths 5-7.1m; e.g., length 7.1m, beam at gunwale 1.6m, 1.13m at bottom, depth 0.5m. Name variant: **bateira caçadeira**

cacam See **hoa-hang**

cacapo See **kakap**

cachamarín See **quechemarín**

cachamarina See **quechemarín**, **quetx**

cache See **ketch**

cache-marée See **chasse-marée**

cachemarina See **quetx**

cacilheiro See **bote cacilheiro**

cacisheiro See **canoa cacilheira**

caddy See **drogher**

cadeï See **kadei**

cadger *England, SW:* Term applied at St. Ives to the small boats that gathered outside a pilchard seine in

order to "cadge" fish from the meshes of the net, hiding them beneath the floorboards.

Cadgwith Cove crabber See **West Country crabber**

caechio See **caicco-1**

caécio See **caique**

caerschip See **watership-1**

cag, caga See **kaag-2**

cage **1.** *Canada, E:* Term for a **log** or **timber raft***. **Cage** is the term used by the lumbermen. Merchants often called it a **dram***, although a **dram** can also be a unit of the **cage**. **Drams** and **cribs*** may be united, side by side or one behind the other, to form a **cage**. Equipment includes cables, chains, anchors, **canoes***, supplies, a 2-man house, and a cookhouse. Crew generally ca. 30. A **cage** may contain ca. 2,400 square meters of wood. Name variant: **cage à bois**
2. *United States:* A French dialect term for a simple **raft*** that ferried people and merchandise in the Mississippi Valley. Four pieces of wood formed a square; overlapping ends lashed with rope or vines. Buffalo skin stretched over the frame. Propelled by swimmers or towed by waders. Spelling variant: **cageux**. Note also **cajeu**.

cage à bois See **cage**

cageux See **cage-2**

cagh, cágua, cague See **kaag-2**

čaḥčūr See **šaḥtūr**

cahic See **caique**

cahique See **caique**, **caique-8**

caiac See **caique**

caiacco See **kayık**

caiaco, caiak See **kayak**

caiasso See **kayık**

caic See **caique**, **kaik-3**, **kayak**, **kayık**

caica See **caique-8**

caicche See **kayık**

caicchi See **caicco-1**

caicchio See **caicco-1**, **kayık**

caicci See **caicco-1**, **kaiki**

caiccio See **caicco-1**

caicco *Italy:* **1.** A long, slender **ship's boat*** that transports people, provisions, and water between shore and the ship. Term 1st used in the 16th century. Early boats employed 10-12 oars. Spelling variants: **caechio, caicc(h)io, caichio, caicio**; pl. **caicc(h)i**. Note also **kaić**.
2. On the Adriatic coast, a small, open multipurpose boat that may be rowed or sailed. In places, when rowed with 4 oarsmen, called a **caicco**; when rowed with 1-2, it is called a **passera**. Sharp bow, square stern. Mast stepped well forward. Length 3.8m, beam 1.4m.
3. One of 2 small rowboats that help with the Sicilian tuna trap operation.
Further references: **caique, kaiki**

caïch See **kayık**

caiche See **caique**, **ketch**

caichio See **caicco-1**

caicho See **kayık**

caicio See **caicco-1**, **caique**

caick See **kayık**

caíco *Portugal, N:* Very small open boat that fishes for pout and other small inshore fish and harvests seaweed.

Double-ended, raked stem and sternpost; carvel-planked; keel. Some similar to the **Banks dory★**. Rowed with 4-6 oars and sailed, setting a sprit- or lug-sail. Crew of 1-4. Reported lengths 2-4m; e.g., length 3.6m, beam 1.5m, depth 0.7m.

caico See **caique, kayık**

caicq, caicque See **caique**

caik See **kayık**

cái mảng *Vietnam, N:* Annamese term for a **raft★**, usually of bamboo.

cái mảng Lu'o'ng-nhiệm, cái mảng Sâm-so'n, cái mảng Thanh-hóa See **ghe bè**

čainyi kliper See **tea clipper**

caïq See **caique**

caique 1. Longboat★ or **pinnace★** that accompanied a **galley★**, often transporting munitions; some carried on board. Portrayed in the 17th and 18th centuries as both sharp- and transom-sterned; rowed double-banked, and might set 1-2 lateen sails. Reported lengths 7-8.5m; e.g., length 8m, beam 2m, depth 1.3m.

2. A **caique** may be considered, especially by the Portuguese, to be a vessel rigged in a particular manner, namely with lateen sails to the fore- and main-masts, and a large jib run on a stay fastened to an iron bayonet at the end of the bowsprit; sometimes used a small lateen mizzen. These were **coasters★**, although smaller types with this rig were used for racing and recreation.

3. Also reported as a small, shallow-draft vessel armed with a bow cannon. In the Black Sea, armed **caiques** served Cossack corsairs, employing 30-50 soldiers. Decked over with cowhides. Rowed. Note also **kaiki, kayık**.

4. A small, oared vessel that accompanied an 18th-century Mediterranean **tartane★** or **barque★**. Open, flat floors, transom stern. Name variant: **lanche★**

5. *Brazil, SE:* Small boat used in Rio Grande do Sul for fishing in shallow waters. Double-ended, raked stem and sternpost, short foredeck, bench around the stern. Mast stepped in the bow, fitted with a standing lugsail; some 2-masted. Also rowed.

6. *France:* **a.** Term first reported from France in late 16th century. **b.** Beamy lug-sailed **fishing boat★** that worked from the steep cobble beaches of Yport and Étretat on the Normandy coast. A few motorized

caique-6

caïques still operated in the 1970s. Clinker-built; bluff bow; heavy stem with rounded forefoot; wide wine-glass transom, slightly raked; low rise to the floors;

soft round bilges; drag to the straight keel. Decked forward; loose planking laid across the thwarts. Capstans on the beaches hauled the boats from the water by a rope run from a hole in the stem. A small type was brightly painted above the waterline, the larger mainly black. Various combinations of sails employed, even in the same period. Prior to 1900, mainly set 3 sails: a forelug tacked to a long bumkin that slanted downward sharply; an enormous mainsail, above which a topsail was sometimes set; and a small lug mizzen, sheeted to an outrigger on the starboard side of the transom. In strong wind, mainmast lowered to a crutch on the port quarter and the fore lug tacked to the stemhead and sheeted aft. Masts raked aft. Mainmast about 1-1/2 times the length of the boat, but dispensed with ca. 1912. Sometimes rowed to the fishing grounds using 5-7 oars (4.9m long) worked through holes in the bulwarks. Vessels motorized after World War II. Crew of 6-8, 3-4 on the small type. Reported lengths 5-9m; e.g., length 7.47m, beam 2.9m, depth 1.52m; the smaller boats were called **demi-caïques**. Other recorded names: **caïque d'Étretat (or d'Yport)**

7. *Mozambique:* **a.** Lateen-rigged cargo and passenger boat of the Mozambique Island area in the north. Carvel-planked; sweeps up to a sharp bow, straight vertical stem; wineglass transom. Often has a castellated ornamentation on each quarter. Open or decked with a central hatch. Steps 2 vertical masts; the foremast stepped well forward; the after mast about a third in from the stern, stayed aft. Lateen sails; after sail sheeted to an outrigger. Crew of 3-4. Reported lengths 10-14m. **b.** In the south, near Inhambane, the **caíques** are smaller and differ slightly. Transport passengers and firewood. Carvel-planked; straight plumb or raked stem; wide wineglass transom. Generally flush-decked; some open. Outboard rudder; short tiller. Lateen sails set to 2 vertical masts. Yard of foremast tacks to the stem; mainsail has a short luff and tacks just forward of the mast. Crew of 1-2. Reported lengths 8-10m; e.g., length 9m, beam 1.0m. A single-masted type, 6-8m long, is called a **lancha**.

8. *Portugal:* **a.** Fishing and cargo **caiques** are used from the Algarve to north of the Tagus River, but their home ports are in the Algarve. Some fish for bonito off Morocco. Carvel-planked; slightly curved stem with tall stemhead; most transom-sterned, some sharp- or counter-sterned; deep keel, with drag; steep floors; high sheer. Decked, with 3-4 hatches, or decked forward and aft with an open waist. Painted black, red, or reddish brown, with contrasting bands; sometimes a triangular patch at bows and oculi painted just below the gunwale. Shredded wool on stemhead reduces chafing of the luff. Outboard rudder; tiller; rudder-stock comes up through counter on counter-sterned type. At Olhão on the south coast, sometimes armed to help protect the coast against pirates; called a **caique bombarda**. Two pole masts; the forward one may rake forward, the after mast raking aft. Generally sets tall quadrilateral lateen-type sails with a short luff, but in bad weather a loose-footed gaff or triangular storm sail substituted on the after mast. Rowed in calms.

Crew of 5-8; fishing **caiques** might employ 25-30 men, 4 boys, and 2 water dogs to retrieve unhooked fish. Reported lengths 15-18m; e.g., length 17.5m, beam 4.7m, depth 1.56m; deep draft. Other recorded names: **barco de pesca de alto**, **cahique**. **b.** In the north, the **caique** of the Douro River is used for ferrying, fishing, and recreation. Clinker-built, flared sides, triangular stern, stemhead generally flush with the gunwales, flat bottom. Mainly rowed; occasionally sailed, setting a spritsail. Reported lengths 5-6m; e.g., length 5m, beam 1.57m, depth 0.62m. Name variant: **caica**. **c.** At Viana do Castelo on the north coast, a type of **caique** accompanies the **barco do pilado** in searching for small crabs. Lightly built, carvel planking with 2 planks per side; straight flaring sides; wide, flat bottom with slight rocker. Lightly curved raked stem; raked transom. Three thwarts set onto the ribs. Rowed with 2 pairs of oars; sculled from the stern. Also sailed. Length 4.5m, beam 1.8m.

Spelling variants: **caécio**, **cahic**, **cahique**, **caiac**, **caïc**, **caicco⋆**, **caiche**, **caicio**, **caico⋆**, **caicq(ue)**, **caïq**, **cayc**, **kaič⋆**, **kaick**, **kaik⋆**, **kajič**, **q̣aîq** (pl. **q̣ùyâq**). Note also **kaiki**, **saique**. Further references: **balıkçı kayığı**, **balancelle-1**, **bateira ílhava**, **kaiki**, **kajjik**, **kayık**, **shakhtura**, **trechandiri**

caïque bombarda See **caique-8**

caïque de carga See **caixamarim**

caïque d'Étretat, **caïque d'Yport** See **caique-6**

caïque viajeiro See **caixamarim**

caïquo See **chaloupe**

cái thúng chài See **thúng chài**

cái thuyền *Vietnam, central:* A **sampan⋆** in Annamite, although the words mean merely "large boat" (**thuyền**).

caixamarim *Portugal:* Late 19th-century **coaster⋆**. Quadrilateral lateen-type sail with a short luff, the foresail having a deep luff (*caixamarim* or *cachamarim* sail), the after sail a shallow luff; a later vessel employed a boomed gaff sail on the after mast (a **macho-fêmea**). Foremast raked slightly forward, the after mast strongly aft. Plumb stem with tall stemhead, counter stern. Other recorded names: **caïque de carga**, **caïque viajeiro**. Note also **quechemarín**.

caïyq See **kayık**

čaja See **czajka-2**

cajak See **kayak**

cajeu *Canada/United States, central:* French dialect term for a light temporary **raft⋆** assembled for a river crossing. A larger, more substantial **raft** transported furs downstream at high water levels. Other recorded names: **cajot⋆**, **cayeu**. Note also **cage**.

čajka See **czajka-2**

cajot *France, N:* Small open boat that worked from the north coast beaches of the Cotentin Peninsula in western Normandy. Engaged originally in fishing, especially for crustaceans; more recently used as an **annexe⋆** to larger craft. Probably extinct. Carvel-planked; sharp bow, narrow transom; ends straight and raked. Flat bottom with rocker matching sheer. Hard chine; straight, slightly flared sides; maximum beam in forward third. Stern seat, with floor extending to near amidships. Two rowing thwarts forward of amidships, with 2 oarports per side; 2 pairs of oars. Oarports and

a hole for a cable in the stem aided in hauling the boat ashore. Outboard motor used later. Length ca. 5m, beam 1.65m, depth 1.0m. Further reference: **cajeu**

Cajun pirogue, **Cajun skiff** See **pirogue-4**

čakhtūr See **šaḫtūr**

calabaza **1.** In Spanish, a poor, cumbersome ship, especially one in bad condition.

2. *Mexico:* Spanish term for a Mayan craft composed of calabash gourds set beneath a bamboo frame. Note also **balsa-8**.

calan, **caland** See **chaland**, **chelandia**

calandra See **chelandia**

calandre See **chaland**, **chelandia**

calannus See **chelandia**

calavela See **caravel-1**

calea See **galley**

calen See **chaland**

calendra See **chelandia**

calera *Spain, north coast:* Lug-rigged offshore **fishing boat⋆**, mainly from Vizcaya and Guipúzcoa, constructed of oak and white pine. Vertical stem, sharp stern; rudder extends ca. 1.0m below keel; centerboard. Open or half-decked. Foremast stepped at bow, mainmast amidships. Also rowed, double-banked. Crew of 8 when trolling, 21 when line fishing. Length 14.2m, beam 2.96m, depth 1.45m, 8t disp. Name variant: **lancha calera**. Note also **bonitera-2**.

calevat See **galley-9**

calf See **coble-1b**

calia See **kalia-1**

Calicut manché See **manji**

calie See **kalia-1**

California clipper *United States:* Term given to **clippers⋆** that sailed around Cape Horn during the mid-19th century. Carried travelers and cargo to California from the east coast; many of them went on to China for tea before returning. Square-rigged. Reported lengths 41-92m.

calima, **calimeira** See **barca da arte xávega**

caliotta, **caliotus** See **galiot**

čallābīje See **chalabiya**

callan See **chaland**

calup *France, SW:* Open **fishing boat⋆** of the Pauillac area in the Gironde Estuary; length 5m, beam 1.5m, depth 0.5m. Also a term for an inland boat of the Gascony region as early as the 16th century. See also **galupe**.

calupus See **galupe**

calvette See **gallivat**

čamac Serbo-Croatian generic term for a **boat⋆**, **skiff⋆**, or **canoe⋆** (**lak čamac**). Spelling variants: **čamičic** (dim.); pl. **čamaci**

čamaci See **čamac**

čamac na vesla See **rowboat-1**

čamac za spasavanje See **lifeboat**

camakau *Fiji, central Pacific:* Fast, seaworthy single-outrigger sailing **canoe⋆** still in use on some of the outer islands in the 1960s. Served mainly for transporting ceremonial exchange items, for fishing, and, in early days, for war. Generally owned by a chief, community, or family group. Hull a single greenheart log, but when enlarged by butting 2 logs together, the craft becomes a **veikoso**. Hull oval in cross section;

outrigger (weather) side straight, lee side bowed; stern elongated and pointed; bow sharp and vertical. Ends decked over, often ornamented; high washstrakes added, originally sewn, later nailed. Caulked with gum from the breadfruit tree. Three primary booms extend to the float; supplemental booms and stringers provide strengthening. Float, roughly half the length of the hull, connected to booms by pairs of stanchions that cross above the booms. Outrigger kept to windward. Platform covers hull and extends out each side slightly; a small thatched hut for provisions and gear might be placed on the platform. Steered with a long, heavy oar attached with a rope tied to holes at upper end of the blade. Mast stepped amidships on platform, pivoted to rake in direction of travel; braced by curved stick from the central boom; stayed fore and aft, 2 shrouds. Shrouds passed through holes at the masthead. Triangular sail, apex down; yard rests in a special slot on deck; tack shifted from end to end when going about; foot boomed. Sail originally of woven pandanus leaves. Also sculled or poled. Lengths of early **canoes** to 30m, later 8-15m; e.g., length 14m, beam 0.64m, depth 0.5m. Other recorded names: **beam float, thamakan, thamakathu, thamakau, waqa ni Viti, zamakau**

camaronero See **shrimper**

čamičic See **čamac**

camin *France, N:* Developed in the 19th century in the Baie de la Seine area as a small beached **fishing boat***. Became a pleasure boat, especially for private fishing. Clinker-planked of elm; flat floors initially, later more deadrise; rounded bilges; some had heavy fixed ballast, others used sacks of disposable beach cobbles. Plumb stem, rounded forefoot; high raked transom with deadwood below; keel and grounding keels. Open; outboard rudder; tiller; centerboard on some. Mainmast stepped on the stem, raking aft; mizzenmast at the sternpost. Both set lugsails, the mizzen sail sheeted to a long jiggerboom. Jib to a long, bowsed-down bowsprit. Working boats 4-6m, pleasure boats 3-5m; e.g., length 4.5m, beam 1.6m, depth 0.67m. Name variants: **camin du Havre, picoteux***

camin du Havre See **camin**

campboat See **chalan, shanty boat**

campo See **chalan**

camus *France, SW:* **Skiff***-like craft used mainly as a **ferry*** on the Garonne River. See also **chenière**.

Canadeesche kano See **Canadian canoe**

Canadian boat See **batteau-2a, St. Lawrence skiff-1**

Canadian canoe 1. Term sometimes applied loosely to any open North American birchbark **canoe***. More generally refers to **canoes** built on the same lines.

2. *Canada, E:* Developed in the mid-19th century on Rice Lake in southern Ontario Province to meet the needs of duck hunters, although it became primarily a pleasure craft. Might be rib-and-batten-built or smooth inside and outside. Sharp lines; broad, flat floors; quick turn of the bilges; slight tumble home to topsides. Bow and stern decks. Generally paddled with a single- or double-bladed paddle, but could be sailed, at which time leeboards were employed. Length typically 4.9m, width 0.76m, depth 0.3m. Note also **Rice Lake canoe**.

3. In the United Kingdom, **Canadian canoe** refers to an open boat with rounded bottom and small decks at bow and stern. Built on the lines of a birchbark **canoe**, as distinguished from the enclosed **kayak***. May be canvas-covered or of wood.

Other recorded names: **Canadeesche kano, Canadian model, canadien, Canadier, canoë canadien, kanadensare, Kanadier; canadienne** (erroneously)

Canadian model See **Canadian canoe**

Canadian pinky See **pinky**

canadien See **Canadian canoe**

canadienne *Canada, E:* Term used by French Canadians of the St. Lawrence River and Estuary for a type of Canadian-built **banker*** that was slightly smaller and less heavily rigged than the regular oceangoing **banker**. Generally transported merchandise and farm produce. Superseded by the **goélette*** of the same area. See also **Canadian canoe**.

Canadier See **Canadian canoe**

canagua, canahua See **canoa-17**

canal boat 1. Navigates on canals and is usually sized to meet the limitation of the locks on a particular canal system. Generally long and narrow, with bluff, nearly vertical ends. Other recorded names: **canaler, canaller*, kanalbåt, Kanalboot**. Note also **flyboat-3a, Lake Champlain canal boat, narrow boat, packet boat**.

2. *United States, NE:* Heavy-duty, square-ended boats used by the ice industry on the Kennebec River in Maine. These large craft kept the channels cut in the ice open at night for the passage of ice blocks next morning. Boats were pulled along by picks and rocked from side to side to keep ice from forming on the sides of the channel. Strapped with iron or covered by sheets of metal.

canaler See **canal boat, canaller**

canal flat See **Mersey flat**

canaller *Canada, S/United States, N:* A Great Lakes vessel designed to traverse St. Lawrence canals and the Welland Canal between Lakes Erie and Ontario when the locks were only 4.3m wide. Blunt, straight stem; flat stern. The sailing ships were followed by powered **canallers**, a few of which still operate. Other recorded names: **canaler, Welland canaller**. Note also **Great Lakes schooner**. Further reference: **canal boat**

canal schooner See **Great Lakes schooner**

cañalucho See **mola, mon-3**

canaoa See **canoa-17, canoe-6, gommier**

canaoua See **canoa-17**

canard See **pile driver-2**

canardi *France, N:* Vessel used by Normans of the Middle Ages to raid the English coast.

canardière *Switzerland:* Lightweight open boat used for duck hunting and fishing on several Swiss lakes. Carvel-planked; flat, keelless bottom, planked fore-and-aft, with slight rocker at ends. Flared sides, no gunwales; 2 ribs; numerous floor frames. Bow shape varies: at Geneva, the bow is square; at Lake of Neûchatel, it is sharp and strongly raked; those used mainly for hunting provide a nearly horizontal support at the bow for the gun. Stern square and low, some with a gun support. One or 2 thwarts forward. Rowed, usually standing, with a pair of oars, but hand paddles used when approaching the ducks. Reported lengths 4.75-5.1m; e.g., length overall 4.75m, on bottom 4.30m, beam 1.0m, depth 0.15m. Name variant: **loquette de chase**

canaua See **canoa-17**, **canoe-6**
Cancale bisquine See **bisquine**
candibá See **ubá**
candil See **barco do candil**
candimaram See **catamaran**
candura See **gundra**
cane See **Kahn-1**, **Kahn-5**
canga, **cange** See **cangia**
cangia *Egypt:* Fine-lined Nile vessel used mainly for transportation since at least the 17th century. Large vessels had 1-2 elaborately furnished cabins on the high poop deck; the smaller, more modest boats were undecked and had only an awning aft. Curved bow;

cangia

large rudder. When rowed, alternate deck planks were removed and the oarsmen sat on the remaining planks, rowing double-banked. Set 1-2 lofty lateen sails. The larger mast stood amidships, the smaller in the bow. Reported lengths 9-20m. Other recorded names: **baş kanca**, **canga**, **cange**, **canja**, **cingia**, **ganga**, **ganja★**, **gemge**, **ghanja**, **kandsje**, **kānga**, **kangia**, **kanj(i)a**, **qāndja bāch**, **qanğa**, **qangeh**. Note also **dahabiyah**, **sandal-2**.
canhonheira See **gunboat**
canja See **cangia**
cannaoiia See **canoe**
cannery tender See **packer**
canneur See **tuna boat-1**
cannew See **canoe**
canning vessel See **factory ship**
canno, **cannoa** See **canoe**
cannoe See **canoe**, **canot**
cannoniera See **gunboat**
cannow *United States, E:* Word used by the early colonists for a **dugout canoe★**, except in northeastern New England, where **cannows** were of birch or elm bark. Term used for those made by Native Americans and by the colonists themselves. The dugouts generally had sharp ends with cutaway forefoot and heel, straight sides. Dugouts to ca. 12m. Other recorded names: **canoe★**, **canow**, **conow**, **water horse**. See also **canoa-1**, **canoe-7**.
cannowa, **cano** See **canoe**
canoa 1. Arawak word for **dugout canoe★**. Term used throughout the West Indies and much of Latin

America, although it may merely mean a **boat★** in general terms. **Piragua★** was the term used by the Caribs of the area (see **pirogue-1**). The **canoas** of the Tainos of the northern islands could hold up to 150 people; sails introduced by the Spaniards. Spelling variants: **cannow**, **canow**. Note also **almady**, **canoa-7a**, **canoe**.
2. In the Portuguese navy, a light, narrow **pulling boat★**, or **gig★**, assigned to a captain, is also called a **canoa**. Name variant: **canoa do comandante**
3. *Brazil:* **a.** In the Amazon basin, **canoa** is a generic term for a keelless **dugout canoe** ranging from a small single-person craft to a large 2-masted vessel such as the **gambarra★**. In some areas, **canoa** may designate a **canoe** with a sail. Small types not plank-extended. On the larger boats, the lower hull has been expanded by heat and pressure, and planks raise the sides. Ends, which flare up due to the pressure exerted in the middle of the hull, are fitted with V-shaped planks. Bottom flattened. Some have overhang aft for steersman. May be open or decked. Paddled, poled, and sailed. Early boats reported as long as 26m; very narrow. Spelling variants: **canoão**, **kanoa**. Note also **bote-3b**, **casco**, **igá**. **b.** Fast open boat found in the Salvador (Bahia) area in northeast Brazil. Plank-extended dugout hull;

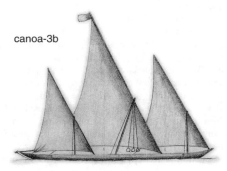

canoa-3b

long overhanging bow and stern help with operation from the beach; flared sides. Propelled by oars and sail. One to 3 masts; the former, now the more common, mainly conveys passengers; 2-masted type serves primarily as a fishing craft and sets tanned lateen or spritsails; the 3-masted boats used for racing at Salvador, setting lateen sails and using slings from the masthead for hiking out. The lateen yards often longer than the craft itself. Some use leeboards. Reported lengths 6-22m, beam 0.5-1.5m, depths 0.35-0.7m. Small type, with large beam and depth in relation to its size, called a **batalão**; occasionally used as a **ship's boat★**. **c.** Three types of **canoas** are used in Paraná State in the south—two for cargo, one for fishing. The **fishing boat★** is a sharp-bowed, single-piece dugout; adapted for working from the beaches; rowed and sailed. One cargo **canoa** is plank-built, with sharp ends, and reinforced with ribs; 2 masts stepped into thwarts, setting triangular sails. The other cargo type is a plank-extended dugout, and mainly rowed.
4. *Chile, S:* Colonial Spanish term for the indigenous **dugout canoe** of the Chiloé Archipelago. Rowed with short, wide-bladed oars; no oarlocks. Still used; locally called **bongos★**; to 6m.

5. *Colombia:* The large **canoa** of the Caribbean coast is a plank-extended dugout with sharp raked ends. Outboard rudder; long tiller. Set 2 boomed leg-of-mutton sails and a large staysail. Foremast, the shorter, stepped well back or gaff sails set to masts of equal height, the foresail loose-footed, the mainsail loose-footed but boomed; staysail. Now mainly motorized.

6. *Colombia, central:* On the inland waterways, the term **canoa** can apply to a plank-extended **canoe**, but more often to a **dugout canoe**. Mainly transports cargo, sometimes cattle. Blunt ends; bottom flattened on the dugouts, flat on the plank-built **canoes**; ends have rocker on both types. Plank-built boats have widely spaced ribs, usually in 3 pieces. The term **canoa** is widely used, but in some places it is called a **barqueta★** and in others a **piragua** or **cayuco★**. The small types (7m long, 0.9m wide, and 0.45m deep) may be called **potro★**, **champa★**, or **macho**; a short, narrow **canoe** is a **potrillo**. Large **canoes** (15m long) may be classed by length: the **tres** (13m), the **quatro** (14m), and the **cinco** (15m); a large **canoe** with an outboard motor is a **motorcanoa** and sometimes a **chivo**.

7. *Cuba:* **a.** The **canoa** of the early Tainos peoples was a **dugout canoe**. Long and narrow; flattened bottom, no keel; hull tarred. Small single-person **canoas** were used, but the boats were also reported by Columbus to have employed as many as 80 paddlers. Note also **canoa-1**. **b.** One-man boat used in line fishing along the south-central coast, especially at the mouth of the Río Guaurabo. Flat bottom, cross-planked; at the stern a plank keel extends forward for ca. 91cm; transom width less than half the maximum beam; sharp, raked stem. A few ribs strengthen the flared sides. Small live well amidships. Open; benches at each end and amidships. Caulked with fiber from the banana tree. Rowed; oarlocks formed by scooped blocks set vertically on the gunwales; oars held with a rope loop. Reported lengths 4.27-5.5m, widths 1-1.47m, depth ca. 0.74m.

8. *Mexico, west coast:* **a.** Beamy **dugout canoe** used for ocean work and, in the Sea of Cortés, for fishing and frequently to carry heavy cargo and passengers; some larger **canoas** served as **lighters★**. Double-ended with rounded bow and stern, mild sheer, vertical sides, flat floors, short entrance and run; sometimes bow built up on smaller craft. Most had heavy gunwales and were fitted with 2-3 frames. Some fishing **canoas** had a live well. Early boats of the Seri people fashioned of many pieces of driftwood, nailed, using barbed wire; coated and caulked with a tar-like substance. Generally rowed, but often sailed, employing a quadrilateral, boomed spritsail. Reported lengths 5-7.3m, widths 0.86-1.5m. Spelling variant: **canóaa** (Seri). **b.** With the decline of suitable trees for dugouts, **canoas** are now plank-built, with hard chines that phase out at the ends. Sharp ends; slight deadrise; frames bent against a triangular chine piece; straight, mildly flared sides. Occasionally round-bottomed. Mainly rowed, but when sailed sets a low leg-of-mutton sail with a long foot; some set a boomed standing lugsail with a short yard. Those fitted with outboard motors have a narrow transom. Length ca. 7.6m.

9. *Mexico, SW:* Dugout used for lagoon fishing in the Chiapas area. Hewn from the trunk of the *huanacaxtle* tree. Characterized by an overhanging extension at the stern on which the fisherman stands. Stern strongly raked below the platform, bow rounded. Mainly poled.

10. *Philippines:* A widely used term for a **dugout canoe** capable of carrying only 1-2 persons.

11. *Portugal, SW:* From north of the Tagus River to the Algarve in the south, a type of small **fishing boat** goes by the general name **canoa**. Being fast sailers, some also serve as **market boats★**, and may be called **enviadas★**. On the Algarve coast, some carry small fish taken from tunny nets to shore at regular intervals. Carvel-planked; strongly raked transom stern; plumb stem, sometimes topped with a mop of wool; straight keel with deadwood aft; round bottom; high sheer. Painted oculi often at the bows. Generally open or with a foredeck. Single mast carries a lateen sail with a short luff. Some small boats set a spritsail. Reported lengths 9-11.6m; e.g., length 9m, beam 2.97m, depth 1.35m. Note also **canoa do alto**, **enviada-2**.

12. *Portugal, central:* Within the Tagus Estuary, a type of **canoa** ferried passengers between Lisbon and Cacilhas across the river; when motor **ferries★** replaced them, the **canoas** began carrying local produce. Set a single lateen sail, with the yard generally to starboard. Reported lengths 6-9m. Other recorded names: **bote-canoa**, **lancha★**

13. *Portugal, Madeira Islands:* Small, transom-sterned inshore **fishing boat**. Carvel-planked; curved or straight raked ends; keel, with grounding keels on the rounded bilges; rudder hangs below the keel. Hole in stem for rope to haul boat onto the beach. Foredeck, with locker below. Generally rowed with 4 oars, asymmetrically placed; block on oar fits over a tholepin. Also employs a dipping lugsail. Reported lengths 2.4-4.3m; e.g., length 4.3m, beam 1.68m, depth 0.57m. Name variant: **lancha** (at nearby Porto Santo Island)

14. *South America, NW:* **Canoas** were noted by early explorers along the coasts of northern Ecuador and southern Colombia. Reported in later years from Panama to south of Callao in Peru, and still found along tributary rivers in Ecuador and adjacent Peru. River dugouts mostly double-ended, with a thick flat bottom, round bilges, flat sides, and generally fine

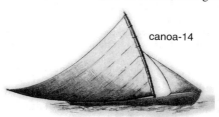

canoa-14

lines and run. Most distinguishing feature is their ends; those of the Cayapa of northwest Ecuador (called **kū'le★**) are flattened and turn up, with a notch; the gunwale is flat and thickened for some distance from the end. The platform on the Colombian **canoa** lacks the notch and is wider; generally the sheer is flatter. Those of Manabí Province in Ecuador have no platform and their almost plumb ends terminate in blunt points. The popular **kū'le** is found throughout the northwest coast; all the Peruvian dugouts come from Ecuador. Oceangoing sailing **canoas** are modified by adding a strake. Most use a leg-of-mutton cotton sail with a long boom that extends well beyond the stern; sometimes a small jib. The light mast steps through a thwart into a block or a piece of cane with a hole cut into it. Some use a short, very high-peaked gaff sail or a loose-footed square sail. The **canoas** of Puerto Pizarro in northern Peru set a spritsail. May use a balance board. River craft paddled or poled; some offshore sailing dugouts hitch a ride behind motorized **fishing boats**. On some river and oceangoing dugouts, a sponson of balsa wood along each side increases stability and buoyancy. Used mostly for transportation, ferrying, and fishing. In some parts of Peru, the bow and stern extensions may serve as platforms on which to stand while harpooning sharks; the harpoon line is attached through a hole in the platform, and the shark, often bigger than the **canoe**, tows it until exhausted. Reported lengths 1.83-18m, with a general length-to-beam ratio of 10:1. Other recorded names: **champa** (north of Buenaventura, Colombia); the small Colombian **canoas** are known as **chingas**, **potrillo**, and **potro**. Further reading: Clinton R. Edwards, *Aboriginal Watercraft on the Pacific Coast of South America* (Berkeley: University of California Press, 1965), 40-50. Note also **cayuco**, **imbabura**, **panga**.

15. *Spain, E:* The racing **canoas** of the Barcelona area were popular in the 1st half of the 20th century. Rowed by 12 men, usually fishermen and the working class. The coxswain used a steering oar.

16. *Venezuela:* **a.** Large dugout reported by Columbus and still used on rivers and occasionally at Isla de Margarita. Hewn with fire and axe. Lighter construction in the interior of the country because sometimes they must be portaged around rapids. The **canoita**, a 1-man type on the lower Orinoco River, was reported as 1.4m long, 0.22m wide, and 0.12m deep inside. **b.** The Lake Maracaibo **canoa** is plank-built, has a square stern, rounded sides, hard chines, small flat bottom. Used for net fishing. Most now have engines. Reported lengths 4.5-10m. **c.** Along the eastern part of the north coast, the **canoa** is a plank-extended dugout. Used for fishing in lagoons, mangrove swamps, and other shallow areas. Sharp overhanging bow, square stern, considerable sheer. Single plank added to each side, strengthened with ribs. Paddled, and sometimes sailed.

17. *West Indies:* **a.** Expanded **dugout canoe** of the West Indies and northeastern South America. Most sharpended and swept up at the ends. Generally plank-extended, the planks sewn on. Breakwater at each end. Multiple benches; close behind each bench was a thwart that braced the sides and served as a backrest. Mainly paddled, but also sailed, setting a single sail. Steered with a paddle. Lengths to ca. 10m; beam ca. 2.4m. A small size, 2.5-6m long, might be called a **couliala** and is not plank-extended. Other recorded names: **canagua**, **canahua**, **canáoa**, **canaoua**, **canaua**, **canot★**, **canoua**, **couíllara**, **coulialla**. Note also **canoe**,

corial, **piragua**. **b.** In the Netherlands Antilles, a **canoa** is an open double-ended **fishing boat**. Sailed, setting a mainsail and headsail. Uses sandbag ballast. Generally 4 in crew. Average length 6m; 4-6grt. **c.** On the island of Nevis in the Leeward Islands, a **canoa** is a blunt-ended two-hulled boat used for pleasure. Sets a leg-of-mutton mainsail and large jib. **d.** In Puerto Rico, **canoa** describes a very small boat propelled by oars.

Further references: **bongo-3**, **bote-3**, **canoa do baleeiro**, **canoe**, **canoe-6**, **canot**, **cayuco-3**, **kanu**, **kunu**, **lippee-lippee**, **vigilenga**

canóaa See **canoa-8**, **panga-3**

canoa a motor See **motor boat-1**

canoa bordada *Brazil, E:* Small boat of the Rio de Janeiro area on which a supplemental strake (*bordada*) raises each side. Blocks on the gunwales hold tholepins. When sailed, mast stepped through a bench forward. Halyard for the square sail is placed a third of the distance along the yard, passed through a hole in the mast, and secured to the bench. Name variant: **canoa de voga**

canoa cacilheira *Portugal, central:* Fine-lined open boat that carried passengers and light merchandise across the Tagus River from Lisbon. Raking transom stern, plumb stem with cutaway forefoot. Continuous bulwarks, marked sheer, single wale along each side. Loose-footed gaff sail and foresail. Length 9.83m, beam 3m, depth 1.38m. Other recorded names: **cacisheiro**, **cano cacisheira**. Note also **bote cacilheiro**.

canoa coberta See **coberta**

canoa con lanciafuori See **outrigger canoe**

canoa da picada *Portugal:* Developed in the late 19th century as a fast, seaworthy vessel to carry the catch from **fishing boats★** to the Lisbon market. Also fished, and in modified form has been a pleasure craft; reported also as a cargo carrier from south coast ports. Typical features include a long, rounded counter stern above a sharply raked sternpost, maximum beam abaft amidships, and a gaff mizzen stepped on the counter and sheeted to an outrigger. Plumb stem, deep drag to the keel, round bottom with slack bilges. Shredded wool on the stemhead prevents chafing of the sail. Decked, 3 hatchways. Inboard rudder; tiller. May tow a small **tender★** called an **aiola★**. Sets a large quadrilateral lateen-type sail with a short luff as a mainsail to a forward-raking or vertical mast; yard, carried generally to starboard, extends beyond the bow; tack to stemhead. Might also set a foresail and a mizzen staysail. Rowed in calms, oars stropped to tholepins. Crew of 15-18 when serving as a **market boat★**. Reported lengths 13.7-18m; e.g., length 18m, beam 5.5m, depth 1.5m. Note also **enviada**.

canoa de corteza See **anan**, **bark boat**

canoa de embondo See **canoa de embono**

canoa de embono *Brazil, NE:* **Coaster★** of the Pernambuco and Alagoas areas; extinct. Dugout bottom, planked-up sides; keel sometimes added to the bottom; spoon bow, square stern. Decked at bow and stern, open waist. Stability and buoyancy provided by log sponsons set along the sides. Wide-bladed rudder; tiller. Stepped 2 flexible masts, the small foremast in the eyes, the mainmast just abaft the foredeck; masts unstayed, curved aft. Set boomed leg-of-mutton sails, cut with narrow cloths. Length 13.4m, beam 1.0m, depth 0.6m. Spelling variant: **canoa de embondo**. Note also **embono**.

canoa de voga See **canoa bordada**

canoa do alto 1. *Brazil, NE:* Large decked boat employed in offshore fishing and in transporting the catch to market. Used particularly out of Salvador (Bahia). **2.** *Portugal:* Engaged in offshore fishing in the area from the Tagus River to the south coast. Straight stem, curved forefoot; shredded wool on stemhead reduces sail chafing; wide raked wineglass transom. Drag to the straight keel; bilge keels; high sides; strong sheer; 2 wales. Some fully decked; more often only a foredeck; enclosed bench aft. Outboard rudder; tiller. Set a lateen sail or quadrilateral lateen-type sail with a short luff. Forward-raking mast stepped on keelson. Some also employed a sprit-rigged, aft-raking mizzenmast sheeted to an outrigger. Rowed in calms and when shooting the net. Crew of 11-13, plus 1-2 boys. Reported lengths 6.58-8.5m; e.g., length 7.7m, beam 3m, depth 1.0m.

canoa do baleeiro *Azores, northern Atlantic:* Slender open **whaleboat★** imported into the islands from the United States until 1894; thereafter built locally. Launched from the beaches. Double-ended with sharp entrance and run; carvel-built, sheer strake may be lapped; frames of 1 piece; rounded bottom; slack bilges; flared sides; whalebone rubbing strakes. When whale strikes, tiller unshipped and rudder swung clear of the water by means of a lanyard that pulls the pintles free of the gudgeon pins. Then a steering oar (ca. 7m long) employed, supported by an iron brace on the port side; wooden peg on oar loom provides a better grip. Chock forward of harpooner's platform; 6 thwarts. Hull white, sheer strake a bright color,

canoa do baleeiro

designating island of origin. 19th-century boats set a boomless gunter lugsail with sprit; subsequently used a high-peaked boomed gaff sail and jib, some club-footed. Heavily canvassed. Mast lowers by a hinge. Relied solely on sail and oar (using oars of 6 different lengths, single-banked) until 1909, when motor **launches★** began towing boats to the whaling grounds. Paddles used in addition to sail when in close range of the whale. Crew of 7. Reported lengths 9-12m; e.g., length 11.6m, beam 2m, depth ca. 0.76m, draft 0.76m. Other recorded names: **baleeira★**, **baleinière**, **bote**, **canoa★**, **whaleboat★**. Note also **tow boat-1**.

canoa do comandante See **canoa-2**, **gig-1**

canoa do Seixal See **enviada-2**

canoa égaritea See **igarité**

canoa grande 1. *Brazil, S:* Large boat used on rivers of Rio Grande do Sul State. Concave stem terminates in a tall stemhead; counter stern, vertical sides. Decked; house abaft the mast. Vertical mast, with topmast, stepped amidships. Sets square sails and sometimes a foresail and fore-topsail. Poled when necessary. **2.** *Portugal, central:* Black-hulled boat from Trafaria on the south shore of the Tagus Estuary that engaged in ocean fishing. Vertical stem; swept up sharply at the bow; raked transom. A low quadrilateral lateen-type sail with a short luff set to a vertical mast stepped about a third in from the bow. Length 8.9m, beam 2.9m, depth 1.2m. Name variant: **canoa grande da trafaria** See also **champa-1**.

canoa grande da trafaria See **canoe grande**

canoa monoxila See **dugout canoe**

canoão See **canoa-3**

canoas See **canot**

cano cacisheira See **canoa cacilheira**

canoe Broadly speaking, a narrow, elongated, open, lightweight craft that may be hewn from a log (**dugout canoe★**); may consist of a framework covered with bark, cloth, skins, or a light wood; or may be constructed of a light metal or fiberglass. Used primarily on inland or sheltered waters for traveling, fishing, exploring, racing, and pleasure. Generally sharp at each end and round-bilged. May or may not have a keel. Most open, but may be decked, with a small cockpit. Propelled and steered by a single- or double-bladed paddle, held in a near-vertical position without use of a fixed fulcrum, the paddler(s) facing forward. Generally paddled by 2 people or solo. Also sailed. Stabilizing devices may be employed: the **balance canoe** uses a board laid athwartships; the **double canoe** is 2 parallel **canoes** united by one or more beams; the **outrigger canoe★** has 1-2 outriggers consisting of multiple booms attached to a float(s). Shallow draft. Selected spelling variants: **caano**, **cannaoiia**, **cannew**, **canno(a)**, **cannoe**, **cannow★**, **cannowa**, **cano(o)**, **canoa★**, **canoë**, **canou(a)**, **canow**, **kano★**, **kanoe**, **kanot★**, **Kanu★**, **kenu★**. Note also **bark boat**, **Canadian canoe**, **kayak**, **piragua**, **pirogue**. **1.** In 19th-century England, the term **canoe** referred to a **kayak★** used for pleasure. By the latter part of the century, a **canoe** was any craft light enough to be portaged by 2 men. **2.** *Dominica, West Indies:* A large open craft used along the protected west side of the island, especially in off-loading ships in the open roadstead at Roseau. **3.** *England, NE:* The fishermen of Hartlepool called their small clinker-built boats **canoes**. Ends sharp; keel ca. 15cm deep; 2 grounding keels enabled the boats to sit upright when the tide was out. Ballasted with sandbags. Carried a lugsail. Length ca. 5.5m, beamy. **4.** *England, E:* Small transom-sterned rowboat that carries mussels to shore at Cley and Blakeney in Norfolk. Each side constructed of 3-5 planks, laid clinker-fashion. Bottom flat except for a slight fore-and-aft rocker and athwartship camber; hard chines; rubbing strakes added to the bottom. Transom has heel of 20-22cm; some heart-shaped. Little freeboard when loaded. Some decked forward. Rowed against tholepins originally, later with oarlocks; also poled and sailed. Sets a loose-footed standing lugsail, steering with an oar. Reported

canoe-4

lengths 4.11-4.88m, widths 1.47-1.75m. Other recorded names: **flatbottom** (at Wells), **flattie***. Note also **mussel boat**.

5. *England, S:* Popular craft on the Dorset coast for wildfowling, winkling, oystering, and other uses; most owner-built and varied accordingly. Flat bottom, hard chines, 1-2 strakes to each side, centerboard or daggerboard, cambered deck. Transom stern; early boats reported as sharp-ended. Rowed or set a spritsail. Length 4.57m, width 1.52m, depth 0.2m, draft 0.1m. Name variant: **Poole canoe**

6. *Guyana:* Word applies to the native **dugout canoe** that is closed at each end by a triangular insert. Hewn where tree felled; at water's edge, expanded by placing over a fire, by filling with wet sand, or by submerging in the river; held open with lashed-on rods and benches. End pieces generally arch above gunwale level and may be fancifully painted. Plank often added to each side when used in an area of rough water. Seams caulked with shredded bark and coated with resin. On long journeys, an arched tent protects the cargo. Generally paddled but may also set a tall

canoe-6

rectangular sail of split palm or a spritsail. Reported lengths 5.7-12.8m; e.g., length 5.7m, beam 1.0m, depth 0.46m. Other recorded names: **canaoa**, **canaua**, **canoa***, **carib**, **paragua**, **piragua***, **pirogue***. Note also **corial**, **falca**.

7. *United States:* Colonial term designating a **dugout canoe** that served as a **ship's boat***; also used for fishing, hunting, and general transportation. Those on Chesapeake Bay were hewn mainly from the durable pitch pine. Reported to have had a flat bottom, square stern, sharp bow. Often rowed, using as many as 5 oars; also sailed. Reported lengths 4-9m; e.g., length 6m, beam 1.2m, depth 0.46m. Name variant: **water horse**. Note also **cannow**.

8. *United States, north-central:* Double-ended open boat used mainly by commercial fishermen. Sometimes served as a **tender*** to larger boats. More common term now is **cutter***, **duck boat***, or **pirogue**. Planked or of plywood; flaring sides. Sharp raked ends; the **canoes** of the Tennessee River had blunt ends. Paddled or poled by 12 men.

9. *West Indies, Cayman Islands:* Used for turtling by the inhabitants of these islands northwest of Jamaica.

Blunt-ended dugout with 2 strakes added to each side. Strengthened with thwarts and a few frames. Rowed with 4 oars and sailed, setting a mainsail and jib. Typically 6.7m long, 1.8m wide; shallow draft.

10. *West Indies, Virgin Islands:* Plank-extended **dugout canoe** of the French fishermen on St. Thomas. Logs obtained from the Dominican Republic; ribs added to the hollowed-out log and to these, planks were nailed. Sharply pointed bow; narrow, V-shaped raking transom stern. Gaff sail set to mast stepped at the bow; also rowed. Reported lengths 4.6-6m, widths 0.9-1.22m, depths 0.6-0.76m.

Further references: **boat-1, canoe-yawl, canot, Chesapeake Bay log canoe, curragh, falouche-1, gommier, kayak-2, pirogue-4, Tortola sloop, York boat**

canoë canadien See **Canadian canoe**

canoë français *France:* Outrigged **scull***-type boat popular on the Seine River in the late 19th century. Could be rowed by 1 or 2, or by 1 with a coxswain; also paddled or sailed. Sharp ends; narrow.

canoe-kayak Produced where Native Americans and Eskimos (Inuit) live in adjacent areas, especially in eastern Canada and Greenland. Pointed ends; ends decked, remainder either open or enclosed. Covered with bark or skins. Name variant: **qajariaq**

canoe-yacht See **canoe-yawl**

canoe-yawl *England:* Basically a **canoe***-shaped boat with sharp ends, but was larger than most sailing **canoes**, beamier and heavier, and was about the same size as a ship's **yawl***. Developed in the 1870s for both sea and inland use as a small, easily handled cruising boat. Usually **ketch***-rigged, with the mizzenmast just forward of the steering device, but some were **yawl**-rigged with the mast abaft the tiller. Some were raced. Popular mainly in the late 19th century. Carvel- or clinker-planked. Fine hollow entrance; most had a plumb stem, generally cutaway forefoot; straight sternpost, sometimes raked, or might have an overhanging stern. Bottom rocker on some and drag to keel; firm or slack bilges. The **Mersey canoe-yawl** of northwestern England had a deep keel, while the **Humber canoe-yawl** of northeastern England usually had a centerboard. Open or half-decked; ample cockpit; the larger generally had a trunk cabin (the **canoe-yacht**). Outboard rudder; tiller might have a bend to clear the mizzenmast; some used a yoke and rods or chains to the tiller. Considerable variation in rig. Usually employed lug mainsail, some battened; larger boats might be gaff-rigged. The mizzen was a lug, gunter-lug, or leg-of-mutton with a sprit, often boomed out. Jib might run to a small horizontal bowsprit. A few **sloop***-rigged. Also rowed. Crew of 1-3. Reported lengths 4-9m; e.g., length on deck 6m, on waterline 5.3m, beam 1.8m, draft with centerboard up 0.53m. Beam of those that raced in the late 19th century could not exceed 0.9m. Other recorded names: **canoe; Humber** or **Mersey yawl**. Further reading: Dick Phillips, "Building a Victorian Canoe Yawl," *Classic Boat* 31 (1991), 105-108; 32 (1991), 59-63; 33 (1991), 54-57; John Leather, "Canoes? Perhaps; Yawls? Hardly," ibid., 40 (1991), 43-48.

canoino See **scull**

canoita See **canoa-16**

cañonera, cañonero, canonnière See **gunboat**

canoo See **canoe**

canot 1. French generic for a small, open, general-purpose **boat★** or **skiff★**. Constructed of wood, metal, or synthetic material. Hull features vary, but generally has a curved stem, small transom, round bottom with strong rise to the floors, straight keel. May have a built-up strake around the stern bench. Special bumpers on those that deliver pilots to ships or retrieve them. Usually rowed, but may be sailed; now often propelled by outboard motor.
2. A light, fast **ship's boat★** used for ship-to-shore and ship-to-ship communication; sometimes towed sailing vessels in calms, or raised anchors. The **canot** of a **galley★** might be carried aboard but is more generally towed. The **grand canot** (English **barge★** or **first boat**) was designated for the admiral (**canot amiral** or **canot de l'amiral**), commandant (**canot du commandant**), or captain (**canot du capitaine**); the **canot amiral** had canopies at bow and stern and might be rowed by 14 men. Next in rank was the **second canot** or **canot de l'etat major** (**pinnace★**). 18th-century **grand canot** was sharp-ended and 7.6-11.9m long, 1.88-2.4m wide, and 0.9-1.0m deep; the **petit canot★** ranged from 6.1-8.5m long, 1.7-2m wide, and 0.69-0.86m deep. The **canots** carried aboard **bisquines★** were 4.4-4.6m long. Note also **barge-11**.
3. *Canada, E:* Long, narrow, open boat used on rivers of the Gaspé Peninsula. Planked, 3 planks per side; closely spaced ribs. Curved stem and sternpost; greater sheer toward the bow.
4. *France:* Small, open lug-rigged boat that works close inshore, generally for shrimp and crabs; some collect seaweed. Transom stern, straight stem. Foremast stepped close to the bow; mainmast amidships, often raking aft. Might step a mizzen, raise lug topsails, and run a jib to a slender bowsprit. Spelling variant: **canotte★**. Note also **annexe**.
5. *United States, central:* To early French-speaking peoples of the Mississippi Valley, a **canot** might be either a birchbark or a **dugout canoe★**. The 18th-century plank-built **ship's boat** had a rounded hull, hourglass transom, shallow keel; set a lugsail or rowed. During the 19th century, lug-rigged **canots** provided general transportation and fished. Note also **pirogue**.
6. *West Indies:* Open transom-sterned **fishing boat★**. In Les Saintes (where it is called **canot saintois**), Guadeloupe, Saint Martin, and Saint Barthélemy, it is plank-built with pronounced flare to the bow, maximum beam well forward, straight raking stem, and broad raked transom. Rising floors, several thwarts, wide gunwale. Rowed and sailed. The foot of the large triangular mainsail is longer than the luff; also sets a jib. When sailed, 2-3 men serve as ballast. In Haiti, the term designates a boat engaging in line, basket, or net fishing; lengths given as 3.66-6m and cap. as 1-3t, the one-ton size predominating. Overall length of the **canot saintois** 5m, on keel 3.5m, beam 1.6m, depth 0.65m. Name variant: **le saintois**. Note also **pirogue**.
Spelling variants: **cannoe, canoa★, canoas, canoe★, canota, canote★, canotte★, canoua, canoue**. Further

references: **annexe, bag, barque sablaise, canoa-17, gommier, kannòt, kanot-3, New Orleans lugger, petit canot, pirogue-4, sardinier breton**

canota See **canot**

canot à avirons See **rowboat**

canot à couple See **double-banked boat**

canot à crevette *Belgium:* Small boat used mainly for shrimping. Local variations, but usually open or half-decked, straight ends, bluff bow, outboard rudder. Sets a dipping lugsail or gaff sail; also rowed. Crew of 1-2 on the open boats and 5-6 on the half-decked types. Reported lengths 6-9.5m. Name variant: **crevettier★**. Note also **Nieuwportse garnaalboot, Oostendse garnaalboot, shrimper**.

canot à glace *Canada, E:* Built in the Magdalen Islands in the Gulf of St. Lawrence for hunting seals. Clinker-planked; ironshod curved keel; skeg; elongated curved bow merges smoothly with the keel; narrow raked transom. Open; some have a small foredeck. Crew of 5-7, four of whom may pull the boat over the ice with ropes secured to the 2 thwarts. Four oars. Length ca. 3.5m. Note also **flat-2, iceboat-1, sealing punt, sealing skiff**.

canot à l'aviron See **pulling boat**

canot allège See **canot léger**

canot amiral See **canot-2**

canot à moteur See **motor boat-1**

canot annexe See **annexe**

canot armé à couple See **double-banked boat**

canot armé en pointe See **single-banked boat**

canot automobile See **motor boat-1**

canot bâtard 1. Term for a **ship's boat★** that is mid-sized between the largest and smallest on board.
2. *Canada, S/United States, N:* Fur trader's birchbark **canoe★**; many used around Great Lakes trading posts. Versatile, as it falls between the **canot du maître★** and the **canot du nord★** in size. Sometimes used as a **canot léger★**. Crew of 10. Reported lengths 9.1-9.8m; cap. 2t. Other recorded names: **ba(s)tard canoe, le bâtard**

canot caseyeur *France, NW:* Small, open lobster boat of the Seine Estuary. Small transom. Rowed with 2 pairs of oars between tholepins. Crew of 4. Note also **caseyeur**.

canot couvert See **houseboat-1, tilt boat**

canot creux mytilicole See **canot mytilicole**

canot d'apparat See **barge-2**

canot d'écorce See **bark boat**

canot de charge See **canot du maître, canot du nord**

canot de chasse *France, N:* Small open boat that engaged in hunting seals on the sandbanks of Baie de Somme in the 19th century. Clinker-planked; sharp, straight stem cutaway into the keel; narrow transom. Outboard rudder, tiller. Ballast of large cobbles. Mast stepped near the bow, setting a dipping lugsail tacked to the stemhead or a gaff sail. A standing lugsail might be set to a mizzenmast on the transom and a jib to a long bowsprit. Also sculled. Length 6m; shallow draft. Note also **sealer**.

canot de l'amiral See **barge-2, canot-2**

canot de l'arrière See **stern boat**

canot de l'etat major See **canot-2**

canot de ligne See **bisquine**

canot de maître See **canot du maître**

canot de Mauritanie See **langoustier-2**

canot de parade See **barge-2**

canot de portemanteaux See **stern boat**

canot de ronde See **guard boat-1**

canot de Saint-Briac, canot de Saint-Cast See **canot de Saint-Jacut**

canot de Saint-Jacut *France, NW:* Small, robust **fishing boat*** of Saint-Jacut, west of Saint-Malo. Mainly of the 19th and 1st half of the 20th centuries. Carvel-planked; straight, nearly plumb stem; transom stern, wineglass-shaped on the early boats. Strong drag to the straight keel, deep skeg; considerable rise to the floors, soft turn of the bilges; swept up forward. Open; tiny foredeck; stern bench. Outboard rudder; tiller. Early boats stepped a vertical foremast in the eyes, setting a standing lugsail. Mainmast stepped about amidships, raking aft, setting a boomed dipping lugsail and a topsail. Jib to bowsprit. By 1925, forward mast became the mainmast, setting a loose-footed dipping lugsail; the mizzen, stepped against the transom, set a standing lugsail sheeted to an outrigger. Reported lengths 3.7-7m; e.g., length 6.6m, beam 3m, depth 1.6m, draft 1.25m. Other recorded names: **canot jaguen** (or **jaguin**); the **canot de Saint-Briac** and **canot de Saint-Cast**, from these nearby communities, were similar.

canot de sardine See **sardinier vendéen**

canot de sauvetage See **lifeboat**

canot de secours See **accident boat**

canot de senne Seee **gommier**

canot de service See **cutter-2**

canot de veille See **guard boat-1**

canot des vivres See **market boat-4**

canot du capitaine See **canot-2**

canot du commandant See **canot-2, gig-1**

canot du gouverneur See **canot léger**

canot du maître *Canada, S/United States, N:* Largest of the fur traders' birchbark **canoes*** that transported supplies and fur on the larger lakes and rivers of the Great Lakes Basin from the 17th to the end of the 19th century. Many also carried express cargo and messages down the Mississippi to New Orleans. Narrow flat bottom, with slight rocker at ends; straight flaring sides; sheer might hog amidships. Stem curvature varied with date and place of construction, but all turned up sharply; inner stem piece either joined to recurved outer stem or was free-standing and braced to the outer stem. Ends generally decorated, the bow usually carrying the symbol of the 4-**canoe** fur brigade. Bark sewn with spruce roots and caulked with spruce and pine gum; sheathed between ribs and bark; hardwood ribs 6-8cm wide. Crew size ranged from 6-18, depending on the difficulty of the trip, cargo size, and number of passengers; paddlers sat 2 to a thwart; bow and sternmen paddled standing, using extra-long paddles. Sometimes sailed, or tracked from shore. Nailing a flat section from a tree with a branch at right angles to the gunwale and attaching a rawhide loop through which the oar was inserted equipped it for rowing. Portaged by 4 men. Reported lengths 9-12m; e.g., length overall 11m, width inside gunwales 1.82m, depth 0.84m;

as little as 15cm freeboard when fully loaded. Other recorded names: **canot de charge, canot de maître, canot maître, double north canoe, five-** (or **six-**) **fathom canoe, freight canoe***, **fur-trade canoe, grand canot, Grand River canoe, great Montreal canoe, Hudson's Bay canoe, large canoe, maître canot, master's canoe, Montreal canoe, Ottawa River canoe.** Further reading: D. A. Gillies, "Canot du Maître or Montreal Canoe," *Canadian Geographical Magazine* 56 (1958), 114-119. Note also **canot bâtard, canot du nord, canot léger, voyageur canoe.**

canot d'un navire See **ship's boat**

canot du nord *Canada:* French, and later British, fur traders' **canoe***. Used on waterways too small and shallow for the similar but larger **canot du maître***. Worked into the early 20th century. Cover of birchbark, sewn with split spruce roots and caulked with spruce and pine gum. Bottom narrow and flattened, no keel; sides straight, flared, and tumble home on some. Sheer swept up slightly toward ends, then curved up sharply to inner stem and sternpost. Shape of curvature at the ends varied with locale, being modified to compare with local Indian types. Hardwood ribs capped by gunwales that extended beyond curved ends. Split cedar flooring. Those of the Hudson's Bay Company had bright blue designs painted on the sides. When running with the wind, a temporary square sail might be raised, but mainly paddled; those in the middle sat 2 to a thwart; bow and sternmen stood while paddling, using a longer paddle. Averaged 8 in crew; portaged by 2 men; when running with minimum load as a **canot léger***, crew numbered 8-10. Reported lengths 6-11m, widths 1.2-1.8m, depths 0.6-0.9m. Other recorded names: **canot de charge, freight canoe***, **fur-trade canoe, light canoe, north(ern) canoe, Northwest canoe, N.W. canoe, Rebecca.** Note also **canot bâtard, voyageur canoe.**

canote *Portugal, NW:* Small, beamy boat used for inshore fishing and seaweed collecting. Carvel-planked, with 3-4 strakes per side; lens-shaped flat bottom, longitudinally planked; keelless; strong sheer. Flat raked ends, with the bow rake greater than the stern; flared curving sides; 14-15 ribs. One type, the **canote de popa aberta**, has the upper part of the sternpost cut to form a small transom. Three or 4 thwarts set on stringers, which also support small end decks. Outboard rudder when sailed; transom-sterned type uses a steering oar. Mast stepped through bench, setting a quadrilateral lateen-type sail with a short luff. Also rowed; block on oar loom slipped over the tholepin. Crew of 2. Reported lengths 3.5-4.15m; e.g., length overall 4.15m, on bottom 2.93m; maximum beam 1.68m, on bottom 1.0m; depth 0.54m. Other recorded names: **barco de fundo de prata, batel.** See also **canot.**

canote de popa aberta See **canote**

canot goëmonier *France, NW:* Small open boat used by seaweed (*goëmon*) gatherers along the western part of the northern coast of Brittany. Plumb stem, raked wineglass transom. Carvel-planked; flat floors, easy turn of the bilges into vertical sides; straight keel, with drag. Worked mostly by 2 men, one using an oar forward, the other sculling from the stern. An engine or outboard motor now installed. Those working on off-shore islands set a fore-and-aft mainsail and a foresail, tacked to the stemhead (the **sloup goëmonier** or **skloup**). Small boats might be sprit-rigged. Reported lengths 4-7m; e.g., length 6.4m, beam 2.52m, depth 1.0m, draft 0.76m. The offshore boats use a small stubby **punt★** as a **dinghy★**, called a **plate★**. These boats may also engage in collecting the seaweed. Flat bottom, sharp bow, narrow transom. Reported lengths 3.5-4m, draft 0.6-0.8m. The modern **bateau goëmonier** is

canot goëmonier

totally motorized, with a pilot house either in the bow or stern; works with a special boom and large hook. Length 10.3m. Other recorded names: **canot goëmonnier**, **goëmonnier**. Further reading: Jean Le Bot, *Les Bateaux des Côtes de la Bretagne Nord*, 2nd ed. (Grenoble: Éditions des 4 Seigneurs, 1984), 165-178.

canot goëmonnier See **canot goëmonier**

canot Indien See **pirogue**

canot jaguen, canot jaguin See **canot de Saint-Jacut**

canot lâche See **canot léger**

canot léger *Canada:* A lightly laden fur traders' birch-bark **canoe★** of the 18th-19th centuries that carried mail, orders, inspection personnel, etc.; might be a **canot du maître★**, a **canot du nord★**, or a specially built narrow-bottomed **canoe**. Used particularly on the western Canada pass routes. Generally manned with a larger than usual crew to permit portaging the **canoe** and contents simultaneously. Reported lengths 3-4.6m. Other recorded names: **canot allège, canot du gouverneur, canot lâche, express canoe, light boat★** (or **canoe**). Note also **canot bâtard**.

canot maître See **canot du maître**

canot mytilicole *France, W:* Centerboard boat that worked the mussel beds of the Baie de l'Aiguillon. Wide, raked wineglass transom; flat floors; low freeboard aft. Decked to mast, side decks. Set a loose-footed gaff sail, foresail. Length 8.47m, beam 2.85m, draft 0.6m. Name variant: **canot creux mytilicole**. Note also **plate de l'Aiguillon, yole-2**.

canot saintois See **canot-6**

canot sardinier See **sardinier vendéen**

canots de bossoir See **davit craft**

canot serreur See **charoi**

canot sur la porte manteaux See **quarter boat**

canot tambour See **paddle-box boat**

cânott See **kannòt**

canotte *United States, south-central:* **1.** In the lower Mississippi Valley, an Acadian term designating a lug-rigged boat.
2. In southern Louisiana, in Terrebonne and adjacent parishes, a **canotte** is a flat-bottomed boat with a sharp bow and flat stern. Open, decked at bow and stern, or decked with a cabin. Inboard engine. Length generally over 4.6m.
See also **barque sablaise, canot, canot-4**.

canotte di salvataggio See **lifeboat**

canotti See **canotto**

canotto **1.** Italian word for the smallest of a merchant **ship's boats★**. Used when the larger **lancia★** is not required. Term may also be used for a **punt★**. One type, the **canotto da regata**, races. Other recorded names: **gozzo★, guzzo★**. Note also **bovo**.
2. *Italy:* One of the small boats that forms a quadrangle at the time of the kill during a tuna fishing operation. Note also **muscaria**.
3. *Italy, N:* Sailing boat used on Lago di Garda for a variety of purposes, but especially for longline fishing. Name variant: **gondola de la colomba**
4. *Malta:* Lightly constructed boat used for fishing and sponging along the coast of Tunisia. Sharp bow with plumb stem; square stern; outboard rudder; moderate sheer. Set a single quadrilateral lateen-type sail with a short luff or square sail to a short vertical mast. Also rowed, standing and facing forward; 2-4 oarsmen. Length 5.1m, beam 1.8m, draft 0.6m.
Spelling variant: pl. **canotti**

canotto da regata See **canotto**

canou See **canoe**

canoua See **canoa-17, canoe, canot**

canoue See **canot**

canow See **cannow, canoa-1, canoe**

cantherius See **barge de cantier**

cantimaran, cantimaron See **catamaran**

Canton sampan See **sha ting**

cánu See **kánu-2**

cao chuan *China:* **1.** River craft that plies the Liao He in Liaoning Province. Reported as very numerous at the beginning of the 20th century.
2. Double-ended craft used on the Chang Jiang (Yangtze), putting in at such ports as Wuhu. Had a low house. Crew of 3-6. Reported lengths 10.4-12.8m.
3. Best known was the seagoing trader out of Chao'an (Ch'ao-chou) in northeastern Guangdong (Kwangtung) that worked along the coast, some going to Southeast Asia. Narrow square bow formed a "T" at the top to meet the flared top strakes; elliptical transom; strong sheer at the stern. Wooden deckhouse aft. Top strake painted red at the bows, with oculi; lower strakes white. Three masts; small foremast set a northern-type square-headed rectangular lugsail; tall mainmast employed a southern high-peaked lugsail with rounded leech; mizzen similar to mainsail. Length 40m, beam 10m, hold depth 5m. Other recorded names: **Ch'ao-chou junk, Chao-chow trading junk, pai-t'ou ch'uan, pak-tow-sun, pih-tow chuen, white-headed junk**
Spelling variants: **ts'ao-ch'uan★** (or **tch'ouan**), **tsao-shuan**

caorlina *Italy, NE:* Elongated boat that plies the Lagoon of Venice in the northwest Adriatic and the Po River; dates to the 14th century. Used for fishing, especially with the *seragia* net (**caorlina da seragia**), and to carry cargo and local produce; also used during traditional regattas, when it may be fancifully decorated or may be a special light type, the **caorlina da regata**. Those that transport casks of wine on the Sile (the **caorlina del Sile**) have a heavier hull. The fishing type lacks rubbing strakes for easier net handling. Double-ended, bluff. Flat bottom curves up above the water-line at ends; ribs curved at chine plank. Curved stem and sternpost extend above the sheer strake; slightly rounded sides; abrupt rise to sheer at ends. The cargo type on the Po had a straight vertical sternpost and lacked the sharp sheer at the stern. Decked at ends; side decks common; a low-roofed stern cabin on some; bitt on each side at the ends. Rudder shipped when sailing; heel hangs below the bottom. Rowed (some by 4-8 men during regattas), sailed, and now some use an outboard motor. May set 1-2 trapezoidal lugsails. On the single-masted boats, mast stepped through thwart in after third. Reported lengths 8-16m, beam 1-1.7m, depth 0.6m. Other recorded names: **battello***; pl. **caorline**. Note also **corallina**.

caorlina da regata, **caorlina da seragia**, **caorlina del Sile**, **caorline** See **caorlina**

cao zi *China, central:* **Junk*** that traded along lower Chiang Jiang (Yangtze) ports and into Poyang Hu (lake), carrying local products such as fish spawn, chinaware, paper, and bamboo, and returning with salt. 20-70t. Spelling variants: **tsao ch'uan**, **ts'ao tse**

cao zi chuan *China, N:* A jointed river cargo vessel of the Hai He (or Paiho or Peiho) in the Tianjin (Tientsin) area. Built in 2 watertight sections joined with wooden pins and rope lashings. Sharp overhanging bow; square stern; straight sides. Balanced rudder. Open hold in forward half, cabin in after part. Mast stepped in a short tabernacle; raised by sheerlegs and windlass. Also poled and sculled. Crew of 6. Reported lengths 15-46m, widths 4.9-5.5m. Spelling variant: **tsao-tsze ch'uan**. Other recorded names: **double boat**, **grass boat**, **snake boat**. Note also **cao zi**, **liang jie tou**.

capalanier See **capelanier**

Cape Ann dory *United States, NE:* Fast, seaworthy sailing **dory*** developed on the Cape Ann peninsula in eastern Massachusetts in the 1870s, especially for inshore fishing and lobstering. Lapstrake construction with 3-5 strakes to each side; flat bottom with slight rocker, planked longitudinally. Straight flaring sides; good sheer. Ends strongly raked; sharp bow with lightly curved stem; V-shaped transom; rudder hung out. Open except for short foredeck; full-length coverboards supported by short, deep deck beams or knees; centerboard, with rounded case. Mainly set a loose-footed spritsail and jib; lifting strap forward used to hook in the jib tack, and one aft substituted for a mainsheet horse. Some stepped 2 masts setting leg-of-mutton sails. Also rowed. Reported lengths 5.2-7.3m; e.g., length 6.4m, beam 1.5m, depth 0.55m. Other recorded names: **New England sailing dory**, **shore dory**. Note also **banks dory**.

Cape Ann sloop boat See **sloop boat**

Cape boat **1.** *Canada, E:* Used for inshore bank trawling off the south coast of Newfoundland, especially on the Cape St. Marys' grounds. Operated until ca. 1925. Open; fore-and-aft rigged. Largest were **three-dory boats**, with a crew of 7. 15-30t. Note also **Cape Island boat**.

2. *South Africa:* Beamy, open **fishing boat*** that varies somewhat from port to port. Stem and stern almost vertical, broad transom stern, apple bows. Sandbag ballast, jettisoned as fish brought on board. Steered by rudder. Set a large spritsail and jib. Those that worked through the surf, **trek boats**, were mainly rowed, operated seine nets, and were steered with a large sweep. Oars as long as 6.4m. Engines installed early in the 20th century. Crew of 3-5. Reported lengths overall 4.9-7.6m, widths 1.6-2m.

Cape cat, **Cape Cod catboat** See **catboat-2a**

Cape Cod dory See **Banks dory**

Cape Cod Power dory See **dory-6**

Cape Island boat *Canada, E:* Ubiquitous motorized **fishing boat*** of the Atlantic coast. Developed early in the 20th century, probably at Cape Sable Island in southern Nova Scotia. Modified as the type spread along the Maritime Provinces and use requirements varied. Engages in most types of fishing and in inshore lobstering. High flaring bow, low stern. Stem plumb or slightly forward raking, cutaway forefoot. Counter stern, with transom slightly raked forward. Sharp entrance, long flat run, deep "V" in cross section amidships, easing out to flat at the stern. Slight drag to keel. Carvel-planked; now of fiberglass. Small boats open; raised deck forward on the larger, often with cuddy below; some fully decked; wheelhouse common. Powered by diesel or gas engine. Reported lengths 5.5-18m; early boats quite slender, now beamier; 1951 boat 11.8m long, 3.9m wide, ca. 1.6m deep, 0.76m draft. Other recorded names: **Cape Islander**, **Hutt boat** (at Prince Edward Island), **quarante-cinq pieds** (in Magdalen Islands), **Robar-type longliner**. Note also **Cape boat**, **Strait boat**.

Cape Islander See **Cape Island boat**

Cape Kiwanda dory See **Oregon dory**

capel See **kapal**

capelanfisker, **capelanié** See **capelanier**

capelanier *Canada, E:* Small double-ended boat used for coastal fishing off Newfoundland, notably for capelin, which served as bait for the cod fishermen, as well as food and fertilizer. Cited in 18th-century literature. Set a square sail to a short mast stepped well forward. Also rowed. Crew of 5. Other recorded names: **capalanier**, **capelan-fisker**, **capelanié**, **capelannier**, **caplanier**, **echeur**, **kaplaanvisser**, **kaplaanzaaier**, **Kaplanfänger**, **loddefisker**. Note also **baiter-1**, **baitskiff**.

capelannier See **capelanier**

capell See **kapal**

caper *Europe, N:* 17th-18th-century lightly armed vessel that served as a **privateer***. Commonly double officered and crowded with men with a purpose of boarding an enemy. Other recorded names: **Auslieger**, **caper vessel**, **capre**, **caraba**, **catturatore**, **Dutch caper**, **kapara-skip**, **kapare**, **kaparefartyg**, **kapare-skepp**, **kapari**, **ka(a)per**, **kaperbåd**, **Kaperschiff**, **kaperschip**, **predatore**. Note also **corsair**, **Duinkerker**, **sea rover**. Further reference: **catboat-2a**

Cape Roseway wherry See **Cape Rosier wherry**

Cape Rosier wherry *United States, NE:* Open lobstering and inshore **fishing boat*** used in the Castine area of Penobscot Bay in Maine. Lapstrake planking, sharp bow, narrow heart-shaped transom, plank keel; bent-frame construction. Primarily rowed with a single pair of oars. Reported lengths 3.7-5.5m. Name variant: **Cape Roseway wherry**. Note also **salmon wherry**.

caper vessel See **caper**

Cape Sable skiff See **gunning skiff-1**

capitaine, capitainia See **capitane**

capitana See **capitane, flagship**

capitana generale See **patronne**

capitane The **flagship*** of a **fleet***. Applied most often to the principal **galley***, being comparable to the **real***. Richly ornamented with paintings and carvings. Might have ca. 30 oars per side, with 7 men on the after oars and 6 on the forward oars. Length ca. 53m, beam at waterline 7.6m. Other recorded names: **capitaine, capitainia, capitana, capitanea, capitanessa, capitania, capitan(ni)o, capitanya, flag galley, gale(r)a capitana, galère capitane, gallere capitaineresse, Hauptgaleere, hoofdgalei, kapetavia, kap(i)tana, kapitavia, kapudana, kaputana**. Note also **bâtard, Galeere, patronne**.

capitanea See **capitane, Galeere**

capitanessa, capitania, capitannio, capitano, capitanya See **capitane**

caplanier See **capelanier**

caporais *Italy:* One of the team of boats used in operating the large net employed by tuna fishermen. Open boxy craft, similar to the **vascello***. Aids in closing the net. Towed to and from the site. Reported lengths 15-20m; e.g., length 15m, beam 4m, depth 0.8m. Note also **barcareccio, cabanella, musciara, palischermo-3**.

cappella, cappella galleggiante See **church boat**

capre See **caper**

capre dunkerquois See **Duinkerker**

capro *Libya:* Vessel that had the head of a goat (*capro*) sculpted on the bow.

capstan boat See **horse-machine boat**

captain boat See **number one**

captain's boat See **whaler-3**

captain's galley See **galley-7**

captain's gig See **gig-1**

car See **fish car, fisherman's car**

carab *British Isles:* Small wicker boat covered with hides. Cited as early as the 14th century. Large enough to have required 2-1/2 hides. One in the early 17th century reported to have sailed from Ireland to southwestern England. Spelling variants: **carabum, carogh**. Note also **carabus**.

caraba See **caper, carabus**

carabe See **carabus, qârob**

carabel See **caravel-1**

carabela See **caravel-1, caravel-3, crevelle**

carabela de armada See **caravel-1, caravela redonda**

carabela latina See **caravel-1**

carabela redonda See **caravela redonda**

carabella See **caravel-1**

carabelón Usually considered a small **caravel***. In the mid-16th century, some were built on the west coast of Mexico and used in trade with Peru. Probably 2-masted. Crew of 6. Ca. 60t.

carabi, carabia, carabion See **carabus**

carabo See **agherrabo, carabus**

carabos See **carabus, jábega**

carabulus See **carabus**

carabum See **carab**

carabus 1. Ancient craft, usually considered to be Roman. Probably circular or elongated, consisting of a light lath frame covered with skin or basketwork. Paddled. Note also **carab**.

2. Small, light vessel generally attributed to the Moors in the Mediterranean, dating from at least 700 A.D. Variously reported to have carried cargo, served a larger ship, fished, and been used as a **corsair***. A 14th-century citation indicates that some transported as many as 60 horses. Rowed with 2 banks of oars and sailed, setting lateen sails. Note also **qârib**.

3. A 14th- and 15th-century sailing ship of the eastern Mediterranean that had a high poop. Probably single-masted.

Spelling variants: **caraba, carabe, carabion, carabo, carabulus, càravo*, caravus, caretone, caribus, caro*, carovus, corab(is), covabis, currabius, curracium, curuca, ghareb, karabia, karabion*, karabos, karabus**; pl. **carabi, carabia, carabos, karaboi**

caraca 1. *France, SE:* Vessel that transported mud in the harbor of Nice.

2. *Indonesia, central/Philippines:* Reported as an oared boat of Sulawesi (Celebes) and the Philippines. See also **carrack**.

caracara See **korakora-1**

caracca See **carrack, tarida**

caracche See **tarida**

carack, caracke See **carrack**

caracoa, caracol, caracola, caracole, caracolle, caracor, caracora, caracore, caracoro, caracoure See **korakora-1**

caracque, carague, carake, caraque, caraquon, carasce See **carrack**

carauel, carauela, carauelle, caraval, caravall See **caravel-1**

caravane flottante See **houseboat-1**

caravel 1. Mentioned as early as the 13th century, but most often described as a vessel of the 15th to early 17th century. Earliest vessels probably **fishing boats***, open except for a covered space forward, setting a single lateen sail. Ranged from the Mediterranean to northern Europe, but most frequently identified as a Portuguese or Spanish vessel, with Christopher Columbus' *Niña* and *Pinta* the best known. Important in 15th-century Portuguese exploration to India, as an auxiliary to the main **fleet*** (**carabela de armada** or **caravella d'amata**), for carrying despatches (**caravela mexeriquira**), and for undertaking inshore reconnaissance, being relatively shallow-draft. Locally, mainly a trading vessel. Stepped 2-4 masts with lateen sails until the end of the 15th century (**caravela [or carabela] latina, lateen caravel**); in the 16th century, employed 2 square sails on the foremast and lateen sails on the other 2-3 masts (**caravela redonda**). Bowsprit on those with a square sail forward. Relatively long and narrow hull, carvel-built. Bluff bows above the waterline, sharp below, strongly curved stem; some early drawings show a beak. Raked transom above a sharp stern; overhanging poop deck.

Strong sheer, low sides, straight keel, flat floors. Long quarter-deck. Rudder came up inboard. Usually armed. Crew of 10-45. Reported lengths 15-30m; length-to-beam ratio 3.3:1; ratio of early types as great as 7:1. Selected spelling variants: **calavela**, **carabel**, **carabel(l)a**, **carauel(a)**, **carauelle**, **caraval(l)**, **caravela**, **caravelão** (aug.), **caravell(a)**, **caravelle**, **caraveletta** (dim.), **caravellone** (aug.), **carueille**, **carvel(le)**, **escarvelle**, **escrevelle**, **karabela**, **karavela**★, **karavell(a)**, **Karavelle**, **karawela**, **karveel**★ (pl. **karvelen**), **kraweelboot**, **Kraweelschiff**, **qaravél(l)a**, **qarrabīla**, **qarrabilla**. Note also **buyscarveel**, **carabelón**, **cáravo**, **crevelle**, **karabel**.

2. *France, SW/Spain, N:* The Basques of the 13th-16th centuries used **caravels** for whaling on the high seas. Beamy vessel, with high bow and towering poop; heavily ballasted. Single deck initially, with the try-works below deck on the sand ballast; later 3 decks. Initially a single **txalupa** (see **chalupa-10**) carried on board; later 5 boats might be carried. Mainmast, amidships, set a large square sail with square topsail; elaborate crow's nest above. Foremast set 1-2 square sails; mizzen set a square, lateen, or fore-and-aft sail. Long bowsprit might set a watersail. Crew of 50. Early vessels 15-18m long; shallow draft.

3. *Turkey:* Large, cumbersome **man-of-war**★ equipped with as many as 60 cannons; 200 in crew. Some carried passengers making the pilgrimage to Mecca. High stern and sides; ornate. Three masts, lateen sails. Cap. 1,200t. Spelling variants: **carabela**, **caravela**, **caravelle**, **karavela**, **qaravéla**

caravela See **caravel-1**, **caravel-3**
caravela da armada See **caravela redonda**
caravela latina, **caravela mexeriquira** See **caravel-1**
caravelão 1. Mentioned in 15th- and 16th-century literature, initially from the Atlantic islands, western Africa, and then from East Africa, India, and Brazil. Most flush-decked, but some smaller **caravelões** (pl.) had a quarter-deck. Lateen-rigged on 2-3 masts. Rowed in calms. Shallow draft.

2. *Azores:* Reported as a light vessel having a very narrow stern below with a small square overhang above.

3. *Brazil:* In common use in the 16th century and still reported in the mid-18th century, especially on the northeast coast. Considered good for coastwise navigation, being suitable for working to windward. Roughly built. 40-50t.

See also **caravel-1**.

caravela redonda A **caravel**★ rigged with square (*redonda*) sails on the main- and foremast and a lateen mizzen. Bowlines from the foresail to a sharply rising bowsprit; mizzen sheeted to a jiggerboom. Mainmast stayed to stemhead. Might also be rigged with a square sail on the foremast and lateen sails on the after 2-3 masts or fully square-rigged. The **caravela da armada** was auxiliary to a **man-of-war**★; fitted with a top on the mainmast. Other recorded names: **carabela de armada**, **carabela redonda**, **round caravel** (incorrectly), **caravela redunda**

caravel redunda See **caravela redonda**
caravell See **caravel-1**
caravella See **caravel-1**, **crevelle**

caravella d'amata See **caravel-1**
caravelle See **caravel-1**, **caravel-3**, **crevelle**
caravelletta, **caravellone** See **caravel-1**
caravelões See **caravelão**
caravenne See **brigantine-2**
cáravo 1. Reported as a small **caravel**★ used in the Mediterranean. Spelling variant: **carevo**

2. In early Portuguese, a **cáravo** was an Asiatic ship employing lateen sails.

càravo See **carabus**
caravus See **carabus**
car'away boat See **menhaden carry-away boat**
car boat See **dipper**
carbonaio, **carbonero**, **carboniera** See **collier-1**
carcoa, **carcolle** See **korakora-1**
carcon See **carrack**
carèbe See **qârob**
caretone See **carabus**
càreu See **caro**
carevo See **cáravo**
car ferry See **ferryboat**, **horse boat-2**, **tongkang-2**
car float A decked **barge**★ or **scow**★-type craft fitted with tracks to transport railroad cars from one railhead to another or to shipside for direct cargo transfer. Usually works within a harbor. Moved by a **tug**★. In the late 19th century, those in New York were owned by the railroad companies; originally 8-car **floats**★, later a 2-car type was 32m long, 3 tracks wide, and carried 22 cars. Name variant: **Wagenfährprahm**

cargo See **freighter-1**
cargo boat See **freighter-1**, **runner**
cargo carrier See **freighter-1**
cargo lighter 1. *Belize:* Sturdy **sloop**★-rigged boat that carries bulk cargoes from the mainland to the offshore islands. A few still operate. Hull shapes vary but most have a sharp bow and wineglass transom stern; a few have a sharp or counter stern. Marked sheer; some slab-sided with hard chine. Decked at ends, narrow side decks, open waist. Mast stepped just abaft the foredeck; sets a boomed gaff mainsail, jib to a short bowsprit; both have a single row of reef points. Boom a heavy bamboo spar. Some gunter-rigged. Crew of 2-3. Reported lengths 9.7-11.7m; e.g., length 11.7m, beam 3.3m, depth 0.76m; shoal draft. Name variants: **sailing barge**, **sand lighter**

2. *Myanmar (Burma):* Carried general cargo at various ports. Sharp ends, stem curled aft above the top strake. Decked at ends. Two masts, the foremast and mizzen stepped about a quarter in from each end. Mainsail a high-peaked dipping lugsail, the mizzen a boomed gaff sail. Reported lengths 15-24m, widths 4.3-5.2m, draft laden 2-3m.

cargo liner See **liner-1**
cargo ship, **cargo vessel**, **carguero** See **freighter-1**
carguero de pescado See **fish carrier-1**
cāri See **taghari**
carib See **canoe-6**, **qārib**
Caribbean sloop See **sloop-10**
caribe *Venezuela, E:* Motorized boat that engages in open sea fishing. Sharp bow, square stern, steep rise to the floors, narrow. Wet well amidships. See also **qârob**.
Caribou kayak See **kayak-5**

caribus See **carabus, curragh**

Carley float See **life raft**

caro *Spain, NE:* Sturdy **rowing boat**★ that fished with a seine net from beaches of Cataluña. Dates to the 12th century. Boat revived for regattas. Bow full, stern sharp but narrower; curved ends; tall stemhead. Flat floors, soft turn of the bilges; strong keel with bilge keels. Foredeck; sometimes a small stern deck, with storage space below; washboards forward; several thwarts; rowed double-banked. Reported lengths 5-8.6m; e.g., length 7m, beam 2m, depth 0.75m. Name variant: **càreu**. Further reference: **carabus**

carogh See **carab**

Carolina sharpie See **sharpie-4**

Carolina sharpie-schooner See **sharpie-schooner-1**

Carolina skiff See **North Carolina sail skiff**

Carolina Sounds sharpie See **sharpie-4**

Carolina spritsail skiff See **North Carolina sail skiff**

caronnière See **whale catcher**

carovus See **carabus**

carrac See **carrack**

carraca See **carrack, tarida**

carracão, carracca, carracó See **carrack**

carrack 1. Burdensome **merchantman**★ of the Mediterranean and western Europe. Reported from the 14th to the 17th century. Mainly a long-distance bulk cargo carrier; often armed against pirates. Some **carracks** were prizes of Mediterranean vessels captured in northern waters. Hull profile changed from relatively low-sided with a poop deck to very high-sided with towering castles at bow and stern by the late 15th century; forecastle could be higher than the after castle. Bluff bows, curved stem; rounded stern, with 1-2 square counters; on later ships, tumble home sides on the castles. Deep hull; high bulwarks. Carvel-planked in the Mediterranean, often clinker in northern Europe. Stern rudder. Rigging also changed markedly as the ships became larger and higher. Originally 2-masted with a square foresail and lateen mizzen; later 3 masts, with square sails on the fore- and mainmasts and lateen mizzen; some employed a 2nd lateen mizzen. Topsails and watersails might be set. Large crews. Reported lengths 30-74m; 1500 Venetian **carrack**: length overall 30m, on keel 21m, beam 10m, depth 6.5m; deep draft; most ca. 1200t. Note also **argosy, great ship**.

2. The Portuguese merchant **caraque** of the late 18th century was much reduced in grandeur. Greater depth provided more capacity but made the vessel unstable.

3. The Saracen **karaque** was reported as early as the mid-13th century as a small ship and as a **corsair** of Salé in Morocco as late as the mid-17th century.

Other recorded names: **caraca**★, **caracca** (pl. **carrache**), **carack(e), cara(c)que, carake, carasce, carrac, carrac(c)a, carrak(e), carraqua, carraque, carreque, carricke, carryk, crack, craque, hulk**★, **karacke, Karak(e), karāka, karràka, kraak**★ (pl. **kraken), kracke, kraeck, nao, nef**★, **qarāqir** (pl.), **quaraque, qurqūr(a)**. Diminutives: **car(r)con, car(r)aquon, carracão, carracó, carraquillon, demi-car(r)aque, demi-carracque, demye-carraque, demyi-carraque**. Further references: **nau, tarida**

carrak, carrake, carraqua, carraque, carraquillon, carraquon See **carrack**

carraway See **carry-away boat, menhaden carry-away boat**

carrcon, carreque, carricke See **carrack**

carrida See **tarida**

carrier 1. Generalized term for a cargo ship.

2. A vessel that transported the catch from a fishing **fleet**★ back to market. In the United Kingdom, **carriers** were often equipped with trawls in order to be classified as **fishing boats**★, thereby avoiding regulations applicable to merchant ships. Note also **carry-away boat, carrying boat, fish-carrying boat**.

3. An **aircraft carrier**.

Further references: **cutter-7, freighter-4, menhaden boat**

carrier boat See **buy boat-1, garvey**

carrocium See **curragh**

carrot See **scute-2b**

carry-away boat One that meets **fishing boats**★ at sea or travels with them in order to convey the catch rapidly to market or to a processing plant. Spelling variant: **carraway**. Note also **market boat, plunger-2, run boat, sardine carrier**. Further references: **menhaden carry-away boat, Quoddy boat, seine boat-5c**

carry-away sloop See **menhaden carry-away boat**

carrying boat *Canada:* Large boat designated to transport fish from smaller **fishing boats**★ to a processing plant. Other recorded names: **bateau transporteur, fish collector** (or **packer**). Note also **packer, bád iomartha**.

carryk See **carrack**

cartier-marron See **catamaran**

carueille See **caravel**

caruka See **zaruq**

carveel, carveelschip See **karveel**

carvel See **caravel-1**

carvelle See **caravel-1, chaloupe-6, crevelle**

Carver boat See **Huron boat**

cáscara See **concha-2**

cascarón de nuez See **cockleshell**

casco 1. *Brazil, central:* Term used by some native groups of the Amazon Basin for a **canoa**★. Dugout, excavated, and spread by fire. Sides flared, bow and stern rounded, some fitted with a V-shaped transom piece at each end; in some non-native areas, may have a strake added to each side. Generally several benches. Paddled from the bow and poled. Shorter than the **ubá**★ but wider amidships. Length 5.2m, beam 1.22m. On the island of Marajó in the Amazon Delta, a small **casco**, called **jacuma**, has 2 seats and is used for fishing. Cap. ca. 200kg of fish. Name variant: **casquinho** (small type)

2. *Philippines:* A type of **lighter**★ that serves ships lying at anchor, usually as a floating home. Rectangular in shape, with sheer line turning up slightly at overhanging bow; raked stern; flat bottom. Sides and bottom planking secured with heavy knees; wide lapped strakes were sewn originally; 2 rattan lashings, athwartships near ends. Hull further strengthened with 3-4 crossbeams in pairs, one above the other resting on residual lugs or projecting outboard. These beams support platforms of bamboo that permit access from one end to the other and provide a place

to stand while paddling or poling. Very wide-bladed rudder; inner edge vertical, not following rake of the stern. On those without sails, hull covered with arched and segmented mat roofing that slides aside to provide access to the cargo. Covered living quarters aft. Oculi painted on sides. Sailing **cascos** set Chinese battened lugsails to a tall mainmast and a shorter foremast, or a single rectangular lugsail to a mast stepped in the forward quarter. Spelling variants: **cascoe**, **caso**
  Further reference: **montaria-2**

casco arrumbado See **hulk-3**

Casco Bay boat, **Casco Bay double-ender** See **Hampton boat**

Casco Bay pinky See **Crotch Island pinky**

cascoe See **casco-2**

caséieur See **caseyeur**

caseyeur *France, W:* Small lobstering, shrimping, and crabbing and **fishing boat**★ of the south Britanny coast. Works mainly with special nets or pots. Plumb stem, raked transom, deep keel, outboard rudder. Variously rigged as **sloops**★, **cutters**★, or 2-masted **luggers**★. Crew of 1-2. Modern motorized boats require 3-4 men. Reported lengths 6-10m; e.g., length 6m, beam 2m, depth 1.0m. The **caseyeur-coquilleur** also drags for scallops. The large **caseyeur-palangrier** works farther offshore, with a crew of 5-6, and average length of 15.5m. Other recorded names: **caséieur**, **sloup caseyeur**. Note also **canot caseyeur**, **coquillier**, **langoustier**, **pot vessel**.

caseyeur-coquillier See **caseyeur**, **coquillier-2**

caseyeur-palangrier See **caseyeur**

caso See **casco-2**

casquinha *Mozambique:* **1.** Generic term for a small boat, particularly a **dugout canoe**★ used from northern coastal beaches. Often stabilized with double outriggers. Mostly paddled.
  2. At Vila de António Enes on the north-central coast, the **casquinha** is a fine-lined sailing **canoe**★. Popular for local racing, but the working craft sail to offshore islands for firewood, chestnuts, and fish. Short mast, raked strongly forward, sets a quadrilateral lateen-type sail with a short luff. Length 4m, beam 1.5m.
  3. For fishing in lagoons and lakes, a bark **casquinha** may be used. The hull is composed of 2 pieces of bark, the natural curve of the bark forming the sides. Held open by spreaders. Length ca. 2.5m.

casquinha-3

casquinho See **casco-1**

cat **1.** *Mediterranean:* Large, fast **galley**★ used until the 16th century for military expeditions and commerce. Sharp beak. Rowed with as many as 50 sweeps to a side, each manned by 2-3 oarsmen. Steered with quarter rudders. Length to 43m. Other recorded names: **catta**, **cattus**, **gat**, **gat(t)a**, **gatos**, **gat(t)us**
  2. *Europe, N:* The 17th- to early 19th-century **cat** was a heavily built **merchantman**★ that transported coal, timber (the Dutch **houthaalder**), masts, tar, etc. Some

served as **whalers**★. Bluff ends; straight stem; flat floors; straight sides with tumble home topsides; narrow counter stern; marked sheer, especially at the stern. Lacked figurehead of the period. Decked; raised quarter-deck and cabin aft, forecastle. Tall, narrow square sails set to the fore and main pole masts; topsails; mizzen set a gaff sail; topgallants by the end of the 18th century. A 30m-long English **cat** carried a crew of 17. Reported lengths 29-46m; e.g., length 39m, beam 10m, depth 5.2m; comparatively shallow draft. Other recorded names: **bark**★, **cat bark**, **cate**, **cat-schip**, **chat**, **chata**★, **chatte du nord**, **coal cat**, **gate**, **gatto**★, **kat**★, **katboot**, **kats(c)hip**, **katt**, **Kat(t)schiff**, **kattskepp**, **shat**; pl. **katchepen**. Note also **chatte**, **collier-2**.
  3. *United States, NE:* A simple **raft**★ of 2-4 logs, spiked together.

  Further references: **catamaran-6**, **catboat-2**, **Deal lugger**

català See **catalana**

catalan See **catalana**, **catalane**

catalana *Spain, NE:* Double-ended **fishing boat**★. Carvel-planked; grounding keels, level with the keel; some have a flat bottom and use a centerboard. Rudder extends below bottom; heavy rubbing strake. High-crowned deck. Sets a large lateen sail to a forward-raking mast. Also rowed; now usually motorized. Reported lengths 10.7-13.4m; e.g., length 13.4m, beam 4.52m, depth 1.63m. Other recorded names: **català**, **catalan**, **catalano**★

catalane *France, Mediterranean coast:* Beamy anchovy and sardine **fishing boat**★ of the Languedoc and Roussillon coasts; used from the early 18th century to the present, now mainly as restorations. Sharp ends; curved stem extends well above the gunwale before being cut to a point; moderate sheer; flat floors; rounded bilges; grounding keels. Narrow, deep outboard

catalane

rudder, hangs below the bottom; tiller. Cambered half deck; removable washboards extend along most of the length, generally slotted for oars. Single relatively low lateen sail set to a strongly forward-raking mast. Halyard run through a longitudinal sheave at the masthead. Yard, longer than the boat, rests in a crutch aft when lowered. Sail has 2-3 reef bands, or it may be reduced in strong winds by setting the yard horizontally and tying sail ends to the yard. Jib may be run to a bowsprit. Also rowed, with single tholepin set into cut in washboards. Crew of ca. 5-6. Reported lengths

6-11m; e.g., length 10.3m, beam 3m, draft 0.58m. Early boats (13th century) by this name or its variants appear to have been **galleys★**. Other recorded names: **barca catalana** (or **catalanesche**), **barco catalano**, **barque catalane**, **bateau catalan**, **catalan**, **catalane languedocine**

catalane languedocinne See **catalane**

catalani See **catalano**

catalano *Italy, NW:* Vessel of the Sestri Levante coast; reported mainly in the 16th-17th centuries. Probably derived from the Spanish **catalana★**. Sharp ends; straight, forward-raking stem, slight tumble home to sternpost, moderate sheer, deep bulwarks. Decked; deep outboard rudder; tiller. Single unstayed mast, strongly raked forward; lateen sail. No jib; when jib and bowsprit employed, the vessel was considered to be a **leudo★**. Cap. 30t. Other recorded names: **rivano**; pl. **catalani**, **rivani**. Further reference: **catalana**

Catalina Channel felucca See **felucca-3**

catamaram See **catamaran**

catamaran **1.** Generic term for a shaped **raft★** of bamboo or logs fastened together in various ways. Found in numerous parts of the world; used mainly for inshore fishing and local transportation. Generally equipped with sails.
2. Small rectangular wooden or steel craft that lies alongside a wharf to keep ships from rubbing against the wall or pilings; some have a scaffolding to aid in painting the ship.
3. In early usage, sometimes a makeshift **float★** of poles on which a platform was placed. Conveyed passengers and goods when no boat was available.
4. British term in brief usage for a vessel that was filled with explosives and fireworks to be sent against the French during the Napoleonic Wars.
5. Sometimes mistakenly applied to an **outrigger canoe★**.
6. Two boats joined together to gain stability in rough water. Recently, a twin-hulled pleasure or racing craft. Also called a **cat★**. Other recorded names: **Doppel-(rumpf)boot**, **double-bottom★**, **double coque**, **double-keel vessel**, **two-hull boat**. Note also **patín**.
7. Lifesaving **raft** aboard a ship, composed of a slatted floor separating parallel cylindrical air tanks. Note also **balsa-12**.
8. **Raft** used to raise sunken logs; fitted with a windlass and grapples.
9. *Canada:* **Raft** fashioned by fastening 2 boats together; popular on the St. Lawrence River.
10. *Egypt:* Craft of the middle Nile River constructed from 2-3 date palm logs lashed together, or used singly. Bow ends of logs generally shaped to lessen resistance. Paddled with hands or with a double-bladed paddle. Reported lengths 1.22-1.52m.
11. *England:* Name applied by fishermen from Hastings to French 3-masted **luggers★**, especially the **chasse-marée★**.
12. *India, E:* Log **raft** used off the open beaches by Tamil and Telegu fishermen for line and net fishing. In early days also transported merchandise along the coast. Called **kattumaram** (or **kathu maram**), which in Tamil means "tied logs." The number of logs and construction details vary. Those of the more southerly

Tamils are generally better made. Some roughly shaped, with as few as 3 logs, lashed together at the ends. Others add a stem piece built of several wedges to form a pointed, upturned bow. Many have rocker, and the bottom rounds transversely. Some use a raised rail along one side as a rest for oars; others have a low washboard along each side to aid in hauling in fish; a single strake may be added on one side as a seat. The **kola maram★** is used only seasonally, for catching flying fish, and is put together from logs of other local **catamarans**. The **periya maram★** works with a smaller **raft**, the **chinna maram**, and when under sail, the two link together to form a single craft. The similar **irukka maram** works alone, and is sailed and paddled; at the stern the logs vary in length. The **thundil maram** is used in line fishing, does not sail, and lacks the stem piece. To the north, the Telegu fishermen employ the **teppa★** in which the logs and stem piece are both pegged and lashed together; still farther north, some **catamarans** are beamier, shorter, and entirely pegged. All types are paddled and/or rowed. When sailed, employ 1-2 lateen-type sails. Sails often boomed at the foot, have a short luff, and are tanned. Those that sail generally employ leeboards or a balance board. Some now fitted with outboard motors. Crew is often the fisherman and a young son. Reported lengths 2.4-4.6m. Further name variants: **katteamarouw**, **raft catamaran**. Note also **boat-catamaran**.
13. *Sri Lanka:* This **catamaran** has been described in several forms. Some are composed of a large center log, flanked by 2 shorter and lighter logs that are sometimes raised to form a trough; bow curves up. Logs squared and secured by crosspieces and lashings. A mat or cotton sail is set to a bamboo mast and yard. When sailed, employs an outrigger, consisting of a small float attached by 2 booms. Crew of 1-2. Reported lengths 5-7.6m, widths 0.8-0.9m. Another type uses 3-4 logs, 0.6m in circumference. These pieces are skewered together in 3 places and then lashed. Those constructed of 5 logs have a supplemental turned-up bow piece fitted to the center and adjacent logs; center logs extend aft to form a platform for the helmsman; logs pegged and lashed. Sometimes employs a centerboard. Except for the smallest, the **teppam**, they set a large triangular sail with yard at top and bottom. A 5-log type fitted with a back for an outboard motor is a **kattumaram maramma** (or **maramma**). Crew of 2-3. Reported lengths 5-9m. The west coast **teppam** of the Sinhalese is made from 4 shaped logs, lashed at each end; bow turns up. Rarely sailed, being used to set traps and for reef fishing. Reported lengths 2.7-4.6m. Other recorded names: **kattamaran**, **kat(t)ou-maram**, **kattumaram**, **kattumaran**, **theppam(a)**

Selected name variants: **candimaram**, **cantimaran**, **cantimaron**, **cartier-marron**, **catamaram**, **catamarão**, **catamaron**, **catameron**, **catamoran**, **catemaron**, **catimaran**, **catimaron**, **catimoran**, **cattamaran**, **cattaraman**, **cattlemaran** (in jest), **cutmurram**, **gatameroni**, **gatimaron**, **katamaran**, **katimaran**, **kattamaram**. Further references: **balsa-12**, **oruwa**, **sinker boat**

catamarão, catamaron, catameron, catamoran See **catamaran**

catapanel See **kaṭapannay, tony-1**

cataponel, cataponey See **kaṭapannay**

catara See **zattera**

cat bark See **cat-2**

catboat 1. *Colombia:* Small, open **fishing boat*** of the Colombian island of San Andrés off the Nicaraguan coast. Double-ended, raked bow and stern. Deep keel with some drag. Decked at bow; 2 thwarts. Short mast stepped about 90cm from the bow. Sliding gunter rig; heel of boom held by becket. Also rowed. Length 4.9m, beam 1.2m; shallow draft.
  2. *United States:* Developed in the mid-1800s for shoal-water fishing and lobstering along the shores of Cape Cod and became a widely used pleasure and racing craft. Characteristically shallow, very beamy, and cat-rigged with a stout, unstayed mast stepped well forward and fitted with a boomed gaff mainsail. Clinker- or carvel-built; plumb stem, later tumble home; fine bow. Hollow waterline; shallow V-shaped midsection; wide transom stern, counter on some; high rounded bilges; strong sheer toward bow. Usually a large oval cockpit with high coaming, some open or half-decked; often a cabin forward. Wide-bladed rudder on transom type; tiller used initially, later a wheel common, especially on pleasure boats. Centerboard with a high centerboard box; some have full keel in lieu of a centerboard. In summer, some workboats **sloop***-rigged, with the unstayed mast stepped farther aft, and a jib to a long bowsprit. Racing boats commonly **sloop**-rigged, and occasionally **ketch***- or **yawl***-rigged. Mainsail laced to the long overhanging boom and hooped to the mast. Engines added to working boats after ca. 1910. Crew of 1-2. Reported lengths 3-13.7m; beam almost half length; shallow draft. Other recorded names: **cat***, **eastern catboat**. Further reading: John M. Leavens, *The Catboat Book* (Camden, Maine: International Marine Publishing Co., 1973). Note also **Bubfisch Boot, una boat, waterboat**.
  Regional adaptations met local needs and preferences of the many builders and owners. **a.** The **Cape Cod catboat** was the prototype from which subsequent models were derived. Gaff sail high-peaked. Those working off the more exposed eastern shore of Cape Cod were generally more seaworthy. Other recorded names: **Cape cat, caper***, **Crosby (cat)boat, Martha's Vineyard cat, packet cat, two-beamed cat. b.** Those that worked the area of Narragansett Bay in Rhode Island in the late 19th century were deeper bodied, had a straighter sheer, a wide V-shaped transom, and more deadrise amidships. On some, the transom was raked and the forefoot was sharply cut away. Most lap-straked; shallow keel. Small live well amidships on workboats and dry covered fish compartments along the sides. Early boats had a full keel; later ones, such as the **Newport catboat**, had a centerboard. Other recorded names: **Narragansett Bay point boat, Narragansett cat, Newport (fishing) boat, Newport fish and lobster boat, point boat, Providence River boat. c.** The **Beetle cat** or **catboat**, designed in 1921 by John Beetle in New Bedford, Massachusetts, has been a popular racing class and pleasure boat. Large foredeck, short afterdeck; cockpit ceiled; full bow. Tiller comes in through the transom. Classic **Beetle catboats** 3.76m long, 1.8m wide, 0.13m draft with centerboard up, down 0.61m. Name variant: **Concordia Beetle catboat. d.** Those on Great South Bay on the southern shore of Long Island were proportionally larger but narrower on the average than the Cape Cod boats. Mainly built as workboats in the 1860s to 1880s, although baymen often raced them. Many had a raked "V" stern, curved plumb stem, hollow entrance and run, slack bilges, drag to the keel, inboard rudder. Larger boats had a trunk cabin aft and a portable cabin over the hold. Some re-rigged seasonally as **sloops**, with mast stepped farther aft, to provide better oyster dredging capabilities. Reported lengths 6-11m. Other recorded names: **Great South Bay, Long Island**, and **South Bay catboat**. Note also **bay boat-3. e.** The **catboats** of the New Jersey coastal bays were active in the oyster and crab industries and were similar to the classic **catboat**, except for having a comparatively large transom and lower freeboard. Sometimes called **Barnegat Bay catboats** or **Barnegatters**. Some to 13m long. **f.** A variety of **catboat** was used for shrimping out of Biloxi, Mississippi, on the Gulf of Mexico. **g.** The San Francisco crab fishery **catboat** of the late 19th century was similar to the eastern boat but might set a sprit-sail instead of a boomed gaff sail.
  3. *West Indies, Cayman Islands:* Fast boat designed early in the 20th century for turtling off these islands northwest of Jamaica; extinct. Carvel-built, with 7-8 strakes per side; 11-15 frames, fastened to the keel, inserted after hull completed. Sharp ends; raked ends, the sternpost raking sharply, curved heels. Moderate rise to the floors, vertical sides. Open; 4 thwarts, the forward thwart reinforced to hold the mast. Steered with rudder and yoke and lines, but by oar when rowing. Always painted bright blue. Mast raked slightly aft; no standing rigging, so easily unshipped. Set a sprit- or leg-of-mutton sail; occasionally a small jib. Two oars, worked through a loop fastened to a block on gunwale. Crew of 2. Typical: 4.9m long, 1.2m wide, ca. 0.76m deep. Name variant: **Caymanian catboat**. Further reading: R. C. Smith, "The Caymanian Catboat: West Indian Maritime Legacy," *World Archaeology* 16 (1985), 329-336.
  Spelling variants: **Kat(boot)**. Further references: **Deal lugger, party boat-1**

catch See **Humber keel, ketch, Lincoln catch, Trent catch**

catch boat See **luring boat, rua kread, rua pheelawk, yaw ngat**

catcher See **whale catcher**

catcher boat See **cray boat, factory ship, gyosen, tow boat-3, whale catcher, whaler-2**

catcher vessel *Canada:* A **fishing boat*** that operates with a **mother ship***. Name variant: **unité de pêche**

catch-fish boat See **tiao yu chuan**

catch-marin See **chasse-marée, quechemarín**

cate See **cat-2**

catemaron See **catamaran**

cathar, cathur, cathuri, cathuro See **catur**
catimaran, catimaron, catimoran See **catamaran**
catiolo See **katyolo**
cat-ketch Type of **ketch★** with its mainmast stepped in the eyes; comparatively tall mizzenmast stepped just forward of the helm. No headsails.
catraia 1. In Portuguese, the word may refer in general to a small, 1-man **rowing boat★**, a **whaleboat★**, a **surfboat★**, or a **pilot boat★**, especially one that precedes a ship, directing it through a channel. The word also denotes a rowing **shell★**, a 1-man shell called a **catraia simple**, a 2-man shell, a **catraia dupla**. Spelling variant: **catraio★**. Note also **barcaça-2, bote catraio.**
2. *Angola, SW:* Open **fishing boat★**. Introduced into the Moçâmedes area by emigrants from northern Portugal. Stemhead taller than the sternpost. Lugsail set to an aft-raking mast; sail tacked to the stem.
3. *Brazil:* Small **jangada★** that serves as a **dinghy★** aboard a **barcaça★**. When used for fishing or turtle hunting, is called a **bote★** and works with a crew of 2-3 within 16km of shore. Composed of 4 logs, often double-ended. Equipped only with a basket, forked staff, anchor, and bench. Rowed or sailed; steered with an oar. Reported lengths 3-4m, widths 0.8-1.0m. Other recorded names: **bote de remo, bote de vela**
4. *Brazil, SW:* Small passenger boat used in the territory of Acre. Characterized by a diamond-shaped awning.
5. *Portugal, N:* Works from the beaches between Vila do Conde and Viana do Castelo; type also seen at Buarcos to the south. The smaller boats fish and gather seaweed in the inshore area only. Double-ended, carvel-planked, strongly raked ends, keel, flat floors, straight flared sides, flat sheer. At Povoa de Varzim, rougher surf conditions require waterways and scuppers; foredeck. Sides painted white, often with designs at the bow, dark sheer strake or dark-hulled with white strake. Mainly rowed. When sailed, sets a dipping lugsail; short luff tacked to stemhead. Crew of 7-15 on large type, 4-11 on the small. **Catraia pequena**: lengths 4-6m, widths 1.5-2.35m, depths 0.53-0.85m; **catraia grande**: 6-7.5m by 2-2.7m by 1.0m. Name variant: **catraia poveira**. Note also **poveiro-2**.
6. *Portugal, N:* Former **pilot boat** over the bar at the mouth of the Douro below Porto; also used by fishermen. Strongly constructed, open, considerable sheer. Rowed double-banked. Also set a large quadrilateral lateen-type sail with a short luff, tacked to a hook inside the stem, sheeted to stern. Length 8.5m, beam 2.65m, depth 0.8m. Spelling variant: **catria**
7. *Portugal, central:* At Nazaré, the **catraia** works off the beach with a seine net. Carvel-planked. High-peaked bow, stemhead sheathed in metal; black circles at bows. Square stern; flat bottom; high gunwales; strong sheer, especially toward the bow. Rowed with a single pair of oars. Small size: length 4.7m, beam 2.2m, depth 0.75m. Other recorded names: **barco de arte de xávega, catraio, chata da xávega★, (barco da) neta, xávega**
catraia dupla See **catraia-1**
catraia grande, catraia pequena, catraia poveira See **catraia-5**
catraia simple See **catraia-1**

catraieiro See **bote catraio**
catraio *Portugal:* **1.** Small, light **ship's boat★**, kept ready for quick lowering.
2. Small boat, used mainly on rivers for transporting people and light cargo. Spritsail set to a short mast. Also rowed.
Further references: **bote catraio, catraia-1, catraia-7**
catrajo See **bote catraio**
catria See **catraia-6**
cat-schip See **cat-2**
cat-schooner *United States:* Usually considered a fore-and-aft **schooner★** rig that lacks headsails, with the foremast stepped very far forward. Masts may be vertical or both rake forward; foresail may be loose-footed. Often used for inshore fishing in New England. The **Block Island boat★** and **Chebacco boat★** are generally considered **cat-schooners**. Note also **periauger-2**.
catt See **chatte-1**
catta See **cat-1**
cattamaran, cattaraman See **catamaran**
cattle boat See **flatboat-4, mrw**
cattle carrier See **cattle ship**
cattle ferry 1. Any craft designed to transport cattle across a waterway, often to island pastures. Usually **scow★**-shaped, with low sides, flat bottom, square raked ends. Cattle protected by railings. Note also **cattle ship, cot-2, ekstock, horse boat-3, kadei, prämm-1**.
2. *Canada, E:* Such **ferries★** on the Saint John River in New Brunswick are decked-over **scows**, with a railing along the sides and a rope or gate at each end. Carry as many as 10 head of cattle. Propelled by rope or bottom cable, or towed.
cattleman *United Kingdom:* Small **schooner★** that sailed from Channel ports to La Coruña in northwest Spain to collect cattle. Chartered between 1855 and 1880 for the Army and Navy commissariat. Carried 60 head of cattle. Note also **cattle ship**.
cattlemaran See **catamaran**
cattle scow See **scow-7**
cattle ship Specially designed to transport livestock. Fitted with suitable partitions, feeding troughs, etc. Other recorded names: **cattle carrier, Kuhtrans-porter, Viehdampfer, Viehtransporter, Viehtrans-portschiff**. Note also **cattle ferry-1, cattleman, couralin-3, flatboat-4, gambarra, horse carrier, scow-7**.
catturatore See **caper**
cattus See **cat-1**
catur 1. *India, W:* Reported by early explorers along the Malabar coast as a long, fast dugout. Several would band together for piracy. Sharp at both ends, especially at the bow; ends curved; sewn-on supplemental planking raised the sides. Propelled mainly by oars with small oval blades; rowed single-banked, being too narrow to sit abreast. Also set a square sail. Reported lengths 19.5-27m; e.g., length 26m, beam 2.4m. Other recorded names: **almadia★, almadie, cat(h)uri, cathuro, chaturi, katur★**. Note also **almady-1**.
2. *Indonesia, central:* Large vessel used mainly for war by kings of Bantam, the ancient capital of Java. Sharp ends, curved; strong sheer. Carried a single mat sail; also rowed with multiple oars. Other recorded names: **cathar, cathur(i), caturi, caturia★, caturs, katoer, kàtturi**

caturi See **catur**

caturia Term for a **dugout canoe*** or for a **raft*** on some parts of the African coast. Further reference: **catur-2**

caturs See **catur-2**

catxmarina See **quechemarín**

cat-yawl 1. A twin-hulled **catamaran*** rigged as a **yawl***. **2.** *United States:* Two-masted boat, with the mainmast stepped in the bow and a mizzen stepped on the transom or, on a counter-sterned boat, stepped halfway out onto the counter. Generally sets gaff sails, sometimes battened. Large size ca. 9m. Name variant: **periauger gig**

cauf See **coble-1b, corf**

cavafango, cavafondo See **dredger-1**

cà vom See **ghe cà vom**

cawf See **corf**

ca-yak, ca-yak-bak See **kayak**

Cayapa canoe See **kule-1**

cayc See **caique**

caych See **ketch**

cayeu See **cajeu**

cayicc, cayique See **kajjik**

Caymanian catboat See **catboat-3**

Cayman schooner *West Indies, Cayman Islands:* Popular vessel used for hunting turtles from these islands northwest of Jamaica. Virtually gone by the 1950s. Strongly raked ends; curved stem; either wide transom or counter stern; strong rise to the floors; drag to the keel. Decked; trunk cabin amidships. On some, masts raked aft. Boomed gaff sails, topsails, 2 headsails. Length 21m, beam 6m, draft 2.4-2.7m. Name variant: **Grand Cayman schooner**

cayuca See **cayuco-5**

cayuco 1. *Latin America:* Generic term for a general-purpose **dugout canoe*** in South America. Range from one-man boats to those able to carry 20 people. May be double-ended or, as on the Pacific coast of Panama and northern Colombia, have a wineglass transom. Bottom usually round; some have a residual shallow keel. Small dugouts open, large types often decked. Thwarts and ribs common. Small **cayucos** paddled or poled; the larger may be rigged with gaff or spritsails. Outboard motors now common. Reported lengths 1.8-14m, widths 0.6-1.5m. **2.** *Dominican Republic, S:* On the Río Ozama, charcoal was transported to Santo Domingo in long, narrow **dugout canoes** called **cayucos**. The charcoal, wrapped in packets created from the bark of a palm tree, was stacked athwartships. Overhanging bow rounded or sharp; square stern; bottom flattened. Paddled from a seat at the stern and often from the bow area. Length ca. 6-7m. **3.** *Honduras:* Dugout canoe used mainly for native fishing. Hewn with very sharp raked ends, residual keel, S-shaped curve to bottom amidships, plumb sides. Open, 3 thwarts. Generally paddled, but occasionally sailed. Mast stepped through forward thwart; small triangular sail, sometimes a jib. Steered with yoke and lines to a rudder when sailing. Length 4.5m, beam 0.68m, depth 0.5m; some to 10m. Name variant: **canoa** **4.** *Mexico, SW:* Dugout canoe used for lagoon fishing in the Chiapas and Oaxaca areas, especially for

prawns. Hewn by axe from the trunk of a *huanacaxtle* tree in the mountains. Sharp ends; the stern rakes and sweeps up sharply. Sailed; early sail a cotton blanket, now of nylon sugar sacks. Mast stepped amidships, against a thwart. Steered with an oar when sailing. Also rowed and poled. Crew of 2. Reported lengths 5.6-10.4m. **5.** *Panama, E:* Well-built seagoing **dugout canoe** of the San Blas de Cuna tribe. Suitable logs are felled and roughly hollowed out on the mainland, now well inland. Vertical ends meet a rising sheer at a slightly recurved point. Thick rounded bottom; hard bilges; sides flare. Skeg, bolted onto bottom or carved into it about a third in from the bow, extends forward, and is deepest at the bow. Gunwales thickened and rounded on the outside. Thwarts set on brackets that are left when the hull is dug out; thwarts removable to provide sleeping space on a long trip. Interior may be brightly painted in abstract designs. Sets a boomed spritsail; jib to bow. Sprit set high-peaked snotter about halfway up the mast. In strong wind sprit may be dropped to create a triangular sail. Light mast supported by a block of wood ca. 30cm square at the base and tapering to ca. 15cm; thwart notched at hull to prevent shifting. Mast usually stepped 1.8m in from the bow. When sailing, helmsman works a steering paddle and the sail; 2nd man hangs out to windward on a rope from the masthead. When laden, freeboard as little as 5-8cm. Those using an outboard motor are modified to support the engine. Reported lengths 2.7-8.9m; length-to-beam ratio 7:1. The coastal Cuna use a small **cayuco** for river travel, fishing, hunting, and transporting crops. Paddled and poled. Narrower than the seagoing **canoe**, having been adapted for river work. Other recorded names: **cayuca, Cuna(h) canoe**; Cuna: **hulú*, hulúgua, Kuna canoe, ulu, ulumola**. Note also **imbabura, piragua-2**. **6.** *United States, Puerto Rico:* Small **dugout canoe** of the early indigenous peoples. Used mainly on quiet waters and rivers. **7.** A **cayuco** has on occasion also been described as a West African **dugout canoe**, an Eskimo **kayak***, and a canvas boat used by expedition groups. Further references: **batelu, canoa-6, dori, jukúa**

cayunera See **panga-6**

Cedar Keys sharpie See **sharpie-5**

çektiri, çektirir, çektirme See **tchektirme**

celandra, celandria, celandrium, celendria See **chelandia**

cempan See **sampan**

centerboard schooner See **Chesapeake Bay schooner**

centine See **sentine**

ceol, ceola See **keel**

cerador, cercador See **seine boat-1**

cerme See **djerme**

cerquero See **seine boat-1**

cetea See **'etea-2, saettia**

cettea See **saettia**

chabâk, chabbâk See **xebec**

chabec 1. *Tunisia, S:* A local version of the **xebec*** used until at least the 1940s. Black circles were painted on the hull, vestigial markings of the gunports of the former pirate craft. Fast, narrow, and relatively deep draft.

2. *United States, south-central:* Dialect term for a **boat**★ in the Bayou Lafourche region of southeastern Louisiana. Generally small with a sharp bow, although the word may imply a **lugger**★.

chabeck, chabek, chaboûk See **xebec**

chabu See **ch'a-pu**

cha chuan *China:* Class of **tea boat**★ of the area west of Poyang Lake, carrying tea from Jiangxi (Kiangsi) Province. More recently carries general cargo also. Most common type is the long, low **sha ba chuan**. Relatively high deckhouse with an arched roof; cargo area covers most of the hull. Attenuated ends terminate in a small square bow and an equally narrow but upturned square stern. Flat bottom, flaring sides. Balanced rudder, stock comes up through the stern; slender tiller. Sometimes sails, the masts stepped forward and aft of the house, setting large rectangular sails. Length 24m, beam 3.7m, depth ca. 1.3m; 35-70t. Spelling variant: **sha-pa ch'uan**

chaderqa See **kadırga**

chai ban zi *China, central:* Commercially important reeds from along Dongting (Tung T'ing) and its tributaries off the Chang Jiang (Yangtze) are transported on old **junks**★ modified to carry these oversized loads. Balks of timber are laid across the deck and well out beyond the sides, with restraining "gunwales," to form a platform on which the reeds are stacked ca. 7m high. Sometimes boats work in pairs, connected by spars at the bow and stern; the reeds are stacked between and out over each side. Thatched top layer forms a covering. A hole cut into the reeds provides shelter. Balance lugsail set above the stack; when the stack is too tall, a topmast and small sail are used. The 2-boat carriers each set a sail, unless one boat is much larger, in which case only that one sets its sail. Rowed when necessary. Steered from a flying bridge atop the stack, with extended rudderpost coming up through the stack. Tobacco common cargo on upstream trip. Reported lengths 9-21m. Other recorded names: **ch'ai-pan tzŭ**, **floating reed stack**, **reed plank-boat**. Note also **reed boat-2**.

chaika See **saique**
chaïke See **shaikŭ**
chaïko See **saique**
chaikŭ See **shaikŭ**
chain boat See **anchor hoy**
chain ferry See **ferryboat**
chain lighter See **anchor hoy**
chainyi kliper See **tea clipper**
ch'ai-pan tzŭ See **chai ban zi**
chaiqa, chaique See **saique**
Chaisson dory-tender See **dory-skiff**
chalabia See **chalabiya**
chalabiya *Iraq, S:* Cigar-shaped reed **raft**★ that is poled or paddled in the marshes of the lower Tigris River. Used mainly for hunting and fishing by 1-2 men. Coated with asphalt. Reported lengths 2.44-3m; a larger type is called an **'abādī je**. Other recorded names: **čallābīje, chalabia, chalabiyya, chelabiza, niğ eme**; pl. **z'ē me** on the Euphrates. Called **zā'ima**

chŭleka in the al Muntafiq area of the lower Euphrates. Note also **zaima**.

chalabiyya See **chalabiya**

chalan *Mexico, NE/United States, SW:* Transom-ended **fishing boat**★ occasionally found on the Mexican part of Laguna Madre; works a seine net. Also reported from the adjacent Texas coast until the 1950s. Roughly built and finished; plank keel; mostly V-bottomed, some with moderate deadrise, others with none. Bottom planked fore-and-aft; with rocker toward the bow; shallow skeg aft. Wales just below the sheer and above the chines. On present-day Mexican craft, the bow transom is the narrower; some sharpended. Ends rake, sides flare. Drop-blade rudder; long centerboard. Decked; 1-2 trunk cabins, the 2nd one often portable. In Mexico, they work in pairs: the beamier **campo** has 2 cabins, the **mercado** (or **mercadero**) one. Deck, transom, and topsides of Mexican boats generally painted greenish-blue, accented in white on upper wale. Accompanied by 2 **tenders**★ to lay out and store nets. Mast stepped in forward third, usually stayed with head bent forward. Gaff mainsail with long boom; web of lazyjacks. Jib to square bowsprit, extended by a sprit. Could be sailed with crew of 2. Reported lengths 8-12m; e.g., length 9m, beam 3.7m, depth aft 0.9m, draft with centerboard up ca. 30cm. Other recorded names: **butthead**★, **Laguna Madre (Port Isabel** or **Texas) scow-sloop, mullett masher, scow-sloop**★; **campboat**. Further references: **chaland, chaland de Loire**

chalana 1. Spanish term applied loosely to a **wherry**★, **lighter**★, or **scow**★. Flat bottom, ends vertical. Often towed. Note also **chaland-1**.

2. Slender-bowed and square-sterned craft used in working careened vessels and in transporting supplies and men to vessels under repair. Flat bottom. Note also **punt-2**.

3. *Argentina/Uruguay:* A common **riverboat**★ seen on the Río de la Plata until the mid-19th century.

4. *Brazil:* Small flat-bottomed boat used to carry light cargo and passengers on rivers and narrow waterways, especially in the Amazon Basin. Straight sides and raked ends. One reported as 2m long and 1.0m wide; low freeboard; shallow draft.

5. *Colombia, central:* Blunt-bowed, plank-built inland waterways boat. No keel. Transports up to 15t of cargo.

6. *Peru, Pacific coast:* Term loosely applied to a plank-built **skiff**★ that engaged mainly in inshore fishing, transporting fishermen to their larger boats, and in minor lightering at major ports. The **fishing boat**★ classed as a **chalana** is open, has a flat or V-bottom, pointed bow, tucked-up transom stern, and sometimes washstrakes. Although mainly rowed, some employ a sail. Length 6m, beam 1.3m, depth 0.5m. Name variant: **bote chalana**. Note also **zapato chalana**.

7. *Philippines:* Large flat-bottomed **lighter**, found mainly in the Manila area.

8. *Spain:* **a.** Small boat used for fishing in shallow waters and for light transport on rivers and in ports, especially on the north and northwest coasts. Design varies. Some have accommodation for the crew at the stern. 1-2t. Other recorded names: **bateira⋆** and **chamala** (Galicia); **bejú** (Montañas dialect); **berdí** (Gypsy); **xalana** (Catalan). **b.** The **chalana gallega** of northwestern Spain engages mainly in fishing in sheltered waters. Some 1- and 2-man boats work in mussel cultivation. Others are **tenders⋆** to larger craft. Sharp raked stem; raked transom stern; a small number of side planks, lapped; flat bottom; plank keel. Generally fore- and stern decks. When sailed, sets a vertical mast; 2 shrouds per side; sateen sail. Also rowed. Reported lengths 2-4m, beamy.

9. *Venezuela, W:* Flat-bottomed boat of Lake Maracaibo. Double-ended with strongly raking bow and stern; rounded bilges; centerboard. Mast, sharply raked aft, stepped through a thwart. Sets a spritsail, with sprit secured by a snotter about a third of the way

chalana-9

up the mast. Reported lengths 4-10m. Sailing **chalanas** mostly manned by 1 and typically 5m long, 0.8m wide, and 0.35m deep. Further references: **falua-3, gánguil-2, prancha**

chalana basculante See **dump barge**

chalana gallego See **chalana-8**

chalana para lestre See **ballast boat**

chaland 1. French generic for a **barge⋆** or **lighter⋆**. Primarily transfers merchandise and supplies between ships and the shore; in arsenals, such craft may transfer materiel to naval vessels. Straight sides, flat bottom. Self-propelled or towed. Note also **allège, chalana-1**.

2. *Canada, E:* Quebec lumbering industry term for a **barge** used to haul men, horses, and supplies.

3. *France:* **a.** Large cargo **barge** that plies French rivers and canals; originated on the Loire River in the early 15th century; later an important craft on the Seine. Propelled by oars, sail, and towing; motorized **barges** go by the name **péniche**. Those on the Rance were 26m long, 4.5m wide, 1.3m deep; the **chalands** of the Garonne Basin were 20-100t. Name variant: **bac**. Note also **chaland de Loire, train de bateaux, waal. b.** Term also applies to a box-like craft, pierced with holes, that holds alive the fish catch, oysters, mussels, etc. Note also **vivier. c.** May now be a naval landing craft, as **chaland de débarquement.**

4. *France, SW:* **a.** On the Adour River, above the bridges at Bayonne, fishermen used a small, 2-man **dugout canoe⋆** called a **chaland**. Flared sides, sharp ends. Sculled from the stern or set a tiny lugsail in the bow. Length 4.5m, beam 0.8m, depth 0.35m. **Chalands** on the Adour are also plank-built, sharp at

the ends, flat bottom turns up as a flat surface to high, swept-up ends. Rowed. Length 6.6m, beam 1.25m, depth 0.5m. **b.** The **chaland** of the Lot River carried Cahors wine. Sharp ends. Steered with a long sweep at the stern. Towing mast. Rigged with lugsails.

5. *United States:* French term for a small, plank-built, flat-bottomed boat of the Mississippi Valley. In the southern Louisiana bayous, the **chaland** is used principally to cross waterways. A large size aids in moss gathering; some were stores. Rectangular; sides and ends vertical; flat sheer; bottom has rocker at ends. Small triangular external keel on some. Decked at ends. Reported lengths 3.1-4.3m, widths 0.76-0.9m, depths 0.2-0.3m. Name variant: **bateau plat⋆**. Note also **shanty boat.**

Other recorded names: **cal(l)an, caland, calen, chalan⋆, c(h)alandre, chalant(a), chaleng, challan, chalon, skâf** (pl. **skâfiou, skefien**), **tchialan, xalanta**. Further references: **chelandia, shalanda**

chaland à vase See **marie-salope**

chaland basculeur See **dump barge**

chaland-citerne See **tank barge**

chaland de Berre *France, S:* **Barge⋆** of the lower Rhône River, especially in the Étang de Berre. Developed early in the 20th century to transport local cargo and petroleum products. Heavily constructed and beamy. Comparatively small rigging, setting a lateen sail, but they were mostly towed.

chaland de charbon See **coal lighter**

chaland de débarquement See **chaland-3c**

chaland de Loire *France, central:* Canal and **riverboat⋆** of the lower Loire River and the Nantes to Brest canal used until the latter half of the 19th century. Averaged 40-60t, maximum 120t; one mid-19th-century boat was 26.6m long and 4.5m wide. Narrow, square, overhanging bow; wide curved transom; flat bottom; straight clinker-planked sides; wood or metal; open waist. The 17th-century **chaland** had an upturned stern from which a long sweep was worked; set a square sail; crewed by 3 men and a boy; carried ca. 50t. The early 19th-century boat also set a square sail to a tall mast; mast lowered to a crutch forward and raised by a hand winch aft. Wide-bladed axial rudder with tiller that sloped upward at ca. 45° and could be turned and lifted out of the water. Some worked the waterways of the upper Loire and Allier Valleys, carrying wine and produce; these were smaller because of lock limitations. Towed by horses or men; later boats motorized. **Chalands** traversing the lower Loire in the early 20th century were modified with nearly plumb bow and transom, cabin aft, and an iron rudder; lengths to 40m. Other recorded names: **chalan⋆, chaland de Nantes, bateau** (or **chaland**) **nantais**. Further reading: François Beaudouin, *La Marine de Loire et Son Chaland* (Conflans-Sainte-Honorine, Amis du Musée de la Batellerie, 1989). Note also **bé de cane, train de bateaux.**

chaland de Nantes See **chaland de Loire**

chaland d'Oise See **picard-2**

chaland-mère See **train de bateaux**

chaland nantais See **chaland de Loire**

chaland normand See **besogne**

chaland percé See **vivier-2**
chaland ponton See **dummy barge-1**
chalandre See **chaland**
chalangu See **masula**
chalanik See **chaloupe**
chalannus See **chelandia**
chalan percé See **vivier-2**
chalant, chalanta See **chaland**
chalão *Angola, SW:* Open **fishing boat★** that works with a net off the beaches in the Namibe (Moçamedes) area. Flat bottom, sharp ends. Rowed. Note also **chatão**.
chalek See **xebec**
chalendra See **chelandria**
chaleng See **chaland**
Chaleur Bay schooner See **Gaspé schooner**
chali See **bhelā**
chalibardon *France, SW:* Large boat that transported heavy cargoes, notably Chalosse wine, on the Adour River. Known to have worked in the 17th and early 18th centuries, and, slightly modified, in the 19th century. Flat bottom curved up at each end, the flat bow terminating in a point, the stern in a wide, shallow transom. Sides curved slightly, and the later type had a distinct bulge where the bottom and sides met. Decked at the ends, with a steering platform aft. Maneuvered and steered with a long sweep set over a pin on the stern. Also stepped a towing mast, which probably set a sail. Reported lengths 14-22m; very shallow draft. Spelling variant: **charibardon**
charibardon See **chalibardon**
chalingue See **masula**
chalk See **tjalk-3**
challan See **chaland**
challupe, challuppe See **chaloupe**
chaloep See **sloep-2**
chalon See **chaland, Saint Lawrence barge**
chalonnius, chalonus See **chelandia**
chalop See **chaloupe**
chaloup See **chaloupe, chaloupe-10, Schaluppe**
chaloupa *Turkey:* Two-masted vessel that participated in Turkish naval encounters. Note also **chaloupe**.
chaloupe **1.** French word often synonymous with the English word **shallop★**.
2. A **ship's boat★**, usually the largest and strongest. In France, it was comparable to the **longboat★** of the British navy. Open, flat floors, wide raked transom stern. Usually rowed double-banked, but also sailed, setting lug- or lateen sails; more recently motorized. Might require 18-20 rowers. Those aboard French **men-of-war★** of the 18th century were armed. The **double chaloupe** or **chaloupe pontée** of the 17th-18th centuries was larger and either fully decked or half-decked. Name variant: **grande chaloupe**
3. The **chaloupe en fagot** of 16th-century explorers was carried aboard unassembled, being too large to carry on deck.
4. The 18th-century **chaloupe à puits** had a well through which the anchor rope passed.
5. *Canada, E:* **a.** At Newfoundland and the French islands of St. Pierre et Miquelon, **chaloupes** engaged in handline fishing for cod on the Grand Banks from the 16th into the 19th century. Off Isle Royale (Cape

Breton Island), they worked inshore, salting the cod ashore. Mainly brought from France knocked down; **flûtes★** of the 17th century carried as many as 10 **chaloupes**. Double-ended, strong rake at ends, round-bilged, scantling keel. Both open and decked. Might have canvas weatherboards; the larger boats had as many as 6-7 fish rooms. The Isle Royale boats compartmented by bulkheads into 6 rooms, one for the fishermen plus a room each for stowing the catch. Set a lugsail or was rowed. Crew of 3 on the 9.8m undecked boats and 5 on the decked craft. Note also **charoi, chaloupe-6. b.** In the Magdalen Islands in the Gulf of St. Lawrence, the **chaloupe** serves as a support boat in the herring net operation. Clinker-planked; sharp, slightly raked ends; flat floors; main strength provided by 2 bulkheads and 2 frames; flared sides; beamy. Open, painted gray. Rowed.
6. *France:* **a.** Small vessel used for fishing, coasting, piloting, and port work from at least the late 17th to the early 20th century. Worked out of ports along the Bay of Biscay (**chaloupes du golfe**), often taking the name of their home port. Carvel-planked; fine run; deep drag to the keel; rounded bilges, floors flat or rose steeply. Straight or lightly curved stem; raked sternpost; rounded stern in later boats, early type sharp-sterned. Outboard rudder, on some extending well below the keel. Undecked until the early 19th century (**chaloupe creuse**), then decked, with 2 hatches, cuddy forward, small cockpit aft (the **pontée**). Originally set 2 square sails; changed to standing lugsails in the 19th century; some small local types set only one sail. Jib run out on long bowsprit; sometimes used a jiggermast with a small lugsail. Topsails common. Early masts vertical; later might rake aft, the mainmast raking the most. Early boats mainly rowed; the tholepins on the Arcachon **chaloupes** were fixed between the top strake and an external stringer. Engines installed in later boats. During fishing season, early 18th-century vessels might carry 12 in crew, later 4. Reported lengths 6-15m; e.g., length overall 9.2m, on waterline 8.7m, beam 3.2m, draft 1.4m. Other recorded names: **bag-lestr, bateau à franc-bord, carvelle, picoteuse; chaloupe arcachonnaise, chaloupe de Fouras, chaloupe de la Rochelle** (or **chaloupe rochelaise**), **chaloupe de Noirmoutier, chaloupe de Royan** (or **chaloupe royannaise**), **chaloupe des Sables, chaloupe du Bassin, chaloupe graisilonne** or **groisilonne, chaloupe sablaise**. Further reading: Marc Gauvin, "René-Joseph alias La Pendule, Dernière Chaloupe Pontée de la Baie de Bourgneuf," *Petit Perroquet* 24 (1978), 29-46. Note also **chalutier, sardinier breton, thonier. b.** The **chaluppe** was an inland boat of the Gascony region of southwest France in the early 16th century.
7. *Haiti:* In the Creole dialect, a **chaloupe** may be a **ship's boat**, but more commonly a small **motorboat★**.
8. *Seychelles:* A small boat fabricated from the materials left over after the construction of a larger craft. Spelling variant: **saloup**
9. *Switzerland, W:* **a. Chaloupes** on Lake of Geneva (Lake Léman) in the late 18th century took depth soundings and meteorological observations. One

reported as 7.5m long, another 12.5m long and 2.2m wide. Some 17th-century boats were used for fishing. An 18th-century **chaloupe** carried orders between other naval vessels. **b.** Also a general term for the pleasure **sailboats** of Lake of Geneva.

10. *United States, south-central:* Used by the French along the Gulf of Mexico and on the lower Mississippi River in the 1st half of the 18th century. Larger vessels (ca. 60t) carried passengers and cargo. Smaller types (ca. 4t) assisted ships by laying anchors and performing ship-to-shore duties; often 1-3 carried on board. Spelling variant: **chaloup**. Note also **shallop-8**.

Other recorded names: **caïquo, chalanik, challup(p)e, chalop, chaloup(pe), chalup** (pl. **chalupper**), **chloup, skloup, xalupa**. Note also **chaloupa, chalupa, Schlup, scialuppa, sloep, sloop, slup**. Further references: **bag, chaloupe de Plougastel, Gaspé schooner, sardinier breton, sloep**

chaloupe à gazoline See **goélette-2**

chaloupe à puits See **chaloupe-4**

chaloupe arcachonnaise See **chaloupe-6**

chaloupe biscayenne See **biscayenne**

chaloupe bretonne See **sardinier breton**

chaloupe cannonière See **gunboat**

chaloupe creuse See **chaloupe-6**

chaloupe de guerre See **sloop-1**

chaloupe de Fouras See **chaloupe-6**

chaloupe de la rade, chaloupe de la Rade de Brest See **chaloupe de Plougastel**

chaloupe de la Rochelle, chaloupe de Noirmoutier See **chaloupe-6**

chaloupe de Plougastel *France, W:* Strong, 2-masted, lug-rigged boat of the Rade de Brest area. During the 18th and 19th centuries, engaged in multiple activities, transporting produce, people, sand, granite, seaweed, and also fishing and scallop dredging. Worked off the beaches. Carvel planking; sharp ends, stern rounded above the waterline; slightly curved ends; high freeboard; maximum beam forward of amidships; keel; soft turn of the bilges. Small deck forward and aft initially, later fully decked. Outboard rudder; tiller. Mainmast raked sharply aft, foremast either vertical or raked. Foremast stepped close to the stem. Set dipping lugsails; yards set at right angles to the masts. Mainsail halyard to an iron traveler; spar might extend the luff on each sail. Later boats carried a jib to a bowsprit. Could be rowed with 2 pairs of oars between double tholepins. Crew of 2-5. Reported lengths 7-10m, beam 2.5-3m, depth forward 1.4m, aft 1.15m, draft ca. 1.0m; cap. 8-9.5t. Other recorded names: **bag Plougastel, bateau de Plougastel, bateau breton, chaloupe*, chaloupe de la rade, chaloupe de la Rade de Brest, chaloupe Plougastel, Plougastel (chaloupe)**. Further reading: Bernard Cadoret, et al., *Ar vag, Voiles au Travail en Bretagne Atlantique*, vol. 3 (Douarnenez: Éditions de l'Estran, 1985), 7-40.

chaloupe de Royan, chaloupe des Sables See **chaloupe-6**

chaloupe double See **barque longue**

chaloupe du Bassin, chaloupe du golfe See **chaloupe-6**

chaloupe en fagot See **chaloupe-3**

chaloupe flamande See **sloep-1**

chaloupe graisillone, chaloupe groisillonne See **chaloupe-6**

chaloupe pilote See **pilot boat**

chaloupe Plougastel See **chaloupe de Plougastel**

chaloupe pontée See **chaloupe-2, chaloupe-6**

chaloupe rochelaise, chaloupe royannaise, chaloupe sablaise See **chaloupe-6**

chaloupe sardinière See **sardinier breton**

chaloupe thonier See **thonier**

chalouppe See **chaloupe**

chaloutière See **chalutier**

chalup See **chaloupe**

chalupa 1. In Portuguese and Spanish, **chalupa** refers to a wide variety of small boats propelled by motor, sail (usually gaff-rigged), or oar. Aboard a ship, it is the largest **ship's boat***, although in the 16th century, it was one of the smaller boats. Other recorded names: **chalupea** or **txalupa** (Basque), **xalupa** (Catalan); **chalupeta** (dim.). Note also **chaloupe, scialuppa**.

2. May also be a small cargo vessel, generally with topmast and topsail above the gaff mainsail; gaff mizzen, staysail, and jib to a bowsprit.

3. *Colombia:* Along the Caribbean coast, the **chalupa** is a **dugout canoe*** used mainly for fishing. Rounded stern; sharp plumb bow, flared topsides; sheer turns up sharply at the bow. Lengths under 8m. On inland waterways, the **chalupa** is either a dugout or a plank-built **canoe*** with narrow square ends.

4. *Mexico:* Term for a small **canoe**.

5. *Panama, S:* Double-ended **fishing boat*** of the Bay of Panama area. Decked except for a small cockpit; hold space for nets and iced fish. Sets a lateen-type sail. Reported lengths 8-9m.

6. *Peru:* Small, beamy, double-ended **fishing boat** used off the coast. Plumb stem with high stemhead, outboard rudder. Decked. Spritsail set to a midship mast, jib to a short bowsprit.

7. *Puerto Rico:* A small **narrow boat***, scarcely able to transport 2 persons.

8. *Spain:* May designate a craft serving guard duty at an arsenal or naval station.

9. *Spain, north coast:* **a.** Small open boat used to catch sea-bream and other types of fish. Rowed and sailed. The 16th-century **rowing boats*** of the north coast might have 15 oars per side and were ca. 21cm long. **b.** Sharp-ended **whaleboat*** used by Basque whalers of Spain and southwestern France. Some were carried aboard **galleons*** and **caravels*** for use in Newfoundland and Labrador. Armed **chalupas** supported some of the naval operations of the 2nd half of the 16th century; these have been variously called **chalupas, txalupak,** or **galiones**. Open boat with 3 thwarts and end decks; strongly curved and swept-up ends, some with tumble home. The harpoon line was threaded through a hole in the stem and ran aft to the timberhead on the after deck. Rowed with 6-8 oars on each side; sailed, with 2 masts. Crew of 8. Whaling boats reported as 5-8.5m long, 1.7-1.8m wide, 0.45m deep. Note also **txalupa handi**.

Further reference: **falua-3**

chalupa grande See **txalupa handi**

chalupa lagosteira See **langoustier**

chalupea, chalupeta See **chalupa-1**

chaluppe See **chaloupe-6, Schlup**

chalupper See **chaloupe**

chalutier   **1.** *Algeria:* Locally built, motorized **fishing boat**★ that is ca. 13m long and carries a crew of 7. Sharp plumb bow; wide square stern permits easier handling of trawl net lines. Decked; cabin house forward, leaving the stern area for net handling.
   2. *Canada, E:* In Quebec, the designation **chalutier** is reserved for **trawlers**★ greater than 16m long and over 25grt.
   3. *France:* Seaworthy vessel designed to trawl with a net (*chalut*). Those that sailed exclusively were called **drogueurs**★; others include the **bateau bœuf**★, **bisquine**★, **chaloupe**★, **harenguier**★, **langoustier**★, and **lougre**★. Large **chalutiers** stayed away from their home ports for 8-10 days, the small vessels 2-4 days. Sailing **chalutiers** required crew of 6-12; motorized **chalutiers**, 5-6. Other recorded names: **chaloutière**; Breton: **bag-rouederez, lestr-roueder, roueder**
   Further reference: **trawler**

chalutier arrière See **trawler**

chalutier de Berck See **bateau de Berck**

chalutier de traille, chalutier latéral See **trawler**

chamala See **chalana-8**

chambequín A **xebec**★-type vessel of the late 17th and early 18th centuries rigged with 2-3 square sails on the fore- and mainmasts and a lateen on the mizzenmast, above which might be 2 square topsails. Other recorded names: **chanvequi, jabequín, xambequi**

Chamberlain dory-skiff See **dory-skiff**

chambo See **chombo**

champa   **1.** *Colombia, west-central:* **Dugout canoe**★ of the indigenous peoples of Chocó Department. Hewn with ax and adze. Sharp ends. Mainly paddled, but poled when water shallow or swift. Paddles painted or varnished. Reported lengths 3-7m, beam ca. 0.8m. Other recorded names: **canoa grande**★; **hapu-mámu** by the Noanamá
   2. *Panama:* Reported by early explorers as a **dugout canoe** of modest size.
   Further references: **canoa-6, canoa-14**

champagne, champaigne See **sampan**

champán   **1.** *Argentina:* Vessel that plied the Río Paraná.
   2. *Colombia:* **a.** Very large **dugout canoe**★ used to carry passengers on the larger rivers, especially the Magdalena. Ends sharp and elongated. Most of the hull covered with a mat house, compartmented into rooms and stores. Poled from the roof, or paddled. Averaged ca. 22 in crew. Steered with a large oar from a stern platform. Reported lengths 20-25m, beam ca. 3m. **b.** Term also applied to a 3-masted merchant vessel.
   Further reference: **sampan**

champana, champanaa, champane, champaneta, champann, champanne, champão, champara, champaulu See **sampan**

champ de vigne See **Bornachen**

champenas See **sampan**

champita pequeña See **potro**

champlong See **chĕmplong, tjemplon**

changādam See **jangar**

ch'ang-k'ou ma-yang tzŭ See **chang kou ma yang zi**

chang kou ma yang zi *China, central:* **1.** Very old cargo **junk**★ that became the prototype for the other **ma yang zi**★ of the Chang Jiang (Yangtze) valley. Designed to traverse the rapids of the Yuan Jiang in Hunan, but proceeded to ports on the Chang Jiang, carrying oil in large oil-proof baskets. Heavily constructed, with as many as 13 bulkheads, several deck beams, and 2 strengthening wales along each side. Sides curved in to square bow and stern, both transversely planked. Flat bottom, longitudinally planked, curved sides. Shallow sheer forward, marked toward the stern. Decked, narrow waterways forward of the house; woodsided house covered with an arched mat roof. Fanshaped rudder, with stock coming up inboard; tiller. Foremast stepped well forward, roughly amidships. Set tall lugsails. Reported lengths 11.6-33m; e.g., length 28m, beam 5.6m, depth 2m. Other recorded names: **ch'ang-k'ou ma-yang tzŭ, open mouth ma-yang tzŭ**
   2. A **chang kou ma yang zi** also operates in Fuling (Fou Chow) and Wanxian (Wan Hsien) below Chongqing (Chungking) on the upper Chiang Jiang. Crew of 7-11, plus 25-40 trackers. Spelling variant: **tch'ang k'eou ma-yang tzŭ**

chang long *China, S:* Long, narrow, swift craft used by pirates and smugglers in the Guangzhou (Canton) delta area. Square raked ends, bow narrower than stern; flat bottom, cambered, planked longitudinally; straight sides. Open. Steered with an oar over the stern, but might ship a rudder with a wide fenestrated blade below the waterline. Generally paddled, the smaller craft having crew of 5-8, the larger 25 or more. Sailed when wind from astern, using a mat sail. Reported lengths 7.6-15.2m; e.g., length ca. 7.9m, beam 1.0m, depth 0.6m; shallow draft. Other recorded names: **ch'ang lung, snake boat, tch'ang long**

ch'ang lung See **chang long**

Changsha dao ba zi, Changsha tao-pa-tzŭ See **dao ba zi-2**

Changshu chuan, Changzhou chuan See **mi bao zi-2**

Channel barge *England, SE:* Term given to a **Thames sailing barge**★ type modified to make it more seaworthy for work in the English Channel and North Sea; extinct. Frequently of steel; flat bottom, no keel; wallsided. Full bow with vertical stem; broad, shallow transom; moderate sheer. Decked; often had wheelhouse aft; fairly deep bulwarks; leeboards. Sprit mainsail set to a short mast, topsail to a tall topmast. Large staysail; 2 jibs to a bowsprit that could be topped up in congested areas. Mizzenmast stepped inboard, generally sprit-rigged; called a **mulie** when the mizzen was a boomed gaff sail brailed to the standing gaff. Some were **ketch**★-rigged **boomies**★. Auxiliaries installed on later vessels. Crew of 3. Reported lengths 24-30m; e.g., length 27m, beam 6.4m, depth 2m.

Channel Islander See **Guernsey mackerel boat**

chanpan See **sampan**

ch'an-tzŭ See **chan zi**

chanvequi See **chambequín**

chany See **ghurāb**

chan zi *China, central:* Salt carrier on the Chang Jiang (Yangtze) from Yueyang (Yochow) west to Shashi (Shasi). Well-built, with features designed to protect the salt, which was carried in large baskets. Hull of fir;

chan zi

relatively few bulkheads, but strengthened by several wales along each side. Raked, square ends; short foredeck; balanced rudder came up inboard. Small mat-roofed cabin at the stern; main house solid wood, with removable panels in the roof through which cargo was loaded. One or 2 masts, setting tall balance lugsails. Also rowed and poled. Crew of 3-5. Reported lengths 15-20m, widths 3.6-4.6m, depths 1.4-1.7m. Spelling variants: **ch'an-tzŭ, tch'an-tse**

ch'ao-chou junk, Chao-chow trading junk See **cao chuan-3**

chap-ats, chap-atz See **West Coast canoe**

chapel boat, chapel hulk See **church boat**

chapel ship See **church ship**

ch'a-pu *China:* Small flat-bottomed **skiff***-like boat. Spelling variant: **chabu**

chapú See **kishti-3**

chá-pŭts See **West Coast canoe**

charbonnier See **collier-1**

chāri See **taghāri**

charibardon See **chalibardon**

charigma *India, Bay of Bengal:* **Outrigger canoe*** of South Andaman Island in the Andaman group. Dugout hull 4-8cm thick, rounded at the ends; shelf-like overhang at bow or at each end serves as a platform for a harpooner. Outrigger float attached by 3 or more light booms that cross the hull and pierce the opposite side; generally 3 crossed connectives attach booms to the float. Often propelled by the haft of the harpoon spear. Other recorded names: **charigma-da, chrok-che, chrok-lekile**

charigma-da See **charigma**

Charleroi bak, Charleroi baquet See **baquet de Charleroi**

Charles Mary See **chasse-marée**

Charleston bateau *United States, SE:* **Punt***-like craft used to guide **timber rafts*** downstream to Charleston, South Carolina. Shallow square ends; flat bottom, longitudinally planked, rocker at ends; straight vertical sides; flat sheer. Cleats nailed to the bottom; no thwarts or seats. Propelled by 1-2 paddles. Length 4.3m, width 0.8m, depth 0.38m. Name variant: **South Carolina logging bateau**

charoi *Canada, E:* One of the several **chaloupes*** used by the **terreneuviers*** while cod fishing off Newfoundland. Designated to make the rounds of the **chaloupes**, carrying the catch back to the **mother ship*** or to the shore processing plant. Also transported the crew to and from shore, and some engaged in coastal fishing. Heavy, lumbering vessel. Sides raised with weather cloths. Some used for hunting and fishing on the St. Lawrence River during the 18th century. Reported lengths 9-12m. Other recorded names: **canot serreur, charroi, char(r)oy, séreur, serreur**. Note also **bateau charroi**.

charoy, charroi, charroy See **charoi**

charrua See **flûte**

charterer See **freighter-1**

chartouch See **šaḥtūr**

chase boat See **layout boat-1**

chaser See **chasseur-2**

chaser ship See **whale catcher**

chasse-marée *France, NW:* Lug-rigged vessel, principally from Brittany. Mainly a **coaster***; renowned for its privateering and smuggling activities, but initially designed to transport fish quickly to shore. Used by the French customs service toward the end of the 18th century. Large vessels crossed the Atlantic. First reported in the late 17th century; some converted to motor, transporting wine and wood until the mid-20th century. A few sailing **chasse-marées** were working in the 1960s. Hull varied with locale, period, and size. Common features were bluff bows, curved stem, rounded stern, with straight vertical sternpost or a counter and raking post. Long straight keel, generally with drag; sides vertical or tumble home to topsides; strong sheer forward. Small boats had an open waist, larger were decked; small cabin aft, and sometimes also forward. Largest 3-masted. Foremast stepped just abaft the stem, setting a large standing lugsail that usually extended abaft of the mainmast. Aft-raking mainmast set a narrower standing lug. Small lug or leg-of-mutton mizzen on the aft-raking mast that pressed against the sternpost, sheeted to a long outrigger. Light standing rigging of one stay and 2-3 halyards; deep bonnet on the fore- and mainsails. Topsails might be set on some or each of the masts; jib run out on a bowsprit that was frequently half the length of the hull and could be topped up in close quarters. On the smaller 2-masted boats, spar bowlines extended the lugsails. Mainsail brailed to one end of the yard; foresail yard lowered and sail wrapped around mast and yard. Crew of 3 on the smaller boats, but as many as 75 on the **privateers***. Reported lengths 10-20m; e.g., length 11m, beam 4m, draft 2m. Other recorded names: **cache-marée, catch-marin, Charles Mary, chasse-marie, chommery, kas-maread, quache-marée, risque-tout, sea-hunter, slash-marée, tide chaser** or **tide racer**. Note also **catamaran-11, lougre, quechemarín**.

chasse-marie See **chasse-marée**

chasseur **1.** French term used since the late 17th century for a fast naval vessel that gives chase to other vessels or engages in reconnoitering activities. Name variant: **bâtiment chasseur**

2. Term for a fast sailing vessel (often a **schooner***) that contacted **fishing boats*** staying away from their home ports for extended periods, the **chasseur** collecting and transporting the catch to market and carrying supplies, salt, mail, and news to and from home. Most fetched cod from the Newfoundland and Iceland fishing banks. By extension, any craft that serves this function. Crew of 5-6. Name variant: **chaser**. Note also **chasse-marée, jagger**.
3. Submarine chaser of World War I.
Further references: **fish carrier, jäger, packer-1, whale catcher**

chasseur-baleinier See **whale catcher**

chat See **cat-2**

chata **1.** In Portugal and Spain, refers broadly to a boat with a flat bottom. May be a **lighter***, a **barge***, or a **monkey boat***. One type aided in careening ships, another served as a pontoon between a vessel and quay.
2. In Latin America, a **chata** might be a 2-masted vessel with a capacity of 60-100t.
3. *Angola:* Small, open boat used primarily for inshore fishing along the central and southern coasts. Plank-built; flat bottom; sharp, relatively plumb stem; wide raked transom; wide gunwales. Rowed with single pair of oars. Ca. 3.7m long.
4. *Brazil:* **a.** In the Brazilian navy, a **chata** was a strongly built, double-ended boat with a flat bottom. Such boats were used as **floating batteries*** in the war between Brazil and Portugal. **b.** Small general utility **rowing boat*** from the upper Paraguaí River in Mato Grosso and Mato Grosso do Sul in southwestern Brazil. Plank-built, with frames; open. **c.** Flat-bottomed, shallow-draft motorized vessel of the Amazon Basin. Small types called **chatinhas**.
5. *Ecuador:* Flat-bottomed **barge**-type craft reported in use on the rivers in the Guayaquil area in the early 18th century.
6. *Mozambique:* Small flat-bottomed boat used for net fishing from beaches in the vicinity of Maputo (Lourenço Marques) on the south coast. Overhanging bow terminates in a raked bow transom that rises in a semicircle above the gunwale; wide, shallow square stern; wale along each side. Open; 3-4 benches; stern notched for the steering oar used when sailing. Generally rowed; also poled. When sailed, sets a lateen sail well forward, uses an oar as a rudder. Reported lengths 5-8m.
7. *Portugal:* **a.** Term for an open **rowboat*** used for recreation, especially off beaches. Length ca. 3m, beam 1.35m, depth 0.4m. **b.** Small **ship's boat*** used for cleaning and painting the sides of ships. Clinker-built, flat bottom. Rowed with a single pair of oars. **c.** In central Portugal on the Vouga River, the **chata** is a local craft that engages in ferrying, fishing, and carrying cargo. Almond-shaped, with slightly raked sharp ends. Flat bottom, plumb sides of a single plank. Completely open, with no thwarts; numerous ribs. Poled. Length 5.5m, beam 1.35m, depth 0.35m. **d.** Small, lightly built **fishing boat*** that works from beaches seaward of Lisbon on the Tagus River as well as from other beaches along the coast. Carvel-

chata-7d

planked; flat bottom with rocker; plank keel; wide raking transom stern; sheer sweeps up at the bow, the curved stem sometimes ending in a knob; 2 wales. May have a short foredeck and a live well; stern sheets. Often painted with oculi on the bows. Deep rudder shipped when sailed; tiller. Mostly rowed. May set a wide dipping lugsail or a quadrilateral lateen-type sail with a short luff. Crew of 2-3. Reported lengths 3.85-5m; e.g., length 4.35m, beam 1.65m, depth 0.55m; a large type, 6.5m long, tends fish traps in the Tagus area.
Further references: **cat-2, chatte-1, dummy barge-1**

chata da xávega See **catraia-7**

chata de alijar See **flat-1**

chatão **1.** Portuguese term given to a boat that has the general form and dimensions of a **whaleboat***, but with a flat bottom to enable it to work easily from beaches. Or, it may be a square-sterned, flat-bottomed boat that can be rowed or sculled, but is somewhat larger than the typical **rowboat***.
2. *Angola:* Common type of flat-bottomed boat used as a general workboat and **fishing boat***, especially off the beaches. Note also **chalão**.

cha tch'ouan See **Kiangsu trader**

chate *Haiti:* A flat-bottomed, undecked boat. See also **chatte-1, chatte-2**.

cha t'ing See **sha ting**

chatinha See **chata-4**

chato *France:* A **lighter*** used to load and unload ships. Spelling variant: **tsato**. Note also **chatte-1, chatte-4**.

chatte *France:* **1.** From the 16th to the 18th century, assisted in the transfer of cargo to and from ships off west coast ports; sometimes employed as a **coaster***. Bluff bows and quarters. Decked, with a small, low cuddy forward; hatches located on either side of the midship mast. Lugsails set to the 2 masts; bonnets on the bottom. Crew of 2. A similar, but undecked, vessel transported artillery. Reported lengths 18-25m, widths 5-7m, depth ca. 2.5m. Spelling variants: **catt, chata*, chate**. Note also **cat, chato**.
2. Fishing boat* used until the latter part of the 19th century, particularly in the Loire Estuary and the area to the south. Drifted broadside while fishing with a drag net held open by long poles extending from the bow and stern. Double-ended, flat bottom. Demountable rudder shifted from one end to the other to avoid tacking. Large trapezoidal sail; foot almost as long as the boat; tacked to windward side. Tall mainmast

stepped amidships. At each end, stepped a small mast with an inboard rake, each setting a small square sail.

chatte-2

Crew of 4 in early 18th century. Reported lengths 9.7-15m, beam 2-4m, depth ca. 1.5m, draft 0.76-0.9m. Other recorded names: **chate★**, **chatte de Bourneuf**, **chatte de la Bernerie**, **chatte du Croisic**

3. A boat that carried fresh water from the Charente River on the west coast to ships lying at anchor off Île d'Aix.

4. At Marseille on the Mediterranean, a type of **lighter★** or a floating wharf. Still in use. Note also **chato**.

5. Vessel with a reinforced hull, enabling it to be armed with heavy cannon in order to defend the entrance to a port.

chatte de Bourneuf, chatte de la Bernerie, chatte du Croisic See **chatte-2**

chatte du nord See **cat-2**

chattee, chattti, chatty See **chatty raft**

chatty raft 1. A craft composed of earthernware pots lashed together with poles to form a **raft★**, but could be a single pot. Other recorded names: **chattee, chatti, chatty, pottery raft, Topfboot, Topffloss**. Note also **mu ying, palla chatty, taghāri**.

2. *Bangladesh/India/Pakistan:* A widely used craft that uses pots (*ghara*) for flotation. Probably now rare, but served as a **ferry★** to cross non-rocky streams, as temporary transportation during periods of inundation, and as a **raft** for wildfowling, fishing, and transporting mail. Also used by raiding parties to cross rivers. The unglazed pots, varying in number but generally 6-15, are open or sealed with leaves, depending on the locale. Bamboo poles are lashed on each side of the

chatty raft-2

mouths of the pots. A light bamboo or woven mat platform, laid across the top, supports passengers, baggage, and merchandise. Sometimes a single pot may be used to ferry a person across a small watercourse. Propelled by swimmers or punted. Pots ca. 76cm in diameter. Other recorded names: **gharnai, gharnao**

3. *Egypt:* A similar **raft** in Upper Egypt served as a **ferry**, to carry produce, and at times, as a means of transporting the pots themselves (see **ramūs**). Mouths of the pots left open or plugged with clay or leaves; a

light platform was laid atop the lashed layer of pots. In use until at least the mid-20th century.

chaturi See **catur-1**

chaucha See **cog**

chaveco In Portuguese, word may refer to a poorly constructed, worthless vessel. Spelling variant: **xaveco**. See also **xebec**.

chayny kliper See **tea clipper**

chébac See **xebec**

Chebacco boat *Canada, E/United States, NE:* Narrow, sharp-sterned boat developed in the latter part of the 18th century in Chebacco Parish, northeastern Massachusetts. Worked until the mid-19th century. Engaged mainly in offshore fishing; some carried produce and cargo south along the coast and to the West Indies, and in Canada a few served as fishery patrol craft. Full round bow; stem mostly curved. On those in which bulwarks stopped short of the stem, grooved stemhead served as a bit for the mooring line; these were generally called **ram's head boats**. **Fishing boats★** often had an open rail rather than bulwarks. Sternpost raked; bulwarks at the stern swept up sharply and continued beyond the post, ending in a V-shaped board that was notched on top to hold the lowered mainsail boom. Deep drag to the straight keel; hard, high bilges. Slender rudder, narrowing toward the top; tiller passed inboard below the top of the bulwark. Small sizes had 1-2 transverse standing rooms for fishing and one for the helmsman (**standing room boat** or **standing roomer**); larger vessels fully decked, small raised cuddy forward. Foremast stepped well forward, mainmast just abaft amidships. Set square-headed gaff sails, initially loose-footed, later boomed; gaffs long, with separate throat and peak halyards. No headsails or topsails. Rowed when necessary. Crew of 2-4. Lengths in the 18th century 10.7-11.6m on deck; after 1800, mostly 12-14m overall; e.g., length between perpendiculars 11.5m, beam 3.4m, hold depth 1.78m. Other recorded names: **Chebacco pinky, Chebbacco boat, Chebucto boat, Gebacca boat, Gebacco boat, Jebacco boat, pinkey, pinkie**. Further reading: William A. Baker, *Sloops & Shallops* (Barre, Mass.: Barre Publishing Co., 1966), 82-91. Note also **cat-schooner, dogbody, pinky, two-mast boat**.

Chebacco dogbody See **dogbody**

Chebacco pinky, Chebbacco boat See **Chebacco boat**

Chebeague stone sloop See **stone sloop**

chébec See **xebec**

chebec à pible See **velacciere**

chebeck, chebek See **xebec**

chébéka See **shebek, xebec**

Chebucto boat See **Chebacco boat**

checce, checchia, checchie, checcia, checcie, chece, chechia, checia See **ketch**

checkdeme See **tchektirme**

checking-up boat Term for a boat that carries supporters of a particular crew in a rowing regatta.

cheemahn, cheeman, cheemaun See **tsiman**

Chefsboot See **barge-2**

chefenschaloupe See **chefensslup**

chefensslup *Denmark:* The **ship's boat★** designated for the use of the commanding officer. Spelling variant: **chefenschaloupe**. Note also **canot-2**.

chekdirme See **tchektirme**

chekeleve See **sakoleva**

chektirmè See **tchektirme**

chelabiza See **chalabiya**

cheland, chelande See **chelandia**

chelandia **1.** *Mediterranean:* Oared Byzantine naval vessel comparable to, but smaller than, the **dromon★**. Reported as early as the mid-8th century, and continued as a **galley★** type until the 11th century. Important as a **horse carrier★** into the 13th century, but as a sailing vessel. Also used to transport troops, to defend rivers, and to seek out pirate haunts. Usually considered to have been flat-bottomed, decked; had 1 or 2 banks of oars, a single lateen sail, and carried as many as 150 in crew. Length 42m, beam 7m, depth 4.2m. **2.** *Mediterranean:* From the 11th to the 13th century, the **chelandia** was a round-hulled sailing **merchantman★** often found in the western Mediterranean. Adopted by the crusaders, especially to carry horses. Deep hull, flat floors, rounded ends, castles at bow and stern, quarter rudder. Two masts, setting lateen sails. Foremast stepped well forward and might rake over the bow; the mainmast was stepped in the forward third or just abaft amidships. A 1269 ship was 30.6m long overall, 21.3m on keel, 6.57m wide, 2.73m deep. **3.** A **chelandia** might also be a large **ship's boat★** designed to transport a large number of troops. **4.** *France:* On the Loire River, **chelandia** might denote a small boat.
Spelling variants: **calan(d), calandra, calandre, calendra, celandr(i)a, celandrium, celendria, chaland★, c(h)alannus, chalon(ni)us, chelande, chelandie★, cheland(ion), cheland(r)ium, chelandra, chelandre, chelandrum, chelijs, chelindra, chelindrus, chilandr(i)a, chilandre, chylandria, galander, galandria, galandrie, ghelandre, k(h)elandrion, palandaria, palandárie, palander, palandrána, palandre, palandrea, pálandr(i)a, palandrie★, palandrina, salandr(r)ium, salandr(i)a, salandre, salandr(in)us, schelander, selander, sélandre, selandro, shalandi(yyat), zalandium, zalandria, zélande, zelander, zelandie, zelandriae**. Note also **palandra, shalanda**.

chelandie *France:* Type of river craft used in the early 17th century. Sailed. Note also **chaland**. Further reference: **chelandia**

chelandion, chelandium, chelandra, chelandre, chelandrium, chelandrum, chelijs, chelindra, chelindrus See **chelandia**

chelinga, chelinge, chelingo, chelingue, chellingue See **masula**

cheloup See **sloop-2**

chemahnans, che'man, chē'manis, chē ma'nisis See **tsiman**

chemboke See **kettuvallam-2**

chemmeen vallom See **vallam-1a**

chĕmpĕlong See **chĕmplong, tjemplon**

chĕmplong *Peninsular Malaysia:* Term applied to small, indigenous **dugout canoes★**. Generally sharp at

the ends and deep-bodied. More sophisticated types may have decking aft, weatherboards, and a well or

chĕmplong

small hold forward. Paddled. Name variants: **champlong, chĕmpĕlong**

chemplong See **tjemplon**

chenard See **chênière**

chenbozi See **shen bo zi**

chêne See **chênière**

cheneque See **esnecca**

Chengtu cormorant fishing punt See **lu ci chuan-2**

Chênhai chuan *China, E:* Slender 3-masted **junk★** that accompanied the Zhoushan (Chou-shan or Chusan) Archipelago fishing **fleet★** to carry the iced catch to markets in Ningbo (Ningpo) and Shanghai. Most built at Zenhai (Chênhai). V-shaped bow transom; high, raked oval stern transom. Flat bottom; vertical sides; 5 heavy wales provided longitudinal strength, merging at the ends; sheer strakes at the bow flared out to form an open area. Two holes in the bottom permitted flooding for better riding in head seas. Hatchet-shaped rudder, hung below the bottom. Decked; 5 hatches in the foredeck provided access to fish holds; additional hatches abaft the mainmast, below a raised deckhouse. Generally vividly painted. Foremast in the eyes, raked forward; vertical mainmast about a third in from the bow; both in tabernacles; aft-raking mizzen stepped to starboard, stayed to an outrigger. Each set battened lugsails. In calms, propelled by 2 *yulohs*, special sculling-type oars. Small **sampan★** hung from stern davits. Crew of 10. Length 21m, beam 4.6m, depth 2.4m. Other recorded names: **bing xian chuan, Chusan ice boat, ping-hsien ch'uan (iceboat★), Zenhai chuan**. Note also **green eyebrow**.

chênière *France, central:* **1.** General term for the 19th-century heavily constructed inland waterways freight carriers built of oak (*chêne*). Reported lengths 18-30m; cap. 50-200t. Other recorded names: **barque chênière, camus★, chenard, chêne** **2.** The **chênières** of the upper Loire Basin and the Canal du Centre were similar to the **toue★**. Flat bottom; straight parallel sides that curved in near the bow; closely framed. Square stern; curved flat bow, the bottom planking turning up to cross-planked top strakes. Generally carvel-planked, although the **chênière roannaise** was clinker-planked, reinforced by a stringer. Rudder wide-bladed below the waterline; tiller. Decked at bow, stern decking formed roof of the cabin. On the canal, pulled by 2 men, one on each bank. Other recorded names: **auvergnat★, roannaise★**

chênière roannaise See **chênière**

ch'enpotzu See **shen bo zi**

cheou k'eou ma-yang tse See **shou kou ma yang zi**

cherec See **xebec**

cherme See **djerme**

Chesapeake Bay bugeye See **bugeye**

Chesapeake Bay clipper-schooner See **Baltimore clipper**

Chesapeake Bay crabbing skiff See **crabbing skiff**

Chesapeake Bay log canoe *United States, E:* Long, narrow log-hulled craft used mainly for oyster tonging and crabbing; evolved during the 18th and 19th centuries, becoming a defined sailing type by the 1850s. Also raced by the watermen and bay area residents. A few still built in the 20th century. Early **canoes**★ constructed of 1-2 logs (or chunks), but by the mid-1800s, they were built of 3, 5, or 7 logs. Sharp ends; straight vertical or raked stem, some with a clipper bow; raked sternpost. Hollow waterlines; straight rise to the floors, often with hard bilges; false keel created by a deep plank set on edge; later boats had large centerboards; one or more hiking boards used while racing. Half-decked; width of side decks varied; larger **canoes** had a small portable cuddy for winter. Smaller **canoes** had a single mast, larger stepped two. No standing rigging, and mast rake adjustable. The taller foremast was stepped well forward, the mainmast just abaft amidships; masts struck while working. Some early boats used lateen sails; later boats employed leg-of-mutton sails with horizontal sprits. Racing boats set topsails and square sails. Club-footed sails popular, especially on those that raced. Some set a flying jib, sometimes with a club, run to a bowsprit; might extend a spar at a 40° angle off the bow to which a triangular sail was laced. Engines installed on later boats. Crew mostly 1-3. Reported lengths 3.6-12.2m; e.g., length 8.4m, beam 1.6m, depth 1.0m; shallow draft. Other recorded names: **Chesapeake Bay oyster boat**, **chunk boat**, **cunoe**, **log canoe**, **oyster canoe**. Further reading: M. V. Brewington, *Chesapeake Bay Log Canoes and Bugeyes* (Cambridge, Md.: Cornell Maritime Press, 1963). Note also **brogan**, **chunk boat**. The boats were never standardized, but regional characteristics and construction methods permit grouping into 3 classes:

1. Poquoson canoe. Built in the southwestern part of Chesapeake Bay. Working in more open water than to the north, they tended to be more weatherly, having higher freeboard and a stronger sheer. Hull shaped by eye from logs (2-7) without the addition of further strakes; ends fastened on. The side from which the waterman tonged might have a flatter section. Natural knees supported the side decks. Moderate deadrise. At one period, they had a ram bow, but a clipper bow was more common later. Most stepped a single mast to which a spritted leg-of-mutton sail was set. Jib, to a small bowsprit, often club-footed or boomed. Generally 5-10m long. Other recorded names: **canoe**, **co(o)nner**, **connur**, **cunner**, **cun'r**, **kay-noo**, **kinoo**, **kunnah**, **kunner**★, **Virginia log canoe**

2. Pocomoke canoe. Used along the lower eastern shore of the bay, both in Virginia and southern Maryland. Generally longer, beamier, and lower-sided than those of the western Virginia shore. Usually built from half models, employing 3-5 logs; timbers inserted on completion of the log hull, and a sheer strake added lapstrake-fashion. Stem straight or slightly curved; sternpost straight and raked. Coaming high

and prominent, running nearly full length. In addition to 2 spritted leg-of-mutton sails, a very small forward-raking spar might be rigged forward of the foremast to which a small version of the larger sails was laced. Some single-masted, with jib. Length 10.4m, beam 2m. Other recorded names: **Eastern Shore canoe**, **Nanticoke canoe**, **Pocomoke River canoe**, **rising strake canoe**

3. Tilghman Island canoe. Representative of the upper bay area, these **canoes** had a "longhead" bowsprit assembly, trail boards, billet head or a small figurehead, headrails, a sharply raked sternpost, and taller masts. Raced from the mid-19th century, and developed into a racing class of the 20th century. Generally of 5 logs and built from half models; top strakes were either short log "chunks" pieced together or rising planks fitted edge-to-edge; strengthened by knees and breast hooks. Trimmed to have some drag to the keel. Wide side decks, low coaming. Reported lengths 9.5-9.8m; e.g., length 9.8m, beam 1.5m. Name variant: **Upper Bay canoe**

Chesapeake Bay oyster boat See **Chesapeake Bay log canoe**

Chesapeake Bay oyster schooner See **Chesapeake Bay schooner**

Chesapeake Bay pilot boat See **pilot boat model**

Chesapeake Bay pungy See **pungy**

Chesapeake Bay schooner *United States, E:* Developed ca. 1835 and worked until ca. 1920. Dredged for oysters; when dredging, propelled by a **yawl boat**★. Also served as a **buy boat**★ carrying oysters to Baltimore, New York, and New Jersey, as a freight and produce carrier, and occasionally entered into the fruit trade between Florida and the Bahamas. Fast, with fine entrance and run, maximum beam forward of amidships, carvel-planked, slight to moderate sheer. Raked curved stem; after the mid-19th century, had a clipper bow; fitted with trail boards, headrails, and billets. Wide, square stern, with upper and lower transoms; raked sternpost. Flat floors; large centerboard, replaced by keel by 1840s. Decked, low quarter-deck; trunk cabin. The slower **clump schooner** was more fully built to carry more freight. The 2 masts raked aft; mainmast set to the side opposite the centerboard. Reported lengths 19.2-22.8m; e.g., length 21.6m, beam 6.8m, depth 1.6m; shoal draft. Other recorded names: **centerboard schooner**, **Chesapeake Bay oyster schooner**, **Chesapeake centerboarder**, **Chesapeake schooner**, **schooner**★. Further reference: **Baltimore clipper**

Chesapeake Bay schooner-clipper See **Baltimore clipper**

Chesapeake Bay sharpie See **sharpie-3**

Chesapeake Bay sneakbox See **dink**

Chesapeake Bay terrapin smack See **terrapin smack**

Chesapeake centerboarder See **Chesapeake Bay schooner**

Chesapeake flattie See **flattie-4**

Chesapeake schooner See **Chesapeake Bay schooner**

Chesil Bank lerret See **lerret**

cheytych See **djerme**

chhatákí See **ekta**

chhip *Bangladesh/India, NE:* Long, narrow, swift boat that plies the Ganges and its lower tributaries, including the Sundarbans. Initially the favored craft of pirates who plundered villages along small waterways and attacked slow-moving freight boats on the main rivers. Popular **fish carrier★**, and the larger boats carried perishable produce to market and passengers. Plank-built; little sheer, with stern only slightly elevated. The **fish carriers** propelled by 6 rowers; some boats used as many as 30 oarsmen. One type is a popular racing craft during an August festival in Jessore District of western Bangladesh. Heavily built, with no overhang. Paddled by as many as 100 men, sitting double-banked. Reported lengths 21-30m. Other recorded names: **chiip, dacoit's boat**

chhuan See **chuan**

chiampana See **sampan**

ch'iang hua tzŭ See **qiang hua zi**

Chiangsu freighter See **Kiangsu trader**

ch'iao See **ni mo chuan**

chiao-hua ch'uan See **jiao hua chuan**

ch'iao-yen ch'uan See **nan he chuan**

chia-pan ch'uan See **lorcha-3**

chiatta *Italy:* Term for a **raft★**, **barge★**, **lighter★**, or **dumb barge★**. May serve to off-load ships in ports or transport merchandise, military personnel, or passengers on canals or rivers; or as a **ferry★** (**chiatta del passo**), or for fishing in shallow waters. Flat bottom, no keel, decked or undecked. No mechanical propulsion. Spelling variants: **chjattë**, **ciattë**, **ciattónë**; pl. **chiatte**. Note also **ciatta**, **zattera**.

chiatta carboniera See **coal lighter**

chiatta da zavorra See **ballast barge**

chiatta del passo See **chiatta**

chiatta per trasportare See **ferryboat-1**

chiatte See **chiatta**

chicabaud, chic-à-bos See **chicabot**

chicabot *France, N:* Small lug-rigged boat that fished for herring out of Réville and Barfleur on the northwest coast of Baie de la Seine. Extinct. Clinker-planked, plumb stem, transom stern, flat bottom, outboard rudder. Stepped the foremast in the eyes, the slightly taller mainmast amidships. Mainmast set a standing lugsail, the foremast a dipping lugsail tacked to a jibboom. Spelling variants: **chicabaud, chic-à-bos**; pl. **chicabots, chics-à-bos**

chicabots See **chicabot**

chicken thief See **flatboat-4**

chics-à-bos See **chicabot**

Chiemsee-Plätte See **Plätte-b**

ch'i-fa See **bi fa zi**

chih ch'uan See **chi shuen**

Chihli trader See **Kiangsu trader**

chiip See **chhip**

chikiri-ikada See **kurèki-ikada**

chilandra, chilandre, chilandria See **chelandia**

Chili Bay trader See **Kiangsu trader**

chiling, chilinga, chilingoe See **masula**

Chilmark boat See **Nomans Land boat**

chiman See **tsiman**

chinchorra *Portugal:* Small boat used in casting the *chinchorro* net. See also **chinchorro-2**.

chinchorro **1.** Smallest of the rowed boats aboard some ships, a **jolly boat★**. Generally for 1-2 persons.
2. *Portugal, central:* Boat from Murtosa and other communities on the Ria de Aveiro that uses a *chinchorro* and similar seine nets. Also found as far north as Porto and at points as far south as Nazaré. Flat bottom with rocker; carvel-planked. Long rising bow, recurved stemhead; stern similar but less extreme. Foredeck provides emergency shelter for the crew. Bow and stern decorations like the **moliceiro★**, but **chinchorro** paintings are restricted to religious personages. Tall lugsail set to a mast stepped just forward of amidships.

chinchorro-2

Rudder shipped when sailed. Also rowed with long curved oars and poled. Crew of 2-6. Reported lengths 7.6-10m; e.g., length 8.14m, beam 1.74m, depth 0.5m. Other recorded names: **bateira chinchorro** (or **murtoseira**), **chinchorra★**, **esguicha**, **esguicho**, **murtozeira**; **barco★** (at Porto)
3. *South America, Pacific coast:* A **balsa★** used for fishing by coastal indigenous peoples. Formed by 2 rolls of reeds tied together.
4. *Spain:* Carried aboard or accompanies the **pareja★** to assist in working nets. Open; mainly rowed, but larger types may set a single lateen sail. Reported lengths 5.49-8.84m, widths 1.25-2m, depths 0.41-0.54m.
5. *Spain, Canary Islands:* Raked bow and stern, high stem and sternpost. Uses oars and sets a lateen sail. Crew of 3. Ca. 2t.
Further reference: **bateira do Mondego**

chinchorrohan *Philippines, central:* A type of **banca★** that uses the *chinchorro* seine off the coasts of Iloilo, Capiz, Negros, and Cebu. Dugout hull; strong sheer to narrow overhanging ends that are cut square; full-bodied above the waterline. May have double outriggers consisting of 2 widely spaced booms that attach directly to long floats. Open; short end decks. Paddled; paddles have long shafts with oblong blades. May also be rowed; oars tied to a pole placed parallel to each side or worked against tholepins. Steered with a large paddle or oar. Some set a spritsail. Reported lengths 6-10.7m; shallow draft.

Chinchou chuan See **hong tou san ban**

Chinchow trader See **hong tou chuan**

Chincoteague skiff See **Sinepuxent skiff**

chinedgeran, chinedkeran See **chñedkeran**

chinedkhulan *China, SE:* Narrow, high-ended **fishing boat★** used from the beaches on the island of Lan Yu (Hung-t'ou or Botel Tobago). Plank-built with 4 three-piece strakes on each side, edge fastened; caulked with fiber and coarse putty. Two frames, spaced at about a third and two-thirds of the length, fastened with rattan lashings to longitudinal lugs along one side; 5 horizontal crossmembers serve as thwarts and as lateral thrusts to the flaring sides. Slightly recurved ends may be as high as 2m; ends shaped from buttress roots and scarfed to a narrow keel. Hull a deep "V" in cross section. Wide side decks; bulwarks as high as 23cm. A type with its hull carved and elaborately painted is called an **ipanitika**; one with no carvings is an **ipiroaun**. A long steering oar, set through a circular

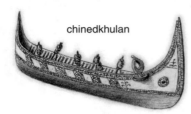

chinedkhulan

rowlock, is used on the quarter. Oarsmen, seated on the side decks, work a single oar (bowman works a pair) secured to a tall rattan grommet. If sailed, employs a violin-shaped sail, with a short horizontal yard on top and a longer boom at the foot. Mast stepped into a hole on the bottom near the bow, stayed aft to the nearest oarlock. Sail originally of matting, later of cotton. Largest require 8-9 in crew. Known lengths 4.6-7.6m; e.g., length 7.5m, width 1.35m, depth 0.75m; early boats reported to 11m. Other recorded names: **Botel Tobago canoe**, **chinurikuran**, **ćineðekulan**. Further reading: E. R. Leach, "Boat Construction in Botel Tobago," *Man* XXXVII (1937), 185-187. Note also **chñedkeran**, **tatara**.

chinedqueran See **chñedkeran**

Chinese dragon boat See **dragon boat-3**

Chinese fishing canoe See **shrimp canoe**

Chinese fishing junk See **lorcha-8**

Chinese seine boat See **phang chun**

Chinese shrimp boat See **shrimp canoe**

ching *United States, SE:* Used for handlining for red snapper off Pensacola in western Florida and adjacent inshore areas. Term applied to a variety of small craft engaged in this fishery. Sail and power. Crew of 5-7. Reported lengths 9-12m. Note also **snapper boat-4**.

chinga See **canoa-14**

chingo See **kü'le-1**, **potro**

chingos See **piragua-2**

ching-pang ch'uan See **jing bang chuan**

ching-pang hua-tzŭ See **hua zi-2**

chinna maram See **catamaran-12**, **periya maram**

chinna padava See **masula**

chinna teppa See **teppa**

Chinook canoe See **West Coast canoe**

chinurikuran See **chinedkulan**

ch'iong See **chuan**

chip *Japan, N:* Term used by the Ainu people of Hokkaidō for their **dugout canoes***. Note also **mochip**, **yachip**. Further reference: **ship**

chip carrier See **timber carrier**

chipe, **chipe de Saint-Suliac** See **ship-4**

Chipewyan canoe *Canada, north-central:* Spruce- or birchbark **canoe*** of the Chipewyan of the area west of Churchill to Great Slave Lake. Stem profile angular at

the foot, tumble home above the outside curve, and flattened across the top. Rather flat sheer but curved up sharply at ends; short end decks. Sides straight and flared; bottom has slight rocker at the ends. Rib spacing varied with type of bark used, ribs might number 30-40; sheathing of short strips; in- and outwales. Occasionally set a small square sail, sometimes a blanket; sapling used as a temporary mast. Reported lengths 3.6-6.7m; e.g., length overall 4.9m, width 1.0m, depth 0.36m. Other recorded names: **tsli**, **tzee**; **kitsi** (birchbark **canoe**). Note also **ghuljai-ts!i**.

chippe See **ship**, **ship-4**

Chippewa canoe, **Chippeway canoe** See **wigwas tsiman**

chi shuen *Hong Kong:* A colorful paper (*chi*) boat made by the boat people at the Chinese New Year. Such boats are set on fire as an offering to the gods of the sea. Other recorded names: **chih ch'uan**, **paper boat***

chitatar, **chitatarro** See **xi-tataru**

chitia See **saettia-2**, **shẹtêya**

chitiha See **shẹtêya**

chi-tong-t'eang *Macau:* Boat on which religious festivals, weddings, etc. were celebrated. Rounded bow and stern; square, upswept gallery aft. Most of hull covered by a house, generally elaborately decorated both inside and out. Crew of 3-8. Towed by a **launch***. Length ca. 16m, beam 4m, depth ca. 0.8m. Other recorded names: **barco de festejos**, **flower boat**. Note also **hua chuan-1**.

Chittagong sampan See **sampan-2**

chiule See **keel**

ch'iu-tzŭ See **qiu zi**

chivo See **canoa-6**

chjattë See **chiatta**

chkof See **skafi**

chkounna See **schooner**

chloup See **chaloupe**

chloupe See **sloup à tape-cul**

chñedkeran *Philippines, N:* Large open boat of Itbayat that provides transportation between islands in the Batan Archipelago, north of Luzon. Accommodates ca. 10 passengers plus the crew of 6-10. Strakes adzed to shape and pegged edge-to-edge; sharp ends. Rowed and sailed. Oars (3-5 per side) worked between double tholepins. Spelling variants: **chinedgeran**, **chinedqueran**, **chinekeran**. Note also **chinedkhulan**.

chneque, **chniaka** See **shnyaka**

chocca, **chocha** See **cog**

cho-gi cham-nan pa *South Korea:* Large 2-masted vessel engaged in netting the popular *cho-gi* fish. Gangways extended ca. 1.2m outboard on each side for the use of the fishermen, who numbered as many as 20. Large rudder. Crew of 25. Length to ca. 22.8m, beam 7.3m, depth 3.7m.

chogi p'asi See **pasi-1**

chombo *East Africa:* In Swahili, general term for a **boat***, **vessel***, or **ship***, ranging from a **dugout canoe*** to a single-masted **dhow***-type vessel that is East African built. In southern dialects, a small **dhow**-type is called a **kičombo**; a large one is a **dyõmbo**. The Zambian **launch***-type **chombo** is used on several lakes to transport fish and passengers. Introduced in the 1930s by Greek traders. Flat bottom. To 60t. Other recorded names: **chambo, cŏmbo, ichombo, kyombo, sambo⋆, sambu, sambwe, tambo**; pl. **ifyambo, vyo**; very large **dhow** might be a **jombo**; pl. **majombo**

chommery See **chasse-marée**

Chongming chuan See **Tsungming chuan**

choonda maram *India, SW:* A **catamaran⋆** of the Kerala coast constructed of 4-5 thin logs; outside logs shaped slightly at the ends. Generally works a seine net in pairs, but may also work singly with hooks and line. Propelled by split bamboo paddles. Crew of 2. Reported lengths 3.6-6m, width ca. 1.0m. Name variant: **maram**

chopping tray See **punt-13**

Choptank River shad skiff *United States, E:* Netted shad, herring, rockfish, and perch on this eastern Chesapeake Bay tributary. Bow sharp, stern sharp or with a narrow transom. Cross-planked flat bottom. Open, narrow side decks. Initially sailed, later employed an outboard or inboard motor. Length ca. 6m, beam 1.5m. Note also **gilling skiff**.

chorwc See **coracle-3**

chouany See **ghurāb**

chrok-che, chrok-lekile See **charigma**

chuan Generic Chinese term for a **boat⋆** or **ship⋆**. Spelling variants: **chhuan, ch'iong, ch'uan, chuen, chun, chuuan, ch'wan, shuen, suēn, sün, tch'ouan, tchuen**

Ch'üanchou Dschunke See **Fukien trader**

chuck boat See **wanigan**

chuen See **chuan**

chu fa See **chu-p'ai**

chu-fa chhuan See **fa zi**

Chukchi skin boat See **kayak-11**

chum boat See **striker boat-2**

chun See **chuan**

Ch'ung-ming ch'uan See **Tsungming chuan**

chunk boat *United States, E:* On Chesapeake Bay, a boat constructed with a log bottom composed of several "chunks," or a boat with major parts, such as the transom, hewn from a log. Found mainly on **bugeyes⋆** and **Chesapeake Bay log canoes⋆**. Name variant: **chunk-built boat**

chunk-built boat See **chunk boat**

chunker *United States, E:* **Barge⋆** that carried coal in the 19th century on the Lehigh River and the Delaware & Raritan Canals from the mines at Mauch Chunk in eastern Pennsylvania. Might run as a 2-section boat. Maximum width 3.2m.

chu-p'ai *China, west coast:* Taiwanese bamboo **raft⋆** used at sea for fishing, for local coastal transport, and in the past for transferring passengers from off-lying ships, especially at Kao-Hsiung (Takow). Smaller, simpler **rafts** ply rivers and lakes. The seagoing craft is constructed of very stout bamboo poles, ranging from 6-14 poles, but mainly 9-11; poles arranged so that the smaller ends are at the front, making the **raft** narrower at the bow. Multiple transverse poles secure the long poles and create a dished effect; smaller poles serve as gunwales and support the tholepins; plastic tubing now popular for the gunwales. Equipped with as many as 6 daggerboards, but generally only 3 employed at a time. Steered with 1-2 sweeps. On those that transferred passengers, a wooden tub was added

for the use of the passengers and/or luggage and a woven weatherscreen might be set up forward; fishing **rafts** have woven mats to hold the nets. A tall pole mast steps into a securely fastened block; sets a chocolate-colored battened lugsail. Also rowed, but now generally motorized. Reported lengths 3.7-12.2m; e.g., length 7m, width 1.2m. Other recorded names: **chu fa, chu-phai, fan fa, katamaran, tek-p'ai, teppai, tray boat**. Further reading: S-S. Ling, "Formosan Sea-Going Raft and Its Origin in Ancient China," *Bulletin, Institute of Ethnology, Academia Sinica* (Taiwan 1956), 1-54. Note also **fa zi**. Further reference: **zhu pai**

chu-p'ai wang See **zhu pai wang**

chu-phai See **chu-p'ai, zhu pai**

chŭ-pŭts See **West Coast canoe**

churchán See **curragh**

church boat A vessel designated to serve as a place of worship, either specially designed for this purpose or a converted **hulk⋆**. Some may have hospital facilities. Term may also apply to a special boat used to transport members of the congregation to a distant church. Other recorded names: **bethel ship, cappella (galleggiante), chapel boat (or hulk), church ship⋆, floating bethel, gospel boat, Kapellenschiff, kerkschip, Kirchenschiff, kyrkbåt⋆**. Note also **boeier-2, kirkebåt, kirkkovene, meeting boat, Methodist canoe, mission boat, mission smack, parish boat**. Further reference: **Adirondack guideboat**

church ship *British Isles:* Vessel used as a place of worship. In the 19th century, converted vessels belonging to religious organizations were anchored at locations on the Thames and various coastal communities. Other recorded names: **chapel ship, floating church**. Note also **church boat**.

Chusan ice boat See **Chênhai chuan**

chuuan, ch'wan See **chuan**

chylandria See **chelandia**

ci *Indonesia, E:* Long, very narrow **dugout canoe⋆** of the Asmat of Irian Jaya. Used for headhunting forays, but also for fishing and collecting sago. Hull spread and tempered by fire; rounded bottom and sides. Pointed, overhanging ends; the bow may have a humped area or elaborately carved recumbent figure. Sides often decorated with vertical stripes. Paddled standing, single file. Reported lengths 12-18m. Name variant: **tiú**

ciampana See **sampan**

ciampane *India, W:* Name given by 15th- and 16th-century explorers to small vessels found on this coast. Rounded bottom. Other recorded names: **ciampanetta** (dim.), **ciampano**. See also **sampan**.

ciampanetta See **ciampane**

ciampanne See **sampan**

ciampano See **ciampane**

ciatta *Italy, NW:* In the Genoa area, a small boat. Note also **chiatta**.

ciattë, ciattóne See **chiatta**

çikirne See **tchektirme**

čiličc See **kelek**

čiliče See **shashah-2**

Cille, Cillen See **Zille**

ĭ·ma·n See **tsiman**
cinagé See **'etea-4**
cinco See **canoa-6**
ĭineðekulan See **chinedkulan**
cingia See **cangia**
cinquante cinquante See **sailer**
ciotaden See **barquette-2**
circus boat *United States:* Plied the Erie Canal in central New York State in the 2nd quarter of the 19th century. The entourage included dormitory, livestock, and equipment boats. Large **circus boats** operated on the Ohio and Mississippi Rivers and some of their tributaries. These had a performance arena with seats. Part of the boat was compartmented into cabins for performers, kitchen, dining room, and cages and stalls for the animals. Pushed from city to city by a **steamboat**.
cisterna See **tanker, water boat-1**
Cisternenschiff See **tanker**
citerne See **tanker, water boat-1**
ciu an See **fassone**
Claddagh hooker See **Galway hooker**
clam boat See **bay boat-3**
clam digger See **clam dredger-1**
clam dredger **1.** Equipped with a hydraulic dredge to commercially harvest soft-shell clams from sandy bottoms. Name variant: **clam digger**
  2. *United States, E:* In Chesapeake Bay since the early 1950s, both conventional **workboats** and special flat-bottomed boats (which compensated for weight of the dredge and conveyor on the starboard side) have been used. Water under pressure cuts a trench in the bottom, and larger objects, such as the clams, are brought by conveyor belt to the boat's side, where the clams are hand extracted. Length ca. 12m.
clammer's dory *United States, NE:* Small, light type of **dory** used on Nantucket Island and Cape Cod in southeastern Massachusetts by clam diggers, and sometimes by inshore fishermen. Lapstrake planking; straight flared sides; narrow flat bottom with rocker; sharp, raked stem; narrow V-shaped transom. Rowed. One-man boat. Length overall 5m, beam across the top 1.2m, across bottom 0.76m, depth 0.46m. Name variant: **Nantucket dory**. Note also **mud sled**.
clamming boat See **mussel boat-4**
clamming skiff *United States, NE:* Sought shellfish, primarily clams, and fish off the Connecticut coast. Dated from the 19th century. Heavily built, carvel planking. Flat bottom; after two-thirds had strong rocker toward the shallow raking transom; slight rocker toward the sharp plumb stem; when light, both stem and stern were above water. Mainly open; small foredeck; narrow side decks, with coaming, along the after two-thirds. Mainly rowed, but might set a small sail. One-man boat. Length 4.6m, beam ca. 1.5m, maximum depth, at stem, ca. 0.15m.
clam skiff See **hand-raker's clam skiff**
Claremont canoe See **tango-1**
Claspar-built boat See **outrigger**
Clayton skiff See **Saint Lawrence skiff**
cleanser boat See **hopper-1**
clee hollaga See **cliath thulca**
cleftrine See **cocoreli**

clene coghe See **cog**
Clevedon boat See **Weston-super-Mare flatner**
cliath thulca *Ireland, central:* **Reed boat** of the River Suck area. Used mainly during winter floods, and for fishing and wildfowling. Extinct. Construction details varied locally and with the skill of the builder. One type was composed of 2 bundles of reeds, narrow at the bow, wider toward the stern. An open, boat-shaped lath framework contained the bundles and provided sides on which to fasten the tholepin for rowing. A reed or wooden seat was set athwartships. Some used wickerwork around the sides to contain the reeds rather than a wood frame. Length ca. 1.5m. Name variant: **clee hollaga**
'cliff boat See **barracouta boat**
clinker eight See **shell-2**
clinker four See **shell-1**
Clinton's Ditch scow See **scow-11**
cliper See **clipper**
clipper A sailing ship specifically designed for speed; only those that proved to be fast were correctly called **clippers**. The **clipper** era was between 1840 and 1870; mainly built in the United States and the United Kingdom. Term not used prior to this time, but the so-called **Baltimore clipper** is considered a prototype for the later true **clippers**. Hulls varied with the attempts to gain speed, but all were narrow, sharp-lined, usually concave-bowed, deep-hulled, with drag to keel; flush-decked. A **clipper** with extra-sharp lines, built until 1855, might be called an **extreme clipper**. Various rig types used, but best known are the 3-masted, square-rigged ships. Streamlining the hull reduced cargo space and heavy canvassing required large crews, so **clippers** carried mainly high-value cargoes, e.g., opium, tea, and wool, and some engaged in the slave trade. Keel lengths 51-92m; length-to-beam ratio 5:1 or 6:1. The **half** (or **medium**) **clipper**, popular in the United States during the 1870s and 1880s, was slower but could carry more cargo. Smaller than the true **clippers**, they worked secondary routes. Other recorded names: **cliper, clipper-ship, kliper(nava), klipper, Klipperschiff, klipperskepp, skyscraper, Halbklipper, half-clipper barque**. Further reading: David R. MacGregor, *Fast Sailing Ships: Their Design and Construction, 1775-1875* (Lymington: Nautical Publishing Co., Ltd., 1973). Note also **California clipper, clipper-schooner, opium clipper, tea clipper**.
clipper banker *United States, NE:* Mid-19th-century **fishing boat** popular for mackerel fishing where speed was important. Had features of the **clipper-schooner** but was less sharp. Further reference: **banker**
clipper barge See **luff barge**
clipper dory See **Nahant clipper dory, Shelburne clipper dory, Swampscott dory**
clipper fisherman, clipper fishing schooner See **clipper-schooner**
clipper-goélette See **Baltimore clipper**
clipper-pinky See **pinky**
clipper-schooner **1.** *Canada, E/United States, NE:* Type of **market schooner** developed to provide rapid transport of freshly caught fish to markets along the northeast coast. Worked mainly out of Gloucester,

Massachusetts; in winter, these vessels might carry oysters from Chesapeake Bay. Replaced the earlier **clipper-schooners** that were built in Baltimore and often went to Cape Cod for oysters. Predominated for ca. 25 years, lasting until the 1880s. Beamier, with lower freeboard than other **schooners** of the period. Hollow bow and stern and long hollow run. Heavy concave bow; stem slightly raked, with curved forefoot; shallow counter stern, vertical sternpost. Long straight keel with some drag; moderate to slight rise to the floors, commonly with hard bilges; vertical or slight tumble home to the sides. Decked; trunk cabin on quarter-deck. Hull painted black and/or dark green, often with stripes along the sheer in red, white, or yellow. Heavily canvassed, with a very large mainsail. Fore and main topmasts, which, with the long jibboom, were unshipped for winter fishing. Staysail with bonnet and club; large jib and jib topsail. Reported lengths 18-30m; e.g., length 21.6m, beam 6.8m, depth 1.6m; shallow draft. Other recorded names: **clipper fisherman**, **clipper fishing schooner**, **Klipergoleta**. Note also **clipper banker**, **sharpshooter**.

2. *United Kingdom:* Developed in the 1820s for use in transporting highly perishable fruit, particularly pineapples from the West Indies; also engaged in opium trade (**opium clipper★**). Length-to-beam ratio greater than that of the American **clipper-schooner**, maximum beam farther aft, less rise to the floors, little drag to the keel. Rabbet at the bow followed the rake of the stem to form the characteristic clipper bow. Hollow lines. Large square foresail below square topsails; loose-footed, boomed gaff sail to fore- and mainmast. Yard topsail on mainmast. 1838 vessel 18.2m long, 4.8m wide, 2.5m deep. Note also **fruit schooner**. Further references: **Baltimore clipper**, **sharpshooter-2**

clipper ship See **clipper**
clipper skiff See **cabin skiff**
closed mouth ma-yang tzŭ See **shou kou ma yang zi**
cloth boat See **narrow boat**
Clovelly picarooner See **picarooner**
clump schooner See **Chesapeake Bay schooner**
Clyde gravel smack *Scotland, W:* Small **coaster★** of the Clyde Estuary that specialized in transporting gravel. Built of wood, iron, or steel; rounded bottom; plumb stem; counter stern. Decked. Set a gaff sail and jib; later, auxiliaries installed. Crew of 2-3.
Clyde nabbie See **nabbie**
Clyde puffer See **gabbart-3**
cnarr See **knarr-1**
coaching gig See **Thames gig**
coalannito See **barca di guardia-1**
coal barge See **coal lighter**
coal boat See **broadhorn**, **coal box**, **dao ba zi**, **red bow**, **shen chuan**
coal box 1. *England, central:* On some canals, **narrow boats★** were loaded with as many as a dozen boxes filled with coal. On a section of the Bridgewater Canal, the **coal boxes** were part of a **fleet★** of maintenance craft. Note also **box boat-1**.
2. *United States, central:* Originally a lightly constructed wooden **barge★** that carried coal down the Ohio and

Mississippi Rivers from the Pittsburgh area. Sold with the cargo at its destination. Square ends, slightly overhanging; flat bottom. Later of steel. Reported lengths 24-53m; e.g., length 53m, beam 8m, depth 3-3.7m. Name variant: **coal boat**
coal brig See **collier-2**
coal bunker *United States, E:* Carried coal in the early 19th century on the Delaware and Hudson Canal in eastern Pennsylvania to the Hudson River. Sharp ends, flat floors. Decked at bow and stern; small cabin aft; open waist generally but might be covered by hatches. Length 28m, beam 1.2m, depth 1.8m. Large boats carried 40t; smaller boats that increased their capacity by building up the sides were known as **hipped boats**. Further name variant: **Delaware and Hudson barge**
coal carrier See **collier-1**
coal cat See **cat-2**, **collier-2**
coal flat See **broadhorn**
coal gabbart See **gabbart-3**
coalier See **collier**
coalinna See **corallina**
coal keel See **Tyne keel**
coal lighter **Barge★** or **lighter★** that transferred coal (generally in sacks) from off-lying **colliers★** to the quay or beach. On the east coast of the United States, coal was hauled in cut-down **schooners★**; more recently coal was transported by **tug-barges** from ports on Chesapeake Bay to powerplants along the coast. Other recorded names: **chaland de charbon**, **charbonnière**, **chiatta carboniera**, **coal barge**, **Kohlenkahn**, **Kohlenleichter**. Note also **coal box**, **Tyne keel**, **Tyne wherry**.
coalman See **collier-1**
coal schooner *United States, E:* Coal sent by **canal barge★** and rail to Georgetown and Alexandria, near Washington, D.C., was often transshipped by **schooner★** to northern ports during the latter part of the 19th century. Smaller **schooners** from other coal terminals on the western side of the Chesapeake Bay supplied coal to towns and factories on both sides of the bay. Many carried coal from bay ports to the West Indies. Coal carried loose in the holds. Most 4- to 5-masters. A 700t burden vessel carried 500t coal. Further reference: **collier-2**
coal scow See **scow-7**
coal scuttle, **coal ship** See **collier-1**
coal slacker *England, central:* Special **barge★** for carrying coal on the upper Trent system. Built with the largest hold capacity possible; no accommodations.
coal smack *Scotland, W:* Carried coal to larger communities in the Loch Fyne area from Glasgow and Ardrossan. These were often surplus fishing craft. Worked until the 1920s. The coal was discharged at a jetty or into small boats to be carried to the beach. Lengths ca. 11m.
coal supply ship See **collier-1**
coal trow See **trow-1**
coastal defense ship See **coast guard ship**
coastal motor boat See **scooter-2**
coastal packet *Canada, E/United States, E:* Vessel of the late 18th and 19th centuries (and until World War I in the Canadian Maritime Provinces). Sailed on an

advertised schedule carrying passengers and freight supplied by the public rather than on the owner's account. Generally built for the trade, they were fast sailers. Cabin aft; passenger accommodations on vessels making longer trips; some equipped to handle horses and carriages. Usually a **schooner*** or **sloop***, but some were square-rigged; heavily canvassed. Lengths generally under 30m. Other recorded names: **constant trader, schooner packet, water stage**. Note also **packet boat**.

coastal patrol vessel, coast defense ship See **coast guard ship**

coaster A small cargo vessel that generally trades along the coast of its home country, usually staying within sight of land. In the United States, the term may include vessels in the West Indies trade. Usually have their own cargo-handling gear, and may take cargo directly from oceangoing ships. Sail or motor-powered. Selected name variants: **barco costeño, buque costero, caboteur*, cabotier(o), cabotor, coast hugger** (a small type), **coasting vessel, costero, costiere, cotier*, cot(t)ière, cottere, coutière, kabotazhnoe sudno, kustboot, Küstenfahrer, Küsten(segel)-fahrzeug, Küsten(segel)schiff, kustfarare, kust-fartyg, kustvaarder, kystfartøj**. Note also **borneur**.

coast-guard cruiser, coast-guard cutter See **revenue cutter-1**

coast guard ship Small, fast, armed vessel, of no specific type, that guards coastal waters against illegal activities. May have special duties in wartime. In the West Indies in the 17th century, they were assigned to preserve the Spanish monopoly in that area. Selected name variants: **buque de guarda-costas, coast(al) defense ship, coastal patrol vessel, coast guard vessel, garde coste, garde côte(s), guarda-coasta, guardacosta(s), guardacostes, guard de costa, Küstenschutzschiff, Küstenwach(t)schiff, Küsten-wächter, navire guard côtes**. Note also **balandra, fishery guard ship, patache-2b, revenue cutter**.

coast guard vessel See **coast guard ship**

coast hugger See **coaster**

coasting schooner *United States, SE:* Served the riverine and coastal plantations of the Carolinas from the late 17th to mid-19th century. Carvel-planked of pine, frames of live oak and cypress. Flat bottom, plank or shallow keel. Transom stern. May have used leeboards. Beamy, shallow draft, 20-50t. See also **freighter-4**.

coasting vessel See **coaster**

Coast Salish canoe *Canada, SW/United States, NW:* **Dugout canoe*** of the Coast Salish Native Americans, characterized by a long overhanging bow with a horizontal notch cut in below the gunwale and a sharp cutwater below the overhang. Used primarily in the Strait of Georgia, Puget Sound, and the lower and middle Fraser River, mainly for transportation and carrying supplies. Gone by the mid-20th century. Dugout hull expanded by pouring water over hot rocks. Overhanging stern raked up in a slightly convex line from the bottom. Moderate sheer; deep sheer "strake" cut into the dugout hull served as a kind of sponson; sides flared below; thwarts rested on the inner part of

this "strake"; shallow gunwale strip added on. Flattened bottom might be slightly deeper near the bow; sat low in the water, especially at the stern. Hull rubbed with oil or fish eggs. Used a pointed-blade paddle. Sometimes sailed. Reported lengths 7.6-10.7m; e.g., length 8.4m, beam 1.0m. Other recorded names: **Salish canoe; nukwil** (or **nakwiL, nokwil**) by mainland Coast Salish; **yiceLt** (or **yichelt, yishelt**) by the Salish of Vancouver Island; **xwagelitcim** (or **Xwo'kintcîm**) on the middle Fraser River; **sdǎwēlth** by the Upper Skagit. Note also **sda'kwihl, tl'ai**.

cobble See **coble-1, coble-6**

cob boat See **cog boat**

coberta *Brazil, central:* Transported cargo and merchandise in the Amazon Basin. Planked up from a minimal dugout base, strengthened with frames; flooring above the waterline. Elongated bow narrowed to blunt end; overhanging stern, raked above the waterline. Wood and palm structures formed cabins forward and aft or amidships. Undecked except for narrow space between the houses for cooking area. Rudderpost extended up through poop roof to tiller. One or 2 masts, lug- or spritsails on each; sometimes a square topsail. When rowed, oarsmen might stand on roof of forward cabin. Reported lengths 8.8-13.2m, widths 2.2-3.3m, depths 1.1-1.6m. Other recorded names: **canoa coberta, cuberta**

cobil, cobill See **coble-1**

coble 1. *England, NE:* Open **beach boat*** with a long ancestry, that still operates in some areas; now primarily motorized. Concentrated during the latter part of

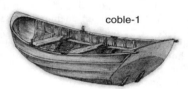

coble-1

the 19th and early 20th centuries from central Northumberland to just north of the Humber Estuary, although some were used as far south as Yarmouth. Within this stretch of coast, there were subtle differences in the boats, and even within the same community, function created different size classes. Large **cobles** (ca. 12m long) were used mostly for herring drifting, medium sizes (ca. 8m) for longlining, and small ones (under 7m) for salmon fishing and as **tenders*** and **pilot boats***. Clinker-built with broad strakes; marked tumble home on the top strake for most of its length. Those with 3 strakes on the bottom and 3 on the side were called **three-stroke cobles**. Forward part of **coble** wineglass-shaped with ample flare to bows. Stem height almost twice that of the stern; sheer nearly straight almost to amidships, then curves up strongly to the stern. Most types have a sharply raked, narrow transom stern; some double-ended. Stem slightly inclined on top, curvature increased to below the waterline and then flattens out and runs straight to midships to form a deep forefoot. Plank or ram keel continues aft and floors become flat; ironshod bilge keels run from forward of amidships to the stern and curve up around the transom for a short distance. Beached types usually hang a narrow rectangular rudder that extends well below the bottom, but a shorter one in summer; easily unships on grounding; long tiller. Tiny cuddy on larger boats; modern motorized **cobles** decked forward; transom board at stern; some have a wheelhouse. Early motorized **cobles** generally **four-strake cobles**, with 4 strakes on the bottom only or 4 on side and bottom. Most single-masted, with tanned dipping lugsail. A 2nd shorter mast might be used when sail reefed or as a temporary bowsprit when setting a jib. Weatherboard, between the transom and after thwart, shifted to windward on a new tack and the sandbag ballast placed between the board and the weather side. Southern **cobles** had a single mast step, northern boats three; mast raked aft; no standing rigging. Larger **cobles** and the **herring mule** used a mizzen sheeted to an outrigger, and a bowsprit for the jib. Rowed with narrow-bladed oars, pivoted over a single tholepin, using a push stroke, two men to starboard, one on port quarter. Launched from the beach bow-first, landed stern-first, the deep forefoot swinging the stern inshore. Other recorded names: **cobble, cobil(l), cobyll, copill, couple, cutwater, kobil, Filey coble, Northumberland** or **Northumbrian coble; Scarborough coble; Whitby coble**

Various types went by special names, a few of which follow: **a. big coble**: Either a large or medium-sized **coble**. Used mainly for longlining and beam trawling, to service ships offshore, and later primarily for pleasure. Square ends; cuddy forward; carried a **corf**★ when longlining for cod. Crew of 3 men and a boy. Typically 10.7m long overall, 7.37m (on ram), beam 2.74m. **b. corf**: A **tender** to a big **coble**, **mule**★, or **yawl**★. Generally a small **coble** but might be a tubby, square-sterned, clinker-built boat with a keel. Would also tow a big **coble** in port or when wind failed. Usually built with 3 side strakes. Carried 3 men. Reported lengths 3.66-4.88m. Other recorded names: **calf, cauf, corfe. c. herring coble**: Name used in the harbor at Filey for a large double-ended boat that mainly drifted. Ram keel initially, later a true keel, consequently sometimes called **mules**. Cuddy forward. Set a dipping lug mainsail and sometimes a mizzen. Reported lengths overall 8-12.8m, beam ca. 4m. Name variant: **Filey herring coble. d. mule**: Sharp-sterned **coble**, used primarily for herring drifting at Scarborough, Filey, Staithes, and Sea Houses; also popular with pilots. The **Scarborough mule** was often varnished above with a white or blue bottom; in

coble-1d

summer took out pleasure parties; gone by 1920. Stern sharply raked. Built with either a ram keel or a true keel, curving up toward the stern. Deep rudder. Normally set a single narrow dipping lugsail. Crew of 4-5. Reported lengths overall 8-12.2m; e.g., length 10m, beam 3m, depth 1.4m. Also called **burro**★, **fiman boat, five-man coble, five-men boat, fyve-man coble, herring coble, herring mule, hulk**★, **mule coble, plosher, splosher** (see **splosher** below). Note also **double-ender-2. e. salmon coble**: A small, heavy **coble** used from May to late August. Generally sailed single-handed. Reported lengths overall 6.9-10.7m, the smaller working inshore; e.g., length overall 6.91m, on the ram 4.88m, beam 1.83m. **f. splosher**: A large square-sterned **coble** used mainly for herring drifting at Staithes. The ram keel turned up at the stern. Manned by 3 men when drifting, 2 when lining or crabbing, and when fully manned was rowed by 6 men. Attachment to the oar loom slotted over a tholepin. Set a high-peaked lugsail. Reported lengths overall 9-9.75m, on the ram 7-7.3m. Also spelled **splasher** or **plosher**; further variant: **Staithes herring drifter. g. winter coble**: A medium-sized **coble** used at Bridlington until the 1930s. Primarily double-ended. Worked longlines and trawls. No shelter. Set a single lugsail unless trawling, when mizzen might be added. Laid up in summer. Reported lengths overall 8-9.14m, on the ram 5.79-6.1m. **h. winter fishing coble**: Filey name for a square-ended open **coble**. Launched from a pair of wheels drawn by horses originally, now by tractor. Crew of 3 when working under sail, 2 when tending pots and once they were motorized. Length overall 8.53m, beam 2.13m. Further reading: J. E. G. McKee, ed., *The English Coble* (Greenwich: National Maritime Museum, 1978).

2. *England, E:* A type of small boat carried aboard 17th- and 18th-century **cod smacks**★. Two men shot and hauled the baited lines.

3. *Scotland:* Local term for a **ferryboat**★.

4. *Scotland, E:* **a.** Small, open **fishing boat**★, used mainly for salmon netting from May to August; also employed

coble-4a

in line fishing on rivers and lakes. Clinker-built with broad strakes; fitted with 3-piece frames. Hull generally deeper forward; bottom flat-floored, generally with rocker; plank keel forward, keelless aft. Some now of fiberglass. Strongly raked and curved stem; wide, vertical square stern, now often sharp-ended. Transom board at stern. Propelled by 4-6 oars, double-banked; oars pivot on single tholepins. Some employ a standing lugsail. Engines now often installed or a small outboard used. Reported lengths 3-9m; length of 4-oared **coble** 6.8m, beam at gunwale 2.6m, depth 0.75m. Other recorded names: **cowble, culaidh**★, **eathar, salmon cobble, salmon coble**★, **Scottish coble. b.** In the Tweed Estuary, a smaller **salmon coble** with a rounded bottom is used. Clinker-built; beached boats may be double-planked. Bow slightly raked and upturned. Flat sheer except forward. Platform at wide stern holds the net. Those used on the upper part of the estuary are propelled by a single pair of oars, while those at the mouth use 2 pairs. Reported lengths 4.3-6m, the shorter used upriver. The **sea coble**, ca. 6.7m long, worked along the coast off the estuary mouth. Other recorded names: **Berwick sea salmon coble**; **punt★** (at Spittal)

5. *Scotland, W:* Worked with a bag net in the West Highlands, especially on the Isle of Skye. Wide wine-glass transom, rounded bottom. Open. Rowed with 4 oars; oar loom fitted with an iron gudgeon slotted over a single tholepin. Now motorized. Crew of 4. Name variant: **bag-net coble**

6. *Virgin Islands, American and British:* Small **sailboat★** used locally in Tortola and in others of the Virgin Islands. Some specialize in carrying charcoal. Term used from at least the early 19th century. Sets a mainsail and jib tacked to the stem. Crew of 2. Other recorded names: **cobble, Tortola coble**

Further references: **foyboat, Hartlepool pilot coble, salmon coble, Wye coracle**

cobyll See **coble-1**
coca See **cock boat-1, cog**
cocca, coccae, coccha, cocche See **cog**
cocchetta, cocchina See **cog-2**
coccho, cocco See **cog**
coccona, coccone See **cog-2**
cocghe See **cog**
cocha See **coche, cog**
cocham See **cog**
coche 1. In French, an inland **barge★** or **track boat★**. Spelling variant: **cocha**. Note also **coche du Rhône**.
2. *Angola:* Small, indigenous cargo vessel.
3. *Mozambique:* Large, light boat with strong bottom rocker.
Further references: **coche d'eau, cog**
coche d'eau *France:* Passenger and merchandise **barge★** that plied rivers on a regular schedule until the early 20th century; one reserved exclusively for passengers was called a **diligence d'eau**. Bow elongated and overhanging; narrow square counter stern; flat bottom. Decked; large central cabin; some carried as many as 100 passengers who usually stayed ashore at an inn overnight. Employed a very heavy, wide-bladed rudder, which sometimes came up through the stern house, and an exceptionally long tiller. Generally towed by horses from a central towing mast. Reported lengths 25-30m, beam 5m. Other recorded names: **bateau coche, coche★, patache★**. Note also **bateau mouche, cabane, flûte-2, flyboat-3a, galiot-4, Wasser-Diligence**.
coche du Rhône *France, S:* **Barge★**-type vessel that transported merchandise on the river, mainly between Lyons and Avignon. Bottom flat with sharp rocker to a small, high bow transom. Full lines at the stern. Strong sheer. Decked except forward; low house. Massive rudder with wide blade; long tiller. Maneuvered with a sweep at the bow and amidships.
cochère *France, E/Switzerland, W:* Small open boat of Lake of Geneva (Lake Léman). Early boats hauled

firewood. Flat bottom, flaring sides, high sheer forward, straight raking bow, square stern. Small cuddy forward; 2 rowing thwarts between the masts; on the later boats, the decking extended to the mainmast and the forward thwart was omitted. Two very large lateen sails set to masts of about equal height. Foremast stepped in the bow, mainmast a little forward of amidships. When necessary, rowed with long oars, one to each thwart. Called **cochère** or **corsaire** from at least the 15th century to the mid-19th century. Cap. 15-40t. Other recorded names: **barque cochère, corseyre, coursière**; small type used for fishing called a **naus**. Note also **barque du Léman**.
cochet See **coquet**
cochetta See **cog-2**
cochina Cited in the early 15th century as a small boat. Spelling variant: pl. **cochinae**. See also **cog-2**.
cochinae See **cochina**
Cochin bandar manché, Cochin manché See **manji**
cochis, cocho See **cog**
cock *England, south coast:* Used at Brighton in the 16th century, particularly for herring fishing but also for inshore mackerel fishing. Sailed. Crew of 6. 2-6t. Spelling variants: **cok★, kog, kogge★**. Further references: **cock boat-1, cog, coggle**
cocka See **cog**
cock boat 1. A small open boat that provides ship-to-shore communication from a **yacht★** or small vessel; in some places refers merely to small boats used on rivers and protected waters. Usually rowed but sometimes sailed. Early British navy **cock boats** employed as many as 12 oars and were steered by a cockswain (now coxswain). Term used from at least the early 15th century; synonymous with **yawl★** in early days. Other recorded names: **coca, cock★, cocke, cockle boat, cockleshell, cog★, cog boat★, cogbo(o)te, cogge, coggle★, cok★, cokke, cok(ke)bote, cook boat, coque, coquet★**. Note also **Fenland lighter, Mersey flat, tender**.
2. *England, SW:* At Sennen, assisted the pilchard **seine boats★**. The **cock boats** of Mounts Bay transferred fish from the mackerel seine nets to shore.
3. *England, W:* **a.** The **flats★** of the Mersey Estuary carried or towed a **cock boat**; called a **punt★** at Liverpool and Birkenhead. Served as a **lifeboat★** and aided in handling lines. Carvel-planked; wide transom stern. Sculled. Length 4m, beam 1.6m, depth 0.6m. **b.** Public **ferry★** on the Manchester Ship Canal. Some were large enough to carry horses and a wagon. Sculled.
Further references: **lurker, perahu ayam**
cocke See **cock boat-1, coggle**
cockle 1. Colloquial term for a small, shallow shell-like boat. Name variant: **cockle boat**. Note also **cockleshell**.
2. A 2-man collapsible boat used by the British Royal Marines in World War II to enter enemy-held rivers and estuaries in order to attach mines to ships.
3. *England:* Term applies in some areas, notably on the east coast, to any boat that collected cockles. Those working in The Wash were either double-ended or had a square counter stern. Low freeboard aft; straight stem; clinker- or carvel-built; generally open. Usually

towed a large **rowboat★** that grounded on the cockle sandbanks at low tide. Loose-footed, boomed gaff sail with 2 headsails; running bowsprit. Now mainly motorized. Crew of 4. Reported lengths 9-12m; e.g., length 11m, beam 3.4m, draft 1.0m. Name variants: **cockle boat, cockler**

cockle boat See **cock boat-1, cockle, cockle galley**

cockle-fishing boat See **hong rou chuan**

cockle galley *England, SE:* Fast, shallow-draft centerboard boat, built on the general lines of the **bawley★**, that raked up cockles in the Thames Estuary, especially out of Leigh on the north shore. Very strong bottom and flat floors enabled it to dry out at low tide; carvel- or clinker-planked. Square stern with rake to sternpost; plumb straight stem. Raised foredeck; limited accommodations in the forecastle. Large open well; on some a movable bulkhead down the midline kept the cockles from shifting, otherwise the centerboard case served this purpose. Some were old naval **galleys★**. Set a lofty, loose-footed, boomless mainsail with a long gaff; foresail, working jib. Auxiliaries added after World War I, becoming fully powered after 1945, and by 1967, mechanical dredging had replaced over-the-side raking. Crew of 3-4. Reported lengths 7-12m; typically 8.5m long, 2.7m wide, 0.76m draft. Other recorded names: **cockle boat, cockler, cockler galley, Leigh cockle galley, Leigh cockler, Muschelkratzer**. Note also **cockle-3**.

cockler See **cockle, cockle galley**

cockler galley See **cockle galley**

cockleshell A light, often cranky boat. Other recorded names: **cascarón de nuez, Nußschale, Seelenverkäufer**. See also **Adirondack guideboat, cock boat-1**.

cocko, coco See **cog**

cocoreli *Greece, S:* Trader, mainly from Maní and the Khóra Sfakíon area in southwestern Crete. A small version, the **cleftrine**, was a local pirate's craft. Double-ended, strong sheer, slightly curved stem with high stemhead, tall rudder. Temporary weathercloths

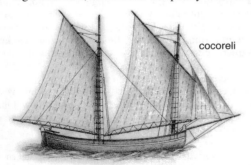

cocoreli

raised the sides. Mainmast, stepped close to the bow, set a large boomed lugsail; mizzenmast stepped about a third in from the stern, setting a boomed gaff sail. Slender, rising bowsprit held 2 headsails. Length ca. 15m. Other recorded names: **kokkoreli, malteza(na), thieves' boat**

cocquet See **coquet**

codbanger *England, E:* Term given to 19th-century **cod smacks★** that had live wells. When sold in port, the cod would be killed with a bludgeon known as a cod-

knocker. Most were **cutters★**; later larger boats were **ketch★**-rigged.

cod boat See **codling boat**

codco See **cog**

cod cutter *England, E:* A popular type of **cod smack★** along east coast ports in the 18th century. Fished for cod off the Suffolk and Norfolk coasts in December, on the Dogger Bank from January to April, and off Iceland and the Faroe Islands the remainder of the year. Fish kept fresh in a live well. **Cutter★**-rigged. Crew of 8. Length to ca. 24m.

cod dory See **Banks dory**

cod fisher See **cod-fishing boat**

cod-fishing boat One that engages principally in hand or longline fishing for cod. Originally worked under sail, usually using **dories** (see **dory**) for the actual fishing; now a motorized vessel. Other recorded names: **bacalhoeiro★, barge à morue, barque morutière★, cod fisher, cod hooker, morutier★, Steinfischer, Stockfischfangboot, Stockfischfänger, torskebåt**. Note also **baccalieu skiff, banker, codbanger, cod cutter, codling boat, codman, cod smack, Oostendse sloep, terreneuvier, torskegarnsbåt, torsköka**.

cod hooker See **cod-fishing boat**

codling boat *Scotland, Shetland Islands:* Sharp-ended open boat that sought codling, a small cod. A type of **sixareen★**. Constructed with 7 lapped strakes per side. Rowed and sailed, setting a low-peaked, dipping square sail with a very long yard. Length on keel ca. 5m. Name variant: **cod boat**

codman *England, E:* **Smacks★** that engaged in handlining for cod out of Grimsby. Those fishing in the late 19th century had a crew of 10. Further reference: **cod smack-1**

cod-net boat See **fembøring-1**

cod-seine boat See **cod-seine skiff**

cod-seine skiff *Canada, E:* Employed along the Newfoundland coast to set and haul cod-seines. Catch might be carried ashore by a **buyer boat★**. Open; sharp, curved, raking stem; transom stern. Nets stowed aft. Mainly rowed, single-banked, with 6 oars. Might also sail. Crew of 6-7. Reported lengths 7.6-9m, beam ca. 2.4m. Other recorded names: **cod-seine boat, cod-seine skift**

cod-seine skift See **cod-seine skiff**

cod's head A fishing vessel with its beam well forward, like a cod fish. Those that also have a slender stern are said to be cod-headed and mackerel-tailed.

cod smack *England, E/Scotland:* **1.** Welled vessel that line-fished for cod in the North Sea and off Iceland. Worked mainly out of ports in the Thames Estuary, Essex, and Suffolk during the 18th-19th centuries. An active **fleet★** worked out of the Shetlands and east coast Scottish ports. Some, such as the **Barking smacks**, served as **fish-carriers** and later engaged in Mediterranean fruit trade. Cod caught early in a voyage were salted; at the end of a trip, the live fish were put in the well. Mainly carvel-planked to permit easier boring of holes for the wet well. Generally a counter stern; decked; davit over the bow for securing the anchor stock. Two watertight athwartship bulkheads contained sea water. The **ship's boat**★, used in hauling the line, also had a wet well. Mainly single-masted, setting a loose-footed or boomed gaff sail, 2-3 headsails, and a topsail. In the latter part of the 19th century, a small lug or gaff mizzen was added to longer vessels. A square sail and square topsail were set to the mainmast when running before the wind. Steam employed in the latter part of the century. Crew of 8-12, plus 2-4 boys. Reported lengths 12-27m; e.g., length 14m, beam 4.4m, depth 3.4m. Other recorded names: **Aldeburgh smack**, **Barking well smack**, **cod cutter**, **liner**★, **welled smack**. Note also **coble-2**, **codbanger**, **codman**, **smack**.

2. Some early **Harwich smacks** set 2 large lugsails. Having 5 in crew (plus a cook), they were called **five-men boats**.

3. In the mid-19th century, the **cod smacks** fishing center moved northward to Grimsby, where the fish could, by that time, be shipped by rail to London. The **Grimsby smacks** were initially **cutter**★-rigged, but by the 1870s, most were **ketches**★. The sailing **smacks** that served as **fish-carriers** from the fishing grounds were called **cutters**, regardless of rig. Counter stern, plumb stem, deep drag to the keel. Carried a beamy **boat** on the starboard deck for use in transferring the catch to a **fish-carrier**. Characteristically, the forestay ran from the collar of the mizzenmast to the deck for a mizzen staysail. Crew of 9-11. Length of ketches ca. 23-25m.

cod-trap boat See **Saint John's trap boat**, **trap skiff**

coff *Australia, Tasmania:* Boat-shaped craft pierced to hold live crayfish awaiting transport to market. Sharp at one end so it will point up into the current and wind. Several moored in a line. Hold 16-20 dozen crayfish. Note also **corf**, **fish car**. Further reference: **kof**

coffin boat See **fei teng**, **guan cai chuan**, **sinkbox**

coffin brig See **packet boat-1**

coffin ship A vessel lacking adequate safety features. Term applied especially to worn-out vessels that were intentionally overloaded to cause foundering in order to collect insurance. Others were exceptionally narrow and prone to capsizing. Note also **Newfoundland coffin**. Further reference: **timber drogher-1**

cog 1. A principal ship type of northern Europe from the late 12th to the 15th century, but reported built as far south as northern Spain. Mainly a capacious merchant vessel but also a **man-of-war**★ and troop carrier; survived as a Dutch inland trader until the 17th century. Initially clinker-built sides; flat, flush-laid bottom; later fully carvel-planked; no keel or plank keel; heavy crossbeams; deck beams pierce side planking. Deep, full hull on later **cogs**; sharp chines initially; each frame supported bottom and one side. Sharp, long, straight raked ends, curved on English vessels; sternpost the taller. Steering oar, then long stern rudder. High-sided. Usually decked, but some small types undecked; later vessels had castles forward and aft to serve as platforms for dispatching armament; high gunwales. Most stepped a single mast, which carried a large square tanned sail; bowlines extended the sail forward to a bowsprit. One or 2 bonnets added in good weather. The stout mast had a platform for archers.

Later enlarged to 2- and 3-masted vessels, the latter having a lateen mizzen. Rowed when necessary. Crew of 20-60. Known lengths 16-30m; e.g., length 23.5m, beam and depth 7.47m; deep draft.

2. The **cog** was also used in southern Europe from the early 14th century until ca. 1600 in the same general form, but modified for local conditions—mainly lighter winds and lower seas—especially in the Mediterranean. The term **cocha**, however, was gradually replaced by **navis** by the end of the 14th century. Primarily a **merchantman**★, occasionally a military transport. Clinker-built, then carvel; bluff ends; shallow keel; deadwood aft. Fore and aft castles generally lower than on those in the north, or none on early vessels. Deck beams pierced the side planking; 1-3 decks; some small vessels were open. Early vessels used either a quarter rudder or a stern rudder. Early single square-sailed ship altered by the 15th century to a multimasted vessel, some with a large square mainsail, small square foresail, and a small lateen mizzen. Generally a bowsprit. Mast also had a cage from which arrows and stone-shots were discharged. Carried as many as 500 men, but as few as 35; the larger ships also carried archers. Reported lengths 20-30m, widths 6-10.6m, depths amidships 2.6-2.7m. Other recorded names: small: **coc(c)hetta**, **coc(c)hina**; **nave quadra**; largest: **coccona**, **coccone**

3. *England, NE:* Small sailing vessel used on the Humber and Ouse Rivers in the 16th century. Other recorded names: **cock**, **cogones**

Selected name variants: **chaucha**, **chocca**, **chocha**, **coc(c)a** (pl. **cocche**), **coccae**, **coccha**, **cocc(h)o**, **cocghe**, **cocha** (pl. **coche**★), **cocham**, **cochis**, **cocho**, **cock**★, **cocka**, **cocko**, **co(d)co**, **cog(g)a**, **cogam**, **cogcho**, **coge**, **cogg(h)e**, **coggis**, **coggo(nis)**, **cog(g)onibus**, **cogko**, **cog(g)ue**, **cogo(nes)**, **cogschip**, **cogscult**, **coka**, **coke**, **conca**, **concha**★, **coqua**, **coque**, **cot(t)a**, **coucha**, **göge**, **gogo**, **g(u)ogue**, **Hansekogge**, **kocg(h)e**, **koche**, **kock(e)**, **kocko**, **kog(a)**, **koge**, **kogg**, **kogga**, **kogge** (pl. **koggen**), **ko(g)cho**, **kogje**, **Kogschip**, **kok**, **koka**★, **köke**, **kroska**, **krosko**, **kugga**, **kuggr**, **kuka**, **nave rotonda**, **quoca**, **quoque**; dimunitives: **clene coghe**, **coquete**, **cuquete**. Note also **cog à bec**, **kåg**. Further references: **cock boat-1**, **coggle**

coga See **cog**

cog à bec *Europe, NW:* A 13th-14th-century sailing vessel distinguished from the **cog**★ by its sharp bow. One in 1340 had a crew of 118, and was 240t burden. Spelling variant: **cogue à beque**

cogam See **cog**

cog boat *England, NE:* Small **tender**★ towed astern a **Humber keel**★ or **Humber sloop**★, other river vessels, and some inshore **fishing boats**★. Sometimes raced, often by wives. Usually clinker-planked of larch or elm; wineglass transom, stern bench. Bow much fuller than stern. Sculled; sculling notch in transom. Length 3.6m, beamy. Other recorded names: **cob boat**, **coggie** (or **coggy**) **boat**, **Kogge**. Further reference: **cock boat-1**

cogboote, **cogbote** See **cock boat-1**

cogcho, **coge**, **cogga** See **cog**

cogge See **cock boat-1**, **cog**

cogghe See **cog**

coggie boat See **cog boat**

coggis See **cog**

coggle *England, E:* Cited during the 16th-18th centuries as a **fishing boat★** along the Yorkshire coast and on the Thames. Other recorded names: **cock★**, **cocke**, **cog★**, **kokke**. Further reference: **cock boat-1**

coggo, coggonibus, coggonis, coggue See **cog**

coggy boat See **cog boat**

cogie See **Deal lugger**

cogko, cogo, cogones, cogonibus, cogschip, cogscult, cogue See **cog**

cogue à beque See **cog à bec**

coïro *Ivory Coast:* Lightweight **dugout canoe★** used for sea and lagoon fishing in the areas to the east and west of Abidjan. Braced by multiple ligatures of palm fiber at bow and stern instead of by thwarts. Stern wider than bow and rounded, with shelf-like extension. Bow rounded and overhanging. Seat for fisherman on the bottom just abaft amidships. Length 5m, beam 0.6m. Spelling variant: **koiro**

coit See **cot**

coite *Ireland:* In old Irish, a **dugout canoe★**. See also **cot**.

cok *England, SW:* Small, open 17th-century boat that engaged in drift fishing for pilchard and mackerel off the Cornish coast. Reportedly set square sails on main- and foremasts. Name variant: **cokyn** (dim.). See also **cock**, **cock boat-1**.

coka See **cog**

cokbote See **cock boat-1**

coke See **cog**

coket See **coquet**

cokke 14th-century term for a British naval **ship's boat★**. Pulled 14 oars and carried 20 men. Further reference: **cock boat-1**

cokkebote See **cock boat-1**

cokong See **jukung**

cokyn See **cok**

Colchester smack See **Essex smack**

colé See **culé**

Colin Archer pilot boat, Colin Archer-skøyte See **losbåt-2**

collar boat, collar punt See **off-and-on boat**

collecting boat 1. *Australia, N:* Small **cutter★**-rigged boat that collects trochus shells for mother-of-pearl from the scattered **fleet★** of **pearling luggers★**. Shells from each **lugger★** carefully segregated on the **floating station★** for accounting purposes. Half-decked, broad-beamed, centerboard. Crew of 3.

2. *United States, south-central:* Company-owned boat that buys shrimp and oysters from individual fishermen and takes the catch directly to the company's packing plant.
See also **cut boat, smack-2, tow boat-2**.

collector boat See **smack-2**

college barge *England, south-central:* Large **houseboat★** moored along the banks of the Isis (upper Thames) that served as headquarters for an Oxford University rowing club. Used mainly from the 1840s until the end of the century, but still found. Square ends, flat bottom. Early boats opulent, with a high stern poop, sitting and dressing rooms, upper deck that

served as a promenade or grandstand, and a tall flagpole forward. Gangway connected with shore, and on the river side, a landing stage served the rowing **shells★** and other club craft. Name variant: **varsity barge**

collier 1. Burdensome vessel fitted to carry coal, either for industrial or home consumption, or earlier to provide coal to ship coaling stations around the world. Generally heavily constructed, roughly maintained, and slow. Those of the 18th-19th centuries were mainly sailing vessels, usually **brig★**- or **bark★**-rigged. More modern vessels steam powered; later diesel, with cap. to 60,000t. Selected name variants: **battello carbonaio** (or **carboniere**), **carbonaio**, **(buque) carbonero**, **(nave) carboniera**, **(bâtiment** or **navire) charbonnier**, **coal carrier**, **coalier**, **coalman**, **coal scuttle**, **coal (supply) ship**, **collier ship**, **Kohlendampfer**, **Kohlen(transport)schiff**, **koolhaalder**. Note also **coal lighter**.

2. *England:* Traded mainly along the east coast, carrying coal from northeast England to London during the 17th to the end of the 19th century. Most returned north in ballast, many using chalk ballast. Some were owned by small ports to provide coal to the community. Many were old merchant vessels relegated to carrying coal. Mostly a summertime trade, so also served as general traders. Those with collapsible funnels and low bridge work for passing under London bridges were called **flat-irons★**. **a. Collier brigs** were bluff-bowed, high-sided. Fairly flat floors enabled them to take the ground. Straight stem, high transom or wide counter; flush deck; flat sheer on some. **Brig**-rigged, with square sails on the foremast and gaff sail on the mainmast, with large square topsails. Several headsails. 1805 vessel 23.7m long between perpendiculars, 18.3m on keel, 7m wide, 3m hold depth. Other recorded names: **coal brig**, **geordie** (**collier brig**), **frying pan** (the **Whitby collier brig's** windvane resembled a frying pan). Further reading: Walter Runciman, *Collier Brigs and Their Sailors* (London: T. F. Unwin, 1926). **b.** The **collier barks** set square sails on the fore- and mainmasts and a gaff, or occasionally a lateen, mizzen sail. A popular type in the 18th century. **c. Schooner★**-rigged **colliers** were favored at Maldon and Whitstable. Requiring a smaller crew, they generally superseded the square-rigged types. **d.** Some British merchant **cats★** were built primarily to carry coal. In the late 17th century, some vessels were sharp-ended; raised quarter-deck. Other recorded names: **coal cat**, **collier cat**, **collier cat-bark** (**bark-rigged**)

collier bark, collier brig, collier cat, collier cat-bark See **collier-2**

collier ship See **collier-1**

Collingwood boat *Canada, SW:* Gaff-rigged **gillnetter★** that fished for salmon on the Fraser River and in Georgia Strait. Stayed mast; jib to a short bowsprit. Further reference: **Mackinaw boat-1**

Collingwood skiff See **Mackinaw boat-1**

Colne punt See **gun punt**

Colne smack See **Essex smack**

Colne watch boat See **watch boat**

čoln na jadra See **sailboat**

colonial barge See **barge-11g**

colt See **timber raft-2b**

Columbia River boat, Columbia River gillnet boat, Columbia River salmon boat See **gillnetter-2**

Columbia River skiff *United States, NW:* Used in gill netting and trolling for salmon; larger than the **gillnetter★** and the **salmon troller★**. Sharp ends; rounded bottom; carvel-planked, with steam-bent oak frames. Small fore and aft decks, washboards. Powered by a small engine.

combàj, combàl See **combàll**

combàll *Italy, N:* Long, narrow cargo boat of Lake Como (Lario); a small type, the **comballino**, travels the Adda River and canals to Milan. Transports produce, animals, and general cargo. In the 17th century, the **comballone** was used in naval skirmishes on Lake Como and nearby lakes. Overhanging ends, slightly raised, especially at the stern. Flat bottom, turns up to a point at the bow and to a blunt curved stern; flared sides. Decked at ends; small cabin at the stern; cargo may be protected by an arched awning. Long steering oar, weighted at inner ends of shaft. On the lake, steps a tall mast well forward, amidships earlier. Sets a rectangular sail; mast unstepped for river travel. On rivers, 2 oars used at the bow and 2 at the stern. Auxiliary now common. Originally towed by horses upstream and on canals. Length 28.2m, beam on gunwale 5.8m, on bottom 5m, depth 1.85m. Other recorded names: **combàl, combàll lariano, comballo**; pl. **combàj, comballi**

comballi, comballino, combàll lariano, comballo, comballone See **combàll**

cõmbo See **chombo**

Combwich flattener See **Parrett flatner**

commercial vessel See **merchantman**

common barge See **Gravesend barge**

commoner's boat See **junk**

compartment boat *England:* One of a train of oblong or roughly square boats that work the canals, mainly carrying coal; some modified to carry pitch. Early boats hauled by men or horses. Later, the iron or steel boats pushed by a **tug★**, the train comprising as many as 32 boats at times. At the head of the train was a wedge-shaped boat called a **dummy bow** that carried no cargo; in severe winters this lead boat (also called **Jabez's head** and **jebus**), when suitably ballasted, might be pushed by a **tug** to break up the ice. A catwalk along one side of the train permitted movement from one end to the other. An earlier system was to push the train, steering by 2 wire ropes, one at each side, that ran the length of the train. Boat was lifted and inverted to discharge the cargo into a seagoing **collier★**. Length 6m, widths 1.93-4.88m, depths 2.13-2.44m. Modern **compartment boats,** 17m long and 5.26m wide, are propelled by a **push tug**. Other recorded names: **(Bartholomew's) bread pan, pan★, pudden, Tom pudden** (or **Pudding**). Note also **tub boat.**

compreng *Indonesia, central:* **1.** Javanese word for **boat★**.
2. Along the north Java coast, **compreng** meant a multi-purpose, small to medium-sized boat without outriggers.
3. At Surabaya, a **barge★**-like craft that traversed the Brantas and Solo Rivers. Cabin aft, lateral rudders. Walkway along the sides for poling. Single mast.

comprèng See **jukung compèng**

compromise boat See **half skipjack**

conca See **cog**

Concarneau tunny boat See **thonier**

concha **1.** *Peninsular Malaysia:* Two-masted trader of Johore. Sharp bow and stern; straight ends. Gallery, with carved railing, extended beyond quarters at the stern; decked; divided cabin at stern. Masts stepped in forward half of the vessel; short bowsprit.
2. *Venezuela:* Bark **canoe★** of the Orinoco River Native Americans; a **concha** is also reported used by the Oyapock on the western side of Lake Maracaibo. Ends tied with rattan, outer rim reinforced with laced-on sticks, and spread with additional sticks. Mud is placed as ballast at the stern to raise the bow a little. Boat portaged around short rapids, but if the walk is long, a new **canoe** is made downstream. A **canoe** 3m long and 80cm wide can hold 5 men. Name variant: **cáscara** See also **cog**.

Concordia Beetle catboat See **catboat-2c**

condo boat See **Delaware River oyster schooner**

condelette See **gondalette**

condora See **condura**

condura 13th- and 14th-century merchant vessel of the Dalmatian coast, especially from Dubrovnik. Largest ca. 18m long. Spelling variants: **condora, conduria, gondura, kond(o)ura, kontoūra**; pl. **kondure.** See also **gondola-1**.

conduria See **condura**

Congo barque See **barque-5**

Connecticut canoe *United States, NE:* Dugout **canoe★** employed in oyster tonging in the New Haven area. Originally obtained from the Native Americans, but in time hewn by the settlers themselves, sometimes of white pine from the headwaters of the Connecticut River and from Cayuga Lake in New York. Used until ca. 1900. Flattened bottom ca. 8cm thick, sides ca. 6-8cm; if bottom wore too thin, replaced by planks laid athwartships. Spoon-ended, with stern cut square at upper third; sides vertical or with slight tumble home; generally a cap rail added. Usually painted and well-maintained. Propelled from the stern by a long sculling oar or stepped a mast (sometimes 2) through a thwart in the forward third, setting a leg-of-mutton sail with a horizontal sprit. Single leeboard, ca. 1.22m long and 0.61m wide, hung by a rope from a bar just abaft the thwart. Known lengths 8.2-10.7m; e.g., length 8.5m, beam 0.9m, depth 0.46m; draft loaded 0.23m; cap. ca. 30-50 bushels of oysters. Other recorded names: **Fair Haven dugout, New Haven dugout** (or **oyster canoe**), **oyster canoe**

Connecticut lobster boat See **Noank sloop**

Connecticut River boat See **Connecticut River drag boat**

Connecticut River drag boat *United States, NE:* Found along the lower Connecticut River and the coast of Long Island Sound from Guilford east to Stonington during the latter part of the 19th and into the 20th century. Engaged in net fishing, especially for shad in season, and in lobstering. Lapstrake or carvel construction; plumb stem, mildly cutaway; high, slightly raked transom; moderate sheer. Wide plank keel with skeg aft; deadrise either moderate or strong. Half-decked; side decks ran to transom; no stern deck to allow nets to be handled over the stern. Centerboard; rudder wide-bladed below waterline; steered with yoke and rudderlines while fishing. Single portable mast stepped well forward, setting a loose-footed, boomed spritsail. Boats over 6m generally **sloop**★-rigged, with the jib to a small plank bowsprit; a few were 2-masted. Also rowed, and the few remaining by the mid-20th century were motorized. Crew of 2. Reported lengths 5-7.3m; e.g., length 5.3m, beam 1.8m, depth 0.7m; shallow draft. Other recorded names: **Connecticut River (shad) boat, drag boat**★, **dragnet boat, Guilford drag boat**

Connecticut River duck boat See **Connecticut scull boat**

Connecticut River shad boat See **Connecticut River drag boat**

Connecticut scull boat *United States, NE:* Waterfowling boat propelled mainly by sculling through a hole in the transom. Elongated sharp bow; shallow hull. Long foredeck, narrow side and stern decks; cockpit shape varied. Those that sailed to and from hunting sites had a centerboard. Reported length 3.8m, beam 1.0m. Other recorded names: **Connecticut River duck boat, Connecticut sculler**

Connecticut sculler See **Connecticut scull boat**

Connecticut sharpie See **sharpie-2**

Connemara hooker See **Galway hooker**

Connemara nobby See **nobby-2**

conner, connur See **Chesapeake Bay log canoe-1**

conoa, conoo See **kunu**

conow See **cannow**

constant trader See **coastal packet**

contact boat See **runner**

Continental galley See **galley-9**

conveyance boat See **skyssbåt**

convoyer See **buis-2, hoy-1**

cook boat See **badjra, cock boat-1, pallar, scow-5**

cookery crib See **crib**

cook scow See **scow-5**

cook wanigan See **wanigan**

coolie ship One that transported indentured Chinese from south China ports and Hong Kong to California, the Chincha Islands off Peru, and the West Indies, especially in the 1850s. So-called **coolie ships** also transported indentured emigrants from Calcutta to Surinam from the late 18th century until World War I; prior to 1906, mainly **clippers**★, then **steamers**.

Coombe Kaffir See **Falmouth oyster punt**

coonner See **Chesapeake Bay log canoe-1**

coonoo See **kunu**

coorial See **corial**

copill See **coble-1**

Copper canoe See **kayak-form canoe**

coppering punt See **copper punt**

Copper kayak See **kayak-7**

copper punt **Raft**★ or small boat used while cleaning a ship's copper sheathing, caulking, and painting the boot topping. The **rafts** were of the **balsa raft**★ type—2 elongated hollow floats secured by a platform. Various types of boats were used: square-ended, flat-bottom **punts**★; boxy, almost hexagonal craft; and

planked double-ended boats. Lengths 3-4.3m. Other recorded names: **coppering punt, plat de calafat, platillo de calafate**

coqua See **cog**

coque See **cock boat-1, cog**

coquet *France:* **1.** A small boat, sometimes defined as a **cock boat**★.
   2. In the 15th century, the **coquet** fished for herring in the English Channel, and some served as small **coasters**★.
   3. A small 18th-century **coquet** carried merchandise on the Seine from the coast to Paris.
   Other recorded names: **batelé, cochet, cocquet, coket, goguet**★, **quocquet, quoquet(a)**

coquete *Spain:* A small, handy boat; may also refer to a **jolly boat**★ or a particularly small **cock boat**★. Further reference: **cog**

coquilleur See **coquillier**

coquillier *France, W:* **1.** Dragged for scallops (*coquilles*) in the Rade de Brest, mainly during the 1st half of the 20th century; last working boat under sail in 1984. Carvel-planked; straight keel with deep drag aft; S-curve to the floors. Low stern, strongly raked; comparatively narrow transom. High bow, relatively plumb stem. Early boats half-decked, then fully decked. Narrow rudder followed rake of the sternpost; tiller came in below the gunwale. Black hull with colored bands. Stepped 2 masts prior to the 20th century, setting lugsails; then **sloop**★-rigged, with boomed gaff mainsail, yard topsail, staysail to stem. Motors installed beginning in the 1920s. The present-day boat is an entirely different craft. Reported lengths 7.7-12m; e.g., length 8.8m, beam 3.16m, maximum depth 2.4m. Other recorded names: **bag-kregina** (Breton), **coquilleur, coquillier de la rade, sloop coquillier brestois, sloup coquillier (de la Rade de Brest)**. Further reading: Bernard Cadoret, et al., *Ar Vag, Voiles au Travail en Bretagne Atlantique*, vol. 3 (Douarnenez: Éditions de l'Estran, 1988), 106-153. Note also **scalloper**.
   2. The **caseyeur-coquilleur** fishes for both shrimp and scallops, especially in the Courreaux de Belle-Île, off the coast west of St. Nazaire. Fully motorized. Reported lengths 9-12m.

coquillier de la rade See **coquillier**

corab, corabis See **carabus**

coracán See **curacán**

corach See **curragh**

coracle **1.** *British Isles:* Small basket-like boat used on rivers, lakes, and quiet tidal waters for ferrying, fishing, wildfowling, and transporting light goods. Of very early origin. Design adapted to meet the physical aspects of particular bodies of water and individual preference. May be oval, round, pear-shaped, or roughly rectangular. Constructed of loosely woven longitudinal and transverse laths or radiating laths through which concentric withes are woven. Bottom generally flat or slightly dished; sides vertical, flared, or have tumble home. Initially covered with a skin, later with waterproofed canvas or oilcloth. Paddled by 1-2 people seated on a wooden board. Average ca. 1.5m in length and 13.5kg in weight. Other recorded

names: **coricle**, **corougle**, **corracle**, **curricle**, **korak(e)l**. Note also **basket boat**, **bouco**, **Boyne curragh**, **bullboat**, **corita**, **curragh**, **dhoni-4**, **ku-dru**, **pelota**, **quffa**, **vitile**.
2. *Scotland:* Information is limited, but this **coracle** appears to have been more basket-like, with rods radiating across the bottom to form the warp, and woven concentric rings of split withes forming the weft. The fresh hide covering (with tail) turned over the stout gunwale and was secured with twisted horsehair lacings. A wide seat spanned the middle. Used for ferrying, fishing, wildfowling, and to guide **timber rafts**★ until at least the

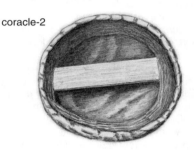

coracle-2

end of the 19th century. Ca. 1.2-1.5m long and 0.9-1.4m wide. Other recorded names: **courach**, **curach(an)**, **currach**, **curro(c)k**, **currough**, **cwrwgle**
3. *Wales:* Here, and in adjacent parts of England, the **coracle** can be traced back to at least the 7th century and is still in limited use on 3 Welsh rivers for salmon fishing. The **coracle** mentioned by Roman writers, however, was a seagoing craft with a keel, similar to the Irish **curragh**★. In some areas, they were used to assist in washing sheep prior to shearing. Design and construction varied with the type of river on which they were used, and their size was frequently based on the stature and weight of the owner; initially the size of the hide was a limiting factor. In general, a skeleton frame of transverse strips is interwoven with longitudinal strips to form a wide, shallow, oval craft; some almost square, with vertical or in-sloping sides. Strengthened around the top by several rows of plaited withes lashed to the frame. Originally the frame was built with branches, later sawn laths were used, and in a recent innovation aluminum frames are being used. Originally covered with a hide, later by flannel saturated with tar and rosin, and more recently by tarred canvas. Various **coracle** types have been identified, the best known being the **Dee**, **Ironbridge**, **Teifi**, **Tywi**, and **Wye coracles**. Other recorded names: **c(h)orwc**, **corwg(l)**, **cwrwg(l)**, **gwrwgl**. Further reading: James Hornell, *British Coracles and Irish Curraghs* (London: The Society for Nautical Research, 1938); J. Geraint Jenkins, *Nets and Coracles* (Newton Abbot: David & Charles, 1974).
4. *India, S:* Generally circular, with either a flat or rounded bottom; a few areas used a quadrilateral shape with rounded corners. Ferries passengers and goods and may engage in fishing. The flat type has a meshwork bottom of split bamboo and curved sides of concentric woven split bamboo. Kept rigid with a rim of unsplit bamboo. The bowl-shaped **coracle** was

generally larger and constructed of unsplit bamboo; ribs crossing the interior added strength. Both types hide-covered, but oiled cloth used on some; now may be covered with a double layer of plastic sacks, sewn

coracle-4

together and tarred. Small types carry a single person, the largest noted conveyed 50 men plus cargo. Generally paddled or poled. Diameter of a small one 1.8m, depth 0.36m, weight dry 20kg; large size ca. 4.27m in diameter, 1.07m deep, but reported to 9m. Other recorded names: **arégolou**; **argī lī**, **arigōlu**, **harigólu**, **and puṭṭi** (in Telugu); **haragalu**, **haragólu**, **harigōlu** or **buṭṭi** (in Kanarese); **para(s)chal**, **paracil**, **parical**, **parisal**, **parisil**, **paricu**, **tokrá** (in Hindi); **dony**
Further references: **bouco**, **ku-dru**, **quffa**
coracora, **coracore** See **korakora-1**
coraillère, **corailleur**, **coraillière** See **corallina**
coral See **courau**
coralan, **coral boat**, **coraleiro**, **coralière**, **coralina**, **coraline** See **corallina**
corallain *West Indies:* Small general-purpose boat used on rivers and sheltered waters, especially in Haiti. Flat bottom, transom stern. Name variant: **couralin**★
corallière See **corallina**
corallina *Mediterranean:* **1.** In the 18th century, a naval and merchant vessel propelled mainly by oars, but also sailed. Sharp ends, flat floors, slightly flared sides. Rowed with 6-8 oars per side. Stepped 2 masts, setting lateen sails or a lateen and a spritsail. Reported lengths 9-12m, widths 1.8-2.4m, depths 0.6-0.76m.
2. A more recent **corallina** worked coral beds off Sicily, Sardinia, the west coast of Italy, eastern Algeria, and Tunisia; also used for fishing and cargo. Also worked out of southeastern French ports. An early type in Algeria was called a **satteau**. Carvel-planked; double-ended; flat floors; rounded bilges; keel; moderate sheer; deep rudder. Straight vertical stem on older boats; later, stems were curved and overhanging.

corallina-2

Some open, but mainly decked; crew quarters aft; also a forward cabin. Large windlass amidships worked the coral dredge. One or 2 masts; square, sprit-, or lateen sails reported; jib set flying, and a spinnaker used when winds favorable. Now mainly motorized. Small boats had a crew of 5-6, larger to 15. Reported lengths 12-14m, widths 3.2-4m, depth ca. 1.0m; many smaller. Other recorded names: **barca corallina, coalinna, corailleur, coraill(i)ère, coralan, coral boat, coraleiro, coral(l)ière, coralina, coralline*, coralure, couraill(i)ère, koralina**; pl. **corallini**. Note also **caorlina, galea di corallo**.

coralline *France, Corsica:* This small open boat gathered coral out of Ajaccio on the west coast. Narrow elongated bow, rounded stern. Length ca. 7m. See also **corallina**.

corallini, coralure See **corallina**

corau See **courau**

corbeta *Spain:* 19th-century **bark***-rigged merchant vessel. Frequently sailed out of north coast ports, carrying barrels of flour and sacks of beans to Cuba, returning with sugar, coffee, tobacco. Square sails on the fore- and mainmasts, fore-and-aft sail on the mizzenmast. An 1840 vessel was 30m long overall, 8.8m wide, 4.6m deep. See also **corvette**.

corbeta aviso, corbeta de guerra See **corvette-1**

corbette *Belgium, W:* Small **fishing boat*** at Ostend cited in the 17th century. Note also **corve**.

corbita Large, full-bodied Roman vessel of the 1st-3rd centuries A.D. Believed to have carried mainly grain, and reported to have traveled from Red Sea ports to India as well as in the Mediterranean. Sharp, curved ends extended above the deck; bottom had rocker. Cabin house aft; heavy quarter rudders. Mainmast stepped amidships, setting a large square sail, sometimes with a triangular sail above. A small square sail might be suspended out over the bow. One estimated to have been 25m long and 6-7m wide; cap. to ca. 400t. Spelling variants: **corbito**; pl. **corbitae**. See also **corvette**.

corbitae, corbito See **corbita**

corcoa See **korakora-1**

cordier *France:* A term used in the north for any boat engaged in bottom fishing, using lines with multiple hooks (*cordes*). In the Mediterranean, the term **palangrier*** is used. Motorized **cordiers** worked generally without sail, with a crew of 9-11 and were ca. 12-20m long; used until World War II. Some **cordiers du Cotentin** were plumb-stemmed, counter-sterned and set a boomed gaff sail and jib to a long bowsprit; others had a curved stem, raking sternpost, flat floors. Name variant: **bateau cordier**. Note also **bateau de Berck**. Further reference: **longliner-2**

cordier berckois See **bateau de Berck**

cordier du Cotentin See **cordier**

Core Sounder *United States, E:* Powered boat that works with sinknets out of Core Sound in the North Carolina bays or on the ocean. "V" bottom of the **deadrise boat*** type. Rounded stern; plumb stem. Smaller types have a logging-type forefoot; planked forefoot on the larger. Originally a slight flare to the bow, later marked flare. Low freeboard. Raised cabin in forward half, open aft. Reported lengths 11-12m; beam ca. one-fourth length; became beamier as engine power increased. Name variants: **Core Sound sinknetter, drop-net boat, Hatteras boat**

Core Sound sharpie See **sharpie-4**

Core Sound sinknetter See **Core Sounder**

corf *England, E:* A large floating box, often boat-shaped, or a basket or cage designed to hold live fish, lobsters, crabs, or bait. Those of wood perforated to permit sea water to flow freely. The **corfts** at Harwich were ca. 5m long. Further spelling variants: **cauf, cawf, corfe, corve***. Note also **coff, fish car**. Further references: **coble-1a, coble-1b**

corfe See **coble-1b, corf**

corft See **corf**

cori *Solomon Islands, western Pacific:* Term given to a **dugout canoe*** of New Georgia Archipelago, especially on Marovo Island. In adzing the hull, lugs are left to which ribs are lashed and on which thwarts are set; round in cross section. Similar peaked-up ends. When sailed, mast either placed into a large bamboo segment lashed to the thwarts and to a rib on the bottom, or the mast steps through a thwart and into a residual socket on the bottom. Sets a triangular sail with the apex down. Also paddled, employing a T-grip or a circular handle. Other recorded names: **hore, hori**

corial *South America, NE:* **Dugout canoe*** of the lower rivers and coastal zone. Design and size vary with tribal group (see **curiara**). Hull may be expanded or not; may be adzed or burned out with coals; thwarts usually used as spreaders. Those of the Bush Negroes of Suriname often have a single washstrake on each side. Generally ends are narrow and pointed, slope upwards, and overhang; if stern end flattened, it may be ornamented. Caulked with cotton, rags, and gum. Paddled primarily, but sometimes sets a small palm or cloth sail. Generally 3-7.6m long, largest ca. 15m; widths mainly 0.45-0.6m, largest 1.8m; depth ca. 0.3m. Other recorded names: **coorial, corjaal, couillara, coulial(l)a, culiàla, culjar, culyara, curial(a)** (Guaraúno); **korial, korjaal*, korjar, koryáli, kuliala, luampo** (Galibi). Note also **canoa-17, canoe-6, falca**.

coricle See **coracle-1**

corita *United States, SW:* Term applied to a **coracle***-like craft of the Native Americans of the lower Colorado River area or to a trough-like **dugout canoe***. Used mainly for ferrying. Constructed of reeds and coated with mud or bitumen. Other recorded names: **bullboat*, corrido**

corjaal See **corial**

corme See **djerme**

cormorant boat See **lu ci chuan, ukai-bune**

corner boat See **half skipjack**

corn hoy *England, SE:* A vessel that carried corn from Kent and Essex to London during the 16th century. Note also **hoy-3a**.

Cornish crabber *United Kingdom:* A small pleasure boat designed in the early 1970s as a modification of the **West Country crabber***. Reported lengths 7.3-9.5m; e.g., length 9.5m, beam 2.44m, depth 0.8m.

Cornish driver See **West Cornish lugger**

Cornish gig *England, SW:* Fast, light, open boat used from Falmouth to Padstow and in the Isles of Scilly for piloting, salvaging, lifesaving, smuggling, fishing, and in the Scillies, for interisland transportation. Provided service from the 18th century until 1929, but several still exist, and these, plus reproductions, race regularly. In general, the **pilot gigs** had narrow clinker planking of elm; a long, straight keel; easy turn of the bilges; slight sheer; thin gunwales; 8 light thwarts, bowed up slightly and supported by a pillar. Bow full; stem straight or slightly rounded; stern narrow, vertical or slightly raked, with a small high transom. Short tiller, often worked with lines. Rowed mostly, usually with 6 oars, each oarsman manning one oar, but might be worked double-banked; used tholepins, the forward pin often of iron or ironwood. Most **pilot gigs** painted black. Rig varied with time and place; Newquay favored a dipping forelug and standing lug mizzen, but a spritsail also used; the south coast employed a sprit or standing lug mizzen with a dipping lug foresail and a jib tacked to the stemhead. At the Isles of Scilly, a leg-of-mutton mizzen was popular. The **pilot gigs** were 5.8-9.75m long; typically 9.12m long, 1.45m wide, and 0.75m deep; proportions varied with primary purpose. Other recorded names: **Cornish**, **Newquay**, **Penzance pilot gig**; also **Falmouth**, **Mounts Bay**, **Newlyn (pilot)**, **Penzance**, **St. Ives**, **Scillonian** (or **Scilly Isles**) **gig**. Further reading: A. J. Jenkins, *Gigs and Cutters of the Isles of Scilly* ([n.p.] Integrated Packing Group and Isles of Scilly Gig Racing Committee, 1975).

Cornish lugger See **East Cornish lugger**, **West Cornish lugger**

Cornish pilot gig See **Cornish gig**

Cornwall driver See **West Cornish lugger**

Cornwall lugger See **East Cornish lugger**, **West Cornish lugger**

corocora, corocore, corocoro, coroquora See **korakora-1**

corougle See **coracle-1**

corracán See **curaćán**

corrach See **curragh**

corracle See **coracle-1**

corragh See **curragh**

corrau, correau See **courau**

correira See **barca correire**

correo, correo maritimo See **packet boat-1**

corrido See **corita**

corsair Armed vessel of the Mediterranean that was most often licensed and encouraged by the Turkish and North African governments to prey upon merchant ships, especially of Christian countries. Operated until the early 19th century. In certain periods, such as the 14th century, the terms corsair and pirate were used interchangeably; later a corsair presumably obtained permission from his government and acted only in times of war against enemy vessels. Selected name variants: **corsale, corsali(u)s, Corsar, corsa(i)re, corsar(i)o, corsary, corser, corsory, cossari, cou(r)saire, coursal, cursalis, cursare, cursarius, cursaro, cursary, cursayre, cursore, cursour, gursar, gusa(r), gusarin, korsan, Korsar(enschiff), korsari(kon), korsere, korzar, koursar(os), kūrsar, kusa(a)r, pirato, quorsan, raider**. Note also **bovo, buccaneer, caper, carabus, freebooter, galiot-7, lancha-11, privateer, sea rover**.

corsaire See **cochère, corsair**

corsale, corsalis, corsalius, Corsar See **corsair**

corsara *Italy:* Customs boat of the Papal States that also patrolled the coast to prevent smuggling. Other

recorded names: **legno corsaro, nave corsara**. Note also **revenue cutter**.

corsare, corsario, corsaro, corsary See **corsair**

corselet box See **berrichon**

corser See **corsair**

corseyre See **cochère**

corsory See **corsair**

cortiçeira *Portugal, N:* One-man **raft**★ used in the rocky areas at Marinhas to catch shellfish and octopus. Strips of cork are spiked together and wedged into a wooden framework; wire network further contains the cork. The vertical side pieces continue at each end to create carrying handles. **Raft** set on a rack on the beach, with the octopus laid out to dry. Poled. Length ca. 1.5m. Note also **cortiço, jangada-4**.

cortiço *Portugal, N:* At Aver-o-mar, just north of Povoa de Varzim, seaweed was collected on **rafts**★ made from 3-4 rolls of cork. Each roll lashed with wire, then skewered with transverse wooden pegs. A slender board sometimes fastened on top at each end. Poled by one man. Ca. 1.3m on each side, 0.33m deep. Name variant: **jangada de cortiço**. Note also **cortiçeira, jangada-4**.

corve *France, N:* A vessel similar to, but smaller than, a **chatte**★ of the period. Term reported from the 14th to at least the 17th century. Some fished locally along the Picard and Flemish coasts for herring, others fished for cod in the North Sea. A small type, the **corvette**★, fished out of Dunkerque until the end of the 19th century; length ca. 10m, beam 4.5m, depth of hold 2.7m. Name variant: **korf**. Note also **corbette**. Further reference: **corf**

corvet, corveta, corvete, corvetta See **corvette**

corvette **1.** Armed vessel of the 17th-19th centuries, classed just below a **frigate**★. Generally used for reconnaissance and as an **advice boat**★; some carried materiel from one port to another (**corvette de charge**). Until 1800, armed with fewer than 20 guns, all on one deck; in the 19th century, they had as many as 30 guns. Generally 3 tall masts. Rigged as a **ship**★ (**ship corvette**), **brig**★ (**brig corvette** or **corvette brig**), or **barque**★. A type of **corvette** with 14-26 guns and a flush deck was called a **corvette sans gaillard** (or **du 2ᵉ rang**), **gladdekskorvet, Glattdeckskorvette**. The type with 28-30 guns and forecastle and quarterdecks was a **corvette à gaillard** (or **du 1ᵉʳᵉ rang**), **kuilkorvet, Kuhlkorvette, well-deck corvette**. Other recorded names: **corbeta de guerra, sloop-of-war** (U.S.); **corbeta** (or **corvette**) **aviso**. Note also **snow**.

2. In the 1870s, the British navy used the term for a steam **frigate**. During World War II, the term was revived for a fast escort vessel that accompanied convoys. Armed with anti-**submarine** depth charges and anti-aircraft weapons. The British **corvettes** bore the names of flowers illustrated in Mr. Middleton's seed catalogue, thereby earning the nickname **Mr. Middleton's light horses**.

3. *France:* Some early 18th-century sources portrayed the **corvette** as an oared vessel that stepped a small foremast and tall mainmast, both setting square sails. Selected name variants: **corbeta**★, **corbita**★, **corvet, corvet(t)a, corvete, courvette, korvet', korvet**

(pl. **korvetten**), **korvet(t)a, korvetenn, Korvette, korweta, light frigate, quorvet.** Further references: **barque longue, corve**

corvette à gaillard, corvette aviso, corvette brig See **corvette-1**

corvette de charge See **corvette-1, gabare-3a**

corvette du 1ere rang, corvette du 2e rang, corvette sans gaillard See **corvette-1**

corwc, corwg, corwgl See **coracle-3**

cosa See **kosha**

Cossack canoe See **czajka**

cossari See **corsair**

costero, costiere See **coaster**

cot 1. *Ireland:* Gaelic and Irish word for a flat-bottomed, keelless **punt★** or small boat. From early times until at least the late 17th century, the boat was primarily a crude **dugout canoe★**. Later planked, often clinker-built. Used on rivers, lakes, and estuaries for day-to-day transportation, fishing, collecting seaweed, transporting cattle to pasture, attending moored boats off shore, etc. Modern **cots** may be of steel, but retain early shapes. Sharp-ended on rivers, square-ended on lakes. Half-decked **cots** used for wildfowling were called **shooting cots**. Most propelled by oars, but some large 19th-century inland transport **cots** carried a mast and large gaff sail in addition to as many as 6 oars and a steering paddle. Lengths mostly 3.3-5.5m; transport **cots** ca. 16.7m long, 3m wide, and 1.7m deep; shallow draft. Spelling variants: **coit, coite★, cot(t)e, cott(ye), coytte**

2. *Northern Ireland:* Name variant: **Derry cot. a.** The open **shooting cot** of the eastern side of Lough Foyle, in the northwest, employs a long-barreled muzzle-loading gun. A few still used in the 1960s. Flat bottom of 3 deal planks, joined inside by 8-9 laths. Sides a single deal plank, slightly flared, supported by L-shaped willow knees. Sharp ends, slightly flared; almost flat sheer. Rudder wide front-to-back and shallow. Propelled with 1.8m-long pronged pole by the single occupant, or hand-paddled. Length 3.7m, beam 0.76m, depth 0.23m, draft ca. 0.6m. A sailing **cot** was also used for wildfowling. Decked for ca. 1.5m forward and 0.61m aft; narrow side decks. Flat bottom curved up to a long overhanging bow. Slightly raked sternpost. Short mast stepped just abaft the foredeck. Small loose-footed gaff sail bent directly to the mast. When stowing the sail, gaff swung down and sail wrapped around the mast, which might then be unstepped and stowed. Also poled and paddled. Length ca. 4.6m. **b.** The fishing **cots** worked on the River Roe, which empties into Loch Foyle. This open **cot** is similar to the **shooting cot** except that willow timbers cross the hull. Still used in the 1960s; in the past also collected seaweed for fertilizer and gathered winkles. Length to 5.5m. Those engaged in salmon netting on the Roe were developed in the mid-19th century to use a special draught-net. Forward three-quarters decked to carry the net; small triangular cockpit aft surrounded by 7.5cm coaming. Sharp ends, raked; flat bottom, longitudinally planked; slightly flaring sides, Deal planking laid edge-to-edge; willow knees; tarred annually. One man carries and shoots the

net from the **cot**, 1-2 work from shore. Length overall 4.8m, beam 1.0m, depth 0.23m. **c. Cots** on Lough Erne in southwestern Northern Ireland transported people and farm animals between the numerous islands. Some participated in regattas. The transport **cots** were larger, as long as 16.8m, 3m wide, and 1.7m deep; carried up to ca. 14t. Employed a single sail and 4-6 oars; a paddle fixed to a pivot served as a rudder. Further references: **gabbard-1, naomóg, Wexford cot**

cota See **cog**

cote See **cot**

cotea, cotia See **kotia**

côtier 1. *Canada, E:* Cod-fishing vessel that remained on the Grand Banks off Newfoundland during an entire season. Note also **banker-2.**
  2. *France:* Term sometimes applied in the 17th century to a person qualified as a coastal pilot, and, by extension, to a vessel directed by such a person.
  3. *France, W:* In Brittany, a small boat engaged in coastal fishing. In the 1930s, such boats were often small, open, and set a large lugsail. Present-day **côtiers** are motorized.

cotier See **coaster**

cotière See **coaster**

cotiyah See **kotia**

cotre *France:* **Cotres** (sometimes **côtres**) served during the 18th and 19th centuries as armed **privateers★**, **advice boats★, trawlers★** (cotres chalutiers), and small **coasters★** (cotre de cabotage) on the Normandy and Brittany coasts. Sharp bow, counter stern. Gaff mainsail; topsail originally square, then set a lug topsail, and later a jib-headed topsail; 2 headsails. Early **coasters** were **brigantine★**-rigged. Low stern on **trawlers** facilitated net handling. A small transom-sterned **cotre** was used in line fishing and collecting seaweed off the north Breton coast and was a popular pleasure boat in the early 20th century. Other recorded names: **cottre, cutter★** (spelling used by the French until the mid-19th century)

côtre See **cutter-1, sinaper**

cotre à corne See **cutter-3**

cotre à tape-cul See **yawl-2**

cotre chalutier See **cotre**

côtre-dandy See **yawl-2**

cotre de cabotage See **cotre**

cotre de Carantec *France, NW:* Fished out of Carantec in Baie de Morlaix on the north Brittany coast. Worked with nets, hooks and lines, and lobster traps. A few restored or newly built as pleasure craft. Carvel-planked; deep keel with strong drag; S-curve to the floors; soft turn of the high bilges. Sharp entrance; plumb stem with curved forefoot. Raked counter stern above a sharply raking sternpost; deep deadwood. Rudderpost comes up inboard; tiller. Decked at bow, stern, and along the sides; may employ legs at low tide. Boomed gaff mainsail, staysail, jib to long bowsprit, gaff topsail. Some later working boats had auxiliaries. Crew of 2 when handling lobster traps. Reported lengths 4.5-9.2m; e.g., length 8m, beam 3m, draft 1.3m.

cotre homardier See **langoustier**

cotre langoustier See **langoustier-1**

cott See **cot**

cotta See **cog**

còttaru See **cutter-1**

cotte See **cot**

cotter See **cutter-1**

cottere See **coaster**

cottero See **cutter-1**

cottière See **coaster**

cotton boat See **padow, Tsungming chuan**

cotton box See **flatboat-5**

cotton prow See **padow**

cottonwood canoe *Canada, W/United States, central:* A **canoe*** hewn from a cottonwood log. Commonly used by traders on the Missouri River; sets a small square sail at times; length to 10m, width 1.2m. Name variant: **cottonwood dugout**

cottonwood dugout See **cottonwood canoe**

cottre See **cotre, cutter-1**

cottro See **cutter-1**

cottye See **cot**

cotya See **kotia**

couanga See **juanga-1**

coucha See **cog**

couffa, couffin See **quffa**

couillara, couliala, coulíalla See **canoa-17, corial**

country boat *Bangladesh/India:* A native-built sailing craft, especially in the colonial period. Also called **country ship***, it may be one privately owned by Indians, or one engaged as a **coaster***. Some, under license from the British East India Company, carried opium to China. In the mid-19th century, some were beautifully appointed and **ship***-rigged. Increasingly mechanized, especially the passenger vessels. Other recorded names: **country wallah**; **mār nu** by the Dibongiyas of eastern Assam. Further references: **Wuhu xiang xia chuan, xiao xiang xia chuan**

country-built ship See **country ship**

country ship A vessel working solely along the coast of its home country. Sometimes a merchant ship registered in one country but working mainly out of a colonial port elsewhere. May also refer to a domestically built ship. Name variant: **country-built ship**. Note also **country boat**.

country wallah See **country boat**

couplage *France:* On the Loire River, term for 2 vessels, such as **toues*** and **sapines***, roped side-by-side, with one ahead by 2-3 meters. Note also **train de bateaux**.

couple See **coble-1**

courach See **coracle-2**

courache See **curragh**

couraillère, couraillière See **corallina**

coural See **courau**

couralin *France:* **1.** Small **passage boat*** serving on rivers and in ports.

2. Open **trawler*** used on the lower parts of the major rivers emptying into the Bay of Biscay and around Île d'Oléron in western France. Set a square sail. Ca. 4t.

3. The Dordogne River **couralin** in southwestern France was a small boat that accompanied a **courau*** during the late 18th and 19th centuries. On the nearby Garonne River, the **couralin** was reported as a craft for transporting cattle.

4. On the Adour River, near the southwest border, the **couralin** was a small, flat-bottomed, square-ended craft that tended salmon nets. Also used by sports fishermen. Bottom curves up above the water to the raked bow transom and curves up to the waterline at the stern. Straight, nearly vertical sides; open; stern seat. Steered with an oar. Poled, rowed, and set a small lugsail. Two pairs of oars worked against single tholepins. Tall mast stepped through forward thwart. Now motorized. Reported lengths 4-6m; e.g., length 4.5m, beam 1.35m, depth 0.67m.

Spelling variant: **courallin**. Further reference: **corallain**

courallin See **couralin**

courant See **filadière**

courau *France, SW:* **1.** Cargo **riverboat*** cited in the 13th and 14th centuries. Square ends with short rise to the flat bottom at each end; clinker-built; open. Some set a standing lugsail.

2. The 17th-century **courau** of the Gironde Estuary and tributary rivers carried produce, wine, firewood, etc. Sharp raking bow; long, overhanging square stern; flat bottom. Decked at bow and stern, open waist. Maneuvered with a tremendously long sweep. Lugsail set to mast stepped in forward half; stayed to stemhead. Crew of 7-8. Cap. 10-50t.

3. Later, the **courau** of the Gironde Estuary and the Dordogne and Charante Rivers was a heavily constructed, bluff-bowed **gabare***. Square or rounded stern; flat bottom with slight rocker; marked sheer toward the bow; slightly flared sides; low freeboard. Outboard rudder, retractable on the upper Dordogne; long tiller; railing along sides and at stern. Cambered hatches; open hold on the upper Dordogne; cabin aft. In the estuary, commonly employed a high-peaked, loose-footed gaff sail and jib to a bowsprit (the **courau sloup**). Elsewhere, originally set a large mainsail and very small foresail, both standing lugsails; later, added a small lug mizzen, sheeted to a jiggerboom. Mainmast stepped into a tall tabernacle and could be lowered. Crew of 2. 25-90t; shallow draft. Note also **sloop-8**.

4. The **courau de l'Isle** was adapted for use on the canals of this Dordogne tributary, also carrying heavy cargo. Similar to the river vessels, but less massive and sides vertical.

5. Sometimes described as a small **yawl*** on the Garonne River; some were used in discharging ships.

6. One type was a local **coaster***. Length 29.6m, beam 6.25m, depth 1.86m; cap. 160t.

7. A small sailing **trawler*** by this name was used between La Rochelle and Île d'Oléron. Ca. 4t.

8. On the Adour River, a square-ended, open **courau** served as a **ferry*** and **lighter*** at Bayonne. The 18th-century boat was flat-bottomed with strong rocker and planked fore-and-aft; wide floor frames extended across the bottom; knee-like ribs set onto the frames. Slightly flared side planks; sheer strake lapped; shallow end transoms. Those of the early 20th century were 3 planks deep and had deeper end transoms, the bow transom shallower; mainly transported cargo. Reported lengths 8-13.5m; e.g., length 13.5m, beam 4.5m, depth 0.75m.

Spelling variants: **coral, corau, corr(e)au, coura(u)l**,

couraud, courau(l)t, cour(r)eau, courrault; pl. **cour(re)aux.** Note also **couralin.**

couraud See **courau**

courau de l'Isle See **courau-4**

couraul, courault, courau sloup, couraut, couraux, coureau, courrault, courreau See **courau**

courrier *France:* Small armed vessel. See also **packet boat-1.**

coursaire, coursal See **corsair**

coursière See **cochère**

courvette See **corvette**

cousaire See **corsair**

'couta boat See **barracouta boat**

coutière See **coaster**

coutter See **cutter-1**

covabis See **carabus**

covered sled *United States, central:* A rectangular, shallow craft that carried short-distance freight on the Ohio and Mississippi Rivers until ca. 1815. Cargo protected by shedlike structures. Rowed. Many were **ferries★**, some **pull flats★**, employing a cable to pull the craft across a river. Carried ca. 8-12t. Other recorded names: **ferry flat, scow★, scow-boat, sled.** Note also **flat, scow ferry.**

cowble See **coble-4**

cow canoe See **kadei**

Cowes boat See **Cowes ketch**

Cowes ketch *England, S:* Trader that worked between the Isle of Wight and the mainland from the early 19th century to the 1930s. Clinker-planked originally, then carvel, finally steel; slack sheer; straight vertical stem; straight keel with deep heel; flat floors; round bilges.

Cowes ketch

Initially double-ended, later counter- or transom-sterned. On early vessels, the timberheads came through a covering board at the bow and stern and were capped by a rail; later built with bulwarks. Large hatch amidships; crew's cabin aft. Some early boats used leeboards. Might be steered by lines from the tiller. **Ketch★** rig characterized by gaffs nearly as long as their booms; sails loose-footed; yard topsail to mainmast. Running bowsprit; jib, staysail. Short mizzenmast, without topsail, set well aft. Sails tanned. Crew of 2. Reported lengths 12-19m; e.g., length overall 15.5m, beam 3m, hold depth 1.8m. Other recorded names: **Cowes boat, Solent (ballast) barge**

Cowes scow See **scow-10**

Cowes skiff *England, S:* Waterman's boat of Cowes and Ryde on the Isle of Wight. Ferried crew and passengers to and from **yachts★** and ships; fished in winter. Late 19th-century boats had a moderately raked stem, turning at a well-rounded forefoot; straight keel with slight drag; tucked-up transom stern; centerboard. Wooden fenders protected boat when lying alongside other craft. Set spritsails on the fore- and mizzenmasts and a staysail. Foremast stepped through the forward thwart. Mizzen sheeted to a short outrigger. More often rowed, with boatman standing and facing forward. Length 4.57m, beam 1.42m, depth 0.56m.

cowhorn See **Block Island boat**

coxed double scull, coxed single scull See **scull**

coytte See **cot**

crab *United States, N:* Small **raft★** used to move rafted logs upstream or across a lake by means of a windlass and anchor.

crabber General term for a craft that sets crab trotlines, traps, or pots; may catch other shellfish seasonally. Usually small and open, being used in local waters; those traveling greater distances larger and decked. Generally low sides for ease of hauling in the traps. Variously rigged: lug, **sloop★, cutter★**; now generally motorized. Other recorded names: **crab boat, crab catcher** (or **trapper**), **crabier, krabb(e)fiskebåt, Krabbenfangboot, Krabbenfänger, Krabbenfischer(boot), Krabbenkutter★, krabber, kraboler, krabschuit★, kranketer.** Note also **small bateau.** Further references: **crabbing skiff, Guernsey crab boat, Norfolk crabber, West Country crabber**

crabbing bateau *United States, E:* A small-scaled **skipjack★** from the central part of the Eastern Shore of Chesapeake Bay. Popular in the early 20th century. Served as a general workboat, and in some areas, they dredged and tonged for oysters. Usually half-decked and lacked the permanent trunk cabin of the **skipjack.** Single or double leg-of-mutton sails; sail extended by a horizontal sprit; clew sometimes carried a club; no shrouds. Reported lengths 6.7-8.8m; e.g., length 8.4m, beam 2.3m, depth ca. 0.67m, draft at skeg 0.43m. Note also **bateau-7.**

crabbing punt *United States, E:* Small rectangular craft used in the Chesapeake Bay area for trotline crabbing. Open; flat bottom; low vertical sides; shallow overhanging transoms. Crew of 2. Length ca. 3m.

crabbing skiff *United States, E:* Popular on Chesapeake Bay from the 1880s through at least the 1940s as a waterman's boat for crabbing, oyster tonging, terrapin scraping, and illegal wildfowling. Design and rig varied somewhat with builder, period, and locale. A shallow plank-built boat, with a flat or "V" bottom; raked ends; sharp bow; rounded, square, or sharp stern; maximum beam forward of amidships. Later boats employed a centerboard. Outboard rudder; tiller. Decked at bow or at both ends; some had side decks. Often had a wet well amidships. Most had a single aft-raking, unstayed mast, stepped well forward; some 2-masted. Usually set a leg-of-mutton sail with a horizontal sprit boom; some had a vertical club on the leech. Jib set flying, often with a club laced to the foot. Easily sculled or poled. Some had an engine. Most under 8.5m long; e.g., length 5m, beam 1.6m, draft 0.5m; shallow hull. Other recorded names: **bateau★**, **Chesapeake Bay crabbing skiff**, **crabber★**. Further reading: Howard I. Chapelle, *Chesapeake Bay Crabbing Skiffs* (St. Michaels, Md.: Chesapeake Bay Maritime Museum, 1979). Note also **Hooper Island crab skiff**, **Smith Island skiff**, **trotliner**.

crab boat See **crabber**, **Guernsey crab boat**, **Norfolk crabber**

crab catcher, **crabier** See **crabber**

crab scraper *United States, E:* The present-day **crab scraper** of the lower Chesapeake Bay is a beamy, shallow-draft, motorized boat that tows a small dredge. Originally cat-rigged. Used for crab scraping and for hand and patent tonging for oysters. Sharp, straight bow; low, shallow square stern. Low freeboard amidships, high sheer forward. Wide "V" bottom that flattens aft; herringbone bottom planking. Decked at bow, stern, and along the sides; low coaming. May have crab holding boxes on the bottom, with holes to permit water to flow in and out. Reported lengths 5-9m; e.g., length 8.5m, beam 3m, draft 0.46m. The earlier **skipjack★**-rigged **crab scrapers** were usually half-decked, had no trunk cabin, and lacked shrouds. Other recorded names: **bar cat** (on Tangier Island), **Jenkins creeker** (on Smith Island)

crab skiff See **Shrewsbury River crab skiff**

crab trapper See **crabber**

crab wincher See **billyboy**

crack See **carrack**

craft 1. During the 15th-17th centuries, the term applied to any kind of net, line, or hook used to catch fish, and consequently also applied to **fishing boats★** of the period.
  2. In the 18th century, a general term for **vessels★** engaged in loading and discharging merchant ships. Also applied to those carrying stores to **men-of-war★**, such as **lighters★**, **hoys★**, and **barges★**.
  3. In the mid-19th century, might also apply to small **vessels** tending a **fleet★**, such as **cutters★**, **schooners★**, and **gunboats★**. Generally commanded by a lieutenant.
  4. Ship★ or **vessel**, individually or collectively. May be any **vessel** or **boat★** transporting cargo. Term is sometimes limited to one larger than a **boat** but smaller than a medium-size **vessel**. May convey the idea of a favorite **vessel** or can be a catchall term with no precise meaning.
  5. The term **small craft** is usually reserved for watercraft operating near shore or on inland waters with no size criteria. Often user-owned.
  6. *Nicaragua:* To the Miskito, a small seagoing **canoe★**.

craque See **carrack**

craveel See **karveel**

Cravel-Galliot See **galiot-5**

cravelschip See **karveel**

cray boat *Australia, S/W:* Set pots for rock lobster off Tasmania and Western Australia. Used from the mid-19th century. Generally fast and weatherly. Fitted with a wet well. Early boats open except for foredeck; narrow side decks; short deck aft for a locker. Clinker-planked, with battened seams; double-ended.

Centerboard raised and lowered by hand. Small boats **cutter★**-rigged, with a topsail; larger **yawl★**- or **ketch★**-rigged. Reported lengths 7.6-11.2m. Those built in the early 20th century were carvel-planked, with the top 3 strakes clinker; counter stern. Now mainly fiberglass, with water-circulating tanks. Decked; raised deck around the mast; low cabin abaft the wet well. Carried a **dinghy★** for handling the pots. Tiller on smaller boats, wheel on the larger. Mizzen on the **ketches** carried a topsail. Crosstrees fitted forward of the mast. Motorized, but some sailed until the 1950s. Length to ca. 21m. The Western Australian boats fish for rock lobster in season and shark and tuna at other times. Other recorded names: **crayfish boat**, **(rock) lobster catcher boat**

crayfish boat See **cray boat**, **lobster boat**

creau *Belize:* Double-ended sailing boat; still used by the Black Carib fishermen. Basic **dorey★** modified by adding gunwale planks, stem and sternpost, and short

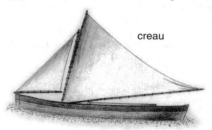

creau

decking forward and aft. Gunter-rigged mainsail set to an aft-raking mast; foresail club-footed. Steered with a yoke to the rudder; movable ballast. Reported lengths 4.6-8.5m. Name variant: **dugout dory**

Cree canoe *Canada, north-central:* The bark **canoe★** of the Cree of the area west of James Bay had a slightly pointed end profile formed by 2 flattened curves. Rounded forefoot; flat floors, slight rocker at ends; fairly vertical sides. Used birch- or sprucebark, the latter thinned at the edges to make a smooth joint. Rounded gunwales; sheer swept up at the ends; stem piece laminated or of spruce root; narrow headboards. Reported lengths 4-4.5m; e.g., length 4.5m, width 0.86m, depth 0.38m. Other recorded names: **oo'se**, **o-síy**; birchbark **canoe**: **wuskwīoose**. Note also **sprucebark canoe**, **wigwas tsiman**.

Cree crooked canoe See **crooked canoe**

Creole skiff See **esquif-2**

creuer See **cruiser-2**

crevella pescereccia, **crevella peschereccia** See **crevelle**

crevelle *France, N:* Seaworthy **fishing boat★** of Normandy and Picardy that fished for herring and mackerel in the English Channel from the 15th to the 18th century. Carvel-planked; low freeboard raised by deep gunwales; open. Two masts; reported as having a square main- and topsail, a square topsail on the mizzen, and a lateen spanker, or a similar mainsail but a foremast that set a square sail. Headsails to a bowsprit. Also rowed. Reported lengths 10-13m overall, widths 3.6-4.2m, depths 1.5-1.8m. Other recorded names: **carabela**, **caravella**, **car(a)velle**, **crevella pesc(h)ereccia**. Note also **caravel-1**.

crevettier French term for a shrimp boat with a beam trawl. Now generally motorized. Those used in the Baie de Seine at the beginning of the 20th century were ca. 6.3m long. Fished from April to October. The Dunkerque **sloop*-**, **cutter*-**, and lug-rigged boats were 8-10m long, 2-3m wide, 1-1.6m deep. Note also **shrimper**. Further references: **canot à crevette, plate-4, shrimper**

crevettier de Nieuport See **Nieuwpoortse garnaalboot**
crevettier ostendais See **Oostendse garnaalboot**
crib A self-contained unit of a lumber **raft*** or **timber raft*** sent down a river to market; may also be a unit of a seagoing **timber raft**.
 1. *Canada, E:* On the Ottawa River, where most rapids were bypassed by slides, a **crib** comprised logs, squared timber, or lumber, and the resulting **raft** (sometimes called a **cage***, **dram***, or **band**) might be of one kind or a combination. Last one delivered to Quebec in 1908. Each **crib** was 7.3m wide and 12m long, and a **raft** might be composed of as many as 100 **cribs**, more often 25-30. The **crib** had a rudimentary mortar-and-tenon framework in which the timbers were lined up. One especially well-made **crib** was the **cookery crib**, with crude shanties for sleeping space. Each **raft** flew a banner identifying its owner's timber mark. Maneuvered by sweeps, a raft drifted or sailed downstream, carrying as many as 12 sails. In heavy whitewater, the **raft** was broken apart and individual **cribs** were worked through the rapids. Other recorded names: **bond, cribe, lumber raft, timber crib**
 2. *United States, central:* A lumber **crib** on Wisconsin rivers was 4.9m by 4.9m, with 24 layers of 5cm lumber. Seven **cribs** made one **rapids piece**, generally 36m long; three **rapids pieces** made one **Wisconsin raft**. Name variant: **boom of logs**
 See also **dram, timber raft-2b, timber raft-3**.
cribe See **crib-1**
crimps' boat See **Whitehall boat**
Croatan boat, Croatian boat See **North Carolina shad boat**
croiseur See **cruiser-3**
croiseur d'escadre See **advice boat**
croiseur leger See **cruiser-2**
Cromer crabber See **Norfolk crabber**
Cromer pinker See **pinker**
crooked canoe *Canada, E:* Bark **canoe*** (**oot**—Eastern Cree generic) of the Eastern Cree, Naskapi, and Montagnais of the Labrador-Ungava peninsula; used on rivers and in open water. Characterized by marked

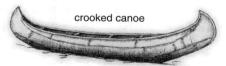
crooked canoe

fore-and-aft bottom rocker without comparable sheer, making the **canoe** deeper amidships than near the ends. Most covered with birchbark (**wiiswaawoot**); covered with canvas (**piicooianiwoot**) from ca. 1908. Generally bottom wide and sides vertical. Stem and gunwales meet in a slightly rounded peak. Gunwales, longer than the bottom, have a light cap pegged or

nailed on, no outwale; bark attached to gunwales by continuous spruce-root lashings. External battens stiffened the ends. Frame of spruce, larch, white cedar; some in the south had maple ribs. Frequently decorated with red paint. Reported lengths 4.34-6.1m; e.g., length 5.5m, width 1.0m, depth 0.58m. Other recorded names: **Cree crooked canoe, Montagnais crooked canoe, Nascapee** (or **Naskapi**) **crooked canoe**; large Cree **canoe: mistoo't**, small **canoe: oo'tisis**. Further reading: J. Garth Taylor, *Canoe Construction in a Cree Cultural Tradition* (Ottawa: National Museums of Canada, 1980). Note also **Cree canoe**.
crooked junk See **qiu zi**
crooked stern junk See **wai pi gu**
Crosby cat or **catboat** See **catboat-2a**
cross-handed dory *Canada, E:* In Newfoundland, a **dory*** equipped to be rowed by one man.
Crotch Island Hampton boat, Crotch Island pinkie See **Crotch Island pinky**
Crotch Island pinky *United States, NE:* Small, beamy, double-ended fishing and lobstering boat developed in the Casco Bay area of southeastern Maine in the 1st half of the 19th century. Extinct by the late 1920s.

Crotch Island pinky

Lapstrake; straight stem with deep forefoot; strongly raked sternpost; broad amidships. Long straight keel; steep rise to the floors; low waist, strong sheer. Open; narrow side decks; centerboard. Characteristically painted bottle green. Rowed and sailed. Masts stepped through thwarts, the taller foremast well forward. Set spritsails, the sprits held high by snotters; foresail loose-footed, mainsail boomed. Sometimes a light jib ran to a temporary bowsprit. Crew of 4. Reported lengths 5.5-8.5m; e.g., length 6.2m, beam 1.7m, depth ca. 0.76m. Other recorded names: **Casco Bay pinky, Crotch Island Hampton boat, Crotch Island pinkie**. Note also **Hampton boat**.
crucero, cruciatore, crucişetor See **cruiser**
cruiser 1. In general, a boat or vessel designed for short- or long-distance cruising. Most now **motor cruisers**. With regard to **yachts***, the term is in contradistinction to a boat designed to be raced. A **day cruiser** lacks accommodations, returning to home port at night. Other recorded names: **battello da crociera, cabin cruiser, crucero, Fahrtenkreuzer, kajut-kruzer, Kreuzer(jacht), navire de croisière**. Note also **vedette**.

2. A fast, well-armed sailing vessel ordered to conduct independent scouting, patrolling, dispatch carrying, blockade duty, etc., mainly in the 18th century. **Frigate***-sized or smaller. Selected name variants: **adviesjacht, barco crucero, bâtiment croiseur, creuer, croiseur leger, crucero, cruizer, cruzador, Kreuzerfregatte, krydser, kryssare, light cruiser, scout***.

3. With the advent of steam propulsion and steel armor, a **cruiser** became a fast small warship which, while still engaging in advance scouting duties, is capable of taking its place in a battle line. Other recorded names: **battle cruiser, croiseur, crucero, cruciatore, crucişetor, cru(i)zer, incrociatore, kreiser, krejser, Kreuzer, kreyser, krstárica, krstaš, krui(s)ser, kruvazor, krysser, nave di crociera, Schlachtkreuzer**

4. *England, S:* Term used by early Sussex smugglers for a revenue vessel. Other recorded names: **Barking tartar, tartar***.

See also **fishery guard ship, privateer**.

cruzador See **cruiser-2**

cruizer, cruzer See **cruiser-2, cruiser-3**

csaike See **saique**

cuberta See **coberta**

cuciforno See **kuserofne**

cufa See **quffa**

culaidh *Scotland, N:* Term for a small boat in the Reay area at the northeast tip of Scotland. See also **coble-4**.

culé *Portugal, central:* Flat-bottomed cargo vessel that brought produce, cork, grain, and passengers from the shallow upper waterways of the Tagus Estuary to the Lisbon area. Double-ended; bottom swept up at the ends, the bow curving up smoothly to a slightly recurved ornamental stemhead, the stern rounding up more vertically. Shallow rudder, wide-bladed below the waterline, narrower above, terminating in a tall rudderhead; tiller worked by block and tackle from a horizontal peg run through the top of the rudder. Leeboards used when sailing. Lateen sail set to an aft-raking mast. One or 2 headsails. Average 30t, some to 100t. Other recorded names: **colé, monaio**

cule See **kule-1**

culiăla, culjar, culyara See **corial**

cumacèna *Italy, NE:* Slender, swift boat used for fishing and hunting in the Valli di Comacchio (lagoon) off the northern part of the Adriatic. Sharp ends; tall, straight, raked stem and sternpost; flat bottom with rocker at ends; flared sides; top strake stops short of the stem; strong sheer. Open except for short decks at the ends that terminate in shallow breakwaters; 1-2 thwarts; bulwarks narrow toward the ends. Hull tarred; bulwarks and sides may be ornamented. Rowed standing, with 2-4 oars worked against tall oar forks; also poled. Occasionally sailed, stepping a light mast through the thwart, setting a lugsail, and using an oar as a rudder. Crew of 2. Reported lengths 4.6-8m; e.g., length 6.5m, beam 1.6m, depth 1.2m. Other recorded names: **battèlla***, **battèllo comacchiese** (pl. **battelli comacchiesi), volizèpid**

Cumberland River drift *United States, central:* Term given to a **timber raft*** on the upper river, in Kentucky and Tennessee. Used above Nashville between the 1870s and 1930s. Logs tied together with hickory

strips, preferably with softwoods and hardwoods alternating, each secured by wooden pins or iron chains. Usually maneuvered by 5 oars set onto rods, 3 in front and 2 in back. On tributaries, small **blocks** were constructed, which in turn might be combined into **drifts**; **blocks** needed only a single oar at each end. A shack provided shelter for the crew and supplies on the drifts; also carried a **johnboat*** or **skiff***. Most **drifts** were three 4.9m-long logs wide and as long as 85m; the **blocks** were a single 4.9m log wide.

Cuna canoe, Cunah canoe See **cayuco-5**

cundara See **gundra**

cunner See **Chesapeake Bay log canoe-1**

cunner boat See **paddy boat-4**

cunno See **kunu**

cunoe See **Chesapeake Bay log canoe**

cun'r See **Chesapeake Bay log canoe-1**

cuquete See **cog**

curac, cura a See **curragh**

curaċ án *Ireland:* Irish term for a small **boat*** or **skiff***. Spelling variants: **coraċ án, corracán**. Note also **curragh**.

curach, curachan See **coracle-2, curragh**

curagh See **curragh**

curaporti, cure-môle, curemolle See **dredger-1**

curial, curiala See **corial**

curiana See **curiara-2**

curiara **1.** *Brazil, W:* **Canoe*** hewn from the *cajuacu* tree. Used by the Crichana of the state of Amazonas.

2. *Venezuela:* **Dugout canoe*** used mainly on rivers. Built and used by the Guarao (Warao) of the Orinoco Delta, but exported to other parts of Venezuela. Basic dugout carefully prepared to achieve a pleasant sheer and length/width proportion. When plank-extended, added plank was lapped. Expanded sides flare; raised, overhanging ends may have a platform; low freeboard; thwarts or round block inserted to maintain flare. Sharply turned-up bow may be cut square to form a small triangle. Gunwale piece may extend beyond the square stern. **Canoes** made by the Makiritare in southern Venezuela have a notch at the stern, and the bow

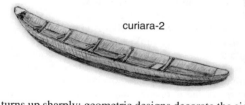

curiara-2

turns up sharply; geometric designs decorate the sides. Those at Isla de Margarita modified for sea fishing; sides raised; stern altered for outboard motor attachment. In places, a small triangular sail set, sometimes of strips of bamboo or of bushy leaves. Large river **canoes** may be 10-16m long, width ca. 1.5m; family boats 2-6m long. Other recorded names: **curiana, koriara** (Carib), **koryári, kuliára, kuriára, kuriera, gwa** or **wa*** (by the Guarao). Further reading: Albert & Philippe Manhuzier, *Chez les Indiens Guaraos du Delta de l'Orénoque* (Paris: Société d'Éditions Géographique et Touristique, 1961). Note also **corial**.

curiará See **ubá**

currabius See **carabus**
currac See **curragh**
currach See **coracle-2**, **curragh**
curracium See **carabus**
curra-curra See **korakora-1**
curragh *Ireland, W and NW:* Hide- and now cloth-covered boat that works from the coastal beaches; of very early origin but still used for sea and inshore fishing and for general transportation. Early versions making oceangoing voyages were covered with 2-3 layers of hide (using 20-30 oxhides) and had a mast and a crew of ca. 20. Numerous local variations, but most had withe or lath frames covered with skin until the mid-19th century; now usually covered with tarred calico. Most elongated, with sharp or blunt bow and flat shallow transom. Gunwale made first and then bottom and sides attached while upside down; strengthened by inserting U-shaped thwarts. Propelled generally by oars, although some set a small sail. Most less than 7.6m long; some early boats much larger. Other recorded names: **canoe***, **caribus**, **carrocium**, **churchán** (dim.), **cor(r)ach**, **corragh**, **courache**, **curac(h)**, **curachán** (dim.), **curagh**, **currac(h)**, **curuca**, **curuch**, **kuruch**, **pirogue***; pl. **curać a.** Further reading: James Hornell, *British Coracles and Irish Curraghs* (London: Society for Nautical Research, 1938); Richard Mac Cullagh, *The Irish Curragh Folk* (Dublin: Wolfhound Press, 1992). Note also **Achill Island curragh**, **Aran Islands canoe**, **Boyne curragh**, **carabus-1**, **coracle**, **curać án**, **Donegal curragh**, **naoṁóg.**
currant schooner See **fruit schooner**
current ferry See **ferryboat-1**
curricanero See **troller**
curricle See **coracle-1**
Currituck hunting skiff, Currituck push boat See **push boat-3**
currock, currok, currough See **coracle-2**
cursalis, cursare, cursarius, cursaro, cursary, cursayre, cursore, cursour See **corsair**
curuca See **carabus**, **curragh**
curuch See **curragh**
cuseforne, cuserofne, cusiforne See **kuserofne**
Custom House boat See **revenue cutter-1**
custom-house galley See **galley-7**
customs guard vessel, customs sloop See **revenue cutter-1**
cut barge *United Kingdom:* One designed to traverse the "cuts" or narrow inland canals. See also **stumpy barge**.
cut boat *Canada, E:* One of the team of boats used in working mackerel trap nets off Cape Breton Island. Towed to the site by the **tow boat***. Works inside the net, pulling and cutting strategic lines to drive the fish toward the **collecting boat***. Open, clinker-planked, closely framed. Name variant: **cutter boat**
cúter See **cutter-1**
cut flat See **Mersey flat**
cutmurram See **catamaran**
cutt See **team boat-4**
cutter **1.** The **cutter** of the 18th and early 19th centuries was rigged with a gaff mainsail, loose-footed or

boomed, a topsail that was jib-headed or set with a yard, and 2 or more headsails. Mast generally stepped roughly a third in from the bow and inclined aft; topmast usually fidded. Jib set flying to a long running bowsprit. Originally carried one or more large square sails, staysail, and a jib to a horizontal or bowsed-down reeving bowsprit; term now includes a vessel with leg-of-mutton mainsail, staysail, and jib to a bowsprit. Some naval **cutters** were rigged as **ketches*** but retained the designation **cutter**. Hull generally deeper, narrower, and with less freeboard than a **sloop***. Early vessels clinker-built. Being fast, often used to combat smuggling and as **advice boats***; heavily armed. Reported lengths 12-18m on the gun deck; beamy. Selected name variants: **côtre**, **còttaru**, **cotter(o)**, **cottre**, **cottro**, **coutter**, **cúter**, **cùttere**, **kater**, **kòter**, **kotter***, **kottr**, **kûter**, **Kutter***. Note also **revenue cutter**.
2. A naval **ship's boat***, especially in the British Royal Navy; used both in England and colonial America. Rowed with 8-14 oars, 1-2 men to an oar, or set 1-2 lugsails or were **ketch**-rigged. Oars worked in cuts in top strake. Mostly lapstrake construction; flat floors; curved keel; sharp entrance; transom stern with reverse chine on the tuck; rounded bilges. Steered with a rudder; centerboard on some. Used as an armed **tender*** for chasing privateers and smugglers, carrying dispatches, and protecting fisheries. Reported lengths 5-10.4m; e.g., length 8.5m, beam 2.3m, depth 0.77m. Other recorded names: **canot de service**, **gèarradair**. Note also **cutter-gig**.
3. A pleasure craft that has a mainsail and 2 headsails, the outer sail set from the bowsprit. Such a rig sometimes called a **sloop** in the United States, where the **cutter** has a gaff mainsail, forestaysail and flying jib to a long bowsprit (**gaff cutter**), but more recently it sets a leg-of-mutton sail (**cutter-yacht**). The mast is stepped ca. 2/5th back from the bow end of the waterline length. Other recorded names: **cotre à corne**, **gaffelkotter**, **gaffelkutter**, **Kutteryacht**
4. Pilot cutters were usually rigged with a gaff mainsail and 2 foresails. Size varied widely; frequently had living accommodations. Now may apply to a **yacht***-like craft used in the pilot service. Note also **pilot boat**.
5. May be a craft carrying officials, trainers, etc., associated with a boating race.
6. *Australia, South Australia:* From the late 19th to the mid-20th century, a decked **fishing boat*** was known as a **cutter**, regardless of rig.
7. *United Kingdom:* **a.** The present-day British navy **cutter** carries a mainsail and jib, pulls 4 or 8 oars, has a high transom stern, and a drop keel. Cap. 29 men. Lengths 7-9.8m; e.g., length 9.8m, beam 2.6m. Note also **black cutter**. **b.** English smuggling **cutters** of the late 18th century were especially fast, armed, well-manned, relatively short-hulled, sharp forward, flush-decked, and well-timbered; traditional **cutter** rigging. **c.** Trinity House in England used steam and diesel **cutters** to service navigation lights and as **pilot boats**. **d.** In England, the term may be used for the **boats** that brought the catch from the fishing **fleet*** to market. In the 19th century, they were **fishing boats** rigged with

a gaff mainsail, foresail and jib to a bowsprit. Name variant: **carrier**★. **e.** Strong long-oared **cutters**, for 4, 6, and sometimes 8 rowers, were raced on the Thames. Blunt bow. One type was called a **half-decker**★. Eight-oared boats were 2lm long. **f.** The fast **Admiralty cutter** pulled 12 oars, while other **cutters** were restricted to 6 oars, following an 18th-century edict to prevent smuggling. Used to at least the early 20th century. Clinker-planked, sharp bow, high-tucked transom stern. Outboard rudder; tiller, manned by the helmsman. **8.** *United States:* **a.** The U.S. naval **cutter** of the late 19th and early 20th centuries was carvel-planked, with a plumb stem, flaring bow, high transom stern, long straight keel. Six thwarts, stern sheets; rowed double-banked with 5-6 pairs of oars, with oarlocks or with rowlocks notched into the washboards. Set 2 sliding gunter lugsails and a foresail. Standard lengths 6.1m, 7.3m, 7.9m, 8.5m, 9.1m; e.g., length 7.9m, beam 2.1m, depth 0.76m. Name variant: **service cutter**. **b.** A **cutter** can be a motorized patrol vessel in the Coast Guard or the Weather Patrol.
Further references: **cod smack**, **cotre**, **groundnut cutter**, **revenue cutter**, **Yarmouth shrimper**

cutter boat See **cut boat**

cutter-brig In the late 18th and early 19th centuries, a large **cutter**★ that became unwieldy might be altered to a **brig**★ rig, with square sails on the mainmast and fore-and-aft and topsails on the mizzen. Retained the comparatively large beam, deep hull, and steep mid-section deadrise of the **cutter**. Other recorded names: **brig-cutter**, **Briggkutter**, **brigkutter**, **Kutterbrigg**

cùttere See **cutter-1**

cutter-gig Term given to a **ship's boat**★ sized between a **cutter**★ and a **gig**★. Employs 2-3 pairs of oars. Lengths 6-7m. Other recorded names: **cutter-gigg**, **Kuttergig**

cutter-gigg See **cutter-gig**

cutter suction dredger See **dredger-1**

cutter-yacht See **cutter-3**

cutter-yawl A mid-18th-century **ship's boat**★ of the British navy that was probably built along **cutter**★ lines, but had the carvel planking of the **yawl**★.

cuttle-fish boat See **mo you chuan**

cutwater See **coble-1**

cwch gwrw See **male boat**

cwrwg, cwrwgl See **coracle-3**

cwrwgle See **coracle-2**

cybaea, cybaea, cybea See **kybaia**

cychod banw See **female boat**

cylinder See **double-bottom-2**

cyule, cyulis See **keel**

czaike, czaiken See **saique**

czajka 1. *Poland, E:* **a.** A popular clinker-built boat used on inland waters, especially in the area of the Masurian lakes, the Pripet Marshes, and the Neman River. Used until World War II. Mainly rowed. **b.** A Cossack **canoe**★ of the 17th-18th centuries.
2. *Slovakia:* A **fishing boat**★. Other recorded names: **čaj(k)a**
Spelling variant: **tshayka**. See also **saique**.

czesekan See **Zeeskahn**

czullen See **Zille**

Dachschiff *Germany, S:* 19th-century cargo boat of the Bavarian part of the Rhine Valley and the Frankenthaler Canal, northwest of Mannheim. Characterized by its movable wooden house. Name variant: **Frachtschiff**

dack See **dawk boat**

däcksbåt *Sweden, W:* Beamy cargo and **fishing boat**★ built mainly between 1880s and 1920s. Most clinker-planked, sharp ends, curved stem and sternpost, straight keel with drag, soft turn of the high bilges, marked sheer, especially toward the bow. Decked, steering well, low cabin on sailing type. Outboard rudder. Mast stepped a little forward of amidships; set loose-footed, boomed leg-of-mutton sail or tall spritsail. Most late boats motorized. Reported lengths 6.7-9.4m; e.g., 8m long, 3m wide, 2m deep. Other recorded names: **stranningen** (from Stranninge), **vrakbåt**; pl. **däcksbåtar**, **däcksbåten**. See also **fiskebåt-3**.

däcksbåtar, däcksbåten See **däcksbåt**

dacoit's boat See **chhip**

daé *Cameroon, north-central:* Small, rough, flat-bottomed **dugout canoe**★ used in the basin of the Benue/Mayo Kabi Rivers.

dåë See **düe**

dæksfartöj fra Hornbæk See **Hornbækbåd**

da fu chuan *China, central:* Very old type of **salt junk**, transporting salt from the Chang Jiang (Yangtze) estuary to ports in Hunan and Jiangxi (Kiangsi) Provinces, where they were built. Carried local products downstream. Low square bow; high square stern. Mat houses covered most of the hull. Three- or 4-masted, the 4th mast raking over the bow. Small mizzen on the transom, sheeted to an outrigger. Set battened lugsails. Crew of 14. Cap. ca. 270-405t. Spelling variant: **ta-fu ch'uan**

dagabia See **dahabiyah**

dagbarge See **trekschuit-2**

dagger *West Indies, Barbuda:* Simple **raft**★ constructed by lobstermen of this Leeward Island. Composed of stalks of the mature dagger (century) plant, ca. 16-17cm in diameter at their wider ends. Stalks secured by a wooden pole that passes through a hole bored at each end of the 12 stalks, held tight by lashings. A pole, ca. 4.5m long, propels the **raft** in deeper water, while a shorter pole is used near shore. Reported lengths 4.5-6m, width 2m.

daggerboot See **dogger**

dago In English-speaking North America, a **vessel**★ from Italy, Spain, or Portugal might be called a **dago**. Note also **Guinea boat**.

Dago fishing boat See **felucca-3**

dagschuit See **trekschuit-3**

da gu chuan *China, E:* **Fishing boat**★ from Hangzhou Wan (Hangchow Bay), south of Shanghai. Employed a bag net for shrimp and jellyfish. Flat keelless bottom with rocker; rounded sides, strengthened with 2 wales of half-round logs. Sharp bow, with cutaway forefoot; square, raked stern; strong sheer. Flush deck. Large

oculi at bows. Mainmast stepped forward of amidships; small mizzenmast abaft the rudder; set battened canvas lugsails. Length overall ca. 16m, beam 3.4m, depth 1.7m. Spelling variant: **ta-ku ch'uan**

dahabeah, dahabeeah, dahabeeyah, dahabeiah, dahabia, dahabiah, dahabieh, dahabiya See **dahabiyah**

dahabiyah *Egypt:* Nile passenger vessel used principally during the 19th century, often having luxurious accommodations. Originally a gilded royal **barge**★, but now may be a small canal boat. Most had a low bow and higher stern; keel; flat bottom; long cabin aft. For upstream travel the foremast, stepped close to the bow, set a high-peaked lateen sail with a very long, tapering yard that rested on a saddle at the top of the mast. Yard fitted with 2 single halyards, each passing through a single sheaved block on each side of the mast. On large vessels, a small lateen sail at the stern aided steering. On the downstream run, the foresail was often taken down and the small stern sail substituted. Large, powerful rudder. Large vessels employed 12-14 huge oars; counterbalance weights sometimes lashed to the loom. Decking lifted to provide seats on the crossbeams when rowed; rowers stood on inclined planks, taking 3 steps forward as they dipped the sweeps and then stepping back as they pulled. Later boats motorized. Small vessels had 8-10 in crew. Averaged ca. 30m long and 4.3m wide; small size 14.3m long, 3.23m wide, 1.0m deep. Spelling variants: **dagabia**, **dahabe(e)ah**, **dahabe(e)yah**, **dahabeiah**, **dahabia(h)**, **dahabieh**, **dahabiya**, **dahabiye(h)**, **Dehabiya**. Note also **cangia**.

dahabiye, dahabiyeh See **dahabiyah**

dahoep See **daoep-daoep, perahu kajangan**

da hong chuan *China, N:* Originated at Dandong (Antung), near the Korean border, trading along the coast. Dated back at least 2,500 years. Flat keelless bottom, longitudinally planked; flat bow and stern, strongly curved and transversely planked; numerous bulkheads formed watertight compartments; longitudinal strength provided by 3 heavy wales. Nearly straight run to the stern; considerable sheer; high poop. Deck usually awash when loaded, there being no bulwarks. Flush deck; hatch for ca. two-thirds of the length of the vessel, high coaming; low deckhouse aft, behind which was a short gallery that terminated in a false transom. Rudderpost came up forward of the gallery; post had 2 sockets for different tiller levels. Hull stained black, with touches of red and green; on some, stern transom ornately painted. Towed or carried aboard a miniature of the **junk**★ as a **tender**★. Fore- and mainmasts in tabernacles; no shrouds or stays; raked slightly in opposing directions. Two quarter masts available, but generally only one stepped at a time. Lugsails of cotton or matting; large number of horizontal battens. Cotton sails dyed in mixture of mangrove bark and pig's blood. Crew of 15-20. Reported lengths 21-33.5m; e.g., length 21.6m, beam

4.6m, hold depth 2m; shallow draft. Other recorded names: **Antung trader**, **big red boat**, **Dandong chuan**, **ta-hung (ch'uan)**, **ta hung-t'ou yang ch'uan (big red-headed oceangoing boat)**. Further reading: D. W. Waters, "Chinese Junks: The Antung Trader," *The Mariner's Mirror* XXIV (1938), 49-68.

dai chuan See **liu wang chuan**

dâiso See **dghajsa-1**

dak See **dawk boat**, **pallar**

da knoren Collective term for small open **boats★** and for **vessels★** in the Shetland and Faroe Islands. Note also **knarr**.

dalama See **dalámas**

dalámas *Philippines, S:* Type of **baroto★**. Simple dugout hull without decoration. Double outriggers. Some set a quadrilateral sail, set fore-and-aft, to a tripod mast. Spelling variant: **dalama**

dalca *Chile:* Pre-Columbian plank-built boat used into the 19th century from north of the Archipélago de Chiloé to the Strait of Magellan and on some Andean

dalca

lakes. The larger boats were seagoing; the smaller ones, used on interior waterways, were sometimes disassembled and portaged across peninsulas. Initially made of 3 planks—bottom and 1 each side, but under Spanish influence some were constructed of 5 and later 7 planks. In each, the bottom plank was longer and narrower at the ends and, following softening by fire and water, was forced up to form a raked bow and stern. In the earlier models the planks were pierced and sewn with shredded saplings; later secured with pegs. Ribs and thwarts were added; on some, multiple thwarts extended outboard below the top strake. On later types, stout timbers affixed at ends formed false stem and sternpost, and some had runners on the bottom for beaching. At the stern, a pair of ribs projecting above the gunwales served as a fulcrum for a steering oar. Shipped a rudder on many 7-plank **dalcas**; worked with yoke and lines. Open; some had raised floorboards on which a turf fireplace was placed. Probably initially paddled; later, mainly rowed by 6-12 oarsmen; round-loomed oar, to which a squared blade was fastened. Large boats could transport as many as 25 persons. With favorable winds, set a sealskin sail; later of cloth. Sometimes portrayed with 2 masts setting square sails. Reported lengths 3.4-20m; e.g., length 16m, beam 1.8m, depth 1.0m. Other recorded names: **dalka**, **dallca**, **guampu**, **piragua★** (colonial term), **vuta guampu** (large type). Further reading: Manuel Puente Blanco, "La 'Dalca' de Chiloé. Su Influencia en la Exploración Austral...," *Revista de Historia Naval* (Madrid) IV (1986), 19-44. Further reference: **anan**

da libo See **libo**

dalka, **dallca** See **dalca**

dambåd See **sjægt**

Damenschiff See **Leibschiff**

damjolle See **smakkejolle**

Dampfbarkasse See **launch**

dandie See **dandy**

Dandong chuan See **da hong chua**

dandy Imprecise term, but originally applied most often to a vessel with a loose-footed fore-and-aft mainsail, 1-2 headsails, and a standing lug mizzen. In time, term also applied loosely to boats that had converted the mizzen to a boomed gaff sail, rigged either as a **ketch★** (sometimes called a **big mizzener**) or a **yawl★** (**little mizzener**). In some areas of England, a **dandy** was a **ketch**-rigged **fishing boat★** with a running bowsprit, such as the **Brixham smack★**, **Lowestoft trawler★**, and **Ramsgate smack★**. In southwest England, the term **dandy** applied to **ketch**-rigged vessels under 18m, the term **ketch** being reserved for larger vessels. Spelling variant: **dandie**. Note also **Manx lugger**, **Nieuwpoortse dandy**. Further references: **dundee**, **Yarmouth shrimper**

dandy au commerce See **dundee**

dandy smack *Ireland, E/Northern Ireland:* In some areas, the **dandy smack** replaced the **Irish wherry★** over the course of the 19th century. Rounded stern. Set a boomed gaff mainsail, a standing lug mizzen, sheeted to an outrigger, and 2 headsails. Name variant: **lugger★**. Further reference: **Manx lugger**

dandy thonier See **thonier**

danga *India, E:* Used by the fishermen of Chilka Lake, near the Orissa coast. Low, open craft with overhanging bow; clinker-planked. Steered and sculled with a long paddle. Tall rectangular mat sail hung from 2 light masts stepped athwartships close to the bow; 2 forestays to the bow from height of ca. 2m. Reported lengths 7.6-10.7m, widths 0.9-1.22m, depths 0.6-0.9m. See also **dhangi**.

dangi *Kuwait:* Cargo vessel similar to the **boom★** except for having the bird's head stem ornament of the **kotia★**. Reported lengths 9-21m. Further reference: **dhangi**

dangiyah See **dhangi**, **dingi**

dang wai *China, S:* Generic term used in the south, especially at Fort Bayard (now Zhanjiang), for several types of Chinese boats, notably the **koupang★**. Unique in having a centerboard placed in the forward third of the vessel, sometimes well forward so that it dropped out at the forefoot. Other recorded names: **tang vay** (**wai** or **way**)

dänische Deke See **Quase**

Danks' trow See **trow-1**

dao *Comoro Islands, western Indian Ocean:* Roughly constructed vessel that carried cargo to the west coast of India, taking advantage of the monsoon winds. Slightly raking stem, square stern. Decked or open. Set a large lateen sail to a forward-raking mast; yard supported by a jibboom. Reported lengths 13.7-15.2m, beamy; 50-60t. Name variant: **boutre★**

dao

dão See **dhow**

dao ba zi *China, central:* Large family of river **junks***, mainly of Hunan Province. Many carry coal to Wuhan on the Chang Jiang (Yangtze). In general, long, narrow, square-ended, and flat-bottomed, but with widely varying features. Reported lengths 13.7m-24.4m. Other recorded names: **scratch back boat, tao-pa-tzŭ**
1. The **Xiangxiang dao ba zi** carries coal and minerals on the Xiang (Siang) Shui to Wuhan, returning with general cargo. Built on the tributary Lian (Lien) Shui. Flat bottom curves up gently at the bow and abruptly at the high stern. Curved sides; 11 bulkheads. Wooden house at stern; cargo in midsection covered by a low house; bow open. Balanced rudder comes up in the house; distinctive wales along the sides terminate before the ends. Mainmast stepped just forward of amidships; light foremast in the bow. Sets high-peaked rectangular sails. Crew of 7. Length 24.4m, beam 3.7m, depth 1.7m. Other recorded names: **Lian (Lien) River coal boat, Siangsiang tao-pa-tzŭ**
2. The **Changsha dao ba zi** transports coal on the upper Xiang Jiang to Changsha. Sides flare from the flat bottom and then become vertical. Overhanging bow, stern curves up; flat sheer except for a hump along the mat-covered area abaft amidships; elsewhere the sides may be raised with sectional washboards. Narrow square ends, the stern narrower. Balanced rudder, raking post comes up inboard; tiller; stick-in-the-mud anchors. Single mast sets a high-peaked battened rectangular sail; mast stepped just forward of amidships. Length 13.7m, beam 1.7m, depth 0.6m; shallow draft. Other recorded names: **Changsha tao-pa-tzŭ, humpback junk**
3. The Lo River **dao ba zi** carries coking coal from mines in western Jiangxi (Kiangsi) Province, via Liling, the Xiang Shui, and the Chang Jiang to Wuhan. Narrow square ends; curved-up bow, more vertical stern; flaring sides. Wooden house abaft the mast, mat roof; open forward and aft. Rudder post from balanced rudder comes up inboard; tiller. Mast stepped just forward of amidships. Crew of 4. Length 18.6m, beam 2.5m, depth 1.0m; shallow draft. Name variant: **Liling tao-pa-tzŭ**

daoeb, daoep See **daoep-daoep**

daoep-daoep *Indonesia:* Very large river craft used in Kalimantan (Borneo) and Sumatra. Characterized by the wooden house that protects passengers. To assist in negotiating sharp river bends, maneuvered by 2 very long oars, one forward, the other aft. Name variant: **daoeb**. For the Kajan-Dayaks of northeastern Kalimantan, **daoep** or **dahoep** is a generic for **perahu***. Note also **perahu kajangan**.

daoi See **düe**

dãou See **dhow**

dapang 1. *East Malaysia:* Long, narrow **outrigger canoe*** of Sabah. Bifid bow. Employs 1-2 outriggers; 3 or more booms attach directly to a bamboo float. Single sail set to a tripod mast. Spelling variant: **dopong**
2. *Philippines, S:* In the Sulu Sea area, **dapang** may apply to any small **dugout canoe***. Plank-extended; no outriggers.
Further references: **kabang, vinta**

darai, daraīm See **sarnái**

daré *Cameroon, N:* Fishing dugout of the Kotoko and Mousgoum peoples. Employs a large hand net. Flat bottom; bluntly pointed bow; overhanging platform for the paddler at the stern. Residual projection, facing inward, at each end of the hull. Crew of 2. Ca. 8m long. Name variant: **houloum** (by the Mousgoum)

dåre See **dory-4**

darewal battella See **bohatja**

darrling See **eka-2**

dã:s See **bã:s**

dau 1. General term used on the East African coast, especially along Kenya, for all small sharp-ended boats. Most used for fishing, some for hunting turtles. Long overhanging bow with sharp forefoot characteristic; raked sternpost; plank-built; most flat-bottomed. Along the northern coast, the rudder is hung by lashings or grommets and the tiller slots over the rudderhead; farther south, rudder is attached by gudgeons and pintles and helm is inserted. Most undecorated except for occasional oculi. Employs a lateen sail; may also be poled or rowed. Generally under 10t. Other recorded names: **daura, idau**. Note also **mtepe**.
2. *Mozambique, N:* Double-ended boat that transports produce in the Pemba (Porto Amelia) area. Carvel-planked; slightly curved stem; raked sternpost; sheer line rises toward the bow. Decked at ends. Full-cut quadrilateral lateen-type sail with a short luff set to a forward-raking mast; luff boomed out over the bow. Crew of 2-3. Reported lengths 10-12m. Note also **n'galawa-3**.
3. *Tanzania, E:* Small open boat of northern Zanzibar Island that collected firewood in mangrove swamps, especially on the mainland coast. Still active for seining off Zanzibar and Pemba. Plank-built with sharp stem and curved stern. Oculi at bows and stern, placed in a triangular "moustache." Occasionally set a square mat sail, later of canvas. Crew of 11-16 for fishing. Other recorded names: **sambuk*, sanbuq;** pl. **madau**
Further references: **dau la mtepe, dhow, kotia, tanga**

daugre, daugrebot See **dogger**

dau la juga See **dau la mtepe**

dau la kuni See **dau la mataruma**

dau la mataruma *East Africa:* Bajun-built **dau*** found mostly between Lamu in Kenya and Kismaayo in Somalia, but also occurs in harbor areas to the south and on northern Zanzibar Island. Plank-built with ribs; flat floors. Sharp raking bow and stern, with heavy stem and sternpost. Usually bossed oculi forward.

dau la mataruma

Short deck at bow and stern. Large rudder, ornamented and carved, angles downward at bottom and at head, and curves partly over the sternpost; tiller slants upward. Forward-raking mast supported against the mast beam. Yard in one piece, often of bamboo. Lateen sail tacks to bowsprit. May also be rowed or poled. Crew varies from 2-6, depending on mission. Maximum length ca. 9m. Designation may relate to the occupation the boat is engaged in at the time, e.g., called **dau la tata** when tending fish traps; **dau la mti** or **dau la kuni** when collecting firewood. Other recorded names: **kuni dau, mti dau, tata dau**

dau la mtepe   *East Africa:* Found sporadically from southern Somalia to southern Tanzania and on northern Zanzibar Island from early 19th century to early 1930s. Transported mangrove poles mainly. Sharply raked, elongated, straight pointed bow and sharp stern; slight sheer. Carvel-planked hull fastened with pegs and coir rope; ribs lashed on later. Slightly curved

dau la mtepe

forefoot. Wedge-shaped blocks sewn onto the stem, then strakes set into the triangle and sewn on. Hull strengthened with 5-7 pairs of thwarts, the lower thwart lashed to the upper; thwarts pierced the hull. Boat resewn each year. Short decks forward and aft; light cabin for crew aft. Oculi at bows, painted or bossed; bowsprit often carried fringe of reeds or flags. Notches for a tassel or small bag cut into the upper part of the strongly raked outboard rudder; tiller slotted over rudderhead. Vertical pole mast stepped into keel and lashed against 2nd or 3rd thwart; secured by 2 stays. Set large square mat sail with top and bottom yards; 2 reef points; some set a canvas sail. Used forward and stern sheets; bowline passed through hole in bowsprit and back to forward thwart. A spar might be run out forward for a jib. Oars used in light winds or in lee areas. Reported lengths 18.3-20.4m; e.g., length overall 18.3m, on keel 10.7m, beam 5.5m, depth 1.85m. Other recorded names: **dau★** (Bajun), **d(h)au ya mtepe, idhau, luzio, mtepe dau, muntafiyah, zambuco**; pl. **madau la** (or **wa) mtepe**. When fishing with a seine net, called **dau la juga** or **dau la yau**. Further reading: A. H. J. Prins, *A Handbook of Sewn Boats* (London: National Maritime Museum, 1986), 64-92. Note also **mtepe**.

dau la mti   See **dau la mataruma**
dau la mtumbwi   See **mtumbwi**
dau la tata   See **dau la mataruma**
dau la yau   See **dau la mtepe**

daura   See **dau-1**
dau ya mtepe   See **dau la mtepe**
dãva   See **dhow**
davit boat   A **ship's boat★** that hangs on davits. Other recorded names: **boissoir de canot, bote de pescantes, canot de bossoir** (or **portemanteau), Davitboot, davit craft, davitsloep, drôme, pescant(e), Seitenboote**. Note also **quarter boat**.
Davitboot, davit craft, davitsloep   See **davit boat**
daw   See **dhow**
dawk boat   *Bangladesh:* Rowing/sailing boat of the 19th century that carried the mail (*dawk* or *dak*) and passengers to and from ships lying off the mouth of the Ganges. Slender double-ended craft with curved, overhanging stem and sternpost; bottom copper-sheathed. Decked; several hatches. When rowed, oars inserted in a forked device so that they were supported well above the gunwale, clearing the washstrake. When sailed, set 1-2 lugsails. Masts stepped in tabernacles. Reported lengths 14-16m; e.g., length 16m, beam 2.5m. Other recorded names: **dack, dak, mail boat★**
day boat   **1.** Small sailing or powered boat that is undecked and suitable mainly for daytime use, although it may have a cuddy forward. Other recorded names: **bateau (vedette** or **voilier) de promenade, day cruiser, day sailer, imbarcazione da giorno, Tagessegler, voilier de promenade**
   2. *British Isles:* Term given to canal **barges★** that engaged in short-haul traffic, carrying bulk cargoes that needed no protection from the weather; horse-drawn boats worked well into the 20th century. Most open, with no sleeping accommodations, although many had shelter. A **narrow boat★** on the Birmingham Canal Navigations that had a small cabin was known as a **Joey** (or **Joey boat**); others with a cabin might be called a **box cabin boat**. In northern England the cabins could be dismantled to clear under bridges. Some English boats were double-ended so that the rudder could be hung at either end, eliminating the need to turn around. **Joeys** were more cheaply built, but had square bilges, vertical sides, and near-vertical stem and sternpost. In south Wales, the **day boats** of the late 18th and early 19th centuries were **passage boats★**, with 1-2 cabins, carrying passengers and parcels on a regular schedule. The **barges** were towed from a towing mast by a single horse. Reported lengths 12.2-22m; **Black Country day boats** were 22m long, 2.2m wide, ca. 1.17m deep. Other recorded names: **market passage boat, open boat★**. Note also **cabin boat**.
   3. *England, SW:* Open carvel-planked boat of Polperro on the southern Cornish coast that handlined for whiting and mackerel. Set a loose-footed gaff mainsail and a staysail. Reported lengths 6.0-7.3m. Name variant: **Polperro day boat**
   4. *United States, E:* On the Chesapeake & Ohio Canal, in the 1st quarter of the 20th century, a **day boat** was one that tied up for part or all of the night, while a **night boat** ran around the clock.
day cruiser   See **cruiser-1, day boat-1**
day sailer   See **day boat-1**
day tar boat   See **black boat**
deadrise   See **deadrise boat, skipjack-1**

deadrise bateau *United States, E:* Small, light craft that was built for wildfowling on the bays of coastal Virginia, especially at Chincoteague. V-bottom; sharp forward; flat from midsection to stern. Oval cockpit; low coaming. Reported lengths 4.0-4.3m; sides 25-31cm deep. Note also **skipjack-1**.

deadrise boat **1.** General term for a boat in which the floor rises to meet the sides at a sharp angle at the bilges to create a wide "V." Bottom flattens toward the stern, sharp forward; most cross-planked, although in North Carolina the bottom planks run fore-and-aft. Other recorded names: **deadrise, double-wedge boat, file-bottom, Spitzbodenboot, V-bottom, vee-bottom boat** or **skiff, V-Spantboot, V-Spantschiff, Wellenbinder**. Note also **Core Sounder, sharpshooter, skipjack**.
  2. *United States, E:* **a.** Term given to the popular shallow-V-bottomed oyster, clamming, and crabbing boats on Chesapeake Bay. Stern may be counter, square, round, or "V." Typically 9-10.7m long, beam 1.8-2.7m in the 1970s, now to 13.7m long and 3m wide. Name variant: **oyster boat★**. Note also **buy boat-2, tonger. b.** The **deadrises** used by upper Chesapeake Bay duck hunters had centerboards and set leg-of-mutton sails.

deadrise sail skiff, deadrise skiff See **North Carolina sail skiff**

Deal cat See **Deal lugger**

Deal galley *England, SE:* Fast **pulling boat★** that took pilots, mail, and supplies to ships lying in the Downs off Deal; some engaged in smuggling activities. Known in the late 18th century, but mostly used in the 19th century; a few remained until World War II. Clinker-built with narrow planking; light framing; straight stem; narrow, tucked-up transom stern; fine lines; washstrake forward; bilge keels. Rudder heel just above the keel to protect it during beaching, which was executed broadside; steered with yoke and lines. Five or 6 thwarts; small watertight locker beneath one thwart; shingle ballast; mainly varnished. Rowed, single-banked; 6-8 oars used until the mid-19th century; later with 4-5 oars; coxswain manned the rudder lines. When sailed, a slightly aft-raking mast was stepped at center thwart, setting a dipping lugsail; shorter mast and sail used in winter. In summer, 2nd mast stepped forward of the mainmast. On occasion, mainmast and sail would be dropped when coming about and an identical sail raised forward. Short, upright timber placed near bow for a towing line from a ship. Reported lengths 8.23-9.75m; e.g., length 9.14m, beam 1.52m, depth 0.82m. Name variant: **pilot galley**

Deal galley punt *England, SE:* Fished and serviced ships with supplies and pilots but mainly engaged in salvage work on the Downs. Worked off the open beaches at Deal from the mid-18th into the early 20th century. Similar boats used at Dover and Walmer. Strongly built of oak planking, clinker fashion, ash frames, and ash or oak keel; heavily ballasted. Vertical stem, bow full-bodied forward; moderately wide transom stern; straight keel; flat floors amidships; 4-5 thwarts; hull varnished. Steered with a tiller. Mainly sailed; mast unstepped when rowed; 3-6 oarsmen rowed standing and facing forward; later equipped with

engines and considerably modified. Had a post forward or hook at the bow for the ship's towing rope. Generally set a single square-headed lugsail to a short unstayed mast stepped roughly amidships. In light winds, a 2nd mast was stepped forward. Three hooks along each side took the tack for the different sail sizes used; had winter and summer sails and masts. Crew of 2-6, attired in top hats in the early 19th century. The smaller **two-handed punt** was 6.4-7m long; e.g., length overall 6.86m, beam 2m, inside depth 0.86m. The 1st-class **galley punt** was 8.2-9.lm long and was narrower in proportion to length. The **great galley**, which was the early name, was 9-11m. Other recorded names: **hoveller★**, **knock-toe** (those with little foot room)

Deal galley punt

Deal hooker *England, SE:* Grappled for slipped anchors and chains on the Downs off Deal.

Deal lugger *England, SE:* Assisted ships, particularly in bad weather, in the area to the north and south of Deal, by providing stores and pilots, and by replacing slipped anchors and chains. Well known for their hovelling of wrecked ships and lifesaving activities; small **luggers★** also fished. Operated from medieval times; most numerous during the 19th and early 20th centuries. Clinker-built, with narrow planks; designed to work off the beaches. Straight, ironshod keel with an eye at each end for a capstan cable; bilge keels; rudder could be triced up during the bow-first launching. Straight stem and bluff bow, hollow below waterline; firm bilges; small square transom stern. Large size decked from bow to mast and were called **forepeakers**; small type, called **cats★**, undecked but had a portable caboose between the fore and main thwarts. A still smaller type, the **half boat★**, was used primarily for sprat, mackerel, and herring fishing; carried an iron lantern forward to aid in fishing. Hull varnished, gunwales and sternboard black. To clear the mizzenmast, the iron tiller had a half-circle indentation. The large vessels that engaged in pilot work carried a small transom-sterned **cogie** that could be rowed or sailed; others carried a **Deal punt★**. Some consider the **half boat** to be a **Deal galley punt★** rather than a **Deal lugger**. Initially 3-masted with dipping lugsails on fore- and mainmasts and standing lug mizzen; mainmast omitted ca. 1850. Mizzenmast stepped at the transom, and sail sheeted to a long horizontal outrigger. Jib ran out on a traveler to a short running bowsprit. Some larger boats had 2 sets of foresails and when going about the sail would be lowered, unhooked from the traveler, and another sail hooked and quickly hoisted on the other side. Rowed in calms; crew stood, pushing the long oars. The **cat** worked with a crew of 3-7; the **forepeaker** required 7 men in summer and 8-12 in winter;

big **hovellers**⋆ might work with 30 men. Rarely exceeded 9m in length in early 19th century, later to 14m; e.g., length 7.39m, beam 1.9m, depth 0.9m. Other recorded names: **cat boat**⋆, **Deal cat**; **last or lasting boat** (medium size); also **Kent**, **Kingsdown**, and **Walmer lugger**. Note also **lug boat-2**.

Deal punt *England, SE:* Open inshore **fishing boat**⋆ in the Deal area; also used as a **ship's boat**⋆ aboard the larger **Deal lugger**⋆. Clinker-built, straight stem, wide transom stern, slight rise to the floor amidships, straight keel, bilge keels. Foremast set a square-headed dipping lugsail, tacked to the stemhead and sheeted at the stern; many lines of reef points; no shrouds, the burton being set up as a backstay. Standing lug mizzen sheeted to a long outrigger. Some had a bowsprit and jib. Also rowed. Reported lengths 3.66-5.49m; e.g., length 4.43m, beam 1.52m, depth 0.67m. Other recorded names: **fore-mizzen punt**, **foresail-and-mizzen punt**, **Kingsdown punt**, **paddle punt**. Note also **sprat punt**.

Deal yall, **Deal yawl** See **yawl-1**

death boat See **death galley**

death galley *England, SE:* Fast, frail, and vulnerable craft that carried gold for profit between Kent ports and France during the latter part of the Napoleonic Wars; also engaged in other smuggling. All ordered seized and destroyed in 1812. Mainly rowed, by 10-20 men; also lug-rigged. Mostly ca. 12m long, some to 24m, very narrow. Other recorded names: **a death**, **death boat**, **guinea boat**, **money boat**

deck boat See **buy boat-2**, **dredge boat-1**, **Tancook schooner**

deck handliner See **handliner**

Decksboot See **boom boat-1**, **waist boat**

deck scow 1. A harbor **scow**⋆ that carries its load on deck.
2. *United States, NE:* On the Erie Canal in central New York State, the so-called **deck scows** hauled bulk cargo. Flat sheer; square sloping ends; phased out in the early 1860s.
Further references: **scow-7**, **scow-11**

Decksprahm See **Prahm-2**

Decktjalk See **dektjalk**

Dee coracle *Wales, N:* Used for salmon netting on the upper River Dee (**Bangor coracle**) until 1920 and for angling on the lower river to the 1950s. Function and water conditions determined the design of the **coracle**⋆, but in both areas they were squarish with somewhat rounded and upturned ends. On the upper river the

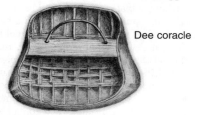

Dee coracle

bilges turned sharply inward from a flat bottom, giving them a strong tumble home and, consequently, more stability for the usual crew of 2. Both types had a frame of longitudinal and transverse laths, the lower river boat having a fairly solid woven bottom; on the

upper river an aluminum frame became popular. Seat supported by a latticework partition on the lower Dee and a strut extended from the seat to the stern; upper river **coracles** used 2 rows of pillars to support 1-2 seats. Covered with tarred canvas or sailcloth. Lower Dee boats were ca. 1.4m long, 1.19m wide at the bilge, and 0.36m deep, weighed 11kg; upper Dee boats (**Llangollen coracles**) were 1.45m long, 1.4m wide on the bottom, 0.97m on the top, and 0.43m deep, 22kg.

Dee jigger boat *England, W:* Trawled for shrimp out from north bank ports of the Dee Estuary into Liverpool Bay. Mainly clinker-built; plumb stem; wide transom above slightly raked sternpost; slight drag to keel. Most decked, with open well; centerboard. Loose-footed, boomed gaff mainsail; jackyard topsail; sprit mizzen, sheeted to jigger boom; jib to short bowsprit. Crew of 1-2. Length overall 7.1m, beam 2.3m, depth 1.2m.

deengee See **dingi**

deep sea boat See **sixareen**

deer canoe, **deerhead canoe** See **West Coast canoe**

Deer Isle peapod See **peapod**

Dee salmon boat *Wales, N:* Clinker-built boat used in River Dee salmon fisheries. Net plays out over the transom stern while the fisherman rows. Plumb stem, low freeboard; the trammel net boats (used on the lower river) have a stern deck. Outboard or inboard engine has replaced a sail. Originally set a small spritsail to a stout mast stepped well forward; sail brailed around the mast while fishing. Reported lengths 5.2-5.5m; e.g., length 5.5m, beam 1.8m. Name variant: **Dee trammel net boat**

Dee trammel net boat See **Dee salmon boat**

Dehabiya See **dahabiyah**

dekenpunter See **zeepunter**

dekhektjalk See **hektjalk**

dekschuit *Netherlands:* **Barge**⋆-type vessel that carried its main cargo on deck, the space below practically unused. Popular in the Amsterdam and Rotterdam areas for transporting cargoes along the waterways. Old types built of wood, with soft turn of the bilges. The later iron or steel vessels had a flat bottom and angular chines. Usually had a heavy wale along each side. Round bow and stern, the latter with a skeg for the rudder; flat sheer; bottom raked up in flat surface at the ends. Open cargo deck with small hatch; end decks, each with a small hatch. Length 16m, beam 5m, depth 1.25m. The **motordekschuit** had a higher bow, counter stern over the rudder, moderate sheer. Low cabin aft of the cargo deck, over the engine. Steered with a horizontal wheel. Length 18m, beam 1.75m, depth 1.25m. Present-day container ships are a type of **dekschuit**. Other recorded names: **Amsterdamsche dekschuit** (or **zolderschuit**), **zolderschuit**. Note also **zolderbak**.

dektjalk *Netherlands:* Member of the **tjalk**⋆ family identified by the lack of a deckhouse. Cabin below the deck, with access through a hatch under the tiller; earlier **dektjalken** had access abaft the main hatch. Windows or ports at the stern provided additional light; low headroom. Built of wood, iron, or steel, mainly in Groningen and Drenthe in the northeast, but also in South Holland. Bluff, rounded ends, sharp tumble home at the ends above the wale; flat bottom, with the strakes rounding up at the bow. Leeboards. Gaff-rigged, with a loose-footed boomed mainsail; gaff generally curved; staysail. Large **dektjalken** employed a running bowsprit and jib. Later vessels motorized; these generally had a wheelhouse. A 1912 vessel was 23m long, 4.67m wide, 1.53m deep. Spelling variant: **Decktjalk**

délasteur See **ballast barge**

Delaware and Hudson barge See **coal bunker**

Delaware Bay masthead sloop See **oyster sloop-2**

Delaware Bay oyster schooner *United States, E:* Dredged for oysters along the southern New Jersey shore of Delaware Bay from the late 19th century to the early 1940s, when most were cut down and motorized. Early vessels had a long, exaggerated cutwater (**long-headed oyster schooner**); during the 1920s, spoon bows adopted; catheads popular. Sternpost vertical or slightly raked; some had very long counters; others had an elliptical raked transom. Straight keel with slight drag; between 1880 and 1900, had an outside keelson. Centerboard cut through the garboard strake, with the mainmast stepped aft of the centerboard case on the opposite garboard. Moderately rising, straight floors with hard or full round bilges. Decked, some with low quarter-deck; low pilot house common. Early boats had carved trailboards, moulding, and figureheads. Monkey rail from midships to stern; continuous scupper from foremast to within a few feet of the stern; rubbing strake set off with beading. Employed a **garvey★** as a **yawl boat★**, hung on davits aft. Older boats set a tall main topsail in order to catch light air; later vessels lacked topmasts; often both masts the same height. Boomed gaff sails, the mainsail often high-peaked; foresail narrow; large jib to a long bowsprit. After the 1920s, the bowsprit was heavy, round, and heavily chain-rigged; a few carried a jibboom with a dolphin-striker. Crew of 2-4. Reported lengths 18-31m; e.g., length overall 23m, beam 6m, molded depth 2m, draft aft 1.8m. Other recorded names: **dredge boat★**, (**New**) **Jersey oyster schooner**, **oyster schooner**; **condo boat** (a motorized type modified by a tall pilothouse)

Delaware Bay railbird boat See **Delaware ducker**

Delaware ducker *United States, E:* Especially stable craft of market gunners and sportsmen for hunting rail and duck in the riverine marshes south of Philadelphia; similar types used along the New Jersey shore of the Delaware River and Bay and on Chesapeake Bay. Popular mainly from the 1870s to the early 1900s; served also for fishing, pleasure boating, and racing. Lapstrake construction; sharp ends; rounded forefoot; slack bilges; plank keel, rounded bottom; no thwarts. Platform aft for the pusher; side decks; daggerboard placed well forward; rudder, often large and curved to match the sternpost, shipped when sailed; removable tiller. Rowed or sailed to hunting site, then poled among the tall reeds. When sailed, mast stepped through the foredeck, setting a small boomed spritsail or a gaff sail. Also rowed. Used by a

hunter and a pusher. Reported lengths 4.5-5m; e.g., length 4.6m, beam 1.0m. Other recorded names: **Delaware Bay railbird boat**, **Delaware River duck boat**, **ducker**, **pole skiff★**, **push skiff**, **railbird boat**, **rail gunning skiff**, **reed-bird boat**

Delaware River duck boat See **Delaware ducker**

Delaware River shallop *United States, E:* Carried freight on the lower river and its major tributaries into the 19th century. Bluff bow with curved stem; square raking counter above a raking sternpost; flat floors; rounded bilges. Decked; quarter-deck, might be surrounded by a low rail. Rudder came up inboard. Single tall mast stepped well forward; some in a tabernacle, enabling the mast to be lowered for bridges. Set a gaff mainsail with a long gaff; jib to a short bowsprit. Also maneuvered by sweeps. Crew of 3. Length 16.5m, beam 6.4m, depth 1.32m; shallow draft.

Delaware River tuckup See **tuckup**

Delaware sloop See **oyster sloop-2**

delibat See **kolek gelibat**

demi-barque *France, N:* **Cutter★**-rigged **fishing boat★** of the eastern part of Baie de la Seine. Popular in the 1st quarter of the 20th century. Plumb stem; raked sternpost below a raked transom or counter. Steep rise to the floors; very deep drag to the straight keel. Low at stern, sheer sweeps up forward. Decked; deep bulwarks. Narrow rudder, post came up inboard. Mast stepped in forward third, setting a loose-footed, boomed gaff sail, topsail, staysail, jib to light bowsprit. Length overall 11.5m, on keel 9.66m, beam 4m. Name variant: **barquette★**

demi-bâtarde See **pinasse-1a**

demi-bélandre See **bilander**

demi-caïque See **caique-6**

demi-caraque, **demi-carracque**, **demi-carraque** See **carrack**

demi-chébec See **xebec-2**

demi-galère *United States, central:* Early naval vessel used on the Mississippi River. Note also **galère**. Further reference: **half galley-1**

demi galley See **half galley-1**

demi-gondola See **gondola-4**

demi-picoteux See **picoteux de plage**

demi-véro See **gabare de la Rance**

demy bellandre See **bilander**

demye-carraque, **demyi-carraque** See **carrack**

demy-galère See **half galley-1**

dengee, **dengey** See **dingi**

dengi See **dhangi**, **dingi**

dengium See **dingi**

depechebaad, **depeschbåt**, **Depeschenboot** See **advice boat**

deposit boat See **sponge boat**, **sponge schooner-2**

deposito See **sponge boat-2**

Depotschiff See **store ship**

depot ship See **mother ship**, **store ship**

depotskip See **store ship**

deregiye, **deregija**, **dereglija** See **barge-1**

dereglja Croatian term for a **bark★**, **longboat★**, **pontoon★**. Further reference: **barge-1**

dériveur *France:* **1.** Initially, any boat that used drift nets while fishing. Now principally a motorized vessel that fishes for herring with a trawl or drift net. English term **drifter★** has now been adopted. Spelling variant: **driveur**

2. A small racing craft that has no keel but relies on a centerboard; transom stern; easily beached; length ca. 4m, beamy. At La Rochelle in western France, it is a flat-bottomed centerboard boat of 3-5t that tends the mussel beds and goes by the name **driveur**.
Further reference: **harenguier**

derrick boat 1. *England:* Of various designs and construction but uses a crane to lift canal lock gates, transport pilings, clear debris from canal bottoms, and perform other canal maintenance operations. Cranes now diesel powered. Other recorded names: **crane barge** (or **boat**). Note also **derrick flat**.
2. *United States, E:* Those on the Erie Canal in New York State cleared sunken wrecks from the channel.
3. *United States, S:* The Spanish moss gatherers in the Louisiana bayous had **derrick boats** to reach the moss hanging in the trees. The tall, spindly derrick was set out onto a **skiff★**. Towed to the site by a **gas boat★**.

derrick flat *England, W:* A type of **Mersey flat★** that transported coping stone for Liverpool docks. Note also **derrick boat**.

Derry cot See **cot-2**
despatch boat, despatch vessel See **advice boat**
dëua See **düe**
deux de couple See **double scull**
deux de pointe See **pair-oar-2**
deux mâts See **two-master**
deux ponts See **two-decker**
devil's coffin See **Barnegat sneakbox**
Devon crabber See **West Country crabber**
de wang *Papua New Guinea, Bismarck Archipelago:* Large 2-masted **outrigger canoe★** of the villages at the western end of New Britain Island, the Siassi Islands to the west, and the Tami Islands off the mainland. Dugout hull, with rounded sides and bottom; 2-3 wash-

de wang

strakes sewn onto each side, strengthened by pairs of knees that joined at the middle. High breakwaters closed the ends. Bow and stern thin and greatly elongated, often carved and painted, as were the washstrakes and sides. The single outrigger comprised 3 very long, sturdy booms, set close together, reached to the stout float; booms crossed on top of the washstrakes and extended out the opposite side. Booms connected to the float with undercrossed stanchions. Atop the booms, centered over the hull, a 2-story platform was constructed, the lower level for cargo, food, and baggage, the upper level for the crew. A mast stepped at each end of the platform, with opposing

rakes. Set a type of lugsail of pandanus leaves. Crew of 6. Reported lengths 9-21m, most ca. 15m. Other recorded names: **na-auga**, **oga**, **wang★**, **wang la**

dgaisa See **dghajsa-1**
dgerme See **djerme**
dghaisa See **dghajsa-1**
dghaisa tal-pass See **dghajsa tal-pass**
dghajjes See **dghajsa-1**
dghajsa 1. *Malta:* Generic term for any small **boat★**, but more specifically, a popular **water-taxi** and general-purpose craft of the Valetta harbors. Virtually extinct except for a modified type used in regattas. Sharp

dghajsa-1

ends; newer boats carry maximum beam well forward; stem and sternpost extend high above gunwale level, with slight tumble home, the taller stemhead cut scimitar-shaped, the sternpost cut horizontal. Early types had a straight raked stem. Usually marked sheer at ends; low rise to the floors amidships; planking ignores end sheer lines; straight keel. Ribs fastened with single nail; washstrake along after half. Open except for short decks at ends; seats along the sides; canopies common in the late 19th century. Brightly painted, with white line at boot top; sheer planks and ends varnished; most have other decorations. Rowed, using single tholepin and grommet; 3 tholepins to starboard, 1 to port. Oarsman stands facing forward, crossing oar looms; sometimes 1 oarsman pushes while another pulls. Some now have engines. Reported lengths 6-7.6m, beam ca. 1.7m. Four-man racing craft, known as **dghasja tal-Midalji (fancy boat)**, to 7.32m long; lightly built; painted in colors of the competing districts. Other recorded names: **barca del passo**, **dâiso**, **dgaisa**, **dghaisa**, **dghajsa tal-pass★**, **diso**, **dra(h)issa**, **dysa**, **dysov**, **ferilla**; pl. **dghajjes**, **dghayyes**. Note also **dghajsa tal-pass**. Further reading: Joseph Muscat, "The Dghajsa—in Memoriam," *The Mariner's Mirror* 77 (November 1991), 389-405.
2. Term sometimes used in the British navy for any ship-to-shore boat, Maltese or not. **Dghajjes** were often carried aboard warships.

dghajsa tal-latini See **dghajsa tal-pass**
dghajsa tal-Midalji See **dghajsa-1**
dghajsa tal-pass *Malta:* Brilliantly painted boat of early origin that carries passengers and produce between the islands of Gozo and Malta. Sharp ends; carvel-planked; heavy construction. Flat floors; keel secured directly to the ribs; sheer especially steep toward the bow; deep washstrakes have removable panels for loading and oar ports. High stemhead, some tumble home; sternpost somewhat lower; tiller passes over top of sternpost; rudder extends below keel. Cambered decks at the ends, narrow waterways. Color wedges at the bows indicate port registry. Sets 1-2 spritsails or 2 quadrilateral lateen-type sails with a short luff. Sprit

heel held by one of the notches cut into a bench (3 on each side), permitting variable positions for the sprit. Forward lateen-type sail might be set to port, the mainsail to starboard. Jib to a long bowsprit; inhaul bent to the middle of the luff. Now motorized. Crew of 4-5. Reported lengths 6-12m; e.g., length 7m, beam 1.35m, depth 0.75m. Other recorded names: **barca del Gozo**, **barca del passo grande**, **dghaisa tal-pass**, **dghajsa tal-latini**, **dghajsa t'Ghawdex⋆**, **dhaisastal latini**, **draissa-tal-pass**, **fregata del passo del Canale**, **Gozo boat** (or **dghaisa**), **gozzo⋆**, **maghdija**, **taffarel**. Note also **dghajsa-1**, **madia-1**.

dghajsa t'Ghawdex See **dghajsa tal-pass**

dghayyes See **dghajsa-1**

dhaisastal latini See **dghajsa tal-pass**

dhangi *India, NW/Pakistan, SE:* Fast double-ended trader built in the Kutch and Sind areas. Sailed to Arabian and East African ports; engines now universal. Characterized by sharp stern and by short timbers that extend forward horizontally beyond the stem just below the stemhead. In the past, a downsloping tiller that passed over the high rudderhead was also characteristic but not prevalent now; motorized **dhangis** steered by yoke and wheel. Stem and sternpost straight and strongly raked; slight sheer. Carvel-built, generally of teak; strakes bolted to the ribs and caulked with raw cotton. Keel, with forward part forming a gripe; soft turn of the bilges. Bottom coated with *chunam* and *dammar*; broad white band painted at waterline; oiled above this; wide, painted triangle at each end below the band. Loose decking of split bamboo; poop occupies about one-third of the stern area; cargo hatch triangular in shape; high bulwarks. Carries a **muchwa⋆**. Generally sets a high-peaked lateen or quadrilateral lateen-type sail with a short luff to 2 short masts, one or both masts raking forward. Tack of mainsail may be brought to stemhead or to a bumkin. Light square topsails may be carried. Masts supported by a forestay and a pair of shrouds on each side. Crew of 8-15. Reported lengths 12-56m; e.g., length overall 21.2m, on keel 14m, beam 6.8m, depth 3.14m. Other recorded names: **boom⋆**, **danga⋆**, **dangi⋆**, **dangiyah**, **dengi**, **dhanji**, **dhungi**, **dhungy**, **dingee**, **dingi⋆**

dhanji See **dhangi**

dhatti hora *Pakistan, SE:* Inshore **fishing boat⋆** of the Karachi and Sind areas. Originally the dugout bases

dhatti hora

were obtained from the Malabar coast of India and planks added locally. Name also applies to a completely

carvel-planked boat. Characterized by an outrigger (*dhatti*) and 1-2 balance boards. Float, ca. 3m long, is thicker at its upward-curving ends; 2 booms lash directly to float; booms extend across hull, lashed to each gunwale. Sharp ends; straight stem with curved forefoot; long straight keel; strongly raked sternpost. Rudder extends below keel and above gunwale; worked with yoke and lines. Small quadrilateral lateen-type sail with a short luff or a simple lateen sail set to a forward-raking mast. Employs oars for short trips. Crew of 4. Reported lengths 9-12m; e.g., length overall 10.21m, beam 1.0m, depth 0.7m. Note also **ekdar**, **gharat hora**.

Dhau, Dhauen See **dhow**

dhau ya mtepe See **dau la mtepe**

dhaw See **dhow**

dhengi See **dingi**

dhindet See **dundee**

dhjukong See **jukung**

dhondho See **dundo**

dhoney See **dhoni-1**, **yathra dhoni**

dhoni 1. Generic term for **boat⋆** in some languages of India, ranging from a **coracle⋆** to a 3-masted **coaster⋆** of the **dhow⋆** type. Spelling variants: **dhon(e)y**, **dhonie**, **don(ah)**, **done(y)**, **doni⋆**, **don(n)y**, **drona**, **drōṇi**; **thoni** (in Tamil), pl. **thonigals**; **tona**, **tone(e)**, **toni**, **tonny**, **tony⋆**, **tune**. Note also **Pamban dhoni**, **shoe dhoni**.

2. *India, SE:* The well-known **Tuticorin thoni** evolved from an open ship-to-shore **lighter⋆** about the time of World War I. These large vessels, built primarily at Tuticorin, still serve as **coasters** along the southern

dhoni-2

coast of the Indian peninsula and off Sri Lanka, and some go as far as Myanmar. Squarish hull, little deadrise; heavy carvel planking, generally with one of the poorer types of teak. Double-ended; slight rake to stem; stern more plumb. Broad keel scarfed in 2-3 places; bottom sheathed with copper, or more recently with an aluminum alloy. Decked; no bulwarks; outboard rudder; tiller may be as long as 5.2m. Characteristically painted black, with large white registration numbers on the bows and aft. Various combinations of rigging adopted, originally carrying a single quadrilateral lateen-type sail with a short luff; now usually steps a heavy mainmast and a small mizzenmast, with the lateen-type sail on the former and a boomed gaff sail on the latter. Topsail may be hoisted to a light topmast, and 2-3 jibs and a water sail run below the long bowsprit. One lateen-type sail set to port, the other to starboard, enabling the vessel to tack. Some 3-masted. Yards usually kept hoisted when sails are furled. Can set as many as 13 sails. Engines now common, with a wheelhouse instead of the mizzen-mast. Crew of 5-17. Reported lengths 21-40m; e.g., length 21.6m, beam 6m, depth 3.7m, draft ca. 2.7m loaded. Other recorded names: **boatu**, **Tuticorin lighter** (or **lugger**). Note also **yathra dhoni**.

3. *India, E:* **a.** On rivers such as the Godavari, **dhonis** transport goods and passengers. Sailed, poled, or towed upstream; drift downstream with the current. Cap. to ca. 35t. **b.** North of Madras (Chennai) on coastal Pulicat Lake, **dhonis** use a type of drag net, the boats working in pairs, each boat carrying half the net. Plank-built, flat bottom; ca. 6.1-7.3m long. Mainly poled, but may set a lugsail to a demountable mast, stepped amidships. Crew of 10 in each boat.

4. *India, W:* In Mysore (now Karnataka State) **coracle**-like **dhonis** ferried people and goods across rivers. Circular baskets, 2.4-3.1m in diameter, covered with leather. Rowed, using a grommet pivot.

5. *India, Lakshadweep Islands:* In the Lakshadweep (Laccadive) Islands lying well off the mainland coast, **thonis** fish within the reefs. Three classes—the **ettu-valikkunna thoni** using 8 oars, the **aruvalikkunna thoni** using 6 oars, and the **naluvalikkunna thoni** using 4 oars. Built of a hard wood and last 20-25 years. Reported lengths 5-8m. Note also **jeha dhoni**, **kuda dhoni**.

6. *Maldive Islands:* Fishing (**mas dhoni**) and trading boat still in use. Rounded stem; some have a unique high, recurved stemhead that may be detached while working. Raked sternpost. Tiller, set over tall rudder-head, may be straight or strongly S-curved. Sharp ends; low stern; a wide platform on which helmsman stands extends out beyond gunwales. Carvel-planked, mainly of coconut, initially sewn; now treenailed; frames inserted later. Sharp entrance; strongly flared amidships; little sheer. Small foredeck, partial deck amidships. Pole mast bowed forward by a rope stay that is lashed to an arched beam ca. 61cm from the stem. Originally set a tall square sail, now mainly a lateen sail; tall crutch at forward end of the platform supports lowered yard. In failing wind, rowed double-banked with broad-bladed oars. Many now propelled by an inboard engine. Crew of 4-6. Reported lengths 5-15m; e.g., length 7.3m, beam 2.44m. Other recorded names: **dhooni**, **dohni**, **dōni***, **donny**, **drona**, **dronī**, **machua***, **mas dhoani**, **mas doni**. Note also **oruva**.

7. *Singapore:* Based on the **dhoni** of southeastern India. The Singapore **dhoni** was owned and operated by Indians during the 2nd quarter of the 19th century. Carried cargo from vessels lying off Singapore River to the quay. Sharp ends.

8. *Sri Lanka:* Term used for a variety of boats, with the Sinhala spelling (**dhoni**) mainly in the south and the Tamil spelling (**thoni**) in the north. A 19th-century **coaster** on the west coast had a small outrigger; sewn planks; 2-masted.

Further reference: **padagu-3**

dhonie, **dhony** See **dhoni-1**

dhooni See **dhoni-6**

dhou, **dhouw** See **dhow**

dhow **1.** Collective term of English-speaking peoples for the Arab-built and Arab-manned lateen-rigged vessels that have sailed the Indian Ocean, the Red Sea, and the Persian (Arabian) Gulf for centuries. The French use the word **boutre***. The Arab word is **markab***, although this is a broader term that includes small boats and modern ships. In the Persian Gulf area, the term **gharāb*** is used in official documents, while the sailors use **lashāb**. Most **dhows** are cargo vessels, although some were used for war and piracy, while many were active in slave trading. In general, **dhows** have long overhanging bows, raking transom sterns, and often high poops. The larger oceangoing vessels were generally 2-masted, the **coasters*** single-masted. All set a quadrilateral lateen-type sail with a short luff. Most now completely motorized. Other recorded names: **bout***, **butră**, **dâo**, **dãou**, **dau***, **dăva**, **daw**, **Dhau** (pl. **Dhauen**), **dhaw**, **dhou(w)**, **diw**, **dow**, **tava**, **qārib shirā'ī**

2. *East Africa, Lake Victoria:* An important trading vessel on the lake beginning ca. 1880. Use declined toward the mid-20th century, but some now serve as feeders to rail lines, especially in the shallow southern part of the lake. Built mainly by shipwrights brought from the Indian Ocean coast, primarily from Lamu. Besides carrying miscellaneous cargoes, the **dhows** engaged in fishing and at one time were active in smuggling. Open or half-decked; wide transom stern; curved and raked stem; flat floors; maximum beam well forward; outboard rudder. Planking fastened with large iron spikes. Shelter provided by sheets of corrugated iron. Single quadrilateral lateen-type sail with a short luff set to a forward-raking or vertical mast. Large vessels employed crew of 14-20; the **fishing boats*** ca. 5. Capacity varied with their fluctuating popularity, ranging from ca. 8-70t; fishing **dhows** were ca. 7.6m long, 1.8m wide, draft 0.76m.

3. *Malawi, E:* Crudely made passenger and cargo sailing **dhows** ply the southern part of Lake Nyasa. Originally an Arab craft, but now African-built and -owned. Planked and framed with the hard, strong *mlombwa* wood; caulked with kapok and resin. Decked or half-decked.

4. *United Arab Emirates:* A type of **man-of-war*** that was an important vessel of the sheikdoms of the south shore of the Persian (Arabian) Gulf.

Further references: **boti-1**, **pangaio-2**

dhunda, **dhúnde**, **dhundhi** See **dunda**

dhungi, **dhungy** See **dhangi**

diahu See **perahu-1**

diamond bottom See **skipjack-1**

diamond bottom bateau *United States, SE:* Beamy **sloop***-rigged boat of the Georgia and South Carolina coasts. Originally a work boat, but in the 1880s became a popular racing craft. V-bottom, longitudinally planked; heavy log chine piece; shallow hull; centerboard. Racing boats had a large sail area, crew of 10; lengths to 10m. Note also **bateau-7j**.

diao chuan *China, E:* 16th-century seagoing vessel from Huai-an that sold rice at Ninghai in Shandong. Name variants: **eagle boat**, **tiao ch'uan**

diao gou zi *China, E:* Carried salt upstream on the Siang River between Shiherwei and Changsha, making 2 trips a year. Downstream, carried local products, such as chinaware, paper, wood oil, alum. Bottom of *sha-mu* wood, sides of camphor wood. Low bow, high stern. House covered after two-thirds, small foremast in the bow, mainmast amidships. Spelling variant: **tiao-kou-tzǔ**

diao ting *China, SE/Hong Kong/Macau:* Two- or 3-masted vessel that serves as a **mother ship★** for 1-5 pairs of **sampans★** that fish with long lines (see **long-liner**). Also stores the catch. In Hong Kong one carrying 4 pairs of **sampans** is called a **see pei**; one with 3 pairs of **sampans** is a **sam pei**; the smaller 2-pair vessel is a **leung pei**, and the 1-pair type is a **yat pei**. Most constructed of fir, a few of teak; beams, rudder, and keel of camphor wood. Sharp raked bow; square stern curves up. High poop deck; fenestrated rudder comes up inboard. Open rail extends outboard along the sides and across the bow. Decked; living quarters on the middle deck, poop deck, and main deck. Sets battened lugsails. Crew of up to 40, plus family members. Lengths to 21m, beam to 6.4m, depth to 2m. **Sampans** are 4-5m long, 1.2-1.5m wide; the larger haul the lines, the smaller pay out the lines; sculled or rowed. Spelling variants: **tiu t'éang, tiu teng**

dickie See **billyboy**

didal boat *England, E:* Worked along the Broads of Norfolk and other rivers; employed a scoop to clear weeds and soft mud, which were deposited in a large central well area. In winter some transported cut ice to storage houses. Watertight bulkhead at each end; a pump on the aft bulkhead helped empty the load; mast stepped on the forward bulkhead. Also poled. Crew of 1-2. Length 7.6m, beam 1.2m. Name variants: **didle boat, didling boat, dydle boat**. Note also **weed cutter**.

didle boat, didling boat See **didal boat**

Dielenfloss See **Bretterfloss**

Dienerschiff, Dienstbotenschiff See **Leibschiff**

diesona, diesone See **gondola da regata**

diftherinon ploion See **ploion**

Digby Neck tub punt See **tub punt-1**

diggelschip, dijnop See **pot-2**

dihènge See **dihengué**

dihengué *Cameroon, SW:* One-man **dugout canoe★** used by the Batanga for sea fishing. Built of a light local wood; very narrow since hull not expanded. Sharp ends rise slightly; rounded bottom with some rocker. Made rigid by light thwarts; the occupant sits astride on a bulkhead, with feet in the water for stability and propulsion. Carried to and from the water on the head. Also paddled, using a short spoon-like paddle. Reported lengths 24.4m, beam 0.3-0.5m. Other recorded names: **dihènge, iyènge, pirogua mosquito, pirogue moustique**; erroneously **moussique**

diligence See **Wasser-Diligence**

diligence d'eau See **coche d'eau**

dinapalang *Philippines, central:* Open **banca★**-type boat of western Negros Island that tends fish corrals, works with nets, and carries cargo and passengers along the coast and on rivers. Dugout hull, flattened bottom; narrow, rounded, overhanging ends. Short end decks; rudderpost comes up through the stern deck; tiller.

Rowed by as many as 10; slender-bladed oars, secured to tholepins by stout cords.

dindet Old French term for a type of **yawl★** in which the jigger mast was somewhat forward and set a single headsail. Sometimes refers, erroneously, to a **yawl**-rigged **thonier★**. Spelling variant: **dinguet**. Note also **sloup à tape-cul**.

dingá *India, NE:* In Bengali, a vessel engaged in the coasting trade. Curved keel. Single forward-raking mast carried a lateen sail. Name variant: **dingua**. Note also **dingi**.

dinga See **dinghy-4**

dingee See **dhangi, dingi, dingy-1**

dingey See **dinghy-1, dinghy-6**

dinggi, dinghee See **dingi**

dinghey See **dinghy-1, dinghy-4**

dinghi See **dinghy-1, dingi**

dinghie See **dinghy-1**

dinghy 1. **Tender★** to a **yacht★** or **fishing boat★**, or the smallest boat on a merchant ship. Most commonly transom-sterned, sharp-bowed, and round-bottomed; undecked. May be constructed of wood, metal, or synthetic materials; some must be inflated. Generally rowed, single-banked, or sets a sail to a portable mast; usually has a centerboard if sailed; the **motor dinghy** has a small outboard. May be towed, hung from stern davits, or carried on board. Reported lengths 2-6m, mostly ca. 3; beamy. Selected name variants: **dingey, ding(h)ey, dinghi(e), dingui, dingy★, dink★, dinkey, dinky (-boat), punt★, yacht tender**. Note also **bij-boot, breu, flattie, jolly boat, patalya, petit canot, pram-2, ship's boat★, youyou**.
2. **Dinghies** comprise a number of classes of **sloop★**-rigged centerboard racing boats.
3. Small collapsible boat used by downed airmen.
4. *India, W:* Slender craft that served as a **water-taxi** in Bombay (Mumbai) and along the Malabar Coast. Raked stem, considerable hollow to the keel, with deep forefoot. Decked or half-decked. Forward-raking mast stepped about one-third in from the bow.

dinghy-4

Set a lug-type sail tacked to the stemhead and sheeted to the heel of the mast; short luff and roached foot; yard about the same length as the boat. Also paddled. Crew of 3-4. Reported lengths 3.7-6m, widths 1.52-1.83m, depths 0.46-0.6m. Other recorded names: **Bombay bark, bumboat★, dinga★, dinghey, ḍiṅgi★, dingua, dingy**

5. *Northern Ireland, central:* Sailing and **pulling boat★** of Lough Neagh that worked to the mid-20th century, catching eels, freshwater herring (pollan), and trout. Clinker-planked, keel, full bilges, slightly hollow entrance, clean run aft. Lightly curved stem; raked transom stern, deadwood below; sternpost outboard. Open except for a short foredeck; low working platform aft; single thwart; rudder and tiller. Long oars pivoted on an outrigged iron pin. Mast stepped through the foredeck. Set a spritsail, with sprit held high; small jib to bowsprit. Length 5m, beam 1.8m, draft 0.46m.

6. *United Kingdom:* Smallest of the **pulling boats** in the Royal Navy; first used in 1825. Clinker-built, bluff bow, small transom stern. Some rowed with 3 pairs of oars. Late 19th- and early 20th-century boats also set a small spritsail and foresail. The 19th-century pleasure **dinghies** of the Thames employed sculls (**sculling dinghies**); usually had a single pair of flared rowlocks. Reported lengths 2.7-4.8m; e.g., length 4.27m, beam 1.57m, depth 0.66m. Spelling variants: **dingey**, **dingy**

7. *United States:* A class of **ship's boat** in the U.S. Navy. Clinker- or carvel-planked, plumb stem, shallow transom, straight keel. Three or 4 thwarts, stern sheets. Rowed, single-banked, with 2-3 pairs of oars. Spritsail set to a light portable mast. Standard lengths 4.27m, 4.88m, 5.49m, 6.1m; e.g., length 4.88m, beam 1.37m, depth 0.56m.

8. *West Indies:* Small **fishing boat** found on the Leeward Islands of St. Kitts, Nevis, Montserrat, and Guadeloupe. Mainly sailed.

Further references: **Bahama dinghy**, **Bermuda dinghy**, **dingi**, **longboat-7**, **skiff-1**, **sponge dinghy**

dingi *Bangladesh/India:* **1.** Generic term in Hindi for small inland boats; sometimes a **dugout canoe★**.

2. Small craft of Bengali rivers and estuaries used for fishing, ferrying, transporting produce and cargo, and as a **water-taxi**. Carvel-planked, frequently with short planks; clinker construction in some areas. Where 9 strakes are used on each side, the boat is known as a **nāotakhtā**. Rounded in cross section; strong sheer, with bow often higher than stern. In most areas, ends pointed, with long overhang; stern may rise more

dingi-2

sharply than the bow. Frequently lacks interior framing, but may have as many as 8 strong thwarts that pierce the strakes; sometimes washstrakes added; no keel. Small types open, larger are loosely decked with split bamboo or similar material; passenger **dingis**

have an arched mat or bamboo cabin amidships, some with sliding doors. Hull usually oiled, producing a dark color. Steered mainly with a long oar, which works against a peg at the stern, held by a loop. When sailed, generally sets a square sail, sometimes with a topsail, or uses a spritsail. Foot of square sail usually narrower than the head and raised high to enable helmsman to see ahead. Sails of light cotton, frequently dyed blue. Mast may be a flexible bamboo pole. More often paddled, sculled, or rowed; 4-5 rowers generally, who sit on the deck with legs extended. Oars lashed to a bamboo frame fitted to the gunwale. In the **tey-mallai** 2 men work as oarsmen and 1 as helmsman. Reported lengths 3.6-15.2m, widths 0.76-2.44m, depths 0.3-1.52m. **Jalia** (**jaile**, or **jaliyā**) **dingi** (or **jele**) is a general term given to **dingis** that engage in fishing with a net; called **parokia** off Contai in southwestern West Bengal. Generally conform to the foregoing description. Those engaging in special fishing may bear specific names, e.g., **bhesal dingi** (uses a dip net); **patam dingi** (uses a seine or other nets depending on the district; ends terminate in rectangular blocks, the bow higher than the stern). **Shangla** or **saingla dingi** fishes with a clap net for hilsa. The **talal dingi** sets a drift net.

3. In the Bengal area, **dingi** may be the smallest of the **ship's boats★** in the navy and merchant marine.

Spelling variants: **dangiyah**, **de(e)ngee**, **dengey**, **dengi(um)**, **dhengi**, **dingee**, **dinggi**, **dinghee**, **dinghi**, **dinghy★**, **dinglie**, **dingue**, **dingui**, **dinguy**, **dingy★**. Further references: **dhangi**, **dinghy-4**

Dingle curragh See **naomhóg-2**

dinglie See **dingi**

dingua See **dingá**, **dinghy-4**

dingue See **dingi**

dinguet See **dindet**

dingui See **dinghy-1**, **dingi**

dinguy See **dingi**

dingy **1.** *India, NW/Pakistan, S:* Cargo vessel with sharp lines, indigenous to the Makran, Sind, and Kutch coasts. High square or rounded stern, stemhead coiled back. Undecked except for split bamboo laid across removable beams. Rudder hung so that there was considerable space between sternpost and rudderpost. Two flagstaffs at the stern, each having weathercocks. Stepped main and mizzenmasts setting lateen sails; mainsail boomed out beyond the bow. Crew of 10-25. Spelling variant: **dingee**; pl. **dingies**

2. *United States, SE:* A small boat that worked around oyster grounds and shuttled back and forth between anchored vessels. Sharp bow, flat bottom, small centerboard, half-decked.

See also **dinghy-1**, **dinghy-4**, **dinghy-6**, **dingi**.

dink *United States, E:* Popular waterfowl gunning craft of Chesapeake Bay. Shallow boat with sharply pointed bow and oval transom stern, flat bottom. Cambered deck, small cockpit with high coaming. Wooden strips on the bottom enabled the craft to slide across the mud and ice. Length 4m. Other recorded names: **Chesapeake Bay sneakbox**, **gunning dink**, **sneak boat★**, **sneakbox**. Note also **Barnegat sneakbox**. Further reference: **dinghy-1**

dinkey See **dinghy-1**

dinkeye See **Bermuda dinghy**

dinkey vallom See **vallom-1b**

dinky See **dinghy-1**, **punt-12a**

dinky-boat See **dinghy-1**

dinky skiff, dinky skift See **Smith Island skiff**

dinner pail boat *United States:* Term given to a **tug**★ or other small working craft that lacked a galley, the crew carrying their own food aboard.

dipper *England, SW:* Shallow boat of the Cornish pilchard fisheries that transferred fish from a tuck net to shore. Other recorded names: **car boat, dipper boat, tuck boat** (at St. Ives). Note also **lurker, seine boat-3, tuck-net boat.**

dipper boat See **dipper**

dirt boat *England, SE:* Term applied in the 17th century to small boats that carried away trash and waste from ships lying in the Thames River. Name variant: **bumboat**★

dirt gabard, dirt gabbard See **ballast barge**

Disappearing Propeller See **Muskoka Lakes skiff**

discovery ship See **rowbarge**

disdotona, disdotone, disdottona See **gondola da regata**

diso See **dghajsa-1**

dispatch boat See **advice boat**

DisPro See **Muskoka Lakes skiff**

ditch box *United States, E:* Narrow **garvey**★-type craft of southern New Jersey used by hunters on narrow waterways. Heavily cambered side decks sloped to low sides; cockpit accommodated 2 gunners. Handrails along sides aided in carrying the boat. Propelled by pole, oar, or outboard motor.

diving boat See **sponge boat-3**

diw See **dhow**

djali boet See **jolly boat-1**

djalō, djaloeë, djaloer See **jalor**

djaloer malieng See **jalur maling**

djalor See **jalor**

djalur maling See **jalur maling**

djanggolan, djangölan See **janggolan**

djarm See **djerme**

djatèn See **jaten**

djehaz See **jahazi, jase**

djěnggolan See **janggolan**

djěnging *Philippines, S:* Outrigged **houseboat**★ of the Bajau peoples of the southern Sulu Archipelago. Generally moored in harbors and creeks. Plank-extended dugout hull; sharp overhanging ends, which may be elaborately carved. Some have a bifid bow with long

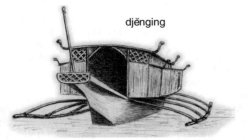

djěnging

rising projection and ram; others have 2 decorative recurving pieces plus a winged shield held aloft over

the stem by shafts from the bow area. Planks secured by edge pegging. Usually stabilized by 2 slender outrigger floats; 3 booms curve down to attach directly to each float. A low house occupies most of the hull; may be merely a flimsy covered area or may be equipped with door, windows, and interior amenities; roof covered with thatch, corrugated iron, sacks, or only cardboard. A **vinta**★ for transportation and fishing is generally tied to the **djěnging**. Reported lengths 3.7-18m, widths of hull 0.6-1.8m, deep-hulled. Other recorded names: **Bajau houseboat, house canoe, lepa-lepa**★, **lipa**★

djenné See **barque Djenné**

djerm, djerma See **djerme**

djerme *Egypt:* A non-specific type, but variously described as a 2-masted cargo vessel of Alexandria and the Nile Delta that was prominent into the early 19th century, but dates at least from the 7th century. Used as an armed vessel, as a boat transporting passengers on the

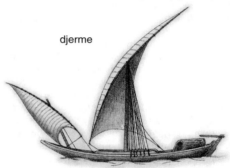

djerme

Nile during high water, and as a **lighter**★ for discharging cargo from ships. Some traveled to Turkey. The cargo vessel had fine lines, long overhanging bow, rounded stern, washboards amidships, flat floors. Most decked; some had a cabin aft. Long lateen yard set atop a vertical mainmast stepped amidships; multiple shrouds. Small foremast raked sharply forward, also setting a lateen sail. Some stepped 3 masts. Reported lengths 15-21m. Other recorded names: **c(h)erme, cheytych, corme, dgerme, djarm** (pl. **djurum**), **djerm(a), Dscherm, garm, germa**★, **germe, germetta** (dim.), **jarm, sarme, Scherm, serme, surme, yerme, zerma**

djiman' See **tsiman**

djoanga, djoeanga See **juanga-1**

djoekoeng See **jukung, jungkung**

djoekoeng pantjing See **jukung pantjing**

djoekoeng tambangan, djoekoeng tembangan See **tambangan**

djoekoeng tembon See **tjemplon-2**

djoekoeng tjompreng See **tjompreng-2**

djoekong See **jukung, jungkung, pajang**

djoeloeng See **julung**

djoeloeng-djoeloeng See **julung-julung**

djoeng *Indonesia:* One of the terms for a child's toy boat. Note also **jong-4**. Further reference: **junk**

djoengkoe *Indonesia:* **1.** One of the terms for a Chinese **junk**★.
2. In some dialects in the Moluccas, refers to a **canoe**★, sometimes a large cargo-carrying **canoe**. Stem and stern may be raised.

djoengkoeng See jungkung

djoenkoeng, djokong See jongkong

djong See jong-2, junk

djongkang, djongkoeng, djongkong, djonkong See jongkong

djouloeng See julung-2

djuanga See juanga-1

djukkung, djukong, djukung See jukung

djukung tambangan See tambangan

djung, djunku See junk

djurum See djerme

doanga See donga-1

dobbele chaloupe See barque longue-1

doble England, E: Shallow-draft craft, with a flat bottom and sharp ends, that fished in embayments in northeastern Essex. Survived to the 1960s. Clinker-planked, transom stern. Wet well divided the boat, hence **double boat**. Spelling variant: **dovel**

doble boat See Medway doble

dodesona, dodesone, dodiciona See gondola da regata

dogbody Canada/United States: Considered to be a square-sterned **Chebacco boat★** with some modifications; called a **jake** in Canada. Used throughout the 19th century for offshore fishing and as a **coaster★**; a few built in Canada into the 20th century. Curved, raking stem; some had a prominent stemhead, and some were **clipper★**-built. Short full entrance and short run; straight keel with drag; full bilges; moderate sheer. Transom on early vessels in 3 sections, the rudderstock passing through the middle transom. Cuddy deck forward; standing well for helmsman. Foremast stepped in the eyes; mainmast raked aft. Square-headed gaff sails; no headsails. Reported lengths 11-12.2m; e.g., length 11.8m, beam 3.4m, hold depth 1.75m. Other recorded names: **Chebacco dogbody, dogbody Chebacco**. Note also **pinky**.

dogbody Chebacco See dogbody

dogboot, dogboten, doger, dogerbot, dogge, doggeboot See dogger

dogger Seaworthy **fishing boat★** used in England, France, Belgium, and Denmark, but primarily a Dutch and Flemish vessel. Reported from the 14th into the 19th century, the last mainly as a cargo vessel. Data are scarce, and it may not be a specific vessel type, but merely a widely used term. Fished mainly on the Dogger Bank in the North Sea for herring, mackerel, and cod; many went to Iceland for cod. Portrayed with a bluff bow, square stern, strong sheer; small vessels clinker-built, large carvel-built. Those fishing in the North Sea might have a live well, but most salted their fish. Usually decked, low bulwarks. Stepped 1-2 masts, the pole mainmast amidships. Mainmast set 2-3 square sails, and depending on the period, the mizzenmast set a square, gaff, lug-, or lateen sail. A Danish **dogger** is shown with loose-footed, boomed gaff sails, plus 2 square sails on the mainmast. Generally several headsails. A 3-masted type, the **dogschip** or **doggerschip**, was a small 17th-century trader. **Fishing boats** might carry a crew of 12. Size varied, with references to 30-150rt and cap. to 350t. At Dunkerque, ca. 1800, one was 14m long, 4.2m wide, and 1.8-2.1m deep. French boats were narrow, English

beamier. A small 17th-century Dutch **dogger**-type was also called a **puye** (pl. **puyen**). Relatively few produced. Sharp bow, with high curved, raking stem; round stern; low bulwarks stopped before the rudder to permit the tiller to pass below the bulwarks. Moderate sheer; narrow leeboards. Decked, with wide hatch; cuddy forward. Set a large square mainsail; small foremast, stepped on the stem, set a small square sail; both masts raked forward. Some sprit-rigged. Ca. 16t. Other recorded names: **daggerboot, daugre(bot), dogboot** (pl. **dogboten**), **doger(bot), dogge(re), doggerbåd, doggerbåt, Doggerboot, dogg(h)e-boot, doggher, dogh-boot** (pl. **dogh-boten**), **dog(h)schuit, dogr, dogre(bot), dougre, drogger, dugga★**. Note also **jagger**.

doggerbåd, doggerbåt, Doggerboot, doggere, doggerschip, dogghe-boot, doggher, dogh-boot, doghboten See dogger

doghole drogher See doghole schooner

doghole schooner United States, Pacific coast: Small, beamy vessel built in the rocky coves (dogholes) along the Mendocino coast of northern California. Mainly a short-haul **coaster★** that worked in and out of the dogholes in the 2nd half of the 19th century, but some went to the South Pacific. Flat floors. Almost all **schooner★**-rigged, many also employing a steam engine by the late 1880s. Under certain conditions a square sail was set on the foremast. Ranged from ca. 40-192t. Other recorded names: **barge★, doghole drogher, outside porter, scow★**

doghouse See shanty boat

doghschuit See dogger

dogol Peninsular Malaysia/Thailand: Fast, crank handline **fishing boat★** found along the east coast from the Kelantan River north into southernmost Thailand. Carvel-built, well-developed sheer, moderately long keel, angled forefoot and heel. Sets a large, rectangular cloth sail. Crew of 2-3. Reported lengths 4.9-6m, widths 0.9-1.0m. Name variant: **kolek ma' Siam★**

dogr, dogre, dogrebot See dogger

Dogrib canoe Canada, NW: Birchbark **canoe★** of the Dogrib of the Northwest Territories. Two types. The portage or Barren Ground type had long, pointed, upturned ends; a loose piece of bark that curved up over the gunwales served as end decking; wooden stem pieces, bark and stems lashed through holes in the stems; numerous narrow ribs; sheathed with widely spaced narrow splints; lengths 3.66-5.49m, widths 0.66-0.77m, depths 0.23-0.33m. The 2nd type was a family **canoe** designed for long lake trips; rounded end profile had a concave notch on top and a deep forefoot; often set a square sail; length 6.5m, width 1.0m, depth 0.36m. On both types the narrow ribs, gunwales, and widely spaced floorboards were of shaved birch.

dogschip, dogschuit See dogger

dohni See dhoni-6

dolbarka Poland, NE: Fishes for eels in Vislinski Zalev. Clinker-planked, sharp bow, slightly raked stem. Steps single mast, probably setting a spritsail. Length 9m, deep hull.

dolboordgiek See wherry-2

Dollenboot See **pulling boat**
Dollenwherry See **wherry-2**
domik See **umiak-1**
don, donah See **dhoni-1**
Donaufischerzille See **Fischerzille**
Donautschaike See **saique-1**
Donauzille See **Zille**
dondá See **dondi**
dondei *Indonesia, E:* Generic term for a **dugout canoe★** in Manado and the Sangihe-Talaud island group. Name variant: **londo**. Further reference: **londeh**
dondi *Pakistan, NE:* On the Jhelum River, the **dondi** was mainly a **ferry★**. Ends turned up sharply to a point, the stern higher; sides parallel except toward the ends, where they turned inward sharply. Decked at bow and stern. Spelling variants: **dondá**, **dúndi**. Note also **dunda**, **dúndo**.
dondo See **dundo**
done See **dhoni-1**
Donegal curragh *Ireland, NW:* The 2 primary types of **curragh★** found along the northwestern coast are multipurpose craft. The paddled **curragh** is a 1- or 2-man boat, 2.4-3.6m in length, ca. 1.0m at its widest, and less than 0.6m deep. Arched shape with a very bluff bow, nearly parallel sides, and truncated stern.

Donegal curragh—paddling

Originally covered with hide, later with a double layer of tarred cloth secured with double withe ribs and stout scantling gunwale. No thwarts; the paddlers kneel at the bow and sit on the bottom at the stern. Those from Tory Island paddled initially, then rowed, and sometimes sailed, stepping a mast well forward; small sail. The rowing **curragh** is 4.6-7.6m long, 0.9-1.2m wide, and 0.5-0.7m deep. Two to 4 rowers work long oars; a block attaches to the loom, which fits over the tholepin. Bow long, pointed, and curves gently upward, spoon-like. After end curves up sharply into a truncated stern. A stout beam extends the front end.

Donegal curragh—rowing

Broad U-shaped ribs secured by stringers. Tarred layers of cloth, separated by brown paper, cover the boat. Other recorded names: **Downing curragh**, **Dunfanaghy curragh**, **Tory Island canoe** (or **curragh**). Further reading: James Hornell, *British Coracles and Irish Curraghs*, Part II (London: Society for Nautical Research, 1938), 161-175.

Donegal yawl See **drontheim**
doney See **dhoni-1**
donga *Bangladesh/India:* **1.** General term for a **dugout canoe★** used for local transportation and fishing on Bengali rivers. One type formed from the bulbous lower end of a palm, creating a spoon-shaped craft; bow end broader. Sometimes a curved trunk is select-

donga-1

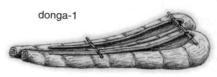

ed so that the stern clears the water, but sheer generally flat. If the soft palm wood deteriorates, a plug of clay is inserted at the "transom." May also be a simple dugout hewn from the trunk of a mango, sal, or cotton tree; sometimes sides raised by planks; rounded bottom. For ferrying, 2 **dongas** are lashed together with connecting poles; a rough platform laid on top increases capacity. Generally poled or paddled. Reported lengths of the palm type 3-7.6m; e.g., length 3.9m, width at bow 0.7m, at stern 0.28m; lengths of the 2nd type to ca. 9m. Other recorded names: **doanga**, **dongha★**, **doo(a)nga**, **dunga**, **pankaī**, **telo dongā**. Note also **sangādam**.
2. In the Pabna area in western Bangladesh, the **donga** is a small flat-bottomed **lighter★**.
3. In northern India, Nepal, and Pakistan, the term **dongā** describes a small boat of native pattern. Spelling variants: **dong'ga**, **dongo★**, **doonga**, **dúga**, **dunga(r)**, **dung'ga**
4. The Kashmiri **donga** of the Jhelum River is a **houseboat★** on which the local peoples live year-round. Those built larger and equipped with suitable accommodations have become popular with summer

donga-4

tourists. In winter, the native boats carry paddy to Srinagar. The native boats may be sharp-ended and selectively called **dungas**. Plank-built of cedar with moderate sheer terminating in overhanging bow and stern; flat bottom. Hull may be completely covered by a cabin; the native boats have a peaked mat roof and mat sides; the tourist boats have wooden house-like structures. The native boats range in length from 7.6-18m and are ca. 1.8m wide; shallow draft. The tourist **houseboats** are 20-29m long and ca. 4.3m wide. Spelling variants: **doonga**, **dungar**. Note also **floatel**. Further reference: **bhelā**
Dongala markab See **markab-2**
dong'ga See **donga-3**
dongha *Somalia:* Somali term for a **canoe★**. Further reference: **donga-1**
Donghala markhab See **markab-2**
dongi See **bhelā**

dongo *Congo:* Term for a **canoe★** or **raft★**. Further reference: **donga-3**

donguri See **kitamae-bune**

doni *Eritrea:* Generic term of the Donkali (Afars) for a sailing ship, especially of the **dhow★** type. Further references: **dhoni-1, dhoni-6**

donny See **dhoni-1, dhoni-6**

dony See **coracle, dhoni-1**

dooanga See **donga-1**

dooey See **düe**

doon-a *Somalia:* Somali term for a **dhow★**.

doondah, doondar See **dunda**

doondee See **dunda, dundo**

doonga See **donga**

door barge See **hopper-1**

door boat *Canada, SE:* Works with mackerel trap nets off Cape Breton Island. Towed to fishing site by a **tow boat★**. Positioned at the trap opening to secure the various parts of the net as it is hauled in. Open, carvel-planked, high-sided. Length ca. 6m.

Doornikenaar See **waal**

dopong See **dapang**

Doppelauslegerboot, Doppelauslegerkanu See **outrigger canoe**

Doppelboden See **double-bottom-1**

Doppelboot See **catamaran-6**

Doppelbugschiff See **liang tou chuan**

Doppeleiner See **double scull**

Doppelender See **double-ender**

Doppelrumpfboot See **catamaran-6**

Doppeltschaike See **saique-1**

Doppelzweier See **double scull**

doppio, doppio canoino See **double scull**

doppio pariglia See **scull**

doppio prora See **double-ender**

doré See **doris-3**

doree See **dory-1**

Dorem boat See **Durham boat**

dorey 1. *Belize:* Double-ended fishing dugout. Stem and sternpost superimposed; fine run; round bottom. Small

dorey-1

deck forward and aft; may have cockpit and live well amidships. Sailing **dorey** called a **creau★**. Crew of 1-2. Reported lengths 5-12.2m. Spelling variant: **dory★**

2. *West Indies:* A small flat-bottomed boat used in fishing and transporting light cargo.

Further reference: **dory**

dori *Honduras/Nicaragua:* Term generally applied by the Miskito of the Caribbean coast to a **dugout canoe★** with a keel, although in some areas it may lack a keel. Used for offshore fishing. Best type hewn from a mahogany, *santa maría*, or *cedro macho* log; strakes of cedar or mahogany added on; ribs of mangrove; stem piece of a softer shock-absorbing wood. Steered with a paddle. Sailed and paddled, the paddles

broad-bladed. Reported lengths 5.5-6m, some to 15m; width ca. 1.0m. Other recorded names: **cayuco★**

dori

(eastern Costa Rica), **doris★, dory★, duerka-taira, duri, dwarka, kuriñ** (Sumu dialect). Note also **Bay Islands dorey**. Further reference: **dory**

Doriboot, dorie See **dory**

dorioh *India, NW:* Indian-built **ketch★** that originated at Surat, north of Bombay (Mumbai); extinct. Narrow stern gallery, surrounded by a low railing, built out several meters beyond the poop. Bluff bow. Other recorded names: **ketch, orioh**

doris 1. *France, N:* The French **doris** was originally carried aboard **morutiers★** and **terreneuviers★** and is still used for fishing inshore, gathering seaweed, and collecting sand. Locally modified to meet special conditions and type of use. Some half-decked; others have a raised cabin forward. Double tholepins used when rowing. Various rigs employed: **ketch★, cutter★, sloop★,** sprit, lug, lateen. Now most use an outboard or inboard motor, and may be constructed of aluminum and have a pilot house. Reported lengths 3.2-7m; e.g., length 7m, beam 2.2m, depth 1.0m.

2. *Norway, SE:* The **doris** of Vestfold County is open and has a cross-planked flat bottom; sharp bow; wide transom stern; carvel-planked. Rowed or has an outboard motor. Length ca. 3.7m, narrow. Note also **dory-3**.

3. *Saint Pierre et Miquelon:* Open boat of these French Overseas Territory islands off the south coast of Newfoundland. Modified from the **Banks dories★** brought from the United States in the 1870s. Those at Canadian Cape Breton Island went by the term **doré**. Motorized **doris** for offshore cod fishing were introduced in the early 1930s. Fishermen often use the term **doris** to designate any **fishing boat★** that engages in coastal fishing. Lapstrake construction with flared sides; longitudinally planked flat bottom with strong rocker. Now often of marine plywood. Sharp bow, raked and slightly curved stem, enclosed by the planking. Trapezoidal transom, mildly pointed at the top; strong sheer. Decked at bow and stern, 3 fixed thwarts set onto sturdy stringers. Outboard rudder hangs below the bottom; tiller on those with an inboard engine. Some of the larger **doris** have a house just abaft amidships. Rowed, using 2 pairs of tholepins; may step a short aft-raking mast through the forward thwart. Reported lengths 6-8.2m; e.g., length overall 7m, on bottom 5.5m, beam at gunwale 2.18m, on bottom 1.1m, depth 0.9m. Other recorded names: **French dory, grand doris, St. Pierre dory, wary★**. Further reading: Eric Rieth, "La Construction des Doris à Saint-Pierre-et-Miquelon," *Neptunia* 175 (1989), 37-44; 177 (1990), 37-44.

Further references: **dori, dory, pinasson**

dorisar See **dory-4**

doris des Bancs See **Banks dory**

dorka See **dory**

Dorm boat See **Durham boat**

dorna 1. General term in Latin American ports for a sailing/rowing boat that transfers passengers and baggage and engages in other harbor work.

2. *Portugal, N/Spain, NW:* **Fishing boat★** employed in protected embayments and rivers since early times. Clinker-planked, with wide strakes. Maximum beam well forward; curved stem, cutaway forefoot, high stemhead; sharply raked, narrow "V" transom; flared sides; flat sheer. Modern **dornas** carvel-planked (**dorna de tope**); S-curve to rising floors; block keel. Usually narrow waterways; larger boats decked in forward third, small boats open; may be divided into compartments for the catch and nets; often a live well.

dorna-2

Two forked poles set along one side hold the oars while fishing. Interior coated with a pitch and sardine oil mixture; exterior black on top, white on bottom. When sailed, ships a rudder that curves under the bottom; tiller slots over the rudderhead. Mostly rowed; block on oar loom slots over the single tholepin. Sets a tall trapezoidal lugsail or lateen sail to an aft-raking mast stepped in forward third of the boat; sometimes 2 lugsails used. Luff may be extended by a spar. Crew of 1-2. Reported lengths 2.5-7.7m; e.g., length overall 6m, on keel 4m, beam 1.75m. The **polveira** (or **polbeira**) is a 1-man open **dorna**, 3-4m long; catches octopi. The **dorna peixeira** engages in general fishing; the **dorna tramalleira** uses a trammel net; and the **dorna xeiteira** fishes for sardines with a *xeito* net. Other recorded names: **barco de dornas**, **dorna galega**, **dornalla**; **dornaxa** (disrespectful diminutive or an old and useless **dorna**), dim. **dornela**, **dorniña**. Further reading: Stefan Mörling, "La Dorna de Galicia," *Chasse-Marée* 69 (1992), 12-29.

3. *Spain, NW:* One type, no longer built, was a **catamaran★** formed by 2 dugouts. Each dugout curved up to the plumb bow; shallower at the square stern; flattened bottom. Narrow opening on each logboat. Platform connected the dugouts, narrower aft, so that the 2 parts were closer at the stern. Worked with 2 oars set over tholepins, which were set into the outer side of the log. Length 3.5m, log width 0.57m.

dorna de tope, **dorna galega**, **dornalla**, **dorna peixeira**, **dorna tramalleira**, **dornaxa**, **dorna xeiteira**, **dornela**, **dorniña** See **dorna-2**

Dorste koolhaler, **Dorsten ake** See **Dorsten'sche Aak**

Dorsten'sche Aak *Germany/Netherlands:* Worked until early in the 20th century, carrying coal (**Dorste koolhaler**), grain, ore, etc., on the Rhine. Built mainly at Dorsten on the Lippe River. An **Aak★** type with a flat bottom that turned up gradually at the bow to form a flat wedge terminating at the gunwale. Sharp stern, nearly vertical, and fairly high. Clinker-planked, later of iron or steel; flaring, curved sides; angular chines.

Flat sheer except toward the stem. Rudder blade wide below the waterline; long downsloping tiller; leeboards. Hold open originally, covered during the 18th and 19th centuries; cuddy forward; deckhouse between the masts; low pavilion aft. Main- and mizzenmasts set loose-footed, boomed gaff sails; sometimes a topsail on the mainmast. Masts could be struck; mizzenmast abaft the hold. Also 2 jibs to a bowsprit, staysail. Reported lengths 30-40m; length-to-beam ratio 7:1. Other recorded names: **Dorsten ake**, **Dorstense aak**, **Dorstenser Aak**, **Dorstsche koolhaler**, **Dorstsche koolhaalder** (or **Koolhaelder**)

Dorstense aak, **Dorstenser Aak**, **Dorste koolhaler**, **Dorstsche koolhaalder**, **Dorstsche Koolhaelder** See **Dorsten'sche Aak**

dory 1. Small wide-board boat with a flat bottom, hard chines, flat flaring sides, and narrow V-transom, making it double-ended on the bottom. Characterized by method of construction. Longitudinal bottom planking cleated together and cut to the shape that determines the shape of the hull; bottom rocker varies. Lapstrake side planking phases into flush planking at the ends; flat pieces sprung into shape; strong sheer. Small number of sawn frames. Some round-sided. Best known as a fishing craft, in North America, France, and Portugal; also widely used as a general-purpose and pleasure boat. Rowed, sculled, and sailed; outboard or inboard engine now popular. The so-called **dory**-rig is a spritsail without a jib. Short mast stepped into a forward thwart; light sprit; no halyards, single sheet. A few set a jib, and some are 2-masted. Length overall ca. 6m. Other recorded names: **fisherman's dory**, **New England dory**; the terms **skiff★** and **wherry★** were used interchangeably with **dory** in early New England reports. Further reading: John Gardner, *The Dory Book* (Camden, Me.: International Marine Publishing Co., 1978). Note also **Banks dory**, **bankskøyte**.

2. Term now often applied to a hard-chined **dinghy★** with flaring sides. Used aboard **yachts★**, small **coasters★**, and some **fishing boats★**. Frequently equipped with an outboard motor.

3. *Norway:* **a.** Used on the west coast fishing banks, working from sailing **smacks★** and larger motorized vessels. The larger, the **Nordnorsk dory**, worked off the northern coast; the smaller, farther south. Developed for Norwegian use in the 1880s, as a stronger boat, capable of carrying heavier loads than the **Banks dory★**. Clinker-planked, deep top strake; flat bottom, narrow "V" transom; numerous curved ribs; deep floor frames. A hand winch at the bow used for handlining. Rowed or sailed. Those used on the **smacks** ranged in length from 4.3-4.9m; on the motorized vessels to 6.4m. Spelling variants: **doryen**; pl. **doryar(e)**, **doryer(e)**. Note also **doris-2**. **b.** A large, open, double-ended **dory** was used to set herring nets prior to ca. 1960. Worked in pairs. Clinker- planked. Length ca. 9m.

4. *Sweden:* Rugged general-purpose boat found mainly along the western and southern coasts, especially in the island groups. Clinker-planked; flaring sides; half and full frames. Flat bottom athwartships with

fore-and-aft rocker; some have a keel; strong sheer. Lightly raked transom, with sculling notch; curved stem; rounded or straight flared sides; maximum beam well forward. Open; thwarts slotted over the frames, resting on stringers. Some have a centerboard. Rowed or sailed, setting a spritsail. Reported lengths 4.3-5.2m; e.g., length 4.6m, beam 1.6m, depth 0.6m; shallow draft. Other recorded names: **dåre***, **doris***, **Kyrkesundsdoris, Nöteyviksdoris, plattboningar, plattbottnad eka, platteka, sköddel, sköddlar**; pl. **dorisar**

5. *United States, Alaska:* The **salmon dory** was a modified **Banks dory** in which the stern was wider, similar to that of the **sharpie***, to provide greater buoyancy aft. Sharp bow, flared sides, great sheer, flat bottom curves up to the square stern. Reported lengths on bottom 3.96-4.88m, the longer lengths being used in cod fishing. Further name variant: **Alaska dory**. Note also **Oregon dory**.

6. *United States, NE:* **a.** Early in the 20th century a **fleet*** of round-sided, motorized **dories** operated off Cape Cod. Best adapted to cod fishing, beam trawling for flounders, and night herring fishing. Most carvel-planked; narrow flat bottom. Considerable overhang at the bow; narrow, V-shaped raked stern; skeg. Short end decking, washboards along the sides. Reported lengths 7.6-10.6m. Name variant: **Cape Cod Power dory**. **b.** In the latter part of the 19th century, Maine lobstermen used the **dory** so much that it almost became a generic term for the **lobster boat***. A few were fitted for power by running the propeller shaft through the boat's bottom. **c.** **Dories** are used in seine-hauling for bass off the exposed south coast beaches of Long Island. Originally of wood and rowed; now motorized and of steel; net payed out from the end of a flatbed truck and hauled back by a second truck located down the beach.
Spelling variants: **doree, dorey***, **dori***, **Doriboot, dorie, doris***, **dorka, Dory Boat**. Further references: **bastard dory, Cape Ann dory, clammer's dory, cross-handed dory, dorey, dori, Lunenburg dory, Parrett flatner, Potomac dory-boat, semi-dory, Shelburne clipper dory, Shelburne dory, Swampscott dory**

doryar, doryare See **dory-3**
dory banker See **dory trawler**
dory-boat See **Potomac dory-boat**
Dory Boat See **dory**
doryen, doryer, doryere See **dory-3**
dory fisher See **doryman**
dory handliner Fishing vessel that employed 12-14 single-man **dories** (see **Banks dory**) in its handlining operation, generally for cod on the North Atlantic banks. Note also **handliner**.
doryman A vessel that carries fishing **dories** (see **Banks dory**) nested on deck. Most often refers to **schooners*** that fished on the Grand Banks off Newfoundland; now motorized. Name variant: **dory fisher**. Note also **dory trawler**.
dory schooner See **dory trawler**
dory-skiff *United States:* Popular all-purpose **rowing boat*** that varies in particulars with area and builder, often assuming a local name. Originated in the late 19th century in Massachusetts. Some built for lifesaving surf work. Lapstrake planking; flat bottom with rocker; stern somewhat wider than the pure **dory***; longitudinally planked. Raked, curved or straight stem; wide, raked transom; lightly rounded sides; considerable sheer. Open; generally a stern seat and 1-2 rowing thwarts. Some use an outboard motor or set a sprit- or gunter sail. Reported lengths 2.7-5.5m; the **dory-skiffs** built at Lowell's in Amesbury, Massachusetts, are 4.3m long, 1.5m wide, and 0.43m deep. Other recorded names: **Amesbury (dory) skiff, Chaisson dory-tender, Lancaster skiff, Lowell dory-skiff**; also **Chamberlain, Marblehead, Swampscott dory-skiff**
dory surf boat See **Sea Bright skiff**
dory trawler Vessel, generally a **schooner***, fitted out to fish with **dories** (see **Banks dory**). Each **dory** carried baited trawl lines. Name variants: **dory banker, dory schooner**. Note also **banker, doryman**. Further reference: **longliner-1**
două ponţi See **two-decker**
Douarnenez lugger See **sardinier breton**
double See **double scull**
double-banked boat One in which 2 oarsmen sit on a thwart, each pulling the oar on his side. Other recorded names: **Boot mit Zweimannduchten, bote de remos pareles, canot (armé) à couple**. Note also **single-banked boat**.
double-banked frigate See **frigate-1, frigate-7**
double barge See **freighter-3a**
double boat See **cao zi chuan, doble, Medway doble**
double-bottom 1. Ship with water ballast tanks in the bottom, covered by a lower deck. A **double-bottomed boat** has a watertight compartment between the bottom and the cabin or cockpit. Other recorded names: **Doppelboden, navire à double fond**
2. *British Isles:* A **catamaran***-type vessel devised in the 17th century. Platform set on 2 cylinders; the largest reported had 2 decks and a 17m-tall mainmast. Other recorded names: **cylinder, sluice boat**
Further reference: **catamaran-6**
double-bottomed boat See **double-bottom**
double bowed See **double-ender**
double canoe See **canoe**
double cat See **Mackinaw boat-1**
double-cedar canoe See **Rice Lake canoe**
double chaloupe See **barque longue, chaloupe-2**
double-coque See **catamaran-6**
double-decker 1. Ship with 2 decks above the waterline.
2. *United States, NE:* Vessel that carried no deck cargo, all its cargo being stowed below, under hatches.
See also **timber raft-3**.
double-ender 1. Boat or vessel that has, or nearly has, symmetrical underwater lines fore and aft. Most often sharp-ended, but may also be round- or square-ended. May be propelled from either end. Other recorded names: **bote con doble proa, canot pointu, Doppelender, doppio prora, double bowed, navire amphidrôme, spitsgatboot, Spitzgattboot**. Note also **ferryboat-1**.
2. *England, NE:* The **double ender** probably descended from the Yorkshire **mule** (see **coble-1d**). Worked off

beaches, notably at Redcar. Differs from the **mule** in that it has steam-bent frames, a conventional keel, and an orthodox rudder.
Further references: **Block Island boat, flatboat-6, paddle boat-7, peapod**

double felouque *Mediterranean:* A 17th-century vessel similar to, but larger and heavier than, the regular **felucca★**. Used as an **advice boat★** and against **corsairs★**. Other recorded names: **dubbele feloek, falucho grande** (or **primero**), **falutx de primer, lanche★, stor felucca** (or **felukk), velika filuka**. Further reference: **felucca-1**

double flyboat See **flyboat-1**

double frigate See **frigate-1**

double-handed punt, double-handed sailing punt See **gun punt**

double-headed ship See **liang tou chuan**

double header *United States:* **1.** Term assigned by bargemen on the Champlain Canal in eastern New York State to 2 **canal boats★** coupled one behind the other.
2. In the Mississippi Valley, a **double-header** was a common **timber raft★**, coupled one ahead of the other. Name variant: **long raft★**

double kayak See **kayak-1**

double-keel vessel See **catamaran-6**

double lay-down battery See **sinkbox**

double loquette See **loquette**

double Moses See **Moses boat-5**

double north canoe See **canot du maître**

double outrigger canoe See **outrigger canoe**

double raft See **timber raft-2b**

double scull Small rowing **shell★** propelled by 2 people, each using a pair of sculls; no coxswain. Frequently raced. No rudder. Length 10.5m, max. beam 0.28m, max. depth 0.2m. Other recorded names: **deux de couple, Doppeleiner, Doppelzweier, doppio** (canoino), **double, double sculler, double skiff, double skull, pair.** Note also **pair-oar, scull.**

double sculler See **double scull, sculler**

double shallop English term for a late 17th- to early 18th-century vessel type found in various European countries, such as England, France, Spain, Sweden, and Belgium. Generally considered a long, low **shallop★**. Often armed. Open, partly, or fully decked. Some were essentially rowing **galleys★**, with supplementary sails (square, lug, lateen). English vessels probably **schooner★**-rigged. Name variant: **double sloop.** Note also **barcolongo, barque longue.**

double skiff See **double scull, Staten Island skiff, Thames skiff**

double skull See **double scull**

double sloop See **barque longue, double shallop**

double topsail schooner See **schooner-1**

double-wedge boat See **deadrise boat**

dou chuan *China, E:* Carried grain on the lower Chang Jiang (Yangtze), originating out of Tungcheng. Strongly built; 7 bulkheads, 3 frames, and 4 half-bulkheads; several wales. Square stern with wide strakes above the curved sternpost; flat bottom; curved, overhanging square bow. House in after third, with tiller extending over the house; wide balanced rudder; 2 masts. Length 16.5m, beam 3.8m,

depth 1.7m. Other recorded names: **rice measure junk, tou ch'uan**

doughnut See **life raft**

dougout See **pirogue-4**

dougre See **dogger**

dovel See **doble**

Dover beach punt See **Dover punt**

Dover punt *England, S:* Open lug-rigged boat common in the 19th century for potting and sprat fishing. Clinker-planked, vertical transom stern, plumb stem. Outboard rudder; tiller; 3 thwarts, side seats. Dipping lug mainsail; standing lug mizzen sheeted to an outrigger. Mainmast stepped in chock; mizzenmast stepped to starboard at the sternpost. When needed, rowed with as many as 3 pairs of oars, worked between double tholepins. 1880 boat 4.4m long, 1.5m wide, 0.66m deep. Name variants: **Dover beach punt, Dover lugger**

Dover lugger See **Dover punt**

dovetail See **Hooper Island draketail**

dow See **dhow, kotia**

Down East blood boat See **blood boat-3**

down easter *United States:* In general, a vessel built in New England. More precisely, a sailing vessel built from the 1860s for west coast grain trade, carrying wheat to the east coast and to Europe. Superseded the **clippers★**, having more capacity, and worked until supplanted by steamships. Most 3-masted, square-rigged **ships★**; some were **barks★**. Almost all of wood. Some built in Canada.

Downing curragh See **Donegal curragh**

down-the-bay sharpie *United States, E:* A **skipjack★** converted to power; centerboard and well removed to enhance shallow-draft qualities. Popular on the Susquehanna Flats on upper Chesapeake Bay to transport waterfowl hunters, a **sinkbox★**, and to provide sleeping accommodations. Usually towed 2 small boats to set the decoys; also aided in putting out the **sinkbox**. Note also **cabin boat-3**.

dozer boat See **boom boat-2**

dozornoe sudno See **guard ship**

draai-over-boord otter See **otter**

Drachenboot See **dragon boat-4, long chuan**

Drachenschiff, draco See **skeid**

drag *England, W:* River Severn **raft★** that transported bulky and heavy cargoes. Name variant: **float★**

draga See **draggarnseka, dredger-1, dredger-2**

drag boat 1. *China, E:* Term sometimes given to a small, indistinctive craft of the Chang Jiang (Yangtze) estuary that was used as a local **ferry★**. Stepped a single mast.
2. *Scotland, Shetland Islands:* A small boat that ferries crews and gear from a **smack★** or **drifter★** anchored offshore.
See also **Connecticut River drag boat, dragger, kosterbåt, tuo wang chuan**.

drage, drageskib See **skeid**

drageur See **dragueur, drogueur**

draggarnseka *Sweden, W:* One-man inland **fishing boat★**, mainly for netting salmon in Halland Province. No longer used. The northern type was square-ended, with shallow, arched, slightly raked transoms; narrower bow. Flat, longitudinally planked bottom; curved up toward the ends, with the bow end terminating above the waterline. Vertical sides; bulkhead just forward of the occupant. Paddled, kneeling; gunwale built up as a fulcrum abreast the paddler. Length 3.7m, beam ca. 1.0m, maximum depth ca. 0.3m. The southern type had sharp ends, the slightly flared sides coming to a raked point in a straight line. The fore-and-aft-planked bottom was totally flat or curved toward the bow. Propelled by a long spiked pole; some used oars to an outrigger device. Length 4m, beam ca. 0.8m, depth ca. 0.2-0.25m. Name variant: **dräga**

dragger 1. *Canada/United States:* Vessel that tows a conical net along the bottom. Includes various trawl nets, scallop drags, and shrimp nets. Motorized; uses a sail mainly for steadying. Length to ca. 40m. Name variant: **draggerman**

2. *United States, NE:* In the late 19th century, mackerel were sometimes caught off the Atlantic coast of New England in small open boats that dragged gill nets, and were therefore called **draggers** or **drag boats***. Plumb stem, transom stern. Boomed gaff sails set to the 2 masts; short topmast; jib to a short bowsprit. Crew of 2. 15-25t.
Further reference: **steam dragger**

draggerman See **dragger-1**

drag-in seine boat *England, SW:* Used for mackerel seining off the southwest coast of Cornwall. Constructed with steamed timbers; 4 thwarts; sharp bow; transom stern. Net stowed aft. Crewed by 4 oarsmen, a helmsman, and 2 net setters. Length 6m, beam 1.5m. Note also **seine boat**.

dragnet boat See **Connecticut River drag boat**, **tuo wang chuan**

dragó See **dragon boat-4**

dragon *France:* **1.** Class of sailing/rowing vessel that was attached to the navy in the mid-17th century, some serving as coastal guard vessels. Carried as many as 16 guns; as many as 120 in crew. Probably also used in the 16th century. To ca. 400t.

2. A **dragon** is also a type of modern pleasure boat. See also **dragon boat-4**.

dragon boat 1. *Indochina:* Reported as early as the 3rd century A.D. from Cambodia and Cochin China.

2. *Indonesia, central:* The Dragon Boat Festival was held at various Javan communities with extensive Chinese populations. Boats raced on the Tji-Sadane, a river at Tangerang, west of Djakarta. Boats long and slender; a dragon's head formed the elongated bow, its tail at the stern; low sides. Raced in pairs to the accompaniment of tambours and cymbals.

3. *East Malaysia:* In Sarawak, a long, slender paddling **canoe*** used in the January 1 regattas. Malay boat but manned by Chinese. A dragon's head is appended to the bow of each **canoe** and simulated scales are painted along the sides. Cadence established by a man with a gong in the bow. Paddled by 20-30 men. Name variant: **Chinese dragon boat**

4. Class of racing boat that originated in Norway in 1929. Popular in Scandinavia, Germany, and the British Isles; Olympic class between 1948 and 1972. **Sloop***-rigged. Usually crew of 3. Length overall 9m, on waterline 5.7m, beam 2m, draft 1.2m. Other

recorded names: **Drachenboot**, **dragó**, **dragon***, **dragon class**, **dragone**
Further references: **fa chuan**, **long chuan**, **perahu naga**

dragon class See **dragon boat-4**, **skeid**

dragone See **dragon boat-4**

dragon sampan See **sampan naga**

dragon ship See **skeid**

drag-seine galley See **shad galley**

drague See **dredger-1**, **drogueur**

drague à godets See **dredger-1**

drague porteuse, **drague porteuse de dèblais** See **hopper**

dragueur *France, SW:* Employed on the Adour to transport sand dredged from the river to the open sea until the mid-19th century. Slightly rounded bottom planked longitudinally, except at the transversely planked ends. Flat bow curved up to a sharp, high point; stern slightly rounded and raked and sheer swept up but to a lesser extent than bow; tumble home sides. Platforms at bow and stern. Rowed, but also towed from a large capstan placed amidships. Length 10m, beam 4m, depth ca. 0.75m. Spelling variant: **drageur**. See also **dredger**, **drogueur**, **saque**.

dragueuse See **dredger-1**, **drogueur**

dragueux See **drogueur**

drahissa, **draissa** See **dghajsa-1**

draissa-tal-pass See **dghajsa tal-pass**

drakar *Denmark:* Employed by Danish kings in raids to the British Isles in the 8th and 9th centuries. Similar in design to the **langskip***; was decorated with a carved dragon head on the bow and tail at the stern. Further reference: **skeid**

drake, **draken** See **skeid**

draketail See **Hooper Island draketail**

drakkar, **drakkare**, **drakker**, **drakon**, **drakr**, **drakskepp** See **skeid**

dram *Canada, E/United States, E:* Detachable unit of logs that formed the **timber rafts*** that floated down the upper St. Lawrence River; constructed until 1914. Staves were also rafted down the river, kept afloat by attaching light timber. Some **rafts*** also carried cargo, such as flour and barrels of pork. Consisted of single tier when built of oak and 3 tiers if constructed of pine or elm; logs squared. Each **dram** tied with birch withes. A **raft** consisted of 8 **drams**, 2 abreast. A wood or canvas cabin for living quarters was set on 2 of the **drams**. A very large **dram**, the **cabin dram**, had a shanty and a cookhouse. Worked with 9m-long sweeps, from the corners; also employed sails. Later **rafts** were towed by a **steamer**, except in heavy rapids. For a run through more dangerous rapids, a **raft** was separated into individual **drams**. Crew of ca. 11 on an 8-**dram raft**. **Dram** 26m wide and 55m long; a 10-**dram timber raft** would be 52m wide and 275m long. Other recorded names: **crib***, **drame**, **Saint Lawrence raft**. Note also **cage**.

drame See **dram**

Dreckprahm See **Mudderprahm**

Dreckschute See **hopper**

Dredfischer See **dredger-2**

dredge See **dredger-1**

dredge boat *United States, E:* **1.** Dredged for hard crabs in Chesapeake Bay during winter months. Freighted in off-season. Employed 2 large dredges, secured to a platform aft. Some log-built. Equipped with both engine and sails in the early part of the 20th century. Reported lengths 15-18m. Other recorded names: **crab dredger, deck boat**
2. Also on Chesapeake Bay, a boat engaging in oyster dredging with heavy iron rakes 1.2-1.5m wide. Harvest conch in summer. Currently a totally motorized **deadrise★**-type vessel and the few remaining **skipjacks★**. Maryland boats work without mechanical propulsion; in Virginia any boat may dredge. Small boats employ a crew of 3, large boats ca. 7. Other recorded names: **dredger★, drudge boat, drudger, oyster boat**
Further reference: **Delaware Bay oyster schooner**
Dredgenfischer See **dredger-2**
dredger 1. Vessel equipped with bucket(s) (**bucket** or **ladder dredger, drague à godets, Eimerbagger**), a grab, a draghead (**trailing dredge**), or suction tubes (**suction dredger** or **cutter suction dredger**) to remove sand and mud from channels, harbors, canals, etc. Some engage in recovering land from the sea (**reclamation dredge**). **Dredgers** were also used to scoop up sand and gravel for ballast. Range from small boats with an attached pump to large seagoing vessels. Towed or self-propelled. Selected name variants: **Bagger, baggerma(s)chine, baggermo(o)len, baggerschuit, bargagno, bargogno, bateau dragueur, cavafango, cavafondo, curaporti, cure-môle, curemolle, draga, drague, dragueur★, dragueuse, dredge, dreg boat★, drudge, Eimerkettenbagger, growler, kavafang(o), moddermolen★, mol, mudderfartyg, Muddermaskine, Mudderprahm, mudderprám, mudderverk, mud dredger** (or **machine**), **mud sucker, Nassbagger, Saugbagger, Schwimmbagger**. Note also **ballast barge, hopper, mariesalope, pontoon-5, spoon dredger**.
2. Type of **trawler★** that scrapes the bottom with a heavy net of rope or chain to scoop up shellfish. Other recorded names: **draga, dragueur★, Dred(gen)-fischer, Dredscher, navio de draga, rastero, Schwimbagger, vongolara**
Further references: **clam dredger, dredge boat, Falmouth oyster dredger, five-finger dredger, watch boat**
dredger boat A boat that fishes for bottom fish, such as turbot and sole, with a dredger net, or for oysters with a scraper.
dredging punt See **ballast punt**
Dredscher See **dredger-2**
dreg boat *Scotland:* Listed among the **fishing boats★** in the official 15th- and 16th-century registers at Edinburgh. May have towed a trawl or seine or perhaps dredged for oysters. Spelling variant: **drag boat**. See also **dredger-1**.
dregeur, drégeux, dreigeur See **drogueur**
dreimastbark See **bark-1**
dreimastbuis See **buis-2**
dreimastschoener, dreimastschoenerbrik See **barkentine**

Dreiruderer See **trireme**
drekar, dreki, drekki See **skeid**
dren See **sarnái**
Drentsche praam See **Drentse praam**
Drentse praam *Netherlands, NE:* A type of **somp★** that carries peat and farm produce on canals and inland waterways in Drente Province. When carrying hay, the hay is stacked high above the deck, the skipper standing on top, steering with a special long tiller. Bluff bow; stem tapers to merge with the wale at a point. Sharp stern, raking sternpost. Flat bottom, with slight rocker toward stern; long skeg; hard chines; straight flared sides up to the narrow wale, tumble home above. Flat sheer, rising toward ends. Decked at bow and stern, with cuddies below; central hold, covered with sloping boards; narrow gangways. In especially shallow waterways, excess peat removed to lighten the vessel. Employs "canal" rig, consisting of a small loose-footed, boomed gaff sail. Mast can be struck. End of boom can be rigged higher to clear deck cargo. Length 18.8m, beam 4.15m, depth 1.48m. Spelling variant: **Drentsche praam**. Note also **praam**.
Dreuch-Ewer See **Ewer**
driever See **drijver-1**
drifkrase See **drivkvase**
drift See **Cumberland River drift**
drift boat *Canada, E:* A small **fishing boat★** that tends drift nets in the Maritime Provinces. In season, fishes for shad. Name variant: **bateau dériveur**. Note also **dériveur**. Further references: **Au Sable River drift boat, drifter, McKenzie River drift boat, party boat-1**
drifter **Fishing boat★**, motorized or sail, that works a wall of drift nets, drifting with the wind or tide, the net to windward. Used especially for surface-swimming fish, such as herring, mackerel, and pilchard. Characteristically sets a sail aft to keep bow into the wind while drifting, but lowers the mast when lying to the nets. Large crew. Other recorded names: **drift boat★, drift fisher, drift netter, drijfnetvisser, driver, driving boat, drover, herring drifter, logger★, mackerel driver, pilchard driver, Treibnetzlogger, steam drifter**. Note also **buss-2, dériveur, drivkvase, harenguier, herring boat**.
drift fisher See **drifter**
drifting boat *United States, central:* Motorized craft of the Mississippi Valley that employed an on-board sawmill to cut up masses of driftwood, especially to saw suitable logs into boards for sale at river towns. Important in the early 20th century.
drift netter, drijfnetvisser See **drifter**
drijfschouw, drijfschuit See **zalmschouw**
drijvende bok See **sheer hulk**
drijvende brandspuit See **fire boat**
drijvende hijbok See **sheer hulk**
drijver *Netherlands:* **1.** A **fishing boat★** that works with a drift net, generally for herring, anchovy, and smelt. Sailed. Spelling variant: **driever**.
2. Small open **fishing boat** used on the Westerschelde in southwestern Netherlands. Bluff ends. Rowed only. See also **kwak, tochtschuit**.

drijversboot, drijverschuit See **zalmschouw**

drive boat See **lumberman's batteau**, **pointer**, **striker boat-1**

driver See **drifter**, **push boat-2**

driver boat See **striker boat-1**

driveur See **dériveur**

drivgarnskøyte See **skøyte-4**

driving bateau See **lumberman's batteau**

driving boat See **drifter**, **pointer**

drivkvase *Denmark:* **Fishing boat★** designed to drift (*driv*) and equipped with a wet well. Introduced from Germany in the 1870s; those retaining the original German characteristics were called **Tyskerkvaser**; others were modified to become a Danish type. Used until World War I. Mainly drifted for eels (**åledrivkvase**), especially in shallow-water areas of southeastern Denmark. Most were built for this purpose, but other types of **fishing boats** were modified to become **drivkvaser**. Clinker-built; full bow with curved stem, some convex; rounded or counter stern; plank keel; low floors, rounded bilges; light sheer. Early boats used 1-2 leeboards, some raised and lowered by a chain attached to the mainmast; later adopted a centerboard. Cabin either aft or forward; elongated open waist bordered by side decks, standing well aft. Set a tall, narrow, loose-footed gaff sail and gaff topsail to the mainmast. Sometimes used a boomed standing lug mizzen sheeted to an outrigger that ran out from the port quarter. Staysail and jib; jibboom and outrigger also used to spread the seine net. Sails tanned. Crew of 2-3. Reported lengths 6.7-9.6m; e.g., length 8.6m, beam 3m, depth 1.0m, draft with centerboard up, 0.84m. Other recorded names: **aaledrivkvase**, **drifkrase**, **Fejødrivkvase**, **Tyske drivkvase**. Note also **drifter**, **kvase**, **Quase**, **treibkvase**. Further reference: **Zeesboot**

droblât See **mahonne-4**

droger See **drogher-1**

drogger See **dogger**, **drogher-1**, **drogueur**

drogh See **drogher**

drogher 1. Term sometimes applied to an old vessel engaged in some disagreeable trade. A slow-moving **coaster★** with bluff lines that carried heavy cargo, such as stone, sand (**sand drogher**), timber (**timber drogher★**), or guano (**dung drogher** or **dung barge**). Some traded between Canada and the United Kingdom. Note also **drogueur**, **sloop drogher**, **wood drogher**. **2.** 18th-century boat that caught herring and cured them aboard. **3.** *West Indies:* **a.** Coasting vessel used in the early sugar trade. Lateen sail. Name variant: **sugar drogher**. **b.** Black **barge★**-like trader that sailed in the Gulf of Paria off western Trinidad. Decked forward. Set a lug- or lateen sail. Crew of 3-4. Length ca. 18m, beamy. **c.** Those in current use in the British Virgin Islands are beamy, slow cargo vessels. Name variant: **droguer-sloop**. **d.** Also reported as an 18th-century **lighter★** that carried sugar and rum to offlying **merchantmen★**.

Other recorded names: **drog(g)er**, **drogh**, **drogner** (erroneously), **droguer★**, **drougher**; **caddy** on Chesapeake Bay

drogheur See **drogueur**

drogner See **drogher-1**

droguer *Canada, E:* Local term in Lunenburg County on the southeast coast of Nova Scotia for a vessel that engaged in droguing, or herring drifting. Most **Tancook schooners★** operated as **droguers** during May and June. Note also **drogueur**, **drifter**. Further reference: **drogher-1**

droguer-sloop See **drogher-3**

drogueur *France, N:* A strong vessel originating from ports in Normandy and Picardy that used a drag net for herring and cod in the North Sea and for mackerel in the Irish Sea. Known from at least the 11th century. The largest also traded with the eastern Mediterranean, carrying salted fish in casks, mainly from Dieppe, returning with drugs and spices. Generally bluff-bowed and counter-sterned. Decked, some with 2 decks. Set a square mainsail and topsail, a square foresail, and at times a mizzen. Later vessels varied greatly in size and capacity, but ranged to as long as 17m; length on keel 11.6m, beam 4.6m. Other recorded names: **drageur**, **drague**, **dragueur★**, **dragueuse**, **dragueux**, **drégeux**, **dre(i)geur**, **drogger**, **drogheur**, **drugger**, **gondole française**, **grand drogueur**. Note also **chalutier**, **drogher-1**.

droitwich trow See **trow-1**

drome 1. French term for a collection of masts and spars consolidated into a **raft★** to preserve them in sea water. Other recorded names: **radeau de mâts**, **train de marine 2.** An assembled group of **ship's boats★** at an arsenal.

drôme See **davit boat**

drona, droni See **dhoni-1, dhoni-6**

drontheim *Ireland, N and NW/Northern Ireland, N:* Double-ended, clinker-built, open fishing and lobstering boat that worked from beaches. Fishermen/farmers also used the boats to transport cattle, produce, seaweed for fertilizer, etc. Essentially extinct, but is being revived as a recreational craft. Known as a **Drontheim boat** in the Greencastle area, but **Greencastle skiff** or **yawl** elsewhere. Some exported to west Scotland towns. Most had sharp, straight, plumb ends; fine ends, with quick rise to the floors; long, slender, slightly curved keel, scarfed toward the

drontheim

ends; frames usually not fastened to the keel; moderate sheer. Outboard rudder; short tiller. Hole in forward 3 thwarts for variable stepping of masts. Mostly single-masted, setting a gaff sail, high-peaked spritsail, or standing lugsail. On 2-masted boats the forward mast might set a spritsail and the after mast a gaff sail. Jib from stemhead or bowsprit. Also rowed, employing 4 very long oars worked between thole-pins; later, engines installed. Crew of 4-7. Reported lengths on keel 7.3-8.5m, widths 1.8-2.6m; 1892 boat length overall 7.3m, beam 2.3m; shallow draft. Other recorded names: **Donegal yawl, Druntheim, Druntin boat, Greenie, Skerries yawl; Westerd drontheim** in Glengad; **skiff*** or **yawl*** or **big salmon boat** (the 8.5m-long boat) at Inishboffin Island; **Dronthiem** (erroneously). The Irish-built boats built on Islay Island, the southernmost of the Inner Hebrides, were known as **sgoth Eireannaich (Irish skiff)**. Further reading: Dónal MacPolin, *The Drontheim: Forgotten Sailing Boat of the North Irish Coast* (Dublin: Playprint, 1992). Note also **Achill yawl**.

Drontheim boat See **drontheim**
drop-net boat See **Core Sounder**
drougher See **drogher-1**
drover See **drifter**
drua *Fiji, central Pacific:* Oceangoing double **canoe*** that was used to the end of the 19th century, mainly for war. The larger craft were plank-built on a dugout-base keel, the smaller used dugout hulls with deep washstrakes; planks sewn on so that no stitching showed on the outside. Caulked with gum from the breadfruit tree. Hulls of unequal size; strengthened with shaped ribs; keels sometimes in 2 pieces, scarfed

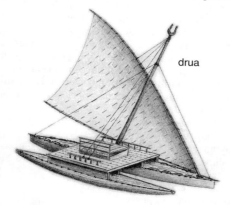

drua

and kept rigid by side planks. Bow of larger hull formed vertical cutwater; stern end small, truncate, and slightly ovate; both ends of smaller hull slender and truncated. Decked at the ends. The 2 hulls connected by numerous crossbeams, made rigid by stout stringers. Platform laid across the beams; often had a deckhouse of plaited palm fronds; bailing hatch at each corner. Steered by large, heavy oars, as long as 6m, one fitted at each end of the larger hull. A lug-lateen mat sail was set to a forward-raking mast stepped in the main hull. On large **canoes** the mast might be 18m tall and the yard 24m long. Halyards ran through a hole near the top of the mast or a fork on the top. No blocks for the sheet, necessitating constant hauling. Smaller hull kept to windward, the sail being reversible. In calms, sculled through a hole in the plat-form. Crews ranged from 40-100; war types carried up to ca. 300. Reported lengths 12-37m; e.g., length 30m, platform length 13.8m, platform width 6.2m, draft 0.75m. Other recorded names: **ndrua, wangga**

ndrua, waqa drua; the **wangga tambu** or **waqa tabu** was a sacred **canoe** reserved for chiefs, and some were built as memorials to the dead. Note also **'alia, kalia**.
drudge See **dredger-1**
drudge boat, drudger See **dredge boat**
drugger See **drogueur**
drum seiner See **seine boat-2**
Druntheim, Druntin boat See **drontheim**
dry boat Term sometimes applied to a **fishing boat*** that does not have a well for holding the catch alive. Other recorded names: **dry-bottomed boat, dry smack**. Note also **well boat**. Further reference: **Belizean smack**
dry-bottomed boat See **dry boat**
dry cargo freighter See **dry cargo ship**
dry cargo ship One that carries only merchandise, no liquids in bulk. Other recorded names: **dry cargo freighter** (or **vessel**), **dry stores carrier, Trocken-fracter**. Note also **merchantman**.
dry cargo vessel See **dry cargo ship**
dry ship One on which abstinence from intoxicating beverages is practiced.
dry smack See **dry boat, lobster smack**
dry stores carrier See **dry cargo ship**
dryver See **tochtschuit**
Dscherm See **djerme**
Dschonke, Dschunke See **junk**
dua See **düe**
duas cobertas See **two-decker**
duas pontas, duas proas See **meia lua-2**
dubbel binlander See **bijlander**
dubbele feloek See **double felouque**
dubbele somp, dubbele zomp See **somp**
dubłanka See **dugout canoe**
duck See **landing craft**
duck boat *United States:* Any small boat pressed into service to hunt ducks and other waterfowl might be called a **duck boat**, but most are specifically designed to move quietly and to support guns, decoys, dogs, and ducks, plus 1-2 hunters. Some designed mainly for marshy areas, others for open water. Hunters shoot from the boat. Lightweight but stable; most low-sided; flat-floored. Generally has a small cockpit with deck-ing forward and aft that may be used for camouflaging grasses and straw. Mostly sculled or hand-paddled. Average length ca. 3-5m; very shallow draft. A **Great South Bay duck boat** was 4.2m long overall, 1.3m wide, 0.36m deep, and had runners for ice sailing. Other recorded names: **ducking boat, duck punt (scow** or **skiff)**. Note also **Barnegat sneakbox, Connecticut scull boat, Delaware ducker, dink, Entenlomme, garvey box, gunning skiff, gun punt, Koshkonong monitor, melon seed, monitor, punt-13, Savannah River duck boat, scooter**. See also **canoe-8, rua pet, scull float, ya ze chuan**.
ducker See **Delaware ducker**
ducking boat See **duck boat**
ducking skiff See **scull float**
duck punt See **duck boat, gun punt**
duck's buttock See **lorcha-3**
duck scow, duck skiff See **duck boat**
ducktail launch See **Hooper Island draketail**

düe *India, Bay of Bengal:* Large single-outrigger **dugout canoe**★ of the Nicobar Islands. Two booms attached to a long float by a double set of 3-stick under-crossed connectives. Ends elongated; bow higher than stern; a tall extension capped with 2 horn-like decorations rose from the bow. Numerous thwarts secured with a wide gunwale strake. Propelled by as many as 20 paddlers; steered with a paddle. Two to 5 short bamboo masts were stepped into thwarts, but did not reach the bottom of the **canoe**. Set short-luffed lateen sails of cotton or pandanus. Length to 20m. Other recorded names: **dāë**★, **daoi**, **dëua**, **dooey**, **dua**, **kōi-la-pū**, **raë**, **rôë**, **rûë**, **rûœ**. Note also **ap**.

due ponti See **two-decker**

duerka-taira See **dori**

dúga See **donga-3**

dugga *Iceland:* Small decked **fishing boat**★, probably a 15th- to 16th-century **dogger**★ from England. Name variant: **fiske-duggur**. Further reference: **duggah**

duggah *Pakistan, N:* Clumsy yet strongly built boat that traversed the rapids on the Indus River between Campbellpore (Attock) and Kalabagh. Most broken up and sold because of the high cost of towing the boat back upstream. No sail. Spelling variant: **dugga**★

duggur See **dugga**

dugout canoe A craft fashioned from a log by hollowing out the center to make it lighter and more buoyant, and to provide a place to sit or stand. Used in most parts of the world where suitable trees are available. Hewn by a tool such as an adze, stone, bone, or ivory, or the interior may be burned out. Drilled or burned holes of appropriate depth enable the builder to know when he has achieved the desired hull thickness, the bottom often being thicker than the sides. Ends rounded, pointed, or left square; on some, mud plugs form the ends. To increase stability, the sides may be flared by soaking and inserting spreaders. Further stability can be achieved by attaching floats to booms and extending them out one or both sides, or setting them against the hull as sponsons. The sides may be increased by adding one or more planks and closing off the ends. On some the dugout part may be minimal, the planking forming the major portion. A **dugout** is generally a single log (a **monoxylon**). In some areas it may consist of 2 halves, sliced longitudinally, the bottom widened by a plank insertion, or 2 hewn logs may be butted end-to-end to form a longer **canoe**★; a few, such as **log canoes**, may be composed of several shaped logs. Although generally the work of primitive peoples, in several societies **dugouts** have achieved a special status, being well-proportioned, designed for speed, elaborately carved, and of tremendous size—54m long from a single log. Most **dugouts** are paddled, although the initial **dugouts** were undoubtedly propelled by hands. Selected name variants: **Baumkahn**, **Baumschiff**, **bohmschep**, **bomkane**, **Boomkahn**, **boomschip(p)**, **boomstamkano**, **boumkane**, **canoa monoxila**, **dublanka**, **Eichbaum**, **Einbaum**, **flotti**, **logboat**, **mandrowner**, **monòssilo** (pl. **monosoli**), **monossilóne**, **monoxila**, **monoxilo(s)**, **monoxyl(o)**, **monoxylus**, **piroga monoxile**, **pirogue monoxyle**, **stammebåd**,

trough; pl. **monoxyla**. Note also **canoa**, **canoe**, **ladva**, **pirogue**.

dugout dory See **creau**

dugout pirogue See **pirogue-4**

Duinkerker *Belgium/France, N:* Fast, maneuverable Flemish **privateer**★ out of Dunkerque, Nieuwpoort, or Oostende. Developed in the 1st quarter of the 17th century, mainly to attack Dutch ships during the Spanish-Dutch wars. Phased out during the 18th century. Two- or 3-masted; also rowed. Other recorded names: **capre dunkerquois**, **Dunkerker**, **dunkirks**. Note also **caper**.

Duiveland platten See **Tholense hoogaars**

dukong *Cocos (Keeling) Islands:* Light open boat developed at the beginning of the 20th century on this Australian island group southwest of Sumatra. Sharp ends; flat floors amidships; keel, ca. 15cm deep, curves up toward the bow. Nearly vertical sides; sharp bilges, with short grounding keels at the turns. Slight inboard rake to stem; sharply raking stern; moderate sheer. Outboard rudder worked with lines. Sets a boomed gunter sail; staysail tacked to stemhead. Crew of 1-2. When sailed by a single adult, children often used as ballast. Reported lengths 4.6-6m; e.g., length 5.2m, beam 1.3m, depth 0.4m. See also **jugong**.

dum See **bom-1**

dumb barge Designed to carry heavy loads but lacks means of self-propulsion and must float with the tide or current, or be towed. Sometimes maneuvered by oars or pole. May have a special design or fittings as required by local ordinance. Usually open and without a rudder. Other recorded names: **barcone a remi**, **barcone d'allibo**, **dumb craft**★, **dumb scow**, **Irish man-o'-war**, **open barge**, **salanda**. Note also **barge**, **dummy barge**, **flat-1**, **lighter**.

dumb craft **1.** Any floating craft that has no self-propulsion, steering, or signalling.
2. Sturdy **barge**★ used for raising heavy objects, especially ships, from the sea or river bottom. Must be towed, having no means of self-propulsion. Further reference: **dumb barge**

dumb hopper See **hopper-1**

dumb lighter See **lighter-1**

dumb scow See **dumb barge**

dummy barge **1.** **Raft**★ or **pontoon**★ placed between the dock and a ship; often receives cargo. Other recorded names: **Anlegeponton**, **barzha plashkoum**, **chaland ponton**, **chata**★, **ponton de largare**, **şlep ponton**
2. Permanently moored **barge**★ or **hulk**★.

dummy bow See **compartment boat**

dummy flat See **pontoon-1**

dump barge Usually, a craft with hinged doors on the bottom enabling the contents, generally dredged or construction materials, to drop through the bottom. Designed with internal flotation for buoyancy when door open. Occasionally, the term may apply to a **barge**★ designed to list in order to permit deck loads to drop over the side. Other recorded names: **chalana basculante**, **chaland basculeur**, **dumping barge**, **dump scow**, **Klapp(en)-prahm**, **Klappschiff**, **Klappschute**, **ponton de fango**, **şalandă basculantă**, **self-dumping barge**. Note also **hopper**, **kantelbak**, **marie-salope**, **scow-1**.

dumping barge See **dump barge**
dump scow See **dump barge, scow-1**
duncan Jamaican term for a **dugout canoe***.
dunda *Pakistan, SE:* Flat-bottomed cargo carrier on the lower Indus River, especially for grain; small **dundas** ply the upper river. Square ends; sloping bow and stern, with stern higher; vertical, straight sides. Constructed by preparing the 2 sides and bottom separately (generally of small pieces) and then uniting the 3 units. Bottom given some fore-and-aft rocker at the ends by applying pressure and a special lubricant, causing planks to curve up. Internal support provided by frames across the bottom, knees, stringers, and athwart beams. Steered with a long, curved oar from an elevated frame, by a rudder and double tillers, or by lines; large rudder, shaped like a "b." Mast lacks standing rigging, so can be easily struck; braced against an athwartships beam in forward part. Sets a huge square sail; those in the delta area set a boomed oblong sail to the after mast and a lateen sail forward. Sails might be hung abaft the mast. When tracked upstream from shore, rope brought inboard to the hauling post before the mast, thence to the area of the helmsman, and then to the masthead. Reported as requiring 1 man for every 3.5t of cargo, plus a cook. Length 24.4m, beam 5.5m; shallow draft; 10-100t. Other recorded names: **dhunda, dhúnde, dhundhi, doondah, doondar, doondee, dund(h)i**. Note also **dondi, dundo**.
dundavoe See **Boston hooker-1**
dundee An early French term for a **ketch***-rigged fishing and cargo boat. In most cases, a mizzenmast was stepped before the helm, but in certain areas, it was abaft the helm, **yawl*** fashion, as in the **thonier***. Originally the mizzen was a lugsail, later a gaff sail. The French usually designate a boat with both masts setting a leg-of-mutton sail as a **ketch**. Other recorded names: **dandy*, dandy au commerce, dhindet** (Breton), **dundi**. Note also **ketch, yawl**.
dundée de la rade de Brest **Coaster*** that operated out of Brest Roadstead, often transporting sand. **Ketch***-rigged but fully motorized by the mid-20th century, in addition to sails. Slightly raked stem, sharply raked transom, drag to the straight keel. Pilot house and small cabin aft. Length 21.7m, beam 6.4m, draft 3m.
dundee du Golfe See **thonier**
dundee harenguier See **harenguier**
dundee langoustier, dundee mauritanien See **langoustier-2**
dundee thonier See **thonier**
dundhi See **dunda, quantel battella**
dundi See **dondi, dunda, dundee, quantel battella**
dúndo *Pakistan, SE:* Small multipurpose boat of the lower Indus River and associated lakes. Smaller but similar to the **dunda***. Convex bottom, stern higher than bow. When fishing, generally worked by a man and wife. Spelling variants: **dhondho, dondo, doondee**. Note also **dondi**.
Dunfanaghy curragh See **Donegal curragh**
dunga See **donga-1, donga-3, donga-4**
dungar See **donga-3, donga-4**
Dungarvan boat See **Boston hooker-2**

dung barge, dung drogher See **drogher-1**
dung'ga See **donga-3**
dung otter See **beerotter**
Dunkerker, dunkirks See **Duinkerker**
Dunrossness yål See **Ness yoal**
Durban surfboat See **surfboat-3**
Durham boat **1.** *United States:* Designed in the early 18th century to transport iron down the Delaware River to Philadelphia. Later carried produce, notably grain, flour, and whiskey, until the 1860s, on the Delaware and other rivers and canals in the northeast, and reported from Ohio and Wisconsin. Lapstrake; bottom flat, with plank keel and rounded bilges.

Durham boat-1

Ends sharp; stern straight and raked; stem curved; vertical sides, parallel for most of their length; ends curve up. Cambered foredeck, stern deck flat and slopes up toward the sternpost to provide better footing for helmsman; living space below decks. Housing amidships protected cargo and passengers on the Wisconsin boats. Running boards bordered the open waist for use of the crew while poling upstream; downstream, the boards were turned up to serve as washboards. Floated downstream, maneuvered by long oars. Steering oar, ca. 9.8m long, with blade 31cm wide; oar had a slight S-curve. Might set a boomed triangular sail to a mast stepped through the forward deck. Crew of 3-5. Reported lengths 12-31m; e.g., length overall 18.2m, beam 2.4m, hold depth 1.0m. Other recorded names: **batteau*, Dor(e)m boat, pole boat***. Further reading: J. A. Anderson, *Navigation of the Upper Delaware* (Trenton, N.J., 1913). Note also **bateau-7**.
2. *United States, E:* In the late 18th century, **Durham boats** were modified to run the Mohawk River in central New York State, from Schenectady to the falls on the Oswego River. Here the cargo was transferred to the smaller **bateaux** (see **bateau-7**) for the remaining downstream run to Lake Ontario. Later improvements enabled the boats to reach Seneca Lake to the south and Lake Ontario without off-loading. Mainly a bulk cargo carrier, working to ca. 1830. Flat oak bottom, plank keel, rounded bilges, vertical sides, closely framed. Sharp bow, curved stem strongly cutaway. Raked sternpost with angle toward the top; wedge-shaped transom. Low sheer except toward the ends. Decked at the ends; side decks cleated for polers; open hold. The long steering oar pivoted on an iron pin on the transom. Tall mast stepped about a third back and could be struck. Square- or **sloop***-rigged. Crew of 5. Reported lengths 15-18m; e.g., length 18m, beam 2.4m, depth ca.1.0m, draft ca. 0.1m light, ca. 0.5m loaded. Name variant: **Mohawk River Durham boat**
3. Canadian adaptation of the Delaware **Durham boat** used in the early 19th century on the St. Lawrence River above Montreal, and on the Ottawa River and

the Rideau Canal. Carried supplies upstream to set-tlements along the St. Lawrence and returned with such items as pork, flour, and potash; some boats ran a regular schedule for passengers. Flat bottom with keel, rounded bow, centerboard, square stern. Decked at bow and stern; small captain's cabin aft; no bul-warks or railings; treads on the side decks aided in poling. Usually propelled by 8 oarsmen, but also sailed and poled, and at times towed from shore by 4-5 yoke of oxen. **Sloop***-rigged, with topsail; the tall mast stepped into a tabernacle ca. 1.2m above the deck; mast lowered to a jury rig aft. Length to 27m; e.g., length 18.2m, beam 3.4-4m, draft 0.76m.

Durham coble See **coble-1**

duri See **dori**

durra raft See **ramūs**

duster See **gold-duster**

Dutch barge See **Thames sailing barge**

Dutch butterbox See **kof**

Dutch caper See **caper**

Dutch hoy See **hoy**

Duwamish shovel-nose canoe *United States, NW:* Riverine **dugout canoe*** of the Duwamish of the Seattle area in northwest Washington State. Square overhanging ends, flat sheer. Hull smoothed with fire, sealed with dogfish oil. Length 6.7m. Note also **shovel-nose canoe.**

duwboot See **push boat**

dvuhpalubnoe sudno See **two-decker**

dwarka See **dori**

dwupokładowiec See **two-decker**

dydle boat See **didal boat**

dÿnop, dynopschuyt See **pot-2**

dyõmbo See **chombo**

dysa, dyso See **dghajsa-1**

dyúkun See **jukung**

dziewiątak, dziewiątkowy galar See **galar**

Eaceac See **kayak-9**

Eagle boat See **diao chuan, iigurutei**

East Anglia beach yawl See **beach yawl-1**

Eastbourne sprat boat See **sprat punt**

East Cornish lugger *England, SE:* Transom-sterned boat that worked out of Cornwall ports east of The Lizard, primarily Mevagissey, Looe, and Fowey; dates to at least the 17th century. Mainly drifted for pilchard, mackerel and, in summer, for herring in the North Sea. Transom raked initially, but became more vertical; counter stern introduced in the 1860s but never popular. Deep heel. Early boats had a very small

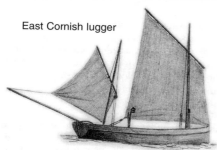

East Cornish lugger

cuddy forward, behind which were the net room and fish rooms; later, hatches covered the rooms, and waterways ran down the sides. Large dipping lugsail set to the mainmast; mast forestay was transferred to opposite deck eyes when going about. Standing lug mizzen, sometimes with a boomed foot; mast set to port; outrigger steeved up. Might carry a jib to a light running bowsprit that ran out through a hole in the port bulwark. Mizzen staysail set at times; topsails used for a short period. Mainmast lowered to a crutch aft of the hold while working the nets. Crew of 3-5. Reported lengths 9.14-13.4m; e.g., length 11.6m, beam 3.38m, hold depth 1.88m, 11rt; counter-sterned boats ran to ca. 16m. Other recorded names: **East Cornwall driver, mackerel driver, pilchard driver**; also **Cornwall, Fowey, Looe, Mevagissey lugger**. Further reading: Edgar J. March, *Sailing Drifters* (Camden, Maine: International Marine Publishing Co., 1972; originally published 1952), 117-137. Note also **Mevagissey tosher, West Cornish lugger.**

East Cornwall driver See **East Cornish lugger**

East Country barge See **swim-headed barge**

East Countryman *England, E:* Term sometimes used for a Lowestoft or Yarmouth boat.

East Country ship See **easterling**

easterling Old term for a ship trading in the Baltic Sea. May also be an early British term for vessels from western German ports. Other recorded names: **Baltic trader★, East Country ship**

eastern catboat See **catboat-2**

Eastern Shore canoe See **Chesapeake Bay log canoe-2**

East-India carrack See **East Indiaman**

East India hoy A **sloop★** licensed to carry stores to the ships of the East India Company. Note also **hoy-3a.**

East Indiaman Ship that went from western Europe to India, the East Indies, and China from the end of the 16th to the early 19th century. Owned by or chartered to the various national East India companies, the most successful operations of which were those of England and the Netherlands. Outbound, carried products and raw materials; returned with spices, tea, coffee, textiles, and porcelain. Passengers included workers supporting the operations, and soldiers protecting the colonies. Heavier and slower than the **men-of-war★** of the periods, but armed against local pirates and ships of competing companies. In general, bluff bows, high and flat stern with windows; fairly angular bilges, flattened bottom. The Dutch ships were double-planked against shipworms. Heavily decorated with gilded carvings; some had dummy gunports to appear more heavily armed. Most 3-masted; square sails on the fore- and mainmasts; mizzen carried a lateen or gaff sail with square topsail. A spritsail might be set below the bowsprit and a square sail above it. One Portuguese vessel required a crew of 120; in the early 19th century others needed as few as 36. Reported lengths 30-50m; 1784 English ship 50m long, 12.8m wide, 5.2m deep. Other recorded names: **East-India carrack, Indiaman, Indien-Schnellsegler, não (or nau) da carreira da India, nau da India, oostindiëvaarder, Ostindiefarer, Ostindienfahrer, retourschip, tea wag(g)on**. In the 18th century, the Portuguese called their ships **náos** or **fragatas★** indifferently, regardless of size. Note also **nau, West Indiaman.**

Eastport carry-away boat See **Quoddy boat**

Eastport pinky See **Eastport pinky-schooner, Quoddy boat**

Eastport pinky-schooner *United States, NE:* Employed in the herring fisheries out of the Eastport area in northeastern Maine during the 1850s and '60s. Clipper bow, sharp entrance; very sharp stern with strongly raked sternpost; deep drag to the keel; hollow floors, hard bilges; flaring sides. Marked sheer; washboards amidships; bulwark continued aft to create the overhang that formed the "pink stern." Rudder hung on sternpost and came up forward of the pink stern. Decked; low, raised deck forward; 3 hatches, the largest being the cargo or fish hold. **Schooner★**-rigged, foremast stepped well forward; masts raked aft. Reported lengths 10-15m; e.g., length overall 15m, on deck 13m, beam 4.3m. Name variants: **Eastport pinky, Eastport schooner-pinky**. Note also **pinky, Quoddy boat.**

Eastport schooner-pinky See **Eastport pinky-schooner**

easy ship See **sea boat**

eathar See **eathrach, coble-4**

eather See **eathrach**

eathrach *Scotland:* Gaelic term that commonly applies to a small boat in the Hebrides.

1. Occasionally, a small **fishing boat★** in the northwest part of Scotland.

2. A **skiff***, **barge***, **vessel***.
Spelling variants: **eathar**, **eather**

ebaeba *Kiribati Islands, central Pacific:* A small outrigger **raft*** used for lagoon fishing. Composed of 2 roughly hewn logs or 2 piles of poles, joined by a raised platform. As many as 3 in crew. Paddled. Spelling variants: **ebeeb**, **ebwaeba**

Ebbekahn See **punt-2**
ebeeb See **ebaeba**
ebri See **'abari**
ebwaeba See **ebaeba**
échébec See **xebec-2**
echeur See **capelanier**
Eckstock See **ekstock-1**
éclaireur See **advice boat**, **scout**
écraseur de crabes See **borneur**
écurie See **horse carrier**
edatharam vallom See **vallam-1b**
Edelleutschiff See **Leibschiff**
Eeakeeak See **baidarka**
Eeber See **Ewer**
Eeberkutter See **Kutter-Ewer**
eela boat *Scotland, Shetland Islands:* Often constructed of materials from a worn-out **sixareen***. Used for inshore fishing for immature staith, as a **tender*** to a **sixareen** (and to catch bait), and to carry sheep to offlying islands. Clinker-planked, sharp ends, marked sheer, curved and strongly raked stem and sternpost. Mostly rowed, one pair of oars, single-banked, or 4 oars, double-banked; narrow-bladed oars worked against tholepins. Might set a square sail. Reported lengths overall 4.57-5.41m, on keel 2.74-3.35m, widths 1.52-1.68m, depths amidships 0.51-0.56m. Name variant: **eella boat**

eel boat *Canada, E/United States, NE:* Floating fish tank that was filled with live eels at St. Jean on the Richelieu River during the summer. In the autumn, groups of tanks were towed to New York City, where the eels were sold directly from the tanks. The empty tanks were towed back to St. Jean in the spring. Last used probably in mid-1930s. Note also **fish car**. Further references: **ma lan**, **palingaak**

eel-fishing boat *Canada, E:* **Punt***-type boat that tends eel traps set in eastern rivers. Wide, flat bottom; square bow strongly raked; vertical stern and sides. Live well below seat just abaft amidships. Small foredeck. Powered by an outboard motor. Crew of 2. Length ca. 4m.

eella boat See **eela boat**
eel schuyt *Netherlands:* Worked the eeling grounds in the Zuiderzee in the 19th century. Open; sharply raked bow; outboard rudder, tiller, leeboards. Mast stepped well forward.

Eemspunt See **Pünte**
een-anan, **een-anèn** See **anan**
eenmansgarnaalbootje, **eenmansgarnaalscheepje** See **Oostendse garnaalboot**
éénmastklipper, **éénmastrivierklipper** See **klipper-1**
eenmastsloep See **Oostendse sloep**, **sloep-1**
eetea See **'etea-2**
eever See **Ewer**
eftirbátr See **skipsbåt-1**
eftirbátur *Iceland:* Towed by the Viking **knarr*** as a

ship's boat* en route from Norway to Iceland in the 9th and 10th centuries. Large enough to carry crew and passengers in an emergency; probably 10- or 12-oared; cap. 8-12t. Subsequently used by Icelanders for transportation and fishing. Name variant: **after boat**. Note also **skipsbåt-1**.

egarité, **égaritea** See **igarité**
ege See **Bornholmsk ege**, **eke**
eger See **Bornholmsk ege**
Egern *Germany, S:* Small **ferryboat*** used on the Tegernsee in Bavaria. Flat bottom, flaring sides, small bow transom. High, crown-shaped stern transom, characteristically painted with a picture. Rowed with a single pair of square-loomed oars slotted over a single tholepin.

egg boat See **sampan Tanka**
Egg Harbor melon seed See **melon seed**
egghen See **ekem**
egg house See **sampan Tanka**
Egmonder pink, **Egmonder zee-pinck** See **pink-5**
ehem *Guinea:* Large native **dugout canoe***. Reported in the 17th and 18th centuries. Constructed of a single log. Some used at sea. Note also **ekem**.

Eichbaum See **dugout canoe**
Eiderbojer See **Bojer**
Eiderbulle See **Eiderschnigge**
Eidergaliot, **Eidergaliot**, **Eiderlotsengaliot** See **galiot-5**
Eiderprahm *Germany, NW:* 19th-century cargo vessel of the Eider River. Sharp ends, full bow, flat bottom. Decked, outboard rudder, leeboards. Strikable mast originally set a spritsail, later a gaff sail; jib to a running bowsprit, staysail. Length 13.46m, beam 4.86m, hold depth 1.16m. Early boats were smaller, open, and carried hay and peat. Note also **Prahm**.

Eiderschnigge *Germany, NW:* Bluff cargo vessel that sailed from ports on the Eider River on the west coast of Schleswig-Holstein from the early 19th century to the 1930s. Traded to the Baltic and England. Full rounded ends; later vessels had a transom or sharp stern; slightly curved raking stem; vertical sternpost; considerable sheer. Flat floors, with rounded bilges; most had a broad plank keel; some had bilge keels. Outboard rudder with embellished head; tiller; generally large leeboards. Decked; deckhouse on some; hatch mildly cambered; often had a white-rimmed window on each side of the sternpost; generally had a steering cockpit forward of the after deck. **Ketch***- or **sloop***-rigged with various combinations of topsails and headsails. Crew of 2-4. Reported lengths 14-20m, widths 3.5-5.5m, depth of hold 1.3-1.8m; very early boats as short as 9m. Other recorded names: **Binnenbulle**, **Bolle**, **Bulle***, **Butenbulle**, **Eiderbulle**, **Hollander***, **Schnigge***, **Schniggschiff**

Eidsvollbåt See **skyssbåt**
eight See **shell-2**
eightereen See **áttamannafar**
eight-handed bateau See **bateau-7e**
eight-man boat See **áttamannafar**
eight-oar See **shell-2**
eight-oared boat See **ba jiang chuan**
eight-oared outrigger, **eight-oared shell** See **shell-2**
eikje See **eke**
Eimerbagger, **Eimerkettenbagger** See **dredger-1**

Einbaum See **dugout canoe**

Einer See **scull**

Einhandschiff *Germany, NW:* Type of vessel that carried such products as peat and potatoes on the Oate River between Bremervördere and Neuhaus. Ends blunt or the bow sharp; flat bottom. Worked single-handed, setting a square sail.

Einmannruderboot See **single-banked boat**

Einmast-Galiot See **galiot-2**

Einmast-Huker See **Huker**

Einmast-Kuff See **Kuff**

Einstellplätte See **Plätte-1**

Eisboot *Germany, S/Switzerland:* Two-man **fishing boat**★ of Lake Constance (Bodensee). Two blades enable the boat to cross the ice. Strongly flared sides; plumb cutwater; narrow, squared, raked ends; flat bottom. Employs oars worked against tholepins. Length 6m, beam 1.3m, depth 0.4m. See also **iceboat**.

Eisbrecher See **ice breaker**

Eisenbahn-Autofähre, Eisenbahnfähre See **ferryboat-1**

Eisewer See **Eiskahn**

Eisjacht See **iceboat**

Eiskahn *Germany, NW:* Iceboats★ were used in the Hamburg area to the end of the 19th century. The **Altenwerder Eiskahn** transported milk in winter between Altenwerder and Altona. Iron runners attached to the narrow flat bottom. Strongly built of oak; 2 wide lapped strakes on each side; heavily framed. Sharp ends strongly raked, the bow slightly curved, the sternpost straight. Decked at the ends. Propelled by sail, oar, or pike poles. Name variant: **Eisewer**

eissago, eissaguero, eissaigo, eissango, eissauga, eissaugero, eissaugo, eissaugue See **palangrier**

Eissig-Waidzille, Eissigzille See **Waidzille**

Eisyacht See **iceboat**

eithrichean mora See **sgoth**

eka 1. *Sweden:* Small, open plank-built boat (of oak—*eka*) used along the coast and on lakes for fishing, local transport of people and produce, hunting (**jakt-eka**), and carrying mail. The inshore boats tend to be round-bottomed and heavily built (**rundbottnad eka**; locally in Dalsand, **båteka**); the lake craft are mainly flat-bottomed (**flateka, flatbottnad eka,** or **platteka**). Bow may terminate in a stem (**stäveka**) or a small transom (**flateka**). Clinker-built for inshore work; carvel or plank-sided on lakes. Strong bottom rocker; may have a small skeg, ending in a partial keel. Those on the west and south coasts are particularly sturdy, similar to a half egg in shape, and transom-sterned (see **blekingseka, orusteka**). The east coast **eka** is keel-built and designed more for sailing (**vindöka** or **vindökstock**). In general mainly rowed, with 1-2 pairs of oars. Lengths mostly 4.6-6m; those for seining and transport to 10-12m. Note also **Bornholmsk ege, eke, ekstock-1, iseka, orusteka, pram-6a, skep, sköteka, stockeka, vadeka, vrakeka.**

2. *Finland:* Here, the Swedish peoples also use the word **eka**, frequently interchangeably with the word **ekstock**★ (in Finnish, **ruuhi**). The boat may be a low **punt**★-like craft with the bottom rising to recurved square ends; 2 strakes on each side; each frame supports one side and crosses the bottom, alternate frames are

attached to opposite side. Others are higher sided, plank-built, have a wide transom and curved stem (**stävekstock** or **darrling**) or may have a bow transom (**gavelekstock, gavelöka, gavelökstock,** or **gluggekstock**). Reported lengths 4.2-5m, widths 1-1.35m. Further name variants: **öka, Wasa punt.** Note also **fäljulle-1, pram-6a.**

3. *Vanuatu (New Hebrides), western Pacific:* Generic term for a boat on Loh Island in the Torres group. Note also **aka.**

Other recorded names: **ekan, ekla, etja, flatesk, ök(i)a, stävöka**; pl. **ekor(na), ökorna**

ekan See **eka**

ekdar *Pakistan, SE:* Plank-built **dugout canoe**★ of the area to the south and west of Karachi; still used for line and net fishing. Originally the dugout base was secured from the Indian Malabar Coast to the south and modified by local fishermen, but the boats are now made in Pakistan. On some **ekdars** the original ends were cut off the dugout and the length increased.

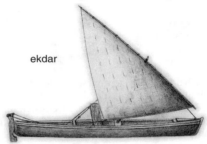

ekdar

Sharp bow and stern; straight stem, rounded forefoot; straight, almost vertical sternpost. Fairly flat floors amidships; long straight keel; flaring sides amidships. Open except at the ends; numerous thwarts and ribs. Rudder extends above the gunwale and below the bottom on some; worked by yoke and lines. Sets a small lateen sail on a short, forward-raking mast. Stabilized by a single outrigger or by 1-2 balance boards. Crew of 4-6. Reported lengths 12-18m; e.g., length overall 14m, beam 1.63m, depth 1.0m. Other recorded names: **ekdar hora, racchan, rachen.** Note also **dhatti hora, gharat hora.**

ekdar hora See **ekdar**

eke *Norway:* **1.** Term for a dugout-hulled craft. A few continued to serve as **ferries**★ into the 20th century.

2. Term used in Østfold County for a **pram**★-type open boat; called an **eka**★ in western Sweden. A general-purpose craft. A large type, the **va-eke**, is used mainly for fishing. Flat bottom rises up toward the ends, especially at the bow. Small bow transom, larger stern transom. Mainly rowed. Spelling variants: **ege, eikje**; pl. **ekene, eker**

'ekea See **wa'a kaulua**

ekem *Ghana:* Name given in the early 18th century to small **dugout canoes**★ used along the central coast for fishing and general transportation. Flattened bottom; long, solid, overhanging, and tapered ends; no thwarts. Used pointed paddles. Reported lengths 4-5m, beam 1.0m. Other recorded names: **almadia**★**, egghen.** Note also **ehem.**

ekene, **eker** See **eke-2**

ekestock See **ekstock-1**

ékhta See **ekta**

eki juftah See **kayık-2**

ekla See **eka**

ek lakdi hodi *India, NW:* Dugout canoe★ used in the Kathiawar Peninsula as an inshore **fishing boat★** and as a **ship's boat★** aboard local vessels. Hewn from trunks of large mango or jack trees. Bow sharp and slightly raised; stern thick, blunt, and curved; bottom nearly flat or curved, generally no keel. Hull (preserved with shark liver oil) lasts as long as 20 years. Usually propelled by oars, but improvised mast may support a trapezoidal sail. **Fishing boats** have crew of 4. Reported lengths 7.3-8.8m, width 1.0m, depths 0.6-0.7m, draft ca. 0.38m. Note also **hodi**.

ekor, **ekorna** See **eka**

ekstock **1.** Swedish word that in precise usage refers to a boat hewn from a single log. Sometimes smaller logs used as sponsons to increase stability. In some

ekstock-1

Swedish dialects, the term may designate a small, low-sided, plank-built boat, round- or flat-bottomed, without keel. Other recorded names: **Eckstock**, **ekestock**, **ekstocken**, **kobb**, **kobbeka**, **ökstock**; pl. **ekstockar(na)**, **kobbar**, **ökstockar(na)**. Note also **eka**, **stockbåt**, **stockeka**.
2. *Finland, W:* The **ekstock** of the Swedish Finns may be a small, low-sided **scow★**-type craft with low square ends. The larger may transport farm animals; the smaller used for fishing. Flat bottom, longitudinally planked; some 3-planked and clinker-laid. One or 2 side boards, flared or vertical. Alternating natural-crook ribs. Rowed, paddled, poled. Reported lengths 4.5-7.3m, widths 2.4-3.7m, depth ca. 0.3m.

ekstockar, **ekstockarna**, **ekstocken** See **ekstock-1**

ekta *India, NE:* Dugout canoe★ of the waterways of Bihar. Provides general transportation, carries grain and in some areas, used for fishing, especially with a bag net. Hewn from a single (*ekta*) tree trunk; flattened bottom and sides; elongated sharp ends, the stern sometimes serving as a platform for paddling or steering. Bamboo protects the gunwales. Paddled from a standing or squatting position. Reported lengths 4.6-9m; e.g., length 7m, beam 0.6m, depth 0.3m. Other recorded names: **bangarā**, **chhatákí**, **ékhta**, **ekthā**, **sahíá**. Note also **sālti**.

ekthā See **ekta**

e kuo *Nauru Island, western Pacific:* Single-outrigger paddling **canoe★** of this island lying to the west of the Kiribati (Gilbert) Islands. Family and fishing **canoe**. U-shaped keel piece curves up slightly at the ends, terminating in a vertical cutwater. Strakes, in multiple pieces, sewn on to form a wide "V" in cross section; thin, solid end pieces; washstrakes have slight tumble home. Short end decks; horn-like bitt projects from each deck. Long, slender outrigger

float connects to 2 thin booms that pierce the washstrake; each boom joined to the float by a forked stick and supplemental bracing; a medial boom crosses to but does not attach to the float; unit strengthened by light stringers. Capacity to ca. 8 people. Reported lengths 3-6m; e.g., length 5.4m, beam 0.66m, depth 0.4m. Spelling variant: **ekwo**

ekwo See **e kuo**

el-běğâl, **el-běğáleh** See **baghla-1**

Elbekahn See **Elbkahn**

Elb-Ewer See **Ewer**

Elbgaliot See **galiot-5**

Elbkahn *Germany, central:* General term for the long, narrow cargo vessels that worked from at least the 18th into the early 20th century. Traversed the Elbe River, mainly from Magdeburg, some going on to Berlin; later vessels worked on the Spree River. Flat bottom, usually of oak; straight, flared pine sides; on some the sides were of iron. Sharp bow and stern, ends raked; the large early vessels on the Unterelbe (below Hamburg) had flat raked ends. Movable decking forward; long peaked hatch extended to the gunwales; trunk cabin at stern. Wide, shallow rudder; on some, the rudderpost was free-standing, working from a pivot on the stern; on early vessels an arm was attached to the outer end of the rudder blade from the tiller. Stepped 1-2 masts. Reported as square-, sprit-, or lug-rigged. Towed upstream. Mast might carry a vane and pennant. Lengths 21m to more than 60m; e.g., length 40m, beam 4.5m, depth ca. 2m; shallow draft. Other recorded names: **Elbekahn**, **Elperkaan**, **Oberländer★**. Note also **Schute-1**.

Elburger bons See **bons**

Elburger pluut See **pluut**

Elbzille See **Zille**

eldijà *Lithuania:* Generic term with wide meaning: **boat★**, **dugout canoe★**, **riverboat★**, **coaster★**, **ship★**. Spelling variants: **aldijà**, **al'dija**, **ajijo**, **edija**, **eldijõs**; pl. **aldijõs**, **edijos**, **eldiju**

edija, **edijos**, **eldijõs**, **eldij** See **eldijà**

elep dušê See **kelek**

eleppu qurqurru See **qurqurru**

eleppu ša dušê, **eleppu ša dušše** See **kelek**

Elk River boat *United States, E:* Type of **railbird skiff★** used on upper Chesapeake Bay for hunting sora. Two planks per side; curved stem and sternpost.

elle'ut See **bat-3**

ellevebordinger, **ellevebordspram** See **pram-6a**

el madi See **maddia**

elm canoe See **bark boat**

Elperkaan See **Elbkahn**

elvabåt, **elvebaad** See **elvebåt**

elvebåt *Norway, N:* Primarily a long, narrow river (*elve*) boat, designed for general travel, freight transport, and salmon fishing on the faster rivers of Finnmark in northeastern Norway. Also built in Finland. Shorter and beamier on slow-moving rivers and lakes. The whitewater boats constructed of 2-3 lapped strakes, with a washstrake filling in the sheer. Block keel, flaring sides, soft turn of the bilges. Sharp ends, curved stem and sternpost, crosspiece near the stemhead; some modern boats have a transom for an outboard motor. No thwarts; the crew and passengers sit on the floorboards. Steered with a short, wide paddle. Rowed with a pair of oars against a natural crook, the oarsman facing foward at the bow. Punted upstream. Reported lengths 7.88-10m; e.g., length 7.88m, beam 0.88m, depth 0.35m. Those used on quieter rivers and on lakes more lightly constructed. More strakes used; garboard strake may be set outside a T-keel; rounded flaring sides; deep frames; stronger sheer. Reported lengths 5.1-5.21m; e.g., length 5.21m, beam 1.55m, depth 0.4m. Spelling variants: **elvabåt**, **elvebaad**. Note also **älvbåt**.

elwậd See **lûd**

embarcação Broad Portuguese term that includes **ships**⋆, **vessels**⋆, **craft**⋆, and **boats**⋆. One that is towed single-banked is an **embarcação de voge**; the **embarcação de palamenta** is rowed double-banked. The **embarcação miuda** is a **ship's boat**⋆. In the dialect of the forecastle crew, a boat in the service of a **man-of-war**⋆ belonging to the Ministerío de Marinha is an **embarcação à paisana**; while one transporting women to a ship is an **embarcação de aqua aberta**. Spelling variant: pl. **embarcações**

embarcação à paisana, embarcação de agua aberta, embarcação de palamenta See **embarcação**

embarcação de pesca See **fishing boat**

embarcação de pilotos See **pilot boat**

embarcação de voge, embarcação miuda See **embarcação**

embarcació menor See **embarcación**

embarcación In Spanish, a general term applied to all types and sizes of floating craft that are capable of navigating. Small craft and **ship's boats**⋆ may be called **embarcaciones menor**. Name variants: **embarcación menor**; Catalan: **embarcació menor**

embarcación con caña y linea See **tuna boat**

embarcación de alijo See **allège**

embarcaciones menor, embarcación menor See **embarcación**

embarcações See **embarcação**

embarcation French generic term applied broadly to small vessels propelled mainly by oar, occasionally by sail, and now by motor. Usually less than 18m long. May be a **ship's boat**⋆. Formerly, term might also apply to larger vessels that were considered old, unseaworthy craft. Spelling variant: **embarquation**

embarcation à l'aviron See **pulling boat**

embarcation à rames See **rowboat-1**

embarcation à voile See **sailboat**

embarcation de côté See **quarter boat-1**

embarcation de pêche See **fishing boat**

embarcation de secours See **accident boat**

embarcation pràtico See **pilot boat**

embarquation See **embarcation**

embono *Brazil, E:* In the dialect of fishermen of the Rio de Janeiro area, a type of boat that has been reinforced and the sides raised to withstand stormy conditions better. Note also **canoa de embono**.

Emder Häringsbuise See **Buise**

emergency boat See **accident boat**

emigrant boat See **line boat-3**

Emspünte See **Pünte**

en-anan See **anan**

encre-poisson bateau See **mo you chuan**

eneche, eneke, eneque, eneske See **esnecca**

engelska kutter See **kutter-5**

Engeyjarsexsæringur See **sexæringur**

engine See **josher**

englische Kuff See **Kuff**

English cutter See **revenue cutter-1**

English Shore schooner See **Gaspé schooner**

English whaleboat See **whaleboat-6a**

enmänning See **gotlandssnipa**

enstockskanot See **kanot-4**

Entenlomme *Poland, N:* Very small, one-man duck-(*Ente*) hunting craft used until the 1970s on the Zalew Wisłany (Frisches Haff, Vistula Lagoon), especially on Jeziero Drużno (Drausensee), south of Elbląg (Elbing). Originally a German craft of East Prussia and later Poland. Double-ended; flat bottom, curved toward the ends; hard chines; flared sides. Heavy, straight, raked stem and sternpost. Short end decks. Hunter lay down to shoot. Hand paddled. Reconstruction: 2.3m long, 0.57m wide at gunwale, 0.37m at bottom. Name variant: **kaczka loma**. Note also **duck boat**.

Enterse somp, Enterse zomp See **somp**

envare See **ever**

enviada 1. In Spain and Portugal, any small boat that accompanies a **fishing boat**⋆ and transfers the catch to shore. Employs sail or motor. Other recorded names: **acostado, escort**. Note also **barca da arte xávega**.
2. *Portugal:* The **enviadas** of the Lisbon area are of 2 types, the **enviada do Barreiro** and the larger **enviada do Seixal**. Each works in association with a particular type of **fishing boat**, generally with similar lines, carrying the catch to market; the Seixal boat works with the **muleta**⋆. Both types have a plumb stem, slightly cutaway at the forefoot; a shredded wool ball on the stemhead keeps the lower edge of the sail from chafing. Wide raked transom; outboard rudder slots over a tall rudderhead. Maximum beam well forward; high sheer toward the bow. May be half-decked or fully decked with open hold. Usually painted with triangular patches at the bows. Large lateen-type sail with a short luff set to a forward-raking mast; the Barreiro type might also set a small, boomed-out headsail. Oars used in calms. Crew of 3-4. Barreiro boat: length 9m, beam 3m, depth 1.35m; Seixal boat 11.6m by 3.8m by 1.42m. Name variant: **canoa do Seixal**. Note also **bote-6, canoa da picada**. Further references: **bateira ílhava, canoa-11**

enviada do Barreiro, enviada do Seixal See **enviada-2**

enxabeque, enxaveque See **xebec**

equif See **skiff**

Equihen fishing boat See **bateau d'Equihen**

équipe See **train de bateaux**

er bai liao yi ke yin xun chuan *China:* Early class of **patrol boat**⋆ built at Nanjing (Nanking); identified by an official customs seal. Boxy shape with small bow transom, curved bottom. High quarter-deck, trunk cabin. Two masts, both forward of amidships. Length on deck 17.5m, on bottom 13m, beam amidships 3.7m, deck height 1.2m. Spelling variant: **erh-pai-liao i-k'o-yin hsün-ch'uan**

Erdlomme *Poland, N:* Strongly built cargo vessel that plied lower Vistula distributaries. Worked at least from the latter part of the 19th century to World War II, initially as a German/East Prussian vessel. Mainly carried raw materials such as sand. Clinker-planked, usually of oak; top strake curved up toward the bow; flat floors; plank keel; rounded bilges. Bottom turned up forward to a wide, slightly raking straight stem. Narrow raked transom; 2 windows in transom. Outboard rudder with wide blade below the waterline; long tiller; leeboards. Decked at ends; cuddy aft; narrow side decks bordered the open waist. Tall pole mast stepped in tabernacle. Tall spritsail; long sprit worked with tackle. Some stepped a small sprit foresail in the bow; others used a staysail. Pennant on masthead. Crew of 3. Reported lengths 15-28m; widths 3-3.5m, some early vessels to 4.3m. Other recorded names: **Böte★**, **Nogat-Lomme**, **Sandlomme**. Note also **Lomme**.

erh-pai-liao i-k'o-yin hsün-ch'uan See **er bai liao yi ke yin xun chuan**

Erie sharpie See **sharpie-8**

Esbjerd cod-fishing boat, **Esbjergkutter**, **Esbjerg fiskekutter** See **bakkebåd**

escafe See **escaffe**, **scaf**

escaffe *France, Normandy and Brittany:* A small, keeled vessel of the 15th century that accompanied a large ship, or served as a **coaster★**. Ca. 10t. Name also given to a small **harenguier★** or to a **dugout canoe★** used as a **ship's boat★**. Spelling variants: **escafe**, **scaff**, **scaphe**, **scaufe**. Note also **escaffié**.

escaffié *France, S:* Used on the lagoons and canals of lower Languedoc in the late 17th and early 18th centuries. Note also **escaffe**.

escaler In Portuguese, designates a **ship's boat★** used for reconnaissance and to transport personnel and supplies. Some early **escaleres** were quite ornate when built for royalty. Constructed of wood, metal, or synthetics. Sharp bow, with straight stem; small raked transom; long straight keel; maximum beam forward of amidships. Open; stern sheets; outboard rudder. Rowed, sailed, and now motorized. Early boats rowed either single- or double-banked against a tholepin or through slots in the washstrake; 8-12 oars. Might have 1-2 masts. The 2-masted boats of Portuguese naval vessels of the late 19th century stepped a mainmast well forward and a mizzenmast against the transom, both setting lugsails; staysail.

escaler do almirante See **barge-2**

escaleres See **escaler**

escampavia *Spain:* Vessel that engaged in scouting, especially in shallow waters, watched for smugglers, and protected fishing vessels. Built to ca. 1920. See also **scout**.

escapadia de maures See **xebec**

escarbilleur See **bette à escarbille**, **tug-1**

escarvelle See **caravel-1**

eschife See **esquife**

eschiffe See **esquife**, **skiff**

esciphe See **esquife**

ésclaireur See **scout**

esclif See **skiff**

escort See **enviada-1**

escort vessel See **consort**

escoute See **escute**, **scout**

escrevelle See **caravel-1**

escuna See **schooner**

escute *France, N:* Small **coaster★** reported from the mid-13th to the early 15th century. Flat floors, low sides. Cap. ca. 60-80t. Spelling variants: **escoute**, **escutte**, **estute**, **scuta**, **scute★**. Further reference: **shout-1**

escute brabançonne See **beurtschuit**

escutte See **escute**

esguicha, **esguicho** See **chinchorro-2**

esguif See **skiff**

esnecca **1.** Term applied in France to an extra-long **langskip★** and later to the Norman version. Served as a raiding and reconnaissance vessel and as a cargo carrier. Full bow and stern. Rowed, employing 20 benches. By the mid-11th century oars had become subsidiary to sail.
2. *England:* **a.** Included among the vessels of Richard I in his crusade to the Holy Land in the late 12th century. Rounded bow and stern. Large enough to transport men, horses, arms, supplies, and often auxiliary craft. Mainly sailed. **b.** Term reported in the 12th and again in the 17th century as a royal **yacht★** in which state voyages were made. Some required as many as 60 sailors. Early vessels stepped a single mast.
Other recorded names: **cheneque**, **ene(s)ke**, **eneque**, **esnecc(a)e**, **e(s)neche**, **esne(c)ke**, **esnège**, **esnèque**, **esnesche**, **esnesque**, **hilnachia**, **hysneca**, **ilnechia**, **isnechia**, **long serpent**, **snaca**, **snacc**, **snake**, **sneccke**, **snékar**. Further reading: R. H. F. Lindemann, "The English Esnecca in Northern European Sources," *The Mariner's Mirror* 74 (1988), 75-82. Note also **skeid**. Further reference: **snekkja**

esneccae, **esnecce**, **esneche**, **esnecke**, **esnège**, **esneke** See **esnecca**

esnèque See **esnecca**, **snekkja**

esnesche, **esnesque** See **esnecca**

esnón, **esnou** See **snow**

Espenboot See **haapio-1**

esperonade, **esperonnade** See **speronera**

espiche See **skiff**

espinace See **pinasse-1b**, **pinnace**

espinasse See **pinasse-1b**

esping See **äsping**, **haapio-1**

espink See **äsping**

espynasse See **pinnace**

esquif **1.** *Switzerland, W:* During the 16th, 17th, and early 18th centuries the **esquif** engaged in naval battles on Lake Geneva (Lake Léman). One report says they were light enough to be carried on a horse, another that they were more modest than the **brigantin★**.
2. *United States, south-central:* Small open boat of the Louisiana bayous, important for transporting local products, for river and lake fishing, and for crabbing and oystering in the bayous. Still in limited use. Sharp bow, narrow transom, flaring sides, flat bottom. Generally a stern seat and sometimes a foredeck. Those used on lakes, especially the coastal lakes, have heavy planking; wide rectangular transom; length ca. 4.3m, fairly beamy. The Mississippi River boats are

about the same length, but slender and the transom slightly V'd. The small, light, narrow **Creole skiff** has a narrow overhanging V-transom and considerable sheer. The **esquifs** are mainly rowed, using a single tholepin, with the oar secured by a strap. The **standing skiff**, mostly the **Creole skiff** type, is rowed standing, facing forward, and employs several designs of outriggers to raise and support the tholepin. Typically 4.9m long. An **esquif** equipped with a motor is generally called a **gas boat★**; fast. May have a cabin or half cabin. Length 6-8m, beam 1.8m, draft 0.5-0.6m. Some large, flat-bottomed boats on the lower Mississippi were called **esquifs** in the 18th century. These were sharp-ended. Later they were called **barges★**, a term describing a heavy vessel capable of handling seine nets and serving as a base for houseboats. See also **esquife, skiff**.

esquife Double-ended craft used in the service of a **nau★**, **galleon★**, or **galley★**. Term reported as early as the 14th century. Either towed or carried on board. Rowed using 4-6 pairs of oars. Also sailed. Reported lengths 6.3-10m on keel, width one-third. Spelling variants: **asquif, eschife, esciphe, esquif★, esquiffe, esquiffon, esquify, esquilfe, esqvy, essquif, squefe, squif(f), esquif(f)o**. Further reference: **skiff**

esquiffe See **esquife**

esquiffon See **esquife, esquifon**

esquiffou, esquifo See **skiff**

esquifon 16th-century term for a small **skiff★**.

esquify See **esquife**

esquifz See **skiff**

esquilfe See **esquife, skiff**

Esquimaux canoe See **kayak**

esqvy See **esquife**

Essex barge See **hay barge**

Essex bawley See **bawley**

Essex oyster boat See **Essex smack**

Essex oyster skiff See **skiff-4**

Essex pinky See **pinky**

Essex punt See **gun punt**

Essex sloop boat See **sloop boat**

Essex smack *England, E:* Fast **cutter★**-rigged boat of the Essex coast that worked until World War II. Now

Essex smack

mainly a pleasure craft. The smallest worked in estuaries, trawling and dredging; others worked offshore; the largest were seagoing; some engaged in salvage work, cargo transport, smuggling and, often in the

winter herring season, were used as **stowboats★**. Design and dimensions varied with their primary activity, but characterized by a plumb stem, slightly curved forefoot; early boats apple-bowed, later had a fine entrance. High freeboard forward, very low aft; graceful sheer; low, shallow counter; arched tiller. Originally clinker-built, later carvel; considerable rise to the floors; moderately hard bilges; long keel, horizontal or with drag; hollow garboard. Beamier and deeper in the mid-19th century. Fine run aft; sternpost raked. Small boats often transom sterned; some of the larger had a type of counter stern; **Maldon smacks** favored an abrupt transom stern. Gear housed in the forecastle, fish hold amidships, cabin aft. Barrel windlass on foredeck, for the anchor, worked with handspikes. Mast stepped well forward; larger boats carried a long housing topmast; characteristically **Tollesbury smacks** housed their topmasts without taking a leg out of the rigging, coiling the wire under the crosstree. Gaff sail high-peaked, generally tanned, loose-footed, but with a boom that extended beyond the stern. Small staysail, jib set flying, sometimes a narrow jib staysail and, in summer, a jib-headed topsail on the larger boats. Long running bowsprit, housed between bits. Later smacks had auxiliaries. Crew of 2-6. Reported lengths 8-21m; e.g., length overall 9.14m, beam 2.74m, depth 1.0m; shallow draft. Other recorded names: **long boomer** (dredged oysters in the Channel Islands and on the Dutch coast), **oyster smack**; also **Brightlingsea** and **Essex oyster boat**; **Colchester, Colne, (West) Mersea, Rowhedge**, and **Wivenhoe smack**; by Kent fishermen: **boomsail boat**. Further reading: John Leather, *Smacks and Bawleys* (Lavenham: Terence Dalton, Ltd., 1991). Note also **skillinger, Whitstable oyster smack**.

essquif See **esquife, squiff**

estate junk See **tongkang-3**

estute See **escute**

étadier *France, N:* Inshore **fishing boat★** of the Baie de Somme area in northeastern Normandy that fished for herring and shrimp with an *étade* net; also engaged in line fishing. Worked mainly in the 19th century. Those

étadier

from St. Valéry were carvel-planked and decked; Étretat boats were clinker-built and open. Bluff bows, stem lightly curved; raked square, plumb, or counter stern. Moderate rise to the floors; round bilges. Mainmast stepped well forward, setting a dipping lugsail sheeted to a high traveler at the stern. Mizzenmast stepped to one side at the transom and set either a standing lugsail or a triangular sail laced to the mast. Jib run out to a running bowsprit. Later boats motorized. Crew of 8-12. Reported lengths 6-10.8m; e.g., length 8m, beam 3.35m, depth 1.52m.

'etea *Solomon Islands, western Pacific:* **1.** In parts of San Cristobal and Florida Islands, **'etea** is a generic for an **outrigger canoe★**.
2. One specific type is a light, single-outrigger paddling **canoe★**. Dugout hull; each end sharp, relatively straight, and raked; bottom curved. Gunwale lath runs full length; open; wide midships seat; 2 thwarts forward. Long, slender float made from the middle rib of a sago palm leaf; positioned so that forward tip lies ahead of the **canoe's** bow and planes up; float 1.2-1.5m from the hull. Two booms cross the hull; the forward boom is a light, flexible pole attached near the bow. After boom, located just abaft the seat, is heavier. Each boom connects to the float by a pair of U-shaped withes. Long-bladed, narrow paddles. Reported lengths 4-5m; widths 0.23-0.5m, depth ca. 0.5m. Other recorded names: on Ulawa Island, **eetea**; by the Bauro peoples, **geetea**, **gétéa**. **3.** On San Cristobal, the **'etea** may be a plank-built **canoe** with similar ends that recurve above the gunwale. Three light strakes to each side; flat sheer. Short decking at each end; wide bench thwarts. Length 5.3m. **4.** The **'etea** on the east coast of Guadalcanal Island is a simple **dugout canoe★**. Sharp, raked ends; curved bottom, wide "U" in cross section. Name variant: **cinagé**

etja See **eka**

ettu balikkandathu See **odam-1b**

ettuvalikkunna thoni See **dhoni-5**

ever *Belgium:* Flemish seagoing vessel and **fishing boat★** recorded as early as the mid-13th century. Reported in the mid-15th century as resembling the early **boeier★**. Name variant: **envare**. See also **Ewer**.

Ever-Galeasse See **Galeass-Ewer**

evert *Norway, W:* Built in the Bergen area in the early 19th century, based probably on the German **Ewer★**. Flat bottom, no keel; often had leeboards. Loose-footed, boomed gaff mainsail, yard topsail; square sails might be set forward of the mast; several foresails.

Ewer *Germany, NW:* Common flat-bottomed cargo and fishing vessel that dated from at least the 13th century. A few have been restored, but essentially extinct. Originally a Dutch type. Worked primarily out of the Elbe Estuary and tributary rivers, the largest sailing into the North Sea (the **See-Ewer★**) and to the Baltic (the **Ostsee-Ewer**); some went to England and Rotterdam. An **evert** was used in Denmark, but those known by that term were German-built. **Ewern** (pl.) were often differentiated by their place of origin or their main area of operation, e.g., **Altenwerder Ewer**, **Blankeneser Ewer**, **Elb-Ewer**, **Finkenwerder Ewer**, **Hamburger Ewer**, **Lühe Ewer**, **Niederelbe Ewer**, **Rhin-Ewer★**, etc. Each had some small feature that

identified the type. The **Fracht-Ewern** carried a variety of cargoes—bunkering coal (**Kohl-Ewer**), peat (**Torf-Ewer★**), straw and hay (**Stroh-Ewer★**), milk (**Milch-Ewer★**), potatoes (**Kartoffel-Ewer**), vegetables (**Gemüse-Ewer**), bricks (**Stein-Ewer★**), etc. Initially cargo carriers had hard bilges, generally with vertical chine planks; later omitted and bilges rounded; bottom rocker on those grounding at low water; no keel on early vessels. Raked transom, usually heart-shaped; name board and windows painted on transom; early vessels often sharp-ended (**Spitzgatt-Ewer**). Stem raked, more curved later; some clipper-bowed. Moderate sheer forward. Open early, later decked; short quarter-deck; cabin usually aft; large central hatch; lacked the wet well of the fishing type and hence called a **Trochen-Ewer** (dry boat). Large leeboards; mostly an outboard rudder; long tiller. Carvel-planked wood hull to latter quarter of the 19th century, then wood bottom and deck, with iron/steel sides; by 1900 most all steel; stern became more rounded. **Coasters★** generally **ketch★**-rigged (the **Besan-Ewer★**); the smaller inland vessels were **cutter★**-rigged (the **Giek-Ewer★**). Gaff topsail on mainmast. Mast(s) could be struck on those working in waterways with low bridges. Crew of 2. Later vessels had auxiliaries. The **Fischer-Ewer** worked mainly with drift nets off Finkenwerder and Altenwerder below Hamburg, and in the Watt River to the west (**Watten-Ewer** or **waddenever**). The **Seefischer-Ewer** worked offshore. Flat bottom narrower than the cargo type; a few river craft V-bottomed. Chine planks vertical or slightly flared, then strong flare to turn of the bilges, continuing vertically or rounded to gunwales; bottom on the **Hochseefischer-Ewer** quite narrow. Moderate sheer. High bow, stem sharply cutaway below the waterline; narrower transom; earlier a sharp stern. Flush deck; steering well, motorized type had a wheelhouse; wet well ran under the deck and accessed through a hatch. No leeboards; some had a centerboard. **Ketch-** or **cutter**-rigged; a few small boats sprit-rigged. Crew of 3-4. Reported lengths of cargo and fishing types 7-20m, the size dependent on rig, the 2-masted generally being the largest. Other recorded names: **spitsgatever**, **spitzgat-ever**; cargo carriers: **Dreuch-Ewer**, **Lasten-Ewer**, **vrachtever**; fishing vessels: **Fischereeber**, **Fischer-Ever**, **Fischerei-Ever** (or **Ewer**), **Fisch-Ewer**, **Hochfisch-Ewer**. Spelling variants: **Eeber**, **eever**, **Ever**, **Evert★**; pl. **Ewern**. Note also **Fähr-Ewer**, **Föhringer Ewer**, **Galeass-Ewer**, **Galiot-Ewer**, **Kutter-Ewer**, **Pfahl-Ewer**.

Ewer-Kutter See **Kutter-Ewer**, **Rhin-Ewer**

Ewern See **Ewer**

Exe salmon boat *England, S:* Open, clinker-built boat used on the River Exe in Devonshire. Sharp bow with vertical stem; narrow square stern; 5 benches; fully floored. Employed 4 oars. Length 6m, beam 1.45m.

explorador See **scout**

express boat See **flyboat-3a**, **packet boat-4**

express canoe See **canot léger**

extreme clipper See **clipper**

F

fa *China:* General term for a large **raft*** of bamboo or timber. Note also **fu**, **pai**.

fâ See **fak**

fabrica flotante, **fabriekschip** See **factory ship**

Fabrikmutterschiff See **mother ship**

Fabrikschiff See **factory ship**

face barge See **tug-2**

fa chuan *China:* A type of **dragon boat*** launched on rivers during the Festival of the Lanterns. The craft, constructed of bamboo covered with multicolored paper, floated with the current on a light bamboo **raft***. The bow formed a dragon's head, the stern the tail. Various structures, similar to those of early imperial **junks***, covered the deck. Costumed people lined the sides, and thousands of miniature lighted ships accompanied the larger craft. Reported lengths 8-10m. Spelling variant: **fa tch'ouan**

factory processor See **factory ship**

factory ship Large vessel equipped with a plant to process and preserve fish brought by its **fleet*** of **catcher boats**. Some both fish and process the fish. Other recorded names: **bateau-usine**, **bâtiment usine**, **canning** (or **tinning**) **vessel**, **buque factoria**, **fabrica flotante**, **fabriekschip**, **Fabrikschiff**, **factory processor**, **nave fattoria**, **navire-usine**, **plavuchaya fabrika**, **processing ship**, **usine flottante**. Note also **mother ship**, **whaler-1**.

factory whaler See **whaler**

færdersnekke See **snekke**

færeng See **færing**

færge, **færgebåd**, **færgekaag** See **ferryboat-1**

færing *Norway:* A small open boat that is rowed with 2 pairs of oars. The Gokstad **færing**, one of the small boats found at the Viking burial mound south of Oslo, is very similar to the present-day **færing** of some parts of the west coast. An all-purpose boat, used for handline fishing, travel, and transporting produce; some are **tenders*** or **seine boats*** aboard **fishing boats***. The large **storfæring** (or **havfæring**) is built for sea work. Clinker-planked of pine or spruce, with frames, stem, sternpost, and keel of pine, birch, or oak; shell-built, with the frames inserted. Flaring curved sides; sharp ends. Most are fuller forward, tapering toward the stern. Thwarts notch over the frames; at each end, an inclined breasthook provides strengthening. Mainly rowed, but also sail. Newer boats that have been modified for outboard motors, with a transom replacing the sharp stern, are called **gavlbåt** (or **gavlbaat**); those retaining the sharp stern, hanging the motor on the quarter, are known as **spiss-stemming**.

1. The **færingar** (pl.) of Hordaland in southwestern Norway include boats from the Hardanger, Sunnhordland, Strandebarm, and Os areas. Constructed of 3 wide pine planks; keel, stem, and sternpost of oak. T-keel; rising floors to flaring sides; moderate sheer; ends cutaway below the waterline. Oars worked between a naturally shaped oak crook and a single tholepin or held by grommets. Sometimes sailed, originally setting a square sail, more recently a spritsail and jib. Reported lengths 4.4-6.3m; a **hardangerfæring** was 5.55m long, 1.6m wide, 0.5m deep. Note also **Oselver**.

2. The **færing** type of **sognebåt*** of the Sognefjorden area is used within the fjord. There are two types: a light, general-purpose boat and a heavier, beamier one for carrying heavy loads. Low rise to the flat floors, with soft turn of the bilges. Top strake narrows sharply toward the stem and sternpost; stem plumb above the waterline, cutaway below; stern lower and markedly curved. Reported lengths 5.45-5.6m; e.g., length 5.6m, beam 1.38m, depth 0.46m. Name variant: **sognefæring**

3. The **nordfjordfæring** is markedly fuller forward, tapering toward the stern. Stem and sternpost curved, the sternpost more undercut; deep keel; strong sheer toward the bow. Top strake wide amidships, very narrow at the ends. The large **storfæring** has an extra rib between the 2 thwarts. Rowed against shaped oarlocks; the oar held by loop. Set a square sail until the 1860s, then an asymmetric dipping lugsail and, late in the 19th century, adopted a gaff rig. Reported lengths 4.8-5.65m; a standard **lisjefæring** would be 5.02m long, while the **storfæring** was 5.6m long; e.g., length 5.35m, beam 1.45m, depth 0.4m.

4. The general-purpose, inshore **færing** of Sunnmøre District has unusual planking—4 of the forward strakes are very narrow, and about a third of the way in from the bow, 2 strakes are each scarfed to a single wide strake that continues to the sternpost. Bow fuller and has a higher sheer than the stern. Curved stem and sternpost; rising floors; high, soft bilges. Rowed against a shaped oarlock, with grommets. The extra large, but unusual, **kjempefæring** was rowed with 6 oars. Some sailed, employing a trapezoidal lugsail and a single-arm yoke from the tiller to the rudder. Reported lengths 4.45-6m; e.g., length 4.45m, beam 1.44m, depth 0.46m. Name variant: **sunnmørsfæring**

5. The **færing** of the Trøndelag area has a number of sub-types, based on the number of spaces (rooms) between the frames supporting the thwarts. The smallest, ca. 4.2-5.4m long, has 2 rooms, and is called a **småfæring**, **to-kne-færing**, **tvi-spenning**, or **kokse***. One with two-and-a-half rooms, the half room a fish room placed amidships, is called a **hundromsfæring** or **storfæring** and ranges between 5.5m and 6.2m long. In Åfjord Township, a 3-room or 6-oared boat may also be called a **storfæring** or **tre-manns færing** (see **seksæring**). Stem generally vertical or with a slight tumble home; plumb sternpost. Wide sheer strake that almost phases out at the stem and sternpost. Steps a mast amidships, setting a square sail. Reported size of an **åfjordsfæring** (from Åfjord Township) was 5.02-5.33m long and 1.57m wide.

6. The **færing** from the Nordland area has the characteristic northern tall, straight stem with slight tumble home and tall, mildly raked sternpost. Bow somewhat fuller than the stern, S-curve to the floors amidships.

Strong sheer toward the ends. A washstrake may be added. Those with the normal 2 "rooms" between the ribs may also be called a **toroms** (**torømming**), or **to-roring**. A **nordlandsfæring** with the middle room divided, creating 2¹/₂ rooms, may be called a **hund-romsfæring** (or **to-roms færing**). The term **kjeks** (or **kjæks**) may be used in the Lofoten Islands for a **2-** or **2¹/₂-romsbåt**. Some set a square sail. Reported lengths 4.5-5.6m; e.g., length 5m, beam 1.26m, depth 0.4m. Other recorded names: **halvtredierømming, halvtre-dierumbsbåd, hundromsbåt, toromsbåt**. Note also **bindalsbåt, ranværingsbåt, straumbåt**.

Other recorded names: **færeng, færingen, færring, faring, ferærõr** (Old Norse), **fjæring** (probably erroneously); pl. **færingar**. Small size: **smaafæring, små-færing**. Note also **feræringur, fourareen**. Further reference: **seksæring-7**

færingar, færingen See **færing**

færingerbaad, færingerbåd, færobaad See **færobåd**

færøbåd *Denmark, Faroe Islands:* General term for the open, double-ended **pulling boats*** of these North Atlantic islands. Designated by size as reflected in the number of men required to man the boats: **tríbekkur*** (2 men), **tristur*** (3 men), **fýramannafar*** (4 men), **seksmannafar*** (6 men), **áttamannafar*** (8 men), **tíggjumannafar*** (10 men), **seksæringur*** (12 men). Characterized by strongly curved stem and sternposts that recurve at the top. Deep oak keel; natural crook ribs and knees treenailed to the clinker planking. Considerable sheer. Narrow, deep rudder; formerly worked with a single-arm yoke to a tiller, now by 2 lines to a yoke running through the rudderhead. Narrow-bladed oars worked against an oak slab slotted into the gunwale; oar held by a rope loop. Most Faroe boats set a square-cut dipping lugsail to a mast stepped in the 1st thwart; early boats set a narrow-headed square sail. Now outboard motors placed inside the well on the smaller boats and inboard engines on the larger. Other recorded spellings: **færingerbaad, færingerbåd, færobaad, Faroese boat, føroysk båt**. Further reading: Morten Gøthche, *Færobåden* (Roskilde: Vikingeskibshallen, 1985).

færring See **færing**

Fahr *Germany, S:* Large cargo vessel that transported wood and coal on Starnberger See in Bavaria in the early 20th century. Spelling variant: pl. **Fahren**

Fährboot See **ferryboat-1, passage boat-1**

Fähre See **ferryboat-1**

Fahren See **Fahr**

fährever See **Fähr-Ewer**

Fähr-Ewer *Germany, NW:* Square-sailed **Ewer***-type vessel that provided passenger service to points along the Elbe River below Hamburg from the 17th into the 19th century. Supplanted by **steamboats**. Decked forward; small deckhouse. Tapered hull; transom by the mid-19th century. Length 19.8m, beam 5m, depth 1.14m; cap. 11-20t. Spelling variant: **fährever**

Fahrgastdampfer See **liner-1**

Fährkahn See **ferryboat-1**

Fahrm See **Farm**

Fahrn See **Bucentaur**

Fährprahm See **ferryboat-1, Prahm-2**

Fährschiff See **Farm, ferryboat-1**

Fährschmack *Germany, NW:* Type of **ferryboat*** used in the North Sea in the early 19th century. Clinker-built, with full lines, sharp stern; open. **Cutter***-rigged, with a loose-footed, boomed gaff mainsail, 2 headsails, and a topsail. Rowed when wind failed.

Fahrtenkreuzer See **cruiser-1**

Fahrzeug See **ship**

Fair Haven dugout See **Connecticut canoe**

Fair Haven sharpie See **sharpie-2**

Fair Isle jol, Fair Isle skiff See **Fair Isle yoal**

Fair Isle yoal *Scotland, N:* Long, lean, very shallow boat used mainly for fishing throughout the Shetland Islands until the mid-19th century, and thereafter only at Fair Isle (between the Shetlands and Orkneys). Initially imported unassembled from Norway.

Fair Isle yoal

Clinker-built, traditionally with 5 strakes per side, although later boats had 6 strakes. Flat sheer amidships and high at ends; long straight keel, earlier short and curved; ribs connected to the keel only at the garboard strakes. Steep rise to the floors, slack bilges. Sharp ends; slightly curved stem; raked sternpost. Rudder, shipped when under sail, curved under the stern; short tiller. Rowed with 6-8 oars, either single- or double-banked, or in combination; oars worked against a single flat tholepin. Sometimes sailed, setting a square sail bent to a horizontal yard; weather leech extended by a bowline when going to windward. Lightly stayed mast, about the same length as the keel, stepped in a square socket amidships. Outboard motors common after World War II. Crew of 3-6. Reported lengths overall 5.79-6.93m, on keel 4.42-5.48m, widths 1.68-1.93m, depths amidships 0.46-0.74m. Other recorded names: **Fair Isle jol** (**skiff** or **yole**), **three-man boat**. Further reading: Adrian G. Osler, *The Shetland Boat: South Mainland and Fair Isle* (London: National Maritime Museum, 1983 [Maritime Monographs and Reports No. 58]). Note also **Shetland model**.

Fair Isle yole See **Fair Isle yoal**

fairy boat See **Adirondack guideboat**

fak *Cameroon, N/Chad, SW:* **Dugout canoe*** used for fishing with a large, baggy net in the basin of the Logone and Chari Rivers. Called a **fak** by the Kims, a **fâ** by the Kabalais, and a **touo** by the Gambayes. Bow curved and blunt, stern extended aft to form a short seat for the stern paddler. Low platform, ca. l.0m long, set into the bow for the net handler. When underway, the net carried like a sail, with one light vertical yard inserted into the platform, the lower yard resting on a forked branch abaft the platform. Crew of 2. Length 5m, beam 0.6m.

falaik See **fäljulle-1, falukah, fụlūka**

Fal barge *England, SW:* The term **barge*** was applied to at least 2 types of sailing vessels that plied the Fal Estuary and upper River Tamar. The **inside barge*** dredged sand for farmers within the estuary in the early 19th century and later transported produce, grain, stone, bricks, timber, etc. The **outside barges** were seagoing and sought cargoes at English and Bristol Channel ports and crossed to the Channel Islands, working until the early 1950s. The **inside barges** usually had decks forward and aft, no bulwarks, a fine entry and run, and fairly flat floors. The **outside barges** were decked and had a cabin aft and a large hatch amidships. They had little deadrise, slack bilges, and hollow run. Both types had a transom stern, either plumb or raked, and generally a straight vertical stem. The **inside barges** towed their boat, while the seagoing type carried it on board. Both set a gaff mainsail and staysail; a jib was usually tacked to the stemhead or, on the larger type, to a running bowsprit. Both carried a jib-headed topsail set to a fidded topmast. Later motorized. Crew of 2. **Outside barge** dimensions: length 9.4m, beam 4m, to 16.7m by 5.2m; draft 1.3-2.3m. **Inside barge** dimensions: 17.9m long, 5.2m wide, 2m hold depth. Other recorded names: **Falmouth stone barge, Fal smack, old salters** (late **barges** that lightered cargo to and from ships). Note also **West Country sailing barge**.

fälbåt **1.** *Finland:* Deep-hulled boat used in winter in the Gulf of Bothnia for hunting seals, and in summer as a general workboat. Double-ended; clinker-planked; bow shallow and rounded; stern deep and strongly raked. T-keel; curves up gently at the stem; broad from midships aft the keel. Strong sheer, partly reduced by washstrakes; hull may be ceiled. Rowed, with 3 places, and sailed. Crewed by 3 or more. Reported lengths 7.3-12m, beamy. Other recorded names: **fälstjivon** (large size), **hylkivene, sälbåt, sälfangstbåt**
2. *Sweden:* Two types worked from the Swedish coast of the Gulf of Bothnia—the Finnish type described above and a newer type with a raked transom stern, rounded stem, and flatter floors. A small edition of the latter sometimes called a **julle** or **fäljulle★**. Generally smaller in the northern part of the gulf than in the south and set 2 spritsails or a lugsail forward and a sprit mizzen; some used a single gunter lug- or gaff sail and staysail. The Öland Island boats set 2 spritsails and a staysail; often carried the mail between Öland and Gotland. Reported lengths 7-9.6m, widths 2-3m. The **fälbåt** was generally accompanied by an **iseka★** or **isjolle★** on sealing trips. Other recorded names: **färd(e)båt, färdesbåt, sälbåt, själabåt**
Further references: **iseka-1, sealer**
fälbåtsjulle See **isjolle**
falca In some areas of northern South America, notably Guyana, Suriname, and eastern Venezuela, an expanded **dugout canoe★** that has had 1-3 planks permanently added on is called a **falca**; elsewhere it would be a **canoe★**

falca

or **corial★**; and in Brazil it would be a **montaria★**. Ends generally closed off by boards; thwarts and ribs

usually added to brace the planks. Frequently has a thatched house aft. Reported lengths 6-7m. Other recorded names: **arosutáhu** (by the Arawak), **sumáripa** (by the Makusi). Note also **barca de falca**. Further reference: **bote-4**
Fale-Brëëm See **Brëëm**
fäljulla See **fäljulle-1**
fäljulle **1.** *Finland, W:* Round-bottomed **eka★** used for hunting seals and for local travel on the Gulf of Bothnia coast. The broad bottom board curves up strongly to the bow and stern, protected by 2 moldings. Clinker-planked. An outboard motor now hung from the transom stern. Modern term for the boat is **själasmacko**. Reported lengths 3.7-4.6m. Other recorded names: **fälaik, fäljulla, fälöik, fälöitjo, färdjulle**
2. *Sweden:* A small version of the **fälbåt★**. Transom stern, rounded stem, fairly flat floors. Name variant: **julle**
Further reference: **fälbåt-2**
Fall boat See **mountain boat-1a**
fallua See **felucca-1**
Falmouth gig See **Cornish gig**
Falmouth oyster dredger *England, SW:* Local design for this boat has varied, and some have been converted from other craft. Dates to at least the early 19th century; some still work in the Falmouth area. Dredge

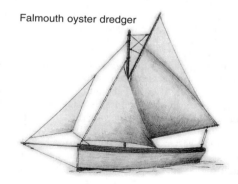

Falmouth oyster dredger

for oysters from October through March. Now has a vertical stem, wide raking transom stern, and a long deep keel; keel irons. Prior to World War II, most had a square counter stern. Originally clinker-built, later carvel; some now of fiberglass; plumb sides. Small forecastle; wide side decks for working the dredges; short stern deck. Large loose-footed or boomed, high-peaked gaff mainsail, with boom overhanging the stern, set to a pole mast. Jib hauled out on a traveler; staysail; at times a jackyard topsail. Bowsprit long and bowsed down by a chain bobstay. Most now have an auxiliary, but their use is prohibited while dredging. Smaller boats work single-handed; crew of 2-3 on the larger. Reported lengths 6-10.7m; 1840 boat: length overall 8.66m, beam 2.7m, molded depth 1.63m; deep draft. Other recorded names: **Falmouth working boat, Fal oyster boat, harbour boat, oyster dredger, Truro River oyster boat**; also **Fal** or **River Fal oyster dredger**
Falmouth oyster punt *England, SW:* Small open boat that works around the upper, shallow parts of the Fal

Estuary oyster dredging, line fishing, lobstering, and conducting general watermen's activities; a few still work. Generally carvel-planked, some clinker; sawn frames; some now of fiberglass. Plumb stem with

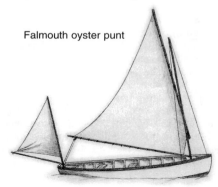

Falmouth oyster punt

rounded forefoot, fine lines forward; transom stern; flat floors, with hard turn of the bilges. By law, work mainly under oars while dredging, employing an anchor and winch to haul the dredge. High-peaked standing lugsail set to a light mast stepped well forward. A triangular sail or standing lug set on the mizzenmast at the transom; sheeted to an outrigger. Sail rarely used now, most employing a small outboard motor. Crew of 1-2. Reported lengths 3.66-4.88m, a few to 5.18m; beamy; shallow draft. Other recorded names: **Coombe Kaffir**, **Fal oyster punt**, **haul-tow punt**, **punt**⋆

Falmouth quay punt *England, SW:* Small **yawl**⋆-rigged boat that serviced sailing ships "awaiting orders" off the port of Falmouth. Worked during the 19th century and until the 1920s; a few remain as pleasure craft. In addition to ferrying provisions, mail, personnel, and ship chandlers, they fished, crabbed, carried light cargo, and took out pleasure parties. Early boats clinker-planked, later carvel. Deep hull with high freeboard; cross sections wineglass-shaped; flat sheer after the 1890s. Straight keel until late 19th cen-

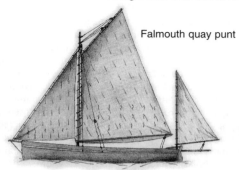

Falmouth quay punt

tury, after which a curved keel predominated; deep draft aft. Straight plumb stem, then rounded forefoot; bow sharp and narrow. Transom stern; raked sternpost in later types. Small cuddy forward; a short deck aft and wide waterways on later boats. Tiller, bent to work around the mizzenmast, often offset from centerline. Winter rig consisted of a small loose-footed, boomed

gaff sail set to a comparatively short mast; triangular mizzen, and staysail. Mizzen loose-footed, boomed, and sheeted to an outrigger that ran through the transom on the starboard side; mast unstayed and stepped originally against the transom. Staysail extended to a bumkin. In summer, a running bowsprit added, with jib, larger mainsail, and often a large standing lug mizzen. Early boats lug-rigged. By World War I auxiliaries were being installed. Crew of 1-2. Reported lengths 4.6-13.2m; the smaller boats used early in the period were called, merely, **punts**⋆. Typically 8m by 2.44m by 2.2m; draft aft 0.9-1.83m. A few fully powered boats, usually referred to as **quay punts**, still run from the Custom House Quay to off-lying ships, carrying passengers and minor supplies.

Falmouth stone barge See **Fal barge**

Falmouth working boat See **Falmouth oyster dredger**

fälöik, **fälöitjo** See **fäljulle-1**

falouca See **felucca**

falouche *United States, south-central:* **1.** Term applied in the Louisiana area in the early 19th century to a small sailing craft of crude construction. Alternately called a **canoe**⋆.

2. In the same period and area, a lug-rigged vessel called a **falouche** was popular with privateers, and at least one served as a U.S. naval vessel between 1813 and 1822; 2 guns; crew of 15. Speed, shallow draft, and ability to resort to oars in calms made the **falouche** easily maneuverable in the coastal waterways and bayous. Strongly curved sides, with tumble home; square tuck at stern. Open except for short end decking. Two forward-raking, demountable masts stepped against transverse beams, shored against the keelson. Some single-masted vessels could change the rake of the mast to aft, and carried fore-and-aft sails to become a **sloop**⋆. Name variant: **felucca**⋆

falouque See **felucca-1**

Fal oyster boat, **Fal oyster dredger** See **Falmouth oyster dredger**

Fal oyster punt See **Falmouth oyster punt**

Fal smack See **Fal barge**

fälstjivon See **fälbåt-1**

falua **1.** Spanish term for an open boat used in ports and rivers to transport important personages and port officials. Varied in grandeur and importance. Early boats reportedly employed 20 or more oars, 2 lateen or quadrilateral lateen-type sails with a short luff, and had a covering at the stern. Spelling variants: **falúa**, **faluca**, **faluga**, **feluga**. Note also **barge-3**, **feluca**.

2. *Canary Islands:* Round-bowed, **cutter**⋆-rigged **fishing boat**⋆ that worked out of the islands, but by the early 1920s, the **falúa** was found only at La Palma Island. Set a large gaff sail; also motorized. Crew of 10. Local name variant: **balandra**⋆

3. *Chile/Peru:* The lateen-sailed **falúa** of European fishermen was introduced from Italy and Dalmatia during the late 19th century. Double-ended, round bottom, carvel-built. Usually decked at bow and stern, some fully decked with one or more hatches; limited accommodations in the forepeak. Yard tacked to stem or a small boom. While scallop fishing, mast stepped well forward and a boomed gaff sail used. When rowed, oarsman stood at stern and faced forward. Now motorized and without sail. Crew of 6-10. Reported lengths 5.5-11m; e.g., length 5.5m, beam 1.8m, depth 0.9m. Other recorded names: **chalana***, **chalupa*** (generally in Chile), **falucho*** (in northern Chile and Peru)

4. *Philippines:* Early **gunboat*** used by anti-piracy forces. Armed with 18- to 24-pound cannon in the square bow. Sailed and rowed. Stepped 2 masts, setting lateen sails, the mizzen well aft, boomed. Reported lengths 16.8-18.2m.

5. *Portugal, central:* 19th-century vessel of the Tagus River that ferried passengers across the river and transported produce from the upper river basin. Last sailing **falua** sank in 1968. Carvel-planked; keel; fine lines forward, with rounded forefoot, high stemhead; long run; rising floors; round bilges; small, narrow raked transom. Most decked to about amidships and open to a stern deck; 2 hatches. Two heavy wales ran down each side; brightly painted. Outboard rudder; tiller. Lateen sails set to 1-2 masts supported by a pair of shrouds; mainmast rake ranged from vertical to aft-raking. Sail proportion also varied, and some had a short luff; sails might be set to opposite sides of the masts; on the last boats, the yard on the mainmast was the longer. On single-masted boats, a small jib ran to a rising bowsprit. Also rowed, using 4 oars. Crew of ca. 5. Reported lengths 13.6-20m; e.g., length overall 13.6m, beam 4m, depth 1.4m.

Further references: **felucca-1**, **palua**

falúa del almirante See **barge-2**

falúa del comandante See **gig-1**

falua do Bugio *Portugal, central:* Round-bottomed boat that serviced the Bugio lighthouse at the mouth of the Tagus River. Name **falua*** given to the boat although it was not a true **falua**.

faluca See **falua-1**, **falucho-3**, **feluca**

faluche See **feluca**

falucho **1.** *Chile, central:* Double-ended **barge***-type craft that was built from the mid-19th century at Constitución on the Río Maule. Decked; designed to carry coal, vegetables, and firewood north to Valparaiso, taking advantage of the prevailing southerly winds. Sold at the end of a single trip, becoming a floating warehouse. The crew of 4 returned home by train. Two small square sails set on short masts. 60-200t.

2. *Cuba:* Small cargo vessel built locally in the 18th century. Set a single high-peaked lateen sail and a jib.

3. *Spain:* Vessel of the **xebec*** family found in Mediterranean waters until the late 19th century. Served for coastal defense, and as a fish and cargo carrier. Stem curved, stemhead tall; stern might overhang, counter-fashion. Decked forward and aft, strong camber; some had a low poop. Rudder and tiller. Most stepped 2 masts, setting lateen sails; also known to use 1 or 3 masts; the **fishing boats*** generally single-masted. Mainmast stepped a little forward of amidships and inclined forward; mizzenmast vertical. Jib on long bowsprit. Reported lengths 12-18m, widths 3.35-5.95m. Other recorded names: **bondo** (Basque), **faluca**, **faluk**, **Falukke**, **felouque***, **felucca***. Note also **barca de mitjana**, **barquilla-2**, **laúd**.

4. *Spain, NW:* Small, single-masted **fishing boat** of western Galicia. Extinct since the mid-20th century. Sharp ends; curved stem, sometimes with tumble home; curved bottom. Deep outboard rudder; tiller. Lateen sail set to a forward-raking mast. Reported lengths 8-10m; e.g., length 7m, beam 2.78m, depth 0.96m. Name variant: **bote falucho** (small size)

Further references: **falua-3**, **lancha-2**

falucho grande, **falucho primero** See **double felouque**

falucque See **felucca-1**

faluga See **falua-1**

faluk See **falucho-3**

faluka See **felucca-1**, **gaiassa**

falukah *Yemen, N:* A rather unstable craft built at Al Luayyah. Wide transom, no sternpost, flaring sides. Spelling variant: pl. **fala'ik**

Falukke See **falucho-3**

falutx See **barca de mitjana**

falutx de primer See **double felouque**

falutxo See **barca de mitjana**

falūwa Cited in late 14th-century Arabic literature as a term for **boat***, perhaps one designated to transport provisions.

fălûxĕ See **lancha-2**

fämbälbåt See **storbåt-1**

fa mei koo See **hua pi gu**

family boat **1.** An easily handled, commodious pleasure boat. Name variant: **family cruiser**

2. *United Kingdom:* Colloquial British term for a **smack*** worked by members of one family.

Further references: **flatboat-4**, **narrow boat**, **Rodney boat**, **showboat-1**

family canoe See **northern-style canoe**, **umiak-1**

family cruiser See **family boat**

family punt See **punt-7**

family ship One in which the crew comes from the same town or area.

fancy boat See **dghajsa-1**

fan fa See **chu-p'ai**

fang *China:* One of the terms for a **raft***.

fang tou *China, E:* Seaworthy boat that transports passengers in the Woosung area. Straight, raking square ends; false bow; flat bottom athwartships, cants up toward the bow; straight sides; 2 bulkheads. Decked forward or might be fully decked; removable awning. Two people plus a child work the long, heavy sculling oar. Sometimes sailed. Other recorded names: **fang t'ou**, **square-headed boat**, **Woosung fang tou**

fanny See **zalmschouw**

fan-tail boat See **shen bo zi**

fantom ship See **ghost ship**

faotasi See **fautasi**

far *Denmark, Faroe Islands:* Term for a **vessel*** or **craft***. Also, a suffix designating a boat of a specific size, as **seksmannafar***. Spelling variant: **før**. See also **farkost**.

ferærör See **færing**

farcoast See **farcost**

farcost *British Isles:* Usually considered a small cargo vessel of the 13th-17th centuries. Some vessels fished; others carried stone, especially in the Thames area. Other recorded names: **farcoast**, **farcosta**, **farcoste**, **farecost**, **farkost***, **fercest**, **fercost(a)**, **fercoste**, **ferr cost**, **ffarecost**, **foriscotia**, **var(e)cost**, **vare coste**

farcosta, farcoste, farecost See **farcost**
färdbåt, färdebåt, färdesbåt See **fälbåt-2**
färdjulle See **fäljulle-1**
farella *Malta:* Fast, robust **fishing boat★** that also serves as a fish carrier and, at times, as a cargo boat, going to Tunisia. Most common in the 19th century. Carvel-planked, low rise to the floors, keel, rounded bilges. Sharp ends; fairly plumb stem that recurves slightly toward the top of the very tall stemhead; sternpost lower. Considerable sheer; removable washboards that stop short of the stem. Outboard rudder; tiller passes over the sternpost. Cambered decks at ends and along the sides; rectangular hatch amidships; small hatchway at stern leads to the hold, but opening used by helmsman in bad weather. Brightly painted, often with allegorical figures; oculi. Short, stout mast, stepped well forward. Sets a rectangular spritsail. Notches for the sprit on the thwart just abaft the foredeck. Small jib to a long bowsprit. Crew of 3-4. Reported lengths 4-9m; e.g., length 5m, beam 1.5m, depth 1.0m. Spelling variants: **ferilla, firilla** (pl. **firelli**)
Faren See **Bucentaur**
fargata See **fragata-1, fragata-4**
faring See **færing**
färja, färjbåt See **ferryboat-1**
farkost *Norway/Sweden:* Collective term for small **boats★** or **vessels★**. Spelling variants: **far★, farkosten, farkoster(na), farr.** See also **farcost**.
farkosten, farkoster, farkosterna See **farkost**
Farm *Austria/Germany, S:* Term applied to large cable **ferryboats★** on the Danube, Salzach, and Isar Rivers. Transported people, animals, vehicles, and cargo. Flat bottom turned up at the open ends to serve as ramps at the shore. Low, parallel, vertical sides. Some narrow at the ends (**Spitzfahrm, Spitzfarm**). Employed a sweep at the stern. Reported lengths 15-30m; e.g., length overall 17.8m, on bottom 8.8m, beam 4.6m. Other recorded names: **Fahrm, Fährschiff, Farmb, Farmplätte, Formplätte, Stockplätte, Überfuhrfarm, Urfahrfarm, Varbm**; pl. **Farmen.** Further reference: **Yorkshire lugger**
Farmb See **Farm**
farm barge See **hay barge**
farm boat See **Yorkshire lugger**
Farmen, Farmplätte See **Farm**
Farmschiff See **Bucentaur**
Faroese boat See **færobåd**
faro flotante See **lightship**
farr See **farkost**
farskip See **ferje**
farteh *Bahrain:* Palm-stalk boat used by local fishermen, especially on the southwest coast; rarely used now. Bottom, sides, and flooring constructed from the stripped ribs of the coconut palm; each stalk sewn to its neighbor. Interior filled with palm bark fiber. Sharp ends. Rowed, but some formerly sailed, employing a trapezoidal sail. Length ca. 3.6m. Note also **hurija, shashah-1**.
farthing ferry See **traghetto-1**
fa-schuen See **hua chuan-2a**
fase See **fa zi**
fasone See **fassone**

fassone *Italy, Sardinia:* **Reed boat★** of the marshy lagoon on the west coast. Popular for wildfowling and fishing. Some of 3 bundles—2 large ones, with a smaller one below to serve as a keel; slender bundles along the sides serve as sponsons and along the top as gunwales. Others formed by 4 bundles on the bottom and one raising each side. Designed to taper at the bow, turning up before being tied to a point. Stern cut square. A bundle lashed athwartships serves as a seat. Rowed, the oars working against tholepins inserted in the side bundles, or set on outriggers; also poled. Reported lengths 2.6-4m, width ca. 0.9m; some early **fassoni** (pl.) were as long as 6m and transported 8 people. Other recorded names: **ciu an, fasone, schilf, šíu, vašni, vassóni.** Further reading: Edoardo Riccardi, "'Fassone,' l'Embarcation de Jonc de Oristano-Sardaigne-Italie," in: *International Symposium on Boat and Ship Archaeology,* 4th, Porto, 1985, Local Boats, (vol. II), 275-285; (Oxford, B.A.R., 1988 [BAR International Series 438]), 275-285.
fassoni See **fassone**
fast boat 1. A **whaleboat★** with a harpoon and line "fast" to a whale; one that was unsuccessful is said to be a **loose boat.**
2. *China, E:* Common 19th-century fishing and cargo vessel of the central coast. Sharp bow and rounded stern, with the maximum beam aft of amidships; strongly curved ends; small wedge-shaped stem; very small high transom. Bottom curved fore-and-aft; keel under forward two-thirds; low rise to the floors with soft bilges; bold sheer. Decked; square platforms extended over the bow and stern. Fenestrated square rudder hung inboard; raked. Some armed. Foremast stepped in the eyes; mainmast amidships. Equipped with battened balance lugsails. Length overall 27.5m, on waterline 21m, beam 6m, depth 2.6m. Other recorded names: **bateau rapide, k'oai tch'ouan, kuai chuan, k'uai ch'uan.** Note also **feng kuai chuan.** Further references: **banting-2, go-down, ha kou ting, hong boat, sampan panjang, Wuxi kuai**
fast crab See **fei xie**
fast express See **ma ling ting**
fast patrol craft See **swift boat-2**
fa tch'ouan See **fa chuan**
fatemari See **pattamar**
fa teng *Hong Kong:* An elaborate paper boat of the boat people, who set it afloat with candles burning inside. Used to appease the sea gods before setting off on a long water journey. Other recorded names: **flower boat, paper boat★.** Further reference: **hua chuan-2a**
fa-t'ing See **hua chuan-2a**
fattehmar See **pattamar**
fa-tzŭ See **bi fa zi, fa zi**
Faue See **Fischerkahn**
fautasi *Samoa, central Pacific:* Exceptionally long, narrow **rowing boat★** used mainly to transport people and produce to market centers; also raced. Generally communally owned. Often crossed through surf. Double-ended; carvel-planked; fine entrance and run; heavy keelson; low rise to the floors; straight, slightly raked stem and sternpost. Open; closely spaced rowing benches; rowed double-banked by as many as 40

oarsmen. Steered with an oar. Reported lengths 15-21m; e.g., length 20.4m, beam 1.45m, depth amidships 0.7m. The present-day craft that are used in inter-country racing are of fiberglass, rowed with 46 oarsmen, and are 27m long. Spelling variants: **faotasi, fautisi, pautasi, poutasi**

fautisi See **fautasi**

fava See **soro**

fa zi *China, W:* Flexible bamboo **raft*** employed to transport cargo on the shallow, turbulent Moron Us He (Ya River) north to Ya'an (Yachow). Nodes planed off the bamboo poles, ca. 13cm in diameter, then oiled. Bow poles bent up by heat, then weighted with stones, and finally the bow end is supported by a bridle to retain the sheer effect. Lashed together with cane withes to numerous crosspieces; bamboo fender runs along each side. Platform for the cargo built up in the center and runs most of the length. Crew's hut aft. Maneuvered with a stern or bow rudder and 3 oars; towed and poled upstream. Crew of 6-8 for upstream trip, 4 for downstream. Reported lengths 7-40m, widths 3-5m, draft 7-15cm. Other recorded names: **bamboo cargo-carrying raft, chu-fa chhuan, fase, fa-tzŭ, pa ts'ien ch'uan, Yachow raft, Ya River raft**. Note also **bi fa zi, chu-p'ai, zhu pai**.

feeder *Myanmar, central:* A fast passenger-carrying **paddle boat*** that operated as part of the Irrawaddy Flotilla between Prome and Mandalay prior to World War II. Length ca. 61m. Name variant: **ferry***

feeder boat See **liu wang chuan, sin-tor-chai**

Fehnmutte See **Spitzmutte**

fei-hsieh See **fei xie**

fei teng *China, S:* Special boat for carrying coffins at Guangzhou (Canton) but initially, because of their speed, transported the sick to hospitals. Sharp, overhanging, slightly curved bow; flat curved stern; maximum beam abaft amidships; 4 bulkheads; moderate sheer; flat floors. Outboard rudder; long tiller. Cabin for relatives amidships; mat roof over the helmsman. Single square sail. Crew of 6 oarsmen. Length ca. 12m, beam 2.7m, depth 1.34m. Other recorded names: **coffin boat, fy t'eng, quick boat**. Note also **guan cai chuan**.

fei xie *China:* A class of police patrol **junk*** that operated throughout China to 1911, primarily to curtail smuggling. Size and style adapted to the nature of the waters on which they operated. On the middle Chang Jiang (Yangtze), identified by a single high-peaked, blue-and-white-striped balance lugsail and pennants at the bow and high stern. Captain's cabin aft; galley forward of the mast; when anchored, a blue and white awning was hung between the mast and cabin. Square ends, with long counter and raked bow; flat bottom; shallow rudder came up inboard; tiller worked from forward of the cabin; cannon at the bow. Rowed, employing 10 oars; also poled. Single high-peaked balance lugsail set to mast stepped just forward of amidships. Crew of 12-47. Reported lengths 6-20m; e.g., length 12.2m, beam 2.7m, depth 0.76m, draft 0.25m. Other recorded names: **fast crab, fei-hsieh, gunboat*, police boat, river police boat, shui bao jia fei xie, shui-pao-chia fei-hsieh**

Fejødrivkvase See **drivkvase**

feleok See **felucca-1**

felete See **flette**

felibot See **flibot**

felibote See **vlieboot**

feliouka See **felucca-1**

felladière See **filadière**

Fellboot See **skin boat-1**

felloucque See **felucca-1**

Fellows boat, Fellows Morton boat See **narrow boat**

felluca See **felucca-3**

felluce See **feluca**

feloca See **felucca-1**

felouka See **felucca-1, felukka-2**

feloukah See **fụlūka**

feloukah-soghayrah See **fụlūka-2b**

felouque *United States, south-central:* Used by the French on the lower Mississippi River and the Gulf of Mexico during the early 18th century for transport service and as **coasters***. Small and swift. Propelled by 2 lateen sails or oars. Helm at either end as needed. Name variant: **felucca***. Further references: **billuga, falucho-3, felucca-1, fụlūka**

felouque corse *France, Corsica:* Open inshore **fishing boat***. Sharp ends; narrow bow, higher than the stern; plumb stem, curved sternpost. Mainly rowed, using as

felouque corse

many as 6 oars, but also set 1-2 high-peaked spritsails or lateen sails. Stubby foremast stepped in the bow. Also a small jib. May be motorized now. As many as 9 in crew, plus 2 boys. Reported lengths 4.5-9m. Note also **billuga**.

felouque provençale *France, Mediterranean coast:* Long, narrow 17th- and 18th-century **fishing boat*** of Provence. Double-ended; curved and raked bow and stern; some had a bow ram; strong sheer. Washstrakes stop before the stem and sternposts. Outboard rudder; tiller. Designed to be rowed, working through oarports. Also used a spritsail and jib. Running rigging ran to iron hooks on the gunwales outside the washboards. Short mast stepped well forward; some 2-masted.

feluca *Italy:* **1.** The 16th-century **feluca** of Venice was a small, swift craft used in war. Rowed by 10 oarsmen; also set as many as 3 lateen sails.

2. A modern-day Sicilian and southern Italian **feluca** engages in swordfishing in the Strait of Messina. Steps a pole that may be as tall as 20m on which a spotter stands; an equally long "bowsprit" serves as a platform for a harpooner. Sharp ends; raked stem with cutaway forefoot, nearly vertical sternpost; flat floors; shallow keel; newer motorized boats have fuller ends and a small counter. Decked fully or only at the ends. Early type rowed. The small, fast **londra**★ waits nearby to pursue the fish. Reported lengths 8.5-14m; widths 2.2-4m, depths 1-2m. Other recorded names: **spada boat**, **swordfish searcher boat**. Note also **ontro**.

3. Sailing vessel prominent in the 18th century; 2 lateen sails set to vertical masts; no bowsprit. Type no longer used.

Spelling variants: **faluca**, **felluce**, **filuca**★, **filuga**; pl. **faluche**, **felloucque**, **feluc(c)he**, **filuc(c)he**, **flouque**. Note also **felucca**.

felucca 1. *Mediterranean:* Served as a cargo carrier, passenger vessel, **man-of-war**★, **corsair**★, and guardian of ports. Term has been applied to a number of different types of vessels during a long history that ended in the 19th century. Small types generally both rowed and sailed; large vessels only sailed, stepping 1-3 masts; an especially large vessel might be called a **double felouque**★. Generally set lateen sails, although a sprit rig was common on some small open **feluccas** in the 17th century. Some Greek **feluccas** set square topsails. As many as 20 banks of oars used and, on older types, outboard gangways supported standing rowers. Sharp ends, flat floors, shallow keel, flared sides. Most had a low beak. The later Spanish craft had a very tall stem extension. Most had an overhanging poop deck, some had a cabin aft, and larger vessels were fully decked. On some, the helm could be placed at either end as needed. The **corsair** carried ca. 20 men. Reported lengths 9-19m, widths 1.8-3.7m, depths 0.7-1.12m. Spelling variants: **fallua**, **falouca**, **falouque**, **falua**★, **falucque**, **faluka**, **feleok**, **feliouka**, **feloca**, **felouka**, **felouque**★, **féluguone**, **feluka**, **felukk(e)**, **feluque**, **filjuga**, **filucca**, **fil(y)uga**, **filuka**★, **f(o)ulouqa**, **fuluka**. Note also **falucho**, **feluca**, **filughetta**, **filva**, **fu̯lūka**, **gaiassa**.

2. *Mexico, W:* At Mazátlan, fishermen raced 4- and 6-oared **feluccas**. Fixed seats, with 2 men to a bench.

3. *United States, W:* **a.** Lateen-rigged **fishing boat**★ of San Francisco Bay area; popular from the latter part of

felucca-3

the 19th to the early 20th century; 3 still working in the mid-1980s. Carvel-planked; sharp ends with stern slightly finer than bow; stem straight or curved, plumb

or had tumble home, terminating in a knob ca. 20cm above gunwale; sternpost usually straight. Deep keel, with slight drag; rounded midsection, moderate to strong rise to the floors; most ceiled. Decked, with low bulwarks, high camber forward; wide waterways; long hatch; small cockpit for helmsman; some open amidships, with rowing thwart. Large rudder, hung on pintles; long tiller. Usually painted white, some with broad colored bands along the top strake. Short, stout, unstayed mast stepped amidships; sharply raked forward. Swelling at top for halyard sheave. Lateen yard, in 2 pieces, longer than the boat. Light bowsprit run through a hole in the starboard gunwale; jib set flying. When rowed, the stroke faced forward, others faced aft; tholepins chocked on bulwarks. Gasoline engines installed about the turn of the century, earning them the name **perfume boats**. Crew generally 2-3. Reported lengths 5.5-12.2m; e.g., length 8.2m, beam 2.89m, depth 0.76m; shallow draft. Other recorded names: **Dago fishing boat**, **felluca**, **Frisco felucca**, **Italian boat**, **San Francisco felucca**. **b.** The **felucca** that fished in the Gulf of Santa Catalina off southern California was similar in hull design, but had a long, straight plank keel, ca. 30cm deep, often of iron or steel; the iron shoe followed the curve of the forefoot and ran to the stemhead. White hull; characteristically, decks and interior were red and waterline a dark green; individuality created by colored railings, coamings, and substantial bulwarks. About the turn of the century adopted a high-peaked gaff rig. Short mast, stepped about one-quarter in from the bow; mainsail boom equaled or exceeded the boat length; staysail ran to a bowsprit. Engines installed at the beginning of the 20th century. Average length 8m, beam 2.7-3m. Other recorded names: **Catalina Channel** (or **San Pedro**) **felucca**

Further references: **falouche**, **falucho-3**, **felouque**, **fu̯lūka**, **galiot-6**

felucche, **feluche** See **feluca**

feluga See **falua-1**

félugoune See **felucca-1**

feluka See **felucca-1**, **felukka-2**

felukah See **fu̯lūka**

felukk See **felucca-1**

felukka *Sudan:* **1.** Pearling, fishing, and **shore boat**★ of the coastal area. Lightly constructed, fine-lined, cutaway forefoot, raked transom; low-sided. Decked at bow and stern. Lateen-rigged; also rowed. Those that pearled were manned by non-Sudanese. Reported lengths 5-7.6m.
2. On the upper Nile River, the **felukka** is a **gharab**★ that attends a **naggr**★. Spelling variants: **felouka**, **feluka**

felukke, **feluque** See **felucca-1**

female boat *Wales, NW:* Term given to a small centerboard boat used in local herring fisheries. Built of larch planking. Set a mainsail and jib, or rowed with 4 oars. Reported lengths 3.7-5m; deep draft. Name variant: **cychod banw**. Note also **male boat**.

female pungy See **pungy**

femboering See **fembøring**

membordsbåt See **storbåt-1**

fembøring *Norway, N:* Large, mostly open boat found from Trondheim northward. Initially transported merchandise, but ca. 1830 became more important as a fishing craft. Clinker-built, originally with 5 (*fem*) strakes per side; long keel; wide, flaring, slightly S-curved sides. Sharp ends; plumb or slightly recurved stem and sternpost, the stem often quite tall. Rudder worked with a single-arm yoke and a long, slender tiller; tall rudderhead permitted tiller to clear the cabin roof. Some had a turtleback cabin aft, which might be set ashore while fishing. Rowed with 8-12 oars; when rowed with 5 oars, 4 men sit forward, rowing double-banked, the 5th man working a single oar aft. Set a large square sail and often a square topsail; some later boats adopted a gaff mainsail, and some larger boats added a gaff mizzen. Polemast stepped roughly amidships. (Features of 2 main types follow.) Other recorded names: **femboering**, **femböring**, **fembøringane**, **femböringsbaad**; pl. **fembøringar**, **fembøringer**; small size **småfembøring**

1. The **fembøring** from Åfjord District, just north of Trondheim, was mainly a 10-oared boat. The smallest, also called a **torskegarnsbåt*** (cod-net boat) and **vinterbåt**, had 6 "rooms" and ranged in length from ca. 10.5-12.6m; the next category had 6 1/2 to 7 "rooms" (the **storfembøring**) and ranged from 12.6-13.8m long; the largest, with 8 "rooms," were the **storbåten*** and the **lofotbåten**, to ca. 16m long. The **lofotbåt** fished principally off the Lofoten Islands. The stem might be quite tall on the **åfjordsfembøring**. Often had extra ribs amidships to take the weight of the ballast stones or heavy cargo. When sailing, washboards might be added amidships. Crew of ca. 7. Reported lengths 10-15m; 1892 boat: 12.27m long, 3.12m wide, and 0.85m deep. Note also **lestabåt**.

2. The **fembøring** of Nordland County was similar but worked mainly with 6 pairs of oars, although some boats omitted one pair. Most boats compartmented into 7 or more "rooms" (the **storfembøring**), but some had as few as 6 (**seksroring*** or **små-seksroring**) or as many as 8 (**storfembøring** or **storbåt***). Oars worked against natural crooks until the mid-19th century; later used tholepins. Most employed crew of 5-7. Lengths of the **seksroring** ca. 11-13m, the regular **fembøring** ca. 13-14m, and the **storfembøring** ca. 14-15.6m; e.g., length 11.6m, beam 1.86m, depth 0.86m. Other recorded names: **nordlandsfembøring**, **Nordlandsk femböringsbaad**. Note also **bindalsbåt**.

femböring, fembøringane, fembøringar, fembøringer, femböringsbaad See **fembøring**

fembørings-jolle See **jolle-6**

femkeiping *Norway, W:* **1.** The **femkeiping** of Sunnfjord normally had 5 pairs of oarlocks (*keipar*), but for gill net fishing for herring, one after pair would be removed to avoid snagging the nets. Also caught cod and shark. Open; sharp ends; curved stem and sternpost. Also sailed, setting a square sail with a short yard and long foot. Large size: 9.28m long, 1.32m wide, 0.84m deep.

2. In Nordfjord, the **femkeiping** employed 5 pairs of oarlocks. Used for fishing, carrying light freight, hay, and church-goers. When employing a trapezoidal lugsail, steered with a single-arm yoke to a long tiller. Mast stepped amidships against a thwart. Reported

lengths 8.58-9.41m; e.g., length 8.58m, beam 2.1m, depth 0.68m.

3. The **femkeiping** of Sognefjord was mainly a **church boat***; also served as an auxiliary craft. Spelling variant: **femkjeiping**. Note also **femroring**.

femkjeiping See **femkeiping**

fem-manns båt *Norway:* A boat that has a crew of 5 most of the time.

femrøing See **femrøring**

femrømming, femrömming See **fem-roms båt**

fem-roms båt *Norway:* A boat compartmented into 5 spaces (*roms*) and employing 5 pairs of oars. Reported lengths ca. 8-10m. Spelling variants: **femrømming**, **femrömming**. Note also **åttring-3**.

femroring *Norway, west-central:* In Nordmøre District, a boat having places for 5 oarsmen (**femroring**), rowing with 5 pairs of oars (**femroing**). Note also **femkeiping**, **femrøring**, **nordmørsbåt**.

femrøring *Norway, west-central:* Term used in some communities in Nordmøre District for a boat with thwarts compartmenting the boat into 5 spaces. Used mainly for cod fishing. Employs 4-6 pairs of oars. Crew of 4. Reported lengths 7-9.4m. Spelling variant: **femrøing**. Note also **fem-roms båt**, **femroring**, **nordsmørsbåt**.

Fen barge See **Fenland lighter**

Fen boat *England, E:* Transported cut peat for fuel and sedge for thatching in The Fens. Small version of the **Fenland lighter***, being used on the lesser waterways. Flat bottom, double-ended, curved stem and sternpost. Towed in **gangs*** of 3. Length 6m, draft 30cm, cap. 2.5t. Name variant: **Fen butt**

Fen butt See **Fen boat**

fen chuan *China, E:* Transported human waste from Shanghai to farmers inland, often returning with vegetables. Square ends curved up from a flat bottom. Crew of 4 accommodated below the short foredeck; owner and family lived aft. High coaming, which extended beyond the stern. Raked rudder. Propelled by a type of sculling oar at the starboard stern; one at the port bow was fixed to a bumkin, activated by ropes to produce a sculling motion. Also sailed, the tall mast being struck for low bridges. Reported lengths 12-15m; e.g., length 15m, beam 3m, depth 0.76m. Name variant: **fu-fu boat**. Note also **night flower boat**, **ordure boat**.

feng chuan See **junk**

Fenland barge See **Fenland lighter**

Fenland lighter *England, E:* Worked in **gangs*** of 5-6 usually, traversing the drainage channels of the Fen Country and surrounding waterways. History goes

Fenland lighter

back to the late 17th century, with declining use toward the end of the 19th century, but transported sugar beets until shortly after World War II. Sides slightly flared and clinker-planked with wide strakes; on some, strakes lapped only at the ends. Bottom flat with only a slight rise to the floors, which were planked longitudinally, clench-fashion; chines lost toward the ends and sections became rounded. Some fully carvel-planked and these might be called **Fenland barges**. Rounded ends with heavy, curved stem and sternpost, faced with wrought iron; oak keel and frames. At bow and stern one set of frames extended above deck level to serve as bitts; 3 transverse beams; 2 large stringers ran full-length on each side. Steel **lighters★** superseded the wooden vessels. Bow and stern sometimes decked; some completely open. Sometimes a special **horse boat★** was towed at the end of the line; generally smaller than the **lighters**; these were also used to collect goods from distant farms. Or, the last boat of a **gang**, the **butt boat**, ca. 9m long, had raking ends to permit the horse to be ferried from one bank to the other. The **dinghy★** was called a **cock boat★**. **Gangs** were coupled together with a pole from the stem of one boat to the sternpost of the boat ahead. The **fore lighter** (or **forebarge**) had a towing mast with lines to men or horses. Helmsman steered from the **fore lighter** by pushing on a long pole that extended well forward. Open, with narrow walkways along the sides or decked at the ends; a **house lighter** had a small cabin at the stern for the crew. The 3rd **lighter**, the **hollip**, had a small cabin in the bow for the horse boy. A large square sail could be set to the **fore lighter**; mast in a tabernacle. By the 19th century the **gangs** (as many as 18) were towed by a small diesel **tug**. Most 12-21m long, 3.0-3.5m wide; shallow draft. Further name variant: **Fen lighter**. Note also **Fen boat**.

Fenland punt *England, E:* Craft of very early origin used in the Fen Country for general work and for eeling along the marshy channels. Clinker-built, sharp ends mostly, but may have a transom stern. To prevent the boat from grounding fast, the flat bottom may have a rocker or hog, or the stem and sternposts curve under the ends; sharp chines. Fishing **punts★** usually have a wet well. Propelled with a 3.7m-long pole. Reported lengths 4.9-5.5m; e.g., length 4.9m, beam 1.34m, depth 0.4m; shallow draft. Other recorded names: **Fen punt, marshman's punt**

Fen lighter See **Fenland lighter**

Fen punt See **Fenland punt**

ferærdr See **færing**

feræringr See **feræringur**

feræringur *Iceland:* A 4-oared boat. Spelling variant: **feræringr**. Note also **færing, fourareen**.

fercest See **farcost**

fercost, fercosts, fercoste See **farcost**

fergata See **fragata-1, frigate-1**

ferge, feria See **ferje**

feribot, ferie, ferigo See **ferryboat-1**

ferilla See **dghajsa-1, farella**

ferjä *Iceland:* Term for a **ferryboat★**, but may also describe a **wherry★**, or a **boat★** in general. Name variants: **feria, ferju-skip**

ferja See **ferje**

ferje Norwegian word for a **ferryboat★**. In the Viking period the term included boats used for transport and victualing as well as rowed **ferries★**. **Ferries** that crossed fjords were usually beamy and had a low freeboard to provide stability and easier access to and from shore. Some are owned by farmers who use them to go to neighboring islands to fetch hay and produce. Name variants: **farskip, ferge, ferja★, róðrarferja, småferja**

ferju-skip See **ferjä**

ferkada, ferkata See **frigate-1**

ferr cost See **farcost**

ferrie, ferrie boit, ferro See **ferryboat-1**

ferry *Myanmar:* On the Irrawaddy, the term **ferry** may mean a boat used to cross the river, but also a vessel that transports local passengers and cargo along the river. In the 1st half of the 20th century, such boats carried the mail (see **mail boat**). See also **feeder, ferryboat-1**.

ferryboat 1. A boat or vessel designed to transport passengers, merchandise, cattle, and vehicles over relatively narrow stretches of water. Operates on a schedule or on demand. Simple **ferryboats** may be poled, paddled, or rowed; others sail; some may employ an overhead or submerged cable (**cable ferry★** or **pull ferry**) or chains (**chain ferry, Kettenfähre**, or **Seilfähre**) by which the craft can be warped across (sometimes called a **floating** or **flying bridge, Rollfähre**), or assumes a 30° angle to the current, utilizing current pressure to slide the boat across (**current ferry**). Early boats twin-hulled to provide a platform for vehicles. Large modern **ferries** are sophisticated motorized ships, some with overnight accommodations. Some specially designed to carry automobiles (**Autofähre, auto ferry, car ferry, Fuhrwerksfähre, vehicular ferry**) or railway cars (**Eisenbahnfähre, railway ferry** or **railway ship, train ferry**). Most **ferryboats** double-ended, with a rudder at each end; the larger have 2 pilot houses. Other selected names: **bac★, barca da traghetto, bat' aiseig, chiatta per trasportare, færge(båd), færgekaag, Fährboot (-kahn, -prahm, -schiff), Fähre, färja, färjbåt, ferga, feribot, ferie, ferigo, ferjä★, ferje★, ferrie, ferrie boit, ferro, ferry★, feryboot, ferybote, fferybarge, fferybote, nave traghetto, paróm★, tragetto, tragheto, traghetto★, tragillo, tragitto, traille, trajekt, transbordador, transbordeur, trapassamento, traversier★, va-et-vient, veerboot, veerpont; pons ductorius, pont volant**. Note also **Fährschmack, Farm, fifie-2, flat-6, flatboat-1, foot boat, Fuhrwerkponte, horse boat, passage boat, pont, paso de barca, scow ferry, team boat**.

2. *British Isles:* Name applied, especially in East Anglia, Yorkshire, and at Hastings, to a small boat that ferried fresh fish to shore, particularly when conditions did not permit the **luggers★** and **yawls★** to land. Strongly built, open, ample cargo space. The east coast boats were similar to **beach yawls★**, but shorter and beamier; also provisioned ships lying at anchor. Some were **cobles★**. Name variant: **bullock boat**

Further reference: **coble-3**

ferry flat See **covered sled, scow ferry**

ferry scow See **scow ferry**

feryboot, ferybote See **ferryboat-1**

Feuerlöschboot, Feuerlöschschiff See **fire boat**

Festmachebooot See **stake boat-2**

Feuerschiff, feu flottant See **lightship**

ffalua See **falua-1**

ffarcost, ffarecost See **farcost**

fferybarge, fferybote See **ferryboat-1**

fflotte See **fleet**

fflye, fflye-boat See **flyboat**

Fiefmannsboot See **Garnboot-1**

fife *Wales, N/Scotland, SW:* Class of pleasure craft, based at Anglesey Island, and raced especially in Menai Strait. Lightly built, originally of wood, now of fiberglass. Long counter stern, long curved stem. Rectangular cockpit; rudder, worked by a tiller, comes up through the after deck. Boomed leg-of-mutton sail, jib to stem. Crew of 3. Length overall 7.3m, on waterline 4.9m, beam 1.9m, draft 1.0m. The **Fairle fifes** of the River Clyde were much larger **yachts***. Other recorded names: **Bangor fife, Conway (or Menai) One Design**. Further reference: **fifie-1**.

Fife skiff *United Kingdom:* A variety of pleasure **yacht***'s **dinghy***. Sharp ends. Rowed, with single pair of oars. Note also **fifie skiff**.

Fife yawl See **fifie yawl**

fiffie See **fifie-1**

fifie *Scotland, east coast:* **1.** Powerful, double-ended drift net **fishing boat*** (especially for herring) that was built until ca. 1912; motorized version still used in 1950s.

fifie-1

Some worked out of west coast ports. Clinker-built until the latter part of the 19th century, then carvel. No set design, but characteristically stem and sternpost near vertical; deep forefoot; long keel; hollow, rising floors. Some fine-bodied with full sections; others sharp, often fuller at the stern; flat sheer; some steep-floored; bilge keels. Open or half-decked (**half-decker***) until mid-1800s, then generally fully decked with long hatch amidships and crew's cabin aft; low bulwarks; steered with a horizontal wheel. Steam capstan hoisted sails and hauled the drift nets; a hand winch aided in lowering and raising the mainmast. Colorfully painted, and scrolls and emblems decorated the bows. In general, the dipping lug foresail was tall, high-peaked, and bent to a heavy yard; standing lug mizzen, sheeted to an outrigger, size varying with weather conditions. Heavy foremast stepped into tabernacle, crutch aft of mizzenmast held the lowered fore-mast; masts may rake forward. Jib sometimes set to a

long running bowsprit. On the west coast, a few small **fifies** set a single dipping lugsail. Oars used in calms or to clear the harbor. Crew of 5-8. In 1850s ca. 7.6-10.9m in length, increased to 13-22m by late 19th century; e.g., length overall 15.2m, beam 4.88m, depth of hold 2.13m. Other recorded names: **fife, fiffie, Scotchman**. Note also **baldie, lang boomer, mule**.

2. *Scotland, E:* Local name for **ferryboat*** plying between Fife and Dundee.

3. *England, NE:* Those from the Yorkshire coast were rigged with a gaff mainsail, foresail, and jib. Generally called **keel boats***.

fifie skiff *Scotland, E:* Small version of the **fifie***. Used mainly for inshore fishing, catching bottom-feeding fish, long-lining for cod, and creel-hauling for lobsters. Sharp ends, vertical stem and sternpost; straight keel; open. Single mast set a lugsail and jib. Note also **Fife skiff**.

fifie yawl *Scotland, east coast:* Small, inshore line-**fishing boat***. Clinker-built; later, some carvel-planked. Double-ended; stem initially raked forward, later more plumb. After the mid-19th century, adopted a forecastle; remainder open. Outboard rudder; tiller. Raking, strik-able mast stepped in forward quarter; set a dipping lugsail. Some installed an engine early in the 20th century. Reported lengths 4.9-9.1m. Name variant: **Fife yawl**

fifty-fifty Term sometimes applied to a boat that moves equally well by paddle or sail. See also **sailer**.

fiir-røing See **firroring**

filadeira, filadiera See **filadière**

filadière *France, SW:* Fishing and oystering boat of protected waters, especially in the outer Gironde Estuary. Dates from at least the early 16th century. Clinker- or carvel-planked; sharp bow; sharper stern, later rounded; raked stem and sternpost. Pronounced sheer, especially toward the stem, which is considerably higher than the sternpost. Straight keel; bow deeper than the stern; low rise to the floors; rounded bilges. Cuddy forward, short stern deck; side decks on some. Tall, unstayed mast stepped in the eyes; set a very large standing lugsail. Some also used a jib to a small bowsprit and/or a mizzen. Also rowed, with 1-2 pairs of oars. Crew of 2-4. Reported lengths 5.2-8m; e.g.,

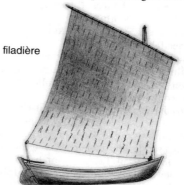

filadière

length 7m, beam 2.3m, depth 1.0m; shallow draft. Other recorded names: **felladière, filadeira, filadiera, filardière, filhadeyre, filladière courant, gabaret***, **lanche***. Note also **yole-filadière**.

file-bottom See **deadrise boat, sharpshooter-2**

filete See **flette**

Filey herring coble See **coble-1**

Filey yawl See **Yorkshire yawl**

filhadeyre See **filadière**

filibote See **vlieboot**

filibustero See **freebooter**

filibustier A class of racing boats. Length overall 4.8m, beam 1.65m. See also **freebooter**.

filibustiere See **freebooter**

filika See **filuka-2**

filipote, filipotto See **vlieboot**

filjuga See **felucca-1**

filladière courant See **filadière**

fillette See **flette**

filuca *Italy, W:* Used for fishing from the Tuscany coast for tunny with a trawl line. See also **feluca**.

filucca See **felucca-1**

filucche, filuche See **feluca**

filuga *Italy, Sardinia, N:* Type of **gozzo***, but term may apply to other boat types elsewhere on the island. Mainly used to fish for coral. Characterized by a sharp cutwater. Stem may be tall and vertical or concave. Sharp stern; outboard rudder; tiller. Those in coral work have a large windlass to handle special equipment. Sailing type sets a lateen sail and a jib to a short bowsprit. Others rowed, employing single tholepins. Spelling variant: pl. **filughe**. Further references: **feluca, felucca-1**

filughe See **filuga**

filughetta Small **felucca***, especially of the 17th century.

filuka 1. *Lebanon:* Beamy, double-ended **fishing boat***. Curved, strongly raked stem; raked sternpost; straight keel; considerable sheer. Decked at ends; outboard rudder; tiller slots through rudderhead. Rowed and sailed; now mainly motorized. Crew of 1-3. Reported lengths 3-9m, beam ca. 3.3m. Spelling variants: **filukah**; pl. **filukata**.
2. *Turkey:* The Turkish **filuka** may be a naval **ship's boat***, or any boat of western design. The **admiral's filuka** was heavily carved and inlaid with mother-of-pearl. Term also applied to the **state barge*** of the sultan during his visits to the **fleet***. Spelling variant: **filika** Further references: **felucca-1, taka-3**

filukah, filukata See **filuka**

filukayı hümayun See **saltanat kayığı**

filyuga See **felucca-1**

fi-man boat See **coble-1d**

Finanzfahrzeug, Finanzschiff See **revenue cutter-1**

Finkenwerder Buttjolle See **Buttjolle**

Finkenwerder Ewer See **Ewer**

Finkenwerder Pfahl-Ewer See **Pfahl-Ewer**

finn A class of single-handed Olympic racing craft. Round bilges; wood or fiberglass; centerboard. Stepped a single adjustable mast well forward, setting a leg-of-mutton sail. Length 4.5m, beam 1.51m, draft with centerboard down 0.86m, weight 150kg. Name variant: **finn dinghy**

Finn boat See **bar boat-2**

finn dinghy See **finn**

Finnmarks-åttring See **åttring-3**

firæring See **firroring**

firanziera See **gondola-4**

fire boat Harbor craft equipped with powerful pumps to provide water to the multiple nozzles used to fight fires on the waterfront and on ships. Some have emergency medical facilities and can undertake rescue work. May have a **ship's boat*** ready for quick launching. Usually multi-engined to permit special maneuverability. Selected recorded names: **barca** (or **battello**) **pompa, barco-bomba, bateau-pompe, blusboot, brandblusboot, buque-bomba, drijvende brandspuit, Feuerlöschboot** (or **schiff**), **fire float, Löschboot, motobarca pompa, motopompa, Pumpenboot** (**dampfer** or **schiff**), **pump vessel, Spritzen Prahm**

fire float See **fire boat**

firemandsfar See **fýramannafar**

fire raft Loaded with various combustibles, the **raft*** was set afire and allowed to drift with the current down onto an enemy vessel. Sometimes towed in chains (or trains), as many as 12. Late 18th-century type reported as 9-10.6m long each, 3.4-3.9m wide. Note also **fire ship**.

fireromsbåt, fire-roring See **firroring**

fire ship Special ship packed with combustible materials that sailed down on an enemy ship disabled in battle, grounded, or trapped in a port, in order to set it afire. **Fire ships** were either built for this purpose or were converted older vessels. Grappling hooks on the yardarms designed to tangle with the rigging of the enemy vessel and hold it alongside. When the **fire ship** was set afire it produced a conflagration on the other vessel. At the last minute, the **fire ship** crew took to their **tender***, which had been towed behind. Used as early as the 12th century, and some limited use into the early 19th century; a few small vessels were employed during the American Revolution. **Fire vessels** were smaller and usually converted merchant ships. A small variation, called a **machine**, was designed to produce an explosion with gunpowder. Other recorded names: **barca** (or **nave**) **incendiaria, brander, brandschip, Brandschiff, bränuare, brûlot*, bruloto, brulotte, brulotto** (pl. **brulotti**). Note also **fire raft**. Further reference: **lightship**

fire tug See **tug-1**

fire vessel See **fire ship**

firewood fleet See **onker**

firgate See **frigate-4**

firilla, firilli See **farella**

firing *Norway, north-central:* In the Trøndelag area, open boats rowed with 4 (*fir*) pairs of oars are locally called **firinger**, while elsewhere they are called **ottringer** (8-oared) (see **åttring**). Engage in herring (**sildegarnsfiring**) and cod fishing, and the largest transport farm produce to Trondheim. Clinker-planked in spruce, with deep keel and stem and sternpost of pine; top strake wide amidships and phases out at the ends; flat floors amidships, soft bilges; strong sheer. Sharp ends; ends relatively plumb with rounded foot; stem taller and may recurve slightly. Compartmented by thwarts into 4 or 5 "rooms." Outboard rudder, with carved head on early boats; long tiller. Some employed 5 pairs of oars. Oarlocks consist of a block forward and tholepin aft. Light mast stepped amidships and stayed forward. Sets a square sail; reef points at top and bottom. Reported lengths 7.5-9.25m; e.g., length 9.2m, beam 2m, depth ca. 0.8m; the **storfiring** (or **lestafiring**) is 9.4-9.5m long and 2.2m wide. The smallest is the **rora-firing**. Spelling variants: **fyreng**, **fyring**; **læstafyreng**; **rora-fyreng**, **rora-fyring**; **storfyring**. Note also **åfjordsbåt**, **firkeiping**, **firroring**, **nordsmørsbåt**. Further reference: **firrroring**

firinger See **firing**

firkata See **frigate-1**

firkeiping *Norway, west coast:* Term given to a sharpended open boat with 4 (*fir*) oarlocks (*keiping*) on each side. Designation may be used in Sognefjord, Sunnfjord, Nordfjord, and Osterfjord. Frequently put to use as a **church boat★**. When sailed, sets a trapezoidal lugsail. One in Osterfjord reported as 6.65m long, 1.88m wide, and 0.68m deep. Note also **sognebåt**.

firMandfar See **firroring**

firmandsfar See **fýramannafar**

firqâta See **frigate-1**

firrøing See **firroring**

firrømming See **firroring-4**

firroring *Norway:* An open boat of the northern half of Norway that was rowed with 4 (*fir*) pairs of oars. Mainly a **fishing boat★**, but also served as a **church boat★** (**kirkebåt★**) and for general transportation. Other recorded names: **fiir-røing**, **firæring**, **fieromsbåt**, **fire-roring**, **firing★**, **firMandfar**, **firrøing**, **fyreng**, **fyring**, **skotkjeiping**, **skotkjeiving**. Note also **åttring**, **firkeiping**.

1. The Nordfjord boat was clinker-built with 4 wide strakes. Sharp ends, the bow fuller; curved stem and sternpost; shallow keel; rounded flaring sides. Curved outboard rudder maneuvered with a slender rightangle tiller. The 8 oars, each held by a loop, worked against a natural crook in the gunwales. Mast stepped amidships; set an asymmetric square sail, tacked at the bow. Average size: 8m long, 1.80m wide, 0.62m deep, draft 2.9m.

2. In Sunnmøre, the original boats were enlarged, but early name retained so that what was called a **firroring** elsewhere was a **seksring** (or 6-oared boat) in Sunnmøre, despite having 8 oars. Sharp ends, with full bow and tapering stern. Clinker-planked.

3. Farther north, in Nordmøre, the clinker-built **firroring** (here spelled **fyring** or **fyreng**) had a short, narrow garboard strake above which were fairly wide strakes. Elongated, curved stem with cutaway forefoot; less raked sternpost. Short, relatively deep keel. Strong sheer at the bow; some had a washstrake aft. Rightangle tiller activated the curved outboard rudder. Oars held with a loop against natural crooks. Asymmetric square sail tacked just in from the bow. Reported lengths 7.5-8.2m; e.g., length 7.64m, beam 1.87m, depth 0.66m.

4. In the Nordland area, this 8-oared boat is known as a **firrømming**, or 4-room boat, the 4 "rooms" being the space between the rowing thwarts. Clinker-planked, with a wide top strake; flaring sides; soft turn of the

bilges. Stem plumb and slightly recurved at the top, sternpost vertical. Outboard rudder worked with a right-angle tiller. Oars pressed against natural crooks. Mast stepped roughly amidships, setting a square sail. Reported lengths 7.3-8m; e.g., length 7.3m, beam 1.8m.

first boat See **canot-2**

first cutter See **quarter boat-1**

Fisaler *Germany, S:* Fast, late 18th-century boat, similar to the Venetian **gondola★** but larger. Part of the **fleet★** that accompanied **Leibschiffe★** on some larger Bavarian lakes, probably serving hunters and beaters. Tall vertical stem and sternpost. Rowed by 3-4 men, standing; stern man stood on a short deck. Note also **fisolera**.

Fischaufkäufersicken See **zig**

Fischerboot See **fishing boat**

Fischerbotter See **botter**

Fischereeber See **Ewer**

Fischereiboot See **fishing boat**

Fischerei-Ever, Fischerei-Ewer See **Ewer**

Fischereifahrzeug See **fishing boat**

Fischereiflotte See **fleet-1**

Fischereikreuzer See **fishery guard ship**

Fischereikutter See **kutter-2**

Fischereischutzboot, Fischereischutzkreuzer, Fischereiüberwachungschiff See **fishery guard ship**

Fischer-Ever, Fisch-Ewer See **Ewer**

Fischerfloss *Austria/Germany:* **Raft★** of early origin, used in fishing on quiet waters. Reported in the 19th century as working with nets on the canals of Ostfriesland in northwest Germany. As recently as the 1980s, a type was used on the Grundlsee in central Austria; 5 logs were secured by pegged crosspieces; bow end tapered and faced with 2 logs; a seat was placed amidships.

Fischerkahn *Germany, N/Lithuania/Poland/Russia, W:* General term for a **fishing boat★**; mostly small, flat-bottomed, and open. May be rowed, sculled, sailed; now mainly motorized. In the Kurski Zaliv (Kurisches Haff) in southwestern Lithuania and western Russia and in the Zalew Wiślany (Frisches Haff) between Poland and western Russia, several similar **Fischerkähne** types are distinguished by the type of gear used, as **ķudilvalts★** (**Keitelkahn**), **Kurnevalts★** (**Kurrenkahn**). Other recorded names: **Faue**, **Fischerkohn**, or **Kohn** at Finkenwerder near Hamburg; **Kurischer Fischerkahn**. Further reference: **żakówka**

Fischerkähne See **Fischerkahn**

Fischerkohn *Germany, W:* Local term for a small, flat-bottomed open boat of the Finkenwerder area on the lower Elbe River. Name variant: **Kohn**. See also **Fischerkahn**.

Fischerkutter See **kutter-2**

Fischerlomme See **żakówka**

Fischernachen See **Nachen-2**

Fischerplätte See **Plätte-3**

Fischerplättel See **Plätte-2**

Fischerquase See **Quase**

Fischerquatze See **Quatze**

Fischersicken See **zig**

Fischerslup See **Helgoländer Schlup, Schlup-1**

Fischerzille *Austria, E:* Small, **punt★**-like fishing craft that worked on the Danube in the Vienna area.

Fischerzille

Fisherman anchored and used handlines. Flat bottom, rising bow cut square, wider square stern, straight sides. Midship area covered by an open-sided shelter. Name variant: **Donaufischerzille**. Note also **Zille**. Further reference: **Waidzille**

Fisch-Ewer See **Ewer**

Fischhändlersicken See **zig**

Fischhuker See **vishoeker**

Fischjäger See **jäger**

Fischkasten See **fish car**

Fischkutter See **kutter-2**

Fischsicken See **zig**

Fischtransporter See **fish carrier-1**

fish boat *United States:* **1.** On Chesapeake Bay, some large **fishing boats★** tow a **fish boat** to hold live fish. Name variant: **fish box★**. Note also **fish car**.
2. On the Louisiana bayous, **luggers★** were sometimes merely called **fish boats**.
3. Term given to the small **submarine** used in Charleston, South Carolina, in 1864 in an effort to break the Union blockade of the harbor. Propelled by a human-powered crankshaft. A spar torpedo projected from the bow. Speed ca. 2.5 knots.

fish box *Canada, E/United Kingdom, W:* Term used by merchant seamen for the small vessels, usually **schooners★**, that carried salted fish from Newfoundland to southern Europe, returning with salt. Some sailed to the West Indies and South America. Owned by merchants from western England, northern Wales, and Newfoundland; operated mainly in the 2nd half of the 19th century. Called **fruiters** when they carried fruit from the Mediterranean. Name variant: **Newfoundland fish box**. Note also **fruit schooner, sack ship**. Further references: **fish boat-1, fish car, tow car**

fish car A box, sometimes boat-shaped, or a derelict boat, which is flooded with water by means of holes or slits along the sides and on the bottom. May be carried aboard a **fishing boat★** and floated alongside while fishing; may be independent and serve to transport the catch to market or to a processing plant; or may be a holding tank from which fish are sold or in which fish are placed to mature. Some float, others submerged by weights. Other recorded names: **caisse à poisson, caja de pescado, canastra, caixa, cassa per pesce, coffre à poisson, Fischkast(en), Fischkiste, fish box★, fiske-kasse, fishing-crib, live boat** (or **car**), **viskist**. Note also **barka-3, bata-1, coff, corf, eel boat, fish boat, fisherman's car, jonque vivier, kaar, maròta, sumbad, sump, tow smack, vivero, vivier-2, vivier flottant**. Further reference: **tow car**

fish carrier **1.** Used exclusively to transport fish. Modern vessels large and equipped with refrigerated holds. Small types lack refrigeration, but quickly transport iced fish to port. The **live-fish transporter** carries fish live in special tanks. Other recorded names: **carguero de pescado, Fischtransporter, fisketransportskib, nave per transporto di pesce, navio de transporte de peixe, navire transporteur de poisson, transporter de poisson, vistransportschip**. Note also **carry-away boat**.
2. *Canada:* Small **tender★** that collects the catch from a **fishing fleet★** and transfers it to shore. Name variant: **chasseur★**. Note also **packer-1**.
Further references: **jäger, jagger, liu wang chuan, sekochi-5a**

fish-carrying boat *England, E:* Designed to transfer the catch from a North Sea **trawler★** to a waiting motorized vessel that, in turn, carried the fish to market; belonged to the **trawler**. Special air tanks provided buoyancy to the heavily laden boat. Clinker-built. Reported lengths 5.2-5.5m, beam 2m, depths 0.75-0.83m. Note also **fleeter**.

fish collector See **carrying boat**

fish dhow See **bedan-2**

fisher bott See **fishing boat**

fisherman **1.** *Canada, E/United States, NE:* Term often given to Canadian and United States **schooners★** specially designed to fish on the Grand Banks off Newfoundland. Other recorded names: **Bank(s) fisherman, fisherman schooner**; by French Canadians: **américaine, goélette américaine, goélette pêcheuse, pêcheuse**. Note also **banker, market boat-3, salt fisherman**.
2. *United Kingdom:* During World Wars I and II, **trawlers★** and **drifters★** that were actively engaged in fishing were called **fishermen**. Those engaged in anti-**submarine** or mine demolition work were called **white ensigns**.
Further reference: **fishing boat**

fisherman's car *United States, NE:* Container for holding fish and crustaceans alive at market or while awaiting transfer to market or canneries. Lobster fishermen may use old leaky boats, especially **dories**, for this purpose, or they may employ specially built slatted boxes ca. 4.6m by 3.1m by 1.0m. Staked out in shallow water, some on the bottom, others floating. Other recorded names: **car, floating car, lobster car**. Note also **fish car**.

fisherman schooner See **fisherman-1**

fisherman's dory See **Banks dory, dory-1**

Fisherman's Reserve Service See **gumboot**

fisherman's skiff See **Mackinaw boat-1**

fishery control vessel, fishery cruiser See **fishery guard ship**

fishery guard ship Designated for surveillance of fishing activities in territorial waters and to preserve order in the **fishing fleets★**. May be lightly armed. Selected recorded names: **bateau de patrouille, bogeyman, (buque** or **nave) guardapesca, Fischereikreuzer, Fischereischutzboot, Fischereischutzkreuzer, Fischereiüberwachungschiff, fisheries protection vessel, fishery control vessel, fishery (protection) cruiser, fishery patrol ship, fiskeri inspektions skib, Government boat, guardapescas, navio (lancha) de**

fiscalização da pesca, navire garde-pêche (or patrouilleur), visserijinspectievaartuig, visserijpatrouillevaartuig, watcher
fishery patrol ship, fishery protection cruiser, fishery protection vessel See **fishery guard ship**
fishery vessel See **fishing boat**
fish hoy See **Southampton hoy**
fishing barge See **barge-7**
fishing bateau See **Chesapeake Bay fishing bateau**
fishing boat In the broadest sense, any boat or vessel that engages primarily in catching fish for profit. Most designed and equipped to meet the needs of a particular type of fishing. Sometimes the term limited to vessels that fish at sea, and sometimes excludes those engaged mainly in whaling or sealing. Term may include vessels that process the catch and those that transport the catch to shore. Other selected names: **barca peschereccia, barco pescador (de pesca), bateau de pêche, bateau pêcheur, battello da pesca, bote de pescador, buque pesquero (de pesca), embarcação de pesca, embarcation de pêche, Fischer(ei)boot, Fischereifahrzeug, fish boat★, fisher bott, fisherman★, fishery vessel, fiskarebåt, fiskerbaad (or båt), fysher boate, fysherbot, łódź rybacka, nave da pesca, navio de pesca, pêcheur, peschereccio, pesquero, promyslovoe sudno, ribarica, rybach'ya lodka, rybač'ja lodka, rybolovnoe sudno, vischboot, visserman, vissersboot**. Note also **fiski-skip**.
fishing-crib See **fish car**
fishing fleet See **fleet-1**
fishing shallop See **shallop-4**
fishing skiff *Canada, E:* In Newfoundland, an open boat used to set and haul nets or traps. Length to 9.14m. See also **Chesapeake Bay log canoe-3, Mackinaw boat-1.**
fishing smack *British Isles:* Generalized term for a decked, fore-and-aft-rigged vessel that engaged mainly in trawling, as distinguished from drifting. Worked mainly during the 19th and into the 20th century. Hulls varied, but the stem was mostly straight or slightly curved and stern was rounded or had a raked transom. Some had live wells. Most **cutter★**-rigged, but as they worked farther from home ports, they became mainly **ketch★**-rigged. Those with anchor chain fairleads to starboard were called **right-handed smacks**; those with fairleads to port were **left-handed smacks**. See also **smack**.
fishing tug See **gill net tug**
fish lighter See **Potomac fish lighter, sharpie-2**
Fishmongers' Company barge *England, SE:* One of the ceremonial **barges★** of the Livery Companies of London. Used until the mid-19th century to accompany royalty downriver, to participate in the annual Lord Mayor's procession, and for outings of company members. The flag-bedecked **barge** had a long, stepped, canopied cabin over most of the hull, a high, ornate stern, and an inboard rudder. Rowed from the open bow area. Note also **barge-3, Stationers' barge.**
fish packer See **carrying boat**
fish skiff See **pound net boat-1**
fish tug See **gill net tug**

fishwheel scow *United States, NW:* Wooden **scow★** with a wheel at the stern activated by the current. Stationed at a projecting point in the Columbia River to catch salmon swimming upstream. **Scow** secured to the bank and shifted as desired. Fish dropped from the wheel's net into a box at the stern. Scow cross-planked on bottom and deck, square ends. Awning protected crew and fish. Wheel held out from the **scow** by 6m-long supports. Name variant: **scow wheel**. Note also **pick-up boat.**
fiskabåt See **gotlandssnipa**
fiskarbåt See **fiskebåt-1**
fiskarebåt See **fishing boat**
fiskebåt 1. Swedish term for a **fishing boat★**. Spelling variants: **fiskarbåt, fiskefartyg**
  2. *Finland, SE/Russia, W:* Built on the north shore of the Gulf of Finland, catching mainly whitefish. Clinker planking, wide flare from keel to gunwale. Strongly raked stem, sharp stern, strong sheer. Reported lengths 6-9m. Name variant: **flatbåt**
  3. *Sweden, SE:* Heavy, decked, clinker-built boat. Curved and raked stem and sternpost; drag to straight keel; soft turn of the bilges. Outboard rudder; short tiller; standing well. Wide side decks; low cabin roof aft. Loose-footed, boomed gaff sail; topsail, staysail, jib to bowsprit. 1888 boat 9.5m long. Name variant: **däcksbåt★**
fiskebåt See **fiskiskip-2**
fiske-duggur See **dugga**
fiskefläde See **fleet-1**
fiskerbåt See **fiskiskip-2**
fiskerfartøj See **fishing boat**
fiskerflåde See **fleet-1**
fiskehukkert See **hukkert**
fiskejolle See **jolle-1**
fiskekutter See **kutter-5**
fiskekvass *Sweden:* Small **fishing boat★** designed to transport live fish. Some specialized in fishing for and transporting eels. One or 2 masts. Note also **kvass.**
fiskeöka See **sköteka**
fiskerbaad See **fishing boat, fiskiskip-2**
fiskerbåt See **fishing boat, fiskskip-2**
fiskerfartøj See **fishing boat**
fiskefartyg See **fiskebåt-1**
fiskerhukkert See **hukkert**
fiskeri inspektions skib See **fishery guard ship**
fiskerkvase See **kvase**
fiskesmakke See **smakke-4**
fisketransportskib See **fish carrier-1**
fiskibátr See **fiskiskip-2**
fiskiskip 1. Icelandic term for a **fishing boat★**.
  2. Fishing boat in Norwegian. Spelling variants: **fiskerbaad, fiske(r)båt**; Old Norse: **fiskibátr**
fiskiskúta See **skuta-2**
fisksump See **sump**
fisolara, fisolare, fisoler See **fisolera**
fisolera *Italy, NE:* 16th- and 17th-century waterfowling boat of the Lagoon of Venice used especially to hunt the elusive *fisolo* (a shoal-nesting bird with a tapering body). Sometimes participated in regattas. Long, slender, and extremely light. Sharp at the ends, with curved stem and sternpost that turned up sharply;

open. Hunter shot with bow and arrow from the bow or rested a gun on the stemhead. Rowed, by 3-8 rowers, standing. Length ca. 5.5m, beam 1.0m. Spelling variants: **fisolara, fisoler(o), fisoli(era), fusoliera**; pl. **fisolare, fisolere**. Note also **Fisaler**.

fisolere, fisolero, fisoli, fisoliera See **fisolera**

five-board bottom See **wu ban**

five-fathom canoe See **canot du maître**

five-finger dredger *England, E:* A **smack**★ that sailed out of Tollesbury in Essex to dredge for starfish, which were used as fertilizer. About 90 worked until World War I and a few to World War II. Employed 4 while dredging.

five-handed bateau See **bateau-7e**

five-handed boat *United States, E:* Sharp-ended boat of Cape Cod and Maine. When name is applied to a **whaleboat**★, there are 4 rowing thwarts, the 5th man being the mate; on a **six-handed boat**, there are 5 rowing thwarts.

five-man boat See **skothomlin, Yorkshire lugger**

five-man coble See **coble-1d**

five-men boat See **coble-1d, cod smack-2**

five-plank junk See **wu ban**

fixed tub See **tub-2**

fjæring See **færing**

fjordajakt, fjordajekt See **jakt-2**

fjouwer-acht tjotter See **tjotter**

flaade See **fleet, raft-2**

Flachboot See **flat, Sohlboot**

fladbåd *Denmark, W:* Flat-bottomed, beamy **barge**★-like craft used to unload **coasters**★, **smacks**★, and stranded ships lying off the flat beaches of northwestern Jutland. Extinct as a working vessel. Clinker-built double-ender, with very bluff bows; massive stem and sternpost; strongly curved stem; straight and sharply raked sternpost. Thwarts heavily braced. Rudder also

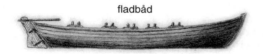

fladbåd

raked, with flare at the lower end; tiller set over rudderhead. Coated with tar. Rowed with 4 pairs of oars. Length 10m, beam 3.4m, depth 0.94m, draft 0.3m.

flåde See **fleet**

flag galley See **capitane**

Flaggschiff, Flaggenschiff, flagmanskiy korabl' See **flagship**

flagship **1.** In navies, this is the command ship of a **fleet**★ or squadron. Carries the highest ranking officer, flies his flag or command, and is provided with suitable accommodations for him and his staff.

2. In the merchant marine, the **flagship** is the most important or famous ship of a shipping company, and is usually commanded by the senior captain, often known as the commodore.

Other selected names: **admiral(e), Admirals(s)chiff, admiral's ship, a(d)miraalschip, amiral(e), amiraljica, amiralskepp, ammiraglia, bâtiment amiral, buque almirante (amirante** or **insignia), Flagg(en)schiff, flagg-skeppet, flagmanskiy korabl',**

flagskibet, nauarchis, nave ammiraglia, navio capitânia (or **comandante), navire amiral** (or **major), praetoris navis, vaisseau amiral** (or **commandant), vascello ammiralgio, vlagg(e)schip**. In early Spanish, **capitana** referred to the supreme commander's vessel, **almiranta** to the vice-admiral's ship. Note also **bâtard-1, capitane, real-1**.

flag-skeppet, flagskibet See **flagship**

flakajekt See **jekt**

Flamänder See **péniche-4a, waal**

flamart, flambar, flambard See **flambart**

flambart 1. *France:* In the late 14th and early 15th centuries the **flambart** was reported as being in the service of **nefs**★, often being towed behind. Sturdy, clinker-built boat; employed numerous oars.

2. *France, N:* In Normandy, on the Manche and Baie de Seine coasts, **flambart** became more a type of rigging than a type of hull. Mainly of the 18th-19th cen-

flambart-2

turies. Two masts, although some single-masted. Some sprit-rigged, most lug-rigged; later boats set a loose-footed, boomed gaff mainsail and lug foresail; topsail on the main common. Foremast might be close to the bow; 1-2 headsails to a long bowsprit. Open or decked. Raked sharp or square stern; plumb stem. Clinker-planked. Deep drag to keel on some. Outboard rudder. Used mainly for fishing, especially for mackerel and herring. Some were **pilot boats**★. In the late 19th century, built as **yachts**★; now enjoying a revival as a pleasure craft. **Fishing boats**★ employed 3-4 in crew. Reported lengths 3.7-13m; e.g., length 8m, beam 2.6m, depth 1.3m.

Other recorded names: **batiau flambar, bateaulx flobars, batel flambart, flamart, flambar(d), flobard, flobart**★; **flambillon** (dim.)

flambart goemonier See **gabare à goémon**

flambillon See **flambart**

Flanders galley Especially large vessel of Venetian origin that engaged in trade with England and Flanders from the 14th to the 16th century. Manned by as many as 180 oarsmen. Also sailed, generally setting 3 lateen sails. Being subject to piracy, the **fleet**★ carried 30 archers. Employed quarter rudders. Length on deck 41.4m, beam on bottom 3.52m, depth 2m. Other selected names: **Flemish galley, galea de Fiandra, galère de Flandre**. Note also **galeazza, galley**.

flat 1. Term loosely applied to a **lighter*** or **dumb barge*** engaged in river or harbor work. Sometimes applied to a craft with floors flat enough to enable it to sit upright when grounded by low tide. Term has also been used for seagoing craft up to ca. 190t. Low freeboard, broad beam, shallow draft. Other selected names: **chata de alijar, Flachboot, flatt, Plattboot, Plätte***
2. *Canada, E:* **a.** Flat-bottomed **rowboat*** used in late 18th-century Newfoundland fisheries. Brought from France knocked down. Square ends; crew of 2. Term still used by fishermen for a **tender***, and sometimes for a **fishing boat*** employed in protected waters; square stern; length ca. 3m. **b.** General-purpose, oystering, lobstering, and sealing boat used in the southern part of the Gulf of St. Lawrence and around Prince Edward Island. Those at the Magdalen Islands have

flat-2b

been described as clinker-built, generally of spruce; one-piece frames from gunwale to gunwale. Narrow bottom, longitudinally planked with birch; flat transversely; fore-and-aft rocker; bottom may extend slightly beyond garboard strakes and stem and sternpost, but this feature was lacking on Prince Edward Island **flats**. Sharp bow, curved stem; broad transom stern, some on 2 planes, lower 15cm angling more sharply than the remainder; planked-up or box skeg. Runners often added to aid in crossing ice when sealing. Rowed. One-man craft; 4-5 needed when sealing. Reported lengths 3-4.3m; e.g., length 3.94m, beam 1.22m, depth 0.4m. Other selected names: **Magdalen Islands flat** (or **ice boat**). Note also **canot à glace**. **c.** On the Gaspé Peninsula in southern Gulf of St. Lawrence, the **flat** was an open, heavily built fishing and general-purpose boat. Flat, almond-shaped bottom, planked fore-and-aft. Curved sides, planking overlapping; floor frames and ribs alternated. Lightly curved stem; strongly raked, narrow V-transom, sculling notch. Mainly rowed, 3 pairs of double tholepins. Length 5.56m, beam 1.52m, depth 0.38m. Name variant: **Gaspé flat. d.** The fishing and lobstering **flat** of the Lahave Islands off the east coast of Nova Scotia was lapstrake-built, with a wide raked transom, onto which the rudder was hung. Centerboard, raised or lowered by an iron staff; washboards. Two masts, initially sprit-rigged, later gaff-rigged. Length ca. 5.5m.
3. *England:* **a.** Shallow **punt*** or **raft*** used for canal and lock maintenance or for work alongside a larger vessel when making repairs or painting. **b.** A **flat** was a towed or sailing **barge***, mostly on rivers or canals, but some large vessels went into open waters. Flat bottom; transom stern initially, double-ended by mid-19th century. The canal **flats** were unrigged. The river **flats** were square-rigged at the beginning of the 19th century, then sprit-rigged with forestaysail, then gaff-rigged. Those on the River Severn were designed for

shallow-water work, drawing only 46cm. Reported lengths 13-22m; the **flats** of the Bridgewater Canal in west-central England were 21m long and 4.3m wide. Note also **Mersey flat, Weaver flat.**
4. *India:* In the late 19th century, 1-2 **flats** would be conveyed upstream by **side wheelers** (see **paddle boat-3**) on rivers such as the Bramaphutra; others were self-propelled river **steamers**. Mainly collected cargo for export. Towed or lashed to the **steamer's** sides by strong hawsers and wire cables, creating one extremely wide craft. Similar to the **steamer**, but often bluffer at the bow. Slightly cambered deck fore-and-aft; might have a fixed awning. Reported lengths 36-40m, widths 6.7-7.3m, draft loaded ca. 0.9m; one was 76m long. Note also **accommodation boat, flat-5.**
5. *Myanmar:* Shallow-draft craft towed by a **steamer** on the Ahrewady (Irrawaddy) River, serving as a bazaar to citizens of river towns in Upper Burma. Some were hulls of old **steamers**, divested of their engine, boiler, and upper works. The **bazaar flats** (or **boats**) were divided into stalls, which were rented by shopkeepers who lived aboard with their families. Special types transported bullocks and buffaloes, and a few carried elephants. A **steamer** might have a **flat** along each side. Note also **flat-4.**
6. *United States:* **a.** In the early 19th century, **flats** moved freight on the Merrimack River in New Hampshire and through the Middlesex Canal in northeastern Massachusetts. Shallow craft; bottom curved up to square ends; vertical sides; flat sheer. Drifted on the river, controlled by sweeps both forward and aft; towed by mules or horses on the canal. Sometimes set a square sail. Cap. 20-25t. Name variant: **New Hampshire flatboat. b.** The **flat** of the Mohawk River in central New York State in the early 19th century was used in quieter stretches. Square ends; flat bottom, transversely planked; low sides. Sometimes sailed. Name variant: **Mohawk flat. c.** Some **flats** were modified to serve as **ferryboats***, as on the Delaware River. Long and narrow; vertical sides, ca. 30cm high. Flat bottom sloped up at the ends to the height of the sides. A hinged flap at one or both ends was turned inboard during the crossing and was lowered onto the riverbank on landing. Steered with sweeps. Usually poled; some utilized the river's current to ferry across while secured to a rope or wire stretched across the river. Size and proportions varied with requirements of a particular crossing. **d.** The 19th-century **cargo flats** of the James River and Kanawha Canal in central Virginia were long and narrow. They traveled in groups of 3-4. Sharp bow; low cabin aft. Crew of 3, 2 to pole and one to steer. Name variant: **bateau***. Note also **James River bateau. e.** On Chesapeake Bay the **cargo flat** was popular until the 1860s. Blunt, rounded ends; flat bottom; ceiled. Platform at each end; leeboards. **Sloop***- or **schooner***-rigged. Also used sweeps. **f.** The **flats** in the lowlands of North Carolina served not only as **ferryboats** but provided produce, timber, and naval stores to river ports downstream. Some, by the early 1900s, were decked over to the height of the sides, with internal girders providing more strength. Floated downstream, aided by long oars. Those moving back

upstream often warped from tree to tree, aided by poling. Reported lengths 9-12m, beam varied according to use; an early **ferry*** on the Trent River was 9.4m long and 3.6m wide. **g.** The term **flat** was given to a large **barge** of the Black River basin in central Louisiana. One function was to transfer livestock from flooded to higher land. Rowed by 4-8 seated or standing oarsmen. The 2.4m-long oars were tied to a plank that extended gunwale to gunwale. By 1910, used in seine fishing.

Further references: **baggeraak**, **covered sled**, **flatboat**, **flatboat-6**, **punt-1**, **scow-11**, **speedboat-2**

flatbåt See **fiskebåt-2**

flat batteau *Canada, E:* Term applied to a late 17th-century craft built to cross the St. Lawrence River. Planked, flat-bottomed, double-ended boat of the **batteau*** type. Some equipped with cannon. Loaded disp. ca. 2-3t.

flatboat **1.** A flat-bottomed, square-ended craft used mainly on shallow, protected waters. Often served as a **ferry***, being rowed, pushed by long poles from the stern, or pulled across by a rope or chain.
2. A craft used for amphibious operations during the 18th and early 19th centuries. Flat bottom; rowed or lug-rigged. Capacity to 30 men plus light field artillery. In northern France in the mid-18th century, they were ca. 30m long, 8m wide, and 2.5m deep. The British **flatboats** of the same period were clinker-built, ca. 11.6m long, 3.4m wide, shallow draft, and carried 50-60 men.
3. *Canada, central:* The Canadian **flatboat** of the 19th century was an inland freight carrier. Sharp ends, flat bottom. Those on the Red River south of Lake Winnipeg were rectangular in shape, ca. 4.6m long and 2.4m wide. Square ends, very low sides. Run in trains; one might have a low-peaked house covering the hull. Maneuvered by sweeps.
4. *United States, central:* **a.** Boxy, flat-bottomed, keelless boat used on the larger rivers by early settlers and traders. Term often used interchangeably with **ark***,

flatboat-4a

broadhorn*, **Kentucky boat** (if destination was along the Ohio River), **New Orleans boat** (when destination was along the Mississippi River); their differences, if any, are now blurred by time. Developed toward the end of the 18th century and used until the latter part of the 19th century in a few areas. Limited use as a cargo craft reported on the upper St. Lawrence River. Many later boats carried livestock to market. Some served as itinerant stores (**store boat***) or for floating tradesmen—cobblers, barbers, tinsmiths, etc. Many ended their days as floating businesses serving those living along the rivers. Built of heavy squared timbers, secured by treenails and strengthened with sleepers; sides added on, 30-60cm high; bow raked. The **ark** was sometimes distinguished by having sharp

ends. Some were roughly built with tent-like shelters; others had substantial structures that housed families and livestock, and were built to withstand attacks from Native Americans. Guided downstream with long oars (called broadhorns), a stern sweep (as long as 12m), and a short bow oar. Those not broken up at their destination returned upstream with double the crew to aid in poling, sailing, and tracking from shore. Occasionally sailed downstream, using 1-2 square sails; some **schooner***-rigged. A few were propelled by a wheel driven by cattle en route to the New Orleans market. **Cargo flatboats** required a minimum of 5 in crew. Dimensions dictated by river conditions, distance to be traveled, family size and/or wealth, and cargo requirements; reported lengths 7-46m, the larger being the **arks**; typically 16.8m long, 5m wide, depth ca. 1.0m, draft 0.9m. Other recorded names: **Arkansas boat**, **box**, **broadbeam**, **broadhorse**, **cattle boat**, **chicken thief**, **family boat***, **flour boat**, **horse boat***, **Kentucky broadhorn** (or **flat**), **Louisiana boat**, **Mississippi boat**, **Missouri boat**, **New Orleans broadhorn**, **Orleans boat***, **produce boat**, **raft***, **shanty boat***, **sneak boat***, **sneakbox**, **tobacco boat***. Note also **keelboat-4**, **shed**. **b.** Special **flatboats** moved barrels of oil on the Allegheny River and Oil Creek in western Pennsylvania to Pittsburgh beginning in 1860. Flat bottom, square ends, low flat sides. Compartmented by numerous bulkheads. Floated downstream at high water or with the assistance of artificial freshets.
5. *United States, SE:* Important in the 18th and 19th centuries for transporting to coastal towns such products as rice and cotton from inland plantations, deerskins for leather, and barrels of turpentine. Some were merely built-up **rafts***, while others, such as the **cotton boxes** (or **box boats***) of the Santee Canal in South Carolina, were high-sided to contain their cargo. The **cotton boxes** were designed to nest inside each other to save tolls on the return trip. In South Carolina, cross-planked flat bottom, with stringers along chine; raking ends also cross-planked. Those that worked in tidal areas were more boat-shaped and were often sailed, sometimes being **schooner***-rigged; some **riverboats*** might set a square or spritsail to a stubby mast. Those working above tidal waters were poled or towed by **steamboats**, and were called **tow boats***. By the mid-19th century, many **flatboats** were powered. Reported lengths 12-15m, beam 4.6m; **cotton boxes** ca. 18m long and 7.6m wide (15m by 3m on the Santee Canal); shallow draft. Muskogee tribesmen of this area called the **flatboat** a **perro-tvpékse**. Note also **plantation boat**.
6. *United States, south-central:* **a.** In the early 18th century, **flatboats** built by the French at Biloxi and Mobile transported inhabitants and supplies throughout the lower Louisiana territory. Those built in 1738 were 12m long, 2.7m wide, and 1.2m deep. Name variants: **bateau***, **bateau plat**, **double-ender***, **flat***, **paddle boat***, **skiff***. **b.** Small, roughly constructed boat currently in use, especially by fishermen, on the Mississippi River and the Louisiana bayous. Flat bottom, curved up at the bow, longitudinally planked;

now of plywood. Slightly raked flat bow; somewhat wider transom stern; sides nearly parallel, but flared. Heavy gunwales; strengthened by 3-piece frames. Fish well common. May carry a **pirogue**★ for work in densely wooded parts of the swamps. Initially designed to be rowed; now employs an outboard motor; sometimes still rowed. Average 3.66-4.27m long, 0.91m wide.

7. *United States, north-central:* An amphibious type of **flatboat** of the upper Mississippi is able to traverse both water and ice. Sides and bottom covered with sheet metal. Square ends; runners on the strongly curved bottom. Small cabin. Employs an airplane engine and propeller.

8. *United States, NE:* **Flatboats** provided an important means of merchandise transport in the 18th and early 19th centuries on the Connecticut River from Hartford, Connecticut, to the Wells River in Vermont. Square-ended, the bow overhanging; low parallel sides. Might have a low cabin athwartships at the stern. Poled upstream, drifted downstream. Averaged 21m in length; cap. 30t.
Other selected names: **flat**★, **flatt**, **Plattboot**. Further references: **batteau-4b, bian zi, gundalow-2, King's boat, Koshkonong flatboat, Parrett flatner, shanty boat, shed, yu maya**

flatbottnad eka See **eka-1**

flatbottom A boat with a flat bottom; especially suitable for shallow, quiet waters. Rowed, poled, sailed. Name variants: **platbodem, Platbodenboot**. See also **canoe-4, mussel boat-4**.

flat-bottomed boat See **guard boat-3a, ping di chuan**

flatchie See **North Isles yole**

flåte See **fleet**

flateka See **eka-1, pråmm-2**

flatesk See **eka**

flathead See **zeeschouw**

flat iron **1.** A shallow-draft naval vessel designed for river and coastal work. Name variant: **river gunboat**. Note also **gunboat, monitor**.
2. May describe a vessel that lies low in the water. Further reference: **collier-2**

flatiron boat See **New Haven flatiron boat**

flatiron skiff *United States:* Easily constructed, general utility boat shaped like an old-fashioned flatiron. Best suited for protected waters. Flat bottom, planked athwartships or longitudinally, may have a slight rocker aft; may have a small skeg. Built upside down, the sides joined to the completed bottom; often 2 planks to each side; sides flare, especially from amidships aft to the stern. Mainly plumb, sharp bow; square raked transom. Most open, but some half-decked or with a foredeck. Rowed, sculled, sailed, or may use an outboard motor. Rudder on those that sail. Rig varies with size and purpose of the boat. Some **sloop**★-rigged; others use a single sail; a few 2-masted. Reported lengths 1.8-6m; beam ca. one-third the length. Other recorded names: **flattie**★, **flattie skiff**★, **sharp-bowed skiff, sharpie rowboat**. Note also **New Haven flatiron boat, Noank sharpie**. Further reference: **sharpie-1, sharpie-2**

flatner *England, W:* Term given to a group of small flat-bottomed boats, especially in the Somerset area bordering the Bristol Channel. No longer built as a working craft. Many had a retractable board or a deep rudder to combat leeway when sailing. Shallow draft. Name variant: **Somerset flatner**. Note also **Parrett flatner, Weston-super-Mare flatner**. Further reference: **Bridgwater boat**

flats boat Used for fishing in shallow water. Employs an outboard motor. Length ca. 4.9m.

flatt See **flat-1, flatboat**

flatte *Canada, E:* Used in seal netting on the north shore of the lower St. Lawrence River. Designed to be winched ashore on a log ramp across low riverbanks. Beamy forward, tapering aft; shallow transom, deadwood below; flat bottom. Propelled by 3 oars, 2 to port forward, a much longer one to starboard aft. On the starboard side, 2 blocks on the gunwale in front of the oarsman for the cable used in raising the net. A large **flatte** can carry 20 seals. See also **flattie**.

flattener See **Parrett flatner**

flattie General term sometimes given to flat-bottomed craft, but may be limited to a flat-bottomed **dinghy**★.
1. *Australia, NE:* In Queensland, any **dinghy** is usually called a **flattie**.
2. *England, E:* Sailing boat used on creeks and estuaries, especially on the Norfolk Broads and in Essex. Shallow draft. The **Brancaster flatty** fished for whelks and mussels in this area on the north Norfolk coast. Heavily constructed, with clinker planking; wineglass transom; fairly straight stem, the lower part sheathed; steam-bent timbers. Open, bulkhead in after third. Usually towed behind a larger boat to the site. Mainly rowed, using a single pair of oars, but could be sailed, albeit poorly. Length ca. 4.6m, beam 1.5m. Other recorded names: **Brancaster** or **Norfolk canoe**. Note also **canoe-4**.
3. *England, W:* Term sometimes given to a **barge**★-like, shallow-draft **steamer** used on the River Mersey.
4. *United States, E:* **Sharpie**★-type boat that mainly transported produce on tributary streams of Chesapeake Bay until the 1860s. Later, the larger ones dredged oysters; the smaller engaged in crabbing; some, unrigged, were used by market gunners. A few still work. Bottom flat forward, becoming V-bottomed aft of amidships; bottom planking fore-and-aft, herringbone, or combination of the two; frequently had a plank keelson; deep drag aft. Straight stem; straight flaring sides; wide, raked transom; strengthening provided by heavy bulkhead just forward of the mast. Centerboard; outboard rudder. Half-decked; occasionally a cabin. Originally a gaff-rigged **sloop**★ (the **Hampton flattie** or **flatte**); boom laced to mainsail; jib generally tacked to stemhead. After 1890s leg-of-mutton sail adopted, extended by a horizontal sprit; similar small sail forward; called a **stick-up flattie** (or **stick-up skiff**). A few crabbing boats carried a single spritsail. Single rowing station. Crew of 4-6. Lengths 4.3-12.2m; e.g., length 8.4m, beam 2.6m, depth ca. 1.4m, draft aft with centerboard up 0.7m. Other recorded names: **Chesapeake flattie**,

flattie sloop, handscrape flattie, Norfolk flatte. Note also **flattie skiff**.

Spelling variants: **flatte★, flatty**. Note also **flat, flatboat, flatner**. Further references: **canoe-5, flatiron skiff, sharpie-3**

flattie skiff *United States, E:* Sprit-rigged **flattie★** that engaged in oystering, crabbing, and transporting produce on Chesapeake Bay. Developed in the late 1890s with a so-called stick-up rig. Leg-of-mutton sail with a horizontal sprit set to an aft-raking mainmast. Small forward-raking mast stepped at the bow, setting a small leg-of-mutton sail that sheeted aft to the helmsman. Mainmast stepped through a thwart in forward quarter. Wide flat bottom, sharp bow, wide transom, deadrise aft. Short foredeck and side decks. Outboard rudder; tiller; centerboard. Could be sailed singlehanded. Length ca. 5m. See also **flatiron skiff**.

flattie sloop See **flattie-4**

flatty See **flattie, Watchet flatty**

flaut, flauta, flàuto See **flûte**

flecte See **flette**

flee-boate See **flyboat**

fleet 1. At one time **fleet** was a generic for **ship★** or **vessel★**. May now be a group of vessels engaging in a particular activity, e.g., **whaling fleet**. May apply to a group of pleasure craft traveling together. May also refer to the collective vessels, both naval and commercial, of a particular country, or to those of a single company. Other recorded names: **Fischereiflotte, fishing fleet, fiske(r)fläde, flota pesquera, flotille de pêche, flotta da pesca, flotte de pêche, flottiglia da pesca, frota de pesca, vissersvloot**
2. *Naval:* **a.** Early designation for a number of naval vessels carrying armed men, under a single command. **b.** More recently, a **fleet** has been a number of armed ships, each under its own commanding officer, the group of ships under orders from an admiral-in-chief. **c.** Collective term for a country's naval vessels, or to any part of it employed in a particular service or expedition.
3. *United States:* In general, a **fleet** was composed of several **rafts★** of lumber fastened together to be floated down a river.
4. *United States, central:* A 19th-century **lumber** or **timber raft★** on the Allegheny River in western Pennsylvania. Composed of platforms, 1.1 square meters, which in turn were coupled tandem to form **pieces**, 22m or 28m long; 4 **pieces** then made up the **fleet**, 9.7m wide and 45m or 56m long. On reaching Pittsburgh, 4 or more of these were assembled into a single **raft** for the trip down the Ohio River, covering nearly one hectare. Each had a hut for shelter. The small **pieces** on the tributaries employed a sweep at each end, pulled by 2 men.

Other recorded names: **fflotte, flaade, flåde, flåte, fleete, fleot(e), flete, flote★, flo(i)t, flot(t)a, Flotte★, flotti, frot(t)a, laivasto, vloot**. Further references: **timber raft-2a, timber raft-3**

fleete See **fleet**

fleeter *United Kingdom:* **Fishing boat★** that operated as part of a fishing **fleet★**. Might consist of 50-60 vessels.

Those on the North Sea were **steam trawlers★** that stayed on the fishing grounds for extended periods, delivering the catch in boxes to a **fish-carrying boat★** for transport to market. Activity directed by an admiral and centered around a **mark boat★**. Name variants: **boxman, Flotillenboot**

Fleet trow *England, SW:* Small flat-bottomed **rowing boat★** used for fishing, ferrying the catch, and as a **gun punt★** on the Fleets, the lagoon backing Chesil Bank (Beach). Narrow, tucked-up transom stern or sharpended; lapped strakes, flared sides. False keels at

Fleet trow

chines and 1-2 along the bottom. Propelled with a pole used both to punt and to paddle; also used up to 3 pairs of balanced oars, working against single metal tholepins. Reported lengths 3-5.5m, beam ca. 1.37m; draft as little as 10cm. Other recorded names: **backwater boat(t), Fleet Water trow**

Fleet Water trow See **Fleet trow**

Fleetwood shrimper See **Morecambe Bay prawner**

fleit See **fluit**

fleitte See **flette**

Flemish galley See **Flanders galley**

Flemish lugger See **panneschuit**

fleot, fleote See **fleet**

Flet 1. *Germany:* Small vessel that served as a **ferry★** or for transport along a river; reported in the early 18th century.
2. *Russia, W:* Small, keeled boat that attended pilots at Pillau (now Baltisk) in former East Prussia in the late 19th century.
Spelling variant: **Flette★**

flete See **fleet, flette**

fletta See **flette**

flette *France, N:* Decked boat that traversed rivers and canals, especially on the upper Seine. Reported as early as the 14th century. Might carry passengers, vehicles, cargo. Sometimes a **ship's boat★**. Some employed 8 oars. Dimensions depended on river size, some ca. 6m long. Other recorded names: **felete, filete, fillette, flecte, fleitte, flet★, flete, fletta, folette, xata**. Note also **flûte-2**. Further references: **baggeraak, Flet**

Fleute, Fleutschiff See **fluit, flûte**

fleysh' See **flûte**

flibaad, flibåt See **vlieboot**

flibot *France:* Small 18th-century vessel of 50-100t reported to have engaged in cod fishing in the North Sea and off Newfoundland, and in transporting cargo to the Iberian Peninsula and probably to the Antilles. Sometimes considered a small **fluit★**, possibly as early as the 14th century. Often armed for protection. Full body, high stern, rounded buttocks, flat floors. Twomasted, setting square sails, and on the 3-masted vessels, a lateen mizzen. Crew of 8-12. Reported length on keel 18.2m, beam 10m. Other recorded names: **felibot, flotebate, flutbot, navicula flotans.** Note also **flûte.** Further references: **buss-2, vlieboot**

flibote See **flyboat, vlieboot**

fliboto, flibotto See **vlieboot**

flibuste See **freebooter**

flibustier *France:* Class of racing **sailboats***. Rounded hull; centerboard; length overall 4.74m. Further reference: **freebooter**

flibutor See **freebooter**

flicker *United States, NE:* Term given to a **canal boat*** used until the mid-19th century on the Delaware and Hudson Canal in southeastern New York State. Carried cargo and provided maintenance. Square ends, flat bottom. Many of the later boats had their sides raised to increase capacity. Reported lengths 5.5-6m, beam 1.2m. On the Morris and Delaware Canals in northern New Jersey, the **flicker** was a company-owned boat. Round stern. Rowed and poled. Length 23m, beam 2.7m. Also called a **stiff** or **stiff boat** (as opposed to the **hinge boat***), or **lighter***. **Flickers** were also used on the Lehigh Canal in eastern Pennsylvania.

flie-boate See **flyboat**

Flieboot *Germany:* Employed in the dried fish industry; cited in the late 1700s. Rounded hull and stern. Three masts with no topmasts; bowsprit. See also **vlieboot.**

flie-bote See **flyboat**

Fliegender Holländer See **flying Dutchman**

Flieger *Germany:* **1.** General term for a fast vessel.
2. On the Rhine and several other rivers, the **Flieger** serves as a **tender*** or **ship's boat*** to large vessels. Sturdily built, with narrow flat bottom, wide garboard strake, and lapped topstrake that turns inward. Flat bow rakes up to a point at the top, no stem; sharp stern, with skeg. Sculled from the stern or rowed with one pair of oars from amidships. Reported lengths 4.5-5m. Name variants: **Beiboot*, Kölner Jolle**

Fliete See **fluit**

flight *Netherlands:* English-language term for a flat-bottomed **passage boat*** used on canals and rivers. Name variant: **flyboat***. Further reference: **fluit**

flipot See **vlieboot**

float 1. Rectangular decked craft or **raft***; often transports cargo to and from ships in a harbor.
2. The term **float** may apply to a **life raft***, to a platform on the water to support people, and sometimes to an inflated or grass-stuffed skin that supports the body, immersed or ridden astride. It may apply to the outside hull of a **trimaran***. Name variants: **skin float, swimming float.** Note also **burdjuk, hun tuo, sarnái.**
3. *Canada, W:* A cedar-log platform that provided support for a building or equipment, one of as many as 20 **floats** that comprised a logging camp in coastal British Columbia, as well as other logging sites with logging camps adjacent to water. Entire camp moved to a new site as needed. Some provided living areas for managers and their families; others had the cookhouse, bunkhouses, tool shed, winch, etc. Constructed by lashing lengthwise logs across a smaller log at each end; live-aboard

floats might have plank decking and fencing. Lasted 20-25 years. Note also **float house.**
4. *England:* **a.** Large flat-bottomed boat used to carry blocks of stone. In some areas, as on rivers in the southwest, **float** may designate a rowed **ferry*** suitable for carrying wagons, horses and riders, cattle. **b.** A fully decked **barge*** of the Bridgewater Canal in west-central England that carried only deck cargoes, such as logs, steel rods, etc. Sharp ends, straight sides, raised deck aft, large rudder.
5. *United States:* **a. Raft** used to store culled and cleaned oysters temporarily. In the San Francisco area they were **barge**-like craft with open bottom planking to permit water circulation, the flotation provided by airtight compartments; 7-12m long. In southwestern Washington State, **floats** were made of heavy unhewn logs and lacked flotation compartments; ca. 9m long and 3.7m wide. The **sink float** of Washington was composed of 2 logs joined on the bottom by crosspieces over which a floor was laid, and the whole covered with ca. 46cm of water for washing purposes. Also used in the New England and southern New Jersey oyster industries; 24m long, 6m wide. Name variant: **oyster float. b.** Oysters dredged on the east and south coasts may be put into a wooden **float** through which water flows freely. Used as temporary storage and to purify and cleanse the oysters. Rectangular framework 6-9m long, 3.6-4.6m wide. Note also **oyster barge. c.** On the Erie Canal in central New York State, a **float** is a **barge** and its **tug*** combined.; length ca. 91m.
6. *West Indies, Virgin Islands:* Local dialect term for a **boat*** or **bateau*.**
Spelling variants: **flota, flote, flotteur.** Further references: **balsa-1, car float, catamaran-3, drag, oyster barge, raft, timber raft-1, Wexford cot**

float boat *United States:* **1.** In a broad sense, a boat that proceeds at a leisurely pace, for pleasure, fishing, etc. Usually flat-bottomed. Some may be inflatable rubber craft, mainly for river running.
2. In Florida, sport fishermen cruise backwaters and swamps in a **float boat** equipped with an airplane engine. Built of wood, square ends, shallow, steered with a long rudder. A similar craft works the cranberry bogs in eastern Massachusetts.
3. Also in Florida, it may be a **party boat***, carrying 40-50 people, that goes offshore and then drifts slowly back to land while the group fishes.
Further reference: **gundalow-2**

floatel A floating hotel. Name variant: **float-inn.** Note also **donga.**

floater *Canada:* **1.** A vessel that anchors on the fishing grounds and uses small boats to catch the fish. May stay out a week or two before returning to home port.
2. Schooner* that engages in summer fishing off Newfoundland and Labrador, especially for cod. As many as 15 in crew. Name variant: **Labrador floater.** Note also **Baccalieu skiff.**

float house *Canada/United States:* A **raft*** of 2 or more large logs on which a house is set. The large logs aligned side-by-side; several smaller logs lashed crosswise by cable or nailed with huge spikes. In large tide areas, moored to shore by a long, or stiff, log. Note also **float-3**, **shanty boat**.

floating academy See **hulk-3**

floating battery 1. In general, a mortar-carrying vessel; sometimes described as a **raft**★ or **barge**★, or as a cut-down, sailing **man-of-war**★ with a mission of bombarding coastal installations or defending a port. By the mid-19th century, they had become ironclad to the waterline. Usually shallow draft. Other recorded names: **batteria (galleggiante)**, **batterie flottante**, **(schwimmende) Batterie**. Note also **chata-4**.

   2. *United States, E:* **Floating batteries** were used during the American Revolution, but details are scarce and conflicting. One Massachusetts vessel was strongly planked, pierced at the waterline for oars (5 per side), and carried 2 cannon and 4 swivel guns. Those working out of Philadelphia mounted 18 pounders (reports vary from 10-18); only a plank parapet protected the crews; rowed and/or sailed; 30m or longer. Name variant: **battery**

floating bethel See **church boat**

floating boat See **kabang**

floating bridge See **ferryboat-1**, **pontoon-2**

floating car See **fisherman's car**

floating chapel See **church boat**

floating church See **church ship**

floating coffin A vessel that is rotten and hence unseaworthy. Name variant: **Sargschiff**. Note also **timber drogher**.

floating dishpan *United States, central:* An extremely shallow-draft **steamboat** used to navigate the many sandbar-filled rivers of the Mississippi Basin. First built in 1818.

floating funeral See **shark-2**

floating light See **lightship**

floating mill A **barge**★ or **raft**★, anchored in a river, that supported a vertical wheel used to drive millstones. Dates to at least the 6th century A.D. Some were a **catamaran**★ type, with the wheel between the **barges**. Often moored under bridges at medieval European cities to take advantage of the faster water, thereby creating a navigational hazard. House covered the millstones. Note also **moulin-bateau**, **mulino galleggiante**.

floating net boat See **liu wang chuan**

floating palace *United States:* Term given to river and bay **steamboats** of the 2nd half of the 19th century; had ornate saloons and passenger cabins and elaborate deck fixtures. See also **packet boat**.

floating pile driver See **pile driver-1**

floating post office See **mail boat-5b**

floating reed stack See **chai ban zi**

floating stage See **punt**, **raft-2**

floating station *Australia, N:* Vessel that accompanies a **fleet**★ of **pearling luggers**★ to supply fresh water, firewood, stores, and miscellaneous luxuries. Also serves as a base for opening the oyster shells, which may contain pearls. Ca. 150-200rt.

floating theatre See **showboat-1**

floating wheelbarrow See **Mersey flat**

float-inn See **floatel**

floaty ship A vessel that draws little water.

flobar See **flobart**

flobard See **flambart**

flobart *France, N:* Very seaworthy **fishing boat**★ that worked from the Picardy and northern Normandy coasts. First mentioned in mid-17th century; now mainly motorized, but a few still sail. Light clinker planking, wide top strake; many now of fiberglass. Flat bottom, straight keel, sharp turn of the bilges into deep vertical sides. Full bows; plumb stem; deep raking transom stern; strong sheer; open. Outboard rudder; tiller; centerboard. Mainmast stepped well forward setting a loose-footed dipping lugsail; mast unshipped while tending the nets or pots. Small mizzenmast at the stern carried a standing lugsail sheeted to a long outrigger; mast stepped off center to enhance tiller handling. Jib to a long rising bowsprit lashed to the mast. Oarports cut into gunwales. Crew of 5-6. Reported lengths 3.25-9m, length-to-beam ratio 2:1; shallow draft. Spelling variants: **flobar**, **flobard**, **vlootbar**. Further reading: Bertrand Louf and François Guennos, *Les Flobarts de la Côtes d'Opale. Bateaux d'Échouage de Boulonnais, de Wissant à Equihen*, XIXème et XXème (l'Ermitage: Punch Éditions, 1998). See also **flambart**.

flodpråm See **barge-1**

floit See **fleet**

fløite See **fluit**

flöjt See **flûte**

fløjte See **fluit**

Florida mullet skiff See **mullet boat-2b**

Florida sharpie See **sharpie-5**

Florida sponge schooner See **sponge schooner-2**

Florida-type shrimp boat See **shrimp boat-1**

flors See **punt-2**

Floss See **raft**, **timber raft**, **zattera**

Flossboot See **life raft**

flot See **timber raft**, **fleet**

flota See **float**, **fleet**, **galleon-1**

flota pesquera See **fleet-1**

flote *England, W:* Term used on the River Severn in the 15th century for a **timber raft**★. See also **fleet**, **float**.

flotebate See **flibot**

flotiha, flotila See **flotilla**

flotilla Term for a group of small naval ships under the command of a captain. Individual ships commanded by a lieutenant-commander or lieutenant. **Squadron** is now the more usual term. Spelling variants: **flotiha**, **flotila**, **flotille**, **Flotte**★, **flottiglia**

flotille See **flotilla**

flotille de pêche See **fleet-1**

Flotillenboot See **fleeter**

flotta See **fleet**

flotta da pesca See **fleet-1**

flottage See **timber raft**

flotte *France, central:* In 17th-century Paris, the boats of master ferrymen were called **flottes**. See also **fleet**, **flotilla**.

flotte de pêche See **fleet-1**

flotteur See **float**

flotti See **dugout canoe**, **fleet**

flottiglia See **flotilla**
flottiglia da pesca See **fleet-1**
Flottmutte See **Mutte frigate**
flouque See **feluca**
flour boat See **flatboat-4**
flower boat See **chi-tong-t'eang, fa teng, hua chuan**
flubust'erskoe sudno See **freebooter**
fluit *Netherlands:* Long-distance bulk-cargo vessel that was well established by the late 16th century; original design so successful that it was widely copied—in France, where it is sometimes known as a **flibot★**; in Germany as the **Fleute**; in England as the **flyboat★** or **flute★**; in Denmark as a **fløjte** (or **fløite**). Also adapted for privateering, as a hospital ship, and as a **hulk★**. Those sailing to the Mediterranean and India were larger and stronger; hold above a lower deck. The Dutch vessels were modified for use in particular areas and over their long history (to the 19th century), lost most of their original characteristics. Being designed to carry cargo, they were full-bodied with strong tumble home to the topsides. Wide flat floors; almost angular bilges, becoming rounded toward the stern; broad buttocks below a high, narrow counter; vertical stem and sternpost. Bluff bows, curved stem; strong sheer. Fully decked; very large hold; high poop on 17th-century vessels. Deck very narrow originally, wider later. Some had a forecastle. Those used for whaling had extra-thick bows. Foremast stepped just behind the stem, setting 1-2 square sails; mainmast set 2 square sails; mizzenmast on the poop deck, setting a lateen, later a gaff sail. Some carried a spritsail below the bowsprit. Crew of 10-19, plus 1-3 boys. Length-to-beam ratio 4:1, later 6:1; reported lengths 30-43m. Mostly 200-500t burden. Other recorded names: **fleit, Fleutschiff, Fliete, flight★, fluite, fluitschip, fluste, fluta, Flüte,** (or **flûte★**), **flute hollandoise, flute-ship, flutte, fluy(u)t, gaing, hollandais, Hollander★, hollandois, Hoorensche gaings, vliet(bot), vliete;** pl. **fluiten.** Note also **noordvaarder, pink-3, vlieboot.**
fluite See **fluit, flûte**
fluiten, fluitschip See **fluit**
Flunderlomme See **żakówka**
flush-decked trow See **trow-1**
Flushing mussel boat See **mosselaar**
Flußschiff See **riverboat**
fluste See **fluit, flûte**
fluta See **fluit**
flutbot See **flibot, vlieboot**
flûte 1. Term used, especially in France during the 17th and 18th centuries, for a cargo ship designed to carry construction timber and naval stores and troops. Popular in the western Mediterranean, and used during the French regime in Canada, some as fishing vessels. Many were **East Indiamen★.** Described as carvel-planked, having flat floors, full, robust build, and a high rounded stern. Three-masted, setting square sails, although the mizzen might set a gaff or lateen sail. A vessel was said to be armed *en flûte* when a ship of the line had had some of the lower deck guns removed to provide more space for personnel and storage.

2. *France, N:* Canal and river vessel used from the early 19th century until at least the 1950s; mainly transported heavy cargo. Pointed bow, square stern, flat bottom, vertical and parallel sides. Wide-bladed rudder, with hinge at outer part. Undecked or with a cabin at the stern; stable amidships. Generally towed, sometimes from a rigged mast. On the Ourcq they usually worked in pairs, side by side; one boat had the cabin. Reported lengths 28.5-38.6m, widths 3-6m, depth ca. 1.8m. Note also **coche d'eau, flette, flûte de Bourgogne, flûte du Berry.**
3. *France, SE:* The **flûte** of the Saône River was introduced in the mid-19th century to dredge and carry sand. Built until the late 1930s. Flat bottom, straight vertical sides, plumb stem; square stern, became more rounded and later heart-shaped. Bow may round up from the bottom and end squared off (the **toue★**), or it may be sharp (the **rackette** or **Spitzkadole**). Outboard rudder. Stable amidships, cabin for family at the stern; later vessels had engines. Reported lengths 13-28m, widths 3.3-5m.
4. *United Kingdom:* A beamy, lightweight **flute** was a **coaster★** and river craft of the 14th century. Two masts. Name variant: **fluve**
5. *Vietnam, N:* Name given to a type of 2-masted **junk★** that superficially resembled the French **flûte.** Transported salt and lime in the Red River (Song Hong) delta area. Square counter stern; rounded stem, considerable sheer; rudderpost came up inboard. Finely woven mat lugsails, strengthened with battens, set to aft-raking masts. Brick-colored sails hung from their leading edge; often set winged out. The 2 shrouds from the mainmast led forward; foremast unstayed. Also towed from the riverbank. Name variant: **fluve**
Other recorded names: **charrua, flaut(a), flàuto, Fleute, Fleutschiff, fleysh', flöjt, fluite, fluste, fluyte, flyboat★, hubot, store ship★.** Note also **chaloupe-5a, fluit.**
flûte berrichonne See **flûte du Berry**
flûte de Bourgogne *France, central:* Highly successful vessel built, beginning in the early 19th century, for use on the Canal de Bourgogne, between the Yonne and Saône Rivers. Carried such items as wine and cut stone to river towns in central France. Blunt bow, with mildly curved stem; flat sheer increased toward the bow. Square stern originally quite concave, later flatter. Longitudinally planked flat bottom; straight sides. Towing mast in a high tabernacle roughly amidships, folded down over the stable house. Cabin adjacent to the stable or at the stern. Balanced rudder with forward part extending to the concave stern; long tiller. Mainly towed, rarely motorized. Reported lengths 20.55-38m; e.g., length 34.6m, beam 5m, depth 2.1m. Note also **flûte-2, flûte-3.**
flûte de Canal du Berry See **flûte du Berry**
flûte du Berry *France, central:* 19th-century cargo boat that carried local industrial products, mainly on the Canal du Berry. Plumb bow, wide, heavy wales at the bow on later vessels; flat stern; straight sides. Flat bottom turned up slightly at the bow. Single or double rudder(s), wide-bladed below the waterline; tiller(s).

Towed by a team of donkeys and/or mules from a tall mast on rivers or 2 short masts on the canal; team housed in stable amidships. Cabin aft. Tarpaulin covered the cargo. Towed a **tender**★. Size dictated by lock dimensions: 28m long, 2.8m wide, cap. 100t. Other recorded names: **flûte berrichonne, flûte de Canal du Berry**. Note also **berrichon**.

flûte hollandaise See **vlieboot**

flute hollandoise, flute-ship See **fluit**

flutte See **fluit**

flutte hollandoise See **vlieboot**

fluve See **flûte-4, flûte-5**

fluyt See **fluit**

fluyte See **flûte**

fluyut See **fluit**

flyboat 1. Described in the 16th century as a shallow-draft cargo vessel of European origin; often served as a **store ship**★. Those that had increased in size by the end of the century warranted the name **double flyboat**. Some 17th- and 18th-century **flyboats** were **men-of-war**★, a kind of **frigate**★; others worked as **privateers**★. Considered excellent for whaling, these having doubled bows. Note also **vlieboot**.
2. A **flyboat** was also described as a small, fast boat, especially a **ship's boat**★, or as a **tender**★ to a **fleet**★. They were also small vessels used off the Shetland Islands, especially by the Dutch, as part of 17th-century fishing **fleets**.
3. *British Isles:* **a.** Term for special **canal boats**★ that provided scheduled express service, carrying light freight, mail, and passengers (the **packet boats**★), beginning in the 1790s. Although generally of lighter construction with finer lines and rounded bilges, some were ordinary **narrow boats**★ with identifying markings. Such boats were permitted through locks at night and were given precedence over the freight carriers at other times; some had a knife-edge scythe on the bow to cut tow ropes of slower craft that failed to give way. Tow rope ran to the mast. Used special relays of horses, sometimes pulling at a gallop; some worked in pairs, each with its own tow horse. Those catering to passengers provided refreshments and other amenities; enclosed cabin area covered most of the boat. Originally term applied only to horse-drawn boats (**horse boats**★), but by the 1830s, some were pulled by a tug. Some later boats operated with a steam engine. A slower type that carried heavier loads was called a **stage boat**. Generally crew of 3 and a boy. Other recorded names: **express boat, fly-out, gigboat, Guinness fly** (working between the Royal Park Brewery and Birmingham), **Scotch boat**★, **Shroppie fly, Shropshire fly**. Note also **cabin boat-1, coche d'eau, swift boat**. **b.** During the 14th-17th centuries, term also applied to small, swift-sailing boats that conveyed mail, goods, and passengers, mainly along the coast, but some crossed the Atlantic. By the 16th century, these boats had a gaff mainsail and jib.
Spelling variants: **fflye(-boat), flee-boate, flibote, fliebo(a)te, flyboate, flyeboat(e)**. Further references: **buss-2, flight, fluit, flûte, market boat-5, vlieboot**

flyboate See **flyboat**

flybooter See **freebooter**

flyeboat, flyeboate See **flyboat**

flyer *United States, E:* Variety of **canal boat**★ used on the Susquehanna Canal System in eastern Pennsylvania in the 1880s. Presumed to be a **freight boat**★ for small consignments, traveling more rapidly than other **freighters**★. Cabin at each end. Further references: **parinda, privateer**

flying bridge See **ferryboat-1**

flying Dutchman 1. Phantom ship that, by tradition, sails the waters south of Cape of Good Hope (sometimes Cape Horn), never making port. Considered a bad omen when "seen." Other recorded names: **Fliegender Holländer, Hollander, vliegende Hollander**. Note also **carmilhan**.
2. Fast mono-hull centerboard sailboat. Raced worldwide. Length overall 6.05m, beam 1.8m.
3. Round-hulled **dinghy**★ intended for inland waters; later sailed and raced on coastal waters.

flying-fish boat See **Barbados flying-fish boat, poti marara**

flying-fish catamaran See **kola maran**

flying-fish dugout See **gommier**

flying prao See **flying proa**

flying prau *Indonesia/Malaysia/Philippines:* Heavily armed pirate vessel that preyed on merchant sailing ships in Southeast Asia, especially those becalmed. Large **fleet**★ worked out of the southern Philippines; others from Java, Sumatra, and Malaysia. Design and rigging dependent on the area of origin. Those of the 19th century showed evidence of western influence in hull and sails. Most 2-masted, setting one of the varieties of eastern lugsail. Also rowed. After their piratical activities were curtailed, vessels were often modified as local cargo carriers. Length roughly 15m. Other recorded names: **prahu, proa**. Note also **flying proa**.

flying proa 1. *Kiribati (Gilbert) Islands, central Pacific:* Modern racing craft of the **wa-ririk**★ type. Plank-built with a deep symmetrical "V" hull and sharp raked ends. Planks originally sewn with sennit, now with nylon fishing line. Single-outrigger **canoe**★, with a small float that usually rides about 60cm above the water. Three booms, strengthened with crosspieces and diagonals, secured to the float by 2 "Y" connectives. Heavily canvassed, employing a triangular nylon sail with the apex down. Mast stepped into one of several cups on the longitudinal stringers that rest on the hull.
2. *Mariana Islands, western Pacific:* Exceptionally fast, interisland, cargo-carrying single-outrigger **canoe**. Reported by early explorers, but extinct toward the end of the 18th century. Dugout hull; large **canoes** made in 2 halves, butted and sewn together. Asymmetric "V" in cross section, with the lee side flat vertically and horizontally; washstrake might raise freeboard. Ends curved up and elongated; cut vertically to form a narrow, flat surface. Thin planking along the windward side reduced spray. Generally 3 booms attached to the short, heavy float by means of stanchions; further strengthened with struts to the ends of

the hull. Outrigger kept to windward; later boats had 2 outriggers. Steered with a paddle; a helmsman at each end, the one at the stern on a particular tack doing the steering. Partly decked; house covered the remainder on later **proas**; some had a bamboo platform over the outrigger booms. Pole mast stepped in a socket on the central outrigger boom, supported by a short prop from the outer end of the boom. Triangular mat sail, hung lateen fashion; boomed at the foot; heel of the yard rested in a socket at the forward end. Crew of 3-7. Reported lengths 5.5-21.3m; e.g., length 9m, beam 0.6m, depth 0.9m. Note also **flying prau**.

Other recorded names: **flying prao, flying prow, proa volant.** Further reference: **popo**

flying prow See **flying proa**
fly-out See **flyboat-3a**
flyte Anglo-Saxon term; cited in the 9th century as a **lighter★** employed in harbor work.
FMC boat See **josher**
fné, fnee See **fune**
Föhringer Ewer *Germany, NW:* Very shallow-draft **Ewer★** built on the island of Föhr off the west coast of Schleswig-Holstein during the latter part of the 19th century. Carried stone, wood, peat, grain, and general cargo. Sharp stern below a low raked transom. Outboard walkway. Small, slender rudder; leeboards. Tall mast set a gaff sail. Length 14m, beam 4.6m, depth 1.2m.
foirine See **moulin-bateau**
Fokien trader See **Fukien trader**
folette See **flette**
follier See **follower-2**
follower **1.** *England:* In the early 15th century, a boat that acted in concert with a large vessel of the King's navy. **2.** *England, SW:* **a.** On the south Cornwall coast, the **follower** worked with a **seine boat★**, carrying the stop net, which was used to close the principal seine net, or carrying the tuck net, depending on the area. Similar to, but often smaller and lighter than, the **seine boat.** Length to ca. 7m. Spelling variants: **follier, fol(l)yer, volyer** (in East Cornwall). Note also **lurker, tuck-net boat. b.** At St. Ives, the term **follower** was used mainly for the small boat that carried men between shore and a pilchard **seine boat.** Rowed or sailed by 2 boys. Might also be a square-sterned boat that carried the small stop net; also called a **tow boat★**. **3.** *Ireland, SW:* Worked with a larger **seine boat** during pilchard fishing, picking up the free end of the net to close the circle. Used into the 19th century. Manned by 5-6.
follyer, folyer See **follower-2**
foncé See **foncet**
foncet *France, N:* Used for local transport of wine, wood, produce on the Seine and Oise Rivers, and for herring fishing on the English Channel. Reported from the 14th into the 18th century. The river craft were sharp-ended, clinker-planked, flat-bottomed, with a strongly raked stem, less raked stern; beamier forward, high-sided, with keel. Strong sheer toward the stern; very large trapezoidal rudder; tiller; decked at ends; cabin at stern. Stepped single mast. Sometimes

towed by a horse. Varied from 18-40t. Those used on the rivers were reported to have been as long as 52m. Other recorded names: **bateau foncet, foncé, fons(s)et, fousse, fo(u)sset**
fonset, fonsset See **foncet**
Foochow junk See **Fukien trader**
Foochow pole junk, Foochow stock junk See **hua pi gu**
Foochow trading junk See **Fukien trader**
foot boat *United Kingdom:* **1.** Term for a heavy **dinghy★** of a **Thames sailing barge★** or **bawley★**. **2.** A **ferry★** used solely for the conveyance of foot passengers.
foot-paddling boat See **jiao hua chuan**
før See **far**
foraine See **moulin-bateau**
forban *France:* **1.** An early term for a ship armed by pirates. Spelling variants: **forbanni, fourban.** Note also **freebooter. 2. Fishing boat★** of the Golfe du Morbihan area on the south Brittany coast and to the south. Worked with lines or a trawl net. Extinct by the 1930s; a few recently reproduced. Carvel-planked; straight, slightly raking stem; high raking transom above a strongly raked sternpost. Deep drag to the straight keel; S-curve to the floors, soft turn of the bilges; low freeboard aft. Narrow rudder; long tiller to clear the after deck. Short deck aft, cuddy below. Two tall, unstayed masts set standing lugsails; jib to bowsprit; foremast stepped close to the bow, raking slightly aft; mainmast stepped roughly amidships. Small boats might be gaff-rigged. Crew of 3 plus a boy. Reported lengths 9-11.2m; 1910 boat 11.2m long, 3.4m wide. Name variant: **forban de Bono**
forban de Bono, forbanni See **forban**
forceur de blocus See **runner**
fore-and-after In general, a sailing vessel with sails roughly aligned parallel with the keel. Employs no square sails. Term most often applied to a **schooner★**, as a **fore-and-aft schooner**, with either gaff or leg-of-mutton sails. Can also refer to a **ketch★** or **yawl★**; and in the broadest sense includes lug- and lateen-rigged vessels. See also **sloop-9**.
fore-and-aft schooner See **schooner-1**
forebarge See **Fenland lighter**
fore boat See **Parrett flatner**
fore lighter See **Fenland lighter**
fore-mizzen punt See **Deal punt**
forenagterskonnert See **schooner**
forepeaker See **Deal lugger**
foresail-and-mizzen punt See **Deal punt**
forest products carrier See **timber carrier**
fore topsail schooner See **schooner**
forine See **moulin-bateau**
føringsbåt See **storbåt-2**
foriscotia See **farcost**
forkita See **frigate-4**
Formplätte See **Farm**
føroysk båt See **færøbåd**
forsbåt **1.** *Finland, N:* Open boat used in running rapids (*fors*). A large, beamy type carries tar (see **paltamo**). Carvel-planked, with 4 strakes per side; closely spaced,

single-piece curved ribs; sharp ends; raked stem and sternpost; low freeboard. Rowed with single pair of oars against natural-crook tholepins. Length 4.3m, beam 1.0m.

2. *Sweden, N:* **Riverboat★** used to transport cargo to the coast, and for fishing. Sharp ends, strongly curved stem and sternpost, strong sheer toward the ends. Clinker-built, lightly planked for flexibility; widely spaced ribs; flaring sides; curved keel. Floats downstream with the current; upstream, poled or sets a square sail to a mast stepped through a thwart. Reported lengths 4.2-12m; e.g., length 6.65m, beam 1.0m, depth 0.35m.

Fort Rupert canoe See **northern-style canoe**

fōrua *Solomon Islands, western Pacific:* Generic term for an **outrigger canoe★** or a **boat★** in the Lau language of northern Malaita in the southeastern islands. See also **porua**.

fosset See **foncet**

fou See **fu**

Fouchou-Pfahl-Dschunke See **hua pi gu**

foulouqa See **felucca-1**

four See **shell-1**

fouræring See **fourareen**

fourareen *Scotland, N:* Open, 4-oared boat of the Shetland Islands, but may be found throughout Scotland. Principally used for day fishing, but also serves as a general workboat, for interisland transportation, and as a popular racing craft. Initially imported from Norway (note **færing**). Sharp ends; clinker-built; graceful sheer, low waist. Frames not usually attached to the keel but arch from one garboard strake to the other; shallow rise to the floors;

fourareen

short, slack bilges. Stem and sternposts raked and somewhat curved, slight extension of the posts; flared ends. Divided into 5 compartments; loose stone ballast in the reinforced center room. Long tiller; high rudderhead. Many gaily painted. Mostly rowed, mainly with 4 oars, but the large **haddock boats★** used 6. When sailed, originally set a single square sail, then a standing lugsail, later a dipping lug. Mast stepped amidships in square-rigged boats and in forward thwarts on the lug-rigged craft. Some sails boomed; at times extended by a bowline; jib occasionally used. Crew of 3-4 for summer fishing (the **summer boat**). Reported lengths 3.66-6.7m overall, 2.44-4.88m on

keel; typically 5.94m overall, 3.58m on keel, beam 1.75m, depth 0.6m, draft ca. 0.38m. Other recorded names: **fouræring, four earing, foureen, fourer(e)n, four-oared boat, fouroarn, fower(er)een, fowereren, haerenger, peerie fourareen** (small), **whilli(e)** or **whilly** (small size, using 1-2 oarsmen). Note also **Shetland Model.**

fourban See **forban-1**

four earing, foureen, foureren, fourern See **fourareen**

fourgaden See **frigate-1**

four-masted bark Sometimes described as a vessel that was square-rigged on the 2-3 forward masts and fore-and-aft rigged on the remaining mast or masts. Note also **bark, shipentine.**

four-masted barque See **bark**

four-master Sailing vessel that steps 4 masts. May be **ship★**-rigged with square sails on each mast or may set a combination of square and fore-and-aft sails. Other recorded names: **four poster, quatre-mâts, Viermaster**

four-oar See **shell**

four-oared barge See **barge-11e**

four-oared boat See **fourareen, whaleboat-4**

four-oared outrigger See **shell-1**

four-oared race boat See **gig-3**

four-oared shell See **shell-1**

fouroarn See **fourareen**

four poster See **bark**

four-stroke coble See **coble-1**

fousse, fousset See **foncet**

Fou tcheou pole See **hua pi gu**

fowereen, fowerereen, fowereren See **fourareen**

Fowey lugger See **East Cornish lugger**

fowling punt See **gun punt**

fox terrier See **spits**

foy See **foyboat**

foyboat 1. One used to assist ships in harbors, for a fee (*foy*), to provision them, and to help if in distress. Small, narrow, and worked with oars or a lugsail. Passenger and watermen's boats may also be **foyboats.** Name variant: **foy**

2. *England, NE:* Small **coble★**-type boat used on the northeast coast, especially in the Tyne Estuary, to attend ships, ferry men and stores, supply bunkering coal, serve as a **pilot boat★**, and assist in warping to the dock. Some engaged in salmon fishing. Hull varies somewhat with the port. Clinker-built; heavily strengthened; straight keel; flat floors; rounded bilges amidships. Open, might have landing boards at bow and stern; vertical stem; narrow, raked wineglass stern. Outboard rudder; long tiller. Tyne craft characteristically have black hulls with black-and-white painted port design on top strakes; also wooden fenders on the sheer strake. Rowed with 2 oars or sculled from the stern. Also sailed, setting a dipping lugsail. Mast raked aft at ca. 20°, stepped on keelson, and secured by hoop on forward thwart. The few remaining boats on the Tyne have diesel engines, but retain the traditional black hull. Reported lengths 4.57-6m; e.g., length overall 5.6m, on keel 4.27m, beam 1.57m, depth 0.53m. Other recorded names: **foy(boat) coble, half**

coble; also **Sunderland, Tyne,** and **Wear foyboat.**
Note also **hoveller.**

foyboat coble, foy coble See **foyboat-2**
Frachter See **freighter-1**
Fracht-Ewer See **Ewer**
Frachtlomme See **Lomme**
Frachtschiff See **Dachschiff, freighter-1**
fragada See **fragata-1**
fragatte See **frigate-1**
fragata 1. Small member of the **galley*** family. Long
projecting bow. Open except for poop deck; carried 2
cannon. Rowed single-banked from 6-12 benches;
might set a lateen sail. Crew of 11-28. Length-to-
beam ratio on some 7:1. Spelling variants: **fargata,
fragada, fregata**
2. *Portugal, central:* Term loosely applied to all the
large **sailing barges*** of the Tagus Estuary, but only
one type correctly bears the name **fragata.** Gaff-
rigged vessel used primarily to carry ship's cargo to
and from outlying areas of the estuary. Some still
work, but last one built in 1928. Carvel-planked; full
bow; plumb stem with rounded forefoot; straight
raked transom stern. Long straight keel; flat floors
with rounded bilges; sheer mostly flat but rises at the
bow; 2 heavy wales along each side; pair of bitts at
bow and stern quarters. Massive rudder, heel hangs
below keel; hung by gudgeons slipped over a long iron
bar; tiller. Decked at bow and stern, open waist;
accommodations in forecastle and aft. Sides black,
with colored band (usually green) below the rail cap;
green on top of stem and rudder; decks and interior
gaily painted in red and green. On older vessels aft
bulkhead elaborately decorated; owner's colors painted
in bands at masthead and on gaff end. Pole mast rakes
aft; gaff sails loose-footed; staysail. Some early **fragatas** pictured with 2 lateen sails, or with a spritsail
and jib. Size range: length 16.2m, beam 4.6m, depth
1.78m to 27m by 7.5m by 3.2m; shallow draft. Other
recorded names: **barca de agua abaixo, fregat(t)a,
frigata.** Note also **bote fragata, lancha-8.**
3. *Portugal, N:* At Porto, the **fragata** was a strongly
built **lighter*** designed to handle ship's cargoes. Flush
deck. Two masts, equipped with cargo booms. Towed.
Reported lengths 23-45m, widths 5-9m, depths 2.5-4m.
4. *Spain:* Fast, armed vessel of the 16th to the early 18th
century that traveled between Spain and the New
World, especially to carry treasures and to police sea
routes to Spanish possessions. Several poop decks;
ram at bow. Forward 2 masts set square sails; the
mizzenmast carried a lateen. Length ca. 31m. Spelling
variants: **fargata, fregata**
5. *United States, SE:* **Fragatas** were purchased in
Havana in the late 16th century and were also built in
South Atlantic ports; some sailed as far north as
Chesapeake Bay. Usually heavily armed. Square sails
on the fore-, main-, and mizzenmasts, plus a spritsail
beneath the bowsprit to offset the high poop. Many
lateen-rigged. A **batel*** might serve as a **ship's boat.**
Also rowed. Keel length of a 1586 vessel 20m, beam
ca. 4.6m.
Further references: **East Indiaman, frigate-1**

fragata aparejada de cruz See **ship-2**
fragatas de força, fragatas ligeiras, fragate See **frigate-1**
fraguate Small **ship's boat***, especially of a 17th-cen-
tury French **galley***. Curved stem, raked transom
stern, flat floors, soft bilges. Length ca. 8m. Name
variant: **frégate.** Further reference: **frigate-1**
fraktångare See **freighter**
frakteskøyte See **skøyte-4**
fraktjakt See **jakt-3**
frame boat See **bugeye**
Frauenzimmerschiff See **Leibschiff**
frebetter See **freebooter**
freebooter A 17th- and 18th-century term applied to
both vessel and men engaging in acts of piracy, especially against Spanish **galleons*** in the West Indies.
Other recoded names: **barque flibustière, bastimento filibustiere, flibuste, flibustier*, filibustiere, filibustero, flibutor, flubust'erskoe sudno, flybooter,
frebetter, fr(e)ibustier, fribust, rozbojnik morski,
sjörövarfartyg, sjørøverskip, sørøverskib, vrijbuiter.** Note also **corsair, forban-1, freiboteros, sea
rover.**
freezer See **ice schooner**
fregaat See **frigate-1**
fregada See **frigate-1, frigate-4**
fregade, fregaden See **frigate-1**
fregadina See **fregatina**
frégat See **frigate-1**
fregata *Malta:* Early lateen-rigged boat, predating the
similar **speronara*.** See also **fragata-1, fragata-2,
fragata-4, frigate-1, frigate-4.**
fregata del passo del Canale See **dghajsa tal-pass,
madia-1**
frégatar See **palangrier**
frégate See **fraguate, frigate-1, frigate-3, frigate-4,
frigate-5, frigate-6**
frégate de ronde See **frigate-5**
frégate légère See **frigate-1**
fregatim See **brigantine**
fregatina 1. *Italy:* **a.** Diminutive for **frigate*. b.** Type of
18th-century **corvette***; built in the Venice area. **c.** A
naval **ship's boat***, often of a **galley*. d.** *Sardinia, SW:*
A large **bilancella*** that transports galena ore to the
mainland. Reported lengths 10-12m; cap. 10-20t.
2. *Malta:* Tiny, colorful harbor boat used for handline
fishing and going out to moorings. Carvel planking.
Rowed mainly, but sailed with a lateen rig in regattas.
Spelling variants: **fregadina, frigadina;** pl. **fregatine,
fregatini**
fregatine, fregatini See **fregatina**
fregatjacht, fregatschepen, fregatschip, fregâtt See
frigate-1
fregatta See **fragata-2**
**Fregatte, Fregattschiff, fregot, fréguate, fréguatte,
fréguete** See **frigate-1**
Freibeuter See **privateer**
freiboteros *Haiti, N:* Term given to the men and to the
lug-sailed boats in which they carried supplies and
hides between the cattle hunters of the northwest
peninsula and Tortuga Island in the late 17th century.
Note also **freebooter.**

freibustier See **freebooter**

freight boat *United States, E:* On lower Chesapeake Bay and the Potomac River in the 1920s, **freight boats** (later called **barges***) carried produce, coal, lumber, and especially seed oysters. Sharp bow, rounded stern; decked, pilot house aft. Engine; also set a gaff sail to a mast stepped in forward third. Length ca. 20m, beam 5.5-6m. Further references: **Adirondack guideboat, box boat-2b, freighter, New Orleans lugger**

freight canoe *Canada, N:* General term applied to the large **canoes*** designated to carry cargo or luggage. Square stern; canvas covered the cedar stripping. Some recent **canoes** employ outboard motors. Reported lengths 6-9m, beam ca. 1.8m, depth ca. 1.0m. Other recorded names: **freighter***, **freighter canoe, freighting canoe, luggage canoe**. See also **canot du maître, canot du nord, Nor'Wester canoe, shitlats, West coast canoe**.

freighter 1. Seagoing vessel designed and constructed to carry cargo safely and economically from one port to another. **Tween deckers** carry general cargo on various levels of the holds. Other selected names: **affréteur, Befrachter, cargo, cargo boat** (or **carrier, ship, vessel**), **carguero, charterer, Frachter, Frachtschiff, fraktångare, fréteur, gruzovoe sudno, Güterschiff, kargo(bot), lastfartyg, lastilaiva, navire de charge, noleggiatore, teretni brod, teretnjak, tovorna ladja, vrachtschip, vrachtvaarder**. Note also **merchantman**. **2.** *Canada, E:* A **freighter** on the Labrador coast was a **schooner*** that took many passengers north in the spring. **3.** *United States:* **a.** A heavy **canal barge*** that carried freight and, ordinarily, no passengers. Operated on many of the canals, but were most numerous on the Erie Canal, where they were divided into company-owned, long-haul and independently owned, short-haul boats. Flat bottom (some with a double bottom); straight sides. Open **barges** carried bulk cargo, while decked boats carried more vulnerable items; living quarters at the stern for the crew and forward for the animals. Towed by horse or mule, and sometimes oxen. On the Erie Canal, 2-section freight boats were called **squeezers** (or **double barges**); roped together in tandem; sent through the locks singly. Empty **barges** were towed in long strings and, on the Erie Canal, were called **hoodledashers**; more recently, a **hoodledasher** is a powered **barge** that pushes one **barge** and tows 1-2 behind. Generally had a crew of 2, the captain as steersman and a horse or mule driver, or a family. Dimensions dictated by minimum lock size; those on the Union Canal in eastern Pennsylvania were 20m long and 2.5m wide. The Chesapeake and Ohio Canal boats were 28m long, 4.4m wide. Note also **hinge boat, sectional boat. b.** Those on the Ohio & Erie Canal had 3 cabins after the early 1870s, the stern cabin for the captain and his family, the smaller bow cabin for crew members. The reserve 3-mule team was housed in the central cabin. Cargo carried between the cabins; sometimes catwalks extended full length. Bluntly pointed bow; square stern, merged

with the raised after deck; heavy rubbing strakes along the sides. Reported lengths 21-24m, width 4.3m, draft less than 0.9m. **4.** *United States, E:* A type of large **schooner** that carried oysters to markets along the east coast in the 19th century was called a **freighter**. Often carried various cargoes and some fished in the off-season, but they rarely dredged for oysters. As distances from the oyster beds to market became greater, faster vessels were developed. Some on Long Island Sound had centerboards and carried their cargo on deck. The Chesapeake Bay **freighters** had clipper bows and wide square sterns (see **pungy** and **Chesapeake Bay schooner**). Other recorded names: **carrier***, **coasting schooner, Long Island Sound freighter, oyster freighter, runner***

Further references: **freight canoe, oyster sloop-1**

freighter canoe, freighting canoe See **freight canoe**

freight sloop See **Hudson River sloop**

freight vessel *United States, central:* Major boat type on the Ohio Canal in the early 19th century. Towed by team of 2 horses or mules at ca. 4.8km per hour. Teams changed every 16-24km. Carried cargoes in relatively small containers. Some built to sleep and feed as many as 20 passengers. Crew comprised the captain, 2-3 deck hands, and a boy to tend the animals. Length under 23m and 4.3m wide to fit within the locks.

French dory See **doris-3**

French Shore schooner See **Gaspé schooner**

frère See **mother**

fresh-buyer See **buyer smack**

fresh fisherman See **market boat-3**

fréteur See **freighter-1**

fribust, fribustier See **freebooter**

fricket See **frigate-1**

fridge ship See **refrigerated ship**

Friendship sloop *United States, NE:* Weatherly, stable, fast lobstering and **fishing boat***. Although now generally named for the town of Friendship on Muscongus Bay on the south-central Maine coast where many were built, they were locally called **sloop boats***. Built all along the bay beginning in the early 1890s; virtually extinct as a working sailing craft by the 1920s. Now the sailing types are restored or replicated pleasure boats. Distinctive features are a deep, full-length sloping keel; hollow garboards; high firm bilges; sharp clipper bow, with billethead and trailboards; a few had spoon bows (the **round-bowed sloop**). Overhanging stern with elliptical transom. Gaff mainsail with a long boom and long gaff; jib or jib and staysail; bowsprit ca. one-third boom length. Other features include a strong sheer and low freeboard abeam the cockpit to aid in handling lobster pots. Half-decked, large cockpit, wide side decks, high coaming, cuddy forward. Broad fin to the rudder, post came up inboard; tiller or wheel. Some larger boats had a fidded topmast with gaff topsail; topmast sent down in winter. Small auxiliary on later boats. Crew of 1-4. Reported lengths 4.6-13.7m, mostly 7.2-9m; length-to-beam ratio ca. 3:1. Other recorded names: **Maine sloop boat, Morse sloop, sloop b'ot**. Further reading: Roger F. Duncan, *Friendship Sloops* (Camden, Maine: International Marine Publishing Co., 1985). Note also **Muscongus Bay sloop**.

Friesche jacht See **Fries jacht**

Friesche palingschuit See **palingaak**

Friesche praam See **praamschuit**

friesches Aalboot See **palingaak**

Friesche schouw See **Friese schouw**

Friese aak, **Friese aakje** See **visaak**

Friese hoy See **praamschuit**

Friese klipper See **klipper-1**

Friese maat, **Friese maatkast**, **Friese maatkastje** See **kast-b**

Friese palingaak, **Friese palingschuit** See **palingaak**

Friese praam See **praamschuit**

Friese punter See **Hoornse punter**

Friese schouw *Netherlands, N:* This member of the **schouw★** family was initially a workboat on inland waters; now a pleasure craft and often raced. Carvel-planked; now often of steel. Flat bottom curves up forward and aft, ending above the waterline in hexagonal bow and stern transoms, with false stem and sternpost; raked ends; hard bilges. Straight flaring sides; deadwood aft. Almost flat sheer; sides may be raised by washboards; planking turns inward above the wale.

Friese schouw

Small boats open, with steering seat; larger decked forward. Wide-bladed rudder; tiller slotted over rudderhead; fan-shaped leeboards. Mast in a tabernacle. Larger boats fitted with a loose-footed, boomed gaff sail with short curved gaff; staysail to small iron bumkin. Smaller sprit-rigged. Reported lengths 4.5-8m; medium size (**middenschouw**): length 5.5m, beam 1.55m. Other recorded names: **Friesche schouw**, **Friese sprietschouw**; large size **grote schouw** or **lelieschouw**; small size **kleine schouw**

Friese snik See **snik-3**

Friese sprietschouw See **Friese schouw**

Friese tjalk *Netherlands, N:* Cargo vessel of the **tjalk★** family that worked until the end of World War II, but some have been converted to **yachts★**. Built of wood until ca. 1900, then steel. Differs from the **Groninger tjalk★** in having a more elegant shape, less sheer, and on the older types, by the position of the tiller, which came in through a triangular hole in the wide top strake (the **hektjalk★**); steel vessels lack this feature. Bow rounded; stem curved and raked, gripe. Stern rounded; sternpost vertical on after edge. Slight tumble home above the wale, increasing toward the ends. Rudder had a wide fin below the waterline; tiller; wide leeboards. Decked; low deckhouse; large hatch abaft the mast; cabin aft. Most painted brown. Tall lowering mast set a loose-footed gaff sail with a long boom. Staysail; jib to a running bowsprit. Some mid-19th-century vessels set a square topsail. Sails tanned. Generally crewed by a man and wife and a boatman. Reported lengths 16-24m, widths 4.7-5.5m; 15-35t.

Friese tjalkje See **Friese tjalk**

Friese turftjalk *Netherlands, N:* **Tjalk★**-type vessel that carried peat (*turf*) on the Zuiderzee from the Friesland area south to Holland in the 18th century. Unlike the **tjalks** of the period, the tiller worked freely above the gunwale rather than through a helm port. Heavily built; bluff bows and stern with curved stem and nearly vertical sternpost. Moderate sheer; top strake of uniform width and turned inward above the heavy wale. Foredeck; long, high hatch coamings; stern deck; windlass on each deck. Set a type of large spritsail, staysail, and jib to a running bowsprit; square topsail. Note also **turftjalk**.

Friesische Jacht See **Fries jacht**

Fries jacht 1. *Germany, NW/Netherlands, N:* Small, fast **market boat★** of the East and West Frisian Islands. A member of the **tjalk★** family. Flat floors; rounded bilges; flaring sides; varying degrees of tumble home above the wale. Full bows, recurving next to the tall stem; vertical sternpost. Long foredeck, with windlass and hatch; peaked covers over the hold; open steering platform abaft the hold. When built with a raised deck aft (the pavilion) for a cabin below, it was known as a **Fries pavilionjacht**. Wide, round leeboards. Strikable mast stepped forward of the hold, supported by a single shroud. Set a loose-footed boomed mainsail with curved gaff; staysail to bumkin. Reported lengths 15-17m; e.g., length 15m, maximum beam 4.32m, depth 1.65m. Other recorded names: **Ostfriesische Jacht**, **Jacht★**

2. *Netherlands, N:* Open pleasure boat, mainly of the protected waters of Friesland. Originated in the 1860s. Carvel-built, with narrow planking. Flat floors, wide skeg; soft turn of the bilges; full rounded sides that start to turn inward below the wale; flat sheer. Curved stem ends in a point; straight sternpost, nearly vertical. High, narrow rudder, with ornament on top; iron tiller; large rounded leeboards. Removable deck forward; when built with an additional cabin may be called a **boeier★**. Usually lavishly decorated. Tall strikable mast stepped against a heavy thwart at end of foredeck. Loose-footed, boomed mainsail, with curved gaff; staysail to small bumkin. Reported lengths 5-7.6m; e.g., length 7m, beam 2.9m, depth 0.6m; the larger sizes were produce carriers. Other recorded names: **aalboeier**, **Friesche jacht**, **Frische Jacht**, **Friese jacht Friesische Jacht**,

Fries jachtje, jacht*. Further reading: J. Vermeer, *Het Friese Jacht* (Leeuwarden: Hedeby, 1992).

Fries jachtje See Fries jacht
Fries skûtsje See skûtsje
frigada See frigate-4
frigadina See fregatina
frigat See frigate-1, frigate-4, zabra
frigata See fragata-2
frigate 1. European man-of-war* or merchantman* of the 16th-19th centuries; used also in the colonies. In the 17th and 18th centuries, often synonymous with nau*. As a naval vessel, it became a standard class and was a light, fast, medium-sized vessel that served mainly for scouting and escort duty, as a lookout and signal repeater, and to engage privateers*. Generally 2 gun decks, double-banked, double frigate or two-decker, but during the 18th century, all the armament was on the so-called gun deck (above the waterline); the lower deck was for crew and stores. Large frigates carried light guns or carronades on the gun deck and forecastle. Smaller single-decked vessels were called light frigates. The cargo-carrying frigates were more full-bodied than the naval vessels. Rigging changed through the period, square-rigged on 3 masts or square sails on the forward 2 masts and a lateen (later gaff) sail on the mizzen. Some early types also used oars (galley frigate), rowing from 8-14 benches per side. Reported lengths 27-96m; length-to-beam ratio of English vessels 4-4.75:1. Selected name variants: fergata, fer'kada, ferkada, ferkata, firkata, firqâta, fourgaden, fragacte, fragata*, fragatas de força (60 guns), fragatas ligeiras, frag(u)ate, fragatte, fregaat, fregada, fregade(n), fregat(a), frégat(t)e, frégate légère, fregatjacht, fregatscheep, fregatschip (pl. fregateschepen), fregâtt, Fregatte, Fregattschiff, fre-got, fréguat(t)e, fréguete, fricket, frigat(te), frigate galley, frig(g)ot, frygatte, furqâta, fyrqateïn, galleon-frigate, leichte Fregatte, lille fregat, liten fregat(t). Note also flyboat-1, nau-1.
2. Modern navies have revived the word for a class of medium-speed vessels that engage in deterrent activities, for example, anti-submarine service, patrol, and escort duties.
3. Advice boat* that was auxiliary to a light naval galley*; some carried munitions or patrolled coasts. Reported in the Mediterranean as early as the 14th century, and used into the early 17th century. Decked or open; low poop deck. Set 1-2 lateen sails. Six to 12 benches, with one oarsman per bench, although large vessels might employ 2 banks of oars. Reported lengths 10.7-21m; e.g., length of 16th-century vessel 10.7m, beam 2.2m, depth 0.8m; by the 17th century, some French frégates were 21m on the keel and 6.4m wide. Name variant: galley frigate
4. *Mediterranean, E:* The frigate of the Byzantine period was a warship, employing ca. 200 oarsmen in 2 tiers, plus a crew of deck fighters. Lacked the usual ram, lying alongside the enemy ship during battle; after the 7th century, liquid fire was introduced. Single square sail or 2 triangular sails supplemented the rowers. Length to ca. 14m. Spelling variants: bregada, firgate,

forkita (dim.), fregada, fregata (pl. fregate), frigada, frigat, frigot
5. *France:* a. In the west, in the 17th and 18th centuries, the armed naval frégate légère conducted coastal reconnaissance and protected convoys. Small vessel, very maneuverable. Two decks. b. From the 14th to the 16th century, naval frégates were assigned to Lyons to maintain order on the Rhône and lower Saône Rivers.
6. *Switzerland, W:* Oared frégates fought on Lake Geneva (Lake Léman) during the 16th-17th centuries.
7. *United States:* The late 18th- and early 19th-century naval frigates were generally larger and faster than their European contemporaries. Carried 24-44 guns, some placed on the forecastle. After 1812, the guns were also placed on the gangways, giving them 2 armed decks and earning the name double-banked frigates. In addition to being ship*-rigged, some used sweeps. Reported lengths on lower deck 35-49m, longest 62m overall.
8. *United States, E:* The 18th-century boats of the Schuylkill Fishing Company, a sport-fishing club on the Schuylkill River in the Philadelphia area, were called frigates. Sharp raked bow; decked forward. Rowed. Reported lengths 3.7-4.3m, narrow.
Further references: barge-8, butthead
frigate galley See frigate-1
frigatte, frigot, friggot See frigate-1
Frisco felucca See felucca-3
Frisian eelboat See palingaak
frota See fleet
frota de pesca See fleet-1
frotta See fleet
frozen and chilled cargo chip See refrigerated ship
Fruchtfahrer See fruit ship
Fruchtjager See fruit schooner
Frucht-Schaluppe See Schlup-1
Fruchtschiff See fruit ship
fruit carrier See fruit ship
fruit clipper See fruit schooner
fruiter See fish box, fruit schooner, fruit ship
fruiterer See fruit schooner
fruitier See fruit ship
fruit or air-cooled ship See fruit ship
fruit schooner Small, fast, sleek vessel that procured oranges, lemons, grapes, and other perishable cargoes from the Azores and the Mediterranean area. Carried the cargo to England and the Continent from the mid-19th century. Those carrying currants from the eastern Mediterranean became known as currant schooners. At off-seasons, North Atlantic fishing schooners* might serve the fruit trade, as did Baltimore clippers*. Kept small to reduce stacking of the fruit and to shorten loading and unloading times. Very high coaming on aft hatch enabled the cover to be removed for ventilation on most days. Clipper bow, generally a long square counter, moderately sharp sections, fine run aft, deep hull, copper-sheathed. Rigged as 2- and 3-masted top-sail schooners, carrying square sails on the fore top-mast; heavily canvassed. Some were barkentines*. Large crew for size. Lengths mostly 25-30m, beam ca.

one-fifth. Other recorded names: **Fruchtjager, fruit clipper, fruiter(er), South Spainer**. Note also **clipper-schooner, fish box, fruit ship**.

fruit ship Vessel that mainly transports fruit. Usually designed or modified to carry a particular type of fruit. Often carries general cargo outbound and fruit home; passengers common. May be company-owned and operate on a regular schedule, or be a **tramp steamer**, traveling to various areas according to season. Usually fast and of small tonnage. Holds designed to ensure good ventilation; now generally refrigerated. Early vessels sailed; now fully motorized. Selected name variants: **air-cooled ship, bateau fruitier, fruit transport vessel, Fruchtfahrer, Fruchtschiff, fruit carrier, fruit(i)er, fruktfartyg, frutero, nave trasporto frutta, Obstschiff, transport de fruits**. Note also **banana boat, fish box, fruit schooner, refrigerated ship, sack ship**.

fruit transport vessel See **fruit ship**

fruktfartyg, frutero See **fruit ship**

frygatte See **frigate-1**

frying pan See **collier-2**

fu *China:* One of the terms for a wooden **raft⋆**. Often used at sea since very early times. Spelling variant: **fou**. Note also **fa, pai**.

Fuchow pole junk, Fuchow timber freighter See **hua pi gu**

Fuderplätte See **Plätte-1**

fu diao zi *China, central:* Cargo vessel, dating from the 14th century, that plied Poyang Hu (lake) and lower Chang Jiang (Yangtze) tributaries. Crudely built of camphor wood. Flat bottom; narrow, square bow overhanging; bottom turned up sharply to the square stern;

fu diao zi

rudder hung beneath overhang. Maximum beam abaft amidships; strong sheer aft. One or 2 houses covered most of the vessel. Tiller controlled by ropes and pulleys. Stepped 1-4 masts, but mainly 2, with foremast the taller. Set balance lugsails. Capstan hoisted sails and weighed anchor. Crew of 16-24. Reported lengths 18-30m; e.g., length 25.8m, beam 5.8m, depth amidships 2.3m. Other recorded names: **fu-tiao tzŭ, hung-hsieh tzŭ, hung-hsiu-hsieh, red slipper junk**

fuel ship Serves as an auxiliary to naval vessels, originally to provide coal, later oil. Note also **tanker**.

fu-fu boat See **fen chuan**

Fuhrwerksfähre See **ferryboat-1**

Fuhrwerksponte *Germany, W:* A **ferryboat⋆** that transported mainly horses and wagons. A type that crossed the Rhine at Emmerich in the 17th century could carry 2 wagons, each with a team of horses, or 15 passengers. Flat bottom; square, transversely planked, overhanging ends; low sides. Poled and steered with a sweep.

fuikenjol See **Staverse jol**

Fujian junk, Fukien junk, Fukien sea-going junk See **Fukien trader**

Fukien trader *China, E:* The strong, seaworthy trading vessels that worked out of the ports in this province (now spelled Fujian). Fine lines forward, with full beam running almost to the raked stern transom; narrow bow transom; bulwarks extended forward of the bow face. Flat floors; no keel; strong sheer; considerable tumble home; low strengthening wales served also as bilge keels. Decked; cargo spaces divided into several watertight compartments; 15 full bulkheads; foremost compartment pierced to permit flooding to reduce pounding. Some had a spacious house for passengers; captain's quarters in the high poop. Highly decorated oval transom. Deep balanced rudder, retractable; some fitted with sockets and secured by a rope that passed under the bottom to the bow; handled by a windlass; **sampan⋆** hung from stern davits. At Xiamen (Amoy), bottom and lower sides whitened and protected with a coating of lime and oil, earning them the name **pai-ti ch'uan** or **white-bottomed boat**. Bulwarks generally black with green border; color of bow piece indicated the home port. Oculus on each bow. Stepped 3 masts, the fore- and mizzenmasts being small. Set brown balance lugsails, of matting until end of the 19th century, then cotton, and later canvas. Crew of 6-8, 25 on the Amoy junks. Reported lengths 18-27.5m, widths 3.7-10m. Other recorded names: **Amoy junk, Ch'üanchou Dschunke, Fokien trader, Foochow junk** (or **trading junk**), **Fujian junk, Fukien (sea-going) junk, pai-ti shuan, pe-ti tch'ouan, Quanzhou chuan**. Note also **Amoy fisher, pai ti chuan**.

fuldrigger See **ship-2**

full-load boat See **reed boat-2**

full raft See **timber raft-2a**

full-rigged ship, full-rigger See **ship-2**

fulouqa See **felucca-1**

fu̠lūka **1.** General term in Arabic for **boat⋆**, and consequently often applies to the Nile **gaiassa⋆**.
2. *Egypt:* **a.** Small boat found between Aswan and Cairo, originally for fishing and cargo, more recently for tourists and local party groups. Hull form not standardized, but usually transom-sterned, high-bowed, partly decked. Very large rudder; heavy tiller; centerboard. Sets a single boomed lateen-type sail with a short luff. Reported lengths 5-6m. **b.** The **fu̠lūka** of Upper Egypt was reported as an open boat that navigated the Nile for 5 months of the year. Length 11.4m, width 3.6m, draft 1.6m. Smaller size, lateen-rigged, went by the name **nousf-feloukah** or **feloukah-soghayrah**. **c.** The large **fu̠lūka**, to 20m long, transports many kinds of cargo, often long distances on the Nile. Originally of wood, now mostly of iron, with

marked change in hull design. Sharply rising bow, low freeboard toward the square stern. Wide rudder, heavy tiller. Mast stepped forward, small mizzen on stern. Lateen sail boomed or loose-footed. Crew of 2. **d.** Swift boat used on very shallow Lake Manzala in the Nile Delta, west of Port Said. Transports people, animals, dung, bricks, sand, and stone, working around the clock. Many engage in fishing. Hull very modern in appearance with sharply pointed, strongly raked wide stem; sharp stern; very flared sides; comparatively narrow bottom. Wide rudder; long tiller. Cuddy forward. Sets a large lateen sail. One crew member may climb out on a hiking board, holding a stay from the mast. Length ca. 12m.

Other recorded names: **feloukah**, **felouque***, **felucca***, **felukah**, **kayasse**; pl. **fạlāik**

Fuluka See **felucca-1**

funce See **fune**

fune *Japan:* Generic term for a **ship***, **boat***, **vessel***, **lighter***, etc. Described in the 18th century as a single-masted **coaster*** capable of carrying heavy cargoes. Spelling variants: **bune(y)**, **fné**, **fnee**, **funce**, **funea**

funea See **fune**

Fünferin, **Fünferl**, **Fünferzille** See **Salzzille**

Furkelzille See **Plätte-1**

furqâta See **frigate-1**

fur scow See **scow-5**

fur seal canoe See **sealing canoe**

fur-trade canoe See **canot du maître**, **canot du nord**

fusoliera See **fisolera**

fu-tiao tzŭ See **fu diao zi**

Futterplätte See **Plätte-1**

Fuzhou pole junk See **hua pi gu**

fýramannafar *Denmark, Faroe Islands:* Small open boat rowed by 4 (*fýra*) men with 3 oars per side, the middle 2 men rowing a single oar each, the other 2 each rowing with a pair. Used for summer handline fishing and trawling for coalfish in narrow straits. Clinker-planked; oak keel and stem and sternposts; 2 end ribs natural crooks, the others 2-piece ribs. Sharp ends; strongly curved stem and sternpost; tall stem. Narrow, deep rudder, worked with a single-arm yoke to a tiller. If sailed, steps a mast through the 1st thwart setting a square-cut dipping lugsail, or may use an outboard motor placed in a well. Length ca. 6.3m. Spelling variants: **fir(e)mandsfar**, **fýramannafør**. Note also **færobåd**.

fýramannafør See **fýramannafar**

fyräringar See **kyrkbåt**

fyreng, **fyring** See **firing**, **firroring**

fyrqateïn See **frigate-1**

fyrskepp, **fyrskib**, **fyrskip** See **lightship**

fysher boate, **fysherbot** See **fishing boat**

fy t'eng See **fei teng**

fyve-man coble See **coble-1d**

G

gaal See **gal**

gaarib See **qārib**

gaba *Martinique, West Indies:* Creole term for a **lighter★** or **barge★**. Square ends. Name variant: **gabarre★**

gabanne See **gribane**

gabara 1. *Bulgaria:* In Bulgarian, **gabára** is a **barge★**.
2. An 18th-century naval vessel of the Dalmatian coast. Armed with 10-20 guns. Sailed and rowed.
3. *Greece:* A 3-masted vessel built in Greek shipyards during the period of Turkish rule. Set square sails on the fore- and mainmasts and a fore-and-aft sail on the mizzenmast.
4. *Philippines:* A type of freight **barge**.
See also **gabare, gabarra**.

gabard See **gabbart, hopper**

gabare 1. French term for a decked **lighter★**, **barge★**, or **scow★** that primarily handles cargo for ships lying at anchor, often transferring the cargo upriver. Term appeared at least as early as the 14th century. Sailed, rowed, or motorized. Note also **gabaret, gabarot**.
2. *Canada/United States, NE:* Term used by the French in the 17th-18th centuries for a wide, flat craft that carried freight on the shallower rivers and assisted in transferring cargo to and from large ships. Some routinely brought firewood, hay, and produce down a river to a town. Those on Lake Champlain in the 17th century were both rowed and sailed.
3. *France:* **a.** Naval transport ship for munitions and supplies in the 18th-19th centuries, often traveling to the colonies. Three masts, square sails to each mast, plus a gaff sail on the mizzen. Capacity to 600t. Other recorded names: **corvette de charge, grande gabare. b.** In the 15th century, a **gabare** could be a **dugout canoe★. c.** In the 18th century, a **gabare** might be a vessel belonging to the customs office.
4. *France, Mediterranean coast:* In the Languedoc area, **gabares** served as **tenders★**.
5. *France, SW:* **a.** General term for a small, basically flat cargo craft; some designed solely for river use, others for river, sea, or ocean use. Generally open, often with extended square bow, flat bottom, square sail. Note also **bot-2, courau, gabare de Charente, sloop-8. b.** In the mid-17th century, **gabarres** were **fishing boats★** in the Gascony area. **c.** Local cargo vessel that served towns along the Gironde River and its tributaries. Massively built with bluff bows and rounded stern; generally marked sheer to the higher bow; low rise to the flat floors; straight keel; deep forefoot; low freeboard when loaded. Upper river types steered with a sweep, otherwise by a strongly raked outboard rudder; tiller. Long, covered hatch abaft the mast; railing around many. Towed a 4.3-4.6m **yole★**. Cargo boom anchored to the mast. Most **sloop★**-rigged (the **gabare à quille**); loose-footed, gaff mainsail, sheeted to a traveler; long gaff. Sail furled to mast. Large foresail to a rising bowsprit or the stemhead; supported by a gammon knee. Mast stepped in a high tabernacle, easily lowered, especial-

ly for maneuvering between bridge piers. Early **gabares** of this area set a square sail in an open waist. Many also set a lugsail to a mizzenmast stepped at the sternpost. Crew of 2-3. Reported lengths 12.6-28m, widths 3.6-5.2m, draft 1.3-2.35m. Name variant: **gabare de Gironde**
6. *France, W:* **a.** Early **gabares** of the Loire River valley were large and set a tall square sail to a strikable mast. Clinker-planked with green oak; treenailed until the end of the 18th century, then bolted, and finally built with iron spikes. Flat bottom; long, raking bow cut square; wide, slightly curved stern. Bow and stern decks. Employed a large-bladed rudder, the tiller for which sometimes passed through a hole in the stern, angling up to crossed supports; worked by a vertical piece that hung down from the tiller. Might have a low house at the stern. As few as 3 in crew. Reported lengths 20-28m; e.g., length 24m, beam 4m, depth 1.2m. Smaller **gabares** on tributary rivers were ca. 10-12m long and ca. 2.5m wide. Note also **train de bateaux. b.** In Brittany, a small type carries local products along the coast. Those at the Rade de Brest date to the 18th century. On Île Molène, **gabares** of 30-40t cap. collected seaweed for fertilizer. Raked, rounded stern; curved stem; flat floors; the latest have plumb stem and counter stern. Decked; large central hold; raked transom stern; **ketch★**-rigged. 18th-century vessels were square-rigged on 1-2 masts with a small jib to a rising bowsprit. Reported lengths 9-22m. Other recorded names: **bateau★, gabare de la Rade de Brest**
7. *French Guiana:* Flat, beamy vessel that transported cargo from ships along the coast and up rivers during the 18th century. Sailed and rowed.
Other recorded names: **gabara★, gabarra★, gabarre★, gabarro, gabart, gabbare, gauarra, gobar, guabarra, kobar**

gabare à clapet See **marie-salope**

gabare à goémon *France, N:* General term given to the vessels along the Perros-Guirec coast that collected seaweed (*goémon*) and sand. Worked mainly in the latter part of the 19th and early 20th centuries. High sides, vertical stem, slightly rounded and raking transom. Foredeck with hatch. Foremast stepped through the deck with 2 movable shrouds; mainmast raked forward. Sails hung to high-peaked yards. Jib to long bows down bowsprit. Crew of 2-3. Other recorded names: **ar vag dor gommon, flambart goémonnier, gabare des goémonier, gabare de Trélévern, gabare du Tréou, gabare goëmonière**. Note also **canot goëmonier**.

gabare à quille See **gabare-5c**

gabareau 1. *France, W:* In the Rennes area, **gabareaux** transported sand and gravel. Rounded bow, flat stern. Hold divided in two to assist in draining the vessel, using a long scoop. Reported lengths 18-20m. Name variants: **gabareau de Vilaine, gabareau rennais**
2. *France, SW:* Small, flat-bottomed **fishing boat★** of the Gironde Estuary. Reported in the late 18th century.
See also **gabarot**.

gabareau de Vilaine, gabareau rennais See **gabareau-1**
gabare à vase See **marie-salope**
gabare de Charente *France, SW:* **1.** Vessel that traversed the Charente River carrying salt, wine, firewood, cut stone, etc. In the 17th-18th centuries, the vessels were open except for a low cabin aft; 19th-century vessels were decked except for large open holds. Sides and frames of oak; square or sharp, raked ends; flat bottom. Wide-bladed rudder; long tiller. Single mast amidships, probably setting a square sail; later a gaff sail. Crew of 3 plus a boy. Reported lengths 20.5-26m, beam 2.5-5.8m; e.g., length 26m, width 5.8m, depth 1.34m, draft 1.14m; 10-50t, depending on the stretch of river normally frequented.
  2. The 19th-century **gabare**★ was a large, fully decked vessel. Flat floors, full bow and stern, plumb sternpost, slightly curved stem, low freeboard. Massive rudder had a wide blade below the waterline; heavy tiller that slotted through the white rudderhead. **Sloop**★-rigged or stepped 2 masts setting lugsails; masts could be struck. Reported lengths 8-32m, widths 1.25-6m, draft 0.54-1.35m.
  Name variant: **gabare de Saint-Simon**. Note also **gabare de Port d'Envaux**.
gabare de Gironde See **gabare-5c**
gabare de la Rade de Brest See **gabare-6b**
gabare de la Rance *France, NW:* Small, beamy boat of an estuary of the Rance River on the north coast of Brittany. Transported firewood to the inhabitants of Saint-Malo and Dinard until World War I. Carvel-planked, straight stem, raked sternpost, transom or counter stern. Rectangular lugsail set to a tall unstayed mast

gabare de la Rance

stepped well forward; sail sheeted to a traveler on the transom; small staysail. Sails russet colored. Crew of 2-3. Length 9.5m, width 4.5m. Other recorded names: **gabare de Pleudihen, véro; demi-véro** (small size)
gabare de Plancoët *France, NW:* A small, open **lighter**★ of Plancoët and the Arguenon River southwest of Saint-Malo on the north Brittany coast. Primarily transports sea sand inland for improving the area's clay soils. Heavily constructed; double-ended; flat floors permit grounding at low tide; short deck aft. Rowed or sculled by crew of 2. Length ca. 9m; widths 3.5-4m.
gabare de Pleudihen See **gabare de la Rance**
gabare de Port d'Envaux *France, SW:* Clinker-planked river craft of the Charente River in the area of Port d'Envaux. Flat bottom; stern narrowed to a flat, V-shaped

transom. Decked with hatches. Wide-bladed rudder; long tiller that slotted into rudderhead. Note also **gabare de Charente**.
gabare de Saint-Simon See **gabare de Charente**
gabare des goémonier, gabare de Trélévern, gabare du Trévou, gabare goëmonière See **gabare à goémon**
gabaret *France:* Term applied in the 18th century to a small **gabare**★. Other recorded names: **gabarote, gabarruella, gavareta, gobarig**. See also **filadière**.
gabarot *France:* **1.** Term sometimes applied to a small, undecked **gabare**★.
  2. Long, low, 19th- and early 20th-century cargo vessel of the Loire River and some of its tributaries in western France. Flat bottom; straight, vertical sides; swept up at the bow, ending in curved, blunt stem. Square stern, heavy rudder with wide blade below the water-

gabarot-2

line. Low, full-width cabin aft; open amidships. Square sail set to a mast stepped amidships. Crew of 2. Reported lengths 14-27m; e.g., length 14m, 17m with rudder, width 2.5m, depth 1.1m.
  3. In the southwest on the Dordogne River, a small boat that accompanied **gabares** in the 18th-19th centuries. The **gabarot** of the Haute-Dordogne was a small, open, sharp-ended boat. Popular for fishing. Some had a small transom. Flat bottom; very elongated, rising ends; stern higher; low, flaring sides; alternating natural crooks formed ribs and floor frames. Lengths of the cargo type 8.75-12.25m, the fishing type 5.5-15m.
  4. The 19th-century **gabarot** of the Garonne River was ca. 12-15m long and carried 10,000kg. Worked until ca. 1930. Loose-footed gaff sail set to a strikable mast; staysail. Crew of 5-9.
  Spelling variants: **gabareau**★, **gabarreau, gabarotte, gabar(r)otus, gabarrot(te), gaboriot, guabarrot**
gabarote, gabarotte See **gabaret**
gabarotus See **gabarot**
gabarra **1.** Italian and Spanish term for a **barge**★, **lighter**★, or military transport vessel. Spelling variants: **gabara**★, **gabarroto**★ (dim.); **gabbarra**; pl. **gabarre**★. Note also **gabare**.
  2. *Italy:* **a.** Small 16th-century river craft used for fishing, pleasure, and transporting cargo. The present-day **gabarra** on the Po River in the Cremona area has a flat bottom and curved sides. Length 22.3m, beam 5m, depth 1.4m. **b.** The 19th-century **gabarra** might be a 3-masted, square-rigged naval vessel that transported troops, supplies, and munitions.
  3. *Italy, N:* On Lake Como (Laria), a large, flat vessel; initially of wood, later of iron or steel.
  4. *Portugal:* Vessel that transports cargo and people. Design varies, but generally flat-bottomed. Rowed and sailed.

5. *Spain:* **a.** Generally a large **barcaza**★ that assists in unloading ships in ports. Towed, pushed, or rowed. Those working as **coasters**★ are decked and use sails. Length ca. 12m. Other recorded names: **lancha gabarra**; **kabarra**★ and **soka-gabarra** (Basque); **gavarra**, **kavarra** (Catalan). **b.** A **gabarra** type at La Coruña on the northwest coast transports stone, sand, and logs to sawmills. Sharp bow, rounded stern, curved stem and less curved sternpost; straight keel. Decked forward, along the sides, and aft. May have a cabin aft. Now motorized. Some early sailing types to 15.5m long.
Further reference: **gabare**

gabarra-tanque See **tank barge**

gabarre *Canada, E:* In the Magdalen Islands in the Gulf of St. Lawrence, a crudely constructed craft loaded with herring transferred from the net. Towed to and from shore by a **botte**★. Blunt bow; vertical sides; wide, square stern. See also **gaba**, **gabare**, **gabarra**, **gabbart**.

gabarreau See **gabarot**

gabarre à vase See **marie-salope**

gabarro See **gabare**

gabarrón Spanish term for a large **barge**★-like vessel that supplies ships with fresh water. In the Galicia area, these vessels have 2 lugsails. An 1838 boat was 12.8m long and 3.6m wide. Spelling variant: pl. **gabarrones**. Note also **aljibe**, **water boat-1**.

gabarrones See **gabarrón**

gabarrot, gabarrotte See **gabarot**

gabarroto *France, SW:* A small **fishing boat**★ of the Gironde Estuary. See also **gabarra**.

gabarrotus See **gabarot**

gabarruella See **gabaret**

gabart See **gabare**, **gabbart**

gabbard 1. *Ireland, SE:* Flat-bottomed cargo boat of the River Slaney developed in the early 19th century and worked until the late 1920s. Carvel-planked, sharp ends, no keel. Set a large lug-, sprit-, or gaff sail. Also poled from catwalks on the gunwales. Mast could be struck to pass under bridges. Crew of 2. Reported lengths 12-18m; e.g., length 12.2m, beam 3.7m; shallow draft. Other recorded names: **Slaney cot**, **Wexford cot**★ (or **gabbard**)

2. *Northern Ireland:* An early 18th-century sailing trader on Lough Neagh; carried mainly coal. Name variant: **gablard**
Further reference: **gabbart**

gabbare See **gabare**, **gabbart**

gabbarra See **gabarra**

gabbart *Scotland:* **1.** Local cargo vessel that traveled from Glasgow to the Isle of Arran, up into Loch Fyne, and through the Forth and Clyde Canal. Used mainly from the late 18th through the 19th century, but term reported from at least the late 16th century. Double-ended with full lines, flat floors, round bilges. Long central hatch bordered by narrow side decks; no bulwarks, but a railing around the stern was common; often had heavy wooden fenders. Outboard rudder. Crew housed aft. Towed by horses when on the canal; sailed elsewhere. Rig varied with the period, but later vessels were either **cutter**★- or **sloop**★-rigged; mast

could be struck. Crew of 2-3. Reported lengths 14-20m; e.g., length 18m, beam 4m, draft loaded to 1.8m. Name variant: **Clyde gabbart**

2. A **dumb barge**★ of small capacity that worked on the Firth of Clyde between Glasgow and Greenock early in the 19th century.

3. Ketch★-rigged **coaster**★ that continued sailing into the early 20th century, carrying coal, merchandise, and livestock on the Crinan Canal. The later **coal gabbarts** were **steamers** and were usually called **puffers**★, carrying coal, timber, gravel, and sand.
Spelling variants: **gabard**, **gabarre**, **gabart**, **gabbard**★, **gabbare**, **gabberd**, **gabbert**, **gabbord**, **gaber(t)**, **gaboard**, **gaboate**

gabberd, gabbert, gabbord See **gabbart**

gabeque See **xebec-2**

gaber, gabert See **gabbart**

gablard See **gabbard-2**

gaboard, gaboate See **gabbart**

gaboriot See **gabarot**

gadhu, gadu See **balam**

gaeta Gill net **fishing boat**★ of the Istrian and Dalmatian coasts dating from at least the 14th century. In recent years, used more for cargo. Double-ended; stem rounded and stemhead projects ca. 45cm above the gunwale; sternpost vertical; bow and stern full; rounded bottom into flaring sides; deep hull; straight keel; narrow rudder extends below keel. On the **gaeta falkuša**, freeboard increased by movable washboards. Decked to mast with space for gear below, and for ca. 1.0m at the stern.

gaeta

On the Dalmatian coast, some decked types may be called **leuto**★. The Dalmatian boat often sets a fire on the foredeck grating to attract sardines at night. Sets a single lateen sail or a quadilateral lateen-type sail with short luff; sometimes a jib to a long bowsprit, and in very light winds, a mizzen. Also rowed with 3-8 oars single-banked, standing and facing forward; now mostly motorized. Some Dalmatian boats employed an outrigger-type device with a tholepin at each end for solo rowing. Crew of 3-5; early 18th-century boats that carried mail required 8 men. Reported lengths 3-9m; e.g., length 5m, beam 2m, depth 1.5m; as long as 12m in Dalmatia. Other recorded names: **gaeta ribarica** (fishing type), **gaita**★, **gaieta** (**falkusha**), **gajeta**, or **gojeta** (on the Dalmatian coast); **Trieste barge**; pl. **gaete**, **gajete**. Note also **traget**.

gaeta falkuša, gaeta ribarica, gaete See gaeta
gaff cutter See cutter-3
gaffelaar *Netherlands:* Gaff-rigged inland vessel with a standing gaff sail. Rounded hull with a strong sheer. Decked; hatches abaft the mast. Tiller came inboard below the deep top strake. Also set a jib to a jibboom, staysail, and topsail to a topmast. Note also **gaffelkaag, gaffelschuit**.
gaffelkaag *Netherlands, S and central:* **Kaag★** type of the late 18th and early 19th centuries. Designed mainly for the larger rivers. Used for lightering and to carry stone for the Dutch dikes; some served as **passage boats★**. Bluff bow with high, pointed stemhead; rounded stern; flat floors. Flat sheer amidships, rising toward the ends. Two heavy wales; rounded leeboards. Tall rudder; tiller came inboard through a triangular hole in the top strake. Decked; low deckhouse aft; peaked hatches. Mast stepped forward of hatches. Long standing gaff; sail brailed to the mast. Jib to a running bowsprit. Might set a topsail. Crew of 3. One reported 18m long, beam 5.2m, depth 2m. Other recorded names: **gaffelschip, lichter, ligter**; pl. **gaffelkagen**
gaffelkagen See **gaffelkaag**
gaffelkotter, gaffelkutter See **cutter-3**
gaffelschip See **gaffelkaag, gaffelschuit**
Gaffelschlup See **Schlup-2**
gaffelschoener, Gaffelschoner See **schooner**
gaffelschuit *Belgium:* Solidly built cargo and passenger vessel of Belgium and Dutch waterways. Related to the **otter★**. Extinct by the end of the 19th century. Bluff bow and stern; deep curved stem; straight sternpost. Flat bottom, angular bilges. Medium tumble home on top strake at bow. Some rose sharply at the stern to enable the tiller to pass through below the top strake. Decked; large central hatch with rounded cover; cabin aft with a roof flush with the steering deck. Wide, rounded leeboards. Loose-footed gaff sail had a long standing gaff; tall, strikable mast. Jib to a running bowsprit. Supplemented in the early 19th century by a "falling gaff." Reported lengths 10-20m; 43-140t. Other recorded names: **gaffelaar, gaffelschip, Gaffelschute, scute à corne**. Note also **schuit**.
Gaffelschute See **gaffelschuit**
gaffer Colloquial term for a boat rigged with a gaff sail, i.e., a fore-and-aft, roughly rectangular sail supported by a spar at the head of the sail and hung from the after side of the mast. Sail can have a boom at the foot to which it may or may not be laced, or be entirely loose-footed with no boom. See also **Polperro gaffer**.
gaff ketch See **ketch-2**
gaff-rigged schooner, gaff schooner See **schooner**
gaffy See **Polperro gaffer**
gaff yawl See **yawl-2**
gagalı *Turkey:* Two-masted **coaster★** of the Black Sea and Istanbul; worked until the early 20th century. Sharp bow with strongly curved stem; small, V-shaped transom; long, straight keel; flat floors; rounded bilges; vertical sides; strong sheer, especially at the bow where it rose to meet the stemhead in a point. Narrow outboard rudder; short tiller. Flush deck; large central hatch; freeboard increased by weathercloths

amidships. Square sails on the fore- and mainmasts and a boomed gaff sail abaft the mainmast. Long, rising bowsprit. Reported lengths 12-24m, beam 4-6m, depth 2-3.2m, draft 1.8-3m. Other recorded names: **marticana, martıka, martingana, martıqa, martuka**
gagap See **kapap**
ğahāz See **jahazi**
gaiassa *Egypt:* Bulk cargo vessel of the Nile that sails upstream with the prevailing northerly wind and drifts downstream with the current; also used on the Suez Canal and the Red Sea. Flat bottom; bottom planks brought up about halfway up the stem; keel at ends only. Bow blunt to almost flat; height varies greatly; now generally a slight sheer at bow. Sides flared; flat sheer and low freeboard. Maximum beam well forward, tapers aft to a transom stern. Thin planking nailed to stout ribs; sheathing of planks over the ribs forms a hold. Some now made of steel and are called

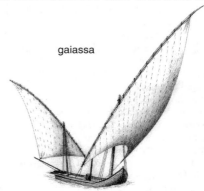

gaiassa

sandals★. High bulwarks stop before the transom proper, ending in a sort of false transom; bulwarks may be set back for polers. Huge rudder controlled by a long, thick, 2-piece tiller that lashes to the rudder. Individual boats identified by colored bands on the mast and yard top. One to 3 masts; most have steps on the side to enable crew to climb aloft. Some masts can be struck, especially on the single-masted craft. Lateen sails; on some, the foresail and mizzen are quadrilateral lateen-type sails with a short luff, or the mizzen may be a quadrilateral sail. The exceedingly long main yard is in 3 pieces, lashed together. Sail may be boomed out forward; outrigger aft. High point of the bow holds the lifting tackle. On recent steel-hulled vessels, the lateen sail may be boomed at the foot. Also poled or rowed. Crew of 2-3. Reported lengths 7.6-24m; e.g., length 17m, beam 3.7m, depth 1.0m. Other recorded names: **'aiyassa, ayasah** (Cairo); **ayassa, gayas(s)a, ghayassah, ghiasha, giyassa, gyassa, qayas(s)ah; faluka, felucca★,** or **fụlūka★**. Note also **markab-1, qatrah**.
gaibao See **ghe bâ'u**
gaï caou See **ghe câu**
gaieta, gaieta falkusha See **gaeta**
ğaijārīje See **qaiyarīyah**
gaillotte See **galiot**
gaing See **fluit**
gaï oko *Solomon Islands, western Pacific:* Simple, undecorated **dugout canoe★** used on the west coast of

Guadalcanal. Hull rounded in cross section; double-ended; sharp cutwater; curved bottom. Other recorded names: **gaï okoa, gie oko(a), gie orkoa, uaga, waga***
gaï okoa See **gaï oko**
gaita 1. *Greece:* **a.** Two-masted ship cited in the early 19th century. Raised poop deck; tall, recurved stem. Foremast raked forward and set a lateen sail; mainmast raked aft and set a lug- or gaff sail with topsail. Jibs to rising jibboom. Reported lengths 15-20m. **b.** Relatively small, sharp-ended **fishing boat*** that worked in the 20th century in the Aegean Islands. Curved stem; raked, straight sternpost; keel.
2. *Indonesia, central:* Term for **raft*** in the Atinggola dialect of northeastern Sulawesi (Celebes).
See also **gaeta**.
gajeta, gajete See **gaeta**
ğajjārīje See **qaiyarīyah**
gal *Guinea-Bissau/Senegal:* **1.** Generic term of the Wolof peoples of Senegal for a **boat*** or **ship***.
2. More specifically, a plank-extended **dugout canoe*** with ram-type ends used for fishing on coastal Senegal; type also seen on the Guinea-Bissau coast (the **pirogue***). Construction details vary somewhat from area to area; some are sewn (**gal u bêtêni**), others nailed (**gal u mbul**). Dugout base elongated at each end by as much as 2.5m; bottom flattened transversely and curved longitudinally; each ram bottom notched at hull end. Two or 3 strakes added to the basal dugout; some strengthened inside by a longitudinal plank. Two to 5 low seats; may be decked at ends, terminating in breakwaters. Coated with tar inside and out and decorated with names and designs. Steered with a paddle.

gal-2

Bamboo or wooden mast stepped forward or roughly amidships, stayed to forward ram. Sets a boomed, loose-footed spritsail; rope snotter holds sprit high. Paddled; sometimes rowed with rowers facing forward. Most large types now modified for a motor. Crew of 5-6. Reported lengths overall 3-15m; e.g., length overall 14m, usable length ca. 8m, beam 1.4m, depth 0.6m. Other recorded names: **gal bumak** (large), **gal gundao** (small). Further reading: G. Balandier and P. Mercier, *Les Pêcheurs Lebou du Senegal* (Saint-Louis, Senegal: Institut française Afrique Noire, 1952).
Other recorded names: **gaal, galle, lith**
galaboot See **barge-2**
galander, galandria, galandrie See **chelandia**
galanzieri See **galanziero**

galanziero *Italy, Sardinia:* Type of **battello*** that specialized in transporting galena ore mined on the Sulcis coast. Spelling variant: pl. **galanzieri**
galar *Poland:* **Barge***-like craft that transported grain and other products on Polish rivers, especially on upper Vistula River tributaries, into the 1950s. Long and low with rise to the flat bottom at the ends. Lightly flared sides, each consisting of 2 planks, caulked with moss; wide, flat stern transom; bow transom common. Ends strengthened by a crossbeam. Alternating single frames of natural-grown crooks and floor timbers. Some rowed by the crew aft and steered with long sweeps at bow and stern. Crew of 4-9; special names given to boats, depending on the number in crew; e.g., one with 6 crew members was a **szóstkowy**; one with 9 was a **dziewiątkowy galar**. Reported lengths 18-36m, widths 5.7-9m, low sides; very shallow draft. Other recorded names: **dziewiątak, galler(a), krakowski galar, piątak, piątkowy galar, siódmek, ulanowski galar**; pl. **galary**
galär See **galley**
galäräsping See **äsping-2**
galarek *Poland, SE:* Transported goods and recently served as a **ferryboat*** on the Wisłoka River; prior to the 20th century, could also be found on other rivers. Some designed to carry horse-drawn carts. Carvel-planked; sparsely timbered, floor and side timbers of natural crooks. Sides slightly flared; flat bottom curved up slightly; recently planked athwartships. Low end transoms. Lengths to 6m; e.g., length 5.74m, width 1.6m, depth ca. 0.6m.
galary See **galar**
ğalâsa See **galeass**
galata *Mediterranean:* Pre-10th-century vessel similar to, and possibly the precursor of, the **tarida***. Cited as late as the early 14th century. Spelling variant: pl. **galatae**
galatae See **galata**
galava, galawa See **ngalawa**
galay See **panco**
galbat *India, W:* **1.** At Bombay (Mumbai) in the late 19th century, might refer to a large vessel of foreign origin. One that was armed was a **sileposa-galbat**.
2. A beamy **fishing boat*** of the Satpati area north of Bombay. Carvel-planked, sharp bow, straight keel, high gunwale. 5-30t disp. Note also **bot-3**.
Further reference: **gallivat**
galbote See **galiot**
gal bumak See **gal-2**
gālbūt See **jalbūt-1**
gale *Indonesia, central:* Long, slender, oared craft of early 17th-century rulers of Gowa, southern Sulawesi (Celebes). Employed a stern rudder and lateral rudders.
galé See **galley**
galea See **galley**
galea ad corallos See **galea di corallo**
galeaça See **galeass**
galea capitana See **capitane**
galeace See **galeass**
galea coralorum See **galea di corallo**
galea de Fiandra See **Flanders galley**

galea di corallo *Italy:* In the 15th century, special Venetian **galleys**⋆ were assigned to transport coral from the leased coral fisheries off Tunisia to the eastern Mediterranean. Name variants: **galea ad corallos**, **galea coralorum**. Note also **corallina**.

galeae See **galley**

galea grossa See **galeazza**

galeai See **galley**

galeam See **galleon**

galeão *Portugal:* **1.** One of a team of boats working out of the Tagus Estuary, employing the large ring net. The rest of the team includes the motorized **mother ship**⋆, also called **galeão**, several **buques**⋆, and 1-2 small **botes**⋆ to serve the **mother ship**. The sailing **galeão** transports the net and aids in setting and hauling it. Carvel-planked; sharp ends; curved stem with shredded wool on the stemhead to reduce chafing of the sail; curved sternpost; keel. Decked, 5 hatches. Outboard rudder; tiller. Mainly rowed; 7 rowing benches along each side; 2 men on each of the 6 oars forward of the mast, and 2 on the 8 oars abaft the mast. Oars held to tholepins by strops. Quadrilateral lateen-type sail with a short luff used when going to and from the fishing grounds. Forward-raking mast secured by single shrouds. Crew of 40 men and 4 boys. Length 15.7m, beam 4m, depth 1.0m, 13.65rt.
2. To the south and off the Algarve coast, the **galeão** is similarly employed and aided by smaller, similar boats, the **galeonetes**. Decked. Lateen sail or quadrilateral lateen-type sail with a short luff set to a forward-raking mast; mast vertical on the **galeonetes**. Reported lengths 16-20m, widths 3-4m, inside depths 0.9-1.52m.
3. The **galeão** out of Setúbal to the south of Lisbon engaged in fishing for tuna and served as a small **coaster**⋆, carrying salt and cork oak. Worked until the early 1960s. Sharp ends; raked bow; slightly raked sternpost; moderate sheer; outboard rudder; tiller. Set a large lateen sail originally, later a gaff sail with foresail. Reported lengths 15-20m; e.g., length 18m, beam 1.5m. Spelling variant: pl. **galeões**. See also **galleon**.

galea oberte per popa See **huissier**

galeas 1. *Finland:* **Topsail schooner** of the Åland Islands that made regular trips to Stockholm across the southern Gulf of Bothnia during the 19th and early 20th centuries. Carried cargo, particularly firewood. Clinker-built; wide transom stern; sharp bow; decked. Tall masts; standing gaff sails; very tall topmasts with long, narrow gaff topsails. Crew of 2-4. Reported lengths 20-30m, length-to-beam ratio ca. 3.5:1; relatively shallow draft. Other recorded names: **ålands-galeas, kaljaasi, vedgaleas**
2. *Norway:* Two-masted cargo vessel popular during the 19th century for carrying, among other things, salted and dried fish to the Mediterranean, the Baltic, and in mid-century, to Latin America. Dated from the mid-18th century; extinct. In general, the hull followed the lines of the **jakt**⋆, and it was not unusual for a **galeas** to be created by lengthening a **jakt** and stepping a 2nd mast. Bow sharp with a straight stem; wide, raked, square stern; steeply rising floors; strong sheer. Flush deck; deep bulwarks; outboard rudder.

Ketch⋆-rigged, the tall mainmast setting both a boomed gaff sail and 2-3 square sails on crosstrees forward of the mast. Mizzenmast set a boomed gaff sail. Both masts carried topsails and 3-4 headsails. Last vessels motorized. Crew of 4-7. Reported lengths 15-27m; e.g., length 21m, beam 6m, depth 4m. Name variant: **galéasse norvegiénne**
3. *Sweden:* Trader that worked until the 1930s. Older vessels clinker-built; later carvel or a combination of clinker and carvel. Most double-ended with well-rounded quarters; stem straight, raked, or rounded with a cutaway forefoot. Strongly curved or straight, raked sternpost; some transom-sterned. Early vessels open; later decked with trunk cabin aft. Outboard rudder; tiller came in below the gunwale. During the 19th century, the rigging was modified from square sails on both masts, the mizzen being shorter, to gaff-rigged, with the foremast sometimes slightly shorter. Set gaff topsails on both masts and 2-3 headsails. Sometimes 3- or 4-masted. Also rowed in the 16th-17th centuries. Many later **galeaser** (pl.) motorized. Reported lengths 13.6-17m; widths 4.25-6.5m. Note also **ålandsskuta**.
Spelling variants: **galease**⋆, **galeasen**, **galjas**, **galleass**, **gallias**; pl. **galeaser**. See also **galease**, **galeass**, **galley**.

galease *Denmark:* Beamy, **ketch**⋆-rigged vessel used for fishing and cargo transport locally and on the North and Baltic Seas. Early vessels also went at least as far as the Mediterranean and to Greenland. Several still sail as **yachts**⋆; these vessels are frequently lengthened and re-rigged from **jagten** (see **jagt**). Lightly built hull with square, rounded, or counter stern. Decked, some with deckhouse; early boats had a taffrail; later types had deep bulwarks; generally hung a boat on aft davits. Main- and mizzenmasts carried running topmasts. Set loose-footed, boomed gaff sails and 3 headsails. Topsails were square on the earlier boats, gaff later. Some employed a leg-of-mutton sail on the mizzen and occasionally on the mainmast also. Auxiliary motors installed on most in later years. Later boats ranged from 10-29m in length, 3-7.6m in width, 0.9-3.45m in draft. Spelling variant: **galeas**. See also **galeas**, **galeass**.

galeasen, galeaser See **galeas**

galeases See **galeazza**

Galeas-Ewer See **Galeass-Ewer**

galeasia See **galeazza**

galeass 1. *Mediterranean:* Developed toward the end of the 15th century from the Venetian **galeazza**⋆ as a large, heavy oared and sailing vessel. Some conducted naval excursions into the Atlantic. Some built on the northwest coast of Spain. Distinguished from the **galley**⋆ by its decking, a type of grating that covered the rowers; this decking made handling the sails and launching weapons easier since the **galeass** was more heavily armed than the ordinary galley. High poop, raised deck forward; recurved or a ram beak at the bow; square stern. Mostly 3-masted, setting all lateen sails or a combination of square and lateen. Rowed with 3-7 men to an oar, 25-32 oars per side, requiring as many as 343 rowers. In addition, there would be ca. 120 sailors and perhaps 170 soldiers. Reported lengths 47-80m; length-to-beam ratio ca. 5:1.

2. *British Isles:* The large English **galeass** came into prominence in the 16th century but was used only a short time. More heavily built than the Mediterranean vessel, as rowing was secondary. Square stern, beak. High freeboard; oarports below the gun deck. Square-rigged on 3-4 masts, the after 2 considered mizzens and rigged with lateen sails. Crew of 100-220 mariners and 16-20 gunners. One reported as 24m long on keel, 6.7m wide, 3.4m hold depth.

3. Also in the 16th century, a **galeass** of northern Europe might be a moderately sized ship that worked without oars.

4. In the Baltic Sea area, **galeass** (also spelled **galeas★** or **galease★**) means a **ketch★**-rigged cargo vessel of the mid-18th century to the 2nd quarter of the 20th century; some now sail as pleasure craft. Carried bulk cargo throughout the Baltic and northern Europe. Generally set a boomed, loose-footed gaff sail; the mizzen fairly large; a small, square topsail on the mainmast; and 3 headsails. Some 3-masted **topsail schooners**. Square stern, deep deadwood; moderate rise to the floors, soft bilges; vertical stem or clipper bow with cutaway forefoot; strong sheer. Decked; some carried leeboards. Reported lengths 20-30m. Other recorded names: **Baltic dandy (ketch,** or **trader),** pl. **galeaser**

5. *Germany:* The German **Galeass** served as a **coaster★** mainly in the Baltic from the mid-18th into the early 20th century; some worked out of the Elbe Estuary on the North Sea coast. Mainly identified by its **ketch** rig since the hull design varied during its period of operation. Early vessels had full bows and a lightly curved stem; later, were sharper forward with a straighter or slightly convex stem. Stern rounded with a flat transom (**Heckgaleass**) or had a short counter. Long, straight keel; most with a bar keel; steep rise to the floors on early vessels, later rather flat; strong sheer on the older craft. Decked; generally high coaming around a central hatch; deckhouse aft. Some employed leeboards. In addition to boomed, loose-footed gaff sails, topsails, and multiple headsails, the **Galeass** characteristically set square sails forward of the mainmast. Most later vessels had auxiliaries. Crew of 4-10. Reported lengths 13-27m; e.g., length on keel 22m, beam 7m, hold depth 2.4m. Other recorded names: **Heckschiff;** pl. **Galeassen.** Note also **Galeass-Ewer, Hukergaleass, Jachtgaleass.**

Selected name variants: **ĝâlâsa, galeaça, gal(l)eace, galeas, galease, galeassa, Galeasssschiff, galeasse, galeatzarra, galeaza, galeaze, galeazza★, galeona, gal(l)iace, galiache, galias★, galiassa, galiasse, gal'-jas, galjass, galleas, galleass(e), gallias(s), galliasse, gallyace, gallyasse, galyas, gauliache, gaulleace, gauliasse, ghalias.** Note also **nef-1.**

galeassa See **galeass, galeazza**

galeasse See **galeass**

Galeassen See **galeass-5**

galéasse norvegiénne See **galease-2**

Galeass-Ever See **Galeass-Ewer**

Galeass-Ewer *Germany:* Two-masted 19th-century cargo vessel of the Baltic and North Seas. Some carried oranges from the Mediterranean. Narrow, flat bottom; lowest side strakes joined the bottom at right angles; subsequent strakes flared out before the turn of the bilge. Full bow, lightly rounded stem; some adopted a clipper bow in the 2nd half of the 19th century. Stern varied; some an oval transom with windows and ornamentation; others a wide flat transom; in later years, stern lightly rounded. Sharp underwater lines, full above; strong sheer forward; high sides. Some employed leeboards, others had bilge keels; by the end of the century, most had a shallow keel. Rudder came up inboard or was hung out with the tiller passing through the taffrail. Decked; generally had a deck-house. The **ketch★** rig of the mid-19th century consisted of square sails set forward of the mainmast and a gaff sail aft; gaff sail to the mizzen, sometimes with a topsail; 3 headsails. Generally a crew of 3. Reported lengths 16-20m; 1835 vessel: 16.75m long, 5.17m wide, and 2m deep. Other recorded names: **Ever-Galeasse, Galeas-Ewer, Galeass-Ever, Galeasz-Ever, galjasever.** Note also **evert, Ewer, galeass-5.**

Galeasslomme See **Lomme**

Galeasssschiff See **Galeass**

Galeasz-Ever See **Galeass-Ewer**

galea tarida See **tarida**

galea triremis See **trireme**

galeatzarra See **galeass**

galeaza See **galeass, galeazza**

galeaze See **galeass**

galeazza *Italy, NE:* Large **galley★** built by the Venetians from at least the 13th into the 18th century. Also built in Spain and France. Served both in naval engagements and as a commercial vessel (**galeazza di mercanzia**). The merchant vessels mainly sailed because of the limited endurance of the oarsmen; rowed with as many as 30 oars per side. The 17th-century **galeazza** had a strongly curved stem, full bow, curved keel, elaborately decorated counter, moderate sheer, raked sternpost, flat floors; rudderpost came up inboard. When sailing, set 3 large lateen sails plus a jib to a long bowsprit. Crew of 1,000-2,000. Reported lengths 40-52m; widths one-fifth or one-quarter of length; up to 250t burden. The Genoese **galeazza** was smaller than the regular **galley** and required a smaller crew. Other recorded names: **galea grossa, galeas★, galeasia, galeass★, galeassa, galeaza, galera grossa, galia gros(s)a, galiazza, galijaca, galleas(s), galleaz(z)a, great galley;** pl. **galeases, galeazze.** See also **mahonne-2.**

galeazza di mercanzia, galeazze See **galeazza**

galecta See **galiot**

galée See **galère-1, galley**

galée huissiere See **huissier**

Galeere *Austria:* This **galley★** type was the largest of the vessels comprising the Danube **fleet★** of the 16th and first half of the 17th century. The strongest, the **flagship★**, was called the **Capitanea** or **Imperiala;** luxurious with special amenities. Long, narrow; has keel; stepped 1-2 masts. Rowed from 16-22 thwarts with 1-2 oarsmen on each oar. A 16-bank **Galeere** had a crew of 80. Spelling variant: pl. **Galeeren.** See also **galley.**

Galeeren See **Galeere**

galée ussiere See **huissier**

galei See **galley**, **galley-5**, **galley-6**

galeia, galeide See **galley**

galeien, galeitje See **galley-5**

galej, galeja, galeje See **galley**

galeo See **galio-1**, **galleon**, **galley**

galeões See **galeão**, **galleon**

galeoia See **galleon**

galeola *Brazil, central:* Itinerant store boat of the Amazon Basin. Very large **dugout canoe★** that is covered, except at the bow, by a shelter that protects the store forward and living quarters aft. Now motorized, but formerly poled or rowed. Cap. 2-4t. Note also **igarité**, **regatão**.

galeón *Spain:* **1. Coaster★** of Galicia in northwestern Spain. Sharp ends. Set 2 lugsails; also rowed with 4-6 oars.
2. Boat used in sardine fishing, holding one end of a ring net (the *tarrafa*) while a motorized vessel closes the other end. Used mainly along the coast of Huelva in the southwest and southern Portugal. Low, slender bow, curved stem; narrow, square counter. Mainly rowed, but may also set 2 lugsails and foresail. Crew of 18-20. Reported lengths 11-30m; e.g., length-to-beam ratio ca. 3.3:1. Spelling variants: **galió**; pl. **galeones**
3. Lateen-rigged vessel. Low sides; transom stern; head cheeks. Armed with as many as 18 cannons. Low sides; transom stern; ornamented knees between the upper bow planking and the stem (head cheeks).
Further reference: **galleon**

galeona See **galeass**, **galleon**

galeone *Italy, NE:* Fast **rowing boat★** that conveyed important Venetian residents. Clinker-built below an elaborate bulwark. Figurehead on the strongly raked stem; square, tucked-up stern; rudderhead came up inboard of a stern gallery; tiller. Rowed with 4 pairs of oars. See also **galleon**.

galeones See **galeón-2**, **galleon**

galeonete See **galeão-2**

galeoni See **galleon**

galeoot See **galjoot**

galeot See **galiot**

galeota **1.** *Brazil:* **a.** In the 19th century, in the Bahia area off northeastern Brazil, a **galley★**-type craft used to transport officials and wealthy persons, and to convey holy statues during festival processions. **b.** In the Amazon Basin, a large **dugout canoe★**. Most of the hull covered by a wooden house. Square sail set in favorable winds, but mainly propelled by an engine. Spelling variant: **galiota★**
2. *Portugal:* **a.** For 16th-century Portuguese in South and Southeast Asia, a **galley**-type vessel. Generally rowed with 15-20 oars per side, 1 man to an oar. Also sailed, stepping 1-2 masts, setting lateen sails. An awning protected the stern area. Note also **brigantine-5**. **b.** In 18th- and 19th-century Portugal, the **galeota** was a vessel used by officials and sometimes by royalty. Elaborately ornamented with an awning aft. Propelled with 12-20 oars per side rowed single-banked, although the largest required 2 men per oar. Some also set a lateen sail. Reported lengths 11.5-25m, widths 2.3-3.3m.

3. *Spain:* Lesser **galley** type. Employed 15-23 banks of oars, 1 man to an oar. Lacked the forecastle of the larger **galleys**. Stepped 1-2 masts, setting lateen sails. The **galeota bombarda** was more heavily constructed and armed with 2 mortars.
Further references: **bi-mastako**, **galiot**, **galley-5**, **masta biko**

galeota à rames, galeota a remo See **galiot-1**

galeota bombarda See **galeota-3**

galeota de remos See **galiot-1**

galeota real, galeotas reaes See **real-3**

galeote See **galiot**, **galleotta**

galeoto See **galiot**, **pinnace**

galeotta *Italy:* **1.** A small, light **galley★** used mainly for war, and especially as a pursuit vessel in the eastern Mediterranean. **Galeotte** (pl.) of the 14th century employed both oars and sail. A lateen sail was set to a vertical mast. Rowed with 16-30 oars, single-banked.
2. The name reappeared during the 17th and 18th centuries for a vessel with different proportions. Rowed when necessary, but mainly sailed, setting lateen sails to 2-3 masts. The foremast was stepped in the eyes, often forward-raking; the mizzen might be fore-and-aft rigged. Bow carried a beak, and the stem might extend well above gunwale level. Ornamented, flat or rounded counter stern, and windows opened out along the sides of the poop deck. Flat or rising floors; sides might be strongly flared. Bow low and lacking a forecastle. Single deck; rudder came up through the poop. Rowed with 1-3 per oar.
3. The **galeotta piccola**, a favorite of pirates, had 10 rowing benches and a crew of 30; the **galeotta grossa** required up to 20 oars per side and a crew of 60. The **galeotta bombardiera** (see **bomb vessel**) of the period had a mortar on each side of the stem and small arms along the sides.
Other recorded names: **galeote**, **galeotta**, **galeotta da bombe**, **galiot(t)a**; pl. **galeotte**. Note also **galeota**, **galiot**, **galeotto**.

galeotta barbaresca See **galiot-7**

galeotta bombardiera See **bomb vessel**, **galeotta-3**

galeotta da bombe See **bomb vessel**, **galeotta**

galeotta grossa, galeotta piccola See **galeotta-3**

galeotte See **galeotta**

galeotto *Italy, N:* A type of **galeotta★** used on the Po River.

galeova, galeoya See **galleon**

galer *Poland, SE:* Rectangular **fishing boat★** used on lakes in the southeastern part of the country. See also **galley**.

galera *Ukraine:* Large and roughly built **barge★** that transported grain on the Dnieper (Dnepr) and Dniester (Dnestr) Rivers. Name variant: **galerka** (dim.). See also **galley**.

galera capitana See **capitane**

galera da cerimonia See **bucintoro-2**

galera grossa See **galeazza**

galera holandesa See **galley-5**

galera patrona See **patronne**

galera real See **real-1**

galère **1.** *France, E/Switzerland, W:* Oared **galley★** that patrolled Lake Geneva (Lake Léman) from the 13th to the 17th century. Early vessels were constructed by Mediterranean shipbuilders, and some were copies of the **galère réale** (see **real**). Might carry a troop of archers. Most mounted cannon forward. Poop deck, some with a cabin or tent; might also have a tent forward. Rowed by 2 men per oar with as many as 25 pairs of oars, although one large **galère** of the early 14th century, the **magna galea** (or **grande galère**), is reported to have required 116 rowers. On some, a mast was stepped amidships. One large vessel of the mid-17th century was 27m long and 5.3m wide. Other recorded names: **galée, gualee**

2. *Switzerland, W:* On Lac de Neuchâtel, a present-day **galère** is an open boat used for net fishing. Flat bottom, curved fore-and-aft; sharp bow, strongly raking stem; square, slightly raked stern, narrow stern deck; strong sheer toward the bow. Straight, flared sides; maximum beam forward of amidships; widely spaced oak ribs, numerous floor timbers. Rowed by 3 men forward on the starboard side, and a 4th rower on the port quarter. Might set a small square sail. Reported lengths 4.8-7.9m; e.g., length 7.9m, beam 2m, depth ca. 0.65m.

3. *United States, central:* Armed vessel of the French used on the Mississippi River during the 18th century. Carried ca. 50 men. Type might also be called a **galiote** (or **galliot***). Note also **demi-galère**. Further references: **galley, galley-9**

gale real See **real-1**

galère algérienne *Algeria:* Fast **galley*** of the 16th-18th centuries used in pursuit and boarding. Sat low in the water; narrow bow. Single cannon at bow and sometimes stern armaments. Mainly rowed with 6-8 oarsmen per bench. Single mast.

galère à rames See **row galley**

galère capitane See **capitane**

galère de Flandre See **Flanders galley**

galère patrone, galère patronne See **patronne**

galère réale See **real-1**

galère savoyarde *France, E/Switzerland, W:* In the late 16th-17th centuries, **galleys*** were used to protect the Savoy shores of Lake Geneva (Lake Léman). Rowed with 17-20 pairs of oars, 2 men per oar. Reported lengths 29-31m, widths 5.5-5.8m.

galère taride See **tarida**

galerka See **galera**

gales reaes See **real-1**

galetta See **galiot**

galey See **galley, galley-5, panco-1**

galeya See **galley**

galezabra See **galizabra**

gal gundao See **gal-2**

galia See **galley**

galiace, galiache See **galeass**

galia grosa, galia grossa See **galeazza**

galías *Iceland:* A **ketch***-rigged vessel of 20-100t cap.

galias See **galeass**

galiassa, galiasse See **galeass**

galiazza See **galeazza**

galibata See **gallivat**

galie, galiérs See **galley**

galiette See **galiot**

galija See **galley**

galijaca See **galeazza**

galîjca, galijica See **galley**

galijun, galijunčič See **galleon**

galio **1.** A small **galley*** of the 12th century. Other recorded names: **galeo, galionis**

2. Large 13th- and 14th-century cargo vessel of the Dalmatian coast. Other recorded names: **gallionus, gallonus**

galió See **galeón-2, galleon**

galiocta See **galiot**

galioen See **galleon**

galion *France, SW:* 18th- and 19th-century vessel of the Charente River working below Cognac. Open except for low cabin aft. Stern rudder, midship mast. Under 30t. Name variant: **galiot***. See also **chalupa-9b, galleon**.

galiona, galione, galioni See **galleon**

galionis See **galio-1, galleon**

galionus See **galleon**

galioot See **galjoot**

galiot **1.** A subclass of **galley***, mainly of southern Europe. Reportedly used from the 12th to the 18th century. A fast vessel, initially mainly rowed and later, more often sailed. Speed made them desirable as chase vessels, especially by corsairs (see **7** below), and as despatch vessels. Lacked the bow platform of larger **galleys**. Usually one man per oar; most had 16 or 20 oars per side. Usually set a single lateen sail. Armed with 1-2 bow cannons, and each oarsman was also a soldier and equipped with a musket. A 20-bank **galiot** of the 17th century was reported to be 32m long, 4.4m wide, 1.6m deep; a mid-18th-century vessel was 15m long, 3.6m wide. Other recorded names: **galeota a remo, galeota à rames, galeota de remos, galiote à rames, light galley, rowing galiote**. Note also **half galley**.

2. The northern **galiot** was an entirely different vessel: a **barge***-like sailing trader. Especially popular in the Netherlands (see **galjoot**), Germany, and Scandinavia, working during the 17th-19th centuries; a few still reported from these areas. Main areas of operation were the North and Baltic Seas; a few made oceanic voyages, some for whaling; and some were used on rivers and lakes. Clinker- or carvel-built; bluff bow, rounded stern; flat floors; straight sides; greatest beam forward of the mainmast; marked sheer. Usually leeboards; outboard rudder; tiller. Bilge keels helped reduce drift. Decked; often had a deck house. Mainly 2-masted, the mainmast setting a square sail forward and a gaff behind; one or more square topsails or a gaff topsail. Mizzenmast set a lateen or gaff sail. Several headsails; long bowsprit and jibboom; watersail used at times. The **schooner***-rigged **galiot** became popular, especially in Germany (the **Schunergaliot**); these usually set topsails on both masts and had a clipper bow. Reported lengths 7-23m, widths 5-8m, hold depths 1.7-2.2m, draft 1.4-1.8m; cap. to 160t. Other recorded names: **Einmast-Galiot, Galiotschiff, hoy***

3. *England, W:* **Galliots** were built on the Rivers Weaver and Mersey in the latter part of the 18th and into the early 19th century. Served as **coasters***.

Similar rounded and bluff ends; flat bottom. **Ketch**★ rig; square topsail on the mainmast until the mid-19th century. Reported lengths 19.2-20.7m, widths 4.9-5.6m, depths 2.1-2.3m. Name variant: **galliot-flat**

4. *France, north-central:* During the 18th and into the 19th century, long, covered **galiotes** provided transportation on the upper Seine River, running from Paris to Versailles or Saint-Cloud. Attracted a clientele from the general populace, as they were less expensive than the **coche d'eau**★.

5. *Germany:* **a.** Important **coaster** along the North Sea; built especially on the Eider River (the **Eidergaliot**), the right-bank tributaries of the Elbe River (the **Elbgaliot**), and the Weser River. Built until the early 19th century; on the Eider to the 1930s. Smaller than the Baltic Sea **Galiot**. Also served as **pilot boats**★ off the Eider (**Eiderlotsengaliot**). Flat floors or low deadrise; straight keel, sometimes bilge keels. Mainly carvel-planked (**Kraweel-Galiot** or **Cravel-Galiot**), some clinker (**Klinker-Galiot**). Sharp bow; some a clipper bow; rounded stern; moderate sheer; relatively low freeboard. Decked, usually with a deck cabin. Outboard rudder; a few steered with a wheel; rarely used leeboards. Mainly **ketch**-rigged with loose-footed, boomed gaff sails; gaff topsail to the mainmast and sometimes on the mizzenmast. Yard on mainmast might carry a square sail. One or 2 jibs to a rising bowsprit and jibboom; staysail. Crew of 3-4. Reported lengths 15-23m; length-to-beam ratio ranged from 3.5:1 to 4.2:1. Other recorded names: **Eidergaljoot, Wewelsflether Galiot. b.** Post-World War I German **Galioten** (pl.) were mainly bulk cargo carriers on rivers and canals. Constructed of steel; flat-plate keel; grounding keels; elliptical counter stern; leeboards. Foresail set flying; sometimes topsail on the mainmast, none on mizzenmast. Reported lengths 20-28m; shallow draft.

6. *Italy, W:* The so-called 18th-century **galiote** in the Naples area is considered a type of **felucca**★. A private craft designed to transport passengers locally. Carvel-planked with sawn frames; shallow keel; low rise to the floors; soft turn of the bilges. Sheer higher at the stern, which had a cabin. Small high transom; beakhead at the bow. Rich ornamentation included a figurehead. Outboard rudder; tiller. Rowed with 9 oars per side, double-banked. Also sailed, probably setting a spritsail. Length ca. 14m, beam 2m, depth 1.0m.

7. *Mediterranean:* The **galiot** was a major type of vessel of the North African Barbary corsairs into the 18th century. Rowed with 12-23 banks of oars, the larger vessels requiring as many as 3 men per oar. Also sailed, setting a single lateen sail. Armament set forward. Carried 50-150 people. Other recorded names: **Barbary galiote, galeotta barbaresca, galiote barbaresque, quarter galley**. Note also **corsair, galiote**.

8. *Russia, E:* The **galiot** in the Russian-American trade of the late 18th century was a capacious, roughly built **coaster**★. Carried passengers in addition to cargo. Full-bodied, beamy. Stepped 2 short, heavy masts; rigged in the manner of the northern **galiot**; employed a watersail to the bowsprit.

9. *Switzerland, W:* Armed **galiots** were part of the **fleet**★ on Lake Geneva (Lake Léman) in the 16th-17th centuries. Rowed by 2 men per oar; 36- and 40-oared vessels reported. Carried a large cannon on the poop, 2 smaller ones at the bow, and 6 small pieces along the sides. Reported lengths 29.3-30.8m, widths 5.5-5.9m, depth 3.3m. Name variant: **parve galée**

10. *United States, E:* In the colonial period, a **ferry**★ on Virginia's Eastern Shore in Chesapeake Bay might be called a **galliot**. Economically built.

Selected name variants: **caliotta, caliotus, galbote, galecta, galeot(e), galeota**★, **galeoto, galeotta**★, **galetta, galiette, galio(c)ta, galiote, galiotta, galjoot**★, **galjot, Galjote, Galjottschiff, galleot(a), galleoth, galleotte, galliot(h), galliota, galliote, galliott(e), galyet, galyott, ghaliot, gualiot, gualveta, huma fandarga**. Note also **kalita**. Further reference: **galion**

galiòta *France, S:* In the language of Languedoc, a small **galley**★.

galiota See **galeota-1, galeotta, galiot**

galiota de bombas See **bomb vessel**

galiote *Algeria:* Small, light, Algerian-built **galley**★ of the 17th- and 18th-century Algerian **fleet**★. Rounded ends. Rowed; 14-25 benches. Also sailed. Note also **galiot-7**. Further references: **galère-3, galiot, galiot-4**

galiote à bombes, galiote à mortiers See **bomb vessel**

galiote à rames See **galiot-1**

galiote barbaresque See **galiot-7**

galiote de Holland See **trekschuit-3**

galioten See **galjoot**

galiotever See **Galiot-Ewer**

Galiot-Ewer *Germany, N:* Large, flat-bottomed vessel built occasionally on the Ems, Weser, and Elbe Rivers in the latter part of the 19th century. Sharper lines than the **Ewer**★; rounded stern; decked; leeboards. **Ketch**★-rigged. Beamy. Spelling variants: **galiotever, galjootever, Galliot-Ewer**

Galiotschiff See **galiot-2**

galiotta See **galeotta, galiot**

galiotte See **galiot**

galiotte Hollandoise See **galjoot**

galioun, galiouni See **galleon**

galioute See **galiot**

galippe *France, SW:* Reported on the Dordogne River in the 15th century as a rowed vessel, apparently used for pillaging. May have been covered with leather. See also **galupe**.

galisabra See **galizabra**

galita See **kalita**

galite *Venezuela, E:* Term applied in the 16th century to the native **dugout canoes**★ of the eastern coastal area. See also **galiot**.

galito *France, S:* **Fishing boat**★ of the Sète area. Popular in the late 19th century, with 153 boats employing 595 fishermen. Also participated in regattas. Length 5m, beam 2m, draft 0.5m.

gal'iun See **galleon**

galivat See **gallivat**

galizabra *Mediterranean:* Armed vessel of the 16th-17th centuries that combined characteristics of the **galley**★ and the **zabra**★. Beak projected ca. 4.5m beyond the stem; square stern. Sometimes a platform extended outboard along the sides and aft. Decked; raised poop; 2 hatches, one forward, the other abaft the mast. When rowed, employed 14 oars per side. Stepped a single mast setting a quadrilateral lateen-type sail with a short luff. One reported as 29m long overall, 21m on keel, 8m beam. A 1568 Spanish **galizabra** had a keel-to-beam ratio of 2.5:1 and length-to-beam ratio of nearly 3.7:1. Other recorded names: **galezabra, galisabra, galleyzabra, gallizabra, treasure frigate**

galjas See **galeas, galeass**

galjasever See **Galeass-Ewer**

galjass See **galeass**

galjoen See **galleon**

galjoot *Belgium/Netherlands:* **Coaster★** and seagoing ship developed in the late 17th century. Probably the forerunner of the **galiot★** built elsewhere in northern Europe. Used through the 19th century. Some were lean, fast, and heavily canvassed **advice boats★**; many of these served the Dutch Company in the Far East. A variety carried the mail, and many regularly transported passengers between the Netherlands and England, having appropriate accommodations and a crew of 7. The type was also seen on the Great Lakes. One type engaged in fishing; these were smaller and had a fish hold. Bluff, rounded ends; flat floors; flat sides; strong sheer, especially at the stern. The fast **hardloper-galjoot** had sharper lines at the stern. Used leeboards in the 17th century; later, large vessels had a keel and no leeboards. Decked, usually with a deckhouse amidships and cabin aft. Outboard rudder; tiller. The small 17th-century **galjoot** employed a standing gaff mainsail and numerous headsails; long, rising bowsprit. **Ketch★**-rigged by the 19th century with gaff or lateen mizzen. The Groningse **galjoot** of the 19th century was a **topsail schooner**; these **schoenergaljooten** had a sharper bow and narrower stern. Some were **brigantine★**- or **brig★**-rigged; later vessels were 3-masted and **ship★**-rigged. Reported lengths 18-30m; an 1830 vessel was 27m long, 7.2m wide, and 3.8m deep; shallow draft. Other recorded names: **galeoot, galioot, galiot(t)e Hollandoise, gal(l)iot hoy, Groningen** (or **Groninger) galjoot**; pl. **galioten, galjoten**. Note also **galiot**.

galjootever See **Galiot-Ewer**

galjot, Galjote See **galiot**

galjoten See **galjoot**

Galjottschiff See **galiot**

gal'jun See **galleon**

galladella See **half galley**

gallaire, gallayre See **galley**

galle See **gal, galley**

gallea See **galley**

galleace See **galeass**

galleae See **galley-5**

galleão See **galleon**

galleas See **galeass, galeazza**

gallease See **galley-5**

galleass See **galeas, galeass, galeazza**

galleasse See **galeass**

galleaza, galleazza See **galeazza**

gallée See **galley**

galleggiante *Italy:* **1.** An Italian word that can mean a **raft★, float★, lighter★,** or **craft★**. Spelling variant: pl. **galleggianti**. Note also **mulino galleggiante**.
2. In Venice, the **galleggianti** were special ceremonial **barges★** that floated along the Grand Canal at night, providing music, opera, and theatrical performances.

galleggianti See **galleggiante**

gallei See **galley-5**

galléole See **barque longue**

galleon **1.** Variously described as a small, single-banked, 12th-century **galley★**; as the largest of the boats carried aboard a ship (16th century); and as a **merchantman★** or **man-of-war★** of the 16th-17th centuries, the latter use more prevalent in the 17th century. Some confusion arises from the looseness of terminology in the period and by the alteration of a particular ship from one type to another. Although best known as a Spanish vessel, it is reported to have originated in England and ranged from the Mediterranean to the Baltic. The term **galleon** (or the Spanish **galeón★**) was also given to each vessel, large or small, that set sail annually from Spain to Cartagena (Colombia) and Portobelo (Panama) with supplies, returning with silver, gold, and other precious merchandise from Peru. Vessels of the **fleet★** that went to Mexico were given the name **flota**. The **galleon** of the Basques engaged in whaling off Newfoundland and Labrador and was sometimes called a **nao**. The merchant and man-of-war **galleon** had a relatively low forecastle, set back from the bow; the after decking stepped up in a series of half and quarter-decks to a very high, square poop. Marked tumble home. A long, low beakhead extended forward from the bow. Narrower and lower than earlier vessels, with reduced fore- and aft castles. Square sails were set to the forward 2 masts and a lateen sail to the 1-2 mizzenmasts; spritsail rigged below the bowsprit. As many as 600 in crew. Early 16th-century merchant **galleons** had a length-to-beam ratio of 3:1. One English **galleon** of 1590 was 18.2m long on keel, 7.9m wide, with a 4m hold depth. Built to over 1200t after 1639. 17th-century Turkish **galleons** were 35-50m long. Note also **argosy, whaler-2**.
2. A 15th-century cargo vessel that worked on European rivers under oar and sail. The **galleoni** (pl.) of Venice were used for river patrols.
3. *Philippines:* A **fleet★** of Philippine-built, Spanish royal **galleons** (or **naos**) sailed between Manila and Acapulco on the Mexican coast during the latter half of the 16th century and into the early 19th century. Carried oriental treasures eastward and silver westward, the latter called **silver galleons**. Heavy, beamy vessel with high forecastle and poop; stoutly planked, framed, and sheathed; some had 4 decks. Mounted 50-60 guns. Crew of 60-300, and often had many passengers. Square sails set to the 3 masts. One mid-18th-century vessel was 57m long overall, 47m on keel, 15m wide, and 7.9m deep. Other recorded names: **adjung, galéon★, Manila (Acapulco,** or **Philippine) galleon, nao de China.** Further reading: William Lytle Schurz, *The Manila Galleon* (New York: E. P. Dutton & Co., 1939).

Selected name variants: **galeam**, **galeão**★ (pl. **galeões**), **galeo(na)**, **galeoia**, **galeón**★ (pl. **galeones**), **galeone**★ (pl. **galeoni**), **galeova**, **galeoya**, **galijun**, **galijunčič**, **galio**★, **galioen**, **galion(a)**, **galione**, **galioni(s)**, **galioun(i)**, **gal'iun**, **galjoen**, **gal'jun**, **galleão**, **gallion**, **galloon**, **gallyon**, **galouni**, **galûn**, **galyon**, **gal'yun**, **geliong**, **guallion**, **nau**★; in England: **king's** or **queen's ship**

galleon-frigate See **frigate**

galleoni See **galleon**

Galle oru See **oruwa**

galleot See **galiot**

galleotta See **galeotta**, **galiot**

galleoth, **galleotte** See **galiot**

galler, **gallera** See **galar**

gallere See **galley**

gallere cappitaineresse See **capitane**

gallevat See **gallivat**

galley 1. In a broad sense, a **galley** of the Mediterranean area could be a warship of any description, but generally one that was rowed.

2. In the Greek, Roman, and Phoenician periods, a long, narrow vessel, mainly rowed, using one or more tiers of oars when engaged in battle. Some had 2 hulls, joined **catamaran**★-fashion. Those serving as **merchantmen**★ were beamier and often sailed. Steered by the oars and side rudders.

3. Long, low, open vessel used in the Mediterranean, mainly in the Middle Ages but lasting into the 19th century. Beginning in the 15th century, many cargo **galleys** were state-owned, but were often chartered to merchants. In the early period, **galley** building spread to France; Spain also became important in **galley** traffic. In the Baltic, Swedish and Russian naval **galleys** were important in the 18th century. Carvel-planked; single deck; transom stern; flat bottom; long straight keel; flared sides; some had a ram bow; generally a high, covered poop. Turkish **galleys** were heavily built and relatively high out of the water, and were used mainly to transport siege forces to their destinations; one midline and 2 side rudders. **Light galleys** were mainly warships and had a length-to-beam ratio of 8:1. The heavier, more seaworthy cargo **galleys** (or **great galleys**) worked into the 15th century, mostly under sail (usually 2-3 lateen sails). Oars predominated on the fishing and naval **galleys**, which might set 1-2 lateen sails to very tall masts. Some ran on a regular schedule between ports. The 16th-century **galley** had at least 21 rowing benches and at least 3 oarsmen to a bench. Large **galleys** had over 250 in crew; the scouting vessels had a crew of ca. 70. To combat piracy, archers were included on both naval and merchant vessels. Reported lengths 27-55m; a 13th-century Italian **galley** was 38.6m long, 5.2m wide, draft ca. 1.3m. Further reading: Richard W. Unger, *The Ship in the Medieval Economy, 600-1600* (London: Croom Helm, 1980).

4. *Canada:* Used by the British in the siege of Montreal in 1760. Curved stem with projecting stem piece; square counter stern; tiller. Small quarter-deck with taffrail, windowed cabin below; elevated forecastle. Propelled by as many as 11 oars per side. Also set a

gaff mainsail, triangular studding sail, and staysail. Length ca. 18m overall, 15m on keel, depth of hold 1.2m, 30t. Name variant: **row galley**★

5. *Netherlands:* Until the mid-17th century, the Dutch and Flemish **galei** was a rowing/sailing vessel for warfare and official use (**roeibargie**). Reported as early as the 10th century. In the 16th century, some city governments used an official **stadsbargie** (or **stadsgalei**). Until the 19th century, the Dutch navy used a **galley**-like craft rowed by 30 men; also sailed, setting 2 lateen sails; 2-4 guns. The **kanoneergalei** was longer, had more oars, and was rigged as a **topsail schooner**. Some 16th-century **galeien** (pl.) had a beakhead, rounded bows, curved stem; sheer rose toward a poop deck; flat transom. Foremast close to the stem; mainmast, with topmast, stepped amidships; both strikable; set square sails; bowsprit. Later, keel added and slight rise to the narrow floors; slack bilges, flaring sides. Sharp bow; narrow square stern. Cabin at stern; 14 rowing thwarts to port, 13 to starboard. Lateen sails to 2 masts. Small type: 21m long, 4.9m wide, rowed with 2 men per oar. Large type: 37m long, 6.1m wide with 19 oars per side and crew of 60 sailors and 100 soldiers. Other recorded names: **galeitje** (dim.); **galera holandesa**, **galey**, **gallei**, **galleae**, **galeota**★; pl. **galeien**. Further reading: L. Th. Lehmann, *Galleys in the Netherlands* (Amsterdam: Meulenhoff, 1984). Note also **baardse**, **Flanders galley**.

6. *Norway:* The 17th- and 18th-century **galei** was 2-masted, setting gaff sails. Low bow with strongly raking, mildly curved stem. High, sharp, and slightly concave stern. Wooden house toward the stern. Armament forward. Rowed, between the masts, with at least 3 oars per side. Two headsails to the bowsprit.

7. *United Kingdom:* **a.** In general, a small, light, open boat that worked under oars and sail. In the latter part of the 19th century, they were carried aboard large naval vessels and were designated for the captain's use (**captain's galley**); 2-masted with dipping lugsails; 10.7m long, 1.8m wide. Used by the coast guard (lengths 6-9m, widths 1.2-1.5m), by the London River police, custom-house officers (**custom-house galley**), press-gangs (**press galley**), and as 6- or 8-oared pleasure boats. Name variant: **row galley**★. Note also **gig-2**. **b.** Heavy **galleys** were used in school rivalries, notably between Eton and Westminster. Rowed with 4-8 oars.

8. *United Kingdom/Ireland:* As early as the 13th century, single-decked **galleys** were used to combat piracy, prevent illegal trading, and monitor foreign vessels fishing inshore. In the latter half of the 16th century, the naval **galley** was rowed and sailed. Those of the 17th century were rowed from the lower deck. As many as 20 guns were positioned on the upper deck, and several were placed aft of the oarsmen on the lower deck. Crews of the 16th-century vessels ranged from 160-400 men, tonnage from 80-250t.

9. *United States:* **a.** Naval vessel of the Continental Army during the American Revolution, especially on Lake Champlain in northeastern New York State; also used on Delaware and Chesapeake Bays. **Galleys** also saw river and harbor service as **gunboats**★. Flat or round bottom, sharp or square stern, and generally had a poop deck. Many set 2 lateen sails. Also rowed, double-banked, using 14-32 oars. Reported lengths 12-32m; on the Delaware River, length on keel 16.7m, beam 4m, depth 1.37m; shallow draft. Other recorded names: **calevat, Continental galley, galère⋆, galliot, gondola⋆, row galley⋆**. Note also **guard boat-3. b.** In the late 17th and early 18th centuries, shipbuilders in America constructed **ship⋆**- and **brigantine⋆**-rigged **galleys** (or **gallies**) as armed merchant vessels that traveled to England and the Mediterranean. Flush-decked with rowing deck below; oar ports located between the gun ports or on a lower deck, although not all were suited for rowing, and the term **galley** merely indicated a hull designed for speed. Some fished on the Grand Banks. Other recorded names: **gallie, gally, runner⋆. c.** A small boat used on Narragansett Bay in Rhode Island in the mid-18th century. **d.** In a general sense, a boat of large dimensions on the Delaware River in the 19th century.

Selected name variants: **calea, galär, galé⋆, galea** (pl. **galeae, galeai,** or **galeas⋆**), **galée, Galeere⋆** (pl. **Galeeren**), **galei, galeia, galeide, galej(a), galeje, galeo, galer⋆, galera⋆, galere⋆, galey(a), gallia, galie, galiérs, gali(j)a, galîjca, galijica** (dim.), **gallaire, gallayre, gallea, gallé(e), gallere, galleya, gal(l)ie, gal(l)ya, gellée, ghalea, goleja, golija, gralai, gualee, gualere, gualie, jalie, row galley⋆**. Note also **barce, bâtard, brigantine, capitane, Flanders galley, fragata-1, galeass, galeota, galeotta, galiot, galizabra, gallivat, ghurāb, golafrus, gourabe, half galley, katorga, long ship, markab-1, real, revenue cutter-2, saettia-1, saique-1**. Further references: **Deal galley, death galley, gig-2, Mohawk boat, packet boat-4, row galley, Selsey galley, shad galley**

galleya See **galley**
galley bateau, galley batteau See **row galley**
galley boat See **row galley-2b**
galley frigate See **frigate-1**
galley gunboat See **gunboat-3**
galley keelboat See **packet boat-4**
galley punt See **Deal galley punt**
galleywat, galleywatt See **gallivat**
galleyzabra See **galizabra**
gallia See **galley**
galliace See **galeass**
gallia di condennati *Italy:* A 16th-century oared **galley⋆** crewed by slaves and indentured persons.
gallia libera *Italy:* An oared **galley⋆** manned by free men.
gallias See **galeas, galeass**
galliass, galliasse See **galeass**
gallibat See **gallivat**
gallie, gallies See **galley**
gallion See **galleon**
gallionus See **galio-2**
galliot See **galère-3, galiot, galley-9**
galliota, galliote See **galiot**
galliote à bombes See **bomb vessel**
Galliot-Ewer See **Galiot-Ewer**
galliot-flat See **galiot-3**
gallioth See **galiot**
galliott, galiotte See **galiot**

gallivat *India, west coast:* **1.** Naval vessel of the late 17th-18th centuries that carried a cannon at the bow. Elongated, raking, straight stem, curved vertically above the gunwale and capped with a globe-like ornament. Raked stern. Low sheer. Outboard rudder; tiller. Large quadrilateral lateen-type sail with a short luff set to a nearly vertical mast. Also rowed, with as many as 14 oars per side.
2. Swift **galley⋆**-type craft that was a favorite of the Maratha pirates until the latter half of the 18th century. Probably adapted from early Portuguese vessels. Term or its variants continued to be used by later Europeans for their own small craft, possibly for a **jolly boat⋆** used for reconnaissance and landing men. Armed, generally at bow and stern; split-bamboo deck, largest had fixed deck. Rowed, employing as many as 50 oars. When sailed, set a large lateen-type mainsail and a small similar-type mizzen. Shallow draft; 50-70t.
3. Later cited as a trader. Low bow with raking stem, rounded or square stern, galleries. Lateen-type sails set to 2 masts, often with headsails. Crew of 6-15. Length overall 23.5m, on keel 13.4m, beam 6m, depth 4m, 110t.
See also **jalba**.
gallizabra See **galizabra**
gallonus See **galio-2**
galloon See **galleon**
galloper *Canada, E:* Small, sharp-ended **schooner⋆** from Newfoundland that engaged in hunting seals and cod fishing, and served as a coastal trader through the 19th century. Carvel-planked; curved stem, heart-shaped transom; both raked. Sharp rise to the floors; round bilges. Flush deck, accommodations in forecastle and aft. Masts loosely stayed; single jib to bowsprit. Crew of 5-7. 1878 boat length 15.7m, beam 4.6m, depth of hold 2m; ca. 30-40t. Note also **boëtteur**.
gally See **galley-9**
gallya See **galley**
gallyace, gallyasse See **galeass**
gallyon See **galleon**
galoper See **boëtteur**
galopini, galopino See **galopinus**
galopinus *France, SE:* Type of boat that transported salt on the Rhone River. Cited in the early 14th century. Spelling variants: **galopini, galopino**
galopper See **boëtteur**
galouni See **galleon**
galta See **navata**
gal u bê-têni, gal u mbul See **gal-2**
galûn See **galleon**
galup, galupa See **galupe**
galupe *France:* **1.** Flat-bottomed cargo carrier of the Adour and Garonne Rivers in southwest France. Used from the 17th into the 20th century, but term appears as **galupus** and **galupi** in the 14th century. The largest, the **galupes sablières**, carried sand until the 20th century; the **grande galupes** carried poles for the mine at Dax and sand in the 19th-20th centuries. Sharp, upturned bow with long overhang; square, raked stern; vertically planked. Bottom planked fore-and-aft; hard chine; closely spaced heavy floor frames. Parallel

sides; irregular strakes lapped; sides lightly curved on the small boats. Flat sheer amidships, swept up at ends. Open except for a small cuddy at stern. Towing mast stepped in forward third. Steered with a heavy sweep, counterweighted with stones on the inner end; helmsman stood on a bench cleated athwartships, forward of a cuddy. Towed from shore or poled. Reported lengths 6.5-24m, depth ca. 0.6-0.8m; cap. to 50t.

2. A small **galupe**, associated with the **accon***, engages in the oyster culture industry in the embayment of Arcachon, and also fishes in other bays along the west coast. Sharp bow; square stern; flat bottom; 4 strakes along each side. Crew of 2, one at the helm, the other forward to handle the nets. Reported lengths 2.1-2.4m; e.g., length 2.3m, beam 1.2m, depth 0.56-0.6m. Name variant: **acone**

3. The **galype** is reported as a **fishing boat*** in Brittany during the Middle Ages.

4. In the vocabulary of Languedoc in southern France, a **galup** is a small **boat***, and the **galupsa** a flat-bottomed boat engaged in cargo work.

Spelling variants: **calup***, **calupus**, **galippe***, **galup(us)**, **galupa**, **galupi**, **galuppe**, **galupsa**, **galupse**, **galype**, **kaluppe**

galupe sablière See **galupe**

galupi, **galuppe**, **galupsa**, **galupse**, **galupus** See **galupe**

galveta, **galvetta**, **galvette** See **gallivat**

Galway gloachoag See **gleóiteog**

Galway hooker *Ireland, W:* Heavily built, multipurpose boat of the Galway Bay area. Probably developed in the 18th century for hook-and-line fishing; a number survive as restored recreational craft. Carvel-built with a high, rounded bow; hollow entrance; curved stem, false stem piece with strong gripe; sternpost set to a sharply raked transom. Deep drag to the long, straight keel. Depending on use, floors either low and rounded or steep with high bilge; closely spaced oak frames;

Galway hooker

strong tumble home. Cuddy forward; open waist for cargo, although some fully decked. Low freeboard aft; washboards run from transom to just forward of the foredeck break. Sharply raked, narrow, outboard rudder; short tiller. Hull tarred. Short, heavy mast that rakes aft slightly, held by an iron strap to the main beam; 2 single shrouds and forestay. High-peaked gaff mainsail loosely laced to the mast; loose-footed with boom secured to the mast well below deck level and raked upward to clear the cargo; long gaff; sheet belayed around a timber post on the quarter. Jib on long, unstayed bowsprit run out to port of the stem;

sometimes just a large staysail. Sails tanned red or black, originally with tar and butter. An 1849 boat reported as requiring 6 men; later, crewed usually by the skipper and a boy. Reported lengths 8.2-13.4m, widths 2.7-3.4m, hold depth ca. 2.1m; draft aft 1.4-1.8m. The **bád mór**, or **big boat**, was 10.6-13.4m long; the **leath bhád**, or **half boat***, was ca. 9.6m long. **Turf boats*** (**bád móna**) were usually in the larger range, but were especially shallow-draft. Other recorded names: **na hucaeri**, **turf trader**; **Claddagh** (and **Connemara**, **Rosmuc**) **hooker**. Further reading: Richard J. Scott, *The Galway Hookers, Working Sailboats of Galway Bay*, rev. ed. (Limerick: the Author, 1996). Note also **Boston hooker**, **gleóiteog**, **hooker**, **Kinsale hooker**, **púcán**.

Galway pookaun See **púcán**

galwet, **galwette** See **gallivat**

galya See **galley**

galyara See **lighter-1**

galyas See **galeass**

galyet See **galiot**

galyon See **galleon**

galyott See **galiot**

galype See **galupe**

gal'yun See **galleon**

gāmalā See **taghari**

gambara See **bark-1**

gambarra *Brazil, E:* Large 2-masted vessel of the Amazon Delta area that transports cattle, logs, etc. A

gambarra

few still used. Clipper-type bow, raked stern. Those carrying cattle have stalls for the animals; an awning between the masts protects the crew of (usually) 5. Gaff-rigged; mainmast boom extends well beyond the stern. Sometimes sets 2 jibs. Note also **canoa-3**.

gamela **1.** *Portugal, N:* Simply built, open boat used on northern rivers, especially right-bank tributaries of the Douro. Probably extant only in the extreme north. Flat bottom, flatiron shaped. Bow sharp and strongly

gamela-1

raked; on some, stem extended beyond the gunwale. Less-raked transom with tall interior sternpost. Sides straight and flared with sharp angle from the roughly parallel sides to the elongated bow. Sparsely framed;

two ribs extended above the gunwales to serve as tholepins. Stern bench, single thwart. Rowed with a pair of oars secured to the tholepin by a loop. Reported lengths 3-4.6m; e.g., length 4.6m, beam across gunwales 2.7m, on bottom 1.8m; depth 0.6m. Spelling variant: **gamella**

2. *Spain, NW:* The **gamela** of Galicia is still used. Flat, strongly raked ends, bow slightly narrower than stern; may have false stem on upper part of the bow transom.

gamela-2

Carvel-planked with 2 planks per side; sides flared; moderate sheer. Flat bottom with rocker; bilge keels. Open; some with side decks. Ships a rudder when sailing. Mainly rowed; 1-2 pairs of oars set over tholepins; some oars have a bulge at the inner end of the loom. When sailed, mast stepped into forward thwart; sets a tall, dipping lugsail. Some now have an outboard motor. Crew of 2-3. Reported lengths 3.2-5.3m; e.g., length 4.2m, beam 1.65m, depth 0.54m.

See also **masseira**.

gamella See **gamela**

gamla See **taghāri**

Gamsplätte, Gamsplette See **Plätte-1**

gan See **gan chuan**

gan chuan *China, central:* Trader that worked through the rapids on the Gan (Kan) Jiang, across Poyang Hu (lake), and as far as Nanjing (Nanking) on the Chang Jiang (Yangtze). Well-constructed; oiled hull; strong, flat bow turned up sharply to form an enclosed forecastle; stern similar but higher; flat bottom; low freeboard when loaded. Distinctive catheads for working the anchors. Wide-bladed, shallow, balanced rudder; rudderpost passed through a hole in the counter; single pair of sweeps pivoted on beams that swung out. Decked; wooden or mat house; poop roofed over. Tall masts stepped just forward and aft of the cabin; stowed on lumber irons when on the Gan River. Set battened, balance lugsails with a straight luff and rounded shoulder to the leech. Mizzen sheeted to a long outrigger. Crew of 6-14. Reported lengths 9-36.5m, widths 2.3-8.3m, depth ca. 1.7m; shallow draft. Spelling variants: **gan, Gan-Dschunke, kan★, kan chuan, kan-ch'wan, Kan-Dschunke, kan-tch'ouan**

gandoo *Myanmar:* Two-masted trader built mainly in the Henzada District northwest of Yangon (Rangoon); worked along the coast and up the Ganges River to Dhaka (Dacca). Dugout base; ribs inserted, then planks raised the sides. Generally set 2 large, square sails. Crew of 40-50. Reported lengths 16-18m, beam 7m, depth 3.7m.

gandra See **gundra**

gandra toni See **padavu**

Gan-Dschunke See **gan chuan**

gang *United States:* **1.** Term for a group of boats that engaged in menhaden seining in the latter part of the 19th century at the eastern end of Long Island. Early **gangs** composed of 4 **rowing boats★**; later they might consist of several double-ended boats towed behind a **sloop★**. Crew of 4 on each **rowing boat**; ca. 7m long and 2.4-2.7m wide. Note also **menhaden boat**.

2. A **gang boat** in Mississippi in the early 20th century was a partnership vessel, owned by several fishermen. Further reference: **Fenland lighter**

ganga See **cangia**

Ganges boat See **bāulīa**

gánguil *Spain:* **1.** Double-ended **fishing boat★** of the Cataluña coast. Sets a single lateen sail.

2. A **lighter★** that transported dredged mud and refuse from ports to the open sea. Flat bottom with trap door to disperse the dredged materials. Self-propelled or towed. One without a mast might be called a **chalana★**. Spelling variant: **gangul**. Note also **hopper**.

gangul See **gánguil**

ganja **1.** *Arabian Peninsula:* Trader resembling the **baghla★**; built at Sur on the Oman coast. In the past, often a slightly modified **kotia★** built in the Kutch area of northwestern India but operated by Arabs. Frequently used by pirates in the early 19th century. Probably extinct. Characteristically had the **kotia's** parrot's head on the long stemhead, which was modified by the addition of a trefoil crest; at the base of the stemhead, a short bar extended out each side of the bow. Stern transom less ornate than the **baghla** and may lack the vestigial quarter galleries, stern windows, and counter, but generally brightly painted designs decorate the poop. Sides flared at the poop to compensate for the wide transom. Fully decked; late 19th-century vessels had an open waist, but freeboard raised by mat weathercloths. Rudder passed through the poop or hung out when there was no counter; steered with a wheel. **Ship's boat★**, usually a **mashua★**, hung from stout catheads at the stern. Hull coated with fat and lime mixture. Normally stepped 2 masts, but might also use a jigger. Forward-raking mainmast set a large lateen sail; the vertical mizzenmast hoisted a smaller sail. Some employed a leg-of-mutton mizzen. Engines installed on most later vessels. Crew of 15-20. Reported lengths 21-39m, widths 5.5-8m, depths 2.6-4m.

2. *India, NW/Maldives:* Reported in the inventory of traders along the northwest coast of India and from the Maldive Islands off the southwest coast. Considered to be a **kotia★** with the name **ganjo** as a prefix to the ship's name.

Other recorded names: **ganjah, ganjawar, ganji, ganjo, ghancha, Ghandscha, ghangi, ghanja(h), ghuncha(h), gunja, gunjo(o), gūnyā, khansha, rand'ja, ranjah, ranji.** See also **cangia.**

ganjah, ganjawar, ganji, ganjo See **ganja**

Ganztschaike See **saique-1**

garabot See **garrabot**

garagar *Marshall Islands, northwestern Pacific:* Small, single-**outrigger canoe★** used for lagoon and inshore fishing. Mainly a paddling **canoe★**, but modified for sailing on some islands. Dugout hull with solid end pieces and washstrakes added. End pieces either cut horizontally or extend to a thin, raking projection. Bottom curves fore-and-aft; V-shaped in cross section; those that sail are flattened along the lee side. Short, stout outrigger float, kept to windward, joined by as many as 6 light booms that curve down at the ends to peg directly into the float. Two straight central booms supported by single vertical stanchions, which are driven into the float; numerous stringers and braces. Steered with a paddle. The sailing type has a small, counterbalancing platform on the lee side. A forward-raking mast is stepped amidships onto the outrigger platform, and stayed to the outer end of the main booms. Sets a triangular sail with its apex tacked to the forward end of the **canoe**; boomed at the foot. Reported lengths 3.5-6m. Spelling variants: **gargar, karegar**

garaku, garakuh See **zaruq**

garapo See **grab-4**

garay See **panco**

gâr˘b See **mahonne-4**

garbage scow See **scow-1**

garde coste, garde côte, garde côtes See **coast guard ship**

Garden Island ice boat See **ice punt-2**

garden punt *England, east-central:* Box-like craft of the River Cam in the Cambridge area. Used by a gardener to cut weeds along the bank, but popular with the young people as a general boat. Square, plumb, similar ends; sides straight or slightly curved; flat bottom, cross-planked. Wide ends could be used as seats. Punt pole also used in steering.

garde-pêche See **fishery guard ship**

garéb See **qārib**

gargar See **garagar**

garib See **qārib**

garibaldie See **baldie**

garm See **djerme**

garnaalschuitje See **garnalenschuit**

garnaatvisser See **Zeeuwse schouw**

garnalenboot See **Nieuwpoortse garnaalboot, Oostendse garnaalboot, shrimper**

garnalenkotter, Garnalenkutter See **shrimper**

garnalenpinkje See **garnalenschuit**

garnalenschuit *Netherlands, W:* Egg-shaped boat that caught shrimp (*garnaal*), working with a trawl net off the beaches of Zandvoort and Katwijk, from the beginning of the 19th century. Gone by 1940. Clinker-planked with heavy, narrow, flat floors; curved bilges and sides. Curved stem, bluff bow, narrow transom stern, low sheer, rising forward. Decked forward to the mast; some had a live well; leeboards. Gaff-rigged with loose-footed, boomed mainsail, straight gaff; foresail; jib to running bowsprit. Some installed auxiliaries. Reported lengths 7-8.5m, widths 3.2-3.85m; draft light 0.9m. Other recorded names: **garna(a)lschuitje, garnalenpinkje, garnalenschuyt, garnalenvisscher, garnelenboot, garneschuit, Zandvoortsche garnalenschuit**. Note also **Nieuwpoortse garnalenboot, Oostendse garnalenboot, schuit**.

garnalenschuyt, garnalenvisscher See **garnalenschuit**

garnalenvisser, garnalenvissersboot See **shrimper**

garnalschuitje See **garnalenschuit**

garn-åttring See **åttring-3**

garnbaad See **garnbåt-1**

garnbåt 1. *Norway, W and N:* Designation for a boat that uses a net (*garn*) in fishing, primarily for herring. Most older boats had a roller attached to the gunwale to aid in playing out and hauling the net. Clinker-planked; keel. Sharp ends; strongly raked, straight or curved stem and sternpost; sheer increased toward the curved stem; some large boats from the Hardanger area had a tucked-up, raked transom. Outboard rudder; tiller; in some districts, the tiller was attached to a single-arm yoke. Might be square-, sprit-, or gaff-rigged, depending on the period and area. The gaff-rigged Hardanger boat had a staysail, and the jib might be boomed out. Also rowed. Crew of 6-7. Reported lengths 8.5-11m; e.g., length 8.5m, beam 2.35m. Name variants: **garnbaad**. The early **garnbåt** from the Rana area in the north was called a **slagbaad** or **slagbåt**. Note also **torskegarnsbåt**.

2. *Sweden, W:* Plump **fishing boat★** of the 19th century that used a net for herring (**sillgarnbåt**) and mackerel (**makrillgarnbåt**) fishing along the coast. Clinker-planked with rounded sides, soft bilges; straight, deep keel. Similar full ends; raked stem, slightly curved; raked sternpost; considerable sheer. Outboard rudder; tiller. Cambered deck; steering well; small, open hold; cuddy forward below a raised hatch. Loose-footed, boomed gaff mainsail; sometimes a yard topsail; staysail; on some, a jib ran to a slender bowsprit. Length ca. 11m, beam 4.7m, depth 2m.

Garnboot *Germany, Baltic coast:* **1.** Rowing boat★ that fished for herring near the beaches, especially on Rügen Island, with a special net. After ca. 1900, some attended weirs, working until the late 1950s. Clinker-planked with 7 strakes per side; flat, almond-shaped box keel. Most sharp-ended; curved stem and sternpost. Open; several thwarts. Reported lengths overall 5.8-6.4m, on keel 4.15-4.95m, beam 1.83-2.55m, depth ca. 0.7-0.9m. Name variant: **Fiefmannsboot** (at Vitt bei Arkona)

2. At Neuendorf on the northwest side of Rügen, a **Garnboot** was designed for sailing and had a raking, U-shaped transom with deadwood below. Also clinker-planked; well-framed; box keel. Employed leeboards until ca. 1895, then a centerboard. Covering board along each side, low coaming. Until 1890, sprit-rigged to 2 masts, the shorter foremast stepped against the stem; thereafter gaff-rigged. Lengths overall 7-8.12; e.g., length overall 8.12m, on keel 6.3m, beam 2.66m.

Garneelenboot See **shrimper**

garnelenboot See **garnalenschuit, shrimper**

Garnelenfischer See **shrimper**

garneschuit See **garnelenschuit**

garnkwak See **kwak**

Gårnprahm See **Prahm-2**

gårnpram *Sweden, S:* Used primarily in net (*gårn*) fishing, some to carry the equipment; some equipped with a spool on which to wind the nets. Design not standardized: some sharp-ended, some square-ended, others with a wide transom. Clinker-planked with wide strakes; lightly framed; some of plywood. Flat bottom with slight rocker; slightly flaring sides. Open. Reported lengths 4.6-7.6m; e.g., length 5.8m, beam ca. 2.4m, depth ca. 0.75m. Note also **garnbåt-2**, **pålpråm**, **pråmm**.

Garnsicke See **Garnsicken**

Garnsicken *Poland, NE:* Worked a drag net in pairs on the Zalew Wiślany (Frisches Haff or Vistula Lagoon). Belongs to the **barkas★** family. Clinker-planked with narrow strakes; keel; strong sheer. Deep, lightly curved stem; rounded stern. Open; outboard rudder; tiller. Tall square sail set to the mast stepped about a third in from the bow. Reported lengths 9-10m, widths 2.9-3.5m. Other recorded names: **Garnsicke**, **Kielsicken**, **Steuersicken**

garokuh, **garooku**, **garookuh** See **zaruq**

garoupeira *Brazil, E:* Found along the coast between Salvador (Bahia) and Rio de Janeiro until the end of the 19th century. Used primarily for grouper (*garoupa*) fishing on the Abrolhos reefs off southern Bahia State. Carvel-built; fine run; sharp ends; fairly full bow; strongly raked, slender stern. Decked; crew housed forward; 2nd hold for fish. Aft-raking mainmast set a lugsail tacked to stemhead; leg-of-mutton mizzen sheeted to a jiggerboom that went through the starboard gunwale. Jib ran out on a bowsprit. No standing rigging; halyards served as backstays. One that set a gaff mainsail was called a **perné** in Salvador. Salvador craft larger than those from Espirito Santo and Rio de Janeiro. A small **canoa★** carried on board. Crew of 6-10. Reported lengths 10-18m. Further name variant: **lancha garoupeira**

gar-pike See **havbåd**

garrabot *France, south-central:* A type of small boat reported from the Languedoc and Gascony areas. See also **gabare**.

garrooka, **garukha**, **garúku**, **garúkuh** See **zaruq**

garvey *United States, E:* Type of small **scow★** used in the shallow coastal waters from southern New Jersey to Chesapeake Bay for oystering, clamming, crabbing, tending fish traps, transporting produce, and sometimes as a **schooner's★** **yawl boat★**. Larger boats

garvey

served as **carrier boats** or **buy boats★**. Marked variation in design, dictated by their use, builder's preferences, and nature of the water body. Rowing **garveys** had a wide, flat bottom brought up to shallow, raked bow and stern transoms; sides tapered slightly toward the ends and flared slightly. Usually decked at bow and stern and along the sides. Sailing **garveys** generally similar in hull form, with a large centerboard or a single leeboard that usually hung to starboard. Rudder, attached to the skeg, was hung either outboard or inboard. Smaller boats set 1-2 spritsails with long sprits. Larger boats were gaff-rigged with a jib to a

short bowsprit; these often had a V-bottom. Motorized **garveys** have a deeper stern and are used over a wide area on the east coast. Rowing **garveys**: 3.7-7m in length, 1.2m wide at chines and 1.5m at gunwale, depths 0.36-0.46m; sailing type: 5-12.2m in length, beam one-fifth overall length. Other recorded names: **garvie**, **New Jersey garvey**, **scow★**, **V-bottom garvey**. Note also **Delaware Bay oyster schooner**, **ditch box**, **garvey box**.

garvey box *United States, E:* **Skiff★** of the marshes and creeks of southern New Jersey. Flat bottom generally cross-planked; some V-bottomed with longitudinal planking in the after three-quarters. Bottom turned up forward and aft to shallow transoms; skeg on those that sailed; flared sides. Forward and after decks flat or cambered; high coaming around the cockpit. Those that sailed had daggerboard forward of the cockpit. Mostly poled, rowed, or towed; some set a boomed spritsail. Reported lengths 3.2-4.3m; e.g., length 3.7m, beam 1.2m. Other recorded names: **garvey gunning box**, **garvey skiff**, **gunning skiff★**. Note also **ditch box**, **garvey**, **melon seed**.

garvey gunning box, **garvey skiff** See **garvey box**

garvie See **garvey**

gas boat **1.** *Canada:* General term for a boat powered by a gasoline engine. Might be powered by such fuels as gasoline, benzene, naptha, or kerosene. A **gasoline canoe** would be driven by an outboard motor. Name variant: **gasoline boat**

2. *United States, Alaska:* Small, all-purpose **launch★** powered by gasoline or similar volatile fuel. Popular along the inland waterways of southeastern Alaska early in the 20th century. Many were conversions from small sailing or steam craft. Deckhouse for passengers could run full length; others had a small cabin. Those that fished might be **ketch★**- or **sloop★**-rigged.

3. *United States, north-central:* Fishermen of northwestern Lake Superior, especially of Isle Royale, used **gas boats** in spring and early summer to line for lake trout and in the fall to work gill nets. The boats were also used to seine for herring for bait. After 1900, the **schooner★**-rigged **Mackinaw boats★** were modified to be gasoline-engine powered, with the engine placed amidships. Used through the 1950s. High, sharp bow; plumb stem; wide, U-shaped or narrow, raked transom or sharp ends. Open except for short foredeck; narrow side decks with high coaming. Outboard rudder; tiller. Crew of 2. Reported lengths 6-8.5m; beam ca. one-third.

4. *United States, south-central:* Local designation for a **bateau**-type (see **bateau-7n**) employed only in seining operations of the Black River basin of central Louisiana. Larger than the Atchafalaya **bateau** and powered by an inboard engine. Developed early in the 20th century. Called a **Joe boat** by people from outside the basin.

5. *United States, SE:* On the Kanawha River in western West Virginia, any boat propelled by a gasoline engine was called a **gas boat**.

6. *United States, W:* Small, heavy wooden **launch★/tug★** of the San Francisco Bay area that provided numerous harbor services. Became popular in the early 20th century with the advent of light, powerful gasoline engines; ultimately replaced by diesel power. Plumb stem, deep forefoot, fantail stern.

Further references: **esquif-2**, **launch-8**, **tar boat**

gashi See **ghashi**

gas-oil boat See **tar boat**

gasoline boat, **gasoline canoe** See **gas boat-1**

gasolin-lancha See **tow boat-1**

Gaspé boat See **Gaspé schooner**

Gaspé flat See **flat-2**

Gaspé longliner See **longliner-2**

Gaspé pink See **pinky**

Gaspé schooner *Canada, E:* **1.** Small, sharp-ended **coaster★** introduced to the Gaspé Peninsula in the mid-18th century and, except for the addition of auxiliary motors, still basically unchanged. Still operating in the 1960s, engaging mainly in longline fishing. Other recorded names: **chaloupe★**, **Gaspé boat**
2. One type, operating from the south-facing Chaleur Bay coast, is clinker-built, has a strongly raked sternpost, curved stem, some hollow to the garboards, low and hard bilges. Topsides flare considerably; steep rise to the sheer toward the stern. Decked; cabin forward. Short pole masts, the foremast stepped well forward; taller mainmast stepped roughly amidships. Square-cut sails with long gaffs, almost parallel to the foot of the sail; foresail loose-footed; short bowsprit. Reported lengths 6-13.7m; e.g., length 11.3m, beam 3.7m, depth 1.2m. Other recorded names: **Chaleur Bay schooner, French Shore schooner**
3. A type working between the towns of Gaspé and Percé, usually off beaches; more finely built and may be either clinker or carvel. Stem curved with cutaway forefoot; sternpost sharply raked; mild flare to the sides. Drag to the long, straight keel; considerable rise to the floors; high, hard bilges; sheer sweeps up aft. Some vessels beached by means of a capstan made fast to a line fitted to a hole in the after end of the keel. Raised cuddy deck; rails extend aft to the stern; 2 standing wells for fishermen, another for helmsman. Two pole masts, each stayed with a pair of shrouds, forestay, and stay between the mastheads. Gaff sails, foresail loose-footed. Jib to a short, light bowsprit run out on starboard side of the stemhead. Generally an auxiliary motor. Length 10.8m, beam 3m, depth 1.14m, draft 1.16m. Name variant: **English Shore schooner**

gaspésienne See **longliner-2**

gat See **cat-1**

gata See **cat-1**, **gato**

gatameroni See **catamaran**

gate See **cat-2**

gate ship, gate vessel See **boom defense vessel**

gaṭîjir See **gaṭîra**

gatimaron See **catamaran**

gaṭîra *Red Sea/Arabian Peninsula, S:* **1.** Small, beamy pearling and **fishing boat★** similar to the **sambûq★**. Raked transom stern; often elbow bend on the top of the curved, raking stem. Steep rise to the floors; straight keel; considerable sheer. Decked at bow and stern; 2 loose planks laid across the open waist. Outboard rudder; tiller. Mainmast stepped amidships into a keel block and lashed to a beam. On some, a mizzenmast steps through the forward part of the after

deck. Sets lateen sails. A small **houri★** serves as a **ship's boat★**. Reported lengths 4.3-12.5m; e.g., length 12.5m, beam 3.55m, draft 1.4m.
2. A Red Sea vessel by this name was portrayed as a **ketch★** in the late 19th century. Straight stem, counter stern, topsails, staysail, jib to a long bowsprit.
3. Term may also apply to a **dinghy★** towed behind a larger craft.
Spelling variants: **attirah**, **ghatira**, **k(h)atira**, **qatira**, **qattirah**; pl. **gaṭîjir**

gato *France, S:* Flat **canal boat★** of French Catalonia. Spelling variant: **gata**

gatos, gatta See **cat-1**

gatti See **cat**, **gatto**

gatto *Italy:* Medieval armed **barge★** used on lakes and rivers in war and against bandits and smugglers. Rowed, possibly employing as many as 100 oars. Narrow. Spelling variant: pl. **gatti**. See also **cat-2**.

gattus, gatus See **cat-1**

ga'twaat *Russia, E:* **Umiak★**-type **skin boat★** used by the Koryaks of easternmost Siberia for hunting sea mammals and carrying cargo. Might use a **kayak** (see **kayak-10**) as a support boat. Strongly raked ends, flaring at gunwale; flared sides. Inner frames consisted of a flat keel timber that rounded up to form the stem; sternpost might be part of the same timber or a separate piece lashed on; doubled bilge stringers; numerous half ribs. Gunwale and the stringer below it curved around at each end; 4-5 thwarts. Bow sheer sweeps up gently; boat wider near the stern. Originally covered with split walrus hide, later with sealskins.

ga'twaat

Platforms at ends used by the harpooner and helmsman. Rowed double-banked. Tripod mast set a rectangular sail, intially of reindeer skins. Sail lashed to yard at mainmast; could revolve around the masthead. Crew of 8-10. Length 9m, beam 2.5m. Other recorded names: **ne'lge ga'twaat**; **baidara★** (by the Russians)

gauarra See **gabare**

gaudy boat See **hua chuan-2a**

gaulée See **galley**

gauliache, gaulleace, gaulliasse See **galeass**

gavarra See **gabarra-5a**

gavarreta See **gabaret**

gavelekstock, gavelöka, gavelökstock See **eka-2**

gavlbaat, gavlbåt See **færing**

gawaarib See **qārib**

gawālbît See **jalbût-1**

gay See **ghe**, **smack-5**

gayasa, gayassa See **gaiassa**

gay bao See **ghe bâ'u**

gay diang See **ghe diang**

Gay Head boat See **Nomans Land boat**

gay you, gay yu, gay yus See **ghe you**

gazelle, gazelle des sables See **barque sablaise**

gazolina See **motor boat**

G boat See **horse boat-3**

geàrradair See **cutter-2**

Gebacca boat, **Gebacco boat** See **Chebacco boat**

gebeng *Malaysia:* Reported as a vessel with a European-type rudder. Note also **sampan gĕbing**.

gedeckter Prahm See **Prahm-2**

gedekte somp See **somp**

geernaarsboot See **Oostendse garnaalboot**

geetea See **'etea-2**

gehazi See **jahazi**, **Zanzibar jahazi**

geh täh See **ghe trê**

geitbåt, **geitbåter** See **nordmørsbåt**

Geisterboot See **spirit boat**

Geisterschiff See **ghost ship**

gejaras See **mahaila-2**

gĕlabūt See **jalbūt-1**

geleira *Brazil:* Plank-built **market boat**★ that transports iced fish from **fishing boats**★, especially in the Amazon Delta area. Bow and stern square, or bow may be sharp and strongly raked. Low house amidships. Variously rigged, but most set 2 high-peaked, boomed gaff sails and a long, flat jib. Masts rake aft. Cap. 5-10t. Spelling variant: **geliera** (probably erroneously)

geleischip See **convoy ship**, **escort vessel**

Geleitschiff See **convoy ship**

gelia *Ukraine:* Armed **galley**★ of the Cossacks of the Dnieper area that raided and plundered ships in the Black Sea. Rowed with 15 men on each side. Generally carried 50-60 men, some to 100. Reported lengths ca. 15-18m, widths 3.7-4.6m. See also **jalia**.

gelibat See **kolek gelibat**

geliera See **geleira**

geliong See **galleon**

Gelle See **Jolle-5**

gellée See **galley**

gellywat See **gallivat**

gellywatte See **gallivat**, **jolly boat-1**

gemge See **cangia**

Gemüse-Ever See **Gemüse-Ever**

Gemüse-Ewer *Germany, NW:* Vegetable (*Gemüse*) boat of the Hamburg area and farther upstream on the Elbe River. Sharp ends, the stem curved and cutaway, the sternpost strongly raked; later boats had a transom. Narrow, flat bottom; longitudinally planked; separate floor frames and ribs. Foredeck with small cuddy below; short stern deck. Narrow leeboards; triangular rudder; tiller. Strikable mast stepped against the thwart. Early 19th-century boats sprit-rigged; later set a loose-footed sail with a long gaff. Reported lengths 8.33-16m, beam 2.2-5m, depth 1-1.5m. Other recorded names: **Gemüse-Ever**, **Groente-Ever**. Note also **Ewer**, **Rhin-Ewer**.

gentleman's pleasure gig See **gig-3**

gentleman's pulling boat See **barge-11g**

gentleman's wherry See **wherry-5**

geordie, **geordie collier brig** See **collier-2**

Georges banker See **Georgesman**

Georgesman *United States, NE:* A type of **schooner**★ that mainly handlined for cod and halibut on Georges Bank, east of Cape Cod, during the latter half of the 19th century. Moderately sharp lines, curved stem with gammon knee; slightly raked sternpost; low, easy bilges amidships; slight tumble home to sides; heavily

ballasted. Special joists, with pegs run through, were nailed to the rail along most of the vessel's length to prevent the fishing lines from slipping. Narrow rudder came aboard below a small, raked counter. Originally carried a **yawl boat**★ on stern davits; later a **dory**★. Summer rig included a main topmast with gaff topsail, and staysail; in winter, topmast sent down and no jib-boom used. While riding at anchor, mainsail reefed to about one-fifth its normal size, serving as a steadying sail. Crew of 6-8 originally, later 8-12 on the larger vessels. 40-85rt. 1848 vessel 19m long between perpendiculars, 5.6m wide, 2.4m deep. Other recorded names: **Georges banker** (or **schooner**), **Gorgaman**. Note also **banker**.

Georges schooner See **Georgesman**

Gepäckschiff See **Leibschiff**

gerba See **germa**

germa Eastern Mediterranean term used in the Middle Ages for a merchant vessel. Short, beamy, low sides, decked; carried 4 large sails. Reported also as a 16th- and 17th-century vessel from the Bandar 'Abbās area of southeastern Iran; a small one was called a **germetta**. Also cited as an early ship on the East African coast. Spelling variants: **gerba** (Catalan), **germundus**, **zerme**, **zerme**. See also **djerme**.

germe See **djerme**

germetta See **djerme**, **germa**

germundus See **germa**

Gerrans crabber See **West Country crabber**

gétéa See **'etea-2**

Getränkschiff See **Bucentaur**

Getreideschiff See **grain carrier**

Gettersche praam See **Giethoornse praam**

gewone tjalk See **tjalk-3**

ghalawa See **ngalawa**

ghalea See **galley**

ghalias See **galeass**

ghaliot See **galiot**

ghancha, **Ghandscha**, **ghangi** See **ganja**

ghanja See **cangia**, **ganja**

ghanjah See **ganja**

gharab *Sudan:* A loosely applied term for a beamy, shallow craft of the Nile that may be used for fishing

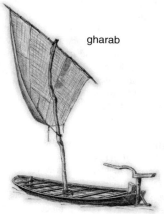

gharab

or ferrying, or as a **tender**★ (**felukka**★) to a **naggr**★. Hull constructed carvel-fashion of short lengths of a very hard wood; without ribs but with numerous transverse beams; flat sheer. Sharp overhanging bow; gener-ally triangular transom stern. Undecked; large mooring bitt forward. Large rudder blade; sturdy tiller set over the rudderhead and humped in the middle. The single sail varies with the stretch of river—lateen, obliquely hung rectangular, or square; the latter is the more common and is made of thin, poor material, often of flour bags, hung from a yard at the top, and controlled by a vang at each end. Mast, secured to a beam, may be an irregularly shaped pole. **Fishing boats**★ also use oars. Crew of 2-5. **Fishing boats**: lengths 7.25-8.2m, beam ca. 2m; **ferries**★ range to 11.7m and are proportionately narrower. Spelling variant: **gharib**. Note also **ghurāb**, **qārib**. Further references: **dhow**, **grab-3**

gharat hora *Pakistan:* Long, narrow, shallow **fishing boat**★ of the Indus River delta and Karachi areas. Large type line fishes offshore; the smaller fishes for sardines and prawns in protected waters. Carvel-planked, frames inserted later; almost flat sheer. Long, straight keel; rising floors; full midships section.

gharat hora

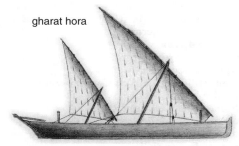

Sharp ends, especially at the stern; vertical stem, rounded forefoot; sharply raking sternpost. Rudder secured with rope lashings; heel flush or slightly above the keel; may be worked with yoke and lines or by a downward-sloping tiller. Lacks continuous decking, but temporary deck may be laid on the thwarts. Stanchions, with crossbar at bow and stern, hold the lowered yard. Generally carefully painted and oiled. Sets a quadrilateral lateen-type sail with a short luff or, during the light wind season (October to March), sets 2 sails. Mainmast stepped about midships, mizzenmast roughly midway between mainmast and the stern; both rake sharply forward. May also set a jib to a temporary bowsprit and triangular topsails. Crew of 8-10. Reported lengths 9-20.7m; e.g., length 14.7m, beam 2m, molded depth 0.84m. Name variant: **hora**. Note also **dhatti hora**, **ekdar**.

gharawa See **ngalawa**

ghareb See **carabus**

gharib See **gharab**

gharnai, gharnao See **chatty raft-2**

gharrabu See **agherrabo**

ghashi *Bangladesh:* Long, narrow vessel, mainly of the Dhaka (Dacca) area, that transports produce and other light cargo as well as passengers; also used for fishing. Characterized by a bow projection that extends for about a meter above the water; stern projection may be backed by a narrow transom. Low bow; sheer rises at

stern to a high point; platform for helmsman at stern. Very low freeboard when loaded. Long, arched bamboo shelter amidships; crew housed at the rear; passenger compartment forward, sometimes with brightly painted doors. Those that carry jute and produce have only an aft cabin; the forward area used for cargo. Twin steering or sculling oars worked from the same side; no rudder. Mast stepped forward of the cabin; no standing rigging. The large, square mainsail can be shifted from side to side or run fore and aft. Square topsail sometimes laced to mainsail. Small **ghashis** might set a spritsail. Rowed from the foredeck. Crew of 3-6. Length to ca. 21m. Spelling variants: **gashi**, **ghasi**, **ghazi**

ghasi See **ghashi**

ghātbāri See **saranga**

ghatira See **gaṭīra**

ghayassah See **gaiassa**

ghazi See **ghashi**

ghe *Vietnam:* Generic term for a **boat**★; in northern Vietnam, this becomes **thuyền**★. May be applied to small craft or to a variety of **barges**★ and **tugboats**★. Spelling variant: **gay**

ghe bao See **ghe bâ'u**

ghe bâ'u *Vietnam:* A term that translates as "cargo-carrying **junk**★" and refers to a number of quite different craft. One type, working out of Qui Nhon on the central Annam coast, carries salt, coconut-fiber rope, coconuts, and fish sauce; some still sailed in the 1980s. Noted for its high freeboard. Hull to waterline built of a gray hardwood fastened with wooden pegs and iron spikes; bottom of woven bamboo made watertight by coating with resin, lime, and wood oil. Compartmented with bulkheads; deck beams extended outboard. Strongly curved stem and sternpost; marked sheer forward; massive rudder curved under the stern, worked by a tiller. Low mat cabin covers most of the deck, gunwale to gunwale, or just at the stern. Generally decorated with oculi on a black triangle. Foremast in the eyes; mainmast forward of amidships; when stepped, mizzenmast outboard of the gunwale, on either side; masts rake aft; mizzenmast unstayed. Boomed standing lugsails set to the 3 masts; sails often of coconut-palm fiber. Also rowed. Crew of 8. Length 14.6m, beam 2.7m, draft 0.48m loaded. Name variants: **gaibao**, **gay bao**, **ghe bao**, **ghe buon**

ghe bè *Vietnam, central:* **1.** Bamboo **raft**★ used mainly for inshore and river fishing, mostly in northern Annam. On some, the poles are arranged so that the smaller upper ends of the bamboo are placed toward the bow, making the bow narrower than the stern. The bamboo may be beveled to permit overlapping of the poles; by applying pressure, bow ends are bent upward. Gunwales formed by bundles of bamboo. Poles secured by green bamboo thongs made supple by boiling. May use as many as 3 daggerboards, mostly in forward part. One to 3 masts generally raked forward; stepped into a block of bamboo root, an arched crossbeam, or a type of tripod resting on a small platform on the floor. Usually multiple positions for each mast. Lugsails predominate, others lateen. Helmsman steers from a bench at the stern, manning a sweep lashed to a post; also may steer by a single oar held in

to a post roughly amidships. Crew of 2-3. Length 7.66m, width 1.5m. Other recorded names: **cái mảng Lu'o'ng-nhiệm**, **cai mảng** (or **radeau de**) **Sâm-so'n**, **cai mảng Thanh hóa**. Further reading: J. Y. Claeys, "L'Annamite et la Mer: Les Radeaux de Pêche de Lu'o'ng-nhiệm (Thanh-hóa) en Bambous Flottants," *Bulletin et Travaux*, 1942, Institut Indochinois Pour l'Étude de l'Homme, Fasc. 1 (1943), 17-28.
2. An Annamite **ghe be** was a small river craft constructed of a single keel piece to which 1-2 planks were added on each side.

ghe bê' See **ghe biê'n**

ghe biê'n *Vietnam, SW:* Term for a seagoing **junk***. Those along the Gulf of Siam side of Cochin China are relatively simple craft. Double-ended with inserted plank posts at the curved bow and stern, widening at the top. Plank keel, flat floors, rounded sides. Side and bottom frames not connected; stringer along each side supports crossbeams that are inserted later. Low washstrake extends almost to the ends. Cabin aft with planked sides and bamboo roof. Cleaver-shaped rudder hung with pintles and gudgeons; when raised, rudder supported to one side by a decorative rest. Often unpainted except for elongated eyes and a green triangle at the bow and stern. Mainly rowed. When sailed, a mast is stepped through a thwart, stayed at each side. Sets a boomed standing lugsail. A small mast, to which a triangular sail is hung, may be stepped in the eyes. Reported lengths 8-15m; e.g., length 9m, beam 2m, depth 1.3m. Other recorded names: **barque de mer**, **ghe bê'***, **ghe hái**, **thuyền bê'**, **thuyền hải**. Further reading: Jean Poujade, *Les Barques de Mer de Rachgia* (Paris: Gauthier-Villars, 1946 [Centre de Recherche Culturelle de la Route des Indies. Documents d'Ethnographie Navale. Fasc. 3]).

ghe buon See **ghe bâ'u**

ghe câu *Vietnam:* Term meaning **fishing boat***; consequently, numerous local types go by this term. The one described here is found along the central coast in the Da Nang (Tourane) area: Side planking constructed first, followed by the addition of 2 stringers, and then the woven bamboo bottom is forced between the planking and the stringers and the whole pegged together. Bottom sealed with a compound of ground bamboo and resin and coated with a vegetable oil. Crossbeams pierce the top planking. Sharp ends curved; each end grooved—at the stern for the large sliding rudder, at the bow for the sliding stemboard that serves in lieu of a centerboard. Decked; protection provided by arched mat roofs that are sectional and may be stacked while fishing. Unpainted except for oculi. Steps 1-3 masts, depending on size; mainmast on larger boats stayed; otherwise masts unsupported. High-peaked balance lugsails; sometimes a trysail hung between the main- and foremast or set forward to one of the fishing spars. A hiking board often used, at times requiring most of the crew, or may be weighted with stones. Depending on size and operation, crew numbers 3-11. Reported lengths 4-20m; e.g., length 12m, beam 3m, draft loaded 0.37m. Other recorded names: **gaï caou**, **thuyền câu**

ghe cà vom *Vietnam, S:* **Riverboat*** of the Cochin China area that mainly transported rice and charcoal. Hull built up from a high-ended dugout obtained from Cambodia; as many as 4 strakes, often in multiple pieces, added to each side. The high ends of the dugout became the broad, heavy stem and sternpost of the finished craft. Bottom rounded in cross section and fore-and-aft. Rudder followed the curve of the raked stern; high rudderpost through which the tiller passed. Lightly planked house ran most of the length and from gunwale to gunwale. Bow generally painted green and red with small oculi on the stem. Set a single high-peaked, balanced lugsail to a short pole mast; yard hung near its forward end making it almost a gaff. Halyard rove through a hole at masthead; 2 shrouds on each side. Also rowed. Reported lengths 6.8-13m; e.g., length 6.8m, beam 1.0m. Name variant: **cà vom**. Further reading: Jean Poujade, *Pirogues et Cà-vom de l'Ouest Cochinchinois* (Paris: Gauthier-Villars, 1946 [Centre de Recherche Culturelle de la Route des Indies. Documents d'Ethnographie Navale. Fasc. 2]).

ghe cu'a *Vietnam, S:* Several types of craft by this name worked from the area east of Cambodia to the Mekong River. One type, found on the island of Phuquoc in southwestern Vietnam, was primarily a **coaster***, transporting jars of brine. Probably extinct. Planked vessel with sharply raking bow and stern; stem flat and widening at the gunwale. Poop built out over sides and beyond the sternpost with a taffrail and arched mat house; high gunwales. Decked; cargo protected by a roof extending forward to the mainmast. Heavy rudder, held by gudgeons and pintles, was raised in shallow water and hung by a rope from the poop crossbeam abaft the rudderpost. Large circular oculi. Two masts stepped in tabernacles; foremast placed against the forefoot; 2 shrouds to each side of mainmast. Set 2 tall, high-peaked, balance lugsails. Fore part of main yard secured to the mast by special tackle; lines from lee end of yard ran to after end of the poop rail. Cap. 24-45t.

ghe cui *Cambodia:* Inland craft, notably on Tonle Sap (lake), for fishing and transporting the catch. Carvel-planked; narrow and curved, overhanging, low bow; curved end on the higher, broader stern; flat floors.

ghe cui

Maximum beam ca. two-thirds aft on the smaller boats, and the freeboard forward is lower than at the stern. On the larger craft, the maximum beam is amidships; freeboard lower forward than at the stern. Open waist; wet well on larger vessels. Identified by tall rudderpost, at least 1.0m above the gunwale; rudder follows sternpost curve; tiller slopes downward. Small boats sailed and rowed (8-12 rowers); the large sizes either sail or are towed. Reported lengths 10-28m; small size: length 12m, beam 3.5m, depth 1.3m, draft light 0.4m; large size: 20m by 4.3m by 1.75m, draft light 0.5m. One type works the *day* net, a conical net 20-25m in diameter and 30-40m long. The **ghe cui**, positioned at the open end of the net, is crossed at the bow and stern by bamboo "booms" that connect with bamboo **rafts**★, each 15-18m long and 20-25m apart. These **rafts** hold the net open. Another **ghe cui** supports the narrow trailing end of the 60-100m-long net.

ghe diang *Vietnam:* Three-masted **coaster**★ and **fishing boat**★; probably no longer in use. Double-ended with strongly raked and flattened stem and sternpost; curved bottom. Cambered deck from stem to mainmast. Thatched coach roof covered part or all of the vessel. Sail data vary: some reported as setting 3 tall, gunter lugsails forward of amidships, the mainsail boomed; others depicted as having boomed, standing lugsails with a small sail in the bow and at the stern. Lengths 12-20m; e.g., length 15m, beam 4.6m, molded depth 2.3m. Note also **rua pet**.

ghe hái See **ghe biê'n**

ghelandre See **chelandia**

ghe luó'i rùng *Vietnam, S:* Gunter-rigged **fishing boat**★ that works with a *rùng* net. Double-ended; may be completely planked with a flat bottom or planked along the sides with a woven bamboo bottom. Ends rake; stem sometimes has an additional decorative piece at the top through which the stay from the mainmast runs; sternpost grooved to hold the rudder. Marked sheer at the ends; sheer strake supplemented by a bulwark, which reduces sheer considerably. Decked; movable gratings on some; may have an arched house. Usually a black band at bow and stern, white beneath; elongated oculi plus *yin* and *yang* motifs. Most step 3 masts, all in forward third of the boat; mainmast, raking slightly aft, stepped through bench; stayed forward, 1-2 shrouds to each side. On the basket-bottom type, the shrouds fasten inside the hull; mainmast yard as long as the boat. Two unstayed forward masts, the foremast ca. 2m high, stepped up against the stem. Each mast sets a gunter-type lugsail, the foresail yard held vertically against the mast. Length to 12m.

ghe nan See **ghe nang**

ghe nang *Vietnam:* General term for basket-hulled **fishing boats**★, particularly of the Annam coast. Some made entirely of woven bamboo; others have a bamboo bottom and planked sides. Resilient, rounded, keelless bottom easily beached; last about 5 years. Small types used to cross flooded rice paddies. On the plank-extended type, the planks are edge-fastened and secured to the stem and sternposts; stringer attached along the inside of the basket, and wooden pegs then driven through the plank, basket, and stringers. The all-basket type has a split-bamboo gunwale. Frames or half frames inserted; larger boats have movable decks. May be round (**thúng chài**★) or **canoe**★-shaped. Various compounds used to waterproof the basket.

Some have a sliding rudder and a stemboard. May have oculi. Sailed, poled, and many now equipped with engines. Lugsails set to 1-3 masts; of woven fiber or cloth. Small boats generally round and under 1.5m in diameter; larger boats, the planked types, run to 15m long. Other recorded names: **basket boat**★, **bateau pannier**, **ghe nan**, **nacelle**★, **pan(n)ier**, **thuyền nan**, **thuyền thúng**; **ghe túng chài**. Further reading: R. F. Cairo, "A Note on South Vietnamese Basket Boats," *The Mariner's Mirror* 58 (1972), 135-153. Note also **song-vành**, **thúng chài**.

ghe nò See **rua chalom**

gherrabu See **agherrabo**

ghe thúng chài See **thúng chài**

ghe trê *Vietnam:* Small, low boat used in several areas. Uses a white board to attract fish by means of the sun's reflection during the day or torches at night. The board rests at an angle, usually along the side but may be at the bow. As the fish jump up, they are swept into the boat; on some, they are caught by a net placed

ghe trê

along the opposite side of the boat and are then flipped into the bottom. The boats themselves have been variously described and may be long, narrow **dugout canoes**★ or bamboo, basket-type boats. One type reported as 2.5-3m long, 0.5m wide. Name variants: **geh täh**, **gué-tré**. Note also **luring boat**.

ghe túng chai See **thung chai**

ghe xuồng Vietnamese term used throughout the Indochina Peninsula for a small, light boat. May be a **dugout canoe**★, a basket-bottom craft, or a planked boat. Generally rowed or paddled; a few sail. The basket type may be coated with a rancid fish oil. The type at Qui Nhon on the central Vietnam coast has a woven bottom and planking above. A special rubstrake at the waterline protects the planking from rocky shores on off-lying islands where the fishermen collect shellfish. Sets 2 small gunter lugsails in the forward part of the boat; extremely small foresail. Employs a large-bladed rudder. Reported lengths 3-6m, widths 0.6-1.0m.

ghe you *Vietnam, central:* Two-masted, flat-bottomed **fishing boat**★ of the Gulf of Tourane (now Da Nang); may be extinct. Bottom planked longitudinally in the middle and transversely at the rising bow and stern. Broad side strakes pegged and fastened with coir; inside seam battens; no frames, deep bulwarks. Movable mat house amidships; temporary decking. Rudder set in a simple rudder trunk and used as both rudder and centerboard when sailed; otherwise rudder secured by a bolt and boat steered with a long oar. Sometimes a balance board, weighted with stones, rigged on the weather side. Generally set 2 boomed lugsails. In light winds, a square sail might be set from the foremast and boomed out with a bamboo pole, and

ghe you

another might be hung between the masts. Sails of matting or cloth. Crew of 8-10. Reported lengths 12-15m; e.g., length 14m, beam 2.3m, depth 1.14m. Spelling variants: **gay yu**, **gay yus**

ghiasha See **gaiassa**

ghirbān See **grab**

ghobang, **ghobong** See **gobang**

ghobun *Papua New Guinea, E:* **Outrigger canoe★** of the Astrolabe Bay area; used principally in the pottery trade. Dugout hull; solid, tapered ends; round in cross section; bottom curved fore-and-aft. High washstrakes sewn on, extending almost to the ends; tall, angled breakwaters; washstrakes and breakwaters decorated. Small **canoes★** stepped one mast and had a single platform atop the washstrakes that extended onto the outrigger booms; platform either edged with solid decorated sides or with railings. Two-masted **canoes** had a bi-level open platform. Two or 3 booms, set close together, extended to the long, slender, pointed float. Booms horizontal or curved downward. Double under-crossed stanchions connected float and booms. On single-masted **canoes**, mast raked forward; on the 2-masted boats, one raked forward, the other aft; stepped at end of the platform. Rectangular or nearly square mat sails hung lug-fashion; boom at foot of sail forked against the mast. Steered with a paddle. Reported lengths 6-12m.

ghondol, **ghondola** See **gondola-4**

ghoráb See **ghurāb**

ghost ship An apparition of a ship, manned by ghosts. Other recorded names: **fantom ship**, **Geisterschiff**, **phantom ship**, **spirit ship**, **spookschip**. Note also **flying Dutchman**.

ghoulet, **ghouleta**, **ghouletta** See **schooner**

ghourab See **ghurāb**

ghrab See **grab-2**, **grab-3**

ghuljai-ts!i *Canada, north-central:* Skin-covered **canoe★** of the Chipewyan. Framework covered with dehaired caribou skins. Name variant: **rawhide canoe**. Note also **Chipewyan canoe**.

ghuncha, **ghunchah** See **ganja**

ghurāb 1. *Mediterranean:* Term used by the Arabs for a merchant **galley★** that was both sailed and rowed. Possibly mainly a **corsair★**. Other recorded names: **al-ghurâb**, **chany** (pl. **chouany**), **ghoráb**, **ghourab**, **gorab★**. Note also **gharab**, **golafrus**, **grab**, **qārib**.

2. *Persian (Arabian) Gulf:* Synonym for a mercantile **steamship**.
Further reference: **grab**

ghurub See **gourabe**

gichka, **gička** See **gig-1**

giek See **gig-1**, **skiff-2**, **wherry**

Giekeeber See **Giek-Ewer**

Giek-Ewer *Germany, NW:* **Cutter★**-rigged **Ewer★** of the lower rivers flowing into the North Sea, mainly in the 19th century. Some enlarged to become the **ketch★**-rigged **Besan-Ewer★**. Wooden hull initially, then iron or steel. Flat bottom; sharp stern until mid-century, then transom; curved stem, some clipper-bowed. Early boats open, then decked; quarter-deck with cabin below; strong sheer. Heavy rudder; long tiller worked from forward of the quarter-deck; leeboards. Pole mast with loose-footed gaff sail, gaff topsail; staysail, usually jib to bowsprit. Mainsail sheeted to a traveler arched over the tiller. Crew of 1-2. Reported lengths 7.3-15.6m; e.g., length 14.34m, beam 4.14m, depth 1.25m. Other recorded names: **Giekeeber**, **Gieksegelewer**

Gieksegelewer See **Giek-Ewer**

gie-maun See **tsiman**

gie oko, **gie okoa**, **gie orkoa** See **gaï oko**

gierpont See **pont**

Gieterse kaarpunter See **Giethoornse punter**

Gieters vlot See **vlot**

Giethoornsche punter See **Giethoornse punter**

Giethoornse praam *Netherlands, E:* Carries hay in the Giethoorn area and collects cattle from outlying meadows. Dates to the 17th century. Sharp ends, flat bottom, open. Length ca. 10m, beam ca. 3m. Name variant: **Gettersche praam**

Giethoornse punter *Netherlands, E:* An important **punter★** type built at Giethoorn to transport produce and people, and to fish in the narrow waterways of the area. Flat bottom longitudinally planked, curved fore-and-aft; low sheer. Sharp ends; slightly fuller forward of amidships; raked, straight stem and sternpost. Wide lower strake on each side, narrow top strake turns inward and stops before the ends; hard chines. Widely spaced, 3-piece frames extend to top of top strake with no gunwale. Open except for a short fore- and/or stern deck; floor boards. The fishing **punters** have a live well box amidships (**Gieterse kaarpunter**). Outboard rudder with high head; downsloping tiller. One or 2 leeboards on the sailing type. Single unstayed mast stepped through the forward thwart. Mainly sprit-rigged, but some use a leg-of-mutton sail. Also punted or rowed with 2 pairs of oars; now may employ an outboard motor. Reported lengths 6-8m; e.g., length overall 6.3m, on bottom 5m; maximum width 1.45m, on bottom 1.0m; depth 0.5m. Other recorded names: **Giethoornsche punter**; at Giethoorn: **boerenpunter**. Further reading: Gait L. Berk, *De Punter* (Weesp: De Boer Maritiem, 1984), 33-43, 73-102.

gig 1. Most often considered a **ship's boat★** used by the commanding officer and therefore smaller, lighter, and more skillfully manned than the other boats. Formerly clinker-built, now carvel; high, narrow, square stern and sharp bow; curved stem cutaway at forefoot; rising sheer at ends; keel; often flat-floored. Some fitted with brass mountings and mahogany benches. Originally rowed with 4-8 oars, with one man to a thwart, pulling a single oar. Rudder worked with ropes by a coxswain. Sometimes sailed, setting a lateen sail (18th century) or 1-2 dipping lug- or gunter sails. Centerboard lowered if sailing. More recently motorized. Reported lengths 4.9-9.7m; e.g., length 8.5m, beam 1.67m, depth 0.66m, draft 0.6m. Other recorded names: **canoa do comandante, canot du commandant, captain's gig, falua del comandante, gichka, gička, gi(e)k, gigg, guig(ue), gui(he), iola*, iole, Kapitänsgig, kik*, Kommandantenboot, motoscafo comandante, paşa fılukası, saettia*, scappavia*, sia-ràmhach, vedette du commandant**. Note also **canoa-2, cutter-gig, quarter boat**.

2. Seagoing **gigs** used by the British coast guard are sometimes called **galleys***. May set 1-2 lugsails. Reported lengths 6-9.14m, widths 1.22-1.52m.

3. A **gig** similar to the **ship's boat**, but larger, was used as a pleasure craft, and racing crews trained in wall-sided **gigs**. Became a popular racing boat on the Thames in England beginning in the 1830s, and in the United States in the mid-19th century, where they were also known as **race barges**. Initially clinker-built, later carvel. Rowed double-banked with as many as 10 oars. The fast, narrower **half-outrigged gig** set its oars on outriggers rather than on the gunwales; raced and cruised. Variously rigged when sailed. Those that raced might be called **four-** or **six-oared race boats**. Reported lengths 6.7-7.6m, width 1.0m. Other recorded names: **gentleman's pleasure gig, Gigvierer** (4-oared), **guiga***. Note also **shell, Thames gig**.

4. *England, SW:* Along Somerset and the north coasts of Devon and Cornwall, the term applies to a small, open sailing/**rowing boat*** mainly employed in herring fishing. Carvel- or clinker-planked. Fine bow; wide transom stern, some with a small, tucked-up transom. Those at St. Ives decked, others generally have a foredeck. St. Ives boats set a large, dipping lugsail and a standing lug mizzen. Now mainly motorized. Lengths to ca. 9.7m; e.g., length 8.1m, beam 2m, depth 0.76m. Name variants: **Port Isaac gig, St. Ives gig**

5. *Scotland:* A light iron vessel that carried passengers on the Glasgow, Paisley & Johnstone Canal in the 1830s. Basically **gig**-shaped; a long awning was spread over a light framework. Some could carry as many as 90 passengers. Towed by 2 horses. Reported lengths 18-21m; e.g., length 21m, beam 1.4m, depth 0.7m.
Further references: **Cornish gig, cutter-gig, shell, sia-ràmhach, swift boat**

gigboat See **flyboat-3a, Mersey gig**
gigg See **gig-1**
gigue à porte nages See **wherry-2**
Gigvierer See **gig-3**
gig whaleboat See **whaleboat-7b**
gik See **gig-1**
giki *Netherlands Antilles, southern group:* Small, flat-bottomed boat carried aboard local **sailboats*** and **motor boats***; undertakes ship-to-shore duties. No keel. Small types rowed using 2 oars; the larger types, carrying 6 people, use paddles. Length 6m, beam 3m, depth 0.6m.

gill boat See **gillnetter-3**
Gille See **Jolle-5**
gilling skiff *United States, E:* Found on tributary rivers of Delaware and Chesapeake Bays; imported to the upper Chesapeake area from the Delaware ca. 1885, the earlier type on the Chesapeake being non-distinctive. Employed several types of gill net to catch a variety of fish; the **shad boats*** on the Delaware were sometimes called **gillnet shad boats**. Carvel-planked; straight, slightly raked stem; might use a pin of wood or pipe extending for ca. 30cm from the bow as an aid in guiding the boat. Transom stern, originally wineglass, later full "U" shape. Keel; round bottom; slack bilges; curved, flaring sides; skeg. Decked forward and along the sides, some at stern; cockpit coaming ran to just abaft amidships; some have a small, 3-sided house or frame shelter. Centerboard; outboard rudder; tiller. Rowed and sailed. Set a spritsail or 1-2 leg-of-mutton sails extended by horizontal sprits. Engines or outboard motors on later boats. Crew of 2-3. Reported lengths 5.5-7.6m, beam ca. 1.5-1.8m. Other recorded names: **gill(net) skiff, shad skiff**. Note also **Choptank River shad skiff**.
gillnet boat See **gillnetter-2**
gillnet shad boat, gillnet skiff See **gilling skiff**
gillnetter 1. General term for any fishing vessel that sets gill nets. A boat that handles the net over the bow is a **bow picker**; a **stern picker** sets and hauls the net over the stern. Additional recorded name: **netter**

2. *Canada, W/United States, W and Alaska:* Open, double-ended boat used in the Pacific salmon fisheries from San Francisco north to the Fraser River in Canada, and in Bristol Bay in Alaska. Most leased to the fishermen by the canneries. Dates from 2nd half of

gillnetter-2

the 19th century; some still operated as sailing craft until the 1950s in Bristol Bay; now completely modern, motorized boats. Carvel-planked with considerable rise to the floors; the Columbia River boats became flat-floored and square-chined. Bow and stern strongly convex above the waterline, sharper below, with hollow lines; stem and sternpost nearly vertical; moderate sheer. Some drag to the shallow, straight keel; fitted with a large centerboard. Initially entirely open; by 1880, decked for ca. 60-90cm at each end; narrow waterways around the large, oval cockpit, which was divided into net and fish rooms; washboards along each side or only at the bow. Spread a tent over the unstepped mast when out at night. Original boats only rowed, often being towed to the fishing grounds by a **monkey boat★** from the cannery. Hull color schemes distinguished boats from the various canneries. Present-day boats recognizable by the large net reel in the cockpit. When sailed, set a leg-of-mutton sail or a boomed quadrilateral sail with a high-peaked sprit that was sometimes dropped in strong winds to form a triangular sail. On the Columbia River boats, 2 spritsails were set to the mast. Some gaff-rigged and some set a foresail tacked to the stemhead. Unstayed mast stepped through forward thwart. If caught upwind, the **monkey boats** would tow them back to the **tally scow★**. After 1900, engines gradually installed, but not until 1951 in Bristol Bay. Some **Bristol Bay gillnetters** were carried aboard square-riggers from Northwest Coast ports for the fishing season. Crew of 2 primarily. Reported lengths 4.6-9.7m, the largest found in Alaska; e.g., length 8m, beam 2.3m, depth 0.84m. Other recorded names: **British Columbia double-ender, British Columbia gillnetter, Columbia River (gillnet) boat, Columbia River salmon boat, gillnet boat, Pacific gillnetter, salmon boat★**; also **British Columbia, Puget Sound, Sacramento River,** and **salmon gillnet boat.** Note also **Columbia River skiff, scow-11h, skiff-3, Whitehall skiff.**

3. *United States, E:* The **gillnetter** of the Potomac River was an open boat with a keel. Worked mainly at night in order to get their catch to Washington markets by morning; net either staked out or set between the boat and a buoy. Sharp ends. Sailed and rowed. Reported lengths 5.5-6m. Name variant: **gill boat**

gill net tug *United States, north-central:* Powered fishing vessel working out of Great Lakes ports during late autumn and early spring. The gill nets were handled off the stern of this completely enclosed boat. Sharp, high bow; square, raked or counter stern; rounded bottom; strong sheer. Wheelhouse on the upper deck. Reported lengths 8-21m; 1910 boat was 17m long, 4.6m wide, 2m deep. Name variants: **fish(ing) tug, steam tug**

gill skiff See **gilling skiff**

gišr See **mahaila-2**

gitting barge See **sand barge-3**

giudizio See **mark boat-1**

giunca, giunche, giunco See **junk**

giyassa See **gaiassa**

gjeitbåt See **nordmørsbåt**

gladdekskorvet, Glattdeckkorvette See **corvette-1**

gladiateur *France, SE:* Developed in late 19th century for regular passenger service on the Rhone River. Worked until 1905. Equipped with suitable amenities for passengers. Propelled by paddlewheels; sometimes a separate boat by the paddlewheel section, either to pull or push. Huge tiller for the balanced rudder. Reported lengths 56.5-80.65m, widths 4.6-5.5m, draft ca. 1.0m.

gleatog See **gleóiteog**

gleóiteog *Ireland, W:* **Fishing boat★** and **Galway hooker★**-type peat, seaweed, and cargo carrier; a few still being built, others restored as pleasure craft. Heavily constructed with stout frames and heavy crossbeams.

Maximum beam well forward; strong stem with wide forefoot; strongly raked transom. Most have a foredeck; low washstrakes along the open waist; sides have strong tumble home. Mast stepped about a third of the way in from the bow. High-peaked, loose-footed, boomed gaff sail; boom extends well beyond the stern, and gaff is more than three-quarters the length of the boom. Staysail; jib to running bowsprit. A few set a lugsail. Sails tanned with a mixture of tar and butter. Reported lengths 4-9m; e.g., length 9m, beam 2.7m, draft 1.0m. Spelling variants: **Galway gloachoag, gleatog, gleoto(i)g, gloachoag, glotaga, glothague, glothogue**

gleóiteog beag See **púcán**

gleotog, gleotoig See **gleóiteog**

glibat See **kolek gelibat**

gloachoag, glotaga, glothague, glothogue See **gleóiteog**

Gloucester dory See **Banks dory**

Gloucester sloop, Gloucester sloop boat See **sloop boat**

Gloucester water boat See **water boat-3**

glow-worm boat *New Zealand, N:* Strong, open boat used in the Waitomo glow-worm grotto in western North Island. Flat bottom; straight, flaring sides; clinker planking. Sharp, raking bow; square, raking transom. Maneuvered by pushing and pulling on wires strung across the grotto. Capacity ca. 25 people. Length 5.5m, beam 1.8m, depth 0.51m.

Glückstadter Ewer See **Rhin-Ewer**

Glückstädter Heringslogger See **Logger**

Glückstadt Prahm See **Störprahm**

gluggekstock See **eka-2**

goat boat See **nordmørsbåt**

gobang *Brunei/Indonesia, Kalimantan/East Malaysia/Philippines, S:* General term for a **dugout canoe★**. Used mainly for river travel but may be seagoing.

gobang

Some simple dugouts, others plank-extended. Usually double-ended with the ends overhanging and cut horizontally on top. A protective rattan hut may extend from gunwale to gunwale. Paddled; sometimes sailed. One reported as 8.5m long, 1.07m wide. Spelling variants: **ghobang, ghobong, gobong, gubang★**. See also **gubang-1**.

gobar See **gabare**

gobarig See **gabaret**

gobong See **gobang**

godiet See **goguet-2**

go-down *China, E/Hong Kong:* Boat used in the Opium War era to carry opium from foreign ships to Guangzhou (Canton). Name variant: **fast boat★**

godyè See **goguet-2**

goebang See **gubang-1**

goeleta, goeletta See **schooner**

goélette 1. *Canada, E:* **a.** Small, 2-masted ship used by the French prior to the 1760s. Many were cod **fishing boats★** carrying 10-11 men, only 3-4 of whom were ailors. Full, bluff bows; keel; raised quarter-deck. Set lateen or fore-and-aft sails. Length ca. 15m; cap. 20-60t. **b. Goélettes** came from France during the 19th century to fish on the offshore banks; others were owned and operated by the inhabitants of the French territory of St. Pierre and Miquelon off southern Newfoundland. Fore-and-aft rigged. The French vessels measured 120-130t; those of the islands were 30-50t. Name variant: **goélette Saint-Pierraise. c.** At the end of the 19th century, special whaling **schooners**★ operated along the north shore of the Gulf of St. Lawrence. Hung a 6m-long **berge baleinière** over each side, ready to be lowered quickly. Crew aboard the **goélette** was 15 men; 6 of these men and a helmsman composed the crew of each **whaleboat**★.

2. Canada: Cargo vessel that traveled the St. Lawrence River and its tributaries until the 1940s; some went to the Great Lakes. Carvel- or clinker-planked. Flat bottom (**goélette à fond plat** or **bateau**★) or has a keel (**goélette à quille**). Straight, raked bow; counter or raked stern; rounded bilges, vertical sides. The **schooner**★-rigged vessels (**goélette à quille**) set loose-footed or boomed gaff sails to 2 aft-raking masts; gaffs long and low-peaked; long mainsail boom. Jib to a short bowsprit. The **goélette à fond plat** was **ketch**★-rigged. Long poles helped maneuver away from shore; later used a motorized **ship's boat**★ (**chaloupe à gazoline**). Auxiliaries on later vessels. Reported lengths 9.5-38m; e.g., length 18m, beam 6m, depth 2.5m. Beginning ca. 1920, another trader worked in the same area, retaining the term **goélette** but never designed to be sailed; last built in 1959. Rounded sides; completely flat, longitudinally planked bottom; no keel; raked stem; counter stern. Pilot house aft. Reported lengths 12-35m. Name variants: **St. Lawrence goélette** (or **schooner**). Further reading: Alain Franck, *Les Goélettes à Voiles du Saint-Laurent, Pratiques et Coutumes du Cabotage* (L'Islet-sur-Mer: Musée Maritime Bernier, 1984).

3. Malagasy Republic: **Schooner** that serves as a **coaster**★ along the Madagascar coast, especially for those west coast ports lacking wharfage. Some receive cargoes from **stationnaires** anchored off a town, transferring the cargo to land. Cabin for crew abaft the mainmast; cooking done on deck behind the mainmast. Carries an **outrigger canoe**★ as a **ship's boat**. Sets loose-footed gaff sails; jib to bowsprit. Capacity of the smallest at Morombe 10t, largest 50t. Shallow draft. Other recorded names: **botry** (pl. **botries**) Further references: **petite goélette, schooner**

goélette à deux huniers, goélette à deux mâts See **schooner-1**

goélette à fond plat See **goélette-2**

goélette à hune, goélette à huniers See **schooner-1**

goélette à mât à pible See **bald-headed schooner**

goélette à quille See **goélette-2**

goélette américaine See **fisherman-1**

goélette à quille See **goélette-2**

goélette aurique See **schooner-1**

goélette baldhead See **bald-headed schooner**

goëlette Bermudienne See **Bermuda schooner-2**

goélette brick See **hermaphrodite brig**

goélette carrée, goélette franche See **schooner-1**

goélette islandaise *France, N:* **Schooner**★ engaged in line fishing for cod off Iceland. Operated out of Normandy and Brittany ports until the 1930s. Deep hull, drag to straight keel, soft turn of the bilges into vertical sides. Concave stem, square counter stern, bow higher than stern. Rudderpost came through the counter; tiller. Cabins forward and aft. Masts set loose-footed gaff sails, gaff topsail on the mainmast, square topsail on the foremast; 3 jibs to the bowsprit and jibboom; staysail. Smaller early vessels had a crew of as few as 6, later larger vessels as many as 27. Reported lengths 33-40m; e.g., length 35m, beam 7.53m, depth 3m, draft 4.5m. Other recorded names: **goélette islandaise de Dunkerque (de Paimpol), goélette morutière, Icelander, Iceland schooner, islandaise, Islandschoner, paimpolaise, Paimpol-Schoner, Paimpol schooner.** Further reading: Jacques Guéguen, "Les Paimpolais à Islande," *Chasse-Marée* 108 (1997), 16-43. Note also **morutier.**

goélette islandaise de Dunkerque, goélette islandaise de Paimpol See **goélette islandaise**

goélette morutière See **goélette morutière, morutier**

goélette pêcheuse See **fisherman-1**

goélette Saint-Pierraise See **goélette-1b**

goélette terre-neuvière See **terreneuvier**

goéliche *France:* Occasionally a familiar term in the early 19th century for a small **schooner**★. Note also **petit goélette.**

goëmonnier See **canot goëmonier**

göge, gogo, gogue See **cog**

goguet *France:* **1.** Reported in the late 15th century as a type of **ship**★.

2. Small, open boat found mainly in the marshy areas of Baie de Seine. Used primarily for eeling, but also to seek mussels, cockles, and at times, waterfowl. Simple construction, with oak or elm planking, treenailed; flat bottom with no keel. Sharp ends, lightly flaring sides, widely spaced frames and ribs. Hull generally tarred. Rowed, poled, and sometimes sailed. Reported lengths 4.11-4.5m, widths 1.2-1.52m. Other recorded names: **godiet, godyè; plate**★ (at Barfleur, St. Vaast, St. Marcouf) Further reference: **coquet**

gojeta See **gaeta**

golabi, golabio, golabis, golabro, golabros, golabus, golafri, golafio, golafrio, golafro See **golafrus**

golafrus *Italy, NW:* Small 11th- and 12th-century **galley**★ that the Genoese adapted from the Moorish **ghurāb**★. Used for whaling and to carry pilgrims to the Holy Lands. Spelling variants: **golabio, golabis, golabro, golabus, golaf(r)io, golafro, gollabro, gorab(i)o, gulafrus;** pl. **golabi, golabia, golabros, golafri, gulafri**

gold-duster *England, E:* Small, open boat of the Humber Estuary that tended ships, primarily sailing vessels, by passing lines to buoys, docks, etc. Met an incoming ship at the mouth of the estuary and was towed to port. The Hull boats were clinker-built with little sheer, flat floors amidships, frames ca. 15cm apart, plumb stem, and narrow stern with tucked-up transom. Those built at Grimsby were carvel-planked with moderate rise to the floors and fine lines, and were fitted with a deep, curved, false keel. Four thwarts; stout fenders. At Hull, generally set 2 equal, high-peaked spritsails; brails ran to block at top of mast; masts shorter than the boat itself so they could

gold-duster

be lowered and stowed inside while the boat was towed astern a ship. The Grimsby boats set 2 standing lugsails initially; later, a lofty dipping lugsail set to a single mast stepped amidships. Also rowed against tholepins. Crew of 2. Hull boats typically 5.5m long and 1.68m wide; Grimsby boats: 6.4m by 2.08m. Other recorded names: **duster, Hull (gold-)duster, Humber gold-duster**

Golden Swan See **rua ballang**

golé'an See **golekan**

goleja See **galley**

golekan *Indonesia, central:* General term for a **boat★**, but more specifically refers to a type built almost exclusively on Madura and still found on the north coast of the island and around the Kangean Islands to the east. Once sailed widely in the Indonesian Archipelago; now, smaller types principally transport fish from the **mayang★** to market. Sharp ends; carvel planking doweled; no ribs or floors on early vessels, so strengthened by numerous crossbeams that pierced the hull; some now have ribs in addition to the beams; wide, smooth curve in cross section. A short, wide keel merges with a deep, raked and mildly curved stem and a straight sternpost. Strong sheer; each endpost terminates in a black-painted point; the sheer strake ends in a scroll form. Decked; low, mat-roofed house extends full width; Y-shaped, carved spar rest at the stern. One or 2 quarter rudders, with short tiller, worked against an outboard crossbeam and held by a rope secured to a vertical piece that serves as the helmsman's back-rest. Most step 2 thick-set masts of roughly equal height, both forward of the house. Sets 2 boomed, triangular sails, their apexes down. Large mainsail hung well forward on the long yard; light pole from the windward side of the after deck helps support the yard. Outrigger boom, abreast of the mainmast, holds the headstay and yardarm sheets. Crew of 6-9. Reported lengths 7.5-18.2m; e.g., length 11m, beam 3m, depth 1.5m. Other recorded names: **golé'an, golekkan, lè-golé'an, Madura prau** or **trader, perahu golekan**

golekkan See **golekan**

goleta 1. *Canary Islands/Western Sahara:* **Schooner★**-

rigged **fishing boat★**. Beamy with wide, shallow transom, clipper or straight bow; live well. Boomed gaff sails, gaff topsails, multiple headsails to a long bowsprit. Crew of 16-20. About 45-90t. Name variant: **pailebot★**
2. *Chile:* Term now applied to a large, motorized craft. May also apply to a sailing vessel of the **schooner** type; formerly numerous. Fine-lined with slightly raised sides. Prior to being modified for an engine, stepped 2-3 vertical masts, setting gaff sails and headsails. Another type is a **sloop★**-rigged cargo carrier found mainly in the Chiloé Archipelago of southern Chile.
3. *Spain, N:* Plainly built, **schooner**-rigged **coaster★**. Set gaff sails, jibs, and gaff topsails. 50-100t. disp.
4. *Venezuela:* **Sloop**-rigged cargo and **fishing boat.** Some now motorized. Lengths 12-15m; 10-30t. Spelling variant: **goletta★**
Further reference: **schooner**

goleta de dos gavias, goleta de velachero See **schooner-1**

goleta košna, golete See **schooner**

goletta 1. Italian term for a **schooner★**. The 18th-century Venetian type was an armed naval and merchant vessel with 2 aft-raked masts. In the late 19th century, **golette** (pl.) were among the sponging vessels off Lampedusa Island in the middle of the Mediterranean.
2. *Malta:* Term given to a **brigantine★**-rigged vessel. See also **goleta-4**.

goletta a gabbiola, goletta a vele auriche See **schooner-1**

golette See **goletta-1**

golija See **galley**

gollabro See **golafrus**

gölle See **Jolle-5, jolly boat-1, Schute-3**

golo See **kru canoe**

golondrina *Spain, E:* At Barcelona, a type of boat that transports passengers within the port area. Name variant: **oranyola** (Catalan)

gommier *West Indies, E:* Plank-extended **dugout canoe★** of Dominica, Martinique, and St. Lucia; a few may be found on Guadeloupe, St. Barthélemy, and St. Vincent. Those under 7.6m mainly fish; larger boats carry freight; a large size that carries a net is called a **canot de senne** on the French islands. Generally launched from beaches. In Martinique, a modified type is raced. A feature of the **gommier** is the bow extension of the dugout part, which on St. Lucia is a

gommier

vertical spade shape that extends for ca. 45cm beyond the stem and is capped with a metal shoe; on Dominica and Martinique, the top of the blade slopes back toward the hull, ending close to the stem. Hull most often made from the *gommier* tree; expanded with hot water and held in position with grown frames. The St. Lucia boats have a higher proportion of dugout to strakes. Bottom generally V-shaped in cross section and flat fore-and-aft. One, sometimes 2, strakes added, often clinker fashion. Most have a small, wedge-shaped transom; some have a stern blade similar to the bow, but shorter. Steered with a narrow, deep rudder; those on the windward coasts usually cross the reefs and use only a steering oar. Gaily painted and bear fanciful names that are often chosen to protect the fishermen against evil spirits. Generally sailed, setting 1-2 square-cut spritsails of cotton or flour bags. In a strong wind, one of the 2 crew members hikes out, sitting or standing on the windward gunwale, holding a rope from the masthead. Sprit and masts of bamboo; no shrouds or halyards; sail and sprit may be brailed to the mast and tied with the sheet, the whole then unstepped and placed in the bottom of the boat. When rowed single-handed, oarsman rows stern first using the ram as a rudder; with 2 men, one rows and the sternman paddles; many now use an outboard motor. Reported lengths 2.74-10.67m, widths 0.76-1.3m. Other recorded names: **bwa-fouyé**, **canáoa**, **canoe***, **canot***, **gonmie**, **kannot**, **oucounni**, **piraugue**, **pirogue***, **St. Lucia flying-fish dugout**. Further reading: J. Morice, "Les Gommiers," *Revue des Travaux de l'Institut des Pêches Maritimes* XXII (Mars 1958), 64-84. Note also **yole-4**.

gonda 1. *Indonesia, central:* Small **dugout canoe*** of Butung Island off southeastern Sulawesi (Celebes). Used for harpoon fishing in quiet waters. One or 2 outriggers. Paddled only. Reported lengths 3.7-5.5m. **2.** *Italy:* The Italian **gónda** is a small lake boat. See also **gondola-4**.

gondalow See **gundalow**

Gondel 1. *Germany, S:* **a.** Term sometimes applied to a **ferryboat*** on the upper Elbe River, and in the 18th century, it was a vessel of the Elector of Saxony. **b.** The Starnberger See and Chiemsee **Gondeln** (pl.) of the 16th to the early 19th century were pleasure boats of the nobility and often were part of the entourage that accompanied **Leibschiffe***. Most were ornate with a glass cabin abaft amidships. Rowed with 2-3 pairs of oars forward of the house; helmsman aft. Reported lengths 10-12m, beam 1.5-1.8m. **c.** A pleasure craft of the Starnberger See. Flat bottom turns up at the bow to form a high, overhanging end; some ornamented with a horn-like piece. Seats along the vertical sides. Propelled by a single oar against a fork-like fulcrum. Ca. 7m long. **2.** *Germany, S/Switzerland, N:* Used on Lake Constance (Bodensee) for fishing and pleasure. Clinker-built, flat bottom; sharp, upturned bow; square stern. Rowed with a pair of oars; tholepins set into the gunwales. **3.** *Poland:* **a.** Small, open, general-purpose boat of the Gulf of Danzig (Gdańsk) before 1945. Clinker-planked, straight stem, wide transom, flat bottom, keel. **b.** The **gonduła** was a small, pre-20th-century pleasure boat. See also **gondola-4**, **grundel**, **Leibschiff**, **Noordhollandse gondel**.

gondela See **gundalow**

gondele See **gondola-4**

gondelette Diminutive of the Venetian **gondola***. Term popular in the 15th century. Some towed behind a vessel. Other recorded names: **condolette**, **gondoletă**, **gondoletta**, **gôndolazinha**

gondell *United Kingdom:* A 15th-century term for a small **ship's boat***.

gondol *Australia, S:* Term for a **canoe*** by the aborigines of Moreton Bay, South Australia.

gondola 1a. The smallest of the boats in the service of a **nef*** or **galley*** during the Middle Ages. Employed 12 oars. Length ca. 10m, narrow. Spelling variants: **condura**, **gondole***, **gondolla**, **gondora**, **gondre***, **gondura**, **gonxdola**, **grandola**, **grondola**, **grundula**; pl. **gondolae**. **b.** Small oared boat used for pleasure outings. **2.** *France, S:* **a.** A small, general-purpose boat popular in the 18th century on Corsica. **b.** At Toulon, an open, lateen-rigged boat. Curved stem, tall rudder worked with lines, rowed with 2 pairs of oars. **3.** *Italy, N:* Rough, heavy boat of Lake Como (Laria) used for general transportation as well as carrying merchandise and the mail. Shell-built with the stem and sternpost and ribs inserted later. High, wide, rounded sides; sharp, strongly raking bow; stern less raked, posts extend above the gunwales. Flat bottom. Cabin aft or an arched canvas covering; decked at ends. Rudder wide-bladed below the waterline; tiller. Propelled by oar, sail, and more recently by auxiliary motor. Mast stepped in shoe in forward third. Tall, narrow, square sail. A 16th-century boat was steered with quarter sweeps and rowed with as many as 6 oars per side. Reported lengths 13-25m; e.g., length 17.6m, beam 5.23m, depth 1.4m. Name variants: **gondola comasca**, **gondola lariana**; dim. **gondoletta 4.** *Italy, NE:* **Water-taxi** of Venice that has undergone a long period of evolution, but has been fairly standard since the late 19th century. In the 13th century, they were **barge***-like and employed numerous oarsmen; during the 16th-17th centuries, they became increasingly ornate, but by later decree they were simplified and painted black. Estimated to have numbered as many as 10,000 in the late 15th century, but only a few now built; almost entirely supplanted by motorized craft. Prior to the end of the 18th century, were rowed by 2 oarsmen, one at each end, and the boats were symmetrical. When reduced to a single oarsman, the port side was made fuller and deeper and the starboard shorter so that the oarsman, standing on the port side with the oar to starboard, is able to keep the boat from swinging to the left. As many as 8 different kinds of wood used in their construction; thin planking bent over ca. 40 sawn frames; bottom flat transversely, curved fore-and-aft, no keel. Sharp ends overhang, especially at the stern; stem inclines ca. 10° to starboard; considerable sheer, especially aft. Open except for a cambered foredeck, which is often decorated; earlier boats had a small, covered compartment amidships; one lacking this cabin was called a **firanziera**. Characteristic iron work (now aluminum) fitted to the bow and stern; the tall bow piece consists of a flat piece shaped like an axe head, with 6-7 teeth facing

forward and one aft. Oarsman stands on a small platform, working a 3.2-4.2m-long oar against a tall, con-
torted oar fork; oar held against the fork at various
points for specific maneuvers. Reported lengths 8-15m,
now mainly ca. 11m; e.g., length 10.87m, beam 1.5m,
depth 0.5m. Several varieties have been identified. The
gondola da fresco (sometimes **demi-gondola** or **summer gondola**) is a small, 2-person pleasure boat. The
gondola de casada (pl. **gondole di casada**) was privately owned. A **gondola di posto** (**gondola da poste**)
is one available for hire. The **gondola a coa de gambero** (**gondola falcada** or **falcata**), which carried people and cargo, had a sharply raked bow, flared rubbing
strakes that joined the stem with a hollow, and a
wrought-iron piece that projected forward at the bow.
Other recorded names: **ghondol(a), gonda★, gondel★,
gondele, gondolla, gondolya, gondora, gondre,
gondula, gróndola, grundola, grundula, gundalo,
gundelo(e), gundelow, gundilo, gundola, gundua,
kondola**; pl. and French **gondole**; dims. **gondolet(t)a,
gondolette**. Further reading: G. B. Rubin de Cervin,
Bateaux et Batellerie de Venise (Paris: Vilo, 1978), 91-
130; Carlo Donatelli, *The Gondola, an Extraordinary
Naval Architecture* (Venice: Arsenale Editorice, 1994).
Note also **barchetta, battellina-2, Fisaler, gondelette,
gondola da regata, sandolino, traghetto**.
5. *Italy, NW:* The **gondola** of the Ligurian coast was a
straight-stemmed, double-ended boat with a keel. Used
for light cargo, passengers, and fishing during the 18th-
19th centuries. Carvel-planked; long, straight keel; stem
lightly raked, sternpost plumb, open. Propelled by oars,
generally 6, or set a spritsail. Length to ca. 10m.
6. *Malta:* Old type of rowing craft characterized by spi-
raled stem and sternposts, both coiling aft. Type used
mainly by the Governor, high-ranking naval officers,
and customs officials. Sharp-ended; at times, fitted
with a rudder.
7. *United States, NW:* **Gondolas** were built by the
Americans during the Revolution for engagements on
the St. Lawrence River and Lake Champlain. Flat bottom, longitudinally planked, some with a slight deadrise and mild fore-and-aft rocker; most had a heavy
keelson. Full bow; narrow, sharp, raked stern. Bottom
and sides separately framed. Maximum beam well forward; sides flared and lightly curved. Smaller vessels
had a forecastle only; larger boats decked with raised
quarter-deck; deep bulwarks; gunports; weathercloths.
Outboard rudder, wide-bladed below the waterline;
tiller. Stepped a tall mast; jib set flying from stemhead
on smaller vessels, 1-2 headsails to a reefing bowsprit
on the larger ones. One captured by the British would
be rerigged with a gaff mizzen, creating a **bomb
vessel★**. Also rowed. Crew of ca. 45. Reported lengths
12-21m; e.g., length 16.5m, beam 4.5m, depth ca.
1.5m; shallow draft. Other recorded names: **gundalo,
gundalow★, praam★, prame★**. Further reading: Lorenzo
F. Hagglund, *A Page From the Past: The Story of the
Continental Gondola "Philadelphia"* (Whitehall,
N.Y.: The Whitehall Times, 1936).
Further references: **galley-9, grondola, gundalow,
gundalow-2, gundula**
gondola a coa de gambero See **gondola-4, row galley**

gondola comasca See **gondola-3**
gondola da fresco See **barchetta-3, gondola-4**
gondola da Mestre See **gondola da regata**
gondola da poste See **gondola-4**
gondola da regata *Italy, NE:* Several special types of
gondolas★ are reserved for racing. Built of mahogany.
Usually very lightweight, necessitating special bracing along the sides, and a cable may run from stem to
stern. Painted in one of several traditional colors. The
disdotóna (pl. **disdotone**) employs 18 standing oarsmen and is ca. 24m long. The **dodesona** (pl. **dodesone**)
is 12-oared, the **diesona** (pl. **diesone**) is 10-oared,
while the **quatordesona** is 14-oared. The lightly built
gondolin (or **gondolino, gondolone★**; pl. **gondolini**)
employs 2 oarsmen and is ca. 9.65m long, 1.12m
wide, and 0.39m deep; like the regular **gondola**, it is
asymmetrical—fuller and deeper on the port side and
with less sheer. The **gondolon(e)** (pl. **gondoloni**) is
heavier and stronger, employing 8 oarsmen, and is
13m long and 1.6m wide; often used to travel to
Mestre and Fusina; also called a **gondola da Mestre**.
Further spelling variants: **disdottona, dodiciona**
gondola da tragheto, gondola da traghetto See **traghetto**
gondola de casada See **gondola-4**
gondola de la colomba See **canotto-3**
gondole di casada See **gondola-4**
gondola di posto See **gondola-4**
gondolae See **gondola-1**
gondola falcada, gondola falcata See **gondola-4**
gondola lariana See **gondola-3**
gondola piana *Italy, north-central:* Small **fishing boat★**
of Lago di Garda. Low ends, flat bottom. Spelling
variant: **gondola piano**
gondola piano See **gondola piana**
gôndolazinha See **gondelette**
gondole *France:* **1.** Cited as a **canot★**, a service boat of
the 13th-18th centuries.
 2. Mediterranean coast **fishing boat★** of the 18th century.
Sharp ends; curved bow; tall stem and sternpost that,
on some, recurved at the top. Rowed or set a lateen sail;
on some, a jib tacked to the stemhead. Crew of 3-6.
 3. During the 17th-18th centuries, the **gondole coraline**
worked off Corsica from March to September; also
sought coral off the North African coast. Sharp-ended,
therefore easily maneuverable. Capstan on deck.
Rowed; also sailed, setting a lateen sail. Crew of 8-12.
Reported lengths 8-13m.
 4. At Bordeaux, in the southwest, small **steamers** ferried
across the Garonne River, providing service from the
early 19th century until World War II. Two cabins: one
for 1st class, the other for 2nd class. Crew of 3.
Lengths 15-20m.
 5. At Grandcamp on the western shore of Baie de Seine
in Normandy, the **gondole** served as a **tender★** to **fishing boats**, anchoring the fishing lines and transferring
the catch to shore. Clinker-planked of fir, flat bottom,
plumb or raked stem, raked transom, flaring sides.
Rowed using 5.5-6m-long oars; also sculled. Reported
lengths 4.2-6.5m; e.g., length 6.5m, beam 2.2m, depth
0.7m, shallow draft.
Further references: **gondola-1, gondola-4**

gondole coraline See gondole-3
gondole di casada See gondola-4
gondole française See drogueur
gondoleta See gondelette, gondola-4
gondoletta See gondelette, gondola-3, gondola-4
gondolette See gondola-4
gondolin See gondola da regata
gondolini See gondola da regata, gondolone
gondolino See gondola da regata
gondolla See gondola-1, gondola-4
gondolo Term applied to a 16th-century **ship's boat***. See also **gundalow**.
gondolo boat See gundalow-2
gondolon See gondola da regata
gondolone *Italy, NE:* Transported people and goods in the Lagoon of Venice. Characterized by the iron piece that ran along the ridge of the vaulted foredeck, projecting beyond the stem. Spelling variant: pl. **gondolini**. See also **gondola da regata**.
gondoloni, gondolino See gondola da regata
gondolya See gondola-4
gondora See gondola-1, gondola-4
gondre Skiff* or ship's boat* serving a **galley***. Reported from the 14th and 16th centuries. Spelling variants: **gondres, gondrez**. Further reference: **gondola-4**
gondres, gondrez See gondre
gondula See gondel-3b, gondola-1, gondola-4, gundalow, gundula
gondulica, gondulina See gundula
gondulo See gundalow
gondura See condura, gondola-1
gonk See junk
gónka See timber raft-1
gonmié See gommier
gonoûk See junk
gonxdola See gondola-1
goods barge See hoy barge
good ship A seaworthy ship for carriage of goods as acknowledged for marine insurance policies, contracts of affreightments, bills of lading, etc.
goofah See quffa
goofer See bumboat-1
Gooier botter, Gooise botter See botter
goose boat See sneak boat-1
Gooysche vischbotter See botter
goozieboat See goozing boat
goozing boat *England, SE:* A large, open **Thames wherry*** that provided pilots and ferrying service to ships arriving at Gravesend. Rigged with a standing lug foresail and a small sprit mizzen. Name variants: **goozieboat, Gravesend goozieboat**
gopalpuri See pallar
gopher See quffa
gorab *Indonesia:* A large, **galley***-type rowing vessel, locally built but of Arab origin; used during the early colonial period. Spelling variant: **gorap**. Further references: **ghurāb***, **grab***
gorabio See golafrus
gorabo See golafrus, grab-3
gorap See gorab, grab-4
gore boat See Parrett flatner
Gorgaman See Georgesman

Gorleston shrimper See Yarmouth shrimper
goro See Kru canoe
gorso See gourse-1
gosha See kosha
goso See gozzetto-2, gozzo
gospel boat See church boat
gospel ship *United States, north-central:* Vessel whose captain provided church services, mainly ashore, at lumber and iron ore harbors in the northwestern Great Lakes during the 1870s and 1880s. First three vessels sailed; the 4th was steam powered. Reported lengths 5.8-24.4m. Name variant: **bethel ship**
gossetto See gourse-2
gosso See gourse-2, gozzo
gotlandssnipa *Sweden, E:* Works off the beaches of Gotland Island, fishing mainly for herring with gill or drift nets, primarily from April to December. Dates to the 1600s. The largest, the **tremänning**, works with crew of 3-4. The **tvåmänning** employs 2 men, and the **einmänning** works single-handed. Lightly built with narrow clinker planking. Sharp ends, strongly curved stem and sternpost. Rounded bottom, deep keel, soft turn of the bilges. Open; strong sheer toward the ends; outboard rudder; long tiller. The 3-man boat steps 3 unstayed masts through the thwarts. Sprit-rigged, staysail to stemhead; sometimes sprit topsails on the main- and foremasts. In brisk winds, the mainsail may be dropped and the smaller mizzen substituted. The 2-man boats set 2 spritsails and a staysail; the 1-man boats set a single spritsail and a staysail. Jib sometimes run to a light bowsprit. The larger boats may be motorized. The oar blades flat on one side, beveled on the other; narrow. Loom square, filling out toward the top to fit over the single tholepin. The 3-man boat, also called **treroning, tre-maenning**, or **storbåt***, is 7-8m long, 1.8m wide, and 0.8m deep. The 2-man boat is 6-6.5m long and 1.5-1.65m wide. The 1-man boat, sometimes called **fiskabåt**, is 3.9-5.3m long and 1.3m wide; the smallest of these is the **torsk(a)båt**. Note also **snipa**.
goualette See gouèlette, schooner
gouèlette *Haiti:* Small, 2-masted vessel that carries cargo locally. Carvel-planked, raked stem, wineglass transom. Decked forward and on the quarter. Stubby masts stepped against massive thwarts. Sets very high-peaked, boomed, loose-footed spritsails. Booms and sprits very long. Length ca. 12m. Other recorded names: **goualette, Haitian schooner**. See also **schooner**.
goufa See quffa
goulette See schooner
gourabe *Maldives:* Term for a **galley***, the royal **galley** called an **ogate gourabe**. Spelling variants: **ghurab***, **gourrabe**. Further references: **grab-1**, **grab-3**, **salah-salah**
gourable See grab-3, salah-salah
gourrabe See gourabe
gourse 1. *France, Mediterranean coast:* Working **gourses** were small, open boats that gathered sardine fry with a beach seine; a few were still working in the 1980s. Sharp ends with full lines; lightly curved stem and sternpost; stemhead often characteristic of a particular port; some had a clipper bow that ended in a beak and

a tall stemhead. Three grounding keels, the lateral keels attached to ends; flat floors; soft turn of the bilges; slight tumble home to topsides; moderate sheer. Working boats open, pleasure craft half-decked. Mainly rowed using a single tholepin; loop secured the oar. When sailed, set a lateen sail to a forward-raking mast. Now motorized and modified considerably. In the late 19th century, the **gourse cannoise** was popularized at Cannes by the British; these boats were sailed, setting lug- or gaff sails. Reported lengths 4-6m; e.g. length 5.75m, beam 1.96m, depth 0.72m. Other recorded names: **gorso, gourse niçoise (or provençale), gourso, gousso, gussou**

2. *Italy, NW:* Along the Gulf of Genoa, the **gourse** is used for both fishing and pleasure. Double-ended, vertical stem and sternpost, no tumble home. Pleasure craft are decked. Rowed using 4 oars. Also sailed, setting a lug- or lateen sail to a mast stepped amidships. Length 5.8m, beam 2m, depth 0.7m. Spelling variants: **gossetto, gosso, gousse, guscio**

gourse atarguié *France, Mediterranean coast:* Small, slender **fishing boat★**. Rounded ends. Mast stepped close to the bow; vertical or raked forward. Sets a small quadrilateral sail, often made of sacking or rags. Reported lengths 2.75-4m.

gourse cannoise See **gourse-1**
gourse de régate See **barquette-2**
gourse niçoise, gourse provençale, gourso See **gourse-1**
gouso See **gozzetto-2, gozzo**
gousse See **gourse-2**
gousso See **gourse-1**
Government boat See **fishery guard ship**
gozo *France, Corsica:* Used by residents of the Ersa area to fish for picarel. Considered a large **gozzo★**. Name variant: **gozzo corse**
Gozo boat, Gozo dghaisa See **dghajsa tal-pass**
gozu See **gozzetto-1**
gozzetta, gozzetti See **gozzetto-1**
gozzetto *Italy:* **1.** Small, open **fishing boat★** principally from Sicily but also reported from the Genoa area and Sardinia. Term sometimes applied to a small **ship's boat★**. Stemhead as much as 75cm above the gunwale; sternpost about half as high. Two or 3 thwarts. Rowed or sailed, setting a lateen sail. Crew of 1-2. Length 4.5m, beam 1.5m. Other recorded names: **gozu, gozzetta, vuazzètèillë, vuzzëtillë, vuzziteddu**; pl. **gozzetti**. Note also **gozzo**.

2. A small pleasure craft propelled by 2-4 oars. Spelling variants: **góso, góuso**
gozzi See **gozzo**
gozzo *Italy:* Found all along the Italian coast, but most notably off the Ligurian shores in northwestern Italy, Sicily, Naples, and Sardinia; also reported from the Dalmatian coast. General-purpose boat that engages in fishing, transporting produce, or working as a **pilot boat★, bumboat★**, or serves as a pleasure craft. Many variations, but characteristically open, beamy, and with a wedge-shaped stern. Stem may rake forward, or be concave or rounded with marked tumble home; high stemhead, recurved on the sharp-sterned type. Carvel-planked; now often of fiberglass. Keel, frequently bilge keels; strong sheer. Those used in open

waters are fuller and higher-sided. Two benches; grating at the bow. Some designed to be rowed only, by 3-4 people; others may set a lateen, sprit-, or lugsail to a portable mast, and occasionally a jib to a slender bowsprit; now mainly motorized. Reported lengths 3.7-12m; e.g., length 3.75m, beam 1.5m, depth 0.65m; the larger boats are known as **anime perse (lost souls)** and search for coral along the African coast. Other recorded names: **bordonaro, gos(s)o, gouso, gozo, guscio, guso, guzo, guzzo★, guzzu, pernacce, vuzzariello, vuzzarìidde, vuzze, vuzzo**; pl. **gozzi**; in Croatian **guc,** dim. **gučić** and **guculić** and in Slovenian, also **lupina**. Note also **gozu, gozzetto, gussi latina.** Further references: **canotto-1, dghajsa tal-pass**
gozzo corse See **gozo**
graanschip See **grain carrier**
grab 1. *Arabian Peninsula:* Persian (Arabian) Gulf and Arabian Sea vessel reported as early as the 16th century. Sewn hull; elongated bow; probably sharp stern; low sides. Appears to have been a **galley★** type, but probably also sailed. Other recorded names: **ghurāb, gorab★, gourabe★, groráb, kurāb, qārib★**; pl. **aghribah, ghirbān**

2. *Bangladesh/India, NE:* Used in naval operations on Bengali rivers in the mid-17th century. Spelling variant: **ghrab**

3. *India, west coast:* Trader that worked at least from the late 16th into the 19th century. Some were **riverboats★**, part of imperial **fleets★**. In the 17th-18th centuries, also popular as a vessel of corsairs, carrying as many as 18 guns; the 2 cannons could be fired over the bow. Extended, low bow with straight stem; high poop ended in a square counter. Flush decked; foredeck not fixed to the sides to permit drainage in head seas; inboard rudder. The 3-masted vessels were rigged in the European manner with square sails on the forward 2 masts and a gaff mizzen. The 2-masted vessels were lateen-rigged or had square sails forward and a fore-and-aft mizzen. The single-masted vessels were lateen-rigged. Sweeps used in calms, employing as many as 50, with one man per sweep. The armed vessels might carry 60 soldiers. Beamy, light draft, 100-300t. Other recorded names: **gharáb, ghrab, ghurab★, gorabo, gourab(l)e, grabh, gurab(a), gurabo**. Note also **salah-salah.**

4. *Malaysia:* Large, 2-masted trader. Mainmast to 30m tall. Rigged with fore-and-aft sails. Crew of 30. Length 91m, beam 9m, depth 6m. Other recorded names: **garapo, ghurab★, gorap, grob, grub, gurab, gurap**
grabh See **grab-3**
grain boat *United States:* **1.** Built to carry grain in the 19th century on the Erie Canal in central New York State. Initially towed singly by a team, then in pairs, and by 1870, steam was introduced. Hold lined with high-grade lumber to prevent seepage into the cargo; the decks were watertight and the hatches tightly covered. Spacious cabin aft. Crew of 2 drivers, 2 helmsmen, and a cook.

2. In the mid-19th century, worked along the Illinois and Michigan Canal. Grain put into 2 covered holds. Some were later converted to **steamboats**. Reported lengths 21-32m.

grain carrier Vessel with a cargo of grain (barley, corn, nuts, oats, pulses, rice, rye, wheat, etc.) equaling more than one-third of its net registered tonnage. Other recorded names: **barco para transporte de cereales**, **céréalier**, **Getreideschiff**, **graanschip**, **grain-laden vessel**, **grain ship**, **Kornschiff**, **transporteur de blé**, **trugero**. See also **sitegos**.

grain-laden vessel, **grain ship** See **grain carrier**

gralai See **galley**

grand banker See **banker-2**

Grand Banks dory See **Banks dory**

Grand Banks schooner See **banker-2**

grand-barque *France, N:* Term given to the large **fishing boats*** that adopted a trawl net in the area around the mouths of the Seine and Orne Rivers. Type spread westward in the 19th century. Note also **grande barque**.

grand bateau *France:* **1.** Type of **barge*** used on the Moselle River in northeastern France and in Germany in the 2nd half of the 19th century. Downstream cap. 220t, upstream 120t. Towed by 6 horses. Name variant: **Großschiff**
2. Barge type of the Dordogne River in southwestern France in the mid-19th century. Draft 1.05-1.1m; 60-80t. Further reference: **plate-9**

grand canot See **canot-2**, **canot du maître**

Grand Cayman schooner See **Cayman schooner**

grand doris See **doris-3**

grand drogueur See **drogueur**

grande barque 1. *France, S:* **Nau*** type used mainly for cargo on the Lot River. Extinct by the end of the 19th century. Flat bottom turned up to shallow end transoms. Some had a small, raised cabin at the stern; otherwise open. Rudder hung on gudgeons and pintles. Note also **grand-barque**.
2. *Switzerland, W:* Used in the late 19th century on Lake Neuchâtel and other lakes in the area to carry stone and wine. Flat bottom, curved up toward the raking stem; wide, square stern. Flared, carvel-planked sides; open; twin rudders. Tall mast could be lowered for bridges. Set 2 square sails and a foresail. In calms, propelled by forked poles (the *tchauques*). Length overall 23.5m, on bottom 22.2m, beam 5.5m, depth aft 2m. Other recorded names: **Barke** (or **barque**) **à tchauque**, **grosse Barke**

grande chaloupe See **chaloupe-2**, **longboat-1**, **txalupa handi**

grande dundee See **langoustier-2**

grande gabare See **gabare-3a**

grande galere See **galere-1**

grande galupe See **galupe**

grande kayasse See **markab-2**

grande plate *France, SW:* Broad, flat-bottomed craft of the Bassin d'Arcachon. Mainly used in the oyster industry, but the few remaining in the early 20th century served as **houseboats***. Ends sharp or square, raked; strong sheer. Set a lugsail. Now mainly of synthetic materials and equipped with a motor. Shallow draft. Name variant: **plate d'Arcachon**. Note also **plate**.

grande plate senegalaise *Mauritania/Senegal:* Passenger vessel of the Senegal River bordering the 2 countries. Flat bottom, raked ends, marked sheer. Raised cabin

with wood or cloth sides. Sets a very large lugsail to a long yard; raised by 2 halyards.

grande tartane See **tartane provençale**

Grand Haven ketch *United States, north-central:* Lumber carrier of the Great Lakes, especially on Lakes Michigan and Huron. One used until the 1930s. Sturdily built because of the heavy equipment they carried. Clipper bow, broad counter stern. **Ketch***-rigged with topsail, mizzen staysail, and as many as 4 headsails. On the Grand Haven rig, the mainmast was stepped well forward, and foreboom extended only to amidships; many were converted **schooners*** that had had their mainmasts removed. Reported lengths 24-30m. Other recorded names: **Lake Michigan ketch**, **schooner**

grandola See **gondola-1**

Grand River canoe See **canot du maître**

granite sloop See **stone sloop**

Granville bisquine See **bisquine**

grass boat *United States:* A market gunner's boat that has been camouflaged with grass. See also **balsa-7**, **cao zi chuan**.

grasshopper-head boat See **perahu kepala kelalang**

gravel barge *England, SW:* An **inside barge*** type that collected sand and gravel in the Taw/Torridge Estuary on the northern Devonshire coast until the mid-20th century. 19th-century **barges*** had higher sides and finer lines and were used mainly for lightering ships, but as the demand for gravel grew, a more specialized **barge** with fuller lines and flatter bottom was developed. Carvel-planked with heavy timbers; stem vertical and straight; transom broad and sloping. Some had hinged rudders. Decked; low or no bulwarks; large hatchways, low coaming; cuddy forward; gear compartment aft. Squarish gaff mainsail, loose-footed with boom, set on a short mast stepped in a tabernacle; staysail. Sails tanned. Motorized later. Crew of 2. Reported lengths 6-15m. Other recorded names: **Appledore gravel barge**, **Bideford sand barge**, **sailing barge***, **sailing lighter***, **sand barge***, **Taw gravel barge**, **Torridge sailing lighter**. Note also **rowing lighter**, **West Country sailing barge**.

Gravelines lugger See **lougre flamand**

gravel wagon See **sandbagger**

Gravesend barge *England, SE:* Chartered to provide passenger and freight service from Gravesend to London, especially to incoming ships in the Thames Estuary. Reported from the 11th century to the 1630s, running the route that became known as the **long ferry**. By the 17th century, they were commanded to serve every tide and were known as **tide boats***. Early boats decked at the stern, with the forward part for cargo. Rowed (by 4-5 men) and sailed; sprit-rigged. 60-85t burden. Other recorded names: **common barge**, **Gravesend ferry barge**. Note also **tilt boat**.

Gravesend bawley See **bawley**

Gravesend ferry barge See **Gravesend barge**

Gravesend goozieboat See **goozing boat**

Gravesend tilt boat See **tilt boat-2**

Gravesend waterman's wherry *England, SW:* Until the 1930s, ferried passengers and merchandise to shore from ships lying in the Thames Estuary and assisted in mooring operations. In the 16th century, provided service between London and Gravesend, carrying a maximum of 5 passengers. Open, clinker-built,

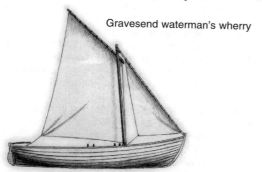

Gravesend waterman's wherry

maximum beam aft of amidships, rounded stem and forefoot; small, raked, transom stern. Mostly rowed with 2 pairs of oars; tholepins. Also set a sprit- or standing lugsail and staysail. Reported as **ketch**★-rigged in the late 19th century. Reported lengths 6-8m; e.g., length 6.4m, beam 1.6m, depth 0.6m. Note also **Thames wherry**.

gre *Australia, SE:* Bark **canoe**★ of the indigenous peoples of Gippsland in southeastern Victoria. Made from a single piece of bark softened by fire; tied at each end with thick fiber rope. Held open by several stretchers secured by lashings. Propelled by poling, or in deeper water, by 2 scoop-shaped pieces of bark. Reported lengths 2.3-5.5m. Other recorded names: **gree, gri, yuro**

great boat *British Isles:* **1.** Served as a **tender**★ to ships of the late 16th-17th centuries; towed behind the ship. Probably bluff-ended. Often armed. Variously reported as 2- or 4-masted. Rowed with as many as 60 oars. Also reported in the mid-17th century as a 14t open boat that carried lumber to Liverpool from north Wales. **2.** *England, E:* **a.** Term applied to the 2-masted **luggers**★ registered at Cromer and Sheringham on the north coast of Norfolk; engaged in fishing for herring, cod, mackerel, whelk, and crabs until the early 20th century. Many were built at Great Yarmouth and were similar to the **Yarmouth lugger**★. When fishing for crabs and cod, they generally carried a **Norfolk crabber**★ on board. Transom stern with an overhang. Cuddy shipped forward when herring fishing. Most converted to gaff mainsail and large, standing lug mizzen in the 1870s. Crew of 10-12. Length ca. 21m. **b.** In the early 17th century at Harwich, a **greate boate** was a large **ferry**★ used especially on heavy traffic days. **3.** *England, SW:* At Cremyll, on the lower River Tamar, **great boates** ferried vehicles and horses across the river in the 16th-17th centuries. **4.** *Northern Ireland, SW:* Reported in the 16th century as a clinker-built boat used on Lough Erne. Some had a cabin. Rowed with 6-7 oars to a side; also sailed. **5.** *Scotland:* Boat of the 17th-century lairds. Either 8-oared (**auchtoaring**) or 12-oared (**twaloaring**). The 8-oared boats transported fish oil, dried fish, butter, etc. Heavy strake below the gunwale, decked at bow. Two-

masted with square sails. Length overall ca. 12m, on keel 9m; cap. 6-7t.
Further references: **kirkkovene, longboat-1**
greate boate See **great boat-2b**
great galley See **Deal galley punt, galeazza, galley-3**
Greathead lifeboat See **lifeboat**
Great Laker See **laker-1**
Great Lakes bateau See **batteau-2**
Great Lakes layout boat See **layout boat-2**
Great Lakes Mackinaw See **Mackinaw boat-1**
Great Lakes pound net boat See **pound net boat**
Great Lakes schooner *Canada/United States:* Special **schooners**★ were built from the early 19th century until 1889 to meet the needs of traffic on the lakes; last used in the 1920s. The so-called **schooners** built after 1889 were merely **tow barges**. Carried mainly bulk cargo—lumber, iron ore, grain, coal—but some of the smaller vessels served as traveling stores. Design depended somewhat on the major cargo. Most had flat floors, little or no drag to the keel, low freeboard. Sharp bow, some clipper-bowed; sharp stern with transom above; inboard rudder. Thin planking; frames alternated between single and double. Often flat-sided, flat-bottomed, and little draft in order to pass through the locks of the Welland Canal (usually called **canallers**★ or **canal schooners**); these had a centerboard. Mainly 2- or 3-masted, although late in the period, 4- and 5-masted vessels were built. On the 3-masted vessels, the mainmast was the tallest; mizzenmast quite short, coming up through the cabin on the **three-'n-afters**. Early vessels carried square topsails, and the foremast set a square sail forward of the gaff sail and a topsail. Several headsails to a bowsprit and jibboom; jibboom might be 18m long. The bowsprit and jibboom of the **canallers** canted up at a steep angle. **Barkentine**★- and **brigantine**★-rigged vessels were locally called **schooners**. Sails on the early gaff-rigged **schooners** were raised by horses or mules working a windlass; later hoisted by donkey engines. Crew of 3-12. Lengths 14-85m; e.g., length 32m, beam 7m, depth 2.8m; shallow or medium draft. **Tow barges** to 130m. Note also **laker, scow-schooner**.
Great Lakes sharpie See **sharpie-8**
great line boat See **handline boat**
great Montreal canoe See **canot du maître**
great ship *United Kingdom:* Large, heavily armed **man-of-war**★ of the 17th century. Similar to the merchant **carracks**★ but modified for extra armament. Initially 2 and later 3 gun decks. Quarter-decks became progressively narrow as they went up; square stern; several foredecks. Outboard rudder; tiller came in below the quarter-decks. Square sails on the main and foremasts, lateen sails on the 2 mizzenmasts. Long, rising bowsprit. Average length 31m, beam 11m, depth 5m.
Further reference: **nau-1**
Great South Bay catboat See **catboat-2**
Great South Bay duck boat See **duck boat**
Great South Bay scooter See **scooter-2**
Great South Bay sloop See **oyster sloop-1**
Great Yarmouth herring drifter See **Yarmouth lugger**
Great Yarmouth shrimper See **Yarmouth shrimper**

grebnaia sliupka, **grebnaya lodka** See **pulling boat**

gree See **gre**

Green Bay boat, **Green Bay hunting boat** See **monitor-3**

green boat See **badjra**

Greencastle skiff, **Greencastle yawl** See **drontheim**

green eyebrow *China, E:* Trader built at Ningbo and operated in the Shanghai area. Type of **chênhai chuan★**. Name derived from the splash of green above the wales just abaft the oculus; when black, called the **black eyebrow**. Originally exclusively an **ice boat★** serving **fishing boats★**. Black hull, numerous wales; green patch just forward of the mizzen. Sharp, curved bow painted red; semi-closed stern also painted red; flat bottom. Three masts; battened lugsails set to starboard; mizzen sheeted to an outrigger. Length 20m, beam 4.6m. Other recorded names: **big bird boat**, **lu mei mao**

Greenie See **drontheim**

Greenland whaleboat See **whaleboat-4**

green parrot See **barge-2**

Greifswalder Leichterboot See **Treckschute**

grete boat See **longboat-1**

gri See **gre**

griban, **gribana** See **gribane**

gribane *France, N:* **Coasters★** of the 15th-17th centuries found in Normandy, Picardy, and Flanders; also river craft of the 19th century, especially on the Seine and Somme Rivers. The **coasters** were clinker-built, double-ended, flat-floored, 2-masted **luggers★**; no topmast. The river craft were sharp- or transom-sterned; flat-bottomed, decked, and had shallow draft; some jury-rigged a collapsible mast. The lug-rigged **coasters** stepped a foremast and set a topsail to the mainmast. Others were gaff-rigged **cutters★** or **sloops★**. Reported lengths 18-34m; river vessel length 18.2m, beam 5.2m, depth 2.3m. Spelling variants: **bribane**, **bribenne**, **gabanne**, **griban(a)**, **gribanne**, **gribarne**, **gribenne**. Further reading: Benoît Morel, "La Gribane de Basse Seine," *Chasse-Marée* 26 (1986), 16-29.

gribanne, **gribarne**, **gribenne** See **gribane**

griendaak *Netherlands, SW:* **Aak★**-type craft that transported osiers, hay, etc. on the rivers in the Biesbosch region southeast of Dordrecht. Built until 1925. Beamy, iron hull designed to carry a light deck cargo. A small type carried fresh-cut osiers to temporary storage houses. Rounded ends, but fine fore and after body. Flat bottom, curved chines. Curved stem with forefoot, straight sternpost. Wale followed sheer. Winch and sheerlegs on foredeck; steering platform forward of raised stern deck. Leeboards; outboard rudder; tiller. Lowering mast stepped forward of hatch; set a boomed, loose-footed gaff sail with straight gaff. Staysail; jib to reefing bowsprit. Length to 20.74m, beam 5.11m, depth 1.44m. Other recorded names: **Biesboschaak**, **rietaak★**, **slechtaak**, **Zuiderwalse aak**. Note also **chai ban zi**, **reed boat-2**.

Griffin wherry See **salmon wherry**

Grimsby smack See **cod smack-3**

grisbåt *Norway, NW:* Fishermen of Nordmøre District gave the nickname **grisbåt** (**pig boat★**) to a boat from neighboring Trøndelag, especially a **åfjordsbåt**. Note also **nordmørsbåt**.

grob See **grab-4**

Groenlandse boot, **Groenlandse sloep** See **whaleboat-4**

Groenlandsvaarder See **whaler-1**

Groenlandtsche sloep See **whaleboat-4**

Groente-Ever See **Gemüse-Ewer**

groin de cochon See **mourre de pouar**

grondola *Spain, NE:* Small boat of the 14th and early 15th centuries used in harbors, especially at Tarragona. Tall stem. Spelling variants: **gondola★**, pl. **grondole**. See also **gondola-1**, **gondola-4**.

grondole See **grondola**

Groningen galjoot, **Groninger galjoot** See **galjoot**

Groninger koftjalk See **koftjalk**

Groningerlander tjalk See **Groninger tjalk**

Groninger slijkpraam See **slijkpraam**

Groninger snik See **snik-2**

Groninger tjalk *Netherlands, NE:* Built to carry bulk cargo on the inland waterways of Groningen Province, although some went to Scandinavia, England, and France. Narrower and lighter draft than other **tjalken** (pl.) to meet local requirements. Worked from the late 19th into the early 20th century. Initially of wood, later of iron or steel. Clinker-planked below the wide, heavy wale, carvel above; later all carvel. Full, rounded ends; heavy stem with cutaway forefoot; deadwood at stern. Flat bottom, longitudinally planked, with forward end curving up to about midway along the stem. Rounded sides, sharp tumble home above the wale at the ends; flat sheer. Curved tiller slotted over the rudderhead, which in early days was carved; wide leeboards. Decked, deckhouse aft, small chimney abaft the deckhouse; covered hold between mast and deckhouse. A square decoration flanked the stem above the wale, each with decorative hawser holes and a vertical piece that ended above the gunwale as a bitt. A window was set on each side of the sternpost; replaced by painted circles on the metal vessels. Early vessels sprit-rigged. Later set a loose-footed, boomed gaff sail to a strikable mast. One or 2 headsails and sometimes a topsail. Length 21m, beam 4.3m; 70-150t. Spelling variants: **Groningerlander tjalk**, **Groningische tjalk**. Note also **Friese tjalk**, **tjalk**.

Groningische tjalk See **Groninger tjalk**

Groningse galjoot See **galjoot**

Groningse snik See **snik-2**

Groomsport yawl *Northern Ireland, E:* Open, double-ended boat of the mouth of Belfast Lough used for longline fishing and pilot work. Clinker-planked;

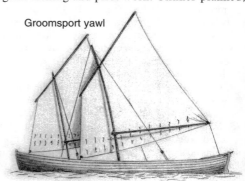

Groomsport yawl

curved, sharp stem with rounded forefoot; slightly raked stern; keel. Outboard rudder; tiller. Stepped 1-2 forward-raking masts close together on the keelson, fitted into half circles on aft side of a thwart. Set overlapping dipping lugsails with high-cut clews; sails could be extended by a boom. Sometimes steered with a yoke and long lines. Also rowed. Auxiliaries supplemented sails on some boats after ca. 1908. Crew of 5. Reported lengths 3.6-9.7m; e.g., length 9.7m, beam 2.7m; shallow draft. Name variant: **Belfast yawl**

groote boot See **longboat-1**, **sloep-2**

groote sloep See **barge-2**

groot sloep See **vishoeker**

groráb See **grab-1**

gros bois *West Indies:* A type of **accon⋆** that transferred provisions, water, and cargo to ships lying in a roadstead. Sharp ends, flat bottom, 3 strakes per side increased capacity. Decked at bow and stern, sometimes with a shelter at the stern. Outboard rudder; tiller. Mainly rowed by ca. 6 oarsmen. Some sailed, employing a lug foresail and a mizzen. Reported lengths 10-15m, widths 2.4-2.7m, depth ca. 1.8m.

Grossboot See **longboat-1**

grosse Barke See **grande barque-2**

grosse barque See **grande barque-1**

Grosse Boot See **longboat-1**

grosse Jagd See **Jagd**

Grosse Nauen See **Nauen**

Großschiff See **grand bateau-1**

grote boot See **longboat-1**, **sloep-2**, **tjotter**

grote jol See **Staverse jol**

grote punter See **zeepunter**

grote schouw See **Friese schouw**, **schouw**

grouin de cochon See **mourre de pouar**

groundnut cutter *Gambia:* The sailing boats (also called **groundnutters**) used to transport groundnuts (peanuts) down the Gambia River to Bathurst (now Banjul) are of 2 types, both designated **cutters⋆**. The **canoe⋆** type is characterized by a keel piece projecting from both the bow and stern. Bottom curved fore-and-aft; moderate sheer; flared sides. Raked end transoms. Rudder post offset to avoid the stern extension; rudder blade pivots below the extension; tiller. Hull gaily painted. Open hold; wide side decks; groundnuts, usually in sacks, piled above deck level. Sets a baggy spritsail, staysail, jib to a short jibboom. Length on deck 18.3m. The 2nd type is a gaff **cutter**. Plumb stem; straight, raked transom, topstrake curves up toward the bow. Crew live on deck. Long gaff, tall topmast, long bowsprit.

groundnutter See **groundnut cutter**

growler See **dredger-1**

grub See **grab-4**

grundel *Netherlands, SW:* A small, flat-bottomed boat that fished and transported local products. Especially popular around Aalsmeer, where it originated in the mid-19th century, although it is called a **punter⋆** or **landschuit** there. Recently enlarged, becoming a popular pleasure craft, the **grundeljacht**. Bottom curves up toward the flat ends; skeg at each end; hard chines; sides flare to the wale, then have tumble home; maxi-

mum beam well forward. Strongly raked, straight stem carries above the sheer strake, some ironclad. Narrow raked transom, roughly hexagonal. Strong sheer, especially forward; considerable freeboard. Short end decks; rowing thwarts in open waist; pleasure boats have a cabin abaft the mast. **Fishing boats⋆** had a live well (the **visschuit van Aalsmeer**). Large-bladed rudder; tiller. Smaller boats used a single narrow leeboard that was shifted as needed; larger used 2 leeboards; **yachts⋆** may have a centerboard. Single strikable pole mast stepped against the forefoot; on the pleasure craft, the mast is just forward of the cabin. Initially employed a spritsail; later a leg-of-mutton sail, loose-footed but with a boom as long as the boat. The **grundeljacht** sets a gaff sail with a short gaff and a staysail. Generally a large jib to an iron bumkin. Also rowed, the oars working in slots in built-up blocks on the gunwales. Some motorized. Crew of 2. Reported lengths of working boats 5-6.5m, beam 1.75m, depth 0.7m. The similar **Zaanse gondel** from the Zaandam area northwest of Amsterdam had a lower freeboard, an even greater rake to the stem, and an oval leeboard. The mast was stepped farther aft and 2 headsails might be set. Lengths overall ca. 5.8m, on keel 4m, beam 1.8m, depth 1.0m. A new pleasure **yacht**, the **zeegrundel**, was developed in 1964 along the lines of the **grundel**. Stem has a break in the rake below the wale; square stern, 2 slender leeboards. Open cockpit, cabin. Sets a leg-of-mutton mainsail and 1-2 headsails. Reported lengths 7-9m; e.g., length 7.5m, beam 2.8m, depth 0.9m. Other recorded names: **Aalsmeers(ch)e grundel**, **gondel⋆**, **vischgondel**, **vischschuit**. Note also **Noordhollandse gondel**.

grundeljacht See **grundel**

grundola See **gondola-1**, **gondola-4**

grundula See **gondola-4**

gruzovoe sudno See **freighter-1**

guabarra See **gabare**

guabarrot See **gabarot**

guadaño 1. *Cuba/Mexico/Spain:* Small harbor craft. Cited from Havana, Mexico, and Cádiz. Awning covered the stern. Rowed with 2 pairs of oars or set a spritsail.

2. Small boat attached to a Spanish **man-of-war⋆** for transferring goods and men between ships and to and from shore.

guaira, **guaire** See **houari**

guairo *Latin America:* Small 2-masted **coaster⋆** that employed a houari rig (see **houari**) on both masts. See also **wherry**.

gualee See **galère-1**, **galley**

gualere, **gualie** See **galley**

gualiot, **gualiote** See **galiot**

guallion See **galleon**

gualveta See **galiot**

guampu See **dalca**

guan cai chuan *China:* Many types of boats used to carry the dead to their ancestral homes for final burial. In Shanghai, the most prevalent type was an old and decrepit **xiao ma tou chuan⋆**. Other recorded names: **coffin boat**, **kuan ts'ai ch'uan**. Note also **fei teng**.

guan chuan See **junk**

guarda-coasta, guardacosta, guardacostas, guarda-costes See **coast guard ship**

guardaostruzioni See **boom defense vessel**

guardapescas See **fishery guard ship**

guardaporto See **balandra-2**, **guard ship**

guard boat 1. One that patrols the activities in a harbor. Some carried an officer of the guards who made night-time rounds of ships of the British navy to test the alertness of watch personnel. May be attached to a **guard ship★**. Other recorded names: **barca di ronda, bote de ronda, canot de ronde** (or **de veille**), **lancia di ronda, watch boat★**
2. A boat used by health officials enforcing quarantine regulations.
3. *United States, E:* **a. Guard boats** served during the American Revolution on the Delaware River and Bay to prevent contact between British sympathizers and the British army at creek mouths and to protect various alarm posts. Built as a small **galley★**; sharp ends, flat bottom, low freeboard. Open, but crew might be protected by an awning. Usually armed with a 4-pound cannon and 2 swivel guns. Mainly rowed using 10-12 oars; probably set a single lateen sail at times. Crew of ca. 12. Reported lengths on keel 9.6-11.7m. Other recorded names: **flat-bottomed boat, half galley★**.
b. Used by oyster growers on Chesapeake Bay in the late 19th century to patrol their private oyster beds to prevent poaching.
Further reference: **picket boat**

guard de costa See **coast guard ship**

guard ship 1. Ship of the British Royal Navy that received men impressed into naval service.
2. Naval or official vessel stationed at a port to defend it or to superintend ships in the harbor. Might defend against pirates and smuggling in colonial areas. May also serve as a school ship for naval cadets. Selected name variants: **bastimento guardaporto, buque de guardia, dozornoe sudno, guardaporto, Hafenpolizei Fahrzeug, harbor ship, navire de garde, patache de police** (or **de surveillance**), **police vessel, station-naire, stazionario, uitlegger, vaisseau de garde, vardacosta, Wach(t)schiff, Wachtboot, Wachtkutter, wachtschip**
3. Name sometimes given to the **flagship★** of the port admiral.
See also **balandra-2, seki bune**.

guari See **houari**

gubang 1. *Indonesia, central:* Small, seaworthy **coaster★** and passenger vessel of the Bugis peoples of south-western Sulawesi (Celebes). Plank-built; sharp clipper bow; full amidships; narrow stern with considerable deadwood; vertical sternpost; keel; midline rudder and tiller. Decked; house aft. Set a modified leg-of-mutton sail, loose-footed; large jib. Long bowsprit, projected from below gunwale level, supported on heavy gammon knee. Crew of 3. Length ca. 7.3m. Other recorded names: **gobang★, goebang, perahu gubang**. Note also **gubang besar**.
2. *Indonesia, W/Peninsular Malaysia:* **Fishing boat★** of the nomadic Orang Laut peoples of the west coast of the Malay Peninsula and the Riau-Lingga Archipelagoes

off Sumatra. Long, overhanging ends. Open or decked with loose planking. Thatched- or wooden-roofed house, sides of bark; often serves as living quarters; house may be dismantled when under sail. Mast stepped just forward of amidships and easily struck. Mat sail with yards at top and bottom; can be worked as a square sail or lugsail. Reported lengths 6-8m; beam ca. 2m. Other recorded names: **Orang Laut boat, perahu gubang, prahu gebang, sampan gĕbèng** (or **gĕbing**). Note also **kakap-1**.
3. Malay pirate craft that was chiefly rowed. Raked bow; small quarter galleries. Decked with house. Breastwork forward protected crew during raids. Swivel guns at the bow. Name variant: **gubang Laut**
Further reference: **gobang**

gubang besar *Indonesia, central:* Large (*besar*), 3-masted vessel of the Buginese of Sulawesi (Celebes). Concave bow terminating in pronged figurehead; long, straight keel; sharp stern; outboard rudder. Decked. Mainmast stepped roughly amidships, foremast about one-quarter in from the bow, mizzenmast well aft. Set lugsails. Jib is run out on light bowsprit inserted into a post on the foredeck.

gubang Laut See **gubang-3**

guc, gučić, guculić See **gozzo**

Gudenåkåg See **kåg-1**

gudiyÉ, gudyiyi See **sealing canoe-2**

gudzu See **guzzo-1**

guenille See **berrichon**

Guernsey crabber See **Guernsey crab boat**

Guernsey crab boat *United Kingdom:* Tended crab trot lines and lobster pots and engaged in inshore fishing from the island of Guernsey off the French coast. Carvel-planked with relatively few planks. Straight stem; raked transom; deep drag aft, but when engines installed, drag eliminated. Open. Usually green or white outside; inside painted according to fancy. Two or 3 masts. Fore- and mainmasts set high-peaked spritsails or changed to gaff sails during the 1870s. Mizzenmast, if used, stepped to port with outrigged lugsail. Jib to bowsprit. Reported lengths 3.7-9m; beamy. Name variants: **Guernsey crabber** (or **lobster boat**)

Guernsey drifter See **Guernsey mackerel boat**

Guernsey lobster boat See **Guernsey crab boat**

Guernsey mackerel boat *United Kingdom:* Fast, powerful boat from the Channel Island of Guernsey that drifted for mackerel and fished for conger eels. Most gone by the mid-20th century. Carvel-planked of pine; straight, plumb stem and fine entrance; counter or square stern; oak frames. Decked to mainmast, open aft. Legs commonly employed when grounded at low tide. Initially set 3 standing lugsails; later adopted a fore-and-aft **schooner★** rig but often retained the standing lug mizzen. Gaff sails high-peaked and boomless; initially laced to masts, later hoops adopted. In good weather, also set a large gaff topsail on one or both masts. Masts struck while fishing. Mizzenmast stepped on the port quarter; omitted ca. 1880. Crew of 5-6. Large size: length 11m, beam 3.66m, depth 2.44m, 12-15t. Name variant: **Channel Islander**

gué-tré See **ghe trê**

gufa, gufah, guffa, guffur See **quffa**
gui See **gig-1**
guideboat See **Adirondack guideboat**
guig See **gig-1**
guiga *Portugal, N:* General-purpose boat used on the Rio Tamega, a right-bank tributary of the Douro River. Sharp ends; flat bottom; vertical stem, sternpost, and sides; about a dozen frames. Open; seats at bow and stern, 2 thwarts. Rowed or poled by one person. Length 4.95m, beam 1.1m, depth 0.4m. See also **gig-3**.
guigue, guihe See **gig-1**
Guilford drag boat See **Connecticut River drag boat**
Guinea boat *United States, NE:* Term given by the Gloucester, Massachusetts, townspeople to the **fishing boats**★ operated by the local Italian immigrants. Brightly painted. Motorized. Length ca. 9m. Note also **dago**. Further reference: **death galley**
Guinea-Kutter See **sinaper**
guineaman, Guinea-ship See **slaver-1**
guineevaarder *Netherlands:* A vessel that went to the Guinea coast.
Guinness fly See **flyboat-3a**
gul *Australia, NE:* Double-**outrigger canoe**★ found on the islands of Torres Strait. In the western islands, the **canoe**★ is called a **gul**, while in the eastern group, it is a **nar**; on the Papua New Guinea side of the strait, a basically similar **canoe** is called a **moto-moto**★. Dugout hull, round in cross section; crossed struts maintain shape; on most, sides raised by full-length washstrakes sewn on with sennit lashings over split bamboo; short deck forward. At ends, bottom extended, terminating in a vertical transom piece; additional triangular strake at the ends sheers up to join the top of these pieces. Richly decorated with a carved figurehead at the bow and a tall, carved board at the stern; other parts ornamented with feathers, tassels, and shells. Two booms, lashed at the center, extend to short, pointed floats; booms and floats joined by 2 pairs of stanchions. Bamboo platform laid across hull and onto booms. Originally set 1-2 tall, rectangular mat sails, the after sail somewhat shorter; light yards threaded through each side maintained shape. Sail supported halfway up each side by a pair of divergent masts, stepped into a shoe near the bow; forward rake controlled by backstays. Struts set the angle of the sails. Now fore-and-aft rigged. Also punted and paddled, the paddles having oval or elongated blades. Reported lengths 9-21m; e.g., length 21m, beam 1.0m, depth 0.8m.
gulafri, gulafrus See **golafrus**
gulbut See **gallivat**
Gulf of Siam trader *Peninsular Malaysia/Thailand:* Chinese **junk**★ built along the Gulf of Siam coast and the east coast of the Malay Peninsula. Traded throughout the area; only a few left by the late 1960s. High, raked, sharp bow; sharp stern, nearly plumb; straight keel. Raised poop; rectangular, balustraded platform extended beyond the stern, often with a mat hut for the helmsman. Gunwale as high as 61cm. Projecting crossbeam fitted at bow, over which the anchor rope ran. Rudder shipped in sockets and raised and lowered

by a tackle. Decked forward; main living quarters provided by a mat house just abaft the mainmast; some carried a small boat. Generally painted black with red gunwale. Mostly 2-masted; foremast stepped in the

Gulf of Siam trader

bow; mainmast just forward of amidships, raking slightly aft. Set battened lugsails; some sails lashed separately to one or more of the battens. On some, a mizzen was stepped on the poop. Crew of 4-5. Reported lengths 9-25m; e.g., length 20m, beam 5m, draft 1.8m. Name variants in Malaysia: **perahu (ma')** **Siam, wangkang**★, **wangkang Siam**. Further reading: Jean Poujade, *Les Jonques des Chinois du Siam* (Paris: Gauthier-Villars, 1946 [Centre de Recherche Culturelle de la Route des Indes. Documents d'Ethnographie Navale. Fasc. 1]).
Gulf scow-schooner See **scow-schooner-2**
guli *Solomon Islands, western Pacific:* Bark **canoe**★ reported from Rua Vatu Mission and Avu Avu on Guadalcanal and Auki on Malaita. Constructed of a single piece of bark; ends made supple by heating with fire; vertical seam sewn with lianas, then cut so that the ends rake sharply, and sewn along the edge; pandanus leaves add stiffening to the ends. Two spreaders create a rounded bottom. Moss and banana tree fiber used for caulking along the vertical seam. Laths sewn along the top form gunwales. Short, ornamental masts, with flowers on top, set against the vertical seams; stayed fore-and-aft with braided lianas. Carry 4-5 people; last about a month. Other recorded names: **lola**★ (at Auki), **makamakatalo** (at Avu Avu)
gumboot *Canada, W:* One of the small wooden boats of the Fisherman's Reserve Service. Composed of west coast **seine boats**★ and **packers**★ used for reconnaissance during World War II. Lightly armed. The service was disbanded in May 1944. Name variant: **Gumboot Navy**
Gumboot Navy See **gumboot**
gunboat Small, relatively heavily armed vessel used in a variety of naval and policing pursuits, especially in shallow coastal areas and inland waterways. Some were a **galley**★ type, setting lateen or square sails and

employing numerous oars. Early Dutch **gunboats** were gaff-rigged. Often converted from other types. Modern **gunboats** are more heavily armed and used mainly by smaller navies. Selected name variants: **barca cannoniera, barco cañonero, bateau cannonier, battello cannoniere, canhonheira, cannoniera, cañonera** (small), **cañonero** (large and modern), **canonnière, chaloupe cannonière, gun vessel, kalunera, kanon(n)eerboot, kanonbåd, kanonbåt, kanonchalouppe, kanonchalup, Kanonenboot, Kanonenschaluppe, kanoner(k)a, kanonerskaya lodka, lancha canone(i)ra, lancha cañonera, lančûn, langûn, obusera, scialuppa cannoniera.** Note also **flat iron, lancione.**

1. *Canada, E/United States, E:* Numerous **gunboats** used by the British and Americans during the American Revolution and in the 1812-1817 period were built on Lake Champlain, on the Richelieu River to the north, and on the upper St. Lawrence River. Carvel-planked; bluff bow with curved stem, rounded or transom stern, flat floors, straight keel. Open or decked; generally carried 3 brass howitzers. Outboard rudder; tiller. Mainmast, stepped in forward third, set a standing lugsail; the mizzenmast, stepped off-center, set a dipping lugsail sheeted to a jiggerboom. Also rowed using as many as 36 oars. Crewed by 25 seamen plus 15 marines. Reported lengths 14-19m; e.g., length 14m, beam 3m, depth 1.5m, depth ca. 0.6m.

2. *United States:* **a.** In the early 19th century, built for the U.S. Navy mainly for coastal defense, although several fought in the Mediterranean. Varied in design, but most had a square stern and flat floors; low sides; decked. Both rowed and sailed. Armed with 1-4 guns. Rigged as **sloops*, cutters*, schooners***, or with a lateen or lugsail. Reported lengths 13.7-23m. Name variant: **galley gunboat.** Note also **row galley-2b.** **b.** During the Civil War (1861-65), sternwheel **gunboats** were used on the Ohio and Mississippi Rivers and some Georgia rivers. These were either converted wooden **steamboats** or specially built ironclad vessels that averaged 600t cap, had sloping sides, and were 23-61m long, 15.6-18m wide, with draft of 1.8-2.4m. Name variants: **ironclad*, timberclad**
Further references: **barge-11a, fei xie, gun punt**

gunboat galley See **row galley**

gun brig Naval vessel rigged as a **brig*** with square sails on 2 masts plus a gaff sail on the mainmast. Primarily of the 18th century, but used into the 19th, mainly as conventional **brigs**. Carried as many as eighteen 18-pound carronades, 9 to each side. Raked stern, overhanging poop deck; curved stem, gammon knee; steep deadrise. Outboard rudder. Could be rowed with as many as 8 long oars per side, worked by standing oarsmen, the oars passing through ports in the bulwarks. Crew of 50 plus boys. Length to ca. 23m.

gundalo See **gondola-4, gondola-7**

gundaloa, gundaloc, gundaloe See **gundalow-1**

gundalow *United States, E:* **1.** In northern New England: **Scow***-like vessel of the swift rivers and some lakes of Maine, Massachusetts, and New Hampshire, the best known being that of the Piscataqua River in New Hampshire. First mentioned in the latter part of the 17th century, and a few worked until the end of the 19th century. Mainly a bulk cargo carrier, transporting hay and thatch, marsh grass for fodder, bricks, coal, cordwood, farm produce, and occasionally passengers when space permitted. Some were **ferries***, and many actively engaged in raids during the American Revolution. Locally built, often by their farmer-skippers. Early vessels were open, square-ended **dumb barges*** propelled by poles and steered with a sweep. By the early 19th century, they were partly decked, had a cuddy, were steered by a wheel attached to the rudder, and the bow and stern had become more rounded. The last vessels had a spoon bow and more rounded stern, were fully decked, and set a lateen sail. The **gundalows** on the Kennebec River in Maine remained square-ended. Flat bottom, longitudinal planking turned up to the sheer strake at each end; deep, false stem in later years followed the sharp rake of the bow before it angled inboard; deadwood aft. Heavy planking laid edge-to-edge; straight, flaring sides; hard chines. When decked, much of the cargo was carried on deck; house either forward or aft; low rail. Balanced outboard rudder, or rudder stock came up inboard; worked by ropes to a wheel; rudder very wide-bladed. Early vessels probably set a square mainsail and topsail. Later, a very large, high-peaked lateen-type sail was set to a stump mast that could be pivoted by means of tackle, enabling mast and sail to be lowered quickly to pass under the many low bridges. Sail brailed to the yard, which was usually as long as the vessel; sail hung from close to the forward end of the yard with a counterbalance on its lower end. Also used sweeps, generally 2, which were as long as 12m. Engines on some later vessels. Crew of 2-3. Reported lengths 15-21m; e.g., length 18.2m, beam 4.6m, hold depth 1.0m; very shallow draft. Other recorded names: **gondalow, gondela, gondola*, gondolo, gondula, gundela, gundola, gundolula, gundaloc, gundaloe, gundel(o)a, gundelo(e), gundelow, gundilo, gundlo(e), gundola, gundolo, gundulow, gunelo, gun'low, Portsmouth pleasure boat, square-toed frigate, sufficient boat;** also **Kennebec River, Merrimac River,** and **Piscataqua River gundalow.** Further reading: Richard E. Winslow, III, *The Piscataqua Gundalow, Workhorse for a Tidal Basin Empire* (Portsmouth, N.H.: Portsmouth Marine Society, 1983).

2. On the Shenandoah River in western Virginia, roughly planked **flatboats*** called **gundalows** carried local products from Port Republic to the Chesapeake and Ohio Canal at Harper's Ferry. Earlier, they had continued down the Potomac River to the Washington, D.C., area. Broken up and sold as lumber at the terminal point. Main side planks 5cm thick and 35cm high; splash board sometimes added. Controlled by a rudder at each end. Poled by 4-6 men. Reported lengths 16-27m, widths 2.7-3m, depths 0.5-1.2m, draft 0.3m. Other recorded names: **floatboat*, gondola, gondolo boat**
Further references: **gondola-7, row galley**

gundara See **gundra**

gundela See **gundalow-1**

gundelo See **gondola-4, gondola-7, gundalow-1**

gundeloa See **gundalow-1**

gundeloe, gundelow, gundilo See **gondola-4, gundalow-1**

gundlo, gundloe See **gundalow-1**

gundola See **gondola-4, gundalow-1**

gundolo See **gundalow-1**

gundra *Maldives:* Vessel constructed of coconut palm. Reported from the 14th to the mid-19th century. Carried cargo, notably locally produced textiles, coir, and cowry shells, to the west coast of India and Calcutta. Planking pegged with treenails. Set a large, square sail and topsail to a single mast. Other recorded names: **candura, cundara, gandra, gundara, kundura**; pl. **kanādir**

gundua See **gondola-4**

gundula Croatian term for a small **boat★**. May sail or be propelled by oars or paddles. Spelling variants: **gondola★, gondula**; dim. **gondulica, gondulina, gundulica**

gundulica See **gundula**

gundulow, gunelo See **gundalow-1**

gung See **junk**

gunja, gunjo, gunjoo See **ganja**

gun'low See **gundalow-1**

gunning dink See **dink**

gunning punt See **gun punt**

gunning punty See **punt-12a**

gunning scow See **cabin boat-3**

gunning shout See **shout-2**

gunning skiff 1. *Canada, SE:* Double-ended boat used for waterfowling in sheltered waters along southeastern Nova Scotia. Carvel-planked; garboard strakes rabbeted into the top of the keel, making the planks flush with the top; closely spaced, 1-piece frames from gunwale to gunwale; curved stem and sternpost. Thwarts set low; no stern seat. Steered with an oar when sailing. Set a spritsail. Also rowed. Reported lengths 3.7-4.5m. Other recorded names: **Cape Sable skiff, Port Mouton skiff**

2. *United States:* General term for a small **skiff★**, usually locally built, used by 1-2 hunters. Sharp bow, square stern, flat bottom. Cockpit; coaming height and hull depth vary with preferences of the owner. Plank-built, but now often of plywood or fiberglass. Rowed, or more recently uses an outboard motor to go to and from the hunting site. Reported lengths 3-4.5m.

3. *United States, E:* Light, one-man, sport wildfowlers' craft on Chesapeake Bay and its tributaries, especially in the late 19th century. Sharp, raked ends; sides a single plank; flat bottom, longitudinally planked; short fore- and stern decks; very slight sheer. Sides and bottom copper-sheathed to prevent damage by ice, and runners affixed to the bottom. Painted white. Largest guns 5cm in diameter, supported on the thwart and foredeck. Mainly use hand paddles, sculls, or oars; sometimes set a portable spritsail. Ice creepers used over ice. Reported lengths 4.3-5.5m, widths 0.6-1.2m; draft ca. 5cm when light. Name variant: **punt★**. Note also **Hooper Island crab skiff**.

Further references: **garvey box, yole de chasse**

gun punt *United Kingdom:* A small, cigar-shaped **punt★** popular for hunting waterfowl, both professionally and for sport, with a long-barreled punt gun; in summer, often used for fishing, especially for eels, and for racing. Mainly built by the hunters themselves so design and construction vary, but follow some regional preferences. The lightly built **duck punt** was more for transportation than for shooting. Might be carvel or clinker; the vertical sides of the **Maldon punts** were created with 2 broad strakes. Recent boats of plywood. The **Hickling Broads punt** had clinker sides and carvel bottom and was decked. Most flat-bottomed or flat-floored; some had a curved profile and transverse camber to aid in crossing mud. Low sides, but the professional **Humber punt** was deep enough to hide the hunter and the gun. Mostly sharp-ended, but in Hampshire, rounded sterns popular. Some completely open (such as the **Blackwater** and **Colne punts**), more commonly decked forward, and often a small stern deck, as on the relatively beamier **Norfolk punt★**; **Manningtree punts** decked at bow and along the sides. Later sailing models might have a centerboard. In Essex, a rudder made from a curved branch and board was worked by the gunner's feet. **Norfolk punts** might hang a small rudder worked with lines and a yoke. Generally used by one hunter, but **two-handed punts** were popular in the early 19th century; in the latter, one hunter knelt or sat on the stern and sculled; the 2nd attended the gun, its long barrel resting on the foredeck. Often rowed to the hunting area and then maneuvered with hand paddles or push-sticks. Those designed to be sailed (**sailing gun punt**) were variously rigged with a light, portable mast and a sprit-, lug-, lateen, leg-of-mutton, or gaff sail; the latter **sloop★**-rigged boat worked large rivers and estuaries. Dimensions often dictated by the gun and hunter size, but reported dimensions range from 4.27-7.49m long and 0.76-1.13m wide; sides as low as 20cm; shallow draft. Other recorded names: **double-handed (sailing) punt, Essex punt, fowling punt, gun boat★, gunning punt, Hampshire gun punt, Hampshire punt★, Humber gun punt, Lymington punt, Maldon gun punt, Poole punt, shooting boat, wildfowling punt**. Note also **Fleet trow, shout, wildfowl canoe**.

gun sampan See **qiang hua zi**

gun vessel See **gunboat-1**

gūnyā See **ganja**

guogue See **cog**

gurab See **grab-1, grab-3, grab-4**

guraba, gurabo See **grab-3**

gurap See **grab-4**

gurgurru See **qurqurru**

gursar See **corsair**

gurūti See **mahaila-2**

gusa, gusar, gusarin See **corsair**

guscio See **gourse-2, gozzo**

gusi See **gussi**

guso See **guzzo**

gussetta, gussette See **guzzo-2**

gussi *Spain, E:* Small, beamy boat that engages in line fishing on the Cataluña coast and in the Balearic Islands. Employs a large light at the stern. Tall, curved stem terminates in a bulging stemhead; low sternpost, turns inward. Moderate sheer. Keel and bilge keels. Washboards along the sides; stern bench; 2 thwarts. Rowed and sailed, setting a tall lateen sail. Length 5m, beam 1.5m, depth 0.55m. Other recorded names: **bote de luz, busi*, buso, bussi, gusi, xaica**. Note also **gozzo, guzzo, teranyina**.

gussou See **gourse-1**

Güterschiff See **freighter-1**

guzo See **gozzo**

guzzetta *Italy:* One of the terms for a **dinghy***. See also **guzzo-2**.

guzzette See **guzzo-2**

guzzi See **guzzo**

guzzo **1.** *France, Corsica:* Heavy **fishing boat*** of the southwestern part of the island. Slightly raked, sharp ends; tall stem. Spritsail set to a small mast stepped in the forward quarter, long sprit; jib to a bowsprit. Also rowed. Length ca. 6m. Spelling variants: **gudzu, guzzu**; pl. **guzzi**

2. *Italy, Sardinia:* Open **fishing boat**. Plumb sternpost. Sets a small lateen sail to a vertical mast. About 10m long; the **guzzetto** is ca. 5m long. Other recorded names: **gussetta rivanetto, guzzetta**; pl. **gussette, guzzi**. Note also **gozzo, gussi, guzzetta**.

Further references: **canotto, gozzo**

guzzoni See **guzzono**

guzzono *Italy, NW:* Fished for sardines and tunny off the Ligurian coast. Sharp ends, raked stem, vertical sternpost, flat floors, half-decked. Lateen sail set to a single forward-raking mast. Crew of 5. Length under 13m. Spelling variant: pl. **guzzoni**

guzzu See **gozzo, guzzo**

gwa See **curiara-2**

gweletten See **schooner**

gwrwgl See **coracle-3**

gyassa See **gaiassa**

gyaẍ See **baidarka**

gyorōsen See **gyosen**

gyosen *Japan:* Generic term for a **smack***, a **fishing boat***, or a **catcher boat**; the last used for whaling. Name variant: **gyorōsen**

Haaf boat See **sixareen**
Haak, Haaken See **aak**
haaparuuhu See **haapio**
haapio 1. *Finland/Russia, N/Sweden:* Expanded **dugout canoe⋆** of inland waters. Adzed from the aspen (*haapa*) tree, sides ca. 2cm thick, bottom 3cm. Sides

haapio-1

expanded by being warmed from the outside and forced wider by inserted poles; bottom expanded by placing poles athwart on the bottom, weighted down with large stones. Shape sustained by ribs. Sheer minimized by addition of shaped side strakes that lap over the lower hull; ends project slightly above the strakes; strongly flaring sides. Propelled with double-bladed paddle or a single short, large-bladed paddle (in Siberia). Length 4.8m, beam 1.12m. Other recorded names: **äsping⋆** (Swedish), **Espenboot, esping, haaparuuhi, resäsping.** Further reading: E. Nikkilä, "En Satakundensisk Äsping och des Eurasiska Motsvarigheter," *Folk-liv* (Stockholm) XI (1947), 33-46. Note also **håp.**
2. *Finland, SE:* A plank-built boat engaged in sealing in the Gulf of Finland, between Kotka and Vyborg, Russia.

haaringschuitje See **haringschuit**
habara *Nigeria, S:* This **dugout canoe⋆** of the Niger Delta area is also used by people upriver. Log hollowed by fire, then spread with sticks; later spread by stone weights hanging from forked sticks wedged over the gunwale. Solid stern platform is used by the steersman; bottom rises gradually to the overhanging, pointed bow. Lashed-on thwarts for the paddlers are set into the sides or laid atop the gunwales. A clay mound at the stern is used for cooking. Some have an arched covering. May set a rectangular sail. Large **canoes** (ca. 15m long) transport produce and fish as well as providing living accommodations; small types (4-5m long) used for fishing.

hacon See **accon**
hacua See **anan**
haḍaga See **padagu-1, pattamar**
haagu See **padagu-1**
haddock boat *Scotland:* General term for boats engaged in line fishing for haddock, mainly during autumn and winter. Early boats of the Shetland Islands were open, 6-strake, clinker-built boats; sharp, curved, raking ends; low rise to the floors. Rowed with 4-6 pairs of oars. Also sailed, setting a low-peaked, dipping square sail. Engines installed after ca. 1910, and later **haddock boats** were fully decked and motorized. Crew of open boats 4-7. Lengths of Shetland open

boats 5.5-7m overall; e.g., length 6.7m, beam 2m, depth 0.7m. Note also **fourareen.**
haddock dory See **Banks dory**
ha dinghy See **ha ting**
hækjolle See **stern boat**
haerenger See **fourareen**
Háf boat See **sixareen**
Hafenbarkasse See **launch-4**
Hafenpolizei Fahrzeug See **guard ship**
Hafenschute See **Schute-1**
Hafflomme See **akókwa**
Haffquatze See **Quatze**
hafskip Scandinavian merchant vessel of the late 8th to the 13th century. Beamier, deeper, and with higher freeboard than the **langskip⋆.** Clinker-built, sharp ends. Decked at ends; cargo stowed in the open hold. Set a square sail to a midship mast. Three basic types: **knarr⋆, buza⋆,** and **byrðingr⋆.** Name variant: **ocean-ship**
hai See **hajer, slup-1b**
haiboot *Finland:* Class of racing boats that resembled the **dragon boat⋆,** but were smaller and less expensive. Name variant: **shark.** See also **hajer.**
hai cutter See **hajer**
Haida canoe, Haidah canoe, haidats See **northern-style canoe**
Haikutter See **slup-1**
Hainan junk See **Hainan trader**
Hainan trader *China, S:* Strongly built, 3-masted **junk⋆** from the island of Hainan that traded widely in southeastern Asia, but also engaged in fishing and piracy. A few still work. Raked bow sharp at the cutwater, blunt above; framework projected forward from abreast the foremast and connected across the bow to hold the anchor, running rigging, etc. Stern rounded up, ending in a high, wide transom; gallery along the quarters and stern. Flat floors; long, straight keel; more recently a drop keel; strong sheer; deep bulwarks; sometimes portable washboards. Fenestrated rudder hung below the bottom; stock came up inboard; tiller controlled by ropes and blocks; many had centerboards. Decked; long hatch amidships; cabins on either side of rudderhead and tiller. **Sampan⋆** hung from aft davits, another carried on deck. Foremast stepped in the bow, raking forward; mainmast roughly amidships; mizzenmast on the stern gallery. Battened, balance lugsails with curved leech; originally of matting, later cloth. Crew of 16-20. Reported lengths 12-37m; e.g., length 25.6m, beam 5.5m, depth 1.6m. Other recorded names: **Hainan junk, Hylam junk**
Haisla canoe See **northern-style canoe**
haitama See **kayak-9**
haitara See **baidara**
Haitian schooner See **gouèlette**
haj See **hajer**
hajer *Denmark:* **Seine boat⋆** of the **kutter⋆** type that worked mainly in the North Sea. Developed prior to World War I and still seen, although many now converted to **yachts⋆.** Carvel planking, transom stern, decked forward and aft. **Cutter⋆**-rigged; some rigged

as **ketches*** after World War I; auxiliaries also installed. Length 12m, beam 4m, deep hull, draft 2m; to 40t. Other recorded names: **hai, haiboot*, hai cutter, haj, hajkutter, hayer, shark**. Note also **slup-1b**.

hajkutter See **hajer, slup-1b**

ha kau *China, S/Hong Kong/Macau:* Category of seagoing fishing vessel that works along the Guangdong (Kwangtung) coast. Mainly trawled, working in pairs; the smaller **ha kau chai** works alone. Low, narrow, and raked bow; stern rounded up, ending in a wide, high, overhanging gallery. Greatest beam just abaft the break of the poop; projecting stem starts below the waterline and joins shallow keel piece that runs to amidships. Decked; numerous fish holds; crew quartered below deck; owner's family lives aft. Catwalk runs fore-and-aft outside the hull, supported on crossbeams; terminates in wide framework below. Capstan in forward third used to raise anchors and nets. Carries a small boat on deck. Fenestrated rudder; stock comes up through poop; long tiller. Usually 3-masted, only 2 on small vessels. Foremast generally rakes slightly forward; mizzen on gallery. Sets battened lugsails with rounded leech; originally of matting, later cloth. Generally motorized since 1947. Crew of 20-25. Reported lengths 15-27m, widths 4.6-6.4m, depths 1.5-3.4m; deep draft. Other recorded names: **ha kau shun, ha kau tor** (or **tow**). Note also **há ku**.

ha kau chai, ha kau shun, ha kau tor, ha kau tow See **ha kau**

ha kou ting *China, S/Hong Kong:* Fast 2-masted **junk*** popular with pilots, company agents, and especially with local pirates of the Hong Kong area. Lug-rigged. Other recorded names: **fast boat*, hia keou t'ing, hia kow t'ing, hsia kou t'ing, shrimp boat**

há ku 1. *Hong Kong/Macau:* Beam **trawler*** that fished for shrimp, working 7-10 trawls at a time. Low, sharp bow; high, rounded stern. Stepped a short foremast in the eyes, tall mainmast amidships; cloth sails, battened, rounded leech. Now motorized. Crew variously reported as 5-6 or 10-15, the larger crew for Macau vessels. Reported lengths for Hong Kong boats, 9.8-10.7m; for Macau boats, 13.5-17.3m, beam 4.5-5.3m, draft 0.75-1.1m. Note also **ha kau**.
2. *Japan:* **Haku** is an early term for a merchant vessel. Name variant: **tsuku no fune**

Halbdecktes Boot See **half-decker**

Halbe Mutte See **Spitzmutte**

halb Galeere *Baltic Sea:* Early small **galley*** propelled with 15-20 pairs of oars. Note also **half galley**.

Halbklipper See **clipper**

Halblädi, Halblädine See **Lädine**

Halbsegelkutter See **yawl-2**

Halbtschaike See **saique-1**

half and half boat See **half and halfer**

half and halfer *England, E:* Boat for which the earnings were divided equally between owner and crew. Term used in Suffolk in the 2nd half of the 19th century for small **drifters*** and **trawlers*** that fished for herring in spring and early summer and for mackerel in autumn. Lug-rigged. Crew of 8. 20-25t. Name variant: **half and half boat**

half a raft See **timber raft-3**

half boat *China, central:* Chinese **houseboat*** created from one half of a Chang Jiang (Yangtze) **junk***. House erected on part or most of the hull, with an open kitchen area at one end. "Ballasted" by careful placement of furniture, washing stones, and water jugs. A 6.5m **half boat** might be occupied by 2 families. Further references: **Deal lugger, Galway hooker, Porthleven half boat**

half box trow See **trow-1**

half brig See **hermaphrodite brig**

half clipper, half-clipper barque See **clipper**

half coble See **foyboat-2**

half-decked boat See **half-decker, halvdæksbåd, Morecambe Bay prawner**

half-decker 1. A boat that has a deck only over its forward part or has short decks forward and aft and an open waist that is generally bordered by narrow waterways. Other recorded names: **bateau mi-ponté, Halbdecktes Boot, half-decked boat**. Note also **Deal lugger, Porthleven half boat**.
2. *Scotland/Shetland Islands:* Imported by Shetland herring fishermen from the east coast of Scotland in the 2nd quarter of the 19th century. Subsequently built locally more along the lines of other Shetland boats. Long raking ends; deck covered the forward third. Lugsails set to 2 masts. Crew of 5. Reported lengths on keel 7.6-10.7m. Further references: **cutter-7, fifie-1, Morecambe Bay prawner**

half dory See **semi-dory**

half galley 1. *Mediterranean:* Presumed to have been a small **galley***, although many were larger than the average **galley**, and the term has sometimes been attributed to a rowed **galiot*** or **brigantine***. Vessels of this type worked the Caribbean area and were popular with pirates. Used into the early 19th century after a long history. Probably 3 men to each oar (17-20 to a side); oars worked on tholepins set to an outrigger parallel to the vessel. Lateen sails set from 2-3 masts. Reported lengths 30-32m, beam 4m. Term has also been applied to an Italian vessel with a crew of half volunteers and half convicts. Other recorded names: **demi-galère*, demi galley, demy-galère, galladella, mezza gale(r)a**. Note also **halb Galeere, skampaveya**.
2. *United States, SE:* Small, heavily armed **galley*** built at Charleston, South Carolina, in the 1740s. **Schooner***-rigged; also rowed. Crew of 50. Further reference: **guard boat-3a**

half-load boat See **reed boat-2**

Halfmutte See **Spitzmutte**

half-outrigged gig See **gig-3**

half outrigger See **outrigger**

half pointer See **pointer**

half raft See **timber raft-2a, timber raft-3**

half shebek See **shebek**

half skipjack *United States, NE:* Developed ca. 1885 on Martha's Vineyard Island, off southeastern Massachusetts; relatively few built. Rounded bottom forward, V-bottom with chines in after half. Some lapstrake; straight, plumb stem; V-shaped, raked transom; strong sheer. Rudderpost entered hull forward of heel of the transom; centerboard. **Sloop***-rigged. Length on deck ca. 6.4m, beam 2.2m, draft aft 0.53m. Other recorded names: **corner boat** (at Provincetown, Mass.), **Martha's Vineyard compromise skipjack**, **Vineyard Haven half skipjack**. Note also **skipjack-1**.

half spreetie See **stumpy barge**

half-York See **York boat**

halibut dory See **Banks dory**

halk See **hulk-1**

Halleiner Plätte, Haller Plätte See **Plätte-1**

Hallsands crabber See **West Country crabber**

Hallstattersee Plätte See **Plätte-2**

haloque See **barca de mitjana**

halque See **hulk-1**

halvdæksbåd *Denmark:* General term for a half-decked boat. Those working the deep waters of eastern Denmark were clinker-planked; bluff-bowed with lightly curved stem; sharp or rounded stern; marked sheer forward. **Fishing boats*** had a wet well. Outboard rudder; tiller. Decked to mast. Single mast set a spritsail or loose-footed, boomed gaff sail, staysail, jib to bowsprit. Some had auxiliaries. Reported lengths 5.8-8m; e.g., length 7.3m, beam 2m, draft 0.9m. On the west coast, where the water is shallower and the boats worked off the beaches, they had flatter floors, often carvel-planked, and might have a centerboard. More fully decked with numerous hatches and a steering well. Note also **Bornholmsk laksebåd**.

halvdekker See **snekke**

halve binlander See **bijlander**

halvege See **Bornholmsk ege**

halvfjer-romming See **seksæring-6**

halvknärr See **knärr-2**

halvsjægt See **sjægt**

halvtredierømming, halvtredierumsbåd See **færing-6**

hamatafua, ha'matefoo'a, hama te fua See **vaka-6**

Hamburger Ewer See **Ewer**

Hamburger Hafenschute, Hamburger Schute See **Schute-1**

hamnpråm See **lighter-1**

Hampden boat See **Hampton boat**

Hampshire gun punt See **gun punt**

Hampshire punt *England, S:* May be either a **gun punt*** or, more recently, a flatiron-shaped pleasure boat. The latter has a slightly raked, straight bow; wide transom, small foredeck; single rowing thwart.

Hampton Beach whaler See **Hampton boat**

Hampton boat *Canada, E/United States, NE:* Reported in the early 19th century as a double-ended boat (**Hampton whaler**); toward the end of the century, transom sterns became more common (**Hampton boats**). Popular along the New England coast and spread to the Canadian Maritime Provinces, Newfoundland, and Labrador, having been sold from **schooners*** that carried them aboard for use by the fishing **fleet***; later built locally, becoming known as **Labrador boats** or **Labrador whalers** and also as **Newfoundland boats**. Lapstrake, carvel, or lapstrake above and carvel below; straight or curved stem; raked stern; deep forefoot. Hollow lines forward and aft; high bilges; strong sheer; outboard rudder. Generally open but some half-decked; washboards on later boats; canvas hood forward might reduce spray. Centerboard on later boats. Rowed and

sailed, generally by 2 people. Most stepped 2 portable masts to which spritsails were permanently secured; a few rigged with leg-of-mutton or gaff sails. Fore spritsail might carry a club laced to its clew; mainsail sometimes boomed. Jib to a plank bowsprit set over the stem. Foremast stepped well forward. Most converted to motor in the early 20th century. Reported lengths 5-8m; e.g., length overall 6.4m, on keel 5.8m, beam 1.8m, depth 1.0m; shallow draft. Other recorded names: **Casco Bay boat, Casco Bay double-ender, Hampton Beach whaler, New England boat, pinky***, **whaleboat***; **Hampden boat** (erroneously). Further reading: J. Gardner, "The Elusive Hampton Boats," *Small Boat Journal* 4 (1979), 13-18. Note also **Crotch Island pinky, Matinicus boat**. Further reference: **wharf boat**

Hampton flattie See **flattie-4**

Hampton whaler See **Hampton boat**

handelkvase See **kvase**

handelsfartyg See **merchantman**

handelskvase See **kvase**

Handelsschiff See **merhantman**

Handkahn **1.** *Poland, NE/Russia, W:* Popular **tender*** to **fishing boats*** and other larger boats in the Vislinki Zaliv (Frisches Haff). Often carried and set the nets. Straight, slightly raked stem; wide "V" transom. Mainly sculled, facing aft; also rowed, employing 2 pairs of tholepins. Other recorded names: **łódź podjazdowa, Plattstevenkahn, podjazdówska**
2. *Russia, W/Lithuania, SW:* Small open boat of the Kurski Zaliv (Kurisches Haff). Often a **ship's boat***. Carvel planking, slightly raked inner stem, flat bottom, flat sides. Rowed. Other recorded names: **Kurisches Handkahn, luõtas, luo(a)ts**
See also **kleiner Kahn, scheike**.

handliner A vessel that engages in fishing over the side with hand lines, often a **schooner***, fishing for cod on the North Atlantic banks. Note also **dory handliner, longliner**.

Handlomme *Poland, N:* Open, general-purpose boat found along the Gulf of Danzig, rivers entering the bay, and on some lakes. Of German origin; used until the 1970s. Served as a **ship's boat*** on small vessels; some towed, others carried aboard. Popular with farmers and as a pleasure craft for family outings. Some, especially at Elbląg (Elbing), served as **ferries***, earning the name **Pfennigfähre**. Some scavenged coal being loaded onto steamships. Clinker-planked with 3-6 strakes per side; sides rounded up from a plank keel; bottom curved up at each end; widely spaced ribs and floor frames. Straight, raked bow, ending in a narrow transom that rose above the gunwale; heart-shaped transom; skeg holds the rudder. Two or 3 thwarts. Tarred; top strake painted in gray, green, or brown. Rowed, sculled, and sailed. When sailed, mast stepped through the forward thwart, setting a gaff or spritsail. Length ca. 4.6m, beam 1.7m, depth 0.6m. Note also **Lomme**.

hand-rakers clam skiff *United States, E:* Worked the clam beds in northern New Jersey's Raritan and Sandy Hook Bays in the early 20th century. When not working, moored out to poles. Open, flat bottom, centerboard. Gaff-rigged; also rowed or poled. Reported lengths overall 4.9-5.5m, shallow draft.

handscrape flattie See **flattie-4**

hand scraper See **skipjack-1**

hand troller See **troller-2**

hangada See **jangada**

Hangchow Bay trader, **Hangchow trader** See **Shaoxing chuan**

hang-chwen See **hong boat**

Hansekogge See **cog**

håp *Sweden, N:* Early Same (Lapp) term for their light, easily portaged, river-running boats. Sharp ends, sewn strakes, stem and keel nailed; wide, flat keel piece. 1732 boat ca. 3.6m long, 1.5m wide, 0.6m deep. Spelling variant: **håpar**. Note also **haapio**.

hápa See **potro**

ha´pa See **wa'k·ai**

hapar *Indonesia, W:* Term for **raft**★ in the Batak Toba dialect of northern Sumatra.

håpar See **håp**

hapu-mámu See **champa-1**

haragalu, **haragólu** See **coracle-4**

haranga See **saranga**

harârîq See **harrâqa**

harbor ship See **guard ship**

harbour boat See **Falmouth oyster dredger**

hardangerbaad See **hardangerbåt**

hardangerbåt *Norway, SW:* Name given to the open boats built in the Hardanger region of Hordaland. Includes the small 4-oared **færing**★ that fished inshore, carried local passengers, and transported produce; the 6-oared **seksæring**★ fished farther offshore with hand- and longlines; the 8-oared **åttring**★ fished for herring in winter; the 8- and 10-oared boats were popular as **church boats**★ (see **kirkebåt**) and were fast under oars. Clinker-planked with pine, the smaller sizes using only 3 strakes per side; stem, sternpost, keel, and oarlocks of oak. Mainly sharp-ended, although some later boats adopted a transom, especially those employing an outboard motor. Gunwales set inside top strake. Originally square-rigged, but during the 19th century, shifted to a spritsail. Spelling variants: **hardangerbaad**, **hardingbåt**. Note also **jakt-2**, **listerbåt**, **notbåt**, **skøyte-5**.

hardangerfæring See **færing-1**

hardangerjakt See **jakt-2**

Hardanger notbåt See **notbåt-2**

hardingbåt See **hardangerbåt**

Harderwijker pluut See **pluut**

hardlopergaljoot See **galjoot**

Harener Pünte See **Pünte**

harenger See **harenguier**

harengueux See **harenguier**

harenguier *France, N:* Worked from Normandy ports, drifting or trawling for herring (*hareng*) from June to January and mackerel from March to June. Primarily under sail until the the end of the 19th century; now motorized and more commonly called **dériveurs**★. The sailing type characterized by square-rigging on fore- and mainmasts, and on the **ketch**-rigged vessels (the **dundee harenguier**, or **pêqueux** at Fécamp), a forward-raking mizzenmast. While fishing, either the mainmast or both the main- and foremast were struck and lowered to an athwartship crutch aft. Also had a large hold forward of the mainmast from which the nets played out over a rack along the side. Decked, cabin aft, fish hold amidships. Hull particulars varied, but generally they had a square or counter stern, rounded forefoot from a straight stem, straight keel with drag, steep rise to the floors; capstan used to haul in the net. Lug- or gaff-rigged; long bowsprit, with large jib; staysail and topsails. Crew of 12-25. Reported lengths 15-35m; e.g., length on keel 25m, beam 7m, depth 3.6m; average 100-110t. Other recorded names: **bateau** (or **lougre**) **harenguier**, **harenger**, **harengueux**, **harenguier de Boulogne** (and **de Fécamp**), **herengueux**. Note also **chalutier**, **drifter**, **escaffe**, **herring boat**.

harenguier de Boulogne, **harenguier de Fécamp** See **harenguier**

Harense punt See **Pünte**

harigōlu See **coracle-4**

harinck-buyse, **haringbuis** See **buis-2**

Häringbuise See **Buise**

Häringbüse See **buis-2**

haringjäger See **jäger**

haringlogger See **logger**

haringschuit *Netherlands:* Small, open boat of the Zuiderzee that fished for herring (*haring*). Sharp ends; straight, raked stem and sternpost; low freeboard. Half-decked, live well; narrow leeboards; outboard rudder; tiller. Sailed, employing a gaff or leg-of-mutton sail. Length 8m, beam 2m; 5-11t. Spelling variants: **haaringschuitje**, **haring schuyt**, **heringsjute**

haring schuyt See **haringschuit**

Häringslogger See **logger**

harok See **alut**

ḥarraka See **harrâqa**, **zauraq-2**

ḥarrâq See **harrâqa**

harrâqa **1.** Arabic term for a ship of the Byzantine period that employed devices for throwing fire on the enemy. Propelled by as many as 100 oars.

2. *Egypt:* Described initially as a small naval vessel, both on the Nile and the Mediterranean. Later, term applied to a pleasure craft for local dignitaries, ornamented in gold and having a cabin.

Spelling variants: **'aqaba**, **ḥarraka**, **harrâq**, **ḥerrāqa**; pl. **harârîq**, **ḥarrâqât**. See also **zauraq-2**.

ḥarrâqât See **harrâqa**

Hartjesvelder See **zalmschouw**

Hartlepool mule See **Hartlepool pilot coble**

Hartlepool pilot coble *England, NE:* **Pilot cobles**★ of the Hartlepool area were designed with sharp sterns so the boats would handle better when towed by the ship. Towed stern first with only the apprentice pilot aboard. Used until the 1920s. Deep forward, shallower at the raking stern; strong tumble home to sheer strake; side keels hung below the normal keel. Deep rudder; long tiller. Mast raked strongly aft; carried 2 masts, the shorter for bad weather or as a bowsprit. Set a tanned dipping lugsail with as many as 4 reef points. Length overall ca. 7.6m, narrow. Name variant: **Hartlepool mule**

Harwich barge See **Thames sailing barge**

Harwich bawley See **bawley**

Harwich smack See **cod smack-2**

hascám See **balsa-7**
hásh ma hata See **sealing canoe-1**
Hastings beach lugger, **Hastings drifter** See **Hastings lugger**
Hastings lugger *England, SE:* Beamy **fishing boat**★ that works off the beach at Hastings, fishing initially in the North Sea and along the western south coast, later working more locally. Clinker-built with full lines; some drag to the straight keel; broad bottom, low rise to the floors; vertical stem. Square transom initially; in latter half of the 19th century, overhanging transom popular; by the turn of the century, elliptical counter adopted. Beached by capstan, launched over greased skids; keel and bilge keels iron shod; 2 projections on port side enabled crew to climb aboard when beached. Leeboards

Hastings lugger

until 1880s, then an iron centerboard until motorized, ca. 1910. Decked; crew quartered in foreroom. Narrow rudder; tiller bent to clear mizzenmast. Characteristically a large brass lantern hung on the forward side of the mizzenmast. Crewed by 6-9 plus a boy when drifting for herring. Three-masted until mid-19th century. The later 2-masted **lugger**★ (known as a **trawl boat**) set a large dipping lug foresail, a standing lug mizzen, and a jib; in favorable winds, might set a mizzen staysail, fore topsail, and mizzen topsail. Reefing bowsprit ran out on the port side of the stem, and a mizzen outrigger on the starboard side at the stern. Mast crutch on the port side of the mizzenmast supported the lowered mainmast; mizzenmast also in a tabernacle. Now motorized with no sails. Known keel lengths 8-14m; 1849 three-master: 15.8m length overall, 13.7m on keel, beam 4.55m, hold depth 1.9m; 1870 two-master: 9.96m overall, 8.8m on keel, beam 3.66m, hold depth 1.45m. The **bog**, or **three-quarter boat**, was similar in design and rig to the **lugger** (or **big boat**), but ranged between 4-7t. The open **punt**★ was smaller still, less than 4t and less than 6m in length overall; the mizzenmast was shorter and sometimes set a spritsail; no topsails or mizzen staysail used. The **punt** retained its centerboard and overhanging transom stern. Other recorded names: **beach punt**★, **Hastings beach lugger**, **Hastings drifter**, **Hastings punt**. Further reading: J. Hornell, "The Fishing Luggers of Hastings," *The Mariner's Mirror* XXIV (1938), 259-274, 409-428.
Hastings punt See **Hastings lugger**
hästransportfartyg See **horse carrier**
hatch boat 1. In general, a small boat on which the deck is composed almost entirely of hatches.
   2. *England, SE:* Beamy, double-ended craft used on the lower Thames Estuary in the first part of the 19th

century for fishing, shrimping, and carrying stores to ships. Some went to south coast ports to sell fish. A wet well amidships permitted transport of the catch live to market; also carried fish from larger vessels for transfer to London. Clinker-built. Cambered decks forward and aft and wide waterways; roomy cockpit; cuddy, later a small cabin with a coach roof. Early boats sprit-rigged with staysail. Later a sprit mizzen added, sheeted to rudderhead; rudder worked with yoke and lines. The larger boats later set a standing gaff mainsail, retaining the sprit mizzen. Mainsail loose-footed, brailed, fitted with vangs, sheet worked to a horse. Topmast added, square-headed topsail. Generally 2 headsails. Rowlocks built into the upper strakes or had tholepins. Reported lengths 5-11m; shallow draft. Other recorded names: **hutch boat**, **Thames hatch boat**
   3. *United States:* A **fishing boat**★ with one or more hatch-covered wet wells. Usually half-decked.
   See also **Tancook schooner**, **West Cornish lugger**.
há-teang, **ha teng**, **ha theng** See **ha ting**
ha ting *Hong Kong:* Small beamy shrimp (*ha*) boat (**ting**★) that operates a shrimp beam trawl near shore. Sharp bow; wide, square stern; low sides; open. Beams cross atop the hull to support a low outboard rail. House aft on some. Bamboo poles, one at the bow and another near the stern on the opposite side, hold towlines to which a net is attached. Mainmast stepped just forward of amidships; some also had a small foremast in the bow and a mizzen; battened lugsails. Motorized by the 1970s. Crew of 2-5, usually a family. Typically 9.4m long, 2.7m wide. Other recorded names: **ha dinghy**, **há-teang**, **ha t(h)eng**, **hsia t'ing**, **shrimp beam trawler**, **shrimp boat**
hat kosha See **kosha**
Hatschierschiff See **Leibschiff-1**
Hatteras boat See **Core Sounder**
haul-tow punt See **Falmouth oyster punt**
haul-tow skiff *England, E:* Small, sharp-ended boat that hauled an oyster dredge in the creeks of the Whitstable and Colchester areas.
Hauptgaleere See **capitane**
Hausboot See **houseboat-1**
Hautboot See **skin boat-1**
havbaad See **havbåt**
havbåd *Denmark, W:* Used for sea fishing from the west coast beaches of Jutland from at least the early 18th century. Flat floors with long plank keel. Clinker-built; early boats had a strong sheer; double-ended with marked flare; ends straight and sharply raked; rounded bilges. Open; usually 5 thwarts; some decked. Rudder often wide below the waterline; on early boats, the tiller reached about one-third of the way in from the stern. Larger boats, called **havskib** (or **gar-pike**), used leeboards. Single mast stepped against a thwart, setting a spritsail and jib; some also used 2 headsails, with jib tacked to short jibboom. Also rowed by as many as 4, one person to an oar and a 5th at the helm. Reported lengths 7.3-10.7m, widths 3-3.2m, depth 1.2m; shallow draft. Other recorded names: **hornfisk**, **hwongjævere**, **koltringer**, **vesterhavsbåd**. Note also **Skawbrig**.
havbåt *Norway:* Boat designed to work at sea, in contrast to one built for protected waters. The **fishing**

boats★, mostly those after cod, are specially outfitted for this sea work. Spelling variant: **havbaad**. Note also **seksæring-5**.

Havelzille See **Zille**

havfæring See **færing**

havpram See **Norsk pram**

Havre de Grace schooner See **scow-11d**

havskib See **havbåd**

hawaari See **houri-3**

hawâra, hawári See **houri-1**

hawayriyah See **hurija**

hawker See **hooker**

haxar See **haxe**

haxe *Sweden, E:* Generic term for a locally built and operated **storbåt★** of the northern Gulf of Bothnia; worked mainly from the mid-16th into the 18th century. The **malmhaxe** carried ore, the **vedhaxe** transported wood; the **strömmingshaxe** fished for herring. Some deep-hulled with steep, rising floors; sharply cutaway stem below the waterline; high transom, raked below. Decked at bow and stern; outboard rudder; tiller. Might set a gaff sail to the main- and mizzenmasts with square sails forward on the mainmast; large jib to a long, rising bowsprit. Also **sloop★**-rigged, according to the standards of the period. The small, boxy **malmhaxe** was also rowed, by 6 men with 6 oars; 5m long, 2.2m wide, 0.75-0.8m draft. Other recorded names: **storhaxe** (large size); pl. **haxar**

haya bune *Japan:* Term given to early boats used for official business, such as **advice boats★** and naval craft. Name variant: **swift boat★**

hay barge *England, SE:* A beamy type of **Thames sailing barge★** that sailed from Essex and Kent with hay or straw for London horses, returning with manure for the fields. A few continued to work until World War II. Very shallow draft; flat bottom enabled them to enter shallow creeks, and a sharply raked, blunt bow on some permitted nosing into riverbanks. Flat sheer; long chine; leeboards. Special gear handled the hay.

hay barge

Hay might be stacked as high as 3m above the deck and 30cm outboard on each side. **Yawl★**-rigged with a high-peaked sprit mainsail. A deep bonnet enabled the mainsail to be shortened when the hay was stacked on board. Some set a jib to a long bowsprit; tiny sprit mizzenmast sometimes stepped on the rudderhead. Mainmast and sprit could be lowered into an alleyway in the cargo stack. At times set a topsail. When loaded, the helmsman required guidance from the mate atop the stack. Crew of 2-3. Length 25m; cap. ca. 50-60t.

Other recorded names: **Essex barge**, **farm barge**, **stackie**, **stacky barge**, **straw barge**

hay boat 1. *England, W:* Type of **narrow boat★** (here called a **longboat★**) that transported meadow hay from River Severn fields between Gloucester and Worcester. Traveled to the Midlands, returning with coal for domestic use and stone. Important in the 1920s. Hay loaded up to ca. 2.4m above the gunwales; cloths along the sides and on the flattened top secured the hay. Towed, close-hauled, to Worcester by a **tug★** and by horse thereafter. Cabin aft. Crew of 3. **2.** *United States, E:* **a.** Generally farmer-built to transport salt hay harvested from the wetlands bordering Great South Bay on Long Island in New York State. Hay used as bedding for animals. Frequently a rectangular, flat-bottomed craft rigged with a spritsail. Name variant: s**alt hay boat. b.** Term given to a **barge★** that transported agricultural produce by means of a **towboat★** down the Hudson River, especially hay for New York City horses in the 19th century. Note also **towboat-4**.

Haydah canoe See **northern-style canoe**

hayer See **hajer**

hay hack See **scow-schooner-3**

hay schooner *United States, NE:* Beamy vessel that carried bales of hay as deck cargo from Maine to Boston in the late 19th and early 20th centuries. Bales lashed down with a tarpaulin, and the crew used ladders to move over the cargo. Sails reefed to clear the cargo, and the helmsman steered by directions from forward. Note also **hay barge**, **scow-schooner-3**, **Stroh-Ewer**.

hay scow See **scow-schooner-3**

haystack A vessel on which poorly set sails resembled a haystack.

Haywood boat See **Huron boat**

head boat *England, S:* In a college rowing race for **shells★** on the Thames, the winner of the previous contest becomes the **head boat**, as it is top-seeded against the other competitors. See also **party boat-1**.

head-hunting canoe See **tomoko-1**

heck boat See **pink-3**

Heckboot See **stern boat**

Heckgaleass See **galeass-5**

Heckmaster See **yawl-2**

heckre See **vishoeker**

Heckschiff See **galeass-5**

Hecktjalk See **hektjalk, Tjalk-2**

Hecktrawler See **trawler**

Hedelsche aak, Hedelse aak See **bovenmaase aak**

heeler A craft with good sailing qualities, having a good pair of heels. Usually light and fast. See also **Baltimore clipper**.

heere jacht, heere jagt See **jacht-3**

heijnst See **hengst**

Heiste kottersgetruigde schuit, Heistenaar, Heisterschuit, Heister vischsloep See **Heiste schuit**

Heiste schuit *Belgium:* Prior to 1895, this **fishing boat★** was similar to the 2-masted, lug-rigged **Blankenbergse schuit★**, although somewhat smaller and with finer lines (**Heiste tweemastschuit**). After 1895, a **cutter★** rig was adopted, and the boats became keeled, carvel-planked, fully decked, and known as

sloepen (pl.). Extinct. The earlier boat had heavy clinker planking; deep top strake; flat bottom with no keel to permit landing on the beach. Mildly curved and slightly raked stem and sternpost. Outboard rudder, unshipped while on the beach; large leeboards. Loose-footed and boomed gaff sail; also set a staysail and 1-2 jibs to a bowsprit. Many added a topmast and topsail. Lug-rigged boats ca. 9m long; gaff-rigged were 10.3m long, 4m wide, and 1.7m deep. Other recorded names: **Heiste kottersgetuigde schuit, Heistenaar, Heisterschuit, Heister vischsloep, Heists(ch)e schuit, Heistsche sloep, Heyst barge, Heystsche schuit, kottergetuigde Blankenbergse schuit Heiste tweemastschuit, Heistsche schuit, Heistsche sloep, Heistse schuit** See **Heiste schuit**

hekjacht *Netherlands:* Pleasure craft of the 17th-18th centuries characterized by a high, flat stern with window-shaped fretwork. Carvel-planked; full, round build. Deep, curved stem; raked stern below a small transom. Rounded leeboards. Some open except for foredeck; small cuddy forward of the cockpit on others. Older types lateen-rigged with no mast, the forward end of the yard stuck into the foredeck, serving as a mast. Larger ones set 2 lateen sails. Later set a loose-footed gaff sail with short gaff to a lowering mast; staysail; jib to a reefing bowsprit. Larger boats set 2 sails and no headsails. Reported lengths 7-9m. Spelling variant: **hekjagt**

hekjagt See **hekjacht**
hekkbåt See **stern boat**
hekkotter See **kotter**
hekre See **vishoeker**
hektjalk *Netherlands:* Robust inland trader of the **tjalk*** family that worked mainly during the 18th and 19th centuries. Characterized by its *hek*, a triangular hole in the upswept taffrail through which the curved tiller passed. Mainly of wood; some 19th-century vessels of iron or steel. Rounded ends; curved stem cut to form a point at the top; straight, vertical sternpost; flat floors; keel; deadwood; soft turn of the bilges. Slight tumble home amidships, increasing at the ends. Swept up at the ends, especially at the stern. Narrow, high outboard rudder with fin on after end below the waterline; early vessels had an elaborately carved rudderhead; heavy leeboards. Decked; windlass on foredeck; cuddies forward and aft; early vessels had distinctive, vaulted hatch covers; a window flanked each side of the rudder. Stern area often colorfully decorated. Might have a deckhouse aft; one without this feature was called a **dekhektjalk**. Early 18th-century **hektjalken** (pl.) employed a large spritsail to a short mast; a bonnet was removed in heavy weather; staysail, jib to reefing bowsprit. Later vessels of the period might also use a topsail. A standing gaff later in the century was replaced by a regular gaff in the 19th century; mainsail loose-footed and boomed; jib to a reefing bowsprit; staysail. Most masts could be struck. Reported lengths 16-29m; 1855 vessel 18.6m long, 4.1m wide, and 1.63m deep. Some old **hektjalken** were **coasters*** for cargo and passengers. Deeper hull, 2 heavy wales, higher ends, pronounced sheer. Sunken passenger cabin abaft the hold. Set a sprit mainsail, square topsail, jib to reefing bowsprit. Other recorded names: **Hecktjalk,**

staatsietjalk, statietjalk (erroneously). Note also **Hollandse tjalk.**
hektrawler See **trawler-1**
hektreiler See **kotter**
Helderse vlet See **vlet**
Helgoländer Fischerschlup See **Helgoländer Schlup**
Helgoländer Hummerboot See **Hummerboot**
Helgoländer Kuff See **Helgoländer Schnigge**
Helgoländer Schlup *Germany, NW:* Small, sprit-rigged **fishing boat*** from Helgoland Island. Dates to the 18th century; only 6 left by the early 20th century. Clinker-built; bluff bow, with maximum beam well forward, tapering to narrower, rounded stern; curved ends. Flat floors amidships with shallow keel; marked sheer. Outboard rudder with tiller slotted over rudderhead; long, very narrow leeboards. Decked at bow; cuddy at stern; fish well amidships. Spritsail narrow and high-peaked; large staysail, and sometimes a jib to a bowsprit. Also rowed with 2 men to an oar; oarlocks slotted on gunwale. Crew of 4. Reported lengths 7-10m; e.g., length 8.82m, beam 3.42m, depth 1.0m. Other recorded names: **Fischerslup, Helgoländer Fischerschlup, Helgoländer Sloop.** Further reading: W. Jaeger, "Die Helgoländer Sloop," *Das Logbuch* I, II, III, IV (1966). Note also **Schlup.**
Helgoländer Schnigge *Germany, NW:* Transported freight, fish, and passengers between Helgoland Island and mainland ports from the 18th to the early 20th century. Also served as a **mother ship*** for two **jollen** (see **jolle**). Carvel-planked; full bow with curved, upright stem; rounded stern; semicircular cross section amidships; broad, shallow keel. The later iron-hulled vessels had sharper lines. Narrow outboard rudder; leeboards. Cambered deck; trunk cabin, 2 hatches; square stern windows. **Ketch***-rigged; sails loose-footed and boomed; staysail to stemhead, jib to long bowsprit. Reported lengths 16-19.4m; length-to-beam ratio 3.75:1. Other recorded names: **Helgoländer Kuff, Helgoländer Sneg.** Note also **Kuff, Schnigge.**
Helgoländer Sloop See **Helgoländer Schlup**
Helgoländer Sneg See **Helgoländer Schnigge**
helk See **hulk-1**
hen boat See **hong tou san ban**
hengst *Belgium, NW/Netherlands, SW:* Important boat that engaged mainly in shrimping, oystering, and musseling (**mosselhengst**), but also fished, and carried cargo, mail, and passengers. A small type, the **hengstje**, assisted in dike work. Type probably worked as early as the 16th century, but name mentioned from the mid-17th century; some working as sailing craft until 1940, are now **yachts***. Built in Zuid-Holland in the 18th century, along the lower Schelde and in the Zeeuwsch Vlaanderen area during the 19th-20th centuries. Flat bottom, slight rocker aft; low keel; hard chines. Sharply raked (ca. 45°), straight stem with gripe; angled tumble home near the top. Sternpost raked and straight. Early **hengsten** (pl.) were broad forward and sharp at the stern. Some early types clinker-planked; later carvel-planked except for the lapped top strake; top strake tumble home at the stern; vertical, discontinuous wale at lower edge of top strake. Curved sides on early **hengsten**, later flared. Strong sheer on

early boats higher toward the stern; later lower aft. Early boats open, later decked to the mast; those with a fish well decked abaft an open waist, with a steering well. Cabin abaft the mast on **yachts**. Oval leeboards, later long and narrow; rounded on Vlaamse boats. Wide rudder hangs below the bottom, lifting when grounded; tiller slots over rudderhead. Hull tarred. Fishing craft without a wet well might tow a **kaar★**, a small, sharp-bowed, square-sterned, flat-bottomed craft pierced with holes. Early boats sprit-rigged with topsail, jib to a reefing bowsprit, and staysail. Some may possibly have been 2-masted (the so-called **henst** or **henstije**). By the 19th century, most set a tall gaff sail, loose-footed and boomed; staysail to stemhead, sometimes a jib. Some masts strikable. Motorized during the 2nd quarter of the 20th century (the **motorhengst**). Crew of 1-3. Reported lengths 9-14m; e.g., length 10.2m, beam 3.4m, depth 1.4m. Other recorded names: **heijnst, henkst, heynst**. Note also **lemmerhengst, mosselaar**.

hengsten, henkst See **hengst**

hen peeked boat See **Yorkshire keel**

henst See **hengst**

hen's tail smack See **skøyte-5**

henstije, henstje See **hengst**

herfstjol See **Staverse jol**

Heringbuise See **Buise**

Heringbüse See **buis-2**

Heringbuyse, Heringsbüse See **Buise**

Heringsboot See **herring boat-1**

Heringsbuyse See **Buise**

Heringsjäger See **jäger**

heringsjute See **haringschuit**

Heringslogger See **logger**

Heringswaadenboot, Heringswadenboot See **Wadenboot**

hermafrodite bark See **jackass bark**

hermafrodite brik, Hermaphrodit-Brigg See **hermaphrodite brig**

hermaphrodite brig Term used in the late 18th and early 19th centuries for a vessel that carried as many as 5 square sails on the foremast and a fore-and-aft mainsail with a gaff topsail. Numerous staysails between the masts and jibs to a long bowsprit. Now usually called a **brigantine★**. When a square topsail was added to the mainsail, the vessel became a **jackass brig★** or **jackass★**. Other recorded names: **bergantí(n)-goleta, bric-goleta, brick-goélette, brick scuner, brigantino goletta, brig goélette, brig goletta, Briggschoner, brig schooner, brigškuner, brigue-escuna, brikškuna, goélette brick, half brig, hermafrodite brik, Hermaphrodit-Brigg, morfidite, Schoenerbrik(ken), Schonerbrigg, schooner-brig, Schooner-brigg, Skonnertbrig**. Note also **brig, skúna**.

herna *Belgium/Germany, W/Netherlands, SE:* Lightly built 17th- to 20th-century **aak★**-type bulk-carrier of the Maas (Meuse) Valley. Also ran the lower Rhine River. Constructed initially of wood in the 17th-19th centuries, later of iron or steel. Double-planked, flat bottom, swept up at each end, terminating at the deep top strake, creating trapezoidal ends; narrower forward. Sides slightly curved, parallel for most of their length, and then tapered in at each end; marked sheer

at the ends; angular chines. Flush deck; winch and hatch in foredeck; sunken deckhouse amidships. Rudderpost passed through the stern deck; the forward part of the rudder followed the curve of the stern; the after part very wide and frequently hinged so it could be folded, reducing its surface in quiet waters. A beam attached to the after end of the rudderhead and the tiller arched up to set over the rudderhead and was

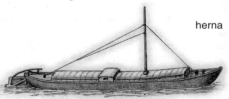

herna

loosely connected with the handle; the tiller activated the rudderpost and the outer end of the rudder blade at the same time. Mast, in a tabernacle stepped about a third of the way from the bow, was designed mainly for towing, but might set a square, dipping lug-, or gaff sail and sometimes a topsail or staysail. Mizzenmast occasionally stepped on the larger vessels. Crew of 2-3. Reported lengths 30-50m; e.g, length with rudder 39.35m, without rudder 38.75m, beam 5m, depth 3.5m, draft loaded 2m. Other recorded names: **bovenlander, hernat, hernnaz**. Note also **spitsbek**.

hernat, hernnaz See **herna**

ḥerrāqa See **ḥarrāqa**

herring boat   1. One that primarily fishes for the pelagic herring, usually with a drift or seine net. Other recorded names: **harenguier★, Heringsboot, herring fisher, navire harenguier**. Note also **drifter, West Cornish lugger**.

    2. *Scotland, NE:* Those that trawled for herring in the 19th century were clinker-built and prior to 1855, were open. Sharp ends, the stern fuller, with maximum beam abaft amidships; curved stem and sternpost; flat sheer; moderate rise to the floors. Outboard rudder. Lug- or gaff-rigged to 2 masts, the foremast stepped well forward. Crew of 5. Reported lengths on keel 9.7-12m; e.g., length overall 11.9m, beam 3.8m, depth 1.3m. Name variant: **Aberdeen boat**

herring buss See **buis-2, buss-2**

herring coble See **coble-1c, coble-1d**

herring cot See **Wexford cot**

herring drifter See **drifter**

herring fisher See **herring boat-1**

herring mule See **coble-1, coble-1d**

herring scoute See **herring scowte**

herring scowte *United Kingdom, Isle of Man:* Used from at least the late 16th through the 18th century, working with a long drift net. Open boat with marked sheer; clinker-built, caulked with wool saturated with tar; sharp, raked bow and stern. Outboard rudder and tiller, or steered with a short oar. Square sail bent to a centered yard; pole mast stepped amidships. Also rowed using 4 sweeps. Early reports cite a crew of 4, later 8. In the late 18th century, keel lengths 6-7.3m; 2-12t burden. Other recorded names: **herring scoute, Manx scowte, Manx squaresail, scoute, squaresail**. Note also **scout, shout**.

herring skiff See **Mackinaw boat-1**

he-sloop See **sloop-9**

hessan See **quffa**

heu *France, N:* **Fishing boat**★ of the English Channel and North Sea that fishes for shrimp near shore and fish farther offshore. Also serves as a **coaster**★. Flat floors, leeboards. Sets a spritsail; mizzen and 2 jibs on the largest. Reported lengths 8-12m. See also **hoy**.

heucre See **howker**

heude, heuden, heudenaar, heudenaer, heudeschip, heue heue See **hoy**

heurque See **howker, hulk-1**

heus, heuscepe, heut, heux, heuz See **hoy**

heynst See **hengst**

Heyst barge, heystsche schuit See **Heistse schuit**

hia keou t'ing, hia kow t'ing See **ha kou ting**

hiate *Brazil, NE:* Large cattle boat used between the island of Marajo and Belem in the Amazon Delta. Both sailing and motorized types. See also **iate-1, yacht**.

Hickling Broads punt See **gun punt**

high deck boat See **cabin boat-1**

high rat *Canada, E:* Large, undecked **fishing boat**★ of Newfoundland that had a washboard, ca. 10cm deep, on each gunwale, permitting the boat to carry a heavier load. Steered by rudder or sculling oar. Mainsail set to a movable mast; small mizzen at the stern. Crew of 2 plus a boy. Cap. 6 or 7 barrels of cod.

high sternsheet wherry See **Norfolk wherry**

high-tailed ship See **seki bune**

hiker *United States, E:* Lightly built, open **catboat**★ type that raced on the Delaware River in the late 19th century. Clinker-planked; flaring sides; slack bilges; plumb stem and transom. Centerboard or daggerboard dropped through the plank keel; wide rudder. Foredeck and side decks; narrow stern deck on the larger. Gaff sail; boom extended over the stern; stayed to bumkin. Larger boats had outriggers to the shrouds. Crew hiked out using short ropes with toggle handles. 1870s boats 4.5m long, 1.3-1.8m wide, depending on the class; later boats 4.9-5.2m long. Further references: **kolek-4, tuckup**

hikinawasen See **troller**

hilnachia See **esnecca**

hinaaja See **tug**

hinge boat *United States, E:* Canal **barge**★ constructed in 2 sections, the bow box and the stern box, each having its own cargo area. Hinging enabled the **barge** to navigate over the top of the inclined planes on the canals. Used on several Pennsylvania and New Jersey canals in the 19th century. A few became floating storage areas for oysters in the New York City market district. Coupled with movable bars and ropes around cleats. Flat bottom; sharp or somewhat blunt bow; square or rounded stern; straight sides. Generally towed by a mule that was stabled at the rear of the bow section. Used a long tiller when light and a short one when loaded; wide-fin rudder, hinged to lift. Small stern cabin. Cargo protected by hatch covers. Length of a recovered single section on the Lehigh Canal 12m, width 3.2m, depth 2m; elsewhere, the total length might be 27m, width 3m, draft loaded with coal 1.5m. Other recorded names: **lemon squeezer, sectional boat**★**, section boat, squeezer.** Note also **flicker.**

Hinterhang See **Bock**

hippagogoi, hippagagus, hippagines (naves), hippagini, hippaginis, hippaginum, hippāgō See **hippagogos**

hippago See **horse carrier**

hippagogae See **hippagogos**

hippagogi See **horse carrier**

hippagogoi, hippagogorum See **hippagogos**

hippagogos **1.** *Greece:* **Galley**★ of the Athenian navy of ca. 500-323 B.C. that transported horses. Used any type of ship until ca. 430 B.C., when **triremes**★ were modified for this purpose. By eliminating the lower 2 banks of rowers, 30 horses could be stabled below the top tier of 60 oarsmen.
2. *Italy:* **a.** The Romans also transported horses by ship. **b.** In the 9th century, the Venetians had ships that were used exclusively for horse transport. Popular with the crusaders. Horses probably arranged in double rows on 2 decks. Also had space for fodder and accommodations for the crew of 50. Probably set a single sail in addition to being rowed.
Spelling variants: **hippagagus, hippaginum, hippāgō, hippagogorum, hippagorum, hippagos, hippagum, hippegos, hippegus, ippagoga, ippagoghi, ippagogo, ippagagos, ippigos**; pl. **hippagines (naves), hippagini, hippaginis, hippagogae, hippagagoi, hippagos, ippegi, ippigi.** Note also **horse carrier, huissier.**

hippagorum, hippagos, hippagum See **hippagogos**

hipped boat See **coal bunker**

hippegos, hippegus See **hippagogos**

hippi, hippoi See **hippos**

hippogabis See **horse carrier**

hippos Class of oared Phoenician **merchantman**★. One of the tall ends depicted a horse, hence the name. Small vessels hauled logs along the Syrian coast. Toward the end of the period some fished along the African Atlantic coast. Other recorded names: **hippi, hippoi** (pl.), **horse, ippoi**

hisbiya See **isbije**

Hjertingepram, Hjerting-kane See **Hjertingpram**

Hjertingpram *Denmark, SW:* A **dory**★-type **fishing boat**★ of the Hjerting area of Jutland. Spruce planking lapped, using 4-5 planks; flared sides; flat bottom with slight fore-and-aft rocker. Sharp bow; straight, raked stem; sharply raked, flat, "V" stern; slight sheer. Round-bladed rudder extends below bottom; broad daggerboard. Length 5.75m, beam 1.57m, depth 0.6m, draft with daggerboard down 0.8m. Other recorded names: **Hjertingepram, Hjerting-kane, pram fra Hjerting.** Note also **pram-4.**

hlaung See **laung**

hleypi-skip, hleypi-skúta See **skuta-1**

hnörr See **knarr-1**

hoa-hang *China:* In ranking of ships during the 12th century, this was the smallest of the three major categories. Other recorded names: **cacam, kakam**

Hoang-ho ch'uan See **Huang He chuan**

hoa-tch'ouan See **hua chuan-1**

hoa t'ing See **lorcha-3**

hoa-tse See **hua zi**

Hobart ketch See **barge-6**

hobble See **hoveller**

hobbler See **hoveller, number one**

Hochfisch-Ewer, Hochseefischer-Ewer See **Ewer**
Hochseefischerkutter, Hochseekutter See **kutter-2**
Hochtakeltschuner See **Bermuda schooner-2**
hoda *India, NW:* One of the generic terms for **boat★**, and in Gujarati, refers to a medium-sized **fishing boat★**. The **Malia hoda** of the inner part of the Gulf of Kutch is used for prawn fishing. Carvel-built of teak, flat bottom, sharp ends, small rudder; open, oiled and tarred hull. Generally rowed or paddled, but may step a bamboo mast with a trapezoidal sail. The **Navlakhi hoda** (also of the Gulf of Kutch) is sturdier, with a keel and a raked bow; full, square stern; decking at bow and stern; painted hull. These raise a lateen sail. On the south side of the Gulf of Cambray, the sea-fishing boats are double-ended, plank-built. Oiled hull; tiller slots through rudder. Sets 2 lateen sails, but also rowed from either end. Some employ a crew of 7-9. Gulf of Kutch boats range from 4.9m long, 1.2m wide, and 0.91m deep to 6.4m by 1.4m by 0.76m; the Malia boats are the longest. Other recorded names: **hodi★, navadi**. Note also **batel, malia**. Further reference: **lodhia**
hode See **hoy**
hodi *India, NW:* Gujarati word for a **dugout canoe★**. Paddled, one man at the bow, the 2nd at the stern, facing each other. No outrigger. Note also **ek lakdi hodi**. Further references: **hoda, hody**
hody *India, W:* Single-masted, plank-built boat used by drift-net fishermen on the west coast and its backwaters, especially at Bombay (Mumbai). Most double-ended, some with a rounded stern; stem curved, stern straight and raked. Open or decked at bow and stern; sometimes weatherboards installed in forward part.

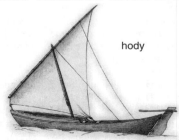

hody

Rudder lashed on or secured by gudgeons and pintles. Some fitted with a single outrigger. A quadrilateral lateen-type sail with a short luff is set to a forward-raking mast and tacked to stemhead. Also rowed. Larger types have as many as 15 in crew. Reported lengths 6.7-12.5m; e.g., length 9m, beam 1.4m, depth 0.43m. Spelling variant: **hodi★**; word considered a corruption of the Kanarese **odi★**. Note also **akada hody**.
hoe See **hoy**
hoecher, hoecker, hoecker-schip, hoeckscepe, hoecschip, hoekboot See **howker**
hoeker See **howker, koopvaardijhoeker, vishoeker**
hoekerbuis *Netherlands:* **Fishing boat★**, employing both nets and hooks and lines, that had the hull characteristics of the **buis★** and the rig of the **howker★**. Worked from the 18th into the 19th century. Carvel-built, strong keel, heavy wale just below the top strake, curved stem, rounded bow. Early types had a flat counter stern, later were round-sterned. Decked; fish

well. Large rudder; one on which the tiller came in directly over the gunwale was sometimes called a **kwee**. Mainmast stepped amidships set a large, square mainsail and small, square topsail; mizzenmast set a small, triangular or gaff sail. Long bowsprit and jib-boom. Crew of 5-6 on the smaller boats, 8-12 on the larger. Length 22m, beam 5.4m, depth 3.1m; 15-20t cap. Other recorded names: **bunhoeker, Hukerbuise**. Further reference: **buis-2**
hoekerschip See **howker**
hoescepe, hoey, hoeye See **hoy**
hogaers See **hoogaars**
hog boat *England, south coast:* Fished out from the beaches between Eastbourne and Shoreham-by-Sea during the 18th-19th centuries. A flat-floored, tubby, clinker-built boat; slightly raking stem with cutaway forefoot; apple bows; small transom stern; 2 strong bilge keels; leeboards. Early boats half-decked; later fully decked, with decks on 3 levels; small hatch in middle of foredeck led to the cuddy; long hatch amidships, small hatch aft. Most stepped 2 masts, setting a large,

hog boat

loose-footed sprit or gaff mainsail and a sprit or lug mizzen; mizzen sheeted to a long outrigger. Heel of sprit set high. Foresail run out on a flat, bowsed down, wooden bumkin; in addition, a large jib sometimes bent to a running bowsprit which passed through a ring on the bumkin. Mast stepped in a tabernacle; 2 shrouds to a side, forestay to bumkin. Crew of 3. Lengths to 10.7m; e.g., length 8.53m, beam 4.88m, depth 1.37m; 8-12t. Other recorded names: **hoggie, hoggy**; **Brighton, Shoreham hog boat**
hogdaling, hogdalseka See **vadeka**
Hogeveense praam See **Hoogeveense praam**
hoggie, hoggy See **hog boat**
hoicbort See **howker**
hoie, hoigh See **hoy**
hoissier See **huissier**
hokkoku-bune See **kitamae-bune**
hola *India, NE:* Cargo boat of the Hooghly and Ganges Rivers. Mainly transports coal and bricks, but also carries straw, sometimes on 2 boats joined **catamaran★**-fashion. Bluff ends; dugout base; each plank curves upward and then is cut off by the top strake. Flat bottom. Stern higher than the bow. May have a straw hut aft. Steered with a long, wide-bladed sweep on the quarter. Rowed; rower sits near the bow when boat is loaded, stands when light. May set a square sail to a pivoting mast. Crew of 4-6. Cap. ca. 24t. Other recorded names: **hollah, lowcoe, saltee**. Note also **sālti**.
holche See **hulk-1**
hold scow See **scow-7**
holeche See **hulk-1**

holi See **barque Djenné**
holic, holik, holk, holke, holker, holkr See **hulk-1**
hollah See **hola**
hollandais *Belgium/France, N:* Term for 19th-century inland waterways craft. Carried cargo. Length 22.5m, beam 4.87m. Spelling variant: **hollandois**. See also **fluit**.
Holländer 1. German designation for a vessel or a person from the Netherlands. Name variant: **holländisches Schiff**
   2. *Germany, NW:* A type of boat from Holland that joined the fishing **fleet*** of Finkenwerder in the 16th century and became a distinctive **Kutter*** build.
Hollander See **Eiderschnigge, fluit**
Holländerfloss See **Rheinfloss**
Holländer Aak See **aak**
Holländisches Schiff See **Holländer-1**
hollandois See **fluit, hollandais**
Hollandsche schechtaak, Hollandsche schlechtaak,
   Hollandse aak See **aak**
Hollandse schouw See **zeeschouw**
Hollandse tjalk *Netherlands, SW:* Built in the South Holland area to carry heavy cargo such as sand and gravel. Some built in the late 1970s. Carvel-planked; flat bottom, full lines below the waterline, curved chines, rounded ends. Narrow wale; tumble home to top strake at the ends; sides parallel for most of their length. Wide, curved stem; sharp, salient stemhead; straight sternpost. Bitts do not come up above the gunwales. Outboard rudder with wide fin below the waterline; some unshipped by chain tackle; heavy tiller. Some early **Zuidhollandse tjalken** (pl.) were **hektjalken*** with the tiller coming inboard below the top strake. Wide, rounded leeboards. Decked; winch and hatch on foredeck; long hatch; some had a cabin house abaft the hatch. Loose-footed, boomed gaff sail stepped to mast about one-quarter in from the bow; straight gaff. Staysail, jib to jibboom. Long pennant from the masthead. Mast in tabernacle, struck by sheerlegs. One built early 20th century was 94t.
Hollandse zoomaak See **aak**
hollich, hollih, hollik See **hulk-1**
hollip See **Fenland lighter**
holmedaljekt See **jekt**
holmsbupram See **pram-6a**
Holvikjekt See **jekt**
Holy Island keelboat See **keelboat-3a**
Holzbarke See **barke-3**
Holzfloss See **raft, timber raft-1**
Holzfrachter See **timber carrier**
Holzgelle, Holzjolle See **Jolle-5**
Holzplätte See **Plätte-1**
Holzschiff See **Ladeschiff**
Holzspäneschiff See **timber carrier**
Holzstammfloss See **raft**
Holzstammschute, Holztransporter,
Holztransportschiff See **timber carrier**
homardier See **langoustier-1, smack-2**
home boat *Canada, E:* Term given, especially in Newfoundland, to a ship from the United Kingdom.
home-trade passenger ship See **home-trade ship**
home-trade ship *United Kingdom:* Ship that trades between ports in the United Kingdom, Channel

Islands, Isle of Man and the Continent between the Elbe River and Brest. Name variant: **home-trade passenger ship**
home trading vessel See **riverboat**
hØneræva, hØnerævskØyte See **skØyte-5**
honey barge See **scow-1**
hong boat *China:* Special boat that, because of its speed, carried passengers and, on occasion, patrolling police and revenue officers. Wooden cabin covered most of the hull, sometimes richly appointed. Propelled by a single large scull made fast to the sternpost, by as many as 6 rowers, or by sail. Reported lengths 7.6-15m. Other recorded names: **fast boat***, **hang-chwen, hong-mee-teng, hong-tch'ouan, k'oai-t'ing, kong se tch'ouan, koon-sze teng, kw'ai t'ing**
hong chuan *China:* **1.** A boat used by several lifesaving associations along the Chang Jiang (Yangtze) to rescue persons involved in capsizings or those who had fallen overboard, and to search for bodies; in the rapids, one of these boats would accompany a **junk*** that was tracking upstream. Worked until World War II. Generally called **hong chuan** for their red color, but a small type used by the association at Zhenjiang (Chenchiang) on the lower part of the river was called **hsun-ch'uan**, while those at the rapids above Yichang (I-ch'ang) were sometimes called **kan-ssŭ-tang**. Besides their red color, the boats, which differed somewhat in style, were identified by lettering along the sheer plank on the stern quarter and generally by a flag at the stern.

hong chuan-1

Most square-ended with the stern swept up. A house of mat or wood covered part of the boat. Steered with a stern sweep and sometimes a bow sweep; rudder on those that sailed on the lower river. On the upper river, mainly rowed, from near the bow. Downstream, they stepped 1-2 masts, setting lugsails. Those above Yichang employed 4 oarsmen and a helmsman. Reported lengths 9-13m; e.g., length 10.7m, beam 2.3m. Other recorded names: **hong-tch'ouan, hung ch'uan, kieou-min tch'ouan, life-boat*, red boat**
   2. Large, robust cargo vessel that plied the lower Chang Jiang and Poyang Hu (lake) carrying tea, paper, porcelain, and vegetable oil downstream, returning with foreign merchandise and salt. Stern swept up sharply to a very high poop; rudderpost for the wide-bladed, balanced rudder came up through the after house, with the tiller worked from the roof. Square bow and stern; marked bulge to sides at the waterline. Shiny hull, liberally oiled. Some employed 2 leeboards. Second house abaft the mainmast. Mainmast and small foremast

stepped in forward half of the vessel; mainmast might be in 2-3 pieces and 25m long. Cotton lugsails. Reported lengths 35-40m, widths 6-7m. Other recorded names: **hong tch'ouan**, **hung ch'uan**, **red boat**

Hong Kong sampan See **ku tsai ting**

hong-mee-teng See **hong boat**

hong rou chuan *China, SE:* Dredged for cockles with a net around Shantou (Swatow). Catch stowed in built-in compartments. Length 8.5m, beam 2.4m. Other recorded names: **cockle-fishing boat**, **hung jou ch'uan**

hong-tch'ouan See **hong boat**, **hong chuan**

hong-t'eou tch'ouan See **hong tou chuan**

hong tou *China, SE:* Worked out of Shantou (Swatow). Identified by a red block at the bow on which an oculus was painted. Bluff bow, narrowing at the waterline; oval transom. Flush deck; high poop. The non-lifting rudder was streamed when not in use. Bottom painted white, remainder unpainted. Most 2-masted; some also stepped a mizzen. Battened balance lugsails set to starboard; curved leech. Length 21m, beam 4.4m. Name variant: **hung-t'ou**, **red bow junk**. See also **hong tou san ban**.

hong tou chuan *China, N:* Cargo vessel that carried grain and produce between ports in Bo Hai (Gulf of Chihli). Solidly constructed with watertight compartments and a series of half-round log wales that paralleled the sheer strake. Flat, raked bow; oval transom; rudderstock fitted into a slot in the transom; high freeboard; strong sheer. Decked; high bulwarks and hatch coaming; arched mat roof abaft the mainmast protected the cargo, then open space for helmsman; wooden cabin aft. Tiller worked with block and tackle; windlasses raised the mainsail, rudder, and anchor; mooring spar extended out over the bow. Decorated along the sides and on the bow and stern; oculi, plus a special eye at the bow. Three masts: a forward-raking foremast at break of the forecastle, mainmast amidships, light mizzen on port quarter sheeted to a jigger boom that braced against the mast. Tanned cloth mainsail, mat fore- and mizzen sails. Crew of 6-8. Reported lengths 24-27m, widths 5.5-5.8m; draft 2m loaded. Other recorded names: **bateau à tête rouge**, **Chinchow trader**, **hong-t'eou tch'ouan**, **hung-t'ou ch'uan**, **red-headed junk**, **Rot-Kopf-Dschunke**. Note also **da hong chuan**.

hong tou san ban *China, E:* Ferried passengers in Shanghai harbor. Operated by 2 main groups of people, those from Ningbo (Ningpo) to the south of Shanghai, and those from Suzhou (Soochow) to the west, but the **sampans**★ were essentially the same. Longitudinally planked, flat bottom that curved up toward the bow, ending in a small, raked bow transom; after fourth of the bottom rose in a straight line to above the waterline. Flared sides; sheer strake curved up sharply at the stern, terminating in wings beyond the U-shaped, raked transom. Foredeck; small, arched house of woven matting amidships; passengers sat in the forward area; family (in the Ningbo **sampans**) lived in the after part of the house. Bow painted red, hence the name **hong tou**★ (translated **red head**); the Ningbo boat had oculi, and the stern transom was gaily painted. Propelled by a sculling oar that pivoted

from the port side of the transom on the Ningbo boats, and the starboard side for the Suzhou boats. Reported lengths 3.5-8m; e.g., length overall 5.5m, beam 1.5m, depth 2m. Other recorded names: **Chinchou (Zinzhou) chuan**, **hen boat**, **hsiao san-pan ta-k'o**, **hung t'ou san-pan**, **mu-chi**, **muji**, **Ningpo sampan**, **Shanghai Harbor sampan**, **Zinzhou chuan**

hoockboot See **howker-1**

hoodledasher See **freighter-3a**

hoofdgalei See **capitane**

hoogaar See **hoogaars**

hoogaars *Belgium/Netherlands, SW:* Sharp-bowed, beamy boat of Zeeland, especially on the lower Scheldt and the Maas, and in Zuid-Holland. Engaged in fishing, oystering, musseling, shrimping, and occasionally in carrying cargo and produce, and served as a **ferry**★. Probably in use by the 16th century as a lightly built cargo carrier different from the fishing **hoogaars** that developed during the 18th century. Extinct as a working craft by the l960s, but converted or newly built as a **yacht**★ (the **hoogaarsjacht** or **jachthoogaars**) since the 19th century. Long, straight bow that overhangs as much as 45°; flat, broad shovel bow. Older boats clinker-planked, generally with 3 flaring strakes below the wale; top strake carvel-planked and has tumble home; S-shaped wale at the stern; considerable sheer forward. Carvel-built boats were **yachts**. Heavy, flat bottom to take the ground, planked fore-and-aft; bow deeper in the water than the stern; bottom fuller forward, sharper aft; sharp chines. Wide, rounded, raked stern. Large outboard rudder followed the rake of the sternpost at the forward edge; after edge roughly vertical with a small extension below the waterline; lifts on grounding. Early leeboards wide and round; deep and narrow since 19th century; rested on top strake when not in use; some boats had alternate positions for the leeboards. Older types completely open, later built with removable foredeck, then fully decked with steering well aft; small cuddy abaft the open waist. Originally sprit-rigged, then a large, loose-footed, boomed gaff mainsail with curved gaff; staysail; jib to bowsprit. Sprit-rigged boats usually carried a topsail. No shrouds or stays to the mast, which stepped just forward of amidships. Most had engines by the 1930s. Also rowed, with a block attached to each side of the loom where it was set into the oarlock. Crew of 2-4. Reported lengths 8-17m; average length 13.45m, beam 4.5m, depth 1.76m; shallow draft. Other recorded names: **hogaers**, **hoogaar(ts)**, **hoogaerts**, **hooge(e)rs**, **jachthoogaars**, **jachtboot**★, **Zeeland hoogaars**, **Zeeuws(ch)e hoogaars**; pl. **hoogaarsen**, **hoogaartsen**, **hoogaarzen**; small **oogaars(e)**. In Zeeland: **schuutje**. Further reading: Jules Van Beylen, *De Hoogaars, Geschiednis en Bouw* (Bussum: De Boer Maritiem, 1978); ibid., *De Hoogaars en de Visserij van Arnemuiden* (Leeuwarden: Hedeby Publishing, 1993). Note also **Arnemuidense hoogaars**, **Kinderlijkse hoogaars**, **Tholense hoogaars**, **Zeeuwsvlaamse hoogaars**.

hoogaarsen See **hoogaars**

hoogaarsjacht See **hoogaars**, **Tholense hoogaars**

hoogaarts, **hoogaartsen**, **hoogaarzen**, **hoogaerts**, **hoogeers**, **hoogers** See **hoogaars**

Hoogeveensche praam See **Hoogeveense praam**

Hoogeveense praam *Netherlands, E:* Peat and produce carrier from Hoogeveen; last built at the beginning of the 20th century. Flat bottom; sharp bilges; sides flared to the wale, vertical above; washstrake above the wale ran from near the stern to the bow in a straight line, making the bow higher than the stern. Semicircular bow, fuller than the stern; mildly sharp stern. Large-bladed rudder; long tiller slotted over rudderhead; oval leeboards. Most undecked but may have a cambered deck extending full beam; cabin forward, central hatch. Set a gaff mainsail and foresail. Length 17.35m, beam 3.52m, depth 1.5m. Other recorded names: **Hoogeveensche praam, marktpraam**. Note also **praam**.

hooibotter See **Marker botter**

hook boat See **Rhode Island hook boat, sponge dinghy, whiting boat**

hooker **1.** Sailor's term for his vessel, usually one past its prime. Can be used affectionately or contemptuously. Note also **howker**.
2. A **fishing boat**★ that employs long lines with hooks, as opposed to nets. Weatherly and handy for picking up end buoys. Other recorded names: **Angel(fischer)boot, Hukboot, Huker**★. Note also **longliner-1**.
3. *Iceland, south coast:* Reported as a single-masted **fishing boat**★.
4. *Ireland:* Used along the west and southeastern coasts from the early 17th to the mid-20th century, primarily for trading, transporting kelp and peat, piloting, and fishing. Characteristically **cutter**★-rigged, heavily built, open or partly decked with full, rounded bow; straight keel; either flat, raked, transom or counter stern. Strong tumble home to top sides. Traditionally black-hulled; red sails. A 10-ton **hooker** of the 1850s was 6.5m long on the keel, 2.7m wide, and 1.8m deep. Other recorded names: **Irish hooker, West Coast hooker**. Note also **bád iomartha, Galway hooker, gleóiteog, Kinsale hooker, púcán**.
5. *United States:* **a.** On the Great Lakes, lumber **steamers** of the late 19th and early 20th centuries were called **hookers** or **lumber hookers**. Most of the rafted logs were towed by **barges**; the finished lumber was loaded on the **hookers** for further transport. Length to 61m. Note also **timber drogher**. **b.** In the dialect of the Maine coast, any good workboat.
Other recorded names: **hawker, hookerman, howker**★.
Further references: **Deal hooker, hooking boat, Plymouth hooker, Polperro gaffer**

hookerman See **hooker**

hooking boat *Canada, NE:* In Newfoundland, a small, single-masted **fishing boat**★ employing hand lines. Name variant: **hooker**★.

hooluck, hoolyck See **ulakh**

Hooper Island crab skiff *United States, E:* Double-ended boat of the Eastern Shore of Chesapeake Bay. Designed originally for commercial crabbing, then used as a **gunning skiff**★, and subsequently for racing. Plank-built, initially with a flat bottom, later with a long, low deadrise; flared, straight sides; maximum beam forward of amidships; some had a deep forefoot and heel; centerboard. Decked at bow and stern; narrow side decks. Aft-raking mast stepped well forward.

Set a leg-of-mutton sail with a sprit boom to a small club at the clew; when working, sail rolled around the sprit and stowed inboard with the unstepped mast. Balance boards used when racing. Reported lengths 4.8-8.5m. Other recorded names: **Hooper Island sharpie, lilliputian**. Note also **crabbing skiff**.

Hooper Island sharpie See **Hooper Island crab skiff**

hoor See **houri-1**

Hoorensche gaings See **fluit**

hoori *India:* Western-style **coaster**★ built mainly in the Bay of Bengal, but also on the west coast. Keel; rounded or square stern. Generally rigged as a **brig**★ or **brigantine**★, but sometimes as a 2-masted **schooner**★. Cap. 300-500t. See also **houri**.

Hoornse punter *Netherlands, NW:* Fished for herring out of Hoorn and Edam on the west side of the Zuiderzee. Open except for a short stern deck. Clinker-built with 3 strakes; flaring sides. Sharp bow, raked stem; narrow, square stern. Flat, lancet-shaped bottom, longitudinally planked, with transverse boards on top; angular chines. Small live well amidships. Rowed, the oars working over a single tholepin. Length ca. 5m. Other recorded name: **Friese punter**

Hoornse schouw, hoornsman See **zeeschouw**

hooy-schip See **hoy**

hopal, hopal api See **kapal**

Hope Cove crabber See **West Country crabber**

hopper **1.** General term for a wooden or steel craft that takes on mud and sand from a **dredger**★, and in early days, received ballast from ships. Invented in mid-18th century. May also be used for sewage disposal. Belt bucket conveyors or trap doors in the bottom release the load; buoyancy tanks are positioned at the ends or along the sides. Often without self-propulsion (**dumb hopper**), therefore towed. A **hopper dredge** may combine the actual dredging with transporting the spoils; the ultra-modern **trailer hopper dredge** can be split into 2 hulls to release its dredged load. Selected name variants: **Baggerprahm, Baggerschute, barca tramoggia, barzha, cleanser boat, door barge, drague porteuse (de déblais) Dreckschute, gabard, Hopperbagger, hopper barge**★, **Hopperboot, hopper dredger, hopper punt, mud boat**★, **mudderprăm, mud hopper**★, **mud lighter, porta-fango, shalanda**★. Note also **beta, beunschip-2, dump barge, gánguil, kantelbak, marie-salope, modderschouw, Mudderprahm, Prahm-1**.
2. May designate a simple, double-hulled **barge**★ that carries dry bulk cargo. Mainly open cargo hold, but sometimes decked. Up to 88m long, and 15m wide.

Hopperbagger See **hopper-1**

hopper barge *Canada:* A floating structure designed to transport fish. Name variant: **hopper punt**. See also **hopper-1**.

Hopperboot, hopper dredge, hopper dredger See **hopper-1**

hopper punt See **hopper-1, hopper barge**

hora See **dhatti hora, ekdar, gharat hora**

hore See **cori**

hori See **cori, houri, shū·ai, tony-2**

Hornbækbåd *Denmark, E:* Decked **fishing boat**★ working out of Hornbæk on the north coast of Sjælland.

Clinker-built with marked sheer and hollow lines. Sternpost straight and sharply raked below the waterline, rounded above; sternpost extends only to top

Hornbækbåd

strake; tiller passes through the bulwark below the gunwale. Stem rounded; bow sharp and flared. **Cutter***-rigged with loose-footed, boomed gaff mainsail. Gaff topsail set to pole mast. Length 11m, beam 4.2m, depth 1.5m. Name variant: **dæksfartöj fra Hornbæk**

hornfisk See **havbåd**

horse See **hippos**

horse boat In general, a boat propelled by one or more horses (or mules or donkeys), either by towing or by walking on a platform that activates a paddle wheel. Note also **team boat**.

1. *Canada, E:* A **horse boat** operated across the St. Lawrence River between Quebec and Levis from ca. 1812 to 1840. Propelled by a paddle wheel turned by 2-4 horses. Laid up by ice in winter; at other times, at the mercy of tides and strong currents.

2. *England:* **a.** In eastern England, a small, open **horse boat** that ferried towing horses from one side of a canal or river to the other; sometimes served as a public **ferry***. Usually towed behind a gang of **barges***. Common in The Fens country (see **Fenland lighter**). **b.** In the southwest, **horse boats**, used to cross many of the rivers and estuaries, were usually distinct from exclusively passenger **ferries** of the same area. Some had unique properties. On the lower River Tamar, the Cremyll Passage **ferry** was towed by a **steamer** from the late 19th to the early 20th century; by 1934, it became known as the **car ferry**. The boat was fully employed carrying horse-drawn bread vans, coal carts, and brewery wagons, as well as livestock, to market. After being cast off by the **steamer**, the **ferry** was maneuvered by the rudder and by poling before being winched ashore. A ramp for loading and unloading was lowered onto the beach. The **horse boat** that crossed the River Lynher, in the same area, conveyed no wagons—only horses, sheep, and cattle; operated until 1910. An opening in the side made transfer of the animals more convenient. Propelled by long sweeps. The **horse boat** at Salcombe worked until 1919 and was always known as the **scow***. Note also **horse ferry**, **pontoon-3**.

3. *Ireland, E:* Wooden, horse-drawn **barge*** built during World War II to transport peat to Dublin and to power stations. Also called **G boats** because the letter "G" was added to their identifying number.

4. *Northern Ireland, SE:* A local **ferry** transported horses and cattle across the tidal inlet between Strangford and Portaferry in County Down. Extinct. Clinker-built. Used both a dipping lugsail and 2 pairs of oars.

5. *United States:* **a.** Term applied in the American colonies and into the early 19th century to a **ferryboat*** large enough to carry a horse. Might be rowed or sailed. In the canal period of the early and mid-19th century, a **horse boat** was one towed by a team of horses or mules, generally stabled in the bow. On some canals, 2 teams were carried because relay barns with relief teams were not available. Note also **team boat**. **b.** The greatly indented coastline of Narrangansett Bay in the Rhode Island area necessitated numerous **ferries**. In the 1st half of the 19th century, some were **horse boats**. On one type, a horse walked a treadmill to turn a wheel; on another, one or more horses walked on a circular platform that was geared to cogs that rotated a horizontal shaft connected with paddle wheels. **c.** Horse-powered boat used on Lake Winnipesaukee in New Hampshire between 1850 and the late 1880s. Mainly carried cordwood and lumber. Two horses drove a pair of paddle wheels. The wheels could be raised on approach to land, and an overhanging bow enabled direct access to shore. Steered with a 5.5m-long sweep. Bunkhouse aft on one side and a cookhouse on the other. Normal crew of 2. Length overall 18.2m, on bottom 12.2m, beam 3.35m, depth 0.9m. Name variant: **Lake Winnipesaukee horse boat**. **d.** *United States, E:* On the Delaware River in the vicinity of Philadelphia, sharp-bowed, square-sterned **ferries** used horses to work a pair of paddle wheels on each side of the boat. On another type, the paddle or bucket wheels were set between a double-hulled craft, and 8-10 horses walked around in a circle on a large, revolving wheel that was geared with the paddle wheels. Poles and sweeps aided the crossing through winter ice. These **ferries** carried single horsemen, stage coaches, farmers' carts, pack trains. **e.** Some **horse boats** were small **keelboats*** that used 6 horses to drive a pair of paddle wheels on an upstream run, progressing at ca. 9-11km per hour. On one type, 2 **keelboats** were connected by a platform on which the horses walked around a wheel. Used on the Mississippi River for a brief period. Carried relief horses.

Further references: **at kayığı, Barton horse boat, flatboat-4, flyboat-3a, horse carrier, narrow boat, team boat-3, team boat-4**

horse carrier A vessel built or modified to carry horses. Stable area in the hold or between decks. Each horse had its own stall, and either stood or was supported by a sling. One 13th-century **nef*** carried 100 horses on 2 decks; later vessels, often military transports, carried varying numbers of horses. Some were **barge***-like for river work; others were seagoing vessels. Other recorded names: **alogocharavo, alogokharavo, (bâtiment) écurie, hästransportfartyg, horse boat*, horse transport, ippagogo** (pl. **ippagoghi**); pl. **ippegi; navire écurie, paardenschip, pasacaballo, passacavalli, passacavallos, stall på båt, statek stajnia, trasporto da cavalli**. Note also **at kayığı, banawa, chelandia-1, chelandia-2, hippagogos, Leibschiff-1, ma chuan, palandrie, tafurea**. Further reference: **huissier**

horse dung box See **berrichon**

horse ferry *England, E:* **Ferries★** in the Norfolk Broads were of 2 types—pedestrian and **horse ferries**. The latter were distinguished by their ability to carry a horse and cart. These consisted of a large, wooden **pontoon★** hauled across the river by a hand-cranked chain system; the surviving **ferry** has a diesel-hydraulic winch. Further reference: **team boat-1**

horse-machine boat An **anchor boat★** on which horses walked around a capstan that kedged an anchor to draw a river vessel upstream. Originated in early 19th century in France, but most widely used on the Volga River in Russia. Might be large enough to accommodate 150 horses and an equal number in crew. Would pull 7-8 vessels, one behind the other. Superseded by the **capstan boat**, which was steam-powered.

horse packet **1.** *England, E:* A **team boat★** that ran from Yarmouth to Norwich in the early 19th century. Four horses, walking in a circle, drove small paddle wheels. Cabin forward and aft. Crew of 4. Length 18m, beam 5.5m.
   2. *United States, NE:* **Horse packets**, carrying mainly passengers, worked the Erie Canal in New York State prior to the introduction of **steam packets★** in the 1870s. Horses drew the boats at a trot, as opposed to pulling the **barges★** at a walk. Sharp bow; fitted with berths and cabins.

horse raft See **lumberman's batteau**

horse transport See **horse carrier**

hottsu See **iso-bune**

houari **1.** French term for a **wherry★**-like craft used for transportation and fishing, and as a **ferryboat★**.
   2. A 1- to 3-masted boat using what became known as a **houari** rig. A tall, triangular sail was set to a short mast and a sliding or gunter yard topmast. The lower part of the sail was hooped to the mast. The upper part laced to the topmast, which slid up and down the lower mast. Sail generally loose-footed; furled to the lower mast by lowering the topmast. Jib to a rising bowsprit. Used as a **coaster★** and for pleasure boating in the Mediterranean.
   Spelling variants: **guaira, guaire, guairo★, guari, hou(r)ario, houri★, houary, huari, wari**. See also **houri-1, houri-4, wherry**.

houario, houary See **houari**

houa-tch'ouan See **hua chuan-1**

houa ting See **lorcha-3**

houcboot, houckboot See **howker**

houcker See **howker, vishoeker**

houcre See **howker, hulk-1**

houkare, houkeboot, houker See **howker**

houlc, houlel See **hulk-1**

houloum See **daré**

houlque See **hulk-1**

hountin See **huntin**

hou-pan See **wai pi gu, wu ban**

hou-pan ch'uan See **wai pi gu**

hourario See **houari**

houri **1.** *Arabian Peninsula:* **a.** **Dugout canoe★** used in the Red Sea, southern part of the Arabian Peninsula, and the Persian (Arabian) Gulf, as a **ship's boat★**, for fishing, and for harbor work. Most imported from the

Malabar Coast of India (where they are called **tony★**), and modified locally. May be retained as simple dugouts, dugouts with one or more strakes added on, clinker-style, or may have a dugout bottom and planked sides. Widely spaced sham ribs often carved into the original dugout, but sides spread and ribs employed when a washstrake is added. Thwarts inserted. Bow and stern rounded or pointed; bottom flattened, some with keel runners. Those used for fishing usually only oiled; others painted and may include oculi. Steered with a paddle consisting of a rounded blade nailed to a shaft. If sailed, rudder added, hung by gudgeon and pintle, and false keel nailed on. Sailing rig might be lateen, gaff, or square sail raised to a short mast. May also be poled or paddled, and many now use an outboard motor. Crewed by 1-3. Reported lengths 3-11m, ca. 0.5m in width. Spelling variants: **hoor(i), hori, houari★, houry, howa, hūri**. **b.** At Qatar, very fast **hawári** race on the anniversary of the emir's accession. Crew of 48 row 2 to an oar. Length 20m. **c.** On the northeast coast of Oman, may denote any small, double-ended boat. Name variants: pl. **hawâra, hawári**
   2. *East Africa:* Small **dugout canoe★** still in use, mainly as a **ship's boat★**, but in some places, for inshore fishing. Imported from the Malabar Coast of India, sometimes by way of Persian (Arabian) Gulf **dhows★**. In Somalia, the tree trunk is often imported and the boat carved locally. Slight differences in construction are reported from various points along the coast. At Dar es Salaam, hull is semicircular in cross section and reinforced with ribs; when converted for sailing, a strake and outriggers added. At Mombasa, one type—a well-finished pure dugout—has a round bottom and curved ends; when sailed, hangs a rudder worked by a tiller or a system of tackles. A 2nd type has stem and stern pieces added to a flat-bottomed dugout. At Zanzibar, the bow and stern are raised and a wedge decorates the bow. Those along the Somalia coast usually have a broad washstrake sewn on and have a pointed bow and stern to aid in handling in the surf; paddled using a mangrove pole with a flat, round blade, or sets a small lateen sail. Reported lengths 3-8m, widths ca. 0.7-0.9m. Other recorded names: pl. **mahori**; dim. **kihori**. Note also **mtumbwi, vallam-1a**.
   3. *Dijbouti:* For inshore fishing, a one-man **houri** is used. Originally a **dugout canoe★**, the log imported from the mountains of the Hadhramaut on the southern Arabian Peninsula. Now plank-built, using a special hard wood for the flat bottom; 4-8 frames. Sharp ends; very narrow and stabilized with a paddle from the stern. Vividly painted. Short mast, braced by 2 thwarts, sets a lateen sail; also paddled. Reported lengths 4-6m. The **houri** that travels offshore has a truncated stern for an outboard motor; small keel; a crew of as many as 6. Reported lengths 7-8m. Other recorded names: by the Afar of Djibouti, Eritrea, Ethiopia: **huuri**, pl. **hawaari**
   4. *France, N:* Lug-sailed **fishing boat★** that worked out of Normandy ports. Fished mainly for mackerel and herring until the mid-19th century, some traveling as far as Scotland. Bluff bow, straight or curved stem, counter stern. Decked, deep bulwarks. One to 3 masts;

mainmast stepped amidships, foremast well forward. When present, mizzenmast vertical or raked aft with sail sheeted to a bumkin. Topsail set to mainmast on larger vessels. Crutch at stern supported lowered mainmast. Crew of 14-15 at Honfleur. Cap. ca. 60t. Spelling variants: **houari***, **houry**, **oury**

5. *Sudan, E:* The **houri** of the Red Sea coast is similar to those found elsewhere, having been obtained from India. Used mainly for handline and small net fishing in shallow, protected waters. Dugout hull; sharp, fine ends cut square on top; flattened bottom. Paddled only. Reported lengths 3-6m, width ca. 0.6m.
Further reference: **houari**

hourque See **howker**, **hulk-1**

houry See **houri-1**, **houri-4**

houseboat In broad terms, a boat with a cabin.
1. A boat that serves principally as a dwelling rather than for transportation. May be built for this purpose or be a converted vessel, such as an old **barge***. Usually found in sheltered waters, moored with direct access to land. In several eastern areas, there are **houseboat** colonies, as in Hong Kong, Kashmir (see **donga**), and the Philippines (see **djěnging**). Modern **houseboats** in the West are well outfitted, commodious, and usually propelled by low-powered engines. Other recorded names: **bateau logement** (or **maison**), **bote de carroza**, **canot couvert**, **caravane flottante**, **Hausboot**, **husbåd**, **husbåt***, **Wohnboot**, **Wohnschiff**, **woonschip**. Note also **ark-5**, **float-3**, **kabang**, **shanty boat**.
2. *United States, NW:* In the Willapa Bay area of southwestern Washington State, the **houseboat** was a single **scow***, decked, and with a house to protect workers culling oysters in winter. Might have a stove.
Further reference: **oyster barge**

house canoe See **djěnging**

house lighter See **Fenland lighter**, **Stour lighter**

Houston scow See **scow-schooner-2**

houte-paard See **bã:s**

houthaalder See **cat-2**

houtvlot See **timber raft-1**

hou uá See **vaka tou uá**

hoveler See **hoveller**

hoveller *England:* A freelance boat used off the south and east coasts to provide passing ships with pilots, supplies, new anchors, and other gear. Some helped sailing ships and **barges*** get underway. Generally lug-rigged. Term also applied to the small boats that sought plunder from wrecks, and on occasion, to a small **coaster***. Later, the primary work of some east coast **hovellers** was cod and herring fishing, crabbing, and whelking. Raked ends. Half decked; some had a portable cabin forward. Oarports in top strakes. At Wells, a motorized version still works. About 6m long. Other recorded names: **hobble(r)**, **hoveler**, **hubbler**, **huffler***. Note also **Deal lugger**, **foyboat**, **lurky**, **Norfolk crabber**. Further reference: **Deal galley punt**

howa See **houri-1**

howker 1. Small- to medium-sized vessel that operated in northern Europe from the Middle Ages into the latter part of the 19th century. Early boats mainly used for fishing, later were also important as **merchantmen***. 16th-century vessels had curved, vertical stem; flat,

vertical transom below flat counter; flat sheer. Later, full bodied forward, square or rounded stern; curved stem, straight sternpost; round bottom; keel; deep hull. Open until the 16th century, then flush-decked. Early boats rowed or set a tall, square mainsail and small mizzen. During their primary period, they set square sails on the pole mainmast and sometimes a topgallant. At first, the mizzen was lateen-rigged, then gaff, often with a square topsail sheeted to a boom. Some had a third mast, a foremast stepped close to the bow, that also set square sails. Two or 3 jibs ran out on a long reeving bowsprit. Note also **hoekerbuis**, **jäger**, **koopvaardijhoeker**, **vishoeker**.
2. The term is sometimes used to describe a vessel with poor qualities, especially in France, where they were called **hourques**. Note also **hooker-1**.
Other recorded names: **heucre**, **heurque**, **hoecher**, **hoeckscepe**, **hoecker(-schip)**, **hoekboot**, **hoecschip**, **hoeker(schip)**, **hoicbort**, **hoockboot**, **hooker***, **houc(k)-boot**, **houcre**, **houkare**, **houkeboot**, **hou(c)ker**, **hourque**, **hukare***, **hukboit**, **Huker***, **hukker**, **huquer**, **Hurke**, **hurque**, **orca**, **oucre**, **ou(r)que**, **ucaro**, **urca***, **urque**

hoy 1. Small, sturdy **coaster*** that worked out of English Channel and North Sea ports and on navigable tributary rivers during the 15th-18th centuries. At the end of the 15th century, 2 Dutch/Belgian types, one with a single or no top strake above the wale, and a large, fully planked vessel of 80-100t (also known as a **bark*** or **berk**), served as offical communication vessels for Antwerp. Some early Dutch ships were naval vessels, and some did convoy duty in the late 17th century, going by the name **uitlegger** or **convoyer**. The 16th-century Dutch **heuden** (pl.) were carvel-planked, with bluff round bows, and probably a round stern. Low castle forward. Top strake extended beyond stern to form a triangular helm port. Large hatches. Spritsail to single mast, later added a topsail and a lateen mizzen; short bowsprit supported a flagstaff. Shallow draft. Early **hoys** carried a sprit mainsail and sprit or lateen topsail and 2 headsails; or might be square-, lug-, or gaff-rigged; a few were 3-masted. Leeboards might be employed, especially on the **heuden**. Some 17th-century inland vessels of the Low Countries set a single large spritsail. Called a **sloop*** in one place, a **smack*** in another, or even a **jacht***. Shallow draft; ca. 100-300t.
2. Term used in parts of Europe for a **barge*** or **lighter*** that transferred goods to and from ships close inshore.
3. *United Kingdom:* **a.** Early English **hoys** transported passengers and cargo along the coast and to the Continent; some were fishing **smacks***, and others small naval vessels serving as dockyard craft. Dated from at least the 15th to well into the 19th century. Some were Dutch **heuden** used by the Admiralty. English **hoys** were also employed in the American colonies. Because of their long period of operation and diverse uses, there was a great deal of variation in hull shape, dimensions, and rigging. Generally beamy with rounded bilges and marked tumble home; strong sheer. Bluff bow; pronounced stem and sometimes a fiddlehead; rounded counter; pronounced raked transom or pink stern; passenger **hoys** generally had a square stern. The cargo vessel had a very large main

hatch and a small after cabin. Steered with a tiller. Elizabethan **hoys** employed a high-peaked sprit mainsail, and on some, a lateen mizzen; later they set a standing-gaff mainsail with a long gaff, mainly loose-footed. Also hoisted a staysail, jib, and on some, a square topsail. Some later **hoys** stepped 2 masts. Maneuverability aided by oars, especially in late 16th-century vessels. Crew of 3-5. Reported dimensions range from 10.7m long, 3.5m wide to 23.5m by 5.7m by 2.4m deep. Note also **corn hoy, East India hoy, Margate hoy, Southampton hoy. b.** Can also be a large, rowed boat that ferried passengers between ships lying at anchor and shore.

4. *United States, E:* Term sometimes applied in the 19th century to a type of small boat on the Delaware River. Other recorded names: **bateau de passage, boyart, Dutch hoy, heu**★ (pl. **heus** or **heux**), **heude** (pl. **heuden**), **heudenaar, heudenaer, heudeschip, heue, heuscepe, heut, heuz, hode, hoe(scepe), hoey(e), hoie, hoigh, hooy-schip, hoye, hoyscepe, hu, hue(scepe), huedescepe, hueyscepe, hui, hulk**★, **hus, huy(e)**. Further reference: **Thames sailing barge**

hoy barge *United Kingdom:* A **barge**★ of the **Thames sailing barge**★ type that made regular trips, carrying a mixed cargo. Other recorded names: **goods barge, passage barge**

hoye See **hoy**

Hoylake nobby See **nobby**

hoyscepe See **hoy**

hsia kou t'ing See **ha kou ting**

Hsiang-chi bean pod, Hsiang-chi tou-k'ou, Hsinghsi-touk'ou See **Xiangji dou kou**

Hsiang-yang pien tzŭ See **bian zi**

Hsianmen chuan See **Amoy fisher**

hsiao-ch'i-pan See **hua chuan-3b**

hsiao-hsiang-hsia ch'uan See **xiao xiang xia chuan**

hsiao-hua ch'uan See **xiao hua chuan**

hsiao-ma-t'ou ch'uan See **xiao ma tou chuan**

hsiao san-pan ta-k'o See **hong tou san ban, sampan-3**

hsia t'ing See **ha ting**

hsia-yu ch'uan See **sampan-3**

hsin hua tzŭ See **hua zi-4**

hsun-ch'uan See **hong chuan**

hu 1. *India, NE:* Hü is a generic term for **boat**★ of the Khamti peoples of Arunachal Pradesh.
2. *New Caledonia, western Pacific:* Single-outrigger sailing **canoe**★ on the south part of Uvea (Ouvéa) Island in the Loyalty Islands group.
See also **hoy**.

huabigu See **hua pi gu**

hua chuan *China:* **1.** Generic term for a pleasure boat, notably those used by courtesans and for entertaining guests, widely known as **flower boats**. Early **hua chuans** described as small, **punt**★-like **fishing boats**★. Other recorded names: **bateau de fleurs, ho(u)a-tch'ouan, hwa ch'uan, pleasure boat, siao-houa tch'ouan**. Note also **chi-tong-t'eang**.

2a. Best known are those that lined the shores of the Zhu Jiang (Pearl River) at Guangzhou (Canton). The large type was an elaborate craft hired for festivals and banquets; singing girls provided entertainment. Low boat with blunt bow and swept-up stern. Ornate house covered

most of the hull, with a large salon, sleeping cabins, kitchen, etc. Propelled by 1-2 sweeps from the stern, or poled. Length ca. 25m, beam 5m. Other recorded names: **fa-schuen, fa teng**★, **fa t'ing, gaudy boat, ornamental boat**. Further reading: G. Schlegel, "A Canton Flower-Boat," *Internationales Archiv für Ethnographie* VII/I (1894), 1-9. **b.** Another type at Guangzhou was the **one-girl flower boat**, a brightly colored **sampan**★ that traveled the harbor in search of trade. Sculled from the stern by an elderly man. A similar type was used at Nanjing (Nanking).

3a. In the Nanjing area, a large type of **hua chuan**, called a **lou-zi** (or **-tzŭ**), was an open-sided "cafe" hired by the wealthy during the summer to traverse nearby lakes and rivers. Equipped with kitchen and tables, and in early days, with a bed. Flat bottom, snub nose, counter stern; rudder. Length ca. 10m. **b.** Also at Nanjing, there was a smaller type called **xiao qi ban (hsiao-ch'i-pan)** that had a single table. Length ca. 5.5m.
4. On the waterways surrounding Chengdou (Chengtu) on the Min Jiang and the upper Chang Jiang (Yangtze) tributary, a type of **hua chuan** was used to provide relief from the summer heat. Open deckhouse amidships, after part enclosed for the women. Gangway along the sides for the rowers; shallow but wide rudder came inboard on the open after deck. Length ca. 11m, beam 2.7m.
Further references: **long chuan, xiao hua chuan**

huampo *Chile, central:* **Dugout canoe**★ of the Araucanian people. Pointed and raised bow and stern. Maneuvered by 2 paddlers and a helmsman, all standing. Largest could transport as many as 30 persons. Spelling variants: **huampu**★, **wampu**

huampu *Bolivia/Peru:* Term for a **boat**★, **canoe**★, or **ship**★ by the Quechua and Aymara Indians. See also **balsa-4, huampo**.

Huang He chuan *China, N:* Roughly constructed vessel of the middle Huang He (Hwang-ho or Yellow River). Iron-clamped planking of irregular lengths and shapes; caulked with jute; strengthened with longitudinal beams and 2 bulkheads. Bow and stern flat, cross-planked, and raked inward; bottom flat. Open, but center compartment covered with matting when carrying passengers. Steered with a very long, crude sweep. Irregularly shaped mast stepped well forward; set a square sail, boomed at bottom. Tracked back upstream. Reported lengths 10-14m; e.g., length 13.7m, maximum beam 6m, depth 1.8m, shallow draft; cap. ca. 20t. Other recorded names: **Hoang-ho ch'uan, Hwang-ho ch'uan, Yellow River junk**

Huangho Dschunke See **Huang He chuan**

huang-shan See **wai pi gu**

hua-phi-ku See **hua pi gu**

hua pi gu *China, E:* Large **junk**★ designed to transport pine poles for scaffolding and pit props to ports north and south of Fuzhou (Foochow) in Fujian (Fukien) province; general cargo carried on the return trip. Short logs placed in the holds, longer poles on deck; still others were bundled up over the sides and secured by a hawser that ran under the hull and attached to the mainmast. Identified by the flared gunwales at the bow that formed wings as high as 3m above the deck;

flat bow terminated at deck level, leaving an open area between the wings; solid stemhead piece covered by an iron plate. Also characterized by its ornately decorated, elliptical, flat stern, earning the nickname **fa mei koo** (flowered buttocks); ornamentation style varied with the home port; large oculi. Hull constructed of a soft wood, frames and knees of a hard wood. Watertight compartments formed by transverse and longitudinal bulkheads; further strengthened by heavy wales at the waterline, which also served as bilge keels; lighter wales above. Fine entrance, sharp forefoot; flat floors; raked transom planked transversely for about half its depth. Rudder trunk ran up forward of this planking; when the large, very heavy, square rudder was lowered, it was secured by chains leading to a windlass at the bow. When raised, rudder stowed in the after castle. Deckhouse aft; high poop. Stepped 3 masts: forward-raking foremast in the eyes, mainmast amidships, light mizzen off midline aft of the poop. Set balanced lug-sails of white or brown cloth; boomed at the foot; rounded leech, straight luff; foresail hung to port side of the mast, main and mizzen to starboard. Crew of 20-35. Reported lengths 18-62m, widths 5-9m. Other recorded names: **Foochow pole** (or **stock**) **junk**, **Fouchou-Pfahl-Dschunke**, **Fou tcheou pole**, **Fuchow pole junk**, **Fuchow timber freighter**, **Fuzhou pole junk**, **huabigu**, **hua-phi-ku**, **hua-p'i-ku**

hua-p'i-ku See **hua pi gu**

huari See **houari**

hua thing See **lorcha-3**

hua-tzŭ See **hua zi**

hua zi *China:* A term meaning literally "small boat," and accordingly applied to a variety of smaller Chinese craft, a number of which fall into the **sampan★** category, while others are small **junks★**. A few types are described below: Spelling variants: **hoa-tse**, **hua-tzŭ**

1. A 2-masted trading **junk** of Jiangxi (Kiangsi) province that carries local products, tobacco, medicines, bamboo, ramie, etc., to and from central Chang Jiang (Yangtze) ports and Poyang Hu (lake). Square ends; stern sweeps up sharply, low freeboard amidships. Cabin house aft. Masts stepped in forward third of the vessel, setting tall, straight-leeched lugsails. 7-30t.

2. The **jing bang hua zi** (**ching-pang hua-tzŭ**) group works out of the middle Chang Jiang port of Shashi (Shasi), and includes quite small craft to medium-sized trading **junks**. One of the larger types is a sturdy, beamy vessel with square ends, the bow shovel-nosed and the stern swept up with a high sheer. High sides; flat bottom; heavy wales along the sides; inboard balanced rudder. Decked; wooden cabin with mat roof covers after two-thirds of the hull and is divided into two. Mainly sailed; single mast sets a tall, balance lug-sail with straight leech and curved luff. Often poled, the polers walking along the side decks; also rowed using long sweeps. Crew of 2-10. Reported lengths 16-24.5m; e.g., length 16.8m, beam 3.4m, depth 1.4m, cap. ca. 20t. Name variant: **Shasi trader**

3. The **Yichang** (**I-Ch'ang**) **hua zi** works in this central Chang Jiang port ferrying passengers across the river and between shore and the large **junks** anchored in the river; type found as far east as Shashi. Constructed mainly of cypress; narrow, square, overhanging bow; wings extend beyond the transom stern; flat bottom with rocker; hull becomes shallower toward the bow. Decked forward; shallow hold aft; mat awning, set on poles, covers the hold area. Propelled by 2 long stern oars and a bow oar; rudder shipped when working close to shore. Reported lengths 6.4-9m, beam ca. 1.8m. Name variant: **I-ch'ang sampan**

4. The **xin hua zi** (**hsin hua tzŭ** or **sin hua tzŭ**) was a post boat that worked downstream on the upper Chang Jiang until 1905; the trip took 12-15 days to Yichang (I-Ch'ang), where the boat was sold. Narrow square bow; raked transom stern. Watertight, wooden house amidships; crew lived aft of the house in a mat shelter. Steered with a long sweep; rowed from the bow. Crew of 4-5. Note also **jiao hua chuan**.

hubbler See **hoveller**, **Norfolk crabber**

hubot See **flûte**

huche, hucheste, huchet, huchette See **vivier**

húŏ-keipr See **kayak-3**

Hudson River brick schooner *United States, NE:* **Scow-schooner★** type built and operated in the late 19th century, mainly on the Hudson River; some in New England. Square-ended; flat-bottomed; many flush-decked, the bricks carried on deck. Some employed leeboards or a centerboard. **Schooner★**-rigged with large jib to a bowsprit. Beamy; shallow draft. Other recorded names: **bricker**, **North River bricker**

Hudson River shad boat *United States, E:* **1.** Round-bottomed **rowing boat★** of the 19th and early 20th centuries that worked nets staked out in the river to catch the spring shad run. Carvel-planked except for the sheer strake that lapped the adjacent strake. Very fine bow with hackmatack knee stem that curved in its lower half; slightly raked, wide wineglass transom secured to a hackmatack knee. Outer part of stem and sternpost shod with iron for protection in beaching; full afterbody. Moderate sheer, low freeboard, with stern higher on some. Oak keel, sharply rounded at heel, deadwood aft, moderate deadrise, hard bilges. Open; natural crook frames; net box placed at the stern. Crew of 1-3. Reported lengths 5.5-5.8m; e.g., length 5.6m, beam 1.48m, depth 0.8m, draft light 15cm. Name variant: **shad skiff**

2. Present-day **shad boats★** are flat-bottomed, beamy **skiffs★** powered with an outboard motor in a forward well. Square stern, high sides, wide side decks. Crew of 3. Length 6m.

Hudson River sloop *United States, E:* Beamy, low-sided vessel that dominated traffic on the Hudson River from the mid-17th to near the end of the 19th century. Some were fast, elegant **packet sloops** running passengers and light freight to points along the river on a regular schedule; others carried mainly cargo (**freight** or **market sloops**). Toward the end of the period, some traded with the West Indies. Most carvel-planked. Bluff bows flared at the waterline; raked stem; long, flat run aft; wide, flat transom with windows; high stern provided cabin headroom. Flat floors with keel; early boats used 1-2 leeboards; centerboard adopted during the 18th century. Rudder worked through rudder trunk by a tiller. Decked;

passenger cabin aft, crew's quarters in forecastle; main hatch abaft the mast; taffrail around the stern; **yawl boat★** hung from stern davits. Upper strake painted in contrasting colors; characteristic red and white pennant flown from masthead. Tall mast stepped well forward. Large mainsail, with short gaff and long boom, sheeted to a traveler at taffrail; lazy jacks confined lowered sail; large jib, often boomed; heavy bowsprit. Originally used a square topsail, later a gaff topsail. Last vessels built were **schooner★**-rigged. Crew of 2-6, more required for long voyages. Reported lengths 16-27m; e.g., length 20.4m, beam 7.6m, depth 1.8m. Other recorded names: **market boat★**, **North River sloop**. Further reading: Paul E. Fontenoy, *The Sloops of the Hudson River. A Historical and Design Survey* (Mystic, Conn.: Mystic Seaport Museum, 1994).

Hudson's Bay bateau, Hudson's Bay boat See **York boat**

Hudson's Bay canoe See **canot du maître**

Hudson's Bay pointer See **pointer**

hue, huedescepe See **hoy**

huelec See **hulk-1**

huescepe, hueyescepe See **hoy**

huffler *England, SE:* Worked until the mid-20th century, providing a person to assist (huffle) in the passage of **Thames sailing barges★** through the bridge at Rochester on the River Medway. The boat came alongside the **barge** and was towed, while the boatman went aboard to help lower and raise the mainmast at the bridge. Clinker-built, curved stem, straight sternpost. Open; outboard rudder; tiller. Painted black, white top strake; individual insignia on mainsail. Standing lugsail set to the mainmast stepped through a forward thwart. Balance lug mizzen to the mizzenmast which stepped on the after side of the rudder; after end of boom lashed to the tiller. Also rowed with single pair of oars through double tholepins. Sails abandoned by 1920s. Average length 4.3m. See also **hoveller**.

hugette See **vivier**

huhunu See **waka unua**

hui See **hoy**

huideschip, huisier, huisiere, huisserium, huisserius See **huissier**

huissier General term in medieval French for a vessel designed primarily to transport horses. In the Mediterranean area, the spelling was **usciere★** (or variants), while **visser** was the more common word in English. Usually referred to in association with naval operations, but some carried passengers with their horses and carriages, or might transport cattle, sheep, and sometimes lumber. Existed to the end of the Middle Ages. The basic **huissier** was the primary type vessel in use at the time. Often modified for specific purposes (see **chelandia** and **tarida**). In order to maneuver the vessel stern-first to the beach, oars were preferable and a stern port and ramp enabled the horses, sometimes with the cavalrymen mounted, to exit directly to the shore (the **galea oberte per popa**). The port was blocked and sealed during the voyage. Later sailing vessels offloaded directly onto a wharf from the side and were

used for more peaceful purposes. Generally 2 decks—the horse stalls on one deck, and the provisions, wheeled vehicles, siege equipment, and supplies on the other deck. In later years, the horses were supported by slings. In the late 13th century, the vessels also had a poop and forecastle. The sailing vessels had 1-2 masts, setting lateen sails or a square foresail. Carried ca. 40 horses, but reported to carry as many as 100. Other recorded names: **at gemisi, hoissier, horse carrier, huideschip, huisier(e), huisserium, huisserius, nave trasporto cavalli, nave uscheria (or usellería, usseria, usuraria), navire huissier, oissier, oxir, portechevaux, ueserius, uffer, uis(s)er, uissiere, uissieré, uixer, 'usārī, usario, usarius, uscerium, usc(h)e-rius, uscheri(a), usciera, usciero, usiae, usicherius, ussaria, usscher, usser(ia), usserie, usserius, ussler, usuraria, uxel, ux(l)er, uxorius, vissier, vuissier**; pl. **oxirii, uscerii, uscieri, usseri, usuriae, uxerii**. Further reading: J. H. Pryor, "Transportation of Horses by Sea During the Era of the Crusades: Eighth Century to 1285 A.D.," *The Mariner's Mirror* 68 (1982), 9-27, 103-125. Note also **nef-1, tafurea**.

huit de couple See **scull**

huit de pointe See **shell-2**

Huizer botter See **botter**

hukare *Sweden:* Type of 18th-century merchant **howker★**. Stepped 2 masts, the mainmast carrying 3 square sails and a gaff sail; the mizzen a gaff sail and on the large vessels, a topsail. Two jibs to a long, rising bowsprit. An 1750s vessel was ca. 120rt. Name variant: **hukare jagt**. Further reference: **bilander-1**

hukare jagt See **hukare**

hukboet See **Huker**

hukboit See **howker**

Hukboot See **hooker-1, Huker**

Hukeboht, Hukeboot See **Huker**

Huker *Germany:* Seaworthy cargo vessel employed in the North and Baltic Seas. Some served as **lighters★**. Recorded from the mid-12th century. Full ends with sharp waterline; straight sides; long keel; flat floors with short, rounded bilges; strong sheer. Decked; generally a trunk cabin; planked bulwark or open railing; 2 windows at the stern. Narrow outboard rudder. Variety of rigs. On the so-called **Einmast-Huker**, the mainmast carried top- and topgallant masts to which square sails were set forward and a gaff sail abaft the mast; a short mizzen set a gaff sail and topsail. Others set square sails on the fore- and mainmasts, plus a gaff sail on the mainmast. Some 3-masted. Length on keel of a 1795 vessel 27m, beam 7m, hold depth 2.5m. Other recorded names: **hukboet, Hukboot, Hukeboht, Hukeboot, Hukkerschiff, Hukkert★**; pl. **Hukern**. Note also **hooker, Hukergaleass, Hukerjacht**. Further reference: **howker**

Hukerbuise See **hoekerbuis**

Hukergaleass *Germany, Baltic coast/Poland:* Cargo vessel, especially of Pomerania, including present-day western Poland; first cited in the mid-18th century and used through the 19th century, mainly to carry timber. Largest type of **Galeass★**. Sharp, keel-built vessel along the lines of the **Huker★**. Stepped a tall mainmast, usually with topmast, and topgallant mast; square sails bent to yards forward of the mast and a gaff sail abaft the mast. Mizzenmast carried gaff sail and topsail. Also set a staysail, jibs, and studding sail. Crew of 8. Length 22.8m, beam 6.8m, depth 3.63m, 169rt. Spelling variant: **Hukergaleasse**

Hukergaleasse See **Hukergaleass**

Hukerjacht *Germany:* A single-masted boat, cited in the 19th century, that engaged in lobster fishing. Mast carried both a square and gaff sail. Note also **Huker**.

Hukern See **Huker**

hukker See **howker**

Hukkerschiff See **Huker**

hukkert *Denmark:* 19th-century 2- or 3-masted **hooker★**. Rounded stern; strong sheer. The **hukkertgalease** had main- and mizzenmasts, jiggerboom and bowsprit. The mainmast set square sails plus a gaff sail. The mizzenmast set a gaff sail; when topsails were set to a mizzen topmast, the vessel became a **krydshukkert-galease**. When a foremast was stepped, it was square-rigged. A fishing **hukkert** with similar but lower rigging was a **fiskerhukkert**. 18th-century vessels 60-120t; fishing type ca. 40t. See also **Huker**.

hukkertgalaease See **hukkert**

hukunu See **waka unua**

hulc, hulce, hulch, hulci, hulck See **hulk-1**

huliya *Bangladesh, SW/India, NE:* Large, beamy, open boat that transported timber and other cargo. Some worked in the Sundarbans area. Bluff bow and stern; heavy, elongated, block stem turned up at each end and notched at the top. Numerous beams crossed the hull and projected out below the top strake. Hand windlass spanned the bow end. Steered with a large sweep. Other recorded names: **khoolea, wood boat★**

hulk 1. Merchantman★ or man-of-war★ of northern Europe, first mentioned in the 8th century. Underwent considerable transformation up to the 16th century. Initially a **coaster★** and local **riverboat★**. The oldest type had rocker in a bottom rising to narrow ends; by the 14th century, had a keel with stem and sternpost; floors later became flat and wide. Probably clinker-planked initially, carvel by the 15th century. Hinged, stern rudder as early as the 12th century. Loose superstructure or castles forward and aft by the 13th century; decked during the 14th century; castles incorporated into the hull construction by the 15th century and built with several decks and flat stern. Rigged with up to 4 masts, the fore- and mainmasts setting square sails, the after 2 masts setting lateen sails. Topsails on 3 or 4 masts. Reported lengths 15-33m; cap. 1,200t by the 16th century. Spelling variants: **halk, halque, helk, heurque, hol(e)che, holic, holke, holk(er), holkr, holli(c)h, hol(l)ik, houcre, houlc, houlel, houlque, hourque, huelec, hulc(e), hulch, hulci, hulck, hulke, hullich, hulloc** (dim.), **hulque, hurte, khul'k, oulque, skáfos**; Dutch and German pl. **hulken**. Note also **hooker**.
2. A large and heavy ship of clumsy build may be spoken of as a **hulk**.
3. An old vessel that is no longer seaworthy, generally stripped of rigging and other means of propulsion. Such a vessel may serve as a store ship, temporary accommodation for seamen, a training ship, a quarantine station, or a prison (**prison hulk** or on the Thames

in England, **floating academy**). Other recorded names: **Blockschiff, blokschiv, casco arrumbado, Lagerhulk, navire condamné, ponton★, Speicherschiff**. Note also **pontoon-6, sheer hulk**.
4. Term applied in the 18th century to a square-rigged vessel engaged in herring fishing.
5. *Netherlands:* The **hulk** of the 8th-10th centuries was a round-bottomed, keelless boat probably used primarily on rivers. Loaded and off-loaded its cargo from the beach or riverbank. Bottom a single expanded log, curved up smoothly to small end transoms well above the waterline; strong sheer. Side planks lapped and tapered toward the transom, pegged; heavy wale covered the seam; multiple heavy floor timbers. Probably decked. Stepped a single mast, either for sailing or towing; employed 2 quarter rudders. The **Utrecht ship**, considered a **hulk**, is 17.8m long, 4m wide, 1.3m deep, draft 0.8m.
Further references: **carrack, coble-1d, hoy**

hulke, hulken See **hulk-1**

Hulk mit Mastenkran See **sheer hulk**

hullich See **hulk-1**

Hull lobster boat See **lobster boat-4b**

hulloc, hulque See **hulk-1**

hulu See **barque Djenné, cayuco-5**

hulúgua See **cayuco-5**

huma fandarga See **galiot**

Humber canoe-yawl See **canoe-yawl**

Humber gold-duster See **gold-duster**

Humber gun punt See **gun punt**

Humber keel *England, NE:* Bluff, square-sailed **lighter★** of the Humber Estuary and Yorkshire waterways and canals. Carried raw materials inland and manufactured goods downstream for export. Probably dates to the 13th century; worked until World War II. Initially clinker-built sides, later carvel; some reported clinker-planked except for the top 3-4 strakes; last constructed of iron or steel. Flat bottom; massive keelson, wide keel extended ca. 76cm below the bottom; hard, round bilges; straight sides; ceiled. Rounded ends; deep, vertical stem and sternpost. Stem projected above the deck; a hawser hole to starboard, anchor hole to port. Alternate timberheads at bow and stern formed stanchions capped by a rail; intermediate timberheads served as bitts. Decked at bow and stern; long cargo hold between, cambered cover and tarpaulin; narrow waterways; cabins forward and aft. Outboard rudder; long tiller, but on canals substituted a short iron tiller to avoid fouling lock sides. Triangular leeboards unshipped in shallow waterways. Tarred below the waterline; gunwales and freeboard brightly varnished; rails and timberheads painted. Those working in non-tidal waterways did not sail, but were horse- or man-towed, leaving their masts ashore. Elsewhere, a very tall pole mast stepped onto the bottom a little forward of center; fitted into a tabernacle, and was raised or lowered by a winch or roller. Pennant atop the mast. Large, white square sail edged with rope and stropped to its yard; some carried a topsail, set flying, and occasionally a topgallant. Sail could be shortened by clewlines to haul the sail up toward the yard. Standing rigging consisted of a heavy forestay (which was also used to lower and raise the mast), a backstay, 2 main shrouds, and one topmast shroud. In the 19th century, a bowsprit and jib occasionally used; some on the River Trent set a lug mizzen. Crewed by a family or a man and boy.

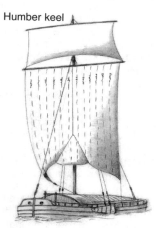

Humber keel

Reported lengths 17-25m, the size determined by the dimensions of the locks in the vessel's area of operation; typically 19m long, 4.7m wide, and 2.44m deep. The tidal **keels** of Yorkshire waterways were shallower than the Humber vessels. Smaller upriver **keels**, with a lighter mast and no topsail or leeboards, were known as **catches** or **ketches***; cap. ca. 65t. Other recorded names: **Humber ship**, **Sheffield boat** or **keel** (designed to travel inland to Sheffield); the **Lincoln(shire) keel** had dimensions to fit those waterways; the **Beverley keel** traversed the upper River Hull; the **Barnsley keel** fit the Barnsley canal requirements. Further reading: Fred Schofield, *Humber Keels and Keelmen* (Lavenham: Terence Dalton, Ltd., 1988). Note also **cog boat**, **Yorkshire keel**.

Humber ship See **Humber keel**

Humber sloop *England, NE:* Plied the Humber Estuary and Lincolnshire waterways and coasted as far as the Thames. Dredged for sand and gravel and carried bulk cargo and produce. Developed in the late 18th century; some were **Humber keels*** that had exchanged their square rig for a fore-and-aft rig. A few survived through World War II. Double-ended, boxy shape of the **Humber keel**, carvel- or clinker-planked, flat floors, wall-sided; most of oak, some of steel; the latter less blunt in form. Pronounced sheer, especially forward; little freeboard when loaded. Generally a long cambered hatch amidships; on some, the hatch continued forward of the mast or was a separate hatch; decked at bow and stern, narrow side decks; stores housed in the forecastle; tiny cabin aft. **Sand sloops** had an open hold. Leeboards worked with tackles; heavy rudder; strong, arched, and carved tiller; taffrail. Hulls made glossy with a coat of coal tar; deck fittings brightly colored, some gilded. Towed a **cog boat***. Boomed, loose-footed gaff mainsail hooped to the mast, sheeted through 2 blocks, and secured just forward of the helmsman; raised by winches; later steel vessels used roller halyards; sail flat-peaked prior to 1914. Gaff almost as long as the boom. Foresail sometimes fitted with a boom and traveled across an iron horse. Mast in tabernacle above the deck. Early **sloops*** fitted with a heavy bowsprit, and jib ran on a stay; also used a flying jib; bowsprit could be run in or swung up when in dock. Some added a jackyard topsail to a short topmast. On canal trips, they might stow the mast ashore and hoist a square sail to a derrick pole. Main-

sail dressed with mixture of horse fat and ochre. Crewed by 2-3 or sometimes by a family. Reported lengths 17.3-20.7m; e.g., length 20.7m, beam 5.26m, depth 2.5m; light draft; average cap. 160t. Other recorded names: **Barton sloop** (one built at Barton-upon-Humber), **Lincolnshire sloop**

Humber yawl See **canoe-yawl**

Hummerboot *Germany, W:* Caught lobsters, in baskets, off Helgoland Island as late as the 1960s. Open, strongly built, partly clinker. Flat floors, chines, parallel sides, deep gunwale, heavy frames. Bluff, flaring bows; plumb stem, rounded stern. Two thwarts; sometimes a small cuddy. Originally set a small lugsail, but rowed at the lobstering sites. Motors installed during the 2nd quarter of the 20th century. Reported lengths 4.64-6.1m; large types to ca. 10m; 1945 boat 4.64m length overall, 4.45m on keel, beam 1.55m, depth 0.6m. Name variant: **Helgoländer Hummerboot**

humpback junk See **dao ba zi-2**

Humpelnachen *Germany, SW:* Cumbersome, boxy cargo vessel of the Main, Neckar, and middle Rhine Rivers. Dated from at least the mid-15th and lasted until the mid-19th century. Flat bottom; shallow draft made them suitable for fluctuating water levels. Ends curved up; low sides raised with washboards; open. Cap. 20-60t. Note also **Nachen-1**.

hun See **huntin**

Hundestedbåd See **Isefjordbåd**

hundred-and-twenty piece boat See **York boat**

hundromsbåt See **færing-6**

hundromsfæring See **færing-5**, **færing-6**

hung ch'uan See **hong chuan**

hung-hsieh tzŭ, **hung hsiu-hsieh** See **fu diao zi**

hung jou ch'uan See **hong rou chuan**

hung t'ou See **hong tou**

hung-t'ou ch'uan See **hong tou chuan**

hung-t'ou san-pan See **hong tou san ban**

hung-tu-shuan See **Kiangsu trader**

hunten See **huntin**

huntin *Benin (formerly Dahomey):* **Canoe*** (*hun*) hewn from a log (*tin*) cut in the forest and carried out to the

huntin

water, accompanied by special rituals. Log now often obtained from southern Nigeria. Used mainly for family fishing and transportation. Overhanging extension at the stern; pointed bow; usually no thwarts. Poled by the husband, paddled by his wife; when sailed, sets a small, square sail to a "V" mast. Reported lengths 4-5m, widths 0.5-0.6m; some to 12m long. Spelling variants: **hountin**, **hun**, **hunten**

hunting kayak See **kayak-3**

hunting punt *United States, E:* Used to hunt game on shore in the Chesapeake Bay area. Gun mounted near the bow, often behind a light used to illuminate the game. Square-raked ends, flat bottom, straight sides, end decks. Poled and rowed. Length ca. 4.6m, narrow.

hunu, hunua See **waka unua**

huquer See **howker**

hurca See **urca-2**

hūri See **houri-1, shū·ai**

hurija *Kuwait:* Craft constructed of midstems of date palm leaves. Stalks buried in moist beach sand for many days to make them pliable. Bottom and flooring created by bundles of stalks, with layers of the butt

hurija

ends of the palm leaves placed in between to serve as flotation. Sides built up onto bamboo "ribs." Pointed ends formed by drawing bottom stems upward and bundling them together with the side stems. Boat not caulked, and water seeps in between the bottom and the floor. Generally rowed with 2 oars, each secured by a rope to a tholepin. Lateen sail may be set to a light mast; sailed in either direction. Reported lengths 2-3m. Spelling variations: **hawayriyah, huwairiyah, huwayriyah, wahriyah, wairjíyah, warjiwa, warraga**; pl. **waráji, wargiyeh**. Further reading: R. LeB. Bowen, "Primitive Watercraft of Arabia," *American Neptune* XIII (1952), 194-196. Note also **farteh, shashah-1**.

Hurke See **howker**

Huron boat *Great Lakes of Canada and United States:* Roomy, 2-masted boat used for gill net fishing in the latter part of the 19th and early 20th centuries. Used on most of the lakes, but was especially popular on the eastern shore of Lake Michigan. Most clinker-built, although the **Carver** and **Haywood** boats were carvel-planked. Generally a high, wide, plumb transom, but some had a short counter, and a few had fantail sterns. Plumb stem, a few clipper bows. Slight drag to the keel; short run. Open or half-decked; stern sheets; centerboard. Foremast stepped in the eyes and slightly taller than the mainmast. Most gaff-rigged; generally boomed, but foresail might be loose-footed; a few sprit-rigged. Jib to a bowsed-down bowsprit popular on the Canadian side. Sails usually tanned after a few years. Reported lengths 6-12m; e.g., length 10m, beam 2.8m, depth 1.2m; light draft. Other recorded names: **Lake Huron boat, square-stern boat, Wheeler boat**

hurque See **howker**

hurte See **hulk**

hus See **hoy**

husbåd See **houseboat-1**

husbåt *Norway, N:* Built in the first half of the 19th century in the Rana district. Large living quarters aft enabled touring government officials to live aboard. Oarsmen sat forward of the cabin, usually on 6 rowing benches. Spelling variant: **huusbaad**. Note also **skyss-båt**. Further reference: **houseboat-1**

hutch boat See **hatch boat-2**

Hutt boat See **Cape Island boat**

huuri See **houri-3**

huusbaad See **husbåt**

huwairiyah, huwayriyah See **hurija**

huy, huye See **hoy**

hvalbåd See **whaleboat-1**

hvalbåt See **whale catcher**

hvalerbaat See **hvalerbåt**

hvalerbåt *Norway, SE:* General term for boats built in the Hvaler Islands, but boats of the type were also found on the west side of the Skaggerak. The **kosterbåt*** in adjacent Sweden is essentially the same type. Used mainly in the 19th century for fishing in the North Sea, for local piloting, and for cargo transport. Also a popular pleasure craft. Decked boats of the latter half of the 19th century may be called **hvaler-skøytene** (pl.). Clinker-planked with treenails. Drag to the keel; garboards almost vertical, then planking flattened out with a soft turn of the bilge into flaring sides. Sharp, full ends; curved stem with cutaway forefoot; curved sternpost, raking sharply below the waterline. Outboard rudder; tiller might be worked from a steering well. Originally open, later decked or half-decked. Usually had a low railing or washstrake along the sides; **fishing boats*** might have a roller forward for the nets. Early boats set a spritsail, staysail, and jib. Later, adopted a loose-footed, boomed gaff sail, topsail, staysail, jib to a long bowsprit. Reported lengths 8.5-10.6m; 1860s boat 8.5m long, 3m wide, 0.9m draft. Other recorded names: **hvalerbaat, hvaloerbåt, hvalöer-sköite, hvalorbaad, hvalörbåt, hvalörsjote, hvalørskjøite, hvalorskøyte, valörbåt, Whale Islands boat**. Note also **losbåt-1, redningsskøyte, skøyte-1**.

hvalerskøyte See **hvalerbåt**

hvalfanger See **whaler**

hvaloerbåt, hvalöer-sköite, hvalorbaad, hvalörbåt, hvalørsjoite, hvalörsjote, hvalorskøyte See **hvalerbåt**

hvassing *Sweden, SW:* Open boat of Bohuslan that assisted the **bankskuta*** in setting trawl lines. Also engaged in coastal fishing for haddock and bait. Clinker-planked; rising floors; sharp bow; curved, raking stem, V-shaped transom; square-footed outboard rudder, tiller. Set a rectangular spritsail, jib to small, adjustable bowsprit. Also rowed with long oars. Length 6.6m, beam 2.5m, depth 1.1m. Other recorded names: **kak, kvassing**

hwa ch'uan See **hua chuan-1**

Hwang-ho ch'uan See **Huang He chuan**

hwa t'ing See **lorcha-3**

hwetakla, hwetukla See **northern-style canoe**

hwongjævere See **havbåd**

hyac See **yacht**

Hylam junk See **Hainan trader**

iac See **yack**

iacco, iachet, Iacht See **yacht**

iachte See **jakt-2**

iacq See **yacht**

iaegschuytie See **trekschuit-3**

iakatoi See **lakatoi**

ialik See **yalik**

ialoer *Indonesia, W:* Boat used on Simeulue Island off the west coast of Sumatra for transportation on rivers and at sea. One type is a plank-extended **dugout canoe★** that is paddled. Blunt, raised ends. On the west coast, another type is a planked craft propelled by long oars from 4-5 thwarts. Spelling variant: **ialur**. Note also **jalor**.

ialur See **ialoer**

iama See **wa'a kaulua**

ianga See **janga**

iangada See **jangada-2, jangar**

iangar See **jangar**

iaque See **yacht**

iar See **igá**

iar-uhu See **batelão-4**

iat *Brazil, NE:* **Bark canoe** of the Emerillon, a Tupí tribe.

iate 1. *Brazil, NE:* Two-masted trader that sails out of Salvador (Bahia) and other ports on the northeast coast. Term now used loosely for any pleasure craft. Raked stem with gammon knee; sheer sweeps up toward the bow; raked transom stern. Flat bottom, some with keel; hard turn of the bilges. Outboard rudder; tiller. Decked;

iate-1

sometimes 2 deckhouses, 1 forward and 1 abaft the mainmast. Boomed gaff sails, gaffs sometimes almost horizontal; at times, gaff topsails on one or both masts. Two headsails, the foresail boomed. Reported lengths 14-23m; e.g., length 14.6m, beam 4m, depth 1.0m.

2. Portuguese generic for **yacht★**; also spelled **hiate★**.

3. *Portugal:* A 2-masted **coaster★** that reportedly still works out of several ports, notably Setúbal on the central coast. Sweeps up to a clipper-bow; sharp stern. Mainmast rakes aft; sometimes carries an extension used for signal flags; foremast vertical. Mainmast sets a boomed, loose-footed gaff sail; foresail loose-footed. May use a single jib to a bowsprit or multiple headsails to bowsprit and jib-boom. Some lateen-rigged with 2 masts, the mainmast raking aft. Crew of 6-8. About 120t cap.

iato *Samoa, central Pacific:* Term for a small **dugout canoe★**. Used mainly for fishing inside reefs.

'iato fa, 'iato lima, 'iato ono, 'iato va See **soatau**

iba See **ubá-1**

ibabura See **imbabura**

ib-gá See **igá**

iblâm See **belem**

ibri See **'abari**

ičájuta *Mexico, central:* Small **dugout canoe★** found at Lake Pátzcuaro and nearby lakes. Made from fir or pine and used by the Tarascan Native Americans for inshore fishing and transportation. Bottom flat fore-and-aft and athwartships; sides unparallel with slight

ičájuta

tumble home. Square ends overhang. Carries 1-4 people. Paddled solo with a round-bladed paddle. Reported lengths 2.4-6.4m, beam ca. 0.6m, depth 0.4m. Spelling variants: **icháruta, ycha-ruta**. Note also **tepári**.

iceboat 1. A boat with runners on the bottom designed to cross both water and ice. More often refers to a very fast 1- or 2-man racing craft used solely on ice; early **iceboats** might require a crew of 10. The early type consisted of a cross or T-shaped framework mounted on 3 metal runners, one at each end of the crossbar, that creates a double outrigger. The 3rd, either at the front or back, serves as a rudder and is maneuvered by a tiller. Racing boats usually **sloop★**-rigged with shrouds from the masthead to the outer end of the runner plank. Used mainly in the northeast and north-central United States and adjacent Canada; also in northern Europe. Largest might be 15m long; most ca. 3.7-4.6m. Other recorded names: **bateau brise-glace** (or **traineau**), **battello a slitta** (or **da ghiaccio**), **Eisboot★, Eisjacht, Eisyacht, ice yacht, iisjagt, isjakt, ispigg, jääpursi, Schlittenboot, Segelschlitten, sledge boat, slitta a vela, traineau à voile, voilier à patins** (or **sur glace**), **ys-jacht**. Note also **canot à glace, Eiskahn, flat-2, ice canoe, iessjuut, ijs-schuitje, isbåt, iseka, scooter, wind sled**.

2. A commercial **fishing boat★** equipped with facilities for icing or refrigerating fresh fish or crustaceans.

3. *Barbados, West Indies:* Offshore **fishing boat** equipped with an insulated ice hold, enabling the boat to stay at sea. Developed in the 2nd half of the 20th century. Sharp, concave bow; square stern, deck- and wheelhouse forward. Inboard engine. Length ca. 12m.

4. *United Kingdom:* Used on the smaller canals to break up winter ice. Dates from at least the early 19th century; originally of sheathed wood, then iron, and by the mid-20th century, of steel. Generally sharp-ended with cutaway forefoot; bow reinforced; some square-ended with considerable bow rake. Sharp-ended boats rounded in cross section; square-ended had a flat bottom. Flat sheer; open. Some had a single sturdy post amidships, others had 2 posts with a rail or taut rope

between; post or rail used by crew, standing on planking, to rock the boat and break the ice. Some boats were rocked by shifting weight against side railings. Long tiller; rudder wide-bladed below the waterline. Towed, mainly by horses; sometimes as many as 26; a few had engines. Crew of 3-8. Reported lengths 4.6-14.6m; shallow draft. Other recorded names: **ice breaker***, **rocking boat**
Further references: **Chênhai chuan, mail boat-2, New Orleans lugger**

ice box See **sinkbox**

ice breaker Vessel designed and constructed to enable it to forge a navigable channel, generally by riding up onto the ice with a specially shaped bow and crushing the ice. Heavily plated and with special strengthening; powerful engine. Those used on canals were towed by horses. Usually relatively beamy. Some **tugs*** have ice-breaking capabilities. Modern **ice breakers** may have a screw forward to pull the water out from under the ice to help collapse it. Selected name variants: **brise glace, Eisbrecher, ice breaking tug, iisbräkker, ijsbreker*, isbryder, isbrytande bogserbåt, isbrytare, isbryter, lekokol, uitbijten**. Note also **iceboat-3, scow-brig**. Further reference: **iceboat-4**

ice breaking tug See **ice breaker**

ice canoe *Canada, E:* Amphibious craft used in winter to ferry passengers, mail, and freight. Use dates at least to the mid-17th century. Popular on the St. Lawrence River; one reported to have carried 20 passengers. Sturdily built; iron runners on the bottom. Sometimes raced. **Dugout canoes*** called **ice canoes** were used by the fur traders in the fall months when ice had formed. Name variant: **winter canoe**

ice punt *United States, NE:* **1.** On Raquette Lake in the Adirondack Mountains of northern New York State, a special **ice punt** transported supplies to winter camps. Square ends; 2 runners attached to the edge of the flat bottom. Pushed by a skater who held a type of raised handle bar. Length 3.7m, beam 1.0m, depth 0.46m.
2. On the upper St. Lawrence River, **ice punts** crossed the river between the U.S. and Canada and provided communication in winter and summer with the Thousand Islands; some carried mail (**mail punt**). Usually built by farmers on both shores. Generally had square ends of roughly equal width, although some later boats had a wide transom to support an outboard motor for crossing open water. Bottom often had rocker and was sheathed with metal; also had runners. Projecting handles at the stern used to push the boat across the ice, or the craft might be "walked" by 4 men holding handles at each corner and by others pushing athwartships poles. In open water, some set a sail; spritsail common but also used a gaff sail. Often rowed, the oars slotted over tholepins. Reported lengths 4-6.7m; dimensions of one that worked between Kingston, Ontario, and Garden Island: length 6.7m, beam 1.4m, depth 0.5m. **Ice punts** are now sleek boats powered by an airplane engine at the stern; square bow curves up smoothly from the wide, flat bottom; decked forward, terminating in a windshield. Other recorded names: **Garden Island ice boat, in and outer, in and out ice boat, punt*, push punt**

ice schooner *United States, E:* **Schooners*** carried ice cut from Maine rivers to ports along the east coast in

the 19th century. Ice packed in sawdust; for ports north of Cape Hatteras, a thick layer of meadow hay was spread on top. Average trip took 2 weeks. Many returned to New England with coal. Mainly 3- and 4-masted. Name variant: **freezer**

ice schooner-barge See **schooner-barge-2**

ice scooter See **scooter-1**

ice skiff *Canada, E:* Seal-hunting boat used during the 19th century in Newfoundland coastal waters from March to June. Usually open. Reported lengths 9-12m.

ice yacht See **iceboat-1**

I-Ch'ang bo chuan See **bo chuan-2**

I-Ch'ang hua-zi See **hua zi-3**

I-Ch'ang lung ch'uan See **long chuan**

I-Ch'ang po-ch'uan See **bo chuan-2**

I-Ch'ang sampan See **hua zi-3**

icháruta See **ičájuta**

ichikondo *Zambia, N:* Bark craft of the Lamba and Lala peoples. Ends of a roll of bark of the *umuputu* tree, ca. 3.66m long, are placed in fire to soften. When pliable, the ends are doubled up and secured with wooden skewers. Sticks inserted transversely at intervals along the top edge keep the craft open. Cracks plugged with clay.

ichombo See **chombo**

idau See **dau-1, mtepe**

idhau See **dau la mtepe**

iecht See **jakt-2**

ielaeck, ielaek, ielaken See **palingaak**

ierdappelskûtsje See **skûtsje**

iessjuut, iessjuutje See **ijsschuitje-2**

ifyombo See **chombo**

igá Guaraní and Tupí term applied to one-man **canoes*** used by these natives of the Amazon Basin, southwestern Brazil, northeastern Argentina, and Paraguay. Hewn from the trunk of the *igá, hyary,* or *timbo* tree. Paddled and poled. Other recorded names: **iar, ib-gá, igár, igara*, yga(r), ygara, ygat***. Note also **canoa-3, igaraçu**.

igapeba See **jangada-2**

igár See **igá**

igára *Peru, north-central:* A **dugout canoe*** of the Kokamilja of the Marañón River area. Note also **ogára**. Further reference: **igá**

igaraçu *Brazil:* One of the generic terms for a large **dugout canoe***. Some employ 1-2 sails, sometimes of leather or straw. Spelling variants: **igarassú, igaruçu** (Guaraní), **igarauçu, ygarassu** (Tupí). Note also **igá**.

igarapeba See **jangada-2**

igarassú See **igaraçu**

igaratá See **igaraté**

igaratim, igaratins See **igarité-1**

igareté, igaripé See **igarité**

igarité *Brazil:* **1.** In the language of the Tupí, an authentic **canoe***, namely one hewn from a single tree trunk. One used by a Tupí chieftain is called an **igaratim** (pl.

igarité-1

igaratins); an especially strong one, an **igaraté**. Note also **igaraçu**.

2. Some writers distinguish between sizes of **dugout canoes***, the **igarité** being larger than the **montaria*** and smaller than the **galeola***. Others, especially at Belem near the mouth of the Amazon, make a distinction between the **montaria** and the **igarité** by the permanance of the cabin, the latter having a fixed cabin aft.

3. One type found throughout the Amazon Basin, including Bolivia and Peru, has an overhanging bow that curves up smoothly from the bottom, ending in a raking transverse board; stern cut square also. Pronounced sheer forward. Dugout hull raised with planking; some strengthened with ribs and thwarts. Awning or cabin near the stern and sometimes forward; usually thatched. Steered with a paddle, sometimes at both bow and stern. Most single-masted, generally setting a spritsail; sometimes spar is extended forward for a jib; some 2-masted, also setting spritsails. Also portrayed as setting a tall, square sail. Those that sail have a rudder and keel. Also paddled, poled, or equipped with a motor. May have as many as 8 polers or paddlers. Capacity might be 7-8t.
Other recorded names: (**canoa**) **égar[téa, egarité, igareté, igaripé**. Note also **galeota, vigilenga**.

igaruçu, igarussú, igarusu See **igaraçu**

igat *Brazil, central and SE:* Native **canoe*** made from the bark of the *jatobá* tree, using bark from half the girth of the tree. The bark, softened by fire, is crimped upward at the bottom to form a square stern. Bow low,

igat

tapered, and usually open at the end. Bark at stern thinned to aid in bending up. Stretchers may be inserted. Cracks caulked with clay or soft inner bark. Occupants sit toward the stern, raising the bow clear of the water. Reported lengths 5-7.3m, widths 0.6-0.77m, depths 0.24-0.3m. Name variant: **jatobá**. Note also **woodskin**.

igherruba See **agherrabo**
Iglulik-Caribou kayak See **kayak-5**
iguerruba See **agherrabo**
iisbräkker See **ice breaker**
iis-jagt See **iceboat-1**

ijsbreker *Netherlands, central:* In order to supply fresh water to Amsterdam breweries from the 17th to the mid-19th century, special **ice breakers*** were constructed to keep the canals clear for the **waterschuiten** (see **waterschip**). Seven iron cutters on the wide, square bow broke up the ice and forced it under the hull. The vessel was pulled by 40 horses and maneuvered by a rudder and tiller from its sharp stern. Pipes to carry fresh water replaced the vessels in 1853.

ijsschuitje *Netherlands:* **1.** Small **iceboat***. Those of the 18th century were **sloop***-rigged, open boats. Runners were outrigged on each side, and a steering runner was on the bottom of the rudder. Used for pleasure, transportation, and to carry cargo on the frozen waterways. Generally crewed by 2. Loose-footed mainsail had a small, curved gaff; jib to a bowsprit. A 17th-century

ysschuyt was portrayed with a spritsail and jib to the stem; this North Holland boat had the forward runners under the hull. Spelling variant: **ysschuitje**

2. The blunt-bowed, amphibious **iessjuut** at Spankenburg, southeast of Amsterdam, set nets for smelts under the ice. Small bow transom, larger stern transom, both raked. Bottom curves up toward the bow; runners placed in after two-thirds. Pulled and pushed over the ice by 2 men, the man at the stern pushing against a crossbar. Under the right conditions, may be rowed or employ a small leg-of-mutton sail. Length ca. 3m, beam 1.0m. Name variant: **iessjuutje** (dim.)

ijzeren aakje, ijzeren aakske See **klipper-1**

ikada *Japan:* Generic term for a **raft***, dating from at least the 7th century. On the Hida and Mishida Rivers northeast of Nagoya, **rafts** composed of squared timbers were lashed with wisteria vines. The **sangenikada** was 5.4m long and 2.3m wide. The single-length logs were further secured by 2 longitudinal logs and a single transverse log. The **tsugi-ikada** comprised 2 sections, making a **raft** 7.2m or 9m long and 2.3m wide; in addition, two longitudinal strengthening logs were placed at the ends. Note also **kurèki-ikada**.

ikakh See **kayak-9**
iki tchiftè See **kayık-2**
ikkumaligdjuark See **Peterhead boat-1**
ikyak See **kayak-9**
ílhava, ílhavo, ílhavo da tarrafa See **bateira ílhava**
ilnechia See **esnecca**

imbabura *Colombia/Ecuador:* Very old, seagoing **dugout canoe*** of the coastal natives. In the 19th century, served as cargo carriers from coastal rivers and larger ports between Panama and Guayaquil; seen occasionally as late as the 1950s. Stability sometimes provided by 1-3 large balsa sponsons laid adjacent to the hull and lashed to 3 athwartship poles. Rib-supported strakes added to the dugout base; ends might be closed with washboards. Bow and stern usually overhanging, flattened platforms; or bow might be sharp

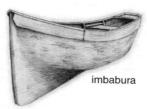
imbabura

and stern a transom type. No keel. Early indigenous craft used sails of unknown design. Steered with a long oar set through a hole in the transom. European adaptations included gaff or spritsails, decking, cabins, rudder, and sometimes leeboards; some early types were **schooner***-rigged; many retained their sponsons. Reported lengths 7.6-13.7m. Term also applied to a large dugout of Panamanian **cayuco*** design used on these coasts. Other recorded names: **balandra*** (in southern Ecuador), **ibabura**. Note also **canoa-14**.

imbarcazione Italian generic term for **boat***, including a **ship's boat***. May be propelled by oar, sail, or motor. Spelling variant: pl. **imbarcazioni**

imbarcazione a remi See **rowboat-1**

imbarcazione a vela See **sailboat**
imbarcazione da giorno See **day boat-1**
imbarcazione dell'anca See **quarter boat-1**
imbarcazione pilota See **pilot boat**
imbarcazioni See **imbarcazione**
Imperiala See **Galeere**
imperial caique See **saltanat kayığı**
in and outer, in and out ice boat See **ice punt-2**
incrociatore See **cruiser-3**
Indiaman See **East Indiaman**
Indian Header *United States, New England:* A fast **schooner*** characterized by a spoon bow with bowsprit and an exaggerated cutaway forefoot. Developed in 1898, they soon became known as **Indian Headers** because the early vessels of the type bore Native American names. Keel formed a continuous curve from stemhead to sternpost; later keels short and straight; steep rise to the floors; moderate sheer; low freeboard. Raked counter had an elliptical transom; raked sternpost; inboard rudder. Gaff-rigged on both masts; staysail, forestaysail, jib, and gaff and jib topsails. Reported lengths overall 29-31m; e.g., length overall 29m, beam 6.4m, depth 3.3m; moderate draft.
Indian trade boat *United States, SE:* Used by the English in the 18th century to transport furs obtained from the Native Americans in the interior to Georgia and South Carolina coastal towns. Dugout hull, some of 2 logs; bow might be sharp or blunt and overhanging. Cabin aft; outboard rudder; tiller. Rowed single-banked by 4-6 men sitting forward of the cargo. Reported lengths 8.5-12m, widths 1.5-2.4m.
Indien-Schnellsegler See **East Indiaman**
Indus punt See **quantel battella**
inflatable life raft, inflatable raft See **life raft**
ingalao See **ngalawa**
inland boat *Canada:* The Hudson's Bay Company employed 3 categories of so-called **inland boats**: the **York boat, sturgeon-head**, and the **scow***. The term was frequently synonymous with **York boat**.
inland lake scow See **scow-11**
inland navigation vessel, inland vessel See **riverboat**
Innersi-åttring See **åttring-3**
inrigged boat See **inrigger**
inrigged wherry See **wherry-2**
inrigger Term sometimes used to describe a boat with its oarlocks set into the gunwales. Name variant: **inrigged boat**. Note also **outrigger**.
inside barge See **Fal barge, gravel barge, Plymouth barge, West Country sailing barge**
inside flat See **Mersey flat**
ioinct See **junk**
iol See **yawl**
'iola *Solomon Islands, western Pacific:* Generic term for a **canoe*** on the islands of Maramasike and Ulawa in the southern part of the archipelago. One inlaid with cone (*la'o*) shells is called an **'iola la'o**; the **'iola raku** seats four. The **'iola sarasara** is a **bonito canoe** inlaid with nautilus shells and may be used in the initiation rites of young boys; tall ends turn up sharply; may be 7.3m long, 0.71m wide, and 0.36m deep. Note also **agai-ni-waiau**. Further reference: **gig-1**
iola atoato See **lisi**

'iola la'o See **'iola**
iola pwau k'ou See **lisi**
'iola raku, 'iola sarasara See **'iola**
iole See **gig-1**
iolla See **yawl**
ionc See **junk**
ioncaro See **jukung**
ionchi See **junk**
ionco *Indonesia, central:* In the late 16th and early 17th centuries, reported as a 2-masted sailing vessel of Java, used both as a merchant and fighting ship.
ioncque, ionque See **junk**
iot See **yacht**
ipanitika, ipiroaun See **chinedkhulan**
ippagagos, ippagoghi, ippagoga, ippagogo, ippegi, ippigi, ippigos See **hippagogos**
ippoi See **hippos**
iqaX, iqjax, iqyar, igyaẋ See **kayak-9**
irilar See **umiak-4**
Irish boat, Irish cutter See **Boston hooker-1**
Irish hooker See **Boston hooker-1, hooker**
Irish man-o'-war See **dumb barge**
Irish skiff See **drontheim**
Irish wherry *Ireland, E:* **Schooner***-rigged boat from the coast north of Dublin. Used for fishing originally and later for trading; most gone by the 1860s. Clinker-planked; curved or straight stem; raked sternpost.

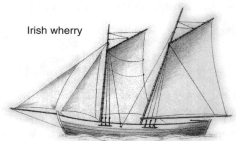

Irish wherry

Decked or half-decked. Aft-raking mainmast set a loose-footed, boomed gaff sail; foremast more vertical; no boom on the foresail; staysail and jib. Crew of 7-8. 20-50t. Other recorded names: **Rush wherry, Skerries hooker** (**wherry** or **whirry**). Note also **dandy smack**.
Ironbridge coracle *England, W:* A shallow, bowl-shaped craft used on the River Severn in the Ironbridge area for ferrying, transporting light goods, fishing, and game poaching. Now illegal for fishing, but a few still made. Nearly oval in shape with ends equally rounded. Framework built of 10 longitudinal and 10 transverse sawn ash laths; 2 short laths cross diagonally from the extremities. Gunwale formed by lath hoops. Board seat set aft of amidships, supported by transverse battens and vertical pillars. Canvas covering made watertight with pitch and tar mixture; a few newly constructed boats skin-covered. Originally paddle was one piece, more recently 3 pieces, consisting of grip, loom, and rectangular blade. Size and weight vary to accommodate owner; length 1.45m, width 0.9m, depth 0.4m; some as broad as 1.0m; mostly under 9kg. Name variant: **Severn coracle**. Further reading: Nic Compton, "Callico Boats, the Ironbridge Coracle," *Classic Boat* 64 (1993), 34-39. Note also **coracle**.

ironclad 19th-century term for naval vessels, either of wood and protected by iron plates or built of iron or steel. See also **gunboat-2**.

iron pot See **Thames sailing barge**

irukka maram See **catamaran-12**

isbåd *Denmark, central:* Open sailing/**rowing boat★** that maintained winter ferry service in the Store Bælt; the boat was pulled and pushed across frozen sections,

isbåd

while the passengers walked. Strong clinker construction of oak; ironshod keel; cutaway forefoot. Top strake continued aft to form a small transom that also served as a name board. When being maneuvered across the ice, the oars were placed across the gunwales to keep the boat on an even keel. Exterior painted black. Sailed with spritsail, staysail, and jib. Crew of 5-6. Length 6.6m, beam 2m, depth 0.84m, draft 0.47m.

isbåt 1. *Finland/Sweden:* During the winter, mail was carried by **isbåtar** (pl.) between the Swedish mainland and the Åland Islands in the southern Gulf of Bothnia. In the 1st half of the 19th century, these boats were clinker-planked with a strongly curved, ironshod keel, reducing the surface on the ice. Sharp ends with deeply curved stem and sternpost. Three thwarts. Generally handled by 6 men who pulled at the bow and pushed from the stern and against an athwartships pole restrained in the oarlocks. Three pairs of oars. In open water, sailed; initially with a square sail, later with gaff or spritsail and jib. Rudder shipped when sailing. Length 8.5m, beam 1.8m. Note also **isöka, postbåt-1**.

2. *Norway, W:* Special boat designed for winter use in the inner part of Sognefjorden. **Pram★**-type bow transom; raked stern transom. Clinker-planked, bottom curves up to long, overhanging bow; slight rocker at stern; wide "U" in cross section. Pushed over the ice on a pair of sled-like runners on the bottom; might be pulled by a horse. Rowed in open water with 2 pairs of oars worked against shaped oarlocks. Also set a square sail. Length 4.4m, beam 1.5m, depth 0.38m.

Further reference: **iseka-2**

isbia See **·isbije**

·isbije *Iraq, central:* Large **basket boat★** built at Hit on the Euphrates River for the transport of bitumen. Flat, roughly oval bottom of interwoven branches, straw, and reeds, across which poles were lashed. Uprights spaced ca. 30cm apart to form the sides with reeds, straw and branches woven between the uprights. Coated inside and out with a mixture of bitumen, sand, and earth. Length ca. 3m; shallow draft. Spelling variants: **hisbiya, isbia, ·isbiya**

·isbiya See **·isbije**

isbryder, isbrytare, isbryter See **ice breaker**

Isefjordsbåd *Denmark, NE:* 19th- and early 20th-century boat built in the Ise Fjord of northern Sjælland Island. Used for herring fishing in the Kattegat and to transport produce, especially potatoes, to Copenhagen; also used in southern waters. Clinker-built with fine lines below the waterline and plumb above; ceiled; very beamy. Full, rounded ends; curved stem, strongly raked sternpost below the waterline. Considerable sheer with bow higher than stern. Decked except for amidships and helmsman's cockpit; low bulwarks; cabin aft. **Cutter★**-rigged with boomed, loose-footed gaff mainsail; gaff topsail, 2 headsails. Later, engines installed; wet well often

Isefjordsbåd

added at this time; those built initially with engines were 1.2-1.8m longer than sailing types. Reported lengths 7-12m; e.g., length 9.7m, beam 4.5m, depth 1.5m; draft 1.5m. Other recorded names: **Hundestedbåd, Issefjordsbaad, Liselejebåd**; pl. **Isefjordsbåden**

iseka 1. *Finland:* Small, open boat, primarily a help boat for the **fålbåt★**, used both in the water and over the ice. Hull essentially the same as the **orusteka★** of Sweden. Small bow transom, larger stern transom. Rounded bottom with plank keel to which runners attached on outer edge. Flaring sides; clinker planking rounds up from the bottom and gathers in at the bow. Length ca. 4m, beam 1.4m, depth 0.5m. Name variant: **tvåköling** (on the south coast). Note also **eka, isöka**.

2. *Sweden:* The **iseka** that served for local transport along the ice-bound coast was similar to the Finnish type. Those used on open or ice-covered lakes for fishing and hunting had a flat bottom with marked rocker; 2 wood or metal runners were set on the bottom. Double-ended; raked transoms; carvel-planked. When rigged as an **isjakt**, set a small, boomed lugsail tacked to the mast. Also rowed. Length ca. 3.5m. Name variant: **isbåt★**. Note also **fälbåt**.

Spelling variants: pl. **isekor, isekorna**

isekor, isekorna See **iseka**

isikoeri, isikoeti, isikoetji See **sekochi**

isja *Indonesia, E:* Small, narrow, elegant **dugout canoe★** used by the men of Lake Sentani to the west of Kayo (Humboldt) Bay in Irian Jaya (New Guinea). Hull round in cross section; recurved, high bow; stern more blunt. Very unstable; single occupant uses paddle blade to brace against capsizing or sits astride the **canoe** using his legs to stabilize it. Waterline length 3.7m, maximum beam 0.25m, 0.15m between gunwales. Note also **kai**.

isjakt See **iceboat-1, iseka-2**

isjollar, isjollarna See **isjolle**

isjolle *Sweden, NE:* Principally a support boat to the **fälbåt**⋆ during sealing operations in the Gulf of Bothnia; also used to catch seals close inshore. Bottom strakes extra heavy; generally had a keel; 2 side keels served as runners on the ice. Heavy, curved stem; similar or transom stern. Hull ceiled in central part; stern bench. When sailed, set small spritsail and steered with an oar. Also rowed. Reported lengths 3-4.3m. Other recorded names: **fälbåtsjulle, isjulle, skibsjolle**; pl. **isjollar(na), isjulln**

isjulle, isjulln See **isjolle**

iskoeti, iskoetji See **sekochi**

island boat See **Nomans Land boat**

Isle of Lewis sgoth See **sgoth**

Isle of Man lugger See **Manx lugger**

Isle of Man nobby See **nobby-3**

Isles of Shoals boat *United States, NE:* **Fishing** and **party boat**⋆ used around these islands off the New Hampshire coast from the mid-19th to the early 20th century. Worked off the beaches. Lapstrake planking; bent frames; straight keel with drag; steep rise to the floors; soft turn of the bilges; moderate sheer. Sharp, hollow ends; cutaway forefoot; straight, raked sternpost. Outboard rudder; tiller slotted over rudderhead. Forward third decked and at the stern; cuddy on some. Two unstayed masts raked slightly aft, the taller foremast well forward, the mainmast through a midship thwart. Sails raised by single halyard from masthead block slung from an iron rod. Mainsail boomed, foresail loose-footed; head and foot of sails nearly parallel. Generally no bowsprit or headsail. Reported lengths 6.7-9m; e.g., length 8.8m, beam 2.6m. Name variant: **Isles of Shoals shay**

Isles of Shoals shay See **Isles of Shoals boat**

isnechia See **esnecca**

iso-bune *Japan:* Open **rowing boat**⋆ commonly found in coastal fisheries, especially for collecting snails and seaweed. Long, sharp bow with strongly raking stem; open V-stern; side planks extend beyond the stern; narrow, flat bottom curves up at the stern; no keel; flat sheer. Long, wide rudder. May be rowed with one pair of oars, paddled, or poled. Length 6.2m, width 1.14m, inside depth 0.46m. Called **hottsu** on Hokkaido.

isöka *Finland, SW:* As late as 1896 in Kumlinge Island in the eastern Åland archipelago, the mail was carried by an **isöka** during winter. Lightly built with clinker planking, flat floor, sharply upturned ends to small bow and stern transoms, strong sheer. Twin runners along the bilges. Length 5m, beam 1.5m. Note also **isbåt-1, iseka-1, postbåt-2**.

ispigg See **iceboat-1**

issago See **palangrier**

Issefjordsbåd See **Isefjordbåd**

Issi-Watzille See **Waidzille**

Italian boat See **felucca-3**

itápába See **jangada-2**

Itchen Ferry boat *England, S:* Workboat of the Solent area. Probably originated on the River Itchen in the 18th century, initially as the small **Itchen Ferry punt**. Both the **punt**⋆ and the larger **Itchen Ferry cutter** (or

smack) trawled for fish and shrimp, dredged oysters, transported passengers, and were raced; some are now built specifically for racing. Several revived and still afloat in the 1990s. Very early boats mainly clinker-built, carvel by 1850s; deep keel with drag; S-curve to the garboards; soft turn of the bilges; slight tumble home to topsides; low sheer, especially on the **punt**. Plumb stem, rounded foot; slightly raked, wineglass transom. Outboard rudder with wide blade below the waterline; tiller. **Punts** open but had a tray set slightly below the gunwales for the nets and fish-sorting. **Cutters**⋆ decked to just abaft the pole mast; wide side decks; similar tray aft; small cuddy forward. Some **punts** had a centerboard; the **cutters** employed either inside ballast or outside, such as an iron keel shoe. Hull gray or black. The **punts** primarily rowed, but when sailed, set a loose-footed spritsail with a long sprit and a staysail initially; later employed a high-peaked

Itchen ferry boat

lugsail or gaff sail. The **cutters** originally had a long gaff that created a nearly vertical leech to the boomless mainsail; later the gaff was shorter and the sail had a boom that extended well beyond the stern. Staysail originally tacked to the stemhead, then to an iron bumkin, and then a long, running bowsprit was added to which a jib was run out on a traveler. Topsail sent up on a pole mast for racing. Later many motorized. Crew of 1-2. The **punts** were 3.66-7.5m long; e.g., length 3.96m, beam 1.52m, depth 0.76m. **Cutters** 5-9m; e.g., length 5.8m, beam 2.5m, depth 1.0m, draft 1.3m. Other recorded names: **Itchen punt, Solent fishing boat** (or **cutter**); **Solent punt** (or **smack**); **Southampton punt**. Further reading: John Leather, *Gaff Rig* (London: Adlard Coles, Ltd., 1970), 168-180.

Itchen Ferry cutter, Itchen Ferry punt, Itchen Ferry smack, Itchen punt See **Itchen Ferry boat**

itsas-ontzi See **barco-1**

itutaralutik See **kayak-8**

iuiú See **youyou**

iunck, iunco, iunk See **junk**

IV See **shell-1**

iweg See **iweng**

iweng *Loyalty Islands, New Caledonia, western Pacific:* On Lifou Island, a **raft**⋆ of thick poles secured by a bar lashed across each end. Sculled with a long pole or an oar. Spelling variants: **iweg, iwenge**

iwenge See **iweng**

iyĕnge See **dihengué**

iyĝax̂ See **kayak-9**

jaagschip See **jäger**

jaagschuit See **trekschuit-3**

jääpursi See **iceboat-1**

jábeca See **jábega**

jábega *Spain, S:* Colorful, open **rowing boat★** that works off Malaga beaches with the *jábega*, a type of drag net; in the Balearic Islands, they are called **laúds★**, and on the opposite coast of Morocco, **cárabos**. Nearly extinct. Ram, supported by a gammon knee, extends forward from just below the rubstrake; the slightly recurved stem projects above the gunwales. Sternpost as tall or higher than the stem and serves as a "hook" for the nets and oars; a special spar at the stern is used as a fulcrum for the steering oar. Washstrake extends from stem to near the stern. The **jábegas** of the Cádiz area also have a high stemhead, but the sternpost is low; 4 evenly spaced thwarts. A special oar with a basket on top is erected in the bow to summon the men who will draw the net onto shore. Elsewhere, 3 rowing thwarts forward of amidships; a washstrake extends for a short distance from just forward of amidships; stemhead also tall. Double-ended with vertical sides; plank keel; flat floors amidships; rounded bilges. Two grounding keels run parallel to each other ca. 25cm apart and join at the heel of the stem and the sternpost. Foredeck. Hulls mostly white but decorated with oculi and other designs. Single tholepins. Crew of 7-12. Reported lengths 7-9m; e.g., length 7.6m, beam 2.37m, depth 1.0m. Other recorded names: **aixàvega** (Catalan), **barca★**, **barca de jábega**, **jábeca**, **jábega malagueña**, **jabeque★**, **xabega**, **xávega★** (pl. **xávegues**). Further reading: Xavier Pastor, "Spanish Coastal Craft, the Jábega of Malaga," *Model Shipwright* 44 (1983), 35-39. Note also **barca da arte xávega**.

jábega malagueña See **jábega**

jabeque *Spain, Balearic Islands:* Three-masted, lateen-rigged **coaster★** that operated until at least the 1940s. Foremast raked forward, main- and mizzenmasts plumb. Mizzen yard held nearly vertical, and sail sheeted to an outrigger. Further references: **jábega**, **laúd**, **xebec**

jabeque redondo See **xebec**

jabequín See **chambequín**

Jabez's head See **compartment boat**

jac See **yack**

jach See **yacht**

jacht **1.** *Germany:* **a.** The **Jacht** of the North Sea and western Baltic ports was a fast, **cutter★**-rigged **coaster★** dating to the 16th century. Gone by World War II. Most carvel-built with sharp floors, deep keel, strong sheer, curved stem. Stern varied with period and locale; some had a rounded stern or a sloping, flat transom; others a small, tucked-up counter (the **Spiegeljacht★**) and a heart-shaped transom, or they might have a sharp stern (the **Spitzgattjacht**). Decked; usually had a cabin, large hatches, and high bulwarks. Tall pole mast; generally set a narrow-headed, loose-footed, boomed gaff mainsail; 3 headsails; some used a square foresail and a jackyard topsail. Engines on later vessels. Crew of 2-5. Reported lengths 8-20m, widths 2.5-6m, depths 1-3m; deep draft. Other recorded names: **Jachtschiff**, **Jagd★**, **Jagdt**, **Jageschiff**, **jagt★**. Note also **Jachtboot**. **b.** The **Staaten-Jacht** of the 17th century was a single-masted government vessel known for its speed.

2. *Germany, E/Poland:* **Barge★** of the Oder River that carried cargo from Szczecin (Stettin) to Berlin in the late 1800s. Built of oak and pine. Length overall 25m, on bottom 19m, beam 2.8m, depth 1.25m.

3. *Netherlands:* The Dutch **jacht** has been used since at least the 16th century for a variety of activities: commerce, war (**oorlogsjacht**), privateering, state missions, fishing, pleasure. Noteworthy originally for its speed. Those active in the East Indian trade were as long as 49m; the **statenjacht** or **prinsenjacht** was an ornate vessel used for entertaining dignitaries, carrying dispatches, collecting revenues, etc. Others were owned by wealthy citizens (the **heere jacht** [or **jagt**]). Those employed in fishing were frequently pleasure **jachten** (pl.) that had been enlarged and their fancy work removed. **Speeljachten** were fast pleasure craft of wealthy merchants and lesser government officials, and a number of these are still afloat; carvel-built with keel, rounded hull, decorative counter, open waist with seats abaft foredeck; estimated length 12m. The East India vessels were 3-masted and full-rigged with a transom stern. The small **coasters** that worked into the 20th century were clinker- or carvel-built with full bows; raked, curved stem; sharply raking stern with a small transom; later vessels were clipper-bowed. In general, **jachten** of Dutch waters had transom sterns, raked and curved stems, flat floors, and considerable sheer, and used leeboards; 17-20m long. **Speeljachten** carried a spritsail, later changing to a gaff sail on a strike mast and staysail; some employed 2 masts, both stepped well forward, each setting loose-footed gaff sails with very short gaffs. Other recorded names: **jag(h)d**, **jaght(e)**, **jaght schip**, **jagt★**, **jagtje**, **pinas★**, **yaegt**; **staaten jagt**. Further reading: Bernard Wuillaume, "Essai dur l'Origine du Statenjacht," *Le Petit Perroquet* 22 (1978), 20-39; ibid., "Le Yacht Hollandais de Charles XI, Roi de Suède," ibid., 25 (1979), 37-49; 27 (1980), 50-65. Note also **bezaanjacht**, **Blokzijlder jacht**, **Fries jacht**, **hekjacht**, **jachtboot**, **spiegeljacht**.

4. *Poland:* A general term for a sport boat.

5. *Poland, NW:* The German **Jacht** of the Pomeranian coast (now Poland) was a small cargo vessel prominent in the late 19th and early 20th centuries. Some worked around the island of Rügen. Clinker-built, sharp bow, concave stem; sharp, transom or counter stern. Inboard rudder, steering well. Flat floors, shallow keel. Decked, cabins forward and aft; deckhouse on some. Pole mast, often longer than the vessel; some had a fidded topmast. Boomed, loose-footed gaff sail, or a tall, loose-footed, rectangular gaff sail (**Jachtquatze**); gaff topsail, staysail, and jib. Later vessels motorized. Crew of 3. Reported lengths 15-16.6m; e.g., length 15m, beam 5.3m, hold depth 1.7m, 31rt. Other recorded names: **Jagt★**, **Pommersche Jacht**; at times **Warp'sche Boot**. Note also **Jachtgaleass**, **Schlup**.

6. *United States, NE:* 17th-century Dutch colonists in the Nieuw Amsterdam (New York) area used small, **sloop***-rigged **jachts** for local trading and to bring furs collected by the Native Americans along the Hudson River to the city. Some also served as **packet boats*** to Albany. A gun was set on a rest on deck. Spelling variant: **yacht***
Further references: **Fries Jacht, hoy-1, jagt-1, Schlup-2, yacht**

jachtboot 1. *Germany, NW:* The **Jachtboot** of the Kiel area in the late 19th century was reported to be a small trader of the **Jacht*** type but was decked only to the mast. Carried 2 men. Cap. 7-9t. Name variant: **Jagdboot**
2. *Netherlands, S:* A type of **hoogaars*** with a distinctive rounded bow and stern. Carvel- or clinker-planked; oblong hatch forward.

Jachtgaleass *Germany/Poland, W:* Developed for trading in the Baltic Sea in the mid-19th century, largely along the then German Pomeranian coast; also found in the North Sea. Considered a **Jacht*** with a **ketch*** rig. Worked until the mid-20th century. Rounded stem; raked wineglass or oval transom. Carvel-planked; straight keel; considerable rise to the floors; soft turn of the bilges. Generally no transom windows. Decked, with quarter-deck; deckhouse amidships. Outboard rudder. Most painted black. Narrow gaff sails, loose-footed and boomed; topsails, staysails, 2-3 jibs. Long, rising bowsprit. A small type with pole masts sometimes called a **Pfahlgaleass**. Later vessels motorized. Crew of 2-4. Reported lengths 18-23m; e.g., length 18m, beam 6m, depth 3.6m. Note also **galeass**.

jachthengst See **lemmerhengst**
jachthoogaars See **hoogaars**
Jachtquatze See **jacht-5**
Jachtschiff See **jacht-1a**
jachtschokker See **schokker**
Jacht Schoner See **schooner**

jack *Canada, E:* Small **schooner*** that fished the inshore grounds of Newfoundland and Cape Breton Island for cod until the 1960s. Characterized by its wide, beet-shaped or square transom from which the rudder was hung in a split rudderstock. Some early boats apple-bowed, later sharp stem enabled them to ride onto ice floes. Raked ends; gentle run aft at the quarter beam buttocks; deep drag to the heavy, straight keel. Forward and aft standing wells for the fishermen; small cuddy; movable-board decking. Outrigged fishing poles might be set from the quarters. Larger **jacks** decked with trunk cabin aft. Generally painted green with black bulwarks. Carried up to 3 single-man **dories** (see **dory**) on deck. Boomed or loose-footed gaff sails; 2 jibs run to a long bowsprit. Sails sometimes tanned. Masts often unstayed, except for jibstay; masts raked. Later boats motorized. Crew of 3-6. Reported lengths 7.6-15.2m; e.g., length overall 14.2m, beam 4.2m, draft 1.88m. Other recorded names: **bateau jack, bummer, jack boat** (or **schooner**), **Southern Shore bummer, two-spar boat, two-sticker**; those from the south coast of Newfoundland, west of Burin Peninsula, called **western boats**. Note also **schooner-2**. Further reference: **yacht**

jackass 1. Term applied to a sailing vessel whose rig deviates from the established norm, such as the standard **bark***, **brig***, or **schooner***. Note also **jackass schooner**.
2. *Canada, E:* **a.** Roughly built **shore boat*** of Newfoundland. **b.** Two-masted sailing vessel from New-

foundland rigged so that the gaff topsail on the mainmast could be temporarily changed to a square sail; foremast square-rigged. Name variant: **jackass brig** Further reference: **hermaphrodite brig**

jackass bark Three-masted vessel rigged with square sails on the foremast, gaff sails on the mainmast with square topsails above, and gaff sail only on the mizzenmast. On the 4-masted type, the forward 2 masts were square-rigged. Popular in the late 19th and early 20th centuries. Other recorded names: **barque jackass, hermafrodite bark, hermaphrodite barque, jackass barque, jigger bark** (or **barque**), **Polkabark, Polka Barque**. Note also **bark**.

jackass barque See **jackass bark**
jackass brig See **hermaphrodite brig, jackass-2b**
jackass schooner 1. Term may apply to a **schooner*** that lacks a main topmast, or to a 3-masted **schooner** employing square topsails on the 2-part foremast.
2. In England in the mid-1800s, might be a vessel square-rigged forward like a **topsail schooner** (see **schooner**), but with a small **ketch's*** mizzen. Note also **billyboy**. Further reference: **schooner-barge-1**

jack barquentine See **schooner-1**
jack boat, jack schooner See **jack**
Jack Sharp See **little packet**
jackstaff barge See **tug-2**
jact See **jakt-2**
jacuma See **casco-1**
jadrenica, jadrilica See **sailboat**
jaegschuitje See **trekschuit-3**
jægt See **jagt, jekt**
jægtbaad See **skipsbåt-2**
jaegte-baade See **jekt**
Jafarabadi hody, Jafarabadi nauri See **batel-3**
Jaffna dhoni, Jaffna doni See **padagu-3**
jagada See **jangar**
jaganda See **jangada**
jagar See **jagger**
Jagd *Germany, S:* The Main River **Jagd** of the 18th and early 19th centuries carried passengers; the larger type called a **grosse Jagd**, the smaller type, the **kleine Jagd**. See also **jacht-1a, jacht-3**.
Jagdboot See **jachtboot-1**
Jagdlomme See **Schiesslomme**
Jagdt See **jacht-1a**
jäger *Netherlands:* Vessel assigned to a herring **fleet***; cited from at least the late 16th century. Principal duty was to collect the early catches and transport them quickly to market. Outbound, took supplies of salt and casks and might also peddle provisions, clothing, ropes, and anchors (often stolen). Originally fast sailing Dutch **howkers***, especially the larger, more heavily canvassed cargo type; later, when steam vessels were fishing, the **jägers** were also steam-propelled. Some sailed out of Belgium also. Other recorded names: **chasseur***, **Fischjäger, fish carrier, haringjäger, Heringsjäger, jaagschip, ventjager, yager**. Note also **jagger**.
Jageschiff See **jacht-1a**
jaggar See **jagger**
jagger *United Kingdom:* A fast sailing vessel of the 17th-18th centuries associated with the herring **fleets***. Primary function was to carry the 1st catch to

United Kingdom and Continent markets in order to get the best price. Also provided the **fleet** with provisions, barrels, nets, etc. Sometimes a special vessel, but usually the fastest vessel of a particular **fleet** type, such as **buss**★ or **dogger**★. Spelling variants: **jag(g)ar**, **jager**★, **jagger-boat**, **jawger**, **yag(g)er**. Note also **chasseur**.

jagger-boat See **jagger**

jaghd See **jacht-3**

jaght, jaghte See **jacht-3**, **yacht**

jaght schip See **jacht-3**

jagt *Denmark:* **1.** Trading **smack**★ that has carried cargo between Danish ports and other Scandinavian countries since the end of the 18th century. Strongly built with heavy oak frames; carvel or clinker planking; marked

jagt-1

sheer on some; rounded bilges; tumble home to sides. Maximum beam well forward, tapering aft to transom stern; bluff bow and strongly curved stem. Older types had a broad, ornamented transom; later transoms heart-shaped; some round- or sharp-sterned. A **dinghy**★ may hang from stern davits. Decked; raised deck aft, crew's quarters forward. Outboard rudder; tiller comes in below the gunwale. A loose-footed, boomed gaff sail is set to a pole mast; 2 headsails and sometimes a flying jib and gaff topsail; some early vessels also set a square sail to the mainmast. Later boats employ auxiliaries. Crew of 2-3. Reported lengths 8.8-16.5m, widths 2.7-6.5m, depths 2.2-2.5m, draft 1-2.5m; many lengthened and changed to **ketch**★ rig, becoming **galeaser** (see **galease**). Spelling variants: **jacht**★, **jægt**; pl. **jagter**
2. One type carried local fruit from the small island of Tåsinge, just south of Fyn, to Copenhagen, earning the name **pæreskude** (**pear boat**). Returned with other produce and supplies. Worked mainly from the late 18th into the early 20th century. Wide transom, often with square windows; curved stem; straight keel; high, rounded bilges with tumble home above; strong sheer. Decked, cabin aft; deep bulwarks. Outboard rudder; long tiller. Carried a small boat on aft davits. Set a boomed gaff mainsail, gaff topsail; staysail, jib to rising bowsprit. Rowed in calms. 1794 boat 13.86m long, 4.13m wide, 2.41m deep, 1.57m draft.
Further references: **jacht-1a**, **jacht-3**, **jacht-5**, **jakt-1**, **jakt-2**, **yacht**

jagter See **jagt**

jagtje See **jacht-3**

jaguanda See **balsa-11**

jahazi *Kenya/Tanzania:* Trader built chiefly at Lamu and Zanzibar but also at towns along the Tanzanian mainland and at Pemba. Vary in design from place to place, but the stem is usually vertical and the stern a small, shield-shaped transom. Open except for a light palm decking at the stern. Employs a single quadrilateral lateen-type sail with a short luff. Some now have an engine. Crew of ca. 7. The major types are the **Lamu jahazi**★ and the **Zanzibar jahazi**★. Other recorded names: **djehaz** and **ǧahāz** (Arabic); **gehazi**; **jehazi** (Swahali); **pangayo** (Portuguese); **zázio**; pl. **jahazia, majahazi**. Note also **mashua-3**.

jahazia See **jahazi**

jaht, jahta See **yacht**

jaile dingi See **dingi-2**

jaique See **kayık**

jaitero See **xeito**

jak See **northern-style canoe**, **yacht**

jake See **dogbody**, **Saint John River woodboat**

jakhta See **yacht**

jakt **1.** *Finland/Sweden:* Cargo vessel of the southern part of the Gulf of Bothnia, especially out of the Åland Islands of Finland and the Roslagen region of Sweden. Those from the Stockholms Skargard (archipelago)

jakt-1

were termed **slup**★. During the 18th and through the 19th century, they carried freight, produce, and especially firewood. Clinker-built; generally a transom stern; most decked with a deckhouse aft. Set a boomed, loose-footed, standing gaff mainsail; could be brailed. Square or gaff topsail run up at times. Staysail might be boomed; 1-2 jibs to a long bowsprit. The **Roslagen jakt** had slightly more freeboard and smaller mainsail than the others. Generally 3 in crew. Reported lengths 14-20.4m, widths 6-7.7m; carried 10-25 cords of firewood. Other recorded names: **jagt**★, **jaktbåt**, **roslagsslup**; pl. **jakter**, **slupar**. Note also **roslagsjakt**.
2. *Norway, W:* Evolved from the **jekt**★ as a gaff-rigged **coaster**★ by the 2nd half of the 18th century. In the Rogaland area of western Norway, the spelling **jekt** was retained. Essentially extinct except for restorations. Actively traded southwestern Norway products to the Lofoten Islands in the north, returning with cod and herring (**sildejakt**) that were salted and then carried to the Baltic and Mediterranean. Some fished off Iceland in summer and locally for herring in winter. Some traveled into the Arctic for seals. The smallest vessels worked the protected coasts (the **fjordajakt**, **fjordajekt**, or **småjakt**); the larger traveled offshore. Originally clinker-planked, gradually adopting carvel planking in the 19th century. Straight keel, some drag aft; flat to moderately rising floors; plumb sides; maximum beam well forward; strong sheer. Stem curved, straight, or clipper. Stern square and raked; often stern windows. Decked;

cuddy forward, deckhouse aft. Outboard rudder, or rudderpost came up inboard; tiller. **Ship's boat*** hung from stern davit. Lofty pole mast stepped just forward of amidships. Set a loose-footed, boomed mainsail, long gaff and boom; yard topsail. One or 2 wide, square sails hung from yards forward of the mast. Long rising bowsprit with jibboom; 2-3 headsails. Some larger **jakter** (pl.) stepped a mizzenmast, becoming **ketch***-rigged (the **jaktgaleas**). Later vessels motorized. Crew of 4-6. Reported lengths 15.5-24.8m; e.g., length 18m, beam 5m, depth 1.8m. Other recorded names: **bomsegljakt, bomseil-jægt, bomseiljakt, bomseiljekt, bomsiglar(jekt), hardang-erjakt, iacthe, iecht, jact, jægt, jagt*, jakta, jekt***; pl. **jaktene, jakter**

3. *Sweden:* Term for a **yacht***. May also designate a small, single-masted cargo (**fraktjakt**) or fishing vessel. Well established by the 18th century. The cargo type of the west coast might be 13.7m long and beamy; sharp ends; cutaway stem; keel; outboard rudder; tiller; gaff-rigged with topsail and 2-3 headsails; square sail hung forward of the mast. Spelling variants: **jakten**; pl. **jakter** Further references: **galeas-2, yacht**

jakta See **jakt-2, yacht**
jaktbåt See **jakt-1**
jakteka See **eka-1**
jakten See **jakt-3**
jaktene See **jakt-2**
jakter See **jakt**
jaktgaleas See **jakt-2**
jaktkanot See **kanot-5**
jal *Yemen:* A craft that ran between off-lying islands and shore. See also **yalik**.
jala *East Malaysia:* Sharp-ended **dugout canoe*** of stilt villages along the Brunei River in northern Borneo. Several thwarts. Paddled. See also **kotak-1, sal-1**.
jālah See **sal-1**
jalak *Peninsular Malaysia:* One- or 2-masted trader that worked along the east coast of the Malay Peninsula; known as a **jalak** at Pahang and as a **payang*** at Trengganu. Raised foredeck and gallery; loose lath decking; awning at the stern. Set mat lugsails. Crew of 8. Length 22m, beam 2.7m, freeboard 1.2m, cap. 5t. Further name variant: **jalak Pahang**
jalak Pahang See **jalak**
jalba *Bangladesh:* In the 1660s, the Viceroy of Bengal used the long, narrow **jalba** as part of his expeditionary river **fleet***. Term also applied to the boats of pirates who ravaged inland as far as Dakha (Dacca). Employed as many as 40 oars. Other recorded names: **gallivat*, jalbah**. See also **jalbūt-1**.
jalbah See **jalba, jalbūt-1**
jalbaut, jalbhūt, jalboot See **jalbūt-1**
jalbosh' See **yalik**
jalbūt **1.** *Arabian Peninsula:* Plumb-stemmed vessel of the Persian (Arabian) Gulf; reported also from the Red Sea. Used widely for pearling and carrying passengers and cargo, and some of the smaller ones are **ship's boats***. In Bahrain, the term **mashua*** is used for a small fishing **jalbūt**. Carvel-planked, originally sewn; straight stem; transom stern raked ca. 45°; flat sheer; straight keel; flat floors. A recent type at Kuwait has the square stern of the **jalbūt**, but the S-curved stem of a **shū·ai***, and is called

a **jalbūt-shu·ai**. Open or half-decked; captain's bench on a flimsy, flying poop; some may have a deckhouse aft. Small rudder hung with metal rings onto the transom; tiller. Usually steps a single forward-raking mast. A

jalbūt-1

quadrilateral lateen-type sail with a short luff tacks to the bowsprit; early boats had mat sails. When equipped with an auxiliary engine, called a **lanch**. Crew of 4-6. Reported lengths 6-30m, beamy; shallow draft. Other recorded names: **gālbūt** (pl. **gawālbī**), **gḍabūt, jalba(h), jalbaut, jalbhūt, jal(i)boot, jalbuti, jālī, jālībōt, jalibut, jelba, jeloa, jilba, jolboat, jōlbūt**. Note also **baghla**.

2. *Iran, Persian Gulf:* Local term for a type of fishing **smack*** on the Dashtestan coast.
3. *Tanzania:* Term sometimes used in Zanzibar and on the mainland outside the Lamu area in referring to the **Lamu jahazi***, which the **jalbūt** resembles.
jalbuti, jalbūt-shu·ai See **jalbūt-1**
jaléa See **jalia**
jaleebote See **jālibōt**
jali *Bangladesh, SE:* **Ketch***-rigged cargo vessel built mainly in the Chittagong and Cox's Bazaar areas. Carvel planking built up on frames and ribs; raked stem sheer sweeps up forward; sharp stern. Leg-of-mutton sails, jib to long, slender spar. Many reconstructed to take an engine. Cap. to ca. 160t. Name variant: **sulluk**. Note also **trawler-2**.
jālī See **jalbūt-1**
jalia *India/Peninsular Malaysia:* Reported in 17th-century Portuguese documents as a small, light **galley*** rowed with 15 oars to a side; used in commerce and war in India and at Malacca. A late 19th-century study cites the **jalia** as a small vessel built to transport salt in India. Those from the Arakan coast (now part of Myanmar) were reported as employing 38-40 oars. Very long and narrow; tent over the stern. Commonly under the command of a Portuguese captain. Spelling variants: **gelia*, jaléa, jaliya, jelia**
jalia dingi See **dingi-2**
jaliboot See **jalbūt-1**
jālibōt *India, W/Pakistan, SE:* A brightly painted harbor craft of Bombay (Mumbai) and Karachi. The Karachi boats were more stoutly built, and the hull was ceiled with light teak planking; stem rounded, stern square; 3 beams served as thwarts. The lighter, finer Bombay boats had a straight stem, square stern, and light decking forward that formed a cuddy; seats at the stern. Outboard rudder; tiller. Both types set a lateen or quadrilateral lateen-type sail with a short luff to a forward-raking mast

stepped amidships; single shroud to each side. The tack on the Karachi boats was secured to a spar rigged out over the bow; on the Bombay boats, it went to a ring bolt on the stem, and a jib was sometimes run to a bowsprit. Smaller rig used during the monsoon season. Crew of 5-7. Bombay boats: reported lengths 7.3-9.4m; e.g., length 8.5m, beam 2m, depth 0.66m. Karachi boats: reported lengths 10-12.2m; e.g., length 10.7m, beam 2.8m, depth 1.12m. Other recorded names: **jaleebote, jolly boat★**

jālībōt, jalibut See **jalbūt-1**

jalie See **galley**

jalik See **yalik**

jaliya See **jalia**

jaliyā dingi See **dingi**

jalk See **tjalk-2**

jaloer See **jalor**

jalor *Indonesia/Malaysia:* Generic term given to several types of craft, but mainly to a small, plank-extended **dugout canoe★**. Other recorded names: **djalō, djaloeë, djalo(e)r, jaloer, jalur, perahu jalur**. Note also **sampan jalur**.
1a. In western Sumatra, a shallow, plank-extended dugout employing an outrigger. Sharp or square stern. A long shelter projects out over the stern. Rowed by 1-4 persons using short, scoop-shaped oars, or rectangular sails set on 1-3 masts. Steered with a short oar. **b.** The **djaloer** of the Telukbetung area at the south end of Sumatra is a relatively large craft with a high, sharp bow and low, square stern. Marked bottom rocker, especially aft. Peaked shelter amidships.
2. On rivers along the east coast of Peninsular Malaysia, transports cargo and passengers. Reported lengths 4-6m; 1.0m wide.
3. In East Malaysia, found on all rivers. Range in length from 3-46m. Note also **alut**.

jalora *Peninsular Malaysia:* Fine, fast **fishing boat★** of northern Pahang on the east coast. Bow well flared; maximum beam just forward of amidships. Long, straight keel. Raked, projecting ends; open. Spar crutch at bow.

jalora

Steered with a paddle. Single aft-raking mast sets a large, rectangular lugsail. In strong wind, 1-2 crew members swing out on ropes attached to the masthead, serving as live ballast. Crew of 3-4. Reported lengths 7.3-8.5m, beam 1.2-1.4m. Spelling variant: **jalorar**

jalorar See **jalora**

jalur See **jalor, phang chun**

jalur maling *Indonesia:* **Dugout canoe★** of Java and Sumatra used as a water-taxi, but name means "thieves' boat," implying nefarious activities. Hewn to even thick-

ness by drilling holes in the log to desired thickness and inserting pegs; inside removed down to the pegs. Ends vertical and U-shaped; no keel. Some required 5 paddlers. Reported lengths 1.8-11.7m, widths 0.6-0.9m. Spelling variants: **djaloer malieng, djalur maling**

jalyanao See **balam**

Jamaica sloop *West Indies:* Small, fast, weatherly vessel that was popular in the islands, especially Jamaica, with buccaneers, smugglers, and traders prior to the mid-18th century. Thereafter it was built and modified in Bermuda, becoming known as the **Bermuda sloop★**. Marked sheer with low freeboard amidships, raked ends, considerable rise to the floors, drag to the straight keel. Loose-footed gaff mainsail and square topsails set to a sharply aft-raking mast. Long bowsprit with multiple headsails. About 18m long. Name variant: **West Indies sloop**. Note also **sloop-10**.

jam boat See **lumberman's batteau**

James River bateau *United States, E:* Carried hogsheads of tobacco or barrels of flour down this Virginia river, other tributaries of Chesapeake Bay, and other southeastern rivers in the late 18th and early 19th centuries. **Bateaux★** (pl.) continued in use on the James River and Kanawha Canal until at least the mid-19th century; these were wider than the earlier **tobacco boats★**. Plank-built, curved stem and sternpost, flat bottom; sharp ends, but original type **scow★**-ended; low sheer. Decked at each end for steersman, and platforms ran outboard along each side for the polers. Temporary awning on hoops might be set up. Crew of ca. 3. Reported lengths 9-27m, widths 1.2-2.4m, depths 0.46-0.61m; draft ca. 30cm. Other recorded names: **bat(t)eau★, market boat★, patented bateau, Rucker (tobacco) bateau, tobacco boat, Virginia tobacco boat**. Further reading: Bruce G. Terrell, *The James River Bateau: Tobacco Transport in Upland Virginia 1745-1840.* (Greenville, N.C.: East Carolina University, 1991). Note also **flat-6**.

jamppu See **balsa-4**

jancada See **jangar**

jandi *Ethiopia, W:* Ox-skin **float★** used by the Galla of Gojam Province for river crossings. Tanned skin perforated around the edges, laid flat, filled with dry grass, and then laced together with hide thongs. Possessions or goods may be placed inside; passenger sits astride. Propelled by a swimmer. Dismantled on the opposite bank. Note also **jendi**.

jang See **jong-1**

janga *Portugal:* Beamy, shallow-draft boat used to transport wood. Spelling variant: **ianga**. See also **jangada de tabuas, jong-1, juanga-1**.

jangada **1.** Portuguese and Spanish term that may refer to a **raft★** of logs lashed together to transport people and merchandise, generally on rivers; to a **raft** using barrels or casks as flotation beneath a platform of poles or boards; or to a ship's **life raft★**.
2. *Brazil, NE:* **Catamaran★** used for fishing and transportation off Ceará and Bahia States. The small **rafts** from Ceará consist of 4-5 *peúba* or *piuba* (balsa-type wood) logs; largest use 8. Logs pointed at ends or blunt; slightly upturned, staggered to form a point, or cut square; doweled together. Chafing pieces affixed to 2 logs. Rocker bottom; may have a short keel or a daggerboard

fitted just abaft the mast, either between the center logs or into a slot cut through the center log. **Raft** usually awash; food and fresh water kept on a tripod or forked stick or hung from the mast; mast crutch aft. Shelter aft on some larger craft. Helmsman sits on a bench to work a 3m-long steering oar that fits into a slot to port or starboard, depending on the tack; the central logs at the stern are strengthened against the oar pressure by a Spanish windlass. Light, curved mast, one-third in from the bow, supported by a sturdy, benchlike rest. May be stepped in one of several fore-and-aft and athwartship steps; secured by a single shifting backstay and a mast partner; some stepped through a raised bench. Baggy, triangular sail, initially with a boom at the foot; more recently, held out with a sprit boom placed well up the mast. Lacing starts above the boom so that it can be unshipped and sail wrapped around the mast while fishing. Carries a long scoop for dousing the sail to improve its wind-holding abilities. Some now also use an outboard motor. Launched from beaches; quickly waterlogged and must be dried out between trips; last about a year. Crew of 2-4, some of whom may hang from straps to windward. Reported lengths 3-8.7m, widths 1-1.6m. The **jangadas** of Bahia State were relatively poorly constructed, using 5-6 logs. Set a lugsail from the mainmast and a small, triangular sail from the after mast. Extinct by end of the 19th century. Other recorded names: **iangada, iga(ra)peba, itápába, jangada de pau, peúba jangada; piperis** (indigenous name at Rio de Janeiro). Further reading: Nearco Barroso Guedes de Araújo, *Jangadas* (Fortaleza: Banco de Nordeste do Brasil, 1985). Note also **burrinha, catraia-3, jangada-bote, jangada de tábuas, jangada do alto, paquete-3**.
3. *Paraguay:* **Rafts** of commercially important logs were floated from upper tributaries of the Río Paraná to Asunción, especially in the late 18th and early 19th centuries. If not broken up at Asunción to be sawn into lumber and beams, continued to the Río de la Plata to be disassembled there. Some carried cargo. Reported lengths 17-27m.
4. *Portugal:* **a.** Log **raft** used in the Viana do Costelo area in the north to collect seaweed. Most composed of 9 logs, roughly squared and pegged together, the central and outer logs extending beyond the bow and stern. A smaller variety consists of 7 planks with the outer 2 longer at each end. Slight upturn at the bow. An additional slender log adds freeboard to each end. Rolled to and from the water on wheels secured under the center. Poled. One-man craft. Reported lengths 1.6-2.5m, widths 1-1.6m, depths 0.2-0.3m. At Anha just across the Rio Lima, the **jangada** (locally called **Anha**) was made of level logs except for the 2 outer logs, which arched up to form wheelbarrow-like handles used to bring the craft from the water. Logs pegged together. **b.** At Marinhas, just north of Esposende, the **jangada** was a covered, box-like craft filled with cork. Used mainly to fish for octopus among the nearby rocks. Handles at each corner aided in carrying the craft. The **jangada de cortiço**, composed of strips of cork contained in a wood framework, is still used at Marinhas. Wheels transport the craft to and from the water. Similar **jangadas** were used at Esposende. Note also **cortiçeira,**

cortiço. c. At Apúlia, south of Esposende, a box-like, wheelbarrow **jangada** was used to collect seaweed and octopus. Cork filled the insides; wooden wheels were placed at one end or under the hull, handles at the other end. Also at Apúlia, bound rolls of cork were pegged together to form a **raft**. Locally called **barca★**. Spelling variant: pl. **jangadas de cortiça**
Spelling variants: **hangada, jaganda, jangade, jangoda, zangada**. Further references: **balsa-11, jangar, life raft, timber raft-1**
jangada-bote *Brazil, NE:* Planked **fishing boat★** that has the **jangada★** rig and general boat design. Rounded hull, keel. Removable rudder in lieu of the steering oar. Waterproof hatch abaft the daggerboard trunk. Sets a baggy, triangular sail to a curved mast. Reported lengths 6-7m, width 1.5m.
jangada de cortiço See **cortiço, jangada-4**
jangada de dormida See **jangada do alto**
jangada de pau See **jangada-2**
jangada de tábuas *Brazil, NE:* Planked facsimile of the log **jangada★**. Used mainly for fishing. Space between bottom and deck stores supplies and fish; access through a hatch. Bow and stern curve up to aid in launching from and landing on the beach; skegs common or may have a keel. Shallow stern transom above deadwood; shallow bow transom. Equipment and rigging similar to the **jangada**, but adds a rudder and a jib. Frequently employs an outboard motor in addition to sails. Crew of 3. Reported lengths 5-8m, widths 0.7-1.8m, depths 0.30-0.35m. Name variant: **janga★**
jangada do alto *Brazil, NE:* Largest of the **jangadas★**, fishing at the edge of the Continental Shelf. These **rafts★** are made of logs 1.1-1.3m in circumference; usually 8 logs. They have a salting platform for fish preservation, which, when it is necessary to stay out at night, is used as a sleeping bench. Last about a year. Crew of 2. Length to ca. 8m. Name variant: **jangada de dormida**
jangada salva-vidas See **lift raft**
jangadas de cortiça See **jangada-4**
jangade See **jangada**
jangala See **jangar**
jangar *India:* A pontoon **raft★** formed by placing a platform across the top of 2 large **dugout canoes★**, generally as a temporary arrangement to ferry bulky goods, vehicles, or cattle, as well as troops and supplies. Reported as early as the 16th century, mainly from the Malabar Coast. Sometimes a bamboo railing surrounded the platform. Other recorded names: **iangada, iangar, jagada, jancada, janga★, jangada★, jangala, janjar, jungar;** in Tamil: **changādam, sangādam★, shangādam;** in Sanskrit: **samghādam**
janggolan *Indonesia, central:* **1.** Trader of southwestern Madura and the Java coast to the west; also serves as a carrier for the larval milkfish that are placed in local fishponds. Important as a bulk carrier, especially for salt, and now timber on the larger vessels. Extant, but relatively few now being built. Solid, plank-built vessel; closely spaced frames inserted later; massive beam ends projected through the sides, now seen only on the smaller boats. Flaring sides; strong sheer. Bottom curves fore-and-aft; keel extends ram-like beyond the bow and stern. Raked, wedge-shaped transoms at each

end, the bow quite tall; both transoms elaborately carved and painted. Large ones decked, small ones undecked; most of hold area protected by a low, peaked-roof deckhouse. Employs 2 massive quarter rudders lashed against a crossbeam and worked against a heavy, H-shaped support on the after deck. Two short masts stepped forward of the deckhouse. Support triangular sails, apexes down. Yards at top and bottom; bamboo spar from the deck braces outer end of the upper yard at the proper angle; yards also stayed from a boom set out over each side. Ring on the end of the upper yard of the smaller foresail runs over the bowsprit as the tack. A 3rd temporary sail may be raised from the deckhouse. Poled in narrow waterways. Crew of 6-7 on a large vessel, 3 on the smaller. Average length ca. 15m; length of a large **janggolan** 20m, beam 7m, hold depth 2.3m. Other recorded names: **djanggolan, djangölan, djěnggolan, jangolan, perahu janggolan, prahoe djanggolan**. Further reading: B. Kaiser, "The Janggolans of Madura," *Wooden Boat* 77 (1987), 52-59.
2. Small boat with a western-style hull that ferries passengers in the Benoa area in southern Bali and undertakes long trips in search of turtles. Carvel-planked; slightly raked, straight stem and sternpost; sharp stern, above which a wide platform for the helmsman rests on 2-3 transverse beams. Straight keel; hull circular in cross section amidships; ribs scarfed at about the turn of the bilges; marked sheer. Open or have a house amidships; midline or quarter rudder; tiller worked by foot. Those catching turtles have fish tanks. Short, vertical mast stepped through a thwart about one-third in from the bow. Sets an elongated, boomed triangular sail, apex down, tacked to one of two bitts near the bow. Tall mast. Also poled. Length 11m, beam 2.75m, depth 0.76m.

jangoda See **jangada**
jangolan See **janggolan**
janguada, janguda See **balsa-11**
janjar See **jangar**
jaola *Solomon Islands (Santa Cruz Group), western Pacific:* Small, single-outrigger paddling **canoe★**. Dugout hull, round in cross section; narrow opening, just wide enough for one leg, and flattened on top permitting the paddler to sit on both gunwales. Raked ends, rounded forefoot. Hull coated with lime. Two squared outrigger booms set close together; become thicker where they cross the hull, shaped to fit into the opening, and lashed to a stick wedged beneath the gunwale lips; also support a small, solid platform on the opposite side. Booms do not connect directly with the short, sharp-ended float; multiple connectives, consisting of straight and curved sticks and stringers, attach to the float; another platform is set on outrigger booms. Sometimes 2 light floats, joined side by side, provide additional support. Paddles have long, slender blades and very long looms. Length ca. 4m. Other recorded names: **téaco, tealo**
jarm See **djerme**
jase *India, W:* Reported as an indigenous vessel of the Portuguese district of Diu; sewn hull. Rowed and sailed. Spelling variants: **djehaz** (Arabic); **jasy**
jasy See **jase**

jatan See **jaten**
jaten *Indonesia, central:* Term applied to **fishing boats★** found at several locations on Java. Word probably derived from the *jati* wood of which the dugout hulls are made. In the Surabaja area on the north coast, these boats are double-**outrigger canoes★**. Small, upturned piece at the bow; straight, slightly raked stern. Two horizontal booms cross atop the hull and connect by vertical stanchions with slender floats. Boomed, triangular sail is tacked to the bow and set to a light, stubby mast. Reported lengths 6-9m. On the south coast, especially in the Kediri and Madiun areas, the **jaten** is a simple **dugout canoe★** used in offshore fishing by 1-2 persons. Sharp ends with tops cut horizontally to form platforms for inshore fishing, or on those fishing offshore, the bow may turn up to a sharp point. No outriggers or washstrakes. Length ca. 3m. Other recorded names: **djatèn, jatan, prahoe** (or **praoe**) **djatèn**
jatobá See **igat**
Java trader See **mayang-1, pencalang-1**
jawger See **jagger**
jaxta See **yacht**
Jebacco boat See **Chebacco boat**
jebeque See **xebec**
jebus See **compartment boat**
jeha dhoni *India, Minicoy Island:* Village-owned **snake boat** used for ceremonial occasions on this island off the west coast. Long, narrow boat painted with scrollwork and interlacing patterns. Twelve oarsmen, uniformly dressed, sit 2 abreast when racing; oars distinctively painted. Note also **dhoni-5**.
jehazi See **jahazi, Zanzibar zahazi**
jeitera, jeito See **xeito**
jekt *Norway, W and N:* Square-sailed **coaster★** that worked from the 14th into the early 20th century. Primary port of call was Bergen; carried local produce, dried fish, firewood, and cattle. Those with a quarterdeck were popular for wedding parties, the ceremony held on the after deck. Hauled on shore for the winter.

jekt

Mainly clinker construction (**klinkajekt**), some carvel (the **klavertjekt**); flat floors amidships, sharp rise at the ends; rounded bilges; straight keel; marked sheer; maximum beam forward of amidships, tapering toward stern. Tall stem, sometimes recurving above the gunwales; curved below the waterline. Cabin at stern ending flush with the transom, which was plumb or slightly raked. Outboard rudder; tiller worked from cabin roof. Open waist, later a fixed deck (the **flakajekt**). A **ship's boat**★ was hung from davits, carried atop the cargo, or towed. Pole mast, stepped roughly amidships; stayed fore-and-aft and with 6-8 shrouds. Sail shape, either rectangular or quadrilateral, varied with the district. Bonnets permitted raising sail to clear cargo or to shorten sail in rough weather. Some ran up topsails. Oars used when necessary. Auxiliaries on many later boats. Crew of 2-35; averaged 5. Reported lengths 10-22m; e.g., length 18m, beam 6.4m, depth 3.7m. One less than 400t was a **småjekt**, between 400 and 800t was a **myllåjekt** (or **mellomjekt**, **mellajekt**), larger than 800t was a **storjekt**. Other recorded names: **jægt, jakt**★, **jekta, råseiljekt**; pl. **jektene, jekter**. Most designated by place of origin: **holmedaljekt, Holvikjekt, nordfarar, nordfarjekt, nordfjordjekt, nordlandsjægt** or **-jekt, nordmørsjekt, Norwegian jekta, sognejekt, sunnfjordjekt, sunnmørsjekt, trønderjekt, vestlandsjekt**. The small Masfjord boat was called a **småjekt**; one from Osterfjord was an **ostreskuta**. The **ship's boat** was a **skipsbåt**★, **skibbåt**, or in Sunnmore, a **jektebåt(or), Jægte-Baade**, or **jekt-skjebåt**. Further reference: **jakt-2**

jekta See **jekt**
jektbåt See **skipsbåt-2**
jektebåt, jektene, jekter, jektskjebåt See **jekt**
jektskjebåt See **jekt**
je-kukltai See **kukltai**
jelba See **jalbūt-1**
jele See **dingi-2**
jelias See **jalia**
Jelle See **jolle-1**
jeloa See **jalbūt-1**
jendi *Ethiopia:* Round, leather-covered craft that ferried passengers across the Blue Nile River. Propelled by wading or swimming. Note also **jandi**.
Jenkins creeker See **crab scraper**
jĕram, jeram scouter See **kakap jĕram**
Jersey bankskiff, Jersey beach skiff See **Sea Bright skiff**
Jersey Coast sneakbox See **Barnegat sneakbox**
Jersey oyster schooner See **Delaware Bay oyster schooner**
Jersey sea skiff See **pound boat-1, Sea Bright skiff**
Jersey skiff See **Sea Bright skiff**
jhong See **jong-1**
jiabanchuan See **lorcha-3**
Jiangsu trader See **Kiangsu trader**
jiao hua chuan *China, E:* Fast craft that carried mail and messages on the lower Chang Jiang (Yangtze) basin prior to the advent of **steamers**. May still be found occasionally in adjacent Zhejiang (Che-Chiang or Chekiang) province as a passenger and light freight transport. Helmsman, seated against a back rest, propels the boat by a foot-operated oar on the starboard side and a paddle held under the arm on either side. The oar, ca. 3.66m long and secured by a tholepin and a grommet, has a long blade, a short loom with a depression for the right foot, and a block-type grip for the left foot. Boat divided into 7 bulkheads, the 2 midship wells reserved for passengers. Narrow, square ends; stern sheers up sharply; flat bottom; deck at stern for helmsman.

Rudder available but seldom used; tiller worked by movement of the helmsman's back. Sectional mat house covers most of the boat. Generally painted, inside and out; oculi added. Reported lengths 7-12m; e.g., length 7m, beam 1.2m, depth 0.53m; shallow draft. Other recorded names: **bateau pédale, bateau pied, bateau poste, chiao-hua ch'uan, foot-paddling boat, kio-t'a tch'ouan, post boat**★. Note also **hua zi-4**.
jibla See **jalbūt**
jigger **1.** A vessel, especially a **fishing boat**★, that has a small mast (a jigger mast) fitted to its rudder, although may otherwise be **sloop**★-rigged.
2. *United States, NE:* A vessel that used weighted hooks, called "jigs," in fishing for mackerel. Generally a small **schooner**★ or **sloop**.
See also **pinky**.
jigger barque See **jackass bark**
jigger flat See **Mersey flat, Weaver flat**
jigger sloop *England, W:* Term applied to a **ketch**★-rigged **Mersey flat**★ that sailed along the coast. Counter stern, bulwarks, bowsprit.
jiman See **tsiman**
jing bang chuan *China, central:* Carried cargo on the Chang Jiang (Yangtze), mainly between Wuhan and Yichang (I-Ch'ang). Broad, flat, raked bow and stern, transversely planked; swept up at ends; often had a heavy beam at bow. Flat bottom, longitudinally planked; heavy wales along the sides; inboard rudder. Flush deck; main and stern cabins wood-sided and mat-roofed. Poling gangway along each side; crossbeam forward of cabin held sweep pivots; on trips above Yichang, additional crossbeams lashed on; a pair of lumber irons held sweeps when not in use. Two masts set balance lugsails; mainmast stepped through house or forward of it; small foremast. Reported lengths 17-23m, widths 3-4.2m, depths 1.2-1.5m; shallow draft. Other recorded names: **ching-pang ch'uan, Kingchow River junk**
jing bang hua zi See **hua zi-2**
joal See **Ness yoal**
joamgua, joanga See **juanga**
jo-boat See **johnboat-1**
Joe boat See **bateau-7n, gas boat-4, johnboat-1, launch-8**
joelong-joelong See **julung-julung-2**
Joey, Joey boat See **day boat-2**
johnboat *United States, central:* **1.** Small, shallow, boxy craft that dates to the early settlers in the Ozark Mountains of Arkansas and Missouri, who used it mainly for fishing and hunting. Some early boats in the Ozarks hauled freight and were used in the logging industry. Flat bottom; longitudinal or athwartships planking, usually

johnboat-1

curved, ending above the water; bow and stern square; often a shallow bow transom. Sides straight or tapered and vertical or flared. May have a double keel. Generally short end decks; 1-2 benches. Most now have bottoms of plywood or aluminum. Might be rowed, poled, paddled,

sculled, or use an outboard motor. Special inboard boats can work through muddy marsh passages only a few cm. deep. Lengths from 3m (for pond use) to as long as 9m; e.g., length 4.3m, beam 1.22m, depth 0.3m; shallow draft. The aluminum fishing types are shorter and beamier. In the early 20th century, a special type was developed for night spear fishing: over 9m long and 0.61m wide; called **redhorse runners** after a preferred fish, the redhorse sucker. Other recorded names: **jo-boat, Joe boat, jon-boat, punt★**. Note also **scow-2**.
   2. The Illinois River **johnboat** was mainly a fishing craft. Adopted an inboard engine in the 1920s. Reported lengths 5.5-6m. Further references: **bateau-7n, launch-8**

Johnny boat, Johnny woodboat See **Saint John River woodboat**
joinct See **junk**
jointed canal boat See **liang jie tou**
jo'kong See **jongkong, kolek ma' Siam**
jol *Belgium/Netherlands:* Small, open boat used as a **dinghy★**, as a small-scale **fishing boat★** (**visjol**), and as a general-utility boat for farmers (**boerenjol**). Usually transom-sterned. The **fishing boat** might have a small live well. Mainly rowed, but some set a sail. Spelling variant: pl. **jollen**. Note also **Staverse jol**. Further references: **beach yawl-1, Fair Isle yoal, jolle, jollyboat-1, Ness yoal, vlet, yawl**
jola *Netherlands Antilles, southern group:* Term for a common flat-bottomed, keelless **rowboat★**. See also **yawl**.
jolboat See **jalbūt-1**
jolbut See **jalbūt-1, Lamu jahazi**
jole See **Ness yoal, shell**
joletta See **scull**
joliwat See **jolly boat-1**
jöll See **jolle, Sandboot**
jolla, jollar, jollarna See **jolle**
jollawatte See **jolly boat-1**
jolle 1. Scandinavian and German term for a **dinghy★**, **jolly boat★, skiff★**, or **yawl★**. May be used for lake or inshore fishing (the Danish **fiskejolle**), for pleasure, or as a **ship's boat★**. Transom or sharp stern; usually without a keel; rowed or sculled, and frequently sets 1-2 spritsails. Usually beamy. Spelling variants: **Jelle, jol★, Jöll, joll(a), Jollenboot, julla** (dim.), **julle, skibsjolle**; pl. **jollar, jollarna, jollen, joller, jullar, jullarna, jullen**. Note also **kadrejerjolle, kragejolle, smakkejolle, sumpjolle, sundjolle**.
2. *Finland, S:* Here the **julle** is a sharp-ended boat with a keel used as a small **skötbåt★**. Heavy stem and sternpost, wide strakes. Reported lengths 4-5.5m, widths 1.2-1.3m.
3. *Finland, SW:* The **julle** of the Åland Islands is carvel-planked and has a transom stern. Sets 1-2 spritsails and occasionally a staysail. Mainsail boomed.
4. *Finland, W:* The **jolle** from the Österbotten (Pohjanmaa) region is clinker-built with broad strakes that abut against the stem and sternpost obliquely, the top 2 strakes on each side terminating at the gunwale. Rounded bottom, flaring sides, T-keel; lightly framed except for several major frames that cross the bottom without being attached to the keel or garboard strakes. Double-ended; on some, the bow is slightly fuller than

the stern. Stem curves and overhangs; sternpost straight and strongly raked; open. Mainly rowed, using double tholepins. May set a sprit mainsail and foresail. Length 5.3m, beam 1.62m. Note also **roddjulle**.
   5. *Germany:* **a.** In the North Sea, the small, open **Jolle** of Helgoland Island fished for lobsters. Some assist the **Helgoländer Schnigge**. Single mast, stepped through a forward thwart, sets lugsails. Rowed with a pair of oars. **b.** On the lower Elbe River, the Spree, and along the North Sea Schleswig-Holstein coast, the **Jolle** transported farm produce and lumber (the **Holzjolle**). Some **Jollen** served as water taxis in ports, notably Hamburg. Flat floors, keel, curved stem, sharp stern. Half or fully decked; outboard rudder. Those that fished had a live well. Sprit- or **cutter★**-rigged when sailed. Reported lengths overall 8.2-8.5m; beamy. Other recorded names: **Gelle, Gille, Gölle; Holzgelle. c.** The small, open **Jolle** of the middle Weser River has a small bow transom and a wider stern transom. Maximum beam well forward, tapering sharply to the bow; low sheer. Single thwart; wide rudder blade partly activated by a bar to the outer end; tiller. **d.** Open **fishing boat★** that worked off Baltic Sea beaches from about the 16th century. The **Warnemünder Jolle** had sharp ends, keel; lightly raked, curved stem; more strongly curved sternpost, strong sheer. Outboard rudder; tiller. Stepped 2 sprit-rigged masts: the taller mainmast set in about a quarter from the bow, the after mast stepped roughly amidships; staysail to jibboom. The **Jolle** of the Wismar area set 2 lugsails. Also rowed. Length ca. 8.4m. Other recorded names: **Jöll, Warnemünder Fischerjolle**
   6. *Norway:* Smallest of the **ship's boats** (see **skipsbåt-2**). Often carried aboard a **femböring★** (**femböringsjolle**), a large **åttring★**, or a **storbåt★**. Clinker-planked usually, flat floors amidships, T-keel, slack bilges, marked sheer. Full bow, curved stem, sometimes a bow transom (**pram★** type); raked transom stern. Open; stern seat; 1-3 thwarts. Rowed with l, 2 (**to-rors jolle**), or 3 (**tre-rors jolle**) pairs of oars. Reported lengths 2.82-3.44m; e.g., length 2.82m, beam ca. 1.3m, depth 0.5m. Spelling variants: **jolla, jollen(e)**; pl. **joller**
   7. *Sweden:* The west coast boat may be a bluff-bowed, open boat with a transom stern (see **bohusjulle**) or sharp-ended; the east coast boat is double-ended. Clinker-planked. Used for fishing, as a general workboat, or as a **dinghy**; some types form racing classes. Sailing boats (the **segeljulle**) have a steep rise to the floors, creating a deeper hull. Heavy, motorized boats (the **motorjulle**) have a deck forward. Set 1-2 spritsails with a staysail or jib and occasionally a topsail. Mast generally stepped through a thwart. Also rowed. Reported lengths 2-6m.
   Further references: **Buttjolle, isjolle, yawl**
jolle fra Snekkersten See **sundjolle**
jollen See **jol, jolle**
Jollenboot, jollene, joller See **jolle**
jolly See **jolly boat-1**
jolly boat 1. Beamy **ship's boat★** carried aboard or on stern davits. May serve as the captain's boat or as a general-purpose craft. Generally strongly built with clinker planking, often with a wide transom; flat floors; strong

sheer. Usually rowed, the number of oars depending on the size of the boat. Reported lengths 3.7-8.5m. Selected name variants: **bărcŭta, djali boet, gelly-watte, gölle, jol*, joliwat, jollawatte, jolly, jollyvatt, jollywatt, jolywat(t), skiff*, šl(j)upka, stern boat*, yole*, yolly boat**. Note also **blood boat, canot, dinghy, gallivat, petit canot, whaler-2**.

2. *United Kingdom:* Although the name appears as early as the late 15th century, in the British navy of the late 18th-19th centuries, the **jolly boat** was a small **cutter***-type pulling 4 oars, sometimes 10, double-banked. Single- or double-masted, setting lugsails. Reported lengths 3.7-10.4m.

3. *England, NE:* At Staithes, a double-ended, clinker-built boat with a keel that engages in fishing, the type of fish dependent on the season. Reported lengths from 3.7-5.5m. Name variant: **Staithes jolly boat**

4. *England, SW:* **a.** In western Cornwall, a **jolly boat** was a long, narrow, clinker-built craft that served a particular **lugger*** (see **West Cornish lugger**). The small, open boat was sculled out to meet the **lugger** and towed back to port while fish were unloaded into it so it could arrive early to market. Four-oared at Newlyn and 3-oared at Mousehole. Some fitted with sails. **b.** The **jolly boats** of the Isles of Scilly and Mounts Bay, locally called **shadrons**, formed a racing class in the 1930s. Carried a gunter rig; drop keel. Generally raced with a crew of 3. Lengths 3.7m, 4.3m, and 5.5m.

5. *Scotland, S:* In the 2nd half of the 19th century, 8.2m-long **jollyboats** were raced on the Firths of Forth, Clyde, and Tay.

Further reference: **jālibōt**

jollyvatt, jollywatt See **jolly boat-1**
jolong See **julung**
jolong-jolong See **julung-julung-2**
jolywat, jolywatt See **jolly boat-1**
jombo See **chombo**
jonboat See **johnboat-1**
jonc See **junk**
joncaro See **jukung**
jonck See **junk**
jonco See **jong-2, junk**
joncque See **junk**
Jonesport peapod See **peapod**

jong 1. *Bangladesh:* Large **riverboat*** capable of transporting 8-20t of produce, jute, and merchandise. Used mainly in the rainy season. Stem and sternpost formed by heavy, squared blocks; high bow; bottom flattened toward the front. Oarsmen stand on a platform above the arched bamboo roof that covers most of the hull. Mast stepped amidships. Crew of 10 or more. Shallow draft. Average cap. 10t. Spelling variants: **jang, janga*, jhong**

2. *Indonesia/Myanmar (Burma):* Trading vessel cited in 16th- and 17th-century reports. Built mainly on the north coast of Java, south coast of Kalimantan, and at Pegu in Myanmar. Planking set edge-to-edge, dowelled; usually had multiple sheathing; crossbeams pierced the sides. Bow raked, with a curled-up, ram-like projection just above the waterline; stern raked and swept up with high transom. Employed quarter rudders. Some triple-decked. Set a combination of mat lateen-type sails to 3 masts plus a boomed-out, triangular sail (apex down)

at the bow or tall, rectangular, battened lugsails. Crew of ca. 24. Length ca. 16m, beam 8.8m, depth 5.5m; to ca. 700t. Other recorded names: **djong, jonco, junco**

3. *Indonesia, NW/Peninsular Malaysia/Singapore:* A model boat, along the general lines of the racing **kolek***, actively raced in Singapore, Johore, and the nearby Indonesian islands. Three types: those used by children, those sailed in calm waters, and a type used in rougher or open waters. May reach speeds of 32km per hour. Hollowed out of a single piece of very light wood to a thickness of 3-15mm. Forefoot and heel rounded and extend in **kolek** style; flat sheer; keel. Decked. Large, high-peaked spritsail set to a mast stepped about a third of the way from the bow. Large jib run to a long bowsprit. Mainly sailed across the wind. Unusual feature for a Malay Peninsula craft is the outrigger, which substitutes for the **kolek's** live ballast. When used as a rudder, the float is set at the required angle and held with diagonal struts. Reported lengths 0.8-2.54m, widths 0.11-0.22m, depths 0.06-0.09m; length of outrigger boom 1.41-2.03m.

4. *East Malaysia:* Toy boat used by children of the Sarawak coastal area. Bow sharp; stern also sharp but with a horizontal, shelf-like extension. One or 2 booms connect directly into the side of the outrigger float. Booms either lashed across the top of the gunwales or pierce the side of the hull. A **jong** may also be a symbolic craft, employed by some indigenous peoples in an exorcism ceremony to cast out diseases. Note also **djoeng**.

5. *Singapore:* The peoples of Pulau Brani (island just south of the main island) made a model **jong** that incorporated features of several local craft, but like the racing **jong**, had an outrigger. Carved from a single piece of wood except for the endpost heads, which were added on. Sharp ends with curved forefoot and heel that angles in a raked, straight line. Mildly curved bottom, keel only at ends. Marked sheer; slightly flared sides; washboards fitted; decked in forward quarter. Single long boom attached directly to a small float. Two masts that set gunter sails; wide jib to a bowsprit. Reported lengths 82.5-92cm. Name variant: **nadeh**

Further reference: **junk**

jongkong *Indonesia, W/Peninsular Malaysia:* **1.** Malay word applied to any undecked boat without built-up ends. Found in the southern part of the Malay Peninsula and the adjacent Riau-Lingga Archipelagoes. Most are **dugout canoes*** with a washstrake added; fastened inboard, outboard, or set edge-to-edge. Small types paddled with a single-, and occasionally, a double-bladed paddle. Larger boats frequently set a small, triangular sail. One-man boats 2.7-3.1m in length; larger types to 4.27m.

2. *Peninsular Malaysia:* **a.** A small **dinghy*** carried athwart the **payang*** and the **perahu buatan barat***. **b.** May also refer to a small iron or steel **barge*** designated to carry ballast, or to one made of tin.

Other recorded names: **djoenkoeng, djokong, djong-kang, djongko(e)ng, (d)jonkong, jo'kong, jukong, jukung*, juncabo**

jonk See **junk**
jonkong See **jongkong**
jonkos, jonque See **junk**

jonque à carène See **tu ti chuan**
jonque de Hangtcheou See **Shaoxing ch'uan**
Joppa shay *United States, NE:* Type of flat **skiff**⋆ indigenous to the Joppa Flats off the mouth of the Merrimack River in northeastern Massachusetts.
josher *England:* **1.** Named for Joshua Fellows of the **canal boat**⋆ firm of Fellows, Morton and Clayton. A **narrow boat**⋆ that operated from London north to Preston on the Hill from the mid-19th to the mid-20th century. Hull sides generally of iron; bottom crossplanked of elm. Front finer and more raked than true **narrow boats**; longer counter, cabin sides have more tumble home. Those powered by steam were called **engines**; counter is "tipped up" to accommodate the 1.0m-diameter propeller; a few still operate. Some converted to pleasure craft and others are now being built along **josher** lines. Length 22m, beam 2m. Further name variant: **FMC boat**
2. After ca. 1920, diesel-powered **narrow boats**⋆ commonly worked with former **horse boats**⋆ and were known collectively as a **josher** (or **pair**); the **horse boat** was called the **butty** (a buddy).
jotter See **tjotter**
joung, jounque See **junk**
Juan de Fuca sharpie See **sharpie-schooner**
juanga 1. *Indonesia, E:* Largest and most important of the **galley**⋆-like vessels of early royalty of the Moluccan islands; used mainly for war and piracy. Double-ended; ends curved up; figurehead at the bow, often of a bird. Keel, ribs, and strakes lashed from inside so that cording did not show outside; strakes pegged. Upper deck reserved for royal personages and armed soldiers; covered with an awning. Some paddlers sat below inside the craft; the remainder were outside on a cane platform constructed on 10-12 crossbeams that extended as far as 1.8-5.5m beyond each side; some may have rowed while others paddled. Smaller types employed ca. 150 paddlers, larger ca. 200; paddle blades mostly spear-shaped; a crosspiece formed the grip. Also sailed using mat or sackcloth sails, probably rectangular. Reported lengths on keel 18-37m; e.g., length 32m, width 3.3m, hold depth 2m. Other recorded names: **djo(e)anga, djuanga, janga**⋆, **joamgua, joanga**; probably also **bo(a)nga, booanga, b(o)uanga, couanga.** Note also **korakora.**
2. *Philippines, S:* A heavily armed vessel, especially of the Iranun (or Illanun) pirates of Jolo; adopted by the Spanish during the 17th century. Planking added to a dugout keel piece; sharp, overhanging ends or tall stems; top strakes extended beyond the bow as 2 wings; steep rise to the floors. Cabin extended out over the quarters. Breastwork at bow mounted 2 swivel guns, and a long gun projected through the breastwork. May have had double outriggers. Two or 4 quarter rudders. Rowed double- or triple-banked with oarsmen pulling a single oar; used as many as 34 oars per side. Stepped 2-3 strikable masts that set wide lugsails. Crew of 50-300 rowers and soldiers. Reported lengths 16-40m; e.g., length 25m, beam 2.5m, depth 2m. Other recorded names: **boanga, joanga, lanoen, lanong**
jugong *Cocos (Keeling) Islands, E Indian Ocean:* Small, sharp-ended sailing boat used for interisland commuting,

fishing, and pleasure. Straight, plumb stem; raked sternpost; short fore- and stern decks; keel curved toward the bow; hard, high chines. Outboard rudder worked with lines. Mast stepped through thwart. Sets a boomed gunter mainsail and a large jib tacked to stemhead. Reported lengths 3-6m, narrow; very shallow draft. Spelling variants: **dukong**⋆, **jukong, jukung**⋆
jukong See **jongkong, jugong, jukung**
jukúa *Guatemala:* **Dugout canoe**⋆ that carries people and cargo on Lake Atitlán; also a 1-man boat used for fishing. The relatively flat-bottomed hull is shaped from a cedar trunk halved lengthwise, retaining the full width of the tree; maximum beam well forward, achieved by using lower end of the tree trunk as the bow end; bottom flares up at ends. Bows cut flat and

jukúa

sheer up to form a raised point above the waterline. Washboards nailed to the sides, stern, and bows; boards follow the line of the dugout base and sheer up to a point. Stern washboard rounded on top, or where lacking, rounded end of the log serves this purpose. To aid in beaching, 2 handles are created by residual extensions at the stern; large boats have one at the bow also. Seams caulked with pitch. No seats, thwarts, or braces. Mostly paddled, standing. Range from 3-10m long and 0.66-1.6m wide; average length 5.8m, beam 1.2m. Other recorded names: **cayuco**⋆, **xku**
jukung *Indonesia, central:* **1.** General term in Java and the Seribu Islands to the northwest for a **boat**⋆. Range from small, inshore fishing craft to seagoing cargo vessels. May have 1-2 outriggers, or none. Generally can be sailed.
2. In eastern Java, Madura, Bali, and Lombok, identified as a **dugout canoe**⋆ extended by a plank on each side and by an end piece at the bow and stern. Some in Bali fashioned from a single log, without added planks.
3. On Madura, Bali, and Lombok, a double-outrigger sailing **canoe**⋆. Sharp ends vary, but bow frequently bifurcated with the upper jaw curving upwards to a sharp point. On Bali, a **jukung** with large, gaping jaws is a **jukung mulut** or **jukung bungut**. Stern usually a blunt point. The so-called female **jukung** ends curve up smoothly to a point. Bottom curves fore-and-aft. Quarter

jukung-3

rudders, but only on port side on Bali. Some gaily painted. Series of rounded thwarts wedged into hull sides; used to lash down the outrigger booms. Two straight booms cross the hull near the ends to connect directly with the float; in some parts of Bali, these rise upward before curving down to connect with each float. Float as long or longer than the hull and projects forward of the bow. Lateen-type sail set to a very short, vertical mast on Bali or a forward-raking mast on Madura. Flexible spar at top and bottom of sail; spar rest at the stern. At one time, some set a spritsail. Reported lengths 4.2-9m, very narrow. Fur-ther reading: Richard D. Herron, "Balinese Jukung: Vestiges of an Ancient Past," *Nautical Research Journal* 38 (1993), 152-162; *ibid*, "A Personal Look at Some Traditional Vessels of Bali and Madura, Indonesia," *INA Quarterly* 21/1-2 (1994), 20-28.

4. Plank-extended **dugout canoe** of the Dayak peoples of southeastern Kalimantan (Borneo). Sharp ends, cut-away forefoot; ends may be shaped above the gunwale to look like a stemhead; wide strake added; consider-able flare to the sides. Several major thwarts; some have additional light crosspieces. Sometimes as many as 20 **jukungs** are joined by a light platform, forming a long **raft★**. Length ca. 7.6m.

5. In the Tambelan Islands, west of Kalimantan, the **jukung** was a small, open, plank-built boat with sharp, moderately curved ends; usually without outriggers. Sailed and paddled. Length ca. 3.5m.
Other recorded names: **cokong, d(h)jukong, djoeko(e)ng, djuk(k)ung, dyúkun, ioncaro, joncaro, jukong, prau djukung**. Note also **jungkung, sekong**. Further references: **jongkong, jugong**

jukung bungut See **jukung-3**

jukung comprèng *Indonesia, central:* Sprit-rigged **fishing boat★** of the Cirebon area on the north coast of Java. Two masts stepped through thwarts and easily demountable. Tall, roughly triangular end pieces. Color-fully painted. Name variant: **comprèng★**

jukung mulut See **jukung-3**

jukung tambangan See **tambangan**

jukung tembon See **tjemplon-2**

julla, jullar, jullarna See **jolle**

julle See **bohusjulle, fälbåt-2, fäljulle-2, jolle, skötbåt-2**

julle från Orust See **bohusjulle**

jullen See **jolle-1**

julung *Indonesia, central:* **1.** Common term for a **boat★**, but especially one with a vertically forked stern.

2. Large cargo vessel of eastern Madura and Banjuwangi at the east end of Java. Decked with bamboo.

3. Double-outrigger **fishing boat★** of the same area that worked until the early 20th century. Sharp bow raked inboard from the waterline; sharp, curved stern; on some, the upper part of the bow extended forward to a point, and the stern was forked. Bottom rounded. Some had a wooden house. Two booms supported the bamboo floats. The forward boom either bowsed down to connect directly with the float or to a curved stick that attached to the float. The aft boom flared upwards, stopping just short of the float and from there, connected to the float. Very short mast supported a triangular sail that had yards at top and bottom; apex of sail tacked downward. Some also set a very small sail of similar design at the bow. Length 9.4m, beam 0.4m, depth 0.6m.
Other recorded names: **djoeloeng, djouloeng, jolong, prahoe djoeloeng**. Note also **julung-julung**.

julung-julung 1. *Indonesia, central:* Double-outrigger cargo vessel of Sulawesi (Celebes). Bow higher than stern. Sail set to a bipod mast of bamboo. Other re-corded names: **djoeloeng-djoeloeng, prao julung-julung**. Note also **julung**.

2. *Malaysia:* Large craft with a long, projecting prow (*julung*). Clipper stem; cutaway forefoot. Decked; ornate, square galleries aft. Set lugsails on 1-2 masts. Other recorded names: **djoeloeng-djoeloeng, jo(e)long-jo(e)long, perahu jalong-jalong, prahu jolong-jolong, prao julung-julung**

junc See **junk**

juncabo See **jongkong**

junck See **junk**

junco See **jong-2, junk**

juncque See **junk**

jung See **junk, tongkang-2**

jungar See **jangar**

jungku See **lambo-1**

jungkung 1. *Indonesia, central:* Long, narrow **dugout canoe★** mainly of southeastern Kalimantan (Borneo). Varies in size and construction details. Some are sim-ple dugouts with sharp ends that curve up before being cut square on the top. Others have a beak-like stern design and are cut square at the bow. Washstrake may be added. Bottom generally curved and may have a keel cut out. Usually open; multiple thwarts. Protec-tive roof at the stern or amidships common. Generally paddled, but some are rigged for sailing.

2. Term designates a boat type in the Sakra area of Lombok in the Lesser Sunda Islands.
Spelling variants: **djoeko(e)ng, djoengkoeng**. Note also **jukung**.

junk A term of broad or narrow meaning, depending on one's depth of experience with native craft, ranging from "odd as a Chinese **junk**" and "sailing vessel of Oriental build" to "if a craft is large enough to carry a water buffa-lo standing athwartships, it is clearly a **junk**. If the animal must assume some other position, or perhaps cannot even make the voyage, the vessel is a **sampan★**." Officially in China, a **junk** or **min chuan** (**commoner's boat**) refers to privately owned sailing, sculling, or rowing craft, as opposed to a motorized vessel; government-owned **junks** are called **guan chuan** (**kuan chuan**). The term can be broadly applied to native sailing vessels of the Far East; Chinese **junks** going to Japan and Southeast Asia were commonly called **sommes** or **sommas**. Usually have a high poop, no keel, high sheer, bulkheaded hull; large-bladed, retractable, mid-line rudder or quarter rudders; and sets 2-5 battened lugsails to raking, unstayed pole masts. May be oceangoing or river craft and have served as traders, fishing vessels, **men-of-war**, and pirate craft. Other recorded names: **a(d)jong, djo(e)ng, djoengkoe★, djung, djunku, Dschonke, Dschunke, dzonka, feng chuan** (or **wind boat** in the Zhujiang Kou [Canton Estuary] area), **giunca** (pl. **giunche**), **giunco, gonk** (pl. **gonoûk**), **gung, ionc** (pl. **ionchi**), **ionct, ionque, iun(c)k, iunco, joinct, jonc(o), jonck, joncque, jong★, jonk(os), jonque, j(o)ung, jounque, junc(o), juncque, junck, yunk, zoncho**. Note also **chuan, shrimp junk**.

kaag 1. *Germany, NW:* The **Kaag** is a sharp-ended, open boat from the Schlei area of northeastern Schleswig-Holstein. Used for fishing and sometimes tows a **fish car★**. Curved stem, raked stern, flat bottom, centerboard. Outboard rudder; tiller. Two light masts step through thwarts, setting tanned spritsails.

2. *Netherlands, W and N:* Sprit-rigged vessel cited from the 15th into the 19th century, but mainly of the 17th century. The earliest boats served as **ferries★**

kaag-2

(the **veerkagen**), carrying passengers to various inland cities, and some (the **beurtkagen**) provided regular service for passengers and cargo. Clinker- or carvel-built with sharp bow; lightly curved or straight, raked stem; curved, raked sternpost; flat floors; rather flat sheer. Leeboards, outboard rudder, and tiller. Decked forward with an open waist; some had a passenger cabin aft. Cambered hatch covers, helmsman's cockpit in after deck. One or 2 headsails. Later vessels were **lighters★** (the **kaaglichter**), crossing the Zuiderzee to Amsterdam carrying cargo to and from ships lying off the coast; some were **coasters★** going to German ports, and others were **fishing boats★**. Heavily built; carvel-planked, bluff at the bow and stern; lightly curved stem; straight, vertical sternpost; strong sheer, flat floors with angular chines. Tumble home of top strake at stern created a triangular opening for tiller; tall, narrow rudder with sculpted head; round leeboards. Decked with cabin house aft; cambered hatch covers; 2 hatches on foredeck. Decorated taffrail. Set a spritsail with bonnet; sprit topsail, jib to jibboom, staysail. Sprit of early vessels could be used as a cargo boom. Length 20.7m, beam 5m, depth 2.4m; shallow draft. Other recorded names: **caga, cag(h), cágua, cague, ka(a)gh, kaagschip, kaagschuit, kaeg(h), kaegschuit, kaegschuyt, kag** (and **kåg★**), **kagg, kag(h)e, lichter, veerkaghe, vrachtkaag;** pl. **Kaagen, kagen.** Note also **gaffelkaag.**
Kaagen, kaagh, kaaglichter, kaagschip, kaagschuit See **kaag-2**
kaaidraaier, kaaidraaijer See **kadraai**
kaan *Netherlands:* Phonetic spelling for the German **Kahn★**.
kaaper See **caper**

kaar *Netherlands:* Used by fishing vessels that lack a live well; towed or placed in still water. Square box types used to store the fish. Bottom and sides bored with holes; top closed over with access through a hatch. Flat bottom, flaring sides. From the Middle Ages to the 19th century, a boat-shaped, lidded basket was used as a **kaar**. Other recorded names: **beun, vis(ch)kaar;** pl. **karen.** Note also **fish car, hengst.**
kaarboot *Netherlands, NE:* Term given in the Noordwesthoek area of the eastern Zuiderzee to a small, light, **punter★**-type boat with a live well. Flat bottom, with rocker toward the stern; sharp bow, strongly raked; wide, raked, flat sternpost; straight, flared sides; low sheer. Well just forward of amidships. Open. Length ca. 5m, beam 1.2m, depth at well 0.4m. Name variant: **kaarbootje.** Note also **kaar, kaarpunter.**
kaarbootje See **kaarboot**
kaarpunter *Netherlands:* Special designation for a **punter★** with a fish well. The covered well, roughly amidships, spans the open boat, creating a small deck. On some, the well box forms part of the mast brace; on others, it is used as a rowing seat. Note also **Giethoornse punter.**
kabang *Myanmar (Burma), S:* Boat of the nomadic Selong (Salon, Selung, or Moken) of the Mergui Archipelago; the boat is their primary home, and from it they engage in fishing, pearling, egg collecting, etc. Lower hull formed from a log that is hewn and then expanded by alternate soaking and heating; wooden thwarts inserted; pressure turns up ends. Flared sides built up with stems of palm or a buoyant, thorny plant tied together with thicker bundles amidships so that the sheer is flat; stayed along the sides by natural crooks. Caulked with a beeswax paste. Sharp bow and rounded stern have deep cavities cut into dugout part to serve as steps for boarding the boat. Decked with split bamboo; house supported by 2 hoops; open on sides; roof of palm leaves stitched together. House may be moved ashore to provide temporary shelter there. Employs a quarter rudder when sailing. Also uses 2 rough oars, with 1 oarsman standing in the bow, the other at the stern. A tall, portable mast steps through a hole in planking to a socket at the bottom; 2 rattan shrouds and a backstay. Sets a lugsail of leaves, either woven or laced into strips. Reported lengths 4.6-9m; e.g., length 7.6m, beam 1.4m. Other recorded names: **dapang★, floating boat, k'bang, kebang, Mergui kabang**
kabaros See **kabarra**
kabarra *France, SW:* Type of boat found in the Garonne area. Spelling variant: **kabaros.** See also **gabarra-5a.**
kabotazhnoe sudno See **coaster**
kachchana thoni See **varakan-oruwa**
kachchha *India, north-central:* Large, burdensome boat of the Bihar area. Square ends, low sides. Steered with a pair of rudders. Shoal draft.
kaczka loma See **Entenlomme**

kadai See **kadei**

kadei *Africa, central:* Papyrus craft of Lake Chad and the delta of the Shari (Chari) River. The papyrus (occasionally ambatch) is bound together with palm frond ropes. Stern cut square, usually with minimal upsweep. Tapered bow on small types drawn out to a fine end and stayed back into a recurving point; on larger **rafts***, the bow stands free in a narrow, vertical

kadei

point. On small fishing **kadei**, small bundles form the bottom, and one along each side provides freeboard. Large **kadei** that transport potash have 2 large, flattened bundles for primary flotation, and small bundles along their inner sides form a protective trough for the cargo. Those that carry cattle have an additional thick bundle on each side at water level, about a meter thick at the middle; these **rafts** also erect a rough pen. A very primitive type of **kadei** is made of a single bundle, the occupant stretching out along the bundle and paddling with his hands. Lasts about 3 months. Gradually being replaced by planked craft. Mainly poled. Reported lengths 2-9m; potash **rafts** may carry 2t. Other recorded names: **cadeï**, **cow canoe**, **kadai**; **kadey** (by the Buduma); **karr** (by the Kotoko); **kedeï** (by the Kouri); **talé**, **taléï**, **tale kotolobe**, **teï-teï** (by the Arabs).

kadey See **kadei**

kadırga *Turkey:* **1.** General term for a **galley*** dating to the mid-13th century. Primarily a fighting vessel until the 17th century. Rowed mainly; sometimes sailed, setting a lateen sail. Note also **kalita**.
2. Best known is the 17th-century **kadirga**, which was rowed with 24 outrigged oars per side with 3 men to each oar. A 3-lantern vessel, indicating its rank. Narrow bow; curved, raking stem; higher, fuller stern; raking sternpost. Flat floors; rudder curves under the keel. Elaborately ornamented, canopied cabin at the stern. Length 40m, beam 5.7m, depth 2m. Spelling variants: **chaderqa**, **kadriga**, **kadyrgha**, **katrygha**, **khadirgon**, **qadergha**, **qadighy**, **qadyrġa**, **qadyrghâ**, **quadergha**, **quadrequa**; pl. **kadirge**

kadirge See **kadırga**

kadjak See **kayak**

kadjangan See **perahu kajangan**

kadraai *Belgium/Germany/Netherlands:* Term given to a boat that sold fresh produce, bread, milk, small articles, clothing, and tobacco in harbors and along rivers and canals. Often worked on a regular schedule. Some in the Netherlands that worked on inland waterways were painted with green and white stripes. Sailed or towed. Those working small waterways were long and narrow. Other recorded names: **kaaidraaier**, **kaaidraaijer**, **kadraaier**, **kai-drai**, **Kajedraier**, **parlevinker**, **Proviantboot**, **scheepzoetelaar**. Note also **bumboat**, **kadrejerjolle**.

kadraaier See **kadraai**

kadrejerbaad See **kadrejerjolle**

kadrejerjolle *Denmark:* Sturdy **bumboat*** that frequented shipping channels, especially between Denmark and Sweden. Also worked as a fish-carrier from the island of Bornholm and served as a general-purpose workboat. A non-specific type, but in general, had clinker planking, sharp ends, curved stem and sternpost, straight keel, round bottom. Open with flooring; partly ceiled; marked sheer; low, removable washboards. **Bumboats** carried a fender forward. Generally set a spritsail, yard topsail, staysail, and jib to a long bowsprit. Reported lengths 5.4-6m; e.g., length 5.8m, beam 2m, depth 0.7m, draft 0.5m. Other recorded names: **kadrejerbaad**, **kai-drai**

kadrejerjolle

kadriga, **kadyrgha** See **kadırga**

kaeg, **kaegh**, **kaegschuit**, **kaegschuyt** See **kaag-2**

kaep *Palau, western Pacific:* Single-outrigger sailing **canoe*** of Palau in the western Caroline Archipelago. Known especially for its racing qualities. Extinct, but a few replicas now being built. Dugout hull a narrow "V" in cross section; sides slightly curved; residual gunwales thickened to form waterways; bottom strongly curved, the ends rising above the waterline; strong sheer. Double-ended to be sailed in either direction; ends raked with a slight forefoot; might have tall endpieces. Thick, triangular pieces formed small fore- and stern decks. Six thwarts that projected outboard on the outrigger side; cowry shells dangled from ends of the thwart bars. Two closely spaced, heavy booms extended to the small, squared float; sharp ends. Float and each boom connected by a vertical stanchion from which an angled piece ran to the boom; 1-2 yokes connected outer ends and supplemental pieces crossed between the booms. Platform covered most of the outrigger unit. Mast, pivoted toward direction of movement, stepped on the inner edge of the platform. Triangular mat sail; apex tacked to forward thwart; spars at the foot slotted into the luff spar. Also paddled. Crew of 4. Reported lengths 7.25-10.5m; e.g., length 10m, beam 0.36m, depth 0.94m. Further reading: J. S. Kubary, *Ethnographische Beiträge zur Kenntnis des Karolinen Archipels* (Leiden, Netherlands: P. W. M. Trap, 1889), 270-286.

ka fadule See **wa fatúl**

Kaffenkahn *Germany, NE/Poland, NW:* Cargo vessel that worked in Stettiner Haff (Zalew Szczeciński) and tributary rivers and canals in Pomerania. Most active in the 1890s, but lasted into the early 20th century. Upper strakes clinker, lower carvel. Wide, flat bottom;

planked longitudinally, the planking rounding up sharply at the bow, butting herring-bone fashion; no stem. Bow terminated in a flat oak block that extended above gunwale level; a similar craft lacking this feature was called a **Bukkahn**. Stern sloped up gradually, the upper strakes continuing aft to form a small transom. Sides vertical; 2 leeboards on each side. Very wide, trapezoidal rudder extended beneath the deeply raked stern; suspended by an arched plank over a pin at the stern; long tiller. End decking only, or decked with a house aft and a covered hatch. Stepped 1-2 strikable masts that set spritsails. Reported lengths 23-30m, some to 40m; widths 4-4.6m, hold depth 2m. Other recorded names: **Bockkahn, Buck(kahn), Scharend-Kahn**; on the Warthe (or Warta) River, **Warthekahn**

Kaffenzille See **Zille**

kåg 1. *Denmark:* **a.** The term designates several types of craft, generally flat-bottomed. Spelling variants: **kaag***; pl. **kåge**. **b.** A seagoing **kåg** was developed in the early 17th century from the Dutch **kog** (see **cog**). Spelling variants: **kog(g)e**. **c.** Some served as **lighters*** and **barges***, helping to load and unload ships. Other recorded names: **lægterkåg, ligterkaag**. **d.** Word has been applied to a long, narrow **barge**-like craft that worked the channels and fjords of Jutland carrying bricks, peat, and other bulk cargo. Primarily used from 1800-65. Clinker-planked, flat bottom, flared sides; sharply raked, straight stem; sharp stern; shallow, wide-bladed rudder. Decked at bow and stern and along the sides; some had a deckhouse forward. Sailed, poled, or towed from shore. Length 25m, beam 5m, depth 0.86m, draft 0.37m. Other recorded names: **Gudenåkåg, kåg fra Randers**. **e.** The open fishing **kåg** of the Limfjorden in northern Jutland is smaller and tends lines, traps, and pound nets. There are local variations, but basically clinker-built; sharp ends; flat bottom, wide or quite narrow; straight or curved sides, generally flared. A single leeboard prevents drifting when under sail. Some only rowed. Those that sail set a small, square spritsail and a staysail. Reported lengths 6.3-8m, widths 1.7-2m, depth 0.58-0.73m, draft 0.18-0.26m. Name variant: **Limfjordskåg**. Note also **Schlei Kahn**.

2. *Sweden, west coast:* Beamy, open boat that engaged in herring seining. Double-ended; clinker-built of wide planks fastened with wooden trunnels; rounded bilges; flared sides; strong sheer.

kåg-2

Rowed by 4 men, single-banked. Customarily single-masted, but might step 2-3. Set spritsails, the mizzen very narrow; triangular topsail hung by a yard lashed to the mast. Some carried a foresail tacked to the stemhead, others added a jib to a rising bowsprit. Reported lengths 5-6.7m; e.g., length 5.5m, beam 2.5m, depth 1.2m. Other recorded names: **tågkåg**; pl. **kågen**

kag See **kaag-2**

kage See **kaag-2, kåg**

kagen See **kaag-2, kåg-2**

kagenaar *Netherlands, W:* Used by farmers and market gardeners of the Kaagpolder and Leiden areas to transport produce, bulbs, and manure. Iron hull; flat bottom; flaring sides curve or have multiple chines; flat sheer except at ends; slight tumble home above the wale. Bottom rounds up forward to decorative stem plate; vertical stern with octagonal transom. Some open; most have a foredeck with hatch; flat hatch cover; small, low cabin forward of steering platform. Wide rudder, iron tiller. Quanted or sailed. Heavy iron brace for quant on fore- and after decks. Strikable mast stepped abaft the foredeck; sets a loose-footed, boomed sail; the very short gaff creates a nearly triangular sail. Also pushed with the quant from shore in narrow waterways. Length ca. 18m, beam 2.5m, depth 1.0m. Name variant: **vlet***

kåg fra Randers See **kåg-1**

kåg fra Slien See **Schlei Kahn**

kagg, kagh, kaghe See **kaag-2**

kagoena, kaguna See **bangko**

kahlua See **kaloa**

Kahn *Germany:* **1.** Term that has a wide range of meanings: small **boat***, **barge***, **lighter***, **canoe***, **skiff***, **wherry***. In a more limited sense, may refer to an open, flat-bottomed **barge** used on inland or protected waters. A few more specific types are described below. Spelling variants: **cane, kaan*, kān, kane, kohn**; pl. **kanen, Kähne**. Note also **Elbkahn, Kaffenkahn, kleiner Kahn, Nachen, Schlei Kahn, tub**.

2. Some **Kähne** were **coasters***, often working out of the Weser Estuary. Others on the Weser transported cargoes from seagoing ships to Bremen. Worked into the 1930s. Clinker- or carvel-planked; flat bottom, keelless; large transom stern; beamy amidships, narrowing aft; marked sheer forward. Decked; large, high-peaked hatch; taffrail on some; square stern windows. Outboard rudder, leeboards. Largest **ketch***-rigged; smaller were **cutters***. Running bowsprit. Some early vessels had topmasts. Sails often tanned. Crew of 2-4. Reported lengths 12-25m, widths 4-7m, hold depths 1.25-2.75m. The present-day **barge** type on the Weser runs to 60m long. Other recorded names: **Bremerkahn, Weserkahn**

3. A **Kahn** of the Rostock area on the Baltic Sea was a small, open **fishing boat***. Clinker-planked with wide strakes. Bottom hewn from a log; flattened, narrow, and curved fore-and-aft. Sharp ends; narrow bow with curved, raked stem; stern fuller with heavy sternpost scarfed onto bottom. Maximum beam in after third; sides curved and greatly flared. Rowed or sculled; stern oar curved with a T-grip, used standing. Length ca. 6.6m, beam 1.4m, depth 0.7m. Further reading: W. Rudolph, "Die Boote der Gewasser um Rügen" in: Reinhard Peesch, ed., *Die Fischerkommünen auf Rügen und Hiddensee* (Berlin: Akademie Verlag, 1961), 18-29.

4. Small, open **fishing boat** on the Havel River at Potsdam, southwest of Berlin. Wide, flat bottom; longitudinally planked, with rocker. Straight, flared sides constructed of 2 lapped strakes; sides roughly parallel along central third. Strongly raked, straight, sharp ends, the stern more attenuated; heavy plank stem and sternpost. Marked sheer forward. Wide sorting tray amidships; end thwarts. Poled, rowed, sailed, and later boats used an outboard motor. Oars had slender blades. Light mast braced against bulkhead in forward third; set a spritsail. Length ca. 7.5m, beam 1.3m, depth 0.6m.

5. Shallow, open **fishing boat** of the Domkeitz area in east-central Germany. Wide, flat bottom, planked longitudinally with 2 planks, curved at the ends. Sides flare, with a single wide plank below and a narrower top strake, lapped and set vertically. Three 2-piece frames; bulkhead foward. Sharp ends, strongly raked; no stem and sternpost, the strakes secured to an inner oak block. A thwart at each end. Steered with an oar. Poled, paddled, rowed, sailed; after 1925, many had engines. Mast stepped through a 3rd thwart, well forward; set a spritsail. Crew of 1-3. Reported lengths 7-8m; e.g., length ca. 7.2m, beam 1.0m, depth 0.45m. Other recorded names: **cane**; those made by F. Mette were called **Mettekahn**. Further reading: See **3** above, pp. 104-108.

6. On the Steinhuder Meer west of Hannover, the open, sprit-rigged **Kahn** transported grass, hay, and peat. Flat bottom, longitudinally planked. Straight bow created from a shaped block; square stern with counter. Sides parallel with tumble home. Anchored by a pole inserted through the counter; quarter rudder. Single thwart. Two masts, the foremast stepped at the bow and raked forward, the mainmast amidships. Crew of 2. Length 8.2m, beam 1.15m, depth 0.7m. Further reference: **barge-1**

Kahnbrücke See **pontoon-2**

Kähne See **Kahn-1**

kai *Indonesia, E:* A large **canoe★** designated for use by the women and children of Lake Sentani in northeastern Irian Jaya. Constructed of a single tree trunk. Spelling variant: **ka'ji**. Note also **isja**. Further reference: **kayak**

kaiak See **kayak, kayık**

kaiangvak See **kayak-9**

kaić Croatian term for a **boat★** or **wherry★**. May designate a **ship's boat★**. Open or partly decked. Spelling variants: **kaičac, kaik★, kàjić, kājik★**. Note also **caicco**.

kaić See **caique**

kaičac See **kaić**

kaiče, kaiche See **kaik**

kaick See **caique, kayak**

kai-drai See **kadraai, kadrejerjolle**

kaik 1. *Albania:* Term applied to a **kayak★, boat★**, or **canoe★**. Spelling variant: **kaik(j)e**

2. *Bulgaria:* General term for a **boat** or **wherry★**. Other recorded names: dim. **kaiče** or **kaiche**

3. *Romania:* An old term meaning **boat, ship's boat★, wherry, skiff★**, or **caique★**. Spelling variant: **caic**

Further references: **caique, kaić, kayak, kayık, kayuk**

kaika See **kayık**

kaikaki See **kaiki**

kaike See **kaik, kayık**

kaikhi See **kaiki**

kaikhpak See **kayak-9**

kaiki Greek generic for a small wooden sailing boat, the term is used broadly for a number of types, known locally by such names as **bratsera★, trechandiri★**, and **tchektirme★**. Sails now auxiliary to an engine. Length range ca. 6-21m, the smaller type used for fishing, the larger type for commerce throughout the Mediterranean and Black Seas. Spelling variants: **caique★, kaikaki** (dim.), **kaikhi**; Italian: **caicco**, pl. **caicci**

kaikje See **kaik**

kaiok, kaiouk See **kayuk**

kai pouke, kaipuke See **puke**

kaique See **kayık**

ka'it See **boom**

kai-yah See **kayak-6**

kaiyak See **kayak, kayak-6**

kaiyariyeh See **qaiyarīyah**

kaiyuh See **kayak, kayak-6**

kajak See **kayak, kayak-3**

kajakker See **kayak-3**

Kajedraier See **kadraai**

ka'ji See **kai**

kajic See **caique, kaić**

kajik *Albania:* One of the terms used for a **boat★** or **launch★**.

kājik See **kaić**

kajjik *Malta:* Inshore **fishing boat★**. Carvel-planked; sharp bow with high stemhead; square stern with sharp sheer at bow. Washboards removable in sections as needed. Generally does not sail, but may set a spritsail. Two- and 4-oared types raced. Other recorded names: **caique★, cayicc, cayique, kajjikk** (pl. **kajjikki**)

kajjikk, kajjikki See **kajjik**

kajk See **kayık**

kajuchka, kajučka See **kayuk**

kajuitschouw *Netherlands:* A **schouw★** larger overall than the average to accommodate a trunk cabin (*kajuit*). Serves as a **fishing boat★** or **yacht★**. Bow and stern transoms; slight sheer. Fan-shaped leeboards; outboard rudder; tiller. Loose-footed gaff mainsail set to a mast stepped forward of the cabin; jib to jibboom. Reported lengths 6-8m; e.g., length 7.16m, beam 2.4m.

kajuk See **kayuk**

kajutbåt See **storbåt-1**

kajutkruzer See **cruiser-1**

kak See **hvassing**

kakaap See **kakap**

kakaap oendoe oendoe See **kakap unduk unduk**

kakala See **oága**

kakam See **hoa-hang**

kakap 1. *Indonesia:* **a.** Cited as early as the 10th century as a trader along the north coast of Java. **b.** Fast rowing vessel popular with sea pirates, particularly as a reconnaissance boat. **c.** Boat of the Riau Archipelago, off Sumatra. Crew of 6-32. Reported lengths 3.7-9m, width ca. 3.7m, depths 1.2-2.2m. **d.** The mid-19th-century **houseboat★** of the Orang Laut peoples of the Riau/Lingga Archipelagoes could be rowed and sailed. Open except for matting used at night or in bad weather. Galley area aft. Large vessels were armed for warlike purposes. Single large sail; also paddled. Note also **gubang-2**.

2. *Peninsular Malaysia:* A **riverboat★**, often belonging to local rulers. High ends. Crew of 5. Length probably ca. 9m.

Spelling variants: **cacapo, gagap, kakaap**. Further references: **kakap jĕram, perahu kakap, salisipan**

kakap jĕram *Peninsular Malaysia:* Coastal **fishing boat★** found along Selangor District. High, ornamented, raked ends; stem may carry a figurehead. Sides raised by a washstrake of woven bamboo filled with palm leaves; washstrake lashed to knees brought up from the ribs. Loops along the starboard side hold punt poles and other spars. Open, but grating may be laid atop thwarts; some raise an awning. Steered with 1-2 long paddles. An athwartships balk forward used for winding the cable. Pole mast sets a battened lugsail. Also paddled. Crew of 3. Length 5.5m, beam 2m, depth 1.0m. Other recorded names: **jĕram, jeram scouter, kakap★, kekap tĕram**. Note also **perahu kakap**.

kakap naga *Peninsular Malaysia:* A type of **riverboat★** of Perak District ornamented with a dragon (*naga*) figurehead.

kakap unduk unduk *Peninsular Malaysia:* Boat of the **kakap★** type belonging to the Sultan of Johore. Red seahorse (*unduk unduk*) figurehead; stern adorned with a red tail. Armed along the sides with 2 swivel guns and 2 blunderbusses. Rowed with 20 oars, and stepped 2 masts. Length 7.3m, beam 2.7m, depth 1.5m. Spelling variant: **kapaap oendoe oendoe**

kakua anĕn See **anan**

kalaba *Indonesia, E:* Term for an ordinary fishing **canoe★** in the Alor/Solor Islands of the Lesser Sunda Archipelago.

ka-laba See **kalabba**

kalabba *Indonesia, W:* Large double-**outrigger canoe★** of the Mentawai Islands off the west coast of Sumatra; similar craft found on nearby Nias Island were called **kalamba** or **owo**. Mainly traders, but also used for fishing, crabbing, collecting coconuts, and in early days, for war. Planked-up hull from a dugout base. Decked forward; shelter of palm leaves over most of the hull. Stepped 1-2 very tall, slender masts; used mat sails. Capable of carrying 20 or more people. Other recorded names: **ka-laba★, owōh**. On Nias Island, **ōwō** also means **ship★**.

kalak *Egypt:* A **raft★** of thick planks. See also **kelek**.

kalakkā, kalakku See **kelek**

kalala See **oánga**

kalamba See **kalabba**

kalār bhelā See **bhelā**

kalia **l.** *Tonga, central Pacific:* Double **canoe★** with dugout hulls connected by crossbeams on which a platform was placed. Used from the late 18th to the latter part of the 19th century for fishing, for transporting produce and passengers, and for war. Ends of hulls originally pointed, but later, influenced by Fijian **canoes**, adopted a vertical cutwater. Sewn planking raised the sides along the central part of each hull to support the platform. The shorter hull set to windward, outrigger fashion. Steered by paddles from both sides. Forward-raking mast, stayed forward and aft,

stepped on the platform deck of the larger hull. Heel of the yard of the lateen-type sail was set in an angular socket at the end of the hull. Reported lengths 15-27m. Spelling variants: **calia, calie, kalie**. Note also **'alia, drua**.

2. *Wallis Islands, central Pacific:* Also a large double **canoe★**; extinct since the early 20th century. Two plank-extended, U-shaped hulls, one longer than the other, were secured ca. 1.8-2m apart by crossbeams on which a large platform was set. House built on the platform, and as many as 100 people could be transported. Hull ends elongated and pointed; bottom sharply curved; ends enclosed. In the area of the platform, the dugout was raised above gunwale level; a transverse coaming closed off the hull at the edge of the platform; a central hatch over each hull permitted bailing. Steered with a long paddle. Raised a single lateen-type sail to a sharply forward-raking mast stepped into the larger hull; a replica, wrecked in 1965, carried 2 leg-of-mutton sails. Reported lengths 15-18m.

kalie See **kalia-1**

kalieta See **kalita**

kalita *Turkey:* A subclass of **kadırga★**. A smaller than average **galley★**; comparable to the **galiot★**. Favorite of Mediterranean corsairs. Spelling variants: **galita, kalieta, kalite, kaliyota, kalyota**

kalite, kaliyota See **kalita**

kaljaasi See **galeas-1**

Kalkplätte See **Plätte-1**

kalla dhoni *India, SE:* Fast vessel that traded between India and Sri Lanka until the early 20th century. Carvel-planked, roughly. Heavy bow with curved stem ending in a scroll; cutaway forefoot; oculi at the bows. Nearly vertical transom stern; a broad rudder hung from a wide, false sternpost; steered by tiller. Low, decked-in poop; remainder generally open but usually covered with a mat awning. The 3 masts set lugsails; very short foremast stepped close to the bow and raked sharply forward; mainmast and mizzen vertical. To compensate for large sail area, balance board laid across the gunwales and extended for a short distance out each side. Reported lengths 15-18m, widths 5-5.5m, depths 2.4-3m. Other recorded names: **boatila manché, bōttellamañci, kalla doni, kaḷḷattōṇi, thief** (*kaḷḷa*) **boat**

kalla doni, kaḷḷttōṇi See **kalla dhoni**

kaloa *Australia, NW:* One of the terms given to a type of fishing **raft★** constructed by several tribal peoples of the West Kimberly area. Six to 12 straight mangrove poles are shaped to a club-like form and laid side-by-side with the large ends together, fan-like, then staked together. A 2nd similar, but generally smaller, **raft** is run beneath the 1st **raft**, the wide ends opposing. Pegs or lashings secure the 2 parts, or they may be superimposed without fastening, the weight of the paddlers holding the 2 parts together. Reed cushions may be laid on top for "dry" seating, and a penned-off area is created at one end for gear and the catch. Paddled. Combined length ca. 5m. Other recorded names: **biel biel, kahlua, 'kalum, kalwa, mi'alba, 'pililim**

kalra See patela

'kalum See kaloa

kalunera See gunboat

kaluppe See galupe

kalwa See kaloa

kalyota See kalita

kamašua See mashua-3

kamé-no-ko-bune *Japan:* Early naval vessel with a thick, protective decking reminiscent of a turtle (*kamé*) shell. Crew and fighting forces worked below decks. Other recorded names: **blind boat**, **mekura bune**, **turtle-shell boat**. Note also **kamé-no-sé**.

kamé-no-sé *Japan:* Craft in which the occupant rides on a turtle (*kamé*) shell; considered a mythical craft by some, perhaps one with a turtle shape; others believe that this boat did exist. Further reading: Shinji Nishimura, *A Study of Ancient Ships of Japan, Pt. IV: Skin Boats* (Tokyo: Society of Naval Architects, 1931), 61-114. Note also **kamé-no-ko-bune**, **kikko-sen**.

kamia 1. *Tuamotu Islands, eastern Pacific:* The **kami'a** of the Gambier (Mangareva) Islands, southeast of the main group, is a single-outrigger **canoe★** of the Tahitian type. Spelling variant: **kamiha**

  2. *Tubuai (Austral) Islands, central Pacific:* Single-**outrigger canoe★** of Rapa Island, southeast of the main chain, used for fishing. Ancient type constructed of short lengths of planking sewn together; the modern **canoe** has a 1- or 2-piece dugout hull. Washstrakes raise the sides of the newer boats; loose thwarts laid atop the gunwale molding; bottom flattened slightly. Sharp, plumb bow; some employ a squared coverboard; stern rounds up. Two widely spaced booms attach to a long, slender float. On some, the float extends forward of the bow. Boom may attach directly to the float by means of a natural fork; on more recent boats, a stout, curved foreboom is attached by 4 stanchions fore-and-aft along the float. Mainly paddled, using lanceolate-bladed paddles. Lengths to ca.12.2m. Other recorded names: **vaka★**, **yaka**

kamiha See kamia-1

Kammerherrenschiff See Leibschiff

kan *Papua New Guinea, Bismarck Archipelago:* Bamboo **raft★** of the island of Watom and the Rabaul area of northern New Britain Island. Constructed of 6-8 bamboo poles tied together, strengthened by 3-4 transverse poles.

kān See gan chuan, Kahn-1

kanadensare, Kanadier See Canadian canoe

kanādir See gundra

kanalbåt, Kanalboot See canal boat

Kanalzille See Krenzille

kanawa, kanáwayishchiputüre See woodskin

kan chuan, kan-ch'wan, Kan-Dschunke See gan chuan

kandsje See cangia

kane, kanen See Kahn-1

kānga, kangia, kanja, kanjia See cangia

kannòt *Haiti:* Creole term for a small **boat★**. Many engage in fishing, mainly with handlines, nets, and lobster baskets. Sharp ends. 1-3t cap.; the larger (and less numerous) type has a keel length of ca. 5.5m. Spelling variants: **canot★**, **cânott**, **kânot★**

kannot See kanot-3

kano 1. *Malta:* A **box boat★** built and used by small boys to develop their boating skills.

  2. *Peru, N:* The **káno** of the Aguaruna peoples in the vicinity of the upper Marañón River is a **dugout canoe★**. Narrow; bow cut square; overhanging square shelf at the stern; rounded bottom. Short-loomed paddle with pointed blade. Small **canoes★** used by 1-2 people, others by as many as 20. Length 10.3m, beam 1.0m, depth 0.42m.

  3. *Suriname:* Bark **canoe** used by the natives of upper rivers. Paddled or poled.

kanoa See canoa-3

kanoe See canoe

Kanoe mit Ausleger See outrigger canoe

kanonbåd, kanonbåt, Kanonenboot, Kanonenschaluppe, kanonera, kanonerka, kanonerskaya lodka See gunboat

kanonneergalei See galley-5

kanot 1. *Montenegro:* A type of small **boat★**, reported especially on Boka Kotorska on the Montenegran coast.

  2. *Réunion:* A creole term for a **fishing boat★** on this western Indian Ocean island.

  3. *Seychelles:* Term for any small **boat**. Most are used by 1 person for fishing (**kanot pwasõ**), either inside the reef or out, but they are also general-purpose craft and **tenders★** to larger vessels. May be lapstrake or carvel-planked of *takamaka* or *calise du pape*; fastenings copper nails clenched over roves; round bilges. Mainly rowed; some now have outboard motors. Lengths to 3.7m. Spelling variants: **canot★**, **kannot★**

  4. Swedish generic term for a **canoe★**. One that sails may be called a **segelkanot**. A simple **dugout canoe★** is an **enstockskanot**.

  5. *Sweden, SE:* Along the Blekinge coast, the **jaktkanot** is a popular wildfowling craft; especially popular during the 19th and early 20th centuries. Sturdily built with clinker planking. Sharp ends, some with maximum beam abaft amidships; strong sheer. Stem and sternpost curved and raked. Straight keel with slight drag. May have low or steep rise to the floors; soft turn of the bilges. Deck flat or cambered; high coaming around the cockpit. Rowed, paddled, or sailed. When sailed, shipped a rudder with tiller. Most stepped a single mast, setting a lug- or spritsail. One making long trips, the **långfärdskanot**, might use 2 lugsails, the mizzenmast stepped through the after deck. Generally 1-man boats. Reported lengths 4-4.2m; e.g., length 4m, beam 1.22m, depth 0.46m. Further reference: **kannòt**

kanot pwasõ See kanot-1

kan-ssŭ-tang See hong chuan

kan-tch'ouan See gan chuan

kantelbak *Netherlands:* A special vessel that empties its deck load of mud or stone by filling a side tank with water, causing the vessel to list and dump its load. Note also **bak**, **dump barge**, **hopper**, **modderschouw**.

kanu 1. *Papua New Guinea:* Pidgin English term for a **canoe★**. River-dwelling peoples apply the word to all types of **canoes**, while to some coastal residents, it denotes sailing and **outrigger canoes***; the term **por*** preferred for river **canoes**.

2. *Peru, NW:* The **kánu** of the Jivaro (Chíwaro) people is a **dugout canoe***. Hewn with fire and axes; sides spread with wedges. Narrow, square stern; in creating the dugout, the stern area may be left thick to make a ledge on which a man stands to spear fish and sits to paddle. Mystical designs incised along the sides with fire. Reported lengths 6-9m. Spelling variants: **canoa***, **cánu**
Further reference: **kū'le-1**

kapa See **kapal**

kapaj, kapaj apoej See **kapal**

kapal 1. In general, a large seagoing vessel found in the area from India to the Philippines. The word, however, usually means any Asian or European ship of the area that has a permanent deck, or a European-rigged, 2- or 3-masted vessel with square sails and top- and topgallant masts. Special types may be designated, such as: **kapal api**, a **steamship***; **kapal layar**, a sailing vessel; **kapal mel**, a mail **steamer**; **kapal perang** (or **parang**), a **warship**. Note also **perahu**.
2. *Indonesia, central:* At Udjung Pandang (Makassar) on the southwest coast of Sulawesi (Celebes), the **kapal** (or **kapala**) is a small, open boat that sets an elongated, rectangular lugsail tacked to the stemhead.
Other recorded names: **capel(l), hopal, hopal api, kapa, kapal(l)a, kapal ai', kapal(a) api, kapala apoe, kapal banak, kapal dagang, kapale, kapal ėpi, kapaj, kapaj apoej, kap(p)al lāyaq, kapala-praou, kapali api kapalo, kapal p'rang, kapan, kâppalá, kappal(i), kappalᵤ, kăpĕn, kĕpal**. Further reference: **ship**
kapala, kapal ai', kapala api, kapal api, kapala apoe, kapala-praou, kapal banak, kapal dagang, kapale, kapal ėpi, kapali api kapalo, kapalla, kapalla dagang, kapal lāyaq See **kapal**

kapal layar, kapal mel See **kapal-1**

kapal parang, kapal perang, kapal p'rang See **kapal**

kapal tambangan See **tambangan**

kapan See **kapal**

kapara-skip, kapare, kaparefartyg, kapareskepp, kapari See **caper**

Kapellenschiff See **church boat**

kāpeniekevalts See **kurnevalts**

kaper, kaperbåd, Kaperschiff, kaperschip See **caper**

kapetavia See **capitane**

kaphala *India, W:* Early Marathi term for a group of vessels, a **fleet***.

kāpili *United States, Hawaii:* Early type of fishing **canoe***. Carried only 1-2 fishing poles.

Kapital-Floss See **Rheinfloss**

kapitana See **capitane**

Kapitänsgig See **gig-1**

kapitavia See **capitane**

kaplaanvisser, kaplaanzaaier, Kaplanfänger See **capelanier**

kappal, kâppalá, kappali, kappal lāyaq, kappalᵤ See **kapal**

kaptana, kapudana, kaputana See **capitane**

karaak See **kraak**

karabel *Ukraine, S/Russia, SW:* Sturdy **schooner***-rigged vessel of the Black Sea. Well-shaped ends, low free-board. Low peak to the sails. Beamy.

karabela See **caravel-1**

karabia See **carabus, karabion**

karabion *Greece, N:* Plank-built craft used on Lake Kastoria. Blunt, raked ends; on some, the ends are about the same breadth and cut square; on others, each end is composed of a wedge-shaped block, one end narrower. Flat bottom with rocker; vertical sides; transverse strength provided by a beam beneath the

karabion

outrigger. Rowed with a pair of long oars supported by an outrigger; a tholepin for the oar is fastened out-board. Length ca. 5m, beam 1.3m, depth 0.7m. Spelling variant: pl. **karabia**. See also **carabus**.

karaboi, karabos, karabus See **carabus**

karacke, Karak, karāka, Karake See **carrack**

karakoa, karakor, Karakore See **korakora-1**

karaque See **carrack, carrack-3**

karavela Trader built at the shipbuilding center of Kotor on the southern Montenegran coast until at least the mid-18th century. Some bows low, others raised for a forecastle; curved stem. Slightly raked, square stern; high poop deck. Hull rounded in cross section. Lateen sails set to 3 vertical masts; mizzenmast stepped on the sternpost, sail sheeted to a jiggerboom. Cap. ca. 100t. See also **caravel-1, caravel-3**.

karavell, karavella, Karavelle, karawela See **caravel-1**

karegar See **garagar**

Karelian ladja See **lodka-3a**

karen See **kaar**

karfar, karfe See **karve**

karfi *Iceland:* Small **rowing boat***. When used in regattas in fjord areas, they are highly decorated. Term may also apply to a fast **galley***-type vessel, probably of early origin; rowed with 6, 12, or 16 oarsmen per side; light and easily portable. Further reference: **karve**

kargo, kargobot See **freighter-1**

karib See **qārib**

karkâra See **korkâra**

karkol, karkolle See **korakora**

karomon See **kroman**

karookuh See **zaruq**

Karpfenprahm See **Prahm-2**

karr See **kadei**

karrāka *Egypt:* A **dredger***.

karràka See **carrack**

Kartoffel-Ewer See **Ewer**

karv See **karve**

karve *Scandinavia:* Lightly built vessel mentioned as early as the 9th century and as late as the 14th century. Used by kings and important personages as a **yacht***, for defense, and as a **coaster*** working mainly in sheltered waters. Designed to be portaged when necessary. Narrow strakes lapped; bottom strake nailed to keel; strakes riveted with iron nails over square roves on the inside. Sharp ends; tall, curved stem and sternpost. T-keel; frames secured to the strakes by lashing, but not fixed to the keel. Numerous athwartship beams; additional strakes above the beams, secured by hanging knees. Loose decking between the beams. Mainly rowed, single-banked, 6-16 oars per side. Narrow oars run out through closable ports. Also sailed, setting a square sail; mast could be struck. Length 23m, beam 5.2m, depth 1.6m. Spelling variants: **karfar**, **karfe**, **karfi***, **karv**

karvebåt *Norway, N:* In the 1700s, a light cargo boat that worked out of Vast Fjord, near Narvik. Probably open, sharp-ended, and both sailed and rowed.

karveel *Netherlands:* Term given to large **coasters*** and inland vessels that are carvel-planked (*karveel*). Reported as early as the mid-15th century. Two types were recognized in the 17th century: the **wijdkarveel** (see **wijdschip**) and the **smalkarveel** (sometimes **smalschip***). Spelling variants: **carveel(schip)**, **craveel**, **cravelschip**, **karveelschip**, **karviel**, **kerfiel**, **kerveel**, **kervielschip**, **wijdkarviel**; pl. **karvelen**. Further references: **boeier-1**, **caravel-1**

karveelbuis See **buis-2**
karveelschip See **karveel**
karvelen See **caravel-1**, **karveel**
karviel See **karveel**
Kasemattschiff See **monitor**
kashti *Iran:* Generic term for **boat*** or **ship*** in Parsi. A sailing vessel is a **kashtī 'i bādī**. Spelling variants: **kastī**, **keshtī**, **kishti***, **kixti**, **quiste***
kashtī See **kishti-1**
kashtī'i bādī See **kashti**
kas-maread See **chasse-marée**
Kastenschute See **Schute-1**
kastī See **kashti**
kāt *Papua New Guinea, NE:* Simple **outrigger canoe*** of the Schouten (Le Maire) Islands. Single outrigger with 2-4 booms spaced fairly closely together. Undercrossed sticks connect booms to float. Float may have a carved crocodile's head at each end, and hand grips aid in carrying the **canoe*** to and from the beach. Platform across the **canoe** and halfway out on the booms; seats on the platform. Sailed with a quadrangular, boomed mat sail that hangs lug-fashion; boom wider at the foot. Simple vertical mast. Steered with a paddle. Length ca. 7m. Name variant: **kíata**
kat See **cat-2**, **catboat**
katak See **kotak-1**
katamaran See **catamaran**, **chu-p'ai**
kaṭapannay *Sri Lanka (Ceylon):* Small inland boat of the 17th-18th centuries that transported cargo from ships. Other recorded names: **catapanel**, **cataponel**, **cataponey**, **kattapannay**
katboot See **cat-2**, **catboat**
kater See **cutter-1**
kathu maram See **catamaran-12**
katimaran See **catamaran**

katimaruk See **kayak-4**
katiolo See **katyolo**
katir See **perahu katir-1**
katira See **gaṭîra**
kátora See **patela**
katrā *India, north-central:* Cargo vessel of the middle Ganges River carrying cotton, stoneware, and local products during the monsoon season. Sharp, high bow; low, sharp stern. Clinker-planked; crossbeams pierce the sides; flat bottom. Cargo covered by a crude house. Steered with a sweep. Floated with the current, rowed from under the roof, or towed. Cap. 4-100t; beamy; shallow draft. Spelling variants: **káturá**, **kutora**, **kuttrey**. Note also **patela**.
katschepen, **Katschiff**, **katschip**, **katship** See **cat-2**
katsuo-bune See **katsuo-tsura**
katsuo-tsura *Japan:* Bonito **fishing boat*** of generally standard hull form but variously rigged; works mostly out of southern Japanese ports. Flat bottom, fine lines forward with projecting bow, square stern, straight sides, deep rudder. Crossbeams project beyond hull to hold sculls, spare spars, and fishing poles. Deck generally formed by portable panels, but some have a permanent deck forward. Live well for bait. Steps 1-3 masts, according to locale, each setting lugsails of appropriate sizes depending on mast height. General range: lengths 11-15m, widths 2.2-3.2m, depth 1-1.3m. Name variant: **katsuo-bune**
katt See **cat-2**
kattamaram See **catamaran**
kattapannay See **kaṭapannay**
katteamarouw See **catamaran-12**
kattou-maram See **catamaran-13**
kattrejarbåt See **bumboat**
Kattschiff, **kattskepp** See **cat-2**
kattumaram See **catamaran-12**, **catamaran-13**
kattumaram maramma, **kattumaran** See **catamaran-13**
kàtturi See **catur-2**
katu-ontziska See **laúd**
katur *Iran:* In Persian, a small vessel armed in times of war. See also **catur**.
káturá See **katrā**, **patela**
Katwijk-pom, **Katwijkse bom**, **Katwijkse bomschuit** See **bom-1**
katyolo *Seychelles:* Popular open boat for fishing within or close to the reefs. Constructed of the local *takamaka* wood. Flat bottom consists of 2-3 wide boards; battened seams rabbetted to be flush. Outer board curves up to form lower strake. Sides clinker-planked with copper nails rove-clenched. The 12 grown frames per side start just below the turn of the bilge and run to the gunwale; alternate floor frames. Similar sharp, elongated ends. Two thwarts, 2 end benches, and a small shelf at one end for the stone anchor. Brightly painted, usually blue with red gunwales. Rowed by 1-2 people, each working a single oar against a tholepin. Length ca. 4m, beam 1.0m; shallow draft. Spelling variants: **catiolo**, **katiolo**
katyrgha See **kadırga**
Kauffahrer, **Kauffahrteischiff** See **merchantman**

kaukāhi See **wa'a kaukahi**
kaukunlott See **kayak-9**
Kaulbarssicken See **zig**
kaulua See **wa'a kaulua**
kauppalaiva See **merchantman**
kavafang, kavafango See **dredger-1**
Kavalierschiff See **Leibschiff**
kavarra See **gabarra-5a**
kawali pathei See **paruwa**
kawārib See **qārib**
kawasaki *Japan, N:* A **sampan***-like boat used off
Hokkaido and Akita Prefectures, mainly for cod fishing but also to transport merchandise and fish to market. Design varied to meet local conditions, and those
that worked off open beaches were especially heavily
built. Common features were a flat bottom and wide,
flat floors; slight sheer, often with washboards; long,
sharp, and overhanging bow; bottom curved up aft.
Stern varied, but mostly flared, either V-shaped or
with a shallow transom. Generally 3 beams projected
beyond each side on which tholepins were inserted for
oars or sculls. Deep, narrow rudder on some; projected
below the bottom. Mostly open, but later models
decked. Early boats stepped a single easily struck mast
on which a tall lugsail was set; later **cutter***-rigged.
Subsequent boats **schooner***-rigged without headsails; employed a centerboard. Crew generally 4-8.
Reported lengths 10.6-15m; e.g., length 12.6m, beam
3m, depth 1.1m.
kayack See **kayak**
kayak 1. Narrow, skin-covered craft found across the
North American Arctic, Greenland, Aleutian Islands
of Alaska, and northeastern Siberia. Used on the
coasts for hunting sea mammals and in the interior
for caribou; also transports passengers and goods;
sometimes several lashed together for greater stability and capacity. Known to have been used for at
least 2,000 years. Light, relatively rigid wooden
frame formed of single pieces of wood, fastened with
sealskin strips and bone or wooden pegs. Main
strength provided by stout gunwales connected by
crossbeams. Ends vary in shape from area to area;
some sharply pointed, others have hornlike, upturned
ends, some with a bifid bow. Covered with seal or
caribou skins, the latter on the inland **kayaks**; hair
removed from the skins, which are removed and
stored in winter. Seams may be waterproofed with
seal blood. Rounded, oval, triangular, or "D"-shaped
cockpit rimmed with coaming; most have a single
opening, some two (**double kayak**), and occasionally three. Waterproof apron enclosing cockpit may be
worn by the paddler. Propelled with a double- or single-bladed paddle, the paddler sitting on the bottom
with legs outstretched. Only rarely sailed. Lengths
range from 2.2-10.4m, but most fall within the 4.6-
8m range; widths 0.3-0.74m; hull as little as 0.15m
deep. Further reading: David W. Zimmerly, *Qajaq:*
Kayaks of Siberia and Alaska (Juneau: Division of
State Museums, 1986).
2. May now be a small pleasure craft built along the
lines of the Eskimo boat. Folding **kayaks** generally of

canvas; racing boats now usually of synthetics; open,
racing **kayaks** of wood. Propelled by double-bladed
paddle. In Britain, the term **canoe*** may designate a
pleasure **kayak**.
3. The Greenland **kayak** is as little as 15-20cm deep
amidships, and the ends are needle-like. The eastern
Greenland **kayak** is shallower and sharper than that
of the west coast. Still a few in use on both coasts,
but nails have replaced wooden or bone pegs; now
sewn with nylon thread, and frames are sawn rather
than shaped from driftwood. On one type (the **pequngasoq**), the ends turn up; most have low ends, following the line of the flat deck; some have bone
knobs on the ends. Bottom curved fore-and-aft, the
bow having a larger angle than the stern; bottom a
shallow "V" transversely; rakes up to terminate in a
straight line. Round or oval, slightly tilted cockpit of
the floating type, resting only against the deck
stringers and held in place by the sealskin covering
(mostly harp seal). Many now canvas-covered, painted white. Some had a folding rudder to increase
directional stability. Short-shafted, double-bladed
paddle used. Lengths of adult **kayaks** 5-6m; e.g.,
length 5.55m, beam 0.5m, depth forward of cockpit
0.23m, aft 0.175m. The lightweight, portable **kayak**,
the **qajaq maqittagaq**, of the northwestern coast is
portaged to the edge of the ice; the heavier hunting
kayak is the **qajaq imarsiut**. The so-called **storm**
kayak (or **qajaq kujaa[gi]nnalik**) has a keel. Other
recorded names: **kajak** (pl. **kajakker**), **qajaq**; **húð-
keipr** (early term used by Icelanders for the
Greenland **kayak**). On the east coast, a **kayak** is also
called a **sakkit, saqqit** or **sarquin**, signifying a craft
for traveling or work. Further reading: P. Scavenius
Jensen, *Den Grønlandske Kajak og Dens Redskaber*
(København: Nordisk Forlag Arnold Busck, 1975); H.
C. Petersen, *Skinboats of Greenland* (Roskilde: Viking
Ship Museum, l986), 15-116.
4. The **kayak** of eastern Canada varies somewhat in
details but generally has a flat bottom, becoming a
"V" toward the bow; greatest beam abaft the cockpit.
Bow long, straight or concave, and rises to the top of
the flat deck; bow much higher than the stern, which

kayak-4

may have a horn. Multi-chined; wide, flat stern.
Framework originally of driftwood; most now of
milled lumber. Deep gunwale planks; heavy, curved
crossbeams amidships spread the planks and raise the
front of the cockpit coaming. Three-piece ribs or else
heavily notched at the chines. Covered with sealskins,
some now with canvas. Double-bladed paddle has a
thick shaft and a long, narrow blade. Averages 6.2m
long, 0.62m wide, and 0.23m deep. A relatively beamy
and slow **kayak** might be called a **usiyat**, while a narrower, tippy **kayak** is a **sukaut**. An extinct 2-hole
kayak, called **pacalik** (or **kayapaakalik**), was limited

to the Belcher Islands on the eastern side of Hudson Bay; length 7.6m. In these islands, 2 **kayaks** lashed side-by-side created a **katimaruk**; the **catamaran⋆** formed by connecting 2 boats by spars was a **krilimitok**. Other recorded names: **agyakruk** (in Cumberland Sound, Baffin Island), **kravak**, **krayak**. Further reading: E. Y. Arima, *Inuit Kayaks in Canada: A Review of Historical Records and Construction* (Ottawa: National Museums of Canada, 1987) [Canadian Ethnology Service Paper No. 110].

5. The light, fast inland **kayak** of the Caribou Eskimos from the west side of Hudson Bay was used for hunting caribou and was covered with caribou or deer skins. Not used in winter. Very attenuated ends; both ends turned up equally, or the bow was horizontal and the stern raked up sharply. Rounded bottom, flat deck, canted cockpit. Ends served as handles. Propelled by a double paddle. Reported lengths 5-10.4m, widths 0.38-0.61m, depths 0.2-0.33m. When rafted for stability, called a **pauvigi:k**. Name variant: **West Hudson Bay kayak**. Further reading: Eugene Y. Arima, *A Contextual Study of the Caribou Eskimo Kayak* (Ottawa: National Museums of Canada, 1975 [Canadian Ethnology Service Paper No. 25]).

6. The relatively small Mackenzie Eskimo **kayak** of the western Northwest Territories is narrow, multi-chined, and full at the ends. Ends terminate in short, vertical horns; flat sheer, strong end rocker. Usually wide but thin keelson and bilge and side stringers; high deck stringer results in a slight deck ridge. Ribs oval-sectioned. Frames lashed with baleen, sinew, and roots. Oval cockpit, slightly tilted. Beluga skin cover. Double lanceolate paddle with thick shaft. Average length 4.78m, width 0.48m, depth 0.2m. Other recorded names: **kai-yah**, **kai-yak**, **kai-yuh**. Further reading: See **4** above.

7. The **kayak** of the north coast of Alaska and the north to central coast of western Canada (except for the Mackenzie Delta area) was long, narrow, and had a tilted cockpit. Flat deck; multi-chined, rounded bottom; moderate rocker. Ends curved up smoothly from the flattened bottom. Round or oval cockpit. Lightly framed; gunwale plank thin but deep. The stringers fastened to the closely spaced ribs with continuous ties. Alaskan boats had a longer curve to the hump before the cockpit; flat aft, short floor stringer. The Canadian boat flatter forward of the cockpit. Most covered with skins of ringed seals, but inland boats might use caribou skins. North Alaskan boats employed a single or double paddle; double-bladed paddle used to the east. Average size of north Alaskan **kayak** 5.28m long, 0.47m wide, 0.19m deep; Canadian boat averaged 6.62m long, 0.46m wide, 0.25m deep. A similar, but late 19th/early 20th-century development on the north coast was the **retrieval kayak**—a small, chunky boat called **qayapauraq** (or **qayapak**). Used to retrieve seals and caribou shot from shore or an ice floe edge. Lengths 2.7-3.7m, widths 0.5-0.76m. Name variant: **Copper kayak**

8. The Bering Sea **kayak** of coastal southwestern Alaska is often characterized by a hole in the bow, an extension of the deck stringer beyond the vertical stern, and its relative beaminess. Gunwales strongly bowed, joined at a sharp point at each end; multichined bottom, smoothly curved or flattened; high-ridged deck; reverse sheer; bow plate rounds up from the bottom in an even curve with a slight hump at top. Large round or oval cockpit can accommodate 2 people; supported by stanchions on each side and 2 deck beams. Formerly covered with sealskins, now with canvas. Individual markings identify each **kayak**. Single-bladed paddle most common. Average length 4.7m, width 0.72m, depth 0.4m. Other recorded names: **ax·ut, qayaq**; at Hooper Bay: 2-holed is an **paitaalik**; two **kayaks** lashed together as a **catamaran** is an **itutaralutik**. Further reading: David W. Zimmerly, *Hooper Bay Kayak Construction* (Ottawa: National Museums of Man, 1979 [Canadian Ethnology Service Paper No. 53]).

9. The **kayaks** of the Aleutian Islanders, the Pacific Eskimos of Koniag (Kodiak) Island, and the Chugach Eskimos of the head of the Gulf of Alaska had 1-3 cockpits. Following Russian usage, it is customary to call an Aleut or Pacific Eskimo **kayak** a **baidarka**. Developed to satisfy Russian needs for seal and sea otter skins. In the 2-cockpit boat, the paddler sat in the after hole, the hunter in the forward hole. The 3-cockpit type was used for cruising and transporting passengers. Bifid bow of varying shape. Short, almost vertical stern; sharp on the Pacific Eskimo **baidarka**. Greatest beam forward of the cockpit; flaring sides. Frame lightly constructed; bottom curved fore-and-aft and rounded over a fairly deep, 3-piece keelson. Aleuts used a lanceolate, double-bladed paddle; the Pacific Eskimos preferred a single blade. Aleut 2-hole **baidarka** averaged 6.6m in length, 0.6m in width, 0.3m in depth; 3-hole boats 7.5m by 0.72m by 0.34m. Single-hole boats 5.3m by 0.49m by 0.3m. Pacific Eskimo boats tended to be shorter and beamier. Other recorded names: **bajdarka, baydarka, baydarque, bidarka, bidarkee, bidarki, bidarky, by-darkey; haitama**. Aleut terminology: 1-hole **iqaX** (**Eaceac, Eaakeeak, ikakh, ikyak, iqjax, iqyar, iqyax, iyĝax̂, qiyax̂, qyax̂**); and **tshinatak** (one with a turned-up bow); 2-hole **ullaXtadaq** (a[a]lax-uluẋtax̂, **alagulot**); 3-hole **ullaxtaq** (**ulaXtaX** or **kaukunlott** a[a]nkun-uluẋtax̂). Koniag terminology: 1-hole **kaiangvak**; 2-hole **kaikhpak** (**kaukunlott**); 3-hole **paitaalek, paita(a)lik, paixalik**; 2- or 3-hole shortened to **uluẋtax̂**. Further reading: George Dyson, *Baidarka* (Edmonds, Wash.: Alaska Northwest Publishing Co., 1986); Joëlle Robert-Lamblin, "Le Kayak Aléoute," *Objets et Mondes* 20 (1980), 5-20.

10. The **kayak** (**mā'to**) of the Koryak (Kamshadal) peoples of eastern Siberia was crudely made and heavy. Short, wide, and shallow; large cockpit extended full width. Cockpit placed a little forward of amidships. Bottom curved up at ends; wide "V" in cross section; the gunwales provided the main strength. Deck slightly cambered. Covered with 2 sealskins; hair not always removed. Hand loops at bow and stern. Kayaker paddled with a pair of short wooden hand paddles; sat on a board on the bottom. Average length 2.8m, width 0.7m, depth 0.26m.

11. The **baidarka** of the Maritime Chukchi of the eastern end of Siberia was covered with sealskin; those of the Inland or Reindeer Chukchi with reindeer skin. Wide cockpit, triangular forward and rounded behind; Maritime Chukchi boat had no cockpit coaming even though used in open waters. Bow and stern strongly raked; deck flat on inland boat. Greatest beam forward of the cockpit. Rounded "V" bottom; a wide "U" on maritime boat. Reindeer Chukchi used a long-shafted, double-bladed paddle with a small, oval blade; one paddle had a pike-like extension to spear reindeer crossing a lake or river. Average length 4.62m, width 0.56m, depth 0.26m. Other recorded names: **anatkuat** (by the Maritime Chukchi); **bajarka**, **baydarka**, **Chukchi** (or **Tchuktchi**) **skin boat**

Selected name variants: **caiaco, caiak, caic, cajak, ca-yak** (2-man: **ca-yak-bak**), **Esquimaux canoe, kadjak, kai*, kaiak, kaick, kaik*, kaíyak, kaíyuh, kajak, kayack, kieyak, kya(c)k, man's boat, qajaq, qayak, qayaq, quayak**[w], **skin boat*** (or **canoe**).
Further reference: **cayuco-7**

kayak-form canoe *Canada, NW/United States, Alaska:* Light, handy, fast bark **canoe*** of general **kayak*** shape made by Eskimos and other indigenous peoples. Design and construction varied somewhat with the tribe, and dimensions were usually dictated by the owner's preference. Amount and shape of end overhang differed; bow and stern varied slightly on many **canoes**; usually raked and curved up at the ends. Bottom flat fore-and-aft and athwartships, slightly hogged before loading; hard chines common. Sides usually straight and flared; greatest beam often abaft amidships. Covered by birch or spruce bark; one or both ends usually decked with bark. Gunwales composed of inwales and outwales lashed continuously or in groups; small, widely spaced ribs; 3-6 thwarts; incomplete sheathing inserted; flooring consisted of 4-6 fore-and-aft battens. Paddled seated, mostly with single-bladed paddles, occasionally with double blade. Might also set a square sail. Reported lengths 3.66-7.62m, widths 0.6-0.8m, depths 0.2-0.3m. Other recorded names: **Athabascan, Beaver, Copper, Nahane, Sekani canoe**

kayapaakalik See **kayak-4**

kayasse See **fulūka**

kayığı See **kayık**

kayık *Turkey:* **1.** Generic for a **boat***, **skiff***, even a **coaster***.

2. On the Bosporus, a slim **rowing boat*** that ferries passengers along and across the waterway; especially common during the 19th century, but an elaborate type served 16th- and 17th-century sultans. Carvel-planked with thin strakes; long, sharp, overhanging ends; often upswept and frequently carved; rocker to keel, rounded bilges; flaring sides; wider at the stern. Sometimes a

light awning covers part of the boat; may have an ornamented foredeck. Generally painted black outside with an ornament at each end. Steered with a sweep or rudder and tiller. Rowed by 1-6 oarsmen, the number generally depending on the rank of the occupant. The **bir juftah** (or **bir tchiftè**) employs a single pair of oars; the **eki juftah** (or **iki tchiftè**), 2 pairs; the **üç çifte**, 3 pairs; and the **beş çifte** (or **bech tchiftè**), 5 pairs. One royal craft used as many as 144 rowers. A bulbous section on the inboard part of the oar loom serves as a counterbalance. Sometimes sailed, setting one or more lateen or spritsails. Reported lengths 5-32m; length-to-beam ratio 5:1; a 1670 sultan's **kayık** was 40m long, 5.7m wide. Further reading: Çelik Gülersoy, *The Caique* (Istanbul: Istanbul Library, 1991). Note also **balıkçı kayığı, kayığı, pazar kayığı, perama-2, piyade, saltanat kayığı**.

3. One type of **kayık** is a double-ended **coaster**. Curved stem, straight or curved sternpost, strong sheer, flat floors, rounded bilges. Waist raised with portable weathercloths on those that sailed; decked. Large spritsail with a very long sprit- or a lateen-type sail extended by a jigger; square sails set forward of the mast; forestaysail; 1-2 jibs to a long, rising bowsprit. Frequently accompanied by a large boat that carries cargo ashore and tows the **kayık** in calms. Ca. 15m long.

Spelling variants: **caiacco, caiasso, caïc, caicche, caicchio, caïch, caicho, cai(c)k, caico*, caique*, caïyq, jaique, kaiak, kaik*, kaika, kaïke, kaique, kajk, kayığı, qaïkia, qaïq(ia), qayiq, quaiq**; pl. **kayıklar**

kayıklar See **kayık**

kay-noo See **Chesapeake Bay log canoe-1**

kayoisen See **shore boat-1**

kayuchka, kayučka See **kayuk**

kayuk *Russia:* **1.** Open **riverboat*** used by the Sakha (Yakut) of northern Russia for fishing expeditions and carrying freight. Rowed and sailed. Length to ca. 15m.

2. Cargo vessel of the Amu Darya River in central Siberia. Stoutly planked, flat bottom; wide, shallow

kayuk-2

transom; decked. Sets a huge square sail to a pole mast. Length 20m, beam 3m, depth 2m.

3. Term used by 18th-century fishermen of the Volga River for a **dugout canoe***.

4. The **kayuk** of the Evenki of the Altai Mountains area in south-central Russia is a bark **canoe***.

5. On the Don River in southwestern Russia, the **kayuk** had a sharply raking stem and raking, wineglass transom. Flat bottom, strongly flaring sides. Washboards at bow and stern. Set a quadrilateral lateen-type sail with a short luff to a short mast in forward third.

6. On the Northern Dwina River, flowing into the White Sea, the **kayuk** was a large, flat-bottomed craft. High, slightly raking stem, recurving at the top; vertical transom above the sternpost. Great sheer to the top strake; filled in along the sides by the full-width hold, terminating aft to form a poop deck. Sides flare to the waterline and are vertical above. Entire hull covered; windows in transom. Outboard rudder, wide blade supported by a brace from the slender rudderstock; tiller. Stepped a tall mast to which a square sail was set.

Other recorded names: **kaik★, kaio(u)k, kajuk, xayik**; dim. **kajuchka, kajučka, kayuchka, kayučka**

k'bang See **kabang**

keama *Papua New Guinea, SE:* Single-outrigger traveling **canoe★** of Goodenough Island in the d'Entrecasteaux Archipelago. Dugout hull built up with 2 washstrakes along each side; ends generally enclosed by carved breakwaters; secured by paired, elbow-shaped braces with holes at the bend through which rods pass. Ends of hull taper to a point. Multiple booms pierce the lower washstrakes; long, sturdy float; booms pass above 2 pairs of crossed-stick connectives. Platform covers entire outrigger area. Paddled, poled, and sailed. Generally sets a palm-leaf lateen-type sail, boomed at the bottom and tacked to the bow. Stout mast stayed fore-and-aft through a prong near the masthead. Small **canoes** may use a temporary mat sail, rectangular in shape and supported by 2 vertical spars, or merely palm leaves or a blanket. Large boats may carry as many as 14 people.

Other recorded names: **kema★, waga★**

keatch See **ketch**

kebang See **kabang**

keč, kech, kecz See **ketch**

kéda See **roko-2**

kedeï See **kadei**

keel *British Isles:* **1.** Earliest usage probably refers to skin-covered boats. Then applied to the **longboat★** (see **langskip**) of the Saxons who landed on the English coast, their boats called **kelen**. A modification of the **langskip** became a merchant vessel in the 12-13th centuries, spelled **ceol** in this period. Heavy keel piece in the 9th-10th centuries. Set a square sail in addition to being rowed at times. Side rudder. At times, term may also apply to a ship in general. Length probably ca. 15m; length-to-beam ratio 3.5-4.5:1.

2. Flat-bottomed, clinker-planked vessel of early origin that transported heavy cargoes on rivers and estuaries; still used in some places, but now motorized. Most rounded at the bow and stern, although Norfolk boats had transom sterns. Characteristically set a large, square sail amidships and at times, a topsail. Note also **Humber keel**, **Lincoln catch**, **Norfolk keel**, **Teign keel**, **West Country boat**, **Yorkshire keel**.

3. Sailing **lighter★** that worked at Yarmouth and on the River Yare on the east coast of England until the mid-19th century. Mainly off-loaded coal from **colliers★** lying either in the roads or the harbor. Also transported barley and malt from inland and provided ballast sand to ships. Clinker-built, flaring bow, pleasing sheer. Open hold, accommodations forward. Square sails set to a midship pole mast; also towed, tracked, and poled. Crew of 2-3. Cap. to 80t. Note also **Tyne keel**.

4. Term that the fishermen of Crail on the east Scottish coast used for their larger **luggers★**. Propelled by as many as 6 oars and sailed.

Other recorded names: **ceol(a), chiule, cyule, cyulis, keele, kiel(e)**. Note also **keelboat-2**.

keelboat 1. A boat that has a keel but is not flat-bottomed. Generally has a single ballast keel, either as an integral part of the hull or bolted on. Name variant: **Kielboot**

2. *England:* Reported as a small **keel★** as early as 1695. Name variant: **keil-boat**

3. *England, NE:* **a.** Open **double-ender★** that fished for herring off the Northumberland coast. Carvel- or clinker-planked, deep hull, straight keel. Bulkhead separated helmsman from the rest of the boat. Set a lofty, square-headed, dipping lugsail to a mast stepped at the bow; 7-8 reef points. Some also set a small lug mizzen. Crutch on bulkhead held lowered mast. Crew of 2. Reported lengths 9-11m, beam 3.4m, depths 1.37-1.52m. Name variant: **Holy Island keelboat. b.** Wooden **fishing boat★** of Yorkshire. Slightly curved stem, **canoe★** stern, low bulwarks. Decked; small wheelhouse aft; fish hold. Mainly propelled by an engine; steadying sail and mast could be struck. Crew of 5. Length 15m, beam 4.8m, shallow draft. Name variant: **Whitby keelboat**

4. *United States:* Popular craft of American rivers, especially those of the Mississippi Basin, from the latter part of the 18th to the early 19th century; some continued to work on the smaller rivers into the 20th century. Designed to travel both up- and downstream, carrying cargo and travelers. Distinguished from other **riverboats★** of the period by their broad plank keel, usually external, designed to absorb the shock of hitting submerged objects; sharp ends; relatively narrow beam. Stem generally rounded,

keelboat-4

stern straight and raked, sides low and strengthened by ribs. Narrow, cleated walkways, either within the hull or set outboard, used by the polers. Waist undecked on the cargo boats, but on those carrying passengers, a low house might cover a major part of the boat. Steersman stood on the roof or on a stepped block at the stern, working a long oar attached to a pivot post. Traveled upstream by poling, rowing, being towed by a rope from shore, warping, bushwacking from tree to tree, or setting a tall square sail. Some small

keelboats, ca. 9m long, were **sloop*-**rigged (**keelboat sloop**). Bench thwarts for rowers forward. Crew of 3-6 on downstream run, as many as 40 upstream. Reported lengths 9-24m, widths 1.8-3.7m, but reported to 5.5m, hold depth 0.9-1.2m; shallow draft. Note also **barge-11h, flatboat-4, horse boat-5e, Mohawk boat, packet boat-4**.
Further reference: **fifie-1**

keelboat sloop See **keelboat-4**

keele See **keel**

Keelung coal boat See **red bow**

keel-wherry *England, NE:* 18th-century vessel similar to the **Norfolk wherry***, but the accommodations were in the forecastle rather than aft. May be an early term for a **Norfolk keel***. Mast stepped amidships and carried a main course bent to a yardarm.

keil-boat See **keelboat-2**

Keitelkahn See **kudilvalts**

kekap tĕram See **kakap jĕram**

kelandrion See **chelandia**

kelate, keleck See **kelek**

keleh lichang See **kolek lichang**

kelek 1. Generic for **raft*** in Arabic, Kurdish, Persian, Syrian, and Turkish.
2. *Iraq:* Square or rectangular **raft** of inflated goat, and sometimes camel, skins. Found mainly on the Tigris River, but also on the Euphrates. In use for at least 2,700 years, carrying produce, firewood, grain, pottery, wool, and people. Also used in eastern Turkey, sometimes to transport military personnel and equipment. Range from 1-family **rafts** of 4-6 skins to larger **rafts** of as many as 1,600 skins that plied the Tigris between Mosul and Baghdad. Usually dismantled upon completing a trip, the poplar framework sold for lumber or firewood, and the skins deflated, retanned, and transported back upstream; donkeys might be carried on board to serve as transportation home. Skins lashed to a poplar pole platform or layers of crossed branches on top of which are placed straw mats or a wooden floor. A hut may be constructed for the crew or when carrying special passengers. Skins positioned so they can be re-inflated en route by means of a reed pipe. In hot weather, the skins must be constantly splashed with water to keep them from bursting. Steered with long sweeps. Oars of split willow. Crew of 2-4. Average 3.6-4.6m long, 4.4-4.9 wide; one with 200 skins would be ca. 9m by 6m. Other recorded names: **čilĭčc, elep dušê, ellepu ša dušê, eleppu ša dušše**
Spelling variants: **kalak*, kalakka, kalakku, kelate, keleck, kelekat, kell(c)k, kielek, kilet;** pl. **aklāk**

kelekat See **kelek**

kelen See **keel-1**

kelleck, kellek See **kelek**

Kellerschiff See **Bucentaur, Leibschiff**

kemà *Indonesia, E:* **Outrigger canoe*** of the Sorong area of northwestern Irian Jaya. Sailed.

kema See **keama**

Kennebec River Gundalow See **gundalow**

Kent lugger See **Deal lugger**

Kentucky boat, Kentucky broadhorn, Kentucky flat See **flatboat-4**

kenu 1. *Solomon Islands, western Pacific:* Narrow single-**outrigger canoe*** of Roboine on the east coast of Bougainville Island. Sharp, overhanging ends; rounded hull. Short, sharp-ended float connected by multiple closely spaced booms. Employs round-bladed paddles. Probably also sails. Name variant: **kenugele**
2. *Vanuatu (New Hebrides), western Pacific:* Generic term for **canoe*** in Bichemamar, the lingua franca of the islands. One with an outrigger is a **plong kenu**.

kenugele See **kenu**

ke-nuh See **kunner**

kĕpal See **kapal**

kerfiel See **karveel**

kerkâra See **korkâra**

kerkscheepje See **boeier-2**

kerkschip See **church boat**

Kerry canoe, Kerry curragh See **naomóg**

kerveel, kervielschip See **karveel**

keshtī See **kashti**

ketch 1. The 17th- and 18th-century European **ketch** was a trader, distinguished by the lack of the usual foremast. The tall mainmast, stepped just abaft amidships, set square sails, plus a fore-and-aft sail, and the mizzen also set a square sail plus a fore-and-aft lower sail (originally lateen, later gaff) and a square topsail. Long bowsprit, with 2-3 jibs. Stoutly built. An armed 1674 English **ketch** was 16m long, 5.5m wide, 2.7m deep, 3m draft, with 30-50 men and 10 guns. Further reading: William A. Baker, *The "Mayflower" and Other Colonial Vessels* (Annapolis, Md.: Naval Institute Press, 1983), 119-144.
2. In modern usage, a 2-masted craft setting fore-and-aft sails on both masts. Identified by the size and position of the mizzenmast, which is shorter than the mainmast and generally stepped just abaft the main boom and forward of the steering device; the mizzen sail area is roughly one-half that of the mainsail. A **gaff ketch** has a gaff mainsail, but the mizzen may be a spritsail; the **Bermudian ketch** employs leg-of-mutton sails. A popular fishing, trading, and yacht rig. Note also **cat-ketch, dandy, dundee**.
3. *Australia, South Australia:* Until about the mid-20th century, the term was applied to local trading vessels to distinguish them from **cutters***, which were always decked **fishing boats***.
4. *England, SE:* In the early 17th century, might designate a small boat that conveyed fish and oysters to the Billingsgate market near London.
5. *United States:* A colonial American offshore fishing **ketch** was more a hull type than a rig; some also engaged in local trading, and a few carried salt cod to the West Indies, returning with sugar. Double-ended, or with a rounded or square stern; strongly built, flush deck. Believed to have been fore-and-aft rigged, the smaller sizes setting a single spritsail and staysail, the larger adding a square topsail on the mainmast and a lateen or gaff mizzen. In the later period, some probably gaff-rigged. Crew of

ca. 4-6. Reported keel lengths 10.4-13.4m; e.g., length on keel 10.4m, beam 3.7m, hold depth 1.8m. Selected recorded names: **Anderhalbmaster, anderhalfmaster, Besankutter, ca(i)che, catch, caych, checc(h)ia** (pl. **checc(h)ie), chec(c)e, chec(h)ia, keatch, keč, kech, kecz, Ketsch, kitchi, kitja, kitji⋆, kits, one-and-a-half master, quaich(e), queche⋆**. Further references: **dorioh, Humber keel, quetx**

ketch-barge *United Kingdom:* **Coaster⋆** that engaged mainly in the coal trade, both along the east coast and from Wales to London. Appeared in the mid-19th century. **Ketch⋆**-rigged, both sails boomed; early vessels set square sails to the main topmast. Long, rising bowsprit with multiple headsails. **Barge⋆**-built without an external keel. Clipper bow; rounded counter stern on the larger, transom on the smaller. Many employed leeboards. Crew of 4-5.

keti See **tony-2**

ketīre See **belem-1**

Ketsch See **ketch**

kettingpont See **pont**

kettuvallam *India, SW:* **1.** Cargo boat that travels the backwaters of the Kerala coast. Planks sewn with coir; double-ended. Central part covered by a rounded, mat-roofed house. Reported lengths 6-18m; widths 1.6-2m, depth to 2.4m. Name variant: **baggage boat**
2. Name given to a coastal **fishing boat⋆** of Alleppey and Quilon Districts in Kerala; along other stretches, known generally as a **tōni**. Those using the *thanga vala* net are known as **thangavallams**. Plank-built, with as many as 18 planks per side, but generally fewer; strakes secured with coir rope, then nailed with copper or iron nails. Caulked with cloth saturated with a gum mixed with coconut oil. Double-ended with upturned, curved stem and sternpost; bottom curved fore-and-aft; 9 thwarts. Steered with a triangular-bladed oar. Small lateen sail set to a stout, vertical mast lashed to a thwart. Also rowed using pointed oars. Outboard motors now common. Crew of 4-15. Reported lengths 8.5-15m, the larger boats found in the south. Other recorded names: **chemboke, tankuvallam, Tānūr tōni, thanguvallom**. Note also **vallam-1a**.

Keulenaar See **Samoreus**

Keulsche Aak, Keulse aak, Keulsze Aek See **Kölner Aak**

Keutelkahn See **udilvalts**

kewo'u *Papua New Guinea, SE:* Small, light, single-**outrigger canoe⋆** found on several of the Trobriand and Amphlett Islands. Used primarily for lagoon fishing and transportation. Simple dugout hull; round in cross section; bottom curves up at ends. Five or 6 evenly spaced booms cross atop the hull and extend to a long, slender float. Booms and float connected by pairs of stanchions that cross beneath the booms. Sometimes a platform is laid across the booms. Reported lengths 1.8-3m.

keyle See **Tyne keel**

Key West smack See **schooner smack**

Key West smackee See **smackee**

Key West sponge schooner See **sponge schooner-2**

Key West sponge sloop *United States, SE:* Engaged in shoal-water sponge fishing in the Florida Keys in the late 19th century. Hull design not standard, but in general, these carvel-planked boats had a fine entrance with a plumb, straight stem and transom stern, some above a vertical sternpost. Straight keel, often with drag; rising floors, strong sheer. Some employed a centerboard. Decked; helmsman's cockpit, oval or rectangular, abaft a trunk cabin. Rudder came up inboard on some; tiller. Mast stepped in forward quarter or third. Gaff mainsail, long boom, some loose-footed. Bowsprit held 1-2 jibs. Might run a topsail to a topmast. Crew of 2-5. Length 7.4m, beam 3.12m, molded depth 0.76m. Name variant: **sloop boat⋆**

khadirgon See **kadırga**

khæper nouka See **nouka**

khansha See **ganja**

khasaba See **baghla-1**

khashab See **khashabah**

khashabah *Arabian Peninsula:* Common term for a sailing vessel in the Persian (Arabian) Gulf; in the Aden area, it may designate a more specific type of vessel. Occasionally considered a synonym for a **baghla⋆**. Spelling variant: pl. **khashab**

khashbah See **Lamu jahazi**

khisti See **kishti**

khatgiri *Bangladesh/India, NE:* Type of **riverboat⋆** widely used in Assam, Bengal, Bihar, and Orissa during the 17th century.

khatira See **gatîra**

khelandrion See **chelandia**

khoolea See **huliya**

khotia See **kotia**

khul'k See **hulk-1**

kiãk See **kik-2**

kialoa *United States, Hawaii:* Small, light, sleek single-**outrigger canoe⋆**. Early boats probably used mainly for racing and display by local chiefs, and today's **canoes⋆** by this name form a local racing class. Details of the early **canoes** unknown. May also be a fishing and general-purpose boat used in sheltered waters. Mainly a single-person **canoe**, although some paddled and/or sailed by 2-3 persons. Other recorded names: **kioloa, wa'a kioloa**

kialu *Chile, S:* Planked **canoe⋆** of the Alaculuf people of the eastern part of the Strait of Magellan. Bottom plank bends upward to form ends that rise above the gunwales. Side strakes lashed together and to the bottom with saplings and vines, now nailed; caulked with moss and fat. Gunwales and thwarts of small sticks. Propelled by 3 long oars and steered with a short one. For long trips, may set a gunter-type, full-cut sail laced to a very long, light boom.

Kiangsu trader *China, E:* Family of **junks⋆** built mainly at Shanghai and other ports of Jiangsu (Kiangsu) Province. Traded principally to the north, but noted in the western Indian Ocean in early times; rarely seen by the 1950s. Characterized by 5 masts and a long stern gallery. Stoutly built; many watertight bulkheads; sides reinforced with heavy wales;

strong tumble home amidships above the wales. Flat bottom, longitudinally planked except where the bottom curved up at the square ends; central plank thicker, forming a sort of plank keel; flared, raked bow. Broad and deep counter stern, sometimes carved in geometric and floral designs; conspicuous poop. Rudderstock came up into the house; rudder worked with tiller and tackles and hoisted by a windlass. Decking made level above the cambered side decks created by the tumble home; row of hatches amidships led to the holds; cabin aft. **Sampan*** stowed on deck or slung beneath the gallery. Forward mast stepped outboard against the port bulwark, raking forward; fore- and mainmasts on the centerline, the foremast raking slightly forward. Small mizzenmast offset slightly to port, raking forward; taller quarter mast, stepped against the port bulwark, used mainly when tacking. No standing rigging. In early drawings, portrayed with 2 masts forward in order to meet government regulations on the number of masts used. Sometimes a staysail was hung between the fore- and mainmasts, and in light air, a topsail on the mainmast. Narrow, tanned, rectangular sails; stiffened vertically with ropes and battened horizontally; system of sheets controlled the leech for reefing. Crew of 20-30. Lengths of the largest class 37-55m, widths to ca. 10.6m; shallow draft. A smaller, generally similar type, called **sha chuan (sand boat*)**, was 30m long, beam 5.6m, depth 2.4m, cap. ca. 40t; crew of 7. Other recorded names: **Beizhili junk, cha tch'ouan, Chiangsu freighter, Chihli trader, Chili Bay trader, hung-tu-shuan, Jiangsu trader, northern trader, Pechili trader, Peichihli Dschunke, Petchili jonque, Petschili, sand ship, sha-chhuan**. Further reading: D. W. Waters, "Chinese Junks: The Pechili Trader," *The Mariner's Mirror* XXV (1939), 62-88.

k'iao-yen tch'ouan See **nan he chuan**

kíata See **kāt**

kiBatela, kibetala See **betala**

ki-bune *Japan:* Wood-carrying boat prevalent throughout Japan, but particularly numerous on Hiuga and Shikoku Islands. Name variant: **wood boat***

kičŏmbo See **chombo**

kičumbwi See **mtumbwi**

Kiedelkahn See **kudilvalts**

kiel See **keel**

kielbom See **bom-1**

Kielboot See **keelboat-1**

kiele See **keel**

kielek See **kelek**

Kiel-Ewer See **Besan-Ewer**

Kielsicken See **Garnsicken**

kieou-min tch'ouan See **hong chuan**

kieyak See **kayak**

kiftis See **kishti-2a**

kihori See **houri-2**

kii See **barque Djenné**

kik 1. *Egypt:* Reported as a cargo vessel of the Damietta (Domyat) branch of the Nile Delta. Sharp bow, flat bottom, lateen-rigged.

2. *Israel, NE:* Small **fishing boat*** of the Sea of Galilee (Tiberias). Decked at each end, 2 bitts on each side of the foredeck for the anchor chain; keel. Mast stepped through thwart in forward quarter, setting a triangular sail, probably a lateen. Spelling variant: pl. **kiāk**

3. *Syria:* **Fishing boat** that fishes for bonito and sardines. Originally sailed, now propelled by motor.

4. *Turkey:* A **skiff***-type boat.
Further reference: **gig-1**

kikko-sen *Japan:* Early, fully enclosed naval craft designed to protect the warriors and sailors. Propelled by crew-driven wheels suspended in a centerboard-like trunk in the flat bottom. In an emergency, the vessel could be paddled. Built of camphor wood; strongly cambered deck covered with copper or iron; no bulwarks; holes along the sides for use of the archers. A rudder at each end. Ca. 14t. Name variant: **turtle-shell boat**. Note also **kamé-no-sé, kwi-son**.

Kilakarai canoe See **kulla-2**

kilet See **kelek**

Kilkeel nickey See **nickey-2**

killer boat See **whale catcher**

kiln-coaster See **Saint John River woodboat**

kiln-wood coaster *United States, NE:* Any craft that carried wood to fuel the lime kilns on the Maine coast, particularly to Rockland. Other recorded names: **kiln-wooder, wooder**. Note also **Maine wood scow, St. John River woodboat**.

kiln-wooder See **kiln-wood coaster, Saint John River woodboat**

kimarkebu See **markab**

kimashua See **mashua-3**

kin See **barque Djenné**

Kinderlijkse hoogaars *Netherlands, SW:* A small, open **hoogaars*** found in the Kinderlijk area east of Rotterdam until the beginning of the 20th century. Mainly used for fishing, hence had a live well amidships; also served as a **ferry*** and for transporting cargo. Bottom flat, no rocker; straight stem, overhanging less than most **hoogaarsen** (pl.); rounded stern, wide sternpost. Sides straight and flared to the wale, with tumble home above; moderate sheer. Outboard rudder, wide fin below the waterline; tiller; rounded leeboards. Pole mast stepped through a thwart about a third in from the bow. Set a spritsail, staysail, jib to bowsprit, topsail. Reported lengths 7-10m; e.g., length 8m, beam 2.1m, depth 0.67m.

Kingchow River junk See **jing bang chuan**

King's boat *Canada, E:* A type of **flatboat***, built during 1776 at Three Rivers on the Saint Lawrence River for use in British naval engagements on Lake Ontario. Designed for landing operations; bow had a broad gangboard pierced with holes for musket fire. Carried 30-40 people with stores and provisions. Name variant: **royal boat**

King's cutter See **revenue cutter-1**

Kingsdown lugger See **Deal lugger**

Kingsdown punt See **Deal punt**

King's Lynn yoll See **yoll-1**

king's ship See **galleon**

Kingston lobster boat See **lobster boat-4b**

kinoo See **Chesapeake Bay log canoe-1**

Kinsale hooker *Ireland, SE:* Deep-hulled boat that traded, carried passengers, fished, and collected seaweed from the late 17th into the early 20th century. Carvel-built; very full bows; lean quarters;

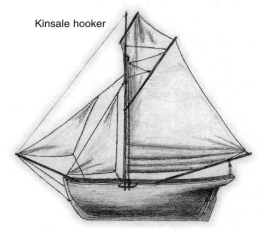

Kinsale hooker

rounded sections; sharp, rising floors; long keel with drag. Rounded stem; raked sternpost below a long, shallow counter. Partly decked. **Cutter★**-rigged with high-peaked gaff; long boom attached to mast below deck level. Jib to long, rising bowsprit, topsail, staysail. Crew of 3-6. Reported lengths 9-12m; typical: length overall 12m, on keel 9.8m, beam 3.4m, depth 2.3m. Smaller **Kinsale hookers** are similar but with a raking transom and partial decking, marked tumble home, and no mast worked until recently. Note also **hooker**.

Kinsale lugger *Ireland, SE/Scotland, W:* Mackerel and herring **fishing boat★** derived from the **West Cornish lugger★** and the **Manx lugger★**. Used originally out of Kinsale, and by the last quarter of the 19th century, at Campbeltown on the west coast of Scotland. Decked; lug-rigged. Length ca. 16m, beam 4.57m, draft 2.13m.

kint'alaŋ See **pencalang**

kioloa See **kialoa**

kio-t'a tch'ouan See **jiao hua chuan**

Kirchenschiff See **church boat**

kirkebåd See **kirkebåt**

kirkebåt *Norway:* Transports parishioners and the minister to and from church. Generally large, well built, well maintained, and easily rowed. Often owned jointly by several farms. Many used at times for fishing. The Hordaland boats of the southwest coast were used in several of the fjords of this county, and boats of this type sometimes carried produce to Bergen. Clinker-built; keel; round bottom with low rise to the floors amidships, flared sides. Sharp ends, curved stem, curved and raked sternpost. Narrow outboard rudder followed the rake of the sternpost. Long tiller connected with a peg set at right angles from the top of the rudder, continuing to forward of the after thwart. Some employed 4-6 pairs of oars. When sailed, set a single trapezoidal sail hung from the center of the yard; bowlines extended the leech to the stemhead. Reported lengths 6.6-9.2m; e.g., length

6.64m, beam 1.88m, depth 0.58m. Spelling variants: **kirkebåd, kyrk(j)ebåt**. Note also **firroring, kyrkbåt, Oselver, sekskeiping, skyssbåt**.

kirkkovene *Finland:* Long, heavy boat used to transport people to church and for other communal travel on Finnish lakes. Most owned by several families. One reported as early as the 13th century: the **usiko** of Häme Province in central Finland. Phased out by the availability of other means of transportation; now being built for regattas. Broad clinker planking; strakes, keel, stem, and sternpost of pine; old boats usually had ribs for every pair of oars plus a seat at each end. Curved ends, flaring sides, low sheerline. Steered with rudder and tiller. Oars, of fir, secured by a loop to the single tholepin; rowed single- or double-banked. A boat with 10 pairs of oars might be 15-18m long. Largest, in eastern Finland, reported as 40m long and 3m wide; used 60 oars and carried 100 people. Name variant: **great boat**. Note also **church boat, kyrkbåt**.

kirska ladja See **zoppolo**

kishtee See **kishti**

Kiste See **tub-1**

kishti **1.** In Hindi, **boat★, ship★**, or **vessel★**. May also refer to an ornamented **raft★** or **float★**. Spelling variants: **kashtī, khisti, kishtee**
   2. *India:* On some rivers, such as the Ganges, a large passenger vessel with cabins. Some reported to have had an elongated bow in the shape of an animal's head and a high stern. May set a square or lugsail forward, small sprit mizzen, and a staysail. Also tracked from shore, and rowed. Length 20m, beam 4m, draft 1.0m. Spelling variants: **kiftis, kisti. b.** May also refer to one of the boats that make up a pontoon bridge on larger Indian rivers. Basically European in design. Name variant: **navak**
   3. *India/Pakistan:* **Punt★**-like **ferry★** of northern India and Pakistan. Characterized by a sharply upturned, flat bow; prow secured to sides by curved clamps of a hard wood. Bottom flat, broader toward the stern. Sides low, straight, and vertical. Steered with 2 sculls at each end. 10-16t burden. Name variant: **chapú**
   4. *India, NW/Pakistan, NE:* A small, flat-bottomed boat propelled by heart-shaped paddles on rivers and lakes in Kashmir.

kishtī See **kashti**

kisti See **kishti-2a**

kistie *Myanmar (Burma):* Beamy craft that transports rice to mills. Double-ended hull built up from a dugout base by adding side planks. Ends turn up. Steered with a quarter rudder. Square sail set to a pole mast; also rowed with as many as 20 men. Reported lengths 10.6-12.2m.

kitamae-bune *Japan, N:* North country **coaster★**, traveling at times to Osaka in southern Honshu; last used in the late 19th century. Long, raking stem; narrow stern swept up sharply; low rise to the floors. Decked forward; roof over the hold; inboard rudder. Tall square sail set to mast stepped abaft amidships. Other recorded names: **donguri, hokkoku-bune, kitamaefune, kitamaye-bune, north country boat★, northern front ship**

kitamaefune, kitamaye-bune See **kitamae-bune**

kitchi See **ketch**

kitepe See **mtepe**

kitja See **ketch**

kitji Malay word in Indonesia for a **ketch***-rigged craft. Word sometimes combined, as in **kitji dagang**, a trader, and **kitji pěrang**, a naval vessel.

kitji dagang, kitji pěrang See **kitji**

kitoboïnoe sudno See **whaler**

kitolovac, kitolovka See **whale catcher**

kits See **ketch**

kitsi See **Chipewyan canoe**

k'i t'u ela *Canada, NW:* Slavey tribe birchbark **canoe***. End profile deep, rounded, and often has a hump on top in which the headboard stands high to form a double hump with the stem. Gunwale may be secured with closely spaced lashings; rail cap often lacking. Wide, flat ribs set over inner sheathing. Bark caulked with spruce gum. On open water, a square sail may be set. Length 5.5m, beam 0.74m, depth 0.38m. Name variant: **Slavey canoe**

kixti See **kashti**

kjæks See **færing-6**

kjæmp-sækstreng See **seksæring-6**

kjeks See **færing-6**

kjempefæring See **færing-4**

kjempe-seksring, kjemp-string See **seksæring-6**

Klappenprahm, Klappprahm, Klappschiff, Klapp-schute See **dump barge**

klaveraak See **palingaak**

klavertjekt See **jekt**

kleine Jagd See **Jagd**

kleine Kahn See **Oberländer-4**

kleiner Kahn *Germany:* Term sometimes given to the **ship's boat*** of a **barge***-type **Kahn*** of the lower Elbe River. By the early 20th century, they were small, 2-man boats; earlier they were much longer, one reported in the late 18th century as 11m long and 1.0m wide. Constructed of oak or pine. Rowed. Now about 3m long. Other recorded names: **Handkahn, neuer Kahn**; in Saxony, usually called a **Schlup***. Note also **Beiboot**.

kleine schokker See **bons**

kleine schouw See **Friese schouw, schouw**

kleine schuit, kleine schute See **bons**

klinkajekt See **jekt**

Klinker-Galiot See **galiot-5**

kliper See **clipper**

Klipergoleta See **clipper-schooner**

klipernava See **clipper**

klipper **1.** *Belgium/Netherlands:* Cargo carrier, mainly of the larger inland waterways. Developed in the latter part of the 19th century, built until the 1930s; a few still worked into the 1970s. Many traveled the Rhine River into Germany. The 1-masted vessel, the **éénmastklipper**, worked the Waddenzee, Zeeuwse streams, and the larger canals; the 2-masted vessel, the **tweemastklipper**, worked on the larger rivers and some became **coasters*** (**zeeklippers**) traveling to the North Sea (**Noordzeeklipper**) and to the Baltic Sea (**Oostzeeklipper**). A few, between 25-30m long, were built as **yachts*** (the **klipperjacht**), and some cargo

vessels were converted to pleasure craft. Characterized by their flared and concave clipper bow, from which they derive the name. Built of iron or steel. Flat bottom with drag aft; quick turn of the bilges; straight, vertical sides. Plumb sternpost, above which was a rounded counter (the so-called **Zeeuwse klipper**) or less frequently a shallow transom (the **Friese klipper**). Strong sheer; low freeboard, especially when loaded. Decked; long hatches before and abaft the mainmast; cabin house aft. Leeboards on the inland vessels, worked generally with a winch; rudder came up inboard, worked by a wheel; vertical on sailing types, sometimes horizontal on motorized **klippers**. The single-masted **klippers** set a loose-footed, boomed mainsail and 2 headsails; long gaff. The 2-masted vessels were **ketch***-rigged, the mizzenmast stepped either before or aft of the house; generally 1 or both masts had topmasts. Masts on both types could be struck to clear bridges; 2 spars below the staysail formed a sheerlegs to aid in raising or striking the mast. Bowsprit could be topped up. Many had engines in addition to sails, but those built entirely for power were called **sleepklippers** (**klippersleepboot** or **klippersleepschip**). Reported lengths 15-46m; e.g., length 38m, beam 6.1m, depth 2.1m; shallow draft; **sleepklipper** to 62m. Other recorded names: **Benedenlander** (from Dordrecht), **Klipperschiff, rivierclipper, rivierklipper, zeilklipper, éénmastrivierklipper, tweemastrivierklipper**. In Belgium, the single-masted vessel might be called an **ijzeren aakje** or **ijzeren aakse**. Note also **klipperaak**.

2. *Netherlands, W:* Also reported as an anchovy **fishing boat***. Crew of 3; 3t. Name variant: **klipperkotter**. Further reference: **clipper**

klipperaak *Netherlands:* Inland vessel that works throughout the Netherlands carrying peat and general cargo. Also found in Belgium. Originated in the late 19th century and built of iron or steel. A few still working, but now entirely motorized. Concave, flared, clipper or plumb bow. Fuller stern than the **klipper*** to provide greater capacity aft. Those built at Waspik in southern Netherlands (the **Waspikker** or **Waspikse klipperaak**) have a full, rounded, handsome stern; tumble home above the wale. Another type has a **tjalk***-type stern; a 3rd type has a stern that resembles a horse's rump. Sheer sweeps up sharply toward the bow; low freeboard amidships. Heavy, plumb rudder; tiller S-shaped and slots over the rudderhead; leeboards. Long, cambered hatches; house aft on most; window on either side of the rudder. Loose-footed, boomed gaff sail set to a heavy, strikable mast; jib to a long bowsprit, staysail. Length of 1915 vessel 23m, beam 5.14m, depth 1.86m.

klipperjacht See **klipper-1**

klipperkotter See **klipper-2**

Klipperschiff See **clipper, klipper-1**

klipperskepp See **clipper**

klippersleepboot, klippersleepschip See **klipper-1**

knar See **knarr-1**

knarr **1.** Viking merchant vessel that traded to Iceland, Greenland, England, and southern Europe from the 8th century until the end of the Middle Ages. Some carried settlers and their belongings and cattle to Iceland and Greenland. The smaller sizes were **coasters**★. Clinker-built, narrow strakes; strengthened by frames and double thwarts; separate futtocks and knees. Double-ended with tall, curved stem and sternpost; high, rounded sides; straight keel. Steered with a large quarter rudder; tiller brought in over the gunwale at right angle to the center line. Decked forward and aft with open hold amidships; some medieval vessels had castles forward and aft. Mast stepped amidships; woolen square sail reinforced with strips of walrus or sealskin; tacking spar extended the sail. Also rowed through oar ports. Crew to ca. 50. Reported lengths 13-34m; e.g., length 25m, beam 6.2m, depth 3m. Other recorded names: **cnarr, knar(rar), knör, knörr, knörr(ur)**; pl. **knerri(r), knörrer; knarrar-skip** (Icelandic). Note also **da knoren, hafskip**.

2. *Finland, W:* This **knärr** is a sharp-ended herring-**fishing boat**★ mainly of the coast north of Vaasa. Clinker-built, steep rise to the floors, T-keel, strong sheer, flooring along the central part. Plumb stem, curved forefoot. The **lillknärr** has a curved sternpost, while the **halvknärr** (also called **knärrjulle**) has a strongly raked, straight sternpost. Outboard rudder; small tiller. The **lillknärr** sets a spritsail and jib to the stemhead; the **halvknärr** steps a mast in the eyes and sets only a spritsail. Some 2-masted. Also rowed, the oars working against single or double tholepins. Reported lengths 5.2-7.3m. Other recorded names: **knärrbåt; pesäpaatti** (Finnish)

3. *Norway:* Name of a popular racing class.

knarrar, knarrar-skip, knärrbåt See **knarr**
knärrjulle See **knärr-2**
knerri, knerrir See **knarr**
knivsviksnekke See **snekke**
knobstick See **narrow boat**
knockabout 1. Word applied, especially in North America, to a sailing vessel rigged without a bowsprit, the jib stayed from or near the stemhead. Type found on **schooners**★, **sloops**★, and **yawls**★.

2. A colloquial term given to a general-purpose boat that handles well and can be sailed or rowed as needed.

3. *Canada/United States:* **a.** Fishing **schooner**★ of the early 20th century that had no bowsprit. Elongated bow curved up from the straight keel and might be nearly plumb or tumble home at the stemhead; counter stern. Strong sheer on early vessels, flattened in later types; fine lines; drag to keel. Low deck house. Masts often stepped close together, necessitating a narrow foresail. Most used topsails. Jib-to-fore-topmast stay attached from the stemhead, which terminated at stemhead; forestaysail, foresail. Most set gaff topsails. Fully motorized by 1930, but continued to fish under sail. Reported lengths 26-38m. **b.** A variation, the **semi-knockabout**, had a short, spike bowsprit from its elongated spoon bow, and the forestay was brought down inboard. Other recorded names: **knockabout banker** (**fisherman** or **schooner**). Note also **banker-2**.

4. *United States, NE:* A small, **sloop**-rigged **yacht**★ of the 1890s popular in New England. Characterized by

lack of a bowsprit or a very short one. Generally full keel; some had a centerboard. Decked or half-decked; sometimes a small cabin. Those that raced had to be under 6.4m on the waterline.

knockabout banker, knockabout fisherman, knockabout schooner See **knockabout-3b**
knock-toe See **Deal galley punt**
knör, knörr, knörrer, knörrur See **knarr-1**
k'oai tch'ouan See **fast boat-2**
k'oai-t'ing See **hong boat**
koak See **mon-3**
kobar See **gabare**
kobåt *Sweden, N:* Type of **storbåt**★ that transports animals on inland waters. Term also used in the Swedish-speaking part of Finland. Strongly constructed; sharp ends; flat bottom reinforced by the bottom framing; flat sheer. Animals restrained by poles along the sides and athwartships. Rowed with a pair of oars forward and another pair at the stern. Length 10m, beam 3.5m.
kobaya See **seki bune**
kobb, kobbar, kobbeka See **ekstock-1**
Kobelzille See **Mutzen-4**
kobil See **coble-1**
kočar See **trawler**
kocge, kocghe See **cog**
koch 1. *Bangladesh/India:* **Dugout canoe**★ used for net and line fishing in several inland districts. Lies flat in the water. Length ca. 4m.

2. *Russia, N:* Other recorded names: **koch', kocha, kochi, kotch(a), kotchamar, kotche, kotchi, ko(t)chmara, kotsa, kotsche, kotschmara. a.** Vessel of the 16th-17th centuries used along the northern coast and the White Sea; designed to withstand ice abrasion. Reportedly built without nails or caulking; sharp ends; bow strongly raked, stern less so; maximum beam well aft; flat floors. Sides rounded; extra protection along the waterline. Decked; low poop; long tiller on an outboard rudder. Set 1-2 square sails. Also rowed. Crew of 10-15. Large size 19m long, beam 5m, draft 1.5-2m, cap. 40t. A small size, the **volokovye**, was 7m long, 2.5m wide, with 7t cap. This craft was designed with side keels in order to be pulled overland between 2 rivers. **b.** The **kochmara** of the 18th-19th centuries was a high-sided vessel. Sharp, raking bow; raking transom above the sternpost; windows in transom. Flat floors, rounded bilges, strong sheer. Outboard rudder; tiller worked from the poop deck. Square sail set to tall mast stepped in after third; mizzen set a loose-footed, boomed gaff sail. Foremast, in the eyes, set an equilateral sail. Headsails to a slender rising bowsprit.

koch', kocha See **koch-2**
koche See **cog**
kochi, kochmara See **koch-2**
kocho See **cog**
kochuvallam, kochuvallom See **vallam-1a**
kock, kocke, kocko See **cog**
Koedijker schuitje *Netherlands, NW:* Small, open boat of Koedijk. Used mainly to carry produce and light goods, but also for inland fishing. Strongly built;

widely spaced, heavy ribs ran to the top of the sheer strake. Flat bottom; raked, heavy stem and sternpost; sheer strake terminated before the ends; light sheer. **Fishing boats*** had a wet well. Propelled mainly by a forked pole. Some sailed, employing a loose-footed leg-of-mutton sail and a single leeboard. Length 5.5m, beam 1.6m.

kof *Netherlands, NE:* A square-hulled vessel that served as a **coaster*** in the late 17th and 18th centuries. By the 19th century, they were constructed on finer, but still full, lines and traveled widely, being nicknamed **Dutch butterboxes**. Last built in the 1890s. Some built in Belgium. Very bluff bow initially; later became finer; heavy stem; round stern, sharper below the waterline; straight sides strengthened by heavy wales. Flat floors, heavy keel; round bilges; strong sheer. Small outboard rudder; early vessels and later smaller models employed leeboards. Fully decked; trunk cabin; stern windows. Variously rigged, but all were 2-masted. Early vessels portrayed with large spritsails abaft the square sails, topsails, and 2-3 jibs. Later, rigged as a gaff **ketch*** and as a **topsail schooner** (schoenerkof) with a topgallant above the topsail. Crew of 7-9. Early vessels built three lengths to one beam, later 4:1. Reported lengths 12-30m, widths 3-7m, hold depths 1.16-3.45m. Other recorded names: **Brabantse schoenerkof, coff*, koff(e), kofke, kofscheepje, kofschip(je), kofschuite, kop*, kuf*, kuffe, kuffschip**; pl. **koffen, koppen**. Note also **koftjalk**.

koff, koffe, koffen See **kof**

Kofftjalk See **koftjalk**

kofke See **kof**

kofscheepje, kofschip, kofschipje, kofschuite See **kof**

koftiya See **kotia**

koftjalk *Netherlands, NE:* A type of **tjalk***, but larger, heavier, and with **kof*** features. Originated as a **coaster*** out of Groningen, although later iron- and steel-built vessels made ocean voyages. Last built ca. 1925. The German **Kufftjalk** was essentially the same. Rounded bow and stern; curved stem, plumb sternpost. Little rise to the floors; rounded cross section; often swept up at the bow to form a pointed stemhead. Deadwood at bow and stern; keel. Wide, continuous rubbing strake characteristic; strong tumble home above the strake along the sides and at the ends; small porthole on each side of the rudder. Large leeboards; rudderhead usually decorated; some had washboards. Decked; deckhouse and 1-2 cambered hatches; cuddy aft. Some 18th-century **koftjalken** (pl.) were portrayed with a spritsail, staysail, and square topsail. Later vessels employed a boomed, loose-footed gaff mainsail, 1-2 jibs, and staysail; many **ketch***-rigged. Long, rising bowsprit sometimes supported by a concave gammon knee. Single-masted **koftjalken** had pole masts; the 2-masted vessels added topmasts. Crew of 2-4. Reported lengths 15-25.8m, widths 4-5.8m, depths 1.4-2.4m; shallow draft. Other recorded names: **Groninger koftjalk, Kofftjalk** (incorrectly). Note also **kof**.

koftjalken See **koftjalk**

kog See **cock, cog**

koga, kogcho See **cog**

koge See **cog, kåg-1**

kogg See **cog, snekke**

kogga See **cog**

kogge See **cock, cog, cog boat, kåg-1**

koggen See **cog, snekke**

koggene, kogger See **snekke**

kogje, Kogschip See **cog**

kohaya *Japan:* Small, swift ship of the 17th century that mainly transported *sake* and various other commodities. Note also **wine ship**.

kohbukson See **kwi-son**

Kohlendampfer See **collier-1**

Kohlenkahn, Kohlenleichter See **coal lighter**

Kohlennachen See **Ruhraak**

Kohlenprahm See **Prahm-2**

Kohlenschiff, Kohlentransportschiff See **collier-1**

Kohl-Ewer See **Ewer, Rhin-Ewer**

kohn See **Fischerkahn, Kahn-1**

kōi-la-pū See **düe**

koiro See **coïro**

kok *Netherlands:* Small inland **fishing boat*** reported from the 17th century. Spelling variant: **koksje**. See also **cog**.

koka *Australia, NE:* Bark **canoe*** used on the Fitzroy River in central Queensland. Constructed in 3 pieces of iron-bark; bottom sometimes of blue gum. Pointed ends, rounded from the bottom; side and bottom pieces sewn together, a roll of paper tea tree bark serving as caulking for the seams. Top strengthened with saplings, also sewn. Reported lengths 1.8-2.1m. Name variant: **okka**. See also **cog**.

Kokar sköt See **skötbåt-1**

köke See **cog**

kokke See **coggle**

kokkoreli See **cocoreli**

kokse *Norway, NW:* A recent small, flat-bottomed boat of Nordmøre district. Often used to travel to and from motorized vessels moored offshore. Raked ends, flaring sides. Bottom planked athwartships. Rowed with a single pair of oars. Length ca. 3m. See also **færing-5**.

koksje See **kok**

kola-catamaran See **kola maram**

kola maram *India, SE:* Sails from the south Coromandel coast during July and August fishing for *kola* (flying fish). Seven logs, often taken temporarily from other types of **catamarans***, are lashed together and held in position by a crosspiece at each end; a supplemental plank lashed along one side provides a seat while the fish are hauled aboard. A shaped, upturned bow is formed by 5 stem pieces lashed to the forward end of the logs. Two strong leeboards (2.7-3.2m deep) lowered when beating; one abreast the mast, the other near the stern, and the steering paddle (ca. 3.7m long) serves as a 3rd. Steps 2 short, forward-raking masts on the leeward side, stayed forward and aft. Brown lateen-type sails; boomed abaft the mast with a rope continuing forward to the yard; reefed by rolling around the boom. Four paddles and 3 oars also available for the 7 crew members. Reported lengths 9-11m, widths 2.1-2.4m. Other recorded names: **flying-fish catamaran, kola-cata-maran**. See also **catamaran-12**.

ko lang ting See **ma ling ting**

kol' See **kolek-2**

koleh See **kolek-3, kolek-4**

koleh chiau See **kolek chiau**

koleh kelibat See **kolek gelibat**

koleh lichung See **kolek lichang**

koleh Malacca See **Malacca kolek**

koleh panjail See **kolek-4**

koleh selat See **kolek šĕlat**

kolek 1. *Christmas Island:* Double-**outrigger canoe★**, of fairly recent origin, used mainly for fishing off the steep beaches of this Australian-administered island south of Java. The solid, sharp ends curve up above gunwale level. Two booms, 2.4-3.1m long, cross the hull and attach to the slender floats (2.2-2.9m long) with ring-shaped connectives. Designed for use by 1-3 people. Reported lengths 4-6m, width 0.5m, depths 0.31-0.36m. **2.** *Indonesia:* One of the Malay terms for **boat★**. A 2nd word following **kolek** generally indicates a specific use, such as **kolek pukat★**, a boat that uses a particular type of fishing net. However, **kolek** alone may designate a specific type of boat, a few of which follow. Spelling variant: **kol'**. **a.** Engaged in fishing and transporting the catch to auction along the western Java coast until the turn of the 20th century; similar to the **mayang★**. Now tends V-shaped fish traps (*séro*) and is called a **sampan séro**. Since the turn of the 20th century, the **kolek** has also carried cargo to the Kepulauan Seribu (Thousand Islands), northwest of Djakarta. In general, long, narrow, plank-built craft; flat floors; ends either narrow and elongated out over the water or strongly curved with very deep, solid, recurved stem and sternpost. Open or partly covered with a house. Employs 1-2 quarter rudders. Steps 1-4 light masts, the **fishing boats★** generally omitting the mast amidships because of a large fish hold. Triangular or quadrilateral sails; leech boomed out with sprits. The single sail of the Kepulauan Seribu type was very large, but made of a light, loose material. Other recorded names: **kolek séro, kolik★, kollek, prau kolek. b.** One variety of Javanese **kolek** was a large traveling vessel. Hull built up from a dugout base that projected forward and aft to form bifid ends; keel. Ends above the rams raked up in flat, ornamented surfaces. Rounded bottom; interior beams provided strengthening; considerable sheer. Decked for a short distance at bow and stern; 2 open wells for cargo; house in after half. Rudder, suspended from a post lashed to a crossbeam, worked on the quarter. Stepped 2 short masts in the forward half; a long bowsprit projected through the bow transom. Set boomed lateen-type sails, the foresail smaller. Name variant: **prahoe kolek. c.** Flat-bottomed, sprit-rigged **fishing boat** of the Djakarta area of western Java. Plank-built, vertical ends. Long and slender; flat sheer. **d.** Crank, 1-man fishing **koleks** were reported from the larger islands between Sumatra and Kalimantan (Borneo). Well-constructed of a light wood; plank keel; curved stem extended well above the gunwale; reverse S-curve to the equally tall sternpost. Short, slender mast stepped

in forward part; triangular sail. A hook for the sheet, carved to resemble a duck's head, was positioned aft and to starboard. Also employed double paddles. Length ca. 3.5m, beam 0.5m. **e. Fishing boat** of the Riau Archipelago off eastern Sumatra. Planked up from a dugout base; sharp bow and stern; raised ends, truncated on top. Temporary decking. Set a boomed, trapezoidal lugsail to a mast stepped well forward. Length 7.2m, beam 2m, depth 0.9m. Other recorded names: **kolek Riouw, kolik★, prahoe kolek**

3. *Peninsular Malaysia/Singapore/Thailand, SE:* Generic term for several types of boats of the Malay Peninsula. Generally any small, open boat that is narrow, crank, and has a longitudinally curved bottom. Hull, size, rig, and use vary; those from the south and west coasts of the peninsula are quite different from those on the east coast. Other recorded names: **koleh, kule★, sampan★**. Note also **Malacca kolek**.

4. *Singapore:* Long, narrow, open boat used for net fishing and, in a specialized form, for racing. Light carvel planking over 1-piece, heavy, natural frames (ca. 90cm apart) held by a single stringer on each side; the racing **kolek** is more heavily planked. Easy turn of the bilges to rounded, flaring sides. Ends sharp; ends convex above and concave below the waterline; shallow notch on upper surface; on some, a carved projection extends above gunwales at each end. Generally deep keel but shallow draft. Steered with a paddle; propelled by 2 sculling oars worked by a standing man; also uses long, lanceolate-bladed paddles. Originally set a high-peaked spritsail with bamboo sprit and boom; later a tall, boomed leg-of-mutton sail with a

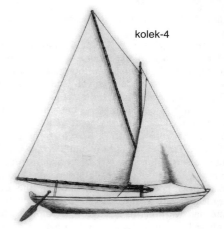

kolek-4

wide, overlapping jib on larger boats. Mast stepped into a single thwart. When racing, the crew hike out, placing their feet on the gunwale and leaning to windward, supported by a sling from the mainmast. Crew of 3-14 when racing. Lengths range from 3-14m. **Fishing boats** typically 6m long, 1.1m wide, 0.48m deep; racing sizes 7m long, 0.8m wide, 0.5m deep to 13m by 0.9m by 0.4m. Other recorded names: **koleh, koleh panjail, koley**. Note also **jong-3**.

5. *Thailand, SW:* In the Malay fishing villages just north of the eastern Malaysia-Thailand border, the **kolek** remains an important boat. These **koleks** retain the

elaborate carvings and painting rarely found now farther south. Near the bow on the port side, a tall wooden arm, representing an abstract dragon head, holds spars when not in use. At the stern, a forked, upright support holds the furled mast and sail; this may be omitted on boats with inboard motors. Near the stern, there is a strong, carved rudderpost to which the heavy rudder is lashed. Sides usually brightly painted, sometimes in intricate designs. Sharp-ended with tall, concave stem and sternpost. Crew of 7. Length ca. 8.5m.
Further references: **kolek lichang, kule-2, Malacca kolek, sampan-6, sampan Riau**

kolek buatan barat, kolek buatan Siam See **perahu buatan barat**

kolek chiau *Peninsular Malaysia/Singapore:* Chinese-built and -operated boat, mainly as a **ferry★** but also for inshore fishing and to tend traps off southern Malay Peninsula. The distinctive rectangular stem and sternpost rake at 45°, the free edges cut convexly just above gunwale level; strakes fit into grooves in side of stem and sternpost. Sharp ends; keel short and straight with well-rounded forefoot and heel; ribs one piece; marked sheer. Steered with oars or a short paddle. Propelled with a pair of long-shafted oars by standing oarsman who faces forward. When sailed, generally sets a jib-headed sail, but may employ a spritsail or loose-footed standing lugsail. Crew of 1-3. Reported lengths 4.9-6.7m; e.g., length 6.7m, beam 1.0m, depth 0.5m. Other recorded names: **koleh chiau, kolek chio(u)w**

kolek China See **phang chun**

kolek chiouw, kolek chiow See **kolek chiau**

kolek gelibat *Peninsular Malaysia:* Boat of the east coast, especially off Pahang, that generally fished with a drift net for a herring-like fish. Characterized by S-shaped stem and sternpost, frequently with carved ornamentation. Plank-built; long keel, almost straight, and sharply angled at forefoot and heel. Stem and stern sharply raked. Steered with a rudder, usually with yoke and lines. Propelled by 3 paddles or with a small gaff or lugsail, usually tanned. Crew of 2-3. Reported lengths 4-8m, widths 0.76-1.4m. Other recorded names: **delibat, gelibat, glibat, koleh kelibat, kolek kelibat**

kolek kelibat See **kolek gelibat**

kolek kue *Peninsular Malaysia:* **Fishing boat★** of the east coast; varies somewhat in size and design from area to area. Generally fairly long keel, cutaway forefoot and heel, endpost extensions high and curved forward. Some have elaborate, bird-like spar rests. Partly decked. Crew of 5. Those used for line fishing 5-6m long, 1.07m wide; a large type that used nets 7.9-8.5m long, 1.52m wide. Other recorded names: **kolek kueh, kolek linchang, kue(h), kueh kepalo panjang** (in Kelantan); **kuek, lichung** (small type to the south of Trengganu). Note also **kueh buteh ketiri**.

kolek kueh See **kolek kue**

kolek lichang *Peninsular Malaysia/Thailand, S:* Graceful craft that fishes from east coast beaches. Called **kolek lichang** or **kolek★** in Kelantan, but only **kolek** in Trengganu. Similar to a small **payang★**. Fine, upturned ends give it a crescent shape; usually painted and sometimes ornamented with Islamic motifs; sternpost deeper and carries a break in the sheer. Well-rounded stem, cutaway forefoot and heel, short keel. Often an ornate crutch supports the lowered spars. Larger types raise 2 lugsails, usually with a staysail; smaller varieties set a single sail, the tack of which is fastened to the mast to serve as a modified lugsail. Oars used when necessary. Crew of 5-10 on larger types; small craft may be used by 1 man. Reported lengths 9-12m, beam 1.8m. Other recorded names: **keleh lichang, koleh lichung, kolek linchong, lichang, lichung, perhau kolek**

kolek linchang See **kolek kue**

kolek linchong See **kolek lichang**

kolek Malacca See **Malacca kolek**

kolek ma' Siam *Peninsular Malaysia:* Undecked **fishing boat★** of the Kelantan coast, having spread southward from southern Thailand. Wide range of sizes, the larger types often referred to as **jo'kong**. Stem and sternpost markedly raked, extending above washstrakes; little sheer. Recurved rudder; tiller. Steps 2 masts; foremast near the bow, the mainmast about a third of the way aft. Crew of 2-3. Maximum length 9.1m, beam 0.76m. See also **dogol**.

kolek Mělaka See **Malacca kolek**

kole kole 1. *Africa, W:* Small **dugout canoe★** of the peoples of the middle Niger River from southeastern Mali, Niger, and northwestern Nigeria. Used mainly for local fishing and transportation. The dugout made in 2 halves, the bow and stern halves then joined by rope lacings through drilled holes. Should one half become worn, a replacement is prepared, but in the meantime, the good half is made usable by plugging the open end with a mixture of mud and grass. Flat bottom; bow end sharp and raked; stern has a square, handle-like extension. Other recorded names: **kwalle kwalle, kwolle kwolle**
2. *Indonesia, E:* The **kolé kolé** of the Moluccas, notably from Ambon, Banda, and Ceram, is mainly a plank-extended **dugout canoe** with or without double outriggers. Outrigger floats attached with U-shaped connectives; booms secured at the hull by 2 lashings that reach down to a rod wedged beneath residual lugs left in the dugout. Some reported as plank-built with tall stem and sternpost. Sprit- or gaff-rigged. Note also **perahu-2**.

kolek pěngayer *Peninsular Malaysia:* Crescent-shaped, open **fishing boat★** used along the east coast. Tall, decorated stem and sternpost follow the curve of the bow and stern. Long keel; angled forefoot and heel; moderate sheer. Carvel planking fastened to heavy, grown frames nearly up to the gunwale; frames connected by a single stringer on each side. Large curved crutch holds lowered spars. Mast stepped through the single thwart; larger types have 2 masts. Single-masted boats set a boomed standing lugsail; 2-masted boats set Malay-type dipping lugs. Also employs spear-shaped paddles; steered with an oar. Crew of 3-4. Reported lengths 7-8m, widths 1.2-1.4m, depth ca. 0.6m, draft 1.0m. Other recorded names: **kolek pengayoh, kolek sa'hari bulan, new-moon boat, pengail★, pěngayer**

kolek pengayoh See **kolek pĕngayer**

kolek poekat See **kolek pukat**

kolek pukat *Indonesia, central:* Large **fishing boat★** of the Bantam area at the northwest end of Java. Employed a net (the *pukat*) in fishing for a type of mackerel. Deep, heavy stem and sternpost that usually recurve above the gunwale line. Generally painted in bright colors. Quarter rudder. Tall crutch at stern supports lowered spars and mast stays. Aft-raking mast stepped about a third in from the bow; sets a trapezoidal sail. Also rowed with the oarsmen forward of the mast. Crew of ca. 11. Spelling variant: **kolek poekat**. Note also **perahu pukat**.

kolek Riouw See **kolek-2**

kolek sa'hari bulan See **kolek pĕngayer**

kolek sĕlat *Indonesia, W/Peninsular Malaysia/ Singapore:* Roughly finished Chinese craft used for small-scale fishing and ferrying in the southern part of the Malay Peninsula and the adjacent Indonesian islands. Double-ended; false stem and sternpost, straight and raking, added after planking completed. Long, slightly curved keel with hard-angled forefoot and heel. Considerable sheer; ribs in 3 pieces; "V" cross section. Sailed with a square-headed standing lugsail, but also rowed, Chinese-fashion, with the oarsman standing and facing forward. Reported lengths 4.8-7.3m; e.g., length 4.8m, beam 1.22m, depth 0.46m. Other recorded names: **koleh selat, sampan★, Straits kolek**

kolek séro See **kolek-2**

kolet See **shakhtura**

koley See **kolek-4**

kolik *Indonesia, central:* Small, narrow, 1-man boat of southwestern Kalimantan (Borneo). Four strakes added to the narrow keel; bow turned up to form a bird's head; stern formed the tail. Four beams supported a planked deck. Single mast stepped through a hole in the forward beam. Cotton sail. Also paddled. See also **kolek-2**.

kolla teppa See **teppa**

kollek See **kolek-2**

Kölner Aak *Germany, W:* Vessel of Cologne that carried wine on the lower Rhine River to the Netherlands, returning with colonial wares, from at least 1530 into the 18th century. Clinker-built; flat bottom, no keel until the mid-17th century. At the bow, the bottom turned up, creating a flat surface partway up before becoming sharp with tumble home; stern remained flat to the gunwale, narrowing to a point, or was similar to the bow. Decked; raised section at the stern until the beginning of the 17th century; arched hatch; gangways along the sides. Heavy rudder; tiller; leeboards employed in the 17th century. Sturdy mast, generally stepped forward of the hatch. Set a spritsail and staysail. Square topsail on later vessels. Also rowed and towed. Reported lengths 16-25m, beam ca. 4m. Other recorded names: **acque de Cologne, Keulsche Aak, Keulse aak, Keulsze Aek, Kölsche Aak**. Note also **aak, Samoreus**.

kolpråmm See **pråmm-4**

Kölsche Aak See **Kölner Aak**

koltringer See **havbåd**

Kommandantenboot See **gig-1**

kommercheskoe See **merchantman**

kondola See **gondola-4**

kondoura, kondura, kondure See **condura**

konebåd, konebåt See **umiak-3**

kong-hói-tói *Macau:* Three-masted **fishing boat★** that remained at sea 4-5 days. Curved bow, high counter stern, strong sheer. Very tall mainmast stepped amidships; much smaller foremast in the eyes; small mizzenmast on the counter. Set battened lugsails. Motors used when going to and from the fishing grounds. Crew of 12-15. 36-60t.

kong se tch'ouan See **hong boat**

kontoūra See **condura**

kooffa See **quffa**

Koolever See **Rhin-Ewer**

koolhaalder See **collier, Dorsten'sche Aak**

koolhaelder See **Ruhraak**

koondoo, koondool See **kundal**

kooner See **kunner**

koong-sze teng See **hong boat**

koopbotter *Netherlands:* A large **botter★** that served as a **buy boat★**, mostly for flounder, herring, and shrimp, transporting the catch to fish auctions. Centered mainly at Huizen, on the south shore of the Zuiderzee. Those that worked on the Shelde River carried Dutch eels to Antwerp. The live wells on **koopbotters** were divided into 3-4 compartments. Carried a large sail area; long jibboom. Other recorded names: **koopschuit, koopsjuut, koper**

koopschuit, koopsjuut See **koopbotter**

koopvaarder See **merchantman**

koopvaardijhoeker *Netherlands:* Dutch merchant **howker★**, mainly of the mid-18th century, but developed during the 17th century. Some owned by the Dutch East India Company; these were heavily armed, carrying 6-14 cannon. Also served as convoy vessels and **privateers★**. In general, hull design similar to the **vishoeker★**, but the **koopvaardijhoeker** was larger and set a larger topsail and a topgallant above the square mainsail. Gaff sail to the mizzen with square topsail. Pole masts. Some 3-masted; the fore- and mainmast square-rigged, the mizzen gaff-rigged with square topsail; the main carried a topgallant. Staysail; very long bowsprit supported 2 jibs. Bluff bows and quarters; square or rounded stern; flat floors that curved toward the bow but were sharp below the waterline at the stern; strong sheer. Lengths to 30m; 1695 vessel 25m long, 6.6m wide, 3.4m deep.

koopvaardijschip See **merchantman**

Kootenay canoe See **tci'k'Enō**

kop *Papua New Guinea:* Small, double-outrigger **dugout canoe★** of the Green (Nissan) Island group in the southeastern Bismarck Archipelago; used in the lagoons and for short coastal trips. Narrow opening, just wide enough for 1 leg. Blunted, overhanging ends with short platforms; small barb beneath each end; U-shaped cross section. Two booms, 2-5m long, cross from side to side, passing through holes just below the gunwales. Fairly long floats, mainly of bamboo, lashed directly to the booms. Sometimes a platform of sticks is lashed across the booms to support a box. Propelled by paddle only. Spelling variant: **kup**. See also **kof**.

kopal See **kapal**

kopboot See **boeier-2**

koper See **koopbotter**

kopjacht, kopjagt See **boeier-2**

koppen See **kof**

kora² See **korakora**

korakel, korakl See **coracle-1**

korakora *Indonesia/Philippines:* **1.** Vessel of local potentates of the eastern Malay Archipelago, especially of the Moluccan Islands; widely used in pillaging and slaving forays. Also cited in the Sulu Sea area of southern Philippines. Early reports describe it as a double-outrigger craft propelled by paddles and supplemented by sail. Type adopted by western colonists for local surveillance duties. Later, broader vessels were built, and the outriggers were often abandoned. Both types became notorious pirate craft. Details vary widely, but the classic **korakora** is portrayed as a narrow, high-ended, low-sided, plank-built vessel. The planks pegged edge-to-edge; frames and thwarts were lashed to residual lugs on the planks. Double-ended; flat floors; keel curved smoothly into the tall stem and sternpost. Multiple S-curved booms crossed the hull to the bamboo floats; stringers were lashed across the booms. The paddlers, as many as 4 ranks, sat on the outrigger components. Vessels without outriggers had a platform out each side for the oarsmen and paddlers. On the largest, a deck was erected over the hull for the warriors. On some, a thatched cabin covered much of the hull. Steered with a paddle or rudder on each quarter. One or 2 oblong lug-type sails were hung from tripod masts; yard at top and bottom. Carried 40-70 paddlers and 25 warriors. Reported lengths 10-40m, widths 3-4m; 1780 vessel 27m long, 8m wide with outriggers, 2.5m hold depth; shallow draft. other recorded names: **caracara, car(a)coa, caracol(a), caracol(l)e, caracor(a), caraco(u)re, caracoro, carcolle, coracora, coracore, corcoa, corocora, corocore, corocoro, coroquora, curra-curra, karakoa, karakor, Karakore, karkol(le), kora★, korkor★** (pl. **korkorren), korra-korra, korre-korre, korrokor** (pl. **korrokorren), krokurre, kura-kura**. Further reading: W. H. Scott, "Boat-Building and Seamanship in Classic Philippine Society," *Philippine Studies* 30 (1982), 335-376. Note also **juanga, korkora**.
2. *Indonesia, central:* In the Lesser Sunda Islands, a small outrigger **korakora** is used for whaling. Harpooner stands on a bow extension. Crew of 8-10.
3. A small dugout **korakora** in the Moluccas served mainly to transport agricultural products.

koralina See **corallina**

korari See **waka korari**

Korbboot, Korbgeflechtboot See **basket boat**

korf See **corve**

korial See **corial**

koriara See **curiara-2**

korjaal *Suriname:* Straight-sided, open boat of Paramaribo shrimp fishermen. In other localities, the boats transport people and fish. Mostly an expanded, plank-extended **dugout canoe★**. Usually poled, but many now have an outboard motor. Reported lengths 5-13.7m; average 7.3m; largest size requires a crew of 5. See also **corial**.

korjar See **corial**

korkâra *Greece/Tunisia:* Name given in Tunisia to a Greek **sakoleva★** that engages in sponge fishing, employing a *korkâra* net to haul the sponges up from the bottom. Two-masted, both the main and mizzen carrying lugsails and the mainsail boomed; 2 headsails. Spelling variants: **karkâra, kerkâra**; pl. **krâker**

körköka See **kyrkbåt**

korkor *Marshall Islands, northwestern Pacific:* Small **canoe★** used mainly in lagoons. In some areas, designates a **canoe** without sails, while those traveling between lagoons have a sail. Solid ends rake up before being truncated. Dugout keel piece to which planking is lashed with sennit. Bottom curves fore-and-aft. The small **canoes** have a larger proportion of dugout to planking. Employs a single outrigger always carried to windward; 4 closely spaced booms curve down to attach directly to a short float. Outrigger side of the hull rounded; lee side flat. A counterbalancing platform extends beyond the lee side on those that sail. Sail set to a strongly forward-raking mast; shrouds lashed to the outrigger booms. Sets a triangular sail with the apex tacked to the bow. Small **canoes** paddled. Length of sailing **canoe** ca. 6m. See also **korakora-1**.

korkora *Indonesia, SE:* Generic term of the Tetun-speaking peoples of Timor for a sailing vessel. Note also **korakora**.

korkorren, korra-korra, korre-korre, korrokor, korrokorren See **korakora-1**

korsan, Korsar, Korsarenschiff, korsari, korsarikon, korsere See **corsair**

korsha See **kosha**

korvenvisser See **pot vessel**

korvet, korvet', korveta, korvetenn, korvetta, Korvette, korvetten, korweta See **corvette**

koryáli See **corial**

koryári See **curiara-2**

korzar See **corsair**

kosa, kosah, kose, kosh See **kosha**

kosha *Bangladesh/India, NE:* A **riverboat★** that serves in a variety of capacities—for ferrying, net fishing, produce and jute transport, as a **houseboat★**, and occasionally as a **ship's boat★** aboard larger river craft.

kosha

The largest, the **militari kosha**, carries mainly sand. In the 17th century, they were the most numerous of the vessels in imperial river **fleets★**. Constructed of broad planks, usually carvel-fashion, occasionally clinker, fastened with boat nails; some built with sheet tin sides. Bottom flat, generally curved at the ends; longitudinal bottom planking. Ends raked, similarly sharp or blunted; stern slightly higher than bow but generally a low sheer; straight, flaring sides; hard bilges. Decked with split bamboo or planks; most have a removable arched or peaked bamboo hut aft or amidships. Fishing **koshas** have a live well. Steered with a paddle. May be propelled by bamboo-shafted oars with wooden blades or set a square or triangular sail to a light mast. Crew of 1-6 when fishing; cargo carriers require a crew of 10 or more. Engines are now being fitted on the cargo boats. Reported lengths 3.7-15m, widths 1-3m, depths 0.2-0.9m; shallow draft. Recent versions of the **kosha**, using traditional methods and materials but cheaper to produce, have been designed for use on the smaller rivers. Other recorded names: **cosa**, **gosha** (erroneously), **korsha**, **kosa(h)**, **kose**, **kosh**, **kusa**; large **koshas** called **hat kosha**, **pātkoshā**, or **pēt kōsā**

Koshkonong flatboat *United States, north-central:* Double-ended wildfowler's boat of the Koshkonong area in southern Wisconsin. Deck cambered both athwartships and fore-and-aft; small, elongated cockpit. Mostly awash when hunter on board. Usually towed to shooting site. Length 3.7m, beam 2.4m.

Koshkonong monitor *United States, north-central:* Late 19th-century **duck boat★** of Koshkonong and other Wisconsin lakes. **Kayak★**-shaped with long, sharp ends and low sides. Wood hull, usually tin-sheathed; deck of wood, canvas, or tin; heavy. Canvas around the elongated cockpit protected the hunter; low freeboard. Rowed.

köşklü kayık See **saltanat kayığı**

kosterbåt *Sweden, W:* Primarily a coastal **fishing boat★** of the 19th-20th centuries that originated in the Kosteroarna (islands), but modified types spread to Norway and the east coast of Sweden. Also served as pilot and customs craft and for smuggling; now a popular pleasure boat. When worked with a drag net for mackerel and herring, was locally called a **drag boat★**. Below the waterline, the hull is short, sharp, and deep; above it is broad, flat, and roomy, especially forward. Clinker-built until ca. 1900, now carvel. Double-ended; heavy and raked curved stem and sternpost; S-formed timbers; strong bilges; deep, straight keel. Open until the 1850s, then half-decked with cuddy forward; fully decked after 1880s; **fishing boats** had a live well amidships. Early boats sprit-rigged with a staysail; some 3-masted. Modified to a boomless gaff mainsail, topsail, and jib to bowsprit. Later, 2-masted with tall, gaff-rigged mainmast and sprit mizzen. Motors adopted later. Reported lengths 6-12m; e.g., length overall 10.7m, on keel 7.6m. Other recorded names: **kostrar**; pl. **kosterbåtar**. Note also **hvalerbåt**.

kosterbåtar, kostrar See **kosterbåt**

kotah See **kotak**

kotak 1. *Indonesia, W/Peninsular Malaysia/Singapore:* Chinese craft used in sheltered waters on the south and west coasts of the Malay Peninsula and the east coast of Sumatra. Used for fishing, carrying cargo, and ferrying. Many variations within the type, but all relatively shallow-draft; strongly raked, "V" bow transom; marked sheer. At the stern, the sides carry aft of the raked "V" transom to form high, pointed wings. Bottom curved; false keel usually added. Oculi on the bows. May be partly decked; generally compartmented with fish lockers or holds. Largest boats (lengths 7.6-9m, widths 2.7-3m, depths 1-1.14m) step a tall mast slightly forward of amidships; 2nd mast, shorter and heavier, in bow; set battened lugsails of Chinese design. Crew of 2-3. Middle-sized boats (6.7-7.6m long) carry a single Chinese lugsail. The smallest (5.5-6.1m long) have a narrow bow transom; frequently propelled by 1-2 pairs of long-shafted oars; a single lugsail is often set, although other types of sail are also used. Motors are now being installed. Three types reported at Singapore: **kotak jala** (or **jala**), which operates the *jala* cast net, is usually under 6.7m long; the **kwah tow** and **tiang pang tow** work a drift net; the latter may exceed 9m in length. Other recorded names: **katak**, **kotah**, **sampan kotak**

2. *East Malaysia:* Chinese-operated craft used in drift net fishing off the Sarawak coast. Carvel-planked; strakes joined by edge nailing through notches cut into upper strakes; natural timbers; keel; flat floors; hard chines aft common; bluff bow; broad, raked transom. Fully decked; transverse deck beams supported by 2 fore-and-aft beams. Early sailing **kotaks** had a Chinese lift-type, perforated rudder; some reported to have had daggerboards. Sheer strake painted in diagonal colors with bulbous eyes. Sets Chinese battened lugsail to single mast; now mostly motorized with a more rounded bottom and longer keel to protect the propeller. Crew of 2. Reported lengths 7.6-9m, beam 2m. Spelling variants: **kotah**, **kutak**

kotak jala See **kotak-1**

Kotak yen-chuan See **yan chuan**

kotch, kotcha, kotchamar, kotche, kotchi, kotchmara See **koch-2**

kòter See **cutter-1**

kothia See **kotia**

kotia *India, NW:* Large, fast, mainly Indian-built trader reported as early as the 16th century. In a modified form, still plies the waters of the Arabian Sea, traveling to the east coast of Africa, into the Persian (Arabian) Gulf, and along the Indian coast. A few built in Sri Lanka and at Persian Gulf ports. The **kotia** is similar to the Arab-built **baghla★**, and is often called a **baghla** and its variant names. A superficially modified **kotia** used by Arabs is called a **ganja★**. The **kotia** of the Maldive Islands was called a **buggalow** (see **bangala**). An aft-facing, stylized parrot's head on the stemhead, a castellated poop, raked transom stern with vestigial quarter galleries, and the 5 stern windows of the **baghla** were distinctive of early **kotias**. Modern craft often have painted scenes in place of the stern carving and windows. Hull strongly built, bottom sometimes coppered; heavily oiled and stained above the waterline; bottom coated with white pitch. Topsides were often gaily painted. Modern **kotias** not oiled but painted in a variety of colors, and the stemhead is painted white. Long grab stem, strongly raked; bow low, considerable sheer. Rudder passed through the poop in the older vessels; on new models, it is lashed to the sternpost. Steered with either tiller or wheel. Fully decked; square hatches; an undecked **kotia** may be called a **pahala**. Generally carries a large **muchwa*** and a small **dhoni*** on deck. Two-masted mainly, but some also step a small mast outboard over the stern. The main- and mizzenmasts may both rake forward, or the mizzen may be vertical. Square topsail set from a light, short topmast. Large masts rigged with a forestay and a pair of shrouds on each side. Lateen sails; main yard may be longer than the vessel; mainsail tacked to a spar rigged out over the bow. Several spars at the stern serve as outriggers to the mizzen sheet and the small transom sail. Some set a jib. Most now have engines also. Crew of 8-20, depending on size. Reported lengths 9-20m; e.g., length 15m, beam 7m, depth 3m. Other recorded names: **bag(g)ala**, **bagalo**, **bagla**, **budgerow**, **bugalilo***, **budgerow**, **buggelow**, **cotea**, **cotia**, **cotiyah**, **cotya**, **dau***, **dow**, **khotia**, **koftiya**, **kothia**, **koṭiyu**, **kottiah**, **kutia**, **kutiyah**, **kutiyya**, **quṭīya**. Further reference: **boutre**

koṭiyu See **kotia**

kotoko *Chad, west-central:* **Dugout canoe*** in the area bordering northeastern Lake Chad. Used mainly for fishing. Lasts ca. 10 years.

Kotoko pirogue, kotokos See **markaba**

kotsa, kotsche, kotschmara See **koch-2**

kotter *Belgium/Netherlands:* Engages in fishing, mostly in trawling. No clear distinction in the past between the **sloep***, **logger***, and **kotter**. Today, in the Netherlands, the term **kotter** is often reserved for motorized vessels under 27m long, while in Belgium, such a craft would be called a **treiler**. Those fishing over the stern are **hekkotters** (or **hektreilers**). The 19th-century **kotter** had sharp lines, straight stem, wide, flat counter stern, and a "V" cross section. Generally **ketch***- or **cutter***-rigged; a 3-masted, lug-rigged type went under the name **Maaskotter**. Further name variant: **viskotter**. Further reference: **cutter-1**

kotterever See **Kutter-Ewer**

kottergetuigde Blankenbergse schuit See **Heistse schuit**

kottiah See **kotia**

kottr See **cutter-1**

kouffa See **quffa**

koupang *China, S:* Smallest of the **dang wai*** type that fished out of Fort Bayard (now Chang-Chiang). Crescent-shaped with flat floors; bottom planks forced up at ends by fire or pressure; resulting sheer negated by setting side strakes horizontally. Sharp bow; flat stem curved and overhanging; flattened stern, the 2 sides left with a gap on the outer side to accommodate the rudderstock; massive, wide-bladed

rudder. Centerboard slotted in forward third of the vessel, sometimes so far forward that it dropped through the forefoot. Decked; cabin for family aft; several hatches; numerous fish compartments. Single battened lugsail raised to a heavy pole mast stepped in forward third; sails of woven straw. Length 28m, beam 6.5m, depth 2m.

koursar, koursaros See **corsair**

kowo See **ku-dru**

kraak *Netherlands:* Inland cargo carrier of the **tjalk*** family that dates to at least the 17th century. Wooden vessels extinct shortly after World War II. Originally carvel-planked of oak. Flat bottom, low sheer; bluff bow and stern; curved stem; straight, nearly vertical sternpost. Outboard rudder; tiller. Decked; long hatch with cambered covers, some running full width; low cabin aft by the 19th century. Wide leeboards. Rigged with a spritsail or standing gaff mainsail; boomed in the 19th century. Forestaysail and jib to jibboom. Reported lengths 16-18m; cap. 40-50t. Iron **kraken** (pl.) had a flat bottom, rounded bilges, vertical sides, slight tumble home above the wale. Straight or slightly curved stem recurved at the top; rounded counter. Outboard rudder; tiller or horizontal wheel. Decked; long hatch abaft the mast, small cargo hatch on foredeck; low cabin below the tiller, low deckhouse. Large leeboards. Mast stepped well forward; strikable with sheerlegs and windlass. Boomed gaff mainsail, straight gaff; narrow staysail. Short topmast on some. Reported lengths 20-25m; 1896 vessel 24.5m long, 5m wide, 1.85m deep. Other recorded names: **karaak**, **kraakschip**. Further references: **carrack**, **Rheinfloss**

kraakschip See **kraak**

krabbefiskebåt See **crabber**

Krabbenfangboot See **crabber**, **shrimper**, **trotliner**

Krabbenfänger See **crabber**

Krabbenfischer, Krabbenfischerboot See **crabber**, **shrimper**

Krabbenkutter *Germany, NW:* Those engaged in inshore crabbing with nets off the North Sea coast in the early 20th century were **cutter***-rigged, decked boats. Plumb stem; bluff bow; raking counter stern and sternpost; moderate sheer. Flat floors enabled them to dry out or work from beaches; shallow keel; rounded bilges; vertical sides. Rudderpost came up inboard of the counter; tiller. No live well, the crabs often steamed on board. Gaff mainsail loose-footed but boomed; topsail; 2 headsails to a long bowsprit. Reported lengths 9-12m; e.g., length overall 11.5m, on the waterline 10.3m, beam 3.8m, draft 0.95m. The later **crabbers*** were larger, motorized vessels.

Krabbenschute See **krabschuit**

krabber See **crabber**

Krabbfangboot See **shrimper**

krabbfiskebåt, kraboler See **crabber**

krabschuit *Netherlands:* Used for fishing and carrying cargo on inland waters. Spelling variant: **Krabbenschute**. See also **crabber**, **panneschuit**.

kracke, kraeck See **carrack**

kragejolle *Denmark:* Lightly built, sprit-rigged craft used especially in the Øresund Strait off the east coast.

Clinker-planked; sharp-ended; fine lines below the waterline; flaring sides; long, straight keel. Curved stem and sternpost, the latter recurved at top. Rudder extends below keel. Decked at ends and along the sides. Set a gaff topsail and 1-2 headsails; largest sometimes stepped a jigger mast. Reported lengths 4.8-9m, beam ca. one-third.

krajbryezhna ládija See **ládija**

kraken See **carrack**, **kraak**

krâker See **korkâra**

krakowski galar See **galar**

kranketer See **crabber**

Krautplätte See **Plätte-1**

kravak See **kayak-4**

kraveelbuis See **buis-2**

kraweelboot See **caravel-1**

Kraweel-Galiot See **Galiot-5**

Kraweelschiff See **caravel-1**

krayak See **kayak-4**

kreeftenbark *Belgium:* **Ketch***-rigged vessel that transported lobsters and oysters from England to Ostend. Usually a discarded **sloep*** of the mid-19th century with a wet well. Length on keel ca. 25m. Spelling variant: **kriftebarke**

kreeftenboot *Netherlands:* Small boat that used baskets to catch lobsters. Worked by 3-4 men.

kreeftenkotter *Belgium:* Transported lobsters, mainly from Norway and France, to Ostend. Wet well dimensions ca. 4 by 4m. Crew of 7-8. Length on keel ca. 25m; 75t.

kreiser, **krejser** See **cruiser-3**

Krennzille See **Krenzille**

Krenzille *Austria/Germany, S:* Transported horseradish (*Kren* or *Krenn*) on Ludwigs Canal and the Danube until World War I. Made a single trip. Staff on each end; steered with a sweep; covered area at the stern for the helmsman. To fit in the canal locks, the maximum length was 32m, beam 4.5m, depth 1.6m. Other recorded names: **Kanalzille**, **Krennzille**

Kreuzer See **cruiser-1**, **cruiser-3**

Kreuzerfregatte See **cruiser-2**

Kreuzerjacht See **cruiser-1**

kreyser See **cruiser-3**

Kriegsloop, **Kriegsschaloupe** See **sloop-1**

Kriegsschiff See **man-of-war**

kriftebarke See **kreeftenbark**

krilimitok See **kayak-4**

križna ladja, **križnjak** See **ship-2**

krogsjægt See **sjægt**

krokurre See **karakora-1**

kroman *Indonesia, central:* Mainly a trader that works the area of eastern Java, southern Madura, and to the east. Early boats carried salt from the evaporation pans in the Gresik and Kalimange areas of eastern Java and eastern Madura, respectively, and as far east as Timor, returning with cattle feed. Some fish, others transport the catch. Carvel-planked; similar squared and raking ends with projections forward just above the waterline; curved bottom. Portable decking; large, peaked house amidships. Employs a quarter rudder held by a strap. Early **kromons** were beautifully decorated, now less

well-made and less colorful. 19th-century boats of the Sapudi Islands had an outrigger. Steps 2 short masts, the foremast in the eyes, the mainmast just forward of the house. Sets triangular sails, the apex of the forward sail tacked to the bowsprit. Yards hung near their forward end and supported at desired angle by a crutch. Boomed at the foot. Length 11.5m, beam 3m, depth 1.0m. Other recorded names: **Madura trader**, **praauw karomon**

Kroo canoe See **Kru canoe**

kroska, **krosko** See **cog**

krstárica, **krstaš** See **cruiser-3**

Kru canoe *West Africa:* **Dugout canoe*** of the West African coast. Used especially by the Kru peoples of Liberia and Sierra Leone for inshore fishing. Dugout hewn to ca. 13cm thickness by fire and adze. Ends finely tapered, terminating in a knob used for beaching the **canoe***. Marked sheer forward, slight aft. Decked aft for ca. 60-75cm, ending in a small breakwater.

Kru canoe

Braced with several thin, transverse gunwale struts of bamboo. Uses an oval-bladed or pronged paddle with a short loom; often decorated with incised designs. Also sets a small spritsail. Crew of 1-4. Reported lengths 3-9m, widths 0.3-0.7m. Other recorded names: **Kroo canoe**; locally called **golo** or **goro**

kruisbrik See **brigantine**

kruiser, **kruisser**, **kruvazor** See **cruiser-3**

krydser See **cruiser-2**

krydshukkert-galease See **hukkert**

krydstoldjagt See **revenue cutter**

krypa 1. *Czech Republic:* A **boat*** or **canoe***.

 2. *Poland:* A **boat*** or **scow***. The small, low-sided, open boat of the lower Wisłoka River in southeastern Poland is a **scow**-type craft. Used mainly for excavating gravel and for ferrying. Flat bottom, transversely planked and reinforced with 1-2 longitudinal battens; bottom turns up slightly, especially at the bow end. Wide, square ends, the bow somewhat narrower than the stern. Two or 3 side planks, slightly flared, fastened carvel-fashion. Caulked with moss, hemp, oakum, sometimes rags; secured by battens. Gunwales designed to be replaced when worn by the gravel shovels. Poled. Reported lengths 7-9m, widths 2-2.2m. Other recorded names: **krypka**, **sand boat***; pl. **krypy**

krypka, **krypy** See **krypa-2**

kryssare See **cruiser-2**

krysser See **cruiser-3**

K.S.-Boot See **patrol boat**

kuai ban *China, E:* Fast **passage boat*** that operated along the creeks of the Pudong (P'utung) area, near Shanghai. A similar, but larger, boat carried cargo. Sharp, raked bow; high, tapered stern with shallow transom; flat bottom, longitudinally planked, raked up to the transom; rounded bilges; vertical sides.

Arched mat house covered most of the open waist; poling gangway along each side. Rudder canted inward, but did not follow the stern line; stick-in-the-mud anchor. Propelled by poles, sails, and 4 sculling-type oars (*yulohs*): 2 over the stern and 2 on the quarters. Two light, curved masts: one near the bow, the other about two-thirds in from the bow; set spritsails. Later models motorized. Length 10.7m, beam 2m, depth ca. 1.5m. Other recorded names: **k'uai-pan, quick plank-boat, speedboat**★

k'uai ch'uan See **fast boat-2**

k'uai-pan See **kuai ban**

kuan chuan See **junk**

kuan ts'ai ch'uan See **guan cai chuan**

kuba See **oánga**

kubbenvisser See **pot vessel**

ku-chai *Macau:* Long, narrow boat used in night fishing. A white board extends the length of the open hull, reflecting the moonlight and enticing the fish to jump into the boat. Square, raked bow and stern; small mat house aft. Poled. Spelling variants: **ku-tchai, ku-tsai**. Note also **luring boat**. Further reference: **ku tsai ting**

Küchenmeisterschiff See **Leibschiff**

Küchenschiff *Austria:* Cook vessel, one of those supporting the late 17th-century Danube **fleets**★. One was assigned to the admiral, another was part cook and part stores vessel. See also **Bucentaur, Leibschiff**.

Kuchlschiff See **Bucentaur**

kuda-dhoni *Maldive Islands, S:* A 6-oared boat of the lagoon at Addu Atoll. Curved stem; may terminate in a tall, recurved stemhead or lack stem extension; square stern. Tall rudder with S-shaped tiller; helmsman sits against the sternpost, working tiller with his foot. Crutch aft for the lowered mast. Mast bowed forward by stay to stemhead. Square sail; boom slots into cringle in the luff, creating a fore-and-aft sail. Length ca. 8m.

kudastre *Philippines, central:* Two-masted, double-outrigger vessel of the western Visayan Islands. Transported merchandise, passengers, and especially fish products between the islands. Heavily built, raked bow with cutaway forefoot, rounded counter stern, strong sheer. Decked; trunk cabin aft; railing ran along sides and around stern. Three outrigger booms on smaller sizes; 4 on the larger, the middle booms placed close together, often with a platform built over them. Booms connected directly to long, slender floats. Pole masts of equal height, the mainmast stepped amidships. Standing lugsails, sometimes strengthened with 2 battens. Jib to rising bowsprit. Reported lengths 10.7-15.2m.

kudilvalts *Lithuania/Poland, NE/Russia, W:* Gaff-rigged **fishing boat**★ of the Kurski Zaliv. Also seen on Zalew Wiślany (Frisches Haff or Vistula Lagoon). Mainly used in the 19th and early 20th centuries with the *kudil* (or *keitel*) bottom trawl net. Heavily built; clinker planking; keelless, flat bottom curved up in forward third; full lines; angular sides; strong sheer; full, rounded stern. Open except for cuddy at one or both ends on the larger boats. Wide rudder blade below the water line; tiller notched for various positions; 1-2 leeboards; later a centerboard. Tall pole mainmast; tall, narrow, loose-footed gaff sail; curved gaff. Early boats

square-rigged, later sprit-rigged in many areas. Very small sprit foresail set to a short mast just forward of the mainsail. Jib to stemhead. Special elaborate pennant flown from the mainmast. Also sculled. Crew of 2. Reported lengths 9-15m; e.g., length overall 11.4m, on the bottom 10.5m, beam 3.3m, depth 1.0m; shallow draft. Other recorded names: **Fischerkahn, Keitelkahn, Keutelkahn, Kiedelkahn**. Note also **kurnevalts**.

ku-dru *China, SW:* A yak-hide craft that serves as a **ferry**★, for carrying goods, and for fishing in parts of Xizang (Tibet). Hides are stretched over a light frame of bent willow, strengthened at the top by a piece of wood, to which the skins are sewn. Seams waterproofed with butter. Rectangular in shape, slightly narrower at the bow; curved sides; flat bottom. Propelled by a short paddle or short oars, the oars secured by rope loops. Reported lengths 1.5-1.8m, maximum width 1.33m, depth 0.76m. Other recorded names: **coracle**★, **kowo**

kue See **kolek kue**

kū'ē'ē See **wa'a kaulua**

kueh See **kolek kue**

kueh buteh ketere, kueh buteh keterch See **kueh buteh ketiri**

kueh buteh ketiri *Peninsular Malaysia/Thailand, S:* Short, squat fishing craft of the east coast of the Malay Peninsula and adjacent Thailand. Called **kueh buteh ketiri** in Kelantan, **kueh jambu golok** and **lichung** in southern Trengganu. Double-ended with wide ends forming a slight S-curve; fairly long keel; rounded forefoot. Length ca. 6.7m. Other recorded names: **kueh buteh ketere(h)**

kueh kepalo panjang See **kolek kue**

kueh jambu golok See **kueh buteh ketiri**

kuei chhuan See **kwi-son**

kuek See **kolek kue**

kuf Danish version of the Dutch **kof**★. Full-bodied with strong sheer, flat floors, shallow keel. Perpendicular stern, stem had triangular gripe below the waterline to improve maneuverability. Very broad rudder; leeboards; some had a centerboard. Decked; raised cabin. Might be 1- or 2-masted, setting loose-footed, boomed gaff sails, topsails, and generally 3 headsails. Two-masted type often called a **kufgalease**. Crew of 2-3. 30-60rt. Spelling variant: pl. **kuffen**.

kufa, kufah See **quffa**

Kuff *Germany, NW:* Trader that worked out of North Sea ports, sailing as far as the Mediterranean and the Western Hemisphere during the 19th century. Also traveled as far as Mainz on the Rhine River. Extinct by World War II. Full, rounded bow and stern, straight sides; long, straight keel; strong sheer on early vessels. Convex curve to the strong stem above the waterline, extra deadwood at forefoot. Straight, slightly raked sternpost; rounded stern above the waterline, sharp below; flat floors; rounded bilges. Deep bulwarks are tumble home at bow and stern; windows on either side of the sternpost. Narrow outboard rudder; long tiller; some employed leeboards. Early vessels decked only at the ends; later fully decked; 2 hatches; raised cabin toward the stern. Variously rigged as a **brig**★ (**Kuff**brigg), **bark**★ (**Barkkuff** or **Kuffbark**), **ketch**★, or **schooner*** (**Schonerkuff**). One type was single-masted (**Einmast-kuff**). Crew of 2-6. Reported lengths 16.8-23.5m; e.g., length 17m, beam 4.18m, depth 2m. Other recorded names: **englische Kuff**, **Pfahl(mast)kuff** (with pole masts), **Schoonerkuff**, **Schunerkuff**, **Toppmastkuff** (with topmasts), **Toppsegelkuff** (with topsails); pl. **Kuffe**. Note also **Helgolander Schnigge**, **kof**, **kuf**, **Koftjalk**.

kuffa See **quffa**

Kuffbark, **Kuffbrigg** See **Kuff**

kuffe See **kof**, **Kuff**

kuffen See **kuf**

kuffschip See **kof**

Kufftjalk See **koftjalk**

kufgalease See **kuf**

kug See **slup-2**

kugga, **kuggr** See **cog**

Kuhlkorvette See **corvette-1**

Kuhtransporter See **cattle ship**

Kuilkorvet See **corvette-1**

kui-son See **kwi-son**

kuka See **cog**

kukltai *Chile, S:* Large, expanded **dugout canoe*** of the Alacaluf peoples of the western part of the Strait of Magellan. Sides usually extended by uncaulked wash-strake; one end might be cut square. Steered with a paddle. Rowed from inserted thwarts. Reported lengths 4-5m, but early boats larger. Name variants: **je-kukltai**; **jekúktại** (in the Tawóksere dialect of the central Alacaluf)

kule 1. *Ecuador, NW:* The **kū'le** of the Cayapa is a well-made **dugout canoe***; often "exported" to other parts of the coast. Characterized by narrow (ca. 20cm) ends that are concave transversely, notched at the end, and flare up abruptly. Distinguished by a longitudinal ridge on the top side of the bow platform and by a hole for a painter. Sides ca. 2cm thick, bottom 5-7.5cm. Coated with hot beeswax; geometric patterns decorate

kule-1

the sides; ends black. Balsa wood sponsons sometimes attached to increase buoyancy when transporting heavy loads; front ends shaped like the bow of the **canoe*** and bound to a transverse pole lashed across the gunwales, using the holes that were previously drilled to aid in transporting the rough-hewn **canoe** from its inland building site. Reported lengths 2.44-10.67m, widths 0.24-1.0m. Other recorded names: **Cayapa canoe**, **cule***, **Kánu***; **chingo** in the delta of the Río Guayas. Further reading: Samuel A. Barrett, *The Cayapa Indians of Ecuador* (New York: American Museum of the American Indian, 1925 [Monograph 40]).

2. *Indonesia, W:* Two-masted, lug-rigged trader from Atjeh (Achin) at the north end of Sumatra. Employed quarter rudders. Cap. 20-40t. Name variant: **kolek***
Further references: **canoa-14**, **kolek-3**

kuliala See **corial**

kuliára See **curiara-2**

kulla *India:* **1. Raft*** or **boat*** in the Dravidian language of Parji in southwestern Orissa in eastern India.

2. At Kilakarai on the northwest coast of the Gulf of Mannar, the **kuḷḷa** is a fishing **outrigger canoe***.

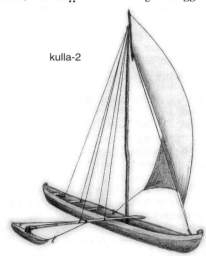
kulla-2

Narrow washstrakes added to an unexpanded, double-ended dugout that has been imported from the Malabar Coast; characteristic Malabar coiled ornament retained on the stem and sternpost. Normally fitted with an outrigger extended by 1-2 booms that attach directly to the short float; designed to be quickly unshipped and moved to the opposite side as required. Rudder hung with gudgeons and pintles to the curved sternpost; worked with a short tiller. The single vertical mast steps aft of the forward (or single) outrigger boom. Sets a low lugsail. Length ca. 6m. Name variant: **Kilakarai canoe**

kūlla, **kūllan** See **oruwa**

kullatoni See **padavu**

kulu See **barque Djenné**

kumei *North Korea, E:* Found in the area of Songjön-man (Syöng-jin) until the early 19th century. Bottom a thick, triangular plank. Sides formed by 2 hollowed logs, ca. 48cm in diameter, nailed to the bottom; a

kumei

plank added to each side increased freeboard. Transom stern formed by a single board. Length 7.2m, width at stern 2.6m, depth ca. 0.7m.

ku'mtsała See **West Coast canoe**

kun See **barque Djenné**

Kuna canoe See **cayuco-5**

kundal *Australia, E:* Indigenous bark **canoe*** from the areas north and south of Brisbane. Made from a single piece of bark (*kundal*), mainly from the bulurtchu tree; rendered pliable by a fire set inside the bark funnel. Ends folded into a pleat to create a sharp bow and stern. Gunwales strengthened along the inner edge with a lashed-on withe. One or more transverse sticks kept the sides from curling in. Propelled, standing, by 1-2 long poles used as paddles. Large **canoes** could carry as many as 10. Reported lengths 3.7-6m. Other recorded names: **koondoo(l), kundole, kundool**

kundole, kundool See **kundal**

kundura See **gundra**

kuni See **barque Djenné**

kuni dau See **dau la mataruma**

kunnah See **Chesapeake Bay log canoe-1**

kunner *United States, E:* Open fishing and general-purpose boat found on the coastal bays of North Carolina and elsewhere along the coast from the late 17th century to ca. 1880. Constructed of 1 or more logs; single-log boats might be split longitudinally and joined to keel, stem, and sternpost; when made of 2, the logs were joined and then dug out. Sometimes 2 logs were set side-by-side. Shallow transom stern; sharp bow; top strake added to dugout base; inserted frames; centerboard; stern bench. Stepped 1-2 masts. Probably set spritsails. Also rowed with as many as 6 oars. Reported lengths 4.3-7.6m, beam ca. 1.75m, low-sided. Other recorded names: **ke-nuh, kooner.** See also **Chesapeake Bay log canoe-1**.

kunte *Norway:* Small **ship's boat★**. Carvel-planked; flat bottom planked athwartships with fore-and-aft strips nailed on; hard chine. Sharp bow, transom stern. Name variant: **pram★**

kunu *Jamaica:* Dialect term for a **fishing boat★**, generally a **dugout canoe★**. Some early boats were quite large and ventured well offshore. Other recorded names: **canoa★, conoa, co(o)noo, cunno**

kunun *Africa, W:* Calabash float used by the Kanuri peoples west and south of Lake Chad. Two large calabashes, covered with a very loosely woven net, are connected by a log; the calabashes serve to hold fish

kunun

and other objects and each has a lid. Paddled by hand with the "boatman" sitting astride the log. Sometimes a single calabash is used, with the occupant draped over the float, paddling by hand. Similar craft are found elsewhere on African lakes and rivers. Name variant: **ngębu**

kup See **kop**

kurāb See **grab-1**

kura-kura See **korakora-1**

kurèki-ikada *Japan, central:* One of the types of **rafts★** (**ikada★**) used to transport lumber on the Hida River to Nagoya. Rectangular in shape. The lower, longitudinal layer lashed close together, the upper level

placed more widely athwartships. Larger logs raised the sides. Steered with a long oar. A special raft, the **chikiri-ikada**, transported larger logs, frequently for masts, on the same river. Four small **rafts** of 10 logs each were lashed on either side to form sponsons. Two men rowed from each raft. Note also **timber raft-1**.

kurenas See **kurnevalts**

Kurenkahn See **kurnevalts**

kuriára, kuriera See **curiara-2**

kuriñ See **dori**

Kurischer Fischerkahn See **Fischerkahn**

Kurisches Handkahn See **Handkahn-2**

kurnevalts *Lithuania/Russia, W:* **Fishing boat★** that employed a beam trawl (the *kurn* or *Kurre*) and was used on the Kurski Zaliv, a lagoon shared by Lithuania and the western exclave of Russia. Clinker-planked of oak; flat pine bottom, no keel; nearly vertical sides; angular bilges; strong sheer forward. Sharp, slightly curved ends; internal stem and sternpost. Open; cuddy forward; may have house abaft the mast. Hatchet-shaped outboard rudder; curved tiller. Mainmast stepped in forward third. Set a tall, narrow spritsail; reef points at upper edge. Jib tacked to stemhead. A tiny foremast stepped just forward of the mainmast; also sprit-rigged; overlapped by the jib. Sometimes a boomed-out jigger sail was hung from the top of the sprit and tacked to the clew. Elaborate, distinctive pennant atop the mainmast. Reported lengths 8-12m; e.g., length 8m, beam 2.5m, depth 0.6m; shallow draft. Other recorded names: **kāpeniekevalts, kurenas, Kurrankahn, Kur(r)enkahn**; the lighter **Braddenkahn** used a drag net. Note also **kudilvalts**.

Kurrankahn, Kurrenkahn See **kurnevalts**

kūrsar See **corsair**

Kursschiff See **Ordinarischiff**

kuru See **barque Djenné**

kuruch See **curragh**

kurz Schiff See **Mutte**

kusa See **kosha**

kusaar, kusar See **corsair**

kuserofne *Japan:* Small, open vessel that hunted whales. Sharp below the waterline; long, narrow. Large crew. Rowed with oarsmen standing. Spelling variants: **cuciforno, cuseforne, cuserofne, curiforne, Kuserosne**

Kuserosne See **kuserofne**

kuşlu kayık See **saltanat kayığı**

kustboot, Küstenfahrer, Küstenfahrzeug, Küstenschiff See **coaster**

Kustenschnellboot See **patrol boat**

Küstenschutzschiff See **coast guard ship**

Küstensegelfahrzeug See **coaster**

Küstenwachboot See **patrol boat**

Küstenwachschiff, Küstenwächter, Küstenwachtschiff See **coast guard ship**

kustfarare, kustfartyg See **coaster**

kustreddingboot See **lifeboat**

kustvaarder See **coaster**

kustvisser *Netherlands:* A coastal **fishing boat★**.

kutak See **kotak-2**

ku-tchai See **ku-chai**

kutchudjik guèmi *Turkey:* Term given to a particularly small boat.

Kutenai canoe See **tci'k'Enō**

kûter See **cutter-1**

kuthir-pānsi See **panshi**

kutia, kutiyah, kutiyya See **kotia**

kutora See **katrā, patela**

ku-tsai See **ku-chai, ku tsai ting**

ku tsai teng See **ku tsai ting**

ku tsai ting *Hong Kong:* Principally a **fishing boat**★ that operates a purse seine, but when used for ferrying and general harbor work, is known as the **Hong Kong sampan**. Fir carvel planking; camphor and lichee wood used for frames; rounded stem, bluff bow; square or slightly rounded counter stern. **Fishing boats** have fish and net holds forward, living accommodations amidships, galley and head aft; arched shelter of mats or oilcloth cover stern or wooden house amidships. Horizontal railing extends outside the gunwale line on the **fishing boats**. Little freeboard when loaded. The very small sizes propelled by 1-2 sculls; others set Chinese lugsails of cotton to 1-2 masts. When motorized, often called a **walla-walla boat**. Some carry 1-2 small **sampans**★, 3-3.5m long, to aid with fishing operations. As many as 18 people live aboard. Reported lengths 3-10.7m, widths 1.83-3.66m, depths 0.9-1.22m. Other recorded names: **ku-chai**★, **ku tsai (teng)**, **small purse seiner**

kutter **1.** *Denmark:* Used in several capacities—for fishing, passengers, mail, pilots, customs (**zollkutter**), naval service, and pleasure. Vertical stem above the waterline curved sharply into a long, straight keel.

kutter-1

Broad, deep, carvel-planked hull; flat sheer. Stern elliptical, sharp, or a flat transom (on older types). Decked with a cabin forward and a hatch; fishing **kuttern** (pl.) had a wet well. **Cutter**★- or **ketch**★-rigged; auxiliaries introduced at the beginning of the 20th century. Originally crewed by 5-6, later only 3. Reported lengths 8-17m, widths 2.7-5m, depths 1.5-2m, draft 1.2-2m. Note also **bakkebåd, revenue cutter-1**.

2. *Germany:* Used on both the North and Baltic Sea coasts, especially by fishermen (**Fisch(erei)kutter**, **Fischerkutter**), pilots (**Lotsenkutter**), and customs officials (**Zollkutter**), for cargo transport, and as a **yacht**★. **a.** The North Sea vessels were **cutter**- or

ketch-rigged. Usually set gaff topsails, staysail, and a jib to a long, running bowsprit. Carvel-planked, later vessels of steel; moderate to steep rise to the floors; deep keel, straight or curved; drag aft. Sharp bow; slightly curved stem, cutaway below the waterline. Sharply raking counter stern; **canoe**★ stern on some later boats. The **Hochseefischerkutter** (or **Hochseekutter**), which fished some distance offshore, had a rounded or sharp stern. Decked; wheelhouse common; **fishing boats** had a live well. Auxiliaries added ca. 1900; later boats used 2 steadying sails, plus a forestaysail. Reported lengths 13-23m; e.g., length 18m, beam 5.7m, depth 2m; deep draft. Note also **hajer, Kutter-Ewer**. **b.** The Baltic Sea **kutter** (**Ostseekutter**) was similar to the North Sea vessel or to those used in Denmark. Locally called merely **Boot** or sometimes **Schlup**★. Carvel-planked; bar keel; deep hull. Stem straight or curved; stern flat and slightly raked above a raking sternpost, or rounded. Decked; rudder came up below the transom or was outboard. Generally employed a single gaff sail; some also stepped a mizzenmast. Long bowsprit, 2 headsails. Crew of 2 fishermen on sailing vessels, 3 on later motorized vessels. Reported lengths 10-15m.

3. *Iceland:* The Icelandic **kútter** was a **ketch**-rigged vessel with a long counter, plumb stem, and deep drag to the long, straight keel. Short mizzenmast. Loose-footed, boomed gaff sails; staysail; jib to a long bowsprit. Length ca. 15m.

4. *Norway:* **Kuttere** (pl.) were also built in Norway. Those built in the north were fuller-bodied. Larger types carvel-planked; smaller were clinker; sharp lines; moderate sheer; vertical stem; raking counter. Decked; wheelhouse forward of mizzenmast. Most **ketch**-rigged, some single-masted. Gaff sails relatively narrow, loose-footed, boomed; gaff topsail. Small mizzen pole mast; long, running bowsprit. Largest 21-24m long on deck.

5. *Sweden:* The Swedish fishing **kuttrar** (pl.) were imported from England (the **engelska kutter**) from the late 19th into the early 20th century and then were built locally. Worked mainly in the North Sea. Carvel-planked, nearly plumb stem; raked, rounded counter or transom stern, drag aft. **Ketch**-rigged; replaced by the larger motorized **kutter**. The term **kutter** may also designate a **cutter**-rigged **yacht**. Further name variant: **fiskekutter**. Note also **lotskutter**.

Further references: **cutter-1**, **whaleboat-1**

Kutterbrigg See **cutter-brig**

kuttere See **kutter-4**

Kuttereeuber, Kutter-Ever See **Kutter-Ewer**

Kutter-Ewer *Germany, NW:* Hybrid vessel combining the above-water lines of the **Kutter**★ and the underwater lines of the **Ewer**★. First built in the last quarter of the 19th century, last built in the mid-20th century; worked out into the North Sea. Wooden hull initially, then steel. Flat bottom, slightly flared chine planks, rounded bilges; bar keel. Plumb stem; raked counter stern. Decked, cabin forward; those with an auxiliary might have a wheelhouse; fishing vessels had a wet well. Leeboards or centerboard on some. Rudderpost came up inboard. **Cutter**★- or **ketch**★-rigged. Set loose-footed, boomed gaff sail(s), gaff topsail(s), staysail, jib to bowsprit. Crew of 3. Reported lengths 16.7-22m; e.g., length 17.6m, beam 5m, depth 1.72m. Other recorded names: **Eeberkutter, Ewer-Kutter, kotterever, Kuttereeuber, Kutter-Ever, Platter Kutter**

Kuttergig See **cutter-gig**
kuttern See **kutter**
Kutteryacht See **cutter-3**
kuttrar See **kutter-5**
kuttrey See **katrā**
kūū See **barque Djenné**
Kuwait boat See **boom**
kvalbåt See **whale catcher**
kvase Danish term for a boat that has a wet well, engaging either in fishing or transporting the catch to market. Most common in the late 19th century. They were **cutter★-, ketch★-,** and **schooner★-**rigged; auxiliaries installed in later years. 1914 boat: 19.5m long, 6.25m wide, draft 2.5m. Other recorded names: **fiskerkvase, handel(s)kvase**; pl. **kvaser**. Note also **drivkvase, kvass, Quase, treibkvase, well boat.**
kvaser See **kvase**
kvass Swedish term for a medium-sized **fishing boat★** that has a wet well. One important type fished for plaice in the Kattegat, an arm of the North Sea between Sweden and Denmark. **Cutter★-**rigged, worked with a crew of 5-6, and was 5-10t burden. Spelling variants: **kvasse**; pl. **kvassar**. Note also **fiskekvass, kvase, well boat.**
kvassar, kvasse See **kvass**
kvassing See **hvassing**
kwah tow See **kotak-1**
kw'ai t'ing See **hong boat**
kwak *Netherlands:* A large type of shrimping **botter★** that used the *kwakkuil*, a bag-type net held open by 2 special booms extending out each side of the boat at the stern. Also fished for eels. Used on the Zuiderzee. Built mainly at Volendam. Full bow that swept up sharply to a high stem; little sheer aft; low rise to the floors, shallow keel; low, rounded stern. Carvel-planked; strongly raked sternpost, deadwood; keel; top strake has tumble home. Decked; without bulwarks on foredeck; open waist; cuddy forward; low steering deck; live well in 3-4 compartments. When fishing, a spare deck was laid atop the well box and the sides. Two narrow leeboards; outboard rudder, large-bladed below the waterline. Windlass on heavy stern thwart. Gaff-rigged with short, curved gaff on the loose-footed, boomed mainsail; in addition to foresail, a tall, narrow square sail might be boomed out forward of the foresail when running downwind. Mast stepped forward of the breakwater at end of foredeck. Jib to bowsprit, large staysail. Crew of 1-2. Reported lengths 10-18m; **Volendammer kwak** (or **botter**): 16.4m long, 5m wide, 2m deep. Other recorded names: **drijver★, garnkwak, kwakbotter, quack(el), quak, Volendamse botter**; pl. **kwakken**. Further reading: Peter Dorleijn, *Van Gaand en Stand Want, de Zeilvisserij Voor en na de Afsluiting van de Zuiderzee* (Bussum: Van Kampen & Zn., 1982), 129-143; Jules Van Beylen, *De Botter—*

Geschiedenis en Bouwbeschriving van een Nederlands Visschersschip (Weesp: Unieboek, 1985), 209-215.
kwakbotter See **kwak**
Kwakiutl canoe See **northern-style canoe**
Kwakiutl war canoe See **mE'nga**
kwakken See **kwak**
kwalle kwalle See **kole kole**
kweden See **buis-2**
kwee See **buis-2, hoekerbuis**
kwɪnɪɭ See **mE'nga**
kwi-son *Korea:* Naval vessel created in the late 16th century in the form of a turtle (*kwi*). Featured a domed roof for protection of the crew and a turtle's head (or heads) at the bow, that was filled with burning sulphur and gunpowder to emit a confusion of smoke. Some ironclad. A railing and ports protected the archers and oarsmen. Flattened bottom longitudinally; blunt bow; double "wings" extended beyond the rounded stern. Heavy, deep rudder; tiller manned by 8 men. Mainly rowed, employing 10 oars to each side; oars worked through oar ports from an enclosed lower deck. Also sailed using 2 masts that could be struck; square sails. Reported lengths 27-33m, maximum width ca. 9m. Other recorded names: **kohbukson, kuei chhuan, kui-son, tortoise** (or **turtle**) **boat.** Note also **kikko-sen.**
kwolle kwolle See **kole kole-1**
kwots See **mE'nga**
kyack, kyak See **kayak**
kybaia *Mediterranean:* Greek and Roman **galley★** that carried wine, grain, and other cargo on open waters and rivers until the 1st century B.C. Boxy shape forward; 4 awnings; one forward awning could be enclosed to accommodate 5 beds. Reported lengths 18-37m; length-to-beam ratio 5.5:1. Other recorded names: **cybaea(e), cybea, kybaidion** (small); pl. **kybaiai.** Note also **wine ship.**
kybaidion, kybaiai See **kybaia**
kyombo See **chombo**
kyrkbåt *Sweden:* Boat that took people to church; sometimes devoted solely to this function. Used widely in Sweden, mainly on lakes and rivers, but also between some coastal islands. Reported from at least the 15th century. Design varied regionally, and in some areas, even within the same lake system where village traditions fostered local designs. Most large boats had special boathouses. Best known are the very large boats of the Dalecarlia (Dalarna) region in central Sweden, especially of Lake Siljan. A few boats remain, and they are raced on special occasions. Some reached a length of 18.5m and required 20 oarsmen manning 10 pairs of oars; 14 pairs are cited, and the largest is reported as carrying 90 people. Sharp ends; curved stem and sternpost, scimitar-shaped at the top; keel; rounded bottom, steep floors; flaring sides; sheer sweeps up at one or both ends. Clinker planking fastened with staples; 1-piece frames. Oarlocks cut into the top strakes and shaped into a specially cut gunwale. Rowed double-banked. Steered with an oar. At Lima on the Västerdälälven River in western Sweden, the **kyrkbåtar** (pl.) were

smaller, mainly worked with 3-5 pairs of oars (the **treäringar** and **fyräringar**) by 5 and 7 oarsmen, respectively. The stem and sternpost more curved but vertical; the stem protected by a metal band. Carvel-planked, fastened with staples; top strake phased out into the end sheer; outwale; middle ribs scarfed; bulkhead at each end. Wide, low benches; flooring at the stern. Crescent-shaped oarlocks with the notch at the top of the crescent; fastened to top strake. Length ca. 7.25m, beam 1.5m, depth 0.33m. The boats of Dälalven Lake, northwest of Uppsala, can be rowed and sailed. Clinker-planked; T-keel; flat, S-shaped bottom; wide, flaring sides. Strongly raked, straight stem; greatest depth at the heel of the stempost; tapers up toward the stern, merging into the sharply raked, elongated sternpost. Rudder follows angle of the sternpost, flaring sharply at the bottom; curved tiller. Oars held to natural crook oarlocks by rope grommets. The **storbåt*** employed 3 pairs of oars, the **tvårodd** 2 pairs. Length 9.4m, beam 2.4m. A type at Väringen Lake in the southeast was a small, flat-bottomed dugout called an **ökstock** (see **ekstock-1**). The boat at Sundby on this lake, called a **körköka**, was twice as large as the others, using 7 oars. The same term was used for a flat-bottomed 3-oared boat on Råsvalen Lake in central Sweden. In southeast Sweden, some of the boats were of the **eka*** type (**kyrkeka**), with a narrow, raked bow transom, raked stern transom, flat bottom, flaring sides, 2-piece frames. Used 4-5 pairs of oars. Rudderpost had a blade only toward the bottom; tiller. Length ca. 6m, beam 2m, depth 0.6m. Further reading: Albert Eskeröd, *Kyrkbåtar och Kyrkbåtsfarder* (Stockholm: LTs Förlag, 1973). Note also **kirkebåt, torsköka**. Further reference: **church boat**

kyrkbåtar See **kyrkbåt**

kyrkebåt See **kirkebåt**

kyrkeka See **kyrkbåt**

Kyrkesundsdoris See **dory-4**

kyrkjebåt See **kirkebåt**

kystfartøj See **coaster**

L

Labberboot, Labberlot See **barge-2**
Labrador boat See **Hampton boat**
Labrador floater See **floater-2**
Labrador whaler See **Hampton boat**
labrega *Portugal, central:* Open boat found from north of Porto to the southeast border, working in coastal inlets. Used mainly for fishing, but on the Ria de Aveiro, they also carry people and cargo, such as dried seaweed for fields. When used for cargo, it is known as a **bateira mercantel★**. Carvel-planked; flat bottom athwartships, slight rocker; straight, flared sides. Long, rising bow terminates in a point; stern more rounded and lower. Decked at the bow. Ships a small rudder worked with lines when sailing. Painted black. Mainly rowed, but sets a tall lugsail at times. Crew of 1-7, depending on the activity. Some are floating homes for the crew and their families. Reported lengths 7-9m; e.g., length 8.14m, beam at gunwale 1.74m, on bottom 1.12m, depth 0.5m. Other recorded names: **bateira labrega, bateira murtoseira, murtoseira, murtozeira; bateira★** (at Porto)
laca See **lākanā**
laccon See **accon**
laccone See **bilancella**
laccun, lacoun See **accon**
lađa See **ladja-1**
ladder bucket dredger, ladder dredger See **dredger-1**
lade See **Oberländer**
lađe See **ladja-1**
ladejka See **lodka-3**
Ladenkarl See **Bretterfloss**
Ladeschiff *Germany, S:* Long, narrow **rowing boat★** of the Tegernsee in Bavaria. Transported mainly produce and wood. Plumb bow, stern, and sides. Length ca. 8m. Name variant: **Holzschiff**. See also **Lädine**.
Ladi See **Lädine, ladja-1**
lađia See **ládija, lodka-3**
lađica See **ladja-1**
Ladie See **Lädine**
ladies' barge See **barge-11f**
ladies' skiff See **Saint Lawrence skiff-1**
ladiia See **lodka-3**
ládija Generic for **ship★** or **vessel★** in some Slavic languages. Spelling may vary, depending on the system used in transliterating from the Cyrillic alphabet. Word often combined to describe a type of vessel, as in the Bulgarian **ribolóvska ládija** (fishing vessel), or **krajbryezhna ládija** (**coaster★**). Spelling variants: **al''dija, alūdiya, ladi(y)a**; dim. **ladijka, ladiyka**. Note also **ladja-1**.
Ladija See **ladja-1, lodka-3**
ladijka See **ládija**
Lädin See **Lädine**
Lädine *Austria/Germany/Switzerland:* Open freight vessel that plied Lake Constance (Bodensee) from the latter half of the 16th to the end of the 18th century, carrying salt (**Salzlädine**), stone, sand, and gravel. A small boat retaining the same features and identified

by the same name served as a farm boat in the 1930s. Longitudinally planked, flat bottom turned up to the gunwale at each of the pointed ends; bow very elongated, stern turned up more sharply. Each rib extended across 2 bottom planks and alternated left and right; between each pair, a flat, transverse frame crossed the bottom. Strong, carvel-planked sides, rounded and flared. A wide-bladed rudder hung from the port quarter from a crossbeam and was worked with a horizontal pin. Solid platforms at the ends. Mast, as tall as 23m, stepped about a third in from the bow. A tall, trapezoidal sail hung, the long side at the top, from a horizontal yard; the sail on a recent small boat was more rectangular. Blue cloth created distinguishing designs. Crew of 3 on the cargo vessel. Reported lengths of cargo vessels 30-40m; e.g., length 31.5m, width on bottom 4.34m, depth amidships 2.26m. A smaller version of the early vessel, called a **Halblädine**, was reported ca. 24m long and 3m wide. Other recorded names: **Halblädi, Ladeschiff★, Lädi(n), Ladie, Lädinne, Ledin, Leede, Leedi, Lödi(ne), Lödin-Schiff**
Lädinne See **Lädine**
lad'ishcha, lad'iskha See **lodka-3**
ladiya See **ládija, lodka-3**
ladiyka See **ládija**
ladja 1. Croatian and Slovenian term for a **ship★** or **vessel★**, but more frequently for a boat that is used on rivers and lakes or one that may ferry passengers to and from ships in port. Word often combined to further describe a craft, as **ladja jedrenjača** for a **sailboat★**; **trgovačka** (or **trgôvaska**) **ladja**, a merchant vessel; **riječna ladja**, a **riverboat★**.
2. The word may also designate a unique craft, such as the open boat used by the inhabitants of the lower Neretva River, on the central Dalmatian coast, to carry bulk cargo. Sharp ends with marked fore-and-aft curve to sides and strong flare from the narrow bottom.

ladja-2

Stringer along top of the natural frames forms an inner gunwale. Rowed with 2 oars. Crew of 3. Length overall 8m, on bottom 3.3-4.1m; widths 2.4-3.1m; draft light 0.25m.
Spelling variants: **lađa, ladi, ladija, lâdja, làdjina, ladva★, lägja, laguiia, laja, lascha**; dim. **lađica, lâdjica, lâjdica; lajica; loja**; pl. **lađe, ladve**. Note also **ládija, zoppolo**.
Lad'ja See **lodka-3**
ladja jedrenjača See **ladja-1**
ladja na kolesa See **paddle boat-3**
lâdjica, làdjina See **ladja-1**

ladva Croatian generic term for a **dugout canoe★** or small **boat★**. Includes plank-extended, dugout craft. Dugouts were common on many lakes and rivers. Note also **zoppolo**. Further reference: **ladja-1**

ladve See **ladja-1**

lad'ya See **lodka-3**

lægter See **lighter-1**

læstabåt See **lestabåt**

læsta-fyreng See **firing**

lægterkåg See **kåg-1**

lagatoi See **lakatoi**

Lagerhulk See **hulk-3**

lägja, laguiia See **ladja-1**

Laguna Madre scow-sloop See **chalan**

lahut *France, Mediterranean coast:* **1.** An early vessel of the western part of the coast, sometimes armed for war. Rounded form; small. Rowed with as many as 12 oars. Spelling variants: **lehut, lut**
  2. Fishing **boat★** of the **tartane★** type used in the Gulf of Lions on the southwest coast. Towed a net that was also called a *lahut* or *lauto*. Set a single lateen sail. Spelling variant: **lavut**. Note also **laúd, leuto**.

L!ai See **tl'ai**

Laira barge See **Plymouth barge**

laiva See **ship**

laivasto See **fleet**

laja See **ladja-1**

lajbot, lajbota See **lifeboat**

låjdica, lajica See **ladja-1**

lak, laka See **lākanā**

lakadrao See **lakandrao**

lakam See **lākanā**

lākanā *Malagasy Republic:* Generic term for an expanded **dugout canoe★**, especially along the east coast. Constructed of a very hard, heavy wood. Expanded by fire. Some are thin with rounded, upturned ends; these sometimes venture out to sea. In the 17th century, some very large **canoes★** made annual visits to the Comoro Islands to the northwest. Other types thick and roughly hewn with elongated horizontal platforms at each end. These are longer and the sides are pierced for an outrigger. Paddled, seated at the stern, and poled from the bow. Protuberances left in the sides support the thwarts. Reported lengths 1.5-20m, widths under 60cm. Other recorded names: **laca, lak(a), lakam**

lakandrao *Malagasy Republic, NW:* Single-outrigger fishing **canoe★** of the lagoons of the northwest coast and nearby Nosse-Bé Island. Dugout hull (called **roko★** or **roka**) raised by planking; numerous half ribs and thwarts strengthen the hull; rounded "V" in cross section. Sharp ends; bow curves up to a point, or the top is truncated like the stern. May be decked between the outrigger booms and at the bow. Slender, sharp-ended float supported by 2 widely spaced booms lashed to a rod that pierces the hull and extends slightly outboard. Each boom inserted in a small stanchion in the float. Booms extend out the opposite side, where they are connected by a light pole, the unit serving as a counterbalance. Steered with a paddle. A rectangular sail supported by 2 light spars, one before the sail, the other aft of it. Fore-and-aft sail created by tacking to the end of the forward outrigger boom and

sheeting to the end of the after counterbalance boom. Spars stepped into a block along the midline; various holes used, depending on wind direction. Some employ a quadrilateral lateen-type sail with a short luff on a forward-raking mast. Spelling variant: **lakadrao**

lakaoi See **lakatoi**

lakatau *Solomon Islands, western Pacific:* Generic term for **ship★** in the Mo-ngiki language of Rennell Island in the southern part of the archipelago. Originally, probably referred to a trading (*tau*) vessel. Note also **lakatoi**.

lakatoi *Papua New Guinea, SE:* A **raft★**-like craft of the Motu people for their annual trip northwestward from the Port Moresby area to the Purari Delta area, sailing before the southeast trade winds, and returning on the northwest monsoon, trading cooking pots for sago and rough-hewn dugouts. An assemblege of 3-14 large, closely spaced **dugout canoes★** (called *asi*) were lashed together, the greater number required for the homebound trip. For local use, a **lakatoi** comprises 3 (*toi*) **canoes★** (*laka*). Secured by heavy beams passing through gunwale holes in the dugouts; a sturdy platform was lashed atop the beams, projecting beyond both sides of the unit. Sides protected by weatherscreens of woven palm, but a staging area ran outside for the crew. Platform partitioned to protect the pottery; shelters at each end. Steered with a heavy paddle at midline and on the quarter, requiring as many as 8 men in heavy weather. Craft might be disassembled at the sago-collecting site, and individual **canoes** used for fishing. Most stepped 2 masts, although 1-3 are reported. Tall, V-shaped or crab claw mat sails set with apex down; bent to 2 yards. Could sail in either direction. Later craft adopted rectangular spritsails of canvas. Now propelled only by outboard motors. Reported as long as 20m and 15m wide. Other recorded names: **bevaia** (an imitation by the Orokolo peoples), **iakatoi, lagatoi, lakaoi, lakéà-vi'i, yagatoi**. Note also **lakatau**.

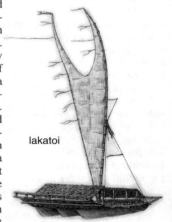

lakatoi

lak čamac See **čamac**

lakéà-vi'i See **lakatoi**

lake boat See **laker-1, Reelfoot stumpjumper**

lake carrier See **laker-1**

Lake Champlain canal boat *United States, NE:* During the 19th and into the 20th century, **schooner★**-rigged boats carried cargo on Lake Champlain and the Champlain Canal, some continuing down the Hudson River to New York. Long, narrow, and straight-sided, having been designed to traverse the canal locks. Flat floors; rounded, bluff bow; straight stem, flat stern above deadwood. Decked; trunk cabin aft; centerboard. Masts set in tabernacle for lowering on the canal, where towed by mules. Loose-footed, boomed gaff sails, long gaffs; jib to stemhead. Length 27m, beam 4.3m.

Lake Erie pound net sharpie See **sharpie-8**

Lake Huron boat See **Huron boat**

Lake Michigan ketch See **Grand Haven ketch**

laker 1. *Canada, S/United States, N:* General term given to vessels that ply the Great Lakes. Mainly bulk carriers with long cargo holds; pilot house well forward and engine room far aft. Most now diesel-powered. Operate for only the roughly 9 ice-free months. Other recorded names: **Great Laker, lake boat** (or **carrier**). Those working mainly on Lake Superior called **upper lakers**. Note also **Great Lakes schooner**.

2. *United States, E:* The **laker** of the Erie Canal in central New York State not only traversed the canal but might cross Lake Ontario, travel on Lake Champlain, and carry freight down the Hudson River to New York City. Flat bottom, square bilges, plumb sides protected by horizontal fenders, bluff bow, slightly overhanging stern swept up at the stem. Decked; high hatch coaming; stable forward for horses, crew accommodations aft. Mainly towed on the canal; rafted and towed by a **steamer** on the lakes; later boats steam-powered. Length ca. 29m, beam 5m, depth 3m.

Lake Winnipesaukee horse boat See **horse boat-5c**

läktare See **barge-1, lighter-1**

lambia See **pirogue-6**

lambo 1. *Indonesia:* Term applied to a relatively recent boat type with an outwardly European-style hull and rig. Built and manned by the Butung people of Sulawesi (Celebes), some of the islands to the east, and in the Riau Archipelago off Sumatra. Used for interisland trading. **Lambo** may refer only to the rig or to the combination of western rig and a hull with a long, straight keel that joins the stem and sternpost at an angle. Hull constructed of long lengths of planking adzed to shape and joined edge-to-edge with dowels. Single-piece cap rail trunnel-fastened through every 2nd rib, which protrude above deck level. Heavy ribs and floors added later. Sharp (**lambo soppe**), elliptical, counter (**lambo pantak**), or transom stern; overhanging poop deck follows sheer line. Rudder hung from the sternpost, or quarter rudders may be supported on athwartship beams (**lambo palari**). Sweeps up at the bow to a straight, raked stem; low freeboard. Decked at bow and stern; bamboo deckhouse amidships has loose planking; toilet box hangs out over the stern. One- or 2-masted with pole masts stepped on the keel. The single-masted boats set a boomed gaff or gunter sail; 1 or 2 headsails; sometimes a topsail. A **lambo** with a gunter rig is called a **prahu nadé**. Two-masted vessels are **ketch**-rigged. Large, boomed jib runs to a long bowsprit that may be supported on each side by a beam that extends to the end; heavy crosspieces form a catwalk. Oars, when used, work on a crossbar joining them to a steering cabin aft. Crew of 2-4, or a family. Reported lengths 6.4-21.3m; e.g., length 14m, beam 4.5m. Other recorded names: **arbor-bot** (in Kai Islands); **Buton** (or **Butung**) **lambo; jungku** (in Moluccas); **lamboe(t), lamboh, lambok, lambo sloop, lambot(e), lambu★, lambut, lombo;**

palari★ (erroneously); **prahu bot** (one of good quality on Ambon); **perahu lambo(t), perahu pantat kedera.** Further reading: G. Adrian Horridge, *The Lambo or Prahu Bot: A Western Ship in an Eastern Setting* (London: National Maritime Museum, 1979 [Maritime Monograph and Reports No. 39]). Note also **bago, lete-lete, sekochi-1**.

2. *Peninsular Malaysia:* At Penang on the northwest coast, a **lighter★** that unloads cargo from ships. Note also **lambu.**

lamboe, lamboet, lamboh See **lambo-1**

lamboh Bali *Indonesia, central:* Well-made and lightly constructed boat built along European lines, used for collecting turtles off some small islands north of Bali. Carvel-planked, then ribs and floors inserted and scarfed together; strakes become wider toward the stern as they run under the counter. Straight, raked stem; low freeboard aft. Decked at bow and stern; portable flooring under the central deckhouse, which has wooden sides and a palm-leaf roof; turtles carried in the hold with some sea water. An aft-raking mast stepped against the keelson in the forward quarter. Sets a boomed gunter sail with a gaff as long as its boom. Large, boomed jib runs from a long bowsprit made of 1-3 squared poles. Some have engines. Lengths 9-12m, widths 2.7-3m. Name variant: **turtle boat.** Note also **lambo.**

lambok, lambo palari, lambo pantak, lambo sloop, lambo soppe See **lambo-1**

lambot See **lambo-1, lete-lete-1**

lambote See **lambo-1**

lambu 1. *Indonesia, central:* One of the Javanese words for **boat★.**

2. *Malaysia:* A term sometimes used by the Chinese to describe a non-traditional type of **boat.**

See also **lambo.**

lambut See **lambo-1**

la mère See **train de bateaux**

lampar, lampara See **lamparo**

lampara boat *United States, W:* Fishes in California for sardines and mackerel with a seine net. Double-ended; decked; some carry the catch on deck, others in a small hold; pilot house forward or amidships. Mast, with derrick, stepped amidships. Motorized. Reported lengths 10.7-18.2m.

lampare See **lamparo**

lamparo *Mediterranean:* Small boat used for fishing with a seine net, employing lamps at night to attract the fish. Varies with the locale. Most Italian boats have a tall stemhead, as high as 58cm, cut horizontally; some Sicilian boats have a ram bow and are highly decorated. On the east coast of Italy, the **lamparo** is a small, open **rowboat★** that has a flush stemhead and a very flat sheer. Spanish boats beamier and the stemhead cap may be oval; transom or sharp-sterned. In Algeria, the general term for these boats is **palangrier★.** Some partly decked, others open. Now motorized, but some set a lateen sail and jib. Recent French boats are as long as 14m. Other recorded names: **bot de llum, lampar(a), lampare**

lampuguera See **llampuguera**

Lamu dhow See **Lamu jahazi**

Lamu jahazi *Kenya, NE:* Lamu-built trader that works along the East African coast from Mogadisho in Somalia to Tanzanian ports; sailed to Bombay (Mumbai)

Lamu jahazi

with ivory until the late 1950s. Distinctive sharp, vertical stem; mat weather cloth raises its low freeboard. Stem has cutaway forefoot and short stemhead projection. Carvel-planked; sewn with braided fibers and caulked with pitch; little sheer, round bottom, and a long, straight keel. Flat, generally wineglass transom. Undecked except for short apron forward and a larger quarter-deck; cargo may be covered by a mat roof that is lifted, wing-fashion, to the shrouds during loading and unloading. Quarter-deck protected while in port by a tarpaulin thrown over the lowered yard. Deep rudder worked by a wheel and a system of ropes and pulleys. Brown color of hull heightened by fish oil varnish; quickwork white, and rubbing strake black and red; oculus motif at bows and carved and painted boards at bow and stern. Toilet box often elaborately decorated. Flags flown from pole at stern and from rudderhead, and a long pennant from the masthead. A **houri★** towed or carried on board. Heavy, forward-raking mast secured against a beam just forward of amidships. Occasionally steps a mizzenmast during fine weather. A large lateen or quadrilateral lateen-type sail with a short luff, with vertical cloths, lashed to a long, multipiece yard and the stemhead. Sail tacks to the end of a long, fixed bowsprit; bowsprit lashed to the mast. A pair of shrouds on each side attach to the masthead by a rope that surrounds the top; lower ends secured to the gunwale and ribs; may be used as a derrick during unloading. Oars also available. Crew of ca. 12. Reported lengths 15-21m, widths 4.3-4.8m, depths 2.1-2.4m; draft ca. 2.13m. Other recorded names: **buti★** (in Mombasa), **jalbūt★**, **jolbut**; **khashbah** (large size); **Lamu dhow**; **nusf khashbah** (small); **safīna**. Further reading: A. H. J. Prins, *Sailing from Lamu* (Assen: Van Gorcum & Co., 1965). Note also **jahazi**, **jalbūt-3**, **Zanzibar jahazi**.

Lancashire nobby See **Morecambe Bay prawner, nobby-1**

Lancaster skiff See **dory-skiff**

lance See **lancia-1**

lanch See **jalbūt-1**, **launch**

lancha 1. *Brazil, NE:* Trader from Bahia. Narrow, raked stern had overhanging upper stern piece. River craft had a strongly raked, slightly curved or clipper bow. Decked forward; cabin aft on some. Two pieces of

wood fitted to the keel served as a lead for the bow hawser. Rudder; tiller. The 3-masted boats set 2 loose-footed gaff sails on aft-raking main- and mizzenmasts, a square sail on the foremast, and 2 headsails run out on the bowsprit, which could be canted upward when anchored; mizzen sheeted to a jiggerboom; fore- and mainmasts stepped close together. The smaller 2-masted type had no mizzen; the mainmast stepped close to the foremast; the square foresail held to wind-

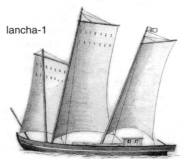

lancha-1

ward by a spar bowline. No standing rigging. Also propelled by oars. Reported lengths 14.7-20m; e.g., length 15.4m, beam 4.2m, depth 0.8m. Other recorded names: **barco★**, **lancha de Barra-For(r)a**, **launcha**, **peru**, **perua★**. Note also **lanche**.

2. *Cape Verde Islands:* One type of **lancha** is a small boat used for fishing at São Nicolau. Another type is a single-masted, open boat of 10-15t that trades between the islands of São Vicente and Santo Antão. Other recorded names: **falucho★**; in local Creole: **láxă** or **fălûxĕ**

3. *Colombia, Pacific coast:* Fishing **dugout canoe★** found north of Cape Corrientes. Well-developed keel, sharp bow, square stern. Sets a spritsail.

4. *Indonesia, W/Peninsular Malaysia:* Large cargo vessel of the late 19th and early 20th centuries that showed European influence. Used particularly along the Sumatra and Malaysia sides of the Strait of Malacca; said to have been built originally in the Lingga and Riau Archipelagoes off central Sumatra. Also reported as a **light cruiser** (see **cruiser**), a **yacht★**, and a vessel used by royalty. Often armed. Carvel-planked; clipper bow and straight, sharp stern. On some, a deep sheer strake extended forward to provide a platform for anchor-handling and to serve as a tack for the foresail or headsails. At the stern, the strake formed quarter galleries, terminating in a square, overhanging poop. Sides might be raised with temporary mat or straw weather boards. Some had temporary decking and a mat-roofed house; others fully decked with a wooden deckhouse aft. Quarter rudders. The main- and foremasts set fore-and-aft sails or lugsails; the mizzen raised a standing gaff sail; 2 headsails. Sails of woven palm or canvas. Some were basically oared vessels, employing as many as 50 men, using long sweeps with small, round blades. Reported lengths 13-16m; one Sumatran vessel was 13m long overall, 9.8m between perpendiculars. Other recorded names: **lanchang★**, **lanciang**, **lantcha**, **lantcia**, **lantja(ng)**, **perahu lancha** (or **lantja**)

5. *Malta:* Shallow-draft boat originating at Malta but found working elsewhere in the Mediterranean. Those reported in Tunisia in the late 19th century discharged ships in roadsteads. Sharp, plumb bow; mainly a square stern, sometimes rounded; flat floors. Partly decked; large hold with high coaming; series of small scuppers along each side. Large-bladed rudder worked by wooden or iron tiller. Brightly painted. Two masts, the foremast slightly shorter. Set lateen or square sails; lateens had 2 reef bands, one running roughly parallel to the yard, and 3 brails. Crew of 5. Length 15.4m, beam 4.2m, depth 1.8m, draft loaded 0.8m. Spelling variant: **lantcha**

6. *Mozambique:* **a.** Transports cargo and passengers in the vicinity of Maputo (Lourenço Marques) in the south. Plumb stem; transom stern; keel; moderate rise to the floors, soft turn of the bilges. Decked with a central hatch. Long boom to the gaff sail, and long, slender bowsprit carries 2 headsails; sometimes a topsail. Crew of 1-2. Reported lengths 9-10m. **b.** At Praia da Costa do Sol, near Maputo, the fishing **lancha** carries a single lateen or quadrilateral lateen-type sail with a short luff. Full-bodied; straight or slightly curved, raked stem; transom stern. Carvel-built; rough frames; caulked with old cording covered with tar. Now generally decked with a central cockpit. Short, vertical mast stepped well inboard; bamboo yard. Reported lengths 6-7m. **c.** In the vicinity of Mozambique Island, in the north, there is a fishing **lancha** of ca. 2-3t and a cargo **lancha** (called also a **lanchão★**) of similar design but with ca. 30t disp. The cargo vessel is used to unload and load ships and to transport cargo to nearby ports; beamy and may be open or have a flush deck with 1-2 hatches. The **fishing boat★** is slender, fast, and open. Both have a transom stern and a sharp, vertical stem. Set a large, quadrilateral lateen-type sail with a short luff or lateen sail to a mast stepped well forward. Bamboo yard and sail hung forward of the mast, with the tack boomed out over the bow.

7. *Philippines, N:* The Itbayat of the Batan Islands, north of Luzon, use the term **lañcha** for a **barge★** or a **ferryboat★**.

8. *Portugal:* **a.** The small, inshore fishing **lancha** of the central coast to the north and south of the Tagus River employed a trammel net. Carvel-planked, keel, raked transom stern, mildly curved stem, full bow, strong sheer, outboard rudder. Open except for foredeck and stern bench; 2 thwarts. Rowed (2-4 oars with block on loom to slot over a tholepin), sailed (quadrilateral lateen-type sail with a short luff), and some now motorized. Reported lengths 4.75-6.20m; e.g., length 4.75m, beam 1.9m, depth 0.65m. **b.** At Vila Franca de Xira in the inner estuary of the Tagus, there is a flat-bottomed **lancha** used for shad fishing. Carvel-planked; curved stem ends in high stemhead; strong sheer toward the bow; wide-bladed rudder. Cambered foredeck with a pair of bitts; stern deck. Rowed, poled, and sailed, setting a lateen sail. Other recorded names: **lancha de Vila Franca**, **praieira de ribatejo**. **c.** A **lancha** may also be the service boat of the Tagus **fragata★**. Open boat with rounded bilges, keel, heart-shaped transom with inner and outer sternposts, and

raked stem. Foredeck has hole for towing line; stern sheets, side benches, and 2 rowing thwarts. Uses 2 short and 4 long oars. Black hull except for light patch at bows. Length 5m, beam 1.95m, depth 0.75m. **d.** At Póvoa de Varzim in the north and at points along the coast to the south, there are 2 sizes of **lancha**: the **lancha grande** that fishes offshore for whiting, and the **lancha pequeña** that usually fishes for sardines. Open boat with keel; carvel-planked; flat floors; sharp-ended with straight, raked stem and sternpost. Reinforced with numerous ribs and heavy benches; small deck at the bow, larger at the stern. Those at Póvoa de Varzim that sailed shipped a rudder and set a quadrilateral lateen-type sail with a short luff or a lugsail to an aft-raking mast. Engines now employed on the larger type. **Lancha grande** lengths 12.4-13.6m; e.g., length 13.6m, beam 3.4m, depth 1.25m, crew of 18-25, 12 oars. **Lancha pequeña** lengths 7.48-11.8m; e.g., length 10.15m, beam 2.25m, depth 1.12m. Other recorded names: **lancha poveira**, **poveira**. Further reading: O. L. Filgueiras, "Barcos" in: *Art Popular em Portugal*, 1962, vol. 3, 353-357. Note also **poveiro. e.** At Caminha on the northern border, a small, extinct **lancha** trawled well offshore. Sharp ends with straight, raking stem and sternpost. Single mast raked strongly aft; struck while fishing, the yard placed in a pair of crutches on one side. Set a large, quadrilateral lateen-type sail with a short luff. Name variant: **lancha caminho**

9. *Portugal, Madeira:* Carried passengers and merchandise on the east coast between Funchal and Machico and on the west coast between Funchal and Paul do Mar. Employed 4 oars. Note also **canoa-13**.

10. *Puerto Rico:* General term applied to small boats used to transport merchandise (rowed) or passengers (motorized).

11. *Spain:* Word applied to several kinds of boats, including a small, 2-masted, lug-rigged boat dedicated to fishing, especially for sardines; an open sailing/**rowing boat★** used in interport traffic on the north coast; and a motorized **launch★**. An armed **lancha corsaria** of the early 19th century had a crew of 38. Other recorded names: Catalan: **llanxa**; pl. **llanxe**. Note also **bonitera, calera, xeito**.

12. *Venezuela, E:* **a.** Flat-bottomed cargo boat of the Orinoco basin. On its upstream trip, taking advantage of the trade winds, the boat set a very large, square mainsail and 2 square topsails. For the trip downstream, the sails were dropped and the boat used the current, aided by large sweeps. Lightly constructed to facilitate refloating after running aground on sandbars. Well-caulked in order to protect

lancha-12a

the cargo, especially the hides it often carried. Length ca. 10m; beamy. **b.** Term also applies to a **canoe**★-type river craft with a deep cockpit covered partly or fully by a barrel-shaped, thatched house. Heavily planked to withstand passage through rapids. **c.** One of the several types of **fishing boats** used on Isla de Margarita and the north coast, mainly trawling and fishing with hooks and lines. Keel with steep rise to the floors. May have a wet well. Motorized.

Further references: **barcachina, bote-4, caique-7b, canoa-12, canoa-13, launch, ngalawa-3**

lancha bombardeira, lancha bombardera See **bomb vessel**

lancha bonitera See **bonitera-2**

lancha calbucanas See **lancha velera**

lancha calera See **calera**

lancha caminho See **lancha-8**

lancha cañonera See **gunboat**

lancha chilota See **lancha velera**

lancha corsaria See **lancha-11**

lancha da pescada See **barco da pescada**

lancha de fiscalização de pesca See **fishery guard boat**

lancha de jeito See **xeito**

lancha del práctico See **pilot boat**

lancha de Vila Franca See **lancha-8**

lancha de xeito See **xeito**

lancha fletera *Spain, north coast:* Swift cargo vessel of the Vizcaya and Guipúzcoa areas. Carried 18-25t.

lancha gabarra See **gabarra-5a**

lancha garoupeira See **garoupeira**

lancha grande See **lancha-8**

lancha jeitera See **xeito**

lanchang *Malaysia:* Sometimes refers to a model boat constructed as an offering to spirits. Some modeled after the 2-masted armed **lancha**★. See also **lancha-4, sampan pukat.**

lanchang To'aru *Peninsular Malaysia:* Fore-and-aft-rigged trading vessel. Named for an early chief of Selangor on the west coast. Short and beamy with raked stem and sternpost and sharp stern; carvel-planked. Bow and stern galleries, the fore gallery used for the anchors; rudder and tiller came up inboard of the end of the stern gallery. House abaft the mainmast. Short masts with long topmasts, the foremast shorter. Both set boomed gaff sails.

lanchão Portuguese word used to describe a **lighter**★, **barge**★, or large-sized **lancha**★. Spelling variant: pl. **lanchões**. Further reference: **lancha-6**

lancha pequeña, lancha poveiro See **lancha-8**

lancha sávara *Portugal, central:* Open **fishing boat**★ used in the vicinity of the mouth of the Tagus River. Carvel-planked, flat floors. Rowed. Length 5m, beam 1.85m, depth 0.7m.

lancha trainera See **trainera**

lancha velera *Chile, S:* Vessel of the Archipelago de Chiloé and the adjacent mainland coast that still transports produce, timber, shellfish to canneries, and livestock. Roughly constructed, beamy boat with soft or hard turn of the bilges; long, straight keel; short, steep run; slight sheer, increasing sharply at the bow. Bluff bow, usually vertical, some raked;

transom stern, generally vertical. Outboard rudder has a high stock; worked with a tiller. Moderately high crown to flush deck, low bulwarks. Small, square hatch may be set into the foredeck; high coaming surrounds the main hatch; athwartships opening at the stern on the larger boats. Hull tarred; deck and hatch unpainted. Bilge keels on those that are beached. **Sloop**★-rigged with a high-peaked, boomed mainsail and a large jib that tacks to a short bowsprit. Many now motorized; these have a wheelhouse aft. Crew of 1-2, or a family. Reported lengths 8-12m, beam ca. 4m, depth 2m; shallow draft. Other recorded names: **lancha calbucanas** (or **chilota**)

lanche 1. At the beginning of the 18th century, cited as a 2-masted, square-rigged ship used in the Mediterranean and sailed to South America.

2. *Brazil:* A **ship's boat**★ of the early 19th century that employed 16-18 oars on each side. Note also **lancha.**

3. *France, W:* Sharp-sterned coastal **fishing boat**★ that worked until the mid-19th century. Two masts of roughly the same height: the foremast well forward and vertical, the mainmast raking aft. Lugsails of similar cut; foresail tacked to stemhead.

4. *Mauritania, W:* Open **fishing boat** developed in the early 20th century in the Canary Islands, often working with a **mother ship**★ off the African coast. About mid-century, the boats were sold to Imragen fishermen of Mauritania, who found them eminently suitable for inshore fishing. Sharp, somewhat convex or curved bow; raked stern. Outboard rudder; tiller. Lateen-rigged. Crew of 2. Reported lengths 8-11m; shallow draft. Name variant: **lanche Imragen**

5. *South America:* A vessel similar in rigging to the French **fishing boat** is reported on this continent for the same general period.

Further references: **caique-4, double felouque, filadière, lânsa, launch**

lanche Imragen See **lanche-4**

lancheta See **launch**

lanchia See **lancia-1**

lanchões See **lanchão**

lanchón *Spain, N:* Cargo vessels by this name were built at various Vizcayan ports in the first half of the 19th century. Usually employed as **lighters**★. Some decked. Reported length 18.2m, beam 3.6m, depth 2m. Spelling variant: pl. **lanchones**. See also **lighter-1.**

lanchones See **lanchón**

lancia *Italy:* **1.** Designates a **ship's boat**★ or **launch**★, especially for naval and merchant marine use. Transom stern. Rowed, double-banked, using 4-8 pairs of oars. Also sailed. Length ca. 10m. Other recorded names: **lanchia, landchia, lando, lanze**; pl. **lanc(i)e**; **prima lancia.** Note also **canotto, palischermo.**

2. Along the central Adriatic coast, the **lancia** is a **fishing boat**★; a more elongated version, used in Sicily, is called a **lancidda** or **lancitedda.** Double-ended, slightly sharper forward; straight, lightly raked or plumb stem; vertical sternpost. Straight, slightly raked keel; flat floors; well-rounded bilges; slight sheer. Open or half-decked, with cockpit amidships; ballast stowed in locker along each side. Rudder extends well below the keel; long, straight tiller. Some colorfully painted. Most set a high-peaked, dipping lugsail with a short luff; 2-piece yard; boomed at foot. Sail becomes more lateen-like to the south. Mast stepped through a thwart just aft of amidships. A 2-masted **lancia** is called a **schilètto** at Ancona and other ports in this area. Crew of one and a boy. Reported lengths 5-13m, the longer having 2 masts; widths 1.65-3.8m; depths 0.85-1.3m. Spelling variant: **lanze**; pl. **schilètti**

3. Lateen-rigged, square-sterned boat found on Sardinia. Further references: **launch, ship's boat**

lancia ammiraglio See **barge-2**

lancia dei viveri See **market boat-4**

lancia de poppa See **stern boat**

lancia de salvataggio See **lifeboat**

lancia di ronda See **guard boat-1**

lancia di spenditori See **market boat**

lanciang See **lancha-4**

lancidda See **lancia-2**

lancie See **lancia-1**

lancione *Italy:* **1.** Type of **gunboat★** used mainly to patrol the coast. Decked. Sailed, using 2 lateen sails, or rowed. Crew of 20. Other recorded names: **lancun, lancuo**

2. A large **raft★**-type craft used in loading and unloading heavy equipment, cables, anchors, arsenals, and hydraulic works. Note also **anchor hoy**.

3. Large ship's **launch★**.

lancitedda See **lancia-2**

lançonnier See **ship-4**

lancun See **gunboat, lancione**

lancuo See **lancione**

landchia See **lancia-1**

landdragningspram See **pram-4**

Landesübliches Boot See **shore boat-1**

lando See **lancia-1**

landschuit See **Aalsmeerse punter, grundel**

Land's End crabber See **West Country crabber**

langabote *India:* Early term used in Portuguese India for a small boat propelled mainly by oars. Probably a corrupt form of **longboat★**. Spelling variant: **lang bot** (Hindi)

langard See **brig**

langbomer See **Oostendse sloep**

lang boomer *Scotland, N:* Term given to the **fifies★** bought by Shetland Islanders after 1877 for line fishing for cod, ling, and halibut. Converted the **fifie** lug rig to a **cutter★** rig with a boomed gaff mainsail, staysail, and jib to a bowsprit. Tanned sails. Reported keel lengths 12.2-13.7m. Other recorded names: **big boat, buckie boat**. Note also **long-boom smack**.

lang bot See **langabote**

lang bote See **longboat-1**

långfärdskanot See **kanot-5**

Langleinen chaluppe See **sloep-3**

Langleinenfischereiboot, Langleiner, langlinefartøj, langlinefisker See **longliner-1**

langostero *Spain:* General term for boats engaged in fishing for rock lobster (*langosta*). Spelling variant: **llagoster** (Catalan). Note also **langoustier, lobster boat-1**.

langoustier 1. *France, W:* Boat of the north and west coasts of Brittany, working frequently off the Scilly Isles and Land's End, fishing for lobster (*homard*) and rock lobster (*langouste*). Many of the larger boats worked off Spain and Portugal. Fish for part of the year. Operated as sailing vessels until World War II.

langoustier-1

Catch held in a wet well that was as long as a third of the waterline of the boat. High bow; straight, slightly raked stem; low aft with broad counter stern above a strongly raked sternpost on the larger boats and severely raking transom on the smaller. Steep rise to the floors, straight keel with deep heel. Decked; cabin aft, store room forward; small boats undecked. Rudderpost comes up inboard on the counter-sterned boats. Smaller boats **cutter★**-rigged, the larger (ca. 21m or more) **ketch★**- or **yawl★**-rigged. Mainsail boomed; also set a lug topsail. **Brigantine★**-rigged at Roscoff. Larger boats employed an auxiliary. Crew of 5 and a boy; the small boats working inshore require only 1-2 men. Reported lengths 5-26m; e.g., length overall 14m, on keel 9m, beam 3.9m, depth 1.7m, draft aft 2.8m. Other recorded names: **cotre langoustier, (cotre) homardier, langoustier camarétais, langoustinier, sloop** (or **sloup**) **langoustier; chalupa lagosteira** by the Portuguese. Note also **caseyeur, chalutier, langostero, lobster boat-1**.

2. *Mauritania/Morocco, W:* Those vessels that fished for lobster, crabs, and crayfish off these coasts were similar to the **thoniers★** of Concarneau and often originated there or at Douarnenez. Developed ca. 1910. Strongly constructed with full lines; straight, slightly raked stem; strongly raked sternpost below an elongated counter stern; vertical sides; strong turn of the bilges; deep drag to the straight keel. Decked with poop or raised deck aft. Each had a large live well. **Ketch**-rigged with heavy mizzenmast, or **yawl**-rigged. Mainsail boom generally supported by a tackle from the mizzenmast. Sails either loose-footed or laced to their booms. Topsail on one or both masts; 2 headsails. By 1930s, engines installed and now fully motorized. Carried 1-2 heavy boats, 6-6.5m long, that helped in tending the nets and were called **canot de Mauritanie**. Crew of ca. 12. Reported lengths overall 23-33m; e.g., length overall 24.4m, beam 8.28m. Other recorded names: **dundee langoustier, dundee mauritanien, grande dundee, langoustier de Douarnenez, langoustier mauritanien, mauritien(ne)**

langoustier camarétais See **langoustier-1**

langoustier de Douarnenez, langoustier mauritanien
See **langoustier-2**

langoustinier See **langoustier-1**

Langschiff, långskepp, langskib, langskibet See **langskip**

langskip Generic term for a long, narrow Viking warship; major period 600-1,000 A.D., but were used in Scandinavia as late at the first quarter of the 15th century. Also used on the east coast of England. At least 2 types: the **snekkja*** and the **skeid***. Although considered unsuitable for ocean voyages, the vessels were reported from Iceland and the Mediterranean. Designed primarily to be rowed, with a square sail used only under favorable wind conditions. Double-ended; clinker-built; usually a low, T-shaped keel; quarter rudder; open; low freeboard. Pulled 50-80 oars, possibly with as many as 4 men per oar; oars worked through oar ports. Pole masts housed in a step. Sails hoisted by a halyard; held in position by bowlines and a spar. Length to 44m, but one reported as 60m. The size of the vessels was designated by the number of "rooms" or rowing thwarts. Other recorded names: **Langschiff, långskepp, langskib(et), long ship***. Note also **byrðing-1, drakar, esnecca-1, hafskip, keel-1**.

langûn See **gunboat**

Langwaidling, Langweidling See **Weidling**

langzat See **laung-zat**

lanoen, lanong See **juanga-2**

lânša *Tunisia:* Two-masted cargo and passenger vessel. Gone ca. 1940. Plumb stem, counter stern, little sheer. Hull usually black. Lateen sails; smaller sail on the after mast, boomed out from stern. Jib run to bowsprit. Reported lengths 10-15m. Other recorded names: **lanche*, lencha, lenche**; dim. **lwînša**

lansh 1. *Lebanon:* Motorized **fishing boat***. Generally longer than 9m. Spelling variant: **lensh**
2. *Oman, NE:* Any small, double-ended boat. Term in use from Majīs northward along the coast.

lantcha See **lancha-4, lancha-5**

lantcia, lantja, lantjang See **lancha-4**

lantjang poeket See **lantjang pukat, sampan pukat**

lantjang pukat *Indonesia:* Short, beamy cargo vessel that set a single square sail to a mast stepped well forward and a jib to the bowsprit. Sharp ends; decked except for the hold, which was roofed over. Steered with a sweep. Armed with a swivel gun. Spelling variant: **lantjang poeket**. See also **sampan pukat**.

lanze See **lancia**

la'o See **lisi**

laoutelle, laoutello See **leuto**

lapataganan *Chile, S:* A **dugout canoe*** of the Yahagan of the eastern part of the Strait of Magellan. Ends rounded; broad washstrakes added. Ca. 5m long.

Lappbåt *Sweden, N:* The small, open boat of the Lapps (Same) has raking stem and sternpost that curve smoothly to the keel. Clinker-planked with 4 wide strakes; strongly flaring sides amidships; one-piece curved frames, deep across the bottom. Some have a washstrake amidships. Rowed with a single pair of oars, against blocks, well forward. Length ca. 3.75m,

beam 1.25m, depth amidships 0.32m. Name variant: **Samebåt**. Note also **bask**.

Lapp boat See **bask**

larboard boat See **whaler-3**

largarete *Philippines, S:* Double-**outrigger canoe*** of the Visayan Islands that provides interisland transportation. Also fishes, dragging a large gill net hung fore-and-aft beneath the **canoe***. Dugout base with mortised and nailed wood ribs; sides raised with planking. Vertical stem and sternpost inserted; narrow ends; flared "U" in cross section; end rocker above the waterline. Decked at the ends, and bamboo strips form light platforms on the outriggers for gear. Three booms, bowed down slightly, connect directly with bamboo floats. Floats curve up slightly at their forward end. Propelled by a small engine, earning the universal name of **pump boat***. Reported lengths 9-12m; e.g., length overall 9.8m, on waterline 8.5m, beam 0.68m, depth 0.78m, draft 0.31m.

large bateau See **pungy**

large canoe See **canot du maître**

Largs line skiff See **line skiff**

larker See **lurker**

larnch See **launch, launch-7**

lascha See **ladja-1**

lashāb See **dhow**

last boat See **Deal lugger**

Lasten-Ewer See **Ewer**

lastfartyg, lastilaiva See **freighter-1**

lasting boat See **Deal lugger**

Lastkahn See **szkuta**

Lastponton, lastprám See **lighter-1**

lateen See **lateener**

lateen caravel See **caravel-1**

lateener General term applied to a vessel whose primary sail is a lateen: a triangular sail hung essentially fore-and-aft, with the luff lashed to a long yard. Sail topped over the stubby mast in going about. Other recorded names: **bâtiment latin, lateen, Lateinsegelboot, latin(a), latine, latino***. See also **Broads lateener**.

Lateinsegelboot, latin, latina See **lateener**

latina See **latino**

Latin barge See **barque du Léman**

latine See **lateener**

latini See **latino**

latino *Italy, NW:* Lateen-rigged **fishing boat*** of the **gozzo*** type of the eastern Ligurian coast. Also transported olives. Carvel planking of pine; sharp, straight ends; frames of acacia. Mast sharply raked forward. Yard in 2 pieces, the 2nd piece overlapping all but the upper end. Also rowed; most now have motors. Reported lengths 8-10m. Spelling variants: **latina;** pl. **latini**. See also **lateener**.

laúd *Spain, S and E:* Small, beamy, lateen-rigged boat used for fishing and transporting the catch to market. Some serve as **coasters***. Used since the Middle Ages, but now nearly extinct. Long and narrow; curved stem and high stemhead, sharp stern, flat floors, deep drag aft. Grounding keels on those that work from beaches. Rudder extends below keel. Smaller boats open; larger may be decked forward and aft and along the sides, or fully decked with low bulwarks; hold amidships. Outboard rudder; tiller. Colorfully painted, white triangle forward, oculi. On smallest types, the sharply

laúd

forward-raking mast is stepped in the eyes; larger boats step mast amidships, forward-raking, and run a jib to a bowsprit. Engines installed in later boats. As many as 8 in crew plus a boy. Reported lengths 3.6-9.6m, widths 1.1-2.3m; shallow draft. Other recorded names: **laúde, laút, llagut, llahut, llaúd, llaút; jabeque*** (Andalucia); **katu-ontziska** (Basque). Note also **falucho, jábega, lahut, leuto.**

laúde See **laúd**

laudo See **leuto**

laudus *Mediterranean, NW:* **1.** Reported in 14th- and 15th-century literature as the 2nd of a **ship's boats***, between the **chaloupe*** and the **petit canot** (see **canot**); employed one sail. When serving as the principal boat, 2 sails were used. Also rowed.
2. A small ship with rounded form, reminiscent of a lute. Name variant: **lut.** Further reference: **leuto**

Laufener Plätte See **Plätte-1**

launch 1. A small boat that works under oars, sail, or power.
2. In most western navies, the largest of the **ship's boats***. Especially seaworthy because in early days, they warped anchors and brought drinking water, munitions, and provisions from shore. Those fetching water were sometimes fitted with a large plug that was removed when the boat was in fresh water, permitting the boat to flood. Frequently armed and sometimes supported landing operations. Bluff bow, wide transom stern, some ceiled, flat floors. Open or half-decked. Large **launches** worked with as many as 16 oars, single- or double-banked. Variously rigged: 2 loose-footed gaff sails with 2 foresails; 2 standing lugsails with 2 foresails; as a **sloop***; or as a **ketch***. Converted to power in the latter half of the 19th century. Reported lengths 4.9-12.8m, beamy; shallow draft. Note also **barce, lancione-3, vedette.**
3. During the 18th-19th centuries, the French, Italian, Spanish, and Turkish navies used an open, flat-bottomed **launch** as a **gunboat***.
4. Generally now a small power boat serving as a **tender*** to **yachts*** and **merchantmen*** or as a larger craft for transporting passengers or officials, especially in a port. Usually open or half-decked; some have a cabin. Other recorded names: **Hafenbarkasse, stoombarkas**
5. *Barbados, West Indies:* Diesel-powered boat used for

day fishing. Clipper bow, transom stern. Pine planking, mahogany ribs and frames; some now of fiberglass. Cabin and pilot house forward of amidships, open aft. Engine amidships. Reported lengths 6-12m.
6. *England, SW:* The wooden **beach boats*** that worked out of Lyme Bay were called **launches**. Used for fishing and commercial trips. Carvel- and clinker-planked; bilge keels; transom stern. Open except for short foredeck; pilot house on some. Inboard engine, but most also stepped 1-2 masts, setting a dipping lug mainsail and a mizzen used for steadying. Length to ca. 7.9m; e.g., 6.7m long, 2.4m wide, 0.7m draft. Name variant: **beach launch**
7. *Pakistan:* **Launch** (or **larnch**) is a stubby motorized vessel that steps a mast to which a sail may be set; however, mast's main purpose is to avoid the survey required for fully motorized vessels. Mainly a **coaster*** trading in the Persian (Arabian) Gulf from Karachi. Also built on the Indian west coast. Sharp, raking stern or pointed counter. Decked with poop deck and wheelhouse. Crew of 8. Reported lengths 18-33.5m; dimensions of an Indian-built vessel: length 33.5m, beam 8.22m, depth 4.87m.
8. *United States, central:* Square-ended, open boat of the Mississippi Valley used by commercial fishermen; nearly extinct. Shallow, plumb transoms extended out over the water, especially at the bow. Low, flaring sides; flat bottom. Originally propelled by a single-cylinder engine; by the 1920s, employed an automobile engine. Length ca. 8.5m, narrow. Other recorded names: **bateau*, gas boat*, joe boat, johnboat*, put-put**
Additional recorded names: **äkatos, barcaccia*, barcass, barcasse*, barkača*, barkas*, barkasa, Barkass(e), barkaz", barkoz, lanch, lancha*** (dim. **lancheta**), **lanche*, lancia*, larnch, palischermo*, Ruderkarbasse; motor launch, Motorbarkasse; Dampfbarkasse, steam launch, stoombarkas.** Note also **longboat, sloep-2, tender.**

launcha See **lancha-1**

launch tug See **tug-1**

laundry barge See **bateau lavoir**

laung *Myanmar (Burma):* **1.** General Burmese term for an expanded, plank-extended **dugout canoe***, regardless of size. Expanded by fire and pressure to almost flat before thwarts are placed in recesses and the shell is permitted to close to desired beam. Planks and ribs added; on large cargo boats, an upper tier of thwarts inserted. Seams caulked with a bee dammar. Long, low bow; high stern; often a deckhouse, behind which is a platform for the helmsman. Quarter rudder on large sizes. Larger ones may be sailed, stepping the mast in a tabernacle. Spelling variants: **hlaung, loung.** Terms in several dialects: **malong, m'loung, paleong, p'loung, talong.** Note also **laung-gô, laung-zat.**
2. A type of **laung** is raced. The single-log, plank-extended dugout is paddled by 25 or 40 men, depending on size, which ranges from 9-12m.

laung-gô *Myanmar (Burma):* Cargo-carrying **riverboat***. Plank-extended, expanded dugout; held open by heavy thwarts; round bottom. Heavy, concave bow terminates in bluntly cut bow extension; abaft the bow section is a carved bulkhead. Stern turns up in a carved "duck's tail" as high as the original log permits. Decked with loose bamboo; arched mat cabin aft for family and crew. Guided downstream with 3-4 sweeps; poled upstream. May step a bipod mast for a square sail. Crew of 3-5. Length ca. 12m. Spelling variant: **loung go**. Note also **laung**.

laung-zat *Myanmar (Burma):* Old vessel of the Ahrewady (Irrawaddy) River; used especially between Prome and Mandalay to transport rice, taking advantage of the southerly winds to set enormous square sails; poled or pulled in calms; floated downstream. Old type seen at least until World War II. Hull long and narrow; formed by soaking, steaming, and shaping soft wood logs to spread the sides; planks raised the sides. Strong sheer to the characteristically high stern; carved on the older vessels. Bow much lower, but swept up from the bottom to a broad, forked top; generally a fine entrance. Helmsman sat on a sheltered seat, sometimes elaborately carved, at the after end of the house, working a quarter rudder on the port side. Cabin extended from abaft the mast, the roof following the sheer. Broad gangways bordered each side at gunwale level. Mast usually bipod and stepped in the forward third in a tabernacle. Tremendous standing yard supported by multiple halyards; ends turned upwards. Sail, bent to rings on the yard, often different colors on port and starboard sides. Older boats also set a pair of square topsails. Both pairs of sails brailed to the mast when furled. Crewed by members of a family, all of whom lived aboard. Reported lengths 15-23m; beamy. The modern **laung-zat** is double-ended, low at bow and stern, and decked at bow and along the sides; low house aft. Not sailed. Other recorded names: **langzat, rice boat**

laurette See **lerret**

laút See **laúd**

lauteddu, lautello, laùto See **leuto**

lavut See **lahut**

lawitan See **baroto**

láх̇ä See **lancha-2**

laxfiskbåt See **Bornholmsk laksebåd**

lay boat *United States, E:* **1.** Term given to the boats that carried iced shad from Delaware Bay upriver to Philadelphia markets. Boats not standardized until gasoline engines adapted ca. 1900. Some **sloop**⋆-rigged, some cat-rigged, and some also stepped a small mizzen. The cat-rigged boats were carvel-planked, had a centerboard, and were ca. 9m long. Name variant: **market boat**⋆. Note also **seine boat-5b**.
2. May also describe a boat that transported and set out a **sinkbox**⋆ for a waterfowl hunter. Used off the mouth of the Susquehanna River on upper Chesapeake Bay. More recently, since the banning of the **sinkbox**, the term **lay boat** has applied to a boat that deposits a hunter in waders onto a bar and surrounds him with decoys. Note also **battery boat, layout boat**.
Further references: **cabin boat, oyster barge**

lay-down battery See **sinkbox**

layout boat *United States:* **1.** On Chesapeake Bay, especially off the Susquehanna River, a **layout boat** was manned by 4 goose hunters: 2 lying facing and firing forward, 2 working aft. Curved decks at ends. Operation supported by a **cabin boat**⋆, to transport decoys and provide shelter for the hunters, and a **chase boat** with an outboard motor to retrieve the downed birds. The low freeboard, ca. 25cm, was further camouflaged by decoys. Note also **bushwack boat, lay boat**.
2. The **Great Lakes layout boat** is a small boat designed to permit a hunter to sneak up on ducks that have been attracted to decoys. Full bow; narrow, sharp stern. Teardrop-shaped cockpit. Blind erected just forward of the cockpit.

leath bhád See **Galway hooker**

leather coffin See **timber drogher-1**

Lebanese schooner See **shakhtura**

le bâtard See **canot bâtard**

lebec See **xebec**

Lebensmittelboot See **market boat**

Lederboot See **skin boat-1**

Ledin, Leede, Leedi See **Lädine**

Leeds and Liverpool long boat See **longboat-4**

Leemster aak See **lemmeraak**

left-handed smack See **fishing smack**

leggio See **lighter**

legno a vela See **sailer**

lagno corsaro See **corsara**

lè-golè'an See **golekan**

legut See **leut**

lehut See **lahut-1**

Leibjagdschiff See **Leibschiff**

Leibschiff **1.** *Austria:* Term given a vessel that transported high-ranking personages on the Danube River. Reported as early as the mid-16th century. On at least one occasion, an entourage of 6 vessels proceeded to Istanbul, while a trip by Queen Maria Theresa in 1745 from Ulm to Vienna involved 32 vessels. Sharp, upturned ends; flat-bottomed. Deckhouse with suitable amenities covered most of the vessel. The Danube vessels were maneuvered by sweeps at each end; also sailed. A flotilla of accompanying vessels might include some of the following: the **Beichväterschiff** for the priest, the **Damenschiffe** for the ladies, the **Kavalierschiffe** for the knights, the **Ministerschiffe** for government ministers, the **Offizierschiff** for military officers, the **Küchenmeisterschiff** and **Küchenschiff**⋆ for the chief chef and as the kitchen and the **Bäckenschiff** for baking, the **Dienerschiffe** (or **Dienstbotenschiffe**) for the servants, the **Wagenschiff** and **Pferdeschiff** (or **Roßschiff**) for the carriages and the horses, the **Proviantschiff** and **Gepäckschiff** (or **Bagageschiff**) for provisions and baggage, the **Musikschiff** for the musicians, and the **Hatschierschiff** for bodyguards.
2. *Germany, S:* Special vessels of noblemen used on Starnberger See from the 16th to the early 19th century. Elegantly appointed and ornately decorated. Flat floors; house aft of amidships; rowed with as many as 42 oarsmen; also sailed, setting a single square sail. Reported lengths 15.5-23m, beam ca. 2.5-4m. Accompanied by a flotilla of smaller vessels: the **Leibjagdschiff** for hunting parties, the **Edelleutschiff** for lesser

dignitaries, the **Frauenzimmerschiff** for the women, the **Küchenschiff** for cooking, the **Silberschiff** and **Kellerschiff** for tableware and beverages, the **Kammerherrenschiff** for the chamberlain, the **Abortschiff** for sanitary facilities, and several small **Gondeln** (see **Gondel-1b**). Note also **Bucentaur, Fisaler.**

leichte Fregatte See **frigate-1**
Leichter See **lighter-1**
Leichterprahm See **Prahm-2**
Leichterschiff See **lighter-1**
Leigh bawley See **bawley**
Leigh cockle galley, Leigh cockler See **cockle galley**
leighte Fregatte See **frigate-1**
Leigh pink *England, E:* 19th-century **fishing boat★** out of Leigh on the north shore of the Thames Estuary. Considered to be a large **Peter boat★**. Double-ended; decked with a small cabin forward, or protection provided by tarpaulins; wet well amidships. Set a loose-footed, boomed spritsail, staysail, and jib; topsail run to topmast. Length ca. 6m. Name variant: **pinkie**. Note also **pink.**
Leigh shrimper See **bawley**
leighter, leiter See **lighter-1**
Leith baldie See **baldie**
léju See **te-puke**
lekokol See **ice breaker**
Lekse schouw See **zalmschouw**
lelieschouw See **Friese schouw**
Lelybom See **bom-2**
lembetto See **lembo**
lembi See **lembo, lembos**
lembo Term with long usage and wide geographical distribution in southern Europe. Italian sources cite the **lembo** as a fast, maneuverable, 14th-century naval vessel with flat floors; rowed and sailed. Merchant **lembi** (pl.) capitalized on the speed and maneuverability of the naval vessel, carrying passengers and cargo in the Mediterranean. During the same period, a **lembo** was a **barge★**-like river craft that carried heavy cargoes. The word seems to have had the same meaning on the Danube River. Other recorded names: **lembetto** (dim.), **libo★** (pl. **libi**), **limba, limbe, limbo**. Note also **lembos.**
lemboi See **lembos**
lembos 1. In early Greek and Roman writings, **lembos** and **lembus**, respectively, meant merely **skiff★**. Term also used for a harbor craft (especially one serving an anchored vessel), river craft (cited on the Rhône River in southern France), and **fishing boat★**.
2. From the mid-3rd to the mid-2nd century B.C., the Illyrians of the Adriatic created the fast, highly maneuverable **lembos** for minor warfare and particularly for piracy. Also used when speed was important for carrying dispatches. Produced with numerous variations by the Illyrians and Romans. Open; sharp bow, some with a ram; slender. Mainly rowed by 16-50 oarsmen, rowing from l-2 levels. Might also carry soldiers and a few horses.
Other recorded names: **lembum, lembus**; pl. **lembi, lemboi**; dim. **lembunculus, lemnunculus, lémuncule, lenuncolo, lenunculus** (pl. **lenunculi**). Note also **lembo.**

lembum, lembunculus, lembus See **lembos**
lemmeraak *Netherlands, N:* Built initially in the late 1870s at Lemmer for trawling in the Zuiderzee and Waddenzee. One type (the **mosselaak**) fished for mussels. Later boats mostly built as pleasure craft, and many **fishing boats★** were converted to **yachts★**, the **lemmeraakjachten** (pl.). Initially of wood, carvel-planked, but by the end of the 19th century, most of steel. Rounded ends; deep, curved stem with bow skeg; straight, raking stern with deep skeg. Low rise to the floors; slack bilges; shallow keel. Greatest beam near the mast, narrowing slightly toward the stern. Top strake widest with tumble home near the mast. Some with strong sheer toward the ends. Wide rudder; tiller slots over rudderhead; narrow leeboards; live well on **fishing boats**. Decked to mast, open waist; **yachts** decked except for cockpit aft, low cabin. Originally a single unstayed mast stepped in a tabernacle. Set a loose-footed, boomed gaff sail with a short, curved gaff. Jib to jibboom, staysail, and sometimes a boomed-out, triangular sail set abaft the mast. Engines occupied the live well space on later boats. Crew of ca. 3. Reported lengths 9-17.5m; e.g., length 14m, beam 4.75m, depth 1.0m; the longer boats were generally **yachts**; shallow draft. Other recorded names: **Leemster aak, lemmerjacht, lemsteraak**; pl. **lemmeraken, lemsteraken**; those out of Bruinisser were called **Bruinisser jachten**. Further reading: T. Huitema, *Lemsteraken van Visserman tot Jacht* (Weesp: Uitgeverij Heureka, 1982). Note also **lemmerhengst, visaak**. Further reference: **wieringer aak**
lemmeraakjacht, lemmeraakjachten, lemmeraken See **Lemmeraak**
Lemmer beurtman, Lemmer beurtschip See **beurtschip**
lemmerhengst *Belgium/Netherlands, SW:* Developed by Zeeland fishermen who went to the Waddenzee in their **hengsten** (pl.) seeking mussel seed and noted the better sailing qualities of the **lemmeraak★**. First modified **hengst★** built in 1899; no longer used. Fully carvel-planked; flat bottom; rounded sides; tumble home to top strake above a continuous wale. Rounded stern of the **lemmeraak**; raked, straight sternpost; stem raked ca. 45° and ended in the angled stemhead of the **hengst**. Maximum beam in forward third; strong sheer toward stemhead. Long leeboards; outboard rudder; tiller. Decked to mast, open waist, decked aft, with steering well. **Lemmerhengsten** set a boomed, loose-footed gaff sail; staysail; jib to bowsprit on some. Mast strikable. Motors installed on some (the **motorlemmerhengst**). Reported lengths 12.2-13.5m, widths 3.9-4.3m, depths 1.1-1.7m. Other recorded names: **jachthengst, lemsterhengst**
lemmerhengsten See **lemmerhengst**
Lemmerhoogaars See **Tholense hoogaars**
lemmerjacht See **lemmeraak**
lemmerschouw See **zeeschouw**
lemnunculus See **lembos**
lemon squeezer See **hinge boat**
lemsteraak, lemsteraken See **lemmeraak**
Lemsterhengst See **lemmerhengst**
Lemsterhoogaars See **Tholense hoogaars**

Lemster schouw See **zeeschouw**
lémuncule See **lembos**
lencha, lenche See **lânša**
lenho Portuguese term for a small 13th- and 14th-century **galley***. Mainly rowed with as many as 18 oars, but might set 1-2 lateen sails. Lacked the forecastle of the larger **galley**.
lensh See **lansh-1**
lensmannsbåt See **seksæring-3**
lento See **leuto**
lenuncolo, lenunculi, lenunculus See **lembos**
lepa See **lepa-lepa, lipa**
lepa², lepah-lepah See **lepa-lepa**
lepa-lepa *Indonesia, E:* Generic for a flat-bottomed **dugout canoe*** found from Sulawesi (Celebes), east through Halmahera, the Moluccas, to Timor. Some carried as a **ship's boat*** aboard a **pinisi***, especially on their trapang-seeking expeditions to northern Australia, where they were adopted by the indigenous peoples, who call their version **lippa-lippa***. When serving as a ship-to-shore **tender***, they are termed **sampan*** by the Bugis peoples of Sulawesi. Also used for fishing, lightering, and at times, several might serve as the base for a **ferry***. Found without outriggers and with one or two. Some plank-extended; ends turn up and overhang. Larger boats have a cabin. Might set a horizontally elongated lugsail or a boomed leg-of-mutton sail. Reported lengths 3.7-4.3m, beam ca. 0.6m. Other recorded names: **lepa, lepa***, **lepah-lepah, lepe lepe, leper-leper, lipa-lipa***, **lip-lip, perhau lepalepa, prahoe lepa-lepa**. In Buginese, one with a single outrigger is a **lêpa-lêpa riyatîri-siwâli**; one with double outriggers is a **lêpa-lêpa riyatîri**. Note also **kole kole, pakur**. Further reference: **djěnging**
lêpa-lêpa riyatîri, lêpa-lêpa riyatîri-siwâli See **lepa-lepa**
lepap *Peninsular Malaysia/Singapore:* Chinese **fishing boat*** found around Singapore and along the west coast of the Malay Peninsula. Sharp and heavily raked ends; light sheer; flat bottom; hard chines. Decked for 60-76cm at stern; short platform above gunwale level at bow. Generally rowed, but may set a rectangular lugsail. Usually steered with a paddle, but sometimes fitted with rudder and lines. Reported lengths 3-6m, widths 1.2-1.5m, depths 0.4-0.6m. Name variant: **perahu lepap**
lepelbaggeraar See **spoon dredger**
lepe lepe, leper-leper See **lepa-lepa**
lerret *England, S:* Beamy, open boat that works off Chesil Beach near Portland. Used since at least the late 17th century for smuggling and later for mackerel or whiting seining and tending crab pots. Essentially

lerret

extinct. Clinker-built; sharp ends, but stern deeper and fuller than bow. Flat floors; rounded bilges; slight drag to the keel. Slightly raked stem with curved forefoot;

sternpost taller, straight, rounded below, and sometimes raked. Rope inserted through hole in keel just forward of sternpost for launching and recovery on the steep shingle beach; grounding keels fitted. Usually steered with an oar when sailed. Small platform at the stern used when setting the seine; small locker aft. Rowed, double-banked, with 2-8 oars, but in the 20th century, mostly with 4. Oars have an elongated block with one or more holes, attached near the grip, fits over a tholepin. Known to have been sailed, setting 2 spritsails or a lugsail forward and sprit mizzen. Six-oared boats required a crew of 12, the 4-oared needed 8. Four-oared boats range in length from 4.88-5.49m; 6-oared from 5.79-6.71m; e.g., length 5.23m, beam 2.13m, depth 1.17m. Other recorded names: **Chesil Bank lerret, laurette, lerrit, lirret, Portland lerret**. Further reading: E. McKee, "The Lerrets of Chesil Bank," *The Mariner's Mirror* 63 (1977), 39-50; Keith Pritchard, "Death or Glory," *Classic Boat* 66 (1993), 31-34.
lerrit See **lerret**
lesovoz See **timber carrier**
lestabåt *Norway, north-central:* Collective term for a boat with a capacity of 12t (1 *lest*). Built in the Åfjord area north of Trondheim, especially to transport farm products to Trondheim and to fish. Clinker-planked with wide strakes; keel; sharp ends, vertical stem and sternpost with rounded forefoot. Open; rock ballast amidships; outboard rudder; very long tiller. Rowed with 2 pairs of long oars worked through oarports. Polemast stepped amidships; trapezoidal square sail, topsail. Engines installed in the 1930s and hull design modified. Crew of 2 when rowing, 4-5 when fishing. Reported lengths 9.8-10.7m. Other recorded names: **læstabåt, lesterbåt; to-lestabåt** (cap. 2 *lester*); **tre-lestabåt** (cap. 3 *lester*), actually a **fembøring***. Note also **listerbåt**.
lestafiring See **firing**
lesterbåt See **lestabåt**
lesteur See **ballast barge**
lestr-roueder See **chalutier**
lete*, **leteh-leteh** See **lete-lete**
lete-lete *Indonesia:* **1.** Sturdy, fast bulk carrier of eastern Madura that has been seen at Singapore; some also fish off Australia. Dates from ca. 1900. Plank-built; sharp ends; curved keel; fairly flat floors, rounded bilges; many ribs, multiple longitudinal stringers. Strong sheer forward; very little freeboard when loaded. Deep, curved, fairly vertical stem and sternpost terminate in tall points. Decked except for short sections at each end. Bamboo-sided, canvas-roofed house amidships extends to gunwales; long railing along this house; most have protective shelter or cabin at the stern. A curved crutch atop the roof ridge serves as a sail rest. Small, undecked **lete-lete** fish in nearby waters for local consumption. Employs 1-2 long, narrow rudders lashed against a crosspiece set on vertical posts at the stern; if single rudder used, it is shifted after each tack. Hull frequently painted white with bright tops to the stem and sternpost. Sets a very large, boomed lateen-type sail tacked to the stemhead. Yard

composed of bamboo poles lashed together. A boom set out to windward extends the line used to adjust the angle of the yard. Mainsail brailed to the fixed yard by wrapping around lower boom and yard. Unstayed mast stepped well forward; may be short and stout, tall, or merely a loose prop; access aloft provided by treads tacked to the mast. May also set a small, similar foresail to a light mast lashed to the stemhead and tacked to a short outrigger; occasionally a 3rd sail set either forward or abaft the house. Crew of 5-10. Reported lengths 9-20m; e.g., length 17m, beam 4m, draft 1.5m. A **lete-lete** hull with a gaff or gunter sail is called a **lambot**.

2. A modified **lete-lete** has been adopted by the Mandar of western Sulawesi (Celebes). Generally smaller. Ends lower and more raked; short planking at ends shaped to fit directly to the stem and sternpost. Strong sheer, especially forward; little freeboard. House flat-roofed. Enormous, flat-bladed rudder supported by an elaborate framework on the overhanging poop. Also sets a large, boomed lateen-type sail.

Spelling variants: **lete***, **leteh-leteh**, **leti-leti**
leti-leti See **lete-lete**
letter of marque ship See **privateer**
létti-skip See **létti-skúta**
létti-skúta *Iceland:* A light, fast vessel often used in rescue work. Name variant: **létti-skip**. See also **skuta-1**.
Leuchtschiff See **lightship**
Leuchtturm-Tender See **beacon boat**
leudi See **leudo**, **leuto**
leudo *Italy, NW:* Robust cargo vessel of the Ligurian coast, carrying casks of wine from Elba and Sardinia, and other cargoes locally and from North Africa; some fished, and early vessels transported ballast. Only a few remained by the mid-1970s. Many launched from beaches, bow first. The sand-carrying vessels were large but with a low deck line. The wine-carrying

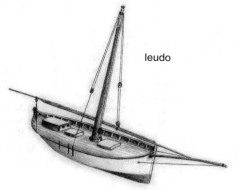

leudo

leudi (pl.) had a higher deck line and stowed the casks below and on deck. The cheese carriers also had a high deck line; also carried firearms, cloth, handmade goods, and agricultural implements. Carvel-planked; tall, straight, raked stem cut obliquely at the top; sharp stern, sternpost vertical or has slight tumble home. Flat floors; long, straight keel; considerable sheer. Narrow outboard rudder extends below the keel. **Fishing boats*** half-decked, highly cambered; full

deck on cargo vessels; capstan forward; low cabin aft. Small boat towed astern. Single forward-raking mast stepped amidships. Lateen sail bent to a 2-piece yard, which is a little longer than the hull. Light bowsprit run through the starboard gunwale; jib may be small or large, overlapping the mainsail. Masthead somewhat bulbous for the sheaves. Many converted to power. Crew of 7 on **fishing boats**. Reported lengths 10-17m, beamy. Other recorded names: **leudo rivano**, **liuto**, **rivano**; pl. **rivani**. Note also **catalano**.
leüdo See **leuto**
leudo rivano See **leudo**
leudus See **leuto**
lèuge See **allège**
leung pei See **diao ting**
leut Mainly a **fishing boat*** of the eastern Adriatic coast, but a 2-masted type served as a trader. Reported as early as the 16th century. Sharp ends; curved stem terminates in a tall stemhead, often with a forward-projecting beak; straight, vertical sternpost; straight keel; deep rudder, with tiller. Half-decked; steering well at the stern and scuttle hatch, or decked to just abaft the mast, with stern bench. The 2-masted traders set lugsails, the foremast stepped well forward. The **fishing boats** set a lateen sail and sometimes a flying jib to a light bowsprit and also used oars; now employ auxiliaries; crew of 5-7. Reported lengths 6-12m, widths 2-2.8m; traders ca. 30-60t. Other recorded names: **legut**, **leuto***, **lèuto dàlmata**, **lev(u)t**, **liuto**; pl. **leuti**
leuti See **leut**, **leuto**
leuto *Italy:* **1.** Beamy 19th-century sponge-**fishing boat*** and **coaster***; most often reported from Trapani in western Sicily. Full hull, especially above the waterline. Straight stem, raked inboard; narrow stern with a small transom, top strake at stern extended aft, creating a raised, false overhang. Keel; flat floors. Pronounced camber to deck; 2 hatchways; rudder outboard or came up through a hole inboard. Crew came aboard through this hole. Anchored from stern. Lateen sails set to 2 masts: the mainmast raking forward, the jigger mast vertical; 2 headsails run to bowsprit. Crew of 6 and a boy. Reported lengths 15-20m, beam one-third. The sharp-sterned cargo **leuti** (pl.) from Liguria and Tuscany employed a loose-footed gaff mainsail and a large, roughly square spinnaker hung from a tall boom at the bow. Carried various cargoes, but mainly wine. Reported lengths 15-20m, widths 4.34-4.48m, depth ca. 1.48m.
2. May also be a small **fishing boat** working out of Sicily and along the northern end of the Adriatic; still working in the 1960s. Sharp ends with curved stem; beak extends forward for ca. 75cm; vertical sternpost. Decked with long central hatch, or half-decked with large cockpit. Set a single lateen sail to a vertical or forward-raking mast; small jib to a jibboom. Also rowed with 4 or more oars. Crew of 5-10. Reported lengths 6-8m, widths 2-2.5m, depth 1.5-2m.
3. The term **liuto** may describe a ship with masts and sail taken down and employed as a **lighter***.
Other recorded names: **laoutelle**, **laoutello**, **laudo**, **laudus***, **lauteddu**, **lautello**, **laùto**, **lento**, **leüdo**, **leudus**,

leutu, liuta, liúto, lodo; pl. leüdi, liuti. Note also lahut, leut. Further references: gaeta, leut

leùto dàlmato See **leut**

leutu See **leuto**

Levant schooner See **shakhtura**

levt, levut See **leut**

le wary See **wary**

leythere See **lighter-2**

lgāreb See **agherrabo**

liang-chieh-thou, liang-chieh-t'ou See **liang jie tou**

liang jie tou *China, E:* Two-section vessel of the Grand Canal (Da Yunhe), operated mainly by northerners but traveling sometimes to Shanghai, carrying produce and grain. Constructed of complete halves, joined by iron pins, that were separated when negotiating sharp bends, when being hauled over obstacles, or when nosed against a bank to load or unload. Double-ended; bottom essentially flat but slightly athwartships as well as longitudinal rocker toward the ends; transverse planking at bow and stern ended in stem and transom beams; strengthened with bulkheads and strong frames. Hatch covered only with matting; crew accommodated in small compartment forward and low house aft. Wide, shoal-water, balanced rudder; post secured to an athwartship beam; long tiller extended to forward of the house; small leeboards in forward section. Tracked from shore or sailed; long bow and stern sweeps employed. Battened, rectangular sail hung from yard; mast easily struck by means of sheerlegs. Crew of up to 10. Reported lengths overall 27-46m; e.g., length ca. 27m, beam 3.5m, hold depth 1.1m, draft ca. 0.9m. Other recorded names: **articulated junk, jointed canal boat, liang-chieh-thou** (or **t'ou**), **two-section boat**. Note also **cao zi chuan**.

lia no *Papua New Guinea, SE:* Single-outrigger traveling **canoe*** of Rossel Island, the easternmost of the islands in the Louisiade Archipelago. Slender dugout hull with sharp, attenuated ends; hull round in cross section. Sides raised along the central portion by 2 lapped washstrakes; the side opposite the outrigger is vertical, the inner strakes slant outward; athwartships cane ties brace the strakes. Carved breakwaters at each end. Eight closely spaced booms extend to the float, which is about half the length of the hull. Most of the outboard area covered by a horizontal platform; in addition, a narrower platform slants downward from the side opposite the outrigger to the lower platform; supported by a gunwale rail on the outer washstrake and by knees braced into the hull. Each boom attached to the float by 2 pairs of undercrossed stanchions. Single mast stepped through the angled platform onto a shoe-spar that extends out across the horizontal platform to the float or may be steadied by a horizontal pole. Sets an oval mat sail (*lia*), lug-fashion. Steered with a paddle. Reported lengths 10-12m. Note also **no-1**.

Lian River coal boat See **dao ba zi-1**

libi See **lembo**

libo *Italy:* Early term for a **lighter*** used on rivers, canals, and in shallow ports to transfer cargo from larger vessels to shore. Name variant: **da libo**. See also **lembo**.

lichang See **kolek lichang**

lichter See **gaffelkaag, kaag-2, lighter-1**

Lichterboot See **lighter-1**

lichtschip See **lightship**

lichung See **kolek kue, kolek lichang, kueh buteh ketiri**

lie-down box See **sinkbox**

liendi See **londeh**

Lien River coal boat See **dao ba zi-1**

lifeboat Any craft used to save lives may be considered a **lifeboat**, although a more encompassing term is **survival craft**. Generally, however, the term applies to a boat built to rigid specifications and deployed either from a ship or from a house on shore by means of a slipway. Fully equipped with survival gear. Double-ended; wooden boats clinker or diagonally planked; also of steel. Buoyancy tanks at bow and stern and sometimes also beneath the thwarts; cork belts along the gunwales were used on some earlier craft. May be self-righting and/or self-bailing; some permanently inflated. Rowed, double-banked; mast and sail usually available. Generally 5.5-10.4m long. Modern shore-based **lifeboats** mostly motorized and employ sophisticated equipment. Selected name variants: **bajbot, baleinière de sauvetage, barco salvavidas, bateau de sauvetage, battello di salvataggio** (or **salvamento**), **bote***, **bote salvavidas, čamac za spasavanje, canot de sauvetage, canotte di salvataggio, Greathead lifeboat, kustreddingboot, lajbot(a), lancia de salvataggio, łódź ratunkowa, reddingsbaad** (or **-båd**), **redding(s)boot, redningsbåt, rescue boat, rešlni čoln, Rettungsboot, salvavidas, spasatel'naia** (**shliupka**). Note also **accident boat, life raft, paat, sea boat, ship's boat, surfboat**. Further reference: **hong chuan**

life float See **life raft**

life raft A buoyant craft, designed to support a number of people, placed aboard a vessel, generally in such a position that it will slide quickly overboard in an emergency. Usually designed to meet standard specifications. Now frequently an inflatable variety, some automatically inflating on contact with the water. A large, oval, ring-type **raft*** with a net suspended below it is called a **life float** or **Carley float** (nicknamed **doughnut**). Other recorded names: **balsa***, **balsa de salvamento, balsa salvavidas, Flossboot, inflatable (life) raft, jangada***, **jangada salvavidas, life-saving raft, pontoon raft, radeau pneumatique (de sauvetage), radeau de sauvetage gonflable, raft boat, redding(s)vloot, redningsfläde, rešilni splav, Rettungsfloss, salvagente collettivo, splav za spasavanje, zattera***, **zattera di salvamento** (or **di salvataggio**). Note also **ship's boat**.

life-saving raft See **life raft**

light boat **1.** Among rowed racing boats, one with a smooth skin might be called a **light boat** as distinct from the heavier clinker-built boats.

2. A boat that fishes with lights. Name variant: **bateau porte-feu**

3. *England, W:* So-called **light boats** were canal boats belonging to the Shropshire, Worcestershire, and Staffordshire Electric Power Company and carried coal to canalside power stations, beginning in 1915. Later, operated under different nationalized names. Traffic ceased in 1965.

4. *Scotland, S:* **Light boats** were introduced on the Monkland Canal in 1830. Carried ca. 150 passengers and were towed by 2 horses at ca. 11.3km per hour. Length 26m, beam 2m.
See also **canot léger, lightship.**

light canoe See **canot du nord, canot léger**
light cruiser See **cruiser-2**
lighter 1. Broadly, any small vessel employed in lightering goods. A strongly built, rectangular craft, open and flat-bottomed; used for short-haul work, especially for transferring cargo to and from a ship lying at anchor. Usually not self-propelled (**dumb lighter**), depending on the tide or a **tug★**. Sometimes a **lighter** may be designed to carry its load on deck only. Word dates at least from the late 15th century, when such vessels were needed to lighten ships, enabling them to cross harbor or river mouth bars. Selected name variants: **al(l)eggio, alibbo, alijador, al(l)ibo, allievo, barcassa, barcaza★, barcon★, hamnpråm, lægter, läktare, lanchón★, Lastponton, lastpråm, leggio, Leichter (schiff), lei(gh)ter, Lichter(boot), li(g)ter, likhter, liktare, limb, lixter, ly(gh)ter, mahona, moana, peniša, vlek.** Note also **allège, bacassa, barge, bo chuan, chiatta, dumb barge, gabare, gabarra, hoy-2, mavna, pram.**

2. *British Isles:* Term for a variety of open-hold vessels used on English rivers and canals. Averaged ca. 12m in length and 3m in breadth, but those on the Bridgewater Canal were as long as 23m. Term may also include sailing **barges★** with masts that can be lowered onto the deck. Spelling variant: **leythere.** Note also **Fenland lighter, Thames lighter.**

3. *England, SW:* In the Fal Estuary, a special open **lighter** transferred cargo from ships up to Truro after the mid-19th century when the Truro River was silting up. Propelled mainly by tide, a sweep, or poles, but set a standing lugsail when racing. 15-20t disp.

4. *Ireland, SW:* The **lighters** of the River Shannon in the late 17th and early 18th centuries were propelled by 4 men with 2 oars. Steered by a sweep. 12-16t.

5. *Northern Ireland:* Term given to an inland waterway **barge**, especially on the Lagan Navigation and the Newry and Ulster Canals. Most round-sterned, a few square. Constructed of pitch pine; some of steel in the late 19th century. Except for colored bulwarks and top strakes, generally painted white below gunwale level. Those on the Lagan had wide side decks, and a board and cloth covered the hatch. During the 19th century, many families lived on board. Motors installed on most, although some used horses until the 1950s. Tall square sails used in crossing Lough Neagh, but some were towed across the lake. Length of Newry vessels 18.9m, beam 4.4m, cap. to 80t; those on the Ulster Canal had to be narrower. Name variant: **barge**
Further references: **flicker, New York sailing lighter, Potomac fish lighter, sailing lighter, scow-1**

lighterman See **picard-1**
lighter of the gods See **shen bo zi**
light frigate See **corvette, frigate-1**

light galley See **galiot-1, galley-3**
lighthouse peapod See **peapod**
lighthouse tender See **beacon boat**
lighting skiff See **sneak skiff**
lightship 1. A strong, seaworthy vessel anchored near a shoal, ship channel, or wreck to serve as an aid to navigation. Ancient **lightships** used fires or torches, later lanterns or oil lamps. Now, like lighthouses, the beacon, set at the top of a mast, transmits in recognizable pulses, using a fixed code. Modern **lightships** also equipped with fog and underwater signaling equipment and radar beacons. Most lack self-propulsion and are towed to the site, although early vessels had a sail available should the vessel's anchor chain break. Gradually being replaced by buoys with automatic beacons. Those also serving as a pilot station called a **pilot lightship.** Selected name variants: **barco faro, barque faro, bateau feu, bateau phare, buque faro (or valiza), Feuerschiff, feu flottant, fireship★, floating light, fyrskepp, fyrskib, fyrskip, leuchtschiff, lichtschip, light boat★, light vessel, luz flotante, nave faro, navire balize, plavuchiy mayak, ponton phare, purbshrits, vuurschip.** Note also **beacon boat, mark boat-1.**

2. A **light ship** is one not carrying cargo or fuel.

light vessel See **lightship**
ligneur *France, W:* Small, solid boat that trawls for sea bass and mullet off the south Breton coast; may work lobster pots in summer. Sharp bow, transom stern. Originally sailed, now mainly motorized. Crew of 2 on motorized boats. Reported lengths 6.2-8m. See also **longliner-1.**
ligter See **gaffelkaag, lighter-1**
ligterkaag See **kåg-1**
liketta See **loquette**
likhter, liktare See **lighter-1**
Liling tao-pa-tzŭ See **dao ba zi-3**
lillbåt See **lillebåt**
lillebåd See **lillebåt-2**
lillebåt 1. *Finland:* Small, open boat used for fishing and general transportation. Clinker-built with broad strakes, hull ceiled amidships. Sharp, strongly raked ends; bow full, stern more tapered; stem mildly curved and cutaway below the waterline; sternpost straight. Rounded in cross section; short "T" keel; strong sheer. Reported lengths 4.5-5.3m; e.g., length overall ca. 5m, on bottom 2.2m, beam 1.4m, depth 0.5m. Spelling variant: **lillbåt**

2. *Norway, S:* General term applied to small, open boats between 4.6 and 5.8m long, especially those along the Kattegat, Skaggerak, and North Sea coasts. Popular as **ship's boats★** and general-purpose craft. Bluff bow, curved stem and sternpost, straight keel, flat floors. When sailed, set a spritsail and foresail. Mid-19th-century boat 4.9m long, ca. 2.2m wide, 0.75m deep. Spelling variant: **lillebåd**

3. *Sweden:* Sturdy, beamy boat built along the west coast and on Öland Island off the east coast. Frequently carried aboard **fishing boats★**; those from Öland Island used in herring fisheries. Double-ended with strong sheer; stem and sternpost straight below the waterline, curved above; straight keel. Clinker-built, narrow strakes; stern almost round; fairly flat floors. Mostly rowed, but at times, sets 2 spritsails. Small foremast stepped against the stem; mainmast a little forward of amidships. Reported lengths 4.8-5.85m, beam about one-half length. Other recorded names: **lillbåt; skebåt** (at Mollösund). Further reading: O. Hasslöf, *Bankskutor och Sjöbåtar i Bohuslän* (Skärhamn: Förlag Båtdokumnentations-gruppen, 1987), 38-44. Originally published 1939.

lille fregat See **frigate-1**
lilliputian See **Hooper Island crab skiff**
lillknärr See **knärr-2**
lil swimp boat See **lugger-3**
Lima-båt See **älvbåt**
limau wangkang See **wangkang**
limb See **lighter-1**
limba, limbe, limbo See **lembo**
lime-wooder See **Saint John River woodboat**
Limfjordskåg See **kåg-1**
Limfjordssjægt See **sjægt**
lin-åttring See **åttring-3**
Lincoln catch *England, E:* **Keel**★-type vessel used on the River Witham in Lincolnshire. Sharp bow; overhanging, sharp stern; tiller came in over the rail. Set square sails to a single mast. Length on keel 19m, maximum draft 1.68m. Name variant: **Lincoln ketch**
Lincoln keel See **Humber keel**
Lincoln ketch See **Lincoln catch**
Lincolnshire keel See **Humber keel**
Lincolnshire sloop See **Humber sloop**
Lincolnville wherry See **salmon wherry**
line-åttring See **åttring-3**
line boat 1. *England, E:* The **line boats** out of Lowestoft fish for cod from October to early June. Some have automatic line-haulers for the 30 longlines used. May be fitted in summer with a small winch for trawling for sole. Length ca. 9m.
2. *Scotland:* **a.** Small Shetland Island boat used for line fishing and local transportation. Open; sharp, raked ends; marked sheer. Length on keel ca. 3m. **b.** The **line boat** at Ardrishaig on Loch Fyne in western Scotland was open with sharp, curved ends. Low locker at the stern; outboard rudder; tiller. Rowed and sailed. Oars worked against single tholepins. Mast stepped against forward thwart. Set a lugsail. Bowsprit braced against a forward crossbeam. Length 5.2m. Note also **line skiff. c.** The **Portpatrick line boat** in southwestern Scotland was a 2-masted, lug-rigged **fishing boat**★ designed to take the ground in the harbor. Clinker-built; sharp but full ends, both raked; beam keel; open. Foremast stepped well forward, mainmast amidships; both strikable. Dipping forelug; boomed, standing main lug. Also rowed, 4 paired tholepins. Reported lengths 5.5-6.1m; e.g., length overall 5.5m, on keel 4.7m, beam 2.03m, depth with keel 0.96m. Name variant: **Portpatrick line skiff**
3. *United States:* An early 19th-century corporation-owned **canal boat**★ that carried both passengers and small, mixed express freight. Smaller, often less elaborately appointed, and slower than the **packet boats**★. Some on the Erie Canal had a galley and tables in a

stern compartment, freight area amidships, and space for sleeping and sitting at the bow. Pairs of fresh horses and mules and crews available at shore relay stations; on some midwestern canals, mules were transported on board. Many converted to steam by the mid-19th century. **Line boats** on the Erie Canal carried about 20 passengers. Name variant: **emigrant boat**
Further reference: **nabbie-1**
line fisher, linefiskebåt See **longliner-1**
liner 1. In a precise sense, a ship or vessel belonging to a particular shipping company, but the term now applied more broadly to those sailing on a regular schedule and following a specified route. Vary from carrying mostly cargo with a few passengers (**cargo liner**) to primarily passengers with little cargo. Other recorded names: **Fahrgastdampfer, Linienfahrer, Linienschiff, linjalaiva, linjefartyg, Passagier-dampfer, transatlántico, Überseedampfer, Überseefrachter**
2. A line-of-battle ship, generally wooden. Term used in the mid-19th century.
See also **cod smack-1, longliner-1, packet boat-1**.
line skiff *Scotland, W:* Small, open boat that fished with long lines off beaches in the western fjords. Line often shot and hauled from a **line skiff** towed by a larger, motorized craft. Sharp ends, curved and raked; clinker-built; narrow washstrake. Set a standing lugsail, jib to bowsprit. Strikable mast stepped against the forward thwart. Rowed with as many as 6 oars. Reported lengths 5.18-5.5m; e.g., length overall 5.18m, on keel 4.9m, beam 1.5m, inside depth 0.5m, draft 0.43m. Name variant: **Largs line skiff**. Note also **line boat, Loch Fyne skiff**. Further reference: **trotliner**
line trawler, linfiskebåt See **longliner-1**
li niao *China, E:* 1. **Fishing boat**★ of the Shantou (Swatow) area. Worked with a bamboo **raft**★, the **zhu pai**★, suspending a net between them. Crew of 3. Other recorded names: **loi chiu, loi jiu**
2. Cargo boat of the Shantou River. Stepped 2 masts to which mat sails were hung. Crew slept on deck, the full area below consigned to cargo.
Linienfahrer, Linienschiff, linjalaiva, linjefartyg See **liner-1**
Linzerzille See **Zille**
lipa *East Malaysia/Philippines, S:* Plank-extended **dugout canoe**★ of the Bajau of Mindanao, the Sulu Archipelago, and the northeast coast of Borneo. Lacks the outriggers of similar craft of the area. Used for transportation and fishing. One or 2 planks added to the dugout base; broad, spatulate, upturned stem piece, some with an inboard rake; steep rise to the floors; low freeboard, considerable sheer forward. Long, straight keel may extend forward to form a bifid bow. Some have a thatched-roof hut, often serving as a permanent home. May be carved at the ends or along the sides. Steered with a paddle on the quarter. Pole mast on which an oblong, boomed, lug-type sail is set. Reported lengths 6.1-12.5m. Name variant: **lepa, lipa-lipa**★. Note also **vinta**. Further reference: **djênging**
lipa-lipa *East Malaysia:* **Outrigger canoe**★ of the Bajau peoples of eastern Sabah State. Uses a single- or double-outrigger, with direct attachments. Dugout hull with

rounded bottom, gunwales elaborately carved, steered with a paddle on the quarter. Horseshoe-shaped sail, square top; sail often adorned with various devices. See also **lepa-lepa**, **lipa**.

lip-lip See **lepa-lepa**

lippa-lippa *Australia, N:* Adapted by the aborigines of Arnhem Land from the **lepa-lepa***, which was brought by Indonesians for their trepang-collecting forays. Now used for transportation, for carrying shellfish from beds, and as a platform for spearing fish. Bluff-ended **dugout canoe*** excavated and shaped by burning and carving; on some, residual stem and sternpost flatten at the top and recurve; flat floors. Lacks outrigger of the Indonesian **canoes***. Paddled; may be sailed, setting a square sail of woven pandanus leaves. Large **canoe** 7m long, beam 1.0m, cap. 1.0t. Note also **lippee-lippee**.

lippee-lippee *Australia, N:* Bark **canoe*** of the indigenous peoples of Coburg Peninsula, Northern Territory. Constructed of a single piece of bark; ends joined with a vine-like rope. Shape preserved by poles laced to the gunwales, bark strips that stretched from one side to the other, and short pieces of bark laid transversely across the bottom. Could transport about 8 people. Length 5.5m, beam 0.6m. Name variant: **canoa***. Note also **lippa-lippa**.

liquette, liquette genevoise See **loquette**
liquid cargo barge See **tank barge**
liquiette See **loquette**
liquor boat See **tank boat**
lirret See **lerret**
lis-alis See **alis-alis**
Liselejebåd See **Isefjordsbåd**

lisi *Solomon Islands, western Pacific:* Reported as a class of large, plank-built **canoes*** originating in the southeastern part of the archipelago, notably on San Cristobal, Ulawa, Malaita, and Guadalcanal. Characterized by raised washstrakes at each end and usually by tall end pieces of roughly the same height. Most are seagoing and used in trading and conducting official visits to neighboring islands. Built up from 1-2 bottom planks. On the larger **canoes**, keel added to beveled garboard strakes; 2-3 beveled strakes form the sides, sewn on. Single-piece ribs, lashed to eyed cleats, also form the support for seats. Special gunwales of palm wood protect top strake from wear by the paddles. Rounded bottom, soft turn of the bilges. Ends curve up from below the waterline, terminating in tall, plank end pieces; inboard, the end pieces form the washstrakes and continue for a short distance toward the middle. **Canoes** that remain in sheltered waters generally lack end pieces. Those belonging to chiefs are inlaid with several thousand pieces of cone shell and decorated with tassels and nautilus shells; such a boat is called a **la'o**, and in order to collect money for its construction, a specially decorated **canoe**, an **iola atoato**, is sent on a fund-raising mission. Paddles have long, narrow blades and a crutch grip; steered with longer paddle from a seat on the gunwale. Length 12.8m, beam 1.5m, depth 0.9m. An ordinary **canoe** of this type is called **lisi nima**, **lisi nume**, **lusuinima**, or

lusuinume; one without end pieces may be called **iola pwa k'ou**, **soro***, **sorosoro**, or **suro**. Note also **sosoro**.
lisi nima, lisi nume See **lisi**
lisjefæring See **færing-3**
listabåt, listerbaad, listerbaat See **listerbåt**
listerbåt *Norway:* Term applied to the fast, seaworthy boat that originated ca. 1830 on the Lista Peninsula on the south coast, as a modification of the **hardangerbåt*** of the west coast and of the east coast boats. Adopted elsewhere to the west and north and called a **listring** in the Nordland area. Mainly a **fishing boat*** for mackerel and herring, working until the end of the 19th century. Clinker-planked with 6 frames and breasthook at the ends; concave waterlines; sharp ends. Curved stem, cutaway forefoot; straight or slightly curved sternpost. Outboard rudder; tiller. Open with narrow side decks until ca. 1860; later half-decked, with cabin forward, or fully decked (see **skøyte-4**). Early boats stepped a mast through a forward thwart, setting a square- or spritsail, staysail, jib to a running bowsprit, and sometimes a topsail. Later substituted a gaff sail. Also rowed. Crew of 4 in the south, 4-7 in the north. Reported lengths overall 7-12m; e.g., length overall 12m, on keel 9m, beam 4.6m, depth 1.4m. Other recorded names: **listabåt**, **listerbaad**, **listerbaat**, **listringer**, **lysterbåt**, **lystreng**, **lystring**. Note also **lestabåt**, **seksæring-1**.
listerskjøite, listersköite, listerskøyte See **skøyte-4**
listring, listringer See **listerbåt**
liten fregat, liten fregatt See **frigate-1**
liter See **lighter-1**
lith See **gal**
little boat *United Kingdom:* **1.** Term sometimes used by trawlermen for their **dinghy***.
2. Off Sheringham on the east coast, the so-called **little boats** worked inshore drifting for herring, mainly for bait, during the early part of the 20th century. Set a single lugsail and jib, the latter used alone while the nets were set.
See also **seine boat-5a**.
little mizzener See **dandy**
little packet *England, west-central:* Term given to the small, elegant **tugs*** used on the Bridgewater Canal to tow the **barges***, towing 4 at once. Dated from the 1870s to ca. World War II. Name variant: **Jack Sharp**
liuger See **lugger-1**
liu peng *China, SE:* A thinly planked boat that carried passengers up many of the rivers on the southeast

liu peng

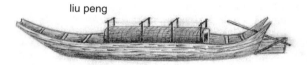

coast. High bow. Large bamboo house amidships. Oars stowed on a framework above the house when not in use. Shallow draft. Other recorded names: **liu p'eng ch'uan**, **paper boat***, **six mat boat**
liu p'eng ch'uan See **liu peng**
liuta, liuti See **leuto**

liuto See **leudo, leut, leuto**

liu wang chuan *China, central coast:* Fast, sprit-rigged **fishing boat★** from Ningbo (Ningpo) that worked mainly in pairs: the **fishing boat**, called **wang chuan (net boat★)**, and the **feeder boat** (called **wei chuan★**) that carried food, water, and other supplies. A similar boat working in the nearby Zhoushan (Chusan) Islands has been called **dai chuan**. Wedge-shaped, raking stem; raked stern with oval transom; abrupt sheer at the stern; flat bottom; flared sides; several heavy wales along each side. Hull strengthened with multiple bulkheads and frames. Decked; arched mat cabin or planked house abaft the mast. Outboard rudder worked with a special sculling device, the *yuloh*; used in calms, with the high planking at the stern removed. Short, forward-raking foremast stepped in the eyes; mainmast stepped about one-third inboard. Staysail between the masts. Crew of 7-8. Reported length 17.4m, beam 3.8m, depth 1.14m, cap. 50t. Other recorded names: **fish carrier, floating net boat; tai ch'uan, tai tch'ouan**

live barge *United States, central:* Large, **barge★**-like craft of the Mississippi River area. Served as a **fish car★** or might be moored at a fish market to store live fish. Watertight bulkhead at each end; compartmented area between had slotted sides to permit fresh water circulation. Fish removed by pumping the bulkheads dry and scooping them out. Name variant: **bulkhead**

live boat See **fish car, tow car**

live box See **tow smack**

live car See **fish car, pasni, tow car**

live-fish car See **tow car**

live fish-carrier See **yu chuan-2**

live-fish transporter See **fish carrier**

Liverpool sider See **longboat-4**

live-well boat See **well boat**

living boat See **sponge boat-3**

living buoy See **mark boat-1**

lixter See **lighter-1**

ljuger See **lugger-1**

llagoster See **langostero**

llagut, llahut See **laúd**

llampuguera *Spain, E:* Boat used in fishing for pompano dolphin, mainly out of Cartagena and the Balearic Islands. Spelling variant: **lampuguera**

Llangollen coracle See **Dee coracle**

llanxa, llanxe See **lancha-11**

llaúd, llaút See **laúd**

llondro See **londra-2**

lobster and sprat punt See **sprat punt**

lobster boat **1.** Tends lobster traps. Often has a live well. Clinker- or carvel-planked; open or half-decked. Rowed, sailed, or motorized. Note also **dory-6, Hummerboot, Kreeftenbark, Kreeftenboot, Kreeftenkotter, langostero, langoustier, lobsterman, lobster smack.**
2. *Canada, E:* The type used in the 1930s in Northumberland Strait, between Prince Edward Island and the mainland, was a fast, open boat powered by a gasoline engine. Sharp entrance, plumb stem, square stern. Usually wide side decks and short fore- and stern decks. Lengths to ca. 12m.

3. *England, SE:* Small, open boat found on the beach at Rottingdean, east of Brighton. Carvel-planked with wide top strake, bluff bow; deep, curved stem; transom stern. Rowed, sculled, and sailed. Note also **sprat punt**.
4. *United States, NE:* **a.** Several types of small boats have tended lobster traps in the New England area; some built exclusively for this purpose; others also engaged in fishing. Before 1900, **sloop★**-rigged boats were popular on the Maine coast, as were the open, double-ended **peapods★**, and **dories** (see **dory-6b**). The **sloop**-rigged boats generally had a sharp bow and shallow transom, and employed a centerboard. Half-decked with a large cockpit that might be used in winter to store the lobsters to keep them from freezing. Gaff-rigged with the mainsail boomed; jib to a light bowsprit. Most **lobster boats** now of wood or fiberglass and fully motorized with hull modifications to accommodate the engine. Generally worked single-handed, but sometimes with a 2nd man. Reported lengths 5.5-12m; e.g., length 7.6m, beam 2.4-3m. Name variant: **lobster sloop**. Note also **Friendship sloop, Matinicus boat, Muscongus Bay sloop, Noank sloop, Nomans Land boat, two-sail lobster boat. b.** The 2-masted, sprit-rigged **lobster boats** of Massachusetts and Cape Cod Bays had a reputation for being fast, weatherly, and handy. Developed at Plymouth in the early 19th century; as working boats, remained essentially the same into the 20th century. Became popular as a local racing boat, with modifications to increase their speed. Lapstrake or carvel planking depending on the builder; some Kingston boats were strip-planked. Hollow garboards; slight drag to the keel; low or steep rise to the floors; moderate sheer. Bluff bows, later sharper; slightly raked stem. Mainly counter-sterned; the racing models had extreme counters. Oval cockpit; centerboard. Rudderpost came up through the counter; tiller. Foremast (often called the mainmast when **ketch★**-rigged) stepped well forward; sail loose-footed and overlapped the after mast. Smaller after sail boomed. Used only the foresail when picking up lobster pots. Sprits held to strops high on the masts. Boats from Hull had a taller rig than to the south. Rowed easily. Crew of 1-2 on workboats. Reported lengths 4.9-6.1m; e.g., length between perpendiculars 5.3m, beam 1.5m. Other recorded names: **Hull, Kingston, North Shore**, or **Plymouth lobster boat**. Note also **two-sail lobster boat**. Further references: **Guernsey crab boat, lobster smack**

lobster car See **fisherman's car**

lobster catcher boat See **cray boat**

lobsterman *United States, E:* Type of fast **Sea Bright skiff★** of the early 1920s used on the northern New Jersey coastal bays. Vertical transom. Reported lengths 7.9-8.5m.

lobster sloop See **lobster boat-4a, Muscongus Bay sloop**

lobster smack *United States, NE:* Vessel that collects lobsters from local fishermen and carries them to canneries or market. May be **dry smacks** with no well, being close to markets or able to transport the lobsters packed in ice. **Wet** (or **well**) **smacks** have a well that can be flooded for carrying lobsters to distant distribution centers. Many of the **smacks**★ engage in off-season fishing. **Schooner**★- or **sloop**★-rigged; then motorized with a steadying sail. Crew of 2-7. Measured 6-45t. Between ca. 1915 and 1970, Maine **lobster smacks** were built with engines. Mainly transported lobsters from offshore islands to mainland distribution and/or processing centers. Trunk cabin aft; mast and loading boom forward. Name variant: **lobster boat**★

Loch Fyne line skiff See **Loch Fyne skiff**

Loch Fyne nabbie, Loch Fyne nabby See **nabbie-1**

Loch Fyne skiff *Scotland, W:* Found in the Firth of Clyde, especially in Loch Fyne, where it was used for herring fishing during the late 19th and early 20th centuries. Originally small and open (the **Loch Fyne line skiff**), but as they increased in size and became half-decked and resembled the **nabbie**★, they were sometimes called **nabbies** in this area. Worked in pairs. Originally clinker-planked, later carvel; double-ended with the stern fuller than the bow; bold sheer. Stem vertical with cutaway forefoot; sternpost sharply raked. Drag to the deep keel, steep rise to the floors, soft bilges. Half-decked **skiffs**★ had a small cuddy forward; carvel-built boats generally fully decked with fish hold amidships; net laid on the stern sheets.

Loch Fyne skiff

Carried movable sandbag ballast. Early boats 2-masted, the lug mizzen serving as a steadying sail; later single-masted. Mast stepped well forward and raked aft sharply, but angle adjusted as the standing lugsail was reefed; mast stepped through slot in deck and could be lowered. Running bowsprit, long on the later boats; carried 3 jibs, setting the one most suitable. The smaller **Loch Fyne line skiff** carried no jib. Sails tanned. Also used oars, some 7.6m long, worked between double tholepins. Later boats had auxiliaries and were **canoe**★-sterned. Crew of 4 and sometimes a boy. Reported lengths overall 9-12m, widths 2.74-3.66m, depths 1.52-1.91m; deep draft aft; early **skiffs** ca. 4.57-7.62m long. Further reading: Angus Martin, *The Ring-Net Fishermen* (Edinburgh: John Donland Publishers, Ltd., 1981), 76-97. Note also **line skiff, ring-net boat, zulu skiff**.

lod' Czech generic term for **boat**★, **vessel**★, or **ship**★. A large vessel is a **lodiště**, and a small boat is a **lodice**. Spelling variants: **lodi**; pl. **lodě**.

lodde See **lodka-3**

loddefisker See **capelanier**

Loddinger See **lodka-3**

lodě See **lod'**

łódeczka See **lodka**

łódek, lodge, lodgen See **łódź**

lodger, lodgie See **lodka-3**

lodhia *India, NW:* Gill net **fishing boat**★ of the coastal waters of southwestern Kathiawar Peninsula. Carvel-planked, raked bow with deep forefoot, sharp stern, strong keel, small rudder. Decked at stern. Mainmast stepped in bow quarter, mizzen in stern quarter. Sets lateen sails. Also rowed. Reported lengths 6.1-7.6m, widths 1.4-1.7m, depths 0.84-0.91m, draft 0.38-0.53m. Other recorded names: **hoda**★, **Verāval lodhia**. See also **lodka-3**.

lodi See **Lädine, lod', lodka-3**

lodia See **lodka-3**

lodice See **lod'**

lodička See **lodka**

Lodie, lodija, lodika See **lodka-3**

Lödine, Lödin-Schiff See **Lädine**

lodiště See **lod'**

lodiya See **lad'ya**

lodja *Estonia:* A beamy, square-sailed craft of Lake Peipus (Chudskoye Ozero) on the eastern border of Estonia. Early boats transported bulk cargo and passengers; only cargo in the 20th century. Worked to World War II. Clinker-planked with treenails, ribs set ca. 75cm apart; keel; rounded bilges with flared sides; double-ended; raked, straight stem and sternpost. Outboard rudder, wide-bladed below the waterline. Decked at ends and along the sides; open waist covered with detachable hatches. The tall, square sail was boomed and loose-footed; raised with a hand winch. Could also be towed from the mast by as many as 10 men. Later vessels operated by steam. Length 23m, beam 14m, depth 2m. See also **lodka-3a**.

lodje See **lodka**

lodjor See **lodka-3a**

lodka In several eastern European languages, the word **lodka** and its related spellings designate a **boat**★, **canoe**★, or **wherry**★. May be rowed, paddled, or sailed.
1. Those used in the eastern Baltic Sea area resembled a small **cog**★. Most were river craft, but those with deeper hulls served as **coasters**★. Worked under sail, stepping a single mast or **ketch**★-rigged, but could be towed by horses. Crew of 3-4.
2. *Romania:* A frequently identified **lodka** is a long, narrow, **canoe**-type craft popular in the Danube Delta area. Used for transportation, carrying produce, and fishing, notably for sturgeon. Curved stem and sternpost, the bow reaching higher than the stern; flat floors; considerable flare topsides. Generally a heavy outwale, the widely spaced ribs extending to top of the sheer strake. Mainly rowed, usually against a single tholepin; steered with a paddle with a T-grip. Sometimes sets 1-2 spritsails to stubby masts. Those used in sturgeon fishing are towed to the offshore sites. Reported lengths 4.6-7.6m. Spelling variant: **lotca**
3. *Russia:* Several types, described below, existed throughout Russia at different times. Other recorded

spellings: **ladi(i)a**, **ladija**, **lad'ishcha**, **ladiya**, **lad'ja**, **lad'ya**, **lodde**, **loddinger**, **lodger**, **lodgie**, **lodhia**, **lodi**, **lodia**, **lodie**, **lodija**, **lodika**, **lodiya**, **lodja**, **lodje**, **lodjor**, **lodk(e)y**, **lod'ya**, **lotia**, **lotkey**, **lydjor**; dim. **ladejka**, **lad'iskha**; pl. **lodki**. Further reading: Carl Olof Cederland, "The Lodja and Other Bigger Transport Vessels Built in the East-European Clinker-Building Technique" in: Sean McGrail and Eric Kentley, eds. *Sewn Plank Boats* (Greenwich, England: National Maritime Museum, 1985 [BAR International Series 276]), 233-252.

lodka-3

a. From the 15th to the early 17th century, the northern vessels were clinker-built, the planks sewn with willow and caulked with moss; top strake might be set flush. High sides; double-ended with a strong sheer; bluff bows; curved or straight, raked stem; flat floors; tall, narrow rudder; decked. Set a square sail amidships or spritsails; staysail. Often poled. Used for trading and fishing. Crew of 8-10. Reported length 30m, beam 5-6m. Similar vessels (the **lodja★** or **lodjor**) were used by the Swedish navy in the Baltic in the 16th-17th centuries to transport troops, supplies, and plunder; to scout; and to engage in local shipyard work. Some 2-masted. Name variant: **Karelian ladja**. **b.** An 18th- and 19th-century 3-masted **coaster** operated in the White Sea area, some traveling to Norway. In summer, might hunt walrus and seals. Keel; bluff bows, strongly rounded stem; oval transom stern with windows. Decked, with poop deck. The fore- and mainmast set square or lugsails; foremast stepped in the bow and the sail tacked to a bumkin. Mizzenmast set a boomed gaff sail or a lugsail. Manned by as many as 80 men. Reported lengths 11-22m, widths 3.1-5.3m, depths 2.1-3.4m. Name variants: **pomor ladia**, **pomor lodja**. **c.** Cargo vessels of the 18th-19th centuries were mainly river craft. Flat bottom, decked, **sloop★**-rigged. **d.** A **lotka** might be a coastal or river vessel, generally transporting merchandise and passengers, but also used for fishing. Some sailed on the Black and Caspian Seas. One type had a sharp, raking bow; stem ran to just above the waterline. Sharp stern with small, high transom; straight keel; flat floors; strong sheer, especially forward. Decked; low poop deck. Mainmast set a gaff sail with 2 square sails forward of the mast; mizzenmast stepped forward of the poop with a gaff sail sheeted to an outrigger. Sharply rising bowsprit with jib. Some merely 4-oared **rowboats★**. **e.** A 19th-century Siberian river **lodka** utilized a dugout hull to which planks were added; ribs of fir fastened with osier lacing. Midships area covered by a tarpaulin or tarred cloth or skins. Set a square sail amidships. Crew of 2. Reported

lengths 6.4-8.5m, widths 1.1-1.5m, draft 0.6m. **f.** On the lower Yenisei River in central Russia, a **lodka** was a sharp-ended **rowing boat★**. Planks fastened with wooden pegs. Flat bottom, fair sheer. Length to ca. 7m.
4. *Sweden:* See **3a** above.
5. *Ukraine:* The Don River **lodka** of the 17th century had a long, raking bow and a narrow, raked, V-shaped transom. Dugout hull; flat bottom, flaring sides, moderate sheer, open. Set a square sail amidships. Length ca. 13.7m, beam 3.1m, depth 1.4m.

Further references: **lad'ya**, **łódź**. Spelling variants: Bulgarian: **lódka**, **lótka**; Czech/Slovak: **lod'★**, **lod´ka**, **lodička** (dim.); Polish: **łódka** (pl. **łódki**), **łódeczke** (dim.); Romanian: **lodka**, **lotcă**, **lotka**; Russian: **lodka**, **lodochenko** and **lodochka** (dims.); pl. **lodki**, **lodky**; Ukrainian: **lódka** (pl. **lódki**); Slovonic: **ladiji** or **aludiji**

lodki, **lodky** See **lodka**

lodo See **leuto**

lodochenka, **lodochka** See **lodka**

lodra See **moliceiro**

lodsbaad See **losbåt-1**

lodsbåd   *Denmark:* Provided pilots to ships passing through the Øresund Strait between Denmark and Sweden. Strongly built with clenched planking; sharp forward, fuller at stern; strong sheer; deep, straight keel; some with drag; soft bilges, flared sides. Decked after 1860; open waist, semicircular cockpit aft.

lodsbåd

Motorized boats fully decked with wheelhouse aft. Hewn rudder; tiller. Painted red below the waterline, green above; vertical red stripe on the sail and letter H (for Helsingør) identified the craft as a **pilot boat★**. Stepped a single short mast with loose-footed gaff mainsail, 2 headsails, and sometimes a topsail. Crewed by a single man and carried 1-5 pilots. Worked as a sailing craft until the 1930s. Reported lengths 8.8-10m, widths 3.2-3.6m, depth 1.4m, draft 1.3-1.5m. Name variant: **lodsdæksbåd**. Note also **smakkejolle**.

lodsbåt See **losbåt-1**

lodsche See **łódź**

lodsdæksbåd See **lodsbåd**

lodsskøite, **lodsskøyte** See **losbåt-1**, **skøyte-3**

lod'ya See **lodya-3**

lodyga   *Poland, N:* Open boat used for fishing on the lower reaches of the Vistula to the early part of the 20th century. Sharp rising ends, flat bottom, lapped planking, flaring sides. Relatively large, narrow, shallow.

łódź   *Poland:* General term for a **boat★**. Combines with other terms, such as **łódź rybacka** (**fishing boat★**) and

łódź ratunkowa (lifeboat★). A small boat or **dinghy★** is a **łódka★** (pl. **łódek**). Spelling variants: **łodzi(a)**, **ludeczka**, **ludka**; German: **Lodgen, Lodsche**

lodzi, lodzia See **łódź**

łódź podjazdowa See **Handkahn-1**

łódź ratunkowa See **lifeboat, łódź**

łódź rybacka See **fishing boat, łódź**

löffelbagger See **spoon dredger**

lofotbåt See **fembøring-1**

log barge See **barge-11j**

logboat See **dugout canoe**

log boom See **boom-2**

log bronc See **boom boat-2**

log canoe See **Chesapeake Bay log canoe, dugout canoe**

log-driving batteau See **lumberman's batteau**

loger See **lugger-1**

logger *Netherlands:* **1.** Large **fishing boat★** imported from France in the early 1860s but subsequently built and modified in the Netherlands. Mainly drifted and trawled (**treillogger**) for herring in the North Sea, but some transported fish (**vrachtlogger**). Initially built of wood; after 1890, built of steel. Sharp lines, especially above the waterline; straight, vertical stem; raked, flat or elliptical counter; steep rise to the floors. Decked; deep bulwarks; no live well, the fish being salted down. Initial vessels stepped 3 lug-rigged masts; when trawling became important, adopted a **ketch★** rig. Mainmast set a loose-footed gaff sail and could be struck; fidded topmast carried a jackyard topsail. Mizzen boomed but loose-footed; topsail. Long, running bowsprit; 2-3 headsails; mizzen staysail. Engines adopted around the beginning of the 20th century (**stoomlogger** or **motorlogger**). Crew of 10-15. Reported lengths 17-29m; e.g., length 24.2m, beam 6.5m, depth 3.1m. The German **Logger** is essentially the same, but some were **coasters★**, often going into the Baltic. Last wooden fishing **Logger** built in 1910. Other recorded names: Netherlands: **haringlogger, loggerman, loggerschip, vislogger, Vlaardingen herringlogger** (incorrectly), **Vlaardinger logger** (or **Heringslogger**), **Vlaardingse häringlogger, zeillogger**; Germany: **Glückstädter Heringslogger, Härings-logger, Heringslogger, Segellogger**
2. Also a small warship. Clinker-built; deep draft aft. Stepped a main- and foremast and a small mizzen; topsails.
Further references: **drifter, kotter, lugger**

loggerbom See **bom-2**

loggerman, loggerschip See **logger**

loggher See **lugger-1**

logging bateau See **Charleston bateau, lumberman's batteau**

lógo-sáka See **wo´te**

log raft See **timber raft**

logre See **lugger**

lohor See **perahu buatan barat**

loi chiu, loi jui See **li niao-1**

loja See **ladja-1**

loju See **te-puke**

loketta See **loquette**

lola *India, NW:* An early oceangoing ship of the Konkan area. One of the **long ship★** types; considered a bad-luck vessel. Length 19.3m, beam 3.7m, depth 2.9m. See also **guli**.

loma See **Lomme**

lombo See **lambo**

Lomm See **Lomme**

Lomme *Poland, NE/Russia, Kalingrad Oblast:* Full-bodied vessel from Zalew Wiślany (Frisches Haff or Vistula Lagoon) that traded to Gulf of Danzig (Gdańsk) and Baltic ports until World War II. Majority built at the East Prussian town of Tolkemit (now Tolkmicko), and are thus called **Tolkemiter Lomme**. Clinker-planked, T-keel, flat floors, rounded bilges. Full bow; wide, flat stem; raked counter stern, often with windows. Rudder stock came up through the counter; tiller; leeboards. Decked; cabin aft; hatch abaft the mainmast; largest had 2nd hold; low bulwarks. Variously rigged, depending on size. Smallest as a **cutter★**, larger as a **ketch★** (**Galeasslomme** or **Lommgaleasse**), largest as a **schooner★** (**Schonerlomme, Schunerlomme**). Sails tanned yellow or dark brown. Carried a blue and red pennant. The **Lomme-yacht** usually had a keel and single mast; later **ketch-**rigged. Motorized in early 20th century. Reported lengths 15-20.5m, widths 5.6-6.8m; a small type ranged from 3-3.7m long. Other recorded names: **loma, Lomm, lomy, Frachtlomme, tolkmicko loma, Tolkmitter Lomme**. Further reading: Siegfried Fornaçon and Gerhard Salemke, *Lommen und Buxer. Volkstümliche Schiffe in Ost- und Westpreussen* (Brilon-Gudenhagen: Selbstverlag Historischer Schiffbau, 1988). Note also **Entenlomme, Erdlomme, Handlomme, Schiesslomme, żakówka, zig**.

Lommenfischer See **żakówka**

Lommeyacht See **Lomme**

Lommgaleasse See **Lomme**

Lommsicken See **zig**

lomy See **Lomme**

londe *Indonesia, central:* Generic term for a **perahu★** in the Masenrempulu dialect of southwestern Sulawesi (Celebes).

londé See **londeh**

londeh *Indonesia, central:* Double-**outrigger canoe★** that works with lines and cast nets off northeastern Sulawesi (Celebes) and the Sangihe and Talaud Islands to the northeast. Dugout hull; long ram projection at the bow and a shorter one at the stern. On some large **canoes★**, a strake raises the sides; bottom flat athwartships, rocker fore-and-aft; strong sheer at the ends. Two widely spaced booms cross the hull; the forward boom curves down to attach directly to the floats; the after boom is straight and connects to the floats by means of a stick that curves upward from the middle of the boom before dropping down to attach to the float. Floats set well forward, and bow ends sharp. Mast braced against the forward boom. Small, boomed, oblong sail; angle and position of each end controlled by ropes to the yard, made fast to belaying pins on the outriggers. Crew of 3. Reported lengths 6-9m, widths 0.61-0.76m, depth ca. 0.15m. Other recorded names: **dondei, liendi, londé, lond(e)i**

londei, londi See **londeh**

londo See **londra-1**

London River lighter See **Thames lighter**
London River sailing barge See **Thames sailing barge**
London tilt boat See **tilt boat-2**
London wherry *United States, NE:* **Rowing boat**★ built largely in the Boston area in the late 19th century. Designed for 3 oarsmen, the middle man rowing with 2 oars, the others with one oar each. Name variant: **randan**★. See also **Thames wherry**.
londra **1.** *Italy:* Lightly armed ship engaged in commerce of the 14th-17th centuries and capable of making long voyages. A **galley**★ type, they were low-sided and undecked. Large types rowed with as many as 25 oars on each side; also set lateen sails. Spelling variants: **londo**, **londre**, **londrum**, **londrus**, **lontra**★, **lontro** (pl. **lontri**); Catalan: **llondro**. Note also **feluca-2**.
  2. *Turkey:* Ship of the 17th-18th centuries; a large, fast, oared vessel used by the Turks to patrol the Black Sea coast and to make raids against the Cossacks. Crew and soldiers numbered ca. 150. Spelling variants: **lountra**, **lundra**★; pl. **londre**
  Further reference: **lundra**
londre, **londrum**, **londrus** See **londra**
lôndwin See **lundwin**
long Gaelic term for a **ship**★, either merchant or naval. May specifically designate a 3-masted, square-rigged ship. Spelling variant: pl. **longa**.
longa See **long**
longa navis See **long ship**
long barque See **barque longue**
longboat **1.** A **ship's boat**★, generally the largest aboard a **man-of-war**★ or **merchantman**★. Reported as early as the 15th century; in the British Royal Navy, it was superseded by the **launch**★ in the late 18th century. Originally it was the boat stowed forward of the mainmast. Used mainly to lay anchors and to carry drinking water, stores, and ballast, and as a **lifeboat**★; sometimes armed. Often had a davit in the bow to assist in working the anchor. Strong, generally open boat of carvel or clinker construction; some as long as half the length of the ship and consequently towed. Slightly raked transom stern, curved stem, full bow, flat floors, deadwood aft. Steered by tiller and rudder from stern bench. Rowed, 2 men to each thwart, with as many as 18 oars, either between double tholepins or oarports. Lug- or gaff-rigged; initially loose-footed, then boomed; 2 headsails. Lengths 6-16m; generally the shorter lengths were in later years, but size usually commensurate with ship size. Mid-18th-century boat 8.5m long, 2.4m wide; length generally 3.5-3.8m times the breadth. Other recorded names: **barkas**★, **Barkass(e)**, **bote lancha**, **grande chaloupe**, **great boat**★, **grete boat**, **gro(o)te boot**, **Grossboot**, **Grosse Boot**, **lang bote**, **longbo(a)te**. Note also **chaloupe-2**, **langabote**, **Schlup-1**, **scialuppa**, **sloep**, **sloop-4**.
  2. *British Isles:* A collegiate racing craft of the late 19th century employing 6 or more oars. Currently, an open, sailing pleasure craft is also called a **longboat**.
  3. *England, central:* A cargo **barge**★ on some of the narrow tributary canals of the River Severn. Worked singly when towed by a horse, but later were towed in 2 parallel lines by a **tug**★. Bluff bow; substantial timberheads. Length 22m, beam 2.18m, draft to 1.14m, cap. 45t.

  4. *England, west-central:* Horse-towed, coal-carrying **barge** that worked the Leeds and Liverpool Canal as far as Wigan, as they were too long to go farther. After 1822, however, they could use the Leigh Branch to Manchester. Planked with pine; frames, keel and keelson of oak; iron or steel hull by the late 19th century. Bluff bow, square or rounded stern, rounded bilges, flat bottom longitudinally planked. Family lived in cabin aft, mate forward; open hold between, covered with tarpaulin except for the coal boats; narrow side decks. Length 22m, beam 4.34m, draft ca. 1.5m; cap to 70t. Other recorded names: **Leeds and Liverpool long boat**, **Liverpool sider**
  5. *Pitcairn Island, eastern Pacific:* Modified British navy **longboat**, one having been presented to the islanders by Queen Victoria; others were donated by passing whaling vessels, so that the resulting boats bear a resemblance to both the **longboat** and the **whaleboat**★. Transports visitors to and from ships and carries timber and supplies around the island. Carvel-planked; planks of local wood or imported pine; the frames of natural timbers; ceiled; keel timber imported. Shaped piece added to gunwale increases bow sheer to ride the breakers better; sharp stern; stem almost plumb and forefoot not cutaway. Short, enclosed end decks; 5-8 thwarts. Steered with a sweep while crossing the surf; rudder shipped when sailed. Rowed with 14 oarsmen, but currently only one boat is rowed; the others now have diesel engines. Early boats set a lugsail; later a gaff sail with a long boom and jib. Reported lengths 9.3-13.1m; e.g., length 9.3m, beam 2.6m, depth 0.86m. Other recorded names: **olwe boat**★, **oroe boat**, **whaleboat**★, **whaler**★
  6. *St. Helena Island:* **Longboats** are also used on this South Atlantic island. Sharp bow, narrow transom stern. Rowed with 4 oars, single-banked.
  7. *Tristan da Cunha, S Atlantic:* Open, canvas-covered boat; made in 2 sizes, the **big boat** and the **dinghy**★. The former travels to the outer islands for guano, bird oil, and eggs; the smaller boat fishes, collects firewood, and transports livestock. Double-ended; stem, sternpost, and keel from driftwood and wrecks; timbers and knees were made from a small, local tree, but now from steamed oak. Stem slightly curved, stern straight and raked; strong flare to the sides; external chine rubbing strake; coverboards fitted outside the canvas along the outer side of the gunwales.

longboat-7

Traditionally, hull blue on top, red stripe, and white on bottom. The **big boat** rowed with 6 oars, the **dinghy** with 4; steering oar on the stern employed when landing on a beach. Sails are a lug mainsail or leg-of-mutton shape with the foot laced to a boom on a traveler; secured to the mast by bands; tack made fast to foot of mast and clew secured to a spar that swings out over the side, the inner end held by a rope strop to the middle thwart. Small jib. Crew of 6-7 in the **big boat**, 4 in the **dinghy**. **Big boat**: length overall 8.53m, on keel 7.92m, beam 2.44m, depth amidships 0.69m; **dinghy**: length overall 6.1m, on keel 5.49m, beam 1.98m, depth amidships 0.69m.

8. *United States, E:* Shallow centerboard **schooner★** of Chesapeake Bay and the Potomac River that transported cordwood to Chesapeake communities and Washington, D.C. Some carried sand for glassmaking, and on the downriver run, produce and bulk cargoes. Developed in the 19th century; last used in the 1930s. Open amidships with short deck forward and small deck aft; walkway along the hatch. Sharp cutwater, square stern, flat floors, rounded sides; some had single bent-timber frames from gunwale to gunwale. Painted with a wide green stripe bordered by brown stripes, with white along the sheer strake; white or light pink below. Originally used leeboards, 2 along each side. Set 2-3 fore-and-aft sails and after 1870, a large jib to a short bowsprit on some. Reported lengths 15-25m; e.g., length 23.5m, beam 4.42m, hold depth 0.79m; draft light 0.46m, loaded 0.91m; cap. 60-80 cords of wood. Other recorded names: **Potomac longboat, woodboat★**

9. *United States, NE:* 19th-century freight and passenger vessel used on the middle reaches of the Kennebec River in Maine. Low and square-ended; flat bottom; steered with a sweep. Accommodations included passenger cabins and dining saloon. Sailed upstream, being tracked from shore when the wind failed and at low water, pulled through a rapids section by oxen; drifted downstream with the current. Reported as having 1-2 masts; set 3-4 square sails. To pass under bridges, the masts, on pivots, could be jackknifed. Reported lengths 18-29m, widths 4.6-6.1m; shallow draft; cap. to 100t.

Further references: **hay boat-1, langskip, narrow boat, sampan panjang**

longboate See **longboat-1**

long boomer See **Brixham smack, Essex smack, long-boom smack, Ramsgate smack, smack-5**

long-boom smack *United Kingdom:* A **cutter★**-rigged fishing **smack★** with a boom at the foot of the mainsail that was exceptionally long for the length of the boat. As the boats became longer in the 2nd half of the 19th century, so did the booms, but at 12m in length, they became dangerous, and rigs employing a mizzen became more practical. Name variant: **long boomer**. Note also **lang boomer**.

longbote See **longboat-1**

long chon See **long chuan**

long chuan *China/Hong Kong/Macau:* **1.** During the Dragon Boat Festival in early summer, many river and coastal ports celebrated either with special boats or with local craft that were suitably decorated. In some places, races were held in long, slender craft as they are today in Hong Kong, where they employ a crew of

22 and a drummer. Well-known were the racing boats of Yichang (I-Chang), on the middle Chang Jiang (Yangtze), which were from 13.4-33.5m long, ca. 1.1m wide, and as shallow as 0.46m deep. A long fir pole formed the keelson; to this, bulkheads were slotted and thin side planking added; poles slotted on top of the bulkheads were capped with planking to form gangways. Bow and stern swept up from the water, supported by braided bamboo ropes that ran from bow to stern and were kept taut in a tourniquet fashion. A carved dragon's head was attached to one end and a tail at the other. Paddled with 20-100 men, sitting 2 abreast; short paddles. A coxswain manned a long steering sweep that either pivoted on an athwartship beam over one side, or rested on a notch in the aftermost bulkhead and passed through a hole aft. On some, a man standing amidships signalled directions to the helmsman by means of flags. A drummer or gong-beater stood at the bow and a standard bearer at the stern. Those at Guangzhou (Canton) were 21-30m long and 0.91m wide; the largest on the Hunan-Hubei (Hunan-Hupeh) plain were ca. 40m long with a crew of 80. The Fuzhou (Foochow) boats were 12-18m long and required a crew of 28-36. On the Hunan-Hubei plain, the boats were organized by region and apparently by family lineage, each boat designated by a color and bearing appropriate names, e.g., **bo chuan★** (**white boat**); such a boat was painted white, its crew wore white uniforms, and its decorative flags were white. Special multicolored boats (**hua chuan**) also participated. Further reading: Y. Ssu-ch'ang, "The Dragon Boat Race in Wu-ling, Hunan," *Folklore Studies* (Catholic University of Peking, Museum of Oriental Ethnology) II (1943), 1-18.

2. The Miao people of southeastern Guizhou Sheng (Kweichow Province) in southwestern China celebrate a Dragon Boat Festival on the Qingshui (Chingshui) Jiang. Here, the boats are constructed of hollowed cedar logs; the middle log, ca. 20m long, is flanked by 2 logs, each 12-15m long. The prows have elaborately carved and painted dragon heads. Bow extends out over the water, low stern; low freeboard. Rowed, standing, by 30-76 oarsmen. Narrow.

Other recorded names: **Drachenboot, dragon boat★, I-Ch'ang lung ch'uan, long chon, long ch'uan, longhschon, lông-sün, long tch'ouan, lung chou, lung ch'uan, po ch'uan, serpent boat**

long ferry See **Gravesend barge, tilt boat-2**

long-headed oyster schooner See **Delaware Bay oyster schooner**

longhschon See **long chuan**

Long Island catboat See **catboat-2**

Long Island scallop boat *United States, E:* Dredged for scallops by sail in Great South Bay on the south coast of Long Island. Employed 6-35 dredges, depending on the boat's size. Centerboard; cabin aft on some. Cat- and **sloop★**-rigged. Reported lengths 5.5-13.7m; freeboard 0.3m; draft 0.6-0.9m.

Long Island scooter See **scooter-2**

Long Island skiff See **skiff-9**

Long Island Sound freighter See **freighter-4**

Long Island Sound sharpie See **sharpie-2**

Long Lake boat, Long-Laker See **Adirondack guide-boat**

longliner **1.** A boat or vessel that engages in hook and line fishing, setting baited hooks weighted near the bottom (**line trawler**) or to lines buoyed near the surface. May also describe a rod and line fishing craft, such as the tuna vessels. Range from small, open boats to large, modern, oceangoing vessels. Other selected names: **Angelleinfahrzeug, beugschip** (or **visser**), **dory trawler★, Langleinenfischerboot, Langleiner, langlinefartøj, langlinefisker, ligneur, linefartøj, line fisher, lin(e)fiskebåt, liner★, navio de pesca à linha, palangreiro, palangrero mercanizado, palangrier, perschereccio (con palangari, con ami, con lenze).** Note also **cordier, handliner, hooker, palangrero, palangrier, tuna boat-3.**
    2. *Canada, E:* **a.** Off Newfoundland, may be a vessel fishing with lines and hooks, or more recently, with gill nets. Small cabin forward, wheelhouse, deep well amidships. Formerly rowed, now have engines. Crew of 5. Reported lengths 13.7-19.8m; e.g., length 13.7m, beam 3.7m. **b.** Nova Scotian **longliners** are presently either double-ended or square-sterned, motorized craft employing lines and hooks. **c.** The **Gaspé longliner** is also known as a **gaspésienne, cordier★,** or **palangrier.** Generally longer than 16m and more than 25grt.
    3. *Canada, N:* The **longliner** of Arctic waters is similar to the **Peterhead boat★** but slightly beamier. Decked; small cabin. Propelled by a 65-80hp engine. Reported lengths 12.2-13.7m.
    Further reference: **diao ting**

long-net salmon punt See **salmon punt-2**

long-nose canoe *Canada, central:* Birchbark **canoe★** of the Ojibwa (Chippewa) Native Americans of the area west and northwest of Lake Superior; used especially for harvesting wild rice. Characterized by its elongated end profile in which the ends rounded up strongly from the bottom and then recurved sharply to meet the end sheer. Bottom flat transversely, rocker at ends;

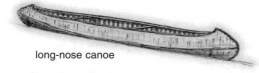

long-nose canoe

well-rounded bilges; sides tumble home toward the ends. Narrow headboards; often merely light sticks, curved sharply, matching the end profile. Bark secured to the rounded gunwales by continuous lashings; cap rails then brought up over the gunwales. Reported lengths 4.5-4.9m; e.g., length 4.9m, beam 0.86m, depth 0.39m. Name variant: **Ojibway long-nose canoe.** Note also **tsiman, wigwas tsiman.**

long-ràmbach See **pinnace**

long serpent See **esnecca, snekkja**

long ship **1.** Term often applied to seagoing vessels propelled primarily by oars (especially to Greek and Roman **galleys★**) or simultaneously by oars and sail. Fast and principally used for war. Length-to-beam ratio ca. 6:1. Other recorded names: **barco longo★, bâtiment** (or **vaisseau**) **long, longa navis, makra**

naus or **naus makra, navi lunghe, navis longa** (pl. **naves longae**), **navis lunga.** Note also **round ship.**
    2. In the British navy, one aboard which there were long intervals between drinks.
    Further references: **langskip, lola**

longshore Term sometimes given to a boat or vessel that fishes mainly in coastal water.

longshore punt See **beach punt-1**

lông-sün, long tch'ouan See **long chuan**

lontra *Romania, E:* Small **dugout canoe★** used on the lower Danube River for fishing and general transportation. Some strengthening provided by ribs. Other recorded names: **lontré, lontro, lountre, vraiits', vranitze.** See also **londra-1.**

lontré See **lontra**

lontri See **londra-1**

lontro See **londra-1, lontra**

lood See **lûd**

loodsboot See **loodsvaartuig, pilot boat**

loodsgalley See **loodsvaartuig-3**

loodsjol *Belgium/Netherlands:* Small, very seaworthy boat used to transfer pilots from **pilot boats★** or shore stations to and from ships. Now mainly built of synthetic materials; formerly of wood. Note also **loodsvaartuig.**

loodskotter See **loodsvaartuig**

loodsrinkelaar, loodsschoener See **loodsvaartuig-1**

loodschokker See **schokker**

loodsschuit See **loodsvaartuig-1**

loodssloep See **loodsvaartuig-2**

loodsvaartuig *Belgium/Netherlands:* The shallow Belgian and Dutch coastal river mouths required early pilotage assistance. By the early 19th century, there was some standardization of the pilot service and the vessels used. Note also **loodsjol, pilot boat.**
    1. An important type, the **loodsrinkelaar,** worked off the Belgian and Dutch coasts until ca. 1880. These were strong, round-built vessels with keel, blunt bows, rounded stern, curved stem, and straight, raked sternpost. Clinker- or carvel-planked; low sheer; decked; leeboards. Early boats gaff-rigged with a single boomed, loose-footed sail with a short gaff. Later **ketch★**-rigged with a short gaff on the mizzen and a longer gaff on the mainsail; mizzen sheeted to an outrigger. Replaced by **schooners★** (the **loodsschoener**) and **cutters★** (the **loodskotter**). Reported lengths 15-21m; e.g., length 16.98m, beam 5.37m, depth 2.6m. Other recorded names: **loodsboot, loodsschuit, rinkelaar**
    2. The Belgian **loodskotter** of the 19th century had a straight or lightly curved stem with a rounded foot; a straight, raked sternpost with a flat counter stern. Deep hull, long keel and little sheer. Decked; accommodations for 4 people. During the 19th century, employed a variety of rigs—**cutter, yawl★, ketch, sloop★ (loodssloep),** and **schooner** (the **schooners** had rounded sterns). Reported lengths 17-21m.
    3. On the Schelde Estuary, the Dutch and Belgian pilot services at Vlissingen used the **loodsgalley** until ca. 1930. Clinker-planked, open boat with lightly curved, vertical stem and small, heart-shaped transom. Six thwarts and stern bench. Rowed with 6 oars or set a wide, dipping lugsail to a mast stepped in the 3rd thwart. Length 6.5m, beam 1.61m, depth 0.61m.

Looe lugger See **East Cornish lugger**
look out See **scout-1**
lookout boat See **scout-1**, **seine boat-5b**, **shad galley**,
   vedette
Loots-Jolle See **pilot boat**
lootspaat See **paat**
loquette *Switzerland, W:* Found on lakes and rivers in
   the Jura region, mainly for fishing, but also as a
   dinghy★ to larger boats and as a **ferry★**. Dated from at
   least the 18th century; now extinct. Carvel-planked
   with 2-3 flaring side strakes; 6-7 ribs; flat bottom of 3-
   4 planks with rocker, usually no keel; sharp bilges.
   Ends sharp or cut square, raked, and swept up. No gunwales or bulkheads; sometimes a single seat. Fishing
   type had a wet well forward. Rowed standing with a
   pair of oars by a single man. Reported lengths 4-7.3m;
   e.g., length overall 7.3m, on bottom 4.9m, beam
   1.55m, depth 0.67m. Other recorded names: **liketta**,
   liqu(i)ette, **liquette genevoise**, **loketta**, **neyeu périssoire**; **noie-chrétien** (small size); fishing type sometimes called **double loquette**. Note also **périssoire**.
loquette de chase See **canardière**
lorch See **lorcha-3**
lorcha 1. In the Far East, a vessel with a western hull
   and an eastern rig.
   2. *Chile, N:* A **lighter★** that carried bags of nitrate to
   ships lying at anchor. Long, low, open craft; sharp,
   plumb stem; square counter stern; swept up at the bow.
   Steered and occasionally propelled by a long sweep.
   Set a single lugsail to mast stepped in forward third.
   Length ca. 13m.
   3. *China:* Modified **junk★** still found in parts of
   Southeast Asia. Developed in the 16th century by the
   Portuguese to suppress Chinese pirates that hounded
   the coast. Later used extensively by European companies in the opium trade and as a cargo vessel along the
   South China coast to north of the Chang Jiang
   (Yangtze). Hull basically European in style, but many
   had characteristics that reflected their place of origin.
   Built largely of teak and camphor wood; sharp, raked
   bow; counter stern, but some had the local flat, oval
   stern; flat floors with easy bilges; straight keel; moderate sheer. Heavy, deep rudder worked with a wheel;
   carried running lights, contrary to Chinese practice.

lorcha-3

Decked, generally with poop and forecastle; many had
a trunk cabin aft of the mainmast. Some hung a boat
from stern davits. Painted brick-red with yellow poop
and forecastle; deckhouse white. Early boats had 2
masts, later 3. Rigging reflected a combination of

Chinese and European origins. Set balance lugsails;
sometimes in good weather, a jib was run to an otherwise useless bowsprit, and topsails reported. Some
had an elaborate windvane. Now fully motorized.
Crew of ca. 20. Approximate range: length 20m, beam
5.8m, depth 1.8m to 40m by 7.3m by 2.1m. Other
recorded names: **bai ao ch'iao, bai ao qiao, chia-pan
ch'uan, hoa t'ing, houa ting, hua thing, hwa t'ing,
jiabanchuan, lorch, pai-ao-ch'iao (white shell fish),
yabigu, ya-p'i-ku (duck's buttock)**
   4. *Peninsular Malaysia:* A sailing craft from Trengganu
on the east coast. Raked stem and counter stern. Sets
Chinese lugsails.
   5. *Mediterranean:* Lateen-rigged ships of the Mediterranean
were sometimes called **lorchas**.
   6. *Philippines:* Trader that carried bags of sugar from
the island of Negros to Iloilo on Panay in the 2nd half
of the 19th century. Modified in the 1860s to a fairly
flat-floored craft able to take the ground at low tide
while loading. Western-style planking. Reported
lengths 20.5-21.3m; e.g., length 20.5m, beam 4.7m,
depth 1.6m. Note also **palowa**.
   7. *Thailand:* Cargo **lighter** manned by Chinese that
worked out of Bangkok taking local produce over the
river mouth bar to off-lying ships. Hull of European
design, generally of teak and camphor wood. Straight,
plumb or raked stem; counter stern; painted brick-red
with yellow poop and forecastle. Generally set 2-3
Chinese battened lugsails; originally of matting, later
of cotton. Sometimes a jib was run to a bowsprit.
Reported lengths 24-60m. Name variant: **bai-ao-shiao**
   8. *United States, W:* Chinese-owned vessel that fished
off the coast of California, especially for barracuda and
abalone, in the latter half of the 19th century. Modeled

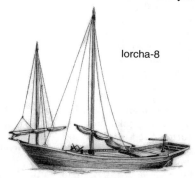

lorcha-8

after the boats used in China, they were carvel-built of
California redwood with a strong sheer, raking stem;
sharp, flaring bow; and rounded bilges. Extending
beyond the narrow stern was a wide, overhanging
counter, beneath which hung a wide rudder perforated
with diamond-shaped holes. Hatches aft and amidships;
some had a makeshift cabin. Outside normally painted
black, with oculi; deck and inside unpainted. Two or 3
masts of imported ironwood. Foremast stepped close
to the stem and raked forward slightly; 2 backstays.
Mainmast vertical and stepped amidships, supported
on each side by 2 shrouds. Set battened lugsails; the
smaller foresail tacked to a bumkin. Motorized about the
turn of the century. Averaged 4 in crew. Dimensions:

length 9m, beam 3.4m, hold depth 0.9m to 16m by 3.7m by 1.22m. Name variant: **Chinese fishing junk**. Note also **shrimp junk**.

9. *Vietnam:* Word has been applied to a 3-masted, square-rigged vessel that was part of the Indochinese **fleet*** in the late 19th century.
Further reference: **palowa**

Lo River dao ba zi See **dao ba zi-3**

losbåt *Norway:* **1.** General term for a boat used by pilots (*los*). Used all along the coast, but mainly in the Skaggerak area to the southeast. Traditionally lapstrake construction, later carvel; deep keel; sharp ends, curved stem and sternpost, often strongly cutaway forefoot; steep rise to the floors. Decked (**losskøyte**) or open; outboard rudder; tiller. Some of the small boats were rowed (see **seksæring-1**). Sprit- or gaff-rigged, the latter sometimes 2-masted. Mainsail usually had a colored vertical stripe, identifying the boat as a **pilot boat***. Crew of pilot and a boy. Reported lengths 8.2-10m. Other recorded names: **lodsbaad, lodsbåt, lo(d)sskøite, lo(d)sskøyte**. Note also **hvalerbåt**.
2. Best-known are the modified **pilot boats** by Colin Archer for use in the southeast, but also used in Sweden and Denmark. Designed and built in the late 19th and early 20th centuries. Carvel-planked; deep iron keel with marked drag aft. Decked; steering well aft; low rail along the sides; outboard rudder; tiller. Set loose-footed, boomed gaff sails to 1-2 masts; topsail on mainmast, staysail, jib to bowsprit. Reported lengths overall 10-13m; e.g., length overall 10m, on waterline 9.1m, beam 3.5m, draft 1.27m. Other recorded names: **Archerskjøite** (or **skøyte**), **Colin Archer pilot boat, Colin Archer-skøyte**. Note also **redningsskøyte**.
Further references: **pilot boat, seksæring-1**

Löschboot See **fire boat**

losskøite See **losbåt-1**

losskøyte See **losbåt-1, skøyte-3**

lost soul See **gozzo**

lotcă See **lodka-2**

lotia See **lodka-3**

lotka See **lodka**

lotkey See **lodka-3**

lotsbåt, Lotsenboot, Lotsenfahrzeug, Lotsenjacht, Lotsenjolle See **pilot boat**

Lotsenkutter See **kutter-2**

Lotsenschiff, Lotsenversetzschiff, Lotsenyacht See **pilot boat**

lotskutter *Sweden:* The modern **lotskutter** is a powerful, seaworthy **pilot boat***. May be of wood or steel. Motorized. Reported lengths 10-14m, widths 3.5-5m.

lotsmanskiy bot See **pilot boat**

loud, loude, loudre See **lûd**

lougher See **lougre**

lougre *France, N:* Fast, robust, lug-sailed vessel that was armed during the 18th century and served as a **privateer*** or **corsair*** and as a naval vessel in the early 19th century. Later **lougres** were **fishing boats***, some going into the North Atlantic for cod; those that trawled might be called **lougres chalutiers**. Clinker-built, square-sterned. Foremast stepped close to the bow, mainmast amidships and raked aft, and when

used, the mizzen was stepped on the rudderhead and sheeted to a jiggerboom. Some lacked the mainmast. Also set lug topsails to topmasts that were stepped abaft the lower masts. Several jibs ran to a long bowsprit. Some **schooner***-rigged. Reported lengths 20-26m. A small type was called a **chasse-marée***. Other recorded names: **lougher, lugre**; a lug-rigged **fishing boat** at Boulogne was called a **scutte** or **schuyt**. Note also **bateau de Berck, bisquine**. Further reference: **lugger-1**

lougre chalutier See **lougre**

lougre de Dunkerque, lougre de Gravelines, lougre dunkerquois See **lougre flamand**

lougre flamand *France, NE:* Three-masted, transom-sterned **lugger*** that fished principally in the North Sea. Phased out in the early 20th century. Deep hull with considerable drag to the straight keel; straight sides, flat floors. Bluff bows; straight or slightly curved stem; raked transom stern. Decked. Shallow lugsails used on those from Gravelines, taller on the Dunkerque boats; forelug overlapped the mainsail. Sails set to opposite sides of the masts. Jib run out on a reefing bowsprit. Mizzen set a standing lugsail (at Gravelines) or a triangular sail (at Dunkerque). Various combinations of sails used for different types of fishing. Reported lengths overall 10-15m, widths 3.3-4.6m, depths aft 2.3-3.3m. Other recorded names: **Gravelines lugger, *lougre de Dunkerque, lougre de Gravelines, lougre dunkerquois***

lougre harenguier See **harenguier**

lougre perlier See **pearling lugger**

Louisiana boat See **flatboat-4**

Louisiana lugger See **lugger-3**

Louisiana pirogue See **pirogue-4**

loung See **laung**

loung go See **laung gô**

lountra See **londra-2**

lountre See **lontra**

lourde See **lûd**

loutre See **otter**

lou tse tch'ouan See **lu ci chuan**

lou-tzŭ, lou-zi See **hua chuan-3a**

lowcoe See **hola**

Lowell dory-skiff See **dory-skiff**

Lowestoft pilot gig, Lowestoft pilot skiff See **Yarmouth pilot gig**

Lowestoft shrimper *England, E:* Worked out of Lowestoft on the Suffolk coast. Hull and rigging not standard, borrowing from designs to the north and south. Best known as a beamy, clinker-built boat with a transom stern. Straight keel, slight drag; vertical stem and sternpost; soft turn of the bilges; slight tumble home to topsides. On some, washstrakes extended from the bow to about amidships. Cuddy below forward deck; aft two-thirds open; floorboards covered the iron ballast; some fully decked. Some **sloop***-rigged, others 2-masted **luggers***. Most set a dipping lug mainsail on a vertical mast and a very small, standing lug mizzen to a forward-raking mast stepped on the transom. Mizzen had a very short yard, was loose-footed with a boom held by a snotter, and was sheeted to a short outrigger from about midpoint on the boom. When **sloop**-rigged, might set a jackyard topsail. Sails tanned with red ochre and fish oil. Engines on all later

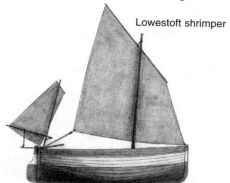

Lowestoft shrimper

boats. Crewed by 1-2. Length 6.25m, beam 2.44m, depth 1.22m. Note also **Yarmouth shrimper**.

Lowestoft smack See **Lowestoft trawler**

Lowestoft trawler *England, E:* **Trawler★** of Lowestoft on the Suffolk coast used from the 1860s until World War II, trawling mainly in the North Sea. Carvel-planked; sharp bow; straight, vertical stem; wide counter stern, either square or elliptical. Long, straight keel with strong drag; steep rise to the floors, rounded bilges; plumb sides. Decked; cabin aft; deep bulwarks; steam capstan worked nets, set sails, etc. Hull painted black and had a distinctive gold decoration below the bowsprit hole. The beam trawl carried along the port side. **Ketch★**-rigged with fidded topmast and jib-head-ed or yard topsail, 2 headsails. Mizzen staysail set with beam wind. Sails tanned. Gaffs almost as long as their booms; loose-footed. Mizzenmast raked forward. Bowsprit run out to starboard side of stem through the bulwark. Crew of 4-5. Reported lengths overall 20.7-23.9m; e.g., length overall 22.9m, on keel 19.1m, beam 5.7m, depth 2.8m. The small **toshers★** were 15m long, worked closest to port, and had a crew of 3-4. Name variant: **Lowestoft smack**

Lowestoft yawl, Lowestoft yoll See **beach yawl**

low sternsheet wherry See **Norfolk wherry**

lozzu See **luzzu**

luampo See **corial**

Lubec boat, Lubec carry-away boat See **Quoddy boat**

lūcenuk See **shitlats**

lucìa See **battèll**

lu ci chuan *China:* **1.** Small, light, open boat that uses cormorants to catch fish in the Ningbo (Ningpo) area, south of Shanghai. The cormorants sit on the rails; cords around their necks prevent the birds from swallowing the fish they catch. Flat bottom, sharp bilges; stern curves up sharply to a point; bow rounds up but much lower than the stern; oculus at bow. Straight sides. Bench at stern; propelled by a *yuloh* (type of sculling oar); anchored by a pole. Length 5.5m, beam 0.7m.
2. In the waterways surrounding Chengdu (Chengtu) of the upper Chiang Jiang (Yangtze) basin, the boat that works with cormorants is **punt★**-shaped with square, cross-planked, sloping ends. Flat bottom, planked

longitudinally. Works with 2 men. Poled; pole also serves as a perch in retrieving the birds. Length 4.9m, beam 0.6m, depth 0.2m, draft 0.07m. Name variant: **Chengtu cormorant fishing punt**
3. In some areas, the fishing is done from a bamboo **raft★**. Square ends turn up. Sculling oar fixed to a tripod at the stern.
Other recorded names: **bateau cormoran, cormorant boat, lou tse tch'ouan, lu-tzŭ ch'uan**. Note also **ukai bune**.

lûd *Tunisia:* Characterized by its tall lug mainsail and black hull. Used mainly for sponge fishing, but also for transporting merchandise and contraband. Few still working. Slightly raked stem and sternpost curve under the bottom to form short keel pieces; flat floors amidships. Fine entrance and run; slight or reverse sheer. Generally double-ended; some small types had a small transom stern and vertical bow; a few cargo boats had a clipper-type bow. Decked forward of the mast. On **fishing boats★**, a raised platform aft facilitated handling the equipment and divers; raised gunwale around after third that extended beyond the hull at the stern. Large-bladed rudder. Mainmast longer than the boat, raked aft at 30°, the angle adjustable; set a tall, rectangular, narrow lugsail with 6-8 reef bands. Foremast almost vertical and set a very small lateen or leg-of-mutton sail, but rarely used. Crew of 2. Reported lengths 8-14m; e.g., length 11.3m, beam 2.6m, depth 0.9m, draft 0.5m. Other recorded names: **lood, loud(e), loudre, lourde, lweid** (dim.), **sandal★, sandale, sandalo**; pl. **elwậd, lwậd**. Further reading: André Louis, *Les îles Kerkena (Tunisie). I, Les "Travaux"* (Tunis: Impr. Bascone & Muscat, 1961), 214-220.

ludeczka, ludka See **łódź**

luff barge *England, central:* A small, squat sailing **barge★** of the upper Thames and the River Medway, manned principally by Irishmen. Transported goods into areas where the larger **Thames sailing barges★** could not go; used into the 20th century. Rounded bow, slightly raked; square stern; round bottom; leeboards. Set a brailed spritsail and foresail. Ca. 60t. Other recorded names: **clipper barge, Paddy boat**

lugaro See **lugger-1**

lug boat *England:* **1.** A lug-rigged **Thames sailing barge★** of the late 19th century. Set a standing lug mainsail that could be brailed, a staysail, and a small sprit mizzen to a mast stepped on the rudderhead.
2. A general term applied to the family of **Deal luggers★**.
Further reference: **umiak-2**

luggage boat 1. *Ireland, central:* A boat of 60-70t towed by a River Shannon **steamer**, carrying the passengers' luggage.
2. *United Kingdom:* **a.** An inland waterways craft that carried produce and parcels but had no accommodations for passengers. Reported on the Thames at least as early as the 13th century. **b. Luggage boats** crossed the River Mersey from Liverpool to Seacombe. Various vessels were built or modified for this service from the late 19th to the mid-20th century. Early **ferries★** carried mainly horse-drawn wagons and

continued to do so even after the tunnel was built. Later vessels transported motor vehicles as well. Pedestrians were also carried. Name variant: **Wallasey luggage boat**

See also **market boat-5, umiak-2**.

luggage canoe See **freight canoe**

lugger 1. A vessel that sets standing or dipping lugsails on each mast, commonly 2, although a mizzenmast also stepped on those requiring extra speed. Occasionally a topsail is run up to a topmast, and often sets 2-3 jibs to a long, running bowsprit. Modified from square-rigged vessels during the latter part of the 17th century because of greater ease of handling and speed. Popular on both sides of the English Channel during the 18th century as **coasters★, privateers★, advice boats★**, and for smuggling. Became a popular **fishing boat★** rig in the 19th century, but in some areas of England, the term **lugger** has been applied to boats engaged in drift-net fishing, even though not specifically lug-rigged. Elsewhere the term may refer merely to a working **sailboat★**, regardless of rig. Spelling variants: **liuger, ljuger, loger, logger★, loggher, logre, lougre★, lugaro, lugre(ro), lyuger**

2. Sometimes a general term, especially in the 18th century, for a multipurpose harbor or coastal craft.

3. *United States, south-central:* In the Louisiana bayous, small shrimp and **oyster boats★** may be called **luggers**. Sailing types have round bottom, hour-glass transom, centerboard. Reported lengths 10.7-15.2m; e.g., length 10.7m, beam 4m; shallow draft. Motorized types have a rounded, fantail transom. Engine aft, fish hold forward; some have an engine forward, are high-sided, and can be as long as 26m. Other recorded names: **lil swimp boat, Louisiana lugger**. Note also **chabec, fish boat, New Orleans lugger**.

Further references: **dandy smack, Deal lugger, Hastings lugger, Manx lugger, pearling lugger, Swansea pilot schooner**

lugre See **lougre, lugger-1**

lugre bacalhoeiro See **bacalhoeiro**

lugrero See **lugger-1**

Lühe Ewer See **Ewer**

Luhü mi chuan *China, E:* Carries rice (*mi*) from Luhü on Dianshan Hu (Tienshan Lake) in southern Jiangsu (Kiangsu) province to Shanghai. Strongly constructed of *shu mu* wood with 5 bulkheads and 7 frames. Flat bottom, rounded bilges; top strakes extend beyond the stern to form short wings. Sides taper in toward the ends. Square bow curves up and overhangs; square stern curves up more sharply. Athwartship deck planking; house covers midship area; small leeboards for lake crossings. Cleaver-shaped rudder; tiller. Short mast, stepped forward of house, sets a square-headed lugsail. Also propelled by a *yuloh*, a balanced sculling pole that pivots on a fulcrum and is worked with ropes. Crew of 3. Length 12.5m, beam 2.1m, depth 1.1m. Name variant: **Luhü rice boat**

Luhü rice boat See **Luhü mi chuan**

lumber boat *United States, E:* Lumber was moved on the Erie Canal in central New York State by special

barges★ coupled together and towed by 3 span of mules. Centerboard helped keep the barge in mid-channel; some used a leeboard. Lumber piled as high as 1.2m on the cabin roof; helmsman stood on a platform; S-shaped tiller. Animals stabled in the bow. Length 29m, beam 4.9m, depth 2.7m, draft light 0.4-0.46m, loaded 1.8m. See also **pointer**.

lumber carrier See **timber carrier**

lumber drogher See **timber drogher**

lumber hooker See **hooker-5**

lumberjack See **timber drogher-2**

lumberman See **timber drogher**

lumberman's batteau *Canada, E/United States, N:* Built to run shallow whitewater rivers; prominent in the 19th century; some worked until the 1950s in New England. Short, flat, narrow bottom with rocker, longitudinally planked. Most had finely pointed ends, straight and sharply raked; bow frequently

lumberman's batteau

more elongated than the stern; ends had an iron band. Strongly flared, straight sides; considerable sheer, often greater at the bow. Some had a sharp bow and square stern, others square at both ends. Lapstrake construction, generally with 3 strakes (on the Penobscot River in Maine, 3-strake boats were called **maynards**, 2-strake boats were **two-streakers**). Michigan and Wisconsin boats were round-sided, and the frames were shimmed rather than notched inside; the laps died out at the ends, becoming flush at the stem and sternpost. Steered with a paddle from the stern. Captain at the bow used a paddle to steer around obstacles. Rowed single-banked; also poled. Crew of 6 on the larger boats: 4 oarsmen, 2 polers. Reported lengths 4.6-15.8m; e.g., length overall 10m, on bottom 6.5m, beam on gunwale 1.7m, on bottom 0.73m, depth 0.48m. In New England, the log drive might be accompanied by a **horse raft**. Four teams of horses rode on a log **raft**; used to twitch stranded logs off shores and meadows. A cook shack called a **Mary Ann★**, also on a log **raft**, went along with the drive. Other recorded names: **drive boat, jam boat, log-driving batteau, logging bateau, Maine batteau, river-driving batteau**; pl. **batteaus**. Further reading: Scott E. Hastings, Jr., *The Last Yankee. Folkways in Eastern Vermont and the Border Country* (Hanover, N.H.: University Press of New England, 1990), 40-47. Note also **bateau, batoe, batteau-4a, pointer**.

lumber raft See **crib-1, fleet, timber raft-3**

lumber schooner See **timber drogher-2**

lumber skiff *Canada, E:* In Newfoundland, a flat, shallow-draft boat that transports lumber.

lu mei mao See **green eyebrow**

lundër See **lundra**

lundra *Albania:* **1.** May signify a **boat★, rowboat★, canoe★, barge★**, or **ferryboat★**. A small boat is a **lundricë** (pl. **lundrica**).

2. A simple **dugout canoe★** of the Kënet'e Kakariqit (lagoon northwest of Lesh). Ends slightly pointed. Length ca. 4m, beam 0.5m. Note also **trap**.

lundra-2

3. Long, narrow, open boat of Lake Scutari in north-western Albania; principally a cargo craft. Plank-built; sharp ends; long, tapering, overhanging bow; stern curves up to a small, square end; flat bottom. Tarred black. A gangway forward permits landing on low shores. When sailed, sets a small sail, or may be pro-pelled by 1-12 oarsmen, standing and facing forward. Reported lengths 15-20m, beam 2-5m.
4. Motorized cargo vessel built for use on Lake Scutari and the Buene (Bojana) River. Flat bottom. Reported lengths 16-18m, beam 5m; shallow draft. Spelling variant: **londra★**
Spelling variants: **londra, lundër, l'undrë, lundrëz(ë), lunner, lunnriza, lunter, luntre★**. Further reference: **londra-2**

l'undrë, lundrëz, lundrëzë, lundrica, lundricë See **lundra**

lundwin *Myanmar (Burma):* Common **riverboat★** that carries light cargo and passengers; shallow draft enables it to work many reaches in low water. Expanded dugout hull to which a variable number of strakes are added. Bottom sweeps up at ends to pro-duce long overhangs, higher at the stern; bow plumb

lundwin

and low; on some, a spoon-like extension is added onto the stern. Steersman works a long sweep on the quarter from a seat at the stern. Long, arched bamboo and mat house covers central part of the boat. Poled upstream. Reported lengths 6.8-15.2m; draft 46-61cm. Spelling variant: **lôndwin**

Lunenburg dory *Canada, SE:* Type of **Banks dory★** built at Lunenburg on the south coast of Nova Scotia. Served aboard codfishing **schooners★**, as **lifeboats★**, and as **tenders★** to fishing vessels. Sharp, raked bow; wedge-shaped, raked transom; planks lapped along the sides, becoming flush at ends; straight, flared sides; narrow, flat bottom, rocker to the fore-and-aft plank-ing; grown-knee frames scribed into the sides and bot-tom; strong sheer. Removable thwarts. Painted a char-acteristic buff color. Crew of 2. Reported lengths over-all 3.4-7.9m, on bottom 2.4-6.1m; e.g., length overall 5m, on bottom 4m, beam at gunwale 1.5m, on bottom 0.76m, depth 0.69m.
lung chou, lung ch'uan See **long chuan**
lunner, lunnriza, lunter See **lundra**

luntre *Romania:* Term for a **barge★** or **boat★**. See also **lundra, ontro**.
luntru *Italy, Sicily:* Small boat used by customs authori-ties. Name variant: **untru**. See also **ontro**.
luoats, luōtas, luots See **Handkahn-2**
lupina See **gozzo**
lurcher See **lurker**
luring boat General term given to the small boats that use a white board to attract small fish by moonlight or torch, as well as during the day. Found mainly in Southeast Asia and southern India. The board is attached to one side while a net on the opposite side catches those fish that jump over the boat. Fish jumping into the boat become entangled in brush or leaves strewn on the bottom. Name variant: **catch boat**. Note also **ghe trê, ku-chai, rua pheelawk, tiao bei, tiao yu chuan**.
lurker *England, SW:* Smallest boat of the pilchard fishery teams that worked off eastern Cornwall. Carried the master seiner who inspected the school of fish and directed the net-setting operation. Curved stem, tucked-up transom stern, straight keel, flat floors, rounded bilges. Centerboard, if sailed. Rowed by 2-4 men. Sprit- or gaff-rigged; mast stepped through for-ward thwart. Might step a mizzenmast at the transom with sail sheeted to an outrigger. Some motorized. Reported lengths 5-6m; e.g., length 5.18m, beam 1.7m, depth 0.69m. Other recorded names: **cock boat★, larker, lurcher**. Note also **dipper, follower, seine boat-3, tuck-net boat**.
lurkie *Scotland, N:* Small, square-sterned, open boat of the Orkney Islands that set a standing lugsail. Known as **lurkie** in the southern islands and **sooie** in the northern group.
lurky *England, NE:* Term applied to a **shore boat★** or **hoveller★** in Northumberland.
lusuinima, lusuinume See **lisi**
lut See **lahut-1, laudus**
lu-tzŭ ch'uan See **lu ci chuan**
luz flotante See **lightship**
luzía See **battello-2**
luzio See **dau la mtepe**
luzzijiet See **luzzu**
luzzu *Malta:* Inshore **fishing boat★** of the 20th century; also used for interisland transport. Double-ended; carvel-planked of imported timber; light ribs, closely spaced amidships. Vertical stem and sternpost project high above the gunwales; the stem twice the height of

luzzu

the stern. Bow flares and sweeps up sharply. Flat floors amidships; low freeboard except at ends. Short decks at bow and stern, narrow side decks. Bulwark a single piece; washboards originally in sections, removed as needed when handling nets; now permanent except on the quarters. Cuddy or wheelhouse. High rudderhead; tiller. Brightly painted; oculi; triangular drain holes in bulwarks often outlined in contrasting colors. Originally sailed, setting a lateen or spritsail; now engines installed and mast not stepped. Crew of 2 on small boats, up to 7 on large. Reported lengths 4.6-13.7m; length-to-beam ratio 3.1 or 3.5:1; shallow draft. Spelling variant: **lozzu**; pl. **luzzijiet**

lwậd, **lweid** See **lûd**

lwînša See **lânša**

lydjor See **lodka-3**

lyghter See **lighter-1**

Lymington punt See **gun punt**

Lymington scow See **scow-10**

Lynæsbåd *Denmark, E:* Some fished for herring out of the Isefjord area in northern Sjælland; others carried cargo, especially potatoes to Copenhagen. A few remain as pleasure craft. Beamy with full bow and stern, low freeboard. Clinker-planked, steeply rising floors, high bilges. Stem strongly curved; sternpost curved above the waterline, straight and raking below. Decked, large hold, low bulwarks. Square-heeled rudder; tiller comes in through bulwark to the small standing well. Tall pole mast. Loose-footed, boomed gaff mainsail, high-peaked topsail, staysail; jib run out on a long, steeved-up bowsprit. Reported lengths 8-11.7m; e.g., length 9.9m, beam 4.2m, depth 1.4m. Other recorded names: **Lynæsbåt**, **Lynæs herring boat**

Lynæsbåt, **Lynæs herring boat** See **Lynæsbåd**

Lynn yoll See **yoll-1**

lysterbåt, **lystreng**, **lystring** See **listerbåt**

lyter See **lighter-1**

lyuger See **lugger-1**

M

ma'addīya See **ma'addiyya**

ma'addiyya *Egypt:* Term for a **ferryboat★**. Most are still being built of wood, but steel hulls are becoming more common. Many still sail, but some are being equipped with diesel engines. Spelling variants: **ma'addīya, maadéëh**; pl. **ma'ādi**

maadéëh, ma'ādi See **ma'addiyya**

Maaskotter See **kotter**

Maasspits, Maasspitz See **spits**

mabagala See **baghla-2**

mabuti See **buti-1b**

macalet *France, SW:* Early 19th-century vessel of the Garonne River between Agen and Langon. Crew size varied with the section of the river: 6-22 downstream, 15-17 upstream. Length 20m; 30t. Spelling variant: **macallet**

macallet See **macalet**

Macassar prahu See **pinisi**

macchawa See **muchwa-1**

macchina See **sponge boat-2**

machava See **muchwa-1**

machhavo, machhawa, machhwa See **muchwa-1**

Machinac boat See **Mackinaw boat**

machina flotante See **sheer hulk**

machine See **fire ship**

machine boat See **sponge boat-3**

macho See **canoa-6**

macho-fêmea See **caixamarim**

machoua See **muchwa-1**

machua *Mozambique, N:* Transports produce in the Pemba (Porto Amélia) area. Carvel-planked; sharp bow; slightly raked stem; wide transom, vertical above, raked below; full-bodied amidships; outboard rudder. Decked at bow and stern. Large quadrilateral lateen-type sail with a short luff set to a slightly forward-raking mast; luff boomed out over the bow. Crew of 2-3. Reported lengths 10-12m. Note also **n'galawa-3**. Further references: **dhoni-6, muchwa-1**.

ma chuan *China:* Horse carrier★ of ca. 15th century that stepped 8 masts.

machuvo See **muchwa-1**

machuwa See **mashua-2, muchwa-1**

machva See **muchwa-1**

machwa See **mashua-2, muchwa-1**

machwah See **muchwa-1**

Mack See **Mackinaw boat**

Mackenzie kayak See **kayak-6**

Mackenzie River drift boat See **McKenzie River drift boat**

Mackenzie River moose-skin boat See **moose-hide canoe**

mackerel driver See **drifter, East Cornish lugger, West Cornish lugger**

mackerel tuck-net boat *England, SW:* Fished for mackerel and mullet in Mounts Bay in western Cornwall. Sometimes worked with a smaller boat as a team. Reported lengths 7.92-8.53m. Note also **tuck-net boat**.

Mackinac bark See **Mackinaw boat-1**

Mackinac boat, Mackinaw, Mackinaw barge See **Mackinaw boat**

Mackinaw boat **1.** *Canada/United States:* **a.** Plank-built boat used on northern rivers, mainly by fur traders. By the late 18th century, the term was frequently applied to a flat-bottomed, **bateau★**-type craft with tapered ends. Rowed or **sloop★**-rigged, with centerboard. Cap. ca. 5t. Other recorded names: **bateau, Mackinaw skiff. b.** In the 1st half of the 19th century, round-bottomed, sharp-ended boats appeared on the upper Great Lakes and adopted the name **Mackinaw**

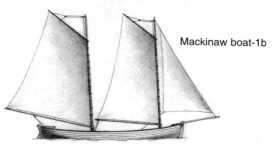

Mackinaw boat-1b

boat. In addition to fishing and moving supplies, the boats were used as **lifeboats★** and as pleasure craft, and they spread to the Fraser River in British Columbia, Lake Winnipeg, and Hudson Bay. Several types were developed during the period of their popularity, until about World War I. Beyond their name, common features are hard to establish. Carvel- or clench-built; some had maximum beam well forward; others, especially the fishing type, carried their maximum beam close to the ends; most flat-floored; some had very hollow garboards; usually a plank keel. Stem ranged from vertical and straight to slightly raked and curved; most had a straight, raked sternpost; sheer moderate, but little sheer on the **Collingwood boats** that originated in Georgian Bay off Lake Huron. Generally half-decked; some with narrow side decks; often a fish well amidships; frequently a centerboard. Early boats rigged with single sail to a mast stepped at the bow. Some **sloop**-rigged, especially on Lake Michigan, but most were 2-masted **schooners★** or **ketches★**; some, like the **Collingwood boats**, had a sprit mizzen. Foremast stepped well forward. Masts generally unstayed and could be struck. Long gaffs; in some areas, sails tanned. The plank bowsprit generally bowsed down. Reported lengths 7.3-13.4m; average ca. 7.9m; e.g., length 8.9m, beam 2.5m, depth 1.2m. Other recorded names: **Collingwood skiff, double cat, Great Lakes Mackinaw, Mackinac bark, Mackinaw fish boat** (sail boat, schooner), **ranger boat.** Further reading: R. C. Swanson, "'Edith Jane': A Search for the Real Mackinaw Boat," *WoodenBoat* 45 (1982), 100-106. Note also **gas boat-3. c.** The rowed **Mackinaw skiff** of the western Great Lakes was a small version of the **Mackinaw boat** used for inshore fishing and recreation. Sharp ends, high sides; flat bottom with rocker. Deep transom stern adopted when outboard motors used. Reported lengths 4.9-5.5m;

beam a little less than one-third. Other recorded names: **fisherman's** (or **fishing**) **skiff**, **herring skiff**
2. *United States, central:* **a.** Broadly speaking, any small sailing craft used in the Straits of Mackinac area, between Lakes Huron and Michigan. **b.** A **barge***-like craft that supplanted the fur traders' **canoes*** on the Great Lakes and other interior waterways during the early 19th century. Carried provisions

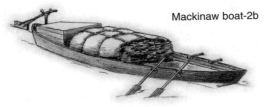

Mackinaw boat-2b

westward and fur eastward, hauling as many as 60 bundles of fur. Built of oak or of cedar frames strengthened with gunwales and crosspieces; covered with layers of birch bark sewn together with roots. Flat bottom; blunt ends. Rowed, paddled, or when conditions suitable, might step a mast amidships setting a square sail. Crew of 7-8 camped ashore at night. Largest ca. 9m long, beam 1.8-2m; shallow draft. Additional recorded name: **barge**. **c.** On the Missouri River and other large rivers in the central basin, a **Mackinaw boat** was a cross between a **flatboat*** and a **bateau**. Used on a downstream run only, transporting cargo; mainly furs. Reported as late as 1870 on the upper Missouri. In some areas, it might be more of a shaped log **raft***. Flat bottom; pointed bow; stern sharp, rounded, or square; sides flared or vertical. Cargo carried amidships on a platform or in cargo boxes. Guided downstream by 4-5 oarsmen with long sweeps; helmsman stood on a tower, working a large oar. Reported lengths 6-21m; e.g., length 15m, beam 3.7m, depth of hold amidships 1.0m, cap. ca. 15t. Name variant: **bateau***
Other recorded names: **bateau Mackinaw**, **Machinac boat**, **Mack**, **Mackinac boat**, **Mackinaw (barge)**, **McKinnaw**
Mackinaw fish boat, **Mackinaw sailboat**, **Mackinaw schooner** See **Mackinaw boat-1**
Mackinaw skiff See **Alleghney skiff**, **Mackinaw boat-1**
macule See **masula**
ma-däl oruwa See **madel-oruwa**
ma-däl paruwa See **paruwa-2**
madau See **dau-3**, **tanga**
madau la mtepe, **madau wa mtepe** See **dau la mtepe**
maddia *Morocco:* Reed **raft*** used to cross rivers and for fishing. Those on the Oued Loukkos (Lucus) in northwestern Morocco employed 4 tied bundles for the bottom of the craft; at the bow, the bundles turned upwards; stern cut square. Shorter bundles placed along the sides. An athwartship stick was inserted at the after end of the "gunwale" bundles to serve as a rowing thwart and as a stiffener for the craft. Towed, poled, rowed, and a lateen sail set in light winds. Employed double tholepins, one pair aft, the other forward. Length ca. 2.5m, beam 1.2m, depth 1.0m. A simpler **raft** was made at the Ras-el-Duro lagoon in which 2 bundles formed the floor and 2 shorter ones

were laced along the sides, all tapering at the bow. Name variants: **el madi**, **madi**. Note also **almady**.
madel-oru See **madel-oruwa**
madel-oruwa *Sri Lanka, S:* Rowed **fishing boat*** of the **oruwa*** family. Uses the *madel* seine net, working in the shallower, calmer nearshore areas. Dugout base with rounded bottom and sides; deep, vertical washstrakes sewn to inner edges, creating a very narrow opening. Raked, flat ends; 2nd strake creates sheer at each end; on larger craft, 2 parallel rails project forward beyond the bow. Outrigger set mostly to starboard; set to port where prevailing winds make this more suitable. Sharp-ended float secured by 2 booms that curve downward to be lashed directly to the float. A local 3-oared type has a platform on the booms for the net. Rowed with 2-5 oars secured by loops; longshafted oars with slightly trapezoidal blades stitched on. Steering oar a single piece, held to starboard. Crew of 5-8, depending on size, includes oarsmen, steersman, and fishermen. Reported lengths overall 10.2-12.5m. Spelling variants: **ma-däl oruwa**; pl. **madel-oru**. Further reading: Gerhard Kapitän, "Records of Native Craft in Sri Lanka—I: The Single Outrigger Fishing Oruwa—Part 2:1 Rowed, Paddled and Poled Oru," *International Journal of Nautical Archaeology and Underwater Exploration* 17 (1988), 223-235. Note also **paruwa**.
madel paru, **mādel paruwa** See **paruwa-2**
madi See **maddia**
madia **1.** *Malta:* Reported in 13th-century literature as a **ferry*** between Malta and Gozo Islands. A 17th-century source infers the boat was double-ended, was rowed, and set lateen sails. Other recorded names: **fregata** (or **bergantino**) **del passo Canale**. Note also **dghajsa tal-pass**.
2. *Mozambique, NE:* The **mádia** is a **lancha*** type found in the Cabo Delgado and Nampula provinces. Sharp, vertical stem; transom stern. Sailed, setting a large lateen or quadrilateral lateen-type sail with a short luff.
madjäng prahu See **mayang**
Madura prau See **golekan**
Madura trader See **golekan**, **kromon**
magazijnschip See **store boat**
Magdalen Islands flat, **Magdalen Islands ice boat** See **flat-2**
maghdija See **dghajsa tal-pass**
maghona, **maghūna** See **mavna**
magna galea See **galère-1**
mahaelah See **mahaila-2**
mahaila **1.** *Bahrain:* Term may apply to a high-sided square-ended pearling vessel. The single mast set a lateen sail.
2. *Iraq, S:* Cargo vessel of the lower Tigris and Euphrates Rivers carrying hay, reed mats for mud walls and roofs, bitumen, stone, and passengers. Some travel to Kuwait, where they go by the name **belem***; may also be called a **sefīne**, but these are generally smaller. Roughly built, often of waste lumber; strengthened by 3-4 stout crossbeams; numerous ribs; no keel; steep rise to the floors; almond-shaped bottom. Sharp ends rise as high as 3.1-3.7m above the

waterline; stem straight and greatly elongated, often terminating in a hook; sternpost straight or lightly curved and less raked; low waist. Generally open except for a steering platform aft; small forecastle for the small clay oven; larger vessels have a stern house of reeds or wood; one without such accommodations is called a **mesih**. Usually a tall, slender rudderpost supports a wide-bladed rudder; tiller inserted through rudderhead. Generally coated with asphalt; on the type found below Kut, the house, top strakes, and bow are decorated. Some employ a small **quffa★**, called a **gišr**, or **belem ·ashuri** (see **belem**) as a **tender★**. Single tall mast stepped in forward third. Sets a large quadrilateral lateen-type sail with a short luff bent to a scarfed yard, raised by an enormous wooden block. Staysail used when wind too strong for the mainsail. In calms or in strong currents, towed by 8-10 men by a line run from the masthead to shore. Crew of ca. 15, or at times, a family. Reported lengths 5-24m, beam ca. one-third. Other recorded names: **mahaelah**, **mahailah**, **maheila(h)**, **mahela**, **mohalla**, **muhāila**, **muheile**, **muhēle**; pl. **mehāil**, **mhēlen**; **safīnah**, **safī neh**; pl. **sefinen**, **sufun**. Locally: **gejaras**, **gurūti**, **tarādah**, **tarārid** (pl.). Further reading: H. Ritter, "Mesopotamische Studien... Arabische Flussfahrzeuge auf Euphrat und Tigris," *Der Islam* IX (1919), 122-134.

mahailah See **mahaila-2**

mahame See **mahonne-2**

maha oruwa See **yathra dhoni**

Maharashtra boat See **pattamar**

maheila, maheilah, mahela See **mahaila-2**

máhi-kush batél See **bedi**

mahn See **mon-3**

mahon See **mahonne-2**

mahona See **lighter-1**, **mahonne-2**, **mavna**

mahone See **mahonne-2**, **mahonne-3**

mahonne 1. *Egypt:* Large cargo vessel used along the Mediterranean coast and in the Turʿat al Maḥmūdīyah (canal). Spelling variants: **mahoun**, **maʿūna**

2. *Mediterranean:* Used in the eastern part, especially by Turkey. Reported in the 15th and 16th centuries as a vessel similar to a large **galley★** that was both rowed and sailed (3-masted with lateen sails). In the 16th century, some were supply vessels to Turkish **fleets★**; rowed with as many as 26 benches, each oar pulled by 7 men. Some were open at stern to load horses and camels. The 17th-century **mahonne** served primarily as a cargo vessel or **lighter★** of 20-30t; set 2 lateen sails or was rowed, each oar manned by 5-6 oarsmen; sometimes 2 decks. In Venice at this period, the vessel was known as a **galeazza★**. In present usage, the term usually refers to a **scow★** or **lighter** used in ports and with no means of self-propulsion (see **mavna**). Other recorded names: **bœurtun**, **mahame**, **mahon(a)**, **mahone**, **mā(h)ūnah**, **majona**, **makhona**, **maʿon**, **maona**, **maon(n)e**, **mâoûna**, **maûn**, **mauna★**, **mauné**, **mawuna**, **moana**

3. *Mediterranean, W:* Small, wooden **coaster★** of France, Spain, and North Africa. Present-day Tunisian vessels carry a variety of rigs—the smallest **cutter★**-rigged, the largest **schooner★**- or **ketch★**-rigged, or they may be lug- or sprit-rigged. Early boats set lateen sails.

Those built in Tunisia in the mid-19th century had a capacity of 5-40t; one was 15m long, 4.5m wide, 1.4m deep. Spelling variant: **mahone**

4. *Morocco, W:* Robust, open craft used along the Atlantic coast to off-load cargo from ships lying at anchor or to lighten one so that it could cross a harbor bar. Sharp ends, high freeboard, vertical stem and sternpost; high bow at Safi because beach landing necessary. Old boats at Rabat had very heavy rubbing strakes. Most had a keel; those at Casablanca also had grounding keels. Decked at ends, the stern forming a low poop; cuddy beneath. At Rabat, the helmsman had a raised seat set into the triangle formed by the gunwale and sternpost. Large rudder with long tiller. Known

mahonne-4

to have been rowed by as many as 32 men, double-banked, usually standing; mostly 12-14 men at Rabat. Long oars, held by a strop, worked against a tholepin; often towed. At Rabat: length 15m, beam 3m, depth 3m. Other recorded names: **barcasse★**; **ḍroblât** (at Casablanca); **gârˇb** or **qârˇb** (at Rabat and in Algeria), pl. **guârˇb**; **tšata** (large type at Essaouira [Mogador]). Further reading: Louis Brunot, *La Mer dans les Traditions et les Industries Indigenes à Rabat et Salé* (Paris: E. Laroux, 1921), 248-279, 302-305.

mahori See **houri-2**

mahoun See **mahonne-1**

mahovna, mahowna, mahownah See **mavna**

máh-ṭi See **bullboat-1**

māhūnah See **mahonne-2**

mail boat 1. Boat or vessel designated to carry the mail, usually under contract with the post office department. Selected name variants: **barco correo**; **bidai-ontzi** (Basque); **mail carrier** (or **ship**); **pacaid** (Gaelic); **postale**, **Postboot**. Note also **barca correire**, **barque-2**, **ice punt**, **isbåt**, **isöka**, **packet boat-1**.

2. *Canada, E:* Began operating in 1828 between Prince Edward Island and the mainland, running across the ice in winter. Clinker-planked, curved stem with wedge-shaped bow transom and strongly cutaway forefoot, high transom stern, marked sheer. Runners, ca. 30cm apart, fitted to the bottom on either side of the keel. Straps along the side used by both crew and passengers to aid in hauling the boat over the ice and for safety, should the boat break through. Set a wide dipping lugsail. Crew of 6. Length 5.5m, beam 1.5m. Name variant: **iceboat★**

3. *St. Lucia, West Indies:* Conveyed passengers and freight along the lee side of this island in the Windward group. Plank-extended **dugout canoe★**; sharp cutwater formed by a knife-like projection; sharp stern.

Employed a spritsail with a long, high-peaked sprit. Length ca. 9m, beam 1.2-1.5m. Name variant: **male boat***

4. *United States, E:* On the North Carolina bays, **mail boats** also carried light cargo, and in the 1920s, transported locally produced illegal alcoholic beverages. Rounded bottom; hull wide and full amidships; plumb stem; round or fan-tail stern. House covered most of the hull. Powerful engine.

5. *United States, north-central:* **a.** Amphibious craft that carried mail and an occasional passenger in the late 19th century from the Ohio mainland to the islands in the western part of Lake Erie. Designed to be sailed and pushed over the ice in winter. Sharp bow; raked transom stern; flat bottom; rocker at ends, especially at the stern. Light mast stepped well forward; boomed gaff sail. Length ca. 4.5m. **b.** Serves the Detroit River area as a **floating post office**. Steel construction, diesel powered. Length 18.6m, beam 4.3m, depth 1.8m.

Further references: **dawk boat**, **packet boat-1**, **Saint Kilda mail boat**

mail carrier See **mail boat-1**
mail packet See **packet boat-1**
mail punt See **ice punt-2**
mail ship See **mail boat-1**
Maine batteau See **lumberman's batteau**
Maine peapod See **peapod**
Maine pinky See **pinky**
Maine sloop boat See **Friendship sloop**
Maine wherry See **salmon wherry**
Maine wood scow *United States, NE:* Square-ended vessel that carried cordwood and local produce to larger towns downriver, especially on the Kennebec and Sheepscot Rivers. Worked into the 1st half of the 20th century. Flat bottom, straight sides, moderate sheer, raked ends. Steered with block and tackle to a wheel. No bulwarks; cordwood piled high on deck and restrained by stakes. Small cabin aft. Large rudder attached to the skeg. Most **sloop***-rigged with boomed gaff sail; large jib to a squared bowsprit. Some set a gaff topsail. Crew of 2. Reported lengths 13.7-18.2m, beam ca. one-third, depth 0.91-1.22m. Name variant: **wood scow**. Note also **kiln-wood coaster**.

maintenance scow See **scow-11f**
main topsail schooner See **schooner-1**
Mainzer Lade, **Mainzer Laden** See **Oberländer**
mai shun *China, E:* Common trader in the Guangzhou (Canton) area. T-head bow, square counter stern, high poop. No outboard gangway; anchor platform forward. Rudderstock came up forward of mizzenmast. Forward-raking mainmast, small mizzen on counter. Battened balance lugsails. Triangular headsail to a plank bowsprit. 70-120t.

maître canot See **canot du maître**
majahazi See **jahazi**
majang, **majangan**, **majang prau**, **majang prauw** See **mayang-1**
majol See **walenmajol**
majole, **majolle** See **spitsbek**
majombo See **chombo**
majona See **mahonne-2**
majorquin See **pilobote**

Makah whaling canoe See **pa-dá-wahl**
makamakatalo See **guli**
Makassaarsche prauw, **Makasser schooner**, **Makasser trader** See **pinisi**
makhona See **mahonne-2**
makora, **makoro** See **mokoro**
makra naus See **long ship**
makrellskøyte *Norway, S:* Used in the late 19th and early 20th centuries for mackerel fishing; built on the south and southeast coasts. After serving as **fishing boats***, they became popular with nomadic groups as living quarters. Carvel- or clinker-planked; beamy; sharp ends; decked; roller for nets forward; outboard rudder; tiller. Sprit- or gaff-rigged. Note also **skøyte-4**.
makrillgarnbåt See **garnbåt-2**
Malacca kolek *Peninsular Malaysia:* Handline fishing craft used along the west coast to the north and south of Malacca. Characterized by a small, transverse block above the bow for the cable when anchored at the fishing grounds and a unique wing-like decoration that rises above the stern. Straight keel; sharp, strongly raked stem and stern; lightly planked; flat floors amidships; deadwood at each end. Hull stained dark brown or black. Steered with a paddle, but may take a rudder and lines. Crew of 1-4. Reported lengths 3.7-6.7m, widths 0.91-1.14m. Other recorded names: **koleh Malacca, kolek*, kolek Malacca, kolek Mëlaka**
ma lan *China, central:* Strongly built, 3-masted vessel from Fuzhou (Foochow); those from Wenzhou (Wenchow) were similar and were called **eel boats**. The Fuzhou vessel worked to the north as far as Shanghai and to Taiwan; the Wenzhou boat traded locally. Strongly raked, flat bow narrowed at the waterline; decorated. Stern higher, round or oval, raked; also decorated. "V" bottom in cross section. Decked; long, low wooden house forward; another house aft, mat-covered on the Fuzhou vessel. Vertical mainmast stepped about one-third in from the bow; foremast strongly raked over the bow; vertical mizzenmast well aft. Set battened balance lugsails. A blue horse was painted on the foresail of the Fuzhou boat, earning the name **blue-horse junk**. Reported lengths 19-23m, widths 4.3-5.2m.
Malay lighter See **tongkang Mëlayu**
Maldon barge See **Thames sailing barge**
Maldon bawley See **bawley**
Maldon gun punt, **Maldon punt** See **gun punt**
Maldon smack See **Essex smack**
male boat *Wales, NW:* A shallow **rowing boat*** used in herring fishing. Oars heavy, squared, and a minimum of 4.3m long. Length ca. 4.3m; fairly shallow draft. Name variant: **cwch gwrw**. Note also **female boat**. Further reference: **mail boat-3**
Malecite moose-hide canoe See **moose-hide canoe**
Malecite river canoe *Canada, E/United States, NE:* Birchbark **canoe*** of the Malecite (or Maliseet) tribes of New Brunswick, part of Quebec, and northern Maine. Flat sheer except at ends, which were sometimes high-peaked; upper part of ends straight and either vertical or overhanging. Well-rounded bilges; marked tumble home, continuing into the ends. Bottom rather flat transversely, fore-and-aft rocker of

ca. 5cm. Gunwales joined to the stem pieces by the outwales and gunwale caps. Ribs wider amidships than near the ends. Headboard straight and vertical.

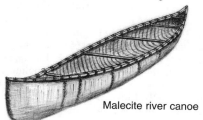

Malecite river canoe

Later types had no tumble home, lacked marked end sheer, and had narrow headboards with a slight forward bulge. Those running white water had temporary battens along the sides and bottom, tied up to the thwarts; also known to use rolls of spruce bark around the bottom for the same purpose. Reported lengths 4.42-5.64m, widths 0.84-0.93m, depths 0.27-0.33m. Other recorded names: **Maliseet river canoe**, **Milicite canoe**, **St. Lawrence canoe**. Further reading: Edwin A. Adney and H. I. Chapelle, *The Bark Canoes and Skin Boats of North America* (Washington, D.C.: Smithsonian Institution, 1964), 36-57, 70-88.

malia *India, NW:* **Dugout canoe**★ used for stake-net fishing in the Gulf of Kutch. Reported lengths 5.4-6.6m, widths 0.9-1.3m, depths 0.5-0.6m.

Malia hoda See **hoda**

malinèla See **sandón**

ma ling ting *China, S:* Popular, fast river **ferry**★ of the Guangzhou (Canton) area. Low, elongated bow, usually square; higher stern, also overhanging and square. Passengers sit forward, protected by an open-sided house; family lives in enclosed wood house aft. Bamboo-mat roof characteristically follows the conical shape of the bow. Propelled by 2-5 oarsmen who work standing, facing forward. Steered by a sweep from the port quarter. Length ca. 6m, narrow. Other recorded names: **fast express**, **ko lang ting**, **ma ling t'ing**, **slipper boat**

Maliseet river canoe See **Malecite river canoe**

mallion boat See **mud hopper**

malmhaxe See **haxe**

malong See **laung**

malonnier, malonnière See **tartane de l'Estaque**

malteza, maltezana See **cocoreli**

mampaboot See **Bullom boat**

manaide *Italy:* Long, slender, inshore **fishing boat**★ found in the Bay of Naples and on the south coast, engaging mainly in sardine and anchovy fishing. Sharp ends; tall, thin stemhead; outboard rudder; tiller; open. Propelled by 6-8 oars or by sail. Sets a sprit- or lateen sail to a portable mast. Reported lengths 7.3-10.4m; e.g., length 10.4m, beam 2.6m, depth 0.75m, draft 0.35m. Other recorded names: **barca de menaide**, **menaida**, **menaide**; pl. **manaidi**

manaidi See **manaide**

manché, manché de Mangalore, manchica, manchou, manchu See **manji**

manchua *Macau:* Small, elaborately ornamented and carved recreation vessel of the Portuguese cited in the 17th century. See also **manji**.

manci, mancia See **manji**

mancina See **mancive**

mancíva See **manji**

mancive *Africa, E:* Oared craft of Indian origin reported in the 17th century. Wide stern; house over the deck; bulwark amidships. Propelled by 20-24 oars. Spelling variant: **mancina**

man-drowner See **dugout canoe**

mangá See **pelota-4**

mangá-îg-cîg See **pelota-2**

Mangalore manche, manieve See **manji**

Manila galleon See **galleon-3**

maniuche See **manji**

manji *India, W:* A term applied along the Malabar Coast to several types of boats, ranging from **dugout canoes**★ to sewn **lighters**★ to **coasters**★. Also reported from Sri Lanka. At Cochin, ranges from a waterway **barge**★ to a seagoing 3-master. Early reports describe a dugout with a thick, round bottom; rounded sides; broad, widely spaced ribs; similar bluntly pointed ends. Sailed, rowed, or paddled. Reported lengths 6-15m. The Mangalore **manji** was a flat-bottomed, sewn **lighter**. Conveyed cargo and passengers from ships anchored off the river mouth; poled up the shallow river. Reported lengths 7.6-10.7m, widths 1.8-2.1m, depths 1.2-1.5m. Those at Calicut (now Kozhikode) were similar but had a raked stem because they worked from the beach. Paddled and sailed. Crew of 8. The **manji** that serves as a fair weather **coaster** may go as far as Aden and occasionally to the East African coast. Has a long, straight, raking bow; raked stern; frames spiked to the carvel planking; considerable sheer forward; deep forefoot. Outboard rudder; tiller. Sometimes decked; mats cover the cargo. Sets 1-2 lateen sails. Crew of ca. 12. Reported length 15.2m, widths 3.1-3.7m, depths 1.52-2.13m. Other recorded names: **bandar manché**, **bateau de charge de Cochin**, **Calicut bandar manché**, **manché**, **manché de Mangalore**, **manchica**, **manch(o)u**, **manchua**★, **manci(a)**, **mancíva**, **manieve**, **maniuche**, **manjua**, **menji**, **mota**, **munchua**, **vañ ci**; Calicut, Cochin, **Mangalore manché**. Note also **kalla doni**, **pambán manché**, **pattamar**.

manjua See **manji**

manka See **mE'nga**

Manningtree punt See **gun punt**

man-of-war General term applied to armed ships of war that belong to the navy of a country. Includes ships of the line and support vessels. Early ships sailed, now have engines. Selected name variants: **bâtiment (navire, vaisseau) de guerre**, **buque** (or **nave**) **de guerra**, **Kriegsschiff**, **man-o'-war**, **navio de guerra**, **oorlog(s)schip**, **örlogsfartyg**, **Orlogsman**, **Orlogschiff**, **orlogsskib**, **örlogs-skepp**, **orlogsskibe**, **orlog vessel**, **ship of war**, **vascello da guerra**, **warship**; pl. **men-of-war**

man-of-war brig See **snow**

man over boord boot See **accident boat**

man-o'-war See **dumb barge**, **man-of-war**

man-o'-war yager *Jamaica:* Old term for a ship of chase or for a **galley**★ with many oars.

man's boat See **kayak**

Manssenboot See **Netzboot**

mantis-head boat See **perahu kepala kelalang**
Manx dandy See **Manx lugger**
Manx lugger *United Kingdom, Isle of Man:* **Dandy★**-
rigged **drifter★**; locally called **lugger★** despite a gaff
mainsail and a standing lug mizzen. Rig adopted in the
early 19th century and persisted until about the end of
the century. Most double-ended, but some had a counter
or rounded stern by the 1880s. Clinker-built originally,
then carvel; full, round quarters. Stem straight and
slightly raked;
sternpost vertical.
Accommodations
in the forecastle;
larger boats ful-
ly decked by the
1880s. Mainsail
generally loose-
footed with boom.
Large gaff top-
sail set to a pole
topmast. Jigger-
boom extended
the mizzen. Bow-
sprit run out
through hole in
the starboard bul-
wark; 2 head-

Manx lugger

sails. Mainsail generally lowered while drifting.
Crew of 7-8. Reported lengths 11.3-15.5m; 1848 boat:
length overall 11.4m, on keel 9.8m, beam 3.51m, hold
depth 1.98m, draft light 0.91m, loaded 1.68m. Other
recorded names: **dandy smack**, **Isle of Man lugger**,
Manx dandy
Manx nickey See **nickey-2**
Manx nobby See **nobby-3**
Manx scowte, Manx squaresail See **herring scowte**
Manx wherry *United Kingdom, Isle of Man:* A double-
ended, 2-masted craft that accompanied **herring boats★**
in the late 18th and early 19th centuries as a so-called
buyer smack★. Also found in Irish Sea estuaries serving as **ferries★**, **tenders★**, and **fishing** and **pilot boats★**.
Some carried cargo to the Continent and North America.
Marked sheer; open or half-decked. Gaff-rigged with
loose-footed, boomed sails; jib to small, bowsed-down
bowsprit; foremast much shorter than mainmast.
Manx yawl See **baulk yawl**
ma·on, maona, maone, maonne See **mahonne-2**
maota *Tuamotu Archipelago, eastern Pacific:* Single
outrigger canoe★ of Napuka Island (Isle of Disappoint-
ment) in the northern group. Primarily collected giant

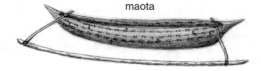

maota

clams from the lagoon. Dugout base in 2 or more pieces,
sewn together; keel piece carved out at each end. Strakes,
generally 3, also in more than one piece and sewn
together and to each other. Solid end pieces came to a
swept-up point, the bow end slightly lower; washstrakes

forward. Loose thwarts sometimes laid across the gunwales. Outrigger comprised 2 booms lashed directly to
a thin float, which might be longer than the **canoe★**;
lashed directly to both gunwales. Propelled with a
scooped paddle, generally by one man; capable of carrying 2-3 people. Reported lengths 3.7-6.7m; e.g., length
5.2m, beam 0.43m, depth 0.66m. Spelling variant:
mota. Further reading: Kenneth P. Emory, *Material
Culture of the Tuamotu Archipelago* (Honolulu: Bernice
P. Bishop Museum, 1975 [Pacific Anthropological
Records No. 22]), 150-153.
maouna See **mahonne-2**, **mavna**
maphrodite See **polacca**
maqoru See **tomoko-1**
maquois See **masula**
maraakib, marâkeb, marakib See **markab**
maram See **choonda maram**
maramma See **catamaran-13**
māran *Japan, S:* Two-masted cargo vessel of the
yanbaru★ type from Okinawa. Plank-built; sharp cutwater, square above; rising counter stern; very strong

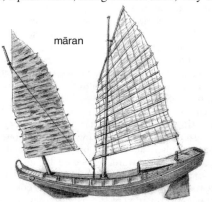

māran

sheer. Decked; low cabin aft; wide rudder hung below
the bottom; oculi at bows. Foremast raked forward
over the bow, mainmast vertical. Set tall, battened lugsails with curved leech. Length ca. 23m.
maran See **marano**
marana, marani See **marano**
marano *Italy, NE:* A small ship cited from the 11th-15th
centuries. Little is known about it except that it carried
firewood and was the main carrier for stone from Istria
for the breakwaters off Venice. Ranged farther in the
Mediterranean at times, and some carried munitions or
horses. Lacked the forecastles of the period; probably
undecked; oared and lateen-rigged; most under 100t cap.
Other recorded names: **maran★**, **marana**, **maranus**,
marr(a)ano, **marranu**, **nave marana**; pl. **mar(r)ani**
maranus See **marano**
Marblehead dory-skiff See **dory-skiff**
marchand See **merchantman**
Margate bawley See **bawley**
Margate hoy *England, SE:* Heavily built, **cutter★**-
rigged vessel that plied the Thames Estuary carrying
as many as 70 passengers between Margate and London,
probably beginning in the late 16th century and continuing until ca. 1825. Carried some light cargo. Bluff
bow, heavy transom stern, with quarter windows; deep

bilges. Decked; one or more cabins. Gaff mainsail loose-footed with boom; square topsail to fidded top-

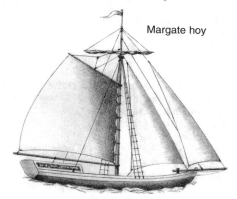

Margate hoy

mast, 2 headsails. Crew of 4-10. Reported lengths 21-24m; e.g., length 24m, beam 5.64m. Note also **hoy-3a.**

Margate row-boat See **Margate wherry**

Margate wherry *England, SE:* Local pleasure and **fishing boat★** used until the 1970s. Launched off the beach using a sling between 2 wheels. Sharp bow, flat transom, fine run, 2 thwarts, and a stern bench. Steered with yoke and lines to an outboard rudder. Mainly rowed using 1-2 pairs of spoon-bladed oars. Dipping lugsail used when fishing; mast stepped through a thwart well forward. Length ca. 5m, beam 1.2m, deep hull. Name variant: **Margate row-boat.** Note also **Thanet wherry.**

margota See **margotat**

margotat *France, central:* Family of square-ended, flat-bottomed craft that may still be found in some sections of the upper Seine River. The largest carry charcoal, wood, grain, and produce on the Haute Seine and the Yonne, a left bank tributary. The smallest are used on riverine lakes and marshes. Fore-and-aft planking of the flat bottom turns up to straight, overhanging ends. Sides parallel for most of their length, then narrow slightly toward the ends. Small boats open; larger open but may have had a small cabin amidships or near the stern. The cargo carriers had a shallow balanced rudder extending under the stern overhang; long tiller slotted through the rudderhead. Large vessels towed by a **tug★**, often in tandem. Very small craft propelled by the standing occupant with a double-bladed paddle; somewhat larger size rowed. Crew of 3 on towed vessels. Reported lengths 2.5-30m; e.g., length 21.8m, beam 5m, depth 1.42m, 85t. Other recorded names: **margota, plate★**

marie-salope *France:* Vessel designed to receive mud and sand from a **dredger★**. In general, each of its holds had a trap door on the flat bottom that opened to release its load. Might set a square sail or 2 gaff sails; also poled, but usually towed. Crew of 2-3. Length ca. 15m, beam 4.3m. Term also used by the early French in Louisiana. Other recorded names: **barca a tramoggia, bette★, chaland à vase, gabare à clapet, gabar(r)e à vase, porta-fango, trébuchet.** Note also **beta, bette à escarbilles, dump barge, hopper.**

marinhoa See **bateira marinhoa**

markab **1.** Arabic generic term for any craft, ranging from an ordinary boat to a modern oceangoing vessel; word used along the North and East African coasts, the eastern Mediterranean, and the Arabian Peninsula. In places, the word has become synonymous with a specific type of vessel, such as the Egyptian **gaiassa★** and the Sudanese **markab.** In early times, the term might refer to a **galley★** or naval vessel, especially in the eastern Mediterranean. Word may be used as a prefix, such as **markab er-rašāida** (boat from Rosetta), **markab el ma'as** (small boat that carries fruit and vegetables), and **markab kulu** (in East Africa, a vessel that sails).
2. *Sudan:* Spoon-shaped cargo craft of the upper Nile between the 3rd and 4th cataracts. Carvel-planked, using relatively short lengths of sunt wood to form 10 strakes for each side; flat sheer. No ribs; strengthened by a variable number of transverse beams that pierce the top strake. Shallow, V-shaped transom stern; full, rounded bow; sharply raked stem. Open waist, decked at ends; stout midline

markab-2

bitt on the forward of the mast; bitt sometimes on the quarters. Rudder blade one-third to one-half the length of the boat; horizontal, arched tiller; amulets often hang from the tiller. Sets a long, narrow, obliquely hung sail with yards at top and bottom; transverse cloths. Vertical mast, lashed to afterside of the extra-strong midships beam, held by 2 cleats; 2-4 forestays amidships and 3 shrouds to a side. Upper end of top yard capped with black goat skin, and an amulet often tied on; also uses a small wind vane and at times, a long pennant. Crossbar at the lower end of the lower yard serves as a handle for furling the sail. When needed, sweeps used, and may also be rowed, poled, or tracked from shore. Wide size range: average length 10.21m, beam 4.88m, depth 1.22m. Other recorded names: **Dong(h)ala mark(h)ab, grande kayasse;** incorrectly **naggr★** or **nuggar.** Further reading: J. Hornell, "The Frameless Boats of the Middle Nile," *The Mariner's Mirror* XXV (1939), 417-432; XXVI (1940), 125-155.

Other recorded names: **kimarkebu** (dim.), **markab shirai, markabu, márkeb, markebu, markhab, markib, markwa, marqab, merākib'', merikabu, merikebu, merkab, mérkĕb, merkib, mīrkab, mórkọb, murkab;** pl. **maraakib, marâkeb, marakib, markâbi, merakib, mrâk˘b, mrakdb, mrākūb.** See also **dhow.**

markaba *Cameroon, N:* Sewn plank boat of the Kotoko peoples south of Lake Chad. Flat bottom and vertical sides made of 16-18 irregularly shaped pieces; sewn with hide; sheer may be quite uneven; seams caulked with fiber. Bow square, low, and raised above cutwater.

markaba

Stern elongated with raised overhang; end narrow and cut square. When used for fishing, a huge net, supported between 2 long multipiece poles, extends from the bow; lowered and raised by ropes, cantilever fashion. Small auxiliary **canoes*** attempt to drive the fish toward the lowered net. An arched mat cabin is placed amidships when boat used for transportation. Reported lengths 10-15m; e.g., length 12.5m, width at bow 1.55m, at stern 0.35m. Other recorded names: **Kotoko pirogue, kotokos.** Note also **kotoko, zemy.**

markab el ma'as, markab er-rašāida, markâbi, markab kulu, markab shirai, markabu See **markab**

mark boat 1. A boat moored in a particular spot to serve as a channel marker or to mark a race course. Other recorded names: **battello giudice, giudizio, living buoy, Zielboot;** also **seamark,** when referring to a boat such as a **lightship*.** Note also **stake boat.**

  2. *North Sea:* A vessel, usually an old **trawler*,** that serves as a central point for a fishing **fleet*,** anchoring and shifting position as directed by the **fleet** admiral. Note also **fleeter.**

mȧrkeb, markebu See **markab**

Marker See **Marker botter**

Marker botter *Netherlands, central:* Smallest of the **botters*.** Generally had an especially low, raked stern that swept up sharply at the strongly raked bow. Built at Monnikendam on the west coast of the Zuiderzee, but worked out of Marken Island opposite. Either fished singly or used a drag-net with another **botter** for herring, flounder, and smelt. At the time of the hay harvest on Marken, many carried hay piled high in the waist and on the foredeck (**hooibotters**). Tiller extended by a rope to the helmsman who stood atop the haystack. Some towed; both vessels sailed, the sail of the **hooibotter** reefed above the stack. Some carried peat for winter fuel in the waist (**turfbotter**). Three live wells. Gaff-rigged with jib to a long, running bowsprit; staysail. Reported lengths 12-13m; 1889 vessel: length 13m, beam 3.9m, depth 1.7m. Other recorded names: **Marker, Marker sleepbotter, Noordwalbotter.** Further reading: Peter Dorleijn, *Van Gaand en Stand Want, De Zeilvisserij Voor en na de Afsluiting van de Zuiderzee,* II (Bussum: Van Kampen & Zn., 1982), 280-297.

Marker sleepbotter See **Marker botter**

Marker Wasserschiff, Marker waterschip, Marker waterschuit See **waterschip**

market See **buy boat**

market boat 1. Any boat that transports local products to market or that sells directly from the boat itself.

  2. A **ship's boat*** used by the steward to bring provisions from shore.

  3. A **fishing boat*,** usually relatively small, that works nearby fishing grounds, returning to shore to sell the catch while still fresh. Called a **fresh fisherman** in the Canadian Maritime provinces. Other recorded names: **Marktboot, portolata*, portolatto.** Note also **carry-away boat.**

  4. A **shore boat*** that carried fresh produce and other supplies to ships lying in a roadstead. Other recorded names: **bateau à marché, canot des vivres, lancia dei viveri (di spemditori), Lebensmittelboot, Marketenderboot, poste au(x) choux, Proviantboot.** Note also **beef boat-1.**

  5. *British Isles:* During the 18th and into the 20th century, some inland waterways craft were designated as **market boats,** carrying produce and packages to market towns. Most also carried passengers, and some, such as the paddle-wheeled **Tamar market boat** on the Tamar River near Plymouth, had a dining saloon. **Ferries*** that carried produce from Lincolnshire villages along the Humber Estuary to Hull were called **market boats.** Other recorded names: **flyboat*** (in south Yorkshire); **luggage boat***

  6. *Canada, SE:* Large, open boat that transported produce, reeds, and merchandise down rivers from clearings to towns in colonial New Brunswick.

Further references: **beurtschip, buy boat, Hudson River sloop, James River bateau, lay boat, marktschuit, Quatze, Quoddy boat, Schiesslomme, warka-moowee**

market caique See **pazar kayığı**

Marketenderboot See **market boat-4**

market fisherman *United States:* A fast vessel, especially a **schooner*,** developed in the 1830s to fish farther out to sea yet be able to bring the catch back to market while still fresh. The carrying of ice on board also encouraged short, quick trips. Note also **clipper-schooner, market schooner.**

market float See **oyster barge**

market passage boat See **day boat-2**

market schooner *United States, E:* A fast, **schooner***-rigged fishing vessel, especially the **sharpshooter*** and the **clipper-schooner*.** Developed in the mid-19th century to transport the catch to market, either iced or kept alive in a wet well, rather than salted.

market sloop See **Hudson River sloop**

market smack See **smack-6**

markhab, markib See **markab**

marknadsbåt See **torsköka**

Marktboot See **market boat, Scheisslomme**

marktpraam See **Hoogeveense praam**

Marktschiff 1. *Germany:* Transported people and merchandise on the major rivers on a regular schedule, beginning in the 12th century. Those on the Rhine River in the early 19th century were 1- or 2-masted, setting spritsails, but they were often towed by horses from shore. Sharp ends, but some had a blunt **pram*** bow. Wide-bladed rudder below the waterline; long tiller; leeboards on some. Cabin covered most of the midship area. Length ca. 25m. Note also **Ordinari.**

  2. *Germany, S/Switzerland, N:* Also used on Lake Constance (Bodensee) to go to and from weekly markets. Considered a "medium large" craft, with a capacity of ca. 300 casks of salt.

marktschip See **beurtschip**

marktschuit *Netherlands:* Boat that transports people from small communities to weekly markets at larger centers. Note also **beurtschip, market boat.**

Marktzille See **Zille**

markwa See **markab**

mār nu See **country boat**

maròta *Italy, NE:* Enclosed, boat-shaped craft perforated to hold live fish; either held the catch from a fishing vessel or was used as a holding tank in which small fish were able to grow, especially eels. Small sizes (**burci** and **burcieli**) carried aboard such fishing vessels as the **bragagna⋆** and **bragozzo⋆**. Most double-ended; flat bottom; many built with ribs. One to 3 hatches. Reported lengths 6-14m; **burcio** ca. 5m long, **burciel** ca. 4m. Other recorded names: **maròtta**; pl. **maròte, maròtte; burchio⋆**, pl. **burchi; vùrchj⋗**. Note also **fish car.**

maròte, maròtta, maròtte See **maròta**

marqab See **markab**

marraano, marrani, marrano, marranu See **marano**

Marsegelschoner See **schooner-1**

Marseille dory See **bette**

marshman's punt See **Fenland punt**

Martha's Vineyard boat See **Nomans Land boat**

Martha's Vineyard cat See **catboat-2a**

Martha's Vineyard compromise skipjack See **half skipjack**

marticana, martíka, martingana, martıqa, martuka See **gagalı**

maru *Japan:* Term customarily appended to the names of Japanese merchant ships, although until 1869, it was appended only to warship names.

Mary Ann A small boat that delivers mail and provisions to a **fleet⋆** while in a harbor. See also **lumberman's batteau.**

Maryland fishing sharpie See **sharpie-3**

Maryland terrapin smack See **terrapin smack**

Maryport shrimper See **Morecambe Bay prawner**

masalah See **masula**

masauwa, masavauha See **masawa**

masawa *Papua New Guinea:* **Outrigger canoe⋆** that trades and fights in the area of the Trobriand and D'Entrecasteaux Islands, off southeastern New Guinea. Special communally owned **canoe⋆** built with great ceremony. Round-bottomed dugout hull; tapered, elongated ends. Two washstrakes, sewn on lapstrake fashion, raise each side; elaborately carved breakwaters. Paired, L-shaped frames are wedged into the upper part of the hull, the vertical half supporting the washstrakes. Multiple booms, often 20 or more, cross to the long float. Booms pass through the lower washstrake and abut against the opposite side, resting on longitudinal stringers that pass through the frames. Tall, crossed stanchions connect float and booms, forcing the booms downward to the hull. Float charred to make it more impervious to the water. **Canoe** double-ended, the outrigger kept to windward. Platform, slanting inward, covered the outrigger unit. Simple, short mast, vertical or raked forward, stepped in forward quarter. Large, triangular pandanus leaf sail hung from the forward part of the

yard; boomed at the foot. Yard hoisted by a halyard that goes through a hole at the base of the fork supporting the yard; tack runs to outer edge of forward outrigger boom. Carries as many as 35 people. Length ca. 10.7m. Spelling variants: **masauwa, masavauha**

maschhuf See **mashhûf**

Maschwa See **mashua-2**

mascula See **muscolo**

mas dhaoni, mas dhoni, mas doni See **dhoni-6**

mash'ahif, mashhoof See **mashhûf**

mashhûf *Iraq, S:* **1.** Beamy, shallow workboat of the Marsh Arabs; carries cargo and passengers. Its high, pointed bow designed to part the tall marsh grasses; somewhat lower stern. Plank-built of a thin wood; strongly flared sides; curved stem and sternpost. Ribs terminate about halfway up the sides and are covered by a stringer, or they continue to the heavy gunwale, covered by inner planking. Narrow, almond-shaped, flat bottom. Open except for short end decks; no floorboards; at least 2 crossbeams and a thwart. Inside undecorated, outside coated with bitumen. Poled or paddled, from each end; towed upstream from shore when traversing a major waterway. Reported lengths 4.6-9.8m; e.g., length 5.6m, beam 1.27m, inside depth 0.43m. Note also **qaiyarīyah. 2.** May also be a **canoe⋆** made of reeds.

Other recorded names: **bārkaš⋆, maschhuf, mash(h)oof, mašḫūf, maškûf, mašôf, meschhuf, mesh(h)ūf**; pl. **mash'ahif**

mashoof See **mashhûf**

mashua 1. Swahili term for a **ship's boat⋆** of European origin, or may mean merely **boat⋆. 2.** *Arabian Peninsula:* In the Persian (Arabian) Gulf, southern Arabia, and Oman, used mainly as a **ship's boat**, usually aboard a **baghla⋆** or **ganja⋆**. Term, however, may apply to a **coaster⋆**, especially from Iranian ports, or loosely to any open, square-sterned boat, even those of aluminum. Generally heavily built of rough-hewn timber with raked, straight or curved stem and usually with a transom stern; considerable deadwood aft; strong sheer. Often decked at bow and stern; **coasters** fully decked. Topsides usually black or oiled, bottom whitened with mixture of oil and lime. Steered with rudder and wheel or tiller. Mostly propelled by oars (generally 6), but may set a lateen sail to a forward-raking mast; traders often 2-masted. Some have bowsprit and jib. Crew of 6-12. Reported lengths 4.5-12.2m; e.g., length 7.6m, beam 1.4m, depth 0.36m. Spelling variants: **mach(u)wa, Maschwa, mashueh, mashuw(a), mashúwah, mashva, mashwa, māšúa, mauchua, muchva, muchwa⋆**; pl. **mwāši 3.** *Kenya/Tanzania:* Small all-purpose boat still in use in protected waters along the mainland coast and at Zanzibar and Pemba. Essentially a small **jahazi⋆**. Beamy, plank-built craft with a keel, a vertical or sharply raking stem, and a wineglass transom stern; hollow entrance. Often built of short planking salvaged from another boat. Rudder operated with lines. Open or decked at bow and poop; sides may be raised with mat weathercloths. Usually has oculi on the bows in Zanzibar. May be rowed only, or sets a lateen sail of cheap cotton with tack extended to bowsprit. Mast stepped against a thwart and an

mashua-3

athwartship beam lashed to the thwart. Many now fitted with an engine. Crew of 2-6. Averages 7.6m in length; shallow draft. Other recorded names: **almache**, **al-mashueh**, **māšua**, **mashuwa**, **mashwa**; dim. **kimashua**, **kimašua**

See also **jalbūt-1**.

mashueh See **belem-3**, **mashua-2**

mašḥūf See **mashhûf**

mashuw, mashuwa, mashúwah, mashva See **mashua**

mashwa See **mashua**, **muchwa-1**

maškûf See **mashhûf**

mas-odi 1. *India, W:* A boat that uses poles and lines for tuna fishing for the preparation of dried tuna (*mas*) in the Lakshadweep (Laccadive) Islands and Minicoy off the mainland coast. Carvel-planked of coconut or local laurel, fastened with copper nails. Sharp bow; high, recurved stem; stern low and full. The larger boats have a platform aft on which the crew and helmsman stand; platform rounded on the sides and extends out beyond the hull. A mast crutch, ca. 1.25-1.5m tall, is set into the platform; also used to support the helmsman. Nine compartments, 4 of which have holes and serve as wet wells for the bait. Rudder has a reverse "S" shape; short, S-shaped tiller. Those with one mast set a tall, narrow, square sail of matting forward of the mast and a boomless gaff sail aft. On the 2-masted boats, the after mast is stepped amidships and the foremast is about midway between the after mast and the bow; after mast is shorter. Also rowed using 7-9 oars per side; shaft ca. 3.5-4m long, blade ca. 30cm long. Reported lengths 8-12.5m; e.g., length 12.5m, beam 3m; shallow draft. Note also **odi-1**.

2. *Maldive Islands:* **Fishing boat**★ of 2.5-3t burden. Early boats had sewn planking and set a small mat sail; present boat sets a tall square sail to a centrally stepped mast. Crew of 9.

mašôf See **mashhûf**

masoola, masoolah See **masula**

masseira *Portugal, NW/Spain, NW:* Small, open, square-ended boat used for sea fishing and in estuaries, for harvesting seaweed and swimming crabs, for recreation, and as a **tender**★ to larger fishing craft. Flat bottom; rocker at ends; bottom and ends planked longitudinally. Ends rake, bow narrower than stern, sides flare, 3-4 thwarts. Hull tarred inside and out; often

decorated with designs and symbols. Sailed and rowed. Mast, raked aft, stepped through forward thwart, setting a lugsail. Rowed from 2 after thwarts with 2 pairs of oars. Mostly 2 in crew. Reported lengths 2.6-4.7m; e.g., length 4.7m, beam on bottom 1.44m, l.9m on gunwale. Name variant: **gamela**★

massoola, massula, massulah See **masula**

masta-bakar See **balandra-1**

Mastenprahm See **sheer hulk**

master's canoe See **canot du maître**

mast flat See **Mersey flat**

mastīku See **mistico**

māšua See **mashua-3**

māšúa See **mashua-2**

masula *India, E:* Famous Madras (Chennai) **surf boat**★ that transferred passengers and cargo between ships and the beach. Now works a huge beach seine, and some engage in other fishing. Identified as early as the 16th century. The present-day boats are found in 3 sectors along the east coast, each with slightly different features, but all have sewn flush strakes, sharp ends, and flat floors amidships, and lack framing; most strengthened by multiple crossbeams that extend beyond the sides; essentially open. The sewing patterns vary somewhat, but basically use a cross stitch on both sides, with vertical bars; most holes plugged with balls of coconut fiber. Reported lengths 4.5-10.5m; early **lighters**★ at Madras as long as l2m. The northern **masulas** of the Telegu fishermen of Orissa and northeasternmost Andhra Pradesh have 5 strakes

masula

per side; plank keel; slightly curved stem and sternpost adzed to shape from a log. Coir stitching and grass wadding must be renewed annually. Six or 7 rounded crossbeams on which benches are laid for the oarsmen. Bow oar pulled by single man, 2nd oar by 2-3 men, 3rd and 4th oars by 3-4. Inside lengths 7.5-8m, length-to-beam ratio ca. 3.5:1, beam-to-depth ratio ca. 2:1. In the central area, in northeast Andhra Pradesh, **masulas** come in 3 sizes: the 6-strake beach seiner and the smaller 3- and 4-strake boats engage in general fishing. More rounded bottom; curved stem and sternpost; restitched annually. Beach seiner has 7 crossbeams, while the 2 smaller types have none. Length-to-beam ratio 5:1 on the large 10m boats. The southern type exists mainly in Tamil Nadu, from Madras south of Karikal. Mostly 6 strakes: 2 bottom and 4 side strakes. Seams wadded with coir, lasting ca. 3 years. Ends straight and strongly raked. At Madras, the 10 crossbeams are used as thwarts; 7 beams to the south. Generally 6-8 oarsmen, each manning an oar, except at Kavali, where the arrangement is similar to that of the northern **masula**. The backwater boats, of 3-4 strakes, set gill nets. Now modified for local conditions. May set a flimsy triangular sail. About 7m long. Other recorded names: **bar boat★** or **ber★** (in Orissa area), **calañku, chalangu, chalingue, chelinga, chelinge, chelingo, chel(l)ingue, chiling(a), chilingoe, chinna padava** (small size), **macule, maquois, masalah, masoola(h), massoola, massula, mas(s)ulah, masula-manc(h)é, masula-mancha, masuli(t), masull, mausolo, mossel, mossula, musoola, mussolo, mussoola(h) mussoolee, mussula(h); padagu★** (in Tamil Nadu area); in Adhra area: **padava, padavu★, paṭaku; pedda padava** (large size). Further reading: Eric Kentley, "Some aspects of the Masula Surf Boat" in: Sean McGrail and Eric Kentley, *Sewn Plank Boats* (Oxford, 1985 [National Maritime Museum, Archaeological Series No. 1. B.A.R. International Series 276]), 303-317.

masulah, masula-mancé, masula-mancha, masula-manché, masuli See **masula**

Masulipatam nava See **nava-3**

masulit, masull See **masula**

matafa, mataffa See **mtepe**

matahiti *Marquesas Islands, eastern Pacific:* Small single-**outrigger canoe★** that fishes in protected waters. Reported as late as the 1920s. Dugout hull; vertical, slightly concave cutwater; rounded up, sharp stern; ends decked. Two widely spaced booms, lashed across the gunwales, extended to the long, pointed float; each boom inserted into a vertical block set into the float. Used by 1-2 men.

matanga See **tanga**

matapa *Somalia:* A **canoe★**-type **fishing boat★** with a deep forefoot. Sets a square sail with tack to the stem. Spelling variant: **matepe**

matchwa See **muchwa-1**

mate boat *United States, NE:* Term given to an early **ferryboat★** in Rhode Island that was paired with another boat on the opposite side of the crossing. Such boats were separately franchised. Further reference: **seine boat-5c**

matepe See **matapa**

Materialtransportschiff See **store ship**

Matinicus boat *United States, NE:* Fast, open lobstering and **fishing boat★** that was important at this offshore island and on the adjacent central Maine coast in the late 19th century. Considered a local version of the **Hampton boat★**. Lapstrake construction; very sharp bow; straight stem above the waterline, curved below; raked, heart-shaped transom, occasionally a counter stern. High, round bilges; strong sheer, especially aft, slight reverse sheer forward. Decked forward of the mast and around the stern; side decks; generally 2 thwarts; centerboard. Outboard rudder; inboard on the counter-stern type. Rowed and sailed. Spritsail carried a short club on the clew; jib to bowsed-down bowsprit. Mast stepped well forward. Reported lengths 6.4-6.7m; e.g., length 6.4m, beam 1.9m, depth 1.1m, draft 0.91m with centerboard up. A recent Matinicus-type, powered **lobster boat★** has a cuddy forward with open cockpit. Steering wheel partway back in the cockpit.

Matinicus Island peapod, Matinicus peapod See **peapod**

mā'to See **kayak-10**

matola See **moliceiro**

ma tou chuan *China, E:* Important vessel used as a **lighter★** in the area between Shanghai and Ningbo (Ningpo) and associated waterways. The **Shanghai ma tou chuan** and the **Ningpo ma tou chuan** are basically similar but retain slight individuality. Strong hull with 3 solid bulkheads, and on the Shanghai **lighters**, a 4th bulkhead has a sliding door. Further strengthening provided by multiple wales along the sides. Flat bottom, longitudinally planked. Square, raked ends; the stern narrower, both planked horizontally. The top planking at the stern extends outboard to create a gallery. Open hold; living quarters at the ends. Cleaver-shaped rudder; tiller; may employ leeboards. Propelled by 2 *yulohs* (type of sculling oar) forward and one aft. Also sailed, setting a tall, square-headed, balance lugsail; sometimes a sprit foresail set to a bamboo mast. Lengths to ca. 18m; one from Ningpo was 18m long, 4.6m wide, 2.1m deep. Name variant: **wharf boat★**. Note also **bo chuan**.

matsyavah See **muchwa-1**

mauchua See **mashua-2**

ma·ûn *Morocco, Atlantic coast:* Generic term for **boat★** or **ship★** at Rabat. Spelling variant: pl. **mawâ'în**

maûn See **mahonne -2**

mauna *Bulgaria, E:* Heavy, open boat that fishes with the *dalian* net. The primary boat is assisted by 2 smaller boats that set and retrieve the net. Rowed double-banked. Operation requires 12-14 men, plus a "captain." Reported lengths 11-13m, beam 2-3m, depth 1.5-1.8m. See also **mahonne**.

ma'una See **mahonne**

māūnah, mauné See **mahonne-2**

mauritien, mauritienne See **langoustier-2**

mausolo See **masula**

mavna *Turkey:* **1.** Term for a **barge★** that transports heavy materials. One that transports coal is a **mavnası**.

2. Those on the Bosporus, especially at Istanbul, are double-ended with easy run, long, overhanging, straight stem; vertical or slightly raked stern; outboard rudder; tiller. Stubby mast with light topmast fitted to starboard side. Lateen sail set to a yard that is counterpoised and steadied by stay and backstay; at times, sail bent to yard with hoops on lower part and hanked on upper. Sail and topmast easily struck. Generally sets a

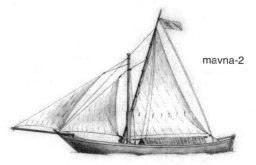

mavna-2

foresail tacked to the long stemhead and sometimes a jib to a rising bowsprit. Cap. 30-40t. Other recorded names: **maghona, maghūna, mahona, mahovna, mahowna(h), maouna, mavona, mav(o)una, mawuna**. Note also **mahonne**.

mavnası, mavona, mavouna, mavuna See **mavna**

mawâ'în See **ma'ûn**

mawato See **wato**

mawuna See **mahonne-2, mavna**

mayang *Indonesia, central:* **1.** A class of boats found in large numbers off the north coast of Java and off Madura. Primarily **fishing boats**★ working offshore with the *payang* (a bag-type net), although in the off-season, they may troll or handline. Some that no longer operate were small **coasters**★ (the **Java trader**). Vary somewhat from district to district, often known by special names. Distinguished by a very large, flat, recurved stemhead and a similar but generally smaller sternpost; size and shape of ends vary regionally. Carvel-planked, the planks merging in a smooth curve with the sharp, raked ends. Lack ribs but strengthened with bulkheads that divide the hull into fish rooms. Flat floors amidships; low freeboard; **coasters** had raised sides. **Fishing boat** often decked only at the ends; cargo carriers generally decked and might have a bamboo house abaft the mast. In some Maduran areas, decorative "horns" extended outboard at the ends to support the nets. Steered with 1-2 quarter rudders or a sweep. Early **mayangs** had outriggers. Single tall mast, stepped forward of amidships, supported by a rattan or pole backstay and by 1-2 horizontal bars from the mast to a crutch aft. Most set an oblong, lug-type sail with a boom at the foot; sail rotated around the mast. The **Java trader** carried a jib to a slender bowsprit. The Madura **mayang** sets a triangular sail with a long yard and boom, both tacking at the bow. Crew of larger vessels ca. 10-20. Reported lengths 6-20m; e.g., length 12m, beam 3m, depth 1.0m; shallow draft. Other recorded names: **madjăng prahu, majang(an), majang prau(w), mayangan, mayang proa, pajangan, pamayang, pěmajang, pemayang, perahu majang, perahu mayang, perahu pemayang, permajang, prahoe majang, prahau mahiang, prahu madjang, prao mayang, prau mayang.** Note also **golekan, kolek-2**. **2.** A modern, motorized **mayang**, used for trawling, is a bluff-bowed, beamy, square-sterned vessel.

mayangan See **mayang**

Mayang ba gan *China, central:* Dedicated mainly to carrying passengers from Mayang in the Yuan Jiang basin, on Dongting (Tungting) Lake, and to ports on the Chang Jiang (Yangtze). Extinct by the early 20th century. Bow square and sharply turned up; stern high and formed the after part of the main cabin; flat bottom. Decked; cabin abaft the mainmast; some had elaborate accommodations. Poling gangway along the sides; 3 crossbeams served as pivots for sweeps; balanced rudder, post coming up inboard. Stepped 1-2 masts, the foremast in the bow. Set balance lugsails. Crew of 7-10. Reported lengths 18-40m, widths 4.6-7.2m, depths 1.2-1.5m. Spelling variant: **Ma-yang pa-kan**

ma yang chuan *China, S:* Large salt-carrying vessel of the Guangzhou (Canton) area. High sides, square bow, high poop, raked ends. House covered most of hull; flooring inside easily removed for cargo stowage. Gangway along the sides for polers. Tripod mast could be lowered. Family lived on board. Length 36.6m, beam 6.1m, hold depth 2.4-2.7m, draft loaded 1.5-

2.1m. Other recorded names: **ma yang tch'ouan**, salt boat★, **West River salt boat**. See also **ma yang zi**.

Ma-yang pa-kan See **Mayang ba gan**

mayang proa See **mayang**

ma yang tch'ouan See **ma yang chuan**

ma-yang tse, ma-yang tseu See **ma yang zi**

ma-yang tzŭ See **ma yang zi, Zhiajiang ma yang zi**

ma yang zi *China, central:* **1.** Developed to carry cargo on Hunan waterways, especially on the Yuan Jiang, which is narrow and swift. Main center initially was Mayang. Boat's success caused the type to spread, in a modified form, to other areas, notably on the middle and upper reaches of the Chang Jiang (Yangtze) and into Sichuan (Szechuan). On most, the maximum beam, although slight, is well aft. The term *ma-yang* generally means "hemp sprout," which is more pointed at one end. Other recorded names: **ma yang chuan**★, **ma-yang tse, ma-yang tseu, ma-yang tzŭ**. Note also **chang kou ma yang zi, shao ma yang, shou kou ma yang zi, Yuanling ma yang zi, Zhijiang ma yang zi**. **2.** One type became important for passage through the Chang Jiang rapids above Yichang (I-ch'ang). Carried such items as oil, paper, charcoal, rice, and cloth. Stoutly built with numerous strong bulkheads and transverse beams; heavy wales. Flat bottom, longitudinally planked; some had midline or side keelsons; half frames strengthened the bottom. Markedly bulging sides with strong tumble home. Square, cross-planked bow; sharply upturned stern. Truncated, fan-shaped, balanced rudder; stock came up inboard; very long tiller reached into a raised part of the cabin and required 3 men to handle it in the rapids. Decked; cross planking removable; low coaming from bow to deckhouse; wooden cabin occupied after half. Rowed, tracked from shore, and sailed. As many as 6 men on each oar at times, using the projecting deck beams as fulcrums. Generally stepped a single tall mast, setting a balance lugsail with a rounded shoulder on the leech; mast in a tall tabernacle. Permanent crew of 8; engaged 50-60 to man the sweeps when needed, and 50 more for tracking from shore. Reported lengths 11-34m, some early vessels to 46m; e.g., length 31m, beam 5.8m, depth 2.6m. **3.** Some **ma yang zi** were passenger vessels. Most of these traveled on the upper and middle Chang Jiang and often on Dongting Hu (lake) in Hunan. A house with suitable amenities covered most of the hull. Some set a single lugsail with a curved leech; others 2-masted, the foremast well forward. Also propelled by sweeps or tracked. Reported lengths 15-18m, beam 3.5m.

maynard See **lumberman's batteau**

ma₂:ga *Iraq, S:* Term in the Babylonian kingdom for a **milk boat**★.

mbaeapu'a See **pelota-4**

mbembéo *Vanuatu (New Hebrides), western Pacific:* Small single-**outrigger canoe**★ of Île Tomman, off south Malekula. Dugout hull; rounded in cross section; pointed ends, with bow having a slight projection. Light poles lashed along the gunwales, across which are laid 4 short poles to support 2 narrow platforms that extend out each side; hull cavity open. Four evenly spaced booms, lashed atop the platforms, extend to the float. Relatively long float, flattened on top, connected to each boom by 2 pairs of under-crossed sticks. Paddled, but probably also sailed, employing the local type of woven pandanus sail, with 2 spars forming a wide "V." Length ca. 7.3m.

mbimba See **bimbá**

mbinambina See **binabina**

McKenzie River boat See **McKenzie River drift boat**

McKenzie River drift boat *United States, NW:* Light, open, **dory***-type boat modified to traverse rapids on this Oregon river and other rivers in the northwest. Used mainly for sport fishing and for river running. Drifts stern first, the oarsman pulling with a pair of long oars against the current to control course. Initially built of thin planks, later of plywood, and now often of fiberglass. Early boats had a wide transom stern (**stern-ender**), then were double-ended, and later had a sharp stern and narrow bow transom. Sweeps up sharply at the stern (downstream end). Wide, flat bottom with strong rocker; high, straight, flared sides, strengthened with frames. Seats removable to permit stacking; some have a rope seat on the upriver end for the steersman. Reported lengths on bottom 4.3-5.5m; e.g., length 4.9m, beam 1.7m. Other recorded names: **drift boat***, **Mackenzie River drift boat** (erroneously), **McKenzie River boat**

McKinnaw See **Mackinaw boat**

mčumbwi See **mtumbwi**

Mecklenburger Sandboot See **Sandboot**

medium clipper See **clipper**

Medway barge See **Thames sailing barge**

Medway bawley See **bawley**

Medway doble *England, SE:* Small, beamy, sharp-ended fishing and general-purpose boat. Some were **tenders*** to **bawleys***; later helped set long dragnets. Used in the Medway and Thames Estuaries into the 20th century; almost all motorized by the 1930s. Clinker planking, widely spaced, strong frames; fuller

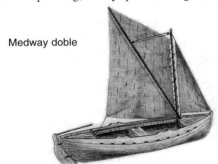

Medway doble

forward than aft; curved stem and sternpost; straight or curved keel. Low freeboard; some later boats had a daggerboard. A few had a square stern. Decked at bow and stern, wide waterways along the sides; at times, a tarpaulin draped over a pole provided shelter. **Fishing boats*** have small live well amidships; overflow of catch towed in a **fish box***. Outboard rudder; tiller. Spritsail set to a short, portable mast stepped well forward; heel of sprit raised on hoop with tackle at masthead; some boomed but loose-footed. Foresail set fly-

ing, tacked to stemhead; sheeted to an iron horse. Occasionally a main horse also. Some later boats used standing lugsails. Also rowed, using 1-2 pairs of oars; oarsman sat on a movable box. Size range: length 3.66m, beam 1.32m, depth 0.46m to 5.95m by 2.69m by 1.07m. Other recorded names: **doble***, **doble boat**, **double boat**, **Medway peter boat**, **Strood doble**

Medway peter boat See **Medway doble**

meerkoet See **zalmschouw**

meeting boat *China, east-central:* Conveys a bridegroom to his future father-in-law's home to meet his bride. Her father places her in a bridal sedan chair for the boat trip to her new home. Custom prevails only in the Suzhou (Soochow) area, and the boat is probably of no specific type. See also **church boat**.

mehãil See **mahaila-2**

mehsangi *North Korea:* Small boat used mainly in noncommercial river fishing. Very narrow, flat bottom; strongly flared sides, flat ends. The planking on those from P'yongyang was twisted so that the port quarter extended just abaft the starboard quarter, and at the bow, the starboard planking extended forward of the port strakes, creating an angle to the bow and stern transoms. Propelled by an oar in a type of sculling motion from the port quarter. Used by 1-2 persons. Length to ca. 4.3m.

meia lua 1. *Indonesia, E:* An old craft of the Sunda Isles, so designated because of its strongly curved bow and stern.

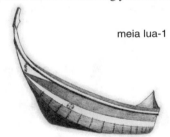

meia lua-1

2. *Portugal:* Shaped like a half moon (*meia lua*); probably extinct. Worked off Atlantic coast beaches with a seine net. Carvel-planked of local pine; planking horizontal at the high ends. Framed with single timbers, 36cm apart; planking pegged to frames. Bottom flat for half its length and then curved up in a graceful sweep, recurving at the top; stem higher than the sternpost. Strong sheer; heavy rubbing strake outside the gunwale. Open except for short deck at bow; usually 7 thwarts. Hull painted in dark color; oculi and religious symbols at ends. Steered with an oar bearing against a wooden post. Rowed with 2-4 oars (10m long), each manned by 5-7 men; wooden blocks on the oar loom slotted over a single tholepin. Reported lengths 8.2-16.5m; e.g., length 16.5m, beam 3.8m, depth 1.5m. Other recorded names: **barco de duas proas**, **barco do mar** (in the north), **duas pontas**, **duas proas**. Note also **bateira do mar-2**, **xávega**.

mekoro See **mokoro**

mekura bune See **kamé-no-ko-bune**

melkbootje *Netherlands, N:* Motorized vessel, mainly of Friesland, that transports milk. In the Waddenzee area, the term may be used disparagingly for a very small motor vessel. Note also **melkschuit**.

melkever See **Milch-Ewer**

melkschouw *Netherlands:* Open boat of the **schouw★** type that transported milk to processing plants. Sometimes built of steel; raked bow and stern transoms. Flat bottom, with rocker toward the bow; skeg at stern to support rudder. Angular chines; sides flare initially, then are vertical. Wide-bladed rudder, especially below the waterline; tiller slots over the rudderhead; leeboards. Light mast stepped in thwart in forward third; set a spritsail. Small **melkschouwje** ca. 4.75m long, 1.2m wide, 0.4m deep. Note also **milk boat**.

melkschouwje See **melkschouw**

melkschuitje *Netherlands, W:* Used by a farmer making his milking rounds; towed by him from the bank or poled along the interior waterways. Those at Assendelft in Nord Holland were carvel-planked of oak; sharp ends, flat bottom, flared sides, widely spaced frames. Decked at ends with bitt-like projections on each side of the inner end of the decks. Length 4.5m, beam 0.6m. Name variant: **Assendelfter melkschuitje**. Note also **melkbootje, milk boat, schuitje**.

mellajekt, mellomjekt See **jekt**

melon seed *United States, E:* **Skiff★** of commercial wildfowlers of New Jersey. Developed in the 1880s; now sometimes built as a pleasure craft. Flat floors, slack bilges, sharp bow with curved stem, sharply raked transom stern, skeg with flat plank keel. Decked except for rectangular cockpit; small hatch forward.

melon seed

Outboard rudder worked with lines or tiller. Employed a dagger-shaped or conventional centerboard. When sailed, set a boomed spritsail or a gaff sail. Mast stepped well forward. Also rowed. Reported lengths 4-4.8m; e.g., length 4.1m, beam 1.3m, depth 0.34m. Other recorded names: **Egg Harbor melon seed, punkin seed**. Note also **garvey box, pumpkin seed**. Further references: **Barnegat sneakbox, Seaford skiff**

menaida, menaide See **manaide**

menaka See **bullboat-1**

mE'nga *Canada, W:* Large, heavy **war canoe** of the Kwakiutl of northern Vancouver Island and the adjacent mainland. Besides raiding forays, transported groups of people and went to the fishing grounds. Extinct by the end of the 19th century. Thick dugout hull, not expanded; high prow, reportedly a stylized eagle's head but form varied; prow might stand 2.5m high, lashed on; straight, raked cutwater. Stern cut square, vertical or raked, raised above gunwale level, and

formed a seat for one or two men. Highly decorated. Crew of 12-25. Length to ca. 15m. Other recorded names: **Kwakiutl war canoe, kwɪniɪL, kwots, manka, mE'nk·a, munka, war canoe**

menhaden boat *United States, E and S:* Steam- and diesel-powered vessel that supports coastal menhaden fishing operations, carrying the gear, auxiliary boats, and crew to the fishing grounds. Actual fishing conducted by the **seine boats★** (also called **purse boats**) and the **striker boat★**, which were sometimes carried aboard the **menhaden boat**. Many equipped to carry crude menhaden oil to refining ports. May have a tall mast for spotting schools. **Menhaden boats** 23-59m long. In the New York Harbor area, the **seine** (or **bunker**) **boats** seined for menhaden for use as chum by **schooners★** fishing for bluefish. Other recorded names: **bony boat, carrier★, menhaden fisher**. Note also **bony-fish boat, gang-1, sail gear**.

menhaden carry-away boat *United States, E:* **1.** Those working off Rhode Island and in eastern Long Island were beamy boats. Part of the team that fished for menhaden, the **carry-away boat★** transported the fish caught by the **seine boat★** to market. Used in the latter part of the 19th century. Carvel or lapstrake construction; early boats double-ended, later transom-sterned. The double-ended boats were open, carvel-planked, with curved stem and sternpost. The later craft were decked centerboard boats with a cargo hold amidships and cabin aft. Open boats fitted with a single gaff sail, and the mast was stepped well forward. **Sloops★** also set a gaff topsail, jib, and jib topsail. Open boats 10.9m long, decked boats 13.2m long; shallow draft. Other recorded names: **car'away boat, carraway, carry-away sloop, menhaden carry-away sloop**. Note also **menhaden boat, sail gear**.
2. In the Delaware Bay area by 1860, small, burdensome **carry-away boats** were accompanying **schooners★** that carried 2 **seine boats** for the actual fishing.

menhaden carry-away sloop See **menhaden carry-away boat**

menhaden fisher See **menhaden boat**

menhaden purse seine boat See **seine boat-5a**

menhaden striker boat See **striker boat-1**

mëniebēib, méniebëp See **meniepep**

meniepep *Micronesia (Caroline Islands), Truk group, western Pacific:* A paddled outrigger **war canoe**; now extinct. Double-ended dugout hull, probably plank-extended; U-shaped hull with residual keel; gunwales strengthened with supplemental strips. Ends extended with lashed-on, ornamental stem pieces. Two or 3 booms pierced the hull and led to the float (ca. 9.5m long); connected by paired stanchions inserted into the float; outrigger kept on the lee side. A rising platform was constructed on opposite side, where some of the crew sat, probably to counterbalance the heavy outrigger; supports for the platform wedged under the opposite gunwale. Some carried 60 men. Length 21m, beam 0.55m, inside depth 0.72m. Spelling variants: **mëniebāb** (on **Lósap Atoll**); **méniebëp**. Note also **wa fötyn**.

menji See **manji**

mE'nk·a See **mE'nga**

men-of-war See **man-of-war**

Meppeler praam *Netherlands, NE:* Carried peat and wood on the smaller Meppel area waterways, mainly in the 19th century. Clinker-planked; sharp, vertical ends; flat bottom; hard chines; wide bulwark. Outboard rudder; tiller. Long, covered hatch; very small cabin below at each end; oval leeboards. Mast stepped about a third in from the bow, lowered forward when struck. Set a loose-footed, boomed, standing lugsail; staysail. Cap. 40-70t; narrow, earning the nickname **snijboon★**, or **string bean**. Length with rudder 19m, beam 3.9m, depth 1.3m; cap. 40-70t. Other recorded names: **Bohne, Meppelsche** (or **Meppelse**) **praam; snijbonen** (pl.)

Meppelsche praam, Meppelse praam See **Meppeler praam**

merakib, merākib′′ See **markab**

mercado, mercadero See **chalan**

mercante, mercanteis, mercantel See **bateira mercantel**

merchantman A privately owned vessel engaged in commercial pursuits, carrying cargo and passengers. May be classed as **dry cargo vessels** or **tankers★**. Selected name variants: **bâtiment de commerce, bâtiment marchand, commercial vessel, handelsfartyg, Handelsschiff, Kauffahrer, Kauffahrtei-schiff, kauppalaiva, kommercheskoe, koopvaarder, koopvaardijschip, marchand, merchant ship** (or **vessel**), **nave di commercio, nave mercantile, navire de commerce, navire marchand, shōsen, torgovoe sudno, trading vessel, trgovački brod** (or **ladja**), **trgôvaska ladja, vaisseau marchand, vaixell mercant**

merchant ship, merchant vessel See **merchantman**

merdeux See **picard-2**

mère See **train de bateaux**

mère-gigogne See **mother ship**

Mergui kabang See **kabang**

méricain See **américain**

merikabu, merikebu, merkab, mérkĕb, merkib See **markab**

Merrimack River wherry *United States, NE:* Small **rowing boat★** of the Merrimack River in northeastern Massachusetts. Often used as a **tender★** in the 19th century. Lapstrake construction; narrow, curved transom, deadwood below; curved stem in 2 pieces, the inner part receiving the planking and an outer false stem. Wide bottom board, sometimes hogged; sharp deadrise; strong sheer, the stern higher. Grown-knee frames; 2 thwarts with a hole in the forward thwart for a mast. Generally rowed, however, using oar straps. Length ca. 3.7m, beam 1.4m, depth ca. 0.5m.

Merrimac River gundalow See **gundalow**

Mersea smack See **Essex smack**

Mersey barge, Mersey barrow See **Mersey flat**

Mersey canoe-yawl See **canoe-yawl**

Mersey flat *England, NW:* Two types of **flats★** traveled the river and canal network of Cheshire and Lancashire, the **canal** or **cut flats**, which were unrigged and towed, and the **mast flats**, which sailed, some working out along the coast and crossing to Ireland. Often carried cargo, bunker coal, and sand ballast to ships. Some **sand flats** obtained sand in the estuary and carried it farther up the estuary for glass makers. Distinctive type developed by the early 18th century

and worked until the 1960s, but later only as **dumb barges★**. Carvel-planked, many of oak; bottom flat with short, slightly projecting keel; deep internal keelson; hard, round bilges; slab-sided, but **Rochdale flats** had rounded sides. Short but fine run; flat sheer. Initially sharp- or transom-sterned, then a square stern until ca. 1850, and finally rounded. Bluff bow, stem and sternpost slightly raked. Timber heads brought up above the deck at bow and stern to serve as bitts; those working in open waters (**outside flats**) had a railing full length or just at the stern (**bare or naked flats**); a few had bulwarks. Massive rudder; iron rod passed through the 2 gudgeons, enabling rudder to lift if vessel grounded; very long, curved tiller. **Canal flats** had a single long hatch; the apple-cheeked **mast flats** also

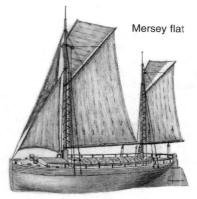

Mersey flat

had a small fore hatch; small cabin below after deck and also forward on some. The **open flats** lacked hatch covers. Heavy windlass at the bow handled the anchor and running lines. The vessel's **tender★** was called a **cock boat★**, ca. 4.9m long, carvel-planked, and generally towed on the starboard quarter. Originally square-sailed, then sprit, and lastly set a high-peaked gaff sail, loose-footed with long boom and gaff, and jib. Some late 18th-century **flats** carried bowsprits, generally of the lifting type. The latter were called **single-masted flats** to distinguish them from the **ketch★**-rigged vessels. Foresail sheeted to an iron traveler forward of the mast. Mast stepped slightly more than a quarter of the way aft. Those with tackle on the forestay for lowering the mast were **inside flats** or **up-river flats**. Sails tanned deep red. **Ketch**-rigged types, known as **jigger flats**, were larger, and in addition set a small jib topsail and a yard topsail; most were **coasters★**. Propelled by sweeps in calms; auxiliaries fitted in later vessels. The unrigged vessels were towed by horses, men, or tugs; sometimes makeshift tarpaulin sails set up. Crew of 2; 3-4 when going to sea. **Canal flat** lengths 20-22m, 4.1-4.5m wide, depth ca. 1.6m; sailing **flats** were 15-27m long; e.g., length 25m, beam 6.1m, depth 3.1m; **jigger flats** ca. 22m long, 4.7m wide, and 2.7m deep. Other recorded names: **floating wheelbarrow; Mersey barge, Mersey barrow** (both erroneously); **sand hooker**. Further reading: John Leather, *Barges* (London: Adlard Coles, Ltd., 1984), 198-214; Michael Stammers, *Mersey Flats and Flatmen* (Lavenham:

Terence Dalton Ltd. and Liverpool: National Museums and Galleries on Merseyside, 1993). Note also **flat-3b**, **jigger sloop**, **number one**, **Weaver flat**.

Mersey gig *England, NW:* Small, heavily built boat that worked from the 18th to the early 19th century out of Liverpool, serving ships, transporting passengers and luggage, ferrying across the River Mersey, and later passing lines from docking vessels. Clinker-built with narrow strakes, thick gunwales, transom stern; open. Hull generally varnished. Set 2-3 spritsails and sometimes a foresail. Easily rowed. Crew of 3. Later boats had engines and were carvel-built. Reported lengths 6.1-8.5m; e.g., length 6.1m, beam 2m. Name variants: **gigboat**, **Mersey gigboat**

Mersey gigboat See **Mersey gig**

Mersey yawl See **canoe-yawl**

meschhuf See **mashhûf**

mesciara See **musciara**

meshhûf, **meshûf** See **mashhûf**

mesih See **mahaila-2**

messenger boat See **sponge schooner-2**

metafa, **metaffy** See **mtepe**

Methodist canoe *United States, E:* A log **canoe★** of the early 19th century that transported a Methodist preacher to services on the islands of lower Chesapeake Bay. Typical of the working vessels of the region. Open. Set 2 leg-of-mutton sails with horizontal sprits. Also rowed. Length ca. 9m, beam 1.5m, depth 0.46m. Note also **church boat**.

Mettekahn See **Kahn-5**

Mevagissey lugger See **East Cornish lugger**

Mevagissey tosher *England, SW:* Lug-sailed mackerel **fishing boat★** of Mevagissey on the southern Cornwall coast. Many present-day **toshers★** use gill nets instead of lines. Characterized by being smaller than the **Mevagissey lugger**, hence a **tosher**. Hull design varied, and they might be open or decked forward and aft with compartments between. Usually transom-sterned; tiller passed through the transom. Lug- or **cutter★**-rigged. Engines installed later, with steadying mizzen. Generally lengths under 6.07m to keep within harbor dues limits; now as long as 9m. Name variant: **tosser**. Further reading: Percy Mitchell, *A Boatbuilder's Story* (Mevagissey: Kingston, 1968). Note also **East Cornish lugger**.

mezza galea, **mezza galera** See **half galley**

mezza gondola See **barchetta-3**

mhēlen See **mahaila-2**

mi'alba See **kaloa**

Miao boat See **Miao chuan**

Miao chuan *China, S:* Slender **riverboat★** of the Miao peoples of Guizhou (Kweichow) Province. Long, tapered, and rising ends; narrow end transoms; narrow, flat bottom; rounded, flaring sides; compartmented by bulwarks. Decked except for forward compartment; arched house covers central section from gunwale to gunwale. Steered with a bow sweep pinned to an athwartships beam that extends out to one side; shallow, balanced stern rudder comes up inboard. Tracking mast stepped in forward third; also poled. Crew of 3-5. Length 14m, beam 1.5m, depth 0.61m. Name variant: **Miao boat**

mi bao zi *China, E:* **1.** Well-made and well-maintained boat that carries rice to Shanghai from the lake area along the lower Chang Jiang (Yangtze). Narrow, square bow turns up sharply; 2 prominent bitts slightly inboard; square stern. Low sides; top strake extends beyond the rudder; washstrakes aft of the house protect the crew. Arched, wooden shelter amidships; matting slides over the open section of roof when necessary; cargo in forward hold and beneath the roof. Leeboards; outboard rudder; tiller. Tall mast stepped forward of the house; sets a rectangular lugsail or spritsail. Crew of 4-5. Reported lengths 15-20m.
2. A type that navigates down Suzhou (Soochow) Creek to Shanghai from Changzhou (Changshu) has a flatter sheer and steps the mast farther aft. The house extends forward and aft of the mast. Bottom flat, bilges rounded, sides tumble home. Nine bulkheads, the 6th and 7th fitted with sliding doors; 3 frames. Marked taper toward the square ends; top strake extends aft of the raked, hatchet-shaped rudder; long, cocked-up tiller. House removable; gaps in the roof covered by tarpaulins in bad weather. Owner lives aft; crew of 3 live forward. Length 16.5m, beam 3.2m, depth 1.4m. Other names: **Changshu (Changzhou) chuan**
Spelling variants: **mi pao tse**, **mi pao tzǔ**

Micmac basket canoe See **basket canoe**

Micmac big-river canoe See **big-river canoe**

Micmac moose-hide canoe See **mu'su u'lk**

Micmac rough-water canoe See **rough-water canoe**

Micmac woods canoe See **woods canoe**

middenschouw See **Friese schouw**, **schouw**

mignole, **mignolle** See **spitsbek**

mijole See **walenmajol**

mijolle See **spitsbek**

Milchboot See **Schiesslomme**

Milch-Ever See **Milch-Ewer**

Milch-Ewer *Germany, NW:* Special fast boat that transported milk on the lower Elbe River, mainly to Hamburg; worked from at least the 17th to the end of the 19th century. Also carried passengers. An **Ewer★** type, but most sharp-sterned and square- or sprit-rigged. Flat bottom with chine planks; decked forward with cabin below; leeboards. Spelling variants: **melkever**, **Milch-Ever**

Miles River cabin skiff See **cabin skiff**

Milicite canoe See **Malecite river canoe**

militari kosha See **kosha**

militia galley See **scout boat**

milk boat *England, central:* Cadbury Brothers, the chocolate company, maintained several **horse boats★** in the early 20th century to transport milk collected from farms along the Shropshire Union Canal to the evaporating factory at Knighton. The churns were set up on stands in the boats. Note also **Eiskahn**, **ma$_2$:ga**, **melkschouw**, **melkschuitje**, **Milch-Ewer**, **Schiesslomme**.

mille-guenille See **berrichon**

minahouët See **sardinier breton**

mǐ-ná-ki See **bullboat-1**

min chuan See **junk**

Minenprahm See **Prahm-2**

Ministerschiff See **Leibschiff**

miopar See **mioparo**

mioparo Craft reported as used by the Phoenicians, Veneti Celts of northwestern France, and the Saxons, mainly for piracy along coasts, rivers, and on lakes. Framework of wicker covered with skins. Other recorded names: **miopar, mioparon, Veneti boat**. Note also **myparon, paro, paron, skin boat**.

mioparon See **mioparo**

mi pao tse, mi pao tzŭ See **mi bao zi**

mirante See **moliceiro**

mīrkab See **markab**

misciaretta See **cabanella**

mission boat 1. *Canada:* Provided religious and medical services to isolated communities along coastal areas and inland waterways. Some also carried freight. Other recorded names: **mission scow** (or **ship**)
2. *England:* A converted **narrow boat★** of the Salvation Army plied the Midlands canals as a **mission boat** for several years after World War II. Renovated to include a small meeting room. Motorized; later engine removed, creating a **butty boat** while a new boat provided the power. The **butty** was fitted with bunks for young people. In the late 19th century, **mission boats** affiliated with other groups ran some of the canals. Name variant: **Salvation Army mission boat**. Note also **church boat**.

mission scow, mission ship See **mission boat**

mission smack *England, E:* Vessel that sailed out of Yarmouth to join the fishing **fleets★** on the Dogger Bank in the North Sea in the late 19th century. Engaged in fishing, but its primary purpose was to provide aid and comfort to the crews of the **fleets** in the form of religious services and reading materials, medical assistance, tobacco, and warm clothing. Some went as far as Newfoundland. Generally **ketch★**-rigged; reported lengths 14-24m. By the early 20th century, they were modern **steamers**. Name variant: **bethel ship**

Mississippi boat See **flatboat-4**

Mississippi scull boat *United States, central:* Stubby, low-lying duck-hunting boat of the upper Mississippi Basin. Well-built; full bow; wide, shallow transom with 2 sculling notches; bottom and sides formed a wide, smooth arc; shallow keel. Wide side decks, small foredeck, low coaming around the cockpit. Decking often piled with brush, grass, or ice to create a blind.

Missouri boat See **flatboat-4**

misṭeh, mistic, misticho See **mistico**

mistico *Mediterranean:* An 18th- and 19th-century vessel, mainly a **coaster★**, but served for armed surveillance off the Spanish coast, as a pirate ship in the Greek archipelago, and for landing operations and carrying despatches. Some used into the 20th century. Generally sharp lines with flaring sides and marked sheer; rounded stem or clipper bow; counter stern. Decked at stern; while at anchor, a tent was rigged over this area. In general, set 2 quadrilateral lateen-type sails with a short luff (*mistico*): high-peaked with the luff cut square; tacked fairly close to the mast. Mizzenmast, used on the larger vessels, set lug- or square sails. Long bowsprit, 2-3 headsails. Fore- and mainmast raked forward. On the Catalan vessels, the lateen sails were set to vertical main- and foremasts; also set a gunter-type leg-of-mutton mizzen. Also

rowed, through oarports; 18-40 oarsmen. Reported lengths 15-40m. Other recorded names: **mastī ku, misṭeh, mistic(ho), mistic(o)u, mistik(o), mistika, mistique, mystaco, mystic, veliero misto**

misticou, misticu, mistik, mistika, mistiko, mistique See **mistico**

mistoo't See **crooked canoe**

mitepe See **mtepe**

mitjang *Australia, N:* Term for **ship★** by the aborigines of Arnhem Land.

mitjiang See **pinisi**

Mittelkahn See **Oberländer-4**

mitumbuí *Mozambique, N:* Double-**outrigger canoe★** that fishes in the Porto Amelía (Pemba) area. Hewn from a single log; sharp, raised, raked ends; vertical sides; flat bottom. Open; 2 benches. Two straight booms cross the hull, lashed to the gunwales. Booms slot into small, vertical blocks which, in turn, peg into slender floats that curve up at the ends. Mainly poled and paddled, but may set a lateen sail to a short mast stepped in forward third. Sail hung outside the 2 shrouds. Length 3.5m, beam and depth 0.4m.

mitumbwi See **mtumbwi**

m'loung See **laung**

moagie See **mohiki-1**

moana See **lighter-1, mahonne-2, vascello-2**

m.o.b. boot See **accident boat**

mochip *Japan, N/Russia, E:* Plank-extended **canoe★** constructed by the Ainu peoples of the Japanese island of Hokkaido and the Russian island of Sakhalin. Planks sewn on. Note also **chip**.

mociara See **musciara**

moddermolen *Netherlands:* **Dredger★** using a wheel or wheels to raise mud in shallow channels or harbors. Initially operated by hand, later by horses; an 18th-century type used a pair of men each walking atop 2 wheels. Mud deposited into waiting **barges★**. Best known in Amsterdam, where they were used as early as 1575. Later, the various types were operated by steam. Other recorded names: **moddermolenschip, moddermoolen, modderschüyt, molen-schip**. See also **dredger-1**.

moddermolenschip, moddermoolen See **moddermolen**

modderpraam See **modderschouw, slijkpraam**

modderprahm See **Mudderprahm**

modderschouw *Netherlands:* Vessel that transported dredged mud. On some, trap doors on the bottom enabled the vessel to release its load. A 17th-century **modderschouw** was 16.3m long, 3.9m wide, 0.8m deep. Name variant: **modderpraam**. Note also **hopper, kantelbak**.

modderschüyt See **moddermolen**

modderskûtsje See **skûtsje**

moderskib See **mother ship**

model-parawa, model paruwa See **paruwa-2**

modhyam balam *Bangladesh, SE:* **Fishing boat★** that operates gill nets in the area between Cox's Bazaar and Chittagong. Usually built up from a dugout base, with the planking either sewn or nailed; strengthened with ribs. Raked bow transom; sharp, raked stern. Short foredeck, larger deck aft, open waist. Employs a quarter rudder. Single mast stepped through a hole in a transverse beam; sets a square sail. Crew of 4-6. Reported lengths 9.1-12.2m; e.g., length overall 12.2m, on keel 8.1m, beam 2.44m, depth 1.83m. Note also **balam**.

moggie See **mokihi-1**

mohalla See **mahaila-2**

Mohawk boat *United States, E:* Used in the Mohawk Valley in central New York State from the late 18th century. Provided transportation and carried supplies and produce. Use spread westward beyond the valley, some traveling to the Niagara River on Lake Ontario. Slightly rounded ends, flat bottom with hard chines, broad plank keel, straight sides, small foredeck, short afterdeck for helmsman. Steered with a long oar. Poled from cleated side decks; poles 5.5-6.7m long. Also rowed, or set a square sail and topsail; mast stepped in the forward half. Crew of ca. 8. Reported lengths 12-15m; narrow; shallow draft. Other recorded names: **galley***, **Mohawk regulator**, **Schenectady boat***, **Schenectady Durham**. Note also **Durham boat**.

Mohawk flat See **flat-6**

Mohawk regulator See **Mohawk boat**

Mohawk River bateau See **bateau-7e**

Mohawk River Durham boat See **Durham boat-2**

mohiki See **mokihi-1**

Möja-skärbåt See **skärbåt**

Moken boat See **kabang**

moki See **mokihi-1**

mokihi *New Zealand:* **1.** A reed craft that provided transportation on inland waters for the Maoris and for European settlers. Constructed of a type of flax stalk; details vary somewhat from area to area. One made from a type of bulrush called *raupoo* might be called a **puhau** or **puwahau**. Most sharp-ended, although one type had a truncated stern. Some were merely a cigar-shaped bundle on which the occupant sat astride. Others were composed of several bundles; many were shaped so that a series of small bundles formed the bottom and sides. Mainly paddled with the hands or a piece of wood, or poled. Reported lengths 3.6-18m. Other recorded names: **moagie**, **moggie**, **mohiki**, **moki**, **mooki(h)i**. Note also **amatiatia**.
2. On the east coast, was sometimes a small, 1-man **canoe***.

mokoro *Botswana, N:* The **water-taxi** of the Okovango Swamp; also used for hunting and fishing. **Dugout canoe*** hewn with an adze to as thin as 5cm on the sides. Shape depends on the original tree and might not be straight if the tree had a bend. Bottom flattened; tapered, solid ends. Mainly poled. Reported lengths 3.7-7.6m, width 0.6m or less. Spelling variants: **makora**, **makoro**, **mokorro**; pl. **mekoro**

mokorro See **mokoro**

mol See **dredger-1**

mola *Solomon Islands, western Pacific:* Plank-built **canoe*** of the **mon*** type found on several of the central islands of the archipelago. In some areas, the end pieces are tall, while elsewhere the ends may be low, or one end may be lower than the other. Built of 6 strakes; thinned edges permit easier boring for stitching; inner side of the strakes may have ridges with cleats to which the ribs are fastened. Keel piece terminates before the ends; bow and stern pieces attached by interlocking stitching. Caulked with putty from a nut, which is also used to coat the outside, making it black. Ordinary **canoes** undecorated; others may have one or both of the erections ornamented with shells. Mainly paddled, but may employ a sail, stepping the mast through a forward thwart. Length ca. 13.7m, beam 1.1m. Name variant: **cañalucho**. Further reference: **mon-3**

molen-schip See **moddermolen**

moleta, **moletta** See **muleta**

molette See **muleta-2**

moliceiro *Portugal, central:* Boat of the lagoon at Aveiro that works from late July to late March collecting seaweed (*moliço*) to be used for fertilizer; occasionally transports merchandise and livestock. Carvel-planked of white pine with pine-root ribs, 19-24 bottom and side frames. Sharp ends; bottom flat for about three-quarters of its length, then rises in a long, low rake. No keel; strongly flared sides; considerable sheer and very low freeboard amidships; wide gunwales. Portable bulwarks raise sides as the seaweed is collected. Characterized by a sharply recurved stem joined by

moliceiro

the sheer strake; hinged upper portion permits lowering while passing under low bridges; sternpost curved. Large, tall, strongly curved rudder attached with pintles; tiller fitted athwartships on rudderhead; rope from one end carries forward, reeves through the stem, and runs back to the tiller. May use a leeboard looped to the mast; 3 of different widths carried. Cuddy forward; storage locker beneath seat at the stern. Bow and stern patches generally elaborately painted, usually in traditional designs; red stemhead; hull ochre with black gunwale initially, then hull entirely black. A small type built at Salreu is black with no ornamentation. A small **tender***, called a **matola**, **lodra**, or **trambolim**, is used in very shallow water. May be sailed, rowed, poled, or towed. Slender, unstayed mast stepped through a thwart roughly amidships; occasionally a 2nd smaller mast is braced against the forecastle. Sets a lugsail; luff extended by 2 bowlines with bridles leading to the stemhead. The Salreu boats are only poled. Crew of 2-3. Approximate size range: length 9.3m, beam 1.35m, depth 0.42m to 17m by 2.7m; shallow draft. Other recorded names: **barco moliceiro**; **mirante** (one from the Mira area). Further reading: José de Castro, *Aveiro. I Tômo. Moliceiros* (Porto: Instituto Para a Alta Cultura, 1943); John Eide, "The Moliceiros of Aveiro Lagoon," *WoodenBoat* 95 (1990), 48-54.

mon 1. *Indonesia, E:* Light, plank-built **canoe★** of the Moluccan Islands. Slender, sharp ends; vertical stem and sternpost rise above gunwale level; U-shaped in cross section; ribs attached to cleats on the multipiece strakes.

2. *Papua New Guinea, Bismarck Archipelago:* Term for a plank-built paddling **canoe** found on several of the islands. One cited for New Ireland had the upturned ends of the Solomon Islands **mon**; no outrigger. On the Tanga Islands to the east, the **mon** lacks the end pieces. Some step 2 masts.

3. *Solomon Islands, western Pacific:* Class of plank-built paddling **canoes** found in the northwestern two-thirds of the archipelago. Characterized by rounded-up, tall end pieces of roughly the same height, although in some areas, one end may be taller. Used mainly for interisland communication, fishing, and war. At Buka and adjacent smaller islands and northern Bougainville, generally built of thin planks of varying widths and lengths, sewn on; specially carved, short upper strakes at each end merge into the sheer line. Washstrakes at each end generally; some have short end decking. Frames, created from buttress roots, lashed to residual cleats inside each strake. Bottom rounded in cross section, flat longitudinally. A modified **mon** on Buka Island has low ends formed by the continuous curve of the bottom; bottom a wide "V" in cross section. No sheer to the planking; ends decked with breakwaters; separate gunwale strips. Number of seats varies with length, each accommodating 2 people; seats laid atop the ribs. Except for carving, most undecorated but coated with a putty from a nut, which blackens the hull; **war canoes** were inlaid with mother-of-pearl, and shells ornamented the erections, which might be topped with feathers. Recently, some step 1-2 masts, setting sprit- or lug-sails. Regular **canoes** carry from 1 to 30 people; **war canoes** as many as 40. Reported lengths 4.6-18.2m, width ca. 1.0m. Special terms designate size, by the number of seats: one—**koak**; two—**poboak**; three—**pokukan**; four—**potana**; five—**potonim**; six—**potonom**; ten—**posawun**. Other recorded names: **cañalucho, mahn, mola★, mona★, muna.** Further reading: Beatrice Blackwood, *Both Sides of Buka Passage* (Oxford: Clarenden Press, 1935), 369-381; O. Finsch, "Ein Plankenboot von Buka...," *Globus* XCV/24 (1909), 275-320.

mon'á *Brazil, central:* **Dugout canoe★** of the Puruborá of the Amazon Basin.

mona See **mon-3**

monaio See **culé**

money boat See **death galley**

monitor 1. An armored naval vessel that originated in 1862 during the American Civil War. Used mainly for coastal bombardment and river duties. During World Wars I and II, updated **monitors** were in use, and the class of vessel was adopted by other nations. In the United States/Vietnam conflict, the term applied to a type of sophisticated craft used against the Viet Cong in the Mekong Delta. **Monitors** were characterized by their heavy armor, revolving turret, and very shallow draft. The Civil War **monitors** on the Mississippi

River were **sternwheelers.** Other recorded names: **Kasemattschiff, pontone armato.** Note also **flat iron-1.**

2. *United States, E:* On Chesapeake Bay, **monitors** are large, wooden, flat-bottomed, rectangular craft that haul oyster shells. In the early 1900s, they also hauled produce from farms to wharves for transfer to a **steamer.** In each corner is a well through which a pole is thrust to anchor the craft, yet permit it to rise and fall with the tide. Towed. Note also **shell boat.**

3. *United States, north-central:* Boat popular with duck hunters in the shallow streams and marshes of the Green Bay, Wisconsin, area during the late 19th and early 20th centuries. Double-ended; flat bottom; lapped cedar strakes. Decked at the ends, narrow side decks; high coaming around a long, oval cockpit. Propelled by a punting pole or push-paddle. Length 4m, beam 0.86m, depth 0.18m; very light. Other recorded names: **Green Bay** (**hunting**) **boat, monitor marsh boat**

Further references: **Koshkonong monitor, sinker boat**

monitor marsh boat See **monitor-3**

monkey 1. A vessel rigged too lightly or in an unorthodox manner.

2. *England:* A single-masted **coaster★** of the 16th and 17th centuries. Set a square sail and sometimes a topsail. Ca. 40-50t burden.

monkey barge See **monkey boat-3b**

monkey boat 1. Small boat used at a dock, especially as a platform from which to paint and clean the sides of ships, or for ferrying across the harbor. Note also **chata.**

2. *Canada:* Term sometimes given to a small, flat-bottomed craft used for fishing.

3. *England:* **a.** A **narrow boat★** that is longer than usual but with a beam of 2.1-2.4m, enabling it to pass through especially narrow waterways. **b.** On the Thames and Severn, 2 **canal boats★** lashed together. Name variant: **monkey barge**

4. *England, SE:* **a.** London term for a **narrow boat★. b.** Half-decked boat on the Thames, particularly above London Bridge.

5. *United Kingdom:* Ships of the Elder-Dempster Line that carried a cargo of nut kernels.

Further reference: **gillnetter-2**

monluçon See **berrichon**

Monomoy *United States:* Double-ended **surfboat★** built along **whaleboat★** lines. First used as a working boat off southeastern Cape Cod, later as a lifesaving boat, and subsequently as a **ship's boat★.** Originally only lapstrake, then also carvel-planked. Partly ceiled, high freeboard, round bilges, heavy stem and sternpost, centerboard. Rudder and tiller. Stations for 6-10 rowers; also equipped with a lugsail, usually with a sliding gunter. Reported lengths 7-8m; e.g., length 7.9m, beam 2.1m, depth 0.7m.

monosoli, monossillóne See **dugout canoe**

monòssilo See **almadia-2, dugout canoe**

monoxila, monoxilo, monoxilos, monoxyl, monoxyla, monoxyle, monoxylo, monoxylon, monoxylus See **dugout canoe**

monsoon canoe See **varakan-oruwa**

Montagnais crooked canoe See **crooked canoe**

Montagu whaler, **Montague whaler** See **whaleboat-6b**
montaria *Brazil:* **1.** Large, flat-bottomed **dugout canoe**⋆
used on rivers, principally for transporting produce, but
also for fishing and hunting. Bow usually has a long overhang; stern square; sides straight and vertical. Paddled.

2. General-purpose **canoe**⋆ of the upper tributaries of
the Amazon Basin, including those originating in
Bolivia. Especially for use through rapids. Small
types are expanded **dugout canoes** with V-shaped
end pieces inserted. Most have a wide bottom onto
which a plank is added along each side; triangular or
semicircular end pieces, the bow piece more elaborate than the stern. One type of **montaria** built of 5
planks; one lacking additional strakes may be called
a **casco**⋆. Bow and stern characteristically narrow
and raked; sides flare and are strengthened with
frames. Temporary lath and palm hut at the stern on
some. May be paddled alone from the bow or stern;
also poled. A large **montaria** propelled by oars is
called a **montaria-possante**; one propelled by a
motor is a **motogodile**. Average 6-8m long. Note also
falca, **igarité-2**.
montaria-possante See **montaria-2**
Monterey squid skiff See **squid skiff**
montluçon See **berrichon**
Montreal canoe See **canot du maître**
mookihi, **mookii** See **mokihi-1**
mooring boat, **mooring hulk**, **mooring lighter** See
anchor hoy
moose-hide canoe *Canada/United States:* Made mainly
for emergency or temporary use, especially by Native
American hunters needing to transport game by water.
Gunwales, framing, stem, sternpost, and sheathing
generally of green saplings. Gunwales often merely
crossed at the ends and lashed. Skins sewn longitudinally, shaped, and secured by lashings; if hair not
removed, it is usually placed on the exterior; skins
later used for other purposes. Reported length 3.8m,
beam 1.02m, depths 0.36-0.48m. On the Mackenzie
River in northwestern Canada, moose-skin craft were
more boat-like. Large cargo-carrying capacity; rowed.
Other recorded names: **Malecite** (or **Penobscot**)
moose-hide canoe. See also **mu'su u'lk**.
moose-skin boat See **moose-hide canoe**
Moray Firth herring boat See **scaffie**
Morbihan lugger, **Mor Bihan sinago** See **sinago**
Morecambe Bay prawner *England, NW:* Class of
nobby⋆ developed in the 2nd quarter of the 19th century to work the shallow inshore waters of Morecambe
Bay for brown shrimp; the larger pink shrimp (locally
called prawns) were sought farther offshore. Last built
ca. 1920. Plumb stem with an almost square-toed foot
on early boats; after ca. 1896, stem was rounded above
the waterline and sharply cutaway below; sharp bow.
Straight keel initially, later slight rocker; shoe keel fitted on underside. Early boats carried inside ballast,
later a large iron casting was let into the keel. Transom

stern followed by rounded or square counter above a
sharply raking sternpost. Stern low in order to work
the shrimp trawl; sheer line rose gradually to the bow.
Carvel-planked; hollow garboards, sharp floors, well-
rounded bilges, maximum beam well forward. Rudder
hung below and forward of the counter. Smallest boats
open abaft the mast; others had a long, narrow cockpit
that was off center to provide more shrimp-sorting
space on one side. Some had a boiler for the shrimp in
the cockpit. Cuddy forward. Set a well-peaked gaff
mainsail, loose-footed with boom. Staysail sometimes
run up on an iron-rod stay; lofty jib. Long, heavy
bowsprit ran out through a gammon iron on the stemhead. At times, used a rectangular yard topsail hoisted
at the end of the pole mast. Sails tanned. Mast stepped
either on the keelson or in a tabernacle. Modern
prawners⋆ are motorized. Crew of 1-4. Reported
lengths 7.6-14.6m; typically 9.1m length overall, 7.2m
on waterline, beam 2.95m, depth 1.32m. Other recorded names: **Bay boat**, **half-decked boat**, **half-decker**⋆,
Lancashire nobby, **nobby**⋆, **prawner**⋆; **Fleetwood**,
Maryport, **Morecambe Bay**, **Southport shrimper**;
smack⋆ at Maryport
Morecambe Bay shrimper See **Morecambe Bay**
prawner
morfidite See **hermaphrodite brig**
mórkob See **markab**
moro, **Moro vinta** See **vinta**
mörsarfartyg See **bomb vessel**
Morse sloop See **Friendship sloop**
mortar boat *United States, central:* Devised during the
Civil War for use on the Mississippi River. Set on a
raft⋆ of lashed logs or on a low **barge**⋆-like craft.
Mortar (33cm) placed amidships within a sloping,
wooden housing. When being fired, crew stood on end
decking. Length ca. 21m, beam 6.4m. **Schooners**⋆
were also used in this period on western rivers. Mortar
was placed amidships. See also **bomb vessel**.
mortar vessel, **morteerchaloupe** See **bomb vessel**
morutier General term in French for a vessel that fishes
for cod (*morue*), especially off Newfoundland, Greenland, Iceland, and Spitzbergen. Variety of hulls and
rigs used; one with a **schooner**⋆ rig was called a
goélette morutière. Now are motorized **trawlers**⋆.
Note also **cod-fishing boat**, **doris**, **terreneuvier**.
mōsca See **advice boat**
mosciara See **musciara**
Moses See **Moses boat**
Moses boat 1. Term often used for a small **ship's boat**⋆,
especially in the 17th and 18th centuries, but still
applied in Germany to the smallest **ship's boat**. In
Denmark, it may be a **norsk pram**⋆, having small
bow and stern transoms. Name variants: **Moses**,
Mosesboot
2. *Barbados, West Indies:* Small, roughly constructed
rowboat⋆; term still used by local fishermen. Works
mainly over the reefs. Sharp bow, transom stern, V-
bottom. Usually rowed, but may use an outboard motor.
Lengths to 6m, shallow draft.
3. *England, SE:* 17th-century **lighter**⋆ on the Thames.
4. *United States, E:* Name appears in literature of the
tobacco industry of Maryland and Virginia.

5. *United States/West Indies:* Heavy, beamy **rowboat** used as a **tender★** or **lighter** to ships lying at anchor in New England and Chesapeake Bay ports, especially during the 17th-18th centuries. Usually clinker-built with a marked sheer, flat floors, curved keel. Bottom pitched, sides varnished. Some reported rigged for sailing. The **single Moses** was square-ended, the **double**

Moses boat-5

Moses double-ended. Many were transported to the West Indies, where they lightered hogsheads of molasses from shore to off-lying ships; the single model, manned by one oarsman, carried one cask in a special cradle; the double type carried 2 casks. V-shaped timbers fit the hogsheads. Reported lengths 2.4-5.5m; e.g., length 4.88m, beam 1.83m, depth 0.81m; shallow draft.

Mosesboot See **Moses boat**

mosquito boat Fast, lightly armed vessel designed for quick maneuvering. Often a river craft. Other recorded names: **mosquito** (or **musquito**) **craft**, **Schnellboot**. Note also **mosquito fleet**.

mosquito craft See **mosquito boat**

mosquito fleet 1. A **fleet★** of **mosquito boats★**.

2. *Australia, SE:* The small trading vessels that plied the inlets and lakes on the south coast of New South Wales comprised the **mosquito fleet**. Sailed in the 2nd half of the 18th century, later motorized. Cap. to 40t; draft 1.2-1.5m.

3. *United Kingdom:* Fast World War II boats of the Royal Navy Light Coastal Forces.

4. *United States:* **a.** On the Maine coast, the small boats manned by youngsters who tended their few lobster pots during the summer made up the **mosquito fleet**. **b.** Term given to the motley collection of small, open boats working out of Charleston, South Carolina, that supplied coastal communities in summer with fresh fish caught within the 10-fathom curve. Varied in type and size. Generally employed a sprit mainsail, and whatever other sail could set. Rowed in calms, using double tholepins. Under 5t. **c.** In Puget Sound in the northwest, the **mosquito fleet** was composed of small **steamers** that provided services to early settlers along the numerous inlets and islands of the bay. Sometimes farmers shipped their livestock together with their produce on these boats.

Spelling variants: **musquito(e) fleet**. See also **yole-3**.

mossel See **masula**

mosselaak See **lemmeraak**

mosselaar *Netherlands, SW:* Gaff-rigged boat of the mussel industry of the Westerschelde area. May also go to the Waddenzee on the north coast for mussel seed. Boat used is frequently a **hengst★**. Other recorded names: **Flushing (Vlissingen) mussel boat**, **mosselkrabber**, **mosselman**, **mosselschip**, **mosselschuit**, **mosselvisser**. Note also **lemmeraak**, **mussel boat**.

mosselhengst See **hengst**

mosselkrabber, **mosselman**, **mosselschip**, **mosselschuit**, **mosselvisser** See **mosselaar**

mossula See **masula**

mot See **Mutte**

mota See **manji**, **maota**, **mut-1**

mother A successful model of a particular type of vessel that becomes a prototype for others. These subsequent vessels built on the same model become **sisters** (also **frères**). Other recorded names: **bateau jumeau**, **buque gemelo**, **nave gemella**, **navio geméo** (or **irmão**), **nave gemella**, **navire frère** (or **jumeau**), **Schwesterschiff**, **sister ship**, **søsterskib**, **zusterschip**

mother ship Term loosely applied to a vessel that serves as home base for a **fleet★** of smaller craft, some of which may be carried aboard. In the British navy, it may be a **depot ship** for a **destroyer** or **submarine**, either a converted vessel or one built for this purpose. Among fishing **fleets**, it may be the one that carries **dories** stacked on deck or one carrying supplies and equipped to process the catch. Other recorded names: **bateau gigogne** (or **mère**), **bâtiment dépôt**, **buque nodriza**, **Fabrikmutterschiff**, **mère gigogne**, **moderskib**, **mum**, **Mutterschiff**, **nave chiocca** (or **madre**), **navire d'entreposage**, **navire de ravitaillement**, **navire mère**, **navire soutien**, **navire usine**, **parent ship**, **visserij-moederschip**. Note also **annexe**, **charoi**, **factory ship**, **terreneuvier**, **whaler-1**.

motobarca See **motor boat-1**

motobarca pompa See **fire boat**

motogodile See **montaria-2**

moto-moto *Papua New Guinea, SW:* Double-**outrigger canoe★** found among the islands in the Fly River delta. Fishes with harpoons and transports passengers. Dugout hull; round in cross section; ends elongated and truncated. Washstrakes raise the sides, sewn on with rattan over split bamboo; washboard at each end. One that had highly ornamented ends is called a **burai**; some of these have a tall, carved erection at the stern. Short, raised platform at bow for harpooner. Pointed floats, thick through the center, are connected by 2 long booms. Floats and booms attached with paired, divergent stanchions that cross above the booms. Light platform laid on the booms, crossing the hull and extending out each side. Steered with a board amidships shifted from side to side as needed (2 used when wind from astern) and a paddle at the stern. Until the turn of the 20th century, the **canoe★** was rigged with 2-3 tall, narrow mat sails, each supported by a pair of light, divergent masts. Sails clustered just forward of the platform. Masts stepped in a shoe in the bottom. Vertical sides of each sail skewered with bamboo to create yards. Complex system of stays, guys, and struts. Later vessels **schooner★**-rigged. Reported lengths 13-18m; narrow. Note also **gul**.

motopompa See **fire boat**

motor *Philippines, N:* Term given to any small or medium-sized boat with an engine, especially in northeastern Luzon. See also **automoteur**.

motoråttring See **åttring-3**

motorbarkasse See **launch**

motor boat 1. Pleasure or work boat propelled by an internal combustion engine. Selected name variants:

auto boat, automobile, bateau à moteur, bateau automobile, canoa a motor, canot à moteur, canot automobile, gazolina, motobarca, Motorboot, motoscafo, vedette à moteur, vedette automobile

2. *Canada, E:* Specific term applied since ca. 1920 in Newfoundland to a boat with a single-cylinder "make or break" engine. In pre-engine days, known as a **big punt**. Used for fishing, birding, and sealing. Carvel-planked; slightly curved, raking stem; raked transom stern; rounded bottom; strong sheer. Open; partitioned into 3 "rooms" by watertight bulkheads; the forward and aft for standing while fishing, the midships space for the catch. Small storage area forward; engine housed just abaft the midship room. Retained sails, employing a loose-footed gaff mainsail, sprit mizzen, single headsail tacked to stemhead. Also carries a long sculling oar that passes through a hole in the stern. Steered by a tiller. Crew of 2-3. Reported lengths 6-10.4m, the larger ones called **trap skiffs⋆**.

See also **narrow boat**.

Motorboot See **motor boat-1**

motorcanoa See **canoa-6**

motor cruiser See **cruiser-1**

motordekschuit See **dekschuit**

motor dinghy See **dinghy-1**

motorhengst See **hengst**

motorjulle See **bohusjulle, jolle-7**

motor launch See **launch**

motorlemmerhengst See **lemmerhengst**

motor lifeboat See **surfboat-6b**

motorlogger See **logger**

motorpont See **pont**

motor sailer See **sailer**

Motorschiff See **automoteur**

motorschokker See **schokker**

motorsnekke See **snekke**

motorspits See **spits**

motortrekschuit See **trekschuit-3**

motorvlet *West Indies, Netherlands Antilles:* Motorized wooden **fishing boat⋆**. Transom stern, decked. Cap. 1-5grt. Note also **vlet-2**. Further reference: **vlet-1**.

motosailer See **sailer**

motoscafo See **motor boat-1**

motoscafo comandante See **gig-1**

moto-topo See **topo**

motshi-so-bune *Japan, SW:* Open boat from Hirado Island on Tsushima Strait. Used for whaling, working in groups of 4. Had tackle for towing a dead whale. Rowed with 8 main oars and 1 small oar. Crew of 12 plus the captain. Reported lengths 12.5-12.8m, beam 2m.

motten See **Mutte**

mouche **1.** Old term, sometimes applied to an **advice boat⋆**, derived from *moucher*, to spy. Name variant: **spy boat**

2. *Turkey:* A variety of luxuriously appointed **steam launch** on the Bosporus.

See also **bateau mouche**.

moulette See **muleta**

moulin à bac, moulin à chalan, moulin à chalon, moulin à nef See **moulin-bateau**

moulin-bateau *France:* A **floating mill⋆** that used the current of a river to turn a single or double waterwheel to grind grain, or in places, to press grapes. Reported from at least the 10th to the end of the 19th century. Anchored to the riverbed or moored to bridge piers. The boat on which the mill house and wheel were set might be called a **forine** or **foraine**. On a two-boat mill, with the wheel between, the larger craft would be called a **bateau cabine**; the smaller, a **bateau du large** or **bateau secondaire**. Other recorded names: **bac(h) de moulin**, **moulin à bac**, **moulin à chalan** or **chalon**, **moulin à nef**, **sentine de moulin**. Further reading: A. Peyronel, "Les Moulins-bateaux Immobiles sur les Fleuves d'Europe," *Chasse-Marée* 11 (1984), 36-51. Note also **mulino galleggiante**.

mountain boat **1.** *United States:* **a.** In Georgia, long, narrow **mountain boats** transported cotton and tobacco downstream to the coast in the early 19th century. Returned with groceries and farm supplies. Could carry 50-100 bags of cotton. Reported lengths 15-23m, beam ca. 2m. Other recorded names: **Fall boat, tobacco boat⋆, upland boat⋆. b.** A type of **mountain boat** was the **Petersburg boat** that carried baled cotton and tobacco in hogsheads down the Savannah River above Augusta in the latter part of the 19th century (Petersburg, about 6.5km above Augusta, now flooded out by a reservoir). Pine-planked; flat bottom; sharp, elongated ends; sides parallel for most of their length. Decked at ends only. Maneuvered downstream with a long sweep; rowed in slack water; poled upstream with 5.5m-long iron-tipped poles, the polers walking on a plank around the gunwale. Crew of 5-8. Reported lengths 7.6-26m, widths 1.8-2.1m, draft 0.25-0.46m.

2. On tributaries of the Ohio, Mississippi, and Missouri Rivers, special shallow-draft **stern wheelers** carried cargo and passengers in the 19th century. Spoon bow for crossing shoals. Lower cargo deck open, passenger cabins on the top deck. Some had 4 rudders just forward of the paddle wheel; the 2 inboard rudders were balanced rudders; the 4 were connected to operate as a single rudder, steered by a wheel from the wheelhouse. Wheelhouse covered with boiler iron to protect the occupants from Native American gunfire. Length 58m, beam 10m, draft light 0.51m, laden 1.37m. Note also **paddle boat-3**.

Mounts Bay crabber See **West Country crabber**

Mounts Bay driver See **West Cornish lugger**

Mounts Bay gig See **Cornish gig**

Mounts Bay lugger, Mounts Bay mackerel driver, Mounts Bay pilchard driver See **West Cornish lugger**

mou-p'ai See **mu pai**

mouré de porc, mouré de pouar, mourré de porc See **mourre de pouar**

mourre de pouar *France, Mediterranean:* Found on the Provence coast, where the boat was used mostly for fishing but also as a **pilot boat⋆** for Marseille. Mainly used until the end of the 19th century, but seen today in isolated areas and as a pleasure craft. Notable was its residual ram bow, inelegantly called pig's snout (*mourré dé pouar* in Provençale). Solidly constructed, double-ended, beamy, flat floors, sharp bilges, straight keel, considerable sheer. Stem flattened and slightly curved and raked, sternpost vertical. Frames in 3 pieces: floor and 2 ribs. Rudder extended well below the bottom; unshipped in shallow water. Movable washboards. Stone ballast carried in wooden boxes. Smaller boats undecked; larger had a cambered deck except for a large hatch amidships and a steering well. **Pilot boats** painted black, with blue and white on the gunwales; others brightly painted. High-peaked lateen sail set to a centrally placed, aft-raking mast; yard, in 2 pieces, about the same length as the boat. A jib might be set to a long bowsprit or from the stem, or 1-2 spritsails to a forward-raking mast stepped in the eyes. Also rowed; some motorized. Crew of 2-4. Reported lengths 4-9m; e.g., length 7.5m, beam 2.35m, depth 1.3m. Other recorded names: **bateau à éperon, gro(u)in de cochon, mourres de pouar** (pl.), **mour(r)é de porc, mouré de pouar, museau de porc.** Further reading: Jules Vence, *Construction & Manfiuvre des Bateaux & Embarcations à Voilure Latine...* (Grenoble: Terre et Mer, 1982, originally pub. 1897), 9-75.

mouse See **topo**

Mousehole drift boat, Mousehole lugger See **West Cornish lugger**

moussique, moustique See **dihengué**

moving canoe See **shitlats**

mo you chuan *China, E:* Seaworthy vessel that engages in catching cuttle fish (*mo you*) with nets off Hangzhou Wan (Hang-chow Bay) and the Zhoushan (Chusan) Archipelago. When night fishing, sets a fire on deck to attract the fish. Flat bottom, double keel; oval transom, slotted for the rudder. Narrow bow transom that terminates short of the flaring upper strakes; ends raked. High sheer, especially at the stern. Portable deck planking provides access to the hold; forward compartment for fresh water, galley aft; deckhouse for the crew. When new, colorfully painted; oculus at each bow. Two or 3 masts; small foremast rakes forward; masts easily unstepped. Balance lugsails, battened and with slightly curved leech; bonnet laced to mainsail; early sails of tanned matting. Crew of 5-6. Reported lengths 15-20m; e.g., length 17m, beam 2.5m. A small variety, the **wu zei chuan**, catches an inshore type of cuttle fish and is closer to 9m long and sets 1-2 sails. Other recorded names: **cuttlefish boat, encre-poisson bateau, mo-yu ch'uan** (or **tch'ouan**), **wu-tsei ch'uan** (or **shuan**).

mo-yu ch'uan, mo-yu tch'ouan See **mo you chuan**

mrâk˘b, mrakđb, mrāküb See **markab**

mrežarica See **seine boat-1**

Mr. Middleton's light horse See **corvette-2**

mrw *Egypt:* Early term for a boat that transported cattle.

mtafieh, mtapa See **mtepe**

mtepe *Kenya, NE/Somalia, SE:* Built in the Lamu Archipelago from at least the 13th until the early 20th century to transport firewood, mangrove poles, cattle, and produce, mainly to Zanzibar. Most prominent feature was its projecting stemhead, which has variously been called the head of a camel or a bird. Sharp ends; built up on a relatively short, straight keel; stem and sternpost scarfed to the keel. The planks (12 to each side) vertically pegged edge-to-edge; initially sewn over a fiber caulking placed inside, then pegged

horizontally on each side of the lashings; pegs and lashings are cut smooth on the outside. Following completion of the hull, frames, stem, and sternpost lashed on; some thwarts double, with the lower thwart resting on the 10th strake and the upper thwart on the wale strake; these were secured together with lanyards. Short deck at bow and stern; shelter aft covered with palm fronds and sticks. Stem and sternpost strongly raked; bow decorated with flags, a coir tassel, and a charm. Large, carved and painted rudder suspended by rope grommets from an equally decorated sternpost. Tiller slotted over wide rudderhead; tassel also hung from rudder. Pairs of stylized oculi at bow and stern. Boat characteristically painted in red, white, and black. A single pole mast stepped a little forward of amidships, supported by a forestay, 2 backstays, and 1-2 shrouds and by an upper and lower thwart.

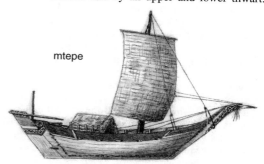

mtepe

Mast vertical or raked forward. One to 3 white pennants flew from the masthead. A large mat sail, hung with upper and lower yards and held out with 2 bowlines to the prow, was hoisted by means of a halyard and 2 lateral tackles. Also rowed and poled. Crew of 13-20. Average length 18.2m overall, 10.6m on keel, beam 5.5m, hold depth 2m, draft 1.8m. Other recorded names: **kitepe** (dim.), **mataf(f)a, metafa, metaffy, mtapa, muṭepe, ṇtepe;** pl. **mitepe, mtafieh, mtepi.** Locally may be called an **idau** (see **dau-1**). Further reading: Robert M. Adams, "Designed Flexibility in a Sewn Boat of the Western Indian Ocean" in: Sean McGrail and Eric Kentley, eds. *Sewn Plank Boats* (Greenwich: National Maritime Museum, 1985 [BAR International Series 276]), 289-302; A. H. J. Prins, *A Handbook of Sewn Boats* (Greenwich: National Maritime Museum, 1986 [Maritime Monographs and Reports 59]), 64-92.

mtepe dau See **dau la mtepe**

mtepi See **mtepe**

mti dau See **dau la mataruma**

m'tombui, mtumbi, mtumbwe See **mtumbwi**

mtumbwi *East Africa:* Swahili term for a **dugout canoe***, but exact connotation varies from place to place. Constructed along the East African coast and on Zanzibar and Pemba beginning in the early 1930s and still used in isolated areas for fishing and transporting light cargo and passengers. Word also used for a dugout on Lake Tanganyika. Some are simple dugouts with a flattened bottom, others have rounded block ends fitted to an open-ended dugout hull. Some sail with the addition of a small square or lateen sail and rudder. Sail may be hung from crossed poles. Also rowed, paddled, or poled. Generally small, ranging from ca. 3.5-6m in length, but known to have been large enough to convey 20-40 passengers. Other recorded namess: **dau la mtumbwi, kičumbwi, mčumbwi, m'tombui, mtumbi, mtumbwe, mučumbwi; nchumbwi** (in Kitikuu); **nčumbwi, ntumbwi;** pl. **mitumbwi.** Note also **houri-2, mitumbuí.**

muchewa See **bedi**

mu-chi See **hong tou san ban**

muchoo, muchra See **muchwa-1**

mu chuan See **sampan-3**

muchuo See **muchwa-1**

muchva See **mashua-2, muchwa-1**

muchwa *India:* **1.** Cargo and **fishing boat★** of the north-west coast; serves as a **ferry★** in some areas. Some large early vessels converted to armed naval craft. Hulls differ in slight details with the locale, and rigging varies with boat use. All have a long, straight, markedly raked stem; some have an ornamental parrot's head stemhead, but those engaged in fishing may leave the ornament ashore and use stem sheaves while setting nets. The raked stern may be sharp, truncated, or rounded; outboard rudder; tiller slots over rudderhead. Teak planking cut with zigzag groove and set flush with caulking between, then lashed, and finally nailed. Bombay (Mumbai) area boats have a distinctive hogged keel with a deep forefoot. Low in the waist, and those carrying cargo may use bulkheads and weather screens to increase freeboard; sweeps up forward. Open, but a short stern deck on some, and some have light bamboo temporary decking. Hulls oiled to nearly black, or they may be painted; some with designs. Steps 1-2 masts, depending on area and use; fishing **muchwas** may lower mast to a stern crutch while fishing. Sets high-peaked quadrilateral lateen-type sail with short luff. May now be powered by a diesel engine. Sometimes 4-6 oars used; early boats used as many as 9 oars per side. Cargo boat has a crew 8-12; more on **fishing boats** to handle the nets. Reported lengths 5.5-24m; Bombay cargo **muchwa**: length overall 15.8m, on keel 6.6m, beam 4.3m, depth amidships 1.6m; a Kathiawar Peninsula boat might be 7.9m by 1.8m by 1.14m. Spelling variants: **macchawa, machava, machhavo, machh(a)wa, mach(o)ua, machuvo, machuwa, machva, machwa(h), mashwa, matchwa, matsyavah, muchoo, muchra, muchuo, muchva.** Further reading: Jean Poujade, *La Machoua de Versova* (Paris: Gauthier-Villars, 1948 [Documents d'Ethnographie Navale, Fasc. 4]).
2. A **ship's boat★** aboard seagoing Indian cargo boats. Further reference: **mashua-2**

mučumbwi See **mtumbwi**

mud boat **1.** *China, E:* Special designation for a **xiao ma tou chuan★** of Shanghai which, due to a poor state of repair, was relegated to collecting mud from the Huangpu (Whangpoo) Jiang for use in plastering the inside of Chinese houses. Mud was collected at low tide when the boats were grounded.
2. *United States, south-central:* Flat-bottomed boat for hunting, fishing, and crabbing in Louisiana marshes. Blunt-ended. Air-cooled inboard motor for passage through very shallow marsh trails. Reported lengths 4.3-4.9m, width ca. 1.0m.
Further references: **hopper-1, mud hopper**

Mudde See **Spitzmutte**

mudderfartyg, muddermaskine See **dredger-1**

Mudderprahm *Germany:* Old term for a large, flat **barge★** used in collecting and transporting mud, sludge, and dirt. Other recorded names: **Dreckprahm, modderprahm, Schlammbagger.** Note also **dredger-1, hopper.**

mudderpram See **dredger-1, hopper**

mudderverk, mud dredger See **dredger-1**

mud hopper *United Kingdom:* Type of maintenance vessel that transported dredged materials along inland waterways. Materials not emptied through doors on the bottom like the regular **hopper★**, but emptied by a grab or suction pump. Originally many were worn-out canal **barges★**, but are now specially constructed, usually of steel. Most were towed by a **tug** and now many are push-towed. Other recorded names: **mud boat★, slutch boat** (in the north), **spoil barge** (or **boat**); the **mallion boat** of the Yorkshire area also transported stone. See also **hopper-1.**

mud horse See **mud sledge**

mudian See **Bermudian**

mud lighter See **hopper-1**

mud machine See **dredger-1**

mud sled *United States:* Small, flat-bottomed craft used by soft-clam farmers, especially in the San Francisco Bay area. Pushed by the occupant over the mudflats at low tide to the digging site. Clams are placed in bags on the sled, washed at high tide, and then the sled is pushed ashore. Rectangular shape with low sides. Handles supported by vertical planking at the "stern." Note also **accon, clammer's dory, mud sledge, ni mo chuan, pousse-pied, Schuiten.**

mud sledge *England, W/Wales, SE:* Along the wide mudflats of the eastern Bristol Channel shore, **mud sledges** have been used to cross to the low water line to hang nets. Used as late as the 1990s on the northern Somerset coast. A rectangular wooden framework, 0.9-1.2m high, fastens to a ski-shaped craft of pliable wood; 2 ropes keep the bow upturned. Fisherman leans on the crossbar and pushes with his foot. A basket or net bag holds nets outbound and the catch homeward. Reported lengths 2-2.3m, widths 0.46-0.48m. Name variant: **mud horse.** Note also **mud sled.** Further reference: **ni mo chuan**

mud-sucker See **dredger**

mud-touching boat See **ni mo chuan**

Mufferdeibrigg See **brigantine**

muffie See **polacca, swim-headed barge**

muffy, muffye See **polacca**

muggu nava See **muggu padava**

muggu padava *India, NE:* Well-constructed boat that transports lime (*muggu*) in Andhra Pradesh. Carvel-built of teak planks; sharp ends; flat floors. Long foredeck; arched shelter protects the cargo. Name variant: **muggu nava**

mugian See **Bermudian**

muhāila, muheile, muhēle See **mahaila-2**

Mühlheimer Aak See **Ruhraak**

muji See **hong tou san ban**

mule *United Kingdom:* Usually a hybrid type, bearing the major characteristics of 2 different boats. The **mule** of the east coast of Scotland may be a cross between a **fifie**★ and a **zulu**★. In some cases, the term is assigned to a boat that has only a minor deviation from the usual type, such as the **mule** of the **Yorkshire coble**★, or the **mule** may be smaller than the standard, such as that of the **Brixham smack**★. See also **coble-1b, coble-1c, coble-1d, Hartlepool pilot coble**.

mule coble See **coble-1d**

mulet *Portugal:* A **coaster**★ with rounded stem and sternpost, strong sheer, outboard rudder. Two or 3 masts; the forward mast(s) raking strongly forward, the mizzen aft, each setting lateen sails. Cap. to ca. 150t. Spelling variant: **muleto**. Note also **muleta**.

muleta 1. *Portugal, central:* **Fishing boat**★ based on the south bank of the Tagus River working offshore fishing grounds with a net. A modified form still operates. The catch is transported to Lisbon markets by **enviadas**★. Some served as **pilot boats**★ at the mouth of the Tagus and on the Douro River to the north. When employing the beamless trawl, the vessel spread an array of "balance" sails to regulate its broadside drift; otherwise a single lateen with a short luff and a jib were used. On some, the stem was almost a half circle, most of which was above the waterline. On older boats, the stem was studded with spikes that may have served as fairleads for the sheets of the water sails; often portrayed with a triangular extension above gunwale level that served to secure the forestay; hollow entrance at the sharp bow. Tall sternpost also curved, but stern sat lower in the water; transom stern; large outboard rudder worked with lines. Bottom flat or concave amidships; keel did not extend below the well-rounded bilges; sides had tumble home. Wales reinforced the solidly built hull. Decked with small central hatch and steering well or decked forward and aft with open waist and an athwartships gangway; movable bulwarks; narrow leeboard hung toward the stern on the lee side to reduce drift. Short mast, strongly inclined forward originally, now rakes aft. Long, slender bowsprit; when fishing, spar fitted into a socket at the bow to support the extra sails; jiggerboom aft for trysails. Sails yellow or ochre. Oars used in calms. Crew of 6-18, depending on activity. Reported lengths 12-20m; e.g., length 15m, beam 3.7m, hold depth 2m. Other recorded names: **bean cod, molet(t)a, moulette, muletta, mulette; bote do arrasto** (term used for the newer type of **muleta** when both the old and new types were operating concurrently). Note also **bote-7, mulet**.
2. *Spain, E:* **Fishing boat** of the Cataluña and Valencia coasts. Straight, raked stem and sternpost; stem may be quite tall. Foredeck and a narrow deck crosses forward of a standing well at the stern. Light masts stepped through thwart in forward third. Sets a lateen sail and jib; yard longer than the boat. Also rowed against a single tholepin. Length ca. 4.6m; narrow in proportion to length. Spelling variants: **moletta, mo(u)lette, mulete** Further reference: **bateira do Mondego**

mulete See **muleta-2**

muleto See **mulet**

muletta, mulette See **muleta-1**

mulie See **Brixham smack, Channel barge, Thames sailing barge**

mulie barge See **Thames sailing barge**

mulinèla See **sandón**

mulini galleggianti, mulino, mulino ad acqua See **mulino galleggiante**

mulino galleggiante *Italy:* **1.** The 19th-century **floating mill**★ in Rome consisted of a rectangular **barge**★ along the riverbank, a water wheel activated by the current, and still farther out, a smaller **barge** supporting the outer end of the shaft. The house on the inner **barge** was several stories high. The complex was connected to the shore by cables and a walkway.
2. The mill at Pontelagoscuro, on the lower Po River in north-central Italy, consisted of 2 boats of the sharp-bow **sandón**★ type with the water wheel between them. A house covered most of each boat, and a covered walkway connected them. Boats decked forward. Length of each boat 14m, beam 3.9m, depth 1.4m. Other recorded names: **mulino, mulino ad acqua, mulino natante;** pl. **mulini galleggianti**. Note also **galleggiante, moulin-bateau**.

mulino natante See **mulino galleggiante**

mullet boat 1. *New Zealand, North Island:* Initially a **fishing boat**★ of the Auckland area, but adopted as a popular racing class. Used from ca. 1880 for netting mullet in creeks bordering Hauraki Gulf; superseded by motorized craft. The racing **yachts**★ (the **mullety**) were divided into 4 classes by length; the longest class is still racing. Plumb stem; wide, vertical, tucked-up transom. Well-curved keel, wide keelson; low deadrise, fairly hard turn of the bilges at the waterline; low freeboard; some ceiled. Originally open, then decked forward of the mast and at the stern, narrow side decks; raised coaming. Centerboard initially a rectangular steel plate controlled by a chain or wire rope; later a projecting arm was introduced. Wide rudder hung on pintles; heavy tiller or rope purchase system. **Cutter**★-rigged, most with gaff, but later a leg-of-mutton sail laced to a long boom; 2 headsails. Pole mast. Bowsed-down bowsprit ca. 2.5m long. Rowed when school of fish sighted. Crew mostly 2-3. Reported lengths 5-10m, the working boats mainly 7.9-8.5m, diesel-powered boats to 18m; e.g., length 6.7m, beam 2.7m, depth 0.84m; shallow draft.
2. *United States, S:* **a.** In the Apalachicola area of Florida, mullet caught with seine nets during the late 19th century was salted and transported to market in special boats, the **mullet boats**. Carvel-planked; flat floors; sharp bow with plumb stem; transom stern with skeg. Decked forward, waterways extended to the stern. Lateen sail set to a short mast. Also rowed. Reported lengths 6.1-6.7m, widths 1.8-2.1m. Note also **pilot skiff. b.** A modern type, using gill nets, is widely used from Georgia to Texas. Generally of plywood; slightly raked, straight stem; straight, flared sides. Open; low platform at the square stern for the nets. Outboard motor mounted forward of amidships. Crew of 3. Length 5.9m, beam 2.1m, depth 0.56m. Name variant: **Florida mullet skiff**

mullett masher See **chalan**

mullety See **mullet boat-1**

Mulmsche Aak See **Ruhraak**

mum See **mother ship**

mumble bee, mumbleby, mumbles bee, mumbles boat
See **Brixham smack**

Mumbles dredging boat, Mumbles oyster dredger See
Mumbles oyster skiff

Mumbles oyster skiff *Wales, S:* **Oyster dredger** that
worked out of the towns of The Mumbles and nearby
Oystermouth on the Welsh side of the Bristol Channel
until ca. 1930. Similar boats used at Port-Eynon to the
west. Early boats open, clinker-built with bluff bows
and a transom stern, and stepped 1-2 masts. By the
mid-19th century, they were decked and **cutter***-rigged.
The **cutters** had a straight stem with rounded forefoot;
straight keel with deep drag; steep rise to the floors;
raked sternpost and square counter. Low freeboard aft
swept up to a high bow. Hold abaft the mast; on the
port side at the bow, a roller served the anchor and
mooring cable; steam capstan for the dredge fitted in
the early 1870s. Early 2-masted boats stepped a foremast in the eyes and a mainmast midway between the
foremast and the stern. Various combinations of sails
used: 2 gaff-headed sails of equal size with the mainsail boomed; lugsails; dipping forelug and sprit
mizzen; some set a single dipping lugsail. The **cutters**
varied somewhat in rig but favored a short mainmast
stepped well forward and a light topmast; supported
by a forestay and 2 shrouds. Mainsail loose-footed and
boomed, the boom extending well over the stern;
luff secured to mast hoops. Long bowsprit run out to
starboard; jib set flying. Crew of 3; 4 at Port-Eynon.
Reported lengths 11.3-12.2m; e.g., length overall
12.2m, on keel 11.3m, width 3.23m, hold depth 1.6m.
Other recorded names: **Mumbles dredging boat** (or
oyster dredger), **Oystermouth lug boat, Port-Eynon
oyster skiff, Swansea Bay dredging skiff**

muna See **mon-3**

munatapu See **nuñatapu**

munchua See **manji**

munka See **mE'nga**

Münstersche Pünte See **Pünte**

muntafiyah See **dau la mtepe**

mu pai *China, central:* Very large **raft*** created to float
timber downstream on some of the tributaries of the
lower Chang Jiang (Yangtze). Most had cabins on top,
and some were floating villages, complete with shops
and small vegetable gardens. Construction varied,
depending on the local tradition and river size and
depth; deeper in the center than on the sides. Often
double, the smaller **raft** lashed on behind. Floated
with the current using sea anchors to maintain the
raft's heading; anchors controlled by a huge capstan.
Might be towed in difficult stretches. Some early **rafts**
had masts and sails. Accompanied by numerous
sampans* that helped with maneuvering the anchors
and their hawsers. Crew of as many as 200 men. Reported lengths 54-300m, widths 15-21m, depths 2.4-3.1m.
Other recorded names: **mou-p'ai, mu phai, timber raft***

mu phai See **mu pai**

muri vallom See **vallam-1b**

murkab See **markab**

Murphrydite See **polacca**

murtoseira See **labrega**

murtozeira See **chinchorro-2, labrega**

Muschelkratzer See **cockle galley**

musciara *Italy, SW:* Smallest of the main boats used in
a Sicilian tuna fishing operation; the one from which
the head fisherman directs the activities is called a
musciara da rais, the 2nd in command is in the so-
called **pitarchia**. Four to 6 of these boats are required.
Double-ended, the bow sharper than the stern; raked
stem with high stemhead; vertical sternpost. High rudderhead to clear sternpost; deep rudder. Flat bottom,
rounded bilges, straight keel, slight sheer. Decked at
ends; those engaged in night watch have a longer stern
deck. A stub mast at the stern supports a bad-weather
awning and holds the corners of the net. Rowed by as
many as 6 men. May step a vertical mast for a lateen
sail. Reported lengths 8-15m; e.g., length 9.8m, beam
2.5m, depth 0.8m, draft light 0.4m. Other recorded
names: **mesciara, mo(s)ciara**; pl. **musciare**. Note also
barcareccio, cabanella, canotto, caporais, vascello.

musciara da rais, musciare See **musciara**

musciaretta See **cabanella**

muscle boat See **mussel boat-3**

muscoli See **muscolo**

muscolo *Italy:* A small commercial ship of the Roman
period. Sometimes attributed to the Venetians. Short
and rounded. Spelling variants: **mascula, muscoli,
musculus***. See also **topo.**

Muscongus Bay boat, Muscongus Bay lobster smack
See **Muscongus Bay sloop**

Muscongus Bay sloop *United States, NE:* Centerboard
lobstering boat built at towns around Muscongus Bay
on the central Maine coast from the 1860s until the
end of the century. Superseded by the deeper and larger
Friendship sloop*. Also engaged in hand-lining and
transporting lobsters. Lapstrake or carvel planking;
straight keel with drag; moderately rising floors; sharp
turn of the bilges; strong sheer. High bow, relatively
plumb stem into a rounded forefoot; clipper bow with
simple longhead. Short counter stern with curved transom; a few sharp-sterned. Inboard rudder; tiller. Half-
decked, cuddy abaft the mast; small, oval cockpit. Live
well on each side of the centerboard. Mast stepped well
forward; no shrouds. Boomed gaff sail with long gaff
was raised by a single halyard. Jib to the bowsprit.
Reported lengths 4.9-8.7m, a few to 10.7m; e.g., length
8m, beam 2.4m, draft with centerboard up 0.86m.
Other recorded names: **lobster sloop, Muscongus Bay
boat** (or **lobster smack**), **Muscongus sloop boat**

Muscongus sloop boat See **Muscongus Bay sloop**

musculus *Mediterranean:* A small, rounded **rowing
boat*** with a projecting cutwater and high, recurved
sternpost. Used as early as 200 A.D. as an auxiliary
craft. Name variant: **mydion**. See also **muscolo.**

museau de porc See **mourre de pouar**

musetto See **musseto**

Musikschiff See **Bucentaur, Leibschiff**

muskweakwitan See **rough-water canoe**

musoola See **masula**

musquito craft See **mosquito boat**

musquito fleet, musquitoe fleet See **mosquito fleet**

mussack, mussak See **mussuck**

mussel boat 1. *England, E:* Small boat towed by local **smacks★** to mussel beds and used to collect the mussels in The Wash. Flat bottom, plumb stem, raked transom, beamy. Name variant: **mussel flat**

2. *England, NW:* Morecambe Bay boats were clinker-planked, plumb-stemmed, transom-sterned, flat-bottomed. No keel; used a centerboard. Set a boomed, standing lugsail; foresail to a short, metal bowsprit. When raced in local regattas, set a big foresail. Reported lengths 4.9-6.1m, beamy.

3. *England, SE:* Taxes in the form of a peck of mussels were levied on **mussel boats** as they passed beneath the bridge at Rochester, at least as early as 1463. Name variant: **muscle boat**

4. *United States, central:* Small, flat-bottomed **mussel boats** of the Mississippi River and lower tributaries fished for freshwater mussels in the late 19th century, for their shells to be made into buttons. A rack was placed over the hull from which hung 2 iron bars with a hundred or more crow-foot hooks suspended by trotlines. The mussels, which lay in the mud with their valves open, would close tightly around the hooks when disturbed. Square ends; flat bottom turned up above the water at the ends; low sides. Length ca. 5m. Some larger boats with deck space had a windlass and dredge. Name variant: **clamming boat**

5. *Wales, NW:* Small, open boat that works in the Conway Estuary raking for mussels. Until the 1880s, the mussels collected were checked for pearls and the meat used for duck food; now collected for human consumption. Boats go out on the ebbing tide, working in at least 1.2m of water, returning on the flood. Clinker-planked, plumb stem, narrow transom stern. Carry 2 long-handled rakes of different lengths. Rowed, or now employ an outboard motor. Manned by 1-2. Reported lengths 4.3-4.9m.
Note also **canoe-4, canot mytilicole, chalana-8, dériveur-2, mosselaar, plate de l'Aiguillon, varke a véle de le kòzze, yole-2.**

mussel flat See **mussel boat-1**

mussel-harvesting boat *Canada, E:* Square-ended, heavily built craft used by mussel farmers in the quieter waters of maritime Canada. The mussels, grown on strings or long sacks, hang in buoyed rows. Flat bottom, nearly plumb, flat sides; strong frames and bracing. Hydraulic hauler at the stern raises the strings. Outboard motor. Length 6m, beam 4.3m, depth 0.74m.

musseti See **musseto**

musseto *Italy, NE:* A type of **topo★** used in tending fish nets and eel pots in the Venetian lagoon. Teardrop-shaped with rounded stern and very narrow bow; raked and lightly curved stem; curved sternpost. Flat bottom, slight rocker toward the ends; flaring sides. Tiller slots over the deep-heeled rudder. Decked at the ends. Steps a single mast through a thwart in after third, setting a lugsail and wide jib, or steps a 2nd mast abaft the foredeck, also carrying a lugsail. May be rowed standing and facing forward; oars worked against tall oarlocks. Mainly 2 in crew. Reported lengths 5.6-6.8m; e.g., length 6.2m, beam 1.55m, depth ca. 0.52m. Other recorded names: **musetto, musso, topo veneziano**; pl. **musseti, mussi**

mussi, musso See **musseto**

mussolèra *Italy, NE:* A boat that works mussel beds, especially in the Trieste area. Uses a capstan. Name variant: **mùssolo**

mussolo See **masula, mussolèra**

mussoola, mussoolah, mussoolee See **masula**

mussuck *India, NW/Pakistan:* Inflated skins of buffaloes, goats, or sheep tied together to form a craft for local river transportation. Other recorded names: **buffalo boat★, mussa(c)k.** See also **burdjuk-1.**

mussula, mussulah See **masula**

mu'su u'lk *Canada, E:* **Moose-hide canoe★** of the Micmac of the Maritime Provinces. Hides of one-and-a-half or two moose were scraped free of hair and formed into a **canoe★** ca. 76-91cm wide and 25cm deep. Used mainly by winter hunters as a temporary craft to transport the game and their possessions from the woods to their camp. Name variant: **Micmac moose-hide canoe**

mut 1. *Bangladesh:* Stout, little boat that plies rivers with passengers and goods. Knob on the prow. Spelling variant: **mota**

2. *Papua New Guinea, Bismarck Archipelago:* Single-**outrigger canoe★** of the Duke of York Islands off the northeast coast of New Britain Island. Elongated, angular bow extension which is cut square inboard; lacks the similar stern piece common in the area. Dugout hull; in the Rabaul area of New Britain, **mut** is a **canoe** hewn from a single log. Multiple booms secured to a very long float.
See also **Mutte.**

muṭepe See **mtepe**

muterere *Mozambique, N:* Bark **canoe★** still used at several coastal embayments for fishing and local transportation. Constructed of multiple pieces of bark with generous overlaps; sewn with sisal. Numerous ribs extend from gunwale to gunwale; pairs of supple stringers along the bottom and sides. Sharp, raked ends, and on some, the sheer sweeps up sharply at the bow; ends held rigid by an internal, vertical batten. Semicircular or oval in cross section. Gunwales formed by bamboo poles. Two seats and several thwarts; interwoven shoots create flooring. Poled, paddled, and at times, sets a small lateen sail boomed at the foot.

muterere

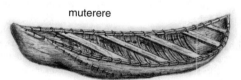

Outrigger in some areas. Reported lengths 3-4m; e.g., length 3m, beam 0.8m, depth 0.4m. A large seagoing type is found just north of Amgoche (António Emes). Paddled or sets a lateen sail. Length 6m, beam and depth 0.9m.

Mutje, Mutschip See **Mutte**

Mutte *Germany, NW/Netherlands, N:* Narrow boat of Friesland and Oldenburg on the North Sea coast; reported from the late 18th century into the 1930s. Type of **tjalk★**. Primarily a peat-carrier, and as such, was an inland boat (**Binnenmutte** or **binnenmot**); some large types worked outside and were called

Butenmutte. Characterized by a rounded stern (**runde Mutte**). Flat bottom, rounded bilges; hull ceiled; bluff bow, lightly curved stem; straight sternpost, rounded quarters, window on each side of the post. Heavy rudder; tiller set over rounded head; leeboards. Decked; wide, long, low hatch; some seagoing

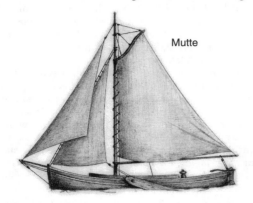

Mutte

vessels had a small deckhouse. Low bulwark or an open railing. Pole mast set in a tabernacle, to which a tanned, boomed gaff sail and staysail were set; seagoing craft added a jib and gaff topsail and sometimes a mizzen. Early **Mutten** (pl.) probably used a spritsail. One or 2 in crew on smaller vessels. Reported lengths 11-19m; e.g., length 14.75m, beam 3.75m, depth 1.25m. Other recorded names: **Aussenmotte, Binnenfahrer, Binnenmotte, buitenmot, Buitenmutte, Flottmutte, kurz Schiff, mot** (pl. **motten**), **Mut**⋆, **Mutje, Mutschip, Muttschiff, Ostfriesische Mutte, Pogge, Schiff, Seilmutte, Tjalk**⋆, **Torfschiff**. Note also **Spitzmutte**.

Mutten See **Mutte**
Mutterschiff See **mother ship**
Mutte-tjalk See **Spitzmutte**
Muttschiff See **Mutte**
Mutt-tjalk See **Spitzmutte**
Mutze See **Mutzen**
Mutzen *Austria/Germany, S:* **1.** Described as a flat-bottomed workboat on the Danube River and its tributaries and some Tirolian lakes. Considered a type of **Plätte**⋆. Ends generally wide and open. Built of wood, often of spruce. Vary widely in size. Some, especially those serving as river **ferries**⋆ (**Überfuhrmutzen**), still operate. Term dates from at least the late 17th century. **2.** On the Inn River, between Austria and Germany, the flat bottom turned up to a narrow bow; stern square and overhanging. Towed by men or horses, with the tow rope set to a post in the forward part. Also rowed.

Steered with a sweep set on an iron crutch at the stern. Some **Mutzen**, carrying sand and gravel, were 12.8m long overall, 4.7m on the bottom, 2.35m wide, 0.7m deep. A towed **ferry** that was not open aft was called a **Seilmutzen** (**Seilplätte**, or earlier **Seilbuche**); 7.5-9.5m long. **3.** On the Danube, large **Mutzen** transported anchors, chains, sails, and heavy machinery. Elsewhere, some small **Mutzen** raised anchors (**Ankermutzen**); others carried ropes. **4.** On Halstätter See in Austria, large **Mutzen** transported salt. Some would return with coal, earning the name **Kobelzillen**. **5.** The **Mutzenzille** was small with square, overhanging ends and flared sides. Length 7.5m, beam 2.1m on top, 1.4m below, depth 0.5m. Other recorded names: **Mutze, Muze, Stutzen, Tiroler Mutzen, Zille**⋆, **Zustutzen**

Mutzenzille See **Mutzen-5**
mu ying *China:* **Raft**⋆ composed of a platform lashed to rows of clay pots; used notably on the upper Chang Jiang (Yangtze) as a **ferry**⋆. Reportedly used in early military operations as well as for local transportation. Some rowed with a pair of oars and steered with an oar at each end. Name variant: **chatty raft**⋆
Muze See **Mutzen**
mwanda *Zaire, E:* Large **dugout canoe**⋆ used by the Boloki peoples of the upper Zaire (Congo) River for traveling, fishing, and warfare. Sharp ends, bottom flat transversely with longitudinal rocker, sides tumble home. Hull ornamented along the top edge with incised patterns. **Canoe**⋆ trimmed so that the stern is at water level and the bow high. Paddlers, 30-50, stand along each side using pointed, spatulated paddles with incised lines along the blade; handle often has a brass knob. Sometimes use steering paddles at both stern and bow. Length to 15m, width to 0.9m, depth to 0.6m.
mwāši See **mashua-2**
mydion See **musculus**
myllåjekt See **jekt**
myopara, myopare See **myoparon**
myoparon *Mediterranean:* Fast, seaworthy oared **galley**⋆ that was a favorite of pirates of the 1st-3rd centuries A.D. Type also used by a number of navies. Data on appearance scarce, but seems to have had a high, recurved stem and a beaked prow. Mast stepped amidships, but sail used for cruising was lowered while fighting. Spelling variants: **myopara, myoparo**; pl. **myoparones**. Note also **mioparo, paro, paron**.
myoparones See **myoparon**
mystaco, mystic See **mistico**

na See **bangala**, **nau-6**

na-ak *Vanuatu (New Hebrides), western Pacific:* **1.** Generic for a **canoe*** on parts of the northeast coast of Malekula and the adjacent small islands. Also a toy **canoe**.
2. The large coastal **na-ak** is formed from a dugout hull on which a multipiece strake is sewn; holes plugged with coconut fiber and seams protected with split bamboo. Raised, elongated bow, terminating in a stylized bird's head; tumble home to blunt stern. Numerous thwarts; breakwater at bow and stern. Three booms cross the gunwales to the slender, sharp-ended float; 2 booms abaft amidships, one forward; employs multiple undercrossed stanchions. Early boats set a woven pandanus sail with 2 spars that formed a wide "V"; no mast; the spars secured to the thwarts. Length 9m, beam 0.5m.
Spelling variants: **n-ak**, **na-wak**, **n-oak**, **nuak**, **nu-angk**, **nuanka**, **nu-wak**. See also **na-ak wala**.

na-ak wala *Vanuatu (New Hebrides), western Pacific:* Single-**outrigger canoe*** built in the small islands off the northeast coast of Malekula; last reported in the early 20th century. Originally built by all coastal peoples of north and east Malekula. This seagoing **canoe***, capable of transporting 20-30 people, was called **rangot** when on a long voyage. Dugout hull with bottom rocker. Plank sewn on raised sides and extended well beyond the dugout section, creating a raked appearance; a 2nd strake was added to each side and to this, stylized bird's heads were appended. Multiple benches laid atop the gunwales. Sharp ends, slightly convex float connected to the **canoe** by 4, occasionally 5, very long booms set close together. Booms pierced the hull below the gunwale and extended out the lee side. Platform laid atop the booms. Sailed with the outrigger on the weather side. Raised a wide, V-shaped sail of strips of woven pandanus, dyed red. The spars forming the sides of the sail crossed at the apex and were made fast to the forward outrigger boom inside the hull. No mast; the sail held by forked pieces inserted into the ends of each spar. Length ca. 13m. Other recorded names: **na-ak***, **naungk wala**, **na-wak wala**

naao See **nau**

na-auga See **de wang**

nabbie *United Kingdom:* **1.** Scottish **herring boat***, especially of Loch Fyne and the Firth of Clyde. Developed in the early 19th century with a transom or counter stern. Later sharp-ended; either carvel- or clinker-built. Stem straight and vertical; forefoot shallow; sternpost raked; keel straight with marked drag. Open except for small foredeck that sheltered the crew of 3-4. Outboard rudder; tiller. Early boats gaff-rigged, then set a high-peaked, standing lug-sail set to aft-raking mast; tacked to the mast. Large jib on reefing bowsprit. Mizzen added in summer. Those still working in the 20th century had engines. Reported lengths overall 9.8-12.3m,

on keel 7.3-10.3m; widths 2.1-3.8m; depth forward 0.3-0.6m, aft 1.07-1.83m; draft ca. 1.12-1.41m. Other recorded names: **Clyde nabbie**, **line boat***, **Loch Fyne nabby**
2. The **nabbie** of Northern Ireland was similar in hull and rig and was used in the same general period. Reported lengths 12-15m.
Spelling variants: **nab(b)y**. See also **Loch Fyne skiff**, **nobby-1**.

nabby See **nabbie**, **nobby-1**

na binabina See **binabina**

nabio See **nave**

naby See **nabbie**

naca See **nacelle-1**, **Nachen-1**

nace See **Nachen-1**

nacela See **nacelle-1**

nacella Reported as a northern European vessel, probably from the 12th-14th centuries. Filled with combustibles and designed to explode on impact. In the latter period, the vessel might carry a crew of 200. See also **nacelle-1**.

nacelle *France:* **1.** A French generic term for a **skiff***, **wherry***, or **cockle***; used primarily on rivers. Dates to the 12th century, when it was apparently skin-covered. Rowed or sailed. Later depictions show a clinker-planked, crescent-shaped boat steered with a sweep. Other recorded names: Italian: **naca**, **nacela**, **nacella***, **nacelo**
2. The **nacelles** of the lagoons of the south coast are used for transport, fishing, clamming, and conch culture. Some served as **tenders*** to the **bateau-bœuf***. Last constructed of wood in the 1960s. Vary slightly, but those of the central lagoons have sharp ends with strongly raked stem and sternpost; marked sheer. Bottom flat athwartships, with fore-and-aft rocker; longitudinal planking extends ca. 2cm beyond the lower side plank; sides flare evenly at ca. 60°; mostly strong, 2-piece natural frames. Narrow, deep rudder hung with pintles; tiller slotted through rudderhead. Open with raised flooring at ends; some have a short foredeck. Short, light, vertical or aft-raking mast stepped through forward thwart. Sets a high-peaked lateen sail; some small **nacelles** set a spritsail. Halyard runs through athwartship hole in mast. Also rowed using a single pair of oars; some with a square loom on the inner end. Completely motorized by the 1960s. Reported lengths 5-6.9m; width ca. 1.5m. Further reading: Bernard Vigne and Christian Dorques, "Nacelles du Languedoc, Bateaux des Pêcheurs des Étangs," *Chasse-Marée* 62 (1992), 28-41.
3. A small river craft reported on the Dordogne River in southwestern France and at Paris. Used mainly as a **ferry***. No sails.
4. Nacelles were common on the upper Meuse River in northwest France and Belgium for fishing, carrying produce, and assisting in loading and unloading larger river vessels. Used mostly in the 17th-18th centuries. Steered with a stern oar.

5. *France/Switzerland:* General term used into the 18th century for a small boat on the Lake of Geneva (Lake Léman). Rowed by 2-4 oarsmen. In the mid-13th century, one served Pierre de Savoie at the castle of Chillon, going by the special term **barga domini** or **barque du seigneur**; this flat-bottomed boat was small enough to be carried up to a boathouse. Other recorded names: **nagella**, **nagelle**, **navicella⋆**

Further reference: **ghe nang**

nacelo See **nacelle-1**

nache, **Nächel** See **Nachen-1**

Nachen **1.** A German term for several types of inland craft. The larger **aak⋆** of the lower Rhine River was called a **Nachen** in old German. Farther inland, the term still applies to craft of the **Kahn⋆** and **Zille⋆** families and may loosely describe small boats or **skiffs⋆**, especially those that are rowed or poled. Probably originally a **dugout canoe⋆**. Other recorded names: **naca**, **nac(h)e**, **nahho**, **nâho**, **nakwa**, **Nauen⋆**, **Rhein-nachen**; **Nächel** (dim.). Note also **Bornachen**, **Humpel-nachen**, **Weidling-5**.

2. The fishing **Nachen** of the lower Rhine is a heavily built, open boat. Sides built up of 2 planks, the lower strake flares outward, the top strake has sharp tumble home. On the middle Rhine, the top strake is either vertical or continues the flare. Flat bottom, heavy frames, strong gunwales. Ends sharply raked; spoon bow and on the middle Rhine, a small transom. May employ washstrakes. When used, the rudder is small, and the rudderpost and tiller may be in one piece, curving over the stern. Rowed, poled. Length ca. 8m. The **Fischernachen** is also found on the Neckar, middle Rhine, and Main Rivers.

Further reference: **aak**

nachtbarge See **trekschuit-2**

nachtschuit, **nachtschuyt** See **trekschuit-3**

nackt Zille See **Zille**

nād See **taghāri**

nadeh See **jong-5**

nadipi teppa See **teppa**

naf See **naue-l**, **nef-1**

naffe See **naue-1**

nagella, **nagelle** See **nacelle-5**

naggar See **naggr**

naggr *Sudan:* Beamy cargo carrier of the upper Nile, south of the Fourth Cataract. Carvel-planked without benefit of ribs but supported by multiple transverse beams; strakes made up of short lengths of thick sunt wood, held together by oblique spikes. Curved, raking stem; heavy keel, greatest depth forward when afloat; transom stern; flat sheer, low freeboard when loaded. Massive rudder, composed of as many as 12 vertical boards; tiller slopes downward with a marked hump just forward of the rudderhead. Weatherboard forward on some. Open; a light cabin of matting may cover part of the midships section. Under adverse wind conditions, an outrigger frame is fitted forward and aft of the mast, projecting out each side; 2 very long sweeps attach to each. Single mast steps vertically and is supported by as many as 11 stays and shrouds on each side; a halyard abreast the mast serves as an additional shroud; these help pre-

vent hogging and spreading of the hull when heavily loaded. Sets a lateen sail bent to a very long, spliced yard; may be boomed at the foot; short luff. Early

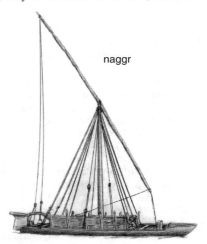

naggr

naggrs had a boomed square sail. On small and medium-sized boats, 2 vangs used; 4 on large craft. Crew of 3-8. Dimensions and proportions vary widely; reported lengths from 8.4-16.35m, widths 3.8-6.4m. Spelling variants: **naggar**, **negg(h)er**, **noggar**, **nog(g)ur**, **nuggah**, **nuggar**, **nuger**, **nuggur**. Further reading: S. Clarke, "Nile Boats and Other Matters," *Ancient Egypt* (1920), Pt. I & II, 2-9, 40-51; J. Hornell, "The Frameless Boats of the Middle Nile," *The Mariner's Mirror* XXV (1939), 417-432, XXVI (1940), 125-155. Note also **felukka**, **gharab**. Further reference: **markab-2**

Nahane canoe See **kayak-form canoe**

Nahant clipper dory *United States, E:* A racing **dory⋆** of the end of the 19th and early 20th centuries. Popular at Nahant, northeast of Boston. Clinker-planked; flat bottom, with rocker; high, soft turn of the bilges; sharp bow; raking, curved stem; strongly raked V-transom. Centerboard; outboard rudder. Mast stepped in forward third, setting a leg-of-mutton mainsail, small foresail. Crew of 4. Length overall 7m, beam to 1.8m, depth 0.6m.

nahho See **Nachen-1**

nahiot See **naviot**

nâho See **Nachen-1**

na hucaeri See **Galway hooker**

n-ak See **na-ak**

naked flat See **Mersey flat**

nakwa See **Nachen-1**

nakwiL See **Coast Salish canoe**

nalu balikkandathu See **odam-1b**

naluvalikkunna thoni See **dhoni-5**

nancies See **nancy**

nancy *United States, E:* Craft used mainly on the lower Potomac River, where they tonged for oysters and crab-scraped. During the Civil War, some engaged in smuggling and were stained black inside and out; color retained later, hence the name **black nancy**. Last built in 1890. Flat bottom; cross-planked on the smaller boats and fore-and-aft on the larger boats, which also had frames; keel. Sides a single plank ca. 76cm deep; topped with narrow washboards. Plumb stem; slightly raked transom stern on most. Open; centerboard; outboard rudder, wide below the waterline; tiller. Two masts; the forward mast at the stem, the aftermast shorter and raked aft; both stepped through thwarts. Set leg-of-mutton sails held out with horizontal sprits; sails wrapped around mast when working. Reference made occasionally to single-masted **nancies** of a **bugeye★** design used on the western shore of Chesapeake Bay. Reported lengths 5.5-8.2m; e.g., length 8.2m, beam 3m, depth 0.6m. Further name variant: **nancy boat**

nancy boat See **nancy**

nan he chuan *China:* **1.** Class of cargo vessel of central China used on the Min Jiang and other tributaries of the upper Chang Jiang (Yangtze). Constructed of *nan mu* wood; flat bottom; sides flare sharply and then have tumble home; heavy wale follows the edge of the foredeck, then curves up sharply abaft amidships and merges with deckhouse planking. Narrow, square ends; bow turns up gradually from bottom; stern turns up sharply; compartmented with watertight bulkheads; heavy athwartship beams, the central one supporting bearing pins for oars, the forward beam carrying heavy bitts. Wide, shallow, balanced rudder.

nan he chuan-1

Flush deck; deckhouse in after half, interrupted to provide area for helmsman. Crew of ca. 6; 23-50 upstream haulers might be hired. Lengths vary widely: large craft 26m long, beam 3.8m, depth 1.8m. Other recorded names: **nan-ho ch'uan** (or **tch'ouan**); salt carriers called **qiao yan chuan** (**chiao-yen ch'uan, k'iao-yen tch'ouan**) **2.** Generic term in the north for **junks★** that traded to Tianjin (Tientsin). Name variant: **wei chuan★**

nan-ho ch'uan, nan-ho tch'ouan See **nan he chuan**

Nanticoke canoe See **Chesapeake Bay log canoe-2**

Nantucket dory See **clammer's dory**

nao See **carrack, East Indiaman, galleon-1, galleon-3, nau-1, nef-1, nouka**

não da carreira da India See **East Indiaman**

nao de China See **galleon-3**

naodee See **nauri**

naomhóg See **naomóg**

naomóg *Ireland:* **1.** A small **boat★, cot★,** or **curragh★.** Often a small **fishing boat★** that sails.
2. In County Kerry on the southwestern coast, the **curragh** is called a **naom óg.** Of relatively recent origin and still used for fishing, lobstering, and local transportation. Pleasant sheer with corresponding bottom

lines. Fine entrance; transom stern less than one-half the beam. Racing boats more slender, narrower at the stern, and lower at the bow. Upper and lower gunwales held apart by struts. May have as many as 43 ribs; stringers or bottom strakes placed 2.5-3.1cm apart.

naomóg

Frame covered with tarred cotton duck. When sailed, 1-2 large leeboards sometimes hung from lee tholepins. Short mast stepped to mast shoe through a hole in forward thwart. Sets small lugsail. Rowed by 3-4 men, single-banked; triangular piece with hole fixed to oar loom slips onto the tholepin. Reported lengths 6.1-7.6m, widths 1.2-1.5m, depths 0.53-0.61m. Other recorded names: **Blasket Island curragh, Dingle curragh, Kerry canoe** (or **curragh**), **neamhóg, nevóg** (at Dingle). Further reading: James Hornell, *British Coracles and Irish Curraghs* Pt. III (London: Society for Nautical Research, 1938), 29-35. Spelling variant: **naomhóg**

náon See **no-2**

náotakhtā See **dingi-2**

naparotatualik See **Peterhead boat-1**

nar See **gul**

ŋardän See **ngardän**

na roko See **roko-2**

Narragansett Bay point boat, Narragansett cat See **catboat-2b**

narrow boat *United Kingdom:* **Canal boat★** used particularly on the English Midlands canal system and designed to negotiate low bridges, tunnels, and narrow locks. Used from the late 18th century to the present; most built to meet local needs or carry special cargoes, so they varied considerably. Worked generally in pairs; the lead boat powered (called the **motor boat★**), the 2nd, or **butty** boat, towed; those pulled by horses, mules, or donkeys were called **horse boats★.** The original wooden boats were carvel-built with oak sides, elm bottom, and wrought-iron knees; strengthened by thwarts; more recent **barges★** of steel. Flat bottom, planked athwartships, with the lowest strake nailed on top rather than along the edge. Double-ended; bow plumb or slightly raked, bluff, and upturned; stem protected by an iron band. Stern raked; motorized boats have a counter stern over the rudder. Wide rudder blade; strong rudderhead into which a massive, down-turned tiller is socketed; tiller cocks up when not in use; those with engines have reverse "S" in the tiller. Rudder can be lifted off or folded against the stern in locks. Long hold begins where full beam achieved; the forward end characterized by a high, trapezoidal board backed by a tarpaulin-covered framework ca. 90cm deep; unit often ornately decorated. Area between stem and hold decked; space beneath used for gear or sometimes as additional living area (called a **family boat★**). On older boats, a long plank sometimes extended from the forward end of the hold to the aft cabin and supported struts for the tarpaulin or canvas hatch covers; modern boats use fiberglass hatch covers. On **butty boats**, a towing mast comes up through the plank from a mast box below. Walking planks are laid atop the hatch cloths. Cockpit aft gives access to a raised cabin. The main living quarters for the operating family usually on the **butty boat**. Hull tarred, but topsides fancifully painted, and often elaborate rope-work protects the painted and vulnerable areas. Lengths vary with the canal system, but all **narrow boats** are less than 2.21m wide. Lengths mostly 21-22m; widths from 1.88-2.21m; depth ca. 1.37m. The Yorkshire **narrow boats** were ca. 17.68m long. Other recorded names: **boat*** (one that was less than 2.13m in width); **knobstick** (round-hulled boat of the Anderton Company that carried mostly finished pottery); **long boat*** (West Country and West Midland term); **cloth** and **open boats** (those with or without tarpaulin rigging, respectively); relatively narrow-ended, barrel-sided **Potteries boat** (transported raw materials for pottery manufacture as well as finished ware on the Trent & Mersey Canal); **salt boats*** were employed by several companies; **town boat** or **town class** (steel boat, wider and deeper and able to work tidal areas also); **watercress** or **bed boat** (contemptuous term for leaky boats, especially the salt carriers of the Mersey Weaver Company); **wooser**, **worser**, or **wusser** (a South Midlands term). **Butty boat** types in the Tyne/Trent area: **butty collier**, **butty gang**, **butty pal**; called a **trailer** on the River Severn. Many **narrow boats** were named for the owning company, such as **Barlow boat**, **Fellows** (**Morton**) **boat**, **Nurser boat**, **Ricky** (**Rickmansworth**) **boat**, **Runcorn boat**, **Walker boat**; each had some distinctive construction feature. Further reading: Tom Chaplin, *Narrow Boats* (London: Whittet Books Ltd., 1989). Note also **admiral class**, **barge-10**, **black boat**, **cabin boat**, **day boat**, **flyboat-3a**, **hay boat**, **josher**, **monkey boat-3a**, **monkey boat-4a**, **number one**, **reserve boat**, **Rodney boat**, **single pup**, **starvationer**, **tar boat**, **wide boat**.

Nascapee crooked canoe, Naskapi crooked canoe See **crooked canoe**

Nassbagger See **dredger-1**

ñataċ See **pelota-4**

natae See **pelota-3**, **pelota-4**

Natal surfboat See **surfboat-2**

natante posa nasse See **pot vessel**

na-tiaka See **aka-3**

nätibåt See **skötbåt-1**

nattnotbåt See **notbåt-3**

nau 1. Generic term for a 14th- to 16th-century **ship***; the term still signifies ship in Catalan. During the 15th-17th centuries, could be synonymous with **nef***, **carrack***, or **galleon***; later with a **frigate***-type vessel. Sometimes term was given to the major ship in a convoy. Some scholars include in the term all vessels of western origin with keels. Many Basque-built in the 16th century. In general, high-sided with castles forward and aft, 2-3 decks, beamy, short keel; deep hull and a midline rudder. Estimated to have been 120-500t. Other recorded names: **great ship***, **naao**, **náo**, **nauf**, **nav***, **nava***. Note also **batel-2**.

2. *France, south-central:* **a.** 19th-century cargo boat of the upper Lot River. Sharply raking, square ends; stern sometimes ended in a transom; flaring sides. Flat bottom, longitudinally planked, bent up to the ends; sheer swept up at the bow and stern; wide frames. If sailed, mast stepped well forward; generally poled and paddled. About 7m long, 1.6m wide, 0.5m deep. **b.** The **nau** was the largest of the upper Dordogne River vessels. Constructed mainly of oak, heavily reinforced; flat bottom; elongated, sharp ends. Length 20m, beam 4.5m, cap. 30t.

3. *India:* **Náū** is a **boat*** or **vessel*** in Hindi and Sanskrit.

4. *Italy, NW:* Common flat-bottomed lake and river craft of the Piedmont region. One type, originating in Lake Maggiore, plied the river system to Venice until World War II. Large, open cargo boat with sharp bow and stern; strong sheer. Steered with a large sweep and 2 side helms. On the lake, they sometimes used a temporary leeboard. Set a square sail.

5. *Nepal:* In the language of the Thāru group, **náu** means **boat**.

6. *Switzerland, S:* A small boat or **ferry*** on the upper Rhône River. Other recorded names: **na**, **nauha**

Further references: **bangala**, **naue-2**

nauarchis See **flagship**

naucella See **navicella**

nau da carreira de India, nau da India See **East Indiaman**

naue 1. *France, E/Germany, S:* During the 15th-16th centuries, a small, flat-bottomed **rowing boat***. Known also as a **naf** or **nawe** in Alsace, and as a **naffe** in Bavaria.

2. *France, E/Switzerland:* Predecessor of the **cochère*** of Lake of Geneva (Lake Léman) and other Alpine lakes. A few worked on Lake Léman and several other lakes into the later part of the 19th and until the beginning of the 20th century on Lakes Mojeur and Lugano. In the 16th and 17th centuries, the boat was a naval vessel. Flat bottom; vertical, square stern; sharp, raked bow; parallel, vertical sides. Undecked, covering board extended aft where the steersman worked 2 oars. Carried a square sail to an unstayed mast or 2 spritsails. Also rowed forward of the midship mast. Length 13m, beam 4.5m. Other recorded names: **nau***; pl. **naus**

Nauen *Switzerland, central:* Large, open boat of Lake of Lucerne. Operated as early as the 13th century. Long, overhanging, square bow and stern enable it to load and unload at the shore. Flat bottom, flared sides. Stern deck; low house at the stern on the largest boats. Originally rowed and sailed, setting a square sail; now motorized. Early boats used 10-20 oarsmen. Length ca. 18m. Other recorded names: **Grosse Nauen**, **nawen**. Note also **naue**. Further reference: **Nachen-1**

nauf See **nau-1**, **nef-1**

nauha See **nau-6**

nauka See **nouka**

naungk wala See **na-ak wala**

nauri *India, NW/Pakistan:* Fast, decked **coaster*** built at Sind and Baluchistan ports of Pakistan and the

Kathiawar coast of northwest India. Trades along Arabian Sea ports and the west coast of India. Sharp-ended; raised stern; poop deck fitted with rails, and poop has carved ornamentation. Strongly raked stem; stemhead mounted with a carved "parrot head" piece,

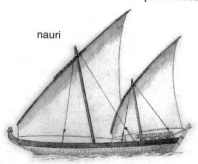

nauri

some with a crest on top. Tiller slotted through the rudderhead and brought in under the poop deck, where it is connected with ropes to a winch barrel worked by a steering wheel. On others, tiller slots over an outboard rudder. Oiled and painted topsides; some have painted portholes. Stout mainmast raked sharply forward, stepped approximately amidships; mizzen smaller or the same height and less raked. Pair of shrouds and a forestay support mainmast. Sets quadrilateral lateen-type sails with a short luff. Crew of 10-12 on some. Reported lengths 8-30m; e.g., length 18.2m, beam 5.18m, depth 2.64m, 80t burden. Spelling variants: **naodee**, **navdi**, **navri**, **nooree**, **nurih**. Note also **batel-3**.

naus See **cochère**, **naue-2**

naus makra See **long ship**

nautella See **navicella**

nav 1. *Italy, north-central:* Long, narrow river craft of the Ticino River between Lago Maggiore and Pavia. Sharp ends, flat bottom. Decked at ends, the after deck having a rounded shelter. Steered with a balanced rudder on the quarter. Spelling variants: **nave**★; pl. **navi**
2. *Turkey:* Armenian generic term for **ship**★.
Further references: **battello-2**, **nau-1**, **nava-1**, **nava-4**

nava 1. Croatian term for a **ship**★ during the 14th to the 18th century. Other recorded names: **nav**★, **navina**; pl. **nave**★
2. Czech word for **ship** or **boat**★. Spelling variant: **nave**
3. *India, E:* **a.** In the Telugu language, **nāva** means **ship**, **boat**, or **vessel**★. Spelling variant: **navi**. **b.** In the vicinity of the Godavari Delta and to the northeast, the **nāva** is an important net **fishing boat**★. The larger boats (**peddanāva**) work offshore, the smaller boats in estuaries and rivers. Carvel-planked; heavily framed with 3-4 strong stringers. Double-ended; bottom rounded or flat with fore-and-aft rocker and rounded bilges; no keel; considerable sheer; low coaming. Bow flared with overhanging edge above the stem piece. Teak planking caulked with coconut fiber and coated on the bottom with tar. Employs a portable leeboard. Short foredeck and longer afterdeck on which the helmsman squats to steer

with tiller and rudder. Some form of oculus on the stem piece. Sets 1-2 quadrilateral lateen-type sails with short luff; after sail quite small. Reported lengths 6.1-10.7m; e.g., length 8.8m, beam 1.8m, depth 0.84m. Name variant: **Masulipatam nava**. **c.** **Nāvas** traversing the Kurnool-Cuddapah Canal northwest of Madras (Chennai) in the 1930s could carry 10 people and averaged 6m long and 1.1m wide, with draft of 0.38m.
4. *Sri Lanka:* **Nāva** is a term for **ship** in Sinhala. Spelling variant: **nāv**
See also **muggu padava**, **nau-1**.

navadi See **hoda**

navak See **kishti-2b**

naval store ship See **store ship**

navata See **almady**

navdi See **nauri**

nave 1. French, Italian, Spanish, and Turkish generic term for a **ship**★ or **vessel**★. More specifically, **navi** (pl.) were large, round-bottomed sailing vessels of the Mediterranean, dating to the 13th century. Mainly used for cargo but also as a naval transport. Constructed with 2-4 decks. Three masts. Lengths ca. 15-25m.
2. *Italy, central:* **a.** A small, open, 3-plank craft of Lake Posta Fibreno southeast of Rome. Bottom, sides, and square ends assembled, then sparse framing inserted. Bottom flat transversely, strong rocker toward the ends. Sides and transoms vertical. Propelled with a long-shafted paddle or poled. Length 4.7m, beam 0.95m, depth 0.35m. **b.** At Rovezzano, near Florence, an overhead cable **ferry**★ across the Arno River. Square, open, sraight, raked ends; flat bottom, flat sheer; sides curved inward to the narrower ends. Length overall 7.4m, beam 3.1m, depth 0.75m.
3. *Italy, NE:* In Venice, used during the 13th-16th centuries to carry cargo on long voyages. Originally 2-masted, later 3- to 5-masted; lateen-rigged.
Other recorded names: **nabio**, **navis**; Spanish dim. **navecilla**; pl. **naves**. Note also **nef**. Further references: **battello-2**, **nav**, **nava-1**, **nava-2**, **ship**

nave ammiraglia See **flagship**

nave bombardier, **nave bombardiera** See **bomb vessel**

nave buzio See **bucia**

nave carboniera See **collier-1**

nave chiocca See **mother ship**

navecilla See **nave**

nave cisterna See **tanker**

nave corsara See **corsair**, **corsara**

nave da guerra See **man-of-war**

nave da pesca See **fishing boat**

nave della dogana See **revenue cutter-1**

nave de Pavia See **rascona**

nave di commercio See **merchantman**

nave di crociera See **cruiser-3**

nave faro See **lightship**

nave fattoria See **factory ship**

nave gemella See **mother**

nave goletta See **barkentine**

nave guardpesca See **fishery guard ship**

navei See **navío-1**

nave incendiaria See **fire ship**

nave latina *Italy, E:* An early 15th-century vessel that set 2 lateen sails. Foremast raked forward, shorter mainmast vertical. As many as 12 shrouds per side on the foremast and 5 on the mainmast. Curved stem and sternpost; steep rise to the floors; slack bilges; low sheer. Steered with a quarter rudder. Length 27.6m, beam 8.3m, depth 3.3m.

nave marana See **marano**

nave mercantile See **merchantman**

nave madre See **mother ship**

nave negriera See **slaver-1**

nave pattuglia See **patrol boat**

nave per trasporter di pesce See **fish carrier-1**

nave pilota See **pilot boat**

nave quadra See **cog-2**

nave rotonda See **cog**

naves See **nave**

naves baragniatae See **navis baragniata**

navesela See **navicella**

naves longae See **long ship**

naves tabellaria See **advice boat**

nave traghetto See **ferryboat-1**, **traghetto**

nave trasporto cavalli See **huissier**

nave trasporto frutta See **fruit ship**

nave uscheria, **nave uselleria**, **nave usseria**, **nave usuraria** See **huissier**

navi See **battello-2**, **nava-3**, **nave**

navicella *Italy:* **1.** Term used variously for a small **ship***, **boat***, **wherry***, or **ferryboat***. Also, a small naval vessel; a **gunboat***, **advice boat***.
2. The **navicella** of Lake Como in northern Italy is a **fishing boat*** with a low bow and a square sail.
Other recorded names: **naucella**, **nautella**, **navesèla**, **navisèla**, **navizèlla**; **navicellette**, **navicellina** (dim.); pl. **navicelle**. See also **nacelle-5**, **navicello**.

navicelle See **navicella**, **navicello**

navicellette See **navicella**

navicelli See **navicello**

navicellina See **navicella**

navicellino See **navicello**

navicello *Italy:* **1.** A **coaster*** that carried mainly marble from the Carrara quarries to Rome and Marseille; seen occasionally as late as the mid-20th century. Heavily constructed with a full hull, especially toward the stern; mainly sharp-ended, although some had a rounded stern; late 18th-century vessels depicted with a counter stern. Flat bottom with a sharp turn of the bilges. Straight, raked, or slightly curved stem; ball on stemhead common; straight sternpost. Decked; small, raised forecastle deck flush with the rail; large hatch abaft the mainmast; early vessels had a low quarterdeck. Outboard rudder; tiller. Mainly 2-masted. The mainmast, stepped a little forward of amidships, originally set a lateen sail; later a standing gaff employed with a loose-footed sail laced to the gaff for about two-thirds of its length, and the peak sheeted to the end through a sheave; topsail to the tall, unstayed topmast. The small foremast raked forward, paralleling the stem; to this a trapezoidal staysail was laced, above which might be an upper main staysail. Jib set to a light bowsprit run out to starboard of the stem. Small

lateen mizzen portrayed on early vessels. Long sweeps employed in calms. Crew of 4. Reported lengths 16.6-24.1m; e.g., length 17.9m, beam 5.4m, depth 2.15m. Further reading: M. Bonino, "Notes sur les Navicelli Italiens," *Le Petit Perroquet* 20 (1976-77), 46-77; 21 (1977), 62-63.
2. An important river craft on several western rivers carrying sand, marble, and agricultural products since the 17th century. Sharp ends with plumb or raked stem and sternpost; flat bottom with strong rocker toward the ends; longitudinally planked; strongly flared sides. Strong sheer at bow and stern. Decked at the ends; open waist; sail might be used as an awning. Deep outboard rudder; tiller slotted over rudderhead. Mainly poled or tracked from shore or rowed, but early drawings show a square or lateen sail. Reported lengths 7.9-16.8m; e.g., length 12.9m, beam 3.1m, depth 0.66m.
Other recorded names: **navicella***, **navicelle**, pl. **navicelli**; **navicellino** (small); **navicellone** (large), pl. **navicelloni**. See also **nef-1**.

navicellone, **navicelloni** See **navicello**

navicula flotans See **flibot**

navi golette See **barkentine**

navili See **navío-1**

navi lunghe See **long ship**

navina See **nava-1**

navío 1. A Spanish term for a **ship***. Term in use from at least the 13th century. In the 16th century, some were **coasters*** on the north coast, and some went to the Grand Banks for cod; 80-120t. At times, may also designate a boat that is decked. Spelling variants: **navei**, **navili**, **navio**, **navyo**
2. The 18th-century **navío** was a large **man-of-war*** equipped with as many as 60 cannons on 2 decks. Full-bodied; high-sided; deep keel; elaborate poop deck. Square sails set to 3 masts; multiple headsails to a long, rising bowsprit. Name variant: **navío redondo**

navio capitânia, **navio comandante** See **flagship**

navio de draga See **dredger-2**

navio de fiscalização See **fishery guard ship**

navio de guerra See **man-of-war**

navio de pesca See **fishing boat**

navio de pesca a vara, **navio de pesca com canas** See **tuna boat-2**

navio de pesca de camarão See **shrimper**

navio de transporte de peixe See **fish carrier-1**

navio geméo, **navio irmão**, **navio-mãe** See **mother**

navio negrero See **slaver-1**

navío redondo See **navío-2**

naviot *France, E/Switzerland, W:* A small **boat***, **skiff***, or **wherry***. Some were sturdy **tenders*** to the **barques du Léman***. Towed the **barques*** in calms and transferred the crew and cargo to shore when there was no suitable landing place. Flat bottom; double frames crossed the bottom, each with a single rib. Sharp bilges; straight, flaring sides; sharp, strongly raked bow; wide, plumb or slightly raked transom. Short foredeck, stern seat. Rowed by 3 men; 2 sat well forward, each pulling a single long oar on the same side, the 3rd at the stern worked a single oar on the opposite side, either rowing or sculling. Reported lengths 5-7m; e.g., length 6.25m, beam 2.05m, depth 0.64m. Spelling variant: **nahiot**

navire *Canada, E:* In Quebec, classification for a **fishing boat★** longer than 12m and greater than 10grt. A **navire hauturier** works on the high seas for periods longer than a day; length over 16m; more than 25grt. See also **ship**.

navire à double fond See **double-bottom-1**

navire amiral See **flagship**

navire amphidrôme See **double-ender**

navire baleinier See **whaler**

navire balize See **lightship**

navire chai See **wine ship**

navire charbonnier See **collier-1**

navire cisterne See **tanker**

navire condamné See **hulk-3**

navire de charge See **freighter-1**

navire de commerce See **merchantman**

navire de croisière See **cruiser-1**

navire de garde See **guard ship**

navire de guerre See **man-of-war**

navire de la douane See **revenue cutter-1**

navire d'entreposage, navire de ravitaillement See **mother ship**

navire de surveillence des pêches See **fishery guard ship**

navire du Ponant See **nef-1**

navire écurie See **horse carrier**

navire frère See **mother**

navire garde côtes See **coast guard ship**

navire garde-pêche See **fishery guard ship**

navire harenguier See **herring boat**

navire hauturier See **navire**

navire huissier See **huissier**

navire jumeau See **mother**

navire major See **flagship**

navire malouin *France, NW:* Term given to the late 19th- and early 20th-century vessels from Saint-Malo that fished for cod off Newfoundland and Iceland. Variously rigged as **barks★**, **hermaphrodite brigs★**, **barkentines★**, and **ships★**. Note also **terreneuvier**.

navire marchand See **merchantman**

navire marin See **sea boat**

navire mère See **mother ship**

navire négrier See **slaver-1**

navire soutien See **mother ship**

navire transbordeur See **tender**

navire transporteur de poisson See **fish carrier-1**

navire usine See **factory ship, mother ship**

navis See **cog-2, nave**

navis baragniata *France, E:* The largest of the naval **galleys★** belonging to Philippe I, Count of Savoy. Built for use on Lake of Geneva (Lake Léman) in 1283. Distinguished by its railings, possibly a taffrail. Eighteen oars per side, each manned by two men. Also carried 10-20 archers and numerous officers. Other recorded names: **barque à barrière**; pl. **naves baragniatae**

navisèla See **navicella**

navis longa, navis lunga See **long ship**

navis sagittaria See **saettia**

navis tabellaria See **advice boat**

navito barco *Puerto Rico, West Indies:* **Sloop★**-rigged **fishing boat★** that worked mainly off the eastern end of the island. Carvel-planked; fine ends; raking stem; high-tucked transom above a raking sternpost. Deep drag to the straight keel; high, rounded bilges. Bold sheer, low freeboard amidships. Decked; open fish hold amidships. Large rudder; tiller comes in through the transom. Leg-of-mutton sail set to an aft-raking mast. Boom extends well aft of the transom. Jib to stemhead. Reported lengths 5.5-10.4m. With the decline of fishing by sail, this boat has been modified for racing, becoming known as a **Puerto Rico sailing sloop**. Raced in 3 sizes: 5.5-6.1m, 7.9-8.5m, 9.1-10.lm; beam ca. one-half keel length. Note also **balandra-9**.

navizèlla See **navicella**

Navlakhdi hoda See **hoda**

navoi See **navío-1**

navri See **nauri**

navyo See **navío-1**

na-wak See **na-ak**

na-wak wala See **na-ak wala**

nawangk ambu *Vanuatu (New Hebrides), western Pacific:* Flexible **raft★** of Malekula Island in the central part of the group; used for short seagoing voyages. Bamboo poles of equal length lashed together; sides and ends raised by 2-3 poles. Length ca. 10m.

nawe See **naue-1**

nawen See **Nauen**

nawire See **ship**

nchumbwi, nčumbwi See **mtumbwi**

ndrua See **drua**

neamhóg See **naomhóg**

Neckaraak *Germany, S:* Long, narrow, lightly built cargo vessel of the Neckar River. Clinker-planked; flared, rounded sides. Flat bottom raked up to a flattened bow; stern rounded with plumb sternpost. Sheer swept up at the ends. Tall rudder with wide blade below the waterline; curved tiller; no leeboards. Decked; peaked hatch; tall pilot house; crew housed either forward or aft. Usually stepped a single mast, but some had a small mizzen also. Reported lengths 25-45m; length-to beam ratio ca. 6.5:l. Name variant: **Neckarschiff**. Note also **aak**.

Neckarschiff See **Neckaraak**

neef See **nef-1**

nef **1.** A poorly defined ship of the Middle Ages. The French term **nef** was used for those employed on the Atlantic, while the term **nave★** was common in the Mediterranean, although use of the words overlapped. The English referred to them as warships. Both terms could be generic for all large sailing vessels of the period, and in the 15th century, **nefs** were sometimes called **pinnaces★**, **balingers★**, and **galeasses★**. Most were **merchantmen★**, carrying cargo and passengers; others were troop carriers; some served the crusaders. Since the end of the 16th century, the term **nef** has passed mostly into poetic language. In general, depicted as a heavy, cumbersome vessel that sat high in the water with prominent castles at bow and stern, the latter often very high and elaborate. On those specializing in passenger transport, the area between the castles might be lined along the sides with cabins. Double-ended with bluff bow and stern; after the adoption of the midline rudder in the 14th century, the stern became sharp. Tiller came inboard to, or below, the poop deck. Earlier, 2 quarter rudders used. Clinker- or carvel-planked; flat floors; tumble home sides. On the **nefs huissiers**, horses could be loaded through a side door and were stabled below decks. Often heavily armed to protect the cargo from pirates. Mediterranean ships mostly set lateen sails to 2 masts. Atlantic vessels adopted square sails, stepping 1-4 masts; some set lateen sails on the after 2 masts. Combined crews and warriors were reported up to 1,500. Reported lengths 18-43m; 16th-century ship 25m long, 8.36m wide, 2.5m deep, 2.95m draft. Other recorded names: **nao***, **nau***, **na(u)f**, **nave**, **navicello***, **navire du Ponant**, **neef**; **nefz** (pl.); **nief**; **nef écurie**. Note also **barge de cantier**.

2. A **nef** can be an elaborate ship model, sometimes in silver, that decorates a dining room table. May also be a ship-shaped salt container.

3. *France:* Type of river craft in use during the early 19th century.

4. *France, N:* Reported as a **fishing boat*** in Normandy and Brittany in the 13th-15th centuries. Fished for herring, mackerel, and cod; some traveled to the Newfoundland fishing grounds; also transported salt. Apparently 2-masted, setting square sails, and some raised a topsail on the mainmast. Averaged 48t in the 14th century.

5. *Switzerland, W:* In the 16th century, reported to have engaged in naval action on the Lake of Geneva (Lake Léman).

Further reference: **carrack**

nef écurie, nef huissier, nefz See **nef-1**
negger, neggher See **naggr**
negreiro, negrero, négrier, negriere See **slaver-1**
negro boat See **almady**
negro ship See **slaver-1**
neighbor boat See **ring-net boat**
ne'lge ga'twaat See **ga'twaat**
Ness joal, Ness jol, Ness jole See **Ness yoal**
Ness sgoth See **sgoth**
Ness yål, Ness yawl See **Ness yoal**
Ness yoal *Scotland, N:* Light, supple, open boat of the southern Shetland Islands; engaged in inshore fishing, sealing, and general transportation; very few left by

Ness yoal

1930. Imported dismantled from Norway until the late 18th century, then only the lumber was imported.

Light clinker construction; 5-6 planks to a side; 3 main timbers, each crossed by a light athwartships beam on which a thwart rested; 2 short timbers stiffened the bottom up to the waterline; timbers bolted to the garboard strakes. Gunwale tapered off ca. 15cm short of the breasthook at each end. Double-ended with bold sheer; soft turn of the bilges amidships; sharp at bow and stern; stem and sternpost raked; low freeboard. Straight keel; demountable rudder hung slightly below the heel; tiller. Set a large, square sail or a dipping lugsail; bowlines extended the luff. Mast stepped just aft of amidships, stayed by a shroud on each side and a forestay. Curved piece of wood or a horn held the yard against the mast. Rowed by 3-4 men using 3 pairs of oars; loom square for about one-third of its length; flat wooden or iron tholepins. Some converted to motor by adding a strake and fitting an outboard well at the stern. Standard sizes: length overall 6.55m, on keel 4.57m, beam 1.67m, depth amidships 0.64m; and 7m by 4.57m by 1.73m by 0.51m; shallow draft. Other recorded names: **Ness joal** (**jol, jole, yål, yawl*, yole, yoll**); **Dunrossness yål**. Further reading: Adrian G. Osler, *The Shetland Boat, South Mainland and Fair Isle* (London: National Maritime Museum, 1983 [Maritime Monographs and Reports 58]). Note also **Shetland model**.

Ness yole, Ness yoll See **Ness yoal**
nesting dory See **Banks dory**
neta See **catraia-7**
net boat **1.** May be used in trawling with another boat; sometimes a **seine boat***. Name variant: **Netzboot***

2. *Australia, SE:* Worked with mesh nets in bays and estuaries of Victoria. Clinker-built until 1890s, then some clinker above the waterline and carvel below; by early 1900s, fully carvel. Sharp bow with stem cutaway; stern sharper than bow; straight sternpost, somewhat raked; skeg ran under the rudder. Those working on the Gippsland lakes had a fuller stern and shallower draft. Large, oval cockpit. Outboard rudder and tiller; centerboard after 1850. Mast, in tabernacle, stepped in forward third. Set a boomed, standing lugsail, 1-2 headsails. Reported lengths 6.7-8.7m; e.g., length 8.5m, beam 2.6m, draft 0.6m.

3. *United States, NE:* Small, open boat used for handline and gill net fisheries. Locally built, generally by the owner; lapstrake construction. Mainly rowed. Reported lengths 5.5-6.1m.

Further references: **ami-bune**, **liu wang chuan**, **phang chun**, **ring-net boat**, **sin-tor-chai**, **whiting boat**

netinha *Portugal, central:* Short, beamy boat that works a type of seine net (*netinha*) off Nazaré. Flat bottom rises sharply at the bow, ending in a triangle; bow continues upward to a point without an external stem; longitudinal bottom planking curves up at stern to a flat, slightly raked transom. Strong sheer; slightly flared sides, strongly curved fore-and-aft; gunwale strake stops short of the beak. Decked for about a third of the length, no camber; 2 rowing benches. Often painted with a large circle or star at the bow and other simple paintings at the stern. Hook at the bow for oxen or tractor to pull boat up onto the beach. Length 4.8m, beam 2.4m, depth ca. 0.85m. Name variant: **barco de bico**

Nettenboot See **Netzboot**
netter See **gillnetter-1**
Nettnboot See **Netzboot**
Netzboot *Germany, NE:* Boat of the Baltic Sea islands of Rügen and Hiddensee that engaged in drift net fishing for herring or perch in the fall, and for other fish during other seasons. Usually worked from beaches. Reported from ca. 1875 to the 1950s. Clinker planking; transom or sharp-sterned, curved stem; straight T-keel. Some had a centerboard. Transom boats usually undecked; sharp-sterned boats decked at ends and along the sides. Some older boats set 2 spritsails. Others gaff-rigged with a loose-footed, boomed mainsail, staysail, jib to a long bowsprit, topsail. Engines installed on later boats. Reported lengths 5-8m, widths 2.8-3.2m, depths 0.8-1.1m. Other recorded names: **Manssenboot, Nett(e)nboot, Seeboot.** See also **net boat.**
Neuendorfer Garnboot See **Garnboot-2**
neuer Kahn See **kleiner Kahn**
Neufundlandschoner See **banker-2**
neure, neurre See **buis-2**
Nevis lighter See **sailing lighter**
nevodnik *Russia, south-central:* Sets and hauls a seine net for sturgeon on the lower Volga River and coastal Caspian Sea. Flat bottom, wedge-shaped stem; narrow, V-shaped transom; flaring sides. Open except for a cuddy at each end; 3 thwarts well forward, one aft; midship area for the nets. Rowed and sailed, directed by the pilot who spots the fish. Crew of 8-12. Reported lengths 9-11m; e.g., length 11m, beam 2m, depth 1.0m.
nevōg See **naoṁóg-2**
nevre See **buis-2**
New Bedford whaleboat See **whaleboat-7a**
Newcastle keel See **Tyne keel**
New England boat See **Hampton boat**
New England dory See **dory-1**
New England pinky See **pinky**
New England sailing dory See **Cape Ann dory**
New England sharpie See **sharpie-2**
New England surfboat See **surfboat-5**
New England Whitehall See **Whitehall boat**
Newfanlan man See **Newfoundlander**
Newfoundland boat See **Hampton boat**
Newfoundland coffin *Canada, E:* Name given to locally built seagoing ships of the early 19th century that proved to have a relatively short lifespan. Note also **coffin ship.**
Newfoundlander An English vessel, especially one from the west of England, that engaged in seasonal fishing or in fish trade at Newfoundland. Other recorded names: **Newfanlan man, Newfoundland man, Newlander.** Note also **terreneuvier.**
Newfoundland fish box See **fish box**
Newfoundland man See **Newfoundlander**
Newfoundland sealing punt See **Toulinguet boat**
Newfoundland skiff See **Toulinguet boat, trap skiff**
Newfoundland trap skiff See **trap skiff**
New Hampshire duck boat, New Hamshire ducking skiff See **scull float**
New Hampshire flatboat See **flat-6**
New Hampshire scull float See **scull float**
New Haven dugout See **Connecticut canoe**

New Haven flatiron boat *United States, NE:* Open, **skiff***-type boat used in the local oystering industry at New Haven on the Connecticut coast during the 19th century. Popular earlier for carrying goods and passengers, and for fishing. Plank-built, sharp bow; wide, square stern; flat bottom, almost vertical sides; 2-3 thwarts. Mainly rowed. Reported lengths 4.6-5.5m, beam ca. one-third of length; shallow draft. Name variant: **flatiron boat.** Note also **flatiron skiff.**
New Haven flatiron skiff See **sharpie-2**
New Haven oyster canoe See **Connecticut canoe**
New Haven sharpie See **sharpie-2**
Newhaven yawl See **baldie**
New Jersey beach skiff See **Sea Bright skiff**
New Jersey garvey See **garvey**
New Jersey oyster schooner See **Delaware Bay oyster schooner**
New Jersey oyster skiff See **Staten Island skiff**
New Jersey oyster sloop See **oyster sloop-2**
New Jersey pilot schooner See **Sandy Hook pilot schooner**
New Jersey pirogue See **periauger-3**
New Jersey sea skiff See **pound boat-1, Sea Bright skiff**
New Jersey skiff See **Sea Bright skiff**
New Jersey sneakbox See **Barnegat sneakbox**
Newlander See **Newfoundlander**
Newlyn gig See **Cornish gig**
Newlyn lugger See **West Cornish lugger**
Newlyn pilot gig See **Cornish gig**
new-moon boat See **kolek pĕngayer**
New Orleans boat, New Orleans broadhorn See **flatboat-4**
New Orleans lugger *United States, S:* Single-masted boat that worked at sea and on backwaters along the Gulf of Mexico coast from Mobile to Galveston, engaging seasonally in fishing, shrimping, oystering, and transporting local produce. Operated from the mid-19th to the mid-20th century. Oyster beds often worked by a **skiff*** or **johnboat***, and the **lugger*** served as a **buy boat*.** Hull lines varied, but bow mostly sharp with plumb stem; wide V-transom; plank keel; floors fairly flat to moderately rising. Carvel planking of cypress or longleaf pine; maximum beam generally well forward; bold sheer. Large centerboard; rudder broad below the waterline, easily unshipped. Cuddy forward of the mast; high coaming around the elliptical cockpit, which extended almost to the stern; hatch covers available for the cockpit; fishing craft had an ice box on each side of the centerboard. The motorized **shrimp luggers** had a fish hold forward. Tall pole mast stepped about one-third abaft the stem, single shroud on each side. Long yard secured by an iron ring and hoisted by a halyard and rove through double blocks. Large dipping lugsail, generally reddish brown, tacked to a traveler near the bow and sheeted to an iron horse at the stern. Also rowed and poled; later boats had an auxiliary in the stern. Crew of 2. Some large **luggers** served as **ice boats*** or **freight boats***, collecting the catch from the smaller **shrimp boats**, icing down the shrimp, and proceeding to port. Reported lengths 4.8-16.8m; e.g., length

11.4m, beam 3.7m, hold depth 0.97m; shallow draft. Name variants: **canot★**, **oyster lugger**. Note also **lugger-3**, **oyster runner**.

Newport boat, **Newport catboat**, **Newport fish and lobster boat**, **Newport fishing boat** See **catboat-2b**

Newquay pilot gig See **Cornish gig**

New York Bay skiff See **Sea Bright skiff**

New York Harbor sailing lighter, **New York lighter** See **New York sailing lighter**

New York oyster smack *United States, NE:* Mainly dredged for oysters in Raritan Bay and Kill van Kull to the south and north of Staten Island. Sometimes carried cargo or engaged in smuggling. Had a live well. **Sloop★**- or **ketch★**-rigged. Crew of 5-6. Length to 18m.

New York pilot schooner See **Sandy Hook pilot schooner**

New York pirogue See **periauger-3**

New York sailing barge See **New York sailing lighter**

New York sailing lighter *United States, NE:* Beamy, **sloop★**-rigged vessel that transferred cargoes to and from ships in New York Harbor during the 19th century; phased out in the early 20th century. Sharp or bluff bow; straight or curved, vertical stem; vertical, square stern; shallow keel; flat floors; round bilges; straight sides; maximum beam well forward; flat sheer. Wide-bladed outboard rudder; tiller; heavy wales. Decked, two hatchways; cargo often carried on deck, sometimes handled with a boom and hand winch, or the mast might be used. Tall pole mast stepped well forward, raking aft. Set a loose-footed gaff sail with a short standing gaff; mainsail brailed, hooped to the mast. Staysail to a stout bowsprit. Crew of 2. Reported lengths 14.9-29.3m, widths 7.5-12.5m, depths 2-2.2m. Other recorded names: **New York Harbor (sailing) lighter**, **New York sailing barge**, **sailing lighter★**, **sail lighter★**

New York Whitehall See **Whitehall boat**

New Zealand scow See **scow-7**

neyeu périssoire See **loquette**

ngalawa **1.** *Africa, E:* Fast, double-**outrigger canoe★** used for line fishing and setting fish traps in Zanzibar and Pemba and on the adjacent mainland coast. Hull quite deep with a narrow but flattened bottom. Plank washstrake pegged on. Considerable overhang to the sharp cutwater; since early 1960s, freeboard might be increased forward by building up and extending the washstrake to form a raised, flattened spoon bow.

ngalawa-1

When sailed, rudder attached by pintles and gudgeons to an almost vertical, sharp stern. Shark's liver oil used on the bottom as a preservative and to reduce friction. Some have oculi, and those with a disk-shaped prow have a motif painted on the bow. Two 1.83-2.24m-long booms attach to double-ended, ski-shaped floats that are 2-3m long. Booms set in middle third of the

hull, each crossing the hull horizontally; booms pierce struts that are secured by lashings; struts set vertically or obliquely and pass through the floats. Floats recently modified so that when craft heels over, they plane just below the surface. Forward-raking mast stepped into a shoe nailed to the bottom of the **canoe★** and stayed to the aft boom. Quadrilateral lateen-type sail with short luff of cheap cotton bent to a bamboo yard; some held loose-footed to a boom. May also be paddled or poled; outboard motors now common. Crew of 1-4; when sailing, one person steers and another stands on windward boom. Reported lengths 3-9.14m, widths 0.26-0.76m, depth ca. 0.7m, draft ca. 0.46m. Other recorded names: **galava**, **g(h)alawa**, **gharawa**, **ingalao**; **ngarawa★** (in Kimvits and Kimrima dialects); **nghulawa**, **ngrauwa** (by the Swahere of Zanzibar); **u(n)galawa**

  2. *Africa, SE:* The **ngalawa** numbered in the thousands on Lake Malawi.

  3. *Mozambique, N:* In some coastal areas, notably at Pemba (Porto Amélia), the term **n'galawa** is used for several types of local **lanchas** (see **machua**, **dau**, **lancha**). Spelling variant: **galava**

ngarawa *Zimbabwe (Rhodesia):* Bark **canoe★** used on rivers along the eastern border. Made from a single piece of bark, sewn at the ends. Sides held open by transverse bamboo thwarts and by 2 long, crossed pieces lashed in place with bark string. Poled. One reported as 3m long and 1.0m wide. See also **ngalawa**.

ngardän *Australia, N:* Bark **canoe★** of the indigenous peoples of northeastern Arnhem Land who use it to collect goose eggs. Constructed of a single sheet of eucalyptus bark, smoked to prevent cracking; inner side of the bark forms the outer surface of the **canoe**. Bow end stitched back at an angle to form a wedge; caulked with clay. Stern end laced vertically along the outer edge, and an inner seam made ca. 30cm inboard, creating a flat fin; tea bark plug wedged into the forward seam. Sides held open with transverse sticks, but excessive spreading prevented by athwartship thongs above these spreaders; thongs tied so that adjustments can be made as necessary. Bottom generally flattened. Mainly poled by a single occupant; paddled with the hands in open water. **Canoe** brought ashore to harden between expeditions. Reported lengths 2.7-3.4m. Spelling variant: **ŋardän**

ngębu See **kunun**

nghulawa, **ngrauwa** See **ngalawa**

nibording, **nibordspram** See **pram-6a**

nickey *British Isles:* **1.** A fast **drifter★** adapted ca. 1870 on the Isle of Man from the **Cornish luggers** that fished in the Irish Sea. Used until ca. 1920. Also used north to the Shetland Islands and on the Irish coast. Distinctive feature was a large dipping lug mainsail set to the lee side of the mast and a high-peaked, standing lug mizzen. Early boats had a sharp, raking stern, but some later boats adopted an elliptical counter or rounded stern. Straight, almost vertical stem; straight keel with moderate drag; easy turn of the bilges; vertical sides; fairly full buttocks. Decked; large fish hold amidships; cabin between mizzenmast and the hold; net room forward of the hold. Carried a small boat.

nickey-1

Mainmast raked aft slightly when afloat and was stepped off center so it cleared the mizzenmast to port when lowered while drifting. Mizzenmast tall and stepped with forward rake but stood vertical when afloat; mizzen sheeted to a long outrigger. Large mizzen staysail common, and high-peaked, jackyard topsail set to mizzenmast in good weather; canvas changed rather than being reefed. Sails generally tanned. Might be rowed by 2 long sweeps; auxiliaries installed on most by World War I. Crew of 7 plus a boy; after installation of steam capstan for the nets, crewed by 6-7. Reported lengths 12-17m; e.g., length 14.6m, beam 4.6m, depth 2.8m.

2. Kilkeel fishermen of southeastern Northern Ireland continued to call their **West Cornish luggers★** by the name **nickey** whether built at Kilkeel, the Isle of Man, or Cornwall. Other recorded names: **nickie, nicky; Manx** and **Skibbereen nickey**. Note also **Manx lugger, nobby-3**.

nickie, nicky See **nickey-2**

nidiliq See **umiak-4**

Niederelbe Ewer See **Ewer**

nief See **nef-1**

nieu, nieu iré See **niu**

Nieuwpoort garnaalboot, Nieuwpoort Garnelenboot, Nieuwpoortsche garnalenboot See **Nieuwpoortse garnaalboot**

Nieuwpoortse dandy *Belgium:* **Fishing boat★** that worked out of Nieuwpoort on the southwest coast until the early 20th century. Carvel-planked; straight stem; transom stern, slightly raked; long, straight keel; rounded bilges; sheer swept up at bow; outboard rudder. Decked; large donkey engine amidships; black hull. **Ketch★**-rigged with loose-footed, boomed sails, 2 headsails, topsails. Crew of 5. Reported lengths 14-18m; e.g., length 15.5m, beam 4.65m, depth 2.6m. Other recorded names: **Nieuwpoortse dandy-kotter** or **dandy-cutter; Nieuwpoortse sloep**. Note also **dandy**.

Nieuwpoortse dandy-cutter, Nieuwpoortse dandy-kotter See **Nieuwpoortse dandy**

Nieuwpoortse garnaalboot *Belgium:* Beamy, **cutter★**-rigged shrimping boat of the Flemish coast; some also served as excursion boats in the summer. Extinct as sailing craft by the 1930s. Carvel-planked; sheer swept up toward the sharp bow; lightly curved stem;

small transom. Decked to the mast; outboard rudder. Loose-footed, boomed gaff or leg-of-mutton sail set to a pole mast; yard topsail, staysail, jib to a light bowsprit. Most motorized by the 1930s. Crew of 1-2. Length 9.4m, beam 3.2m, depth 1.3m. Other recorded names: **crevettier de Nieuport, Nieuwpoort garnnaalboot, Nieuwpoort Garnelenboot, Nieuwpoortsche garnalenboot**. Note also **canot à crevette**.

Nieuwpoortse hoeker See **vishoeker**

Nieuwpoortse sloep See **Nieuwpoortse dandy**

niğeme See **chalabiya**

night boat See **boat-1, day boat-4**

night flower boat *China, S:* Term applied in the Guangzhou (Canton) area to boats that carried overnight human waste. Note also **fen chuan, hua chuan, ordure boat**.

night scraper See **skipjack-1**

nigilag See **umiak-4**

ni mo chuan *China, E:* One-man craft propelled by foot across tidal mudflats in search of small mollusks or fish. In the Qing Dynasty era, some were used to fight pirates stranded on the mudflats. Now also found

ni mo chuan

on many shallow lakes; some used for duck hunting. Reported in very early Chinese literature and probably still in use. In the Shanghai area, they are long, narrow, shallow craft built of 3 pine planks, one for the bottom, and one along each side. Ends closed off with transoms, the bow transom narrow; bottom forward sweeps up slightly. Occupant kneels, holding a transverse bar, one leg inside the craft, his shin in a notch in the stern transom; the other leg pushes along the side. Reported lengths 1.8-2m, widths 0.2-0.24m, depth ca. 1.0m. In the Ningbo (Ningpo) area, the term applied to an oval, bucket-type craft. The fisherman sat at one end holding a transverse brace and pushed with one leg outside. Pushing foot might have an oversized, flat sandal strapped on. Other recorded names: **bou-écran, ch'iao, mud sledge★, mud-touching boat, ni-m(o)u**. Note also **accon, mud sled**.

ni-mou, ni-mu See **ni mo chuan**

Ningpo ma tou chuan See **ma tou chuan**

Ningpo sampan See **hong tou san ban**

niu *New Caledonia, western Pacific:* Single-**outrigger canoe★** of the southern part of the main island and the Isle of Pines. Dugout hull with fore-and-aft bottom rocker; ends narrow and beveled. Deep washstrakes, sewn on; ends decked and often decorated. Three booms extend to a slender float connected by pairs of forked sticks; outrigger kept to windward. Large platform covers inner part of booms and hull and extends out the lee side. Steered with a paddle. Single triangular sail, apex down at the forward end, set to a forward-raking mast. Mast pivots and sail secured to opposite end when tacking. Masthead flattened to lozenge shape and pierced to accept the halyard. Reported lengths 3-8m. On the Isle of Pines, the **canoe**★ is called a **nieu**, and an undecked type is a **nieu iré**.

no   **1.** *Papua New Guinea, SE:* Generic term for a family of **canoes**★ from the western end of Rossel Island, easternmost of the Louisiade Archipelago. Note also **lia no**.

   2. *Peru, N:* **Nó** is the term for a **canoe** of the Cahuapana (Kahuapana) group. Name variant: **náon**

n-oak   See **na-ak**

Noank boat, Noank lobster boat   See **Noank sloop**

Noank sharpie   *United States, NE:* Local term given by Noank, Connecticut, fishermen to the **flatiron skiff**★ type they used to go to and from their **fishing boats**★. Open; sides lapstrake- or carvel-planked; sharp bow; wide, square stern. Rowed. Length ca. 3.7m, beam 1.3m.

Noank sloop   *United States, NE:* Used in commercial fisheries on Long Island Sound from the mid-19th century to the mid-1960s. Built mainly at Noank, Connecticut, but type constructed elsewhere on the Sound. Engaged in a variety of fishing, mainly for lobsters, oysters, and mackerel; some were trading vessels. Sharp bow with plumb or clipper stem. Raked sternpost with broad, raked transom above. Carvel-planked; rising floors; hard bilges; keel. Wet wells on one or both sides of the centerboard. Smaller boats had an oval cockpit with raised cuddy forward; some half-decked with a quarter-deck and low trunk cabin. Rudder hung on transom or came up inboard. Pole mast stepped in forward quarter. Large, boomed mainsail; long gaff. Either large jib to the long bowsprit or 2 smaller jibs. Larger boats might set a topsail. Engines installed by the beginning of the 20th century; early boats retained their sails, though modified; the engines also aided in hauling lobster pots. Crew of 1-2. Reported lengths 5.5-14m; e.g., length 7.5m, beam 3.2m, depth 1.37m, draft with centerboard up 0.76m. Other recorded names: **Connecticut lobster boat**, **Noank boat** (**lobster boat, smack**, or **well-smack**). Note also **lobster boat-4a**.

Noank smack, Noank well-smack   See **Noank sloop**

nobbie   See **nobby-1, nobby-2**

nobby   **1.** *England, W/Wales, W:* From Annan, near Carlisle, to Aberdovey, in Cardigan Bay, Wales, refers to a particular shape of hull. Characteristically, these **nobbies** have a counter stern ending in a narrow, elliptical transom; originally a short, vertical sternpost; later raked. Early models had a vertical stem, but on later boats, a rounded stem graded into a cutaway forefoot; sharp turn of the bilges. Keel initially straight, later had slight rocker; grounding keels common because they worked in shallow tidal waters. Full-bodied to the rudderpost; rudder raked slightly, ending forward of the counter. Freeboard low aft; the sheer line rising gradually to the bow; outside ballast. Decked except for a long, narrow cockpit; some had a wheelhouse in the forward part of the cockpit; now covered. Usually **cutter**★-rigged, but now generally motorized and sails dispensed with. Most **trawlers**★ engaged mainly in shrimping and flatfish fishing. Crew of 2. Vary in size, but generally under 12m;

length on waterline 9.75m, beam 2.74m, draft 1.14m. Other recorded names: **Hoylake nobby, Lancashire nobby, nabbie**★**, nabby, nobbie**

2. *Ireland:* Deep-sea **fishing boat**★ built locally until World War I; others in use were Isle of Man **nobbies**. Double-ended with a high, straight stem and a 30° rake to the sternpost; sweeping sheer; drag to the straight keel. Deep hold on the foredeck; some open. Standing lugsails set to 2 masts, the mizzen sheeted to an outrigger. Foremast raked forward ca. 15°, mizzen vertical. Jib to a very long bowsprit that ran out on the starboard side. Reported lengths 12-14.3m; e.g., length 14.1m, beam 4.3m, depth 1.93m. Other recorded names: **Connemara nobby, nobbie, nobí**

3. *United Kingdom, Isle of Man:* This **nobby** evolved from the **nickey**★ in the late 19th century, setting a tall, standing lugsail on a raking mainmast and a staysail instead of a large dipping lug tacked to the stemhead. Some built in Northern Ireland until World War I. Used for herring drifting in the Irish Sea, but known to work in other parts of the British Isles, and the larger type engaged in spring mackerel fishing off Spain. Many were converted **nickeys**, but others (generally smaller) were newly built. Carvel planking with sharp bow and somewhat rounded, raking stern or elliptical counter; **canoe**★ stern on motorized **nobbies** (which were used until World War II). Maximum beam nearly amidships; sharp, rising floors. Stem fairly straight, rounded forefoot common; sternpost sharply raked. Decked; small cabin forward of the mizzenmast. Larger type carried a small boat on deck. White, wedge-shaped cutwater painted in. Tanned, standing lugsails set to both masts, the small mizzen sheeted to an outrigger. Narrow staysail; a flying jib ran out on a reefing bowsprit that pierced the gunwale; no topsails. Foremast raked aft. Crew of 7 plus a boy; only 6 needed after installation of steam capstans to haul the warps on the larger boats. Reported lengths 7.6-14m; e.g., length overall 12.4m, on keel 9.6m, beam 3.63m, depth 1.88m. Other recorded names: **Isle of Man nobby, Manx nobby**. Further reading: Edgar J. March, *Sailing Drifters* (London: Percival Marshall & Co., 1952; reprinted 1972), 179-222.

Further reference: **Morecambe Bay prawner**

nobí   See **nobby-2**

nodebåt   See **notbåt-2**

Nogat-Lomme   See **Erdlomme**

noggar, noggur, nogur   See **naggr**

noie-chien   *France:* Familiar term for a **skiff**★-like boat. Initially used for hunting on rivers. Spelling variant: **noye-chien**

noie-chrétien   See **loquette**

n-ok   See **ok**

nokwil   See **Coast Salish canoe**

noleggiatore   See **freighter-1**

Nomans Land boat   *United States, NE:* Principal name given to a boat used in the waters off the Massachusetts island of Martha's Vineyard, the tiny island of Nomans Land (or No Mans Land) 4.8km to the southwest, and to some extent, along the south shore of Cape Cod. In use by the mid-19th century, and a few still worked in the 1930s. Primarily a lobstering and **fishing boat***, but some, especially the larger, ferried supplies and residents to and from the mainland. Sharp-ended; mainly lapstrake, a few carvel-planked. Stem curved with cutaway forefoot; sternpost sharply raked; deep keel with drag, generally ironshod; firm, round bilges; marked sheer. Centerboard, common by the 1880s, dropped through the garboard strake alongside the keel; rudder hung from sternpost. Evolved progressively from completely open to decked forward, aft, and along the sides with high coaming around an oval cockpit; live well in a few. Most launched stern-first from the beaches and retrieved bow-first by means of a cable attached to a hole in the stem; at Nomans Land, the boats were hauled up a "ladder" with wooden rollers. Worked with oars, sail, and later by motor. Stepped 2 unstayed masts that could be easily stowed; the foremast well forward, the shorter mainmast just abaft amidships. Most commonly set spritsails with varying combinations of booms and clubs along their lower edges. Foresail usually overlapped the after sail; sheeted to pegs on underside of gunwale. Some later boats adopted a gaff foresail. Crew of 1-2. Reported lengths 4.3-7.6m; e.g., length 5.7m, beam 1.9m, depth 0.74m. Other recorded names: **Chilmark boat**, **Gay Head boat**, **island boat** (at Nomans Land), **Martha's Vineyard boat**, **Vineyard (Sound) boat**

nonpareil sharpie *United States, NE:* Fast, weatherly **sharpie*** developed in the late 1870s on the north shore of Long Island, mainly for yachting, although a few were built as workboats. Distinctive features were a plumb stem that cut below the waterline to reduce hammering; shallow, square transom; a slight deadrise at the bow and later also amidships; angular bilges. Variously rigged: leg-of-mutton sails with horizontal sprit on 2 masts; **sloop***-rigged, or **yawl***-rigged with a sliding gunter forward and leg-of-mutton jigger. Reported lengths 11.6-18.6m; e.g., length 11.6m, beam 2.6m, draft 0.64m. Other recorded names: **Roslyn sharpie** (or **yawl**)

Noordhollandse gondel *Netherlands, N:* Engaged in fishing on inland waters and along the coast, mainly during the 19th century. Flat bottom; straight, raking stem and transom; lightly curved sides, strong turn of the bilges. Decked to the mast, fish well amidships; narrow leeboards. Set a leg-of-mutton or gaff sail to a lowering mast and a jib. Length 14.2m, beam 3.8m. Other recorded names: **Nord-Holländische Gondel**, **North-Holland gondola**, **vischgondel**. Note also **grundel**.

noordsvaarder See **noordvaarder**

noordvaarder *Netherlands:* Term applied to a merchant vessel that traveled to northern ports or engaged in whaling during the 17th-18th centuries. Such vessels were frequently 3-masted **fluits***. Those designed to carry timber had a loading port at the stern. Length-to-beam ratio commonly 5:1. Other recorded names: **noordvaerder**, **noordsvaarder**, **noortsche deel-haalder**, **noortsvaerder**. Note also **whaler**.

noordvaerder See **noordvaarder**

Noordwalbotter See **Marker botter**
Noordzeebotter See **botter**
Noordzeeklipper See **klipper-1**
Noordzeeschokker See **schokker**
nooree See **nauri**
noortsche deel-haalder, noortsvaerder See **noordvaarder**
Nootka canoe See **West Coast canoe**
Nootkan sealing canoe See **sealing canoe-1**
noravee yawl See **Norway yawl-1**
nordfarar, nordfarjekt See **jekt**
nordfjordbaad See **nordfjordbåt**
nordfjordbåt *Norway, west-central:* Term applied to the small, open boats built in the Nordfjord area. They were considered excellent **sea boats*** and were sold elsewhere along the coast. Ranged from 4- to 12-oared, but of special interest is the 4-oared **færing***, the 6-oared **seksæring***, the **firrøring*** (or **firkeiping***) that was rowed with 4 pairs of oars, and the **femkeiping*** that used 5 pairs. Boats steered with a single-arm yoke to an outboard rudder when sailing. Spelling variant: **nordfjordbaad, Nordfjords-båt**. Note also **jekt, notbåt**.
nordfjordfæring See **færing-3**
nordfjordjekt See **jekt**
Nordfjords-båt See **nordfjordbåt**
Nord-Holländische Gondel See **Noordhollandse gondel**
Nordische Boot See **Norsk pram**
nordischer Kahn See **Norsk pram-2, pram-6a**
nordlandsåttring See **åttring-3**
nordlandsbaad, nordlandsbåd See **nordlandsbåt**
nordlandsbåt 1. *Norway, N:* Collective term for the boats built in northern Norway, especially those of Nordland County. Specific types designated by the number of oars used (or originally used) or by the number of compartments into which the bulkheads divide the boat. Includes the 4-oared **færing***, the 6-oared **seksæring***, the **fembøring*** with 6 pairs of oars; the ten-oared **åttring***, which normally has 8 oars elsewhere; and the **firrømming** (see **firrøring-4**), which uses 8 oars. In addition, the boats include those named for the place of origin, such as the **bindalsbåt*** (from Bindal), the **ranværingsbåt*** (from Rana), and the **saltværingsbåt** (from Salta). Used mainly for cod fishing, but larger boats carried freight. **Nordlandsbåter** (pl.) are characterized by tall, square-heeled stem and sternpost, slightly recurving at the top. Sharp-ended; clinker-planked of pine or spruce; rather flat floors; flaring sides. Steered with a single-arm yoke from a long tiller; rudder rakes away from the sternpost at the top, following the lower part of the post. Open; larger boats had a portable cabin aft which was set ashore while fishing. Besides being rowed, also set a tall square sail and sometimes a topsail. Spelling variants: **nordlandsbaad, nordlandsbåd**. Note also **straumbåt**.
2. *Sweden, N:* Boats of the Nordland type were sometimes found on lakes in Lappland.
nordlandsfæring See **færing-6**
nordlandsfembøring See **fembøring-2**
nordlandsjægt, nordlandsjekt See **jekt**
Nordlandsk fembøringsbaad See **fembøring-2**
nordlandsottring See **åttring-3**

nordmörbaad, nordmörebaad, nordmørsbåd, nordmörsbåt See **nordmørsbåt**

nordmørsbåt *Norway, north-central:* Overall term given to the boats produced in the Nordmøre district, mainly for fishing. In general, these slender, clinker-planked boats were full toward the bow, had strongly curved stem and sternpost, hard bilges, and a fairly deep T-keel. Rowed and sailed, setting a trapezoidal-type, square sail. Specific types that have been described are: **femroring, femrøring, firroring**, and **torskegarnsbåt**. Fishermen from Trøndelag, especially from Åfjord to the northeast, tauntingly called the Nordmøre boat **geitbåt (goat boat)**, and the term was ultimately adopted by the people of Nordmøre for their boats. Other recorded names: **geitbåt, gjeitbåt, nordmör(e)baad, nordmørsbåd, nordmörsbåt, nordmørsgeita**. Note also **grisbåt**.

nordmørsgeita See **nordmørsbåt**

nordmørsjekt See **jekt**

Nordnorsk dory See **dory-3**

Nordzeebotter See **botter**

Norfolk beach punt See **beach punt-1**

Norfolk beach yawl, Norfolk beach yoll See **beach yawl-1**

Norfolk canoe See **flattie-2**

Norfolk crabber *England, E:* Small, sharp-ended, beamy boat that engages in crabbing, lobstering, herring and cod fishing, whelking, and, in the early days, in hovelling from the beaches on the north coast of Norfolk. Dates from at least the Middle Ages. Some were taken aboard local herring **luggers★** to the Yorkshire coast for crabs and from these, a line of similar boats, the **Yorkshire crab boats**, developed. Clinker-built with very wide planks; natural frames fitted after planking completed, closely spaced amidships, wide at the ends. Abrupt entry and run; hollow sections; steep rise to the floors; chafing pieces added to the bottom and bilges. Rounded stem and sternpost, straight sternpost on those built with engines. Long, curving rudder projected below the keel; now hung on the straight endpost; tiller. No gunwale; top strake capped with iron to reduce chafing of gear. Oar ports (2-3 to each side) cut into top strake; also, oars inserted athwartships aided in carrying the boat to and from the water; now hauled out by winch or tractor. Open; 3 thwarts; parting board ran fore-and-aft amidships to keep the bagged shingle ballast from shifting; floorboards at stern sheets only. The larger boats, the **hovellers★**, added a temporary cuddy forward when used for fishing. Painted in combinations of red, white, and blue; tarred black below the waterline. Now built mainly of fiberglass, using a traditional hull as a mold, with a hole for the propeller; these have become popular pleasure craft. Set a short, wide, high-peaked dipping lugsail; white the first year, then tanned to almost black. Tacked outside the stemhead, but when running, tack secured to an iron hook just forward of the mast on the weather side; sheet passed through hole in top of sternpost and then through an aft oar port. Short

mast stepped well forward; stowed when working, and the sails rolled around the yard. No shrouds; halyard set to weather side. **Hovellers** also set a jib and mizzen. More recently, some use gaff and gunter rigs. Engines installed since World War I, at which time rollers were used in beaching the boat. Crew of 2-3; 6-8 in a **hoveller**. Reported lengths 4.9-6.7m; longer and beamier after engines installed; e.g., length overall 5.66m, on keel 4.27m, beam 2.08m, depth 1.07m; **hoveller** ca. 5.5-7.6m overall. Other recorded names: **crabber★, crab boat, Cromer crabber, hubbler, Sheringham crabber**. Note also **beach punt-1, great boat-2a**.

Norfolk fishing punt See **beach punt-1**

Norfolk flatte See **flattie-4**

Norfolk keel *England, E:* A shallow-draft cargo carrier used on the Norfolk and Suffolk Broads. Reported as early as the mid-16th century, the last one gone ca. 1890. Clinker-built; raked bow; narrow transom stern, some sharp-sterned. Late 18th-century vessel flat-floored, later had well-rounded sections. Open hold amidships with high coaming; raised cabin forward. Outboard rudder with cleaver-shaped blade; tiller.

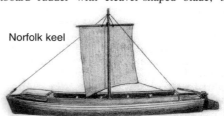

Norfolk keel

Hull tarred. At one time, some used 2 masts, but most stepped a single pole mast amidships into a tabernacle built onto the keelson. Set a tanned square sail; single block in the middle of the yard. Also quanted. Crew of 2-4. Lengths to 21m; e.g., 16.6m long, 4.42m wide, 1.24m deep, draft 1.22m. Other recorded names: **Norwich keel, Yarmouth keel**. Note also **keel, keelwherry, Norfolk wherry**.

Norfolk punt *England, E:* The wildfowling **gun punt★** of the Norfolk Broads occasionally participated in regattas. Proving fast, they were modified and by the late 1930s, became a 6.7m racing class. Sharp ends; flared, flat sides; low freeboard, flat bottom, centerboard. Early working boats were open with broad strakes on sawn frames; no gunwales. Set a small balance or standing lugsail or **sloop★**-rigged with sliding gunter mainsail.

Norfolk wherry *England, E:* Double-ended passenger, and later cargo, vessel of the Norfolk and Suffolk Broads. Used from the 16th century until the 1930s. Some converted to pleasure craft for hire by the late 19th century. Clinker-built, later of iron or steel; hollow entrance; low freeboard when loaded. Rounded buttocks and bottom; considerable sheer; false keel bolted on at times; usually only 2 transverse beams. A few transom-sterned. Massive rudder extended 1.8-2.1m aft; tiller ca. 1.8m long; a **high sternsheet wherry** was steered from the deck; on a **low sternsheet wherry**, the helmsman stood in a small well. Short foredeck; long hatch with overlapping, wooden, cambered covers; narrow side decks; small, raised stern cabin. Hull tarred below deck level except for 2 white quadrants at the bow on Waveney vessels, and all black on the Yare; forward end of main hatch and cabin top gaily painted. Heavy mast stepped in massive tabernacle well forward; pivoted above deck level and counterbalanced with a lead weight; forestay the only standing rigging. Boomless gaff mainsail with long gaff; windlass used for the single rope halyard that hoisted peak and throat at the same time; sheeted to a horse on cabin roof. Bonnet laced on in light wind. Sail usually dressed with fish oil and tar to make it black. Distinctive vane and streamer on masthead. Also poled with a 7.3m-long pronged quant. Crew of 1-2. Reported lengths 10.7-19.8m, widths 2.7-5.8m; e.g., length 17.7m, beam 4.6m, depth 1.37m, draft 1.52m. The **Bure** and **North River wherries** were smaller, had a white transom and tiller, and a white sail; those built as **yachts★** had counter sterns; the **Yare** and **Waveney wherries** were sharp-sterned. Early passenger **wherries** had a blunt, raked bow and sharp stern; by the early 19th century, these boats had a full raking bow, small transom, and set a spritsail and foresail. Lengths to ca. 10.7m. During the latter half of the 19th century, some were converted to **yachts**, becoming **wherry yachts**; some still operate. Other recorded names: **black-sailed trader**, **Broadland wherry**, **Broads wherry**, **North River barge**. Further reading: George Colman Green, *The Norfolk Wherry, Its Construction, Evolution, and History* (Wymondham: George R. Reeve, 1953); Roy Clark, *Black-Sailed Traders: The Keels and Wherries of Norfolk and Suffolk* (London: Putnam, 1961). Note also **keel-wherry**, **Norfolk keel**, **reed boat-2**.

Norfolk yoll See **yoll-1**

Norische Boot See **Norsk pram**

norska eka See **orusteka**

Norsk pram **1.** *Denmark:* Small, open, inshore **fishing boat★** used off beaches, especially along the northwest coast of Jutland. Based on the **pram★** of Norway. Characterized by a raked transom stern and a long, rising bow that ends in a small, raked, flat stem piece.

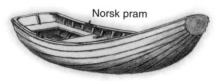

Norsk pram

Clinker-built; no gunwale strake; bottom strakes round up to the bow transom. Round bottom with skeg aft; may also have side keels aft. Sailing **prams** have a broad rudder and may use a detachable fin forward or a centerboard. Double tholepins when rowed. Sets a spritsail with 1-2 headsails and sometimes a yard topsail. Reported lengths 3-7m; e.g., length 4.7m, beam 1.65m, depth 0.63m, draft 0.31m. The **havpram** line

fished farther offshore for cod, haddock, and sole. Decked with steering well aft; keel; rounded sternpost. Sometimes used both motor and sail. A 1905 boat was 7.35m long, 2.52m wide, 1.4m draft. Note also **Moses boat**.

2. *Germany, NW:* The so-called **nordischer Kahn** was a **Norwegian pram★**-type boat used for fishing on the North Sea coast, working under sail and oar; some served as **ship's boats★**.
Other recorded names: **Nor(d)ische Boot**, **nordischer Kahn**, **Norwegian pram**

north-away yawl See **Norway yawl-1**

north canoe See **canot du nord**

North Carolina sail skiff *United States, E:* Used for oyster tonging, clamming, tending crabpots, fishing, and as transportation on the sounds behind the North Carolina seacoast. Developed in the mid-1800s and worked into the 1940s; presently a pleasure craft. Varied somewhat in design in the various sounds. Carvel-built, wide planks; sharp, vertical stem; transom stern; easy run. Flat or "V" bottom; chine piece. Short foredeck; narrow, side decks on some. Adjustable centerboard; sandbag ballast; hiking boards used when raced. Outboard rudder; tiller. Set a spritsail, either high or moderately peaked, and a jib to the stemhead. Larger boats carried a sprit topsail and flying jibs. Topsail set on its own mast, hauled up by a halyard and separately sheeted. Crew of 1-2. Reported lengths 4.2-7.3m; beam one-quarter; depth ca. 0.41-0.56m. Other recorded names: **Beaufort skiff**, **Carolina (spritsail) skiff**, **deadrise (sail) skiff**, **North Carolina spritsail skiff**, **sharpie★** (erroneously), **sharpie-skiff★**

North Carolina seine boat See **North Carolina shad boat**

North Carolina shad boat *United States, E:* Worked out of the sounds bordering the North Carolina coast setting pound and seine nets from the latter part of the 19th century. Extant but not as a sailing craft, having been converted to motor by the early 20th century. Carvel-planked; sharp bow; straight, raking stem; raked transom stern; keel shaped from a log with some drag; rising floors; stern planked and shaped, deadwood; natural frames, curved; strong, graceful sheer. By the end of the 1st quarter of the 20th century, the customary round hull was replaced by a V-bottom hull of similar profile. Open; narrow waterways with low coaming. Centerboard, outboard rudder, sandbag ballast. Short, unstayed mast stepped through a thwart; pole topmast. High-peaked spritsail; jib tacked to stemhead. Jib-headed, sprit topsail set with the mainsail or alone. Also rowed. Crew of 2-3. Reported lengths 5.5-9.8m; e.g., length 7.4m, beam 2.24m, depth 0.9m; shallow draft. Other recorded names: **Albemarle Sound shad boat**, **Croatan** (incorrectly **Croatian) boat**, **North Carolina seine boat**, **Pamlico Sound seine boat**, **Roanoke Island (shad) boat**, **round-bottom shad boat**, **round-chine shad boat**

North Carolina sharpie See **sharpie-4**

North Carolina spritsail skiff See **North Carolina sail skiff**

north country boat See **kitamae-bune**

North Country coble See **coble-1**
North Devon polacca See **polacca**
North Ender See **Yarmouth shrimper**
northern canoe See **canot du nord**
northern-style canoe *Canada, W/United States, Alaska, S:*
Cedar **dugout canoe★** made by a number of Native
American tribes on the northern coast of British
Columbia and southeast Alaska. Those of the Haida
(Queen Charlotte Island) were best known and widely
traded. Similar, but with some modifications, were
those of the Bella Bella, Haisla, Kwakiutl, Tlingit, and
Tsimshian peoples. Divided into four classes—the
light, portable hunting **canoe★** that had relatively simple lines and was used by 1-3 men; the family **canoe**,
5.5-10.7m in length; and the voyaging (freight) and
war **canoes** that ranged up to 28m in length and could
hold up to 100 men. Most familiar were the large
canoes with long, overhanging ends, similarly truncated; sometimes elaborately carved at the bow; on
the largest **canoes**, the end pieces were added on.
Hewn from a single cedar log expanded by water
heated with hot stones; gunwales left thicker than the
sides. Bottom usually rounded in cross section with
slight rocker toward ends. Sides flared above the
waterline; a near-vertical cutwater fin extended for
about one-half the hull length; hollow entrance and
run; strong sheer. Many elaborately carved and painted, and gunwales might be inlaid with otter's teeth.
Primarily paddled, but later **canoes** adapted cloth
spritsails set onto 2 masts. Typically: length 10.9m,
beam 1.83m, depth 0.64m. Other recorded names:
Alaskan canoe, **Fort Rupert canoe** (also **que'taqtla**), **hwetakla**, **hwetukla**, **Queen Charlotte Island
canoe**, **tsaba'xad**; **hai'dats** (by the Kwakiutl); **jåk**,
yäk, or **yàk** (by the Tlingit); **Bella Bella**, **Haida** (or
Haydah), **Kwakiutl**, **Tlingit**, **Tsimshian canoe**. Note
also **mE'nga**.
northern trader See **Kiangsu trader**
north front ship See **kitamae-bune**
North-Holland gondola See **Noordhollandse gondel**
North Isles yawl See **North Isles yole**
North Isles yole *Scotland, N:* Open boat used until the
late 19th century for interisland transport, fishing, and
lobstering from the northern Orkney Islands. Also
reported from Moray Firth to the south. Clinker-built
of imported Norwegian pine on oak frames. Sharp
ends, but stern fuller; drag to keel. Full lines; hollow,
rising floors; wide, round bilges; strong sheer. Stem
lightly curved and raked; stern straight and sharply
raked. Outboard rudder; tiller slotted into rudderhead.
Hull tarred originally, later painted green or black.
Two masts of about equal height; mainmast raked
slightly aft. Set 2 standing lugsails; the mainsail loose-
footed with boom, foresail sometimes had a boom.
Mainsail extended by a traveler fitted with a goose-
neck on the boom. Reefing bowsprit ran through a
gammon iron either to port or starboard of the stemhead, depending on the locale; heel fixed by an iron
on the foremast; set single foresail. Also rowed
using 2 pairs of oars worked between double
tholepins and held by a wide grommet. Last boats

motorized. Reported lengths 3.4-9.1m; e.g., length
overall 5.8m, on keel 4.3m, beam 2.9m, depth 0.8m.

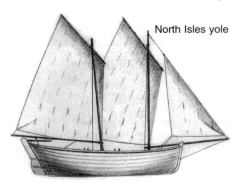

North Isles yole

Other recorded names: **flatchie** (Shetland Islander
term); **North Isles yawl**, **Orcadian yol(e)**, **Orkney
flatchie**, **Orkney yole**, **Westray yole**. Note also
South Isles yole.
North Jersey skiff See **Sea Bright skiff**
northland boat See **rua nua**
North River barge See **Norfolk wherry**
North River bricker See **Hudson River brick schooner**
North River sloop See **Hudson River sloop**
North River wherry See **Norfolk wherry**
North Sea botter See **botter**
North Shore canoe *Canada, E:* Clinker-built boat mod-
ified from the birchbark **canoe★** of the Montagnais of
the northern shore of the St. Lawrence River. Used as
an all-purpose boat to carry mail, for fishing, pleasure,
etc. Coarsely fashioned with 5 planks to a side; heav-
ily timbered. Rowed using a pin oar. Length 4.3m,
beam 0.8m.
North Shore dory See **Swampscott dory**
North Shore lobster boat See **lobster boat-4b**
North Strait boat See **Strait boat**
Northumberland coble See **coble-1**
Northumberland Strait boat, **Northumberland
Strait fisherman** See **Strait boat**
Northumbrian coble See **coble-1**
Northwest canoe See **canot du nord**
norvégien Term sometimes applied to a **sailboat★** rigged
with a tall, narrow leg-of-mutton sail. Generally rounded, tumble home stern.
norvégienne **1.** *France, N:* Small pleasure and **fishing
boat★** found on the lower Seine River from at least the
end of the 19th century. Clinker-planked, small bow
transom. Set a lugsail to a mast stepped well forward.
Also rowed.
  2. *Norway:* Used by whalers to quickly maneuver a har-
pooned whale alongside before it sinks. Rounded,
raised bow.
Norway skiff Light, buoyant, swift boat, especially a
ship's boat★. Considered particularly safe in severe
weather. Rowed. Name variant: **Norwegian skiff**. See
also **Norway yawl-2**.
Norway vlet See **vlet**
Norway yawl **1.** British term for an open boat that
resembled some of the small Norwegian fishing craft.

Term sometimes applied to British Royal Navy **yawls*** despite the fact that these had square sterns, whereas the **Norwegian yawls** did not. Some sources describe the **Norway yawl** as having a shovel-like **pram*** bow, square stern, and setting a lugsail, like the **Arendal yol**. Also rowed. Length-to-beam ratio ca. 4:1. Other recorded names: **noravee yawl**, **north-away yawl**, **nuravee yawl**. Note also **yawl-1**.
2. *Ireland/Northern Ireland:* Imported from Norway in the early part of the 19th century but often modified by the addition of 1-2 strakes. Found mainly along the north and northeast coasts of Ireland, engaging in line fishing into the 20th century. Clinker planking; sharp, strongly curved ends; open; low amidships. Rowed with 4 oars. When sailed, set a sprit- or lugsail. Reported lengths on keel 5.5-6.1m, widths 1.67-1.83m. Name variant: **Norway skiff***
3. *United States, NE:* Used in the Boston area in the early 18th century.

Norwegian boat *United States, north-central:* Heavy boat used by enclaves of Scandinavian fishermen on Lake Michigan. Clinker- or carvel-built; flaring sides; sharp stern or narrow transom; keel; hollow floors; strong sheer. Occasionally had a centerboard. Decked at bow and stern or bow only; washboards along the sides. Gaff mainsail, forestaysail, jib; sometimes a gaff topsail. Crew of 3-5 mainly. Reported lengths 7.6-12.2m; e.g., length 10.7m, beam 2.6m, depth 1.07m.

Norwegian jekt See **jekt**
Norwegian pram See **Norsk pram**, **pram-6a**
Norwegian skiff See **Norway skiff**
Nor'Wester canoe *Canada, central:* General term for the birchbark **freight canoes*** of the North Western Company. Superseded in 1821 by the **York boat*** when the company merged with the Hudson's Bay Company. Cedar planking and ribs. Length 8m, beam 1.4m. Note also **canot du nord**.
Norwich keel See **Norfolk keel**

notbåt **1.** *Finland, S:* Open, clinker-built boat used for herring seining (*not*). Double-ended; flat floors; stem curved at upper end, straight and strongly raked below; straight, vertical sternpost. Short deck at each end. Rowed with long, heavy oars that have a bulbous loom at the end but terminate in a small grip. Also sailed, setting a square sail to a midship mast. Reported lengths 7.6-9.1m, widths 2.4-3m. In the Åland Islands, the term has been applied to a transom-sterned **storbåt*** also engaged in herring fishing.
2. *Norway, W:* Used in coastal seine-net fishing, mainly for herring. Many built in the Hardanger area. Popular as a pleasure craft in some places. Clinker-planked, rising floors; sharp bow, square or sharp stern, maximum beam abaft amidships. Net paid out over a roller on the transom. Outboard rudder; tiller came in below the roller. Movable, cambered deck abaft the mast protected the nets. Rowed with 4 pairs of oars or set a loose-footed gaff sail. Main sheeted to a traveler across the stern. Large staysail; jib set flying to a reefing bowsprit; yard topsail. Reported lengths 9.9-12.1m; e.g., length 9.9m, beam 3m, depth 1.4m. A small, beamy Nordfjord type had strongly flaring,

curved sides and raking, curved stem and sternpost. Wide floorboards aft or permanent floor protected the net; also had a roller. Rowed with 3 pairs of oars. Might set a sprit- or gaff sail; older boats square-rigged. Recent boats may have a small house forward and an engine. A small 1890 boat was 7.38m long, 2.52m wide, 0.75m deep. Other recorded names: **Hardanger notbåt**, **nodebåt**, **notebaad**, **seine boat***
3. *Sweden, central:* **a.** Small, open boat used in net fishing for salmon and whitefish (**siknotbåt**). Mainly a river craft. Some specialize in night fishing (**nattnotbåt**). Clinker-planked; flat floors; very flared, curved sides; 2-piece frames. Slightly raked transom; bow turns up into a long overhang. Rowed using one pair of oars. Length ca. 8.4m, beam 1.9m, depth 0.5m; whitefish boats shorter. **b.** Up to the end of the 18th century, **notbåtar** (pl.) fished for herring along the central Baltic coast. Presumed to have been sharp-ended, low-sided, and ca. 6m long.

notebaad See **notbåt-2**
Nöteyviksdoris See **dory-4**
Notfallboot See **accident boat**
notfartøj See **seine boat-1b**
not-og-vodfartøj See **seine boat-1a**
Nottingham pan See **pan**
nouka *Bangladesh/India, NE:* Bengali word for **boat***, especially a plank-built boat characterized by heavy, raked end pieces. Pieces most often a single block of wood but may be formed by planks, creating a hollow box; taper to a point well above gunwale level, but may also be blunt, rounded, or low and cut flat. Large boats of this class are called **boro** (big) **noukas**, while those engaged in commercial pursuits may be specifically called **khæper noukas**. These latter are self-contained since they travel long distances. Many **noukas** are **fishing boats***. A **nouka** may also be a boat of dugout construction. Other recorded names: **nao**, **nauka**
nousf-feloukah See **fulūka-2b**
noye-chien See **noie-chien**
ntepe See **mtepe**
ntumbwi See **mtumbwi**
nu **1.** *India, NE:* Term for **boat*** or **canoe*** by the Deoria Chutiya of northeast Assam. Name variant: **nung**
2. *United States, W:* **a.** The **nu'** of the Patwin of central California was a tule grass **raft***. Small **rafts** were used to cross rivers, large ones for downstream travel. Composed of thick bundles wrapped and lashed with grapevines. Edges built up to form gunwales. Turned up at the bow, stern flat. Paddled with willow poles without blades or poled. Downstream **rafts** ca. 6.1m long, 1.8m wide. Name variants: **balsa***, **tule balsa**. **b.** To the southern Wintun of northern California, **nu** is the generic term for a **boat**.
nü See **wa´k·ai**
nua See **rua nua**
nuak, **nu-angk**, **nuanka** See **na-ak**
nuggah See **naggr**
nuggar See **markab-2**, **naggr**
nugger, **nuggur** See **naggr**
nukwil See **Coast Salish canoe**

number one *England/Wales:* River and **canal boat★** that was owner-operated. Most were **narrow boats★**, although family-owned **Weaver flats★** were called **number one flats**. Most frequent cargo was coal. Might work under contract to a large **canal boat** operator. Usually well-maintained and finely decorated. Horse-drawn until the 1930s, when most were motorized. Name variants: **captain boat** (a boat on the Leeds & Liverpool system worked by a single captain who was not necessarily the owner); **hobbler** (South Wales term for a **number one**)

number one flat See **Weaver flat**

nuñatapu *Solomon Islands (Santa Cruz Group), western Pacific:* Single-outrigger paddling **canoe★** in which the hull consists of a simple unexcavated log. Shaped at the ends, flattened on top. Two closely spaced, horizontal booms rest on pegs set into the hull. At the float end, several stanchions and curved braces support the booms. Float sharp-ended. Light platform set onto the booms, extending a short distance out the outrigger and opposite sides. Spelling variant: **munatapu**

nung See **nu-1**

nuravee yawl See **Norway yawl-1**

nurih See **nauri**

Nurser boat See **narrow boat**

nusf khashbah See **Lamu jahazi**

Nussschale See **cockleshell**

nuu-chah-nulth, nuu-chah-ulth See **West Coast canoe**

nu-wak See **na-ak**

N. W. canoe See **canot du nord**

ōă *Indonesia, E:* A double-**outrigger canoe★** in the area of Windesi in Sarera (Geelvink) Bay on the north coast of Irian Jaya. Paddled and sailed.

oa See **wa-1, wa-2, wa-ririk**

oai *Papua New Guinea, Bismarck Archipelago:* Single-outrigger fishing **canoe★** of the Kaniet Islands in the northwest part of the group. Massive dugout hull; sides generally raised with washstrakes, sewn on. Raked ends elongated, terminating in a platform that might be carved along the top and sides. Thwarts rested on notches in the hull or, where present, in the washstrakes; a gunwale pole rested on the thwarts and outrigger booms. An open framework at each end was used by the fishermen. Sharp-ended float, about two-thirds the length of the hull, attached by 3-5 booms. Each boom flanked by flexible spars along its outer part; spars turned down toward the ends and were lashed outside the multiple vertical stanchions that connected the booms and float. Single mast raked forward, stepped between the gunwale pole and the hull and braced from the platform. Set a rectangular mat sail lug-fashion; boom at the foot forked against the mast, holding the sail up obliquely. Halyard passed over a decorative crutch at the top of the mast. Name variant: **oaihút**

oaihút See **oai**

oak See **wa-2**

o-ak See **ok**

oáṅga *Papua New Guinea, Bismarck Archipelago:* Single-**outrigger canoe★** produced on the island of Watom off the north end of New Britain Island. Often found on New Britain, having been traded to this island. Primarily a fishing and turtle-hunting craft.

oáṅga

Characterized by extensions that lashed to the raked ends of the dugout hull; sharp spur projects from the inner side of the end piece, and the end terminates fiddlehead fashion; bow end lower and more vertical. Several outrigger booms cross atop the gunwales to the very long, slender float on the port side. End booms attached by means of branches lashed to the float; medial booms forked at the float end and clamped between a pair of tall sticks that insert into the float; stringers strengthen the outrigger unit. Lime used to whiten hull; outrigger black. Mainly paddled. Large **canoes★** ca. 9-12m long, very narrow. Other recorded names: **a kuba, kakala, kalala** (erroneously), **kuba, oáṅga tuna, peu** (one without end pieces). Note also **waqa.**

oáṅga tuna See **oáṅga**

oared boat See **rowboat**

obangga See **bangka**

Oberländer *Germany, S/Netherlands, SE:* **1.** Term given to cargo vessels of the upper Rhine River basin, upper reaches of major tributaries, and the Meuse (Maas) River. Term dates to the 13th century. Some well-known types were the **beitelaak★, Dorsten'sche Aak★, herna★, Hollandse aak** (see **aak**), **spitsbek★**; sometimes called **oberländer** or its variants. Other recorded names: **bovenlander, Lade, Mainzer Lade(n), ofenlander, overlander, overlandre**

2. The earliest form was a split **dugout canoe★** with planks inserted to create a flat bottom and ends. Fuller toward the stern, where the tree trunk had a greater dimension.

3. By the 17th century, the Rhine vessel, working above Cologne, had a trapezoidal shape with clinker planking. The bow narrow and low, the curved stern wider and high. Ends and bottom flat; bow overhanging. High sides; roughly constructed. The stern might be built up to provide a small shelter for the helmsman. Some vessels covered amidships. Stern quarter rudder, bow sweep. Towed from a mast; might also set a sprit-sail and later a square sail. Also rowed. Length to ca. 25m, width at stern 6.5m, at bow 3.5m Further reading: K. Schwarz, *Die Typenentwicklung das Rheinschiffs bis zum 19 Jahrhundert* (Karlsruhe: Bad Technischen Hochschule "Friedericiana," 1926), 65-71.

4. *Poland, SW:* On the Oder River, above Wrocław, a type of **Oberländer** operated in the latter part of the 19th century (at that time, part of Germany). Constructed of oak and pine. The **Mittelkahn** was 37-38.5m long overall, 29-30m on the bottom, 4.25m wide, 1.6m deep; draft light 0.36m, laden 1.28m. The **kleine Kahn** was 31.4m long overall, 24.5m on bottom, 3.3m wide; draft light 0.31m, laden 1.1m. Name variant: **Scheitniger Oderkahn**
Further reference: **Elbkahn**

Oberländer Kahn *Poland, N:* An important German vessel of the 19th century that worked the canal/river system from Elbląg (Elbing) southward, on the route generally called the Oberländischer Kanal (Kanal Elbląsko-Ostródzki). Flat bottom; plumb sides; curved stem; shallow, wineglass transom. Decked; long hatch. Outboard rudder with wide fin; tiller; leeboards abreast the mast. Stepped the mainmast in forward third, setting a loose-footed, boomed gaff sail. Mizzen a standing lugsail. Large staysail. Reported lengths 24.5-30m; e.g., length 24.5m, beam 3m, depth 1.2m. Name variant: **Oberländische Canalschiff**

Oberländische Canalschiff See **Oberländer Kahn**

Oberländische Saalschiff *Germany, SE:* Flat-bottomed 19th-century cargo vessel of the Unstrut River, a tributary of the Saale. Constructed of fir. Length 37m, beam 4.6m; cap. 50-125t.

Obstplätte See **Plätte-1**

Obstschiff See **fruit ship**

Obstzille See **Zille**

obusera See **gunboat**

oça See **balsa-4**

ocean canoe See **Passamaquoddy ocean canoe, rough-water canoe**

ocean-ship See **hafskip**

octuple scull See **scull**

odam 1. *India, Lakshadweep (Laccadive) Islands:*
a. Transports cargo between these islands and the Indian west coast. A few still used, but most are **pattamars*** modified to island tradition. Planks still sewn edge-to-edge with coir; stitches recessed on the outside and sewn over coir wadding on the inside; garboard strakes are both pegged and sewn to the keel. Stemhead varies slightly in design, but characterized by a high extension that usually recurves; stem strongly raked. Early boats reportedly had high poops, now low; gallery decorated with individual motifs. Roomy toilet box hung across the stern, also painted. Hull tarred black with a wide white band on top strake and narrow band below. Peaked, thatched roof covers the cargo amidships; small, square cabin at the stern; some have a cookhouse amidships. Carries wooden water tanks with up to a two-month supply of fresh water. May be single-masted or also step a mizzen; mainmast rakes forward. Lateen rigged; sometimes with a boomed-out jib. Uses a sweep when becalmed. Crew of ca. 11. Reported lengths 11.3-18.2m; e.g., length overall 18.2m, on keel 14m, beam 5.18m. Other recorded names: **odom, ōṭi, pattamar***. **b.** May also be a small **fishing boat***. Built with 5-6 planks to a side. Steered with a rudder or oar. May be sailed or rowed, the oars working against a tholepin and secured by a coir loop. A craft with 8 oarsmen is identified as an **ettu balikkandathu**, one with 6 oarsmen as an **aru balikkandathu**; these 2 types have 2 sails. A 4-oarsmen boat is a **nalu balikkandathu** and sets one sail.
2. *India, SE/Sri Lanka:* A **boat*** or **raft*** in the modern Tamil language; **pakada** in ancient Tamil. Spelling variant: **ōṭam**
3. *India, SW:* The fishing **odam** of the Malabar and Kerala coasts is a large, well-made **dugout canoe***. Ends may be low and identical, or one may extend upward and recurve to form a knob-like decoration. Round in cross section; bottom curved longitudinally. Steered with a long sweep. Paddled with long, rectangular-bladed paddles. Occasionally sets a small spritsail. Crew of 7-12. Lengths vary regionally, ranging from 9.5-12.8m; widths 0.9-1.3m, depths 0.64-0.94m. Other recorded names: **vanchi, vañci, vanji** (may also mean merely **boat***)

odi 1. *India, Lakshadweep (Laccadive) Islands/Maldive Islands:* Generic term for several types of carvel-built boats used in these islands off the west coast of India. Some bluff-bowed, others have a hollow waterline and a high, recurved stem. Most are sewn boats. Larger boats have a house amidships and step 2 masts. A large type from southern Maldives might be 27.4m long. Spelling variant: **ody**. Note also **mas-odi**.
2. *India, SW:* The **oḍi** from Kerala is a narrow racing boat with a high, upturned prow.
3. *India, W:* **a.** Large vessel that was part of the **fleet*** of the ruler of Minicoy Island off the west coast. Until the mid-19th century, **ódis** sailed as far as Bengal, carrying Minicoy nuts and returning with rice; some still sail, but few are locally made. Hull resembles western vessels. Decked; outboard rudder; tiller. Foremast carries 2-3 square sails, the after mast either lateen-, square-, or gaff-rigged. Small square sail hung from a forward-raking mast; tacked fore-and-aft to a light bowsprit. Cap. ca. 200t. **b.** In the Kanarese language, **oḍi** means a long, narrow sea boat. Note also **hody**.

odom See **odam-1a**

ody See **odi-1**

oeresundboot See **sildebåd**

ofenlander See **Oberländer**

off-and-on boat *Canada, E:* In Newfoundland, a small **rowboat*** that plies between the shore and moored craft. Locally, a mooring is called a collar. Generally ca. 3.7-4.3m long. Name variant: **collar punt** (or **boat**), **off-and-on punt**. See also **Bermuda dinghy**.

off-and-on punt See **off-and-on boat**

Offizierschiff See **Leibschiff**

og See **ok**

oga See **aidedeya, de wang**

ogára 1. *Brazil, W/Peru, north-central:* Dugout canoes* of the Cocama of the Marañón and Ucayali River areas. Paddles have short loom with crutch grip and long blades, tapering at the end.
2. *Peru, NE:* Dugout canoe of the Omagua of the upper Amazon River. Early paddle blades wide, later blades more elongated.
Note also **igára**.

ogate gourabe See **gourabe**

Ohio packet boat See **packet boat-4**

Ohio pound net boat, Ohio pound net sharpie, Ohio sharpie See **sharpie-8**

oil barge See **tank barge**

oil boat See **tar boat**

oil carrier, oil tanker See **tanker**

oissier See **huissier**

Ojibway canoe See **wigwas tsiman**

Ojibway long-nose canoe See **long-nose canoe**

ok *Vanuatu (New Hebrides), western Pacific:* Term for a **canoe*** on several of the islands in the northern part of this archipelago, especially in the Banks group. Most have a single outrigger. Spelling variants: **ak*, n-ok, o-ak, og**. Note also **aka**.

öka See **eka**

okhotnich'e sudno See **sealer**

ökia See **eka**

okka See **koka**

ökorna See **eka**

ökstock See **ekstock-1, kyrkbåt**

ökstockar, ökstockarna See **ekstock-1**

olan mesa *Indonesia, central:* Double-**outrigger canoe*** of the Gulf of Mandar in southwestern Sulawesi (Celebes). Wall-sided, flat-bottomed dugout hull; light sheer amidships, ends turn up with stem higher than the stern. Bamboo lattice work raises sides at each end. Two booms cross the hull by internal and external lashings to a rod that pierces the hull and by a short brace atop the booms. Each horizontal boom connects with the float by a single curved piece. Quarter rudder. Single mast sets a large, boomed rectangular sail; mast crutch stepped on each gunwale. Length to ca. 10m.

old hooker See **whaler-1**

old salter See **Fal barge**

oljefartyg See **tanker**

oloako, olocko See **ulakh**

Ölprahm See **Prahm-2**

Öltanker, Öltankschiff See **tanker**

olwe boat *Pitcairn Island, eastern Pacific:* Small **dugout canoe*** used for fishing. Shaped like the dried casing of the coconut palm flower, the *oroe*. Sharp, overhanging, curved ends; narrow, residual keel; flattened bottom. Seams caulked with banyan tree resin. Crew of 1-2. Reported lengths 5.5-6.1m, widths 0.76-0.86m. Name variant: **oroe boat**. See also **longboat-5**.

omenak See **umiak-1**

one-and-a-half master See **ketch**

one-day boat See **smackee**

one-girl flower boat See **hua chuan-2b**

one hundred and fifty bushel sharpie, one hundred bushel sharpie See **sharpie-2**

100-piece boat See **York boat**

one-lunger A boat powered by a single-cylinder engine; usually noisy. See also **St. Lawrence skiff-1**.

one-man sharpie See **sharpie-2**

one-sail bateau *United States, E:* **1.** In Chesapeake Bay waters, any V-bottom or flat-bottomed boat that has a single mast and sail and exceeds 6m in length.
2. In the areas of Smith Island and Crisfield on the Eastern Shore of Chesapeake Bay, the term refers to a specific type of shallow, beamy crabbing and oyster-tonging boat. Sharp bow with straight, wide stem; shallow transom; bottom planked fore-and-aft or in a herringbone pattern; moderate deadrise; slight flare to side decks; longer boats had portable trunk cabin; open rails. Tall mast stepped well forward; leg-of-mutton sail with horizontal sprit. Most later boats powered. Lengths mainly 5.8-8.2m; beam a little more than one-third length. Name variant: **one-sail dinghy**

one-sail dinghy See **one-sail bateau**

120-piece boat See **York boat**

onker Term given in England to wooden Scandinavian vessels in the Baltic timber trade. Familiarly called **onkers**, presumably because of the grunting and groaning noises made by the deck windmill pumps. Often returned to Scandinavia with coke. Gone by World War II. Most **bark***- or **schooner***-rigged. Other recorded names: **firewood fleet, split-wood fleet**. Note also **timber carrier**.

ontri See **ontro**

ontro *Italy, Sicily and Sardinia:* Small, fast swordfishing boat found mainly in the Strait of Messina, but also on the east coast of Sardinia. Worked into the 1970s. Some assisted the larger **feluca***. Design of boat varied but characterized by a short pole stepped roughly amidships on which a spotter stood. Fine lines; light scantlings. Double-ended; stem and sternpost rounded or might have a clipper bow and an inward-raking sternpost; some ends tall. Decked at bow for the harpooner. Mainly rowed with 4 oarsmen standing, facing either forward or aft; the midship pair of oars might be outrigged. Motorized by the 1960s. Crew of 4-5 plus harpooner. Length 6.9m, beam 1.22m. Other recorded names: **luntre*, luntru*, ontro lanciatore, untra, untru;** pl. **ontri**

ontro lanciatore See **ontro**

ontzi See **barco-1**

ontziño, ontziska See **barqueta**

onwaro, ooaro See **ouaro**

oogaars See **hoogaars**

oolack, oolak, oolank See **ulakh**

oome'ak, oomiack, oomiak, ooniak See **umiak-1**

oorlogsjacht See **jacht-3**

oorlogschip, oorlogsschip See **man-of-war**

oorlogssloep See **sloop-1**

oo'se See **Cree canoe**

Oostendsche boot See **Oostendse garnaalboot**

Oostendsche sloep See **Oostendse sloep**

Oostendse boot See **Oostendse garnaalboot**

Oostendse dandy sloep See **Oostendse sloep**

Oostendse garnaalboot *Belgium:* Originally fished for shrimp (*garnaal*) and later also for sprats and herring. Worked mainly out of Ostend from ca. 1860. Extinct by 1930, by which time most were motorized (**eenmansgarnaalbootje**). Originally the size of a large **rowboat***. Clinker-planked prior to World War I, then carvel; usually a plumb stem; small, heart-shaped, vertical transom or sharp stern; full in cross section. Deep keel; sheer swept up toward the bow; soft turn of the bilges. Rudder; tiller. Small foredeck; stern seat. Pole mast set a large dipping lugsail; jib to a light bowsprit on the larger boats. Also rowed. Crew of 1-2, the one-man boats called **eenmansgarnaalscheepje**. Reported lengths 6-13m; e.g., length 9m, beam 3m, depth 1.2m; shallow draft. Other recorded names: **crevettier ostendais, garnalenboot, geernaarsboot, Oostends(ch)e boot, Oostendse garnalenboot, open garnaalboot, schover(tje)**. Note also **canot à crevette**.

Oostendse garnalenboot See **Oostendse garnaalboot**

Oostendse sloep *Belgium:* Heavily built cod and herring fishing vessel that worked out of Ostend into the North Sea from the 18th into the 1st quarter of the 20th century. First vessels gaff-rigged with a boomed, loose-footed mainsail; staysail; and jib to a long bowsprit. Modified in the 19th century, when the mast was stepped close to the bow and the mainsail carried an exceptionally long (up to 12.5m) boom (the **langbomer**). The **ketch***-rigged vessel, or **tweemastsloep**, dominated in the 20th century. Initially clinker-planked, later carvel. The earlier boats had full lines, rounded bow and stern, slightly curved stem and straight sternpost, rounded bilges, and long keel. Later 2-masted boats had a sharper bow, and the maximum beam was aft of amidships; the straight keel had some drag. Decked; some had a live well amidships; deep bulwarks; steam winch introduced in the 1880s; narrow rudder; tiller slotted over ornamental rudderhead. Often colorfully painted, and later boats had a triangular white patch at the bow. Distinctive vane at masthead. Crew of 5-6. Reported lengths 17.5-18.9m; **langbomer**: length 18m, beam 5.8m, depth 3.1m. Other recorded names: **dandy*, eenmastsloep, Oostandsche sloep, Oostendse dandy sloep**. Further reading: Gaston and Roland Desnerck, *Vlaamse Visserij en Vissersvaartuigen*, Vol. 2 (Oostende: R. Desnerck, 1976), 158-192.

oostindiëvaarder See **East Indiaman**

Oostwalbotter See **botter**

Oostzee-Ever See **See-Ewer**

Oostzeeklipper See **klipper-1**

Oostzeetjalk See **zeetjalk**

oot, oo'tisis See **crooked canoe**

open barge See **dumb barge**

open boat One that is essentially undecked. See also day boat-2, narrow boat.

open bolpraam See **bolpraam**

open flat See **Mersey flat**

open garnaalboot See **Oostendse garnaalboot**

open mouth ma-yang tzŭ See **chang kou ma yang zi**

open schouw See **schouw**

open somp See **somp**

open-water canoe See **rough-water canoe**

opgeboeide bol See **bol-2**

opium clipper Very fast, small **clipper**★ that carried opium to China from India, where many were built in the 2nd quarter of the 19th century. Some returned to Europe with Chinese tea. Subject to piracy, consequently carried only a small cargo; heavily armed. Cargo usually transferred to Chinese boats for transport up local waterways. Most were **brigs**★, **barks**★, and **schooners**★ (these latter often **brigantine**★-rigged, although called **schooners**). Also rowed. Large crew. One built in 1832 was 43m long, 9.4m wide, with 5.2m draft aft. Note also **clipper-schooner**.

ora *Solomon Islands, western Pacific:* On San Cristobal Island, a generic term for a plank-built **canoe**★. Term may also designate a class of **canoes** found on this and adjacent islands in the south end of the archipelago. Characterized by crescent-shaped ends, roughly the same height, and a bow erection that flares out to form short washstrakes. Used for fishing, transportation, and ceremonial functions. Planks of a semi-hard, rot-resistant wood; 2 keel pieces, laid side-by-side, form a flattened bottom; 2-3 side strakes; planking sewn together; no stem or sternpost, the ends merely bound together; caulked with the pulp of parinarium nuts. Three or more ribs inserted, lashed to residual cleats in the strakes. Generally coated with the putty of a nut and polished down; often decorated with black paint in the fore part, and inlaid with shell; carved birds and animals may adorn the bow erection and elsewhere along the ends. Primarily paddled by 3-6 paddlers. Reported lengths 4.6-10.7m; e.g., length 10m, beam 1.0m, depth 0.48m; shallow draft. Note also **agai-ni-waiau**.

oram-bi, oramby, oranbai, oranbaik, orangbaay, orang baik See **orembai**

Orang Laut boat See **gubang-2**

oranyola See **golandrina**

orca See **howker, urca-2**

Orcadian yol, Orcadian yole See **North Isles yole, South Isles yole**

Ordinari *Austria/Germany, S:* A variety of **Marktschiff**★ used on the Danube River to transport passengers, light freight, and often the mail, on a regular schedule. Dated from ca. 1670. They were often designated by the name of the city from which they originated or to which they were going, e.g., **Ulmer Ordinari**, although in Ulm, they would be called **Wiener Schiffe**. Those traveling from Ulm to Vienna in the 18th century were **rafts**★ with straight sides scored with firemarks; flat bottom and wide stern. Generally broken up at Vienna for firewood and other purposes. Cabin amidships; open forward and aft. Regular crew of 2 plus working passengers. Steered with long bow and stern sweeps. Vertical black and white stripes painted along the sides. Lengths 16-34m; e.g., length 30m, beam 7m, depth 11.2m, 150t burden. Later Ulm boats were called **Ulmer Schachteln**, a name still in use. The **Ordinarischiffe**★ traveling from Regensburg to Vienna in the 19th century were boat-like with proper planking and amenities. Other recorded names: **Schwaben, Schwabenplätte, Schwabenzille, Schwabinnin, schwäbische Zille, Ulmer Plätte** (or **Schiff**), **schlechtweg Zille, Ulmer Schachtel, Wiener Zille**

Ordinarischiff *Switzerland, NE:* 17th-century boat that provided messenger service to Lake of Zurich residents. Name variant: **Kursschiff**. See also **Ordinari**.

ordinary tjalk See **tjalk-3**

ordure boat *China, E:* The Anhui (Anhwei) boat traversed inland waterways in the Wuhu area, carrying overnight human waste for farmers. Flat bottom; curved sides tapered in a straight line toward square, elongated ends. Open; high coaming. Wide-bladed, balanced rudder; tiller. Sailed. Length ca. 10.6m, beam 1.8m, depth 0.43m. Name variant: **Wuhu ordure boat**. Note also **fen chuan, night flower boat, Tsungming chuan**.

Oregon dory *United States, NW and Alaska:* Modified **dory**★ developed for tending a salmon set-net (a gill net anchored perpendicular to the shore). Works out from the beaches along the Oregon coast. Broad, plumb transom; very full, raked bow; flat sheer except toward the bow. Flat bottom; on some newer types that troll for salmon, the bottom curves up at the bow. Now built of marine plywood. Propelled mainly by a powerful outboard motor. Reported lengths 6.1-6.7m; e.g., length 6.7m, beam 1.5m, draft 0.1-0.15m. Other recorded names: **Cape Kiwanda dory, Pacific City dory**. Note also **salmon troller**.

orembaai See **orembai**

orembai *Indonesia, E:* Lightly built boat of the Moluccan Islands. During its long history, has been used as a trader, **fishing boat**★, and state **barge**★, and now often transports children to school and people to places of worship. Carvel-planked; originally sewn, now dowelled edge-to-edge; planks of irregular lengths but with prescribed pattern, each of the 7 strakes becoming progressively longer above the keel; planks fitted directly to the stem and sternpost without an apron. Ribs originally lashed to residual lugs, now treenailed. Curved ends; tall sternpost, often taller and narrower than the stem; in some areas, both capped by a knob. Sides rounded in cross section. May be lightly decked. Some had a quarter rudder. Prior to ca. 1910, they had double outriggers; now none. Some mainly paddled with 40-100 paddlers on ceremonial occasions; at Ambon, may now be a sophisticated craft with 22 oarsmen. In some areas, set a broad, boomed, rectangular sail to a tripod mast; fore-and-aft rigged with jib and staysail; bowsprit. Reported lengths 8.5-12.2m; e.g., length 8.5m, beam 1.7m, depth 0.69m. Other recorded names: **arobail, āròebāil, aroe(m)bai, aroepae, ar(oe)pai, arubai(llo), arumbae, arumbai, oram-bi, oramby, oranbai(k), orangbaay, orang baik, orembaai, orinbaire, orobail, rambaïa, rambâja, rembaja**

orembai belan *Indonesia, E:* Large, plank-built boat of Banda, in the Moluccan group, that had 18 thwarts for paddlers. Tall ends. Note also **bélang**.

Öresundboote, Øresundsbåd See **sildebåd**

orinbaire See **orembai**

orioh See **dorioh**

Orkney flatchie See **North Isles yole**

Orkney yole See **North Isles yole**, **South Isles yole**

Orleans boat *United States, central:* Colloquial term for a Mississippi River **steamboat** bound for New Orleans. See also **flatboat-4**.

örlogsfartyg, orlogskib, Orlogsman, Orlogsschiff, orlogs-skepp, orlogsskibe, orlog vessel See **man-of-war**

ornamental boat See **hua chuan-2a**

orobail See **orembai**

oroe boat See **longboat-5**, **olwe boat**

orou *Papua New Guinea, SE:* Double **canoe*** of Mailu Island, close off the eastern end of the south coast. Used mainly for trading. Dugout hulls; the main hull larger, the somewhat smaller hull serving as an outrigger. Hulls almost round in cross section; center hewn out. Sides raised with vertical planks to form washstrakes, and ends closed off with breakwaters; often carved; washstrakes and breakwaters lashed to dugout. Caulked with scraped inner bark of a special tree. **Canoe** ends bluntly pointed. Hulls set ca. 1.2-1.5m apart; multiple transverse poles connect the 2 hulls, passing through holes in the washstrakes. Poles extend outboard on the main hull. Planking laid atop the poles; portable shelter might be placed on the platform; fireplaces at either end. Rudder lashed to one of the poles near the stern. Mast lashed to bracing along inner side of the main hull; stayed fore-and-aft from outrigger hull. So-called crab-claw sail raised by a halyard rove through a hole in the masthead, and secured about midway along one yard close to the mast. Lower end tacked at foot of mast. Yards as long as 13.5m along both sides of sail; these bend inward at the top. Mat sail made in vertical strips with deep curve at the top. Sailed with outrigger hull to windward. Rowed when becalmed, poled in shallows. Crew of 6. Most 9-10.6m long. Further reading: W. J. V. Saville, *In Unknown New Guinea* (London: J. B. Lippincott Co.; 1926, reprint New York: AMS Press, 1979), 120-142.

oru See **oruwa**

orusteka *Sweden, W:* Small, beamy, open boat that is a member of the **eka*** family. Main center of construction on Orust Island on the central coast, but widely built elsewhere along the west coast. General-purpose boat, but also popular as a **ship's boat***, often towed

behind. Sometimes described as having the shape of half an egg. Clinker-planked; wide, rounded bottom (**rundbottnad eka**) with rocker; plank keel, many with a short keel piece at the stern. Bow and stern transoms; the bow transom small, raked, and well above the water; stern transom wide and raked and often notched for a sculling oar. Single- or 3-piece frames. Strong sheer toward the bow. Stern seat, 3-4 thwarts. Mainly rowed with 2-3 pairs of double tholepins. Some step a light mast through a thwart, setting a spritsail. Reported lengths 4.3-4.6m; e.g., length 4.6m, beam ca. 1.9m, depth ca. 0.7m. Other recorded names: **bohuseka, bohuslänska, norska eka**. Note also **iseka-1, pråmm-1**.

orustsnipa See **snipa**

oruva *Maldive Islands:* Word for **boat*** on some of the islands, while the term **dhoni*** is preferred on others. May also designate a **dugout canoe***. Spelling variant: **oruvai**. Further reference: **oruwa**

oruvai See **oruva**

oruwa *Sri Lanka:* **1.** Sinhala word for **boat*** or **canoe***. Other recorded names: **arua, catamaran*, Galle oru, oruva***; pl. **oru**. In Tamil: **kūlla, kūllan**.

2. Term frequently describes a very narrow single-**outrigger canoe*** of western and southern Sri Lanka that engages in several types of fishing, going as far as 40km from shore. Dugout base to which a vertical or tumble home washstrake, ca. 38cm deep, is sewn to each side; replaced by fiberglass hulls. Washstrake extends beyond the dugout and continues the raking line of the ends for ca. 61cm; closed at the ends; bow slightly fuller than the stern; gunwales beaded with shells. Since the opening at the top is only 27-38cm wide, the paddlers may sit on a bamboo platform outboard with just one leg inside the boat. Strengthened by stout battens toward the ends and by rods that serve as thwarts and as tacks for the sail. Two down-curving, flexible booms connect directly with the cigar-shaped float, which is about half the length of the boat; one boom set toward the bow, the other roughly amidships

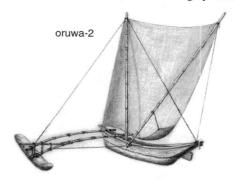

oruwa-2

and on the outer end, a raised piece serves as a foothold for 1-2 men who may ride the boom as ballast. Also has 2-3 leeboards. Waterproofed with a black gum; protective coating of coconut oil applied weekly. Steered by foot with a heavy oar that may pass through a hole in the gunwale. Sets a square sail to a single mast stepped amidships or a rectangular sail supported at the top corners by 2 light masts; one forward of the sail, the other aft; one mast fitted into a thick ring of coir while the other steps into a wooden shoe. The outrigger remains on the same side and the V-mast is twisted around, the backstay shifted, and the sail moved to the other side of the mast when sailing in the opposite direction. Sails usually tanned. Rowed when wind fails. Crew of 4-8. Reported lengths 4.6-5.9m. Note also **äng-oruwa**, **madel-oruwa**, **palu-oruwa**, **varakan-oruwa**.

Oselvar, Oselvarbåt, Oselv boat See **Oselver**

Oselver *Norway, SW:* General term for the triple-plank, finely finished boats built in Os Township, south of Bergen. Design essentially unchanged for many centuries. Now largely pleasure boats, but they also engage in fishing, transporting farm produce, and travel, and the larger size may serve as **church boats★** (**kirkebåt★**). Rowed with 4 oars (**færing★**), 6 oars (**seksæring★**), or 8 oars (**church boat**). Sharp ends with the curved stem and sternpost cutting away to a relatively short keel. Three lapped strakes, the sheer strake as wide as 30cm amidships. Frames inserted after shell formed; garboard strake hewn, the ends created from twisted roots. Open; thwarts slot over the frames. May also be sailed, setting a sprit-, gaff, or leg-of-mutton sail. When sailed, ships a rudder with a right-angle yoke to the tiller. Reported lengths 4.9-6.2m. Other recorded names: **Oselvar(båt)**, **Oselv boat**, **Oselverbåt**, **Oselvere**, **Oselving**

Oselverbåt, Oselvere, Oselving See **Oselver**

o-síy See **Cree canoe**

Ostebulle *Germany, NW:* Low, open cargo boat of the Oste, a tributary of the Elbe Estuary. Sharp bow; raked, flat stern. Set a tall square sail to a mast 6-7m high. Reported lengths 9-10m, beam 3m. Note also **Bulle**.

Ostfriesische Jacht See **Fries Jacht**

Ostfriesische Mutte See **Mutte**

ostindiefarer, Ostindienfahrer See **East Indiaman**

ostregher da mar See **topo**

ostreskuta See **jekt**

Ostsee-Ever See **See-Ewer**

Ostsee-Ewer See **Ewer, See-Ewer**

Ostseekutter See **kutter-2**

Ostseetjalk See **zeetjalk**

ōṭam See **odam-2**

oti *Indonesia, E:* Term for an **outrigger canoe★** in the Moluccan islands of Ternate, Tidore, and at Roni and Akeselaka on northeastern Halmahera. Plank-extended dugout hull; those that lack a washstrake may be called an **oti** (or **otti**) **ma-héra**. Usually double outriggers; 2 booms attach to the long, slender floats with U-shaped connectives.

ōṭi See **odam-1a**

oti ma-héra See **oti**

o tsang See **ao zeng**

Ottawa River canoe See **canot du maître**

ottemandsfar, ottemansfar See **áttamannafar**

otter *Belgium:* Wooden inland boat of the Schelde River and its tributaries that carried freight to the Netherlands, France, and on the Rhine and Ruhr Rivers from the early 18th to the early 20th century. Bluff bow; rounded stern lower and narrower than the bow; heavy stem terminated at a point; maximum beam well for-

ward. Flat bottom; shallow or no keel, the stem and sternpost continuing under the bottom for a short distance; flat sheer except toward the ends; heavy wale; round leeboards. Some built of iron or steel. Rudder wide-bladed at and below the waterline; on the largest, the tiller came in through a triangular opening in the stern; on others, it could swing freely over each side (**draai-over-boord otter**). Decked; most had a deckhouse aft; rounded hatches; one with a deck level with the gunwale at the stern was called a **paviljoenotter**. Usually high rudderhead; tiller; occasionally the hawser holes painted green. Small types stepped a single mast to which a loose-footed, boomed gaff sail and 1-2 headsails were fitted. When employed, stepped a mizzenmast just behind the hatch setting a boomed gaff sail, or a jiggermast was placed against the rudderhead, using a small gaff or spritsail sheeted to an outrigger. Crew of ca. 3. Reported lengths 16-35m; e.g., length with rudder 22.3m, without rudder 21m, beam 5.43m. Other recorded names: **loutre**, **Otterschiff**, **otterschip**, **Vlaamse otter**. Note also **beerotter**, **gaffelschuit**.

Otterschiff, otterschip See **otter**

otter trawler See **trawler**

otti ma-héra See **oti**

otto See **shell-2**

ottring See **åttring**

ottringer See **firing**

ottringsbaad See **åttring**

ou, oua See **wa-2**

ouaro *Gabon:* **1.** Generic term for a **canoe★** in the dialects of some of the coastal peoples. Spelling variants: **onwaro**, **ooaro**, **oworo**, **uaro**

2. Long, narrow **dugout canoe★** used for coastal fishing. Stern sweeps up from the bottom, ending in a squared, overhanging platform. Forward, a keel-like projection terminates in a sharp cutwater above which is a similar square platform or a slightly pointed end. Two or 3 thwarts. When sailed, mast stepped through forward thwart, setting a very large sail. Paddled with sharp-bladed paddle. Length to ca. 5m, mostly 3-4m.

oucounni See **gommier**

oucre See **howker**

oueris See **wary**

ouimiack See **umiak-1**

oulque See **hulk-1**

oumiak See **umiak-1**

ou-pan See **wu ban**

ouque, ourque See **howker**

oury See **houri-4**

Outer Isle sgoth See **sgoth**

outrigged wherry See **wherry-2**

outrigger A boat equipped with extended brackets on which oarlocks are fastened, permitting extra oar leverage on a very narrow boat. Designed on the River Tyne in northeastern England in the late 1820s, but became popular elsewhere. Mainly a racing craft; raced in classes for 2, 4, 6, and 8 oars. Early boats clinker-built, some with folding outriggers. May be rowed with one person to each very long oar, alternating sides; if rowed by a person using 2 shorter oars, or sculls, it is called an **outrigger scull**. A boat with short outrigger brackets might be called a **half outrigger**. Other recorded names: **Claspar-built boat, rigger★**; those serving as **wager boats** were called **wager outriggers**. Note also **inrigger, shell**.

outrigger canoe Generally a narrow dugout or dugout-based craft that requires an outrigger on one or both sides to provide stability. Areas of concentration: East Africa, South and Southeast Asia, and Oceania. Each outrigger unit is composed of 2 or more booms that extend at right angles from the hull and attach to a float lying generally parallel to the hull. Such **canoes★** may be paddled or sailed. In a few cases, outriggers have been attached to large vessels, such as the Sri Lankan **yathra dhoni★** and the Indonesian **korakora★**. Selected name variants: **Auslegerkanu, balance-log canoe, canoa con lanciafuori, Kanoe mit Ausleger, pirogue à balancier, vlerkprauw, double outrigger canoe, Doppelauslegerboot, Doppelauslegerkanu, pirogue à double balancier, twin-outrigged canoe**. Note also **perahu katir-1**.

outrigger scull See **outrigger**

outside barge See **Fal barge, Plymouth barge, West Country sailing barge**

outside boat *United States, E:* A **freighter★** on the Delaware and Hudson Canal, between Kingston on the Hudson River and eastern Pennsylvania, that was not the direct responsibility of the Delaware and Hudson Canal Company. These boats belonged to other companies using the canal.

outside flat See **Mersey flat**

outside porter See **doghole schooner**

outside schooner See **scow-schooner-3**

overhaalpont, overhaalpontje See **pont**

Overijsselsche pot See **pot-2**

Overijselsche praam, Overijsselsche praam See **Overijsselse praam**

Overijsselse praam *Netherlands, E:* Robust peat-carrier from Overijssel Province. Used especially during the 19th century, but worked at least into the 1930s. Also carried hay and stone. Similar rounded ends with deep stem and sternpost; flat bottom, protective planking extended under the ends and along the bottom for a few meters; no keel. Heavy wale paralleled the flat sheer midway along the sides, curving up sharply at the ends to merge with the stemhead. Sides flared out below the wale, vertical above, had tumble home at ends. Decked; large central hatch; some had a cuddy, others a full cabin aft. Wide fin at lower part of the rudder, curved tiller, leeboards. Loose-footed gaff mainsail with bent gaff, foresail, and jib; mast could be struck. Reported lengths 19-21m; e.g., length 21m, beam 4.5m, depth 1.9m; to 100t. Name variants: **Overijs(s)elsche praam**. Note also **praam**.

Overijsselse tjalk See **pot-2**

overland barge See **Thames sailing barge**

overlander, overlandre See **Oberländer-1**

Overzeesche turfpont See **pot-2**

owo, owōh See **kalabba**

owon See **pumuk o'wan**

oworo See **ouaro**

oxir, oxirii See **huissier**

oyafune *Japan:* Cargo vessel of the 19th century. Long, raked stem; raked stern; sides extended beyond stern with large-bladed rudder set in between; long tiller. Sheer swept up to high stern. Decked. Stout mainmast stepped abaft amidships and stayed to the stem; mizzenmast at stern; foremasts, both raking forward, stepped in the eyes and slightly aft. Each set a square sail with yards almost to masthead. About 225t.

oyster barge *United States, E:* Floating oyster market moored between similar **barges★** along various sections of the New York City waterfront and other ports in the New York area. Popular in the late 19th and early 20th centuries. House, generally 2 stories high, built over the hull; deep hold below for oysters (cap. ca. 700 bushels). Strongly built, flat bottom; square ends. Average length 23m, beam 7.3m, hold depth 1.8m. Other recorded names: **ark★, float★, houseboat★, lay boat★, market float, oyster boat★, oyster float, oyster scow★, scow★**

oyster bateau See **bateau-7p, skipjack-1**

oyster boat *United States:* General term for any craft associated with the oyster industry: in cultivation of the beds, harvesting, or transportation to market. See also **bay boat-3, deadrise boat-2a, oyster barge, Pensacola oyster boat, ponton**.

oyster buckeye See **bugeye**

oyster canoe See **Chesapeake Bay log canoe, Connecticut canoe**

oyster dredge boat See **dredge boat-2**

oyster dredger See **Falmouth oyster dredger, Mumbles oyster skiff, sinago, skipjack, Whitstable oyster smack**

oyster dredging sloop See **oyster sloop-1**

oyster flat See **scow-11c**

oyster float See **float-5, oyster barge**

oyster freighter See **freighter-4**

oyster lugger See **New Orleans lugger**

oysterman's bateau See **Staten Island skiff**

Oystermouth lug boat See **Mumbles oyster skiff**

oyster navy *United States, E:* To enforce an 1865 law permitting only vessels licensed in Maryland to dredge for oysters, a **fleet★** of armed **patrol boats★**, mostly fast **schooners★**, cruised its Chesapeake Bay waters searching for violators, who were usually armed. Also tried to prevent the larger **dredge boats★** from encroaching on the shallower water reserved for the **tongers★**. Name variant: **oyster police**. Note also **watch boat**.

oyster pirate See **skipjack-1**

oyster police See **oyster navy**

oyster pungy See **pungy**

oyster punt See **Falmouth oyster punt, punt-5**

oyster runner *United States, S:* Vessel that takes iced oysters from buyers on the Gulf Coast oyster grounds to markets or packing plants. In the 1920s, they were **schooners★** or **luggers★** converted from sailing to motorized craft. Schooner lengths 12-24m, **lugger** 9-18m. Note also **New Orleans lugger, run boat★**.

oyster schooner See **Chesapeake Bay schooner, Delaware Bay oyster schooner, freighter-4**

oyster scow *United States:* **1.** A type of craft used in the oyster industry of Chesapeake Bay.

2. Pacific coast oyster **tonger*** of the late 19th century, especially in San Francisco Bay. A roughly built, square-ended, flat-bottomed craft. Sides tapered slightly toward the ends. Cambered deck ended in a low railing. Large iron ring at each end, through which anchoring poles were driven. The **tongers** also used a moored, open **scow*** to store supplies and as a working area for culling the oysters. Reported lengths 5-7m, widths 2.1-2.4m; shallow hull.
See also **butthead-2**, **oyster barge**, **scow-11c**.

oyster skiff See **skiff-4**, **Staten Island skiff**

oyster sloop *United States, E:* **1.** Dredged for oysters until the 1960s, especially in eastern Long Island Sound and Great South Bay of Long Island; some early boats worked in lower New York Bay. The larger served as **buy boats*** or **freighters***. Sharp bow; generally a wide, square, raked stern; some rounded; rounded bottom, low freeboard. Centerboard; inboard rudder. Decked; trunk cabin forward or aft. Gaff-, cat-, or **sloop***-rigged with mast steps to accommodate particular rigging. When gaff-rigged, the mainsail was large, boomed, and had a long, high-peaked gaff; jib to bowsprit; gaff topsail and jib topsail used when running to market or in light air. Later boats used power going to and from the oyster beds. Crew of 2-3. Reported lengths 9-15m; e.g., length 11.5m, beam 3.9m; shallow draft. Other recorded names: **oyster dredging sloop**, **south sider** (**Great south Bay sloop**). Note also **bay boat-3**, **sandbagger**.
2. Dredger* that worked the beds off the New Jersey side of Delaware Bay until the mid-1900s. Also used in coastal trade. Clipper bow, square stern, strong sheer. Open railing from bow to stern until 1900; small boat hung from aft davits; inboard rudder. Decked, cabin forward. Boomed leg-of-mutton or gaff sail, jib to bowsprit; some gaff-rigged boats used a topsail. Other recorded names: **Delaware Bay masthead sloop**, **Delaware sloop**, **New Jersey oyster sloop**
3. Shallow, boxy craft used in the oyster industry from South Carolina to northern Florida into the mid-1900s. Smaller boats had a flat bottom, the larger a "V" bottom, and a few were round-bottomed. Wide, raked transom stern; plumb stem; straight sides. Decked; low trunk cabin aft. Prior to 1905, the oysters were stowed in the 2 holds, but thereafter, were piled high on the deck with boards added along the sides to contain them. Oysters generally gathered by an accompanying small **bateau***, but the **sloop** itself was sometimes called a **bateau**. Gaff sail with long gaff and boom; jib to short bowsprit. Reported lengths 9-15m; dimensions of flat-bottomed type: length 10.7m, beam 4.1m, depth 0.7m.
Further reference: **plunger-2**

oyster smack See **Essex smack**, **New York oyster smack**, **watch boat**, **Whitstable oyster smack**

oyster steamer *United States, E:* Company-owned boat that dredged for oysters and clams on Great South Bay on Long Island in New York State in the early 1900s. A few were steam-powered, but mainly gasoline- or naphtha-powered. Plumb or raked stem, rounded counter stern. Pilot house and cabin aft; dredge post on forward deck. Beamy, draft 0.9-1.5m.

oyster-tonging boat See **tonger-1**

oyster watch boat See **watch boat**

pä See **pae**

paalever See **Pfahl-Ewer**

paalmastschoener See **schooner-1**

paardenschip See **horse carrier**

paaruwa See **padda boat**

päästepaat See **paat**

paat *Estonia:* Term for **boat★**. Frequently used in combined form, such as **lootspaat** (**pilot boat★**), **päästepaat** (**lifeboat★**), and **veepaat** (**water boat★**).

pacaid See **mail boat-1**

pacalik See **kayak-4**

pacchebotto, pacchetto See **packet boat-1**

pa-chiang chhuan, pa-chiang ch'uan See **ba jiang chuan**

Pacific City dory See **Oregon dory**

Pacific gillnetter See **gillnetter-2**

Pacific Whitehall See **Whitehall boat**

pack canoe See **woods canoe**

packer 1. A boat that buys fish from fishermen out on the fishing grounds, ices the catch, and delivers it to the fish-processing plant. Other recorded names: **bateau collecteur, bateau de transport, chasseur★**. Note also **carrying boat**.
2. *Canada, W/United States, Alaska:* A boat from a packing company that buys salmon from fishermen, ices the catch, and delivers it to the cannery. Motorized. Other recorded names: **cannery tender, pick-up boat, tender★**

packet *England, west-central:* Term given to the steam and motor vessels that operated on the Weaver Navigation. Carried salt or chemicals downstream and coal for the salt works upstream from the latter half of the 19th century until the 1980s. Towed up to 3 **barges★**. Wood or iron; round stern. Long single hatch with boards and cloth to protect the salt. Crew of 3 quartered forward; largest type had an extra hand. Those owned by the Salt Union were tarred black and called **black flats** or **salties**. The short mast used for the masthead light when under tow; also had a cargo derrick. Length 27m, beam 6.4m; cap. 80-250t. Name variant: **Weaver packet**. Note also **Weaver flat**. Further references: **horse packet, little packet, packet boat-1**

packet boat 1. Vessel that operated on a stated schedule between specified ports carrying mail, passengers, and express freight. As early as the 16th century, designated by a government to carry the "packet" of official letters and dispatches. Frequently operated under the direction of the postal service. Many lightly armed to ward off **privateers★**. Usually **cutter★-, brig★-,** or **schooner★**-rigged, but later vessels were **steam packets**. Many smaller **brig**-rigged **packets** were overrigged, earning the name **coffin brigs**. Selected name variants: **barco de correo, correo (maritimo), courrier, liner★, mail boat★, mail packet, pacchebotto, pacchetto, packet★, packet ship, pacquetbot, paketbåd, Paketboot, paketbot, pakket(boot), paquebot(e), paquebouc, paquete★, pochtovoe sudno, postale, post-bark, post boat★, postmaster's frigate, Post**

Office packet. Note also **coastal packet, passage boat, smack-1**.
2. Sometimes a term of endearment for a particular ship.
3. *United States:* **Canal boat★** of most long-distance canals in operation in the 1st half of the 19th century, carrying as many as 100 passengers and premium freight; traveled at ca. 2.5km per hour (1.55 knots). Bow sharp or blunt; stern rounded; bottom flat.

packet boat-3

Constructed of either wood or iron. Cabin covered most of the length and extended full beam; some richly appointed, although sleeping accommodations were in converted salons. Steered by tiller and rudder. Generally towed, some by 3 horses, others by 2 teams, with the spare team carried on board forward. A small cuddy forward housed the crew of ca. 5-10, including a cook and occasionally a chambermaid. Reported lengths 18-30m, widths 3.6-4.8m. Name variant: **floating palace★**. Note also **line boat**.
4. *United States, central:* Regularly scheduled **keelboat★**-type craft that carried passengers and light freight on the Ohio and Mississippi Rivers in pre-**steamboat** days. Later, **paddle boats★** served as **packet boats**. Stoutly built and heavily armed; ends sharp, bottom flat with keel. Long, sweep-type rudder had a flat, squared blade. Passenger cabin generally in after half. Poled, rowed, towed from shore by the crew, and sailed. Rigged as a **sloop★**, schooner, brig, or set a tall square sail. Reported lengths 23-31m; e.g., length 24.8m, beam 5m, depth 1.5m. Other recorded names: **express boat, galley★, galley keelboat, Ohio packet boat**
Further reference: **flyboat-3a**

packet cat See **catboat-2a**

packet cutter See **smack-5**

packet ship See **packet boat-1**

packet sloop See **Hudson River sloop**

pacquetbot See **packet boat-1**

pacquetbot à roues See **paddle boat-3**

pada See **padagu-1**

pada boat See **padda boat**

padagu 1. A **boat★** or **ship★** in some of the Dravidian languages of southern India and northeastern Sri Lanka. Spelling variants: **aḍagu, haḍaga, haḍagu, paḍa, paḍahu, paḍangu, paḍava, padavu★, paṭaku, paṭavu**. Note also **akada hody, padhagi**.
2. *India, W:* In some areas, as in the South Kanara District of Karnataka State, designates a specific type of boat that operates the *rampani*, a very large shore seine. Plank-built boat; single outrigger float joined by 2 booms. Reported lengths 15.2-16.8m.
3. *Sri Lanka:* Coasting vessel from the Tamil area, working until the 1930s. Carvel planking of Malabar

teak with a sharp, raked stem and stern; stem recurved on the Hindu-owned vessels, ending in a coiled, ornamental head; lacking on the Moslem vessels. Short deck at each end, terminated in a high breakwater; open waist covered by a sliding roof of palm leaves secured by closely spaced battens. Usually painted or tarred black, ornamented with 2 white lines; Hindu vessels had carved oculi on bows. Foremast much the taller of the two; square masthead with 2 sheaves. Long, high-steeved bowsprit ran out on starboard side; 5 headsails used regularly. Reported lengths 20-30m; e.g., length overall 20.4m, on keel 11.7m, beam 6.6m, depth 3.4m. Other recorded names: **dhoni***, **Jaffna d(h)oni**, **thoni**

Further reference: **masula**

paḍahu, paḍangu See **padagu-1**

padao, padau See **padow**

pa-dau-t'hl See **pa-dá-waħl**

padav See **padow**

padava See **masula, muggu padava, padagu-1**

padavu *Sri Lanka, NW:* A long, planked boat used in beach seine operations along the coast. Planks ca. 5cm thick and frames ca. 13cm square. Vertical white stripes painted along each side. Steps a single aft-raking mast. Reported lengths 9.1-13.7m, beam ca. 2.44m. Other recorded names: in the south: **gandra toni, kullatoni**. See also **akada hody, masula, padagu-1**.

pa-dá-waħl *United States, NW:* Oceangoing **canoe*** used for whaling by the Makah of coastal Washington. Dugout of Nootka style (see **West Coast canoe**). Flat bottom; separate end pieces, the stern sharp, vertical and tall, the concave bow projecting forward and terminating in a stylized animal head. Sides flared sharply just below the gunwale. Thwarts divided the hull into 5 compartments. Might set a cotton spritsail to a light mast; originally used a woven square sail. Crew of 8. Reported lengths 9-12m. Other recorded names: **Makah whaling canoe, pa-dau-t'hl, pa-dow-t'hl**

padda boat *Sri Lanka:* **Scow***-like craft that conveys passengers (not rice) on the coastal canals between Colombo and Puttalam to the north. Also used for throwing large nets in shore fishing. Flat bottom; square, raking ends; plumb sides, vertical ribs and right-angled knees. Arched mat roof covers most of

padda boat

the boat. Some writers report the boat to have sewn planking; others describe it as a double **dugout canoe***. Towed, rowed (with heavy oars with looms that merge into the square-ended blade), poled, or sailed. Steered, and probably sculled, with a long sweep. In favorable winds, sets a square sail or rectangular spritsail. Reported lengths 5.5-15.2m; e.g., length 8.7m, beam 1.9m, depth 0.8m. Other recorded names: **paaruwa, pada boat, paddy boat***, **paruwa*** (pl. **paru**), **patai, rice boat** (erroneously)

Paddelboot See **paddle boat-2**

paddewakan, paddewakkang See **padewakang**

paddle boat **1.** Small boat driven by paddle-fitted wheels. Sometimes found as a recreational craft in parks, propelled by foot power. Other recorded names: **patí de pedals, patín de pedales**

2. A small, light, usually narrow boat maneuvered by paddles, especially a **kayak*** or **canoe***. Paddled with single- or double-bladed paddles, standing, kneeling, or sitting. Spelling variant: **Paddelboot**

3. A steam vessel propelled by paddle wheels. One with wheels along the side is a **side wheeler**; when the wheel is at the stern, it is a **stern wheeler** (sometimes disparagingly a **wheel barrow**). Some designed for ocean crossings, but most worked in sheltered waters. Other recorded names: **barco de ruedas, bateau à aubes** (or **à roues**), **brod na točkove, buque de ruedas, ladja na kolesa, pacquetbot à roues, paddler, paddle ship** (steamer or wheeler), **Raddampfer, splasher**. Note also **flat-4, mountain boat-2, paddle-box boat, raft boat-2, swift boat**.

4. *China, SE:* On the Zhu Jiang (Pearl River) in the early 20th century, passengers might choose a **paddle boat**. The stern wheel was turned by coolies on a treadmill with irregularly spaced pedals to prevent their keeping in step. Passengers might earn their passage by joining the coolies. Depending on tide and weather, the boats made 4.8-8km per hour (3-5 knots). Name variant: **stern-wheel boat**

5. *United States:* Small, double-ended, open boat suitable for waterfowling on inland streams and protected waters. Flat bottom; single-plank sides or lapstraked if several planks; flat sheer. May have end decking of canvas. Length overall 4.57m, beam 1.0m, depth 0.23m.

6. *United States, E:* The eastern **paddle boat**, used on rivers, lakes, and bays from Maine to Georgia, had a single-cylinder beam engine with both paddle wheels on one shaft. (The western boats used 2 single-cylinder engines that worked independent wheels.) Most eastern boats had only 1 stack. Reported lengths 54-67m.

7. *United States, NE:* Small, open, **canoe**-like boat designed for fishing on small ponds in the Franklin County area of northwestern Maine. Lapstrake planking; sharp, plumb ends with rounded forefoot; flat floors with soft turn of the bilges; closely spaced ribs. Short end decks. Propelled by a single paddle.

Further references: **pirogue-6, sandall, team boat**

paddle-box boat A **ship's boat*** designed in England in the early 19th century to be carried, upside down, on top of the paddle box that covered the paddle wheels of a **paddle steamer** (see **paddle boat-3**). Carvel-planked. Other recorded names: **barco copriruota** (or **tamburo), bote de rueda a popa, bote salvavidas de los tambores, canot tambour, Radkastenboot**

paddle punt See **Deal punt**

paddler, paddle ship See **paddle boat-3**

paddle steamer See **paddle boat-3, push boat**

paddle wheeler See **paddle boat-3**

paddy boat **1.** May refer in general to a Chinese rice-carrying craft.

2. Term applied to the **steamers** of Henderson's line running from Scotland to Myanmar (Burma).

3. *Myanmar (Burma):* Transported rice for export down the Ahrewady (Irrawaddy) River to Yangon (Rangoon) in long, narrow, expanded dugouts. Bow very low; stern rose above the water, terminating in a truncated end. Arched mat hut covered central part of the hull. Quarter rudder. Set a wide square sail with vertical cloths. Bipod mast, stepped forward of the hut, could be struck. Spelling variant: **pady boat**. Note also **laung-zat**.

4. *United States, NE:* The **Paddy boat** of the Irish of the Boston area was a **fishing boat★** of the 2nd half of the 19th century. Nearly vertical stem, raked transom stern, high freeboard, slight tumble home to topsides, hard bilges, considerable drag to the keel. Gaff sail set to an aft-raking mast that was stepped well forward. Sail loose-footed and carried a long boom; 1-2 headsails. Name variant: **cunner boat**. Note also **Boston hooker**.
Further references: **luff barge**, **padda boat**

paddy gig See **thón-kin**

padewahkan, padewaka, padewakan See **padewakang**

padewakang *Indonesia, central:* Large 18th- and 19th-century trading vessel developed by Bugis and Makassarese shipbuilders on southwestern and western Sulawesi (Celebes); some built in Java, and known on the Mandar coast as **padewakang abi jawa**. Traveled widely, going beyond Malacca, to northern Australia, and to Manila. Sharp ends; plank-built of teak or giam, with the strakes doweled; keel curved up smoothly into the stem and sternpost, creating a superstructure that terminated in a bulkhead before the stem and extended aft to quarter galleries and a transom. On early boats, this addition produced a sloping deck; the strakes were carved, and a railing ran along the sides. On later vessels, sides plainer and the deck flush before the mast; these were called **padewakang abi tarus**. On some, mainly those built at Makassar (now Ujung Pandang), there was a split-level deck just forward of the opening from which quarter rudders were worked, earning the name **padewakang abi jumpandan**, and there was no decking around the masts. Rudders secured by rattan to a crossbeam that extended 61-91cm out each side. 18th-century anchors were of a hard wood, with a large stone fastened to the stocks. Initially had 1-3 tripod masts, each carrying elongated, rectangular sails, lug-fashion. Various combinations of sails and sizes were tried, ending in a **ketch★** rig toward the end of the 19th century; these were smaller and became the **palari** (see **pinisi**). Also rowed, the early boats having 2 banks of oarsmen. Crew of 8-13. Reported lengths 8-30m, the smaller sizes becoming more prevalent in later years; e.g., length 15m, beam 4m, depth 2.4m. Other recorded names: **Bugis paduakan, paddewakan, paddewakkang, padewahkan, padewaka(n), padewakkang, padoe(w)akang, padouacan, padou(c)ane, padoucann, padouhan(n), paduacan, padu(w)akan, pedebakah** (island of Kangean), **pediwak, perampok-laut, praauw padoeakan; padewakang abi djawa (abi djoempandan, abi taroes)**

padewakang abi djawa, padewakang abi djoempandan, padewakang abi jawa, padewakang abi jumpandan, padewakang abi taroes, padewakang abi tarus, padewakkang See **padewakang**

padhagi *India, NW:* Usually associated with European vessels, especially of the Portuguese, but sometimes those of the Maratha. Might refer to an auxiliary naval vessel, or to a **merchantman★** (the **savakari-padagu**). Spelling variants: **padhagu**; pl. **padhagya**. Note also **padagu**.

padhagu, padhagya See **padhagi**

padi *Bangladesh, S:* Carries red clay for pottery in the Barisal area. Heavy block ends, both tall and truncated on top. Very low freeboard amidships. Covered area over most of the hull. Quarter rudder. Mast stepped in forward third. Crew of 2. Length ca. 13m.

padjala See **pajala**

pado See **perahu-1**

padoeakang, padoewakang See **padewakang**

padoewang See **paduwang**

padouacan, padouane, padoucane, padoucann, padouhan, padouhann See **padewakang**

padow *India:* **1. Coaster★** found mostly along the northwest coast, but sometimes seen in Arabian Peninsula ports and reported from Malaysia; small sizes were important cargo carriers in Bombay (Mumbai) harbor. **Coasters** distinguished by a parrot's head stem ornament, and by an anchor cable sheave on each side of the stemhead; the Bombay vessels lack the ornament, but often have a rope fender on the stemhead. Fine lines forward, beamy aft; hull strengthened with athwartships beams. Long, straight, raking stem; square or rounded stern, raked; stern low on Bombay vessels, high and sometimes decorated on **coasters**. Very short, hogged keel; rising floors, soft turn of the bilges. Short decking at ends, and decked amidships for cooking and sleeping area, which is tented over. Low waist sweeps up toward the bow; on **coasters**, sides protected by full-length weather screen of bamboo and split palm, sometimes plastered with mud. Outboard rudder; tiller. Hulls oiled or painted black. May carry a **muchwa★**. Sets quadrilateral lateen-type sails with a short luff to 1-2 forward-raking masts; Bombay vessels mostly single-masted. Sometimes a jib runs out to a long, raking bowsprit. Rowed in calms. Later vessels motorized. Crew of 5-11. Reported lengths 15.2-24.8m; e.g., length overall 20.8m, between perpendiculars 11.3m; beam 7.5m, depth 2.2m. Other recorded names: **cotton boat** (or **prow** at Bombay), **padao, padau, padav, parao★, pelo, pilau★, pilu(r), prao, pros, prow**. A small Bombay **padow** is called a **ballao**.

2. In southern India, the **parao** appears to have been of dugout construction. Rowed with bamboo oars and sailed using a bamboo mast. Length ca. 10m.

pa-dow-t'hl See **pa-dá-waHl**

paduacan, paduakan See **padewakang**

paduang See **paduwang**

paduwakan See **padewakang**

paduwang *Indonesia, central:* Seaworthy trader and **fishing boat★** of Madura, the northeast coast of Java, and the Sapudi Archipelago, east of Madura. Sides planked up from a keel balk that extends 61-91cm beyond the bow and stern, creating a bifid bow; ribs strengthen the planking. Sharp ends rake up in a straight line; no stem or sternpost, the planking closed off at each end by a board. Decked; bamboo shelter amidships. Double outriggers; 2 booms extend to the floats, which may consist of 2 lengths of bamboo, one thicker than the other and lashed together. Forward boom straight and slants down to the float; after boom curves downward; narrow platform may be set close to the hull over the booms. Quarter rudder. Traders had a cargo hold. Sets 2 sails. The small foremast, stepped in the eyes, sets a triangular sail with the apex tacked to a spar out from the bow or an oblong sail. The larger, triangular mainsail is supported by a long spar; apex tacked forward of the shelter, spar stepped aft of it. Both sails boomed at the foot. On some, a long bowsprit projects through a hole in the bow piece and braces against the foremast. Mainsail stayed from the outer part of each boom. Length ca. 10.4m, narrow. Other recorded names: **padoewang, paduang, pedoe(w)ang, peduang, praauw pedoewang, prahu paduwang, prahu peduang**

pady boat See **paddy boat**

pae *Korea:* Generic term for **ship** or **boat**. Spelling variants: **pä, pai, pei**

pæreskude See **jagt-2**

pagaia See **pangaio**

pahala See **kotia**

pahee See **pahi-3, pahi-4**

pahi 1. *Cook Islands, central Pacific:* Large, oceangoing double **canoe** used mainly by chiefs and their retainers; more recently, a generic term for **ship** or a sprit-rigged, single-outrigger fishing **canoe**. Hulls set side by side, secured by 3 booms that extended outboard and were braced by stringers; port hull slightly smaller. Dugout hulls generally of several pieces sewn together; washstrakes added; bottom rounded with rocker at ends; very tall, decorative stern pieces. Platform laid between the hulls; house set at stern. Sailed and paddled, but last vessels were apparently rowed. Two sails, probably triangular with the apex down. Reported lengths of the larger hull 18.2-24.4m. Spelling variants: **pai** or **pa'i**
2. *New Zealand:* An old Maori term for a large, seagoing **canoe**. Spelling variant: **pahii**. Note also **waka pahii**.
3. *Society Islands, southeastern Pacific:* Spelling variants: **pahee, pahie, prahic, prahik**. **a.** General term for a plank-built **boat** or a **ship**. One that sails is a **pahi ie**; a **steamboat** is a **pahi auahi**. **b.** Early travelers described the **pahi** as an oceangoing double **canoe**. Plank-built of short lengths sewn together; washstrakes added; strengthened with frames; "V" cross section; shallow keel. Hulls equal or unequal, secured by discontinuous platforms and braces at each end or by a large, open platform that covered most of the hulls; on the former, 2 platforms extended outboard on each side. On some, both ends were tall, terminating in stylized tiki figureheads; on others, only the stern was tall. One or 2 huts on the platform. Steered with a sweep. Generally stepped 2 vertical masts between the hulls; some placed both masts forward of amidships; on others, the masts were on the 2 platforms that extended outboard on each side, one about a third of the way in from the bow, the other near the stern. Tall, narrow sails extended well above the masts; luff above

the mast was crescent-shaped; boomed at foot and vertically along the leech. Feathers ornamented the mastheads and chains of feathers or leaves served as wind vanes from the top of the vertical booms. Reported lengths 9-23m. **c.** One variety of older **pahi** was similar in hull design to the above vessel, but was an outrigger craft. Plank-built with upturned, ornamented ends. The single long float, paralleling the forward two-thirds of the hull, was secured directly to 2 widely spaced booms. An open platform rested on the inner part of the booms and extended for an equal distance out the opposite side; a large, thatched house sat on the platform. Probably set a single sail. **d.** A modern adaptation of the **pahi** is found in the western group, the Leeward Islands. Hull built up from a 2-piece dugout base; multipiece strake sewn onto each side. Bow sharp with vertical cutwater; stern rounds up from the bottom to a pointed and elongated end; bottom rounded in cross section, sides relatively straight; open. Single slender float projects forward of the bow; 2 booms extend to the float; after boom turns down and either connects directly to the float or by a pair of arched sticks; forward boom heavier, straight, and connected by 2 arched sticks and secondary supports. As a counterbalance, a plank or light poles bound together projects out the opposite side as an extension of the forward boom. Sets a boomed spritsail; heavy sprit. Mast stepped in the bottom, stayed forward; 2-3 shrouds lead from the forward boom and the counterbalance to the masthead; aft stay runs from a spar set out from the stern to the top of the sprit. Steered with a paddle. Crew of at least 3. Length ca. 5.5m.
4. *Tuamotu Islands, eastern Pacific:* In present-day usage, **pahi** means a **ship** or **vessel**. Earlier, the word referred to a large, seagoing double **canoe** that was extinct by the late 19th century. Details given in the few reports vary, probably due to local differences in this long archipelago. Earlier hulls planked in short lengths sewn together, and sometimes joints were covered with tortoise shell. One hull somewhat shorter than the other; slightly asymmetric in shape longitudinally; mainly V-shaped in cross section; bottom curved toward the sharp ends. On some, the sheer strake extended beyond a breakwater to join a supplemental endpost forming an open, triangular area at each end. Hulls joined by a number of stout booms that passed through the top strakes; solid platform covered the area between the hulls as well as part or all of one or both hulls. Steered with 1-2 long oars with a loom that flared at the blade and was then cut square; oar fixed by a short crossbar on the end of the platform, or by a crutch across the end of the hull; steering oar shifted when sailed in the opposite direction. A shelter was placed on the windward side of the platform. Stepped 1-2 masts on the platform, setting V-shaped sails or a single large sail on either mast, depending on the direction. Reported lengths 9-30m; e.g., length of hull 14.5m, beam 1.05m, depth 1.4m. Spelling variant: **pahee**

Further reference: **waka pahii**

pahi auahi, pahie See **pahi-3**

pahii See **pahi-2, waka pahii**

pahi ie See **pahi-3**

pahi tama'i *Society Islands, southeastern Pacific:* Very large, double-hulled **war canoe**; probably gone by the end of the 18th century. Two types, both built up with 2-3 wide strakes from a dugout base; the **pahi tama'i** had a V-shaped hull that curved in at the top to take on the strakes; the **va'ai tama'i** had a round bottom and slab sides. On the former, the sterns swept up as high as 7.3m, while on the latter the bows were higher. The 2 hulls were joined by as many as 18 strong transverse beams. Platform, raised on pillars, was set near the bow; used by chiefs and warriors. The end erections carved at the top or otherwise ornamented; some carried carved pillars at the ends or elsewhere on the craft. Paddled, the largest by as many as 144 men; some sat beneath the platform. Reported lengths 15-33m; each hull ca. 1.0m wide and 0.9-1.2m deep.

pahu See **perahu-1**

pai *China:* One of the terms for a **raft**★, especially in the south. Constructed of logs or bamboo. Spelling variant: **phai**. Note also **fa, fu**. Further references: **pae, pahi-1**

pai-ao-ch'iao See **lorcha-3**

pailabot In Italian, the word referred, particularly in the late 19th century, to a 2-masted **schooner**★ or to a **pilot boat**★, the confusion deriving from the use of **schooners** as **pilot boats** in United States ports. Spelling variant: **palabot**. See also **pilot boat**.

pailão *Guinea-Bissau (Portuguese Guinea), SE:* **Dugout canoe**★ of the Bijagos Islands. Used primarily for fishing with traps, lines and snares, hand-cast nets and small gill- and entangling nets. Reported lengths 5-10m; cap. to 1t.

pailebot **1.** *Argentina, NE:* A popular vessel type in the Río de la Plata in the 1st half of the 19th century. **Schooner**★-rigged.

2. *Ecuador:* Large, 2-masted **coaster**★; decked. **Schooner**-rigged, setting gaff sails.

See also **goleta-1, pailebote**.

pailebote *Spain:* Small, **schooner**★-rigged **fishing boat**★ and **coaster**★. Virtually extinct by the 1980s. Square or counter stern; concave cutwater with scroll work; decked. Those fishing for *langosta* in the Balearic Islands had a live well. Generally without topsails after the introduction of auxiliaries in the early 20th century. Some 3-masted. **Schooner** types had a crew of ca. 6. Reported lengths 18.9-28.3m; e.g., length 18.9m, beam 4.6m, depth 2.13m. May also designate a **pilot boat**★. Spelling variant: **pailebot**. Note also **palhabote**. Further reference: **pilobote**

pai-mu ch'uan See **shou kou ma yang zi**

pair See **double scull, josher-2, pair-oar**

pairau See **perahu-1, prow-1**

pair-oar *England, S:* **1.** Large **water-taxi** of the 17th-19th centuries in London. Rowed by 2 licensed watermen, each pulling a single oar. Note also **sculler, Thames wherry**.

2. A class of collegiate racing boats employing 2 oarsmen, each manning an oar, with or without a coxswain. Also used in France, where they were known as **deux de pointe**, in the Netherlands (as **tweeriemsgiek**), and in Italy. Oars generally outrigged; usually no rudder. Sometimes converted for

double sculling (see **double scull**). Reported lengths 9.75-11.28m, beam ca. 0.4m, depth amidships ca. 0.25m. Other recorded names: **pair-oared outrigger, racing pair**

Other recorded names: **pair (of oars)**

pair-oared outrigger, pair of oars See **pair-oar**

pair of pups See **timber raft-2a**

pair of scullers See **sculler**

paitaalek See **kayak-9**

paitaalik See **kayak-8, kayak-9**

pai-tai ch'uan See **Amoy fisher**

paitalik See **kayak-9**

pai ti chuan *China, E:* Generic term for a group of handsome, white-bottomed vessels that worked along the coasts of Zhejiang (Chekiang) and Fujian (Fukien). Some fished (see **Amoy fisher**), others traded (see **Fukien trader**). Other recorded names: **jonque à carène blanche, p'ai ti ch'uan, pei ti tch'ouan, white-bottomed boat**

pai-ti shuan See **Fukien trader**

pai-t'ou ch'uan See **cao chuan-3**

pai-tu ch'uan See **bai du chuan**

Paiute tule balsa See **saKi**

paixalik See **kayak-9**

pajala *Indonesia, central:* Double-ended craft built on the eastern tip of the southwestern peninsula of Sulawesi (Celebes) for use in coastal trading, conveying passengers, fishing, and at one time, piracy. The **pajala lompo** engages in seining with the *lompo* net. In southeast Kalimantan, the **pajala** transports coral for building foundations. Centuries old and still used. The sides may be raised and an overhanging poop installed, creating the **pinisi**★. Shell constructed carvel-fashion with pegged planking; planks carved to shape, not bent. Ribs inserted later; floors attached to ribs only toward the bow and stern; curved sides. Curved and strongly raked stem and sternpost merge smoothly with the relatively short, shallow, and curved keel; on some, the stem and sternpost extend well above the gunwales. Open except for a short bamboo foredeck; may have a house aft or a temporary shelter amidships. Short, high washboards behind the foredeck. Quarter rudders worked from the open stern extension. One or 2 tripod masts, of bamboo, pivot in tabernacle to permit lowering. Generally sets a wide, rectangular, lug-type sail boomed at foot. Reefed by rolling around the boom by means of a crossbar through the end of the boom. Sails originally of woven leaf matting, more recently of cotton. Reported lengths 7-12m; e.g., length 11.2m, beam 3m, depth 1.0m. Other recorded names: **padjala, pedjala**★. Further reading: G. Adrian Horridge, *The Konjo Boatbuilders and Bugis Prahus of South Sulawesi* (London: National Maritime Museum, 1979 [Maritime Monographs and Reports, 40]). Note also **bago-1, palari**.

pajala lompo See **pajala**

pajang *Indonesia, central:* **Fishing boat**★ of northwest Madura that sometimes traveled to the island of Barwean for the *ikan pèndang*. Hull painted red; stem and sternpost black except for red stemhead and the red, fishtail-shaped stern. Crew of 5. Sailed and paddled. Name variant: **djoekong**. Note also **sampan payang**.

pajangan See **mayang-1**

pakada See **odam-2**

pakasse See **woodskin**

paketbåd, Paketboot, paketbot, pakket, pakketboot
See **packet boat-1**

pakoer See **pakur**

pakschuit See **trekschuit-3**

pak-tow-sun See **cao chuan-3**

pakur *Indonesia, central:* Double-outrigger trading **canoe**★ of the west coast of southern Sulawesi (Celebes); a small type also tended special fishing platforms. Sometimes allied with the **lepa-lepa**★. Plank-extended dugout with sharp, upturned, vertical ends; ribs hold the gunwales in place. Sharp bottom. Long, heavy bamboo floats secured to the 2 booms by elbow-shaped connectives; booms cross the hull at bow and amidships. Steered with a quarter rudder. Some have a built-up structure amidships for cargo and passengers that extends full beam or even beyond. Single pole mast stepped forward of amidships. Variously rigged: large, generally rectangular lugsail with luff shorter than leech and light boom at foot; a spritsail; a wide sail to an aft-raking mast, which required that the floats be moved forward; or a vertical-gaff, triangular sail with a very long boom. When rigged as the latter, the boat is called a **sandé**. Crew of 3-4. Reported lengths 7-10m; e.g., length 7m, beam 0.5m, depth 1.0m. Other recorded names: **pakoer, soppé**★

palabot See **pailabot, pilot boat**

palacca See **polacre**

palagai kattu vattai *India, SE:* Narrow, 3-masted **lugger**★ that fished out of Adirāmpatnam and environs. Plank-built, double-ended, rounded stem; straight, raked sternpost. Used a long, compound balance board forward of the mainmast that was bent down at the ends, stayed to the mast, and weighted; or else some of the crew might be assigned to the weather end. A 2nd balance board, ca. 2.13m long, was placed abreast the mizzenmast and was neither stayed nor weighted. Quarter steering boards used in lieu of a rudder, loosely lashed under the stern thwart, worked by the helmsman's feet; an additional steering board might be placed forward of the mainmast. Crew of 4-5. Reported lengths 5.5-11.3m, widths 0.6-0.9m, depth 0.76m. Spelling variant: **palagai kattu vattal**. Note also **Adirāmpatnam boat**.

palagai kattu vattal See **palagai kattu vattai**

palandaria See **chelandia, palandra**

palandárie, palander See **chelandia**

palandra *Italy:* **1.** Term used by 16th-century Venetian writers for a fairly large vessel from the eastern Mediterranean, especially one carrying horses. Note also **chelandia**.

2. Naval vessel of 17th-century Venice designed to bombard coastal positions. Bow and stern of roughly equal height. Open forward for the mortars; accommodations and storerooms abaft the mainmast. Two or 3 vertical masts and another light mast raked over the bow. Crew of ca. 30. Length 18.2m, beam 6.7m, depth 3.7m. Spelling variants: **pal(l)andaria, palandrea, palandria, palandrie**★, **parandaria, polandra; palandrina** (small). Further references: **bilander-1, chelandia**

palandrána See **chelandia**

palandre See **chelandia, palandrie**

palandrea, palandria See **chelandia, palandra**

palandrie *Turkey:* French term for a moderately sized 15th- and 16th-century cargo ship in the eastern Mediterranean. Often served as a **horse carrier**★. Flat floors. Spelling variants: **palandre, palandrio**. See also **chelandia, palandra**.

palandrina See **chelandia, palandra**

palandrio See **palandrie**

palangre See **palangrero**

palangreiro See **longliner-1**

palangrera See **palangrero**

palangrero **1.** *Spain, NE:* Used on the Cataluña coast with *palangre* gear consisting of a fish line with multiple hooks at the end. Generally worked from beaches. Sharp ends; curved stem, high stemhead; strong tumble home to sternpost. Flat floors, straight keel, grounding keels; soft turn of the bilges; flaring sides.

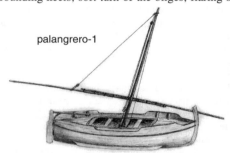

palangrero-1

Slender outboard rudder dropped below the bottom; tiller. Decked at ends and along the sides; narrow, open hold; steering well. Washstrakes along each side, terminating at the stern washboard and before the stem. Lateen sail set to a forward-raking mast. Also rowed from 3 rowing thwarts working over single tholepins. Reported lengths 10.2-11.4m; e.g., length 10.2m, beam 2.8m, depth 1.2m. Also used in the Balearic Islands—the **barco de palengre mallorquina**. Other recorded names: **barca de palangra** (or **palengre**), **barque de palangre, buque palangrero, palangre(ra)**. Note also **longliner, palangrier**.
2. *Venezuela:* Locally built, modern, motorized vessel used mainly for tuna fishing, the **palangrero atunero**.

palangrero atunero See **palangrero-2**

palangrero mercanizado See **longliner-1**

palangrie See **palangrier**

palangrier **1.** *France, Mediterranean coast:* General term for a boat that uses long, multihook lines for bottom fishing. Small boats lay the lines by hand; large, modern craft, using lines several kilometers long, use windlasses. Physical characteristics vary with locale. The sailing types of the 17th-19th centuries set a lateen mainsail and perhaps a mizzen or a lateen foresail to a sharply forward-raking mast stepped in the eyes; bow usually had a beak. Special local names have also been applied to **palangriers**; e.g., at Saint-Tropez, the boats were called **frégatars**; at Agde, they were **sardinayes**; elsewhere they might be **aissaugues**. Other recorded names: **palangrie, palangrin; ayssangue, eissa(i)go, eissango, eissauga, eissaugo, eissaugue, issago;**

dim. **eissaguero, eissaugero; saugo, savego**. Note also **cordier, longliner, palangrero**.
2. *Morocco, Mediterranean coast:* Small boat for fishing with long lines or nets. Sharp ends, plumb stem with high, scimitar-shaped stemhead, low stern. Highly cambered deck. Sets a lateen sail to a portable mast. Also rowed. Crew of 2. Reported lengths 5.5-6m. Other recorded names: **pointu** (by the French), **sardinal★** (by the Spanish)
Further references: **cordier, lamparo, longliner-1**
palangrin See **palangrier**
palari *Indonesia, central:* **1.** Vessel built along **pajala★** lines, but now rigged as a gunter or gaff **sloop**. Has the **pinisi★** overhanging, square poop above a sharp stern. **2.** A fast, 2-masted pleasure craft of southwestern Sulawesi (Celebes). Elaborately carved cabin. Sat low in the water. Rowed in calms, having as many as 12 oarsmen.
See also **lambo-1, pinisi**.
palari penis, palari pinisi, palari sompot See **pinisi**
palascarmo, palaschermo, palaşkerma See **palischermo-1**
paleong See **laung**
palesquarme, palestarme See **palischermo-1**
palhabote *Portugal:* Type of gaff-rigged **schooner★** used for cargo and recreation. Generally carries topmasts to which gaff topsails are set. Mainsail boomed, foresail sometimes boomed. Foremast may set a square sail in heavy winds. **Yachts★** carry a staysail and large jib to a long bowsprit; working vessels set smaller multiple jibs and a staysail. Usually clipper-bowed and counter-sterned. Note also **pailebote**.
palingaak *Netherlands, N:* Sturdy Frisian vessel that transported eels (*paling*) in its large wet well to London from the early 15th century almost until World War II. Some were permanently moored off Billingsgate on the Thames as receiving vessels for the eels. A member of the **tjalk★** family. Rounded, bluff ends; deep, curved stem terminated in a point; generally had a gripe below the waterline; sternpost straight, considerable deadwood aft. U-shaped in cross section, flat floors; tumble home to top strake; considerable sheer. Decked; steering cockpit aft; leeboards. Large outboard rudder; tiller slotted over rudderhead and sloped downward. Carried a boat on deck. Mainly set a tall mainsail with a loose-footed, boomed, curved or straight gaff. Staysail, jib to bowsprit; sometimes a topsail. Early vessel sprit-rigged. Crew of 3-5. Reported lengths 18.5-21m; e.g., length 18.5m, beam 4.85m, depth 2.4m. Other recorded names: **aalaak, Fries(ch)e palingschuit, Friese palingaak, friesche Aalboot, Frisian eelboat, ielae(c)k, klaveraak, palingschuit, Palingschute, paling schuyt**; pl. **aalaken, ielaken, palingaken**. Further reading: Jan Zetzema, *De Friese Palingaken* (Amsterdam: A. J. Hilgersom, 1976).
palingaken, palingschuit, Palingschute, paling schuyt See **palingaak**
paliscalmo, paliscarmo See **palischermo-1**
paliscarmotto See **palischermo-3**
paliscelmo, paliscermo, palischermi See **palischermo-1**
palischermo 1. Italian generic term for a small, open **boat★**, although it is often a shipboard designation for

the **ship's boat★**. Term, in its local spelling variations, is found widely in the Mediterranean area. Other recorded names: **balaşkerma, barca de paliscalmo** (or **de panescal, de parascalmo, de parescalmo, de parischalmo, de penescalm**), **barcha de parescalmo, palascarmo, palaschermo, palaşkerma, palesquarme, palestarme, paliscalmo, paliscarmo, palischermo, paliscermo, pallascarmus, panescal(m), (barque de) parascalme, parascalmo, parascalmus, paraschelmus, paraşkerma, parescaume, pareschelmo, parischalmo, pariscalmus, perascaline, poliscalma, poliskalmos**; pl. **palischermi, barce de parischalmo**. Note also **lancia**.
2. The word also appears in literature of the 15th-17th centuries, designating a large cargo vessel.
3. Two **palischermi** participate in Italian tuna trap-netting during the kill, one on each side of the **caporais★**. Open boat; capstan available for lifting the net. Length 12m. Other recorded names: **paliscarmotto, palischermo d'entrara** (or **d'entrata**), **palischermotto**
4. Term may designate a single **scull★** (**singolo**) or racing **skiff★**.
Further references: **launch, ship's boat**
palischermo del luogo See **shore boat-1**
palischermo d'entrara, palischermo d'entrata, palischermotto See **palischermo-3**
pålkran See **pile driver**
palla See **pallar**
palla chatty *Pakistan, SE:* An open, spherical, earthen jar on which a fisherman of the Indus River balanced while working a large dip net (*palla*) or using a spear. The jars (*chatties*) were made especially for this use. The fisherman sprawled across the mouth of the jar, propelling the craft with his legs and guiding it with his hands. Fish placed in the jar as caught. In some, the fisherman sat within the jar. Note also **chatty raft, taghāri**.
pallandaria See **palandra**
pallar *Bangladesh:* Shallow-draft lower Ganges River **riverboat★** used primarily for cargo; may designate a small, single-person craft, a passenger vessel, or an accompanying **cook boat**. In the Pūrnia district of Bihar, **pallar** designates a **pilot boat★**. Dates at least from the

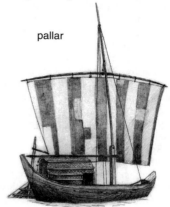

pallar

mid-17th century. Full lines; keel piece bends up to form a flush stem and sternpost; typical of most boats of the area, the bottom strakes run roughly parallel to the keel line except for the top 4-5 strakes, which are roughly horizontal, following the sheer line. Elongated, pointed block stem composed of several plank extensions; sternpost, also a block, higher than bow. Very low free-board when loaded. Washstrake may raise sides. Fully decked; deck beams pierce the hull; large, central cabin of palm or bamboo; high steering platform aft. Use either a fixed steering oar, or a balanced rudder, a major part of the rudder forward of its turning axis; rudder worked on the port side. Some small **pallars** are **skiff**★-like without cabins or sails and sometimes assist larger vessels in working through narrow passages. Large vessels set a single square sail and frequently a square topsail. Mast stepped forward of the cabin and can be lowered from a high tabernacle. Average 7-9 in crew. When rowed, standing oarsmen use 6m-long sweeps; sweeps rest on a bamboo "rail" and are lashed to an upright. Larger **pallars** 12-20m long; e.g., length 15.2m, beam 3.66m, depth 1.83m; average cap. 56t. Other recorded names: **dak**, **palla**, **palowari**, **palowary**, **palvār**, **palwa(h)**, **palwâr**, **palwarah**, **pollari**, **palouar**, **paloyār**, **pouloua**, **pulva**, **pulwá**, **pulwar**; **gopalpuri** (in Mānikganj subdivision). Note also **badjra**.

pallascarmus See **palischermo**

pallone *Italy:* Small boat assigned exclusively to official personages. Rowed with 2 oars. See also **rua ballang**.

palori See **pinisi**

palouar See **pallar**

palowa *Philippines, central:* **Schooner**★-rigged **coaster**★. Double-ended, flat floors, marked sheer, European-type rudder, trunk cabin aft. Gaff sails loose-footed and boomed; 2 headsails run to a long bowsprit. Length ca. 21m. Name variant: **lorcha**★

palowari, **palowary**, **paloyār** See **pallar**

pålpråm *Sweden, S:* Used in southwestern Skåne and Blekinge to drive stakes for nets used to catch bottom fish. At other times, may transport farm animals. May be **scow**★-like with the pile-driving apparatus at the stern; some are **catamarans**★, with the **pile driver**★ set between the 2 hulls. Flat bottom(s), square stern(s), sharp bow(s). Towed to the site. Reported lengths 6-7m. Name variant: **bottengarnpråm**. Note also **garnpråm**, **pound boat**, **pound net scow**.

pal-san *South Korea, S:* Around Nam-hai and Chyou-jyu, a log **raft**★ used for fishing and collecting seaweed along the coast. Generally formed of an odd number of logs laid side-by-side with 2 poles passed through holes made in the logs. A small platform of slender poles might be lashed on top; others had railings along each side or a light frame flooring of bamboo. Propelled by a sculling oar or by a rectangular, battened, mat sail. A 7-log **raft** reported as 6.9m long and 1.5m wide. Spelling variant: **pal-son**

pal-son See **pal-san**

paltamo *Finland, central:* Tar exported from Oulu (Uleåborg) was transported in barrels through the rapids on the Oulu (Uleå) River in these long, narrow, open boats. Planked with 3 wide, lapped strakes; rounded bottom; closely spaced frames; sharp ends; heavy stem and sternpost. When carrying a load, sides raised with an additional sewn strake. Mainly rowed with a single pair of oars, each man handling an oar.

Steered with a long paddle. Might also set a square sail. Crew of 3. Length 13.7m. Other recorded names: **tar boat**★, **teravene**, **tjärbåt**. Note also **forsbåt**.

palua *Philippines, N:* Provides transportation for ca. 20-30 passengers among the Batan Islands, north of Luzon. Plank-built; strakes adzed to shape and pegged edge-to-edge; sharp ends; curved stem and sternpost. Rudder and tiller used when sailed. Rowed with 6 oars per side; employs double tholepins set into a block on the gunwale. Mast stepped through a thwart; sail originally of pandan leaves, now cotton. Crew of 12. Name variant: **falua**★

palu-oruwa *Sri Lanka, S:* Sailing **outrigger canoe**★ of the **oruwa**★ type; used mainly for fishing. Dugout hull; sides raised by deep, vertical washstrakes; bottom and sides of dugout rounded. Ends flat, high, and strongly raked; sails out to fishing grounds with bow forward, returns "stern first." Outrigger to starboard; long, sharp-ended float connects directly to 2 downward-curving booms. Two narrow leeboards hang along the port side. On some, in the after part, a rectangular, transverse beam extends through the washstrakes to support an outboard motor. In some places, a horizontal rail set on the booms forms the top of a mat weatherscreen. Mast, either vertical or raked slightly forward, held by ropes against the after boom; 4 stays. Trapezoidal lateen sail hung from a 2-piece yard. Also uses 2 oars. Crew of 3. Length ca. 7m.

palvār, **palwa**, **palwah**, **palwâr**, **palwarah** See **pallar**

pamacari *Brazil, west-central:* Family boat used on the upper Amazon River to transport supplies, wood, fruit, and rubber. Characterized by a palm-leaf roof over

pamacari

most of the hull. Pointed, overhanging bow and narrow, raked transom stern. Hitches a tow from a **steamer** on the upstream trip; floats downstream. Reported lengths 6.1-7.6m. Spelling variant: **pamacaris**

pamayang See **mayang**

Pamban dhoni *India, SE:* Roughly built, open boat that ferried pilgrims between the shrine on Rameswaram Island and Pamban on the mainland. Carvel-planked, high bow, straight stem and stern, square stern, high freeboard. In brisk weather, a balance board seating 1-3 men was thrust to windward; crossed abaft the mast and was wedged between 2 stringers on the lee side. Single mast stepped amidships; sail type might be a quadrilateral lateen-type with a short luff or fore-and-aft. Reported lengths 9.2-10.3m; e.g., length 9.2m, beam 2.26m, depth 0.84m, draft loaded 0.6m. Name variant: **Rameswaram dhoni**

pambán-manché *India, W:* Long and very narrow **dugout canoe**★ used on the coastal lagoons of Kerala as an escort boat to rajahs. Also found on the island of Minicoy to the west of the mainland. During the 19th century, they also conveyed passengers, and their design and opulence were commensurate with the rank of the owner; some had ornate ends and a cabin of grass or wood. Most were generally of a single log. Those of Cochin were noteworthy for their length, being as long as 20m, 0.94m wide, and 0.4m deep. The Travancore

pambán-manché

boats, which are now raced at festivals, have a very long, overhanging bow, often capped with a bronze spur; the stern rises in a crescent shape, providing a vantage point for the helmsman. All types paddled, by 30-40 paddlers, double-banked. Other recorded names: **bateau serpent**, **pamban-manchúa**, **pambo-manché**, **serpent boat**, **snake boat**. Note also **manji**.

pamban-manchúa, **pambo-manché** See **pambán-manché**

Pamlico Sound seine boat See **North Carolina shad boat**

pamunuanan See **boteng pamunuanan**

pan *England, central:* Term assigned to steel or iron dumb **lighters★** on the River Trent. The open-hold **Nottingham pan** was horse-pulled and worked between Nottingham and Burton; length 22m, beam 4.3m. The decked **Trent pan** was towed by a **tug★** in the area between Hull and Nottingham; length 25m, beam 4.4m, depth 1.6m, draft 1.5m. See also **compartment boat**.

pānasī See **panshi**

panaval *India, NW:* A type of small, fast **pattamar★** that transported fruit and vegetables to Bombay (Mumbai).

pan boat See **Tyne keel**

panca *Philippines:* Plank-extended **dugout canoe★** used mainly for fishing. The booms of the double outriggers pass beneath the strake. May have an awning of bamboo and rattan. Large **pancas** capable of carrying 15 people. Paddled and sailed. Reported lengths 4.6-7.3m. Note also **banca**. Further reference: **panco-2**

panchi, **panchway** See **panshi**

panco *Philippines, S:* **1.** Fast pirate vessel of the Moros and Malays. Plank-built; no keel; sharp ends with cutaway or tall stem and sternpost; steep rise to the floors. Square poop deck out over the sharp stern. Light bamboo decking; breakwater forward pierced with a cannon. Quarter rudders. Rowed in 2 banks, 13-30 oars per side, the upper tier working from a platform out each side. Wide lugsail set to a tripod mast. Crew to ca. 100. Reported lengths 15-24m, beam of largest 6m; draft 1-1.5m. Other recorded names: **galay**, **galey**, **garay**, **penjajap★**. Note also **salisipan**.
2. **Coaster★** of the southern islands and adjacent Indonesia. Plank-built along western lines; some bottoms copper-sheathed. Square stern. Two tripod masts; fore-and-aft sails. Length 24m, widths 5.5-6.1m. Other recorded names: **auang-galay** (on Mindinao); **panca★**

panego See **peingaw**

panescal, **panescalm** See **palischermo-1**

panfilo See **yacht**

panga **1.** *Central America:* General term applied to a **dugout canoe★**, especially in Panama, where they transport bananas from the interior to the coast. Some plank-extended. Ends usually pointed and rising. May have platform at the stern for the steersman. Bottom

flat for most of its length. Paddled, rowed, and sailed. Length ca. 5-6m, beam 1.4m. Name variant: **bongo★**
2. *Ecuador:* The relatively new plank-built **panga** serves as a **dinghy★** to **fishing boats★** along the coast in the San Pedro area, west of Guayaquil (see also **6** below). Some fish inshore for shrimp. Vary in design, but most sharp-bowed and plumb-transomed, creating a triangular boat; small keel; rounded hull. Many have an outboard motor. Generally a one-man craft.
3. *Mexico, NW:* Double-ended, plank-built boat used for fishing by the Seri of Tiburon Island in the Gulf of California. Replaced the reed **balsa★**. Frames of local mesquite wood, other materials purchased. Piece added to stern to support an outboard motor; also paddled. Reported lengths 5-6m. Name variant: **canóaa**
4. *Mexico, W:* Small, modern, beamy workboat found on many beaches in the Gulf of California and to the south. The smaller boats fish locally; the larger fish for shark offshore. Sharp, raked bow; transom or sharp stern, strong sheer, flat bottom. On some, fins extend laterally just below the waterline from each side of the skeg. Open except for foredeck. Now mainly of fiberglass. Powered generally by an outboard motor. Reported lengths 7-9m, widths 1.7-2.3m; shallow draft. Spelling variant: **ponga**. Note also **pongo**.
5. *Philippines:* In the Tagalog language, a well-made and well-outfitted boat used by 17th-century friars and clergy.
6. *South America, NW:* Used by coastal fishermen from Panama to Ecuador (see also **2** above). Sharp-ended **dugout canoe** with fine entrance; straight, raked bow and stern; mild sheer except at the ends, no keel. Balsa logs sometimes fixed along the sides for stability. Occasionally a small sail hoisted. Length ca. 4.6m. Name variant: **cayunera**. Note also **canoa-14**.
Further reference: **pango**

pangai, **pangaia** See **pangaio**

pangaio **1.** *Africa, E/India:* Variously described in the 16th and 17th centuries as a **raft★**, a small sailing **canoe★**, and a single-masted vessel with a coconut-mat sail and sewn planking. Mainly attributed to the eastern African coast, but also described as an Indian trader that procured cargo from the African coast. These slender vessels had a high poop and set 2 large lateen sails to forward-raking masts.
2. *Mozambique:* At least until the 1950s, an updated version of the **pangaio** worked from northern ports. Low sides, flush deck, square stern. Set a large lateen mainsail to a forward-raking mast, a boomed gaff mizzen, and a jib to a bowsprit. Name variant: **dhow★**
Spelling variants: **pagaia**, **pangai(a)**, **pangara**, **pangaye**, **pangayo**, **panguage★**. Note also **panguay**.

pangajaoa See **penjajap-3**

pan gan zi *China, central:* Long, narrow boat designed to work the shallow rapids of the Xiang (Siang) Chiang in Hunan Province. Snubbed-up, tapered bow with straight lines; rounded-up, pointed stern; flat bottom. Fitted with 11 bulkheads. Forward of after cabin, a long, full-width mat house covers the cargo; poling walkways extend outboard. Large-bladed rudder. Steps 2 masts, both forward of amidships, and a battened lugsail with curved luff. Length 19.4m, beam

2.4m, depth 1.4m, cap. 22t. Other recorded names: **pan-kan-tzŭ, pole boat★**

pangara, pangaye See **pangaio**

pangayo See **jahazi, pangaio**

pange *Tuamotu Islands, eastern Pacific:* Small single-**outrigger canoe★** of Reao, an island in the eastern part of the archipelago. Used especially for turtle hunting. Built of irregular lengths of wood on a deep, narrow keel piece; strakes sewn. Distinguished from similar **canoes★** by a walestrake that thickens toward the top; thin washstrake then sewn on the inner side of the walestrake. Sharp, generally solid end pieces; ends rake and curve toward the bottom. Outrigger set to starboard; 2 light booms cross the hull to the float at the ends of the **canoe**. Angled connective scarfed onto the outer end of the boom and leads down to the outer edge of the plank float, to which it is lashed; a 2nd, lighter connective, bound on to this angled piece, leads to the inner edge of the float; float may tilt toward the hull. Length 3.1m, beam 0.38m, depth 0.46m.

pangipitan See **buralan**

pango *Philippines:* Large, plank-extended **dugout canoe★** that served mainly as a **coaster★**. Also reported from China. Some had outriggers. Set mat sails to 3 masts spaced evenly from bow to stern. Rowed in calms, the rowers working in 2 banks. Spelling variant: **panga★**

panguay *Comoro Islands, western Indian Ocean:* Reported in the late 18th century as a large craft that made lengthy voyages to sea. Sides raised with reeds and branches bound together and made waterproof with a resinous substance. Mainly single-masted, setting a mat sail. Note also **pangaio**.

panguaye *Maldive Islands:* A **raft★** constructed of light, pliable branches. See also **pangaio**.

panier See **ghe nang**

panjajaap See **penjajap-2**

pankaī See **donga-1**

pan-kan-tzŭ See **pan gan zi**

pan keel See **Tyne keel**

panneman, pannenaar, pannepot See **panneschuit**

panneschuit *Belgium, SW:* Heavily built boat that worked initially off the beaches at De Panne but later out of Nieuwpoort; some built at Ostend. Extinct by

panneschuit

ca. 1918. Fished mainly for shrimp, but in winter, fished for herring and sprat. Carvel-built with thick planking, some clinker; straight or slightly curved, thick stem; rounded bow; straight or mildly raked, U-shaped transom. Keel with slight drag, U-shaped in cross section, lightly rounded floors; maximum beam well forward; rather flat sheer. Some decked at bow and stern, open well behind the mainmast; others fully decked; winch on after deck; largest type had a donkey. Most lug-rigged with a vertical foremast stepped against the stem, the mainmast raking slightly aft, and the vertical or aft-raking mizzen standing off-center against the transom. Early boats carried tall, high-peaked lugsails on the fore- and mainmasts and a smaller lugsail on the mizzen; then shorter lugsails set with a lug topsail on the mainmast; later vessels used triangular topsails and a triangular mizzen. Mainsail sheeted to a traveler. Flying jib to running bowsprit. Mizzen outrigger and bowsprit were run from port side of the stem and sternpost. The **panneman** set a gaff mainsail, triangular mizzen, and 2 headsails. Sails mostly tanned. Crew of 5 initially, later 3; vessels fishing for herring off Iceland carried 7-8 men. Reported lengths 8.5-15m; e.g., length 10.5m, beam 3.4m, depth 1.65m. Other recorded names: **barque pannoise, crabschuit, Flemish lugger, krabschuit★, Oostendse pannepot(ten), pannenaar, pannepot, Panse schuit, scute de la Panne**. Note also **schuit**.

pannier See **ghe nang**

Panse schuit See **panneschuit**

panshi *Bangladesh/India, NE:* **Water-taxi, fishing boat★, ferryboat★,** and produce carrier of the Ganges River and Delta. Carvel planking fastened with staples; sides teak, bottom ironwood; rounded hull without keel. Long, overhanging spoon bow and stern formed from heavy, squared stem and sternpost; bow low, stern higher and broader. Generally undecked except at the ends. Those carrying jute and rice have a large, built-up house; cargo area lined with tin sheets; sides and roof of bamboo. Passenger **panshis** have a cabin with sides of wood or tin; a large type may be called a **kuthir-pānsi**. Steered with either an oar or tall, balanced rudder; steering platform built above the cabin. Rowed by 6 oarsmen seated forward, poled, or sailed, setting 1-2 square sails. Average 5-6 in crew. Reported lengths 6-20m; West Bengal fishing **panshi**: length 8.2m, beam 2.28m, depth 0.9m; shallow draft. The Pabna **panshi** is a long, narrow boat used in local boat races. Other recorded names: **pānasī, panchi, panchway, panshway, pānsi, pansoī, pansūhī, panswae, panswah, panswai, pānsway, passage boat★, paunchway, paunsway, paushway, pausi, permit boat, pons(a)y, ponsway, punshi, punsoee, punsui**. Note also **badjra, bhedi**.

panshway, pānsi, pansoī, pansūhī, panswae, panswah, panswai, pānsway See **panshi**

pantjalang, pantjallang See **pencalang**

paopao 1. *Kiribati (Gilbert Islands), central Pacific:* Sailing **outrigger canoe★** with platform cantilevered out the lee side. Plank-built on a hollowed-out keel piece; planks lashed edge-to-edge, with the lashings let into the planks and smoothed over with a fiber putty; deep, V-shaped hull, slightly curved on the outrigger side; double-ended. Straight, raked ends terminate in a stylized frigate bird or in taller, unornamented ends.

Short, heavy outrigger float attached to 2 closely spaced booms by multiple stanchions; braces extend from hull ends to the booms. Large platform on lee side for cargo space, the navigator, and a small hut. Mast socketed amidships but slightly to the hull's weather side; rakes forward, but pivots to the opposite end when tacking. Small crook at top of mast permits air to pass between sail and mast. Triangular sail with apex tacked to stemhead; yard bowed, boom S-curved; sail of woven pandanus until World War II, now of cotton. Steering oar braced against an outboard thwart section; handle lashed to oar for leverage; helmsman's foot presses vertically held blade in and out. Length overall 7.6m, beam 0.4-0.5m, draft 1.02m.

2. *Micronesia (Caroline), western Pacific:* Single-outrigger paddling **canoe** of Nukuoro, an isolated island group south of the main chain. Double-ended dugout; deep hull, slight tumble home to topsides; ends raked; slight forefoot; gunwale sheer sweeps up abruptly at each end. Two booms extend to a medium-long, sharp-ended float bending downward at about midpoint; partly supported by a stringer that parallels the hull. Each boom connects to the float by 2 pairs of tall stanchions crossed below the boom and lashed directly to the hull; may have a supplemental fore-and-aft brace atop the outer part of the booms. Small, light platform laid across the booms outboard of the stringer. Paddled with lanceolate blade. Crew of 1-2. Length ca. 4.6m. Note also **waka-1**.

3. *Samoa, central Pacific:* One-man, paddling **outrigger canoe** used for lagoon fishing and harbor transportation. Fine-lined dugout hull; tumble home to topsides, sometimes with an inside flange to aid in supporting the booms. Bottom rocker toward the stern, deeper at the bow; sharp, concave bow generally has small, raised, square-cut knobs on top surface; block left as handle at the tapered stern. Two or 3 booms extend out port side to the slender float; connected with 2 pairs of divergent stanchions, or pegged directly into the float from a fork in the boom. Float tapered to chisel point forward, the end roughly aligning with the bow. Sometimes has a small spritsail. Reported lengths 3.1-5.5m; e.g., length 5.1m, beam 0.37m, depth at bow 0.36m. Spelling variant: **pau-pau**. Further reading: Peter H. Buck, *Samoan Material Culture* (Honolulu: Bernice P. Bishop Museum, 1930 [Bulletin 75]).

4. *Solomon Islands, western Pacific:* Designated as a non-sacred **canoe** on Anuta, an isolated eastern island.

5. *Tokelau Islands, eastern Pacific:* One- or 2-man single-**outrigger canoe**; worked in the lagoons. Dugout hull with rounded or U-shaped cross section. Bow varies among the islands from a sharp, plumb, or slightly concave cutwater to a blunt and raked form; stern generally elongated to a point. Solid ends ornamented on top. Two widely spaced booms extend to the slender, pointed float; float connected by 2 pairs of divergent stanchions that join above the booms; a strengthening stringer laid across booms near the float.

6. *Tuvalu (Ellice Islands), western Pacific:* Single-**outrigger canoe** used for lagoon fishing and transportation. Slight differences between northern and southern island types. Dugout hull, generally of rough construction; fuller

in cross section on the outrigger side. Vertical cutwater in the north, shallower in the central islands, and bow pointed in the south. Stern drawn out to a point. Float toes in at the forward end. Two or 3 booms connect directly with the float; in the north and central islands, booms parallel the water and then branch down in a straight line to the float. In the south, the booms curve down at the ends. Usually a single stringer braces the booms. Reported lengths 4.1-5.4m; on Vaitupu Island: length 4.6m, beam 0.33m, depth 0.38m.

7. *Wallis and Futuna Islands, central Pacific:* Simple **outrigger canoe**. One-piece dugout hull with U-shaped cross section; bottom has rocker; sharp ends cut vertical above the waterline. Two straight booms, lashed to the gunwales, extend to a fairly long, pointed float that toes in slightly; 2 pairs of undercrossed sticks connect the booms with the float; several light stringers lashed across the booms. Uses oval-bladed paddles. On Futuna Island, **pa'opa'o** may refer to a European-type boat or to a **whaleboat** type. Name variant: **vaka tafua**

papao See **baobao**

Papa Westray skiff See **Westray skiff**

paper boat 1. Term sometimes used for a boat with very thin planking.

2. *United States:* Boats made of paper were produced in the latter half of the 19th century. Especially popular were **paper canoes** and racing **shells**. Three layers of thick manila paper that had a hemp content were fitted over a mold; laminated with fish or hide glue. Waterproofed with shellac or varnish, then fitted with ribs, seats, etc.
See also **chi shuen**, **fa teng**, **liu peng**.

paper canoe See **paper boat-2**

paquebot, paquebote, paquebouc See **packet boat-1**

paquete 1. Portuguese word for a fast vessel used for passengers and mail or a small boat carrying orders or communications.

2. *Brazil, E:* Ferried cargo and passengers between Juàzeiro and Petrolina on the Rio São Francisco; in use until a bridge was built in the mid-20th century. Flat bottom, flared sides, small keel. Set a large, triangular sail. Two in crew. Average length 9m.

3. *Brazil, NE:* A medium-sized **jangada** that fishes mostly inshore but in good weather, sails to the edge of the Continental Shelf. Crew of 2. Its logs (usually 6) are ca. 6-7m long and have a circumference of 1.1-1.3m; widths of the craft 1.5-2m.
See also **batelão-3**, **packet boat-1**.

para See **paruwa-1**

parachal, paracil See **coracle-4**

paragua See **canoe-6**

paraho, parahoe See **perahu-1**

parama See **perama**

paranca, parancella, parancelle See **paranza**

parandā See **parinda**

parandaria See **palandra**

paranza *Italy, E:* Beamy **fishing boat** of the lower Adriatic Sea and Sicily that works mainly with another boat pulling a trawl net (the *paranza*) between them. Some fish for coral, and in winter, may engage in commercial traffic. Carvel-planked; full bow; strongly curved stem with a knob or hank of wool on the recurved top; rounded stern, curved sternpost; long, straight keel; flat floors. Decked; central hatch for ropes, nets, and fish. Very long, heavy rudder that extends well below the bottom, raised by tackle from the mast; worked with a long tiller. Often brightly painted, including oculi at the bows. Lateen or a large lugsail with a short luff set to a vertical mast; boomed at the foot; long 1- or 2-piece yard. Sail may be tanned and some have decorative bands or designs. A large jib runs to a slender bowsprit. Rowed in calms using 8-10 oars. Crew of 2-11. Reported lengths 8.45-14.75m; e.g., length 12.4m, beam 4.1m, depth 1.3m, draft 0.7m. The **paranzella** of the Naples area was ca. two-thirds the length of the **paranza**, sharp-ended, and lateen-rigged. Some were armed and, in the late 19th century, served for coastal defense. Other recorded names: **balancelle★**, **baransèlla**, **barca paranza**, **bilancella da pesca**, **paranca**, **parancella**, **paranziello**; pl. **parancelle**, (**barche**) **paranze**, **paranzelli**. Note also **bilancella**.

paranze, **paranzella**, **paranzelli**, **paranziello** See **paranza**

parao   **1.** *China/Vietnam:* Poorly described **coaster★** of this area. Flat floors with no keel; relatively low sides; rudder and tiller; house amidships. A battened mat sail was laced to the mast. Also rowed, both forward and abaft the house. Some armed. Spelling variants: **parau★**, **paro★**, **parro**

2. *Indonesia, central:* Reported as a small Javanese war vessel in the late 16th century. Some employed a sail.

3. *Philippines, central:* Double-outrigger **coaster** that moved goods, fish products, and passengers between the Visayan Islands. Raked stem; square, raked stern; steep rise to the floors; keel. Decked, cabin abaft the mainmast; open railing. Quarter rudder. Four, sometimes 3, light booms crossed the hull to the 2 long, slender bamboo floats; central booms placed close together. Two masts stepped in the bottom and secured on deck by stocks; mainmast roughly amidships, foremast well forward. Sails originally battened lugsails; later cotton sails that were a cross between standing lugsails and gaff sails, boomed at the foot. Jib to a rising bowsprit. Also employed large oars with rounded blades. Reported lengths 9-21m. A similar type, the **binabaeng parao**, was used in the same area. Stem more rounded and cutaway, greater sheer toward the bow, narrower aft, rounded counter. Midline rudder; tiller worked with block and tackle. Spelling variants: **parau★**, **paraw★**

See also **basnigan**, **padow**, **perahu-1**, **prow-1**.

paraoe For terms beginning with **paraoe**, see **perahu**.

parascalme, **parascalmo**, **parascalmus** See **palischermo-1**

paraschal See **coracle-4**

paraschelmus, **paraškerma** See **palischermo-1**

paraskmalia See **paraskmalion**

paraskmalion *Turkey, Black Sea coast:* Heavy, round-bottomed **lighter★** that worked off beaches; of early origin, but extinct by the 1930s. Carvel-planked; bow and stern curved up sharply, creating a strong sheer; sheer strake continued beyond the stem and sternpost to form leads for the tow rope; grapnel at the bow, and

rudder iron distinguished the stern. Deep washboards stopped inboard from the bow to permit space for rowers; steered at stern with a fixed sweep or by the stern oarsman; also rowed and towed. Reported lengths 6-12m. Spelling variant: **paraskmalia**

paraskmalion

parau   **1.** *Indonesia, W:* Term for a **canoe★** by the Batak of northern Sumatra.

2. *Papua New Guinea, Bismarck Archipelago:* Designates a **boat★** or **ship★** in the Rabaul area of New Britain Island.

See also **basnigan**, **parao**, **paraw**, **perahu-1**, **prow-1**.

parau pinsalang See **pencalang**

Parava vallam See **vallam-2**

paraw *Philippines, S:* Small, light **fishing boat★** commonly found around Siasi Island in the Sulu Archipelago. Plank-built onto a dugout base; slender, 25cm-tall pegs inserted into the top strake to support the gunwales; resulting open space filled with tightly woven, painted bamboo strips to form a type of washstrake. In some areas, plywood is substituted for the woven gunwale and short end decks may be of plywood. Slender bow turns up, raking forward; on some, the bow piece is flat. Stern straight with fan-shaped extension. "U" shape in cross section. Thwarts placed between gunwales provide strengthening and support for the mast. Ends painted in bright colors; gunwale strake curves up onto the bow piece. Double outriggers connect directly to bamboo floats by 2 booms that bend down at their outer ends. Floats aligned with the bow. Light mast stepped just forward of amidships; sets a boomed leg-of-mutton sail. Crew of 2. Length overall 7.7m, on waterline 5.4m, beam 0.36m, depth 0.46m, draft 0.2m. Spelling variant: **parau★**. See also **parao-3**, **perahu-1**.

parcel tanker See **tanker**

parchment canoe See **bullboat-3**

paredgia, **paregge** See **pareggia**

pareggia *Italy, NW:* Lateen-rigged vessel that worked out of the Ligurian area until the end of the 19th century, especially from Sestri Levante to Riva-Trigoso. Mainly a trader carrying general merchandise, wine, and passengers; also fished, some off the Tunisian coast. Carvel-planked. Stem straight, slightly raked, and with a high stemhead, which had a hole for the yard guy; square or rounded, raked counter stern. Deep bulwark; long, straight keel; flat floors. Rudder came up inboard. Cambered deck, large hold with 2 cargo hatches; crew's quarters forward. Carried a **lancia★**. Short mainmast stepped roughly amidships; forward rake adjustable. Mizzenmast stepped at the sternpost, also raked. Large mainsail, small mizzen, sheeted to a jiggerboom. Long bowsprit secured a wide-footed jib. Some later vessels had engines. Crew of 6 when fishing. Reported lengths 15-19m; e.g., length 16.9m, beam 5.47m, hold depth 2.25m. Other recorded names: **bovo**⋆, **paredgia**; pl. **paregge**. Further reading: G. Morino, "The Ligurian Pareggia," *Model Shipwright* 30 (1979), 58-70.

pareille See **balancelle-1**

pareja *Spain:* **1.** Offshore **trawler**⋆ of the eastern and southern coasts and the Balearic Islands; may be either a sailing craft or motorized vessel. Works in pairs towing the *pareja* net from the stern. Some sailing **parejas** have a deep keel, others are flat-floored and use a centerboard; bilge keels common for protection in landing on beaches and as stabilizers at sea. High stemhead; sternpost curves inward. Decked; 3 hatches, the larger near the mast and small ones at the bow and stern. Some carry an **enviada**⋆. Most set a single lateen sail on a forward-raking mast; mast inclination can be altered. Some set a jib to the bowsprit; others may use 2 triangular pollaca sails, one boomed out forward to one side, the other aft to the opposite side, plus a large lateen sail, the yard of which is set more horizontally. Crew of 7-8. Length 14m, beam 5m, depth 1.8m. Other recorded names: **barca** (or **barco**) **de pareja, barca de parella, parella**. Note also **barca del bou, chinchorro-4**.

2. Used on the north and Galician coasts to catch tunny. In addition, they engaged in pair fishing and drifting in winter for sardines. Straight stem; strong sheer forward, little aft. Platform at the stern used for tunny lines and for net operation. Fish wells just forward of the platform; small fish hatch forward of amidships. Crew of 12-15 housed in forecastle. Wheelhouse amidships. Carried a small boat. Two masts, one forward and one aft, but mainly operated by an engine. Reported lengths 20-24m, beam 5.5-6.1m.

parella See **pareja**

parenda, parendah See **parindah**

parent ship See **mother ship**

parescaume, pareschelmo See **palischermo-1**

parical, paricu See **coracle-4**

parinda *India, NW/Pakistan, N:* Long, light, narrow **state barge** used on the Jhelum River and lakes in Kashmir. Also recorded as a hunting boat. Fast, employing 30-50 paddlers using heart-shaped paddles, sitting in 2 rows. As many as 4 passengers sat on a raised seat forward; some boats had a canopy covering most of the hull. Name variants: **flyer**⋆, **parindā**. Note also **parindah**.

parinda boat See **parindah**

parindah *Bangladesh/India, NE:* Type of **riverboat**⋆, especially of Bengali rivers. Some were part of the mid-17th-century imperial **fleet**⋆. Long and narrow, some with a cabin aft. Other recorded names: **parenda(h), parinda boat**. Note also **parinda**.

parisal See **coracle-4**

pariscalmo, pariscalmus See **palischermo-1**

parish boat *Canada, E:* In Newfoundland, a vessel that transports members to their church or in which a clergyman travels to visit parishioners. Note also **church boat**.

parisil See **coracle-4**

parlvinker See **kadraai**

parme See **perama-2**

paro *Mediterranean:* Cited as an early Greek **rowing boat**⋆; also as a 14th-century pirate boat out of Zadar on the Dalmatian coast. High, recurved bow. Note also **mioparo, myoparon**. Further references: **parao-1, perahu-1, prow-1**

paroe See **perahu-1**

parokia See **dingi-2**

paróm In Russian, a **ferryboat**⋆. May be a type of **raft**⋆, especially one formed by **canoes**⋆ joined together **catamaran**⋆-fashion. Spelling variants: **porom**⋆; **porón** (Ukrainian).

paron *Greece:* Early vessel believed to have been built on Parian Island in the Aegean. Among the more numerous of their large but light vessels. Name variant: pl. **parones**

paròn See **briki, rascona**

parones See **paron**

paròni See **rascona**

paroo See **prow-1**

paroowa, parre See **paruwa-1**

Parrett flatner *England, SW:* Small, open boat of the River Parrett and Bridgwater Bay on the southeast coast of the Bristol Channel. Used mainly for local fishing, but also for withy gathering around Bridgwater. Active during the 19th century, but a few remained until the mid-20th century. Flat bottom with rocker athwartships and fore-and-aft. Double-ended, but later boats had transom sterns for outboards; sides a single plank or of 2 planks scarfed vertically in the middle; sides flared 70°, resulting in considerable sheer; natural knees fitted. Sternpost straight, stem

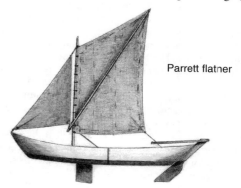

Parrett flatner

curved, both raked. One type, the **gore boat**, had washstrakes, which distinguished it from a 2nd type, the **Bay boat**⋆. Tanned spritsail bent to unstayed, short mast; sprit approximately the length of the boat. Headsail set from a pronged pole wedged against the forward thwart; pole also used for holding to a mudbank and hauling the net. Rowed with 2 pairs of squared oars that tapered down without a blade; worked between double tholepins. Crew of 2. Reported lengths 4.57-6.4m; e.g., length 5.94m, beam topsides 1.67m, at bottom 1.17m, depth 0.53m, draft 10cm. The so-called **Combwich flattener** operated as a **ferry**⋆ in the 19th century. The crossing at Combwich was undertaken later as a do-it-yourself activity. Other recorded names: **Bridgwater flatner;**

dory* (at Weston-super-Mare); **flat boat***, **flattener**, **fore boat**, **vlatner**

parro See **parao**

parrua See **prow**

partaich See **patache**

party boat *United States:* **1.** Boat that takes out groups of sport fishermen for a day's fishing on an individual paid basis. Some large **catboats*** were built in the late 19th century expressly for this purpose; also used by summer visitors for an hour or so of sailing. On Chesapeake Bay, watermen sometimes referred derogatorily to Bay **schooners*** used for pleasure parties as **head boats***. Another recorded name: **drift boat***. Note also **tripper boat**.
2. Term applied to **scooters*** used primarily by non-**scooter** owners.

pāṛu *India, S:* A **ship***, especially a sailing ship in Tamil and Kannada languages; a small **boat*** or **catamaran*** in the Malayalam language.

paru See **padda boat**, **paruwa**, **prow-1**

parund See **shikara**

parus See **paruwa**, **sailer**

parusnoe sudno See **ship-2**

paruwa *Sri Lanka:* **1.** A "floating aid" in Sinhala. May be a twin-hulled **riverboat*** that carries passengers (see **padda boat**), or one that collects and transports sand. The latter boats are beamy, heavily constructed, fastened with metal rather than sewn, **scow***-ended, with chine strakes, and a flat sheer, but are basically similar to the seining boats described below; poled. Other recorded names: **para**, **paroowa**, **parre**; pl. **paru***, **parus**; in Tamil: **patai**, **pathei**
2. Long, narrow, sewn boat used in beach seining along the west, south, and northeast coasts. Bottom planked longitudinally, concave transversely. Split, hollowed-out log forms the bilges and lower sides; deep washstrake raises each side, battened internally; rail lashed on top. Flat ends rise at 30-45° to or above the washstrakes, the bow sometimes higher; wedge-shaped pieces may be added to meet the rising bottom planking; strengthened at the join by heavy, vertical pieces. Sides straight but slightly narrower at the ends, the bow somewhat narrower than the stern. Two rowing thwarts set into the gunwales near the bow; a crossbeam abaft the after thwart extends outboard to provide handles for lifting the boat to and from the water. A single outrigger is used along a short stretch of coast south of Colombo, where the boats work a net in pairs; 2 booms arch over the hull and bend down to attach directly to the small, curved float. Steered with a paddle or oar. Mainly rowed; long-loomed oars with spade-shaped blades; poled in some shallow areas. Reported lengths 5.5-10.7m, the shorter types found on the northeast coast; e.g., length 9.4m, beam 1.0m, depth 0.9m. The **mādel-paruwa** sets a long *mādel* seine net and the **barudel paruwa** sets the smaller *barudel* net (in Tamil, **kawali pathei** and **perumwaral pathei**, respectively). Other recorded names: **ma-däl paruwa**, **model-parawa** (pl. **madel paru**), **model paruwa**. Further reading: Eric Kentley and Rohan Gunaratne, "The Madel Paruwa—A Sewn Boat With Chine Strakes,"

International Journal of Nautical Archaeology and Underwater Exploration 16 (1987), 35-48. Note also **madel-oruwa**.
Further reference: **padda boat**

parve galée See **galiot-9**

pasacaballo See **batea**, **horse carrier**

paşa fılukası See **gig-1**

pasi 1. *South Korea, SW:* The **p'asi** is a floating fish market found off parts of the southwest coast; patronized by middlemen from the mainland. The location of the boats varies with the availability of fish at different seasons; whale **p'asi** operate in winter, mackerel **p'asi** in autumn. A small type, the **chogi p'asi**, works around Kagodo Island selling *chogi*, the yellow corvina. Note also **cho-gi cham-nan pa**.
2. *Society Islands, southeastern Pacific:* In Tahitian, a **ship*** or **boat***. Note also **pahi**.

pasni *Pakistan, W:* Type of **tow car*** used by shark gill net fishermen off the western coast. Small fish such as sardines, used to attract the sharks, carried in the car; towed behind to the fishing grounds. Made of palmyra leaves, which are sewn together to create the sides; several stringers provide strengthening. Sharp ends; flat bottom. Length ca. 3.2m. Name variant: **live car**

passacavalli, **passacavallos** See **horse carrier**

passage barge See **hoy barge**

passage boat 1. One that regularly plies between two places on a sea, river, or canal, carrying passengers, animals, or merchandise. Form varies. Other recorded names: **barco de pasage**, **bateau de passage**, **Fährboot**, **passage packet**, **passagier**. Note also **ferryboat**, **packet boat**.
2. *Australia, Tasmania:* Small, **cutter***-rigged freight boat that made the passage through the D'Entrecasteaux Channel at the south end of the island in the late 19th century. Also fished. Double-ended; plumb stem, slightly raked sternpost, clinker-built. Half-decked; outboard rudder; tiller. A **ketch***-rigged boat 11.6m long, 3m wide, 1.1m deep. Name variant: **South Arm boat**
Further references: **bāūlīa**, **panshi**

passage packet, **passagier** See **passage boat**

Passagierdampfer See **liner-1**

Passamaquoddy ocean canoe *United States, NE:* Porpoise and seal hunting birchbark **canoe*** of the Passamaquoddy of northeastern Maine. Early types had strong end sheer terminating in high ends; sheer much reduced or non-existent in later models. Tumble home close to gunwale. Bottom athwartships rounded or rounded "V"; end rocker 10-12cm; bilges slack. End profile straight on top and rounded below. Bark brought up over the gunwale and pegged down onto it. Usually sets a dory spritsail. The mast is stepped in the bow with the mast heel braced against a notched stick lashed to thwart and gunwales. Also rowed. Decorations mostly along the gunwales and at the ends. Reported lengths 5.28-7.62m, widths 0.64-1.12m, depths 0.33-0.53m.

passe-cheval See **team boat-1**

passera See **caicco-2**

passerelle volant, **passerelle volante** See **pontoon-2**

patača, **patacchia**, **pataccio**, **patach** See **patache**

patacha *Portugal, central:* Small, light river craft that transports produce, salt, seaweed, etc. Built of pine. Flared sides; may have sharp, raked ends or a wide transom stern; those lacking futtocks are strengthened with thwarts. Lightly tarred to a golden color initially, then blackened after the first repairs. Rowed by 2 men. Average length 4.4m, beam 1.28m. See also **patache**.

patache **1.** *Argentina/Honduras/Mexico:* Term for a small **boat**★.

2. *Southern Europe:* **a.** A fast, armed **tender**★ to larger ships of a squadron, carrying orders between ships, reconnoitering, guarding ports; those from Portugal often carried gold and treasures. Rowed and sailed. Ranged from a small boat to a 2-masted vessel with gaff or lateen mainsail and square foresails. Length of a 1585 Spanish vessel 16m; length-to-beam ratio ca. 3.54:1; breadth-to-depth ca. 0.66:1. Name variant: **patache d'avis**. Note also **advice boat**. **b.** A vessel of customs services that worked along the coast and larger rivers, checking commercial vessels, sometimes leaving a guard on board. 16th-century French boats were rowed with as many as 18 oars per side; later boats were small, open, **sloop**★-rigged craft. Name variant: **patache de la douane**. Note also **coast guard ship**, **revenue cutter**. **c.** A **barge**★-like craft used by port police as nighttime quarters. **d.** One type was an armed, oared **galley**★ of the **fleet**★ of Spain's Philip II in the late 16th century. **e.** A deprecatory term for a cumbersome vessel lacking seaworthy qualities.

3. *Spain, N:* **a.** A variety of **patache** was a 2-masted **coaster**★ of the late 19th century. Mainmast set a fore-and-aft sail and no topsail; the foremast, in 3 sections, set square sails and no topgallant. Capacity ca. 26-76t. **b.** The **patache** of northwest Spain is a motorized craft that transports sand. Full bow, transom stern. Decked forward and aft, open waist. Also rowed.

Selected name variants: **partaich, pataca, patacchia, pataccio, patacha**★**, patach(ea), patachia, patach(i)o, patage, pataggio, pataiche, pataje, patakija, Patasche, patas(c)ia, patas(sa), patasse, patatchio, patatxo, pataxe, patax(o), pataxos, patazzio, pattache, petača, petach(e), petaix, petaknon, petas**. Further references: **balandra-2, balsa-6, caballit-1, coche d'eau**

patachea See **patache**

patache d'avis See **patache-2a**

patache de la douane See **patache-2b, revenue cutter-1**

patache de police, patache de surveillance See **guard ship-2**

patachia, patachio, patacho See **patache**

pataely See **patela**

patage, pataggio See **patache**

patai See **padda boat, paruwa**

pataiche See **patache**

pataili See **patela**

pataje, patakija See **patache**

pataku See **masula, padagu-1**

patalā, patalia, patallah See **patela**

patalya *Turkey:* Variously designated as a naval **ship's boat**★ (with 1-3 oars), **dinghy**★, **punt**★, or **jolly boat**★. Spelling variant: **batalya**

patam *Bangladesh, NE:* **1.** Large **riverboat**★ from Bajitpur that carries sand and stone from Sylhet to Dhaka. Long and narrow; ends terminate in heavy, squared blocks; bow high and extends out over the water; stern low. Little freeboard when loaded. Arched mat roof covers much of the boat; roof decorated along the sides. Poled or tracked from shore; steering sweeps. Cap. 32-40t. Other recorded names: **bajit-puri, bazitpuri, sylheti**

2. A smaller **patam** carries agricultural products in the Dhaka and western Mymensingh areas. High bow, lower stern, heavy block stem and sternpost. Plank keel; planking parallels the keel, with the sheer strake cutting across the side planking at an angle; circular in cross section; no framing. Open; arched mat house covers the stern area. Maneuvered with a heavy sweep. Towing mast for tracking set up in forward third. May set a light spritsail to a slender mast. Averages 4 in crew. Length to ca. 15m; cap. averages 10t. Name variant: **pati**. Note also **dingi**.

3. At Brahmanbaria, long, narrow **patams** are featured at races held in conjunction with an August festival. Musicians stand on the high, sloping stern encouraging their crews. Name variant: **pattan**

Spelling variant: **patham**

patamar, patamarin See **pattamar**

patam dingi See **dingi-2**

patas, Patasche, patascia, patasia, patassa, patasse, patatchio, patatxo See **patache**

paṭavu See **padagu-1**

patax, pataxe, pataxo, pataxos, patazzio See **patache**

patela *Bangladesh/India, NE:* Beamy cargo vessel still used in the lower Ganges River basin. At times, reported to have transported soldiers, and in the mid-17th century, engaged in naval operations. One variety has a flat bottom, planked longitudinally, with athwartships planking over it, the 2 layers bolted together. The sides clinker-built above hard chines; square stern; floor forced up at the bow and stern to produce a pronounced rocker. Another type reported to be smooth-skinned with stapled strakes; these are double-ended and beamier. Crossbeams extended through hull just below the top strake. A thatched deckhouse protects the cargo for most of the vessel's length; above it is a platform from which the boatmen work. Uses a triangular, balanced rudder. Rowed, poled, or tracked from shore. Sometimes sets a rectangular sail. Crew of 10-12. Reported lengths 12-20m; shallow draft. Other recorded names: **baggage boat, kalra, kátora, káturá, kutora, pataely, pataili, patalā, patalia, patallah, patelee, paṭelī, patella, patello, patila(h), patil(e), patillé, patli, patunga, petile, puteli, putel(l)ee**. Note also **katrā**.

patelee, paṭelī, patella, patello See **patela**

patemar See **pattamar**

patented bateau See **James River bateau**

patent-stern bugeye See **bugeye**

patham See **patam**

pathei See **paruwa**

pathemar See **pattamar**

pati See **patam-2, patín**

patí de pedals See **paddle boat-2**

patí de vela See **patín**

patil, patila, patilah, patile, patillé See **patela**

patimar See **pattamar**

patín *Spain, E:* A **catamaran**★-type craft propelled by 1 or more double paddles or by a tall, triangular sail. Developed in the Barcelona area in the late 1920s. The sailing type (**patín a vela**), ca. 5.5m long, became a popular local racing type. Slightly aft-raking mast stepped well forward. Other recorded names: **patí** (**de vela**)

patín à vela See **patín**

patín de pedales See **paddle boat-2**

patjalang See **pencalang**

pātkoshā See **kosha**

patli See **patela**

patmar See **pattamar**

patrol boat Small naval craft used for patrol or blockade duty. Some served as a convoy escort. Other recorded names: **Küstenschnellboot (K.S.-Boot)**, **Küstenwachboot**, **nave pattuglia**, **patrol vessel**, **Patrouillenboot**, (**bateau de**) **patrouilleur**, **patrulheiro**, **patrullero**, **Rondeboot**, **Streifenboot**, **Vorpostenboot (Vp-Boot)**, **Wachboot**. Note also **picket boat**, **swift boat-2**. Further reference: **vedette**

patrol craft fast See **swift boat-2**

patrol vessel See **patrol boat**

patrona See **patronne**

patronne Large **galley**★ that followed the **capitane**★ or **real**★ in rank, carrying the second-in-command of a major **fleet**★. Sometimes the term was used for the principal **galley** of small states or republics. Length ca. 47m; 28 or 29 rowing benches with 6-7 men per oar. Also sailed, stepping 2 masts, the foremast well forward, setting lateen sails. Other recorded names: **capitana general**, **galera patrona**, **galère patron(n)e**, **patrona**

Patrouillenboot See **patrol boat**, **picket boat**

Patrouillentschaike See **saique-1**

patrouilleur See **fishery guard boat**, **patrol boat**

patrulheiro, **patrullero** See **patrol boat**

pa tsiang tch'ouan See **ba jiang chuan**

pa ts'ien ch'uan See **fa zi**

pattache See **patache**

pattamá, **pattamach** See **pattamar**

pattamar *India, W:* Lateen-rigged cargo vessel that works out of coastal ports, especially Bombay (Mumbai). Sails along the coast and across to eastern Africa and the Arabian Peninsula; reported as early as the 16th century; some still sailing in the 1970s. Characterized by a high sheer and a long, slightly curved stem (same length as the keel) surmounted by a globe, sometimes gaily painted. Square stern on larger vessels, rounded on the smaller; outboard rudder; tiller. Planked with teak; fastened with nails and bolts on the larger vessels, although some still sewn with coir. Generally oiled to a dark red with black gunwales; coated below the waterline with lime mixed with coconut oil and damar. Keel often concave, the forefoot deeper; of 2-3 pieces. Sharp forward; beamy on the quarters. Open except for short area forward and larger section aft; a light, tent-shaped bamboo shelter covers the waist; those carrying timber between the Malabar Coast and Bombay have short, raised poops. When laden, weatherscreen of matting and bamboo set up. Small **pattamars** often have a

single mast; large vessels have two with a small mizzen set in good weather. Masts rake strongly forward except for mizzen, which is vertical. Haul yard to triple block from masthead aft; serves also as backstay; 2 shrouds; jib set to an in-and-out jibboom. Early vessels might set quadrilateral, lateen-type sails with a short luff to a vertical mainmast. Crew of 10-20. Reported lengths 22.8-37.4m; e.g., length overall 28m, on keel 10m, beam 6.6m, depth 2.5m; now generally more beamy. Other recorded names: **fatemari**, **fattehmar**, **Maharashtra boat** (Malabar coast term), **patamar(in)**, **pat(h)emar**, **pat(i)mar**, **pattamá**, **pattamach**, **pattemar**, **pattima(r)**, **patumar(e)**; **hadaga** (Alibag name). Note also **panaval**, **sambuk**. Further reference: **odam-1a**

pattan See **patam-3**

pattemar, **pattima**, **pattimar**, **patumar**, **patumare** See **pattamar**

patunga See **patela**

Patuxent rail skiff, **Patuxent River skiff** See **railbird skiff**

Paudel See **zig**

Pauite tule balsa See **saKi**

Paull shrimper *England, NE:* **Cutter**★-rigged boat that worked out of Paull on the north shore of the Humber Estuary from the 19th to the mid-20th century. Carvel- or clinker-planked, mostly boxy lines, rounded stem, counter stern, considerable drag to the straight keel. Long, narrow well; facilities for

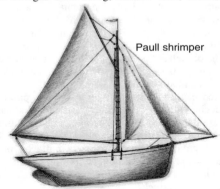

Paull shrimper

boiling the shrimp. Loose-footed gaff mainsail; boom extended to the end of the counter. Forestaysail; jib to a long bowsprit. Worked mostly single-handed, crew of 2 on the larger boats. Length overall 9.85m, on waterline 8.61m, beam 2.9m, draft 1.37m; 6-20t disp.

paunchway, **paunsway** See **panshi**

pau-pau See **paopao-3**, **popo**

paushway, **pausi** See **panshi**

pautasi See **fautasi**

pauvigi:k See **kayak-5**

pavilion caique See **saltanat kayığı**

paviljoenjacht See **spiegeljacht-2**

paviljoenotter See **otter**

paviljoenpraam See **praam**

paviljoenschuit See **paviljoentjalk**

paviljoentjalk *Netherlands:* A **tjalk**★ characterized by a raised after deck that was level with the top of the bulwark, the *paviljoen*. Built of wood, iron, or steel, mainly in South Holland and Noordbrabant in the south and in Friesland in the northeast. Carried cargo on inland waters from the 18th to the mid-20th century. Flat bottom; sheer swept up to boxy ends; curved stem that did not follow the tumble home of the top strake; vertical sternpost. Living quarters beneath the *paviljoen* lit by a skylight and 2 windows in the stern. Long hold amidships. Outboard rudder; very long tiller worked by the helmsman forward of the *paviljoen*; wide leeboards. Early vessels sprit-rigged. Later set a large, boomed, loose-footed gaff mainsail. Staysail might also be boomed and loose-footed. Some had a jib to a running bowsprit that could be triced up. Lowering mast. Engines in some later **paviljoentjalken** (pl.). Reported lengths 14-23m; e.g., length 19.6m, beam 4m, depth 0.54m. Other recorded names: **paviljoenschuit, Pavillontjalk**

Pavillontjalk See **paviljoentjalk**

paxiuba *Brazil, SW:* **Canoe⋆** of the Arawak of the Madeira River basin. Made by digging out the core of a palm, leaving the ends intact. Center spread open and reinforced with thwarts; one variety of palm has a natural bulge that forms the mid-section.

payang *Peninsular Malaysia:* **1.** Trading vessel popular at the end of the 19th century. Carvel-planked; sharp ends; strongly raked stem, sternpost less raked; long, straight keel; sharp rise to the floors. Considerable sheer; top strakes continued roughly parallel at both the bow and stern to terminate in squared ends beyond the stem and sternpost; extensions decked and bordered by shallow bulwarks. Waist decked; house toward the stern, some divided into parts along the midline. Outboard rudder, often worked with yoke and lines. Slender pole masts stepped amidships and in the forward quarter; employed palm-leaf lugsails. Also rowed. Crew of 4-15, 40 when engaged in piracy. Reported lengths 9-22m; e.g., length 22m, beam 3.7m, depth 1.5m. Spelling variant: **payong**
2. Brightly painted east coast boat that uses a large purse seine, the *pukat payang*. Distinguished by its outward-curving, white stem and sternpost that extend 60-90cm above the gunwale; also by its 2 carved spar rests, the bow rest being used to hold the lowered spar and the stern rest to hold the long steering paddle when it is shipped. A stout bitt against the starboard gunwale amidships takes the anchor cable when work-

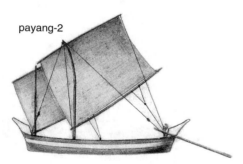
payang-2

ing the net. Straight keel and garboard cut from single log; carvel planking; fairly full bilges; little sheer.

A loose plank decking covers most of the boat. Steps 1-2 masts; foremast close to the stem; the mainmast about a third in from the bow, bending forward at the top. Boomed lugsails of black cloth; boom may be set at a high angle, forming a "V" with the mast; sail rolled onto the boom as it is lowered. Rowed with 13-18 long oars in calms; also paddled. Steered with a paddle over the lee quarter. Now most are fitted with an engine. Crew of 15-20, 2 of whom man a **jongkong⋆** or **sampan payang⋆** when working the seine. Reported lengths 10-15m, widths 1.8-2.4m, depth ca. 0.9m. Other recorded names: **perahu** (or **prahu**) **payang⋆**, **perahu pukat payang**. Note also **kolek lichang**.
Further reference: **jalak**

payong See **payang-1**

pazar kajk See **pazar kayığı**

pazar kayığı *Turkey, NW:* Large, open boat that ferried passengers and merchandise to Istanbul markets (*pazar* or *bazar*) from villages bordering the Bosporus. Mainly used during the 17th-19th centuries. Could carry 50-60 passengers. Double-ended; tall, curved stem and sternpost; strong sheer toward the ends; long, straight keel; decked at bow and stern. Rowed with 3 pairs of oars, the oarsmen standing; steered with a sweep or rudder. Length roughly 12m. Other recorded names: **bazar caique, Bazar-Kaik, bazar qaïghy, market caique, pazar kajk, pazar kayık**. Note also **kayık**.

pazar kayık See **pazar kayığı**

PCF swift See **swift boat-2**

pe *Papua New Guinea:* **1.** Term for a **dugout canoe⋆** by the Kiwai and Mawata Papuans of the Fly River delta and coastal areas in the southwestern part of the country. Spelling variants: **pei, peri**. Note also **peére**.
2. A single-**outrigger canoe⋆** at the stilt village of Leitere on the northwest coast. Washstrakes fixed to a dugout hull; bow overhangs, stern turns up more sharply. Two booms connect with the float by crossed sticks. Other recorded names: **pérau, péso**

peapod *United States, NE:* Popular sharp-ended lobstering and **fishing boat⋆** in the 2nd half of the 19th

peapod

and early 20th centuries; many served as official **tenders⋆** to lighthouses. Developed around Matinicus on the Maine coast. Now mainly a pleasure craft, although some still used in lobstering. Being locally built, there was considerable individuality in their design and construction. Double-ended; lapstrake, carvel, or strip-planked; stem plumb or rounded with cutaway forefoot; sternpost rounded like the stem or straight and raked. Keel straight or slightly curved, often with a deep, false keel on sailing models; the **Washington County peapod** had a 15cm oak keel. Low or ample rise to the floors; strong sheer. Open; early boats had natural crook sawn frames, later steam-bent, running from gunwale to gunwale.

Steered with an oar or by rudder. Lobstering boats mainly rowed standing and pushing the oars, employing raised oarlocks. When sailed, set a spritsail to a short mast stepped through the forward thwart. Some lighthouse **tenders** used a gaff sail raised with a single halyard. Some larger **peapods** modified to take an engine. Reported lengths 3.7-6m; e.g., length 4.6m, beam 1.4m, depth 0.46m. Other recorded names: **double-ender★**, **lighthouse peapod**, **pod**; also **Deer Isle**, **Jonesport**, **Maine**, and **Matinicus (Island) peapod**

pear boat See **jagt-2**

pearling lugger *Australia, N:* Works mainly from Broome on the northwest coast and from Thursday Island (**TI lugger**) off the tip of Cape York Peninsula in the northeast. Sought pearls initially, later mainly mother-of-pearl shell, since the mid-19th century. Retain the term **lugger★** although currently **cutter★-**, **ketch★-**, **brigantine★-**, or **schooner★-**rigged. Now mainly **ketch**-rigged and supplemented by an auxiliary engine. Hull design modified as diving techniques developed, but since the vessels still drift broadside over the pearling grounds, they must be designed to remain stable with little rise and roll that would jerk the divers along. Deep forefoot, **yacht★**-like counter stern, deep keel sections, moderate sheer, low freeboard, straight sides, bottom copper sheathed; early **TI luggers** were sharp-sterned. Those working out of Broome were more heavily built because of the need to dry out on the mud. Teak deck, low bulwarks; on the Thursday Island vessels, the anchor chains kept in boxes on deck; heavy rudder. Several boats carried on board. Particularly sturdy mast steps and strong standing rigging. Crew of 6-8. Reported lengths 9-32m; e.g., length overall 13.7m, on keel 11.6m, beam 4m, draft 1.8m. Other recorded names: **barque perlière**, **lougre perlier**, **trochus lugger**. Note also **collecting boat-1**, **floating station**.

peata *Italy:* **1.** Peata or piatta can be a general term for a **barge★** or **lighter★**.
2. More specifically, **peata** (or in earlier form **piatta**) designates a **barge**-like craft used in the Venetian lagoons to transport local produce, serve as an itinerant store, and initially, to lighter cargo from ships serving Venice. Dates at least to the 13th century; none now being built. On the 21st of November each year, some anchor side-by-side to create a pontoon bridge across the Grand Canal, enabling the citizens to participate in ceremonies at the Church of Santa Maria della Salute. Flat bottom; rounded bow and stern, stem plumb above the waterline, cutaway below; vertical sternpost; sheer sweeps up at each end; sides almost parallel. Decked at each end with small, square hatches; open waist, hull ceiled; outboard rudder drops below the bottom; long tiller, slotted over the rudderhead, slants sharply down to the deck; sturdy towing bitt at each end. Originally painted in bright colors, later black. Rowed, using 3 long oars, with rowers facing forward; now occasionally seen being towed in trains. As many as 16 oarsmen used during rowing events. Length 15.2m, with rudder 16.4m, beam 3.64m, depth 1.53m, cap. 45t; shallow draft. Other recorded names: **piat(t)a**, **piato**, **piatto★**, **plat(a)★**,

plate★, plato, platta, platus; pl. peate, piatte, plati. Note also **peatone**, **peota**.

peata da ormeggio See **anchor hoy**

peate See **peata**

peatone *Italy, NE:* A large-sized **peata★** designated for the ceremonial use of the 13th- and 14th-century Venetian Doge and the Senatori. The flat-bottomed **barge★** was richly ornamented with gold and silver carvings and tapestries. Most of hull covered by arched house. Snub bow; narrow, raked, square stern. Propelled by 4-8 gaily attired rowers, or might be towed. Other recorded names: **piattone**, **plate★**; pl. **peatoni**, **piattoni**

peatoni See **peatone**

pêcheur See **fishing boat**

pêcheuse See **fisherman-1**

Pechili trader See **Kiangsu trader**

peddanāva See **nāva-3**

pedda padava See **masula**

pedda teppa See **teppa**

pedebakah, **pediwak** See **padewakang**

pedjala *Indonesia, central:* Term for a small **canoe★**, without outriggers, in the Salayar dialect of the Ujung Pandang (Makassar) area of southwestern Sulawesi (Celebes). See also **pajala**.

pedoeang, **pedoewang** See **paduwang**

pedota Lateen-rigged, 16th- and 17th-century vessel of the eastern Adriatic. Note also **peota**.

pedòtta See **peota-1**

peduang See **beduang**, **paduwang**

peenus See **pinash**

peére *Papua New Guinea, SW:* Kiwai Papuans of the Fly River delta islands create a **peére**, or "half canoe★," by removing the worn upper half of a **dugout canoe★**. Such a craft is poled or paddled in creeks. May be as long as 10m. Note also **pe**.

peerie fourareen See **fourareen**

peeryaugo See **periauger**

pègahoe See **perahu**

pegge See **somp**

pei See **pe-1**, **pae**

Peichihli Dschunke See **Kiangsu trader**

peingaw *Myanmar (Burma):* **1.** Carried crude petroleum in jars on the central Ahrewady (Irrawaddy) River and

peingaw-1

other rivers. Lower hull constructed of 2 hollowed logs with thick planking between to form a flat bottom;

additional planks extended the sides. Bow and stern turned up spoon fashion. Long, arched bamboo and mat house covered most of the hull; outboard on each side, bamboo galleries served as rowing or poling platforms and occasionally as storage areas for additional cargo. Sailed upstream, spreading a large square sail bent to a very long yard; the bipod mast stepped forward of amidships; square topsails also used. Crew of 6-8. Reported lengths 12-18m; e.g., length 15m, width without galleries 2.2m, depth 1.22m.
2. Term may also apply to a small, simple **dugout canoe★**. Spelling variants: **panego, peingo, peinjo**

peingo, peinjo See **peingaw**

pekadjangan See **perahu kajangan**

pekart See **picard**

pelagic sealing boat See **sealing boat-2**

pĕlari See **pinisi**

pelele *Indonesia:* **1.** Small **dugout canoe★** of the Djakarta area used for fishing. Lacks the usual washstrakes; sheer sweeps up toward sharp ends. Paddled and sailed.
2. Fast, passenger-carrying river **canoe★** of the west side of Kalimantan (Borneo). Dugout hull, flattened bottom, no washstrakes. Mainly paddled. Length to ca. 18m; very narrow.

peleleh *East Malaysia:* Small, slender, fast boat of Sarawak. Tall, pointed, and raked endposts. Freeboard often increased by demountable washstrakes, which are pegged to the hull timbers. Rudder hung from the lee quarter. Pole mast stepped through a thwart about a quarter of the way in from the bow; no standing rigging. Halyard rove through sheave at masthead and made fast to a windward timber, serving as a shroud. Sets a dipping lugsail. Name variant: **bandong temuai**. Note also **pelele**.

pelele laoet See **pelele laut**

pelele laut *Indonesia, central:* **Dugout canoe★** used in sea (*laut*) fisheries off western Kalimantan (Borneo). Generally strengthened with ribs; sides raised by broad washstrakes; bottom curved fore-and-aft. End shapes vary, some cut flush with the gunwale; on others, the cutwater is blunt at one end and slightly concave at the other end; on other types, the stern projection is tall and slender while the bow is fiddle-shaped. May have a small deck at the stern. Paddled, rowed, or sailed. Mast, stepped through a thwart, sets a rectangular sail. Spelling variant: **pelele laoet**

pelić See **pelig**

pelig Two-masted **coaster★** of the eastern Adriatic that has similarities to the Italian **pielago★** and **trabaccolo★**, but developed along local lines. Dated from at least the early 18th century and worked into the 20th century. Some bluff-bowed with curved stem, wide gripe, and rounded stern; others had a straight, raked stem with gammon knee supporting the bowsprit and a counter stern. Decked; heavy bulwarks; taffrail on the counter-sterned type. Set either 2 large, boomed lugsails or a boomed lug foresail and a boomed gaff mainsail. Long, rising bowsprit carried 1-2 jibs. Auxiliaries on the later vessels. Crew of ca. 4. Reported lengths 11-28m; e.g., length 18m, beam 5.25m, depth 2.15m, draft 1.7m. Spelling variants: **pelić, peliga, peligo**

peliga, peligo See **pelig**

pelo See **padow**

pelota **1.** Primitive craft created from the skin of an animal. Skin usually stretched over a light framework and lashed or sewn on. In some cases, there is no framework, the stiffness of the hide serving instead. Might be square, triangular, oval, or round. Towed by a swimmer, wader, and sometimes by holding the tail of a horse. Assisted by 1-2 paddles, sometimes made from the bladebone of an animal lashed to a stick. Note also **bangué, bouco, bullboat, coracle**.
2. *Argentina/Uruguay:* Used by local native groups and early Spanish settlers to ferry over waterways in the lower Paraná Basin. Deer, cow, guanaco, or vicuña skin laced to the square framework that formed the gunwale edge; resulting bowl shape held firm by "timbers" of bushes, inserted with the leafy ends downward and lashed to the gunwale. To keep the craft from spreading, a lariat or rawhide rope was lashed across the top. Other recorded names: **balsa★, mangá-îg-cîg**
3. *Bolivia, central:* The Mojo of lowland Bolivia are known to have used an oxhide **pelota**. Skin stretched over framework of reeds and rods to create a basin ca. 15cm deep. Name variant: **natae** in the Chiquitos region
4. *Brazil, SW/Paraguay:* Ferried a passenger, saddles, or light goods across rivers. Occupant sat on the bottom, giving a "V" shape to the craft, or on a board set

pelota-4

atop a pair of flexible stick thwarts. Usually made from a single undressed skin, turned up at the edges to form the craft. Dismantled on opposite shore, packed up, and reused at the next crossing. Depth ca. 46cm. Other recorded names: Guaraní names: **mangá, mbaeapu'a** (rounded sides), **yoki**; Abipone of Paraguay: **ñatać, natae**. Note also **bangué**.

pĕmajang, pemayang See **mayang-1**

pen See **sardinier breton**

penajap See **penjajap-1**

Penang sailing lighter, Penang tongkang See **Tamil tongkang**

penawał, penawathl See **shitlats**

pencalang *Indonesia:* **1.** 19th-century trader that worked out of western Java; also reported from northwest Sumatra and from Makassar (now Ujung Pandang) in Sulawesi (Celebes). Double-ended; strongly curved stem and sternpost; round bottom with keel; low freeboard, raised slightly by washstrake amidships; heavy athwartships beams. Partly or wholly decked; deckhouse over most of the hull; helmsman protected by a roof. Steered with quarter rudder that could be worked from a hook on either side. Stout mast, stepped against a bulkhead forward, could be lowered to a mast crutch. Very wide, shallow lugsail boomed at the foot. Jib set to a long, plank bowsprit. Crew of 8-20. Reported lengths 10.7-16.5m, widths 3.7-5.5m, depths 1.8-3.7m. Name variant: **Java trader**

2. At Palembang on the southeast coast of Sumatra, transported local officials on inland waters. Dugout hull; narrow, overhanging, square-ended bow fitted with a copper band; stern might turn up sharply and bifurcate. Generally not plank-extended, but if planked, the vessel was called a **pencalang èbèk**. Decked; house in after half. Steered with an oar on the quarter. Paddled, using 24-30 men. Further name variant: **residentiepraauw**

3. Also reported as a **man-of-war★** and as a pirate vessel. Other recorded names: **béntjalang** (at Atjeh), **kint'alaŋ** (at Simeulue Island), **pantjal(l)ang**, **parau pinsalang**, **patjalang**, **pent'alaŋ**, **pinsalang**, **pint'alaŋ**, **praaw** or **prahoe pentjalang**, **prahu pencalang**, **tjalang**. Note also **penchalang**, **perahu tinda**.

pencalang èbèk See **pencalang-2**

penchalang 1. *Indonesia, central:* Seagoing vessel of the Bugis traders of southwest Sulawesi (Celebes). Two masts, furnished with ratlines. Length 24.4m, beam 4.6m, depth 2.7m. Note also **pencalang**.

2. *Peninsular Malaysia:* Provided transportation out of Johore at the southern tip of the Malay Peninsula, or served as a **scout boat★**. Sharp ends, hollow entrance with raked and curved stem, curved sternpost, full amidships, straight sheer. Carved bulwarks. House abaft amidships. Light mast stepped in forward thwart. Square lugsail, boomed at foot. Length 9.6m, beam 2.3m, depth 1.0m.

pendjadjab See **penjajap-2**, **perahu penjajab**
pendjadjap See **penjajap-2**
pendjaleng See **perahu penjaleng**
pendžadžap See **penjajap-3**
pénèle See **penelle**

penelle *France, Mediterranean coast:* Cargo boat of the lower Rhône and Isère Rivers and along the adjacent coast; phased out during the latter half of the 19th century. Built of pine; square ends swept up; flat bottom. On the rivers, employed a huge rudder and long tiller, but replaced at sea by 2 rudders that were paired so that they worked together from the tiller. Partly decked. Generally towed in a train on the rivers, but sailed when at sea, setting a large lateen mainsail and a jib. Late 18th-century vessel ca. 18m long. Other recorded names: **barque du Rhône**, **pénèle**, **penello**, **pennelle**, **pinello**

penello See **penelle**
penes See **perahu pinas**

pengail 1. *Indonesia, central:* The **pěngail** of western Kalimantan (Borneo) is a small boat that engages in line fishing. Spelling variant: **pěnggail**

2. *Peninsular Malaysia:* The Malaccan **pengail** fishes along the west coast. Sharp ends, raked stem and sternpost, keel; hollow, rising floors; light sheer. Partly decked. Outboard midline rudder. Light mast stepped in thwart near the bow. Sets a square-headed lugsail, originally of woven leaves. Paddles lanceolate-bladed with cross grip. Length overall 6.6m, beam 2m, depth 0.84m. Note also **sampan pengail**.

Further reference: **kolek pěngayer**

pěngayer See **kolek pěngayer**
pěnggail See **pengail**
pénhulu See **barque Djenné**

penice *Italy, NW:* Regional term for a type of **lighter★** or **barge★** that transported small items within a port or at an arsenal. Spelling variant: **pennice**. Note also **péniche-1a**.

péniche 1. *France:* **a.** Term sometimes applied to a service craft in a seaport that lacks means of propulsion. **b.** During the 18th-19th centuries, the term might refer to a fine-lined, fast boat of the French navy that both sailed and rowed well. Generally set lugsails. Clinker-built. Two primary lengths: 12.5m and 18m. **c.** May also be a military landing craft for personnel and materiel.

2. *France, E/Switzerland, W:* **Rowing boat★** used on Lake of Geneva (Lake Léman) for sport fishing, duck hunting, and pleasure boating. Straight or slightly curved stem; raked, wineglass transom; flat or S-curve to the floors. Decked forward and deck or seat aft.

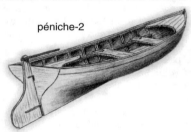

péniche-2

Those used for duck hunting were painted blue-gray and had a large, slotted shield forward for protection and to support the gun; these were propelled by 2-3 pairs of oars and a hand-cranked propeller; steered with a yoke and lines to the rudder. Reported lengths 5-8m; e.g., length 7.25m, beam 1.37m, depth 0.75m. Note also **6** below.

3. *France, Mediterranean coast:* One type transported merchandise along the coast. Lateen sails set to 2 masts. Reported lengths 18-26m; shallow draft.

4. *France, N:* **a.** Decked canal and river **barge★**. Constructed of wood prior to World War I, of steel thereafter. Rounded bow and stern; blunt, vertical stem and sternpost; flat bottom, sharp chines. Small cabin forward, large one aft, covered hold between; on early boats, cabin amidships with an adjacent stable for the towing animals. Large-bladed rudder; on wooden boats, long tiller worked from the cabin roof. Large towing mast for river work, 2 smaller masts for canal passage. Later **barges** towed in groups or self-propelled. Those with diesel engines, **automoteurs★**, have finer lines. Tows or carries a **bachot★**. Reported lengths 12.5-40m; e.g., length 38.5m, beam 5m, depth 2.4m. Other recorded names: **bateau de canal**, **Flamänder**, **Penische**. Note also **waal**. **b.** The **péniche de flotille** was one type of ca. 400 armed vessels that Napoleon planned to use as troop transports in an invasion of England in 1803. Employed 40 oars; also set 3 lugsails and a jib to a long bowsprit. Length 19.5m, beam 3.25m, depth 1.63m.

5. *France, S:* Flat-bottomed **rowing boat** of Arles, northwest of Marseille. Oculus-type star nailed to the bows.

6. *Switzerland, W:* A small, keeled pleasure craft at Geneva. Sometimes sailed. Note also **2** above.

7. *Tunisia, S:* A variety of **péniche** patrolled the sponge-fishing grounds. Sharp ends, plumb stem and sternpost, decked, long hatch, outboard rudder and tiller. Set a lateen sail to a mast stepped in forward third; jib to a bowsprit. Crew of 5 plus the captain. Length 11m, beam 3.5m, draft 0.9m.

8. *United States, central:* Small vessel used in Gulf of Mexico coastal waters and on the tributary rivers. Flat floors, sharp bow, squared stern. Sailed and rowed.

9. *Vietnam, central:* The **peniche** of Tourane (now Da Nang) was pictured in the early 19th century as a long, narrow **rowing boat**. Transported important officials to and from off-lying vessels. Sharp bow elongated; elaborate, raised platform above a sharp stern. Wide-bladed rudder worked from the platform. Rowed by 14 men per side, standing and facing forward; tholepins set into the gunwales. Reported lengths 18-20m, beam 3-4m.

Further references: **chaland-3a**, **pirogue-4**, **train de bateaux**

péniche de Barfleur *France, N:* Line-**fishing boat★** of Barfleur on the western coast of Normandy. Bluff bows with straight, vertical stem; counter stern. Deep hull with drag to keel; steep floors; straight, rising sheer forward. Hung oil lamps or candles in the shrouds. **Cutter★**-rigged; large jib run to a long bowsprit.

péniche de flotille See **péniche-4b**

péniche du Nord, **péniche flamande**, **péniche van Doornik** See **waal**

penis 1. *Indonesia:* The cargo **pénis** was found in many parts of the archipelago. Built and rigged along European lines. One or 2 masts. Other recorded names: **perahu pinas**, **praoe pinis**

2. *Seychelles:* A sailing vessel, probably an early trading **schooner★**. Also a long, narrow, open **fishing boat★**. Sailed, stepping a light mast in the forward quarter. Also rowed. About 7.6m long. Other recorded names: **penniche**, **pinnace★**

See also **pinisi**.

peniša See **lighter-1**

Penische See **péniche-4a**

penisse See **pinash**

penjajaap See **penjajap-2**

penjajap 1. *Indonesia, central:* Term has been applied to the light vessels of the Bugis raiders of southwestern Sulawesi (Celebes). Two-masted; also rowed. According to the type of quarter-deck, the vessels were designated **penjajap kepala kakatua** or **penjajap pagar tengga-long**. Spelling variants: **penajap**, **pinjajap**

2. *Indonesia, W:* Initially a state vessel of the princes of the Lingga and Riau Archipelagoes, but later their swiftness made them notorious pirate vessels. Long, narrow, and lightly built. Besides swivel guns, two 12-pounders pierced a wooden breastwork forward. Open except for an awning for the helmsman. Rowed, double-banked, with 24 short oars. Stepped 2 masts setting square mat sails. Crew of 20-30. Other recorded names: **panjajaap**, **pendjadjab**, **pendjadjap**, **penjajaap**, **perahu penjajap★**, **prahoe pendjajap**

3. *Peninsular Malaysia:* Slender trader used chiefly along the east coast and the Strait of Malacca. Essentially a wall-sided hull with marked sheer; low freeboard, at times raised by matting or wooden washboards. Bundles of bamboo often placed below each gunwale to enhance stability and serve as spare spars.

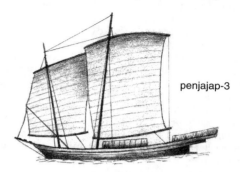

penjajap-3

Clipper-type bow. Small transom stern, almost obscured by an overhanging gallery. Mat shelter in waist and over the stern, or a deckhouse. Usually 2 tall, slender masts, both stepped forward of amidships; foremast placed in the bow, raked over stem. Lattice platform in lieu of bowsprit. Set large Malay or Chinese lugsails, the former with long leech and with foot tacked to a light boom. Crew of 25. Reported lengths 15-20m; e.g., length 17m, beam 3.4m, depth 2.13m. Other recorded names: **rua yayap** (on east coast of Gulf of Siam); **pangajaoa**, **pendžadžap**, **pindgiapiap**, **pindjadjap**. Note also **perahu penjajap**.

Further reference: **panco**

penjajap kepala kakatua, **penjajap pagar tenggalong** See **penjajap-1**

penjaleng *Indonesia:* Trader of the Malay Archipelago area. Sharp ends; flat in cross section amidships; poop. Decked at ends; roof amidships protected cargo. Quarter rudder. Stepped 1-2 tripod masts to which trapezoidal or triangular mat sails were hung. Crew of 8-20. Reported lengths 11-24m, widths 3.7-4.6m, depths 1.4-2.7m; average cap. 36t. Note also **perahu penjaleng**.

pennelle See **penelle**

pennice See **penice**

penniche See **penis-2**

pennis See **pinnace**

Penny-Bridge boat See **sandbagger**

penny ferry See **traghetto-1**

pennys See **pinnace**

Penobscot Bay salmon dory See **salmon wherry**

Penobscot canoe *United States, NE:* Birchbark hunting and fishing **canoe★** of the Penobscot Native Americans of northeastern Maine. Round bottom athwartships, V-section toward the ends. Bottom straight fore-and-aft until ca. 10cm from the ends. Tumble home to topsides. Slight curve to raking bow and stern, ending in point at end sheer; ends stuffed with shavings, and headboards inserted; 5 thwarts. Originally, seams caulked with spruce gum, then with pitch, and later with commercial resin. Later **canoes** had cloth pieces affixed to ends with pitch. Small circle or star painted at the bow end. Oceangoing types generally had a modified "V" bottom, moderate fore-and-aft rocker, and higher ends than the river **canoes**. Typically 5.66m long, 0.94m wide, and 0.38m deep.

Penobscot moose-hide canoe See **moose-hide canoe**

Pensacola oyster boat *United States, S:* Used for oyster tonging in the Pensacola area of western Florida. Carvel-planked of yellow pine. Flat bottom, planked athwartships, with camber aft; skeg. Sharp bow, wide transom stern. Decked forward and at stern; washboard along each side; centerboard. Boomed gaff mainsail to a mast stepped in the bow, or if stepped farther aft, carried a foresail. Crew of 2. Reported lengths 6.4-7.9m, beam 2.1-2.4m.

pen sardine See **sardinier breton**

pent'alaŋ See **pencalang**

pentjalang See **perahu tinda**

Penzance gig See **Cornish gig**

Penzance herring boat, Penzance lugger See **West Cornish lugger**

Penzance pilot gig See **Cornish gig**

peota 1. *Italy, NE:* A light, fast boat used into the 19th century at Venice and in the northern Adriatic to carry messages and special passengers. Best known, however, as one of the types used at regattas, being elaborately ornamented, with a central awning or cabin, fanciful bow and stern decorations, and draperies along the sides. Rowed by 4-10 men standing on the end decks. Might set a single sail. In the 17th century, some were round-ended river **barges★**, probaby **peate** (see **peata**) that were pressed into service. Length 12.8m, beam 1.8-2.1m, depth 0.9m. Other recorded names: **pedòtta**, **peotta**, **piota**; pl. **peote**, **peotte**
2. A small vessel used on the Dalmatian coast. Reported in the early 17th century. Sailed and rowed. Averaged 4 in crew. Ca. 30t. Other recorded names: **peote**; dim. **peotina**. Note also **pedota**.

peote See **peota**

peotina See **peota-2**

peotta, peotte See **peota-1**

pepe See **waka pahii**

pêqueux See **harenguier**

pequngasoq See **kayak-3**

peragio See **periagua**, **pirogue-3**

peragua See **pirogue**

perahoe For terms starting with this spelling, see **perahu**.

perahu 1. Malay generic term for a native boat or vessel; sometimes a **houseboat★**. Term widely used, in its various spellings, throughout Southeast Asia and the western Pacific. Word originally applied to any undecked, native, seagoing vessel, but current usage fails to make this distinction. In some locales, the term may designate an outrigged craft. In Indonesia, the term generally implies a craft on which the sail is raised by a halyard. Usually combined with a word signifying use or construction. Other recorded names: **diahu**, **pado**, **pahu**, **pairau**, **paraho(e)**, **parao★**, **paraoe**, **parau★**, **paraw**, **paro(e)**, **pègahoe**, **perahoe**, **perau'**, **perehoe**, **piyahu**, **praauw**, **prahau**, **praho(e)**, **prahu(k)**, **prao(e)**, **praou**, **prau(h)**, **prauw(e)**, **praw(e)**, **pro**, **proa(h)**, **proe**, **pros**, **provoe**, **prow★**; pl. **prau prau**, **prau²**, **prauwen**. Note also **kapal**, **pilau**.

2. *Indonesia, E:* At Ambon and Banda Islands, a heavy type of **kolé kolé★** with double outriggers was merely called a **perahu**. Might or might not be plank-extended or have tall stem and sternpost.
Further references: **sampan-6**, **sampan Riau**

perahu alis-alis See **alis-alis**

perahu ayam *Peninsular Malaysia:* River craft; name derived from its cock-shaped figurehead. Name variant: **cock boat★**

perahu (prau) bago See **bago-3**

perahu (perahoe) bandoeng, perahu bandong See **bandong**

perahu (prahoe) bangko See **bangko**

perahu beda See **bedar**

perahu (prau) bedang See **beduang**

perahu bedar See **bedar**

perahu (prao) bedouang, prau beduang, prau beduwang See **beduang**

perahu belan, prahu bélang See **bélang**

perahu bĕlongkang *Peninsular Malaysia:* A cargo-carrying **riverboat★**. Strakes added to a dugout hull to increase the freeboard. Name variant: **perahu timbau**

perahu bĕlungkang See **belongkang**

perhau berkatir See **perahu katir-2**

perahu (proa) bero, prahu bérok See **bero**

perahu besar 1. *Indonesia:* In Malay, means a big **boat★**; now increasingly motorized. **Fishing boats★** in Irian Jaya known by this term are longer than 9m.
2. *Peninsular Malaysia:* Cargo vessel owned by Chinese or Malays; used along the east coast. Two masts; foremast stepped in the bow, mainmast stepped just forward of amidships. Long bowsprit on a clipper bow. Length 24m.

perahu (perau', prāhu) bidar See **bidar-1**, **bidar-3**

perahu binta See **binta**

perahu bintak See **bintak**

perahu (praauw) bloengkang See **belongkang**

perahu (prahu) bot See **lambo-1**

perahu buatan barat *Peninsular Malaysia:* Undecked **fishing boat★** of the east coast and adjacent Thailand. Double-ended; vertical cutwater, but above the waterline; stem and sternpost flare outward and extend

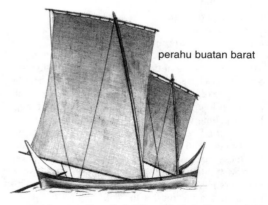

perahu buatan barat

upward as much as 1.5-1.8m. Plank-built on a dugout base, which forms a broad keel. A spar rest, often elaborately carved, extends outboard on the port side abaft the stem; in some areas, a similar piece extends out the starboard side and serves to secure the anchor. Boats colorfully painted. In the monsoon season, substitution of short, stumpy stem and sternpost permits better handling through the surf. Some have an aft-raking stick amidships to which the steering oar is affixed. Normally steps 2 masts, each setting a rectangular mat or canvas sail. Foremast stepped in the eyes, as is a single mast. Crew of 5-7, but some exceptionally large boats may employ 30 men. Reported lengths 9.8-10.4m, beam ca. 1.83m, depth 0.76m; in northern Kelantan, only ca. 5.5m long. Other recorded names: **kolek buatan barat, kolek buatan Siam, lohor** (in Pahang). Note also **jongkong-2**.

perahu Bugis *Singapore:* A local type that went by the same name as the Sulawesi (Celebes) traders (see **pinisi**), but the Singapore craft is a different vessel. Used extensively to transport pineapples to Singapore canneries. Sharp ends; nearly vertical stem and sternpost; wide, U-shaped cross section with flared sides; keel. Decked; some open amidships; hatch leads to galley forward of the mast; arched mat house aft accommodates crew. Single mast raked slightly aft. Boomed leg-of-mutton sail set to gunter yard, hoisted by 2 halyards. Crew of 4. Reported lengths 10.8-15.2m; e.g., length 10.8m, beam 3.8m, depth 1.7m; shallow draft. Spelling variant: **pra(h)u Bugis**

perahu (prahoe) djanggolan See **janggolan**
perahu (prahoe, praoe) djatèn See **jaten**
perahu (prahoe) djoeloeng See **julung-2**
perahu (prau) djukung See **jukung**
perahu (prahu) gebeng See **gubang-2**
perahu golekan See **golekan**
perahu gubang See **gubang-l, gubang-2**
perahu jalong-jalong See **julung-julung**
perahu jalur See **jalor**
perahu janggolan See **janggolan**
perahu (prahu) jolong-jolong, prao julung-julung See **julung-julung**
perahu (and prahoe, prau) kadjangan See **perahu kajangan**
perahu (prahoe) kagoena, perahu (proa) kaguna See **bangko**
perahu kajangan *Indonesia, W:* Transported merchandise and people on the waterways in the Palembang area of southeastern Sumatra; also reported as a fishing craft. Identified by a saddle-shaped mat roof (*kajang*) that covered all but the bow area and sloped down to the gunwales; might be in several telescoping sections. Dugout hull, truncated at the ends; sides raised by a wide strake; bottom flat athwartships, with fore-and-aft rocker. At the stern, the strake might be cut lower to provide for the triangular quarter rudder. Gunwale pieces swept up on each side to form a raised area for the helmsman and to support the stern awning. Light bamboo decking. Rowed. Reported lengths 11-15m; e.g., length 15m, beam 3m. Other recorded names: **dahoep, kadjangan, pekadjangan, perahoe kajoe agoeng, perahu** (also **prahoe, prau) kadjangan, perahu kaju agung, prahoe pekadjangan.** Note also **daoep-daoep.**
perahu (perahoe) kajoe agoeng, perahu kaju agung See **perahu kajangan**

perahu kakap *Peninsular Malaysia:* A narrow boat with high ends and low freeboard. Name variant: **kakap*.** Note also **kakap jĕram.**
perahu (praauw) karomon See **kromon**
perahu katir 1. *Indonesia:* Term given to an **outrigger canoe*,** *katir* meaning outrigger float. **a.** On the eastern part of the north coast of Java, the **perahu katir** is comparable to the double-outrigger **jukung*.** Distinguished by its western-style, leg-of-mutton-type sail. Bow curves up smoothly or is forked; deep sternpost rises sharply and may end in a point or be notched on the top. Flattened bottom with slight rocker. Washstrake along the sides. Two booms curve up after they cross the hull and then down to connect directly to the floats; floats extend well forward of the bow and flare outward. Bench-like quarter rudder support. Carved mast rest at stern; ends of hull decorated. Tall, slender mast stepped into a residual block on the bottom, close to the bow, stayed to ends of the forward outrigger booms. Mast rake adjusted by blocks wedged into the tabernacle-like support. Sail raised by a halyard run through a pully on the masthead; boom set at a high angle. Length ca. 4.6m, narrow. **b.** The Bawean peoples of Pulau Belitung (Billiton) off southeastern Sumatra obtain their fishing **katirs** from Pulau Bawean, north of Java. Sharp ends, the bow curving up to a deep notch above the waterline, the stern more erect and tall. Bottom flattened. Two booms cross the hull; the forward boom is secured beneath the gunwale and connects directly with the floats. The much heavier after boom curves upward and is lashed to an athwartship rod set into the hull; the separate connectives angle down to the floats. Bamboo floats toe in slightly. Quarter rudder braced against a bench-like fixture. Short mast stepped into a block, through a thwart forward. Sets a boomed rectangular or trapezoidal sail that cants up, being tacked down from the yard to the hull.

2. *Malaysia:* A **catamaran*.** Name variant: **perhau berkatir**
perahu (prahu) kepala belalang See **perahu kepala kelalang**
perahu kepala kelalang *Peninsular Malaysia:* Rounded figurehead, similar to a mantis or grasshopper head, characterizes this long, narrow boat. Used in Kelantan District in the northeast, mainly to carry rice. Broad bottom; sharp bow. Decked below water level; sides built up with planks; awning of palm leaves. Shallow draft. Other recorded names: **grasshopper-head boat, mantis-head boat, prahu kepala belalang**
perahu (prahoe, prau) kolek See **kolek-2, kolek lichang**
perahu lambo, perahu lambot See **lambo-1**
perahu lancha, perahu lantja See **lancha-4**
perahu (prahu) layar motor See **pinisi**
perahu (prahoe) lepa-lepa See **lepa-lepa**
perahu lepap See **lepap**
perahu (prahu) madjang, perahu (prahau) mahiang, perahu (prahoe) majang, perahu mayang See **mayang-1**
perahu ma' Siam See **Gulf of Siam trader**
perahu (prao, prau) mayang See **mayang-1**
perahu (prahu) nadé See **lambo-1**

perahu naga *Malaysia:* Two-masted boat of Malay rajahs that had a figurehead of a dragon (*naga*). Bow and stern rounded; galleries forward and aft; deckhouse. Rigged with square-headed dipping lugsails. Also paddled. Name variant: **dragon boat★**. Note also **sampan naga**.

perahu (praauw) padoeakan See **padewakang**

perahu (prahu) paduwang See **paduwang**

perahu (perahoe, prahoe, praoe) pajang See **perahu payang**

perahu (prahu) palari, perahu palari penis See **pinisi**

perahu pantat kedera See **lambo-1**

perahu payang *Indonesia, central:* **1.** Double-outrigger **fishing boat★** of the southwest coast of Java in the area of Pelabuhan (Wijnkoops) Bay. Uses the *payang*, a seine-type net. Plank-extended dugout hull; wales cover the outside of the seam. Sharp ends with tall, curved stem and sternpost. Two long and widely spaced booms rest atop the gunwales; at the float end, a stanchion curves down directly to the long bamboo float. Single mast sets an oblong sail. Length 12m, beam 1.25m, depth 0.5-0.7m.
2. On the northeast coast of Java, a plank-built boat with a large stem that is wide, flat, and recurves above the gunwale; post at the stern is lower and smaller. Boat also fishes with the *payang* net. Single mast sets a type of boomed, elongated lugsail. Crew of ca. 10-12. Spelling variants: **perahoe (perahu, prahoe, praoe) pajang**. See also **payang-2**.

perahu (praauw) pedoewang See **paduwang**

perahu (prahu) peduang See **beduang, paduwang**

perahu (prahoe) pekadjangan See **perahu kajangan**

perahu pemayang See **mayang-1**

perahu (prahu) pencalang See **pencalang**

perahu (praauw) pendjadjab See **perahu penjajap**

perahu (prahoe) pendjadjap See **penjajap-2**

perahu (proa) pendjaleng See **perahu penjaleng**

perahu (perau') pengayau See **bangkong**

perahu penjajap *Indonesia, W:* Small cargo vessel used along the Sumatra coast and around the island groups to the east. Popular also as a **houseboat★** with the Orang Laut peoples, who live by fishing for trepang and collecting seaweeds that produce agar-agar. Sharply built with straight, raking ends; gunwale strakes extend aft, terminating beyond the sternpost; low freeboard raised by mat or plank weatherboards. Bamboo lath decking supported by athwartship beams; mat house amidships. Hull oiled. Rowed and sailed; steered with lines attached to a rudder. Slender mast stepped amidships; stayed forward. Tall, narrow sail hung above the house. Other recorded names: **pendjadjab, perahu** (and **praauw**) **pendjadjab**. See also **penjajap-2**.

perahu penjaleng *Indonesia, central:* Double-outrigger cargo vessel reported from Java in the early 19th century. Plank-extended dugout; ends elongated; shield-shaped breakwater, with a sharp beak extending forward, enclosed the bow; sharp spur extended upward from the stern. Bottom flat amidships, with rocker toward the ends; wide "V" in cross section. Light platform laid across central part of the hull and for a short distance out along the sides. Two widely spaced

booms extended out each side; set parallel to the water for most of their distance, then turned down to attach directly to long, slender floats. Quarter rudder. Tripod mast stepped well forward. Elongated mat lugsail boomed at the foot. Also rowed, one group of oarsmen working from the outer part of the platform, the 2nd bank working from along the gunwale; employed a type of tholepin. Lengths 12-15m. Other recorded name: **(proa) pendjaleng**. Note also **penjaleng**.

perahu (praauw, prahoe) pentjalang See **pencalang**

perahu pinas *Peninsular Malaysia:* **Coaster★** built along the Trengganu River on the east coast from the mid-19th century; a few still operate. Traveled mainly to Bangkok and Ho Chi Minh City (Saigon) and to Singapore. Built along European lines with well-molded counter stern; clipper bow terminated in a characteristically upturned beak; good sheer; full turn of the bilges; straight sides. The straight-stemmed type is called **perahu pinas dogor**. Planked deck; 2 hatches cover hold; large mat deckhouse aft on most vessels; assorted smaller houses on others. Steered with rudder; tiller set ca. 15cm above the deck, being pushed away by the seated helmsman's feet and brought back by pulleys. **Schooner★**-rigged until ca. 1900 with long topmasts and short crosstrees; set jib-headed topsails; gaff sail brailed to the mast. Later used 2 large, polygonal Chinese lugsails strengthened with bamboo battens. Canvas or gunny sack jib sometimes set on long, bowsed-down bowsprit. Crew of 5-7. Mostly 18-21m long, 4.5-5.2m wide, and 2.1-2.4m deep. Other recorded names: **penes, perahu pinas gobel, pinas, pinas dogor (gobel** or **golok), Trengganu perahu pinas** (or **schooner**). Note also **perahu pinnace**. Further reference: **penis-1**

perahu pinas dogor, perahu pinas gobel See **perahu pinas**

perahu (prau) pinisi See **pinisi**

perahu pinnace *Peninsular Malaysia:* Small, 2-masted **coaster★** that transported rice along the east coast. Sharp clipper bow, strongly raked sternpost, considerable sheer, outboard rudder; long, downward-slanting tiller. Mainmast vertical, foremast raked forward. Set polygonal, battened Chinese lugsails. Long poles propelled the boats in and out of rivers. Crew of 6-8. Small size ca. 7.6m long, 1.8m wide. Note also **perahu pinas**.

perahu (perahoe, prahoe, praauw) poekat See **perahu pukat, sampan pukat**

perahu (praou) poukat See **sampan pukat**

perahu pukat *Indonesia/Malaysia/Singapore:* Vessel that carried cargo between the Riau Archipelago off east-central Sumatra and Singapore and along the Strait of Malacca until ca. 1860; sometimes engaged in piracy. A smaller and later variety, the **sampan pukat★**, engaged in deep-sea fishing, but terms used interchangeably. Sharp, raked bow; square counter stern, vertical sternpost; flat floors. Loose decking; house for passengers; seats along the sides for rowers. Open-sided room for the helmsman, who worked quarter rudders. Mainly rowed using 20-28 small-bladed oars. Also sailed, stepping 2 masts to which lugsails were set; mast struck when vessel rowed.

Crew of 30-40, mainly Chinese. Reported lengths 12.2-17.7m, widths 2-3m, depths 1.2-2.4m. Other recorded names: **p(e)rahoe poekat**, **praauw** (and **sampan**) **poekat**, **sampan poucatt**. Note also **kolek pukat**. Further reference: **sampan pukat**

perahu pukat payang See **payang-2**

perahu (prahoe) sagoer, (prahu) sagor, perahu sagur See **sagur**

perahu sasak *Indonesia, central:* A double-hulled craft used mainly for river crossings on the north-central coast of Java. Dugout hulls have flat bottoms that sweep up to inward-raking, blunt ends. Similar bulkheads located near the ends of each **canoe★**. Hulls joined by a woven platform laid amidships; bamboo-sided house may be added. Other recorded names: **praoe sasak, sasak, sasak tambangan**

perahu (prahoe) sekong See **sekong**

perahu séman *Indonesia, E:* General term for a double-**outrigger canoe★** of the Moluccan Islands. Ranges from a simple dugout hull to one planked up from a dugout keel piece. Two light booms attach to the floats (*séman*) by U-shaped connectives. May also sail. Crew of 2-3 when fishing. Length ca. 6m; width of plank-built boats ca. 1.4m, dugouts 0.75m wide. Other recorded names: **prahoe, prahu, praoe,** or **prau séman; prahoe semang, prau semban, séman**

perahu (prahoe) semang, prau semban See **perahu séman**

perahu Siam See **Gulf of Siam trader**

perahu (praauw) soepe, perahu (and **prahoe, prahu**) **sopé, prahu sopee** See **soppé**

perahu sopi *Indonesia, E:* Plank-built boat of the Aru Islands in the eastern end of the Malay Archipelago. Planks treenailed; heavy floors; stiff ribs inserted into planked-up hull; straight keel. Long, curving stem and sternpost rise well above the gunwales at the sharp ends. Open with a few thwarts, or decked with split bamboo. Generally has a quarter rudder, although some hang a rudder on the sternpost. May set a lateen sail, a triangular sail with a vertical gaff, or a rectangular gaff sail and jibs. Length ca. 7.6m. Spelling variant: **prahu sopi**. Note also **soppé**.

perahu sumbawa *Indonesia, W:* Small **dugout canoe★** that earned the name **thieves' boat**, although they appear to have engaged primarily in carrying local produce on inland waterways. Other recorded names: **praauw sumbawa, sampan sĕmbawa**

perahu (perau') tambang See **tambang, tambangan**

perahu (prahoe) tambangan See **tambangan**

perahu timbau See **perahu bĕlongkang**

perahu tinda *Indonesia, W:* Transported officials on southern Sumatran rivers. Dugout hull; truncated bow; flattened bottom; wide crossbeams. Cambered deck; washstrake raised the sides along after half. Central part protected by a wide awning (the *tinda*), which was supported by sturdy poles. Rowed. Name variant: **pentjalang**. Note also **pencalang**.

perahu tjompreng See **tjompreng-2**

perahu (praauw) tjompring See **tjompreng-1**

perahu (praauw) toop, perahu (and **prahoe**) **top** See **top**

perahu (prao, proa) volant See **wa lap**

perama **1.** *Greece:* Term applies to a hull shape, i.e., one having a sharp bow and similar stern. Dates to the Byzantine period; still carried cargo in the 1980s. Other hull features include a strong sheer; strongly raked, straight stem; slightly curved sternpost, flat floors, multiple keelsons; outboard rudder; decked. Characteristically, a bulkhead at bow creates a bow transom behind the stem; a similar bulkhead lies forward of the sternpost. Colorfully painted. Mainly stepped 2 masts of about equal height and were rigged as gaff **schooners★**, as **brigantines★**, or with a dipping lugsail forward and standing lugsail aft. Two headsails to a long, rising bowsprit. Now motorized with no sails. Reported lengths 16-31m; e.g., length overall 25m, on keel 20m, beam 6m, depth 2m. Spelling variants: **parama, peramo, perema**; pl. **peramata**

2. *Turkey:* **a.** Trader of the 17th-19th centuries that plied the Mediterranean. Marked sheer, rounded stem, sharp stern, straight keel, hold amidships. Set 2 large lugsails and 2 headsails to a long bowsprit. Reported lengths 14-15m; e.g., length 14.4m, beam 3.6m, depth 1.8m. Spelling variants: **bereme, pereme, perime, perm(a), prama, prema, preme**. **b.** A long, narrow, heavy type of **kayık★** that ferried passengers and light cargo on the Bosporus. Curved, raked stem. Rowed with 2 or 4 oars; also sailed. Spelling variants: **parme, perame, pereme**; pl. **peremeler**

peramata See **perama**

perame See **perama-2**

peramo See **perama-1**

perampok-laut See **padewakang**

peraouger See **pirogue**

perascaline See **palischermo-1**

perau' For Malay names beginning with the word **perau'**, see **perahu**.

pérau See **pe-2**

peraugua See **periauger**

perau' tambang See **tambang**

pereago See **pirogue**

pereauger See **periauger**

perehoe See **perahu-1**

perema, pereme See **perama-2**

peremeler See **perama-1**

perfume boat See **felucca-3**

pergantini, pergende See **brigantine**

peri See **pe-1, piperi**

periaga See **periagua, pirogue**

periago, periagoe See **periauger, pirogue**

periagua *West Indies:* Designated as a small **dugout canoe★**, generally by the Carib peoples, or as a large craft capable of carrying as many as 50 passengers or transporting artillery. The larger type, ca. 12m long, became extinct ca. 1800, and descriptions vary. Some reported to have been constructed of 2 tree trunks, others were plank-extended dugouts, the planks sewn on and pitched with bitumen. Some wholly or partly decked; a flat-pooped stern carved with an animal's head was reported. Stepped 1-3 masts plus a bowsprit and jib. Leg-of-mutton sails were noted. Also rowed, using 8-10 oars. Spelling variants: **peragio, periaga, pirágua★**. See also **periauger, pirogue**.

periaguay See **pirogue**

periaguer See **periauger, pirogue**

periamaram See **periya maram**

periauger *United States:* **1.** Word widely used in colonial times for a variety of craft. Originally probably large, sailing **dugout canoes★**. Some were fast under oars, for they are known to have challenged a **whaleboat★**. Varied in size. In the early 1800s, some were built as **gunboats★** for the navy. Almost flat bottom; rounded bilges. Length 14.6m, beam 5.5m, hold depth 1.7m.
2. Term frequently applied to a boat rigged with 2 masts about the same height, sometimes raked in opposing directions, and carrying no headsails. Foremast stepped near the bow. Sails generally loose-footed or mainsail boomed; short gaffs.
3. In New York Harbor, a type of **periauger** served as a passenger **ferry★** from the mid-18th century until ca. 1830. High-sided, **scow★**-like craft; keelless, flat bottom. Some had a cabin aft for passengers and were decked forward. Used leeboards. One or 2-masted; also could be rowed. 1788 **ferry** ca. 9m long; shallow draft. Other recorded names: **New Jersey** (or **New York**) **pirogue, pirogue ferry**
4. Periaugers continued to work during the 19th century in the New York Bay area as sailing **lighters★** or **market boats★**. Also reported in use on the Mississippi River. Flat bottom with no keel; probably sharpended; open or decked at the ends; sometimes used oval leeboards. **Schooner★**-rigged; also employed sweeps. Reported lengths 15.5-19m; one in New York was 19m long, 7m wide, and 1.5m deep; shallow draft.
5. In the southeastern United States, a general freight boat used from Georgia north to the North Carolina sounds and the associated tributary rivers. Transported produce, hogsheads of tobacco, animals between plantations, and passengers. Worked mainly from the early 18th into the early 19th century; some served as military craft (see **scout boat**). Proportions varied, with the beamier and deeper boats used in more exposed waters. Constructed of several shaped logs; some were a log split down the middle with several boards inserted; some were planked up from a log base. Most flat-bottomed, some round-bottomed; sharp bow; transom stern; washstrakes often ran along the sides. Cabin aft, forecastle, generally open waist. Two unstayed masts; sails probably sprit, leg-of-mutton, or gaff-headed. Also rowed by as many as 12 oarsmen and poled. Reported lengths 9-18m, widths 1.2-4.3m.
Spelling variants: **peeryaugo, peraugua, pereauger, periago(e), periagua★, periaguer, periaugo, perigua, perriauger, perry-auger, petitaugre, pettiagua, pettiaguer, pettiauger, pettiaugre, petty-(y)auger, piragua★, pirogue★, pittyauger**

periauger gig See **cat-yawl**

periaugo See **periauger**

perieago, perigua See **pirogue**

perime See **perama-2**

periogue, perioque See **pirogue**

periperi See **piperi**

périssoire *France:* **Canoe★** or **kayak★** that comes in a variety of models. Mainly employ a double-bladed paddle, used either sitting or standing. Decked or semi-decked. Long, narrow, light. Note also **loquette**.

periyago See **pirogue**

periya maram *India, E:* Log **raft★** used in net fishing along the Coromandel coast. The 2 middle logs of the 4 that compose the **raft** extend as much as 1.22m beyond the stern to form an area for the paddling helmsman. Forward, the marginal logs taper to form a bow, with an addition of 2 wedge-shaped pieces that turn up sharply. **Raft** pieces lashed together at each

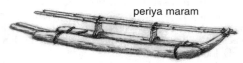
periya maram

end. Bottom has rocker. Fixed to one side is a rowing rail of bamboo on which a protective strake is lashed; held at proper height by a stretcher. Rowers sit on small, transverse seats; 1-2 paddle on the opposite side. When working the *thuri valai* net, the **raft** is assisted by a **chinna maram**, which has only 3 logs and a single bow piece; crew of 2. If a small sail is set by the **periya maram**, the **chinna maram** ties alongside the larger craft. **Periya maram** lengths 7.6-7.8m, widths 1-1.07m; **chinna maram** length 6.4m, width 0.7m. Other recorded names: **periamaram, thuri valai catamaran**. See also **catamaran-12**.

perm, perma See **perama-2**

permajang See **mayang-1**

permit boat See **panshi**

pernacce See **gozzo**

perné See **garoupeira**

pēro See **pirogue-4**

perogue, peroqua, peroque, perriago, perriagua, perriaguer See **pirogue**

perriauger See **periauger, pirogue**

perriaugre, perriaugua, perriawger See **pirogue**

Perrine See **Barnegat sneakbox**

perrogue See **pirogue**

perro-tvpékse See **flatboat-5**

perry-auger See **periauger**

peru See **lancha-1, perua**

perua *Brazil, E:* Large, open, plank-extended dugout that transports produce and firewood from rivers in the Rio de Janeiro area. Blunt bow enables the boat to nose onto shore for loading and unloading. Large square sail, hung from the middle of the yard, set to a mast stepped through the center thwart. Stay and 2 braces, one for each end of the yard, fasten to the stemhead. Halyard extends aft to the helmsman, as do 2 sheets. Also rowed or poled, the crew standing nearly in the bow; more recently towed. A large size from Campos is called **prancha★**. Other recorded names: **barco da roça, peru**. See also **lancha-1**.

perumwaral pathei See **paruwa-2**

perý See **piperi**

peryago See **pirogue**

pesäpaatti See **knärr-2**

pescantina *Italy, NE:* Boat of the Adige River. Sharp ends, the stern finer; ends curve and rake up to a point. Flat bottom; flaring sides to the top strake, then vertical. Decked at ends; small steering well on the port side. Steered with a wide-bladed rudder on the port quarter. Mast stepped at end of foredeck. Length 30.38m, beam 4.72m, depth 1.33m. Name variant: **barca pescantina**

peschereccio See **fishing boat, trawler**

peschereccio a cianciolo See **seine boat-1b**

peschereccio con lenze e canne See **tuna boat-2**

peschereccio con palangeri See **longliner-1**

peschereccio gamberi See **shrimper**

peschereccio per sciabeca See **seine boat-1a**

péso See **pe-2**

pesqueresse See **sardinier breton**

pesquero See **fishing boat**

pesquero al cerco See **seine boat-1**

pet See **rua pet**

petača See **patache**

petacchi See **petacchio**

petacchio *Italy:* Fast 17th- and 18th-century 4-masted vessel used as an advance guard and scouting vessel; 4-5 accompanied a **fleet⋆**. Carried up to 20 cannons. Relatively small. Spelling variants: **pettachio**; pl. **petacchi**. Note also **patache**.

petach, petache, petaix, petaknon, petas See **patache**

Petchili jonque See **Kiangsu trader**

Peter boat *England, SE:* **1.** Beamy, double-ended boat with a history of fishing in the Thames River and Estuary, possibly from the 14th until the beginning of the 20th century. Clinker-built; fuller stern on those below London Bridge. Stem curved; sternpost usually less rounded and raked; steep rise to the floors; curved keel; flat sheer. Some later boats transom-sterned.

Peter boat-1

Decked forward and aft; waterways sat low along the sides; live well amidships; canvas shelter abaft the mast on the larger boats. Outboard rudder; small tiller. Upriver boats mostly rowed or set a spritsail and foresail, but later some added a sprit mizzen. On the lower river, they originally used a loose-footed gaff mainsail and 2 headsails, evolving into the **bawley⋆**. Sprit held high and when detached, sail was rolled around the mast. Heavy oars; rectangular loom inboard of the oarlocks, which were built into top strake, there being no gunwale. Crew of 2. Dimensions above London Bridge ranged from less than 3.66m to 5.49m in length; e.g., length 4.27m, width 1.5m, depth 0.6m. Below the bridge, they ranged from 5.49-9.14m long; e.g., length 5.8m, beam 2.13m, depth 1.0m. Note also **Leigh pink**.

2. A small, **bawley**-type boat imported into the Mersea area in Essex in the 1880s. **Sloop⋆**- or **cutter⋆**-rigged. Further reference: **Medway doble**

Peterboro canoe See **Peterborough canoe**

Peterborough canoe *Canada, SE:* Plank **canoe⋆** built in the Peterborough area of south-central Ontario from the 1850s. Principally built by the Peterborough and Canadian Canoe companies until the 1930s. Initially constructed of cedar or basswood; 3 thin planks per side, later 4. Curved stem and sternpost; flat floors, slight rocker toward the ends; keel strip; soft turn of the bilges; ends and sides have slight tumble home. Planks clench-nailed to bent ribs, set 15cm apart; battens covered the inter-rib spaces. Some rigged for sailing. Length overall 4.8m, beam 0.83m, depth 0.3m. Spelling variant: **Peterboro canoe**. Note also **Rice Lake canoe**.

Peterhead boat **1.** *Canada, N:* Two prototypes were built for the Hudson's Bay Company at Peterhead, Scotland, and transferred to Fort Chimo in northern Quebec Province (either in 1911 or 1919) for use by the Eskimos in seal and walrus hunting and as supply boats. Subsequent boats built in Newfoundland and Nova Scotia and recently at Selkirk in southern Manitoba. Carvel-planked; raked stem, hollow entrance; wide, U-shaped transom; moderate rise to the floors. Decked; cabins forward and aft; large hold amidships. Now generally has an engine and sail; originally only sailed, setting a boomed gaff mainsail and jib, even though sometimes called a **Peterhead schooner**. Reported lengths 9.7-12.8m. Other recorded names: **ikkumaligdjuark, naparotatualik, Peterhead launch, umiardjuk**

2. *Scotland:* Used in the herring fisheries until about the mid-19th century. Clinker-built; hollow lines forward and aft; steep rise to the floors; straight keel. Lightly curved stem, mildly raked sternpost. Undecked. Set 2 lugsails. Crew of 5. Length 11.4m, beam 4.1m, depth 1.4m, 5t disp.

Peterhead launch, Peterhead schooner See **Peterhead boat**

Petersburg boat See **mountain boat-1b**

petiaguay, petiaugre See **pirogue**

petile See **patela**

petit bateau de dragage See **bâche-2**

petit canot French term for a **jolly boat⋆** or **dinghy⋆**. Also a **ship's boat⋆** of an 18th-century French **man-of-war⋆** (see **canot-2**).

pe-ti tch'ouan See **Amoy fisher, Fukien trader, pai ti chuan**

petitaugre See **periauger**

petite goélette *Canada, E:* Small fishing **schooner⋆** that worked off northeastern New Brunswick from the late 19th into the early 20th century. Varied somewhat in design, but generally had a raked stem; straight, raked transom; deep drag to keel, narrow outboard rudder. Aft-raking masts, topmast on mainmast. Boomed gaff sails, jib to short bowsprit, main staysail. Reported lengths 9.5-18m, mostly 10.4-11.6m; widths 3.5-4.4m; to 21rt. Name variant: **petite goélette du Nord Est**

petite goélette du Nord Est See **petite goélette**

pēt kōsā See **kosha**

petroler, petrolero See **tanker**
pétroleuse See **pinasse-1a**
pétrolier, petroliera See **tanker**
Petschili See **Kiangsu trader**
pettachio See **petacchio**
pettiagua See **periaguer, pirogue**
pettiaguay See **pirogue**
pettiaguer See **periauger**
pettiauger, pettiaugre See **periauger, pirogue**
pettiaugua, petty-auga See **pirogue**
petty-auger See **periauger, pirogue**
petty augre, petty-oager See **pirogue**
petty-yauger See **periauger**
peturusan *Indonesia, central:* **Fishing boat★** of eastern
    Java that used the *turu* net. Boat similar to the
    alis-alis★.
peu See **oánga**
peúba jangada See **jangada-2**
peydè See **piyade**
pfahl-ever See **Pfahl-Ewer**
Pfahl-Ewer *Germany, NW:* Pole-masted, square-sailed
    fishing boat★ of the lower Elbe River area; the larger
    types worked out into the North Sea. Some built to
    carry cargo. Reported from the 17th to the end of the
    19th century. Sharp ends, stem curved, sternpost strong-
    ly raked; hull fuller forward; some had a transom stern
    above the sternpost. Flat bottom; garboard strakes
    flared out in a straight line; top strake vertical. Strong
    sheer, especially toward the high bow; low amidships;
    long, narrow leeboards. Wet well (**Bünn-Ewer**) abaft
    the mast. Originally open, later decked almost to the
    mast; cabin below. Outboard rudder; forward edge fol-
    lowed rake of the sternpost, after part less raked; tiller
    slotted over rudderhead. Pole mast (*Pfahlmast*) stepped
    in thwart just forward of amidships; forestay to stem-
    head, backstay to starboard side. On some, mast raked
    aft. Set a tall square sail; bowlines to stemhead; multi-
    ple reef points on upper half; 1-2 foresails. Crew of 2-
    3. Reported lengths 13.2-18.6m; e.g., length 13.86m,
    beam 4.46m, depth 1.58m, draft 1.0m. Other recorded
    names: **Blankeneser-Ewer, Blankeneser Pfahl-Ewer,
    Finkenwerder Pfahl-Ewer, Paalever, pfahl-ever,
    Pohleeber, pole ewer;** pl. **Pfahl-Ewern.** Note also **Ewer.**
Pfahl-Ewern See **Pfahl-Ewer**
Pfahlgaleass See **Jachtgaleass**
Pfahlkuff, Pfahlmastkuff See **Kuff**
Pfahlmastschoner See **schooner**
Pfennigfähre See **Handlomme**
Pferdeschiff See **Leibschiff**
Pferdplätte See **Plätte-1**
phai See **pai**
phang chun **1.** *Indonesia, W/Peninsular Malaysia/
    Singapore:* Engaged in seine net fishing in the Riau
    and Lingga Archipelagoes and on the southern coasts
    of the Malay Peninsula. Probably extinct. Very narrow
    and sharp-ended; originally carvel-planked on a
    dugout base, later built up from a broad plank bottom.
    False keel; strong bottom rocker that rises above the
    water at each end; top sheer similar; rounded bottom
    curved up smoothly into flaring sides. Ends raked, the
    bow more than the stern; flattened stem and sternpost
    terminated above the gunwale. Fitted with ribs, either

naturally grown or of irregularly shaped pieces; forward 2 extended above the gunwale to serve as spar
rests; open. Shipped a deep rudder when sailing, and
at times, a crew member would serve as ballast, hanging to windward from a rope secured to the mast.
Generally rowed. When sailed, stepped 1-2 short
masts. On the single-masted boats, the mast was
stepped amidships or about one-third in from the bow;
on the 2-masted type, the foremast was close to the
bow and the mainmast amidships. Some used irregularly shaped spritsails with the luff of the foresail forward of the mast and tacked to the stem; others set a
type of wide lugsail. Crew of ca. 7. Reported lengths
9-16m; e.g., length 11.4m, beam 1.45m, depth 0.6m.
Other recorded names: **bang choon, Chinese seine
boat, jalur, kolek China, net boat★, sampan★, seine-
net boat, Teochew seine boat**
2. *Peninsular Malaysia:* At Penang on the northwest
coast, the **phang ch'un** was a 2-masted trader. Raked
ends; a broad, convex counter supported a gallery;
some small vessels had a mock counter and more vertical ends. Large vessels had yin and yang symbols on
the stern. Hatches forward of and abaft the mainmast.
Mainmast stepped almost amidships; taller foremast.
Large, battened lugsails. Reported lengths 15-24m,
widths 3.7-8.3m, inside depths 1.5-2.7m. Name variant: **tongkang★**
3. *Singapore:* Local Chinese use the term **phang ch'un**
for most seagoing sailing vessels.
pharao See **prow-1**
phi-fa tzŭ See **bi fa zi**
Philippine galleon See **galleon-3**
p'hineez See **pinash**
phing-ti ch'uan See **ping di chuan**
phinisi See **pinisi**
phoquier See **sealer**
piade, piadet See **piyade**
piakka *Suriname, E:* Expanded and built-up **dugout
    canoe★** used for coastal fishing off the Maroni River.
    Hollowed log expanded with fire and held in position
    with thwarts; trimming boards added to the plank-
    extended sides. High, squared bow; planked, truncat-
    ed stern. Propelled by paddle, sail, or outboard motor.
    Reported lengths 3.7-10.7m.
piata See **peata**
piątak, piątkowy galer See **galar**
piato, piatta, piatte See **peata**
piatto Italian term for a flat-bottomed vessel. See also
    peata.
piattone, piattoni See **peatone**
picard **1.** *British Isles:* Initially, in the 14th-15th cen-
    turies, the term was associated mainly with the herring
    fisheries. The **pickards** would carry salt to the **fleet★**
    and return with the catch. Crew of 4. Probably sailed
    employing a single mast. Irish **picards** were probably
    less than 12t. Later, their primary function appears to
    have been lightering cargo to and from ships. Sailed,
    stepping at least 2 masts. Those carrying grain on the
    River Severn in the 16th century were reported as 15-
    36t burden. A modified type, the **lighterman,** helped
    load and unload ships on the River Dee in western
    England into the 18th century.

2. *France, N:* River and canal **barge★**, mainly of the Seine, Oise, and Aisne Rivers. Compartmented to carry sewage. Carvel-planked, flat bottom; straight, vertical sides; rounded ends. Plumb, vertical stem and sternpost; cutaway forefoot. Decked; cabin house at stern or abaft amidships. Very wide rudder with fin-like extension that could be raised when necessary; very long tiller. Early vessels might raise a square sail. Reported cap. 250-375t. Other recorded names: **bateau picard, chaland d'Oise, merdeux** (pl.) Spelling variants: **pekart, pic(c)arde, picarte, pi(c)kard, pi(c)ker, pycar(d), pyckarde, py(c)ker, pykard, pykkert**

picarde See **picard**

picaron See **picaroon**

picaroon Small pirate vessel of the 17th-18th centuries, especially in the Caribbean area. In Chesapeake Bay, picarooners sided with the British during the Revolutionary War, and their ships effectively blocked shipping on the bay. Spelling variants: **picaron, pic-caroon, pickaroon, pickero(o)on, Pikaroon**

picarooner *England, SW:* Small, lug-rigged **beach boat★** from Clovelly on the south shore of the Bristol Channel. Fished for herring in winter and carried passengers in summer; popular in the late 19th century. Carvel-planked with grown frames; sharp bow, plumb stem, fairlead block on stem; heart-shaped transom, painted white. Flat floors; fine run. Many half-decked. Outboard rudder; tiller slotted through rudderhead. Dipping lug foresail; standing lug mizzen sheeted to an outrigger; some had stern sheets. Also rowed; sculling notch in transom. Crew of 2. Reported lengths 4-6m.

picarte, piccarde See **picard**

piccaroon See **picaroon**

pich-li See **pith-lo**

pickard See **picard**

pickaroon See **picaroon**

picker See **picard**

pickeron, pickeroon See **picaroon**

picket boat Fast, naval motor **launch★** that stands guard in a harbor or close inshore. Some employed for reconnaissance in advance of the **fleet★**. Those attached to the British navy are carried aboard 1st class ships. Other recorded names: **guard boat★, patrol boat★, Patrouillenboot, Sicherungsboot, Vorpostenboot (Vp-Boot), Wachboot**

pick-up boat See **packer**

picot, picoteur See **picoteux**

picoteuse See **chaloupe-6**

picoteux *France, N:* Flat-bottomed, lug-rigged **fishing boat★** of the western Normandy coast that dates at least to the early 18th century; modern **picoteux** are motorized. Often fished for *picot* or flounder. Mainly clinker-built with broad strakes; bluff bows; sharply curved, salient stem, recurved on top; rounded or sharp stern, some more recent boats have transoms; strongly raked sternpost. Moderate sheer, rising at the bow; narrow, almond-shaped bottom; slack bilges. Washboards removed while fishing or rowing; small boats open, larger decked. Rudder extended below the bottom on some; short tiller. Sail plan varied: lugsails on a foremast stepped in the eyes, on an aft-raking mainmast,

and on a small mizzenmast stepped outside the stern; others had a large lug mainsail in the bow and a small lug mizzen; occasionally a lug mainsail was set to a mast a little forward of amidships plus a mizzen; or a standing lugsail with topsail and 1-2 headsails. All

picoteux

employed a jib to a long bowsprit. A small spritsail is used on the Orne River near Caen, where they transport sand (**picoteux sablonniers** or **sabliers**). Also rowed, the oars working between tholepins. Crew of 1-3. Reported lengths 4.2-7.9m, widths ca. 1.18-2.99m, depths 0.62-2.2m. Other recorded names: **picot(eur), sablonnier**. See also **camin**.

picoteux sabliers, picoteux sablonniers See **picoteux**

piece See **fleet-4, timber raft-3**

pielaghi See **pielago**

pielago *Italy, E:* **1.** **Coaster★** of the Adriatic. Considered to be a type of **trabaccolo★** from the 17th to the mid-19th century, the terms essentially synonymous in this period. Worked until the early 20th century, many fishing on the Istrian and Dalmatian coasts. Full bow, curved stem, some with cutaway forefoot; round counter stern, flat floors; sheer swept up at bow. Outboard rudder, some extending well below the bottom and above the gunwale; tiller. Decked, central hatch, poop deck. Two or 3 masts, the foremast either vertical or raked forward. Jibs to a long, rising bowsprit. Early vessels set lateen sails; later vessels used a lug foresail and gaff mizzen, both boomed. Crew of 8 when fishing. Reported lengths 16-19m; e.g., length 17.3m, beam 5.24m, depth 2.26m; most under 100t.

2. A **tartana★** engaged in fishing with a *parangalo* (*palangrese*) net. Teams with a **topo★**; operation requires crew of 7 and a boy. Works out of the Lagoon of Venice, especially from Chioggia. Also reported engaging in sponge fishing off Lampedusa Island in the central Mediterranean. Open boat with a flat bottom. Reported lengths 6-9m.

Spelling variants: **pielego**; pl. **pielaghi, pieleghi**. Note also **pelig**. Further reference: **trabaccolo**

pieleghi, pielego See **pielago**

pien-tan, pien-tzŭ See **bian zi**

pi-fa, pi-fa tzŭ See **bi fa zi**

pig boat 1. Name sometimes given to a **submarine** by its crew.

2. *Canada/United States, north-central:* A popular term on the Great Lakes for iron or steel, round-decked or whaleback cargo **steamers** of the late 19th century. The vessels were able to run the St. Lawrence River rapids; some also worked along the east coast. Flat floors, spoon bow, raked stern. Towed or self-propelled. 1890 ship 83m long, 11m wide. Other recorded names: **turtleback**, **whaleback***. Note also **schooner-barge-2**.

3. *China, SE:* Cargo boat of the Zhu Jiang (Pearl River), initially carrying pigs downriver to Hong Kong, and more recently rice to the Guangdong (Kwangtung) hinterland. Square-ended, straight-sided hull. Open aft, arched house forward. Two masts stepped fairly close together, forward mast taller. Set tall, rectangular, battened sails. Also employed long oars. Crew of 2. Further references: **grisbåt**, **yao wang chuan**

piggskuta See **roslagsskuta**

pih-tow chuen See **cao chuan-3**

piicooianiwoot See **crooked canoe**

piitau See **waka pitau**

pikard See **picard**

Pikaroon See **picaroon**

piker See **picard**, **Stornoway yawl**

pilang See **vinta**

pilau *Indonesia:* The pronunciation used by local Chinese for the Malay generic term **perahu***. See also **padow**.

pilchard boat See **West Cornish lugger**

pilchard driver See **drifter**, **East Cornish lugger**, **West Cornish lugger**

pilchard seine boat See **seine boat-3**

pile driver 1. A floating support for the equipment used in driving pilings into the mud for a dock, retaining wall, etc. Early craft often twin-hulled with a tripod on each hull to support the pile hammer; hammer might be activated by a waterwheel. Now activated by steam or air pressure. Other recorded names: **bateau sonnette**, **battipalo**, **floating** (or **pontoon**) **pile driver**, **pålkran**, **pile driving barge**, **Ramme**, **Rammponton**, **Rammprahm**, **Schwimmramme**, **sonnette flottante** (or **nautique**)

2. A ship that characteristically pounds heavily when pitching. Other recorded names: **bâtiment canard**, **canard** See also **pålpråm**, **pound net scow**.

pile driving barge See **pile driver-1**

'pililim See **kaloa**

piling raft See **timber raft-2b**

pilobote *Spain, Balearic Islands:* **Schooner*** that carried oranges to Marseille and other parts of the Mediterranean. Clipper bow, counter stern. White hull, poop decorated in blue and gold. Rigged fore-and-aft; some 3-masted. Originally lateen-rigged. Employed an auxiliary. Extinct. Other recorded names: **balancela***, **balancelle***, **majorquin**, **pailebote***

pilot boat Vessel that ferried pilots to and from incoming and outbound ships. May be anchored off a port, channel, or canal, transferring the pilot from a **launch***, or a vessel from a shore-based pilot station may go alongside. Local conditions and working distance offshore greatly affected vessel size and design. Pilots working inside harbors or rivers go to a ship by **launch** when needed; **pilot boats** working offshore have full accommodations for as many as 30 pilots. Generally distinctively marked. Prior to the 20th century, it was not unusual for several **pilot boats** to approach a ship, each offering its services. In some strategic locations, early **pilot boats** would carry company orders informing a particular ship to which port it should proceed. Now motorized, but early vessels sailed. Variously rigged, but mainly as **schooners*** or **cutters***; generally heavily canvassed. Selected name variants: **barca (di) piloti**, **barco** (or **lancha**) **del práctico**, **barco de pilotos**, **bateau pilote***, **battello di piloti**, **battello pilota**, **bote de práctico**, **chaloupe pilote**, **embarcação de pilotos**, **embarcation prático**, **imbarcazione pilota**, **lodsbåd***, **loodsboot**, **loodsvaartuig***, **Loots-Jolle**, **losbåt***, **lotsbåt**, **Lotsenboot**, **Lotsenfahrzeug**, **Lotsenjacht**, **Lotsenjolle**, **Lotsen(versetz) schiff**, **Lotsenyacht**, **lotskutter***, **lotsmanskiy bot**, **nave pilota**, **pailabot***, **pailebote***, **palabot**, **pilot cutter**, **pilot(e)-bot**, **pilote-both**, **pilotina**, **pilotine**, **pilot schooner***, **pilot vessel**. Note also **Boston pilot schooner**, **canoe-9**, **catraia-1**, **cutter-4**, **lightship**, **paat**, **Sandy Hook pilot schooner**, **Swansea pilot schooner**, **Virginia pilot schooner**.

pilot boat model *United States, E:* Term sometimes given to the fast **schooners*** developed in lower Chesapeake Bay in the early 19th century for use as offshore **pilot boats***. The type was also used by New York and Boston pilots and was popular with privateers. Distinguishing feature was the lack of ornamental features at the bow and very low freeboard. Name variant: **Chesapeake Bay pilot boat**. Note also **Virginia model**, **Virginia pilot schooner**.

pilot-bot See **pilot boat**

pilot canoe See **pilot yawl**

pilot coble See **Hartlepool pilot coble**

pilot cutter See **cutter-4**, **pilot boat**

pilote-bot, **pilote-both** See **pilot boat**

pilot galley See **Deal galley**

pilot gig See **Cornish gig**, **pilot yawl**, **Yarmouth pilot gig**

pilotina, **pilotine** See **pilot boat**

pilot lightschip See **lightship**

pilot punt See **punt-9**

pilot schooner *United States, SE:* Pilot service was well established at ports from South Carolina to northern Florida by the mid-18th century. Sailed until the early 20th century. Most were fast, weatherly **schooners*** that sailed out to meet incoming ships. Occasionally carried passengers and light freight on coastwise runs; in the mid-19th century, many became **privateers***. Decked, cockpit; shallow, square-tucked stern; rudder came up through the counter. Early boats carried the pilot and an apprentice, the latter returning to port alone after transferring the pilot. 1760s boats reported as 8.5-9.7m long on keel; by mid-19th century, vessels reported as 15-18m on keel. Note also **pilot boat**.

pilot skiff *United States, SE:* Used in mullet fishing from the exposed beaches on the North and South Carolina coasts during the 19th century. Lapstrake construction; round bottom; keel; square or sharp stern. Steered with an oar. Reported lengths 7.6-8.5m, widths 1.2-1.8m, depth ca. 0.5m. Note also **mullet boat-2a**. Further reference: **Yarmouth pilot gig**

pilot vessel See **pilot boat**

pilot yawl *United States:* Shuttled pilots between the **pilot boat**★ and the vessel being piloted. Designation varied with the port: those in Boston were sometimes called **pilot canoes**; on the west coast, they were called **pilot gigs**. Rowed to and from the client **schooner**★ or **steamer** until the mid-20th century; thereafter the boat type changed, though it was still called a **yawl**★. Round bottom, the amount of deadrise varying with the length-to-beam ratio. Mainly lapstrake or a combination of lapstrake and carvel; west coast boats carvel. Keel, relatively plumb stem, wide transom stern. Rowed single-banked by 2 men. Reported lengths 4.3-5.3m, beam 1.8-1.9m. Note also **Boston pilot schooner, Sandy Hook pilot schooner**. Further reference: **beach yawl**

pilu, pilur See **padow**

pinaça See **pinaza, pinnace**

pinacce, pinaccia, pinaccio, pinace See **pinnace**

pinacea *Mediterranean:* Small, oared boat with 5-6 rowing benches. Constructed of spruce. See also **pinnace**.

pinanyo See **sibidsibiran**

pinardier *France, S:* **Tanker**★ that transports wine, especially on the Canal du Midi. Note also **wine ship**.

pinas *Papua New Guinea:* Pidgin-English term for a **motor boat**★. See also **jacht-3**, **perahu pinas**, **pinash, pinisi, pinnace**.

pinasa See **pinnace**

pinas dogor, pinas gobel, pinas golok See **perahu pinas**

pinash *Bangladesh/India:* Flat-bottomed vessel of the **badjra**★ type used by English merchants and planters for short trips and for pleasure on Bengali rivers. Most of hull covered by a house; living quarters aft, servants forward. Early 19th-century **pinashes** were square-rigged,

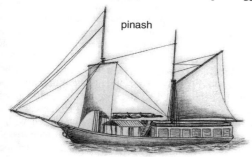

pinash

usually as **brigs**★; later adopted large gaff sails on the 2 masts, the forward mast taller; keel. Rowed when necessary, using as many as 16 oars. Crew of 12-20. Reported lengths 12-15m; shallow draft. Spelling variants: **peenus, penisse, p'hineez, pinas**★, **pinish, pinnace**★

Pinass See **pinnace**

pinasschip See **pinnace-2**

pinasse 1. *France, SW:* **a. Canoe**★-shaped **fishing boat**★, especially in the Bassin d'Arcachon. Dates from at least the mid-16th century; last working boats under sail in the early 1930s; motorized **pinasses** have been

modified considerably and go by the names **pinasse à moteur, pinasse automobile**, and **demi-bâtarde**. The sailing **pinasse** originally clinker-built, later of light carvel construction. Early flat bottom evolved to flat floors amidships and a V-bottom at bow and stern.

pinasse-1a

Flared sides; on some, narrow side decks extended beyond the gunwales. Low sheer amidships, raised at bow and stern with maximum beam aft of amidships; rudder followed sternpost curve and extended well below the bottom; also used a daggerboard. Decked at ends. Mast inserted through thwart, and longitudinal and lateral rake could be modified by placing the mast heel pin into various holes in the step. Lugsail sheeted to the stern, passed through the top gudgeon, and secured by the pintle. Also rowed, using 2-3 pairs of oars. Crew of 2-3 in the bay, 5-8 at sea, 14-15 when sardine fishing. Reported lengths 6.5-14m; e.g., length 8m, beam 1.0m, depth 0.6m; shallow draft. A small **pinasse**, called **pinasse de Parc** or **pétroleuse**, works oyster beds in the lagoons; small motor, although sailed while oystering. Other recorded names: **bâtarde, pinasse d'Arcachon**; **pinassote** (local term for a small, non-motorized **pinasse**). Note also **pinasson**. **b.** Long, narrow vessel that carried pilgrims from Bayonne to Santiago de Compostela, in northwest Spain, from at least the 15th to the 19th century. Clinker-built with a sharp stern. Decked; cabin located in the central part. Rowed and sailed; square sail set to a mast stepped in the forward part of the vessel. Spelling variants: **espinace, espinasse**. **c.** On the lower Adour River, a similar vessel of the same general period transported passengers, especially during the 17th and 18th centuries. Clinker-planked; rounded sides, blunt bow and stern, curved stem, straight sternpost, probably a flat bottom. Outboard rudder; tiller. Open-sided cabin amidships. Square sail set to a mast well forward. Rowed by 4 oarsmen forward of the mast, each manning a single oar. Lengths ca. 7-9m. **2.** *France, W:* Flat-bottomed, motorized vessel that served as a **mother ship**★ in the mussel culture industry in the Pertuis Breton, an embayment north of La Rochelle. Sharp bow; very wide, square stern; cabin house forward. Later types have a derrick to help in handling the stakes, the baskets of young mussels, and the nets full of harvested mussels. Towed 1-2 **yoles**★ and carried 1-4 **accons**★; these small boats are used for the actual planting and harvesting operations. Reported lengths 12-15m; e.g., length 15m, beam 5m, draft loaded 0.48m.

3. *Morocco, Atlantic coast:* **Schooner***- or **sloop***-rigged boat used by privateers of Salé. Length 15.2m, beam 3.7m.

Further references: **barque Djenné, pinnace-2**

pinasse à moteur, pinasse automobile, pinasse d'Arcachon, pinasse de Parc See **pinasse-1a**

pinasson *France, W:* A **dory***-type boat carried aboard motorized **fishing boats*** and **pinasses***, from St. Nazaire southward along the coast. Assists in setting sardine nets; 5-12 boats may be carried. Name variant: **doris***

pinassote See **pinasse-1a**

pinaza *Spain:* **1.** A light, 17th-century rowing/sailing vessel that had 3 masts, a high bow, and a square stern. Length ca. 40m, beam 7m.

2. An old **fishing boat*** (especially for sea bream) or **coaster*** of the Cantábrica coast of northern Spain. Undecked; flat bottom. Length ca. 20m; narrow.

3. The Basque **pinazas** ranged from 4-man, 8-oared, 10m-long boats that hunted whales to 16m-long vessels that sailed to northwestern Spain and Ireland with a crew of 14.

Spelling variant: **pinaça**. See also **pinnace**.

pinazza See **pinnace**
pinchi See **pink-2**
pinck See **pink-5**
pincke See **pink-1, pink-5**
pinco See **pink-2**
pindgiapiap See **penjajap-3**
pindis See **pinnace**
pindjajap See **penjajap-3**
pinease See **pinnace**
pine boat See **bote de pinho**
pinello See **penelle**
pinesse See **pinnace**
pinewoł, pinewuł See **shitlats**
pingarde See **pripri**
ping di chuan *China, E:* One of the types used in coastal defense by Fujian (Fukien) provincial authorities; cited in the mid-18th century. Flat bottom; hull compartmented into as many as 15 sections; bow transom; high, overhanging poop; strong sheer. Decked; high bulwarks sheltered the guns. Rudder stock came up inboard; also used a bow sweep. Oculi on the bows. Set rectangular, battened sails; the small foremast stepped well forward, the mainmast amidships. A 3rd mast stood on the port side of the poop. Mainmast in a tabernacle and had a crow's nest. Reported lengths 12.8-14.6m, widths 3.3-4.5m. Name variant: **flat-bottomed boat, phing-ti ch'uan**

pingey *Canada, E:* Large **skiff*** of the raftsmen of the St. Lawrence River; used also by the Caughnawaga Native Americans in the latter part of the 19th century. Sides generally built up 0.91-1.22m, lapstrake fashion. Painted red.

ping-hsien ch'uan See **Chênhai ch'uan**
pingos, pingue See **pink-2**
piniace See **pinnace**
pinis See **perahu pinas, pinnace**
pinish See **pinash**

pinisi *Indonesia:* Refers to a style of hull built by the Konjo and Bugis peoples on the southwestern peninsula of Sulawesi (Celebes) and more recently on Kalimantan (Borneo). A **pajala*** becomes a **pinisi** by adding 60-90cm to the sides and adding a stern gallery. Used by the Buginese and Makassarese peoples for trading and traveling to Singapore and northern Australia, where they were called **mitjiangs**.

pinisi

Through the years, the **pajala** hull has undergone relatively few changes, while the **pinisi** features have been modified as a result of outside contacts. Mainly sharp-ended. Prior to the mid-20th century, the bow was square abaft the curved stem; carvel planked, treenailed, with the starboard side slightly higher than the port side to provide intentional asymmetry; closely spaced treenailed ribs fitted after the hull completed; keel shallow, short, and slightly curved fore-and-aft. Present-day stem straight and overhanging; sternpost curved. Until the 1930s, two galleries extended out over the stern, now only one; sheer sweeps up at the stern. Decked, generally nailed down, but early boats had a loose bamboo deck; at the bow, deck is ca. 60cm lower to permit the lateral supports for the bowsprit to run inboard; bulwark abaft this deck. Hold extends full length; steering cabin aft. Mainly employs quarter rudders, requiring 2 helmsmen at times, but actual steering may be done by the set of the sails. The initial single-masted boats carried a large, oblong sail set fore-and-aft (the **palari sompot**); some carried 2 sails on the same mast. Then, **sloop***-rigged with a boomed gaff sail and large, boomed jib. Later vessels were **ketch***- or **schooner***-rigged, and now set leg-of-mutton sails. Mainsail carried on a tripod mast, set in pivots for lowering; gaff and boom fixed; sail extended with outfall of rattan hoops; mainsail boom often dispensed with; luff fastened to a vertical bamboo sprit that in turn is fastened to the rungs of the tripod mast. Tall, fixed topmasts with crosstrees serving as platforms for sail handling, not as spreaders for the topmast shrouds; jib-headed topsails. Three jibs to the very long, heavy bowsprit, supported by timber guys. Some 3-masted. Recent vessels mainly motorized (**prahu layar motor**), with masts down and hull modified. Crew may row or pole sitting on the bowsprit timbers. Up to 20 in crew. Lengths overall 12-45m, on waterline 8-25m, widths 2.4-8.5m. Other recorded names: **Bugis prahu** (or **schooner**), **Macassar prahu**, **Makassaarsche prauw**, **Makasser schooner** (or **trader**), **palari★**, **palari penis** (or **pinis, pinisi**), **pĕlari, penis★, perahu palari penis, phinisi, pinas★, pinisik, prau Bugis★, prau pinisi**. Further reading: G. Adrian Horridge, *The Konjo Boatbuilders and the Bugis Prahus of South Sulawesi* (London: National Maritime Museum, 1979 [Maritime Monographs and Reports, No. 40]). Note also **padwakang**.

pinisik See **pinisi**

pinjajap See **penjajap-1**

pink 1. *Europe, NW:* Term loosely applied to sharp- or pink-sterned vessels; in the 18th century, considered one of the principal hull types. Sail plan varied and number of masts ranged from 1-4. Reported from the 15th-19th centuries. Generally a merchant ship, but also a naval vessel or **fishing boat★**. Most frequently cited as a vessel with a narrow stern that extended out beyond the rudderpost, terminating in a small, simple square transom or a decorative poop with stern and quarter windows. Considerable deadrise; rounded hull. One having leeboards was called a **sword pink**. Reported lengths 16.5-34.5m, widths 5.2-9.3m, depths 2.45-4.85m. Spelling variants: **pincke, pyncke**

2. *Mediterranean:* **Merchantman★** and **coaster★**, especially along the Italian and Dalmatian coasts. Operated during the 17th and 18th centuries; most gone by the mid-19th century. Ample hull, full bows, sharp stern with a shallow transom above the sternpost or a square stern. Flat floors; wide keel; hull might be shallow or deep. Decked; rising or raised poop, hold amidships. Beak at bow supported by a lattice-work platform. Some armed, especially those from Spain and from Safi on the Atlantic coast of Morocco, the latter carrying 10-20 cannon and 200 men. Mostly 3-masted, the foremast raking forward, the mizzenmast sometimes raking aft. Primarily lateen-rigged, but also substituted square sails on the fore- and mainmasts when running before the wind, laying the lateen yards on deck, especially in heavy weather. The 17th-century Genoese vessel set square sails on the foremast. Long bowsprit and jibboom. Reported lengths 23-34.5m; e.g., length 34.5m, beam 5.55m, depth 3.6m. Other recorded names: **bi(n)k, pinco** (pl. **pinchi**), **pingos, pingue, pinka, pinke, Pinkschiff, pinque, pinque genois, pinquet, vinco**

3. *British Isles:* Popular in the late 17th and 18th centuries, but reported as early as the 15th century. Word usually applied to a vessel with a stern that was narrow on top, becoming broader below. Many were very similar to the Dutch **fluit★**. Most carried cargo, but also cited as a **fishing** and **passage boat★**. Clinker-built; fully decked or decked only at the bow. One to 3 masts. One reported as 18.7m long, 5.8m wide, 2.3m deep at hold; cap. ca. 200-400t. Name variant: **heck boat**. Note also **Leigh pink, pinky**.

4. *Denmark:* Small naval vessel with a narrow stern; considered suitable for quarter cannon. Continued in use after the northern **merchantmen** had been phased out. Reported capacity 104-220t. Name variant: **pinkskib**

5. *Netherlands:* **a.** Reported in the early 15th century as a **merchantman** that traded to England and France, carrying such items as linen, salt, and salted fish. **b.** The fishing **pink** was quite different, working from coastal beaches out as far as the Orkneys; first mentioned in the late 15th century and used into the 18th century. A type that specialized in fishing for plaice (*schol*) was called a **scholschuit**; the small, deeper Zeeuwse **pinkje** fished for mussels on muddy foreshores and rivers in Zeeland. Clinker-built sides

pink-5b

and carvel bottom; heavy planking; mostly flat-floored; rounded sides. The larger herring boats had deeper hulls. Curved, raked stem; straight, strongly raked sternpost; rounded bows and full buttocks. Some open, others half or fully decked; the larger, deeper boats had a cabin under the foredeck and a low cabin aft; open waist for nets and fish. Narrow leeboards. Variously rigged during its long history: normally 1-2 masts with tall, narrow square sails; the small foremast, raking forward, stepped just behind the stem; the mainmast behind the foredeck. Single-masted types mainly gaff-rigged with staysail and jib to a long bowsprit. Sometimes a mizzen used. Mainmast struck while fishing. Also rowed. Reported lengths 9.3-12.5m; beam one-third; depth one-quarter beam; shallow draft. **Egmonder pink:** 9.8m long, 3.36m wide. Other recorded names: **Egmonder zee-pinck, pinck(e), pinkje, pinkschip, pinque, pynck(e), scholschuitje, scholschuyt, Sheveningen pink, viss(ch)erspink, zeeboot, zeepink;** pl. **pinken**. Note also **bezaanschuit, schuit**.

6. *United States, NE:* In colonial New England, **pinks** were widely used for offshore fishing, and some carried cargo and passengers to Europe and the West Indies. Characterized by bulwarks that extended beyond the sharp stern. Variously rigged, but chiefly a **ketch★** rig that included yards for square sails. Size varied, but most ca. 14-15m long. Note also **pinky**.
Further reference: **schuit-1**

pinka, pinke See **pink-2**

pinken See **pink-5**

pinker *England, E:* Narrow-sterned boat that fished for cod out of North Norfolk beaches in the mid-19th century. Half-decked, lug-rigged. Name variant: **Cromer pinker**

pinkey See **Chebacco boat, pinky**

pinkie See **Chebacco boat**, **Leigh pink**, **pinky**

pinkje See **pink-5**

pinks See **pinky**

Pinkschiff See **pink-2**

pinkschip See **pink-5**

pinkskib See **pink-4**

pink-snow See **snow**

pinkstern *England, W:* A small vessel having a narrow stern. Also, an exceptionally narrow boat type that plied the River Severn.

pink-sterned schooner See **pinky**

pinky *Canada, E/United States, NE:* Weatherly, **schooner***-rigged vessel of the Maritime Provinces and New England that was a popular **fishing boat*** and occasionally a cargo carrier in the latter half of the 18th and the 1st half of the 19th century. Due to their durability, a few were still working into the 20th century; some built in Canada in the 20th century. Those

pinky

that towed a mackerel jig were called **jiggers***. Stern feature distinguished this **pinky** from others of similar name—the swept-up extension of the bulwarks aft of the rudder joined in a narrow, false transom that was notched to serve as a crutch for the main boom. Carvel-built; some in Canada lapstrake. Full, round bow; curved stem, small gammon knee; some had a clipper bow (the **clipper-pinky**). Sharp stern; straight, raked sternpost; full buttocks. Straight keel with deep drag; steep rise to the floors; easy bilges; rounded sides. The Canadian **pinky** had more deadrise and was beamier. High bulwarks, considerable sheer; fully decked, raised forward; cabin in bow, some with brick fireplace. Small **pinkies** had a helmsman's standing well. Tiller or wheel. Aft-raking pole masts; lacked shrouds on early boats; main topmast struck in winter; foremast stepped over the forefoot. No bowsprit originally, then steeved-up bowsprit; at least one jib, sometimes club-footed. In light weather, gaff topsail and a main topmast staysail used. Crew of 5-10. Reported lengths 9-22m; e.g., length overall 15.5m, on waterline 13.9m, beam 4m, depth 2m, draft aft 2.6m. Other recorded names: **Canadian pinky**, **Essex pinky**, **Gaspé pink**, **Maine pinky**, **New England pinky**, **pinkey**, **pinkie**, **pinks**, **pink-sterned schooner**, **pinky-schooner**, **red stem boat**, **schooner-pinky**, **Yarmouth pinky**. Further reading: Howard I. Chapelle, *The American Fishing Schooners, 1825-1935* (New York: Norton & Company, 1973), 36-57. Note also **Crotch Island pinky**, **Eastport pinky-schooner**,

pink. Further references: **Hampton boat**, **Quoddy boat**, **Strait boat**

pinky-schooner See **Eastport pinky-schooner**, **pinky**

pinnace 1. A **ship's boat***, especially of a naval vessel, that was generally assigned to lesser officers; term as a **ship's boat** came into use in the 17th century. Heavy, clinker- or carvel-built boat; small, high-tucked transom stern; considerable deadrise; curved stem; moderate sheer. Decked forward; stern bench; coxswain sat behind the bench. Sometimes armed. At various periods, rowed by 6-16 oarsmen; originally single-banked, later double-banked. In the 18th and early 19th centuries, often portrayed with 2 equal-sized spritsails; in late 19th century, adopted a single loose-footed gaff sail and foresail with option to set a topsail and topmast staysail; sometimes shown lateen-rigged on 2 or 3 masts. Sliding gunter sails also used. Later motorized. Reported lengths 5.8-16.5m; e.g., length 9.75m, beam 2.84m, depth 0.96m. Other recorded names: **barcă de serviciu**, **boat-pinnace**. Note also **canot-2**, **scorridora**.

2. A fast, maneuverable, relatively narrow, square-sterned vessel of the late 17th through the 18th century. Used by the English, French (**pinasse***), Dutch (**pinasschip***), and Portuguese (**pinaça**) as a **merchantman*** and **man-of-war***. Some small **pinnaces** were carried knocked down aboard discovery vessels and reassembled for use in exploring the coast. Some were **whalers***. Resembled the **jacht*** and was often confused with it. The 17th-century vessels had 2 decks, a forecastle, and a half deck at the stern. Soft, V-shaped bottom; angular bilges, tumble home to sides above the waterline. Ornamented beakhead and stern. Armed with ca. 18 guns. **Frigate***-rigged with square lower sails, topsails at the fore- and mainmast, lateen and mizzen topsail on the mizzen mast. Large ships had a spritsail and a sprit topsail below the bowsprit. Crew of 60-70. Averaged 35-45.7m long, 7.6-11.6m wide. Those used by the English against the Spanish in the West Indies were nicknamed **Spanish frigates**.

3. Term sometimes applied to a double-banked, carvel-planked **rowboat***, or may describe a small **motor boat***.

4. *Italy:* A boat of the custom's service may be called a **pinaccia** (pl. **pinacce**).

5. *United States, E:* The colonial **pinnace** of the early 17th century might be a **pulling boat*** or a small vessel employed in fishing, scouting, trading, or as a cargo carrier going to England and the West Indies. Frequently similar to, and designed to accompany, a larger vessel. Term applied only to **pulling boats** by the end of the 17th century. The smaller craft were reported as open or half-decked; the larger were decked with forecastle and poop. Probably lapstrake construction; most had square sterns. Stepped 1-2 masts, occasionally 3. Sail types reported as sprit, lateen, or gaff; transatlantic vessels were square-rigged. Fishing **pinnaces** had a crew of 5-6. Length of pulling type 8.5m, beam 2m, depth 0.8m; 3-masted traders might be 13.7m long.

Selected name variants: **espinace**, **espynasse**, **galeote**, **galeoto**, **long-ràmbach**, **pennis**, **pennys**, **pinaça**, **pinaccia** (pl. **pinacce**), **pinaccio**, **pinace**, **pinacea***, pinas*, pinasa, pinash*, Pin(n)ass, pinaz(z)a, pindis, pinease, piniace, pinnasse, pin(n)esse, pinniccia, pin(n)is, pinus, pynace, pynas (pl. **pynassen**), **pynas-schip**, pynnes(se), **Ruderpinnase**, spinaccia, spinace, spinacium, spinazza, spynagtz, spyn(n)es. Further references: **nef-1, penis-2, perahu pinnace, pinash, scorridora-1**

Pinnass, pinnasse, pinnesse, pinniccia, pinnis See **pinnace**

pinque See **pink-2, pink-5**

pinque genois, pinquet See **pink-2**

pinsalang, pint'alaŋ See **pencalang**

pinus See **pinnace**

pĭ-nŭ-wŭhī See **shitlats**

piota See **peota-1**

pipante See **pitpan-2**

piperi 1. *Brazil, NE:* Small **raft*** used for fishing by the coastal Tupí tribes (southeast of the Amazon Delta). Constructed of 4-5 thick lengths of wood bound together with vines. Propelled with a flat stick.
  2. *West Indies:* In the French islands, a 1-man fishing **raft**. Three to 6 short logs are arranged side-by-side. Length 1.65m, width 0.7m. Note also **pripri**.
Spelling variants: **perí, periperi, perý, piperie, piri**

piperie See **piperi**

piperis See **jangada-2, pripri**

pipirit See **pripri**

piragoua See **pirogue**

piragua 1. *Nicaragua, S:* Used in the mid-19th century on Lake Nicaragua and tributary rivers. Two planks raised each side of the dugout. Mainly rowed, double-banked, by as many as 10 people. Also sailed. Length 12m, beam 2.4m.
  2. *Panama, SE:* **a.** This **dugout canoe*** of the Chocó peoples is used mainly to transport plantains to market, a 15m **canoe*** carrying 10,000 plantains. Semicircular bottom; overhanging, squared ends that form short end decks. Small logs on the bottom serve as seats. Hull hollowed by axe and smoothed by adze; ca. 5cm thick on the bottom and 1.25cm at the gunwale. Poled and paddled; lanceolate paddle blades with longitudinal ridge. Stern sawed off for an outboard motor on some large **canoes**. Reported lengths 7.6-15.2m, average 10.7m; e.g., length 9m, beam 0.74m, inside depth 0.33. A small size, the **chingos**, is ca. 4m long and 0.9-1.2m wide. **b.** In addition to the **cayuco***, the Cuna of the San Blas Islands have a **piragua**-type **canoe** called a **uluchuwis**. Serves as a trough for fermenting *chica* from sugarcane and for carrying the dead to the mainland for burial. Carved of cedar or oak; shallow hull; low bow and stern. Spelling variants: **ula chúi, ulachuwi**
  3. *Paraguay, SE:* Built at Asunción to transport 9,000-14,000kg of cargo down the Río Paraná, especially in the 18th and 19th centuries. One cargo, *yerba maté*, a type of tea, was packed into bullhide bundles and sewn up. Vessel composed of a rectangular box set upon 2 large dugouts, sawed in two lengthwise, serving as floats. Cargo piled onto the box and covered by a temporary decking. Benches along the sides provided seats for the oarsmen.
  4. *Venezuela, NE:* **a.** Transom-sterned, plank-built **fishing boat*** of Isla Margarita and the eastern part of the

north coast. On some, the transom forms a high, oval counter; on others, a wide "U"; exterior sternpost may extend partway up or to the top of the transom. Stem plumb above the waterline, curved below; keel; high sheer. On some, the sheer plank extends just abaft the transom. Small boats open with a wide stern bench; larger boats decked, low cabin in after third. Oculi on many boats, either bossed pieces or elaborately painted. Larger boats **sloop***- or lateen-rigged; sturdy bowsprit. Now mainly motorized. Reported lengths 7-14m. **b.** A type of **piragua** served as a **passage boat*** on the Orinoco River. Plank-built. High-peaked gaff sails with a very long, light boom. Light, flexible mast stepped well forward. Might also set a square sail if running before the wind. Length ca. 6m.
Further references: **canoa-1, canoa-6, canoe-6, dalca, periagua, periauger, pirogue**

pirahua See **pirogue**

pirateer See **privateer**

pirato See **corsair**

piraugue See **gommier**

pirauguer See **pirogue**

piri See **piperi**

pirlo See **bote-8**

pirog 1. *Réunion:* Creole term for a **fishing boat*** on this western Indian Ocean island.
  2. *Seychelles:* Black-hulled fishing and transport boat; no longer being built, but many still fish for mackerel and sardines. Well-suited for work off beaches. Traditionally a dugout base to which a deep strake has been added; some plank-built; others merely **dugout canoes***. In the plank-extended type, the strake is set into the base and the joint covered with a broad copper strip. Early large **pirogs** constructed of 2 dugout halves joined by putting the halves into recesses and covering the joint with copper strips. White, lanceolate bow weatherboards are characteristic. Sharp ends with strongly raking, curved stem and sternpost; pronounced sheer; flat bottom, no keel. Widely spaced half ribs on alternate sides provide strength and rigidity. Thwarts set into horizontal slots left when the base is hewn out, or on stringers. Tray-type decking at the ends. Generally anchored from the stern with a large stone. Steered with an oar held against a post on the starboard side. Rowed, usually single-banked; single tholepins, intermediately spaced. Large early boats required 10 or more oarsmen, often carrying copra from island to island. When sailed, set a spritsail or leg-of-mutton sail; no longer sail. Mast stepped into a block. The current **fishing boats** are ca. 7m long and require a crew of 7. Originally 5-12m long. Spelling variant: **pirogue***
See also **pirogue**.

pirog" See **pirogue**

piròga *France, Corsica:* A very small **fishing boat*** that worked the Étang de Biguglia on the northeast coast of the island. See also **pirogue**.

piroga monoxile See **dugout canoe**

piroge, piroghe, pirogua See **pirogue**

pirogue 1. Broadly speaking, a long, narrow, fast, native **dugout canoe***. A French word adopted into English; Spanish uses the variant spelling **piragua***, which was the word used by the Caribs; the Arawaks used **canoa**★. Usually spoken of in association with dugouts of the Caribbean area, the Gulf of Mexico, and the west coast of South America, but may include African and Pacific **canoes**★. Generally a single hewn tree trunk, or constructed of 2 or more logs lashed together end-to-end; some are made wider by inserting a flat plank bottom between 2 rounded sides. May be expanded, sides raised by planking, and may employ outriggers or sponsons. Sailed or paddled.

2. *Canada, E:* **Dugout canoe** of white pine used in the Acadian region between the St. Lawrence River and the Atlantic. On the French islands of St. Pierre and Miquelon off southern Newfoundland, **pirogues** similar to **whaleboats**★ were used in coastal fishing as late as 1900.

3. *United States, S and central:* **a.** The **pirogue**, adapted from the Native American dugouts, was a popular craft from the colonial period until the early 19th century, and was used on quiet waters from the east coast across to the midwest. Used by settlers, fishermen, trappers, and fur traders; as **freighters**; and for local transportation. Varied widely in type of wood used, design, and size. Constructed in various ways: hewn from a single log; 2 logs might be suitably shaped or a single log split lengthwise and the two parts joined, spiking or binding bottom planks between; 2 logs might be set side-by-side with a plank on top; or 2 logs or dugout hulls set parallel, **catamaran**★-fashion, with a platform between, sometimes with a house on top. On many cargo **pirogues**, transverse bulkheads strengthened the hull. On the Missouri River, early boatmen distinguished a **pirogue** from an ordinary **dugout canoe**, the former having a square stern. Rowed, poled, and sometimes sailed. Reported lengths 4.5-15.2m. Note also **shallop-8**. **b.** On the Georgia and Carolina coasts, a type of **pirogue** (interchangeably **piragua**, **peragio**, or **canoe**) engaged in scouting work against the Native Americans as well as in cargo transport. Constructed by sawing a dugout lengthwise and treenailing and stapling a plank between the 2 halves; wide strakes raised the sides. Timbers fitted to close bow and create a square stern. Decked at bow; a longer deck extended out over the rudder, with cuddy below. Mainly **schooner**★-rigged with short gaffs; rarely rowed. Reported lengths 12-15m, beam 2.1-2.4m, depth 1.2-1.5m. Note also **scout boat**.

4. *United States, south-central:* **a.** On the bayous and rivers of southeastern Louisiana, **pirogues** are still in use, but here the term may apply to any kind of small boat. A general-utility craft, but most popular with trappers working in the swamps and marshes. Early **pirogues** were dugouts hollowed from a single cypress log, but now made from a log sawed in half lengthwise with a plank bottom inserted; these are called **dugout pirogues** to distinguish them from entirely plank-built **pirogues**. Sharp, raked ends, the bow more deeply hollowed; flattened bottom with slight rocker; some had a residual ridge on the bottom at each end. Round bilges, slightly flared sides; fuller forward than aft; flat sheer. Molding strip added below the gunwale. Two thwarts. Mostly

rowed, but may be poled, or paddled, and now frequently use an outboard motor. The larger early **canoes** set a leg-of-mutton sail. One-man boat. Lengths usually 1.8-4.6m, rarely more than 9m; average ca. 3.7m long after about 1910; widths 0.51-1.02m; depths 0.25-0.76m. Other recorded names: **Cajun pirogue**, **canot**★, **dougout**, **Louisiana pirogue**, **pēro**. **b.** The plank-built **pirogue**, introduced early in the 20th century, has replaced the dugout in most areas and is found across southern Louisiana. Locally, it may be called a **plank pirogue**, **plank boat**, **pirogue en planche**, and sometimes a **péniche**★. In southwestern Louisiana, it may be called a **skiff**★, **canoe**, or **Cajun skiff**. In the north of the state, it is called simply a **pirogue**. Shape very similar to the **dugout pirogue**, but with distinct local traits and qualities of construction. Bottom planked with 2-3 longitudinal planks. Single side planks, either nailed together at the ends or to triangular stem and sternpost; flared sides. Elbow braces added to each side and horizontally across the bottom. Some now of plywood. Most painted green. Reported lengths 4.3-4.9m, width 0.7m. Further reading: W. B. Knipmeyer, "Folk Boats of Eastern French Louisiana," in: Don Yoder, ed. *American Folklife* (Austin: University of Texas, 1976), 108-130.

5. *United States, west-central:* Two plank-built **pirogues** were used by the Lewis and Clark Expedition of 1803-1805 in traversing the Missouri River. Planking of cottonwood, bottom flat, ends sharp. Open except for an awning at the stern. Outboard rudder. Square sail set forward of the short mast, a spritsail behind. Probable sizes 12 and 13m long and 2.5m and 2.8m wide, respectively. Other recorded names: **red pirogue**, **white pirogue**

6. *West Indies, Lesser Antilles:* The light, fast Trinidad and Grenada **pirogues** show more European influence than those of the islands to the north. The dugout portion consists of the keel and garboard in one piece, to which 3-4 planks are added to each side, lapstrake fashion. Straight, sloping stem; transom stern, marked sheer forward, flaring sides. Fishing **pirogues** have a live well amidships. Most rowed double-banked, with a 3rd man trolling. When sailed, sets a triangular sail; now inboard engines common. Reported lengths 4.6-7.3m; e.g., length 7m, beam 1.9m, depth amidships 0.7m. Other recorded names: **lambia**, **shellboat**, **Trinidad pirogue**

Other recorded names: **canot Indien**, **peragua**, **peraouger**, **pereago**, **periaga**, **periago(e)**, **periagua**★, **periaguay**, **periaguer**★, **perieago**, **perigua**, **periogue**, **perioque**, **periyago**, **perogue**, **peroqua**, **peroque**, **perriago**, **perriagua**, **perriaguer**, **perriauger**, **perriaugre**, **perriaugua**, **perriawger**, **perrogue**, **peryago**, **petiaguay**, **pettiagua(y)**, **pettiauger**, **pet(t)iaugre**, **pettiaugua**, **pettiawga**, **petty-auga**, **pettyauger**, **petty augre**, **petty-oager**, **piragoua**, **piragua**★, **pirahua**, **pirauguer**, **pirog**★, **pirog"**, **piròga**★ (Italian pl. **piroghe**), **piroge**, **pirogua**, **piroque**, **pyrage**, **pyraugua**, **pyraugue**, **pyrog(u)e**. Further references: **canoe-6**, **canoe-8**, **curragh**, **gal-2**, **gommier**, **periauger**, **pirog**, **whaleboat-1**, **whaler-2**

pirogue à balancier, pirogue à double balancier See **outrigger canoe**

pirogue de barre See **baleinière de barre**

pirogue de voyage See **amatasi-1**

pirogue Djenné See **barque Djenné**

pirogue en planche See **pirogue-4**

pirogue ferry See **periauger-3**

pirogue monoxyle See **dugout canoe**

pirogue mosquito, pirogue moustique See **dihengué**

piroque See **pirogue**

Piscataqua River gundalow See **gundalow**

Piscataqua River gunning skiff See **scull float**

Piscataqua River wherry *United States, NE:* Open **dory★** type used along this Maine river. Lapstrake sides, flat bottom, curved stem; strongly raked, narrow V-transom. Rowed. Reported lengths 4.3-5m, widths 1.19-1.24m.

pitarchia See **musciara**

pitau See **waka pitau**

pitban See **pitpan-2**

pith-lo *United States, SE:* Sharp-bowed **dugout canoe★** of the Seminoles of southern Florida. Hewn by adze from a log of bald cypress which has been buried in the mud to gain flexibility and reduce splitting; another technique roughs out the exterior shape with an axe before severing the hull from the log, hollowing the hull away from the tree site. Bow angles in to a sharp cutwater in a straight line; sheer sweeps up abruptly; gunwale cap at bow; stern rounded and overhanging. Sides straight and tapered toward the stern. Short, planked end decks may be added. Mainly poled, but occasionally sets a small, boomed gaff sail and is steered with a paddle. Also paddled. Reported lengths 4.2-9.4m; e.g., length 7.3m, beam 0.61m. Other recorded names: **pich-li, p'thlee, Seminole canoe**

pitpam See **pitpan-2**

pitpan 1. *Belize:* Type of river **dugout canoe★** seldom seen now. Bottom generally flattened. Ends have a platform on which a man stands when poling, but the boat is mostly paddled, also standing. Often has an awning and side curtains on rollers. As many as 8 paddlers. Reported lengths 11-15m; e.g., length 11m, beam 1.2m, depth 0.5m. Note also **batteau-1**.

2. *Honduras/Nicaragua:* Narrow, keelless **dugout canoe** used by the Miskito mainly for river travel, but also for nearshore fishing and turtling. Thick, flat bot-

pitpan-2

tom; long overhang at bow and stern; squared ends, flat on top. Some have sides raised with planking and a small bulwark at each end. Platform at the stern for poling or for sighting fish. May be moored at a river-bank by inserting a pole perpendicularly through a hole in the bow. Poled, paddled, or may set a crude sail. Paddles broad-bladed. Length to ca. 19m, width ca. 1.2-1.5m. Other recorded names: **pipante, pitban, pitpam**. Note also **bateau-5**.

pitpante *Costa Rica:* Flat-bottomed **dugout canoe★** used particularly for transportation from the mountains to the coast in southern Costa Rica. Sharp ends; parallel,

vertical sides. Steered with a sweep in the upper reaches and poled in shallow coastal areas. Length ca. 2m.

pittyauger See **periauger**

piyade *Turkey, NW:* This fast, light **kayık★** transported passengers in the Istanbul area. Available for hire or privately owned. The smallest carried 2 passengers and was rowed by a single oarsman; larger boats carried 5-6 passengers and were rowed, usually single-banked, by as many as 6 oarsmen. Phased out after the introduction of motorized craft. Lightly planked; shallow keel. Early boats had a low, elongated, sharp, iron-tipped bow; higher, fuller stern. Later boats double-ended. Some ornamented, others only varnished. Some had end decks; oarsmen sat on benches forward; passengers aft, seated on the bottom, on a padded bench, or along the sides. Bulbous inner end to the long oars served as a counter-balance. Loom secured by a leather loop to a tholepin. Sometimes sailed on longer trips; mast stepped well forward. Reported lengths 4.6-9.1m, widths 0.6-1.1m. Other recorded names: **biade, peyade, piade(t), piyade kayığı**; a 3-oared boat would be a **ür çifte piyade**; a 5-oared boat, **beş çifte piyade**.

piyade kayığı See **piyade**

piyahu See **perahu-1**

Pläcke See **Plätte-4**

plaisancier See **yacht-2**

plaite See **pleit-1**

plancha See **prancha-2**

plancha See **punt-2**

plank boat *Canada, NW:* A roughly constructed, flat-bottomed craft used for transportation on the Yukon River. See also **pirogue-4**.

plank pirogue See **pirogue-4**

plantation barge See **plantation boat**

plantation boat *United States, SE:* Ubiquitous boat of the plantations from North Carolina to Georgia during the 1800s. Provided transportation for people and produce. A **dugout canoe★**, either a single log or multi-log; some plank-extended. Sharp, plumb bow; high-tucked transom stern, low sheer; flat floors amidships, soft turn of the bilges into vertical sides. Awning often covered part of the hull. Rowed with 6, 8, or 12 oars, usually by slaves. Reported lengths 9-15m. Name variant: **plantation barge**. Note also **flatboat-5**.

plat 1. *British Isles:* Cited during the 15th-17th centuries as a small, flat-bottomed vessel. Served as a **coaster★** and **fishing boat★**. Spelling variants: **plate★, playte**

2. *Canada, E:* Small boat of French fishermen at the mouth of the St. Lawrence River; numerous by the mid-17th century. Constructed of 3 wide planks: single plank on the bottom and one on each side.

3. *Netherlands:* Small **fishing boat** with a 2-3 cubic meter capacity.

Further references: **peata, plate**

plata *France, Corsica:* Small, local **fishing boat★** of the Étang de Biguglia on the northeast coast of the island. See also **peata**.

plat de calafat See **copper punt**

plate *France:* 1. A small, open, flat-bottomed boat that is rowed, sculled, or poled in quiet waters. Of no specific shape, generally being built by the owner, but usually angular with little sheer, shallow keel, wide bottom, frequently a vertical transom stern, trapezoidal cross section. Called a **bachot★** when used on rivers.

2. A large, flat-bottomed **barge★**.

3. Term may apply to a **punt★** used in shipyards while caulking, cleaning, and painting the sides of ships. Other recorded names: **baleinière du calfat**, **bâtiment de servitude**, **platte de travail**. Note also **balsa raft**, **copper punt**.

4. Boat of the Normandy coast, particularly around Bay of the Seine, that dates to the 18th century. Trawled inshore, especially for shrimp. Extinct by the 1930s.

plate-4

Bluff bow; sharp, raked stern; lightly curved stem, flat floors. Initially open, later decked. Outboard rudder; short tiller. Small live well or towed a boat-shaped **fish car★**. Originally set 1-2 square sails. Later a lug- or loose-footed, boomed gaff mainsail or lug- or gaff foresail, topsail on mainmast. Long, running bowsprit; foresail. Crew of 3-4. Reported lengths overall 9.35-9.86m, on keel 7.45m, beam 3.15m, depth 1.27m, draft aft 1.6m. Other recorded names: **crevettier★**, **platte de Honfleur** (or **du Havre**). Note also **platte d'Arromanches**, **platte de Villerville**.

5. Early **plates** carried wine along the Seine River.

6. Very small, stubby boat of the north coast of Brittany, often serving as a seaweed collector's **dinghy★** and for small-scale fishing. Square stern, notched for a scull. Bow also flat, either quite narrow or about half the width of the stern; vertical or raked. Bottom flat, usually with

plate-6

athwartships planking. Sides vertical. One or 2 seats. Scull may also serve as a yoke for carrying the boat up the beach. Coated with coal tar. Crew generally 1 man and a boy or 2 men. Reported lengths 1.2-4m. Other recorded names: **ar plato**, **plate des goëmonniers**, **plate goémonière**

7. On the south coast of Brittany, at Etel, the flat-bottomed seine-net **plate** may have a raked, rounded stern composed of 3 flat surfaces. Flared sides, raked stem. Foredeck with locker beneath; large stern deck with

low bulwark. Rowed or uses an outboard motor. Length ca. 3.6m.

8. The **plate** that works the cultivated oyster beds on the Morbihan coast is a small, open boat. Also used for fishing and as a general-purpose boat. Flat bottom with rocker; carvel planking; sharp bow, slightly raked transom stern. Traditionally painted a pale blue. Rowed but now many hang an outboard motor on the transom. Length to 6.5m; e.g., length 3.8m, beam 1.5m. Name variant: **plate morbihannaise**

9. On Lac de Grand-Lieu, southwest of Nantes, a small **fishing boat★** of early origin. Constructed of oak with a 3-plank flat bottom with rocker; small grounding keels. Sides flare; top strake lapped. Sharp, straight, raked bow; planking fastened outside the stem. Bottom planks bent up at stern to form a narrowing, overhanging stern; square across the top. Widely spaced frames. Open except for small foredeck and larger stern deck; live well beneath midships bench. Hull tarred. Propelled by pole, oar, sail, and recently by outboard motor. Square sail hung between 2 divergent, light poles. Main pole lashed to one gunwale. Sail position varied by adjusting the secondary, lighter pole, which is forked against the base of the main pole. Length ca. 5.5m, beam 1.65m, depth 0.5m. Name variant: **grand bateau**

10. In the lagoons along the western Mediterranean coast, used for fishing with a hoop net, the *trabac*. Sharp, raked ends, stern taller. Flat bottom; high, flaring sides. Short end decks. Generally rowed, but may be poled. Length 3.8m; beamy; shallow draft.

Other recorded names: **bateau plat★**, **plat★**, **platte**, **plecte**, **plet(t)e**, **pletre**, **pleyte**. Note also **grande plate**. Further references: **bateau lavoir**, **canot goëmonier**, **goguet**, **margotat**, **peata**, **peatone**, **plat**

plate à derive See **plate de l'Aiguillon**

platea skaphe See **punt**

plate chaude See **bateau lavoir**

plate d'Arcachon See **grande plate**

plate de l'Aiguillon *France, W:* Used for mussel cultivation in the Aiguillon embayment north of La

plate de l'Aiguillon

Rochelle. Introduced at the end of the 19th century; extinct. Carvel-planked, mostly of oak; floor timbers not fastened to bottom. Flat bottom, tightly planked, no caulking. Wide, raked transom stern; sharp, raked bow; foredeck with breakwater; daggerboard. Hull blackened with coal tar. Pivoting centerboard. Steered with an oar except when they stepped a mizzen, at which time shipped a lifting rudder hung on rings. Initially set a large lugsail tacked to the foot of the mast. Later added a jib and a mizzenmast stepped against the transom, setting a lugsail sheeted to a jiggerboom. Also rowed or poled; now motorized. Reported lengths 4-9m. Other recorded names: **plate à derive**, **plate mytilicole**. Note also **canot mytilicole**, **yole-2**.

plate des goëmonniers See **plate-6**
plate froid See **bateau lavoir**
plate goémonière See **plate-6**
plate morbihannaise See **plate-8**
plate mytilicole See **plate de l'Aiguillon**
platform See **fleet-4**
plati See **peata**
platillo de calafate See **copper punt**
platkop See **zeeschouw**
plato, platta See **peata**
plattboningar See **dory-4**
Plattboot See **flatboat**
plattbottnad eka See **dory-4**

Plätte *Austria/Germany, S:* **1.** A flat-bottomed craft that ranges from small 6m boats to long, narrow vessels of 38m. The largest were found mainly on the Danube River and its tributaries, the smaller on a number of Tirolian lakes. Relatively crudely made, since they were used for only a short time, often for a single downriver trip, the planking then sold at its destination. **Plätten** (pl.) were often **ferries*** (**Überfuhrplätten**), transferring people, horses, and wagons. Dates to at least the early 17th century; most gone by the end of the 19th century, but a few small boats are still found on lakes (**Seeplätten**). Some **Plätten** were distinguished by their use, with suitable design and size. The **Einstellplätte** (also called **Rossplätte**, **Pferdplätte**, **Buesenzille** for the towing post, or **Furkelzille** for the pivoting crutch for the tow rope) was ca. 13m long, 2.5m wide, and 0.7m deep; 30-50 horses, with riders, towed the boat back upstream. The **Futterplätte** (27.5m by 4m by 1.3m), **Obstplätte**, and **Krautplätte** transported fodder, fruit, and vegetables, respectively; the **Futterplätte** continued downstream from Budapest with chinaware. The **Steinplätte** carried stone; the **Kalkplätte** carried lime. Danube mail might have been sent in the fast **Postplätte**. Wood was carried on the long, **barge***-like **Holzplätte**, cattle in the **Viehplätte**. Frequently the boats bore the name of their town or region of origin, and many of these were passenger vessels. The **Tiroler Plätte** of the Inn River (25-30m by 6m by l.6m) carried mainly lime and cement. The **Salzburger Plätte** carried rock salt, gypsum, and wood, and ranged from 18-27m in length, to 7m wide, and ca. 0.8m in depth. The **Rosenheimer Plätte** freighted lime and gypsum and was ca. 30m long, 8.2m wide. The **Ulmer Plätte** originated at Ulm, carrying passengers to Vienna (See **Ordinari**). The **Haller Plätte** (from Hall in the Tirol) traversed the Inn and the Danube; reported lengths 12-35m, widths 3-5m. **Plätten** had a wide, flat bottom and low, straight sides. The **Spitzplätte** had a low, square stern created by 1-2 horizontal logs, while the bow was sharp and upturned. The **Stockplätte** (also called **Stockplette**, **Gamsplätte**, or **Gamsplette**) was square at each end, the planking at the

bow vertical; carried lumber and firewood on the Inn to Hungary. Flush-planked of oak and spruce; caulked with moss; no keel; open. Upper river boats drifted downstream, maneuvered by sweeps or a rudder; those returning upstream were tracked from shore. On the larger rivers and lakes, a single sail might be set; a few later vessels motorized. Other recorded names: **Blätte**, **Blette**, **Blödte**, **Plet(t)e**, **Plötte**; dim. **Plättel**, **Plettl**, **Plöttel**; **Fuderplätte**, **Unterplätte**; **Berchtesgadener**, **Halleiner**, **Laufener Plätte**. Note also **Mutzen**.
2. A small type on the Traunsee in Austria and nearby lakes still operates. These have a greatly elongated, slender, high bow; some have a small bow transom. Slightly raked, square stern; flared sides. Rowed standing or poled. Some were called **Ufahrplättel** or **Uferplättel** (8m long, 1.28m wide, 0.47m deep), and those fishing in pairs are called **Fischerplättel**. The long neck on the **Hallstattersee Plätte** ended in a scroll; sharp stern; 3-4 rowing positions, the oars resting on raised gunwales.
3. The shallow **Fischerplätte** of the Chiemsee in southern Germany is an open 2-man boat used for fishing and transporting local produce. Sharp, raked bow with short foredeck; raked transom stern. Planking lapped but shaped to produce a smooth surface; nailed or riveted. Rowed standing with single pair of oars; oars inserted through a rope loop. Reported lengths 7-10m; e.g., length 7.1m, beam 1.5m, depth 0.5m.
4. At Prien on the western side of Chiemsee, the **Plätte**, here called a **Pläcke**, was originally a dugout, but more recently carvel-planked; 4 or more ribs; no gunwale. Flat bottom, rocker follows the sheer; flaring sides. Ends raked, the bow sharp and higher than the square stern. Short end decks; 3 thwarts. Rowed; oars worked over an iron pin fastened inside the top strake. Length overall 6.3m, beam 1.3m, depth at stern 0.35m.

platte See **bateau lavoir**, **plate**
platte bol See **bol-2**
platte bolle See **bolpraam**
platte d'Arromanches *France, N:* Three-masted, lug-rigged boat that worked out of Arromanches on the south shore of the Bay of Seine. Fished for herring, but carried cargo and oysters in the off-season. Extinct by the 1840s. Flat floors enabled boat to be beached. Clinker-planked with 6 strakes forward; 7th strake inserted as top strake along after two-thirds; deep washboards. Decked at ends. Curved stem, cutaway below the waterline; straight, raked sternpost; full bows and quarters. Large outboard rudder followed rake of the sternpost; triced up when ashore. Foresail tacked to a bumkin; mizzen to an aft-raking mast, sheeted to a jigger. Reported lengths 12-15m. Note also **plate-4**.
platte de Honfleur See **plate-4**
platte de travail See **plate-3**
platte de Villerville *France, N:* Boat type that abandoned the flat bottom of the area in the 1830s in favor of a deep keel, but retained the term **plate***. Trawled for shrimp and small fish in the Bay of Seine, working until the early 20th century. Usually built at Honfleur for Villerville fishermen. Straight, slightly raked stem; rounded stern with raking sternpost. Drag to keel; steep rise to the floors; high, soft turn of the bilges.

Narrow outboard rudder; short tiller. Initially open, decked by 1850; cabin abaft the mainmast. Painted black with coal tar; colored, triangular wedge extended from the bow. Originally dipping lugsails set to 2 aft-raking masts, the foremast in the eyes, the mainsail loose-footed but boomed. Evolved to 2 large lugsails, topsail and jib to a long, running bowsprit, then a lug foresail and gaff mainsail, and by 1892, set 2 gaff sails and 2 headsails, plus a top mainsail. Crew of 3 and a boy. 1862 boat 10.3m long, 3.54m wide, 1.5m deep. Note also **plate-4**.

platte du Havre See **plate-4**
platteka See **dory-4**, **eka-1**
Plättel, Plätten See **Plätte-1**
Platter Kutter See **Kutter-Ewer**
Plattstevenkahn See **Handkahn-1**
platus See **peata**
plavuchaya fabrika See **factory ship**
plavuchiy mayak See **lightship**
playte See **plat-1**
pleasure boat See **hua chuan-1**, **xiao hua chuan**, **yacht-2**
pleasure punt See **punt-7**
pleasure wherry See **Thames wherry**
pleasure yoll See **yoll-2**
plecte See **plate**
pleit *Belgium/Netherlands:* **1.** Dating at least to the mid-13th century, was initially a Flemish **coaster★** (**zeepleit**) and lasted as such until the end of the 19th century. The inland **pleit** (**binnenpleit**) was modified to travel the waterways of Belgium and the Netherlands. Other recorded names: **plaite**, **pleite**, **pleyt**, **Vlaams(ch)e pleit**, **Vlaemsche pleit**; pl. **pleiten**, **pleyten** **2.** In the Middle Ages, the **zeepleit** sailed to France, England, Norway, and the Baltic with a crew of 16; cap. ca. 60-70t. Some 17th-century vessels required only a crew of 3. 18th-century vessels employed 5; cap. 70-105t; low-sided with flat sheer, long covered hatches and gangways along each side; sprit-rigged. Later vessels had a strong sheer; steep, curved stem; triangular helmport for the tiller; high, recumbent rudder. Cuddy below steering deck. Mainmast set a standing gaff sail, square topsail; forestaysail, jib to a long, running bowsprit. Mizzen stepped close to helmport, setting a boomed gaff sail sheeted to an outrigger. By the end of the period, stepped only a boomed gaff mainsail. Helmport disappeared during the 19th century, substituting a flush bulwark. Reported lengths 23-35m, beam 4.8-5m; cap. 43-197t. A 1900 iron vessel was 35m long, 5m wide, 270t. **3.** The 16th-century **binnenpleit** was long and flat; long cargo hold covered with cambered hatches. Built of steel after ca. 1900. Low cabin aft with flush deck on top of the sheer strake. Wide rudder lacked rudderhead. Small mast stepped amidships, setting a small spritsail; on rivers and canals, mostly towed by horses or manpower. The 18th-century **binnenpleit** had a triangular helmport for the tiller. Name variant: **bélandre hollandais** See also **spits**.
pleite, pleiten See **pleit-1**
plete See **plate**, **Plätte-1**
pletină *Moldova/Romania, NE/Ukraine, W:* Small **barge★**

that transported 250-400t of grain on the Prut River. Most of hull covered by an arched roof; house aft. Large rudder activated from the house roof. Probably towed, having no self-propulsion. Length 9.5m, beam 1.3m. Name variant: **şlepul de Prut**
pletre See **plate**
plette See **plate**, **Plätte-1**
Plettl See **Plätte-1**
pleyt See **pleit-1**
pleyte See **plate**
pleyten See **pleit-1**
pleziervaartuig See **yacht-2**
ploia, ploiaria rhapta, ploiarion, ploiarion raphton See **ploion**
ploion *Greece:* In early Greece, a general term for a **ship★**, either a sailing or a **galley★** type. A **ploiarion**, however, might be merely a **skiff★**-type craft; a **ploiarion rhapton** was a sewn boat, a **diftherinon ploion** was a skin-covered boat, and a **ploion zeugmatikon** may have been a twin-hulled **catamaran★**. In Egypt, a **ploion Hellenikon** appears to have been a Nile vessel built in the Greek style. Other recorded names: **ploia**, **ploja**, **rhapta** (**ploiaria**), **rhaptôn ploiariôn**; pl. **ploiaria rhapta**. Note also **round ship**.
ploion Hellenikon, ploion zeugmatikon, ploja See **ploion**
plong kenu See **kenu-2**
ploščak See **batana**
plosher See **coble-1d**, **coble-1f**
plot 1. Russian term for a **ferryboat★** or **raft★**. **2.** *Poland, N:* Primitive craft found in the Vistula/Nogat Delta area. Clinker-planked with 3 wide strakes; flat bottom; straight sides; small bow transom; wide, slightly raked, flat stern. Open; single thwart. Length ca. 5m; narrow.
See also **timber raft-1**.
Plötte, Plöttel See **Plätte-1**
Plougastel, Plougastel chaloupe See **chaloupe de Plougastel**
p'loung See **laung**
pluit, pluiten, pluiter See **pluut**
plunger 1. A type of fast **cutter★** that had a centerboard. **2.** *United States, W:* **Plungers** used in the San Francisco oyster industry were cat-rigged. The **plunger** of

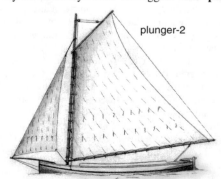
plunger-2

Washington State was **sloop★**-rigged (**Willapa oyster sloop**) with a short gaff and very long boom; jib ran to a bowsed-down bowsprit. Both types were also called **sloops**. Some flush-decked, others had a large, oval, cockpit, and a large one had a low deckhouse. Carvel-planked; sharp bow, cutaway forefoot, rounded bilges, centerboard. Oysters generally carried to market on the deck; the Washington boats appear to have been **carry-away boats*** for the salmon industry. Popular in the late 19th century. Crew of 1-2. Reported lengths 9-12m; length of a Columbia River boat ca. 11m, beam 3.7m, draft 0.9m. One in San Francisco was 11m long, 4.7m wide, 1.3m deep. Other recorded names: **oyster sloop***, **San Francisco oyster sloop**

pluta Generic term for a **raft*** in Bulgarian (**plúta**) and Romanian (**plutǎ**). On some in Romania, the logs were laced together with freshly cut branches of a fir tree, making the **raft** supple; **raft** in 2 sections, one behind the other; steered from both the bow and stern. Spelling variant: **plutu**

Plüte, pluten See **pluut**

plutu See **pluta**

pluut *Netherlands:* **Fishing boat*** of the southeastern part of the Zuiderzee that initially fished for flounder and later for eels. Workboats built from the mid-19th to the mid-20th century; some now built as pleasure craft,

pluut

of steel. Carvel-planked with a flat bottom, hard chines, and lightly rounded sides below the wale. Bottom curved slightly at the stern with skeg continuing to the sternpost. Stem and sternpost straight and sharply raked; rounded but slender bow and stern. Little sheer amidships, but at each end, the narrow wale swept up to sharply reduce the sheer strake width, especially at the bow. Forward edge of rudder follows line of sternpost, after edge vertical; tiller; long, narrow leeboards. Decked to mast, with cuddy; small locker below stern planking; open amidships, with or without a live well. Pole mast stepped just forward of amidships, raking slightly aft. Narrow, loose-footed, boomed gaff mainsail; short, curved gaff; wide forestaysail, the sheet overlapping the mast; sometimes a jib to a running bowsprit. Crew of 2. Reported lengths 8-12m; e.g., length overall 9.44m, on keel 6.71m, beam 2.74m, depth 1.33m. Other recorded names: **Elburger pluut**, **Harderwijker pluut**, **pluit(er)**, **Plüte**, **pluutje** (dim.); pl. **pluten, pluiten**

pluutje See **pluut**

Plymouth barge *England, SW:* The sailing **barges*** of the Plymouth area fell into 2 main categories: **inside barge** and **outside barge**. The **inside barges** traded along the River Tamar and in the estuary, carrying limestone, produce, oak bark, manure, etc., until ca. 1930. Also called **Blue Elvan barge**, **Laira barge**, **Plymouth sloop**, **Plymouth stone barge**, **river barge**, **Tamar (gravel) barge**, and **Tamar River sloop**. Flat on the bottom to withstand grounding, but with well-rounded bilges; keel ca. 21cm deep; straight. Originally open; later, forecastle housed the galley and stores with a cabin aft; long hatch. Stem generally straight and vertical; stern usually a shallow, flat transom, occasionally rounded. Loaded, freeboard as little as 50cm. Some had a centerboard. Set a loose-footed gaff mainsail with a very long boom and gaff and short luff; large staysail and, when used, a jib ran from the running bowsprit. Mast short and heavy; no shrouds; could be struck. A few **ketch***-rigged. Towed a **punt*** or **boat***; also poled or tracked from shore from the masthead; engines installed later. Crew of 2. Average: length 13.7m, beam 4.6m, depth of hold 1.5m. **Outside barges**, also called **smacks*** or **trading smacks***, worked both within the estuary and along the coast, going to the Bristol Channel and across the English Channel; last vessel gone by 1953. They were longer, deeper, and fully decked; large central hatch; cabin aft. Some had a broad counter through which the rudderpost ran, or they had a shallow transom with the rudder hung outboard to a bolted-on sternpost. Main distinction in their rigging was the addition of a long, fidded topmast and a square-headed gaff topsail; some **ketch**-rigged. Jib hauled out to the end of a long bowsprit by tackle and a traveler. Crew of 2. Reported lengths 15.2-19.2m; e.g., length 19.2m, beam 5.7m, depth 2m. Note also **West Country sailing barge**.

Plymouth hooker *England, SW:* **Cutter***- or **dandy***-rigged **fishing boat*** used out of ports in the Plymouth area. Straight, plumb stem; raked transom stern, straight keel with drag, full midship section, hard turn

Plymouth hooker

of the bilges, carvel planking. Smaller types decked forward and for a short distance at stern; open well abaft the mast, bordered by waterways; accommodations forward. Larger boats fully decked with a long hatch amidships; cabin aft. Mostly **cutter**-rigged; mainsail had a long gaff, high peak, no boom, almost vertical leech, and clew was sometimes sheeted by a long hook. Also set a staysail, large jib, and jackyard topsail. Stubby pole mast stepped almost at midline and supported by 2 shrouds to a side. The larger, **dandy**-rigged boats had a small mizzenmast on the sternpost, setting a lugsail sheeted to an outrigger. Reefing bowsprit ran out port side of stem; none on later boats. Crew of 2-6. Reported lengths 7.9-12.5m; typical 9.45m long, 2.9m wide, 2.4m deep aft. The **hookers★** employed methods other than hooks and lines, especially the **dandy**-rigged boats that engaged in drift-net fishing in winter and line fishing at other times. Larger **hookers** that used long lines were called **boulter boats**. **Whiting boats★** were smaller **hookers** that used hand lines. Note also **Polperro gaffer**.

Plymouth lobster boat See **lobster boat-4b**

Plymouth sloop, **Plymouth stone barge** See **Plymouth barge**

poboak See **mon-3**

pochtovoe sudno See **packet boat-1**

po ch'uan See **bo chuan**, **long chuan**

Pocomoke canoe, **Pocomoke River canoe** See **Chesapeake Bay log canoe-2**

Pocomoke round-bottom See **skipjack-1**

pod See **peapod**

podjazdówka See **Handkahn-1**

poepoe See **báka poe-poe**

Pogge See **Mutte**

Pohleeber See **Pfahl-Ewer**

point boat See **catboat-2b**

Point de Galle canoe See **warka-moowee**

pointer *Canada:* **1.** A smaller and more refined **lumberman's batteau★** designed in the late 19th century to aid in rounding up logs on tributary lakes and rivers of the Ottawa River watershed. Still used for lumbering, mining, and construction, including work on the St. Lawrence Seaway. Sharply pointed and raked bow and stern; wide, flat bottom; flared sides; strong sheer forward; planked with white pine, frames cut from white cedar roots. Distinctive brick-red color. Steered with a 2.7m-long paddle. Rowed by 4-10 men; also paddled. One designed to take an outboard motor has a square stern, the **half pointer**. Reported lengths 6.1-16.8m; shallow draft; an 8-man **pointer** could float on 13cm of water. Other recorded names: **bonne**, **bun**, **drive boat**, **driving boat**, **Hudson's Bay pointer**, **lumber boat★**, **pointer boat**
2. May also be a river freight **bateau★** used in the fur trade. Square stern for an outboard motor; pointed bow. Length 6.4m; shallow draft.

pointer boat See **pointer**

pointu See **palangrier-2**, **rafiau-1**, **spits**

poisson-sauter bateau See **tiao yu chuan**

pokrissa-oruwa See **äng-oruwa**

pokukan See **mon-3**

pol See **polacca**

polaak, **polaca** See **polacre**

polacca *England, SW:* Small, 2-masted **coaster★** that worked out of the Taw/Torridge Estuary during the late 18th through the 19th century, mostly carrying limestone from south Wales; some, however, made ocean voyages. Characteristically rigged on pole masts with square foresail, topsail, and topgallant, and loose-footed, boomed gaff mainsail and jackyard topsail;

2 staysails between the masts. Topsails and topgallant lowered to the foreyard when stowed. Carvel-planked; bluff bow, generally counter stern, round bottom, moderate sheer. Decked. Hull tarred, with white or blue stripe. Generally crew of 3, 5-6 on the larger **polacca brigs**. Reported lengths 12-23m; e.g., length 15.5m, beam 4.6m, depth of hold 2.3m. Other recorded names: **Bar muffie**, **Bideford polacca** (or **polacker**), **maprodite**, **muffie**, **muffy(e)**, **Muphrydite**, **North Devon polacca**, **pol**, **polacca brigantine**, **polacca schooner**, **polacco**, **polacker**, **polacre★**, **polaker**, **poleacre**, **pole-hacker**, **stonehacker**, **Torridge polacker**. Further reading: V. C. Boyle, "The Bideford Polackers," *The Mariner's Mirror* 18 (1932), 109-124. See also **polacre**.

polacca brig, **polacca brigantine**, **polacca schooner** See **polacca**

polacche See **polacre**

polacco See **polacca**

polaccre, **polacka** See **polacre**

polacker See **polacca**, **polacre**

polaco See **polacre**

polacra *Argentina:* Small, seagoing ship of the late 18th century; survived into the early 1800s as a **riverboat★** of the Río de la Plata estuary and as a **coaster★**. See also **polacre**.

polacre *Mediterranean:* Merchant vessel of the 16th to early 20th century with widely varied characteristics. In Spain in the late 17th century, the **polacra★** was an armed vessel; the corsairs of Salé, Morocco, used **polacres** in their raids, carrying as many as 200 men. Name believed to have been derived from the long beak that projected from the bow. Depicted with a high poop that extended beyond the rudderpost or with a small, square stern; flat floors; generally a fine bow; decked. Typically had 2-3 masts, the mainmast being a pole (or *polacre*) mast without crosstrees. Sail plan varied with time and place. Might set square sails on the main and mizzen or a lateen mizzen with a square topsail (**brig polacre**); others stepped a forward-raking foremast to which a large lateen sail was set with the yard tacked to the beak, square sails on the mainmast, and a lateen mizzen with a square topsail (**ship polacre** or **polacre xebec**); or lateen sails on all 3 masts. Some polemasted vessels set a gaff sail to the mizzen (**polacre bark** or **polacre brigantine**). The small **polacron** of Provence could also be rowed. A 3-masted, lateen-rigged, French vessel of the late 17th century required 21 men; 112t. A late 18th-century Italian vessel was 200t; one of the mid-19th century was 33m long, 8.9m wide, 5.4m deep. Spelling variants: **palacca**, **polaak**, **polaca**, **polacca★**, **polaccre**, **pola(c)ka**, **polacker**, **polac(r)o**, **polakker**, **polaque**, **poleacre**, **poliakra**, **pollacha**, **pollac(r)a**, **polyakra**, **poulacro**, **pulaka**; Italian pl. **polacche**

polacre bark, **polacre brigantine** See **polacre**

polacre settee See **velacciere**

polacre xebec, **polacro**, **polacron**, **polaka** See **polacre**

polaker See **polacca**

polakker See **polacre**

polandra See **palandra**

polaque See **polacre**

półbarkas See **barkas**

polbeira See **dorna-2**

poleacre See **polacca, polacre**

pole-and-line schip, pole-and-line tuna vessel See **tuna boat-2**

pole barge *United States, SE:* Carried merchandise up the Oklawaha (Ocklawaha) River from Palatka in northeastern Florida and transported regional products downstream in the mid-19th century. Propelled by a gang of men, each equipped with a long pole set into the bottom from the bow; each man pushed on his pole walking to the stern and then returned to the bow to repeat the process.

pole boat *United States:* **1.** Plank-built, flat-bottomed craft common on American rivers into the early 1800s. Was floated downstream and poled upstream. Sharp ends; some had a shallow keel; sometimes decked at the ends. Men worked from narrow side decks or from walkways constructed out along each side. Poles usually iron-spiked at one end. Bow and stern steering sweeps common. Sometimes warped upstream. Might have as many as 20 in crew, especially for upstream trips. Reported lengths 6-9m, some to 21m; widths 1-1.5m; depths 0.6-0.9m; shallow draft. Some in Georgia could transport 400-700 bags of cotton or 70-80t of freight.
2. Used on the Grand River above Grand Rapids in western Michigan in the 1830s.
See also **Au Sable River drift boat, Durham boat, pan gan zi, railbird skiff**.

pole ewer See **Pfahl-Ewer**

pole fisher See **tuna boat**

pole-hacker See **polacca**

pole junk See **hua pi gu**

pole-masted barge See **stumpy barge**

pole skiff *United States, E:* Used in net fishing on tributary creeks of the bays of North Carolina. Lightly built with sharp, vertical stem; wide transom stern, flat bottom. Short foredeck and sometimes side decks. Generally poled, sometimes rowed. Length 4.9m, beam 1.4m, depth 0.31-0.36m. See also **Delaware ducker**.

poliakra See **polacre**

police boat See **fei xie, soon son**

police vessel See **guard ship**

poling boat *Canada, NW/United States, Alaska:* Double-ended, open boat used on rivers for freight and general transportation. Propelled by 2 men poling from each end. Narrow, flat bottom; sharp, raked ends; strongly flared sides, marked sheer. Reported lengths 3-9m, beam 0.76-1.52m.

poliscalma, polskalmos See **palischermo-1**

Polkabark, Polka Barque See **jackass bark**

pollaca, pollacha, pollacra See **polacre**

pollari See **pallar**

Polperro crabber See **West Country crabber**

Polperro day boat See **day boat-3**

Polperro gaffer *England, SW:* Gaff-rigged boat of Polperro on the southern Cornwall coast. Used for drift-net and longline fishing from the latter half of the 19th century. Carvel-built; straight, vertical stem; curved forefoot, straight keel with deep heel; wide, raked transom with sculling notch; sharply rising floors. Cuddy forward, open fish room abaft the mast,

hatched-over net room, short deck at the stern, narrow waterways. Tiller passed through transom. **Cutter**-rigged with high-peaked, boomless mainsail laced to the mast; staysail; very large jib, sheeted aft; yard topsail, usually set to port. Short pole mast; single shrouds; bowsprit run out through the gunwale. Engines installed during World War I. Reported lengths overall 7.5-9.1m; e.g., length overall 8.1m, on keel 7.9m, beam 2.74m, depth 1.65m. Other recorded names: **gaffer***, **gaffy, Polperro hooker**

Polperro hooker See **Polperro gaffer**

polveira See **dorna-2**

polyakra See **polacre**

pomarynk See **pomeranka**

pomeranka *Poland, N:* Open **fishing boat*** of the coastal Kashubians of eastern Pomerania; worked until the mid-20th century. Those used on the Baltic were **fish carriers*** and their hulls and rig were heavier than those used in the sheltered Bay of Danzig (Gdańsk). Sharp ends, both strongly raked; clinker-planked; wide, vertical top strake amidships; alternating ribs and floor frames inserted after hull planked. Strong sheer, especially at the ends. Long, straight, plank keel; flat floors just forward of amidships, steeper aft; sharp entrance and run. Slender daggerboard; earlier, leeboard hung from leeward side when tacking. Raked outboard rudder; tiller. Rowed when fishing inshore; 2 pairs of oars worked between oarlocks or double tholepins; set in openings in the bulwark; openings could be closed when sailing. Initially set a spritsail, later a boomed, loose-footed gaff sail; foresail, jib, topsail. Small types might set a lugsail. Special lines from the mast to a tackle on the sideboards substituted for shrouds; easily loosened for lowering the mast. Crew of 5. Reported lengths 8-9m, widths 2.5-3m. Spelling variants: **pomarynk, pommerenke**

pommerenke See **pomeranka**

Pommersche Jacht See **jacht-5, Schlup-2**

Pommersche Schlup See **Schlup-2**

Pomo balsa See **tō´ xana**

pomor ladia, pomor lodja See **lodka-3b**

pond boat See **boom boat-2**

pondt See **pot-2**

ponga See **bongo-1, panga-4**

pongee See **pungy**

pongo *Mexico, S:* Used by the natives to ferry passengers across the Río Valle Nacional, north of Oaxaca. **Dugout canoe*** to which double outriggers were placed close to the hull as sponsons. Rounded ends swept up from a flattened bottom. Length ca. 8m, beam 1.0m. Note also **bongo**.

ponsay See **panshi**

pons ductorius See **ferryboat-1**

ponsway, ponsy See **panshi**

pont *Netherlands:* **Ferryboat***, generally open, that transported passengers (the **stadspont**), horses, and vehicles across a river or along a canal. Square, overhanging ends; flat bottom. Could be rowed or sailed, setting a spritsail and forestaysail; mast stepped to one side. Now motorized (**motorpont**). Term also applies in general to a square-ended, flat-bottomed, shallow-draft boat. The **overhaalpont** was towed by the skipper, who pulled the vessel along a cable fixed to both riverbanks. The **kettingpont** was connected to a chain running over a cogged warping drum of a steam engine. The **gierpont** used the force of the current and a long cable anchored in midstream to cross from one side to the other; employed 4 leeboards. Other recorded names: **overhaalpontje, veerpont;** pl. **ponten; spoorpont** for railway cars. **Stadspontje** (dim.). Note also **ferryboat**. Further references: **pot-2, Prahm-2, punt.**

pontão See **pontoon**

pont de bateaux See **pontoon-2**

pont de calafat See **punt-2**

pont de pontons See **pontoon-2**

ponte, pontebot See **punt**

ponte di barche, ponte di chiatte, ponte di pontoni See **pontoon-2**

pontée See **chaloupe-6**

pontem See **punt**

ponten See **pont, pontin, pot-2**

pont flottant See **punt-2**

ponti See **ponto**

pontin *Philippines:* Stoutly built interisland trader common in northern Luzon. European-type hull; either open or decked at ends. Large headrails provided stowage for the wooden anchors. Local **dugout canoe*** served as the **ship's boat***. Two masts set fore-and-aft sails of either matting or canvas. 80-150t. Spelling variants: **ponten, ponting**

ponting See **pontin**

ponto 1. A 7th-century rectangular **rowing boat*** with a flat bottom and sloping sides.
  2. *France, Mediterranean coast:* Heavily built, 2-masted Roman transport vessel of the 1st century B.C. High, recurved prow; a lower, sharp stern; heavy gunwale. Flat floors carvel-built of oak; quarter rudder. Set a square mainsail and a triangular foresail to the forward-raking foremast; leather sails. Beamy.
Spelling variants: pl. **ponti, pontones.** See also **pontoon, punt.**

pontões See **pontoon**

ponton 1. *France, W:* Low, stable craft developed in the mid-20th century for the oyster culture industry of the Morbihan and Arcachon embayments. Metal construction with flat bottom; wide, square stern; straight, raked bow ending in a shallow transom. Pilot house aft. Cargo booms and other mechanical equipment on deck; inboard engine. Reported lengths 15.5-17m, beam 5-5.5m, draft ca. 0.4m. Other recorded names: **ponton arachonnais, ponton dragueur, ostréicole**
  2. *Mauritania, N:* Spanish vessel that anchors in the Baie du Lévrier to store a **trahina's*** catch and dry and repair its nets.
See also **hulk-3, pontoon.**

pontona See **pontoon**

ponton a biga See **sheer hulk**

ponton-allège See **pontoon-1, sheer hulk**

ponton à mâter See **sheer hulk**

ponton arachonnais See **ponton**

ponton-bigue See **sheer hulk**

Pontonbrücke See **pontoon-2**

ponton de carénage See **pontoon-1**

ponton de fango See **dump barge**

ponton de largare See **dummy barge-1**

pontón de limpie See **pontoon-5**

ponton dragueur ostréicole See **ponton**

pontone See **pontoon**

pontone à biga See **sheer hulk**

pontone armato See **monitor-1**

pontone-biga See **sheer hulk**

pontone a salpare, pontone d'ormeggio See **anchor hoy**

pontones See **ponto, pontoon**

pontone salpa-ancore See **anchor hoy**

pontoni See **pontoon**

ponton-mâture See **sheer hulk**

ponton mouilleur See **anchor hoy**

ponton phare See **lightship**

pontoon 1. Flat-bottomed, rectangular craft that transports heavy objects in a harbor and cargo to and from ships, or serves as a base for a floating crane or as a landing stage for a **ferry*** or pier where the tide variation requires vertical flexibility. Sometimes equipped to assist careening ships (**ponton de carenage**), especially sailing vessels along the Mediterranean coast of France. Other recorded names: **alzacaballo, Brückenkahn, Brückenponton, Brückenschiff, dummy flat, ponton-allège.** Note also **sheer hulk.**
  2. A boat that, when joined with similar boats, forms a temporary bridge. Sometimes merely a bridge of logs. Other recorded names: **bridge of boats, floating bridge, Kahnbrücke, passerelle volant(e), pont de bateaux, pont de pontons, ponte di barche, ponte di chiatte, ponte di pontoni, Pontonbrücke, pontoon bridge, puente flotante, Schiffsbrücke.** Note also **tombaz.**
  3. A **ferryboat*** or other boat used in river transport. The **Higher Ferry** at Dartmouth in southwest England in the early 19th century was a horse-propelled **pontoon.** The horse, housed within a square shelter, paced around a winch that wound a rope, propelling the vessel. Note also **horse boat-2.**
  4. A vessel designed and equipped to raise wrecks.
  5. A flat-bottomed, square-ended craft used to dredge channels, ports, and rivers. Name variant: **pontón de limpie.** Note also **dredger-1.**
  6. A ship or **hulk*** that serves as a store ship, hospital, or prison ship.
  7. *England:* Surplus World War II bridging **pontoons** were converted to canal pleasure boats; especially popular during the late 1940s and early 1950s. Generally a homemade cabin was built on the basic hull. Hull of plywood on softwood frames with angle irons. Square bow raked, transom stern plumb; straight sides. Original hulls had a grab rail along each side and 12 large oarlocks. Usually propelled by an outboard motor. Length ca. 6m, beam 1.8m, depth 0.6m. Name variant: **Bailey bridging pontoon**
Other recorded names: **pontão** (pl. **pontões**), **ponto***, **ponton, pontón, pontona, pontone** (pl. **pontoni**), **pontones, puntone, tombaz***. Further reference: **sinker boat**

pontoon bridge See **pontoon-2**

pontoon pile driver See **pile driver-1**

pontoon raft See **life raft**

pont volant See **ferryboat-1**

pookaun, pookawn, pookhaun See **púcán**

Poole canoe See **canoe-5**

Poole punt See **gun punt**

pool tow boat See **push boat-2**

pooti See **poti**

popao See **baobao**

popo *Micronesia (Caroline Islands), western Pacific:* Fast sailing **canoe***, mainly of the central island group, known to Europeans as the **flying proa***. The larger boats made long voyages, but most served for interisland transport; only the small types remain. Plank-extended **dugout canoe***; where timber was scarce, the dugout portion was merely the keel piece; planking, of irregular lengths, sewn on and caulked with a lime mixture. Hull a deep V-section, the weather side curved and the lee side lightly curved, but more often flat both vertically and longitudinally; weather gunwale slightly higher. Bottom curved fore-and-aft. Double-ended; the cutwaters and tall, bifurcated, bird-shaped figureheads were single pieces attached to the hull. Solid bulkheads and thwarts strengthened the **canoe**. Two stout booms curved downward to a short float; booms pierced the 2 washstrakes; braced by spars that ran from the outer part of the booms toward each end of the hull. Booms connected to the float by Y-shaped crutches, braced by a yoke between, or connected by 4 stanchions. A platform was built out on the booms, and on the larger **canoes**, light decking continued out beyond the solid platform. The larger **canoes** also had a canted, lightly decked platform that acted as a counterpoise on the lee side; small huts on both platforms. Hull generally painted black and burnished to a high gloss. Steered with a quarter rudder maneuvered with a tiller and by the helmsman's foot against the rudder blade. Sailed with the outrigger to windward. Single mast stepped in a socket on the platform close inboard; always raked forward, the rigging and sail being shifted from end to end with each tack. Triangular sail hung with the apex tacked to the forward end; yards at forward edge and foot. Lanceolate paddle blades. Crew of 5-6. Reported lengths 6.6-13m; e.g., length 9.1m, beam 0.91m, depth 1.2m; some small **canoes**, 5-7m, lacked the lee platform. Other recorded names: **pau-pau, prao volant, pros, pros volant**. Further reading: Thomas Gladwin, *East is a Big Bird; Navigation and Logic on Puluwat Atoll* (Cambridge: Harvard University Press, 1970).

popow *Micronesia (Caroline Islands), western Pacific:* One of the so-called albatross-tail **outrigger canoes*** extant on Yap Island, in the western group. Mainly used for local fishing. Ends extend above gunwale level in a recurved, 2-pronged fork. Dugout hull. Simple outrigger unit: 2 closely spaced, squared booms cross atop the hull, ending in a lashed stringer; vertical stick connective from each boom inserts directly into the short float; connectives braced back to the booms.

Poquoson canoe See **Chesapeake Bay log canoe-1**

por *Papua New Guinea:* **1.** Pidgin English word for a **dugout canoe*** without an outrigger. Term used mainly by coastal natives for river **canoes***.
2. Some in the northeast are beamy, heavy, and crudely built; others narrow, light, and well-shaped. After being adzed and carved, the better craft are burnished with fires of palm leaves and faggots to make them watertight and to reduce the oozing of a noxious resin. Punted with long bamboo poles, or paddled with as many as 10 standing paddlers. Name variant: **pro**

pora 1. *Easter Island, southern Pacific:* Reed **raft*** used to travel to a nearby island and to visit ships. Also used on the volcanic lake. Reeds tied into a conical bundle, turned up at the bow end. Side bundles fatter, forming "gunwales." Some were a single bundle on which the user reclined on the widest part and paddled with his feet. Reported lengths 1.5-2.1m.
2. *New Zealand:* Maori term for a **ship***, especially one of European origin. Same designation used by the Moriori of the Chatham Islands to the east.
3. Also a Maori term for a large, seagoing **canoe***, probably a double **canoe** with a platform between.

porgoe, porka See **purgoo**

porom *Balkan Peninsula:* In the language of Illyria, a **raft***, flat-bottomed **boat***, or **ferryboat***. See also **paróm**.

porón See **paróm**

portable boat See **sectional boat**

portable kayak See **kayak-3**

porta-fango See **hopper, marie-salope**

portage canoe See **woods canoe**

portanova See **barca di guardia-1**

porte-chevaux See **huissier**

portellata See **portolata**

porte-poisson See **balancelle-1**

Port-Eynon oyster skiff See **Mumbles oyster skiff**

Porthgwarra crabber See **West Country crabber**

Porthleven half boat *England, SW:* **Fishing boat*** of this community in the Falmouth area. Decked to the mast. Plumb stem, square stern, outboard rudder, tiller. Originally lug-rigged, later set a boomed gaff sail with jib to a bowsprit. Length 9.3m. Note also **half-decker**.

Porthleven lugger See **West Cornish lugger**

Port Isaac gig See **gig-4**

Port Isabel scow-sloop See **chalan**

Portland lerret See **lerret**

Port Mouton skiff See **gunning skiff-1**

portolada See **portolata**

portolata *Croatia/Italy, N:* In the Gulf of Venice and along the Dalmatian coast, term given to a **market boat*** or **fish carrier***. One will support 5-6 **braggozzi** (see **bragozzo**) or on occasion, may serve as a substitute during the trawling operation; **portolate** (pl.) also serve the **tartana***, the **bragagna***, and the **topo***. Type not specific, but those serving **bragozzi** are sharp-ended, flat-bottomed, decked at the ends, and ca. 9-10m long. Older boats stepped 3 masts, setting dipping lugsails; now employ a single mast and an engine, or are entirely motorized (the **portolato**). Spelling variants: **portellata, portolada, portulada, portulata**

portolate, portolato See **portolata**

portolatto See **market boat-3**

Portpatrick line boat, Portpatrick line skiff See **line boat-2**

Portsmouth pleasure boat See **gundalow**

Portsmouth wherry *England, S:* Fast waterman's and **passage boat**★ used during the 19th and early 20th centuries off Portsmouth and Southampton. The smaller boats worked mainly in the harbor; the larger, or First Class, conveyed officers and baggage between ships lying in Spithead and the shore or ran to the Isle of Wight with passengers and merchandise. Clinker-built, oak planking; double-ended, sharper forward; greatest beam forward of amidships; straight stem and sternpost; almost circular midship section. Side benches; thwart seat at the stern; washboards added in foul weather; small cuddy on the larger boats. Some passenger **wherries**★ ornamented with carving on the inside of the top strake and florid paintings on the stern seat backboard. Steered with yoke and rudder lines. Spritsails set on short masts; foresail tacked to stemhead. Sprits of different lengths used on main-mast, depending on weather conditions; sail brailed to mast. Mizzenmast stepped well inboard; sail sheeted to sternpost. On some, the mizzen set a lugsail. Small **wherries** set a standing lugsail. Staysail used on the 2-masted boats. Mast unstepped when rowed. Crew of 2. Reported lengths 8.23-10.46m, widths 2.51-2.74m, depths 1.45-1.68m; the Second Class boats were narrower but of normal depth for their beam. Other recorded names: **Ryde wherry**, **Spithead wherry**

portulada, portulata See **portolata**

porua *Solomon Islands, western Pacific:* Single-**outrigger canoe**★ of Ndai Island in the southeast part of the archipelago. Simple dugout hull with similar pointed ends that curve up gently from the bottom; hull round in cross section. Coverboards at the ends may be ornamented. Two widely spaced, straight booms cross the top of the hull to the long, slender float; booms and float connected by 4 light stanchions, 2 raked outward and 2 inward. Now sets a boomed spritsail and headsail. Spelling variant: **forua**

posawun See **mon-3**

postale See **mail boat-1**, **packet boat-1**

post-bark See **packet boat-1**

postbåt 1. General term in Swedish for a boat that carries the mail. Note also **isbåt**, **postjakt**.

2. *Finland:* The smaller **postbåtar** delivered the mail to areas too difficult for the **postjakter** to go. One type in the Åland Islands was a small, open boat with sharp ends; outboard rudder; tiller. Set 2 spritsails, the mainsail boomed; jib to small bowsprit. Also rowed. Note also **isöka**.

Further reference: **seksæring-2**

post boat *Scotland, W:* Small, open boat that delivered the mail in some of the more remote lochs. An early 20th-century boat on Loch Broom was a sailing/**rowing boat**★ with a curved stem; raked, wineglass transom; deep keel, clinker planking, soft turn of the bilges, moderate sheer. Tiller slotted over the raked rudder. Three thwarts, the forward one grooved for the mast partners. Set a single dipping lugsail. Rowed with a pair of oars between double tholepins. Length

4.3m, beam 1.8m, depth 0.4m. See also **jiao hua chuan**, **packet boat-1**.

Postboot See **mail boat-1**

poste au choux, poste aux choux See **market boat-4**

Postjacht See **advice boat**

postjakt 1. *Finland, Åland Islands:* Good sailing boat that carried mail between the Åland Islands and the Swedish coast. Portrayed as early as the late 17th century, and worked into the 19th century. Most built at Eckero on the western coast of Åland Island. Oak-built with counter stern and an essentially plumb stem. Maximum beam well forward, tapering aft; straight keel with drag. Decked; low house amidships. Boomed gaff sail set to mast forward of house. Topsail; 2 headsails to bowsprit, the staysail boomed. Reported lengths 10-12m; e.g., length 12m, beam 4.2m, draft 1.5m. Note also **postbåt-1**.

2. *Sweden:* Carried mail and passengers since at least the latter part of the 17th century. Some went from southern Sweden to the northern German coast. In the latter half of the 19th century, crown-owned **postjakten** (pl.) operated mail service across the strait to the Åland Islands; these were heavier than those built in the islands. Square-sterned, full bowed, poop deck. The early vessels depicted with 1-2 gaff sails, square topsails on the mainmast, 2 headsails.

postmaster's frigate, Post Office packet See **packet boat-1**

Postplätte See **Plätte-1**

post-ship *United Kingdom:* Term given to rated sailing ships (as defined by the number of guns carried), which were in the command of a post-captain and carried a master responsible for navigation.

pot 1. *Micronesia (Caroline Islands), western Pacific:* Term given to a European-type **boat**★.

2. *Netherlands:* **a.** The **pot** of northeastern Netherlands was mainly a peat carrier. Cited as early as the 15th century, working into the 19th century, but in altered forms. Some early small types, used on the smaller waterways, were lightly built, open boats with clinker planking; some with 3 planks per side; generally boxy. Some larger but still lightly built; clinker-planked craft had curved sides, a sharp rise to the bottom, and closely spaced ribs; flooring laid on the ribs; raked ends. Later boats heavier and carvel-planked (of oak); bow and stern rise from a strong sheer; flat floors, bluff bows. On some, tiller passed below a triangular helmport at the sharp stern. Decked; long hatch; long, narrow leeboards. Sprit-rigged. Early 17th-century vessels worked with 1-2 men. Reported lengths 16.5-18m; e.g., length overall 16.5m, on bottom 13.8m, beam 3.6m, depth 1.2m. Other recorded names: **Overijsselsche pot**, **pondt**, **pont**★, **poth**, **pott**, **turfpont**, **turrif pott**, **veenpont**; pl. **ponten**, **potten**. **b.** By the mid-16th century, the large **potschip** carried peat across the Zuiderzee to Amsterdam, and by the 18th century, these were similar to the **tjalk**★. Use as peat carriers discontinued during the 19th century, but those carrying porcelain and stoneware from northeastern Netherlands continued into the 20th century (the **diggelschip**); others

transported and sold small merchandise en route. Solidly built with carvel planking; heavy, curved stem; raked sternpost to a rounded stern; flat floors. Decked; long, rounded hatch; rounded leeboards; outboard rudder; tiller came inboard below the gunwale. Sprit-rig with standing sprit, jib to a running bowsprit, staysail; later boats set a gaff mainsail. Other recorded names: **Overijsselse tjalk**, **Overzeesche turfpont**, **zeegaande pot**; pl. **potschepen. c.** The 17th-century vessel of South Holland carried peat, sand, and ballast on inland waterways to Amsterdam. Full, sharply raked ends; long hatch; outboard rudder; tiller; leeboards. Sprit-rigged; staysail. Sprit raised and lowered with the aid of a windlass at the stern. Reported lengths 15.6-17m; e.g., length 15.6m, beam 3.5m. Other recorded names: **dijnop**, **dÿnop**, **dynopschuyt**, **veense turrif pondt**

3. *Papua New Guinea, Bismarck Archipelago:* Term used for a western-style **boat** in the Rabaul area of northeastern New Britain. See also **bot-9**.

potana See **mon-3**

pot boat 1. *England, S:* Works with woven pots to catch lobsters and prawns along the seaward coast of the Isle of Wight. Older boats worked 24 pots with 2 men, one to row and one to haul. Recent larger boats designed to handle as many as 100 pots. Work off beaches. Traditional open boat ca. 4.3m long.
2. *Wales, NW:* A few **pot boats** are still used from beaches along the Anglesey coast.

poth See **pot-2**

poti *Pacific Ocean:* Term used by indigenous peoples in widely separated island groups for a boat constructed along western lines; sometimes for one built on **whaleboat**★ lines. Spelling variant: **pooti** (on Nanumea in the Tuvalu Islands). Note also **poti marara**, **vaka poti**.

poti marara *Society Islands, southeastern Pacific:* Special type of boat developed on Tahiti to catch flying fish (*marara*); now used for other fishing as well. Fast and very maneuverable. Motorized. Originally 4-5m long, now ca. 6m. Name variant: **flying-fish boat**

poti vaka See **vaka poti**

Potomac ark See **ark-4c**

Potomac dory See **Potomac dory-boat**

Potomac dory-boat *United States, E:* V-bottomed boat developed at the mouth of the Potomac River in the late 1870s to dredge oysters; only a few survive. Carvel-planked; bottom fore-and-aft planked; closely spaced ribs; high chines, especially aft; straight, plumb stem; slightly raked, shield-shaped transom; centerboard. Decked forward; side decks; small cabin forward on larger boats. Painted white with colored stripes. Stepped 2 slightly aft-raking masts, the foremast taller and stepped in the eyes. Set boomed leg-of-mutton sails, or on larger boats, employed sprit booms. Last boats had engines. Crew of 3. Reported lengths 5.5-12.8m; e.g., length 10.3m, beam 3.5m, depth 0.94m. Other recorded names: **dory**★, **Potomac dory**

Potomac fish lighter *United States, E:* Transported the catch from boats fishing on the lower Potomac River to markets in the Washington, D.C., area. Operated

from the late 19th century until World War II. On the downriver trip, carried bulk cargo such as bricks, building stone, and salt. Towed by a steam **tug**★ in groups of as many as 15 vessels. Some flatiron-shaped; sharp bow, slightly raked stem; wide, vertical stern; the maximum beam just forward of the transom. Flat bottom with rocker aft; slightly flared, straight sides. Small cuddy aft for the one-man crew; long, wide hatch with 4 covers; outboard rudder; tiller; towing bitt at bow. Hull tarred. Reported lengths 13.7-18.2m; e.g., length 15.9m, beam 4.47m, depth 1.63m. Name variant: **barge**★. Note also **sharpie-2**.

Potomac longboat See **longboat-8**

Potomac River shad seine boat See **shad galley**

Potomac sharpie See **sharpie-3**

potonim, potonom See **mon-3**

potrillo See **bote-4, caballito-1, canoa-6, canoa-14**

potro *Colombia, west-central:* Small **dugout canoe**★ of the natives of Chocó Department. Square ends terminate in a platform that rises toward the ends. Paddled, the men standing, the women seated; also poled. May be anchored by inserting a pole through a hole in the bow platform. Reported lengths 2.7-4.5m, beam ca. 0.6m. Other recorded names: **champita pequeña**, **chingo**; **hápa** by the Noanama. Note also **canoa-6**, **canoa-14**.

potschepen, potschip, pott, potten See **pot-2**

Potteries boat See **narrow boat**

pottery raft See **chatty raft**

pot vessel Sets pots to catch lobsters, crabs, crayfish, etc. **Pot vessels** range from open boats for inshore work to larger vessels of 20-50m that operate at the edge of the Continental Shelf. The inshore boats are mainly rowed; fast. Other recorded names: **cayeyeur**★, **korvenvisser**, **kubbenvisser**, **natante posa nasse**, **Reusenfischer**. Note also **pot boat**.

pouce-pied See **pousse-pied**

poulacro See **polacre**

pouloua See **pallar**

pound boat *United States, E:* **1.** Used along the New Jersey coast from the 1870s until the early 1960s to empty the pound nets that were staked offshore. Two, coupled **catamaran**★-fashion, formed a platform for driving the stakes that secured the nets. The early boats were ordinary **Sea Bright skiffs**★, but these were gradually enlarged and modified for pound net work. Clinker-built; vertical stem, curved forefoot, raked transom built with lapped seams. Plank keel, initially curved, later flat; narrow, flat bottom with slack bilges; steam-bent, one-piece frames set 30cm between centers; planked-up skeg. Foredeck; raised floor in after third. Rudder replaced steering oar when engines installed (ca. 1908); rudder hung vertically, supported by a tripod strut or an iron shoe from the skeg. Launched from the beach using rollers and horses; when in the surf, the boat was hauled through by a rope to an offshore piling. Originally rowed. Six oarsmen plus the captain. Reported lengths 6-11m; e.g., length 10.7m, beam 3.1m, depth ca. 1.4m. Other recorded names: **Jersey sea skiff**, **New Jersey sea skiff**, **sea-skiff**

pound-boat. Further reading: Peter J. Guthorn, *The Sea Bright Skiff and Other Shore Boats*, rev. ed. (Exton, Pa: Schiffer Publishing Ltd, 1981).
2a. On the western shore of Chesapeake Bay, local **pound boats** were square-sterned craft powered by an old automobile engine. Flat bottom, planked athwartships with rocker at ends; plank keel; straight, flaring sides. Open; narrow coverboards with coaming. Outboard rudder. The pound nets were hauled ashore by oxen working a capstan. Length 9.4m, beam 2.3m, depth 0.66m. Name variant: **bateau***. Note also **pound net boat**. **b.** May also be used as a platform for driving the poles for the nets. Most boats of the **deadrise*** type and built in the 1920s; a few still operating in the 1990s. High, relatively sharp bow; low, square stern. Half-decked, house aft. Crew of 3. Reported lengths 12.8-14.6m; e.g., length 14.6m, beam 4.2m.
Further references: **pound net boat, sharpie-8**
pound net boat *United States:* **1.** Tended pound nets on the eastern side of Chesapeake Bay. Sometimes used as a **fish carrier*** and towed back to port. Sharp-ended, slightly curved stem and sternpost, lightly flared sides, flat floors, low freeboard. Open; narrow covering boards, bench down each side on which to kneel when hauling the nets. Towed to nets, then sculled. Length 9.5m, beam 2.5m. Other recorded names: **fish skiff, pound net skiff**. Note also **pound boat**.
2. Several types of boats were used on the Great Lakes to tend pound nets. Best known was the **pound net sharpie**. There was also a 2-masted, flatiron-shaped boat with a wide, flat bottom that turned up sharply at the stern; carvel- or clinker-built; centerboard; balanced rudder; set modified leg-of-mutton sails with batten-like gaffs. The Lake Michigan boats might be sprit- or **sloop***-rigged, and some were **scow***-like. At Waukegan, on the west shore of the lake, a type of **pound net boat** lacked sails, and was either rowed, or more often towed, to and from the nets by a horse; these were flat-bottomed with a sharp bow and broad, square stern; natural ribs with crosspieces between each frame on the bottom (length 7.6m, beam 2.4m). The so-called **pound net dinghy** (or **pound net dinkey**) was used as a **tender*** and ranged from 4.9-5.5m in length and was 1.5m wide; flat bottom with rocker; sharply raked stem; narrow, square stern; 3 rowing benches. Other recorded names: **Great Lakes pound net boat, pound boat***
pound net dinghy, pound net dinkey See **pound net boat**
pound net scow *United States:* Used for setting and pulling poles for the pound nets and weirs on the Great Lakes and on Chesapeake Bay, Cape Cod, and the Maine coast. Rectangular hull; flat bottom curved up to shallow transoms; skeg at stern for the rudder; sides flared on the east coast boats, vertical on the Great Lakes. Decked; some had a small hatch aft for gear. Often had 2 projecting timbers at the bow to hold the pile-driving rig and steady the poles; the Great Lakes and Chesapeake boats generally had a notch at the stern to facilitate pulling out the stakes, placing the rudder off center. Rudder on northern boats hung off-center and

often had an auxiliary blade that served as a supplementary centerboard. Both areas employed a large centerboard. Great Lakes boats were cat-rigged with boomed gaff sail; some **schooner***-rigged. Northern boats were cat- or **sloop***-rigged. Reported lengths 7.6-15.2m; Cape Cod boat: length 11m, beam 2.9m, depth 1.0m. Other recorded names: **pile driver*, stake boat***. Note also **pålpråm, pound boat, pound net boat**.
pound net sharpie See **pound net boat-2, sharpie-8**
pound net skiff See **pound net boat-1**
pousse-pied *France:* **1.** A 2-man craft used at Rochefort on the southwest coast to clear mud from the holds of ships, inspect mast footings, etc. Length 2.74m, width 0.9m, depth 0.3m.
2. Another type used on the tidal flats north of the Gironde Estuary by fishermen and mussel and oyster collectors. Rectangular box; cross-planked, flat bottom curves up at the bow; plumb, square stern. May

pousse-pied-2

have 2 uprights at the stern to facilitate pushing. Propelled by a man kneeling with one leg inside and pushing over the mud with the other. Reported lengths 1.2-3m; e.g., length 1.83m, width 0.46m, depth 0.3m. Other recorded names: **acon, pouce-pied**. Note also **accon-2, mud sled, ni mo chuan, Schuiten**.
pousseur See **barge-9, push boat**
pousseur-barge See **barge-9**
poutasi See **fautasi**
poveira See **lancha-8d, poveiro-2**
poveiro **1.** *Brazil, E:* Large, beamy boat that fished off Cabo Frio in Rio de Janeiro State. Very raked bow with pronounced stemhead. Set a large, quadrilateral, lateen-type sail with a short luff tacked to stemhead and sheeted to rudderhead. Also rowed.
2. *Portugal, N:* Category of beamy, sharp-ended boat found mainly in Povoa de Varzim, but ranges as far south as Sesimbra, where it is larger and heavier, and north into Spanish Galicia. Best-known are the **barco poveiro**, the **catraia***, and the **lancha***. All used principally for fishing. The **barco*** has a straight stem, the amount of rake varying with the locale; sternpost somewhat raked; outboard rudder; tiller. Lightly planked; closely spaced ribs; flat floors; keel; bold sheer on some. Either open with triangular bench at each end, or decked at bow and stern with waterways along the open waist. Most step a single mast, although at Buarcos, may step 2. Mast rakes aft on the lug-rigged boats, and forward on the lateen craft. Also rowed, against tholepins, mainly with 4 oars. Crew of 2 on the smaller boats. Reported lengths of **barco poveiro** 5.2-8.7m. Other recorded names: **poveira, povera**. Sometimes the boat takes the name of its primary activity, e.g.: **sardinheiro** for one fishing for

sardines, **troleiro** for line fishing close to shore. Note also **batel-6**.

povera See **poveiro**

pówbarkas See **barkas-3**

power boat See **tow boat-2**

power dory See **Swampscott dory**

praam *Netherlands:* Collective term for a number of long, narrow, inland cargo and produce carriers; developed in the 17th century. One type used for fishing. Clinker-built, later carvel; many of iron or steel. Longitudinally planked, flat bottom with, on the small types, rocker at the ends; plank keel; right-angle bilges into vertical sides. Bluff bow, finer stern; stem and sternpost vertical, or on some small types, sharply raked. Low sheer; large **pramen** (pl.) use leeboards. Decked, some with a cuddy forward; small, local produce carriers open. One type with a large cabin aft, often for passengers, is called a **paviljoenpraam**. Some have a wet well. Wide rudder; tiller slotted over rudderhead. Larger boats generally sailed, setting a gaff sail and foresail. Small, open **pramen** rowed and sometimes sailed, setting a spritsail. Rowed from near the bow to permit maximum space for the cargo. Outboard engines now prevalent. Large types 17-22m long; e.g., length 19m, beam 3m, depth 1.05m; shallow draft. Small **pramen** ca. 6.8-8.5m long. Other recorded names: **praamschip**, **pram***, **prame***. Note also **bolpraam**, **Drentse praam**, **Giethoornse praam**, **Hoogeveense praam**, **Meppeler praam**, **Overijsselse praam**, **praamaak**, **praamschuit**, **slijkpraam**, **spitspraam**, **Utrechtse praam**, **veense praam**. Further references: **gondola-7**, **Prahm**, **pram-1**, **pram-4**, **pram-6**

praamaak *Netherlands:* Inland vessel, considered a hybrid, with an **aak***-type bow and a **praam***-type stern. Flat bottom that turned up at the bow to the bulwarks in a flat wedge. Stern rounded; vertical sternpost. Vertical sides and bulwarks, sharp turn of the bilges. Low sheer; wide top strake above a full-length wale. Outboard rudder with fin below the waterline; tiller. Decked, long hatch. Cabin beneath the deck aft; some **praamaken** (pl.) had a deckhouse. Leeboards. Lowering mast in forward third; set a gaff sail with a very long boom. Reported lengths 23-27m; e.g., length 23m, beam 5m, depth 2.2m.

praamaken See **praamaak**

praamschip See **praam**

praamschuit *Netherlands, NE:* **Tjalk***-like boat that carried cargo and served farmers in Friesland in the 19th century. Built of wood, iron, or steel. Curved stem, straight sternpost, flat floors, rounded bilges. Only a slight sheer; lacked fixed bulwarks but had removable washstrakes. Outboard rudder, decorative rudderhead; tiller passed inboard through the top strake. Open, or decked to the mast; leeboards. Strike mast set a loose-footed, boomed gaff mainsail; very long boom; staysail, jib to a bowsprit. Crew of ca. 2. Ca. 20t. Name variants: **Friese hoy**, **Fries(ch)e praam**

praauw For all terms beginning with the word **praauw**, see **perahu**.

praem See **pram-1**

praetoris navis See **flagship**

prahau See **perahu-1**

prahic, prahik See **pahi-3**

Prahm 1. *Czech Republic, NW:* In the late 19th century, at Ústi nad Labem (formerly Aussig) on a tributary of the Elbe River, large cargo **Prahme** (pl.) were built for a one-way trip downstream, then broken up at destinations in Germany.

2. *Germany:* Note also **Eiderprahm**, **Störprahm**. **a.** Serves mainly as a heavy-duty **lighter*** or **scow*** on rivers and in ports. Dates from at least the 13th century. The **Kohlenprahm** transported bunkering coal, the **Ölprahm** carried oil, the **Minenprahm** was a mine carrier, the **Wasserprahm** supplied fresh water to ships (see **water boat**), **Salzprähme** carried salt. The small, flat-sided **Scheuerprahm** serves as a floating stage during painting and cleaning of ships. **Baggerprähme** have a trap door in the bottom to release ash and mud (see **hopper**). Some serve as **pontoons*** for raising and lifting heavy objects. The **Fährprahm** (or **Prahmfähr**) ferries automobiles. Most have low, straight sides; flat bottom. Constructed of wood or steel. May have square or sharp ends. Generally open, but some decked (**gedeckter Prahm** or **Decksprahm**). Early boats rowed. Other recorded names: **Leichterprahm**, **Pont**. Note also **Mudderprahm**. **b.** On the Baltic coast, especially in the area of Rügen Island, **Prähme** were mainly sturdy **ferryboats*** (**Fahrprähme**) until ca. 1930. **Viehprähme** ferry cattle to fields, even today. Cross-planked, flat bottom with rocker; 2-3 side planks; heavily timbered; blunt, raked ends; open. Most poled, occasionally rowed; some of the larger had a motor. Reported lengths 4-20m; widths 1.25-7m. **c.** In the area of Mursewiek, a net-fishing **Prahm** is occasionally seen. May also be called a **Gårnprahm** or **Sohlenboot**. **d.** On the upper and middle Elbe, special wooden **Karpfenprähme** were constructed for live carp being taken down the river to Hamburg.

Spelling variants: **Praam***, **pram***, **Prame***, **prôm**; pl. **Prähme**, **pramen**. Further references: **Brëëm**, **Schute-6**

Prähme See **Prahm**

Prahmfähr See **Prahm-2**

praho See **perahu-1**, **sampan-4**

prahoe For all terms beginning with the word **prahoe**, see **perahu**.

prahoe djaten See **jaten**

prahu For all terms beginning with the word **prahu**, see **perahu**. See also **flying prau**, **tongkang Mělayu**.

prahuk See **perahu-1**

praieira de ribatejo See **lancha-8**

pram 1. May refer to a flat-bottomed craft, **barge***, or **lighter***, or to a small boat with a small bow transom and larger stern transom. On occasion, may be a disparaging term for a small boat or for a clumsy and unsightly vessel. In Slavic languages, designates a large **ferryboat***; in Bulgarian, may merely imply a large, decked craft. Slavic **prams** characteristically used an L-shaped bilge plank. Spelling variants: **praam***, **praem**, **Prahm***, **pråm**, **prám**, **prama**, **pramče** (Croatian dim.), **prame***, **pram(m)ŭpramm***, **prámr**, **praum**, **prom(ik)**, **prum**

2. A **yacht's* dinghy***. Distinguished from other types by having the small **pram** bow. Clinker-built, square stern, deadrise or rounded bottom that sweeps up at the bow. Generally no keel. Lengths ca. 1.96-4.88m. Other recorded names: **pram dinghy, pram dingi, pram jolle**
3. Small **ship's boat*** during the 16th-18th centuries.
4. *Denmark, W:* Clinker-built **fishing boat*** of the west coast of Jutland, often working off beaches (**land-dragningspram**). Characterized by its **pram** bow: the side and bottom strakes are gathered together to form an overhanging, tapered bow, ending in a small, flat stem piece. Raked stern mostly sharp, but may be a transom type. Wide, rounded bottom; skeg aft; may have grounding keels; some flat-floored. Many use a centerboard; large rudder. Open or half-decked, usually with side decking. When sailed, steps a single pole mast to which a spritsail, 1-2 headsails, and sometimes a topsail are set; reefing bowsprit. Also rowed, and engines recently installed. Crew of 4. Reported lengths 5-7m, widths 1.7-2.6m, depths 0.66-0.86m. Spelling variants: **praam***; pl. **pramme(n)**. Note also **Hjertingpram, Norsk pram**.
5. *England:* A late 19th-century English **pram** was used for racing, and the larger sizes carried 2 lugsails. Planks treenailed, fastened to the keelson and timbers. Flat floors, deep keel aft, bottom curved up at bow.
6. *Norway:* Spelling variants: **praam*, prahm*, prame norvégienne, pramm(en), prom**; pl. **prammar**.
a. Small open boat, mainly of southeastern Norway, that has been popular as a **ship's boat**, but also engages in local fishing, hunting, and transportation. Adapted in Denmark as the **Norsk pram***, in Sweden as the **eka***, and in Germany as the **nordischer Kahn**. Clinker-built; strong bottom rocker, the bow ending well above the water. Greatest beam abaft amidships. Semicircular cross section amidships, at the raked transom, and at the small bow transom. Plank keel on those mainly rowed; keel or centerboard on those that also sail. Two to 4 thwarts; may have a stern seat. Mainly rowed or sculled. When sailed, sets 1-2 small sprit- or lugsails. Outboard motors prevalent. Reported lengths 2.4-9.1m; e.g., length 5.2m, beam 1.6m, depth 0.49m. Two major types—one from the Arendal area, the other from Holmsbu. The **holmsbupram** is more elongated, has finer lines, and the garboard strakes have no deadrise, being set above the bottom plank; protective laths tacked along the garboard strakes. The **arendalspram** laps the garboard under the bottom plank and has a small skeg aft. A 9-strake Holmsbu boat may be called a **nibordspram** or **nibording**; the larger, 11-strake **pram** is an **ellevebordspram** or **ellevebordinger**. Other recorded names: **Norwegian pram, pram norvégien(ne). b.** In Finnmark in northern Norway, a **todeltpram** is used for lake fishing. This boat can be bisected (*todelt*) to permit easier portaging. Double bulkheads secured on the outside with metal clasps; full-length gunwale strips come off separately. Carvel-planked; raked end transoms, flat bottom.

7. *United States, E:* A variety of **pram** was used on the Eastern Shore of Chesapeake Bay as a **tender*** to a **yacht**. Steel-shod runners on each bilge enabled it to cross the ice with a push pole. Square, raked ends; flat bottom cross-planked, single plank on each side. Mainly rowed. Length 2.5m, beam 0.9m. Further references: **kunte, praam, prahm, prame-2, pråmm**
prama See **perama-2, pram-1, prame-2**
pråmar, pråmarna See **pråmm**
pramče See **pram-1**
pram dinghy, pram dingi See **pram-2**
prame 1. *England, E:* In the dialect of Suffolk, a flat-bottomed boat or **lighter***.
2. *France:* During the 18th and early 19th centuries, heavily armed **prames** defended the coast, especially the harbors of the north coast. Flat-floored, some with 3 parallel keels; vertical stern. Some had space for as many as 50 horses. **Ketch***- or **bark***-rigged; also rowed. Reported lengths 29-37m; e.g., length 37m, beam 8m, draft 2.5m. Spelling variants: **pram*, prama** See also **gondola-7, praam, Prahm, pram-1**.
pramen See **praam, Prahm**
prame norvégienne See **pram-6**
pram fra Hjerting See **Hjertingpram**
pram jolle See **pram-2**
pråmm *Sweden:* **1.** On the Baltic coast, a simple, flat-bottomed boat that transports animals between the mainland and off-lying island pastures; also transfers produce and fishing gear. In the area of the Øresund on the southwest coast, the word may be applied to any flat-bottomed boat, while to the north on this coast, it may be synonymous with the **eka** (see **orusteka**).
2. The typical **prömm** (or **flateka**) in Dalsland in southwest-central Sweden has square, raking ends, the bow relatively narrow. Wide, lapped or carvel strakes; flaring sides; strong rocker to flat bottom, rising to bow transom. Rowed with single pair of oars. Lengths 4.6-4.9m; e.g., length 4.9m, beam 1.6m, depth 0.4m.
3. The **pråmmar** (pl.) in the Skane area of southwestern Sweden are open **rowing boats***. Clinker-planked, rocker to bottom. Some round-bottomed, but with flat floors, skeg aft, and a small bow transom. Others flat-bottomed with sharp bow and raked or curved stem. Transom stern. Frames in 3 parts—across the bottom and down each side. Stern seat, 1-2 thwarts. Rowed with 1-2 pairs of oars, between double tholepins. Reported lengths 4-4.3m, widths ca. 1.5-2m, depths ca. 0.5-1.0m.
4. On inland waterways in the south, the **pråmm** is mainly a **barge***, the **kolpråmm** carrying coal, for instance. Might be poled in confined areas, tracked by oxen from shore, or towed on lakes by a motorized craft, often in trains. Clinker-planked; flat bottom; sharp ends, often raked; open. When poled, employs 2-4 men. Reported lengths 13-15m; e.g., length 15m, beam 3.5m, depth 1.4m.
Spelling variants: **pram***; pl. **pråmar(na), pråmmarna**. Further reference: **pram**
prammar See **pram-6, pråmm**
pråmmarna See **pråmm**

pramme See **pram-4**

prammen See **pram-4**, **pram-6**

prammŭ See **pram-1**

pram norvégien, pram norvégienne See **pram-6a**

prámr, pramŭ See **pram-1**

prancha *Brazil:* **1.** A long, wide, flat-bottomed boat from Campos in the Rio de Janeiro area with a dugout base to which 1-3 planks (*prancha*) and ribs are added. Raking stem terminates in a tall stemhead; vertical stern. Transports produce and firewood from tributary rivers and carries passengers and cargo to and from ships. Name variant: **chalana⋆**
2. In Mato Grosso in western Brazil, has been used for river travel since the 19th century. Bow bluntly pointed and overhanging; stern squared. Flat-roofed house amidships; rudderpost comes up inboard. Floats downstream; upstream, uses a cone-ended pole, but when water is too deep, the poler uses the hook on the other end to catch onto tree branches. Spelling variant: **plancha**
See also **perua.**

prao For all terms beginning with the word **prao**, see **perahu.** See also **padow.**

praoe For all terms beginning with the word **praoe**, see **perahu.**

praoe pinis See **penis**

praou See **perahu-1**

prao volant See **popo, wa lap**

prau For all terms beginning with the word **prau**, see **perahu.**

prauh See **perahu-1**

praum See **pram-1**

prau prau, prau², prauw, prauwe, prauwen See **perahu-1**

praw See **perahu-1**, **prow-1**

prawe See **perahu-1**

prawn boat See **shrimper**

prawner General term for a craft that fishes for prawns, usually with pots. Note also **shrimper.** Further reference: **Morecambe Bay prawner**

prawn-tailed batela See **batela-2**

praw tampanggan See **tambang**

predatore See **caper**

prema, preme See **perama-2**

prèr *Palau, western Pacific:* **Raft⋆** used for fishing in the lagoon on Palau Island. Nine or 10 large poles were laid side-by-side, secured by lashings and thin strakes driven through the poles. Better **rafts** had a platform to protect men and gear. Reported lengths 6-8m, width 1.0m.

press galley See **galley-7**

press tender See **tender**

presteskyssbåt See **skyssbåt**

Presto ketch See **sharpie-5**

prima lancia See **lancia**

Prince Edward Island surfboat *Canada, E:* Strong, light boat found on isolated and recreational beaches of the island and on the north coast of Nova Scotia. Used for communication, fishing, and rescue. Originally 4 lapped cedar or redwood strakes on each side, now of plywood planking. Narrow, flat bottom; shallow keel; curved sides. Curved stem with cutaway forefoot; wide transom stern. Buoyancy tanks beneath the 3 thwarts on the rescue boats. Painted white with red gunwales. Rowed with 2 pairs of oars. Length 4.3m, beam 1.4m.

Prince's Bay oyster skiff See **Staten Island skiff**

prinsenjacht See **jacht-3**

pripri *West Indies:* A bamboo or log **raft⋆** used mainly for fishing; some carry produce, often on a one-way trip. Some are simple **rafts** of 4-6 logs placed side-by-side and secured at each end by a metal pin run through the logs, or lashed with cord or fibers. Haitian craft use bamboo poles arranged to form a blunt bow; a 2nd, larger pole may add freeboard, and a seat may be erected aft. In addition to being rowed, they sometimes sail, setting a farina sack or mat sail to a short pole mast. Some employ a spritsail. Haitian **rafts** reported ca. 2.44m long and 0.9m wide. Other recorded names: **pingarde, piperis, pipirit, pyperi.** Note also **piperi.**

prison hulk See **hulk-3**

privateer A privately owned, outfitted, and manned armed vessel officially commissioned by virtue of a letter of marque or similar document to take merchant enemy ships as prizes in time of war. Built and operated strictly as vessels of war. The underwriters, the crew, and the government claimed shares of the spoils. Instituted in 1293; abolished in 1856, but abolishment not acknowledged by a number of countries. Word often used synonymously with **corsair⋆.** The late 18th-century **private man-of-war** (or **flyer⋆**) was usually a heavily armed, converted **merchantman⋆.** The **letter of marque ship** was a less well-armed merchant vessel that could lawfully capture enemy vessels encountered while en route. Rig and size varied. Selected name variants: **buque armado en corso, cruiser⋆, Freibeuter, pirateer, raider, sea wolf.** Note also **caper, freebooter, sea rover.**

private man-of-war See **privateer**

Privater *Germany:* Designates a vessel that is privately owned and operated as opposed to one owned by a company.

pro See **perahu-1, por-2**

proa For terms using **proa** in combined form, see **perahu.** See also **flying prau.**

proah See **perahu-1**

proa volant See **flying proa, wa lap**

processing ship See **factory ship**

procession barge See **barge-3**

produce boat See **flatboat-4**

proe See **perahu-1, prow-1**

prom See **Prahm, pram-1, pram-6**

promik See **pram-1**

prömm See **pråmm-2**

promyslovoe sudno See **fishing boat**

prorĕz *Russia:* **1.** A vessel with a wet well (see **well boat**).
2. Those on the lower Volga River transported fish to market and canneries at Astrakhan at the northern end of the Caspian Sea. Wells occupied a major part of the vessel; water entered through a series of long, narrow slits. Flat bottom; sharp bow, slightly concave; decked. Two-masted, the small foremast stepped in the

eyes; set lugsails. Now motorized. Other recorded names: **Astrakhan river smack**; **proreze, prorezi, prorezy, tank boat**★

proreze, prorezi, prorezy See **prorěz**

pros See **padow, perahu-1, popo**

pros volant See **popo**

proviantbåt See **bumboat-1**

Proviantboot See **kadraai, market boat**

Proviantschiff See **Leibschiff, store ship**

Providence River boat See **catboat-2b**

provo See **prow-1**

provoe See **perahu-1, prow-1**

prow 1. An Anglo-Indian word for a variety of ill-defined native vessels, cited especially in references to the west coast of India. Early explorers to the Indian Ocean used several allied spellings for these vessels. Some of the variants overlap with terms used in the Malay Archipelago (see **perahu**), the Philippines, and Micronesia. Those on the Indian coast ranged from large, simple **dugout canoes**★ to small, rowed and sailed vessels used in commerce and war. Some of the large Indian pirate vessels were manned by 500-600 men. Spelling variants: **pairau, parao**★, **parau**★, **paro(o), parrua, paru**★, **pharao, praw, proe, provo(e)**
2. In poetry, a **ship**★.
Further references: **padow, perahu-1**

prum See **pram-1**

p'thlee See **pith-lo**

púcán *Ireland, W:* Open **Galway hooker**★-type boat used mainly for fishing, transporting peat, and collecting seaweed; a few remain as pleasure craft. Heavy carvel planking with stout frames; long and straight keel with drag. Full bow with either a straight and plumb or a rounded stem; strongly raked transom hung with a narrow outboard rudder.

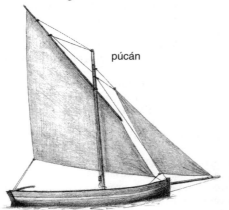

púcán

Marked sheer; tumble home to topsides; low free-board with weatherboards installed abaft the mast on some; hull tarred. A stout, unstayed mast stepped about a third of the way aft of a slot across the keelson, supported against the 2nd thwart by an iron band. Sets a high-peaked, loose-footed, tanned dipping lugsail, triangular in shape, with a partial yard; hoisted by 2 halyards and tacked to posts on either side of the breast stock; peak halyard supports outer

end of the yard. Small jib may be set flying from a bowsprit run out through the port gunwale. Also rowed. Crewed by a man and a boy. Reported lengths 6.1-8.5m, widths 1.8-2.4m, depths 1.2-1.5m, draft aft 0.8-1.1m. Other recorded names: **Galway pookaun, pook(h)aun, pookawn; gleóiteog beag** (small size)

pudden See **compartment boat**

puente flotante See **pontoon-2**

Puerto Rico racing sloop See **navito barco**

puffer *United Kingdom:* In the Royal Navy, a heavily built, fishing-type vessel. Multipurpose craft that, among other things, served to land armed parties and functioned as a supply boat. Fitted with a single-cylinder engine. See also **gabbart-3**.

Puget Sound gillnet boat See **gillnetter-2**

puhau See **mokihi-1**

pu hoe *Society Islands, southeastern Pacific:* Single-outrigger paddling **canoe**★ used on most of the islands, mainly for fishing. The simple, single-piece dugout hull is called a **pu hoe**, or **va'a**★, while a **canoe** constructed of 2 or more pieces butted together is a **tipai hoe**. Square molding added along the gunwale; some large **canoes** have washstrakes; bottom rounded transversely; generally slab-sided. Concave, vertical, or raked cutwater; some have a square bow platform

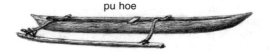

pu hoe

sewn on. Stern rounds up on the bottom and tapers to an overhanging point; on one kind, the **pu vohé**, the stern terminates in a raking, U-shaped transom. Slender float connected by 2 booms on the port side; extends up to or forward of the bow; terminates just behind the after boom. Foreboom, forming a reverse curve, attaches to the float with 2 pairs of stanchions; boom extends beyond starboard side; after boom connects directly with float. Paddled or poled. Used by 1-6 persons. Reported lengths 4.6-10m, widths 0.41-0.48m, depths 0.31-0.46m.

pukat See **sampan pukat**

puke *New Zealand:* Maori term for a **ship**★, especially one of European origin. Other recorded names: **kai pouke, kaipuke**. See also **te-puke**.

pukei, puki See **te-puke**

pukutan See **baroto**

pulaka See **polacre**

pullboat *United States, SE:* Type of **barge**★ used in cypress and swamp hardwood operations. A steam cable skidder mounted on board is used to extract logs from the swamp and place them on the **barge**, which then transports them out through the narrow passageways. Floated or towed to and from the site. Name variant: **pulling boat**★. See also **skipjack-1**.

pull ferry See **ferryboat-1**

pull flat See **covered sled**

pulling boat One designed to work under oars or sculls. Term more likely to be used for seagoing craft, as opposed to inland **rowboats★**, and is preferred in naval terminology. Other recorded names: **canot à l'aviron, Dollenboot, embarcation à l'aviron, grebnaia sliupka, Ruderboot**. Note also **barge-2, rowing boat**. Further reference: **pullboat**

pulpwood barge See **barge-11j**

pulva, pulwá, pulwar See **pallar**

pump boat 1. *Canada, SE/United States, NE:* Used in conjunction with herring weirs. The boat enters the weir and pumps the fish out of the enclosure into its own hold or into another vessel that transports the catch to shore. The **pump boat** sells the herring scales to a processing plant making paint, jewelry, buttons, and cosmetics, the scales having been filtered out and deposited into containers on deck. Name variant: **pumper**

2. *England:* Used to empty the water from canal locks and pounds and to assist in salvaging sunken vessels from the canal waterways.

See also **banca, largarete**.

Pumpenboot, Pumpendampfer, Pumpenschiff See **fire boat**

pumper See **pump boat**

pumpkin seed A beamy **dinghy★**. Note also **melon seed**.

pump vessel See **fire boat**

pumuk o'wan *United States, W:* A **balsa★** of the Yokut of central California. Made from 3 bundles of tule sedge; long central bundle; the outer 2, smaller and fatter, created slightly raised sides. Bow end bent up and tied in a point. Poled on Tulare Lake (now dry) and surrounding waterways, using one pole when traveling with a single passenger, or 2 when more people were on board; held up to 6 comfortably. Other recorded names: **owon, tuwipē**

pungee, pungee boat, pungie, pungo See **pungy**

pungy *United States, E:* An important **schooner★** type on Chesapeake Bay in the 2nd half of the 19th century, a few working until the late 1940s. In winter, dredged for oysters, and in other seasons, engaged in general freighting. Some served as **packet boats★**, and a few briefly carried pineapples from the Bahamas. Those active in menhaden fishing that were not owned by a fish plant were called **snappers** or **snapper rigs**. Differed from other Bay **schooners** by having drag to the keel, greater mast rake, log rail, stepped transom, maximum beam farther forward. One variety had a centerboard and was called a **she-pungy**. Carvel-planked; amount of deadrise varied, the earlier vessels having considerable rise to the floors; round bilges; drag to the keel; maximum beam well forward; moderate sheer. Raked stem with strongly curved rabbet; full bow on deck, sharp below; head long and pointed in profile; elaborate trailboards. Raking sternpost; square stern with shallow upper and lower transoms; bottom of lower transom characteristically formed a cross seam at right angles to the sternpost. Rudderstock passed through the massive transom beam; steered with a wheel; on one type, the **beanie**, the rudderstock was outboard. Flush deck, trunk cabin, small main hatch; stanchion and cap rail aft, log rail forward. Most painted with a

bottle-green sheer strake, flesh pink below, white rail. The 2 masts raked aft; mainmast carried a topmast that was bowed forward slightly. Gaff mainsail boomed; gaff foresail originally lapped the main and was loose-footed, later boomed. Short, stout bowsprit supported by forestay; large jib, generally club-footed. The small **pungy** from Tangier Island was single-masted, and a particularly small one was called a **large bateau**. Crew of 1-2. Reported lengths 9-24m; 1871 vessel 16m long, 5.6m wide, 1.7m deep. Other recorded names: **Chesapeake Bay pungy, oyster pungy, pongee, pungee (boat), pungie, pungo; pungyboat** (the smaller sizes). Type with a centerboard also called **female pungy, pungy-schooner, square-sterned bugeye**. Note also **bugeye, small bateau**.

pungyboat, pungy-schooner See **pungy**

punkin seed See **melon seed**

punshi, punsoee, punsui See **panshi**

punt 1. A simply constructed craft, generally with a flat bottom athwartships and rockered at the ends, longitudinally planked. Square ends, generally raked to permit nosing onto river or lake banks; may have coverboards at ends. Low, straight, flared sides, either parallel or curved; flat or slight sheer. Poled (punted) or rowed; occasionally sailed, in which case a centerboard is added; now frequently propelled by an outboard motor. Currently used mainly for pleasure. Reported lengths 3.7-6.1m; shallow. Other recorded names: **accon★, flat★, scow★**

2. A rectangular floating platform on which workmen stand to caulk, paint, or clean a ship's sides. Generally sculled, sometimes rowed. Other recorded names: **batea★, floating stage, plancha de agua, pont de calafat, pont flottant, ras de carène, side punt**. Note also **bac, balsa raft, chalana-2, plate-3, raft**.

3. A loose term for a small, beamy boat, especially a **dinghy★**.

4. Term has at times been applied to a **ferryboat★, barge★, raft★, dugout canoe★, lighter★, ship's boat★,** and inshore **fishing boat★**.

5. *Australia, SE:* Worked the oyster farms along the Hunter River, north of Sydney; the boats were also used to cut mangrove poles for the oyster stakes. Flat bottom; wide, square ends; low sides, little sheer. Mainly poled, but rowed in open areas. Length 4.3m.

6. *Canada, E:* Round-bottomed keel boat employed in coastal fishing off Newfoundland. Basically open, although loose planking may be laid across the thwarts amidships; standing room for the fishermen at both bow and stern. Propelled by oars (**row punt**), sail, or motor. Generally single-masted, setting low mainsail, jib, and driver. Crew of 2. Reported lengths 4.9-7.6m.

7. *England, SE:* **a.** From the late 19th century, the **pleasure punt** on the Thames was fairly beamy and flat-bottomed. The flat sides are joined by cross boards supported by braces; each end slants to permit easy access to the boat from the bank. Decked at the stern, from which end it is punted. Traditionally painted green. Sometimes fitted with mast and sail. The earlier **punts** were used mainly for fishing and had a live well; the **rough punt** was also used for weeding and de-silting; popular also on the east coast. Other recorded names: **family punt**, **Thames punt**. Further reading: R. T. Rivington, *Punting, Its History and Techniques* (Oxford: R. T. Rivington, 1983). **b. Racing punts** were popular with both amateurs and professionals in the mid-19th century. Lightly built; similar, square, overhanging ends; poled from amidships in either direction; ends one-half the width of the widest beam. Flat, vertical sides; hard chines. Floor ribs provided traction for the punter. Reported lengths 7-10.7m; e.g., length 8.5m, beam 0.68m. Those as wide as 91cm were sometimes called **barges**; the **semi-racer** might be as narrow as 46cm. Note also **best and best punt**. Further reading: See Rivington above.

8. *England, SW:* The West Country **punt** is a round-bottomed **rowing boat***. Used generally as a work boat or a **ship's boat**, as on the **Brixham smack***. Clinker-built; transom stern with deadwood below, bluff bow; may have bilge keels. Also sculled from the stern. Ca. 3m long.

9. *England, W:* The small, heavily built boats that served **pilot cutters** of the Bristol Channel were called **punts**. Clinker-built; flat floors; transom stern. Carried aboard on the port side; on the **cutters*** out of Bristol, the **punt** was launched through a section of gunwale that was unshipped; on the Welsh **cutters**, the **punt** was handled over the lower gunwale. Painted white for visibility. Reported lengths 3.8-4m; e.g., length 3.8m, beam 1.44m, depth 1.14m. The small **rowing boats** of the River Mersey **pilot cutters** were also called **punts**. Other recorded names: **boarding punt**, **pilot punt**

10. *Northern Ireland:* In general, a small, clinker-built, open boat with transom stern. Between Bloody Bridge and Cranfield on the south County Down coast, the term applies to any craft under 5.5m long. Elsewhere along the coast, used mainly in connection with lobstering and fishing; towed by, or carried aboard, a **lugger*** to the fishing grounds. On returning, if low tide prevents entry to the harbor, the **punt** ferries the catch to shore. Sculled from the square stern, oar feathered in a scull hole. Also rowed or sets a single lugsail; lobstering boats may have outboard motors. Length ca. 3.7m. Name variant: **yawl***

11. *United States:* **a.** A class of workboat in the U.S. Navy. Square and slightly raked ends; maximum beam amidships; flat bottom, slight rocker toward ends; plank keel; bilge battens; straight sides. Two thwarts and covering boards. Rings on gunwales and stringers for hoisting aboard. Rowed and sculled. Length 3.7m, beam 1.27m, depth 0.5m. **b.** One form of shallow-water **shooting punt** consisted of a canvas-covered, rectangular framework that was collapsible. Diagonal bottom frames were fastened with wingnuts and hinges, enabling the craft to be folded flat. Generally poled. Length 4.3m, beam 0.9m, depth 0.3m. Note also **gun punt**. **c.** Another type of **shooting punt** had a cambered bottom with rocker at the bow that meets the foredeck. Rounded bow; shallow, square stern.

Low coaming surrounded the square cockpit; stern deck could carry decoys. A pair of oarlocks fitted to side decks. Length 3.7m, beam 1.2m. **12.** *United States, E:* **a.** Small fishing and duck-hunting craft used in the 19th century on Long Island in New York State and elsewhere along the Atlantic coast. Shallow hull; flat bottom transversely planked; usually a sharp bow; square or rounded stern; low, vertical sides. Some had a centerboard or daggerboard. Fairly flat decks; the foredeck ca. 1.2m long, the after deck ca. 0.62m long and enclosed by a bulwark that provided space for the catch; cockpit coaming ca. 10cm deep. While underway, the gunner sat on the watertight hatch, and the guide stood on the deck to pole. Also rowed. Crossed both ice and open water; curved, brass-sheathed runners on those used over the ice. Might set a spritsail to a portable mast. Steered initially by dragging the pike pole, a long pole with a vertical blade; later steered by a spiked wheel. Length 3.9m, beam 1.3m. Other recorded names: **dinky**, **gunning punty**, **puntie**, **punty**. Note also **dink**, **gun punt**. **b.** On Chesapeake Bay, a modified **dugout canoe** of the colonial period might be called a **punt**. Sides softened with hot water, and thwarts inserted to maintain the expanded width. Ends spoon-shaped. Reported lengths 3.7-4.6m, widths 0.61-1.22m. **c.** A large type of **punt** searched the western shores of Chesapeake Bay for cobbles to be used as street paving. **d.** Also on Chesapeake Bay, the fisherman's **punt** had a covered well amidships in which live bait was placed, and where crabs and eels could be held. Oystermen found the **punt** handy for shallow water hand picking.

13. *United States, NE:* Used by lobstermen to go out to their moored **lobster smacks***. Straight sides; flat bottom that curves up at each end. Sometimes called a **chopping tray** because of its resemblance to an old-fashioned kitchen chopping tray. Small, but has a large capacity.

Other recorded names: **platea skaphe**, **pont***, **ponte-(bot)**, **pontem**, **ponto***, **punt-boat**, **punte***, **punte boot**, **punto**. Note also **beach punt**, **gun punt**. Further references: **ballast punt**, **beach punt**, **best and best punt**, **coble-4b**, **cock boat-3**, **crabbing punt**, **dinghy-1**, **Falmouth oyster punt**, **Falmouth quay punt**, **Fenland punt**, **gunning skiff-3**, **Hastings lugger**, **ice punt-2**, **johnboat-1**, **Plymouth barge**, **rodney**, **scow-2**, **sealing punt**, **skiff-6**, **skiff-8**, **Thames lighter**, **West Cornish lugger**, **Weston-super-Mare flatner**

punt-boat See **punt**

Pünte *Germany, NW/Netherlands, NE:* Flat-bottomed, wooden **barge*** of the Ems Estuary and connecting canals and the East Frisian Islands, carrying wood, stone, straw, cattle, etc. Mainly built at Haren; reported as early as 1800 and used into the 1930s. Flat, square bow enabled the craft to nose onto riverbanks to load and unload. Sharp, vertical sternpost (**Spitzpünte***), or rounded stern (**Rundpünte**); angular bilges; straight, sloping sides; little sheer. Large outboard rudder, wide below the waterline; used large leeboards when sailing. Open, or decked forward with lockers for cables and rigging; towing horses housed forward; cabin aft. Early boats poled, later towed, using the mast as a purchase. When sailed, set a tanned square, lug-, or spritsail. Pole mast secured between 2 bitts; could be struck. Crew of 2. Reported lengths 14-28.5m; e.g., length 25m, beam 4.25m, depth 1.5-2.2m; shallow draft. Other recorded names: **Eemspunt, Emspünte, Harener Pünte, Harense punt, Münstersche Pünte**

punte See **punt, Schute**

punte boot See **punt**

punter *Netherlands:* Graceful, slender boat of the narrow waterways bordering the Zuiderzee, especially the southeastern part. Transports produce, thatching hay, cattle, and cargo (**vrachtpunter**), and fishes for flounder and eels (**vispunter**). In the 17th century, known as a **weyschuit**★. Sharp ends, with strongly raked, straight stem and lower, straight, raked sternpost. Flat bottom, longitudinally planked; may be curved fore-and-aft; keel piece runs under bow and stern; sharp bilges. Tumble home to top strake. Large, triangular rudder easily unshipped so that the boat can be backed into narrow passages; long, downsloping tiller. Small boats open with short end decks, stern bench, and mast thwart; larger boats half-decked. One or 2 leeboards. **Fishing boats**★ have a live well (**kaarpunter**★). Originally sprit-rigged to a mast stepped well forward; later employed a wide foresail, the sheet of which extended beyond the mast. Large **punters** set a gaff sail with the gaff almost vertical; large staysail. Boomed-out, triangular sail may be run up aft of the mast. Also rowed, punted, or pushed; the punting pole has a cross-piece for the shoulder; punted from the stern. Outboard motors common. Crew of 1-2. Reported lengths 3.4-12m; length-to-beam ratio 4.2:1; shallow draft. Further reading: Gait L. Berk, *De Punter* (Weesp: De Boer Maritiem, 1984). Note also **Aalsmeerse punter, Giethoornse punter, Hoornse punter, kaarboot, vlot, zeepunter**. Further reference: **grundel**

puntie See **punt-12a**

punto See **punt**

puntone See **pontoon**

punty See **punt-12a**

pup See **single pup, timber raft-2a**

puparin *Italy, NE:* A member of the **sandolo**★ family. Originally a private passenger craft (**puparin da casada**) at Venice and also used for hunting in the lagoon. Now mainly raced (**puparin da regata**). Very light hull. Long, straight, narrow, pointed bow with an iron thimble capping the stem. Wedge-shaped, overhanging transom; stern sheer sweeps up smoothly and is considerably higher than the bow. Flat bottom with rocker; flaring sides; ribs set abaft the floor timbers in the after half of the boat and forward of the timbers in the forward half. Hull asymmetric, the port side fuller. Arched deck at the bow; stern deck has a block on the port side from which the oarsman works the oar to starboard with his right foot; side deck wide toward the stern on the port side. Propelled by 2-3 oarsmen, standing. Reported lengths 7-10m; e.g., length 9.25m, beam 1.22m, depth ca. 0.3m. Other recorded names: **barca da casada, puparino, pupparin, sandolo pup(p)arin**; pl. **puparini**

puparin da casada, puparin da regata, puparini, puparino, pupparin See **puparin**

puré See **roko-2**

purbshrits See **lightship**

purga, purgo, purgoe See **purgoo**

purgoo *Bangladesh/India, NE:* High-sided, beamy craft that anchored off the Ganges Delta to serve as a **lighter**★ to assist in off-loading ships; cited in 17th-century reports. Rowed with as many as 5 oars to a side; oars had heart-shaped blades. Anchored from the stern. Other recorded names: **byrogoe, porgoe, porka, purga, purgo(e)**

purjelaiva See **sailer**

purse boat See **bait boat-2, menhaden boat, seine boat-1, seine boat-5a**

purse-seine boat, purse seiner See **seine boat-1**

push boat 1. Designed with a powerful engine to push one or more **barges**★ rather than towing them. Mainly rectangular, but some present-day **push boats** are constructed so that the bow wedges into a V-shaped stern on the **barge**, thereby becoming, essentially, a single unit. On some, the pilot house is raised to enhance visibility forward. Some designed to either push or pull according to need. Other recorded names: **buksir-tolkach, duwboot, pousseur, pusher, pusher boat**★, **push(er) tug, push tow, Schubboot, Schubschlepper, Schubschiff, spintore, tow boat**★. Note also **tug**.

2. *United States, central:* Push-type boats on the Ohio and Mississippi Rivers, often called **tow boats**, were stern-wheel **paddle steamers** with multiple rudders. Developed in the mid-19th century. Most narrow with low freeboard. Pilot house generally amidships. **Pool tow boats** were those with pilot house forward and low smokestacks to permit passage beneath bridges across the pools above dams. Living space for crew of ca. 28. The arrangement of the **barges** might vary according to the swiftness of a particular stretch of river, a single-file arrangement being used in the quieter stretches. On some, a **barge** was made fast to each side of the **tow boat** to assist in pushing the tow, and was called a **driver**. Modern **tow boats** may have three 2.7m-long propellers and push a line of **barges** 0.4km long. The tunnel type had twin propellers in tunnels at the stern; 4 rudders; length 61m, beam 12.2m. Other recorded name: **rafting boat**. Note also **bow boat**.

3. *United States, E:* Hunting boat of the coastal sounds of North Carolina. Propelled by poling. Those designed to carry decoys were open with a sharp bow, wide transom stern; straight, flared sides; flat bottom, narrow side decks. Some were shallow craft with a sharp, elongated bow; cambered deck, cockpit; length 4.3m, beam 1.67m. Other recorded names: **Currituck hunting skiff** (or **push boat**)

4. *United States, NW:* **Push boats** handle as many as 5 **barges**, laden with grain, on the Columbia/Lewis River system. Some **barges** refrigerated for transporting frozen foods. Pilot house set high to enable crew to see in all directions, in order to negotiate locks. Four barges are pushed, the 5th secured alongside. Crew of 4-5. Length of **push**

boat 28m, beam 9m, draft 3.8m. Other recorded names: **riverboat***, **tow boat**
Further references: **bugeye, skipjack-1**

pusher See **push boat, skipjack-1**

pusher boat *United States, NE:* Small, open boat used on logging lakes to corral logs into a **timber raft***. Operation facilitated by a blade 3.7-4.7m long and 0.46m wide that projects from the bow. Motorized. Length 6.1m, beam 2.4m. See also **push boat**.

pusher tug See **push boat**

push punt See **ice punt-2**

push skiff See **Delaware ducker, railbird skiff**

push tow See **push boat**

push tug See **compartment boat, push boat**

putelee, puteli, putellee See **patela**

put-put See **launch-8**

Puttershoeker See **zalmschouw**

puṭṭi See **coracle-4**

pu vohé See **pu hoe**

puwahau See **mokihi-1**

puye, puyen See **dogger**

pwan ré ouwéa *New Caledonia, western Pacific:* Term for a sailing double **canoe*** at Nakéty on the east coast of New Caledonia.

pycar, pycard, pyckarde, pycker, pykard, pyker, pykkert See **picard**

pynace, pynas, pynas-schip, pynassen See **pinnace**

pynck See **pink-5**

pyncke See **pink-1, pink-5**

pynnes, pynnesse See **pinnace**

pyperi See **pripri**

pyrage, pyraugua, pyraugue, pyroge, pyrogue See **pirogue**

Q

qadergha, qadirghy, qadyirġa, qadyrghâ See **kadırga**

qaïkia See **kayık**

qaiq See **caique, kayık**

qaïqia See **kayık**

qaiyarīyah *Iraq, S:* Considered to be a larger but inferior type of **mashhûf***. Bitumen-covered, thin planking; numerous ribs of rough-cut sticks; heavy beam athwartships. Sharp ends, the stem as long as 8m, the sternpost ca. 6m; strong sheer; flaring sides; flat bottom with rocker. Tall rudderhead, wide blade; tiller bends downward. Sailed; mast stepped in a shoe. Spelling variants: **ǧaijārīje, (sefine) ǧajjāriyeh, kaiyariyeh, qajjārīje**

qajaq See **kayak, kayak-3**

qajaq imarsiut, qajaq kujaaginnalik, qajaq kujaannalik, qajaq maqittagaq See **kayak-3**

qajariaq See **canoe-kayak**

qajjārīje See **qaiyarīyah**

qāndja bach, qanga, qangeh See **cangia**

qarab See **qârob**

qarāqir See **carrack**

qaravéla See **caravel-1, caravel-3**

qaravélla See **caravel-1**

qârˇb See **mahonne-4**

qârˇb *Morocco, NW:* Large, open boat used at Rabat and Casablanca. Similar to the **agherrabo***, but larger and lacking the ornamentation of the Berber boat. Rowed using 14 oars. Length 15m.

qāreb See **qārib**

qārib **1.** Generic Arabic term for **boat***, especially a small **rowboat*** used close to shore. Early literature also refers to the **qārib** as a **ship's boat*** carrying as many as 33 men, or as a small boat that accompanied a ship, sometimes carrying extra cargo. Note also **ghurāb, grab.**
2. *Egypt:* One of the smaller Nile sailing craft. Note also **gharab.**
3. *Mediterranean:* Arab warship of the Byzantine era; a 2-banked **galley***. Also reported as a seagoing **barge*** that carried heavy loads.
4. *Tunisia:* On the island of Djerba (Jerba) off the southern coast, the **qarib** is a wide-beamed vessel of shallow draft with a flat bottom, overhanging bow, and raking mast.
Other recorded names: **carib, gaarib, garéb, garib, karib, qāreb;** pl. **aqrab, gawaarib, kawārib, qawāreb, qawārib.** Note also **carabus, gharab.** Further references: **boat-1, grab**

qārib shirā'ī See **dhow**

qârob *Tunisia, E:* Vessel, mainly from Kerkenna Islands, that engaged in fishing, sponging, cargo transport to and from the mainland, and in early days, lightering cargo from ships. A wale ran fore-and-aft, above which a weatherboard extended from the stern almost to the stem. Hull of spruce, frames of olive wood. Sharp bow with clipper or curved stem; beamy and flat-floored amidships; square stern, or sharp with platform that extended beyond the sternpost and

quarters. Rudder outboard or came up through the platform. Decked forward of mainmast and aft at the poop deck, open waist. Black hull; wale often painted in green and red-brown. Stepped 2-3 masts. The tall mainmast raked strongly aft and set a lugsail; a small vertical foremast set a lateen sail, as did the smaller mizzenmast, when used. Mizzen sheeted or tacked to an outrigger. Crew of 4-8. Reported lengths 8-15m; e.g., length 15m, beam 5m, depth 1.5m. Other recorded names: **caràbe, carèbe, caribe*, qarab;** pl. **qwårob**

qarrabīla, qarrabilla See **caravel-1**

qatira See **gaṭîra**

qatrah *Egypt:* **Tender*** to larger Nile boats, especially the **gaiassa***. Generally miniatures of the type and material of the **mother ship***. Always towed behind. Name variant: **atrah**

qattirah See **gaṭîra**

qawāreb, qawārib See **qārib**

qayak See **kayak**

qayapak, qayapauraq See **kayak-7**

qayaq See **kayak, kayak-8**

qayasah, qayassah See **gaiassa**

qayāwaq See **qāyeq**

qāyeq *Egypt:* An open pleasure boat; rowed. Spelling variants: **qāyiq;** pl. **qawāyeq**

qāyiq See **kayık, qāyeq**

qiang hua zi *China, central:* Small, open wildfowling craft of the lower and middle Chang Jiang (Yangtze). Flat bottom curved up gently to square ends; bow slightly higher than stern; flaring sides. Bulkhead at each end; forward bulkhead supported the 1.8m-long shotgun, which extended well beyond the bow. Floated downstream, maneuvered by hand paddling. Crew of gunner and oarsman. Length 4.3m, beam 0.9m, depth less than 0.31m. Other recorded names: **ch'iang-hua tzŭ, gun sampan**

qiao yan chuan See **nan he chuan**

qishir See **quffa**

qiu zi *China, central:* Class of Hubei (Hupeh) Province cargo **junk*** that operated on the Han Shui, a left-bank tributary of the Chang Jiang (Yangtze). Varied somewhat with town of origin, but the sides tapered toward the ends, the main cabin was wood-sided, and several protective wales ran along the sides. Built of fir, strengthened by numerous bulkheads; mainly flat-bottomed, but some upper river boats had a slightly rounded bottom. Flat, raked stern turned up sharply to form a high post, some recurved. On the so-called **crooked junk**, the **wai qiu zi (wai-ch'iu tzŭ)**, the stern twisted to one side. Bow square; some had protective bumper timbers. Decked; main cabin roofed with wood or matting; after part open-sided or enclosed. Rudderpost came up inboard; forward crossbeams provided pivots for the sweeps, supported the main tabernacle, or were pierced to take a mud anchor. Poled, tracked from shore, or sailed. Stepped 1-2 masts, both in the forward half, setting tall, low-peaked balance lugsails. Crew of ca. 7. Reported lengths 15-22m, widths 3-5m, depths 1.2-1.5m. Other recorded names: **ch'iu-tzŭ, wood-roofed boat**

qiyax̂ See **kayak-9**

quache-marée See **chasse-marée**

Quack *Germany, central:* Narrow **barge*** or **lighter*** reported from the 17th to the mid-18th century, especially at Magdeburg on the Elbe River. Reported lengths 15.4-17.1m; 1752 **Quack** 17.1m long, beam on bottom 2.4m, depth 1.1m. Selling variants: **Quak, Quakel.** See also **kwak.**

quackel See **kwak**

quad See **scull**

quadergha, quadrequa See **kadırga**

quadruple, quadruple scull See **scull**

quaffa See **quffa**

quaich, quaiche See **ketch**

quaiq See **kayık**

quak See **kwak, Quack, tochtschuit**

Quakel See **Quack**

quantel battella *Pakistan, SE:* **Punt***-like boat of the Indus River, marshes, and irrigation canals. Small boats engage in ferrying and fishing, the larger in

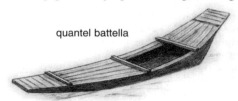

quantel battella

transporting cargo. Bottom composed of odds and ends of used pieces, flat amidships and forced up at ends to create a long, overhanging bow and the higher stern. Square ends; sides flare slightly; sides and bottom joined with sawn knees; floor timbers do not fasten to the sides. Decked at ends; open area corresponds with the flat bottom run; large boats have a framework over the open area, covered with matting, to provide living quarters. Small boats are unpainted; cargo vessels have bright woodwork and a carved and decorated bow. Larger craft steered with a tall, narrow rudder and downward-sloping tiller; rudder hung from massive framework. Sometimes sculled on the quarter. Large boats set a lateen or wide, boomed lugsail to a light mast. Lengths of **fishing boats*** ca. 4.9m; cargo boats more than 15m. Other recorded names: **dund(h)i, Indus punt**

Quanzhou chuan See **Fukien trader**

quarante-cinq pieds See **Cape Island boat**

quaraque See **carrack**

quarter boat **1.** Term given to a **ship's boat*** hung on davits on one of the quarters, ready for immediate use. Large vessels may carry one on each quarter. Used by officers and crew; may be the captain's **gig***. Some sailed, employing lug main- and mizzen sails. Reported lengths of early U.S. Navy boats 6.7-8.5m; e.g., length 7.6m, beam 1.8m, depth 0.69m; pulled 12 oars. Other recorded names: **bota da popa, bote de los pescantes del costado, bote de popa, canot sur la**

porte manteaux, imbarcacione dell'anca, Quarter-boot; sometimes **first** and **second cutter**. Note also **davit craft.**

2. *United States, central:* Long, 2-storied vessel used as rudimentary living quarters for workmen of the U. S. Corps of Engineers engaged in maintaining the levees along the Mississippi River. Moved by a **tow boat***. About 60m long.

Quarterboot See **quarter boat-1**

quarter galley See **galiot-7**

quarter-wheel tug See **tug**

Quase *Germany/Poland:* **Fishing boat*** of the Baltic coast; adapted from the Danish **drivkvase***, which had originated from the German **Zeesboot***. Spread during the early 20th century from west to east, being known in the west as a **Quase**, along the central coast as a **Quatsch**, and in Pomerania as a **dänische Deke**. Last built in 1946. Clinker- or carvel-planked; full forward; raked, straight or curved stem; straight raked or tucked-up transom; flat floors; drag to keel. Decked; centerboard; live well. Early boats sprit-rigged to 2-3 masts; later **cutter***-rigged. Some motorized. Reported lengths 9-12m; **cutter**-rigged boat 11.7m long, 3.75m wide, draft with centerboard up 0.8m. Other recorded names: **Fischerquase, Quaze**; pl. **Quasen**. See also **Quatze.**

Quasen See **Quase**

quatordesona See **gondola da regata**

quatre de couple See **scull**

quatre de pointe See **shell-1**

quatre-mâts barque See **bark-1**

quatro See **canoa-6**

Quatsch See **Quase**

quattro See **shell -1**

Quatz See **Quatze**

Quatze *Germany/Poland:* A fast Pomeranian **market boat*** that transferred the catch from around the Baltic to shore, some going up the larger inland waterways. In some areas, mainly a **fishing boat***. Built until the beginning of the 20th century; last one destroyed in 1960. Clinker-built; sharp stern, concave stem, full bows. Open, half-decked, or fully decked; trunk cabin aft on some; wet well. Loose-footed gaff mainsail; topsail, staysail, jib to a long bowsprit. Low mizzenmast on larger vessels. Also **schooner***-rigged (**Schunerquatze**). Last vessels motorized. Crew of 2-3. Reported lengths 7-18m; e.g., length 18m, beam 5.8m, depth ca. 2.5m. Other recorded names: **Fischerquatze, Haffquatze, Quase*, Quatz, Quets(ch)e, Seequatze**; pl. **Quatzen**

Quatzen See **Quatze**

quayak See **kayak**

quay punt See **Falmouth quay punt**

Quaze See **Quase**

Quebec batteau *Canada, E:* Craft of the lower St. Lawrence River that transferred cargo to sailing ships at anchor. Designed to be fully loaded on the riverbank at low tide; heavy, flat bottom with longitudinal planking. Double-ended; strongly flaring sides, bow and stern decked, outboard rudder. Initially set a standing lugsail, later gaff-rigged with staysail. Crew of 2. Ca. 50t.

Quebec pilot boat *Canada, E:* Three-masted, open boat of the lower St. Lawrence River. Heavily constructed; generally carvel-planked, but sometimes lapstrake. Full lines above the waterline at bow and stern; straight plank keel extended 23-25cm below garboard strakes; deadrise ca. 5° with hard bilges; transom stern. An iron bar with a shoe was shackled to the gunwale to aid in beaching the boat. Foremast stepped through foredeck, mainmast through bench amidships; mizzen stepped off-center at the transom. Set spritsails; jib to a light bowsprit. Length-to-beam ratio 3:1. Note also **Saint Lawrence yawl.**

queche Portuguese and Spanish word for a **ketch***, but also reported as a small fishing **smack***. See also **quetx.**

quechemarín *Spain, N:* **Coaster*** dating from at least the late 18th century. Concave cutwater, deep forefoot; curved sternpost. Set lugsails on the fore- and mainmasts; sometimes a small mizzen, a jib to a bowsprit, and topsails. Also used a lateen mainsail and boomed leg-of-mutton mizzen. Reported lengths 12-15m, widths 4-7.7m, depths 2-3m. Other recorded names: **cachamarín, cachamarina, catch-marin, catxmarina, quetxmarí.** Note also **caixamarín, chasse-marée.**

Queen Charlotte Island canoe See **northern-style canoe**

Queenscliff couta boat See **barracouta boat**

queen's ship See **galleon**

quenouille *France, N:* 18th-century square-sailed boat that engaged in line fishing out of Dieppe and along the coast of Calvados Department to the southwest. A large type was called **bâtard du Pollet**, and a small one was sometimes called a **batelet***. Crew of 4-5. Reported lengths 4.6-8.5m, widths 1.95-2.28m.

Quersegelschiff See **ship-2**

quẽ'taqtla See **northern-style canoe**

Quetsche, Quetse See **Quatze**

quetx *Spain, NE:* Catalan term that may apply to a vessel rigged as a **ketch*** (**queche**). Some have 2 masts; foremast is raked forward and sets a lateen sail; after mast gaff-rigged. One or 2 jibs to a long bowsprit. Clipper bow and counter stern. A **fishing boat*** or **coaster***. Ca. 150t. Other recorded names: **cachamarina*, cachemarina**

quetxmarí See **quechemarín**

quffa *Iraq:* Round basket (*quffa*) boat still seen occasionally on upper parts of the Tigris and Euphrates Rivers. The craft has had at least a 2,500-year history.

quffa

An all-purpose boat for carrying produce, merchandise, minerals, passengers, and livestock, and for use as a **ferryboat***, **lighter***, or **tender***. Formed by concentric coils of interwoven layers of straw and palm fronds bound with palm-fiber rope; strengthened by curved, closely spaced ribs of split withes sewn to the walls. Large boats coated with hot bitumen outside and on the inside to level the floor; to ward off the "evil eye," cowrie shells and blue beads may be pressed in before the bitumen hardens; small boats not coated. Originally leather-covered. Bottom nearly flat; tumble home to sides; stout, cylindrical gunwale; short, wooden bars spaced along the inside on which the paddler may kneel. Paddled in deep water, stroking to left and right; poled in shallow water; going downstream, straw bumpers may be placed at the "bow," and a stone may be dragged behind to keep its heading. Crew of 1-2. The large class (the **hessan**) is 4.9-5.5m in diameter and has a capacity of 12-16t; the medium size ranges between 2.1-4.6m in diameter; the smallest (the **qishir**), used mainly for fishing, is 0.91-1.8m in diameter and 0.76m deep. Other recorded names: **basket boat***, **coracle***, **couffa, couffin, cufa, goofah, gopher, goufa, gufa(h), guffa, guffur, kooffa, k(o)uffa, kufa(h), quaffa, quffah, quffeh, quppu** (*ša šūri*); pl. **quffât.** Note also **mahaila.**

quffah, quffât, quffeh See **quffa**

quick boat See **fei teng**

quick plank-boat See **kuai ban**

quillat *Spain, E:* **1.** Large **fishing boat*** of the Mediterranean coast, especially the Valencia and Cataluña area, that serves as a **drifter*** using a *bou* net; some carry cargo. Sharp ends; stem and sternpost meet the keel at right angles; tall stemhead. Straight keel, steep rise to the floors, merging with flaring sides. Rudder hangs well below the bottom. Lateen sail set to a forward-raking mast; small jib run out on a rising bowsprit. Modern motorized **quillats** are a very different vessel.

2. A small **fishing boat** of the Levant and Ponent coasts. Deep hull, creating a high-sided craft. Plumb stem; slender.

Other recorded names: **aquillado, barca quillada**

quiste *Maldive Islands:* Small sailing vessel reported in the early 19th century. Spelling variant: **quyste.** See also **kashtī.**

quoca See **cog**

quocquet See **coquet**

Quoddy Bay double-ender See **Quoddy boat**

Quoddy boat *Canada, SE/United States, NE:* Tended weirs and seines and served as a **carry-away boat*** to the herring, sardine, and mackerel fisheries and as a **market boat*** to lobstermen of Passamaquoddy Bay along the northeastern border of the United States and adjacent Canada. Popular from the 1870s to the 1890s. Two size ranges with minor differences in hull design and rigging. Sometimes locally called a **pinky***, despite lacking the pink stern and **schooner*** rig. Carvel-planked, although lapstrake reported in the early period; the smaller boats had a rounded stem, the larger a straight, raked stem. Sharp, raking stern; deep drag to keel; high bilges; sweeping sheer with low freeboard amidships; heavy interior ballast. Smaller boats had a large cockpit and small cuddy. The larger boats were decked and had a raised foredeck and trunk cabin; fish hold entered through a hatch in the deck amidships, and a standing well aft for the helmsman; low rails, no bulwarks. Long tiller. Smaller boats fitted with a loose-footed, boomed gaff sail with a short gaff to an aft-raking mast; sometimes a jib set flying to a light bowsprit. The larger type has a longer gaff and standing bowsprit. Crew of 1-2. Reported lengths 6-12m; e.g., length 10.2m, beam 3.4m, hold depth 1.37m, draft aft 1.52m. Other recorded names: **Eastport carry-away boat**, **Eastport pinky**, **Lubec (carry-away) boat**, **Quoddy Bay double-ender**, **Quoddy Head sloop**, **Quoddy pilot**, **Quoddy pinky**, **sardine carrier***, **trap sloop**. Note also **Eastport pinky-schooner**.

Quoddy Head sloop, Quoddy pilot, Quoddy pinky See **Quoddy boat**

quoque See **cog**

quoquet, quoqueta See **coquet**

quorsan See **corsair**

quorvet See **corvette**

quppu, quppu ša šuri See **quffa**

qurqūr, qurqūra See **carrack**

qurqurru *Iraq:* Assyrian word for a type of large Mesopotamian **riverboat***. Other recorded names: **eleppu qurqurru**, **gurgurru**

quṭîya See **kotia**

qůyậq See **caique**

quyste See **quiste**

qwårob See **qårob**

qyax̂ See **kayak-9**

Raaschaluppe See **Schlup-2**

rabão *Portugal, N:* A general-purpose craft on the lower reaches of the Douro River used as a **fishing boat★** or **ferry★**, or to carry coal (**răbao carvoeiro**) and other cargo. Three basic types—the **rabão de apegadas**, which has a bridge aft from which the helmsman works his long sweep; the **rabão de rabo baixo**, on which the stern is lower than the bow and there is no bridge; and the **rabão de pesca** (or **barquito de pesca**), which is much smaller and used for fishing. All have a long, straight, overhanging stern and a lightly curved bow; flattened end pieces are wider at the bottom. Clinker-planked; narrow, flat bottom; rounded, flared sides; keel. Some have a house or canvas-covered area at the stern. The long, curved steering sweep is set over a peg. Propelled by oars and sail. May set a square, lug-, or spritsail; sometimes twin spritsails set athwartships with the sprits suspended in a common snotter at the base of the mast. Crew of 2-8, the larger number on the **rabão de apegadas**. Reported lengths 9-16.7m; e.g., length 16.7m, beam 3.1m, depth 1.4m, cap. ca. 40t; coal boats 23.1m by 5.5m by 2m. Other recorded names: **barco rabão, rabão branco, rabão de carvão**; **rabãozinho** (dim.); pl. **rabões**

rabão branco, rabão carvoeiro, rabão de apegadas, rabão de carvão, rabão de pesca, rabão de rabo baixo, rabãozinho, rabãozinho See **rabão**

rabelo *Portugal, N:* Carried casks of wine on the Douro River from at least the 9th century, but extinct as a working craft. Clinker-built of local pine, wide strakes; maximum beam well forward; 3-piece ribs. Flat bottom, longitudinally planked; no keel or keelson; rounded bilges. Bow and stern curved up, the stern rising higher; strong sheer; freeboard ca. 13cm when loaded; midsection raised by washboards. Open except for a small, wooden or canvas-covered house aft. Steered from a very tall, open bridge aft using a 10m-long sweep with a wide "S" shape; counterbalance on inner end; fit over a tholepin on a broad, flat piece on the sternpost. On upriver trips, set a large square sail to a tall mast stepped just forward of amidships. Yard usually in 2 pieces; topping lift made fast aft, serving as a backstay. Rope from block on masthead circled the sail, enabling it to be pulled up in the middle for visibility from the bridge. Rowed with 2-4 long sweeps set into raised oar slots near the bow. Also towed by oxen from shore. Crew of 10-12. Reported lengths 12-20m; e.g., length 18.2m, beam 3.7m, depth 1.22m; shallow draft. One carrying fewer than 40 casks of wine was called a **barquinha rabela** and worked with a crew of 8-10. Other recorded names: **barco rabel(l)o**. Further reading: Armando de Mattos, *O Barco Rabelo* (Porto: Junta de Província do Douro Litoral, 1940 [Comissão Provincial de Etnografia e Historía do Douro Litoral. Serie A, I]).

rabões See **rabão**

racchan See **ekdar**

race barge See **gig-3**

Race Point surfboat *United States, NE:* Derives its name from Race Point at the tip of Cape Cod, where it was first used in 1894. Later saw service on the exposed beaches of New England and Long Island. Initially constructed by private builders, later by the U.S. Coast Guard, the last being built in 1958. Lightly constructed with lapstrake planking; stem and sternpost strongly curved below the waterline; flat floors; soft bilges; marked sheer. Early boats had a full, cod's head bow and lean, mackerel tail stern; these features less evident in later models. Open; steered either with a long sweep or when sailing, by a rudder with yoke and lines. Early boats had a centerboard. Rowed single- or double-banked, or a combination. When sailed, mast braced against forward thwart; set a spritsail and jib. Generally crew of 6. Standard length 7.47m, beam 1.85m. Note also **surfboat-1**.

rachen, rachhan See **ekdar**

racing eight See **shell-2**

racing four See **shell-1**

racing pair See **pair-oar-2**

racing punt See **punt-7**

rackette See **flûte-3**

Raddampfer See **paddle boat-3**

raddow See **radeau-2**

radeau 1. *Switzerland, NE:* Mid-l5th-century naval vessels on Lake Zurich that engaged in several battles. These rectangular **rafts★** are variously depicted as having an angled shield at the bow through which a cannon projected; another had curved-up bow timbers, behind which were protective bulkheads; a later type carried as many as 800 men positioned with the musketeers in front, spearbearers aft, and banner-carriers in the center. The **rafts** were rowed, poled, and towed from shore.

2. *United States, NE:* Naval vessel of the French and Indian War and the American Revolution. Used principally in harbor defense and during engagements on Lake Champlain and Lake George. Rectangular in shape with a nearly flat bottom; upper part of raked ends are vertical or have sharp tumble home; curved or flat sides; some had deadrise aft. Some had a sharp bow and an angular stern. High, short quarter-deck; deep bulwarks; gunports. Variously rigged as a **schooner★**, **ketch★**, or **brig★**, or with 2 square sails. Sweeps needed at times. Reported lengths 12-29m; e.g., length on deck 28m, on keel 22m, beam 10.5m, hold depth 2m. Spelling variants: **raddow, radeau de guerre, rideau**

3. *United States, central:* A boat of the Mississippi Valley that transported heavy and bulky merchandise during the mid-18th-century French period. Boxy and flat-bottomed.

See also **raft**.

radeau de guerre See **radeau-2**

radeau de Lu'o'ng-nhiêm See **ghe bè**

radeau de mâts See **drome**

radeau de Sâm-so'n See **ghe bè-1**

radeau de sauvetage, radeau de sauvetage gonflable
See **life raft**

radeau de Thanh-hóa See **ghe bè**

radeau pneumatique, radeau pneumatique de sauvetage See **life raft**

Radkastenboot See **paddle-box boat**

raë See **düe**

rafiau *France:* **1.** Short, beamy boat of the Marseille and Toulon areas on the eastern Mediterranean coast; some found around Corsica. Used by watermen, fishermen, and vacationers. Carvel-planked, double-ended, sides have slight tumble home, flat floors, soft turn of

rafiau-1

the bilges, keel straight or has a slight fore-and-aft rocker. Stem may have tumble home and extend 50-60cm above a flattened cap rail; stemhead sharply angled inward and capped with a bulging piece, often painted red. Sternpost may also extend above the rail if the boat has no rudder. When used, rudder extends below the bottom; tiller. Open or half-decked with side decks; freeboard increased by washstrakes. Painted white or bright colors, the washstrakes a different color. Rowed with 1-2 pairs of oars or sets a lateen or quadrilateral, lateen-type sail with a short luff and a jib to a reefing bowsprit. Slightly aft-raking mast stepped through a thwart. Usually worked by one man. Now motorized. Reported lengths 4.25-9.3m, widths 1.57-2.73m, depths 0.55-1.09m. Other recorded names: **bateau toulonnaise**, **batèou**, **pointu**, **rafiot**; pl. **rafiaux**
2. May apply to a slow vessel that handles badly.
3. Sometimes the fastest of a **ship's boats***, the one most often used.

rafiaux See **rafiau-1**

rafiot See **rafiau-1**, **scute-2b**

raft 1. Flat framework of buoyant material, usually temporary, used to transport cargo, animals, and people. Generally a collection of planks, logs, bamboo, reeds, casks, skins, etc., lashed side-by-side and tier-upontier. Usually rectangular in shape. Poled, paddled, sailed, or drifts with the current. Note also **balsa**, **life raft**, **timber raft**, **zattera**.
2. A rectangular craft designed to support careening sailing ships. Planks laid fore-and-aft formed the bottom; crossbeams, curved at sides, served as ribs; sides and decking planked; caulked to be watertight. Temporary **rafts** for emergency careening were made

from masts and planking. Reported lengths 9-12m, widths 4.6-6.1m, depths 0.6-0.9m. Other recorded names: **flaade**, **floating stage**, **ras de carène**, **ras ponté** (decked type), **sal***, **zattera di carenaggio**. Note also **pontoon-1**, **punt-2**.
3. May also serve as a temporary floating bridge for troops, etc.
Selected name variants: **float***, **Floss**, **Holzfloss**, **Holzstammfloss**, **ikada***, **pluta***, **radeau***, **ras**, **Tornfloss**, **Tornholz**, **vlodt**, **vloet**, **vlot***. Further references: **barque-6**, **Fischerfloss**, **flatboat-4**, **timber raft**

raft boat *United States, NE:* **1.** Wooden **scow*** or large **skiff*** used during the 19th century by the ice and logging industries on the Kennebec River in Maine. Tied up along the shore to provide temporary living accommodations for 1-2 men. Small house built on the craft.
2. *United States, north-central:* A **paddle boat*** that towed pine log **rafts*** downstream to mills during the late 19th century on some Wisconsin rivers.
See also **life raft**.

raft catamaran See **catamaran-12**

rafting boat See **push boat-2**

ragosie, ragusa, ragusce, ragusea, ragusy, ragusye See **argosy**

Rahschlup See **Schlup-2**

Rahschoner See **schooner-1**

Rahsegeler, Rahsegelschiff See **ship-2**

Rahsegelschoner See **schooner-1**

rai 1. *Indonesia, E:* Double-**outrigger canoe*** of Berau Bay in northwestern Irian Jaya (New Guinea). Built up from a dugout keel piece, usually with 2 strakes to a side; separate end pieces curve up from the keel piece, often to tall ends with notched tops. Rounded bottom; sides strengthened by crosspieces, set one above the other into blocks nailed to the sides. Seats at each end for the paddlers. Four horizontal booms cross atop or through the hull; elbow connectives slant down to slender floats; outer ends of the booms held secure by a stringer. Matting may be placed over the booms to provide a platform; on some, an awning covers the hull. Paddled and poled; some provided with a temporary sail. Large **canoes** 6-8m long, 1.5m wide, and 1.0m deep.
2. *Spain, NE:* Catalan term for a **raft***. In western Catalonia, they were **timber rafts*** maneuvered downstream by 2-3 oarsmen. Other recorded names: **barca solera**, **raig**

raider See **corsair**, **privateer**

raig See **rai-2**

railbird boat See **Delaware ducker**

railbird skiff *United States, E:* Special boat for hunting rail in rivers and creeks bordered by meadows of sedge, bulrush, wild rice, etc. Design not standard and varies with the locality, but generally fast to overtake and flush out the swimming birds. Those on the Connecticut River had a wide stern; on the Housatonic River, also in Connecticut, they were sharp-ended. In the Delaware Bay area, they were sharp-ended, while on upper Chesapeake Bay, they had a sharp or wide, raking transom; present-day **Patuxent rail skiffs** (or **Patuxent River skiffs**) on this tributary of Chesapeake Bay have a narrow transom. Planking may be lapstrake or carvel, and plywood has become popular. Heavy bottom is rounded, flat, or has a fore-and-aft rocker. The thin bow may be steeply raked to aid in parting the vegetation. A platform at the stern is used by the standing poler; gunner sits forward. Boats also sculled, rowed, or sailed (usually with a spritsail). The New Jersey boats that sailed had a pivoting centerboard and rudder. Reported lengths 4.3-5m; e.g., length 4.9m, beam 1.08m, depth 0.6m; very light draft. Other recorded names: **pole boat★**, **push skiff**, **rail boat**, **rail (gunning) skiff**, **reedbird skiff**. Note also **Delaware ducker**. Further reading: Robert A. Miller, "The Railbird Skiff: A Boat for Exploring the Saltmarshes," *WoodenBoat* 120, (1994), 78-89.

rail boat See **railbird skiff**

rail gunning skiff See **Delaware ducker**, **railbird skiff**

rail skiff See **railbird skiff**

railway ferry, railway ship See **ferryboat-1**

rak, rakeh, raket, raki See **rakit**

rakit *Indonesia/Malaysia:* Term for a **raft★** of logs or bamboo poles. Used on rivers to transport produce and timber, or in quiet waters as a **houseboat★** (**rakit balai gambang** or **rumah rakit**). Materials lashed together with bark or wood-fiber ropes. Bamboo **rafts** have thicker ends at the bow, tapering toward the stern; square at bow with a long, wooden peg run athwartships through holes in the poles. When carrying a heavy load, 2-3 layers of poles may be bound together. Poles along the sides serve as gunwales; a raised platform covered with palm thatching provides a shelter. Often poled from the bow and stern, supplemented by paddlers. Length may exceed 13m. Other recorded names: **akit, rak(eh), raket, raki(tan), rakot**

rakitan, rakit balai gambang, rakot See **rakit**

ramas 1. *Djibouti/Eritrea/Ethiopia:* A **raft★** in the dialect of the Afar. Spelling variant: pl. **ramàsa**. Note also **ramũs**. **2.** *Sudan:* Sharp-ended, flat-bottomed craft used as a **tender★** to local vessels. Further reference: **ramath**

ramàsa See **ramas-1**

ramasth See **ramath**

ramath *Oman:* A 3-log **raft★** of Muscat and Al Bātinah coastal fishermen; probably extinct. Logs unshaped but chosen for their similar curve, the largest placed in the center; bound with coconut-fiber rope. Propelled by a double-bladed paddle or poled. Reported lengths 1.8-2.7m. Spelling variants: **ramas★, ramasth**

rambaïa, rambāja See **orembai**

rambarga, rambarge, rambargio, rambargo, ramberga, ramberge, rambergo See **rowbarge**

ram-ended canoe See **tci'k'Enō**

Rameswaram dhoni See **Pamban dhoni**

Ramme, Rammponton, Rammprahm See **pile driver-1**

Rammy See **Ramsgate smack**

Ramsgate smack *England, SE:* **Fishing boat★** that worked out of Ramsgate from the mid-19th into the early 20th century. Mainly trawled, using a **cutter★** rig, but when a **ketch★** rig was adapted, the remaining **cutters** became **sack ships★** (or **sackers**), fast **fish carriers★** for the London market. Deep hull with hollow entrance and waterline, and a long, fine run. Straight stem with varying degrees of curve to the

forefoot; raked sternpost; low, rounded or elliptical counter or square stern; steep rise to the floors; straight keel with deep heel. Decked; low bulwarks; small engine powered the trawl capstan. Large rudder. **Cutter**-rigged until the 1880s, although often called **sloops★**; tall topmast with crosstree; long, reefing bowsprit; 2 headsails. The **ketches** set large gaff topsails in the summer on the main- and mizzenmasts and jib topsails when heading for market. Later employed shorter spars, no crosstrees, a jib-headed topsail on the mainmast only, but a bigger gaff and boom on the mizzen. Sails loose-footed, boomed, and tanned. Engines on the later boats. Crew of at least 4. Reported lengths overall 21-27m; e.g., length between perpendiculars 19.4m, beam 5.5m, depth 2.7m. Other recorded names: **long boomer** (the **cutter**-rigged vessels), **Rammy, Ramsgate trawler**

Ramsgate tosher *England, SE:* A small version, hence a **tosher★**, of the **Ramsgate smack★**. Straight, vertical stem; sharply cutaway forefoot, raked sternpost, extended counter. **Cutter★**-rigged until the last quarter of the 19th century, then **ketch★**-rigged. Crew of 3-4. Reported lengths overall 12.5-17.4m; e.g., length overall 14.3m, on keel 12m, beam 4m, depth 2m, draft 1.8m.

Ramsgate trawler See **Ramsgate smack**

ram's head boat See **Chebacco boat**

ramũs *Egypt:* **1.** **Raft★** of the upper Nile used principally to reach the cultivatable islands that appear in receding waters. Three bundles of straw are individually tied around and lengthwise and then secured with 3-4 transverse sticks. Bow end shaped slightly. Some early boats made of papyrus. Paddled with a short stick to which a flat board has been attached. Length ca. 4m, width 0.9m. Note also **ramas-1**.

ramũs-1

2. The potters of Qena used the **ramũs** to transport their pots down the Nile; palm stalks were passed through the handles of the pots to create a **raft**. Other recorded names: **durra raft, rms, roms, rops, rũmes**; pl. **rawamis**

Rana boat See **ranværingsbåt**

randan *England:* Boat employing a system of rowing devised in the mid-19th century for the **Thames wherry★**. The middle person worked a pair of oars while the bow and stern persons each worked a single oar on opposite sides. Might also have a coxswain to steer, using a yoke and lines to the rudder. Popular not only with the local watermen, but also with customs officials and river police. Later became a popular pleasure boat on the upper Thames and on other waterways. Lengths usually 8-9m, widths 1.2-1.5m, depth ca. 0.33m. Name variant: **randan skiff**. Note also **London wherry**.

randan skiff See **randan**

rand'ja See **ganja**

Ranen See **ranværingsbåt**

ranger boat See **Mackinaw boat-1**

rangkang See **bangkong-2**

rangot See **na-ak wala**

rangschiff See **beurtsomp**

ranjah, ranji See **ganja**

rantjang poekat See **sampan pukat**

ranværing See **ranvæingsbåt**

ranværings-åttring See **åttring-3**

ranværingsbaad See **ranværingsbåt**

ranværingsbåt *Norway, N:* General term for the highly regarded, **Nordlandbåt***-type boats built in the Rana area. Used mainly for fishing, especially off the Lofoten Islands. Have the characteristic northern, square-heeled stem and sternpost, recurving at the top. Long keel with slight rocker toward the ends. Clinker-planked with spruce; strong sheer. Sharp ends, although some boats have a transom on which to hang an outboard motor. Rowed and sailed. Open; portable cabin aft on some. Several types are made: the 4-oared **færing***; the **sexring** (see **seksæring**), rowed with 6 oars; the **ottring** (see **åttring**), rowed here with 10 rather than the usual 8 oars; the **fembøring***, which worked with 5-6 pairs of oars; and the 8-oared, 4-roomed **firrømming** (see **firrøring**). Other recorded names: **Rana boat**, **Ranen**, **ranværing(sbaad)**, **ranveirsbaad**

ranværsottring See **åttring-3**

ranveirsbaad See **ranværingsbåt**

rapids boat *Canada, NW:* Marked channels on the Mackenzie River with buoys and stakes between shifting sandbars. A variety of **sturgeon-head*** with special equipment. Shoal draft.

rapids piece See **crib-2**

Raritan Bay oyster skiff See **Staten Island skiff**

ras See **raft**

raschip See **ship-2**

rascona *Italy, N:* Cargo vessel of ancient origin that worked in the Lagoon of Venice, on the Po River and some of its tributaries, and on northern lakes until the early part of the 20th century. Carried mainly grain and produce. Flat bottom, flaring sides. Usually portrayed with overhanging ends that rounded up from the bottom, terminating in a wedge. On a small variety at Bologna (the **paròn**), the bow rose in a straight line terminating in a very small bow transom. Sharp-ended, but on the **paròn**, the bow end tapered more gradually. Marked sheer at the ends; low freeboard when loaded. Decked at bow and stern; some had a cabin aft; open waist, which on some was protected by an arched roof. Steered by an ancient system of 1-2 quarter rudders worked with a shaft attached to the rudderstock; on those with a cabin and roof, the helmsman sat high at the stern, working the rudder with a long rod attached to a lever. Towed by horses from the riverbank, or when the wind was from astern, set 1-2 small lugsails. Masts stepped at the ends of the decking. Reported lengths 18.6-33m; e.g., length 27.6m, beam 6.5m, depth 1.64m, 120t cap. Other recorded names: **nave de Pavia**, **roscona**; pl. **paròni**, **rascone**

rascone See **rascona**

ras de carène See **punt-2**, **raft-2**

råseiljekt See **jekt**

ras ponté See **raft-2**

rastero See **dredger-2**

rauberge See **rowbarge**

rāū-che See **roko-1**

rauó See **ubá-3**

ravitailleur See **store ship**

rawamis See **ramūs**

rawhide canoe See **ghuljai-ts!i**

razvedchik See **scout**

reaes galeotas See **real-3**

real **1.** A royal **galley***, considered the principal **galley** of a monarchy, especially in France (**réale**), Portugal, and Spain. Used during the 16th-19th centuries. Sumptuously decorated with a pavilion aft. Carried as many as 460 people. Some rowed with 60 or more oars, with 5 to 7 men (often slaves) on each oar. Lateen sails might be set to a short foremast and taller mainmast. One of the last 18th-century French **réales** was 56m long, 7.7m wide, and 2.5m in draft; carried 315 people. Other recorded names: **galera real**, **galé real** (pl. **gales reaes**), **galère réale**. Note also **capitane**, **galère-1**, **patronne**.
  2. The Portuguese **real** of the **brigantine*** class used as many as 40 oars and 120 oarsmen. Some also sailed. One reported as 26m long on the keel and 3.8m wide. Other recorded names: **bergantim real**; pl. **bergantine reaes**
  3. The galeota real of the **galeota*** type of Portuguese state vessel was popular in the 18th and early 19th centuries. Used 12-40 oars and rowed mainly double-banked. Some had a central aisle between the rowers. Might set a lateen sail. Reported lengths 12-25m, widths 2.45-2.7m. Other recorded names: pl. **galeotas reaes**, **reaes galeotas**

réale See **real-1**

Rebecca See **canot du nord**

rebocador See **tug**

reclamation dredge See **dredger-1**

Recognoscirungsschiff, reconnoitering vessel See **scout-1**

red boat See **hong chuan**

red bow *China, N:* Carried coal from a mine on the east coast to the Chilung (Keelung) area. Some were used for fishing. Bluff bow, raked bow transom; raked, open transom stern. Flush deck, moderate sheer. Painted black except for red on the upper part of the bow and red and green blocks on either side forward. Single pole mast stepped about a quarter in from the bow. Set a battened lugsail sheeted to the stern. Length 13.7m, beam 3.7m. Name variant: **Keelung coal boat**

red bow junk See **hong tou**

reddingboot, reddingsbaad, reddingsbåd, reddingsboot See **lifeboat**

reddingschokker See **schokker**

reddingsloep See **sloep-2**

reddingsvlot, reddingvlot See **life raft**

red head See **hong tou san ban**

red-headed junk See **hong tou chuan**

redhorse runner See **johnboat-1**

redningsbåt See **lifeboat**

redningsflåde See **lift raft**

redningskoite, redningskøyte See **redningsskøyte**

redningsskøyte *Norway:* Very seaworthy boat used by the life-saving service to safeguard men and vessels at sea, especially **fishing boats***. Since the late 19th century, most were modifications of Colin Archer's design that had been adapted from the **hvalerbåt*** of the Skagerak area. Heavy, carvel-planked hull; steep rise to the floors; deep, ballasted keel with marked drag aft. Sharp bow, curved stem, sharply cutaway forefoot; sternpost curved above the waterline, straight and sharply raked below; some later boats with engines had a counter stern. Decked; steering cockpit; some had a house aft; low bulwark or railing. **Ketch***-rigged; loose-footed, boomed gaff sails, large forestaysail, jib to bowsprit, topsail on mainmast. Identification of R.S. (*Redningselskap*) and number painted on the sail. Crew of 4-6. Reported lengths 11.6-14.3m; e.g., length 13.4m, beam 4.37m, depth 2.4m, draft 2.44m. Spelling variants: **redningskoite, redningskøyte**. Note also **losbåt-2, skøyte-1**.

red pirogue See **pirogue-5**

Red River boat, Red River freighter's boat See **York boat**

red slipper junk See **fu diao zi**

red snapper smack See **snapper boat-4**

red stem boat See **pinky**

reed barge See **reed boat-2**

reed-bird boat See **Delaware ducker**

reed-bird skiff See **railbird skiff**

reed boat 1. A boat constructed of local reeds. Name variant: **Binsen-Floss**. Note also **ashi-buné, balsa, caballito, cliath thulca, farteh, fassone, hurija, kadei, mohiki, ramūs, sarnái, shashah, tankwa, thagi, tule boat**.

2. *England, E:* A boat involved in the collection or transportation of reeds for thatching in the Norfolk Broads area. Some were 9m-long **punts*** paddled or powered by an outboard motor. Others were **Norfolk wherries*** that carried thatch and marsh grasses, and some were **steamers** used in cutting reeds. Also some were small, clinker-built **barges***, similar to the **wherries**, which were only quanted or rowed. Open, double-ended; low, flaring sides; heavy frames. A **full-load boat** was ca. 7.6m long and 2.7m wide; the smaller **half-load boat** held the cuttings of a single man; in between, there was a **three-quarter load boat**. Other recorded names: **reed barge** (**cutter*** or **lighter***). Note also **chai ban zi, griendaak, rietaak**.

reed canoe See **ashi-buné**

reed cutter, reed lighter See **reed boat-2**

reed plank-boat See **chai ban zi**

reed ship See **ashi-buné**

Reelfoot stumpjumper *United States, central:* Locally made and used on Reelfoot Lake, a shallow lake in northwestern Tennessee, for sport and commercial fishing and duck hunting. Sharp ends; flat bottom of 2 planks; curved sides of 2 planks; initially caulked, then tin-sheathed, now usually of fiberglass; heavy scantlings. Open; movable seats. Paddled, sculled, and rowed; special bow-facing oars worked with cast-metal levers and swivels. Most are now motorized with a fan-shaped shoe to protect the propeller and kick-up rudder. Reported lengths 2.7-7.3m; e.g., length 4.7m, beam 1.7m at gunwale, 0.7m at the floor; shallow draft. Other recorded names: **lake boat, stumpjumper**

reeper See **tochtschuit**

regatão *Brazil, NE:* **Sloop***-rigged trader of the lower Amazon River; also served as a medical clinic. Decked from ca. 1.22m abaft the bow to the cabin or storeroom. Wide-bladed rudder governed by a strong tiller. When not under sail, rowed by 4 men; 5th man at the tiller; now mostly motorized. Length ca. 10.67m, beam 2.13m, draft 0.6m. Spelling variant: pl. **regatões**. Note also **batelão-regatão, galeola**.

regatões See **regatão**

Regge somp, Regge zomp See **somp**

reho See **rehu**

rehu *Society Islands, southeastern Pacific:* Term for a **raft***. One variety constructed of long bamboo poles formed into a thick bundle. Lashed with bark rope, the bow end tied to a rough point. Platform of light poles set lengthwise onto 3 transverse poles; 3 poles laid across the top secured the unit. Propelled by wading, poling, and in early days, by means of kites. Spelling variant: **reho**

reis-bidar See **bidar-3**

rejebåd See **shrimper**

rembaja See **orembai**

remberge See **rowbarge**

remolcador, remorcher, remorqueur See **tug**

Rennachter See **shell-2**

Renneiner See **scull**

Renn-Rudderboot See **shell**

resäsping See **haapio-1**

rescue båd See **accident boat**

rescue boat See **accident boat, lifeboat**

reserve boat *England, W:* A very narrow **narrow boat*** that carried local traffic (as opposed to a **flyboat***) between Trench and Shrewsbury on the Shrewsbury Canal. Worked until 1921. Beam only 1.9m. Low cabin. See also **accident boat**.

resesump See **segelsump**

residentiepraauw See **pencalang-2**

rešilni čoln See **lifeboat**

rešilni splav See **life raft**

retourschip See **East Indiaman**

retrieval kayak See **kayak-7**

Rettungsboot See **lifeboat**

Rettungsfloss See **life raft**

Reusenfischer See **pot vessel**

revenue cruiser See **revenue cutter-1**

revenue cutter 1. Owned or chartered by customs and excise authorities and, in the 18th and early 19th centuries, authorized to catch smugglers. Fast, strong, serviceable, armed. In England, they were rigged as topsail **cutters*** or **yawls***, but in the United States, most were **schooner***-rigged. English vessels of the early 19th century were ca. 13m long, 4.4m wide, 2.3m deep. Term currently applies to fully motorized craft. Other recorded names: **bastimento di dogana** (or **bastimento doganale**), **bateau de la douane**, bâtiment de douane, battello della dogana, coast-guard cutter (or cruiser), Custom House boat, customs guard vessel, customs sloop, English (or King's) cutter, Finanzfahrzeug, Finanzschiff, krydstoldjagt, nave della dogana, navire de la douane, patache de la douane, revenue cruiser (or vessel), Zoll(wächter)fahrzeug, Zollkruiser, Zollwächt(er)schiff. Further reading: Graham Smith, *King's Cutters: The Revenue Service and the War Against Smuggling* (London: Conway Maritime Press, 1983). Note also coast guard ship, corsara, patache-2b.

2. *United States:* Fast, weatherly, schooner-rigged vessel. First built at the end of the 18th century under the supervision of the Revenue Marine. In addition to collecting revenue and catching smugglers, the vessels provisioned lighthouses, set channel markers, and were, at times, commandeered for naval action. Gradually replaced by steam vessels by the end of the 19th century. Being locally built, the vessels varied with the builder and period and gradually increased in size; in the early 19th century, some were galleys★. Most sharp-bowed with cutaway forefoot, stern a square or rounded counter, most steep-floored, deep drag aft. Decked; some with a quarter-deck; early vessels had open bulwarks, later generally had deep, solid bulwarks. Almost all were schooners, most with topsails. Lengths on deck mainly 17-33m, beam one-quarter. Name variant: **Revenue Marine cutter**. Further reading: Howard I. Chapelle, Ch. 4, *The History of American Ships* (New York: Norton & Company, 1935).

Revenue Marine cutter See revenue cutter-2
revenue vessel See revenue cutter-1
rhaguse See argosy
rhapta, rhapta ploiaria, rhaptôn ploiariôn See ploion
Rheinaak *Germany, W/Netherlands, SW:* Cargo vessel of the aak★ family that traversed the Rhine River from at least the mid-18th century. Flat bottom; rounded, clinker-planked sides. Bow flat to the gunwale, raked; stern curved with plumb sternpost. Decked with long hatch and narrow side decks; cabin aft; leeboards. Tall rudder; tiller. Two lowering masts. In the 18th century, set a tall square sail with square topsail on the tall mainmast; mizzen set a gaff sail. Later set a gaff mainsail. One or 2 headsails; long bowsprit. Dimensions of l850 vessel: length 28.6m, beam 6m, depth 2m. Recent vessels of steel, fully motorized, with 2,000t cap. Name variant: **Rijnaak** (pl. **Rijnaken**)
Rheinfloss *Germany, W/Netherlands, S:* Enormous timber raft★, mainly of oak and fir from Swiss and German forests, floated down the Rhine River to Dordrecht in the Netherlands, and to other cities along the way. Small rafts★ on the tributaries were combined to make a single raft, as long as 220m and 43m wide. Last of these rafts ran the river in 1964. Oarsmen worked from each end; some oars as long as 14m. Helmsman directed from a platform. Accompanied by several small boats for communication with shore and by **Ankernachen** that carried the anchors and chains needed to guide and stop the raft.

Most were virtual villages with dwelling houses for the crew and their families, cook houses, slaughter houses, etc. In 1875, rafts averaged 520,000 cubic meters of wood. Other recorded names: **Holländerfloss, Kapital-Floss, kraak★**
Rheinnachen See Nachen-1
Rhiner Ever, Rhin-Ever See Rhin-Ewer
Rhin-Ewer *Germany, NW:* Fast, low cargo vessel of the Ewer★ family that mainly carried vegetables on the Rhine River and its tributaries and on the Elbe River during the 18th and early 19th centuries. Most built at Glückstadt near the mouth of the Rhine. Carvel-planked; flat floors, slightly curved stem, heart-shaped transom, strong sheer. Scuttle hatch forward of the mast, large hatch amidships; low poop deck with railing. Leeboards, outboard rudder. Carved and decorated transom, and floral motifs along the bows. Loose-footed, boomed gaff sail set to a strike mast. Jib to bowsprit, staysail, topsail. Reported lengths 12.5-15.2m, length-to-beam ratio ca. 3.8:1; cap. 10-28t; shallow draft. Other recorded names: **Rhin-Ever, Rhiner Ever, Glückstadter Ewer; Kohl-Ewer** or **Koolever** (cabbage **Ewer**). Note also **Gemüse-Ewer**.
Rhode Island hook boat *United States, NE:* Small, open boat used off southwestern Rhode Island for fishing. Lapstrake planking; frames joggle over the laps. Sharp, raked ends. Crew of 2, both of whom rowed, the after man facing forward. Length 4.8m, beam 1.67m.
Rhodes wherry See salmon wherry
ribarica See fishing boat
ribolóvska ládija See ládija
rice boat See laung-zat, Luhü mi chuan, mi bao zi, padda boat, rua kao
Rice Lake canoe *Canada, SE:* Plank-built canoe★ of Rice Lake, just north of Lake Ontario. Followed the general lines of the local native birchbark canoe. Widely used beyond the lake area and sometimes known as the **Canadian canoe★**. Note also **Peterborough canoe**.
Rickmansworth boat, Ricky boat See narrow boat
rideau See radeau-2
rietaak *Netherlands, central:* Aak★ type used to gather and transport reeds (*riet*). Overhanging, rounded ends; high stem, lower stern. Flat bottom, rounded bilges and sides; sheer strake the same width above the wale; soft sheer. The small **rietaakje** open except for short foredeck. On larger types, long hold abaft the short foredeck, covered with peaked hatches; cuddy below stern deck. Medium-round leeboards. Narrow rudder; S-shaped tiller. Mast stepped before the hold; strikable on sheerlegs. Occasionally a jib set to a jibboom. Length ca. 9m; beamy. See also **griendaak**.
rietaakje See reitaak
rigger *England, S:* Term used by Eton College crews for their type of single sculling boat used in all major regattas. Lengths 6.1-6.6m, widths 0.41-0.43m. Note also scull. Further reference: outrigger
right-handed smack See fishing smack
riječna ladja See ladja-1
Rijnaak, Rijnaken See Rheinaak

rimorchiatore See **rimorchio-1**, **tug**

rimorchio *Italy:* **1.** Italian word for a vessel being towed. The vessel doing the towing is a **rimorchiatore**, or a **tug★**.
2. One of the boats employed in Sicilian tunny fishing. Besides towing the other boats to and from the fishing site, a **rimorchio** is stationed on each side of the **vascello★**. Sailed or motorized.
See also **tug**.

rind See **snow**

Rindenboot See **bark boat**

ringdækjolle See **smakkejolle**

ringer See **ring-net boat**

ring-net boat 1. *Scotland:* Employed a ring net (or so-called trawl net) devised in the 1830s for herring fishing. Used mainly on the west coast, but was also found on other Scottish coasts, mainly on **zulus★** and **scaffies★**. Originally worked out from shore, a single boat pulling the net in a large circle, or worked with another boat, the **net boat★** shooting the net while the **neighbor boat** held the end; both hauled in the net. Larger, motorized vessels worked farther offshore by the early 20th century, the net shot by 9-10.7m, motorized **dories** (see **dory**). Early boats were **trawl skiffs**, which were open and rowed (with 4 oars) while working the net, although they usually carried a small lugsail, and some had a jib. Reported lengths 4.6-9.1m, beam ca. 1.8m. By the 1880s, the work was done mainly by **Loch Fyne skiffs★**. The motorized vessels had a plumb stem with cutaway forefoot, **canoe★** stern, slight drag to the keel, rising floors; low freeboard amidships; wheel house generally aft; crew of 5. Had 1-2 masts to which gaff- or lugsails were set. Reported lengths 12-15.6m, beamy. Other recorded names: **ringer**, **ring-netter**
2. *United States, W:* Motorized **ring-net boats** are used in the California mackerel fisheries. In the 1930s, they were operated mostly by Japanese and Italians.

ring-netter See **ring-net boat**

Ringwadenfischer, Ringwadenkutter, Ringwadenlogger See **seine boat-1**

rinkelaar See **loodsvaartuig-1**

rising strake canoe See **Chesapeake Bay log canoe-2**

risørskøyte See **skøyte-2**

risque-tout See **chasse-marée**

rivani, rivano See **catalano, leudo**

rivano-bilancella See **bilancella**

river barge See **Plymouth barge**, **Thames sailing barge**

riverboat 1. Vessel designed to navigate inland waterways, usually with unique characteristics to accommodate conditions on a particular waterway. Generally designed primarily for cargo, passengers, or a combination. Term sometimes restricted to small craft carrying passengers on rivers or in harbors. Usually have a flat bottom and shallow draft. Sides low and straight. Ends often of similar shape, blunt or sharp. Originally floated downstream and tracked from shore upstream, using horses or a team of men. Later steam-powered, then diesel. Selected name variants: **bateau fluvial** (or **d'interior**), **Binnenfahrzeug, Binnenschiff,**

binnenschip, binnenvaartuig, Flußschiff, home trading vessel, inland (navigation) vessel, Stromfahrzeug. Note also **canal boat**.
2. *Canada, E:* **a. Punt★**-like craft of salmon fishermen on the shallow, swift St. Marys River in northeastern Nova Scotia. Flat bottom cross-planked of pine, rising toward the ends, the bow end having a longer rise. Sides a single spruce plank; shallow, square ends, the bow somewhat wider. Sides vertical or slightly flared. Ends decked; single seat. Anchored with a bundle of chains, the cable run out through a small davit and pulley. Mainly poled. Those fitted for an outboard motor have a bracket on the stern transom. Reported lengths 6.1-6.7m. **b.** The sport fishermen's **riverboat** on the Miramichi River in central New Brunswick is **canoe★**-like, but with a transom stern for an outboard motor. Canvas covers the cedar planking; closely spaced ribs. Two chair-like seats for the fishermen. Guide sits at the stern to handle the motor, or paddles or poles. Bundle of chains serves as an anchor and to maintain position on the swift river. Length ca. 6m. **c.** In northeastern Newfoundland, **riverboats** are multipurpose craft transporting sportsmen, trappers, hunters, and supplies in the Gander area. Heavily planked and framed; keel. Sharp bow, deep stem; narrow transom above a sharp sternpost. Foredeck. Employs an outboard motor or poled or paddled. Reported lengths 4.9-7.3m, widths 0.76-0.86m.
3. *Canada, SW:* **Flatiron skiff★** type that fished on the Nicomekl River near Vancouver, British Columbia, in the 1920s. Three-planked, flat bottom and 2-planked sides, of red cedar. Small foredeck, 2 thwarts, sternsheets. Rowed. Length 4.5m, beam 1.3m.
Further references: **bateau-7j, push boat-4**

River dory See **batteau-2**

river-driving batteau See **lumberman's batteau**

River Fal oyster dredger See **Falmouth oyster dredger**

river gunboat See **flat iron-1**

river police boat See **fei xie**

river raft See **timber raft-2a**

River Stour lighter See **Stour lighter**

rivierclipper, rivierklipper See **klipper-1**

rivierpraam See **spitspraam**

rms See **ramūs**

ro *Indonesia, SE:* **1.** Considered by the Tetun-speaking peoples of Timor to be a generic term for **boat★, ship★,** and **vessel★**. A **sailboat★** is a **ro laan**, a steamship a **ro ahi**, and a warship a **ro funu**.
2. On Wetar, to the north of Timor, **rō** is a type of **canoe★**.
See also **roh**.

roā *India, Bay of Bengal:* Generic term of the Onge peoples of Little Andaman Island for a **boat★**. One with a sail is called a **roātotphal**. Note also **roko**.

road-cart *United States, E:* Cited as a colloquial term for a 2-man boat, of no particular type, that sailed across Chesapeake Bay from Tangier Island to crab on the Northern Neck peninsula. Reported lengths 4.9-5.5m. Name variant: **Tangier road-cart**

ro ahi See **ro**

roannaise *France, central:* General term given to the various boats that served the area on the upper Loire River around the manufacturing city of Roanne. One type was the **chênière★**.

Roanoke Island boat, Roanoke Island shad boat See **North Carolina shad boat**

roātotphal See **roā**

Robar-type longliner See **Cape Island boat**

Robbenboot, Robbenfängboot, robbenschip, robbenslager, robbenvaartuig, robbenvangschip See **sealer**

roberge *France:* Comparable to the English **rowbarge★**; used until the end of the 16th century. Lower sides than the **galleon★**, but higher and shorter than the **galley★**. One in the mid-16th century was converted to a royal **galley**. Decked; armed. Fast; usually propelled by up to 26 oars. Short mast. Length on keel ca. 13.7m, beam 5.5m, depth 3.6m. Spelling variant: **robergie**

robergie See **roberge**

Rochdale flat See **Mersey flat**

Rochester bawley See **bawley**

rock-boat See **skärbåt**

rocking boat See **iceboat-4**

rock lobster catcher boat See **cray boat**

Rockport granite sloop, Rockport stone sloop See **stone sloop**

ró-da See **roko-1**

roddjulle *Finland, W:* A small **julle**-type (see **jolle-4**) designed to be rowed. Used for a variety of inshore fishing along the coast—small net, trap, hook and line. Clinker-planked; flaring, curved sides, strong sheer, relatively short keel. Sharp ends; raked, straight sternpost. Rowed with 2 pairs of oars between double tholepins. Occasionally sailed, the light, sprit-rigged mast stepped through a thwart near the bow. Reported lengths 4.6-5.2m; e.g., length ca. 5m, beam 1.45m, depth 0.6m. Further reference: **bohusjulle**

roddsnipa See **snipa**

roddsump **1.** *Finland:* Double-ended **fishing boat★** that has a live well (*sump*) and is mainly rowed (*rodd*). Used chiefly for local fishing, especially for *fjällfisk* and pike. Clinker-built; beamy with full bow, narrower at the stern; curved stem and sternpost. Fish well forward. Shallow draft.
2. *Sweden:* **a.** On the east coast in the Roslag and Småland areas, the **roddsump** is double-ended; curved stem, straight sternpost, deep keel, strong sheer. Live well at the stern. Rowed with 2 pairs of oars, some by one man in the bow using 2 oars while 2 others use a single long oar each. On occasion, might set 2 spritsails. Reported lengths 4.2-5.8m; e.g., length 5.8m, beam 1.67m. **b.** In the west-central interior bordering Lake Vanern, a similar **roddsump** is used. Sharp ends, curved stem, sternpost more sharply curved below the waterline. Clinker-planked; smooth turn of the bilges; drag aft; sharp sheer, especially toward the bow. Decked at stern over the live well. Rowed with 2 pairs of oars. Also sailed. Length 6m, beam ca. 1.5m, depth amidships ca. 0.7m.
Other recorded names: **somp★, sump★, sumpbåt**. Note also **segelsump, sumpjolle**.

rodney *Canada, E:* Small, sturdy, open **Newfoundland boat** used for general fishing, birding, sealing,

lobstering, and single-handed cod fishing, and as a **tender★**. When cod fishing, it is towed by a **motorboat** to the grounds. Carvel-planked; wineglass transom with sculling notch; curved stem; round bottom, double-ended on the waterline. Fish well amidships. Rowed and sculled at the same time; also sailed, stepping a portable mast, setting a spritsail and jib. Most now have a small outboard motor. Crew of 1-3. Reported lengths 3-5m; e.g., length 4.3m, beam 1.2m, depth 0.5m. Other recorded names: **punt★, rondey**. Further reading: David R. Taylor, *Boat Building in Winterton, Trinity Bay, Newfoundland* (Ottawa: National Museums of Canada, 1982), 67, 69-72, and Chapter VI. Note also **Baccalieu skiff, bay punt**.

Rodney boat *England:* A **narrow boat★** of the **family boat★** type that has been let go to wrack and ruin by an irresponsible crew.

róðrarferja See **ferje**

róðrarskúta See **skuta-1**

rôë See **düe**

roeibaarze, roeibaerdtze See **baardse**

roeibargie See **galley-5**

roeiboot *Netherlands:* **1.** Generic term for a **rowboat★**.
2. Best known is the **schouw★** type with raked, hexagonal bow and stern transoms. Flat bottom, longitudinally planked with 3-4 planks, with rocker at bow, skeg at stern. Sides of 2 lapped strakes; the lower strakes flare outward, the upper have tumble home at the ends; strong sheer forward. Sparsely framed; external stem and sternpost. Two thwarts; stern seat; some have a wet well. Rowed with a pair of oars set over a single tholepin or worked with oarlocks. Other recorded names: **roeischouw**; pl. **roeiboten**

roeiboten, roeischouw See **roeiboot**

roeivlet See **vlet-1**

ro funu See **ro**

roh *Indonesia, SE:* Double-outrigger, traveling and fishing **canoe★** of the eastern Lesser Sunda Islands. Dugout hull; sides raised by washstrakes near the stern or by palm weather cloths. Curved bottom rounded up at each end to tall, ornamental end pieces, often recurved, or to a stylized animal's head. Open or had light decking. Each outrigger consisted of 2 floats set side-by-side and joined to 2 widely spaced, paired booms, each pair set one above the other. Two platforms crossed the hull, resting outboard on a stringer laid atop the booms. Employed a quarter rudder. Tripod mast set a boomed, rectangular mat sail. Other recorded names: **bero★, ro★**; local types: **roh dugan** (or **doegan**), **roh talor**

roh doegan, roh dugan, roh talor See **roh**

roka See **lakandrao**

roko **1.** *India, Bay of Bengal:* Indigenous term for a **dugout canoe★** on Little and South Andaman Islands. One variety from South Andaman Island is merely a hollowed-out tree trunk; some have a shelf-like projection at each end. A more elaborate type employs a single outrigger. Three to 8 booms cross to a long, slender float; booms pass between a pair of crossed sticks and a vertical stick; at the hull end, the booms pierce both sides of the hull.

Blunt-ended. Other recorded names: **rāū-che**, **ró-da**, **róko-da**, **ró-lekíle**. Note also **roā**.

2. *Solomon Islands, western Pacific:* Small **canoe★** of the **binabina★** type found on Florida Island in the southeastern Solomon chain; on Guadalcanal and Savo, called a **puré**; at Santa Isabel, a **kéda**; and at Ndai and Malaita, a **béroko**. Used in bonito fishing. Tall sternpost, low bow. Plank-built, U-shaped in cross section; sharp ends; short washstrakes protect the bows; bottom curves up at the ends. Painted black with some strakes left natural; ends decorated with shell inlay and cowrie shells. Mainly paddled; paddle elongated with pointed blades and a U-shaped grip. Boats vary in size to carry 2-6 passengers. Other recorded names: **bena, na roko**
Further reference: **lakandrao**
róko-da See **roko-1**
ro laan See **ro**
ró-lekíle See **roko-1**
Rollfähre See **ferryboat-1**
rollover duck boat See **Susquehanna sneak boat**
Romagna battàna See **battana-3**
roms See **ramūs**
Rondeboot See **patrol boat**
rondey See **rodney**
Roonboot See **boot-2**
rops See **ramūs**
rora-firing, rora-fyreng, rora-fyring See **firing**
roscona See **rascona**
Rosenheimer Plätte See **Plätte-1**
Roslagen jakt See **jakt-1**
roslagsjakt *Sweden, E:* **Sloop★**-rigged trader that worked from the Roslagen coast northeast of Stockholm. Beamy; broad, square stern; curved stem. Cabin aft. Tall mast stepped forward of amidships. Set a gaff mainsail; boom extended beyond the stern; staysail tacked to the stemhead. Note also **jakt-1**.
roslagsskuta *Sweden, E:* **Sloop★**-rigged **coaster★** of the Roslagen and Stockholm areas. Transported heavy cargoes during the latter half of the 1800s until the early 1900s. Clinker-built with a strong sheer at the bow; counter stern, curved or angular stem, straight keel. Open or half-decked; cabin aft. Tall, forward-raking mast. Mainsail laced to a long boom, short gaff; headsail tacked to the stemhead. Reported lengths 11-15m; e.g., length 15m, beam 5.3m, depth 1.3m. Local names: **piggskuta, rospigg, storbåt★**. Note also **skuta**. Further reference: **sandkil**
roslagsslup See **jakt-1**
Roslyn sharpie, Roslyn yawl See **nonpareil sharpie**
Rosmuc hooker See **Galway hooker**
rospigg See **roslagsskuta**
Rosslare cot See **Wexford cot**
Rossplätte See **Plätte-1**
Rossschiff See **Leibschiff-1**
Rostocker Sandboot See **Sandboot**
Rot-Kopf-Dschunke See **hong tou chuan**
Rotterdamer Samoreus See **Samoreus**
roueder See **chalutier**
rough punt See **punt-7**
rough-water canoe *Canada, E:* Seal- and porpoise-hunting birchbark **canoe★** (**muskweakwitan**) of the

Micmac of the Gaspé Peninsula and parts of the Maritime Provinces. Well-built **canoe** characterized by circular bow and stern profiles that curve up from the bottom to merge in a smooth line with the sheer. Strongly hogged sheer amidships; marked tumble home; bottom well-rounded or a slightly rounded "V"; moderate rocker at the ends. Battens outside the bark reinforce the ends, which are stuffed with shavings; light gunwales; guard strips 15-17cm below gunwales; headboards fitted. Five to 7 thwarts; light ribs; narrow, split-cedar sheathing between ribs and bark cover. Hogging achieved by softening bark with boiling water and then staking it out in desired sheer to dry. A temporary sail sometimes made from a densely foliaged, young spruce tree; in early times, a square sail of moose skin or bark was used; by the end of the 19th century, a spritsail was common. Sheet double-ended, one end made fast to the clew and the other to the head of the sprit. Mast secured to a thwart; heel stepped into a block or into a hole in bottom board. Reported lengths 4.88-7.42m, originally probably to 8.5m; modern type: length 6.4m, beam 1.07m, depth 0.4m; earlier **canoes** narrower and deeper. Other recorded names: **Micmac rough-water canoe, ocean canoe, open-water canoe**. Further reading: Wilson D. and Ruth A. Wallis, *The Micmac of Eastern Canada* (Minneapolis: University of Minnesota Press, 1955), 42-50.
round-bottom shad boat See **North Carolina shad boat**
round-bowed sloop See **Friendship sloop**
round caravel See **caravela redonda**
round-chine shad boat See **North Carolina shad boat**
round ship *Mediterranean:* General term applied by the Greeks and Romans to their merchant vessels and to other vessels during the Middle Ages. Mainly sailed, but some were rowed. Reported lengths 15-35m, widths 5-9.5m; 13th-century vessel 21m long overall, 16.5m on keel, beam 5.2m, hold depth 3m. Other recorded names: **stroggylos, strongylē naus, strongylos**. Note also **long ship, ploion**.
round-stern bugeye See **bugeye**
routine boat, Routineboot See **trot boat**
rover See **sea rover**
rowbarge **1.** As implied by the name, a **barge★**-type craft propelled mainly by oars. Also employed sails. But this term, in its variant spellings, has been used for several ill-defined vessel types, mainly in northwestern Europe. A few of these follow.
2. Armed vessel of the 14th-17th centuries that made reconnoitering excursions and served as an **advice boat★** or **tender★**. One to 3 masts, each setting a lateen sail; distinguished by its topmast platforms. Pulled as many as 15-18 oars to a side. Crew of 37-45. Long and low; 120-200t.
3. Second boat of 16th-century **men-of-war**; apparently propelled solely by oars or sweeps.
4. Vessel of the 15th century that transported cargo across the English Channel.
5. Designated as a small river craft as late as the 17th century.
6. An oared craft that carried a sprit mainsail well forward and a lateen mizzen.

7. A **packet boat★**.

Other recorded names: **barge à rames, discovery ship, rambarga, rambarge, rambarg(i)o, ramberga, ramberge, rambergo, rauberge, remberge, rowing barge**. Note also **roberge, row galley**.

rowboat 1. Small, open boat propelled mainly by oars. Some consider a **rowboat** to be round-bottomed as opposed to the flat-bottomed **skiff★**. Sometimes differentiated from a **pulling boat★** if used principally on quiet inland waters. A type used during the American Revolution was armed with a single gun. Other recorded names: **bote de remos, čamac na vesla, canot à avirons, embarcation à rames, imbarcazione a remi, oared boat, roeiboot★, rowing boat★, Ruderboot, vesel'naya shlyukpa, wiosłowa łódź**

2. *United States, SE:* In North Carolina, special large **rowboats** carried produce on the Cape Fear River and provided transportation in the late 18th century. Might have an awning. One such boat was rowed by 6 slaves. See also **barge-11a, troller-2**.

row galley 1. Open boat of the **galley★** type that was principally rowed. Reported from England and America from the 16th-18th centuries. Fine lines, shallow hull. A square-sterned **row galley** with a divided poop was called a **batardelle**, while one with a square stem was a **batardate**. Occasionally sailed, but generally rowed with 6-8 sweeps; some used as many as 36. Other recorded spellings: **bastardella, bastardelle**

2. *United States:* **a.** An important type was built on both the Maryland and Virginia shores of Chesapeake Bay in the late 1770s. Their shallow draft made them suitable for retreat into tributary rivers to evade larger naval ships, but they were seaworthy for action in the Bay. Those that transported troops did not sail. Classified as a 20-gun vessel, but never mounted that many. Most **schooner★**-rigged. Oarports were set between the gunports. Rowed double-banked with 2 men to a sweep. Reported lengths 12-24.7m on keel, beam 4.3-7.6m, depth of hold 1-2.3m. **b.** On the Ohio River, an oared **gunboat★** that patrolled the river in the early days of the country. Strongly built; raked bow, decked; bullet-proof, hinged bulwarks protected the rowers. Also sailed. Largest carried a crew of 110 and employed 40 oars. Reported lengths 13.7-22m; e.g., length 13.7m, beam 3.7m. Other recorded name: **galley boat**

Other recorded names: **galère à rames, galley★, galley bat(t)eau, gondola★, gunboat galley, rowbarge★, row-galley, gundalow★**; pl. **row gallies**. Note also **batard**. Further reference: **barge-11h**

row gallies, rowgalley See **row galley**

Rowhedge smack See **Essex smack**

rowing barge See **rowbarge**

rowing boat General term for a fresh-water racing boat in which each oarsman holds a single sweep oar with both hands. Rowed by 2-8 persons, usually with a coxswain. Note also **pulling boat, shell, ship-3**. Further reference: **rowboat-1**

rowing galiote See **galiot-1**

rowing lighter *England, SW:* Open **barge★** of the Taw/Torridge Estuary on the north Devon coast. Carried bulk cargo—sand, limestone, ceramic clay, and timber—from at least the early 17th to the early 20th

century. Worked with two 3.66-4.88m-long sweeps, relying mainly on the tide and current. Bluff bow, broad transom, almost flat sheer, heavily timbered. Short decks at bow and stern, open waist. Crew of 1-2. Reported lengths 9.1-10.7m, beam 3.66m, depth 1.68m. Name variant: **barge**. Note also **gravel barge**.

row punt See **punt-6**

royal barge See **barge-3**

royal boat See **King's boat**

rozbojnik morski See **freebooter**

rrá-uó-rrikan See **ubá-3**

ršek See **šerk**

rua *Thailand:* Generic term applied originally to inland watercraft, but now may include boats used in the Gulf of Siam. Spelling variant: **ruah**

rua ballang *Thailand:* Ceremonial **barge★**, literally "boat of the throne." The European word **balon★**, however, is often used for other ceremonial **barges**, including those of Myanmar (Burma) and Laos. The king's **barge** is a **rua phrathinang**, and the current **barge** goes by the name **Suphannahong (Golden Swan)**; earlier **barges** of this rank had other specific names. Generally constructed from a single log, the bottom sheer sweeping up to elevated ends, which are intricately carved, often as animals' heads and tails. Low amidships. Usually have a shelter amidships, and on royal **barges**, a pagoda-like shelter protects the important passengers. Entire craft elaborately ornamented and frequently gilded inside and out. Rowed or paddled by a crew of 50-180; oars and paddles may be gilded. The 46m-long **Suphannahong** employs 50 oarsmen. Lengths 20-54m or more; widths 1.37-3.6m. Further spelling variants: **ballang, balloen, ballo(o)n, balloni, pallone★**; **Srisupan(n)ahong, supannahong, suppannahongse**

rua chalawn See **rua chalom**

rua chalom *Thailand:* Double-ended craft of the northern Gulf of Siam. Used mainly for fishing but may also work mussel beds, and some larger, 2-masted vessels are traders. Also used along the Cambodia coast under the name **tuk chap pok** or **tuk chaleum** and on the Annam coast of Vietnam as **ghe nò**. Straight, elongated, raked ends, the stern more vertical; stem and sternpost flattened. Carvel-planked; shallow keel or none. Ribs stop short of the keel piece, and alternate with futtocks that overlap the inner ends of the ribs by 1-2 strakes. Decking consists of a few widely spaced planks; on some larger vessels, a bamboo roof protects the cargo. Use 1-2 cleaver-shaped quarter rudders, depending on size and weather conditions, hung from U-shaped supports at the stern; when fishing, the rudder(s) may be unshipped and used at the stern to keep the head to windward. Most step a single tall, aft-raking mast to which a rectangular lugsail is set; foot may be laced to the boom or loose except at the clew; tacked to the mast. Some use a Chinese lugsail, and the 2-masted type sets one at the bow. Propelled by long sweeps in calms, with crew standing; most now motorized. Crew of 3-5; large vessels may need a crew of 8. Reported lengths 10-19m; e.g., length 13.7m, beam 2.74m, depth 1.37m; the Cambodian vessels are beamier. Spelling variant: **rua chalawn**

rua chang *Thailand:* Small, open boat that serves as family transportation or as a **ferry**★ for local passengers. Squared-off, overhanging ends sweep up from the bottom; low freeboard amidships raised by washstrakes; short bow and stern decks. Some have a semi-circular mat cover amidships. Oar hung from rattan

rua chang

loop near or at the top of a 46cm post stepped to one side at the stern; oarsman stands on opposite side to work the oar. Lengths ca. 3.7-5.5m, beam 0.76m.

ruah See **rua**

rua kao *Thailand:* Graceful **riverboat**★ that transports rice downstream and general cargo upstream. Most Chinese-owned. Strongly built, mainly with teak planking; double-ended; low bow, high stern. Woven bamboo and mat house amidships or at the stern; cargo, mainly on deck, protected by an arched mat covering. Open foredeck permits crew to pole and work long sweeps; footboard along each side for poling. Coated with a red-brown varnish. Quarter rudder or midline rudder hung on sternpost. Tall bamboo mast, stepped well forward, sets a standing lugsail. Reported lengths 9-13.7m, widths 3-4.6m, deep draft. Other recorded names: **rice boat, ru'a khao**

ru'a khao See **rua kao**

rua kread *Thailand, SW:* Long, narrow boat that employs a comb-like device (the *kread* or *kriad*) to scare inshore fish and shrimp into the boat. Operates on both coasts of peninsular Thailand. Long, overhanging ends cut blunt at top, widely spaced ribs. On one side, a fencing of palm leaves keeps the fish from jumping over the boat, and on the other side a bamboo platform serves as a sponson. The comb, ca. 8m long, is set at an 80° angle. Propelled by a single occupant who pushes along the bottom from the stern, with one leg outside and one inside the boat. Reported lengths 9-10m, beam 1.0m. Name variant: **catch boat**

rua nua *Thailand, N:* Cargo craft of northern rivers. Those in the west have a long, ascending bow and stern, while the eastern type is snub-nosed and short-sterned. Bottom flat. Arched mat house extends from roughly amidships to near the stern; on some, a covered structure protects the helmsman and may provide living quarters for a family. Steered with a long, broad-bladed quarter rudder. The long, overhanging bow is used by polers who run forward, set the pole, and walk back on footboards set outboard along the sides; rowed downstream. Crew of 3-4. Size varies with physical aspects of the rivers; typical: length 13.7m, beam 0.9m, depth 0.28m; very shallow draft. Other recorded names: **northland boat, nua**

rua pet *Thailand:* **1.** Deep-hulled, 2-masted boat of the Gulf of Siam; very similar to the Vietnamese **ghe**

diang★. Larger boats engaged in trading, smaller in fishing and transporting local produce; few remain. Carvel-planked; planking finished flush with the stem and sternpost; large, closely spaced timbers. Double-ended; flat stem and sternpost, as wide as 30cm at gunwale; bow curves up spoon-fashion from curved keel; stern straight and raked. Marked sheer; deeper draft aft; rudder curves under hull slightly at the bottom. Light, non-watertight deck from bow to mainmast, beneath which the crew lives; open hold covered by an arched mat roof; grating at stern supports helmsman and crew. Short foremast stepped in the eyes; aft-raking mainmast approximately amidships; foremast unstayed, mainmast supported by 2 shrouds. Sets high-peaked, boomed, standing lugsails of palm matting. Mainsail reefed by lowering the yard to desired height and rolling up the boom with a handspike; foresail seldom reefed, serving as a steering sail. Uses 2 sweeps in harbor. Crew of 3-4. Reported lengths 6-15m; e.g., length 11m, beam 3.4m, depth 1.8m.
2. Another type was a flat-bottomed, teak-built craft used on the lower reaches of rivers.
Other recorded names: **duck (pet) boat**★, **pet**

rua pheelawk *Thailand:* Daytime **fishing boat**★ that works in shallow water, catching the fish in the boat by luring them with a white board along one side. Fisherman rocks the boat violently while paddling, causing the fish to jump up. Board ca. 4-6m long and 0.6m high. Name variant: **catch boat**

rua phrathinang See **rua ballang**

rua pla *Thailand, NE:* **Fishing boat**★ and **fish carrier**★ of the east coast of the Gulf of Siam and on the Mae Nam Chao Phraya near Bangkok. Has a live well. Worked with 4 oars. Spelling variant: **rua plaa**

rua plaa See **rua pla**

rua yayap See **penjajap-3**

Rucker bateau, Rucker tobacco boat See **James River bateau**

rudder-out-door See **sandbagger**

rudder punt See **Thames lighter**

Ruderbarke See **barke-3**

Ruderboot See **pulling boat, rowboat-1**

Ruderkarbasse See **launch**

Ruderpinnasse See **pinnace**

rûë See **düe**

Ruhraak *Germany, central:* Coal carrier of the Ruhr River from the late 17th to the early 19th century. Flat bottom that turned up to narrow, flat ends; low freeboard. Flat, parallel sides narrowed quickly at the ends. Carvel- or clinker-planked. Deadwood at the stern supported the wide rudder that was activated by a humped tiller attached to both the forward and aft parts of the blade; leeboards. Open initially, later most had a cabin house forward. Early boats towed by a single horse. One or 2 lowering masts set gaff sails. Some set a large spritsail on the mainmast and a gaff mizzen. Early vessels ran up a topsail. Crew of 7-10 and a family on the larger vessels. Reported lengths 15-45m; 1800 vessel 33.5m long, 5m wide, 1-1.5m deep, draft light 0.22m, laden 0.8m, cap. 90t. Other recorded names: **Aakschiff, Kohlennachen, Mühlheimer Aak, Mulmsche Aak, Ruhrack, Ruhrkohlenschiff,**

Ruhrnachen, Slof (pl. Sloffen); koolhaelder (Dutch). Note also aak.

Ruhrack, Ruhrkohlenschiff, Ruhrnachen See Ruhraak

rumah rakit See rakit

rum boat See runner

rūmes See ramūs

rum runner See runner, Seaford skiff

run boat *United States, E:* Term for a fast craft that buys fish, crabs, and oysters from fishermen working out on the coastal grounds; boat may be dealer-owned or sell to a dealer ashore. The captain of the run boat receives a commission on the haul. Any local craft—sailing or motorized—may be used. Other recorded names: runner*, running boat. Note also buy boat, carry-away boat, oyster runner. Further reference: bushwack boat

Runcorn boat See narrow boat

rundbottnad eka See eka-1, orusteka

runde Mutte See Mutte

Rundpünte See Pünte

rundstævnede See Bornholmsk laksebåd

runner A vessel that engages in smuggling. Term applied especially to boats that smuggled illicit liquor, such as a rum runner. Word also used for vessels that ran naval blockades (blockade runner); well-armed merchantmen*; and sometimes vessels that sailed without joining a convoy. Such vessels were unusually fast and maneuverable. Other recorded names: cargo boat, contact boat, forceur de blocus, rum boat, running boat (or ship). See also buy boat-2, freighter-4, galley-9b, run boat.

running boat See run boat

running ship *China:* Relatively small vessel that smuggled opium chests into the smaller ports. See also runner.

rûœ See düe

Rush wherry See Irish wherry

russesnekke See shnyaka

ruuhi See eka-2

rybach'ya lodka, rybač'ja lodka See fishing boat

saam paan See **sampan**

saayan See **sakayan**

šabaka See **xebec**

sabani *Japan, S:* **Dugout canoe★** used in the operation of *oikomi* and *ambushi* nets in reef areas of the southern Ryukyu Islands. Blunt, raked bow; square, narrow, raked stern; flat bottom, straight sides. Open. Short mast stepped through a forward thwart sets a battened lugsail; upper part of leech curved. Also paddled.

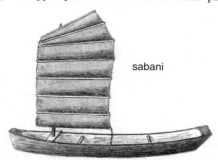

sabani

Worked single-handed or, originally, by a father and son. Length 3m.

šabbâk See **xebec**

sablier non ponté See **bâche-2**

sablonnier See **picoteux**

šabûk See **xebec**

sacaleva, sacalêwa See **sakoleva**

sacáy, sacayán See **sakayan**

saccaleva, saccoleva, saccoleve, sackalever See **sakoleva**

sacker See **Ramsgate smack**, **sack ship-2**

sack ship *United Kingdom:* **1.** Term for an English merchant ship that provided supplies to fishermen working on the banks in the northwest Atlantic Ocean in the 17th-18th centuries; then carried dry salt cod to markets in Spain and around the Mediterranean, and back either to Newfoundland or to British ports with a dry wine (sack) and fruit. Generally ca. 100-200t. Spelling variant: **sac ship**. Note also **by-boat**, **fish box**.
2. Fast-sailing, **cutter★**-rigged vessel that carried fresh fish from 19th-century **smacks★** to market, especially in the English Channel. Name variant: **sacker**. Note also **Ramsgate smack**.

Sacksicken See **zig**

sacolega, sacolege, sacolère, sacolero, sacolèva, sacoleve, sacolevo See **sakoleva**

Sacramento River gillnet boat See **gillnetter-2**

sac ship See **sack ship**

saculeva See **sakoleva**

sadanga See **saranga**

sækstreng See **seksæring-6**

saeta See **saettia**

saëte See **saettia-3**

saetía, saetie, saetta, saette See **saettia**

saettia 1. Attributed mainly to Italy, but appears in literature from other parts of the Mediterranean from the 11th-16th centuries. Fast, narrow boat; rowed and sailed, considered to be a type of **galley★**. Served as a naval vessel, a **corsair★**, a trader, and sometimes a **fishing boat★**. Lightly built, some of cedar, fir, or alder. Square stern; bowsprit supported by a gammon knee. Early boats open, later decked; low sides. In the late 13th century, employed as many as 100 oarsmen; the light patrol **galleys** might use as few as 16 oars. Number of masts varied, but the 3-masted vessels of the 16th century set lateen sails to a forward-raking foremast, mainmast, and a very small mizzenmast. Other recorded names: **cet(t)ea**, **navis sagittaria**, **saetía**, **saet(t)a**, **saetya**, **sagetia**, **sagette**, **sagettia**, **sagitta**, **saghitea**, **sagitaire**, **sagite(d)a**, **sagit(t)a**, **sagittao**, **sagittaria**, **sagittea**, **sagitteæ**, **sagit(t)ia**, **sagittina** (dim.), **sagittiva**, **sahetia**, **saita**, **saitie**, **saitt(i)a**, **sajeta**, **seatia**, **setea**, **setye**, **sithia**, **sittia**; pl. **saetie**, **saettiæ**, **saett(i)e**, **saëtties**, **sagite**, **sagittarii**, **saittie**, **sajete**.
2. *Algeria:* Reported in the 17th century with square sails on the main- and foremasts and a lateen mizzen. Rowed well. Armed with as many as 34 guns. A small type of ca. 15m set a single lateen sail. Other recorded names: **barque★**, **chitia**.
3. *France, Mediterranean coast:* The **saëtes** of Marseille were 30-90t at the end of the 16th century.
4. *Morocco, Atlantic coast:* Long, narrow vessel used by corsairs of Salé and elsewhere along the coast. Reported as early as the mid-14th century. Sailed only, carrying 3-4 sails.
See also **gig-1**.

saettiæ, saettie, saëtties, saetya See **saettia**

safâ'in See **safina**

safety barge See **barge-11f**

safika, safîn See **safina**

safina In old Arabic, a **boat★** or **ship★**; often used in a poetic sense. Also described as a type of **galley★**, especially a **privateer★**, and as a ship carrying "war machines." Spelling variants: **safâ'in**, **safika**, **safîn**, **safînah**, **safiyna**, **sefina**, **sefînâh**, **sefyné**, **suffeenu**; pl. **sufun**. Note also **sēfinē**.

safina See **Lamu jahazi**

safînah See **mahaila-2**, **safina**

safîneh See **mahaila-2**

safiyna See **safina**

sagetia, sagette, sagettia See **saettia**

Sägewarenfloss See **Bretterfloss**

saggita, saghitea, sagita, sagitaire, sagite, sagitea, sagiteda, sagitia, sagitta, sagittao, sagittaria, sagittarii, sagittea, sagitteæ, sagittia, sagittina, sagittiva See **saettia**

sagoer, sagor See **sagur**

sagur *Malaysia:* Malay term for a **dugout canoe★**. In the northeastern part of the Malay Peninsula, the **sagur** is small, plank-extended, and has square-cut ends. Used mainly on rivers. Other recorded names: **perahu** (or **prahu**) **sagor**, **perahu sagur**, **prahoe sagoer**, **sago(e)r**

sagur belahan See **sampan sagur belahan**

sahetia See **saettia**

sahíá See **ekta**

šaḥtūr *Iraq/Syria/Turkey:* Rough, box-like craft used on the upper and lower Euphrates and Tigris Rivers and in the southern Iraqi marshes. In some areas, as in the Syrian segment of the rivers, they hauled firewood from near the Turkish border. Broken up on reaching

šaḥtūr

their destination, towed back upsteam, or served as **ferries★** or **fishing boats★**. Farther downstream, some traveled side-by-side, **catamaran★**-fashion. Plank-built; flat bottom turned up to form square, raking ends; bottom usually logs sawed in half with wide boards on top and below. Strengthened with ribs, stringers, and on some, by athwartship beams. Caulked with rags and asphalt. Floated with the current or rowed, the oarsmen seated in the bow. Steered with a long sweep, which sometimes rested in a fork at the end with a board tied across the fork. Reported lengths 5.5-10m; width ca. 2.5m, depth 1-1.5m. Other recorded names: **čaḥčūr**, **čakhtūr**, **chartouch**, **schachtur**, **shahtur**, **shakhtur**, **shartoush**

šaḥtūra mbaṭṭne See **šaḥtūra mbaṭṭan**

šaḥtūra mbaṭṭan *Israel, NE:* Utilized the *mbaṭṭan* net on the Sea of Galilee (Tiberias). Sharp bow, counter stern. Platform at bow and stern. Net housed at the stern. Set a lateen sail to a slightly aft-raking mast stepped in the forward quarter through a thwart. Also rowed, standing, employing a pair of long oars. Length 5m, beam 1.7m. Spelling variant: **šaḥtūra mbaṭṭne**

saïc, saica, saicca, saicche, saicchisti, saiche, saick, saico, saïcq, saiek, saik, saika, saike See **saique**

sailboat Small craft using sails as its primary source of propulsion. Generally a cruising or racing craft. Selected name variants: **barca a vela★**, **barco de vela**, **barco velera**, **bateau à voiles**, **bote de vela**, **čoln na jadra**, **embarcation à voile**, **imbarcazione a vela**, **jadrenica**, **jadrilica**, **sailing boat**, **sailing craft**, **segelbåt**, **Segelboot**, **sejlbåd**. Note also **sailer**. Further references: **boat-8**, **smack boat-1**

sail cart See **Yarmouth lugger**

sailer A vessel that relies principally on its sails for power. One that relies equally on its engine is often called a **motor sailer**. Selected name variants: **legno a vela**, **parus**, **purjelaiva**, **sailing ship** (or **vessel**), **sailship**, **sayler**, **Segelfahrzeug**, **segelfartyg**, **Segelschiff**, **seglare**, **segler**, **seglskip**, **seglskute**, **seiler**, **sejler**, **sejlskib**, **veler(o)**, **velier(e)**, **veliero**, **voilier**; **cinquante cinquante**, **fifty-fifty**, **motosailer**, **voiliervedette**, **yacht mixte**. Note also **sailboat**.

sail gear *United States, NE:* Name for menhaden **sloops★** at Mystic, Connecticut. Each worked with a "gang" composed of 2 **seine boats★**, a small **striker boat★**, and a small, **sloop**-rigged **menhaden carry-away boat★**. Note also **bony-fish boat**, **menhaden boat**.

sailing barge *British Isles:* General term applied to vessels with **barge★**-like characteristics that sailed coastal waters and inland waterways. Best known are the **Thames sailing barges★**, the **keels★**, **flats★**, **Mersey flats★**, **Norfolk wherries★**, **Plymouth barges★**, **West Country sailing barges★**, and **western barges★**. See also **cargo lighter**, **gravel barge**.

sailing boat See **sailboat**, **smack boat-1**

sailing craft See **sailboat**

sailing gun punt See **gun punt**

sailing lighter *West Indies, NE:* Full-bodied, **sloop★**-rigged cargo vessel of the islands of Nevis and St. Kitts in the Leeward Islands. Straight, raked stem and sternpost; deep hull, flat sheer. Mainsail has a very short gaff and very long boom; staysail. Length ca. 15m, beam 6m. Other recorded names: **Nevis lighter**, **St. Kitts sailing lighter**. See also **gravel barge**, **New York sailing lighter**.

sailing ship, **sailing vessel** See **sailer**

sail lighter See **New York sailing lighter**

sailorman See **Thames sailing barge**

sailor's cradle See **skiff**

sailship See **sailer**

sail skiff *Canada, E:* In Newfoundland, a large boat propelled by sail and oar, and used to carry loads of fish, firewood, etc. See also **North Carolina sail skiff**.

saingla dingi See **dingi-2**

Saint Francis canoe See **Abenaki canoe**

Saint Francis sneakbox See **Barnegat sneakbox**

Saint Ives gig See **Cornish gig**, **gig-4**

Saint Ives lugger, **Saint Ives mackerel driver** See **West Cornish lugger**

Saint John Harbour salmon skiff See **salmon skiff**

Saint John River salmon boat *Canada, E:* Open **fishing boat★** of the St. John River area in New Brunswick. Clinker construction with S-curve to floor amidships, planked-up skeg, natural crook frames. Wide, raked transom. Later boats fitted with a gasoline engine. Note also **salmon skiff-1**.

Saint John River woodboat *Canada, SE:* Boat that traveled the St. John River in eastern New Brunswick carrying cordwood, lumber, and produce to St. John and kiln wood for the lime kilns on the New England coast. Well established by the 1830s; last built in 1917. Carvel-planked of spruce; run either long and fine or short and full; strong tumble home to stem; full bow; wide, shallow, raked transom. Long keel; also generally had bilge keels; low deadrise; strong sheer. Rudder hung out; long tiller; later used a wheel. Low freeboard when loaded. Flush deck; railing ran around bow and stern, open space eased cargo handling; trunk cabin aft; brick fireplace; small hatch for storage forward, main hatch abaft mainmast. Originally tarred, later painted black. **Tender★** hung from stern davits. Bald-headed **schooner★** rigging. On most, foremast stepped in the eyes, mainmast amidships; shoulder on the masts, up ca. 3.1-3.7m, stopped the boom jaws and parrel above the deck cargo. Long gaffs; foresail cut almost square; mainsail extended well beyond the stern. Crew of 2-3. Reported lengths 11-25m; e.g., length 22m, beam 7.6m, hold depth 2m; shallow draft. Other recorded names: **jake, Johnny (wood)boat, St. John woodboat, woodboat★**; those carrying firewood for Maine's lime kilns were known as **kiln-coasters, kiln-wooders**, and **lime-wooders**. Further reading: William A. Baker, *Sloops & Shallops* (Barre, Mass.: Barre Publishing Co., 1966): 92-102.

Saint John's seine boat See **seine boat-2**

Saint John's trap boat *Canada, E:* Hauled coastal cod traps in the vicinity of Saint John's, Newfoundland. Carvel-planked of pine; rounded sides; ceiled amidships; medium sheer. Sharp bow; curved, raking stem; raking, heart-shaped stern. Keel; long run; steep rise to the floors. Open; 5 thwarts, after thwart adjustable. Platform at ends; seat down each side from after thwart to a wide stern seat. Propelled mainly by large oars; sculling hole in transom; rarely sailed. Length 8.5m, beam 1.9m, depth 0.73m.

Saint John woodboat See **Saint John River woodboat**

Saint Kilda mail boat *Scotland, W:* A boat-shaped craft, ca. 60cm long, launched in bad weather from the main Outer Hebrides Islands to drift, it was hoped, to St. Kilda, ca. 68km to the west. Used until the 1920s. Hull hollowed out for the mail and a wooden cover afixed. Iron keel and mast fitted.

Saint Kitts sailing lighter See **sailing lighter**

Saint Lawrence barge *Canada, E:* Transported lumber to oceangoing ships on the St. Lawrence River. Narrow, square bow; transom stern, flat bottom; little freeboard when loaded. Generally painted blue. Originally set 2-3 square sails on the tall mainmast; often a gaff mizzen; later fitted with a gaff mainsail in lieu of the square sails. On the square-rigged vessels, multiple halyards led aft to a large winch atop the cabin. Some had a stubby bowsprit to which a small jib was occasionally set. Colorful vane atop the pole mast. Reported lengths 18-45m. Other recorded names: **bateau★, chalon, St. Lawrence trader**

Saint Lawrence bateau *Canada, E:* **1.** Double-ended, general-purpose **skiff★** used on the river from Montreal to the mouth. Flat bottom, cross-planked, with slight rocker at the ends. Curved stem; mildly curved, raked sternpost, lower than stem. Straight, flared sides; often of a single plank. Rowed using as many as 3 pairs of oars. Length 5.4m, beam at gunwales 1.3m.
2. Early farmer-built boat for general use in the Thousand Islands along the upper river on both the Canadian and U.S. sides. Double-ended; flat bottom, very wide planking nailed to ribs. Length 5.5m.

Saint Lawrence canoe See **Malcite river canoe**

Saint Lawrence goélette See **goélette-2**

Saint Lawrence raft See **dram**

Saint Lawrence River dory See **batteau-2**

Saint Lawrence schooner See **goélette-2**

Saint Lawrence sharpie See **sharpie-7**

Saint Lawrence skiff **1.** *Canada, E/United States, NE:* **Canoe★**-like boat of the upper St. Lawrence River developed in the mid-19th century as a work and family boat for fishing, hunting, and transportation among the Thousand Islands; later became a popular pleasure

Saint Lawrence skiff-1

craft. Copied in many parts of the United States. Lapstraked, white cedar or pine hull, occasionally laps planed to create a smooth skin; 6-7 strakes to a side. Generally varnished; workboats painted. Most double-ended, some sharper aft. The Canadian boats were heavier, built for working; the New York boats were more often pleasure craft. Steam-bent, oak ribs and stems; sawn frames; variety of hardwoods used for trim. Ends curved; sharp turn into the wide, flat keel; rounded bottom. Decked at each end; narrow side decking with shallow coaming; chair seats provided for passengers; fish box in the center. Designed to be rowed, in either direction, using pinhole oarlocks. When sailed, stepped a short mast well forward without shrouds but sometimes with a forestay. Usually set a boomed spritsail. Generally rudderless; steered by trimming the sheet and by shift of the helmsman's weight and the judicious use (after 1880) of a small, metal, folding, fan-type centerboard. Reported lengths 3.6-7.3m, the sailing **skiffs★** longer; the **ladies' skiffs** were 4.9-5.8m long. Typical: 4.88m long, 1.12m wide, 0.45m deep amidships. A larger and heavier boat, built later to incorporate an engine, was called a **skiff-putt** or **one-lunger★**, although some motorized craft were converted **skiffs**. Other recorded names: **Clayton skiff, skief, skift; batwing boat** (used for racing; large sail)
2. *Canada, E:* The **Saint Lawrence skiff** (or **skief**) of the area between Montreal and Quebec was a double-ended, flat-bottomed, working craft; characteristically painted green. Flaring sides, often of a single strake of white pine; bottom, planked athwartships, has slight rocker, with matching sheer. No frames except for stiffening battens. Strong rake to stem, stern generally plumb. Rowed using pin oars or sailed with a small spritsail set to a mast stepped amidships; steered with a rudder.

Saint Lawrence sloop See **sloop-6**

Saint Lawrence trader See **Saint Lawrence barge**

Saint Lawrence yawl *Canada, E:* **Pilot boat★** and pleasure craft of the St. Lawrence River. Carvel-planked with pine; squared ribs; long, straight keel; vertical stem; broad counter. Cabin amidships; roomy cockpit.

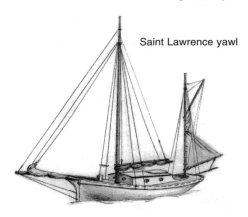

Saint Lawrence yawl

Most employed iron legs with shoes to prevent the beached boat from sinking into the mud. Set gaff sails; the mizzen used a standing gaff, the sail being furled against the mast. Larger boats set 2 headsails and a triangular topsail. The smaller used a single large jib; topmast but no topsail. Engines installed after World War I. Crew of 2. Reported lengths on deck 7.6-15.2m. Note also **Quebec pilot boat**.

Saint Lucia flying-fish dugout See **gommier**

Saint Margarets Bay skiff *Canada, SE:* Beamy, open craft used mainly in fish- and net-carrying for the weir and trap mackerel fishery in St. Margarets Bay near Halifax on the southeast coast of Nova Scotia. Clinker- or carvel-planked; slack bilges; wide, plank keel tapers at each end from 25-31cm amidships, or conventional keel; strong sheer. Sharp or wineglass transom stern. Initially all hulls painted dark green; now turquoise, white, or tan; most tarred inside. Now towed, but originally rowed by 2 fishermen, one at each end, the center reserved for the fish or nets. Reported lengths 8-9m, beam ca. 3m. Other recorded names: **Saint Margarets Bay trap boat**, **seine skiff**, **trap skiff★**

Saint Margarets Bay trap boat See **Saint Margarets Bay skiff**

saintois See **canot-6**

Saint Pierre dory See **doris-3**

Saint-Rambert See **salembarde**

saïq See **saique**

saique 1. *Europe, central:* A variety of **saique** was a small, light, armed **galley★** used on some of the larger central European rivers, notably the Danube, during the 16th-19th centuries. Employed from 18-34 oars; some had oarports. Those attributed to Austria were 1- and 2-masted, setting square, lug-, or spritsails; masts could be struck. **Ganztschaiken** (pl.) were 20-24m long, 3.9-4.1m wide, 0.37-0.65m draft and had 28-32 oarsmen; **Halbtschaiken** were 11-15m by 2-3.5m by 0.37-0.6m, 16-20 oarsmen; **Doppeltschaiken** were 27-28m by 3.76m by 0.57m, 32-36 oarsmen; a **Vierteltschaike** was 10.35m by 2.35m by 0.51m;

Vedettentschaiken or **Patrouillentschaiken** were ca. 10m by 1.6m by 0.4m, 6 oarsmen. Name variant: **Donautschaike**. Note also **shaiku**.

2. *Mediterranean, E:* A transport ship by this name was reported from Venice in the late 11th century. During the 17th-19th centuries, it was a burdensome, 2-masted vessel attributed mainly to Turkey and Greece. Sharp, raked bow; flat stern, either triangular or rectangular in shape; high sheer. Decked; large cabin aft. Outboard rudder; tiller. Vertical mainmast with tall topmast; shrouds to mainmast, topmast stayed to bowsprit. Set square sails of nearly equal depth; bonnet on topsail. Lateen sail to a short mizzenmast. A small square sail hung below the long, rising bowsprit. Some set lateen sails to a vertical mainmast and forward-raking foremast. Reported lengths 18-30m.

Spelling variants: **chaika**, **chaïko**, **chaiqa**, **chaique**, **csaike**, **czaike** (pl. **czaiken**), **czajka★**, **saïc**, **saic(c)a**, **saicche**, **saicchisti**, **saiche** (pl.), **saick**, **saico**, **saï(c)q**, **saiek**, **saik(a)**, **saike**, **sayka**, **sayke**, **Schayke**, **Scheike**, **shaika**, **Tschaike** (pl. **Tschaiken**), **Tscheigge**, **Tscheuke**, **zayke**. Note also **caique**.

saita See **saettia**

saitia *Greece:* Two-masted merchant vessel built by Greek shipwrights in the early 19th century during the period of Turkish rule. Square sails on the foremast, lateen on the mainmast.

saitie See **saettia**

sai ting See **sha ting**

saitta, saïttia, saittie See **saettia**

saiyeh See **shū·ai**

sajeta See **saettia**, **strijela**

sajete See **saettia**

sa-kai-yan See **vinta**

sakajan, sakakyang-dagat See **sakayan**

sakalawât, sakalêwa See **sakoleva**

sakay See **sakayan**

sakaya *Indonesia, central:* Generic term for a **perahu★** in the Sarudu dialect of southwestern Sulawesi (Celebes).

sakayan *Philippines:* **1.** Generic term for a **boat★** or **ship★** in several dialects. In Tagalog, **sakakyang-dagat** implies a seagoing vessel.

2. In the Jolo area of the southern Philippines, a small sailing **canoe★** used for fishing and transportation. Ends bifid with the upper parts flared and recurving. Although generally unadorned, some are elaborately carved at the bow and stern or on a strip running longitudinally along the hull. Booms for the double outriggers may be carved at the ends.

Spelling variants: **saayan**, **sacáy**, **sacayán**, **sakajan** (by the Yami of Lan yu), **sakay**, **sakkayan**, **sarac-yan**, **saraquian**, **sasakayán**. See also **vinta**.

saKi *United States, W:* Simple craft of the Pauite of Honey Lake, California, and the marshy lakes in western Nevada. Used particularly for net fishing and wildfowl hunting. Two bundles of tule grass tied with cattail rope were lashed together at the ends or only at the bow. Gunwales of a tule bundle or cattail leaves formed the sides, and on the square-sterned craft, the bundle would curve around to form a seat. When waterlogged, fresh bundles were added. Poled. Very small boats only carried game and weapons, and were propelled by wading or swimming. Reported lengths 2.6-5.2m; e.g., length 5.2m, width 1.6m, depth 0.6m. Name variant: **tule balsa**. Further reading: Margaret M. Wheat, *Survival Arts of the Primitive Paiutes* (Reno: Univ. of Nevada Press, 1967): 40-47.

sakkayan See **sakayan**

sakkit See **kayak-3**

sakkolefe, sakkoleva See **sakoleva**

sakoesi See **sekochi**

sakoleva *Mediterranean:* Greek word describing a type of spritsail; term has been widely adopted in the eastern Mediterranean as referring to a type of vessel, although hull types vary and many combinations of sails have been employed. Served as a **coaster★** and for fishing and sponging; early boats were often

sakoleva

armed by Greek and Turkish corsairs; some smaller types still exist. Most double-ended, but some have a shallow counter; on early vessels, the poop extended over the sharp stern. Stem raked and either curved or straight; high sheer; low freeboard, often raised with canvas weathercloths. Flat floors, rounded bilges; long, straight keel. Most decked; some with poop deck, others with steering cockpit. Often painted black. Stepped 1-3 masts; the mainmast generally raked sharply forward, the mizzen raked aft. The full-cut, square, sprit mainsail ran out on a wire rope stay or on a gaff from the mainmast to the end of the long, light sprit. Sail brailed in to the mast for stowing. Usually carried 2-3 sails, changing sails to accommodate wind conditions. Sprit controlled by 2 vangs. Some carried a fidded topmast, setting a square topsail and sometimes a topgallant. Mizzen carried a jib-headed or lateen sail sheeted to a bumkin. When 3rd mast used, it was stepped forward of the mizzen and set a small lateen sail. Two or 3 jibs set flying from a long, slender, running bowsprit. Crew of 3. Lengths 7.7-23m; e.g., length overall 12.5m, on keel 9.3m, beam 3.7m, depth 1.25m; shallow draft. Spelling variants: **chekeleve, sacalêwa, sac(c)aleva, saccoleva, sac(c)oleve, sackalever, sacolega, sacolege, sacolère, sacolero, sacolèva, sacolevo, saculeva, sakalawât** (pl.), **sakalêwa, sakkolefe, sakkoleva, sakoleve, sakouleva, saqlāwa, saqualeva.** Note also **korkâra, trechandiri.**

sakoleve See **sakoleva**

sakōtji See **sekochi**

salouleva See **sakoleva**

sal 1. *Afghanistan, E:* The **śāl** is a **raft★** of inflated skins that transports goods and people on the Kabul and associated rivers. Bamboo platform, covered with grass, set atop the skins. Other recorded names: **shāl; jāla★, jālah.** Note also **turssuk.**
2. *Asia, central:* Turkic word for **raft.**
3. *Bulgaria:* Term for **raft** and sometimes **ferryboat★**. Spelling variant: pl. **sálove**
4. *Mongolia:* Also a **raft.**
5. *Romania, E:* A **şal** is a log **raft** from the Galaţi area that is towed downstream on the Danube to the Black Sea.
6. *Russia, south-central:* In the Tyva (Tuva) Autonomous Republic, the Tyvans create a **raft** of tree trunks bound with birchbark or willow for downstream trips.
7. *Turkey:* Term for a **raft.**

salah-salah *Indonesia:* Name given to the **grabs★** of India that traded to the Sunda and Moluccan Islands. Two- or 3-masted, the latter with fore-and-aft sails on 2 masts and a lug- or square sail on the mizzen. Two-masted vessels were **ketch★**-rigged. Generally low at the sharp bow; stern high; others modified with square galleries at the bow and stern extending beyond the sharp ends. Large deckhouse. Crew of 8-20. Length of a 3-master 73m, beam 9m; 2-master 22m long, 3m wide, 4.6m deep. Other recorded names: **gourabe★, gourable, sala-sala**

salambard See **salembarde**

salanda See **bilander-1, dumb barge, shalanda**

şalandă basculantă See **dump barge**

salandium, salandra, salandre, salandria, salandrinus, salandrium, salandrus See **chelandia**

sala-sala See **salah-salah**

sälbåt See **fälbåt**

salembard See **salembarde**

salembarde *France, south-central:* Open cargo boat that carried coal on the upper Loire River to the lower Loire and Paris until the mid-19th century. Built mainly at Saint-Rambert; those built in the region of Brassac in the Auvergne were called **auvergnates★**. Considered a variety of **sapine★** (the **sapine salembarde**). Traveled downstream only and consequently roughly constructed, but strong and light to withstand fast water. Wide, clinker planking secured with treenails. Flat bottom; parallel sides, cut in sharply to the bow. Bottom planking turned up at the bow to form a flat, raking surface. Square, slightly raked stern. House amidships on some. Steered with a sweep at each end. Special crew of 5 to Roanne, then cargo transferred to a larger **salembarde** and coupled side-by-side with another **salembarde**, each having 3 men. Length ca. 28m, beam 4.5m, depth 1.25m, very shallow draft. Other recorded names: **Saint-Rambert, salambard, salembard**

Salem sloop boat See **sloop boat**

sälfangstbåt See **fälbåt-1**

salīna See **saranga**

Salish canoe See **Coast Salish canoe**

Salish shovel-nose canoe See **tl'ai**

salisipan *Philippines, S:* Fast, light, **canoe★**-like vessel that was popular for coastal raids, usually working in association with the **panco***. Plank-extended dugout hull with the planks doweled on and lashed with rattan. Steep floors; sharp ends; the bow sometimes had a carved, ram-like projection; stern sheer swept up, also with a ram. Might have outriggers. Some had a palm washstrake along each side. Quarter rudder. Mainly rowed; some standing oarsmen worked against an oar-fork, others rowed seated. A quadrangular sail might be hung from a single mast. Reported lengths 9-10.6m. Other recorded names: **baroto***, **kakap***, **vinta***

sallop See **shallop**

salmon boat *Canada, E:* Used in the commercial salmon fisheries of Newfoundland. Undecked. Name variant: **salmon punt***. See also **Dee salmon boat**, **Exe salmon boat**, **gillnetter-2**, **Saint John River salmon boat**, **whammel boat**.

salmon cobble See **coble-4**

salmon coble *Northern Ireland:* Open **rowing boat*** used in conjunction with drift net fishing for salmon. Clinker-built; transom stern, curved stem with cutaway forefoot, flat floors. Rowed with 2 pairs of oars, single-banked. Length ca. 5m. See also **coble-1e**, **coble-4**.

salmon dory See **dory-5**, **salmon troller**

salmon drift-net boat See **whammel boat**

salmon gillnet boat See **gillnetter-2**

salmon hang-net boat See **whammel boat**

salmon punt *England:* **1.** On the south coast, the **salmon punts** of the Stour/Avon Estuary served not only for fishing, but in winter, as **ferries*** in the Christchurch and Mudeford areas. Square ends, flat bottom, beamy, ca. 4.6m long. Rowed, requiring 3 men when the water was rough.
2. On the River Severn, in the west, **salmon punts** work with a smaller, transom-sterned boat. The former carries and lays out the net, the latter transfers a person to the opposite shore. The 3 thick, longitudinal bottom planks are tongue-and-grooved and bolted together; single plank along each side; no frames. Square ends curve up from the bottom; strong end sheer. Open; worked with a pair of oars, the oarsman seated well forward; originally used a paddle, which today continues to serve as a bailer. Length 6.8m, beam 1.1m, depth 0.43m. Other recorded names: **long-net salmon punt**, **Severn punt**. Note also **salmon boat**.

salmon seine boat See **seine boat-6**

salmon skiff **1.** *Canada, SE:* Small, open boat that worked in Saint John Harbour in southern New Brunswick until World War II, catching shad and alewives and drift-netting for salmon. Lapstrake planking, natural crook frames, plank keel. Curved stem; raked, wineglass transom. Some decked at ends and along the sides. Rudder hung to split gudgeons that slipped over a flattened section at the top of the rudderpost for easy unshipping. Mainly rowed with 2 pairs of oars. Those that sailed set a spritsail and had a daggerboard. Engine on later boats. Length-to-beam ratio ca. 3.5:1. Name variant: **St. John Harbour salmon skiff**. Note also **St. John River salmon boat**.
2. *Canada, W:* In British Columbia, **salmon skiffs** were affiliated with canneries, and were usually towed to a fishing site by a company **tug***. Lapstrake-planked; V-

transom; straight, raked bow; flat bottom. Open except for temporary canvas shelter at the bow. Nets run through breaks in the top strake at the stern or over a roller on the transom. May have a centerboard. Painted with identifying colors of the cannery that owned it. Rowed and sailed. Crew of 1-2. Length 8.4m, beam 2m.
3. *United States, Alaska:* Those working in commercial salmon fisheries in southeastern Alaska have a wide, raked transom with a full-width roller for setting and hauling the net. Flared sides; open with transverse bulkheads; engine forward. Crew of 1-2. Length 7.62m.

salmon troller *United States, NW:* **1.** Several types of boats troll in Puget Sound in northwestern Washington State. One type is similar to the sharp-ended, round-bottomed **Columbia River skiff***. Work with 1-2 men; some formerly worked with a Native American in a **canoe*** as a **tender***. Decked forward and aft; wheelhouse on some. Four trolling poles fixed to after end of the house; stayed with a fair spreader. Powered with a small inboard engine. Some employ a steadying sail. Generally under 18m.
2. On the Oregon coast, a **dory*** type used for both sport and commercial salmon fishing, working from the beaches. Flat bottom athwartships, with strong rocker; straight, flaring sides; marked sheer. Plywood construction or conventional **dory** planking. Raked ends, either sharp or a **dory** stern. Foredeck; 2 trolling poles amidships; fish well. Rowed through the surf; then an outboard motor, housed in after third, is dropped. Crew of 4. Length 6m, beam 2m, depth 0.94m. Name variant: **salmon dory**. Note also **Oregon dory**, **troller**.

salmon wherry *United States, NE:* Used by farmers/fishermen in the western Penobscot Bay area of Maine from at least the 1st half of the 19th century; extinct as a workboat. Numerous local variations, but characteristically lapstrake construction, nearly double-ended on the waterline. Curved stem; full bow, but degree of fullness varied. Tall, champagne glass-shaped, raked transom (the **Griffin model**) or straight tuck and angular transom (**Rhodes model**); some had a notch for sculling or to facilitate breaking out the anchor. Single bottom board, box stern, slight rocker; soft turn of the bilges; rounded sides; sawn frames of natural crook cedar or hackmatack added after boat planked. Considerable sheer, the stern sometimes higher than the bow. Open; fishermen knelt on a low platform just abaft the stem when hauling in the salmon. Mainly rowed, but those that sailed used a centerboard or daggerboard. Set a single spritsail principally, and occasionally a jib to a short bowsprit. Reported lengths 3.2-5.5m; e.g., length 4.1m, beam 1.3m, depth 0.56m. Other recorded names: **Ash Point**, **Griffin**, **Lincolnville, Maine**, and **Rhodes wherry**; **Penobscot Bay salmon dory**, **Wade salmon wherry**. Note also **Cape Rosier wherry**.

saloup See **chaloupe-8**

sálove See **sal-3**

saltanat kayığı *Turkey:* Elegant **imperial caique** used by the sultan and his family for local travel. Each sultan had one built for his own use; last used during

World War I. Heavily ornamented along the sides and at the bow and stern. Bow elongated and horizontal or upturned and recurved. Commonly had a gilded bird figurehead and was known as a **bird caique** (or **kuşlu kayık**). An ornate pavilion at the stern provided shelter (the **köşklü kayık** or **pavilion caique**) and distinguished the **sultan's caique** from other court **caiques***. Mainly rowed, double-banked, using as many as 26 oars. Steered by rudder and tiller. Early boats equipped with double sails. Reported lengths 30-32m, beam and depth 2.5-3m. Additional name variants: **fılukayı hümayun**; pl. **saltanat kayıkları**. Further reading: Douglas S. Brookes, "The Turkish Imperial State Barges," *The Mariner's Mirror* 76 (1990): 41-49. Note also **kayık-2**.

saltanat kayıkları See **saltanat kayığı**

salt banker See **banker**

salt boat *India, NE:* Conveyed salt from the seacoast to ports along the Hooghly River. Narrow bow and stern transoms; high stern, lower bow; crossbeams extended out below top strake. Mat and thatch house in after half. Steered from a platform atop the house with a very large, wide-bladed sweep. Rowed in forward half, 5 oarsmen per side, each manning a long-shafted, round-bladed oar. Also sailed. Reported cap. 32-150t. See also **buffalo boat, galopinus, ma yang chuan, narrow boat, sentine, yan chuan.**

saltee See **hola, sālti**

salt fisherman *Canada, E:* A term used in Newfoundland for a vessel that fished for cod on the Grand Banks and off Labrador. The fishermen wet salted their catch, taking it to port to dry. Name variant: **salt fishing vessel.** Note also **fisherman, market boat-3.**

salt fishing vessel See **salt fisherman**

salt hay boat See **hay boat-2**

sālti *India, NE:* Term applied in West Bengal to a flat-bottomed, general-purpose dugout of the **ekta*** type and to a larger craft used for foreshore fishing. Cut from the *śāl* tree. Sometimes a small mat roof amidships. The smaller types range from 6-9m in length, 0.3-0.6m in width at the gunwale, and are 0.3m deep; the larger range from 9-13.7m long, 1.8-2.1m wide, and 0.91-1.07m deep. Spelling variant: **saltee.** Note also **hola.**

saltie See **packet**

salt junk See **da fu chuan, yan chuan**

saltværingsbaad See **saltvæingsbåt**

saltværingsbåt *Norway, N:* A sturdy, reliable **fishing boat*** of the **Nordlandsbåt*** type built in the Salten area, mainly in the 19th century. Clinker-planked of pine or spruce; sharp ends; open. Worked under oars and sail. Reported lengths 9.4-12.55m. Spelling variant: **saltværingsbaad.**

salui *East Malaysia:* General term for **canoe*** by the Punan Bah peoples of central Sarawak. Their **canoes** are narrow dugouts, mostly plank-extended, initially by lashing with rattan, now nailed. Some ends sharp and overhanging, others square and raked. Number of thwarts depends on length; slightly flared sides. Paddled. The smallest, for children, are only a few meters long; the largest, to 50m, initially used for

tribal warfare and headhunting, now for regattas. Those between 12-16m are used for long-distance river transportation. Most are 6.5-8m.

salvagente collettivo See **life raft**

Salvation Army mission boat See **mission boat-2**

salvavidas See **lifeboat**

Salzburger Plätte See **Plätte-1**

Salzlädine See **Lädine**

Salzprahm See **Prahm-2**

Salzzille *Austria:* General term for the river **barges*** that carried salt, especially on the Traun (**Trauner Salzzille**) and Danube Rivers. In the late 16th century, the boats were commandeered for use in the war with Turkey, and by the late 19th century, some carried stone on the Danube. Flat bottom turned up to a pointed bow; stern lower. Controlled by dual sweeps at the stern, the men standing on a platform. Mainly open, but those with a covering were called **Sechserkobel** and **Siebnerkobel.** Types designated by the number of bottom boards—4 boards: **Viererl, Viererzille;** 5 boards: **Fünferin, Fünferl, Fünferzille;** 6 boards: **Sechserin, Sechserzille;** 7 boards, the most common: **Siebernin, Siebnerzille;** 8 boards: **Achterin, Achterzille;** 10 boards: **Zehnerin, Zehnerzille.** The **Zwidorzille** fell between the **Siebernin** and **Achterin** in size; by the end of the 18th century, it carried coal to Vienna and was called a **Zwidorkohlzille.** A **Siebernin** employed 10 men. Reported lengths 19-41m; a late **Siebernin** was 35m long, 5m wide, 1.45m deep.

samaki dhow See **bedan-2**

samb See **sambo-2**

samba-bune See **samma-ami-bune**

sambak See **sambūq**

sambecchino, sambecco, sambeco, šambek See **xebec**

Samberspits See **spits**

sambo 1. *Indonesia, central:* Early Javanese vessel.
    2. *Malagasy Republic:* **Sàmbo** is a general term for a **boat*** or **ship*.** A **sàmbo láy** is a sailing ship, while the **sàmbo mpiady** is a naval vessel. Spelling variants: **samb, samb(o)u, tsambou**
    See also **bot-4, chombo.**

sàmbo láy, sàmbo mpiady See **sambo-2**

sambook See **sambūq**

sambou See **sambo-2**

sambouck, sambouk, sambouq See **sambūq**

sambu See **chombo, sambo-2**

sambucco, sambuchi, sambuck, sambuco, sambūg See **sambūq**

sambuk *India, NW:* A small boat, sometimes the **ship's boat*** of a **pattamar***, especially in the Kolaba district of Maharashtra state. See also **dau-3, sambūq.**

sambuki See **sambūq**

sambūq 1. Widely used Arabic term that can refer to a specific class of vessel or **boat***, or to **vessels*** in general. Throughout the Persian (Arabian) Gulf, the term may merely designate a type of medium-size **freighter*** originating in Oman and elsewhere on the Arabian coast. Early reports also refer to it as a **ship's boat*** and as a vessel of the west coast of India (note **sambuk**).
    2. *Arabian Peninsula/Djibouti/Egypt/Eritrea/Somalia/Sudan:* Cargo and passenger vessel found all along

the coasts of the Arabian Peninsula, Iran, both sides of the Red Sea, and Somalia. Wide-ranging, sailing to India and down the east coast of Africa. Popular pearling vessel in the Persian Gulf; in the Red Sea, they are most often fishing craft. The few still operating are mainly motorized, although they may also carry sails. Some are built on the west coast of India for Arab owners. Considerable regional variation, but characterized by a long, curved stem, generally in a smooth arc from the long keel, although in some areas, there is an elbow bend above the waterline. Stem terminates in a deep, scimitar-shaped head, which is more pronounced at Aden and Red Sea areas; tip either oiled wood or painted. Some have oculi on the stemhead, and in the Red Sea, geometric designs may adorn the stem piece. Square-sterned, either with a smooth rake or a shallow counter; stern generally wider in the Persian Gulf area; some had high poops. A double-ended type is called a **zaruq★**. Stern may have simple carvings, and some have 4 small openings. On the smooth-sterned boats, the long rudder extends to just below the poop rail, with an iron tiller shipping inboard; on the counter-sterned type, the rudder is short and the post comes up through the counter, passing to the poop deck. Tiller maneuvered by ropes leading to a wheel. Carvel-planked; strakes nailed; full-bodied amidships; bow low, higher toward the poop; poop highest on Persian Gulf vessels. Strakes along the poop often decorated or painted blue and white and may extend beyond the stern. Large vessels decked; the smaller are open except for working platforms at the bow and stern. Mat weathercloths protect the cargo on the undecked Red Sea boats; later vessels often have a wheelhouse. A **mashua★** is carried as a **ship's boat**; a small, sewn **banouche** is carried on the Aden boats. Bottom coated with a combination of oil and lime; oiled above the waterline. Motorized vessels generally single-masted, but earlier, most were 2-masted: massive mainmast stepped amidships, short mizzen just forward and abaft the poop deck break, both raking slightly forward. Set lateen sails; mainsails tacked either to stemhead or to a spar rigged over the bow. Crew of 3-16 on **fishing boats★**, 9-45 on traders. Lengths: **fishing boat** 11m long, 1.83m wide; trader 23.5-40m; e.g., 25m long overall, 19m between perpendiculars, beam 5.4m, depth 2.6m. Further reading: G. R. Millward, "The Birth of a Dhow," *Sudan Notes and Records* 32 (1951): 197-206; P. Nougarede, "Qualités Nautiques de Navires Arabes," in: International Colloque d'Histoire Maritime VI, Lourenço Marques, 1962, *Océan Indien et Méditerranée*: 95-122. Note also **gatīra, ṭarrādah, zaima**.

3. *Oman/Yemen:* On the southern coast of Oman and adjacent Yemen, a small, double-ended, sewn boat is also called a **sambūq**. Works from the beaches catching sardines, but some transfer cargo to and from off-lying ships. Mango wood planks sewn with coconut fiber; frames lashed in. Very sharp, raked stem; sternpost less raked. Straight keel, strong deadrise amidships to a sharp chine. Rowed and sailed. Generally sets a single lateen sail, but sometimes a square sail is used. Reported lengths 7-12m, narrow. A small

sambūq on the Muscat coast of Oman may be called a **shū·ai★**.
Name variants: **sambak, sambook, sambou(c)k, sambouq, sambuc(c)o, sambuck, sambūg, sambuk★, sambuki, sambuque, sanābīg, sanābī k, sanbak, sanbik, sanbok, sanbūk, sanbūq, sembuk, soemboek, soenboek, sombūq, sonbuk, sumbook, sumbuk, sunbūq, zambuca, zambuche, zambucis, zambuc(c)o, zambuquo;** pl. **sambuchi, zambuc(c)hi.** Further reference: **zaima**
sambuque See **sambūq**
sambwe See **chombo**
Samebåt See **Lappbåt**
Samerös See **Samoreus**
samghādam See **jangar**
saṁghāṭi See **angula**
samma-ami-bune *Japan, S:* Drift-net boat from Wakayama Prefecture in southern Honshū that fishes for mackerel. Strong sheer at ends. Long, narrow rudder. Steps 2 masts. Crew of 16-18. Waterline length 10.7m, beam 2.3m, depth 0.7m. Name variants: **samba-bune, sampa-bune**
Sammereus, Sammoreus See **Samoreus**
Samoreus *Germany/Netherlands:* Cargo vessel of the lower Rhine, Sambre, and Maas Rivers that occasionally went into the Zuiderzee. Dated from the 17th century to ca. 1850, carrying wood initially and later freight and some passengers. The largest and strongest came from Holland, while the lighter vessels worked farther up the Rhine, especially above Cologne. An **aak★**-type vessel with the characteristic flat bow that tapered to a point at the gunwale. Clinker-planked; flat bottom, slightly curved sides, topsides had tumble home, sheer swept up at ends. Those from Rotterdam had a fuller and steeper bow than those built at Amsterdam. Stern sharp and often shallow above the skeg and sternpost that supported the heavy rudder; long tiller; wide, rounded, or narrow leeboards. Decked; usually a deckhouse well aft; long, arched hatch. Loading boom associated with the mast. Early vessels employed one very tall mast, setting a square main, topsail, and forestaysail. Later adopted a boomed, loose-footed mizzen. Some were sprit-rigged to 1-2 masts. Mast stayed by shrouds and backstays. Sometimes 1-2 jibs to a running bowsprit. Crewed by 7-10 or a family. Reported lengths 25-47m, widths 4.4-7.5m, depths 3.2-3.8m, draft loaded 1.8-2.8m. The **Amsterdamer Samoreus** was slimmer than the **Rotterdamer Samoreus** because some of the locks it traveled were narrower. Other recorded names: **bateau de Cologne, Keulenaar, Samerös, Sammereus, Sammoreus, Samoreuse, Samoreux, Samoreuze, Samorose, Samoureus, Samurdin.** Note also **Kölner Aak.**
Samoreuse, Samoreux, Samoreuze, Samorose, Samoureus See **Samoreus**
sampa 1. *Japan:* Boat that operates a purse seine with a 2nd **sampa**. Open; flat bottom has rocker at the stern; strong sheer; sharp bow with curved stem that extends well above the gunwale. Sides curve in sharply and extend aft beyond the bottom to form a V-shaped stern. Several crossbeams pierce the sides. Roller on

forward beam for hauling in the net. Oarlock straps, all forward of amidships. Length 5.6m, beam 1.35m, depth 0.5m.

2. *Macau:* The **sam-p'á** transported diverse cargo and passengers around Macau. Also a popular pirate vessel. Bow somewhat sharp; stern sharp or slightly rounded. Decked; rounded house amidships. Strikable mast set a battened lugsail. Crew of 8-12. Length ca. 12m, beam 1.8m, draft 0.6m.

sampaan See **sampan**

sampa-bune See **samma-ami-bune**

sampam See **sampan**

sampan **1.** Loose term used in east and southeast Asia to designate various small harbor and local coastal craft. Term now often used for small, Chinese-built boats, but early travelers applied the word and its variant forms more widely, even to much larger vessels. Note also **cái thuyền, phang chun, tam ban**.

2. *Bangladesh, SE:* Range from small, open waterman's boats to large, decked cargo carriers that sometimes sail as far as Yangon (Rangoon). Carvel-planked; high, rounded sides; flat bottom, hard chines, strong rise to the bottom at ends. Tall, vertical, hewn stem; high, U-shaped transom stern with twin horns. Frames fitted after hull has been planked. Larger boats have an arched hood over the stern or most of the hull; some have hatch coamings. Stern rudder on the larger types. Gaily painted. Small **sampans**, and at times the larger, are rowed by oarsmen facing forward working the oars cross-loom fashion. Small boats set a high-cut spritsail. The largest boats set a quadrilateral, lateen-type sail with a short luff; originally employed lugsails. Long yard nearly vertical where forward of the mast; sail tacked to stemhead; after part boomed with boom secured to the mast by a rope sling. Mast in a tabernacle, supported by many shrouds and a forestay. Jib may be extended by a spar; very small, triangular mizzen. Rowed in calms with long, pointed oars. Large boats require 10 men. Reported lengths 4.3-18m; e.g., length 10.7m, beam 3.66m or 4.57m, depth 2.44m. Name variants: **Chittagong sampan, shampan**

3. *China:* General term for a small boat that cannot otherwise be classified as a **junk★, barge★,** etc. Word originally used mainly by foreigners, but now frequently used by the Chinese themselves. Design and use vary widely, depending on local needs and customs. Some carry cargo, produce, and livestock; others ferry passengers; some are floating kitchens; many are **fishing boats★**; and often they are **houseboats★**. One very blunt, square-ended type serves as a **dinghy★** on **junks**, characteristically having a plank between the stern wings. In northern coastal areas, the **sampan** is a heavily built longshore boat, and in Sichuan (Szechuan) in west-central China, the word **sampan** denotes a type of large **junk**, while small types are called **hua zi★** (or **mu chuan**), as they are on the lower Chang Jiang (Yangtze), notably in the Shanghai area. The **hua zi** has a flat bottom; square, overhanging bow; characteristic wings that extend beyond the square stern; sides flare from the bottom and then have tumble home; full amidships; sheer sweeps up at stern and frequently at the bow. Decked at the ends, and

often have an arched house for a family over part of the hull. The small passenger **sampan** (**hong tou san ban★** or **hsiao san-pan t'a-ko**) has an arched shelter to protect the passengers. Hull gaily painted. Generally rowed or sculled, but occasionally raises a small, cloth, battened lugsail to a midship mast. Wide size range, but some ca. 6.4m long, 1.5m wide, and 0.61m deep. The upriver Chang Jiang **hua zi** lacks the stern wings, being double-ended with narrow, square, overhanging ends. Flattened bottom, rounded sides, flat sheer. No bulwarks in forward and after thirds, the stern reserved for the helmsman who uses a sweep, and the bow for the one or two oarsmen; pasengers sit in the midships well. Length 12.2m, beam 2.4m. Other recorded names: **xia you chuan** (**hsia-yu ch'uan**)—a generic term for any small **sampan** ca. 4.6m long. Note also **siampan**.

4. *Indonesia:* **a.** Word commonly used in the islands but with varied meanings. Most often refers to a particular type of boat that is not indigenous to that region. May denote a plank-built craft, as opposed to a **dugout canoe★**. In some islands (as on Java and the Aru Islands), it has a single outrigger, and in Sulawesi (Celebes), it is a large **outrigger canoe★** equipped with a cabin. A 16th-century treatise on the Moluccan Islands describes a **sampan** as a large, freight-carrying vessel. Most, however, are single-masted, setting a rectangular or triangular sail. **b.** Large cargo vessel from Atjeh at the north end of Sumatra. Plank-built; sharp, raked bow; decked; stern rudder. Accommodations for passengers at the stern. Stepped 1-2 masts. Single-masted vessels set a spritsail and a boomed staysail. Two-masted boats employed a rectangular or gaff sail and square or gaff topsail. Name variant: **praho. c.** Small **fishing boat** of the Banjuwangi area on the east coast of Java. Sharp ends; plank-built. Boomed, triangular sail set to a short mast; apex tacked to bow. **d.** In the Biak language of Biak Island off the north coast of Irian Jaya, a **sampan** is a **dugout canoe** with 2 plank outriggers.

5. *Japan:* Term applied to a range of craft, from 1-man boats to 3-masted vessels. Generally have a shallow deadrise from a broad, flat keel; hard chines. Bottom rakes up to a shallow, square transom; on some, the bottom planks along each side extend beyond the transom to join the side planking. Sharp bow with long, straight, raking stem; some with recurved stemhead, others greatly elongated. One-man boats sculled from the port quarter or over the transom; larger boats employ multiple sculls, working from both sides. Those that sailed set square sails from 1-3 masts. Now mainly motorized.

6. *Peninsular Malaysia/Singapore:* **a.** Generic term not restricted to a particular type of boat, although it may distinguish a plank-built boat from a dugout-based craft. Often used interchangeably with **kolek★** and **perahu★**. Found along the south and west coasts, used mainly for fishing and ferrying. Those off the west coast are beamier and have more sheer than the Singapore craft, with sharper rise at the stern. Normally rigged with a standing lugsail reinforced with battens; 2-masted at Malacca. Name variant:

shoe boat. b. The Chinese fishing **sampan** of the Singapore area has sharp ends. Crudely built and finished. Ribs in 3 pieces. Outboard rudder; tiller. Light mast stepped in forward quarter. Sets a battened lugsail. Crew of 2. Lengths ca. 4.6-7.6m.

7. *Myanmar (Burma):* Found in the Ahrewady (Irrawaddy) Delta area and along the coast as small, passenger and general-purpose craft and as larger cargo boats. Flat bottom overhangs and rises forward, either to a fairly vertical stem or directly to the top of the sheer strake. At stern, bottom also curves up but is less pronounced; on the small **sampans**, the bow is higher than the stern. Top strakes at stern extend beyond the raking transom to form the characteristic "horns" or "wings"; on the large cargo **sampans**, the

sampan-7

stern is higher than the bow. Small boats have a short, boxed-in area at the bow; larger boats may have an arched mat covering aft and an open hold amidships; narrow side decks or fully decked. Generally rowed with oarsman facing forward; single tholepin. Large boats may be sculled in close quarters. Sometimes steps a pole mast setting a square or lugsail; large, square rudder shipped when sailed. Motors now common. One man works small boats; crew of 3-5 on cargo craft. Small boats 4.6-6.1m long; e.g., length 5.5m, beam 1.9m, draft 0.25m. Cargo boats to 10.7m long.

8. *Thailand:* The seagoing **sampan** of the Gulf of Siam has been replaced by motorized craft. The original small vessel (ca. 9m on the waterline) stepped 2 masts that set battened lugsails. In Bangkok, the small **sampans** are used as **market boats**★, selling merchandise to the boat population of the city. The larger boats set a boomed, rectangular, standing lugsail; the smaller are only paddled. Narrow, square bow; rising sheer to the square stern; washboards increase the low freeboard. Reported lengths 3-6m.

9. *United States, Hawaii:* Japanese-owned **sampans** were prevalent in the Hawaiian group in the 1st quarter of the 20th century. Most fished well offshore, some staying out 2-3 weeks. Those engaging in day trips had a live well for the bait outbound and for the catch on the homeward trip; the deep-water boats packed the fish in ice. Curved stem, shallow transom, overhanging scuppers. Painted a pale blue. Some small types were sailed only. Most were powered but had 2-3 sails they hoisted to very small masts that were unstepped when not in use. Crew of 2-8; slept on the after deck. Reported lengths 9-20m.

10. *United States, W:* Small **fishing boat** of some of the bays where Chinese had congregated—San Diego, Monterey, Carmel, and San Francisco. Used mainly in the latter half of the 19th century. Built Chinese-style of local redwood. Sculled from the stern or set a single sail.

Selected name variants: **cempan, champa(i)gne, champan★, champana(a), champane, champaneta** (dim.), **champann(e), champão, champara, champaulu, champenas, chanpan, c(h)iampana, ciampane★, ciampanne, saam paan, sampaan, sampam, sampana, sampang, sampan(n)e, san ban, sanpan★, Schampan, shan ban** (or **pan**)**, siampan★.** Further references: **kolek-3, kolek sĕlat, lepa-lepa, phang chun, sampan Riau**

sampana See **sampan**

sampan batil Malay term for a small, beamy boat with a markedly rounded form.

sampan bidar See **bedar-2, bidar-3, bidar-4**

sampan Djohor See **tambang**

sampane, sampang See **sampan**

sampan gĕbèng See **gubang-2, sampan gĕbing**

sampan gĕbing *Indonesia, W:* Originally a fighting vessel of northeastern Sumatra and of the Bataks of Lake Toba; later used mainly to transport merchandise and officials. Fine-lined, well made, ornamented vessel. "S" curve to strongly raked stem with figurehead; sharp stern with overhanging poop deck. Rudder secured by gudgeons and pintles; straight keel; beamier toward the stern; strong sheer. Decked; ornamented cabin on poop deck; armed with swivel guns. Two aft-raking masts, one amidships, the other forward. Lateen-type sails set to nearly vertical yards; after sail boomed at the foot. Also rowed. Crew of 15. Name variant: **sampan gĕbèng.** Note also **gebeng.** Further reference: **gubang-2**

sampan jalur *Indonesia, central:* Simple **dugout canoe★** of Kalimantan (Borneo). Small type, often 1-man, used for fishing; larger type, carrying 16-20 people, provides river transportation. Bottom rounded or flattened; some larger types have a broad, keel-like projection. Raked ends, either pointed or blunt. Paddled or rowed. Larger boats 10-12m long, ca. 1.0m wide. Note also **jalor.**

sampan Johore See **tambang**

sampan kotak See **kotak-1**

sampan naga *Peninsular Malaysia:* A long, slender **riverboat★** that conveyed people to and from the coast, especially in Perak on the west coast. Plank-built; sharp bow with concave waterline, ending in a stylized dragon's (*naga*) head. Seams caulked with tree bark or scraped peel of a type of cane; hull coated with a composition of resin and lime. Most of boat covered by a mat awning that swept up over a house at the stern. Propelled by oars and paddles; steered by an oar from a stern platform. Name variant: **dragon sampan.** Note also **perahu naga.**

sampanne See **sampan**

sampan pajang See **sampan payang**

sampan pandjang See **sampan panjang**

sampan pandjang tambang See **sampan panjang tambang**

sampan panjang *Indonesia, W/Peninsular Malaysia/ Singapore:* Long, **canoe★**-like craft of Singapore, neighboring Malaysia (Johore), and the Lingga and Riau Archipelagoes. Used as a **houseboat★**, fast **ferry★**, and ultimately refined in the Singapore area as a racing craft of the elite. Working boats double-ended, sharp-floored, curved at the cutwater, with moderate sheer; keel. Open or partly decked; some in the Riau area had a house aft. Generally rowed, but also sailed using a small lugsail. Reported lengths 7.2-11.3m, widths 1.34-2.02m, depths 0.56-0.84m. Those that raced were open, carvel-planked with sawn frames, clipper-bowed. Used both rudder and steering paddle. Set 2-3 high-peaked lugsails and a jib. Masts were heavy spars stepped through thwarts. Raced with as many as 23 in crew, consisting of bailers, sheet tenders, general hands, steersman, and as many as 8 men who hung out on ropes from the masthead as ballast. Length 14m, beam 2m, depth 0.6m. Other recorded names: **fast boat★**, **longboat★**, **sampan pandjang**

sampan panjang tambang *Indonesia, W:* A craft smaller than the **sampan panjang★** that carries passengers and merchandise over long distances in the Riau Archipelago off eastern Sumatra. Partly covered by an awning. Spelling variant: **sampan pandjang tambang**

sampan payang *Indonesia, central:* Plank-built cargo and **fishing boat★** from Bawean Island in the Java Sea. Some traveled as far as Singapore. Short, vertical ends. Spelling variant: **sampan pajang**. Note also **pajang**. Further reference: **payang-2**

sampan penambang See **sampan Riau**

sampan pengail *Singapore:* A seagoing, **canoe★**-type craft for use by 2-3 persons. Note also **pengail**.

sampan poekat See **perahu pukat**, **sampan pukat**

sampan poekat ikan See **sampan pukat**

sampan poucatt See **perhau pukat**

sampan pukat *Indonesia, W:* Long, narrow **fishing boat★** that uses a type of seine or drag net, the *pukat*, a term sometimes applied to the boat itself. Used on the northern Sumatra coast and in the Riau Archipelago off the east coast. Often work in pairs. Plank-built; keel with rounded bottom; sharp ends, overhanging bow, low freeboard. May have a hold between 2 bulkheads. Three or more rowing benches; rowed facing forward, 1 man to an oar. Steered with an oar supported on a forked rest or by a loop to a post. Steps 1-2 masts stayed fore-and-aft; sets lugsails. Chinese-operated boats manned by 6 rowers and the helmsman. Length 15.8m, beam 3.1-3.7m, depth 3.1m. Other recorded names: **lanchang★**, **lantjang poekat**, **lantjang pukat★**, **prahoe poekat**, **praou poukat**, **prau pukat**, **rantjang poekat**, **sampan poekat**, **sampan poekat ikan**. See also **perahu pukat**.

sampan Rhio See **sampan Riau**

sampan Riau *Indonesia, W:* Double-ended **fishing boat★** and trader of the Riau-Lingga Archipelago off the east coast of Sumatra. Fish and cargo carried to Singapore. Until the 1930s, 2 strakes were added to a dugout base; later boats entirely plank-built. Stem and sternpost straight and strongly raked and terminate flush with the gunwales. Straight keel with angled heel and forefoot; slight sheer. Steered with rudder and lines. Some decked at gunwale level at bow and stern; loosely decked or open waist; sides extended by coaming; peaked-roof mat house set abaft amidships. Larger boats generally set a gaff mainsail to a single mast stepped well forward; jib to a short bowsprit. Lengths of **fishing boats** 6.1-6.7m; traders 9m. Other recorded names: **sampan Rhio**, **sampan Riouw**; locally,

kolek★, **perahu★**, **sampan★**. The people of Pulau Brani, an island off the southern tip of Singapore, call the boat a **sampan penambang** (**ferryboat★**).

sampan Riouw See **sampan Riau**

sampan sagor belahan See **sampan sagur belahan**

sampan sagur belahan *Indonesia, W:* Cargo craft of the Batak peoples of northwestern Sumatra. Dugout hull, rounded bottom, beamy athwartships. Stem curved with a ridge along the midline; stern narrow and cut to fishtail shape. Decked. Pole used to propel the boat and to assist in cargo handling. Spelling variant: **sampan sagor belahan**

sampan sĕmbawa See **perahu sumbawa**

sampan séro See **kolek-2**

sampan tambang *Indonesia, W:* Used by the Chinese in the Riau Archipelago off eastern Sumatra to ferry passengers. Rowed standing. Note also **tambang**, **tambangan**.

sampan tambangan *Indonesia, central:* A narrow fishing craft from the west coast of Kalimantan (Borneo). Sharp, straight, or slightly concave ends; short platform extends out each end; flattened bottom; low washstrakes along the flared sides. Open, decked at ends; may have bulkheads. Paddled. Note also **tambang**, **tambangan**.

sampan tambanggan See **tambang**

sampan Tanka *China/Hong Kong/Macau:* General-purpose harbor boat worked by Tanka boat people, especially to transport passengers from off-lying vessels. Vary somewhat with the locale, but generally a shallow, oval craft with a spoon-shaped bottom. Decked, at least at the bow and stern; 1-2 arched mat and bamboo houses; family lives aboard; separate area for passengers.

sampan Tanka

Rowed and sculled, principally by the women of the family; a single oar, attached by a grommet to a tholepin, used at the bow; a long sculling oar, on a pivot, at the stern. Some employ a rudder with the tiller worked by the sculler's foot. Reported lengths 2.4-10m. Other recorded names: **egg boat**, **egg house**, **tanca(r)**, **tanka**, **tankëa**, **tán-kiá**, **tan k'o**, **tan kou**, **t'éang-chai**

sam pei See **diao ting**

sampierota See **sanpierota**

Samurdin See **Samoreus**

sanābīg, **sanābīk** See **sambūq**

sanādīl See **sandal**

sanbak See **sambūq**

san ban See **sampan**

sanbèco See **xebec**

sanbik, **sanbok**, **sanbūk** See **sambūq**

sanbuq See **dau-3**, **sambūq**

sandaal See **sandal**

sandal 1. In early Arabic, a **ship's boat★**. Spelling variant: **sanādīl**

2. *Egypt:* **a.** Small, open boat similar to a **cangia★**, or a **ship's boat**. **b.** A modern **sandal** in the Cairo area is a steel cargo carrier with a flat bottom, transom stern, sharp bow, flared or vertical sides, and large-bladed rudder. Decked at bow and stern and along the sides. Lateen-rigged, but now mostly motorized.

3. *Egypt/Sudan:* A small, light, flat craft used in the Nubian section of the upper Nile. Often a double-decked **barge***. Sailed or towed, sometimes by a **steamer**.

4. *Mediterranean:* Trader, especially for vegetables, of the eastern Mediterranean and along the North African coast; during the 18th century, the term applied to a craft that served to unload large ships. Length ca. 10m.

5. *Tunisia:* From the early 19th century, **sandals** were built mainly on the island of Djerba off the southwest coast, and at least until the 1940s, ferried passengers to the mainland. Double-ended, flat floors amidships. Decked at bow and stern; open waist. Outboard rudder; tiller. Generally painted black with a white stripe and simulated gunports. Single-masted, lateen-rigged boats set a large jib to a small bowsprit. Two-masted vessels stepped the small foremast in the bow, mainmast about amidships; masts raked forward. Some set a square sail to both masts, others lateen sails, and still others a lateen mainsail and sprit foresail. Crew of 4 generally. One-masted type: length 12m, beam 2.85m, depth 1.3m; 15-50t burden. Name variants: **sendale tunisino**, pl. **šnâdol**

6. *Turkey:* **a.** One of the terms for **boat*** or **barge. b.** May apply to a type of **skiff***-like **rowing boat*** and often to a **ship's boat**. At Istanbul, it may be a boat used by watermen to transport passengers on the Bosporus and the Golden Horn, to carry light cargo, and for handline fishing. Most sharp-ended or have a small transom; graceful sheer; slightly curved, raked stem with rounded forefoot; straight, raked sternpost; straight keel; fairly flat floors. Short deck at bow and stern; those that carry passengers have an elaborate stern bench. Rowed single- or double-banked; swelling in the middle of the oar loom serves as a counterbalance; blade notched at the end. A small dipping lugsail with a very short luff may be set to a mast stepped at the end of the foredeck or into a thwart. Inboard motors now common. Reported lengths 4.5-6.5m; e.g., length 6m, beam 1.14m, depth 0.55m. Spelling variants: **sandali**; pl. **sandallar**. Note also **sandalaya**.

Spelling variants: **sandaal, sandala, sandale, sandalia, sandalo**. Further references: **gaiassa, lûd**

sandala See **sandal**

sandalaya *Turkey, NW:* A large **kayık*** that, with several others, preceded the **sultan's caique** (see **saltanat kayığı**) to clear the route when it went out on the Bosporus.

sandale See **lûd, sandal, sandolo**

sandali See **sandal-6, sandolino-1, sandolo**

sandalia See **sandal**

sandalino See **sandolino**

sandalino da regata See **sandolino-2**

sandall *Albania:* Term for a **canoe*, ferryboat***, or **paddle boat***.

sandallar See **sandal-6**

sandalobatana See **lûd, sandal, sandolo**

sandárí See **sarnái**

sandbagger *United States, E:* Beamy, shallow, centerboard boat that evolved from a type of New York workboat into a fast racing craft of the 2nd half of the 19th century. Most popular on the western part of Long Island Sound, but also found in Boston, Chesapeake Bay, Florida, New Orleans, and the Great Lakes. Later, some of the Long Island Sound craft were converted to oyster dredgers, as were those on the Eastern Shore of Chesapeake Bay. While racing a large boat, an average of fifty 23kg bags of gravel ballast were shifted to windward with each tack. Straight, plumb stem and sternpost; transom stern, strongly flared sides, fully ceiled. Large-bladed, flat, plank rudder. Half-decked; when converted for oystering, cabin erected abaft the mast. **Sloop***- or cat-rigged; heavily canvassed. **Sloops** carried a very long bowsprit and large jib. Reported lengths 4.6-9.5m; e.g., length on waterline 7.2m, beam 3.2m. Other recorded names: **bagger, bag-wagon, Penny-Bridge boat, rudder-outdoor, skimming dish***. Further reading: Rob Napier, "Sandbaggers in General, *Cruiser* in Particular," *Nautical Research Journal* 34 (March 1989): 32-43. Note also **shell kicker**.

sandbank boat See **tan chuan**

sand barge 1. A vessel that transports sand, and often gravel, for construction, industry, and earlier, for ship ballast. May be specifically designed for this purpose or converted from other types. May work under sail with auxiliary, be fully motorized, or be towed. Other recorded names: **sand drogher, Sandkahn, sand scow, Sandsegelkahn**

2. *England:* A mid-17th-century version was full-bodied with maximum beam well forward, flared sides, soft turn of the bilges, low rise to the floors, heavy beams. Curved stem, raked transom stern. Forward and aft cuddies; standing well for helmsman. Outboard rudder; tiller. Aft-raking mast. Length between perpendiculars 12.5m, on keel 8.9m, beam 5.1m, hold depth 1.7m.

3. *England, SE:* The silver sand of the Thames was carried by small sailing **barges*** to London for use in scrubbing floors in taverns and homes from early times until the 1930s. The sand was also used by iron foundries for castings. **Barges** grounded at low tide and the sand was shovelled into the hold, or they were moored to stakes and dredged for the sand, letting the tide wash it into leather scoops. Other recorded names: **gitting barge, sandy** (pl. **sandies**)

See also **gravel barge**.

sand boat 1. A small craft fitted with wheels and a sail for sailing over large sand flats.

2. *Bangladesh:* Some **country boat*** types engage in collection and transport of sand. Mainly collected from river bottoms, often by boat crews who dive in alongside the boat, loading buckets by hand. Poled and sailed, setting a spritsail.

3. *Ireland, SW:* Used on the River Shannon during the late 17th and early 18th centuries, carrying 6-8t.

4. *United States, E:* Name given to the boats that dredged sand from the east branch of the Niagara River in western New York State. The sand washed in from Lake Erie during storms. Used from the 1890s to the 1930s. Name variant: **sandsucker**

See also **Kiangsu trader, krypa-2, sha ting**.

Sandboot 1. *Germany, NW:* Collected sea sand and gravel off the Mecklenburg coast. Some also built as **ship's boats***. Sharp ends, curved stem and sternpost; open or half-decked. Outboard rudder curved under stern, vertical aft. Some designed to be rowed only, by 2 men, a 3rd steering. The sailing type (**Sandsegler**) stepped a single mast that originally set a spritsail and jib, later a loose-footed gaff sail. Sailing boats often worked single-handed. Reported lengths 9-10m, cap. to 25t. Other recorded names: **Boot***, **Jöll**, **Sandkahn**; **Mecklenburger**, **Rostocker**, **Travemünder Sandboot**
2. *Netherlands:* The **sandboot** was reported in the 19th century as a common type of small boat.

sand drogher See **sand barge-1**

sandé See **pakur**

sand flat, **sand hooker** See **Mersey flat**

sandies See **sand barge-3**

Sandkahn See **sand barge-1**, **Sandboot**

sandkil *Sweden, east-central:* **Sloop***-rigged vessel of the Stockholm Archipelago often used to transport salted herring. Some still working in the 1940s. Full bow, curved stem, cutaway forefoot; wide, shallow, raked transom; deep drag to the straight keel; strong sheer. Deep bulwarks, wide side decks, foredeck with anchor windlass; open waist. Low cabin aft with hatch opening facing forward or to the starboard side. Strongly raked outboard rudder, worked with tackle. Tall mast stepped in forward third. Gaff sail, long boom; foresail tacked to stemhead. 1928 boat ca 8.5m long, 3.5m wide, 1.8m deep. Other recorded names: **roslagskuta***, **sandpigg**

sand lighter See **cargo lighter**

Sandlomme See **Erdlomme**

sandol, **sandoli** See **sandolo**

sandolin, **sandolini** See **sandolino**

sandolino *Italy:* **1.** A small boat that is rowed or paddled. Sharp ends, flat bottom. Rowed standing. Word may also designate a **sculler***. Spelling variants: **sandalí**, **sandalino**, **sandolin**, **sandulin**, **sandùlina**; pl. **sandolini**
2. At Venice, the **sandalino da regata** is a small, **gondola***-type boat used in traditional regattas.

sandolo *Italy:* **1.** Light, narrow, open boat common to the Lagoon of Venice from at least the 13th century.

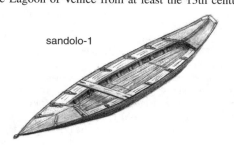

sandolo-1

Form not standardized, being modified to meet the owner's specifications. Used mainly to transport produce and merchandise, to carry passengers (**sandolo da barcariol**) and merchandise, and for pleasure, hunting, racing, and regattas (**sandolo da regata**). Low, sharp, overhanging bow terminates in an olive-shaped, iron knob at the end of a short spike; *fleur de lis* flange on deck. Stern has a very narrow, flat, raked

transom that arches across the top. Bottom, flat transversely, has rocker longitudinally. Sides flare; rubbing strake terminates at the bow in a characteristic hollow at the stemhead; moderate sheer. Decking at bow and stern highly cambered; side decks. Rowed by 2 men standing well aft and facing forward, using tall oar forks. Reported lengths 4.5-10m; e.g., length 6.78m, beam 1.24m, depth 1.4m.
2. A type of **scow***, **dumb barge***, or a **dredger*** in the canals is also known as a **sandolo**.
3. The large **sandolo buranelo** from Burano, northeast of Venice, is used mainly for fishing and sets a small, trapezoidal lugsail. Mast stepped through the middle thwart. Ships a rudder. Stem protected by a wrought iron piece that curls up at the outer end. Length to 9m.
4. The **sandolo** may be used at Italian arsenals to transport anchors and munitions.
5. The flat-floored **sandolo** of Chioggio, south of Venice, engages in lagoon fishing. Sets a single sail. Crew of 2. Reported lengths 5-8m, widths 1-1.5m.
Spelling variants: **sandale**, **sandalo**, **sandol**; pl. **sandali**, **sandoli**. Note also **puparin**, **sandolino**, **sanpierota**. See also **battana-2**, **battello veneto**, **sandal**, **sanpierota**.

sandolo buranelo See **sandolo-3**

sandolo da barcariol, **sandolo da regata** See **sandolo-1**

sandolo puparin, **sandolo pupparin** See **puparin**

sandolo sampieroto, **sandolo sanpieroto**, **sandolo sanpierotta** See **sanpierota**

sandón *Italy, NE:* Term given to the boats that supported floating flour mills (**mulino galleggiante***), especially on the lower Adige and Po Rivers. Of very early origin. The larger mills had 3 boats: the **sandón da tèra**, closest to the shore; the **sandóna** in the middle, the paddle wheel itself; and on the outside in the faster current, the **antàn**. The entire complex was permanently anchored and connected to the river bank by a walkway. The smaller **mulinèla** had only a **sandóna** and an **antàn**. On some, the paddle wheel was on the river side of the unit. These heavy, open boats were flat-bottomed with a square or pointed end on the upstream side and a square stern. The square-bowed boats had a sharply raked bow that was higher than the stern. Straight sides. They were joined by several beams. Length of each boat ca. 10-14m, width 1.8-3.9m, but the **antàn** narrowed to ca. 1.0m at the stern. Other name variants: **sandoncello**, **sandone**; pl. **sandones**, **sandóni**. Further reading: Giovanni Beggio, *I Mulini Natanti dell'Adige* (Firenze: L. S. Olschki, 1969).

sandóna, **sandoncello**, **sandón da tèra**, **sandone**, **sandones**, **sandóni** See **sandón**

sandpigg See **sandkil**

sand scow See **sand barge-1**, **scow-schooner-3**

Sandsegelkahn See **sand barge-1**

Sandsegler See **Sandboot**

sand ship See **Kiangsu trader**

sandskude *Denmark, W:* Local trader that worked off the sandy beaches of northwestern Jutland. From March to July, carried grain and produce to southwestern Norway, returning with timber and some ironware. Phased out early in the 19th century, although the trade continued in other types of vessels. Most built in Norway, remainder in Denmark. Pulled high among the dunes by rollers and ropes in the off-season. Clinker-planked; treenailed for flexibility; keel; raked ends. Decked at ends, hold between. Three pole masts usually, setting square sails; on some, mizzen may have been a lateen sail. Reported lengths 12.2-14.7m, beam 3.6-4.2m, depth 1.2-1.8m. Note also **skude**.

sand sloop See **Humber sloop**

sandsucker See **sand boat-4**

sandulin, sandùlina See **sandolino**

sandy See **sand barge-3**

sand yacht *Northern Ireland, W:* Beginning in the 1840s **sand yachts** owned by Enniskillen merchants carried sand from the Lusty Islands in the lower Lough Erne to Enniskillen and timber, slate, and coal from Belleek.

Sandy Hook pilot schooner *United States, E:* **Pilot boat★** for the port of New York, worked by New York and New Jersey pilots. Their primary development as an acknowledged type was during the 1st half of the 19th century, with individual builders vying to design the fastest, the most seaworthy, and the most weatherly vessels. The efforts produced numerous modifications in hulls and rigging during the 19th century. Sharp bow, later having a hollow entrance; stem usually had a cutaway forefoot; some clipper-bowed. Square transom initially raked, then vertical; later boats had a rounded counter. Deep keel with drag aft; steep rise to the floors, high bilges; sides generally flared, some with tumble home amidships. Slight sheer, the short bowsprit following the sheer. Flush, uncluttered deck; standing well for helmsman; most had no bulwarks, but on some, a quarter rail ran from waist to transom. Crew housed in forecastle, pilots' cabin amidships. Two-man **yawl★** on deck for pilots' use. Masts raked aft on most; topmasts, but rarely set topsails. Until ca. 1845, set gaff mainsail, loose-footed but boomed; large gaff foresail without boom, with clew abaft the mainsail; single headsail. Later, foresail narrower and both sails laced to booms; multiple headsails. Crew of 4 to man the **schooner★**, plus a cook; 6 pilots. Reported lengths 18-26m; e.g., length 23.6m, beam 5.7m, depth 2.4m, draft 2.9m. Name variants: **New Jersey pilot schooner**, **New York pilot schooner**. Note also **pilot yawl**.

San Francicso Bay scow-schooner See **scow-schooner-3**

San Francisco felucca See **felucca-3**

San Francisco oyster sloop See **plunger-2**

sangādam *India:* **1.** Term applied in parts of India to a double **canoe★**, usually 2 dugouts.
2. On the Godavari and Kristna Rivers in eastern India, the double **canoe** was made from a hollowed-out palmyra palm. The bulbous root ends formed the bow. Bamboo poles placed transversely lashed the 2 dugouts together. Note also **donga**, **jangar**.
3. Also reported as a small, **raft★**-type craft to which a single-log outrigger is attached.

sangadam See **angula**, **jangar**, **tarappam**

sangara 1. *India, W:* Reported as a very large, seagoing **dugout canoe★**, a large log **raft★**, or a twin-hulled craft composed of large, hewn logs. Reported from the early part of the Christian era.

2. *Red Sea:* Name given to a craft hewn from a single log. Carried cargo and passengers until the early 19th century.
Spelling variant: **sángaro**. See also **saranga**.

sángaro See **sangara**

sangen-ikada See **ikada**

sanghāṭa *India:* Cited in Vedic and post-Vedic literature as an oared vessel using as many as 100 oars. See also **angula**.

sanpan *United States, Great Lakes:* Small sailing **punt★** peculiar to Put-in-Bay on Lake Erie in the late 19th century. Length ca. 2.4m. See also **sampan**.

San Pedro felucca See **felucca-3**

sanpierota *Italy, NE:* A brightly painted, **sandolo★**-type boat that fishes in and outside the Lagoon of Venice; now also a popular family boat. Flat bottom, with slight rocker fore-and-aft; straight, flaring sides; top 2 strakes lapped. Sharp, raking bow; in profile, slightly curved on top; mildly raked transom stern; strong sheer. Cambered deck in forward third, limited cuddy below; open aft. Raked rudder, deep heel about twice hull depth; tiller. Usually steps a single unstayed mast through a thwart in after third; sometimes 2nd mast stepped just abaft the cuddy. Sets boomed lugsails, jib to stemhead. Also rowed or sculled. Reported lengths 6-7m; e.g., length overall 6.6m, on bottom ca. 5m, beam 1.74m, depth ca. 0.5m. Other recorded names: **sampierota**, **sandolo★** (in the Po Delta area), **sandolo sampieroto** (**sanpierota** or **sanpierotta**), **sanpieroto**, pl. **sanpierote**. Note also **batana**, **topa**.

sanpierote, sanpieroto See **sanpierota**

santenne See **sentine**

sapin, sapina See **sapine**

sapine *France:* **1.** General term for a **barge★**-like vessel built of pine or fir. Reported on the Rhône River as early as the 14th century. Worked in the upper Loire River basin from the 17th to the mid-19th century. Boxy shape, but with a narrowed bow that turned up from the flat bottom to a flattened surface. Many constructed to make a downstream trip only. Reported lengths 17-30m. Other recorded names: **sapin(a)**, **sapinea barca**, **sapine d'Auvergne**, **sapinia**, **sapinière**, **sappine**. Note also **auvergnat**, **salembarde**.
2. In the southwest, the **sapines** of the Garonne Basin and the Canal du Midi carried cargo and produce. On some waterways, they worked into the early 20th century. Flat-bottomed, mainly open craft. Those on the Canal du Midi had a plumb, slightly curved stem; flat, V-shaped stern; maximum beam well forward; slightly flared sides; wide rudder; tiller. Towed, floated downstream, and later vessels on the Canal du Midi had engines. The **canal boats★** were ca. 28.3m long, 5.5m wide, and 2.6m deep; on the Lot River, they were 20-28m by 4.8-5m. Those on the middle Garonne River were up to 100t, while on the Gironde Estuary, they were as much as 200t.
3. On the Adour River in the extreme southwest, a type of **sapine** carried resin to Bayonne.
Further reference: **bâche-2**

sapinea barca, sapine d'Auvergne See **sapine-1**

sapine salembarde See **salembarde**

sapinia, sapinière, sappine See **sapine-1**

saqlāwa See **sakoleva**

saqqit See **kayak-3**

saqualeva See **sakoleva**

saque *France, NW:* A 17th-century **fishing boat*** at Saint Malo. More recently called a **dragueur***.

sarac-yan See **sakayan**

Saranac boat, Saranac Laker, Saranac skiff See **Adirondack guide-boat**

saranga *Bangladesh/India, NE:* Dugout-based craft of Bangladesh, Assam, Bengal, and Bihar. May be simple, all-purpose, flat-bottomed, blunt-ended dugouts; others are **galley***-like boats, seating as many as 50 and used exclusively for racing on ceremonial occasions. Many roughly hewn from logs near Chittagong and then exported to areas where suitable logs are unavailable. In some districts, strakes added on, as in Rangpur in northern Bangladesh, where the **tepatuā** has 3 strakes added, and the **ghātbāri**, a smaller **saranga**, has only one-and-a-half strakes added. The supplemental strakes may be lashed on with cane, caulked inside with straw, and a split bamboo strip lashed outside. Overhanging ends; stern much higher than bow. Large balanced rudder. An arched bamboo cabin may protect passengers and cargo. Some, as at Chittagong and Barisal, set a single square sail to a light mast stepped near the bow. Generally poled or paddled. Small **sarangas** are 1-man boats; large ones may require a crew of 5. Reported lengths 4.6-21m; e.g., length 8.2m, beam 0.7m. Further name variants: **haranga, sadanga, salīna, sangara*****, saranga nauka, sarangga, sarangi, saringa, sarinnā, sarungá, seringee, shad'anga, sharanga, s(h)arenga, sharonga**

saranga nauka, sarangga, sarangi See **saranga**

saraquian See **sakayan**

sardinal A boat primarily employed in fishing for sardines with a special net, the *sardinal*, especially in Spain and along the Mediterranean coast of France. Note also **barco de sardinal**.

  1. *Algeria:* Here, the **sardinal** is half-decked and lateen-rigged. Length 8m, beam 2.5m, depth 0.7m.

  2. *France, Mediterranean:* The **sardinals** working in the lagoons behind the southwest coast work a drag net or a draw net. Originally sailed; now equipped with auxiliaries. Draft 0.50-0.75m; 2-4t. Name variant: **bateau sardinal**.

  3. *Spain, E:* Beamy boat with low rise to the floors, soft bilges. Full, round stern. Sides raised with weathercloths; decked. Lateen-rigged with mast stepped in forward third. Also rowed with 2 pairs of oars. Crew of 6 plus a boy.

Further references: **palangrier, xeito**

sardinaye See **palangrier**

sardine carrier *Canada, SE/United States, NE:* Specially built, fast boat that serves as a **carry-away boat*** for sardine packers, especially off New Brunswick and northeastern Maine. Early boats **sloop***- or **schooner***-rigged; most equipped with an engine by the beginning of the 20th century. Crew of 2. Present-day vessels ca. 15m long. Further reference: **Quoddy boat**

sardinera See **barco de sardinal**

sardinheiro See **poveiro-2**

sardinier French word for a boat that engages primarily in sardine fishing. Now mainly motorized. Spelling variant: **sardinière**. Note also **vedette**.

sardinier breton *France, W:* The sardine boat of south Brittany underwent considerable evolution in addition to varying somewhat from port to port; superseded by motorized craft after World War I. Drifted, towing a gill net. Fish attracted by a **tender***, the **pen** (or **pen sardine**), that scattered a paste of cod's eggs. Basically a fast, beamy, carvel-planked vessel with fine lines forward, flat floors, vertical sides, deep keel with marked drag aft. Straight stem raked inboard slightly; curved until ca. 1865. Type of stern varied from sharp or elliptical, to round (**chaloupes***, or **ar vag** in Breton), to a raked transom (**canots***, **ar c'hanot** in Breton). Early boats open; later decked, although some remained undecked except at the stern. Narrow rudder followed the rake of the sternpost; tiller. Hull tarred black. The pole fore- and mainmasts were stepped in the forward half of the boat and were flexible, unstayed, and raked aft, generally at the same angle. Dipping forelug tacked to the stemhead and overlapped one half of the mainsail; originally forelug was square and much smaller. Mainsail usually a standing lug, somewhat taller than the forelug, tacked to the mast and sheeted to a traveler at the stern. Sails generally black, brown, or ochre. When towing the net, the masts were lowered and the boat was rowed with long, heavy oars, the forward 2 oars much longer. Towed a single **annexe*** which, with an **annexe** from a companion **sardinier**, helped set the nets. Crew generally 6-8 plus 2 boys. Reported lengths 6.7-15m; e.g., length overall 10.4m, on waterline 9.6m, beam 3.2m, depth 1.65m, draft aft 1.55m; modern motorized vessels to 20m long. Other recorded names: **chaloupe bretonne** (or **sardinière**), **Douarnenez lugger, minahouët** (Lorient, Concarneau, Douarnenez area), **pesqueresse, sardinier de Cornouaille** (or **de Douarnenez**). Further reading: Bernard Cadoret, et al., *Ar Vag: Voiles au Travail en Bretagne Atlantique*, vols. 1 & 2 (Grenoble: Editions des 4 Seigneurs, 1978-1979). Note also **trainière-2**.

sardinier de Cornouaille, sardinier de Douarnenez See **sardinier breton**

sardinier des Sables See **sardinier vendéen**

sardinière See **sardinier**

sardinière des Sables, sardinière vendèenne See **sardinier vendéen**

sardinier vendéen *France, W:* Open sardine boat that worked from ports on the Vendée coast, mainly out of Les Sables-d'Olonne; dated from the mid-19th century. Early boats had a rounded stern with deadwood; altered to a raked transom by the end of the century. Vertical stem, or rounded with cutaway forefoot; fine bow with hollow below the waterline; fairly flat floors; deep keel with drag. Some carried 2 boats for use in setting the nets (see **annexe**). Main- and foremast set standing lugsails with lug topsails; standing lug or sprit mizzen. Jib run to a long bowsprit. Early boats carried no topsails. Mainmast struck in rough weather; rowed in calms. Reported lengths 5.8-8.5m; e.g., length 7m, beam 2.5m, depth 1.0m, draft ca. 1.0m. Other recorded names: **canot de sardine, canot**

sardinier, sardinier des Sables, sardinière des Sables, sardinière vendèenne, Vendéen lugger (or sardine boat)

sarenga See saranga

Sargschiff See floating coffin

saringa, sarinnā See saranga

sarme See djerme

sarna See sarnái

sarnái *India, N/Pakistan, N:* Inflated-skin **raft*** used to transport goods, timber, and passengers down rivers. Also a common craft of professional river thieves. The skins (mostly buffalo or goat, occasionally sheep) were tied tightly at the openings except for one leg, reversed, and inflated; the number of skins used depended on the load. Individual skins served as 1-man **floats*** used to free **rafts** caught by rocks and eddies. Also, a man might move his family by riding astride a skin, towing his family on a reed **raft**. A framework platform helped secure the skins. Two men, each supported by an inflated skin, steered the craft on its downstream run. At its destination, the skins were deflated and carried back upstream. When a skin was used singly, loops were attached to the hind legs of a goat skin through which the prone man inserted his own legs and propelled the craft with his hands, while buffalo **sarnái** were propelled by the feet and steered with a paddle. Other recorded names: **sandárí**, **sarna**, **sernai**, **śināj**, **śirnā**; in some districts called **darai**, **daraīm**, or **dren**

sarquin See kayak-3

sar teng See sha ting

sarungá See saranga

sasa-buné *Japan:* Toy boat made from a single bamboo leaf. Leaf folded in such a way as to create a flat-bottomed "boat" with turned-up ends. Name variant: **bamboo-leaf boat**. Further reading: Shinji Nishimura, *Skin Boats*, A Study of Ancient Ships of Japan, Part IV (Tokyo: Society of Naval Architects, 1931): 210.

sasak See perahu sasak

sasakayán See sakayan

sasak tambangan See perahu sasak

sasakyang-dagat See sakayan-1

šāše See shashah-2

sasha See shashah-1

sash-marry See Yarmouth lugger

sàtara, sàtera See zattera

satteau See corallina-2

Saugbagger See dredger-1

säugchen See zig

saugo See palangrier

savakari-padhagi See padhagi

Savannah River duck boat *United States, SE:* Light boat used to shoot wildfowl on the river, mainly in the 1st half of the 20th century. Sharp bow, square stern. Cambered, sliding deck hatch; 15cm coaming. Raised section at the bow for the retriever. Sculled with an oar through a hole in the transom. Length 4.17m, beam 1.5m, depth 0.56m.

savego See palangrier

saveiro **1.** *Brazil, NE:* **a.** Term applies to several varieties of flat-floored, square-sterned boats used for fishing, cargo, passenger traffic, and recently as converted pleasure craft. The fishing **saveiros** were open boats that set 2 lateen sails on aft-raking masts; the forward sail overlapped the after mast, sheeting at the stern; also rowed. The cargo type, known as **saveiro de caes** or **saveiro de carga**, set a single

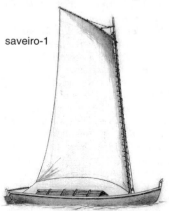

saveiro-1

lateen sail. Present-day vessels at Salvador (Bahia) set a very long, narrow, loose-footed gaff sail on an extremely tall mast; sometimes a jib. Some small boats engaging in local transport were open and used a spritsail. An early 2-masted boat at Salvador set a square foresail, held out by a spar bowline, and a loose-footed gaff mainsail; both masts set into the same step. The cargo **saveiro** employs high washboards or rails set well inboard to restrain the cargo when heeled over. **b.** Trading **schooners*** built at Salvador may be called **saveiros** when working along the southeast coast.

2. *Portugal:* Found at intervals along the west coast working off the open beaches with a long seine net (the *xávega*). Launched bow first, beached stern first. Carvel planking of pine runs horizontal, ignoring the sheer. Bottom flat and horizontal for about half its length, then rises forward over the waterline in a straight line to a short stem that is often diamond-shaped at the top; peak may be as high as 5.2m above the bottom line. At the stern, the bottom rises in a curve, terminating lower than the bow. Marked sheer; sides slightly flared; fitted with 2-piece frames and iron knees; gunwales ironshod to prevent chafing. Short, strongly cambered deck at bow; small stern deck. Brightly painted, especially with religious motifs. Primarily rowed using 2 very large oars north of the Aveiro Lagoon and 4 to the south; oars have a block on the loom that passes over the single tholepin. Crew of 34 on the 2-oared boats and 46 on the 4-oared; crews now greatly reduced. Lengths to 16.7m; e.g., length 16.45m, beam 4.18m, depth 1.28m. Other recorded names: **barco de mar**, **barco do mar**, **barco savaleiro**, **saveiro da costa**, **xávega***

3. *Portugal, south-central:* Engages mainly in river fishing along the inner Tagus River and the Sado River to the south, using gill nets. Shallow hull, flat bottom with strong rocker, especially at the bow where it curves up sharply to a point; bow higher than the stern.

Plank keel; wale extends along each side with more sheer than the top strake. Open except for a forecastle. Wide-bladed outboard rudder worked with yoke and lines. Hull mainly tarred black. When sailing, steps a single mast through a thwart, setting a high-peaked standing lugsail; gear stowed when rowing or fishing. Rowed in calms with 2 oars, either single- or double-banked; oar looms fitted with a piece that slips over the tholepin. Crew of 2 plus a boy. Reported lengths 7.75-7.9m; e.g., length 7.9m, beam 1.65m, depth 0.5m.
See also **alvarenga-2**, **valboeiro**.

saveiro da costa See **saveiro-2**

saveiro de caes, **saveiro de carga** See **saveiro-1**

sa-wanga See **wanga**

sawed-lumber raft See **timber raft-2b**

sax earing, **saxereen** See **sixareen**

say, **sayeh** See **shū·ai**

sayka, **sayke** See **saique**

sayler See **sailer**

sayn boat See **seine boat-3**

šbâbek See **xebec**

scab See **tug-2**

scab-timber raft See **timber raft-4**

scaf *England:* A light **boat★** or **skiff★**. Term dates from the 14th century. Spelling variants: **escafe**, **scaff(e)**, **scaphe**, **scarfe**, **scauphe**, **schaffe**. Note also **scaffie**, **skafi**.

scafa **1.** Italian generic term for a small **boat★**, sometimes a **ship's boat★**, or often a nondescript river or harbor craft that conveys people and goods. In the 14th century, the river **scafa** was used for naval purposes, or as a small, seagoing vessel that accompanied a larger one. In the 16th-17th centuries, **scafe** (pl.) were long, narrow, generally unseaworthy, lateen-rigged ships. The word has also been used for 9th- and 10th-century carvel-built **coasters★** of the Carolingians. The 6th-century **scapha** of the Gauls of western France was a flat-floored, square-sterned trader; large sail. Earlier, the small Roman **scafa** carried passengers on French rivers. Further name variants: **scaffa**, **scafo**; **scafula** (dim.); pl. **scaf(f)e**, **scaphae**. Note also **skafi**.
2. One type of **scafa** on the central Tiber (Tevere) River in west-central Italy was an open **ferryboat★**. Bow square and open; stern sharp. Flat bottom curved up at each end. High bulwarks above the flat flooring. Stern deck for helmsman. Rudder wide below the waterline; tiller slotted through rudderstock. Length 10.2m, beam 3.4m, depth 1.55m.

scafe See **scafa**

scaff See **escaffe**, **scaf**, **scaffie**

scaffa See **scafa**, **scaffie**

scaffe See **scaf**, **scafa**

scaffie *Scotland, NE:* Lightly built, double-ended boat used mainly for herring drifting. Originated toward the end of the 18th century and built into the early 20th century, but most common prior to 1885. Distinctive features were a curved stem, sternpost that raked as much as 45°, and a short, straight, deep keel. Most clinker-built with maximum beam about three-fifths in from the stem; bluff bow; low, raked stern; flat floors; firm bilges. In the mid-18th century, some **scaffies** had a slightly raked, rounded stern. Open until ca. 1850 (these were also called **buckies★**), then decked with a

long central hatchway, or half-decked. Outboard rudder with wide blade below the waterline; tiller. Hull oiled or varnished; white wedge painted above the waterline at bow and stern. Early boats were 3-masted **luggers★** stepping a tall, slightly aft-raking foremast in the eyes, vertical mainmast amidships, and forward-raking mizzen. Fore- and mainmasts set dipping lugsails, mizzen a standing lug. While fishing, foremast lowered to a crutch and mizzen unstepped. Spars sometimes extended the foresail luff. Last boats set a large dipping lugsail with a broad foot on the mainmast and sometimes a smaller standing lugsail on the forward-raking mizzenmast; mizzen was stepped well inboard and sail sheeted to a long outrigger. In light air, a jib was sometimes run out to a light bowsprit. Sails tanned to almost black. Last boats had auxiliaries. Generally crew of 4-5, more in winter. Reported lengths 5.2-18m overall, 4.6-11m on keel, 2-5.3m in width, 1.45-2.74m in depth; some to 21m overall. Other recorded names: **Buckie (herring) boat**, **Moray Firth herring boat**, **scaff(a)**, **scaith**, **scarph**, **scathie**, **skaffie**; inshore **scaffies** up to ca. 6m long were called **skiffs★**. Note also **ring-net boat**.

scaffie

scaffie yawl *Scotland, E:* Small, decked boat. Sharply raked sternpost of the **scaffie★**; rounded stem. Long hatch amidships. Set a short-footed dipping lugsail; jib run out on a long bowsprit. Length overall 7.72m, on keel 4.7m, beam 2.59m, inside depth 1.1m. Name variant: **yawl★**

scafo, **scafula** See **scafa**

scaith See **scaffie**

scallop See **shallop**

scallop boat See **Long Island scallop boat**, **scalloper**, **Tancook schooner**

scallop dragger, **scallop dredger** See **scalloper**

scalloper Vessel that drags for scallops. Distinguished more by its equipment than by vessel type. One or 2 booms handle 1-2 dredges; booms have a working platform aft. Motorized. Vary widely in length: Australian craft reported as 7-28m; Canadian as 29-30m; New Jersey as 26m. Name variants: **scallop boat** (**dragger** or **dredger**). Note also **coquillier**.

scampafie See **skampaveya**

scampavia *Italy, SW:* Fast, sharp-ended, **galley★**-type vessel used by the Kingdom of the Two Sicilies during the Napoleonic War. Armed with a single gun forward of the mainmast. Also reported from Malta, and as a **packet boat★**. Pulled 20 oars on each side; oarsmen slept beneath their rowing benches. Mainmast stepped about a third in from the bow; raised a large lateen sail. Occasionally a jib set on a gaff-like boom. May also have used a lateen mizzen with topsail above. Length to ca. 50m. Spelling variant: **Skampavia***. See also **skampaveya**.

scampavoya See **skampaveya**

scapha, scaphae See **scafa-1**, **skafi**

scaphandre See **skafi**

scaphe See **escaffe**, **scaf**, **skafi**

scaphium, scapho, scaphuba, scaphula See **skafi**

scappavia *Italy:* **1.** Large, flat-floored vessel that transported heavy materials in a harbor.
2. Naval vessel that was part of the **fleet*** of Ferdinando III in the Messina area in the 18th century. Cannon at the bow.
3. Light, narrow **rowing boat*** (see **gig-1**).
Spelling variant: pl. **scappavie**

scappavie See **scappavia**

Scarborough coble See **coble-1**

Scarborough ketch See **Yorkshire yawl**

Scarborough mule See **coble-1d**

Scarborough yawl See **Yorkshire yawl**

scarfe See **scaf**

scarph, scathie See **scaffie**

scath-ros *England, SW:* Obsolete Cornish term for a **seine boat***.

scaufe See **escaffe**

scauphe See **scaf**

scaut See **scout**

ṣcebek See **xebec-2**

scèna See **schooner**

sceola *Italy, NE:* A small 12th-century **ferry*** used on the Grand Canal in Venice. Fare a quarter of a *denero*.

sceort-scip In Anglo-Saxon, a small **vessel***.

sceute See **schuit**

scevo See **vascello-2**

schachtur See **šaḥtūr**

Schäf See **Schiff**

scháfe See **skafi**

Schäff See **Schiff**

schaffe See **scaf**

schafioy, schafís, schafos See **skafi**

Schalk See **tjalk-2**

schallop, schallup, schalop See **shallop**

Schalupe, Schalupen, Schalupp See **Schlup-1**

Schaluppe *Europe, central:* Part of the Danube **fleet*** during the 18th century. Heavily armed; crew of 50-60 plus artillerymen. Spelling variant: **Chaloup**. See also **Schlup-1**.

Schaluppen See **Schaluppe**

Schaluppschiff See **Schlup-1**

Schampan See **sampan**

schancle See **Schinakel**

schanjacka See **shnyaka**

Schärenboot See **skärbåt**

Scharend-Kahn See **Kaffenkahn**

Schasche See **shashah-2**

Schauke *Germany:* May refer to a **ferryboat*** or a **punt***, possibly one used as a **ferry***.

Schayke See **saique**

schebeck See **xebec-3**

Schebecke See **xebec-2**

Schechtaak See **aak**

schedia Cited in early Greek and Roman literature as a **raft*** or a hastily constructed vessel. **Schedia diphtherinai** were **rafts** of hides. In modern Greek, the word may describe a **pontoon*** for transporting heavy objects or a bridge of boats. Spelling variants: **schedium, skedia**; pl. **schedie**

schedia diphtherinai See **schedia**

schedie, schedium See **schedia**

scheep See **ship**

scheepsboot See **ship's boat**

scheepszoetelaar See **kadraai**

Scheerboot *Germany, NE/Poland, NW:* **Cutter***-rigged boat that fished along the Pomeranian coast. Curved stem; sharp, raked stern; rounded bottom; short, flat keel; moderate sheer. Flush deck; cabin from bow to mast, then fish well; helmsman's cockpit and space for gear aft. Tall pole mast stepped ca. one-third in from the bow. Loose-footed gaff sail with long head and short foot. Jib set flying, forestaysail, topsail with long yard. Length overall 11.6m, on keel 8.6m, beam 4m, depth 1.32m. See also **skärbåt**.

Schef, Scheff See **Schiff**

scheik *Russia/Ukraine:* 17th-century troop transport vessel on the Black Sea. Carried ca. 70 people. Single pole mast set a square sail. Also rowed. Length ca. 15m, beam 3.5m.

Scheike *Lithuania, SW/Russia, W:* Small, flat-bottomed boat of the Kurski Zaliv (Kurisches Haff). Originally a German type. Interior stem and sternpost, curved and slightly raked. Carvel planking beveled to fit against the sides of the stem and sternpost. Mainly rowed. Name variant: **Handkahn***. See also **saique**.

scheip, scheipe See **ship**

Scheitniger Oderkahn See **Oberländer-4**

schelander See **chelandia**

Schenectady boat *Canada, E:* A **batteau***-type craft used on the St. Lawrence River in the late 18th and early 19th centuries. Sharp bow and stern, flat bottom. Rowed with 6 oars, single-banked. Some equipped with a sail. Length 9m, beam 2.4m. Further reference: **Mohawk boat**

Schenectady Durham See **Mohawk boat**

schepe See **ship**

schepesbot See **ship's boat**

šcherbot See **skärbåt**

Scherm See **djerme**

Scheuerprahm See **Prahm-2**

scheut See **schuit**

Scheveningische bom See **bom-1**

Schiesskahn See **Schiesslomme**

Schiesslomme *Poland, N:* Light hunting boat used in the eastern Vistula tributaries area. In off-season, also used for fishing, to carry produce semi-weekly to towns such as Elbląg (Elbing), becoming a **Marktboot**, and for going to pastures to milk cows (**Milchboot**). Sharp, raking ends with internal stem and sternpost; narrow, flat bottom with rocker at ends; strong sheer. Two lapped strakes per side; sides rounded. Open; 2 thwarts. Coated with tar; characteristically a white stripe along the side with a large black number of the owner at the bow. Paddled; a 2nd person rowed. When sailed, set a spritsail. Length 4.2m, beam 1.05m, draft 0.16m. Further name variants: **Jagdlomme, Schiesskahn, Streckfusser** (for the town of origin). Note also **lomme, milk boat.**

Schif See **Schiff**

schifetti, schifetto See **schifo**

Schiff *Austria:* On the upper Danube and nearby lakes, might designate a **boat★**, including a **dugout canoe★**. Spelling variants: **Schäf(f), Schef(f), Schif, Schöf, Schoff, Schyff;** pl. **Schiffe(n).** See also **barque des marmets, Mutte, ship, skiff.**

schiffa See **schifo**

schiffe See **Schiff, schifo, skiff**

Schiffen See **Schiff**

schiffi, schiffo See **schifo**

Schiffsboot See **ship's boat**

Schiffsbrücke See **pontoon-2**

schifi See **schifo**

schifo *Italy:* **1.** In 13th-century Venice, a small, seagoing craft attached to a larger, 2-decked vessel.
2. May refer to a large **ship's boat★** belonging to a **merchantman★**.
3. An inshore **fishing boat★**. Sharp bow, rounded stern, keel. Rowed or sailed, setting a lateen sail with spinnaker. Crew of 1-3. Reported lengths 8-12m.
4. A light racing craft rowed by a single oarsman, without helm.
Spelling variants: **schifetto** (dim.), **schiffa, schiffo;** pl. **schifetti, schiffe, schif(f)i.** See also **skiff.**

Schikarra See **shikara**

schilètti See **lancia**

schilètto See **lancia-2**

schilf See **fassone**

Schimackschiff See **Schmack**

schinackel *Hungary:* Small, planked fishing **punt★** of the Rothbach area. Flat bottom of 2 boards; sides vertical; bow and stern square and raked; flat sheer. Seat in the middle and at each end. Poled; steered with a paddle. Length overall 4m, on bottom 3.28m, beam 0.67m, depth 0.3m.

Schinakel *Austria:* Small boat used in the Danube Valley. Referred to as early as the 17th century, often to transport troops. Double-ended; flat bottom; straight, flared sides. Ca. 7m long. Spelling variants: **schancle, Tschenakl, zinakln**

schip See **ship**

schip dat met de hengel vist See **tuna boat-2**

schiph See **skiff**

schipp See **ship**

schip van Doornik See **waal**

Schlachtkreuzer See **cruiser-3**

Schlammbagger See **Mudderprahm**

Schlarren See **tub-1**

Schlechtaak See **aak**

schlechtweg Zille See **Ordinari**

Schlei Kahn *Germany, NW:* Long, narrow, open **fishing boat★** of the Schlei River in eastern Schleswig-Holstein. Sharp ends; 3 lapped planks on each side; 2 planks on the flat bottom. Strongly raked, slightly curved stem and sternpost; moderate sheer. Steered with rudder or a long oar. Rowed, sailed, and now

motorized. When sailed, set 2 small sprit- or leg-of-mutton sails. Length 7.45m, beam 1.4m, depth 0.52m, draft ca. 0.16m. Name variant: **kåg fra Slien.** Note also **Kahn.**

Schleppboot, Schlepper See **tug**

Schleppfischer See **trawler**

Schleppleinenfischerboot See **troller**

Schleppschute See **Treckschute**

Schlickschiff See **tjalk-2**

Schlittenboot See **iceboat**

Schluhp See **Schlup**

Schlup 1. *Germany:* Term, with a variety of spellings, for a **coaster★** and **fishing boat★** from both the North and Baltic Sea coasts, primarily in the 19th century. In early days, the word also designated a ship's **longboat★**.
2. *Germany, Baltic Sea:* A popular vessel of the protected waters around Rügen Island (the **Binnenschlup**) westward to Schleswig-Holstein and eastward into Pomerania. Those that traded more widely in the Baltic were called **Seeschlupen** (pl.). Reported from the late 18th into the early 20th century. Clinker-built until ca. 1870, then carvel, although some were clinker below the waterline and carvel above. Full bow with lightly raked, curved or straight stem; some had a gammon knee. Early vessels had a flat stern, often with stern windows; later mainly a counter stern. Keel; fairly flat floors, straight sides. Cambered deck, some with a quarter-deck; 1-2 hatches; low bulwarks; inboard rudder. After 1860, a sharper type with a clipper bow, strong sheer, and rounded or flat transom was often called a **Jacht★.** Two general sail plans: the **Rahschlup** set a wide, loose-footed gaff mainsail with a long gaff and long boom, a square sail forward of the mast, and 1-2 yard topsails; several headsails. The **Gaffelschlup** set no square sails, substituting a gaff topsail. Both had a tall, heavy topmast. Crew of 2-5. Lengths 10-16.5m; widths 3.5-5.5m; hold depths 1.25-1.5m. Other recorded names: **Pommersche Jacht** (or **Schlup**), **Raaschaluppe**
3. *Germany, North Sea:* The **Schalupen** bore a marked resemblance to the Dutch **tjalk★** and the **kuff★**, especially those originating from Ostfriesland. The **Frucht-Schaluppe** of the 2nd half of the 19th century frequently went to the Mediterranean for fruit and wine. Fast, robust craft with full, rounded bow and a sharper stern. Lightly rounded bottom with shallow keel and rounded bilges. Decked; steering well aft, 1-2 hatches, and a raised cabin; local craft had leeboards. **Fishing boats** might be open but with a live well. Some rigged with a single loose-footed gaff mainsail, large staysail, and jib to the bowsprit; others carried a small gaff mizzen. The mainmast on the **fishing boats** could be struck. Crew of 3 on the **fishing boats.** Reported lengths 11.8-14.4m; e.g., length 14.35m, beam 4.48m, depth 1.4m. Name variant: **Fischerslup.** Note also **Helgoländer Schlup.**
Spelling variants: **Chaluppe, Schalupe, Schalupp, Schaluppe★, Schaluppschiff, Schluhp, Schlupe, Schlupp, Schlupschiff, Sloop★, Slop, Sloup, Slup★, Slupe;** pl. **Schalupen.** Further references: **kleiner Kahn, kutter-2**

Schlupe, Schlupp, Schlupschiff See **Schlup**

Schlurren See **tub-1**

Schmack *Germany, NW:* North Sea **coaster★** of the late 18th-19th centuries. Flat floors with shallow keel; bluff bow and stern; strong sheer, especially toward the stern. Employed leeboards or bilge keels. Tall rudderhead; tiller came inboard beneath the sheer strake. Decked; house aft. Tall mainmast with topmast; set a gaff sail abaft the mast and square sails forward of it. Mizzen carried a gaff sail. Some earlier vessels used spritsails. Jibs to a long, rising bowsprit; staysail. Length ca. 18m, beam 4m. Name variants: **Sch(i)mackschiff**; pl. **Schmacken**. Note also **smack**. Further reference: **smak**

Schmacken See **Schmack**

Schmackschiff See **Schmack**, **smak**

Schmalschiff See **smalschip**, **wijdschip**

schnapper boat See **snapper boat-1**

Schnau, Schnaue, Schnaumastschiff, Schnauschiff See **snow**

Schneck, Schnecken See **Schnigge**

Schnellboot See **mosquito boat**

schniaka See **shnyaka**

Schnick See **Schnigge**

Schnigge *Germany:* Term used from the 10th-19th centuries for different types of rowing and sailing vessels.

1. Reported from the Baltic Sea coast in the Middle Ages both as a small, armed despatch vessel and as a **fishing boat★**. Rowed and sailed.

2. In the 18th-19th centuries, the **Schnigge** was used along the North Sea coast, especially around the islands of Ostfriesland, for fishing and oystering. Flat bottom with no keel, square stern, decked, leeboards. Rigged with a spritsail or a gaff mainsail and topsail to a single mast.

3. 19th-century North Sea **coaster★** that became extinct in the 1940s. Full build, bluff bow, transom or counter stern, flat floors, shallow keel, strong sheer. Leeboards. One- or 2-masted with sprit rig; 3 headsails. Reported lengths 15-17m, widths 4.3-4.9m, hold depths 1.22-1.73m.

4. A long, sharp boat used on the inland waterways of Ostfriesland in the late 19th century.

Other recorded names: **Schneck, Schnick, Schnikke, Snicke, snig, Snigge, Snik★, snikke**; pl. **Schnecken, Schniggen, Sniggen**. Note also **Helgoländer Schnigge**. Further references: **boeier, Eiderschnigge**

schniggen See **Schnigge**, **snekkja**

Schniggschiff See **Eiderschnigge**

Schnikke See **Schnigge**

schnjacta, schnjaka See **shnyaka**

Schocker See **schokker**

schoener See **schooner**

schoenerbark See **barkentine**

Schoenerbrik, Schoenerbrikken See **hermaphrodite brig**

schoenergaljoot See **galjoot**

schoenerkof See **kof**

schoëte See **Schute**

Schöf, Schoff See **Schiff**

Schoker *Germany, S:* Small, open, **punt★**-like craft used in the upper Danube Basin as a general workboat, local **ferry★**, and for fishing. Square, raked ends; flat

bottom with rocker at ends, fore-and-aft planked. One pair of natural frames crossed the bottom; slightly flared sides. Poled or paddled. Reported lengths 3-4m, widths 1-1.1m, depth ca. 0.23m. See also **schokker**.

schokker **1.** *Germany, SW:* Used in fresh-water eel fishing with bag nets on the Rhine, Main, and Mosel Rivers. Sharp lines with transom stern. Length ca. 12m.

2. *Netherlands:* Robust **fishing boat★** mainly of the Zuiderzee, but also worked ca. 1900 on the Scheldt and the Waddenzee in the north. The large **Noordzeeschokker** worked out on the North Sea, not only fishing but also as a specially built life-saving boat (**reddingschokker**) and **pilot boat★** (**loodsschokker**). Trawled and drifted for herring, plaice, sole, cod, eels, etc. Recently modified to become pleasure craft (**schokkerjacht** or **jachtschokker**). Known from at least the 17th century. Main characteristic is the straight stem that rakes as much as 45° and the square stemhead. Stem doubled at the head to create a sheave for the anchor cable. Originally clinker, then carvel-planked, generally of oak; **yachts★** steel-built. Narrow, flat bottom; soft, angular chines; curved sides. Rounded stern on most, though some sharp; straight, raked sternpost. Wide sheer strake with tumble home above a prominent wale; strake cutaway in semi-circle at the stem; partial washstrake; strong sheer toward the bow. Outboard rudder, downward-sloping tiller; long, narrow leeboards. Half-decked with cuddy forward; heavy steering thwart forward of the stern locker; cabin on yachts; North Sea **schokkers** decked. **Fishing boats** had live wells. Sprit-rigged during the 17th-18th centuries, some with a loose-footed, boomed gaff mizzen; staysail, jib to a slender, running bowsprit. Later set a loose-footed gaff mainsail and large forestaysail, which reached abaft the mast, to a tall, slightly aft-raking pole mast. Gaff short and curved. Sometimes a triangular sail was hung from the mast and boomed out over the stern. North Sea boats 2-masted. Some had an engine after 1915 (**motorschokker**). Crew of 2-4. Reported lengths 10-18m, the largest being the **Noordzeeschokker**; the 10-11m size is the **bons★**. Further name variants: **Schocker, schoker★, schokker schuit; schokkertje** (dim.); **Zuiderzeeschokker**

Further reference: **Waalschokker**

schokkerjacht See **schokker**

schokkerschouw See **zalmschouw**

schokker schuit, schokkertje See **schokker**

schollenschute See **bezaanschuit**

scholschuit See **bezaanschuit**, **pink-5**

scholschuitje, scholschuyt See **pink-5**

scholschuyte See **bezaanschuit**

Schoner See **schooner**

Schonerbark See **barkentine**

Schonerbrigg See **hermaphrodite brig**

Schonerkuff See **Kuff**

Schonerlomme See **lomme**

Schonerschute See **schooner-barge-2**

schooner **1.** A vessel with 2 or more masts with sails aligned fore-and-aft, generally setting boomed gaff sails, but leg-of-mutton sails are now common; one or more headsails. On 2-masted vessels, the after mast is

taller, distinguishing the **schooner** from the **ketch**★ and **yawl**★. Rig type dates from the 17th century, although name not adopted until the mid-18th century. Size and number of masts increased, ultimately reaching 7. Many 18th-century **schooners** carried a large square sail forward on the foremast with a gaff sail abaft the mast and at least one square topsail. Naval **schooners** of the 18th century were small, some only 15-18m long. A **schooner** that has all fore-and-aft sails with no square sails is generally called a **fore-and-aft schooner**. Sets gaff sails, often with jib-headed or jackyard topsails, or leg-of-mutton sails. Also called **fore-and-after**★, **forenagterskonnert, gaffelschoener, Gaffelschoner, gaff(-rigged) schooner, goélette (à deux mâts, aurique,** or **franche), goletta a vele auriche, Voor und Achter Schoner, Voor und Hinter Schoner.** Vessels carrying square topsails on the foretopmast are generally called **topsail schooners** (**Bramsegelschoner, bramsejlskonnert, fore topsail schooner, goélette à hune, goélette à huniers, goélette carrée, goleta de velachero, goletta a gabbiola, Marsegelschoner, Rah[segel]schoner, Toppsegel-Schoner, Topsegel-Schoner, topsejlskonnert, topzeilschoener**). One with a topgallant to which a square sail is set is a **topgallant schooner**. Those with square topsails on the mainmast as well are called **main topsail schooners** (**double topsail schooner, goélette à deux huniers, goleta de dos gavias, two-topsail schooner, Zweitoppsegelschoner**). On **staysail schooners** (**stagsegelschoner, stagsejlskonnert, stagzeilschoener**), the gaff or leg-of-mutton foresail is replaced by staysails between the 2 masts. Called a **jack barquentine** at Portmadoc in northwestern Wales. A **schooner** with no topmasts is said to be a **bald-headed schooner** or **baldheader**★ (**goélette à pible, paalmastschoener, Pfahlmastschoner**). Note also **two-master**.
2. *Canada, E:* Two-masted vessel of Newfoundland distinguished from the **jack**★ by having a counter stern and inboard rudder.
3. *Seychelles:* Name variant: **goélette**★. **a.** The fishing **schooner** of these Indian Ocean islands is an old, traditional vessel that is still widely used. Single mast, setting a leg-of-mutton sail; also a foresail. Carvel-planked with copper fastenings; rounded bilges. Decked; cooking done on deck. Also has an engine. Crew of 5-6. Average length 11-12m, beam 3.5m, draft 1.0m. Note also **shark boat-3. b.** The trading **schooners** carry cargo and passengers between the islands of the archipelago and to some farther to the west. Built of local *takamaka* wood; clipper bow, transom stern, rounded bilges. Although most are fitted with a diesel engine, they also sail, stepping 2 masts in normal **schooner** manner. Length overall 17m, beam 4.6m, draft 1.8m; cap. ca. 40t and 55 passengers.
4. *Sri Lanka:* **Schooner** is the common Sri Lankan term for sailing vessels. At Trincomalee on the east coast, the **schooner** is similar to the Arab **boom**★. Transported rice from Muttur on the south side of the bay, but now practically extinct. Raked ends, flat sheer, low freeboard, open. Outboard rudder; tiller. Large, quadrilateral, lateen-type sail with a short luff; with long luff,

mast rakes forward. Length ca. 27m. Other recorded names: **battal** (Sinhala), **vattal** (Tamil).
5. *United States, south-central:* A shrimp **trawler**★ used mainly in the outer bays and along the coastal beaches off Louisiana is known as a **schooner**. Fully motorized. Reported lengths 13.7-16.8m.
Selected name variants: **chkounna, escuna, ghoulet(ta), ghouleta, goelet(t)a, goélette**★, **goleta**★, **goleta košna, golete, goletta**★, **goualette, gouelette**★, **goulette, gweletten, Jacht Schoner, scèna, schoener, Scho(u)ner, škchuna, Schuner, scona, scooner, scuna, scuner, shchuna, shkuna, skôna, skonare, škoner, skonjar, skon(n)ert, skooner, skouna, š(k)uner, szkuna.**
Further references: **américain, Barbados schooner, Bermuda schooner, bote de vela, Cayman schooner, Chesapeake Bay schooner, clipper-schooner, fruit schooner, goéliche, Grand Haven ketch, Indian Header, shebek, West Indies schooner**

schooner-barge 1. *England, E:* Flat-bottomed vessel that was **ketch**★-rigged with square topsails, but since **schooners**★ of the period had no topsails, the term **schooner-barge** was adopted. In **ketch** fashion, the foremast of the **schooner-barge** was the taller, and the mizzenmast was stepped well inboard. Some 3-masted. Worked during the 2nd half of the 19th century, carrying heavy cargo such as coal and bricks. Flat-sided, square or counter stern; many had leeboards. Reported lengths 27-43m; e.g., length 32.8m, beam 7.5m, depth 3.4m. Other recorded names: **jackass schooner**★, **sideboard schooner**
2. *United States, E:* Used from 1860 until the early 20th century, carrying mainly ice from Maine southward and coal northward. Two or 3 towed by a **tug**★, but very large **tugs** might pull 4-6. Reduced **bald-headed schooner** rig used for steadying, for power when wind abaft the beam, or if the tow broke loose. Hull as thick as 61cm, but built less expensively than regular **schooners**. Three-masted vessels had a crew of 5-6; 4-masted had 6-7, but following the advent of steam-hoisting engines, crew reduced by 1 or 2. In the early 20th century, **whalebacks**★ from the Great Lakes were used briefly. Cap. 400-1,000t of ice, which was packed solid with sawdust, straw, or brown paper between. Other recorded names: **barge**★, **ice schooner-barge, Schonerschute.** Note also **ice schooner**.
3. *United States, central:* Vessel of the 2nd half of the 19th century built on the Great Lakes. Carried a variety of bulk cargo—stone, iron ore, lumber, coal, grain, and ice. Mainly built of wood; a few of steel. Flat bottom, square bilges. Some sharp-ended, others counter-sterned. Mainly 3-masted; some 2-masted. Reported lengths 10-103m.
Further reference: **scow-7**
Schoonerbark See **barkentine**
schooner-brig, Schooner-brigg See **hermaphrodite brig**
Schoonerkuff See **Kuff**
schooner packet See **coastal packet**
schooner-pinky See **pinky**
schooner-scow See **scow-7, scow-schooner-1**
schooner-sharpie See **sharpie-schooner-1, sharpie-schooner-4**

schooner smack *United States, E:* A fast, **schooner***-rigged vessel that had a live well. Worked from the 1830s out of ports on Long Island Sound, and in the latter half of the century, from the Key West area of southern Florida. Used for fishing and as a **market boat***; those at Key West supplied fish to Havana. Great similarity between the northern and southern vessels, many of the Key West boats having been brought from New England; others locally built of native woods. Carvel-planked; drag to keel; high, rising floors; rounded bilges; topsides had slight tumble home. Sharp bow; stem either mildly raked or clipper type. Sternpost rake varied; some had a deep, square stern, others a slightly overhanging counter. Flush deck; cabins both forward and aft; some Key West vessels had a trunk cabin; live well amidships. Rudder came up inboard, worked by a wheel. The northern vessels carried a 4.6m **yawl boat***. These 2-masted **schooners** set boomed gaff sails and 2 headsails. Topmast on mainmast or on both masts; long, fixed bowsprit. Reported lengths 15-20m; e.g., length 18.6m, beam 5.56m, hold depth 2.05m, draft aft 2.3m. Other recorded names: **Key West smack, smack schooner**

schooner trow See **trow-1**

Schöörboot See **Strandboot**

schoot See **schuit**

Schörboot, Schörer See **Strandboot**

schorsboot See **bark boat**

schoude See **schouw**

Schouner See **schooner**

schourd See **Zeeuwse schouw**

schout See **scout**

schoute See **shout-1**

schouw *Netherlands:* Dutch generic term for **scow***. Reported as early as the 13th century. There are, however, a number of types of **schouwen** (pl.) in the Netherlands. Characteristically double-ended with overhanging bow. Flat bottom, planked transversely; hard bilges; sides that curve in toward the square ends. Some types have a curved bottom athwartships and sides that flare below the wale with tumble home above. Others have raked bow and stern transoms and vertical sides. Several are a cross between the latter two types. Smallest boats sprit-rigged, larger gaff-rigged. Used for fishing, transporting merchandise and produce, ferrying, and as pleasure craft. Range in length from 4.75m (**kleine schouw**) to 5.5m (**middenschouw**) to 6m (**grote schouw**). For some of the types described, see **boerenschouw, Friese schouw, kajuitschouw, modderschouw, sjouwerman, zalmschouw, zeeschouw**. Further name variants: **bunschouw** (with live well), **open schouw, schoude, schouwe(as), schouwtje, scoude, vischschouw**. Note also **aak, roeiboot, Zeeuwse schouw**.

schouwe, schouweas, schouwen, schouwtje See **schouw**

schouw van Philippine See **Zeeuwse schouw**

schover, schovertje See **Oostendse garnaalboot**

schrobnetvisser See **trawler**

Schubboot, Schubschiff, Schubschlepper See **push boat**

Schuhboot See **shoe dhoni**

schuit *Belgium/Netherlands:* **1.** Dutch and Flemish word used for many kinds of boats, especially inland craft used for fishing (**visschuit**) and cargo handling, but may describe a large, oceangoing ship. The coastal **fishing boats*** of Belgium went by the name **schuit** or **scute***, but in some areas of Holland, the term **pink*** was more common; **Vlaamse schuit** was applied to one working from the Flemish coast. Often, however, the word **schuit** may be used in a pejorative sense or because of ignorance of the vessel's real name. The **speelschuit** is mainly a pleasure craft. Word frequently found in a compound form to describe place or function, and several of these have been described separately, such as **ballastschuit, Blankenbergse schuit, garnalenschuit, haringschuit, Heiste schuit, panneschuit, steekschuit, steenschuit, steigerschuit, tentschuit, tochtschuit, trekschuit. 2.** Several types of strongly built **barges*** of southern Netherlands and northern Belgium in the 19th century served as **packet boats*** or **market boats*** along rivers and canals. Most flat-bottomed; square-ended; straight-sided amidships but rounded elsewhere; leeboards. Largest had a low cabin aft and the tiller passed through a hole in the raised gunwale (**statiepaviljoenschuit**). Originally sprit-rigged with a small mizzen, then gaff-rigged. Mast struck to permit transit under bridges. Crew of 2-3. Reported lengths 10-15.5m, widths 4-5.5m. Other recorded names: **bateau brabaçon, Brabantse schuit, schuit hollandais, Zuidhollandse schuit**. Note also **ballastschuit, bezaanschuit, gaffelschuit, vlotschuit, weischuit**. Other recorded names: **bunschuit** (one with a live well), **sceute, scheut, sc(h)oot, schute*, schuyt(e), schyte, scoute, scuit, scut, scuta-boot, scutscepe, scuttye, skeut, vischschuit, visschuit;** pl. **schuite, schuiten*;** dim. **visschuitje**. Further references: **boerenplat, bolpraam, zalmschouw**

schuite See **schuit, scute-2a**

Schuiten *Germany, NW:* A type of **mud sled*** used by shrimp and flounder fishermen in the Weser Estuary. Pulled by 2-3 large dogs across the mud banks at low tide. Constructed from the end of the 19th century until the late 1960s. Flat, wooden bottom turns up at the front; box for the catch set forward, leaving a short step at the rear on which the fisherman stands. Fisherman holds a crossbar (ca. 96cm tall), which is braced diagonally from the front. Dogs' harnesses fastened to iron hooks at the front. Length 1.6m, width 0.4m. Spelling variant: **schütjen**. Note also **accon-1, ni mo chuan, pousse-pied**. Further reference: **schuit**

schuit hollandais See **schuit-2**

schuitje 1. *Indonesia, E:* One of the terms for a rowed **boat*** on Siau Island in the Sangihi Islands northwest of Sulawesi (Celebes). **2.** *Netherlands:* Dutch for a small **boat**, usually open. Spelling variant: **schuitjen**. Note also **melkschuitje, schuit, skûtsje**.

schuitjen See **schuitje**

šchuna, Schuner See **schooner**

Schunergaliot See **galiot-2**

Schunerkuff See **Kuff**

Schunerlomme See **lomme**

Schunerquatze See **Quatze**

schup See **ship**

schut See **Schute, scout**

Schuta See **Schute**

Schute *Germany:* The **Schute** takes several forms, but the word basically describes a large-capacity **lighter***, **barge***, or **scow***. Usually lacks self-propulsion. Not all of the distinctions are clear since several types are quite old. A few types are described below.

1. In the Hamburg area, transferred cargo to and from warehouses along the Alster River during the late 19th and early 20th centuries. Flat bottom, sharp bow and stern. Generally open, but one decked type (**Kasten-schute**) specialized in handling guano. Unrigged. Poled and towed. Reported lengths 15-20m. **Hamburger Schuten** of the mid-19th century were among the largest **Elbkähne***, carrying products from the inner Elbe River to Hamburg. Oak planking with 4 planks per side. Spacious deckhouse. Largest ca. 46m long, 5.5m wide, 1.5m deep. Other recorded names: **Alsterschute, Hafenschute, Hamburger Hafenschute**

2. In the late 18th century, the **Schute** at Hamburg was a small, decked pleasure craft that was both sailed and rowed. Reported to have had a concave bottom.

3. During the 18th-19th centuries, a large type of **Schute** traversed the Spree, Havel, and Elbe Rivers, traveling as far as Berlin. Sharp bow, broad stern, and a cabin. Length ca. 37m, beam 5.5m, depth 1.6m.

4. There was also a sailing type of **Schute** (**Segelschute**), generally **ketch***-rigged with strike masts. These carried heavy cargoes along the lower Elbe, but some went to Denmark. The **Tonschute** specialized in carrying clay. Carvel-planked; flat bottom, angular bilges; straight, nearly plumb or slightly raked stem; most sharp-sterned; slight sheer. Decked with varied hatch arrangements; cabin forward; low washboards; large leeboards. Reported lengths 18-22m, widths 4.8-5.3m, depths 1.3-1.8m.

5. In East Frisia, the **Schute** was a flat-bottomed sailing craft. Sharp-ended. Ca 10t.

6. The **Schute** on the Baltic was a small, shallow-draft **coaster*** (called **Prahm*** on the Schleswig-Holstein coast). Sharp bow and stern, flat bottom. Some open, others partly decked. Those in Ostpommern set a loose-footed gaff mainsail, gaff topsail, and 2 headsails; often 3-masted. Other recorded names: **Pünte*, Schoëte, Schut(a), Schüte, Schutte, Schüttschiff**; pl. **Schuten**. Note also **Schuit**. Further references: **Bulle, schuit**

Schuten See **Schute**

Schütjen See **Schuiten**

Schutte, Schüttschiff See **Schute**

schuutje See **hoogaars**

schuyt See **lougre, schuit, shout-1**

schuyte See **schuit**

Schwaben, Schwabenplätte, Schwabenzille, Schwab-innin, schwäbische Zille See **Ordinari**

Schwammfischereiboot See **sponge boat**

Schwerterschiff See **mother**

Schwimmbagger See **dredger-1, dredger-2**

schwimmende Batterie See **floating battery**

Schwimmramme See **pile driver-1**

Schyff See **Schiff**

schyp, schype, schypp, schyppe See **ship**

schyppe bot See **ship's boat**

schyte See **schuit**

sciabecchi, sciabecchino, sciabecco, sciabeccu, sciabeco, sciabica See **xebec**

scialuppa Italian and Corsican word designating the largest of a **ship's boats***. In the Italian navy, it would be the **barca a vela***, while in the merchant marine, it would be the **barcaccia***. Formerly provided shore transportation after setting the anchor. Note also **chaloupe, chalupa, longboat**.

scialuppa cannoniera See **gunboat**

sciambecco See **xebec**

sciere See **vascello-2**

sciff, sciffe See **skiff**

Scillonian gig, Scilly Isles gig See **Cornish gig**

scip See **ship**

sciph See **skiff**

scipp See **ship**

scocci See **sekochi**

scona, scooner See **schooner**

scoot 1. *England, E:* Welled **fishing boat*** reported from Harwich in the mid-18th century. Fished for cod and lobsters for the London market. Gaff mainsail set to a single mast, 2 headsails, square topsail. Ca. 40t. Spelling variant: **scoote**

2. *United States, NE:* On the northeast coast of Maine, a **scoot** was a familiar term for a boat that sailed, especially a **fishing boat**.

See also **scout, schuit**.

scoote See **scoot, skuta-4**

scooter 1. Flat-bottomed, amphibious craft with lateral keels that form skates; joined at bow and stern. Easily beached or run up on the ice. Also a small, fast sport craft that skims across the water. Ridden somewhat like a motorcycle. Powered by an outboard motor. Other recorded names: **ice scooter, sea scooter, water scooter**

2a. *United States:* Amphibious craft of Great South Bay on the south shore of Long Island. Used for duck hunting and crossing to the outer beaches for ship salvage work. First built in the late 19th century by local lifesaving stations to cross to the mainland. Also found on the New Jersey bays. A lighter, modified hull is raced.

scooter-2a

Pointed bow with a small, oval transom. Rounded bottom, transversely planked; a pair of long, curved, wooden runners, brass- or steel-bound, and a pair of shorter inner runners enable the craft to sail or be poled over the ice. Oak deck, cambered fore-and-aft and athwartships; cockpit has high coaming; sometimes camouflaged with bundles of grass. Steered initially on water with an oar or pole and over the ice with a pike-pole; later some relied on the balanced jib and shifting of weight to aid in steering, the skipper sitting forward to work the oversized jib. First used spritsail and jib, later gaff mainsail with a very long boom; subsequently a leg-of-mutton sail adopted, some fitted over a crook at the masthead. Large, heavy bowsprit, but size changed with the weather. Crew of 1-4; **duck boats★** were designed for either one hunter or two. Reported lengths 3.7-9.1m, widths 0.91-1.68m, depth ca. 0.25m. Other recorded names: **Great South Bay scooter, Long Island scooter, scooter puntie, South Bay scooter; scow★**, a working **scooter** or one not in top racing form. Note also **party boat-2**. **b.** Term for a fast World War I **motor boat★**. Name variant: **coastal motor boat**

scooter puntie See **scooter-2**

scoridor, scoridora, scorridor See **scorridora**

scorridora *Croatia/Italy:* **1.** A **pinnace★**.

2. A small, fast boat found along the coasts, mainly in the service of customs, police, and health officials. Sharp, clipper-type bow; counter stern. Decked or open. Large lateen sail set to a tall mast stepped just forward of amidships; jib to a long, rising bowsprit. Rowed and more recently motorized. Reported lengths 10-12m, narrow.

Other recorded names: **barca corridoia, scoridor(a), scorridor(e), scorritore, secorridor, skoridor**

scorridore, scorritore See **scorridora**

Scotch boat *Ireland:* Special **flyboat★** used on the Grand Canal in the mid-19th century. First boat obtained from Scotland in 1833. Later built in Ireland and modified by addition of a wooden cabin. So narrow and unstable that the 50 or so passengers had to remain seated while the boat was underway. Length 19.8m, beam 1.8m. See also **flyboat-3a**.

Scotch buck See **buckie**

Scotchman See **fifie-1**

scoth See **sgoth**

Scots buck See **buckie**

Scottish coble See **coble-4**

scoude See **schouw**

scout 1. A small, armed naval vessel designed for special uses, especially reconnoitering. Other recorded names: **Aufklärer, Aufklärungsfahrzeug, Aufklärungsschiff, escampavia★, é(s)claireur, explorador, lookout (boat), razvedchik, Recognoscirungsschiff, reconnoitering vessel, scout boat★ (ship or vessel), spy boat**

2. *British Isles:* Reported in the early 17th century as a salmon-fishing craft.

3. *Canada:* A boat used to locate schools of fish. Other recorded names: **éclaireur, scout(ing) vessel**

Other recorded names: **scaut, sch(o)ut, scoot★, scout boat★, scowt(e), scut, scute★, skeut, skoute, skowt, skut(e)**. Note also **schuit**. Further references: **cruiser-2, shout-1**

scout boat *United States, SE:* 18th-century craft used by military units for river and bay patrol in Georgia and the Carolinas. Dugout hull, either plank-extended or of a single cypress log; double-ended. Ribs and thwarts reinforced the thin hull; stem, sternpost, and keel added. Armed with swivel guns. Some had a cabin aft. Rudder used when sailing. Mainly rowed

with as many as 10 oars. Also sailed using a type of **schooner★** rig; small boats single-masted. Reported lengths 10.7-12.2m; e.g., length 10.7m, beam 1.8m; shallow draft. Smaller craft called **scout canoes**. Another recorded name: **militia galley**. Note also **periauger-5, pirogue-3**. Further reference: **scout**

scout canoe See **scout boat**

scoute See **herring scowte, schuit**

scouting vessel See **scout-3**

scout ship, scout vessel See **scout-1**

scow 1. Large, open, rectangular, flat-bottomed craft that transports such materials as merchandise, coal, gravel, mud, and refuse (**garbage** or **dump scow**, also colloquially **honey barge** or **boat**). Generally work in protected waters. Locally called a **barge★** or **lighter★**. Canal workboats, with the crew living aboard, might be called **scows**. Some serve as the hull for **houseboats★**. Towed or rowed. Other recorded names: **scute★, skow★, square-ender★**. Note also **dump barge**.

2. May also describe a small, simple craft with a flat bottom that rises at each end in a straight line to square, shallow transoms; often called a **punt★**. Sides parallel or may narrow slightly toward the ends. Note also **johnboat-1, pram-1**.

3. A slovenly vessel. Note also **tub-1**.

4. *Canada, E:* On the upper St. Lawrence River near the mouth of Lake Ontario, a **sloop★**-rigged **scow** worked commercially, carrying lumber, etc. Length to ca. 15m.

5. *Canada, N:* Used in the latter part of the 19th century to transport furs and trade goods on the Athabasca/Slave River network, especially by the Hudson's Bay Company. Broken up downstream for lumber. Also used on the north-flowing rivers of northern Ontario. Carvel planking; square ends with shallow, overhanging transoms; straight, nearly vertical sides that curved in toward the ends; moderate sheer. Flat bottom, planked fore-and-aft; close, heavy

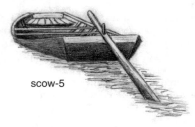

scow-5

timbering crossed the bottom; more widely spaced ribs on the sides; some boats ceiled. Open; numerous thwarts. A **cook scow** (or **cook boat**) accompanied a group of **scows**. Guided by a long sweep set over a pin at the stern; upstream, rowed and tracked from shore, and in later years, towed in groups by a small **steamer** on suitable stretches of river. Required crew of 4-6 on the Athabasca, 2-3 in Ontario. Reported lengths 12-30m; e.g., length 16.8m, beam 3.4m. Other recorded names: **Athabasca scow, fur scow, trading batteau**

6. *Canada, SE:* On the Restigouche River in New Brunswick, carried supplies to lumber camps. Square, slightly tapered ends; very shallow hull with strongly flared sides. Mainly pulled by 3 horses in midstream with a rider up on one horse; when the water was too deep, the horses towed the boat from shore. Long steering sweep at the stern. Length 21m; cap. 6-7t.

7. *New Zealand:* Flat-bottomed, interisland cargo carrier; some made regular trips to Australia. Built from 1873 to the l920s, largely at Auckland. Bottom transversely planked on longitudinal frames; square chines; square stern; flat sheer on early vessels. Deck beams supported by stanchions on longitudinal stringers; some divided into solid compartments by fore-and-aft partitions. Before 1890, all had square bows; later clipper bows. Leeboards on early vessels; later 1-3 centerboards, depending on size and period, the 3rd being a small fin forward of the foremast. The huge rudder worked with steering chains shackled to each side of the after end of the rudder and led inboard to a wheel barrel; rudder raised or lowered depending on water depth. Most had a deckhouse aft. The early vessels were **deck scows★**, carrying mostly logs on stoutly timbered decks; the empty space below added buoyancy for this heavy cargo. **Hold scows** carried the cargo both in the hold and on deck; **cattle scows** were divided into pens; timber vessels had bulwarks only at the ends; **coal scows** required only 3 hands. Employed their own gear to load and unload. Smaller **scows ketch★**-rigged, but most were **fore-and-aft schooners** with 2-3 masts. Some 3-masters had topsails and were called **schooner-scows**. Set 3-4 headsails. Crew depended on size and cargo, ranging from 3-7. Reported lengths 14-40m; typical early **scow**: length 18m, widths 5.5-6m, depth 0.9m; 2-masted logging **scows** 28.8m, beam 7.37m; all shallow draft. Additional name variants: **barge, New Zealand scow, schooner-barge★, scow-schooner★.** Further reading: Percy A. Eaddy, *'Neath Swaying Spars; the Story of the Trading Scows of New Zealand* (Auckland: Witcombe & Tombs, Ltd., 1939); C. W. Hawkins, "The New Zealand Scow," *The Mariner's Mirror* 51 (1965): 221-232.

8. *Northern Ireland:* Workboat on the Lagan Navigation southwest of Belfast; in operation until 1956. Crewed by specialists: carpenter, blacksmith, stone mason, etc., who repaired locks, lock houses, stables, weirs, banks, and such. Square ends, flat bottom. Cabin at stern equipped with work benches, forge, etc. Also had a pile driver on the flat deck. Name variant: **workman's scow**

9. *Scotland:* **a.** General term for canal **barges**. Early craft of wood, then iron or steel. Double-ended; round bilges; heavy wales. Short deck at each end with a day cabin aft; open type carried various minerals; those with a hatch transported perishables; often served as canal maintenance craft; some carried coal in loaded wagons on deck. Last built in 1948. Towed by a horse; later steam-operated. Crew of 3 on horse-towed craft. Length ca. 18m, beam 4m, draft loaded 1.5-1.8m. Name variants: **waggon boat, waggon scow. b.** The 17th-century **scow** of the east coast port of Montrose was a flat-bottomed **barge** of 50t.

10. *United Kingdom:* Small, beamy **dinghy★**, especially common in the Solent area and in scattered pockets along the east coast, on Malta, along the west coast of France, and in America and Australia. A popular racing class. Clinker-planked; bluff bow; shallow, curved stem; slightly raked, wide transom; some with skeg. Strong bottom rocker, flat floors. Decked to mast; centerboard. Outboard rudder, rounded blade; tiller. Sets a standing lugsail. Most 3.5m long, 1.4m wide; draft with centerboard down 0.8m. Other recorded names: **Cowes, Lymington, Solent, West Wight,** and **Yarmouth** (Isle of Wight) **scow; scow-dinghy**

11. *United States:* **a.** Sprit-sailed craft used by wildfowl hunters. Flat bottom, vertical sides, leeboards. Cabin forward; a battery for the hunter carried abaft the mast; towed 1-2 flat-bottomed boats, called **yawls★**, used to help set the battery and decoys. Foresail used in addition to the spritsail. Also carried sweeps and poles. Length 12.2m, beam 2.7m. Name variant: **American shooting yacht. b.** A popular racing craft in the northeast and on the Great Lakes in the late 19th and early 20th centuries. Flat floors, firm bilges, long overhang at the pointed bow or square ends, low freeboard, **canoe★**-shaped waterline, completely open or only at the cockpit. Often fitted with bilge boards; twin rudders on some; others employed a centerboard. **Sloop**-rigged. Shallow draft. Other recorded names: **bilge board scow, inland lake scow. c.** A **scow** was used by 6-8 oyster tongers in shallow waters off northern New Jersey in the late 19th century to transport the oysters ashore. Box-shaped; strongly built; bottom curved up at each end, shallow transoms, platform at each end, keelson formed a longitudinal partition, decked at ends. Poled, sculled, rowed, or towed. Reported lengths 9.1-12.2m; e.g., length 12.2m, beam 2.5m, inside depth 0.6m. Name variants: **oyster flat, oyster scow★. d.** On Chesapeake Bay, **schooner★**-rigged **scows** were developed in the mid-18th century to transport pig iron from the upper to the lower bay. Locally carried salt, fish, grain, produce, stone, railroad ties, and served as **houseboats** for gunners of the late 19th century off Havre de Grace (see **cabin boat-3**). Used on the upper bay until the 1940s. Raked ends square but stern tapered; sides straight and vertical; flat bottom planked athwartships. Employed 1-2 leeboards; some had centerboards. Decked; cabin house forward or abaft the mainmast, long hatches. Steered with a tiller or wheel; rudder usually within a stock. Jib to a long bowsprit. Most painted white. Reported lengths 9-20m; e.g., length 18.3m, beam 4.4m, hold depth 1.12m; shallow draft. Other recorded names: **flat★, Havre de Grace schooner, scow-schooner, scow-sloop★. e.** In central New York State, the **scow** was one of the main Erie Canal types, carrying coal, lumber, barrels of apples, and merchandise unaffected by weather. Most open, but some decked forward, half-decked, or fully decked (the **deck scow**) to protect the cargo. Narrow washboards along the sides. Small stable forward for an extra team; small cabin aft. Straight sides of heavy pine logs; 6-8 oak beams, evenly spaced; flat bottom; short, rounded ends. When framed, they were ceiled. Late 19th-century **scows** 29.8m long, 5.4m wide. Name variant: **Clinton's Ditch scow. f.** The **scows** on the Morris Canal in northwestern New Jersey in the 19th and early 20th centuries were maintenance boats. Crew worked

segments of the canal, returning home each evening. Repaired breaks in canal banks, cut brush from towpath, and did minor dredging. Square ends, bow raked, decked forward; on some, a rough house aft. Open amidships for equipment and debris and brush cleared from the banks. Name variants: **maintenance** (or **work**) **scow**. **g.** Some salmon fishermen on the tributary rivers of San Francisco Bay lived on **houseboats** called **scows**. Varied in shape but generally flat-bottomed, ends square and raked, sides vertical and tapering toward the ends. House covered most of the hull. Length ca. 6m, beam 3.7m. Note also **ark-5**. **h.** In the northwest, the Columbia River **scows** of the late 19th century received salmon from **gillnetters** for counting and recording; special **tugs** transported the fish to the cannery. The **scows** were moved to different parts of the river, depending on the center of activity at the time. Long house covered the craft. Length ca. 9m, widths 3.7-4.6m. Another type of **scow** served the seine fishery and on these, both men and horses might live. Also covered. **i.** In northwest Washington State, the **scow** worked with the Puget Sound **seine boats** in salmon fishing, helping to set the seine. Square ends, roughly built. Iron winch at each end and wooden davit along one side used to purse the seine. Crew of 2. Length 7m, beam 2.43m.
Further references: **ark-3**, **bateau-7**, **box float-2**, **covered sled**, **deck scow**, **dog-hole schooner**, **garvey**, **horse boat-2**, **Maine wood scow**, **oyster barge**, **punt-1**, **schouw**, **scooter-2**, **shed**, **smelt scow**, **tally scow**, **tobacco boat**

scow-boat See **covered sled**

scow-brig *United States, E:* Term given to a 19th-century **canal boat** on the Delaware and Hudson Canal in New York and Pennsylvania that would be heavily loaded in winter with sand and cement in the bow. Boat would then be rammed up onto the ice to break it and keep the canal navigable. Note also **ice breaker**.

scow-dinghy See **scow-10**

scow ferry 1. *Canada:* **Scows** frequently served to ferry people and horses across rivers. Raised sides prevented the horses from stepping into the water.
2. *United States:* Flat-bottomed craft designed to provide service for people, horses, and vehicles. Popular on the smaller tributaries of Chesapeake Bay and on southern and western rivers. Square ends, shallow sides, ends sloped up or were hinged to lower onto the bank. Larger boats might have a cabin. On narrow waterways, propelled by a rope with pulleys to the hull and to a cable stretched over the water, the ferryman pulling on a wooden, notched "heaver." Might be sailed on lakes and other deep water. Name variant: **ferry scow**. Note also **covered sled**.
Further reference: **ferryboat**

scow house See **ark-3**

scow-schooner *United States:* **1.** Centerboard cargo **schooner** of the Great Lakes that came into favor in the 1st half of the 19th century and lasted into the early 20th century. Carried lumber, food, staples, bricks, etc. Most were butt-ended with the planking straight across the bow; some had bent bow planking, others had sharp bows in which stem and cutwater

extended forward of the chine, which had been carried up to the deck; slab-sided. Most had a flat bottom, usually with a keelson; heavy chine timbers ran along both sides of the bilges. Vessels "gunnel-built" with bolts driven edgewise through 2 or more thick side planks; few if any frames. Cabins forward and aft. Rudder often hauled by tackles from a drum on the steering wheel to the outer edge of the rudder. Mostly 2-masted, some with 3. Short boom on jib; some employed multiple jibs. Usually crew of 2-3. Reported lengths 10-40m; e.g., length 27m, beam 7m, depth 2m, 94t; shallow draft. Name variant: **schooner-scow**. Note also **Great Lakes schooner**.
2. Those built on the Gulf of Mexico coast, west of New Orleans, were used for coastal and river work from ca. 1840. Most had a flat bottom, planked fore-and-aft, with moderate rocker; V-bottomed vessels also popular. Bow transom greatly raked. Centerboard; large rudder worked by tiller. Decked; trunk cabin aft. Gaff-**schooner** rig with 1-2 headsails. Lengths mostly 9.8-15.2m; shallow draft. Other recorded names: **butt head**, **Gulf scow-schooner**, **Houston scow**
3. Heavy cargo vessel that worked San Francisco Bay and its tributary rivers in the 2nd half of the 19th century, transporting bulk cargoes such as farm produce, grain, hay, cordwood, gravel, bricks, and sand that was dug by the crew. Last sailing **scow** launched in 1905; adaptations now built as **yachts**. Square ends, most with the bow transom slightly shallower and wider than the stern; both ends raked; the few that served as **coasters**, the **outside schooners**, had sharp bows. Bottom flat for most of its length with an abrupt upward curve aft; mainly fore-and-aft planking; some had a V-bottom with a shallow deadrise; keel ran the full length of the flat part of the bottom; fore-and-aft planked vessels were framed; cross-planked boats lacked frames but had heavy chines and thick strakes. Employed a very large centerboard. Stockless rudder, generally outboard, worked with adjustable tackle. Slightly cambered deck; central hold, but most bulk cargoes carried on deck. Because of high deck cargo, steering wheel was on a small platform that could be raised. Small trunk cabin aft for crew of 2, sometimes 3. Initially painted bottle green with white bulwarks and red sheer strake; some white, others barn red. Mostly **schooner**-rigged with main topsail, boomed forestaysail; sometimes gaff topsail set from both masts plus a main topmast staysail. Heavy bowsprit. Earlier and smaller **scows sloop**-rigged (**scow-sloop**). In confined waters, might be poled, warped upstream by use of riverside pilings, or towed (by its **yawl**, called a **Swedish towboat**); converted to power in later years. Reported lengths 11-27m; e.g., length 18m, beam 6.7m, depth 1.3m; shallow draft. Other recorded names: **brick scow**, **hay hack**, **hay scow** (a general term used regardless of the cargo), **sand scow**, **San Francisco Bay scow-schooner**, **square-toed packet**. Further reading: Roger R. Olmsted, *Scow Schooners of San Francisco Bay* (Cupertine: California History Center, 1988). Note also **ark-5**, **Hudson River brick schooner**.
Further references: **scow-7**, **scow-11d**

scow-sloop *United States:* **1.** Important **coaster★** in the northeast during the late 19th and early 20th centuries. Carried supplies locally and cordwood, bricks, ice, etc., from Maine communities to Boston, working mostly in the more sheltered waters. Some tended fish traps and fished. A present-day **scow-sloop** works in Massachusetts between Martha's Vineyard and the mainland. Raked, square ends; overhanging bow curved up from the flat bottom; skeg aft; some wall-sided, others had flared sides; relatively flat sheer. The fishing **scows★** out of Casco Bay in Maine were planked longitudinally on the bottom; others cross-planked. Bulwarks on larger craft; log rail on the smaller. Decked; trunk cabin aft, hatch amidships. Larger **scows** had stockless, barn-door rudders, hung on the skeg, and worked by ropes from a horn on the outer edge of the blade; stocked, outboard rudder on the smaller vessels. Leeboards, generally double, used on the Maine and lower Bay of Fundy vessels; centerboard elsewhere. **Sloop★**-rigged; large, slightly overlapping jib to bowsprit; gaff topsail. Crew of 2. Reported lengths 9.4-18.2m; e.g., length 12.6m, beam 4m, depth 1.28m.

2. The **scow-sloops** of Chesapeake Bay were built mainly in the 1860s to 1890s, the last operating in 1941. Carried primarily bulk cargoes. Raked, square ends; slightly flared sides narrowed toward each end; flat bottom, planked athwartships; variable sheer. Leeboards or centerboard. Very large inboard rudder, worked with tiller or wheel. Trunk cabin forward of the mast. Large gaff sail with long boom, boomed jib, sometimes a gaff topsail. Engines installed in the 1920s. Reported lengths 12-20m; e.g., length 19m, beam 5.3m, depth 1.2m. As size increased, the type became the **scow-schooner★**. Note also **cabin boat-3**.

3. Used along rivers bordering coastal rice plantations of South Carolina in the mid-19th century. Shallow bow transom, skeg below, nearly plumb stem, shallow stern transom, vertical sternpost. Slight deadrise, flaring sides. Decked; low cabin in after third, hold amidships. Wide-bladed outboard rudder; tiller; centerboard. Mast stepped in forward third; stubby bowsprit. **Sloop**-rigged. Length 10.2m, beam 3.3m, depth ca. 1.2m. Further references: **chalan, scow-11d, scow-schooner-3**

scowt See **scout**

scowte See **herring scowte, scout**

scratch back boat See **dao ba zi**

scuit See **schuit**

scull A **shell★** that uses pairs of long, scoop-shaped sculls on outriggers (see **outrigger**). Mainly used by 2 persons (see **double scull**) or solo (**single scull**); at one time, **sculls** for 4 and 8 people (**quad[ruple] scull** and **octuple scull**) were popular. Each person rows with a scull in each hand. Length of boat commensurate with the number of scullers, but about the same as the **shells**. A solo racing **shell** may be no shorter than 8m, no wider than 0.38m, and must weigh at least 14kg. Other recorded names: **canoino, sculler★, sculling boat** (or **outrigger**), **Skullboot; Einer, Renneiner, Skulleiner; quatre de couple; huit de couple; coxed single scull, joletta; coxed double**

scull, **doppio pariglia**. Note also **canoë français, pair-oar, palischermo-4, rigger**.

scull boat Designed to be maneuvered by sculling with a single oar projecting through a hole or a notch in the stern. Name variant: **Wriggboot**. See also **Connecticut scull boat, Mississippi scull boat**.

sculler *England:* Small waterman's boat operated by a single boatman pulling a pair of oars. Used mainly in the 17th and 18th centuries on the River Thames, but may now refer to the **single-** or **double-sculler** used as a pleasure craft. Other recorded names: **pair of scullers, sculling boat, skoll(o)er, skuller**. Note also **pair-oar, sandolino, Thames wherry**. Further references: **Connecticut scull boat, scull**

scull float *United States, NE:* Duck hunter's craft of coastal New Hampshire. Elongated, narrow bow; square or sharp stern, flat bottom. Low coaming around the rectangular cockpit set in the after third. Movable weight put into the bow. Sculled with a long oar inserted into a leather sleeve through a hole in the transom. Also rowed or powered by a small outboard motor. Length ca. 4.5m, beam 0.86-1.0m, depth ca. 0.38m. Other recorded names: **duck boat★, ducking skiff, New Hampshire duck boat** (**ducking skiff** or **scull float**), **Piscataqua River gunning skiff, sneakbox**

sculling boat See **scull, sculler**

sculling dinghy See **dinghy-6**

sculling outrigger See **scull**

scuna, scuner See **schooner**

scut See **schuit, scout**

scuta See **escute**

scuta-boot See **schuit**

scute 1. In old French, a small **boat★** serving a ship. In Italian, **scuto** has the same meaning.

2. *France, N:* **a.** Open boat that transports local produce and personnel on the small waterways of the Saint-Omer area. Flat bottom, longitudinally planked; long, sharply pointed bow; sharp stern; flared sides, straight along central part; bow sheer sweeps up. Short foredeck ends in curved breakwater; small deck at stern; characteristically has 2 bulkheads. Light sails may be set to a short mast that also may serve for towing. Poled or rowed; now has an outboard motor. Reported lengths 5.7-7m, widths 1.33-1.62m. Name variants: **escute★, schuite**. Further reading: G. L. Berk, "Die Schuite Maker van St. Omer," *De Waterkampioen* (9 Novembre 1973): 2720-2923. Note also **bacop**. **b.** Two-masted **fishing boat★** of the northern coast, working out of harbors or from beaches. Clinker-built; flat floors, rounded bilges, plumb stem; wide, raking transom; flat sheer. Decked. Originally set square sails; later loose-footed, boomed gaff sails with topsail on main topmast. Mizzenmast stepped well aft. Jib to a long bowsprit. Also rowed. Other recorded names: **carrot, rafiot★, sloup** Further references: **bateau de Berck, escute, schuit-1, scout, scow-1**

scute à corne See **gaffelschuit**

scute de Blankenberge See **Blankenbergse schuit**

scute de la Panne See **panneschuit**

scuto See **scute-1**

scutscepe See **schuit**

scutte See **lougre, shout-1**

scutte de Blankenberghe See **Blankenbergse schuit**

scuttye See **schuit**

scuyt See **shout-1**

scyp See **ship**

sda'kwihl *United States, NW:* Fast, light, 2-person **canoe*** of the Coast Salish Native Americans. Mainly a river **canoe** for duck hunting and fishing, but some were used to hunt seals and porpoises on Puget Sound. Elongated and raised prow with stylized animal's head at top; low stern. River **canoes** low-sided; those used on the Sound were plank-extended. Length 5m, beam 0.74m. Other recorded names: **staxwił, traveling canoe.** Note also **Coast Salish canoe.**

sdǎwělth See **Coast Salish canoe**

sea-bat See **boat-1**

sea boat 1. In the broad sense, a boat designed for use at sea. A good **sea boat** is one that behaves well in rough seas. Other recorded names: **easy ship, navire marin**

2. A vessel that works offshore, as opposed to an inshore craft. Other recorded names: **Seeboot, Seeschiff**

3. British Royal Navy term for a **ship's boat*** suspended from davits, ready for immediate use. Mainly for ship-to-shore communication. The same boat is designated as a **lifeboat*** when used to rescue a person who has fallen overboard.

ᵾee also **accident boat.**

Sea Bright dory See **Sea Bright skiff**

Sea Bright skiff *United States, E:* Fished and tended pound nets staked out primarily along northern New Jersey beaches, but also found along the south Jersey coast and on Long Island. Used from about the mid-19th century. Became a popular sport fishing and pleasure craft, and during the Prohibition Era (1919-1933), was used extensively by smugglers. A lengthened version was used for rescues until the 1900s. Light, flexible, and buoyant. Lapstrake planking; narrow, flat bottom formed a "box" keel, tapered toward the ends. Plank-on-edge keel on the southern New Jersey beach craft. Slight bottom rocker; rounded bilges and sides; full aft; strong sheer. The New York Bay oystering **skiffs*** were ceiled. Most had a slight curve to the broad stem, with an iron stem band. Wide, raked, V- or U-shaped transom, the older types having a reverse curve; some south Jersey boats had a sharp stern and were called **sharpies*.** Hollow skeg with reverse chines on most; solid skeg on southern type. Open; short foredeck or fore, stern, and side decks; large boats often fully decked with trunk cabin. Those that sailed had a centerboard or daggerboard placed well forward; generally steered with an oar held in a transom notch. Prior to installation of engines, the **skiffs** were rowed or sailed, setting a boomed spritsail and small, clubbed jib. Sail wrapped around the mast, which was unshipped when fishing. Larger boats 2-masted, employing a sprit or leg-of-mutton rig. Crew of 1-3. Reported lengths 4-12.8m; e.g., length 6.4m, beam 1.8m, depth ca. 0.76m. Other recorded names: **beach dory, beach skiff*, dory surf boat, Jersey bankskiff, (New) Jersey beach skiff, Jersey (sea) skiff, New Jersey (sea) skiff, New York Bay skiff, North Jersey skiff, Sea Bright dory, sea dory, sea**

skiff, skift. Also **Atlantic City skiff, South Jersey beach skiff.** Further reading: Peter J. Guthorn, *The Sea Bright Skiff and Other Shore Boats,* (Exton, Pa.: Schiffer Publishing Ltd., 2nd ed., 1982); Robby Robinson, "The Sea Bright Skiff," *WoodenBoat* 109 (1993): 40-49. Note also **lobsterman, pound boat.**

sea coble See **coble-4**

sea dory See **Sea Bright skiff**

Seaford skiff *United States, NE:* Originated ca. 1870 on Great South Bay on southern Long Island as a **gunning skiff*** for market wildfowlers; also used for fishing, oystering, smuggling from **rum runners** lying off shore, and now as a pleasure craft. Carvel-planked. Hollow entrance; raked, curving stem; flat floors amidships; easy bilges; strongly raked, oval transom; plank keel 31-41cm wide; most had a box skeg. Runners, added in winter, enabled boat to glide over the ice. Decked except for an elongated cockpit; foredeck cambered. Some used a centerboard. Set a high-peaked, boomed spritsail. Also poled or rowed. Reported lengths 3.7-4.9m; e.g., length 4.3m, beam 1.3m, depth amidships 0.33m; shallow draft. Other recorded names: **melon seed*, Verity skiff**

sea-hunter See **chasse-marée**

sealer Strong, heavy boat often resembling a small **whaleboat*** used to hunt seals. Usually carried the crew, skins, and equipment from larger vessels to shore. Other recorded names: **okhotnich'e sudno, phoquier, Robben(fäng)boot, robbenschip (slager, vaartuig, vangschip), seal-hunting boat, Seehund(s)-fänger, soiler, sw(o)iler.** Note also **canot de chasse, falbåt, flat-2, flatte, galloper, haapio-2, ice skiff, isjolle, Toulinguet boat.**

seal-hunting boat See **sealer**

sealing boat *United States:* **1.** The east coast boats, used mainly to hunt seals in the South Atlantic early in the 20th century, were double-ended and open. As many as 9 were carried aboard **sealing schooners,** placed on edge, 3 to a side, one on each side of the mainmast, and the 9th tipped against the cabin aft. Carvel-built with pine planking; keel, stem, and sternpost birch or maple; ash frames. Most gaff-rigged to a light mast. Also rowed; rope-bound oarlocks. Crew of 2-3. Length ca. 5.8m, beam 1.4m.

2. The northwest coast boats engaged in pelagic sealing. Small **whaleboat*** type. Clinker-built with cedar planking, fir frames, sharp ends. Seven might be carried aboard a **schooner*.** Seals shot by the hunter and skinned aboard. Rowed or sailed, setting a gaff or sprit mainsail, jib. Crew of 2-3. Length 5.8m, beam 1.4m.

sealing canoe 1. *Canada, SW:* **a.** The Nootka of the west coast of Vancouver Island used a special **dugout canoe*** for their commercial fur sealing expeditions. Smooth, polished, flat bottom; flaring sides. Keel-like blades at the ends reduced slapping in choppy waters; vertical stern; characteristic dog's head bow. Paddled. Crew of 2-3. The Makah of the Olympic Peninsula in western Washington State used the same kind of **sealing canoe** (the **yE'cabΔqΔdts** or **yecabuquts**), which they obtained from the Nootkas. Reported lengths 6.7-7.3m, beam 1.2m. Other recorded names: **fur-seal canoe, Nootkan sealing canoe, yasha:baXts,**

yashbaqats, yashmaqats, yEcmaqàts. Note also **West Coast canoe. b.** The Claquot Nootkas of the central west coast also used a special **canoe** for sealing. The term applied to them, **hásh ma hats**, has the broader meaning of a general-purpose craft. Similar to other **West Coast canoes***. Carried 3 men and 2 fur seals. Reported length 6.7m, beam on top 1.27m, on bottom 0.8m, depth 0.55m.

2. *United States, Alaska, SE:* The Yakutat used their **sealing canoe** to hunt seals among the ice floes at the heads of Yakutat and Icy Bays. **Dugout canoe** with a short bow projection to fend off icebergs; low, thick, rounded bow; concave stern. Small, residual seat forward. Paddled stern first, the stern being sharp. Steered with a paddle. Held 1-2 hunters. Reported lengths 3.7-4.6m, beam 1.1-1.2m. Other recorded names: **gudiyÉ, gudiyi**

sealing punt *Canada, E:* Open boat used close to the Newfoundland shore to capture seals with nets, working off **schooners***. Some having this designation engaged mainly in fishing. Square stern. Set 1-2 spritsails; on some, the mizzen is on the stern and sheeted to an outrigger. Other recorded names: **punt*, skiff***. Note also **bay punt, canot à glace.**

sealing schooner See **sealing boat, sealing vessel**

sealing ship See **sealing vessel**

sealing skiff *Canada, E:* Large, undecked boat used off Newfoundland in the 18th century to set and haul seal nets. Note also **canot à glace.**

sealing vessel *Canada, E:* Engaged in the annual seal hunt. Strengthened for working among the ice floes. Carried a **whaleboat***-type craft for use at the hunt. Motorized or sailed. Other recorded names: **sealing schooner** (or **ship**)

seaman See **terreneuvier**

seamark See **mark boat-1**

sean boat See **seine boat-3**

searcher boat See **feluca-2**

sea rover A vessel engaging in wide-ranging acts of piracy and plunder. Name variants: **rover, zeerover**. Note also **caper, corsair, forban-1, freebooter, privateer.**

sea scooter See **scooter-1**

sea skiff See **Sea Bright skiff**

sea-skiff pound-boat See **pound boat-1**

seatia See **saettia**

sea tjalk See **zeetjalk**

sea wolf See **privateer**

šebbâk, şebec, sebeco, sebek, sebeka See **xebec**

Sechserin, Sechserkobel, Sechserzille See **Salzzille**

Sechuras *Peru, N:* Log **raft*** of the fishermen of Sechura Bay. Built with 5-8 balsa logs of uniform length and 20-30cm in diameter. Logs lashed in 3 places with cross-ties, and a pair of large-diameter bamboo poles serve as railings along the sides. "Sculled" by means of a 1.8-2.4m-long plank that is thrust down between the logs, one at the stern when passing through the surf and another at the bow when sailing, both of which help in steering and maintaining course. A hardwood block serves as a fulcrum. A high-peaked, cotton lugsail, its luff shorter than its leech, is bent to a bamboo yard, which is slightly shorter than the mast. A light spar may extend the luff, the inboard end lashed to the

mast ca. 1.5m up. Crew of 2. Reported lengths 4.6-6.1m, widths 1.5-1.8m. Further reading: C. R. Edwards,

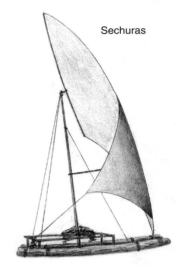

Sechuras

"Sailing Rafts of Sechuras: History and Problems of Origin," *Southwestern Journal of Anthropology* (1960): 368-372. Note also **balsa-11**.

seckochi See **sekochi**

second canot See **canot-2**

second cutter See **quarter boat-1**

secorridor See **scorridora**

sectional boat *United States, E:* A small **canal boat***, built in 2-4 sections, portaged on a railway carriage for passage up an inclined plane, in lieu of a series of closely spaced locks. Used in the 2nd quarter of the 19th century on the Pennsylvania Canal and in New Jersey. Some **sectional boats**, mounted on cradles and supported by double-wheel trucks, made part of the journey across Pennsylvania by railway and part by canal. Developed for both freight and passenger use. Round bottom. Each section 6.3m long. The teams of horses for the canal segments were stabled in the bow or stern section. Name variant: **portable boat**. See also **hinge boat.**

section boat See **hinge boat**

Seeboot See **Netzboot, sea boat-2**

See-Eeber, See-Ever See **See-Ewer**

See-Ewer *Germany, NW:* **Coaster*** that worked out of the Elbe Estuary and the west coast of Schleswig-Holstein ports during the 18th-19th centuries. The **Ostsee-Ewer** traveled to Baltic ports. Largest of the **Ewer*** family; beamier, deeper, and more strongly built than other **Ewern** (pl.). Strong sheer, high bulwarks, transom stern, curved stem, bilge keels. Outboard rudder; tiller; leeboards. Decked; quarterdeck; small hatch; accommodations aft. **Ketch***- or **cutter***-rigged; 2-3 headsails to a fixed bowsprit. Early vessels had fixed topmasts, square foresail, topsail, and topgallant. Crew of 2-4. Reported lengths 15-21m; Length-to-beam ratio 2.3-3:1. Other recorded names: **See-Eeber, See-Ever, Oostzee-ever, Ostsee-Ever**

Seefischer-Ewer See **Ewer**

Seehundfänger, Seehundsfänger See **sealer**

Seelandische Schouw See **Zeeuwse schouw**
Seelenverkäufer See **cockleshell**
see pei See **diao ting**
Seeplätte See **Plätte-1**
Seequatze See **Quatze**
Seeschlup See **Schlup-2**
Seeschiff See **sea boat-2**
sefina, sefinâh See **safina**
sefine *Turkey:* Generic term for a **ship***. One that sails may be called a **sefinesi**. Spelling variants: pl. **sefineler, sufun**. Note also **safina**.
sefîne See **mahaila-2**
sefîne ğajjārīyeh See **qaiyarīyah**
sefineler See **sefine**
sefinen See **mahaila-2**
sefinesi See **sefine**
sefyné See **safina**
segelbåt, Segelboot See **sailboat**
Segelfahrzeug, segelfartyg See **sailer**
segeljulle See **bohusjulle, jolle-7**
segelkanot See **kanot-4**
Segellogger See **logger**
Segelschiff See **sailer**
Segelschlitten See **iceboat**
Segelschute See **Schute-4**
segelskuta See **skuta-4**
segelsnipa See **snipa**
segelsump *Finland, W/Sweden, E:* Transported live fish from the Åland Islands to Stockholm; Åland-built boats also worked out from the Stockholms Stårgård (archipelago). Fish well in after end, cabin forward. Deck over the well lower than the forward deck; stern weighted with large stones to make it lie lower in the water. Clinker-built; double-ended; curved stem; long tiller extended over the well to cockpit aft of the cabin. Set a loose-footed, boomed gaff sail, 1-2 headsails, and sometimes a topsail. Early boats set a square sail to a raking mast. Reported lengths 5.4-13.4m; e.g., length 9.2m, beam 3.8m. Other recorded names: **Ålands sumpar, resesump, somp*, sump***. Note also **ålandsskuta, roddsump, sumpjolle**.
seglare, segler, seglskip, seglskute See **sailer**
Seilbuche See **Mutzen-2**
seiler See **sailer**
Seilfähre See **ferryboat-1**
seiljagte See **sjekte**
Seilmutte See **Mutte**
Seilmutzen, Seilplätte See **Mutzen-2**
sein attau See **sein efief**
seine boat **1a.** Generic term for any craft that catches such fish as mackerel, menhaden, herring, salmon, or tuna, with the small-mesh seine net. Some work a seine net with a weir. Nowadays, **seiners** may also troll, using longlines or gill nets. Other recorded names: **cerador, cerquero, not-og-vodfartøj, peschereccio per sciabica, pesquero al cerco, seine netter, Seinerboot, seine skiff*, seining vessel, (bateau) senneur, seyner, vaartuig voor zegenvisserij, Wadenboot*, Wadenfischer(eiboot), youyou de senne, zegenvisserijvaartuig**. Note also **hajer, net boat**. **b.** Vessel that lays out a vertical purse seine (or ring net) in a circle may be specifically called a **purse**

seiner. Net is drawn together at the bottom to entrap the fish. Other recorded names: **brod plivaričar, buque de pesca al cerco de jareta, cerquero, mrežarica, notfartøj, peschereccio a cianciolo, purse boat, purse-seine boat, Ringwadenfischer (kutter** or **logger), senneur a senne couilissante**. Note also **skiff-8a**.
2. *Canada:* **a.** Open, transom-sterned boat that tends fish traps, notably in St. Margarets Bay on the southeast coast of Nova Scotia. Lapstrake construction, curved stem; raked, wineglass transom; high sheer. Originally rowed, now motorized. Length 8.5m, depth 2.4m. **b.** Seined for cod, herring, and capelin on St. John's and other bays along the Newfoundland coast. Heavily built with carvel planking of pine; moderate sheer; keel; convex floors; rounded bilges. Moderately sharp bow, curved stem; slightly raked V-transom. Open except for a platform forward and a small one aft for helmsman; 2 thwarts forward, one aft; partly ceiled. Rowed with 6 pairs of oars, double-banked; helmsman used a steering oar. Length 9.6m, beam 2.3m, depth 0.7m. Name variant: **St. John's seine boat**. Note also **seine skiff. c.** In British Columbia, on the Pacific coast, **seiners** now use a hydraulically powered drum, on a raised table at the stern, to set and haul purse seine nets. Prior to the early 1900s, nets hauled by hand, then either by winch or on rollers. Early **drum seiners** were rather unstable because of concentrated weight aft and were used mainly for inside fishing; now modified. **Drum seiner** lengths ca. 13-16m, widths 4-4.5m. Name variant: **table seiner**
3. *England, SW:* **a.** Largest of a team of **rowing boats***, transporting and shooting the seine net used in pilchard fishing off the Cornwall and southwest Devon coasts. Worked from the Middle Ages until the early 20th century. Accompanied by 2-4 boats, their number and names varying with the locale. Form of the boat also varied with local needs and preferences. Mostly carvel-planked; generally open, but some had a cuddy forward; others used a canopy in poor weather. Generally sharp bow with maximum beam well aft. Stern sharp; rounded, flat, or square tuck. Net, as much as 3t in weight, housed in area of maximum beam. Some had an ironbound stem and keel to protect against rocky bottoms and beaching. Usually tarred black, often with colorful symbols to denote ownership. Long oars used, mostly worked against tholepins, but at Sennen, oar ports were cut into the bulwarks. Crew of 5-8. Reported lengths 9.14-12.19m, widths 2.74-3.66m, depths 1.09-1.22m. Other recorded names: **pilchard seine boat, sayn boat, sean boat, seine-net boat, seining boat, stop seiner**. Note also **cock boat, dipper, drag-in seine boat, follower, lurker, scath-ros, tuck-net boat. b.** In southwestern Devon, the crab fisheries used 2- and 4-man **seine boats** to catch fish suitable for bait in crab pots or for baiting longlines that caught bait for the pots. Four-man boat rowed by 3 men, the 4th shooting the net.
4. *Ireland, SW:* Large boat, pulling ca. 12 oars, that worked into the 19th century, shooting a seine net to catch pilchard. Teamed with the smaller **follower** (see **follower-3**).

5. *United States, E:* **a.** Strongly built **seine boats** were developed for the mackerel and menhaden industries in the mid-19th century and worked into the 1930s, primarily off New England and the mid-Atlantic coast. Special **seine** (or **purse**) **boats**, working in pairs, still support the now motorized **menhaden boats***. In New England, generally towed behind a **schooner*** (generally known as a **seiner**) to fishing grounds; elsewhere, they were often carried aboard the **menhaden boats**. Initially lapstrake; then smooth, battened seams. Originally square-ended; later sharp ends, the bow sharper; full buttocks to support the long, heavy net carried in the after part; curved stem and sternpost, stern higher than the bow. Raised garboard until 1881, then smooth; those on Chesapeake Bay sheathed. Platform at bow for the crew who hauled the cork line and one at the stern for the helmsman; floored; 4 thwarts. Small engine helped haul in the seine. Usually towed a **dory*** that held one end of the net while the net was being set. Generally, bottom green or blue to just above the waterline, white above. Rowed using 7-9 long oars, single-banked. Steered with a long sweep. In addition to rowers, crew of 3 required to shoot the net, plus the captain. Some had a gasoline engine. Reported lengths 8.5-11.6m; e.g., length 10.4m, beam 2.26m, depth 0.84m. The present-day **purse boats** on the Chesapeake are constructed of aluminum, average 12m long, 3.6m wide, and 0.76m deep. The one carried on the starboard side of a **menhaden boat** is called the **big boat**; the one on the port side is the **little boat***, even though they are the same size. Diesel powered. Note also **sail gear, striker boat. b.** The shad **seine boat** of the Delaware River was used to lay the net in a semicircle from shore; other boats in the operation were the **lookout boat** and the **lay boat***. Lapstrake or carvel-planked; flat bottom with skeg at stern. Long, sharp bow with slightly curved stem; square stern. Roller at stern used in playing out the net. Rowed double-banked with 7-9 oarsmen per side. Reported lengths 9-18m, widths 2.4-3.7m. Other recorded names: **shad flat, shad hall** (or **haul**), **weir haul**. Note also **shad galley. c.** The Long Island Sound **fleet*** was composed of 4 boats: the **seineboat**, the **mate boat***, and 2 **carry-away boats***. These boats all set a single gaff sail. Note also **menhaden carry-away boat, sail gear.**

6. *United States, Pacific coast and Alaska:* Used in the salmon, sardine, and mackerel fisheries. The mackerel boats of southern California used a purse seine or ring net. Open; flat bottom with rocker, sharp bow, square stern, moderate sheer. Net stowed on aft deck. Rowed by 2-6 men. Length 7.6m, beam 2m; shallow draft. Modern, powered **seine boats** to 30m long and crewed by 5-6. Name variant: **salmon seine boat**. Note also **scow-11i.** Further references: **menhaden boat, menhaden carry-away boat, notbåt**

sein efief *Micronesia (Caroline Islands), western Pacific:* Single-**outrigger canoe*** used for lagoon fishing in the Truk group. Dugout hull, generally adzed from a breadfruit log; double-ended; residual barb just above the waterline at each end; rounded "V" in cross section with a slight keel projection. Ends overhang, terminating in a low elevation; earlier, taller, tapered end pieces lashed on; often decorated with cording. Closely spaced thwarts lashed across the gunwales; amidships, the raised gunwales provide recessed areas for the booms. Two squared booms, braced with cross- and longitudinal stringers, extend to the short, tapered float; 2 pairs of angled stanchions, driven into and lashed to the float, secure the booms. Outrigger kept on the lee side. Hull generally painted black; stanchions often carved. Paddled; lanceolate-shaped blade. Small boats employ crew of 1-2, larger 5-6. Reported lengths 2.4-9.2m. Name variants: **sein attau, wa***. Further reading: Frank M. LeBar, *The Material Culture of Truk*, University Publications in Anthropology, No. 68 (New Haven: Yale University Press, 1964): 130-145. Note also **sein maun, wa fötyn.**

seine-net boat See **phang chun, seine boat-3**
seine netter, seiner, Seinerboot See **seine boat-1**
seine skiff 1. *Canada, E:* In Newfoundland, large, open boat that works with seine nets. Sharp bow, square stern. Rowed with as many as 8 very large oars. Note also **seine boat-2.**
2. *United States, W:* Carried aboard **tuna boats*** and used to pull the long, heavy purse seine. Diesel engine. Length 7.3m, beam 3.7m, draft 1.5m. Further references: **Saint Margarets Bay skiff, seine boat-2b**
seining boat See **seine boat-3**
seining vessel See **seine boat-1**
sein kittir See **sein maun**
sein maun *Micronesia (Caroline Islands), western Pacific:* Single-outrigger, paddling **canoe*** of the Truk group used for ceremonial purposes, racing, and warfare. Construction similar to the **sein efief*** except for the addition of washstrakes amidships and tall, stylized bird figureheads at each end. Both washstrakes and figureheads sewn on. Further decoration of young coconut palm leaves was strung along the gunwales. Could carry ca. 20 men. Paddled single-banked. Reported lengths 12-15m. Name variant: **sein kittir.** Note also **wa fötyn.**
Seitenboote See **davit craft**
Seitentrawler See **trawler**
sejlbåd See **sailboat**
sejler, sejlskib See **sailer**
Sekani canoe See **kayak-form canoe**
seki bune *Japan:* **1.** Used for ferry work across Shimonoseki Strait between southwestern Honshu and Kyushu. May be translated as **straits ship**. By the 14th century, they were well-designed and strongly built, finding favor with pirates. Employed 35-60 oars.
2. Oared naval vessel that probably operated into the 19th century. The larger size, with 40 or more oars, went by the term **seki bune** (**guard ship***), while the smaller were called **kobaya**. The **seki bune** had an upper deck, and in the 14th century, they had a tall stern, earning the name **taka ō bune** (**high-tailed ship**). The crew of a 20-oar scouting **kobaya** was 20 rowers, 1 helmsman, 6 armed men; on a 58-oar **seki bune**, there were 58 rowers, 1 helmsman, 1 captain, and 53 armed men. Rowed standing, facing forward.

sekochi   **1.** Malay term for a boat or vessel with a European-design hull, particularly one with stem and sternpost that join the keel at an angle. In many dialects, the word refers broadly to a boat that is rowed. Most double-ended with long, straight keel; straight, raked ends; stern or quarter rudders. Ribs and floor frames alternate or may be continuous. Usually decked. Sometimes likened to a ship's **cutter*** or **gig***. The rig depended on the district or the nationality of the owner, mainly **sloop*** or **cutter**, but early descriptions include lug- and square sails. In Sulawesi (Celebes), a present-day lateen-rigged craft with a western hull is called a **sekochi**, while the same hull carrying a gaff or gunter sail may be a **lambo***.
  2. *Indonesia, central:* The fishing **sekochi** of southwestern Sulawesi has deep, curved stem and sternpost terminating in a point. Wooden structure over the hold has inward-sloping sides and a flat roof; outboard, on each side, a framework holds fish traps. Firebox set on the roof. Decked; overhanging poop. Quarter rudder. Hull dark blue or green; white top strake, with narrow band of color between. **Sloop**-rigged; boomed gaff mainsail; mast in tabernacle. Large, boomed foresail extended forward by a tripartite spar.
  3. *Indonesia, E:* **a.** On Flores and in the Lesser Sunda Islands, the **sekochi** of the 1930s was a transom-sterned boat that worked along the coast, using paddles in calms or setting a sprit- or gaff sail and jib. Reported lengths 4-6m. **b.** At Ternate on western Halmahera, the **sekochi** provides local transportation. Sharp ends, vertical sternpost, ribs and floor timbers alternate, platform extends out over stern quarter. Open with thwarts for seats; midline rudder hung on gudgeons and pintles. Sets a gunter mainsail; large foresail. Reported lengths 9-12m, beam 2m, depth 1.0m.
  4. *Indonesia/Malaysia:* The 19th-century **sekochi** of the Strait of Malacca, between Malaysia and Sumatra, was a Chinese-operated trader. Double-ended, but the

sekochi-4

deep sheer strake was elongated at the bow and extended aft to form quarter galleries and a square counter stern. House in after part. Two tall masts set palm-leaf lugsails. Length 15m, beam 4.6m, depth 1.2m, cap. 27t.
  5. *Peninsular Malaysia:* **a.** Small, plain, European-type boat that has become increasingly popular along the east coast. Used mainly for fishing; large types serve as **fish carriers***; also used as a **ship's boat***. Ends

low and raked, stem slightly rounded, stern straight. Sheer increases along the coast to Kaula Trengganu, then decreases farther northward. Steered with a rudder, either with lines or a tiller; tall rudderhead. Some have short spar rests of an abstract design. Sets mainly a single high-cut lugsail. Mast stepped well forward. Small boats used for line fishing have a crew of 2-3; large types working with nets require a crew of 8-10. Reported lengths 5-16m, narrow. **b.** Chinese boat that mainly transported firewood from Malacca to Singapore. Double-ended; straight keel, nearly vertical stem and sternpost. Stern gallery. Chinese-style rudder. Two masts, each setting a large, high-peaked, battened lugsail. Reported lengths 9-12m. Name variant: **tongkang***
Other recorded names: **isikoeri, isikoet(j)i, iskoet(j)i, sakoesi, sakōtji, scocci, seckochi, sekoci, sekoetji, sekotchi, sekotji(e), sigosi, sikoet(j)i, sī kōsī kōtjī, sikot(j)i, sikuntji, skoe'oetè, skoesi, skoetji, skoitje, sko(t)chi, skotji, s'kuchi, soppé*** (so-called at one time in the Lesser Sunda Islands)

sekoci, sekoetji   See **sekochi**

sekong   *Indonesia, central:* Double-**outrigger canoe*** of the **jukung*** type used along the eastern part of the north coast of Java for fishing, transportation, and pleasure. Also found on Madura, Bali, and Lombok. Dugout hull; ends curved up from the bottom to massive, overhanging, decorative pieces; design varied but bow usually pointed, and stern swept up to a fanciful sort of fish tail. Tumble home to topsides; strong sheer toward the ends. Most open; decorative spar rest aft; quarter rudder. Floats set well forward and connected by 2 booms that crossed atop the gunwales. The forward booms curved down to attach to the end; a single stick, supplemented by lashing, connected the boom and float. Generally set a single triangular sail with the apex down; yard usually supported by a spar from the stern. Some employed a quadrilateral sail to a short mast. Crew of 2-5. Reported lengths 6.1-10.5m; e.g., length 6.6m, beam 0.8m, depth 0.4m, but proportions varied locally. Name variants: **prahoe sekong, soekoeng, sokong, sukung**

sekotchi, sekotji, sekotjie   See **sekochi**

seksæring   *Norway:* Term for a widely used, open boat rowed with 6 (*seks*) oars, by 3 rowers. Term may also designate a boat with a crew of 6, 4 rowing double-banked and 2 at the ends rowing single-banked. Some of the regional variations follow. Spelling variants: **seksæringen, seksäring, seksring, seksroring, sexæringer, sexring**; pl. **seksæringene, seksæringer**
  1. The **seksæring** that operated out of the Lista district (see **listerbåt**) was typical of those of the south and southeast coasts. Used by pilots (**losbåt***) and fishermen. Narrow clinker planking of oak; ribs of pine; caulked with tarred moss; strongly flared, rounded sides. Straight keel; moderate sheer aft, strong sheer forward. Stem and sternpost curved, the sternpost strongly raked; rabbeted. Maximum beam about a third forward, tapering to a sharp stern. Rudder follows the sternpost; downsloping tiller slotted over rudderhead. Oars worked in double tholepins. Light mast stepped through a thwart. Originally set a spritsail,

later a gaff sail; foresail to stemhead. 1850 boat 5.38m long, 1.8m wide, 0.58m deep.

2. The Hordaland area of the west coast developed a fast boat that became a popular pleasure craft, but initially served for fishing, transporting farm produce, travel, and often for carrying the mail (**postbåt**). Clinker-planked with only 3 strakes to the rounded, flared sides. Low sheer, greater aft. Sharp ends, slightly narrower toward the stern; curved stem and sternpost merged smoothly with the relatively short T-keel. Outboard rudder followed the sternpost; slender tiller. Sturdy mast stepped onto the keel; sprit-rigged by the early 19th century, probably a square sail earlier; foresail. Each of the 6 oars worked against a block (*keip*) and were held by an osier ring. Reported lengths 5.8-9.5m; e.g., length 5.8m, beam 1.8m, depth 0.45m; shallow draft. Those used in regattas are Bermuda-rigged, have a fin keel, and carry no ballast except the crew. Name variants: **trek(j)eiping**. Note also **Oselver**.

3. Those built in the Sunnfjord area on the west coast were also used at the islands off Sognefjord to the south. Some served the local police (**lensmannsbåt**). Clinker-planked; wide garboard strake; soft bilges, flaring sides; keel. Strongly curved stem; more elongated, curved sternpost; stern sharper than the bow. The 6 oars were worked against blocks and held by loops. Mid-19th-century boat 6.14m long, 1.68m wide, 0.63m deep.

4. The west coast, Nordfjord-built **seksæring** was popular to the south for offshore fishing, having greater freeboard and a fuller hull aft than those built locally. Also served as a general-purpose boat. Clinker-planked; sharp ends, curved stem and sternpost. Curved outboard rudder maneuvered by a right-angle tiller. The 3 pairs of oars worked against blocks and secured by loops. Mast stepped against a thwart, roughly amidships. Set a dipping lugsail. Reported lengths 5-6.94m; e.g., length 6.94m, beam 1.66m, depth 0.7m.

5. On the Sunnmøre (Sundmøre) coast, an 8-oared boat, which is an enlarged 6-oared boat, may retain the name **seksring**. A true 6-oared boat is more likely to be called a **treroring**★—one rowed by 3 oarsmen, each manning a pair of oars. In the 18th century, a **seksring** might be a **havbåt**★, with 5 pairs of oars. The 6-oared type was used mainly for fishing, sometimes traveling several kilometers out to sea. To achieve flexibility, designed with the maximum beam well forward, tapering to a slender stern; beam achieved by 2 extra strakes on each side, each being scarfed to a wide strake that continued aft. Two pairs of diagonal ribs and midship inwales helped provide strengthening; clinker-planked of pine. Curved stem and sternpost, the sternpost more elongated; keel; curved, flaring sides. Mast stepped through a thwart amidships, setting an asymmetric, dipping lugail. Oars worked against a block and held by a loop. Crew of 5. Inside lengths 7.74-8.7m, widths 2.3-2.96m, depth ca. 0.76m.

6. In the Åfjorden area, north of Trondheim, the fishermen using the **seksring** pulled 3 pairs of oars. Sharp ends, the stern sharper; tall stem plumb or had slight reverse curve at the top, straight or curved; sternpost straight and slightly raked. Clinker-planked; long, slender keel; soft turn of the bilges. Open; compartmented by thwarts in 3 "rooms"; one with a large middle room was a **stor-seksring** or a **små-halfjermeng**. Outboard rudder; right-angle arm to long, slender tiller. One with a bulkhead forward was a **kjempe-seksring** or **halvfjer-rømming**. Oar works against a natural-crook block. Square sail set to pole mast stepped just forward of amidships. Sail extended by bowlines to the tall stemhead. Reported lengths 5.6-7.3m, beam ca. 1.5m. Other recorded names: **åfjordsseksring, sækstreng, sekstring, sexring; kjæmp-sækstreng, kjemp-string**

7. The **seksæring** of the northern coast was also called a **trerømming**, having 3 compartments or "rooms." In the Lofoten Islands, however, this 6-oared boat might be called a **færing**★, the center room enlarged. Commonly used for traveling and fishing and sometimes by officials. Especially powerful under oars. Some motorized. Reported lengths 5-6.9m; e.g., length 6.9m, beam 1.5m. Further name variants: **seksring, tre-roms båt**★, **treroring**★. Note also **straumbåt**.
Further reference: **sexæringur**

seksæringen, seksæringene, seksæringer See **seksæring**

seksæringur *Denmark, Faroe Islands:* Seagoing boat rowed with 6 pairs of oars by 12 men, each manning a single oar. Transports merchandise and government officials between the islands and sometimes to the Shetland Islands. Clinker-built; sharp ends, deep keel. Outboard centerline rudder maneuvered by a single-arm yoke to the tiller. Open, but those now propelled by an inboard engine have a wheelhouse. Those sailing employ a square-cut, dipping lugsail. Mast stepped through the 1st thwart; if mizzenmast used, stepped through the after thwart, also setting a lugsail. Oar blades only a little wider than the shaft; flat piece on the shaft worked against a flat peg set into the gunwale, secured by a thong. Length ca. 8.8m. Spelling variants: **seksæring**★, **seksåringer, seksáringur, sexæingur**★. Note also **færøbåd**.

seksäret sjekte See **sjekte**

seksäring See **seksæring**

seksåringer, seksáringur See **seksæringur**

sekskeiping *Norway, west-central:* Large, open boat equipped with 6 pairs of shaped oarlocks (*keipar*); found in the Vestlandet region. Frequently built as a **church boat**★ (see **kirkebåt**). Clinker-planked; rounded, flaring sides; sharp ends. Also sailed, setting a trapezoidal square sail. Length ca. 9m, Length-to-beam ratio ranges from 1-1.42:1.

seksmandsfar See **seksmannafar**

seksmannafar *Denmark, Faroe Islands:* A six-man, open boat of these North Atlantic islands. Used as a general-purpose boat and for summer handline fishing. Clinker-planked; sharp ends, curved stem and sternpost; keel; 4 thwarts. When sailed, ships an outboard rudder. Mainly rowed with 3-4 pairs of oars. When 3 pairs used, each man rows with a single pair; with 4 pairs, the men on the forward and after thwarts each handle a pair, the other 4 men sit 2 to a thwart and row with a single oar. May also sail, setting a dipping lugsail to a single mast stepped through a thwart. Reported lengths 6-8m. Spelling variants: **seksmandsfar, sexmannafar**. Note also **færobåd, seksæringur**.

seksring See **firroring-2**, **seksæring**

seksroing See **seksroring**, **torskegarnsbåt**

seks-roms båt *Norway:* Large, open boat compartmented into 6 rowing spaces (*roms*) by 7 thwarts.

seksroring *Norway:* Boat rowed with 6 (*seks*) oars; used mainly in line fishing. Relatively narrow for its length. Name variants: **seksroing**, **seksrøring**; dim. **småseksroring**. Note also **fembøring-2**, **seksæring**.

sekstring See **seksæring-6**

selander, sélandre, selandro See **chelandia**

self-dumping barge See **dump barge**

Selong boat See **kabang**

seloup See **sloop-7**

Selsey galley *England, S:* Built to service sailing ships anchored off the protected east side of Selsey Bill. Worked until World War I. Clinker-planked; sharp ends; straight, plumb sternpost. Open; outboard rudder. Rowed with 11 pairs of oars, double-banked; oar ports slotted into gunwale strakes. Set 1-2 lugsails, but might also carry a spritsail. Length 12m, narrow.

semacco See **smack-1**

semale See **smack-1**, **smalschip**

semale-schip See **smalschip**

semalo See **smack-1**

séman See **perahu séman**

semaque See **sloop-7**, **smack-1**, **smak**

sembuk See **sambūq**

semi-dory *United States:* Small, open, flat-bottomed **rowing boat**★. General workboat, but also used for lobstering in New England. Sharp bow; slightly curved, raked stem; wide, raked transom. Narrow, flat bottom; skeg or curved bottom aft; soft turn of the bilges into flaring sides. Maximum beam often abaft amidships. Some modified to sail or to take an outboard motor. Reported lengths 3.7-5m; e.g., length 3.7m, beam 1.3m, depth 0.4m. Name variant: **half dory**

semi-deck boat See **Tancook schooner**

semi-knockabout See **knockabout-3**

Seminole canoe See **pith-lo**

semi-racer See **punt-7**

senale See **snow**

senau *Belgium/Netherlands:* Small, swift Flemish vessel of the 17th-18th centuries used mainly for privateering. Open, armed. Rowed and sailed. Lateen-rigged. Probably similar to, or the same as, the **barque longue**★. Carried 20-25 men. Vessels of this type used by Peter the Great for explorations. Spelling variants: **snauw, snouw**. See also **snow**.

senaut See **snow**

sendale tunisino See **sandal**

seneau See **snow**

sengoku-bune *Japan:* Term given in the Edo period (1600-1868) to a cumbersome cargo vessel of 100t disp. Used until ca. 1900. Suitable mainly for inland water areas, especially the Inland Sea. Sharp, elongated stem, sometimes curving at the top; high, open, square stern above a raking sternpost. Decked, usually removable; cabin amidships; some flush-decked. Huge rudder; very long, downsloping tiller; helmsman located below deck, directed by 2 crewmen. A fore winch unstepped the mast; an after winch lowered and raised the rudder. The heavy mast set a tall square sail.

Might also set a very small, rectangular sail in the bow and a large staysail. Also rowed. Crew of 8-14. Reported lengths 18.5-40m; length of 1992 replicas 18.5m, beam 5.75m. Name variants: **be(n)zaisen**

Sennen Cove crabber See **West Country crabber**

senneur, senneur à senne couillissante See **seine boat-1**

sentaine See **sentine**

sentine *France:* Reported as a small **fishing** or **passage boat**★ on the Loire River. Word also designated a **salt boat**★. Spelling variants: **centine, santenne, sentaine**

sentine de moulin See **moulin-bateau**

sE'qEm See **West Coast canoe**

sequelouppe See **sloop-7**

séreur See **charoi**

seringee See **saranga**

šerk *Albania, N:* Goatskin **raft**★ used for ferrying on the Drin River. A platform of interlaced sticks secured the inflated skins. Usually guided by a swimmer supported by a single skin, a **ršek**. A 4-skin **raft** would be ca 1.5m long and 1.2m wide, cap. 100kg. Spelling variant: **širć**

serme See **djerme**

sernai See **sarnái**

seró *Myanmar (Burma):* Small, fast, paddling boat, especially of Pegu, northeast of Yangon (Rangoon). Spelling variant: **seroo**

seroo See **seró**

serpent boat See **long chuan**, **pambán-manché**

serreur See **charoi**

service barge See **barge-2**

service cutter See **cutter-8**

Sese canoe See **sesse**

sesse *Uganda:* Sewn, plank-extended dugout of the northern shore of Lake Victoria and of Lake Albert. Originally a craft for war and piracy, having been fitted with a ram extension of the keel; later, and when on peaceful missions, a false prow was fitted to the ram, curving up at the same angle as the stem. A cord strung between the end and the stemhead supported feathers, cloth, leaves, etc. The peacetime prow might also be topped with horns or a bird's head. Dugout

sesse

base V-shaped or rounded and to this, 1-2 strakes were added to each side, each slotted into the stem and sternpost; strakes usually in 2-3 pieces. Strakes also slotted for the thwarts, which extended out through the sides; the wide forward thwart provided a handle for beaching. In some areas, small strips inserted under the lashings created a tighter binding; also caulked with fiber, or more recently, with inner tube rubber and tin flashing. Outside might be smeared with red clay. Paddled by 24-30 men with short, stout, spear-shaped paddles, and poled. Reported as long as 24m, but mostly ca. 6-9m; ram ca. 1.0m long. Other recorded names: **Sese canoe**, **Uganda canoe**

setea See **saettia**

sétie See **shẹtêya**

set-up battery See **sinkbox**

setye See **saettia**

seume See **zaima**

seunat See **tongkang-2**

Severn punt See **salmon punt-2**

Severn trow See **trow-1**

Severn wherry *England, W:* Small, 2-man boat for transporting passengers and small loads on the River Severn. Mainly rowed, but also sailed, probably setting a spritsail.

sewche See **zig**

sexærdr See **sexæringur**

sexæring See **sixareen, tristur**

sexæringar See **sexæringur**

sexaeringer See **seksæring, sixareen**

sexæringur *Iceland:* A boat employing 3 pairs of oars. Well established by the 18th century. Used mainly for fishing. Clinker-planked; sharp ends, straight keel. Rudder; tiller. Oars worked between double tholepins. Trapezoidal sail from a yard set to a mast stepped roughly amidships. Average length 7.25m, beam 1.88m. The type from Engey on the southwest coast, the **Engeyjarsexæringur**, has straight, raking stem and sternpost; sets 2 spritsails, staysail, and a jib to a short bowsprit. Other recorded names: **seksæring★, sexærdr, sexaringr, sex manna far★**; pl. **sexæringar**. Note also **seksæringur, sixareen**. Further reference: **seksæringur**

sexaringr See **sexæringur**

sexern See **sixareen**

sex manna far *Iceland:* Small, open, 6-man boat mainly of the northern coast. Dates at least to the early 19th century. Clinker-planked; sharp, strongly curved stem and sternpost. Rowed and sailed, but considered a poor sailer in open waters. Set a trapezoidal sail with a wide foot, hung from a short yard. Spelling variant: **sex manna för**. Note also **sexsæringur**.

sexmannafar See **seksmannafar**

sex manna för See **sex manna far**

sexring See **seksæring, seksæring-6**

seyner See **seine boat-1**

sghiffo See **skiff**

sgoth *Scotland, W:* Gaelic term for **skiff★**. In the Hebrides, they are small, open **fishing boats★** that were most numerous in the late 19th century; virtually extinct. Clinker-planked with alternating ribs and floor frames. Sharp ends, stern somewhat fuller; raked stem with curved forefoot; strongly raked, straight sternpost. Long, straight keel; S-curve to steeply rising floors; sides flare. Outboard rudder; short tiller; short bilge keels. Sand and shingle ballast in bags, dumped before beaching. Aft-raking mast stepped through a thwart; mast struck forward while fishing. Carries a dipping lugsail tacked to stemhead, sometimes a jib. Rowed, with up to 6 oars, while setting the longlines. Crew of 6. Reported lengths on keel 4.3-9m; e.g., length on keel 9m, beam 3.35m, depths 1.3-1.4m. Other recorded names: **eithrichean mora, Isle of Lewis, Ness**, and **Outer Isle sgoth, scoth, sgoth niseach**

sgoth Eireannaich See **drontheim**

sgoth niseach See **sgoth**

shabbâra See **zauraq-2**

sha-chhuan, sha chuan See **Kiangsu trader**

shad'anga See **saranga**

shad battery *United States, E:* On the lower Susquehanna River off upper Chesapeake Bay, the shad industry used a **shad battery** to assist in handling nets. Basically a large log **raft★**. Held a cabin for the crew and large reels for the nets.

shad boat *United States, SE:* Used on rivers from northern Florida to South Carolina for spring shad fishing in the latter part of the 19th century. Probably modified from the boats brought from Connecticut each year; in the 1880s, the **shad boats** formed a racing class in regattas at Savannah, Georgia. Open, probably V-bottomed; centerboard. Sprit-rigged with portable mast. Reported lengths 4.6-6.1m. See also **Bay of Fundy shad boat, gilling skiff, Hudson River shad boat, North Carolina shad boat**.

Shade's ark See **ark-2a**

shad flat See **seine boat-5b**

shad galley *United States, E:* Used in the late 19th and early 20th centuries to seine for shad on tributary rivers of Chesapeake Bay, especially the Potomac and Susquehanna. Open; sharp bow with curved, raked stem; wide transom, raked but sternpost vertical. Long, straight keel with slight drag; rounded bilges; little sheer. Braced longitudinally to prevent hogging. No thwarts in after part where nets were carried; some had a platform aft for the nets and a roller on the transom for playing them out. A short mast held a lamp for night fishing. Rowed using 8-26 oars, mostly double-banked. Seine pulled ashore by horses. Reported lengths 12.2-24.4m; e.g., length 22m, beam 3.66m, depth 1.14m. Other recorded names: **drag-seine galley, lookout boat, Potomac River shad seine-boat**. Note also **seine boat-5b**.

shad hall, shad haul See **seine boat-5b**

shadron See **jolly boat-4b**

shad skiff See **Choptank River shad skiff, gilling skiff, Hudson River shad boat**

shahoof See **shahuf**

shahtur See **šaḥtūr**

shahuf *Oman, NE:* Small, open **fishing boat★** of the Al Bāṭinah coast, where it is known as a **shahuf** south of Majīs, a **baggarah** or **zaima★** near Muscat, and a **zaruq★** near the Strait of Hormuz. Fishes mainly with a beach seine for sardine and anchovy. Sharp bow with a long, straight, raking stem, terminating in a carved and decorated stemhead. Sharp stern with a wide, multipiece sternpost that sweeps up in a truncated head; gunwale strake may extend aft of the sternpost. Short keel angles up toward the stern; maximum beam abaft amidships; low sheer; stem and sternpost may be sewn on. Narrow balanced rudder extends well below the keel and terminates at the top in a point; controlled by lines from a peg on the outer edge of the rudder blade. Decked. Mainly rowed using as many as 28 oarsmen. When sailed, sets a lateen sail to a slightly forward-raking mast. Reported lengths 7.6-10.7m. Spelling variant: **shahoof**

shaika See **saique**

shaikŭ *Bulgaria:* Generic term for a small **rowing boat★**. May also be a military craft for river use. Spelling variants: **chaïke, chaikŭ, shajka, shajtja**. Note also **saique-1**.

shajka, **shajtja** See **shaikǔ**

shakhtoura See **shakhtura**

shakhtur See **šaḥṭūr**, **shakhtura**

shakhtura *Mediterranean, E:* Trading **schooner*** of the Levant coast; some Egyptian. Probably a few still sailing, but with reduced rig and equipped with auxiliaries. Carvel-planked; strong sheer. Generally concave stem; full, flaring bows; mostly raked transom stern; some early vessels had elliptical counters; sternpost comes up outside the transom. Decked; anchor deck at rail level forward, main hatch amidships, deckhouse aft, open railing around the stern, boom crutch at stern, weathercloths common. Generally painted white. Two pole masts, about the same height, raked slightly aft; foremast stepped well forward. Most use leg-of-mutton sails, although some Turkish vessels gaff-rigged; main boom extends out over the stern for half its length; loose-footed foresail, but when sails are set winged out, a spar extends foot of foresail. Exceptionally long bowsprit and jibboom; 3-4 headsails. Crew of ca. 4. Reported lengths 16-30m; e.g., length 16.7m, beam 4.6m, draft light 1.8m. Other recorded names: **caique*** (at Arwad Island [Rouad]), **kolet** (by the Turkish), **Lebanese schooner**, **Levant schooner**, **shakhtoura**, **shakhṭūr**, **sharaka** (by the Egyptians), **Syrian schooner**

shāl See **sal-1**

shalanda 1. In Russian, a **barge***, **lighter***, **wherry***, or **dredger***.

    2. *Russia:* A small, sailing **fishing boat*** with a centerboard.

    3. *Ukraine, SE:* Dialect word for a flat-bottomed **riverboat*** or **ferry*** at Zhdanov on the Sea of Azov off the northern part of the Black Sea. Spelling variant: **šalanda**. Note also **chaland**, **chelandia**.

Further reference: **hopper-1**

shalandi, **shalandiyyat** See **chelandia**

shalloop See **shallop**

shallop 1. An open, 2-masted boat that became common in the 17th century, although reported in the 16th century. Extant in isolated areas. Small foremast, taller mainmast, being **schooner***-rigged without the bowsprit in America, but with a bowsprit and jib in England. Short gaff sails set to both masts, the mainsail loose-footed but boomed; short gaffs. Later boats often single-masted, lug-rigged, sometimes sprit-rigged. Clinker- or carvel-planked or a combination; rounded or flat bottom; T- or plank keel. Most square-sterned; when sharp-sterned, may be called a **double shallop***. Some employed leeboards. Early boats served as **ship's boats*** or **tenders*** and were often carried partially knocked-down, to be assembled at the ship's destination; length ca. 8m. Frequently used by a sailing **man-of-war***; replaced by the larger **longboat***; also a popular fishing type. Often armed. Length roughly 10m, beam 2.8m, depth 1.0m. English **shallops** used for whaling off Greenland in the early 18th century required 6 men: harpooner, steersman, linesman, and 3 rowers. Vessels of 200t employed 4 **shallops**; 250t boats used 5; 300t boats needed 6; 450t boats required 7.

    2. A small, open boat used in shallow waters; may serve as a **dinghy***. Square ends. Rowed or sailed. Crew of 2.

    3. Term sometimes applied to single-masted craft hastily constructed from timbers of a wrecked vessel in order to search for help.

    4. *Canada, E:* One type was used in Newfoundland cod and seal fisheries during the 17th-19th centuries. Decked at the ends, cuddies below; open waist with movable deck boards. The 2 masts set lugsails prior to 1780, then spritsails. Also rowed, 3 oars on one side and a single, very long oar on the other. Crew of 3-5. Reported keel lengths 9-12m, beam ca. 3m. Name variant: **fishing shallop**. Note also **chaloupe-5**.

    5. *Canada, N:* **Shallops** also served the Hudson's Bay Company in the 17th century. These were double-ended and set a spritsail.

    6. *Canada, SE:* Popular inshore **fishing boat*** of the Maritime Provinces, especially in the 17th-18th centuries. Open boat, plumb stem, transom or sharp stern, strong sheer. Stepped 2 masts through thwarts; no standing rigging. Set gaff sails, the mainsail loose-footed but boomed; later boats added a bowsprit and jib. Crew of 3. Length ca. 9m, beamy, shallow draft. A type of **shallop** is still used on the south shore of the Gaspé Peninsula and around the Magdalen Islands in the Gulf of St. Lawrence. Loose-footed gaff sails; furled by lowering the gaff peak and wrapping the sail around the gaff and mast. Some have a short bowsprit. Modern, motorized craft use the **shallop** rig as auxiliary power. Note also **chaloupe-5**.

    7. *England, SE:* On the Thames, the **shallop** was a light rowing craft used to transport a few people. Oarsmen, often 4, rowed single-banked on benches forward of an awning set up to protect passengers; a royal **shallop** of the late 17th century was pulled by 10 oarsmen. Steered with lines to the rudder. Long and narrow.

    8. *United States:* **a.** Popular multipurpose boat of the colonists of New England, southern New Jersey, Chesapeake Bay, and the Potomac River, being among the first locally built craft in the early 17th century. Used until the early 1900s. Heavily constructed with clinker or carvel planking, rounded bottom and bilges, sharp or transom stern. Early boats used leeboards; might be steered with yoke and lines. Open or half-decked, some with a cuddy forward. Two masts of about equal height set square, lug-, or gaff sails with short gaffs; loose-footed with one or both sails boomed. New England boats of the 17th century were also single-masted, setting sprit mainsail and staysail. Also rowed. Crew of 5-14. Reported lengths 5-13m; e.g., length overall 12.8m, on keel 10.6m, beam 3.1m, depth 1.07m. **b.** **Shallops** are mentioned in Louisiana in the late 16th and early 17th centuries in the sense of boats of all kinds, including large **pirogues*** owned by the government. Some were probably of the **flatboat*** type. Note also **chaloupe-10**.

Other recorded names: **sallop**, **schal(l)op**, **schallup**, **shalloop**, **shallope**, **shallopp(e)**, **shalloup**, **shallupp**, **shalop**, **shalupe**, **shawlopp**, **shollup**, **two-mast boat***; erroneously **scallop**, **skallop**. Note also **chaloupe**, **chalupa-9b**, **sloop**. Further references: **chaloupe**, **Delaware River shallop**, **whaler-2**

shallope, **shallopp**, **shalloppe**, **shalloup** See **shallop**

shallow boat See **sha ting**

shallow water boat See **tan chuan**
shallupp, shalop, shalupe See **shallop**
shampan See **sampan-2**
shan ban See **sampan**
shangādam See **jangar**
Shanghai Harbor sampan See **hong tou san ban**
Shanghai ma tou chuan See **ma tou chuan**
shangla dingi See **dingi-2**
shan pan See **sampan**
shanty boat *United States:* **1.** Barge*-like craft used mainly by sport fishermen and hunters. A small house with basic living quarters is built on the rectangular hull. Generally towed to the site and anchored more or less permanently. Many that serve as permanent homes on rivers, lakes, and swamps of central United States are built and furnished from odds and ends, much of it flotsam taken from the rivers. One with only a minimal shelter is called a **doghouse**; often only a tin hut set on a **flatboat***.
2. In the Louisiana bayous, where they are generally called **campboats, chalands***, or **flatboats**, the craft serve mainly as permanent living quarters for moss gatherers, fishermen, and trappers; others house fish markets. Some now have numerous modern amenities. Those of the moss gatherers may be towed to the collecting sites during their week-long forays, but generally they are moored where convenient.
3. The **shanty boats** on New Jersey's Delaware and Raritan Canal between New Brunswick and Bordentown in the 19th century were workboats for the canal crews. **Shanty boats** on the Erie Canal were hovel-type **houseboats***anchored at wide places in the canal.
4. The waterman's **shanty boat** or **ark*** of eastern upper Chesapeake Bay served as living quarters for shad fishermen. The **shad boats*** were too small for adequate shelter, so a shanty, set on a **scow***, was towed to a suitable site and beached until the shad run was over. The one-room temporary home held the necessary amenities plus supplies and tools.
See also **flatboat-4, wanigan**.
shanty raft See **timber raft-2a**
Shaohing ch'uan See **Shaoxing chuan-1**
Shaohing wine boat See **Shaoxing chuan-2**
shao-hsing chhuan, shao-hsing ch'uan See **Shaoxing chuan-1**
shao ma yang *China, central:* Cargo carrier of the **ma yang zi*** family. Trades mainly between Yichang (I-ch'ang) and Shashi (Shasi) on the Chang Jiang (Yangtze). Square, raked ends with heavy transverse beam at the bow; beams cross the hull above the deck, but stop short of the sides, providing a walkway for the polers. Flat bottom; slightly curved sides strengthened on each side by 2 wales. Flat sheer forward, slight upturn at the stern. Fan-shaped balanced rudder; post comes up inboard. Divided house in after half; wood sides, mat roof. Poles of iron-tipped bamboo. Mast stepped just forward of the house, setting a battened balance lugsail. Length typically 30m, beam 5m, depth 2.3m; shallow draft.
shaoshing junk, shaosing See **Shaoxing chuan**
Shaoxing chuan *China, E:* **1.** Name given to traders that worked out of Shaoxing (Shaohsing), at one time on the southern shore of Hangzhou Wan (Hangchow Bay), south of Shanghai. Shaoxing is now inland, having been replaced by the port of Hangzhou (Hangchow). Sturdily built to handle the tidal bore in the bay; carried mainly firewood, coal, cotton, and sand to Shanghai. Identified by their flat, trapezoidal, raked bow that was painted with a stylized dragon's mask; U-shaped transom stern, quarters, and sides of the bow also decorated. Flat floors curved at ends, no keel, ends raked, side planking extended beyond the transom, joined at the top by a crossbar. Strong sheer. Rudder came up within the wings, resting in chocks and knees on the transom; suspended by a tackle pulling on the shoulder, enabling it to be raised and lowered; tiller. Ten bulkheads; longitudinal strength provided by 2 heavy wales. Leeboards 2.4-3m long. Cambered deck; high bulwarks; small deckhouse; some lacked a solid deck. **Sampan***towed or triced up on a quarter. "Stick-in-the-mud" anchors pierced the bottom of the hull. Usually 3 masts, the fore- and mainmasts supported by fore-and-aft props; foremast raked forward slightly; mizzenmast stepped against starboard bulwark. Set battened balance lugsails—high-peaked, set to starboard of the masts, aligned at the foot. Wind vanes on main- and mizzenmasts. Crew of 6-8. Reported lengths 18-30m; e.g., length 23m, beam 6m, hold depth 1.8-2.4m; shallow draft. Other recorded names: **Hangchow (Bay) trader, jonque de Hangtcheou, shaohing ch'uan, shao-hsing chhuan, shao-hsing ch'uan, shaoshing junk, shaosing**
2. Another **Shaoxing chuan** specialized in carrying rice wine from this important wine-making district to Shanghai markets in heavy jars. Boat strongly constructed with 4 bulkheads and 10 thick frames. Flat bottom with slight rocker toward the bow; rounded bilges; plumb sides above the wale. Forward cut square with tumble home, beyond which was a false, raking bow leading to a false stempost. Bottom at stern turned up to a small, hexagonal transom. Hatchet-shaped rudder hung 60cm below the bottom and was lifted vertically. Mat-roofed, open-sided house at the stern. Propelled by 3 straight *yulohs* (type of sculling oar), one at the stern, 2 forward, and by quants worked from platforms that extended outboard along the sides. When sailed, set a small sprit foresail at the bow and a gaff mainsail amidships. Crew of 6. Length 22m, beam 4.3m, depth 1.7m. Name variant: **Shaohing wine boat**
sha-pa ch'uan See **cha chuan**
shapats See **West Coast canoe**
sharaka See **shakhtura**
sharanga, sharenga See **saranga**
shark See **haiboot, hajer**
shark boat **1.** *Australia, SE:* Powered craft, out of Victoria since ca. 1927, that longlines for shark during autumn and winter and fishes for crayfish in summer. Sharp bow, cutaway forefoot; raked counter stern; high, slack bilges; moderate sheer; keel extends beyond propeller. Early boats undecked to mast; later, larger boats decked; small pilot house. Open wet well holds gutted sharks. Sets an auxiliary, boomed gaff sail and jib. Reported lengths 9-18m; length-to-beam ratio often 3:1.

2. *Mexico, W:* Fishes for shark offshore in area south of Mazatlán from December through early June. Mostly sturdy wooden vessels, although some are **dugout canoes***, fiberglass, or steel-hulled. The latter are referred to locally as **floating funerals** because they sink rapidly if broached, lacking flotation. Sharp, swept up, raked stem; square or sharp stern. Powered by an outboard motor or powerful diesel engine. Crew of 3. Length of larger wooden vessels ca. 9m, beam 3m.

3. *Seychelles:* So-called **shark schooner** fishes with longlines out from these Indian Ocean islands. Boats stay at sea ca. 10 days, the crew of ca. 6 gutting, cutting into strips, and salting the meat in the hold. Plumb stem, counter stern. Trunk cabin amidships. Variously rigged, commonly as a gaff **cutter***. Typically 11.6m long. Note also **schooner-3**.

shark schooner See **shark boat-3**

sharonga See **saranga**

sharp See **sharpie**

sharp-bowed skiff See **flatiron skiff**

sharpie *United States:* **1.** Elongated, flatiron-shaped boat used for fishing and local transportation. Developed in the mid-19th century, initially in New England, but the type became widespread with local variations. Popular because of the ease and cheapness of construction. Also a racing class, using a slightly modified hull and rig. An armed **sharpie** appeared in France in the 1880s. Carvel-planked topsides; bottom narrow and flat, planked athwartships; at stern, bottom curves up to above the waterline; some had a skeg. Hard chines; straight, flaring sides; low freeboard; moderate sheer. Sharp bow, plumb stem; square stern originally, later mostly rounded. Generally a centerboard; long, shallow balanced rudder came up inboard; tiller. Oval cockpit. One or 2 unstayed masts, setting mainly leg-of-mutton sails, extended by horizontal sprits. Foremast generally well forward. Small, single-masted boats often called **flatiron skiffs***. Good rowing qualities. Reported lengths 3.7-19.8m; bottom length-to-beam ratio ca. 4 or 6:1. Racing **sharpies** have a flatter run and greater beam than working boats; jib and hiking board common. Further reading: Howard I. Chapelle, *The Migration of an American Boat Type*, U.S. National Museum, Bulletin 228 (Washington, D.C.: Smithsonian Institution, 1961).

2. The **New Haven sharpie** was the progenitor of the **sharpie** type. Easily and cheaply built, developed especially for oyster tonging in the harbor and adjacent areas of this Connecticut town. Except for a revival as a pleasure craft, gone by the mid-20th century. Straight stem had a brass stemband; when light, heel cleared the water. Shallow counter stern; usually rounded, sometimes square. Originally open; later half-decked with wide side decks and low coaming. Balanced rudder could be raised and lowered according to water depth; iron rudderstock. Centerboard housed in long case. When tonging, anchored by means of 2 brass-tipped poles. The large, 2-masted boats had an additional step to permit sailing with a single mast; mainmast normally stepped all the way forward; masts could be rotated in steps. The leg-of-mutton sails were extended by a horizontal sprit from

the clew and held to the mast by a snotter; mainsail might have a small club at the clew. Also sculled or rowed. Crew of 1-2. Reported lengths 6-12m; e.g., length 10m, beam 1.75m, depth at stern 0.9m, at stem 0.3m. A rowing type ranged from 3.7-4.6m in length. Other recorded names: **one hundred (and fifty) bushel sharpie, one-man sharpie, two-man sharpie**; **Connecticut, Fair Haven, Long Island Sound, New England,** or **West Haven sharpie; New Haven flat-iron skiff**

3. The **sharpie** was developed in the 1870s on Chesapeake Bay and the lower Potomac River, mainly for oystering. When past their prime, the Potomac boats became **fish lighters**. Early boats had a flat bottom, but by the 1890s, were built with a low deadrise. Raked transom with skeg on which the rudder hung. A few sharp-sterned **sharpies** were built. Employed a daggerboard with a metal lifting handle or a centerboard. Those in the 7.3-10m range were half-decked; the smaller boats were open. Two unstayed masts were used in summer; in winter, a single mast was stepped through a center thwart. The leg-of-mutton sails were laced to the mast until the 1890s, then hooped. Reef bands parallelled the mast. Some had a club on the clew, and some used a jib to a short bowsprit. Reported lengths 4.8-10.7m; e.g., length 8.5m, beam 2.27m, depth 0.64m. Other recorded names: **Chesapeake Bay** or **Potomac sharpie, Maryland fishing sharpie**. Note also **flattie-4, Hooper Island crab skiff**.

4. Oyster tonging and fishing **sharpie** of the southern North Carolina bays dates from the 1870s; presently enjoying a revival as a pleasure craft. Sharp, plumb stem; stern fuller, rounded and occasionally square; no floor timbers. Balanced rudder; centerboard. Most half-decked with oval cockpit; some have a cuddy forward or both forward and aft. The Core Sound boats stepped 2 masts that set leg-of-mutton sails with long, vertical clubs and horizontal sprits or boomed gaff sails. Occasionally employed only a single mast to which a similar leg-of-mutton sail was set or else a boomed gaff sail and jib. Crew of 2. Reported lengths 4.5-15m; most 7.6-7.9m; pleasure craft 4.5-8m; shallow draft. Other recorded names: **Carolina, Carolina Sounds, Core Sound,** or **North Carolina sharpie; Albemarle Sound skiff**

5. The **sharpie** of South Florida and the Gulf Coast varied widely in size, rig, and hull features, but all were flat-bottomed, hard-chined, centerboard boats. Introduced in the 1880s. Slight tumble home to the straight stem; sharp, square, or rounded stern, generally raked; skeg; a few had fore gripes. The 2-masted **Presto ketch** had soft chines. Half-decked or open; some had a cabin; rudder hung out. Generally single-masted, stepped either in the bow with no headsails or **sloop***-rigged. The 2-masted boats set sprit- or leg-of-mutton sails. Some later boats motorized. Reported lengths 4.9-12.2m; e.g., length on gunwale 6.3m, beam 1.7m, depth 0.57m; shoal draft. Other recorded names: **Biscayne Bay** or **Cedar Keys sharpie, flattie***, **Florida sharpie**. Note also **skiff-12**.

6. The **sharpie yacht** of Lake Champlain in northeastern New York State was similar to the **New Haven**

sharpie. A few non-**yachts**★ were built to carry local products, but most were pleasure craft. Employed a wide range of rigging, some experimental.

7. On the upper St. Lawrence River, the **sharpie** had several forms; a few still in use, mainly as general workboats. One type has a sharp bow and boxy transom stern, both mildly raked; flat bottom, longitudinally planked, with slight rocker toward bow; sides vertical. Short deck at bow. Generally rowed. Reported lengths 3.4-4.9m; e.g., length 3.8m, beam 1.0m, depth 0.37m. Name variant: **Saint Lawrence sharpie**

8. The **pound net sharpie** became popular for tending pound nets on Lake Erie in the last quarter of the 19th century. Used elsewhere on the Great Lakes by commercial hunters and local traders. Built by the fishermen and varied in proportion and with local preferences. Carvel-planked, although sheer strake might be lapped; raked, square or rounded stern; raked, straight stem. Balanced rudder with rectangular blade forward and aft of the narrow rudderpost; others had a skeg and normal rudder; tiller slotted through rudderpost. Large

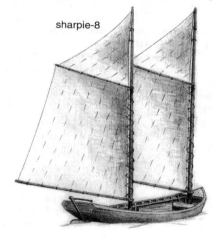

sharpie-8

centerboard. Open; generally 2 thwarts and stern sheets; in some communities, side decks were popular; a step might run along the side to facilitate handling the gear. Two tall, heavy, unstayed masts stepped into blocks that were spiked to the top of the keel members; raked aft to varying degrees; foremast in the eyes. Modified leg-of-mutton sails hooped or laced to the masts; used batten-like sprits set three-quarters up the mast; foremast loose-footed. Some small boats **sloop**-rigged. Reported lengths 6-12.8m; e.g., length 7.5m, beam 3m, depth amidships 0.9m. Other recorded names: **Erie**, **Great Lakes**, or **Ohio sharpie**; **Lake Erie** or **Ohio pound net sharpie**, **Ohio pound net boat**, **pound boat**★. Note also **pound net boat**.

9. **Sharpies** on Great South Bay of Long Island in New York State are merely flat-bottomed, sharp-bowed **rowboats**★. Some sailed, others powered. Reported lengths 3.7-5.5m.

10. The **sharpie** of the Truckee River in western Nevada had a square stern, a raised cabin between the masts, and an open area abaft the mizzen. Very tall mainmast; leg-of-mutton sails.

Spelling variants: **sharp**, **sharpy**. Further references: **batteau-3c**, **down-the-bay sharpie**, **Noank sharpie**, **nonpareil sharpie**, **North Carolina sail skiff**, **Sea Bright skiff**, **sharpie-launch**, **sharpie-schooner**, **sharpshooter-1**

sharpie-launch *United States:* Used mainly for fishing in protected waters of the east coast, the Mississippi River, and some parts of the Pacific coast. Flat bottom, planked athwartships, with rocker at stern; skeg above the propeller. Flared sides; sharp, plumb bow; square stern. Large cockpit. Outboard rudder; inboard engine. Lengths to ca. 15m; length of 1941 boat 6.3m, beam 1.8m, draft 0.43m. Name variant: **sharpie-skiff**★

sharpie rowboat See **flatiron skiff**

sharpie-schooner *United States:* **1.** Developed in the 1880s for oyster tonging and dredging in the coastal bays of North Carolina; served also as a carrier for supplies from the mainland to the barrier islands. Used until ca. 1938. Sharp lines; flat bottom, cross-planked, with rocker; plumb stem; rounded stern, some square. Decked; trunk cabins forward and/or aft; some had only a cuddy; U-shaped hatch; steering cockpit. Balanced rudder; centerboard. Masts raked slightly aft; fitted with boomed gaff sails; the foresail might be loose-footed. Jib, with club, run to bowsprit. Crew of 2-3. Reported lengths 12-15m; e.g., length 13m, beam 3m, depth 0.8m. Other recorded names: **Carolina sharpie-schooner**, **schooner-sharpie**

2. In Florida, served as a **yacht**★ in the 1880s but was taken over as a commercial vessel, carrying fish to market on the west coast and fishing for Spanish mackerel on the east coast. Generally straight, slightly raked stem; many clipper-bowed; raked transom, flat or rounded. Flat bottom, planked athwartships; strong fore-and-aft rocker; marked sheer. Decked; trunk cabins; centerboard. Most set gaff sails, others leg-of-mutton; generally carried a large jib. Reported lengths 15-18m; e.g., length 16.2m, beam 3.6m, depth 1.3m. Note also **sharpie-5**.

3. Popular in the late 19th century on Great South Bay on Long Island in New York State. Wet well created between 2 bulkheads at the ends of the hold with holes drilled into the hull. Name variant: **smack**★

4. In the northwest, used for halibut fishing on Puget Sound in the latter part of the 19th century. Double-ended; flat bottom with marked rocker forward; slightly curved stem; raked sternpost; strong sheer. Centerboard; outboard rudder; tiller. Heavily ballasted. Decked; cabin forward, cockpit on either side of mainmast, and steering well. Fitted with boomed gaff sails and a club-footed jib to the bowsprit. Length 11m, beam 2.7m, depth 0.9m. Other recorded names: **Juan de Fuca sharpie**, **schooner-sharpie**

Further reference: **terrapin smack**

sharpie-skiff *United States, SE:* **Tender**★ for **fishing boats**★ working out of Key West at the southern end of the Florida Keys. Carvel-planked of pine; flaring sides a single plank. Sharp bow; straight, vertical stem; square stern with external sternpost; flat bottom, transversely planked, with rocker toward the stern; long, deep skeg. Open; 2 thwarts. Rowed. Length 2.97m; beam amidships 0.97m, on bottom 0.6m; depth 0.43m.

Spelling variant: **sharpy skiff**. Further references:
North Carolina sail skiff, **sharpie-launch**

sharpie yacht See **sharpie-6**

sharps See **sharpshooter-1**

sharpshooter 1. *Bahamas:* Built originally at Eleuthera
Island in the 1850s to transport produce to Nassau;
also used for fishing. Now widely built and generally
known as a **bare-head smack**. Short, hollow entrance
from a straight or curved cutaway stem; raked transom
stern. Drag to keel; considerable deadrise; strong
sheer; tumble home to topsides; maximum beam forward of amidships. Planked-up deadwood; those built
at Nassau had a skeg. Rudder hung from sternpost,
worked with a tiller. Portable trunk cabin, generally
forward; no bulwarks aft. Mast stepped on stem knee
and raked sharply aft; mast vertical on current
smacks★. No shrouds or stays. Set a boomed, loose-
footed leg-of-mutton sail with a headboard; large
roach to the foot. Sail laced to the mast on small boats;
mast rings used on the larger boats. Sculled in calms.

sharpshooter-1

A few set a foresail to a long bowsprit. Reported
lengths 5.5-12.2m; e.g., length overall 7.4m, on keel
6.1m, beam 2.7m, draft aft 1.3m. Other recorded
names: **Bahama sloop**, **sharpie★**, **sharps**. Note also
smack boat.

2. *United States, NE:* Fast fishing **schooner★** out of
Gloucester, Massachusetts, that worked during the
mid-19th century. A large, commodious type worked
as a **banker★**, staying out on the fishing grounds and
salting down the catch. A shallower, faster type
worked closer inshore as a **market schooner★**, returning daily with the fish iced or in a wet well. Clipper
bow with raking stem; flared bow sharp on the waterline, rounded at the rail. Raked, boxy transom above a
sharp sternpost originally; later an elliptical stern
introduced; rudder stock went through the lower transom face. Slight to moderate deadrise, sharp turn of
the bilges, deep drag to keel, low freeboard. Decked;
low quarter-deck to just forward of the mast; cabin
trunk aft. Masts raked strongly aft. Gaff fore- and
mainsails, 1-2 headsails to heavy bowsprit, 1-2 topsails. Reported lengths 18-23m; beam ca. 30% of
length; hold depth 1.5-2.2m. Other recorded names:
clipper-schooner★, **file-bottom**

sharpy See **sharpie**

sharpy-skiff See **sharpie-skiff**

shartoush See **šaḥtūr**

shash See **shashah-1**

shasha See **shashah**

shashah 1. *Bahrain/Oman, NE/United Arab Emirates, E:*
Canoe★-shaped **reed boat★** still popular for fishing
along the Al Bāṭinah coast. Constructed of the ribs of
date palm leaves sewn together; originally with coir
cording, now nylon. Flat bottom; fairly plumb sides;
ends taper to a point. Reverse curve to the sheer, with
the ends lower than amidships. Deck created of palm
ribs and hogged amidships; low bulwarks; deck
secured by thwarts lashed on top. Cavity originally
filled with coconut bark fiber; now often of styrofoam.
This modification permits the craft to stay at sea
longer, and some now serve as **tenders★**, employed to
fish out from a **mother ship★** farther offshore. Mainly
rowed using long, slender oars worked against tall single tholepins; blades vary in shape regionally. Some
sail, employing a small, quadrilateral, lateen-type sail
with a short luff with a light yard set to a bipod mast.
Crew of 1-3. An outboard motor now fitted occasionally. Reported lengths 3-5.5m, widths 1.0m, depth ca.
0.6m. Spelling variants: **sasha**, **shash(a)**, **shashe**.
Note also **farteh**, **hurija**.

2. *Iraq, S:* Reed **canoe** of the Marsh Arabs. Sharp ends.
Other recorded names: **čiliče**, **šāše**, **Schasche**, **shasha**

shashe See **shashah-1**

Shasi trader See **hua zi-2**

shat See **cat-2**

sha teng See **sha ting**

sha ting *China, S:* **Water-taxi** of the Guangzhou
(Canton) area. Flat bottom, raked ends, transom stern,
high sheer at the stern. Arched mat cabin amidships
for passengers; interior profusely decorated; family
lives in stern section. Rowed, from the bow, by
women; sculled from the stern. Reported lengths 7-
8.5m; e.g., length 7.3m, beam 1.8m, draft ca. 0.25m.
Other recorded names: **Canton sampan**, **cha t'ing**,
sai ting, **sand boat★**, **sar teng**, **shallow boat**, **sha
teng**, **si t'ing**

shaṭṭī See **saettia-4**

shawlopp See **shallop**

shay See **Isles of Shoals boat**, **Joppa shay**

shchuna See **schooner**

shear hulk See **sheer hulk**

shebek *Russia, W:* The Russian version of the
Mediterranean **xebec★** was a heavy and rather clumsy
vessel of the late 18th century used in the Baltic Sea.
Higher sides and flatter sheer; characteristic ram beak;
counter stern. Armed with 32-50 guns. Rowed with ca.
40 oars, but mainly sailed. Rigged with a mixture of
lateen, square, and gaff sails; some set, in that order, on
the forward-raking foremast, mainmast, and mizzen;
also portrayed with 3 gaff sails and square sails. Length
37m, widths 9-10.4m, draft 2.6-3.5m. A **half shebek**
was 2-masted and also known as a **schooner★**,
although not so-rigged. Variously reported as lug-
sailed or carried a lateen on the foremast and a gaff sail
with square topsail on the mainmast. Length 23m,
beam 5.8m. Spelling variants: **chébéka**, **shebeka**

shebeka See **shebek**, **xebec**

she chuan *China, central:* Passenger and cargo craft of the Wu Jiang, a south branch of the upper Chang Jiang (Yangtze). Bow characteristically long, overhanging, and squared-off; stern turns up sharply to a point; bottom slightly concave and strengthened internally by 3 longitudinal planks; only 5 frames. Open except for arched mat house in central part. Propelled by 2 oars at the bow and one at the stern; steered with a long sweep; tracked upstream by a line from a towing mast stepped through a forward thwart. Crew of 5. Length 13.7m, beam 2m, depth 0.7m. Name variant: **snake boat**

shed *United States, central:* Crude type of Mississippi River **flatboat★**. Shallow, rectangular hull on which a flat-roofed house was built to provide shelter for the early settlers. Livestock housed outside. Name variant: **scow★**

sheepskin raft See **bi fa zi**

sheer hulk A **hulk★** or **pontoon★** modified or specifically designed for stepping or removing masts, or lifting heavy weights around a dockyard, by the use of sheerlegs on the beam. Other recorded names: **Bockkranhulk, Bockprahm, Bockschiff, Hulk mit Mastenkran, machina flotante, Mastenprahm, ponton-allège, ponton a biga, pontone-(à-)biga, ponton-bigue, ponton à mâter, ponton-mâture, shear hulk, sheer pontoon**. Note also **sheer vessel**.

sheer pontoon See **sheer hulk**

sheer vessel *United Kingdom:* Naval dockyard craft of the 18th and early 19th centuries built as a mobile crane, as opposed to a converted **hulk★** (see **sheer hulk**). Sheerlegs extended over the bow. Curved stem, counter stern; decked; heavy rubbing strake along sides. Set a loose-footed gaff sail, forestaysail. Also employed at least 2 sweeps. 1815 vessel 20m overall, 16m on keel, beam 6.2m.

Sheffield boat, Sheffield keel See **Humber keel**

Shelburne clipper dory *Canada, SE:* Popular in the Shelburne area of southern Nova Scotia for transportation, inshore fishing, and recreation. Sharp ends; curved internal stems with false external stems. Narrow, flat bottom with rocker; curved, flaring sides. Open; centerboard on those that sailed. Length ca. 5m, beam 1.5m.

Shelburne dory *Canada, SE:* Fishing **dory★** built mainly at Shelburne on the southern coast of Nova Scotia. Distinguished from other **dories** by the 2 galvanized metal clips riveted through each frame section where the bottom and sides meet. Flat bottom with rocker; straight, flaring sides. Sharp, raking bow; inside stem with false stem outside. Narrow, raked V-transom. Open; strong sheer; 3 thwarts set on stringers. Rowed, oars worked between double tholepins. Might have a sculling notch in transom. Boomed gaff sail set to mast stepped through the forward thwart; jib to stemhead. Length overall 4.5m, on bottom 4.3m. Note also **Shelburne clipper dory**.

shell Long and very narrow boat used for racing and exercise. Propelled either by long sculls or sweep oars, the distinction being made that sculls are pulled in pairs by the rowers while oars are pulled singly. However, the same boat may be converted from one type to the other, since all the boats are essentially the same and are modified to carry the desired load. In general, the smaller boats are for 1-2 persons (termed

sculls★), and the larger are rowed by 4-8; the larger usually have a coxswain seated aft to call the stroke and to steer. Some early boats were covered with paper or canvas; now generally of very thin cedar strips or synthetic materials. Early boats clinker-built, now smooth-skinned. Sharp ends, internal struts, no external keel after the mid-19th century. Oarlocks fitted into outriggers after the mid-1800s, the boats initially called **gigs★** (see **outrigger**); the oarlocks are paired on the **scull** and staggered on the oared boats. Most clinker-built boats had fixed seats; smooth-skinned boats had sliding seats. Seats arranged one behind the other, although on the earlier, wider **shells**, the seats were closer to the side opposite the outrigger (**snubby boat**), permitting the boat to be shorter. Early **shells** completely open and relatively wide; later decked at ends and very narrow. Other recorded names: **jole, Renn-Rudderboot, skeleton boat, sweep (boat)**. Note also **catraia-1, double scull, head boat, pair-oar, paper boat-2, rowing boat**.
1. The so-called **four** employs 4 oarsmen, usually with a coxswain; those without a coxswain generally shorter. Lengths 12-13.7m; e.g., length 12.85m, beam 0.53-0.8m, depth 0.18-0.23m. The heavier **clinker fours** ranged between 11.6-12.8m in length, 0.58-0.61m in width, and 0.20-0.23m in depth. Other recorded names: **four-oared outrigger** (or **shell**), **IV, quatre de pointe, quattro, racing four, Vierer, vierriemsgiek**.
2. The **eight** pulls 8 oars, with coxswain. Some early Oxford **eights** had a gangway down the middle to facilitate propelling the boat through locks. Lengths 13.7-20m; e.g., length 20m, beam 0.6m, depth 0.23-0.28m. The heavier **clinker eights** were 17-18m long, 0.61-0.69m wide, and 0.2-0.23m deep. Other recorded names: **Achter, achtriemsgiek, eight-oar, eight-oared outrigger** (or **shell**), **huit de pointe, otto, racing eight, Rennachter**
3. At times, **shells** have been rowed and raced with 6 persons, the **VI**.

shell boat *United States, E:* Carried oyster shells from Chesapeake Bay shucking houses to fertilizer factories in Baltimore, Maryland, or Alexandria, Virginia. Note also **monitor-2**. Further reference: **pirogue-6**

shell kicker *United States, NE:* Boat that used its propellor backwash to flush out oyster shells, which were used by oyster cultivators. Worked in Connecticut river mouths in the 1st half of the 20th century. Boat moored in such a way that it could pivot its stern from side to side to create mounds of shells. Various boat types used, including old **sandbaggers★**.

shen bo zi *China, west-central:* **1.** Lightly built, very shallow-draft vessel designed to negotiate the rapids on the Daling (Taling) in eastern Sichuan (Szechuan). Carried local products. Gone by 1930. Identified by its high, recurved stern formed by extensions of the gunwales, earning the name **fan-tail boat**. Sides tapered at bow and stern, ending in narrow, cross-planked, square ends, the stern flaring outward at the top. Flat bottom; numerous bulkheads; flared sides. Decked; cabin abaft the mast; loose matting covered the roof, and when anchored, mats may have covered most of the boat. Anchored by means of a pole inserted into a hole at the stern and driven into the mud, enabling the boat to rise and fall with the tide. Mainly steered with a sweep fitted into the port stern gunwale, but under suitable conditions, may have used a rudder. Drifted downstream, tracked and rowed upstream; when on the Chang Jiang (Yangtze), a single tall lugsail was set; mast also used for tracking. Basic crew of 3-4. Reported lengths 10.7-16.8m; e.g., length 11m, beam across gunwales 1.7m, on bottom 1.1m, depth 1.1m; draft light 13-18cm, loaded 38cm. Other recorded names: **boat** (or **lighter**) **of the gods, chenbozi, ch'enpotzu, shen potse, shen-po tzŭ, tch'en-po tse, Wushanchenbozi, Wushanch'enpotzu, Wu-shan shên-po tzŭ**

2. On the tributaries to Dongting Ho (Tungting Lake) in Hunan Province, there is a similar craft. This cargo vessel, also designed to run shallow rapids, has a high stern, but the stern planking narrows at the top to form a reverse "V." Long, narrow, square bow; flat bottom; sides have tumble home. Decked at the bow; arched mat cabin amidships; side planking at stern continues up to form a house for the captain and helmsman; rudderpost comes up in this house, with the tiller extending forward of the cabin. Rowed, tracked, and sailed. Mast, stepped a little forward of amidships, sets a tall, square, battened lugsail. Crew of 4-6 plus trackers. Length 12.2m, beam 1.8m, depth 0.9m; lake boats by this name and those on the Chang Jiang in this area are larger.

Shenchow ma-yang tzŭ See **Yuanling ma yang zi**

shen chuan *China, central:* Shallow-draft coal carrier found on the Zi Shui (Tzukiang) in Hunan Province. Flat bottom longitudinally planked; rounded bilges; sides taper toward square, upturned ends; stern higher than bow; large-bladed inboard rudder. House in after half. Tall, rectangular lugsail set to single mast. Length 22m, beam 2.7m, depth 1.14m, cap. 30t. Name variant: **coal boat**

shen potse, shên-po tzŭ See **shen bo zi**

shep, shepe, sheppe See **ship**

she-pungy See **pungy**

Sheringham crabber See **Norfolk crabber**

shẹṭêya *Tunisia:* Fast cargo vessel of the 19th century; similar to the Sicilian **velacciere***. Also found along the Tripolitania coast of western Libya. Set 3 square sails on a tall foremast, a lateen or large gaff mainsail, and a small lateen mizzen that sheeted to an outrigger. Two headsails to a rising bowsprit. Clipper bow, counter stern. Black hull with wide, white stripe on which black rectangles were painted to simulate gunports. Towed in calms. Crew of 6. Length 16.8m, beam 4.5m, draft 1.8-2m. Other recorded names: **chitia, chitiha, sétie, sitie**; pl. **šwâṭẹ**. Note also **saettia-2**.

Shetland boat See **Shetland Model**

Shetland Model *Scotland, N:* A term adopted in the Shetland Islands by the mid-19th century for the locally produced boats built along the lines of those imported from Norway. Included in the term are **sixareens*, fourareens*, Fair Isle yoals***, and Ness **yoals***. Although subject to local modifications, they are open and sharp-sterned (the **square-sterned Shetland Model** is a recent adaptation), have clinker planking, usually a straight keel, flat to well-rounded

bilges, and flare to topsides. Ends curved, the sternpost slightly lower than the stem; strong sheer. Mainly rowed, single-banked, double-banked, or a combination; slender-bladed oars with square looms, worked against a single tholepin held by a grommet. Sometimes sailed, setting a single square sail or a dipping lugsail; rudder shipped when sailed. Many now motorized. Range of 5-10m length overall, 2.7-8.2m on keel; width 1.5-2.7m, depth amidships 0.46-1.07m. **Shetland Model** is a term also applied to a racing type in the area. Name variant: **Shetland boat**. Further reading: Adrian G. Osler, *Open Boats of Shetland: South Mainland and Fair Isle*, Maritime Monographs and Reports, No. 58 (London: National Maritime Museum, 1983).

Shetland sixern, Shetland yawl See **sixareen**

Sheveningen pink See **pink-5**

shewe, shewee See **shū·ai**

shih See **ship**

shikara *India, NW/Pakistan, NE:* Small, plank-built boat used on the lakes of Kashmir as a taxi, general workboat, **bumboat***, sightseeing craft, and **fishing boat***; a small size (**bundūqī shikarī**) is used for wildfowling. Sides taper toward the overhanging bow and stern; one or both ends sometimes open; sides may flare outward at bow; low freeboard. Those used by fishermen have a platform at the stern. Some have a canopy forward. Steered with a scull or small paddle.

shikara

Paddled from the stern. Reported lengths 5-11m; e.g., length 11m, beam 1.0m, depth 0.3m. Other recorded names: **parund, Schikarra, shikarī, shikarra, śikārā, śikörī; bundūqī śikörī**

shikarī, shikarra See **shikara**

shikukul *United States, SW:* **Balsa*** of the Kamia of the lower Colorado River area. Composed of 12-14 bundles of tule tied together with willow bark cording. Paddled with a pole. Capacity ca. 6-7 people. Length ca. 4.5m.

shiletto See **bragozzo**

ship 1. In general, any seagoing vessel, merchant or naval, is a **ship**, as opposed to a **boat***. In earlier days, the term was applied to the highest class of sailing vessel, a different type at any one time. The U.S. Navy classifies a **ship** as a vessel too large to be placed on the deck of another.

2. Vessel with 3 and sometimes 4 masts, each setting square sails. Generally also carries a fore-and-aft sail on the lower mizzenmast; early vessels had a lateen mizzen. Multiple headsails to the bowsprit. Carvelplanked. In colonial days in America, small **ships** were often called **barks***. Early vessels had a length-to-beam ratio of ca. 3 or 3.5:1. Other recorded names: **fuldrigger, full-rigger, križna ladja, križnjak, parusnoe sudno, Quersegelschiff, Rahsegler, Rahsegelschiff, raschip, square-rigged ship, square-rigger, trois-mâts carré** (or **franc**), **Vollgetakeltes Schiff, Vollrigger, Vollschiff**. Note also **shipentine**.

3. Sometimes applied to an 8-oared **rowing boat★**.

4. *France, NW:* Small, double-ended **fishing boat★** of the Rance Estuary on the north coast of Brittany. Worked with a special seine net for sandeels (*lançons*) in the estuary of Baie de Saint-Malo. Mentioned toward the end of the 18th century; gone by World War II. Plumb stem with rounded forefoot; straight, slightly raked sternpost, bluffer forward; flat floors. Small foredeck; outboard rudder; tiller. Mainly rowed using 2 pairs of oars, double-banked; oar blade and rounded loom of fir; scarfed on to the inner part is an oval extension of ash or elm that is set over the tholepin. May be fitted with a lugsail to a mast stepped against the forward bench; now being motorized. Crew of 5. Length 5.4m, beam 2m, depth 1.0m; shallow draft. Other recorded names: **chip(p)e, lançonnier, ship** (or **chipe**) **de Saint-Suliac**

Selected name variants: **bastimen, bastimento★, batimen, bâtiment, buque★, chip★, chippe, Fahrzeug, kapal★, laiva, long★, nava★, nave★, navire, nawire, scheep, scheip(e), schepe, Schiff★, schip(p), schup, schyp(e), schypp(e), scip(p), scyp, shep(e), sheppe, shih, shipe, shipp(e), shup, shyp(e), shyppe, sip, skep★, skip★, ssip, vaisseau, vascello★, vašel(o), vašijo**

ship-boat See **ship's boat**

ship-corvette See **corvette-1**

ship de Saint-Suliac See **ship-4**

shipe See **ship**

shipentine Most often considered a 4-masted vessel with the forward 3 masts square-rigged and the after mast fore-and-aft rigged. Generally called a **four-masted bark★** in Great Britain. Note also **bark**.

ship of war See **man-of-war**

shipp, shippe See **ship**

shippe boate See **ship's boat**

ship polacre See **polacre**

ship's boat Broadly, a **boat★** carried aboard a ship, vessel, or larger boat. Used for communication with the shore and as an emergency craft for crew and passengers should it be necessary to abandon ship. The number of **ship's boats** and special **rafts★** is now usually at least sufficient to hold everyone on board. May be rowed, sailed, or motored. Carried on board, hung from davits over the stern, pivoting davits on the sides, or towed. Selected name variants: **Beiboot★, bijboot** (pl. **bijboten), bote lancha, canot d'un navire, embarcación menor, embarcation★, escaler★, imbarcazione★, lancia★, palischermo★, scheepsboot, schepesbot, Schiffsboot, schyppe bot, ship-boat, shippe boate, shlyupka, shyppe boate, skeppsbåt, skibsbaad, skibsbåd, skipsbåt★.** Note also **accident boat, barge-2, barge-11b, cutter-2, cutter gig, cutter yawl, davit craft, dinghy, jollyboat-1, launch-2, lifeboat, longboat-1, pinnace-1, quarter boat, sea boat, tender.**

ship-sloop See **sloop-1**

shitlats *Canada, W:* Large **dugout canoe★** of the Clayoquot tribe of the central part of western Vancouver Island, British Columbia. Although used for ceremonial occasions, their main function was to transport belongings during seasonal migrations, at which time two might be used **catamaran★**-fashion (termed a **lūcenuk**). Distinguished from similar

canoes★ of the area by 4 narrow rows of fluting around the inside, just below the gunwale. Bow and stern pieces sewn on, the bow elongated and ending in a dog-like head; the sharp stern vertical but flared up sharply to a small platform at the top. Broad, flattened bottom. Dugout hull expanded with water heated to boiling with hot stones. Generally paddled using a blackened paddle with a crutch handle and an elliptical blade. When sailed, used a spritsail in which the sprit pierced the cedar-mat sail; cedar withes served as hoops. Reported lengths 10.7-13.7m, occasionally to 14.6m; widths 1.22-1.83m; depth 0.6m. Other recorded names: **freight canoe★, moving canoe, penawał, penáwathl, pinewoł, pinewuł, pĭ-nŭ-wŭhl.** Further reading: Vincent A. Koppert, *Contributions to Clayoquot Ethnology*, Anthropological Series No. 1 (Washington, D.C.: Catholic University of America, 1930). Note also **West Coast canoe.**

shkuna See **schooner**

shlyupka See **ship's boat**

shmak See **smack-1**

shnaika, shneka, shnekke, shniak, shnjak, shnjaka, shnyak See **shnyaka**

shnyaka *Russia:* **1.** In Russian, any seagoing **vessel★**.

2. On the Kola Peninsula in northwestern Russia, a **shnyaka** was a sewn, clinker-built **fishing boat★** used by both the Russians and Lapps (Same). Sharp stern with straight, slightly raked sternpost; stem raked below the waterline and strongly recurved above or straight. Planking of pine or spruce fastened by a combination of clenching and sewing. Keel, stem, sternpost, and treenailed framing of birch. Moderately flat floors amidships. Most open with tarred canvas covers at each end; some had a cuddy aft. Rudder narrow except at the heel; rudderhead often carved. Rudder activated by a short yoke extending at right angles from the rudder, lashed to a long tiller. Single mast to which a large square sail was set; when close-hauled, a bowline from the foot and a spar to the top extended the luff. Might employ a loose-footed gaff mizzen. Some 3-masted. Rowed with strong, narrow oars, often using 6. One that was rowed only, was called a **brama.** Crew of 4. Reported lengths 7.6-15m; e.g., length 10m, beam 2m, depth 0.74m.

Spelling variants: **chneque, chniaka, russesnekke, schanjacka, schniaka, schnjacta, schnjaka, shneka, shnekke, shnaik(a), shnjak(a), shnyak, snackta, snekke★, snjaka**

Shoalwater Bay boat, Shoalwater oyster bateau See **bateau-7p**

shoe boat See **sampan-6**

shoe dhoni *India, E:* Shoe-shaped boat used for both river and sea fishing in the vicinity of the Godavari Delta. Carvel-planked of thin teak strips nailed to the frames; sides have tumble home. Sharp bow with deep forefoot that merges into a fin keel for about a third of the length; after part of the bottom is flat. Narrows gradually toward the stern, which is generally cut square. Cambered deck forward ending in a high, transverse coaming; after area decked for ca. 1.0m; narrow well in between. Outside of hull coated with tar. Helmsman squats on after deck steering or sculling with a long oar held in a low crutch at the stern; some have a rudder. Also poled, stern first. A lofty square sail may be bent to a bamboo yard.

shoe dhoni

Reported lengths 6.1-9.5m; e.g., length 9.5m, width forward 1.1m, aft 0.8m, depth 0.7m; shallow draft. Other recorded names: **bateau soulier**, **baulea**, **Schuhboot**, **shoe thoni**

shoe thoni See **shoe dhoni**

shola bhelā See **bhelā**

shollup See **shallop**

shooting boat See **gun punt**

shooting box See **sinkbox**

shooting cot See **cot-2**, **Wexford cot**

shooting punt See **punt-11b**, **punt-11c**

shooting yacht See **scow-11a**

shore boat 1. A boat for hire that transports passengers and crew from ship to shore; more specifically, one that is owned ashore rather than a **ship's boat★**. Other recorded names: **barca local**, **bateau de terre**, **kayoisen**, **Landesübliches Boot**, **palischermo del luogo**, **water taxi**. Note also **shore punt**.
2. *Canada, E:* In Newfoundland, a general term for a small, open boat that works inshore fisheries, hauls firewood, etc. Name variant: **shore punt**

shore dory See **Cape Ann dory**

Shoreham hog boat See **hog boat**

shore punt See **shore boat-2**

short ferry See **tilt boat-2**

shōsen See **merchantman**

shot *United States, NE:* A section of a **timber raft★** on the Middlesex Canal in northeastern Massachusetts during the 1st half of the 19th century was called a **shot** or **band**. The sections were sized to fit the 24m by 3m locks. Towed by oxen. The **raft** itself was maneuvered by 4-5 men.

shotter *England, S:* **1.** A boat of 6-26t burden that fished for mackerel off the coast of Brighton during the late 16th century. Employed 8-12 men.
2. Name given to later boats from Chichester and Langston, to the west of Brighton, that scoured the sands offshore for shot fired from **gunboats★**. **Shotters** were licensed for this function and did little else.

shou-k'ou ma-yang tzŭ See **shou kou ma yang zi**

shou kou ma yang zi *China, west-central:* Strongly built freight boat that traversed the upper Chang Jiang (Yangtze) from Shashi (Shasi) to Luzhou (Luchow) in southern Sichuan (Szechuan) province. Built of *bai mu*, a blond cypress, earning the local name of **bai mu chuan** (**pai-mu ch'uan** or **white wood boat**). Hull oval in cross section with flat bottom; recurved, rounded sides and narrow deck; strengthened with strong half frames, sturdy crossbeams, and heavy wales along the sides. Bottom rounded up to a square bow; stern sheer swept up sharply to a narrower, high, square-ended poop; shallow rudder, post came up inboard.

Cabin, in after half, had wood sides and mat roof. Stepped 2 masts and sometimes a very small mizzen, although generally only 2 sails set at a time. Balance lugsails with curved shoulder; mizzen sail sheeted to a slender outrigger. Rowed downstream, employing long oars, as many as a dozen on the large vessels. Sometimes 10 men required to work an oar, which could be as long as 27m. Tracked by 70-100 hired haulers up through the rapids; lines fastened to the mast and down to the crossbeams. Reported lengths 11-46m; e.g., length 37m, beam 6m, depth 2.6m. Other recorded names: **cheou k'eou ma-yang tse**, **closed mouth ma-yang tzŭ**, **shou-k'ou ma-yang tzŭ**, **white wood sparrow-tail boat**. Note also **ma yang zi**.

shout *England:* **1.** Generally transported bulky cargoes and produce on inland waters, but also made short sea trips. Reported as early as the 14th century. Double-ended; bottom nearly flat. Set a single spritsail. Moderate size; shallow draft. Other recorded names: **escute★**, **s(c)houte**, **sc(h)uyt**, **scout★**, **scutte**, **showte**, **shutas**, **shute**; **ysgraflau** (Welsh). Note also **herring scowte**.
2. A light, flat-bottomed duck **punt★** used in The Fens of eastern England. Beamier than the cargo **shout**. Name variant: **gunning shout**. Note also **gun punt**.

shoute See **shout-1**

shovel-nose canoe See **tl'ai**

showte See **shout-1**

Shrewsbury River crab skiff *United States, E:* Developed in the last quarter of the 19th century to meet the needs of commercial crabbers along the northern New Jersey coastal area. Lapstraked; sharp bow; wide transom stern; curved forefoot; flat bottom, usually longitudinally planked; slightly rounded, flaring sides. Thwarts with parting boards forward of a raised section created 2-3 wet wells; small compartment in bow. Length 4.9m, beam 1.2m, depth 0.38m.

shrimp beam trawler See **ha ting**

shrimp boat See **ha kou ting**, **ha ting**, **New Orleans lugger**, **shrimper**

shrimp canoe *United States, W:* Chinese-operated boat that fished and shrimped along the California coast, especially during the latter part of the 19th century. Flat bottom, some with considerable rocker at the ends. Sharp or square ends; sharp-ended type had a

shrimp canoe

straight stem with tumble home; moderately flared sides; strong sheer. Sharp-ended boats had decking only at the ends; square-ended boats were decked with a long hatchway. Steered with a sweep or adjustable rudder. Could be rowed, sailed, or sculled. Square-ended type used a square sail, others a lateen sail that tacked at the bow and at times, was sheeted to an aft bumkin. Reported lengths 4.6-12.2m; e.g., length 6.1m, beam 0.9m, depth 0.5m. Other recorded names: **Chinese fishing canoe, Chinese shrimp boat**

shrimp dragger See **shrimper**

shrimper A boat or vessel that primarily trawls for shrimp. Early boats sailed, but modern **shrimpers** have powerful engines. The Louisiana **trawling skiffs** work both inland and in the Gulf of Mexico; sharp, raked bow; wide transom stern, deep, semi-V hull, cypress- or cedar-planked; lengths 12-21m, beam one-third. Other recorded names: (**buque**) **camaronero, crevettier*, garnalenkotter** (or **kutter**), **garnalenvisser**(**sboot**), **Garne(e)lenboot, Garnelenfischer, Krabbfangboot, Krabben-fischer(boot), navio de pesca de camarão, peschereccio gamberi, prawn boat, rejebåd, shrimp boat** (**dragger** or **trawler**). Note also **bawley, canot à crevette, garnalenschuit, ha kou ting, ha ting, Morecambe Bay prawner, Nieuwpoortse garnaalboot, Oostendse garnaalboot, Paull shrimper, prawner, shrimp canoe, shrimp junk, Yarmouth shrimper**.

shrimp junk *United States, W:* Used in San Francisco Bay by Chinese shrimp fishermen. Blunt bow, square stern, round bottom, no keel. Gear stowed in the bow, net room just aft, then open hold for the catch; after area decked and used as living quarters. Battened lugsail set to a midships mast. Size varied, mostly ca. 15.2m long and 3.7m wide. Note also **junk, lorcha-8**.

shrimp lugger See **New Orleans lugger**

shrimp trawler See **shrimper**

Shroppie fly, Shropshire fly See **flyboat-3a**

shū·ai *Arabian Peninsula:* A Persian (Arabian) Gulf and Omani craft still built in some areas. In Kuwait, a **shū·ai** is a small, single-masted, double-ended **fishing boat*** or a large (23-50m-long) **coaster*** (the **shū·ai saffar**); the Kuwaiti double-ended type of **shū·ai** is called a **hōri*** at Bahrain. The 2-masted Bahraini trader is similar to a **sambūq***; on the Muscat coast of Oman, it is a small **sambūq**, while at Dubai in the United Arab Emirates, a straight-stemmed **sambūq** is a **shū·ai**, ferrying passengers to Bandar 'Abbas in Iran, where it is called an **ābra**. In general, the **shū·ai** has a straight stem, sometimes curved below the waterline, with an S-curve to the stemhead, the top of which is generally painted blue; raked transom stern. Carvel-planked; straight keel, delicate sheer, flared sides. Low bow; upswept poop with a low railing around it and quarter strakes that extend beyond the stem; tall rudder. **Houri*** carried on a platform at the stern. Now mainly motorized, but originally sailed or rowed. Stepped 1-2 masts carrying quadrilateral, lateen-type sails with short luffs; sail tacked to sliding boom that extended beyond the stem. Crew of 6-10, but large vessels employed as many as 40. Reported lengths 4.6-15.8m; e.g., length 13.8m, beam 4.3m, depth 1.8m; generally under 15t. Other recorded names: **sa(i)yeh, say, shewe(e), shuei, shū'i**; small type called a **hūri**

(see **houri**) on parts of the Oman coast. Further reference: **jalbūt-1**

shū·ai saffar See **shū·ai**

shuang peng chuan *China, E:* 17th-century vessel of the Fujian (Fukien) coastal defense **fleet***. Despite being called a **two-master***, the vessel stepped a small mizzen on the poop in addition to a fore- and mainmast. Length 10.4-18.6m, beam 2.7-5m. Spelling variants: **shuang peng chhuan** (or **ch'uan**)

shuang peng chhuan, shuang peng ch'uan See **shuang peng chuan**

shuei See **shū·ai**

shuen See **chuan**

shū'i See **shū·ai**

shui-pao-chia fei-hsieh See **fei xie**

shup See **ship**

shutas, shute See **shout-1**

shuwai'ai, shuwai'i See **baghla-1**

shyp, shype, shyppe See **ship**

shyppe boate See **ship's boat**

siampan *China:* Small, fast vessel, probably a type of **sampan***. Propelled by multiple oars or a single sail. Carried 25-30 people. Spelling variant: **Siampane**. See also **sampan**.

Siampane See **siampan**

Siangsiang tao-pa-tzŭ See **dao ba zi-1**

siao-houa tch'ouan See **hua chuan-1**

sia-ràmhach See **gig-1**

sibidsibiran *Philippines, central:* Open double-**outrigger canoe*** of the **baroto*** type used for longline fishing and trolling (*sibidsibid*) in the Visayan area. Built-up dugout; bow rakes in slight curve, terminating in a point; narrow, overhanging stern cut square. Waterproofed matting may raise sides. Three booms connect directly with long, slender floats. Steered with a quarter rudder on the starboard side; rudder worked against a pin on an athwartships beam. Light mast stepped through a thwart; stayed to 2 outrigger booms. Sets a boomed spritsail; headsail tacked to forward end of top strake. Generally a 1-man boat. Name variant: **pinanyo**

Sicherungsboot See **picket boat**

Sicke, Sicken, Sickenlomme See **zig**

sideboard schooner See **schooner-barge-1**

side-fishing trawler See **trawler**

side punt See **punt-2**

side-set trawler, side trawler See **trawler**

side wheeler See **paddle boat-3**

sidewinder See **trawler-1**

Sidmouth lugger See **Beer lugger**

Siebnerin, Siebnerkobel, Siebnerzille See **Salzzille**

sigosi See **sekochi**

śikārā See **shikarī**

sikbåt *Finland:* Fishes for whitefish (*sik* in Swedish, *silka* in Finnish). Open; sturdily built; 2 strakes per side, lapped; flat bottom; keel; wide transom. Rowed against a pair of double tholepins. Length 5m, beam 2m.

siknotbåt See **notbåt-3**

sikoeti, sikoetji See **sekochi**

śikörī See **shikarī**

sīkōsīkōtjī, sikoti, sikotji, sikuntji See **sekochi**

Silberkammerschiff See **Bucentaur**

Silberschiff See **Bucentaur, Leibschiff**

sildebåd *Denmark:* General term for a herring- (*silde*) **fishing boat★**. Built in several areas, notably in the central part of the country and in the east. Well known was the lightly built boat that worked in the Øresund Strait between Copenhagen and Helsingør. Clinker-planked, double-ended. Sharp bow, curved stem with cutaway forefoot, strongly raked sternpost with tumble home to topsides. Straight keel, some with slight drag; S-shaped midsection; considerable sheer, bow higher than stern. Outboard rudder followed raked contour of the sternpost. Some open and rowed as well as sailed. Later boats half-decked with an oval cockpit and steering well; cuddy forward. Engines installed on many boats, and following modifications, a wet well was added. Most sprit-rigged with a square-headed mainsail; jib-headed topsail, staysail, and jib. Mainsail brailed. Crew of 2-3. Reported lengths 4.9-10.4m; e.g., length overall 9.1m, on keel 5.7m, beam 3.5m, depth 1.5m. Other recorded names: **oeresundboot**, **Öresundboote**, **Øresundsbåd**, **Skovshoved sildebåd**, **sundbåd**

sildegarnsfiring See **firing**

sildejakt See **jakt-2**

sileposa-galbat See **galbat-1**

sillegarnbåt See **garnbåt-2**

silver galleon See **galleon-3**

sinago *France, W:* Fast, seaworthy, south Breton boat from the Golfe du Morbihan; served as a **coaster★**, but more often as an **oyster dredger**. The older, round-sterned type became extinct in the 1920s; replaced by

sinago

a larger, beamier, sharper-sterned craft. Carvel-planked; raked and lightly curved stem; maximum beam well forward; long, straight, sharply raked sternpost. Straight keel with drag; strong sheer and less rise to the floors on later boats. Decked forward, low flooring amidships, stern bench. Tiller slotted over a tall, raked outboard rudder that hung well below the bottom; tiller had to rise over the sternsheet. Hull blackened with coal tar. The 1-2 aft-raking, unstayed masts on the older type set tall, narrow standing lugsails to horizontal yards; on the later boats, they were peaked up and a headsail might be added, tacked to a short bowsprit. Mainsail set to starboard, halyard to port, the foresail opposite. Sails tanned or dyed blue. Engines installed in the late 1940s. Crew of 1-2. Reported lengths 6.5-13m; the larger boats were the later type; e.g., length 9.4m, beam 3m, depth 1.2m; shallow draft.

Other recorded names: **Morbihan lugger**, **Mor Bihan sinago**, **sinagot**

sinagot See **sinago**

śināj See **sarnái**

sinaper *Guinea:* Handline fishes offshore with a crew of 4-5. May also engage in coastal trading. Plank-built; straight sides, sharp bow; full amidships, narrowing to transom stern; low freeboard. Most open; numerous benches; cargo may be carried high on deck, restrained by strakes. Some carry a small, polygonal sail hung from a forward-raking mast, extended with multiple booms and sprits. Others suspend a triangular sail between 2 divergent, light masts. A motor may supplement the sail. Reported lengths 8-9m, beam 2m, depth 1.5m, draft 0.6m. Other recorded names: **côtre★**, **Guinea-Kutter**

Sinepuxent skiff *United States, E:* Beamy, V-bottomed boat that engaged in oyster tonging, crabbing, and party fishing on Sinepuxent and Chincoteague Bays behind Assateague Island on the Maryland coast. Lightly constructed with straight rise to the floors; straight, flaring sides; plank keel, strong sheer. Straight, raked stem; wide, raked, square or rounded stern, vertically staved; outboard rudder; tiller; centerboard. Decked forward and along the sides. Tall, vertical mainmast stepped in the bow; set a large leg-of-mutton sail with horizontal sprit, clubbed clew, and short gunter staff at the head. The aft-raking mizzenmast, stepped well aft, set a small triangular sail with sprit slanting down to clew, sheeted to an outrigger. Reported lengths 5-8m, a few to 12m; e.g., length 6.2m, beam 2.5m, depth ca. 0.6m. Name variant: **Chincoteague skiff**

Singapore lighter See **tongkang Mĕlayu**

Singapore trader *Peninsular Malaysia/Singapore:* A Chinese **junk★** built either at Singapore or at Kuala Trengganu. Hauls cargo in the Singapore area but may travel to Penang on the west coast of Malaysia and to Bangkok. Heavily built, using western methods. Bow pointed and well-raked. Nearly wall-sided with little flare, full bilges; shallow, straight keel. Square-cut stern with overhanging poop. From amidships aft to the stern, bottom almost flat, with the chines rising

Singapore trader

sharply. Hold open or covered with a wooden deckhouse over the hatch. Perforated rudder raised and lowered by a windlass on the poop. A deck windlass used for cargo. Smaller sizes step 2 masts; mainmast usually plumb and roughly the same length as the keel; foremast two-thirds the height of the mainmast and rakes sharply forward. When mizzenmast stepped, it is normally less than one-half the height of the mainmast. Sets Chinese battened lugsails of canvas or sacking. Small boats worked by a crew of 4-5; larger have crew of 12-15. Reported lengths 11.7-27.4m, widths 3.81-5.79m, depths 1.14-3.05m; average 21.54m by 6.3m by 2.13m. Name variant: **tongkang**★

single-banked boat Craft with 1 oarsman to a thwart, pulling a single oar, usually sitting on the side of the boat opposite the oar blade. Other recorded names: **canot armé en pointe**, **Einmannruderboot**. Note also **double-banked boat**.

single-day boat See **smackee**

single-masted flat See **Mersey flat**

single Moses See **Moses boat-5**

single pup *England, central:* A **barge**★ of the canals of the Birmingham area that was propelled by a 9hp Bolinder engine (the "pup") and worked without a **butty**. Note also **narrow boat**.

single scull See **scull**

single-sculler See **sculler**

single skiff See **Staten Island skiff**

singolo See **palischermo-4**

Singora Lake boat *Thailand, SW:* Two-masted, plank-extended dugout that served as a **fishing boat**★, **ferry**★, and cargo craft on this shallow lake in peninsular Thailand. Several strakes added to dugout base, terminating short of the ends and enclosed with breakwaters. Top strakes extended slightly beyond the other

Singora Lake boat

strakes at the bow and turned up; they also projected beyond the stern, serving as a platform for the helmsman. Overhanging bow and strongly raked stern; quarter rudder. Arched mat house amidships and sometimes a shelter at the stern. Set high-peaked standing lugsails to a short foremast and taller mainmast; sails of light yellow matting. Reported lengths 7.6-10.7m.

singri See **ber**

sin hua tzŭ See **hua zi-4**

sink, sink boat See **sinkbox**

sinkbox *United States, E:* Used by wildfowl hunters, especially on Long Island Sound, New Jersey, upper Chesapeake Bay, and in the North Carolina bays. Mainly of the 19th century; banned in the 1930s on Chesapeake Bay. Consisted of a square or oblong box

in which the hunter lay. Wings of wood or canvas-covered slats extended out each side for ca. 61cm. Wings lay flat on the water and usually had iron decoys set onto them to serve as ballast; might be grass-covered. A lead sheet coaming around the box could be raised to hide the hunter or keep water out. Some had runners on the bottom and skated to hunting site when ice thick enough; if set into a hole cut through the ice, the **sinkbox** might be called an **icebox**. Towed to the desired location and anchored. On Long Island Sound, some **sinkboxes** had water compartments that helped sink the box to water level, but if the water became rough, some of the water ballast could be pumped out. This type could be rowed to collect the kill if the compartments were not full, otherwise the craft was towed to the site and other boats collected the kill. Painted a dull gray. Some double **sinkboxes** held 2 hunters. Box itself ca. 1.8-2.1m long. A larger size, usually called a **battery**, was used by as many as 4 hunters and had wider wings, especially the forward one. **Battery**, however, might describe a single-man **sinkbox** and was called a **lay-down battery**; there were also **double lay-down batteries**. The **set-up** or **sit-up battery** held up to 4 hunters. When spread out, these would be ca. 5.5m long and 4m wide. Other recorded names: **box**, **coffin boat**, **lie-down box**, **shooting box**, **sit-down box**, **sit-up box**, **sink (boat)**, **Susquehanna Flats sinkbox**, **tub box**. Note also **battery boat**, **cabin boat-3**, **lay boat-2**.

sinker boat *United States:* A logger's term for a small **raft**★ carrying a windlass and grapple to recover sunken logs; may also serve as a mooring buoy for another boat. Other recorded names: **catamaran**★, **monitor**★, **pontoon**★

sink float See **float-5**

sinknetter See **Core Sounder**

sin-tor-chai *China, SE:* **Fishing boat**★ that operated out of Shantou (Swatow). Generally worked in pairs; the one carrying the nets called the **wang chuan** or **net boat**★, the other, carrying food, water, and fuel, called the **wei chuan**★ (feeder boat). Beamy above the waterline; V-shaped bow transom; horseshoe-shaped stern transom with high wings that supported the rudderhead and windlass. Strong sheer; flush deck; deep rudder. Hull stained brown; forward wales painted red; oculi. Two- or 3-masted; the fore- and mizzen masts usually stepped slightly to port to clear the anchor cable, fishing gear, and tiller. Battened lugsails of matting or brown canvas; slightly rounded leech. Crew of ca. 5. Reported lengths 7-16m; e.g., length 7m, beam 2.7m, depth 0.64m. Other recorded names: **Swatow fisherman**, **Swatow off-shore trawler**

siódmek See **galar**

sip *Vanuatu (New Hebrides), western Pacific:* Term for **ship**★ in Bichelamar, the lingua franca of the islands.

siparoner See **speronara**

širć See **šerk**

śirnā See **sarnái**

sister, sister ship See **mother**

sit-down sinkbox See **sinkbox**

sithia See **saettia**

sitie See **šhẹtêya**

si t'ing See **sha ting**
sittia See **saettia**
sit-up battery, sit-up box See **sinkbox**
šíu See **fassone**
sixaern See **sixareen**
sixareen *Scotland, N:* Shetland Islands, 6-oared, long-line, deep sea (*haaf*) fishing and general-purpose boat. Popular until the 1880s, although a few were used until the mid-20th century; until 1830s, imported knocked-down from Norway. Clinker-built with wide planks; widely spaced, sawn frames connected to the keel only along the deep garboard strakes; flaring sides and low freeboard amidships; sheer reduced through the years. Divided into 6 or 8 compartments, each having a separate function. Double-ended; curved and raking stem and sternpost, but later boats had a straight sternpost; fuller forward than aft; short, straight tiller. Some later and larger boats decked, motorized, and had living accommodations. Stone ballast jettisoned as the boat filled with the catch. Coated with a mixture of tar and fish oil. Oars ca. 4.88m long with a narrow blade and square loom; held to tholepin by a loop; rowed double-banked. A few pulled 8 oars.

sixareen

Mast stepped through a bench slightly forward of amidships; 2 shrouds to a side; single halyard, both ends run through a hole at the top of the mast and secured to the yard. Original square sail replaced by a low dipping lugsail, tack to fore quarter, and bowline extended the luff; 2 reef lines at the head, 2-3 at the foot, and 1 down the after side of the leech. Crew of 6-7. Length overall 7.62-11.28m, on keel 5.18-7m, beam 2.49-3.05m, molded depth 0.76-0.9m. Other recorded names: **deep sea boat, Haaf boat, Háf boat, sax earing, saxereen, sexæring(er), sexern, Shetland sixern** (or **yawl**), **sixaern, sixear-een, sixén, sixer(e)n, six-oared boat, six-oared yawl, six-oarer, sixoarn, sixtreen.** Further reading: Charles Sandison, *The Sixareen and Her Racing Descendants* (Lerwick: Shetland Times, Ltd., 1954; reprint, 1981). Note also **codling boat, eela boat, Shetland model.**
sixear-een, sixén, sixeren, sixern See **sixareen**
six-fathom canoe See **canot du maître**
six-handed boat See **five-handed boat**
six mat boat See **liu peng**
six-oared barge See **barge-11e**
six-oared boat See **sixareen, whaleboat-4**
six-oared race boat See **gig-3**

six-oared yawl, six-oarer, sixoarn, sixtreen See **sixareen**
60-piece boat See **York boat**
sjægt *Denmark, W:* Small **fishing boat*** that worked with hand seines and traps in the Limfjorden area of northern Jutland. Clinker-planked; double-ended; strongly curved and raked stem and sternpost; long, straight keel; considerable rise to the floors; strong sheer. Open; later decked at ends and along the sides. Most had a live well. Outboard rudder, wide blade below the waterline; long tiller on some. Sailed to and from fishing grounds, setting a tanned spritsail, yard topsail, and jib. Mainsail sheeted to a deck horse. A large type set a loose-footed gaff sail and 2 headsails. Also rowed, employing single or double tholepins. Crew of 2-5. Reported lengths 4-6.7m; e.g., length 6.4m, beam 2m, depth 0.7m, draft 0.55m. Those under 5.2m in length called **krogsjægt** or **halvsjægt**. Other recorded names: **dambåd, Limfjordssjægt, sjægte(n), skægte**
sjægte See **sjægt, sjekte**
sjækte See **sjekte**
sjæten See **sjægt**
själabåt See **fälbåt-2**
själasmacko See **fäljulle-1**
sjalupp *Norway:* An open, naval **ship's boat***. Mainly rowed.
sjekta See **sjekte**
sjekte *Norway, SE:* Small boat found in Oslofjorden and on the west coast of the Skagerak, mainly during the 19th century. Served primarily for fishing, but might transport farm produce and hay. Clinker-planked with narrow strakes; steep rise to the floors from a short keel. Sharp ends with cutaway stem and sternpost; solid gunwales of oak. Open, but a large, decked type in Oslofjorden was called a **snekka**. Mainly rowed with 1-3 pairs of oars. When sailed, set a lugsail originally, later a spritsail and jib; steered with an oar. Reported lengths 4.3-8m; e.g., length 5.8m, beam 1.5m, depth 0.38m. Other recorded names: **arendalssjægte, arendalssjekte, sjægte, sjekta, sjækte, sjogte, sjokte, skjegte; seiljagte; pl. sjektene, sjekter.** A 6-oared boat was called a **seksaret sjekte.** Note also **snekke.**
sjektene, sjekter, sjogte, sjokte See **sjekte**
sjomp See **somp**
sjörövarfartyg, sjørøverskip See **freebooter**
sjouwerman *Netherlands:* Small, general-utility boat of the **schouw*** family. Built of wood or metal; flat bottom athwartships curved fore-and-aft to shallow, narrow, rectangular bow and stern transoms; skeg at stern; angular, one-piece frames. Open, generally with 2-3 benches supported on iron knees. Rowed; long oars worked against built-up oarlocks. Roughly 4.6m long.
skægte See **sjægt**
skaerbaat See **skerry-boat**
skaf See **chaland, skiff**
skaffie See **scaffie**
skafi **1.** Greek word initially meaning a **dugout canoe***, or a withy or leather craft. Eventually included oared vessels, and later applied to a **boat*** in general. Might also be a harbor or river **barge*** (**hyperetikai skaphai**). Now may be more narrowly applied to a **dinghy*** or to a small, open, crudely built **rowing**

boat★. Word and its variant spellings used throughout the eastern Mediterranean and on the North African coast. Spelling variants: **chkof, scaphandre, scaphe, scapho, scaphuba, scaphula, scháfe, schafioy, scháfis, schafos, skafion** (dim.), **skâfis, skafos, skaphae** (pl.), **skaphai** (pl.), **skaphē, skaphos**; Latin: **scapha, scaphae, scaphium**. Note also **scafa**.
2. In Greece, sometimes pictured as a beamy, sprit-rigged craft used for sponge fishing or for trading. Last built, on the island of Simi, in the mid-1930s. Transom stern; long, straight, sharply raked stem; tall, raked sternpost; moderate sheer, higher at the bow. Decked at ends; large hold amidships; sides protected by canvas weatherscreens. Tall outboard rudder; tiller. Short mast, sometimes with topmast, stepped in forward third. Large spritsail extends almost to stern; may have a slender gaff; headsail tacked to stemhead; sometimes a jib set to a rising bowsprit; square topsail; small leg-of-mutton mizzen. One type sets a lateen sail, square topsail, and 3 headsails. Sponging boats carry a crew of 5. Reported lengths 10-15m; e.g., length 10m, beam 3m, depth 0.8m.
skâfion See **skafi**
skâfiou See **chaland**
skâfis See **skafi**
skafos See **hulk, skafi**
Skagbobrig, Skagenbåd See **Skawbrig**
skȧin See **skûna-2**
skallop See **shallop**
skammevaya, skampavea See **skampaveya**
skampaveya *Russia:* **1.** An armed vessel that engaged in reconnaissance.
2. A type of **half galley★**, but smaller, used by Peter the Great in the early 18th century in the Baltic Sea. Rowed with 16-18 banks of oars; also sailed, stepping 2 masts. Reported lengths 22-30m; e.g., length 22m, beam 3m. Spelling variants: **scampafie, scampavia★, scampa-voya, skammevaya, skampavea**. Note also **skampavia**.
skampavia *Greece:* Reported as a type of **gunboat★** of the early 19th century. Note also **skampaveya**. Further reference: **scampavia**
skaphae, skaphai, skaphē, skaphi, skaphos See **skafi**
skärbåt *Finland, SW/Sweden, east-central:* Open boat that fished for herring in the Roslagen region, especially from Möja, east of Stockholm. In the 19th century, also transported fresh fish to Stockholm, and some of the larger boats traveled to the Åland Islands. Clinker-planked with low rise to the floors amidships; sheer might be filled in with a washboard along most of each side. Sharp ends, but slightly fuller forward. Stem built with an angle, raking more sharply below the waterline. Sternpost straight and raked. Straight keel with slight drag. Three widely spaced thwarts; outboard rudder; tiller. Rowed with 2 pairs of oars against double tholepins. Also sailed, setting a square sail; mast raked aft. Crew of 5-6. Reported lengths 7.6-11.4m; e.g., length 8m, beam 2.85m, depth ca. 1.0m. Other recorded names: **Möja-skärbåt, rock-boat, Schären-boot, Scheerboot, šcherbot, skerry-boat★**
Skåsheimsbåt See **storbåt-2**
Skawbrig *Denmark, NW:* Two-masted, sprit-rigged boat that engaged in sea fishing off The Skaw at the north end of Jutland; also transported dried fish to Copenhagen. Clinker-built; sharp lines; top strakes continued aft to form a shallow transom; keel. Decked since the latter part of the 19th century. Length to 9m. Other recorded names: **Skagbobrig, Skagenbåd**. Note also **havbåd**.
skebåt See **lillebåt-3**
skedia See **schedia**
skefien See **chaland**
skeid A large Viking **langskip★** that was particularly fast, the word *skeid* meaning a racer. Term sometimes used interchangeably with **drake**, although there may have been a size distinction, the **drake** being larger. The vessel was also used by Viking settlers on the Normandy coast and in the conquest of England in 1066; built until the mid-13th century. Clinker-built; double-ended; flat floors; keel; quarter rudder. Generally open but may have had a raised deck in the forepeak; some later vessels had castles. High stem and sternpost to which decorative finials were added during marauding or conquest missions, generally the head of a fierce dragon. The vessels were classed according to the number of rooms they had, which corresponded with the number of transverse beams or thwarts, and therefore, the number of pairs of oars employed; reported to have had 25-40 rooms. Sailed at times, setting a large square sail to a pole mast stepped amidships. Length to ca. 55m. Other recorded names: **Drachenschiff, draco, drage(skib), dragone, dragon ship, drakar★, draken, drakkar(e), drakker, drakon, drakr, drakskepp, drekar, dreki, drekki** (pl.), **skeidh, skoeid**; pl. **skeider**
skeider, skeidh See **skeid**
skeis *Norway, N:* Trøndelag term for a small, **pram★**-type boat. Used mainly as a **ship's boat★** (see **skipsbåt**). Clinker-planked; rounded sides, beamy; small bow transom, larger stern transom. Rowed with a single pair of oars. Other recorded names: **skeisbåt**; pl. **skeisa**
skeisa, skeisbåt See **skeis**
skeit See **skötbåt-1**
skekta *Iceland, W:* Open, inshore **fishing boat★**. Clinker-built; high sheer; long, raking stem with rounded forefoot, sharp stern, curved sternpost. Narrow rudder, long tiller. Rowed and sailed. Large square sail, and sometimes a small topsail, set to a mast stepped a little forward of amidships. Reported lengths 6.2-7m, widths 2.2-2.5m.
skeleton boat See **shell**
skep *Sweden, S:* Term may be given to an inland boat of the **eka★** type, having a dugout base. Flared, planked sides; sharp bow, square stern. Some have a residual stem piece shaped from the dugout base. Mainly rowed. Note also **skepp**. Further reference: **ship**
skepp Swedish generic term for a **ship★**, especially a sailing vessel with 3 masts and square sails. May also be used in compound form to designate a particular type of ship. Note also **skep**.
skeppsäsping See **äsping**
skeppsbåt See **ship's boat**
Skerries hooker, Skerries wherry, Skerries whirry See **Irish wherry**
Skerries yawl See **drontheim**

skerry-boat Reported in the 18th century as a small, easily maneuvered, inshore **patrol boat★** of the Scandinavian countries. Depicted as a fore-and-aft **schooner** and as a 3-masted vessel with trapezoidal sails hung square from the fore- and mainmasts and a small gaff mizzen. Armed with swivel guns and howitzers. Also employed 10-12 pairs of sweeps. Crew of ca. 50. Reported lengths 16-20m. Name variant: **skaerbaat**. Further reference: **skärbåt**

skeut See **schuit**, **scout**

skibbaad See **skipsbåt-1**

skibbåt See **skipsbåt**

Skibbereen nickey See **nickey-2**

skibsbaad, **skibsbåd** See **ship's boat**

skibsjolle See **jolle-1**

skief See **Saint Lawrence skiff**

skif See **skiff**

skiff **1.** Small, light, fast, all-purpose craft designed primarily for inland use. Term dates from at least the 16th century. In the British Royal Navy, a **skiff** is a 2-man **ship's boat★**; also termed a **dinghy★**. Generally open, but modern, powered **skiffs** may have a cabin. Most flat-bottomed, often with rocker; sharp bow, sharp or transom stern, lapstrake or carvel planking. Usually rowed, but may be sailed using a simple rig. Note also **barge-9**. **2.** Long, narrow racing craft. Generally rowed by a single oarsman on a sliding seat, using long sculls supported on outriggers. Clinker- or carvel-built; keelless. Open except for light covering at the ends. Reported lengths 7-9m. Name variant: **giek** **3.** *Canada:* **a.** A popular term in Newfoundland, and several types have been identified: a small type has been used for inshore fishing, setting nets, traps, and handlining. Clinker-planked; full bow, square stern, keel. Small boats mainly rowed, but also set a spritsail; the larger boats employed 2 spritsails and sometimes a jigger at the stern. Crew of 1-2. Reported lengths 4.6-9m. At Saint John's, the **skiffs** were roughly built, carvel-planked fishing craft. Keel; sharp bow; heart-shaped, raking transom; considerable rise to the floors, rounded bilges. Open; locker aft, cuddy forward, washstrake above the gunwales; outboard rudder; tiller. Rowed, sculled, and sailed. Stepped 2 masts, mainmast amidships, foremast well forward. Set spritsails; small jib tacked to stemhead. Length 5.6m, beam 1.5m, depth 0.7m. The **big skiff** had a keel length of 6m and required a 4-man crew. Set cod and herring seines. Open for ca. 2.4m at the stern; cuddy forward. Worked with 2 large gaff sails and 1-2 headsails. Small auxiliary on some. In the 1930s, small **skiffs** were used in nocturnal drift-net fishing for salmon, going as far as 24km off the Newfoundland coast. In the early 19th century, special **skiffs** served as **packet boats★** in the Conception Bay area of eastern Newfoundland. Employed 6 oars. **b.** On the west coast of Canada, the term was applied to an early type of **gillnetter★**. Cedar-planked, flat-bottomed, double-ended. Used oars or a gaff sail. **4.** *England, E:* Those of Essex, particularly in the Colne River, are used for oystering, going to and from anchored boats, and for off-loading fish, especially sprat from **stowboats★**. Heavy, open, clinker-built

boat with large, grown frames; flat floors, wide keel. Transom stern with sculling notches or sharp-ended. Also rowed and sometimes sailed. Reported lengths 4-7.6m, widths 2.13-2.51m, depths 0.71-0.76m; shallow draft. Other recorded names: **Essex oyster skiff**, **oyster skiff**, **skift** **5.** *Ireland, SE:* Open waterman's boat of Dublin Bay that, until the early 1930s, met inbound ships needing pilot assistance. Set a dipping lugsail. Also rowed with the boatman standing and facing forward, using 4.9m-long sweeps. **6.** *Northern Ireland:* At Newcastle in south County of Down, any sharp-sterned, open craft, regardless of length. To the southwest, a craft under 5.5m would be called a **punt★**, and **skiff** designates fishing vessels between 5.5-10.7m; to the northeast, between St. John's Point and Strangford Lough, the fishing **skiff** is called a **yawl★**. The longline-fishing **skiffs** are clinker-built and open; the herring boats are half-decked with limited accommodations, but include a tiny coal stove, the pipe of which passes through the deck. Mast stepped against a forward thwart or the cuddy bulkhead. Sets a single dipping lugsail hoisted on a yard hooked to a traveler on the mast. Also rowed. The later herring **skiffs** were motorized. **7.** *Scotland:* May be a small version of a larger type of boat. **8.** *United States, NE:* **a.** Maine bluefin tuna **purse seiners** (see **seine boat-1b**) employ a heavy, flat-bottomed boat called a **skiff**. The boat initially pulls the net off the turntable, then supports the net during hauling, and may assist in keeping the **purse seiner** in proper position in relation to the net. Sharp bow, square stern, both lightly raked; open; heavy thwart amidships. Rowed; those used in California have engines. Crew of 2. 1955 boat 6.7m long, 2.6m wide. **b.** The Maine lobsterman's **skiff** is a beamy, flat-bottomed boat that serves as a **tender★**. In some areas of the coast, it may be called a **punt**. Sharp, raked bow; wide transom stern; straight, flared sides. Generally rowed single-banked or employs a small outboard motor. Length ca. 2.5m. **9.** *United States, E:* Baymen on Great South Bay on Long Island in New York State describe a **skiff** as any small, round-bottomed boat. Name variant: **Long Island skiff** **10.** *United States, central:* A small **bateau★** used by early settlers, occasionally for lengthy river trips, but more frequently as a **tender** to larger craft. Flat bottom; ribbed; often square-ended. Rowed. Note also **Mackinaw boat-1**. **11.** *United States, south-central:* In some areas, as on the Texas coast, any craft propelled solely by oars. **12.** *United States, SE:* A local **sharpie★** type in the Pensacola, Florida, area. Roughly built by the fishermen; planked in yellow pine, red cedar frames. Narrow stern with a platform across the gunwales for the seine nets. Flat bottom. Four thwarts for the rowers; rarely sailed. Crew of 6. Lengths 7.3-7.6m, beam 1-2.5m, depths 0.46-0.51m.

Selected name variants: **equif**, **eschiffe**, **esclif**, **esguif**, **esquif★**, **esquife★**, **esquifle**, **sailor's cradle**, **schiff(e)**, **schifo★**, **schiph**, **sciff(e)**, **sghiffo**, **siph**, **skaf**, **skif(fe)**, **skiph**, **skyfe**, **squiffe**. Further references: **baldie**, crabbing skiff, dory-1, drontheim, flatboat-6, jolly boat-1, Loch Fyne skiff, palischermo-4, pirogue-4, Saint Lawrence skiff, Saint Margarets Bay skiff, scaffie, Sea Bright skiff, sealing punt, squid skiff, Westray skiff

skiffe See **skiff**

skiff-putt See **Saint Lawrence skiff-1**

skift See **bawley, Saint Lawrence skiff, Sea Bright skiff, skiff-4**

skillinger *England, E:* A large **smack*** from the Essex coast that engaged in deep-water oyster dredging off Terschelling Light on the northern Dutch coast. Early boats **cutter***-rigged, later **ketch***-rigged. Many were old Lowestoft and Grimsby boats converted for this use. Had live wells. Lengths to ca. 21m; e.g., length 18m, beam 5.2m. Name variant: **skilling smack**. Note also **Essex smack**.

skilling smack See **skillinger**

skimming dish 1. Small racing craft with broad beam, flat floor, deep fin keel, low sides, centerboard. Tends to race on, rather than through, the water. Shallow draft. 2. *United Kingdom:* **Motor launch** of the Royal Navy used for scouting purposes. So called because its speed and design caused it to plane across the water. See also **sandbagger**.

skin boat 1. Boat with a shell framework of lath or bone over which an animal skin has been tightly stretched. Most common in the Arctic, where wood and reeds are unavailable. May also be found in sub-Arctic areas where skins, such as moose, may provide covering for temporary boats to transport furs and meat (see **moose-hide canoe** and **mu'su u'lk**). Other recorded names: **Fellboot, Hautboot, Lederboot**. Note also **baidara, bullboat, coracle, curragh, ga'twaat, kayak, keel-1, mioparo, pelota, umiak**. 2. *Canada, NW:* Temporary craft made by Native Americans and early trappers. Usually covered with uncured moosehide, hair side in. Hide stretched over a spruce frame. Name variant: **skin canoe**. Note also **moose-hide canoe**. 3. *United States, E:* One of the disparaging terms used by Chesapeake Bay watermen for **schooners*** hired for pleasure cruises. Further reference: **kayak**

skin canoe See **bullboat, kayak, skin boat-2**

skin float See **float-2**

skip Generic term in Icelandic and Norwegian for a **ship*** or **vessel***.

skipbåt See **skipsbåt**

skipbåtr See **skipsbåt-1**

skiph See **skiff**

skipjack *United States:* 1. Heavy, **sloop***-rigged, oyster dredging boat that has been used since ca. 1890 on Chesapeake Bay and many of its tributaries; some built in North Carolina. A few still work on the Bay. In summer, occasionally hauled local produce to major markets. Term sometimes applied to its particular type of rig, so hull types may vary along the east coast. Regional differences reflect varying water conditions. The wide, shoal-draft, V-bottom hull type is frequently called a **deadrise bateau*** along the central part of the Eastern Shore of Chesapeake Bay. Bottom planked her-

ringbone fashion; keelson and skeg; hard chines; moderate sheer; low freeboard; maximum beam abaft the midships line. Those built at Pocomoke City, on the eastern side of the bay, had a round-chine hull and were known as **Pocomoke round-bottoms**. Clipper bow with billethead, headrails, and trailboards. Stout bowsprit bowsed down, generally parallel to the waterline; secured by 2 gammoning irons and characteristic knightheads. Broad, raked transom stern, fitted with taffrails; most have an outboard rudder controlled by linkage from rudderhead to a wheel. The large centerboard hangs below skeg when lifted, but designed to rise if the vessel grounds. Decked; small **skipjacks** half-decked with trunk cabin aft, cuddy forward, and cargo hatch amidships. Some early boats had a large, standing well abaft the hatch. Topsides painted white; bottom red or brown. Mast stepped well forward and rakes sharply aft. Leg-of-mutton sail hooped to mast except for upper part between headstay and jibstay; laced to boom that extends beyond the stern. Full-cut jib has a partial club. Mainsail lowered into lazy jacks; 3-4 rows of reef points. A few were 2-masted and termed **three-sail bateau**. A **yawl*** (or **yawl boat***) was carried aboard prior to ca. 1904; now a **push boat*** (or **pusher**) provides the only legal means of motorized propulsion, although it is sometimes used as a **pullboat***, towing from the bowsprit. Can be sailed by one man; 4-6 deckhands used while dredging. Reported lengths 7.3-20.4m; e.g., length on deck 12.3m, beam 4.6m, molded depth 0.86m. Some of the smaller boats used for summer crabbing were 6.7-9m long (**crab scrapers***); a narrower, fast type, called **hand scrapers, night scrapers**, and **oyster pirates**, was developed for poaching. Other recorded names: **bat(t)eau***, **box-built boat, deadrise, diamond bottom, oyster bateau, two-sail bateau, V-bottom**. Further reading: Howard I. Chapelle, "Notes on Chesapeake Bay Skipjacks," *American Neptune* (St. Michaels, Md.: Chesapeake Bay Maritime Museum, October, 1944; reprint, 1981). Note also **crabbing bateau, down the bay sharpie, dredge boat, half skipjack**. 2. In the Jacksonville area of northeastern Florida, the **skipjack** was used for fishing, and some were **yachts***. Dated from about the mid-19th century. Straight, slightly raked stem; plumb stern; V-bottom; considerable deadrise; bottom commonly planked longitudinally; chines rose above the waterline at bow and stern. Centerboard. **Sloop**-rigged with a large, boomed gaff sail; long bowsprit. Some sprit-rigged. Length 6m, beam 2.26m, draft 0.7m.

skipsbåt 1. Icelandic and Norwegian generic term for a **ship's boat***. One that is towed may be called **aftrhlestr** or **eftirbátr**. Spelling variants: **skibbaad, skibbåt, skipbåt, skip(s)bátr**. Note also **eftirbátur**. 2. *Norway:* Small, sturdy, open boat. Primarily carried aboard, on stern or quarter davits, or towed behind a **jekt*** (**jektbåt, jægtbaad**) or a **storbåt***. Clinker-planked; keel; sharp bow with curved stem; slightly raked transom; slack bilges. Rowed with 2-3 pairs of oars. Reported lengths 5.3-5.5m; e.g., length 5.3m, beam 1.84m, depth 0.66m. Spelling variants: **skibbåt, skipbåt**. Note also **jolle-6, kunte, skeis**.

skipsbátr See **skipsbåt-1**

skjegte See **sjekte**

skjøite See **skøyte-1**

Sklavenschiff See **slaver-1**

skloup See **canoe goëmonier, chaloupe**

skochi See **sekochi**

sköddel, sköddlar See **dory-4**

skoeid See **skeid**

skoe'oetè, skoesi, skoetji See **sekochi**

skogsproduktfartyg See **timber carrier**

skøite See **skoyte**

skoitje See **sekochi**

skøjte See **skøyte-1**

skoller, skolloer See **sculler**

Skoltebask See **bask**

Skoltelapsbåt *Norway, NE:* Sewn boat of the Skolte Same peoples of Finnmark. Used for spring cod fishing. Three lapped strakes per side; steep rise to the floors; straight keel; heavy frames treenailed. Strongly curved, sharp stem, recurved above the top strake; sharp, straight sternpost. Open; outboard rudder worked with slender, single-arm tiller. Mast stepped at heavy middle thwart. Set a tall trapezoidal sail, narrower at the foot. Shaped oarlocks with oars (3 per side) held by loops. Length 3.43m, beam 1.1m, depth 0.4m.

skôna See **schooner, skûna-2**

skonare, škoner, skonert, skonjar, skonnert See **schooner**

skonnertbrig See **hermaphrodite brig**

skooner See **schooner**

skoridor See **scorridora**

sköt See **skötbåt-1**

skötbåt 1. *Finland, S:* Strongly built, seagoing **fishing boat★** of the southern part of the west coast, the south coast, and the Åland Archipelago; uses a drift net (*sköt*) for herring; also used for interisland travel. Open boat; clinker-planked; sharp or transom-sterned with bluff lines. Raked, curving stem; rising floors; slack bilges; narrower toward the stern; some ceiled; considerable sheer. Rudder curves under the raking sternpost, vertical on after side; tiller. May have detachable washboards. Spritsails set to 2 masts of roughly equal height, stepped through thwarts, the foremast in the eyes. Mainsail may be boomed; foresail loose-footed. Some employ a single foresail tacked to the stemhead. Early boats set a single square sail. Also rowed, using single and double tholepins. Crew of 2. Reported lengths 6.1-8.2m; e.g., length 7.7m, beam 2.8m, depth 0.8m. Other recorded names: **Kökar sköt, nätibåt, skeit, sköt.** Note also **jolle-2.**

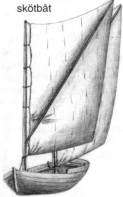

skötbåt

2. *Sweden, E:* Catches herring and salmon along the coast with a drift net; may also carry produce and animals; for the latter, 2 boats are set **catamaran★**-fashion with a penned-in platform between. Sharp-ended; clinker-built, usually with 4 strakes, sometimes 5; some large early boats were double-hulled; smaller types might be ceiled at the bow and stern. Stem rounded; sternpost straight or curved and raked at about 45°; relatively short, straight "T" keel; soft turn of the bilges. Those that carried produce were equipped with a breakwater. Flooring amidships on some. Rudder hung outboard when sailing; tiller. Rowed by 2-3 men; oars worked against a type of tholepin fastened to the inside of the gunwale and restrained by a loop. One or 2 masts stepped through or against the thwarts, position varying with locale. Sets lug-, sprit-, or gaff sails; some also use a headsail and a jib to a bowsprit. Sails may be boomed, loose-footed, or a combination. Some equipped with a motor. Crew of 2-3. Reported lengths 6-9m, widths 1.5-2m; a small type, called a **julle** on Singö, north of Stockholm, is 4.5-4.8m long. Further reading: "Ett Skötbåtsbygge," *Västerbotten* (1986): 115-127.

skotchi See **sekochi**

sköteka *Finland, west-central/Sweden, SE:* Used a drift net (*sköt*) for herring along the coasts. Clinker-built, generally with 5 strakes on each side; curved stem; straight keel; strongly raked transom, often with an external sternpost. Usually open, but the larger boats that stay at sea have a cabin aft. Rowed and sailed. At the turn of the century, set a square sail; later a sprit-sail. Reported lengths 5.4-7.5m; e.g., length 6.5m, beam 2.75m. Other recorded names: **fiskeöka, skötöka, strömmingsöka.** Note also **eka.**

skothomlin *Scotland, N:* Early 19th-century boat of the Shetland Islands rowed by 5 men; 4 double-banked, the stern man rowing single-banked. Sharp-ended, clinker-planked. Name variant: **five-man boat**

skotji See **sekochi**

skotkjeiping, skotkjeiving See **firroring-4**

skötöka See **sköteka**

skouna See **schooner**

skoute See **scout**

Skovshoved sildebåd See **sildebåd**

Skow *Germany, N:* A flat-bottomed craft found in north German rivers. See also **scow-1.**

skowt See **scout**

skøyta See **skøyte-1**

skøyte *Norway, S and SW:* **1.** Designation used since the early 19th century for the large boats of the area that were decked or half-decked. Popular as fishing **smacks★, pilot boats★, coasters★,** fisheries guards and life-saving boats (**redningsskøyte★**). Sharp ends below the waterline with shallow, overhanging transoms above. Clinker- or carvel-planked; sometimes drag to the deep keel; curved stem, often cutaway forefoot. Outboard rudder; tiller. Some had a deckhouse. Gaff-rigged as a **cutter★, sloop★,** or **ketch★**; some sprit-rigged.

2. The **risørskøyte** was built in the Søndeledsfjorden area of southeast Norway, especially at Risør and on Barmen Island. Engaged in drift net fishing and shrimp trawling, and was also used as a **pilot boat**

from ca. 1868. Carvel planking; straight keel with drag; steep rise to the floors; high bilges. Sharp ends, the curved stem strongly cutaway below the waterline. Decked; outboard rudder; tiller. Usually painted white. Loose-footed, boomed gaff sail set to a stout pole mast; large staysail, jib to bowsprit. Reported lengths 9-12m; e.g., length 11.6m, beam 4.12m, draft 1.85m. Other recorded names: **barmenskjøite, barmenskøite, sondeledskøyte**

3. The **arendalsskøyte** was a popular **pilot boat** (**losskøyte** or **lodsskøite**). Built near and to the south of Arendal. Full, high, clinker-planked hull; more roughly built than the boats to the northeast. Strongly curved stem, plumb sternpost; maximum beam forward of amidships, and width retained almost to the stern. Short keel. Decked; outboard rudder; tiller. Boomed, loose-footed gaff sail, staysail, jib to a long bowsprit, sometimes a topsail.

4. Farther west was the beamy **listerskøyte** that was built in the Lister area. The **fishing boats*** drifted (**drivgarnskøyte**) for fresh herring or mackerel (**makrellskøyte***) on the North Sea. Many of the cargo boats (**frakteskøytene**) carried lumber, the smallest ca. 30 cords, the largest 80 cords. Clinker- or carvel-planked; rising floors, soft bilges; especially sharp bow, fuller stern. Ends vertical or slightly curved; the stem might have slight tumble home. Outboard rudder; tiller. Decked, a few half-decked; steering well; later boats had a small trunk cabin aft. The **fishing boats** had a roller for nets at the bow. Most single-masted, setting a sprit- or gaff sail, yard topsail, staysail, jib to a long bowsprit. Mainmast was either a pole mast or had a topmast with topsail; mizzen a pole mast, rarely set a topsail. The occasional 2-masted type was called a **topindere**. Crew of 3-5. Reported lengths 9-12m; e.g., length 9m, beam 3.4m. Other recorded names: **listerskjøite, listersköite**; 2 main sub-types: **bordhaugskøyte** (with vertical stem above the waterline) and **vatneskøyte**

5. On the southwest coast, especially in Sunnhordland and Hardanger, the **høneræyskøyte** was characterized by a square platform above the rounded stern. The so-called **hen's tail smack** carried produce and fresh herring to Bergen. Worked from ca. 1830 and lasted into the 1960s as a **houseboat***. Clinker-built; long keel with drag. Sharp bow at the waterline; stem mildly curved; sternpost straight and raked; soft turn of the bilges. The wide sheer strake continued beyond the sternpost to create an overhanging platform. Rudderpost came up through the platform; tiller. Decked; cabin aft. Most single-masted, setting a loose-footed, boomed gaff sail, topsail, staysail, jib and sometimes a flying jib to the bowsprit. Some also set a square sail to a yard forward of the mast. Another type was 2-masted, the **topinner**. Reported lengths 12-21m. Name variant: **høneræva**

Other recorded names: **skjøite, skøite, sköite, skøjte, skøyta**; pl. **skøytene, skøyter; Vestlandsskøyte; stengeriggskøyte, storskjøite, storskøyte**. Note also **bankskøyte, hvalerbåt, losbåt, makrellskøyte**.

skøytene, skøyter See **skøyte-1**

---

s'kuchi See **sekochi**

skude Danish word for a small **ship*** or **vessel***, especially in a deprecatory sense. Spelling variant: pl. **skuder**. Note also **sandskude**. Further references: **skuta-1, skuta-3, skuta-4**

skuder See **skude, skuta-1**

Skullboot, Skulleiner See **scull**

skuller See **sculler**

skûna 1. *Syria:* Vessel that often carried oranges to Malta, returning with cordage. Also sailed to Odessa on the Black Sea. A **hermaphrodite brig***, the foremast carrying square sails, the mainmast a fore-and-aft sail. Name variant: **brick goélette**
2. *Tunisia:* **Hermaphrodite brig** either bought from Europeans or built at Jerba. Clipper bow; counter stern; long, straight keel. Decked; rudder came up inboard. Square sails on the mainmast. Loose-footed, boomed gaff sail on the mainmast; gaff topsail. Jib to a rising bowsprit. Reported lengths 25-30m; e.g., length 30m, beam 8m, depth 4m. Other recorded names: **brick goélette, skôna**; pl. **skâin**

škuner See **schooner**

skut See **scout**

skuta 1. Small naval craft of the Viking period that conducted coastal missions. Narrow in proportion to length, having been built for speed. Rowed with 10-20 oars on a side; one designed solely for rowing called a **róðrarskúta**. Other recorded names: **hleypi-skúta** (swift **skúta**), **hleypi-skip, létti-skúta*** (light **skuta**), **skude*** (pl. **skuder**); pl. **skutur**
2. *Iceland:* **Skúta** is sometimes given as a general term for a **boat***, **vessel***, or **smack***, but it may also be applied to a **cutter***- or **ketch***-rigged vessel. One engaged in fishing is called a **fiskiskúta**. Early types accompanied a **fleet*** for use in rivers and along the coast.
3. *Norway:* Generic term for a small vessel, especially one that sails. Usually decked. Those working out of Bergen on the west coast in the 19th century were deep, beamy boats that carried produce, firewood, and charcoal from neighboring fjords. Crew of 2. Length ca. 11m. Name variants: **skude***, **skute**; pl. **skutor**
4. *Sweden:* Popular term for a variety of boats. Also a general term for a small cargo boat that was important from at least the 16th century. Early boats probably sewn. Stepped 1-2 masts; more recently motorized. A large sailing vessel may be familiarly called a **skuta**. Other recorded names: **scoote, segelskuta, skude***, **skutan**; pl. **skutor(na)**. Note also **roslagskuta**.
Further reference: **szkuta**

skutan See **skuta-4**

skutar See **szkuta**

skute See **scout, skuta-3**

skutor See **skuta-3, skuta-4**

skutorna See **skuta-4**

skûtsje *Netherlands, N:* In Frisian, a term meaning **boat***. Now more often describes a produce and peat carrier of the Friesland area belonging to the **tjalk*** family. Dates to the mid-15th century. Constructed originally of wood, later of iron or steel. Flat floors with rounded bilges, snub bows with deep curved stem, rounded stern. Strong sheer; top strake above the heavy wale with sharp tumble home at the bow. Wide leeboards hung just abaft the mast. Decked; cambered central hatch; some have a low cabin aft; early vessels had a steering well. Wide rudder; humped tiller slots over rudderhead. Tall, strikeable mast stepped about one-quarter in from the bow. Loose-footed, boomed mainsail; small, curved gaff. Jib to a short jibboom. Crew of 2. Reported lengths 10-18.3m; e.g., length 13.15m, beam 3.02m, depth 1.07m; shallow draft. Other recorded names: **aardappelskûtsje, Fries skûtsje, ierdappelskûtsje** (potato **skûtsje**), **modderskûtsje** (dredged-mud carrier), **skuutje.** Note also **schuit, schuitje.**

skutur See **skuta-1**

skuutje See **skûtsje**

skyfe See **skiff**

skyscraper See **clipper**

skyssbåd See **skyssbåt**

skyssbåt *Norway, W:* Provided transportation for officials, merchants, and wealthy people along the highly indented coastline of western Norway. The **presteskyssbåt** conveyed the minister. Usually a long, sleek hull with a relatively narrow transom or counter. Stem curved and often cutaway; high sheer forward. Clinker planking, flared sides, maximum beam well forward; outboard rudder. The large **vengebåt** had a cabin (*veng*) aft; some cabins portable and used only in bad weather. Usually painted white in contrast to the tarred hulls of other regional vessels. Mainly rowed, but in suitable conditions, might set a small square sail. Used 3-5 pairs of oars. Reported lengths of the **vengebåt** 6.3-9.6m; length-to-beam ratio 3.8:1. Other recorded names: **conveyance boat, skyssbåd, Speiel-Baad** (in Sunnmøre); **vængebaad, vengebaad, vengbåt.** A special boat that carried officials to Eidsvoll was called an **Eidsvollbåt.** Note also **husbåt.**

slaaf haelder See **slaver-1**

slacker See **coal slacker**

slagbaad, slagbåt See **garnbåt-1**

Slaney cot See **gabbard-1**

slash-marée See **chasse-marée**

slavenhaler, slavenschip See **slaver**

slaver 1. Ship that transported slaves, mainly from West Africa. Prior to the ban on the trade in the early 19th century, slaves were carried not only to the Western Hemisphere but also to Great Britain. Following the ban, the trade to the United States, the West Indies, and Brazil continued until the middle of the century. The early vessels were fast for the sake of their cargo and relatively burdensome, but after the ban, speed became a factor in order to avoid detection. Most later ships were built in the United States; the later and smaller **Baltimore clippers*** were the most popular; other building sites included Cuba and Brazil. The slaves, as many as 500, were tightly packed and chained between decks; about half died en route. Later ships were relatively small and of light displacement with sharp waterlines, deep hull aft, slightly hollow floors, low freeboard, unencumbered deck with few openings. Most **brig***-rigged (**brig-slaver** or **slaver-brig**). Some were **topsail schooners.** Long spars

increased sail area. Crew of ca. 40 on the **brigs.** Later vessels mostly 23-30m long between perpendiculars. Other recorded names: **African trader, bâtiment (navire** or **vaisseau) négrier, buque** (or **navío) negrero, guineaman, Guinea-ship, nave negriera, negreiro, négrier, negriere, negrero, negro ship, Sklavenschiff, slaaf haelder, slavenhaler, slavenschip, slave ship, slaveskibet**

2. May refer to a ship on which the crew is required to work exceptionally hard. Name variant: **slave ship**

slaver-brig, slave ship, slaveskibet See **slaver**

Slavey canoe See **k'i t'u ela, tsu'u t'u ela**

slechtaak See **aak, griendaak**

sled See **covered sled**

sledge boat See **iceboat**

sleep-beunschip See **beunschip-2**

sleepboot, sleepbootje See **tug**

sleepbotter See **Marker botter**

sleeper *Netherlands:* **Fishing boat*** that dragged a narrow net to catch smelt.

sleeping wanigan See **wanigan**

sleepklipper See **klipper-1**

sleepspits See **spits**

slep See **barge-1**

slepebåt See **tug**

şlep ponton See **dummy barge**

şlepul de Prut See **pletină**

Sleusenkriecher See **Bojer**

Sliedrechter aak, Sliedrechter aakje, Sliedrechtse aak See **baggeraak**

slijkpraam *Netherlands:* Small, open boat reported from Groningen Province in the northeast and Utrecht Province in the south-central part of the country. Used mainly for dredging, *slijk* meaning mud. Rounded ends with straight sides between; rounded bottom and bilges; narrow. Outboard rudder; tiller. In the Groningen area, a modified type was called a **vlotpraam;** primarily for farm use. Other recorded names: **Groninger slijkpraam, modderpraam, slÿkpraam**

slipper boat See **ma ling ting**

slitta a vela See **iceboat**

šljupka See **jolly boat-1**

sloep 1. Reported initially in the 16th century in the Netherlands as a **ship's boat*** that maintained communication with shore, especially to transport personnel; continues to the present as the **reddingsloep.** Also used in Belgium and was an important vessel on the Hudson River in the 17th century. Early boats clinker-built; cutaway bow, small transom or sharp stern. Generally open with numerous thwarts. Early **sloepen** (pl.) were sprit-rigged with staysail or set a leg-of-mutton sail to an unstayed mast stepped in the eyes; some were 2-masted with square sails. Those carried aboard a naval vessel were also called **barkas*** and were heavy and rowed by 4-6 men, double-banked; on a merchant vessel, they were called a **groote** (or **grote) boot.** By the early 17th century, some were as long as 12.8m and 2.7m wide. Other recorded names: **chaloep, chaloupe*, sloepe.** Note also **longboat.**

2. *Belgium:* Built, beginning in the 18th century, for cod fishing, often going to Iceland and Greenland. One type (the **sloepschip**) carried cargo. Early vessels had a full build, rounded bows, fairly flat floors, flat stern, and set a single boomed gaff sail (the **eenmastsloep**). Later, their characteristics were more varied, some having a counter or rounded stern, and most stepped a mizzen either on the sternpost or well inboard (the **tweemastsloep**) and topsail above the gaff mainsail. Decked; high bulwarks; many had a live well. Crew of 5. Reported lengths 15-18m; e.g., length 17.5m, beam 5.45m, depth 3.25m, cap. 40t. Other recorded names: **chaloupe***, **chaloupe flamande**, **vis(ch)chaloupe**. Note also **Antwerpse sloep**, **Oostendse sloep**.

3. *Netherlands:* From the early 19th century until ca. 1930, the word **sloep** also designated a **fishing boat*** used mainly in the North Sea. One employed in longline (*beug*) fishing was called a **beugsloep**. Carvel- or clinker-built; later of steel. Early vessels had a heavy, curved stem; later straight. Flat stern gave way to a transom or elliptical counter; long, straight keel with drag. Decked, generally with a large live well (**beunsloep**). Rig evolved, being gaff-rigged with 2 headsails, **schooner***- or **ketch***-rigged. A small, sprit-rigged type with a well was called a **sloepke**. Reported lengths 5.8-25m; e.g., length 20.7m, beam 5.8m, depth 3m. Other recorded names: **bünnsloep**, **bunsloep**, **chaloupe***, **Langleinen chaluppe**, **sloepe**, **sloepken**, **vischbunsloep**, **vischchaloup**, **vis(ch)sloep**, **visschersloep**, **vissloep**. Note also **beunschip**, **kotter**, **longboat**, **panneschuit**.

Further reference: **Heistse schuit**

sloepe, sloepen See **sloep**
sloepke, sloepken See **sloep-3**
sloepschip See **sloep-2**
Slof, Sloffen See **Ruhraak**

sloop Term has meant different craft at different times and at different places, referring initially to hull type, to a naval rating, and later to rig. Principal distinctions are as follows:

1. In the British Royal Navy of the 17th-19th centuries, a class of small, square- or sprit-rigged naval vessel (**sloop-of-war**) carrying guns on the upper deck only. Might be rigged as a 3-masted **ship*** (**ship-sloop**), **snow***, 2-masted **brig*** (**brig-sloop**), or **ketch***. The rank of the commanding officer determined the term by which the vessel was called; e.g., the **ship-sloop** was commanded by a captain and carried 24 guns, the **brig-sloop** by a commander. Other recorded names: **chaloupe de guerre**, **Kriegsloop** (or **Kriegsschaluppe**), **oorlogssloep**

2. Prior to the mid-19th century, also a general term for a **coaster*** that was gaff-rigged with 2 headsails, one hanked to a forestay on the stem and the other to an outer forestay on a standing, steeved-up bowsprit; the addition of 1 or more square or gaff topsails created a **topsail sloop**. Distinct from the **cutter*** of the period, which was narrower and built for speed; in the latter part of the period, characterized by the running, more horizontal bowsprit. Other recorded names: **cheloup**, **sloope**, **slop(e)**, **soup(e)**, **slup***

3. Recent terminology becomes further confused with **cutter**. A **sloop** usually carries a single jib to a jibstay, although a temporary headsail may be added. The

sloop's mainsail is generally larger than that of the **cutter**, and the mast is stepped farther forward. British Admiralty terminology describes a **sloop** as having a high-peaked standing lugsail, sometimes loose-footed. Note also **knockabout**, **sloep**.

4. In the 17th century, might be a large, open boat along the general lines of a **longboat***.

5. In World War II, British **sloops** were a class of convoy escort vessels.

6. *Canada, E:* Flat-bottomed boat that transported sawn timber on the middle St. Lawrence River in the second half of the 19th and early 20th centuries; gone by World War II. Mainly flat-bottomed, but a few had keels. Raked, straight stem; high, wide transom above a raked sternpost; flared sides. Open abaft the mast; small cabin forward. Outboard rudder; tiller. Mast stepped against the keel about a third in from the bow. Gaff mainsail, either boomed or loose-footed; jib to stemhead. Crew of 2-3. Reported lengths 9.3-22.8m; 1886 vessel 15.5m long, 6m wide, 1.6m deep. Other recorded names: **bateau***, **St. Lawrence sloop**

7. *France, N:* **a.** The fishing **sloup** of the French Flanders coast mainly stepped a single mast, but some had a mizzenmast also. Gaff mainsail loose-footed but boomed; usually a jib-headed or yard topsail. Mizzen might set a gaff or lugsail. Some ran out a bowsprit with 2-3 jibs, others only a large staysail. Most carvel-planked; square or counter stern; plumb stem; some had a wet well. Name variant: **semaque**. **b.** Small **coaster** of the north coast of Brittany, often carrying apples in season. Plumb stem, counter stern; high freeboard forward, low aft; deep drag to the straight keel; decked. Sets a loose-footed gaff mainsail, jib-headed or lug topsail to a topmast; 2 headsails. Long bowsprit. Length 14.2m, beam 4.35m. Other recorded names: **seloup**, **sequelouppe**, **sloup***

8. *France, SW:* Type of solidly constructed **gabare*** used in the Gironde Estuary. Large capacity to transport heavy cargoes as far as Bordeaux. Gone by World War II. Flat floors, straight keel, quick turn of the bilges; straight, plumb sides. Bluff bow, curved stem; rounded stern; slightly raked, straight sternpost; moderate sheer. Large midships hatch with high coaming. Outboard rudder; short tiller. Mast stepped into a tall tabernacle about a quarter in from the bow. Set a loose-footed gaff sail, jib to bowsprit. Auxiliary installed in 1920s. Reported lengths 18-22m. Spelling variant: **sloup***. Note also **courau**.

9. *United States:* **a.** The small **sloop** of colonial America was used as a trader, traveling frequently to the West Indies, and as a **whaler***, **fishing boat***, or **privateer***. In the American Revolution, was used as an armed fighter. Fine-lined; a lightly curved stem; square, moderately raked stern, though some rounded; strong sheer; heavy wales. The smaller types were open and worked in protected waters; the larger were usually decked and fitted with bulwarks; some had a deck cabin at the stern. Rudder outboard. In Chesapeake Bay, a centerboard was added ca. 1820, and thereafter the vessels became known as **he-sloops**. Single mast generally raked, setting a large, boomed gaff sail with a short gaff; some had 2-3 yards for square topsails. Long, steeved-up bowsprit ran atop the stemhead; 2-3 headsails. Reported lengths on keel 10.4-13.7m; length on keel 12.5m, beam 5m, depth of hold 2.3m. Other recorded names: **fore-and-after***, **sloope**. Note also **Bermuda sloop**. **b.** In the Narragansett Bay area of Rhode Island, **sloop**-rigged boats provided **ferry*** service until the 1870s. Open except for short foredeck on which a small wagon or cart might be placed; livestock contained in the waist amidships, forward of a bulkhead; benches for passengers aft. Heavy oak planking; counter stern. Set a loose-footed, boomed gaff sail to a mast stepped just abaft the foredeck; jib to a short bowsprit. Length ca. 10.7m; shallow draft. **10.** *West Indies:* The **sloop** of the Windward and Leeward Islands is widely used to carry freight, passengers, and for fishing. Most are rigged with a gaff, jib-headed or gunter mainsail, and 1-2 headsails; has an exceptionally long boom. Most roughly built with carvel planking, usually of pitch pine above the waterline, greenheart below; natural crook frames of cedar. Counter or raked transom stern; curved or straight, raked stem; bluff bow; full body amidships; strong sheer. Larger boats decked, often with a trunk cabin in after part. Northern boats that engage in fishing may have a wet well, but in the southern islands, the fish are dried in the rigging. Those with auxiliaries have a double sternpost, the rudder hung from the after post. Crew of 3 plus a boy. Reported lengths 7-30m; e.g., length 8.2m, beam 2.4m, depth 1.2m. Other recorded names: **Caribbean sloop, trading sloop, West Indies sloop**. Note also **Jamaica sloop, Tortola sloop, West Indies schooner**.

Further references: **Belizean smack, hoy-1, Humber sloop, plunger-2, Ramsgate smack, Schlup-1**

sloop à tape-cul See **dindet, sloop à tape-cul**

sloop boat *United States, NE:* A fast, **sloop***-rigged **fishing boat*** developed ca. 1880 by builders on Cape Ann in eastern Massachusetts and known as a **Gloucester sloop boat**. Built on the Maine coast also, where they were known as **Friendship sloops***. Some worked until the 1940s. Sharp bow with either plumb or concave stem; cutaway forefoot; long counter stern. Deep drag to keel; considerable deadrise and generally some hollow in garboard; moderate sheer. Decked; the larger boats with a short quarter-deck and trunk cabin aft; small boats were flush-decked and had the cabin forward. Mast stepped about a third back from the bow. Gaff mainsail with long, overhanging boom; on some, a gaff topsail set from a fidded topmast; fixed bowsprit with staysail and 1-2 jibs. Many had small gasoline engines. Crew of 4. Reported lengths 12-18m; e.g., length 16m, beam 4.6m, depth 2m, draft loaded 2.2m. Other recorded names: **Gloucester sloop**; also **Cape Ann, Essex**, and **Salem sloop boat**. Further reading: Howard I. Chapelle, *American Sailing Craft* (New York: Bonanza Books, 1986): 109-121. Further references: **Friendship sloop, Key West sponge sloop, smack boat-1**

sloop bo't See **Friendship sloop**

sloop coquillier brestois See **coquillier**

sloop drogher *United States, SE:* **Sloop***-rigged vessel that served riverine plantations in the late 18th and early 19th centuries. Some made short coastal trips. Rice a principal cargo. Length 16.5m, beam 6m, hold depth 2.3m. Note also **drogher**.

sloope See **sloop-2, sloop-9a**

sloop langoustier See **langoustier-1**

sloop-of-war See **corvette-1, sloop-1, snow**

sloop sablaise See **barque sablaise**

slop See **Schlup-1, sloop-2**

slope See **sloop-2**

sloup See **Schlup-1, scute-2b, sloop-2, sloop-7**

sloup à tape-cul *France:* Early term for a **yawl*** with a single headsail, usually a large jib to a long bowsprit. Name variants: **sloop à tape-cul**; at Cancale, called **chloupe**. Further reference: **dindet**

sloup caseyeur See **caseyeur**

sloup coquillier, sloup coquillier de la Rade de Brest See **coquillier-1**

sloupe See **sloop-2**

sloup goemonier See **canot goëmonier**

sloup langoustier See **langoustier-1**

sluice boat See **double-bottom-2**

slup **1.** *Denmark:* **a.** Slender cargo carrier that became popular in the early 19th century. Deep hull; generally curved, vertical stem; raked transom or elliptical stern, straight keel, light sheer. Flush deck, deep bulwarks. Mast carried a tall topmast. Gaff mainsail, loose-footed and with a long boom; staysail, jib, and sometimes a flying jib; gaff topsail. Some used a square foresail and square topsail. Crew of 2-3. Reported lengths 10.7-13.7m, widths 4-4.6m, draft 1.7-2.2m. Spelling variants: **sluppe**; pl. **sluppen, slupper. b.** The fishing **slup** of the Faroe Islands was ketch*-rigged with a straight stem and counter stern. In Denmark, this boat, built since 1912, would be called a **hajkutter**; average length 15m. Other recorded names: **Haikutter**; pl. **sluppir**. Note also **hajer**. **2.** *Lithuania:* A **šlūp** was an early type of vessel. Name variant: **kug**

Further references: **jakt-1, Schlup-1, sloop-2, slupp**

slupar See **jakt-1, storbåt-1**

Slupe See **Schlup-1**

sluper See **slupp**

šlupka See **jolly boat-1**

slupp *Norway:* **Coaster*** and **fishing boat*** that dates to the 18th century. Straight, vertical or lightly curved stem; sharp bow; raked sternpost; raked, flat counter stern; long, straight keel. Decked; some had cabin house aft. Rudder; tiller comes up inboard. Stepped a single mast with a long topmast. Loose-footed, boomed gaff mainsail, gaff topsail, forestaysail, jib to jibboom, and at times, a flying jib topsail. Some early vessels set square sails forward of the mast when running free; the large, lower sail fastened only by a ring in the upper corners, and 2 square topsails. Crew of 2-3. Reported lengths 12-23m; e.g., length 18.3m, beam 5m, molded depth 2.4m. Spelling variants: **slup*, sluppen**; pl. **sluper, sluppene, slupper**. Note also **jakt**.

sluppe See **slup-1**

sluppen See **slup-1, slupp**

sluppene See slupp
slupper See slup-1, slupp
sluppir See slup
slúpskip *Iceland:* A type of sloop* that set a boomed
gaff mainsail, staysail, jib to a bowsprit, and sometimes a topsail. Used mostly for line fishing and herring drifting, mainly along the northwest coast.
Decked. Reported lengths 12-15m, widths 4-5m. Note
also skip.
Slüsenkrüper See Bojer
slutch boat See mud hopper
slÿkpraam See slijkpraam
smaafæring See færing
små-åttring See åttring
småbåt 1. *Norway:* Boat that is smaller than the average
size of the same type. Usually compartmented into no
more than 3 1/2 "rooms." In northern Norway, it is one
that is smaller than an åttring*.
2. *Sweden:* General term for a small-sized boat. Usually
rowed, but may be sailed. Term used with the same
connotation by Swedish Finns.
Note also storbåt.
smac, smacco See smack-1
smack 1. The word has been broadly applied to a fishing
boat*, coaster*, packet boat*, or a naval vessel's
tender*. English fishermen may differentiate between a
boat* and a smack, calling a decked craft a smack; others consider a smack to be a fishing boat devoted exclusively to trawling. In the 18th century, smack could be
synonymous with hoy*. Usually fore-and-aft rigged:
cutter*, sloop*, ketch*, or yawl*. The so-called smack
rig of the 18th century set a gaff trysail and a small
square topsail on the forward side of the mast, with a
square course below. Many fishing smacks now fully
motorized. The packet boats could be as much as 20t
burden. Other recorded names: semac(c)o, semale,
semalo, semaque, shmak, smac(co), smack boat*,
smacke, smag. Note also boat-7, cod smack, dry boat,
lobster smack, Schmack, trading smack, well boat.
2. *Canada, E:* In Newfoundland and Labrador, a smack
was a small, decked vessel that sailed between settlements collecting fish, lobsters, etc., for processing or
export; also carried passengers. A motorized vessel
serving the same function might be called a collecting
boat* or collector boat. Name variant: homardier
(French Canada)
3. *Sweden:* Term applied to a sailing craft used either for
fishing or for cargo. Rigged as a yawl, ketch, or galeas*.
4. *Sweden, SE:* On the coast of Småland, a smack is a
type of roughly built, round-bottomed boat. Name
variant: smälla
5. *United Kingdom:* a. Cutter-rigged packet boat popular in the early 19th century for regular crossings of
the English Channel, North Sea, Irish Sea, and from
London to Scotland. Carried both passengers and
cargo. Heavily canvassed. Other recorded names: gay,
long boomer (Newhaven to Dieppe), packet cutter.
b. Fast, weatherly, cutter-rigged boat that worked out
of west coast ports from the Bristol Channel to
Morecambe Bay and the Isle of Man. Fished mainly
for herring from the late 18th century through the 1st

quarter of the 19th century. The larger boats (40-60t)
were buyer smacks*. Clinker-planked; curved stem,
raked stern, half-decked. Loose-footed, boomed gaff
mainsail; long boom. Jib to a long bowsprit; staysail.
Crew of 6. Lengths on keel 7-10m, beam 4m, hold
depth 1.8m. c. By the mid-19th century, northwest
coast smacks were mainly ketch-rigged trawlers*
engaged in bottom fishing. Straight stem, cutaway
forefoot; straight keel. Some cutter-rigged.
Auxiliaries on most boats. Crew of 4. 1893 boat 20.7m
long, 5.1m wide, draft 2.9m.
6. *United States:* Term was applied to fishing vessels
having a watertight compartment for keeping fish
alive, although the distinction was not always maintained. Primarily fore-and-aft rigged. Landsmen may
give the term fishing smack* to any fishing boat.
Also, term usually applied to any boat over 5t—i.e.,
those that must register with U.S. Customs. Other
recorded names: market smack, well(ed) smack.
Note also dry boat, smackee, well boat.
Further references: Belizean smack, Brixham smack,
family boat, hoy-1, lobster smack, Morecambe Bay
prawner, Plymouth barge, sharpie-schooner-3,
smak, terrapin smack, West Country sailing barge
smack boat 1. *Bahamas:* Sloop*-rigged craft built
locally in accordance with the type prevalent in that
community and by builder preference. Used mainly for
fishing, but also as a market boat* and for interisland
transportation. Popular in local regattas. Solid construction, natural crook frames; sharp bilges. Straight,
raked stem with a clipper-style knee; broad, raked,
wineglass transom; deep heel; long, straight rise to the
floors. Outboard rudder; tiller comes inboard below the
gunwale. Decked; small trunk cabin aft; wet well
amidships; cargo hold abaft the mast. Most painted
white with colored trim; wing-like design on transom.
Mast, nearly twice boat length, stepped well forward,
setting a loose-footed, boomed leg-of-mutton sail fitted
with a wooden headboard; those with a jib to a
bowsprit were called locally a sail boat* or sailing
boat. Boom projects 1.8-3m beyond the stern. Deep
roach in the foot of the sail; reefed by a tricing line to
raise the foot. Long, tapering bowsprit mortised to a
samson post. Headsail carries 2 pairs of sheets, the
upper used in strong winds. Crew of 3. Reported keel
lengths 5.5-12.2m; e.g., length on keel ca. 8m, beam
3.4m, depth amidships 1.8m. Other recorded names:
Bahama sloop (or smack), bowsprit sloop, sloop
boat*. Note also Bahama dinghy, sharpshooter-1.
2. *United States, NE:* Small, inshore, New England lobstering and fishing boat*. Design varied with the
builder; lapstrake. Despite name, lacked a wet well.
Further reference: smack-1
smacke See smack-1, smak
smackee *United States, SE:* Fishing or market boat*
that worked out of Key West, Florida, in the late 19th
century. Carvel-planked; straight keel with drag; some
with skeg; high, rising floors; round bilges, flared
above. Sharp bow; rake of stem varied, some plumb;
rounded forefoot; some had a gammon knee head.
Sharply raked, V- or heart-shaped transom; straight

sternpost. Rudderpost came up through a hole in the stern; tiller. Decked; cuddy forward, sometimes a trunk cabin fitted over one of the hatches. Cockpit with coaming; live well. Larger boats **sloop***-rigged, either with a leg-of-mutton mainsail or with a small club at the head of the sail; long boom, sail usually loose-footed. Slender pole mast stepped well forward. Jib to a short, light, fixed bowsprit. The smaller boats went out only for day runs (the **single-day boats** or **one-day boats**) and carried no jib. Crew of 2. Lengths overall 6.4-8.5m, widths 1.96-2.44m, depths and draft 1.22-1.37m. The cat-rigged boats were 4.3-4.9m long by 1.22-1.83m wide by 1.0m deep. Further name variant: **Key West smackee**

smack schooner See **schooner smack**
smack ship See **smak**
småfæring See **færing**
småfembøring See **fembøring**
småferja See **ferje**
smag See **smack-1**
små-halfjermeng See **seksæring-6**
småjakt See **jakt-2**
småjekt See **jekt**
smak *Belgium/Netherlands:* Heavily built cargo vessel that served mainly as a **coaster***, trading as far as the Baltic Sea and Spain; also used on inland waterways and for naval purposes. Basically of similar construction from the 17th to the late 19th century, but with varying rigs. Bluff bow and stern; long, straight keel; deep stem, wide forefoot; deadwood aft; flat floors; rounded bilges. Strong sheer, especially toward the stern; leeboards; outboard rudder with tall rudderhead; on 17th-century vessels, the tiller passed through a triangular opening in the wide top strake. Decked; galley and passenger bunks forward; series of cambered hatches, followed by a cabin for the crew, abaft the mainmast. One windlass forward on sprit-rigged boats and one abaft the cabin. 17th-century vessels set a large spritsail on the mainmast, with a long sprit. Mizzenmast stepped against the taffrail, setting a loose-footed, boomed gaff sail with a very short gaff; staysail and jib, square topsail. By the 18th century, a standing gaff mainsail was substituted, often with a square sail forward of the mast and square topsails. Reported lengths 15-25m; e.g., length 20m, beam 6.8m, hold depth 2.5m. Other recorded names: **Schmack***, **Schmackschiff**, **semaque**, **smack***, **smacke**, **smack ship**, **smakk**, **smak(k)schip**; pl. **smakken, smaks, smakschepen**
smakje See **tjalk-3**
smakk See **smak**
smakke *Denmark:* **1.** Mid-18th- to early 19th-century cargo vessel. Flat floors, generally full bows and buttocks, nearly plumb sides, leeboards. Decked; usually a deckhouse for the crew. Stepped main- and mizzenmasts, the latter close to the stern. Gaff-rigged with a topsail; several headsails.
2. Smakker (pl.) of the early 19th century in the Store Bælt area of central Denmark were square-sterned, gaff-rigged vessels. Some served as **mail boats***. Decked; stern might have windows. Outboard rudder; tiller passed

beneath taffrail. Square sail set forward of mainmast at times; mainsail boomed. Name variant: **bæltsmakke**
3. The **smakke** of the north end of Sjælland is either open or decked; some still sail as pleasure craft. Early boats fished and sold supplies to passing vessels. Clinker-planked; sharp ends; curved stem and sternpost; outboard rudder; tiller. Hull generally tarred. Mast stepped just forward of amidships. Rectangular spritsail laced to mast, staysail, jib to a long bowsprit, jib-headed topsail. Reported lengths 5-6m; e.g., length 5.8m, beam 1.78m, draft 0.63m.
4. *Faroe Islands:* **Ketch***-rigged, seagoing **fishing boat*** of the late 19th century. Straight, plumb stem; square counter stern. Decked; tiller came up inboard. Length 25.6m, beam 6.2m; 50-100rt. Name variant: **fiskesmakke**
smakkejolle *Denmark, S:* Lightly built boat used for small-scale fishing, for ferrying, and as a **pilot boat***. Originated hundreds of years ago; existed until the

smakkejolle

1930s. Clinker-built; double-ended; low freeboard; often had removable washboards. Some had a wet well (**damjolle**). Stem and sternpost curved; often a slight gripe to stem; keel might extend beyond the sternpost. Some entirely open, others decked forward and aft with side decks forming a long, oval cockpit (**ringdækjolle**). Outboard rudder; tiller. Sailed with 1-3 rectangular spritsails (*smakke sejl*), boomed out at times; jib might run to a reefing bowsprit. Masts short, unstayed, and stepped through thwarts or were clamped to them. One with 2 masts was called **to-smakkejolle** or **2-smakkejolle**; a 3-masted boat was called **tre-smakkejolle** or **3-smakkejolle**. Also rowed with 1 man to an oar on different benches. Some motorized. Crew of 2-6. Reported lengths 5-8.8m, widths 1.6-2.8m, depths 0.54-0.97m; draft 0.39-0.71m. Other recorded name: **sprydstagejolle**
smakken See **smak**
smakker See **smakke**
smakschip, smaks, smakschepen, smakschip See **smak**
smalkarveel See **karveel**
smälla See **smack-4**
small bateau *United States, E:* Term applied to a small crabbing boat of Tangier Island on the eastern side of Chesapeake Bay. Equipped with a single sail, detachable tiller, centerboard, and single oar for sculling or poling. Mast inserted through a hole in the heavy foredeck ca. 46cm from the stem to a hole in a strong crosspiece below. Small, boomed gaff mainsail sheeted to pegs near the stern. When not in use, sail

wrapped around the detached mast and unit secured against the gunwale. Length ca. 5m.

small craft See **craft-5**

small pleasure boat See **xiao hua chuan**

small purse seiner See **ku tsai ting**

smalschepen See **smalschip**

smalschip *Netherlands:* Inland vessel that traveled many Dutch and Belgian waterways during the 17th-18th centuries. Maximum beam determined by the lock at Gouda, enabling the vessel to go through the city, while the **wijdschip★** had to use a peripheral waterway. Carvel-planked; full lines; deep, curved stem; straight sternpost; flat floors with keel; rounded bilges; topsides tumble home; strong sheer; heavy wales. Decked; long central hatch, rounded leeboards. Very wide rudder; tiller passed through stern bulwark. Set a large spritsail, foresail, and a small square topsail. Reported lengths 14.5-21.5m; e.g., length 17m, beam 4.5m, depth 2m. Other recorded names: **Schmalschiff, semale, semale-schip;** pl. **smalschepen, smalschipen**. See also **karveel**.

smalschipen See **smalschip**

små-seksroring See **fembøring-2, seksroring**

smelt scow *United States, NE:* Heavily constructed, open boat used in commercial net fishing for smelt on the Penobscot River in northeast Maine. Pine strakes; hackmatack frames supported one side and crossed the bottom; opposite counterpart adjacent so that frames were double across the bottom. Flat bottom longitudinally planked; slightly raked, square ends; mildly flared sides. Hand-operated winch at each end raised the frame and net. Propelled by a stern sculling oar. Crew of 2. Length 9.4m, beam 2.67m.

Smith Island crabbing skiff See **Smith Island skiff**

Smith Island skiff *United States, E:* Built at Smith Island and Crisfield on the Eastern Shore of Chesapeake Bay, especially for crab trotlining. Fast and light; V-bottom, planked fore-and-aft; some have considerable deadrise; straight, raked or plumb stem; shallow, raked transom stern; flat tumble home amidships on later models; widely spaced frames, no longitudinal framing. Centerboard; wide-bladed rudder; tiller. Decked at bow and around the sides. Aft-raking mast stepped well forward; leg-of-mutton sail with horizontal sprit boom. Might have an engine. Reported lengths 4.8-8.5m; e.g., length 6.5m, beam 1.5m, depth ca. 0.67m; shallow draft. Other recorded names: **dinky skiff** (or **skift**), **Smith Island crabbing skiff**. Note also **crabbing skiff**.

snaauw, snaauwschip See **snow**

snacac See **esnecca, snekkja**

snacc See **esnecca, snik**

snacca, snaccha, snace See **snekkja**

snacga See **snik**

snacha See **snekkja**

snäcka, snäckor, snäckorna See **snipa**

snackta See **schnayka**

snâdǫl See **sandal-5**

snaekke See **snekke**

snaekkia See **snekkja**

snake See **esnecca**

snake boat See **cao zi chuan, chang long, jeha dhoni, pambán-manché, she chuan, snekkja**

snäkka, snakr See **snekkja**

snapper *United States, E:* **1.** Nickname given to the double **canal boats★** joined end-to-end on the Pennsylvania Canal in the 2nd quarter of the 19th century. **2.** Served as general workboats in the North Carolina bays. Name derived from the snapping sound made by their single-cylinder engines. Shallow "V" bottom amidships and toward the stern; sharp "V" forward. Square or rounded stern; plumb stem; open. Length ca. 8.5m, narrow.
Further reference: **pungy**

snapper boat **1.** *Australia, E:* Originally, snapper was caught off New South Wales by handlines or longlines from a variety of craft; mostly lug-rigged, some rowed. By the 1920s, the motorized **snapper boats** became fairly standardized, but **canoe★** sterns generally replaced the transoms during the 1930s. Sharp bow; straight, vertical or slightly raked stem. Deadwood aft or planked down to the keel. Raised deck at the bow, followed by wheelhouse/cabin, then open or decked with cockpit aft. Sail mainly for emergency use. Reported lengths 6-10.7m; e.g., length 10m, beam 3.7m, draft 1.37m. Spelling variant: **schnapper boat** **2.** *Canada, E:* **Longliner★** type developed in the 1940s in Newfoundland to catch snapper. Catch sold to fresh-fish processing plants. Reported keel lengths 12.2-13.7m. **3.** *Sierra Leone:* European-type boat that worked near Freetown; now rarely seen. Plank-built with keel; sharp bow, cutaway stem; transom stern. Outboard rudder with wide blade; short tiller. Open; several thwarts; cooking stove at 2nd thwart. Mast stepped through forward thwart. Also paddled. Crew of 3-6. Reported lengths 8-10m. **4.** *United States, SE:* **a.** Two-masted **schooners★** worked out of Pensacola on the western Florida coast at least into the 1940s. Fished off this coast and later off Yucatan. Used mainly hand lines for snapper in winter and grouper in summer. Catch iced in holds. Equipped with auxiliaries. Crew to 12. Reported lengths 15-30m. Name variant: **red snapper smack**. Note also **ching**. **b.** Gasoline-powered **snapper boats** worked out of the Tarpon Springs area on the west coast of Florida beginning in the early 1940s. Crew of 2-4. Reported lengths 9-13.7m.

snapper rig See **pungy**

snau, snaubrig, snauschip See **snow**

snauw See **senau, snow**

snauwschip, snaw See **snow**

sneak boat **1.** *Canada, E:* One-man boat used by market hunters. Now illegal. In the spring, the raised sides were camouflaged with ice. Propelled by a hand-cranked paddle wheel or propeller. Name variant: **goose boat** **2.** *United States, north-central:* Popular wildfowling boat, especially of the early 20th century. Strip-built of 25cm-wide cedar strips; sharp ends; long cockpit. Worked with 2 pairs of oars. Rowed upwind and then drifted down on the ducks, the hunters hidden by a hinged screen that

dropped down for shooting. Steered with a paddle. Length 6m, beam 1.4m; low freeboard; heavy.
See also **Barnegat sneakbox, bushwack boat, dink, flatboat-4, Susquehanna sneak boat.**

sneakbox See **Barnegat sneakbox, dink, flatboat-4, scull float**

sneak skiff *United States, E:* Custom-made, waterfowl gunning boat used on Chesapeake Bay. Often used for crabbing in the off-season. Carvel-planked; sharp, raked ends; flat bottom planked athwartships; flat sheer; slightly flared sides; widely spaced ribs. An early type on the upper bay off the Susquehanna River had a square stern, and the sculling oar extended through the transom. Decked at ends, the foredeck supporting the massive punt gun. Painted white. In winter, runners might be fixed to the bottom for working on ice. Propelled by oars, a sculling oar, hand paddles, or pole. At times, might set a sprit- or gaff sail, and be steered with an oar. Reported lengths 3.7-5.5m; e.g., length 5m, beam 1.0m; shallow draft. When a special lamp was mounted on the bow for night shooting, the **skiff** was called a **lighting skiff.**

sneau See **snow**

sneccke See **esnecca**

sneck See **snik**

sneckia See **snekkja**

sneek, sneeken See **snik**

Sneg See **Helgoländer Schnigge**

snek See **snik**

snekar See **esnecca, snekkja**

snekja See **snekkja**

snekka See **sjekte, snekke**

snekkar See **snekkja**

snekke *Norway, S and SW:* Small, beamy, general-purpose boat found along the coast. Clinker-built; sharp ends; curved stem and sternpost, bow higher than stern; some drag to the deep, straight keel; sometimes weighted with an iron shoe. Rising floors; soft turn of the bilges. Three-piece frames, the floor frame overlapping the ribs. Outboard rudder; tiller. Also rowed, oars working between double tholepins. The **færdersnekke** of Færder Island in Oslofjorden is a popular pleasure craft, having a deep, curved keel with deep drag, high bilges, strongly cutaway forefoot. Decked forward; some have side decks. Sprit-rigged with peak slightly lower than the throat; staysail, jib. Recent boats motorized (**motorsnekke**); the **knivsviksnekke** has been modified for an inboard engine, but may also be sailed. Reported lengths 5-8m. Other recorded names: **halvdekker, snaekke, snekka**; pl. **snekker, snekkerne.** In the Telemark area, the term **kogg** or **koggen** (pl. **kogger, koggene**) is generally used. Note also **sjekte, snekkja.** Further references: **shnyaka, snekkja**

snekker See **snekke, snekkja**

snekkerne See **snekke**

snekkerstenjolle See **sundjolle**

snekkja Type of Norse **langskip★** that was a fast naval vessel until about the 12th century. Clinker-built; high stem and sternpost; frames in pairs and not fastened to the keel; quarter rudder. Fully decked or decked only at the ends. Employed 20-30 oars to a side. Also

sailed, bending a square sail to a mast stepped amidships. Crew of ca. 100. Length ca. 21.6m, beam 5.5m. Other recorded names: **esnecca★, esneque, long serpent, schniggen, snac(c)a, snac(c)ha, snace, snaekkia, snake boat, snäkka, snakr, sneckia, snekja, snek(k)ar, snekke★** (pl. **snekker**)

snick, snicka See **snik**

snicke See **Schnigge, snik**

snig See **Schnigge**

snigg See **snik**

Snigge, Sniggen See **Schnigge**

snijbonen, snijboon See **Meppeler praam**

snik *Belgium/Netherlands:* Very old word that has been applied to several craft employed in a number of capacities:
1. Reported in the 17th-18th centuries as fishing along the Frisian coast in the north and on the Waal River in South Holland and Belgium; some carried fresh fish to market. The northern **zeesnik** was decked with a live well; full build, lightly curved or straight, raked stem. Carried a spritsail on the mainmast; a small, triangular mizzen; staysail; and jib to a jibboom. Similar boats worked in the south. 20-28t.
2. In Groningen in northeastern Netherlands, the **snik** was a **trekschuit★** that was towed along inland waterways carrying cargo and passengers on a regular basis; reported during the 17th-19th centuries. Decked at bow and stern with a long, raised cabin that extended from gunwale to gunwale, or cabin only at the stern. Sharply raked, overhanging bow; narrow, perpendicular stem; narrow wale; small keel; outboard rudder; tiller. Towed by a horse ridden by a boy; boat managed single-handed. Later vessels motorized, of steel, and some became **yachts★.** Other recorded names: **barge★, Groninger** or **Groningse snik**
3. The inland **Friese snik** was a sailing craft that carried cargo and produce; the **aardappelsnik,** for example, transported potatoes. Built of wood or steel; flat floors; sharply raked, straight stem ending in a point; rounded stern. Hatch, abaft the mast, extended full beam. Decked with steering well aft; limited accommodations since captain did not live aboard. Rounded leeboards. Gaff main- and foresail; mast struck to pass beneath the many low bridges. Length 14m, beam 3.2m, depth 1.5m; shallow draft. Other recorded names: **beurtsnik, Warnmonder snik**
Spelling variants: **snacc, snacga, sneck, sne(e)k, snick(a), snicke, snigg, snikke, snyck**; pl. **sneeken, snikken.** See also **Schnigge.**

snikke See **Schnigge, snik**

snikken See **snik**

snipa *Finland, SW/Sweden:* Term applied to a slender, double-ended sailing or **rowing boat★** (**segelsnipa** or **roddsnipa**). Popular on the west coast of Sweden but also found on lakes and along the south and east coasts and in the Finnish Åland Islands (**ålandssnipa**). Design varies somewhat from area to area; some imported from Norway. Used mainly for inshore fishing, but the large sailing types may work along the coast. Strongly built, clinker or carvel construction, with either sharp or slightly rounded ends; generally rounded in cross section, the **roddsnipa** being more rounded. Raked stem curved or straight, and cutaway at forefoot; keel straight; sternpost straight and sharply raked. May be open or partially to entirely decked. Generally an outboard rudder, but some use a steering oar. Those that sail step 1-2 short masts, usually with spritsails, although loose-footed gaff sails also used. Early **sniporna** set square or lugsails. Staysails common; some raise a topsail by blocks on the masthead secured by a spar supported on the sprit. In the Åland Islands, 3-masted boats common. Many now motorized. Reported lengths 4.44-6.57m; e.g., length 5.75m, beam 2m, depth 0.8m. Other recorded names: **orustsnipa, snäcka** (northwest coast of Sweden); pl. **snäckor, snäckorna, snipor, snippar.** Note also **gotlandssnipa.**

snipor, sniporna, snippar See **snipa**

snjaka See **shnyaka**

snoo, snoro See **snow**

snouw See **senau, snow**

snow Two-masted, square-rigged vessel that worked primarily in the 16th-19th centuries as a **merchantman★** and to carry dispatches and mail; usually armed. In the second half of the 18th century, its distinctive feature was a light mast stepped on the deck immediately abaft the mainmast to the height of the main topmast and supported by the mainmast. This mast set a gaff sail, enabling the mainmast to retain its square mainsail. This extra mast distinguished the **snow** from the **brig★** of this period, but gradually the terminology became blurred, first by the term **snowbrig**; the 2 terms ultimately became interchangeable. Armed **snows** were commonly known as **corvettes★** or **sloops-of-war.** In the United States, naval **brigs** were **snow**-rigged until the 1860s but were called **man-of-war brigs.** In general, **snows** were square-sterned, but a few in the 18th century had sterns like **pinks★** and were called **pink-snows. Snows** are also reported as fishing for cod off the North American banks in the 17th century, but details of these vessels are not known. Other recorded names: **esnón, esnou, rind, Schnau(schiff), Schnaue, Schnaumastschiff, senale, senau★, senaut, seneau, snaauw(schip), snau(schip), snauw(schip), snaw, sneau, snoo, snoro, Snouw, snaubrig**

snowbrig See **snow**

snubby boat See **shell**

snyck See **snik**

soatau *Samoa, central Pacific:* Class of single-outrigger fishing **canoes★** that ranged from simple paddling **canoes** to large, multiboomed sailing craft. Special names given to the **canoes** depending on the number of booms connecting the float, one with 4 booms being an **'iato fa;** with 5, an **'iato lima;** with 6, an **'iato ono;** with 9, an **'iato va.** Dugout hull, U-shaped in cross section. Bow sharp and concave in profile; some with a distinct forefoot. Stern curved up gradually, terminating in a small, square end above the waterline. Some larger **canoes** had an elaborate, vertical, decorative piece at the bow, and cowrie shells lined the bow and stern decks. Smaller boats undecked. Straight booms, evenly spaced or clustered in pairs. Cylindrical float,

sharp at forward end, placed so that the blunt after end terminated just behind the after boom. Float and each boom connected by 2 pairs of divergent stanchions and a central rope lashing looped beneath the float. Sailing types employed a boom set at a 60° angle that, with the forward-raking mast, resulted in a V-shaped sail. Mast stayed forward to a boom and to a board out the side opposite the outrigger. Balance board wedged beneath the opposite gunwale. Branched stick placed on a boom supported the fishing poles. Smaller **canoe** lengths ca. 4-7m. Note also **iato.**

šǫbbā̲k See **xebec**

soekoeng See **sekong**

soemboek, soenboek See **sambūq**

soepe See **soppé**

sognabåt See **sognebåt**

sogneåttring See **åttring-1**

sognebaad See **sognebåt**

sognebåt *Norway, W:* General term for the small, open boats designed for use within Sognefjorden, where currents and winds are often difficult. Light and elastic build of clinker construction; deep top strake; sharp ends; strong sheer forward and aft. Mainly rowed, but when sailed, set a wide, low square sail; originally of wool, later of hemp or linen. Well known are the 4-oared **færing★ (sognefæring)** and the 8-oared **åttring★ (sogneåttring)** or **firkeiping★.** Spelling variants: **sognabåt, sognebaad.** Note also **isbåt, jekt.**

sognefæring See **færing-2**

sognejekt See **jekt**

Sohlboot *Germany:* Shallow-draft, flat-bottomed cargo vessel that works protected coastal waters. Name variant: **Flachboot**

Sohlenboot See **Prahm-2**

soiler See **sealer**

soka-gabarra See **gabarra-5a**

sokong See **sekong**

sokori-bune *Japan:* Common dredging boat that uses a comb-like dredge for clams, shrimp, and whitebait. Plank-built; square ends; flat bottom, with strong rocker, terminates in shallow platforms at each end. Marked sheer, the stern lower. Open. Sculled. Length ca. 3.75m, beam 0.9m.

Solent ballast barge, Solent barge See **Cowes ketch**

Solent fishing boat, Solent fishing cutter, Solent punt See **Itchen Ferry boat**

Solent scow See **scow-10**

Solent smack See **Itchen Ferry boat**

soloe See **solu**

soloe bolan, soloe bólon See **solu bólon**

soloe ratsaran See **solu ratsaran**

solu *Indonesia, W:* Batak generic term for their **dugout canoes★;** used on Lake Toba in northwestern Sumatra. Range from simple, 1-man fishing **canoes★** to those capable of carrying 250 people. Many ornamented at bow and stern. Spelling variant: **soloe.** Note also **solu bólon, solu ratsaran.**

solu bólon *Indonesia, W:* Large (*bólon*) trading **canoe★** of Lake Toba in northwestern Sumatra; earlier, the Bataks used them for war. Dugout hull; sharp ends; residual keel piece carved into the bottom, where it curves up toward the ends. On some, the strakes extend beyond the bow, retaining the hull's width. The forward ends of the strakes are joined by a crosspiece and supported by angled pieces to the bow; this small area is decked. A finial-type decoration is mounted to the true bow. Various other decorative bow and stern designs have been noted, including a long projection draped with horse hair. Outriggers reported on some. Mainly paddled, but also steps a single mast through a thwart, well forward. To this, a large, trapezoidal standing lugsail is set, with a very long boom at the foot. Largest could carry 40 men. Reported lengths 9-35m, widths 1.5-2m, depths 1-1.5m. Spelling variants: **soloe bolan, soloe bólon**

solu ratsaran *Indonesia, W:* Light, 1-man fishing **canoe**★ of the Batak of Lake Toba in northwestern Sumatra. Dugout hull with a sharp cutwater at bow and stern; at gunwale level, the hull flares out sharply to form a small platform or decking; decorative piece at the bow. Paddled. Length 3.8m, beam 0.52m. Spelling variant: **soloe ratsaran**

Solway Firth net whammel, Solway whammel boat See **whammel boat**

sombūq See **sambūq**

Somerset flatner See **flatner**

Somerset turf boat See **turf boat**

somma See **junk**

sommar-åttring See **åttring-3**

somme See **junk**

sommer-åttring See **åttring-3**

somp *Netherlands, NE:* Fast, slender cargo boat of the rivers of Overijssel that dated to the Middle Ages. Lightly built; fine bow and stern, the stern sharper; stem rounded and had tumble home, sternpost straight; wide, flat bottom with rocker. Straight sides; strong sheer dipping to just above the waterline amidships; top strake set on vertically and flattened out the sheer, stopping short of the sternpost. Small **sompen** (pl.) had removable washboards. Narrow gangways along each side. Large-bladed rudder; leeboards. The **open somp** had a cuddy forward with removable sides. Cargo covered with cloths. The **gedekte somp** or **brandschuit** had a foredeck with a sloping hatch extending to the sides; open cockpit aft. Single pole mast, in a tabernacle, set a boomed spritsail and forestaysail; some used a triangular sail that required 1-3 sprits. Usually had a foresail. Worked single-handed. Often punted. Reported lengths 7.5-22m; e.g., length 13.5m, beam 2.75m, depth 1.75m; shallow draft. One larger than 24t, with hatches, is a **dubbele zomp** (or **somp**). Other recorded names: **Enterse somp** (or **zomp**), **pegge, Regge somp** (or **zomp**), **sjomp, Vegtschuit, zomp**. Further reading: G. J. Schutten, *Varen Waar Geen Water Is* (Henglo: Uitgeverij Broekhuis, 1981). Note also **beurtsomp, Drentse praam**. Further references: **roddsump, segelsump**

sompen See **somp**

sonbuk See **sambūq**

sondeledskøyte See **skøyte-2**

Söndmöersk baat See **sunnmørsbåt**

Söndmöersk ottringsbaad See **åttring-2**

Söndmöersk yawl, søndmørbaad, Sondmore boat See **sunnmørsbåt**

sondmør-ottring See **åttring-2**

söndmörsbaat See **sunnmørsbåt**

song An-Ģiü See **song-vành**

song-vành *Vietnam, central:* Shark-fishing **basket boat**★ of the Qui Nhon area in An Nhon (Binh Dinh) province. Entire hull composed of woven strips of bamboo; gunwales strengthened with a band of bamboo; frames inserted. Rounded stern; elongated, rounded bow; flattened bottom, especially aft. Very large rudder extends well below the bottom and forward under stern. Decked with woven bamboo. Painted oculi. Set a gunter lug mainsail and standing lug foresail, extended by a bowline. Mainmast, without standing rigging, inclined 30° aft; stepped in shoe on floorboards. Lengths to 8m, width ca. 1.3m. Name variant: **song An-Ģiü**

sonnette flotante, sonnette nautique See **pile driver-1**

sooie See **lurkie**

soon son *Korea:* Reported as a 12th-century **police boat** off the east coast. Decked; rudder projected through a stern platform. Single mast.

sopé, sopeh, sopek See **soppé**

soppé *Indonesia:* A widespread term that describes different craft. Reported from Sulawesi (Celebes), Java, Madura, Sapudi Archipelago, Bali, and the Lesser Sunda Islands, mainly as a small trader, **fishing boat**★, and in parts of Sulawesi, as a lug-rigged, racing **dugout canoe**★ with a single outrigger. The **soppé rumah** of the nomadic Bajaus of eastern Sulawesi serves as a **houseboat**★. On some islands, the word formerly meant a **sekochi**★. Usually plank-built with a long, straight keel; sharp, raked ends; some with a carved transom piece as an extension of the top strake; raked bow. Decked, often with a house amidships or aft. Uses a quarter rudder. Those at Udjung Padang (Makassar) have double outriggers. Rig varies with the district; for the Bajau, it is any craft carrying a tilted, rectangular lugsail. Pole mast stepped forward of amidships to which a lugsail or spritsail is set; some set a triangular sail, others 2 lugsails. Other recorded names: **prahu** (or **prahoe** or **perahu**) **sopé, praauw soepe, prahu sopee, soepe, sopé, sopeh, sopek, soppét**. Note also **perahu sopi**. Further reference: **pakur**

soppé rumah, soppét See **soppé**

soro *Solomon Islands, western Pacific:* **1.** Rectangular **raft**★ of light logs used on Guadalcanal. Logs held in position by a crosspiece at each end. Other recorded names: **tsoro, vorau**; on Malaita, **fava**

2. Also a type of **catamaran**★ on Guadalcanal and on northern Malaita. Design varies, but basically 2 balsa logs, pointed at the bow, and joined by 3 transverse rods; often supplementary converging rods support a raised plank between the logs. Some sail, setting a spritsail and headsail.

Further references: **lisi, sosoro-1**

sorosoro See **lisi, sosoro-1**

sørøverskib See **freebooter**

sosoro *Solomon Islands, western Pacific:* **1. Canoe**★ of the Bugotu peoples of the south end of Santa Isabel Island. Term also used in the 'Āre'āre language of the northwest end of Malaita. Flat sheer; lacks usual tall end pieces found elsewhere in the area. Spelling variants: **soro**★ or **sorosoro** (on Malaita)
2. *Florida Island:* **a.** A **raft**★ of the Nggelu peoples. Employs a frond sail. **b.** A toy **canoe.**

søsterskib See **mother**

sous-tireau, sous-tirot See **train de bateaux**

Southampton hoy *England, S:* **Cutter**★-rigged boat that fished and transported goods from ships lying off Southampton in the early 19th century. Clinker-built; beamy with rounded sections and bluff bow; stem and sternpost raked and heavy. High counter, sharp below. Rounded bilges, steep rise to the floors, drag to keel. Narrow rudder; tiller came in below the counter. Decked; central hatch. Loose-footed gaff sail with long boom; jackyard topsail; 2 headsails; bowsprit. Length overall 8.76m, on keel 5.2m, beam 3.76m, depth 2.62m. Name variant: **fish hoy.** Note also **hoy-3a.**

Southampton punt See **Itchen Ferry boat**
South Arm boat See **passage boat-2**
South Bay catboat See **catboat-2d**
South Bay scooter See **scooter-2**
South Carolina logging bateau See **Charleston bateau**
Southend bawley See **bawley**
South Ender See **Yarmouth shrimper**
southern canoe See **West Coast canoe**
Southern Shore bummer See **jack**
South Isles yole *Scotland, N:* Beamy **passage boat**★ of the southern Orkney Islands. Also used for fishing. Clinker-built, most with 10 strakes on a side. Double-ended with full lines; flat floors; flaring bow and quarters; beam carried well aft. Stern rounder than bow; straight sternpost sharply raked; stem mildly raked; rounded forefoot. Generally open, but some had small bow and stern decks. In contrast to the similar **North Isles yole**★, set 2 high-peaked spritsails and a jib. Sprits, usually set on opposite sides, supported at the heel by a snotter. Foremast vertical, mainmast raked aft; sometimes stepped a single mast. Bowsprit run through gammon iron at stemhead, heel through an iron at foremast. Jib halyards rove through a block fitted with a strop at the masthead; 2 sheets on jib. Two pairs of oars worked between double tholepins; oar held by a wide grommet. Later motorized. Reported lengths overall 4.57-6.1m, on keel 3.35-4.77m; widths 2.13-2.44m; depth 0.8m. Name variants: **Orcadian yol(e), Orkney yole**
South Jersey beach skiff See **Sea Bright skiff**
Southport shrimper See **Morecambe Bay prawner**
south sider See **oyster sloop-1**
South Spainer See **fruit schooner**
Southwold beach punt See **beach punt-1**
Southwold beach yawl See **beach yawl-1**
spada boat See **feluca-2**
Spanish frigate See **pinnace-2**
Spanish vessel See **batelão-4**
span of colts See **timber raft-2b**
spare boat See **accident boat**

Sparendammer visser See **tochschuit**
sparoner See **speronara**
spar raft See **timber raft-2a**
spasatel'naia, spasatel'naia shliupka See **lifeboat**
speedboat **1.** Generally, a small, open pleasure boat designed to skim swiftly through the water.
2. *Canada, E:* A fast fishing and bird- and seal-hunting boat of Newfoundland. Carvel-planked of spruce or fir; steam-bent timbers; flat floors; straight sides; shallow keel; wide, flat stern; raked stem. Open; well amidships; 2 thwarts forward. Large outboard motor; may also be sculled. Reported lengths 4.6-6m; beamy. Name variant: **flat**★
3. *United States, Alaska:* On St. Lawrence Island, a **speedboat** is a small, plywood or aluminum boat. Introduced in the late 1940s. Used only under ice-free conditions. Sharply raked bow below the waterline, square stern, low rise to floors. High coaming around the cockpit. Outboard motor. Reported lengths 4-5m, very beamy.
    See also **kuai ban.**
speeljacht See **jacht-3**
speelschuit See **schuit-1**
Speicherschiff See **hulk-3**
Speiel-Baad See **skyssbåt**
Speightstown schooner See **Barbados schooner**
spekbak See **zeeschouw**
sperona, spéronade See **speronara**
speronara **1.** *Italy:* Vessel of early origin that transported cargo, passengers, and dispatches; probably originated in Malta, and perhaps most were built there. Also used by the Sicilian and Calabrian navies. Bow narrow and sharp, with a ram-like projection; counter stern long and overhanging or short and rounded. Undecked. Propelled by oars and sail. Mostly 3-masted, setting lateen sails; mizzenmast raked aft, sail sheeted to an outrigger. Three-masted vessel 15.5m long, 4.4m wide; cap. 22t.
2. *Malta:* Fast cargo vessel of the central Mediterranean Basin; built until the late 19th century. Sharp bow with curved stem that projected high above the gunwale; ram-like projection extended beyond the stem. Rounded, vertical stern or a long counter. Strong sheer, flat floors, cambered deck; deep, removable bulwarks; small types undecked. Tall rudderhead on round-sterned type. Oculi. Rigged with 1-3 masts. Most set lateen sails; the small, open boats used spritsails. Jib to a very long bowsprit. A 2-masted boat might use 18-20 oars. Reported lengths 8-15m, width ca. 4.5m.
Other recorded names: **esperon(n)ade, s(i)paroner, sperona, spéronade, spéronare, speronéra, speroniera, spronara, xprunára.** Note also **spirunara.**
spéronare, speronéra, speroniera See **speronara**
Sperrbewachter, Sperrfahrzeug, Sperrwaffenschiff See **boom defense vessel**
spiegeljacht **1.** *Germany, NE:* The German **Spiegeljacht** was a **coaster**★ built in Pomerania until ca. 1850. Clinker- and carvel-built. Some raised a topmast. Note also **jacht-1a, jacht-3.**
2. *Netherlands:* Pleasure craft of the late 17th-19th centuries. Characterized by a U-shaped transom (*spiegel*)

and an aft cabin with staterooms (*paviljoen*) and windows at sides and stern. Horseshoe-shaped counter overhung the transom below the extended cabin deck. Full lines forward; rounded, raked stem; raked stern; strong sheer; large, rounded leeboards. Inboard rudderstock pierced the cabin deck; tiller extended to the steering well forward of the cabin. Elaborately carved and appointed. Standing gaff mainsail set to a strike mast; some employed 3 headsails; long bowsprit. Length 9m, beam 2.7m, depth 1.6m, cap. 72t. Other recorded names: **paviljoenjacht**, **spiegeljagte**

spiegeljagte See **spiegeljacht-2**

spigonara See **spirunara**

spinaccia, **spinace**, **spinacium**, **spinazza** See **pinnace**

spintore See **push boat**

spirunara *Italy:* Used to catch anchovies with a *spigone* net and as a small trader off Sicily. Slender, elongated bow. Name variant: **spigonara**. Note also **speronara**.

spiss-stemming See **færing**

spit See **spits**

Spithead wherry See **Portsmouth wherry**

spits *Belgium/France, N/Netherlands, S:* Narrow canal and river vessel. Constructed of wood initially, then with a wooden bottom and iron flanks. By the end of the 19th century, entirely of iron, then steel. Basically boxy in shape; rounded at the stern; straight raking stem; straight, vertical sides swept up at the ends. Flat floors; hard turn of the bilges. Bottom planking on those of wood and iron sloped up at the bow to join a stem that began just above the waterline. Low washboards at bow and stern; towing bitt behind the stem. Decked; long central hold, cambered hatch covers; living quarters under the after deck; motorized vessels (the **motorspitsen**) have a wheelhouse. Leeboards used in some areas. Large rudder with fin below the waterline; some hinged in 2 places to permit folding; ornamental rudderhead; rudder on motorized vessels worked by a wheel. Until 1920, designed to be towed (the **sleepspits**), but some later boats set a small lugsail or a loose-footed, boomed gaff sail with a boomed-out foresail. All had lowering masts. Those over 40m long might step 2 masts. Lengths 20-47m, the longer called the **Samberspits**; e.g., length with rudder 32.6m, without rudder 30m, beam 4.8m, draft loaded 2m. The **Maasspits**, built of iron since the end of the 19th century, had a somewhat different shape. Flat bottom, hard chines, bluff forward and aft. Vertical stem with curved foot; straight, vertical sternpost. Decked; cambered hatch covers. Other recorded names: **bateau pointu**, **fox terrier**, **Maaspitz**, **Maasspitz**; **pleit*** (incorrectly); **pointu** (Walloon French); **spit**, **spitz**; pl. **spitsen**

spitsbek *Belgium, NE/France, N/ Netherlands, SE:* Long, narrow, **aak***-type river vessel related to the **herna*** and the **walenmajol***. Plied the Meuse (Maas) River; first mentioned in the 16th century; gone by the beginning of the 20th century. Built initially of wood, later of iron. Flat bottom rounded up at each end, terminating in a point at the gunwale or in a shallow transom; higher at the bow than the stern. Bow and stern symmetrically blunt; sides slightly flared, rounded, or

straight. Upper strake vertical and clinker-laid. Decked at ends with central deckhouse; on the iron vessels, the ends were decked with living quarters below the after deck. Rudderpost passed through the stern, with the part of the blade forward of the post matching the curve of the stern and a 3.5-4.4m-wide blade aft. A balance beam connected the outer end of the blade and the post; activated by the forward end of the tiller; on some, the blade was hinged to reduce the size of the rudder. Designed to be towed on the upper and middle Meuse. Elsewhere sailed, employing a lowering mast. Single spritsail until the 18th century, later sprit mainsail and mizzen. In the 19th century, rigged with a boomless lug- or gaff sail. Crew of 2-3. Reported lengths 15-38m; e.g., length 30m, beam 4.2m, depth 1.6m. Steel **spitsbekken** (pl.) worked local Walloon rivers and canals. Flat bottom, hard chines; straight, vertical sides. Towed; later motorized. Length 19.4m, beam 2.84m, 40t. Other recorded names: **bovenlander**, **majol(l)e**, **mignol(l)e**, **mijolle**

spitsbekken See **spitsbek**

Spitsche Mot, **Spitsemot** See **Spitzmutte**

spitsen See **spits**

spitse praam See **spitspraam**

spitsgatever See **Ewer**

Spitsmutte See **Spitzmutte**

spitspraam *Netherlands, NE:* Carried potatoes, peat, and bulk cargoes; a few of the later iron-hulled vessels remain, serving as **houseboats***. Characterized by a strongly upturned bow and lightly curved stem with gripe below the waterline. Rounded stern, bow less rounded; raked stem; planking above the wale almost vertical, except at the stern, where it is tumble home; strong sheer at bow. Wide rudder; jog in tiller; leeboards. Decked; central hold; some had a cabin aft, entered by a ladder beneath the tiller; stern windows. Mast, stepped in forward third, could be struck with the help of a counterbalance weight. Length 16.4m, beam 4.02m. Other recorded names: **rivierpraam**, **spitse praam**; pl. **spitspramen**. Note also **praam**.

spitspramen See **spitspraam**

spitz See **spits**

Spitzbodenboot See **deadrise boat**

Spitzfahrm, **Spitzfarm** See **Farm**

spitzgat-ever, **Spitzgatt-Ewer** See **Ewer**

Spitzgattjacht See **jacht-1a**

Spitzgranselzille See **Waidzille**

Spitzkadole See **flûte-3**

Spitzmot, **Spitzmotte** See **Spitzmutte**

Spitzmutte *Germany, NW/Netherlands, N:* Sharp-ended **coaster*** and inland vessel from Oldenburg and Frisian areas on the North Sea coast; built until the 1930s. Flat bottom with hard chines; slightly flared sides; straight, raked stem and sternpost. Narrow leeboards; large-bladed rudder; tiller. Decked; some with a high cabin or a below-deck cabin; 1-2 hatches; steering platform. Gaff or spritsail set to a pole mast; staysail; some employed a gaff topsail and jib. Larger vessels stepped a mizzenmast fitted with a gaff sail. Reported lengths 14.3-18.5m; e.g., length 16m, beam 4.5m, depth 1.6m. Other recorded names: **Fehnmutte**,

Halbe Mutte, Halfmutte, Mudde, Mutt(e)-tjalk, Spitsche Mot, Spitsemot, Spitsmutte, Spitzmot(te); pl. **Spitzmutten**. Note also **Mutte**.

Spitzmutten See **Spitzmutte**

Spitzplätte See **Plätte-1**

Spitzpünte *Germany, NW:* A variety of **Pünte★** built on the Ems River between 1860 and 1902; carried cargo to ports in northwest Europe. Flat bottom; sharp bow and stern; vertical stem, sometimes clipper-shaped. Decked; large hatch; generally a deckhouse. Leeboards, often replaced by bilge keels; outboard rudder; long tiller. Stepped 1-2 masts; variously rigged: **cutter★, ketch★**, and occasionally **schooner★** (**Spitzpünte-Gaffelschuner**). Reported lengths 20-26m; e.g., length 23.8m, beam 5.8m, depth 2.77m.

Spitzpünte-Gaffelschuner See **Spitzpünte**

splasher See **coble-1, paddle boat-3**

splav za spasavanje See **life raft**

split-wood fleet See **onker**

splosher See **coble-1**

spoil barge, spoil boat See **mud hopper**

sponge boat **1.** In general, a boat used for collecting sponges. Other recorded names: **Schwammfischerei-boot, sponger, sponging vessel.** Note also **barchetta-2, korkâra, sponge schooner.**

2. *Greece, E:* The sponging operation of the Aegean area uses 2 boats: a large **mother ship★** (**deposito** in Italian) to house the crew and store the sponges and a small **macchina** (Italian term) from which the divers operate. The large vessel steps 2 masts; the shorter foremast sets a quadrilateral, lateen-type sail with a short luff, the taller mainmast sets a high-peaked gaff sail; also a jib runs to a long bowsprit. The small boat sets a single spritsail to a short, forward-raking mast; exceptionally long sprit. Both boats sharp-ended. Combined crew of 20-40. The **deposito** 35-40rt, the **macchina** 5-10rt. Note also **aktarma.**

3. *United States, SE:* The **sponge boats** of the west coast of Florida were mainly built and manned by Greek sponge fishermen. Early boats closely reflected those built in Greece. A few survive. Sharp ends; carvel-planked without the use of caulking; curved stem with strongly cutaway forefoot; straight, raked sternpost; strong sheer; drag to keel. These decked boats had a low bulwark, weatherboards or cloths, steering cockpit. Later boats had more moderate lines and adopted a square-tuck stern. White hull with colored stripe below the sheer strake. The Greek-type boats were originally sprit-rigged with a very long sprit and forward-raking mast. Sail brailed to mast by means of rings on a stay to the end of the sprit. Later boats might step a short mainmast and a taller foremast, both setting loose-footed, boomed gaff sails; later **yawl★**-rigged with a leg-of-mutton jigger, and auxiliaries added. Reported lengths 8.5-15m; length-to-beam ratio on larger boats 3:1. Early boats also rowed. Later boats had auxiliaries and used the sails mainly for steadying while working. A **deposit** or **living boat**, usually a **schooner★**, served as living quarters for the sponge crew and as a place to deposit the sponges for curing. Those employing pumps to supply air to divers working with helmets might be called **diving** or **machine boats.** Note also **Key West sponge sloop, sponge schooner.**

sponge dingey See **sponge dinghy**

sponge dinghy *United States, SE:* Used in shallow reef areas by 2 men, 1 to scull the boat and the other to hook the sponge after sighting it through a glass-bottomed bucket. Those working in secluded reef areas require only a single person to both hook and scull. Shark oil may be used to smooth the water. Boats worked off the **sponge schooners★** out of Key West at the south end of Florida and along the west coast of Florida, mainly until the beginning of the 20th century. Later, worked off vessels called **hook boats.** Carvel-planked; keel. Straight stem, curved below the waterline; heart-shaped vertical transom above a skeg; sculling notch in transom. Low freeboard swept up at ends. Bow and stern seats; 3 thwarts. Hooking poles as long as 15m. Some rowed, facing forward, instead of sculling. Reported lengths 3.7-4.6m; e.g., length 4m, beam 1.4m, depth 0.43m. Name variants: **dinghy★, sponge ding(e)y**

sponge dingy See **sponge dinghy**

sponger See **sponge boat**

sponge schooner **1.** *Bahamas:* Worked until the mid-1960s collecting sponges, catching turtles, and carrying cargo to the northern West Indian islands and to Florida. Locally built by fishermen. Raked stem with a long head and cutaway forefoot; shallow counter or flat, square transom; raked sternpost. Long, sharp run; drag to the keel; strong deadrise. Flush deck, low trunk cabin aft. Nested 6-8 two-man **dinghies★** on deck; these were sculled to and from the sponging sites. Slight aft rake to the masts. Gaff sails usually loose-footed and boomed, although foresail might not have a boom. Staysail and sometimes a fisherman's staysail between the masts. Jib to a rising bowsprit; sometimes set an extra jib to a jibboom. Ran up topsails until the 1940s. Crew of 10-20. Reported lengths 12-16.5m; e.g., length 16.5m, beam 4.4m, depth 1.5m.

2. *United States, SE:* Engaged in sponge fishing out of Key West in southern Florida in the latter part of the 19th century, serving mainly as a **mother ship★.** Those less than 30t were specially built for this trade, while the larger vessels had been converted from other uses. Planked with local yellow pine and framed with madeira wood; considerable rise to the floors; quick turn of the bilges. Moderately raked clipper bow; wide, rounded or flat counter stern. Flush deck; log gunwale 25-46cm high; larger vessels had a cooking box on deck. Wide centerboard. Used **dinghies** (see **sponge dinghy**) to gather the sponges, one **dinghy** for every 2 crew members, with the cook left aboard to sail the vessel. Boomed gaff sails set to the 2 masts; main topmast; generally no jibboom. Crew of 13. Reported lengths 13-21m; e.g., length overall 21m, on keel 18m, beam 5.6m, hold depth 1.8m, 43t; shallow draft. Other recorded names: **deposit boat, Florida sponge schooner, Key West sponge schooner, messenger boat.** Note also **sponge boat.**

sponge sloop See **Key West sponge sloop**

sponging vessel See **sponge boat-1**

spoon canoe *Canada, W:* Long, slender estuary and river **canoe*** of the Kwakiutl, Bella Coola, and the Gulf of Georgia Salish tribes of northern Vancouver Island and the British Columbia mainland to the north.

spoon canoe

Fast; frequently engaged in inter-village races. Cedar dugout hull rounded in cross section with a thick bottom to provide stability. Tapered ends turn up gracefully. On the Bella Coola **canoes**, the stern rises sharply, and the sides angle in a straight line to a point. Mainly poled, but paddled in deep water. Generally 4 in crew. Reported lengths 6-9m, some to 15m; width ca. 1.22m.

spoon dredger Flat-bottomed boat that scoops up bottom mud from narrow waterways and canals with a large, wooden or iron, spoon-shaped scoop. Mud deposited in an accompanying **barge*** or on the bank. On the waterways in the United Kingdom, the spoons were attached by a chain and pulley to a crane or derrick. Some early **dredgers*** in the Netherlands employed scoops on the ends of poles; these were moved along the bottom by means of a wheel amidships. Other recorded names: **bag and spoon dredger, lepelbaggeraar, Löffelbagger.** Note also **dredger-1**.

spoorpont See **pont**

spouter See **whaler-1**

sprat punt *England, SE:* Small boat that worked off the steep shingle beaches of the coast fishing for sprat and lobster. Popular in the late 19th century, some working to the 1920s. Full lines amidships; clinker-planked; flat floors; sharp bilges. Plumb stem, counter-type (lute) stern above a vertical sternpost. Movable washstrake fitted in winter. Short foredeck with cuddy below. Rudder came up below the counter; tiller curved around the mizzenmast. Large centerboard. Mainmast stepped in forward third; mizzen on the counter, sheeted to a jiggerboom. Jib to a light, reefing bowsprit. Set standing lugsails. Also rowed. Length 6m, beam 1.7m, draft 0.8m. Other recorded names: **Eastbourne sprat punt, lobster and sprat punt.** Note also **Deal punt, lobster boat-3**.

spratter See **beach punt-1, stowboat**

Spratt's ark See **ark-2**

spreetie See **Thames sailing barge**

spritsail barge See **Arun spritsail barge, Thames sailing barge**

sprittie, spritty See **Thames sailing barge**

Spritzen Prahm See **fire boat**

spronara See **speronara**

sprucebark canoe *Canada:* Several native groups across the country used spruce bark for fashioning their **canoes***. Some were for temporary use, as with the Malecites of the Maritime Provinces and northeastern Maine, exhibiting considerable individuality in design. The Cree of central Canada regularly built **sprucebark canoes** along the lines of their birchbark **canoes** (see **Cree canoe**). **Canoes** of spruce bark were

also reported in use by the Kutenai in the Columbia River area. In the northwest, **sprucebark canoes** had a relatively narrow bottom and flared sides. **Canoes** of spruce bark were stiffer and needed fewer ribs. The sapling thwarts of the Malecite **canoes** wrapped around the gunwale and were lashed top and bottom. Note also **tci'k'Enō, ts'u t'u ela.** Further reference: **bark boat**

sprydstagejolle See **smakkejolle**

spy boat See **mouche-1, scout-1**

spynagtz, spynes, spynnes See **pinnace**

sqam See **West Coast canoe**

square-ender *United States, NE:* At New Haven, Connecticut, a **scow***-type boat used in the oyster industry was called a **square-ender** or **batteau***. Further references: **scow-1, Tusket River square-ender**

square-rigged ship, square-rigger See **ship-2**

squaresail See **herring scowte**

square-stern boat See **Huron boat**

square-sterned bugeye See **pungy**

square-sterned Shetland Model See **Shetland Model**

square-timber raft See **timber raft-2b**

square-toe frigate See **butthead, stone sloop**

square-toed frigate See **gundalow**

square-toed packet See **scow-schooner-3**

squeezer See **freighter-3a, hinge boat**

squid skiff *United States, W:* Used by Chinese squid fishermen along the California coast, especially at Monterey. Characterized by its **sampan***-like stern in which the strakes extended beyond the wide, square stern. Sharp bow; flat bottom with sharp rocker at stern; strong sheer; flaring sides. Open except for short platforms at bow and stern. Rowed, sculled, and sailed. Length 6.38m, beam 1.78m, depth 0.7m. Other recorded names: **skiff***, **Monterey squid skiff**

squiffe See **skiff**

Srisupanahong, Srisuppannahong See **rua ballang**

ssip See **ship**

Staaten-Jacht See **jacht-1b**

staaten jagt See **jacht-3**

staatsietjalk See **hektjalk**

stackie, stacky barge See **hay barge**

stadsbarge *Belgium:* In the 15th-16th centuries, some Flemish and Brabant cities maintained an official **rowing barge** to transport high-ranking visitors on rivers and canals. Low forecastle and spacious cabin at the stern. In the open waist, as many as 12 oarsmen worked on 6 thwarts. Note also **barge-3**.

stadsbargie, stadsgalei See **galley-5**

stadspont, stadspontje See **pont**

stage boat See **flyboat-3a**

stagsegelschoner, stagsejlskonnert, stagzeilschoener See **schooner-1**

Staithes herring drifter See **coble-1f**

Staithes jolly boat See **jolly boat-3**

Staithes yacker *England, NE:* Seaworthy, 3-masted, lug-rigged herring boat, mainly of the 1st half of the 19th century. Built and registered at Whitby, owned in Staithes. Clinker planking of oak; bluff bows; square stern; decked. Large sail plan; masts lowered to 20° above the deck while riding to the nets; set the huge yacker sail on the 3rd mast. Running bowsprit. Crew of 7. Beamy. Other recorded names: **Staithes yawl, yacker**

Staithes yawl See **Staithes yacker**

stake boat 1. In a boat race, one that is anchored out to mark the start or a turning point in the course may be called a **stake boat**. Note also **mark boat-1**.
2. *United States, E:* On the lower Hudson River, can be an anchored vessel lacking self-propulsion to which towed **lighters★** make fast. Name variant: **Festmacheboot**
Further reference: **pound net scow**

stale boat, stall boat See **stowboat**

stall på båt See **horse carrier**

stambecchi, stambecchino, stambecco See **xebec**

stammebåd See **dugout canoe**

stand-by boat See **accident boat**

standing room boat, standing roomer See **Chebacco boat**

standing skiff See **esquif-2**

stangfartøj, stang-og-line-båd See **tuna boat-2**

starboard boat See **whaler-3**

starvationer *England, SW:* A particularly slender **narrow boat★** employed on the Bridgewater/Taunton Canal. Those engaged in the underground workings of certain coal mines at Worsley were raised from level to level by inclined planes. Sharp ends. Presumably so called because their massive ribs showed above a low deck. Reported lengths 6-15m; e.g., length 9m, beam ca. 1.2m. Other recorded names: **starver, Worsley mine boat**

starver See **starvationer**

state barge See **barge-3, parinda**

state boat See **boarding boat-3**

statek stajnia See **horse carrier**

Staten Island skiff *United States, E:* Engaged in oyster tonging in the area between Staten Island in southern New York State and Sandy Hook in northeastern New Jersey from the mid-19th century until the 1960s. Also widely used on Chesapeake Bay; many reached the bay originally aboard **schooners★** in the 1870s. Lapstrake construction with white cedar planks and natural oak timbers; box keel; narrow, flat bottom, longitudinally planked, came to a point at each end. Rounded bilges, planked-up skeg. Full bow and slightly curved and raked stem; small wineglass transom with vertical or raked sternpost; moderate sheer. Open; partially ceiled; larger boats had 2 movable thwarts forward of the ceiling and were called **double skiffs**; single-thwart boats were called **single skiffs**. Rowed, towed, and sailed. Those that sailed had a centerboard and set a small spritsail to a mast stepped a little forward of amidships. Crew of 2. Reported lengths 5.5-7.9m; e.g., length overall 6.7m, on bottom 5.5m, beam 1.8m, depth 0.5m; shallow draft. Other recorded names: **oysterman's bateau, oyster skiff**; **Yankee skiff** (more common term on Chesapeake Bay); **New Jersey, Prince's Bay, Raritan Bay oyster skiff**

statenjacht See **jacht-3**

statie-paviljoenschuit See **schuit-2**

statietjalk See **hektjalk**

Stationers' barge *England, SE:* Ceremonial **barge★** built for the Stationers' Company to accompany royalty and the Lord Mayor of London in processions on the Thames. First company-owned **barge** built in 1680; last one operated until 1849. Rowed by 18 oarsmen who sat forward of the well-appointed house, which covered the after half. Boat directed by the barge-master from the bow; mate manned the elaborately carved tiller from the high, decorated stern. Accompanied by 1-2 small **rowing boats★**, called **whifflers**, that helped maneuver the **barge** if necessary. Early type 22.8m long. Further reading: *The State Barges of the Stationers' Company* (London: The Worshipful Company of Stationers and Newspaper Makers, 1972). Note also **barge-3**.

stationnaire See **guard ship**

stäveka, stävekstock See **eka**

Staversche jol See **Staverse jol**

Staverse jol *Netherlands, north-central:* Engaged mainly in anchovy, herring, and eel fishing in the Zuiderzee. Developed in the last quarter of the 19th century and worked until the 1950s; a few remain as pleasure craft. High, bluff bow with strongly curved stem. Narrowed toward the stern, ending in a heart-shaped transom above a vertical sternpost. Initially clinker-planked, later carvel; sometimes of steel; pronounced sheer forward. Light, V-shaped floors with deep, straight keel; no leeboards. High, rounded sides, tumble home over the entire length; some had washboards. Outboard rudder with wide blade below the waterline; tiller slotted over rudderhead. Initially open, later decked to mast; after two-thirds open; open or low cabin amidships on pleasure craft. Some had a wet well. Stepped a single pole mast in forward third. First set a spritsail, then added a forestaysail. Larger **jols** gaff-rigged, loose-footed, with or without boom; gaff originally straight, later curved. Forestaysail set on a short, iron bumkin; jib to light bowsprit. Crew of 2-3. Reported lengths 4-9m, the largest being the **yachts★**; length-to-beam ratio generally 2.5:1. Other recorded names: **grote jol, jol★, Staversche jol, Stavorensche Jol, Stavoren jol**. Three small types also fished: the **ansjovisjol** (the smallest, which fished specifically for anchovies), the **fuikenjol**, and the **herfstjol**.

stävöka See **eka**

Stavoren jol, Stavorensche Jol See **Staverse jol**

staysail barge See **Thames sailing barge**

staysail schooner See **schooner-1**

staxwił See **sda'kwihl**

stazionario See **guard ship**

steam drifter See **drifter**

steam launch See **launch**

steam packet See **packet boat, Weaver flat**

steekschuit *Netherlands:* Small, sprit-rigged **fishing boat★** used on the larger rivers. Sharp ends; straight, strongly raked stem with small, straight, tumble home stemhead; slightly raked sternpost. Wide, flat bottom; sides flared below the wale; top strake had tumble home. Open; leeboards. Length 8m, beam 2m, draft light 0.35m.

steenever See **Stein-Ewer**

steenschip See **steenschuit**

steenschuit *Belgium, N:* Gaff-rigged, brick-carrying **barge*** that worked the waterways of the Antwerp area. 19th-century vessels were double-ended; full, rounded bow and stern; curved stem, pointed on top; straight, vertical stern with deadwood. Flat bottom; hard turn of the bilges; shallow, tumble home to topsides; narrow top strake retained the same width over its length. Fan-shaped leeboards; early boats had a special clamp on the leeboards to protect them from the quay at low water. Decked; steering well aft; hatch abaft the mast had rounded cover; some larger boats had accommodations. Tall, heavy, lowering mast, roughly the length of the vessel, set a loose-footed, boomed gaff sail with curved gaff; staysail, jib to a bowsprit. Manned by captain and a boy. Reported lengths 11-18m; e.g., length 13m, beam 4.25m, depth 1.7m. Also built in the Netherlands. Other recorded names: **steenschip, stone schuit**. Note also **schuit**.

steigerschuit *Netherlands:* 17th-century boat that ferried passengers and cargo between off-lying ships and piers or landing areas (the *steiger*), particularly in the Amsterdam area. Some were small, open, rowed boats; others were partly decked with a hatch, used leeboards, and set a sprit- or gaff sail and staysail. Spelling variants: **steygerschuit, steygerschuyt, stijgerschuit**

Stein-Ever See **Stein-Ewer**

Stein-Ewer *Germany, NW:* A **Ewer*** type designed to transport bricks from kilns to locations along the lower Elbe River during the 19th and into the early 20th century. Carried other bulk cargo at times. Heavily built to withstand drying out at low water; flat bottom. Wide transom; outboard rudder; tiller; leeboards. **Ketch***-rigged with loose-footed, boomed gaff sails. For some routes, masts strikable to pass beneath low bridges. Reported lengths 15-16m, widths 5.06-5.32m, depths 1.59-1.63m; relatively deep draft. Spelling variants: **steenever, Stein-Ever**

Steinfischer See **cod-fishing boat**

Steinplätte See **Plätte-1**

stengeriggskøyte See **skøyte-1**

stern boat A **ship's boat***, mainly of merchant vessels, that hangs on davits over the stern. Other recorded names: **bote de los pescantes de popa, canot de l'arrière, canot de portemanteaux, hækjolle, Heckboot, hekkbåt, lancia de poppa.** Further reference: **jolly boat-1**

stern box See **hinge boat**

stern-ender See **McKenzie River drift boat**

stern picker See **gillnetter-1**

stern trawler See **trawler**

stern-wheel boat See **paddle boat-4**

stern wheeler See **mountain boat-2, paddle boat-3**

stE'tlEm See **tl'ai**

Steuersicken See **Garnsicken**

stevenaak See **aak**

stevenschouw See **zalmschouw**

Stevenzille See **zille**

steygerschuit, steygerschuyt See **steigerschuit**

stick-up flattie, stick-up skiff See **flattie-4**

stiff, stiff boat See **flicker**

stijgerschuit See **steigerschuit**

stockbåt Swedish generic term for boats hewn from a single log, constructed of 2 or more logs, or from a single log with a plank added to each side to increase capacity. Mostly poled, paddled, or rowed. Spelling variant: pl. **stockbåtar**. Note also **ekstock-1, stockeka**.

stockbåtar See **stockbåt**

stockeka *Sweden:* Generally designates a small, shallow craft constructed of 2 or more hewn logs arranged longitudinally. Shape varies with locale and builder. Rectangular **stockeka** type is found in the waters around the islands of Rossö, Älgö, and Galstö in Bohuslän in western Sweden. Used mainly for fishing, often with spears. Flat bottom; vertical sides may be either of a single or multiple planks fastened edge-to-edge. Square ends, slightly rounded on top. Name variant: **stocköka**. Note also **eka, ekstock-1**.

Stockfischfangboot, Stockfischfänger See **cod-fishing boat**

stock junk See **hua pi gu**

stocköka See **stockeka**

Stockplätte See **Farm, Plätte-1**

Stockplette See **Plätte-1**

Stöckzille See **Waidzille**

stonehacker See **polacca**

stone schuit See **steenschuit**

stone sloop *United States, NE:* Transported stone, especially granite blocks, from the Maine coast and from Rockport, Massachusetts, to Boston and farther south along the east coast through the 19th into the early 20th century. Design varied, and some were **scow***-like. Heavily constructed; keelson; often clipper-bowed; raked transom or counter stern. One variety had flat floors and a centerboard. Decked; trunk cabin aft. Special loading boom, usually lowered to the deck when underway. Some had a narrow-gauge track in the hold. Low freeboard when loaded; paving stones might serve as ballast. Most single-masted, but largest stepped 2 masts. Boomed gaff sail with long hoist and short gaff. One or 2 headsails; large staysail hanked to a stay that was carried a short distance out on the heavy bowsprit; gaff topsail to topmast. Reported lengths 10-29m; e.g., length 26m, beam 8.3m, depth 2.2m. Other recorded names: **Chebeague stone sloop, granite sloop, Rockport granite** (or **stone**) **sloop, square-toe frigate**

stoombarkas See **launch**

stoomlogger See **logger**

stop-seiner See **seine boat-3**

stor-åttring See **åttring, åttring-3**

storbaad, storbåd See **storbåt-2**

storbåt 1. *Finland:* Transom-sterned boat used for herring fishing and cargo and passenger transport; small types carried mail. When seining for herring, called a **notbåt***. Characteristically, clinker-built with 5 strakes, earning the local names of **fämbälbåt** or **fembordsbåt**. Curved stem; shallow, raked transom; beamy; considerable sheer. Open or had a cabin aft. Some set a square sail to an aft-raking mast; luff secured by a boomed-out bowline. Others **sloop***-rigged. Reported lengths 7-10m. Other recorded names: **kajutbåt, slupar** (at Lemblad)

2. *Norway:* **a.** Term for a big boat, in excess of 6m long; one larger and with more capacity than average for a particular type. Name variants: **storbaad, storbåd, storebåt.** Note also **åfjordsbåt, åttring, fembøring, småbåt. b.** In Sognefjorden on the west coast, farm-owned freight boats (**føringsbåtar**) carried surplus products to Bergen. The **storebåt** was similar to, but smaller than, the **jekta** (see **jekt**). Open except for a small cabin below a poop. Square stern; tall stem with rounded foot. Clinker-planked; flat floors, low sides. Tall, slender rudder; tiller. Square sail with bonnets; mast stepped amidships. Crew of 2. Dimensions of the boat belonging to Skåsheim farm (**Skåsheimsbåt**): 10.4m long, 3.3m wide, 1.0m deep. **c.** In the Trøndelag area, **storbåt** designates a small, square-sailed cargo vessel with a transom stern.

3. *Sweden:* Strong, heavy boat used around the coast for fishing and for transporting passengers, produce, and fish; reported from ca. 1850. Characterized by a high, raked transom. Clinker-built; heavy keel with drag; curved stem, cutaway forefoot. Shallow deadrise, smooth bilges. Generally open with 3 thwarts. Outboard rudder. Variously rigged: 2 lug- or spritsails, **cutter***, or **sloop***. Rowed when necessary, employing tholepins. Reported lengths 7.3-7.6m; e.g., length 7.3m, beam 2.5m, depth aft 1.2m. Name variants: **storebåt, storöka;** pl. **storökor.** Note also **haxe, kobåt, skärbåt.**

Further references: **gotlandssnipa, kyrkbåt, roslags-skuta, skipsbåt-2, torsköka.**

storebåt See **storbåt-2, storbåt-3**

store boat 1. Carries provisions for sale en route or at a specific destination. Operates along a river, canal, or coast. Some carry supplies to fishing **fleets***. May be operated independently or affiliated with a company. Name variant: **trade boat.** Note also **batelão-regatão, flatboat-4, galeola.**

2. A boat that transports materiel. Name variant: **Train-boot.** Note also **store ship.**

storeka See **vrakeka**

store ship Special auxiliary vessel that carries naval stores and munitions for use of the **fleet***. Other recorded names: **Depotschiff, depot ship, depotskip, magazijnschip, Materialtransportschiff, naval store ship, Proviantschiff, ravitailleur, stores support vessel, supply ship, transport arsenal, transport de matériel** (or **ravitaillement**), **vaisseau de charge, Vorratsschiff.** Note also **flyboat-1, gabarra-1, store boat-2.** Further reference: **flûte**

stores support vessel See **store ship**

storfæring See **færing**

stor felucca, stor felukk See **double felouque**

storfembøring See **fembøring-1, fembøring-2**

storfiring, storfyring See **firing**

storhaxe See **haxe**

storjekt See **jekt**

storm kayak See **kayak-3**

Stornoway yawl *Scotland, NW:* Longline **fishing boat*** on Lewis in the Outer Hebrides. Popular in the mid-19th century. Open, clinker-built, beamy with broad quarters, raked stem and stern. Set 2 short, broad lugsails. Worked with oars while fishing. Crew of 5-6. Reported lengths overall 7.6-9m, on keel 6-7.6m. Name variant: **piker**

Stornowegian *Scotland, NW:* Term applied to craft from the fishing port of Stornoway on the east coast of Lewis in the Outer Hebrides.

storöka, storökor See **storbåt-3**

storottring See **åttring-3**

Störprahm *Germany, NW:* A cargo vessel that worked the Stör River, near the mouth of the Elbe River, carrying lumber, firewood, straw, and grain to Hamburg from the late 18th century to the beginning of the 20th century. Strongly built; flat bottom; straight stem; flat stern with windows; straight sides. Decked; large hatch that went from gunwale to gunwale on some; large leeboards; heavy rudder; tiller. Large spritsail set to a strike pole mast; staysail; 1-2 jibs to a running bowsprit. Crew of 2. Reported lengths 14.7-18m; e.g., length 18m, beam 4.86m, hold depth 1.33m, cap. 45t. The **Glückstädter Prahme,** built at Glückstadt, just upstream on the Elbe, were very similer to the **Störprähme.** Note also **Prahm.**

stor-seksring See **seksæring-6**

storskjøite, storskøyte See **skøyte-1**

Stour barge See **Stour lighter**

Stour lighter *England, E:* A bulk-cargo **barge*** of the River Stour, between Suffolk and Essex, that worked until the 1930s. Coupled into "gangs," the sternpost of the forward **barge** lashed by a seizing chain to the stem of the after boat. Steered from amidships on the forward **barge** by a 9m-long "tiller" that was secured just forward of the hatch on the after **barge,** this **barge** serving as a rudder; long pole used to push the tiller outboard on sharp river bends. Wide clinker strakes; flat bottom, longitudinally planked; closely spaced ribs; vertical sides. Stem lightly curved and raked; sternpost of the forward **barge** similar, but straight and vertical on the after **barge.** Decked; low, covered hatches, the hatch on the forward **barge** divided to permit standing room for the helmsman; after **barge,** known as the **house lighter,** had accommodations for the crew of 2 or a family. Mainly towed by a single horse; platform at the bow used by the horse when towpath changed sides. In tidal areas, might set a crude square sail; also poled. Length 14.2m, beam 3.2m, depth 0.97m; draft loaded 0.84m. Other recorded names: **River Stour lighter, Stour barge**

stovet See **stowboat**

stowboat *England, east coast, Isle of Wight, and Morecambe Bay:* One that fishes, while anchored, for herring (sprat) in winter and for whitebait in August; a long funnel net is slung beneath the boat from the anchor cable. Used from at least the 15th century; a few still worked until the 1970s. Gear used aboard **Essex smacks***, **bawleys***, and some **cutter***-rigged boats in the Solent. Worked with a crew of 2-6. Other recorded names: **spratter, stale boat, stall boat** (original name), **stovet.** Further reading: Hervey Benham, *The Stowboaters* (Colchester: Essex County Newspapers Ltd., 1977).

Strait boat *Canada, E:* Modified **Cape Island boat★** used in Northumberland Strait between Nova Scotia and New Brunswick and the south shore of Prince Edward Island, and in the Gulf of Saint Lawrence. Popular for lobstering. Strong bow flare, earning the name **wedge boat** in places. Plumb stem; now have flat counter stern; some early boats sharp-sterned; a round-sterned type (called a **pinky★**) is used in Newport, Nova Scotia. Lower sheer than the **Cape Island boats** and slimmer. Edge-nailed planking; narrow, almost square planks; no caulking; now mostly of fiberglass, but retain the same shape. Early boats open; now have a small cuddy forward; wheelhouse. Usually painted white. Crew of 2. Reported lengths 10.7-12.2m; e.g., length 11.6m, beam 3.35m. Other recorded names: **North Strait boat, Northumberland Strait boat** (or **fisherman**)

Straits kolek See **kolek sĕlat**

straits ship See **seki bune-1**

Strandboot *Germany, NE/Poland, NW:* Term used for the **fishing boats★** that worked off the beaches of Pomerania until the mid-20th century. The smaller boats tended fish traps. Small boats had a curved stem, narrow transom; partial keel; clinker-planked. Might employ leeboards. Usually decked, but small boats open. Mainly sailed, setting lug-, sprit-, and gaff sails. Outboard motor on some; the large **Schörer** was motorized. Those used in the area of Usedom were 7-8m long. Other recorded names: **Schö(ö)rboot**. Note also **Scheerboot**. Further references: **beach boat, Zeesboot-2**

Strandlomme See **żakówka**

straumbåt *Norway, N:* Built for fishing in the very strong currents near Bodø. A variety of **nordlandsbåt★** but relatively light, of pliable construction, relatively deep hull, beamy, and with a prominent rocker in the keel toward the ends. Clinker-planked of pine, wide top strake, flat floors amidships; tall, slightly recurved stem and sternpost; sharp ends, strong sheer. Rowed with 2 pairs of oars (the **færing★**), or 3 pairs (the **seksæring★**); oars worked against aft-raking blocks and secured by loops. Length 4.76m, beam 1.48m, depth 0.5m. Spelling variant: **strømbåt**

straw barge See **hay barge**

straw boat *England, SE:* Plied the River Thames carrying straw for London's horses. Worked at least during the 17th century. Prohibited from carrying passengers. See also **bote de pinho**.

Streckfusser See **Schiesslomme**

Streifenboot See **patrol boat**

strijela Fast vessel used by the Bokelians of Boka Katorska on the eastern Adriatic and by the Turks in the eastern Mediterranean in the 15th century. Carried cargo and passengers. Strongly curved stem, plumb stern, keel, strong sheer ending in a quarter-deck. Outboard rudder. Armed with 4 guns. Small foremast with square sail; mainmast set a square course and square topsail. Cap. ca. 140t. Name variant: **sajeta**

striker boat *United States:* **1.** In the Atlantic coastal menhaden fishing industry, 1-2 of these boats are sent out to look for schools of fish. When located, the "striker" calls for the **seine boats★** and the **menhaden boat★**, helps to halt the fish by striking the water with his oar, and when inside the net, helps support the floats. Need for the **striker boat** now minimized by use of aircraft spotters. Sharp bow; plumb transom stern; round bottom; shoe keel; sometimes lapstrake sides. Open with stern seat and single thwart. Carried on aft davits or hoisted aboard the **menhaden boat**. Rowed with a single pair of oars, the oarsman usually standing. Reported lengths 3.6-4.1m; e.g., length 3.66m, beam 1.37m, depth 0.53m. Other recorded names: **drive(r) boat, menhaden striker boat**. Note also **sail gear**.

2. The motorized **striker boat** of the Pacific coast is used to catch mackerel with hook and line, the "striker" being the leather lure. Other recorded names: **bait boat★, chum boat**

string See **timber raft-3**

string bean See **Meppler praam**

stro-ever See **Stroh-Ewer**

stroggylos See **round ship**

Stroh-Ewer *Germany, central:* Modified **Ewer★** type for transporting hay and straw on the middle Elbe River to the Hamburg area. Worked mainly during the 19th century. Short end decks, open waist. Employed a loose-footed gaff sail and staysail. Length ca. 20m. Spelling variant: **stro-ever**

strömbåt *Sweden, central:* Sharp-ended, open boat designed to traverse such rivers as the Ljusnan. Clinker-planked; T-keel; rounded in cross section; single-piece ribs. Curved stem and sternpost; low deck at bow. Washstrakes abaft the mast. Outboard rudder; tiller. Mast steps through thwart near amidships. Sets spritsail and foresail. Also rowed; single tholepins.

strømbåt See **straumbåt**

Stromfahrzeug See **riverboat**

strömmingshaxe See **haxe**

strömmingsöka See **sköteka**

strongylē naus, strongylon ploion, strongylos See **round ship**

Strood doble See **Medway doble**

Stümmel See **Bretterfloss**

stumpie See **stumpy barge**

stumpjumper See **Reelfoot stumpjumper**

stumpy barge *England:* A river **barge★** rigged without a topmast, the **Thames sailing barge★** being the most common. The short mast carried a tanned mainsail held in a high peak by a long, heavy sprit. Sail brailed to the mast; a few employed a long, standing gaff to which the sail was brailed, the so-called **half spreetie**. A small sprit mizzen was set to a mast stepped on the rudderhead; single large foresail; others carried no mizzen or foresail. Dates to at least the early 18th century, carrying bulk cargo such as bricks, chalk, cement, gunpowder, and London's refuse in the Thames Estuary and River until the 1930s. The smallest, the **cut barges★**, carried building materials on the Regent and Surrey Canals. Hull form varied. Early vessels were sharp-ended; later, many were **swim-headed barges★** with sharply raked, blunt bows and similar sterns that were elongated by deadwood; flat sheer; leeboards used in a tideway; very low freeboard. Open in early period; later decked around a central hold. Crew of 2. Reported lengths 14-24m; e.g., length 21m, beam 4.3m, depth 1.7m. Other recorded names: **polemasted barge, stumpie, Thames stumpy**. Note also **brickie**.

sturgeon, sturgeon boat See **sturgeon-head**

sturgeon-head *Canada, N:* One of the 3 categories of so-called **inland boats★** used by the Hudson's Bay Company on Canadian rivers, especially the Athabasca in Alberta Province. Made a downriver trip only. Clinker-built; tubby with a blunt bow; transom formed a wide "U"; round bottom, sometimes marked chines; rounded transverse frames. Steered with a long sweep that passed through a ring at the stern. Poled, rowed, and tracked from shore; later used an outboard motor. Might have 7 in crew. Length to ca. 17m, beam 3.4m. Other recorded names: **sturgeon (boat), sturgeon-head boat (or scow), sturgeon (-nosed) scow**. Note also **rapids boat**.

sturgeon-head boat, sturgeon-head scow See **sturgeon-head**

sturgeon-nose canoe *United States, NW:* Sharp-ended lake and river **canoe★** of the Kalispel tribes of northeastern Washington State. Cone-shaped ends, closed on top with external battens; low ends permitted good visibility and minimal wind resistance. Constructed of inner white-pine bark, cedar ribs, sewn with pine roots, sapling gunwales. Bottom rocker at ends. Reported lengths 4.3-4.9m, beam ca. 0.6m. See also **tci'k'Enō**.

sturgeon-nosed scow, sturgeon scow See **sturgeon-head**

Stutzen See **Mutzen**

suction dredger See **dredger-1**

suēn See **chuan**

suffeenu See **safina**

sufficient boat See **gundalow**

Suffolk beach boat, Suffolk beach punt See **beach punt-1**

Suffolk beach yawl See **beach yawl-1**

Suffolk punt See **beach punt-1**

sufun See **mahaila-2, safina, sefine**

sugar drogher See **drogher-3**

sukaut See **kayak-4**

süken See **zig**

sukung See **sekong**

sula See **sule**

sule *Albania, NW:* **Fishing boat★** of Lake Scutari. Open; 3 planks per side, heavy top strake; sides parallel. Flat bottom with straight rocker at each end, the ends terminating above the waterline. Sharp, plumb ends, the bow sharper. Seat at each end for the rowers, who face each other. A block fastened on the port side at each end for an oar. Reported lengths 3-7m; e.g., length 7m, beam 2m, depth 1.5m. Other recorded names: **sulje, sull**; a dugout type: **suli**; pl. **sula**

suli, sulje, sull See **sule**

sullage lighter See **ash boat**

sulluk See **jali**

sultan's caique See **saltanat kayığı**

sumaca *South America, E:* Small, roughly built, flat-bottomed **coaster★** peculiar to the Río de la Plata Estuary, but also used along the east coast of South America in the 18th and early 19th centuries. In the later period, served as a **corsair★** of the Spanish and Argentinians. Set square foresails, gaff mainsail, and gaff topsail; multiple headsails to bowsprit and jibboom. Length overall 20m, on keel 18m, beam 5.2m, depth 2.3m. Spelling variants: **sumack, zumaca, zumeca**

sumack See **sumaca**

sumáripa See **falca**

sumbad *Estonia:* Covered **fish car★** similar to an upside down **flat-iron skiff★**, or is an elongated, double-ended craft. Pierced with holes to permit water to flow freely.

sumbook, sumbuk See **sambūq**

summer gondola See **gondola-4**

sump In Swedish, a boat with pierced sides that permit flooding of a contained area for live fish. It may also be a vessel with a wet well that transports fish to market (**fisksump**) or may be a **fish car★**. Spelling variants: **sumpen**; pl. **sumpar**. Note also **roddsump, segelsump, sumpjolle**.

sumpa *Estonia/Latvia:* Seaworthy craft that transported live fish in its well from offshore islands to cities on the mainland coast; also used to transfer the catch from **fishing boats★** out at sea to land. Decked; some had a cabin aft for passengers. Crew of 1-2. Reported lengths 7.6-15m, widths 4.6-8.3m. Note also **sumppaat**.

sumpar See **sump**

sumpbåt See **roddsump**

sumpen See **sump**

sumpjolle 1. *Finland:* Small **fishing boat★** with a wet well (*sump*) in the after half. Well caused the stern to ride low in the water and the bow high. Clinker-built; round bottom, curved stem; transom stern. When sailed, ballast placed in the well. Small size called a **sumpjulla**.

2. *Sweden, E:* Fished in the home waters of the Stockholm Stårgård (archipelago) for whitefish and pike in particular. Transom stern; wet well. Worked with 2 pairs of oars, or set a spritsail and jib. Reported lengths 4-7.3m; e.g., length 4m, beam 1.5m.
Spelling variant: **sumpjulle**. Note also **roddsump, segelsump**.

sumpjulla, sumpjulle See **sumpjolle**

sumplaev See **sumppaat**

sump otter See **beerotter**

sumppaat *Estonia:* Term for a **fishing boat★** that has a wet well. Name variant: **sumplaev**. Note also **sumpa**.

sün See **chuan**

sunbūq See **sambūq**

sundbåd See **sildebåd**

Sunderland foyboat See **foyboat-2**

sundjolle *Denmark, E:* Small, open boat that fished and tended pound nets in the Øresund Strait off the east coast of Sjælland. Double-ended, clinker-built, marked sheer. Strongly curved stem and sternpost. Sturdy rudder, often shaped from natural curve of timber. Set spritsail, staysail, and topsail. Mast stepped against thwart; no shrouds, easily struck. Also rowed. Crew of 2. Reported lengths 4.2-6.1m; e.g.,

sundjolle

length 5.2m, beam 1.8m, depth 0.7m, draft 0.6m. Other recorded names: **jolle fra Snekkersten, snekkerstenjolle**. Note also **jolle-1**.

Sundmore boat, Sundmoreboot See **sunnmørsbåt**
šuner See **schooner**
Sunnemøre boat See **sunnmørsbåt**
sunnfjordbaat See **sunnfjordbåt**
sunnfjordbåt *Norway, W:* Overall term for the small, open boats produced in the highly indented coastline of Sunnfjord district. The 4-oared boats run errands, while the larger boats are used mainly for herring fishing, having a large capacity, relatively flat floors, and a wider keel. Good sailers, setting a square sail type. Boats are principally 4-oared (**færing★**), 6-oared (**seksæring★**), 8-oared (**firkeiping★**), and 10-oared (**femkeiping★**). Spelling variants: **sunnfjordbaat, sunnfjords-båt**
sunnfjordjekt See **jekt**
sunnfjords-båt See **sunnfjordbåt**
sunnmørsåttring See **åttring-2**
sunnmørsbaad See **sunnmørsbåt**
sunnmørsbåt *Norway, NW:* General term given to the open boats produced in Sunnmøre (earlier Sondmøre) County. Mainly used for fishing, generally offshore. Early boats characterized by 2 pairs of narrow strakes from each bow that were joined to wide strakes that continued aft, creating a full bow and narrow stern. Trapezoidal, dipping lugsail replaced by 2 standing lug- or gaff sails. Many of the boats were enlarged, but the original characteristics were retained. The 10-oared boat was called an **ottring** (see **åttring**), despite not having 8 oars; the 8-oared boat was a **seksring** (see **seksæring**) which has 6 oars elsewhere, and the true 6-oared boat became a **treroring** or **three-rower** (see **seksæring**). The **færing★** remained a 4-oared boat. Spelling variants: **Söndmöersk baat** (or **yawl**), **søndmørbaad, Sondmore** (or **Sundmore**) **boat, söndmörsbaat, Sundmoreboot, Sunnemøre boat, sunnmørsbaad**
sunnmørsfæring See **færing-4**
sunnmørsjekt See **jekt**

sunnmørsottring See **åttring-2**
Supannahong, Suphannahong, suppannahongse See **rua ballang**
supply ship See **store ship**
surfboat **1.** A light, open boat designed and modified to work well through sea and surf conditions off a particular beach. Used to land passengers and goods and as a **lifeboat★**. Term may also describe a craft built for surf-riding. Primarily double-ended; fine entrance; carvel-planked with battens or clinker-built; flat floors; strong sheer; heavy scantlings; often a curved keel. Frequently has a short deck forward and aft; later boats self-bailing. Paddled or rowed using a steering oar. Rarely sailed. Mostly 6.1-8.2m long; shallow draft. Other recorded names: **Brandungsboot, Surfboot**. Note also **Monomoy, Race Point surfboat, whaleboat-1**.
2. *Australia, E:* Primarily a coastal rescue boat built under design rules prescribed by the Surf Life Saving Association. Since early in the 20th century, the local clubs have been highly competitive, resulting in considerable design modifications. Early so-called **banana boats★** were sharp-ended with strongly curved stem and sternpost, bottom rocker, strong sheer. Decked at ends with flotation tanks. Later boats have a very narrow transom stern; maximum beam in forward third. A bar across the gunwales helps stabilize the helmsman, who works a long sweep. Carvel-built with light, narrow planking; now being developed with synthetic materials. Crew of 5 usually, 4 rowing single-banked plus a helmsman. Lengths to 8m.
3. *South Africa, SE:* Craft that worked off Natal beaches, employing a seine net. Carvel-built; longitudinally planked, flat bottom with sharp rocker at bow, following the strong bow sheer; 3-piece frames. Chafing pieces at the bilges. Sharp, plumb stem; raked transom stern. Open. Pulled 4 oars, single-banked, against tholepins. Length ca. 5.5m. Name variants: **Durban** (or **Natal**) **surfboat**
4. *United Kingdom:* Class of boat in the Royal Navy used for surveying. Employs a drop keel. Steered with a sweep. Sets a boomed gunter sail with foresail or a boomed lugsail. Also rowed using 4 or 5 regular oars and from 2 to 10 surf oars. Reported lengths 4.4-8.2m, widths 1.5-2m.
5. *United States, NE:* Type widely used along the Maine coast until ca. 1876 by the old Lighthouse Board and by the Life Saving Service. Lapstrake construction, sharp ends; curved, plumb stem; straight, raked sternpost; straight keel, rising floors, moderately hard bilges. Open; 5 thwarts, horseshoe-shaped stern seat; outboard rudder; tiller. Mainly rowed, using long oars. Length 6.7m, beam 2m, depth 0.6m. Name variant: **New England surfboat**
6. *United States:* **a.** A landing craft used by the army at Veracruz in 1847 during the Mexican War. Sharp ends. Fitted with a bow gun. Made in 3 sizes so they could be nested aboard a transport vessel: 12.2m long, 3.7m wide, 1.33m deep, carrying 45 or more men; 11.5m by 3.4m by 1.22m, carrying 40 men; 10.9m by 3.1m by 1.14m, carrying fewer than 40 men. Sharp ends; flat bottom, lightly planked. Crew of 6 oarsmen, a

coxswain, and a skipper. Name variant: **beach boat★**.
b. The present generation of **surfboats** operated by the Coast Guard engage mainly in rescue work, especially in the surf zone and off mouths of navigable rivers. Mainly of steel and recently of aluminum. Those stationed along the Oregon and Washington coasts are 12.4m long, 5.2m wide, draft 0.91m; crew of 3-4. Name variant: **motor lifeboat**
Further references: **baleinière de barre, Prince Edward Island surfboat**

Surfboot See **surfboat-1**

surme See **djerme**

surnā See **sarnái**

suro See **lisi**

survival craft See **lifeboat**

Susquehanna ark, Susquehanna boat See **ark-4b**

Susquehanna Flats sinkbox See **sinkbox**

Susquehanna sneak boat *United States, E:* Open waterfowler's gunning craft that operated out of the lower Susquehanna River. Sharp, raked ends; canvas-covered, clench-fastened white pine planking. Multiple chines apparently enabled hunter to roll the craft onto its beam, where, hidden by cambered washboards, he could stealthily approach the ducks. Poled and paddled. Length ca. 4.6-4.9m. Other recorded names: **rollover duck boat, turnover sneak boat**

Swampscott dory *United States, NE:* Popular fishing and pleasure craft of the late 19th century; now enjoying a revival. Designed at Swampscott, Massachusetts, northeast of Boston, to work off beaches. Narrow, flat bottom; rounded sides with slack bilges; raked ends, greater at the stern; stem slightly curved; narrow, wedge-shaped transom with sculling notch. Four or more lapped strakes to each side; considerable sheer. Rudder and centerboard used on sailing types. Open; later sailing models half-decked with cockpit. Motorized versions (called **power dories**) decked with standing well amidships and low cabin aft over the engine compartment; transom wider and raked. Rowed or set a leg-of-mutton sail with a long, high-kicked boom; jib tacked to stemhead. Reported lengths 4.6-6.4m; e.g., length 4.9m, beam 1.6m, depth 0.5m; the motorized type ran to 9m. Other recorded names: **clipper dory, North Shore dory**. Note also **dory**.

Swampscott dory-skiff See **dory-skiff**

Swansea Bay dredging skiff See **Mumbles oyster skiff**

Swansea pilot cutter See **Swansea pilot schooner**

Swansea pilot schooner *Wales, S:* Provided service out of Swansea from the late 18th through the 19th century. Early boats open, clinker-built, transom-sterned; 6.4m long and 2m wide. Carvel planking adapted ca. 1840, and after that, the boats increased in length to more than 16m. Hull modified with sharper lines, steeper floors, deep heel, plumb or raked stem and sternpost, slightly rounded counter stern, and full deck. Throughout, retained the basic **schooner★** rig; fore-and-aft sails, employing very short gaffs set to pole masts. No standing rigging. Foremast stepped well forward; mainmast about

amidships with a sharp rake aft. Foresail boomless; mainsail loose-footed with boom; sails laced to the masts. Running bowsprit and flying jib added ca. 1840. Main boom unshipped in harbor since it extended well beyond the stern. Crew of 1-3. Length overall 15.2m, on keel 11.3m, beam 4.1m, depth 3.4m. Other recorded names: **lugger★, Swansea pilot cutter**. Further reading: J. F. Coates, "Swansea Bay Pilot Boats," *The Mariner's Mirror* 30 (1944): 114-122.

šwâte See **šheṭêya**

Swatow fisherman, Swatow off-shore trawler See **sin-tor-chai**

Swedish towboat See **scow-schooner-3**

sweep, sweep boat See **shell**

swift boat **1.** *United Kingdom:* Term applied to a type of fast passenger boat used on some Scottish and English canals in the 1830s; some used as **steamers** until the 1880s. Might have a swan neck at the bow, which was a scythe to cut the tow lines of slower-moving vessels. Lightly built, iron hull; passenger cabins and a pantry. One type was double-hulled with a hand-operated paddlewheel between; also called a **gig★**. Towed by 2 horses. Reported lengths 21-22m; e.g., length 22m, beam 1.8m, depth 0.84m; shallow draft. Note also **fly-boat-3a, paddle boat-3**.
2. *United States:* An inshore **patrol boat★** used extensively in the Mekong Delta during the Vietnam War of 1964-1975. Adapted for naval use from a commercial oil-rig **launch★**. Constructed of aluminum; very small cabin. Crew of 6. Very shallow draft. Other recorded names: **fast patrol craft, patrol craft fast, PCF swift**
Further reference: **haya bune**

swiler See **sealer**

swim bow See **butthead**

swim-headed barge *England, SE:* Type of **Thames sailing barge★** characterized by a 40° rake to the blunt bow, enabling it to nose into riverbanks. Carried heavy cargoes such as ballast and bricks. Flat bottom turned up at the stern like the bow, but a skeg ran aft to form a vertical sternpost, from which hung a large-bladed rudder, the so-called **budgett stern**. **Lighters★** with swim heads and budgett sterns still ply the Thames. Straight sides for most of their length before narrowing to square ends; leeboards. Mainmast stepped almost amidships, carrying a large spritsail, 2 headsails, and occasionally a topsail; the small mizzenmast also set a spritsail. Reported lengths 18-21m. Other recorded names: **budget(t) barge, East Country barge, muffie, swim-header, swim-heads, swimmie, swimmy**. Note also **stumpy barge**.

swim-header, swim-heads, swimmie See **swim-headed barge**

swimming float See **float-2**

swimmy See **swim-headed barge**

swoiler See **sealer**

swordfish searcher boat See **feluca-2**

sword pink See **pink-1**

sylheti See **patam-1**

Syrian schooner See **shakhtura**

szkuna See **schooner**

szkuta *Poland:* The largest traditional river vessel, carrying grain, salt, and other products, especially on the Vistula River, until the mid-19th century. Wide, flat bottom with rocker, longitudinally planked; tapered to a sharp, recurving bow; narrow but flat stern; sides clinker-planked and flared; keelson with mast step.

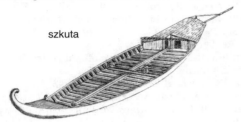

szkuta

Open except for house at the stern. Very wide rudder blade activated from the outer end; tiller extended over house. Oars worked from fore part. Crew of 16-20 on downriver trip. Upstream, square sail set to the single mast stepped amidships; sometimes towed. Reported lengths 30-38m, widths 3.8-9m, molded depth 0.95-1.0m, draft loaded ca. 1.0m. Other recorded names: **Lastkahn, skuta*, skutar, Weichselkahn**; pl. **szkuty**. Note also **szkutka**.

szkutka *Poland, west-central:* Small, open craft of the Warta River. Almond-shaped, flat bottom; 1-3 longitudinal planks; slight rocker. Narrow, raking transom ends. Used natural crooks as floor timbers and side frames, alternating from side to side. Two lapped planks formed the sides; slightly flared; nearly flat sheer. **Fishing boats*** had a covered live well amidships. Sculled, poled, and towed upstream from shore with a line to a mast. Wooden type extinct; some now built of metal. Reported lengths ca. 4.5-5.4m, widths 1-1.2m. Spelling variant: pl. **szkutki**

szkutki See **szkutka**

szkuty See **szkuta**

szóstkowy See **galar**

taawai See **waka tiwai**

tabellaria, tabellaria navis See **advice boat**

tabilai *Fiji, central Pacific:* **1.** Fast, interisland single-**outrigger canoe***; small size extant on some outer islands. Early **canoes*** used for war purposes. Dugout hull left solid at the ends; double-ended with narrow, vertical cutwaters; hull strengthened by gunwale rails. Partly decked. Three main booms extend to the float, plus numerous shorter booms and stringers; platform rests on booms in the hull area. Float and main booms connected by a pair of divergent stanchions. Sets a triangular sail with the apex tacked to forward end; raking mast pivoted to opposite end when tacking, the outrigger kept to windward. Sail boomed at the foot. Also sculled. Early boats exceptionally long. Other recorded names: **tambilai, waqa ni Viti**
   2. The term has also been used for a type of double **canoe**. Joined by a solid platform; one hull slightly smaller. Set a triangular sail.

table seiner See **seine boat-2**

tafa'aga See **vaka tafaanga**

tafaana *Samoa, central Pacific:* Decked **outrigger canoe***. See also **tafa'anga**.

tafa'anga *Tonga, central Pacific:* Seagoing single-**outrigger canoe*** used mainly for bonito fishing. Present-day **canoe*** essentially the same as that described in the mid-17th century. Plank-built of multiple pieces; sewn from the inside through ridges in the edges of the strakes; the few remaining **canoes** have been reinforced with nails. Round in cross section. Vertical or concave cutwater; at the stern, bottom tapers up, ending at the gunwale. Decked at ends; line of cowrie shells may decorate the decking. A trolling pole is set against the stern breakwater. Long, slender float with front end roughly aligned with the bow; aft end truncated just abaft the after boom. Two to 4 booms cross the gunwales; attached to the float by 2 pairs of stanchions, each pair joining above the boom and lashed vertically from boom to the float. Short pseudo-booms may extend partway to the float to hold the fishing poles. Mainly paddled, but some larger **canoes** sailed, employing a triangular sail to a short, vertical mast; sail boomed at the foot and set in a wide "V." When sailed, a counterbalance spar projects out the side opposite the outrigger. Reported lengths 6-9m; e.g., length 6.5m, beam and depth 0.65m. Spelling variants: **tafaana*, taf(ah)anga**. Further reading: M. C. Bataille-Benguigai, "Pirogues Cousues et Pêche à la Bonite aux Îles Tonga" in: Gela Gunda, ed., *The Fishing Culture of the World*, vol. 2 (Budapest: Akadémiai Kiadò, 1984), 991-1023. Note also **vaka tafaanga**.

tafahanga, tafanga See **tafa'anga**

tafarese See **tafurea**

taffarel See **dghajsa tal-pass**

tafforea, tafforée, taforea, taforée, taforeia, taforie, tafourée See **tafurea**

ta-fu ch'uan See **da fu chuan**

tafurca See **tafurea**

tafurea *Mediterranean:* Flat vessel of the 15th-16th centuries that transported horses and artillery, and merchandise in times of peace. Used in France, Italy, Spain, and Portugal; some traveled to the Indian Ocean with expeditionary forces. Low sides; no keel; divided internally to accommodate the horses. High enough at the stern for an opening to discharge horses. 14th-century report cites it only as a small vessel that carried merchandise from one country to another. Spelling variants: **tafarese, taf(f)orea, taf(f)orée, taforeia, taforie, tafourée, tafurca, tafurella, tafurenza, tafurera, tafuresse, tafureya, tafuria, tafurosa**. Note also **horse carrier, huissier**.

tafurella, tafurenza, tafurera, tafuresse, tafureya, tafuria, tafurosa See **tafurea**

tagari See **taghāri**

Tagessegler See **day boat-1**

taghāri *Bangladesh/India, NE:* Clay-pot craft used for local travel in the Ganges Delta area, especially during monsoon flooding. Pots normally used to feed cattle. Often raced during festivals. Slightly conical hemi-

taghāri

sphere with decorated lip; made of fired clay; increase in depth over diameter provided adequate displacement for reasonable stability. Single occupant squatted on a board laid across the bottom or on a bed of grass or straw; freeboard ca. 15cm. Propelled with hands or a single paddle worked on alternate sides. Diameter 76cm, depth 38cm. Other recorded names: **cāri, chāri, gāmalā, gamla, nād, tagari, tigari**. Note also **chatty raft, palla chatty**.

tågkåg See **kåg-2**

tahpooy *Guyana/Venezuela:* **Coaster*** with flat, raked, trapezoid-shaped bow, wider side on top; rounded stern. Outboard rudder. Smaller boats **cutter***-rigged; the larger **schooner***-rigged. Lengths 9.8-25m; widths 3-6.6m; draft aft ca. 1.4m.

tahucup See **acal**

ta-hung, ta-hung ch'uan, ta hung-t'ou yang ch'uan See **da hong chuan**

tai ch'uan See **liu wang chuan**

taipairua See **tipairua**

tai tch'ouan See **liu wang chuan**

taka *Turkey:* **1.** Small Black Sea **fishing boat*** that works from beaches; hauled ashore by a capstan with ropes attached to an athwartships beam about amidships. Straight stem, cutaway forefoot; curved sternpost; curved keel. Strong sheer; washboards in after third; decked at bow and stern; outboard rudder; short tiller. Lugsail set to a vertical mast; sometimes a small jib. Also rowed; now generally motorized. Reported lengths 5.5-7m; e.g., length 5.6m, beam 1.7m, depth 0.7m.

2. The **trawlers★** and **fish carriers★** were **schooners★**, but now are generally motorized. Clipper or "chicken beak" stem; high, flaring bow. High, square transom or rounded counter stern; straight keel; flat floors. Very strong sheer; bulwarks start abaft the stem and run to the stern. Outboard rudder; tiller may pass through the bulwarks; decked, now have a deckhouse. Reported lengths 10-14m.

3. The coasting **takas** of the Black Sea were clinker-built; great sheer resulted in a high bow and high transom; outboard rudder; decked. Now motorized, but earlier set a standing lugsail, occasionally with headsails. Length to 18m. Name variant: **filuka★**

taka ō bune See **seki bune**

takia *Fiji, central Pacific:* Single-**outrigger canoe★** used mainly on rivers of Viti Levu and Vanua Levu islands, although occasionally they worked along the shore, and may still work out from the more southern islands. Roughly hewn dugout, the design of which was dictated largely by the shape of the original tree; ends elongated with small, horizontal shelves; circular in cross section. Low, lashed-on washstrakes raised the sides to support the outrigger booms. Platform extended beyond both gunwales; sometimes a peaked house covered the platform. Three horizontal booms ran to the float; supplemental booms went only to the longitudinal stringers that were laid atop the boom. Float short and bluntly pointed. Booms and float attached by 2 pairs of tall, divergent stanchions. Mainly paddled, a large **takia** requiring 6-8 paddles; might be poled, especially upstream. One variety raises a boomed, triangular mat sail, set with the apex tacked to the bow. Reported lengths 6-10m. Name variant: **velovelo★**

ta-ku ch'uan See **da gu chuan**

Ta-ku fisherman *China, N:* Used by fishermen from Da Gu (Ta-ku) in Bo Hai (Gulf of Chihli). Solidly constructed; box-shaped with flat bow, transom stern, and flat bottom; strong sheer, little or no freeboard amidships; outboard rudder; tiller. Flush deck; high coaming around the central hatch; crew of 5-6 accommodated below decks aft; portable mat house for helmsman. Stepped a tall mainmast amidships setting a large balanced lugsail with a straight leech. In addition, might step a very small foremast setting a tanned lugsail, or set a jib tacked to the anchor davit. Reported lengths 10-15m; shallow draft.

talal dinghi See **dingi-2**

talé, taléï, tale kotolobe See **kadei**

tally scow *United States, Alaska:* Received and counted salmon caught by the **gillnetters★**, transported the catch from the fishing grounds to the cannery, and provided hot meals for the fishermen.

talong See **laung**

talque See **tjalk-3**

t̯al̯t̯âna See **tartane**

tamão See **tambangan**

Tamar barge, Tamar gravel barge See **Plymouth barge**

Tamar market boat See **market boat-5**

Tamar River sloop See **Plymouth barge**

tam ban **1.** *Cambodia:* **a.** A small **tam bản** paddles between shore and large **fishing boats★**. Constructed of 6 planks, 2 on the bottom and 2 on each side, strengthened by ribs; bottom has rocker; square ends; decked at each end. Reported lengths 3-5m; e.g., length 3.5m, beam 0.85m, depth 0.3m. **b.** A sailing type transports dried fish in the coastal waters. Carvel-planked with very flat floors; framed with 3-piece ribs and stringers; plank keel; vertical sides. Bow terminates in blunt stem that widens and becomes concave toward the top; stern raked with strakes ending beyond the transom, the top

tam ban-1b

strake supporting an overhanging transom board; flat sheer. Rudderpost passes inboard of this transom piece to a slotted tiller; rectangular rudder blade with long side perpendicular to the stern. Decked to mast and at stern; house covers undecked area. Short mast stepped about a third in from the bow, setting a boomed gunter lugsail. Reported lengths 8-15m; e.g., length 10m, beam 3.5m, depth 0.8m, cap. 10t.

2. *Vietnam:* Annamite term for a three-plank **sampan★**. Name variant: **thuyền tam ban**

tambaŋan See **tambangan**

tambang *Malaysia:* Generic term for a harbor passenger boat or **ferry★**. Some distinctive, having a narrow bow elongated into a beak. Stern wider, with helmsman's seat rigged outboard; European-type midline rudder. Little sheer except toward the bow. Decked; bulwark forward; decorative washboards abaft the mast on some. Set a leg-of-mutton, sprit-, or lugsail; also paddled. Reported lengths 3.66-4.88m, widths 0.9-1.22m, depths 0.46-0.6m. Other recorded names: **perahu** (or **perau'**) **tambang, praw tampanggan, sampan tambang★, sampan tambanggan, tambanggan, tampanggan**; those at Johore called **sampan Djohor, sampan Johore**. See also **tongkang-2**.

tambangan *Indonesia:* **1.** Generic term for a small **ferryboat★** or **passage boat★** in western Indonesia.

2. Those at Banjarmasin in southern Kalimantan (Borneo) are narrow, double-ended **dugout canoes★** with a slightly convex bottom. Ends turn up; cut square at the top. Paddled. Carry up to 20 passengers. In the same area, could be a coastal craft with a rounded bottom and raked ends. A palm-leaf roof covered part of the hull. Paddled.

3. The **tambangan** of Palembang in southeastern Sumatra is also a **dugout canoe★**. Sharp, overhanging ends; flared sides; flat sheer; no keel. Slatted flooring extends over most of the hull, above which is a shelter. Paddled using a triangular-bladed paddle. Length 7.3m, beam 1.5m.

4. On the north coast of Java, a large type served as a **passage boat** from such ports as Djakarta and Surabaja. Flat floors; keel; curved ends, the bow more than the stern, square cut on top. Loose plank deck; awning aft. One or 2 masts stepped through thwarts. Set trapezoidal or square cotton sails. Also paddled.

Other recorded names: **djoekoeng (djukung) tambangan, djoekoeng tembangan, jukung tambangan, kapal tambangan, perahu tambang, prahoe tambangan, tamão, tambaŋan, tembangan**. Note also **sampan tambang, sampan tambangan, tambang**.

tambanggan See **tambang**

tambilai See **tabilai-1**

tambo See **chombo**

tam'e' *United States, W:* Tule grass **raft★** of the Nisenan of central California. Propelled by 3.7-4.6m-long poles. Also used single-bladed paddles. Name variant: **tule balsa**

Tamil lighter See **Tamil tongkang**

Tamil tongkang *Peninsular Malaysia:* Tamil-operated **lighter★** from Penang. Used along the west coast to transport rubber, timber, and produce to the main ports. Initially double-ended, then transom-sterned. Hull terminated in a raked stem and stern; fiddle-head at top of stem. Steered with a western-style rudder; wide blade below the waterline. Low sheer except at the bow; little freeboard when loaded. Mainmast stepped well forward and carried a dipping lugsail. When used, the mizzenmast set a gaff sail. Jib run to the bowsprit. Later set only a boomed mainsail. Canvas sails tanned with cutch. Reported lengths 16-29m, widths 4-6.7m, inside depths 1.3-2m. Other recorded names: **Penang sailing lighter, Penang tongkang, Tamil lighter**. Note also **tongkang**.

tampanggan See **tambang**

Tanabask See **bask**

tanca, tancar See **sampan Tanka**

tan chuan *China, E:* Flat-bottomed boat designed to traverse quiet waterways of the Chang Jiang (Yangtze) delta and the Ninbgo (Ningpo) area, often carrying local produce. Square, transversely planked ends, turned up from the longitudinally planked bottom; sheer strake extended beyond the stern transom; on some, the stern sheer swept up sharply. Hull strengthened with bulkheads and frames. Portable deck planks; cargo housed forward; crew aft. Worked with a stern oar or poled in shallow water; some had a tracking mast. Lengths to 15m; e.g., length 9m, beam 2m, depth 1.0m, draft 0.8m. Other recorded names: **sandbank boat, shallow water boat**

tancoa See **tankwa**

Tancook scallop sloop *Canada, SE:* Built on Tancook Island off Nova Scotia beginning ca. World War I. Popular for inshore fishing, lobstering, and scalloping until ca. 1940. Some still operate, but unrigged. Curved, raking stem; raking transom, curved sides. Lightweight for easy launching and hauling in winter. **Sloop★**-rigged. Reported lengths ca. 8m; draft 0.6-0.9m. Name variant: **scallop boat★**

Tancook schooner *Canada, SE:* A more burdensome vessel than the **Tancook whaler★**, which the **schooner★** replaced in Canada during the 1920s. Mostly a **fishing boat★**, but some built as **yachts★**. Differed from the **whaler★** mainly by a high, raked, oval transom. Rounded, cutaway stem; steep rise to the floors, deep drag aft. Rudder came up forward of the counter. Set 2 boomed gaff sails, or the mainsail was sometimes a leg-of-mutton. Two headsails, main topsail, top staysail. Designed mainly for power. Reported lengths 9-14m; e.g., length overall 12.2m, on waterline 9.4m, beam 3m, molded depth 1.6m. Special designations were given to the vessels according to size, decking, and fishing types. **Deck boats** were fully decked, over 15m long, and carried 2-4 **dories** (see **dory**). **Hatch boats★**, which were under 15m, had 2-4 prominent, removable hatches that were fitted around the mainmast in the cockpit; open except for foredeck and cuddy. **Semi-deck boats**, 12-15m long, combined the features of the above and carried a single **dory**. Further reading: Wayne M. O'Leary, *The Tancook Schooners: An Island and Its Boats* (Montreal: McGill-Queen's University Press, 1994).

Tancook whaler *Canada, SE/United States, NE:* Developed on Tancook Island near Halifax, Nova Scotia, in the latter half of the 19th century for inshore fishing. Used as a workboat until the turn of the century; became a popular pleasure craft in maritime Canada and New England in the 1920s and 1930s. Sharp, similar ends with deep, raking sternpost and long-reaching, clipper-type bow. Some lapstrake but mainly carvel construction; rising floors from plank keel with considerable drag; low freeboard amidships and swept-up ends, especially at the stern. Half-decked with narrow waterways; cuddy forward and abaft the foremast. Narrow rudder; long tiller passed beneath the traveler; most had a centerboard. Employed a low **schooner★** rig; set a loose-footed, overlapping gaff foresail and a boomed mainsail. Forestaysail often clubbed on the clew; short bowsprit; club-headed staysail set to the main topmast. Sails usually tanned. Often rowed to fishing grounds in calms; auxiliaries in later boats. Crew of 2-3. Reported lengths 7.3-15.2m; e.g., length overall 12.5m, on waterline 10.4m, beam 2.7m, depth ca. 1.6m, draft with centerboard up 1.3m. Name variant: **whaler★**. Further reading: Robert C. Post, *The Tancook Whalers: Origins, Rediscovery, and Revival* (Bath: Maine Maritime Museum, 1985). Note also **Tancook schooner**.

tandem boats *United States, E:* On the Susquehanna River and Tidewater Canal in eastern Pennsylvania, pairs of boats were hitched one behind the other and pulled by a team of mules. Some employed a chain-linkage steering device between the 2 boats so that the rear boat became the rudder. A wheel in the pilot house in the after part of the forward boat activated the chains. A normal rudder also available on the 2nd boat.

tandem team See **timber raft-2b**

tanga *Africa, central:* Sailing craft of Lake Tanganyika. In the early 19th century, worked mainly from towns on the eastern shore. The more common small boats,

8-10m long, were narrow with parallel sides. The larger boats, to 20m, had a more elliptical shape with maximum beam amidships. Both types generally plank-extended dugouts, the planks braced by knees and thwarts. Flat bottom without keel. Straight, slightly raked stem; transom stern. Small boats open; larger boats often decked at the ends. The largest might have a shelter aft. Single mast, stepped slightly forward of amidships, secured against a thwart and 2 longitudinal planks that form a "V." Large lateen sail hung from relatively short yard. Also rowed. On the large type, the oars held by loops to tholepins set into the gunwale. Crew of 12 on the large boats. Other recorded names: **dau***; pl. **madau, matanga**

Tangier road-cart See **road-cart**

tango 1. *Australia, NE:* Double-**outrigger canoe*** of the indigenous peoples of the eastern shore of Cape York Peninsula. Dugout hull, rounded in cross section. Rounded and raked bow with flattened area for use in harpooning dugongs and turtles. Stern vertical, also with a shelf-like extension. Two booms cross atop the gunwales by means of single pegs driven into holes in the hull. Booms lashed directly to the slender floats. Reported lengths 7.3-9m. Other recorded names: **Claremont canoe, tanju, taŋo**
2. *Philippines, central:* Smallest and fastest of the craft used in the Visayan Sea area.
3. *United States:* The slow-moving **tango boat** of the United States' riverine forces during the Vietnam War (1964-1975) was an armored troop carrier (**ATC**). Some modified for a helicopter flight deck and others as first-aid stations. Square bow.

tang vay, tang wai, tang way See **dang wai**

tanju See **tango-1**

tanka See **sampan Tanka**

tank barge An inland waterways vessel designed to carry bulk liquid cargoes. Mid-19th-century **barges*** were rectangular, open vessels holding barrels of crude oil. Modern vessels may be as long as 88m. Other recorded names: **chaland-citerne, liquid cargo barge, Tankkahn, Tankleichter**. Note also **tanker, water boat**. Further reference: **tank boat**

tank boat *England:* **Canal boat*** fitted with special tanks for carrying bulk liquids, mainly acids. Some carried gas water from gasworks for processing as fertilizer. Self-propelled or towed. On the lower Thames, they carried petroleum products from the oil farms to the depots near London; raised a small red flag to warn of dangerous cargo. Other recorded names: **liquor boat, tank barge*, tanker***. Note also **aljibe, tar boat**. Further references: **prorěz, water boat-1, whammel boat**

tankeä See **sampan Tanka**

tanker Special ship designed to carry bulk liquids, now important for petroleum products. Some built to transport liquid chemicals and liquified natural gas; a small type carries wine or molasses. The **bitumen carrier** has heating coils around the holds to keep the cargo liquid. A **parcel tanker** is constructed to carry several grades of liquid cargo, including chemicals and refined oil products. Generally long and low with raised forecastle, bridge, and accommodations either amidships or aft; engines aft. Cargo loaded by gravity and discharged by the ship's pumps. Transverse and longitudinal bulkheads compartmentalize the ship. To ca. 475m long. Selected alternate names: **bateau citerne, cisterna, Cisternenschiff, citerne, nave cisterna, navire cisterne, oljefartyg, Tankfahrzeug, tankfartyg, Tankschiff, tank vessel; fuel ship***, **oil carrier** (or **tanker**), **Öltanker, Öltankschiff, petroler(o), pétrolier, petroliera**. See also **tank boat**.

Tankfahrzeug, tankfartyg See **tanker**

tán-kiá See **sampan Tanka**

Tankkahn, Tankleichter See **tank barge**

tan k'o, tan kou See **sampan Tanka**

Tankschiff See **tanker**

tankuvallam See **kettuvallam-2**

tank vessel See **tanker**

tankwa *Ethiopia, N:* Papyrus-stem **raft*** of Lake Tana. Made by creating a flat floor of small papyrus bundles; near the edge, they turn up slightly and are joined on each side by 2 stout bundles that form the sides and continue beyond the ends, then are lashed together. Both ends turn up, the bow higher. Bunches may overlap on the bottom to form a "keel," or a piece of acacia wood may serve this purpose. Athwartships bundles raise passengers and cargo, as the **rafts** waterlog quickly. When crossing large stretches of water, outriggers may be fixed across the middle; rear paddler varies the outrigger pitch to control stability and speed. Paddled or poled. May carry 8-10 people, but very large **rafts** often carry 20 people or 7t of cargo. Reported lengths 5.5-10.7m, widths 0.9-2.13m. Spelling variants: **tancoa, tanqua**

tank whammel boat See **whammel boat**

taŋo See **tango-1**

tanqua See **tankwa**

Tānūr tōni See **kettuvallam-2**

tao-pa-tzǔ See **dao ba zi**

tapairua See **tipairua**

tarabaccola See **trabaccolo**

tarada See **tarrāda**

tarādah See **mahaila-2**

tarai-bune *Japan, W:* Oval, wooden, tub-like craft reportedly used by fishermen in some areas of northwestern Japan. Flat bottom, planked longitudinally; sides planked vertically and hooped like a cask with bamboo or rattan. Sculled from the stern with a long paddle held against a grooved cleat on the gunwale and secured by a rope loop. Length 1.8m, width 1.4m, depth 0.6m. Other recorded names: **basin boat, tub boat***

tara'id See **tarida, ṭarrādah**

tarappa *India, W:* A **raft***-like **ferry*** of the Thana area northeast of Bombay (Mumbai); transported horses and carts.

tarappam *India, W:* **Raft*** used for lagoon fishing on some of the Lakshadweep (Laccadive) Islands off the west coast. Ten to 16 pieces of light, soft wood are laid parallel and lashed with crosspieces on the top and bottom. The front and back pieces are longer to facilitate carrying the **raft** onto the beach. Crew of 4-8 paddlers, a helmsman, and a harpooner. Length ca. 5.5m, width 1.4m. Single-man **rafts**

ca. 4m long; poled. Other recorded names: **sangadam***, **tharappam**

tarārid See **mahaila-2**, **ṭarrādah**

tarata See **tráta-1**

taratana See **tartana-3**, **tartane**

tarate See **tarida**

tar boat *England, central:* A variety of **narrow boat*** that carried bulk liquids, particularly by-products from gas works, e.g., liquid tar, ammonia water, creosote. Worked the Midlands canal system northwest of Birmingham from the late 19th century until the 1960s. Mainly of wood, a few of iron or steel. Open initially, later decked; hatches or lids provided access for pumping the liquids in or out; tank area baffled. Generally bulk-headed; cabins at bow and stern; some used forward area for storage. Flush-decked. Mast on those towed by a horse; many motorized. Length 21.7m, beam 2.2m, cap. 25t. Other recorded names: **gas boat***; **gas-oil boat**; **oil boat** (those carrying oil from Ellesmere Port to Oldbury). Note also **tank boat**. Further references: **Avon tar boat**, **black boat**, **paltamo**

tareda, **tarede**, **tareta**, **tarete**, **taretta**, **tarette**, **tarica** See **tarida**

tarida *Mediterranean:* Reported from the 7th-14th centuries, mainly as a transport for military personnel, supplies, and munitions, but especially for horses, asses, and cavalry. In battle, they served in the 2nd line. Early vessels of Venice and Genoa traded bulk cargo with eastern Mediterranean countries; some engaged in coastal traffic. Popular with the Arabs in the 12th-13th centuries for transporting horses. Bluff ends; fairly flat floors; rounded bilges; flat sheer. Decked; poop deck; horses stabled below or on deck. To facilitate loading and unloading horses (20-40), the vessels had 1, 2, or 4 stern ports. Rowed single- or triple-banked, with 40-140 oars reported. Mainly 2-masted, setting lateen sails, the larger foresail to a forward-raking mast. Some had platforms for archers on one or both masts. Reported lengths 27-38m; 1246 vessel 35m long, 4m wide, 2.2m deep. Other recorded names: **caracca**, **caracche**, **carraca**, **carrack***, **carrida**, **tarâ'id**, **tareda**, **taret(t)a**, **taret(t)e**, **tarica**, **tarī dah**, **taridam**, **taride**, **tar(r)ita**, **tarite**, **tarrâd(a)**, **tarra'id**, **tarrecta**, **tarrida**, **tauride**, **tereda**, **tereta(m)**, **ter(r)ida**; pl. **tarate**, **tarede**, **tar(r)idae**, **teride**. The **tarrida bahariyya** was a transport ship; the **galea tarida** (or **galère taride**, **taride galère**) had characteristics closer to a **galley***. Note also **galata**, **huissier**.

taridae See **tarida**

taridah See **tarida**, **ṭarrādah**

taridam, **taride**, **taride galère**, **tarita**, **tarite** See **tarida**

tarrad See **tarida**, **terrada**

tarrāda *Iraq, S:* A sharp-ended craft of great antiquity used by the Marsh Arab peoples, mainly for personal transportation. Plank-built of a light wood; timbers cross the flat bottom; short ribs are secured to the sides; floorboards customary. Ends sweep up into a point, the bow rising as much as 1.5m above the water; low freeboard. Distinctive rows of ornamental, flat nails, as large as 5cm across, line the inner planking. Open except for short end decks; thwart across

the center, and crossbeams a third in from bow and stern. May have removable flooring on which mats or rushes can be spread. Exterior coated with bitumen. Mainly paddled, usually by 2 men at each end. Reported lengths 6-11m; e.g., length 7m, beam 0.7m; very shallow draft. In the same area, term may apply to a boat-shaped craft made of reeds. Other recorded names: **black boat***, **tarada**, **terrāde**, **terrata**, **tirada**, **turade**, **ṭyrrâde**, **war canoe**. Note also **ṭarrādah**, **terrada**.

tarrâda See **tarida**

ṭarrādah *Arabian Peninsula:* Poorly defined craft. An early description portrays a barrel-shaped ship for conveying horses and knights. More recently, it is reported as an especially fast **sambūq***. A **ṭaridah** (pl. **ṭararid**) of the 15th century was the largest of the ships carrying the treasure of an expedition. Other spelling variant: pl. **tarā'id**. Note also **tarrāda**.

tarra'id, **tarrecta**, **tarrida**, **tarrida bahariyya**, **tarridae**, **tarrita** See **tarida**

tartaan, **tartan** See **tartane**

tartana 1. *Greece:* **a.** A large, strongly built vessel popular during the period of Turkish rule. Set 2 square sails on the mainmast and a small lateen mizzen. **b.** The present-day **tartana** is generally a small vessel with good lines. Characteristically, a pair of timbers extend beyond the stern and join at a point; this stern "beak" serves to make fast the sheet on a 2-masted vessel and is often gaily painted. Most step a single pole mast to which a lateen or spritsail is set; 2-3 jibs. **2.** *Italy, NE:* One type was used for fishing in the northern Adriatic, working with the *tartana* net singly or in pairs. Extinct by the end of the 19th century. Full bow with high, strongly curved or raked stem; iron band on stem; apron fitted inside the stempost. Full buttocks; curved sternpost; flat bottom, longitudinally planked. Decked; distinctive trapezoidal hatch; large, deep outboard rudder. Black hull; colorful designs on the bulwarks, especially at the stern. Portrayed with 2 masts setting boomed lugsails, or with a single mast to which a lateen sail was hoisted, with a small jib to a long, rising bowsprit. Foremast raked forward. Bowlines extended lugsails forward, the forward lines running to a spar. Colored sails. Might carry a **topo*** to serve as a **fish carrier***. Crew of 4-8. Reported lengths 16-24m; length-to-beam ratio 3.5:1. Other recorded names: **tartana chioggiotta**, **tartana da pesca**, **tartana peschereccia** (pl. **tartane peschereccie**), **tartana procidana**, **tartana veneta**; pl. **tartane***. Further reading: Mario Mazari, "The Tartana de Pesca: A Fishing Vessel from Chioggia," *Mariner's Mirror* 71 (1985), 287-303. Note also **pielago-2**, **portolata**, **tartanella**. **3.** *Spain:* Lateen-rigged vessel of the Mediterranean and southwestern coasts. Those frequenting Seville carried cargo; others engaged in fishing. Presumed extinct. Mainmast stepped amidships; some had a small mizzenmast; both vertical. Bowsprit carried several jibs or one very large jib. The **fishing boats*** that drifted broadsides employed small, rectangular sails at each end and larger, triangular sails with apex down, all boomed out; the lateen mizzen was inverted with the yard parallel to the deck. Name variant: **taratana** Further reference: **tartane**

tartana chioggiotta See **tartana-2**

tartana da guerra See **tartane**

tartana da pesca See **tartana-2**

tartana grossa See **tartane**

tartana peschereccia, tartana procidana, tartana veneta See **tartana-2**

tartane *Mediterranean:* Dates from at least the 12th to about the mid-20th century. Evolved during this long period and was modified to suit local preferences and uses; ranged from small, flat-bottomed **fishing boats★** to 300t **merchantmen★**, and during the 15th-17th centuries, were largely 3-masted vessels of war (**tartana grossa** or **tartana da guerra**); some were employed as **privateers★** on the Atlantic coast of North Africa.

tartane

Most sharp-ended, some with transom stern; marked sheer; rounded midships sections. Raked stern; curved bow with cutaway forefoot; high stemhead; gammon knee supported a beak. Open or fully decked. Rig varied widely with time and use. Coasting **tartanes** generally had 2 masts (**tartane minori**), the strongly raking foremast in the eyes, both setting lateen sails or a square sail forward; some had a lateen mainsail and a small lateen mizzen sheeted to an outrigger. Others set lateen sails on 3 masts; some set only a single lateen with a large jib, but in strong winds, set a square sail. Later **tartanes** had auxiliaries, using sails only for steadying. Reported lengths 8-25m, widths 3-7m; the Adriatic vessels were beamier and of lighter draft than the Mediterranean **tartanes** to facilitate entering Venice and Albanian ports. Other recorded names: **ţáļtâna, taratana, tarta(a)n, tartana★, tartane grosse, tartanétta** (dim.), **tartanne, tertana, trtana**. Note also **barque de mer, caique-4, lahut**. Further reference: **tartana**

tartane de l'Estaque *France, S:* Until 1905, these vessels carried 7,000-8,000 tiles from factories in the l'Estaque area southeast to Marseille for export worldwide. Most were old **bateaux bœufs★** outfitted for this purpose. Sharp ends; outboard rudder; tiller. Set a large lateen sail and large jib to a long bowsprit. Towed by its boat in calms or in negotiating the

harbor. Crew of 2 plus a boy. Continued to the 1930s as unrigged **barges★**, 5-6 being towed with a single crew member aboard. Reported lengths 18-20m. Other recorded names: **malonnier, tartane** (**malonnière**). Note also **tartane de Marseille**.

tartane de Marseille *France, Mediterranean coast:* **Fishing boat★** of the Gulf of Lions that worked from the 17th to the end of the 19th century, employing a large net held open by spars from the bow and stern. One type was a trader with a similar hull, but rig was modified and later motorized. Generally lateen-rigged with 1-2 jibs to a long bowsprit, but to aid its broadside drift while fishing, a kite-like sail was set on the short midship mast and 2 triangular or quadrilateral sails were set at each end, sheeted to spars. Some later boats gaff-rigged. Double-ended; marked sheer; full or clipper bow; decked. Crew of 2-3. Reported lengths 10-20m; e.g., length 12.5m, beam 5m, depth 2.5-3m. Other recorded names: **barque tartane, tartane de pêche à la vache, tartano, tortono**. Note also **lahut, tartane de l'Estaque**.

tartane de pêche à la vache See **tartane de Marseille**

tartane grosse See **tartane**

tartanela, tartanele See **tartanella**

tartanella *Croatia/Italy, NE:* Mainly a **fishing boat★** of the Venetian area and Dalmatia; sometimes considered a small **tartana★**. Reported from the 14th century. Strong sheer forward. Short decks at bow and stern. Rowed and sailed, now motorized. Mainly 2-masted, setting lateen sails, but reported to have also been single-masted in the Šibenik area of Dalmatia. Long bowsprit with large headsail. Cap. 2-4t. Other recorded names: **tartanela, tartanella peschereccia**; pl. **tartanele, tartanelle**

tartanella peschereccia, tartanelle See **tartanella**

tartane malonnière See **tartane de l'Estaque**

tartane minori See **tartane**

tartane peschereccie See **tartana-2**

tartane provençale *France, Mediterranean coast:* **Fishing boat★** and **coaster★** of the eastern coast; large **coasters** worked throughout the western Mediterranean. Used from the 17th into the 20th century.

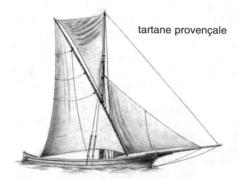

tartane provençale

Double-ended; strong sheer, lessened in later boats; flat floors, easy turn of the bilges; slight tumble home. Recurved stem, rising above the gunwale, or clipper bow; sternpost raked. Outboard rudder; tiller. Decked; cabin aft. Sail plan modified through the years, but they were best known when they carried a large lateen mainsail, a triangular topsail set to the upper half of the lateen yard and tacked just below the masthead, 1-2 headsails to the bowsprit, and a jibboom. Early in the 20th century, gaff mainsail generally adopted. Reported lengths 12-20m; e.g., length 20m, beam 6.2m, depth amidships 3.2m. Other recorded names: **grande tartane**, **tartanne**

tartanétta See **tartane**

tartanne See **tartane**, **tartane provençale**

tartano See **tartane de Marseille**

tartar Reported as a single-masted, lateen-rigged vessel. See also **cruiser-4**.

Tasmanian barracouta boat See **barracouta boat**

Tasmanian ketch See **barge-6**

tata dau See **dau la mataruma**

tatala See **tatara**

tatara *China, SE:* A small, very unseaworthy boat of the Yami of the island of Lan Yü (also called Botel Tobago). Sharp ends rise as high as 1.26m above the waterline, ending in a point; ends formed by the top strake. Narrow keel above which 3 planks are doweled edge-to-edge. Residual lugs on the strakes amidships and at the ends used to lash the frames. Flared sides; greatest beam amidships. Propelled by 1-2 men using short sculls. Reported lengths 3-3.6m; e.g., length 3m, beam 1.2m, depth amidships 0.7m. Spelling variant: **tatala**. Note also **chinedkhulan**, **tataya**.

tataya *Philippines, N:* General term for the plank-built boats of the Batanes Islands north of Luzon. Adzed planks, doweled edge-to-edge or lashed with rattan. Sharp, curved stem and sternpost; gunwale strake projects forward at the bow. Mainly rowed using as many as 3 oars per side. Large type may sail. Note also **tatara**.

tauride See **tarida**

taurua **1.** *Austral (Tubuai) Islands, central Pacific:* Early double **canoe*** of Rapa Island in the southeastern part of the archipelago. Used mainly for fishing; the type used for war was called a **taurua tamaki**. Hulls constructed of short planks sewn to a dugout base; sharp bows probably vertical and convex; the sterns swept up to tall ends. Area between the hulls decked over, and an open house provided shelter. Sailed, probably employing boomed, triangular sails set with the apex down. Could transport 20-30 people, the **taurua tamaki** 40 people.
2. *New Zealand:* **a.** Early Maori double **canoe**, apparently created for temporary stability when undertaking coastal or fishing trips or for raising heavy objects. Two regular **canoes** were lashed together and a platform built on the connecting booms. **b.** A **canoe** in which nets are carried.
3. *Society Islands, southeastern Pacific:* One of the terms given to a double **canoe**, *rua* meaning two.

taurua tamaki See **taurua-1**

tava See **dhow**

tawai See **waka tiwai**

ta-wanga See **wanga**

Taw gravel barge See **gravel barge**

tcektirme See **tchektirme**

tch'ang k'eou ma-yang tzŭ See **chang kou ma yang zi-2**

tch'ang long See **chang long**

tch'an-tse See **chan zi**

tchekdyrmé, **tchektirma** See **tchektirme**

tchektirme *Turkey:* **1. Coaster*** that transported wood from the Black Sea into the Bosporus, but also worked in the eastern Mediterranean. Now mainly powered, but may have auxiliary sails. Carvel-planked; double-ended with bluff bow and stern; curved or straight stem; curved or straight, vertical sternpost. Outboard rudder; tiller. Early vessels elaborately carved at bow and stern. Bold sheer that may dip below the waterline when heavily loaded; high bulwarks amidships, and cargo may be further protected by canvas weather screens. Decked at bow and stern; central hatch. Stepped a stump mast just forward of the cargo hatch. Topmast run through an iron cap on the masthead, with the heel sometimes secured on the deck. Large 19th-century vessels set a square foresail and topsails; large spritsail set aft of the mast, working on an outhaul along a wire from the mast cap to the sprithead. Two jibs hanked to stays set to the bowsprit and jibboom; forestaysail. Smaller craft set a boomed leg-of-mutton sail and 3 headsails. Earlier vessels both rowed and sailed, setting 2 lateen sails. Reported lengths 15-24m.
2. A variety is used for net fishing. Double-ended; raked stem with cutaway forefoot; straight, raked sternpost. Straight keel with some drag; fairly flat floors and soft turn of the bilges into flared sides; full entrance and run. Partly decked; bulwarks raise the central part. Mast stepped in tabernacle. Sets a dipping lugsail with a very short luff. Most now converted to power. Reported lengths 9-16m; e.g., length 9.12m, beam 2.96m, depth 1.42m.
Spelling variants: **cektiri(r)**, **çektirme**, **checkdeme**, **chekdirme**, **chektirmè**, **çikirne**, **tcektirme**, **tchekdyrmé**, **tchektirma**, **tchichernee**, **tchickerné**, **tchikirne**, **tchirme**, **tschektima**, **Tschektirne**, **tschikirne**, **tserkirne**. Note also **kaiki**, **tserniki**.

tch'en-po tse See **shen bo zi**

tchialan See **chaland**

tchichernee, **tchickerné**, **tchikirne** See **tchektirme**

tchiman, **tchimanan**, **tchimanens** See **tsiman**

tchimbala See **bimbá**

tchirme See **tchektirme**

tch'ouan See **chuan**

tchou-p'ai See **zhu pai**

tchou-p'ai wang See **zhu pai wang**

tchuen See **chuan**

Tchuktchi skin boat See **kayak-11**

tci'k'Enō *Canada, SW:* Ram-ended **canoe*** of the Kutenai of southeastern British Columbia and adjacent United States. Made principally of pine or spruce bark, turned inside out; generally had a 10-13cm band of birchbark below the gunwale. Sewn with split root

tci'k'Enō

fibers or rawhide and caulked with pine pitch and plastered with mud; later models reported to have been canvas-covered. Bow and stern formed a cone and raked strongly inward; ends closed by external battens; no internal stem and sternpost. Hull strengthened with ribs of split cedar or vine maple; longitudinal strips fastened along the floor and sides. Three or 4 thwarts on larger **canoes**; gunwale consisted of inner and outer wales and a cap wale. Bottom variously described as flat, rocker, or hogged; the latter 2 possibly the result of heavy use. Reported lengths overall 4.27-7.32m; length overall 4.67m, over the gunwale 4.13m, width 0.65m, depth amidships 0.3m. Other recorded names: **ac-so-molth**, **Kootenay canoe**, **Kutenai canoe**, **ram-ended canoe**, **sturgeon-nose canoe★**. Further reading: O. T. Mason, "Pointed Bark Canoes of the Kutenai and Amur" in: U.S. National Museum, *Annual Report for 1899* (Washington, D.C.: Government Printing Office, 1901), 505-537.

tcimân See **tsiman**

tea boat *England, SW:* **Houseboat★** converted to a floating cafe at Mudeford at the mouth of the River Stour in the 2nd quarter of the 20th century. One had 2 decks. Length ca. 14m, beam 6m. Note also **tea house**. Further reference: **cha chuan**

tea clipper A **clipper★** that carried tea from China to the British Isles during the mid-19th century. As the tea tended to lose flavor in a ship's hold, its value was increased by a quick passage. Some expressly built for this trade, especially in London, Liverpool, and Aberdeen; some American **clippers** also engaged in tea trade. Other recorded names: **čainyi**, **chainyi**, or **chayny kliper**, **Teeklipper**. Further reading: David Roy MacGregor, *The Tea Clippers, Their History and Development, 1833-1875* (London: Conway Maritime Press, 1983; Annapolis, Md.: Naval Institute Press, 1983).

téaco See **jaola**

tea house *China, central:* Those on the middle Chang Jiang (Yangtze) at Yichang (Ichang) row or pole out to meet incoming passenger vessels and secure themselves to the vessel. The house is built out onto a condemned, upper river **junk★**. Family live aft, cafe facilities forward. Note also **tea boat**.

tealo See **jaola**

team boat **1.** One that is drawn or propelled by a team of animals. Proposed as early as the 4th century A.D. as a craft propelled by oxen. Other recorded names: **horse ferry★**, **passe-cheval**. Note also **horse boat-5**.
2. *British Isles:* A paddle-type **ferryboat★** that used one or more teams of horses to work the paddles.
3. *Canada, SE:* Twin-hulled **ferry★** that operated between Halifax and Dartmouth from 1816 to 1830, carrying carriages, horses, cattle, and passengers. Operated by 9 horses, and in one period, by oxen. The horses worked a horizontal cog wheel in the round house amidships. Cabins flanked the house. Rounded, overhanging ends. Later, a mast and square sail were added to assist the horses. Crew of 3. Length 15m, beam 10.6m. Name variant: **horse boat★**
4. *United States:* Horse-powered **ferryboat** used at many locations in the U.S., but specifically in New York City and on the Hudson River in the early 19th century. Found as a single-hulled craft with a paddle wheel on each side, and as a double- or triple-hulled boat with a paddle wheel between the hulls. Generally propelled by a pair of horses or mules,

but one working between Brooklyn and Manhattan used 4 horses to each paddle wheel; 18m long and each of the 2 boats was 3m wide. The animals walked a treadmill or circular track. In the latter, a capstan operated the paddle wheel by means of bevel gears. Usually had a shelter. One working from Manhattan to New Jersey was 27m long. A Boston **team boat** required 25 horses. A double-ended paddle wheel boat ferried across Lake Champlain; 19m long and was probably worked by 2 horses, walking a horizontal wheel to activate twin paddle wheels. Name variants: **cutt**, **horse boat★**
5. *United States, SE:* A horse- or mule-powered craft that transported bales of cotton on the Savannah River in Georgia in the early 19th century. Two boats were united by a type of bridge. Propelled by intermeshing wheels that were set in motion by 4-8 teams of horses, 24 horses being needed for the upstream run. A circular upper deck provided space for the bales and shelter for the horses. Other simpler craft used 8 mules. Length 26m, width overall 17m, draft light 0.5m. Further references: **horse packet-1**, **paddle boat**

t'éang-chai See **sampan Tanka**

tea waggon, tea wagon See **East Indiaman**

te baurua See **baurua**

teddy balam *Bangladesh, SE:* A modernized (*teddy*) **balam★** type of coastal cargo vessel. Carvel-planked; sharp ends. Sets triangular sails. Cap. ca. 40-80t.

Teeklipper See **tea clipper**

téglenica See **barge-1**

Teifi coracle *Wales, SW:* Pear-shaped **coracle★** used for daytime salmon fishing, ferrying, and river-dipping of sheep. A few were still licensed to fish commercially for salmon on the River Teifi in 1991. Work in pairs with a special net between. Broad, blunt bow, relatively plumb and with little curvature; narrow, low, round, raked stern; gunwale pinched in at the midships seat; bottom flat except at the stern where it curves up slightly. Frame composed of 7 steam-bent, U-shaped, longitudinally split willow or hazel laths interwoven with 7 transverse laths; transverse pieces stop just abaft the seat and are doubled up to reinforce the area

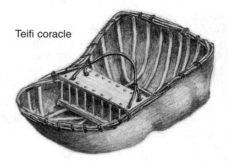

Teifi coracle

under the feet; also 2 diagonal laths. Gunwales raised at the quarters by additional braided withes. Broad seat supported by a series of wooden stanchions; twisted-withe carrying strap attached to the seat. Canvas or twill covering waterproofed with a mixture of pitch and tar, or of pitch, linseed oil, and lard;

originally covered with hides. Paddle, ca. 1.27m long,
manipulated one-armed using a figure-eight motion.
Reported lengths 1.27-1.52m; maximum widths 1-
1.16m, behind the seat 0.84-0.86m; depths amidships
0.34-0.37m; weight 11.8-18kg. Spelling variant:
Teivy coracle

Teign barge, **Teign clay barge** See **Teign keel**
Teign keel *England, SW:* Flat-bottomed craft that mainly
transported pottery clay on the River Teign, its estuary,
and the Stover and Hackney Canals in Devon. Dates

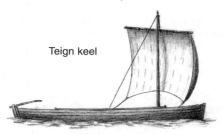

Teign keel

from the late 18th century, working until World War II.
Bluff bow; wide, raked transom stern. Long, wide
hatch bordered by shallow coamings; narrow side
decks, low bulwarks. Timberheads at bow served as
bitts. Wide rudder; long tiller. In the estuary, set a large
square sail on an unstayed mast placed well forward.
At times poled or rowed; also towed, from the bow.
Crew of 2. Reported lengths 15.2-17m; e.g., length
15.2m, beam 4.2m, depth 1.5m. Other recorded
names: **Teign (clay) barge**, **Teignmouth keel**. Note
also **Tyne keel**.

Teignmouth keel See **Teign keel**
teï-teï See **kadei**
Teivy coracle See **Teifi coracle**
tek-p'ai See **chu-p'ai**
telo dongā See **donga-1**
tembangan See **tambangan**
tĕmbon See **tjemplon-2**
temoi See **alut**
tender A small vessel that attends a larger one, carrying
supplies, mail, crew and passengers; services lighthouses, buoys, etc.; and in the case of naval vessels,
relays messages and provides munitions. A **press tender** collected and delivered men impressed into the
British Royal Navy. In the United States, a **tender**
may provide fishing and whaling vessels with supplies
and transfer the catch to ports or landing places; in the
U.S. Navy, a **tender** serves as a support or repair vessel. Term sometimes used for a small boat carried
aboard a **yacht***. Other recorded names: **annexe***,
bateau-annexe, **bijboot*** (pl. **bijboten**), **navire
transbordeur**. Note also **bachot-1**, **cock boat**,
dinghy, **launch**, **patache-2a**, **ship's boat**. Further references: **beacon boat-1**, **packer**, **tug**
teng See **ting**
ten-man boat See **tíggjumannafar**
Tennessee River busthead See **busthead**
tent See **tentschuit**
tent-bidar See **bidar-3**
tentschuit *Netherlands:* **Fishing boat*** of the Zuiderzee
and the North Sea coast. Open or decked. Sailed. Crew

of 2-3. Name variant: **tent**. Note also **schuit**. Further
reference: **trekschuit-3**
Teochew seine boat See **phang chun**
tepári *Mexico, central:* Large **dugout canoe*** of the
Tarascan peoples of Lake Pátzcuaro. Used mainly for
mid-lake net fishing. Log cut and hewn in the mountains and refined by the owner. Flat bottom; vertical
sides except at gunwale, where they turn inwards.
Overhanging stern wider than the bow and provides a
seat for passengers and a paddler. Bow squarish and
more overhanging. Blocks of wood on the bottom
serve as seats and to strengthen the **canoe***. Rowed
from the bow by 1-3 people; round-bladed oar run
through a loop fastened to inverted "V"s, which slot
over the gunwale and lash down from the apex. The
largest known to transport 25 people and rowed by 3
men. Reported lengths 6.7-11.7m. Note also **icájuta**.
tepatuā See **saranga**
teppa *India, SE:* In the Telegu language, *teppa* means
anything that floats. More specifically applied to a
boat-shaped log **raft*** used by Telegu fishermen off
east coast beaches. Designed to be partially dismantled to dry out after use. Usually made from 2-4
squared logs, to which a pointed and rounded-up bow
piece is pegged, or the forward end of each log may be

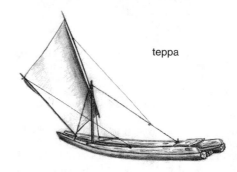

teppa

hewn to produce a suitable bow. Square-cut stern.
Washboards of extra logs may raise the outside edges.
Logs and washboards lashed together at the ends. May
use a balance board, centerboard, or leeboards. Sets a
small sail to a mast stepped just abaft the bow piece.
Small rudder used when sailing. Also paddled. Crew
of 2-3. Reported lengths 4.3-7.6m, widths 0.8-1.5m.
The various sizes have special names: a big one is a
pedda teppa, a medium-sized one is a **nadipi teppa**,
and the **chinna teppa** is a small one. The **kolla teppa**
directs the operation of a shore seine, being similar in
construction but ca. 2.4m long and 0.4m wide.
Spelling variants: **teppalu**, **teppu**, **theppa(lu)**. Note
also **catamaran-12**, **trapa**.
teppai See **chu-p'ai**
teppalu See **teppa**
teppam See **catamaran-13**
teppu See **teppa**
te-puke *Solomon Islands (Santa Cruz Group), western
Pacific:* Interisland **canoe*** renowned for its long voyages. Dugout hull, round in cross section with only a
narrow opening on top; open area covered with a
ridged piece. Ends attenuated and slightly upturned.

Single outrigger always carried to windward; a platform angles upward out the lee side. Cantilever-type pieces support the lee platform and become the outrigger booms, which are lashed to a stick wedged beneath the rounded section of the upper hull. Float

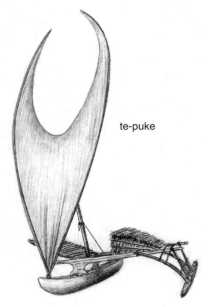

te-puke

may be one piece or several pieces fastened together longitudinally, sharp at both ends and flattened on top. Two sturdy, horizontal booms extend to, but do not attach to, the float. A mat hut is generally set onto the outrigger side. Steered by a long paddle from the lee platform. Short mast, raking strongly forward, supported by a backstay and by 2 shrouds, one to each platform; mast pivoted when tacking. So-called "crab-claw" sail, boomed on luff and leech, tacked directly to the forward end of the hull. Reported lengths 7-14m; very narrow. Other recorded names: **alo folafolau, léju, loju, puke★, puk(e)i, tepuk(e)i**

tepukei, tepuki See **te-puke**

terada See **terrada**

teravene See **paltamo**

tercer bote See **yawl-1**

tereda, terede, tereta, teretam See **tarida**

teretni brod, teretnjak See **freighter-1**

terida, teride See **tarida**

tĕriperi ŏa See **wa-3**

terrada Described as a craft of the Persian (Arabian) Gulf and sometimes the Red Sea, East Africa, and India. Most citations from the 16th-17th centuries. A small, oared type was important in providing supplies and water to the island of Ormuz (now Hormuz) off the Iranian coast; some were official boats of the local iman. A larger type steps 1-2 masts. One is shown as a sharp-ended vessel with a long, raking stem and high, decked poop; the mainmast sets a quadrilateral, lateen-type sail with a short luff; the small mizzenmast, stepped through the poop deck, probably similarly rigged. Some vaguely described as naval vessels. In early India, might be an indigenous **shore boat★**.

Spelling variants: **tarrād, terada, terrāde, terrate**. Note also **tarida, tarrāda, ṭarrādah**.

terrāde See **tarrāda, terrada**

terra-neuva, terraneuvier See **terreneuvier**

terrapin smack *United States, E:* Used on Chesapeake Bay for oystering and hunting terrapin. Used from the 1880s. Plumb stem; square, raked transom; rocker bottom; centerboard. Wet well between the 2 masts; cabin aft. Gaff-rigged; masts might rake aft; club-footed jib to a short, bowsed-down bowsprit. Length 11.3m, beam 2.7m, depth 0.8m. Other recorded names: **Chesapeake Bay terrapin smack, Maryland terrapin smack, sharpie-schooner★**

terrata See **tarrāda**

terrate See **terrada**

terre-neuva, terreneuvain See **terreneuvier**

terreneuvier French term for a vessel that fished for cod on the Grand Banks off Newfoundland (Terre-Neuve). Those that sailed out of French ports until the mid-20th century were mostly 3-masted and fitted with square sails on the fore- and mainmasts and a boomed gaff sail on the mizzen; or square sails on the forward mast and gaff sails on the main and mizzenmast; or gaff sails on each mast. Some 2-masted with square sails plus a gaff sail on the mainmast. Often had a clipper bow, counter stern, straight keel with drag. Carried 10-14 nested **doris★** (see **dory**) on board. As many as 50 in crew. Reported lengths 42.6-54m; e.g., length 43m, beam 8.7m, depth ca. 6m. Other recorded names: **banquetier, banquier, goélette terre-neuvière, seaman, terra-neuva, terraneuvier, terre-neuva, terreneuvain**. Note also **banker, charoi, morutier, navire malouin, Newfoundlander**.

terrida See **tarida**

tertana See **tartane**

tete See **waka tete**

Tête de Boule canoe See **wigwas tsiman-1**

te-wagga See **wang**

Texas scow-sloop See **chalan**

tey-mallai See **dingi-2**

thagi *Chile:* **Reed boat★** used for fishing and transportation in the central and southern provinces and on Andean lakes. Three bundles of *totora* reed are bound together to form a pointed bow and square stern.

thamakan, thamakathu, thamakau See **camakau**

Thames barge See **Thames sailing barge, western barge**

Thames bawley See **bawley**

Thames gig *England, SE:* Pleasure **gig★** of the River Thames that was in vogue in the mid-19th century. Sharp bow, curved stem; high, narrow transom stern; clinker-planked; flat sheer. Rowed generally with 1-2 pairs of sculls, in- or outrigged. Fixed seat. Steered with lines from the rudder. The so-called **coaching gig**, used for exercise and training, was 7.9-8.5m long, 1.01-1.07m wide, and 0.27-0.36m deep; the **tub gig** was inrigged and ca. 5.8m long. Sailing **gigs** became popular in the 1870s, especially as racing craft; these stepped a mast through the forward thwart, setting mostly a lugsail and jib to a bowsprit. A centerboard and rudder were added. Reported lengths 3.7-5.8m. Note also **tub-2**.

Thames hatch boat See **hatch boat-2**

Thames lighter *England, SE:* Moved bulk cargoes along the River Thames from at least the 17th century; now mostly steel **dumb barges⋆**. Characterized by flat, sloping ends (swim-headed); vertical sternpost; flat bottom and wall or flared sides; designed to take the ground at low tide. Decked at bow and stern; long hold amidships; those with recessed deck called **well-deck punts**. Generally lacks a helm, but a vessel with one is called a **rudder punt**. Usually towed, or works the tide with 2 oars (as long as 9m) for propulsion and steering; originally a single man poled or punted the craft. Tholepins or rowing irons set near the bow. Sometimes a square-headed lugsail might be set. Length 19.2m, beam 5.33m, depth 1.52m; cap. 60-250t, the steel **barges** having the larger capacity. Those under 50t called **punts⋆**. Name variant: **London River lighter**. Note also **Thames sailing barge**.

Thames punt See **punt-7**

Thames sailing barge *England, SE:* Handy, seaworthy vessel that carried bulk cargoes in the shoal waters of the Thames Estuary area. Evolved in hull design and rigging from the 16th century, but by the mid-19th century, had become relatively standardized with sub-types designed for special cargoes and local conditions. Working vessels extinct since the 1950s, but some have been restored as pleasure and charter vessels. Majority constructed of wood, although some larger **barges⋆** were of iron (the **iron pots**). Flat bottom; chines softened toward the ends; no keel but strong keelson; wall-sided, narrowing forward and aft to about one-third the extreme width; sharp, vertical stem (see also **swim-headed barge**); transom stern; very low freeboard. Undecked until the early 19th century; then decked with the main hatch abaft the mast; a 2nd hatch forward, both leading to the single hold; aft cabin with raised roof for skipper; crew accommodated in forepeak; low bulwarks. Large, broad leeboards with block and chain tackle falls that led to steersman; tiller until 1800s, then wheel; large, strong rudder. Primary rig was a sprit mainsail with a heavy sprit (**spritsail barge**); sail brailed to mast and worked by a winch; sprit might serve as a cargo boom. Some set a large square sail forward of the mainmast. Short mainmast stepped in tabernacle, about one-third from the stem. Working topsail to a long topmast, remained aloft (the **topsail barge**); one with no topsail was called a **stumpy barge⋆**. A small mizzenmast, also in a tabernacle, was stepped just aft; set a boomed spritsail with its sheet rove through a block on the rudder to aid in heading up into the wind; earlier tiller-operated vessels stepped the mizzenmast against the rudderhead. Those with a boomed, standing gaff mizzen and somewhat smaller mainsail were called **mulies, mulie barges,** or **overland barges**; mast forward of the wheel. Two headsails, 3 if the vessel carried a bowsprit; the **staysail barge** had no bowsprit. Except for the jib and fore topmast staysail, sails were tanned russet, black, or yellow after the 1st year. One type, the **boomy⋆**, was gaff-rigged. Most had a crew of 2; largest might use 4. Reported lengths 12-31m; e.g., length 24m, beam

5.7m, molded depth 2m; shallow draft. Other recorded names: **Dutch barge, hoy⋆, London River sailing barge, river barge, sailorman** (one without an auxiliary), **spreetie, sprittie, spritty**; also **Harwich, Maldon, Medway,** and **Thames barge.** Further reading: Dennis J. Davis, *The Thames Sailing Barge: Her Gear and Rigging* (Camden, Maine: International Marine Publishing Co.; Newton Abbot: David & Charles, 1970); Edgar J. March, *Spritsail Barges of Thames and Medway* (London: Percival Marshall, 1948). Note also **barge-yacht, brickie, Channel barge, foot boat, hay barge, hoy barge, lug boat.**

Thames sculler See **Thames wherry**

Thames shrimper See **bawley**

Thames skiff *England, SE:* Transom-sterned **rowing boat⋆** used by the "below London Bridge" watermen of the River Thames to tend ships and ferry passengers. Some served flounder fishermen of the upper tideway. Used as early as the 10th century; became a popular pleasure boat on the upper Thames ca. 1870; still used. Clinker-built, carvel more recently with bevel-edge planking; rounded bottom and sides amidships; slight rocker to keel; good sheer. Narrow, raked, wineglass transom. Bluff bow; stem curved and raked, the amount of rake varying in different parts of the river. Moderate freeboard, little sheer. Rudder worked with yoke and lines; could be unshipped. Gunwale raised abaft the thwarts to form rowlocks, generally 2 pairs on the pleasure craft (**double skiff**); rowed with single or double sculls. Some **double skiffs** modified for camping by the addition of hoops and canvas covering. Early pleasure boats might step a short mast through a thwart and set a balanced lugsail. Reported lengths 4.3-8.2m; the pleasure craft ranged from ca. 6-9m long, widths 1-1.5m, depth ca. 0.3m.

Thames stumpy See **stumpy barge**

Thames tilt boat See **tilt boat-2**

Thames wherry *England, SE:* **Water-taxi** of the River Thames dating from at least the 10th into the 19th century. Design modified through the period. Open, light, clinker-built. Designed for rowing with oars or sculls:

Thames wherry

rowed single; sculled or rowed double; sculled with 3 pairs of sculls, randan-fashion (see **randan**): the center man pulling 2 oars, each of the other 2 men working a single scull; or rowed with 3 pairs of oars. Most had a sharply raked, straight, elongated stem; sometimes capped with iron; hollow entrance; flat sheer; low freeboard. Flared sides; on some, beam carried well aft. Tapered stern with short, straight, vertical sternpost. V-bottom; 3-piece frames. Varnished; top strakes painted a bright color; chair rail often served as a backrest. Might attach a rudder. Some had a small table. Sometimes set a sprit- or lugsail on a short, light, unstayed mast stepped through a hole in the forward thwart; sprit set well up on the mast. Reported

range: length 5.64m, beam 1.22m, depth 0.44m to
7.92m by 1.76m by 0.48m; the larger **wherries★** might
be licensed to carry 8 passengers. Other recorded
names: **London wherry★**, **pleasure wherry**, **Thames
sculler** and **wager boat** or **wager wherry** (light
wherries used for racing, although initially, **wager
boats** were ordinary **ferries★** raced across the river,
the participating passengers taking odds), **wherry-
bote**. Note also **goozing boat**, **Gravesend waterman's wherry**, **pair-oar**, **sculler**.

Thanet wherry *England, SE:* Small **pulling boat★** used
for fishing and pleasure from the beaches of the
Thanet area at the southeasternmost part of England.
Clinker-planked; small transom stern; double-ended
below the waterline. Hull varnished. The **wherry★** had
high sides, the **wherry-punt** low sides. Length ca.
5.5m; narrow, but those that fished were often a little
beamier. Note also **Margate wherry**.

thangavallam, **thanguvallom** See **kettuvallam-2**

tharappam See **tarappam**

theng See **ting**

theppa, **theppalu** See **teppa**

theppam, **theppama** See **catamaran-13**

thiallick See **tjalk-3**

thick plank boat See **wai pi gu**

thief boat See **kalla dhoni**

thieves' boat See **cocoreli**, **jalur maling**, **perahu
sumbawa**

Tholensche schouw See **Zeeuwse schouw**

Tholense hoogaars *Netherlands, SW:* Elegant, gaff-
rigged **hoogaars★** built at Tholen for fishing, but popular as a pleasure craft (**hoogaarsjacht**). Clinker-
planked below the wale, wide carvel planking above.
Flat, pear-shaped bottom, the round end forward, with
slight rocker at ends. Straight, flared sides; top strake
has tumble home. Flattened bow; strongly raked,
straight stem; short, raking sternpost. From about
1900, built with a rounded stern (the **Lemmerhoogaars** or **Lemsterhoogaars**). Short skegs at bow
and stern. Moderate, elegant sheer. The underrim at
the stern shaped in a moderate but elegant S-line on
both sides of the sternpost. Outboard rudder; inner
edge raked, outer edge vertical but with an extension
below the waterline; heel of rudder flush or hangs
below the bottom; tiller. Long, narrow leeboards.
Decked to mast, open waist, decked forward of a steering well. Cuddy abaft the waist; **yachts★** have cabin
over the waist. Loose-footed, boomed mainsail;
curved gaff; forestaysail; when used, jib run to a jibboom that passes out through a ring on the port side.
Mast stepped about a third in from the bow; fixed or in
a tabernacle; no shrouds. Reported lengths 10-13.4m,
the earlier boats being shorter; length commonly
13.2m, beam 4m, depth at mast 1.74m; greatest draft
at intersection of stem and bottom.

Tholense schouw See **Zeeuwse schouw**

thoni See **dhoni**, **padagu-3**, **tony-1**

thonie See **tony-1**

thonier *France, W:* **Fishing boat★** from the south Breton
coast; fished mainly for tunny, but between seasons,
trawled for other fish. The original boats were
chaloupes★ (**chaloupes thonier**), then **cutters★** or

schooners★ before becoming **yawl★**-rigged (**thonier
dundee**). Last sailing boats operated until the mid-
20th century; now fully motorized. Carvel-planked;
usually flat counter stern, previously rounded or
sharp; raked sternpost; bluff, high bow; straight stem,
rounded forefoot; deep drag to the keel; steep rise to
the floors. Low freeboard aft; sheer swept up at the
bow. Originally undecked; racks amidships for the
tunny. Often brightly painted. In the 19th century, fishing spars, longer than the mainmast, were set to either
side of the mast and swung out at about 45°, and were
supported from the upper part of the mast; each carried multiple lines spaced out along the spar. Gaff
mainsail and mizzen, loose-footed with boom; topsails
and 2 headsails; mizzen sometimes leg-of-mutton.
Sails multicolored in shades of tan, ochre, green, or
blue. The early **chaloupes** carried lugsails on 2 aft-
raking masts. Crew of 4-12. Lengths of sailing
thoniers 12-28m; e.g., length 21.8m, beam 5.82m,
draft 2.74m, 58t disp. Other recorded names: **bateau
thonier**, **Breton tunnyman**, **Concarneau tunny
boat**, **dandy thonier**, **dundee du Golfe**, **dundee
thonier**, **thonier Breton**, **thonnier**, **tunnyman**; erroneously **dindet★**. Note also **dundee**, **langoustier-2**,
tuna boat-1.

thonier à l'appât vivant See **tuna boat-1**

thonier Breton, **thonier dundee** See **thonier**

thonigals See **dhoni**

thón-kin *Myanmar (Burma):* Sturdy, plank-built cargo
boat employed on lower river sections to transport
bulk rice. Wide, flat transom stern; straight, slightly

thón-kin

raked stem. Broad-bladed rudder; long tiller. Rectangular hatch amidships with high coaming; narrow
waterways; small cabin aft. Light mast, stepped well
forward, sets a large lugsail. Crew of ca. 8. Reported
lengths 18-24m, widths 4.6-5.2m. Name variants:
paddy gig, **tonkin**. Note also **paddy boat**.

thonnier See **thonier**

thony See **yathra dhoni**

Thoolsche schoud See **Zeeuwse schouw**

thorrocle See **Wye coracle**

thoue See **toue-1**

three-dory boat See **Cape boat-1**

three handed *Canada, E:* In Newfoundland, a boat or
vessel manned by a crew of 3.

three-handed bateau See **bateau-7e**

three-man boat See **Fair Isle yoal**

three-masted brig, **three-masted schooner** See **barkentine**

three-'n-after See **Great Lakes schooner**
three-quarter boat See **Hastings lugger**
three-quarter load boat See **reed boat-2**
three-sail bateau See **skipjack-1**
3-smakkejolle See **smakkejolle**
three-stroke coble See **coble-1**
thundil maram See **catamaran-12**
Thunfischer, Thunfischerfänger See **tuna boat-1**
thúng chài *Vietnam, central:* Round **basket boat★** of the Annam coast that is popular as a **ship's boat★**.

thúng chài

May also be used for fishing, especially with a cast net, going as far as 3km offshore. Constructed of woven bamboo; largest have 2 pairs of bamboo ribs perpendicular to each other; a single bench is set at one side across the gunwale. Flattened bottom; slack or hard bilges; inner and outer gunwales composed of split bamboo poles. Coated with a mixture of resin, dung, lime, and oils, the combination depending on the locale. May be paddled, the paddler standing and facing forward; sculled; or frequently propelled solely by a unique rocking motion. Sometimes sailed, setting a small lugsail; mast stepped through the bench and lashed to the gunwale. Crew of 1-2. Diameter 1-1.7m, depth 0.46-0.6l. Other recorded names: **cái** (or **ghe**) **thúng chài, thuyền chài**
Thunklipper See **tuna boat-1**
thuri valai catamaran See **periya maram**
Thursday Island lugger See **pearling lugger**
thuyền *Vietnam, N:* Generic term for a **boat★**, **junk★**, or **ship★**. Note also **cái thuyền, ghe**.
thuyền bê' See **ghe biê'n**
thuyền câu See **ghe câu**
thuyền chài See **thúng chài**
thuyền hai See **ghe biê'n**
thuyền lu'o'i *Vietnam, N:* A family **fishing boat★** of the Gulf of Tonkin. Carvel-planked of a local hardwood; flat bottom, with rocker at ends; hard bilges; flattened stem, straight and raked at gunwale strake and curved below; wide, raked transom. Gunwale turns up sharply at transom to form wings; hull black. Rectangular rudder attached to a high post; live well. Most of hull generally covered by rounded roof of bamboo matting, serving as living quarters for the extended family and livestock. Rowed and sailed. Steps 1-2 masts, depending on size; small foremast stepped in the eyes, raked forward. Sets Chinese balanced lugsails of russet-colored cloth, battened. Reported lengths 5.8-8m. Other recorded names: **tuyen dang, tuyen luoi**
thuyền nan See **ghe nang**
thuyền tam ban See **tam ban-2**
thuyền thúng See **ghe nang**
tialk, t'ialka, tialque See **tjalk-3**
tiang pang tow See **kotak-1**

tiao bei *China, S:* A type of **luring boat★** used at night by fishermen along the Guangdong (Kwangtung) coast. Dates at least to 200 B.C. A white board set at an angle out each side lures fish into a net placed in the boat. A comb-like device is used to stir up the water. Some use a single board. Some work in pairs, the 2 boats secured together. May sail to the inshore fishing sites. Length ca. 8m, beam 0.8m; shallow draft. Name variants: **t'iao-pai, tiao-pé tchuen**
tiao bei yu chuan *China, E:* Engages in moonlight river fishing on the lower Chang Jiang (Yangtze). Anchors in such a way that the white board that lies along the side at an angle reflects the light and attracts the fish. A vertical net on the opposite gunwale keeps the fish from jumping over that side. A small scoop on a pole helps to push the fish into the grass-lined bottom. Narrow, square, raking ends. Propelled by a *yuloh* (type of sculling oar). Crew of 2. Reported lengths 8-9m, beam 1.0m, low freeboard. On the Han Jiang in Guangdong (Kwangtung), to the south where the current is strong, 2 boats anchor side-by-side to provide a greater area in which to catch the fish, which usually fall into the 2nd boat. Spelling variant: **t'iao pe yu tch'ou**. Note also **luring boat, tiao bei, tiao yu chuan**.
t'iao-pai, tiao-pé tchuen See **tiao bei**
tiao pe yu tch'ouan See **tiao bei yu chuan**
tiao you chuan, t'iao-you tch'ouan See **tiao yu chuan**
tiao yu chuan *China, E:* Long, narrow boat used in the Ningbo (Ningpo) area to catch fish on moonlit nights. A white board, ca. 30cm wide, is placed at an angle out over one side. The fish, attracted by the white, jump up toward the board and are caught in a net, hung from vertical stanchions on the opposite gunwale, that drops to the bottom of the boat. Length 9m, beam 0.4m; shallow draft. Other recorded names: **catch-fish boat, poisson-sauter bateau, t'iao-you tch'ouan, t'iao-yü ch'uan**. Note also **luring boat, tiao bei yu chuan**.
t'iao-you tch'ouan, t'iao-yu ch'uan See **tiao you chuan**
tiarlec, tiarlk See **tjalk-3**
tide, tide barge See **tide boat**
tide boat *England, SE:* Term given to boats and **barges★** on the Thames with schedules dictated by the tide, moving upstream on the flood and downstream on the ebb. Name variants: **tide, tide barge, tyde boate**. See also **Gravesend barge**.
tide chaser, tide racer See **chasse-marée**
tigari See **taghāri**
tíggjumannafar *Denmark, Faroe Islands:* Ten-man boat used for transportation between these islands in the North Atlantic, for handline fishing in winter, and for hunting the pilot whale. Although relatively small, large crew needed because of difficult currents and wind conditions. Clinker-planked; sharp ends, curved stem and sternpost; 5 thwarts; mainly open. Men sit 2 to a thwart, each manning a single oar. When sailing, sets a dipping lugsail to a short mast stepped into the forward thwart and a spritsail to a mizzenmast into the after thwart. While sailing downwind, mizzenmast unstepped and foremast stepped amidships. Mainsail originally a narrow-headed square sail. Now inboard engine common and wheelhouse installed. Length ca.

8m. Other recorded names: **ten-man boat, tíggjuman-nafør, timandsfar, timannsbåt**. Note also **færøbåd**.

tíggjumannafør See **tíggjumannafar**

tiiwai See **waka tiwai**

Tilghman Island canoe See **Chesapeake Bay log canoe-3**

tilt boat 1. A boat that has an awning, the tilt, to protect fragile or perishable cargoes from the weather. Other recorded names: **bateau** (or **canot**) **couvert, tilt bote, tilte boote, tylt(e) bote**

  2. *England, SE:* Provided ferry service on the Thames, for as many as 40 passengers, between Gravesend and London (the **long ferry**) from the 16th to the early 19th century. One between Gravesend and Tilbury was called the **short ferry**. Departed Billingsgate at high tide and Gravesend at low tide. Passengers protected

tilt boat-2

by an awning. Early 18th-century boats were decked, but being found unsafe, they reverted to open boats with only a short foredeck. Clinker-built with a fine run forward and aft; narrow stern. Set a square sail supported by a halyard and lifted from the yardarm; pole mast amidships stepped with a forestay and pair of shrouds. Later set a boomed gaff sail, staysail, and flying jib from the bowsprit. When rowed, used 4-5 oarsmen. Those operating as **long ferries** were in excess of 15t burden; shallow draft. Name variants: **Gravesend, London,** or **Thames tilt boat**. Note also **Gravesend barge**.

tilt bote, tilte boote See **tilt boat-1**

TI lugger See **pearling lugger**

timandsfar, timannsbåt See **tíggjumannafar**

timber carrier General term for a vessel built to transport logs, cut lumber, shingles, barrel staves, etc., or one that has been modified for this purpose. A **chip carrier** (**Holzspäneschiff**) is designed to carry log chips; some **barge**★ types specially designed to be self-tipping, depositing the logs into the water. Other recorded names: **forest products carrier, Holzfrachter, Holzstammschute, Holztransporter, Holztransportschiff, lesovoz, lumber carrier, skogsproduktfartyg, timberman**. Note also **lumber boat, lumber skiff, onker, timber drogher**.

timberclad See **gunboat-2**

timber crib See **crib-1**

timber drogher 1. *Canada, E:* Worked out of Quebec carrying timber from eastern Canada and the northern United States to English ports during the 19th century. Usually old sailing ships with square ports cut into

their bows and stern for direct loading into the holds. As the waterline rose, the lower ports were closed and the higher ports used. Between 1823 and 1825, two large, **ship**★-rigged vessels were built entirely of squared timbers; designed to be dismantled on arrival in England, to use the timber. Four-masted. Other recorded names: **coffin ship, leather coffin, timber ship**

  2. *United States, E:* Many northern New England **schooners**★ that had served as **coasters**★ carried lumber in their later years, a few working into the 1920s. Some built in New York and New Jersey, initially for the coal trade. Lumber laid fore-and-aft both in the hold and on deck. Stakes along the rail contained the deck cargo. Mostly large, 2-masted vessels; sails reefed above the deck lumber. Some New England vessels sought business from the early 19th to the early 20th century by working out of Chesapeake Bay, going to southern Virginia and North Carolina in ballast, returning with lumber. Delivered to bay ports, Washington, D.C., and Philadelphia. Being mainly an inland trip, the deck cargo, as high as 3m, was often laid fore-and-aft with alternating athwartships layers; an occasional stake was driven through the layers. Loaded over the rail, with some longer pieces handled through ports at the bows. Reported lengths 27-37m. Name variants: **lumberjack, lumber schooner**. Note also **lumber boat**.

  3. *United States, north-central:* A heavily built vessel that carried timber and lumber on the Great Lakes during the 19th century. Those that negotiated the Welland Canal between Lakes Erie and Ontario were straight-sided, flat-bottomed, and fitted with a centerboard. Many carried a team of horses to aid in cargo handling, setting sails, and to assist the local canal horses or mules. Variously rigged; some with square sails on the foremast and a gaff sail on the mainmast. Note also **hooker-5**.

Other recorded names: **lumber drogher, lumberman, timber freighting vessel**. Note also **drogher, timber carrier**.

timber freighter See **hua pi gu**

timber freighting vessel See **timber drogher**

timberman See **timber carrier**

timber raft 1. An assemblage of timber or lumber floated downstream or across a large body of water to a sawmill or to a ship designed to transport it. More broadly, any collection of logs, planks, or casks fastened together to be floated from one place to another. The design and size are determined by the waterway to be navigated. The designation **raft**★ (or **boom**★) may also apply to logs confined by chains, cables, or boom sticks and towed by a **tug**★. Selected alternate names: **Baumfloss, float**★**, Floss, flot(tage), gónka, Holzfloss, houtvlot, kurèki-ikada, log raft, timmerflotte, tømmerflåde, tømmerflåte, vlothout**. Note also **almady-2, balsa-11, bow boat, Bretterfloss, cage, crib, Cumberland River drift, dram, fa, fleet, flote, ikada, jangada, mu pai, plot, plută, pusher boat, rai-2, shot, train de bois**★**, wanigan, zhu pai**.

  2. *United States, E:* **a.** On the upper Susquehanna River, **rafts** consisted of **pups** (or **half rafts**), composed of 10-12 squared logs abreast, lashed with athwartships poles; steered with bow and stern oars set over oarpins. As the river widened, a pair of **pups** were coupled together to form a **river raft** (or **fleet⋆** or **full raft**); a collapsible shanty in the center served as a bunk house and cook shack (**shanty rafts**). The **spar raft** was composed of 9-10 spars tied with hickory withes; kept flexible to reduce damage; spar lengths averaged 27m. The **bill raft** was composed of timbers made to order to a certain size. A **raft** was followed by a **bateau⋆** of ca. 9m. The **raft** crew consisted of a pilot, a steersman, and 4-8 additional men. **b.** Moving timber down the Delaware River to Philadelphia began in the mid-18th century, initially with spars; subsequent **rafts** transported logs, squared timber, sawed lumber, and toggle timber for wharves. Reported as late as the early 20th century. In the **toggle-timber**, **log**, **piling**, and **square-timber rafts**, the poles were set end-to-end and side-by-side; lash poles were laid across the top. Blocks at each end held oarpins for 1-3 oars (9-12m long); others were placed along the sides. For the **sawed-lumber rafts**, 3 heavy logs were laid parallel, the width depending on the length of the lumber; athwartships joists were set over vertical strakes; these units were called **cribs⋆**. The 1st layer of lumber was set crosswise, wedged tightly to form a watertight layer; subsequent layers were laid longitudinally. Four or 5 **cribs** formed a **colt**, although a **colt** might also be a small single **raft** on certain small tributaries, with a single oar at each end. Eight to 10 **cribs** formed a **raft**; 4 **colts** set two-by-two or 2 **colts** end-to-end made a **double raft**, **fleet⋆**, **span of colts**, or **tandem team**. Some **timber rafts** also carried flagstones and building stone. Generally no shelter; an untrimmed sapling was stuck into a log to hold extra clothing to keep it dry during rapids stretches. Special crews often ran the **rafts** through difficult passages. Ordinary **rafts** 46-90m long and to 15m wide.

3. *United States, north-central:* In the 19th century, on the upper Mississippi River and its tributaries, **rafts** of sawed timber and lumber were made up first into **cribs**, shallow frames 9.7m long and 4.9m wide, into which the timber was placed. These in turn were coupled into **strings**, each 122m long and 4.9m wide. The number of **cribs** reached as many as 160 on the Mississippi itself. These **rafts** were maneuvered by huge oars, one at the end of each **string**; looms were ca. 6m long with a 3.7m-long blade pegged on, balanced on a head block. The crew of 20-30 were accommodated in low huts and a cookhouse. Each **raft** was under the direction of a special pilot. By the late 19th century, many of the **rafts** were towed by **tugs**. **Log rafts** were composed of 2 **half rafts** or **pieces**, each consisting of 3 **brails**. A **brail**, loose logs end-to-end in a rectangular frame, was 182m long and 13.7m wide. The full **raft** was composed of 800,000-1,000,000 logs. **Log rafts** had only tents for accommodation of the crew. A **double-decker⋆** had 2 layers of logs. These were pushed downriver by a **steamboat**; a smaller boat at the bow directed its course. Further name variant: **half a raft**, **lumber raft**

4. *United States, SE:* **a.** A single **raft** unit of about a dozen logs in North Carolina was called a **bateau⋆**, the entire **raft** being a **train of bateaux**. These were found on the rivers into the 20th century. On narrow stretches, the **bateaux** were run in chains while on wider rivers, they were fastened in tandem. The timber in each **bateau** was pegged or spiked at each end to batten poles. Chains were linked by a log pegged from one **bateau** to another. Steered by a long oar that extended forward from the lead **raft**; another man worked from the rear raft. **b.** In the late 18th century, the so-called **raft** on the Northeast River in southeastern North Carolina transported as many as 50,000 deals (sawn lumber) and 200 barrels of tar or turpentine along the sides. Passengers sat in the center. Floated down on the tide to Wilmington. **c. Timber rafts** also ran the coastal rivers of Georgia, such as the Altamaha and Savannah, in the latter part of the 19th and early 20th centuries. Generally composed of squared timber (**scab-timber raft**) bound together by slender boards and fastened with pegs. Usually assembled in 6 sections, each ca. 6-9m long; width limited by bridge pilings. The longer outside logs extended aft ca. 6-9cm; each section was nested up between these outside logs and was interlocked by an athwartships binder pole. Ends tapered, the V-bow created by 2 logs that projected forward; entire **raft** tapered toward the stern. The Savannah **rafts** were 1.8m wide at the bow, angled to 7.6m and continued at that width for a length of ca. 54m; logs rolled on after basic **raft** completed. Steered with bow and stern oars, 13.7-15m long, pivoted on wooden blocks. Amenities included a clay hearth for cooking and a brush shelter. Crew of 3. Carried a **bateau**.

timber ship See **timber drogher-1**

timber tongkang *Indonesia, W/Peninsular Malaysia/ Singapore:* Large, open, Chinese-owned vessel of European construction that transports logs from ports in Peninsular Malaysia and northern Sumatra to Singapore. Dates from the mid-19th century; a few still operate. Sharp, high bow with raking stem; vertical sternpost; straight keel; little deadrise; sharp buttocks; wide transom stern. Sheer sharp at the bow. Washboards fitted the length of the hold when loaded. Built with keel and keelson; natural frames, each in 3 pieces. Several external and internal wales provide strength. Open waist from forecastle to poop. Gallery extends abaft the transom for ca. 3m. Huge rudder, often fenestrated, worked with a long tiller. Long, heavy, steeved-up bowsprit with lattice platform below. **Ketch⋆**-rigged; standing gaffs; the mainsail loose-footed; 2-3 headsails; sails tanned; brailed when stowed. Crew of 6-7. Reported lengths 26-30m, widths 8-10m, depths 3.4-4.6m. Name variants: **tongkang⋆**, **tongkong**, **tongkung**

timmerflotte See **timber raft-1**

ting *China, S:* Cantonese term for a large or small **junk⋆**. Spelling variants: **teng**, **theng**

ting-king See **tongkang-2**

tinimbao, **tinimbaw** See **baroto**

tinning vessel See **factory ship**

tipae ʻati rua See **tipairua**

tipai hoe See **pu hoe**

tipairua *Society Islands, southeastern Pacific:* Double-hulled traveling **canoe⋆** used mainly by local chiefs for short and medium-length voyages; extinct. Differed from similar craft of the islands by the flat, horizontal pieces that projected forward as much as 1.5-1.8m from the hulls themselves and the sharply rising stern; generally topped by a tall, vertical ornamentation. Basal dugout hulls raised by 2 broad, sewn strakes in short lengths; deep "U" in cross section. Straight or slightly concave cutwater; bottoms had slight rocker at the bows, but sterns swept up 4.6-5.5m above water level. Stern decorations were carved cylinders, square pieces, or carved, grotesque figures; bows sometimes carried low decorations. The number of crosspieces connecting the 2 hulls varied as to position and number, with as many as 18 in some cases. They were evenly spaced or clustered at the ends with more widely spaced pieces under the hut that spanned the 2 hulls. Bow ends enclosed, terminating in breakwaters. Stepped 1-2 vertical masts: one well forward, the 2nd forward of amidships and abaft the hut. Tall, vertical mat sail; yard extended along the foot and up the leech, recurving at the top, well forward of the mast. Also rowed. Steered with a paddle. Reported lengths 9-24m, beam ca. 0.6m, depths 0.9-1.2m. Spelling variants: **taipairua, tapairua, tipea 'ati rua, tipaitua**

tipaitua See **tipairua**

tirada See **tarrāda**

tirade *France, S:* Traveled on the coastal lagoons and canals of lower Languedoc, carrying merchandise to seaports.

tireau See **train de bateaux**

Tiroler Mutzen See **Mutzen**

Tiroler Plätte See **Plätte-1**

tirot See **train de bateaux**

tiú See **ci**

tiu t'éang, tiu teng See **diao ting**

tiwai See **waka tiwai**

tjalang See **pencalang**

tjalk 1. *Denmark:* Dutch **tjalken** (pl.) were purchased for use in Denmark. Their flat bottoms made them suitable for areas where they had to take the ground. Most had engines installed.

2. *Germany, W:* Low, narrow **coaster⋆** from Ostfriesland and Oldenburg; some traversed the lower Ems and Weser Rivers, and some worked on the Rhine. A German modification of the **Groninger tjalk⋆**. Last wooden vessel built in 1908; one iron-hulled **Tjalk** operated until the 1970s, but without sail. The vessels carried general cargo, and some transported peat for fuel; those that carried mud for fertilizer were nicknamed **Schlickschiffe**. Flat bottom with rounded or angular chines; deadwood aft. Full, rounded ends, the bow generally higher than the stern; curved stem; some iron vessels had a clipper bow. Vessels ceiled. Rhine boats generally stockier than those of other areas, and the inland vessels (**Binnentjalken**) generally had less camber and sheer than the seagoing vessels. Decked, the largest having a quarter-deck; most had 2 hatches; white deckhouse on seagoing vessels, none on inland boats. Outboard rudder; some were **Hecktjalken⋆**, with the tiller passing through the swept-up bulwark. Leeboards common. Sprit-rigged until ca. 1800; then set a gaff mainsail with a short, straight gaff to a pole mast; sail boomed but loose-footed. Also a staysail, gaff topsail, and 1-2 jibs to a long, rising bowsprit. A few stepped a mizzen. Lowering masts. Inland boats used a large mainsail and staysail. Later vessels had engines. Crew of 2-4 or a family. Reported lengths 11.5-25m, the inland boats usually the smaller. 1892 wooden **Tjalk**: 16.9m long, 4.13m wide, 1.92m deep. Other recorded names: **jalk, Schalk, Tjalkschiff**

3. *Netherlands:* Collective term for a number of flat-bottomed vessels with rounded ends. Mainly inland freight carriers (**binnentjalken**), but 2 types, the early **koftjalk⋆** and the later **zeetjalk⋆**, worked at sea. Some have been converted to **yachts⋆** (**tjalkjachten**). Dates to the 2nd half of the 17th century. Some built in Belgium. Constructed of wood until the 20th century; since then, mainly of iron or steel. Full, rounded bow and stern with tumble home top strake along the sides and strong tumble home at ends. Stem curved with a gripe below the waterline; stem wide, ending in an angled point. Straight, almost vertical sternpost. Wide, flat bottom with shallow or heavy plank keel; rounded bilges and sides. Amount of sheer varies, but is higher at the bow; greater sheer on early vessels and those working open waters; low freeboard when loaded. Rubbing strakes may phase out at the ends. Long, wide leeboards; strong outboard rudder; massive tiller; on some, the tiller came in below a triangular helmport (the **hektjalk⋆**). Decked; most, the **gewone** (or **ordinary**) **tjalken**, have a deckhouse aft. One with a cabin below deck level is either a **paviljoentjalk⋆** or a **dektjalk⋆**. Two hatches; small one forward of the mast, main hatch abaft the mast; on early vessels, the hatch was rounded; later a peaked cover opened in the middle. Early **tjalken** sprit-rigged (also called **smakje**); might step a small gaff mizzen. In the 19th century, adopted a gaff rig to a single pole mast stepped in a tabernacle about a quarter in from the bow. Short gaff, curved or straight; mainsail loose-footed but boomed. Large forestaysail; single jib on small vessels, 2 on larger. A few were **ketch⋆**-rigged (the **tweemastkof-tjalk**). Auxiliaries on later vessels. Reported lengths 11-36m; length-to-beam ratio 3.5-4:1; shallow draft, deeper on seagoing vessels. The inland vessels are narrower and lower than the **zeetjalken**. Other recorded names: **chalk, talque, thiallick, tialk, t'ialka, tialque, tiarlec, tiarlk, tjalkje** (small type), **tjalkschip, tyalk**. Further reading: Frits R. Loomeijer, *Met Zeil en Treil: de Tjalk in Binnen- en Buitenvaart* (Alkmaar: Uitgeverij De Alk, 1980); Horst Menzel, *Die Tjalk: das weitverbreitetste Binnenschiff der Niederlande...* (Kiel: Verlag Rolf Kelling-Eischeid, 1986). Note also **aaktjalk, Friese tjalk, Groninger tjalk, Hollandse tjalk, kraak, Mutte, palingaak, skûtsje, turftjalk, waterschip**.

tjalkjacht, tjalkje See **tjalk-3**

Tjalkschiff See **tjalk-2**

tjalkschip See **tjalk-3**

tjärbåt See **paltamo**

tjemploe, tjemploeng See **tjemplon**

tjemplon *Indonesia:* **1.** Plank-built **coaster★** that traded along the north coast of Java. Double-ended; full lines; rounded stem and sternpost curved above the gunwales as oval pieces; keel. Decked; mat house aft. Set a lugsail. Also rowed using tholepins set into a supplemental railing. Length ca. 7.6m.
2. On the Java coast between Rembang and Tjirebon (Cheribon), might be a **dugout canoe★** used for inshore fishing. Employed an outrigger that could be shifted from side to side; long bamboo float attached by a single boom projecting from the bow end; boom pierced a vertical plank set into the float. Hull slab-sided; ends curved and truncated on top. Paddled and sailed. Large size could accommodate 13 fishermen. Reported lengths 4.6-12.2m; e.g., length 4.6m, beam 0.9m. Other recorded names: **djoekoeng tembon, jukung tembon, těmbon**
3. The Sumatran **tjemplon** has also been described as a **dugout canoe.** Paddled. Crew of 12. Length 18.2m, beam 1.6m.
Spelling variants: **champlong, chěmpělong, chemplong★, tjemploe(ng)**

tjompreng *Indonesia, central:* **1.** Short, beamy cargo carrier of some of the coastal rivers of the Surabaja area of Java. Keel; high ends recurved at the top. Steered with a quarter rudder. Decked; cargo hold amidships; cabin aft or over the midship area. Stepped a single short mast forward of amidships; set a rectangular sail. Name variant: **praauw tjompring**
2. In the Tjirebon (Cheribon) area of western Java and the Kendal area of central Java, the **tjompreng** was a plank-built **fishing boat★.** Sharp ends. Some set 2 spritsails; masts in forward third. Length ca. 7.5m. Other recorded names: **djoekoeng tjompreng, perahu tjompreng**

tjotter *Netherlands, N:* Small, beamy boat of the Zuiderzee, especially in the Friesian lake and canal area; a work boat for fishing and cargo in the 19th century. Reported as a pleasure craft at Amsterdam and

tjotter

later in Friesland. Mainly carvel-built of oak, some clinker; apple bows and stern; strongly curved stem extends under the bottom for a short distance; steep

sternpost, with deep deadwood, extends almost to midships. Rounded floors; rounded bilges and sides; S-shaped frames; some built with tumble home top strake, narrowing toward the ends; removable washboards. Large, fan-shaped leeboards; broad rudder often had carved rudderhead; tiller slots over rudderhead. Open forward and abaft the mast; ballast box amidships on older models; bench along the sides. Later half-decked with cuddy forward; some had a wet well. Mostly painted black. Very tall pole mast on pleasure craft; unstayed and can be struck. Tall, narrow gaff mainsail, loose-footed with boom and short, curved gaff. Some sprit-rigged. One or 2 foresails tack to an extendable iron bumkin. Two in crew on the old **fishing boats.** Reported lengths 3.58-5.09m; length-to-beam ratio 2:1; pleasure craft to 4.8m long. In Friesland, a **fjouwer-acht tjotter** is a sturdy craft that carries a large sail area when racing; 4.8m long, 2.5m wide. Other recorded names: **boeiertje, boot, grote boot, jotter**

tl'ai *Canada, SW/United States, NW:* **Shovel-nose canoe★** used by the Coast Salish of the Puget Sound/Georgian Strait basin for river travel and for gathering foods. Several of the inland tribes used the type for spearing salmon. Shallow dugout with squared, overhanging ends; some tribes added a plank platform to the ends of the hull. Flat floors, flaring sides, nearly flat sheer. Several rod-like thwarts. Reported lengths 3-12m; e.g., length 8.2m, beam 0.8m. Other recorded names: **l!ai, Salish shovel-nose canoe; stE'tlEm** (by the Songish of southern Vancouver Island); **tl'ala'i, tłayi, tl'lai, tl'la'i.** Note also **Coast Salish canoe.**

tl'ala'i, tłayi See **tl'ai**

Tlingit canoe See **northern-style canoe**

tl'lai, tl'la'i See **tl'ai**

tō˙ See **tun**

toa See **wa-1**

tôb See **top**

tobacco boat *United States, E:* A boat used on some parts of the James River in Virginia in the early 18th century that consisted of 2 **dugout canoes★** secured with crossbeams and longitudinal pieces. Capable of carrying 5-10 hogsheads of tobacco athwartships. Reported lengths 15-18m, widths 1.2-1.5m; shallow draft. Separated on the return upstream and poled by 2 men. On other western tributaries to Chesapeake Bay, the hogsheads were transported on a **scow★**-type craft. Some 24m long. Other recorded names: **tobacco canoe, tottering vehicle.** Further references: **flat-boat-4, James River bateau, mountain boat-1a**

tobacco canoe See **tobacco boat**

tochener, toch-ever See **tochtschuit**

tochtschuit *Netherlands:* **1.** Small **fishing boat★** that pulled a large, floating net in the Zaandam area and on the Zuiderzee. Reported during the 16th-17th centuries. Carvel-built; tumble home top strake; no wale; keel. Lightly curved stem; gripe at lower end; straight, sloping sternpost; flat floors; hard chines rounding into full ends; strong sheer forward. Decked to just abaft the mast and at the stern; fish well amidships; narrow, rounded leeboards. Outboard rudder; tiller

slotted over rudderhead. Short mast, setting a sprit mainsail, might raise a forestaysail or a tall, rectangular foresail substituted. Other recorded names: **drijver**★, **dryver**, **quak**, **reeper**, **Sparendammer visser**, **tochener**, **toch-ever**, **tocht schuyt**, **toeghe**, **togenaar**, **togenaer**, **tog(h)tschuit**, **toichener**, **Treiber**
2. Also reported as a type of **passage boat**★ similar to a **trekschuit**★.

tocht schuyt See **tochtschuit**
todeltpram See **pram-6b**
todi-todi See **bilolang**
toeghe See **tochtschuit**
toengkang See **tongkang-2**
toep See **top**
toep Siam See **top-3**
togenaar, togenaer See **tochtschuit**
toggle-timber raft See **timber raft-2b**
toghtschuit, togtschuit See **tochtschuit**
togiaki *Wallis & Futuna Islands, central Pacific:* Term for a double **canoe**★. See also **tongiaki**.
toichener See **tochtschuit**
to-kne-færing See **færing-5**
tokrá See **coracle-4**
to-lestabåt See **lestabåt**
Tolkemiter Lomme, Tolkmicko loma, Tolkmitter Lomme See **Lomme**
Tollesbury smack See **Essex smack**
tomako See **tomoko**
tombaz *Turkey:* Small, open boat used on rivers. May also describe a **pontoon**★, especially one used in forming a floating bridge.
tømmerflåde, tømmerflåte See **timber raft-1**
tomoko *Solomon Islands, western Pacific:* **1.** Well-known **war canoe** of the islanders of Santa Isabel, New Georgia, and other nearby islands. Used in head-hunting and slave forays until the early 20th century. Characterized by very tall stem and sternpost that were decorated along their outer edges with cowrie shells. At the bow, a small, carved figurehead was secured just above the waterline to ward off "water fiends" and watch for reefs. Double-ended; plank-built; edges of strakes beveled and sewn together. At the ends, the planks were bound together with 2 or more seizings; ribs lashed through holes bored in the longitudinal ridges left in each strake. A wide, shallow "U" in cross section; ends of hulls curved up from the bottom; vertical end pieces as tall as 3.7m, the stern ca. 46cm higher in order to protect against enemy arrows. Besides the cowrie shells, the end pieces were carved, decorated with feathers, and ornamented with inlaid nautilus shells; outside of hull stained black. Undecked; paddlers sat on the bottom or on thwarts, 2 abreast; in the center of large **canoes**★, a platform held food and often heads of the victims. Number of paddlers ranged from 20-100. Occasionally sailed, using 1-2 demountable masts setting spritsails. Reported lengths 12-18m; e.g., length 13.4m, beam 1.4m, depth 0.7m. Name variants: **head-hunting canoe**; **maqoru** (in the Marovo language of New Georgia)
2. A smaller version in these same islands had lower decorated end pieces. Sharp ends; U-shaped in cross

section; generally 2 longitudinal keel planks to which 3 strakes were sewn; ribs lashed on the larger canoes. Mostly paddled, the paddlers generally seated on the bottom. Might set a spritsail. Length to ca. 10m.
Spelling variant: **tomako**
Tom pudden, Tom Pudding See **compartment boat**
tona, tone, tonee See **dhoni**
toney See **tony-1**
tong boat See **tonger**
tonger 1. *Canada, E:* The oyster-tonging boat of Prince Edward Island and the north shore of Nova Scotia is flat-bottomed, sharp-bowed, and flat-transomed. Rubbing strakes cover the spruce plank seams, helping reduce wear from the scissor-like tongs. Now often of plywood. Sorting trays fastened to one or both gunwales at the bow or stern. Small foredeck. Rowed. Mostly a 1-man operation. Reported lengths 3.7-5m.
2. *United States, E:* Small boat of no specific type that tongs for oysters, generally in water less than 6m deep. Found principally in Chesapeake Bay and North Carolina bays. Low-sided in order to use the paired rakes that are worked with 2 poles as long as 6.7m. Culling board at the stern. Flat-bottomed in North Carolina. Now generally a motorized, **deadrise**★-type boat. Often used for running crab pots in summer. Name variants: **tong boat, tong(ing) skiff**. Note also **oyster scow**.
tongiagi See **tongiaki**
tongiaki *Tonga, central Pacific:* Double-hulled voyaging **canoe**★; extinct since the late 18th century. Plank-built craft with hulls of roughly the same size; connected by a large, heavy platform that rested on washstrakes on each hull and sometimes also on stanchions at each end. On some, the platform sloped upward toward the stern. Hulls reported to have been either a narrow oval or heart-shaped in cross section; ribs lashed to cleats inside the irregular strakes. Rocker bottom; hulls tapered to a sharp point forward and a blunted point aft. Decked at each end; hatches gave access to interiors to permit bailing. Steered with 2-3 oars, each worked by 2 men when seas heavy. Short mast, vertical or raked forward; some notched to form steps. One type employed a bipod mast with each part stepped in a different hull. Set a triangular mat sail with the apex down; boomed at the foot. Mast stayed in various ways, including shrouds that ran from a long balance spar that crossed the platform abaft the mast and extended well out each side. Reported lengths 18.2-21.3m, total widths 4.5-5m. Spelling variants: **togiaki**★, **tongiagi**
tonging skiff See **tonger**
tongkang 1. *Brunei/East Malaysia:* Local Malay cargo vessel, mainly of Brunei Bay. Double-ended; stern gallery. Decked at ends, house amidships. Single mast set a square sail or dipping lugsail. Reported lengths 9-12m.
2. *Indonesia/Singapore:* Term applied to large sailing **lighters**★ used in harbor work at Singapore or to transport cargo between Singapore and ports of Borneo and Sumatra. May also describe a heavy, unwieldy craft; also a **car ferry**. Hull basically of western design, but shape varies, as does the type of rig, carrying gaff sails

or Chinese lugsails. Most Chinese-built and manned, although the **Tamil tongkang**★ is built by Tamils. Term sometimes applied to open **lighters** that are poled in Singapore harbor, but word usually reserved for sailing vessels. Other recorded names: **bangka**★, **jung**, **seunat**, **ting-king**, **toengkang**, **tongkong**, **tongkung**, **tong rung**, **tonkang**, **tungkang**, **wangka**★, **wangkang**★; on the north and east coasts of Sumatra, called a **tambang**★. Note also **Gulf of Siam trader**, **timber tongkang**, **tongkang Mĕlayu**.

3. *Peninsular Malaysia:* Variety of **junk**★ that carried rubber downstream from the rubber-growing estates to main ports on the west coast. Beamy hull with sharply raked stem, square counter stern, very strong sheer, and wide, fenestrated rudder. Deckhouse amidships; crew housed in the poop. Two or 3 masts, the foremast raking forward; set Chinese lugsails. Crew of 6. Length ca. 21m. Name variant: **estate junk**. Note also **Tamil tongkang**.

Further references: **phang ch'un**, **sekochi-5b**, **Singapore trader**, **timber tongkang**

tongkang Malayu See **tongkang Mĕlayu**

tongkang Mĕlayu 1. *East Malaysia:* Lug-rigged trader of eastern Sabah that carried firewood in Sandakan Bay. Transom stern; large, open hold. Wide rudder; tiller. Foremast raked forward; both masts set large, boomed, high-peaked dipping lugsails. Smaller, single-masted boats set a large dipping lugsail and single headsail. In calms, employed long sweeps. Reported lengths 12.2-13.7m, widths 4.9-5.5m, depths 1.5-2m. Name variant: **prahu**

2. *Singapore:* Heavy, **ketch**★-rigged **lighter**★ used in the roads off Singapore. Some had scroll-work on a projecting bow. Double-ended, or some had a rounded counter. Outboard rudder, or on the counter-sterned vessels, the rudderpost came up inboard; tiller. Both rudderhead and tiller might be carved. Some had a deckhouse and hatchway. Mainsail and mizzen set out by an outhaul along the gaff. Sails loose-footed; one or both might be boomed. Topsails, 2 headsails to a bowsprit. Small crew. Reported lengths 11-22m, most 15-22m. Other recorded names: **Malay lighter**, **Singapore lighter**, **tongkang Malayu**

tongkong, tongkung See **timber tongkang**, **tongkang-2**

tong rung See **tongkang-2**

tong skiff See **tonger**

toni See **dhoni**, **kettuvallam-2**, **tony-1**

tonie, tonies See **tony**

tonkang See **tongkang-2**

tonkin See **thón-kin**

tonn *Australia, NE:* Bark **canoe**★ of the Archer River area on the western side of the Cape York Peninsula. Constructed of a single sheet of bark made pliable by

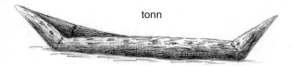
tonn

heating and sewn with split cane. Shape maintained by a pair of crossed sticks that support a raised thwart.

Ends sharp, swept-up, and raked. Bottom reinforced with bark flooring. Paddled. Reported lengths 2-5.5m, beam ca. 0.5m.

tonne See **tony-1**

Tonnenleger See **beacon boat**

tonny See **dhoni**

Tonschute See **Schute-4**

tony 1. *India, W:* General-purpose **dugout canoe**★ of the protected coastal backwaters. Most of teak; double-ended; flat bottom; flat sheer; slight tumble home. Ends sharply curved and formed by separate blocks, some projecting forward and aft as platforms. Usually without keel, but may have a short, curved skeg at each end. Sides often extended by one or more planks. When rudder shipped, worked with yoke and lines. Those that convey passengers, as at Bombay (Mumbai), have a canvas awning over the after part; behind this is a loosely decked area for supplies. At Bombay, usually painted black with a white band; blue inside. Oars consist of a pole with spoon-shaped discs for blades. Sets a small, quadrilateral, lateen-type sail with a short luff to a forward-raking mast; sometimes also a jib to a bowsprit. Crew of 3-4. Reported lengths 3.7-12.2m; e.g., length 6.25m, beam 0.9m, depth 0.46m. The basic dugouts are sold around the Arabian Sea and are known there by the term **houri**★. Sometimes 2 are lashed together, in which case the double boat is called a **catapanel**. Spelling variants: **thoni(e)**, **toney**, **toni(e)**, **tonne**; pl. **tonies**. Note also **beppu toni**, **kettuvallam**.

2. *Pakistan:* Until partition, the **tony** was secured from the Malabar Coast of India, but since then Pakistani

tony-2

tonies have been plank-built, but along the lines of the original dugouts. Used mainly for fishing in backwaters, as **tenders**★ for larger craft, and as **carrier boats**. Called **keti** or **hori**★ on the Makran coast and **hori** in the Sind.

Further reference: **dhoni**

Toolsche schouw, Toolse schouw See **Zeeuwse schouw**

toop See **top**

toothpick 1. *Canada, E:* Old term for a clipper-bowed Grand Banks **schooner**★ with a long bowsprit.

2. *United States:* A very narrow type of **canal boat**★. See also **best boat**.

top 1. *Indonesia/Malaysia:* Large trader that worked the area from Sumatra east to Sulawesi (Celebes); Probably extinct. Western-style hull; bluff bow, curved stem; elaborately carved, square transom or counter; waterline wale. Decked; low poop: some with accommodations below decks, others with a house; hatchways abaft each mast. Heavy gallows forward and abaft the mainmast held lowered sails and rigging. Employed a European-style rudder or quarter rudders. Stepped 2-3 masts; tall mainmast amidships; short mizzen forward of the house. On 2-masted vessels, the mainsail was quadrilateral, the mizzen triangular; some fore-and-aft rigged. Three-masted vessels set tall, quadrilateral main- and foresails and a gaff mizzen. Rowed in calms with 16-20 oars held by loops from tholepins. Reported lengths 12.2-27.4m, widths 2.6-5.7m, depths 3-4m.

2. *Peninsular Malaysia:* Term may also apply to a type of **barge★** employed on sugar estate canals to transport cane to the mills.

3. *Thailand:* Many of the traders originated in Thailand, where their primary cargo was rice. Name variants: **to(e)p Siam**

Other recorded names: **perahu top**, **praauw toop**, **prahoe top**, **tôb**, **toep**, **toop**, **t(o)up**. See also **topo**.

topa *Italy, NE:* A type of **topo★** of the lagoon of Venice that has a transom stern. Popular as pleasure craft, but the largest may serve as light cargo carriers. In Venice, the term also indicates a **topa** that has had a washstrake added to raise the sides. Raked stem, not iron-faced like the **topo**; stern vertical or somewhat raked; the **topa sampierota** of Chioggia has a flat stern rather than a transom. Bottom flat transversely, with longitudinal rocker; moderate sheer. Outboard rudder with deep heel; tiller slots over rudderhead. Hull brightly painted. Propelled by sail or outboard motor. Boomed lugsail set to a stout, unstayed mast stepped through a thwart about one-third in from the stern. Reported lengths 6-8m; e.g., length 7.13m, beam 1.94m, depth ca. 0.55m. Further name variant: pl. **tope★**

topa sampierota See **topa**

top boat *Scotland, SE:* Designation earned by a **fishing boat★** that habitually brought back the largest catch, especially by those from Pittenweem.

tope *China:* Reported as a type of **junk★**. See also **topa**.

Topfboot, Topffloss See **chatty raft-1**

topgallant schooner See **schooner-1**

topi See **topo**

t'o-pien tzŭ See **bian zi**

topindere See **skøyte-4**

topinner See **skøyte-5**

topo *Italy, NE:* Well-known boat of the northern Adriatic area, found mainly in the Lagoon of Venice, but also along the Istrian Peninsula and at Trieste. Most engaged in fishing or transporting fish to market (the **portolata★**). Mainly gone, although the term is used for a fully motorized craft, the **moto-topo**, which has the same general hull design; many transport produce to neighborhood shops in Venice. A few old sailing types have been restored for family use. One variety, the **topo venessian**, was a pleasure craft until World War II, participating in regattas. The boat is enjoying a revival as a **yacht★**. Hull design varied slightly with locale and use. Some sharp-ended; others had a rounded stern; still others had a flat stern. The frames on the round-sterned type diverged up from the floor. Bow sharp in the Venetian models, fuller on the Istrian boats; stem straight and raked or strongly curved; iron piece sheathed the stem. Bottom flat, planked longitudinally, with slight rocker toward the ends; those carrying cargo had flooring, otherwise frames exposed. Sides mildly flared with slight curve just above the chines; sides parallel for most of the hull. On one type,

the **batelo col fio** at Chioggia, a washstrake raised the sides. Those working well offshore had a strong sheer forward. Large rudder; deep heel extended well below the bottom; rudder served as a centerboard and could be raised and lowered by means of a rope to the after thwart. Long, downsloping tiller slotted over the rudderhead. Open, half-decked, or fully decked; decks cambered; when carrying passengers, the area between the masts might be roofed over. Hull generally painted black or varnished with colored bands along the upper strake; pleasure craft were white. Mainly single-masted, but might step a small foremast. Sturdy mast stepped through a thwart about one-third in from the stern; mast portable and fastened with a hasp to the after thwart. Set a boomed balance lugsail with a short luff; often painted in colorful designs; sail always hung to port of the mast; jib from stemhead. Also designed to be rowed, employing 2-4 oars that worked against a local type of oar-fork. Crew of 1-5. Reported lengths 4.5-14m, the larger mostly from the Istrian Peninsula area; e.g., length 10.5m, beam 2.4m, depth 1.0m; length-to-beam ratio varied locally. The **topo da mestiereta** trawled out of Chioggia in the south part of the Lagoon of Venice; the **topo da carico** moved building materials; the large **topo da sabbia** transported river sand; the **ostregher da mar** engaged in oystering; one from Chioggia with a wedge-shaped piece on the stem is called a **batelo a pizzo**. Other recorded names: **mouse**, **muscolo★**, **top★**, **topo chioggioto**, **topo istriano**, **topo mestiereta**, **toppo**; **bateo a chioggia**, **bateo a pisso**; pl. **topi**, **toppi**. Note also **musseto**, **pielago**, **tartana-2**, **topa**, **topo-sorcio**.

topo chioggioto, topo da carico, topo da mestiereta, topo da sabbia, topo istriano, topo mestiereta See **topo**

topo-sorcio *Italy:* Type of **pontoon★** used in careening ships for general bottom repairs.

topo venessian See **topo**

topo veneziano See **musseto**

toppi See **topo**

Toppmastkuff See **Kuff**

toppo See **topo**

Toppsegelkuff See **Kuff**

Toppsegel-Schoner See **schooner-1**

topsail barge See **Thames sailing barge**

topsail schooner See **schooner-1**

topsail sloop See **sloop-2**

Topsegel-Schoner, topsejlskonnert See **schooner-1**

top Siam See **top-3**

topzeilschoener See **schooner-1**

Torfboyer See **Bojer**

Torf-Ewer *Germany, NW:* In the 19th century, collected peat (*Torf*) from the moors along the lower Elbe River, carrying it to major cities where it was used for heating. A **Ewer★** type with a flat bottom and wide transom; leeboards; outboard rudder; tiller. Peat piled man-high on top of the closed hatch and covered with a tarpaulin. Some had a small cabin either forward or aft. **Ketch★**-rigged or stepped a single tall mast that could be struck. Reported lengths 13-16m, widths 3.26-5.23m, depths 1-1.4m. Spelling variant: **turfever**

Torfschiff See **Mutte**

torgovoe sudno See **merchantman**

Tornfloss, Tornholz See **raft**

torømming, toroms, toromsbåt, to-roms færing, to-roring See **færing-6**

Torridge polacker See **polacca**

Torridge sailing lighter See **gravel barge**

torskbåt See **gotlandsnipa**

torskebåt See **cod-fishing boat**

torskegarn See **torskegarnsbåt**

torskegarnsbåt *Norway, NW:* Engaged in cod (*torsk*) fishing with a net; from Nordmøre District. Clinker planking treenailed; open. Sharp ends; curved stem and sternpost. Outboard rudder; long, slender tiller. Rowed single-banked using 4-6 pairs of oars. Also sailed, the older type employing a dipping lugsail; the newer, a gaff sail with staysail and jib. Reported lengths 8.5-12.6m; e.g., length 11.35m, beam 2.75m. Those from the Åfjord area north of Trondheim are also open, sharp-ended, with tall stem and sternpost. Hull compartmented into 7-10 "rooms" by thwarts. Rowed with 6 long oars. Mast struck when working the net. Reported lengths 11.3-12.6m. Name variants: **torskegarn, toskansbåt, toskgarnsbåt**. Note also **garnbåt**. Further reference: **fembøring-1**

torsköka *Sweden, SE:* Heavy **cod-fishing boat★** of the Småland coast. Also used as a **market boat★** and **church boat★** (see **kyrkbåt**). Clinker planking; rounded bottom and bilges; flaring sides. Raking cutaway stem rounded into curved keel; strongly raked transom. Open, 3 thwarts, stern seat, low flooring forward. Mast braced against light forward thwart. Set a spritsail; staysail to stemhead. Also rowed with 2 pairs of oars; block on oar loom set over single tholepin. Length 4.55m, beam 1.47m, depth 0.53m. Other recorded names: **marknadsbåt, storbåt★**

tortoise boat See **kwi-son**

Tortola coble See **coble-6**

Tortola cutter See **Tortola sloop**

Tortola sloop *British Virgin Islands:* Freight and passenger boat of these islands in the northeastern Caribbean. Those rigged as **sloops★** may be called **canoes★** locally, while the **cutter★**-rigged boats are called **vessels★**. Distinguished from other **sloops** of the West Indies by their marked sheer forward, ending in a high bow. Heavily constructed; carvel-planked, unusually large number of butts; S-timbers in after frames. Straight, raked stem; hollow entrance; fine lines aft; curved, overhanging transom stern; strong sheer; high freeboard; deep drag to the straight keel. Small boats open; larger decked with small hatch forward, cargo hatch amidships, trunk cabin, and steering well aft. Outboard rudder; curved tiller. The **sloop**-rigged boats set a boomed leg-of-mutton mainsail and a genoa-type jib; exceptionally long boom. The **cutter**-rigged boats have a boomed gaff mainsail and 2 headsails; mast and boom approximately the length of the boat; sometimes a short bowsprit. The Antigua-built **sloops** are generally similar. Lengths overall 5.5-9.7m; basic dimensions: depth one-fourth the keel length, beam one-half keel length. Additional name variant: **Tortola cutter**. Further reading: E. Doran, Jr., "The Tortola Boat:

Characteristics, Origin, Demise," *The Mariner's Mirror* 56 (1970), supplement.

tortono See **tartane de Marseille**

Tory Island canoe, Tory Island curragh See **Donegal curragh**

tosher *United Kingdom:* **1.** Term used to indicate a boat that is smaller than another of the same type, such as the **Mevagissey tosher★**, which is smaller than the **Mevagissey lugger**. Note also **Ramsgate tosher**.
2. Nickname for a small cargo vessel that carried timber to London. About 100t.
3. Small **fishing boat★** that trolled for mackerel off the west coast of England using long poles. **Yawl★**-rigged. Reported lengths 5.5-6m.
4. Small sailing **smack★** from Southwold on the east coast. Worked from the beach by 3 men.
5. Term sometimes applies to small boats engaged in toshing or scavenging along the Thames.
Further references: **Lowestoft trawler, tug-1**

toskansbåt, toskgarnsbåt See **torskegarnsbåt**

to-smakkejolle See **smakkejolle**

tosser See **Mevagissey tosher**

tote boat See **Adirondack guide-boat**

tottering vehicle See **tobacco boat**

tou, toua See **toue-1**

toucang *Peninsular Malaysia/Singapore:* Lug-rigged **fishing boat★** used in the Strait of Malacca. Sharp ends; bow and stern raked with straight or curved stem and straight stern; keel straight or curved. Short end decks.

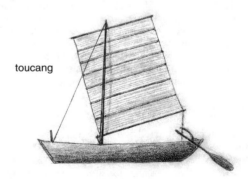

toucang

The single cane sail had parallel battens and was reefed by rolling; boomed. Or set a spritsail. Mast stepped through a thwart. Steered with a paddle or quarter rudder. Reported lengths 5-10m; e.g., length ca. 5, beam 1.0m, depth 0.6m. Other recorded names: **toup, tucang, tukang**

toue *France:* **1.** Term ascribed to a variety of inland craft: **barge★**, small **fishing boat★**, or **ferryboat★**. Mainly of the Loire River valley. Reported during the 17th-19th centuries, but a fishing type is extant. Other recorded names: **cabane★, thoue, tou(a)**
2. The **barge** type carried merchandise and charcoal; some dredged for sand. At the mouth of the Loire, they lightered cargo between shore and off-lying ships. Flat bottom; on some, the longitudinal bottom planking turned up at the bow to, or close to, the top strake. Stern cut square. Straight sides, lapped or smooth; slight sheer at the stern, marked sheer at the bow. The river craft worked generally in pairs (a

couplage⋆), the larger one leading. Steered with an easily demountable rudder that was worked from its outer end; some employed a large sweep, the inner end supported on a tall crutch and maneuvered by lines. Most open, but some had a cabin abaft the tall, strikable mast. Set a square sail; sail held taut by bowlines and spars to the clews. Reported lengths 11-40m; 18th-century boat 15.5m long, 2.2m wide, 1.3m deep. Note also **chênière**.

3. The fishing **toue** that works in the Nantes area on the Loire in west-central France tends barrage nets for salmon. Low boat with long, overhanging bow and raked stern. Those more or less permanently moored had a cabin aft (the **toue cabanée**). No rudder. Crew of 2. One on an upper Loire tributary was 6.5m long, 1.13m wide, and 0.45m deep.
Further references: **flûte-3**, **train de bateaux**
toue cabanée See **toue-3**
touk thnot See **tuk thnot**
Toulinguet boat *Canada, E/United States, Alaska:* Small, open boat popular in the late 19th century for seal hunting off Newfoundland, especially at Toulinguet (Twillingate) on the east coast; off Labrador; and in the Pribilof Islands off southwestern Alaska. Initially clinker-built; later carvel; light, bent frames; long, fine run; moderate sheer; lightly rounded bottom and sides; deep false keel. Raked, curved stem; strongly raked, heart-shaped transom; skeg. Outboard rudder; tiller slotted over rudderhead. Open; 4 thwarts; deep stern seat. Short mast stepped through the 2nd thwart; set a spritsail; jib tacked to stemhead. Also rowed. Reported lengths 4.6-5.5m; e.g., length 5.2m, beam 1.3m, depth ca. 0.64m. Other recorded names: **Newfoundland sealing punt**, **Newfoundland skiff**, **Toulinquet boat**, **Twillingate boat**
Toulinquet boat See **Toulinguet boat**
touo See **fak**
toup See **top**, **toucang**
touque See **buis-2**
Tournai boat, **tournaisien** See **waal**
tovorna ladja See **freighter-1**
tow 1. A vessel or other craft being towed. Note also **tug**.
 2. *United States:* On major waterways, as many as 40 **barges**⋆ may be lashed by wire cables into a solid unit and pushed or pulled by a **tow boat**⋆, becoming a single unit known as a **tow**.
t'o-wang ch'uan See **tuo wang chuan**
tow barge See **Great Lakes schooner**, **tug**
tow boat 1. *Azores, N Atlantic:* Fast, powerful **motor boat**⋆ used in association with whaling operations. Tows the **whaleboats**⋆, 2-3 in line or in tandem, to the area of a sighted whale or may tow the questing **whaleboat** closer. Often tows the dead whale back to the whaling station. Locally made since the early 20th century. Cuddy forward. Mast equipped with a boatswain's chair for a lookout; sail carried but used only if engine fails. Crew of 2. Length 12m, beam 2.4m. Name variant: **gasolin-lancha**. Note also **canoa do baleeiro**.
 2. *Canada, SE:* **a.** Cargo and passenger vessel used on the St. John River in New Brunswick during the 2nd half of the 19th century. Cargo carried amidships; the

2 tow horses housed in the bow. Average cap. 13t. **b.** Motorized craft used off Cape Breton Island to tow the **door boat**⋆, the **cut boat**⋆, and the **dory**⋆ to the site selected for a mackerel trap net. Fish taken to shore by a larger **collecting boat**⋆. Name variant: **power boat**
 3. *Japan:* In coastal whaling operations, the Japanese employ a **tow boat** to tow the whale into the harbor from a **catcher boat**.
 4. *United States:* **a.** On the Hudson River in the late 1830s, steam-powered **tow boats** conveyed 2 **barges**⋆, each lashed to the side of the tow boat. Initially these were obsolete, paddle wheel passenger vessels stripped except for pilot house, boilers, and minimal crew accommodations. Modified with towing hooks and strengthened to protect the paddle wheels. Passengers permitted on the upper deck. Used until the 1880s. By 1846, **tow boats** were towing trains of canal **barges** loaded with goods through the Erie Canal and down the Hudson. **b. Steamboats** served as **tow boats** on the Ohio River in the mid-19th century. Initially either dragged **barges** or **coal boats** behind or placed them along the sides as well as ahead and behind. Later, **sternwheelers** were modified to push groups of boats. Note also **broadhorn**, **push boat-2**.
Further references: **barge-11f**, **flatboat-5**, **follower-2b**, **push boat-2**, **push boat-4**, **track boat**, **tug**
tow box See **tow car**
tow car *United States, central:* **1.** A **skiff**⋆-type craft designed in the latter part of the 19th century to transport live fish from the swamps of Louisiana's Atchafalaya River basin to the railhead at Morgan City. Locally, they were towed by 2 **rowboats**⋆ to market. Loaded, they were transported alongside a **tug**⋆. Sharp ends; flat bottom with slight rocker. Sides formed by slats with space between; bottom either solid or also with open slats. Buoyancy regulated by a watertight compartment at each end that was filled or emptied as required. Well partitioned into compartments and covered by hinged slats. In some areas of northern Louisiana, the craft was rowed. Lengths 5.5-9m, widths 1.5-1.8m, depth ca. 2m.
 2. Those used by seine fishermen in the bays behind the Texas coast were similar to the local rowed **skiffs**, and some were, in fact, old **skiffs** in which holes had been bored and an open slat-top added. Cap. 180-900kg of fish.
 3. Still used in the headwaters of the Mississippi River where cooler summer water prolongs the life of the fish, mainly carp caught in seine nets. Used both to transport fish and as a holding box in ponds. Originally **skiff**-shaped; now more **scow**⋆-shaped. Slatted sides, flat bottom with hinged top sections.
Other recorded names: **fish box**, **fish car**⋆, **live boat**, **love car**, **live-fish car**, **tow box**, **well car**. Note also **fisherman's car**, **pansi**.
town boat, **town class** See **narrow boat**
tow smack *United States, E:* A wooden, slatted box used to hold live crabs. Name variant: **live box**. Note also **fish car**.
Towy coracle See **Tywi coracle**
tō´ xana *United States, W:* **Balsa**⋆ of the Pomo Native Americans; used on Clear Lake in northern California.

Bundles of tule grass fashioned into a double-ended **raft***, or the forward end of the central bundle was forced up into a bow and the stern was cut square. Length ca. 6m. Name variants: **Pomo balsa, tō´ xīna, tsûta´ xīna, xana**

tō´ xīna See **tō´ xana**

trabac *Russia, S/Ukraine, S:* Two-masted vessel of the Black Sea used during the 18th century. Bluff bows, gammon knee; raked counter above a raked sternpost. Straight keel; flat floors; high, vertical sides. Rudder came up inboard. Small trunk cabin forward. Mainmast stepped amidships; shorter foremast stepped close to the bow. Set boomed lugsails; 2 jibs to a jibboom and bowsprit. See also **trabaccolo**.

trabaccola, trabaccoletto, trabaccoli, trabaccolino See **trabaccolo**

trabaccolo   1. *Greece, Aegean Sea:* Modification of the Adriatic **trabaccolo**, one type used for fishing, another for cargo. Rounded ends, strongly curved stem, plumb sternpost, strong sheer. Sets either 2 lugsails or a boomed lug foresail and a boomed gaff mainsail. Jib to a slender bowsprit. Spelling variants: **trabaccola, trambakuolo**

2. *Italy, E:* Vessel associated with the Adriatic, although some sailed to distant parts of the Mediterranean, and others plied the Po River and its tributaries. Reported from at least the 17th century, and a few worked into the 1960s. Primarily a cargo vessel (**trabaccolo da trasporto**), but the smaller types fished on the central east coast and around Istria (**barchetto***). At the beginning of the 19th century, some were armed and served as troop transports. Heavy, full hull; carvel-planked, generally of oak; floors flat or with a low rise; keel; rounded bilges; flaring sides; moderate sheer, rising sharply toward the bow. Full bow, some quite bluff; curved stem, sometimes with a sculptured mop at the head. Rounded stern; straight sternpost, plumb or slightly raked. Some double-ended; others narrower at the stern with the maximum beam well forward. Counter stern on the **riverboats***. Decked; some older vessels had a high poop with a seat for the helmsman; large central hatch; deep bulwarks; rail around the quarters. Narrow rudder extended well below the bottom; long, downward-sloping tiller slotted over the rudderhead; early vessels employed a large quarter rudder. Hull often colorfully painted and usually carried large red oculi; often bossed; bulwark might be carved. The **coasters*** carried a 4-5m-long **battellino** (see **battello**). Mostly 2-masted, setting lugsails on both masts, but occasionally reported with a single mast, and some early vessels had a lateen mizzen. Foresail a large dipping lug; the main a high-peaked standing lugsail; both boomed. One to 2 jibs to a long, rising bowsprit run out to port of the stem. Small square topsails to both masts on the larger vessels. Pennant carried on the mainmast. At the end of the 19th century, some vessels substituted a spanker for the main lugsail. Fishing vessels also used oars. Engines often installed after 1912. Crew of 4-7, 2-8 on the **fishing boats***. Cargo vessels 20-30m long; **fishing boats** 11-21m; beam

roughly one-third length; depth one-third beam; shallow draft. Further reading: Mario Marzari, *Trabaccoli e Pielaghi nella Marineria Traditionale dell'Adriatico* (Milano: Mursia, 1988). Note also **pelig, pielago-1**.
   Other recorded names: **pielago***, **tarabaccola, trabac***; **trabaccoletto** and **trabaccolino** (dims.); **trabàccue, trabaco, trabacola, trabàcolo, trabàcul(o), trabàculu, trabak(o), Trabak(k)el, trabakū, trabäkul, trabakula; trabakulić, trabakulica** (dims.); **trabakuo, trabaque, trabauco, trabbàcculë, trabecol, trambachuolo, trambakuolo, trébac, trebau(co); pl. barchetti, trabaccola, trabac(c)oli, trabachi, trabakuli; trabaccolo da pesca, bacolo (pl. bacoli), barchèt**

trabaccolo da pesca See **bragozzo, trabaccolo**

trabaccolo da trasporto, trabàccue, trabachi, trabaco, trabacola, trabacoli, trabàcolo, trabàcul, trabàculo, trabàculu, trabak, trabako, Trabakel, Trabakkel, trabakù, trabäkul, trabakula, trabakuli, trabakulić, trabakulica, trabakuo, trabaque, trabauco, trabbàcculë, trabecol See **trabaccolo**

track barge See **track boat**

track boat One towed on a narrow inland waterway, especially in the United Kingdom. Generally towed from shore, but may be pulled by a **tug***. Carried goods and had passenger accommodations. Term known to date from the early 17th century. Other recorded names: **tow boat***, **track barge, trakboat, trek boat**. Note also **coche, tochtschuit, Treckschute, trekschuit-1**.

trackonderi See **trechandiri**

track-schyt, track-scout, tract-scout See **trekschuit-3**

trade boat See **Indian trade boat, store boat**

trading batteau See **scow-5**

trading cutter See **trading smack**

trading schooner See **West Indies schooner**

trading sloop See **sloop-10**

trading smack *British Isles:* **Cutter***-rigged vessel that engaged in coastal trading, especially off the west coast of England; a few worked until the mid-20th century. Most deep-hulled and somewhat tubby; flat floors. Bulwarks generally high; often had removable sections on the quarters to assist in loading and unloading, frequently directly onto beaches. Could have a combination windlass and cargo winch. Usually set a topmast and topsail with a short yard. Vessels were often rebuilt and lengthened, necessitating a change in rig, generally to a **ketch***. Crew of 2 and sometimes a boy. Reported lengths 12-20m. Name variant: **trading cutter**. Note also **smack-1**. Further reference: **Plymouth barge**

trading vessel See **merchantman**

traget   1. Croatian term applied at times to a **ferryboat*** or transport vessel. Spelling variants: **treget, trget**

2. Also a large **gaeta*** of the eastern Adriatic. Curved stem with high stemhead, plumb stern, and straight keel. Deep outboard rudder; tiller. Vertical mast set a quadrilateral, lateen-type sail with a short luff. Cap. 8-15t. Name variant: **tragetič**

tragetič See **traget-2**

tragetto, tragheto See **ferryboat-1**

traghetti See **traghetto**

traghetti da soldo, traghetti del bagattino, traghetti de viazzi See **traghetto**

traghetto Italian word meaning **ferryboat★**. Ranges from a small, open boat to an ocean-going ship (**nave traghetto**).

1. In Venice, a heavy-duty **gondola★** used mainly to cross the Grand Canal. The **traghetto da soldo** was a **penny ferry**; the **traghetto del bagattino** was a **farthing ferry**; the **traghetto de viazzi** went to the mainland. Length ca. 10.4m, beam 1.6m. Name variants: **gondola da traghet(t)o**

2. The **traghetto** of the Chiascio in central Italy is a square-ended, completely open craft. Flat bottom with rocker at each end; planking on the straight sides is horizontal and phases out at the open ends. Cleats cross the bottom, vertical ribs. At each end, the ribs extend up through the gunwale to form double tholepins.

3. A 19th-century **traghetto** on the Tiber (Tevere) River at Marsciano was long, narrow, and high-sided. Flat bottom rounded up sharply to form square ends.

4. At Deruta on the middle Tiber, the 16th- and 17th-century **ferry★** had a sharp, raking bow and high-tucked transom above a raking sternpost. Flat bottom, curved sides, rounded bilges, numerous ribs. Top strake continued forward to create a small beak. Stern seat. Probably poled. Length 7.7m, beam 2.5m, depth 1.0m.
Spelling variant: **traghetti** (pl.)

tragillo, tragitto See **ferryboat-1**

trahina *Mauritania, N:* Motorized Spanish vessel that engages in ringnet fishing, beginning in November in some areas, and from January to June in the Baie du Lévier. Length to 30m. Note also **trainera**.

trailer See **narrow boat**

trailer hopper dredge See **hopper**

trailing dredge See **dredger-1**

traille See **ferryboat-1**

traiña *Spain:* Inshore **fishing boat★** used mainly to catch anchovies and sardines on summer nights with the *traiña* (or *traiñon*) net. Those in northwestern Spain have a slightly raked bow; rounded stern higher than the bow; curved sides; clinker-planked. Small foredeck, larger deck at stern, wide side decks. Works with 4 smaller auxiliary boats of similar design; rowed. Maneuvered with a long sculling oar mounted on an iron tholepin at the stern. Originally set a lateen sail or a lug; now motorized. Combined crew of 25-40. Reported lengths 13-14m, beam 3m, depth 1.5m, draft 1.0m. Other recorded names: **barco traiñon, trenyinera**; pl. **barcos trainones**

traina See **trainera**

traina gallega See **trainera**

Trainboot See **store boat**

train de bateaux *France:* A group of river **barges★** (**chalands★**) coupled to form a chain, the lead boat called **chaland-mère**; the 2nd, the **tirot**; and the last, the **sous-tirot**. A **toue★** or **allège★** might be included. Used especially on the Loire River, dating from at least the 17th century. Sharp bow with slight sheer; straight sides; square stern. The **chaland-mère** used its rudder; the others unshipped theirs. This **barge** also had a cabin house aft for the use of the captain; the crew lived on the **tirot**. A plank provided access between each boat. The tall square sail on **la mère** was

hoisted to the masthead, while those on the next boats were set progressively lower. Early **tirots** were reported to be 11.6-23.3m long. On the Loire, special names were assigned: the chain called an **équipe**; the lead boat, a **bateau de tête** or **bateau de mât**; the 2nd boat, a **tireau**; and the last, the **sous-tireau**; Crew of 11 managed the **équipe**. A 2-boat unit was a **couplage★**. Further name variant: **train de chalans**. Note also **bachot-3g, chaland de Loire, péniche**.

train de bois French term sometimes used for a group of **timber rafts★** (individually called a **brelle**) coupled together to form a large single **raft★**. Some carried cargo, and frequently casks of wine, in the 19th century. The term was also used in the Mississippi Valley with the same meaning.

train de chalans See **train de bateaux**

train de marine See **drome**

traineau à voile See **iceboat-1**

traineira *Portugal:* Fishes offshore, north of Cape Roca, with a trawl net, primarily for sardines. Term now applies to a motorized **trawler★**. Formerly the **traineira** of Peniche was a long, narrow, open boat that set 2 high-peaked lugsails, the larger on the foremast. Stem and sternpost curved; rudder extended well below the bottom; decked forward of the foremast. Those working off the mouth of the Mondego River were mainly rowed, employing 3 men to each of the 4 oars, plus a captain and helmsman. With favorable winds, a mast was stepped and a lateen sail set. Reported lengths of the motorized boats at Peniche 12-27m. Note also **trainera, traînière-1**.

trainera *Spain, N:* Slim **rowing boat★** used along the coast for anchovy and sardine fishing with a purse seine; also fished for bonito and tuna. A special light type raced (the **trainerak**). Clinker- or carvel-planked; fine entrance and run; flat floors; rounded stern; slightly curved stem. Mainly open, foredeck, low sides. Generally 7 tholepins to a side; short oars. Sailed at times, setting 2 lugsails to masts stepped against thwarts, or might step just one forward mast. Vertical foremast close to the stem; the aft-raking mainmast amidships. Masts might also incline transversely. Steered with a long oar secured to a thole by a rope, or when under sail, steered with tiller and rudder. Crew of 14-30. Reported lengths 9.3-15m; e.g., length 10.85m, beam 2.95m, depth 1.35m. Other recorded names: **lancha trainera, traina★, traina gallega, trainerilla** (6-oared), **traiñero, treinerua**. Note also **traineira**. Further reference: **traînière-1**

trainerak See **trainera, traînière**

trainerilla, traiñero See **trainera**

train ferry See **ferryboat-1**

traînière **1.** *France, SW/Spain, N:* A long, narrow Basque **pulling boat★**. Fished mainly within sight of shore with a large net until ca. 1912. Carvel-planked; flat floors, rounded bilges, generally little sheer. Rounded stern; straight stem, slight tumble home; very fine run. When sailed, shipped a narrow rudder that extended well below the bottom; tiller slotted over the rudderhead. Heavy sectional weatherboards were removed as needed when rowed; short end decks. Rowed by 12-18 oarsmen on 8-11 benches. Set

2 lugsails when appropriate; foremast stepped through foredeck; mainmast roughly amidships. Now motorized. Crew included a helmsman. Reported lengths 10-14m; e.g., length 10m, beam 1.83m, depth 0.8m. Other recorded names: **trainera***, **treñeros**. Note also **traineira**, **txalupa handi**.

2. *France:* The **trainière à vapeur** had a silhouette similar to the **sardinier breton***. Fished for sardines with a circular seine net.

trainière à vapeur See **traînière-2**

train of bateaux See **timber raft-4**

trajekt See **ferryboat-1**

trakandini See **trechandiri**

trakboat See **track boat**

trakonderi See **trechandiri**

tråler See **trawler**

trambachuolo, trambakuolo See **trabaccolo**

trambolim See **moliceiro**

trammel net boat See **Dee salmon boat**

tramoggia See **hopper**

transatlántico See **liner-1**

transbordador, transbordeur, transfer See **ferryboat-1**

transfer boat See **bo chuan-1**

transport arsenal See **store ship**

transport de fruits See **fruit ship**

transport de matériel, transport de ravitaillement See **store ship**

transporter de poisson See **fish carrier-1**

trap *Albania, N:* Triangular craft consisting of 2 **dugout canoes*** securely fastened together; used to cross rivers, notably the Drin. The single dugout was called a **lundra***. A heavy wooden peg passed completely through the solid bows, holding them side-by-side.

trap

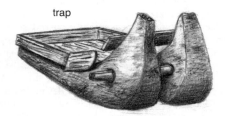

Held apart at the stern by another peg that passed through a sort of sternpost left in the squared-off hulls. Some very simple types were merely lashed together with withes. The bows might be pointed or blunt; generally with sharp sheer; flat bottom. A weatherboard might extend around the combined craft. Paddled by 1-2 men. Reported lengths 7-8m; some larger types ferried horses that stood with forelegs in one **canoe*** and hindlegs in the other. Other recorded names: **barke***, **trapa***, **trapp**, **varke**

trapa *India:* Hindi word for a **raft***. Note also **teppa**. Further reference: **trap**

trapassamento See **ferryboat-1**

trap boat 1. *Canada, N:* Used mainly in Arctic fisheries and as a general-purpose boat by the Hudson's Bay Company. Modeled after the Newfoundland **trap skiff***. Straight, raked stem. Low cabin forward; open aft. Powered by an inboard motor. Reported lengths 7.9-10.7m.

2. *United States, NE:* Specially designed boat used off Cape Cod to work the 97m-diameter traps staked out to catch herring and mackerel. Driven by a 2-cycle engine. Length 9m.
See also **Saint John's trap boat**, **Saint Margarets Bay skiff**, **trap skiff**.

trapp See **trap**

trapping skiff *United States, NE:* A short, narrow boat used by early trappers on the waterways of the Adirondack Mountains in northern New York State. Lapstrake construction with 3 strakes per side; each fastened to a few natural-crook knees; sharp ends. Mainly poled.

trap setter General term for a vessel from which traps, pots, pound nets, stow nets, etc., are set. Note also **pot boat**, **pound boat**, **pound net boat**, **stowboat**, **trap skiff**.

trap skiff *Canada, E:* A fine-lined, inshore **fishing boat*** of the Maritime Provinces, Newfoundland, and Labrador that uses a small seine net (the trap) to catch cod and mackerel. Many home-built with consequent local variations. Carvel or lapstrake construction over natural frames. Strongly raking transom with a high tuck; may have hole in transom for sculling oar. Deep skeg; curved stem; rounded bottom; double-ended on the waterline; considerable sheer. Some now built of steel. Open or half-decked; may have evenly spaced thwarts; others leave waist clear; stern seat. Often compartmented for fish and ballast, covered with movable decking; centerboard on some. Occasionally steered with a rope bridle across the helmsman's waist, freeing his hands. Rowed and sailed. **Ketch***-rigged with short mainmast stepped through a thwart well forward. Sets gaff or spritsails. Most now equipped with engines. Reported lengths 6-10.6m; e.g., length 6.2m, beam 1.5m, depth ca. 0.8m; a large **trap skiff** capable of carrying 5t of fish. Other recorded names: **cod-trap boat**, **Newfoundland (trap) skiff**, **trap boat***. Note also **motor boat-2**. Further reference: **Saint Margarets Bay skiff**

trap sloop See **Quoddy boat**

trasporto da cavalli See **horse carrier**

tráta 1. Aegean craft used both in Greece and Turkey for seine net (*tráta*) fishing until World War II. At times, they were lightly armed and used to chase pirates and on some islands, were used by the pirates themselves. Sharp-ended; clipper bow terminated in truncated beak; high, thick stemhead; marked sheer; high rudderhead; long tiller. Decked; some had a wet well; 2 crutches on each side supported gear and the mast. Large lateen sail, yard about the length of the boat. Also rowed with as many as 12 oars. Crew of 10-12 on large boats. Reported lengths 10-15m; narrow. Name variants: **tarata**, **tratak** (small size), **tratas**; pl. **tratai**, **trates**

2. Name also given to an escape boat (**tráta tou bourlotou**) towed astern a fireship set to sail down on an enemy vessel, and by virtue of its own ignited explosives, destroy the enemy.

tratai, tratak, tratas See **tráta-1**

tráta tou bourlotou See **tráta-2**

trates See **tráta-1**

trauersier See **traversier-2**

trauler See **trawler**

Trauner Zalzzille See **Salzzille**

traveling canoe See **sda'kwihl**, **tripper**, **West Coast canoe**

Travemünder Sandboot See **Sandboot**

traversier 1. *Canada, E:* In French Canada, term may apply to a **ferryboat★**. Name variant: **bateau de passage**
   2. *France, W:* Square-sailed boat of the Loire Estuary and the La Rochelle area that fished and undertook short coasting trips; worked mostly in the 2nd half of the 17th and early 18th centuries. Bluff bow, round stern, curved stem; straight, raked sternpost; flat floors, slight tumble home topsides; considerable sheer. Narrow outboard rudder; tiller. Decked at the ends. Most stepped a mast amidships. Set a large, rectangular mainsail and sometimes 1-2 square topsails. Used 1-2 headsails. Flat bowsprit. Three or 4 men

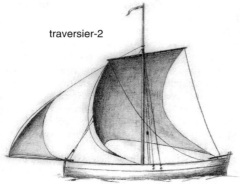

traversier-2

might row, if needed. Generally a crew of 2-4. Reported lengths 9-18m; e.g., length ca. 15m, beam 4.2m, depth 1.8m. Other recorded names: **bateau de Lanvéoc**, **trauersier**, **traversière**. Further reading: Jean Boudroit, "Un Survivance: Le Bateau de Lanvéoc," *Neptunia* 153, 1st trimestre (1984), 1-6.
   3. *United States, south-central:* In the 1st half of the 18th century, the term was applied by the Louisiana French to any vessel that made frequent trips between 2 places, particularly voyages to Mexico and the West Indies. These same vessels might serve as **coasters★** at other times. Some were armed. Cap. ca. 50t.

traversière See **traversier-2**

trawl boat See **Hastings lugger**, **trawler**

trawl dory See **Banks dory**

trawler 1. Loosely, any **fishing boat★**. More precisely, a fishing vessel that tows a trawl net (a large bag net) on or near the bottom, either from the stern (**stern trawler**) or from its side (**side trawler**); such vessels indicate their mode of operation by special lights. May fish inshore or in deep-sea waters. Characteristically a seaworthy and powerful vessel; heavily constructed with a pronounced sheer forward and a low stern. Size and shape vary widely: the former because of trawl dimensions and hold capacity, the latter dictated by the method of handling the trawl. One that uses a beam on the lower opening of the bag-shaped net is called a **beam trawler**, while one that uses boards to spread the wings of the net is an **otter trawler**.

Originally, **trawlers** worked under sail, operating the net to between 30 and 40 fathoms; modern powered **trawlers** can work to 500 fathoms. Selected additional names: **arrastrero**, **arrostrero**, **barco de arrastre** (or **arresto**), **chalutier★**, **chalutier de traille**, **kočar**, **peschereccio**, **Schleppfischer**, **schrobnetvisser**, **tråler**, **trauler**, **trawl boat**, **treiler**; **arrostrero por popa**, **chalutier arrière**, **Hecktrawler**, **hektrawler**; **arrostrero por el costado**, **chalutier latéral**, **Seitentrawler**, **side-fishing trawler**, **side-set trawler**, **sidewinder**, **vrečarica**. Note also **dory trawler**, **dragger**, **fish-carrying boat**.
   2. *Bangladesh:* A collective term for wooden boats that have an inboard diesel engine, either fitted into a reconstructed **balam★** or **jali★** or newly built. Term first used in the late 1960s to distinguish between sailing craft and these motorized boats. Carry cargo, often crude salt or timber. Those crossing the northeastern part of the Bay of Bengal may set a small sail in favorable winds.

trawling skiff See **shrimper**

trawl skiff See **ring-net boat**

tray boat See **chu-p'ai**

treäringar See **kyrkbåt**

treasure frigate See **galizabra**

trébac See **trabaccolo**

trebandiri See **trechandiri**

trebau, **trebauco** See **trabaccolo**

trébuchet See **marie-salope**

trechandira, **trechandiraki** See **trechandiri**

trechandiri *Greece:* Term applied to a sharp-sterned, beamy vessel used for coastal transport, fishing, and sponging. Originated about the mid-17th century as a vessel of 4-5t burden; still built in some areas. Hull specifics vary, but generally have a full, flaring bow and stern; strongly raked, slightly curved stem that extends above the gunwale; straight, raked sternpost; soft turn of bilges; flaring sides; strong sheer. Always decked, and canvas weathercloths may raise the low, midships freeboard. Outboard rudder; tiller. Most painted white with colored stripes or designs along the sides. Might set a square mainsail and lateen mizzen or gaff sails; some small **trechandiris** were **sakoleva★**-rigged with a spritsail; others became **bratseras★** having 2 tall lugsails; still others had two tall lateen sails. With the installation of engines, beginning ca. 1920, adopted gaff sails; now sails rarely seen. Reported lengths 8-12m; general specifications: length overall: keel length plus one-third; width: one-half keel length; depth of hold: one-third width; largest sailing vessels to 250t burden. Other recorded names: **caique★**, **trackonderi**, **trakandini**, **trakonderi**, **trebandiri**, **trechandira**, **trechandiraki** (small), **trechanteri**, **trechantiri**, **trechendiri**, **treha(n)diri**, **trekandian**, **trekandini**, **trekhandiri**; pl. **trechandira**. Note also **aktarma**, **kaiki**.

trechanteri, **trechantiri**, **trechendiri** See **trechandiri**

treckschuit See **trekschuit-3**

Treckschut See **Treckschute**

Treckschute German word for a **canal boat★** or **barge★**. Reported also along the Ryck River between Greifswald and the harbor at Wieck on the eastern

Baltic coast. Popular from the 16th-18th centuries as official and private **yachts**, serving many large European cities. **Treckschuten** (pl.) used in the Berlin area in the 18th century were beamy and flat and made daily runs between Berlin and Charlottenburg. Length to ca. 15m. Other recorded names: **Greifswalder Leichterboot, Schleppschute, Treckschut, Treidelschute, Treckyacht.** Note also **tochtschuit-2, track boat, trekschuit-1.**

treckschuyt, treckschuyte See **trekschuit-3**

Treckyacht See **Treckschute**

treerøing See **treroring**

treget See **traget**

trehaderi, trehandiri See **trechandiri**

Treiber See **tochtschuit**

treibkvase *Denmark/Germany:* A **fishing boat*** that drifts with a seine net (*treib*) and has a wet well. Spelling variants: **Treibquase, Treibquatze.** Note also **drivkvase, kvase.**

Treibnetzlogger See **drifter**

Treibquase, Treibquatze See **treibkvase**

Treidelschute See **Treckschute**

treiler See **kotter, trawler**

treillogger See **logger**

trei-mat See **bark-1**

treinerua See **trainera**

trekandian, trekandini See **trechandiri**

trek boat See **Cape boat, track boat**

trekeiping See **seksæring-2**

trekhandiri See **trechandiri**

trekjacht See **trekschuit-3**

trekjeiping See **seksæring-2**

trekschuit   **1.** *Belgium/Netherlands:* A boat that is pulled (*trek*) along a canal or river, carrying passengers and cargo. Other recorded names: **baardse***, **barge***, **bargie, bark***. Note also **schuit, track boat, Treckschute.**

2. *Belgium:* Carried passengers from Gent to Brugge from the early 17th century. The day boat (**dagbarge**) ceased operation with the opening of the railroad in 1838; the night boat (**nachtbarge**) continued working until the end of the century. Usually towed by 2-4 horses, but under favorable conditions, hoisted a gaff sail. The late 18th-century vessel was flat-bottomed with a full, round bow; curved stem; transom stern; poop deck; tiller passed below the gunwale. Passengers accommodated in large cabins below deck; windows along the side. Length 20m, beam 5m.

3. *Netherlands:* Worked the inland waterway network from the 17th into the 19th century. Can be divided into 2 groups: those used in the southwestern part of the country, which had sharp, straight, overhanging stems and flat bottoms; and the less massive **trekjacht** of the northern area that had blunter, upswept, curved bows and a rounder bottom. Most **trekschuiten** (pl.) followed a regular schedule, and some were night boats (**nachtschuiten**) with rudimentary sleeping accommodations. The smaller **trekjacht** was often a private craft, and some were used for pleasure outings, often being rowed. Early boats were open or only an awning covered the passengers and freight; later vessels had long, window-lined cabins; all had long decks

at bow and stern and a steering well aft. The **pakschuit** was open abaft the cabin, bordered by benches. Might have leeboards. Towed with a line from the skipper in a steering well to a forward towing mast and thence to a horse. Some sailed, setting a sprit-, lug-, or gaff sail. Masts could be struck to pass under the numerous bridges. Later boats motorized (**motortrekschuiten**). Vessel crewed by a helmsman, a man to handle the towline, and a boy on the horse; some large vessels carried 36 passengers. Reported lengths 9-19m; e.g., length 18.6m, beam 3m, draft 0.5m. Further name variants: **dagschuit, galiote de Holland, iaegschuytie, jaagschuit, jaegschuitje, nachtschuyt, tentschuit***, **track-schyt, track-scout, tract-scout, treckschuit, treckschuyt(e), volkschuit.** Note also **snik.**

tre-lestabåt See **lestabåt**

tre-maenning, tremänning See **gotlandssnipa**

tre-manns færing See **færing-5**

treñeros See **traînière-1**

Trengganu perahu pinas, Trengganu schooner See **perahu pinas**

Trent catch *England, NE:* Traversed the River Trent from Hull to Nottingham; some traveled along the coast. Carvel-planked; sharp ends, straight sides, flat bottom with square bilges. Decked; long, covered hold; leeboards. Tiller worked over the rail on the narrow stern. Square main and topsails; mainsail wider at the foot; fore-and-aft or lug mizzen. Length to 22.8m, beam 4.3m, depth to 1.8m. Name variant: **Trent ketch**

Trent ketch See **Trent catch**

Trent pan See **pan**

trenyinera See **traiña**

trerøding, treroing See **treroring**

trerømming See **seksæring-7, tre-roms båt**

tre-roms båt *Norway, N:* An open boat compartmented by 4 thwarts into 3 "rooms" of ca. 66-90cm each. Name variant: **trerømming.** Note also **seksæring-7.**

trerømming See **tre-roms båt**

trerong See **treroring**

treroning See **gotlandssnipa**

treroring *Norway:* Open boat with 3 (*tre*) tholepins or oarlocks per side, usually using 6 oars. Also sailed, setting a trapezoidal square sail to a mast stepped amidships. Reported lengths 5.2-8.7m. Spelling variants: **treerøing, trerøding, treroing, trerong.** Note also **seksæring-5, seksæring-7.**

tre-rors jolle See **jolle-6**

tres See **canoa-6**

tre-smakkejolle See **smakkejolle**

tres-mast See **bark-1**

trget See **traget**

trgovačka ladja See **ladja-1, merchantman**

trgovački brod See **merchantman**

trgôvaska ladja See **ladja-1, merchantman**

tríbekkur *Denmark, Faroe Islands:* The smallest **færøbåd***; mainly fishes, close to shore. Clinker-planked; sharp ends, curved stem and sternpost, deep keel, 3 thwarts. Rowed by 2 men seated on forward 2 thwarts, using 2 pairs of oars. Length ca. 5m.

triera, triere, trieres See **trireme**

Trieste barge See **gaeta**

trim-tram See **beach punt-1**

trincado *Spain, NW:* Small cargo and fishing vessel. Clinker-built; straight rise to the floor; shoe keel; straight, flared sides. Double-ended; strongly curved stem and sternpost rounding smoothly into the keel. Rudder extends well below the bottom. Decked at ends; layers of cork secured beneath the flooring aid in flotation, as do air lockers placed along the sides. Lug-rigged on 1-2 masts; mast on single-masted boats raked sharply aft. Luff extended by bowline and spar. Rowed in calms.

trincadour See **biscayenne**

trincadoure See **biscayenne, trincadura**

trincadura *Spain, N:* Double-ended vessel of the coast around Vizcaya. Used for fishing, cargo, towing ships in harbors, and in places, by customs officials. Extinct. Clinker-planked; flat bottom; high bow. Open; outboard rudder. Sets 2 lugsails; in bad weather, the small *borriquete* is substituted for the regular forelug. Mainmast raked aft; foremast vertical and stepped in the eyes. Also rowed, double-banked. Crew of 16 when armed for surveillence activities. Other recorded names: **Biscayan boat, barca de atoage de Vizcaya, trincadoure; trinkadura** (Basque). Note also **biscayenne**.

Trinidad pirogue See **pirogue-6**

Trinity boat *England, S:* General term given to the racing boats belonging to the boat club at Trinity College, Cambridge University.

Trinity buoy yacht See **beacon boat**

Trinity House barge *England:* One of the corporation **barges*** that lined the route of sculling races and participated in ceremonial processions in the mid-19th century. Note also **barge-3**.

Trinity House boat, Trinity House tender, Trinity House yacht, Trinity sloop, Trinity yacht See **beacon boat**

trinkadura See **trincadura**

tripper *Canada/United States:* A **canoe*** particularly suited to extended inland travel. Double-ended, permitting easy movement from either end; curved stem and sternpost; smooth, symmetrical sheer. Flat floors, rounded bilges, slight tumble home, no keel, bottom has rocker at ends. Paddled or poled. Lengths ca. 5-6m. Other recorded names: **traveling canoe, wilderness tripper**

tripper boat *United Kingdom:* Any boat that mainly provides summer visitors with transportation to off-lying sites or carries them on short outings. Note also **party boat**.

trira, trireis See **trireme**

trireme *Mediterranean:* Fast, light, oared ship-of-the-line of Mediterranean navies that had its height of popularity during the 4th-5th centuries B.C.; continued into the medieval period. Rowed from 3 levels by as many as 150 oarsmen. Two-pronged ram projected forward at the waterline for use in naval operations; the Romans also employed catapults. Probably flat-bottomed, straight-sided both longitudinally and vertically. Sternpost curved up and recurved in high arc. Cables running fore-and-aft provided strengthening. Maneuvered by twin quarter rudders, manned single-banked. Crew slept and ate ashore. An auxiliary sail

set when conditions permitted. Athenian vessel 37m long, 5m wide. Crew of ca. 200. Other recorded names: **galea triremis, triera, triere(s), trira, trireis, triremis, trirene**; pl. **triremi**

triremi, triremis, trirene See **trireme**

tristur *Denmark, Faroe Islands:* Category of **færøbåd*** rowed by 3 men, each pulling a pair of oars. Used for inshore fishing and collecting birds' eggs. Clinker-planked; sharp, curved ends; 4 thwarts. Length 6.7m. Name variant: **sexæring**

Trochen-Ewer See **Ewer**

Trochenfracter See **dry cargo ship**

trochus lugger See **pearling lugger**

trois-mâts, trois-mâts barque See **bark-1**

trois-mâts carré, trois-mâts franc See **ship-2**

trois-mâts goëlette See **barkentine**

troleiro See **poveiro-2**

troller **1.** In a general sense, any boat, powered, sailed, or rowed, that tows baited hooks or lures astern to catch pelagic fish. Popular on the Pacific coast of the United States for salmon, tuna, and albacore. On commercial boats, outrigged poles (usually 4) trail the lines; line rollers are used to pick up a line that has a fish. Managed by 1-2 in crew. Lengths vary, generally between 7.6-13.7m. The largest, the albacore boats, run to ca. 18m and require a crew of 8-10. Other recorded names: **bateau de pêche à traine, curricanero, hikinawasen, Schleppleinenfischerboot, trolling boat**. Note also **salmon troller**.
2. *Canada, SW:* In the 1st half of the 20th century, open **hand trollers** were important craft for inshore hand-lining for salmon. Sharp-ended, carvel-planked. Might set a spritsail, but also rowed. Worked single-handed. Length ca. 4.6m.

trolling boat See **troller**

trønderjekt See **jekt**

trot boat One that plies regularly between a line of anchored ships and the shore, carrying supplies, stores, crew, etc. Other recorded names: **routine boat, Routineboot**

trotline boat, Trotlinenboot See **trotliner**

trotliner *United States, E:* Small, open boat that tends long, baited lines (trotlines) to catch crabs in Chesapeake Bay. Primarily carvel-planked; square stern, sharp bow. Works by hauling the anchored lines hand-over-hand or over a roller on the gunwale; sails to and from the crabbing grounds, employing a small sail set to a portable mast. Also poled. A boat engaged in a similar operation in Germany would be called a **Krabbenfangboot**. Other recorded names: **line skiff*, trotline boat, Trotlinenboot**. Note also **crabbing skiff**.

trough See **dugout canoe**

trow *United Kingdom:* **1.** Trading vessel of the Severn Estuary in western England that was well established by the early 15th century, but underwent considerable evolution of hull and rig as its primary working area shifted from upriver to midriver, then to coastal activities, even working out of the River Parrett on the south shore of the Bristol Channel. Some were vessels imported from other areas and converted to **trow** work. For their early activity on the River Severn watershed and the River Wye, they set a square mainsail and topsail and sometimes a lateen mizzen into the 1st half of the 19th century. Those on the River Avon, which were similar to the **Severn trows**, retained their square sail. Later, a **cutter**⋆ rig was adopted, and small, **sloop**⋆-rigged **trows**, called **'Wich barges**, carried salt from Droitwich to Gloucester. As they moved into open water, the vessels became larger, and a **ketch**⋆ rig with topsails was more common; for a short period, some were reported to be **schooner**⋆-rigged. The **Bridgwater trows** were **ketches**. The **ballast** and **coal trows** stepped their masts in tabernacles. The strongly built **Upper Severn trows** had to be bow-hauled by men through the Severn Gorge. Degree of decking varied from the early open boats to fully decked vessels; on some, sidecloths compensated for the lack of bulwarks.

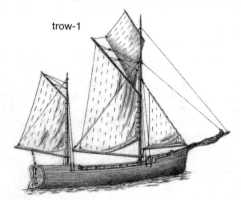

trow-1

Those that went into the Bristol Channel, or even to the Continent, had bulwarks, side decks, and a high coaming around the hatch area, and were called **box trows**. If the waist remained open but bulwarks ran down the sides, and each end of the hold had transverse coamings, they were called **half box trows**. **Flush-decked trows** were fully decked with covered hatches. **Trows** worked until the mid-20th century, but mostly as unrigged **lighters**⋆. Characteristically had a deep, tucked-up, D-shaped transom, but some early vessels were double-ended. Since they often took the ground, flat floors amidships were common; on some, the bottom sloped upwards slightly toward the keel. Some had a removable false keel rigged with chains from the bulwarks; others had fixed keels. Rounded bilges. Bluff bow with curved stem; wall-sided. The 19th-century **trows**, both open and boxed, made of iron for Messrs Danks & Co., were called **Danks' trows**. Crew of 2 mostly, but as many as 4 on the larger vessels. **Trows** overall length 15.9-25.9m, beam 5.4-6.5m, depth 2-2.4m. Other recorded names: **schooner trow**, **witch barge**, **Wye trow**. Note also **Avon tar boat**.

2. A **catamaran**⋆-type **trow** was used for night salmon fishing in southern Scotland and northern England. Two narrow, sharp-sterned boats were set close together, connected on top by a board and at the ends. Salmon, drawn by the light of a torch, were speared in the intervening space. Might be used separately for general fresh-water fishing. Name variant: **trows**

3. A small, flat-bottomed **trow** was used for herring fishing in the area of Sidmouth on the southern coast of England.
Further references: **barge-8**, **Fleet trow**

trows See **trow-2**

trtana See **tartane**

truckle See **Wye coracle**

Truro River oyster boat See **Falmouth oyster dredger**

tsaba'xad See **northern-style canoe**

tsambou See **sambo-2**

ts'ao ch'uan *Hong Kong:* Single-masted **fishing boat**⋆. Sharp, raking bow; rounded stern. Flush deck; house aft. Fenestrated rudder came up inboard. Battened balance lugsail had slight hump on the leech. Length 11m, beam 4.6m. See also **cao chuan**, **cao zi**.

tsao-shuan, **ts'ao-tch'ouan** See **cao chuan**

ts'ao tse See **cao zi**

tsao-tsze ch'uan See **cao zi chuan**

tšata See **mahonne-4**

tsato See **chato**

tsat pon *China, S/Hong Kong/Macau:* **Trawler**⋆ that worked with another vessel in the South China Sea; probably extinct as a sailing craft. Identified by its large centerboard, hung forward of the mainmast; by a heavy wale that ran from bow to near the stern (beyond which the planking became vertical); and by the presence of standing rigging. Constructed of teak; curved stem widened to a small bow transom at the top; square counter stern; small keel; round bilges; strong sheer at the stern. Straight, parallel sides. Large, fenestrated rudder hoisted by tackle to a windlass; post came up inboard. Decked; fish hold amidships; nets carried in a forward hold; crew and owner's family accommodated in aft and midships cabins. Stepped 2-3 masts; foremast raked forward; mainmast vertical or raked; vertical mizzen at taffrail. Deck timbers projected outboard to support the heavy fore-and-aft spars that served as platforms to spread the forward shroud; 3 wire stays. Set battened lugsails of matting. Crew of 20-30. Reported lengths 11-26m; e.g., length 11.3m, beam 4.3m, depth 2.7m. Name variants: **tsat pong tor** (or **tow**)

tsat pong tor, **tsat pong tow** See **tsat pon**

Tschaike, **Tschaiken** See **saique**

tschappits See **West Coast canoe**

Tscheigge See **saique**

tschektima, **Tschektirne** See **tchektirme**

Tschenakl See **Schinakel**

Tscheuke See **saique**

tschikirné, **tserkirne** See **tchektirme**

tsernik See **tserniki**

tserniki *Greece:* Double-ended boat, generally of the eastern Aegean. Mainly used for fishing, but its speed and maneuverability make it popular as an illegal trader. Stem straight and sharply raked. Stern also raked, but subject to local variations. Strong sheer; low washboards amidships. Outboard rudder; short tiller. Large, roughly square mainsail held out by a long sprit. Mast may be vertical or rake forward sharply. One or 2 square topsails and 1-2 headsails. Rising bowsprit. Some employ a small mizzen to a light pole at the stern. Length 10.9m, beam 3m. Other recorded names: **tsernik(ia)**, **tsernikovarka**. Note also **tchektirme**.

tsernikia, tsernikovarka See **tserniki**

tshayka See **czajka**

tshinatak See **kayak-9**

tsiman Generic term for **canoe*** used by a number of native North American groups, such as the Obijwa (Chippewa), Cree, and Algonkin. May refer to a **canoe** with a skin of birchbark (*wigwas*). Hiawatha built a **cheemaun** in Longfellow's "Song of Hiawatha." Further spelling variants: **cheemahn, cheeman, chemahnans** (small), **che'man, che'manis** (small), **chiman, či'ma·n, djiman', gie-maun, jiman, tchiman, tchimanan** (pl.), **tchimanens** (small), **tcimân. Chēma'nisis** is a small **canoe** of little worth. Note also **wabanaki chiman, wigwas tsiman.**

Tsimshian canoe See **northern-style canoe**

tsḷi See **Chipewyan canoe**

Tsongming junk See **Tsungming chuan**

tsoro See **soro**

tsugi-ikada See **ikada**

tsuku no fune See **haku-2**

tsukupin *Micronesia, western Pacific:* Single-outrigger sailing **canoe*** used seasonally for catching flying fish off Yap Island, in the western group. Esteemed as sacred. Dugout hull, strong rocker longitudinally; symmetrical, deep "V" in transverse section; residual, cleat-like projection above the waterline at each end. Double-ended with long, narrow ends that terminate in swan-like heads, symbolizing the frigate bird; large cowrie shells hang from the beaks. Except for white beaks, hull painted red. Short, stout outrigger float connected by 2 closely spaced booms; always set to windward. Booms connect to float by crutch-shaped stanchions or by multiple sticks. Solid platform laid on booms close to hull; lighter-weight platform extends to float; outrigger unit further strengthened by spars angling from ends of hull to outer part of booms. Smaller platform built out on lee side, canting upward. Single triangular sail set to a forward-raking mast stepped amidships; apex of sail tacked down to pegs, one at each end; mast and sail pivoted to opposite end when tacking.

Tsungming chuan *China, E:* Carries baled cotton and passengers from the island of Chongming (Tsungming) in the Chang Jiang (Yangtze) estuary to Shanghai; return cargo often night waste for fertilizer. Sturdily built with numerous bulkheads and 3 heavy wales at the waterline; deck beams project through the sides on some. Bottom flat; bow and stern square and raked; platform extends beyond the stem, holding the tack of the foresail and mainsail. Washboards run from the 1st bulkhead to the stern; some as high as 61cm forward. Rudder in trunk; 2 small leeboards; in heavy weather, large, basket sea anchor employed to further reduce drifting. Loose decking; cabin abaft the mainmast on some; on others, crew accommodated below deck. Painted black. Steps 2-3 masts; mainmast especially tall and is often 2 pieces fished together; some rake aft. Foremast vertical or rakes forward; mizzenmast stepped on transom, slightly to port, raking aft. Square-headed, battened lugsails with straight leech. Crew of 3. Reported lengths 10-25m; e.g., length overall 18m, beam 4m,

depth 2m; light draft. Some much narrower. Other recorded names: **Chongming chuan, Ch'ung-ming ch'uan, Tsongming junk, Tsungming cotton boat, Tsungming trader**

Tsungming cotton boat See **Tsungming chuan**

Tsungming pig boat See **yao wang chuan**

Tsungming trader See **Tsungming chuan**

tsuri-bune *Japan:* Small, coastal **fishing boat*** found throughout the country with local variations. Sharp bow; wide, raking stem; tall stemhead; square stern. Plank keel; rising floors to hard chines; wide, vertical top strake extends beyond transom; bottom has rocker at stern. Decked forward; a wide, tray-like section sits abaft the open waist and extends outboard on each side; standing well aft. Rudder slotted into transverse beam abaft the transom. Mainly sculled, braced against a crutch aft; also poled and sailed. Crew of 1-8. Length mostly 4m, beam 1.25m; under 5gt.

tsûta´ xīna See **tō´ xana**

ts'u t'u ela *Canada, NW:* Sprucebark **canoe*** of the Slavey Native Americans. Ends sharp and sometimes strongly raked; ends closed with lashings of spruce root and caulked with spruce gum. Spruce gunwale, lashed at intervals; sheer at ends varies, some sweeping up sharply. Made from a single piece of bark, the holes plugged with moss and spruce gum; light, widely spaced ribs inserted; several light thwarts. Length 3.7m, beam 0.72m, depth 0.3m. Spelling variant: **tzu tu ela**

tub **1.** An ugly, poorly maintained, and usually old vessel. Term might also describe an uncomfortable, clumsy vessel. Other recorded names: **Kahn***, **Kiste, Schlarren, zossen**

2. *United Kingdom:* A heavy, clinker-planked training craft, although sometimes raced by novices. Rowed by a pair (**tub pair**), by four (**tub four**), and sometimes by eight people. Seat at the stern for helmsman. Originally inrigged, later half-rigged, and then fully outrigged (see **outrigger**). A **fixed tub** is an artificial structure with appropriate amenities, fully anchored, used for practicing movements. Name variant: **tub boat***. Note also **Thames gig.**

tub boat *United Kingdom:* Open, rectangular, box-like **canal boat*** that transported bulk minerals, such as coal and sand. Some canals designed for their use, especially those with inclined planes. Generally towed in trains, as many as 20 at a time; coupled with chains. Some worked in coal mines. Mainly pulled by a horse, with a man on the bank guiding the string with a shaft. Used as early as the 18th century. Built of wood or iron. Wooden boats had a cross-planked bottom and reinforced keelson. Three planks per side. Ends secured by wooden (later iron) knees; stout posts at the corners. On some canals, the lead boat had a sharp bow. On the Bude Canal in southwestern England, some were fitted with wheels that ran in channels on the inclined planes. Reported lengths 4.5-10m; e.g., length 6m, width 1.9m, depth 0.84m, draft loaded 0.6m. Note also **compartment boat**. Further references: **tarai-bune, tub**

tub box See **sinkbox**

tub four See **tub-2**

tub gig See **Thames gig**

tub pair See **tub-2**

tub punt **1.** *Canada, E:* Sharp-ended, open boat of Digby Neck in western Nova Scotia. Carried tubs filled with longlines; towed by the fishing vessel. Often returned with extra catch. Extinct. Stoutly constructed of spruce; slightly flared, straight sides. Flat bottom, longitudinally planked; slight rocker; reinforced with an extra sheathing. Straight, slightly raked stem and sternpost; towing ring set low on the stem. Heavy frames and 4 natural-crook knees. Rubbing rails along the sides at top and bottom protected against damage in rough weather. Two thwarts. Reported lengths 4.3-4.9m; beam ca. 1.2m. Name variant: **Digby Neck tub punt**

2. *United Kingdom:* Square, flat-bottomed, low-sided craft used for river work and occasionally for local fishing.

tucang See **toucang**

tuck boat See **dipper, tuck-net boat**

tuck-net boat *England, SW:* Term given to a boat that entered a drawn pilchard seine net and shot the fine-meshed, smaller tuck net in order to further confine and raise the fish for transfer to a **tuck boat**. Crew of 6-8. Rowed and sailed. Note also **follower-2**.

tuckup *United States, E:* Popular racing and pleasure craft of the Delaware River in the late 19th century. Originally used for fishing, crabbing, trapping, and gunning. Derived its name from the upward turn of the plank keel to a wide, wineglass transom. White cedar planking; white oak frames; gently rising floors; soft, high turn of the bilges. Plumb stem. Foredeck; side decks. Daggerboard; wide outboard rudder; tiller. Heavily rigged with mast stepped in the bow; stayed to a curved bumkin. Long gaff and boom. Smaller rig when not racing. Easily rowed. Racing crew of 3-5. Reported lengths 4.57-4.65m; e.g., length 4.57m, beam 1.4m, depth 0.46m. Name variant: **Delaware River tuckup**

tug **1.** Powerful and highly maneuverable vessel that tows or pushes another vessel. Large, seaworthy, ocean-going **tugs** may tow salvaged vessels, oil rigs, etc., for great distances. Small harbor, dock, and river **tugs** may haul laden **barges*** or **lighters*** or may assist in docking and undocking large ships. **Tug tenders** serve not only to help maneuver a ship, but also to transfer passengers and baggage. Some have fire-fighting equipment (the **fire tug**). Engine power usually out of proportion to the **tug's** size. Most have deep draft aft; high bow. Long, low counter stern to keep a parted or slack tow rope from fouling the propeller. Superstructure set well forward. Small crew; oceangoing **tugs** average 8 in crew. Size commensurate with the **tug's** primary activity. The small **launch tugs** (**toshers***) handle mainly **barges** and similar craft. A special type of **quarter-wheel tug**, used in some river work, had a paddle wheel on each quarter. Selected alternate names: (**bateau) remorqueur, bogserbåt, bukser(båt), buksir, escarbilleur, hinaaja, rebocador, (buque) remolcador, remorcher, rimorchiatore, rimorchio, Schleppboot, Schlepper, sleepboot(je), slepebåt, tow barge, towboat*, tugboat**.

Further reading: M. J. Gaston, *Tugs & Towing* (Sparkford, England: Patrick Stephens Limited, 1991). Note also **ice breaker, push boat, tow**.

2. *United States, central:* On the Mississippi River, **tow boats*** push their **barges**, while **tugs** pull them. The **tow boats** have either **scow***- or **pram***-type hulls. The **barge** made up directly to the **tow boat** is called a **face barge**; the farthest one ahead is the **jackstaff barge** and usually has a jackstaff to steer by. Outboard **barges** are called **scabs**.

Further references: **car float, gas boat-6, gill net tug**

tugantine *United States, E:* Unique, diesel-powered and sail-assisted tug, the *Norfolk Rebel*, working out of Norfolk, Virginia, at the lower end of Chesapeake Bay. Built 1980. Used for salvage and towing work, particularly assisting tall ships plying the eastern U.S. coast. Often participates in maritime festivals from the Gulf of Mexico to the Great Lakes and Canada. Term suggests a **brigantine** rig. Actually a topsail **schooner** with aft-raking main- and foremasts, each setting a boomed gaff sail. Foremast carries a single square sail set just above the throat of the gaff. Two headsails set on masthead stays, 1 stay to stem, 1 to the retractable bowsprit. Steel construction. High bow, rounded stem, full bulwarks. Full box keel; rounded stern; skeg-mounted rudder. Wheelhouse above cabin with galley and captain's quarters, roughly amidships. Crew quarters in forecastle. Deep hold forward of wheelhouse. Lazarette aft. Crew of 4-5. Length 15.72m, on waterline 14.63m; beam 4.65m; draft 1.98m.

tugboat, tug tender See **tug**

tukang See **toucang**

tuk chaleum, tuk chap pok See **rua chalom**

tuk-dœm-thnot See **tuk thnot**

tuk thnot *Cambodia:* A small river craft scooped out of half of a palm tree, the wider end shaped to form a bow, and a transom fashioned with a plug of clay. When paddled solo, at the bow, a leeboard arrangement is

tuk thnot

suspended aft to reduce yawing. Length 2.5m, width 0.4m. Name variants: **touk thnot, tuk-dfim-thnot**

tule balsa See **nu-2a, pumuk o'wan, saKi, shikukul, tam´e', wo'te, tō´xana**

tule boat One constructed from bundles of tule grass. Note also **balsa-1, reed boat-1**.

tun *Liberia:* Deep-water fishing **canoe*** of the Kru peoples. Dugout hull, usually cut and hewn 80-95km in from the coast. Narrow, elongated ends cut square. On some, fan-shaped pieces form washboards forward. Two movable thwarts. Rowed and sailed. Crew of 2. Length ca. 8m. Name variants: **tō˙**; pl. **tunwine**

tuna boat **1.** A vessel that engages in fishing for any of the genera of tuna. Other recorded names: **atuneira*, atunero, barca das portas, pole fisher, thonier a appât vivant, Thunfischer, Thunfischfänger, Thunklipper, Thun-Langleinenboot, tuna clipper, tunbåd,**

tunfiskefartøj, tunny boat, tunnyman. Note also **barcareccio, mas-odi, palangero, pareja-2, thonier, vivero-2**.

2. The **pole-and-line tuna vessel** uses poles to catch tuna. The fishermen stand at the railing or on a platform at the stern, using long poles to which a line with hooks is attached. Other recorded names: **Angelfischereifahrzeug, buque para pesca con caña, canneur, embarcación con caña y linea, navio de pesca à vara, navio pesca com canas, peschereccio con lenze e canne, pole-and-line schip, schip dat met de hengel vist, stangfartøj, stand-og-line båd**

3. The **tuna longliner** is a medium-sized vessel. Winch that hauls the lines is placed on the starboard side forward. Fish preserved in brine freezing tanks.

4. Tuna purse seiners use large and heavy purse seine nets to capture the tuna. Usually carry a boat to assist in working the net.

Note also **seine skiff-2**.

tuna clipper See **tuna boat-1**

tuna longliner See **tuna boat-3**

tuna purse seiner See **tuna boat-4**

tunbåd See **tuna boat-1**

tune See **dhoni**

tunfiskefartøj See **tuna boat-1**

tungkang See **tongkang-2**

tunny boat See **tuna boat-1**

tunnyman See **thonier, tuna boat-1**

tunwine See **tun**

tuo bian zi See **bian zi**

tuo wang chuan *China, E:* One of several types of boats used by professional scavengers along the canals and waterways of the lower Chang Jiang (Yangtze) area. Dragged the bottom with a net. The lightly constructed craft had 6 bulkheads and 8 frames. Bottom flat, longitudinal planking curving up at the bow and stern; square ends, but overhanging extension at the stern formed a platform; sides lightly rounded. Midships house accommodated the owner's family, often 6 or more in the 2.7m by 1.8m area. Rowed with 3 oars, 2 at the bow on the same side and 1 at the stern on the opposite side. Length 8.5m, beam 2m, depth 0.76m. Other recorded names: **drag boat⋆, dragnet boat, t'o-wang ch'uan**

tup See **top**

turade See **tarrāda**

turf boat 1. *England, W:* A farm produce and peat transport boat still used in some areas of Somerset. Individually made and not standardized. Generally, flat bottom made from a single slab of elm, strongly flared sides, strakes clench lapped, knees of grown crooks, flat sheer. Identical low and sharply raked ends formed by a block. Propelled by a forked pole with a transverse grip. Sometimes tracked from shore. Reported lengths 5.2-10.7m; e.g., length 5.26m, beam 1.4m, depth 0.36m.

2. *Ireland:* Boats of various sizes transported peat on the Grand Canal to Dublin in the early 19th century.

See also **Fen boat, Friese turftjalk, Galway hooker, turftjalk**.

turfbotter See **Marker botter**

turfever See **Torf-Ewer**

turftjalk *Netherlands, N:* Collected peat (*turf*) from areas in Groningen, Drenthe, and Friesland for transport on their canals across the Zuiderzee to the southern part of the country. A type of **tjalk⋆**. Lightly built; flat floors; rounded bilges; low sheer except at the ends. Curved stem, vertical sternpost. Decked; low central hatch; deckhouse abaft the hold. Outboard rudder; tiller; narrow leeboards. Mast stepped just forward of the hold. Set a loose-footed, boomed gaff mainsail; may use a very short gaff while traversing canals, longer in open water. Staysail to stemhead. Ca. 50-60t disp. Note also **Friese turftjalk, turf boat**.

turfpont See **pot-2**

turf trader See **Galway hooker**

turnover sneak boat See **Susquehanna sneak boat**

turrif pott See **pot-2**

turssuk *Afghanistan/Tajikistan, Turkmenistan, Uzbekistan:* Goatskin **raft⋆** used on the Amu Darya and other rivers of the western Pamirs. Inflated skins contained by a rectangular framework of thin poles. A 12-skin **raft** could carry 2 men, directed by 3-4 swimmers. Spelling variant: **tursuk**. Note also **sal-1**.

tursuk See **turssuk**

turtleback See **pig boat-2, whaleback**

turtle boat See **kwi-son, lamboh Bali**

turtle-shell boat See **kamé-no-ko-bune, kikko-sen**

turtling canoe See **canoe-11**

Tusket River square-ender *Canada, E:* Small, open craft used on this river in southern Nova Scotia to fish for alewives and eels, as well as for sport fishing. Bow sharply raked, the stern vertical; strongly flared sides of 2 planks, either lapped or flush; flat bottom fore-and-aft planked; sides and bottom framed. Now often of plywood. Poled or rowed; some have an outboard motor on a reinforced stern. Reported lengths 3.7-5.5m, widths 0.76-1.2m.

Tuticorin lighter, Tuticorin lugger, Tuticorin thoni See **dhoni-2**

Tuticorin vallam See **vallam-2**

tutín *Afghanistan, SW/Iran, SE:* Reed boat⋆ used for wildfowling and fishing on Hāmūn-i-Helmand (Daryācheh-ye Sīstan), a marshy lake. Bottom composed of 3 cigar-shaped bundles of bulrush (*tut*) stalks, arranged to be fuller at one end, and bound with a rope of bulrush leaves; each end tapers and turns up slightly. Slender bundles on each side form low bulwarks; connected at the bow end by a transverse bundle. Front end may be fuller to create a raised bow. Last ca. 3 months and capable of carrying 2 people when used only for wildfowling, but last as few as 15 days when conveying heavy loads. Poled. Length 3m, width 0.76m, depth of floor 0.25m. Further reading: N. Annandale, "Note on the Fisheries of the Delta of the Helmand and on the Use of Shaped Rafts of Bulrushes in India and Seistan," *Records of the Indian Museum* XVIII (1920), 192-203.

tuwipē See **pumuk o'wan**

tuyen dang, tuyen luoi See **thuyền lu'o'i**

tvåköling See **iseka-1**

tvåmänning See **gotlandssnipa**

tvårodd See **kyrkbåt**

tvi-spenning See **færing-5**

twakow *Peninsular Malaysia/Singapore:* Beamy Chinese **lighter**★ that combines features of a **junk**★ and a **sampan**★. Developed in the mid-19th century. Flat bottom, curved keel; flaring sides; V-shaped bow transom and wide, raked stern transom; side planking extends beyond transom. Moderate sheer; little freeboard when loaded. Decked at ends; cabin or arched mat roof aft; large central hold. Brightly painted; oculi common. Steered with a very large, fenestrated rudder shipped to sternpost; long tiller. Small foremast stepped against the bow, raking sharply forward; mainmast stepped about a quarter in from the bow.

twakow

Originally set a single loose-footed dipping lugsail; later tanned, battened, Chinese lugsails of canvas. Those without sails propelled by a long stern scull or towed. Now motorized. Crew of 2-3. Reported lengths 15-18m; average length 17.5m, beam 6.7m, depth 2.3m. Name variant: **twaqo**. Further reading: D. W. Waters, "Chinese Junks: The Twaqo," *The Mariner's Mirror* 32 (1946), 155-167.

twaloaring See **great boat-5**

twaqo See **twakow**

tweemastbuis See **buis-2**

tweemastklipper See **klipper-1**

tweemastkoftjalk See **tjalk**

tweemastrivierklipper See **klipper-1**

tweemastsloep See **Oostendse sloep, sloep-1**

tween decker See **freighter**

tweeriemsgiek See **pair-oar**

Twillingate boat See **Toulinguet boat**

twin-outrigged canoe See **outrigger canoe**

twisted-stern junk See **wai pi gu**

two-beamed cat See **catboat-2a**

two-handed punt See **Deal galley punt, gun punt**

two-hull boat See **catamaran-6**

two-man sharpie See **sharpie-2**

two-mast boat *United States, NE:* Late 17th- to late 18th-century term for a small, general-purpose boat. Initially sharp-sterned; later many had square sterns. Open, but later boats decked, with raised cuddy forward. Mainmast stepped approximately amidships; short foremast stepped in the eyes. Set loose-footed gaff sails with very short gaffs; mainsail boomed. In later years, the foremast became almost as tall as the mainmast and the gaffs longer. Reported lengths on

keel 5.5-8.5m; e.g., length overall ca. 6.6m, beam 1.7m, depth 0.8m. Note also **Chebacco boat**. Further reference: **shallop**

two-master A boat or ship having 2 masts. A 2-masted **schooner**★ with topmasts on both masts might be called a **two-topmaster**. See also **shuang peng chuan**.

two-sail bateau See **skipjack-1**

two-sail lobster boat *United States, NE:* Term given to small boats using 2 sails as opposed to the more usual single sail. Worked mostly in Maine and Massachusetts in the late 19th century. Lapstrake construction; deep keel, round bilges, sharp bow, transom stern. Loose-footed lugsail set to the foremast; the smaller mainsail was gaff-rigged with boom. Reported lengths 5-6m.

two-section junk See **liang jie tou**

2-smakkejolle See **smakkejolle**

two-spar boat, two-sticker See **jack**

two-streaker See **lumberman's batteau**

two-topmaster See **two-master**

two-topsail schooner See **schooner-1**

txalupa See **biscayenne, chalupa-9b**

txalupa handi *France, SW/Spain, N:* Basque **fishing boat**★. During the 17th and 18th centuries, formed part of the whaling **fleets**★ going to northeastern Canada and Newfoundland. By the 19th century, they fished closer to home, although some went to Ireland. Fished for tuna from May to October and for local varieties during the winter. Originally open; movable washboards along the sides raised the freeboard when needed; decked by the end of the 19th century. Carvel-planked; slight tumble home at stem; rounded stern; fairly flat floors. Stepped 2 lug-rigged masts: the small aft-raking foremast well forward against the foredeck; the mainmast approximately amidships, also raking aft. Also rowed. Length ca. 13m. Name variants: **chalupa grande, grande chaloupe**. Note also **chalupa-9b, traînière-1**.

txalupak See **chalupa-1, chalupa-9b**

txanel See **batel-7**

tyalk See **tjalk-3**

tyde boate See **tide boat**

tylt bote, tylte bote See **tilt boat**

Tyne foyboat See **foyboat-2**

Tyne keel *England, NE:* **Barge**★ of the River Tyne that carried coal to **colliers**★ from the mid-14th to the mid-19th century, although a few remained in service until the early 20th century. A laden **keel**★ traveled downstream using the current and ebbing tide; upstream, empty and on the flood tide, was aided by sail and oar. Towed in later years. Initially clinker-built, later carvel. Double-ended, but so beamy that they appeared almost oval; stem and sternpost slightly raked. Low freeboard, hold protected by low coamings; flat sheer; flaring sides; flat bottom. Decked forward and aft; small cabin aft; oblong hatch, narrow waterways that were sometimes different widths. No bulwarks; heaped coal restrained by boards surrounding the hatch. Steered initially with a large oar, later by rudder. Painted black with a colored stripe around the hull. Mast stepped in a tabernacle just forward of the hold. Most hoisted a square sail that was sometimes set as a standing lugsail; later often used a spritsail and jib. Sail tanned black. Crew of 2-4 plus a boy. Length 12.8m, beam 5.79m, draft laden 1.27m, cap. 21t. Those that carried the coal in tubs were called **pan keels** or **pan boats**.

Tyne keel

Other recorded names: **coal keel, keyle, Newcastle keel**. Further reading: Eric Forster, *The Keelmen* (Newcastle upon Tyne: Frank Graham, 1970). Note also **keel-3, Teign keel**.

Tyne wherry *England, NE:* Employed in lightering coal and general cargo on the River Tyne from the 1830s; partly supplanted the **Tyne keel⋆**. Mainly clinker planking; strongly built; sharp ends; beamy with flat floors. Decked at bow and stern and along the sides; large, open hold. Heavy rudder and tiller. Usually towed by tugs, but sailed in favorable winds. About 40-60t.

ṭyrrâde See **tarrāda**

Tyske drivkvase, Tyskerkvase See **drivkvase, Zeesboot**

Tywi coracle *Wales, SW:* Salmon-fishing craft of the River Tywi (Towy); a few still licensed in 1991, solely for sport fishing. Bluntly oval in shape with the broader, flatter end forming the bow; relatively straight sides, raked stern, flat bottom. Ash framework of U-shaped laths, 7 lengthwise and 7 across; diagonal laths add strength as do additional short transverse pieces at the forward end. Tarred canvas or twill covering; plaited withy gunwale. The **coracles⋆** are now being made of molded fiberglass. Broad seat supported by a solid bulkhead; leather carrying strap attached to the seat. Propelled with a long, oar-like paddle. Usually "made to measure," the length being the distance from a man's nose to his feet; reported lengths 1.63-1.83m; width forward and at seat 1.0m; depth amidships 0.36-0.6m; weight ca. 13kg. Name variant: **Towy coracle**

tzee See **Chipewayan canoe**

tzu tu ela See **ts'u t'u ela**

ua **1.** *Brazil, SE:* The **ü-a** of the Tupí of the Yvahý River in Paraná is a bark **canoe★**.

2. *Marshall Islands, northwestern Pacific:* Generic term for a **canoe**, especially a small single-**outrigger canoe★**; also a **boat★** or **ship★**. Other recorded names: **wa★**, **we**. Note also **wa lap**.
Further reference: **wa-2**

uá See **wa-4**

uaga See **gaï oko**

uaqa See **waqa-2**

uaro See **ouaro**

ubá *Brazil/the Guianas:* Generic term for native **canoes★**, dugout or bark, of the Amazon Basin. Other recorded names: **candibá, curiará, iba, ubang**. Note also **casco-1**.
1. More specifically, term applies to a **dugout canoe★** with a narrow, slightly rising bow that rounds up gradually from the bottom, either to a point or spoon shape. Square stern that may rise directly from the bottom or overhang to form a small platform.

ubá-1

Rounded bottom; rib-like frames sometimes left during carving; on some, strakes may be added. Arched canopy of palm common. Usually paddled from the bow, or poled. Reported lengths 4.8-13m, widths 0.5-1.2m; typical: length 10.6m, beam 0.95m, depth 0.4m.
2. Among the Carajá of southern Brazil, one type of **ubá** is a single heavy log with booms at each end that cross the log and attach to small floats on each side. Amidships, 2 sponsons lie close to the log and provide foot rests for the polers. All components pointed at each end. Length ca. 2m. Other recorded names: **rauó, rrá-uó-rrikan**

ubang See **ubá**

Überfuhrfarm See **Farm**

Überfuhrmutzen See **Mutzen-1**

Überfuhrplätte See **Plätte-1**

Überfuhrzille See **Zille**

Überseedampfer, Überseefrachter See **liner-1**

ucaro See **howker**

üç çifte See **kayık-2**

uche *Papua New Guinea, E:* **1.** Term for **canoe★** in the Hermit Islands in the northwestern part of the Bismarck Archipelago.
2. The fishing **canoe** has a dugout hull to which one or more strakes are sewn; hull rounded in cross section; ends sharp, overhanging, and round up from the bottom; top strake sweeps up at ends. Thwarts inserted between the hull and gunwale poles. Four booms cross to the sharp-ended float, which is a little less than half the length of the hull. Each boom generally connects to the float by 3-4 pairs of undercrossed sticks; further rigidity provided by a spar that runs from midpoint of the boom to beneath the crossed part of the sticks. Platform of sticks laid atop the booms close to the

hull; rectangular frame between the platform and float strengthens the outrigger unit. Hull may be painted red with black-and-white designs on sides. Mast stepped in a sling between the hull and a boom extension on the off side, braced from the platform. Sets an oblong, lug-type sail; boom at the foot forks against the mast. **Canoe** sailed in either direction, the mast restepped at the opposite end when tacking. Steered with an oar. Length ca. 9m.
3. Another type was a high-sided, 2-masted traveling and ceremonial **canoe**. Dugout hull to which 3 strakes were sewn; sides carved in geometric designs and painted. Ends curved up from the bottom and continued above gunwale level as recurved end pieces; ends decorated with shells and tassels. Single outrigger unit composed of 4 heavy, horizontal booms and a relatively long, sharp-ended float connected by multiple tall stanchions. Some stanchions on the outer booms were taller and partially formed the framework for basket-like devices; platform laid across most of the area between the hull and float; a larger basket was situated at the outer end of the 2 middle booms; there was a smaller, counterbalancing platform on the opposite side. Oblong sails were hung from 2 masts stepped roughly amidships, the forward mast taller; each steadied by a mast shore and 2 stays. Foresail overlapped the after sail by more than half its width. Sails boomed at the foot with the heel of the boom forked against the mast. Steered with a paddle. Length ca. 17m.
Spelling variant: **úxe**

uchi-kai-bune *Japan:* Early **rowing boat★** (*kai* meaning oars). In the 16th century, these boats were oval-shaped naval vessels. Later boats, rowed with 6-8 oars, supported naval craft. In the late 19th century, the **uchi-kai-bune** towed **junks★** in a harbor. Lengths 6-9m.

ueserius See **huissier**

Ufahrplättel, Uferplättel See **Plätte-2**

uffer See **huissier**

ugalawa See **ngalawa**

Uganda canoe See **sesse**

uiser, uisser, uissier, uissiere See **huissier**

uitbijten See **ice breaker**

uitlegger See **guard ship, hoy-1**

uitleggergiek See **wherry-2**

uixer See **huissier**

ukae-bune See **ukai-bune**

ukai-bune *Japan:* Long, narrow, open boat used in fresh-water fishing with cormorants (*ukai*). Tame cormorants, tied to ropes, seek fish for their owners, generally at night; procedure dates to more than 1,000 years ago. Early boats were dugouts; later plank-built with sharp bow; stern square with a long, overhanging platform on which the cormorants ride. Two men manage the cormorants and 2 maneuver the boat with long oars. Length to ca. 13m, beam 1.3m, depth 0.5m.
Spelling variant: **ukae-bune**. Note also **lu ci chuan**.

ula chúi, ulachuwi See **piragua-2**

ulag, ulak See **ulakh**

ulakh *Bangladesh/India, NE:* Cargo and passenger boat of the middle Ganges River basin; still used. Clinker- or carvel-built; sides rounded; bow long, pointed, and overhanging; stern higher than the bow. Partly or wholly decked; large house may occupy most of the boat; protective awning amidships on the cargo

ulakh

boats. Large, triangular, balanced rudder suspended by ropes on the port quarter near the sternpost. Superstructure aft for the helmsman. Rowed, poled, or set a square sail to a pivoting mast stepped roughly amidships. Early boats used as many as 20 oarsmen, rowed from beneath the awning. Crew generally 6-12. Reported lengths 7.9-10.9m; e.g., length 7.9m, beam 4.27m, depth 1.22m. Other recorded names: **baggage boat**, **hooluck**, **hoolyck**, **oloako**, **olocko**, **oola(c)k**, **oolank**, **ulag**, **ulak**, **ulānk**, **ulaoko**, **willock**, **wol(l)ack**, **woolock**

ulānk See **ulakh**

ulanowski galar See **galar**

ulaoko See **ulakh**

ulatoka *Fiji, central Pacific:* **1.** A **raft**★ in which 2 shaped logs were joined by crossed poles or by a raised platform. Transported heavy loads across lagoons and on rivers. Those used for fishing employed a sail, enabling them to drift near fish. One log generally shorter than the other. Name variant: **bakanawa**

2. Single-outrigger craft of Viti Levu. Hull **canoe**★-shaped but not excavated. Three booms attached to both the short float and the hull by pairs of stanchions. A light platform covered the hull portion. Triangular sail set to a forward-raking mast; tacked to the bow end; boomed at foot. Mast stayed to float end of the central boom.

3. Variety of toy **canoe** that uses 2 crossed booms and 2 parallel booms to connect the 2 hulls.

ulaXtaX, ullaXtadaq, ullaxtaq See **kayak-9**

Ulmer Ordinari See **Ordinari**

Ulmer Plätte See **Ordinari, Plätte-1**

Ulmer Schachtel, Ulmer Schachteln, Ulmer Schiff See **Ordinari**

ulu See **cayuco-5**

uluchuwi See **piragua-2**

ulumola See **cayuco-5**

umak See **umiak-1**

umbrella boat See **Yorkshire keel**

umiahaluraq See **umiak-4**

umiak **1.** Skin-covered, open boat employed by Eskimos (Inuit) from Far Eastern Siberia to Greenland as an all-purpose transport craft; used especially for whaling. Construction details varied and size was usually dictated by available materials and intended use. Wooden framework covered with skins of walrus or bearded seal; frame often of driftwood. Western **umiaks** were paddled only, while in the east, they were sometimes rowed and occasionally sailed. Ranged in length from 3-12m, mostly 6-9m; beam ca. one-third. Other recorded names: **an·giar·**, **annisaq, domik, family canoe, omenak, oome'ak, oomia(c)k, ooniak, ouimiack, oumiak, umak, umiaq, umiavik, umjak, umyak, ung'yet, uomiak, yuniak**. Note also **baidara, ga'twaat**.

2. *Canada:* It is probable that in prehistoric times, the **umiak** was used all across the north coast, but explorers and settlers reported them only from the Mackenzie Delta east to Baffin Island, Hudson Strait, the southern coast of Hudson Bay, and Labrador. Early travelers called them **luggage** or **lug boats**★. Those in the west followed the general lines of the northern Alaskan **umiak**. Bottom flattened, stringer along bilges. Hudson Strait boats had vertical stem and sternpost that slotted into the keelson, which was narrower along the central part of the boat than at the ends. On the Labrador coast, the stem and sternpost were lashed to a straight keelson. Sides flared; side battens stopped short of the stem and sternpost. Gunwale pieces extended to the edge of the wide headboards at each end; lashed on to the top of the gunwale were pieces of wood into which rowing notches were cut; usually 4 short oars secured by thong loops. The dehaired sealskin covering, put on green, became taut on drying; skin laced to the battens; skins removed in winter and stored. Steered with an oar principally, but sometimes with a rudder. The Hudson Bay **umiak** set a square sail (originally of seal intestines, later of cotton) to a mast stepped in the bow; Labrador boats not generally sailed. Size varied with available materials and size of the family, but ranged from 4.5-18.2m; small Hudson Strait boat reported as 7.9m long, 1.74m wide, and 0.57m deep.

3. *Greenland (Kâlatdlit-Nunât):* Used principally in seasonal migrations and made long coastal trips accompanied by men in **kayaks**★. Extinct. Rowed by the women, hence called a **konebåd** or **konebåt** or **woman's boat**; men rowed while whale hunting; a man steered on the west coast, a woman on the east coast. Pointed, mildly raked, concave ends; gunwales extended beyond the ends, almost touching; bottom flat with slight rocker or hog; slightly flared sides. Floor timbers set on edge to form keel and chine stringers, creating an arch on the underside; side battens passed through the risers; frames of driftwood lashed and pegged on older boats; later with pegs and iron fastenings; framing generally heavier than the Alaskan **umiak**. Covered with skins of harp, hooded, or bearded seals. Rowed by 4-6, each pulling a single oar. Oars usually had oval blades, the longer oars used by the women; oar passed through 2 loops attached to the inner gunwale; loom thicker in the middle to prevent the oar from sliding out. Might set a square gutskin sail in West Greenland; later a spritsail of cloth; rarely sailed in East Greenland. Reported lengths 7-12m, early boats reported to 18m; e.g., length 8m, width 1.6m, depth 0.56m. Other recorded names: **aaddaarit** (in East Greenland); **umiaq angisooq** (ca. 9m); **umiaq mikisoq** (ca. 6m); **umiarujutaq** (ca. 10m); **women's boat**. Further reading: H. C. Petersen, *Skinboats of Greenland* (Roskilde: Viking Ship Museum, 1986), 117-197.

4. *United States, Alaska:* Vary in form, especially the ends. Those of the Aleut of southern Alaska are directly related to the Russian **baidara*** and are so called in this area; the northern **umiak** is akin to those of northern Canada and Greenland. In all areas, covered with de-haired walrus skins from the less-scarred females or with sealskins, using up to 50 skins. All types mostly rowed or paddled (by 6-8), but a lugtype or triangular sail sometimes employed; early sails of seal stomachs, caribou skin, or grass matting. Early masts might be stepped into the lower jawbone of a walrus; stayed fore-and-aft with thongs of hide. Those used on rivers were tracked upstream from shore, using 4-6 dogs. Outboard motors now common. Reported lengths 4.6-15.2m; e.g., length 10.7m, beam 2.4m, depth 1.2m. The Aleut boat had square ends, one of which turned up sharply; rounded bottom; frame of driftwood, or at times of whale ribs, fastened with seal thongs or whale sinews. Some raised skin "weatherboards" in rough seas and inflated skins might be lashed alongside to increase flotation. The **umiak** of St. Lawrence Island in the Bering Sea was flat-bottomed with straight, flaring sides until ca. 1860. Eskimos used acquired **whaleboats*** from this time until ca. 1930, when **whaleboat** sources dried up; since then, the islanders have built **umiaks** with steam-bent frames and round bottoms. Sharp cutwater on both types; gunwales extend beyond stem and sternpost. The later boats have a keel under the skin covering, but outside there is a false keel usually shod with a bone or ivory runner. Present boats have considerable deadrise and rounded sides. Frames, external and internal stringers, and thwarts of oak or hickory secured from Nome; keel of driftwood; stem and sternpost of suitable tree roots. Skin covering made waterproof by application of animal fat or commercial paint. Now mainly propelled by an outboard motor set into a well amidships or on the stern. Early boats steered with a paddle; now by rudder. The northern **umiak** has sharp ends with the gunwales extending beyond the stem and sternpost; sides markedly flared; bottom flat with an inner keel, sometimes of walrus ivory; sheer sweeps up at the bow. Steered with a paddle. A recent innovation along the north coast is the small, safe **umiahaluraq**, which is replacing the **retrieval kayak** (see **kayak-7**). Other recorded names: St. Lawrence Island: **angyapik** (pl. **angyapiget**) originally referred to the flat-bottom boat, now to the rib-bent boat; Aleut: **irilar, nidiliq, nigilag**; Tanaina: **wádi**; Nunivak: **uṇ-i-yŭh**. Further

reading: Stephen R. Braund, *The Skin Boats of Saint Lawrence Island, Alaska* (Seattle: University of Seattle Press, 1988). Note also **angyaq**.

umiaq See **umiak-1**

umiaq angisooq, umiaq mikisoq See **umiak-3**

umiardjuk See **Peterhead boat-1**

umiarujutaq See **umiak-3**

umiavik, umjak, umyak See **umiak-1**

una boat *United Kingdom:* Pleasure boat descended from the American **catboat*** *Una,* which was taken to England in the mid-19th century. Gaff sail hoisted by a single halyard and trimmed by a single sheet. Note also **Bubfisch boot**.

una rua See **vaka katea**

Unfallboot See **accident boat**

ungalawa See **ngalawa**

ung'yet See **umiak-1**

unité de pêche See **catcher vessel**

uṇ-i-yŭh See **umiak-4**

Unterplätte See **Plätte-1**

untra See **ontro**

untru See **luntru, ontro**

untzi See **barco-1**

unua, unuku See **waka unua**

unu rua See **vaka katea**

uomiak See **umiak-1**

upland boat *Canada, E:* Reported from the Moose River in central Ontario in the late 18th century. Carried goods to fur-trading posts. See also **mountain boat-1a**.

Upper Bay canoe See **Chesapeake Bay log canoe-3**

upper laker See **laker-1**

Upper Severn trow See **trow-1**

up-river flat See **Mersey flat**

up-river trow See **barge-8**

urca 1. *Ireland:* 16th-century Spaniards arriving on the west coast used small boats called **urcas**; rigged with a leg-of-mutton sail.

2. *Spain:* **a.** A lightly armed vessel of the 16th century that transported military stores, chiefly in the Mediterranean. Term also used by the Portuguese. **b.** An armed **flyboat*** that traded along the Spanish coast during the 17th-18th centuries; also used as an **advice boat*** attached to a **fleet***. Flat floors, high stern, wide buttocks. Might be square- or lateen-rigged. To 300t. Other recorded names: **hurca, orca; urche** (Ital. pl.)

Further reference: **howker**

urche See **urca-2**

ür çifte piyade See **piyade**

Urfahrfarm See **Farm**

Urker botter See **botter**

urque See **howker**

'uśārī, usario, usarius, uscerii, uscerium, uscerius, uscheri, uscheria, uscherius, usciera See **huisser**

usciere *Italy:* One of the **barges*** that form the quadrangle of boats in the tunny fishing operation. See also **huissier**.

uscieri, usciero, usiae, usicherius See **huissier**

usiko See **kirkovene**

usiyat See **kayak-4**

ussaria, usscher, usser, usseri, usseria, usserie, usserius, ussier, usuraria, usuriae See **huissier**

utase-ami gyosen *Japan:* **Fishing boat★** that works with a *utase-ami* (trawl net), drifting broadside. One type, found in Ise and Tokyo Bays and the Inland Sea, is plank-built with sharp, plumb bow and shallow, square, overhanging stern. Wide side planks extend

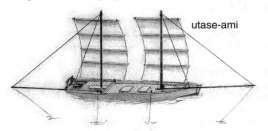

utase-ami

beyond the stern; vertical transom; hard chines; plank keel; bottom may be slightly lower at the bow to facilitate drifting. Decked; low bulwarks; slightly raised quarter-deck with shallow standing room. Deep rudder worked with a short tiller; crutch at stern. Steps 2-3 masts, setting battened lugsails while drifting; engines used when traveling to the fishing grounds. Crew of 3-7. Length 6m, beam 1.22m; 3-15 gt. Other recorded names: **broadside sailing boat, utase-bune**

utase-bune See **utase-ami gyosen**

Utrechtsche praam See **Utrechtse praam**

Utrechtse praam *Netherlands, central:* Slender cargo vessel of the Kromme Rijn and Vecht Rivers in Utrecht Province. Clinker-planked with wide strakes; flat bottom; hard chines; flaring, parallel sides; low sheer. Sharp ends; straight, strongly raked stem and sternpost. Open hold; decked at ends. Outboard rudder follows rake of the sternpost, creating a wide blade below the waterline; tiller. Length 14m, beam 2.15m. Spelling variant: **Utrechtsche praam**

Utrecht ship See **hulk-5**

'uwaisiyyah See **bedan-1**

úxe See **uche-1**

uxel, uxer, uxerii, uxier, uxorius See **huissier**

V

va See **va'a, wa-2**

va'a *Pacific Ocean:* One of several spellings used throughout the area for a **canoe***; sometimes **va**. May refer to single- or double-**outrigger canoes*** or to double **canoes**. Usually a dugout hull. Note also **vaka-1, vaka-2a, vaka-3, wa, waka**. Further reference: **pu hoe**

va'a alo *Samoa, central Pacific:* Fast single-**outrigger canoe*** used in catching bonito and shark beyond the reefs. Mainly plank-built of short, thin lengths, usually of breadfruit; some later **canoes*** built as lightweight dugouts. Strong rocker to the keel piece; keel ends shaped to hold the end pieces. Solid bow piece sharp and strongly concave; stern piece similar but much shorter. Assembled hull components lashed through paired holes and around the flanges on the inside of the hull; smooth outside; strong sheer when completed; caulked with rotted breadfruit. Cover pieces at ends decorated with lines of shells. Two booms, lashed across the wide, flat gunwales, extend to the float, which is positioned so that the forward end is nearly opposite the bow; after end terminates just abaft the connective. A central boom braces the gunwales and serves as a seat but does not extend to the float. Float truncated at the after end, sharp forward. Two pairs of divergent stanchions and lashings connect float and booms. A branch lashed vertically to the outer end of the forward boom supports the fishing pole. Some larger **canoes** set a V-shaped sail or a spritsail. Crew of 2 paddlers and a fisherman. Reported lengths 7.5-18m, the smaller sizes more common; e.g., length 7.5m, beam 0.3m, depth 0.45m. Other recorded names: **alaalafaga, bonito canoe, va'a-alu-atu**. Further reading: Peter H. Buck, *Samoan Material Culture*, Bulletin 75 (Honolulu: Bernice P. Bishop Museum, 1930), 380-404.

va'a-alu-atu See **va'a alo**

vaa hauua, vaa houua See **vaka tou uá**

va'ai tama'i See **pahi tama'i**

va'a katea See **vaka katea**

va'a motu *Society Islands, southeastern Pacific:* Tahitian single-**outrigger canoe*** used for interisland travel. Early boats accompanied warring parties, providing transportation and carrying the dead home. Plank-extended dugout hull, sometimes in sections, sewn end-to-end; rounded bottom; truncated stern swept up strongly. Sharp, concave cutwater; squared coverboard extended beyond the bow cutwater, often with low washboard at after end; sometimes hull raised by washstrakes. Long, slender float on port side of hull connected by 2 booms. Foreboom horizontal and attached to the float by 2 pairs of crossed stanchions; the flexible stern boom curved down and lashed directly to the float. A balance board generally extended out the outrigger side as well as the starboard side. Stepped 1, occasionally 2, portable pole masts in forward half; stayed forward, to outrigger boom, and to the balance board. So-called "crab claw" sail of pandanus leaves had a long boom that curved up to run parallel to and beyond the mast. Frequently paddled. Reported lengths 9.8-12.2m.

va'a poti See **vaka poti**

vaartuig voor zegenvisserij See **seine boat-1**

vaca See **vaka-6**

vadeka *Sweden, SW:* Open **fishing boat*** that works a seine net (*vad*) in Bohuslan coastal waters. Of the **eka*** type, having a small bow transom, but the **vadeka** has a flat bottom with bilge keels. Clinker-planked with 3-4 pegged strakes; bottom planked fore-and-aft, with rocker at each end, especially at the bow. Three-piece frames; some have partly ceiled hull; many have a heavy bulkhead in forward third. Marked sheer. Wooden roller for the net common. Some use a lamp, hung from a short post, for night fishing. Rowed with 2 oars between double tholepins. Reported lengths 4-9m; e.g., length 7.6m, beam 2m, depth 0.6m. Other recorded names: **hogdaling, hogdalseka**

va-eke See **eke-2**

vængebaad See **skyssbåt**

va-et-vient See **ferryboat-1**

va fatin, va fedul See **wa fötyn**

vag See **bag**

vaga *Papua New Guinea, E:* Single-**outrigger canoe*** of the Nukumanu Islands, administered by Papua New Guinea. Basal dugout hull with pieces added on by sewing. Bottom has rocker; small, blunt ends. Small breakwater/coverboard at each end. Narrow washstrakes. Thwarts near the ends. Three to 5 booms extend to the V-shaped connectives; partly covered by stringers. Long, slender float. Bent rod extends over or beneath the booms and is lashed to the float. Other recorded names: **vak***, **vaka***. See also **waga-2a**.

väge See **wache**

vahan *India, NW:* **1.** One of the Gujariti terms for **boat***.
2. Motorized bulk cargo vessel that trades along the Indian coast; some go to Persian (Arabian) Gulf ports. Also engages in smuggling. Built mainly in Mandvi. Sharp-ended. Reported tonnages 250-365.
3. The fishing **vahans** catch various types of fish in several locations, depending on the season. Carvel planking rabbetted. Square, raking stern; raking bow carved with bird or animal head. Keel; deep hull. Fore- and stern decks; temporary bamboo poles increase freeboard. Massive rudder. Steps a single mast a little forward of amidships, setting a quadrilateral, lateen-type sail with a short luff. Crew of 8. Reported lengths 9.8-13.7m, widths 3-3.7m, depths 1.8-2.3m, draft 1-1.8m.

vahka See **báka**

vaisseau See **ship**

vaisseau amiral, vaisseau commandant See **flagship**

vaisseau de charge See **store ship**

vaisseau de garde See **guard ship**

vaisseau de guerre See **man-of-war**

vaisseau long See **long ship**

vaisseau marchand See **merchantman**

vaisseau négrier See **slaver-1**

vaixell See **barco-1, buque**

vaixell mercant See **merchantman**

vak *Fiji Islands, central Pacific:* Single-**outrigger canoe*** of the Rotuma group, north of the main islands. Early type had a sharp-ended hull, the ends covered and lined with shells. Hull planks sewn together on the inside; slight sheer; 4 thwarts. Three unevenly spaced, straight booms crossed the hull and extended to the slender float; attached to float by 2 pairs of oblique stanchions and a vertical support. Reported lengths 5.84-13m; smallest beam 0.38m. More recent **vaks** had a simple dugout hull with sharp, tapered ends; rounded bottom; sides have slight tumble home; bottom rose to the ends; flat sheer. Small mooring cleat at one end. Two outrigger booms crossed the hull, lashed through 2 holes in the hull on each side. Single-piece booms angled down at a natural crook to insert directly into the float; bamboo stringer at outer end of booms rested on natural knobs. Sharp-ended float. Spelling variant: **vaka***. See also **vaga**.

vaka   **1.** *Pacific Ocean:* General term for a single- or double-**outrigger canoe*** or a double **canoe***. Numerous derivatives occur, such as **báka***, **va'a***, **wa'a***, **waga***, **waka***, **waqa***, **war***. In some places, the word has come to describe precise craft, a few of which are described below.

   2. *Cook Islands, central Pacific:* **a.** General term for an **outrigger canoe**; sometimes spelled **va'a** or **waka**. A few local types follow. **b.** On Aitutaki and Rarotonga in the southern group, **canoes** are divided according to the number of pieces that comprise the hull: a **vaka tavai** is made from a single hewn log; the **vaka tutaki tumu** is made in 2 pieces, the bow and stern halves lashed together; the **vaka tamoe** has 2 end pieces and a central section; hole drilled through the sections, sewn together, and caulking material inserted. Planks, sewn on, raise the sides. A

vaka-2b

flat piece may be added to the sharp bow to extend it forward; on some, a similar projection is at the stern. Early travelers reported that the stern on the Aitutaki **canoes** turned up sharply. Thwarts serve as braces for the sides, as seats, and as mast steps. Two booms, extending from near the bow and stern, connect the long float. Type of attachment to the float varies: Y-shaped pegs stuck into the float, pairs of crossed sticks, or a forked boom with one "tine" pegged into the float. Paddle blade pointed; knobbed grip. Also poled. Small, inshore **canoes** step 1 mast; seagoing **canoes** might use 2; on the single-masted **canoes**, the mast is shifted to the opposite end when tacking. Sails were of woven pandanus strips, generally a boomed, standing lugsail or occasionally an inverted triangle. Reported lengths 4-8.8m, widths 0.25-0.43m, depths 0.2-0.5m. **c.** At Pukapuka in the Northern Cook Islands, 2 types of **vaka** have been

described: The small single-**outrigger canoe** for lagoon fishing has a U-shaped dugout hull; bow projects forward as a slender, horizontal cone; slight sheer at stern, ending in a truncated knob. Deep washstrakes sewn on, the outboard side higher; at the bow and stern, cover pieces are sewn on to the ends of the washstrakes; shallow breakwaters enclose the ends of the cockpit. Two booms, lashed across the top of the washstrakes, extend to the short float; booms connect to the float beneath opposing pairs of sticks. Steered with a paddle. Employs a single triangular sail set to a mast stepped in a circular boss, enabling the mast to rake forward at different angles. The early sail had a boom as long as the mast and was often carried apex down; later a leg-of-mutton type adopted. Reported lengths 5.4-7.2m; e.g., length 7.1m, beam 0.38m. A large, 2-masted **vaka** had a similar hull but required 6 booms to secure the float. Transported copra in the lagoon; extinct by the 1930s. The connectives to the float were further strengthened by a light withe from the boom to one of the crossed sticks and by a stringer, lashed to the outer ends of 6 pseudo-booms, that ran fore-and-aft midway between the hull and the float. The forward mast was stepped well forward, the after mast just abaft amidships. Leg-of-mutton sails. Length ca. 18.2m, cap. 1t. Further reading: Gordon Macgregor, *Notes on the Ethnology of Pukapuka*, Occasional Papers, 11/6 (Honolulu: Bernice P. Bishop Museum, 1935), 34-41. **d.** At Manihiki Island in the Northern Cook Islands to the north of the main chain, the **vaka** was a handsome **outrigger canoe** elaborately inlaid with mother-of-pearl. A long, sharp stem piece and a fin-like stern piece gave the hull the appearance of a fish. Dugout hull sometimes in 3 pieces butted end-to-end and sewn together. Bottom flattened in cross section amidships, becoming V-shaped at the ends; shallow forefoot at the bow; long overhang at the stern. End pieces scarfed and sewn to the dugout hull; seat-like decking at each end. Washstrakes fitted by means of flanges that projected inward across the gunwale and downward along the side; battened on the inside. Might use a woven weatherscreen above the washstrake. Small **canoes** had 2 straight outrigger booms; large craft had 3; connected to the sharp-ended float by 4 stanchions. Steered with a paddle. Might step 2 short, forward-raking masts. Lateen-type sails boomed at the lower edge; yard and boom tacked to a crosspiece at the bow. Small **canoes** ca. 4.5m long and 0.3m wide; large craft 8.8m long, 0.36m wide, and 0.51m deep, including the washstrake. Spelling variant: **waka**. Note also **vaka taurua**.

Further reading: Peter H. Buck, *The Material Culture of the Cook Islands*, Memoirs of the Board of Ethnological Research, vol. 1 (New Plymouth, N.Z.: 1927).

   3. *Marquesas Islands, eastern Pacific:* Generic term for a **canoe**. Also spelled **va'a** or **vaa**. Three described under this generic term follow: **a.** The early voyaging **vaka** was a single-outrigger craft constructed from a dugout base with freeboard raised by deep washstrakes, often carved. Stern swept up to a tall, ornamented endpost; bow lower, sometimes in the form of the head of a bird or animal. Two straight, widely spaced outrigger booms crossed to a slender, sharp-ended float; booms and float secured by divergent stick connectives. Used a triangular mat sail, apex down. **b.** The **vaka** of Nuku Hiva was a **dugout canoe*** with a low washstrake lashed on. Blunt bow elongated and horizontal; slender stern rose at ca. 45° from the waterline. Hull round in cross section; bottom rounded up toward the stern to merge with the end piece. Helmsman sat just forward of the stern extension on a raised seat, steering with a paddle. Three light booms crossed atop the gunwales and extended out both sides; on the side away from the outrigger, the booms turned up slightly. Slender float, as long as the hull, connected to the booms by single or double vertical stanchions. Paddled by 4 men seated on thwarts. Reported lengths 5-10.2m; e.g., length 10.2m, beam 0.76m, depth 0.66m. **c.** A modern type is small and has a simple dugout hull to which narrow washstrakes are often added, clinker-fashion. At the ends, the strakes are nailed together without benefit of stem or sternpost. U-shaped in cross section; some have short end decks. Two widely spaced outrigger booms cross to a slender, sharp-ended float. Booms and float connected by a narrow plank that slots into the float, each boom passing through a hole in the plank. Sets a spritsail. Reported lengths 3.7-5.5m, widths and depths 0.31-0.46m.

4. *Solomon Islands, western Pacific:* General term for a **boat*** in a number of the islands. On New Georgia in the central part of the chain, **vaka** refers to a nonnative vessel. Some specific types follow: **a.** Two types are used at Rennell Island in the southeastern part of the archipelago: one at sea, the other on the interior lake. The seagoing **canoe** has a slender, double-ended dugout hull; concave cutwater, ending at the top in a slightly elongated point; gunwale stringers, lashed atop transverse poles, run full length. Outrigger float, nearly as long as the hull, attached by 2-3 light booms. Booms lashed atop gunwale stringers and connect to float beneath 4 pairs of sticks, supplemented by 2 single sticks, or by 2 pairs of crossed sticks. Paddled or poled. On the lake **canoe**, a platform extends out of both sides of the hull, lying atop the booms on the outrigger side; otherwise similar to the seagoing **canoe**. This **canoe** also sails, stepping a single mast amidships, generally raked forward. Two types of sails reported: one is pear-shaped and loosely attached to a yard and boom; the other is an open "V" with a curved yard and a straight boom; both hang from approximately the middle of the yard with the point tacked close to the bow. Sail of woven pandanus palm. **b.** The Tauu (Matlock) Islands in the northwest used both a paddling and a sailing outrigger **vaka**. Reported details vary, but these **canoes** had a fairly broad dugout hull with strong bottom rocker. Sides raised by washstrakes; early boats had elaborately carved end pieces that projected horizontally. Three to 5 booms,

strengthened by a network of stringers and spars, extended to the relatively short float; booms lashed to paired sticks that diverged from the float. On the larger **canoes**, a platform was built outboard opposite the outrigger. Single forward-raking mast stepped amidships. Boomed, V-shaped, cloth sail hung with point tacked near the bow. Sailing **canoes** reported as 12-14m long; largest ca. 1.5m deep. Spelling variant: **waka**. **c.** At Tikopia, an isolated island to the southeast of the main archipelago, the **vaka** is a small single-**outrigger canoe**. Rounded dugout hull; bottom rocker; slight residual keel. Elongated, overhanging ends; the stern truncated vertically, the bow having a thin, trapezoidal form; solid ends flattened on top and often decorated. Cockpit enclosed by washstrakes and washboards that are sewn on. Three to 5 booms cross from atop the gunwales to the long, pointed float; each secured by 3 pairs of crossed stanchions; float set farther back from the bow than the stern. Length 7m, maximum beam 0.5m, opening at top 0.33-0.38m, depth 0.43m.

5. *Tokelau Islands, eastern Pacific:* Small single-**outrigger canoe** used mainly in lagoons for fishing and carrying supplies. Dugout hull, sometimes in multiple lengths, sewn together; washstrake, usually in several pieces, raised each side; the lower edge irregular to fit the top of the uneven dugout hull; residual transverse ridges sometimes strengthened hull. Rounded bottom; sides curved or vertical; cutwater near-vertical; stern tapered on the 4 sides, terminating in a truncated point. Coverboards lashed on at each end, terminating inboard by breakwaters; stern breakwater notched to hold a bonito fishing rod. Coverboards generally decorated with a longitudinal row of knobs into which shells are imbedded. Thwarts rest on gunwales. Outrigger set from the port side; slender, pointed float attached by 3-6 booms lashed to the gunwales; 2 fore-and-aft stringers laid atop booms at the float end. Outside booms connected to float by 2 pairs of divergent stanchions; the shorter inner booms connected by single inward-leaning stanchions. One variety used single stanchions lashed to both the inner and outer stringer. Platform occasionally laid on the booms to carry cargo. Employed narrow-bladed paddles. Sometimes sailed, stepping a single forward-raking mast to which a triangular sail was set, lateen-fashion; lower edge boomed; forward part tacked near the bow. Reported lengths 7-11m.

6. *Tonga, central Pacific:* Term applied originally to a pre-17th-century seagoing **canoe** about which little is known. A later **vaka**, also known as a **hamatafua**, was used until the 1880s. Deep hull, either plank-built or a dugout; sharp ends; ribs lashed to residual lugs along the sides. Three to 7 booms attached to the slender float by means of paired divergent stanchions. Platform built over the hull, part of the outrigger booms, and out the lee side; supplemental booms helped support the platform. One or 2 hatches in the hull area. Steered with an oar attached to a triangular piece on the lee end of the platform. The single mast could be raked in either direction. Probably set a triangular sail with apex down. Sculled in calms. Reported lengths 12-20m. Other recorded names: **ha'matefoo'a**, **hama te fua**, **vaca**, **vaka hama tafua**, **vakka**

7. *Tuamotu, eastern Pacific:* One of the terms for **canoe**, although sometimes limited to one with a single outrigger or to one with a single mast. Term may also designate a **raft***. Specifics vary somewhat from island to island. **a.** The single-outrigger **vaka** of Paraoa, one of the central islands, has been described as a plank-extended dugout with the V-shaped end pieces, planks, and gunwales sewn on. Larger interisland **canoes** might have the keel piece in several sections. The small, light, bonito-fishing **canoe** had a rounded bottom; the depth of the dugout part and strakes nearly equal. Traveling **canoes** had a wide bottom, and the sides flared outward. Long, thin float connected by 2 booms, the outer ends of which forked downward to pierce the float. Brightly painted. Sometimes sailed using a pandanus-leaf sail. Small canoe ca. 5m long. Name variant: **aveka**. Further reading: H. Bodin, "Quelques Souvenirs des Tuamotu. Les Pirogues Cousues des Îles de Corail," *Bulletin de la Société des Études Oceaniennes* V/1142 (1932), 1-9. **b.** On Tatakoto on the eastern fringe of the archipelago, numerous multipiece strakes were sewn on to a multipiece keel. Stem raked up to a pointed bow; triangular sternpost curved up and extended above the gunwale; pierced at the top. Two stout, bowed struts, attached to each side of the sternpost and extended forward to a rear seat, served as a grip in launching and landing. Two widely spaced booms connected to the long, squared float by a forked withe lashed to each boom; outrigger to starboard. Reported lengths 4.6-7.8m. Further reading: Kenneth P. Emory, *Material Culture of the Tuamotu Archipelago*, Pacific Anthropological Records 22 (Honolulu: Bernice P. Bishop Museum, 1975).

Further references: **báka**, **kamia**, **vaga**

vaka hama tafua See **vaka-6**

vaka heke fa *Niue Island, central Pacific:* Four-man fishing **canoe***. Dugout hull; washstrakes and end decking sewn on; slender, elongated ends taper on all sides; rounded bottom. Hull spread with curved pieces lashed to the 3 booms, which also serve as thwarts; stringers cross atop the booms above the washstrakes. Sharp-ended, cylindrical float attached by 2 pairs of oblique stanchions and a single vertical one. Paddled using lanceolate-bladed paddles. Length 7.6m, beam 0.4m, depths 0.46-0.6m.

vaka katea *Cook Islands, central Pacific:* Double **canoe*** of the southern islands used for catching flying fish and for interisland transportation. Dugout hulls of unequal length joined with the bows even or the smaller hull slightly behind. Hulls generally more than one piece; strengthened by ribs, some residual in the dugout itself. Rounded bottoms with strong tumble home; ends curved up, the bows slightly above the gunwale and the sterns quite tall, a piece having been added to the hull. Coverboards at each end; gunwale pieces added; sometimes washstrakes.

Hulls joined by 3 booms that project outboard on either side ca. 76cm; outboard booms might be secured by stringers; platform of poles between the hulls or across both hulls. Generally rowed; double tholepins set into the stringers. Early boats sailed; mast stepped in forward part of the platform; probably V-shaped mat sail. Length of longer, starboard hull averaged 8.2m, the port hull being as much as 25% shorter. Other recorded names: **una rua**, **unu rua**, **va'a katea**, **vaka purua**, **vaka tirua**

vaka pai manu *Solomon Islands, western Pacific:* Small **outrigger canoe*** of Anuta, a tiny island to the east of the main group. Dugout base roughed out in the bush and finished on the beach. Deep "V" in cross section; often asymmetrical; narrow, residual keel. Supplemental strake raises each side; lashed on. Horizontal splash rail added to top of gunwale. Bottom curves up at the elongated, overhanging ends. Decked at the ends; ornamented with barbs. Vertical, decorative end pieces fashioned and lashed on, each end depicting a stylized head of a bird (the *manu*). Outrigger float almost as long as the **canoe***. Three to 7 booms cross the hull and extend out the port side; serve also as thwarts. Vertical wooden "pins" pegged into the float and lashed to the booms. Two stringers atop the booms provide some rigidity. Mast stepped onto the port bow boom, stayed to starboard side. Early **canoes** had a wide, V-shaped pandanus sail. Now set a wide square sail to a vertical mast. Occasionally 2 sails set to a single mast; if 2-masted, both set square sails. Paddles long and heavy with elongated, pointed blades. Lengths to 9.7m, beam 0.66m, depth 1.0m. Further reading: Richard Feinberg, *Polynesian Seafaring and Navigation: Ocean Travel in Anutan Culture and Society* (Kent, Ohio: Kent State University Press, 1988).

vaka poepoe See **báka póe-póe**

vaka poti *Marquesas Islands, eastern Pacific:* Plank-built single-**outrigger canoe*** of recent origin. Generally, strakes added clinker-fashion to a keel piece that is convex on the outside and channeled within; wide "V" in cross section; a few light frames inserted. Some formed from a round-bottomed dugout to which a wide washstrake is added. Double-ended; slightly curved, raked stem and sternpost. Decked at ends; 3 thwarts inserted; midline rudder. Two widely spaced, straight booms extend to a long, pointed float. Booms inserted through a hole in vertical or inward-raking planks, which in turn are slotted into the float and bound together; booms lashed atop the gunwales. When sailed, a light mast steps through the forward thwart. Sets a boomed spritsail or a leg-of-mutton sail and sometimes a small jib. Sprit supported by a line from the mast that fits to a notch at the foot of the sprit. Reported lengths 6-8m, widths 0.6-0.9m, depth ca. 0.74m. Other recorded names: **poti vaka**, **va'a poti**. Note also **poti**.

vaka purua See **vaka katea**

vaka taf'aga See **vaka tafaanga**

vaka tafaanga *Wallis and Futuna, central Pacific:* Single-**outrigger canoe**★ of Uvéa Island, the largest of this group lying between Fiji and Samoa. Basic hull a dugout onto which 1-2 strakes are lashed with sennit; lashing either entirely on the inside or run through to the outside; caulked with small sticks and smeared with a gum. Coverboards, originally with bosses on top, lashed to each end, the stern end sloping downward slightly. Two to 9 booms cross the hull to the long float; booms and float joined by straight, over-crossed sticks; generally 2 pairs. Float toes in slightly at the bow. One or 2 masts stepped through thwarts, stayed to end of boom on port side and to the midpoint of one of the booms on the outrigger side. Originally set mat sails of unknown type; some sails portrayed with a vertical sprit; later cloth spritsails. When paddled, uses paddles with elliptical blades. Length to ca. 14.6m. Other recorded names: **tafa'aga, vaka tafa'aga, waka takaaga**. Note also **tafa'anga**.

vaka tafua See **paopao-7**

vaka tamoe See **vaka-2b**

vaka taurua *Cook Islands, central Pacific:* Extinct double **canoe**★ of Manihiki, one of the northern islands. Dugout hulls, about the same size, constructed in several pieces, butted and sewn together. Each bow had a shallow forefoot raked upward in a straight line; sterns raked up more gently. Hollowed-out end pieces added, the bows terminating in a sharp point, the sterns truncated and scored with notches on top. Deep hull with tumble home; strong bottom rocker, with reverse rocker just abaft the forefoot. Washstrakes, set on flanges, flared out slightly; leaf weatherscreens also used. Hulls elaborately decorated with inlaid mother-of-pearl. Several stout booms connected the hulls that were set parallel, but the bow and stern were opposite so they could sail in either direction; some had a platform laid across the booms. Set 2 sails, probably triangular, apex down. Masts stepped in the same hull or in opposite hulls; one forward, the other aft. Steered with a paddle notched to fit over the boom on the quarter. Other recorded names: **waka taur(u)a**. Note also **vaka-2d**.

vaka tavai See **vaka-2b**

vaka tirua See **vaka katea**

vaka tohua See **vaka tou uá**

vaka tou uá *Marquesas Islands, eastern Pacific:* Extinct double **canoe**★ used for interisland travel, war, and probably migrations. Dugout hulls, of roughly the same length, joined by 3 stout beams; especially large **canoes** required butting 2 logs together; sides raised by washstrakes. Form of ends variously depicted: some projected horizontally at both ends, stern sweeping up to a lofty, stylized bird's head, or both ends curved up to tall end pieces. Some had a platform (*hou ua*) laid atop the booms; often used by warriors. Sailed and paddled. Single V-shaped mat sail set to a mast stepped on forward crossbeam. Length at least 12m. Other recorded names: **hou uá, vaa hauua, vaa houua, vaka tohua**

vaka tutaki tumu See **vaka-2b**

vakka See **vaka-6**

valboeiro *Portugal, N:* Boat of the lower Douro River that is mainly a cargo craft (**barco de frete, barco de toucinheiro**), but may serve as a **ferry**★ (**barca de passagem**) and as a **fishing boat**★ (**saveiro**★) for shad, on both the river and the nearby sea. Most built at Avintes, but name derived from Valbom, where they

valboeiro

congregate. At Avintes, those similar to the **saveiro**, that carry passengers and merchandise, are crewed by women and are called **barcos das padeiras** or **barcos semanais**. Long, rising, tapering bow; stern more curved and lower; block stem and sternpost covered largely by planking; flat bottom with rocker toward the stern; no keel; deep forefoot; flared, curved sides; maximum beam forward of amidships. Clinker-planked; crenulated strake above the sheer strake creates a raised segment for the tholepin; most ribs rise to or above this strake. Short platforms at each end; those used as **ferries** are generally ceiled and have an awning. Rowed standing with 2-4 oars on each side. Steered with a rudder or sweep. On occasion, may set a square spritsail laced to a mast stepped well forward; sprit secured in upper third of the mast; sometimes another sail is spritted out forward from this mast. Crew of 1-3 on **fishing boats**, traditionally dressed. Cargo and **ferryboats**★ ca. 17m long, 3.45m wide, 1.2m deep; **fishing boats** 4-7.3m long; e.g., length 7.3m, width 1.75m, depth 0.67m.

vale See **vallam-1a**

valiya vallom See **vallam-1b**

vallam 1. *India, SW:* **a.** Term used along the coastal backwaters and rivers of the Malabar Coast for a locally produced **dugout canoe**★. Many exported to Persian (Arabian) Gulf countries and to East Africa (see **belem** and **houri**). Used for line fishing and transporting passengers and local produce. Similar, sharp, recurved ends, often distinctively carved; sides parallel; pseudo-ribs left when hull excavated; round bottom. Arched mat house or houses of bamboo and cadjan thatch on the larger boats; some can sleep 6-10 persons. Poled, rowed, or sets a spritsail. Those used in open waters may set a lateen-type sail. Reported range from 5.5m long, 1.07m wide, 0.62m deep to 13m long by 1.14m wide. The **chemmeen vallom** of Trivandrum District may spend as many as 8 days at sea. Two large sails employed on these dugouts. Other recorded names: **balão, balaum, ballam, ballong, bal(l)oon, ballum, baloa, bellum, vale, vallom, vallum, vellam, wallam, wallum; kochu-vallam, kochuvallom** (small **vallam** in Kerala). Note also **balon, kettuvallam. b.** The fishing **valloms** of the Alleppey coast are open, double-ended craft. Crescent-shaped hull; planks sewn with coir; preserved with fish oil. Outboard motor prevalent by the 1980s, increasing overall size. A large boat is a **valiya vallom**; when cut in two and modified to operate a trawl net, they become **muri valloms**. Medium-sized boats are **edatharam valloms**; the smallest are **dinkey valloms**.

2. *India, SE:* On the Tinnevelly coast, the dugout base, imported from the Malabar area, is expanded and the sides raised. Used mainly for fishing, pearling, and collecting coral stone used for building and burned for lime. Curved sternpost; straight stem with cutaway forefoot; rounded bottom; no keel; thwarts set low. Open. Large rudder extends well below the bottom; long tiller slotted over rudderhead. Large types plank-built along the same lines. The larger **vallams** set a short, wide lugsail to a mast stepped nearly amidships; largest may also carry a mizzen. Yard raised by a double pulley set in a square truck on the masthead. Largest crewed by 7-8 men. Reported lengths 8-12m; small sizes used for inshore fishing. Other recorded names: **ballam, boat-canoe***, **Parava vallam, Tuticorin vallam**

3. *Sri Lanka:* Fishing **dugout canoe** of the northern Tamils and east coast Muslims. Used mainly for shore seining with the *madel* net. Generally open, but may have a short deck at each end. Double-ended; rounded bottom; tumble home along the sides; ends vertical above the waterline, curved below; low washstrakes. When sailed, fitted with an outrigger that can be shifted from side to side. Steered by rudder. Motorized boats transom-sterned. Reported lengths 6-10.7m, widths 0.77-1.52m. A planked **vallam** is also used for fishing. Planking 3-4cm wide; frames 1.0cm square, spaced ca. 76cm apart. Now motorized. Reported lengths 9-10.7m, beam 1.5m, draft light 0.15m. Spelling variants: **balham, ballam, wallama** (pl. **wallam**)
Further reference: **beppu tōni**

vallom, vallum See **vallam-1a**
valörbåt See **hvalerbåt**
valsa, valssa See **balsa**
vanchi See **odam-3**
vañci See **manji, odam-3**
vanga See **wanga**
vangboot See **whale catcher**
vanji See **odam-3**
vanka *Micronesia, western Pacific:* **Outrigger canoe*** of Yap, an island of the western Carolines, constructed along European lines. Yap style outrigger unit, having 2 closely spaced, down-curving booms, each supported by 2 crutch-type connectives that peg directly into the short float. See also **waqa-1**.
var See **wa-2**
vāragam-oruwa See **varakan-oruwa**
varakan-oruwa *Sri Lanka:* 1. Large **fishing boat*** of the **oruwa*** type. Fishes offshore from the west coast with hook and lines, mainly for tuna. Double-ended dugout hull; deep, vertical washstrake sewn on. Bottom flat; sides flare and then are tumble home. Elongated, raked ends. Outrigger set to port; 2 stout booms curve upward initially, then downward to the cylindrical float. Double sprits diverge to support the tall, rectangular sail. Heavier sprit stepped in strop lashed to the midship boom; the 2nd sprit is lighter and steps

immediately forward of the same boom into a socket. Steered by a leeboard held by the helmsman's leg outside the hull; in strong winds, a tiller slots into a hole at the upper end of the leeboard. Crew of 4. Length to 10m. Other recorded names: **bala-oruwa; kachchana thoni** (Tamil); **monsoon canoe, vāragam-oruwa, warakan-oruwa**

2. Planked cargo boat. Planks sewn, fitted to a keel piece. Semi-circular deck aft, for the helmsman, extends beyond the gunwales; cargo hold roofed over. Rudder and tiller. Single mast abaft the cabin.

varangay See **barangay**
Varbm See **Farm**
varca See **barca**
vardacosta See **guard ship**
varino See **bateira ílhava**
varke See **barca, barkë-2, trap**
varke a véle de le kòzze *Italy, SE:* Lateen-rigged boat used in the cultivation of mussels (*cozze* or *kòzze*) in the area of Taranto. Open; vertical stem; keel; deep rudder. Lateen yard in 2 parts; sail tacked to stem. Note also **mussel boat**.
varkha See **barkë-2**
varkkas See **barakas**
varsity barge See **college barge**
vascelletto, vascelli, vascellino See **vascello-1**
vascello *Italy:* 1. Generic term for **ship***. Early reports indicate that they were rowed and sailed and might be naval or cargo vessels. Other recorded names: **vascelletto** and **vascellino** (dims.); **vascellum, vascellus, vascìedde, vasculum, vasella, vassello(to), vassellum, vassèlo**; pl. **vascelli**

2. In the Sicilian tuna fisheries, transports the nets and forms one end of the quadrangle during the kill; the similar **caporais*** is located at the opposite end. Bluff bow, plumb stem, square stern, flat bottom, grounding keels. Portable deck at the bow; waist divided into several compartments. Longitudinal bulkhead paralleling each side protects fishermen from the thrashing tuna; raised floor for the crew between the sides and the bulkhead. Freeboard increased by detachable washboards. Equipped with capstan in the bow for raising the net and moorings. Two masts, with booms, are stepped to assist in transferring the catch to other craft for transport to shore. Towed, having no means of self-propulsion. Reported lengths 12-26m; e.g., length 17m, beam 4.4m, depth 1.5m, draft loaded 3m. Other recorded names: **moana** (Tunisia); **scevo, sciere**. Note also **barcareccio, cabanella, musciara, rimorchio**.

vascello ammiraglio See **flagship**
vascello da guerra See **man-of-war**
vascellum, vascellus, vascìedde, vasculum See **vascello-1**
vašel See **ship**
vasella See **vascello-1**
vašelo, vašijo See **ship**
vašǫni See **fassone**
vassello, vasselloto, vassellum, vassèlo See **vascello-1**
vassoni See **fassone**
vastimento See **bastimento**
vatneskøyte See **skøyte-4**

vattai See **palagai kattu vattai, vattal**

vattal *Sri Lanka, N:* Open, inshore cargo vessel of the Tamils; extinct. Carvel-planked; low freeboard. Sharp, convex stem with fiddlehead ornament at the top; sharp stern; sternpost also convex. Brightly painted in blue or green. Single mast stepped just forward of amidships; 2-sheave block at the masthead; one for the main halyard, the other for the peak halyard. Originally set a square sail, then a short, wide lugsail. Beamy; shoal draft. Spelling variant: **vattai**. See also **schooner-4**.

V-bottom See **deadrise boat, skipjack-1**

V-bottom garvey See **garvey**

vedetta See **vedette**

vedette A French term applied mainly to a fast, decked, multipurpose, motorized boat. In English: **vedette boat** or **launch⋆**; in German: **Vedettenboot**; in Italian: **vedetta**. The **vedette-amiral** is the major **ship's boat⋆** of a naval vessel. A **vedette de surveillance** (or **lookout** or **patrol boat⋆**) checks on shipping, coastal activities, etc., while the **vedette de la douane** belongs to the customs service. The **vedette guarde-pêche** monitors fishing activities. Some fishing communities on the west coast of France use **vedettes** in the sardine fisheries (see **sardinier**), employing **doris⋆** for the actual fishing. **Vedettes** may serve as lighthouse or light buoy **tenders⋆**. A **vedette de croisière** (or **vedette habitable**) is a pleasure **cabin cruiser**. A **torpedo boat** is a **vedette porte-torpilles** or **vedette torpilleur**.

vedette-amiral See **barge-2, vedette**

vedette à moteur, vedette automobile See **motor boat-1**

vedette boat, vedette de croisière, vedette de la douane See **vedette**

vedette de l'amiral See **barge-2**

vedette de promenade See **day boat-1**

vedette de surveillance See **vedette**

vedette du commandant See **gig-1**

vedette guarde-pêche, vedette habitable, Vedettenboot See **vedette**

Vedettentschaike See **saique-1**

vedette porte-torpilles, vedette torpilleur See **vedette**

vedgaleas See **galeas-1**

vedhaxe See **haxe**

vee-bottom boat, vee-bottom skiff See **deadrise boat**

veenpont See **pot-2**

veense praam *Netherlands, W:* Small, flat-bottomed boat used by farmers and peat workers. A few still worked in the 1970s. Wooden boats replaced by iron or steel. Full bow and sharp stern, both strongly raked; stem set inside the planking, the bow strengthened by an iron band. Flaring sides. When used to collect mud for use as fertilizer by vegetable farmers, 2 bulkheads compartmented the hull, the waist holding the mud. Decked at ends; top strake along the central part removable. Large, triangular rudder; tiller slotted over rudderhead and curved convexly downward. Might hang a leeboard at the forward bulkhead. Mostly rowed, poled, or pushed, but occasionally set a sprit- or lugsail to a mast stepped in forward third. When rowed, oarsman sat well forward. Length ca. 6.4m.

veense turrif pondt See **pot-2**

veepaat See **paat**

veerboot See **ferryboat-1**

veerkaag, veerkagen, veerkaghe See **kaag**

veerman See **veerschip**

veerpont See **ferryboat-1, pont**

veerschepen See **veerschip**

veerschip *Netherlands:* A vessel that ferried passengers from ports on the Zuiderzee to Amsterdam from the 17th to the mid-19th century. Some open abaft the mast; others decked with raised cabin or cabin below decks; stern windows on some. Bluff bow, rounded stern; deep, curved stem; deadwood aft. Flat floors; keel; straight sides; considerable sheer. Outboard rudder; on some, tiller came inboard below the bulwarks; leeboards. Early **veerschepen** (pl.) set a spritsail, staysail, and often a topsail. Later, set a gaff sail, loose-footed and with standing gaff; 2 headsails. Reported lengths 9.3-21.5m; e.g., length 21.5m, beam 5.66m, depth 2.7m; shallow draft. Name variant: **veerman**. Note also **beurtschip**.

Vegtschuit See **somp**

vehicular ferry See **ferryboat-1**

veikoso See **camakau**

velacciere *Mediterranean:* **Coaster⋆** of Italy (especially Sicily) and Spain that used a combination of square and lateen sails on 3 masts. Mainly of the 19th century. Square sails to the tall pole foremast; usually a lateen to the mainmast, sometimes a gaff sail; lateen mizzen. Mizzen sheeted to an outrigger; several headsails to a long, rising bowsprit. Some 2-masted. Plumb stem below the waterline, concave above or straight and raked; counter stern; decked. Crew of ca. 6. Sicilian vessel of 1866 15.78m long, 4.22m wide, 1.79m deep; cap. 31t. Other recorded names: **chebec à pible, polacre settee, velacera, velachero, velachierro, vélacière, velechero, vellaciere, veloc(h)ero, velociere, velociero;** pl. **velaccieri.** Note also **šhetêya**.

velaccieri, velacera, velachero, velachierro, vélacière See **velacciere**

vel'bot See **whaleboat-1**

velechero See **velacciere**

veler, velero, velier, veliere, veliero See **sailer**

veliero misto See **mistico**

velika filuka See **double felouque**

vellaciere See **velacciere**

vellam See **vallam-1a**

velocero, velochero, velociere, velociero See **velacciere**

velovelo *Fiji, central Pacific:* **1.** Formerly a small, river-going single-**outrigger canoe⋆**. Dugout hull; round in cross section; bottom curved up to sharp, overhanging ends. Three light outrigger booms extended to the short, pointed float; supplemental booms stopped short of the float. Float and main booms connected by 2 pairs of stanchions that crossed above the booms. On some, a solid platform was lashed over the hull, extending out on each side. Paddled. Reported lengths 5-7.3m. **2.** Term now designates a western-style **ship's boat⋆** or keeled **dinghy⋆**.

Further reference: **takia**

Vendéen lugger, **Vendéen sardine boat** See **sardinier vendéen**

Veneti boat See **mioparo**

vengbåt, **vengebaad**, **vengebåt** See **skyssbåt**

ventjager See **jäger**

veppu tōni See **beppu tōni**

Verāval baghla See **batel-3**

Verāval lodhia See **lodhia**

vergantin See **brigantine**

Vergnügsfahrzeug See **yacht-2**

Verity skiff See **Seaford skiff**

véro See **gabare de la Rance**

Vertäuboot, **Vertäuungsprahm** See **anchor hoy**

vesel'naya shlyupka See **rowboat-1**

vessel A nebulous term ranging from any water craft (larger than a **rowboat★**) capable of providing transportation to a decked craft longer than a **boat★** but smaller than a **ship★**. International Rules of the Road assume the broadest possible definition and include such craft as seaplanes, **dumb barges★**, and floating cranes. More generally, however, a **vessel** in the present period would be ca. 12-46m long, capable of navigation at sea or on a large body of water, decked, able to carry at least one service craft, usually owned by a group of people, and transporting passengers and/or cargo. Such a definition requires modification for an earlier period, and in the late 18th century, **vessels** were limited to small, ocean, and inland waterway craft with 1-2 masts. Note also **craft**. Further reference: **Tortola sloop**

vesterhavsbåd See **havbåd**

vestlandsjekt See **jekt**

Vestlandsskøyte See **skøyte-1**

VI See **shell-3**

viehdampfer See **cattle ship**

Viehplätte See **Plätte-1**

Viehprahm See **Prahm-2**

Viehtransporter, **Viehtransportschiff** See **cattle ship**

Vierer See **shell-1**

Viererl, **Viererzille** See **Salzzille**

Viermastbark See **bark**

vierriemsgiek See **shell-1**

Vierteltschaike See **saique-1**

vigilenga *Brazil, NE:* Cargo and passenger vessel of the Pará and lower Amazon Rivers. The more common,

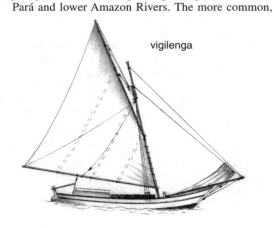

vigilenga

single-masted type is called a **canoa★**; a 2-masted boat is a **barco★**. Now motorized but still carries a sail. Planked boat with frames; keel; deep hull; sharply raking bow and stern; square or rounded stern with outboard rudder; moderate sheer. Low, wooden cabin aft for cargo and passengers. Characterized by tanned, high-peaked gaff sails with very long gaff and boom. Short mast raked aft; mast lowered to crutch when in narrow, vegetation-enclosed waterways, and crew resorts to poling with long poles. Rising bowsprit with large jib. Crew of 3. Length ca. 10m; cap. 15-30t.

villuga See **billuga**

vinco See **pink-2**

vindöka, **vindökstock** See **eka-1**

Vineyard boat See **Nomans Land boat**

Vineyard Haven half skipjack See **half skipjack**

Vineyard Sound boat See **Nomans Land boat**

vinta *Philippines, S:* Very fast double-**outrigger canoe★** of the Samal, Tausug, and Bajau peoples of the Sulu Sea. General utility boat for trading, pearling, transportation and, not infrequently, for smuggling; now mainly for fishing. Some Bajau live on their boats. Vary slightly from island to island, but basically a dugout hull; flat bottom, hard chines, some with a shaped keel; rocker toward the ends. Straight sides; may be raised by washstrakes attached with vertical wooden dowels. Characteristic bifid bow and stern, the upper bow piece turning up in a single flat board; the more elaborate stern in 2 pieces, strengthened with transverse struts. Sides may be raised by washstrakes. Interior divided into several sections, the central part covered with portable, split-bamboo decking; larger boats may have a temporary house of nipa palm matting over bamboo poles. Usually elaborately carved. Steered with a paddle. Two to 4 booms curve down to connect directly with 2 long bamboo floats. The outer booms pass beneath the gunwales and are braced at the hull end by a light bowed support that crosses above the gunwale; at each end of this bowed support, a crutch serves to hold mast, spars, etc. Inner booms may be in 2 pieces. Floats extend forward of the bow and are set so that they are closer to the hull at the stern. May have a cylinder at forward end that curves up to ride over the waves. Tripod or bipod mast, stepped well forward, supports a square or oblong sail hung lug-sail-fashion. Boom at foot lashed to foreleg of the tripod mast. Sail frequently sewn in cloths of different colors, creating individual patterns; often have tassles on ends of the sail. Now mainly use a spritsail to a bamboo mast; sail laced permanently to mast and boom. Some Samal **canoes★** use a triangular sail. Also paddled, worked with one foot and one hand. Reported lengths 6-13.7m; e.g., length 7.4m, beam ca. 0.7m, depth ca. 0.66m. Other recorded names: **binta★**, **bintas**; **dapang★** (at Sibutu); **moro**, **Moro vinta**; **pilang** (in Siasi, Bongo, and Samal areas); **sa-kai-yan**, **sakayan★**

(in Jolo area). Further reading: A. Spoehr, *The Double Outrigger Sailing Canoe of Zamboanga and the Sulu Archipelago...*, Occasional Papers XXIV/7 (Honolulu: Bernice P. Bishop Museum, 1971). Note also **lipa**. Further reference: **salisipan**

vinter-åttring See **åttring-3**

vinterbåt See **fembøring-1**

Virginia-built schooner See **Virginia model**

Virginia log canoe See **Chesapeake Bay log canoe-1**

Virginia model *United States, E:* One of the terms applied to the prototype of the **Baltimore clipper***. Term popular in the early 19th century. Built in both Virginia and Maryland along the Chesapeake Bay. Vessel most often used by privateers. Length on deck of a late 18th-century vessel 24.8m, beam 6.8m, hold depth 2.6m. Name variant: **Virginia-built schooner**. Note also **pilot boat model**, **Virginia pilot schooner**.

Virginia pilot schooner *United States, E:* Fast vessel that worked off the mouth of Chesapeake Bay from the mid-18th century until the 1860s. Built in the bay, both in Maryland and Virginia, but phased out because the main Atlantic shipping moved north. Relatively shallow draft to sail into shallow bay areas when necessary; straight keel with drag; marked deadrise, especially later; easy bilges; flaring topsides; thin quarters, low sheer. Curved stem cutaway below the waterline. Straight sternpost, some with short, shallow counter above. Outboard rudder or rudderstock came up inboard of the counter; tiller. Early boats open except for low quarter-deck; later flush-decked; steering cockpit; no bulwarks, but generally a log rail; prominent knightheads at stem characteristic. Large-diameter masts, both raking aft; some with greater rake to the mainmast; no shrouds or stays. Set large, boomed mainsail; loose-footed foresail lapped the mainmast; short gaffs on early vessels; large jib set flying and a large staysail between the masts. Those converted for privateering carried square sails and topsails. Reported lengths 11-24m; e.g., length 19m, beam 5.5m, depth amidships 1.83m, draft aft 2.13m. Note also **Virginia model**.

Virginia tobacco boat See **James River bateau**

visaak *Netherlands, N:* A general term, but can be characterized as follows: engaged in fishing, especially in Friesland, but some also collected seaweed and served as **fish carriers***. Larger types worked along the North Sea coast. Dated from at least the late 18th century. Full, rounded ends; high, curved stem; flat bottom, no keel; hard turn of the bilges; broad top strake had tumble home; low sides might be raised with a washboard. Early boats of wood; later of steel, becoming the **lemmeraak***. Decked; cuddy forward; live well; narrow leeboards. Rowed and sailed. Set a gaff sail, staysail, and on some, a jib to a running bowsprit. Large types might be **ketch***-rigged. Motorized after World War II. Crew of 2-3. Reported lengths 7.3-12.6m; e.g., length 7.3m, beam 2.94m. Other recorded names: **aak***, **aakschip**, **aek**, **Friese aak(je)**, **vischeraak**, **visser(s)aak**, **vissersmansaak**; pl. **visaken**; dims. **aakje, aekje**. Further reference: **Vollenhovense bol**

visaken See **visaak**

visbotter See **botter**

vischaloupe See **sloep-1**

vischboeieraakje See **boeieraak-1**

vischboot See **fishing boat**

vischbunsloep, vischchaloup See **sloep-3**

vischchaloupe See **sloep-1**

vischeraak See **visaak**

vischgondel See **grundel, Noordhollandse gondel**

vischhoeker See **vishoeker**

vischkaar See **kaar**

vischschouw See **schouw**

vischschuit See **grundel, schuit**

vischsloep See **sloep-3**

visgondel See **grundel**

vishoeker *Belgium/Netherlands:* A type of **howker*** that fished for cod and haddock with hook and lines in the North Sea from at least the 13th to the late 19th century. Last built at Vlaardingen in 1866. Hull and rig relatively standard by 1600. Had a reputation as a good sailer. Heavily built with bluff bow and rounded stern; strong sheer, especially toward the stern. Heavy wales. Deep, curved stem; straight, vertical or raked sternpost. Long, straight, heavy keel; flat or rising floors; rounded bilges. Decked; live well added during the 18th century (the **bunhoeker**). Narrow outboard rudder; long, down-sloping tiller. Stepped a pole mast amidships to which a tall square sail was set; 1-2 square topsails. A small mizzenmast carried a square sail initially; sheeted to an outrigger; later a triangular, boomless mizzen; finally set a standing gaff sail, either boomed or loose-footed. Staysail; sometimes a mizzen staysail. Bowsprit added in the 17th century, running out 1-2 jibs. Crew of 12-24. Lengths 15-24m; an 1845 vessel was 19.8m long, 5m wide, 2.85m deep. Small types might drift for herring. Other recorded names: **Fischhuker, hekre, hoeker, houcker, vischhoeker, Vlaardinger vishoeker**. A **Nieuwpoortse hoeker** of the early 18th century was called a **groot sloep**. Note also **hoekerbuis, koopvaardijhoeker**.

visjol See **jol**

viskaar See **kaar**

viskotter See **kotter**

vislogger See **logger**

vĭsŏ *Papua New Guinea, Bismarck Archipelago:* Type of **raft*** among the Sambuári and Kowamerára peoples of the Tabar Islands off eastern New Ireland. May have a natural-crook support for spears, paddles, and poles secured to one side of the **raft**.

vispunter See **punter**

visschersloep See **sloep-3**

visscherspink See **pink-5**

visschuit, vischuitje See **schuit**

visschuit van Aalsmeer See **grundel**

visser See **huissier**

visseraak See **visaak**

visserijinspectievaartuig See **fishery guard ship**

visserij-moederschip See **mother ship**

visserijpatrouillevaartuig See **fishery guard ship**

visserman See **fishing boat**

vissermanaak, vissersaak See **visaak**
vissersboot See **fishing boat**
visserspink See **pink-5**
vissersvloot See **fleet-1**
vissier See **huissier**
vissloep See **sloep-3**
vista-byrðingr See **byrding-1**
vistransportschip See **fish carrier-1**
vitile A light boat made from tarred withes covered with cloth or skins. Note also **coracle**.
vivaio See **well boat-1**
vivandier See **bumboat-1**
vivero **1.** In addition to designating a Spanish vessel with a wet well (see **well boat**), may describe a special floating or underwater container used to keep fish and shellfish alive. May be box- or boat-like or a basket used to grow or fatten the fish to market size. Name variant: **barco vivero**. Note also **fish car**.
2. *Cuba:* **Tuna boats*** that work out of the southwest and north coasts. Fish relatively close to shore, catching their own live bait, which is held in the wet well amidships. Motorized but carry a gaff sail and flying jib for emergencies. Crew of 7. Reported lengths 10-17m; draft 1.05-1.35m.
3. *Cuba, north-central:* **a.** In the mid-19th century, **sloop***-rigged **viveros** worked out of Havana. The wet well was contained by a false lower deck that was reached by means of a hatch; holes in the bottom provided fresh seawater; compartment lined with zinc. Plumb stem; cutaway forefoot; raked sternpost with shallow counter; straight keel with drag; steep rise to the floors; high, slack bilges. Rudderpost came up through the counter. Cabin aft; low railing. Gaff mainsail laced to a very long boom; yard topsail to topmast; large jib to a very long bowsprit. Crew of 6. Length 14m, beam 4.6m, depth 3.2m. Name variant: **balandro vivero**. **b.** The small **vivero de Caibarién** works out of this port fishing for lobsters, sponges, and moray eels. Employs a centerboard lowered by means of a long handle. Flat bottom, straight stem, slightly raked transom, skeg, outboard rudder, and tiller. Half-decked. Those that sail (the **bote vivero**) set a boomed gaff sail; small jib to jibboom. Now mainly motorized. Length 6.25m, beam 1.52m.
vivero de Caibarién See **vivero-3b**
vivier *France:* **1.** A vessel equipped to transport live fish or crustaceans from the fishing grounds to market. A well amidships is supplied with water by means of holes in the hull, or, more recently, by a pumping system. The small boats used on rivers were often called **bascules**. Other recorded names: **basculle, basouille, bateau vivier**. Note also **bachot-3, bèche, well boat**.
2. Along the coast and on some rivers, floating or fixed containers, also called **viviers**, hold fish, mollusks, or crustaceans being fed and fattened for market. When they also serve as a source for direct purchase of the fish, they may be called **boutiques**. Other recorded names: **banneton, bouticlar(d), chalan(d) perce, huche(ste), huchet(te), hugette, vivier flottant***. Note also **chaland-3b, fish car**.

vivier flottant *Cambodia:* Floating **fish carrier*** that transports live fish down the Mekong River to southern Vietnam. Large, rectangular, **raft***-like craft, the forward end of which forms a small aquarium for the fish; the **raft** itself is supported by bamboo poles along the sides. At the stern, there is a house of straw and wattle. The water in the pool is covered with plants to protect the fish from the heat. Floats downstream with the current, guided by poles. Length 20m, beam and depth 4m. Note also **fish car**. Further reference: **vivier-2**
Vlaamsche pleit See **pleit-1**
Vlaamse beurtschuit See **beurtschuit**
Vlaamse otter See **otter**
Vlaamse pleit See **pleit-1**
Vlaamse schuit See **schuit-1**
Vlaardingen herringlogger, Vlaardinger Heringslogger, Vlaardinger logger See **logger**
Vlaardinger vishoeker See **vishoeker**
Vlaardingse häringslogger See **logger**
Vlaemsche pleit See **pleit-1**
vlaggeschip, vlaggschip See **flagship**
vlatner See **Parrett flatner**
vleet See **vlet-1**
vlek See **lighter-1**
vlerkprauw See **outrigger canoe**
vlet **1.** *Netherlands:* Sturdy **rowing boat*** that serves as a workboat, **fishing boat***, **ferry***, or coastal **lifeboat***; some used as a **dinghy*** for larger craft. Generally clinker-built; later large sizes carvel; strakes wide amidships, becoming narrow toward the bow; rounded sides; some of iron or steel. Circular in cross section; narrow, flat floor; bottom planking bends up sharply to the small bow transom. Skeg aft; strong sheer toward the bow; wide, raked, U-shaped transom stern. Bilge runners on those brought up

vlet-1

onto the dikes. Open with small foredeck and large stern bench; number of thwarts depends on size. May be rowed (**roeivlet**) single- or double-banked; frequently sculled. Some lug- or sprit-rigged; many recent **vletten** (pl.) motorized (**motorvlet***). Wide range in size, depending on use; reported lengths 1.7-12m. Other recorded names: **Helderse vlet, jol***; **Norwegian vlet** (so called in the 19th century); **vleet, vletschuit**
2. *Netherlands Antilles:* Round-bottomed **rowboat***. Note also **motorvlet**.
Further references: **baggeraak, kagenaar**
vletschuit, vletten See **vlet-1**
vlieboot *Netherlands:* Late 16th- and 17th-century vessel that carried bulk cargo in the North Sea area, although some made transatlantic voyages. Initially

built for use through Vliestroom, the shallow passage from the Zuiderzee into the North Sea. Many
were armed during the wars of this period, especially by pirates, and many were secured by the
English, where they were called **flyboats**★ and were
ridiculed for their smallness. Beamy vessel with flat
floors and high, square stern. Two-masted with
square or sprit mainsail, lateen mizzen, and square
topsails on each mast. Capacity 40-140t; shallow
draft. Other recorded names: **felibote, filibote,
filipote, filippotto, flibaad, flibåt, flibot**★**, flibote, flibot(t)o, Flieboot**★**, flipot, flutbot, flûte hollandaise, flutte hollandoise**; pl. **vlieboten**. Note
also **fluit, flûte**.

vlieboten See **vlieboot**
vliet, vlietbot, vliete See **fluit**
Vlissingen mussel boat See **mosselaar**
vlodt, vloet See **raft**
vloot See **fleet**
vlot   1. *Belgium/Netherlands:* **Raft**★ used in harbors
since the Middle Ages as a working platform for ship
repair. Made of logs; with decking. Some large types
have 1-2 sheds for tools, materials, and to provide
shelter. Note also **balsa raft**.
    2. *Netherlands, E:* Open boat used mainly to transport
hay in the Nordwesthoek area. Extant member of
the **punter**★ family. Wide, flat bottom; sharp,
strongly raked ends; flared side; top strake has tumble home. Three-piece frames run to top of the top
strake; no gunwales. May be floored; bulkhead at
each end with no flooring between it and the short
end decking. Punted and sailed. Mast stepped well
forward, setting a high-peaked spritsail. Length
overall 9m, on bottom 7.3m, maximum breadth
1.8m, depth 0.5m. Other recorded names: **Gieters
vlot, vlöt**
Further reference: **raft**
vlote-scute See **vlotschuit**
vlothout See **timber raft-1**
vlotpraam See **slijkpraam**
vlotschuit *Netherlands:* Cargo **lighter**★ that dates to the
11th century; used especially at Amsterdam and on
the Zuiderzee. Sharp, strongly raked ends; deadwood
aft; flared sides. Decked with a small hatch; cargo
carried on deck. Some later boats of iron or steel.
Poled. Various sizes; one reported as 20m long overall,
16.4m on the bottom, beam 4.1m, depth 1.27m.
Spelling variants: **vlote-scute, vlotschuyt, werkschuit**.
Note also **schuit**.
vlotschuyt See **vlotschuit**
vlouwschouw, vlouwschuit See **zalmschouw**
vodoleĭ See **water boat**
voilier See **sailer**
voilier à patins See **iceboat-1**
voilier de promenade See **day boat-1**
voilier sur glace See **iceboat-1**
voilier-vedette See **sailer**
**Volendammer botter, Volendammer kwak,
Volendamse botter** See **kwak**
volizèpid See **cumacèna**
volkschuit See **trekschuit-3**

Vollenhoofse bol, Vollenhovens boljacht See **Vollenhovense bol**
Vollenhovense bol *Netherlands, NE:* Served as a flounder **fishing boat**★ out of Vollenhove on the eastern
side of the Zuiderzee from ca. 1900; last built in 1920
but has since become a pleasure craft (the
Vollenhovens boljacht). Clinker-planked originally;
now steel. Bluff bow with curved and raked stem that
comes to a point; sides taper toward the moderately
rounded stern. Slightly raked, tall sternpost; almost
flat bottom with slight rocker toward the stern; hard
chines; skeg extends to amidships. Flat sheer, but bow
higher than the stern; flaring, curved sides; tumble
home to top strake. Some have a hawser hole on each
side of the stem. Narrow leeboards; outboard rudder;
tiller slots over rudderhead. Decked forward, cuddy
below; wet well; pleasure models have a cabin. Sets a
loose-footed, boomed gaff sail; foresail; and sometimes a jib to a long bowsprit. Short, curved gaff.
Reported lengths 6.4-10m; e.g., length 8.75m, beam
3m, depth 0.7m. Other recorded names: **visaak**★**,
Vollenhoofse bol, Vollenhover bol**. Note also **bol**.
**Vollenhovense bons, Vollenhovense schokker, Vollen-
hovense schuit** See **bons**
Vollenhover bol See **Vollenhovense bol**
Vollenhover bonsje See **bons**
Vollgetakeltes Schiff, Vollrigger, Vollschiff See **ship-2**
volokovye See **koch-2**
volyer See **follower-2**
vongolara See **dredger-2**
Voor und Achter Schoner, Voor und Hinter Schoner
  See **schooner**
vorau See **soro**
Vorpostenboot See **patrol boat, picket boat**
Vorratsschiff See **store ship**
voyageur canoe *Canada, S/United States, north-central:*
Term applied to a **canoe**★ manned by voyageurs, mostly men from Quebec. Transported supplies upstream
and brought back furs. Their principal **canoes** were
the **canot du maître**★ and the **canot du nord**★.
Vp-Boot See **patrol boat, picket boat**
vrachtboeier See **boeier-2**
vrachtever See **Ewer**
vrachtkaag See **kaag-2**
vrachtlogger See **logger**
vrachtpunter See **punter**
vrachtschip, vrachtvaarder See **freighter-1**
vraiits' See **lontra**
vrakeka *Sweden, S:* Open **fishing boat**★ of the south
and southeast coasts, especially from Blekinge and
Skåne; believed to date from the 17th century.
Traveled considerable distances to catch herring; used
a drift net. Clinker-planked; curved, raked stem, some
terminating in a sharp point; shallow, raked transom;
deep keel. Narrow rudder; curved tiller. Early boats
set a tall dipping lugsail to a mast stepped through a
thwart amidships; bowlines and spar extended the
luff. Mast stayed to stemhead, single shroud on each
side, fastened to the frames abaft the mast; rake of
mast adjustable. Also portrayed with a lug mainsail
and sprit fore- and mizzen sails. Sometimes rowed.

Crew of 5-6. Reported lengths 7-9m; e.g., length over-all 7.7m, on keel 7.4m, beam 2.5m, depth 0.86m. The **storeka** ran to 12.2m long. Spelling variants: **brake-ka**; pl. **vrakekor**. Note also **blekingseka, eka**.

vrakekor See **vrakeka**

vranitze See **lontra**

vratsera See **bratsera**

vrečarica See **trawler**

vrijbuiter See **freebooter**

V-Spantboot, V-Spantschiff See **deadrise boat**

vuazzëtèillë See **gozzetto-1**

vuissier See **huissier**

vùrchjɔ See **maròta**

vuta guampu See **dalca**

vuurschip See **lightship**

vuzzariello, vuzzarìidde, vuzze See **gozzo**

vuzzëtillë, vuzziteddu See **gozzetto-1**

vuzzo See **gozzo**

vyombo See **chombo**

wa **1.** *Kiribati (Gilbert Islands), central Pacific:* Small, cigar-shaped **canoe**★ used in lagoons and near shore areas for traveling and fishing. Sewn planks over a keel; strengthened with ribs; hull asymmetrical. Single outrigger; 2 booms cross hull to the small float; forked stanchions inserted into the float and braced by horizontal stringers across the booms. Paddles used for steering and propelling. Carries 2 people. Boomed, triangular sail set to a mast raked sharply forward; yard tacked to bow. Reported lengths 3.7-4.8m, beam 0.38-0.61m. Other recorded names: **oa**★, **toa**

2. *Micronesia (Caroline Islands), western Pacific:* General term for a **canoe**, **boat**★, or **ship**★, especially in the eastern and central islands. Spelling variously reported, mostly by travelers of different periods and different nationalities; e.g., at Kusaie: **oak**, **waag**; Pohnpei (Ponape): **var**, **wah(r)**, **war**★, **wuar**; Mortlock group: **ua**★, **va**, **wa**; Truk: **va**, **wa**; Puluwat: **oa**, **wa**, **waa**★; Satawal: **oa**, **ou**, **oua**; Woleai: **warr**; Ifalik: **wa**. A few that have been described under this generic follow: **a.** The **outrigger canoe**★ of Pohnpei (Ponape) and nearby islands in the eastern group had a dugout hull; rounded in cross section. Flat bottom amidships rising to overhanging, pointed ends; sharp at cutwater. Multiple thwarts; small platform amidships rested on outrigger booms. Exterior smoothed with coral. Two squared booms, set close together, connected with the long float by paired stanchions; on some, a central boom extended to the float. Older boats had a platform for passengers, covered with mats, and protected by an awning. Additional strengthening provided by poles from the ends of the hull to ends of the booms and by 1-2 long stringers, the ends of which were lashed to the float. Paddled or poled, and some set a lateen-type sail; early **canoes** had mat sails. Largest (**wa ma lout**) could carry 10 passengers. Reported lengths 6-9m; e.g., length 8m, beam 0.34m, depth 0.44m. **b.** The **wa** of Puluwat in the central group is also an **outrigger canoe**. Deep hull cut with slight chine to the lee side and with the weather side higher; fastened to booms so that it heels toward the lee side; gunwale sweeps up toward the ends and hogs slightly amidships. Bottom rocker; narrow ends rake and terminate in carved, forked finials. Two heavy booms extend to a short, stocky float; booms straight to the middle and then slope downward to rest on forked stanchions and are secured to them by a yoke lashed to the float at its ends. Additional bracing provided by 2 poles from ends of the hull. Platform laid across the booms. A 2nd platform, separately braced, extends out the lee side, canting upward; large **canoes** may have a hut on this platform. Mast stepped between the booms close to the hull and is raked toward the front end, depending on the direction being sailed. Employs a triangular, lateen-type sail, hung with apex down. Length 7.8m, beam 1.14m, depth 1.22m.

3. *Palau (Belau), western Pacific:* In the small Sonsoral Islands southwest of the main group, the **wa** is a long, narrow single-**outrigger canoe**. Dugout hull shaped into a symmetrical "V" in cross section; strake added to each side increases depth; strong longitudinal rocker to bottom. Slightly raked ends; upper part formed of solid end pieces carved to create vertical projections. Two straight booms, set close together, extend to the short, pointed float; joined by crutch connectives, a yoke between the booms, and several oblique braces. Two spars that run from the ends of the hull to ends of the booms help support a light, triangular platform; small, solid platform near the hull. Diamond-shaped paddles, flat on one side and ridged on the other; as many as 12 on large **canoes**. When sailed, sets a triangular sail with its apex tacked to the forward end; mast pivots toward opposite end when tacking, the outrigger kept to windward. Halyards rove through hole on masthead. Length ca. 8.7m, beam ca. 0.5m. Other recorded names: large: **těriperi ŏa**; small: **χaperi ŏa**

4. *Papua New Guinea, Bismarck Archipelago:* **a.** A slender **canoe** with pointed, horizontal and vertical extensions at each end. Found on the Wuvulu Islands (sometimes called Aru or Maty Islands) at the western end of the archipelago. The small, one-man **canoes** fished for shark and flying fish; the largest were used for interisland transport and for war. Hewn from the breadfruit tree; V-section hull; bottom rocker; elongated, pointed ends; at the end of the cockpit, 2 triangular, vertical spurs were affixed, extending up as much as 1.6m. Single outrigger connected to the short float by multiple booms, 3-4 on the smaller **canoes**, 8-9 on the larger types; booms passed through the hull; outer end might be forked; booms set in crossed connectives. One boom often wide and flat as it crossed the hull, forming a counterbalance seat. Paddled by as many as 22 men on the largest **canoes**; blade pointed; steered with a paddle. Reported lengths 3.5-18m; e.g., length 16m, beam 0.69m, depth 0.66m. Spelling variant: **uá**. **b.** Long, slender **outrigger canoe** of Ninigo Atoll at the northwestern end of the archipelago. Generally hewn from driftwood; bottom flattened transversely; central part flat fore-and-aft but rises in long, straight line at ends, terminating in squared attached blocks; sides vertical. Numerous thwarts; gunwale pole tops the thwarts and outrigger booms. Steered with a paddle.

wa-4b

Hull often painted in wide, vertical stripes. Single outrigger; supported by 4 (sometimes 6) booms that cross the hull and connect to a small, cigar-shaped float; each boom attached with 4 pairs of crossed connectives. Light framework on a platform may lie atop the booms, and a removable platform may extend out the opposite side. Paddled; blades heart-shaped. When sailed, mast stepped in sling outboard, raking over the outrigger; stayed to outer booms and further supported by a crutch from an outrigger boom. Rectangular mat lugsail set nearly vertical, with the sail boom resting against the mast. Some stepped 2 masts. Length of single-sail **canoe** ca. 11m.

5. *Vanuatu (New Hebrides), central Pacific:* One of the terms for **canoe** on some parts of Epi Island.
Note also **wa fötyn**, **waka-1**. Further references: **curi-ara-2**, **sein efief**, **ua-2**, **waga-2a**, **wai-1**

waa   1. *Indonesia, NE:* Term for a small **canoe*** on Amblau in the Moluccas.
2. *United States, Hawaii:* **Wa'a** is a generic term for a **canoe** or small **boat***.
See also **vaka-1**, **wa-2**.

wa'a 'ākea *United States, Hawaii:* A special, unpainted **canoe*** sent to sea at the end of the annual period of prohibition for **canoe** use. See also **wa'a kaulua**.

Waadenboot See **Wadenboot**
waa fétún See **wa fötyn**
waag See **wa-2**

wa'a kaukāhi *United States, Hawaii:* Generic term for a single-**outrigger canoe***. Dugout hull; sides raised by washstrakes, originally sewn on; later, nails driven through the overlap. Washstrake continues to the bow and is cut vertical; at the stern, the strake stops short of the end, creating a short spur. On small **canoes**, 2 booms extend to the slender float and are lashed directly to it. Paddled and sailed. Older types used a V-shaped sail with a tall, vertical, curved boom; more recently a boomed spritsail used. Lengths to 15m, occasionally to 21m; e.g., length 10.8m, beam 0.51m, depth 0.66m. Other recorded names: **kaukāhi**, **waka kaukuhi**

wa'a kaulua *United States, Hawaii:* Large double **canoe*** that was primarily the property of kings and chiefs; used into the early 19th century. Carried cargo and passengers; also used for war. Hulls hewn from single logs that were generally about the same size, but when one was larger, the vessel was called a **kū'ē'ē**; the shorter hull placed to port. Sides vertical; quick turn of the bilges to a rounded bottom. Bottom rocker toward ends, terminating in characteristic high, pointed end pieces, the bow pieces taller; a short spur projected aft from the dugout hull. Sides raised by washstrakes; ends decked with breakwater on foredeck; open waist might have a mat cover to protect cargo. Hulls placed close together, joined by 3-6 poles lashed to spreaders wedged into the hulls; narrow, light platform laid between the hulls. When paddled, crews sat on thwarts in each **canoe**. Also sailed; light, vertical mast stepped forward in the starboard hull; woven pandanus sail laced to the mast; boom vertical and curved, forming a triangular sail. Lengths to 32.5m; average length 14.5m (larger hull), beam 0.57m, depth 1.0m, width across both hulls 2m. Other recorded names: **kaulua**, **waka kaulua**. Starboard

hull called **'ākea**, **wa'a 'ākea***, **wa'a kea**, or **'ekea**; port hull called **ama** or **iama**.

wa'a kea See **wa'a kaulua**
wa'a kioloa See **kialoa**

waal *Belgium/France, N:* Flemish term for a canal and river **barge***; called **bélandre** (see **bijlander**), **péniche***, or **chaland*** in France. Transported various cargoes, especially coal, ore, grain, sand, and stone, from the late 19th to the mid-20th century. Usually constructed of wood. Box-like with straight, parallel, carvel-laid sides; generally flattened bow and stern. Flat sheer, lifting faintly toward ends; flat bottom; square chines. Stem slightly raking; strong bitt behind the bow; 1-2 strong wales (*moustaches*) ran from the stem across the bows and partway along the sides; 2-3 rubbing strakes below the wale at the bow and along the sides. Straight, vertical sternpost. Decked; large, covered hold; cambered hatch covers; generally a cabin amidships; on some **barges**, this area housed the tow horses. Large rudder; older types had a wing device or hinge so it could be folded while negotiating locks; long, very heavy, extendable tiller. Bow rudder under bottom helped prevent the boat from making leeway. Rudderpost and tiller on foredeck. Originally man- or horse-drawn, then towed by a **tug***; later self-propelled. Lowering mast set a lugsail or loose-footed gaff sail and sometimes a narrow square topsail. Lengths 37.5-39m, width ca. 5m, depths 2.4-3.3m; draft loaded 1.8-2.3m. There are several well-known types, distinguished mainly by their bow and stern shapes; e.g., the **bak***, which is still used, has a straight stem; the **Doornikenaar** or **bateau de Tournai** had a very heavy, curved stem and tumble home above the heavy moustache. Other recorded names: **bac***, **baquet wallon**, **bateau Wallon**, **becandre**, **Flamänder**, **péniche du Nord**, **péniche flamande**, **péniche** (or **schip**) **van Doornik**, **Tournai boat**, **touranaisien**, **walenbak**, **walenpont**, **walenschip**, **Wallonenschiff**, **Walloon barge**; pl. **walen**, **walenschepen**. Further reading: J. Van Beylen, "Bouwschrijving van en Houten Walenschip (Waal)," *Mededelingen van de Marine Academie* XXVII (1971-1972), 1-23.

Waalschokker *Germany, W/Netherlands, S:* Name given to a vessel that anchored in the Waal, Maas, and Rhine Rivers in order to catch salmon with a large stow net. Originally they were discarded Zuiderzee **fishing boats***, mostly **botters***; later this special type, the **Waalschokker**, was developed. Flat bottom, high bow. Decked; forecastle; live well. A large winch hauled in the net and the anchor. The mast carried no sail, but might be used for towing and to provide a support for the net hung up to dry. Name variant: **schokker***

waater schep See **waterschip**
wabânäki chiman See **wabânäki tcîmân**
wabânäki tcîmân *Canada, E:* Late Algonkin birchbark **canoe*** of the Ottawa River basin. *Wabinaki* is a corruption of Abinaki (or Abenaki), a tribe from whom the Algonkins apparently obtained the prototype **canoe**. Soaked bark applied with the inside facing

out; caulked with spruce gum. Flattened bottom; ends mostly high-peaked; sheer fairly flat until the ends. Stem and sternpost curved or straight; flat on top or sharp and often with a slight tumble home. In- and outwales lashed on with spruce root. Stem pieces either laminated or cut from a thin board; ribs, gunwales, and sheathing of cedar. Designs may be created along the sides of a winter-bark **canoe** by

wabânäki tcîmân

scraping away the dark layer. Reported lengths 3-5.5m; e.g., length 4.75m, beam 0.85m, depth 0.34m; 24kg. Other recorded names: **Abenaki canoe⋆**, **Algonkin canoe⋆**, **Algonquin canoe**, **wabânäki chiman**, **wabinaki chiman**, **wa·panakki·či·ma·n**. Further reading: David Gidmark, *The Indian crafts of William and Mary Commanda* (Toronto: McGraw-Hill, 1980), 93-136; ibid., *The Algonquin Birchbark Canoe* (Aylesbury: Shire Publications Ltd., 1988). Note also **tsiman.**

wabinaki chiman See **wabânäki tcîmân**

Wachboot See **patrol boat**, **picket boat**

wache *Indonesia, E:* Single-outrigger man's **canoe⋆** of Kayo (Humboldt) Bay on the northeast coast of Irian Jaya (western New Guinea). Washstrakes sewn on to the rounded dugout hull create a very narrow cockpit. Double-ended; elaborately carved figurehead at the bow. Short, pointed float attached by 2 booms amidships; booms connected by 2 pairs of divergent stanchions. Platform, atop the booms, extends out over the outboard side, terminating in a railing. Mast, outboard, supported against the forward boom and platform; when sailing in the opposite direction, mast stepped at the other boom; stayed forward and to the end of one of the booms, or fore-and-aft. Masthead forked to hold the halyard, ornamented with feathers. Boomed, tall, rectangular sail of pandanus leaves; some battened with bamboo. Reported lengths 4.8-9.1m; e.g., length 5.8m, beam 0.15m. Spelling variants: **väge**, **wäga⋆**, **wage**, **wäka⋆**, **ware**

Wachschiff, Wachtboot, Wachtkutter, Wachtschiff, wachtschip See **guard ship**

Wädboot See **Wadenboot**

waddenever See **Ewer**

Wadenboot *Germany, Baltic coast:* Worked a seine net (*Wade*) for herring. Heavily built with clinker planking of oak. Sharp, raked ends; flat floors. Open, with a short deck at the stern and also at the bow on some. Outboard rudder; tiller. On some, an athwartships roller device assisted in pulling in the net. When rowed, worked with oars as long as 7m. Some stepped 2 masts against thwarts in the forward third. Set spritsails. A jib might be run to a small jibboom. Reported lengths 7.65-9.5m; e.g., length overall 9.5m, on keel 7m, beam 2.8m, inside depth 0.79m. Other recorded names:

Heringswa(a)denboot, Waadenboot, Wädboot. See also **seine boat-1**.

Wadenfischer, Wadenfischereiboot See **seine boat-1**

Wade salmon wherry See **salmon wherry**

wádi See **umiak-4**

Wädschelch See **Waidschelch**

wa fatúl *Micronesia (Caroline Islands), western Pacific:* Single outrigger paddling **canoe⋆** of the eastern islands of the State of Yap: Satawal, Woleai, and Ifalik. Double-ended dugout hull with tall, forked, raked ends; V-bottom; flared sides. Two booms cross to the short float, bending down to the slightly divergent connectives. Crew of 4-5. Reported lengths 4.85-5.1m, beam 0.54-0.65m. Spelling variant: **ka fadule** (at Ifalik). Note also **wa fötyn**.

wa fotul, wa fötün See **wa fötyn**

wa fötyn *Micronesia (Caroline Islands), western Pacific:* Generic term in the Truk group for paddling **canoes⋆**. Essentially double-ended with a single outrigger. Small fishing **canoes** are called **sein efief⋆**; the large **war canoe** is a **sein maun⋆**; a 3rd, an extinct type of **war canoe**, was the **meniepep⋆**, which had a rising platform opposite the outrigger. Spelling variants: **va fatin, va fedul, waa fétún, wa fotul, wa fötün**. Note also **wa fatúl**.

wag See **waga-2a**

waga **1.** *Indonesia, E:* General term for a **canoe⋆** or **boat⋆** in some parts of the Moluccan Archipelago. Most Ceram boats have double outriggers with a dugout hull.
2. *Papua New Guinea, SE:* **a.** In the southeastern peninsula, nearby island groups, and parts of the Bismarck Archipelago, **waga** means an **outrigger canoe⋆**, generally single. May also designate a seagoing **canoe**. Spelling variants: **vaga⋆, wa⋆, wag(e), wangga⋆, woga**. **b.** In the Louisiade Archipelago, the long, narrow dugout hull of the **waga** is often blunt at the stern and elongated at the bow. Some carry a carved, finial bow decoration. The planked-up gunwale is closed off at the bow but generally open aft, the back of the stern paddler serving as the closure. The heavy outrigger float equals or exceeds the length of the hull. Six to 8 booms extend through the gunwale and attach to the crossed sticks that are inserted into the float. Poles laid across the booms form a platform. Paddle blade lanceolate. When sailed, the generally vertical mast is stepped forward or amidships. Woven palm sail is either an elongated, oval, boomed lugsail or a type of spritsail, the mast and sprit threaded through the sail. Reported lengths 8-12m. **c.** The **waga** from Woodlark (Murua) Island in the Trobriand group was especially well built and was traded to other parts of southeastern New Guinea. A beautifully carved figurehead characterized this single-**outrigger canoe**. Rounded dugout hull raised by flaring washstrakes; sharp ends swept up from the bottom. As many as 8 booms pierced the washstrake and led to the long float; crossed-stick connectives. Steered with a paddle. The single mast was braced by a forked stick which, in turn, was secured to an outrigger boom. Set an elongated,

oval sail of woven pandanus leaves. Reported lengths 7.5-9m. **d.** The **waga** on Normanby Island in the D'Entrecasteaux Archipelago is a sharp-ended, outrigger paddling **canoe**. Vertical wash-strake along each side raises the sides; carved breakwater at each end. Four booms extend through the washstrake to the crossed-stick connectives on the long float. Longitudinal poles, laid atop the booms, form a wide and long, open platform. Length ca. 4m. **e.** Both the paddling and sailing **wagas** of the southeast end of New Guinea carry a single outrigger, attached with as many as 10 booms to the long, slender float. Two pairs of crossed-stick connectives used; a light platform covers all but the 2 end booms; on some sailing **canoes**, a small platform extends out the opposite side. Dugout hull generally raised on the sailing **canoes** by low wash-strakes and breakwaters; ends elongated. Long, oval, palm-leaf sail hung lug-fashion from a light mast; boomed at bottom. Mast shored by a stick from the outrigger platform and stayed forward and aft; halyard rove through a hole in the masthead, which is forked, often with a carved bird on top. Reported lengths 4.9-7.6m, beam 0.3m.

3. *Vanuatu (New Hebrides), central Pacific:* Generic term for **boat** in some of the islands of the group. Further references: **gaï oko**, **keama**, **vaka-1**, **wache**, **waka-1**, **waqa-2**

waga angina See **waka-1**
waga diu See **waka tiu**
waga langa See **waka-1**
wage See **wache**, **waga-2a**
Wagenfährprahm See **car float**
Wagenschiff See **Leibschiff**
wager boat See **best and best boats**, **best boat**, **Thames wherry**
wager outrigger See **outrigger**
wager wherry See **Thames wherry**
waggon boat, **waggon scow** See **scow-9**
wah, **wahr** See **wa-2**
wahriyah See **hurija**
wai 1. *Indonesia, E:* Double-**outrigger canoe*** of the northern coast of Irian Jaya and some of the off-lying islands. V-shaped dugout hull; may have cover over most of hull. Floats, sometimes double, attached by 2-4 booms with a single connective. Mainly paddled. Larger **canoes** sail, employing a tri-pod mast and boomed, rectangular sail set at an angle. Other recorded names: **wa***, **wei**. At Manokwari, a large **canoe** is a **wai bebă**, while a small one is a **wai kăpĭrărĕ**.
2. *Nepal:* Term for **boat*** by the Kusúnda. Name variant: **wou**

wai bebă See **wai-1**
wai-ch'iu tzŭ See **qiu zi**
Waidling, **Waidnachen** See **Weidling**
Waidschelch *Germany, central:* Smallest of the cargo vessels on the Main River during the 15th-16th centuries; reported again in the 19th century. Clinker-built of oak; flat bottom; no rudder. Capacity ca. 0.8-1.7t. Spelling variants: **Wädschelch**, **Weidschelch**

Waidschiff *Germany, S:* Open, lake **fishing boat***; became extinct during the early part of the 20th century. Carvel-planked with 2-3 bottom planks, 2 strakes on each side, and 3 pairs of ribs. Both ends square; narrow at the bow; bottom curved up to a long overhang. Length 6m, width on bottom 0.8-0.9m, depth 0.55-0.6m. Other recorded names: **Waitschiff**, **Weidschiff**, **Weitschiff**, **Weydschiff**; dim. **Weidschiffal**, **Weydschiffel**

Waidzille *Austria/Germany, S:* Small but sturdy, open-ended boat used on the Danube River, its tributaries, and some Bavarian lakes. Popular with sport fisher-men and hunters; also provided local transportation for people and produce. Some were **ship's boats***, especially for carrying lines to shore (the **Burchzille**). Smallest of the **Zille*** family. Flat bottom planked fore-and-aft with 4 planks that bent up at the ends. Ends either sharp (**Spitzgranselzille**) or narrow, shallow transoms well above the water (**Stöckzille**). Sides a single plank, straight but flared. Moderate sheer at the ends. Open; a seat at each end. Rowed standing or sitting. Reported lengths 5-11m; e.g., length 7m, beam 1.5m, depth 0.4m. On the lower Austrian Danube, the **Eissigzille** (**Eissig-Waidzille**, **Issi-Watzille**) transported vinegar and fruit. These boats had a skeg on the bottom at each end. Lengths 10.4-12.9m. Other recorded names: **Fischerzille***, **Waitzille**, **Wat(z)zille**, **Waydzille**, **Weidzille**, **Weit(z)zille**

wai kăpĭrărĕ See **wai-1**
wai-phi-ku See **wai pi gu**
wai pi gu *China (PRC), central:* **1.** Transports salt up the swift-flowing Wu Jiang. Made mainly at Fuling (Foochow) at the junction with the Chang Jiang (Yangtze). One of at least 3 types of **junks*** with crooked sterns used on several of the tributaries. Transom stern twisted so that the port side is far-ther aft and higher than the starboard, enabling the primary steering oar, which is pinned to a heavy bumkin off the quarter, to align on the central axis. Helmsman stands atop a flying bridge to work the sweep, which is roughly the length of the vessel. A smaller, auxiliary sweep is available on the star-board quarter, and a bow oar is used. Crudely con-structed; flat bottom of thick planking. Square bow, cross-planked, sheer sweeps up in a long overhang; bow strengthened by 2 fore-and-aft frames. Numerous transverse bulkheads, sometimes also off-axis. Central deckhouse with arched mat roof; deck over most of the hull. Tracked upstream from a short mast near the bow. Crew of ca. 6, plus hired trackers at rapids. Reported lengths 15-30m; e.g., length 21m, beam 5m, depth 1.5m. Other recorded names: **crooked stern junk**, **hou-pan** and **hou-pan ch'uan** (**thick plank boat**), **huang-shan** (**yellow eel**), **twisted stern junk**, **wai-phi-ku**, **wai-p'i-kou tch'ouan**, **wai-p'i-ku**, **wai-p'i-ku'rh**. Further reading: G. R. C. Worcester, *Notes on the Crooked-bow and Crooked-stern Junks of the Yangtze*, Miscellaneous Report 52 (Shanghai: Maritime Customs, 1941).

2. A smaller variety on the same river carries general cargo. These employ a single sweep and 2 oars forward. Mat house. Length ca. 12m, beam 2.4m, depth 0.9m.

wai-p'i-kou tch'ouan, wai-p'i-ku, wai-p'i-ku'rh See **wai pi gu**

wai qiu zi See **qiu zi**

wairjíyah See **hurija**

waist boat One carried in the waist of a ship. On early whalers⋆, used by the second mate and housed amidships on the port side. Name variant: **Decksboot**. See also **whaler-3, yao zhou**.

Waitschiff See **Waidschiff, Weidling**

Waitzille See **Waidzille**

waka **1.** *Micronesia (Caroline Islands), western Pacific:* Generic term for a **canoe**⋆ at Kapingamarangi Atoll in western Pohnpei state. One unable to sail close to the wind is a **waga** (or **waka**) **angina**; a **canoe** that rides high in the water is a **waga** (or **waka**) **langa**. Spelling variant: **waga**⋆. Note also **wa-2. a.** Two types were found at the atoll in the 1940s, but only a few of the older 3-boom type were extant. Breadfruit dugout hull with a strong bottom rocker; asymmetric "U" cross section, bulged on the outrigger side. Lashed-on washstrakes raised sides. Strongly raked ends added on above the waterline, curving slightly above the gunwale and cut square. Gunwale rails extended to the end of the washstrake forward and to the top of the stern projection. Three main booms crossed the hull and extended out the port side to the short, pointed float; multiple tall sticks connected each boom to the float. Four additional booms extended out the port side to a stringer midway to the float; platform laid over part of the 3 main booms. Two supplemental booms ran from the stringer along the ends of the platform and curved down to fasten directly to the float. Paddled using sharply pointed paddles or set a boomed, mat, lateen-type sail. Reported lengths overall 6.4-9.4m; width ca. 0.23m. **b.** The Nukuoro (an atoll to the north) **waka** was adopted at Kapingamarangi, being simpler to produce. This **canoe** lacks the washstrakes, gunwale rails, and the bulge to the hull, and only 2 main booms connect the hull and float. End pieces lower, and the sides have tumble home. Short booms extend to the stringer; booms curve upward slightly so that the connectives to the float are quite tall. Platform lies atop the 2 main booms. Sets a similar sail, but mast stepped into a sliding block wedged onto the gunwales, enabling the rake of the mast to be adjusted. Length overall 9.2m, on bottom 8.5m, hull opening 0.21m, depth 0.56m. Further reading: Peter H. Buck, *Material Culture of Kapingamarangi*, Bulletin 200 (Honolulu: Bernice P. Bishop Museum, 1950), 174-209. Note also **paopao-2**.

2. *New Zealand:* General term for a **canoe** by the Maori and by the Moriori of the Chatham Islands to the east. Spelling variant: **whaka**

3. *Papua New Guinea:* The single-outrigger paddling **waka** of Goodenough Bay on the southeast peninsula

has elongated ends that form a small shelf, sometimes arrowhead-shaped. Dugout hull with rounded bottom. Three strong poles pierce the upper part of the hull to which the outrigger booms are lashed. Each boom attaches to the float by a single pair of crossed sticks. A square platform of palm or other light material is set athwart the hull and lashed to the booms. Name variant: **bognono**

4. *Vanuatu (New Hebrides), central Pacific:* One of the terms for a **boat**⋆ or **canoe** on the northern islands of Pentecost and Malekula and on the southern island of Futuna.

Further references: **vaka-1, vaka-2a, vaka-2d, vaka-4b, wache**

waka ama *New Zealand:* Maori term for a **canoe**⋆ with an outrigger (*ama*).

waka-ami-bune See **waku-ami-bune**

waka angina See **waka-1**

waka hunua See **waka unua**

wa'k·ai *United States, W:* Log **raft**⋆ of the Nisenan of central California. Composed of 2 redwood logs lashed together or a single log with a flattened top; ends turned up slightly. Not hollowed out. Paddled or poled. Other recorded names: **ha·pa·, nü**⋆

waka kaukuhi See **wa'a kaukāhi**

waka kaulua See **wa'a kaulua**

waka korari *New Zealand, Chatham Islands:* Moriori fishing craft with a framework of light sticks, stuffed with buoyant flower stalks of a type of flax (*korari*). Worked from the beaches of these islands east of New Zealand; no longer made. Roughly **punt**⋆-shaped with a flat bottom, square ends, and slightly curved and flaring sides. Two keels, ca. 25cm apart, served as runners; these followed the sharp bottom rocker at the stern and continued aft as handles. Bow rocker more attenuated. Carved transom board raked inward; bow narrower and an elongated extension of the bottom. Bottom created by closely spaced sticks laid transversely; sides consisted of an inner framework of vertical sticks to which stalks were bound; gunwale pole lashed on top. Flooring of closely packed stalks, ca. 13cm thick, laid on the bottom. Open construction permitted water to pass through freely; several seats, also of fern stalks; small boats had a single seat aft. Rowed. Reported lengths 2.4-4m; e.g., length 4m, beam aft 0.5m, depth 0.44m. Other recorded names: **korari, waka pu(h)ara**

waka langa See **waka-1**

waka pahi See **waka pahii**

waka pahii *New Zealand, Chatham Islands:* Seagoing, **raft**⋆-like craft used by the Moriori of these islands east of New Zealand. Extinct; originally used for interisland travel. Framework of rods and bundles of fern stalks and flat stems created the sides and bottom; flat bottom had 2 keels made of thin wood lashed together; at each end, these strips curved up to above the gunwale line; ends square and raked. Additional buoyancy obtained from a flooring of layers of a broad, flat kelp (which has air pockets). Multiple seats formed by transverse rods and fern stalks. Rowed using heavy oars against tholepins. Reported lengths 15-18m; e.g., length overall 15.2m, on the keels 9m, beam 2.4m, depth 1.5m. Other recorded names: **pahi★**, **pahii**, **pepe**, **waka pahi**; **waka pata** and **waka patu** (probably erroneously); **waka pepe**, **whaka pahi'i**

waka pata, **paka patu**, **waka pepe** See **waka pahii**

waka pitau *New Zealand:* Largest of the Maori **war canoes**; also used for voyaging. Identified by an elaborate, perforated bow piece that incorporated a full human figure (a *pitau*); slender stern piece, as tall as 3-5.5m, elaborately carved and trimmed with feather streamers. Dugout hull, fashioned from 1-3 pieces, sewn together; sides raised by 1-2 strakes; on some, the 2nd strake formed a bow washboard; seam between the hull and strake was battened. Bottom rocker longitudinally and a wide, shallow "V" athwartships. Ends tapered. Open; some had a floor grating. Most painted red. Mainly paddled, the paddlers sitting 3-5 abreast, the inside paddlers resting. Occasionally sailed, employing 1-3 triangular mat sails, apex down and boomed on both long sides. Averaged ca. 35m in length. Other recorded names: **piitau**, **pitau**. Note also **waka taua**.

waka puara, **waka puhara** See **waka korari**

waka takaaga See **vaka tafaanga**

waka taua *New Zealand:* Generic term for a Maori **war canoe**, although such **canoes★** also made coastal voyages, particularly to pay social visits. On occasion, they were used for fishing, their special bow and stern pieces removed and replaced with those more appropriate to a fishing **canoe** (**waka tete★**); or 2 fishing **canoes** set side-by-side might be used during warring expeditions, and called a **waka taua**. Characterized by a low bow piece and a very tall, vertical stern piece; both perforated and intricately carved. Further decorations included projecting rods at the bow to which bunches of feathers were tied, and long feather streamers at the stern. Painted red and black. Dugout hull, often in 2-3 sections; sides raised with topstrakes. Mainly paddled, some employing • 100 paddlers. Also sailed, using 1-2 triangular sails set with the apex down; when 2 **canoes** joined, only one sail used, the forward-raking mast stepped in one of the hulls. Reported lengths 15-37m, beam 1.2-2.4m. Other recorded names: **waka taua nunui**, **waka tava**. Further reading: Elsdon Best, *The Maori Canoe*, originally published as Dominion Bulletin 7, 1925 (Wellington: Government Printer, 1976), 65-175.

waka taua nunui See **waka taua**

waka taura, **waka taurua** See **vaka taurua**

waka tava See **waka taua**

waka tete *New Zealand:* Maori **canoe★** used for fishing and coastal travel. Dugout hull, raised by a washstrake, ca. 23cm high; strake lashed on, battened both inside and out; stopped just short of the ends where it was shallower. Hull a single piece or lengthened at each end; bottom a wide "U" in cross section; sloped up gently at bow and stern. A low figurehead was slotted on to the bow, merging with the washstrake; frequently had a grotesque head, the tongue hanging out; a small breakwater terminated the bow piece. Tall, vertical stern piece usually unornamented, although it might have a small figure at the base. Open; ca. 8 thwarts; floor-like grating on the bottom. Mainly paddled, but might set a single triangular, boomed, mat sail, apex down. Steered with a paddle. Crew of 10. Reported lengths 11-15m; e.g., length 12.8m, beam 1.3m, depth 0.43m. Other recorded names: **tete**, **waka tetee**. Note also **waka taua**.

waka tetee See **waka tete**

waka tiu *Micronesia (Caroline Islands), western Pacific:* Large **bonito canoe** of Kapingamarangi Atoll in the southwestern extremity of the Pohnpei Island group. Single outrigger, small float. Spelling variant: **waga diu**

waka tiwai *New Zealand:* Class of simple **dugout canoes★** that the Maori used for river fishing and local transportation. One-piece hull excavated by fire; round bottom in cross section; bottom tapered up at ends to join the flat sheer in a point; bow cut square; stern notched. Maximum beam abaft amidships. No thwarts, but some had a type of floor of light sticks laid atop crosspieces that rested on stringers. Paddled. Reported lengths 7-9.5m, beam ca. 0.8m. Other recorded names: **ta(a)wai**, **ti(i)wai**

waka unua *New Zealand:* Small double **canoe★** of the Maori, mainly of South Island, apparently used primarily for local fishing. Dugout hulls, one larger than the other, connected permanently by a series of poles on which a platform was placed. Hulls set close together; the bow ends positioned closer than the stern. A pair of poles at each end crossed both hulls; the poles between were lashed only to the inner gunwales. Sewn washstrakes raised the sides; high end pieces, the bow pieces carved as figureheads. Steered with 2 paddles. Some set a triangular sail to a midships mast, boomed at top and bottom, apex down. Length of larger hull ca. 5.5m, the smaller 4.2m. Other recorded names: **huhunu**, **hukunu**, **hunu(a)**, **unua**, **unuku**, **waka hunua**

waku-ami-bune *Japan, N:* Open **fishing boat★** of Hokkaido, stationed at the exit of a herring pound net suspending a bag net (*waka-ami*) beneath it. Once full, the boat is rowed to shore. Carvel-planked; wide, plank keel; straight, rising floors; hard chines to nearly vertical sides; sharp, flaring bow with strong rake; stem curves at top to tall, coppered stemhead; square stern overhangs. Some have a mat house forward. Rudder hangs below bottom; tiller. Also sailed. Length overall 10.9m, beam 2.86m, depth 0.74m. Spelling variant: **waka-ami-bune**

wa lab See **wa lap**

wa lap *Marshall Islands, central Pacific:* Generic term for a sailing **canoe★**. Most often describes an inter-island single-**outrigger canoe★**; now extinct. Hull built up from a dugout keel piece into an asymmetric "V," the lee side flat and straight, the weather side curved fore-and-aft and rounded vertically. Solid end pieces sewn on, terminating in slender, raked-up extensions; frequently ornamented with fan-shaped pieces. Strong bottom rocker. Five or 6 closely spaced, light booms connected directly to the stout float; 2 sturdy booms near the middle of the unit helped support the lee platform. A weather platform built out over the booms; another out the lee side raked upward; on a very large **canoe** (**wa pap**), a small house was set up on each platform. Stout mast stepped in socket set onto the outrigger close to the hull; stayed fore-and-aft and supported by 3-7 shrouds to the outer ends of the booms. Mast raked forward but pivoted toward the opposite end when tacking, the outrigger always kept to windward. Set a triangular mat sail with apex tacked to the forward end. Sail lashed to yard and boom through holes along one edge. Crew of 3 on smaller **canoes**; some of the largest could carry 50 passengers. Reported lengths 5.3-21.3m; e.g., length 6.7m, beam 0.8m, depth ca. 0.9m. Other recorded names: **prao volant, proa volant, wa lab**

Walberswick beach yawl See **beach yawl-1**

Walboot See **whaleboat-1**

walbuwa See **walpa**

walen, walenbak See **waal**

walenmajol *Belgium, E/Netherlands, S:* Cargo carrier of the Meuse (Maas) River, mainly of the 18th-19th centuries. An **aak**★ type with a flat bottom that curved up slightly to terminate above the gunwale in a point; hard chines. Flaring sides; upper 3 strakes clinker laid, the lower strakes carvel. Flat midships sheer, curving up toward the ends. Wide-bladed, balanced rudder; the forepart extended under the stern; rudderpost came up through the stern. Arched, secondary tiller worked the after part of the rudder, coupled with the regular tiller. Decked; long, arched hatch between gangways extended from main- to mizzenmast; cabin amidships; winch abaft hatches. Tall mainmast, forward of hatch, set a spritsail to a long yard. Mizzenmast, just abaft the hatch, set a small spritsail sheeted to top of rudderpost. Short bowsprit. Other recorded names: **majol, mijole, whalemajol**. Note also **spitsbek**.

walenpont, walenschepen, walenschip See **waal**

Walfangboot See **whale catcher**

Walfangschiff See **whaler**

Walfischboot See **whaleboat-1**

Walfischfänger See **whale catcher**

Walker boat See **narrow boat**

wallam See **vallam-1a, vallam-3**

wallama See **vallam-3**

Wallasey luggage boat See **luggage boat-2**

walla-walla boat See **ku tsai ting**

Wallonenschiff, Walloon barge See **waal**

wallum See **vallam-1a**

Walmer lugger See **Deal lugger**

walpa *Australia, N:* Stable mangrove **raft**★ used by the aborigines in the Wellesley Islands and on the opposite mainland in the southern Gulf of Carpentaria. Logs tied with larger ends together, making the **raft** wider at the stern. Seaweed on top forms a cushion. Name variant: **walbuwa**

Walsay sixern See **sixareen**

walvissloep See **whaleboat-1**

walvisvaarder See **whaler-1**

wa ma lout See **wa-2a**

wampu See **huampo**

waña See **wanga**

wanagan, wanegan See **wanigan**

wang *New Caledonia:* Term for a **boat**★ by the peoples of the northern part of the island. To the Webias and Balad peoples, it may describe a single-outrigger **dugout canoe**★. Spelling variants: **te-wagga; wong** (by the Yengen and Wagap of the east coast); **wonga**★ (by the Ponerihuen, also on the east coast). See also **de wang, waqa-1**.

wanga   **1.** *Indonesia, central:* A **boat**★ at Bolaang Mongondow in the northeastern part of Sulawesi (Celebes).

  2. *Vanuatu (New Hebrides):* Term for a **canoe**★ on some of the central islands of the archipelago. Most single-outrigger **dugout canoes**★. On Epi Island, a **canoe** may be a **ta-wanga** or **sa-wanga**. Spelling variants: **vanga, waña**

See also **waqa-1**.

wangan See **wanigan**

wang chuan See **liu wang chuan, sin-tor-chai**

wangga *Australia, NE:* Single-**outrigger canoe**★ of the Cape Bedford area of northeastern Queensland. **Canoe**★ hull a single hewn log with the bow end frequently wider than the stern, being the lower end of the trunk. Rounded sides; raked and slightly pointed bow; raked and squared stern. On some, a single plank washstrake, lashed on, forms a gunwale; generally caulked with a coil of tea-tree bark. Paired stick-booms (4-8 pairs) pierce each gunwale, merging at the float end with one resting on top of the crossed-stick connective, the other passing below. Float as long as the hull. Poled and paddled. See also **waga-2a, waqa-1**.

wangga ndrua, wangga tambu See **drua**

wangka Early term for **boat**★ in the Austronesian area. Spelling variant: **bangka**★. See also **tongkang-2**.

wangkang *East Malaysia:* Iban term for a large Chinese sailing ship. The **limau wangkang** specialized in importing Chinese oranges. See also **Gulf of Siam trader, tongkang-2**.

wangkang Siam See **Gulf of Siam trader**

wang la See **de wang**

wanigan *Canada/United States:* A boat or **raft**★ that follows a log drive down a river. Some had special functions, such as the **cook wanigan**, which was a **houseboat**★ on which meals were prepared for the drivers. A **chuck boat** carried supplies. The **sleeping wanigan** was a **houseboat** with rudimentary sleeping accommodations. In Oregon, might carry as many as a dozen horses. Some powered by an outboard motor. The term may be used in a more general sense and over a wider geographical area. Some, built onto **barges**★, provided amenities in remote areas, such as Alaska. Other recorded names: **ark**★, **wanagan, wan(n)egan, wan(n)gan, wannigan; shanty boat**★ (southern forests). Note also **timber raft-1**.

wanka See **waqa-1**

wannegan, wanngan, wannigan See **wanigan**

wa·panakki·či·ma·n See **wabânäki tcîmân**

wa pap See **wa lap**

waqa 1. *Fiji Islands, central Pacific:* Generic term for a **canoe***. Spelling variants: **vanka***, **wang***, **wanga***, **wangga***, **wanka**
   2. *Papua New Guinea, Bismarck Archipelago:* On the north end of the island of New Britain, term for a **canoe**, especially one bought or traded from natives of nearby Watom Island. Primarily a multiboomed, single-outrigger, dugout-hulled craft. Spelling variants: **a waqa, uaqa, waga***. Note also **oáṅga**.

waqa bilibili See **bilibili**

waqa drua See **drua**

waqa ni Viti See **camakau, tabilai-1**

waqa tabu See **drua**

war *India, NW:* A variety of small cargo vessel found on Kashmiri rivers. Low at the bow. Capacity ca. 15t. See also **vaka-1, wa-2**.

waráji See **hurija**

warakan-oruwa See **varakan-oruwa**

war canoe See **baurua, mE'nga, meniepep, mon-3, pahi tama'i, sein maun, tarrāda, tomoko, waka pitau, waka taua, West Coast canoe**

ware See **wache**

wargiyeh See **hurija**

warhis See **wary**

wari See **houari**

waria See **wary**

wa-ririk *Kiribati (Gilbert Islands), central Pacific:* Small **outrigger canoe***... [remainder]

warjiwa See **hurija**

warkamoovee See **wark-moowee**

warka-moowee *Sri Lanka, S:* Plank-extended dugout **canoe*** with a single outrigger...

Bottom flattened; top third of **canoe***... Other recorded names: **market boat***, **Point de Galle canoe, warkamoovee, warka-mowe**

warka-mowe See **warka-moowee**

Warnmonder snik See **snik-3**

Warnemünder Fischerjolle, Warnemünder Jolle See **jolle-5**

Warp'sche Boot See **jacht-5**

warr See **wa-2**

warraga See **hurija**

warry See **wary**

warship See **man-of-war**

Warthekahn See **Kaffenkahn**

wary *Canada, E:* Locally made, open **fishing boat***... Other recorded names: **le wary, oueris, warhis, waria, warry, werrie**. See also **doris-3**.

Wasa punt See **eka-2**

Washington County peapod See **peapod**

Waspikker, Waspikse klipperaak See **klipperaak**

Wasserboot See **bumboat-1, water boat-1**

Wasserdepôtschiff See **water boat-1**

Wasser-Diligence *Germany, W:*... Name variant: **diligence**. Note also **coche d'eau**.

Wasserprahm See **Prahm-2, water boat-1**

Wassertanker, Wassertender See **water boat-1**

watch boat *England, SE:* **Oyster smack**... Other recorded names: **oyster watch boat, watch smack**; also **Blackwater, Colne**, and **Whitstable watch boat**.

Note also **oyster navy**, **Whitstable oyster smack**. Further reference: **guard boat-1**

watcher See **fishery guard ship**

Watchet flatty *England, SW:* Sharp-ended, flat-bottomed boat of the Watchet area in southwestern Somerset. Used for salmon and herring fishing. Phased out in the 1930s. Bottom rocker at ends and athwartships; external layer of boards protected the bottom from the local ledges. Flared sides of a single plank. Sailed, setting a spritsail, and rowed. Length ca. 5.5m.

watch smack See **watch boat**

water barge See **water boat-1**

water-bark See **waterschip**

water boat **1.** One that carries fresh water to vessels anchored in the harbor or roadstead. Constructed with special tanks and pumps. Other recorded names: **barcaça d'agua**, **barca cisterna**, **bateau à eau**, **bateau citerne**, **cisterna**, **citerne**, **tank boat***, **vodoleĭ**, **Wasserboot**, **Wasserdepôtschiff**, **Wasserprahm**, **Wassertanker**, **Wassertender**, **water barge**, **water hoy**, **watering boat**, **waterschuit**, **water tender**, **Zisterne**. Note also **aljibe**, **anchor hoy**, **gabarrón**, **paat**, **tank barge**.
2. *United States:* The U.S. Army has used motorized **water boats** to transport fresh water to military installations lacking adequate supplies. Those used in the 1940s were ca. 30m long and had a crew of 11.
3. *United States, NE:* Carried fresh water to ships and **fishing boats*** anchored in New England harbors before deepwater wharves were built. Sharp bow, rounded stern, moderate drag to keel, fairly flat floors, hard bilges. Flush deck; cockpit for helmsman; some had a small cabin aft. Steered by tiller. Water contained in large, built-in, wooden tanks located roughly amidships; discharged by a hand pump; some also carried ice. On the **catboat*** type, the mast was stepped at the bow, setting a boomed mainsail with a short, low-peaked gaff hoisted by a single halyard. Others **sloop***-rigged. The sail was usually lettered "water." Crew of 1-2. Reported lengths 9.1-16.5m; e.g., length 11.3m, beam 3.7m; the Boston boats were generally smaller. Name variant: **Gloucester water boat**

watercress boat See **narrow boat**

waterhaler See **waterschip**

water horse See **cannow**, **canoe-7**

water hoy, **watering boat** See **water boat-1**

waterlegger, **waterman** See **waterschip**

waterman's wherry See **Gravesend waterman's wherry**

waterschepen See **waterschip**

waterschip *Netherlands:* **1.** Fishing **trawler*** of the Zuiderzee, dating from roughly the late 14th to the mid-19th century. Some were modified to carry live fish to market (**caerschip**), and some used their excellent towing qualities to pull seagoing ships over the Pampus shoals near Amsterdam until 1829, when a channel was dredged across the shoals. This towing capability was made possible by their large jib, which was supported by a web of lines between the stays and shrouds. Carvel- or clinker-planked. Bluff ends; heavy sternpost; pronounced, straight and heavy stem; high bow, low stern; long keel; live well. Outboard rudder; tiller; no leeboards. Decked; long deckhouse abaft the mast. Large, high-peaked spritsail or a gaff sail; large jib. Largest of the Zuiderzee **fishing boats***. Reported lengths 16.8-19.6m, widths 5.6-6.3m, depth 2.77m. Further name variant: **Zuyderzese visser**
2. Term also applied to **barges*** similar to the **tjalk*** that carried fresh water to Belgian and Dutch communities requiring it as well as sea water to be distilled into salt, until the beginning of the 20th century. Bluff bow with heavy stem and sternpost; pronounced deadwood; rounded stern. Flat floors; long, shallow keel. Decked with large covered hold for the water; deckhouse. Most lacked leeboards. Early vessels set a high-peaked spritsail, 2 headsails. Gaff-rigged with 1-2 headsails. Length 20m, beam 5m. Name variant: **zoutwaterschip**, **zoetwatertjalk**
3. Another type, a long, flat craft, brought a steady supply of fresh water to Amsterdam brewers. These set a square sail and a large foresail. Sometimes called a **waterschuit** or **waterschuÿt**. Note also **ijsbreker**.
4. An early term referred to any fishing vessel with a live well. Generally sprit-rigged.
Other recorded names: **Marker waterschip** (**waterschuit**, or **Wasserschiff**), **waaterschip**, **water-bark**, **waterhaler**, **waterlegger**, **waterman**; pl. **waterschepen**. Further reference: **beunschip**

waterschuit See **water boat-1**, **waterschip-3**

waterschuÿt See **waterschip-3**

water scooter See **scooter-1**

water stage See **coastal packet**

water taxi See **shore boat-1**

water tender See **water boat-1**

wato *Malawi:* **Dugout canoe*** of the Tonga peoples of Lake Nyasa. Small, square projection at each end. Tree may be felled and the **canoe*** adzed out some distance inland from the lake. Paddled and poled. Paddles carefully made; narrow blade with a ridge worked into each side. Spelling variant: pl. **mawato**

Watten-Ewer See **Ewer**

Watzille, **Watzzille** See **Waidzille**

Waveney wherry See **Norfolk wherry**

Waydling See **Weidling**

Waydzille See **Waidzille**

we See **ua-2**

Wear foyboat See **foyboat-2**

Weaver flat *England, W:* The **Weaver** and **Mersey flats*** were essentially the same craft, and many of the River Mersey vessels were built on the River Weaver. Traded mainly between Liverpool and the Weaver, but some worked along the coast. Towed by men in the upper reaches of the Weaver until 1840, then by horses, and then became steam **barges*** (see **packet***). Salt was a major cargo. Length 17.4m, width 4.57m. Other recorded names: **jigger flat** (**ketch***-rigged), **number one flat** (family-owned), **Weaver sailing barge**

Weaver packet See **packet**

Weaver sailing barge See **Weaver flat**

wedge boat See **Strait boat**

weed cutter **1.** *England:* Cuts weeds from canal bottoms. May be specially designed for this purpose or a modified **canal boat★**. One type employs a V-shaped blade at the bow that can cut a 2.4m swatch, and can be lowered to 3m. Propelled by a gasoline engine that drives paddles at the bow. Flat bottom, sharp stern. Length 6m, beam 1.2m, draft 0.25m. Name variant: **weeder**. Note also **bank boat, bateau faucher, didal boat**.
  2. *United States, E:* Also employed on U.S. canals. Those on the Morris Canal in northeastern New Jersey cut underwater weeds with a gasoline engine-powered sickle appended to the **scow★** bow.

weeder See **weed cutter**

wei See **wai-1**

weiboot See **weischuit**

Weichselkahn See **szkuta**

wei chuan *China, N:* Vessel that carried cargo between Yingkou in Liaoning Province to Tianjin (Tientsin). Spelling variant: **wei tch'ouan**. See also **liu wang chuan, nan he chuan, sin-tor-chai**.

Weidlig See **Weidling**

Weidling *Germany/Switzerland:* **1.** Those on the middle and upper Rhine and Aare Rivers are small, open cargo vessels that carry stone, gravel, and wood. Poled upstream with pronged poles. Bow and stern square and overhanging, the stern more elongated. Flat bottom, longitudinally planked, with strong rocker; strips protect the bilge seams. Flaring sides, considerable sheer. Steered with a long sweep. Also rowed. Reported lengths 10-22m; e.g., length 21m, beam at top 2.5m, depth 0.95m.
  2. On the Lake of Biel in western Switzerland, an open, unrigged, **scow★**-type boat. Reported lengths 10-14m, beam ca. 2m, depths 0.6-1.0m.
  3. In the 17th century, one type centered at Bern, the **Berner Schiff** (or **Berner Weidling**), carried freight on the Aare. Crew of 2. Length ca. 13m, beam 1.0m, depth 1.1m. Spelling variant: **Weidlig**
  4. In Switzerland, the term may also apply to flat-bottomed craft used for hunting on lakes and rivers. Bottom curved up to a square bow; flat sides. Length ca. 10m.
  5. Word was also used by missionaries from southern Germany in the 17th-18th centuries to describe the Latin American **dugout canoe★**.
  6. In southwestern Germany, may be a small, **Nachen★**-type boat of 10-30t cap. used to transport 3-4 people. Also used for fishing. Name variant: **Waidnachen** Other recorded names: **Langwaidling, Langweidling, Waidling, Waidnachen, Waitschiff, Waydling, Weydling**

Weidschelch See **Waidschelch**

Weidschiff, Weidschiffal See **Waidschiff**

Weidzille See **Waidzille**

Weintanker See **wine ship**

weir haul See **seine boat-5b**

weischuit *Netherlands:* Small boat that traversed meadowlands; in the southwestern part of the country, in Zeeland, some were used for mullet fishing. Strongly raked stem; sharp bow and stern;

flat bottom; tall rudder extended below the bottom. Open except for short foredeck; 2 thwarts. Larger boats used leeboards when sailing; might set 2 gaff sails. Reported lengths 5.5-7m; e.g., length 5.5m, beam 1.4m, depth 0.38m. Other recorded names: **weiboot, weischuitje, weyschuit, weyschuyt**. Further reading: Nicolaes Witsen, *Architectura Navalis et Regimen Nauticum...* (Amsterdam: Pieter en Joan Blaeu, 1690; facsimile, Amsterdam, 1971), 179, 188, 189. Note also **schuit**.

weischuitje See **weischuit**

wei tch'ouan See **wei chuan**

weitschiff See **Waidschiff, wijdschip**

Weitzille, Weitzzille See **Waidzille**

welbot See **ballinier**

Welland canaller See **canaller**

well boat **1. Fishing boat★** or **fish carrier★** with a watertight compartment, fed with circulating seawater through holes in the bottom and/or sides, enabling the fish or crustaceans to reach the market alive. Some used mainly to carry live bait. Dates to the 16th century. Pumps now generally circulate the water. Most carvel-planked. Other recorded names: **bateau vivier, beunschip★, brønnbåt, Bünn-Ewer, Bünnschiff, kvase★, kvass★, live-well boat, prorez★, vivaio, vivero★, vivier★, well(ed) smack, wet smack**. Note also **dry boat, smack, tow car, yu chuan**.
  2. A flat-bottomed boat used for landing troops and stores; rowed.
  Further reference: **whiting boat**

well car See **tow car**

well-deck corvette See **corvette-1**

well-deck punt See **Thames lighter**

welled smack See **cod smack-1, smack-6, well boat-1**

Wellenbinder See **deadrise boat**

well smack See **lobster smack, smack-6, well boat-1**

wepipyu'ara See **woodskin**

Werkendammer boot See **zalmschouw**

werkschuit See **vlotschuit**

werrie See **wary**

werÿ See **wherry**

Weserkahn See **Kahn-2**

West Coast canoe *Canada, SW:* General term applied to the **dugout canoe★** made by the Nootkan tribes of the west coast of Vancouver Island. Traded widely and found from the north end of the island south to the Columbia River and into Puget Sound. Characterized

West Coast canoe

by the grooved, deer or wolf head-like prow and the near-vertical, sharp stern capped by a small, elevated platform; bow and stern pieces attached by dowels and lashings. Expanded dugout with flared sides; widest beam amidships; a slight sheer results from the spreading process; bottom flat longitudinally and transversely. Concave bow line presents clipper-bow appearance; chevron-like ornament incised where bow piece joins the hull. Gunwales capped with strips; thwarts of rounded poles. Usually painted; often red inside. Rows of parallel grooves in places along exterior and interior. Those used for whaling ornamented with inset shells or seal teeth. Paddle sharply pointed; dowel crosspiece formed grip. Rudimentary square sail of woven cedar bark used at times; boomed at the foot; mast supported between 2 athwartships rods. Wide size range, depending on whether used for local travel, war, ceremonial occasions, cargo (**freight canoe★**), or whaling. Reported lengths 2.4-18.2m. **Whaling canoe** length 10.67m, beam 1.83m, depth 0.6m; crew of 8: 6 paddlers, harpooner, steersman. Other recorded names: **ao'txs, a'tqEs, big canoe, chap-ats, chap-atz, chă-pŭts, Chinook canoe** (**sE'qEm** or **sqam** by the Kwakiutl), **chu-puts, deer (head) canoe, ku'mtsała, Nootka canoe (nuu-chah-[n]ulth), shapats, southern canoe, traveling canoe, tschap-pits, war canoe**. Further reading: T. T. Waterman, *The Whaling Equipment of the Makah Indians*, Publications in Political and Social Science, 1.1 (Seattle: Univ. of Washington, 1920), 9-29. Note also **pa-dá-wahl, sealing canoe-1, shitlats**.

West Coast hooker See **hooker**

West Cornish lugger *England, SW:* **Double-ender★** that drifted for pilchard and mackerel from the ports west of The Lizard around Land's End to St. Ives.

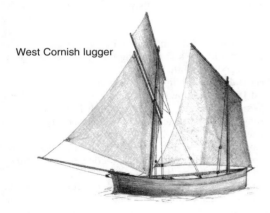

West Cornish lugger

Pilchard boats generally smaller and half-decked, and in addition to pilchard, fished locally for herring. Mackerel boats later decked and characterized by a jackyard topsail set to the mizzenmast; also fished for herring in distant waters during the summer. Although mostly sharp-ended, during some periods, transom and counter sterns were popular. Generally near-vertical stem and raked stern; straight keel with drag. Sharper lines and flatter floors on St. Ives boats. Bilge keels added onto the boats that grounded at low tide. Mostly apple-bowed until ca. 1865, but the lines became sharper and the stem straighter with time. The mackerel boats had a cabin aft with a distinctive skylight forward of the mizzenmast. Those with a long hatchway that could be closed were called **hatch boats★** in the Mounts Bay area. The larger mackerel boats carried a 3.66-5.18m boat, called a **punt★**. In the late 18th and early 19th centuries, some 3-masted

luggers★ worked from Mousehole and St. Ives. Square-headed dipping lugsail on the foremast, tacked to an iron bumkin, and extended forward by a spar. Mainmast also set a dipping lug and a square-headed topsail to a topmast; each sail extended by a bowline. Mizzenmast short or tall, and some raked over the stern; sheeted to an outrigger that extended out from the port side of the sternpost. Jib also used. Later boats 2-masted. Pilchard boats had a tall mainmast (locally called the foremast) to which a dipping lugsail was set. Shorter mizzenmast, raked forward, stepped a standing lugsail that sheeted to a long, steeved-up outrigger; halyard held forward of the mast. On mackerel boats, the mizzenmast was tall to accommodate the yard topsail. Crew of 5-9. Pilchard boats ranged from 9-12m in length; e.g., length overall 10.6m, on keel 9.4m, beam 3.35m, hold depth 1.12m. Mackerel boats 13.7-16.6m; e.g., length 14.8m, beam 4.27m, inside depth 1.98m. Other recorded names: **herring boat★, mackerel driver, Mounts Bay driver** (and **pilchard driver, mackerel driver, lugger), Mousehole drift boat, Penzance herring boat, pilchard boat, pilchard driver, Saint Ives mackerel driver, West country pilchard boat**; also **Cornwall, Mousehole, Newlyn, Penzance, Porthleven, Saint Ives,** and **West Country lugger; Cornish (Cornwall) driver**. Further reading: Edgar J. March, *Sailing Drifters* (Newton Abbot: David & Charles; Camden, Maine: International Marine Publishing Co., 1969/1972), 138-178; R. M. Nance, "West Cornwall Fishing Luggers Before 1850," *The Mariner's Mirror* 30 (1944), 93-108. Note also **East Cornish lugger, jolly boat-4a, nickey-2**.

West Country barge *England, north-central:* A type of coal-carrying **barge★** that worked on waterways in the Leeds area. See also **western barge**.

West Country boat *England, central:* Non-tidal **keel★** of the Calder and Hebble Canal and the Rochdale Canal in Yorkshire; some traveled to Liverpool on the west coast. Rounded ends, straight sides. Fully decked or decked only at the ends. Outboard rudder; iron tiller on the canal, wooden tiller on rivers. Early **barges★** of wood, and horse-drawn; later of steel, and diesel-powered or towed in part by steam **tugs**. Most had a small rig that was used occasionally, and otherwise stowed. Length 17.5m, beam 4.3m, hold depth 2m, draft 1.5m. Other recorded names: **boat★, West Country keel**. Note also **Yorkshire keel**.

West Country crabber *England, SW:* The coves of the south coast of Cornwall and Devon had small boats used principally for crabbing and lobstering, but might also engage in line fishing. Generally similar from place to place but with small variations in hull and rigging. Most carvel-planked; clinker in a few places, as at Polperro and Portloe. Transom stern; plumb, straight stem. Generally open with 4-5 thwarts and bulkheads that compartmented the boat; some later boats had a foredeck and a covered hold amidships. Turn of the bilges generally soft and floors steep. At Sennen, an extra washstrake made the sides too high for rowing, so oar ports were cut into the top strake;

shuttered closed when at sea. Later boats at Polperro and Cadgwith had centerboards; all carried considerable ballast. Early boats favored 2 spritsails, the mizzenmast stepped against the port transom; then the sprit mizzen was retained, but the mainsail (called foresail in this area) was changed to a dipping lugsail. After World War I, the mizzen became a standing lugsail, and the mast was stepped farther for-

West Country crabber

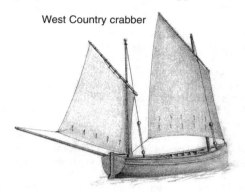

ward. Mizzen sheeted to a very long outrigger. In bad weather, the mizzen sail might be moved to the forward mast and a smaller mizzen run up. In some places, the mainsail was sheeted to a wooden or iron bumkin, and in Hope Cove, a jib was used. No mizzen at Hallsands. Rowed in calms. Motors now common. Crew of 2. Reported lengths 4.8-9.1m, widths 1.75-2.74m, depths 0.76-1.37m; shallow draft. Large, modern **crabbers★**, working well offshore, may be as long as 15m. Other recorded names: **crabber**; also **Cadgwith Cove**, **Devon**, **Gerrans**, **Hallsands**, **Hope Cove**, **Land's End**, **Mounts Bay**, **Polperro**, **Porthgwarra**, and **Sennen Cove crabber**. Note also **Cornish crabber**.

West Country keel See **West Country barge**

West Country lugger, **West Country pilchard boat** See **West Cornish lugger**

West Country sailing barge *England, SW:* Worked within the estuaries and their tributary rivers at Plymouth, Falmouth, and Appledore, or sailed along the coast. **Inside barges** stayed entirely within the estuaries, while **outside barges**, which were longer, deeper, and decked, worked along the coast, and on occasion, crossed to the Channel Islands. Carried various cargoes depending on the locale and demand of the time. Reported from the early 19th century; gone by the mid-20th century. Straight stem; shallow, sloping transom; rounded bottom. **Inside barges** had a high-peaked gaff mainsail, staysail, and sometimes a jib to a bowsprit. **Outside barges** also raised a square-headed gaff topsail to a fidded topmast. Reported lengths 6-15m; e.g., length 12.2m, beam 3.7-3.9m, inside depth 1.8m; shallow draft. Name variant: **West Country smack**. Further reading: H. O. Hill, "West Country Barges," *The Mariner's Mirror* (1962), 205-220. Note also **Fal barge**, **gravel barge**, **Plymouth barge**.

West Country smack See **West Country sailing barge**

Westerd drontheim See **drontheim**

western barge *England, S:* Used on the River Thames west of London from medieval times until the early 19th century to carry timber, faggots, malt, hops, etc. Some provided regular passenger service, but such service was limited to 10 passengers in the 17th century. Initially a simple rectangular shape with vertical sides; flat bottom; raked, **punt★**-like ends; no deck. Evolved into a decked craft with a pointed bow, transom stern, and a more rounded cross section. Employed leeboards and a wide-finned rudder. Towed from the masthead upstream and through canals by as many as 12 horses and occasionally by gangs of men. Early **barges★** set a square sail; high-peaked spritsail adopted in the 18th century. Pole mast stepped in a tabernacle. Early undecked boats had a crew of 3. Dimensions varied widely depending on the period, stretches of river traveled, and lock limitations. Reported lengths 15-39m; e.g., length 26.7m, beam 3.5m, draft 0.9-1.2m. Other recorded names: **Thames barge**, **West Country barge**

western boat See **jack**

West Haven sharpie See **sharpie-2**

West Hudson Bay kayak See **kayak-5**

West Indiaman **Merchantman★** of the latter part of the 18th and early 19th centuries that traveled between Europe and the Caribbean. Smaller than the **East Indiaman★**, and since they carried perishable goods, were generally faster. Many built in the United States. Most **bark★**-rigged with square sails on the fore- and mainmasts; gaff mizzen with a square topsail. Multiple jibs to a long, rising bowsprit. Some armed. Averaged 300-500t.

West Indian beach lighter See **beach punt-3**

West Indies schooner Interisland trader of the southern Windward Islands that carries both freight and passengers. The term **schooner★** is used loosely and frequently applied to **sloop★**- or **cutter★**-rigged vessels. Roughly built with heavy, rough-hewn timbers; bluff bow; curved stem; heavy, raked counter stern; rounded bottom; strong sheer. Generally have a white band along the top strake; hull painted in various colors. On the 2-masted **schooners**, about half carry 2 topmasts; remainder have a topmast only on the mainmast. High-peaked gaff on the single-masted boats; mast short, boom long. Most have auxiliaries. Reported lengths 15-48m; now most ca. 12m; length-to-beam ratio roughly 4:1, depth one-half beam; shoal draft. Name variant: **trading schooner**. Note also **Barbados schooner**, **Cayman schooner**, **sloop-10**.

West Indies sloop See **Jamaica sloop**, **sloop-10**

West Mersea smack See **Essex smack**

Weston-super-Mare flatner *England, SW:* Open, flat-bottomed, clinker-built passenger and **fishing boat★**. Used primarily in Weston-super-Mare Bay, on the south coast of Bristol Channel, from the mid-19th century to the present. Longitudinal bottom planking, usually in 2-3 layers; athwart and fore-and-aft rocker; hard chines. Smaller boats required 6-7 broad strakes, more on the larger; rounded sides; initially, frames sawn or grown; later steam-bent; heavier and more widely spaced than usual. Maximum beam well forward; medium to bold sheer. Stem curved and raked; most had a high-tucked, raked transom. Two or 3 thwarts; for sailing, a portable thwart inserted, level with the sheer, to which the mast was clamped. Two daggerboards sometimes used in tandem on those that sailed. Generally set a single spritsail and jib to an

Weston-super-Mare flatner

unstayed mast; larger boats might be rigged as **sloops★**, **cutters★**, or with 2 masts setting sprit-, lug-, or gaff sails. Rowed with 2 pairs of long oars; engines installed on recent boats. Reported lengths 3-9m; e.g., length 7m, beam topsides 2.13m, on bottom 0.9m, depth 0.84m. The small **dinghy★**-sized **flatners★** were called **punts★**; those in the 4.6-5.2m range were called **Clevedon boats**. Further reading: J. E. G. KcKee, "The Weston-Super-Mare Flatner," *The Mariner's Mirror* 57 (1971), 24-39.

Westray skiff *Scotland, N:* Open boat of the Orkney Islands used for fishing and transportation. Clinker planking, sharp ends. Rowed and sailed. Mast stepped well forward; sets a tanned dipping lugsail. Length overall 5.5m, on keel 4.6m, beam 2m. Name variant: **Papa Westray skiff**

Westray yole See **North Isles yole**

West River salt boat See **ma yang chuan**

West Sulawesi lambo See **bago-1**

Westwalbotter See **botter**

West Wight scow See **scow-10**

wet smack See **lobster smack, well boat-1**

Wewelsflether Galiot See **galiot-5**

Wexford cot *Ireland, SE:* **1.** Employed in Wexford County fisheries, working off the beaches; small **cots★** ferry between shore and the moored seagoing **cots**. These latter carried fish to southwest England in the 15th century and coal from Wales. Sides clinker-planked; widely spaced frames. Sharp, slightly raked ends on older boats; those using outboard motors have a narrow transom stern, but are sharp below. Heavy, longitudinal planking on the flat bottom with rocker; sharp chines. Short lengths of keel at each end; stern keel extends aft to protect the small rudder; grounding keels amidships on some. Older **cots** used a center-board; later a daggerboard. Ballast of heavy stones or

sandbags. Open. Set 2-3 sprit- or gaff sails and often a foresail; mizzensail extended aft by a jigger boom; mainsail tanned. Those under 7m set a single sail. Sometimes poled, sculled, or rowed. Fishing **cots** had a crew of 4. Length to 12m; e.g., length 7.3m, beam 1.8m, depth 0.6m; shallow draft. Other recorded names: **herring cot**, **Rosslare cot**. Further reading: O. T. P. Roberts, "The Cots of Rosslare Harbour and Wexford," *The Mariner's Mirror* 71 (1985), 13-34. **2.** In the latter part of the 19th century, wildfowlers of the Wexford area used lightly built, **punt★**-like **cots**. Open; square ends; flat bottom; sides nearly vertical. Length ca. 4.6m, beam 0.7m, depth 0.25m. Other recorded names: **float★**, **shooting cot**
See also **gabbard-1**.

Wexford gabbard See **gabbard-1**

Weydling See **Weidling**

Weydschiff, Weydschiffel See **Weidschiff**

weyschuit See **Aalsmeerse punter, punter, weischuit**

weyschuyt See **weischuit**

weyschuytje See **Aalsmeerse punter**

whaka See **waka-2**

whaka pahi'i See **waka pahii**

whaleback *United Kingdom:* Torpedo boat built prior to World War I with a curved hull forward that resembled a whale. Name variant: **turtleback**. Note also **schooner-barge-2**. Further reference: **pig boat-2**

whaleboat **1.** A small, sharp-ended, open boat used for harpooning whales, working either from shore or from a **mother ship★**. By extension, any fast, light boat of similar design. Term may also apply to a **ship's boat★**, both naval and merchant, and sometimes to a **surfboat★** launched from shore lifesaving stations. Propelled by oar, sail, and more recently by motor. Other recorded names: **baleazalea** (Basque); **baleeira★**, **baleinier★**, **baleinière**, **balenera**, **balenièra**, **bale-ontzi**, **ballenera★**, **ballen(n)ier**, **barco ballenero**, **hvalbåd**, **kutter★**, **pirogue★**, **vel'bot**, **Walboot**, **Walfischboot**, **walvissloep**, **whaler★**. Note also **canoa do baleeiro**, **chalupa-9b**, **fast boat**, **five-handed boat**, **goélette-1c**, **whale catcher**. **2.** *Australia:* These **whaleboats** had less freeboard than the **Yankee whaleboat** (see **7a**), but otherwise similar. Graceful sheer, no centerboard. Those used for bay whaling were clinker- or carvel-built; crew of 7 at the oars; length 9.8m, beam 1.8m, depth 0.46m. The off-shore type was carvel-planked and worked with 5 at the oars; 8.5m long. When converted for fishing, open well and centerboard fitted; sprit-rigged. **3.** *Cocos Islands, eastern Indian Ocean:* Primarily a workboat with many special modifications, particular-ly a deep keel and tumble home to the sides. **4.** *Greenland (Kalâtdlit-Nunât):* Plans for one, dated 1768, show ends fuller than later boats; sides straighter; keel curved; strong sheer. Carvel-planked; strakes of fir; stem, sternpost, keel, and frames of oak. Cuddy boards at each end. **Six-oared boats** carried a crew of 7; the **four-oared boats** had 5. Reported lengths 7-8.5m; length of 1768 boat 7.5m, beam 1.6m, depth ca. 0.8m. Other recorded names: **Green-land whaleboat**, **Groenlandse boot** (or **sloep**), **Groentlandsche sloep**

5. *New Zealand:* In the early 19th century, locally constructed **whaleboats** were made especially for trade to the Maoris, who used the boats as all-purpose craft. A special feature was the use of natural-crook stem and sternpost; clinker-built of cedar. Those engaged in whaling carried a crew of 6-8 and were hung from davits over the ship's sides. Rowed single-banked. Reported lengths 7.9-9.1m, beam ca. 1.5m.

whaleboat-5

6. *United Kingdom:* **a.** The **whaleboat** of British whalers of the 18th-19th centuries was a long, narrow craft with fine entrance and run at the ends, raked and rounded stem and sternpost, considerable sheer, flat keel, rising floors, and slack bilges. Somewhat fuller forward than aft; some had a small transom. Ends fuller and sides flatter than the American **whaleboat**. Carvel-planked by 1820s; some from Scotland diagonally planked. Loggerhead at the bow or substituted 2 posts. Oars (4-6) were of uniform length. Crew of 5, 7, or 8. Reported lengths 7.6-10m; e.g., length 10m, beam 1.7m, depth 0.47m; small 4-oared boats: 7-7.3m long, 1.6m wide. Name variant: **English whaleboat. b.** The **whaleboats** of the British navy had little sheer, high freeboard, nearly plumb ends, sprung keels, and relatively full lines. Lapstrake planking of elm or oak. Rudder worked with yoke and lines, or long tiller. Pulled 1-5 pairs of oars single-banked. Rig evolved from a single dipping lugsail to 2 short-leeched dipping lugsails set to slightly aft-raking masts. The **Montague whaler** of the 20th century set a gunter or low, standing lug mainsail, small leg-of-mutton mizzen, foresail, and trysail. These had fuller lines, slightly curved keel, rounded stem and sternpost, and a centerboard; the few remaining are used for ceremonial occasions and racing. Two lengths, 7.6m and 8.2m; e.g., length 8.2m, beam 1.8m, depth 0.38m, draft 0.91m. Powered **launches*** of the navy continue to be called **whalers***. Other recorded names: **Montagu whaler, whaler**

7. *United States:* **a.** Those used by American whaling interests evolved from the early 1700s and were standardized ca. 1870. Carried aboard whaling ships or worked from shore, used as **lifeboats***, and during military actions, were important in scouting expeditions. Open; sharp ends; curved stem and sternpost. Hard turn of the bilges with little deadrise; later soft bilges with pronounced deadrise amidships; fine run. On early boats, the keel amidships rounded suddenly to a depth of ca. 10cm to serve as a pivot point and prevent leeway; in the late 19th century, most had a centerboard. Clinker-built until ca. 1852, when a smooth-skinned boat was developed, except for a lapped garboard strake and 2 strakes along the sheer (the **Beetle whaleboat**); hull ceiled. Foredeck and aft cuddy board; long steering oar with short, right-angle grip used for close maneuvering; most rigged for

sailing and fitted with rudder and tiller; loggerhead at stern for belaying the harpoon line. Mainly rowed, single-banked; 5 or 6 oars of various lengths. Variously rigged, setting a dipping lug-; sprit-; quadrilateral, lateen-type sail with a short luff; sliding gunter; or gaff sail and sometimes a jib; mast stepped into tabernacle. Crew of 6. Early boats 4.6-7.9m; later to 9m; e.g., length 8.6m, beam 1.9m, depth 0.87m. Other recorded names: **Beetle boat*, New Bedford whaleboat, Yankee whaleboat**. Further reading: Willis D. Ansel, *The Whaleboat: A Study of Design, Construction and Use From 1850 to 1970* (Mystic, Conn.: Mystic Seaport Museum, 1978). Note also **whaler-3. b.** A **whaleboat**-type craft was used for military purposes, especially scouting, by the British in North America in the second half of the 18th century, and by the revolutionaries for raiding, smuggling, intelligence gathering, etc., especially on Long Island Sound and Chesapeake Bay. Colonial **whaleboats** generally ca. 8.5m long, 1.2m wide; might set a lateen or lugsail. Each carried a crew of up to 30 men with 6-8 at the oars. Standardized type adapted by the U.S. Navy in the 1840s. These had fuller bilges, less rake, mahogany trim, and stern sheets; deadwood aft from ca. 1900. Copper tanks fitted under bow and stern sheets in late 19th-century boats to aid in flotation. Those 9m long were rowed double-banked; shorter boats single-banked. Rigged as a **ketch*** with a sliding gunter sail. Engines installed in the early 20th century. Naval boats: lengths 6-9m; e.g., length 8.5m, beam 2m, depth 0.7m. The **gig whaleboat** was lighter and more cheaply made; some carvel-planked above the waterline and lapstrake below; lengths 8.5-9.1; e.g., length 8.5m, beam 1.8m, depth 0.74m. Other recorded names: **baleinière, berge, whaleboat gig**

8. *United States, E:* The Long Island **whaleboat** worked from south shore beaches into the 20th century. Carvel-planked except for the 2 top strakes, which were lapped; no battens; ceiled; sides flared. Set a small spritsail. Reported lengths 8.2-8.5m.

9. *West Indies, SE:* Introduced into the southern Windward Islands in the mid-19th century, notably on Bequia, St. Vincent, and St. Lucia; a few still used for whaling, but most now fish. Work from the beaches. Beamier than the Yankee boats; some with deadwood at forefoot and aft and a deeper keel. Hand-hewn carvel planking; curved, natural-crook stem, sternpost, and thwart knees; slight sheer; centerboard; 5 rowing thwarts on larger boats; cuddy board and loggerhead aft. Outboard rudder; tiller; steering oar used when rudder unshipped and stowed. Sets a high-peaked, boomed spritsail and very large jib. Those from St. Lucia employ a three-cornered mainsail with a triangular piece of the tack cut away. Bamboo mast. Crew of 3-6. Reported lengths 4.3-9.1m; e.g., length overall 7.6m, on keel 6m, beam 1.93m. Name variant: **whaler***. Note also **billieboat**.

Further references: **baleeira-2, baleinière de Gaspé, ballinier, bonitera-1, canoa do baleeiro, goélette-1c, Hampton boat, longboat-5, whaler-2**

whaleboat gig See **whaleboat-7b**

whale catcher A vessel, generally powered, that attends a modern whale factory ship and is used in the manner of the old **whaleboats*** to harpoon the whale. Other recorded names: **caronnière, catcher (boat), chaser ship, chasseur*, chasseur-baleinier, hvalbåt, killer boat, kitolovac, kitolovka, kvalbåt, vangboot, Walfangboot, Walfisch-fänger, whale chaser, whale killer**

whale chaser See **whale catcher**

whale factory See **whaler-1**

Whale Islands boat See **hvalerbåt**

whale killer See **whale catcher**

whalemajol See **walenmajol**

whaler   1. In general, a vessel engaged in catching whales. Until the mid-19th century, term referred to sailing vessels carrying a complement of **whaleboats***; subsequently these **tenders*** might become known as **whalers**. Sailing **whalers** were often other types of vessels modified for whaling. A **factory whaler** is equipped to process whales. Selected name variants: **baleinier*, balenario, balenière, balenista, balingaria, balingario, balingera, ballanero, ballanero, belingiero, blubber hunter** (or **ship**), **hvalfanger, kitoboïnoe sudno, navire baleinier, norvégienne, old hooker, spouter, Walfangschiff, walvisvaarder, whale ship** (or **factory**), **whaling ship, baleinier-usine**. Note also **cat-2, factory ship, noordsvaarder, pinnace-2, whale catcher**.
    2. *Canada:* **a.** In the Canadian navy, a **whaler** is comparable to a **jolly boat*.** **b.** Term applied to the boats carried aboard the Labrador fishing **fleet*** out of Nova Scotia in the first part of the 19th century. Handlined for cod and other fish. Open; double-ended; rowed and sailed, stepping a single portable mast. Crew of 2. About 5.2m long. **c.** The Basque **whalers** of the 16th century, off Labrador, were a **galleon*** type, being a cross between a **galley*** and a 15th-century whaling ship. Oak-built; long keel. Armed against **privateers*** and the native peoples. Carried up to 10 **catcher boats*** (also called **biscayennes*, boats*, pirogues*, shallops*,** or **whaleboats***). May have towed a **pinnace***, which would have been too large to carry aboard. Mainmast, the length of the keel plus the vessel's rake, set a square sail; similarly rigged foremast, the length of the keel. Lateen mizzen; sprit foresail hung from the bowsprit. Crew of 50-120. Cap. ca. 300-900 cubic meters.
    3. *United States, NE:* The New England **whalers** were originally **sloop***-rigged; later **schooner*-, bark*-,** or **ship***-rigged. The 19th-century vessels usually carried 4 **whaleboats** on davits. The **whaleboat** aft on the starboard side was the **captain's** or **starboard boat**; a 5th boat might be carried forward on this side. The port boats were the **larboard boat** aft (under the first mate), the **waist boat*** (commanded by the second mate) hung abreast the mainmast, and the **bow boat*** forward (with the third mate in charge). Two or 3 spare **whaleboats** were carried as replacements for those damaged in service. Later vessels were smaller and

hung only 2-3 boats on davits. A typical vessel of the 1840s was 32m long, 8.2m wide, and 4.15m deep. Other recorded name: **Yankee whaler**. Note also **Hampton boat**.
 Further references: **Boston whaler, longboat-5, Tancook whaler, whaleboat-1, whaleboat-6b, whaleboat-9**

whale ship See **whaler-1**

whaling canoe See **pa-dá-wahl, West Coast canoe**

whaling ship See **whaler-1**

whammel boat   *England, NW/Scotland, SW:* Inshore and river **fishing boat*** especially for salmon; uses a whammel net, one end of which is staked close inshore, the other aboard the boat. A few licensed to take salmon in the 1990s. Early boats clinker-built, later carvel; moderately heavy scantlings; deep keel; extra iron keel bolted on, creating a rocker. Stem straight above the waterline; rounded forefoot. Sharp stern or a transom, both raked. Initially open; later, when larger, decked forward with cuddy below, small deck aft, and wide side decks along the wet well. Some, called **tank boats***, have a watertight compartment at bow and stern, as they were used in the rougher water at the mouth of the River Lune. Standing lug- or gaff sail set to a short mast, stepped about one-third in from the bow; hinged mast collar permitted lowering of mast while grounded. Boom fitted with jaws; sail sometimes loose-footed. Occasionally set a jib to a light bowsprit. Early boats sprit-rigged. Boats now motorized and built along different lines. Rowed when playing out the whammel net. Crew of 2 on sailing type. Reported lengths 4.27-6.25m; e.g., length overall 5.87m, on keel 5.22m, beam 1.92m, inside depth 0.84m; shallow draft. Other recorded names: **Annan whammel-net boat, salmon boat*, salmon drift-net boat, salmon hang-net boat, Solway Firth net wham-mel, Solway whammel boat, tank whammel boat, whammle boat**. Further reading: P. J. Oke, "Local Types XXVI—Annan Whammel Net Boats," *Yachting Monthly* 66 (1939), 306-307.

whammle boat See **whammel boat**

wharf boat   **1.** A vessel, usually an old **hulk***, moored close to a bank to serve as a wharf or office in an area with marked variation in water level. A platform is usually fixed atop the vessel, and a ramp leads to shore.
    2. *England, central:* Coal-carrying boat of the wider, lock-free waterway between Cannock and Wolverhampton, northwest of Birmingham. Open except for a small cabin aft; flat bottom; straight sides; blunted ends. Pulled singly by a horse or by a **tug*** in a train of 5 boats, each boat snubbed close with stem and stern overlapping. Rudder could be hung at either end. Length 27m, beam 2.6m, cap. 58t. Other recorded names: **'Amptonboat (or flat), boat*, Wolverhampton boat**
    3. *United States, central:* The development of **wharf boats** of the type described in **1** above coincided with the advent of **steamboats** on the Mississippi and its major tributaries. Served both as passenger stations

and storage areas for cargo to be loaded aboard. Some had a 2nd story with beds for passengers awaiting delayed **packet boats***. Could be as large as 109m long and 23m wide.
See also **bo chuan-1, ma tou chuan**.

whary, wheary See **wherry**
wheel barrow See **paddle boat-3**
Wheeler boat See **Huron boat**
wheery, where, wherie, wherrey, wherrie See **wherry**
wherry 1. Light, shallow boat used mainly on inland waters to carry passengers and light goods. Fine entrance and run, rounded bottom, plank keel; most lack gunwale pieces. Usually a high, tucked-up stern but may be double-ended below the waterline. Generally rowed.
2. Term also given to a narrow, open boat used by 1-2 oarsmen for racing and exercising. May have a coxswain. Sharp ends, especially at the bow. Clinker-planked. Propelled by 1 or 2 pairs of sculls or 2 outrigged oars; often equipped with a sliding seat. Some inrigged (the **inrigged wherry, dolboordgiek**, and **Dollenwherry**). May be sailed, using 1-2 dipping lugsails. Reported lengths 6-8m. Other recorded names: **Ausleger gig** (or **wherry**), **outrigged wherry, uitleggergiek**
3. A light, fast, transom-sterned **ship's boat***. Dates from the 15th century. Rowed by 1-3 men, single-banked. Reported lengths 7-7.6m.
4. *England, E:* Large, beamy, **barge***-like craft, especially of the Thames Estuary and the Norfolk Broads. Early use appears to have been mainly for light merchandise and passengers; later transported heavy cargoes. Usually sailed. Note also **Norfolk wherry**.
5. *United States:* The American **wherry** was generally sturdier than the English rowing **wherry**, although the 17th-century boats were probably copied from the English. Some of the initial New England colonists called the **dugout canoes*** they made **wherries**. Popular as a method of transportation, especially for plantation owners bordering Chesapeake Bay. These were lapstrake construction, flat-floored, smartly maintained, brightly painted, rowed by servants, and steered with yoke and lines to an outboard rudder. Some of the 18th-century working **wherries** of New England were flat-bottomed, **dory***-type boats. Fishing **wherries** were often sailed and had a centerboard; usually set 1-2 spritsails. Reported lengths 5.6-6.6m. Name variant: **gentleman's wherry**
6. *United States, E:* In the early 19th century, a type of **wherry** provided transportation across the Delaware River between Camden and Philadelphia. Strongly built; decked at the stern. Runners on each side of the keel permitted the boat to be pulled over the ice in winter.
Selected name variants: **bàtà da chroinn, giek, houari*, werȳ, wh(e)ary, wheery, where, wherrey, wher(r)ie, whery, whirie, w(h)irry, whurry, whyrr(e)y, wyhen.** Note also **wary.** Further references: **Cape Roseway wherry, dory-1, Gravesend waterman's wherry, Irish wherry, Manx wherry, Margate wherry, Piscataqua River wherry,**

Portsmouth wherry, salmon wherry, Severn wherry, Thames wherry, Thanet wherry
wherry-bote See **Thames wherry**
wherry-punt See **Thanet wherry**
wherry yacht See **Norfolk wherry**
whery See **wherry**
whiff *England:* A solo racing and training craft used from the second half of the 19th century on the Thames. Propelled by a pair of half-outrigged sculls (see **outrigger**). Mainly clinker-planked but light; raked bow, plumb stem. Generally a fixed seat. Reported lengths 6.1-7.9m, widths 0.41-0.46m. The **whiff gig** was 5.8-6.1m long, 0.81-0.86m wide, and 0.31m deep.
whiff gig See **whiff**
whiffler See **Stationers' barge**
whilli, whillie, whilly See **fourareen**
whirie, whirry See **wherry**
Whitby coble See **coble-1**
Whitby collier brig See **collier-2**
Whitby keelboat See **keelboat-3b**
whitebaiter See **bawley**
white barge See **barge-7**
white boat See **long chuan**
white-bottomed boat See **Amoy fisher, bai du chuan, Fukien trader**
white bottomed junk See **pai ti chuan**
white ensign See **fisherman-2**
Whitehall boat *United States:* Believed to have originated in New York in the 1820s as a waterman's boat. Shortly thereafter became important in Boston, especially to runners from ship's chandlers and boarding houses, who rowed out to incoming ships seeking business. Local boat races and racing between the 2 cities became popular. The New York boats tended to be slightly beamier and had a shallower deadrise, but during the 1870s to 1890s, the distinctions blurred. The Pacific coast boats were usually longer, beamier, and were more often sailed. Now found as a pleasure craft. The term **Whitehall** is often applied to many small **pulling boats*** with a nearly plumb stem, rounded bilges, and a wineglass transom, but a true **Whitehall** was carvel-planked; the deadwood was a deep single piece, and had its own sequence of framing and planking. Long, fine, slightly hollow run; straight keel; moderate sheer; steep deadrise; slack bilges. Steered with a tiller or yoke and lines; if sailed, a daggerboard or centerboard might be added. Usually painted white with backrest, thwarts, transom, and sheer strake varnished. Rowed with 1-3 pairs of oars, some with spoon blades. When sailed, set a low spritsail or leg-of-mutton sail with headboard. Reported lengths 3.7-6.7m; an 1853 New York boat was 5.8m long, 1.35m wide, and 0.48m deep. Other recorded names: **crimps' boat, Whitehall pulling boat; Boston, New England, New York**, and **Pacific Whitehall**. Further reading: John Gardner, *Building Classic Small Craft* (Camden, Maine: International Marine Publishing Co., 1977), 213-233.
Whitehall pulling boat See **whitehall boat**

Whitehall skiff *United States, NW:* Term for the first **gillnetters★** on the Columbia River in the mid-19th century. Imported from Maine along with the nets used to catch Atlantic salmon.

white-headed junk See **cao chuan-3**

white pirogue See **pirogue-5**

white shell fish See **lorcha-3**

white wood boat, white wood sparrow-tail boat See **shou kou ma yang zi**

whiting boat *Australia, South Australia:* Small, **sloop★**-rigged **fishing boat★** that worked in Spencer Gulf, catching whiting, snapper, and kingfish. Especially popular in the first half of the 20th century. The smaller of the 2 types was the **net boat★**; the larger, the **hook boat**, had a live well and was also called the **well boat★**. Flat floors enabled the boat to sit upright at low tide. Older boats were clinker-built, then carvel below the waterline, and finally all carvel. Decked forward of the mast and along the sides; centerboard. Carried a large sail with high-peaked gaff and a long boom; jib to bowsprit. Rowed with long sweeps while looking for schools of whiting; engines installed on some. **Net boat**: 6.1-6.4m long, 2.1m wide, draft 0.38-0.46m; **hook boat**: 6.7-7.3m long. Note also **net boat-2**. Further reference: **Plymouth hooker**

Whitstable bawley See **bawley**

Whitstable oyster dredger See **Whitstable oyster smack**

Whitstable oyster smack *England, SE:* Strongly built, **cutter★**-rigged **oyster dredgers** designed to withstand grounding off their home port of Whitstable on

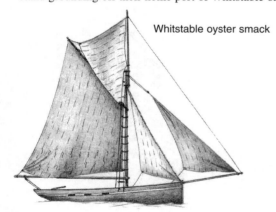

Whitstable oyster smack

the south shore of the Thames Estuary. Worked the oyster beds and did some trawling, shrimping, and freighting from about the mid-19th into the 20th century. Some served as **watch boats★**. Clinker-built until the 1870s, then carvel. Full bilges; some doubled from keel to above the bilge; a few had copper-sheathed bottoms. Horizontal, straight keel on early boats; drag aft later. Straight, vertical stem; most had a boxy, raked counter; some an elliptical stern. Decked with 1-2 hatches. Large ports cut into bulwarks facilitated removing shell and culch. Heavy barrel windlass in bow. Towed a **tender★**. Loose-footed, boomed gaff sail set to a pole mast; some hoisted

a jib-headed or jackyard topsail on a long topmast. Staysail; jib run out on a long bowsprit. A few **ketch★**-rigged. Motors added later. Crew of 3-4. Reported lengths 11-15m; e.g., length 12.3m, beam 4.04m, depth 1.52m, draft ca. 1.8m. Other recorded names: **Whitstable oyster dredger**; locally called a **yawl★**. Note also **Essex smack**.

Whitstable watch boat See **watch boat**

whurry, whurrey, whyrry See **wherry**

'Wich barge See **trow-1**

wickerwork canoe See **basket canoe**

wide boat *England:* Term applied to an open-hold cargo boat used on canals and navigable rivers; wider than the **narrow boat★**. Some sources distinguish between a **wide boat** and a **barge★**, the latter having a beam in excess of 4.27m. Construction and decoration similar to the **narrow boat**. Generally 21.3-21.9m long, 3.05-3.35m wide, draft light 25-28cm. Name variant: **bastard boat** (on the Kennet and Avon Canal)

Wiener Schiff, Wiener Zille See **Ordinari**

wieringen aak See **wieringer aak**

wieringer aak *Netherlands, N:* Heavily built **fishing boat★** of the Waddenzee and around Wieringen. Built at Makkum, Workum, and Hindloopen in the 2nd half of the 19th century; a few still sail, mainly as pleasure craft. Fished for flatfish, and collected periwinkles and seaweed. Carvel-planked; rounded, flaring sides; quick turn of the bilges; wide top strake with sharp tumble home; washboard ends before the bow; broad, flat bottom, rising at ends. Top strake merges with the curved stem to form a point; full, rounded bow. Sternpost straight and mildly raked; deep deadwood below a shallow, rounded stern; maximum beam well forward. Pronounced sheer rising toward the stem; wale follows sheer. Wide, heavy outboard rudder; tiller slots over the rudderhead; narrow leeboards. Decked to the mast, but those also used for cargo had a removable deck aft. Most had a fish well, and those collecting seaweed had special pumps. Slightly aft-raking pole mast. Set a loose-footed, boomed gaff sail with a short, lightly curved gaff. Relatively narrow staysails; jib to a long jibboom, the end of which was lashed to a clamp on the foredeck close to the mast. Reported lengths 10-13m; e.g., length 11.7m, beam 4.4m, depth 1.37m. In some areas, called a **lemmeraak★**, but **wieringer aken** (pl.) were generally shorter, beamier, and swept up less at the bow. Further name variant: **wieringen aak**

wieringer aken See **wieringer aak**

wiguaol See **Abenaki canoe**

wigwahs cheemahn, wigass tchiman See **wigwas tsiman-2**

wigwass tciman See **Algonkin canoe**

wigwas tsiman 1. *Canada, E:* Sharp-lined, well-constructed birchbark (*wigwas*) **canoe★** (*tsiman*) used for hunting and family transportation by the Tête de Boule (Barrière) Native Americans of southern Quebec Province. Bottom and sheer straight for about half the length, then turned up. Ends rounded with stem and sternpost slightly recurved; interior headboards. Flat bottom athwartships; well-rounded

bilges; sides flared slightly. Gunwales composed of main gunwale, cap, and outwale. Thwarts tenoned into the gunwale and secured by a peg and lashing. Thin sheathing and ribs. One-man hunter's **canoe** 2.44-3.66m long; e.g., length 2.95m, beam 0.67m, depth 0.3m. Family **canoes** 4.27-4.88m long; e.g., length 4.47m, beam 0.84m, depth 0.36m. Name variant: **Tête de Boule canoe**. Further reading: Camil Guy, *The Weymontaching Birchbark Canoe*, Anthropological Papers, 20 (Ottawa: National Museums of Canada, 1974). Note also **Cree canoe, crooked canoe, tsiman**.
2. *Canada, central/United States, central:* General term for the finely made birchbark **canoe** of the Ojibway (Chippewa) of western Ontario and the area south and west of Lake Superior. Usually had a flattened end profile with tumble home turning up quickly above the gunwale sheer; end pieces recurved sharply at the top with bellied headboards fastened to them. Flat floors; bow end slightly beamier than the stern; flaring, straight or slightly curved sides; gunwales extended to the top or above the end pieces. Sheathed with long cedar strips. Caulked with pine pitch blackened with powdered charcoal. Reported lengths 3.8-5.7m, early **canoes** to 12m; e.g., length 4.9m, beam 0.94m, depth 0.36m. Spelling variants: **wigwahs cheemahn, wigwass tchiman, wiigwaasijiimaan**. Further reading: R. E. Ritzenthaler, "The Building of a Chippewa Indian Birch-bark Canoe," *Bulletin of the Public Museum of the City of Milwaukee* 19 (November, 1950), 56-98. Note also **long-nose canoe, tsiman**.
3. Term of the Algonquins of western Quebec and eastern Ontario for a birchbark **canoe**. Spelling variant: **wîkwâs tcîman**. Note also **wâbanäki tcîmân**.

wiigwaasijiimaan See **wigwas tsiman-2**

wiiswaawoot See **crooked canoe**

wijdkarveel, wijdkarviel See **karveel**

wijdschepen See **wijdschip**

wijdschip *Netherlands:* Mainly an inland vessel that ran scheduled trips across the Zuiderzee, but some made sea voyages. Although used on many waterways during the 17th-18th centuries, it is referred to most often in connection with the city of Gouda, where it was forced to go around the city while the narrower **smalschip★** could pass through the center. Heavily built with medium bluff lines and wide wales. Keel; flat bottom; rounded bilges; curved, raked stem; slightly raked sternpost. Moderate sheer; one wide and 3 smaller wales, the highest at the rim of the top strake. Flush deck; hold abaft the mast, covered with arched hatches in front of deck house. Tiller from the narrow rudder passed through the triangular helmport. Round leeboards. Set a spritsail with a heavy sprit, staysail, jib to jibboom. Reported lengths 21.3-22.6m; e.g., length 22m, beam with leeboards 6.8m, depth 2.6m. Spelling variants: **Weitschiff, wijtschip, wydschip, wydt-schip, wytschip**; pl. **wijdschepen; Schmalschiff**. Note also **karveel**.

wijtschip See **wijdschip**

wîkwâs tcîman See **wigwas tsiman-3**

wilderness tripper See **tripper**

wildfowl canoe *England:* Clinker-built craft used for hunting in creeks and marshy areas. Slightly rounded

bottom, flat floors, keelson, square stern. Rowed with a pair of oars or sculled from the stern. Occupied by 2 hunters. Length 3.66m, beam 1.0m, depth 0.38m.

wildfowling punt See **gun punt**

Willapa oyster sloop See **plunger-2**

willock See **ulakh**

willock eater *England, S:* Nickname given to both the fisherman of Eastbourne and his boat, willock being another name for the common guillemot.

wind boat See **junk**

wind sled *United States, central:* Type of **iceboat★** used for winter fishing on the Upper Mississippi River. Propelled by an airplane motor and skimmed across ice or water.

wine boat See **Shaoxing chuan-2**

wine ship A vessel that specializes in transporting wine. Modern **wine tankers** can carry several grades of wine at the same time. Other recorded names: **navire chai, Weintanker**. Note also **aak, bateau sétois, Kölner Aak, kohaya, kybaia, pinardier, Shaoxing chuan-2**.

wine tanker See **wine ship**

winkle brig *England, E:* Small, open sailing and **rowing boat★** that frequents the creeks and estuaries of Essex. A general-purpose workboat of the 19th and early 20th centuries, but mainly for winkling (collecting periwinkles) and inshore oyster dredging; now a popular pleasure craft. At times, the term **winkle brig** was applied to any **dinghy★** that engaged in winkling;

winkle brig

recently to any old sailing boat. Hull forms vary, but generally clinker-built, flat-floored, very beamy, transom-sterned. Centerboard on some. Early boats steered with a sculling oar; now by outboard rudder and tiller. Sets a gaff sail with or without a boom; foresail tacked to an iron bumkin. Others set a boomed standing lugsail, or a gunter-lug mainsail and a foresail. Reported lengths 3-8.5m; e.g., length overall 4.6m, on waterline 4.3m, beam 1.6m, inside depth 0.36m, draft 0.6m. Other recorded names: **bumkin, bumpkin**

wink punt See **Falmouth oyster punt**

winter canoe See **ice canoe**

winter coble, winter fishing coble See **coble-1g, coble-1h**

Winterton beach yawl See **beach yawl**

wiosłowa łódź See **rowboat**

wirry See **wherry**
Wisconsin raft See **crib-2**
witch barge See **trow-1**
Wivenhoe smack See **Essex smack**
Woerkommer See **zalmschouw**
woga See **waga-2a**
Wohnboot, Wohnschiff See **houseboat-1**
wolder *England, E:* **Trawler**★ that worked in the Would, a channel at Yarmouth, prior to the 20th century. Might be **cutter**★-, **ketch**★-, or lug-rigged. Lengths to 12m; 3.5-10t.
wollack See **ulakh**
Wolverhampton boat See **wharf boat**
wom *Sierra Leone:* **Dugout canoe**★ of the Shrebro Estuary area on the central coast. Range from 1-man craft used for line fishing within the estuary to boats with crews of 4-6 that work cast nets offshore. Bow elongated to a sharp point; stern truncated, forming a V-shaped transom. Freeboard may be raised by a narrow washstrake. Paddled and poled. Lengths to 9m; e.g., length 6.1m, beam 0.76-0.91m. Name variant: **bonga**★
woman's boat, women's boat See **umiak-3**
wong See **wang**
wonga *Papua New Guinea, E:* Term for the **canoes**★ of the Kelana area on the north coast. **Canoes** in this area have a single outrigger. See also **wang**.
wood boat *United States, NE:* Term given in the 1690s to a ship that, in order to avoid British customs duties, offloaded its main cargo elsewhere along the coast and sailed into Boston with a layer of kindling on top. See also **huliya, ki-bune, longboat-8, Saint John River woodboat**.
wood drogger See **wood drogher**
wood drogher *United States, E:* **Schooner**★ that collected and transported young oysters from Chesapeake Bay to be planted in Delaware Bay, or ran mature oysters to Philadelphia markets. Carried on deck. Light draft; cap. 500-1,500 bushels. Name variant: **wood drogger**
wooden horse See **bã:s**
wooder See **kiln-wood coaster**
wood-roofed boat See **qiu zi**
woods canoe *Canada, E:* Light, birchbark river **canoe**★ of the Micmac. Used on the Gaspé Peninsula, Nova

woods canoe

Scotia, Prince Edward and Cape Breton Islands, and on the north shore of New Brunswick. Sharp lines; torpedo shape; bow and stern almost a circle from bottom around to top sheer. Flat bottom athwartships; moderate rocker at ends; marked tumble home. Shaped ends had no inner framework, but were stiffened by an exterior batten on each side. Bark brought over the light gunwales and lashed; rounded cap placed atop the gunwales. Headboards fitted; 5-7 thwarts; thin ribs; narrow sheathing. Bark gores abutted and sewn with spiral stitching to form a smooth surface. Proportion

and measurements modified between colonial period and the late 19th century; earlier **canoes** narrower in proportion to length. Sometimes sailed using a square sail originally; later a spritsail. Decorated at ends and along gunwales. Reported lengths 2.74-4.59m; e.g., length 4.32m, beam 0.76m, depth 0.33m. Other recorded names: **pack canoe, Micmac woods canoe, Portage canoe**
wood scow See **Maine wood scow**
woodskin *Brazil/Guyana/Venezuela:* Generic term often given to a bark **canoe**★. Design varied somewhat with the method of construction, but each made from a cylindrical piece of bark; usually of the purple-heart or locust tree. Ends often raised by slicing the bark about one-quarter of the way in from each end to form a rough point, then by creating a fold in the softened bark, allowing the ends to lift up; the folds were lashed into position. In others, the insertion of thwarts raised the ends slightly to form an open-ended craft. In another variation, the bow swept up while the stern was closed off by pushing the open end forward to cre-

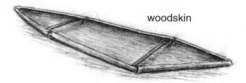
woodskin

ate a "transom." Strengthening sticks were lashed along the top of each side. Small blocks or the thwarts served as seats; cargo kept dry by placing it on a stick platform or pieces of bark. **Canoe** was sunk in the water between outings to prevent cracking and warping; cracks repaired by insertion of a bark piece that swelled on becoming wet. Paddled or poled. Size depended on length and circumference of the initial bark piece; some can carry 5 people, but usually fewer. Some as long as 9m. Possibly still used in very limited areas. Various groups of Caribs and Arawaks have specific names for a **woodskin**; e.g., **attamanmad** (by the Wapisianas of northeast Brazil), **kanawa** (by the Apalaii of northeast Brazil), **kanáwayishchiputüre, yishchiputure**, or **yikchibitiri** (by the Waiwai in southern Guyana), **wepipyu'ara** or **pakasse** (by the Barama River Caribs). Note also **igat**.
woolock See **ulakh**
woonschip See **houseboat-1**
wooser See **narrow boat**
workman's scow See **scow-8**
work scow See **scow-11**
worser See **narrow boat**
Worsley mine boat See **starvationer**
wo´te *United States, W:* The Miwok used a tule-grass boat on the rivers of their area in central California for hunting and when moving camp. Generally composed of 20 cylindrical bundles made rigid by 2 willow gunwale poles and about 8 external willow ribs. Propelled by one or more paddles. Length 4.6m, widths 0.91-1.22m. The tule boat of the Coastal Miwok, called a **lógo-sáka**, was composed of several bundles and was either punted or poled. Other recorded names: **balsa**★, **tule balsa**

wou See **wai-2**

Wriggboot See **scull boat**

wuar See **wa-2**

wu ban *China, west-central:* **1.** Carried coal on a single downstream trip on the Min Jiang, a tributary of the upper Chang Jiang (Yangtze); was then broken up for firewood at its destination. Roughly built of inferior lumber; sharply upturned and elongated, square bow; sheer strake at the square stern turned up to form wings; flat bottom. Square mainsail, often supplemented with the matting from the roof of the temporary cabin. About 15 in crew.

2. The **wu ban** that worked upstream from Pingshan on the middle Jinsha Jiang (Chin-sha-chiang or Kin-cha-kiang), an extension of the Chang Jiang, had little sheer and elongated, square ends. Used a rudder; anchored by a pole inserted through a hole in the bow into the riverbank. House of wood and matting amidships. Square sail set to a mast forward of the house. Crew of 4 or 5.

3. In the Chang Jiang gorges, a **wu ban** type attended **junks**★ passing through the gorges, ferrying trackers and lines to and from shore. Long and low with raked, square bow and stern. Strong rudder; anchored by means of a pole through the bow. Arched mat house. Employed many oars. Set an unbattened cotton sail to a bipod mast when conditions suitable. Crew of 10-18. Reported lengths 12-18m, beam ca. 2.4m, depth 1.2m, draft 0.76m.

4. The cargo-carrying **wu ban** that plied the Chang Jiang and its tributaries between Wuhan and Chongqing (Chungking) was a shallow, open vessel. Flat bottom; square, raked bow; planking at the stern extended beyond the transom; hull strengthened by a heavy wale just below the gunwale. Steered with a long sweep. Tall mast set a narrow lugsail. Also maneuvered with oars or pivoting sweeps. Reported lengths 12.2-19.8m, widths 1.8-2.6m, depths 0.91-1.2m.

Other recorded names: **five-board bottom**, **five-plank junk**, **hou-pan**, **ou-pan**

Wuhu country boat See **Wuhu xiang xia chuan**

Wuhu ordure boat See **ordure boat**

Wuhu xiang xia chuan *China, E:* **Sampan**★ of the Wuhu area on the lower Chang Jiang (Yangtze). Square ends, planked athwartships, raked; bow somewhat narrower than stern. Flat bottom, markedly flaring sides, tumble home to top strakes; maximum beam amidships. Open. Length ca. 7.3m, beam 1.4m, depth 0.46m. Name variant: **Wuhu country boat**

Wushanchenbozi, **Wushanch'enpotzu**, **Wu-shan shên-po tzŭ** See **shen bo zi**

Wusieh k'uai, **Wusih fast boat**, **Wusih-k'uai**, **wusihkui** See **Wuxi kuai**

wuskwīoose See **Cree canoe**

wusser See **narrow boat**

wu-tsei ch'uan, **wu-tsei shuan** See **mo you chuan**

Wuxi kuai *China, central:* **Houseboat**★, built mainly at Wusih (Wuxi) on the Grand Canal (Da Yunhe), hired out to foreigners; the original **Wusih-k'uai**, however, was a native craft. Flat bottom; wide, overhanging, square bow; tapered, square stern that ended in a decked platform out beyond the stern. Three bulkheads and multiple half frames. Wide-bladed rudder could be raised. Two poling gangways along the sides. Elaborate house over most of the hull; Chinese owner lived on board. European sails and leeboards might be added. Reported lengths 14-21m; e.g., length 20.4m, beam 4.3m, depth 1.2m. Other recorded names: **fast boat**★, **Wusieh k'uai**, **Wusih fast boat**, **wusihkui**. Further reading: J. O. P. Bland, *Houseboat Days in China*, 2nd ed. (London: W. Heinemann, 1919).

wu zei chuan See **mo you chuan**

wydschip, **wydt-schip** See **wijdschip**

Wye coracle *Wales, SE:* Engaged in line and net fishing on the River Wye until the end of World War I. Worked singly or in pairs. Elongated craft with bluntly rounded bow and squarish stern. Sides pinched in at the midship seat. Frame of woven ash or willow laths; 7 lengthwise, 7-8 across, 2 set diagonally; extra athwartships laths under the feet. Plaited hazel withy bands formed the gunwale. A vertical partition helped support the seat. Early boats coated with a mixture of pitch and coal tar, then "baked" to saturate mixture into the cloth, and finally re-coated. Propelled with a narrow-bladed paddle ca. 1.5m long; straight loom. Length 1.5m, width at seat 0.97m, maximum width 1.0m, depth 0.37m. Other recorded names: **coble**★, **thorrocle**, **truckle**. Note also **coracle**.

Wye trow See **trow-1**

wyhen See **wherry**

wytschip See **wijdschip**

xabec, xabeco See **xebec**

xabega See **jábega**

xabeque, xabica See **xebec**

xabigu See **lorcha-3**

xa´ bōl xīna See **tō´ xana**

xaica See **gussi**

xalana See **chalana-8**

xalanta See **chaland**

xalupa See **chaloupe**, **chalupa-1**

xambequi See **chambequin**

xana Sęe **tō´ xana**

χaperi ŏa See **wa-3**

xata See **flette**

xavec See **xebec**

xaveco See **chaveco**, **xebec**

xávega Portuguese term for a long seine net (or *chávega*), but name is frequently given to the boats that work the net, such as the **meia lua**⋆, the **catria**⋆, and the **saveiro**⋆. Name variant: **barco da xávega**. See also **barca da arte xávega**, **jábega**.

xávegues See **jábega**

xaveque See **xebec**

xayik See **kayuk**

xebec **1.** *Canada:* During the French regime, the armed, 3-masted, lateen-rigged **xebec** was used against small **corsairs**⋆ on the Great Lakes and on Lake Champlain. Counter stern. Foremast stepped well inboard; mainmast amidships; small mizzen stepped well forward. Foresail tacked to long, rising bowsprit. Spelling variant: **chébec**

2. *Mediterranean:* A slim, swift merchant vessel that became a feared **corsair** of the 17th-century Barbary pirates. Considered mainly a vessel of the 18th and early 19th centuries, but reported as early as the 10th century as a **fishing boat**⋆, and worked as a Tunisian merchant craft into the early 20th century. Mainly associated with the Mediterranean area, but some operated out of Atlantic ports of Morocco and France. Wide geographic and date range resulted in considerable variations in size, use, construction, workmanship, and sail plan. Characteristically had an exaggerated rostrum and a gallery that elongated the counter stern. Curved or straight, raked stem; raked stern; flat floors amidships; soft bilges; low, flaring sides; strong sheer, especially at the stern. Highly cambered deck, but made more tenable by gratings that provided level decking and permitted water to drain to scuppers below; cabin aft. Some carried a boat on deck. Rudder came up inboard. Generally armed, carrying 4-30 cannon. Designed to be both rowed and sailed. Rowed through oarports, some with 15 oars to a side. Sail plan varied with period, area of origin, and especially with wind conditions. Most often portrayed with 3 lateen sails; the mainsail very large, the foremast raking forward. However, they might also set a combination of lateen, square, or gaff sails, and on some, topsails. A bumkin and jib were added. A type that was lateen-rigged on the foremast and square-rigged on

the main- and mizzenmast might be called a **jabeque redondo**. Some smaller sizes were 2-masted. Crew size ranged from 8 on the Tunisian merchant vessels to 450 on the large, armed ships. Reported lengths 15-40m; e.g., length 26m, beam 7.55m, depth 4.28m; length-to-beam ratio 3.5-4:1; shallow draft. Other recorded names: **barbareske**, **barbaresque**, **chab(b)âk**, **chabec**⋆, **chabe(c)k**, **chaboûk**, **chalek**, **chaveco**⋆, **chébac**, **chébec**, **chebe(c)k**, **chébéka**, **cherec**, **échébec**, **enxabeque**, **enxaveque**, **escapadia de maures**, **gabeque**, **jabeque**⋆, **jebeque**, **lebec**, **šabaka**, **śabbâk**, **śabûk**, **sambec(c)o**, **śambek**, **sanbèco**, **scebek**, **Schebecke**, **sciabecco** (pl. **sciabecchi**), **sciabica**, **sciabeco**, **sciabeccu**, **sciambecco**, **šebbâk**, **şebec**, **sebeco**, **sebek(a)**, **shebeka**, **šǫbbâk** (pl. **šbâbek**), **stambecco** (pl. **stambecchi**), **xabec(o)**, **xabeque**, **xabica**, **xavec(o)**, **xaveque**, **xebeck**, **zabecchio**, **zabeco**, **zabeko**, **zambecco**, **zebec**; dims. **demichébec**, **sambecchino**, **sciabecchino**, **stambecchino**, **zambecchino**. Further reading: Wolfram Mondfeld, *Die Schebecke und Andere Schiffstypen de Mittelmeerraumes* (Bielefeld: Verlag Delius, Klasing & Co., 1974). Note also **chambequin**, **falucho-3**, **polacre**, **shebek**.

3. *United States, E:* A few lateen-rigged vessels employing a rig similar to the Mediterranean **xebec** of the 1860s were built on Chesapeake Bay and its estuaries. Used as **slavers**⋆ but also as naval vessels, **privateers**⋆, and smugglers. Also seen patrolling the Gulf of Mexico coast in the early 19th century. Spelling variants: **schebeck**, **zebec**

xebeck See **xebec**

xeito *Spain, NW:* Galician term for a boat that works the *xeito* drift net for sardines and anchovies. Double-ended with pronounced sheer forward. Curved stem; high, recurved stemhead. Hull and decks of local pine.

xeito

Interior divided into 4 compartments: the forward one for ropes, the 2nd for the crew, the next for nets, and the aft one for the catch. Steered with a long oar. Sets a tall lugsail on an aft-raking mast stepped close to the bow; some lateen-rigged. Also rowed; each oar worked against a single heavy tholepin. Crew of 4-8. Reported lengths 6-9m; e.g., length 6m, beam 2.47m, depth 0.77m. Other recorded names: **jaitero, jeitera, jeito, lancha de jeito** (or **xeito**), **lancha jeitera, sardinal★**. Further reading: E. L. Padin, "Jeitos o 'Xeitos'," *Mares* II/19 (Madrid, 1945), 7-9. Note also **bote xeitero, burro**.

Xiamen chuan See **Amoy fisher**

Xiangji dou kou *China, west-central:* Relatively small cargo **junk★** at Xiangji (Hsiang-chi), Zigui (Tzu-kuei), and Fengjie (Feng-ch'ieh or Kweichow). Designed to traverse the Chang Jiang (Yangtze) gorges. Flat bottom; square bow; tapered stern with tall, slightly recurving post; overhanging ends; inboard rudder. Decked; 2 cabins abaft the mast enclosed by raised side planking that fitted to the sternpost; mat roofs. Movable beam between mast and cabin supported fulcrums for 2 long sweeps. Single mast, raked slightly aft, set a balance lugsail. Crew of 3-5. Reported lengths 10.7-13m, beam ca. 2m, depth 0.9m or less. Other recorded names: **Hsiang-chi bean pod, Hsiang-chi tou-k'ou, Hsianghsitouk'ou, Xiangxidoukou**

xiangxiang dao ba zi See **dao ba zi-1**

xiangxidoukou See **xiang dou kou**

Xiang-yang bian zi See **bian zi**

xiao hua chuan *China, west-central:* Open **riverboat★** at Chengdu (Chengtu) in central Sichuan (Szechuan) province that, despite its name (translated literally as **small flower boat**), often carried coal. Flat bottom swept up slightly from the forward bulkhead to a sharp bow above the waterline; longitudinally planked. Square stern; 2 bulkheads aft; narrow decking around the stern. Length 5.9m, beam 1.4m, depth ca. 0.38m. Other recorded names: **hsiao-hua ch'uan, (small) pleasure boat**

xiao ma tou chuan *China, E:* Heavily built cargo boat of Shanghai Harbor. Square ends, the bow slightly narrower and rounded up from the bottom; stern less rounded but extended aft to form a shallow platform. Flat bottom; closely spaced frames; 2 bulkheads. Decked; cargo generally carried below deck; awning provided shelter. Rudderstock came up inboard. Propelled by a *yuloh*, a type of sculling oar, at the stern

and sometimes by 1-2 *yulohs* at the bow. A flexible bamboo mast stepped in forward third, setting a type of spritsail. Crew of 3-5. Length 17.4m, beam ca. 2.7m, depth ca. 1.5m; cap. 28-70t. Name variant: **hsiao-ma-t'ou ch'uan**. Note also **guan cai chuan, mud boat**.

xiao qi ban See **hua chuan-3b**

xiao xiang xia chuan *China, E:* Transported vegetable stalks for fuel in the Shanghai area. Narrow, square ends; bow overhanging and slightly curved; stern curved; projecting gallery. Flat bottom, longitudinally planked; rounded bilges; plumb sides; flat sheer. Decked at ends; small house for the 2-man crew; wooden awning over the stern. Propelled by a sculling oar (the *yuloh*). Length 12m, beam 2.4m, depth 1.0m. Other recorded names: **country boat★, hsiao-hsiang-hsia ch'uan**

xia you chuan See **sampan-3**

xīna See **tō´ xana**

xin hua zi See **hua zi-4**

xi-tatarju See **xi-tataru**

xi-tataru *Mozambique, S:* Fishing **raft★** of the area of Maputo (Lourenço Marques). A few still worked in the 1970s. Composed of stems of palm leaves, the bundles tied with leaves, fiber, copper wire, or nylon thread. A layer forms the flat bottom, and vertical sides are formed by 3-4 bamboo poles. Forward ends may be cut at an angle to create a sharp cutwater; an extension at the stern provides handles for carrying the **raft** to the water. A seat aft supports the sides and closes off the stern; a box holds the gear and the catch. Open at the bow. A type of thwart forward supports a light mast. Sail may be quite rudimentary, but basically a lateen sail; yard suspended by a loop over a fork at the masthead. Steered with a rough paddle. Length ca. 4m. Spelling variants: **chitatar(ro), xi-tatarju**. Further reading: J. P. M. Louro, "'Xi-tataru', Barco Tradicional de Pesca de Baia de Lourenço Marques," *Biomar* 3 (Lourenço Marques, 1973), 1-8.

xku See **jukúa**

xprunára See **speronara**

xulū See **barque Djenné**

xûna´, xûwa´, xīna See **tō´ xana**

xwagelitcim, xwo'kintcîm See **Coast Salish canoe**

yabigu See **lorcha-3**

yac See **yacht**

yachip *Japan, N:* Trough-shaped birchbark craft of the Ainu of Hokkaido Island; extinct. Made from a single piece of bark; squared ends joined to sides by lacing

yachip

over moss. Strengthened with bamboo stems around the gunwale. Branches laid longitudinally along the bottom, secured by crosspieces; cords tied from gunwale to gunwale to prevent spreading. Note also **chip**.

Yachow raft See **fa zi**

yacht 1. During the 17th century, **yachts** were state vessels in Holland, where they originated, and in England. Royal **yachts** became important vessels, serving to convey royalty, distinguished visitors, and at times, to carry important messages. Subsidiary **yachts** of the crown were used by excise commissioners, the navy, and customs. Accommodations and hull decorations usually elaborate. Generally armed. Rigged as **ketches***, **cutters***, and **sloops*** of the period, or as 3-masted, square-rigged ships. The royal **yachts** of the latter part of the 17th century ranged from 9.4 to 24m long.
2. The term gradually came to refer to a privately owned craft. Usually fast and fine-lined, large enough to make extended sea voyages, and one that exceeds the owner's navigational and maneuvering abilities, requiring a crew. **Yachts** are usually licensed, permitting them to call at and depart from home-country ports without clearing through customs. Proceed under sail or power. In wartime, **yachts** may be converted to an auxiliary **fleet***. Racing **yachts** are of any type, but generally built to be raced, with little attention to comfort. Other recorded names: **barque de promenade, bateau de plaisance, plaisancier, pleasure boat, pleziervaartuig, Vernügungsfahrzeug** Selected name variants: **hiate*, hyac, iacco, iachet, Iacht, iacq, iaque, iate*, iot, jach, jacht*, jack*, jaght(e), jagt*, jaht(a), jak(hta), jakt*, jaxta, panfilo, yac(te), yack*, yackt, yagt, yak(h)ta, yaque, yat(e), yatch(t), yauch(t), yaugh*, yaxta, yeach, yeagh, yoath, yolke, yought(e), yuaght, z(e)aught.** Note also **palhabote**. Further reference: **jacht-6**

yacht-barge See **barge-yacht**

yacht mixte See **sailer**

yacht tender See **dinghy-1**

yack *France, W:* At Rochefort, a harbor craft that transported powder in barrels and biscuits in sacks to ships off île d'Aix roadstead in the 1820s. Mast stepped about a third in from the bow; raked aft. Set a fore-and-aft sail. The bowsprit held a jib and a staysail. Length ca. 22m, beam 6m, draft 2.35m. Spelling variants: **iac, jac.** See also **yacht.**

yacker See **Staithes yacker**

yackt, yacte See **yacht**

yaegt See **jacht-3**

yagatoi See **lakatoi**

yager See **jager, jagger, man-o'-war yager**

yagger See **jagger**

yagt See **yacht**

yäk See **northern-style canoe**

yaka See **kamia**

yakhta, yakta See **yacht**

yal See **Ness yoal, yalik, yawl**

yalbosh' See **yalik**

yale See **yawl**

yalik Russian generic term for a small **rowing boat***; may designate a **jolly boat*, skiff*, wherry***, or **yawl***. Frequently used for fishing. When sailed, sets 2 lugsails and a jib. Other recorded names: **ialik, jal*, jalbosh', jalik, yal, yalbosh'**

yall See **yawl**

yampa See **balsa-4**

yanbaru *Japan, S:* Common term in the southern Ryukyu Islands for a **junk*** of Chinese design. Some serve as **ferryboats***, others are cargo carriers (see **māran**).

yan chuan *China:* The great demand for salt in China resulted in the development of a number of specialized **salt boats***. A few follow:
1. In Jiangsu (Kiangsu) Province at the mouth of the Chang Jiang (Yangtze), one type was a long, narrow, and exceptionally well-built craft. Double-ended; flat bottom, longitudinally planked. Bow curved up gently from the bottom, ending in a cross-planked bow transom that had vertical, exterior timbers at midline and corners. Stern square and raked. Side planking extended beyond the transom; rudderpost came up within this extension. Single wale ran full length; graving pieces incised into top strake near the bow. Decked; cabin aft. Propelled by 2 oars on fulcrums forward and a single oar from the starboard stern quarter. Stepped a single mast. Length 23.8m, beam 4m, depth 1.7m.
2. Another variety, with salt evaporators, served a small town on the Chang Jiang between Ichang (I-Ch'ang) and Chongqing (Chungking). These were long, low craft with a tall, lyre-shaped stern. Swept-up, truncated bow. Hut amidships. Used poles for anchoring.
3. On a tributary of the Tuo Jiang, off the upper Chang Jiang, an undecked **yan chuan** relayed salt to larger river craft for the journey downstream. Flat bottom, flared sides. Bottom raked up into a squared bow; flat stern; both bow and stern crooked so that the starboard bow gunwale was higher; the port gunwale was higher at the stern. Strong sheer at bow; top strake wider abaft amidships, creating a reverse sheer. Platform at each end; arched hut might cover the waist. Towing mast. Reported lengths 13-20m; e.g., length 13.1m, beam 2.4m, depth 0.76m.
4. Salt was carried along the south coast from Beihai (Pakhoi or Pei-hai) to Guangzhou (Canton) in boats

built at Gaode (Kao-te or Kotak). Sharp bow, rounded stern, drop keel. Sharp sheer at the stern; interrupted bulwarks. Fenestrated rudder. Generally 2-masted, the foremast raking slightly forward; mainmast stepped roughly amidships. Battened mat lugsails with rounded leech. Length 21.6m, beam 6.4m. Name variant: **Kotak yen-ch'uan**. Note also **ma yang chuan**.
Other recorded names: **salt junk**, **yen-ch'uan** (or **-ch'wan**, **-tch'ouan**)

Yankee skiff See **Staten Island skiff**

Yankee whaleboat See **whaleboat-7a**

Yankee whaler See **whaler-3**

yao chou See **yao zhou**

yao wang chuan *China, E:* A northern-type vessel that was an important carrier of live pigs from ports in the Chang Jiang (Yangtze) delta to Shanghai. Built on bluff lines with rounded sides with tumble home that form a turret-type hull; strengthened by 6 bulkheads, 7 frames, and heavy wales. Flat, cross-planked bow raked up from the flat, longitudinally planked bottom; flat, raked counter stern, also cross-planked; platform projected beyond the counter. Hoisting-type rudder came up inboard; leeboards. Decked; camber along the sides adjusted by planking laid level with the bulwarks; generally had a small house for crew, or lacking a house, crew lived in the forward and aft compartments. Stepped 4 masts; the small fore- and mizzenmasts stepped to port of the midline and easily struck. All carried square-headed lugsails. Crew of 6. Wide range of sizes; typically 15m long, 3.2m wide, 1.2m deep. Other recorded names: **pig boat★**, **Tsungming pig boat**

yao zhou *China:* 12th-century term for buoyant supports—inflated skins, gourds, clay vessels—used by individuals to traverse small water bodies. Other recorded names: **waist boat★**, **yao chou**

ya-p'i-ku See **lorcha-3**

yaque See **yacht**

Yare wherry See **Norfolk wherry**

Ya River raft See **fa zi**

Yarmouth beach yawl See **beach yawl**

Yarmouth dandy, **Yarmouth drifter** See **Yarmouth lugger**

Yarmouth keel See **Norfolk keel**

Yarmouth lugger *England, E:* Drifted for herring in the North Sea until the 1890s. Worked mainly out of Yarmouth, but also from Sheringham, Lowestoft, and Southold. Initially 3-masted, lug-rigged vessels, but by the 1870s, most were converted to gaff **ketches★** while retaining the name **lugger★**. Clinker planking; sharp rise to the floors; plumb stem; rounded counter stern above a raking sternpost on the larger boats; smaller types might have a rounded, plumb stern. Decked; capstan, operated by 4 men, hauled the nets; 6 timberheads forward, above the rail, for belaying rig of mainsail and jib. Carried 1-2 **cobles★** on deck. Originally set dipping lugsails to the fore- and mainmasts; both pole masts; mizzenmast stepped to port, setting a standing lugsail sheeted to a jiggerboom. Topsail on the mainmast and jib to a long, reefing bowsprit. Foremast in tabernacle; lowered while riding to the nets, with sail stowed. Mainmast eliminated

when gaff sail adopted on the forward mast; mizzen retained the lugsail or also adopted a gaff sail. Gaffs high-peaked, and sails loose-footed but boomed. Sails tanned. Used sweeps when necessary. Crew of 8-12 until 1860s, fewer after installation of the capstan. Reported lengths 17.8-20m; 1848 vessel: 18.7m overall, 13.4m on keel, beam 4.5m, depth 2.8m, draft aft 1.6m. Other recorded names: **Great Yarmouth herring drifter**, **sail cart**, **sash-marry**, **Yarmouth dandy** (or **drifter**). Note also **great boat-2a**.

Yarmouth pilot gig *England, E:* Long, narrow **pulling boat★** used from the beaches of Yarmouth, Lowestoft, and other East Anglian communities from the early 1800s. Transported pilots and aided ships in distress. Clinker-built with unscarfed strakes; fine lines; low washboards at bow. Straight, vertical stem; small, high transom. Rudder worked with long lines. Rowed single- or double-banked with 6 or 8 oars; oar lengths varied with position in the boat. Occasionally set a lugsail from a light mast stepped amidships. Other recorded names: **beach gig★**, **Lowestoft pilot gig** (or **pilot skiff**), **pilot skiff★**. Note also **beach yawl**.

Yarmouth pinky See **pinky**

Yarmouth pleasure yoll See **yoll-2**

Yarmouth punt See **beach punt-1**

Yarmouth scow See **scow-10**

Yarmouth shrimper *England, E:* **Sloop★**-rigged boat that fished for shrimp from spring to mid-fall and usually for sole in winter, off Yarmouth; identifiable type by 1870. Generally clinker-built of oak with moderate sheer; hollow entrance; long run. Curved, ironshod keel; rising floors to high bilges; slight tumble home to topsides. Mild rake to stem and sternpost; narrow transom with tuck, sometimes painted white; occasionally sharp-sterned. Outboard rudder; very short tiller passed under the mainsheet horse. Forward third decked with hatch leading to a small cuddy; open aft. Boomed, loose-footed gaff mainsail; snotter held boom to mast; boom generally kept to starboard of mast. Jib from bowsprit; in good weather, yard topsail sent up. Mast in tabernacle, stayed by single shroud on each side and forestay to bowsprit. Bowsprit run through gammon iron on starboard side of stemhead. Sail stowed by casting off the snotter, lowering the peak of the gaff, and furling sail to mast. Also rowed. All employed engines by early 1930s. Crew of 1-2. Reported lengths 6-8m; e.g., length overall 6.5m, on keel 6.3m, beam 2.49m; avg. 2t. Other recorded names: **cutter★** (locally), **dandy★**, **Gorleston shrimper**, **Great Yarmouth shrimper**; **North Ender** (those mooring north of Breydon Water), **South Ender** (the remainder). Further reading: J. Leather, "The Sailing Shrimpers of Great Yarmouth," *The Mariner's Mirror* 56 (1970), 429-437. Note also **Lowestoft shrimper**.

yasha:baXts, **yashbaqats**, **yashmaqats** See **sealing canoe-1**

yat, **yatch**, **yatcht**, **yate** See **yacht**

yathra dhoni *Sri Lanka, SW:* Boat of the Sinhalese pictured as early as the 8th or 9th century; extinct by the early 20th century. Known to have sailed to Malacca and to the Maldives. Sewn planking, caulked with palm and plantain stalks; later, planks nailed. Crossbeams extended beyond hull below the top strake and served to secure the shrouds, sheets, and tacks. Double-ended; sharply raking, curved stem and sternpost; considerable sheer; "V" bottom. Narrow rudder slung from sternpost with rope lashings; tiller sloped downward from the tall rudderhead. Two curved booms connected directly with the heavy outrigger float; booms passed through hull below the gunwale and out the opposite side. Outrigger always positioned to leeward; after adoption of fore-and-aft sails, position became fixed. Partially undecked; cargo protected by a long, curved, bamboo roof. Cargo-handling boom. Generally stepped a main- and mizzen-mast, setting square sails originally, then lugsails, and finally fore-and-aft sails; when lacking a mizzenmast, the mizzen was hung from a large spar stepped against the mainmast. Masts in tabernacles. Jib to steeved-up bowsprit; sometimes a foresail. Reported lengths 18-20m, widths 5.8-6.1m, inside depths 2.7-3.1m; averaged 50t burden. Other recorded names: **dhoney**; **maha oruwa** (Sinhala); **thony, yathra doni, yathra oruwa** (or **oruva**), **yatra dhoni, yatrawe**

yathra doni, yathra oruva, yathra oruwa See **yathra dhoni**

yat pei See **diao ting**

yatra dhoni, yatrawe See **yathra dhoni**

ya-tse ch'uan, ya-tse tch'ouan See **ya ze chuan**

yauch, yaucht See **yacht**

yaugh Early term for a small, square-sterned sailing vessel or for a **yacht***.

yaught See **yacht**

yaul, yaule See **yawl**

yawl 1. Term initially used for one of the smaller **ship's boats***. Those used aboard British Royal Navy ships became standardized in the late 17th century; phased out by the 1830s. Early boats sometimes referred to as **Norway yawls***, although true Norway boats had sharp sterns. The early boats were built at Deal on the south coast of England and were clinker-built; also known as **Deal yawls**. Later **yawls** were carvel-planked, and both types were used interchangeably. Curved stem; narrow transom stern, raked and tucked-up. Mainly rowed, double-banked, employing 6-12 oars; tholepins set into gunwales; grommets on oars. Occasionally sailed, stepping as many as 3 lug-rigged masts. Reported lengths 4.9-10.7m, the length depending on the size of the ship; 1804 **yawl**: 8m long, 2m wide, 0.9m deep. Other recorded names: **tercer bote, Deal yall**. Note also **cock boat, yawl boat**.
2. Yawl now usually describes a type of rig. Traditionally, a 2-masted boat with a small mizzen-mast, stepped abaft the helmsman or the rudder, to which a small sail is set, sheeted to a bumkin. The similar **ketch*** has a taller mizzenmast stepped forward of the rudder and carries a proportionally larger sail. Term for the **yawl** rig initiated in the early 19th century; rig was especially popular in the early 1900s. Mainsail may be a gaff sail (**gaff yawl**) or leg-of-mutton (**Bermudian yawl**). Initially the mizzen was a standing lug with or without a boom; later a gaff and now often a leg-of-mutton. Two headsails common.

Other recorded names: **cotre à tape-cul, cotre-dandy, Halbsegelkutter, Heckmaster, yol**. Note also **dandy**.
3. Term sometimes loosely applied to any double-ended **rowboat***.
4. *Canada, central:* An indigenous type found on Lake Winnipeg. Open. Length ca. 6m.
5. *United Kingdom:* **a.** During the 18th century, the term might be applied to any small boat, especially one that fished. More recently, in some areas, **yawl** described a **cutter***-rigged **smack***. **b.** In northern Scotland, a sharp-ended boat with hollow garboards, some deadrise, with flared sides and raked ends. **c.** On the west coast of Scotland, the term was applied broadly to fishing craft that set a large, dipping lugsail.
6. *United States, central:* Term for all boats carried on a **riverboat***. Hung from davits right-side up. Flat bottom with rocker; skeg at stern. Brightly painted. Two or 3 oarsmen. Reported lengths 4.6-5.5m.

Spelling variants: **iol(la), jol***, **jola***, **Jolle***, **yal(e), yall, yaul(e), yawle, yoal, yol(a), yole***, **yoll***, **yolle, you(gha)ll**. Further references: **barge-9c, baulk yawl, beach yawl, Boston pilot schooner, canoe-9, canoe-yawl, cat-yawl, coble-lb, dindet, drontheim, Ness yoal, pilot yawl, punt-10, Sandy Hook pilot schooner, scaffie yawl, scow-11a, skiff-6, skipjack-1, sloup à tape-cul, Staithes yacker, Whitstable oyster smack, yawl boat**

yawl boat 1. Small, powered boat used to tow or push a vessel. Note also **schooner smack, skipjack-1**.
2. *United States:* Heavily constructed, open, general-purpose **pulling boat*** carried on stern davits of **coasters*** and **fishing boats*** prior to the 1870s. Often used in calms. Carvel-planked; rounded "V" or flat bottom; planked-up deadwood; curved stem; transom stern. Might set a sprit- or leg-of-mutton sail. Reported lengths 3.7-8m; e.g., length 4.6m, beam 1.7m, depth 0.69m. Note also **yawl-1**.

yawle See **yawl**

yaw ngat *Thailand, SW:* Long, narrow **fishing boat*** of the western side of peninsular Thailand. Boat paddled slowly in shallow water at night, the 2 paddlers striking the water repeatedly with their paddles, causing small fish to jump into the boat. A net on the opposite side catches the fish jumping over the boat. Sharp, raked ends terminate in small, squared tops; considerable end sheer. Name variant: **catch boat**

yaxta See **yacht**

ya ze chuan *China/Macao:* A floating duck farm, providing meat and eggs for local consumption and export. Found on many inland waters and along coastal Guangdong (Kwantgung) Province in the south. A flat-bottomed, low-sided craft that generally provided living quarters for the family in the after part, the remainder being occupied by the ducks. A caged area of latticework extended out over each gunwale. The ducks were turned loose each morning down a lowered ramp and were called home in the evening by a gong. A large boat might be 15m long. Other recorded names: **ap-t'eang** (at Macao); **bateau à canards, duck boat***, **ya-tse ch'uan** (or **tch'ouan**)

ybrgq See **brig**

ycharuta See **ičájuta**

yeach, yeagh See **yacht**

yE´cabdΔqΔts, yEcmaqǻts See **sealing canoe-1**

yellow eel See **wai pi gu**

Yellow River junk See **Huang He chuan**

yen-ch'uan, yen-ch'wan, yen-tch'ouan See **yan chuan**

yerme See **djerme**

yga, ygar, ygara See **igá**

ygarassu See **igaraçu**

ygat *Brazil, E:* Carioca dialect term of the Rio de Janeiro area for a small **dugout canoe***. See also **igá**.

yiceLt See **Coast Salish canoe**

Yichang hua zi See **hua zi-3**

Yichelt See **Coast Salish canoe**

yikchibitiri, yishchiputure See **woodskin**

Yishelt See **Coast Salish canoe**

yoal See **Fair Isle yoal, Ness yoal, yawl**

yoath See **yacht**

yoki See **pelota-4**

yol See **beach yawl, yawl**

yola See **yawl**

yole **1.** Light, fast **pulling boat***. Term applies to several types of small boats. In the 18th and early 19th centuries, designated as a class of **ship's boat*** in the French navy. The **ship's boat** and pleasure craft are usually clinker-built; racing **yoles** are smooth-skinned. Narrow transom stern. Oarsmen pulled a single oar (**yole de pointe**) or a pair (**yole de couple**). May also be sailed. An 18th-century boat was 11m long.
2. *France, W:* Participates in the mussel culture industry in the Pertuis Breton, an embayment north of La Rochelle on the Bay of Biscay. One or 2 **yoles** accompany the **mother ship***, a motorized **pinasse***, to the owner's sites, where rows of stakes have been set up to hold the developing mussels. The **yoles** transport the baskets of new mussels to be affixed to the stakes and help to collect the harvest. Flat bottom, sharp bow, transom stern, lightly flared sides. May be of wood or fiberglass. An outboard motor is set into a well at the stern. Crew of 2. Length ca. 3.5m. Note also **accon, canot mytilicole, plate de l'Aiguillon**.
3. *Scotland, NE:* Sharp-ended, motorized boat of the Fraserburg area. Popular for nearshore fishing, especially during the 1920s and 1930s. Still built in the 1960s. So numerous at one time that they were called the **mosquito fleet***. Initially clinker-built and painted green. Plumb stem, deep bulwarks. Small pilot house. Early **yoles** 6m long.
4. *West Indies, Martinique:* Plank-built on a dugout base. Used for fishing, and some are specially built for racing off this island in the Windward group. Racing boats constructed of special woods and prepared with great care. Sharp bow; small transom stern; ribs fixed to the keel piece; flat bottom. Worked with rudder and tiller or a large steering paddle. Carries a large, rectangular spritsail on a light mast stepped well forward and sometimes a foresail. When racing, several balance boards may be employed, with 7 of the 10-man crew exerting weight outboard. Reported lengths 7-9m; e.g., length 7m, beam 1.75m. Note also **gommier, pirogue-6**.

Further references: **Fair Isle yoal, jolly boat, Ness yoal, North Isles yole, South Isles yole, yawl**

yole de chasse *France, W:* Mainly a waterfowl hunting boat used on lac de Grand-Lieu, southwest of Nantes; also used to hunt muskrat and by fishermen working in very shallow water. Carvel-planked of northern fir; flat bottom; sharp, raked stem. Stern decking slopes down and bottom curves up to form a very shallow transom. Also decked forward and along the sides; large cockpit. Runners affixed to bottom when lake frozen. Hull tarred. Poled. Length 4.2m, beam 1.0m, depth 0.35m.

yole de couple See **yole-1**

yole de l'amiral See **barge-2**

yole de pointe See **yole-1**

yole vendéene *France, W:* Shallow, flat-bottomed river craft of the Vendée area. Cross-planked bottom turns up at bow and stern; bow sharp or with a small bow transom; stern wide, often with coverboard; straight, vertical or flared sides. Length ca. 4.3m, beam 1.25m, depth 0.35m.

yolke See **yacht**

yoll *England, E:* **1.** Fished for shrimp, mussels, eels, and cockles in The Wash during the mid-19th century. Sharp, plumb ends; clinker-built; flat floors. Long, open hatchway. Outboard rudder; tiller. Loose-footed, boomed gaff mainsail with long gaff; staysail; jib to horizontal bowsprit. Usually ca. 10.5m long; shallow draft. Other recorded names: **King's Lynn yoll, Lynn yoll, Norfolk yoll**
2. At Yarmouth, some **beach yawls*** were converted to pleasure boats for summer tourists. Later, some were built for this purpose, although they also fished; the last were essentially **motor launches**. The original boats were clinker-planked and double-ended. Decked. Most gaff-rigged. Lengths to 12.8m. Name variant: (**Yarmouth**) **pleasure yoll**
See also **beach yawl, Ness yoal, yawl**.

yolle See **yawl**

yolly boat See **jolly boat-1**

yonson See **bote-4**

York See **York boat**

York boat *Canada, north-central:* Developed by the Hudson's Bay Company to replace their fragile birchbark **canoes***. Carried freight, passengers, and furs from the mid-18th to the first quarter of the 20th century on the larger rivers and lakes. Most built at York Factory, but even these varied considerably in size and detail. A few new boats are being built as community projects. Carvel-planked; ends sharp and raked to ca. 45°; rounded bottom with slack bilges; scantling keel; moderate sheer at ends. Painted dark red. Sharply angled rudder hung out when under sail; downsloping tiller from tall rudderhead. Helmsman sat on a stern platform or a deck. On open water, a tall, portable mast might be stepped amidships and a square sail set; stayed to the stem. Mostly rowed, the crew sitting on the center line, one behind the other, each manning a sweep; some as long as 8.5m. Portaged on wooden rollers. The smaller, early boats used 4 men and a steersman; later boats employed 8 middlemen plus a steersman and bowman who used a hooked pole. Tracked from shore when necessary. Reported lengths 8.5-15.2m; e.g., length 13.7m, beam 2.4m, depth inside 1.2m; shallow draft. A small type might be known as a **half-York**. The **York boat** was also built in the 1840s at the mouth of the Columbia River in northwestern United States for use by the company in its operations in this area. These were more **canoe**-shaped, built of cedar strips, and were called **canoes**. Length ca. 9m. Other recorded names: **bateau★**, **Hudson's Bay bateau** (or **boat**), **inland boat★**, **100-piece boat**, **120-piece boat**, **Red River (freighter's) boat**, **60-piece boat**, **York**. Note also **scow-5**, **sturgeon-head**.

Yorkshire billyboy See **billyboy**
Yorkshire blobber See **blobber**
Yorkshire coble See **coble-1**
Yorkshire crab boat See **Norfolk crabber**
Yorkshire farm See **Yorkshire lugger**
Yorkshire keel *England, N:* Two types: those working the tidal waterways, going out onto the Humber Estuary and River Mersey, and those that did not go out into the Humber. The tidal **keels★** had ca. 30cm less depth than the **Humber keels★** so that they could traverse the Calder and Heble Navigation and the Rochdale Canal. Flat bottom, straight sides, rounded ends, leeboards. Set a square sail; in the canals, stepped a short, horse-towing mast. Crew of 2 or a family. 1850s boat: 17.4m long, 4.2m wide. The non-tidal **keels** were unrigged; the bow was more shaped and employed no leeboards. Many square-sterned. Frequently built of iron or steel. Many had no side decks; the **umbrella** or **hen peeked boats** had iron stanchions on which 3 parallel rails were laid like hen perches, over which cloths were spread. Further name variant: **boat★**. Note also **West Country boat**.
Yorkshire lugger *England, NE:* Fast, 3-masted vessel that primarily fished for herring, but was popular for smuggling and privateering in the late 18th and early 19th centuries. Evolved between the mid-17th and mid-18th centuries. Clinker-built to the wale; carvel-planked bulwarks. Stem curved; raked sternpost; flat or counter stern; considerable rise to the floors; short bilge keels. Decked; long hatch amidships; cabin in stern; carried 1-3 **cobles★** for the actual fishing. Foremast stepped in tabernacle, no shrouds; dipping lugsail tacked to eye in stemhead, sheeted well aft. Mainmast raked aft slightly, stayed forward; dipping lugsail tacked to eye amidships. Topmasts on main- and foremasts fitted to after side; topsails set flying. Mizzenmast stepped to port side and raked aft; sail sharply peaked, sheeted to an outrigger. Bowsprit added after 1820; jib used when fishing. Sails tanned. Mainmast discarded ca. 1840, and larger sails set. Reported lengths 13.7-18.9m; e.g., length overall 18.9m, on keel 13.4m, beam 5.94m, depth 2.29m. Other recorded names: **farm boat** (at Scarborough); **five-man boat** (5 partners, plus 2-3 in paid crew); **Yorkshire farm**
Yorkshire yawl *England, NE:* Lug- or **ketch★**-rigged boat of Scarborough, Filey, and Whitby; engaged in longline fishing from February to July and herring drifting from August to November. Evolved during the 2nd quarter of the 19th century. Clinker-built; old **yawls★** revitalized with an additional layer of carvel

planking. Heavy bow, straight stem; narrow lute stern, rounded at Filey. Straight keel with drag; high, soft bilges; sheer similar to the **coble★**, having a wave profile. Initially partly decked; later fully decked; net room forward, then fish hold, warp room, and cabin.

Yorkshire yawl

Tall capstan just forward of mizzenmast to haul nets. Carried 2 **cobles** when line fishing and one when herring fishing. Early boats set 2 lugsails with fidded mizzen topmast; no jib. Changed to fore-and-aft rig in the 1870s; loose-footed mainsail sheeted to a wide horse; mast in tabernacle. Mizzen boomed; 2 headsails; bowsprit to starboard; yard topsails. Crew of 6 plus 2 boys. Reported lengths 11-20m; e.g., length overall 14m, on keel 13m, beam 4.68m, hold depth 2m; cap. 28t. Other recorded names: **Filey yawl**, **Scarborough ketch** (or **yawl**)
youghall See **yawl**
yought, youghte See **yacht**
youll See **yawl**
youyou **1.** French term for a **dinghy★** used by **yachts★**; the smallest if there are several boats aboard. Generally short, beamy, and transom-sterned, with 1-2 seats for the oarsmen and a seat aft for passengers. Rowed, sculled, or sometimes sets a sliding gunter, leg-of-mutton, or lugsail. May be as small as 2.5m in length.
2. Term is sometimes applied derisively to a very small boat.
3. French word for a small boat found on Chinese rivers and at ports. Propelled by means of a scull worked on a peg.
Spelling variants: **yow yow**, **yuyu**; **iuiú** (Catalan)
youyou de senne See **seine boat-1**
yow yow See **youyou**
ysgraflau See **shout-1**
ys-jacht See **iceboat-1**
ysschuitje, ysschuyt See **ijsschuitje**
ytabába See **ytapá**
ytapá *Brazil, W:* Guaraní word for a **raft★**. The Paumari and Pammary tribes of the upper Rio Purus use the

ytapá

raft during periods of high water when they are forced to abandon their **ubas★**. Two layers of logs are set at right angles and lashed together with lianas. A large house is constructed on top. Poled or paddled. Other recorded names: **balsa dos Paumarys**, **ytabába**

Yttersi-åttring See **åttring-3**

yuaght See **yacht**

yuampu See **balsa-4**

Yüanchow ma-yang tzŭ See **Zhijiang ma yang zi**

Yuanling ma yang zi *China, central:* Cargo **junk★** of the lower reaches of the Yuan Jiang in Hunan. Built at Yuanling (formerly Shenchow). Strongly built and reinforced with 16 bulkheads and 6 wales. Upturned, square bow fitted with 2 removable catheads for the heavy anchors. Square, raked stern. Flat bottom. House covers more than half the hull; storeroom below deck at bow. Angular, balanced rudder comes up inboard; helmsman operates tiller from inside the house, looking forward out a small opening. Foremast stepped well forward; mainmast just forward of house; set battened balance lugsails. Length 30m, beam 4.9m, depth 1.0m, cap. 110t. Name variant: **Shenchow ma-yang tzŭ**. Note also **ma yang zi**.

yu chuan *China:* **1.** Generic term for a **fishing boat★**.

2. One type transports live fish from fish farms to the Shanghai market on the central east coast. Live well in the forward compartment; separated from the rest of the hull by a bulkhead. Water enters this area through square, wooden gratings on the sides and the bow; when the boat is empty, these gratings can be closed off. Large stones provide adjustable ballast since the bow noses down when the well is filled. Square ends; bow markedly raked; small platform extends beyond the stern; house amidships; washboards along the sides. Large, cleaver-shaped rudder hung out. Sets a single square-headed lugsail to a short mast. Also propelled by an iron-rimmed sculling oar, the *yuloh*. Crew of 5. Length 11.3m, beam 2.6m, depth 0.9m. Name variant: **live fish carrier**

3. A fanciful portrayal of an early seagoing **yu chuan** shows a square-bowed vessel with sheer rising abruptly aft to a very tall stern; capped with a crow's nest. Narrow transom stern; rudder came up inboard. Cannon in crow's nest. Rowed and sailed. Arched mat-roofed house amidships. Crew of 5.

Spelling variant: **yu tch'ouan**

yu maya *United States, SE:* Plank-built **canoe★** of the Catawba. Propelled by a 3.1-3.7m-long pole. Name variant: **flat boat★**

yuniak See **umiak-1**

yunk See **junk**

yuro See **gre**

yu tch'ouan See **yu chuan**

yuyu See **youyou**

Zaanse gondel See **grundel**

zabecchio, zabeco, zabeko See **xebec**

zabra *Portugal/Spain:* Small vessel of the 15th-17th centuries, reported from such diverse places as Peru, East Africa, and Goa. Some built for service in Flanders, and Basque-owned boats (**azabra**) fished for cod in the northwest Atlantic. Often described as a vessel from the north coast of Spain, engaging in fishing and privateering; the Portuguese used the **zabra** in minor naval engagements. Rowed and sailed, stepping 2 masts. About 20-170t, but some probably larger, carrying 100 men. Other recorded names: **bergantín cántabro, frigat, zarra, zavra**. Note also **galizabra**.

zaeima, zaim See **zaima**

zaima 1. *Djibouti:* A square-sterned **sambūq★**. The raked, straight stem has an elbow bend before continuing vertically to the scimitar-shaped stemhead. Straight keel; low rise to the floors amidships. Sheer sweeps up to the low poop. Rudder comes up inboard. Designs painted on quarter strakes and the stern. Single forward-raking mast carries a lateen sail; often motorized. Length ca. 20m.

2. *Iraq, S:* Reed **canoe★** of the Marsh Arabs. Constructed of long bundles lashed separately and then together to form the flattened bottom. Sides created by reeds bent U-shaped, reinforced by willow wands. Upper half of the sides "planked up" inside with long bundles. Ends sharp; several stout thwarts fixed in with softened bitumen. Exterior coated with successive layers of bitumen. Last about a year. Length ca. 3.1m, beam 0.76m. Note also **chalabiya**.

3. *Yemen:* **a.** An important **fishing boat★** and **coaster★** in the Red Sea area; essentially a small, sharp-sterned **sambūq**. Rounded stem terminates in a pointed stemhead that is often blue-tipped. Short, straight keel. Slender outboard rudder rises well above the low poop deck; worked with yoke and lines or tiller. Cargo type often employs weathercloths amidships. Steps 1-2 masts, setting lateen sails or quadrilateral, lateen-type sails with a short luff. Reported lengths 6.1-7.6m. **b.** On the south Arabian Peninsula coast, any small, **dhow★**-style boat. At Aden, may be a small, double-ended **fishing boat** with a very long, raked stem or the double-ended **sambūq** found in the Red Sea area.

Spelling variants: **seume, zaeima, zaim, z'imah, zaym, zeima**. Further references: **shahuf, zaruq-2**

zā'ima chūleka See **chalabiya**

za'imah See **zaima**

zak *China/India/Pakistan:* **Raft★** of inflated goat or sheep skins. Provides downstream transportation for people and cargo in Kashmir, the Punjab, and Xizang (Tibet). Skins soaked before being inflated through one leg. Lashed to a light platform of branches and poles. Size varies according to need, but may use as many as 40 skins. Spelling variants: **zakh, zok**

zak

zakh See **zak**

żakówka *Poland, NE:* Small, sprit-rigged **fishing boat★** that towed a net in the Zalew Wiślany (Frisches Haff or Vistula Lagoon); probably also worked in the northern part of the lagoon. One fishing for sprats was called a **Breitlingslomme**. Clinker planking; rounded in cross section; plank keel, flanked by grounding keels. Bottom rocker toward the bow; skeg aft. Slightly raking, straight stem; sharp stern. Outboard rudder; tiller; long, narrow leeboards on some. Open; small storage locker aft; small quarter-deck. Live well. Stepped 1-2 light masts. The shorter mast raked over the bow; the taller, vertical mainmast stepped just forward of amidships. Each set a tall spritsail. The **Strandlomme**, from the mouth of the Vistula River, set a single spritsail to a taller mast, a topsail, and a jib to a small bumkin. Rowed in calms. Employed auxiliaries after 1950s. Crew of 2. Reported lengths 5-7.6m; e.g., length 7.6m, beam 2.1m, depth 0.85m. The **Hafflomme** was 6.5-9m long. Other recorded names: **Fischerkahn★, Fischerlomme, Flunderlomme, Lommenfischer, Zeis'lomme**. Note also **lomme, zig**.

zalandium, zalandria See **chelandia**

zalmhengst See **zalmschouw**

zalmschouw *Netherlands, SW:* **Fishing boat★** designed to catch salmon (*zalm*) on lower rivers, as well as other fish. Through the years, use and place of origin have resulted in variations in details and in a multiplicity of names. Dates from at least the 17th century. Extinct except as a pleasure craft. Built of wood until ca. 1900, then iron or steel. Flat bottom continues in a long, curving stem extending as a flat surface to the gunwale. False stem added; stern pointed with vertical or near-vertical sternpost. Maximum beam well forward; sides flare below the wide wale, are tumble home above; pleasant sheer, rising toward the bow. Open, although larger boats had a cuddy forward. Rudder broad-bladed below the waterline, hung so it lifts on striking bottom; long, rounded leeboards. Most early boats had no live well; later steel boats had one immediately abaft the mast. Short, unstayed mast stepped in thwart fitted with a spritsail and staysail; some pleasure boats gaff-rigged. Also rowed. Crew of 1-2. Reported lengths 5-10.5m; e.g., length 6m, beam 2.1m, depth 1.04m. Other recorded names: **Bergenaar, drijfschouw, drijfschuit, drijversboot, drijverschuit, fanny, Hartjesvelder, Lekse schouw, meerkoet, Puttershoeker, schokkerschouw, schuit★, stevenschouw, vlouwschouw, vlouwschuit, Werkendammer boot, Woerkommer, zalmhengst, zegenschuit**; pl. **zalmschouwen**. Further reading: T. Huitema, *Ronde en Platbodem Jachten* (Amsterdam: Van Kampen & Zoon, 1977), 188-190, 282-284.

zalmschouwen See **zalmschouw**

zamakau See **camakau**

zambecchino, zambecco See **xebec**

zambuca, zambucchi, zambuche, zambuchi, zambucco, zambucis See **sambūq**

zambuco See **dau la mtepe, sambūq**

zambuquo See **sambūq**

Zandvoortsche garnalenschuit See **garnalenschuit**

zangada See **jangada**

Zanzibar jahazi *Tanzania (Zanzibar and Pemba):* Beamy cargo vessel built to trade along the African mainland coast, the Malagasy Republic, and occasionally the

Zanzibar jahazi

Arabian Peninsula. Carvel-built; long, flat keel; slightly curved or strongly raked stem; generally a wide transom stern. Outboard rudder worked with a wheel or by a tiller inserted through the rudderpost. Decked at bow and stern; open waist. Oculi motifs at the bows and sometimes at the stern. Single mast stepped vertically or raked forward. Large lateen sail tacks to the outer end of a light bowsprit. Spelling variants: **gehazi**, **jehazi**. Note also **jahazi**, **Lamu jahazi**.

zapato *Peru, central:* Small, shoe-like (*zapato*) **rowing boat★** used for net handling from the beaches at Huarmey. Still reported in the 1940s. Plank-built; bottom planked athwartships, continuing up at the ends to form a square bow and stern. May use a palm awning. Length 6m, beam 2m, depth 1.0m.

zapato chalana *Peru, central:* Rowing **punt★** characterized by its sharply upturned, square bow. Most numerous between Cerro Azul and Chimbote. Launched

zapato chalana

through heavy surf. Forward sheer terminates in a narrow bow plank, which may be vertical or carry out the upturned chine line. Overhanging stern also square but lower. Midships sheer relatively slight. Mildly flared sides; cross-planked bottom strengthened with flat keel and 2 bilge strakes. Usually 2 thwarts and stern sheets. May have short foredeck. Reported lengths 3.7-5.2m.

zárak See **zohrak**

zarook, zaroug, zarouq See **zaruq**

zarra See **zabra**

zarug, zarugah, zaruk, zaruka See **zaruq**

zaruq 1. *Djibouti:* The fishing **zaruq** employs a large net. Originally set a lateen sail, now usually powered by a diesel engine. Sharp ends with the bow especially sharp and stem straight and elongated; raked sternpost; strong sheer; low sides amidships. Outboard rudder; tiller. Decked at ends and along the sides. Crew of ca. 6. Recorded lengths 10-11m.

2. *Oman/United Arab Emirates:* A class of sharp-ended vessels, generally encompassing the **bedan★**, **batil★**, and **shahuf★**. Characterized by a tall, straight, wide sternpost to which an equally tall rudder is fixed; rudder worked by lines. At times, each of the above was called a **zaruq** or **zaruqah** by 19th-century writers. They were described as **fishing boats★** (**zaruqah**), fighting vessels (**zaruq**), and traders (**zaruqah**). Bow sharp and strongly raked, although one type portrayed as having a vertical stem with a clipper-type addition at the top. Carvel-planked; short keel, generally curved up toward the stern; decked or open. Sailed, setting 1-2 lateen sails to a forward-raking mast. Crew of 7-8 on the smaller vessels. Reported lengths 4.6-25m. Further name variant: **zaima★** (near Muscat). Note also **zauraq**.

3. *Yemen:* Double-ended vessel of the Red Sea and the Gulf of Aden. Light and fast, making it a favorite of smugglers and slave traders in early days; now mainly used for fishing and cargo. Bow sharp and strongly raked, either straight or with a slight curve along the upper part of the stem, or completely straight with the stem stopping abruptly about halfway between the waterline and the top, the upper strakes meeting at a point. Carvel-planked; short keel; considerable sheer forward and aft. Low freeboard amidships; weathercloths and bulwarks forward raise the sides on the traders. Open except for the poop deck and a platform at the bow. Toilet box outboard at forward end of the poop. Outboard rudder, worked mainly by a tiller or by a yoke and steering chains, or earlier by lines leading from the after part of the rudder to an outboard spur and then to a wheel. Generally gaily painted with alternating bands of color along the upper strakes and geometric designs on the quarters. One or 2 masts, raked very sharply forward, backstayed by halyards. Employs lateen sails with a short luff. Auxiliaries now common. Crew of 6-10. Reported lengths 9-21m. Spelling variants: **zarook**, **zar(o)ug**, **zarouq**, **zaruk(a)**, **zaruqah**, **zerog**

Other recorded names: **caruka, garaku(h), garokuh, garooku(h), garrooka, garukha, garúku(h), karookuh, zarook, zarugah, zaruk(a)**. Further references: **bedan-1, sambūq-2, shahuf**

zaruqah See **bedan-1, zaruq**

zata, zátah, zàtara, zatarò, zataròn, zatta See **zattera**

zattera Term for a **raft★**, particularly in northern Italy. Word has also come to mean a **barge★** or **lighter★**. May describe a simple rectangular craft of logs, a log **raft** with planked-up sides and perhaps a shaped bow and/or stern (a **zataròn**), or it may describe a craft of sawn planks. Sometimes applies to a **raft** that is created when logs are floated downstream. Other recorded names: **catara, sàtara, sàtera, zatarò, zatta, zzàttërë**; small: **zatterella**; large: **zatterone, zzattëróné**;

pl. **zattere**; in Spanish: **zata, zatàra**; in Czech: **zátah**; **Floss** by German-speaking peoples on Lake Como. Note also **chiatta**. Further reference: **life raft**

zattera di carenaggio See **raft-2**

zattera di salvataggio See **life raft**

zattere, zatterella, zatterone See **zattera**

zaught See **yacht**

zaurak See **zohrak**

zauraq **1.** *Iran:* A type of **boat★** or **ship★**. Spelling variant: **zawraq★**. Note also **zaruq, zevrakçe**.

2. *Iraq:* Early small boat used for pleasure trips on the lower Tigris and Euphrates River systems, although originally probably an armed craft. Some fancifully designed to represent lions, elephants, birds, dolphins, and snakes. Sometimes referred to as a **shabbâra**. Spelling variants: **harraka, harrâqa★, zawrak**

zavra See **zabra**

zawāriq See **zawraq**

zawrak See **zauraq-2, zawraq**

zawraq Arabic generic for **boat★, rowboat★,** or **skiff★**. Referred to as a **ship's boat★** in some early literature. A **fishing boat★** is a **zawraq aş-şaid**. Spelling variants: **zauraq★, zawrak**; pl. **zawāriq**. Further reference: **zauraq-1**

zawraq aş-şaid See **zawraq**

zayke See **saique**

zaym See **zaima**

zázio See **jahazi**

zeaught See **yacht**

zebec See **xebec**

zeebargie See **baardse**

zeebijlander See **bijlander**

zeeboot See **pink-5**

zeegaande pot See **pot-2**

zeegrundel See **grundel**

zeeklipper See **klipper-1**

Zeeland hoogaars See **hoogaars**

Zeeland scow See **Zeeuwse schouw**

zeepink See **pink-5**

zeepleit See **pleit-1, pleit-2**

zeepunter *Netherlands, E:* Open boat that worked along the southeastern part of the Zuiderzee, mainly fishing near the coast and at river mouths. Considered fast and seaworthy under sail, but usually rowed while fishing. Flat bottom with rocker; hard chines. Sharp ends; maximum beam forward of amidships. Strongly raked, straight stem and sternpost. Hull sheer swept up higher at the bow; straight, flared sides; wide top strake had tumble home and terminated before reaching the stem and sternpost. Frames extended to top of top strake; no gunwale. Outboard rudder with tall rudderhead; long, narrow leeboards. Ends often decked; live well. Those fishing with a drag net equipped with a windlass forward. Set a high-peaked spritsail, often boomed. Wide foresail overlapped the mainsail. Also punted. Crew of 2. Reported lengths 5.6-7m, some to 9m; e.g., length overall 7m, on bottom 5.2m; beam 1.65m; depth 0.8m. Other recorded names: **dekenpunter, grote punter, zegenpunter**. Note also **punter**.

zeerover See **sea rover**

Zeesboot **1.** *Germany, Baltic coast:* Heavily built **fishing boat★** of the shallow coastal areas. Mainly a

trawler★ employing a special net, the *Zeese*. Dates from the mid-19th century, and a few worked under sail until the 1970s; some still participate in regattas. Those imported as **drifters★** into Denmark were known as **Tyskerkvase**. Originally clinker-built, later carvel; on the carvel-planked boats, the sheer strake overlapped the one below; moderate sheer. Flared bow; stem raked and straight, convex, or concave. Sharp, raked stern, elliptical or with a counter.

Zeesboot-1

Straight, plank keel; low rise to the floors. Half-decked; trunk cabin forward; side decks bordered the waist amidships; some had a standing well aft; small, single-masted boats generally open. Early boats used a leeboard; later a centerboard. Outboard rudder; tiller. Long spars rigged out at bow and stern held the drift net open. Those from the western German coast were **ketch★**-rigged with a loose-footed gaff mainsail with long gaff; gaff topsail, 2 headsails, and a standing lug mizzen sheeted to the rudder; some small boats set a single boomed gaff sail and headsail. Very long bowsprit. Eastern boats set a loose-footed lugsail on the mainmast and larger boats also used a boomed-out lug mizzen with boom at the foot. Sails tanned. Small boats equipped for rowing. In later years, many converted to power. Crew of 2. Reported lengths on keel 5.4-12.6m; e.g., length on keel 8.8m, beam 3.14m, depth 1.1m, draft with leeboard up 0.84m. Other recorded names: **drivkvase★, Quase★, Tyskedrivkvase, Zeese(n)boot, Zeisenboot**. Further reading: Timm Stutz, *Braune Segel im Wind—Die Letzen Zeesboote* (Berlin: VEB Verlag für Verkehrswesen, 1988). Note also **Zeeskahn**.

2. *Lithuania, S/Russia, W:* Open **fishing boat** of the Kurski Zaliv (Kurische Haff) that uses the *Zeisen* (*Zeese*) net. Eight or 9 clenched planks to each side; curved stem; straight, raked sternpost; moderate sheer. Outboard rudder; tiller. Rowed and sailed. Tall square sail set to an aft-raking mast stepped amidships; some set a spritsail and jib. Crew of 2. Reported lengths 5.1-5.5m; beam ca. 2m, depth 0.6m. Other recorded names: **Strandboot★, Zeis(en)boot**

zeeschouw *Netherlands:* Built since the beginning of the 20th century in several areas, mainly for fishing, especially on the Zuiderzee, but also for shrimp trawling and recently as a **yacht★**. A small type still accompanies larger fishing vessels. Because of their boxy shape, they were known colloquially as a **spekbak**

(**bacon box**) or **platkop** (**flathead**). Originally built of wood, later of steel. Narrow, flat bottom with rocker toward ends (Lemmer type) or over the entire length (Hoorn type). Forward end butts above the waterline with an angular chine against a six-sided, raked bow transom; stern butts below the waterline with a wider, six-sided transom. Shallow keel extends from stern to mast. Sides flare to wale, then are tumble home; strong sheer, especially at the bow; sheerline more curved on Hoorn type than Lemmer type. Decked to the mast on **fishing boats***; **yachts** have a cabin over the well area. Outboard rudder; tiller slots over rudderhead. Narrow leeboards. Live well on **fishing boats**. Mast unstayed originally; later a forestay set to top of bow transom. **Fishing boats** set a loose-footed gaff sail with a straight gaff, curved on **yachts**; large staysail and sometimes a jib to a jibboom. Originally also hung a boomed-out, triangular sail from the mast. Later motorized. Reported lengths 6-11m; e.g., length 8m, beam 3m, depth 1.1m. Other recorded names: **Hollandse schouw, Hoornse schouw, hoornsman, Lemmerschouw, Lemster schouw**; pl. **zeeschouwen**. Note also **Zeeuwse schouw**.

zeeschouwen See **zeeschouw**

Zeeseboot See **Zeesboot**

Zeesekahn, Zeesekähne See **Zeeskahn**

Zeesenboot See **Zeesboot-1**

Zeesenkahn, Zeesenerkahn See **Zeeskahn**

Zeeskahn *Germany, N/Poland, W:* Sturdy **fishing boat*** that operated in the Stettiner Haff (Zalew Szczeciński) area from the 15th to the early 20th century. Superseded by the **Zeesboot***. Towed the *Zeese* net. Clinker-planked; convex or concave stem; sharp stern with slightly raked sternpost; flat floors amidships; plank keel and sometimes bilge keels. Leeboards; outboard rudder; long tiller. Decked; steering well aft; live well amidships. Stepped 2-3 tall masts, setting spritsails or tall lugsails; staysail. Crew of 3. Reported lengths on keel 9-22m, widths to 7m, depths 1.8-2.8m; shallow draft. Other recorded names: **czesekan, Zeesekahn, Zeesen(er)kahn, Zes(z)ekan, Zesekahn, Zesener-Kahn**; pl. **Zees(e)kähne**

Zeeskähne See **Zeeskahn**

zeesnik See **snik-1**

zeetjalk *Netherlands:* A modified **tjalk*** that was both a **coaster*** and an oceangoing vessel that traveled widely. Proportionally broader and deeper with more sheer than inland **tjalken** (pl.). Built from the 1st half of the 19th century; last one worked until the mid-20th century. Most constructed in Groningen Province in the northeast. Originally of wood, then of iron or steel. Rounded ends with marked tumble home above the wide, heavy wale; slight S-curve to the stem; vertical sternpost; considerable deadwood. Sharp sheer toward the stemhead. Outboard rudder with fin on outer end; tiller; large leeboards. Decked; large hatch abaft the mast; deckhouse aft. Small, single-masted vessels carried a loose-footed, boomed gaff sail; early boats had a curved gaff, later straight. Large staysail; some had a jib. Larger **zeetjalken** rigged as **ketches***; mizzenmast stepped against the deckhouse; long, rising bowsprit held 2-3 jibs. Some

set a square sail forward of the mainmast. Later vessels had auxiliaries. Reported lengths 15-25m, widths 4.5-6m, depths 1.8-2m. Other recorded names: **sea tjalk**; one going mainly to the Baltic was called a **oostzeetjalk** (or **Ostsee tjalk**).

Zeeuwsche hoogaars, Zeeuwse hoogaars See **hoogaars**

Zeeuwse klipper See **klipper-1**

Zeeuwse pinkje See **pink-5**

Zeeuwse schouw *Netherlands, SW:* **Fishing boat*** that worked oyster and mussel beds and fished for flounder in rivers until the 20th century. At times carried freight, and some new, steel pleasure craft have been built. Constructed with 2 overlapping strakes, later 3; broad top strake had tumble home where the wale dipped low amidships; narrow throughout on later boats. Straight, flaring sides. Flat, longitudinally planked bottom curved up and narrowed almost to the top strake at each end and fixed against a short, massive beam; curved, false stem added on some. Raked skeg supported a tall, wide-bladed rudder; tiller slotted through rudderhead. Angular chines; narrow leeboards. Foredeck low, loose on older type, fixed and higher on later; open waist; short deck aft with steering cockpit; cuddy forward of the cockpit. Bilge pump abaft the mast thwart on old type. Unstayed mast stepped in forward third; could be struck. Loose-footed, boomed gaff sail with short, curved gaff; narrow staysail and sometimes a jib to a short bowsprit. Crew of 2. Reported lengths 10-11.6m; e.g., length 10.2m, beam 3.4m, depth 1.3m, draft 1.6m. Other recorded names: **Berg(en)se schouw, botvissertje, garnaatvisser, schourd, schouw van Philippine, Seelandische schouw, Tholens(ch)e schouw Thoolsche schouw, Tools(ch)e schouw, Zeeland scow**. Note also **zeeschouw**.

Zeeuwsvlaamse hoogaars *Netherlands, SW:* A **hoogaars*** type built along the south bank of the Westerschelde River in the late 19th and early 20th centuries. Distinctive feature was the short stern rocker of its flat bottom. Set a loose-footed, boomed gaff sail; 2 headsails. Reported lengths 8.5-11m.

zegenpunter See **zeepunter**

zegenschuit See **zalmschouw**

zegenvisserijvaartuig See **seine boat-1**

Zehnerin, Zehnerzille See **Salzzille**

zeilaak See **aak**

zeilklipper See **klipper-1**

zeillogger See **logger**

zeima See **zaima**

Zeisboot, Zeisenboot See **Zeesboot**

Zeis'lomme See **żakówka**

zélande, zelander, zelandie, zelandriae See **chelandia**

Zelle See **Zille**

z'ēme See **chalabiya**

zemy *Africa, central:* Large, sewn **canoe*** of some of the fishermen of Lake Chad; extinct. Wide forward, where a device was installed to hold a triangular fishing net. Length 12m. Note also **markaba**.

Zenhai chuan See **Chênhai chuan**

zerma See **djerme, germa**

zerme See **germa**

zerog See **zarug**

Zesekan, Zesekahn, Zesener-Kahn, Zeszekan See **Zeeskahn**

zevrak See **zevraq**

zevrakçe Persian term for a small **boat***. Note also **zauraq**.

zevraq Turkish generic term for a small **boat***, or **skiff***. Spelling variant: **zevrak**. Note also **zauraq**.

Zhijiang ma yang zi *China, central:* Slender cargo vessel used on the swift upper reaches of the Yuan Jiang in Hunan. Lightly built, but strengthened with multiple wales, bulkheads, and frames. Sides mildly curved and taper to narrow, elongated, raked, square ends; flat bottom. Wood-sided, mat-roofed house amidships. Angular balanced rudder comes up inboard; tiller; stick-in-the-mud anchor. Mast stepped in forward third; lugsail. Length 18.6, beam 2.3m, depth 1.0m. Other recorded names: **ma yang tzŭ, Yüanchow ma-yang tzŭ**. Note also **ma yang zi**.

zhu pai *China:* **1.** **Rafts*** constructed of bamboo, popular for river and coastal fishing, ferrying, transporting produce, and as **tenders*** to **timber rafts***. In some cases, it may be the bamboo itself that is being transported.
2. At Xiamen (Amoy) on the east coast, 2-12 **zhu pai** are carried aboard the **Amoy fisher***. Work in pairs: one, with a crew of 2, pays out the longlines, while the 2nd, with a crew of 3, collects the catch. Constructed of 10 or more bamboo poles, secured with crosspieces. Propelled by oars worked against a combined tholepin and lumber iron. Length 3.6m, width 1.8m.
3. In the Shantou (Swatow) area in eastern China, works in conjunction with the **li niao*** from March to September. A net is hung between them. Constructed of 10 bamboo poles trimmed hexagonally to prevent splitting. Worked with oars hung in rattan grommets from tholepins.
Spelling variants: **chu-phai, tchou-p'ai**. Note also **chu-p'ai, fa zi**.

zhu pai wang *China, E:* One-man bamboo **raft*** from the Xiamen (Amoy) and Ningbo (Ningpo) areas. At Xiamen, the **raft** worked with a **sampan*** in handling a drift net or lines; the rectangular **raft** was composed of 5-6 thick bamboo poles ca. 2m long, laced together with bamboo fibers; rowed standing with oars nested in tall, forked supports. On the Ningbo **rafts**, a hut sheltered the fishermen. Other recorded names: **chu-p'ai-wang, tchou-p'ai wang**

Zielboot See **mark boat-1**

Ziellen See **Zille**

zig *Poland, N:* **Fishing boat*** and **fish carrier*** of the Gulf of Danzig (Gdańsk) and the Zalew Wiślany (Frisches Haff or Vistula Lagoon). Dates at least to the late 12th century. A type of **Lomme***. Mainly clinker-planked with 3-4 strakes per side; plank keel, rocker at bow; rounded sides. Ends terminate in narrow, raked transoms; skeg aft. Live well. Open except for small stern deck; wet well amidships. Outboard rudder, blade wide below the waterline; tiller slots over rudderhead. Sets spritsails to 1-2 masts. Some motorized. Crew of 2-3. Reported lengths 5-7m; e.g., length 5.5m, beam 1.5m, depth 0.63m. The larger **Sickenlomme** fished out in the Baltic. Some served as fish buyers (**Fischaufkäufersicken**). Numerous clinker-laid strakes; rounded sides. Sharp, raked ends; strong sheer forward. Slightly raised cuddy aft; fish well amidships; leeboards. Gaff-rigged with loose-footed mainsail; staysail. Reported lengths 8.5-9.5m. Other recorded names: **Fisch(er)sicken, Fischhändlersicken, Kaulbarssicken** (to catch brill), **Brillsicken, Lommsicken, Paudel, Sacksicken, säugchen, Sewche, Sicke(n), Süken, ziga**. Note also **garnsicken**.

ziga See **zig**

Zijdse bom, Zijdtsche bom See **bom-1**

Zille Generic term for a flat-bottomed, **barge***-like craft found on many rivers, canals, and lakes of central Europe, notably the Danube and its tributaries, and on the Elbe, Havel, Oder, Main, and Vistula Rivers. Used for cargo (the **Obstzille**, for instance, carries fruit), local transportation, ferrying (**Überfuhrzille**), fishing, and wildfowling. Name dates to at least the early 16th century. Usually open, or with short end decks. The ends of the **Kaffenzille** turn up in a flat surface, terminating in a narrow, flat bow; the **Stevenzille** had relatively sharp ends with stem and sternpost. Long and very narrow; flush-planked; bottom has rocker; some on the Danube were more **skiff***-like with longer overhang and narrower bow. Generally rowed, poled, or floats with the current; some early boats employed sails. Cargo boats were usually towed back upstream by horses. Reported lengths 5-50m, widths 1-6m; very shallow depth. Other recorded names: **Berliner Zille, Böhmisch Zille, Cille(n), czullen, Donauzille, Elbzille, Havelzille, Linzerzille, Marktzille, nackt Zille, Zelle, Ziellen, Zil(l)n, Zuin, zull, Zülle(n), Zülln, züln;** pl. **Zillen**. Note also **Fischerzille, Nachen, Waidzille**. Further reference: **Mutzen**

Zillen, Zilln, Ziln See **Zille**

zinakln See **Schinakel**

Zinzhou chuan See **hong tou san ban**

Zisterne See **water boat-1**

zoetwaterschip See **waterschip-2**

zohrak *Pakistan:* Cargo carrier of Punjabi rivers; still used. Strong, but roughly built of clamped planks. Boxy shape; bow and stern round up to square ends of equal height; nearly flat bottom; flat sheer. Many built of scavenged cedar that was uprooted during floods and floated downstream. On long trips, a thatched hut might be erected on deck. Those in the Multan area had a very low waist and hoisted a mat sail to a small mast. Reported lengths 12-18m, widths 3.5-4.5m; very shallow draft; 40-50t burden. Spelling variants: **zárak, zaurak, zohruk, zoru(c)k**

zohruk See **zohrak**

zok See **zak**

zolderbak *Netherlands:* **Barge*** that carries its cargo on deck, a **dekschuit***, mainly in the Amsterdam area. Built of wood or steel. On larger vessels, the deck is supported by numerous pillars. May be sharp- or blunt-ended; flat bottom; flared sides. Pleasant sheer rising toward the stem. Rudder wide-bladed below the waterline; tiller. Reported lengths 20.5-23.5m, widths 5-5.3m, depth ca. 1.3m. Name variant: **zolderschuit**. Note also **bak**.

zolderschuit See **dekschuit, zolderbak**

Zollkruiser See **revenue cutter-1**

Zollkutter See **kutter-1**, **kutter-2**
Zollwächterfahrzeug, **Zollwächterschiff**,
Zollwächtschiff See **revenue cutter-1**
zomp, **zompen** See **somp**
zoncho See **junk**
zoomaak See **aak**
zòpolo, **zoppo** See **zoppolo**
zoppolo *Croatia/Italy, NE:* Plank-extended, oak dugout
of the northeastern Adriatic and the Dalmatian coast;

zoppolo

used for fishing. Sharp ends with raked bow and vertical stern; flat floors; straight sides. Decked at ends;
2-3 thwarts. Mostly rowed, by 1 or 2 men standing.
Long oar set in oarlock at one end of an outrigged
stablizing plank, ca. 3m long, that crosses the hull
and extends ca. 1.0m out each side. Probably also
used a square sail. Length 4m, beam 1.0m. Other recorded names: **kirska ladja**, **zòpolo**, **zoppo**. Note also
ladja-1, **ladva**.
zoruck, **zoruk** See **zohrak**
Zossen See **tub-1**
zoutwaterschip See **waterschip-2**
Zuiderwalse aak See **griendaak**
Zuiderzeebotter See **botter**
Zuiderzeeschokker See **schokker**
Zuidhollandse schuit See **schuit-2**
Zuidhollandse tjalk See **Hollandse tjalk**
Zuidwalbotter See **botter**
Zuin, **zull**, **Zülle**, **Züllen**, **Zülln**, **züln** See **Zille**
zulu *Scotland:* Herring **drifter**★ used mainly out of
northeastern ports from the 1880s until World War I;
conversion to power began ca. 1906, and of these,
some continue to work at line fishing and lobstering.

zulu

A few built in Ireland. Initially clinker-built, but shifted to carvel construction as length increased; sharp
ends. Characterized by a plumb stem and heavily

raked sternpost; fine, sharp bow with deep forefoot;
fine run aft. Straight keel with drag; rounded bilges.
Decked; hold amidships; small cabin aft; motorized
vessels have a wheelhouse. Capstan used for hauling
nets, raising the mainmast, and tightening halyards.
Initially steered by tiller, later by a horizontal wheel.
Generally painted black, most with a white cutwater;
black, green, and blue topsides; later a varnished hull
was favored. Set a large dipping lugsail to a lofty, massive mainmast; tack usually to stemhead, but could go
to a hook on the mast or an eyebolt on deck. On large
zulus, sails were so large they were raised by steam.
Mast unsupported except for halyards and burton;
lowered to crutch beside the mizzenmast while shooting the nets. High-peaked, standing lug mizzen used
mainly as a steadying sail while fishing; foot extended
by outrigger; mizzenmast stepped midway between
mainmast and stern, raking forward. In light winds, a
jib was run out on a long bowsprit. Sails tanned black.
In confined places, rowed with long sweeps or poled.
Some later **zulus** built as motorized vessels, until ca.
1934. Crew of 8-9. Reported lengths overall 8-27m;
e.g., length overall 16.5m, on keel 11.6m, beam
5.05m, hold depth 2.44m. Further reading: Edgar J.
March, *Sailing Drifters* (Newton Abbot: David &
Charles; Camden, Maine: International Marine
Publishing Co., 1952; reprint, 1969): 274-288. Note
also **mule**, **ring-net boat**, **zulu skiff**.
zulu skiff *Scotland:* Line **fishing boat**★ that worked
around the coasts during the late 19th century and was
exported for use along the northwest coast of Ireland.
Initially clinker-built, later carvel. Straight stem;
curved forefoot; very raked sternpost; flared bow;
rounded stern; straight keel with drag. Large rudder.
Cabin beneath foredeck; open aft; narrow side decks.
Hull varnished to waterline, red or black below. Two
masts, setting standing lugsails; bowsprit common in
the 1880s; later stepped a single sharply aft-raking
mast. Set a high-peaked standing lugsail; tack to short
iron horse at foot of the mast. Mast stepped in trunk,
supported by 2 shrouds to a side; to adjust the rake,
some boats had 3 steps. Long bowsprit. Also rowed
with long sweeps. Crew of 3-4. Lengths overall 6-
12.8m; e.g., length overall 10.7m, on keel 8.1m, beam
3.38m, inside depth 1.9m. Note also **Loch Fyne skiff**,
zulu.
zumaca See **sumaca**
zumbra *Spain:* An early type of **skiff**★ or **yawl**★.
zumeca See **sumaca**
zusterschip See **mother**
Zustutzen See **Mutzen**
Zuyderzeebotter See **botter**
Zuyderzese visser See **waterschip-1**
Zweimastewer See **Besan-Ewer**
Zweitoppsegelschoner See **schooner-1**
Zwidorkohlzille, **Zwidorzille** See **Salzzille**
zzàttërë, **zzattërónë** See **zattera**

Selected Reading

Adney, Edwin Tappan and Howard I. Chapelle. *The Bark Canoes and Skin Boats of North America.* Washington, D.C.: Smithsonian Institution, 1964.

Audemard, L. *Les Jonques Chinoises.* 10 vols. Rotterdam: Maritiem Museum "Prins Hendrik," 1957-1971.

Beaudouin, François. *Bateaux des Côtes de France.* Grenoble: Éditions des 4 Seigneurs, 1975.

———. *Bateaux des Fleuves de France.* Douarnenez: Éditions des l'Estran, 1985.

Chapelle, Howard I. *American Small Sailing Craft: Their Design, Development, Construction.* New York: W. W. Norton & Company, 1951.

Dodd, Christopher. *The Story of World Rowing.* London: Stanley Paul, 1992.

Edwards, Clinton R. *Aboriginal Watercraft on the Pacific Coast of South America.* Berkeley: University of California Press, 1965.

Færøyvik, Øystein and Bernhard. *Inshore Craft of Norway.* Greenwich: Conway Maritime Press, 1979.

Filgueiras, Octavio Lixa. *The Decline of Portuguese Regional Boats.* Maritime Monographs and Reports No. 47. London: National Maritime Museum, 1980.

Gillmer, Thomas C. *A History of Working Watercraft of the Western World.* 2nd ed. Camden, Maine: International Marine Publishing Co., 1994.

Greenhill, Basil. *The Archaeology of the Boat.* Middletown, Conn.: Wesleyan University Press; London: A. & C. Black Limited, 1976.

Haddon, A. C. and James Hornell. *Canoes of Oceania.* Honolulu: Bishop Museum Press, 1975. Originally published 1936-1938.

Holmes, Tommy. *The Hawaiian Canoe.* Hanalei: Editions Limited, 1981.

Hornell, James. "The Origins and Ethnological Significance of Indian Boat Designs" in: *Memoirs of the Asiatic Society of Bengal.* VII/3 (1920), 139-256.

———. *Water Transport: Origins & Early Evolution.* Cambridge: University Press, 1946.

Horridge, Adrian. *The Prahu: Traditional Sailing Boat of Indonesia.* 2nd ed. Singapore: Oxford University Press, 1976.

Kemp, Peter, ed. *The Oxford Companion to Ships & the Sea.* London: Oxford University Press, 1976.

Koch, Gerd. *Boote aus Aller Welt.* Berlin: Museum für Völkerkunde, 1984.

Landström, Björn. *The Ship: An Illustrated History.* Garden City, N.Y.: Doubleday & Co., 1961.

Leather, John. *Gaff Rig.* 2nd ed. Camden, Maine: International Marine Publishing Co., 1982.

———. *Spritsails and Lugsails.* London: Granada Publishing, 1979.

McKee, Eric. *Working Boats of Britain: Their Shape and Purpose.* London: Conway Maritime Press, 1983.

Needham, Joseph. *Science and Civilization in China.* Vol. 4, *Physics and Physical Technology,* Part III, *Civil Engineering and Nautics.* Cambridge: University Press, 1971.

Neyret, Jean. *Piroques Océaniennes*. 2 vols. Supplements in *Neptunia*, 1977-1985. Paris: Association des Amis des Musées de la Marine, 1976.

Nielson, Christian. *Wood Boat Designs: Classic Danish Boats*. New York: Charles Scribner's Sons, 1980.

Paget-Tomlinson, Edward W. *The Illustrated History of Canal & River Navigations*. Sheffield: Sheffield Academic Press, 1993.

Paris, François Edmond. *Essai sur la Construction Navale des Peuples Extra-europeens*. Paris: A. Bertrand, 1832.

⸻. *Souvenirs de Marine: Collection des Plans au Dessins de Navires et de Bateaux Anciens et Modernes....* 6 vols. Paris: Gauthier-Villars, 1886-1910.

Petrejus, E. W. *Oude Zeilschepen en Hun Modellen: Binnenschepen Jachten en Visserschepen*. 2nd ed. Bussum: Unieboek N. V., 1973.

Prins, A. H. J. *A Handbook of Sewn Boats: the Ethnology and Archaeology of Archaic Plank-built Craft*. Maritime Monographs and Reports No. 59. Greenwich: National Maritime Museum, 1986.

Renault, François. *Bateaux de Normandie: de Granville à Honfleur*. Douarnenez: Éditions de l'Estran, 1984.

Roberts, Kenneth G. and Philip Shackleton. *Canoe: A History of the Craft from Panama to the Arctic*. Camden, Maine: International Marine Publishing Co., 1983.

Smyth, H. W. *Mast and Sail in Europe and Asia*. Edinburgh: Blackwood & Sons, 1929.

Suder, Hans. *Vom Einbaum und Floss zum Schiff: Die Primitiven Wasserfahrzeuge*. Veröffentlichen des Instituts für Meereskunde, Neue Folge, B. Historische-volk wirtschaftliche Reihe, Heft 7. Berlin: Verlag E. S. Mittler & Sohn, 1930.

Van Beylen, Jules. *Zeilvaart Lexicon: Viertalig Maritiem Woordenboek*. Weesp: De Boer Maritiem, 1985.

Wilson, N. F. J. *The Native Craft: A General Description of the Native Craft Visiting Bombay Harbour and Particulars as to Their Survey, Registry, Measurement, and Lighting*. Bombay: Bombay Port Trust, 1909.

Witsen, Nicolaes. *Architectura Navalis et Regimen Nauticum: Ofte Aaloude en Hedendaagsche Scheeps-Bouw en Bestier....* Amsterdam: 1690; facsimile 1971.

Worcester, G. R. G. *The Junks & Sampans of the Yangtze*. Annapolis, Md.: Naval Institute Press, 1971.

Geographical Index

AFGHANISTAN
šāl
turssuk
tutín

ALBANIA
barkë
kaik
kajik
lundra
sandall
šerk
sule
trap

ALGERIA
balancelle
bateau bœuf
chalutier
corallina
palangrier
saettia
sardinal

AMERICAN SAMOA
See Samoa Islands

ANGOLA
bimbá
catraia
chalão
chata
chatão
coche

ANTIGUA and **BARBUDA**
dagger
Tortola sloop

ARABIAN PENINSULA
See also Bahrain, Kuwait,
   Oman, Qatar, United Arab
   Emirates, Yemen
'abari
baghla
bârko
batil
bedan
belem
boom
bugalilo
falūwa
gatîra
ghurāb
grab
houri
jalbūt
khashabah
markab

ARABIAN PENIN., *cont.*
mashua
qārib
sambūq
sandal
sangara
shū·ai
tarrādah
terrada
zawraq

ARGENTINA
balandra
ballenera
balsa
barco
bote
brigantine
chalana
champán
igá
pailebot
patache
pelota
polacra

AUSTRALIA
äkälla
barge
barracouta boat
bärwän
bay boat
best and best boat
coff
collecting boat
cray boat
cutter
flattie
floating station
gondol
gre
gul
kaloa
ketch
koka
kolek (Christmas Island)
kundal
lippa-lippa
lippee-lippee
mitjang
net boat
ngardän
passage boat
pearling lugger
punt
scalloper
scow
snapper boat
surfboat
tango

AUSTRALIA, *cont.*
tonn
walpa
wangga
whaleboat (& Cocos/Keeling)
whiting boat

AUSTRAL ISLANDS
kamia
taurua

AUSTRIA
Berghe
Bretterfloss
Bucintoro
Farm
Fischerfloss
Fischerzille
Galeere
Krenzille
Küchenschiff
Leibschiff
Mutzen
Nachen
Ordinari
Plätte
Salzzille
saique
Schiff
Schinakel
Waidzille
Zille

AZORES
canoa do baleeiro
caravelão
tow boat

BAHAMAS
Bahama dinghy
sharpshooter
smack boat
sponge schooner

BAHRAIN
See also Arabian Peninsula
belem
farteh
mahaila
shashah
shū·ai

BANGLADESH
accommodation boat
badjra
baida
balam
barki
berá
bhedí

BANGLADESH, *cont.*
bhelā
bhur
bouri de nage
chatty raft
chhip
country boat
dawk boat
dingi
donga
ghashi
grab
hulíya
jalba
jali
jong
khatgiri
koch
kosha
modhyam balam
mut
nauka
padi
pallar
panshi
parindah
patam
purgoo
sampan
sand boat
saranga
taghāri
teddy balam
trawler
ulakh

BARBADOS
Barbados flying-fish boat
Barbados schooner
bateau
ice boat
launch
Moses boat

BELAU *See Palau*

BELGIUM
aak
ankerschip
Antwerpse sloop
baardse
bache
bachot
bak
ballastschuit
baquet de Charleroi
barque longue
beerotter
beunschip
beurtschip

BELGIUM, *cont.*
beurtschuit
bijlander
bilander
Blankenbergse schuit
blazer
boeier
boeieraak
boot
bovenmaase aak
buis
bunboot
canot à crevette
corbette
dogger
Duinkerker
ever
gaffelschuit
galjoot
Heistse schuit
hengst
herna
hoogaars
jol
kadraai
klipper
kogge
kotter
kreeftenbark
kreeftenkotter
lemmerhengst
loodsjol
loodsvaartuig
Nieuwpoortse dandy
Nieuwpoortse garnaalboot
Oostendse sloep
otter
panneschuit
pleit
schuit
senau
sloep
smak
spits
spitsbek
stadsbarge
steenschuit
trekschuit
vishoeker
vlet
vlot
waal
walenmajol

BELIZE
batteau
Belizean smack
bungay
cargo lighter
creau
dorey
pitpan

BENIN (formerly Dahomey)
huntin

BERMUDA
ballahou
Bermuda dinghy
Bermuda schooner
Bermuda sloop
Bermudian

BOLIVIA
balsa
huampu
igarité
montaria
pelota

BOTSWANA
mokoro

BRAZIL
alvarenga
balandra
baleeira
balsa
bangué
barca
barcaça
barcachina
barco
barco mineiro
bateira
batelão
batelão-regatão
bote
breu
burrinha
caique
canoa
canoa bordada
canoa de embono
canoa do alto
canoa grande
caravelão
casco
catraia
chalana
chata
coberta
curiara
embono
galeola
galeota
gambarra
garoupeira
geleira
hiate
iat
iate
igá
igaraçu
igarité
igat

BRAZIL, *cont.*
jangada
jangada-bote
jangada de tábuas
jangada do alto
lancha
lanche
mon'á
montaria
pamacari
paquete
paxiuba
pelota
perua
piperi
poveiro
prancha
regatão
saveiro
sumaca
ü-a
ubá
vigilenga
woodskin
ygat
ytapá

BRITISH ISLES
See also Ireland & United Kingdom
balinger
ballast barge
barge-yacht
buyer smack
carab
church ship
day boat
double-bottom
farcost
ferryboat
fishing smack
flyboat
flyte
galeass
great boat
keel
lighter
longboat
market boat
nickey
Norway yawl
picard
pink
plat
sailing barge
sceort-scip
scout
tea clipper
team boat
trading smack

BRUNEI
bidar
gobang
tongkang

BULGARIA
alamana
gabára
kaik
ládija
lódka
mauna
plúta
prám
sal
shaikŭ

BURMA *See Myanmar*

CAMBODIA
dragon boat
ghe cui
rua chalom
tam ban
tuk thnot
vivier flottant

CAMEROON
daé
daré
dihengué
fak
kadei
markaba
zemy

CANADA
See also St. Pierre and Miquelon
Abenaki canoe
admiral
Algonkin canoe
ark
Baccalieu skiff
baiter
baitskiff
baleinière de Gaspé
banker
Banks dory
barge
barque
basket canoe
bateau
bateau plat
batoe
batteau
bay boat
Bay of Fundy shad boat
bay punt
Beothuk canoe
big-river canoe
boat
boëtteur

CANADA, *cont.*

boom
boom boat
botte
brigantin
bullboat
by-boat
cabane
caboteur
cage
cajeu
Canadian canoe
canadienne
canaller
canoe-kayak
canot
canot à glace
canot bâtard
canot du maître
canot du nord
canot léger
Cape boat
Cape Island boat
capelanier
carrying boat
catamaran
catcher vessel
cattle ferry
chaland
chaloupe
chalutier
charoi
chasseur
Chebacco boat
Chipewyan canoe
clipper-schooner
coastal packet
cod-seine skiff
Collingwood boat
côtier
cottonwood canoe
Cree canoe
crib
crooked canoe
cross-handed dory
cut boat
dogbody
Dogrib canoe
door boat
dragger
dram
drift boat
drogher
Durham boat
eel boat
eel-fishing boat
fish box
fish carrier
fisherman
fishing skiff
flat
flat batteau
flatboat

flatte
float
floater
flûte
freight canoe
freighter
gabare
gabarre
galley
galloper
gas boat
Gaspé schooner
ghuljai-ts!i
gillnetter
goélette
Great Lakes schooner
gunboat
gunning skiff
Hampton boat
high rat
home boat
hooking boat
hopper barge
horse boat
Huron boat
iceboat
ice canoe
ice punt
ice skiff
inland boat
jack
jackass
kayak
kayak-form canoe
King's boat
k'i t'u ela
knockabout
laker
lobster boat
longliner
long-nose canoe
lumberman's batteau
lumber skiff
Lunenburg dory
Mackinaw boat
mail boat
Malecite river canoe
market boat
mE'nga
mission boat
monkey boat
moose-hide canoe
motor boat
mussel-harvesting boat
mu'su u'lk
navire
Newfoundland coffin
Newfoundlander
North Shore canoe
northern-style canoe
Nor'Wester canoe
off-and-on boat

packer
parish boat
Peterborough canoe
Peterhead boat
petite goélette
pig boat
pingey
pinky
pirogue
plank boat
plat
pointer
poling boat
Prince Edward Island
  surfboat
pump boat
punt
Quebec batteau
Quebec pilot boat
Quoddy boat
rapids boat
Rice Lake canoe
riverboat
rodney
rough-water canoe
sail skiff
Saint John River salmon
  boat
Saint John River woodboat
Saint John's trap boat
Saint Lawrence barge
Saint Lawrence bateau
Saint Lawrence skiff
Saint Lawrence yawl
Saint Margarets Bay skiff
salmon boat
salmon skiff
salt fisherman
sardine carrier
scalloper
Schenectady boat
schooner
scout
scow
scow ferry
sealing canoe
sealing punt
sealing skiff
sealing vessel
seine boat
seine skiff
shallop
Shelburne clipper dory
Shelburne dory
shitlats
shore boat
skiff
skin boat
sloop
smack
snapper boat
sneak boat

speedboat
spoon canoe
sprucebark canoe
strait boat
sturgeon-head
Tancook scallop sloop
Tancook schooner
Tancook whaler
tci'k'Enō
team boat
three handed
timber drogher
tl'ai
tonger
toothpick
Toulinguet boat
tow boat
trading batteau
trap boat
trap skiff
traversier
tripper
troller
tsiman
ts'u t'u ela
tub punt
Tusket River square-ender
umiak
upland boat
voyageur canoe
wabânäki tcîmân
wanigan
wary
West Coast canoe
whaler
wigwas tsiman
woods canoe
xebec
yawl
York boat

CANARY ISLANDS
balandra
balandro
barquillo
chinchorro
falúa
goleta

CAPE VERDE ISLANDS
barquinha
lancha

CAROLINE ISLANDS
See Palau and Micronesia

CAYMAN ISLANDS
canoe
catboat
Cayman schooner

CHAD
fak
kadei
kotoko

CHANNEL ISLANDS
See United Kingdom

CHILE
anan
balsa
bongo
canoa
dalca
falúa
falucho
goleta
huampo
kialu
kukltai
lancha velera
lapataganan
lorcha
thagi

CHINA
Amoy fisher
ao zeng
bai du chuan
ba jiang chuan
bian zi
bi fa zi
bo chuan
buffalo boat
cao chuan
cao zi
cao zi chuan
chai ban zi
cha chuan
chang kou ma yang zi
chang long
chan zi
Chênhai chuan
chinedkhulan (Taiwan)
chuan
chu-p'ai (Taiwan)
da fu chuan
da gu chuan
da hong chuan
dang wai
dao ba zi
dia chuan
diao gou zi
diao ting
dou chuan
drag boat
er bai liao ke yin xun chuan
fa
fa chung
fang
fast boat
fa zi
fei teng

CHINA, *cont.*
fei xie
fen chuan
fu
fu diao zi
Fukien trader
gan chuan
go-down
green eyebrow
guan cai chuan
Hainan trader
ha kau
ha kou ting
half boat
hoa hang
hong boat
hong chuan
hong rou chuan
hong tou
hong tou chuan
hong tou san ban
hua chuan
Huang He chuan
hua pi gu
hua zi
jiao hua chuan
jing bang chuan
junk
Kiangsu trader
koupang
kuai ban
ku-dru
liang jie tou
li niao
liu peng
liu wang chuan
long chuan
lorcha
lu ci chuan
Luhü mi chuan
ma chuan
mai shun
ma lan
ma ling ting
ma tou chuan
Mayang ba gan
ma yang chuan
ma yang zi
meeting boat
Miao chuan
mi bao zi
mo you chuan
mud boat
mu pai
mu ying
nan he chuan
night flower boat
ni mo chuan
ordure boat
paddle boat
paddy boat
pai
pai ti chuan

pan gan zi
pango
parao
pig boat
ping di chuan
red bow (Taiwan)
running ship
sampan
sampan Tanka
shao ma yang
Shaoxing chuan
sha ting
she chuan
shen bo zi
shen chuan
shou kou ma yang zi
shuang pheng chuan
siampan
sin-tor-chai
tatara (Taiwan)
Ta-ku fisherman
tan chuan
tang tou
tea house
tiao bai
tiao you chuan
ting
tope
tsat pon
Tsungming chuan
tuo wang chuan
wai pi gu
wei chuan
wu ban
Wuhu xiang xia chuan
Wuxi kuai
Xiangji dou kou
xiao hua chuan
xiao ma tou chuan
xiao xiang xia chuan
yan chuan
yao wang chuan
yao zhou
ya ze chuan
youyou
Yuanling ma yang zi
yu chuan
zak
Zhijiang ma yang zi
zhu pai
zhu pai wang

COCOS (Keeling) **ISLANDS**
dukong
jugong
whaleboat

COLOMBIA
balsa
bongo
bote
canoa

COLOMBIA, *cont.*
catboat
chalana
chalupe
champa
champán
imbabura
lancha
potro

COMORO ISLANDS
dao
panguay

COOK ISLANDS
pahi
vaka
vaka katea
vaka taurua

COSTA RICA
See also Latin America
pitpante

CROATIA
barkaca
batana
batelin
battellina
bragozzo
brazzera
condura
gabara
gaeta)
galio
gozzo
gundula
kaić
ladja
ladva
leut
nava
pedota
pelig
peota
pièlago
portolata
scorridora
tartanella
trabaccolo
zoppolo

CUBA
balandro
canoa
falucho
guadaño
vivero

CYPRUS
adrya

CZECH REPUBLIC
bárka
krypa
lod'
lodka
nava
prahm

DENMARK
See also Faroe Islands
båd
Bæltsbåd
bakkebåd
Bornholmsk ege
Bornholmsk laksebåd
chefensslup
bysse
doggerbåd (dogger)
drakar
drivkvase
evert
far
fladbåd
galease
hajer
halvdæksbåd
havbåd
Hjertingpram
Hornbækbåd
hukkert
isbåd
Isefjordsbåd
jagt
kadrejerjolle
kåg
kragejolle
kuf
kutter
kvase
lodsbåd
Moses
Norsk pram
pink
pram
sandskude
sildebåd
sjægt
Skawbrig
skude
slup
smakke
smakkejolle
sundjolle
tjalk
treibkvase
Zeesboot

DJIBOUTI
houri
ramas
sambūq
zaima
zaruq

DOMINICA
canoe
gommier

DOMINICAN REPUBLIC
barge
cayuco

EAST AFRICA
baghla
batelo
buti
chombo
dau
dau la mataruma
dau la mtepe
dhow
germa
houri
mancive
mtumbwi
ngalawa
pangaio
sambūq
tanga

EASTER ISLANDS
báka
báka póe-póe
pora

ECUADOR
balandra
balsa
balsilla
barca
bongo
caballito de totora
canoa
chata
imbabura
kü'le
pailebot
panga

EGYPT
baris
cangia
catamaran
chatty raft
dahabiyah
djerme
fulūka
gaiassa
gatîra
harrâqa
kalak
karrâka
kik
ma'addiyya
mahonne
mrw
qārib

EGYPT, *cont.*
qatrah
qāyeq
ramūs
sambūq
sandal
shakhtura

EL SALVADOR
bongo

ENGLAND
See United Kingdom

EQUATORIAL GUINEA
batelu

ERITREA
doni
ramas
sambūq

ESTONIA
lodja
paat
sumbad
sumpa
sumppaat

ETHIOPIA
jandi
jendi
ramas
tankwa

FAROE ISLANDS
áttamannafar
da knoren
færobåd
fýramannafar
seksæringur
seksmannafar
slup
smakke
tíggjumannafar
tríbekkur
tristur

FIJI
ak
bilibili
camakau
drua
tabilai
takia
ulatoka
vak
velovelo
waqa

FINLAND
ålandsskuta
bask

FINLAND, *cont.*
eka
ekstock
fälbåt
fäljulle
fiskebåt
forsbåt
galeas
haapio
haiboot
isbåt
iseka
isöka
jakt
jolle
kirkkovene
knärr
kobåt
lillebåt
notbåt
paltamo
postbåt
postjakt
roddjulle
roddsump
segelsump
sikbåt
skärbåt
skötbåt
sköteka
smabåt
snipa
storbåt
sumpjolle

FRANCE
accon
allège
allège d'Arles
annexe
automoteur
auvergnat
bac
bâche
bachet
bachot
bag
baicha
balancelle
baleinier
balinger
barca
barcasse
barche
barcot
barcu
barge
bark
barka
barque
barque de mer
barque du Léman
barque longue

FRANCE, *cont.*

barque provençale
barquerole
barque sablaise
barquet
barquette
barquille
barquot
bâtard
bateau
bateau bâtard
bateau bœuf
bateau charroi
bateau de Berck
bateau de Lannion
bateau d'Equihen
bateau faucher
bateau lavoir
bateau mouche
bateau pilote
bateau sétois
batel
batelet
bèche
bé de cane
berrichon
besogne
bette
bette à escarbilles
bijlander
bilander
billuga
biscayenne
bisquine
bombotte
bomb vessel
borneur
bot
brigantin
bugalet
buis
cabane
cabotière
caique
cajot
calup
camin
camus
canardi
canoë français
canot
canot caseyeur
canot de chasse
canot de Saint-Jacut
canot goëmonier
canot mytilicole
caraca
caravel
caseyeur
catalane
catamaran
chaland
chaland de Berre

chaland de Loire
chalibardon
chaloupe
chaloupe de Plougastel
chalutier
chasse-marée
chasseur
chato
chatte
chelandia
chelandie
chênière
chicabot
coche
coche d'eau
coche du Rhône
cochère
coquet
coquillier
coralline
cordier
corve
corvette
côtier
cotre
cotre de Carantec
couplage
couralin
courau
courrier
crevelle
crevettier
demi-barque
dériveur
dindet
dogre (dogger)
doris
dragon
dragueur
drogueur
drome
Duinkerker
dundee
dundée de la rade de Brest
embarcation
escaffe
escaffié
escute
esnecca
étadier
felouque corse
felouque provençale
filadière
flambart
flette
flibot
flibustier
flobart
flotte
flûte
flûte de Bourgogne
flûte du Berry

foncet
forban
fraguate
frégate (frigate)
gabare
gabareau
gabare de la Rance
gabare de Plancoët
gabaret
gabarot
gabarroto
galère
galère savoyarde
galiot
galiòta
galito
galippe
galopinus
galupe
garrabot
gato
goguet
gondola
gondole
gourse
grand-barque
grande barque
grande bateau
grande plate
gribane
guzzo
harenguier
heu
hollandais
horse-machine boat
houari
houri
huissier
kabarra
lahut
lamparo
lanche
langoustier
ligneur
lougre
lougre flamand
macelet
mahonne
margotat
marie-salope
morutier
moulin-bateau
mourre de pouar
nacelle
nau
naue
nave
naviot
navire malouin
navis baragniata
nef
noie-chien

norvégienne
pair-oar
palangrier
patache
penelle
péniche
péniche de Barfleur
périssoire
picard
picoteux
pinardier
pinasse
pinasson
pink
pinnace
piròga
plata
plate
plate de l'Aiguillon
plate mytilicole
platte d'Arromanches
platte de Villerville
pointu (spits)
polacre
ponto
ponton
pontoon
pousse-pied
quenouille
rafiau
réale
roannaise
roberge
saettia
salembarde
sapine
saque
sardinal
sardinier
sardinier breton
sardinier vendeén
scialuppa
scow
scute
sentine
ship
sinago
skeid
sloop
sloop à tape-cul
tartane de l'Estaque
tartane de Marseille
tartane provençale
terreneuvier
thonier
tirade
toue
train de bateaux
train de bois
traînière
traversier
txalupa handi

FRANCE, *cont.*
vedette
vivier
waal
yack
yole
yole de chasse
yole vendéene
youyou

FRENCH GUIANA
gabare
ubá

GABON
ouaro

GAMBIA
Barra canoe
groundnut cutter

GERMANY
aak
aaktjalk
Arbeitsboot
Arke
Balinger
Barke
Barse
Beiboot
beitelaak
Bock
Bojer
Boll
Bönder
Boot
Bornachen
Bretterfloss
Bubfisch Boot
Bucentaur
Buise
Bulle
Buttjolle
Dachschiff
Dorsten'sche Aak
Egern
Eiderprahm
Eiderschnigge
Eisboot
Eiskahn
Elbkahn
Ewer
Fahr
Fähr-Ewer
Fährschmack
Farm
Fisaler
Fischerfloss
Fischerkohn
Flet
Flieboot
Föhringer Ewer

GERMANY, *cont.*
Fries Jacht
Fuhrwerkponte
Galeass
Galeass-Ewer
Galiot
Galiot-Ewer
Garnboot
Gemüse-Ewer
Giek-Ewer
Gondel
Helgoländer Schlup
Helgoländer Schnigge
herna
Holländer
Huker
Hukergaleass
Hukerjacht
Hummerboot
Humpelnachen
Jacht
Jachtboot
Jachtgaleass
Jagd
Jolle
Kaag
kadraai
Kaffenkahn
Kahn
kleiner Kahn
Kölner Aak
Krabbenkutter
Krenzille
Kuff
Kufftjalk
Kutter
Kutter-Ewer
Ladeschiff
Lädine
Leibschiff
Logger
Marktschiff
Milch-Ewer
Mudderprahm
Mutte
Mutzen
Nachen
naue
Neckeraak
Netzboot
Norsk Pram
Oberländer
Oberländische Saalschiff
Ordinari
Ostebulle
Pfahl-Ewer
Plätte
Prahm
Privater
Pünte
Quack
Quase
Quatze

Rheinaak
Rheinfloss
Rhin-Ewer
Ruhraak
Samoreus
Sandboot
Schauke
Scheerboot
Schlei Kahn
Schlup
Schmack
Schnigge
Schoker
Schokker
Schuiten
Schute
See-Ewer
Skow
Sohlboot
Spiegeljacht
Spitzmutte
Spitzpünte
Stein-Ewer
Störprahm
Strandboot
Stroh-Ewer
Tjalk
Torf-Ewer
Treckschute
treibkvase
trotliner
Waalschokker
Wädenboot
Waidschelch
Waidschiffe
Waidzille
Wasser-Diligence
Weidling
Zeesboot
Zeeskahn
Zille

GHANA
ahima
ekem

GREAT BRITAIN
See British Isles, United
  Kingdom

GREECE
aktarma
bastimento
bombarda
bratsera
briki
cocoreli
gabara
gaita
kaiki
karabion
korkâra

GREECE, *cont.*
paron
perama
ploion
saique
saitia
sakoleva
schedia
skafi
skampavia
sponge boat
tartana
trabaccolo
tráta
trechandiri
tserniki

GREENLAND
canoe-kayak
kayak
umiak
whaleboat

GRENADA
billieboat
bumboat
pirogue

GUADELOUPE
canot
dinghy

GUATEMALA
jukúa

GUINEA
almady
bark
ehem
sinaper

GUINEA-BISSAU
gal
pailão

GUYANA
canoe
falca
kanawa
ubá
woodskin

HAITI
bak
barge
bateau
batiman
boumba
canot
chaloupe
chate
corallain
freiboteros

HAITI, *cont.*
- gouèlette
- kannòt
- pripri

HONDURAS
- *See also Latin America*
- bateau
- Bay Islands dorey
- bungay
- cayuco
- dori
- patache
- pitpan

HONG KONG
- chi shuen
- diao ting
- fa teng
- go-down
- ha kau
- ha kou ting
- há ku
- ha ting
- ku tsai ting
- long chuan
- sampan Tanka
- ts'ao ch'uan

HUNGARY
- bárka
- schinackel

ICELAND
- balaou
- bússa
- byrðingur
- dugga
- eftirbátur
- feræringur
- ferja
- fiskiskip
- galías
- hooker
- karfi
- kútter
- létti-skúta
- sexæringur
- sex manna far
- skekta
- skip
- skipsbåt
- skúta
- slúpskip

ILLYRIA
- lembos

INDIA
- accommodation boat
- Adirāmpatnam boat
- akoda hody
- almady

INDIA, *cont.*
- ap
- badjra
- balon
- barakas
- bargatim
- batel
- batela
- battela
- bāūlīa
- bedi
- beppu tōni
- ber
- berá
- bhelā
- bhim
- bhimā
- bhur
- boat-catamaran
- bot
- bouri de nage
- bunder boat
- cabin boat
- catamaran
- catur
- charigma
- chatty raft
- chhip
- choonda maram
- ciampane
- coracle
- country boat
- danga
- dhangi
- dhoni
- dingá
- dinghy
- dingi
- dingy
- donga
- dorioh
- düe
- eklakdi hodi
- ekta
- flat
- galbat
- gallivat
- ganja
- grab
- hoda
- hodi
- hody
- hola
- hoori
- hu
- huliya
- jalia
- jālibōt
- jangar
- jase
- jeha dhoni
- kachchha
- kalla dhoni

- kapal
- kaphala
- kettuvallam
- khatgiri
- kishti
- koch
- kola maram
- kosha
- kotia
- ku̱lla
- langabote
- launch
- lodhia
- lola
- malia
- manji
- mas-odi
- masula
- muchwa
- muggu padava
- mussuck
- náū
- nauri
- nava
- nouka
- nu
- odam
- odi
- padagu
- padhagi
- padow
- palaggi kattu vattai
- Pamban dhoni
- pambán-manché
- panaval
- pangaio
- panshi
- parinda
- parindah
- pā̱ru
- patela
- pattamar
- periya maram
- pinash
- pinnace
- prow
- purgoo
- roā
- roko
- salt boat
- sālti
- sambuk
- sambūq
- sangādam
- sangara
- sanghāta
- saranga
- sarnái
- shikara
- shoe dhoni
- tag̱hāri
- tarappa

- tarappam
- teppa
- terrada
- tony
- trapa
- ulakh
- vahan
- vallam
- wai
- war
- zak

INDONESIA
- abak
- alis-alis
- alut
- ârŏ
- arut
- bago
- balinger
- banawa
- bandong
- bangka
- bangkang
- bàngka rī nàngkē
- bangko
- banka
- banting
- bantingan
- batele
- bedar
- beduang
- bélang
- belongkang
- bĕrgas
- bero
- bidar
- bilo'
- bilolang
- binta
- birowah
- birowang
- bot
- caraca
- catur
- ci
- daoep-daoep
- djoeng
- djoengkoe
- dragon boat
- flying prau
- gaita
- gale
- gobang
- golekan
- gonda
- gorab
- gubang
- gubang besar
- hapar
- ialoer
- ionco

INDONESIA, *cont.*
isja
jalor
jalur maling
janggolan
jaten
jong
jongkong
juanga
jukung
jukung comprèng
julung
julung-julung
jungkung
kai
kakap
kalaba
kalabba
kapal
kemà
kitji
kolek
kolekan
kolé kolé
kolek pukat
kolek selat
kolik
korakora
korkora
kotak
kroman
kule
lambo
lamboh Bali
lambu
lancha
lantjang pukat
lepa-lepa
lete-lete
londe
londeh
mayang
meia lua
mon
ōa
olan mesa
orembai
orembai belan
oti
padewakang
paduwang
pajala
pajang
pakur
palari
parao
parau
pedjala
pelele
pelele laut
pencalang
penchalang
pengail

pénis
penjajap
penjaleng
perahu
perahu besar
perahu kajangan
perahu katir
perahu payang
perahu penjajap
perahu penjaleng
perahu pukat
perahu sasak
perahu séman
perahu sopi
perahu sumbawa
perahu tinda
peturusan
phang chun
pilau
pinisi
rai
rakit
ro
roh
sakaya
salah-salah
sambo
sampan
sampan batil
sampan gebing
sampan jalur
sampan panjang
sampan panjang tambang
sampan payang
sampan pukat
sampan Riau
sampan sagur belahan
sampan tambang
sampan tambangan
schuitje
sekochi
sekong
solu
solu bólon
solu ratsaran
soppé
tambangan
timber tongkang
tjemplon
tjompreng
tongkang
top
waa
wache
waga
wai
wanga
wangkang

IRAN
batil
beden

IRAN, *cont.*
belem
boom
germa
jalbūt
kashti
katur
mashua
tutín
zauraq
zevrakçe

IRAQ
ama
baghalah
belem
burdjuk
chalabiya
'isbije
kelek
mahaila
mashûf
ma₂:ga
quffa
qaiyarīyah
qurqurru
šaḥtūr
shashah
tarrāda
zaima
zauraq

IRELAND
See also British Isles
Achill Island curragh
Aran Islands canoe
bád
bád iomartha
bàrc
barge
barki
Boyne curragh
cliath thulca
coite
cot
curaćán
curragh
dandy smack
Donegal curragh
drontheim boat
follower
gabbard
galley
Galway hooker
gleóiteog
hooker
horse boat
Irish wherry
Kinsale hooker
Kinsale lugger
lighter
long
luggage boat

IRELAND, *cont.*
naoṁóg
nobby
Norway yawl
picard
púcán
sand boat
Scotch boat
seine boat
skiff
turf boat
urca
Wexford cot
zulu

ISLE OF MAN
See United Kingdom

ISRAEL
šaḥtūr mbaṭṭan
kik

ITALY
accon
balandra
barca
barcé
barca a vela
barcaccia
barca correire
barca di guardia
barcareccio
barchètt
barchetta
barchetto
barco
barcòn
barcone
barcoso
barcotta
barcù
bargia
bargio
barquerole
bastardo
bastimento
batèl
batela
batelin
batelon
battana
battèll
battella
battellina
battellino
battello
battello veneto
battelluccio
batto
beta
betta
bilancellia
bombarde

ITALY, *cont.*

bota
bovo
bragagna
bragozzo
brazzera
brigantino
bucia
bucintoro
bucintoro del Panaro
burchièlla
burchièllo
burchio
buzo
cabanella
caicco
canotto
caorlina
caporais
catalano
chelandia
chiatta
ciatta
cog
combàll
corallina
corsara
cumacèna
fassone
feluca
filuca
filuga
filughetta
fisolera
Flanders galley
fregatina
gabarra
gaeta
galea di corallo
galeazza
galeotta
galeotto
galiot (galiote)
galleggiante
gallia di condennati
gallia libera
gatto
golafrus
goletta
gónda
gondola
gondola da regata
gondola piana
gondolone
gourse
gozzetto
gozzo
guzzo
guzzono
half galley
imbarcazione
lamparo
lancia

lancione
latino
leudo
leuto
libo
londra
luntru
mahonne
manaide
marano
maròta
mulino galleggiante
musciara
muscolo
musseto
mussolèra
nau
nav
nave
nave latina
navicella
navicello
ontro
pailabot
pair-oar
palandra
palischermo
pallone
paranza
pareggia
peata
peatone
penice
peota
pescantina
petacchio
pièlago
pinaccia
pink
pinnace (pinnaccia)
polacre
portolata
puparin
rascona
rimorchio
saettia
sandolino
sandolo
sandón
sanpierota
scafa
scampavia
scappavia
sceola
schifo
sciabica (xebec)
scialuppa
scorridora
speronara
spirunara
tartana
tartanella

topa
topo
topo-sorcio
trabaccolo
traghetto
usciere
varke a véle de le kòzze
vascello
velacciere
zattera
zoppolo

IVORY COAST

coïro

JAMAICA

bateau
bungay
duncan
Jamaica sloop
kunu
man-o'-war yagar

JAPAN

agetaguri-ami-bune
ami-bune
ashi-bune
chip
fune
gyosen
haku
haya-bune
ikada
iso-bune
kamé-no-ko-bune
kamé-no-sé
katsuo-tsura
kawasaki
ki-bune
kikko-sen
kitamae-bune
kohaya
kurèki-ikada
kuserofne
māran
maru
mochip
motshi-so-bune
oyafune
sabani
samma-ami-bune
sampa
sampan
sase-bune
seki-bune
sengoku-bune
sokori-bune
tarai-bune
tow boat
tsuri-bune
uchi-kai-bune
ukai-bune

JAPAN, *cont.*

utase-ami-gyosen
waku-ami-bune
yachip
yanbaru

KENYA

bedan
dau
dau la mataruma
dau la mtepe
dhow
houri
jahazi
Lamu jahazi
mashua
mtepe

KIRIBATI

aka
baurua
ebaeba
flying proa
paopao
wa
wa-ririk

KOREA

cho-gi cham-nan pa
kumei
kwi-son
mehsangi
pal-san
p'asi
pei
soon son

KUWAIT

See also Arabian Peninsula
belem
boom
dangi
hurija
jalbūt
shū·ai

LATIN AMERICA

See also South America
almady
bongo
canoa
cayuco
chata
dorna
guairo
panga

LATVIA

sumpa

LEBANON

filuka
lansh
shakhtura

LIBERIA
Kru canoe
tun

LIBYA
capro
šḥeṭêya

LITHUANIA
barkas
eldijá
Handkahn
ķudilvalts
kurnevalts
Scheike
slup
Zeesboot

LOYALTY ISLANDS
See New Caledonia

MACAU
chi-tong-t'eang
diao ting
ha-kau
há ku
kong-hói-tói
ku-chai
long chuan
manchua
sam-p'a
sampan Tanka
ya ze chuan

MADEIRA ISLANDS
atuneira
barcaça
barqueta
canoa
lancha
lanchão

MALAGASY REPUBLIC
boutre
lākanā
lakandrao
sàmbo

MALAWI
dhow
ngalawa
wato

MALAYSIA
alut (East)
anak bedar
ballon
bandong (East)
bangkong (East)
bantim
banting
beda
bedar

MALAYSIA, *cont.*
bidar (East)
bintak
bot
chĕmplong
concha
dapang (East)
dogol
dragon boat (East)
flying prau
gebeng
gobang (East)
grab
gubang
Gulf of Siam trader
jala (East)
jalak
jalia
jalor
jalora
jong
jongkong
julung-julung
kakap
kakap jĕram
kakap naga
kakap unduk unduk
kapal
kolek
kolek chiau
kolek gelibat
kolek kue
kolek ma' Siam
kolek pĕngayer
kolek selat
kueh buteh ketiri
lambo
lambu
lancha
lanchang
lanchang To'aru
lepap
lipa (East)
lipa-lipa (East)
lorcha
Malacca kolek
panco
payang
peleleh (East)
penchalang
pengail
penjajap
perahu
perahu ayam
perahu bĕlongkang
perahu besar
perahu buatan barat
perahu kakap
perahu katir
perahu kepala kelalang
perahu naga
perahu pinas
perahu pinnace

perahu pukat
phang chun
rakit
sagur
salui (East)
sampan
sampan naga
sampan panjang
sekochi
Singapore trader
tambang
Tamil tongkang
timber tongkang
tongkang
tongkang Mĕlayu (East)
top
toucang
twakow
wangkang

MALDIVES
bangala
brigantine
dhoni
ganja
gourabe
gundra
kuda-dhoni
mas-odi
odi
oruva
panguaye
quiste

MALI
hulu
kole kole

MALTA
canotto
dghajsa
dghajsa-tal-pass
farella
fregata
fregatina
goletta
gondola
kano
kijjik
lancha
luzzu
madia
scow
skampavia
speronara

MARIANA ISLANDS
flying proa (Ladrone)

MARQUESAS ISLANDS
matahiti
vaka
vaka poti
vaka tou uá

MARSHALL ISLANDS
garagar
korkor
ua
wa lap

MARTINIQUE
gaba
gommier
yole

MAURITANIA
grande plate sénégalaise
lanche
langoustier
ponton
trahina

MEDITERRANEAN
bargatim
barge de cantier
barque
barquerole
besquine
bombarde
brigantine
bucia
carabus
cáravo
cat
chambequín
chelandia
cog
corallina
corsair
double felouque
felucca
frigate
galata
galeass
galiot
galizabra
galley
germa
ghurāb
half galley
kybaia
lamparo
lanche
laudus
lembo
lorcha
mahonne
markab
mistico
musculus
myoparon

MEDITERRANEAN, *cont.*
nave
nef
paro
pinacea
pink
polacre
qārib
round ship
saettia
saique
sakoleva
sandal
shakhtura
skafi
strijela
tafurea
tarida
tartane
trireme
velacciere
xebec
zabra

MEXICO
acal
balsa
calabaza
canoa
carabelón
cayuco
chalan
chalupa
felucca
guadaño
ičájuta
panga
patache
pongo
shark boat
tepári

MICRONESIA (CAROLINES)
See also Palau
meniepep
paopao
popo
popow
pot
sein efief
sein maun
tsukupin
vanka
var
wa
wa fatúl
wa fötyn
waka
waka tiu

MOLDOVA
pletină

MONGOLIA
sal

MONTENEGRO
kanot
karavela

MONTSERRAT
dinghy

MOROCCO
agherrabo
goleta
langoustier
maddia
mahonne
ma'ûn
palangrier
pinasse
polacre
qârĕb
saettia

MOZAMBIQUE
almadia
barca
caique
casquinha
chata
coche
dau
lancha
machua
mádia
mitumbuí
muterere
n'galawa
pangaio
xi-tataru

MYANMAR (BURMA)
cargo lighter
feeder
ferry
flat
gandoo
jalia
jong
kabang
kistie
laung
laung gô
laung-zat
lundwin
paddy boat
peingaw
sampan
seró
thón-kin

NAURU
e kuo

NEPAL
donga
náu
wai

NETHERLANDS
aak
aaktjalk
Aalsmeerse punter
Arnemuidense hoogaars
baardse
baggeraak
balinger
barkas
beitelaak
beunschip
beurtschip
beurtsomp
bezaanjacht
Biesbosschuitje
bilander
Blankenbergse schuit
blazer
Blokzijlder jacht
boeier
boeieraak
boerenplat
boerenschouw
bol
bolpraam
bom
bons
boot
botter
bovenmaase aak
buis
bunboot
buyscarveel
dekschuit
dektjalk
dogger
Dorsten'sche Aak
Drentse praam
drijver
flight
fluit
Friese tjalk
Friese turftjalk
Fries jacht
Fries schouw
gaffelaar
gaffelkaag
galei (galley)
galjoot
garnalenschuit
Giethoornse praam
Giethoornse punter
griendaak
Groninger tjalk
grundel

NETHERLANDS, *cont.*
guineevaarder
haringschuit
hekjacht
hektjalk
hengst
herna
heu (hoy)
hoekerbuis
Hoogeveense praam
Holländer
Hollandse tjalk
hoogaars
Hoornse punter
hourque
hulk
ijsbreker
ijsschuitje
jacht
jachtboot
jäger
jol
jola
kaag
kaan
kaar
kaarboot
kaarpunter
kagenaar
kajuitschouw
kantelbak
karveel
katschip (cat)
Kinderlijkse hoogaars
klipper
klipperaak
Koedijker schuitje
kof
koftjalk
kok
koopbotter
koopvaardijhoeker
kotter
kraak
krabschuit
Kreeftenboot
kustvisser
kwak
lemmeraak
lemmerhengst
logger
loodsjol
loodsvaartuig
Markerbotter
marktschuit
melkbootje
melkschouw
melkschuitje
Meppeler praam
moddermolen
modderschouw
mosselaar
Mutte

NETHERLANDS, *cont.*
Noordhollandse gondel
noordvaarder
Oberländer
Overijsselse praam
palingaak
paviljoentjalk
pinasschip (pinnace)
pink
plat
pluut
pont
pot
praam
praamaak
praamschuit
Pünte
punter
Rheinaak
rietaak
roeiboot
Samoreus (Keulenaar)
Sandboot
schokker
schouw
schuit
schuitje
senau
sjouwerman
skûtsje
sleepers
slijkpraam
sloep
smak
smalschip
snik
somp
spiegeljacht
spits
spitsbek
Spitzmutte
spitspraam
Staverse jol
steekschuit
steigerschuit
tentschuit
Tholense hoogaars
tjalk
tjotter
tochtschuit
trekschuit
turftjalk
Utrechtse praam
veense praam
veerschip
visaak
vishoeker
vlet
vlieboot
vlot
vlotschuit
Vollenhovense bol
Waalschokker

walenmajol
waterschip
weischuit
wieringeraak
wijdschip
zalmschouw
zeepunter
zeeschouw
zeetjalk
Zeeuwse schouw
Zeeuwsvlaamse hoogaars
zolderbak

**NETHERLANDS
ANTILLES**
boat
canoa
giki
jola
motorvlet
vlet

NEW CALEDONIA
botr (Loyalty Islands)
hu (Loyalty Islands)
iweng (Loyalty Islands)
wang

NEW ZEALAND
amatiatia
best and best boat
mokihi
mullet boat
pahi
pora
puke
scow
taurua
waka
waka ama
waka korari
waka pahii
waka pitau
waka taua
waka tete
waka tiwai
waka unua
whaleboat

NICARAGUA
See also Latin America
bateau
craft
dori
piragua
pitpan

NIGER
kadei
kole kole

NIGERIA
aru
bar boat
habara
kadei
kole kole
kunun

NIUE
vaka heke fa

NORTHERN IRELAND
see United Kingdom

NORWAY
åfjordsbåt
attring
bankskøyte
barki
bask
båt
bindalsbåt
búza
byrding
doris
dory
dragon boat
eke
elvebåt
evert
færing
farkost
fembøring
femkeiping
fem-manns båt
fem-roms båt
femroring
femrøring
ferje
firing
firkeiping
firroring
fiskiskip
galeas
galei (galley)
garnbåt
grisbåt
hafskip
hardangerbåt
havbåt
husbåt
hvalerbåt
isbåt
jakt
jekt
jolle
karve
karvebåt
kirkebåt
knarr
kokse
kunte
kutter

NORWAY, *cont.*
langskip
lestabåt
lillebåt
listerbåt
losbåt
makrellskøyte
nordfjordbåt
nordlandsbåt
nordmørsbåt
norvégienne
Norway yawl
notbåt
Oselver
pram
ranværingbåt
redningsskøyte
saltværingsbåt
seksæring
sekskeiping
seks-roms båt
seksroring
sjalupp
sjekte
skeid
skeis
skip
skipsbåt
sloltelapsbåt
skøyte
skuta
skyssbåt
slupp
snekke
snekkja
storbåt
straumbåt
sunnfjordbåt
sunnmørsbåt
torskegarnsbåt
tre-roms båt
treroring

OMAN
'abari
abubuz
batil
bedan
bedan-safar
bedan-seyad
boom
ganja
houri
lansh
mashua
ramath
sambūq
shahuf
shashah
shū·ai
zarūq

PACIFIC
See also major island groups
boat
kalia
poti
vaa
vaka
vaka tafaanga
wangka

PAKISTAN
bedi
berí
bhart
bohatja
bunder boat
chatty raft
dhangi
dhatti hora
dingy
dondi
donga
duggah
dunda
dúndo
ekdar
gharat hora
jālibōt
kishti
launch
mussuck
nauri
palla chatty
parinda
pasni
quantel battella
sarnái
tony
zak
zohrak

PALAU
See also Micronesia
kaep
prèr
wa

PANAMA
See also Latin America
bongo
canoa
cayuco
chalupa
champa
panga
piragua

PAPUA NEW GUINEA
aidedeya
aiyebu
ak
aka
bot

PAPUA NEW GUINEA, *cont.*
bout
de wang
ghobun
kan
kanu
kāt
keama
kewo'u
kop
lakatoi
lia no
masawa
mon
moto-moto
mut
no
oai
oáṅga
orou
parau
pe
peére
pinas
por
pot
uche
vaga
vísŏ
wa
waga
waka
waqa
wonga

PARAGUAY
ahangada
balsa
barco
igá
jangada
pelota
piragua

PERU
balandra
balsa
balsilla
balsita
bergantín
bonitera
bote
caballito
canoa
chalana
chalupa
falúa
huampu
igára
igarité
káno
kánu
nó

PERU, *cont.*
ogára
Sechuras
zapato
zapato chalana

PHILIPPINES
balandra
balinger
balóto
balsa
banca
barangay
baroto
basnigan
batel
batil
bilus
bintak
boteng pamunuanan
buralan
bu-ti
canoa
caraca
casco
chalana
chinchorrohan
chñedkeran
dalámas
dapang
dinapalang
djĕnging
falua
flying prau
gabara
galleon
gobang
juanga
korakora
kudastre
lancha
largarete
lipa
lorcha
motor
palowa
palua
panca
panco
panga
pango
parao
paraw
pontin
sakayan
salisipan
sibidsibiran
tango
tataya
vinta

PITCAIRN ISLAND
longboat
olwe boat

POLAND
barka
barkas
bat
bata
bôt
bote
Bücke
czajka
Entenlomme
Erdlomme
galar
galarek
galer
Garnsicken
gondel
Handlomme
Hukergaleass
Jacht
Jachtgaleass
Kaffenkahn
krypa
ķudilvalts
łódka
łodyga
łódź
Lomme
Oberländer
Oberländer Kahn
plot
pomeranka
Quase
Quatze
Scheerboot
Scheike
Scheisslomme
Strandboot
szkuta
szkutka
żawówka
Zeeskahn
zig

PORTUGAL
See also Madeira Islands
aiola
alvarenga
aveiro
bacalhoeiro
balandra
barca
barcaça
barca da arte xávega
barca da gacha
barca das portas
barca do alto
barco
barco da pescada
barco de lavrador
barco do candil
barco do pilado
barcote
barqueta

PORTUGAL, *cont.*

barquinha
barquinha
barquinho do coberto
bateira
bateira do mar
bateira do Mondego
bateira ílhava
bateira marinhoa
bateira mercantel
batel
batela
batelão
batel da testa
batel do Seixal
bote
bote cacilheiro
bote catraio
bote de pinho
bote do camarão
bote fragata
bote xeiteiro
brigantine
buque
caçadeira
caíco
caique
caixamarin
canoa
canoa cacilheira
canoa da picada
canoa do alto
canoa grande
canote
cáravo
catraia
catraio
chalupa
chata
chaveco
chinchorra
chinchorro
cortiçeira
cortiço
culé
dorna
enviada
escaler
falua
falua do Bugio
fragata
gabarra
galeão
galeón
galeota
gamela
guiga
iate
janga
jangada
labrega
lancha
lanchão

lancha sávara
lenho
masseira
meia lua
moliceiro
mulet
muleta
netinha
palhabote
patacha
patache
poveiro
queche
rabão
rabelo
real
saveiro
traineira
valboeiro
xávega
zabra

PUERTO RICO

balandra
bote de vela
canoa
cayuco
chalupa
lancha
navito barco

QATAR

See also Arabian Peninsula
houri

RÉUNION

bato
kanot
pirog

ROMANIA

kaik
lodka
lontra
luntre
pletină
plută
şal

RUSSIA

baida
baidar
baidara
barka
barzha
bask
bat'
boudarka
flet
galiot
ga'twaat
haapio

RUSSIA, *cont.*

Handkahn
horse-machine boat
karabel
kayak (ma'to, baidarka)
kayuk
koch
ķudilvalts
kurnevalts
lodka
mochip
prorĕz
scheik
scheike
shalanda
shebek
shnyaka
skampaveya
trabac
Zeesboot

SAINT HELENA ISLAND

longboat

SAINT KITTS and NEVIS

canoa
dinghy
sailing lighter

SAINT LUCIA

gommier
mail boat
whaleboat

SAINT PIERRE and MIQUELON

barquette
boëtteur (galoper)
doris
wary

SAINT VINCENT and THE GRENADINES

billieboat
whaleboat

SAMOA ISLANDS

'alia
amatasi
fautasi
iato
paopao
soatau
tafaana
va'a alo

SCOTLAND

See United Kingdom

SÉNÉGAL

gal
grande plate sénégalaise

SEYCHELLES

ballinier
chaloupe
kanot
katyolo
penis
pirog
schooner
shark boat

SIERRA LEONE

Bullom boat
Kru canoe
snapper boat
wom

SINGAPORE

bandong
dhoni
jong
kolek
kolek chiau
kolek sĕlat
kotak
lepap
perahu Bugis
perahu pukat
phang chun
sampan
sampan panjang
sampan pengail
Singapore trader
timber tongkang
tongkang
tongkang Mĕlayu
toucang
twakow

SLOVAKIA

czajka

SLOVENIA

ladja

SOCIETY ISLANDS

pahi
pahi tama'i
pasi
poti marara
pu hoe
rehu
taurua
tipairau
va'a moto

SOLOMON ISLANDS

agai-ni-waiau
binabina
bõnga
cori
'etea
fõrua
gaï oko

SOLOMON ISLANDS, *cont.*

guli
'iola
jaola (Santa Cruz Islands)
kenu
lakatau
lisi
mola
mon
nuñatapu (Santa Cruz Islands)
ora
paopao
porua
roko
soro
sosoro
te-puke (Santa Cruz Islands)
tomoko
vaka
vaka pai manu

SOMALIA

'abari
beden
dau la mataruma
dau la mtepe
dongha
houri
matapa
mtepe
sambūq

SOUTH AFRICA

bã:s
Cape boat
surfboat

SOUTH AMERICA

See also Latin America
balsa
canoa
chinchorro
corial
falca
lanche
panga
sumaca
woodskin

SPAIN

See also Canary Islands
albuferenc
aljibe
balahú
balancela
balandra
barca
barca de falca
barca del bou
barca de mitjana
barcaza
barco
barco de sardinal

SPAIN, *cont.*

barcolongo
barqueta
barquete
barquilla
barquilla de sardinal
barquillo
bastimento
batea
batel
batela
battela
bonitera
bote
bote xeiteiro
bou
brigantine
buceta
buey
buque
burcho
burro
busi
cabana
calabaza
calera
canoa
caravel
caro
catalana
chalana
chalupa
chata
chinchorro
coquete
corbeta
dorna
embarcación
enviada
escampavia
falua
falucho
fragata
gabarra
gabarrón
galeón (galleon)
galeota
galizabra
gamela
gánguil
golondrina
grondola
guadaño
gussi
jábega
jabeque
jangada
lamparo
lancha
lancha fletera
lanchón
landro
langostero

laúd
llampuguera
mahonne
masseira
mistico
muleta
nau
nave
navío
pailebote
palangrero
pareja
patache
patín
pilobote
pinaza
polacre
queche
quechemarín
quetx
quillat
rai
real
sardinal
tartana
traiña
trainera
trincado
trincadura
txalupa handi
urca
velacciere
vivero
xeito
zabra
zumbra

SPANISH SAHARA

See Western Sahara

SRI LANKA

äng-oruwa
angula
brigantine
catamaran
dhoni
katapannay
madel-oruwa
manji
näva
oruwa
padagu
padavu
padda boat
palu-oruwa
paruwa
schooner
vallam
varakan-oruwa
vattal
warka-moowee
yathra dhoni

SUDAN

felukka
gharab
houri
markab
naggr
ramas
sambūq
sandal

SURINAM

corial
falca
kano
korjaal
piakka
ubá

SWEDEN

ålandsskuta
älvbåt
äsping
Baltic trader
bankskuta
båt
blekingseka
bohusjulle
bomb vessel
boyert
dory
draggarnseka
eka
ekstock
fälbåt
fäljulle
farkost
fiskebåt
fiskekvass
forsbåt
galeas
garnbåt
gårnpram
gotlandsnipa
haapio
håp
haxe
hukare
hvassing
isbåt
iseka
isjolle
jakt
jolle
kåg
kanot
kobåt
kosterbåt
kutter
kvass
kyrkbåt
lad'ya
Lappbåt
lillebåt

SWEDEN, *cont.*
lotskutter
nordlandsbåt
notbåt
orusteka
pålpråm
postbåt
postjakt
pråmm
roddsump
roslagsjakt
roslagsskuta
sandkil
segelsump
skärbåt
skep
skepp
skötbåt
sköteka
skuta
småbåt
smack
snipa
stockbåt
stockeka
storbåt
strömbåt
sump
sumpjolle
torsköka
vadeka
vrakeka

SWITZERLAND
almadia
barka
barke
barketta
barque
barque des marmets
barque du Léman
barquette
Böcke
Brëëm
brigantin
canardière
chaloupe
cochère
Eisboot
esquif
frégate (frigate)
galère
galère savoyarde
galiot
gondel
grande barque
Lädine
loquette
Markschiff
nacelle
nau
naue
Nauen

SWITZERLAND, *cont.*
naviot
nef
Ordinarischiff
péniche
radeau
Weidling

SYRIA
bucia
kik
šaḥtūr
shakhtura
skûna

TAIWAN *See China*

TAJIKSTAN
turssuk

TANZANIA
baghla
betala
dau
dau la mataruma
dau la mtepe
dhow
houri
jahazi
jalbūt
mashua
ngalawa
tanga
Zanzibar jahazi

THAILAND
bote
dogol
Gulf of Siam trader
kolek
kolek lichang
kueh buteh ketiri
lorcha
rua
rua ballang
rua chalom
rua chang
rua kao
rua kread
rua nua
rua pet
rua pheelawk
rua pla
sampan
Singora Lake boat
top
yaw ngat

TOGO
ahima

TOKELAU
paopao
vaka

TONGA
baobao
kalia
tafa'anga
tongiaki
vaka

TRINIDAD
bumboat
drogher
pirogue

TRISTAN DA CUNHA
longboat

**TUAMOTU
ARCHIPELAGO**
kamia
maota
pahi
pange
poti
vaka

TUNISIA
bateau bœuf
chabec
corallina
korkâra
lancha
lânša
lûd
mahonne
moana (vascello)
péniche
qarib
qârob
sandal
šḥeṭêya
skûna

TURKEY
aktarma
alamana
at kayığı
balıkçi kayığı
barça
barçe
barquerole
baştarda
buranija
caravel
chaloupa
filuka
gagalı
kadırga
kalita
kayık
kik
kutchudjik guèmi
londra
mahonne
mavna

TURKEY, *cont.*
mouche
nav
nave
pelandrie
paraskmalion
patalya
pazar kayığı
perama
piyade
šaḥtūr
saique
sakoleva
sal
saltanat kayığı
sandal
sandalaya
sefine
shakhtura
taka
tchektirme
tombaz
tráta
zevraq

TUVALU
amatasi
paopao

UGANDA
barque
dhow
sesse

TURKMENISTAN
burdjuk
turssuk

UKRAINE
baida
baidaka
galera
gelia
karabel
pletină
scheik
shalanda
trabac

U.S.S.R. (former)
barkas
bot
caique
nevodnik
paróm
plot
sal
yalik

UNITED ARAB EMIRATES
See also Arabian Peninsula
'abari
boom

UNITED ARAB EMIR., *cont.*
dhow
shashah
shū·ai
zarūq

UNITED KINGDOM
See also British Isles
balsa raft
banana boat
barge
baulk yawl
beach gig
beetle boat
Bermuda sloop
best boat
bilander
blood boat
boarding boat
boat
bomb vessel
bounty boat
box float
bumboat
buss
butterbox
by-boat
Canadian canoe
cattleman
clipper-schooner
cokke
collier
Cornish barge
cut barge
cutter
dinghy
East India hoy
family boat
Fife skiff
fish box
fisherman
fleeter
flute
foot boat
fruit schooner
galley
gondell
great ship
guard ship
gun punt
home-trade ship
hourque
hoy
iceboat
jagger
jolly boat
ketch-barge
little boat
long-boom smack
long ship
luggage boat
monkey boat
mud hopper

UNITED KINGDOM, *cont.*
mule
narrow boat
pinnace
post-ship
puffer
revenue cutter
rowbarge
sack ship
scow
sea boat
sheer vessel
skimming dish
smack
spoon dredger
surf boat
swift boat
tosher
track boat
tripper boat
trow
tub
tub boat
tub punt
una boat
whaleback
whaleboat
yawl

Channel Islands
Guernsey crab boat
Guernsey mackerel boat

England
admiral class
Arun spritsail barge
Avon tar boat
baiter
ballast punt
bank boat
barge
Barton horse boat
batelle
bawley
beach punt
beach skiff
beach yawl
Beer lugger
best and best boat
best and best punt
billyboy
black boat
black cutter
blobber
boat
boomy
bottoms
box boat
brickie
Bridgwater boat
Brighton beach boat
Brixham smack
Broads lateener

cabin boat
cadger
canoe
canoe-yawl
cat
catamaran
Channel barge
coal box
coal slacker
coble
cock
cock boat
cockle
cockle galley
cod smack
cog
cog boat
coggle
cok
college barge
collier
compartment boat
corf
corn hoy
Cornish gig
Cowes ketch
Cowes skiff
cruiser
dandy
day boat
Deal galley
Deal galley punt
Deal hooker
Deal lugger
Deal punt
death galley
derrick boat
derrick flat
didal boat
dipper
dirt boat
doble
dogger
double-ender
drag
drag-in seine boat
East Cornish lugger
East Countryman
esnecca
Essex smack
Exe salmon boat
Fal barge
Falmouth oyster dredger
Falmouth oyster punt
Falmouth quay punt
Fen boat
Fenland lighter
Fenland punt
fifie
fish-carrying boat
Fishmongers' Company
  barge

five-finger dredger
flat
flatner
flattie
Fleet trow
float
flote
follower
foyboat
galiot
garden punt
gig
gold-duster
goozing boat
gravel boat
Gravesend barge
Gravsend waterman's
  wherry
half and halfer
Hampshire punt
Hartlepool pilot coble
Hastings lugger
hatch boat
haul-tow skiff
hay barge
hay boat
head boat
hog boat
horse boat
horse ferry
horse packet
hoveller
huffler
hulk
Humber keel
Humber sloop
Ironbridge coracle
Itchen Ferry boat
jackass schooner
jigger sloop
jolly boat
josher
keelboat
keel-wherry
ketch
Leigh pink
lerret
light boat
lighter
Lincoln catch
line boat
little packet
lobster boat
longboat
Lowestoft shrimper
Lowestoft trawler
luff barge
lug boat
lurker
lurky
mackerel tuck-net boat
Margate hoy

UNITED KINGDOM, *cont.*
Margate wherry
Medway doble
Mersey flat
Mersey gig
Mevagissey tosher
milk boat
mission boat
mission smack
monkey
monkey boat
Morecambe Bay prawner
Moses boat
mosquito fleet
mud sledge
mussel boat
nobby
Norfolk crabber
Norfolk keel
Norfolk punt
Norfolk wherry
number one
onker
packet
paddle-box boat
pair-oar
pan
Parrett flatner
Paull shrimper
Peter boat
picarooner
pinker
pinkstern
Plymouth barge
Plymouth hooker
polacca
Polperro gaffer
pontoon
Porthleven half boat
Portsmouth wherry
pot boat
pram
prame
pump boat
punt
Ramsgate smack
Ramsgate tosher
randan
reed boat
rigger
Rodney boat
row galley
rowing lighter
salmon punt
sand barge
scaf
scath-ros
schooner-barge
scoot
sculler
seine boat
Selsey galley
Severn wherry

shallop
sheer vessel
shotter
shout
skeid
skiff
skillinger
Southampton hoy
sprat punt
Staithes yacker
starvationer
Stationers' barge
Stour lighter
stowboat
straw boat
stumpy barge
swim-headed barge
tank boat
tar boat
Teign keel
Thames gig
Thames lighter
Thames sailing barge
Thames skiff
Thames wherry
Thanet wherry
tide boat
tilt boat
Trent catch
Trinity boat
Trinity House barge
tub
tuck-net boat
turf boat
Tyne keel
Tyne wherry
watch boat
Watchet flatty
Weaver flat
weed cutter
West Cornish lugger
West Country barge
West Country boat
West Country crabber
West Country sailing barge
western barge
Weston-super-Mare flatner
whammel boat
wharf boat
wherry
whiff
Whitstable oyster smack
wide boat
wildfowl canoe
willock eater
winkle brig
wolder
Yarmouth lugger
Yarmouth pilot gig
Yarmouth shrimper
yoll
Yorkshire keel

Yorkshire lugger
Yorkshire yawl

Isle of Man
herring scowte
Manx lugger
Manx wherry
nobby

Northern Ireland
buckie
cot
dandy smack
dinghy
drontheim
gabbard
Groomsport yawl
horse boat
lighter
nabbie
nobby
Norway yawl
punt
salmon coble
sand yacht
scow
skiff

Scotland
baldie
bàrc
bàta
boatie
Clyde gravel smack
coal smack
coble
cod smack
coracle
culaidh
da knoren
drag boat
eathrach
eela boat
Fair Isle yoal
fifie
fifie skiff
fourareen
gabbart
gig
haddock boat
half-decker
herring boat
Kinsale lugger
lang boomer
light boat
line boat
line skiff
Lock Fyne skiff
long
lurkie
nabbie
Ness yoal

North Isles yole
paddy boat
Peterhead boat
post boat
ring-net boat
Saint Kilda mail boat
scaffie
scaffie yawl
scow
sgoth
Shetland Model
sixareen
skiff
skothomlin
South Isles yole
Stornoway yawl
Stornowegian
top boat
Westray skiff
yole
zulu
zulu skiff

Wales
Aberystwyth beach boat
bad
coracle
Dee coracle
Dee salmon boat
female boat
male boat
mud sledge
Mumbles oyster skiff
mussel boat
nobby
number one
pot boat
Swansea pilot schooner
Teifi coracle
Tywi coracle
Wye coracle

UNITED STATES
See also Puerto Rico &
    Virgin Islands
Abenaki canoe
Adirondack guide-boat
áma
anchor boat
angyaq
ark
Au Sable River drift boat
awā'n
bait boat
balsa
Baltimore clipper
banker
Banks dory
barge
bark
Barnegat sneakbox

UNITED STATES, *cont.*

barque
bat
bateau
bateau plat
batoe
batteau
battery boat
bay boat
Bay coaster
bayman
beach punt
beef boat
Bermuda sloop
bethel ship
bilander
Block Island boat
blood boat
boarding boat
boat
boat-canoe
bongo
bony-fish boat
boom
boom boat
Boston hooker
Boston pilot schooner
bo't
bouco
bow boat
box boat
box float
brigantin
broadhorn
brogan
bugeye
bullboat
bullhead boat
bumboat
bushwack boat
busthead
butthead
buy boat
cabin boat
cabin skiff
cable ferry
cage
cajeu
California clipper
canal boat
canaller
cannow
canoe
canot
canot bâtard
canot du maître
canotte
Cape Ann dory
Cape Rosier wherry
car float
cat
catboat
cat-schooner

cat-yawl
chabec
chaland
chaloupe
Charleston bateau
Chebacco boat
Chesapeake Bay log canoe
Chesapeake Bay schooner
ching
Choptank River shad skiff
chunk boat
chunker
circus boat
clam dredger
clammer's dory
clamming skiff
clipper banker
clipper-schooner
coal box
coal bunker
coal schooner
coastal packet
coasting schooner
Coast Salish canoe
collecting boat
Columbia River skiff
Connecticut canoe
Connecticut River drag boat
Connecticut scull boat
Core Sounder
corita
cottonwood canoe
covered sled
crab
crabbing bateau
crabbing punt
crabbing skiff
crab scraper
crib
Crotch Island pinky
Cumberland River drift
cutter
day boat
deadrise bateau
deadrise boat
deck scow
Delaware Bay oyster
  schooner
Delaware ducker
Delaware River shallop
demi-galère
diamond bottom bateau
dinghy
dingy
dink
ditch box
dogbody
doghole schooner
dory
dory-skiff
double-decker
double-header

down-easter
down-the-bay sharpie
dragger
dram
dredge boat
drifting boat
duck boat
Durham boat
Eastport pinky-schooner
eel boat
esquif
falouche
felouque
felucca
fish boat
fisherman
fisherman's car
fishwheel scow
five-handed boat
flat
flatboat
flatiron skiff
flattie
flattie skiff
fleet
flicker
float
float boat
float house
floating battery
floating dishpan
floating palace
flyer
four-masted bark
fragata
freight boat
freighter
freight vessel
Friendship sloop
frigate
gabare
galère
galley
galliot (galiot)
gang
garvey
garvey box
gas boat
Georgesman
gilling skiff
gillnetter (and Alaska)
gill net tug
gondola
gospel ship
Grand Haven ketch
grass boat
Great Lakes schooner
guard boat
Guinea boat
gunboat
gundalow
gunning skiff

half galley
half skipjack
Hampton boat
hand-rakers clam skiff
hatch boat
hay boat
hay schooner
hiker
hinge boat
hooker
Hooper Island crab skiff
horse boat
horse packet
houseboat
hoy
Hudson River brick schooner
Hudson River shad boat
Hudson River sloop
hunting punt
Huron boat
ice punt
ice schooner
Indian Header
Indian trade boat
Isles of Shoals boat
jacht
James River bateau
jigger
johnboat
Joppa shay
kāpili
kayak
kayak-form canoe
keelboat
ketch
Key West sponge sloop
kialoa
kiln-wood coaster
knockabout
Koshkonong flatboat
Koshkonong monitor
kunner
Lake Champlain canal boat
laker
lampara boat
launch
lay boat
layout boat
line boat
live barge
lobster boat
lobsterman
lobster smack
London wherry
longboat
Long Island scallop boat
lorcha
lugger
lumber boat
lumberman's batteau
Mackinaw boat
mail boat

UNITED STATES, *cont.*

Maine wood scow
Malecite river canoe
marie-salope
market fisherman
market schooner
mate boat
Matinicus boat
McKenzie River drift boat
melon seed
menhaden boat
menhaden carry-away boat
Merrimack River wherry
Methodist canoe
Mississippi scull boat
Mohawk boat
monitor
Monomoy
moose-hide canoe
mortar boat
Moses boat
mountain boat
mud boat
mud sled
mullet boat
Muscongus Bay sloop
mussel boat
Nahant clipper dory
nancy
net boat
New Haven flatiron boat
New Orleans lugger
New York oyster smack
New York sailing lighter
Noank sharpie
Noank sloop
Nomans Land boat
nonpareil sharpie
North Carolina sail skiff
North Carolina shad skiff
northern-style canoe
Norway yawl
Norwegian boat
nu'
one-sail bateau
Oregon dory (and Alaska)
Orleans boat
outside boat
oyster barge
oyster boat
oyster navy
oyster runner
oyster scow
oyster sloop
oyster steamer
packer
packet boat
pa-dá-wahl
paddle boat
paddy boat
paper boat
party boat
Passamaquoddy ocean canoe

peapod
péniche
Penobscot canoe
Pensacola oyster boat
periauger
picaroon
pig boat
pilot boat model
pilot schooner
pilot skiff
pink
pinky
pinnace
pirogue
Piscataqua River wherry
pith-lo
plantation boat
plunger
pole barge
pole boat
pole skiff
poling boat
Potomac dory-boat
Potomac fish lighter
pound boat
pound net boat
pound net scow
pound net sharpie
pram
pullboat
pump boat
pumuk o'wan
pungy
punt
push boat
pusher boat
quarter boat
Quoddy boat
Race Point surfboat
radeau
raftboat
railbird skiff
Reelfoot stumpjumper
revenue cutter
ring-net boat
Rhode Island hook boat
road-cart
rowbarge
rowboat
row galley
run boat
sail gear
Saint Lawrence skiff
saKi
salmon skiff
salmon troller
salmon wherry
sampan
sandbagger
sand boat
Sandy Hook pilot schooner
sanpan

sardine carrier
Savannah River duck boat
scalloper
schooner
schooner-barge
schooner smack
scoot
scooter
scout boat
scow
scow-brig
scow ferry
scow-schooner
scow-sloop
scull float
sda'kwihl
Sea Bright skiff
Seaford skiff
sealing boat
sealing canoe
sectional boat
seine boat (and Alaska)
seine skiff
semi-dory
shad battery
shad boat
shad galley
shallop
shanty boat
sharpie
sharpie-launch
sharpie-schooner
sharpie-skiff
sharpshooter
shed
shell boat
shell kicker
shikukul
shot
Shrewsbury River crab skiff
shrimp canoe
shrimper
shrimp junk
Sinepuxent skiff
sinkbox
sinker boat
skiff
skin boat
skipjack
sloop
sloop boat
smack
smack boat
smackee
small bateau
smelt scow
Smith Island skiff
snapper
snapper boat
sneak boat
sneak skiff
snow

speedboat
sponge boat
sponge dinghy
sponge schooner
square-ender
squid skiff
Staten Island skiff
stone sloop
striker boat
sturgeon-nose canoe
surfboat
Susquehanna sneak boat
Swampscott dory
swift boat
tally scow
tam'e'
Tancook whaler
tandem boats
tango boat
team boat
tender
terrapin smack
timber drogher
timber raft
tl'ai
tobacco boat
tonger
toothpick
Toulinguet boat
tow
tow boat
tow car
tow smack
train de bois
trap boat
trapping skiff
traversier
tripper
troller
trotliner
tsiman
tuckup
tug
tugantine
two-mast boat
two-sail lobster boat
umiak
Virginia model
Virginia pilot schooner
voyageur canoe
wa'a
wa'a 'ākea
wa'a kaukāhi
wa'a kaulua
wa'k·ai
wanigan
water boat
weed cutter
whaleboat
whaler
wharf boat
wherry

UNITED STATES, *cont.*
Whitehall boat
Whitehall skiff
wigwas tsiman
wind sled
wood boat
wood drogher
wo'te
xebec
xûna'
yawl
yawl boat
York boat
yu maya

URUGUAY
balandra
ballenera
balsa
chalana
pelota

UZBEKISTAN
burdjuk
turssuk

VANUATU (NEW HEBRIDES)
aka
bilibili
bot
eka
kenu
mbembéo
na-ak
na-ak wala
nawangk ambu
ok
sip
wa
waga
waka
wanga

VENEZUELA
balsa
bombote
bongo
bote
canoa
caribe
chalana
concha
curiara
falca
galite
goleta
lancha
palangrero
piragua
tahpooy
woodskin

VIETNAM
cái màng
cái thuyền
dragon boat
flûte
ghe
ghe bâ'u
ghe bè
ghe biê'n
ghe câu
ghe cà vom
ghe cu'a
ghe diang
ghe luó'i rùng
ghe nang
ghe trê
ghe xuông
ghe you
lorcha
parao
peniche
rua chalom
song-vành
tam ba'n
tango

VIETNAM, *cont.*
thúng chài
thuyền
thuyền lu'o'i

VIRGIN ISLANDS
canoe (U.S.)
coble (British & U.S.)
drogher (British)
float
Tortola sloop (British)

WALES
See United Kingdom

WALLIS AND FUTUNA
kalia
paopao
togiaki
vaka tafaanga

WEST AFRICA
baleinière de barre
boñgo
caturia
cayuco
Kru canoe
kunun

WESTERN SAHARA
balandra
balandro

WESTERN SAMOA
See Samoa Islands

WEST INDIES
See also individual islands
accon
américain
antillais
bacassa
ballahou
barge

WEST INDIES, *cont.*
beach punt
Bermuda schooner
buccaneer
canoa
corallain
dorey
drogher
gros bois
Jamaica sloop
Moses boat
periagua
picaroon
piperi
pripri
sloop
West Indies schooner

YEMEN
See also Arabian Peninsula
jal
sambūq
zaima
zarūq

YUGOSLAVIA (former)
barka
čamac
traget

ZAIRE (now Congo)
barque
dongo
mwanda

ZAMBIA
banana boat
chombo
ichikondo

ZIMBABWE
ngarawa

Notes